The Sporting News

COMPLETE HOCKEY BOOK

1993-94 EDITION

Editors/Complete Hockey Book
CRAIG CARTER
GEORGE PURO

Contributing Editors/Complete Hockey Book
MARK SHIMABUKURO
LARRY WIGGE

WITHDRAWN

The Sporting News

PUBLISHING CO.

Francis P. Pandolfi, Chairman and Chief Executive Officer; Nicholas H. Niles, Publisher and President; John D. Rawlings, Editorial Director; Kathy Kinkeade, Vice President/Production; William N. Topaz, Director/Information Development; Gary Brinker, Director of Electronic Information Development; Gary Levy, Editor; Mike Nahrstedt, Managing Editor; Joe Hoppel, Senior Editor; Craig Carter, Tom Dienhart, Dave Sloan and Larry Wigge, Associate Editors; Mark Shimabukuro, Assistant Editor; George Puro, Production Assistant; Bill Bayer, Kevin Hormuth, Daniel Rezny and Ronald Zizmor, Editorial Assistants; Bill Perry, Director of Graphic Presentation; Mike Bruner, Art Director/Yearbooks and Books; Corby Ann Dolan, Database Analyst; Vern Kasal, Composing Room Supervisor.

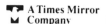 A Times Mirror Company

CONTENTS

1993-94 NHL Season 3
  National Hockey League directory 4
  Individual teams section
     (schedules, directories, rosters, etc.) 5
  Mighty Ducks of Anaheim 5
  Boston Bruins 7
  Buffalo Sabres 10
  Calgary Flames 13
  Chicago Blackhawks 16
  Dallas Stars 19
  Detroit Red Wings 22
  Edmonton Oilers 25
  Florida Panthers 28
  Hartford Whalers 30
  Los Angeles Kings 33
  Montreal Canadiens 36
  New Jersey Devils 39
  New York Islanders 42
  New York Rangers 45
  Ottawa Senators 48
  Philadelphia Flyers 51
  Pittsburgh Penguins 54
  Quebec Nordiques 57
  St. Louis Blues 60
  San Jose Sharks 63
  Tampa Bay Lightning 66
  Toronto Maple Leafs 69
  Vancouver Canucks 72
  Washington Capitals 75
  Winnipeg Jets 78
  Schedule, day by day 81
1992-93 NHL Review 89
  Regular season 90
    Final standings 90
    Individual leaders 90
    Statistics of players with two teams 92
    Miscellaneous 95
  Stanley Cup playoffs 99
    Results, round by round 99

  Games summaries, Stanley Cup finals 100
  Individual leaders 102
  Individual statistics 102
  Miscellaneous 105
  All-Star Game 107
  Awards 108
  Player drafts 109
NHL History 115
  Stanley Cup champions 116
  All-Star Games 117
  Records 119
  Award winners 123
  Team histories 127
Minor Leagues 159
  American Hockey League 160
  International Hockey League 176
  East Coast Hockey League 188
  Central Hockey League 201
  Colonial Hockey League 207
Major Junior Leagues 215
  Canadian Hockey League 216
  Ontario Hockey League 219
  Quebec Major Junior Hockey League 234
  Western Hockey League 243
College Hockey 257
  NCAA Division I 258
  Central Collegiate Hockey Association 260
  Eastern College Athletic Conference 264
  Hockey East 268
  Western Collegiate Hockey Association 271
  Independents 274
  Canadian Interuniversity Athletic Union 275
  Canadian colleges 276
Index of Teams 278
Hockey Register 279
  Players 282
  NHL head coaches 702

ON THE COVER: Buffalo Sabres right winger Alexander Mogilny tied for the NHL lead with 76 goals and finished with 127 points during the 1992-93 season. (Photo by Rick Stewart/Allsport USA)

Editorial assistance provided by Igor Kuperman of the Winnipeg Jets.

ISBN: 0-89204-470-5 (perfect-bound)   10 9 8 7 6 5 4 3 2 1
      0-89204-471-3 (comb-bound)

1993-94 NHL SEASON

GV
847.5
NHL directory   ·C66
Team information   1993/94
Schedule

NHL DIRECTORY

LEAGUE OFFICES

OFFICERS

Commissioner
Gary B. Bettman
Senior vice president
Stephen Solomon
Senior vice president/general counsel
Jeffrey Pash
Vice president, hockey operations
Jim Gregory
Vice president, broadcasting
Glenn Adamo
Vice president, television and team services
Ellis T. "Skip" Prince
Vice president, public relations
Arthur Pincus
Vice president, corporate communications
Bernadette Mansur

MONTREAL OFFICE

Address
1800 McGill College Avenue
Suite 2600
Montreal, Que., Canada H3A 3J6
Phone
514-288-9220
FAX
514-284-0300
Executive vice president
Brian F. O'Neill
Director of administration
Phil Scheuer
Assistant director of administration
Steve Hatzepetros

NEW YORK OFFICE

Address
650 Fifth Avenue
33rd Floor
New York, NY 10019
Phone
212-398-1100
FAX
212-245-8221
Director of broadcasting
Stu Hackel

TORONTO OFFICE

Address
75 International Blvd.
Suite 300
Rexdale, Ont. M9W 6L9
Phone
416-798-0809
FAX
416-798-0819
Vice president of hockey operations
Jim Gregory
Director of officiating
Bryan Lewis
Assistant director of officiating
Wally Harris
Director of central scouting
Frank Bonello
Executive director of communications
Gary Meagher
Director, editorial and information systems
Susan Elliott

Statistician/information officer
Benny Ercolani
Information officer
Greg Inglis

NHL ENTERPRISES, INC.

Address
1633 Broadway
40th Floor
New York, NY 10019
Phone
212-767-4600
FAX
212-767-4646
President, NHL Enterprises, Inc.
Steve Ryan
Senior vice president, general counsel
Richard Zahnd
General manager, publishing
Michael A. Berger

PROMOTIONAL LICENSING DIVISION

Vice president
Steve Flatow
Director, sponsor services
Sarah S. Galvin

RETAIL LICENSING DIVISION

Vice president
Fred Scalera

SPECIAL EVENTS

General manager
Frank Supovitz

BOARD OF GOVERNORS

Anaheim
Michael Eisner
Boston
Jeremy M. Jacobs
Buffalo
Seymour H. Knox III
Calgary
Harley N. Hotchkiss
Chicago
William W. Wirtz
Dallas
Norman N. Green
Detroit
Michael Ilitch

Edmonton
Peter Pocklington
Florida
Bill Torrey
Hartford
Richard H. Gordon
Los Angeles
Bruce McNall
Montreal
Ronald Corey
New Jersey
John J. McMullen
New York Islanders
Bob Rosenthal

New York Rangers
Stanley R. Jaffe
Ottawa
Bruce Firestone
Philadelphia
Jay T. Snider
Pittsburgh
Howard Baldwin
Quebec
Marcel Aubut
St. Louis
Michael F. Shanahan

San Jose
George Gund III
Tampa Bay
David LeFevre
Toronto
Steve A. Stavro
Vancouver
Arthur R. Griffiths
Washington
Abe Pollin
Winnipeg
Barry L. Shenkarow

DIVISIONAL ALIGNMENT

EASTERN CONFERENCE

ATLANTIC DIVISION
Florida Panthers
New Jersey Devils
New York Islanders
New York Rangers
Philadelphia Flyers
Tampa Bay Lightning
Washington Capitals

NORTHEAST DIVISION
Boston Bruins
Buffalo Sabres
Hartford Whalers
Montreal Canadiens
Ottawa Senators
Pittsburgh Penguins
Quebec Nordiques

WESTERN CONFERENCE

CENTRAL DIVISION
Chicago Blackhawks
Dallas Stars
Detroit Red Wings
St. Louis Blues
Toronto Maple Leafs
Winnipeg Jets

PACIFIC DIVISION
Mighty Ducks of Anaheim
Calgary Flames
Edmonton Oilers
Los Angeles Kings
San Jose Sharks
Vancouver Canucks

MIGHTY DUCKS OF ANAHEIM
WESTERN CONFERENCE/PACIFIC DIVISION

1993-94 SCHEDULE

Home games shaded.
* — At Madison Square Garden, New York.
† — At Phoenix.
△ — At Orlando, Fla.

OCTOBER

SUN	MON	TUE	WED	THU	FRI	SAT
					1	2
3	4	5	6	7	8 DET	9
10 NYI	11	12	13 EDM	14	15 BOS	16
17 CAL	18	19 NYR	20 NJ	21	22	23 MON
24	25 OTT	26	27	28 SJ	29 WAS	30
31 SJ						

NOVEMBER

SUN	MON	TUE	WED	THU	FRI	SAT
	1	2	3 DAL	4	5 NJ	6
7 PIT	8	9† DAL	10	11 CAL	12	13
14 VAN	15	16	17 TOR	18	19 VAN	20
21 EDM	22 CAL	23	24 WIN	25	26 SJ	27 SJ
28	29	30				

DECEMBER

SUN	MON	TUE	WED	THU	FRI	SAT
			1 WIN	2 LA	3	4
5 TB	6	7 FLA	8	9	10	11
12 STL	13	14 DET	15 TOR	16	17 DAL	18
19 CHI	20 WIN	21	22 DAL	23	24	25
26 LA	27	28 NYI	29	30 WAS	31	

JANUARY

SUN	MON	TUE	WED	THU	FRI	SAT
					1 FLA	
2△ TB	3	4	5	6 CHI	7	8 STL
9	10 DET	11	12 SJ	13	14 HAR	15
16 VAN	17	18 TOR	19 DET	20	21	22* ALL-STAR GAME
23	24 STL	25	26 WIN	27	28 NYR	29 LA
30	31					

FEBRUARY

SUN	MON	TUE	WED	THU	FRI	SAT
		1	2 CAL	3	4 VAN	5
6 CHI	7	8	9	10	11 LA	12
13 EDM	14	15	16 PHI	17	18 QUE	19
20 STL	21	22	23 BUF	24 PIT	25	26 QUE
27	28					

MARCH

SUN	MON	TUE	WED	THU	FRI	SAT
		1	2 MON	3	4 EDM	5
6 SJ	7	8† CHI	9 BUF	10	11 CHI	12
13 OTT	14	15	16 LA	17	18	19
20	21	22 DAL	23	24 BOS	25	26 HAR
27 PHI	28	29	30 LA	31 EDM		

APRIL

SUN	MON	TUE	WED	THU	FRI	SAT
					1	2 TOR
3	4	5	6 CAL	7	8 EDM	9 VAN
10	11 CAL	12	13 VAN	14	15	16

1993-94 SEASON

CLUB DIRECTORY

President
Tony Tavares
Vice president of finance/administration
Andy Roundtree
Vice president of sales and marketing
Ken Wilson
General manager
Jack Ferreira
Assistant general manager
Pierre Gauthier
Head coach
Ron Wilson
Assistant coaches
Tim Army
Al Sims
Director of hockey operations
Kevin Gilmore
Pro scout
Paul Fenton

Regional scouts
Al Godfrey
Richard Green
Equipment manager
To be announced
Director of sales and marketing
Bill Holford
Director of public relations
Bill Robertson
Controller
Marc Serrio
Manager of marketing services
Monica Spoelstra
Manager of admin./ticket box office
Jenny Price
Manager of premium ticketing services
Anne McNiff

DRAFT CHOICES

1—Paul Kariya	5-10/157	4	F	Univ. of Maine (H. East)
2—Nikolai Tsulygin	6-3/196	30	D	Salavat Yulayev Ufa, CIS
3—Valeri Karpov	5-10/176	56	F	Chelyabinsk, CIS
4—Joel Gagnon	6-0/194	82	G	Oshawa (OHL)
5—Mikhail Shtalenkov	6-2/180	108	G	Milwaukee (IHL)
6—Antti Aalto	6-2/185	134	C	TPS Turku, Finland
7—Matt Peterson	6-2/190	160	D	OSSEO (Minn.) H.S.
8—Tom Askey	6-2/185	186	G	Ohio State Univ. (CCHA)
9—Vitaly Kozel	6-3/187	212	C	Novops, Europe
10—Anatoli Fedotov	178	238	D	Moncton (AHL)
11—David Penney	6-1/175	264	F	Worcester Academy

MISCELLANEOUS DATA

Home ice (capacity)
Anaheim Arena—The Pond
(17,250)
Address
1739 South Douglass
Anaheim, CA 92806
Business phone
714-502-3880

Rink dimensions
200 feet by 85 feet
Club colors
Burgandy, teal, silver and white
Minor league affiliations
TBA

TRAINING CAMP ROSTER

No. FORWARDS	Ht./Wt.	BORN Place	Date	NHL exp.	1992-93 clubs
Antti Aalto (C)	6-2/185	Lappeenranta, Finland	4-8-75	0	SaiPa (Fin.), TPS Jr. (Fin.), TPS Turku (Fin.)
Robin Bawa (RW)	6-2/215	Chemainus, B.C.	3-26-66	3	Hamilton (AHL), Kansas City (IHL), San Jose
Bob Corkum (C/RW)	6-2/212	Salisbury, Mass.	12-18-67	3	Buffalo
Peter Douris (RW)	6-1/195	Toronto	2-19-66	7	Providence (AHL), Boston
Stu Grimson (LW)	6-5/227	Kamloops, B.C.	5-20-65	5	Chicago
Trevor Halverson (LW).	6-1/195	White River, Ont.	4-6-71	0	Baltimore (AHL), Hampton Roads (ECHL)
Paul Kariya (LW)	5-11/157	Vancouver, B.C.	10-16-74	0	U. of Maine (H. East)
Valeri Karpov (LW/RW)..	5-10/176	Chelyabinsk, U.S.S.R.	8-5-71	0	CSKA Moscow (CIS), Traktor Chelyabinsk (CIS)
Steven King (RW)	6-0/195	East Greenwich, R.I.	7-22-69	1	Binghamton (AHL), N.Y. Rangers
Lonnie Loach (LW)	5-10/181	New Liskeard, Ont.	4-14-68	1	Ottawa, Los Angeles, Phoenix (IHL)
Troy Loney (LW)	6-3/209	Bow Island, Alta.	9-21-63	10	Pittsburgh
Joe Sacco (LW)	6-1/195	Medford, Mass.	2-4-69	3	Toronto, St. John's (AHL)
Anatoli Semenov (C/LW)	6-2/190	Moscow, U.S.S.R.	3-5-62	4	Tampa Bay, Vancouver
Jarrod Skalde (C)	6-0/170	Niagara Falls, Ont.	2-26-71	3	Cincinnati (IHL), Utica (AHL), New Jersey
Tim Sweeney (C)	5-11/185	Boston	4-12-67	3	Providence (AHL), Boston
Jim Thomson (RW)	6-1/205	Edmonton, Alta.	12-30-65	6	Ottawa, Los Angeles, Phoenix (IHL)
Shaun Van Allen (C)	6-1/200	Shaunavon, Sask.	8-29-67	2	Cape Breton (AHL), Edmonton
Terry Yake (C).............	5-11/175	New Westminister, B.C.	10-22-68	5	Springfield (AHL), Hartford
DEFENSEMEN					
Bobby Dollas................	6-2/212	Montreal	1-31-65	8	Adirondack (AHL), Detroit
Anatoli Fedotov	5-11/178	Saratov, U.S.S.R.	5-11-66	1	Moncton (AHL), Winnipeg
Mark Ferner	6-0/193	Regina, Sask.	9-5-65	4	New Haven (AHL), San Diego (IHL)
Sean Hill	6-0/195	Duluth, Minn.	2-14-70	3	Montreal, Fredericton (AHL)
Bill Houlder	6-3/218	Thunder Bay, Ont.	3-11-67	6	San Diego (IHL), Buffalo
Alexei Kasatonov	6-1/215	Leningrad, U.S.S.R.	10-14-59	4	New Jersey
Randy Ladouceur..........	6-2/220	Brockville, Ont.	6-30-60	11	Hartford
Myles O'Connor	5-11/165	Calgary, Alta.	4-2-67	3	Utica (AHL), New Jersey
Nikolai Tsulygan	6-3/196	Ufa, U.S.S.R.	5-29-75	0	Salavat (CIS)
David Williams	6-2/195	Plainfield, N.J.	8-25-67	2	Kansas City (IHL), San Jose
GOALTENDERS					
Joel Gagnon	6-0/194	Hearst, Ont.	3-14-75	0	Oshawa (OHL)
Guy Hebert...................	5-11/180	Troy, N.Y.	1-7-67	2	St. Louis
Mikhail Shtalenkov.......	6-2/180	Moscow	10-20-65	0	Milwaukee (IHL)
Ron Tugnutt	5-11/155	Scarborough, Ont.	10-22-67	6	Edmonton

LEADING SCORERS ON FIRST-YEAR EXPANSION TEAMS

Team	Season	Team points leader	G.	A.	Pts.	NHL points leader
Pittsburgh Penguins	1967-68	Andy Bathgate	30	29	59	Stan Mikita, Chicago—87
Los Angeles Kings.........	1967-68	Ed Joyal	23	34	57	Stan Mikita, Chicago—87
Minnesota North Stars◆	1967-68	Wayne Connelly	35	21	56	Stan Mikita, Chicago—87
St. Louis Blues..............	1967-68	Red Berenson*	22	29	51	Stan Mikita, Chicago—87
Philadelphia Flyers.........	1967-68	Lou Angotti	12	37	49	Stan Mikita, Chicago—87
Oakland Seals†..............	1967-68	Gerry Ehman‡	20	25	45	Stan Mikita, Chicago—87
Buffalo Sabres..............	1970-71	Gilbert Perreault	38	34	72	Phil Esposito, Boston—152
Vancouver Canucks.......	1970-71	Andre Boudrias	25	41	66	Phil Esposito, Boston—152
Atlanta Flames§.............	1972-73	Bob Leiter	26	34	60	Phil Esposito, Boston—130
New York Islanders	1972-73	Billy Harris	28	22	50	Phil Esposito, Boston—130
Kansas City Scouts ★	1974-75	Simon Nolet	26	32	58	Bobby Orr, Boston—135
Washington Capitals.......	1974-75	Tommy Williams	22	36	58	Bobby Orr, Boston—135
Edmonton Oilers●	1979-80	Wayne Gretzky	51	■86	x137	Wayne Gretzky & Marcel Dionne, L.A.—137
Hartford Whalers●	1979-80	Mike Rogers	44	61	105	Wayne Gretzky & Marcel Dionne, L.A.—137
Quebec Nordiques●	1979-80	Real Cloutier	42	46	88	Wayne Gretzky & Marcel Dionne, L.A.—137
Winnipeg Jets●	1979-80	Morris Lukowich	35	39	74	Wayne Gretzky & Marcel Dionne, L.A.—137
San Jose Sharks............	1991-92	Pat Falloon	25	34	59	Mario Lemieux, Pittsburgh—131
Tampa Bay Lightning.....	1992-93	Brian Bradley	42	44	86	Mario Lemieux, Pittsburgh—160
Ottawa Senators............	1992-93	Norm Maciver	17	46	63	Mario Lemieux, Pittsburgh—160

*Berenson started season with N.Y. Rangers, gaining three points for a two-team total of 54.
†Became Cleveland Barons after 1975-76 season; Barons merged with Minnesota North Stars after 1977-78 season.
‡Ted Hampson collected 27 points for Detroit and 27 for Oakland for a two-team total of 54.
§Became Calgary Flames after 1979-80 season.
★Became Colorado Rockies after 1975-76 season; became New Jersey Devils after 1981-82 season.
●Entered NHL during a merger with the World Hockey Association.
◆Became Dallas Stars after 1992-93 season.
■Led league.
xTied for league lead.

BOSTON BRUINS
EASTERN CONFERENCE/NORTHEAST DIVISION

1993-94 SCHEDULE

Home games shaded.
* — At Madison Square Garden, New York.
† — At Minneapolis.
Δ — At Cleveland.

OCTOBER

SUN	MON	TUE	WED	THU	FRI	SAT
					1	2
3	4	5 NYR	6	7 BUF	8	9 QUE
10	11 MON	12	13	14	15 ANA	16 SJ
17	18	19 VAN	20	21	22 EDM	23 CAL
24	25	26	27	28 OTT	29	30 STL
31						

NOVEMBER

SUN	MON	TUE	WED	THU	FRI	SAT
	1	2 DET	3	4 CAL	5	6 TB
7 BUF	8	9	10	11 EDM	12	13 NYI
14	15	16	17 HAR	18 SJ	19	20 PHI
21	22	23	24 PIT	25	26 FLA	27 TOR
28	29	30 QUE				

DECEMBER

SUN	MON	TUE	WED	THU	FRI	SAT
			1	2 NYI	3	4 MON
5 BUF	6	7	8	9 VAN	10	11 CHI
12 HAR	13	14	15	16	17	18 TB
19 FLA	20	21	22	23 PIT	24	25
26	27 OTT	28	29	30	31† PHI	

JANUARY

SUN	MON	TUE	WED	THU	FRI	SAT
						1
2 WAS	3	4	5	6 WIN	7	8 FLA
9	10 TOR	11 PIT	12	13 PHI	14	15 DET
16	17 HAR	18	19 MON	20	21	22° ALL-STAR GAME
23	24 HAR	25 WAS	26	27	28 NYI	29 NYI
30	31 QUE					

FEBRUARY

SUN	MON	TUE	WED	THU	FRI	SAT
		1	2	3 NYR	4	5 PHI
6 FLA	7	8 QUE	9	10 BUF	11	12 NJ
13	14 LA	15	16 DAL	17	18 STL	19
20 TB	21	22	23 NYR	24	25 WIN	26
27 CHI	28					

MARCH

SUN	MON	TUE	WED	THU	FRI	SAT
		1	2	3 LA	4	5 OTT
6	7 WAS	8 PIT	9	10 NYR	11	12 NJ
13	14 MON	15	16	17 PIT	18	19 NJ
20	21	22 QUE	23	24 ANA	25	26 MON
27 WAS	28	29	30	31 DAL		

APRIL

SUN	MON	TUE	WED	THU	FRI	SAT
					1 BUF	2
3Δ PIT	4	5	6	7 OTT	8	9 TB
10 PHI	11	12	13 OTT	14 HAR	15	16

1993-94 SEASON

CLUB DIRECTORY

Owner and governor
Jeremy M. Jacobs
Alternative governor
Louis Jacobs
Alternate governor, president and G.M.
Harry Sinden
Vice president
Tom Johnson
Assistant general manager
Mike Milbury
Assistant to the president
Nate Greenberg
Director of administration
Dale Hamilton
Coach
Brian Sutter
Assistant coach
Tom McVie
Coord. of minor league player personnel/scouting
Bob Tindall

Director of player evaluation
Bart Bradley
Scouting staff
Jim Morrison
Andre Lachapelle
Joe Lyons
Don Saatzer
Lars Waldner
Marcel Pelletier
Jean Ratelle
Harvey Keck
Sven-Ake Svensson
Controller
Bob Vogel
Trainer
Jim Narrigan
Athletic therapist
Scott Waugh
Equipment manager
Ken Fleger
Director of media relations
Heidi Holland

DRAFT CHOICES

1—Kevyn Adams	6-1/182	25	C	Miami of Ohio (CCHA)
2—Matt Alvey	6-5/195	51	F	Springfield Olym. (NEJHL)
4—Charles Paquette	6-1/193	88	D	Sherbrooke (QMJHL)
4—Shawn Bates	5-11/160	103	C	Medford
5—Andrei Sapozhnikov	6-1/185	129	D	Chelyabinsk, CIS
6—Milt Mastad	6-3/205	155	D	Seattle (WHL)
7—Ryan Golden	6-3/197	181	C	Reading
8—Hal Gill	6-6/200	207	D	Nashoba
9—Joel Prpic	6-6/200	233	C	Waterloo, Ont. (Jr. B)
10—Joakim Persson		259	G	Hammarby, Europe

MISCELLANEOUS DATA

Home ice (capacity)
Boston Garden (14,448)
Address
150 Causeway Street
Boston, MA 02114
Business phone
617-227-3206

Rink dimensions
191 feet by 83 feet
Club colors
Gold, black and white
Minor league affiliations
Providence (AHL)
Charlotte (IHL)

TRAINING CAMP ROSTER

No.	FORWARDS	Ht./Wt.	Place	BORN Date	NHL exp.	1992-93 clubs
21	Ted Donato (C)	5-10/170	Dedham, Mass.	4-28-68	2	Boston
23	Steve Heinze (RW)	5-11/180	Lawrence, Mass.	1-30-70	2	Boston
42	Brent Hughes (LW)	5-11/180	New Westminster, B.C.	4-5-66	4	Boston
49	Joe Juneau (C)	6-0/175	Pont-Rouge, Que.	1-5-68	2	Boston
10	Dmitri Kvartalnov (LW)	5-11/180	Voskresensk, U.S.S.R.	3-25-66	1	Khimik Voskresensk (CIS), Boston
	James Lavish (RW)	5-11/175	Albany, N.Y.	10-13-70	0	Yale University (ECAC)
27	Steve Leach (RW)	5-11/200	Cambridge, Mass.	1-16-66	8	Boston
	Daniel Marois (RW)	6-0/190	Montreal	10-3-68	6	N.Y. Islanders, Capital District (AHL)
45	Andrew McKim (C)	5-7/170	St. Johns, N.B.	7-6-70	1	Providence (AHL), Boston
44	Glen Murray (RW)	6-2/200	Halifax, N.S.	11-1-72	2	Providence (AHL), Boston
8	Cam Neely (RW)	6-1/210	Comox, B.C.	6-6-65	10	Boston
12	Adam Oates (C)	5-11/190	Weston, Ont.	8-27-62	8	Boston
13	Grigor Panteleyev (LW)	5-9/194	Riga, U.S.S.R.	11-13-72	1	Providence (AHL), Boston
17	David Reid (LW)	6-1/205	Toronto	5-15-64	10	Boston
20	Bryan Smolinski (C)	6-0/185	Toledo, O.	12-27-71	1	Michigan St. (CCHA), Boston
22	Jozef Stumpel (RW)	6-1/190	Nitra, Czech.	6-20-72	2	Providence (AHL), Boston
18	C.J. Young (RW)	5-10/180	Waban, Mass.	1-1-68	1	Calgary, Boston, Providence (AHL)
11	Sergei Zholtok (LW)	6-0/185	Riga, U.S.S.R.	12-2-72	1	Providence (AHL), Boston
	DEFENSEMEN					
77	Ray Bourque	5-11/210	Montreal	12-28-60	14	Boston
43	Denis Chervyakov	6-0/185	St. Petersburg, U.S.S.R.	4-20-70	1	Boston, Providence (AHL), Atlanta (IHL)
6	Glen Featherstone	6-4/215	Toronto	7-8-68	5	Providence (AHL), Boston
14	Gord Roberts	6-1/195	Detroit	10-2-57	14	Boston
	Jon Rohloff	6-0/200	Mankato, Minn.	10-3-69	0	Minn.-Duluth (WCHA)
	Andrei Sapozhnikov	6-1/185	Chelyabinsk, U.S.S.R.	6-15-71	0	Traktor Chelyabinsk (CIS)
	Kurt Seher	6-2/170	Lethbridge, Alta.	4-15-73	0	Seattle (WHL), Providence (AHL)
34	David Shaw	6-2/204	St. Thomas, Ont.	5-25-64	11	Boston
32	Don Sweeney	5-11/170	St. Stephen, N.B.	8-17-66	5	Boston
	Mikhail Tatarinov	5-10/194	Penza, U.S.S.R.	7-16-66	3	Quebec
26	Glen Wesley	6-1/195	Red Deer, Alta.	10-2-68	6	Boston
36	Jim Wiemer	6-4/210	Sudbury, Ont.	1-9-61	10	Boston, Providence (AHL)
	GOALTENDERS					
	Scott Bailey	5-11/185	Calgary, Alta.	5-2-72	0	Johnstown (ECHL)
30	Mike Bales	6-1/180	Saskatoon, Sask.	8-6-71	1	Providence (AHL), Boston
39	John Blue	5-10/185	Huntington Beach, Calif.	2-9-66	1	Providence (AHL), Boston
	Jon Casey	5-10/155	Grand Rapids, Minn.	8-29-62	8	Minnesota
	Joakim Persson	5-11/168	Stockholm, Sweden	5-4-70	0	Hemmarby Stockholm (Sweden)

1992-93 REVIEW

INDIVIDUAL STATISTICS

SCORING

	Games	G	A	Pts.	Pen.	+/-	PPG	SHG	Shots	Shooting Pct.
Adam Oates	84	45	†97	142	32	15	24	1	254	17.7
Joe Juneau	84	32	70	102	33	23	9	0	229	14.0
Ray Bourque	78	19	63	82	40	38	8	0	330	5.8
Dmitri Kvartalnov	73	30	42	72	16	9	11	0	226	13.3
Stephen Leach	79	26	25	51	126	-6	9	0	256	10.2
Dave Poulin	84	16	33	49	62	29	0	5	112	14.3
Vladimir Ruzicka	60	19	22	41	38	-6	7	0	146	13.0
Dave Reid	65	20	16	36	10	12	1	5	116	17.2
Ted Donato	82	15	20	35	61	2	3	2	118	12.7
Don Sweeney	84	7	27	34	68	34	0	1	107	6.5
Glen Wesley	64	8	25	33	47	-2	4	1	183	4.4
Stephen Heinze	73	18	13	31	24	20	0	2	146	12.3
David Shaw	77	10	14	24	108	10	1	1	122	8.2
Cam Neely	13	11	7	18	25	4	6	0	45	24.4
Gord Murphy	49	5	12	17	62	-13	3	0	68	7.4
Gordie Roberts	65	5	12	17	105	23	0	0	40	12.5
Gregori Pantaleyev	39	8	6	14	12	-6	2	0	45	17.8
Darin Kimble	55	7	3	10	177	4	0	0	20	35.0
Glen Featherstone	34	5	5	10	102	6	1	0	33	15.2
Brent Hughes	62	5	4	9	191	-4	0	0	54	9.3
C.J. Young*	15	4	5	9	12	1	0	0	22	18.2
Peter Douris	19	4	4	8	4	5	0	1	33	12.1
Tim Sweeney	14	1	7	8	6	1	0	0	15	6.7
Glen Murray	27	3	4	7	8	-6	2	0	28	10.7

	Games	G	A	Pts.	Pen.	+/-	PPG	SHG	Shots	Shooting Pct.
Jim Wiemer	28	1	6	7	48	1	0	0	39	2.6
Stephane J.G. Richer*	21	1	4	5	18	-6	0	0	22	4.5
Brent Ashton*	26	2	2	4	11	0	0	0	26	7.7
Andrew McKim	7	1	3	4	0	2	0	0	12	8.3
Bryan Smolinski	9	1	3	4	0	3	0	0	10	10.0
Jozef Stumpel	13	1	3	4	4	-3	0	0	8	12.5
Darren Banks	16	2	1	3	64	5	0	0	15	13.3
John Blue (goalie)	23	0	2	2	6	0	0	0	0	0.0
Sergei Zholtok	1	0	1	1	0	1	0	0	2	0.0
Chris Winnes	5	0	1	1	0	1	0	0	2	0.0
Andy Moog (goalie)	55	0	1	1	14	0	0	0	0	0.0
Mike Bales (goalie)	1	0	0	0	0	0	0	0	0	0.0
Denis Cheryakov	2	0	0	0	2	-1	0	0	2	0.0
Bill Huard	2	0	0	0	0	0	0	0	0	0.0
Dominic Lavoie*	2	0	0	0	2	-1	0	0	7	0.0
Rejean Lemelin (goalie)	10	0	0	0	4	0	0	0	0	0.0

GOALTENDING

	Games	Min.	Goals	SO	Avg.	W	L	T	Shots	Sv. Pct.
Mike Bales	1	25	1	0	2.40	0	0	0	10	.900
John Blue	23	1322	64	1	2.90	9	8	4	597	.893
Andy Moog	55	3194	168	3	3.16	37	14	3	1357	.876
Rejean Lemelin	10	542	31	0	3.43	5	4	0	225	.862

Empty-net goals (do not count against a goaltender's average): Bales 1, Blue 1, Lemelin 1, Moog 1.
*Played with two or more NHL teams.
†Led league.

RESULTS

OCTOBER

8—Hartford	W	*3-2
10—N.Y. Islanders	T	*3-3
12—Ottawa	W	6-3
15—At San Jose	W	8-2
17—At Los Angeles	L	6-8
22—At Calgary	W	4-2
23—At Edmonton	W	6-3
25—At Vancouver	W	5-3
29—Los Angeles	W	8-3
31—Chicago	L	2-3

NOVEMBER

5—Quebec	W	6-4
7—N.Y. Rangers	T	*2-2
11—At Buffalo	L	2-7
12—Calgary	W	5-3
14—Toronto	L	1-4
16—At Montreal	L	3-6
19—N.Y. Islanders	W	5-2
21—Philadelphia	W	4-3
23—At Ottawa	W	3-2
25—At Washington	L	2-6
27—Hartford	W	*5-4
28—At Hartford	L	*3-4
30—At Quebec	W	4-3

DECEMBER

3—Montreal	W	4-3
5—At New Jersey	W	4-2
6—At Philadelphia	W	7-1
9—At Buffalo	L	2-5
10—Ottawa	W	4-2

12—At Montreal	L	1-5
15—Buffalo	L	2-3
18—At Detroit	L	1-6
19—Washington	W	4-3
22—Tampa Bay	W	5-3
26—At Hartford	W	9-4
27—At N.Y. Rangers	L	5-6
29—At Winnipeg	L	4-5
31—At Minnesota	L	3-5

JANUARY

2—Hartford	W	*3-2
5—At Pittsburgh	L	2-6
7—Quebec	L	*2-3
9—New Jersey	L	2-6
12—Buffalo	W	5-2
14—Pittsburgh	W	7-0
16—Philadelphia	L	4-5
18—San Jose	W	4-3
19—At N.Y. Islanders	T	*2-2
21—At Philadelphia	W	5-4
23—New Jersey	W	7-5
25—At Montreal	L	*2-3
26—At Quebec	T	*4-4
28—Winnipeg	W	6-2
30—At N.Y. Islanders	W	6-5

FEBRUARY

2—Edmonton	L	3-4
3—At Quebec	W	4-1
8—Pittsburgh†	L	0-4
9—At St. Louis	W	6-1
11—At Chicago	L	3-6
14—At Tampa Bay	T	*3-3

17—At Montreal	W	5-2
20—At Toronto	T	*4-4
25—Minnesota	T	*3-3
27—Washington	W	*5-4

MARCH

1—Montreal	L	2-5
4—Vancouver	W	4-3
6—St. Louis	W	*4-3
9—At Pittsburgh	L	2-3
11—Montreal	W	5-2
13—Ottawa	W	6-3
15—At N.Y. Rangers	W	3-1
16—New Jersey‡	W	3-1
18—At Ottawa	W	4-1
20—Detroit	L	4-7
22—Hartford	W	5-4
24—At Buffalo	W	2-0
25—Montreal	W	2-0
27—Pittsburgh	L	3-5
30—At Hartford	W	3-1

APRIL

3—Buffalo	W	3-2
4—At Buffalo	W	3-0
6—At Quebec	W	7-1
8—Quebec	W	6-2
10—At Montreal	W	5-1
11—Ottawa	W	4-2
14—At Ottawa	W	4-2

*Denotes overtime game.
†At Atlanta.
‡At Providence, R.I.

BUFFALO SABRES
EASTERN CONFERENCE/NORTHEAST DIVISION

1993-94 SCHEDULE

Home games shaded.
* — At Madison Square Garden, New York.
† — At Sacramento, Calif.
△ — At Orlando, Fla.
+ — At Minneapolis.

OCTOBER

SUN	MON	TUE	WED	THU	FRI	SAT
					1	2
3	4	5	6	7	8 BOS	9 MON
10 HAR	11	12 PHI	13	14	15 NYR	16 WAS
17	18 DET	19	20	21	22 PIT	23 HAR
24	25	26	27 CAL	28	29 EDM	30 VAN
31						

NOVEMBER

SUN	MON	TUE	WED	THU	FRI	SAT
	1	2	3† PIT	4	5	6
7 BOS	8	9	10 PHI	11	12	13 PHI
14	15	16	17 NJ	18	19 WIN	20
21 SJ	22 OTT	23	24 NJ	25	26 OTT	27 QUE
28	29 TOR	30				

DECEMBER

SUN	MON	TUE	WED	THU	FRI	SAT
			1 TB	2 FLA	3	4
5 BOS	6	7	8 OTT	9	10 CAL	11 HAR
12	13 NYR	14	15	16 PIT	17 LA	18
19 TB	20	21	22	23 MON	24	25
26 NYI	27 PHI	28	29	30	31 NYR	

JANUARY

SUN	MON	TUE	WED	THU	FRI	SAT
						1
2 TOR	3	4	5	6	7 PIT	8
9 VAN	10	11 CHI	12 WIN	13	14	15 STL
16 DAL	17	18	19 EDM	20	21	22° ALL-STAR GAME
23	24‡ TB	25	26	27 WAS	28	29 MON
30 FLA	31					

FEBRUARY

SUN	MON	TUE	WED	THU	FRI	SAT
		1	2 NJ	3	4 FLA	5
6 NYI	7	8 NYI	9	10 BOS	11 MON	12
13 DAL	14	15	16 HAR	17	18 FLA	19
20 WAS	21 QUE	22	23 ANA	24	25 CHI	26 PIT
27	28					

MARCH

SUN	MON	TUE	WED	THU	FRI	SAT
		1 QUE	2 OTT	3	4 PIT	5
6 DET	7	8 SJ	9 ANA	10	11	12 LA
13	14	15	16	17 NJ	18+ NYI	19
20 OTT	21	22	23 STL	24	25 HAR	26
27 NYI	28	29	30 TB	31		

APRIL

SUN	MON	TUE	WED	THU	FRI	SAT
					1 BOS	2 QUE
3	4	5	6	7	8 MON	9
10 QUE	11	12 NYR	13	14 WAS	15	16

1993-94 SEASON

CLUB DIRECTORY

Chairman of the board and president
Seymour H. Knox III
Vice chairman of the board and counsel
Robert O. Swados
Vice chairman of the board
Robert E. Rich Jr.
Treasurer
Joseph T. J. Stewart
Assistant to the president
Seymour H. Knox IV
Senior vice president, administration
Mitchell Owen
Senior vice president, finance
Robert W. Pickel
Exec. V.P. for sports operations
Gerry Meehan
General manager and coach
John Muckler
Assistant coaches
John Tortorella
Don Lever
Assistant to the general manager
Craig Ramsay
Director of player personnel
Don Luce

Director of scouting
Rudy Migay
Pro scout
Joe Crozier
Scouting staff
Don Barrie
Jack Bowman
Larry Carriere
Boris Janicek
Dennis McIvor
Paul Merritt
Mike Racicot
Frank Zywiec
Director of communications
Paul Wieland
Director of public relations
Steve Rossi
Public relations assistant
Bruce Wawrzyniak
Head athletic trainer
Jim Pizzutelli
Trainer
Rip Simonick
Equipment supervisor
John Allaway

DRAFT CHOICES

2—Denis Tsygurov	6-3/198	38	D	Lada Togliatti, CIS	
3—Ethan Philpott	6-4/230	64	F	Phillips And. Acad. (Mass.)	
5—Richard Safarik	6-3/194	116	F	Nitra, Czech.	
6—Kevin Pozzo	6-1/176	142	D	Moose Jaw (WHL)	
7—Sergei Petrenko	5-11/167	168	F	Dynamo Minsk, CIS	
8—Mike Barrie	6-1/170	194	C	Victoria (WHL)	
9—Barrie Moore	5-11/175	220	F	Sudbury (OHL)	
10—Chris Davis	6-3/177	246	G	Calgary Royals (Tier II)	
11—Scott Nichol	5-8/160	272	C	Portland (WHL)	

MISCELLANEOUS DATA

Home ice (capacity)
Memorial Auditorium
(16,284, including standees)
Address
Memorial Auditorium
140 Main St.
Buffalo, NY 14202
Business phone
716-856-7300 or 800-333-7825

Rink dimensions
193 feet by 84 feet
Club colors
Blue, white and gold
Minor league affiliations
Erie (ECHL)
Rochester (AHL)

TRAINING CAMP ROSTER

FORWARDS

No.	FORWARDS	Ht./Wt.	Place	BORN Date	NHL exp.	1992-93 clubs
28	Donald Audette (RW)	5-8/175	Laval, Que.	9-23-69	4	Buffalo, Rochester (AHL)
36	Matthew Barnaby (LW) ..	6-0/170	Ottawa	5-4-73	1	Victoriaville (QMJHL), Buffalo
	Jozef Cierny (LW)	6-2/176	Zvolen, Czech.	5-13-74	0	Rochester (AHL)
	Jason Dawe (LW)	5-10/195	North York, Ont.	5-29-73	0	Peterborough (OHL)
34	Gord Donnelly (D/RW) .	6-1/202	Montreal	4-5-62	10	Buffalo
12	Bob Errey (LW)	5-10/183	Montreal	9-21-64	10	Pittsburgh, Buffalo
9	Viktor Gordiouk (RW) ...	5-10/176	Moscow, U.S.S.R.	4-11-70	1	Buffalo, Rochester (AHL)
14	Dave Hannan (C)..........	5-10/185	Sudbury, Ont.	11-26-61	12	Buffalo
10	Dale Hawerchuk (C)......	5-11/190	Toronto	4-4-63	12	Buffalo
13	Yuri Khmylev (LW)	6-1/189	Moscow, U.S.S.R.	8-9-64	1	Buffalo
16	Pat LaFontaine (C)	5-10/177	St. Louis	2-22-65	10	Buffalo
44	Doug MacDonald (LW) .	6-0/192	Point Moody, B.C.	2-8-69	1	Rochester (AHL), Buffalo
27	Brad May (LW)	6-0/200	Toronto	11-29-71	2	Buffalo
89	Alexander Mogilny (RW) .	5-11/187	Khabarovsk, U.S.S.R.	2-18-69	4	Buffalo
17	Colin Patterson (RW/C)..	6-2/195	Rexdale, Ont.	5-11-60	10	Buffalo
18	Wayne Presley (RW).....	5-11/180	Dearborn, Mich.	3-23-65	9	Buffalo
32	Rob Ray (LW)	6-0/203	Stirling, Ont.	6-8-68	4	Buffalo
	Todd Simon (C)	5-10/188	Toronto	4-21-72	0	Niagara Falls (OHL)
20	Bob Sweeney (C/RW)....	6-3/200	Boxborough, Mass.	1-25-64	7	Buffalo
21	Scott Thomas (RW)	6-2/195	Buffalo, N.Y.	1-18-70	1	Rochester (AHL), Buffalo
19	Randy Wood (LW/RW).	6-0/195	Princeton, NJ.	10-12-63	7	Buffalo

DEFENSEMEN

No.	DEFENSEMEN	Ht./Wt.	Place	BORN Date	NHL exp.	1992-93 clubs
	Mark Astley	5-11/185	Calgary, Alta.	3-30-69	0	Lugano (Switzerland)
8	Doug Bodger.................	6-2/213	Chemainus, B.C.	6-18-66	9	Buffalo
4	Philippe Boucher	6-2/189	St. Apollnaire, Que.	3-24-73	1	Laval (QMJHL), Rochester (AHL), Buffalo
6	Keith Carney	6-2/205	Pawtucket, R.I.	2-3-70	2	Buffalo, Rochester (AHL)
	David Cooper	6-1/190	Ottawa	11-2-73	0	Medicine Hat (WHL)
3	Grant Ledyard	6-2/195	Winnipeg, Man.	11-19-61	9	Buffalo, Rochester (AHL)
	Dean Melanson..............	6-0/213	Antigonish, N.S.	11-19-73	0	St. Hyacinthe (QMJHL), Rochester (AHL)
24	Randy Moller	6-2/207	Red Deer, Alta.	8-23-63	12	Buffalo, Rochester (AHL)
42	Richard Smehlik	6-3/208	Ostrava, Czech.	1-23-70	1	Buffalo
41	Ken Sutton	6-0/198	Edmonton, Alta.	5-11-69	3	Buffalo
7	Petr Svoboda	6-1/175	Most, Czech.	2-14-66	9	Buffalo
	Denis Tsygurov	6-3/198	Chelyabinsk, U.S.S.R.	2-26-71	0	Lada Togliatti (CIS)

GOALTENDERS

No.	GOALTENDERS	Ht./Wt.	Place	BORN Date	NHL exp.	1992-93 clubs
35	Tom Draper..................	5-11/185	Outremont, Que.	11-20-66	4	Buffalo, Rochester (AHL)
31	Grant Fuhr..................	5-9/190	Spruce Grove, Alta.	9-28-62	12	Toronto, Buffalo
39	Dominik Hasek	5-11/168	Pardubice, Czech.	1-29-65	3	Buffalo
	Markus Ketterer	5-11/169	Helsinki, Finland	8-23-67	0	Jokerit (Finland)
	Bill Pye......................	5-9/170	Royal Oak, Mich.	4-4-69	0	Rochester (AHL)

1992-93 REVIEW

INDIVIDUAL STATISTICS

SCORING

	Games	G	A	Pts.	Pen.	+/-	PPG	SHG	Shots	Shooting Pct.
Pat LaFontaine	84	53	95	148	63	11	20	2	306	17.3
Alexander Mogilny	77	‡76	51	127	40	7	27	0	360	21.1
Dale Hawerchuk	81	16	80	96	52	-17	8	0	259	6.2
Dave Andreychuk*	52	29	32	61	48	-8	20	0	171	17.0
Doug Bodger	81	9	45	54	87	14	6	0	154	5.8
Bob Sweeney	80	21	26	47	118	2	4	3	120	17.5
Randy Wood	82	18	25	43	77	6	3	3	176	10.2
Yuri Khmylev	68	20	19	39	28	6	0	3	122	16.4
Wayne Presley	79	15	17	32	96	5	0	1	97	15.5
Richard Smehlik	80	4	27	31	59	9	0	0	82	4.9
Brad May	82	13	13	26	242	3	0	0	114	11.4
Petr Svoboda	40	2	24	26	59	3	1	0	61	3.3
Ken Sutton	63	8	14	22	30	-3	1	0	77	10.4
Dave Hannan	55	5	15	20	43	8	0	0	43	11.6
Donald Audette	44	12	7	19	51	-8	2	0	92	13.0
Grant Ledyard	50	2	14	16	45	-2	1	0	79	2.5
Gord Donnelly	60	3	8	11	221	5	0	0	38	7.9
Bob Corkum	68	6	4	10	38	-3	0	1	69	8.7
Mike Ramsey*	33	2	8	10	20	4	0	0	27	7.4
Viktor Gordijuk	16	3	6	9	0	4	0	0	24	12.5

	Games	G	A	Pts.	Pen.	+/-	PPG	SHG	Shots	Shooting Pct.
Randy Moller	35	2	7	9	83	6	0	0	25	8.0
Bill Houlder	15	3	5	8	6	5	0	0	29	10.3
Colin Patterson	36	4	2	6	22	-2	0	1	30	13.3
Keith Carney	30	2	4	6	55	3	0	0	26	7.7
Rob Ray	68	3	2	5	211	-3	1	0	28	10.7
Bob Errey*	8	1	3	4	4	2	0	0	9	11.1
Philippe Boucher	18	0	4	4	14	1	0	0	28	0.0
Scott Thomas	7	1	1	2	15	2	0	0	4	25.0
Matthew Barnaby	2	1	0	1	10	0	1	0	8	12.5
Doug MacDonald	5	1	0	1	2	0	0	0	1	100.0
Greg Brown	10	0	1	1	6	-5	0	0	10	0.0
Tom Draper (goalie)	11	0	1	1	2	0	0	0	0	0.0
Daren Puppa (goalie)*	24	0	1	1	0	0	0	0	0	0.0
Pete Ciavaglia	3	0	0	0	0	0	0	0	2	0.0
Dominik Hasek (goalie)	28	0	0	0	0	0	0	0	0	0.0
Grant Fuhr (goalie)*	29	0	0	0	10	0	0	0	0	0.0

GOALTENDING

	Games	Min.	Goals	SO	Avg.	W	L	T	Shots	Sv. Pct.
Dominik Hasek	28	1429	75	0	3.15	11	10	4	720	.896
Grant Fuhr*	29	1694	98	0	3.47	11	15	2	903	.891
Daren Puppa*	24	1306	78	0	3.58	11	5	4	706	.890
Tom Draper	11	664	41	0	3.70	5	6	0	344	.881

Empty-net goals (do not count against a goaltender's average): Fuhr 3, Draper 1, Hasek 1.
*Played with two or more NHL teams.
‡Tied for league lead.

RESULTS

OCTOBER

8—Quebec	L	4-5
10—At Hartford	W	5-2
11—Montreal	W	8-2
13—At Pittsburgh	L	5-6
16—Tampa Bay	W	*5-4
17—At Washington	L	4-6
21—Chicago	W	4-1
23—San Jose	W	5-4
28—At Toronto	T	*4-4
30—Ottawa	W	12-3
31—At Ottawa	T	*2-2

NOVEMBER

2—At N.Y. Rangers	L	*6-7
5—At San Jose	L	5-7
7—At Los Angeles	L	2-5
11—Boston	W	7-2
13—Hartford	W	8-2
14—At N.Y. Islanders	L	5-7
17—At Pittsburgh	L	2-4
18—New Jersey†	L	2-3
21—Minnesota	L	3-4
22—At Philadelphia	T	*4-4
25—Quebec	T	*1-1
27—Ottawa	W	4-1
29—At Ottawa	W	5-2
30—At Montreal	L	0-3

DECEMBER

4—N.Y. Islanders	T	*5-5
6—New Jersey	L	3-7
7—At Quebec	L	3-4

9—Boston	W	5-2
11—Hartford	W	9-3
12—At Hartford	T	*1-1
15—At Boston	W	3-2
19—At Montreal	L	2-4
20—Toronto	W	5-4
23—Washington	W	4-1
27—Pittsburgh	L	2-4
31—N.Y. Rangers	W	11-6

JANUARY

2—At Ottawa	W	7-2
3—St. Louis	W	*6-5
6—At Hartford	W	3-1
8—N.Y. Islanders	W	6-5
10—Calgary	W	5-3
12—At Boston	L	2-5
15—At Vancouver	L	1-4
17—At Edmonton	L	*2-3
19—At Calgary	W	*3-2
22—Quebec	W	6-2
23—At Quebec	L	3-4
26—At Philadelphia	W	*4-3
27—Washington	W	4-3
29—N.Y. Rangers	W	6-4
31—Edmonton	L	*4-5

FEBRUARY

3—Hartford	W	3-2
8—At Ottawa	L	2-4
10—At Winnipeg	W	6-2
12—Vancouver	L	1-3
14—Pittsburgh	W	7-4
17—At Hartford	W	5-3

19—At New Jersey	T	*3-3
24—Detroit	W	10-7
26—Montreal	L	4-6
27—At Montreal	L	4-8

MARCH

1—Vancouver†	L	2-5
3—At N.Y. Rangers	T	*2-2
5—Hartford	L	2-4
7—Winnipeg	W	2-1
10—At Quebec	W	7-4
13—At Hartford	T	*3-3
15—Los Angeles	L	2-4
16—At St. Louis	T	*2-2
20—At Tampa Bay	W	3-1
22—At Montreal	W	8-3
24—Boston	L	0-2
25—At Chicago	W	6-4
28—Ottawa	W	3-1
30—At Washington	L	1-4
31—New Jersey	W	5-2

APRIL

3—At Boston	L	2-3
4—Boston	L	0-3
6—At Minnesota	L	1-3
10—At Detroit	L	5-6
11—Quebec	L	1-3
13—Montreal	L	*2-3
15—Philadelphia	L	4-7

*Denotes overtime game.
†At Hamilton, Ont.

CALGARY FLAMES
WESTERN CONFERENCE/PACIFIC DIVISION

1993-94 SCHEDULE

Home games shaded.
* — At Madison Square Garden, New York.
† — At Saskatoon, Sask.
∆ — At Phoenix.

OCTOBER

SUN	MON	TUE	WED	THU	FRI	SAT
					1	2
3	4	5 NYI	6	7 SJ	8	9 VAN
10	11	12	13	14 SJ	15	16 LA
17 ANA	18	19	20 EDM	21 VAN	22	23 BOS
24	25 WAS	26	27 BUF	28	29	30 EDM
31 WIN						

NOVEMBER

SUN	MON	TUE	WED	THU	FRI	SAT
	1	2	3 HAR	4 BOS	5	6 MON
7	8	9 LA	10	11 ANA	12	13 VAN
14	15 WIN	16	17	18 STL	19	20 DAL
21	22 ANA	23	24 TOR	25	26 CHI	27
28	29	30 DAL				

DECEMBER

SUN	MON	TUE	WED	THU	FRI	SAT
			1	2	3	4 PHI
5	6 OTT	7 QUE	8	9	10 BUF	11
12	13	14 VAN	15	16	17 STL	18 WIN
19	20 LA	21	22 EDM	23† VAN	24	25
26	27	28 SJ	29	30 EDM	31 MON	

JANUARY

SUN	MON	TUE	WED	THU	FRI	SAT
						1
2 STL	3	4	5 NYR	6	7 NYI	8 PIT
9	10	11 QUE	12	13	14	15 OTT
16	17 SJ	18	19 VAN	20	21	22* ALL STAR GAME
23	24∆ LA	25	26 DAL	27	28 NJ	29 STL
30	31					

FEBRUARY

SUN	MON	TUE	WED	THU	FRI	SAT
		1	2 ANA	3	4	5 LA
6	7 EDM	8	9 EDM	10	11 HAR	12 TOR
13	14 CHI	15	16	17	18 DAL	19
20 WIN	21	22 VAN	23	24 TB	25	26 LA
27	28					

MARCH

SUN	MON	TUE	WED	THU	FRI	SAT
		1 DET	2	3 CHI	4	5 NJ
6 WAS	7	8	9 DET	10	11 FLA	12 SJ
13	14	15 TB	16 FLA	17	18	19
20 TOR	21	22 NYR	23	24	25	26 PIT
27	28	29	30	31 PHI		

APRIL

SUN	MON	TUE	WED	THU	FRI	SAT
					1	2 DET
3 CHI	4	5	6 ANA	7	8 SJ	9 DET
10	11 ANA	12	13 LA	14	15	16

1993-94 SEASON

CLUB DIRECTORY

Owners
Harley N. Hotchkiss
Norman L. Kwong
Sonia Scurfield
Byron J. Seaman
Daryl K. Seaman
President and alternate governor
W.C. "Bill" Hay
General manager
Doug Risebrough
Vice president, business and finance
Clare Rhyasen
Director, hockey operations
Al MacNeil
Vice president, broadcasting
Leo Ornest
Vice president, marketing
Lanny McDonald
Assistant general manager
Al Coates
Head Coach
Dave King
Assistant coaches
Guy Charron
Jamie Hislop
Slavomir Lener
Goaltending consultant
Glenn Hall

Director of public relations
Rick Skaggs
Assistant public relations director
Mike Burke
Chief scout
Gerry Blair
Scouts
Ray Clearwater
Jiri Hrdina
Guy Lapointe
Ian McKenzie
Gerry McNamara
Nick Polano
Lou Reycroft
Scouting staff
Ron Ferguson
Glen Giovanacci
David Mayville
Lars Norrman
Pekka Rautakallio
Tom Thompson
Controller
Lynne Tosh
Trainer
Jim "Bearcat" Murray
Equipment manager
Bobby Stewart

DRAFT CHOICES

1—Jesper Mattsson	6-0/176	18	RW	Malmo, Sweden
2—Jamie Allison	6-1/188	44	D	Detroit (OHL)
3—Dan Tomkins	6-2/205	70	F	Omaha (Jr. A, Tier II)
4—Jason Smith	6-4/210	95	D	Princeton University
4—Marty Murray	5-8/164	96	C	Brandon (WHL)
5—Darryl Lafrance	5-11/175	121	C	Oshawa (OHL)
5—John Emmons	6-0/185	122	C	Yale University
6—Andreas Karlsson	6-2/180	148	F	Leksand, Sweden
8—Derek Sylvester	6-2/215	200	F	Niagara Falls (OHL)
10—German Titov	6-0/185	252	C	TPS Turku, Finland
11—Burke Murphy	6-0/180	278	F	St. Lawrence University

MISCELLANEOUS DATA

Home ice (capacity)
Olympic Saddledome (20,230)
Address
P.O. Box 1540
Station M
Calgary, Alta. T2P 3B9
Business phone
403-261-0475

Rink dimensions
200 feet by 85 feet
Club colors
Red, white and gold
Minor league affiliation
Saint John (AHL)

TRAINING CAMP ROSTER

No.	FORWARDS	Ht./Wt.	Place (BORN)	Date	NHL exp.	1992-93 clubs
15	Brent Ashton (LW/C) ...	6-1/200	Saskatoon, Sask.	5-18-60	14	Boston, Providence (AHL), Calgary
	Ted Drury (C)	6-0/185	Boston	9-13-71	0	Harvard University (ECAC)
14	Theoren Fleury (C/RW) ..	5-6/155	Oxbow, Sask.	6-29-68	5	Calgary
27	Tomas Forslund (RW) ..	5-11/200	Falun, Sweden	11-24-68	2	Calgary, Salt Lake City (IHL)
19	Todd Harkins (C)..........	6-3/210	Cleveland	10-8-68	2	Salt Lake City (IHL), Calgary
13	Shawn Heaphy (C)	5-8/175	Sudbury, Ont.	11-27-68	1	Salt Lake City (IHL), Calgary
12	Paul Kruse (LW)	6-0/200	Merritt, B.C.	3-15-70	3	Salt Lake City (IHL), Calgary
38	Patrick Lebeau (LW)	5-10/173	St. Jerome, Que.	3-17-70	2	Salt Lake City (IHL), Calgary
11	Chris Lindberg (LW)	6-1/185	Fort Francis, Ont.	4-16-67	2	Calgary
	Jesper Mattsson (C)	6-0/173	Malmo, Sweden	5-13-75	0	Malmo (Sweden)
	Sandy McCarthy (RW)	6-3/225	Toronto	6-15-72	0	Salt Lake City (IHL)
25	Joe Nieuwendyk (C)	6-1/175	Oshawa, Ont.	9-10-66	7	Calgary
29	Joel Otto (C)	6-4/220	Elk River, Minn.	10-29-61	9	Calgary
23	Greg Paslawski (RW)....	5-11/190	Kindersley, Sask.	8-25-61	10	Philadelphia, Calgary
28	Paul Ranheim (LW)......	6-0/195	St. Louis	1-25-66	5	Calgary
26	Robert Reichel (C)	5-10/185	Litvinov, Czech.	6-25-71	3	Calgary
10	Gary Roberts (LW)	6-1/190	North York, Ont.	5-23-66	7	Calgary
22	Ronnie Stern (RW)	6-0/195	Ste. Agatha Des Mont, Que.	1-11-67	6	Calgary
	Cory Stillman (C)	6-0/174	Peterborough, Ont.	12-20-73	0	Peterborough (OHL)
	Niklas Sundblad (RW) ..	6-1/196	Stockholm, Sweden	1-3-73	0	AIK (Sweden)
	Vesa Vitakoski (LW)	6-2/205	Lappeenranta, Finland	2-13-71	0	Tappara (Finland)
33	Carey Wilson (C/RW) ...	6-2/205	Winnipeg, Man.	5-19-62	10	Calgary
	DEFENSEMEN					
4	Kevin Dahl	5-11/190	Regina, Sask.	12-30-68	1	Calgary
5	Chris Dahlquist	6-1/190	Fridley, Minn.	12-14-62	8	Calgary
34	Roger Johansson	6-4/190	Ljungby, Sweden	4-17-67	3	Calgary
2	Al MacInnis	6-2/196	Inverness, N.S.	7-11-63	12	Calgary
3	Frantisek Musil	6-3/215	Pardubice, Czech.	12-17-64	7	Calgary
4	Michel Petit.................	6-1/185	St. Malo, Que.	2-12-64	11	Calgary
	Ken Sabourin	6-3/210	Scarborough, Ont.	4-28-66	4	Baltimore (AHL), Salt Lake City (IHL)
	Brad Schlegel	5-10/190	Kitchener, Ont.	7-22-68	2	Baltimore (AHL), Washington
20	Gary Suter	6-0/190	Madison, Wis.	6-24-64	8	Calgary
18	Trent Yawney	6-3/185	Hudson Bay, Sask.	9-29-65	6	Calgary
	GOALTENDERS					
	Trevor Kidd	6-2/190	St. Boniface, Man.	3-29-72	1	Salt Lake City (IHL)
35	Jeff Reese	5-9/155	Brantford, Ont.	3-24-66	6	Calgary
1	Andrei Trefilov	6-0/180	Moscow, U.S.S.R.	8-31-69	1	Salt Lake City (IHL), Calgary
30	Mike Vernon	5-9/170	Calgary, Alta.	2-24-63	10	Calgary

1992-93 REVIEW

INDIVIDUAL STATISTICS

SCORING

	Games	G	A	Pts.	Pen.	+/-	PPG	SHG	Shots	Shooting Pct.
Theoren Fleury	83	34	66	100	88	14	12	2	250	13.6
Robert Reichel	80	40	48	88	54	25	12	0	238	16.8
Gary Suter	81	23	58	81	112	-1	10	1	263	8.7
Gary Roberts.............................	58	38	41	79	172	32	8	3	166	22.9
Joe Nieuwendyk	79	38	37	75	52	9	14	0	208	18.3
Sergei Makarov...........................	71	18	39	57	40	0	5	0	105	17.1
Al MacInnis................................	50	11	43	54	61	15	7	0	201	5.5
Joel Otto	75	19	33	52	150	2	6	1	115	16.5
Paul Ranheim	83	21	22	43	26	-4	3	4	179	11.7
Ronnie Stern	70	10	15	25	207	4	0	0	82	12.2
Chris Lindberg	62	9	12	21	18	-3	1	0	74	12.2
Roger Johansson.........................	77	4	16	20	62	13	1	0	101	4.0
Brent Ashton*	32	8	11	19	41	11	0	2	58	13.8
Trent Yawney	63	1	16	17	67	9	0	0	61	1.6
Frank Musil................................	80	6	10	16	131	28	0	0	87	6.9
Gary Leeman*	30	9	5	14	10	5	0	0	49	18.4
Craig Berube	77	4	8	12	209	-6	0	0	58	6.9
Michel Petit	35	3	9	12	54	-5	2	0	58	5.2
Carey Wilson	22	4	7	11	8	10	1	2	30	13.3
Kevin Dahl	61	2	9	11	56	9	1	0	40	5.0
Chris Dahlquist	74	3	7	10	66	0	0	0	64	4.7
Greg Paslawski*.........................	13	4	5	9	0	3	0	0	19	21.1
Alexander Godynyuk......................	27	3	4	7	19	6	0	0	35	8.6
Brian Skrudland*	16	2	4	6	10	3	0	0	22	9.1

	Games	G	A	Pts.	Pen.	+/-	PPG	SHG	Shots	Shooting Pct.
C.J. Young*	28	3	2	5	20	-7	1	0	21	14.3
Todd Harkins	15	2	3	5	22	-4	0	0	17	11.8
Paul Kruse	27	2	3	5	41	2	0	0	17	11.8
Jeff Reese (goalie)	26	0	4	4	4	0	0	0	0	0.0
Greg Smyth	35	1	2	3	95	2	1	0	14	7.1
Tomas Forslund	6	0	2	2	0	0	0	0	3	0.0
Mike Vernon (goalie)	64	0	2	2	42	0	0	0	0	0.0
Shawn Heaphy	1	0	0	0	0	0	0	0	2	0.0
Patrick Lebeau	1	0	0	0	0	0	0	0	0	0.0
Andrei Trefilov (goalie)	1	0	0	0	2	0	0	0	0	0.0

GOALTENDING

	Games	Min.	Goals	SO	Avg.	W	L	T	Shots	Sv. Pct.
Jeff Reese	26	1311	70	1	3.20	14	4	1	629	.889
Mike Vernon	64	3732	203	2	3.26	29	26	9	1804	.887
Andrei Trefilov	1	65	5	0	4.62	0	0	1	39	.872

Empty-net goals (do not count against a goaltender's average): Vernon 4.
*Played with two or more NHL teams.

RESULTS

OCTOBER
6—Los Angeles	L	*4-5
8—Edmonton	W	7-2
10—Toronto	W	3-2
13—Minnesota†	W	4-3
15—At Los Angeles	L	0-4
17—At San Jose	W	6-2
20—Los Angeles	W	6-2
22—Boston	L	2-4
25—At Edmonton	W	4-0
28—At Winnipeg	W	7-5
30—Washington	L	1-3
31—Minnesota	W	5-3

NOVEMBER
2—Vancouver	W	5-3
4—At Vancouver	T	*5-5
5—Ottawa	W	8-4
8—At Quebec	T	*5-5
9—At Montreal	L	2-5
11—At Hartford	W	4-3
12—At Boston	L	3-5
14—At Tampa Bay	W	5-3
19—Vancouver	W	4-3
21—N.Y. Islanders	L	3-4
25—San Jose	L	*3-4
27—Tampa Bay	W	*3-2
28—Chicago	L	2-5

DECEMBER
2—Winnipeg	T	*3-3
4—St. Louis	W	5-3
7—Edmonton	W	6-3

8—At Edmonton	L	1-3
11—At Toronto	W	6-3
12—At Ottawa	T	*1-1
14—At Detroit	W	3-0
15—At N.Y. Rangers	W	3-0
19—Los Angeles	W	5-3
21—Edmonton	W	*3-2
23—At Winnipeg	W	4-3
27—At Edmonton	W	7-3
31—Montreal	W	5-3

JANUARY
2—Philadelphia	W	7-3
5—Winnipeg	L	2-4
7—At St. Louis	L	*2-3
9—At Pittsburgh	L	2-3
10—At Buffalo	L	3-5
12—At N.Y. Islanders	L	2-8
14—At Philadelphia	T	*4-4
16—At Minnesota	L	3-4
19—Buffalo	L	*2-3
22—Winnipeg	T	*4-4
23—Pittsburgh	L	3-4
26—Detroit	L	1-9
28—At Los Angeles	W	2-1
30—At San Jose	W	5-4

FEBRUARY
2—At Washington	W	6-4
3—At New Jersey	W	5-4
10—San Jose	W	13-1
12—Quebec	T	*4-4
13—Hartford	W	*4-3
16—Philadelphia‡	T	*4-4

17—At Toronto	L	2-4
19—At Detroit	T	*3-3
21—At Chicago	L	3-4
23—At San Jose	W	6-3
26—N.Y. Rangers	T	*4-4
27—San Jose	W	5-4

MARCH
2—At Los Angeles	L	2-6
4—At St. Louis	L	1-2
6—At Tampa Bay	L	4-7
11—Detroit	W	6-3
13—New Jersey	W	4-3
14—Vancouver	W	3-2
16—Chicago	L	0-1
21—At Winnipeg	L	2-4
24—St. Louis	L	2-4
26—At Vancouver	W	3-1
28—Toronto	L	0-4
30—Winnipeg	L	4-5

APRIL
1—Minnesota	W	5-3
3—At San Jose	W	*3-2
4—At San Jose	W	4-3
6—At Los Angeles	T	*3-3
9—Vancouver	W	8-1
11—At Vancouver	L	3-6
13—At Edmonton	W	4-2
15—San Jose	W	7-3

*Denotes overtime game.
†At Saskatoon, Sask.
‡At Cincinnati.

CHICAGO BLACKHAWKS
WESTERN CONFERENCE/CENTRAL DIVISION

1993-94 SCHEDULE

Home games shaded.
* — At Madison Square Garden, New York.
† — At Sacramento, Calif.
Δ — At Phoenix.

OCTOBER

SUN	MON	TUE	WED	THU	FRI	SAT
					1	2
3	4	5	6 FLA	7	8	9 TOR
10 WIN	11	12 DAL	13	14 HAR	15	16 WIN
17	18 DAL	19	20	21 QUE	22	23 DET
24	25	26 STL	27	28 TOR	29	30 PIT
31 PHI						

NOVEMBER

SUN	MON	TUE	WED	THU	FRI	SAT
	1	2	3	4 NYI	5	6
7 EDM	8	9	10	11 PIT	12	13 TOR
14 DAL	15	16	17	18 FLA	19	20 TB
21	22	23	24 EDM	25	26 CAL	27
28	29 VAN	30				

DECEMBER

SUN	MON	TUE	WED	THU	FRI	SAT
			1	2	3	4 NJ
5	6	7 STL	8	9	10	11 BOS
12 SJ	13	14	15 DAL	16	17	18 PHI
19 ANA	20	21 DET	22	23 SJ	24	25
26 STL	27 TOR	28	29 WIN	30	31 DAL	

JANUARY

SUN	MON	TUE	WED	THU	FRI	SAT
						1
2 WIN	3	4 DAL	5	6 ANA	7	8 WAS
9 EDM	10	11 BUF	12	13 TB	14	15 NYI
16 NYR	17	18	19	20	21	22* ALL-STAR GAME
23	24	25 DET	26	27 DET	28	29 OTT
30	31 OTT					

FEBRUARY

SUN	MON	TUE	WED	THU	FRI	SAT
		1	2 VAN	3	4 EDM	5
6 ANA	7	8† SJ	9 LA	10	11 SJ	12
13 SJ	14 CAL	15	16	17 VAN	18 WIN	19
20 NJ	21	22	23	24 WIN	25 BUF	26
27 BOS	28					

MARCH

SUN	MON	TUE	WED	THU	FRI	SAT
		1	2	3 CAL	4	5
6 LA	7	8Δ ANA	9 LA	10	11 ANA	12
13 VAN	14 QUE	15	16 MON	17	18 NYR	19
20 STL	21	22 DET	23	24 MON	25	26
27 DET	28	29	30 HAR	31 WAS		

APRIL

SUN	MON	TUE	WED	THU	FRI	SAT
					1	2
3 CAL	4	5 STL	6	7	8 STL	9
10 LA	11	12 TOR	13	14 TOR	15	16

1993-94 SEASON

CLUB DIRECTORY

President
William W. Wirtz
Vice president
Arthur M. Wirtz Jr.
Vice president and asst. to the president
Thomas N. Ivan
Senior vice president/general manager
Bob Pulford
Assistant general manager
Jack Davison
Director of player personnel
Bob Murray
Head coach
Darryl Sutter
Assistant coaches
Rich Preston
Paul Baxter

Scouts
Jimmy Walker
Dave Lucas
Kerry Davison
Michel Dumas
Jim Pappin
Jan Spieczny
Duane Sutter
Steve Lyons
Brian DeBruyn
Russ Huston
Public relations
Jim DeMaria
Trainer
Mike Gapski
Lou Varga
Randy Lacey

DRAFT CHOICES

1—Eric Lecompte	6-4/190	24	F	Hull (QMJHL)
2—Eric Manlow	6-0/190	50	C	Kitchener (OHL)
3—Bogdan Savenko	6-1/192	54	F	Niagara Falls (OHL)
3—Ryan Huska	6-2/194	76	F	Kamloops (WHL)
4—Eric Daze	6-4/202	90	F	Beauport (QMJHL)
4—Patrik Pysz	5-11/187	102	C	Augsburg, Germany
5—Jonni Vauhkonen	6-2/189	128	F	Keikki-Reipas Lahti, Finland
7—Tom White	6-1/185	180	C	Westminster
8—Sergei Petrov	5-11/185	206	F	Cloquet H.S. (Minn.)
9—Mike Rusk	6-1/175	232	D	Guelph (OHL)
10—Mike McGhan	6-1/177	258	F	Prince Albert (WHL)
11—Tom Noble	5-10/165	284	G	Catholic Memorial H.S.

MISCELLANEOUS DATA

Home ice (capacity)
Chicago Stadium (17,317)
Address
1800 W. Madison Street
Chicago, IL 60612
Business phone
312-733-5300

Rink dimensions
185 feet by 85 feet
Club colors
Red, black and white
Minor league affiliation
Indianapolis (IHL)

CHICAGO BLACKHAWKS

1993-94 NHL SEASON

CHICAGO BLACKHAWKS

TRAINING CAMP ROSTER

No.	FORWARDS	Ht./Wt.	Place	Date	NHL exp.	1992-93 clubs
56	Alexander Andrijevski	6-5/211	Minsk, U.S.S.R.	8-10-68	1	Indianapolis (IHL), Chicago
	Shawn Byram (LW)	6-2/204	Neepawa, Man.	9-12-68	2	Indianapolis (IHL)
	Rob Conn (LW/RW)	6-2/200	Calgary, Alta.	9-3-68	1	Indianapolis (IHL)
14	Greg Gilbert (LW)	6-1/191	Mississauga, Ont.	1-22-62	12	Chicago
16	Michel Goulet (LW)	6-1/195	Peribonqua, Que.	4-21-60	14	Chicago
33	Dirk Graham (LW/RW)	5-11/190	Regina, Sask.	7-29-59	10	Chicago
	Bobby House (RW)	6-1/190	Whitehorse, Yukon.	1-7-73	0	Brandon (WHL)
	Sergei Klimovich (C)	6-2/183	Novosibirsk, U.S.S.R.	5-8-74	0	Dynamo Moscow (CIS)
59	Sergei Krivokrasov (RW)	5-11/175	Angarsk, U.S.S.R.	4-15-74	1	Chicago, Indianapolis (IHL)
28	Steve Larmer (RW)	5-10/189	Peterborough, Ont.	6-16-61	13	Chicago
	Eric Lecompte (LW)	6-4/190	Montreal	4-4-75	0	Hull (QMJHL)
26	Jocelyn Lemieux (RW)	5-10/200	Mont Laurier, Que.	11-18-67	7	Chicago
32	Stephane Matteau (LW)	6-3/195	Rouyn, Que.	9-2-69	3	Chicago
17	Joe Murphy (RW)	6-1/190	London, Ont.	10-16-67	7	Chicago
19	Troy Murray (C)	6-1/195	Winnipeg, Man.	7-31-62	12	Winnipeg, Chicago
10	Brian Noonan (C/RW)	6-1/180	Boston	5-29-65	6	Chicago
27	Jeremy Roenick (C)	6-0/170	Boston	1-17-70	5	Chicago
22	Christian Ruuttu (C)	5-11/192	Lappeenranta, Finland	2-20-64	7	Chicago
	Jeff Shantz (C)	6-0/185	Edmonton, Alta.	10-10-73	0	Regina (WHL)
12	Brent Sutter (C)	5-11/180	Viking, Alta.	6-10-62	13	Chicago
	Kerry Toporowski (RW)	6-2/212	Prince Albert, Sask.	4-9-71	0	Indianapolis (IHL)
	DEFENSEMEN					
47	Adam Bennett	6-4/206	Georgetown, Ont.	3-30-71	2	Chicago
4	Keith Brown	6-1/195	Corner Brook, Nfld.	5-6-60	14	Chicago
7	Chris Chelios	6-1/192	Chicago	1-25-62	10	Chicago
	Ivan Droppa	6-2/209	Liptovsky Mikulas, Czech.	2-1-72	0	Indianapolis (IHL)
45	Karl Dykhuis	6-3/195	Sept-Iles, Que.	7-8-72	2	Indianapolis (IHL), Chicago
6	Frantisek Kucera	6-2/205	Prague, Czech.	2-3-68	3	Chicago
2	Bryan Marchment	6-1/198	Scarborough, Ont.	5-1-69	5	Chicago
3	Craig Muni	6-3/200	Toronto	7-19-62	11	Edmonton, Chicago
8	Cam Russell	6-4/175	Halifax, N.S.	1-12-69	4	Chicago
5	Steve Smith	6-4/215	Glasgow, Scotland	4-30-63	9	Chicago
	Mike Speer	6-2/202	Toronto	3-26-71	0	Indianapolis (IHL)
	Neil Wilkinson	6-3/180	Selkirk, Man.	8-15-67	4	San Jose
	GOALTENDERS					
30	Ed Belfour	5-11/182	Carman, Man.	4-21-65	5	Chicago
	Jeff Hackett	6-1/180	London, Ont.	6-1-68	4	San Jose
	Christian Soucy	5-11/160	Gatineau, Que.	9-14-70	0	U. of Vermont (ECAC)

1992-93 REVIEW

INDIVIDUAL STATISTICS

SCORING

	Games	G	A	Pts.	Pen.	+/-	PPG	SHG	Shots	Shooting Pct.
Jeremy Roenick	84	50	57	107	86	15	22	3	255	19.6
Chris Chelios	84	15	58	73	282	14	8	0	290	5.2
Steve Larmer	84	35	35	70	48	23	14	4	228	15.4
Steve Smith	78	10	47	57	214	12	7	1	212	4.7
Brent Sutter	65	20	34	54	67	10	8	2	151	13.2
Christian Ruuttu	84	17	37	54	134	14	3	1	187	9.1
Michel Goulet	63	23	21	44	43	10	10	0	125	18.4
Dirk Graham	84	20	17	37	139	0	1	2	187	10.7
Stephane Matteau	79	15	18	33	98	6	2	0	95	15.8
Greg Gilbert	77	13	19	32	57	5	0	1	72	18.1
Jocelyn Lemieux	81	10	21	31	111	5	1	0	117	8.5
Brian Noonan	63	16	14	30	82	3	5	0	129	12.4
Bryan Marchment	78	5	15	20	313	15	1	0	75	6.7
Frantisek Kucera	71	5	14	19	59	7	1	0	117	4.3
Dave Christian	60	4	14	18	12	6	1	0	75	5.3
Joe Murphy	19	7	10	17	18	-3	5	0	43	16.3
Igor Kravchuk*	38	6	9	15	30	11	3	0	101	5.9
Keith Brown	33	2	6	8	39	3	0	0	47	4.3
Rob Brown	15	1	6	7	33	6	0	0	16	6.3
Mike Hudson*	36	1	6	7	44	-6	0	0	33	3.0
Cam Russell	67	2	4	6	151	5	0	0	49	4.1
Karl Dykhuis	12	0	5	5	0	2	0	0	10	0.0
Troy Murray*	22	1	3	4	25	0	1	0	32	3.1

	Games	G	A	Pts.	Pen.	+/-	PPG	SHG	Shots	Shooting Pct.
Ed Belfour (goalie)	71	0	3	3	28	0	0	0	0	0.0
Stu Grimson	78	1	1	2	193	2	1	0	14	7.1
Adam Bennett	16	0	2	2	8	-2	0	0	15	0.0
Brad Lauer	7	0	1	1	2	-1	0	0	8	0.0
Milan Tichy	13	0	1	1	30	7	0	0	12	0.0
Alexander Andrijevski	1	0	0	0	0	0	0	0	0	0.0
Steve Bancroft	1	0	0	0	0	0	0	0	0	0.0
Steve Tepper	1	0	0	0	0	0	0	0	0	0.0
Rod Buskas	4	0	0	0	26	2	0	0	3	0.0
Sergei Krivokrasov	4	0	0	0	2	-2	0	0	0	0.0
Craig Muni*	9	0	0	0	8	1	0	0	9	0.0
Jim Waite (goalie)	20	0	0	0	0	0	0	0	0	0.0

GOALTENDING

	Games	Min.	Goals	SO	Avg.	W	L	T	Shots	Sv. Pct.
Ed Belfour	†71	†4106	177	†7	2.59	41	18	†11	1880	.906
Jim Waite	20	996	49	2	2.95	6	7	1	411	.881

Empty-net goals (do not count against a goaltender's average): Waite 3, Belfour 1.
*Played with two or more NHL teams.
†Led league.

RESULTS

OCTOBER

7—At Tampa Bay	L	3-7
10—At St. Louis	W	3-0
11—Tampa Bay	T	*4-4
15—Edmonton	L	*3-4
17—At Toronto	L	3-4
18—Vancouver	W	3-1
21—At Buffalo	L	1-4
22—New Jersey	L	*5-6
25—Detroit	W	8-2
29—Philadelphia	T	*5-5
31—At Boston	W	3-2

NOVEMBER

1—San Jose	T	*4-4
3—Washington†	L	1-4
5—Toronto	W	1-0
7—At Quebec	W	7-4
8—Pittsburgh	W	7-2
12—St. Louis	W	1-0
14—At Minnesota	L	0-3
15—Minnesota	W	2-1
17—At Detroit	L	4-5
19—At Los Angeles	L	1-4
21—At San Jose	W	2-1
23—At Vancouver	L	2-5
27—At Edmonton	W	8-1
28—At Calgary	W	5-2

DECEMBER

1—Los Angeles‡	L	3-6
3—Toronto	W	4-3
5—At Toronto	T	*2-2

6—Montreal	W	2-0
8—At Detroit	W	3-2
10—N.Y. Islanders	W	5-3
12—At Minnesota	W	3-0
17—Winnipeg	W	5-1
19—At Philadelphia	L	1-3
20—Minnesota	W	4-0
23—At Ottawa	W	4-2
26—St. Louis	L	*2-3
27—Detroit	L	0-4
29—At Detroit	W	6-3
31—Tampa Bay	W	5-0

JANUARY

2—At Washington	T	*2-2
3—Winnipeg	W	4-1
7—Edmonton	T	*3-3
9—At St. Louis	L	1-4
10—Los Angeles	L	4-5
12—At Minnesota	W	3-1
14—Minnesota	W	3-1
16—At Toronto	W	5-3
17—Toronto	W	5-3
19—At Winnipeg	L	2-5
21—Washington	W	6-2
23—At Hartford	W	6-2
24—Vancouver	W	6-2
27—At Vancouver	T	*4-4
29—At San Jose	W	4-2
30—At Los Angeles	T	*2-2

FEBRUARY

3—At Detroit	L	0-5
11—Boston	W	6-3

13—At Pittsburgh	L	1-4
14—Detroit	L	3-5
18—Los Angeles	W	7-2
21—Calgary	W	4-3
25—At Tampa Bay	W	5-1
27—At Detroit	W	2-1
28—St. Louis	L	1-7

MARCH

4—Quebec	T	*3-3
5—At New Jersey	T	*1-1
7—Ottawa	W	4-2
11—N.Y. Rangers	L	1-4
14—At Edmonton	W	*5-4
16—At Calgary	W	1-0
20—At Montreal	L	2-6
21—Tampa Bay	W	3-2
25—Buffalo	L	4-6
26—At N.Y. Rangers	W	3-1
28—Hartford	W	3-0

APRIL

1—Detroit	L	1-3
3—At St. Louis	T	*3-3
4—St. Louis	W	5-4
8—At N.Y. Islanders	W	3-2
10—At Tampa Bay	W	4-2
11—Tampa Bay	T	*3-3
13—At Minnesota	W	3-2
15—Toronto	W	3-2

*Denotes overtime game.
†At Indianapolis.
‡At Milwaukee.

DALLAS STARS
WESTERN CONFERENCE/CENTRAL DIVISION

1993-94 SCHEDULE

Home games shaded.
* — At Madison Square Garden, New York.
† — At Phoenix.
△ — At Minneapolis.

OCTOBER

SUN	MON	TUE	WED	THU	FRI	SAT
					1	2
3	4	5 DET	6	7 TOR	8	9 WIN
10	11	12 CHI	13	14	15	16 STL
17	18 CHI	19	20 MON	21 OTT	22	23 QUE
24	25 DET	26	27 HAR	28	29	30 OTT
31						

NOVEMBER

SUN	MON	TUE	WED	THU	FRI	SAT
	1 TOR	2	3 ANA	4	5 SJ	6
7 WIN	8	9† ANA	10	11 SJ	12	13 WIN
14 CHI	15	16	17 TB	18	19	20 CAL
21 LA	22	23	24 NYI	25	26	27 DET
28	29 EDM	30 CAL				

DECEMBER

SUN	MON	TUE	WED	THU	FRI	SAT
			1	2	3	4 STL
5 EDM	6	7	8 PIT	9△	10	11
12 FLA	13	14	15 CHI	16	17 ANA	18
19 VAN	20	21	22 ANA	23 LA	24	25
26	27 DET	28	29 TOR	30	31 CHI	

JANUARY

SUN	MON	TUE	WED	THU	FRI	SAT
						1
2 QUE	3	4 CHI	5	6 PHI	7	8
9 STL	10	11 EDM	12	13 TOR	14 DET	15
16 BUF	17	18 LA	19	20	21	22° ALL-STAR GAME
23	24 NJ	25	26 CAL	27 VAN	28	29 EDM
30	31					

FEBRUARY

SUN	MON	TUE	WED	THU	FRI	SAT
		1	2 WIN	3	4	5
6 SJ	7	8	9 WIN	10	11	12 PIT
13 BUF	14	15	16 BOS	17	18 CAL	19
20	21 SJ	22	23 LA	24	25	26 NYR
27	28					

MARCH

SUN	MON	TUE	WED	THU	FRI	SAT
		1	2 WIN	3	4 VAN	5
6 MON	7	8 PHI	9 TOR	10	11	12 HAR
13 NJ	14	15	16	17	18 WAS	19
20 VAN	21	22 ANA	23	24	25 STL	26
27 TB	28 FLA	29	30	31 BOS		

APRIL

SUN	MON	TUE	WED	THU	FRI	SAT
					1 NYR	2
3 WAS	4	5 TOR	6	7	8 NYI	9
10 STL	11	12 STL	13	14 DET	15	16

1993-94 SEASON

CLUB DIRECTORY

Owner and governor
Norman N. Green
President
Jim Lites
Vice president/g.m. and head coach
Bob Gainey
V.P of advertising and promotion
Jeff Cogen
Vice president of finance
Rick McLaughlin
Vice president of marketing
Bill Strong
Assistant coaches
Doug Jarvis
Rick Wilson
Director of player personnel
Les Jackson
Director of amateur scouting
Craig Button

Assistant to the general manager
Doug Armstrong
Assistant to the hockey department
Dan Stuchal
Director of public relations
Larry Kelly
Director of merchandising
Mary Meulman
Director of ticket sales
Murray Cohn
Head trainer
Dave Surprenant
Assistant trainer
Dave Smith
Equipment manager
Lance Vogt

DRAFT CHOICES

1—Todd Harvey	5-11/190	9	C	Detroit (OHL)
2—Jamie Langenbrunner	5-11/180	35	C	Cloquet H.S. (Minn.)
4—Chad Lang	5-10/188	87	G	Peterborough (OHL)
6—Rick Mrozik	6-2/185	136	D	Cloquet H.S. (Minn.)
6—Per Svartvadet	6-1/180	139	F	MoDo, Sweden
7—Jeremy Stasiuk	5-11/189	165	F	Spokane (WHL)
8—Rob Lurtsema	6-5/237	191	F	Burnsville H.S. (Minn.)
10—Jordan Willis	5-9/155	243	G	London (OHL)
10—Bill Lang	5-10/181	249	C	North Bay (OHL)
11—Cory Peterson	6-2/205	269	D	Jeff'son HS, Bl'ton (Minn.)

MISCELLANEOUS DATA

Home ice (capacity)
Reunion Arena (16,814)
Address
901 Main Street
Suite 2301
Dallas, TX 75202
Business phone
214-467-8277

Rink dimensions
200 feet by 85 feet
Club colors
Black, gold, green and white
Minor league affiliation
Kalamazoo (IHL)

TRAINING CAMP ROSTER

No.	FORWARDS	Ht./Wt.	Place	BORN Date	NHL exp.	1992-93 clubs
	Jeff Bes (C)	6-0/185	Tillsonburg, Ont.	7-31-73	0	Guelph (OHL), Kalamazoo (IHL)
28	James Black (C)	5-11/185	Regina, Sask.	8-15-69	4	Minnesota, Kalamazoo (IHL)
7	Neal Broten (C)	5-9/170	Roseau, Minn.	11-29-59	13	Minnesota
27	Shane Churla (RW)	6-1/200	Fernie, B.C.	6-24-65	7	Minnesota
26	Russ Courtnall (RW)	5-11/183	Victoria, B.C.	6-3-65	10	Minnesota
20	Mike Craig (RW)	6-1/180	London, Ont.	6-6-71	3	Minnesota
22	Ulf Dahlen (RW)	6-2/195	Ostersund, Sweden	1-12-67	6	Minnesota
	Dean Evason (C)	5-10/180	Flin Flon, Man.	8-22-64	10	San Jose
15	Dave Gagner (C)	5-10/188	Chatham, Ont.	12-11-64	9	Minnesota
12	Stewart Gavin (RW)	6-0/190	Ottawa	3-15-60	13	Minnesota
41	Brent Gilchrist (C)	5-11/181	Moose Jaw, Sask.	4-3-67	5	Edmonton, Minnesota
	Todd Harvey (C)	5-11/190	Hamilton, Ont.	2-17-75	0	Detroit (OHL)
	Paul Jerrard (RW)	5-10/185	Winnipeg, Man.	4-20-65	1	Kalamazoo (IHL)
29	Trent Klatt (RW)	6-1/210	Robbinsdale, Minn.	1-30-71	2	Kalamazoo (IHL), Minnesota
	Cal McGowan (C)	6-1/185	Sidney, Neb.	6-19-70	0	Kalamazoo (IHL)
17	Mike McPhee (LW)	6-1/203	Sydney, N.S.	2-14-60	10	Minnesota
	Kip Miller (C)	5-11/190	Lansing, Mich.	6-11-69	2	Kalamazoo (IHL)
9	Mike Modano (RW/C)	6-3/190	Livonia, Mich.	6-7-70	5	Minnesota
16	Brian Propp (LW)	5-10/195	Lanigan, Sask.	2-15-59	14	Minnesota, Lugano (Switz.)
44	Reid Simpson (LW)	6-1/210	Flin Flon, Man.	5-21-69	2	Kalamazoo (IHL), Minnesota
21	Derrick Smith (LW)	6-2/215	Scarborough, Ont.	1-22-65	9	Kalamazoo (IHL), Minnesota
	Jarkko Varvio (RW)	5-9/172	Tampere, Finland	4-28-72	0	HPK Hameenlinna (Fin.)
	DEFENSEMEN					
5	Brad Berry	6-2/190	Bashaw, Alta.	4-1-65	7	Minnesota
	Paul Cavallini	6-1/210	Toronto	10-13-65	7	St. Louis, Washington
2	Derian Hatcher	6-5/205	Sterling Heights, Mich.	6-4-72	2	Minnesota, Kalamazoo (IHL)
6	Jim Johnson	6-1/190	New Hope, Minn.	8-9-62	8	Minnesota
3	Craig Ludwig	6-3/217	Rhinelander, Wis.	3-15-61	11	Minnesota
4	Richard Matvichuk	6-2/190	Edmonton, Alta.	2-5-73	1	Minnesota, Kalamazoo (IHL)
38	Roy Mitchell	6-1/200	Edmonton, Alta.	3-14-69	1	Kalamazoo (IHL), Minnesota
23	Mark Osiecki	6-2/200	St. Paul, Minn.	7-23-68	2	Ottawa, New Haven (AHL), Winnipeg, Minnesota
33	Tommy Sjodin	5-11/185	Sundsvall, Sweden	8-13-65	1	Minnesota
24	Mark Tinordi	6-4/205	Red Deer, Alta.	5-9-66	6	Minnesota
	GOALTENDERS					
	Andy Moog	5-8/170	Penticton, B.C.	2-18-60	13	Boston
35	Darcy Wakaluk	5-11/180	Pincher Creek, Alta.	3-14-66	4	Minnesota

1992-93 REVIEW

INDIVIDUAL STATISTICS

SCORING

	Games	G	A	Pts.	Pen.	+/-	PPG	SHG	Shots	Shooting Pct.
Mike Modano	82	33	60	93	83	-7	9	0	307	10.7
Russ Courtnall	84	36	43	79	49	1	14	2	294	12.2
Dave Gagner	84	33	43	76	143	-13	17	0	230	14.3
Ulf Dahlen	83	35	39	74	6	-20	13	0	223	15.7
Mark Tinordi	69	15	27	42	157	-1	7	0	122	12.3
Mike McPhee	84	18	22	40	44	-2	1	2	161	11.2
Mike Craig	70	15	23	38	106	-11	7	0	131	11.5
Tommy Sjodin	77	7	29	36	30	-25	5	0	175	4.0
Neal Broten	82	12	21	33	22	7	0	3	123	9.8
Todd Elik*	46	13	18	31	48	-5	4	0	76	17.1
Gaetan Duchesne	84	16	13	29	30	6	0	2	134	11.9
Trent Klatt	47	4	19	23	38	2	1	0	69	5.8
Jim Johnson	79	3	20	23	105	9	1	0	67	4.5
Shane Churla	73	5	16	21	286	-8	1	0	61	8.2
Derian Hatcher	67	4	15	19	178	-27	0	0	73	5.5
Stewart Gavin	63	10	8	18	59	-4	0	0	114	8.8
Bobby Smith	45	5	7	12	10	-9	3	0	53	9.4
Craig Ludwig	78	1	10	11	153	1	0	0	66	1.5
Brian Propp	17	3	3	6	0	-10	1	0	35	8.6
Richard Matvichuk	53	2	3	5	26	-8	1	0	51	3.9
Dan Quinn	11	0	4	4	6	-4	0	0	20	0.0
James Black	10	2	1	3	4	0	0	0	10	20.0
Darcy Wakaluk (goalie)	29	0	3	3	20	0	0	0	0	0.0
Jon Casey (goalie)	60	0	3	3	28	0	0	0	0	0.0
Brad Berry	63	0	3	3	109	2	0	0	49	0.0

	Games	G	A	Pts.	Pen.	+/-	PPG	SHG	Shots	Shooting Pct.
Brent Gilchrist*	8	0	1	1	2	-2	0	0	12	0.0
Derrick Smith	9	0	1	1	2	-2	0	0	3	0.0
Enrico Ciccone	31	0	1	1	115	2	0	0	13	0.0
Reid Simpson	1	0	0	0	5	0	0	0	0	0.0
Doug Barrault	2	0	0	0	2	-1	0	0	0	0.0
Roy Mitchell	3	0	0	0	0	0	0	0	0	0.0
Mark Osiecki*	5	0	0	0	5	0	0	0	1	0.0

GOALTENDING

	Games	Min.	Goals	SO	Avg.	W	L	T	Shots	Sv. Pct.
Jon Casey	60	3476	193	3	3.33	26	26	5	1683	.885
Darcy Wakaluk	29	1596	97	1	3.65	10	12	5	803	.879

Empty-net goals (do not count against a goaltender's average): Casey 3.
*Played with two or more NHL teams.

RESULTS

OCTOBER

6—At St. Louis	L	4-6
8—St. Louis	W	5-2
10—Tampa Bay	W	2-1
13—Calgary†	L	3-4
15—At St. Louis	W	5-4
17—At Montreal	L	1-8
18—At Toronto	W	5-1
22—Quebec	W	5-2
24—Los Angeles	T	*5-5
28—At Edmonton	L	2-5
30—At Vancouver	W	3-2
31—At Calgary	L	3-5

NOVEMBER

5—N.Y. Islanders	W	3-0
7—Edmonton	T	*2-2
10—Pittsburgh	L	1-4
12—Winnipeg	L	2-7
14—Chicago	W	3-0
15—At Chicago	L	1-2
18—At Washington	W	5-4
19—At Tampa Bay	W	4-1
21—At Buffalo	W	4-3
25—Vancouver	L	2-4
27—N.Y. Rangers	T	*4-4
28—San Jose	W	10-3
30—At N.Y. Rangers	W	4-2

DECEMBER

1—At Ottawa	W	3-1
3—At Detroit	W	4-2
5—At Quebec	W	7-4
10—Edmonton	L	2-3
12—Chicago	L	0-3
15—Toronto	W	6-5
19—Detroit	T	*3-3
20—At Chicago	L	0-4
22—St. Louis	T	*2-2
26—Winnipeg	W	5-4
27—At Winnipeg	L	4-7
31—Boston	W	5-3

JANUARY

2—At N.Y. Islanders	L	2-3
3—At Hartford	T	*6-6
6—At New Jersey	L	1-5
7—At Pittsburgh	W	6-3
9—Tampa Bay	W	6-4
12—Chicago	L	1-3
14—At Chicago	L	1-3
16—Calgary	W	4-3
19—At Tampa Bay	W	4-2
21—Ottawa	W	7-2
23—Vancouver	T	*3-3
24—At Tampa Bay	T	*2-2
26—At Toronto	W	2-1
28—New Jersey	W	4-2
30—Tampa Bay	L	3-4

FEBRUARY

1—At Vancouver	W	5-4
3—At San Jose	W	7-3
9—Washington	L	2-3
11—At Tampa Bay	W	1-0
13—At Toronto	L	1-6
14—Toronto	L	5-6

17—Los Angeles	L	5-10
20—Philadelphia	W	5-2
21—Detroit	L	1-4
25—At Boston	T	*3-3
27—At St. Louis	L	2-3
28—At Winnipeg	L	6-7

MARCH

3—At Toronto	L	1-3
6—Montreal	W	4-3
7—Detroit	L	1-7
9—San Jose	W	4-2
11—Vancouver†	W	4-3
13—At St. Louis	L	2-6
14—St. Louis	L	1-3
16—At Philadelphia	L	3-4
18—At Detroit	L	1-5
21—Detroit	L	2-6
25—Toronto	T	*3-3
27—Hartford	L	1-2
31—At Edmonton	L	2-5

APRIL

1—At Calgary	L	3-5
3—At Los Angeles	W	3-0
6—Buffalo	W	3-1
10—St. Louis	W	4-3
11—At St. Louis	L	1-5
13—Chicago	L	2-3
15—At Detroit	L	3-5

*Denotes overtime game.
†At Saskatoon, Sask.

DETROIT RED WINGS
WESTERN CONFERENCE/CENTRAL DIVISION

1993-94 SCHEDULE

Home games shaded.
* — At Madison Square Garden, New York.
† — At Minneapolis.
∆ — At Cleveland.

OCTOBER

SUN	MON	TUE	WED	THU	FRI	SAT
					1	2
3	4	5 DAL	6	7	8 ANA	9 LA
10	11	12	13 STL	14	15 TOR	16 TOR
17	18 BUF	19	20	21 WIN	22	23 CHI
24	25 DAL	26	27 LA	28	29	30 QUE
31						

NOVEMBER

SUN	MON	TUE	WED	THU	FRI	SAT
	1	2 BOS	3	4 TOR	5	6
7	8	9 EDM	10	11	12	13 PIT
14	15	16	17 WIN	18	19	20 NJ
21 STL	22	23 SJ	24 VAN	25	26	27 DAL
28 NYI	29	30				

DECEMBER

SUN	MON	TUE	WED	THU	FRI	SAT
			1 HAR	2	3 OTT	4
5 WIN	6 WIN	7	8	9 STL	10	11 SJ
12	13	14 ANA	15	16	17 NYR	18 MON
19	20	21 CHI	22	23 PHI	24	25
26	27 DAL	28	29	30	31 LA	

JANUARY

SUN	MON	TUE	WED	THU	FRI	SAT
						1
2	3	4 STL	5	6 TB	7	8 LA
9	10 ANA	11	12 TB	13	14 DAL	15 BOS
16	17† TB	18	19 ANA	20	21	22° ALL STAR GAME
23	24	25 CHI	26	27 CHI	28	29 WIN
30 WAS	31					

FEBRUARY

SUN	MON	TUE	WED	THU	FRI	SAT
		1	2 TB	3	4 PIT	5 TOR
6	7	8 VAN	9	10	11 PHI	12 STL
13	14	15 TOR	16 FLA	17	18 EDM	19
20 FLA	21	22	23 NJ	24∆ HAR	25	26 SJ
27	28					

MARCH

SUN	MON	TUE	WED	THU	FRI	SAT
		1 CAL	2	3	4 TOR	5
6 BUF	7 NYR	8	9 CAL	10	11 EDM	12
13	14	15 VAN	16	17 NYI	18	19 WIN
20	21	22 CHI	23 OTT	24	25 WAS	26
27 CHI	28	29 HAR	30	31 QUE		

APRIL

SUN	MON	TUE	WED	THU	FRI	SAT
					1	2 CAL
3 STL	4	5 VAN	6	7	8	9 CAL
10 EDM	11	12	13 MON	14 DAL	15	16

1993-94 SEASON

CLUB DIRECTORY

Owner and president
Michael Ilitch
Owner and secretary/treasurer
Marian Ilitch
Executive vice president
To be announced
Senior vice president
Jim Devellano
General manager
Bryan Murray
Assistant general manager
Doug MacLean
Head coach
Scott Bowman
Assistant coaches
Dave Lewis
Barry Smith
Pro scouting director
Dan Belisle
Director of amateur scouting
Ken Holland
Admin. assistant/scouting coordinator
Michael Abbamont
USA scouting director
Billy Dea

Western hockey league scout
Wayne Meier
Western USA scout
Chris Coury
Eastern USA scout
Mike Addesa
Ontario scouts
Sam McMaster
Paul Crowley
Eastern Canada scout
John Stanton
European scouts
Hakan Andersson
Vladimir Havluj
Director of public relations
Bill Jamieson
Director of advertising sales
Len Perna
Athletic trainer
John Wharton
Equipment manager/trainer
Mark Brennan
Assistant equipment manager
Tim Abbott

DRAFT CHOICES

1—Anders Eriksson	6-3/218	22	D	MoDo, Sweden
2—Jon Coleman	6-1/190	48	D	Phillips And. Acad. (Mass.)
3—Kevin Hilton	5-11/170	74	C	Univ. of Michigan (CCHA)
4—John Jakopin	6-5/220	97	D	St. Michael's (Jr. B)
4—Benoit Larose	6-0/200	100	D	Laval (QMJHL)
5—Norm Maracle	5-9/175	126	G	Saskatoon (WHL)
6—Tim Spitzig	6-0/195	152	F	Kitchener (OHL)
7—Yuri Yeresko	5-11/178	178	D	CSKA Moscow, CIS
8—Viteslav Skuta	6-0/198	204	D	Tj Vitkovice, Czech.
9—Ryan Shanahan	6-0/161	230	F	Sudbury (OHL)
10—James Kosecki	6-1/170	256	G	Berkshire H.S.
11—Gordon Hunt	6-5/200	282	C	Detroit Compuware (Jr. A)

MISCELLANEOUS DATA

Home ice (capacity)
Joe Louis Arena (19,275)
Address
600 Civic Center Drive
Detroit, MI 48226
Business phone
313-396-7544

Rink dimensions
200 feet by 85 feet
Club colors
Red and white
Minor league affiliations
Adirondack (AHL)
Toledo (ECHL)

TRAINING CAMP ROSTER

No.	FORWARDS	Ht./Wt.	Place	Born Date	NHL exp.	1992-93 clubs
11	Shawn Burr (C/LW)	6-1/200	Sarnia, Ont.	7-1-66	9	Detroit
22	Dino Ciccarelli (RW)	5-10/175	Sarnia, Ont.	2-8-60	13	Detroit
28	Dallas Drake (LW)	6-0/170	Trail, B.C.	2-4-69	1	Detroit
91	Sergei Fedorov (C)	6-1/191	Minsk, U.S.S.R.	12-13-69	3	Detroit
14	Jim Hiller (RW)	6-0/190	Port Alberni, B.C.	5-15-69	1	Los Angeles, Phoenix (IHL), Detroit
	Greg Johnson (C)	5-11/180	Thunder Bay, Ont.	3-16-71	0	U. of N. Dakota (WCHA)
15	Sheldon Kennedy (RW)	5-11/175	Brandon, Man.	6-15-69	4	Detroit
	Kory Kocur (RW)	6-0/190	Kelvington, Sask.	3-6-69	0	Fort Wayne (IHL), Adirondack (AHL)
13	Vyacheslav Kozlov (LW)	5-10/172	Voskresensk, U.S.S.R.	5-3-72	2	Detroit, Adirondack (AHL)
20	Martin Lapointe (RW)	5-11/197	Lachine, Que.	9-12-73	2	Adirondack (AHL), Detroit, Laval (QMJHL)
	Steve Maltais (LW)	6-2/210	Arvida, Ont.	1-25-69	4	Atlanta (IHL), Tampa Bay
	Darren McCarty (RW)	6-1/211	Burnaby, B.C.	4-1-72	0	Adirondack (AHL)
25	John Ogrodnick (LW)	6-0/208	Ottawa	6-20-59	14	Detroit, Adirondack (AHL)
55	Keith Primeau (C/LW)	6-4/225	Toronto	11-24-71	3	Detroit
24	Bob Probert (LW)	6-3/225	Windsor, Ont.	6-5-65	8	Detroit
26	Ray Sheppard (RW)	6-1/190	Pembroke, Ont.	5-27-66	6	Detroit
23	Mike Sillinger (C)	5-10/191	Regina, Sask.	6-29-71	3	Detroit, Adirondack (AHL)
18	Chris Tancill (C)	5-10/185	Livonia, Mich.	2-7-68	3	Adirondack (AHL), Detroit
19	Steve Yzerman (C)	5-11/183	Cranbrook, B.C.	5-9-65	10	Detroit
	DEFENSEMEN					
	Serge Anglehart	6-2/200	Hull, Que.	4-18-70	0	Adirondack (AHL), Fort Wayne (IHL)
	Bob Boughner	5-11/201	Windsor, Ont.	3-8-71	0	Adirondack (AHL)
3	Steve Chiasson	6-1/205	Barrie, Ont.	4-14-67	7	Detroit
77	Paul Coffey	6-0/200	Weston, Ont.	6-1-61	13	Los Angeles, Detroit
4	Mark Howe	5-11/185	Detroit	5-28-55	14	Detroit
8	Steve Konroyd	6-1/195	Scarborough, Ont.	2-10-61	13	Hartford, Detroit
16	Vladimir Konstantinov	5-11/185	Murmansk, U.S.S.R.	3-19-67	2	Detroit
8	Gord Kruppke	6-1/200	Edmonton, Alta.	4-2-69	2	Adirondack (AHL), Detroit
5	Nicklas Lidstrom	6-2/180	Vasteras, Sweden	4-28-70	2	Detroit
	Stewart Malgunas	5-11/190	Prince George, B.C.	4-21-70	0	Adirondack (AHL)
33	Yves Racine	6-0/200	Matane, Que.	2-7-69	4	Detroit
	Aaron Ward	6-2/200	Windsor, Ont.	1-17-73	0	U. of Michigan (CCHA)
38	Jason York	6-2/195	Nepean, Ont.	5-20-70	1	Adirondack (AHL), Detroit
	GOALTENDERS					
32	Tim Cheveldae	5-11/180	Melville, Sask.	2-15-68	5	Detroit
	Chris Osgood	5-10/156	Peace River, Alta.	11-26-72	0	Adirondack (AHL)
37	Vince Riendeau	5-10/185	St. Hyacinthe, Que.	4-20-66	6	Detroit

1992-93 REVIEW

INDIVIDUAL STATISTICS

SCORING

	Games	G	A	Pts.	Pen.	+/-	PPG	SHG	Shots	Shooting Pct.
Steve Yzerman	84	58	79	137	44	33	13	‡7	307	18.9
Dino Ciccarelli	82	41	56	97	81	12	21	0	200	20.5
Sergei Fedorov	73	34	53	87	72	33	13	4	217	15.7
Ray Sheppard	70	32	34	66	29	7	10	0	183	17.5
Paul Ysebaert	80	34	28	62	42	19	3	3	186	18.3
Steve Chiasson	79	12	50	62	155	14	6	0	227	5.3
Jimmy Carson*	52	25	26	51	18	0	13	0	108	23.1
Dallas Drake	72	18	26	44	93	15	3	2	89	20.2
Bob Probert	80	14	29	43	292	-9	6	0	128	10.9
Nicklas Lidstrom	84	7	34	41	28	7	3	0	156	4.5
Yves Racine	80	9	31	40	80	10	5	0	163	5.5
Shawn Burr	80	10	25	35	74	18	1	1	99	10.1
Mark Howe	60	3	31	34	22	22	3	0	72	4.2
Keith Primeau	73	15	17	32	152	-6	4	1	75	20.0
Sheldon Kennedy	68	19	11	30	46	-1	1	0	110	17.3
Gerard Gallant	67	10	20	30	188	20	0	0	81	12.3
Paul Coffey*	30	4	26	30	27	7	3	0	72	5.6
Vladimir Konstantinov	82	5	17	22	137	22	0	0	85	5.9
Mike Sillinger	51	4	17	21	16	0	0	0	47	8.5
Brad McCrimmon	60	1	14	15	71	21	1	0	53	1.9
John Ogrodnick	19	6	6	12	2	-2	4	0	25	24.0
Jim Hiller*	21	2	6	8	19	7	0	0	24	8.3

	Games	G	A	Pts.	Pen.	+/-	PPG	SHG	Shots	Shooting Pct.
Vyacheslav Kozlov	17	4	1	5	14	-1	0	0	26	15.4
Tim Cheveldae (goalie)	67	0	4	4	4	0	0	0	0	0.0
Jim Cummins	7	1	1	2	58	0	0	0	5	20.0
Chris Tancill	4	1	0	1	2	-2	0	0	3	33.3
Steve Konroyd*	6	0	1	1	4	1	0	0	4	0.0
Dennis Vial	9	0	1	1	20	1	0	0	5	0.0
Jason York	2	0	0	0	0	0	0	0	1	0.0
Martin Lapointe	3	0	0	0	0	-2	0	0	2	0.0
Bobby Dollas	6	0	0	0	2	-1	0	0	5	0.0
Gord Kruppke	10	0	0	0	20	1	0	0	7	0.0
Vincent Riendeau (goalie)	22	0	0	0	2	0	0	0	0	0.0

GOALTENDING

	Games	Min.	Goals	SO	Avg.	W	L	T	Shots	Sv. Pct.
Vincent Riendeau	22	1193	64	0	3.22	13	4	2	522	.877
Tim Cheveldae	67	3880	210	4	3.25	34	24	7	1897	.889

Empty-net goals (do not count against a goaltender's average): Cheveldae 5, Riendeau 1.
*Played with two or more NHL teams.
‡Tied for league lead.

RESULTS

OCTOBER
6—At Winnipeg	L	1-4
8—At Los Angeles	W	5-3
10—At San Jose	W	6-3
15—Quebec	L	2-4
17—Edmonton	W	4-2
20—Winnipeg	W	5-3
22—At Pittsburgh	L	6-9
24—At St. Louis	W	6-1
25—At Chicago	L	2-8
28—San Jose	W	4-3
30—Toronto	W	7-1
31—At Toronto	L	1-3

NOVEMBER
4—Montreal	L	3-4
6—Hartford	W	5-2
7—At Montreal	L	1-5
11—At Tampa Bay	L	4-6
13—Pittsburgh	W	8-0
14—At Hartford	W	2-0
17—Chicago	W	5-4
19—Winnipeg	L	3-5
20—At Washington	W	7-5
23—Tampa Bay	W	10-5
25—St. Louis	W	11-6
27—Los Angeles	L	3-5
28—At St. Louis	T	*2-2
30—Washington	L	1-4

DECEMBER
2—At N.Y. Rangers	L	3-5
3—Minnesota	L	2-4
5—At Tampa Bay	W	9-7
8—Chicago	L	2-3
9—At Toronto	L	3-5
11—Philadelphia	W	4-2
14—Calgary	L	0-3
15—At Ottawa	W	*3-2
18—At Boston	W	6-1
19—At Minnesota	T	*3-3
22—Toronto	T	*4-4
26—At Toronto	W	5-1
27—At Chicago	W	4-0
29—Chicago	L	3-6
31—Ottawa	W	*5-4

JANUARY
2—At Quebec	W	6-2
4—Toronto	L	2-4
8—Vancouver	W	6-3
11—St. Louis	L	0-1
13—Tampa Bay	W	5-3
15—San Jose	W	6-3
17—At Philadelphia	W	7-4
19—N.Y. Rangers	T	*2-2
21—St. Louis	W	5-3
23—At St. Louis	L	3-4
26—At Calgary	W	9-1
27—At Edmonton	T	*2-2
30—At Vancouver	T	*4-4

FEBRUARY
3—Chicago	W	5-0
9—New Jersey	W	8-5
11—At Los Angeles	T	*6-6
13—At St. Louis	L	3-4

14—At Chicago	W	5-3
17—Tampa Bay	W	3-1
19—Calgary	T	*3-3
21—At Minnesota	W	4-1
22—Philadelphia†	T	*5-5
24—At Buffalo	L	7-10
27—Chicago	L	1-2
28—At New Jersey	L	3-6

MARCH
2—At N.Y. Islanders	L	2-3
5—Toronto	W	5-1
7—At Minnesota	W	7-1
10—At Edmonton	W	6-3
11—At Calgary	L	3-6
14—At San Jose	W	4-1
16—Washington‡	L	2-4
18—Minnesota	W	5-1
20—At Boston	W	7-4
21—At Minnesota	W	6-2
23—N.Y. Islanders	W	3-2
27—At Tampa Bay	W	8-3
29—Los Angeles	L	3-9

APRIL
1—At Chicago	W	3-1
3—Vancouver	W	5-1
8—At Tampa Bay	W	9-1
10—Buffalo	W	6-5
15—Minnesota	W	5-3

*Denotes overtime game.
†At Cleveland.
‡At Milwaukee.

EDMONTON OILERS
WESTERN CONFERENCE/PACIFIC DIVISION

1993-94 SCHEDULE

Home games shaded.
* — At Madison Square Garden, New York.
† — At Saskatoon, Sask.
△ — At Sacramento, Calif.

OCTOBER

SUN	MON	TUE	WED	THU	FRI	SAT
					1	2
3	4	5	6 SJ	7	8 NYI	9
10	11 VAN	12	13 ANA	14 LA	15	16 VAN
17	18 WIN	19	20 CAL	21	22 BOS	23
24 WAS	25	26 SJ	27	28	29 BUF	30 CAL
31						

NOVEMBER

SUN	MON	TUE	WED	THU	FRI	SAT
	1	2	3 OTT	4	5	6 STL
7 CHI	8	9 DET	10	11 BOS	12	13 HAR
14	15 TOR	16	17 MON	18	19	20 TOR
21 ANA	22	23	24 CHI	25	26	27 VAN
28	29 DAL	30				

DECEMBER

SUN	MON	TUE	WED	THU	FRI	SAT
			1 PHI	2	3	4
5 DAL	6	7 NYI	8 NYR	9	10	11 NJ
12 PHI	13	14	15 VAN	16	17 SJ	18
19 STL	20	21 VAN	22 CAL	23	24	25
26	27 WIN	28	29 MON	30 CAL	31	

JANUARY

SUN	MON	TUE	WED	THU	FRI	SAT
						1
2 SJ	3	4	5	6	7 QUE	8
9 CHI	10	11 DAL	12	13 STL	14	15 PIT
16	17	18 OTT	19 BUF	20	21	22* ALL-STAR GAME
23	24† VAN	25	26 NJ	27	28 STL	29 DAL
30	31					

FEBRUARY

SUN	MON	TUE	WED	THU	FRI	SAT
		1	2 LA	3	4 CHI	5
6 WIN	7 CAL	8	9 CAL	10	11	12 HAR
13 ANA	14	15 WAS	16	17	18 DET	19 TOR
20	21	22	23 TOR	24	25 LA	26
27 TB	28					

MARCH

SUN	MON	TUE	WED	THU	FRI	SAT
		1 VAN	2	3 SJ	4 ANA	5
6	7	9 FLA	9	10	11 DET	12
13	14	15	16 TB	17	18 FLA	19
20 QUE	21	22	23 NYR	24	25 LA	26
27 PIT	28	29	30	31 ANA		

APRIL

SUN	MON	TUE	WED	THU	FRI	SAT
					1	2 LA
3△ LA	4	5	6 WIN	7	8 ANA	9
10 DET	11	12	13 SJ	14 LA	15	16

1993-94 SEASON

CLUB DIRECTORY

Owner/governor
Peter Pocklington
Alternate governor
Glen Sather
General counsels
Bob Lloyd
Gary Frohlich
President/general manager
Glen Sather
Coach
Ted Green
Assistant coaches
Ron Low
Kevin Primeau
Exec. V.P./assistant general manager
Bruce MacGregor
Vice president, finance
Werner Baum
Executive secretary
Betsy Freedman
Director of public relations
Bill Tuele
Coord. of publications & statistics
Steve Knowles

Director of player personnel/chief scout
Barry Fraser
Hockey operations
Kevin Prendergast
Scouting staff
Ace Bailey
Ed Chadwick
Lorne Davis
Harry Howell
Curly Reeves
Jan Slepicka
Brad Smith
Athletic trainer
Barrie Stafford
Assistant trainer
Lyle Kulchisky
Athletic trainer/therapist
Ken Lowe
Massage therapist
Stewart Poirier
Team physicians
Dr. Gordon Cameron
Dr. David C. Reid

DRAFT CHOICES

1—Jason Arnott	6-3/193	7	C	Oshawa (OHL)
1—Nick Stajduhar	6-2/194	16	D	London (OHL)
2—David Vyborny	5-10/172	33	C	Sparta Praha, Czech.
3—Kevin Paden	6-3/175	59	C	Detroit (OHL)
3—Alexander Kerch	5-10/187	60	F	Dynamo Riga, CIS
5—Miroslav Satan	6-1/176	111	C	Dukla Trencin, Czech.
7—Alexander Zhurik	6-3/191	163	D	Dynamo Minsk, CIS
8—Martin Bakula	6-1/190	189	D	Univ. of Alaska-Anchorage
9—Brad Norton	6-4/225	215	D	Cushing Academy (Conn.)
10—Oleg Maltsev	6-3/224	241	F	Chelyabinsk, CIS
11—Ilya Byakin	5-9/183	267	D	Landshut, Europe

MISCELLANEOUS DATA

Home Ice (capacity)
Northlands Coliseum (17,503)
Address
Edmonton, Alta. T5B 4M9
Business phone
403-474-8561

Rink dimensions
200 feet by 85 feet
Club colors
Blue, orange and white
Minor league affiliation
Cape Breton (AHL)

TRAINING CAMP ROSTER

FORWARDS

No.	FORWARDS	Ht./Wt.	Place	Born Date	NHL exp.	1992-93 clubs
	Jason Arnott (C)	6-3/193	Collingworth, Ont.	10-11-74	0	Oshawa (OHL)
16	Kelly Buchberger (RW)	6-2/210	Langenburg, Sask.	12-12-66	7	Edmonton
8	Zdeno Ciger (LW)	6-1/190	Martin, Czech.	10-19-69	3	New Jersey, Edmonton
9	Shayne Corson (LW/C)	6-1/200	Barrie, Ont.	8-13-66	8	Edmonton
	Dan Currie (LW)	6-2/195	Burlington, Ont.	3-15-68	3	Cape Breton (AHL), Edmonton
29	Louie DeBrusk (LW)	6-2/215	Cambridge, Ont.	3-19-71	2	Edmonton
34	Todd Elik (C)	6-2/190	Brampton, Ont.	4-15-66	4	Minnesota, Edmonton
20	Mike Hudson (C/LW)	6-1/205	Guelph, Ont.	2-6-67	5	Chicago, Edmonton
14	Craig MacTavish (C)	6-1/195	London, Ont.	8-15-58	14	Edmonton
	Kirk Maltby (RW)	6-0/180	Guelph, Ont.	12-22-72	0	Cape Breton (AHL)
	Dean McAmmond (C)	5-11/185	Grand Cache, Alta.	6-15-73	1	Prince Albert (WHL), Swift Current (WHL)
	Roman Oksiuta (RW)	6-3/229	Murmansk, U.S.S.R.	8-21-70	0	Cape Breton (AHL)
26	Shjon Podein (LW)	6-2/200	Rochester, Minn.	3-5-68	1	Cape Breton (AHL), Edmonton
12	Steve Rice (RW)	6-0/215	Waterloo, Ont.	5-26-71	3	Cape Breton (AHL), Edmonton
	Juha Riihijarvi (RW)	6-3/205	Salla, Finland	12-15-69	0	JyP HT (Finland)
18	Craig Simpson (LW)	6-2/195	London, Ont.	2-15-67	8	Edmonton
15	Kevin Todd (C)	5-10/180	Winnipeg, Man.	5-4-68	4	New Jersey, Utica (AHL), Edmonton
23	Vladimir Vujtek (C)	6-1/190	Ostrava, S'ravsky, Czech.	2-17-72	2	Edmonton, Cape Breton (AHL)
	David Vyborny (C)	5-10/172	Jihlava, Czech.	1-22-75	0	Sparta Prague (Czech.)
39	Doug Weight (C)	5-11/191	Warren, Mich.	1-21-71	2	N.Y. Rangers, Edmonton
	Tyler Wright (C)	5-11/175	Canora, Sask.	4-6-73	1	Swift Current (WHL), Edmonton

DEFENSEMEN

No.	DEFENSEMEN	Ht./Wt.	Place	Born Date	NHL exp.	1992-93 clubs
	Ilya Byakin	5-9/183	Sverdlovsk, U.S.S.R.	2-2-63	0	Landshut (Germany)
6	Brian Glynn	6-4/220	Iserlohn, W. Germany	11-23-67	6	Edmonton
2	Chris Joseph	6-2/210	Burnaby, B.C.	9-10-69	6	Edmonton
21	Igor Kravchuk	6-1/200	Ufa, U.S.S.R.	9-13-66	2	Chicago, Edmonton
35	Francois Leroux	6-6/221	St. Adele, Que.	4-18-70	5	Cape Breton (AHL), Edmonton
24	Dave Manson	6-2/210	Prince Albert, Sask.	1-27-67	7	Edmonton
	Gord Mark	6-4/210	Edmonton, Alta.	9-10-64	2	Cape Breton (AHL)
22	Luke Richardson	6-4/210	Ottawa	3-26-69	6	Edmonton
25	Geoff Smith	6-3/200	Edmonton, Alta.	3-7-69	4	Edmonton
	Nick Stajduhar	6-2/194	Kitchener, Ont.	12-6-74	0	London (OHL)
36	Brad Werenka	6-2/204	Two Hills, Alta.	2-12-69	1	Cape Breton (AHL), Edmonton

GOALTENDERS

No.	GOALTENDERS	Ht./Wt.	Place	Born Date	NHL exp.	1992-93 clubs
	Wayne Cowley	6-0/185	Scarborough, Ont.	12-4-64	0	Cape Breton (AHL), Wheeling (ECHL)
	Joaquin Gage	6-0/200	Vancouver, B.C.	10-19-73	0	Portland (WHL)
30	Bill Ranford	5-11/185	Brandon, Man.	12-14-66	8	Edmonton
	Andrew Verner	6-0/195	Weston, Ont.	11-10-72	0	Cape Breton (AHL)

1992-93 REVIEW

INDIVIDUAL STATISTICS

SCORING

	Games	G	A	Pts.	Pen.	+/-	PPG	SHG	Shots	Shooting Pct.
Petr Klima	68	32	16	48	100	-15	13	0	175	18.3
Shayne Corson	80	16	31	47	209	-19	9	2	164	9.8
Craig Simpson	60	24	22	46	36	-14	12	0	91	†26.4
Dave Manson	83	15	30	45	210	-28	9	1	244	6.1
Bernie Nicholls*	46	8	32	40	40	-16	4	0	86	9.3
Esa Tikkanen*	66	14	19	33	76	-11	2	4	162	8.6
Scott Mellanby	69	15	17	32	147	-4	6	0	114	13.2
Kelly Buchberger	83	12	18	30	133	-27	1	2	92	13.0
Craig MacTavish	82	10	20	30	110	-16	0	3	101	9.9
Zdeno Ciger*	37	9	15	24	6	-5	0	0	67	13.4
Martin Gelinas	65	11	12	23	30	3	0	0	93	11.8
Brent Gilchrist*	60	10	10	20	47	-10	2	0	94	10.6
Shjon Podein	40	13	6	19	25	-2	2	1	64	20.3
Greg Hawgood*	29	5	13	18	35	-1	2	0	47	10.6
Geoff Smith	78	4	14	18	30	-11	0	1	67	6.0
Rian Glynn	64	4	12	16	60	-13	2	0	80	5.0
Kevin Todd*	25	4	9	13	10	-5	0	0	39	10.3
Luke Richardson	82	3	10	13	142	-18	0	2	78	3.8
Igor Kravchuk*	17	4	8	12	2	-8	1	0	42	9.5
Chris Joseph	33	2	10	12	48	-9	1	0	49	4.1
Vladimir Vujtek	30	1	10	11	8	-1	0	0	49	2.0

	Games	G	A	Pts.	Pen.	+/-	PPG	SHG	Shots	Shooting Pct.
Craig Muni*	72	0	11	11	67	-15	0	0	51	0.0
Louie DeBrusk	51	8	2	10	205	-16	0	0	33	24.2
Todd Elik*	14	1	9	10	8	1	0	0	28	3.6
Brad Werenka	27	5	3	8	24	1	0	1	38	13.2
Doug Weight*	13	2	6	8	10	-2	0	0	35	5.7
Josef Beranek*	26	2	6	8	28	-7	0	0	44	4.5
Brian Benning*	18	1	7	8	59	-1	0	0	28	3.6
Steven Rice	28	2	5	7	28	-4	0	0	29	6.9
Shaun Van Allen	21	1	4	5	6	-2	0	0	19	5.3
Bill McDougall	4	2	1	3	4	2	0	0	8	25.0
Bill Ranford (goalie)	67	0	3	3	10	0	0	0	0	0.0
Tyler Wright	7	1	1	2	19	-4	0	0	7	14.3
David Maley*	13	1	1	2	29	-3	0	0	9	11.1
Mike Hudson*	5	0	1	1	2	-1	0	0	2	0.0
Scott Thornton	9	0	1	1	0	-4	0	0	7	0.0
Francois Leroux	1	0	0	0	4	0	0	0	0	0.0
Dan Currie	5	0	0	0	4	-4	0	0	11	0.0
Ron Tugnutt (goalie)	26	0	0	0	2	0	0	0	0	0.0

GOALTENDING

	Games	Min.	Goals	SO	Avg.	W	L	T	Shots	Sv. Pct.
Bill Ranford	67	3753	240	1	3.84	17	38	6	2065	.884
Ron Tugnutt	26	1338	93	0	4.17	9	12	2	767	.879

Empty-net goals (do not count against a goaltender's average): Ranford 2, Tugnutt 2.
*Played with two or more NHL teams.
†Led league.

RESULTS

OCTOBER
6—Vancouver	L	4-5
8—At Calgary	L	2-7
10—At Vancouver	L	2-5
11—Toronto	T	*3-3
14—At Winnipeg	L	3-7
15—At Chicago	W	*4-3
17—At Detroit	L	2-4
20—At Tampa Bay	L	1-6
23—Boston	L	3-6
25—Calgary	L	0-4
28—Minnesota	W	5-2
31—Washington	W	4-2

NOVEMBER
3—Ottawa	W	5-2
6—At Winnipeg	W	6-1
7—At Minnesota	T	*2-2
10—At St. Louis	T	*4-4
12—At San Jose	W	4-3
14—At Los Angeles	L	2-6
18—Vancouver	W	4-2
21—At Vancouver	L	0-9
22—N.Y. Islanders	T	*5-5
25—Los Angeles	L	1-3
27—Chicago	L	1-8
28—Tampa Bay	W	*4-3

DECEMBER
1—At San Jose	W	3-1
3—At Vancouver	L	1-4
5—St. Louis	L	1-5
7—At Calgary	L	3-6

8—Calgary	W	3-1
10—At Minnesota	W	3-2
12—At Tampa Bay	L	1-3
13—N.Y. Islanders†	L	1-4
16—Vancouver	W	4-2
18—Los Angeles	T	*5-5
21—At Calgary	L	*2-3
23—San Jose	W	4-2
27—Calgary	L	3-7
29—Montreal	L	3-6
31—At Winnipeg	L	2-3

JANUARY
2—Tampa Bay	W	2-1
3—Philadelphia	T	*2-2
5—At St. Louis	L	1-6
7—At Chicago	T	*3-3
9—At Washington	L	3-4
10—At Philadelphia	L	0-4
13—Winnipeg	L	1-4
15—Hartford	W	3-1
17—Buffalo	W	*3-2
19—Los Angeles	L	4-5
22—Pittsburgh	W	2-1
23—At Winnipeg	L	5-8
27—Detroit	T	*2-2
31—At Buffalo	W	^5-4

FEBRUARY
2—At Boston	W	4-3
3—At Ottawa	L	2-3
9—At Los Angeles	W	6-3
12—San Jose	W	6-0
14—Quebec	L	*2-3

16—At N.Y. Islanders	L	2-7
18—At Pittsburgh	W	5-4
20—At Hartford	L	3-7
21—At Montreal	L	3-4
23—At Quebec	L	3-6
27—N.Y. Rangers	L	0-1
28—San Jose	W	4-1

MARCH
4—Winnipeg	L	3-5
6—At Los Angeles	L	1-6
7—At San Jose	L	3-6
10—Detroit	L	3-6
12—New Jersey	W	6-4
14—Chicago	L	*4-5
17—At N.Y. Rangers	W	*4-3
18—At New Jersey	L	1-5
20—At Toronto	L	2-4
21—Pittsburgh‡	L	4-6
26—Los Angeles	L	1-4
27—Toronto	L	2-6
31—Minnesota	W	5-2

APRIL
3—Winnipeg	L	4-6
6—At San Jose	L	2-5
7—At Vancouver	L	4-5
11—Winnipeg	L	5-7
13—Calgary	L	2-4
15—At Winnipeg	L	0-3

*Denotes overtime game.
†At Oklahoma City, Okla.
‡At Cleveland.

FLORIDA PANTHERS
EASTERN CONFERENCE/ATLANTIC DIVISION

1993-94 SCHEDULE

Home games shaded.
* — At Madison Square Garden, New York.
† — At Orlando, Fla.
△ — At Hamilton, Ont.

OCTOBER
SUN	MON	TUE	WED	THU	FRI	SAT
					1	2
3	4	5	6 CHI	7	8	9 TB
10	11	12 PIT	13	14 OTT	15	16
17 TB	18	19 LA	20	21 TOR	22	23 NJ
24	25	26 WIN	27	28 NYI	29	30 TB
31						

NOVEMBER
SUN	MON	TUE	WED	THU	FRI	SAT
	1	2 PHI	3 TOR	4	5	6
7 QUE	8	9	10 MON	11 OTT	12	13
14 QUE	15	16 NYR	17	18 CHI	19	20 WAS
21	22	23 HAR	24	25	26 BOS	27 HAR
28	29	30				

DECEMBER
SUN	MON	TUE	WED	THU	FRI	SAT
			1	2 BUF	3	4
5 SJ	6	7 ANA	8 LA	9	10 WIN	11
12 DAL	13	14	15 MON	16	17	18
19 BOS	20	21	22 NYR	23	24	25
26† TB	27	28 WAS	29 HAR	30	31	

JANUARY
SUN	MON	TUE	WED	THU	FRI	SAT
						1 ANA
2	3 NYR	4	5	6	7 NJ	8 BOS
9	10	11	12	13 PIT	14	15 MON
16	17 NYI	18	19 WAS	20	21	22* ALL STAR GAME
23	24 MON	25	26 TB	27	28 SJ	29
30 BUF	31					

FEBRUARY
SUN	MON	TUE	WED	THU	FRI	SAT
		1 PIT	2 OTT	3	4 BUF	5
6 BOS	7	8	9	10 PHI	11	12 NYI
13 VAN	14	15	16 DET	17	18 BUF	19
20 DET	21	22△ WIN	23	24 WAS	25	26 WAS
27	28 PIT					

MARCH
SUN	MON	TUE	WED	THU	FRI	SAT
		1	2 NJ	3	4 HAR	5
6	7 VAN	8	9 EDM	10	11 CAL	12
13	14 NYR	15	16 CAL	17	18 EDM	19
20 PHI	21 NJ	22	23△ TOR	24 PHI	25	26 NYI
27	28 DAL	29	30 STL	31		

APRIL
SUN	MON	TUE	WED	THU	FRI	SAT
					1	2 OTT
3	4 NYR	5 QUE	6	7 PHI	8	9
10 NJ	11	12 QUE	13	14 NYI	15	16

1993-94 SEASON

CLUB DIRECTORY

Owner
H. Wayne Huizenga
President
William A. Torrey
Vice president and general manager
Bob Clarke
Vice president, business and marketing
Dean Jordan
Vice president, finance and administration
Jonathan Mariner
Consultant
Gary Green
Assistant to the general manager
Chuck Fletcher
Head coach
Roger Neilson
Assistant coaches
Craig Ramsay
Lindy Ruff
Goaltending coach
Bill Smith
Chief scout
Dennis Patterson

Eastern scout
Ron Harris
Director, public/media relations
Greg Bouris
Public/media relations associates
Kevin Dessart
Ron Colangelo
Director, promotions and special projects
Declan J. Bolger
Director, group/season ticket sales
Bill Beck
Director, ticket and game day operations
Steve Dangerfield
Director, corporate sales and sponsorship
Kimberly Terranova
Coord., corporate sales and sponsorship
Eric Bresler
Director, merchandise
Ron Dennis
Controller
Larry Cohen
Athletic trainer
David Settlemeyer

DRAFT CHOICES

1—Rob Niedermayer	6-2/200	5	C	Medicine Hat (WHL)
2—Kevin Weekes	6-0/158	41	G	Owen Sound (OHL)
3—Chris Armstrong	6-0/184	57	D	Moose Jaw (WHL)
3—Mikael Tjallden	6-2/194	67	D	MoDo, Sweden
3—Steve Washburn	6-1/178	78	C	Ottawa (OHL)
4—Bill McCauley	6-0/173	83	C	Detroit (OHL)
5—Todd MacDonald	6-0/155	109	G	Tacoma (WHL)
6—Alain Nasreddine	6-1/201	135	D	Drummondville (QMJHL)
7—Trevoe Doyle	6-3/204	161	D	Kingston (OHL)
8—Briane Thompson	6-3/205	187	D	Sault Ste. Marie (OHL)
9—Chad Cabana	6-1/200	213	F	Tri-City (WHL)
10—John Demarco	6-4/210	239	D	A'bishop W'ms HS (Mass.)
11—Eric Montreuil	6-1/170	265	C	Chicoutimi (QMJHL)

MISCELLANEOUS DATA

Home ice (capacity)
Miami Arena (14,500)
Address
100 North East Third Avenue
10th Floor
Fort Lauderdale, FL 33301
Business phone
305-768-1900

Rink dimensions
200 feet by 85 feet
Club colors
Red, navy blue and yellow-gold
Minor league affiliations
Cincinnati (IHL)
Birmingham (ECHL)

No.	FORWARDS	Ht./Wt.	Place	BORN Date	NHL exp.	1992-93 clubs
	Douglas Barrault (RW)	6-2/200	Golden, B.C.	4-21-70	1	Kalamazoo (IHL)
	Len Barrie (C)	6-0/190	Kimberly, B.C.	6-4-69	2	Hershey (AHL), Philadelphia
	Jesse Belanger (C)	6-0/170	St. Georges Beauce, Que.	6-15-69	2	Fredericton (AHL), Montreal
	Brian Benning	6-0/195	Edmonton, Alta.	6-10-66	9	Philadelphia, Edmonton
	Dallas Eakins	6-2/195	Dade City, Fla.	1-20-67	1	Moncton (AHL), Winnipeg
	Tom Fitzgerald (RW/C)	6-1/197	Melrose, Mass.	8-28-68	5	N.Y. Islanders
	Randy Gilhen (C)	6-0/192	Zweibrucken, W. Germany	6-13-63	8	N.Y. Rangers, Tampa Bay
	Jeff Greenlaw (RW)	6-1/230	Toronto	2-28-68	5	Baltimore (AHL), Washington
	Jody Hull (RW)	6-2/200	Petrolia, Ont.	2-2-69	5	Ottawa
	Mike Hough (LW)	6-1/192	Montreal	2-6-63	7	Quebec
	Darin Kimble (RW)	6-2/205	Lucky Lake, Sask.	11-22-68	5	Providence (AHL), Boston
	Marc Labelle (LW)	6-1/215	Maniwaki, Quebec	12-20-69	0	N.H. (AHL), S.D. (IHL), Th.B. (Col.HL)
	Scott Levins (RW)	6-3/200	Portland, Ore.	1-30-70	1	Moncton (AHL), Winnipeg
	Bill Lindsay (LW)	5-11/185	Big Fork, Mont.	5-17-71	2	Quebec, Halifax (AHL)
	Andrei Lomakin (LW)	5-10/176	Voskresensk, U.S.S.R.	4-3-64	2	Philadelphia
	Dave Lowry (LW)	6-1/195	Sudbury, Ont.	1-14-65	8	St. Louis
	Bill McCauley (C)	6-0/173	Detroit	4-20-75	0	Detroit (OHL)
	Scott Mellanby (RW)	6-1/205	Montreal	6-11-66	8	Edmonton
	Rob Niedermayer (C)	6-2/200	Cassiar, B.C.	12-28-74	0	Medicine Hat (WHL)
	Brian Skrudland (C)	6-0/196	Peace River, Alta.	7-31-63	8	Montreal, Calgary
	Greg Smyth	6-3/212	Oakville, Ont.	4-23-66	7	Calgary, Salt Lake City (IHL)
	Pete Stauber (LW)	5-11/185	Duluth, Minn.	5-10-66	0	Adirondack (AHL)
	Steve Washburn (C)	6-1/178	Ottawa, Ont.	4-10-75	0	Ottawa (OHL)
	DEFENSEMEN					
	Chris Armstrong	6-0/184	Regina, Sask.	6-26-75	0	Moose Jaw (WHL)
	Steve Bancroft	6-1/214	Toronto	10-6-70	1	Ind. (IHL), Moncton (AHL)
	Joe Cirella	6-3/207	Hamilton, Ont.	5-9-63	12	N.Y. Rangers
	Trevor Doyle	6-3/204	Ottawa	1-1-74	0	Kingston (OHL)
	Alexander Godynyuk	6-0/207	Kiev, U.S.S.R.	1-27-70	3	
	Gord Hynes	6-1/170	Montreal	7-22-66	2	Philadelphia, Hershey (AHL)
	Paul Laus	6-2/205	Beamsville, Ont.	9-26-70	0	Cleveland (IHL)
	Gord Murphy	6-1/180	Willowdale, Ont.	2-23-67	5	Boston, Providence (AHL)
	Alain Nasreddine	6-1/201	Montreal	7-10-75	0	Drummondville (QMJHL)
	Stephane Richer	5-11/190	Hull, Que.	4-28-66	1	T. Bay, Providence (AHL), Boston
	Jeff Serowik	6-0/190	Manchester, N.H.	10-1-67	1	St. John's (AHL)
	Briane Thompson	6-3/205	Peterborough, Ont.	4-17-74	0	Sault Ste. Marie (OHL)
	Milan Tichy	6-0/200	Plzen, Czech.	9-22-69	1	Indianapolis (IHL), Chicago
	Mikael Tjallden	6-2/194	Ornskoldsvik, Sweden	2-16-75	0	MoDo (Sweden Jr.)
	GOALTENDERS					
	Mark Fitzpatrick	6-2/190	Toronto	11-13-68	5	N.Y. Islanders, Capital District (AHL)
	Todd MacDonald	6-0/155	Charlottetown, P.E.I.	7-5-75	0	Tacoma (WHL)
	Pokey Reddick	5-8/170	Halifax, N.S.	10-6-64	5	Fort Wayne (IHL)
	John Vanbiesbrouck	5-8/172	Detroit	9-4-63	11	N.Y. Rangers
	Kevin Weekes	6-0/158	Toronto	4-4-75	0	Owen Sound (OHL)

FIRST-YEAR RECORDS OF NHL EXPANSION TEAMS

Team	Season	Games	W	L	T	Pts.	Division, Conference
Philadelphia Flyers	1967-68	74	31	32	11	73	West Division
Hartford Whalers*	1979-80	80	27	34	19	73	Norris Division, Wales Conference
Los Angeles Kings	1967-68	74	31	33	10	72	West Division
St. Louis Blues	1967-68	74	27	31	16	70	West Division
Minnesota North Stars*	1967-68	74	27	32	15	69	West Division
Edmonton Oilers*	1979-80	80	28	39	13	69	Smythe Division, Campbell Conference
Pittsburgh Penguins	1967-68	74	27	34	13	67	West Division
Atlanta Flames†	1972-73	78	25	38	15	65	West Division
Buffalo Sabres	1970-71	78	24	39	15	63	East Division
Quebec Nordiques*	1979-80	80	25	44	11	61	Adams Division, Wales Conference
Vancouver Canucks	1970-71	78	24	46	8	56	East Division
Tampa Bay Lightning	1992-93	84	23	54	7	53	Norris Division, Campbell Conference
Winnipeg Jets*	1979-80	80	20	49	11	51	Smythe Division, Campbell Conference
Oakland Seals‡	1967-68	74	15	42	17	47	West Division
Kansas City Scouts§	1974-75	80	15	54	11	41	Smythe Division, Campbell Conference
San Jose Sharks	1991-92	80	17	58	5	39	Smythe Division, Campbell Conference
New York Islanders	1972-73	78	12	60	6	30	East Division
Ottawa Senators	1992-93	84	10	70	4	24	Adams Division, Wales Conference
Washington Capitals	1974-75	80	8	67	5	21	Norris Division, Wales Conference

*Entered NHL during a merger with the World Hockey Association.
†Became Calgary Flames after 1979-80 season.
‡Became Cleveland Barons after 1975-76 season; Barons merged with Minnesota North Stars after 1977-78 season.
§Became Colorado Rockies after 1975-76 season; became New Jersey Devils after 1981-82 season.
✶Became Dallas Stars after 1992-93 season.

HARTFORD WHALERS
EASTERN CONFERENCE/NORTHEAST DIVISION

1993-94 SCHEDULE

▧ Home games shaded.
* — At Madison Square Garden, New York.
† — At Cleveland.

OCTOBER

SUN	MON	TUE	WED	THU	FRI	SAT
					1	2
3	4	5	6 MON	7	8	9 PHI
10 BUF	11	12	13 MON	14 CHI	15	16 PIT
17	18	19 TOR	20 QUE	21	22	23 BUF
24	25	26	27 DAL	28 STL	29	30 NYR
31						

NOVEMBER

SUN	MON	TUE	WED	THU	FRI	SAT
	1 STL	2	3 CAL	4	5	6 NYI
7	8	9	10 OTT	11	12	13 EDM
14	15	16	17 BOS	18 PHI	19	20 SJ
21	22	23 FLA	24 TB	25	26	27 FLA
28	29 OTT	30				

DECEMBER

SUN	MON	TUE	WED	THU	FRI	SAT
			1 DET	2	3	4 PIT
5	6	7 WAS	8 VAN	9	10	11 BUF
12 BOS	13	14	15 NYR	16	17	18 WAS
19	20	21	22 NJ	23 OTT	24	25
26 OTT	27	28 NJ	29 FLA	30	31	

JANUARY

SUN	MON	TUE	WED	THU	FRI	SAT
						1 NYI
2 PIT	3	4	5 WIN	6† STL	7	8 NYI
9	10	11	12 LA	13	14 ANA	15 SJ
16	17 BOS	18	19 TOR	20	21	22° ALL-STAR GAME
23	24 BOS	25	26 MON	27 OTT	28	29 QUE
30	31					

FEBRUARY

SUN	MON	TUE	WED	THU	FRI	SAT
		1 QUE	2 MON	3	4 WIN	5
6 VAN	7	8	9	10	11 CAL	12 EDM
13	14	15	16 BUF	17 PIT	18	19 NYR
20	21	22	23	24† DET	25	26 NJ
27 WAS	28					

MARCH

SUN	MON	TUE	WED	THU	FRI	SAT
		1	2 LA	3	4 FLA	5 TB
6	7	8	9 TB	10 NJ	11	12 DAL
13 PIT	14	15	16 NYR	17 QUE	18	19 PHI
20	21	22 WAS	23	24	25 BUF	26 ANA
27	28	29 DET	30 CHI	31		

APRIL

SUN	MON	TUE	WED	THU	FRI	SAT
					1	2 PHI
3	4	5	6 NYI	7 QUE	8	9
10 TB	11 MON	12	13	14 BOS	15	16

1993-94 SEASON

CLUB DIRECTORY

Managing general partner and governor
Richard H. Gordon
President and alternate governor
Emile Francis
General manager
Brian Burke
Assistant general manager
Ken Schinkel
Director of hockey operations
Tom Rowe
Special asst. to the managing gen. partner
Gordie Howe
Vice president, marketing and sales
Rick Francis
Treasurer
Michael J. Amendola
Director of advertising sales
Kevin Bauer
Director of ticket operations and sales
Jim Baldwin
Director of public relations
John H. Forslund
Public relations assistant
Mary Lynn Gorman

Chief statistician, assistant director of public relations and archivist
Frank Polnaszek
Coach
Paul Holmgren
Assistant coaches
Pierre McGuire
Kevin McCarthy
Director of pro scouting
Kevin Maxwell
Scouts
Leo Boivin
Roger Borough
Fred Gore
Bruce Haralson
Claude Larose
Willy Lindstrom
Roger Oxborough
Steve Rooney
Trainer
Frank "Bud" Goveira
Equipment manager
Skip Cunningham
Strength and conditioning coach
Doug McKenney

DRAFT CHOICES

1—Chris Pronger	6-5/190	2	D	Peterborough (OHL)
3—Marek Malik	6-5/185	72	D	Tj Vitkovice, Czech.
4—Trevor Roenick	6-1/200	84	F	Boston Jr. Bruins
5—Nolan Pratt	6-2/190	115	D	Portland (WHL)
8—Emmanuel Legace	5-8/180	188	G	Niagara Falls (OHL)
9—Dimitri Gorenko	6-0/165	214	F	CSKA Moscow, CIS
10—Wes Swinson	6-2/183	240	D	Kitchener (OHL)
11—Igor Chibiryev		170	266	F	Fort Wayne (IHL)

MISCELLANEOUS DATA

Home ice (capacity)
Hartford Civic Center (15,635)
Address
242 Trumbull Street
8th Floor
Hartford, CT 06103
Business phone
203-728-3366

Rink dimensions
200 feet by 85 feet
Club colors
Silver, blue, white and green
Minor league affiliation
Springfield (AHL)

TRAINING CAMP ROSTER

No.	FORWARDS	Ht./Wt.	Place	BORN Date	NHL exp.	1992-93 clubs
21	Andrew Cassels (C)	6-0/192	Mississauga, Ont.	7-23-69	4	Hartford
11	Yvon Corriveau (LW)	6-1/195	Welland, Ont.	2-8-67	8	San Jose, Hartford
7	Randy Cunneyworth	6-0/180	Etobicoke, Ont.	5-10-61	10	Hartford
46	Scott Daniels (LW)	6-3/200	Prince Albert, Sask.	9-19-69	1	Hartford, Springfield (AHL)
15	Joe Day (C)	5-11/180	Chicago	5-11-68	2	Springfield (AHL), Hartford
14	Chris Govedaris (LW)	6-0/200	Toronto	2-2-70	3	Springfield (AHL), Hartford
17	Mark Greig (RW)	5-11/190	High River, Alta.	1-25-70	3	Hartford, Springfield (AHL)
22	Mark Janssens (C/LW)	6-3/216	Surrey, B.C.	5-19-68	6	Hartford
38	Robert Kron (LW)	5-10/180	Brno, Czech.	2-27-67	3	Vancouver, Hartford
20	Nick Kypreos (RW)	6-0/195	Toronto	6-4-66	4	Hartford
34	Jamie Leach (RW)	6-1/205	Winnipeg, Man.	8-25-69	4	Pittsburgh, Hartford, Springfield (AHL), Cleveland (IHL)
33	Jim McKenzie (LW)	6-3/210	Gull Lake, Sask.	11-3-69	4	Hartford
	Scott Morrow (LW)	6-1/181	Chicago	6-18-69	0	Springfield (AHL)
68	Barry Nieckar (LW)	6-3/200	Rama, Sask.	12-16-67	1	Springfield (AHL), Hartford
36	Mikael Nylander (C)	5-11/176	Stockholm, Sweden	10-3-72	1	Hartford
39	Robert Petrovicky (C)	5-11/172	Kosice, Czech.	10-26-73	1	Hartford, Springfield (AHL)
24	Patrick Poulin (LW)	6-1/208	Vanier, Que.	4-23-73	2	Hartford
	Barry Richter (D/RW)	6-2/205	Madison, Wis.	9-11-70	0	University of Wisconsin (WCHA)
8	Geoff Sanderson (LW)	6-0/185	Hay River, N.W.T.	2-1-72	3	Hartford
	Jim Sandlak (RW)	6-4/219	Kitchener, Ont.	12-12-66	8	Vancouver
16	Pat Verbeek (RW)	5-9/190	Sarnia, Ont.	5-24-64	11	Hartford
	DEFENSEMEN					
26	Jim Agnew	6-1/190	Deloraine, Man.	3-21-66	6	Hartford, Springfield (AHL)
6	Adam Burt	6-0/190	Detroit	1-15-69	5	Hartford
27	Doug Houda	6-2/200	Blairmore, Alta.	6-3-66	7	Hartford
37	Dan Keczmer	6-1/190	Mt. Clemens, Mich.	5-25-68	3	Springfield (AHL), Hartford
	Brad McCrimmon	5-11/197	Dodsland, Sask.	3-29-59	13	Detroit
41	Allen Pedersen	6-3/210	Edmonton, Alta.	1-13-65	7	Hartford
	Chris Pronger	6-5/190	Dryden, Ont.	10-10-74	0	Peterborough (OHL)
	Todd Richards	6-0/190	Robbinsdale, Minn.	10-20-66	2	Springfield (AHL)
4	Eric Weinrich	6-0/210	Roanoke, Va.	12-19-66	5	Hartford
3	Zarley Zalapski	6-1/210	Edmonton, Alta.	4-22-68	6	Hartford
	GOALTENDERS					
1	Sean Burke	6-4/210	Windsor, Ont.	1-29-67	5	Hartford
35	Corrie D'Alessio	5-11/155	Cornwall, Ont.	9-9-69	1	Springfield (AHL), Hartford
31	Mario Gosselin	5-8/160	Thetford Mines, Que.	6-15-63	8	Springfield (AHL), Hartford
30	Mike Lenarduzzi	6-1/168	Mississauga, Ont.	9-14-72	1	Springfield (AHL), Hartford
40	Frank Pietrangelo	5-10/185	Niagara Falls, Ont.	12-17-64	6	Hartford

1992-93 REVIEW

INDIVIDUAL STATISTICS

SCORING

	Games	G	A	Pts.	Pen.	+/-	PPG	SHG	Shots	Shooting Pct.
Geoff Sanderson	82	46	43	89	28	-21	21	2	271	17.0
Andrew Cassels	84	21	64	85	62	-11	8	3	134	15.7
Pat Verbeek	84	39	43	82	197	-7	16	0	235	16.6
Murray Craven*	67	25	42	67	20	-4	6	3	139	18.0
Zarley Zalapski	83	14	51	65	94	-34	8	1	192	7.3
Terry Yake	66	22	31	53	46	3	4	1	98	22.4
Patrick Poulin	81	20	31	51	37	-19	4	0	160	12.5
Eric Weinrich	79	7	29	36	76	-11	0	2	104	6.7
Michael Nylander	59	11	22	33	36	-7	3	0	85	12.9
Mark Janssens	76	12	17	29	237	-15	0	0	63	19.0
Nick Kypreos	75	17	10	27	325	-5	0	0	81	21.0
Adam Burt	65	6	14	20	116	-11	0	0	81	7.4
Steve Konroyd*	59	3	11	14	63	-16	0	0	62	4.8
Yvon Corriveau*	37	5	5	10	14	-13	1	0	45	11.1
John Cullen*	19	5	4	9	58	-15	3	0	38	13.2
Randy Cunneyworth	39	5	4	9	63	-1	0	0	47	10.6
Robert Petrovicky	42	3	6	9	45	-10	0	0	41	7.3
Jim McKenzie	64	3	6	9	202	-10	0	0	36	8.3
Dan Keczmer	23	4	4	8	28	-3	2	0	38	10.5
Doug Houda	60	2	6	8	167	-19	0	0	43	4.7
Mark Greig	22	1	7	8	27	-11	0	0	16	6.3
Joe Day	24	1	7	8	47	-8	0	0	10	10.0
Robert Kron*	13	4	2	6	4	-5	2	0	37	10.8

	Games	G	A	Pts.	Pen.	+/-	PPG	SHG	Shots	Shooting Pct.
Randy Ladouceur	62	2	4	6	109	-18	0	0	37	5.4
Tim Kerr	22	0	6	6	7	-11	0	0	48	0.0
Jamie Leach*	19	3	2	5	2	-5	0	0	17	17.6
Allen Pedersen	59	1	4	5	60	0	0	0	16	6.3
Paul Gillis	21	1	1	2	40	-2	0	0	8	12.5
Sean Burke (goalie)	50	0	2	2	25	0	0	0	0	0.0
Chris Govedaris	7	1	0	1	0	-2	0	0	6	16.7
Mario Gosselin (goalie)	16	0	1	1	2	0	0	0	0	0.0
Scott Daniels	1	0	0	0	19	0	0	0	0	0.0
Corrie D'Alessio (goalie)	1	0	0	0	0	0	0	0	0	0.0
Barry Nieckar	2	0	0	0	2	-2	0	0	1	0.0
Mike Lenarduzzi (goalie)	3	0	0	0	0	0	0	0	0	0.0
Jim Agnew	16	0	0	0	68	3	0	0	3	0.0
Frank Pietrangelo (goalie)	30	0	0	0	4	0	0	0	0	0.0

GOALTENDING

	Games	Min.	Goals	SO	Avg.	W	L	T	Shots	Sv. Pct.
Corrie D'Alessio	1	11	0	0	0.00	0	0	0	3	1.000
Mike Lenarduzzi	3	168	9	0	3.21	1	1	1	87	.897
Mario Gosselin	16	867	57	0	3.94	5	9	1	499	.886
Sean Burke	50	2656	184	0	4.16	16	27	3	1485	.876
Frank Pietrangelo	30	1373	111	0	4.85	4	15	1	783	.858

Empty-net goals (do not count against a goaltender's average): Burke 4, Pietrangelo 3, Gosselin 1.
*Played with two or more NHL teams.

RESULTS

OCTOBER
6—Montreal	L	1-5	
8—At Boston	L	*2-3	
10—Buffalo	L	2-5	
12—At N.Y. Rangers	L	2-6	
14—Ottawa	W	4-1	
17—Pittsburgh	L	3-7	
20—At New Jersey	W	5-4	
22—At Ottawa	W	5-1	
24—At N.Y. Islanders	L	2-4	
28—New Jersey	L	*3-4	
31—Los Angeles	L	1-7	

NOVEMBER
3—Quebec	T	*3-3	
6—At Detroit	L	2-5	
7—Washington	L	2-6	
11—Calgary	L	3-4	
13—At Buffalo	L	2-8	
14—Detroit	L	0-2	
18—St. Louis	W	5-2	
19—At Ottawa	W	4-2	
21—At Quebec	L	2-8	
25—Montreal	L	1-6	
27—At Boston	L	*4-5	
28—Boston	W	*4-3	

DECEMBER
1—At St. Louis	L	4-8	
3—At San Jose	W	7-5	
5—At Los Angeles	L	3-7	
9—Ottawa	W	6-2	
11—At Buffalo	L	3-9	
12—Buffalo	T	*1-1	
16—Washington	W	6-3	
18—At Washington	L	3-4	
19—N.Y. Rangers	T	*4-4	
21—At Montreal	W	5-2	
23—Tampa Bay	W	3-1	
26—Boston	L	4-9	
27—At New Jersey	L	2-6	
31—Quebec	L	2-6	

JANUARY
2—At Boston	L	*2-3	
3—Minnesota	T	*6-6	
6—Buffalo	L	1-3	
9—Quebec	W	4-2	
10—Montreal	L	5-7	
13—At Montreal	L	3-7	
15—At Edmonton	L	1-3	
16—At Vancouver	L	3-8	
18—Winnipeg†	L	7-8	
21—San Jose	W	4-2	
23—Chicago	L	2-6	
24—At Philadelphia	L	*4-5	
27—At Montreal	W	6-5	
28—At Ottawa	L	2-5	
30—Winnipeg	L	3-6	

FEBRUARY
3—At Buffalo	L	2-3	
8—St. Louis‡	L	1-3	
12—At Winnipeg	W	6-2	
13—At Calgary	L	*3-4	
17—Buffalo	L	3-5	
20—Edmonton	W	7-3	

MARCH
21—Pittsburgh	L	3-4	
24—Philadelphia	L	2-5	
27—At Quebec	W	5-3	
28—N.Y. Islanders	L	*6-7	
3—New Jersey	L	4-7	
5—At Buffalo	W	4-2	
6—Vancouver	W	5-1	
8—At Quebec	W	4-2	
10—At Toronto	L	3-5	
13—Buffalo	T	*3-3	
16—At Tampa Bay	W	*4-3	
19—At Washington	L	2-5	
22—At Boston	L	4-5	
24—Montreal	L	*5-6	
27—At Minnesota	W	2-1	
28—At Chicago	L	0-3	
30—Boston	L	1-3	

APRIL
1—At Pittsburgh	L	2-10	
3—Ottawa	W	7-3	
5—At N.Y. Rangers	W	5-4	
7—At Ottawa	W	6-1	
10—At Quebec	L	3-6	
11—Toronto	L	2-4	
13—At N.Y. Islanders	T	*3-3	
14—N.Y. Islanders	W	5-4	
16—Philadelphia	L	*4-5	

*Denotes overtime game.
†At Saskatoon, Sask.
‡At Peoria, Ill.

LOS ANGELES KINGS
WESTERN CONFERENCE/PACIFIC DIVISION

1993-94 SCHEDULE

Home games shaded.
* — At Madison Square Garden, New York.
† — At Phoenix.
∆ — At Sacramento, Calif.

OCTOBER

SUN	MON	TUE	WED	THU	FRI	SAT
					1	2
3	4	5	6 VAN	7	8	9 DET
10 SJ	11	12 NYI	13	14 EDM	15	16 CAL
17	18	19	20 TB	21	22 WAS	23
24 NYR	25	26 NYI	27 DET	28	29 WIN	30
31						

NOVEMBER

SUN	MON	TUE	WED	THU	FRI	SAT
	1	2	3 NJ	4	5	6 PIT
7	8	9 CAL	10 VAN	11	12	13 STL
14	15	16	17	18 TOR	19	20 STL
21 DAL	22	23	24	25 QUE	26	27 MON
28	29	30 WIN				

DECEMBER

SUN	MON	TUE	WED	THU	FRI	SAT
			1	2 ANA	3	4 TB
5	6	7	8 FLA	9	10	11 STL
12	13 OTT	14 PIT	15	16	17 BUF	18 TOR
19	20 CAL	21	22	23 DAL	24	25
26 ANA	27	28 VAN	29	30	31 DET	

JANUARY

SUN	MON	TUE	WED	THU	FRI	SAT
						1 TOR
2	3	4 QUE	5	6	7	8 DET
9	10	11 SJ	12 HAR	13	14	15 NJ
16 PHI	17	18 DAL	19	20	21	22* ALL-STAR GAME
23	24† CAL	25 WIN	26	27 NYR	28	29 ANA
30	31 VAN					

FEBRUARY

SUN	MON	TUE	WED	THU	FRI	SAT
		1	2 EDM	3	4	5 CAL
6	7	8	9 CHI	10	11 ANA	12 WAS
13	14 BOS	15	16	17	18 PHI	19 SJ
20	21 TOR	22	23 DAL	24	25 EDM	26 CAL
27	28 MON					

MARCH

SUN	MON	TUE	WED	THU	FRI	SAT
		1	2 HAR	3 BOS	4	5
6 CHI	7	8	9 CHI	10	11	12 BUF
13	14	15 OTT	16 ANA	17	18	19 SJ
20 SJ	21	22	23 VAN	24	25 EDM	26
27 VAN	28	29	30 ANA	31		

APRIL

SUN	MON	TUE	WED	THU	FRI	SAT
					1	2 EDM
3∆ EDM	4	5 SJ	6	7 STL	8	9 WIN
10 CHI	11	12	13 CAL	14 EDM	15	16

1993-94 SEASON

CLUB DIRECTORY

Owner/chairman
  Bruce McNall
Assistant to the chairman
  Rogatien Vachon
President
  Roy A. Mlakar
Vice president, public relations
  Scott J. Carmichael
Vice president administration/marketing
  Robert Moor
General manager
  Nick Beverley
Coach
  Barry Melrose
Assistant coach
  Cap Raeder
Administrative assistant to general manager
  John Wolf
Dir. of player personnel and development
  Bob Owen

Scouting staff
  Jim Anderson
  Ron Ansell
  Serge Aubry
  John Bymark
  Gary Harker
  Jan Lindegren
  Mark Miller
  Al Murray
  Vaclav Nedomansky
  Ted O'Connor
  Don Perry
  Alex Smart
Director of media relations
  Rick Minch
Media relations assistant
  To be announced
Trainers
  Pete Demers
  Peter Millar
  Mark O'Neill

DRAFT CHOICES

2—Shayne Toporowski..	6-2/204	42	F	Prince Albert (WHL)
3—Jeffrey Mitchell.........	6-1/175	68	C	Detroit (OHL)
4—Bob Wren..................	5-10/174	94	F	Detroit (OHL)
5—Frederick Baubien	6-1/204	105	G	St. Hyacinthe (QMJHL)
5—Jason Saal................	5-9/165	117	G	Detroit (OHL)
5—Tomas Vlasak	5-10/161	120	C	Slavia Praha, Czech.
6—Jere Karalanti	6-2/180	146	D	Helsinki IFK, Finland
7—Justin Martin	6-4/210	172	F	Essex Junction
8—John-Tra Dillabough ..	6-1/170	198	C	Wexford (Jr. B)
9—Martin Strebak	6-3/198	224	D	Presov, Europe
10—Kimmo Timonen	5-9/180	250	D	Kalpa, Europe
11—Patrick Howald	5-11/185	276	F	Lugano, Europe

MISCELLANEOUS DATA

Home ice (capacity)
  The Great Western Forum (16,005)
Address
  3900 West Manchester Blvd.
  Inglewood, CA 90305
Business phone
  310-419-3160

Rink dimensions
  200 feet by 85 feet
Club colors
  Black, white and silver
Minor league affiliation
  Phoenix (IHL)

TRAINING CAMP ROSTER

No.	FORWARDS	Ht./Wt.	Place	BORN Date	NHL exp.	1992-93 clubs
	Bob Berg (LW)	6-1/195	Beamsville, Ont.	7-2-70	0	Muskegon (Col.HL)
8	Scott Bjugstad (LW)	6-1/185	St. Paul, Minn.	6-2-61	9	Phoenix (IHL)
12	Jimmy Carson (C)	6-1/200	Southfield, Mich.	7-20-68	7	Detroit, Los Angeles
15	Pat Conacher (LW/C)	5-8/190	Edmonton, Alta.	5-1-59	11	Los Angeles
11	Mike Donnelly (LW)	5-11/185	Livonia, Mich.	10-10-63	7	Los Angeles
	John Druce (RW)	6-1/200	Peterborough, Ont.	2-23-66	5	Winnipeg
21	Tony Granato (LW)	5-10/185	Downers Grove, Ill.	7-25-64	5	Los Angeles
99	Wayne Gretzky (C)	6-0/170	Brantford, Ont.	1-26-61	14	Los Angeles
17	Jari Kurri (C/RW)	6-1/195	Helsinki, Finland	5-18-60	12	Los Angeles
13	Robert Lang (C)	6-2/180	Teplice, Czech.	12-19-70	1	Los Angeles, Phoenix (IHL)
28	Guy Leveque (C)	5-11/180	Kingston, Ont.	12-28-72	1	Phoenix (IHL), Los Angeles
	Rob Murphy (C)	6-3/205	Hull, Que.	4-7-69	6	Ottawa, New Haven (AHL)
27	Marc Potvin (RW)	6-1/215	Ottawa	1-29-67	3	Adirondack (AHL), Los Angeles
	Keith Redmond (LW)	6-3/208	Richmond Hill, Ont.	10-25-72	0	Muskegon (Col.HL), Phoenix (IHL)
20	Luc Robitaille (LW)	6-1/195	Montreal	2-17-66	7	Los Angeles
10	Warren Rychel (LW)	6-0/202	Tecumseh, Ont.	5-12-67	3	Los Angeles
7	Tomas Sandstrom (RW)	6-2/200	Jakobstad, Finland	9-4-64	9	Los Angeles
41	Brandy Semchuk (RW)	6-1/190	Calgary, Alta.	9-22-71	1	Phoenix (IHL), Los Angeles
14	Gary Shuchuk (RW/C)	5-11/191	Edmonton, Alta.	2-17-67	2	Adirondack (AHL), Los Angeles
18	Dave Taylor (RW)	6-0/195	Levack, Ont.	12-4-55	16	Los Angeles
	Dave Thomlinson (LW)	6-1/195	Edmonton, Alta.	10-22-66	3	Binghamton (AHL)
	Mike Vukonich (C)	6-2/220	Duluth, Minn.	5-11-68	0	Phoenix (IHL)
9	Sean Whyte (RW)	6-0/198	Sudbury, Ont.	5-4-70	2	Phoenix (IHL), Los Angeles
	DEFENSEMEN					
4	Rob Blake	6-3/205	Simcoe, Ont.	12-10-69	4	Los Angeles
24	Mark Hardy	5-11/195	Semaden, Switzerland	2-1-59	14	N.Y. Rangers, Los Angeles
22	Charlie Huddy	6-0/210	Oshawa, Ont.	6-2-59	13	Los Angeles
	Jim Maher	6-1/205	Warren, Mich.	6-10-70	0	Phoenix (IHL), Muskegon (Col.HL)
33	Marty McSorley	6-1/225	Hamilton, Ont.	5-18-63	10	Los Angeles
25	Darryl Sydor	6-0/200	Edmonton, Alta.	5-13-72	2	Los Angeles
3	Brent Thompson	6-2/200	Calgary, Alta.	1-9-71	2	Phoenix (IHL), Los Angeles
	Dave Tretowicz	5-11/195	Liverpool, N.Y.	3-15-69	0	Phoenix (IHL)
5	Timothy Watters	5-11/185	Kamloops, B.C.	7-25-59	12	Phoenix (IHL), Los Angeles
2	Alexei Zhitnik	5-11/190	Kiev, U.S.S.R.	10-10-72	1	Los Angeles
	GOALTENDERS					
43	David Goverde	6-0/210	Toronto	4-9-70	2	Phoenix (IHL), Los Angeles
32	Kelly Hrudey	5-10/189	Edmonton, Alta.	1-13-61	10	Los Angeles
	Pauli Jaks	6-0/191	Schaffhausen, Switz.	1-25-72	0	Ambri Piotta (Switz.)
1	Rick Knickle	5-11/170	Chatham, N.B.	2-26-60	1	San Diego (IHL), Los Angeles
35	Robb Stauber	5-11/170	Duluth, Minn.	11-25-67	2	Los Angeles

1992-93 REVIEW

INDIVIDUAL STATISTICS

SCORING

	Games	G	A	Pts.	Pen.	+/-	PPG	SHG	Shots	Shooting Pct.
Luc Robitaille	84	63	62	125	100	18	24	2	265	23.8
Jari Kurri	82	27	60	87	38	19	12	2	210	12.9
Tony Granato	81	37	45	82	171	-1	14	2	247	15.0
Mike Donnelly	84	29	40	69	45	17	8	1	244	11.9
Wayne Gretzky	45	16	49	65	6	6	0	2	141	11.3
Rob Blake	76	16	43	59	152	18	10	0	243	6.6
Paul Coffey*	50	8	49	57	50	9	2	0	182	4.4
Tomas Sandstrom	39	25	27	52	57	12	8	0	134	18.7
Alexei Zhitnik	78	12	36	48	80	-3	5	0	136	8.8
Marty McSorley	81	15	26	41	†399	1	3	3	197	7.6
Corey Millen	42	23	16	39	42	16	9	2	100	23.0
Darryl Sydor	80	6	23	29	63	-2	0	0	112	5.4
Charlie Huddy	82	2	25	27	64	16	0	0	106	1.9
Lonnie Loach*	50	10	13	23	27	3	1	0	55	18.2
Jimmy Carson*	34	12	10	22	14	-2	4	0	81	14.8
Pat Conacher	81	9	8	17	20	-16	0	2	65	13.8
Dave Taylor	48	6	9	15	49	1	1	0	53	11.3
Warren Rychel	70	6	7	13	314	-15	0	0	67	9.0
Jim Hiller*	40	6	6	12	90	0	1	0	59	10.2
John McIntyre*	49	2	5	7	80	-13	0	0	31	6.5
Bob Kudelski*	15	3	3	6	8	-3	0	0	12	25.0
Gary Shuchuk	25	2	4	6	16	0	0	0	24	8.3
Robert Lang	11	0	5	5	2	-3	0	0	3	0.0
Brent Thompson	30	0	4	4	76	-4	0	0	18	0.0
Kelly Hrudey (goalie)	50	0	4	4	10	0	0	0	0	0.0

	Games	G	A	Pts.	Pen.	+/-	PPG	SHG	Shots	Shooting Pct.
Guy Leveque	12	2	1	3	19	-4	0	0	12	16.7
Mark Hardy*	11	0	3	3	4	-4	0	0	20	0.0
Peter Ahola*	8	1	1	2	6	-2	0	0	3	33.3
Sean Whyte	18	0	2	2	12	1	0	0	7	0.0
Tim Watters	22	0	2	2	18	-3	0	0	8	0.0
Robb Stauber (goalie)	31	0	2	2	4	0	0	0	0	0.0
Jeff Chychrun*	17	0	1	1	23	-3	0	0	3	0.0
Marc Potvin	20	0	1	1	61	-10	0	0	7	0.0
Brandy Semchuk	1	0	0	0	2	0	0	0	0	0.0
David Goverde (goalie)	2	0	0	0	0	0	0	0	0	0.0
Darryl Williams	2	0	0	0	10	0	0	0	1	0.0
Frank Breault	4	0	0	0	6	-1	0	0	0	0.0
Marc Fortier*	6	0	0	0	5	-2	0	0	2	0.0
Jim Thomson*	9	0	0	0	56	-1	0	0	2	0.0
Rick Knickle (goalie)	10	0	0	0	2	0	0	0	0	0.0
Rene Chapdelaine	13	0	0	0	12	-6	0	0	5	0.0

GOALTENDING

	Games	Min.	Goals	SO	Avg.	W	L	T	Shots	Sv. Pct.
Robb Stauber	31	1735	111	0	3.84	15	8	4	987	.888
Kelly Hrudey	50	2718	175	2	3.86	18	21	6	1552	.887
Rick Knickle	10	532	35	0	3.95	6	4	0	292	.880
David Goverde	2	98	13	0	7.96	0	2	0	51	.745

Empty-net goals (do not count against a goaltender's average): Hrudey 4, Goverde 1, Stauber 1.
*Played with two or more NHL teams.
†Led league.

RESULTS

OCTOBER

6—At Calgary	W	*5-4
8—Detroit	L	3-5
10—Winnipeg	W	6-3
13—San Jose	W	2-1
15—Calgary	W	4-0
17—Boston	W	8-6
20—At Calgary	L	2-6
23—At Winnipeg	L	2-4
24—At Minnesota	T	*5-5
27—At N.Y. Islanders	W	4-3
29—At Boston	L	3-8
31—At Hartford	W	7-1

NOVEMBER

5—New Jersey	W	5-2
7—Buffalo	W	5-2
8—At San Jose	W	11-4
10—At Winnipeg	T	*4-4
12—Vancouver	W	7-4
14—Edmonton	W	6-2
16—At Vancouver	L	3-6
17—At San Jose	L	0-6
19—Chicago	W	4-1
21—Toronto	W	6-4
25—At Edmonton	W	3-1
27—At Detroit	W	5-3
28—At Toronto	L	2-3

DECEMBER

1—Chicago†	W	6-3
3—Pittsburgh	W	5-3
5—Hartford	W	7-3

8—Montreal‡	T	*5-5
10—Quebec	L	4-5
12—St. Louis	W	6-3
15—Tampa Bay	L	2-3
18—At Edmonton	T	*5-5
19—At Calgary	L	3-5
22—Vancouver	L	2-6
26—At San Jose	L	2-7
29—Philadelphia	L	2-10
31—At Vancouver	L	0-4

JANUARY

2—Montreal	T	*5-5
6—Tampa Bay	L	3-6
8—At Winnipeg	L	3-6
10—At Chicago	W	5-4
12—At Ottawa	W	3-2
14—At New Jersey	L	1-7
16—Winnipeg	L	2-5
19—At Edmonton	W	5-4
21—Vancouver	L	4-5
23—N.Y. Rangers	L	3-8
26—San Jose	W	7-1
28—Calgary	L	1-2
30—Chicago	T	*2-2

FEBRUARY

2—At Quebec	L	2-3
3—At Montreal	L	2-7
9—Edmonton	L	3-6
11—Detroit	T	*6-6
13—Washington	L	3-10
15—Vancouver	W	3-0
17—At Minnesota	W	10-5

18—At Chicago	L	2-7
20—At Washington	L	3-7
22—At Tampa Bay	W	5-2
25—At St. Louis	L	0-3
27—Toronto	L	2-5

MARCH

2—Calgary	W	6-2
4—Ottawa	W	8-6
6—Edmonton	W	6-1
9—At N.Y. Rangers	L	3-4
11—At Pittsburgh	L	*3-4
15—At Buffalo	W	4-2
16—Winnipeg	W	8-4
18—N.Y. Islanders	W	7-4
20—St. Louis	W	3-2
24—At Vancouver	L	2-6
26—At Edmonton	W	4-1
28—At Winnipeg	T	*3-3
29—At Detroit	W	9-3
31—At Toronto	T	*5-5

APRIL

1—At Philadelphia	W	3-1
3—Minnesota	L	0-3
6—Calgary	T	*3-3
8—San Jose	W	2-1
10—At San Jose	W	*3-2
13—At Vancouver	L	4-7
15—Vancouver	L	6-8

*Denotes overtime game.
†At Milwaukee.
‡At Phoenix.

MONTREAL CANADIENS
EASTERN CONFERENCE/NORTHEAST DIVISION

1993-94 SCHEDULE

Home games shaded.
* — At Madison Square Garden, New York.
† — At Hamilton, Ont.
Δ — At Orlando, Fla.
+ — At Phoenix.

OCTOBER
SUN	MON	TUE	WED	THU	FRI	SAT
					1	2
3	4	5	6 HAR	7 PIT	8	9 BUF
10	11 BOS	12	13 HAR	14	15	16 QUE
17	18 QUE	19	20 DAL	21	22	23 ANA
24	25	26 NJ	27	28 NYR	29	30 TOR
31						

NOVEMBER
SUN	MON	TUE	WED	THU	FRI	SAT
	1	2	3 TB	4	5	6 CAL
7	8	9	10 FLA	11	12	13 OTT
14	15 OTT	16	17 EDM	18† NYI	19	20 PIT
21	22	23 NYR	24 PHI	25	26	27 LA
28	29	30				

DECEMBER
SUN	MON	TUE	WED	THU	FRI	SAT
			1 OTT	2	3 WAS	4 BOS
5	6 VAN	7	8 NJ	9	10	11 WAS
12	13	14Δ TB	15 FLA	16	17	18 DET
19	20	21	22 NYI	23 BUF	24	25
26	27 STL	28	29 EDM	30	31 CAL	

JANUARY
SUN	MON	TUE	WED	THU	FRI	SAT
						1
2 VAN	3	4 SJ	5+ QUE	6	7	8 NYR
9	10 WIN	11	12 NJ	13	14 NYI	15 FLA
16	17 WAS	18	19 BOS	20	21	22* ALL-STAR GAME
23	24 FLA	25	26 HAR	27	28	29 BUF
30 PHI	31					

FEBRUARY
SUN	MON	TUE	WED	THU	FRI	SAT
		1	2 HAR	3	4 WAS	5 OTT
6	7 PIT	8	9 NYR	10	11 BUF	12 QUE
13	14	15	16	17 TB	18	19 PIT
20	21 PHI	22	23 SJ	24	25	26 TOR
27	28 LA					

MARCH
SUN	MON	TUE	WED	THU	FRI	SAT
		1	2 ANA	3	4	5
6 DAL	7	8	9 STL	10 QUE	11	12 PHI
13	14 BOS	15	16 CHI	17	18	19 QUE
20	21	22	23 WIN	24 CHI	25	26 BOS
27	28 OTT	29 NJ	30	31		

APRIL
SUN	MON	TUE	WED	THU	FRI	SAT
					1 NYI	2 NYI
3	4	5	6 TB	7	8 BUF	9 PIT
10	11 HAR	12	13 DET	14	15	16

1993-94 SEASON

CLUB DIRECTORY

Chairman of the board, pres. and governor
Ronald Corey
V.P. hockey and managing director
Serge Savard
Senior vice president, corporate affairs
Jean Beliveau
Vice president, Forum operations
Aldo Giampaolo
Vice president, finance and administration
Fred Steer
Assistant to managing director
To be announced
Director of recruitment and assistant to managing director
Andre Boudrias
Coach
Jacques Demers
Assistant coaches
Jacques Laperriere
Charlie Thiffault

Goaltending instructor
Francois Allaire
Director of player development and scout
Claude Ruel
Chief scout
Doug Robinson
Director of public relations
To be announced
Director of press relations
Michele Lapointe
Club physician
Dr. D.G. Kinnear
Athletic trainer
Gaetan Lefebvre
Equipment manager
Eddy Palchak
Assistants to the equipment manager
Pierre Gervais
Robert Boulanger

DRAFT CHOICES

1—Saku Koivu	5-9/165	21	C	TPS Turku, Finland
2—Rory Fitzpatrick	6-1/190	47	D	Sudbury (OHL)
3—Sebastien Bordeleau	5-10/176	73	C	Hull (QMJHL)
4—Adam Wiesel	6-3/201	85	D	Springfield (USJ, Jr. B)
4—Jean-Francois Houle	5-8/145	99	F	Northwood Prep
5—Jeff Lank	6-3/185	113	D	Prince Albert (WHL)
5—Dion Darling	6-3/205	125	D	Spokane (WHL)
6—Darcy Tucker	5-10/163	151	C	Kamloops (WHL)
7—David Ruhly		177	F	Culver Military Acad. (Ind.)
8—Alan Letang	6-0/183	203	D	Newmarket (OHL)
9—Alexandre Duchesne	6-0/212	229	F	Drummondville (QMJHL)
10—Brian Larochelle	6-1/185	255	G	Phillips Exeter Acad. (N.H.)
11—Russell Guzior	5-10/165	281	C	Culver Military Acad. (Ind.)

MISCELLANEOUS DATA

Home ice (capacity)
Montreal Forum (16,197)
Address
2313 St. Catherine Street West
Montreal, Que. H3H 1N2
Business phone
514-932-2582

Rink dimensions
200 feet by 85 feet
Club colors
Red, white and blue
Minor league affiliation
Fredericton (AHL)

TRAINING CAMP ROSTER

No.	FORWARDS	Ht./Wt.	Place	Date	NHL exp.	1992-93 clubs
23	Brian Bellows (LW)	5-11/195	St. Catharines, Ont.	9-1-64	11	Montreal
22	Benoit Brunet (LW)	5-11/184	Montreal	8-24-68	4	Montreal
	Valeri Bure (LW)	5-10/160	Moscow, U.S.S.R.	6-13-74	0	Spokane (WHL)
	Jim Campbell (C)	6-1/175	Worcester, Mass.	2-3-73	0	Hull (QMJHL)
21	Guy Carbonneau (C)	5-11/184	Sept Iles, Que.	3-18-60	12	Montreal
20	Patrik Carnback (LW)	6-0/187	Goteborg, Sweden	2-1-68	1	Fredericton (AHL), Montreal
25	Vincent Damphousse	6-1/185	Montreal	12-17-67	7	Montreal
45	Gilbert Dionne (LW)	6-0/194	Drummondville, Que.	9-19-70	3	Montreal, Fredericton (AHL)
15	Paul Dipietro (C)	5-9/181	Sault Ste. Marie, Ont.	9-8-70	2	Fredericton (AHL), Montreal
36	Todd Ewen (RW)	6-2/220	Saskatoon, Sask.	3-26-66	7	Montreal
12	Mike Keane (RW)	5-10/178	Winnipeg, Man.	5-29-67	5	Montreal
	Saku Koivu (C)	5-9/163	Turku, Finland	11-23-74	0	TPS (Finland)
47	Stephan Lebeau (C)	5-10/172	Sherbrooke, Que.	2-28-68	5	Montreal
17	John LeClair (C)	6-2/205	St. Albans, Vt.	7-5-69	3	Montreal
26	Gary Leeman (RW)	5-11/180	Toronto	2-19-64	11	Calgary, Montreal
11	Kirk Muller (LW)	6-0/205	Kingston, Ont.	2-8-66	9	Montreal
6	Oleg Petrov (RW)	5-9/161	Moscow, U.S.S.R.	4-18-71	1	Montreal, Fredericton (AHL)
32	Mario Roberge (LW)	5-11/185	Quebec City	1-31-64	3	Montreal
31	Ed Ronan (RW)	6-0/197	Quincy, Mass.	3-21-68	2	Montreal, Fredericton (AHL)
	Brian Savage (C)	6-1/195	Sudbury, Ont.	2-24-71	0	Miami of Ohio (CCHA)
	Pierre Sevigny (LW)	6-0/189	Trois-Rivieres, Que.	9-8-71	0	Fredericton (AHL)
30	Turner Stevenson (RW)	6-3/200	Port Alberni, B.C.	5-18-72	1	Fredericton (AHL), Montreal
	Lindsay Vallis (RW)	6-3/207	Winnipeg, Man.	1-12-71	0	Fredericton (AHL)
	DEFENSEMEN					
	Brent Bilodeau	6-4/215	Dallas	3-27-73	0	Swift Current (WHL)
43	Patrice Brisebois	6-2/175	Montreal	1-27-71	3	Montreal
48	J.J. Daigneault	5-11/185	Montreal	10-12-65	8	Montreal
	Dion Darling	6-3/205	Edmonton, Alta.	10-22-74	0	Spokane (WHL)
28	Eric Desjardins	6-1/200	Rouyn, Que.	6-14-69	5	Montreal
14	Kevin Haller	6-2/183	Trochu, Alta.	12-5-70	4	Montreal
	Sylvain Lapointe	6-0/190	Anjou, Que.	3-14-73	0	Hull (QMJHL)
24	Lyle Odelein	5-10/206	Quill Lake, Sask.	7-21-68	4	Montreal
5	Rob Ramage	6-2/200	Byron, Ont.	1-11-59	14	Tampa Bay, Montreal
8	Mathieu Schneider	5-11/189	New York	6-12-69	5	Montreal
	David Wilkie	6-2/202	Ellensburg, Wash.	5-30-74	0	Kamloops (WHL)
	GOALTENDERS					
1	Frederic Chabot	5-11/175	Hebertville, Que.	2-12-68	2	Fredericton (AHL), Montreal
	Les Kuntar	6-2/195	Buffalo, N.Y.	7-28-69	0	Fredericton (AHL)
37	Andre Racicot	5-11/165	Rouyn-Noranda, Que.	6-9-69	4	Montreal
33	Patrick Roy	6-0/182	Quebec City	10-5-65	9	Montreal

1992-93 REVIEW

INDIVIDUAL STATISTICS

SCORING

	Games	G	A	Pts.	Pen.	+/-	PPG	SHG	Shots	Shooting Pct.
Vincent Damphousse	84	39	58	97	98	5	9	3	287	13.6
Kirk Muller	80	37	57	94	77	8	12	0	231	16.0
Brian Bellows	82	40	48	88	44	4	16	0	260	15.4
Stephan Lebeau	71	31	49	80	20	23	8	0	150	20.7
Mike Keane	77	15	45	60	95	29	0	0	120	12.5
Denis Savard	63	16	34	50	90	1	4	1	99	16.2
Gilbert Dionne	75	20	28	48	63	5	6	1	145	13.8
Eric Desjardins	82	13	32	45	98	20	7	0	163	8.0
John LeClair	72	19	25	44	33	11	2	0	139	13.7
Matt Schneider	60	13	31	44	91	8	3	0	169	7.7
Patrice Brisebois	70	10	21	31	79	6	4	0	123	8.1
Kevin Haller	73	11	14	25	117	7	6	0	126	8.7
Benoit Brunet	47	10	15	25	19	13	0	0	71	14.1
J.J. Daigneault	66	8	10	18	57	25	0	0	68	11.8
Gary Leeman*	20	6	12	18	14	9	1	0	36	16.7
Paul Dipietro	29	4	13	17	14	11	0	0	43	9.3
Guy Carbonneau	61	4	13	17	20	-9	0	1	73	5.5
Lyle Odelein	83	2	14	16	205	35	0	0	79	2.5
Todd Ewen	75	5	9	14	193	6	0	0	59	8.5
Ed Ronan	53	5	7	12	20	6	0	0	54	9.3
Brian Skrudland*	23	5	3	8	55	1	0	2	29	17.2

	Games	G	A	Pts.	Pen.	+/-	PPG	SHG	Shots	Shooting Pct.
Mario Roberge	50	4	4	8	142	2	0	0	23	17.4
Sean Hill	31	2	6	8	54	-5	1	0	37	5.4
Jesse Belanger	19	4	2	6	4	1	0	0	24	16.7
Oleg Petrov	9	2	1	3	10	2	0	0	20	10.0
Donald Dufresne	32	1	2	3	32	0	0	0	13	7.7
Patrick Roy (goalie)	62	0	2	2	16	0	0	0	0	0.0
Rob Ramage*	8	0	1	1	8	-3	0	0	16	0.0
Andre Racicot (goalie)	26	0	1	1	6	0	0	0	0	0.0
Frederic Chabot (goalie)	1	0	0	0	0	0	0	0	0	0.0
Turner Stevenson	1	0	0	0	0	-1	0	0	1	0.0
Eric Charron	3	0	0	0	2	0	0	0	0	0.0
Patrik Carnback	6	0	0	0	2	-4	0	0	4	0.0
Patrik Kjellberg	7	0	0	0	2	-3	0	0	7	0.0

GOALTENDING

	Games	Min.	Goals	SO	Avg.	W	L	T	Shots	Sv. Pct.
Frederic Chabot	1	40	1	0	1.50	0	0	0	19	.947
Patrick Roy	62	3595	192	2	3.20	31	25	5	1814	.894
Andre Racicot	26	1433	81	1	3.39	17	5	1	682	.881

Empty-net goals (do not count against a goaltender's average): Roy 5, Racicot 1.
*Played with two or more NHL teams.

RESULTS

OCTOBER

6—At Hartford	W	5-1	
8—At Ottawa	L	3-5	
10—Pittsburgh	T	*3-3	
11—At Buffalo	L	2-8	
15—At Pittsburgh	L	2-5	
17—Minnesota	W	8-1	
19—St. Louis	W	6-2	
21—San Jose	W	8-4	
23—At N.Y. Rangers	T	*3-3	
24—At Philadelphia	W	7-6	
28—Tampa Bay	W	4-3	
31—N.Y. Rangers	W	4-3	

NOVEMBER

2—Winnipeg	W	2-1	
4—At Detroit	W	4-3	
7—Detroit	W	5-1	
9—Calgary	W	5-2	
11—At New Jersey	W	8-3	
14—Philadelphia	L	*3-4	
16—Boston	W	6-3	
17—At Ottawa	W	5-3	
19—At Quebec	L	3-4	
21—Ottawa	W	3-1	
23—Washington	T	*1-1	
25—At Hartford	W	6-1	
28—Vancouver	L	5-6	
30—Buffalo	W	3-0	

DECEMBER

3—At Boston	L	3-4	
5—At Winnipeg	W	*3-2	
6—At Chicago	L	0-2	
8—Los Angeles†	T	*5-5	
12—Boston	W	5-1	
13—At N.Y. Rangers	L	5-10	
16—Quebec	L	1-5	
17—At Quebec	W	8-3	
19—Buffalo	W	4-2	
21—Hartford	L	2-5	
23—N.Y. Islanders	L	2-6	
27—At Vancouver	L	2-5	
29—At Edmonton	W	6-3	
31—At Calgary	L	3-5	

JANUARY

2—At Los Angeles	T	*5-5	
4—San Jose‡	W	4-1	
5—At San Jose	W	2-1	
9—Toronto	L	4-5	
10—At Hartford	W	7-5	
13—Hartford	W	7-3	
14—At Quebec	W	5-3	
16—N.Y. Rangers	W	3-0	
20—New Jersey	W	3-2	
22—At New Jersey	L	2-6	
23—At Toronto	L	0-4	
25—Boston	W	*3-2	
27—Hartford	L	5-6	
30—Ottawa	W	5-3	
31—Philadelphia	W	6-4	

FEBRUARY

3—Los Angeles	W	7-2	
9—At N.Y. Islanders	W	5-3	
11—At Philadelphia	T	*0-0	

(continued)

13—At Ottawa	W	4-1	
17—Boston	L	2-5	
20—Ottawa	W	5-4	
21—Edmonton	W	4-3	
23—At St. Louis	W	5-1	
26—At Buffalo	W	6-4	
27—Buffalo	W	8-4	

MARCH

1—At Boston	W	5-2	
3—At Tampa Bay	L	1-3	
6—At Minnesota	L	3-4	
10—N.Y. Islanders	W	5-1	
11—At Boston	L	2-5	
13—Quebec	L	2-5	
18—At Quebec	W	5-2	
20—Chicago	W	6-2	
22—Buffalo	L	3-8	
24—At Hartford	W	*6-5	
25—At Boston	L	0-2	
27—Ottawa	W	*4-3	
31—Quebec	L	2-6	

APRIL

2—At Washington	L	0-4	
3—At N.Y. Islanders	W	3-2	
7—At Pittsburgh	L	*3-4	
10—Boston	L	1-5	
12—Washington	L	*2-3	
13—At Buffalo	W	*3-2	

*Denotes overtime game.
†At Phoenix.
‡At Sacramento, Calif.

NEW JERSEY DEVILS
EASTERN CONFERENCE/ATLANTIC DIVISION

1993-94 SCHEDULE

Home games shaded.
* — At Madison Square Garden, New York.
† — At Halifax, N.S.
∆ — At Minneapolis.

OCTOBER

SUN	MON	TUE	WED	THU	FRI	SAT
					1	2
3	4	5	6 TB	7	8 WAS	9 WAS
10	11	12 WIN	13	14	15	16 NYI
17	18	19	20 ANA	21	22	23 FLA
24	25	26 MON	27	28	29	30 PHI
31† NYR						

NOVEMBER

SUN	MON	TUE	WED	THU	FRI	SAT
	1	2	3 LA	4	5 ANA	6
7 SJ	8	9	10 NYI	11 PHI	12	13 SJ
14	15	16	17 BUF	18 OTT	19	20 DET
21	22	23 QUE	24 BUF	25	26 STL	27
28	29	30 NYR				

DECEMBER

SUN	MON	TUE	WED	THU	FRI	SAT
			1	2 PIT	3	4 CHI
5 NYR	6	7	8 MON	9 QUE	10	11 EDM
12	13	14 NYI	15 BOS	16	17	18 QUE
19 PHI	20	21	22 HAR	23 TOR	24	25
26 NYR	27	28 HAR	29	30	31	

JANUARY

SUN	MON	TUE	WED	THU	FRI	SAT
						1 OTT
2	3	4 NYI	5	6	7 FLA	8
9 WAS	10	11	12 MON	13	14 WAS	15 LA
16	17	18	19 WIN	20	21	22° ALL STAR GAME
23	24 DAL	25	26 EDM	27	28 CAL	29 VAN
30	31					

FEBRUARY

SUN	MON	TUE	WED	THU	FRI	SAT
		1	2 BUF	3	4 OTT	5 PIT
6	7	8	9	10 VAN	11	12 BOS
13 TB	14	15	16	17 TOR	18	19 TB
20 CHI	21	22	23 DET	24 NYR	25	26 HAR
27	28 STL					

MARCH

SUN	MON	TUE	WED	THU	FRI	SAT
		1	2 FLA	3 TB	4	5 CAL
6	7 QUE	8	9	10 HAR	11	12 BOS
13 DAL	14	15 NYI	16	17 BUF	18	19 BOS
20	21 FLA	22	23	24 TB	25	26 PHI
27∆ QUE	28	29 MON	30	31		

APRIL

SUN	MON	TUE	WED	THU	FRI	SAT
					1 WAS	2 NYR
3	4	5	6 PIT	7	8 PIT	9
10 FLA	11	12 PHI	13	14 OTT	15	16

1993-94 SEASON

CLUB DIRECTORY

Chairman
John J. McMullen
President and general manager
Louis A. Lamoriello
Executive vice president
Max McNab
Head coach
Jacques Lemaire
Assistant coach
Larry Robinson
Director, public and media relations
David Freed
Assistant director, media relations
Mike Levine
Director of player personnel
To be announced

Assistant director of player personel
David Conte
Scouts
Claude Carrier
Marcel Pronovost
Milt Fisher
Frank Jay
Ed Thomlinson
Dan Labraaten
Glen Dirk
Les Widdifield
Joe Mahoney
Ferny Flaman
John Cunniff
Bob Sauve

DRAFT CHOICES

1—Denis Pederson	6-2/189	13	C	Prince Albert (WHL)
2—Jay Pandolfo	6-1/195	32	F	Boston University (H. East)
2—Brendan Morrison	5-11/170	39	C	Penticton (Jr. A, Tier II)
3—Krzysztof Oliwa	6-5/220	65	F	Welland (JBR, Jr. B)
5—John Guirestante	6-2/172	110	F	London (OHL)
6—Steve Brule	5-11/184	143	C	St. Jean (QMJHL)
7—Nikolai Zavarukhin	5-9/167	169	F	Salavat Yulayev Ufa, CIS
8—Thomas Cullen	6-1/205	195	D	Toronto Wexford (Jr. B)
9—Judd Lambert	6-0/165	221	G	Chilliwack, B.C. (Jr. A)
10—Jimmy Provencher	6-3/200	247	F	St. Jean (QMJHL)
11—Michael Legg	5-11/165	273	F	London (Jr. B)

MISCELLANEOUS DATA

Home ice (capacity)
Byrne Meadowlands Arena (19,040)
Address
P.O. Box 504
East Rutherford, N.J. 07073
Business phone
201-935-6050

Rink dimensions
200 feet by 85 feet
Club colors
Red, black and white
Minor league affiliation
Albany (AHL)

TRAINING CAMP ROSTER

No.	FORWARDS	Ht./Wt.	Place	BORN Date	NHL exp.	1992-93 clubs
11	Dave Barr (RW)	6-1/195	Edmonton, Alta.	11-30-60	12	New Jersey
24	Doug Brown (RW)	5-10/180	Southborough, Mass.	6-12-64	7	New Jersey, Utica (AHL)
	Sergei Brylin (C)	5-9/176	Moscow, U.S.S.R.	1-13-74	0	CSKA Moscow (CIS)
9	Tom Chorske (RW)	6-1/205	Minneapolis	9-18-66	4	New Jersey, Utica (AHL)
28	Jim Dowd (C)	6-1/185	Brick, N.J.	12-25-68	2	Utica (AHL), New Jersey
18	David Emma (C)	5-11/180	Cranston, R.I.	1-14-69	1	Utica (AHL), New Jersey
12	Bill Guerin (C/RW)	6-2/190	Wilbraham, Mass.	11-9-70	2	New Jersey, Utica (AHL)
	Donevan Hextall (LW)	6-3/190	Wolseley, Sask.	2-24-72	0	Utica (AHL)
16	Bobby Holik (RW)	6-3/210	Jihlava, Czech.	1-1-71	3	Utica (AHL), New Jersey
22	Claude Lemieux (RW)	6-1/215	Buckingham, Que.	7-16-65	10	New Jersey
15	John MacLean (RW)	6-0/200	Oshawa, Ont.	11-20-64	10	New Jersey
21	Randy McKay (RW)	6-1/185	Montreal	1-25-67	5	New Jersey
	Corey Millen (C)	5-7/168	Cloquet, Minn.	4-29-64	4	Los Angeles
17	Jason Miller (C)	6-1/190	Edmonton, Alta.	3-1-71	3	Utica (AHL), New Jersey
19	Bernie Nicholls (C)	6-0/185	Haliburton, Ont.	6-24-61	12	Edmonton, New Jersey
34	Janne Ojanen (C)	6-2/200	Tampere, Finland	4-9-68	4	New Jersey, Cincinnati (IHL)
	Denis Pederson (C)	6-2/189	Prince Albert, Sask.	9-10-75	0	Prince Albert (WHL)
18	Scott Pellerin (LW)	5-10/185	Shediac, N.B.	1-9-70	1	Utica (AHL), New Jersey
	Mike Peluso (LW)	6-4/200	Hibbing, Minn.	11-8-65	4	Ottawa
44	Stephane Richer (RW)	6-2/200	Buckingham, Que.	6-7-66	9	New Jersey
20	Alexander Semak (C)	5-9/190	Ufa, U.S.S.R.	2-11-66	2	New Jersey
25	Valeri Zelepukin (RW)	5-11/180	Voskresensk, U.S.S.R.	9-17-68	2	New Jersey

No.	DEFENSEMEN	Ht./Wt.	Place	BORN Date	NHL exp.	1992-93 clubs
6	Tommy Albelin	6-1/190	Stockholm, Sweden	5-21-64	6	New Jersey
3	Ken Daneyko	6-0/210	Windsor, Ont.	4-17-64	10	New Jersey
23	Bruce Driver	6-0/185	Toronto	4-29-62	10	New Jersey
2	Viacheslav Fetisov	6-1/220	Moscow, U.S.S.R.	5-20-58	4	New Jersey
	Jaroslav Modry	6-2/195	Ceske-Budejovice, Czech.	2-27-71	0	Utica (AHL)
	Christopher Nelson	6-2/190	Philadelphia	2-12-69	0	Utica (AHL), Cincinnati (IHL)
27	Scott Niedermayer	6-0/200	Edmonton, Alta.	8-31-73	2	New Jersey
	Matt Ruchty	6-1/210	Kitchener, Ont.	11-27-69	0	Utica (AHL)
	Jason Smith	6-3/185	Calgary, Alta.	11-2-73	0	Regina (WHL), Erie (ECHL)
4	Scott Stevens	6-2/215	Kitchener, Ont.	4-1-64	11	New Jersey

No.	GOALTENDERS	Ht./Wt.	Place	BORN Date	NHL exp.	1992-93 clubs
	Martin Brodeur	6-1/190	Montreal	5-6-72	1	Utica (AHL)
	Mike Dunham	6-2/170	Johnson City, N.Y.	6-1-72	0	U. of Maine (H. East)
	Peter Sidorkiewicz	5-9/180	Dabrown Bialostocka, Pol.	6-29-63	6	Ottawa
31	Chris Terreri	5-8/155	Warwick, R.I.	11-15-64	6	New Jersey

1992-93 REVIEW

INDIVIDUAL STATISTICS

SCORING

	Games	G	A	Pts.	Pen.	+/-	PPG	SHG	Shots	Shooting Pct.
Claude Lemieux	77	30	51	81	155	3	13	0	311	9.6
Alexander Semak	82	37	42	79	70	24	4	1	217	17.1
Stephane J.J. Richer	78	38	35	73	44	-1	7	1	286	13.3
Valeri Zelepukin	78	23	41	64	70	19	5	1	174	13.2
Scott Stevens	81	12	45	57	120	14	8	0	146	8.2
Bruce Driver	83	14	40	54	66	-10	6	0	177	7.9
John MacLean	80	24	24	48	102	-6	7	1	195	12.3
Peter Stastny	62	17	23	40	22	-5	7	0	106	16.0
Scott Niedermayer	80	11	29	40	47	8	5	0	131	8.4
Bobby Holik	61	20	19	39	76	-6	7	0	180	11.1
Bill Guerin	65	14	20	34	63	14	0	0	123	11.4
Viacheslav Fetisov	76	4	23	27	158	7	1	1	63	6.3
Randy McKay	73	11	11	22	206	0	1	0	94	11.7
Scott Pellerin	45	10	11	21	41	-1	1	2	60	16.7
Bernie Nicholls*	23	5	15	20	40	3	1	0	46	10.9
Tom Chorske	50	7	12	19	25	-1	0	0	63	11.1
Alexei Kasatonov	64	3	14	17	57	4	0	0	63	4.8
Dave Barr	62	6	8	14	61	1	0	1	41	14.6
Janne Ojanen	31	4	9	13	14	-2	1	0	44	9.1
Ken Daneyko	84	2	11	13	236	4	0	0	71	2.8
Zdeno Ciger*	27	4	8	12	2	-8	2	0	39	10.3
Kevin Todd*	30	5	5	10	16	-4	0	0	48	10.4
Troy Mallette	34	4	3	7	56	3	0	0	19	21.1

	Games	G	A	Pts.	Pen.	+/-	PPG	SHG	Shots	Shooting Pct.
Tommy Albelin	36	1	5	6	14	0	1	0	33	3.0
Doug Brown	15	0	5	5	2	3	0	0	17	0.0
Ben Hankinson	4	2	1	3	9	2	0	0	3	66.7
Claude Vilgrain	4	0	2	2	0	-3	0	0	2	0.0
Jarrod Skalde	11	0	2	2	4	-3	0	0	11	0.0
Brian Sullivan	2	0	1	1	0	-1	0	0	2	0.0
Craig Billington (goalie)	42	0	1	1	8	0	0	0	0	0.0
Jim Dowd	1	0	0	0	0	-1	0	0	1	0.0
David Emma	2	0	0	0	0	0	0	0	2	0.0
Jason Miller	2	0	0	0	0	-1	0	0	1	0.0
Jon Morris*	2	0	0	0	0	-1	0	0	1	0.0
Myles O'Connor	7	0	0	0	9	-4	0	0	4	0.0
Chris Terreri (goalie)	48	0	0	0	6	0	0	0	0	0.0

GOALTENDING

	Games	Min.	Goals	SO	Avg.	W	L	T	Shots	Sv. Pct.
Chris Terreri	48	2672	151	2	3.39	19	21	3	1324	.886
Craig Billington	42	2389	146	2	3.67	21	16	4	1178	.876

Empty-net goals (do not count against a goaltender's average): Terreri 2.
*Played with two or more NHL teams.

RESULTS

OCTOBER

6—N.Y. Islanders	W	4-3
9—At Philadelphia	L	4-6
10—N.Y. Rangers	W	4-2
12—Washington	W	4-2
14—At N.Y. Rangers	L	1-6
17—Philadelphia	W	2-0
20—Hartford	L	4-5
22—At Chicago	W	*6-5
24—Pittsburgh	L	3-4
28—At Hartford	W	*4-3
30—N.Y. Islanders	L	1-4
31—At N.Y. Islanders	W	5-3

NOVEMBER

5—At Los Angeles	L	2-5
7—At San Jose	W	6-1
11—Montreal	L	3-8
13—Washington	W	3-0
14—At Washington	W	*4-3
18—Buffalo†	W	3-2
20—Pittsburgh	L	1-4
21—At Pittsburgh	L	0-2
25—At Ottawa	L	1-3
28—At Quebec	W	6-3

DECEMBER

1—Toronto	W	8-3
3—At Ottawa	T	*3-3
5—Boston	L	2-4
6—At Buffalo	W	7-3
9—Washington	L	2-6
11—Pittsburgh	W	2-1
12—At Pittsburgh	L	5-6
15—At Winnipeg	L	3-4
18—At Tampa Bay	W	2-0
21—N.Y. Rangers	L	0-3
23—At N.Y. Rangers	W	5-4
27—Hartford	W	6-2
29—At Quebec	L	1-4

JANUARY

1—At Washington	L	2-9
2—Winnipeg	T	*2-2
4—At N.Y. Rangers	T	*3-3
6—Minnesota	W	5-1
8—Ottawa	W	6-4
9—At Boston	W	6-2
12—Vancouver	W	3-2
14—Los Angeles	W	7-1
16—N.Y. Islanders	L	3-5
20—At Montreal	L	2-3
22—Montreal	W	6-2
23—At Boston	L	5-7
26—At N.Y. Islanders	L	2-8
28—At Minnesota	L	2-4
30—At St. Louis	T	*2-2

FEBRUARY

3—Calgary	L	4-5
8—N.Y. Rangers	W	5-4
9—At Detroit	L	5-8
13—Philadelphia	W	6-4
14—At Philadelphia	W	5-2
17—St. Louis	W	4-3
19—Buffalo	T	*3-3
21—Quebec	L	3-6

MARCH

23—At Pittsburgh	W	3-1
25—At Philadelphia	L	2-6
27—Ottawa	W	5-2
28—Detroit	W	6-3
3—At Hartford	W	7-4
5—Chicago	T	*1-1
7—Philadelphia	W	7-3
9—At Vancouver	L	2-7
12—At Edmonton	L	4-6
13—At Calgary	L	3-4
16—Boston‡	L	1-3
18—Edmonton	W	5-1
20—Quebec	L	1-5
21—At Philadelphia	W	3-2
23—Tampa Bay	W	9-3
25—At Pittsburgh	L	3-4
27—At Washington	W	5-2
29—San Jose	W	5-0
31—At Buffalo	L	2-5

APRIL

3—At Toronto	L	0-1
4—Pittsburgh	L	2-5
7—N.Y. Rangers	W	5-2
10—At Washington	W	5-3
11—N.Y. Islanders	L	1-4
14—Pittsburgh	T	*6-6
16—At N.Y. Islanders	L	4-8

*Denotes overtime game.
†Hamilton, Ont.
‡Providence, R.I.

NEW YORK ISLANDERS
EASTERN CONFERENCE/ATLANTIC DIVISION

1993-94 SCHEDULE

■ Home games shaded.
* — At Madison Square Garden, New York.
† — At Hamilton, Ont.
△ — At Minneapolis.

OCTOBER
SUN	MON	TUE	WED	THU	FRI	SAT
					1	2
3	4	5 CAL	6	7	8 EDM	9
10 ANA	11	12 LA	13	14	15	16 NJ
17	18	19 PIT	20	21 PHI	22	23 OTT
24	25	26 LA	27	28 FLA	29 TB	30
31						

NOVEMBER
SUN	MON	TUE	WED	THU	FRI	SAT
	1	2 VAN	3	4 CHI	5	6 HAR
7	8	9 WIN	10 NJ	11	12	13 BOS
14	15	16	17 OTT	18† MON	19	20
21 PHI	22	23	24 DAL	25	26	27 NYR
28 DET	29	30 WAS				

DECEMBER
SUN	MON	TUE	WED	THU	FRI	SAT
			1	2 BOS	3 QUE	4
5	6	7 EDM	8	9	10	11 PHI
12	13	14	15	16	17 TOR	18
19 PIT	20	21	22 MON	23	24	25
26 BUF	27	28 ANA	29 QUE	30	31	

JANUARY
SUN	MON	TUE	WED	THU	FRI	SAT
						1 HAR
2	3	4 NJ	5	6	7 CAL	8 HAR
9	10 OTT	11	12	13	14 MON	15 CHI
16	17 FLA	18	19 TB	20	21	22* ALL-STAR GAME
23	24	25	26 TOR	27	28 BOS	29 BOS
30	31					

FEBRUARY
SUN	MON	TUE	WED	THU	FRI	SAT
		1 SJ	2 NYR	3	4	5 QUE
6 BUF	7	8 BUF	9	10 PIT	11	12 FLA
13	14	15 TB	16	17	18 WAS	19 OTT
20	21 WAS	22	23	24 PHI	25 PHI	26
27 QUE	28					

MARCH
SUN	MON	TUE	WED	THU	FRI	SAT
		1 STL	2	3	4 NYR	5 NYR
6	7 WIN	8	9 VAN	10 SJ	11	12 STL
13	14	15 NJ	16	17 DET	18△ BUF	19
20 PIT	21	22 TB	23	24	25	26 FLA
27 BUF	28	29 WAS	30	31		

APRIL
SUN	MON	TUE	WED	THU	FRI	SAT
					1 MON	2 MON
3	4	5 WAS	6 HAR	7	8 DAL	9
10 NYR	11	12	13 TB	14 FLA	15	16

1993-94 SEASON

CLUB DIRECTORY

Co-chairmen
Robert Rosenthal
Stephen Walsh
Chief operating officer
Ralph Palleschi
Executive vice president
Paul Greenwood
Senior vice president & CFO
Arthur J. McCarthy
Consultant
John H. Krumpe
General counsel
William M. Skehan
VP hockey operations/general manager
Don Maloney
Assistant general manager
Darcy Regier
Coach
Al Arbour
Assistant coaches
Rick Green
Lorne Henning
Director of scouting
Gerry Ehman
Director of pro scouting
Ken Morrow
Scouts
Harry Boyd
Earl Ingarfield
Gord Lane
Bert Marshall
Mario Saraceno
Vice president/communications
Pat Calabria
Director of media relations
Ginger Killian

Media relations assistant
Eric Mirlis
Dir. of publications/media relations assoc.
Chris Botta
Director of community relations
Maureen Brady
Director of game events
Tim Beach
Dir. of amateur hoc. dev. & alumni relations
Bob Nystrom
Director of ticket sales
Jim Johnson
Director of advertising sales
Glenda Brown
Director of administration
Joseph Dreyer
Controller
Ralph Sellitti
Athletic trainer
Ed Tyburski
Equipment manager
John Doolan
Assistant trainer
Jerry Iannarelli
Team orthopedists
Jeffery Minkoff, M.D.
Barry Simonson, M.D.
Team internists
Gerald Cordani, M.D.
Larry Smith, M.D.
Physical therapist
Steve Wirth
Team dentists
Bruce Michnick, D.D.S.
Jan Sherman, D.D.S.

DRAFT CHOICES

1—Todd Bertuzzi	6-3/227	23	C	Guelph (OHL)
2—Bryan McCabe	6-1/200	40	D	Medicine Hat (WHL)
3—Vladim Cherbaturkin	6-2/189	66	D	Kristall Electrosal, CIS
4—Warren Luhning	6-2/185	92	F	Calgary Royals (Tier II)
5—Tommy Salo	5-11/161	118	G	Basteras, Europe
6—Peter Leboutillier	6-1/198	144	F	Red Deer (WHL)
7—Darren Van Impe	6-0/195	170	D	Red Deer (WHL)
8—Rod Hinks	5-10/185	196	C	Sudbury (OHL)
9—Daniel Johansson	5-11/176	222	D	Rogle, Sweden
10—Stephane Larocque	6-1/214	248	F	Sherbrooke (QMJHL)
11—Carl Charland	5-11/180	274	F	Hull (QMJHL)

MISCELLANEOUS DATA

Home ice (capacity)
Nassau Veterans Memorial Coliseum
(16,297)
Address
Uniondale, NY 11553
Business phone
516-794-4100

Rink dimensions
200 feet by 85 feet
Club colors
Blue, white and orange
Minor league affiliation
Salt Lake (IHL)

TRAINING CAMP ROSTER

No.	FORWARDS	Ht./Wt.	Place	BORN Date	NHL exp.	1992-93 clubs
15	Brad Dalgarno (RW)	6-4/215	Vancouver, B.C.	8-8-67	7	Capital District (AHL), N.Y. Islanders
20	Ray Ferraro (C)	5-10/185	Trail, B.C.	8-23-64	9	N.Y. Islanders, Capital District (AHL)
26	Patrick Flatley (RW)	6-2/200	Toronto	10-3-63	10	N.Y. Islanders
39	Travis Green (C)	6-0/195	Creston, B.C.	12-20-70	1	Capital District (AHL), N.Y. Islanders
	Brent Grieve (LW)	6-1/205	Oshawa, Ont.	5-9-69	0	Capital District (AHL)
33	Benoit Hogue (LW)	5-10/190	Repentigny, Que.	10-28-66	6	N.Y. Islanders
	Steve Junker (LW)	6-0/184	Castlegar, B.C.	6-26-72	1	Capital District (AHL), N.Y. Islanders
27	Derek King (LW)	6-1/210	Hamilton, Ont.	2-11-67	7	N.Y. Islanders
	Martin Lacroix (RW)	5-11/155	Rosemere, Que.	1-4-70	0	Capital District (AHL)
10	Claude Loiselle (C)	5-11/195	Ottawa	5-29-63	12	N.Y. Islanders
18	Marty McInnis (C/LW) .	6-0/185	Weymouth, Mass.	6-2-70	2	N.Y. Islanders, Capital District (AHL)
16	Brian Mullen (RW)	5-10/185	New York	3-16-62	11	N.Y. Islanders
	Zigmund Palffy (LW)	5-10/169	Skalica, Czech.	5-5-72	0	Dukla Trencin (Czech.)
38	Scott Scissons (C)	6-1/201	Saskatoon, Sask.	10-29-71	2	Capital District (AHL), N.Y. Islanders
	Chris Taylor (C)	6-1/190	Stratford, Ont.	3-6-72	0	Capital District (AHL)
32	Steve Thomas (LW/RW) .	5-11/185	Stockport, England	7-15-63	9	N.Y. Islanders
77	Pierre Turgeon (C)	6-1/203	Rouyn, Que.	8-29-69	6	N.Y. Islanders
25	David Volek (LW/RW) ..	6-0/190	Prague, Czech.	8-16-66	5	N.Y. Islanders
12	Mick Vukota (RW)	6-2/215	Saskatoon, Sask.	9-14-66	6	N.Y. Islanders
	DEFENSEMEN					
	Kevin Cheveldayoff	6-0/202	Saskatoon, Sask.	2-4-70	0	Capital District (AHL)
	Dean Chynoweth	6-2/190	Saskatoon, Sask.	10-30-68	4	Capital District (AHL)
11	Darius Kasparaitis	5-11/190	Elektrenai, U.S.S.R.	10-16-72	1	Dynamo Moscow (CIS), N.Y. Islanders
4	Uwe Krupp	6-6/236	Cologne, W. Germany	6-24-65	7	N.Y. Islanders
28	Tom Kurvers	6-1/197	Minneapolis	9-14-62	9	N.Y. Islanders, Capital District (AHL)
7	Scott Lachance	6-2/197	Charlottesville, Va.	10-22-72	2	N.Y. Islanders
	Joni Lehto	6-0/205	Turku, Finland	7-15-70	0	Capital District (AHL)
	Christopher Luongo	6-0/180	Detroit	3-17-67	2	Ottawa, New Haven (AHL)
23	Vladimir Malakhov	6-3/220	Sverdlovsk, U.S.S.R.	8-30-68	1	Capital District (AHL), N.Y. Islanders
	Wayne McBean	6-2/185	Calgary, Alta.	2-21-69	5	Capital District (AHL)
47	Rich Pilon	6-0/211	Saskatoon, Sask.	4-30-68	5	N.Y. Islanders, Capital District (AHL)
37	Dennis Vaske	6-2/211	Rockford, Ill.	10-11-67	3	Capital District (AHL), N.Y. Islanders
	GOALTENDERS					
27	Ron Hextall	6-3/192	Winnipeg, Man.	5-3-64	7	Quebec
	Milan Hnilicka	6-0/180	Kladno, Czech.	6-24-73	0	Swift Current (WHL)
1	Danny Lorenz	5-10/183	Murrayville, B.C.	12-12-69	3	Capital District (AHL), N.Y. Islanders
	Jamie McLennan	6-0/190	Edmonton, Alta.	6-30-71	0	Capital District (AHL)

1992-93 REVIEW

INDIVIDUAL STATISTICS

SCORING

	Games	G	A	Pts.	Pen.	+/-	PPG	SHG	Shots	Shooting Pct.
Pierre Turgeon	83	58	74	132	26	-1	24	0	301	19.3
Steve Thomas	79	37	50	87	111	3	12	0	264	14.0
Derek King	77	38	38	76	47	-4	21	0	201	18.9
Benoit Hogue	70	33	42	75	108	13	5	3	147	22.4
Patrick Flatley	80	13	47	60	63	5	1	2	139	9.4
Vladimir Malakhov	64	14	38	52	59	14	7	0	178	7.9
Jeff Norton	66	12	38	50	45	-3	5	0	127	9.4
Uwe Krupp	80	9	29	38	67	6	2	0	116	7.8
Tom Kurvers	52	8	30	38	38	9	3	0	128	6.3
Brian Mullen	81	18	14	32	28	5	1	0	126	14.3
Brad Dalgarno	57	15	17	32	62	17	2	0	62	24.2
Marty McInnis	56	10	20	30	24	7	0	1	60	16.7
Ray Ferraro	46	14	13	27	40	0	3	0	72	19.4
Tom Fitzgerald	77	9	18	27	34	-2	0	3	83	10.8
Travis Green	61	7	18	25	43	4	1	0	115	6.1
Scott Lachance	75	7	17	24	67	-1	0	1	62	11.3
Dave Volek	56	8	13	21	34	-1	2	0	118	6.8
Darius Kasparaitis	79	4	17	21	166	15	0	0	92	4.3
Bill Berg*	22	6	3	9	49	4	0	2	30	20.0
Claude Loiselle	41	5	3	8	90	-5	0	0	41	12.2
Dan Marois	28	2	5	7	35	-3	0	0	41	4.9
Mick Vukota	74	2	5	7	216	3	0	0	37	5.4
Dennis Vaske	27	1	5	6	32	9	0	0	15	6.7
Iain Fraser	7	2	2	4	2	-1	1	0	7	28.6
Richard Pilon	44	1	3	4	164	-4	0	0	20	5.0

	Games	G	A	Pts.	Pen.	+/-	PPG	SHG	Shots	Shooting Pct.
Rich Kromm	1	1	2	3	0	3	0	0	2	50.0
Gary Nylund	22	1	1	2	43	-2	0	0	19	5.3
Glenn Healy (goalie)	47	0	2	2	2	0	0	0	0	0.0
Mark Fitzpatrick (goalie)	39	0	1	1	2	0	0	0	0	0.0
Greg Parks	2	0	0	0	0	0	0	0	0	0.0
Graeme Townshend	2	0	0	0	0	0	0	0	3	0.0
Danny Lorenz (goalie)	4	0	0	0	0	0	0	0	0	0.0

GOALTENDING

	Games	Min.	Goals	SO	Avg.	W	L	T	Shots	Sv. Pct.
Glenn Healy	47	2655	146	1	3.30	22	20	2	1316	.889
Mark Fitzpatrick	39	2253	130	0	3.46	17	15	5	1066	.878
Danny Lorenz	4	157	10	0	3.82	1	2	0	78	.872

Empty-net goals (do not count against a goaltender's average): Healy 6, Fitzpatrick 5.
*Played with two or more NHL teams.

RESULTS

OCTOBER

6—At New Jersey	L	3-4
8—At Pittsburgh	L	3-7
10—At Boston	T	*3-3
15—At Philadelphia	W	5-4
17—N.Y. Rangers	W	6-3
18—At N.Y. Rangers	L	3-4
20—Philadelphia	W	4-3
23—At Washington	W	5-2
24—Hartford	W	4-2
27—Los Angeles	L	3-4
30—At New Jersey	W	4-1
31—New Jersey	L	3-5

NOVEMBER

3—At Pittsburgh	L	0-2
5—At Minnesota	L	0-3
7—Tampa Bay	L	*5-6
12—At Philadelphia	L	5-8
14—Buffalo	W	7-5
19—At Boston	L	2-5
21—At Calgary	W	4-3
22—At Edmonton	T	*5-5
24—At Winnipeg	T	*3-3
27—At Philadelphia	L	3-6
28—Philadelphia	W	9-3

DECEMBER

1—Pittsburgh	L	3-7
4—At Buffalo	T	*5-5
5—Washington	L	3-5
7—At Tampa Bay	W	6-1
10—At Chicago	L	3-5

12—Winnipeg	L	*3-4
13—Edmonton†	W	4-1
15—St. Louis‡	W	*4-3
17—Ottawa	W	9-3
19—At Pittsburgh	W	4-3
20—At Quebec	L	3-5
23—At Montreal	W	6-2
26—N.Y. Rangers	W	6-4
29—Toronto	L	2-3
31—At St. Louis	L	1-5

JANUARY

2—Minnesota	W	3-2
5—Quebec	L	1-2
8—At Buffalo	L	5-6
9—Vancouver	L	4-5
12—Calgary	W	8-2
14—Washington	L	0-3
16—At New Jersey	W	5-3
17—At Ottawa	W	7-2
19—Boston	T	*2-2
23—Philadelphia	W	8-4
26—New Jersey	W	8-2
28—At Pittsburgh	W	5-2
30—Boston	L	5-6

FEBRUARY

1—N.Y. Rangers	T	*4-4
3—At Toronto	W	3-2
9—Montreal	L	3-5
12—At N.Y. Rangers	L	3-4
13—N.Y. Rangers	W	5-2
16—Edmonton	W	7-2
18—St. Louis	L	2-4

20—Pittsburgh	W	4-2
23—Washington	L	2-4
25—At Quebec	L	4-6
27—At Philadelphia	W	3-2
28—At Hartford	W	*7-6

MARCH

2—Detroit	W	3-2
7—At Washington	W	3-2
9—Philadelphia	W	4-2
10—At Montreal	L	1-5
14—Pittsburgh	L	2-3
16—At San Jose	W	6-0
18—At Los Angeles	L	4-7
20—At Vancouver	W	7-2
23—At Detroit	L	2-3
25—Washington	L	2-5
27—San Jose	W	7-3
30—Philadelphia	W	2-1

APRIL

2—At N.Y. Rangers	W	*3-2
3—Montreal	L	2-3
6—At Washington	W	3-2
8—Chicago	L	2-3
10—Ottawa	L	3-5
11—At New Jersey	W	5-4
13—Hartford	T	*3-3
14—At Hartford	L	4-5
16—New Jersey	W	8-4

*Denotes overtime game.
†At Oklahoma City, Okla.
‡At Dallas.

NEW YORK RANGERS
EASTERN CONFERENCE/ATLANTIC DIVISION

1993-94 SCHEDULE

Home games shaded.
* — At Madison Square Garden, New York.
† — At Halifax, N.S.

OCTOBER
SUN	MON	TUE	WED	THU	FRI	SAT
					1	2
3	4	5 BOS	6	7 TB	8	9 PIT
10	11 WAS	12	13 QUE	14	15 BUF	16 PHI
17	18	19 ANA	20	21	22 TB	23
24 LA	25	26	27	28 MON	29	30 HAR
31† NJ						

NOVEMBER
SUN	MON	TUE	WED	THU	FRI	SAT
	1	2	3 VAN	4	5	6 QUE
7	8 TB	9	10 WIN	11	12	13 WAS
14 SJ	15	16 FLA	17	18	19 TB	20
21	22	23 MON	24 OTT	25	26	27 NYI
28 WAS	29	30 NJ				

DECEMBER
SUN	MON	TUE	WED	THU	FRI	SAT
			1	2	3	4 TOR
5 NJ	6	7	8 EDM	9	10	11
12	13 BUF	14	15 HAR	16	17 DET	18
19 OTT	20	21	22 FLA	23 WAS	24	25
26 NJ	27	28	29 STL	30	31 BUF	

JANUARY
SUN	MON	TUE	WED	THU	FRI	SAT
						1
2	3 FLA	4	5 CAL	6	7	8 MON
9	10 TB	11	12	13	14 PHI	15
16 CHI	17	18 STL	19	20	21	22° ALL STAR GAME
23	24	25 SJ	26	27 LA	28 ANA	29
30	31 PIT					

FEBRUARY
SUN	MON	TUE	WED	THU	FRI	SAT
		1	2 NYI	3 BOS	4	5
6	7 WAS	8	9 MON	10	11 QUE	12 OTT
13	14 QUE	15	16	17	18 OTT	19 HAR
20	21 PIT	22	23 BOS	24 NJ	25	26 DAL
27	28					

MARCH
SUN	MON	TUE	WED	THU	FRI	SAT
		1	2 PHI	3	4 NYI	5 NYI
6	7 DET	8	9† WAS	10 BOS	11	12 PIT
13	14 FLA	15	16 HAR	17	18 CHI	19
20	21	22 CAL	23 EDM	24	25 VAN	26
27 WIN	28	29 PHI	30	31		

APRIL
SUN	MON	TUE	WED	THU	FRI	SAT
					1 DAL	2 NJ
3	4 FLA	5	6	7	8 TOR	9
10 NYI	11	12 BUF	13	14 PHI	15	16

1993-94 SEASON

CLUB DIRECTORY

Governor
Stanley R. Jaffe
President and general manager
Neil Smith
Vice president, finance
Jim Abry
Director of communications
Barry Watkins
Director of marketing
Kevin Kennedy
Director of administration
John Gentile
Alternate NHL governors
Neil Smith
Kevin Billet
Bob Gutkowski
Assistant G.M., player development
Larry Pleau
Coach
Mike Keenan
Associate coach
Colin Campbell

Scouting staff
Tony Feltrin
Herb Hammond
Lou Jankowski
Martin Madden
Christer Rockstrom
Scouting manager
Bill Short
Manager of team operations
Matthew Loughran
Manager of communications
Kevin McDonald
Public relations assistant
John Rosasco
Team physician and orthopedic surgeon
Barton Nisonson, M.D.
Medical trainer
Dave Smith
Equipment trainer
Joe Murphy

DRAFT CHOICES

1—Niklas Sundstrom	6-0/183	8	C	Ornskoldsvik, Sweden
2—Lee Sorochan	5-11/208	34	D	Lethbridge (WHL)
3—Maxim Galanov	6-1/167	61	D	Lada Togliatti, CIS
4—Sergei Olympijev	5-10/172	86	F	Dynamo Minsk, CIS
5—Gary Roach	6-1/180	112	D	Sault Ste. Marie (OHL)
6—Dave Trofimenkoff	6-0/177	138	G	Lethbridge (WHL)
7—Sergei Kondrashkin	5-11/172	162	F	Cherepovets, Europe
7—Todd Marchant	5-10/170	164	C	Univ. of Clarkson (ECAC)
8—Eddy Campbell	6-2/210	190	D	Omaha (Jr. A, Tier II)
9—Ken Shepard	5-10/192	216	G	Oshawa (OHL)
10—Andrei Kudinov	6-0/185	242	F	Chelyabinsk, CIS
11—Pavel Komarov	5-11/176	261	D	Nizhni Novgorod, Europe
11—Maxim Smelnitski		268	C	Chelyabinsk, CIS

MISCELLANEOUS DATA

Home ice (capacity)
Madison Square Garden (18,200)
Address
4 Pennsylvania Plaza
New York, NY 10001
Business phone
212-465-6000

Rink dimensions
200 feet by 85 feet
Club colors
Blue, red and white
Minor league affiliation
Binghamton (AHL)

TRAINING CAMP ROSTER

No.	FORWARDS	Ht./Wt.	Place	Date	NHL exp.	1992-93 clubs
33	Tony Amonte (RW)	6-0/186	Weymouth, Mass.	8-2-70	3	N.Y. Rangers
	Don Biggs (C)	5-8/180	Mississauga, Ont.	4-7-65	2	Binghamton (AHL)
29	Phil Bourque (LW)	6-1/196	Chelmsford, Mass.	6-8-62	9	N.Y. Rangers
37	Paul Broten (RW)	5-11/183	Roseau, Minn.	10-27-65	4	N.Y. Rangers
	Chris Ferraro (RW)	5-10/175	Port Jefferson, N.Y.	1-24-73	0	U. of Maine (H. East)
	Peter Ferraro (C)	5-10/175	Port Jefferson, N.Y.	1-24-73	0	U. of Maine (H. East)
22	Mike Gartner (RW)	6-0/188	Ottawa	10-29-59	14	N.Y. Rangers
9	Adam Graves (LW)	6-0/203	Toronto	4-12-68	6	N.Y. Rangers
18	Mike Hartman (LW/RW)	6-0/192	W. Bloomfield, Mich.	2-7-67	7	Tampa Bay, N.Y. Rangers
26	Joey Kocur (RW)	6-0/209	Calgary, Alta.	12-21-64	9	N.Y. Rangers
27	Alexei Kovalev (RW)	6-1/189	Moscow, U.S.S.R.	2-24-73	1	N.Y. Rangers, Binghamton (AHL)
	Daniel Lacroix (LW)	6-2/188	Montreal	3-11-69	0	Binghamton (AHL)
14	John McIntyre (C/LW)	6-1/175	Ravenswood, Ont.	4-29-69	4	Los Angeles, N.Y. Rangers
11	Mark Messier (C)	6-1/202	Edmonton, Alta.	1-18-61	14	N.Y. Rangers
13	Sergei Nemchinov (C)	6-0/199	Moscow, U.S.S.R.	1-14-64	2	N.Y. Rangers
12	Ed Olczyk (LW)	6-1/200	Chicago	8-16-66	9	Winnipeg, N.Y. Rangers
	Jean-Yves Roy (RW)	5-10/185	Rosemere, Que.	2-17-69	0	Binghamton (AHL)
	Niklas Sundstrom (LW)	5-11/183	Ornskoldsvik, Sweden	6-6-75	0	MoDo (Sweden)
10	Esa Tikkanen (LW)	6-1/200	Helsinki, Finland	1-25-65	9	Edmonton, N.Y. Rangers
8	Darren Turcotte (C)	6-0/178	Boston	3-2-68	5	N.Y. Rangers

DEFENSEMEN

No.		Ht./Wt.	Place	Date	NHL exp.	1992-93 clubs
5	Peter Andersson	6-0/187	Orebro, Sweden	8-29-65	1	N.Y. Rangers, Binghamton (AHL)
23	Jeff Beukeboom	6-4/223	Ajax, Ont.	3-28-65	8	N.Y. Rangers
44	Per Djoos	5-11/196	Mora, Sweden	5-11-68	3	Binghamton (AHL), N.Y. Rangers
32	Mike Hurlbut	6-2/200	Massena, N.Y.	7-10-66	1	Binghamton (AHL), N.Y. Rangers
2	Brian Leetch	5-11/190	Corpus Christi, Tex.	3-3-68	6	N.Y. Rangers
	Doug Lidster	6-1/200	Kamloops, B.C.	10-18-60	10	Vancouver
4	Kevin Lowe	6-2/195	Lachute, Que.	4-15-59	14	N.Y. Rangers
28	Joby Messier	6-0/193	Regina, Sask.	3-2-70	1	Binghamton (AHL), N.Y. Rangers
	Mattias Norstrom	6-1/196	Mora, Sweden	1-2-72	0	AIK Solna (Sweden)
3	James Patrick	6-2/192	Winnipeg, Man.	6-14-63	10	N.Y. Rangers
	Michael Stewart	6-2/197	Calgary, Alta.	3-30-72	0	Binghamton (AHL)
	Brad Tiley	6-1/190	Markdale, Ont.	7-5-71	0	Binghamton (AHL), Phoenix (IHL)
24	Jay Wells	6-1/210	Paris, Ont.	5-18-59	14	N.Y. Rangers
21	Sergei Zubov	6-0/187	Moscow, U.S.S.R.	7-22-70	1	CSKA Moscow (CIS), Binghamton (AHL), N.Y. Rangers

GOALTENDERS

No.		Ht./Wt.	Place	Date	NHL exp.	1992-93 clubs
	Glenn Healy	5-10/185	Pickering, Ont.	8-23-62	7	N.Y. Islanders
31	Corey Hirsch	5-10/170	Medicine Hat, Alta.	7-1-72	1	Binghamton (AHL), N.Y. Rangers
35	Mike Richter	5-11/182	Philadelphia	9-22-66	4	N.Y. Rangers, Binghamton (AHL)

1992-93 REVIEW

INDIVIDUAL STATISTICS

SCORING

	Games	G	A	Pts.	Pen.	+/-	PPG	SHG	Shots	Shooting Pct.
Mark Messier	75	25	66	91	72	-6	7	2	215	11.6
Tony Amonte	83	33	43	76	49	0	13	0	270	12.2
Mike Gartner	84	45	23	68	59	-4	13	0	323	13.9
Adam Graves	84	36	29	65	148	-4	12	1	275	13.1
Sergei Nemchinov	81	23	31	54	34	15	0	1	144	16.0
Darren Turcotte	71	25	28	53	40	-3	7	3	213	11.7
Doug Weight*	65	15	25	40	55	4	3	0	90	16.7
Alexei Kovalev	65	20	18	38	79	-10	3	0	134	14.9
Brian Leetch	36	6	30	36	26	2	2	1	150	4.0
Sergei Zubov	49	8	23	31	4	-1	3	0	93	8.6
Ed Olczyk*	46	13	16	29	26	9	3	0	109	11.9
James Patrick	60	5	21	26	61	1	3	0	99	5.1
Phil Bourque	55	6	14	20	39	-9	0	0	71	8.5
Jeff Beukeboom	82	2	17	19	153	9	0	0	54	3.7
Jan Erixon	45	5	11	16	10	11	0	1	36	13.9
Peter Andersson	31	4	11	15	18	4	3	0	68	5.9
Kevin Lowe	49	3	12	15	58	-2	0	0	52	5.8
Paul Broten	60	5	9	14	48	-6	0	1	57	8.8
Steven King	24	7	5	12	16	4	5	0	42	16.7
Mark Hardy*	44	1	10	11	85	2	0	0	28	3.6
Jay Wells	53	1	9	10	107	-2	0	0	32	3.1
Joe Cirella	55	3	6	9	85	1	0	1	37	8.1

	Games	G	A	Pts.	Pen.	+/-	PPG	SHG	Shots	Shooting Pct.
Joey Kocur	65	3	6	9	131	-9	2	0	43	7.0
Mike Hurlbut	23	1	8	9	16	4	1	0	26	3.8
Esa Tikkanen*	15	2	5	7	18	-13	0	0	40	5.0
Randy Gilhen*	33	3	2	5	8	-8	0	1	34	8.8
Mike Richter (goalie)	38	0	5	5	2	0	0	0	0	0.0
Kris King*	30	0	3	3	67	-1	0	0	23	0.0
Tie Domi*	12	2	0	2	95	-1	0	0	11	18.2
Per Djoos	6	1	1	2	2	0	0	0	4	25.0
John McIntyre*	11	1	0	1	4	-1	0	0	5	20.0
Craig Duncanson	3	0	1	1	0	0	0	0	1	0.0
John Vanbiesbrouck (goalie)	48	0	1	1	18	0	0	0	0	0.0
Dave Marcinyshyn	2	0	0	0	2	-1	0	0	1	0.0
Mike Hartman*	3	0	0	0	6	0	0	0	3	0.0
Corey Hirsch (goalie)	4	0	0	0	0	0	0	0	0	0.0
Joby Messier	11	0	0	0	6	0	0	0	11	0.0

GOALTENDING

	Games	Min.	Goals	SO	Avg.	W	L	T	Shots	Sv. Pct.
John Vanbiesbrouck	48	2757	152	4	3.31	20	18	7	1525	.900
Corey Hirsch	4	224	14	0	3.75	1	2	1	116	.879
Mike Richter	38	2105	134	1	3.82	13	19	3	1180	.886

Empty-net goals (do not count against a goaltender's average): Richter 4, Vanbiesbrouck 3, Hirsch 1.
*Played with two or more NHL teams.

RESULTS

OCTOBER

9—At Washington	W	4-2
10—At New Jersey	L	2-4
12—Hartford	W	6-2
14—New Jersey	W	6-1
17—At N.Y. Islanders	L	3-6
18—N.Y. Islanders	W	4-3
21—Washington	W	2-1
23—Montreal	T	*3-3
24—At Ottawa	W	*3-2
26—Philadelphia	W	8-4
29—Quebec	L	3-6
31—At Montreal	L	3-4

NOVEMBER

2—Buffalo	W	*7-6
4—Philadelphia	W	3-1
7—At Boston	T	*2-2
9—Tampa Bay	L	1-5
11—Washington	L	4-7
14—At Quebec	L	3-6
19—At Philadelphia	L	3-7
21—At Winnipeg	W	5-4
23—Pittsburgh	L	2-5
25—At Pittsburgh	W	11-3
27—At Minnesota	T	*4-4
30—Minnesota	L	2-4

DECEMBER

2—Detroit	W	5-3
4—At Washington	L	4-8
6—Toronto	W	6-0
9—Tampa Bay†	W	6-5
11—At Tampa Bay	W	5-4
13—Montreal	W	10-5
15—Calgary	L	0-3
17—At St. Louis	W	4-3
19—At Hartford	T	*4-4
21—At New Jersey	W	3-0
23—New Jersey	L	4-5
26—At N.Y. Islanders	L	4-6
27—Boston	W	6-5
29—At Washington	L	*3-4
31—At Buffalo	L	6-11

JANUARY

2—At Pittsburgh	L	2-5
4—New Jersey	T	*3-3
6—Ottawa	W	6-2
9—At Philadelphia	L	3-4
11—Vancouver	T	*3-3
13—Washington	W	5-4
16—At Montreal	L	0-3
19—At Detroit	T	*2-2
23—At Los Angeles	W	8-3
27—Winnipeg	W	5-2
29—At Buffalo	L	4-6
30—At Toronto	L	1-3

FEBRUARY

1—At N.Y. Islanders	T	*4-4
3—Philadelphia	T	*2-2
8—At New Jersey	L	4-5
10—Pittsburgh	L	0-3
12—N.Y. Islanders	W	4-3
13—At N.Y. Islanders	L	2-5
15—St. Louis	W	4-1

Feb/March

20—At San Jose	W	6-4
22—San Jose‡	W	4-0
24—At Vancouver	L	4-5
26—At Calgary	T	*4-4
27—At Edmonton	W	1-0

MARCH

3—Buffalo	T	*2-2
5—Pittsburgh	W	3-1
6—At Quebec	L	2-10
9—Los Angeles	W	4-3
11—At Chicago	W	4-1
15—Boston	L	1-3
17—Edmonton	L	*3-4
19—San Jose	W	8-1
22—At Ottawa	W	5-4
24—Philadelphia	L	4-5
26—Chicago	L	1-3
28—Quebec	L	2-3

APRIL

2—N.Y. Islanders	L	*2-3
4—At Washington	W	4-0
5—Hartford	L	4-5
7—At New Jersey	L	2-5
9—Pittsburgh	L	5-10
10—At Pittsburgh	L	2-4
12—At Philadelphia	L	0-1
14—Washington	L	0-2
16—At Washington	L	2-4

*Denotes overtime game.
†At Miami.
‡At Sacramento, Calif.

OTTAWA SENATORS
EASTERN CONFERENCE/NORTHEAST DIVISION

1993-94 SCHEDULE

Home games shaded.
* — At Madison Square Garden, New York.
† — At Minneapolis.

OCTOBER

SUN	MON	TUE	WED	THU	FRI	SAT
					1	2
3	4	5	6 QUE	7	8	9 STL
10	11	12	13	14 FLA	15	16 TB
17	18	19	20	21 DAL	22	23 NYI
24	25 ANA	26	27 PHI	28 BOS	29	30 DAL
31						

NOVEMBER

SUN	MON	TUE	WED	THU	FRI	SAT
	1	2	3 EDM	4	5 WIN	6
7	8	9	10 HAR	11 FLA	12	13 MON
14	15 MON	16	17 NYI	18 NJ	19	20
21	22 BUF	23	24 NYR	25	26 BUF	27 PIT
28	29 HAR	30				

DECEMBER

SUN	MON	TUE	WED	THU	FRI	SAT
			1 MON	2	3 DET	4 WAS
5	6 CAL	7	8 BUF	9†	10	11 QUE
12	13 LA	14	15 TB	16	17 WAS	18
19 NYR	20	21 QUE	22	23 HAR	24	25
26 HAR	27 BOS	28	29	30 TB	31	

JANUARY

SUN	MON	TUE	WED	THU	FRI	SAT
						1 NJ
2	3 PIT	4	5 VAN	6 TOR	7	8 WIN
9	10 NYI	11 PHI	12	13	14 VAN	15 CAL
16	17	18 EDM	19	20	21	22* ALL STAR GAME
23	24	25 PIT	26	27 HAR	28	29 CHI
30	31 CHI					

FEBRUARY

SUN	MON	TUE	WED	THU	FRI	SAT
		1	2 FLA	3	4 NJ	5 MON
6	7	8 PHI	9	10 TB	11	12 NYR
13	14	15	16	17	18 NYR	19 NYI
20	21	22	23	24 SJ	25	26 STL
27	28 TOR					

MARCH

SUN	MON	TUE	WED	THU	FRI	SAT
		1	2 BUF	3	4† WIN	5 BOS
6	7	8 QUE	9	10 PHI	11	12
13 ANA	14	15 LA	16	17 SJ	18	19
20 BUF	21	22	23 DET	24 PIT	25	26
27	28 MON	29	30 QUE	31		

APRIL

SUN	MON	TUE	WED	THU	FRI	SAT
					1	2 FLA
3	4	5	6 WAS	7 BOS	8	9 WAS
10	11 PIT	12	13 BOS	14 NJ	15	16

1993-94 SEASON

CLUB DIRECTORY

Chairman and governor
Bruce M. Firestone
Co-chairman and chief executive officer
Rod Bryden
President and general manager
Randy J. Sexton
Head coach
Rick Bowness
Assistant coaches
E.J. MacGuire
Alain Vigneault
Director of player personnel
John Ferguson

Head equipment trainer
Ed Georgica
Administrative assistant
Allison Vaughan
Vice president of marketing
Jim Steel
Vice president of sales
Mark Bonneau
Director of media relations
Laurent Benoit
Media relations assistant
Dominick Saillant

DRAFT CHOICES

1—Alexandre Daigle	6-0/170	1	C	Victoriaville (QMJHL)
2—Radim Bicanek	6-1/178	27	D	Duklajihlava, Czech.
3—Patrick Charbonneau	5-11/217	53	G	Victoriaville (QMJHL)
4—Cosmo Dupaul	6-0/186	91	C	Victoriaville (QMJHL)
6—Rick Bodkin	6-4/179	131	C	Sudbury (OHL)
7—Sergei Polistchuk		157	D	Soviet Wings
8—Jason Disher	6-2/202	183	D	Kingston (OHL)
9—Toby Kvalevog	5-10/170	209	G	Bemidji H.S. (Minn.)
9—Pavol Demitra	5-11/178	227	F	Dukla Trencin, Czech.
10—Rick Schuwerk	6-1/195	235	D	Canterbury Prep (Conn.)

MISCELLANEOUS DATA

Home ice (capacity)
Ottawa Civic Centre (10,500)
Address
301 Moodie Drive
Nepean, Ont. K2H 9C4
Business phone
613-726-0540 or 613-721-0115

Rink dimensions
200 feet by 85 feet
Club colors
Black, red and gold
Minor league affiliation
Prince Edward Island (AHL)

TRAINING CAMP ROSTER

No.	FORWARDS	Ht./Wt.	Place (BORN)	Date	NHL exp.	1992-93 clubs
15	Dave Archibald (C/LW)	6-1/190	Chilliwack, B.C.	4-14-69	4	Binghamton (AHL), Ottawa
13	Jamie Baker (C)	6-0/190	Nepean, Que.	8-31-66	4	Ottawa
	Alexandre Daigle (C)	6-0/170	Montreal	2-7-75	0	Victoriaville (QMJHL)
	Jake Grimes (C)	6-1/196	Montreal	9-13-72	0	New Haven (AHL)
	Daniel Guerard (C/RW)	6-4/211	Lasalle, Que.	4-9-74	0	Verdun (QMJHL), New Haven (AHL)
25	Tomas Jelinek (RW)	5-10/189	Prague, Czech.	4-29-62	1	Ottawa
26	Bob Kudelski (RW)	6-1/200	Springfield, Mass.	3-3-64	6	Los Angeles, Ottawa
7	Mark Lamb (C)	5-9/180	Swift Current, Sask.	8-3-64	8	Ottawa
28	Jeff Lazaro (LW)	5-10/180	Waltham, Mass.	3-21-68	3	Ottawa, New Haven (AHL)
10	Darcy Loewen (LW)	5-10/185	Calgary, Alta.	2-26-69	4	Ottawa
	Troy Mallette (C/LW)	6-2/190	Sudbury, Ont.	2-25-70	4	New Jersey, Utica (AHL)
20	Andrew McBain (RW)	6-1/205	Toronto	1-18-65	10	Ottawa, New Haven (AHL)
	Shawn McCosh (C)	6-0/188	Oshawa, Ont.	6-5-69	1	Phoenix (IHL), New Haven (AHL)
	Chad Penney (LW)	6-0/195	Labrador City, Nfld.	9-18-73	0	North Bay (OHL), Sault Ste. Marie (OHL)
21	Martin St. Amour (LW)	6-2/195	Montreal	1-30-70	1	New Haven (AHL), Ottawa
	Claude Savoie (RW)	5-11/182	Montreal	3-12-73	0	Victoriaville (QMJHL), New Haven (AHL)
61	Sylvain Turgeon (LW/C)	6-0/200	Noranda, Que.	1-17-65	10	Ottawa
	Alexei Yashin (C)	6-2/189	Sverdlovsk, U.S.S.R.	11-5-73	0	Dynamo Moscow (CIS)

No.	DEFENSEMEN	Ht./Wt.	Place	Date	NHL exp.	1992-93 clubs
6	Gord Dineen	6-0/195	Quebec City	9-21-62	11	San Diego (IHL), Ottawa
	Dmitri Filimonov	6-4/207	Perm, U.S.S.R.	10-14-71	0	Dynamo Moscow (CIS)
5	Ken Hammond	6-1/190	London, Ont.	8-23-63	8	Ottawa, New Haven (AHL)
2	Radek Hamr	5-11/167	Prague, Czech.	6-15-74	1	New Haven (AHL), Ottawa
22	Norm Maciver	5-11/180	Thunder Bay, Ont.	9-8-64	7	Ottawa
3	Kent Paynter	6-0/185	Summerside, P.E.I.	4-27-65	6	New Haven (AHL), Ottawa
34	Darren Rumble	6-1/200	Barrie, Ont.	1-23-69	2	Ottawa, New Haven (AHL)
4	Brad Shaw	6-0/190	Cambridge, Ont.	4-28-64	8	Ottawa
	Patrick Traverse	6-3/173	Montreal	3-14-74	0	St. Jean (QMJHL), New Haven (AHL)
	Dennis Vial	6-1/200	Sault Ste. Marie, Ont.	4-10-69	3	Detroit, Adirondack (AHL)

No.	GOALTENDERS	Ht./Wt.	Place	Date	NHL exp.	1992-93 clubs
32	Daniel Berthiaume	5-9/160	Longueuil, Que.	1-26-66	8	Ottawa
	Craig Billington	5-10/170	London, Ont.	9-11-66	4	New Jersey
30	Darrin Madeley	5-11/165	Holland Landing, Ont.	2-25-68	1	New Haven (AHL), Ottawa

1992-93 REVIEW

INDIVIDUAL STATISTICS

SCORING

	Games	G	A	Pts.	Pen.	+/-	PPG	SHG	Shots	Shooting Pct.
Norm Maciver	80	17	46	63	84	-46	7	1	184	9.2
Jamie Baker	76	19	29	48	54	-20	10	0	160	11.9
Sylvain Turgeon	72	25	18	43	104	-29	8	0	249	10.0
Brad Shaw	81	7	34	41	34	-47	4	0	166	4.2
Bob Kudelski*	48	21	14	35	22	-22	12	0	125	16.8
Jody Hull	69	13	21	34	14	-24	5	1	134	9.7
Mark Lamb	71	7	19	26	64	-40	1	0	123	5.7
Mike Peluso	81	15	10	25	318	-35	2	0	93	16.1
Mark Freer	63	10	14	24	39	-35	3	3	80	12.5
Neil Brady	55	7	17	24	57	-25	5	0	68	10.3
Andrew McBain	59	7	16	23	43	-37	1	0	71	9.9
Laurie Boschman	70	9	7	16	101	-26	0	1	84	10.7
Darren Rumble	69	3	13	16	61	-24	0	0	92	3.3
David Archibald	44	9	6	15	32	-16	6	0	93	9.7
Doug Smail	51	4	10	14	51	-34	0	0	73	5.5
Tomas Jelinek	49	7	6	13	52	-21	0	0	60	11.7
Chris Luongo	76	3	9	12	68	-47	1	0	76	3.9
Jeff Lazaro	26	6	4	10	16	-8	0	1	38	15.8
Rob Murphy	44	3	7	10	30	-23	0	0	55	5.5
Darcy Loewen	79	4	5	9	145	-26	0	0	42	9.5
Ken Hammond	62	4	4	8	104	-42	0	0	64	6.3
Gord Dineen	32	2	4	6	30	-19	1	0	36	5.6

	Games	G	A	Pts.	Pen.	+/-	PPG	SHG	Shots	Shooting Pct.
Mark Osiecki*	34	0	4	4	12	-21	0	0	20	0.0
Brad Marsh	59	0	3	3	30	-29	0	0	35	0.0
Dominic Lavoie*	2	0	1	1	0	0	0	0	8	0.0
Blair Atcheynum	4	0	1	1	0	-3	0	0	2	0.0
Jim Kyte	4	0	1	1	4	0	0	0	1	0.0
Marc Fortier*	10	0	1	1	6	-7	0	0	12	0.0
Jim Thomson*	15	0	1	1	41	-11	0	0	21	0.0
Daniel Berthiaume (goalie)	25	0	1	1	2	0	0	0	0	0.0
Martin St. Amour	1	0	0	0	2	0	0	0	2	0.0
Tony Cimellaro	2	0	0	0	0	-2	0	0	4	0.0
Darrin Madeley (goalie)	2	0	0	0	0	0	0	0	0	0.0
Lonnie Loach*	3	0	0	0	0	0	0	0	3	0.0
Radek Hamr	4	0	0	0	0	-4	0	0	2	0.0
Kent Paynter	6	0	0	0	20	-7	0	0	3	0.0
Steve Weeks (goalie)	7	0	0	0	0	0	0	0	0	0.0
Brad Miller	11	0	0	0	42	-5	0	0	2	0.0
Peter Sidorkiewicz (goalie)	64	0	0	0	8	0	0	0	0	0.0

GOALTENDING

	Games	Min.	Goals	SO	Avg.	W	L	T	Shots	Sv. Pct.
Daniel Berthiaume	25	1326	95	0	4.30	2	17	1	739	.871
Peter Sidorkiewicz	64	3388	†250	0	4.43	8	†46	3	1737	.856
Darrin Madeley	2	90	10	0	6.67	0	2	0	44	.773
Steve Weeks	7	249	30	0	7.23	0	5	0	144	.792

Empty-net goals (do not count against a goaltender's average): Sidorkiewicz 7, Berthiaume 3.
*Played with two or more NHL teams.
†Led league.

RESULTS

OCTOBER

8—Montreal	W	5-3
10—At Quebec	L	2-9
12—At Boston	L	3-6
14—At Hartford	L	1-4
16—At Washington	L	1-5
20—Toronto†	L	3-5
22—Hartford	L	1-5
24—N.Y. Rangers	L	*2-3
27—Pittsburgh	L	2-7
30—At Buffalo	L	3-12
31—Buffalo	T	*2-2

NOVEMBER

3—At Edmonton	L	2-5
5—At Calgary	L	4-8
6—At Vancouver	L	1-4
9—Toronto	L	1-3
11—Quebec	L	3-7
13—At Tampa Bay	L	0-1
15—At Philadelphia	L	2-7
17—Montreal	L	3-5
19—Hartford	L	2-4
21—At Montreal	L	1-3
23—Boston	L	2-3
25—New Jersey	W	3-1
27—At Buffalo	L	1-4
29—Buffalo	L	2-5

DECEMBER

1—Minnesota	L	1-3
3—New Jersey	T	*3-3
5—Philadelphia	W	3-2

7—Washington	L	5-6
9—At Hartford	L	2-6
10—At Boston	L	2-4
12—Calgary	T	*1-1
15—Detroit	L	*2-3
17—At N.Y. Islanders	L	3-9
19—At Toronto	L	1-5
21—Washington	L	3-4
23—Chicago	L	2-4
26—At Quebec	L	2-4
27—Quebec	L	1-6
31—At Detroit	L	*4-5

JANUARY

2—Buffalo	L	2-7
6—At N.Y. Rangers	L	2-6
8—At New Jersey	L	4-6
10—San Jose	W	3-2
12—Los Angeles	L	2-3
14—St. Louis	L	1-4
16—At Pittsburgh	L	1-6
17—N.Y. Islanders	L	2-7
19—Quebec	L	2-5
21—At Minnesota	L	2-7
23—At Washington	L	4-6
26—At St. Louis	L	1-5
28—Hartford	W	5-2
30—At Montreal	L	3-5

FEBRUARY

1—Winnipeg	T	*4-4
3—Edmonton	W	3-2
8—Buffalo	W	4-2
9—At Philadelphia	L	1-8

13—Montreal	L	1-4
17—At Quebec	L	4-6
20—At Montreal	L	4-5
22—At Winnipeg	L	3-6
23—Winnipeg‡	L	2-8
25—Pittsburgh	W	2-1
27—At New Jersey	L	2-5
28—Quebec	W	6-4

MARCH

2—At San Jose	L	*2-3
4—At Los Angeles	L	6-8
7—At Chicago	L	2-4
13—At Boston	L	3-6
18—Boston	L	1-4
22—N.Y. Rangers	L	4-5
25—Tampa Bay	L	*2-3
27—At Montreal	L	*3-4
28—At Buffalo	L	1-3
30—At Pittsburgh	L	4-6

APRIL

1—Quebec	L	2-4
3—At Hartford	L	3-7
4—Vancouver	L	0-3
7—Hartford	L	1-6
10—At N.Y. Islanders	W	5-3
11—At Boston	L	2-4
13—At Quebec	L	2-6
14—Boston	L	2-4

*Denotes overtime game.
†At Hamilton, Ont.
‡At Saskatoon, Sask.

PHILADELPHIA FLYERS
EASTERN CONFERENCE/ATLANTIC DIVISION

1993-94 SCHEDULE

☐ Home games shaded.
* — At Madison Square Garden, New York.
† — At Minneapolis.
△ — At Cleveland.

OCTOBER
SUN	MON	TUE	WED	THU	FRI	SAT
					1	2
3	4	5 PIT	6	7	8	9 HAR
10 TOR	11	12 BUF	13	14	15 WAS	16 NYR
17	18	19	20	21 NYI	22	23 WIN
24	25	26 QUE	27 OTT	28	29	30 NJ
31 CHI						

NOVEMBER
SUN	MON	TUE	WED	THU	FRI	SAT
	1	2 FLA	3	4 QUE	5	6 TOR
7 VAN	8	9	10 BUF	11 NJ	12	13 BUF
14	15	16 PIT	17	18 HAR	19	20 BOS
21 NYI	22	23	24 MON	25	26 TB	27 TB
28	29	30				

DECEMBER
SUN	MON	TUE	WED	THU	FRI	SAT
			1 EDM	2 VAN	3	4 CAL
5	6	7	8	9 WAS	10	11 NYI
12 EDM	13	14	15	16 QUE	17	18 CHI
19 NJ	20	21 WAS	22	23 DET	24	25
26	27 BUF	28 PIT	29	30	31† BOS	

JANUARY
SUN	MON	TUE	WED	THU	FRI	SAT
						1
2	3	4	5	6 DAL	7	8 TB
9	10	11 OTT	12	13 BOS	14 NYR	15
16 LA	17	18	19 STL	20	21	22* ALL-STAR GAME
23	24	25 QUE	26	27	28	29 WAS
30 MON	31					

FEBRUARY
SUN	MON	TUE	WED	THU	FRI	SAT
		1	2△ WAS	3 SJ	4	5 BOS
6	7	8 SJ	9	10 FLA	11 DET	12
13 PIT	14	15 NJ	16 ANA	17	18 LA	19
20	21 MON	22	23	24 NYI	25 NYI	26
27	28					

MARCH
SUN	MON	TUE	WED	THU	FRI	SAT
		1	2 NYR	3	4 WAS	5
6 TB	7	8 DAL	9	10 OTT	11	12 MON
13 TB	14	15	16	17	18	19 HAR
20 FLA	21	22 STL	23	24 FLA	25	26 NJ
27 ANA	28	29 NYR	30	31 CAL		

APRIL
SUN	MON	TUE	WED	THU	FRI	SAT
					1	2 HAR
3	4 WIN	5	6	7 FLA	8	9
10 BOS	11	12 NJ	13	14 NYR	15	16

1993-94 SEASON

CLUB DIRECTORY

Chairman of the exec. committee/owner
Edward M. Snider
President
Jay T. Snider
Chairman of the board emeritus
Joseph C. Scott
Executive vice president
Keith Allen
Chief operating officer
Ron Ryan
General manager
Russ Farwell
Assistant general manager
John Blackwell
Vice president, finance
Dan Clemmens
Coach
Terry Simpson
Assistant coaches
Mike Eaves
Craig Hartsburg
Goaltending instructor
Bernie Parent
Phys. conditioning and rehabilitation coach
Pat Croce
Director of pro scouting
Bill Barber
Chief scout
Jerry Melnyk

Scouts
Inge Hammarstrom
Glen Sonmor
Red Sullivan
Vaclav Slansky
Simon Nolet
Blair Reid
Bill Dineen
Peter Dineen
Jerry Moschella
Doug Overton
Evgeny Zimin
Vice president, public relations
Mark Piazza
Assistant director of public relations
Jill Vogel
Ticket manager
Ceil Baker
Vice president, sales
Jack Betson
Director of team services
Joe Kadlec
Athletic therapist
Gary Smith
Trainers
Jim Evers
Harry Bricker
Team physician
Jeffrey Hartzell, M.D.

DRAFT CHOICES

2—Janne Niinimaa	6-1/196	36	D	Karpat, Finland
3—Vaclav Prospal	6-2/167	71	C	Budejovice, Czech.
3—Milos Holan	5-11/183	77	D	Tj Vitkovice, Czech.
5—Vladimir Krechin	5-11/180	114	F	Chelyabinsk, CIS
6—Mike Crowley	5-11/165	140	D	Jeff'son HS, Bl'ton (Minn.)
7—Aaron Israel	6-2/175	166	G	Harvard University
8—Paul Healey	6-1/174	192	D/F	Prince Albert (WHL)
9—Tripp Tracy	5-10/170	218	G	Harvard University
9—E.J. Bradley	5-10/182	226	C	Tabor Academy
10—Jeffrey Staples	6-2/207	244	D	Brandon (WHL)
11—Kenneth Hemmenway	6-1/175	270	D	Alaska All-Stars

MISCELLANEOUS DATA

Home ice (capacity)
The Spectrum (17,380)
Address
Pattison Place
Philadelphia, PA 19148
Business phone
215-465-4500

Rink dimensions
200 feet by 85 feet
Club colors
Orange, white and black
Minor league affiliation
Hershey (AHL)

TRAINING CAMP ROSTER

No.	FORWARDS	Ht./Wt.	BORN Place	Date	NHL exp.	1992-93 clubs
42	Josef Beranek (RW)	6-2/185	Litvinov, Czech.	10-25-69	2	Edmonton, Cape Breton (AHL), Philadelphia
10	Claude Boivin (LW)	6-2/200	St. Foy, Que.	3-1-70	2	Philadelphia
17	Rod Brind'Amour (C)	6-1/202	Ottawa	8-9-70	5	Philadelphia
21	Dave Brown (RW)	6-5/205	Saskatoon, Sask.	10-12-62	11	Philadelphia
22	Viacheslav Butsayev (C)	6-2/200	Tolyatti, U.S.S.R.	6-13-70	1	CSKA Moscow (CIS), Philadelphia, Hershey (AHL)
46	Al Conroy (LW)	5-8/170	Calgary, Alta.	1-17-66	2	Hershey (AHL), Philadelphia
	Jim Cummins (RW)	6-2/200	Dearborn, Mich.	5-17-70	2	Adirondack (AHL), Detroit
	Eric Dandenault	6-0/193	Sherbrooke, Que.	3-10-70	0	Hershey (AHL)
11	Kevin Dineen (RW)	5-11/190	Quebec City.	10-28-63	9	Philadelphia
	Yanick Dupre (LW)	6-0/195	Montreal.	11-20-72	1	Hershey (AHL)
	Tracy Egeland (RW)	6-1/180	Lethbridge, Alta.	8-20-70	0	Indianapolis (IHL)
9	Pelle Eklund (LW)	5-10/175	Stockholm, Sweden.	3-22-63	8	Philadelphia
36	Andre Faust (C)	6-1/180	Joliette, Que.	10-7-69	1	Hershey (AHL), Philadelphia
18	Brent Fedyk (LW)	6-0/195	Yorkton, Sask.	3-8-67	6	Philadelphia
	Chris Jensen (RW)	5-11/180	Fort St. John, B.C.	10-28-63	6	Hershey (AHL), Knoxville (ECHL)
88	Eric Lindros (C)	6-5/235	London, Ont.	2-28-73	1	Philadelphia
41	Glenn Mulvenna (C)	5-11/187	Calgary, Alta.	2-18-67	2	Philadelphia, Hershey (AHL)
	Pat Murray (RW)	6-3/195	Stratford, Ont.	8-20-69	2	Hershey (AHL)
8	Mark Recchi (RW)	5-10/185	Kamloops, B.C.	2-1-68	5	Philadelphia
	Mikael Renberg (RW)	6-2/183	Pitea, Sweden	5-5-72	0	Lulea (Sweden)
	Ryan Sittler (LW/C)	6-2/185	London, Ont.	1-28-74	0	U. of Michigan (CCHA)
	Dave Tippett (C/LW)	5-10/180	Moosomin, Sask.	8-25-61	10	Pittsburgh
	Claude Vilgrain (RW)	6-1/205	Port-au-Prince, Haiti	3-1-63	4	Cin. (IHL), N.J., Utica (AHL)
	Chris Winnes (RW)	6-0/170	Ridgefield, Conn.	2-12-68	3	Providence (AHL), Boston
	DEFENSEMEN					
28	Jason Bowen	6-4/220	Courtenay, B.C.	11-11-73	1	Tri-City (WHL), Philadelphia
	Aris Brimanis	6-3/195	Cleveland	3-14-72	0	Brandon (WHL)
29	Terry Carkner	6-3/212	Smith Falls, Ont.	3-7-66	7	Philadelphia
44	Shawn Cronin	6-2/210	Flushing, Mich.	8-20-63	5	Philadelphia, Hershey (AHL)
	Jeff Finley	6-2/185	Edmonton, Alta.	4-14-67	5	Capital District (AHL)
	Corey Foster	6-3/204	Ottawa	10-27-69	2	Hershey (AHL)
3	Garry Galley	6-0/190	Ottawa	4-16-63	9	Philadelphia
20	Greg Hawgood	5-10/190	St. Albert, Alta.	8-10-68	6	Edmonton, Philadelphia
	Milos Holan	5-11/183	Bilovec, Czech.	4-22-71	0	TJ Vitkovice (Czech.)
	Dan Kordic	6-5/220	Edmonton, Alta.	4-18-71	1	Hershey (AHL)
27	Ryan McGill	6-2/195	Prince Albert, Sask.	2-28-69	2	Hershey (AHL), Philadelphia
5	Ric Nattress	6-2/210	Hamilton, Ont.	5-25-62	11	Philadelphia
	Toni Porkka	6-2/190	Rauma, Finland	2-4-70	0	Hershey (AHL)
2	Dimitri Yushkevich	5-11/187	Yaroslavl, U.S.S.R.	11-19-71	1	Philadelphia
	GOALTENDERS					
	Yanick Degrace	5-11/175	Lameque, N.B.	4-16-71	0	Hershey (AHL)
	Scott LaGrand	6-1/170	Potsdam, N.Y.	2-11-70	0	Hershey (AHL)
	Ray Letourneau	5-11/190	Lewistown, N.H.	1-14-69	0	Greensboro (ECHL), Roanoke Valley (ECHL)
33	Dominic Roussel	6-1/185	Hull, Que.	2-22-70	2	Philadelphia, Hershey (AHL)
30	Tommy Soderstrom	5-9/163	Stockholm, Sweden	7-17-69	1	Hershey (AHL), Philadelphia

1992-93 REVIEW

INDIVIDUAL STATISTICS

SCORING

	Games	G	A	Pts.	Pen.	+/-	PPG	SHG	Shots	Shooting Pct.
Mark Recchi	84	53	70	123	95	1	15	4	274	19.3
Rod Brind'Amour	81	37	49	86	89	-8	13	4	206	18.0
Eric Lindros	61	41	34	75	147	28	8	1	180	22.8
Kevin Dineen	83	35	28	63	201	14	6	3	241	14.5
Garry Galley	83	13	49	62	115	18	4	1	231	5.6
Brent Fedyk	74	21	38	59	48	14	4	1	167	12.6
Pelle Eklund	55	11	38	49	16	12	4	0	82	13.4
Greg Paslawski*	60	14	19	33	12	0	4	0	90	15.6
Dimitri Yushkevich	82	5	27	32	71	12	1	0	155	3.2
Greg Hawgood*	40	6	22	28	39	-7	5	0	91	6.6
Brian Benning*	37	9	17	26	93	0	6	0	87	10.3
Josef Beranek*	40	13	12	25	50	-1	1	0	86	15.1
Keith Acton	83	8	15	23	51	-10	0	0	74	10.8
Doug Evans	65	8	13	21	70	-9	0	0	60	13.3
Andrei Lomakin	51	8	12	20	34	15	0	0	64	12.5
Terry Carkner	83	3	16	19	150	18	0	0	45	6.7

	Games	G	A	Pts.	Pen.	+/-	PPG	SHG	Shots	Shooting Pct.
Ric Nattress	44	7	10	17	29	1	0	0	57	12.3
Vyatcheslav Butsayev	52	2	14	16	61	3	0	0	58	3.4
Ryan McGill	72	3	10	13	238	9	0	0	68	4.4
Claude Boivin	30	5	4	9	76	-5	0	0	21	23.8
Mark Pederson*	14	3	4	7	6	-2	1	0	21	14.3
Gord Hynes	37	3	4	7	16	-3	0	0	39	7.7
Allan Conroy	21	3	2	5	17	-1	0	0	24	12.5
Len Barrie	8	2	2	4	9	2	0	0	14	14.3
Andre Faust	10	2	2	4	4	5	0	0	11	18.2
Steve Kasper*	21	1	3	4	2	-4	0	1	9	11.1
Shawn Cronin	35	2	1	3	37	0	0	0	12	16.7
Dave Snuggerud*	14	0	2	2	0	0	0	0	10	0.0
Dominic Roussel (goalie)	34	0	2	2	11	0	0	0	0	0.0
Tommy Soderstrom (goalie)	44	0	2	2	4	0	0	0	0	0.0
Dave Brown	70	0	2	2	78	-5	0	0	19	0.0
Jason Bowen	7	1	0	1	2	1	0	0	3	33.3
Stephane Beauregard (goalie)	16	0	1	1	0	0	0	0	0	0.0
Glen Mulvenna	1	0	0	0	2	0	0	0	1	0.0

GOALTENDING

	Games	Min.	Goals	SO	Avg.	W	L	T	Shots	Sv. Pct.
Tommy Soderstrom	44	2512	143	5	3.42	20	17	6	1327	.892
Dominic Roussel	34	1769	111	1	3.76	13	11	5	933	.881
Stephane Beauregard	16	802	59	0	4.41	3	9	0	405	.854

Empty-net goals (do not count against a goaltender's average): Soderstrom 4, Beauregard 1, Roussel 1.
*Played with two or more NHL teams.

RESULTS

OCTOBER
6—At Pittsburgh	T	*3-3
9—New Jersey	W	6-4
10—At Washington	W	4-2
13—At Quebec	L	3-6
15—N.Y. Islanders	L	4-5
17—At New Jersey	L	0-2
18—Winnipeg	W	5-4
20—At N.Y. Islanders	L	3-4
22—Vancouver	T	*4-4
24—Montreal	L	6-7
26—At N.Y. Rangers	L	4-8
29—At Chicago	T	*5-5
31—At St. Louis	L	4-6

NOVEMBER
4—At N.Y. Rangers	L	1-3
7—St. Louis	W	4-2
12—N.Y. Islanders	W	8-5
14—At Montreal	W	*4-3
15—Ottawa	W	7-2
19—N.Y. Rangers	W	7-3
21—At Boston	L	3-4
22—Buffalo	T	*4-4
27—N.Y. Islanders	W	6-3
28—At N.Y. Islanders	L	3-9

DECEMBER
3—Quebec	W	*3-2
5—At Ottawa	L	2-3
6—Boston	L	1-7
11—At Detroit	L	2-4
12—Washington	L	2-5

15—At Pittsburgh	L	2-6
17—Pittsburgh	L	*4-5
19—Chicago	W	3-1
20—At Tampa Bay	L	1-4
23—Pittsburgh	L	0-4
26—At Washington	T	*5-5
29—At Los Angeles	W	10-2
30—At San Jose	W	6-2

JANUARY
2—At Calgary	L	3-7
3—At Edmonton	T	*2-2
7—Washington	W	8-2
9—N.Y. Rangers	W	4-3
10—Edmonton	W	4-0
14—Calgary	T	*4-4
16—At Boston	W	5-4
17—Detroit	L	4-7
21—Boston	L	4-5
23—At N.Y. Islanders	L	4-8
24—Hartford	W	*5-4
26—Buffalo	L	*3-4
28—Quebec	L	3-6
30—At Pittsburgh	L	2-4
31—At Montreal	L	4-6

FEBRUARY
3—At N.Y. Rangers	T	*2-2
9—Ottawa	W	8-1
11—Montreal	T	*0-0
13—At New Jersey	L	4-6
14—New Jersey	L	2-5
16—Calgary†	T	*4-4
18—At Vancouver	W	3-2

20—At Minnesota	L	2-5
22—Detroit‡	T	*5-5
24—At Hartford	W	5-2
25—New Jersey	W	6-2
27—N.Y. Islanders	L	2-3

MARCH
2—Pittsburgh	W	5-4
5—At Washington	W	3-0
7—At New Jersey	L	3-7
9—At N.Y. Islanders	L	2-4
11—Washington	W	6-4
16—Minnesota	W	4-3
20—At Pittsburgh	L	3-9
21—New Jersey	L	2-3
24—At N.Y. Rangers	W	5-4
25—San Jose	W	5-2
27—At Quebec	L	3-8
30—At N.Y. Islanders	L	1-2

APRIL
1—Los Angeles	L	1-3
3—Tampa Bay	W	6-2
4—Toronto	W	4-0
6—At Winnipeg	W	4-2
8—Washington	W	4-3
10—At Toronto	W	4-0
12—N.Y. Rangers	W	1-0
15—At Buffalo	W	7-4
16—At Hartford	W	*5-4

*Denotes overtime game.
†At Cincinnati.
‡At Cleveland.

PITTSBURGH PENGUINS
EASTERN CONFERENCE/NORTHEAST DIVISION

1993-94 SCHEDULE

Home games shaded.
* — At Madison Square Garden, New York.
† — At Sacramento, Calif.
∆ — At Cleveland.

OCTOBER

SUN	MON	TUE	WED	THU	FRI	SAT
					1	2
3	4	5 PHI	6	7 MON	8	9 NYR
10 QUE	11	12 FLA	13	14 TB	15	16 HAR
17	18	19 NYI	20	21	22 BUF	23 STL
24	25	26	27	28 QUE	29	30 CHI
31						

NOVEMBER

SUN	MON	TUE	WED	THU	FRI	SAT
	1	2 SJ	3† BUF	4	5	6 LA
7 ANA	8	9 STL	10	11 CHI	12	13 DET
14	15	16 PHI	17	18 WAS	19	20 MON
21	22	23	24 BOS	25	26 WAS	27 OTT
28	29	30				

DECEMBER

SUN	MON	TUE	WED	THU	FRI	SAT
			1	2 NJ	3	4 HAR
5	6	7	8 DAL	9	10	11 TB
12	13	14 LA	15	16 BUF	17	18
19 NYI	20	21 TB	22	23 BOS	24	25
26 WAS	27	28 PHI	29	30	31 QUE	

JANUARY

SUN	MON	TUE	WED	THU	FRI	SAT
						1
2 HAR	3 OTT	4	5	6	7 BUF	8 CAL
9	10	11 BOS	12	13 FLA	14	15 EDM
16	17	18 QUE	19	20	21	22 ALL STAR GAME
23	24	25 OTT	26	27 QUE	28	29 TOR
30	31 NYR					

FEBRUARY

SUN	MON	TUE	WED	THU	FRI	SAT
		1 FLA	2	3	4 DET	5 NJ
6	7 MON	8	9	10 NYI	11	12 DAL
13 PHI	14	15 WIN	16	17 HAR	18	19 MON
20	21 NYR	22	23	24 ANA	25	26 BUF
27	28 FLA					

MARCH

SUN	MON	TUE	WED	THU	FRI	SAT
		1	2	3	4 BUF	5
6 WIN	7	8 BOS	9	10 TOR	11	12 NYR
13 HAR	14	15 WAS	16	17 BOS	18	19 VAN
20 NYI	21	22 SJ	23	24 OTT	25	26 CAL
27 EDM	28	29	30 VAN	31		

APRIL

SUN	MON	TUE	WED	THU	FRI	SAT
					1	2
3∆ BOS	4 TB	5	6 NJ	7	8 NJ	9 MON
10	11 OTT	12	13	14	15	16

1993-94 SEASON

CLUB DIRECTORY

Owners
Howard Baldwin
Morris Belzberg
Thomas Ruta
Chairman of the board and governor
Howard Baldwin
President
Jack Kelley
Executive V.P. and general manager
Craig Patrick
Head coach
Ed Johnston
Assistant coaches
Rick Kehoe
Bryan Trottier
Scouts
Greg Malone
Gilles Meloche
Les Binkley
John Gill
Charlie Hodge
Ralph Cox
Executive V.P. and chief financial officer
Donn Patton
Senior V.P. marketing and public relations
Bill Barnes

Executive V.P. PHA Sports Marketing LTD
Richard Chmura
V.P. public and community relations
Phil Langan
Vice president, merchandising
Bill Cox
Controller
Kevin Hart
Director of public relations
Cindy Himes
Director of media relations
Harry Sanders
Assistant director of media relations
Steve Bovino
Director of ticket sales
Jeff Mercer
Trainer
To be announced
Strength and conditioning coach
John Welday
Equipment manager
Steve Latin
Team physician
Dr. Charles Burke

DRAFT CHOICES

1—Stefan Bergqvist	6-3/216	26	D	Leksand, Sweden
2—Domenic Pittis	5-11/180	52	C	Lethbridge (WHL)
3—Dave Roche	6-4/224	62	F	Peterborough (OHL)
4—J. Andersson-Junkka	6-2/165	104	D	Kiruna, Sweden
5—Chris Kelleher	6-1/215	130	D	St. Sebastian's HS (Mass.)
6—Patrick Lalime	6-2/165	156	G	Shawinigan (QMJHL)
7—Sean Selmser	6-1/182	182	F	Red Deer (WHL)
8—Larry McMorran	6-3/193	208	C	Seattle (WHL)
9—Timothy Harberts	6-1/185	234	C	Wayzata H.S. (Minn.)
10—Leonid Toropchenko	6-4/235	260	C	Springfield (AHL)
11—Hans Jonsson	6-1/176	286	D	MoDo, Sweden

MISCELLANEOUS DATA

Home ice (capacity)
Civic Arena (16,164)
Address
Gate No. 9
Pittsburgh, PA 15219
Business phone
412-642-1800

Rink dimensions
200 feet by 85 feet
Club colors
Black, gold and white
Minor league affiliation
Cleveland (IHL)

TRAINING CAMP ROSTER

No.	FORWARDS	Ht./Wt.	Place	BORN Date	NHL exp.	1992-93 clubs
16	Jay Caufield (RW)	6-4/230	Philadelphia, Pa.	7-17-65	7	Pittsburgh
20	Jeff Daniels (LW)	6-1/200	Oshawa, Ont.	6-24-68	3	Pittsburgh, Cleveland (IHL)
	Justin Duberman (RW)	6-1/185	New Haven, Conn.	3-23-70	0	Cleveland (IHL)
10	Ron Francis (C)	6-2/200	Sault Ste. Marie, Ont.	3-1-63	12	Pittsburgh
	Daniel Gauthier (C)	6-2/192	Charlemagne, Que.	5-17-70	0	Cleveland (IHL)
68	Jaromir Jagr (RW)	6-2/208	Kladno, Czech.	2-15-72	3	Pittsburgh
66	Mario Lemieux (C)	6-4/210	Montreal	10-5-65	9	Pittsburgh
15	Shawn McEachern (C)	5-11/195	Waltham, Mass.	2-28-69	2	Pittsburgh
7	Joe Mullen (RW)	5-9/180	New York	2-26-57	13	Pittsburgh
	Markus Naslund (LW)	5-11/174	Harnosand, Sweden	7-30-73	0	MoDo (Sweden)
39	Mike Needham (RW)	5-10/185	Calgary, Alta.	4-4-70	2	Pittsburgh, Cleveland (IHL)
26	Mike Stapleton (C)	5-10/183	Sarnia, Ont.	5-5-66	6	Pittsburgh
25	Kevin Stevens (LW)	6-3/217	Brockton, Mass.	4-15-65	6	Pittsburgh
82	Martin Straka (C)	5-10/178	Plzen, Czech.	9-3-72	1	Pittsburgh, Cleveland (IHL)
22	Rick Tocchet (RW)	6-0/205	Scarborough, Ont.	4-9-64	9	Pittsburgh
	Bryan Trottier (C)	5-11/195	Val Marie, Sask.	7-17-56	17	

DEFENSEMEN

No.		Ht./Wt.	Place	Date	NHL exp.	1992-93 clubs
	Greg Andrusak (D)	6-1/195	Cranbrook, B.C.	11-14-69	0	Cleveland (IHL), Muskegon (Col.HL)
	Stefan Bergqvist (D)	6-3/216	Leksand, Sweden	3-10-75	0	Leksand (Sweden)
	Paul Dyck (D)	6-1/192	Steinbach, Man.	4-15-71	0	Cleveland (IHL)
33	Bryan Fogarty (D)	6-2/198	Montreal	6-11-69	4	Pittsburgh, Cleveland (IHL)
3	Grant Jennings (D)	6-3/200	Hudson Bay, Sask.	5-5-65	6	Pittsburgh
55	Larry Murphy (D)	6-2/210	Scarborough, Ont.	3-8-61	13	Pittsburgh
	Patrick Neaton (D)	6-0/180	Redford, Mich.	5-21-71	0	University of Michigan (CCHA)
	Todd Nelson (D)	6-0/200	Prince Albert, Sask.	5-15-69	1	Cleveland (IHL)
2	Jim Paek (D)	6-1/195	Seoul, South Korea	4-7-67	3	Pittsburgh
6	Mike Ramsey (D)	6-3/195	Minneapolis	12-3-60	14	Buffalo, Pittsburgh
28	Kjell Samuelsson (D)	6-6/235	Tyngsryd, Sweden	10-18-58	8	Pittsburgh
5	Ulf Samuelsson (D)	6-1/195	Fagersta, Sweden	3-26-64	9	Pittsburgh
23	Paul Stanton (D)	6-1/200	Boston	6-22-67	3	Pittsburgh
32	Peter Taglianetti (D)	6-2/200	Framingham, Mass.	8-15-63	9	Tampa Bay, Pittsburgh
	Chris Tamer (D)	6-2/185	Dearborn, Mich.	11-17-70	0	U. of Michigan (CCHA)

GOALTENDERS

No.		Ht./Wt.	Place	Date	NHL exp.	1992-93 clubs
35	Tom Barrasso (G)	6-3/211	Boston	3-31-65	10	Pittsburgh
	Rob Dopson (G)	6-0/200	Smith Falls, Ont.	8-21-67	0	Cleveland (IHL)
	Bruce Racine (G)	6-0/178	Cornwall, Ont.	8-9-66	0	Cleveland (IHL)
31	Ken Wregget (G)	6-1/195	Brandon, Man.	3-25-64	10	Pittsburgh

1992-93 REVIEW

INDIVIDUAL STATISTICS

SCORING

	Games	G	A	Pts.	Pen.	+/-	PPG	SHG	Shots	Shooting Pct.
Mario Lemieux	60	69	91	†160	38	†55	16	6	286	24.1
Kevin Stevens	72	55	56	111	177	17	26	0	326	16.9
Rick Tocchet	80	48	61	109	252	28	20	4	240	20.0
Ron Francis	84	24	76	100	68	6	9	2	215	11.2
Jaromir Jagr	81	34	60	94	61	30	10	1	242	14.0
Larry Murphy	83	22	63	85	73	45	6	2	230	9.6
Joe Mullen	72	33	37	70	14	19	9	3	175	18.9
Shawn McEachern	84	28	33	61	46	21	7	0	196	14.3
Ulf Samuelsson	77	3	26	29	249	36	0	0	96	3.1
Dave Tippett	74	6	19	25	56	5	0	1	64	9.4
Troy Loney	82	5	16	21	99	1	0	0	83	6.0
Jim Paek	77	3	15	18	64	13	0	0	57	5.3
Paul Stanton	77	4	12	16	97	7	2	0	106	3.8
Martin Straka	42	3	13	16	29	2	0	0	28	10.7
Bob Errey*	54	8	6	14	76	-2	0	0	79	10.1
Mike Needham	56	8	5	13	14	-1	0	0	49	16.3
Mike Stapleton	78	4	9	13	10	-8	0	1	78	5.1
Jeff Daniels	58	5	4	9	14	-5	0	0	30	16.7
Kjell Samuelson	63	3	6	9	106	25	0	0	63	4.8
Tom Barrasso (goalie)	63	0	8	8	24	0	0	0	0	0.0
Peter Taglianetti*	11	1	4	5	34	4	0	0	18	5.6
Grant Jennings	58	0	5	5	65	6	0	0	32	0.0
Bryan Fogarty	12	0	4	4	4	-3	0	0	11	0.0
Mike Ramsey*	12	1	2	3	8	13	0	0	8	12.5

	Games	G	A	Pts.	Pen.	+/-	PPG	SHG	Shots	Shooting Pct.
Peter Ahola*	22	0	1	1	14	-2	0	0	5	0.0
Ken Wregget (goalie)	25	0	1	1	6	0	0	0	0	0.0
Jeff Chychrun*	1	0	0	0	2	1	0	0	0	0.0
Jamie Leach*	5	0	0	0	2	-2	0	0	2	0.0
Jay Caufield	26	0	0	0	60	-1	0	0	6	0.0

GOALTENDING

	Games	Min.	Goals	SO	Avg.	W	L	T	Shots	Sv. Pct.
Tom Barrasso	63	3702	186	§4	3.01	†43	14	5	1885	.901
Ken Wregget	25	1368	78	§0	3.42	13	7	2	692	.887

Empty-net goals (do not count against a goaltender's average): Barrasso 2, Wregget 2.
*Played with two or more NHL teams.
†Led league.
§Barrasso and Wregget shared a shutout.

RESULTS

OCTOBER
6—Philadelphia	T	*3-3
8—N.Y. Islanders	W	7-3
10—At Montreal	T	*3-3
13—Buffalo	W	6-5
15—Montreal	W	5-2
17—At Hartford	W	7-3
20—Vancouver	W	5-1
22—Detroit	W	9-6
24—At New Jersey	W	4-3
27—At Ottawa	W	7-2
29—At St. Louis	L	4-6

NOVEMBER
1—At Tampa Bay	W	5-4
3—N.Y. Islanders	W	2-0
5—St. Louis	W	8-4
7—At Toronto	L	2-4
8—At Chicago	L	2-7
10—At Minnesota	W	4-1
12—Quebec	T	*4-4
13—At Detroit	L	0-8
17—Buffalo	W	4-2
20—At New Jersey	W	4-1
21—New Jersey	W	2-0
23—At N.Y. Rangers	W	5-2
25—N.Y. Rangers	L	3-11
27—At Washington	L	4-6
28—Washington	W	5-3

DECEMBER
1—At N.Y. Islanders	W	7-3
3—At Los Angeles	L	3-5
5—At San Jose	W	9-4
8—Winnipeg	W	5-2
11—At New Jersey	L	1-2
12—New Jersey	W	6-5
15—Philadelphia	W	6-2
17—At Philadelphia	W	*5-4
19—N.Y. Islanders	L	3-4
21—Quebec	W	7-4
23—At Philadelphia	W	4-0
27—At Buffalo	W	4-2
31—Toronto	T	*3-3

JANUARY
2—N.Y. Rangers	W	5-2
5—Boston	W	6-2
7—Minnesota	L	3-6
9—Calgary	W	3-2
10—At Winnipeg	L	2-3
14—At Boston	L	0-7
16—Ottawa	W	6-1
19—At Vancouver	W	5-2
22—At Edmonton	L	1-2
23—At Calgary	W	4-3
26—Washington	W	6-3
28—N.Y. Islanders	L	2-5
30—Philadelphia	W	4-2
31—At Washington	T	*2-2

FEBRUARY
8—Boston†	W	4-0
10—At N.Y. Rangers	W	3-0
13—Chicago	W	4-1
14—At Buffalo	L	4-7
18—Edmonton	L	4-5
20—At N.Y. Islanders	L	2-4
21—At Hartford	W	4-3
23—New Jersey	L	1-3
25—At Ottawa	L	1-2
27—Tampa Bay	T	*3-3
28—At Washington	W	4-2

MARCH
2—At Philadelphia	L	4-5
5—At N.Y. Rangers	L	1-3
9—Boston	W	3-2
11—Los Angeles	W	*4-3
14—At N.Y. Islanders	W	3-2
18—Washington	W	7-5
20—Philadelphia	W	9-3
21—Edmonton‡	W	6-4
23—San Jose	W	7-2
25—New Jersey	W	4-3
27—At Boston	W	5-3
28—At Washington	W	4-1
30—Ottawa	W	6-4

APRIL
1—Hartford	W	10-2
3—At Quebec	W	5-3
4—At New Jersey	W	5-2
7—Montreal	W	*4-3
9—At N.Y. Rangers	W	10-5
10—N.Y. Rangers	W	4-2
14—At New Jersey	T	*6-6

*Denotes overtime game.
†At Atlanta.
‡At Cleveland.

QUEBEC NORDIQUES
EASTERN CONFERENCE/NORTHEAST DIVISION

1993-94 SCHEDULE

Home games shaded.
* — At Madison Square Garden, New York.
† — At Phoenix.
∆ — At Minneapolis.

OCTOBER
SUN	MON	TUE	WED	THU	FRI	SAT
					1	2
3	4	5	6 OTT	7	8	9 BOS
10 PIT	11	12	13 NYR	14	15	16 MON
17	18 MON	19	20 HAR	21 CHI	22	23 DAL
24	25	26 PHI	27	28 PIT	29	30 DET
31						

NOVEMBER
SUN	MON	TUE	WED	THU	FRI	SAT
	1	2 TB	3	4 PHI	5	6 NYR
7 FLA	8	9 WAS	10	11	12	13 TB
14 FLA	15	16	17	18	19	20 WIN
21	22	23 NJ	24	25 LA	26	27 BUF
28	29	30 BOS				

DECEMBER
SUN	MON	TUE	WED	THU	FRI	SAT
			1	2	3 NYI	4 VAN
5	6	7 CAL	8	9 NJ	10	11 OTT
12	13 WAS	14	15	16 PHI	17	18 NJ
19 SJ	20	21 OTT	22	23 WIN	24	25
26	27	28 TB	29 NYI	30	31 PIT	

JANUARY
SUN	MON	TUE	WED	THU	FRI	SAT
						1
2 DAL	3	4 LA	5† MON	6	7 EDM	8
9	10	11 CAL	12 VAN	13	14	15 WAS
16	17	18 PIT	19	20	21	22* ALL-STAR GAME
23	24	25 PHI	26	27 PIT	28	29 HAR
30	31 BOS					

FEBRUARY
SUN	MON	TUE	WED	THU	FRI	SAT
		1 HAR	2	3 STL	4	5 NYI
6	7	8 BOS	9	10	11 NYR	12 MON
13	14 NYR	15	16	17 SJ	18 ANA	19
20	21 BUF	22	23	24 STL	25	26 ANA
27 NYI	28					

MARCH
SUN	MON	TUE	WED	THU	FRI	SAT
		1 BUF	2	3	4	5 TOR
6	7 NJ	8 OTT	9	10 MON	11	12 WAS
13	14 CHI	15	16	17 HAR	18	19 MON
20 EDM	21	22 BOS	23	24	25	26 TOR
27∆ NJ	28	29	30 OTT	31 DET		

APRIL
SUN	MON	TUE	WED	THU	FRI	SAT
					1	2 BUF
3	4	5 FLA	6	7 HAR	8	9
10 BUF	11	12 FLA	13	14 TB	15	16

1993-94 SEASON

CLUB DIRECTORY

President and governor
Marcel Aubut
General manager and coach
Pierre Page
Assistant to the general manager
Gilles Leger
Assistant coaches
Don Jackson
Clement Jodoin
Andre Savard
V.P./administration and finance
Jean Laflamme
V.P./marketing and communications
To be announced
Director of public relations
Richard Thibault
Director of press relations
Jean Martineau
Coordinator of public relations
Nicole Bouchard
Scouts/pro hockey and special assignment
Orval Tessier
Dave Draper

Scouts
Ross Ainsworth
Don Boyd
Herb Boxer
Roland Duplessis
Yvon Gendron
Mark Kelley
Bengt Lundholm
Don McKenney
Frank Moberg
Don Paarup
Richard Rothermel
Team doctor
Dr. Pierre Beauchemin
Trainers
Rene Lacasse
Rene Lavigueur
Jacques Lavergne

DRAFT CHOICES

1—Jocelyn Thibault	5-11/170	10	G Sherbrooke (QMJHL)
1—Adam Deadmarsh	6-0/195	14	D Portland (WHL)
2—Ashley Buckberger	6-2/200	49	F Swift Current (WHL)
3—William Pierce	6-1/190	75	C Lawrence Academy
4—Ryan Tocher	6-1/194	101	D Niagara Falls (OHL)
5—Anders Myrvold	6-1/178	127	D Farjestad, Europe
6—Nicholas Checco	5-11/185	137	C Jeff'son HS, Bl'ton (Minn.)
6—Christian Matte	5-11/164	153	F Granby (QMJHL)
7—David Ling	5-9/185	179	F Kingston (OHL)
8—Petr Franek	5-11/185	205	G Litvinov, Europe
9—Vincent Auger	5-10/175	231	C Hawkesbury, Ont. (Jr. A)
10—Mark Pivetz	6-3/205	257	D Saskatoon (Jr. A, Tier II)
11—John Hillman	6-1/200	283	C St. Paul (Jr. A, Tier II)

MISCELLANEOUS DATA

Home ice (capacity)
Quebec Colisee (15,399)
Address
2205 Avenue du Colisee
Quebec, Que. G1L 4W7
Business phone
418-529-8441

Rink dimensions
200 feet by 85 feet
Club colors
Blue, white and red
Minor league affiliation
Cornwall (AHL)

TRAINING CAMP ROSTER

No.	FORWARDS	Ht./Wt.	Place	BORN Date	NHL exp.	1992-93 clubs
46	Niklas Andersson (LW)	5-9/175	Kunglav, Sweden.	5-20-71	1	Halifax (AHL), Quebec
	Paul Brousseau (RW) ...	6-2/212	Montreal	9-18-73	0	Hull (QMJHL)
	Stephane Charbonneau	6-2/195	Ste.-Adele, Que.	6-27-70	1	Halifax (AHL)
	Rene Corbet (LW)	6-0/176	Victoriaville, Que.	6-25-73	0	Drummondville (QMJHL)
	Adam Deadmarsh (RW)	5-11/200	Trail, B.C.	5-10-75	0	Portland (WHL)
	Peter Forsberg (C)	6-0/181	Ornskoldsvik, Sweden	7-20-73	0	MoDo (Sweden Jr.)
	Murray Garbutt (C/LW) ..	6-1/205	Hanna, Alta.	7-29-71	1	Quebec
	Martin Gelinas (LW)	5-11/195	Shawinigan, Que.	6-5-70	5	Edmonton
31	Valeri Kamensky (LW) .	6-2/198	Voskresensk, U.S.S.R.	4-18-66	2	Quebec
51	Andrei Kovalenko (RW)	5-9/161	Gorky, U.S.S.R.	7-7-70	1	CSKA Moscow (CIS), Quebec
47	Claude Lapointe (C)	5-9/173	Ville Emard, Que.	10-11-68	3	Quebec
	Paul MacDermid (RW)..	6-1/205	Chesley, Ont.	4-14-63	12	Washington
11	Owen Nolan (RW)	6-1/194	Belfast, N. Ireland	2-12-72	3	Quebec
	Dwayne Norris (RW)	5-10/175	St. John's, Nfld.	1-8-70	0	Halifax (AHL)
9	Mike Ricci (C)	6-0/190	Scarborough, Ont.	10-27-71	3	Quebec
25	Martin Rucinsky (LW) ..	5-11/178	Most, Czech.	3-11-71	2	Quebec
19	Joe Sakic (C)	5-11/185	Burnaby, B.C.	7-7-69	5	Quebec
	Reggie Savage (RW)	5-10/187	Montreal	5-1-70	2	Baltimore (AHL), Washington
12	Chris Simon (LW)	6-3/230	Wawa, Ont.	1-30-72	1	Halifax (AHL), Quebec
13	Mats Sundin (RW)	6-2/190	Sollentuna, Sweden	2-13-71	3	Quebec
15	Tony Twist (LW)	6-1/212	Sherwood Park, Alta.	5-9-68	4	Quebec
	Todd Warriner (LW/C) .	6-1/172	Chatham, Ont.	1-3-74	0	Windsor (OHL), Kitchener (OHL)
48	Scott Young (RW)	6-0/190	Clinton, Mass.	10-1-67	5	Quebec

No.	DEFENSEMEN	Ht./Wt.	Place	Date	exp.	1992-93 clubs
28	Steve Duchesne..............	5-11/195	Sept-Illes, Que.	6-30-65	7	Quebec
29	Steven Finn....................	6-0/198	Laval, Que.	8-20-66	8	Quebec
52	Adam Foote	6-1/180	Toronto	7-10-71	2	Quebec
5	Alexei Gusarov	6-2/170	Leningrad, U.S.S.R.	7-8-64	3	Quebec
2	Kerry Huffman................	6-3/205	Peterborough, Ont.	1-3-68	7	Quebec
	Alexander Karpovtsev ...	5-11/180	Moscow	4-7-70	0	Dynamo Moscow (CIS)
	Jon Klemm	6-3/200	Cranbrook, B.C.	1-6-70	1	Halifax (AHL)
	Janne Laukkanen	6-0/180	Lahti, Finland	3-19-70	0	HPK Hameenlinna (Fin.)
7	Curtis Leschyshyn.........	6-1/205	Thompson, Man.	9-21-69	5	Quebec
6	Craig Wolanin................	6-3/205	Grosse Point, Mich.	7-27-67	8	Quebec

No.	GOALTENDERS	Ht./Wt.	Place	Date	exp.	1992-93 clubs
32	Jacques Cloutier	5-7/168	Noranda, Que.	1-3-60	11	Quebec
35	Stephane Fiset..............	6-0/175	Montreal	6-17-70	4	Quebec, Halifax (AHL)
	Paul Krake	6-0/175	Lloydminster, Alta.	3-25-69	0	Halifax (AHL), Okla. City (CHL)
	Garth Snow...................	6-3/200	Wrentham, Mass.	7-28-69	0	U. of Maine (H. East)
	John Tanner	6-3/182	Cambridge, Ont.	3-17-71	3	Halifax (AHL)
	Jocelyn Thibault	5-11/170	Montreal	1-12-75	0	Sherbrooke (QMJHL)

1992-93 REVIEW

INDIVIDUAL STATISTICS

SCORING

	Games	G	A	Pts.	Pen.	+/-	PPG	SHG	Shots	Shooting Pct.
Mats Sundin..	80	47	67	114	96	21	13	4	215	21.9
Joe Sakic	78	48	57	105	40	-3	20	2	264	18.2
Steve Duchesne	82	20	62	82	57	15	8	0	227	8.8
Mike Ricci	77	27	51	78	123	8	12	1	142	19.0
Owen Nolan	73	36	41	77	185	-1	15	0	241	14.9
Andrei Kovalenko	81	27	41	68	57	13	8	1	153	17.6
Scott Young	82	30	30	60	20	5	9	6	225	13.3
Martin Rucinsky	77	18	30	48	51	16	4	0	133	13.5
Valeri Kamensky	32	15	22	37	14	13	2	3	94	16.0
Claude Lapointe	74	10	26	36	98	5	0	0	91	11.0
Curtis Leschyshyn	82	9	23	32	61	25	4	0	73	12.3
Mike Hough..	77	8	22	30	69	-11	2	1	98	8.2
Alexei Gusarov	79	8	22	30	57	18	0	2	60	13.3
Gino Cavallini	67	9	15	24	34	10	0	0	71	12.7
Kerry Huffman	52	4	18	22	54	0	3	0	86	4.7
Adam Foote	81	4	12	16	168	6	0	1	54	7.4
Scott Pearson	41	13	1	14	95	3	0	0	45	28.9
Steven Finn	80	5	9	14	160	-3	0	0	61	8.2
Bill Lindsay	44	4	9	13	16	0	0	0	58	6.9
Tim Hunter*	48	5	3	8	94	-4	0	0	28	17.9

	Games	G	A	Pts.	Pen.	+/-	PPG	SHG	Shots	Shooting Pct.
Mikhail Tatarinov	28	2	6	8	28	6	1	0	46	4.3
Craig Wolanin	24	1	4	5	49	9	0	0	17	5.9
Chris Simon	16	1	1	2	67	-2	0	0	15	6.7
Tony Twist	34	0	2	2	64	0	0	0	14	0.0
Stephane Fiset (goalie)	37	0	2	2	2	0	0	0	0	0.0
Ron Hextall (goalie)	54	0	2	2	56	0	0	0	1	0.0
Niclas Andersson	3	0	1	1	2	0	0	0	4	0.0
Leonard Esau	4	0	1	1	2	1	0	0	1	0.0
Dave Karpa	12	0	1	1	13	-6	0	0	2	0.0
Jacques Cloutier (goalie)	3	0	0	0	0	0	0	0	0	0.0

GOALTENDING

	Games	Min.	Goals	SO	Avg.	W	L	T	Shots	Sv. Pct.
Stephane Fiset	37	1939	110	0	3.40	18	9	4	945	.884
Ron Hextall	54	2988	172	0	3.45	29	16	5	1529	.888
Jacques Cloutier	3	154	10	0	3.90	0	2	1	65	.846

Empty-net goals (do not count against a goaltender's average): Fiset 3, Hextall 3, Cloutier 2.
*Played with two or more NHL teams.

RESULTS

OCTOBER
8—At Buffalo	W	5-4
10—Ottawa	W	9-2
13—Philadelphia	W	6-3
15—At Detroit	W	4-2
17—St. Louis	L	5-6
21—At St. Louis	T	*5-5
22—At Minnesota	L	2-5
24—At Tampa Bay	L	2-3
27—Tampa Bay	W	4-3
29—At N.Y. Rangers	W	6-3
31—Winnipeg	W	3-2

NOVEMBER
3—At Hartford	T	*3-3
5—At Boston	L	4-6
7—Chicago	L	4-7
8—Calgary	T	*5-5
11—At Ottawa	W	7-3
12—At Pittsburgh	T	*4-4
14—N.Y. Rangers	W	6-3
17—Toronto†	W	3-1
19—Montreal	W	4-3
21—Hartford	W	8-2
22—Washington	L	4-6
25—At Buffalo	T	*1-1
26—At Toronto	W	*5-4
28—New Jersey	L	3-6
30—Boston	L	3-4

DECEMBER
3—At Philadelphia	L	*2-3
5—Minnesota	L	4-7

7—Buffalo	W	4-3
10—At Los Angeles	W	5-4
12—At San Jose	W	*8-7
13—At Vancouver	T	*3-3
16—At Montreal	W	5-1
17—Montreal	L	3-8
20—N.Y. Islanders	W	5-3
21—At Pittsburgh	L	4-7
26—Ottawa	W	4-2
27—At Ottawa	W	6-1
29—New Jersey	W	4-1
31—At Hartford	W	6-2

JANUARY
2—Detroit	L	2-6
5—At N.Y. Islanders	W	2-1
7—At Boston	W	*3-2
9—At Hartford	L	2-4
14—Montreal	L	3-5
16—San Jose	W	4-1
19—At Ottawa	W	5-2
22—At Buffalo	L	2-6
23—Buffalo	W	4-3
26—Boston	T	*4-4
28—At Philadelphia	W	6-3
29—At Washington	T	*3-3

FEBRUARY
2—Los Angeles	W	3-2
3—Boston	L	1-4
9—Vancouver	L	1-5
12—At Calgary	T	*4-4
14—At Edmonton	W	*3-2
17—Ottawa	W	6-4

20—Tampa Bay‡	W	5-2
21—At New Jersey	W	6-3
23—Edmonton	W	6-3
25—N.Y. Islanders	W	6-4
27—Hartford	L	3-5
28—At Ottawa	L	4-6

MARCH
2—At Winnipeg	W	7-4
4—At Chicago	T	*3-3
6—N.Y. Rangers	W	10-2
8—Hartford	L	2-4
10—Buffalo	L	4-7
13—At Montreal	W	5-2
15—Toronto	W	4-2
18—Montreal	L	2-5
20—At New Jersey	W	5-1
23—At Washington	L	1-5
27—Philadelphia	W	8-3
28—At N.Y. Rangers	W	3-2
31—At Montreal	W	6-2

APRIL
1—At Ottawa	W	4-2
3—Pittsburgh	L	3-5
6—Boston	L	1-7
8—At Boston	L	2-6
10—Hartford	W	6-3
11—At Buffalo	W	3-1
13—Ottawa	W	6-2

*Denotes overtime game.
†At Hamilton, Ont.
‡At Halifax, N.S.

ST. LOUIS BLUES
WESTERN CONFERENCE/CENTRAL DIVISION

1993-94 SCHEDULE

▢ Home games shaded.
* — At Madison Square Garden, New York.
† — At Sacramento, Calif.
△ — At Cleveland.

OCTOBER

SUN	MON	TUE	WED	THU	FRI	SAT
					1	2
3	4	5	6	7 FLA	8	9 OTT
10	11	12	13 DET	14	15	16 DAL
17	18	19 SJ	20	21† SJ	22	23 PIT
24	25	26 CHI	27	28 HAR	29	30 BOS
31						

NOVEMBER

SUN	MON	TUE	WED	THU	FRI	SAT
	1 HAR	2	3 WIN	4	5	6 EDM
7	8	9 PIT	10	11 TOR	12	13 LA
14	15	16 VAN	17	18 CAL	19	20 LA
21 DET	22	23	24 WAS	25	26 NJ	27
28 WIN	29	30				

DECEMBER

SUN	MON	TUE	WED	THU	FRI	SAT
		1 TOR	2 TOR	3	4 DAL
5	6	7 CHI	8	9 DET	10	11 LA
12 ANA	13	14	15 SJ	16	17 CAL	18
19 EDM	20	21	22	23 TB	24	25
26 CHI	27 MON	28	29 NYR	30	31 WIN	

JANUARY

SUN	MON	TUE	WED	THU	FRI	SAT
						1
2 CAL	3	4 DET	5	6△ HAR	7	8 ANA
9 DAL	10	11	12	13 EDM	14	15 BUF
16	17	18 NYR	19 PHI	20	21	22* ALL STAR GAME
23	24 ANA	25 VAN	26	27	28 EDM	29 CAL
30	31 NJ					

FEBRUARY

SUN	MON	TUE	WED	THU	FRI	SAT
		1 TOR	2	3 QUE	4	5 SJ
6	7	8 WIN	9	10 WAS	11	12 DET
13	14	15 VAN	16	17	18 BOS	19
20 ANA	21	22	23	24 QUE	25	26 OTT
27	28 NJ					

MARCH

SUN	MON	TUE	WED	THU	FRI	SAT
		1 NYI	2	3 VAN	4	5
6	7 TOR	8	9 MON	10	11	12 NYI
13	14	15	16 WIN	17	18 TOR	19
20 CHI	21	22 PHI	23 BUF	24	25 DAL	26
27 SJ	28	29	30 FLA	31		

APRIL

SUN	MON	TUE	WED	THU	FRI	SAT
					1 TB	2
3 DET	4	5 CHI	6	7 LA	8 CHI	9
10 DAL	11	12 DAL	13	14 WIN	15	16

1993-94 SEASON

CLUB DIRECTORY

Board of directors
Michael F. Shanahan
Jud Perkins
Al Kerth
Ed Trusheim
Andy Craig
Larry Alexander
Chairman of the board
Michael F. Shanahan
President
Jack J. Quinn
Vice president/general manager
Ronald Caron
Vice president/director of sales
Bruce Affleck
V.P./dir. of player personnel and scouting/ assistant general manager
Ted Hampson
V.P./director of player development
Bob Plager
V.P./dir. of broadcast sales
Matt Hyland
V.P./dir. of finance and administration
Jerry Jasiek

V.P./dir. of marketing and P.R.
Susie Mathieu
Head coach/assistant general manager
Bob Berry
Assistant director of scouting
Jack Evans
Western Canada/U.S. scout
Pat Ginnell
Scouts
Yuri Karmanov
Matt Keator
Paul MacLean
Assistant coach
Ted Sator
Assistant directors of public relations
Jeff Trammel
Mike Caruso
Head trainer
Tom Nash
Equipment managers
Frank Burns
Terry Roof

DRAFT CHOICES

2—Maxim Bets	6-0/192	37	LW	Spokane (WHL)
3—Jamie Rivers	6-0/180	63	D	Sudbury (OHL)
4—Jamal Mayers	6-0/190	89	C	Western Michigan Univ.
6—Todd Kelman	6-1/190	141	D	Vernon (Jr. BC A)
7—Mike Buzak	6-3/183	167	G	Michigan State U. (CCHA)
8—Eric Boguniecki	5-8/192	193	C	Westminster
9—Michael Grier	6-1/215	219	F	St. Sebastian's HS (Mass.)
10—Libor Prochazka	6-0/185	245	D	Poldi Kladno, Czech.
11—Alexand Vasilevskii	5-10/165	271	F	Victoria (WHL)
11—Christer Olsson	5-11/187	275	D	Brynas, Europe

MISCELLANEOUS DATA

Home Ice (capacity)
St. Louis Arena (17,188)
Address
5700 Oakland Avenue
St. Louis, MO 63110-1397
Business phone
314-781-5300

Rink dimensions
200 feet by 85 feet
Club colors
Blue, gold, red and white
Minor league affiliation
Peoria (IHL)

TRAINING CAMP ROSTER

No.	FORWARDS	Ht./Wt.	Place (BORN)	Date	NHL exp.	1992-93 clubs
28	Bob Bassen (C)	5-10/180	Calgary, Alta.	5-6-65	8	St. Louis
	Maxim Bets (LW)	6-0/192	Chelyabinsk, U.S.S.R.	1-31-74	0	Spokane (WHL)
36	Philippe Bozon (LW)	5-10/175	Chamonix, France.	11-30-66	2	St. Louis, Peoria (IHL)
39	Kelly Chase (RW)	5-11/195	Porcupine Plain, Sask.	10-25-67	4	St. Louis
7	Nelson Emerson (C)	5-11/178	Hamilton, Ont.	8-17-67	3	St. Louis
9	Denny Felsner (LW)	6-0/195	Warren, Mich.	4-29-70	2	Peoria (IHL), St. Louis
	Tony Hrkac (C)	5-11/170	Thunder Bay, Ont.	7-7-66	6	Indianapolis (IHL)
16	Brett Hull (RW)	5-10/203	Belleville, Ont.	8-9-64	8	St. Louis
15	Craig Janney (C)	6-1/190	Hartford, Conn.	9-26-67	6	St. Louis
12	Vitali Karamnov (LW)	6-2/185	Moscow, U.S.S.R.	7-6-68	1	St. Louis, Peoria (IHL)
38	Igor Korolev (RW)	6-1/176	Moscow, U.S.S.R.	9-6-70	1	Dynamo Moscow (CIS), St. Louis
	Nathan Lafayette (C)	6-1/194	New Westminster, B.C.	2-17-73	0	Newmarket (OHL)
	Ian Laperriere (C)	6-1/195	Montreal	1-19-74	0	Drummondville (QMJHL)
17	Basil McRae (LW)	6-2/205	Beaverton, Ont.	1-5-61	12	Tampa Bay, St. Louis
37	Kevin Miehm (C)	6-2/195	Kitchener, Ont.	9-10-69	1	Peoria (IHL), St. Louis
14	Kevin Miller (RW)	5-9/170	Lansing, Mich.	8-9-65	5	Washington, St. Louis
	Jim Montgomery (C)	5-10/185	Montreal	6-30-69	0	U. of Maine (H. East)
25	Vitali Prokhorov (LW)	5-9/185	Moscow, U.S.S.R.	12-25-66	1	St. Louis
	David Roberts (LW)	6-0/185	Alameda, Calif.	5-28-70	0	U. of Michigan (CCHA)
19	Brendan Shanahan	6-3/210	Mimico, Ont.	1-23-69	6	St. Louis
23	Rich Sutter (RW)	5-11/188	Viking, Alta.	12-2-63	11	St. Louis
22	Ron Sutter (C)	6-0/180	Viking, Alta.	12-2-63	11	St. Louis
	DEFENSEMEN					
34	Murray Baron	6-3/215	Prince George, B.C.	6-1-67	4	St. Louis
	Jeff Batters	6-2/210	Victoria, B.C.	10-23-70	0	Peoria (IHL)
21	Jeff Brown	6-1/204	Ottawa	4-30-66	8	St. Louis
5	Garth Butcher	6-0/204	Regina, Sask.	1-8-63	12	St. Louis
6	Doug Crossman	6-2/190	Peterborough, Ont.	6-30-60	13	Tampa Bay, St. Louis
44	Bret Hedican	6-2/195	St. Paul, Minn.	8-10-70	2	Peoria (IHL), St. Louis
41	Dan Laperriere	6-1/180	Laval, Que.	3-28-69	1	St. Louis, Peoria (IHL)
	Jason Marshall	6-2/195	Cranbrook, B.C.	2-22-71	1	Peoria (IHL)
33	Stephane Quintal	6-3/220	Boucherville, Que.	10-22-68	5	St. Louis
	Steve Staios	6-0/183	Hamilton, Ont.	7-28-73	0	Niagara Falls (OHL), Sudbury (OHL)
	Tom Tilley	6-0/189	Trenton, Ont.	3-28-65	3	Milan (Italy)
4	Rick Zombo	6-1/195	Des Plaines, Ill.	5-8-63	9	St. Louis
	GOALTENDERS					
	Parris Duffus	6-2/192	Denver	1-27-70	0	Hampton Roads (ECHL), Peoria (IHL)
	Jim Hrivnak	6-2/185	Montreal	5-28-68	4	Washington, Winnipeg
31	Curtis Joseph	5-11/182	Keswick, Ont.	4-29-67	4	St. Louis
	Geoff Sarjeant	5-9/180	Orillia, Ont.	11-30-69	0	Peoria (IHL)

1992-93 REVIEW

INDIVIDUAL STATISTICS

SCORING

	Games	G	A	Pts.	Pen.	+/-	PPG	SHG	Shots	Shooting Pct.
Craig Janney	84	24	82	106	12	-4	8	0	137	17.5
Brett Hull	80	54	47	101	41	-27	29	0	390	13.8
Brendan Shanahan	71	51	43	94	174	10	18	0	232	22.0
Jeff Brown	71	25	53	78	58	-6	12	2	220	11.4
Nelson Emerson	82	22	51	73	62	2	5	2	196	11.2
Kevin Miller*	72	24	22	46	65	6	8	3	153	15.7
Rich Sutter	84	13	14	27	100	-4	0	2	148	8.8
Ron Sutter	59	12	15	27	99	-11	4	0	90	13.3
Igor Korolev	74	4	23	27	20	-1	2	0	76	5.3
Bob Bassen	53	9	10	19	63	0	0	1	61	14.8
Ron Wilson	78	8	11	19	44	-8	0	3	75	10.7
Garth Butcher	84	5	10	15	211	0	0	0	83	6.0
Rick Zombo	71	0	15	15	78	-2	0	0	43	0.0
Dave Lowry	58	5	8	13	101	-18	0	0	59	8.5
Philippe Bozon	54	6	6	12	55	-3	0	0	90	6.7
Stephane Quintal	75	1	10	11	100	-6	0	1	81	1.2
Lee Norwood	32	3	7	10	63	-5	2	0	36	8.3
Doug Crossman*	19	2	7	9	10	-3	2	0	24	8.3
Bret Hedican	42	0	8	8	30	-2	0	0	40	0.0
Kelly Chase	49	2	5	7	204	-9	0	0	28	7.1
Vitali Prokhorov	26	4	1	5	15	-4	0	0	21	19.0

	Games	G	A	Pts.	Pen.	+/-	PPG	SHG	Shots	Shooting Pct.
Paul Cavallini*	11	1	4	5	10	3	1	0	22	4.5
Dave Mackey	15	1	4	5	23	-3	0	0	17	5.9
Murray Baron	53	2	2	4	59	-5	0	0	42	4.8
Kevin Miehm	8	1	3	4	4	1	0	0	5	20.0
Basil McRae*	33	1	3	4	98	-13	1	0	22	4.5
Curt Giles	48	0	4	4	40	-2	0	0	23	0.0
Jason Ruff*	7	2	1	3	8	-1	1	0	7	28.6
Denny Felsner	6	0	3	3	2	4	0	0	4	0.0
Curtis Joseph (goalie)	68	0	2	2	8	0	0	0	0	0.0
Dan Laperriere	5	0	1	1	0	-3	0	0	7	0.0
Vitali Karamnov	7	0	1	1	0	-2	0	0	7	0.0
Guy Hebert (goalie)	24	0	0	0	2	0	0	0	0	0.0

GOALTENDING

	Games	Min.	Goals	SO	Avg.	W	L	T	Shots	Sv. Pct.
Curtis Joseph	68	3890	196	1	3.02	29	28	9	†2202	†.911
Guy Hebert	24	1210	74	1	3.67	8	8	2	630	.883

Empty-net goals (do not count against a goaltender's average): Joseph 7, Hebert 1.
*Played with two or more NHL teams.
†Led league.

RESULTS

OCTOBER

6—Minnesota	W	6-4
8—At Minnesota	L	2-5
10—Chicago	L	0-3
13—Tampa Bay	L	1-2
15—Minnesota	L	4-5
17—At Quebec	W	6-5
19—At Montreal	L	2-6
21—Quebec	T	*5-5
24—Detroit	L	1-6
26—San Jose	W	4-1
29—Pittsburgh	W	6-4
31—Philadelphia	W	6-4

NOVEMBER

3—At Tampa Bay	L	4-6
5—At Pittsburgh	L	4-8
7—At Philadelphia	L	2-4
10—Edmonton	T	*4-4
12—At Chicago	L	0-1
14—Winnipeg	W	4-2
16—At Toronto	T	*2-2
18—At Hartford	L	2-5
21—Tampa Bay	W	4-2
25—At Detroit	L	6-11
26—Vancouver	W	7-5
28—Detroit	T	*2-2

DECEMBER

1—Hartford	W	8-4
4—At Calgary	L	3-5
5—At Edmonton	W	5-1
7—At Vancouver	L	3-4

10—At San Jose	W	3-2
12—At Los Angeles	L	3-6
15—N.Y. Islanders†	L	*3-4
17—N.Y. Rangers	L	3-4
19—Winnipeg	L	0-1
22—At Minnesota	T	*2-2
26—At Chicago	W	*3-2
27—Toronto	L	3-6
31—N.Y. Islanders	W	5-1

JANUARY

2—At Toronto	T	*2-2
3—At Buffalo	L	*5-6
5—Edmonton	W	6-1
7—Calgary	W	*3-2
9—Chicago	W	4-1
11—At Detroit	W	1-0
13—At Toronto	L	3-4
14—At Ottawa	W	4-1
16—At Tampa Bay	W	5-3
19—Toronto	L	1-5
21—At Detroit	L	3-5
23—Detroit	W	4-3
26—Ottawa	W	5-1
28—At Tampa Bay	W	4-2
30—New Jersey	T	*2-2

FEBRUARY

1—Toronto	T	*1-1
3—At Winnipeg	W	4-2
8—Hartford‡	W	3-1
9—Boston	L	1-6
11—Washington	L	6-10
13—Detroit	W	4-3

15—At N.Y. Rangers	L	1-4
17—At New Jersey	L	3-4
18—At N.Y. Islanders	W	4-2
21—At Washington	L	2-5
23—Montreal	L	1-5
25—Los Angeles	W	3-0
27—Minnesota	W	3-2
28—At Chicago	W	7-1

MARCH

4—Calgary	W	2-1
6—At Boston	L	*3-4
11—San Jose	W	5-2
13—Minnesota	W	6-2
14—At Minnesota	W	3-1
16—Buffalo	T	*2-2
20—At Los Angeles	L	2-3
22—At Vancouver	W	3-1
24—At Calgary	W	4-2
26—At Winnipeg	L	2-4
30—Vancouver	L	3-6

APRIL

3—Chicago	T	*3-3
4—At Chicago	L	4-5
6—At Tampa Bay	T	*2-2
10—At Minnesota	L	3-4
11—Minnesota	W	5-1
13—At Toronto	L	*1-2
15—Tampa Bay	W	6-5

*Denotes overtime game.
†At Dallas.
‡At Peoria, Ill.

SAN JOSE SHARKS
WESTERN CONFERENCE/PACIFIC DIVISION

1993-94 SCHEDULE

Home games shaded.
* — At Madison Square Garden, New York.
† — At Sacramento, Calif.

OCTOBER

SUN	MON	TUE	WED	THU	FRI	SAT
					1	2
3	4	5	6 EDM	7 CAL	8	9
10 LA	11	12	13	14 BOS	15	16 BOS
17	18	19 STL	20	21† STL	22	23 VAN
24 VAN	25	26 EDM	27	28 ANA	29	30 WAS
31 ANA						

NOVEMBER

SUN	MON	TUE	WED	THU	FRI	SAT
	1	2 PIT	3	4	5 DAL	6
7 NJ	8	9 TOR	10	11 DAL	12	13 NJ
14 NYR	15	16 WAS	17	18 BOS	19	20 HAR
21 BUF	22	23 DET	24	25	26 ANA	27 ANA
28	29	30				

DECEMBER

SUN	MON	TUE	WED	THU	FRI	SAT
			1	2	3 WIN	4
5 FLA	6	7 TB	8	9	10	11 DET
12 CHI	13	14	15 STL	16	17 EDM	18
19 QUE	20	21	22 TOR	23 CHI	24	25
26	27	28 CAL	29	30	31 VAN	

JANUARY

SUN	MON	TUE	WED	THU	FRI	SAT
						1
2 EDM	3	4 MON	5	6 DET	7	8
9	10	11 LA	12 ANA	13	14	15 HAR
16	17 CAL	18	19	20	21	22* ALL-STAR GAME
23	24	25 NYR	26	27	28 FLA	29 TB
30	31					

FEBRUARY

SUN	MON	TUE	WED	THU	FRI	SAT
		1 NYI	2	3 PHI	4	5 STL
6 DAL	7	8† LA	9	10	11 CHI	12
13 CHI	14	15 PHI	16	17 QUE	18	19 LA
20	21 DAL	22	23 MON	24 OTT	25	26 DET
27	28 WIN					

MARCH

SUN	MON	TUE	WED	THU	FRI	SAT
		1	2	3 EDM	4	5
6 ANA	7	8 BUF	9	10 NYI	11	12 CAL
13	14	15	16	17 OTT	18	19 LA
20 LA	21	22 PIT	23	24 TOR	25 WIN	26
27 STL	28	29 WIN	30	31 TOR		

APRIL

SUN	MON	TUE	WED	THU	FRI	SAT
					1	2 VAN
3	4	5 LA	6	7 VAN	8 CAL	9
10 VAN	11	12	13 EDM	14	15	16

1993-94 SEASON

CLUB DIRECTORY

Co-owner & chairman
George Gund III
Co-owner & vice chairman
Gordon Gund
President & chief executive officer
Arthur L. Savage
Exec. vice president, finance
Grant Rollin
Exec. V.P., marketing and broadcasting
Matt Levine
Exec. vice president, building operations
Frank Jirik
Vice president/dir. of hockey operations
Dean Lombardi
Vice president/dir. of player personnel
Chuck Grillo
Head coach
Kevin Constantine
Asst. coach & asst. to dir. of hoc. operations
Wayne Thomas
Scouting coordinator
Joe Will
Executive assistant
Brenda Knight
Director of media relations
Tim Bryant
Assistant director of media relations
Ken Arnold
Media relations assistant
Paul Turner

Scouting staff
Bob Gernander
Ray Payne
Tim Burke
Sakari Pietila
Bob Grillo
Larry Ross
Pat Funk
Tim Gorski
Ben Hays
Thomas Holm
Randy Joevanazzo
Konstantin Krylov
Peter Mahovlich
Jack Morganstern
Joe Rowley
Dan Summers
Deborah Wright
Bob Friedlander
Head trainer
Tom Woodcock
Equipment manager
Bob Crocker Jr.
Assistant equipment manager
Arne Pappin
Team physician
Dr. Arthur Ting
Director of ticket operations
Daniel DeBoer

DRAFT CHOICES

1—Viktor Kozlov	6-5/209	6	F	Moscow, CIS
2—Shean Donovan	6-1/178	28	F	Ottawa (OHL)
2—Vlastimil Kroupa	6-3/176	45	D	Chemopetrol (Czech Jrs.)
3—Ville Peltonen	5-10/172	58	F	Helsinki IFK, Finland
4—Alenander Osadchy	5-11/191	80	D	CSKA Moscow, CIS
5—Andrei Buschan	6-2/194	106	D	Sokol Kiev, CIS
6—Petri Varis	6-1/200	132	F	Assat Pori, Finland
6—Fredrik Oduya	6-2/184	154	D	Ottawa (OHL)
7—Anotoli Filatov	5-9/174	158	F	UST-Kamenogorsk, CIS
8—Todd Holt	5-6/153	184	F	Swift Current (WHL)
9—Jonas Forsberg	5-10/154	210	G	Djurgarden, Sweden
10—Jeff Salajko	6-0/172	236	G	Ottawa (OHL)
11—Jamie Matthews	6-1/200	262	C	Sudbury (OHL)

MISCELLANEOUS DATA

Home ice (capacity)
San Jose Arena (17,500)
Address
525 West Santa Clara Street
San Jose, CA 95113
Business phone
408-287-7070

Rink dimensions
200 feet by 85 feet
Club colors
Pacific teal, gray, black and white
Minor league affiliation
Kansas City (IHL)

TRAINING CAMP ROSTER

No.	FORWARDS	Ht./Wt.	Place	BORN Date	NHL exp.	1992-93 clubs
15	David Bruce (LW)	5-11/190	Thunder Bay, Ont.	10-7-64	7	San Jose
	Jan Caloun (RW)	5-10/176	Usti-nad-Labem, Czech.	12-20-72	0	Chemopetrol Litvinov (Czech.)
9	Dave Capuano (LW/C)	6-2/190	Warwick, R.I.	7-27-68	3	Hamilton (AHL), Atlanta (IHL), Tampa Bay
20	John Carter (LW)	5-10/175	Woburn, Mass.	5-3-63	8	San Jose, Kansas City (IHL)
	Alexander Cherbayev	6-1/187	Voskresensk, U.S.S.R.	8-13-73	0	Khimik Voskresensk (CIS)
39	Ed Courtenay (RW)	6-4/200	Verdun, Que.	2-2-68	2	San Jose, Kansas City (IHL)
33	Dale Craigwell (C)	5-10/180	Toronto	4-24-71	2	San Jose, Kansas City (IHL)
	Gaetan Duchesne (LW)	5-11/200	Quebec City	7-11-62	12	Minnesota
17	Pat Falloon (RW)	5-11/192	Foxwarren, Man.	9-22-72	2	San Jose
10	Johan Garpenlov (LW)	5-11/185	Stockholm, Sweden	3-21-68	3	San Jose
37	Rob Gaudreau (RW)	5-11/185	Cranston, R.I.	1-20-70	1	Kansas City (IHL), San Jose
11	Kelly Kisio (C)	5-9/183	Peace River, Alta.	9-18-59	11	San Jose
	Viktor Kozlov (RW)	6-5/209	Togliatti, U.S.S.R.	2-14-75	0	Dynamo Moscow (CIS)
	Igor Larionov (C)	5-9/165	Voskresensk, U.S.S.R.	12-3-60	3	Lugano (Switzerland)
	Sergei Makarov (RW)	5-11/185	Chelyabinsk, U.S.S.R.	6-19-58	4	Calgary
25	David Maley (C)	6-3/200	Beaver Dam, Wis.	4-24-63	8	Edmonton, San Jose
9	Jon Morris (C)	6-0/175	Lowell, Mass.	5-6-66	5	Utica (AHL), Cincinnati (IHL), New Jersey, San Jose
	Andrei Nazarov (LW)	6-4/209	Chelyabinsk, U.S.S.R.	3-21-72	0	Dynamo Moscow (CIS)
36	Jeff Odgers (LW)	6-0/195	Spy Hill, Sask.	5-31-69	2	San Jose
18	Mark Pederson (LW)	6-2/196	Prelate, Sask.	1-14-68	4	Philadelphia, San Jose
44	Michel Picard (LW)	5-11/190	Beauport, Que.	11-7-69	3	Kansas City (IHL), San Jose
28	J.F. Quintin (LW)	6-1/180	St. Jean, Que.	5-28-69	2	San Jose, Kansas City (IHL)
47	Mike Sullivan (C)	6-2/193	Marshfield, Mass.	2-28-68	2	San Jose
14	Ray Whitney (C)	5-9/165	Edmonton, Alta.	5-8-72	2	Kansas City (IHL), San Jose
45	Dody Wood (C/LW)	5-11/180	Chetywynd, B.C.	5-8-72	1	Kansas City (IHL), San Jose

No.	DEFENSEMEN	Ht./Wt.	Place	Date	NHL exp.	1992-93 clubs
	Link Gaetz	6-2/223	Vancouver, B.C.	10-2-68	3	Nashville (ECHL), Kansas City (IHL)
4	Jay More	6-1/190	Souris, Man.	1-12-69	4	San Jose
	Jeff Norton	6-2/195	Cambridge, Mass.	11-25-65	6	New York Islanders
	Sandis Ozolinsh	6-1/189	Riga, U.S.S.R.	8-3-72	1	San Jose
41	Tom Pederson	5-9/180	Bloomington, Minn.	1-14-70	1	Kansas City (IHL), San Jose
	Mike Rathje	6-5/195	Manville, Alta.	5-11-74	0	Medicine Hat (WHL), Kansas City (IHL)
	Michal Sykora	6-3/195	Pardubice, Czech.	7-5-73	0	Tacoma (WHL)
24	Doug Wilson	6-1/187	Ottawa	7-5-57	16	San Jose
2	Rob Zettler	6-3/195	Sept Iles, Que.	3-8-68	5	San Jose
19	Doug Zmolek	6-1/195	Rochester, Minn.	11-3-70	1	San Jose

No.	GOALTENDERS	Ht./Wt.	Place	Date	NHL exp.	1992-93 clubs
31	Wade Flaherty	6-0/175	Terreace, B.C.	1-11-68	2	Kansas City (IHL), San Jose
32	Arturs Irbe	5-7/180	Riga, U.S.S.R.	2-2-67	2	Kansas City (IHL), San Jose
	Jimmy Waite	6-0/163	Sherbrooke, Que.	4-15-69	5	Chicago

1992-93 REVIEW

INDIVIDUAL STATISTICS

SCORING

	Games	G	A	Pts.	Pen.	+/-	PPG	SHG	Shots	Shooting Pct.
Kelly Kisio	78	26	52	78	90	-15	9	2	152	17.1
Johan Garpenlov	79	22	44	66	56	-26	14	0	171	12.9
Rob Gaudreau	59	23	20	43	18	-18	5	2	191	12.0
Dean Evason	84	12	19	31	132	-35	3	0	107	11.2
Pat Falloon	41	14	14	28	12	-25	5	1	131	10.7
Jeff Odgers	66	12	15	27	253	-26	6	0	100	12.0
Sandis Ozolinsh	37	7	16	23	40	-9	2	0	83	8.4
Ed Courtenay	39	7	13	20	10	-15	2	0	56	12.5
Tom Pederson	44	7	13	20	31	-16	2	0	102	6.9
Doug Wilson	42	3	17	20	40	-28	1	0	110	2.7
John Carter	55	7	9	16	81	-25	0	1	110	6.4
Doug Zmolek	84	5	10	15	229	-50	2	0	94	5.3
Mike Sullivan	81	6	8	14	30	-42	0	2	95	6.3
David Williams	40	1	11	12	49	-27	1	0	60	1.7
Jay More	73	5	6	11	179	-35	0	1	107	4.7
Mark Pederson *	27	7	3	10	22	-20	1	0	42	16.7
Ray Whitney	26	4	6	10	4	-14	1	0	24	16.7

	Games	G	A	Pts.	Pen.	+/-	PPG	SHG	Shots	Shooting Pct.
Yvon Corriveau*	20	3	7	10	0	-7	1	0	32	9.4
Brian Lawton	21	2	8	10	12	-9	0	0	29	6.9
Dave Snuggerud*	25	4	5	9	14	-3	0	1	51	7.8
Hubie McDonough	30	6	2	8	6	-21	2	0	41	14.6
Larry DePalma	20	2	6	8	41	-14	1	0	29	6.9
Neil Wilkinson	59	1	7	8	96	-50	0	1	51	2.0
Petri Skriko	17	4	3	7	6	-8	2	1	35	11.4
Perry Berezan	28	3	4	7	28	-18	1	1	37	8.1
J.F. Quintin	14	2	5	7	4	-4	0	0	12	16.7
David Maley*	43	1	6	7	126	-25	1	0	48	2.1
Rob Zettler	80	0	7	7	150	-50	0	0	60	0.0
Robin Bawa	42	5	0	5	47	-25	0	0	25	20.0
Lyndon Byers	18	4	1	5	122	-2	0	0	18	22.2
David Bruce	17	2	3	5	33	-14	2	0	36	5.6
Peter Ahola*	20	2	3	5	16	-6	0	0	32	6.3
Michel Picard	25	4	0	4	24	-17	2	0	32	12.5
Dale Craigwell	8	3	1	4	4	-4	0	0	7	42.9
Jon Morris*	13	0	3	3	6	-10	0	0	11	0.0
Dody Wood	13	1	1	2	71	-5	0	0	10	10.0
Jaroslav Otevrel	7	0	2	2	0	-6	0	0	4	0.0
Dean Kolstad	10	0	2	2	12	-9	0	0	22	0.0
Mark Beaufait	5	1	0	1	0	-1	0	0	3	33.3
Claudio Scremin	4	0	1	1	4	-1	0	0	4	0.0
Pat MacLeod	13	0	1	1	10	-19	0	0	20	0.0
Brian Hayward (goalie)	18	0	1	1	2	0	0	0	0	0.0
Jeff Hackett (goalie)	36	0	1	1	4	0	0	0	0	0.0
Wade Flaherty (goalie)	1	0	0	0	0	0	0	0	0	0.0
Mikhail Kravets	1	0	0	0	0	-1	0	0	0	0.0
Arturs Irbe (goalie)	36	0	0	0	10	0	0	0	0	0.0

GOALTENDING

	Games	Min.	Goals	SO	Avg.	W	L	T	Shots	Sv. Pct.
Arturs Irbe	36	2074	142	1	4.11	7	26	0	1250	.886
Wade Flaherty	1	60	5	0	5.00	0	1	0	46	.891
Jeff Hackett	36	2000	176	0	5.28	2	30	1	1220	.856
Brian Hayward	18	930	86	0	5.55	2	14	1	559	.846

Empty-net goals (do not count against a goaltender's average): Irbe 3, Hackett 2.
*Played with two or more NHL teams.

RESULTS

OCTOBER
8—Winnipeg	W	*4-3
10—Detroit	L	3-6
13—At Los Angeles	L	1-2
15—Boston	L	2-8
17—Calgary	L	2-6
21—At Montreal	L	4-8
23—At Buffalo	L	4-5
24—At Toronto	L	1-5
26—At St. Louis	L	1-4
28—At Detroit	L	3-4
30—At Tampa Bay	W	2-1

NOVEMBER
1—At Chicago	T	*4-4
5—Buffalo	W	7-5
7—New Jersey	L	1-6
8—Los Angeles	L	4-11
10—At Vancouver	L	2-6
12—Edmonton	L	3-4
14—Vancouver	L	2-5
17—Los Angeles	W	6-0
19—Toronto	L	0-2
21—Chicago	L	1-2
25—At Calgary	W	*4-3
27—At Winnipeg	L	*2-3
28—At Minnesota	L	3-10

DECEMBER
1—Edmonton	L	1-3
3—Hartford	L	5-7
5—Pittsburgh	L	4-9
9—At Vancouver	L	3-8
10—St. Louis	L	2-3
12—Quebec	L	*7-8
16—Tampa Bay	L	*4-5
18—At Vancouver	L	1-8
19—Vancouver	L	3-6
21—At Winnipeg	L	4-5
23—At Edmonton	L	2-4
26—Los Angeles	W	7-2
29—At Vancouver	L	5-7
30—Philadelphia	L	2-6

JANUARY
2—Vancouver	T	*2-2
4—Montreal†	L	1-4
5—Montreal	L	1-2
8—At Toronto	L	1-5
10—At Ottawa	L	2-3
12—At Winnipeg	L	1-4
15—At Detroit	L	3-6
16—At Quebec	L	1-4
18—At Boston	L	3-4
21—At Hartford	L	2-4
23—At Tampa Bay	L	1-5
26—At Los Angeles	L	1-7
29—Chicago	L	2-4
30—Calgary	L	4-5

FEBRUARY
1—Tampa Bay	L	4-5
3—Minnesota	L	3-7
10—At Calgary	L	1-13
12—At Edmonton	L	0-6
14—At Winnipeg	W	3-2
16—Washington	L	3-4
18—Winnipeg	W	5-3
20—N.Y. Rangers	L	4-6
22—N.Y. Rangers†	L	0-4
23—Calgary	L	3-6
25—Toronto	L	0-5
27—At Calgary	L	4-5
28—At Edmonton	L	1-4

MARCH
2—Ottawa	W	*3-2
7—Edmonton	W	6-3
9—At Minnesota	L	2-4
11—At St. Louis	L	2-5
14—Detroit	L	1-4
16—N.Y. Islanders	L	0-6
19—At N.Y. Rangers	L	1-8
21—At Washington	L	3-5
23—At Pittsburgh	L	2-7
25—At Philadelphia	L	2-5
27—At N.Y. Islanders	L	3-7
29—At New Jersey	L	0-5

APRIL
1—Winnipeg	L	5-9
3—Calgary	L	*2-3
4—Calgary	L	3-4
6—Edmonton	W	5-2
8—At Los Angeles	L	1-2
10—Los Angeles	L	*2-3
15—At Calgary	L	3-7

*Denotes overtime game.
†At Sacramento, Calif.

TAMPA BAY LIGHTNING
EASTERN CONFERENCE/ATLANTIC DIVISION

1993-94 SCHEDULE

Home games shaded.
* — At Madison Square Garden, New York.
† — At Orlando, Fla.
Δ — At Hamilton, Ont.
+ — At Minneapolis.

OCTOBER

SUN	MON	TUE	WED	THU	FRI	SAT
					1	2
3	4	5	6 NJ	7 NYR	8	9 FLA
10	11	12	13	14 PIT	15	16 OTT
17 FLA	18	19	20 LA	21	22 NYR	23 TOR
24	25	26	27 WIN	28	29 NYI	30 FLA
31						

NOVEMBER

SUN	MON	TUE	WED	THU	FRI	SAT
	1	2 QUE	3 MON	4	5	6 BOS
7	8 NYR	9	10	11 WAS	12	13 QUE
14	15	16	17 DAL	18	19 NYR	20 CHI
21	22	23	24 HAR	25	26 PHI	27 PHI
28	29	30				

DECEMBER

SUN	MON	TUE	WED	THU	FRI	SAT
			1 BUF	2	3	4 LA
5 ANA	6	7 SJ	8	9	10	11 PIT
12	13	14† MON	15 OTT	16	17	18 BOS
19 BUF	20	21 PIT	22	23 STL	24	25
26† FLA	27	28 QUE	29	30 OTT	31	

JANUARY

SUN	MON	TUE	WED	THU	FRI	SAT
						1 WAS
2† ANA	3	4 Δ TOR	5	6	7	8 PHI
9	10 NYR	11	12 DET	13 CHI	14	15
16 WIN	17* DET	18	19 NYI	20	21	22* ALL-STAR GAME
23	24† BUF	25	26 FLA	27	28	29 SJ
30	31					

FEBRUARY

SUN	MON	TUE	WED	THU	FRI	SAT
		1	2 DET	3	4	5 WAS
6	7 TOR	8	9	10 OTT	11	12 VAN
13 NJ	14	15 NYI	16	17 MON	18	19 NJ
20 BOS	21	22	23	24 CAL	25	26 VAN
27 EDM	28					

MARCH

SUN	MON	TUE	WED	THU	FRI	SAT
		1 WAS	2	3 NJ	4	5 HAR
6 PHI	7	8	9 HAR	10	11	12
13 PHI	14	15 CAL	16 EDM	17	18	19
20† WAS	21	22 NYI	23	24 NJ	25	26
27 DAL	28	29	30 BUF	31		

APRIL

SUN	MON	TUE	WED	THU	FRI	SAT
					1 STL	2
3	4 PIT	5	6 MON	7	8	9 BOS
10 HAR	11	12	13 NYI	14 QUE	15	16

1993-94 SEASON

CLUB DIRECTORY

Pres., Lightning Partners, Ltd.
Yoshio Nakamura
Governor
David LeFevre
Pres., general manager and alt. gov.
Phil Esposito
Executive V.P., treasurer and alt. gov.
Mel Lowell
Executive V.P., alternate governor
Chris Phillips
Vice president, secretary
Henry Paul
Director of hockey operations
Tony Esposito
Head coach
Terry Crisp
Assistant coaches
Wayne Cashman
Danny Gare
Chief financial officer
Mark Anderson
Accounting manager
Vincent Ascanio
Vice president, communications
Gerry Helper
Media relations manager
Barry Hanrahan

Vice president, sales and marketing
Steve Donner
Director of team services
Carrie Esposito
Director of sales
Paul D'Aiuto
Director of merchandising
Kevin Murphy
Director of ticket operations
Jeff Morander
Scouting staff
Angelo Bumbacco
Jacques Campeau
Jake Goertzen
Doug Macauley
Don Murdoch
Richard Rose
Jonathan Sparrow
Luke Williams
Head trainer
Skip Thayer
Assistant trainer
John Forristall
Equipment manager
Jocko Cayer

DRAFT CHOICES

1—Chris Gratton	6-3/202	3	F	Kingston (OHL)
2—Tyler Moss	6-0/168	29	G	Kingston (OHL)
3—Allan Egeland	6-0/184	55	C	Tacoma (WHL)
4—Marian Kacir	6-1/183	81	F	Owen Sound (OHL)
5—Ryan Brown	6-3/215	107	D	Swift Current (WHL)
6—Kiley Hill	6-3/205	133	F	Sault Ste. Marie (OHL)
7—Mathieu Raby	6-2/204	159	D	Victoriaville (QMJHL)
8—Ryan Nauss	6-5/196	185	F	Peterborough (OHL)
9—Alexandre Laporte	6-3/210	211	D	Victoriaville (QMJHL)
10—Brett Duncan	6-0/208	237	D	Seattle (WHL)
11—Mark Szoke	5-9/176	263	F	Lethbridge (WHL)

MISCELLANEOUS DATA

Home ice (capacity)
Florida Suncoast Dome (26,000)
Address
501 East Kennedy Blvd.
Tampa, Fla. 33602
Business phone
813-229-2658

Rink dimensions
200 feet by 85 feet
Club colors
Black, blue, silver and white
Minor league affiliation
Atlanta (IHL)

No.	FORWARDS	Ht./Wt.	Place	BORN Date	NHL exp.	1992-93 clubs
34	Mikael Andersson (LW)	5-11/185	Malmo, Sweden	5-10-66	8	Tampa Bay
21	Tim Bergland (RW)	6-3/194	Crookston, Minn.	1-11-65	4	Atlanta (IHL), Tampa Bay
19	Brian Bradley (C)	5-10/177	Kitchener, Ont.	1-21-65	8	Tampa Bay
28	Marc Bureau (C)	6-1/198	Trois-Rivieres, Que.	5-17-66	4	Tampa Bay
12	Jock Callander (C/RW)	6-1/188	Regina, Sask.	4-23-61	5	Atlanta (IHL), Tampa Bay
24	Danton Cole (RW)	5-11/185	Pontiac, Mich.	1-10-67	4	Tampa Bay, Atlanta (IHL)
10	Adam Creighton (C)	6-5/210	Burlington, Ont.	6-2-65	10	Tampa Bay
18	Rob DiMaio (C)	5-10/190	Calgary, Alta.	2-19-68	5	Tampa Bay
	Gerard Gallant (LW)	5-10/190	Summerside, P.E.I.	9-2-63	9	Detroit
	Aaron Gavey (C)	6-1/169	Sudbury, Ont.	2-22-74	0	Sault Ste. Marie (OHL)
	Randy Gilhen (C)	6-0/192	Zweibrucken, W. Germany	6-13-63	8	N.Y. Rangers, Tampa Bay
	Chris Gratton (C)	6-3/202	Brantford, Ont.	7-5-75	0	Kingston (OHL)
	Brent Gretzky (C)	5-10/160	Brantford, Ont.	2-20-72	0	Atlanta (IHL)
	Petr Klima (LW/RW)	6-0/190	Chaomutov, Czech.	12-23-64	8	Edmonton
16	Chris Kontos (C/LW)	6-1/195	Toronto	12-10-63	8	Tampa Bay
8	Herb Raglan (RW)	6-0/205	Peterborough, Ont.	8-5-67	8	Halifax (AHL), Tampa Bay, Atlanta (IHL)
20	Jason Ruff (LW)	6-2/192	Kelowna, B.C.	1-27-70	1	Peoria (IHL), St. Louis, Tampa Bay, Atlanta (IHL)
	Denis Savard (C)	5-10/175	Pointe Gatineau, Que.	2-4-61	13	Montreal
14	John Tucker (C)	6-0/200	Windsor, Ont.	9-29-64	9	Tampa Bay
7	Rob Zamuner (LW/C) ...	6-2/202	Oakville, Ont.	9-17-69	2	Tampa Bay
	DEFENSEMEN					
	Peter Ahola	6-3/205	Espoo, Finland	5-14-68	2	Los Angeles, Pittsburgh, Cleveland (IHL), San Jose
	Drew Bannister	6-1/193	Belleville, Ont.	9-4-74	0	Sault Ste. Marie (OHL)
2	Bob Beers.....................	6-2/200	Pittsburgh	5-20-67	4	Providence (AHL), Tampa Bay, Atlanta (IHL)
25	Marc Bergevin	6-1/197	Montreal	8-11-65	9	Tampa Bay
	Scott Boston	6-2/180	Ottawa	7-13-71	0	Atlanta (IHL)
	Jeff Buchanan	5-10/165	Swift Current, Sask.	5-23-71	0	Atlanta (IHL)
22	Shawn Chambers	6-2/200	Royal Oaks, Mich.	10-11-66	6	Atlanta (IHL), Tampa Bay
	Eric Charron	6-3/192	Verdun, Que.	1-14-70	1	Fredericton (AHL), Montreal, Atlanta (IHL)
6	Alain Cote	6-0/200	Montmagny, Que.	4-14-67	8	Fredericton (AHL), Tampa Bay, Atlanta (IHL)
34	Donald Dufresne............	6-1/206	Quebec City	4-10-67	5	Montreal
44	Roman Hamrlik..............	6-2/189	Gottwaldov, Czech.	4-12-74	1	Tampa Bay, Atlanta (IHL)
26	Matt Hervey	5-11/205	Whittier, Calif.	5-16-66	3	Atlanta (IHL), Tampa Bay
40	Chris LiPuma	6-0/183	Chicago	3-23-71	1	Atlanta (IHL), Tampa Bay
29	Joe Reekie....................	6-3/215	Victoria, B.C.	2-22-65	8	Tampa Bay
3	Shawn Rivers	5-10/185	Ottawa	1-30-71	1	Atlanta (IHL), Tampa Bay
	GOALTENDERS					
30	Jean-Claude Bergeron...	6-2/192	Hauterive, Que.	10-14-68	2	Atlanta (IHL), Tampa Bay
35	Pat Jablonski................	6-0/178	Toledo, O.	6-20-67	4	Tampa Bay
	Daren Puppa..................	6-3/205	Kirkland Lake, Ont.	3-23-65	8	Buffalo, Toronto
	Manon Rheaume	5-6/136	Lac Beauport, Que.	2-24-72	0	Atlanta (IHL)
1	Wendell Young	5-9/181	Halifax, N.S.	8-1-63	8	Tampa Bay, Atlanta (IHL)

1992-93 REVIEW

INDIVIDUAL STATISTICS

SCORING

	Games	G	A	Pts.	Pen.	+/-	PPG	SHG	Shots	Shooting Pct.
Brian Bradley..............................	80	42	44	86	92	-24	16	0	205	20.5
John Tucker...............................	78	17	39	56	69	-12	5	1	179	9.5
Chris Kontos..............................	66	27	24	51	12	-7	12	1	136	19.9
Rob Zamuner.............................	84	15	28	43	74	-25	1	0	183	8.2
Adam Creighton..........................	83	19	20	39	110	-19	7	1	168	11.3
Shawn Chambers.........................	55	10	29	39	36	-21	5	0	152	6.6
Bob Beers.................................	64	12	24	36	70	-25	7	0	138	8.7
Marc Bureau..............................	63	10	21	31	111	-12	1	2	132	7.6
Doug Crossman*..........................	40	8	21	29	18	-4	2	0	54	14.8
Mikael Andersson	77	16	11	27	14	-14	3	2	169	9.5
Danton Cole	67	12	15	27	23	-2	0	1	100	12.0
Rob DiMaio	54	9	15	24	62	0	2	0	75	12.0
Roman Hamrlik............................	67	6	15	21	71	-21	1	0	113	5.3
Steve Maltais.............................	63	7	13	20	35	-20	4	0	96	7.3
Rob Ramage*..............................	66	5	12	17	138	-21	5	0	115	4.3
Marc Bergevin	78	2	12	14	66	-16	0	0	69	2.9

	Games	G	A	Pts.	Pen.	+/-	PPG	SHG	Shots	Shooting Pct.
Joe Reekie	42	2	11	13	69	2	0	0	53	3.8
Ken Hodge	25	2	7	9	2	-6	0	0	32	6.3
Peter Taglianetti*	61	1	8	9	150	8	0	0	60	1.7
Mike Hartman*	58	4	4	8	154	-7	0	0	74	5.4
Steve Kasper*	47	3	4	7	18	-13	0	0	23	13.0
Jason Lafreniere	11	3	3	6	4	-6	1	0	17	17.6
Tim Bergland	27	3	3	6	11	-5	0	0	44	6.8
Anatoli Semenov*	13	2	3	5	4	-5	0	0	14	14.3
Basil McRae*	14	2	3	5	71	-3	1	0	23	8.7
Chris LiPuma	15	0	5	5	34	1	0	0	17	0.0
Matt Hervey	17	0	4	4	38	-6	0	0	18	0.0
Stan Drulia	24	2	1	3	10	1	0	0	22	9.1
Michel Mongeau	4	1	1	2	2	-2	0	0	2	50.0
Dave Capuano	6	1	1	2	2	-4	1	0	10	10.0
Jock Callender	8	1	1	2	2	-5	0	0	12	8.3
Keith Osborne	11	1	1	2	8	-1	0	0	11	9.1
Shawn Rivers	4	0	2	2	2	-2	0	0	3	0.0
Randy Gilhen*	11	0	2	2	6	-6	0	0	11	0.0
Wendell Young (goalie)	31	0	2	2	2	0	0	0	0	0.0
Pat Jablonski (goalie)	43	0	2	2	7	0	0	0	0	0.0
Shayne Stevenson	8	0	1	1	7	-5	0	0	4	0.0
J.C. Bergeron (goalie)	21	0	1	1	2	0	0	0	0	0.0
Dave Littman (goalie)	1	0	0	0	0	0	0	0	0	0.0
Jason Ruff*	1	0	0	0	0	0	0	0	1	0.0
Alain Cote	2	0	0	0	0	-1	0	0	1	0.0
Herb Raglan	2	0	0	0	2	0	0	0	0	0.0
Stephane J.G. Richer*	3	0	0	0	0	-3	0	0	2	0.0
Martin Simard	7	0	0	0	11	-1	0	0	1	0.0

GOALTENDING

	Games	Min.	Goals	SO	Avg.	W	L	T	Shots	Sv. Pct.
J.C. Bergeron	21	1163	71	0	3.66	8	10	1	574	.876
Wendell Young	31	1591	97	0	3.66	7	19	2	758	.872
Pat Jablonski	43	2268	150	1	3.97	8	24	4	1194	.874
Dave Littman	1	45	7	0	9.33	0	1	0	21	.667

Empty-net goals (do not count against a goaltender's average): Bergeron 3, Jablonski 2, Young 2.
*Played with two or more NHL teams.

RESULTS

OCTOBER

7—Chicago	W	7-3
10—At Minnesota	L	1-2
11—At Chicago	T	*4-4
13—At St. Louis	W	2-1
15—At Toronto	L	3-5
16—At Buffalo	L	*4-5
20—Edmonton	W	6-1
22—Toronto	L	2-5
24—Quebec	W	3-2
27—At Quebec	L	3-4
28—At Montreal	L	3-4
30—San Jose	L	1-2

NOVEMBER

1—Pittsburgh	L	4-5
3—St. Louis	W	6-4
6—At Washington	T	*2-2
7—At N.Y. Islanders	W	*6-5
9—At N.Y. Rangers	W	5-1
11—Detroit	W	6-4
13—Ottawa	W	1-0
14—Calgary	L	3-5
17—Winnipeg	L	5-6
19—Minnesota	L	1-4
21—At St. Louis	L	2-4
23—At Detroit	L	5-10
24—At Toronto	W	3-2
27—At Calgary	L	*2-3
28—At Edmonton	L	*3-4

DECEMBER

5—Detroit	L	7-9

7—N.Y. Islanders	L	1-6
9—N.Y. Rangers†	L	5-6
11—N.Y. Rangers	L	4-5
12—Edmonton	W	3-1
15—At Los Angeles	W	3-2
16—At San Jose	W	*5-4
18—New Jersey	L	0-2
20—Philadelphia	W	4-1
22—At Boston	L	3-5
23—At Hartford	L	1-3
31—At Chicago	L	0-5

JANUARY

2—At Edmonton	L	1-2
4—At Vancouver	L	0-7
6—At Los Angeles	W	6-3
9—At Minnesota	L	4-6
11—At Toronto	L	2-4
13—At Detroit	L	3-5
16—St. Louis	L	3-5
17—Washington	L	3-5
19—Minnesota	L	2-4
21—Toronto	L	1-6
23—San Jose	W	5-1
24—Minnesota	T	*2-2
28—St. Louis	L	2-4
30—At Minnesota	W	4-3

FEBRUARY

1—At San Jose	W	5-4
3—At Vancouver	L	2-4
9—Toronto	W	3-1
11—Minnesota	L	0-1
14—Boston	T	*3-3

17—At Detroit	L	1-3
19—At Toronto	L	1-4
20—Quebec‡	L	2-5
22—Los Angeles	L	2-5
25—Chicago	L	1-5
27—At Pittsburgh	T	*3-3

MARCH

3—Montreal	W	3-1
6—Calgary	W	7-4
9—Winnipeg	L	2-4
12—At Toronto	L	2-8
14—At Winnipeg	L	1-3
16—Hartford	L	*3-4
18—Toronto	L	2-4
20—Buffalo	L	1-3
21—At Chicago	L	2-3
23—At New Jersey	L	3-9
25—At Ottawa	W	*3-2
27—Detroit	L	3-8

APRIL

1—Vancouver	L	3-5
3—At Philadelphia	L	2-6
6—St. Louis	T	*2-2
8—Detroit	L	1-9
10—Chicago	L	2-4
11—At Chicago	T	*3-3
13—At Winnipeg	W	5-3
15—At St. Louis	L	5-6

*Denotes overtime game.
†At Miami.
‡At Halifax, N.S.

TORONTO MAPLE LEAFS
WESTERN CONFERENCE/CENTRAL DIVISION

1993-94 SCHEDULE

Home games shaded.
* — At Madison Square Garden, New York.
† — At Hamilton, Ont.

OCTOBER

SUN	MON	TUE	WED	THU	FRI	SAT
					1 DAL	2
3	4	5	6	7 DAL	8	9 CHI
10 PHI	11	12	13 WAS	14	15 DET	16 DET
17	18	19 HAR	20	21 FLA	22	23 TB
24	25	26	27	28 CHI	29	30 MON
31						

NOVEMBER

SUN	MON	TUE	WED	THU	FRI	SAT
	1 DAL	2	3 FLA	4 DET	5	6 PHI
7	8	9 SJ	10	11 STL	12	13 CHI
14	15 EDM	16	17 ANA	18 LA	19	20 EDM
21	22 VAN	23	24 CAL	25	26	27 BOS
28	29 BUF	30				

DECEMBER

SUN	MON	TUE	WED	THU	FRI	SAT
			1 STL	2 STL	3	4 NYR
5	6	7	8 WIN	9	10	11 CAL
12 WIN	13	14	15 ANA	16	17 NYI	18 LA
19	20	21	22 SJ	23 NJ	24	25
26	27 CHI	28	29 DAL	30	31	

JANUARY

SUN	MON	TUE	WED	THU	FRI	SAT
						1 LA
2 BUF	3	4† TB	5	6 OTT	7	8 VAN
9	10 BOS	11 WAS	12	13 DAL	14	15 WIN
16	17	18 ANA	19 HAR	20	21	22* ALL-STAR GAME
23	24	25	26 NYI	27	28	29 PIT
30	31					

FEBRUARY

SUN	MON	TUE	WED	THU	FRI	SAT
		1 STL	2	3	4	5 DET
6	7 TB	8	9	10	11 WIN	12 CAL
13	14	15 DET	16	17 NJ	18	19 EDM
20	21 LA	22	23 EDM	24	25	26 MON
27	28 OTT					

MARCH

SUN	MON	TUE	WED	THU	FRI	SAT
		1	2	3	4 DET	5 QUE
6	7 STL	8	9 DAL	10 PIT	11	12 WIN
13	14	15	16 VAN	17	18 STL	19
20 CAL	21	22	23† FLA	24 SJ	25	26 QUE
27	28 VAN	29	30	31 SJ		

APRIL

SUN	MON	TUE	WED	THU	FRI	SAT
					1	2 ANA
3	4	5 DAL	6	7	8 NYR	9
10 WIN	11	12 CHI	13	14 CHI	15	16

1993-94 SEASON

CLUB DIRECTORY

Chairman of the board and CEO
Steve A. Stavro
President, COO and general manager
Cliff Fletcher
Secretary-treasurer
J. Donald Crump
Alternate governor
Cliff Fletcher
Alternate governor and counsel
Brian P. Bellmore
Assistant general manager
Bill Watters
Special consultant to the president
Darryl Sittler
Dir. of bus. operations and communications
Bob Stellick
Public relations coordinator
Pat Park
Controller
Ian Clarke
Director of marketing and advertising
Bill Cluff
Box office manager
Donna Henderson
Director of pro scouting
Floyd Smith
Director of professional development
Tom Watt
Coach
Pat Burns

Assistant coaches
Mike Kitchen
Mike Murphy
Goaltending consultant
Rick Wamsley
Director of scouting
Pierre Dorion
Scouts
George Armstrong
Dick Duff
Anders Hedberg
Peter Johnson
Garth Malarchuk
Dan Marr
Ernie Gare
Jack Gardiner
Bob Johnson
Doug Woods
Dick Bouchard
Athletic therapist
Chris Broadhurst
Trainers
Jim Carey
Brian Papineau
Brent Smith
Team doctors
Dr. Michael Clarfield
Dr. Darrell Olgilvie-Harris
Dr. Leith Douglas
Dr. Michael Easterbrook
Dr. Simon McGrail
Dr. Ernie Lewis

DRAFT CHOICES

1—Kenny Jonsson	6-3/187	12	D	Rogle, Sweden
1—Landon Wilson	6-2/202	19	F	Dubuque, USHL (Jr. Tier II)
5—Zdenek Nedved	5-11/179	123	F	Sudbury (OHL)
6—Paul Vincent	6-4/200	149	C	Cushing Academy (Conn.)
7—Jeff Andrews	6-4/196	175	F	North Bay (OHL)
8—David Brumby	6-0/170	201	G	Tri-City (WHL)
10—Kyle Ferguson	6-3/215	253	F	Michigan Tech (WCHA)
11—Mikhail Lapin	6-2/190	279	D	Western Michigan Univ.

MISCELLANEOUS DATA

Home ice (capacity)
Maple Leafs Garden
(15,842, including standees)
Address
60 Carlton Street
Toronto, Ont. M5B 1L1
Business phone
416-977-1641

Rink dimensions
200 feet by 85 feet
Club colors
Blue and white
Minor league affiliation
St. John's (AHL)

TRAINING CAMP ROSTER

No.	FORWARDS	Ht./Wt.	Place	BORN Date	NHL exp.	1992-93 clubs
9	Glenn Anderson (RW) ...	6-1/190	Vancouver, B.C.	10-2-60	13	Toronto
14	Dave Andreychuk (LW)	6-3/225	Hamilton, Ont.	9-29-63	11	Buffalo, Toronto
	Patrik Augusta (RW)	5-10/169	Jihlava, Czech.	11-13-69	0	St. John's (AHL)
22	Ken Baumgartner	6-0/200	Flin Flon, Man.	3-11-66	6	Toronto
10	Bill Berg (LW)	6-1/198	St. Catharines, Ont.	10-21-67	4	New York Islanders, Toronto
16	Nikolai Borschevsky.......	5-9/180	Tomsk, U.S.S.R.	1-12-65	1	Toronto
	Terry Chitaroni (C)	5-11/200	Haileybury, Ont.	12-9-72	0	St. John's (AHL), Baltimore (AHL)
17	Wendel Clark (LW)	5-11/194	Kelvington, Sask.	10-25-66	8	Toronto
	Brandon Convery (C) ...	6-1/180	Kingston, Ont.	2-4-74	0	Niagara Falls (OHL), Sudbury (OHL), St. John's (AHL)
19	John Cullen (C)	5-10/187	Puslinch, Ont.	8-2-64	5	Hartford, Toronto
32	Michael Eastwood (C)	6-2/190	Cornwall, Ont.	7-1-67	2	St. John's (AHL), Toronto
71	Mike Foligno (RW)	6-2/200	Sudbury, Ont.	1-29-59	14	Toronto
93	Doug Gilmour (C)	5-11/164	Kingston, Ont.	6-25-63	10	Toronto
	Todd Hawkins (RW)	6-1/195	Kingston, Ont.	8-2-66	3	St. John's (AHL)
	Darby Hendrickson (C) .	6-0/175	Richfield, Minn.	8-28-72	0	U. of Minnesota (WCHA)
26	Mike Krushelnyski (C)	6-2/200	Montreal	4-27-60	12	Toronto
	Alexei Kudashov (C)	6-0/180	Elekhrostal, U.S.S.R.	7-21-71	0	Soviet Wings (CIS)
18	Kent Manderville (LW) .	6-3/195	Edmonton, Alta.	4-12-71	2	Toronto, St. John's (AHL)
	Grant Marshall (LW).....	6-1/185	Toronto	6-9-73	0	Newmarket (OHL), Ottawa (OHL), St. John's (AHL)
7	David McLlwain (RW/C) .	6-0/190	Seaforth, Ont.	1-9-67	6	Toronto
21	Mark Osborne (LW)	6-2/200	Toronto	8-13-61	12	Toronto
12	Rob Pearson (RW)	6-1/180	Oshawa, Ont.	8-3-71	2	Toronto
	Yanic Perreault (C)	5-11/182	Sherbrooke, Que.	4-4-71	0	St. John's (AHL)
25	Peter Zezel (C)	5-11/200	Toronto	4-22-65	9	Toronto
	DEFENSEMEN					
55	Drake Berehowsky	6-1/211	Toronto	1-3-72	3	Toronto, St. John's (AHL)
	Ted Crowley..................	6-2/190	Concord, Mass.	5-3-70	0	St. John's (AHL)
4	Dave Ellett	6-2/200	Cleveland	3-30-64	9	Toronto
23	Todd Gill	6-0/185	Brockville, Ont.	11-9-65	9	Toronto
	Kenny Jonsson	6-3/187	Angelholm, Sweden.	10-5-74	0	Rogle (Sweden)
2	Sylvain Lefebvre	6-2/204	Richmond, Que.	10-14-67	4	Toronto
34	Jamie Macoun	6-2/200	Newmarket, Ont.	8-17-61	11	Toronto
	Matt Martin	6-3/190	Hamden, Conn.	4-30-71	0	U. of Maine (H. East), St. John's (AHL)
8	Bob McGill....................	6-1/193	Edmonton, Alta.	4-27-62	12	Toronto
55	Brad Miller	6-4/226	Edmonton, Alta.	7-23-69	5	Ottawa, New Haven (AHL), St. John's (AHL)
15	Dmitri Mironov	6-2/191	Moscow, U.S.S.R.	12-25-65	2	Toronto
3	Bob Rouse....................	6-2/210	Surrey, B.C.	6-18-64	10	Toronto
	GOALTENDERS					
29	Felix Potvin...................	6-0/185	Anjou, Que.	6-23-71	2	Toronto, St. John's (AHL)
	Damian Rhodes	6-0/170	St. Paul, Minn.	5-28-69	1	St. John's (AHL)

1992-93 REVIEW

INDIVIDUAL STATISTICS

SCORING

	Games	G	A	Pts.	Pen.	+/-	PPG	SHG	Shots	Shooting Pct.
Doug Gilmour	83	32	95	127	100	32	15	3	211	15.2
Nikolai Borschevsky	78	34	40	74	28	33	12	0	204	16.7
Glenn Anderson	76	22	43	65	117	19	11	0	161	13.7
Todd Gill	69	11	32	43	66	4	5	0	113	9.7
John Cullen*	47	13	28	41	53	-8	10	0	86	15.1
Dave Ellett	70	6	34	40	46	19	4	0	186	3.2
Mike Krushelnyski.................................	84	19	20	39	62	3	6	2	130	14.6
Wendel Clark	66	17	22	39	193	2	2	0	146	11.6
Dave Andreychuk*	31	25	13	38	8	12	12	0	139	18.0
Rob Pearson	78	23	14	37	211	-2	8	0	164	14.0
Peter Zezel	70	12	23	35	24	0	0	0	102	11.8
Dimitri Mironov....................................	59	7	24	31	40	-1	4	0	105	6.7
Mark Osborne	76	12	14	26	89	-7	0	2	110	10.9
Drake Berehowsky	41	4	15	19	61	1	1	0	41	9.8
Jamie Macoun	77	4	15	19	55	3	2	0	114	3.5
Dave McLlwain	66	14	4	18	30	-18	1	1	85	16.5
Mike Foligno	55	13	5	18	84	2	5	0	95	13.7
Bill Berg*	58	7	8	15	54	-1	0	1	83	8.4

	Games	G	A	Pts.	Pen.	+/-	PPG	SHG	Shots	Shooting Pct.
Bob Rouse	82	3	11	14	130	7	0	1	78	3.8
Sylvain Lefebvre	81	2	12	14	90	8	0	0	81	2.5
Joe Sacco	23	4	4	8	8	-4	0	0	38	10.5
Mike Eastwood	12	1	6	7	21	-2	0	0	11	9.1
Kent Manderville	18	1	1	2	17	-9	0	0	15	6.7
Bob McGill	19	1	0	1	34	5	0	0	8	12.5
Ken Baumgartner	63	1	0	1	155	-11	0	0	23	4.3
Felix Potvin (goalie)	48	0	1	1	4	0	0	0	0	0.0
Ken McRae	2	0	0	0	2	-1	0	0	3	0.0
Dave Tomlinson	3	0	0	0	2	0	0	0	1	0.0
Rick Wamsley (goalie)	3	0	0	0	0	0	0	0	0	0.0
Daren Puppa (goalie)*	8	0	0	0	0	0	0	0	0	0.0
Guy Larose	9	0	0	0	8	-3	0	0	8	0.0
Darryl Shannon	16	0	0	0	11	-5	0	0	10	0.0
Grant Fuhr (goalie)*	29	0	0	0	0	0	0	0	0	0.0

GOALTENDING

	Games	Min.	Goals	SO	Avg.	W	L	T	Shots	Sv. Pct.
Daren Puppa*	8	479	18	2	2.25	6	2	0	232	.922
Felix Potvin	48	2781	116	2	†2.50	25	15	7	1286	.910
Grant Fuhr*	29	1665	87	1	3.14	13	9	4	826	.895
Rick Wamsley	3	160	15	0	5.63	0	3	0	91	.835

Empty-net goals (do not count against a goaltender's average): Potvin 3, Fuhr 1, Puppa 1.
*Played with two or more NHL teams.
†Led league.

RESULTS

OCTOBER
6—Washington	L	5-6
10—At Calgary	L	2-3
11—At Edmonton	T	*3-3
15—Tampa Bay	W	5-3
17—Chicago	W	4-3
18—Minnesota	L	1-5
20—Ottawa†	W	5-3
22—At Tampa Bay	W	5-2
24—San Jose	W	5-1
28—Buffalo	T	*4-4
30—At Detroit	L	1-7
31—Detroit	W	3-1

NOVEMBER
5—At Chicago	L	0-1
7—Pittsburgh	W	4-2
9—At Ottawa	W	3-1
14—At Boston	W	4-1
16—St. Louis	T	*2-2
17—Quebec	L	1-3
19—At San Jose	W	2-0
21—At Los Angeles	L	4-6
24—Tampa Bay	L	2-3
26—Quebec	L	*4-5
28—Los Angeles	W	3-2

DECEMBER
1—At New Jersey	L	3-8
3—At Chicago	L	3-4
5—Chicago	T	*2-2
6—At N.Y. Rangers	L	0-6
9—Detroit	W	5-3

11—Calgary	L	3-6
15—At Minnesota	L	5-6
19—Ottawa	W	5-1
20—At Buffalo	L	4-5
22—At Detroit	T	*4-4
26—Detroit	L	1-5
27—At St. Louis	W	6-3
29—At N.Y. Islanders	W	3-2
31—At Pittsburgh	T	*3-3

JANUARY
2—St. Louis	T	*2-2
4—At Detroit	W	4-2
6—Vancouver	L	2-5
8—San Jose	W	5-1
9—At Montreal	W	5-4
11—Tampa Bay	W	4-2
13—St. Louis	W	4-3
16—Chicago	L	3-5
17—At Chicago	L	3-5
19—At St. Louis	W	5-1
21—At Tampa Bay	W	6-1
23—Montreal	W	4-0
26—Minnesota	L	1-2
30—N.Y. Rangers	W	3-1

FEBRUARY
1—At St. Louis	T	*1-1
3—N.Y. Islanders	L	2-3
9—At Tampa Bay	L	1-3
11—Vancouver	W	5-2
13—Minnesota	W	6-1
14—At Minnesota	W	6-5
17—Calgary	W	4-2

19—Tampa Bay	W	4-1
20—Boston	T	*4-4
22—At Vancouver	W	8-1
25—At San Jose	W	5-0
27—At Los Angeles	W	5-2

MARCH
3—Minnesota	W	3-1
5—At Detroit	L	1-5
6—Winnipeg	W	4-2
9—At Washington	L	1-3
10—Hartford	W	5-3
12—Tampa Bay	W	8-2
15—At Quebec	L	2-4
18—At Tampa Bay	W	4-2
20—Edmonton	W	4-2
23—At Winnipeg	W	5-4
25—At Minnesota	T	*3-3
27—At Edmonton	W	6-2
28—At Calgary	W	4-0
31—Los Angeles	T	*5-5

APRIL
3—New Jersey	W	1-0
4—At Philadelphia	L	0-4
8—At Winnipeg	L	3-5
10—Philadelphia	L	0-4
11—At Hartford	W	4-2
13—St. Louis	W	*2-1
15—At Chicago	L	2-3

*Denotes overtime game.
†At Hamilton, Ont.

VANCOUVER CANUCKS
WESTERN CONFERENCE/PACIFIC DIVISION

1993-94 SCHEDULE

Home games shaded.
* — At Madison Square Garden, New York.
† — At Saskatoon, Sask.

OCTOBER
SUN	MON	TUE	WED	THU	FRI	SAT
					1	2
3	4	5	6 LA	7	8	9 CAL
10	11 EDM	12	13	14	15	16 EDM
17	18	19	20	21 CAL	22	23 SJ
24 SJ	25	26	27 WAS	28	29	30 BUF
31						

NOVEMBER
SUN	MON	TUE	WED	THU	FRI	SAT
	1	2 NYI	3 NYR	4	5 WAS	6
7 PHI	8	9	10 LA	11	12	13 CAL
14 ANA	15	16 STL	17	18	19 ANA	20
21	22 TOR	23	24 DET	25	26 WIN	27 EDM
28	29 CHI	30				

DECEMBER
SUN	MON	TUE	WED	THU	FRI	SAT
			1	2 PHI	3	4 QUE
5	6 MON	7	8 HAR	9 BOS	10	11
12	13	14 CAL	15 EDM	16	17 WIN	18
19 DAL	20	21 EDM	22	23† CAL	24	25
26	27	28 LA	29	30	31 SJ	

JANUARY
SUN	MON	TUE	WED	THU	FRI	SAT
						1
2 MON	3	4	5 OTT	6	7	8 TOR
9 BUF	10	11	12 QUE	13	14 OTT	15
16 ANA	17	18	19 CAL	20	21	22° ALL STAR GAME
23	24† EDM	25 STL	26	27 DAL	28	29 NJ
30	31 LA					

FEBRUARY
SUN	MON	TUE	WED	THU	FRI	SAT
		1	2 CHI	3	4 ANA	5
6 HAR	7	8 DET	9	10 NJ	11	12 TB
13 FLA	14	15 STL	16	17 CHI	18	19
20	21	22 CAL	23	24	25	26 TB
27	28					

MARCH
SUN	MON	TUE	WED	THU	FRI	SAT
		1 EDM	2	3 STL	4 DAL	5
6	7 FLA	8	9 NYI	10	11 WIN	12
13 CHI	14	15 DET	16 TOR	17	18	19 PIT
20 DAL	21	22	23 LA	24	25 NYR	26
27 LA	28 TOR	29	30 PIT	31		

APRIL
SUN	MON	TUE	WED	THU	FRI	SAT
					1 WIN	2 SJ
3	4	5 DET	6	7 SJ	8	9 ANA
10 SJ	11	12	13 ANA	14	15	16

1993-94 SEASON

CLUB DIRECTORY

Chairman of the board
Frank A. Griffiths
Vice chairman and governor
Arthur R. Griffiths
President, general manager, head coach
Pat Quinn
V.P./Dir. of marketing and communications
Glen Ringdal
Vice president of finance and administration
Carlos Mascarenhas
Director of media and public relations
Steve Tambellini
Director of hockey operations
George McPhee
Director of player development
Mike Penny
Director of hockey information
Steve Frost
Public relations assistant
Veronica Bateman
Assistant coaches
Rick Ley
Stan Smyl
Strength coach
Wayne Wilson
Director of amateur scouting
Mike Penny

Director of pro scouting
Murray Oliver
Scouts
Ron Delorme
Jack McCartan
Noel Price
Ken Slater
Paul McIntosh
Ed McColgan
Scott Carter
Jack Birch
Thomas Gradin
Ticket manager
Denise McDonald
Medical trainer
Larry Ashley
Equipment trainers
Pat O'Neill
Darren Granger
Team doctors
Dr. Ross Davidson
Dr. Doug Clement
Team dentist
Dr. David Lawson

DRAFT CHOICES

1—Mike Wilson	6-4/180	20	D	Sudbury (OHL)
2—Rick Girard	5-11/180	46	C	Swift Current (WHL)
4—Dieter Kochan	6-1/165	98	G	Kelowna, B.C. (Jr. A)
5—Scott Walker	5-9/170	124	D	Owen Sound (OHL)
6—Troy Creurer	6-1/180	150	D	Notre Dame (SJHL, Jr. A)
7—Jevgeni Babariko	6-1/183	176	C	Nizhni Novgorod, Europe
8—Sean Tallaire	5-10/185	202	F	Lake Superior St. (CCHA)
10—Bert Robertsson	6-2/187	254	D	Sodertalje, Europe
11—Sergei Tkachekko	6-2/198	280	G	Hamilton (AHL)

MISCELLANEOUS DATA

Home ice (capacity)
Pacific Coliseum (16,150)
Address
100 North Renfrew St.
Vancouver, B.C. V5K 3N7
Business phone
604-254-5141

Rink dimensions
200 feet by 85 feet
Club colors
White, black, red and gold
Minor league affiliation
Hamilton (AHL)

TRAINING CAMP ROSTER

No.	FORWARDS	Ht./Wt.	Place	BORN Date	NHL exp.	1992-93 clubs
8	Greg Adams (C)	6-3/198	Nelson, B.C.	8-1-63	9	Vancouver
31	Shawn Antoski (LW/RW)	6-4/245	Brantford, Ont.	5-25-70	3	Hamilton (AHL), Vancouver
10	Pavel Bure (RW/LW)	5-10/180	Moscow, U.S.S.R.	3-31-71	2	Vancouver
14	Geoff Courtnall (LW)	6-1/190	Victoria, B.C.	8-18-62	10	Vancouver
32	Murray Craven (C/LW)	6-2/185	Medicine Hat, Alta.	7-20-64	11	Hartford, Vancouver
	Neil Eisenhut (C)	5-11/190	Osoyoos, B.C.	2-9-67	0	Hamilton (AHL)
26	Tim Hunter (LW/RW)	6-2/205	Calgary, Alta.	9-10-60	12	Quebec, Vancouver
	Dane Jackson (RW)	6-1/190	Winnipeg, Man.	5-17-70	0	Hamilton (AHL)
16	Trevor Linden (C)	6-4/205	Medicine Hat, Alta.	4-11-70	5	Vancouver
	Sandy Moger (RW)	6-2/190	100 Mile House, B.C.	3-21-69	0	Hamilton (AHL)
27	Sergio Momesso (LW)	6-3/215	Montreal	9-4-65	9	Vancouver
19	Petr Nedved (C)	6-3/185	Liberec, Czech.	12-9-71	3	Vancouver
29	Gino Odjick (LW)	6-3/220	Maniwaki, Que.	9-7-70	3	Vancouver
	Mike Peca (RW/C)	5-11/165	Toronto	3-26-74	0	Ottawa (OHL), Hamilton (AHL)
	Libor Polasek (C)	6-3/198	Vitkovice, Czech.	4-22-74	0	Hamilton (AHL)
	Sean Pronger (C)	6-3/195	Thunder Bay, Ont.	11-30-72	0	Bowling Green St. (CCHA)
7	Cliff Ronning (C)	5-8/175	Vancouver, B.C.	10-1-65	7	Vancouver
	Alex Stojanov (LW)	6-4/225	Windsor, Ont.	4-25-73	0	Guelph (OHL), Newmarket (OHL), Hamilton (AHL)
23	Garry Valk (LW/RW)	6-1/195	Edmonton, Alta.	11-27-67	3	Vancouver, Hamilton (AHL)
17	Dixon Ward (LW)	6-0/200	Edmonton, Alta.	9-23-68	1	Vancouver
	DEFENSEMEN					
	Adrian Aucoin	6-1/194	London, Ont.	7-3-73	0	Can. nat. team (Int'l)
44	Dave Babych	6-2/215	Edmonton, Alta.	5-23-61	13	Vancouver
	Jassen Cullimore	6-5/225	Simcoe, Ont.	12-4-72	0	Hamilton (AHL)
4	Gerald Diduck	6-2/207	Edmonton, Alta.	4-6-65	9	Vancouver
22	Robert Dirk	6-4/218	Regina, Sask.	8-20-66	6	Vancouver
21	Jyrki Lumme	6-1/207	Tampere, Finland	7-16-67	5	Vancouver
5	Dana Murzyn	6-2/200	Regina, Sask.	12-9-66	8	Vancouver
6	Adrien Plavsic	6-1/205	Montreal	1-13-70	4	Vancouver
32	Dan Ratushny	6-1/210	Windsor, Ont.	10-29-70	1	Fort Wayne (IHL), Vancouver
24	Jiri Slegr	5-11/190	Litvinov, Czech.	5-30-71	1	Vancouver, Hamilton (AHL)
	Brent Tully	6-3/185	Peterborough, Ont.	3-26-74	0	Peterborough (OHL)
	GOALTENDERS					
	Jason Fitzsimmons	5-11/185	Regina, Sask.	6-3-71	0	Columbus (ECHL), Hamilton (AHL)
1	Kirk McLean	6-0/185	Willowdale, Ont.	6-26-66	8	Vancouver
35	Kay Whitmore	5-11/185	Sudbury, Ont.	4-10-67	5	Vancouver

1992-93 REVIEW

INDIVIDUAL STATISTICS

SCORING

	Games	G	A	Pts.	Pen.	+/-	PPG	SHG	Shots	Shooting Pct.
Pavel Bure	83	60	50	110	69	35	13	‡7	†407	14.7
Cliff Ronning	79	29	56	85	30	19	10	0	209	13.9
Geoff Courtnall	84	31	46	77	167	27	9	0	214	14.5
Trevor Linden	84	33	39	72	64	19	8	0	209	15.8
Petr Nedved	84	38	33	71	96	20	2	1	149	25.5
Greg Adams	53	25	31	56	14	31	6	1	124	20.2
Dixon Ward	70	22	30	52	82	34	4	1	111	19.8
Anatoli Semenov*	62	10	34	44	28	21	3	2	88	11.4
Jyrki Lumme	74	8	36	44	55	30	3	2	123	6.5
Sergio Momesso	84	18	20	38	200	11	4	0	146	12.3
Jim Sandlak	59	10	18	28	122	2	1	0	104	9.6
Adrien Plavsic	57	6	21	27	53	28	5	0	62	9.7
Jiri Slegr	41	4	22	26	109	16	2	0	89	4.5
Doug Lidster	71	6	19	25	36	9	3	0	76	7.9
Robert Kron*	32	10	11	21	14	10	2	2	60	16.7
Gerald Diduck	80	6	14	20	171	32	0	1	92	6.5
Dave Babych	43	3	16	19	44	6	3	0	78	3.8
Gino Odjick	75	4	13	17	370	3	0	0	79	5.1
Dana Murzyn	79	5	11	16	196	34	0	0	82	6.1
Tom Fergus	36	5	9	14	20	1	1	1	29	17.2
Garry Valk	48	6	7	13	77	6	0	0	46	13.0
Robert Dirk	69	4	8	12	150	25	0	0	41	9.8
Murray Craven*	10	0	10	10	12	3	0	0	12	0.0
Tim Hunter*	26	0	4	4	99	1	0	0	12	0.0
Ryan Walter	25	3	0	3	10	-2	0	0	15	20.0

	Games	G	A	Pts.	Pen.	+/-	PPG	SHG	Shots	Shooting Pct.
Kay Whitmore (goalie)	31	0	3	3	2	0	0	0	0	0.0
Stephane Morin	1	0	1	1	0	-1	0	0	3	0.0
Dan Ratushny	1	0	1	1	2	0	0	0	2	0.0
Kirk McLean (goalie)	54	0	1	1	16	0	0	0	0	0.0
Shawn Antoski	2	0	0	0	0	0	0	0	0	0.0

GOALTENDING

	Games	Min.	Goals	SO	Avg.	W	L	T	Shots	Sv. Pct.
Kay Whitmore	31	1817	94	1	3.10	18	8	4	858	.890
Kirk McLean	54	3261	184	3	3.39	28	21	5	1615	.886

Empty-net goals (do not count against a goaltender's average): None.
*Played with two or more NHL teams.
†Led league.
‡Tied for league lead.

RESULTS

OCTOBER

6—At Edmonton	W	5-4
10—Edmonton	W	5-2
12—Winnipeg	W	8-1
16—At Winnipeg	W	6-2
18—At Chicago	L	1-3
20—At Pittsburgh	L	1-5
22—At Philadelphia	T	*4-4
25—Boston	L	3-5
28—Washington	W	4-3
30—Minnesota	L	2-3

NOVEMBER

2—At Calgary	L	3-5
4—Calgary	T	*5-5
6—Ottawa	W	4-1
8—Winnipeg	W	6-1
10—San Jose	W	6-2
12—At Los Angeles	L	4-7
14—At San Jose	W	5-2
16—Los Angeles	W	6-3
18—At Edmonton	L	2-4
19—At Calgary	L	3-4
21—Edmonton	W	9-0
23—Chicago	W	5-2
25—At Minnesota	W	4-2
26—At St. Louis	L	5-7
28—At Montreal	W	6-5

DECEMBER

3—Edmonton	W	4-1
7—St. Louis	W	4-3
9—San Jose	W	8-3

13—Quebec	T	*3-3
16—At Edmonton	L	2-4
18—San Jose	W	8-1
19—At San Jose	W	6-3
22—At Los Angeles	W	6-2
27—Montreal	W	5-2
29—San Jose	W	7-5
31—Los Angeles	W	4-0

JANUARY

2—At San Jose	T	*2-2
4—Tampa Bay	W	7-0
6—At Toronto	W	5-2
8—At Detroit	L	3-6
9—At N.Y. Islanders	W	5-4
11—At N.Y. Rangers	T	*3-3
12—At New Jersey	L	2-3
15—Buffalo	W	4-1
16—Hartford	W	8-3
19—Pittsburgh	L	2-5
21—At Los Angeles	W	5-4
23—At Minnesota	T	*3-3
24—At Chicago	L	2-6
27—Chicago	T	*4-4
30—Detroit	T	*4-4

FEBRUARY

1—Minnesota	L	4-5
3—Tampa Bay	W	4-2
9—At Quebec	W	5-1
11—At Toronto	L	2-5
12—At Buffalo	W	3-1
15—At Los Angeles	L	0-3
18—Philadelphia	L	2-3

20—Winnipeg	W	4-2
22—Toronto	L	1-8
24—N.Y. Rangers	W	5-4
26—At Winnipeg	W	7-4

MARCH

1—Buffalo†	W	5-2
2—At Washington	T	*3-3
4—At Boston	L	3-4
6—At Hartford	L	1-5
9—New Jersey	W	7-2
11—Minnesota‡	L	3-4
12—At Winnipeg	W	3-2
14—At Calgary	L	2-3
18—Winnipeg	L	2-5
20—N.Y. Islanders	L	2-7
22—St. Louis	L	1-3
24—Los Angeles	W	6-2
26—Calgary	L	1-3
30—At St. Louis	W	6-3

APRIL

1—At Tampa Bay	W	5-3
3—At Detroit	L	1-5
4—At Ottawa	W	3-0
7—Edmonton	W	5-4
9—At Calgary	L	1-8
11—Calgary	W	6-3
13—Los Angeles	W	7-4
15—At Los Angeles	W	8-6

*Denotes overtime game.
†At Hamilton, Ont.
‡At Saskatoon, Sask.

WASHINGTON CAPITALS
EASTERN CONFERENCE/ATLANTIC DIVISION

1993-94 SCHEDULE

Home games shaded.
* — At Madison Square Garden, New York.
† — At Cleveland.
△ — At Halifax, N.S.
+ — At Orlando, Fla.

OCTOBER
SUN	MON	TUE	WED	THU	FRI	SAT
					1	2
3	4	5	6 WIN	7	8 NJ	9 NJ
10	11 NYR	12	13 TOR	14	15 PHI	16 BUF
17	18	19	20	21	22 LA	23
24 EDM	25 CAL	26	27 VAN	28	29 ANA	30 SJ
31						

NOVEMBER
SUN	MON	TUE	WED	THU	FRI	SAT
	1	2	3	4	5 VAN	6
7	8	9 QUE	10	11 TB	12	13 NYR
14	15	16 SJ	17	18 PIT	19	20 FLA
21	22	23	24 STL	25	26 PIT	27
28 NYR	29	30 NYI				

DECEMBER
SUN	MON	TUE	WED	THU	FRI	SAT
			1	2	3 MON	4 OTT
5	6	7 HAR	8	9 PHI	10	11 MON
12	13 QUE	14	15	16	17 OTT	18 HAR
19	20	21 PHI	22	23 NYR	24	25
26 PIT	27	28 FLA	29	30 ANA	31	

JANUARY
SUN	MON	TUE	WED	THU	FRI	SAT
						1 TB
2 BOS	3	4	5	6	7	8 CHI
9 NJ	10	11 TOR	12	13	14 NJ	15 QUE
16	17 MON	18	19 FLA	20	21	22° ALL STAR GAME
23	24	25 BOS	26	27 BUF	28	29 PHI
30 DET	31					

FEBRUARY
SUN	MON	TUE	WED	THU	FRI	SAT
		1	2† PHI	3	4 MON	5 TB
6	7 NYR	8	9	10 STL	11	12 LA
13	14	15 EDM	16	17	18 NYI	19
20 BUF	21 NYI	22	23	24 FLA	25	26 FLA
27 HAR	28					

MARCH
SUN	MON	TUE	WED	THU	FRI	SAT
		1 TB	2	3	4 PHI	5
6 CAL	7 BOS	8	9△ NYR	10	11	12 QUE
13	14	15 PIT	16	17	18 DAL	19
20+ TB	21	22 HAR	23	24	25 DET	26
27 BOS	28	29 NYI	30	31 CHI		

APRIL
SUN	MON	TUE	WED	THU	FRI	SAT
					1 NJ	2
3 DAL	4	5 NYI	6 OTT	7	8	9 OTT
10	11	12 WIN	13	14 BUF	15	16

1993-94 SEASON

CLUB DIRECTORY

Chairman and governor
Abe Pollin
President and alternate governor
Richard M. Patrick
Vice president and general manager
David Poile
Legal counselors and alternate governors
David M. Osnos
Peter O'Malley
Vice president of finance
Edmund Stelzer
Vice president/marketing
Lew Strudler
Public relations assistant
Dan Kaufman
Assistant director of marketing
Debi Angus
Director of community relations
Yvon Labre
Director of promotions and advertising
Charles Copeland
Admin. assistant to public relations
Julie Hensley
Admin. assistant to the general manager
Pat Young

Coach
Terry Murray
Assistant coaches
Keith Allain
John Perpich
Strength and conditioning coach
Frank Costello
Dir. of player personnel and recruitment
Jack Button
Scouts
Craig Channell
Gilles Cote
Fred Devereaux
Eje Johansson
Bud Quinn
Hugh Rogers
Bob Schmidt
Dan Sylvester
Niklas Wikegard
Darrell Young
Trainer
Stan Wong
Assistant trainer/head equipment manager
Doug Shearer

DRAFT CHOICES

1—Brendan Witt	6-1/205	11	D	Seattle (WHL)
1—Jason Allison	6-2/192	17	C	London (OHL)
3—Patrick Boileau	6-0/184	69	D	Laval (QMJHL)
6—Frank Banham	5-11/175	147	F	Saskatoon (WHL)
7—Daniel Hendrickson	5-10/180	173	F	St. Paul (Jr. A, Tier II)
7—Andrew Brunette	6-0/212	174	F	Owen Sound (OHL)
8—Joel Poirier	6-0/190	199	F	Sudbury (OHL)
9—Jason Gladney	5-11/198	225	D	Kitchener (OHL)
10—Mark Seliger	5-10/156	251	G	Rosenheim, Germany
11—Dany Bousquet	5-11/175	277	C	Penticton (Jr. A, Tier II)

MISCELLANEOUS DATA

Home ice (capacity)
USAir Arena (18,130)
Address
Landover, MD 20785
Business phone
301-386-7000
Rink dimensions
200 feet by 85 feet

Club colors
Red, white and blue
Minor league affiliations
Portland (AHL)
Hampton Roads (ECHL)

TRAINING CAMP ROSTER

No.	FORWARDS	Ht./Wt.	Place (BORN)	Date (BORN)	NHL exp.	1992-93 clubs
	Keith Acton (C)	5-8/170	Newmarket, Ont.	4-15-58	14	Philadelphia
	Jason Allison (C)	6-2/192	Toronto	5-29-75	0	London (OHL)
	Craig Berube (LW)	6-2/195	Calihoo, Alta.	12-17-65	7	Calgary
	Mike Boback (C)	5-11/180	Mt. Clemens, Mich.	8-13-70	0	Baltimore (AHL)
12	Peter Bondra (RW)	5-11/180	Luck, U.S.S.R.	2-7-68	3	Washington
18	Randy Burridge (LW)	5-9/185	Fort Erie, Ont.	1-7-66	8	Baltimore (AHL), Washington
11	Bobby Carpenter (LW)	6-0/200	Beverly, Mass.	7-13-63	12	Washington
19	Pat Elynuik (RW)	6-0/185	Foam Lake, Sask.	10-30-67	6	Washington
	Martin Gendron (RW)	5-8/180	Valleyfield, Que.	2-15-74	0	St. Hyacinthe (QMJHL), Baltimore (AHL)
32	Dale Hunter (C)	5-10/198	Petrolia, Ont.	7-31-60	13	Washington
	Martin Jiranek (C)	5-11/170	Bashaw, Alta.	10-3-69	0	Baltimore (AHL)
26	Keith Jones (RW)	6-2/190	Brantford, Ont.	11-8-68	1	Baltimore (AHL), Washington
	Kevin Kaminski (C)	5-9/170	Churchbridge, Sask.	3-13-69	3	Halifax (AHL)
8	Dimitri Khristich (LW)	6-2/190	Kiev, U.S.S.R.	7-23-69	3	Washington
22	Steve Konowalchuk (C)	6-0/180	Salt Lake City	11-11-72	2	Baltimore (AHL), Washington
21	Todd Krygier (LW)	5-11/180	Northville, Mich.	10-12-65	4	Washington
16	Alan May (RW)	6-1/200	Swan Hills, Alta.	1-14-65	6	Washington
10	Kelly Miller (LW)	5-11/195	Lansing, Mich.	3-3-63	9	Washington
	Jeff Nelson (C)	6-0/180	Prince Albert, Sask.	12-18-72	0	Baltimore (AHL)
	Pat Peake (C)	6-0/195	Detroit	5-28-73	0	Detroit (OHL)
20	Michal Pivonka (C)	6-2/196	Kladno, Czech.	1-28-66	7	Washington
	Dave Poulin (C)	5-11/190	Mississauga, Ont.	12-17-58	11	Boston
17	Mike Ridley (C)	6-1/200	Winnipeg, Man.	7-8-63	8	Washington

No.	DEFENSEMEN	Ht./Wt.	Place	Date	NHL exp.	1992-93 clubs
	Enrico Ciccone	6-4/200	Montreal	4-10-70	2	Minnesota, Kalamazoo (IHL), Hamilton (AHL)
3	Sylvain Cote	6-0/190	Quebec City	1-19-66	9	Washington
	Sergei Gonchar	6-0/178	Chelyabinsk, U.S.S.R.	4-13-74	0	Dynamo Moscow (CIS)
4	Kevin Hatcher	6-4/225	Detroit	9-9-66	9	Washington
34	Al Iafrate	6-3/220	Dearborn, Mich.	3-21-66	9	Washington
6	Calle Johansson	5-11/205	Goteborg, Sweden	2-14-67	6	Washington
	Ken Klee	6-1/200	Indianapolis	4-24-71	0	Baltimore (AHL)
	Jim Mathieson	6-1/209	Kindersley, Sask.	1-24-70	1	Baltimore (AHL)
	John Slaney	5-11/180	St. John's, Nfld.	2-7-72	0	Baltimore (AHL)
	Brendan Witt	6-2/205	Humboldt, Sask.	2-20-75	0	Seattle (WHL)
25	Jason Woolley	6-0/190	Toronto	7-27-69	2	Baltimore (AHL), Washington

No.	GOALTENDERS	Ht./Wt.	Place	Date	NHL exp.	1992-93 clubs
33	Don Beaupre	5-9/165	Kitchener, Ont.	9-19-61	13	Washington
35	Byron Dafoe	5-11/175	Duncan, B.C.	2-25-71	1	Baltimore (AHL), Washington
	Duane Derksen	6-1/180	St. Boniface, Man.	7-7-68	0	Baltimore (AHL), Hampton Roads (ECHL)
	Olaf Kolzig	6-3/205	Johannesburg, S. Africa	4-6-70	2	Rochester (AHL), Washington
31	Rick Tabaracci	5-11/179	Toronto	1-2-69	4	Winnipeg, Moncton (AHL), Washington

1992-93 REVIEW

INDIVIDUAL STATISTICS

SCORING

	Games	G	A	Pts.	Pen.	+/-	PPG	SHG	Shots	Shooting Pct.
Peter Bondra	83	37	48	85	70	8	10	0	239	15.5
Mike Ridley	84	26	56	82	44	5	6	2	148	17.6
Kevin Hatcher	83	34	45	79	114	-7	13	1	329	10.3
Dale Hunter	84	20	59	79	198	3	10	0	120	16.7
Michal Pivonka	69	21	53	74	66	14	6	1	147	14.3
Dimitri Khristich	64	31	35	66	28	29	9	1	127	24.4
Al Iafrate	81	25	41	66	169	15	11	1	289	8.7
Pat Elynuik	80	22	35	57	66	3	8	0	121	18.2
Sylvain Cote	77	21	29	50	34	28	8	2	206	10.2
Kelly Miller	84	18	27	45	32	-2	3	0	144	12.5
Calle Johansson	77	7	38	45	56	3	6	0	133	5.3
Bob Carpenter	68	11	17	28	65	-16	2	0	141	7.8
Keith Jones	71	12	14	26	124	18	0	0	73	16.4
Todd Krygier	77	11	12	23	60	-13	0	2	133	8.3
Paul MacDermid	72	9	8	17	80	-13	1	0	45	20.0
Alan May	83	6	10	16	268	1	0	0	75	8.0
Paul Cavallini*	71	5	8	13	46	3	0	0	77	6.5
Steve Konowalchuk	36	4	7	11	16	4	1	0	34	11.8
Shawn Anderson	60	2	6	8	18	-2	1	0	42	4.8

	Games	G	A	Pts.	Pen.	+/-	PPG	SHG	Shots	Shooting Pct.
Reggie Savage	16	2	3	5	12	-4	2	0	20	10.0
Kevin Miller*	10	0	3	3	35	-4	0	0	10	0.0
Jim Hrivnak (goalie)*	27	0	3	3	0	0	0	0	0	0.0
Jeff Greenlaw	16	1	1	2	18	-3	0	0	15	6.7
Jason Woolley	26	0	2	2	10	3	0	0	11	0.0
Brad Schlegel	7	0	1	1	6	1	0	0	8	0.0
Don Beaupre (goalie)	58	0	1	1	20	0	0	0	0	0.0
Bob Babcock	1	0	0	0	2	0	0	0	0	0.0
Byron Dafoe (goalie)	1	0	0	0	0	0	0	0	0	0.0
Olaf Kolzig (goalie)	1	0	0	0	0	0	0	0	0	0.0
Randy Burridge	4	0	0	0	0	1	0	0	7	0.0
Rick Tabaracci (goalie)*	6	0	0	0	4	0	0	0	0	0.0
Mark Hunter	7	0	0	0	14	1	0	0	5	0.0
Rod Langway	21	0	0	0	20	-13	0	0	6	0.0

GOALTENDING

	Games	Min.	Goals	SO	Avg.	W	L	T	Shots	Sv. Pct.
Byron Dafoe	1	1	0	0	0.00	0	0	0	0	.000
Rick Tabaracci*	6	343	10	2	1.75	3	2	0	162	.938
Don Beaupre	58	3282	181	1	3.31	27	23	5	1530	.882
Jim Hrivnak*	27	1421	83	0	3.50	13	9	2	677	.877
Olaf Kolzig	1	20	2	0	6.00	0	0	0	7	.714

Empty-net goals (do not count against a goaltender's average): Beaupre 7, Hrivnak 2, Tabaracci 1.
*Played with two or more NHL teams.

RESULTS

OCTOBER

6—At Toronto	W	6-5
9—N.Y. Rangers	L	2-4
10—Philadelphia	L	2-4
12—At New Jersey	L	2-4
16—Ottawa	W	5-1
17—Buffalo	W	6-4
21—At N.Y. Rangers	L	1-2
23—N.Y. Islanders	L	2-5
26—At Winnipeg	L	2-6
28—At Vancouver	L	3-4
30—At Calgary	W	3-1
31—At Edmonton	L	2-4

NOVEMBER

3—Chicago†	W	4-1
6—Tampa Bay	T	*2-2
7—At Hartford	W	6-2
11—At N.Y. Rangers	W	7-4
13—At New Jersey	L	0-3
14—New Jersey	L	*3-4
18—Minnesota	L	4-5
20—Detroit	L	5-7
22—At Quebec	W	6-4
23—At Montreal	T	*1-1
25—Boston	W	6-2
27—Pittsburgh	W	6-4
28—At Pittsburgh	L	3-5
30—At Detroit	W	4-1

DECEMBER

4—N.Y. Rangers	W	8-4
5—At N.Y. Islanders	W	5-3
7—At Ottawa	W	6-5
9—At New Jersey	W	6-2
11—Winnipeg	W	8-6
12—At Philadelphia	W	5-2
16—At Hartford	L	3-6
18—Hartford	W	4-3
19—At Boston	L	3-4
21—At Ottawa	W	4-3
23—At Buffalo	L	1-4
26—Philadelphia	T	*5-5
29—N.Y. Rangers	W	*4-3

JANUARY

1—New Jersey	W	9-2
2—Chicago	T	*2-2
7—At Philadelphia	L	2-8
9—At Edmonton	W	4-3
13—At N.Y. Rangers	L	4-5
14—At N.Y. Islanders	W	3-0
17—At Tampa Bay	W	5-3
21—At Chicago	L	2-6
23—Ottawa	W	6-4
26—At Pittsburgh	L	3-6
27—At Buffalo	L	3-4
29—Quebec	T	*3-3
31—Pittsburgh	T	*2-2

FEBRUARY

2—Calgary	L	4-6
9—At Minnesota	W	3-2
11—At St. Louis	W	10-6
13—At Los Angeles	W	10-3
16—At San Jose	W	4-3
20—Los Angeles	W	7-3
21—St. Louis	W	5-2
23—At N.Y. Islanders	W	4-2
27—At Boston	W	*4-5
28—Pittsburgh	L	2-4

MARCH

2—Vancouver	T	*3-3
5—Philadelphia	L	0-3
7—N.Y. Islanders	L	2-3
9—Toronto	W	3-1
11—At Philadelphia	L	4-6
16—Detroit‡	W	4-2
18—At Pittsburgh	L	5-7
19—Hartford	W	5-2
21—San Jose	W	5-3
23—Quebec	W	5-1
25—At N.Y. Islanders	W	5-2
27—New Jersey	L	2-5
28—Pittsburgh	L	1-4
30—Buffalo	W	4-1

APRIL

2—Montreal	W	4-0
4—N.Y. Rangers	L	0-4
6—N.Y. Islanders	L	2-3
8—At Philadelphia	L	3-4
10—New Jersey	L	3-5
12—At Montreal	W	*3-2
14—At N.Y. Rangers	W	2-0
16—N.Y. Rangers	L	2-4

*Denotes overtime game.
†At Indianapolis.
‡At Milwaukee.

WINNIPEG JETS
WESTERN CONFERENCE/CENTRAL DIVISION

1993-94 SCHEDULE

■ Home games shaded.
* — At Madison Square Garden, New York.
† — At Hamilton, Ont.
∆ — At Minneapolis.

OCTOBER

SUN	MON	TUE	WED	THU	FRI	SAT
					1	2 DAL
3	4	5	6 WAS	7	8	9 DAL
10 CHI	11	12 NJ	13	14	15	16 CHI
17	18 EDM	19	20	21 DET	22	23 PHI
24	25	26 FLA	27 TB	28	29 LA	30
31 CAL						

NOVEMBER

SUN	MON	TUE	WED	THU	FRI	SAT
	1	2	3 STL	4	5 OTT	6
7 DAL	8	9 NYI	10 NYR	11	12	13 DAL
14	15 CAL	16	17 DET	18	19 BUF	20 QUE
21	22	23	24 ANA	25	26 VAN	27
28 STL	29	30 LA				

DECEMBER

SUN	MON	TUE	WED	THU	FRI	SAT
			1 ANA	2	3 SJ	4
5 DET	6 DET	7	8 TOR	9	10 FLA	11
12 TOR	13	14	15	16	17 VAN	18 CAL
19	20 ANA	21	22	23 QUE	24	25
26	27 EDM	28	29 CHI	30	31 STL	

JANUARY

SUN	MON	TUE	WED	THU	FRI	SAT
						1
2 CHI	3	4	5 HAR	6 BOS	7	8 OTT
9	10 MON	11	12 BUF	13	14	15 TOR
16 TB	17	18	19 NJ	20	21	22* ALL-STAR GAME
23	24	25 LA	26 ANA	27	28	29 DET
30	31					

FEBRUARY

SUN	MON	TUE	WED	THU	FRI	SAT
		1	2 DAL	3	4 HAR	5
6 EDM	7	8 STL	9 DAL	10	11 TOR	12
13	14	15 PIT	16	17	18 CHI	19
20 CAL	21	22† FLA	23	24 CHI	25 BOS	26
27	28 SJ					

MARCH

SUN	MON	TUE	WED	THU	FRI	SAT
		1	2 DAL	3	4∆ OTT	5
6 PIT	7 NYI	8	9	10	11 VAN	12 TOR
13	14	15	16 STL	17	18	19 DET
20	21	22	23 MON	24	25 SJ	26
27 NYR	28	29 SJ	30	31		

APRIL

SUN	MON	TUE	WED	THU	FRI	SAT
					1 VAN	2
3	4 PHI	5	6 EDM	7	8	9 LA
10 TOR	11	12 WAS	13	14 STL	15	16

1993-94 SEASON

CLUB DIRECTORY

President and governor
Barry L. Shenkarow
Alternate governors
Bill Davis
Michael A. Smith
Vice president and general manager
Michael A. Smith
Asst. G.M./director of hockey operations
Dennis McDonald
Vice president of finance and adminstration
Don Binda
Exec. asst to V.P. and G.M.
Pat MacDonald
V.P., broadcasting and communications
Mike O'Hearn
Director of community relations
Lori Summers
Vice president of marketing
Madeline Hanson
Director of team services
Murray Harding
Coach
John Paddock

Assistant coaches
Zinetula Bilyaletdinov
Glen Williamson
Director of amateur scouting
Bill Lesuk
Assistant director of amateur scouting
Joe Yanetti
Pro scout
Sean Coady
Scouts
Connie Broden
Larry Hornung
Tom Savage
Charlie Burroughs
Vaughan Karpan
Athletic therapists
Jim Ramsay
Phil Walker
Equipment managers
Craig Heisinger
Stan Wilson

DRAFT CHOICES

1—Mats Lindgren...........	6-1/187	15	C	Skelleftea, Sweden
2—Scott Langkow..........	5-11/180	31	G	Portland (WHL)
2—Alexander Budajev ...	6-2/183	43	F	Kristall Electrosal, CIS
4—Ruslam Batyrshim....	6-1/180	79	D	Dynamo Minsk, CIS
4—Ravil Gusmanov........	6-3/185	93	F	Chelyabinsk, CIS
5—Larry Courville.........	6-1/180	119	F	Newmarket (OHL)
6—Michal Grosek..........	6-2/183	145	F	Zlin, Czech.
7—Martin Woods	5-10/196	171	D	Victoriaville (QMJHL)
8—Adrian Murray	6-3/175	197	D	Newmarket (OHL)
9—Vladimir Potatov.......	6-2/187	217	F	Kristall Electrosal, CIS
9—Ilja Stashenkov........	5-11/178	223	D	Soviet Wings
9—Harijs Vitolinsh	6-3/205	228	C	Chur, Europe
11—Russell Hewson	6-0/190	285	F	Swift Current (WHL)

MISCELLANEOUS DATA

Home Ice (capacity)
Winnipeg Arena (15,393)
Address
15-1430 Maroons Road
Winnipeg, Man. R3G 0L5
Business phone
204-982-5387

Rink dimensions
200 feet by 85 feet
Club colors
Blue, red and white
Minor league affiliations
Fort Wayne (IHL)
Moncton (AHL)

TRAINING CAMP ROSTER

No.	FORWARDS	Ht./Wt.	Place	Date	NHL exp.	1992-93 clubs
14	Stu Barnes (C)	5-10/175	Edmonton, Alta.	12-25-70	2	Moncton (AHL), Winnipeg
38	Luciano Borsato (C)	5-10/165	Richmond Hill, Ont.	1-7-66	3	Winnipeg
11	Evgeny Davydov (LW)	6-1/185	Chelyabinsk, U.S.S.R.	5-27-67	2	Winnipeg
20	Tie Domi (RW)	5-10/198	Windsor, Ont.	11-1-69	4	N.Y. Rangers, Winnipeg
36	Mike Eagles (C)	5-10/180	Sussex, N.B.	3-7-63	9	Winnipeg
18	Bryan Erickson (RW)	5-9/170	Roseau, Minn.	3-7-60	8	Moncton (AHL), Winnipeg
	Jan Kaminsky (LW)	6-2/176	Penza, U.S.S.R.	7-28-71	0	Dynamo Moscow (CIS)
17	Kris King (LW/C)	5-11/208	Bracebridge, Ont.	2-18-66	6	N.Y. Rangers, Winnipeg
	Mats Lindgren (C)	6-1/187	Skelleftea, Sweden	10-1-74	0	Skelleftea AIK (Sweden)
	Pekka Peltola (C/RW)	6-2/196	Helsinki, Finland	6-24-65	0	Lukko (Finland)
21	Russ Romaniuk (LW)	6-0/185	Winnipeg, Man.	5-9-70	2	Winnipeg, Fort Wayne (IHL), Moncton (AHL)
13	Teemu Selanne (RW)	6-0/180	Helsinki, Finland	7-3-70	1	Winnipeg
34	Darrin Shannon (LW)	6-2/200	Barrie, Ont.	12-8-69	5	Winnipeg
25	Thomas Steen (C)	5-10/195	Tocksmark, Sweden	6-8-60	12	Winnipeg
	Jeremy Stevenson (LW)		San Bernardino, Calif.	7-28-74	0	Newmarket (OHL)
7	Keith Tkachuk (C/LW)	6-2/200	Melrose, Mass.	3-28-72	2	Winnipeg
	Dave Tomlinson (C)	5-11/190	N. Vancouver	5-8-68	2	St. John's (AHL), Toronto
	Paul Ysebaert (LW)	6-1/190	Sarnia, Ont.	5-15-66	5	Detroit
10	Alexei Zhamnov (C)	6-1/187	Moscow, U.S.S.R.	10-1-70	1	Winnipeg
	DEFENSEMEN					
3	Sergei Bautin	6-3/185	Murmansk, U.S.S.R.	3-11-67	1	Winnipeg
6	Phil Housley	5-10/179	St. Paul, Minn.	3-9-64	11	Winnipeg
26	Dean Kennedy	6-2/200	Redvers, Sask.	1-18-63	10	Winnipeg
	Dan Lambert	5-8/177	St. Boniface, Man.	1-12-70	2	Moncton (AHL)
	Boris Mironov	6-3/196	Moscow, U.S.S.R.	3-21-72	0	CSKA Moscow (CIS)
	Mike Muller	6-2/205	Minneapolis	9-18-71	0	Dynamo Moscow (CIS)
27	Teppo Numminen	6-1/190	Tampere, Finland	7-3-68	5	Winnipeg
4	Fredrik Olausson	6-2/200	Vaxsjo, Sweden	10-5-66	7	Winnipeg
	Darryl Shannon	6-2/195	Barrie, Ont.	6-21-68	5	Toronto, St. John's (AHL)
5	Igor Ulanov	6-2/202	Kraskokamsk, U.S.S.R.	10-1-69	2	Moncton (AHL), Fort Wayne (IHL), Winnipeg
	GOALTENDERS					
	Stephane Beauregard	5-11/185	Cowansville, Que.	1-10-68	4	Philadelphia, Hershey (AHL)
35	Bob Essensa	6-0/160	Toronto	1-14-65	5	Winnipeg
	Sean Gauthier	5-11/194	Sudbury, Ont.	3-28-71	0	Moncton (AHL)
	Scott Langkow	5-11/180	Edmonton, Alta.	4-21-75	0	Portland (WHL)
	Mike O'Neill	5-7/155	Montreal	11-3-67	2	Moncton (AHL), Winnipeg
	Allain Roy	5-10/165	Campbelltown, N.B.	2-6-70	0	Can. nat. team (Int'l)

1992-93 REVIEW

INDIVIDUAL STATISTICS

SCORING

	Games	G	A	Pts.	Pen.	+/-	PPG	SHG	Shots	Shooting Pct.
Teemu Selanne	84	‡76	56	132	45	8	24	0	387	19.6
Phil Housley	80	18	79	97	52	-14	6	0	249	7.2
Alexei Zhamnov	68	25	47	72	58	7	6	1	163	15.3
Thomas Steen	80	22	50	72	75	-8	6	0	150	14.7
Darrin Shannon	84	20	40	60	91	-4	12	0	116	17.2
Fredrik Olausson	68	16	41	57	22	-4	11	0	165	9.7
Keith Tkachuk	83	28	23	51	201	-13	12	0	199	14.1
Evgeny Davydov	79	28	21	49	66	-2	7	0	176	15.9
Teppo Numminen	66	7	30	37	33	4	3	1	103	6.8
Luciano Borsato	67	15	20	35	38	-1	1	1	101	14.9
Mike Eagles	84	8	18	26	131	-1	1	0	67	11.9
Sergei Bautin	71	5	18	23	96	-2	0	0	82	6.1
Stu Barnes	38	12	10	22	10	-3	3	0	73	16.4
Ed Olczyk*	25	8	12	20	26	-11	2	0	81	9.9
John Druce	50	6	14	20	37	-4	0	0	60	10.0
Kris King*	48	8	8	16	136	5	0	0	51	15.7
Bryan Erickson	41	4	12	16	14	2	2	0	45	8.9
Igor Ulanov	56	2	14	16	124	6	0	0	26	7.7
Tie Domi*	49	3	10	13	249	2	0	0	29	10.3
Mike Lalor	64	1	8	9	76	-10	0	0	75	1.3
Dean Kennedy	78	1	7	8	105	-3	0	0	50	2.0
Troy Murray*	29	3	4	7	34	-15	1	0	45	6.7
Bob Essensa (goalie)	67	0	5	5	2	0	0	0	0	0.0

	Games	G	A	Pts.	Pen.	+/-	PPG	SHG	Shots	Shooting Pct.
Russ Romaniuk	28	3	1	4	22	0	0	0	20	15.0
Randy Carlyle	22	1	1	2	14	-6	0	0	21	4.8
Anatoli Fedotov	1	0	2	2	0	1	0	0	1	0.0
Andy Brickley	12	0	2	2	2	0	0	0	5	0.0
Dallas Eakins	14	0	2	2	38	2	0	0	9	0.0
Mark Osiecki*	4	1	0	1	2	1	1	0	5	20.0
Rob Murray	10	1	0	1	6	0	0	0	4	25.0
Alan Kerr	7	0	1	1	2	-4	0	0	1	0.0
Scott Levins	9	0	1	1	18	-2	0	0	8	0.0
Bob Joyce	1	0	0	0	0	0	0	0	0	0.0
Michael O'Neill (goalie)	2	0	0	0	0	0	0	0	0	0.0
Jim Hrivnak (goalie)*	3	0	0	0	0	0	0	0	0	0.0
John LeBlanc	3	0	0	0	2	0	0	0	5	0.0
Kris Draper	7	0	0	0	2	-6	0	0	5	0.0
Rick Tabaracci (goalie)*	19	0	0	0	10	0	0	0	0	0.0

GOALTENDING

	Games	Min.	Goals	SO	Avg.	W	L	T	Shots	Sv. Pct.
Bob Essensa	67	3855	227	2	3.53	33	26	6	2119	.893
Jim Hrivnak*	3	180	13	0	4.33	2	1	0	96	.865
Rick Tabaracci*	19	959	70	0	4.38	5	10	0	496	.859
Michael O'Neill	2	73	6	0	4.93	0	0	1	34	.824

Empty-net goals (do not count against a goaltender's average): Essensa 4.
*Played with two or more NHL teams.
‡Tied for league lead.

RESULTS

OCTOBER
6—Detroit	W	4-1
8—At San Jose	L	*3-4
10—At Los Angeles	L	3-6
12—At Vancouver	L	1-8
14—Edmonton	W	7-3
16—Vancouver	L	2-6
18—At Philadelphia	L	4-5
20—At Detroit	L	3-5
23—Los Angeles	W	4-2
26—Washington	W	6-2
28—Calgary	L	5-7
31—At Quebec	L	2-3

NOVEMBER
2—At Montreal	L	1-2
6—Edmonton	L	1-6
8—At Vancouver	L	1-6
10—Los Angeles	T	*4-4
12—At Minnesota	W	7-2
14—At St. Louis	L	2-4
17—At Tampa Bay	W	6-5
19—At Detroit	W	5-3
21—N.Y. Rangers	L	4-5
24—N.Y. Islanders	T	*3-3
27—San Jose	W	*3-2

DECEMBER
2—At Calgary	T	*3-3
5—Montreal	L	*2-3
8—At Pittsburgh	L	2-5
11—At Washington	L	6-8
12—At N.Y. Islanders	W	*4-3
15—New Jersey	W	4-3
17—At Chicago	L	1-5
19—At St. Louis	W	1-0
21—San Jose	W	5-4
23—Calgary	L	3-4
26—At Minnesota	L	4-5
27—Minnesota	W	7-4
29—Boston	W	5-4
31—Edmonton	W	3-2

JANUARY
2—At New Jersey	T	*2-2
3—At Chicago	L	1-4
5—At Calgary	W	4-2
8—Los Angeles	W	6-3
10—Pittsburgh	W	3-2
12—San Jose	W	4-1
13—At Edmonton	W	4-1
16—At Los Angeles	W	5-2
18—Hartford†	W	8-7
19—Chicago	W	5-2
22—At Calgary	T	*4-4
23—Edmonton	W	8-5
27—At N.Y. Rangers	L	2-5
28—At Boston	L	2-6
30—At Hartford	W	6-3

FEBRUARY
1—At Ottawa	T	*4-4
3—St. Louis	L	2-4
10—Buffalo	L	2-6
12—Hartford	L	2-6
14—San Jose	L	2-3
18—At San Jose	L	3-5

20—At Vancouver	L	2-4
22—Ottawa	W	6-3
23—Ottawa†	W	8-2
26—Vancouver	L	4-7
28—Minnesota	W	7-6

MARCH
2—Quebec	L	4-7
4—At Edmonton	W	5-3
6—At Toronto	L	2-4
7—At Buffalo	L	1-2
9—At Tampa Bay	W	4-2
12—Vancouver	L	2-3
14—Tampa Bay	W	3-1
16—At Los Angeles	L	4-8
18—At Vancouver	W	5-2
21—Calgary	W	4-2
23—Toronto	L	4-5
26—St. Louis	W	4-2
28—Los Angeles	T	*3-3
30—At Calgary	W	5-4

APRIL
1—At San Jose	W	9-5
3—At Edmonton	W	6-4
6—Philadelphia	L	2-4
8—Toronto	W	5-3
11—At Edmonton	W	7-5
13—Tampa Bay	L	3-5
15—Edmonton	W	3-0

*Denotes overtime game.
†At Saskatoon, Sask.

SCHEDULE

DAY BY DAY

*Denotes afternoon game.

TUESDAY, OCTOBER 5
Boston at N.Y. Rangers
Pittsburgh at Philadelphia
Detroit at Dallas
N.Y. Islanders at Calgary

WEDNESDAY, OCTOBER 6
Quebec at Ottawa
Hartford at Montreal
Tampa Bay at New Jersey
Florida at Chicago
Washington at Winnipeg
San Jose at Edmonton
Vancouver at Los Angeles

THURSDAY, OCTOBER 7
Buffalo at Boston
Montreal at Pittsburgh
Tampa Bay at N.Y. Rangers
Dallas at Toronto
Florida at St. Louis
San Jose at Calgary

FRIDAY, OCTOBER 8
New Jersey at Washington
N.Y. Islanders at Edmonton
Detroit at Anaheim

SATURDAY, OCTOBER 9
Quebec at Boston
Philadelphia at Hartford
N.Y. Rangers at Pittsburgh
Buffalo at Montreal
Washington at New Jersey
Florida at Tampa Bay
Chicago at Toronto
Ottawa at St. Louis
Winnipeg at Dallas
Calgary at Vancouver
Detroit at Los Angeles

SUNDAY, OCTOBER 10
Hartford at Buffalo
Pittsburgh at Quebec
Toronto at Philadelphia
Winnipeg at Chicago
San Jose at Los Angeles
N.Y. Islanders at Anaheim

MONDAY, OCTOBER 11
Montreal at Boston*
Washington at N.Y. Rangers
Edmonton at Vancouver*

TUESDAY, OCTOBER 12
Winnipeg at New Jersey
Buffalo at Philadelphia
Pittsburgh at Florida
Chicago at Dallas
N.Y. Islanders at Los Angeles

WEDNESDAY, OCTOBER 13
Montreal at Hartford
Quebec at N.Y. Rangers
Washington at Toronto
St. Louis at Detroit
Edmonton at Anaheim

THURSDAY, OCTOBER 14
Pittsburgh at Tampa Bay
Ottawa at Florida

Hartford at Chicago
Calgary at San Jose
Edmonton at Los Angeles

FRIDAY, OCTOBER 15
N.Y. Rangers at Buffalo
Philadelphia at Washington
Detroit at Toronto
Boston at Anaheim

SATURDAY, OCTOBER 16
Hartford at Pittsburgh
Quebec at Montreal
New Jersey at N.Y. Islanders
N.Y. Rangers at Philadelphia
Buffalo at Washington
Ottawa at Tampa Bay
Toronto at Detroit
Chicago at Winnipeg
St. Louis at Dallas
Vancouver at Edmonton
Boston at San Jose
Calgary at Los Angeles

SUNDAY, OCTOBER 17
Tampa Bay at Florida
Calgary at Anaheim

MONDAY, OCTOBER 18
Detroit at Buffalo
Montreal at Quebec
Dallas at Chicago
Edmonton at Winnipeg

TUESDAY, OCTOBER 19
Pittsburgh at N.Y. Islanders
Anaheim at N.Y. Rangers
Los Angeles at Florida
Hartford at Toronto
Boston at Vancouver
St. Louis at San Jose

WEDNESDAY, OCTOBER 20
Quebec at Hartford
Dallas at Montreal
Anaheim at New Jersey
Los Angeles at Tampa Bay
Calgary at Edmonton

THURSDAY, OCTOBER 21
Dallas at Ottawa
N.Y. Islanders at Philadelphia
Toronto at Florida
Winnipeg at Detroit
Quebec at Chicago
San Jose at St. Louis†
Vancouver at Calgary
†Game played in Sacramento, Calif.

FRIDAY, OCTOBER 22
Pittsburgh at Buffalo
Los Angeles at Washington
N.Y. Rangers at Tampa Bay
Boston at Edmonton

SATURDAY, OCTOBER 23
Buffalo at Hartford
St. Louis at Pittsburgh
Anaheim at Montreal
Dallas at Quebec
Ottawa at N.Y. Islanders

Florida at New Jersey
Winnipeg at Philadelphia
Toronto at Tampa Bay
Detroit at Chicago
Boston at Calgary
Vancouver at San Jose

SUNDAY, OCTOBER 24
Los Angeles at N.Y. Rangers
Washington at Edmonton
San Jose at Vancouver

MONDAY, OCTOBER 25
Anaheim at Ottawa
Dallas at Detroit
Washington at Calgary

TUESDAY, OCTOBER 26
Philadelphia at Quebec
Los Angeles at N.Y. Islanders
Montreal at New Jersey
Winnipeg at Florida
St. Louis at Chicago
Edmonton at San Jose

WEDNESDAY, OCTOBER 27
Philadelphia at Ottawa
Winnipeg at Tampa Bay
Los Angeles at Detroit
Hartford at Dallas
Buffalo at Calgary
Washington at Vancouver

THURSDAY, OCTOBER 28
Ottawa at Boston
Quebec at Pittsburgh
Montreal at N.Y. Rangers
N.Y. Islanders at Florida
Toronto at Chicago
Hartford at St. Louis
Anaheim at San Jose

FRIDAY, OCTOBER 29
N.Y. Islanders at Tampa Bay
Los Angeles at Winnipeg
Buffalo at Edmonton
Washington at Anaheim

SATURDAY, OCTOBER 30
St. Louis at Boston
N.Y. Rangers at Hartford
Chicago at Pittsburgh
Toronto at Montreal
Detroit at Quebec
Philadelphia at New Jersey*
Tampa Bay at Florida
Ottawa at Dallas
Edmonton at Calgary
Buffalo at Vancouver
Washington at San Jose

SUNDAY, OCTOBER 31
New Jersey at N.Y. Rangers†
Philadelphia at Chicago
Calgary at Winnipeg
San Jose at Anaheim
†Game played in Halifax, N.S.

MONDAY, NOVEMBER 1
St. Louis at Hartford
Toronto at Dallas

— 81 —

TUESDAY, NOVEMBER 2
Tampa Bay at Quebec
Vancouver at N.Y. Islanders
Philadelphia at Florida
Boston at Detroit
Pittsburgh at San Jose

WEDNESDAY, NOVEMBER 3
Calgary at Hartford
Pittsburgh at Buffalo†
Tampa Bay at Montreal
Vancouver at N.Y. Rangers
Florida at Toronto
St. Louis at Winnipeg
Ottawa at Edmonton
New Jersey at Los Angeles
Dallas at Anaheim
†Game played in Sacramento, Calif.

THURSDAY, NOVEMBER 4
Calgary at Boston
Quebec at Philadelphia
Toronto at Detroit
N.Y. Islanders at Chicago

FRIDAY, NOVEMBER 5
Vancouver at Washington
Ottawa at Winnipeg
Dallas at San Jose
New Jersey at Anaheim

SATURDAY, NOVEMBER 6
Tampa Bay at Boston
Calgary at Montreal
N.Y. Rangers at Quebec*
Hartford at N.Y. Islanders
Philadelphia at Toronto
Edmonton at St. Louis
Pittsburgh at Los Angeles

SUNDAY, NOVEMBER 7
Boston at Buffalo
Florida at Quebec*
Vancouver at Philadelphia
Edmonton at Chicago
Winnipeg at Dallas
New Jersey at San Jose*
Pittsburgh at Anaheim

MONDAY, NOVEMBER 8
Tampa Bay at N.Y. Rangers

TUESDAY, NOVEMBER 9
Winnipeg at N.Y. Islanders
Quebec at Washington
Edmonton at Detroit
Pittsburgh at St. Louis
Los Angeles at Calgary
Toronto at San Jose
Dallas at Anaheim†
†Game played in Phoenix.

WEDNESDAY, NOVEMBER 10
Ottawa at Hartford
Philadelphia at Buffalo
Florida at Montreal
Winnipeg at N.Y. Rangers
N.Y. Islanders at New Jersey
Los Angeles at Vancouver

THURSDAY, NOVEMBER 11
Edmonton at Boston*
Florida at Ottawa
New Jersey at Philadelphia
Washington at Tampa Bay
Pittsburgh at Chicago
Toronto at St. Louis
San Jose at Dallas
Anaheim at Calgary

SATURDAY, NOVEMBER 13
Edmonton at Hartford
Detroit at Pittsburgh
Ottawa at Montreal
Boston at N.Y. Islanders
San Jose at New Jersey*
Buffalo at Philadelphia*
N.Y. Rangers at Washington
Quebec at Tampa Bay
Chicago at Toronto
Dallas at Winnipeg
Vancouver at Calgary
St. Louis at Los Angeles

SUNDAY, NOVEMBER 14
San Jose at N.Y. Rangers
Quebec at Florida
Dallas at Chicago
Anaheim at Vancouver

MONDAY, NOVEMBER 15
Montreal at Ottawa
Edmonton at Toronto
Winnipeg at Calgary

TUESDAY, NOVEMBER 16
Philadelphia at Pittsburgh
San Jose at Washington
N.Y. Rangers at Florida
St. Louis at Vancouver

WEDNESDAY, NOVEMBER 17
Boston at Hartford
N.Y. Islanders at Ottawa
Edmonton at Montreal
Buffalo at New Jersey
Tampa Bay at Dallas
Detroit at Winnipeg
Toronto at Anaheim

THURSDAY, NOVEMBER 18
San Jose at Boston
Washington at Pittsburgh
New Jersey at Ottawa
N.Y. Islanders at Montreal†
Hartford at Philadelphia
Chicago at Florida
Calgary at St. Louis
Toronto at Los Angeles
†Game played in Hamilton, Ont.

FRIDAY, NOVEMBER 19
Winnipeg at Buffalo
N.Y. Rangers at Tampa Bay
Anaheim at Vancouver

SATURDAY, NOVEMBER 20
Philadelphia at Boston
San Jose at Hartford
Pittsburgh at Montreal
Winnipeg at Quebec
Detroit at New Jersey*
Chicago at Tampa Bay
Washington at Florida
Los Angeles at St. Louis
Calgary at Dallas
Toronto at Edmonton

SUNDAY, NOVEMBER 21
San Jose at Buffalo
N.Y. Islanders at Philadelphia
Detroit at St. Louis
Los Angeles at Dallas
Anaheim at Edmonton

MONDAY, NOVEMBER 22
Buffalo at Ottawa
Anaheim at Calgary
Toronto at Vancouver

TUESDAY, NOVEMBER 23
New Jersey at Quebec
Montreal at N.Y. Rangers
Hartford at Florida
Detroit at San Jose

WEDNESDAY, NOVEMBER 24
Boston at Pittsburgh
New Jersey at Buffalo
N.Y. Rangers at Ottawa
Montreal at Philadelphia
St. Louis at Washington
Hartford at Tampa Bay
N.Y. Islanders at Dallas
Anaheim at Winnipeg
Toronto at Calgary
Chicago at Edmonton
Detroit at Vancouver

THURSDAY, NOVEMBER 25
Los Angeles at Quebec

FRIDAY, NOVEMBER 26
Florida at Boston*
Ottawa at Buffalo
Tampa Bay at Philadelphia*
Pittsburgh at Washington
New Jersey at St. Louis
Vancouver at Winnipeg
Chicago at Calgary
San Jose at Anaheim*

SATURDAY, NOVEMBER 27
Florida at Hartford*
Ottawa at Pittsburgh
Los Angeles at Montreal
Buffalo at Quebec
N.Y. Rangers at N.Y. Islanders*
Philadelphia at Tampa Bay
Boston at Toronto
Dallas at Detroit*
Vancouver at Edmonton
Anaheim at San Jose*

SUNDAY, NOVEMBER 28
Detroit at N.Y. Islanders*
Washington at N.Y. Rangers
Winnipeg at St. Louis

MONDAY, NOVEMBER 29
Hartford at Ottawa
Buffalo at Toronto
Dallas at Edmonton
Chicago at Vancouver

TUESDAY, NOVEMBER 30
Boston at Quebec
Washington at N.Y. Islanders
N.Y. Rangers at New Jersey
Dallas at Calgary
Winnipeg at Los Angeles

WEDNESDAY, DECEMBER 1
Detroit at Hartford
Ottawa at Montreal
Buffalo at Tampa Bay
St. Louis at Toronto
Philadelphia at Edmonton
Winnipeg at Anaheim

THURSDAY, DECEMBER 2
N.Y. Islanders at Boston
New Jersey at Pittsburgh
Buffalo at Florida
Toronto at St. Louis
Philadelphia at Vancouver
Anaheim at Los Angeles

FRIDAY, DECEMBER 3

Quebec at N.Y. Islanders
Montreal at Washington
Ottawa at Detroit
Winnipeg at San Jose

SATURDAY, DECEMBER 4

Montreal at Boston
Pittsburgh at Hartford
Washington at Ottawa
Vancouver at Quebec
Chicago at New Jersey
N.Y. Rangers at Toronto
Dallas at St. Louis
Philadelphia at Calgary
Tampa Bay at Los Angeles

SUNDAY, DECEMBER 5

Boston at Buffalo
New Jersey at N.Y. Rangers
Edmonton at Dallas
Detroit at Winnipeg
Florida at San Jose*
Tampa Bay at Anaheim

MONDAY, DECEMBER 6

Calgary at Ottawa
Vancouver at Montreal
Winnipeg at Detroit

TUESDAY, DECEMBER 7

Calgary at Quebec
Edmonton at N.Y. Islanders
Hartford at Washington
Chicago at St. Louis
Tampa Bay at San Jose
Florida at Anaheim

WEDNESDAY, DECEMBER 8

Vancouver at Hartford
Buffalo at Ottawa
New Jersey at Montreal
Edmonton at N.Y. Rangers
Winnipeg at Toronto
Pittsburgh at Dallas
Florida at Los Angeles

THURSDAY, DECEMBER 9

Vancouver at Boston
Quebec at New Jersey
Washington at Philadelphia
St. Louis at Detroit
Ottawa at Dallas†
†Game played in Minneapolis.

FRIDAY, DECEMBER 10

Calgary at Buffalo
Florida at Winnipeg

SATURDAY, DECEMBER 11

Chicago at Boston
Buffalo at Hartford
Washington at Montreal
Ottawa at Quebec
Philadelphia at N.Y. Islanders
Edmonton at New Jersey
Pittsburgh at Tampa Bay
Calgary at Toronto
San Jose at Detroit*
St. Louis at Los Angeles

SUNDAY, DECEMBER 12

Hartford at Boston
Edmonton at Philadelphia
San Jose at Chicago
Florida at Dallas
Toronto at Winnipeg
St. Louis at Anaheim

MONDAY, DECEMBER 13

Los Angeles at Ottawa
Washington at Quebec
Buffalo at N.Y. Rangers

TUESDAY, DECEMBER 14

Los Angeles at Pittsburgh
New Jersey at N.Y. Islanders
Montreal at Tampa Bay†
Anaheim at Detroit
Vancouver at Calgary
†Game played in Orlando, Fla.

WEDNESDAY, DECEMBER 15

Hartford at N.Y. Rangers
Boston at New Jersey
Ottawa at Tampa Bay
Montreal at Florida
Anaheim at Toronto
Chicago at Dallas
Vancouver at Edmonton
St. Louis at San Jose

THURSDAY, DECEMBER 16

Buffalo at Pittsburgh
Quebec at Philadelphia

FRIDAY, DECEMBER 17

Los Angeles at Buffalo
Toronto at N.Y. Islanders
Ottawa at Washington
N.Y. Rangers at Detroit
Anaheim at Dallas
St. Louis at Calgary
San Jose at Edmonton
Winnipeg at Vancouver

SATURDAY, DECEMBER 18

Washington at Hartford
Detroit at Montreal
New Jersey at Quebec*
Chicago at Philadelphia*
Boston at Tampa Bay
Los Angeles at Toronto
Winnipeg at Calgary

SUNDAY, DECEMBER 19

N.Y. Islanders at Pittsburgh
Tampa Bay at Buffalo
San Jose at Quebec*
Ottawa at N.Y. Rangers
Philadelphia at New Jersey
Boston at Florida
Anaheim at Chicago
St. Louis at Edmonton
Dallas at Vancouver*

MONDAY, DECEMBER 20

Anaheim at Winnipeg
Los Angeles at Calgary

TUESDAY, DECEMBER 21

Tampa Bay at Pittsburgh
Quebec at Ottawa
Washington at Philadelphia
Chicago at Detroit
Edmonton at Vancouver

WEDNESDAY, DECEMBER 22

New Jersey at Hartford
N.Y. Islanders at Montreal
N.Y. Rangers at Florida
San Jose at Toronto
Calgary at Edmonton
Dallas at Anaheim

THURSDAY, DECEMBER 23

Pittsburgh at Boston
Montreal at Buffalo
Hartford at Ottawa

Toronto at New Jersey
Detroit at Philadelphia
N.Y. Rangers at Washington
San Jose at Chicago
Tampa Bay at St. Louis
Quebec at Winnipeg
Calgary at Vancouver†
Dallas at Los Angeles
†Game played in Saskatoon, Sask.

SUNDAY, DECEMBER 26

Ottawa at Hartford
Buffalo at N.Y. Islanders
New Jersey at N.Y. Rangers
Pittsburgh at Washington
Florida at Tampa Bay†
Chicago at St. Louis
Los Angeles at Anaheim
†Game played in Orlando, Fla.

MONDAY, DECEMBER 27

Philadelphia at Buffalo
Boston at Ottawa
Toronto at Chicago
Montreal at St. Louis
Detroit at Dallas
Winnipeg at Edmonton

TUESDAY, DECEMBER 28

Philadelphia at Pittsburgh
Tampa Bay at Quebec
Anaheim at N.Y. Islanders
Hartford at New Jersey
Florida at Washington
Calgary at San Jose
Vancouver at Los Angeles

WEDNESDAY, DECEMBER 29

N.Y. Islanders at Quebec
Florida at Hartford
N.Y. Rangers at St. Louis
Toronto at Dallas
Chicago at Winnipeg
Montreal at Edmonton

THURSDAY, DECEMBER 30

Tampa Bay at Ottawa
Anaheim at Washington
Edmonton at Calgary

FRIDAY, DECEMBER 31

Philadelphia at Boston†
Quebec at Pittsburgh
N.Y. Rangers at Buffalo
Los Angeles at Detroit
Dallas at Chicago
St. Louis at Winnipeg*
Montreal at Calgary
San Jose at Vancouver
†Game played in Minneapolis.

SATURDAY, JANUARY 1

New Jersey at Ottawa
Hartford at N.Y. Islanders*
Tampa Bay at Washington*
Anaheim at Florida*
Los Angeles at Toronto

SUNDAY, JANUARY 2

Washington at Boston*
Pittsburgh at Hartford
Toronto at Buffalo
Anaheim at Tampa Bay†
Winnipeg at Chicago
Calgary at St. Louis
Quebec at Dallas
San Jose at Edmonton*
Montreal at Vancouver*
†Game played in Orlando, Fla.

MONDAY, JANUARY 3
Pittsburgh at Ottawa
Florida at N.Y. Rangers

TUESDAY, JANUARY 4
N.Y. Islanders at New Jersey
Tampa Bay at Toronto†
Detroit at St. Louis
Chicago at Dallas
Montreal at San Jose
Quebec at Los Angeles
†Game played in Hamilton, Ont.

WEDNESDAY, JANUARY 5
Winnipeg at Hartford
Vancouver at Ottawa
Montreal at Quebec†
Calgary at N.Y. Rangers
†Game played in Phoenix.

THURSDAY, JANUARY 6
Winnipeg at Boston
St. Louis at Hartford†
Ottawa at Toronto
Anaheim at Chicago
Philadelphia at Dallas
Detroit at San Jose
†Game played in Cleveland.

FRIDAY, JANUARY 7
Pittsburgh at Buffalo
Calgary at N.Y. Islanders
Florida at New Jersey
Quebec at Edmonton

SATURDAY, JANUARY 8
Florida at Boston
N.Y. Islanders at Hartford
Calgary at Pittsburgh
Winnipeg at Ottawa
N.Y. Rangers at Montreal
Chicago at Washington*
Philadelphia at Tampa Bay
Vancouver at Toronto
Anaheim at St. Louis
Detroit at Los Angeles

SUNDAY, JANUARY 9
Vancouver at Buffalo
Washington at New Jersey
Edmonton at Chicago
St. Louis at Dallas

MONDAY, JANUARY 10
Toronto at Boston
N.Y. Islanders at Ottawa
Winnipeg at Montreal
Tampa Bay at N.Y. Rangers
Detroit at Anaheim

TUESDAY, JANUARY 11
Boston at Pittsburgh
Ottawa at Philadelphia
Toronto at Washington
Buffalo at Chicago
Edmonton at Dallas
Quebec at Calgary
Los Angeles at San Jose

WEDNESDAY, JANUARY 12
New Jersey at Montreal
Tampa Bay at Detroit
Buffalo at Winnipeg
Quebec at Vancouver
Hartford at Los Angeles
San Jose at Anaheim

THURSDAY, JANUARY 13
Florida at Pittsburgh

Boston at Philadelphia
Dallas at Toronto
Tampa Bay at Chicago
Edmonton at St. Louis

FRIDAY, JANUARY 14
Montreal at N.Y. Islanders
Philadelphia at N.Y. Rangers
New Jersey at Washington
Dallas at Detroit
Ottawa at Vancouver
Hartford at Anaheim

SATURDAY, JANUARY 15
Detroit at Boston
Edmonton at Pittsburgh*
Florida at Montreal
Washington at Quebec
Chicago at N.Y. Islanders
Los Angeles at New Jersey
Buffalo at St. Louis
Toronto at Winnipeg
Ottawa at Calgary
Hartford at San Jose

SUNDAY, JANUARY 16
Los Angeles at Philadelphia
N.Y. Rangers at Chicago
Buffalo at Dallas
Tampa Bay at Winnipeg
Vancouver at Anaheim

MONDAY, JANUARY 17
Hartford at Boston*
Washington at Montreal
Florida at N.Y. Islanders*
Detroit at Tampa Bay†
Calgary at San Jose*
†Game played in Minneapolis.

TUESDAY, JANUARY 18
Edmonton at Ottawa
Pittsburgh at Quebec
St. Louis at N.Y. Rangers
Anaheim at Toronto
Los Angeles at Dallas

WEDNESDAY, JANUARY 19
Toronto at Hartford
Edmonton at Buffalo
Boston at Montreal
St. Louis at Philadelphia
N.Y. Islanders at Tampa Bay
Washington at Florida
Anaheim at Detroit
New Jersey at Winnipeg
Calgary at Vancouver

SATURDAY, JANUARY 22
All-Star Game at Madison Square
Garden, N.Y.

MONDAY, JANUARY 24
Boston at Hartford
Buffalo at Tampa Bay†
Montreal at Florida
New Jersey at Dallas
Los Angeles at Calgary‡
Vancouver at Edmonton§
St. Louis at Anaheim
†Game played in Orlando, Fla.
‡Game played in Phoenix.
§Game played in Saskatoon, Sask.

TUESDAY, JANUARY 25
Ottawa at Pittsburgh
Philadelphia at Quebec
Boston at Washington
Chicago at Detroit

St. Louis at Vancouver
N.Y. Rangers at San Jose
Winnipeg at Los Angeles

WEDNESDAY, JANUARY 26
Montreal at Hartford
Florida at Tampa Bay
N.Y. Islanders at Toronto
Dallas at Calgary
New Jersey at Edmonton
Winnipeg at Anaheim

THURSDAY, JANUARY 27
Quebec at Pittsburgh
Washington at Buffalo
Hartford at Ottawa
Detroit at Chicago
Dallas at Vancouver
N.Y. Rangers at Los Angeles

FRIDAY, JANUARY 28
Boston at N.Y. Islanders
San Jose at Florida
New Jersey at Calgary
St. Louis at Edmonton
N.Y. Rangers at Anaheim

SATURDAY, JANUARY 29
N.Y. Islanders at Boston
Quebec at Hartford*
Buffalo at Montreal*
Washington at Philadelphia*
San Jose at Tampa Bay
Pittsburgh at Toronto
Winnipeg at Detroit*
Ottawa at Chicago
St. Louis at Calgary
Dallas at Edmonton
New Jersey at Vancouver
Anaheim at Los Angeles

SUNDAY, JANUARY 30
Florida at Buffalo*
Philadelphia at Montreal*
Detroit at Washington*

MONDAY, JANUARY 31
Quebec at Boston
Chicago at Ottawa
Pittsburgh at N.Y. Rangers
Los Angeles at Vancouver

TUESDAY, FEBRUARY 1
Florida at Pittsburgh
Hartford at Quebec
San Jose at N.Y. Islanders
Toronto at St. Louis

WEDNESDAY, FEBRUARY 2
Florida at Ottawa
Hartford at Montreal
N.Y. Islanders at N.Y. Rangers
Buffalo at New Jersey
Washington at Philadelphia†
Detroit at Tampa Bay
Dallas at Winnipeg
Los Angeles at Edmonton
Chicago at Vancouver
Calgary at Anaheim
†Game played in Cleveland.

THURSDAY, FEBRUARY 3
N.Y. Rangers at Boston
San Jose at Philadelphia
Quebec at St. Louis

FRIDAY, FEBRUARY 4
Ottawa at New Jersey
Montreal at Washington

Buffalo at Florida
Pittsburgh at Detroit
Hartford at Winnipeg
Chicago at Edmonton
Vancouver at Anaheim

SATURDAY, FEBRUARY 5

Philadelphia at Boston*
Montreal at Ottawa
N.Y. Islanders at Quebec*
Pittsburgh at New Jersey
Tampa Bay at Washington
Detroit at Toronto
San Jose at St. Louis
Calgary at Los Angeles

SUNDAY, FEBRUARY 6

N.Y. Islanders at Buffalo
Boston at Florida
San Jose at Dallas
Winnipeg at Edmonton*
Hartford at Vancouver*
Chicago at Anaheim*

MONDAY, FEBRUARY 7

Montreal at Pittsburgh
Washington at N.Y. Rangers
Tampa Bay at Toronto
Edmonton at Calgary

TUESDAY, FEBRUARY 8

Philadelphia at Ottawa
Boston at Quebec
Buffalo at N.Y. Islanders
Vancouver at Detroit
Winnipeg at St. Louis
Chicago at San Jose†
†Game played in Sacramento, Calif.

WEDNESDAY, FEBRUARY 9

N.Y. Rangers at Montreal
Winnipeg at Dallas
Calgary at Edmonton
Chicago at Los Angeles

THURSDAY, FEBRUARY 10

Buffalo at Boston
N.Y. Islanders at Pittsburgh
Tampa Bay at Ottawa
Vancouver at New Jersey
Florida at Philadelphia
Washington at St. Louis

FRIDAY, FEBRUARY 11

Montreal at Buffalo
Quebec at N.Y. Rangers
Philadelphia at Detroit
Toronto at Winnipeg
Hartford at Calgary
Chicago at San Jose
Los Angeles at Anaheim

SATURDAY, FEBRUARY 12

New Jersey at Boston*
Dallas at Pittsburgh*
N.Y. Rangers at Ottawa
Quebec at Montreal
Florida at N.Y. Islanders
Vancouver at Tampa Bay
Detroit at St. Louis
Toronto at Calgary
Hartford at Edmonton
Washington at Los Angeles

SUNDAY, FEBRUARY 13

Dallas at Buffalo*
Pittsburgh at Philadelphia*
New Jersey at Tampa Bay
Vancouver at Florida

Anaheim at Edmonton*
Chicago at San Jose*

MONDAY, FEBRUARY 14

N.Y. Rangers at Quebec
Chicago at Calgary
Boston at Los Angeles

TUESDAY, FEBRUARY 15

Winnipeg at Pittsburgh
Tampa Bay at N.Y. Islanders
Edmonton at Washington
Detroit at Toronto
Vancouver at St. Louis
Philadelphia at San Jose

WEDNESDAY, FEBRUARY 16

Buffalo at Hartford
Florida at Detroit
Boston at Dallas
Philadelphia at Anaheim

THURSDAY, FEBRUARY 17

Hartford at Pittsburgh
Montreal at Tampa Bay
New Jersey at Toronto
Vancouver at Chicago
Quebec at San Jose

FRIDAY, FEBRUARY 18

Florida at Buffalo
Ottawa at N.Y. Rangers
N.Y. Islanders at Washington
Edmonton at Detroit
Boston at St. Louis
Calgary at Dallas
Chicago at Winnipeg
Philadelphia at Los Angeles
Quebec at Anaheim

SATURDAY, FEBRUARY 19

N.Y. Rangers at Hartford
Pittsburgh at Montreal
Ottawa at N.Y. Islanders
Tampa Bay at New Jersey*
Edmonton at Toronto
Los Angeles at San Jose

SUNDAY, FEBRUARY 20

Buffalo at Washington*
Boston at Tampa Bay
Detroit at Florida
New Jersey at Chicago*
Anaheim at St. Louis
Calgary at Winnipeg*

MONDAY, FEBRUARY 21

Quebec at Buffalo
Washington at N.Y. Islanders*
Pittsburgh at N.Y. Rangers*
Montreal at Philadelphia*
Dallas at San Jose*
Toronto at Los Angeles*

TUESDAY, FEBRUARY 22

Florida at Winnipeg†
Calgary at Vancouver
†Game played in Hamilton, Ont.

WEDNESDAY, FEBRUARY 23

Anaheim at Buffalo
San Jose at Montreal
Boston at N.Y. Rangers
New Jersey at Detroit
Toronto at Edmonton
Dallas at Los Angeles

THURSDAY, FEBRUARY 24

Anaheim at Pittsburgh

San Jose at Ottawa
St. Louis at Quebec
N.Y. Rangers at New Jersey
N.Y. Islanders at Philadelphia
Washington at Florida
Hartford at Detroit†
Winnipeg at Chicago
Tampa Bay at Calgary
†Game played in Cleveland.

FRIDAY, FEBRUARY 25

Chicago at Buffalo
Philadelphia at N.Y. Islanders
Boston at Winnipeg
Los Angeles at Edmonton

SATURDAY, FEBRUARY 26

New Jersey at Hartford*
Buffalo at Pittsburgh
St. Louis at Ottawa
Anaheim at Quebec
Florida at Washington
Montreal at Toronto
San Jose at Detroit*
N.Y. Rangers at Dallas
Los Angeles at Calgary
Tampa Bay at Vancouver

SUNDAY, FEBRUARY 27

Washington at Hartford
Quebec at N.Y. Islanders
Boston at Chicago*
Tampa Bay at Edmonton

MONDAY, FEBRUARY 28

Toronto at Ottawa
St. Louis at New Jersey
Pittsburgh at Florida
San Jose at Winnipeg
Montreal at Los Angeles

TUESDAY, MARCH 1

Buffalo at Quebec
St. Louis at N.Y. Islanders
Tampa Bay at Washington
Calgary at Detroit
Edmonton at Vancouver

WEDNESDAY, MARCH 2

Los Angeles at Hartford
Buffalo at Ottawa
Philadelphia at N.Y. Rangers
New Jersey at Florida
Dallas at Winnipeg
Montreal at Anaheim

THURSDAY, MARCH 3

Los Angeles at Boston
New Jersey at Tampa Bay
Calgary at Chicago
Vancouver at St. Louis
Edmonton at San Jose

FRIDAY, MARCH 4

Pittsburgh at Buffalo
Winnipeg at Ottawa†
N.Y. Islanders at N.Y. Rangers
Philadelphia at Washington
Hartford at Florida
Toronto at Detroit
Vancouver at Dallas
Edmonton at Anaheim
†Game played in Minneapolis.

SATURDAY, MARCH 5

Ottawa at Boston
Toronto at Quebec
N.Y. Rangers at N.Y. Islanders
Calgary at New Jersey*

— 85 —

Hartford at Tampa Bay

SUNDAY, MARCH 6

Calgary at Washington*
Philadelphia at Tampa Bay
Buffalo at Detroit
Los Angeles at Chicago*
Montreal at Dallas
Pittsburgh at Winnipeg*
Anaheim at San Jose*

MONDAY, MARCH 7

Washington at Boston
Detroit at N.Y. Rangers
Quebec at New Jersey
St. Louis at Toronto
N.Y. Islanders at Winnipeg
Florida at Vancouver

TUESDAY, MARCH 8

Boston at Pittsburgh
Ottawa at Quebec
Dallas at Philadelphia
Anaheim at Chicago†
Buffalo at San Jose
†Game played in Phoenix.

WEDNESDAY, MARCH 9

Tampa Bay at Hartford
St. Louis at Montreal
N.Y. Rangers at Washington†
Dallas at Toronto
Detroit at Calgary
Florida at Edmonton
N.Y. Islanders at Vancouver
Chicago at Los Angeles
Buffalo at Anaheim
†Game played in Halifax, N.S.

THURSDAY, MARCH 10

N.Y. Rangers at Boston
Toronto at Pittsburgh
Montreal at Quebec
Hartford at New Jersey
Ottawa at Philadelphia
N.Y. Islanders at San Jose

FRIDAY, MARCH 11

Vancouver at Winnipeg
Florida at Calgary
Detroit at Edmonton
Chicago at Anaheim

SATURDAY, MARCH 12

Dallas at Hartford*
N.Y. Rangers at Pittsburgh*
Philadelphia at Montreal
Boston at New Jersey*
Quebec at Washington
Winnipeg at Toronto
N.Y. Islanders at St. Louis
San Jose at Calgary
Buffalo at Los Angeles

SUNDAY, MARCH 13

Pittsburgh at Hartford*
Dallas at New Jersey
Tampa Bay at Philadelphia
Vancouver at Chicago*
Ottawa at Anaheim*

MONDAY, MARCH 14

Boston at Montreal
Chicago at Quebec
N.Y. Rangers at Florida

TUESDAY, MARCH 15

Washington at Pittsburgh

New Jersey at N.Y. Islanders
Calgary at Tampa Bay
Vancouver at Detroit
Ottawa at Los Angeles

WEDNESDAY, MARCH 16

Chicago at Montreal
Hartford at N.Y. Rangers
Edmonton at Tampa Bay
Calgary at Florida
Vancouver at Toronto
St. Louis at Winnipeg
Los Angeles at Anaheim

THURSDAY, MARCH 17

Pittsburgh at Boston
New Jersey at Buffalo
Hartford at Quebec
N.Y. Islanders at Detroit
Ottawa at San Jose

FRIDAY, MARCH 18

Buffalo at N.Y. Islanders†
Chicago at N.Y. Rangers
Edmonton at Florida
St. Louis at Toronto
Washington at Dallas
†Game played in Minneapolis.

SATURDAY, MARCH 19

New Jersey at Boston*
Vancouver at Pittsburgh*
Quebec at Montreal
Hartford at Philadelphia*
Detroit at Winnipeg
San Jose at Los Angeles*

SUNDAY, MARCH 20

Ottawa at Buffalo*
Edmonton at Quebec
Pittsburgh at N.Y. Islanders
Washington at Tampa Bay†
Philadelphia at Florida
Calgary at Toronto*
St. Louis at Chicago*
Vancouver at Dallas
Los Angeles at San Jose*
†Game played in Orlando, Fla.

MONDAY, MARCH 21

New Jersey at Florida

TUESDAY, MARCH 22

San Jose at Pittsburgh
Boston at Quebec
Tampa Bay at N.Y. Islanders
Hartford at Washington
Chicago at Detroit
Philadelphia at St. Louis
Anaheim at Dallas
N.Y. Rangers at Calgary

WEDNESDAY, MARCH 23

St. Louis at Buffalo
Detroit at Ottawa
Toronto at Florida†
Montreal at Winnipeg
N.Y. Rangers at Edmonton
Vancouver at Los Angeles
†Game played in Hamilton, Ont.

THURSDAY, MARCH 24

Anaheim at Boston
Ottawa at Pittsburgh
Tampa Bay at New Jersey
Florida at Philadelphia
San Jose at Toronto
Montreal at Chicago

FRIDAY, MARCH 25

Hartford at Buffalo
Washington at Detroit
Dallas at St. Louis
San Jose at Winnipeg
Los Angeles at Edmonton
N.Y. Rangers at Vancouver

SATURDAY, MARCH 26

Montreal at Boston*
Anaheim at Hartford
Florida at N.Y. Islanders*
Philadelphia at New Jersey*
Quebec at Toronto
Pittsburgh at Calgary

SUNDAY, MARCH 27

N.Y. Islanders at Buffalo*
Quebec at New Jersey†
Anaheim at Philadelphia
Boston at Washington*
Dallas at Tampa Bay*
Detroit at Chicago*
San Jose at St. Louis
N.Y. Rangers at Winnipeg*
Pittsburgh at Edmonton
Los Angeles at Vancouver*
†Game played in Minneapolis.

MONDAY, MARCH 28

Ottawa at Montreal
Dallas at Florida
Toronto at Vancouver

TUESDAY, MARCH 29

Montreal at New Jersey
N.Y. Rangers at Philadelphia
N.Y. Islanders at Washington
Hartford at Detroit
Winnipeg at San Jose

WEDNESDAY, MARCH 30

Chicago at Hartford
Tampa Bay at Buffalo
Quebec at Ottawa
St. Louis at Florida
Pittsburgh at Vancouver
Anaheim at Los Angeles

THURSDAY, MARCH 31

Dallas at Boston
Calgary at Philadelphia
Quebec at Detroit
Washington at Chicago
Toronto at San Jose
Edmonton at Anaheim

FRIDAY, APRIL 1

Boston at Buffalo
Montreal at N.Y. Islanders
Dallas at N.Y. Rangers
New Jersey at Washington
St. Louis at Tampa Bay
Winnipeg at Vancouver*

SATURDAY, APRIL 2

Philadelphia at Hartford
N.Y. Islanders at Montreal
Buffalo at Quebec
N.Y. Rangers at New Jersey
Ottawa at Florida
Calgary at Detroit*
Vancouver at San Jose
Edmonton at Los Angeles*
Toronto at Anaheim*

SUNDAY, APRIL 3

Boston at Pittsburgh*†

Dallas at Washington*
St. Louis at Detroit*
Calgary at Chicago
Edmonton at Los Angeles*‡
†Game played in Cleveland.
‡Game played in Sacramento, Calif.

MONDAY, APRIL 4

Tampa Bay at Pittsburgh
Florida at N.Y. Rangers
Philadelphia at Winnipeg

TUESDAY, APRIL 5

Florida at Quebec
N.Y. Islanders at Washington
Chicago at St. Louis
Toronto at Dallas
Detroit at Vancouver
San Jose at Los Angeles

WEDNESDAY, APRIL 6

N.Y. Islanders at Hartford
New Jersey at Pittsburgh
Washington at Ottawa
Tampa Bay at Montreal
Edmonton at Winnipeg
Anaheim at Calgary

THURSDAY, APRIL 7

Ottawa at Boston
Hartford at Quebec
Florida at Philadelphia

Los Angeles at St. Louis
San Jose at Vancouver

FRIDAY, APRIL 8

Montreal at Buffalo
Dallas at N.Y. Islanders
Toronto at N.Y. Rangers
Pittsburgh at New Jersey
St. Louis at Chicago
San Jose at Calgary
Anaheim at Edmonton

SATURDAY, APRIL 9

Tampa Bay at Boston*
Pittsburgh at Montreal
Ottawa at Washington
Los Angeles at Winnipeg*
Detroit at Calgary
Anaheim at Vancouver

SUNDAY, APRIL 10

Tampa Bay at Hartford*
Quebec at Buffalo*
N.Y. Rangers at N.Y. Islanders*
Boston at Philadelphia*
New Jersey at Florida
Winnipeg at Toronto
Los Angeles at Chicago*
Dallas at St. Louis*
Detroit at Edmonton
Vancouver at San Jose

MONDAY, APRIL 11

Montreal at Hartford
Pittsburgh at Ottawa
Calgary at Anaheim

TUESDAY, APRIL 12

Buffalo at N.Y. Rangers
New Jersey at Philadelphia
Winnipeg at Washington
Quebec at Florida
Chicago at Toronto
St. Louis at Dallas

WEDNESDAY, APRIL 13

Boston at Ottawa
N.Y. Islanders at Tampa Bay
Montreal at Detroit
Edmonton at San Jose
Calgary at Los Angeles
Vancouver at Anaheim

THURSDAY, APRIL 14

Hartford at Boston
Washington at Buffalo
Philadelphia at N.Y. Rangers
Ottawa at New Jersey
Quebec at Tampa Bay
N.Y. Islanders at Florida
Toronto at Chicago
Winnipeg at St. Louis
Detroit at Dallas
Edmonton at Los Angeles

1992-93 NHL REVIEW

Regular season

Stanley Cup playoffs

All-Star Game

Awards

Player drafts

REGULAR SEASON

FINAL STANDINGS

CLARENCE CAMPBELL CONFERENCE

JAMES NORRIS DIVISION

	G	W	L	T	Pts.	GF	GA	Home	Away	Div. Rec.
Chicago Blackhawks	84	47	25	12	106	279	230	25-11- 6	22-14- 6	22-11- 4
Detroit Red Wings	84	47	28	9	103	369	280	25-14- 3	22-14- 6	22-12- 3
Toronto Maple Leafs	84	44	29	11	99	288	241	25-11- 6	19-18- 5	18-13- 6
St. Louis Blues	84	37	36	11	85	282	278	22-13- 7	15-23- 4	15-15- 7
Minnesota North Stars	84	36	38	10	82	272	293	18-17- 7	18-21- 3	13-20- 4
Tampa Bay Lightning	84	23	54	7	53	245	332	12-27- 3	11-27- 4	7-26- 4

CONN SMYTHE DIVISION

	G	W	L	T	Pts.	GF	GA	Home	Away	Div. Rec.
Vancouver Canucks	84	46	29	9	101	346	278	27-11- 4	19-18- 5	25-10- 2
Calgary Flames	84	43	30	11	97	322	282	23-14- 5	20-16- 6	24- 9- 4
Los Angeles Kings	84	39	35	10	88	338	340	22-15- 5	17-20- 5	17-16- 4
Winnipeg Jets	84	40	37	7	87	322	320	23-16- 3	17-21- 4	19-14- 4
Edmonton Oilers	84	26	50	8	60	242	337	16-21- 5	10-29- 3	10-26- 1
San Jose Sharks	84	11	71	2	24	218	414	8-33- 1	3-38- 1	8-28- 1

PRINCE OF WALES CONFERENCE

CHARLES F. ADAMS DIVISION

	G	W	L	T	Pts.	GF	GA	Home	Away	Div. Rec.
Boston Bruins	84	51	26	7	109	332	268	29-10- 3	22-16- 4	27- 9- 1
Quebec Nordiques	84	47	27	10	104	351	300	23-17- 2	24-10- 8	20-14- 3
Montreal Canadiens	84	48	30	6	102	326	280	27-13- 2	21-17- 4	23-14- 0
Buffalo Sabres	84	38	36	10	86	335	297	25-15- 2	13-21- 8	18-15- 4
Hartford Whalers	84	26	52	6	58	284	369	12-25- 5	14-27- 1	13-21- 3
Ottawa Senators	84	10	70	4	24	202	395	9-29- 4	1-41- 0	4-32- 1

LESTER PATRICK DIVISION

	G	W	L	T	Pts.	GF	GA	Home	Away	Div. Rec.
Pittsburgh Penguins	84	56	21	7	119	367	268	32- 6- 4	24-15- 3	25- 9- 3
Washington Capitals	84	43	34	7	93	325	286	21-15- 6	22-19- 1	13-22- 2
New York Islanders	84	40	37	7	87	335	297	20-19- 3	20-18- 4	22-14- 1
New Jersey Devils	84	40	37	7	87	308	299	24-14- 4	16-23- 3	18-17- 2
Philadelphia Flyers	84	36	37	11	83	319	319	23-14- 5	13-23- 6	14-20- 3
New York Rangers	84	34	39	11	79	304	308	20-17- 5	14-22- 6	12-22- 3

INDIVIDUAL LEADERS

SCORING

TOP SCORERS

	Games	G	A	Pts.	Pen.	+/-	PPG	SHG	Shots	Shooting Pct.
Mario Lemieux, Pittsburgh	60	69	91	*160	38	*55	16	6	286	24.1
Pat Lafontaine, Buffalo	84	53	95	148	63	11	20	2	306	17.3
Adam Oates, Boston	84	45	*97	142	32	15	24	1	254	17.7
Steve Yzerman, Detroit	84	58	79	137	44	33	13	†7	307	18.9
Teemu Selanne, Winnipeg	84	†76	56	132	45	8	24	0	387	19.6
Pierre Turgeon, N.Y. Islanders	83	58	74	132	26	-1	24	0	301	19.3
Alexander Mogilny, Buffalo	77	†76	51	127	40	7	27	0	360	21.1
Doug Gilmour, Toronto	83	32	95	127	100	32	15	3	211	15.2
Luc Robitaille, Los Angeles	84	63	62	125	100	18	24	2	265	23.8
Mark Recchi, Philadelphia	84	53	70	123	95	1	15	4	274	19.3
Mats Sundin, Quebec	80	47	67	114	96	21	13	4	215	21.9
Kevin Stevens, Pittsburgh	72	55	56	111	177	17	26	0	326	16.9
Pavel Bure, Vancouver	83	60	50	110	69	35	13	†7	*407	14.7
Rick Tocchet, Pittsburgh	80	48	61	109	252	28	20	4	240	20.0
Jeremy Roenick, Chicago	84	50	57	107	86	15	22	3	255	19.6
Craig Janney, St. Louis	84	24	82	106	12	-4	8	0	137	17.5
Joe Sakic, Quebec	78	48	57	105	40	-3	20	2	264	18.2
Joe Juneau, Boston	84	32	70	102	33	23	9	0	229	14.0
Brett Hull, St. Louis	80	54	47	101	41	-27	29	0	390	13.8
Theoren Fleury, Calgary	83	34	66	100	88	14	12	2	250	13.6
Ron Francis, Pittsburgh	84	24	76	100	68	6	9	2	215	11.2

The scoring leader is awarded the Art Ross Memorial Trophy.
*Indicates league-leading figure.
†Indicates league-tying figure.

Games
Jimmy Carson, Detroit/Los Angeles.... 86
Many tied with 84

Points
Mario Lemieux, Pittsburgh 160
Pat LaFontaine, Buffalo 148
Adam Oates, Boston 142
Steve Yzerman, Detroit 137
Teemu Selanne, Winnipeg 132
Pierre Turgeon, N.Y. Islanders......... 132
Alexander Mogilny, Buffalo 127
Doug Gilmour, Toronto 127
Luc Robitaille, Los Angeles 125
Mark Recchi, Philadelphia 123

Points by a defenseman
Phil Housley, Winnipeg 97
Paul Coffey, Los Angeles/Detroit...... 87
Larry Murphy, Pittsburgh.................85
Steve Duchesne, Quebec...................82
Ray Bourque, Boston..........................82

Goals
Alexander Mogilny, Buffalo 76
Teemu Selanne, Winnipeg..................76
Mario Lemieux, Pittsburgh 69
Luc Robitaille, Los Angeles................63
Pavel Bure, Vancouver......................60
Pierre Turgeon, N.Y. Islanders...........58
Steve Yzerman, Detroit......................58
Kevin Stevens, Pittsburgh 55
Brett Hull, St. Louis 54
Dave Andreychuk, Buffalo/Toronto.. 54

Assists
Adam Oates, Boston 97
Doug Gilmour, Toronto 95
Pat LaFontaine, Buffalo....................95
Mario Lemieux, Pittsburgh 91
Craig Janney, St. Louis.....................82
Dale Hawerchuk, Buffalo 80
Phil Housley, Winnipeg 79
Steve Yzerman, Detroit......................79
Ron Francis, Pittsburgh....................76
Paul Coffey, Los Angeles/Detroit......75

Power-play goals
Dave Andreychuk, Buffalo/Toronto.. 32
Brett Hull, St. Louis 29
Alexander Mogilny, Buffalo 27
Kevin Stevens, Pittsburgh 26
Pierre Turgeon, N.Y. Islanders...........24
Adam Oates, Boston 24
Luc Robitaille, Los Angeles................24
Teemu Selanne, Winnipeg..................24

Shorthanded goals
Pavel Bure, Vancouver........................7
Steve Yzerman, Detroit 7
Mario Lemieux, Pittsburgh 6
Scott Young, Quebec...........................6
Dave Reid, Boston 5
Dave Poulin, Boston 5

First goals
Jeremy Roenick, Chicago.................... 12
Mario Lemieux, Pittsburgh 11
Mark Recchi, Philadelphia 11
Brendan Shanahan, St. Louis 10
Brett Hull, St. Louis 10
Dave Andreychuk, Buffalo/Toronto.. 10

Game-winning goals
Alexander Mogilny, Buffalo 11
Geoff Courtnall, Vancouver 11
Adam Oates, Boston 11
Mario Lemieux, Pittsburgh 10
Mike Ricci, Quebec 10
Pierre Turgeon, N.Y. Islanders........... 10

Game-tying goals
Martin Rucinsky, Quebec.....................3
Jeremy Roenick, Chicago....................3
Many tied with 2

Shots
Pavel Bure, Vancouver.....................407
Brett Hull, St. Louis 390
Teemu Selanne, Winnipeg................387
Alexander Mogilny, Buffalo 360
Ray Bourque, Boston........................330

Shooting percentage
(84 shots minimum)
Craig Simpson, Edmonton...............26.4
Petr Nedved, Vancouver...................25.5
Dimitri Khristich, Washington.........24.4
Mario Lemieux, Pittsburgh.............24.1
Luc Robitaille, Los Angeles.............23.8

Plus/minus
Mario Lemieux, Pittsburgh 55
Larry Murphy, Pittsburgh.................45
Ray Bourque, Boston.........................38
Ulf Samuelsson, Pittsburgh 36
Lyle Odelein, Montreal 35
Pavel Bure, Vancouver......................35

Penalty minutes
Marty McSorley, Los Angeles...........399
Gino Odjick, Vancouver....................370

(continued top right column)
Tie Domi, N.Y. Rangers/Winnipeg .. 344
Nick Kypreos, Hartford 325
Mike Peluso, Ottawa 318
Warren Rychel, Los Angeles............314
Bryan Marchment, Chicago.............313
Bob Probert, Detroit 292
Shane Churla, Minnesota.................286
Chris Chelios, Chicago 282

Consecutive-game point streaks
Mats Sundin, Quebec 30
Adam Oates, Boston 21
Mark Recchi, Philadelphia 17
Teemu Selanne, Winnipeg................. 17
Dave Andreychuk, Buffalo.................17

Consecutive-game goal streaks
Mario Lemieux, Pittsburgh 12
Mario Lemieux, Pittsburgh 11
Luc Robitaille, Los Angeles............... 10

Consecutive-game assist streaks
Adam Oates, Boston 18
Phil Housley, Winnipeg 14
Dino Ciccarelli, Detroit.....................11
Ray Bourque, Boston......................... 10
Alexei Zhamnov, Winnipeg 10

Most games scoring three or more goals
Alexander Mogilny, Buffalo 7
Teemu Selanne, Winnipeg...................5
Mario Lemieux, Pittsburgh 4
Pierre Turgeon, N.Y. Islanders............4
Many tied with 3

Points by a rookie
Teemu Selanne, Winnipeg................ 132
Joe Juneau, Boston 102
Eric Lindros, Philadelphia.................75
Alexei Zhamnov, Winnipeg 72
Andrei Kovalenko, Quebec 68

Goals by a rookie
Teemu Selanne, Winnipeg...................76
Eric Lindros, Philadelphia..................41
Joe Juneau, Boston 32
Evgeny Davydov, Winnipeg.................28
Shawn McEachern, Pittsburgh..........28
Keith Tkachuk, Winnipeg...................28

Assists by a rookie
Joe Juneau, Boston 70
Teemu Selanne, Winnipeg...................56
Alexei Zhamnov, Winnipeg 47
Andrei Kovalenko, Quebec 41
Vladimir Malakhov, N.Y. Islanders....38

GOALTENDING

Games
Ed Belfour, Chicago........................... 71
Curtis Joseph, St. Louis....................68
Tim Cheveldae, Detroit......................67
Bob Essensa, Winnipeg.....................67
Bill Ranford, Edmonton 67

Minutes
Ed Belfour, Chicago........................ 4106
Curtis Joseph, St. Louis...................3890
Tim Cheveldae, Detroit...................3880
Bob Essensa, Winnipeg....................3855
Bill Ranford, Edmonton 3753

Goals allowed
Peter Sidorkiewicz, Ottawa..............250
Bill Ranford, Edmonton 240
Bob Essensa, Winnipeg....................227
Tim Cheveldae, Detroit.....................210
Mike Vernon, Calgary....................... 203

Shutouts
Ed Belfour, Chicago............................ 7
Tommy Soderstrom, Philadelphia 5
Tom Barrasso, Pittsburgh 4
Tim Cheveldae, Detroit........................4
John Vanbiesbrouck, N.Y. Rangers..... 4

Lowest goals-against average
(25 games played minimum)
Felix Potvin, Toronto.................... 2.50
Ed Belfour, Chicago.......................2.59
Tom Barrasso, Pittsburgh 3.01
Curtis Joseph, St. Louis 3.02
Kay Whitmore, Vancouver.............3.10

Highest goals-against average
(25 games played minimum)
Jeff Hackett, San Jose...................5.28
Frank Pietrangelo, Hartford...........4.85
Peter Sidorkiewicz, Ottawa...........4.43
Daniel Berthiaume, Ottawa...........4.30
Ron Tugnutt, Edmonton.................4.17

Games won

Tom Barrasso, Pittsburgh	43
Ed Belfour, Chicago	41
Andy Moog, Boston	37
Tim Cheveldae, Detroit	34
Bob Essensa, Winnipeg	33

Best winning percentage
(25 games played minimum)

Jeff Reese, Cal. (14-4-1)	.763
Andre Racicot, Mon. (17-5-1)	.761
Tom Barrasso, Pit. (43-14-5)	.734
Andy Moog, Bos. (37-14-3)	.713
Daren Puppa, Buf./Tor. (17-7-4)	.679

Worst winning percentage
(25 games played minimum)

Jeff Hackett, S.J. (2-30-1)	.076
Daniel Berthiaume, Ott. (2-17-1)	.125
Peter Sidorkiewicz, Ott. (8-46-3)	.167
Arturs Irbe, S.J. (7-26-0)	.212
Frank Pietrangelo, Har. (4-15-1)	.225

Games lost

Peter Sidorkiewicz, Ottawa	46
Bill Ranford, Edmonton	38
Jeff Hackett, San Jose	30
Curtis Joseph, St. Louis	28
Sean Burke, Hartford	27

Shots against

Curtis Joseph, St. Louis	2202
Bob Essensa, Winnipeg	2119
Bill Ranford, Edmonton	2065
Tim Cheveldae, Detroit	1897
Tom Barrasso, Pittsburgh	1885

Saves

Curtis Joseph, St. Louis	2006
Bob Essensa, Winnipeg	1892
Bill Ranford, Edmonton	1825
Ed Belfour, Chicago	1703
Tom Barrasso, Pittsburgh	1699

Highest save percentage
(25 games played minimum)

Curtis Joseph, St. Louis	.911
Felix Potvin, Toronto	.910
Ed Belfour, Chicago	.906
Tom Barrasso, Pittsburgh	.901
John Vanbiesbrouck, N.Y. Rangers	.900

Lowest save percentage
(25 games played minimum)

Jeff Hackett, San Jose	.8557
Peter Sidorkiewicz, Ottawa	.8561
Frank Pietrangelo, Hartford	.858
Daniel Berthiaume, Ottawa	.871
Wendell Young, Tampa Bay	.872

STATISTICS OF PLAYERS WITH TWO OR MORE TEAMS

SCORING

	Games	G	A	Pts.	Pen.	+/-	PPG	SHG	Shots	Shooting Pct.
Peter Ahola, Los Angeles	8	1	1	2	6	-2	0	0	3	33.3
Peter Ahola, Pittsburgh	22	0	1	1	14	-2	0	0	5	0.0
Peter Ahola, San Jose	20	2	3	5	16	-6	0	0	32	6.3
Totals	50	3	5	8	36	-10	0	0	40	7.5
Dave Andreychuk, Buffalo	52	29	32	61	48	-8	20	0	171	17.0
Dave Andreychuk, Toronto	31	25	13	38	8	12	12	0	139	18.0
Totals	83	54	45	99	56	4	†32	0	310	17.4
Brent Ashton, Boston	26	2	2	4	11	0	0	0	26	7.7
Brent Ashton, Calgary	32	8	11	19	41	11	0	2	58	13.8
Totals	58	10	13	23	52	11	0	2	84	11.9
Brian Benning, Philadelphia	37	9	17	26	93	0	6	0	87	10.3
Brian Benning, Edmonton	18	1	7	8	59	-1	0	0	28	3.6
Totals	55	10	24	34	152	-1	6	0	115	8.7
Josef Beranek, Edmonton	26	2	6	8	28	-7	0	0	44	4.5
Josef Beranek, Philadelphia	40	13	12	25	50	-1	1	0	86	15.1
Totals	66	15	18	33	78	-8	1	0	130	11.5
Bill Berg, N.Y. Islanders	22	6	3	9	49	4	0	2	30	20.0
Bill Berg, Toronto	58	7	8	15	54	-1	0	1	83	8.4
Totals	80	13	11	24	103	3	0	3	113	11.5
Jimmy Carson, Detroit	52	25	26	51	18	0	13	0	108	23.1
Jimmy Carson, Los Angeles	34	12	10	22	14	-2	4	0	81	14.8
Totals	†86	37	36	73	32	-2	17	0	189	19.6
Paul Cavallini, St. Louis	11	1	4	5	10	3	1	0	22	4.5
Paul Cavallini, Washington	71	5	8	13	46	3	0	0	77	6.5
Totals	82	6	12	18	56	6	1	0	99	6.1
Jeff Chychrun, Pittsburgh	1	0	0	0	2	1	0	0	0	0.0
Jeff Chychrun, Los Angeles	17	0	1	1	23	-3	0	0	3	0.0
Totals	18	0	1	1	25	-2	0	0	3	0.0
Zdeno Ciger, New Jersey	27	4	8	12	2	-8	2	0	39	10.3
Zdeno Ciger, Edmonton	37	9	15	24	6	-5	0	0	67	13.4
Totals	64	13	23	36	8	-13	2	0	106	12.3
Paul Coffey, Los Angeles	50	8	49	57	50	9	2	0	182	4.4
Paul Coffey, Detroit	30	4	26	30	27	7	3	0	72	5.6
Totals	80	12	75	87	77	16	5	0	254	4.7
Yvon Corriveau, San Jose	20	3	7	10	0	-7	1	0	32	9.4
Yvon Corriveau, Hartford	37	5	5	10	14	-13	1	0	45	11.1
Totals	57	8	12	20	14	-20	2	0	77	10.4
Murray Craven, Hartford	67	25	42	67	20	-4	6	3	139	18.0
Murray Craven, Vancouver	10	0	10	10	12	3	0	0	12	0.0
Totals	77	25	52	77	32	-1	6	3	151	16.6
Doug Crossman, Tampa Bay	40	8	21	29	18	-4	2	0	54	14.8
Doug Crossman, St. Louis	19	2	7	9	10	-3	2	0	24	8.3
Totals	59	10	28	38	28	-7	4	0	78	12.8
John Cullen, Hartford	19	5	4	9	58	-15	3	0	38	13.2
John Cullen, Toronto	47	13	28	41	53	-8	10	0	86	15.1
Totals	66	18	32	50	111	-23	13	0	124	14.5

	Games	G	A	Pts.	Pen.	+/-	PPG	SHG	Shots	Shooting Pct.
Tie Domi, N.Y. Rangers	12	2	0	2	95	-1	0	0	11	18.2
Tie Domi, Winnipeg	49	3	10	13	249	2	0	0	29	10.3
Totals	61	5	10	15	344	1	0	0	40	12.5
Todd Elik, Minnesota	46	13	18	31	48	-5	4	0	76	17.1
Todd Elik, Edmonton	14	1	9	10	8	1	0	0	28	3.6
Totals	60	14	27	41	56	-4	4	0	104	13.5
Bob Errey, Pittsburgh	54	8	6	14	76	-2	0	0	79	10.1
Bob Errey, Buffalo	8	1	3	4	4	2	0	0	9	11.1
Totals	62	9	9	18	80	0	0	0	88	10.2
Marc Fortier, Ottawa	10	0	1	1	6	-7	0	0	12	0.0
Marc Fortier, Los Angeles	6	0	0	0	5	-2	0	0	2	0.0
Totals	16	0	1	1	11	-9	0	0	14	0.0
Grant Fuhr, Toronto (goalie)	29	0	0	0	0	0	0	0	0	0.0
Grant Fuhr, Buffalo (goalie)	29	0	0	0	10	0	0	0	0	0.0
Totals	58	0	0	0	10	0	0	0	0	0.0
Brent Gilchrist, Edmonton	60	10	10	20	47	-10	2	0	94	10.6
Brent Gilchrist, Minnesota	8	0	1	1	2	-2	0	0	12	0.0
Totals	68	10	11	21	49	-12	2	0	106	9.4
Randy Gilhen, N.Y. Rangers	33	3	2	5	8	-8	0	1	34	8.8
Randy Gilhen, Tampa Bay	11	0	2	2	6	-6	0	0	11	0.0
Totals	44	3	4	7	14	-14	0	1	45	6.7
Mark Hardy, N.Y. Rangers	44	1	10	11	85	2	0	0	28	3.6
Mark Hardy, Los Angeles	11	0	3	3	4	-4	0	0	20	0.0
Totals	55	1	13	14	89	-2	0	0	48	2.1
Mike Hartman, Tampa Bay	58	4	4	8	154	-7	0	0	74	5.4
Mike Hartman, N.Y. Rangers	3	0	0	0	6	0	0	0	3	0.0
Totals	61	4	4	8	160	-7	0	0	77	5.2
Greg Hawgood, Edmonton	29	5	13	18	35	-1	2	0	47	10.6
Greg Hawgood, Philadelphia	40	6	22	28	39	-7	5	0	91	6.6
Totals	69	11	35	46	74	-8	7	0	138	8.0
Jim Hiller, Los Angeles	40	6	6	12	90	0	1	0	59	10.2
Jim Hiller, Detroit	21	2	6	8	19	7	0	0	24	8.3
Totals	61	8	12	20	109	7	1	0	83	9.6
Jim Hrivnak, Washington (goalie)	27	0	3	3	0	0	0	0	0	0.0
Jim Hrivnak, Winnipeg (goalie)	3	0	0	0	0	0	0	0	0	0.0
Totals	30	0	3	3	0	0	0	0	0	0.0
Mike Hudson, Chicago	36	1	6	7	44	-6	0	0	33	3.0
Mike Hudson, Edmonton	5	0	1	1	2	-1	0	0	2	0.0
Totals	41	1	7	8	46	-7	0	0	35	2.9
Tim Hunter, Quebec	48	5	3	8	94	-4	0	0	28	17.9
Tim Hunter, Vancouver	26	0	4	4	99	1	0	0	12	0.0
Totals	74	5	7	12	193	-3	0	0	40	12.5
Steve Kasper, Philadelphia	21	1	3	4	2	-4	0	1	9	11.1
Steve Kasper, Tampa Bay	47	3	4	7	18	-13	0	0	23	13.0
Totals	68	4	7	11	20	-17	0	1	32	12.5
Kris King, N.Y. Rangers	30	0	3	3	67	-1	0	0	23	0.0
Kris King, Winnipeg	48	8	8	16	136	5	0	0	51	15.7
Totals	78	8	11	19	203	4	0	0	74	10.8
Steve Konroyd, Hartford	59	3	11	14	63	-16	0	0	62	4.8
Steve Konroyd, Detroit	6	0	1	1	4	1	0	0	4	0.0
Totals	65	3	12	15	67	-15	0	0	66	4.5
Igor Kravchuk, Chicago	38	6	9	15	30	11	3	0	101	5.9
Igor Kravchuk, Edmonton	17	4	8	12	2	-8	1	0	42	9.5
Totals	55	10	17	27	32	3	4	0	143	7.0
Robert Kron, Vancouver	32	10	11	21	14	10	2	2	60	16.7
Robert Kron, Hartford	13	4	2	6	4	-5	2	0	37	10.8
Totals	45	14	13	27	18	5	4	2	97	14.4
Bob Kudelski, Los Angeles	15	3	3	6	8	-3	0	0	12	25.0
Bob Kudelski, Ottawa	48	21	14	35	22	-22	12	0	125	16.8
Totals	63	24	17	41	30	-25	12	0	137	17.5
Dominic Lavoie, Ottawa	2	0	1	1	0	0	0	0	8	0.0
Dominic Lavoie, Boston	2	0	0	0	2	-1	0	0	7	0.0
Totals	4	0	1	1	2	-1	0	0	15	0.0
Jamie Leach, Pittsburgh	5	0	0	0	2	-2	0	0	2	0.0
Jamie Leach, Hartford	19	3	2	5	2	-5	0	0	17	17.6
Totals	24	3	2	5	4	-7	0	0	19	15.8
Gary Leeman, Calgary	30	9	5	14	10	5	0	0	49	18.4
Gary Leeman, Montreal	20	6	12	18	14	9	1	0	36	16.7
Totals	50	15	17	32	24	14	1	0	85	17.6
Lonnie Loach, Ottawa	3	0	0	0	0	0	0	0	3	0.0
Lonnie Loach, Los Angeles	50	10	13	23	27	3	1	0	55	18.2
Totals	53	10	13	23	27	3	1	0	58	17.2
David Maley, Edmonton	13	1	1	2	29	-3	0	0	9	11.1
David Maley, San Jose	43	1	6	7	126	-25	1	0	48	2.1
Totals	56	2	7	9	155	-28	1	0	57	3.5

— 93 —

	Games	G	A	Pts.	Pen.	+/-	PPG	SHG	Shots	Shooting Pct.
John McIntyre, Los Angeles	49	2	5	7	80	-13	0	0	31	6.5
John McIntyre, N.Y. Rangers	11	1	0	1	4	-1	0	0	5	20.0
Totals	60	3	5	8	84	-14	0	0	36	8.3
Basil McRae, Tampa Bay	14	2	3	5	71	-3	1	0	23	8.7
Basil McRae, St. Louis	33	1	3	4	98	-13	1	0	22	4.5
Totals	47	3	6	9	169	-16	2	0	45	6.7
Kevin Miller, Washington	10	0	3	3	35	-4	0	0	10	0.0
Kevin Miller, St. Louis	72	24	22	46	65	6	8	3	153	15.7
Totals	82	24	25	49	100	2	8	3	163	14.7
Jon Morris, New Jersey	2	0	0	0	0	-1	0	0	1	0.0
Jon Morris, San Jose	13	0	3	3	6	-10	0	0	11	0.0
Totals	15	0	3	3	6	-11	0	0	12	0.0
Craig Muni, Edmonton	72	0	11	11	67	-15	0	0	51	0.0
Craig Muni, Chicago	9	0	0	0	8	-1	0	0	9	0.0
Totals	81	0	11	11	75	-14	0	0	60	0.0
Troy Murray, Winnipeg	29	3	4	7	34	-15	1	0	45	6.7
Troy Murray, Chicago	22	1	3	4	25	0	1	0	32	3.1
Totals	51	4	7	11	59	-15	2	0	77	5.2
Bernie Nicholls, Edmonton	46	8	32	40	40	-16	4	0	86	9.3
Bernie Nicholls, New Jersey	23	5	15	20	40	3	1	0	46	10.9
Totals	69	13	47	60	80	-13	5	0	132	9.8
Ed Olczyk, Winnipeg	25	8	12	20	26	-11	2	0	81	9.9
Ed Olczyk, N.Y. Rangers	46	13	16	29	26	9	0	0	109	11.9
Totals	71	21	28	49	52	-2	2	0	190	11.1
Mark Osiecki, Ottawa	34	0	4	4	12	-21	0	0	20	0.0
Mark Osiecki, Winnipeg	4	1	0	1	2	1	1	0	5	20.0
Mark Osiecki, Minnesota	5	0	0	0	5	0	0	0	1	0.0
Totals	43	1	4	5	19	-20	1	0	26	3.8
Greg Paslawski, Philadelphia	60	14	19	33	12	0	4	0	90	15.6
Greg Paslawski, Calgary	13	4	5	9	0	3	0	0	19	21.1
Totals	73	18	24	42	12	3	4	0	109	16.5
Mark Pederson, Philadelphia	14	3	4	7	6	-2	1	0	21	14.3
Mark Pederson, San Jose	27	7	3	10	22	-20	1	0	42	16.7
Totals	41	10	7	17	28	-22	2	0	63	15.9
Daren Puppa, Buffalo (goalie)	24	0	1	1	0	0	0	0	0	0.0
Daren Puppa, Toronto (goalie)	8	0	0	0	0	0	0	0	0	0.0
Totals	32	0	1	1	0	0	0	0	0	0.0
Rob Ramage, Tampa Bay	66	5	12	17	138	-21	5	0	115	4.3
Rob Ramage, Montreal	8	0	1	1	8	-3	0	0	16	0.0
Totals	74	5	13	18	146	-24	5	0	131	3.8
Mike Ramsey, Buffalo	33	2	8	10	20	4	0	0	27	7.4
Mike Ramsey, Pittsburgh	12	1	2	3	8	13	0	0	8	12.5
Totals	45	3	10	13	28	17	0	0	35	8.6
Stephane J.G. Richer, Tampa Bay	3	0	0	0	0	-3	0	0	2	0.0
Stephane J.G. Richer, Boston	21	1	4	5	18	-6	0	0	22	4.5
Totals	24	1	4	5	18	-9	0	0	24	4.2
Jason Ruff, St. Louis	7	2	1	3	8	-1	1	0	7	28.6
Jason Ruff, Tampa Bay	1	0	0	0	0	0	0	0	1	0.0
Totals	8	2	1	3	8	-1	1	0	8	25.0
Anatoli Semenov, Tampa Bay	13	2	3	5	4	-5	0	0	14	14.3
Anatoli Semenov, Vancouver	62	10	34	44	28	21	3	2	88	11.4
Totals	75	12	37	49	32	16	3	2	102	11.8
Brian Skrudland, Montreal	23	5	3	8	55	1	0	2	29	17.2
Brian Skrudland, Calgary	16	2	4	6	10	3	0	0	22	9.1
Totals	39	7	7	14	65	4	0	2	51	13.7
Dave Snuggerud, San Jose	25	4	5	9	14	-3	0	1	51	7.8
Dave Snuggerud, Philadelphia	14	0	2	2	0	0	0	0	10	0.0
Totals	39	4	7	11	14	-3	0	1	61	6.6
Rick Tabaracci, Winnipeg (goalie)	19	0	0	0	10	0	0	0	0	0.0
Rick Tabaracci, Washington (goalie)	6	0	0	0	4	0	0	0	0	0.0
Totals	25	0	0	0	14	0	0	0	0	0.0
Peter Taglianetti, Tampa Bay	61	1	8	9	150	8	0	0	60	1.7
Peter Taglianetti, Pittsburgh	11	1	4	5	34	4	0	0	18	5.6
Totals	72	2	12	14	184	12	0	0	78	2.6
Jim Thomson, Ottawa	15	0	1	1	41	-11	0	0	21	0.0
Jim Thomson, Los Angeles	9	0	0	0	56	-1	0	0	2	0.0
Totals	24	0	1	1	97	-12	0	0	23	0.0
Esa Tikkanen, Edmonton	66	14	19	33	76	-11	2	4	162	8.6
Esa Tikkanen, N.Y. Rangers	15	2	5	7	18	-13	0	0	40	5.0
Totals	81	16	24	40	94	-24	2	4	202	7.9
Kevin Todd, New Jersey	30	5	5	10	16	-4	0	0	48	10.4
Kevin Todd, Edmonton	25	4	9	13	10	-5	0	0	39	10.3
Totals	55	9	14	23	26	-9	0	0	87	10.3
Doug Weight, N.Y. Rangers	65	15	25	40	55	4	3	0	90	16.7
Doug Weight, Edmonton	13	2	6	8	10	-2	0	0	35	5.7
Totals	78	17	31	48	65	2	3	0	125	13.6

	Games	G	A	Pts.	Pen.	+/-	PPG	SHG	Shots	Shooting Pct.
C.J. Young, Calgary	28	3	2	5	20	-7	1	0	21	14.3
C.J. Young, Boston	15	4	5	9	12	1	0	0	22	18.2
Totals	43	7	7	14	32	-6	1	0	43	16.3

GOALTENDING

	Games	Min.	Goals	SO	Avg.	W	L	T	Shots	Sv. Pct.
Grant Fuhr, Toronto	29	1665	87	1	3.14	13	9	4	826	.895
Grant Fuhr, Buffalo	29	1694	98	0	3.47	11	15	2	903	.891
Totals	58	3359	185	1	3.30	24	24	6	1729	.893
Jim Hrivnak, Washington	27	1421	83	0	3.50	13	9	2	677	.877
Jim Hrivnak, Winnipeg	3	180	13	0	4.33	2	1	0	96	.865
Totals	30	1601	96	0	3.60	15	10	2	773	.876
Daren Puppa, Buffalo	24	1306	78	0	3.58	11	5	4	706	.890
Daren Puppa, Toronto	8	479	18	2	2.25	6	2	0	232	.922
Totals	32	1785	96	2	3.23	17	7	4	938	.898
Rick Tabaracci, Winnipeg	19	959	70	0	4.38	5	10	0	496	.859
Rick Tabaracci, Washington	6	343	10	2	1.75	3	2	0	162	.938
Totals	25	1302	80	2	3.69	8	12	0	658	.878

†Led league.

MISCELLANEOUS

HAT TRICKS

(Players scoring three or more goals in a game)

Date	Player, Team	Opp.	Goals
10- 7-92	Chris Kontos, Tampa Bay	Chi.	4
10- 8-92	Alexander Mogilny, Buffalo	Que.	3
10-10-92	Owen Nolan, Quebec	Ott.	3
10-10-92	Bobby Holik, New Jersey	NYR	3
10-12-92	Vladimir Ruzicka, Boston	Ott.	3
10-12-92	Pavel Bure, Vancouver	Win.	4
10-14-92	Teemu Selanne, Winnipeg	Edm.	3
10-17-92	Kevin Stevens, Pittsburgh	Har.	4
10-22-92	Claude Lemieux, New Jersey	Chi.	3
10-22-92	Mario Lemieux, Pittsburgh	Det.	3
10-24-92	Benoit Hogue, N.Y. Islanders	Har.	3
10-24-92	Greg Paslawski, Philadelphia	Mon.	3
10-24-92	Steve Yzerman, Detroit	St.L.	3
10-29-92	Adam Oates, Boston	L.A.	3
10-31-92	Vitali Prokhorov, St. Louis	Phi.	3
10-31-92	Sergei Makarov, Calgary	Min.	3
11- 2-92	Joe Nieuwendyk, Calgary	Van.	3
11- 2-92	Pavel Bure, Vancouver	Cal.	3
11- 4-92	Theoren Fleury, Calgary	Van.	3
11- 5-92	Gary Leeman, Calgary	Ott.	3
11- 7-92	Jeremy Roenick, Chicago	Que.	3
11- 7-92	Doug Crossman, Tampa Bay	NYI	3
11- 8-92	Michel Goulet, Chicago	Pit.	3
11- 8-92	Jari Kurri, Los Angeles	S.J.	3
11- 8-92	Luc Robitaille, Los Angeles	S.J.	3
11- 8-92	Mike Donnelly, Los Angeles	S.J.	3
11-11-92	Andrei Kovalenko, Quebec	Ott.	3
11-13-92	Dave Andreychuk, Buffalo	Har.	4
11-13-92	Jimmy Carson, Detroit	Pit.	3
11-15-92	Eric Lindros, Philadelphia	Ott.	3
11-17-92	Evgeny Davydov, Winnipeg	T.B.	3
11-22-92	Pierre Turgeon, N.Y. Islanders	Edm.	3
11-25-92	Vincent Damphousse, Montreal	Har.	3
11-25-92	Adam Graves, N.Y. Rangers	Pit.	3
11-26-92	Owen Nolan, Quebec	Tor.	3
11-28-92	Geoff Sanderson, Hartford	Bos.	3
11-28-92	Steve Larmer, Chicago	Cal.	3
12- 1-92	Kevin Miller, St. Louis	Har.	3
12- 3-92	Rob Gaudreau, San Jose	Har.	3
12- 4-92	Gary Roberts, Calgary	St.L.	3
12- 5-92	Mats Sundin, Quebec	Min.	3
12- 5-92	Brian Bradley, Tampa Bay	Det.	3
12- 8-92	Vincent Damphousse, Montreal	L.A.	3
12- 9-92	Alexander Mogilny, Buffalo	Bos.	3
12-11-92	Teemu Selanne, Winnipeg	Was.	3
12-12-92	Scott Young, Quebec	S.J.	3
12-12-92	Rob Gaudreau, San Jose	Que.	3
12-12-92	Kevin Stevens, Pittsburgh	N.J.	3
12-17-92	Brendan Shanahan, St. Louis	NYR	3
12-23-92	Alexander Mogilny, Buffalo	Was.	3
12-23-92	Steve Larmer, Chicago	Ott.	3
12-26-92	Eric Lindros, Philadelphia	Was.	3
12-27-92	Alexei Kovalev, N.Y. Rangers	Bos.	3
12-27-92	Gary Roberts, Calgary	Edm.	3
12-29-92	Rod Brind'Amour, Philadelphia	L.A.	3
12-31-92	Alexander Mogilny, Buffalo	NYR	3
12-31-92	Yuri Khmylev, Buffalo	NYR	3
1- 2-93	Alexander Mogilny, Buffalo	Ott.	3
1- 7-93	Kevin Dineen, Philadelphia	Was.	3
1- 7-93	Ulf Dahlen, Minnesota	Pit.	3
1-10-93	Pat Lafontaine, Buffalo	Cal.	3
1-10-93	Bob Kudelski, Ottawa	S.J.	3
1-12-93	Joe Juneau, Boston	Buf.	3
1-13-93	Kevin Hatcher, Washington	NYR	3
1-14-93	Stephen Heinze, Boston	Pit.	3
1-16-93	Pierre Turgeon, N.Y. Islanders	N.J.	3
1-16-93	Robert Reichel, Calgary	Min.	3
1-17-93	Michel Goulet, Chicago	Tor.	3
1-21-93	Russ Courtnall, Minnesota	Ott.	3
1-21-93	Tomas Sandstrom, Los Angeles	Van.	3
1-22-93	Bobby Holik, New Jersey	Mon.	3
1-26-93	Kevin Stevens, Pittsburgh	Was.	3
1-26-93	Steve Yzerman, Detroit	Cal.	3
1-28-93	Adam Oates, Boston	Win.	3
1-29-93	Sergei Nemchinov, N.Y. Rangers	Buf.	3
1-31-93	Kelly Buchberger, Edmonton	Buf.	3
2- 9-93	Kevin Dineen, Philadelphia	Ott.	3
2-10-93	Alexander Mogilny, Buffalo	Win.	4
2-10-93	Ronnie Stern, Calgary	S.J.	3
2-10-93	Robert Reichel, Calgary	S.J.	3
2-11-93	Dimitri Khristich, Washington	St.L.	3
2-14-93	Steve Yzerman, Detroit	Chi.	3
2-20-93	Pat Verbeek, Hartford	Edm.	3
2-20-93	Pierre Turgeon, N.Y. Islanders	Pit.	3
2-21-93	Geoff Sanderson, Hartford	Pit.	3
2-22-93	Thomas Steen, Winnipeg	Ott.	3
2-24-93	Alexander Mogilny, Buffalo	Det.	4
2-27-93	Brian Bellows, Montreal	Buf.	4
2-28-93	Pat Verbeek, Hartford	NYI	3
2-28-93	Teemu Selanne, Winnipeg	Min.	4

Date	Player, Team	Opp.	Goals	Date	Player, Team	Opp.	Goals
3- 2-93	Teemu Selanne, Winnipeg	Que.	3	4- 1-93	Rick Tocchet, Pittsburgh	Har.	3
3- 2-93	Luc Robitaille, Los Angeles	Cal.	3	4- 1-93	Johan Garpenlov, San Jose	Win.	3
3- 4-93	Adam Oates, Boston	Van.	3	4- 4-93	Craig Janney, St. Louis	Chi.	3
3- 9-93	Teemu Selanne, Winnipeg	T.B.	3	4- 7-93	Michael Nylander, Hartford	Ott.	3
3-20-93	Mario Lemieux, Pittsburgh	Phi.	4	4- 7-93	Rick Tocchet, Pittsburgh	Mon.	3
3-19-93	Dimitri Khristich, Washington	Har.	3	4- 9-93	Mario Lemieux, Pittsburgh	NYR	5
3-24-93	Ed Olczyk, N.Y. Rangers	Phi.	3	4- 9-93	Joe Mullen, Pittsburgh	NYR	3
3-24-93	Eric Lindros, Philadelphia	NYR	3	4-10-93	Laurie Boschman, Ottawa	NYI	3
4-16-93	Pierre Turgeon, N.Y. Islanders	N.J.	3	4-13-93	Mikael Andersson, Tampa Bay	Win.	3
3-18-93	Mario Lemieux, Pittsburgh	Was.	4	4-15-93	Kevin Dineen, Philadelphia	Buf.	3
3-29-93	Stephane Richer, New Jersey	S.J.	3	4-15-93	Cliff Ronning, Vancouver	L.A.	3

OVERTIME GOALS

Date	Player, Team	Opponent	Time	Final score
10- 6-92	Tomas Sandstrom, Los Angeles	Calgary	3:40	Los Angeles 5, Calgary 4
10- 8-92	Joe Juneau, Boston	Hartford	2:16	Boston 3, Hartford 2
10- 8-92	Kelly Kisio, San Jose	Winnipeg	4:00	San Jose 4, Winnipeg 3
10-15-92	Craig Simpson, Edmonton	Chicago	2:06	Edmonton 4, Chicago 3
10-16-92	Bob Sweeney, Buffalo	Tampa Bay	2:30	Buffalo 5, Tampa Bay 4
10-22-92	Stephane J.J. Richer, New Jersey	Chicago	0:49	New Jersey 6, Chicago 5
10-24-92	Phil Bourque, N.Y. Rangers	Ottawa	4:49	N.Y. Rangers 3, Ottawa 2
10-28-92	Randy McKay, New Jersey	Hartford	0:48	New Jersey 4, Hartford 3
11- 2-92	Darren Turcotte, N.Y. Rangers	Buffalo	0:58	N.Y. Rangers 7, Buffalo 6
11- 7-92	Doug Crossman, Tampa Bay	N.Y. Islanders	1:16	Tampa Bay 6, N.Y. Islanders 5
11-14-92	Kevin Dineen, Philadelphia	Montreal	0:48	Philadelphia 4, Montreal 3
11-14-92	Bobby Holik, New Jersey	Washington	2:09	New Jersey 4, Washington 3
11-25-92	Tom Pederson, San Jose	Calgary	3:53	San Jose 4, Calgary 3
11-26-92	Owen Nolan, Quebec	Toronto	0:23	Quebec 5, Toronto 4
11-27-92	Ted Donato, Boston	Hartford	4:36	Boston 5, Hartford 4
11-27-92	Joel Otto, Calgary	Tampa Bay	1:01	Calgary 3, Tampa Bay 2
11-27-92	Thomas Steen, Winnipeg	San Jose	1:29	Winnipeg 3, San Jose 2
11-28-92	Murray Craven, Hartford	Boston	2:53	Hartford 4, Boston 3
11-28-92	Craig Simpson, Edmonton	Tampa Bay	3:45	Edmonton 4, Tampa Bay 3
12- 3-92	Claude Boivin, Philadelphia	Quebec	2:03	Philadelphia 3, Quebec 2
12- 5-92	Vincent Damphousse, Montreal	Winnipeg	2:18	Montreal 3, Winnipeg 2
12-12-92	Scott Young, Quebec	San Jose	4:19	Quebec 8, San Jose 7
12-12-92	Russ Romaniuk, Winnipeg	N.Y. Islanders	1:41	Winnipeg 4, N.Y. Islanders 3
12-15-92	Sergei Fedorov, Detroit	Ottawa	2:10	Detroit 3, Ottawa 2
12-15-92	Derek King, N.Y. Islanders	St. Louis	2:33	N.Y. Islanders 4, St. Louis 3
12-16-92	John Tucker, Tampa Bay	San Jose	2:53	Tampa Bay 5, San Jose 4
12-17-92	Jaromir Jagr, Pittsburgh	Philadelphia	2:50	Pittsburgh 5, Philadelphia 4
12-21-92	Gary Roberts, Calgary	Edmonton	4:35	Calgary 3, Edmonton 2
12-23-92	Stephane J.J. Richer, New Jersey	N.Y. Rangers	1:33	New Jersey 5, N.Y. Rangers 4
12-26-92	Murray Baron, St. Louis	Chicago	1:35	St. Louis 3, Chicago 2
12-29-92	Michal Pivonka, Washington	N.Y. Rangers	1:28	Washington 4, N.Y. Rangers 3
12-31-92	Sheldon Kennedy, Detroit	Ottawa	0:28	Detroit 5, Ottawa 4
1- 2-93	Gregori Pantaleyev, Boston	Hartford	2:36	Boston 3, Hartford 2
1- 3-93	Brad May, Buffalo	St. Louis	1:20	Buffalo 6, St. Louis 5
1- 7-93	Andrei Kovalenko, Quebec	Boston	1:35	Quebec 3, Boston 2
1- 7-93	Brendan Shanahan, St. Louis	Calgary	2:58	St. Louis 3, Calgary 2
1-17-93	Zdeno Ciger, Edmonton	Buffalo	0:25	Edmonton 3, Buffalo 2
1-19-93	Yuri Khmylev, Buffalo	Calgary	2:07	Buffalo 3, Calgary 2
1-24-93	Ric Nattress, Philadelphia	Hartford	2:37	Philadelphia 5, Hartford 4
1-25-93	Ed Ronan, Montreal	Boston	0:14	Montreal 3, Boston 2
1-26-93	Bob Sweeney, Buffalo	Philadelphia	2:23	Buffalo 4, Philadelphia 3
1-31-93	Kelly Buchberger, Edmonton	Buffalo	0:46	Edmonton 5, Buffalo 4
2-13-93	Gary Roberts, Calgary	Hartford	3:29	Calgary 4, Hartford 3
2-14-93	Mats Sundin, Quebec	Edmonton	2:28	Quebec 3, Edmonton 2
2-27-93	Vladimir Ruzicka, Boston	Washington	2:03	Boston 5, Washington 4
2-28-93	Pierre Turgeon, N.Y. Islanders	Hartford	2:39	N.Y. Islanders 7, Hartford 6
3- 2-93	Johan Garpenlov, San Jose	Ottawa	4:24	San Jose 3, Ottawa 2
3- 6-93	Ray Bourque, Boston	St. Louis	4:39	Boston 4, St. Louis 3
3-11-93	Jaromir Jagr, Pittsburgh	Los Angeles	3:18	Pittsburgh 4, Los Angeles 3
4-16-93	Dimitri Yushkevich, Philadelphia	Hartford	1:25	Philadelphia 5, Hartford 4
3-14-93	Michel Goulet, Chicago	Edmonton	3:09	Chicago 5, Edmonton 4
3-16-93	Murray Craven, Hartford	Tampa Bay	1:03	Hartford 4, Tampa Bay 3
3-17-93	Craig MacTavish, Edmonton	N.Y. Rangers	0:32	Edmonton 4, N.Y. Rangers 3
3-24-93	Vincent Damphousse, Montreal	Hartford	2:01	Montreal 6, Hartford 5
3-25-93	Mikael Andersson, Tampa Bay	Ottawa	0:36	Tampa Bay 3, Ottawa 2
3-27-93	Oleg Petrov, Montreal	Ottawa	1:29	Montreal 4, Ottawa 3
4- 2-93	Pierre Turgeon, N.Y. Islanders	N.Y. Rangers	3:41	N.Y. Islanders 3, N.Y. Rangers 2
4- 3-93	Theoren Fleury, Calgary	San Jose	3:06	Calgary 3, San Jose 2
4- 7-93	Ulf Samuelsson, Pittsburgh	Montreal	2:11	Pittsburgh 4, Montreal 3
4- 7-93	Geoff Courtnall, Vancouver	Edmonton	1:33	Vancouver 5, Edmonton 4

Date	Player, Team	Opponent	Time	Final score
4-10-93	—Tomas Sandstrom, Los Angeles	San Jose	3:22	Los Angeles 3, San Jose 2
4-12-93	—Mike Ridley, Washington	Montreal	4:12	Washington 3, Montreal 2
4-13-93	—Brian Bellows, Montreal	Buffalo	3:50	Montreal 3, Buffalo 2
4-13-93	—Peter Zezel, Toronto	St. Louis	1:46	Toronto 2, St. Louis 1
4-14-93	—Mark Janssens, Hartford	N.Y. Islanders	1:08	Hartford 5, N.Y. Islanders 4

PENALTY-SHOT INFORMATION

Date	Shooter	Goaltender	Scored	Final score
10-22-92	Brian Bradley, Tampa Bay	Felix Potvin, Toronto	No	Toronto 5, Tampa Bay 2
10-28-92	Dave Gagner, Minnesota	Bill Ranford, Edmonton	No	Edmonton 5, Minnesota 2
11- 7-92	Pierre Turgeon, N.Y. Islanders	Pat Jablonski, Tampa Bay	Yes	Tampa Bay 6, N.Y. Islanders 5
11-11-92	Brad May, Buffalo	Andy Moog, Boston	Yes	Buffalo 7, Boston 2
11-12-92	Mike Donnelly, Los Angeles	Kirk McLean, Vancouver	Yes	Los Angeles 7, Vancouver 4
11-18-92	Reggie Savage, Washington	Jon Casey, Minnesota	Yes	Minnesota 5, Washington 4
11-27-92	Paul Ysebaert, Detroit	Robb Stauber, Los Angeles	Yes	Los Angeles 5, Detroit 3
11-29-92	Pat LaFontaine, Buffalo	Peter Sidorkiewicz, Ottawa	Yes	Buffalo 5, Ottawa 2
12-11-92	Theoren Fleury, Calgary	Rick Wamsley, Toronto	Yes	Calgary 6, Toronto 3
12-15-92	Mikael Andersson, Tampa Bay	Robb Stauber, Los Angeles	Yes	Tampa Bay 3, Los Angeles 2
12-19-92	Phil Housley, Winnipeg	Curtis Joseph, St. Louis	No	Winnipeg 1, St. Louis 0
12-26-92	Eric Lindros, Philadelphia	Don Beaupre, Washington	Yes	Philadelphia 5, Washington 5
12-27-92	Brendan Shanahan, St. Louis	Grant Fuhr, Toronto	No	Toronto 6, St. Louis 3
12-27-92	C.J. Young, Calgary	Bill Ranford, Edmonton	No	Calgary 7, Edmonton 3
12-31-92	Brett Hull, St. Louis	Glenn Healy, N.Y. Islanders	No	St. Louis 5, N.Y. Islanders 1
12-31-92	Bryan Marchment, Chicago	Pat Jablonski, Tampa Bay	No	Chicago 5, Tampa Bay 0
1-23-93	Joe Nieuwendyk, Calgary	Ken Wregget, Pittsburgh	No	Pittsburgh 4, Calgary 3
1-25-93	Denis Savard, Montreal	John Blue, Boston	No	Montreal 3, Boston 2
1-26-93	Jaromir Jagr, Pittsburgh	Don Beaupre, Washington	No	Pittsburgh 6, Washington 3
2- 1-93	Laurie Boschman, Ottawa	Michael O'Neill, Winnipeg	Yes	Ottawa 4, Winnipeg 4
2- 2-93	Mats Sundin, Quebec	Kelly Hrudey, Los Angeles	No	Quebec 3, Los Angeles 2
2-16-93	Benoit Hogue, N.Y. Islanders	Ron Tugnutt, Edmonton	Yes	N.Y. Islanders 7, Edmonton 2
2-23-93	Stu Barnes, Winnipeg	Peter Sidorkiewicz, Ottawa	No	Winnipeg 8, Ottawa 2
2-25-93	Steve Maltais, Tampa Bay	Ed Belfour, Chicago	No	Chicago 5, Winnipeg 1
3- 9-93	Teemu Selanne, Winnipeg	Wendell Young, Tampa Bay	Yes	Winnipeg 4, Tampa Bay 2
3-10-93	Alexei Gusarov, Quebec	Grant Fuhr, Buffalo	Yes	Buffalo 7, Quebec 4
3-18-93	Steve Yzerman, Detroit	Darcy Wakaluk, Minnesota	No	Detroit 5, Minnesota 1
3-20-93	Craig Janney, St. Louis	Robb Stauber, Los Angeles	No	Los Angeles 3, St. Louis 2
4- 3-93	Philippe Bozon, St. Louis	Ed Belfour, Chicago	Yes	St. Louis 3, Chicago 3
4- 3-93	Luc Robitaille, Los Angeles	Jon Casey, Minnesota	No	Minnesota 3, Los Angeles 0

TEAM STREAKS

Most consecutive games won

Pittsburgh, Mar. 9-Apr. 10 17
Montreal, Oct. 24-Nov. 11 8
Calgary, Dec. 14-Jan. 2 8
Winnipeg, Jan. 5-19..........................8
Boston, Mar. 30-Apr. 14 8
Philadelphia, Apr. 3-16......................8

Winnipeg, Jan. 5-23.........................10
Toronto, Feb. 11-Mar. 3....................10

Toronto, Feb. 11-Apr. 3 12
Pittsburgh, Oct. 6-Nov. 21 11
Pittsburgh, Feb. 27-Apr. 10...............11

Most consecutive games undefeated

Pittsburgh, Mar. 9-Apr. 14 18
Montreal, Oct. 17-Nov. 11 12
Pittsburgh, Oct. 6-27 10
Calgary, Dec. 11-Jan. 2....................10

Most consecutive home games won

Los Angeles, Oct. 10-Dec. 5 12
Pittsburgh, Mar. 9-Apr. 10 10
Vancouver, Nov. 6-Dec. 9....................9
Winnipeg, Dec. 27-Jan. 23 9

Most consecutive home games undefeated

Vancouver, Nov. 4-Jan. 16................18
Los Angeles, Oct. 10-Dec. 8 13
Washington, Nov. 25-Jan. 31...........13

Most consecutive road games won

Boston, Mar. 15-Apr. 14 8
Minnesota, Nov. 18-Dec. 5 7
Pittsburgh, Mar. 14-Apr. 9 7

Most consecutive road games undefeated

Pittsburgh, Mar. 14-Apr. 14 8
Boston, Mar. 15-Apr. 14 8
Minnesota, Nov. 18-Dec. 5 7
Buffalo, Mar. 3-25.............................7

TEAM OVERTIME GAMES

Team	OVERALL					HOME					AWAY				
	G	W	L	T	Pct.	G	W	L	T	Pct.	G	W	L	T	Pct.
New Jersey	11	4	0	7	.682	4	0	0	4	.500	7	4	0	3	.786
Pittsburgh	10	3	0	7	.650	6	2	0	4	.667	4	1	0	3	.625
Quebec	15	4	1	10	.600	2	0	0	2	.500	13	4	1	8	.615
Detroit	11	2	0	9	.591	4	1	0	3	.625	7	1	0	6	.571
Montreal	14	5	3	6	.571	6	2	2	2	.500	8	3	1	4	.625
Boston	15	5	3	7	.567	9	5	1	3	.722	6	0	2	4	.333
Philadelphia	17	4	2	11	.559	9	2	2	5	.500	8	2	0	6	.625
Vancouver	10	1	0	9	.550	5	1	0	4	.600	5	0	0	5	.500
Los Angeles	13	2	1	10	.538	5	0	0	5	.500	8	2	1	5	.563
Edmonton	17	5	4	8	.529	9	2	2	5	.500	8	3	2	3	.563
Calgary	19	4	4	11	.500	11	3	3	5	.500	8	1	1	6	.500

— 97 —

Team		OVERALL					HOME					AWAY			
	G	W	L	T	Pct.	G	W	L	T	Pct.	G	W	L	T	Pct.
Buffalo	18	4	4	10	.500	6	2	2	2	.500	12	2	2	8	.500
N.Y. Islanders	13	3	3	7	.500	5	0	2	3	.300	8	3	1	4	.625
Toronto	13	1	1	11	.500	8	1	1	6	.500	5	0	0	5	.500
Winnipeg	11	2	2	7	.500	5	1	1	3	.500	6	1	1	4	.500
Washington	11	2	2	7	.500	8	1	1	6	.500	3	1	1	1	.500
Minnesota	10	0	0	10	.500	7	0	0	7	.500	3	0	0	3	.500
Tampa Bay	14	3	4	7	.464	4	0	1	3	.375	10	3	3	4	.500
St. Louis	17	2	4	11	.441	9	1	1	7	.500	8	1	3	4	.375
N.Y. Rangers	17	2	4	11	.441	9	1	3	5	.389	8	1	1	6	.500
Chicago	16	1	3	12	.438	9	0	3	6	.333	7	1	0	6	.571
San Jose	10	3	5	2	.400	7	2	4	1	.357	3	1	1	1	.500
Hartford	18	3	9	6	.333	11	2	4	5	.409	7	1	5	1	.214
Ottawa	10	0	6	4	.200	7	0	3	4	.286	3	0	3	0	.000
Totals	165	65	65	100	1.000	165	29	36	100	.479	165	36	29	100	.521

STANLEY CUP PLAYOFFS

RESULTS

DIVISION SEMIFINALS

ADAMS DIVISION
Series "A"

	W	L	Pts.	GF	GA
Buffalo Sabres	4	0	8	19	12
Boston Bruins	0	4	0	12	19

(Buffalo won Adams Division semifinal, 4-0)

Sun.	April 18—Buffalo 5, at Boston 4 (a)
Tue.	April 20—Buffalo 4, at Boston 0
Thur.	April 22—Boston 3, at Buffalo 4 (b)
Sat.	April 24—Boston 5, at Buffalo 6 (c)

(a)—Bob Sweeney scored at 11:03 (OT) for Buffalo.
(b)—Yuri Khmylev scored at 1:05 (OT) for Buffalo.
(c)—Brad May scored at 4:48 (OT) for Buffalo.

Series "B"

	W	L	Pts.	GF	GA
Montreal Canadiens	4	2	8	19	16
Quebec Nordiques	2	4	4	16	19

(Montreal won Adams Division semifinal, 4-2)

Sun.	April 18—Montreal 2, at Quebec 3 (d)
Tue.	April 20—Montreal 1, at Quebec 4
Thur.	April 22—Quebec 1, at Montreal 2 (e)
Sat.	April 24—Quebec 2, at Montreal 3
Mon.	April 26—Montreal 5, at Quebec 4 (f)
Wed.	April 28—Quebec 2, at Montreal 6

(d)—Scott Young scored at 16:49 (OT) for Quebec.
(e)—Vincent Damphousse scored at 10:30 (OT) for Montreal.
(f)—Kirk Muller scored at 8:17 (OT) for Montreal.

PATRICK DIVISION
Series "C"

	W	L	Pts.	GF	GA
Pittsburgh Penguins	4	1	8	23	13
New Jersey Devils	1	4	2	13	23

(Pittsburgh won Patrick Division semifinal, 4-1)

Sun.	April 18—New Jersey 3, at Pittsburgh 6
Tue.	April 20—New Jersey 0, at Pittsburgh 7
Thur.	April 22—Pittsburgh 4, at New Jersey 3
Sun.	April 25—Pittsburgh 1, at New Jersey 4
Mon.	April 26—New Jersey 3, at Pittsburgh 5

Series "D"

	W	L	Pts.	GF	GA
N.Y. Islanders	4	2	8	23	22
Washington Capitals	2	4	4	22	23

(N.Y. Islanders won Patrick Division semifinal, 4-2)

Sun.	April 18—N.Y. Islanders 1, at Washington 3
Tue.	April 20—N.Y. Islanders 5, at Washington 4 (g)
Thur.	April 22—Washington 3, at N.Y Islanders 4 (h)
Sat.	April 24—Washington 3, at N.Y. Islanders 4 (i)
Mon.	April 26—N.Y. Islanders 4, at Washington 6
Wed.	April 28—Washington 5, at N.Y. Islanders 5

(g)—Brian Mullen scored at 14:50 (2 OT) for N.Y. Islanders.
(h)—Ray Ferraro scored at 4:46 (OT) for N.Y. Islanders.
(i)—Ray Ferraro scored at 5:40 (2 OT) for N.Y. Islanders.

NORRIS DIVISION
Series "E"

	W	L	Pts.	GF	GA
St. Louis Blues	4	0	8	13	6
Chicago Blackhawks	0	4	0	6	13

(St. Louis won Norris Division semifinal, 4-0)

Sun.	April 18—St. Louis 4, at Chicago 3
Wed.	April 21—St. Louis 2, at Chicago 0
Fri.	April 23—Chicago 0, at St. Louis 3
Sun.	April 25—Chicago 3, at St. Louis 4 (j)

(j)—Craig Janney scored at 10:43 (OT) for St. Louis.

Series "F"

	W	L	Pts.	GF	GA
Toronto Maple Leafs	4	3	8	24	30
Detroit Red Wings	3	4	6	30	24

(Toronto won Norris Division semifinal, 4-3)

Mon.	April 19—Toronto 3, at Detroit 6
Wed.	April 21—Toronto 2, at Detroit 6
Fri.	April 23—Detroit 2, at Toronto 4
Sun.	April 25—Detroit 2, at Toronto 3
Tue.	April 27—Toronto 5, at Detroit 4 (k)
Thur.	April 29—Detroit 7, at Toronto 3
Sat.	May 1—Toronto 4, at Detroit 3 (l)

(k)—Mike Foligno scored at 2:05 (OT) for Toronto.
(l)—Nikolai Borschevsky scored at 2:35 (OT) for Toronto.

SMYTHE DIVISION
Series "G"

	W	L	Pts.	GF	GA
Vancouver Canucks	4	2	8	21	17
Winnipeg Jets	2	4	4	17	21

(Vancouver won Smythe Division semifinal, 4-2)

Mon.	April 19—Winnipeg 2, at Vancouver 4
Wed.	April 21—Winnipeg 2, at Vancouver 4
Fri.	April 23—Vancouver 4, at Winnipeg 5
Sun.	April 25—Vancouver 3, at Winnipeg 1
Tue.	April 27—Winnipeg 4, at Vancouver 3 (m)
Thur.	April 29—Vancouver 4, at Winnipeg 3 (n)

(m)—Teemu Selanne scored at 6:18 (OT) for Winnipeg.
(n)—Greg Adams scored at 4:30 (OT) for Vancouver.

Series "H"

	W	L	Pts.	GF	GA
Los Angeles Kings	4	2	8	33	28
Calgary Flames	2	4	4	28	33

(Los Angeles won Smythe Division semifinal, 4-2)

Sun.	April 18—Los Angeles 6, at Calgary 3
Wed.	April 21—Los Angeles 4, at Calgary 9
Fri.	April 23—Calgary 5, at Los Angeles 2
Sun.	April 25—Calgary 1, at Los Angeles 3
Tue.	April 27—Los Angeles 9, at Calgary 4
Thur.	April 29—Calgary 6, at Los Angeles 9

DIVISION FINALS

ADAMS DIVISION
Series "I"

	W	L	Pts.	GF	GA
Montreal Canadiens	4	0	8	16	12
Buffalo Sabres	0	4	0	12	16

(Montreal won Adams Division final, 4-0)

Sun.	May 2—Buffalo 3, at Montreal 4
Tue.	May 4—Buffalo 3, at Montreal 4 (o)
Thur.	May 6—Montreal 4, at Buffalo 3 (p)
Sat.	May 8—Montreal 4, at Buffalo 3 (q)

(o)—Guy Carbonneau scored at 2:50 (OT) for Montreal.
(p)—Gilbert Dionne scored at 8:28 (OT) for Montreal.
(q)—Kirk Muller scored at 11:37 (OT) for Montreal.

PATRICK DIVISION
Series "J"

	W	L	Pts.	GF	GA
N.Y Islanders	4	3	8	24	27
Pittsburgh Penguins	3	4	6	27	24

(N.Y. Islanders won Patrick Division final, 4-3)

Sun. May 2—N.Y. Islanders 3, at Pittsburgh 2
Tue. May 4—N.Y. Islanders 0, at Pittsburgh 3
Thur. May 6—Pittsburgh 3, at N.Y. Islanders 1
Sat. May 8—Pittsburgh 5, at N.Y. Islanders 6
Mon. May 10—N.Y. Islanders 3, at Pittsburgh 6
Wed. May 12—Pittsburgh 5, at N.Y. Islanders 7
Fri. May 14—N.Y. Islanders 4, at Pittsburgh 3 (r)
(r)—David Volek scored at 5:16 (OT) for N.Y. Islanders.

NORRIS DIVISION
Series "K"

	W	L	Pts.	GF	GA
Toronto Maple Leafs	4	3	8	22	11
St. Louis Blues	3	4	6	11	22

(Toronto won Norris Division final, 4-3)

Mon. May 3—St. Louis 1, at Toronto 2 (s)
Wed. May 5—St. Louis 2, at Toronto 1 (t)
Fri. May 7—Toronto 3, at St. Louis 4
Sun. May 9—Toronto 4, at St. Louis 1
Tue. May 11—St. Louis 1, at Toronto 5
Thur. May 13—Toronto 1, at St. Louis 2
Sat. May 16—St. Louis 0, at Toronto 6
(s)—Doug Gilmour scored at 3:16 (2 OT) for Toronto.
(t)—Jeff Brown scored at 3:03 (2 OT) for St. Louis.

SMYTHE DIVISION
Series "L"

	W	L	Pts.	GF	GA
Los Angeles Kings	4	2	8	26	25
Vancouver Canucks	2	4	4	25	26

(Los Angeles won Smythe Division final, 4-2)

Sun. May 2—Los Angeles 2, at Vancouver 5
Wed. May 5—Los Angeles 6, at Vancouver 3
Fri. May 7—Vancouver 4, at Los Angeles 7
Sun. May 9—Vancouver 7, at Los Angeles 2
Tue. May 11—Los Angeles 4, at Vancouver 3 (u)
Thur. May 13—Vancouver 3, at Los Angeles 5
(u)—Gary Shuchuk scored at 6:31 (2 OT) for Los Angeles.

CONFERENCE CHAMPIONSHIPS

PRINCE OF WALES CONFERENCE
Series "M"

	W	L	Pts.	GF	GA
Montreal Canadiens	4	1	8	16	11
N.Y. Islanders	1	4	2	11	16

(Montreal won Wales Conference title, 4-1)

Sun. May 16—N.Y. Islanders 1, at Montreal 4
Tue. May 18—N.Y. Islanders 3, at Montreal 4 (v)
Thur. May 20—Montreal 2, at N.Y. Islanders 1 (w)
Sat. May 22—Montreal 1, at N.Y. Islanders 4
Mon. May 24—N.Y. Islanders 2, at Montreal 5
(v)—Stephan Lebeau scored at 6:21 (2 OT) for Montreal.
(w)—Guy Carbonneau scored at 12:34 (OT) for Montreal.

CLARENCE CAMPBELL CONFERENCE
Series "N"

	W	L	Pts.	GF	GA
Los Angeles Kings	4	3	8	22	23
Toronto Maple Leafs	3	4	6	23	22

(Los Angeles won Campbell Conference title, 4-3)

Mon. May 17—Los Angeles 1, at Toronto 4
Wed. May 19—Los Angeles 3, at Toronto 2
Fri. May 21—Toronto 2, at Los Angeles 4
Sun. May 23—Toronto 4, at Los Angeles 2
Tue. May 25—Los Angeles 2, at Toronto 3 (x)
Thur. May 27—Toronto 4, at Los Angeles 5 (y)
Sat. May 29—Los Angeles 5, at Toronto 4
(x)—Glenn Anderson scored at 19:20 (OT) for Toronto.
(y)—Wayne Gretzky scored at 1:41 (OT) for Los Angeles.

STANLEY CUP FINALS
Series "O"

	W	L	Pts.	GF	GA
Montreal Canadiens	4	1	8	15	12
Los Angeles Kings	1	4	2	12	15

(Montreal won Stanley Cup championship, 4-1)

Tue. June 1—Los Angeles 4, at Montreal 1
Thur. June 3—Los Angeles 2, at Montreal 3 (z)
Sat. June 5—Montreal 4, at Los Angeles 3 (aa)
Mon. June 7—Montreal 3, at Los Angeles 2 (ab)
Wed. June 9—Los Angeles 1, at Montreal 4
(z)—Eric Desjardins scored at 0:51 (OT) for Montreal.
(aa)—John LeClair scored at 0:34 (OT) for Montreal.
(ab)—John LeClair scored at 14:37 (OT) for Montreal.

GAME SUMMARIES. STANLEY CUP FINALS

GAME 1

AT MONTREAL, JUNE 1

Los Angeles 4, Montreal 1

Los Angeles	1	1	2	—4
Montreal	1	0	0	—1

FIRST PERIOD—1. Los Angeles, Robitaille 7 (Zhitnik, Gretzky), 3:03 (pp). 2. Montreal, Ronan 2 (unassisted), 18:09. Penalties—Odelein, Montreal (holding), 2:42; Dionne, Montreal (high-sticking), 6:12; Hrudey, Los Angeles, served by Donnelly (delay of game), 11:03; Kurri, Los Angeles (holding), 15:54.

SECOND PERIOD—3. Los Angeles, Robitaille 8 (Blake, Gretzky), 17:41 (pp). Penalties—Granato, Los Angeles (interference), 5:08; Taylor, Los Angeles (roughing), 6:23; Muller, Montreal (roughing), 6:23; McSorley, Los Angeles (un-

sportsmanlike conduct), 7:16; Odelein, Montreal (unsportsmanlike conduct), 7:16; Damphousse, Montreal (slashing), 10:23; Millen, Los Angeles (high-sticking), 17:23; Desjardins, Montreal (high-sticking), 17:23; Brisebois, Montreal (holding), 17:23; Roy, Montreal, served by LeClair (delay of game), 18:33; Gretzky, Los Angeles (hooking), 19:32.

THIRD PERIOD—4. Los Angeles, Kurri 9 (Gretzky, Granato), 1:51. 5. Los Angeles, Gretzky 14 (Sandstrom), 18:02 (en). Penalties—Huddy, Los Angeles (hooking), 6:41; Daigneault, Montreal (cross-checking), 18:41.

Shots on goal—Los Angeles 11-20-7—38. Montreal 11-10-11—32. Power-play opportunities—Los Angeles 2 of 6; Montreal 0 of 5. Goalies—Los Angeles, Hrudey, 10-6 (32 shots-31 saves). Montreal, Roy, 12-4 (37-34). A—17,959. Referee—Andy van Hellemond. Linesmen—Gerard Gauthier, Ray Scapinello.

GAME 2

AT MONTREAL, JUNE 3

Montreal 3, Los Angeles 2 (OT)

Los Angeles	0	1	1	0—2
Montreal	1	0	1	1—3

FIRST PERIOD—1. Montreal, Desjardins 2 (Damphousse, Lebeau), 18:31. Penalties—Odelein, Montreal (roughing), 5:57; Robitaille, Los Angeles (hooking), 6:40; Brisebois, Montreal (roughing), 7:05; Blake, Los Angeles (tripping), 10:25; Roy, Montreal, served by Bellows (high-sticking), 10:38; Watters, Los Angeles (holding stick), 13:01; Muller, Montreal (tripping), 13:01; Sydor, Los Angeles (holding), 14:44; Schneider, Montreal (holding stick), 17:02; Granato, Los Angeles (holding), 17:53.

SECOND PERIOD—2. Los Angeles, Taylor 3, 5:12 (sh). Penalties—Muller, Montreal (cross-checking), 0:35; Huddy, Los Angeles (cross-checking), 4:20; McSorley, Los Angeles (roughing), 9:43; Damphousse, Montreal (roughing), 9:43; Robitaille, Los Angeles (roughing), 16:02; Dionne, Montreal (roughing), 16:02.

THIRD PERIOD—3. Los Angeles, Conacher 6 (Taylor, Granato), 8:32. 4. Montreal, Desjardins 3 (Damphousse, Schneider), 18:47 (pp). Penalties—Brunet, Montreal (slashing), 1:31; Damphousse, Montreal (cross-checking), 2:13; Zhitnik, Los Angeles (tripping), 4:17; Taylor, Los Angeles (goalie interference), 11:56; Brisebois, Montreal (cross-checking), 13:16; McSorley, Los Angeles (illegal stick), 18:15.

OVERTIME—5. Montreal, Desjardins 4 (Brunet, Ronan), 0:51. Penalties—None.

Shots on goal—Los Angeles 5-9-9-1—24. Montreal 16-12-11-2—41. Power-play opportunities—Los Angeles 0 of 8; Montreal 1 of 7. Goalies—Los Angeles, Hrudey, 10-7 (41 shots-38 saves). Montreal, Roy, 13-4 (24-22). A—17,959. Referee—Kerry Fraser. Linesmen—Kevin Collins, Ray Scapinello.

GAME 3

AT LOS ANGELES, JUNE 5

Montreal 4, Los Angeles 3 (OT)

Montreal	1	2	0	1—4
Los Angeles	0	3	0	0—3

FIRST PERIOD—1. Montreal, Bellows 6 (Haller, Muller), 10:26 (pp). Penalties—Zhitnik, Los Angeles (tripping), 4:23; Bellows, Montreal (cross-checking), 5:21; Desjardins, Montreal (interference), 7:40; Watters, Los Angeles (tripping), 10:21; Ronan, Montreal (goalie interference), 13:09; Lebeau, Montreal (slashing), 16:37; Blake, Los Angeles (roughing), 19:59.

SECOND PERIOD—2. Montreal, Dionne 6 (Keane, Lebeau), 2:41. 3. Montreal, Schneider 1 (Carbonneau), 3:02. 4. Los Angeles, Robitaille 9 (Gretzky, Sandstrom), 7:52. 5. Los Angeles, Granato 6 (unassisted), 11:02. 6. Los Angeles, Gretzky 15 (Donnelly, Hardy), 17:07. Penalties—Ronan, Montreal (slashing), 11:42; Taylor, Los Angeles (slashing), 11:42.

THIRD PERIOD—None. Penalties—Lebeau, Montreal (holding), 6:48; Sandstrom, Los Angeles (goalie interference), 10:50.

OVERTIME—7. Montreal, LeClair 3 (Muller, Bellows), 0:34. Penalties—None.

Shots on goal—Montreal 12-9-12-3—36. Los Angeles 10-13-10-0—33. Power-play opportunities—Montreal 1 of

4; Los Angeles 0 of 5. Goalies—Montreal, Roy, 14-4 (33 shots-30 saves). Los Angeles, Hrudey, 10-8 (36-32). A—16,005. Referee—Terry Gregson. Linesmen—Wayne Bonney, Ray Scapinello.

GAME 4

AT LOS ANGELES, JUNE 7

Montreal 3, Los Angeles 2 (OT)

Montreal	1	1	0	1—3
Los Angeles	0	2	0	0—2

FIRST PERIOD—1. Montreal, Muller 9 (unassisted), 10:57. Penalties—Conacher, Los Angeles (cross-checking), 1:53; Desjardins, Montreal (high-sticking), 4:24; Granato, Los Angeles (roughing), 4:24; Schneider, Montreal (elbowing), 16:50.

SECOND PERIOD—2. Montreal, Damphousse 11 (Keane, Desjardins), 5:24 (pp). 3. Los Angeles, Donnelly 6 (Granato), 6:33. 4. Los Angeles, McSorley 3 (Gretzky, Robitaille), 19:55 (pp). Penalties—Hardy, Los Angeles (holding), 3:32; McSorley, Los Angeles, misconduct, 5:24; Daigneault, Montreal (roughing), 7:37; Rychel, Los Angeles (goalie interference), 7:37; Brisebois, Montreal (roughing), 12:09; Blake, Los Angeles (roughing), 12:09; Sydor, Los Angeles (interference), 15:58; Bellows, Montreal (hooking), 19:10.

THIRD PERIOD—None. Penalties—Daigneault, Montreal (cross-checking), 2:42; Schneider, Montreal (roughing), 19:30; Granato, Los Angeles (roughing), 19:30.

OVERTIME—5. Montreal, LeClair 4 (unassisted), 14:37. Penalties—None.

Shots on goal—Montreal 13-7-12-7—39. Los Angeles 6-11-15-10—42. Power-play opportunities—Montreal 1 of 3; Los Angeles 1 of 3. Goalies—Montreal, Roy, 15-4 (42 shots-40 saves). Los Angeles, Hrudey, 10-9 (39-36). A—16,005. Referee—Andy van Hellemond. Linesmen—Wayne Bonney, Kevin Collins.

GAME 5

AT MONTREAL, JUNE 9

Montreal 4, Los Angeles 1

Los Angeles	0	1	0—1
Montreal	1	2	1—4

FIRST PERIOD—1. Montreal, DiPietro 7 (Leeman, LeClair), 15:10. Penalties—Schneider, Montreal (tripping), 4:35; Keane, Montreal (charging), 10:46; Granato, Los Angeles (tripping), 12:49; Blake, Los Angeles (roughing), 19:23; Sandstrom, Los Angeles (roughing), 19:23; Ronan, Montreal (roughing), 19:23.

SECOND PERIOD—2. Los Angeles, McSorley 4 (Carson, Robitaille), 2:40. 3. Montreal, Muller 10 (Damphousse, Odelein), 3:51. 4. Montreal, Lebeau 3 (Keane, LeClair), 11:31 (pp). Penalties—Leeman, Montreal (tripping), 5:32; Damphousse, Montreal (elbowing), 7:40; Hardy, Los Angeles (holding stick), 10:28.

THIRD PERIOD—5. Montreal, DiPietro 8 (Dionne, Odelein), 12:06. Penalties—None.

Shots on goal—Los Angeles 7-7-5—19. Montreal 10-12-7—29. Power-play opportunities—Los Angeles 0 of 4; Montreal 1 of 3. Goalies—Los Angeles, Hrudey, 10-10 (29 shots-25 saves). Montreal, Roy, 16-4 (19-18). A—17,959. Referee—Terry Gregson. Linesmen—Ray Scapinello, Wayne Bonney.

INDIVIDUAL LEADERS

Goals: Wayne Gretzky, Los Angeles (15)
Assists: Doug Gilmour, Toronto (25)
Wayne Gretzky, Los Angeles (25)
Points: Wayne Gretzky, Los Angeles (40)
Penalty minutes: Marty McSorley, Los Angeles (60)
Goaltending average: Patrick Roy, Montreal (2.13)
Shutouts: Tom Barrasso, Pittsburgh (2)
Curtis Joseph, St. Louis (2)

TOP SCORERS

	Games	G	A	Pts.	Pen.
Wayne Gretzky, Los Angeles	24	15	25	40	4
Doug Gilmour, Toronto	21	10	25	35	30
Tomas Sandstrom, Los Angeles	24	8	17	25	12
Vincent Damphousse, Montreal	20	11	12	23	16
Luc Robitaille, Los Angeles	24	9	13	22	28
Ray Ferraro, N.Y. Islanders	18	13	7	20	18
Wendel Clark, Toronto	21	10	10	20	51
Dave Andreychuk, Toronto	21	12	7	19	35
Mario Lemieux, Pittsburgh	11	8	10	18	10
Glenn Anderson, Toronto	21	7	11	18	31

INDIVIDUAL STATISTICS

BOSTON BRUINS

(Lost Adams Division semifinals to Buffalo, 4-0)

SCORING

	Games	G	A	Pts.	Pen.
Adam Oates	4	0	9	9	4
Joe Juneau........................	4	2	4	6	6
Cam Neely	4	4	1	5	4
Stephen Leach	4	1	1	2	2
Dave Poulin	4	1	1	2	10
Stephen Heinze	4	1	1	2	2
Ray Bourque	4	1	0	1	2
Peter Douris	4	1	0	1	0
Bryan Smolinski	4	1	0	1	2
David Shaw	4	0	1	1	6
Ted Donato	4	0	1	1	0
Brent Hughes	1	0	0	0	2
Jim Wiemer	1	0	0	0	0
John Blue (goalie)	2	0	0	0	0
Andy Moog (goalie)	3	0	0	0	0
Stephane J.G. Richer..........	3	0	0	0	0
Tim Sweeney	3	0	0	0	0
Darin Kimble	4	0	0	0	2
Dmitri Kvartalnov	4	0	0	0	0
Gordie Roberts	4	0	0	0	6
Don Sweeney	4	0	0	0	4
Glen Wesley	4	0	0	0	0

GOALTENDING

	Games	Min.	Goals	SO	Avg.
John Blue	2	96	5	0	3.13
Andy Moog	3	161	14	0	5.22

BUFFALO SABRES

(Lost Adams Division finals to Montreal, 4-0)

SCORING

	Games	G	A	Pts.	Pen.
Dale Hawerchuk	8	5	9	14	2
Pat LaFontaine	7	2	10	12	0
Alexander Mogilny	7	7	3	10	6
Yuri Khmylev	8	4	3	7	4
Doug Bodger	8	2	3	5	0
Randy Wood	8	1	4	5	4
Ken Sutton	8	3	1	4	8
Donald Audette	8	2	2	4	6
Bob Sweeney	8	2	2	4	8
Richard Smehlik	8	0	4	4	2
Keith Carney	8	0	3	3	6
Dave Hannan	8	1	1	2	18
Brad May	8	1	1	2	14
Bill Houlder	8	0	2	2	4
Wayne Presley	8	1	0	1	6
Matthew Barnaby	1	0	1	1	4
Bob Errey	4	0	1	1	10
Colin Patterson	8	0	1	1	2
Dominik Hasek (goalie)	1	0	0	0	0

	Games	G	A	Pts.	Pen.
Bob Corkum	5	0	0	0	2
Grant Fuhr (goalie)	8	0	0	0	2
Grant Ledyard	8	0	0	0	8

GOALTENDING

	Games	Min.	Goals	SO	Avg.
Dominik Hasek..........	1	45	1	0	1.33
Grant Fuhr	8	474	27	1	3.42

CALGARY FLAMES

(Lost Smythe Division semifinals to Los Angeles, 4-2)

SCORING

	Games	G	A	Pts.	Pen.
Theoren Fleury	6	5	7	12	27
Joe Nieuwendyk	6	3	6	9	10
Gary Roberts..................	5	1	6	7	43
Al MacInnis	6	1	6	7	10
Joel Otto........................	6	4	2	6	4
Robert Reichel	6	2	4	6	2
Trent Yawney	6	3	2	5	6
Gary Suter	6	2	3	5	8
Chris Dahlquist	6	3	1	4	4
Greg Paslawski	6	3	0	3	0
Brent Ashton	6	0	3	3	2
Brian Skrudland	6	0	3	3	12
Frank Musil	6	1	1	2	7
Kevin Dahl......................	6	0	2	2	8
Chris Lindberg	2	0	1	1	2
Roger Johansson	5	0	1	1	2
Craig Berube	6	0	1	1	21
Paul Ranheim	6	0	1	1	0
Jeff Reese (goalie)	4	0	0	0	0
Mike Vernon (goalie):	4	0	0	0	2
Ronnie Stern	6	0	0	0	43

GOALTENDING

	Games	Min.	Goals	SO	Avg.
Jeff Reese................	4	209	17 (1)	0	4.88
Mike Vernon..............	4	150	15	0	6.00

CHICAGO BLACKHAWKS

(Lost Norris Division semifinals to St. Louis, 4-0)

SCORING

	Games	G	A	Pts.	Pen.
Brian Noonan	4	3	0	3	4
Jeremy Roenick	4	1	2	3	2
Steve Larmer	4	0	3	3	0
Brent Sutter	4	1	1	2	4
Chris Chelios	4	0	2	2	14
Jocelyn Lemieux	4	1	0	1	2
Michel Goulet	3	0	1	1	0
Stephane Matteau	3	0	1	1	2
Keith Brown	4	0	1	1	2
Dave Christian	1	0	0	0	0

	Games	G	A	Pts.	Pen.
Stu Grimson	2	0	0	0	4
Greg Gilbert	3	0	0	0	0
Ed Belfour (goalie)	4	0	0	0	2
Dirk Graham	4	0	0	0	0
Bryan Marchment	4	0	0	0	12
Craig Muni	4	0	0	0	2
Joe Murphy	4	0	0	0	8
Troy Murray	4	0	0	0	2
Cam Russell	4	0	0	0	0
Christian Ruuttu	4	0	0	0	2
Steve Smith	4	0	0	0	10

GOALTENDING
	Games	Min.	Goals	SO	Avg.
Ed Belfour	4	249	13	0	3.13

DETROIT RED WINGS

(Lost Norris Division semifinals to Toronto, 4-3)

SCORING
	Games	G	A	Pts.	Pen.
Paul Coffey	7	2	9	11	2
Sergei Fedorov	7	3	6	9	23
Steve Yzerman	7	4	3	7	4
Dino Ciccarelli	7	4	2	6	16
Dallas Drake	7	3	3	6	6
Ray Sheppard	7	2	3	5	0
Paul Ysebaert	7	3	1	4	2
Steve Chiasson	7	2	2	4	19
Mark Howe	7	1	3	4	2
Yves Racine	7	1	3	4	27
Shawn Burr	7	2	1	3	2
Gerard Gallant	6	1	2	3	4
Bob Probert	7	0	3	3	10
Sheldon Kennedy	7	1	1	2	2
Vyacheslav Kozlov	4	0	2	2	2
Tim Cheveldae (goalie)	7	0	2	2	2
Keith Primeau	7	0	2	2	26
Nicklas Lidstrom	7	1	0	1	0
Vladimir Konstantinov	7	0	1	1	8
Steve Konroyd	1	0	0	0	0
John Ogrodnick	1	0	0	0	0
Jim Hiller	2	0	0	0	4

GOALTENDING
	Games	Min.	Goals	SO	Avg.
Tim Cheveldae	7	423	24	0	3.40

LOS ANGELES KINGS

(Lost Stanley Cup finals to Montreal, 4-1)

SCORING
	Games	G	A	Pts.	Pen.
Wayne Gretzky	24	15	25	40	4
Tomas Sandstrom	24	8	17	25	12
Luc Robitaille	24	9	13	22	28
Jari Kurri	24	9	8	17	12
Tony Granato	24	6	11	17	50
Warren Rychel	23	6	7	13	39
Mike Donnelly	24	6	7	13	14
Alexei Zhitnik	24	3	9	12	26
Darryl Sydor	24	3	8	11	16
Pat Conacher	24	6	4	10	6
Rob Blake	23	4	6	10	46
Marty McSorley	24	4	6	10	60
Jimmy Carson	18	5	4	9	2
Dave Taylor	22	3	5	8	31
Corey Millen	23	2	4	6	12
Charlie Huddy	23	1	4	5	12
Gary Shuchuk	17	2	2	4	12
Mark Hardy	15	1	2	3	30
Tim Watters	22	0	2	2	30
Lonnie Loach	1	0	0	0	0
Marc Potvin	1	0	0	0	0
Jim Thomson	1	0	0	0	0
Robb Stauber (goalie)	4	0	0	0	0
Kelly Hrudey (goalie)	20	0	0	0	2

GOALTENDING
	Games	Min.	Goals	SO	Avg.
Kelly Hrudey	20	1261	74 (1)	0	3.52
Robb Stauber	4	240	16	0	4.00

MONTREAL CANADIENS

(Winner of 1993 Stanley Cup)

SCORING
	Games	G	A	Pts.	Pen.
Vincent Damphousse	20	11	12	23	16
Kirk Muller	20	10	7	17	18
Brian Bellows	18	6	9	15	18
Mike Keane	19	2	13	15	6
Eric Desjardins	20	4	10	14	23
Paul Dipietro	17	8	5	13	8
Gilbert Dionne	20	6	6	12	20
John LeClair	20	4	6	10	14
Benoit Brunet	20	2	8	10	8
Kevin Haller	17	1	6	7	16
Stephan Lebeau	13	3	3	6	6
Guy Carbonneau	20	3	3	6	10
Lyle Odelein	20	1	5	6	30
Ed Ronan	14	2	3	5	10
Denis Savard	14	0	5	5	4
J.J. Daigneault	20	1	3	4	22
Patrice Brisebois	20	0	4	4	18
Gary Leeman	11	1	2	3	2
Matt Schneider	11	1	2	3	16
Jesse Belanger	9	0	1	1	0
Patrick Roy (goalie)	20	0	1	1	4
Todd Ewen	1	0	0	0	0
Oleg Petrov	1	0	0	0	0
Andre Racicot (goalie)	1	0	0	0	0
Donald Dufresne	2	0	0	0	0
Sean Hill	3	0	0	0	4
Mario Roberge	3	0	0	0	0
Rob Ramage	7	0	0	0	4

GOALTENDING
	Games	Min.	Goals	SO	Avg.
Patrick Roy	20	1293	46 (3)	0	2.13
Andre Racicot	1	18	2	0	6.67

NEW JERSEY DEVILS

(Lost Patrick Division semifinals to Pittsburgh, 4-1)

SCORING
	Games	G	A	Pts.	Pen.
Stephane J.J. Richer	5	2	2	4	2
Scott Stevens	5	2	2	4	10
Bruce Driver	5	1	3	4	4
Scott Niedermayer	5	0	3	3	2
Tommy Albelin	5	2	0	2	0
Claude Lemieux	5	2	0	2	19
Bobby Holik	5	1	1	2	6
Bill Guerin	5	1	1	2	4
Alexander Semak	5	1	1	2	2
Viacheslav Fetisov	5	0	2	2	4
Peter Stastny	5	0	2	2	2
Valeri Zelepukin	5	0	2	2	0
Dave Barr	5	1	0	1	6
John MacLean	5	0	1	1	10
Tom Chorske	1	0	0	0	0
Craig Billington (goalie)	2	0	0	0	0
Alexei Kasatonov	4	0	0	0	0
Chris Terreri (goalie)	4	0	0	0	0
Ken Daneyko	5	0	0	0	8
Randy McKay	5	0	0	0	16
Bernie Nicholls	5	0	0	0	6

GOALTENDING
	Games	Min.	Goals	SO	Avg.
Craig Billington	2	78	5	0	3.85
Chris Terreri	4	219	17 (1)	0	4.66

NEW YORK ISLANDERS

(Lost Wales Conference finals to Montreal, 4-1)

SCORING

	Games	G	A	Pts.	Pen.
Ray Ferraro	18	13	7	20	18
Steve Thomas	18	9	8	17	37
Derek King	18	3	11	14	14
Pierre Turgeon	11	6	7	13	0
Benoit Hogue	18	6	6	12	31
Vladimir Malakhov	17	3	6	9	12
Patrick Flatley	15	2	7	9	12
Brian Mullen	18	3	4	7	2
Tom Fitzgerald	18	2	5	7	18
Uwe Krupp	18	1	5	6	12
Dennis Vaske	18	0	6	6	14
Dave Volek	10	4	1	5	2
Darius Kasparaitis	18	0	5	5	31
Travis Green	12	3	1	4	6
Brad Dalgarno	18	2	2	4	14
Glenn Healy (goalie)	18	0	3	3	0
Claude Loiselle	18	0	3	3	10
Jeff Norton	10	1	1	2	4
Tom Kurvers	12	0	2	2	6
Steve Junker	3	0	1	1	0
Marty McInnis	3	0	1	1	0
Scott Scissons	1	0	0	0	0
Greg Parks	2	0	0	0	0
Mark Fitzpatrick (goalie)	3	0	0	0	2
Richard Pilon	15	0	0	0	50
Mick Vukota	15	0	0	0	16

GOALTENDING

	Games	Min.	Goals	SO	Avg.
Mark Fitzpatrick	3	77	4 (1)	0	3.12
Glenn Healy	18	1109	59 (1)	0	3.19

PITTSBURGH PENGUINS

(Lost Patrick Division finals to N.Y. Islanders, 4-3)

SCORING

	Games	G	A	Pts.	Pen.
Mario Lemieux	11	8	10	18	10
Ron Francis	12	6	11	17	19
Kevin Stevens	12	5	11	16	22
Rick Tocchet	12	7	6	13	24
Larry Murphy	12	2	11	13	10
Jaromir Jagr	12	5	4	9	23
Joe Mullen	12	4	2	6	6
Ulf Samuelsson	12	1	5	6	24
Mike Ramsey	12	0	6	6	4
Jeff Daniels	12	3	2	5	0
Shawn McEachern	12	3	2	5	10
Troy Loney	10	1	4	5	0
Dave Tippett	12	1	4	5	14
Martin Straka	11	2	1	3	2
Peter Taglianetti	11	1	2	3	16
Tom Barrasso (goalie)	12	0	3	3	4
Kjell Samuelsson	12	0	3	3	2
Mike Needham	9	1	0	1	2
Paul Stanton	1	0	1	1	0
Mike Stapleton	4	0	0	0	0
Grant Jennings	12	0	0	0	8

GOALTENDING

	Games	Min.	Goals	SO	Avg.
Tom Barrasso	12	722	35 (2)	2	2.91

QUEBEC NORDIQUES

(Lost Adams Division semifinals to Montreal, 4-2)

SCORING

	Games	G	A	Pts.	Pen.
Joe Sakic	6	3	3	6	2
Claude Lapointe	6	2	4	6	8
Mike Ricci	6	0	6	6	8
Scott Young	6	4	1	5	0
Steve Duchesne	6	0	5	5	6
Mats Sundin	6	3	1	4	6
Curtis Leschyshyn	6	1	1	2	6
Martin Rucinsky	6	1	1	2	4
Andrei Kovalenko	4	1	0	1	2
Owen Nolan	5	1	0	1	2
Alexei Gusarov	5	0	1	1	0
Steven Finn	6	0	1	1	8
Mike Hough	6	0	1	1	0
Adam Foote	6	0	1	1	2
Valeri Kamensky	6	0	1	1	6
Stephane Fiset (goalie)	1	0	0	0	0
Kerry Huffman	3	0	0	0	0
Dave Karpa	3	0	0	0	0
Scott Pearson	3	0	0	0	0
Gino Cavallini	4	0	0	0	0
Craig Wolanin	4	0	0	0	4
Chris Simon	5	0	0	0	26
Ron Hextall (goalie)	6	0	0	0	0

GOALTENDING

	Games	Min.	Goals	SO	Avg.
Stephane Fiset	1	21	1	0	2.86
Ron Hextall	6	372	18	0	2.90

ST. LOUIS BLUES

(Lost Norris Division finals to Toronto, 4-3)

SCORING

	Games	G	A	Pts.	Pen.
Brett Hull	11	8	5	13	2
Jeff Brown	11	3	8	11	6
Craig Janney	11	2	9	11	0
Brendan Shanahan	11	4	3	7	18
Nelson Emerson	11	1	6	7	6
Denny Felsner	9	2	3	5	2
Kevin Miller	10	0	3	3	11
Dave Lowry	11	2	0	2	14
Garth Butcher	11	1	1	2	20
Philippe Bozon	9	1	0	1	0
Kevin Miehm	2	0	1	1	0
Basil McRae	11	0	1	1	24
Rich Sutter	11	0	1	1	10
Rick Zombo	11	0	1	1	12
Guy Hebert (goalie)	1	0	0	0	0
Curt Giles	3	0	0	0	2
Igor Korolev	3	0	0	0	0
Stephane Quintal	9	0	0	0	8
Bret Hedican	10	0	0	0	14
Murray Baron	11	0	0	0	12
Bob Bassen	11	0	0	0	10
Curtis Joseph (goalie)	11	0	0	0	2
Ron Wilson	11	0	0	0	12

GOALTENDING

	Games	Min.	Goals	SO	Avg.
Guy Hebert	1	2	0	0	0.00
Curtis Joseph	11	715	27 (1)	2	2.27

TORONTO MAPLE LEAFS

(Lost Campbell Conference finals to Los Angeles, 4-3)

SCORING

	Games	G	A	Pts.	Pen.
Doug Gilmour	21	10	25	35	30
Wendel Clark	21	10	10	20	51
Dave Andreychuk	21	12	7	19	35
Glenn Anderson	21	7	11	18	31
Dave Ellett	21	4	8	12	8
Bob Rouse	21	3	8	11	29
Todd Gill	21	1	10	11	26
Mike Krushelnyski	16	3	7	10	8
Nikolai Borschevsky	16	2	7	9	0
Mike Foligno	18	2	6	8	42
Sylvain Lefebvre	21	3	3	6	20
Jamie Macoun	21	0	6	6	36
John Cullen	12	2	3	5	0
Rob Pearson	14	2	2	4	31

	Games	G	A	Pts.	Pen.
Peter Zezel	20	2	1	3	6
Mike Eastwood	10	1	2	3	8
Dimitri Mironov	14	1	2	3	2
Mark Osborne	19	1	1	2	16
Bill Berg	21	1	1	2	18
Ken Baumgartner	7	1	0	1	0
Kent Manderville	18	1	0	1	8
Daren Puppa (goalie)	1	0	0	0	2
Dave McLlwain	4	0	0	0	0
Felix Potvin (goalie)	21	0	0	0	6

GOALTENDING

	Games	Min.	Goals	SO	Avg.
Felix Potvin	21	1308	62	1	2.84
Daren Puppa	1	20	1	0	3.00

VANCOUVER CANUCKS

(Lost Smythe Division finals to Los Angeles, 4-2)

SCORING

	Games	G	A	Pts.	Pen.
Geoff Courtnall	12	4	10	14	12
Greg Adams	12	7	6	13	6
Trevor Linden	12	5	8	13	16
Pavel Bure	12	5	7	12	8
Cliff Ronning	12	2	9	11	6
Murray Craven	12	4	6	10	4
Dave Babych	12	2	5	7	6
Gerald Diduck	12	4	2	6	12
Dana Murzyn	12	3	2	5	18
Dixon Ward	9	2	3	5	0
Petr Nedved	12	2	3	5	2
Jyrki Lumme	12	0	5	5	6
Jim Sandlak	6	2	2	4	4
Anatoli Semenov	12	1	3	4	0
Sergio Momesso	12	3	0	3	30
Jiri Slegr	5	0	3	3	4
Doug Lidster	12	0	3	3	8
Kirk McLean (goalie)	12	0	3	3	0
Garry Valk	7	0	1	1	12
Gino Odjick	1	0	0	0	0
Robert Dirk	9	0	0	0	6
Tim Hunter	11	0	0	0	26

GOALTENDING

	Games	Min.	Goals	SO	Avg.
Kirk McLean	12	754	42 (1)	0	3.34

WASHINGTON CAPITALS

(Lost Patrick Division semifinals to N.Y. Islanders, 4-2)

SCORING

	Games	G	A	Pts.	Pen.
Dale Hunter	6	7	1	8	35
Dimitri Khristich	6	2	5	7	2
Al Iafrate	6	6	0	6	4

	Games	G	A	Pts.	Pen.
Mike Ridley	6	1	5	6	0
Peter Bondra	6	0	6	6	0
Pat Elynuik	6	2	3	5	19
Bob Carpenter	6	1	4	5	6
Calle Johansson	6	0	5	5	4
Kelly Miller	6	0	3	3	2
Sylvain Cote	6	1	1	2	4
Todd Krygier	6	1	1	2	4
Paul Cavallini	6	0	2	2	18
Michal Pivonka	6	0	2	2	0
Randy Burridge	4	1	0	1	0
Steve Konowalchuk	2	0	1	1	0
Kevin Hatcher	6	0	1	1	14
Alan May	6	0	1	1	6
Don Beaupre (goalie)	2	0	0	0	0
Rick Tabaracci (goalie)	4	0	0	0	4
Shawn Anderson	6	0	0	0	0
Keith Jones	6	0	0	0	10

GOALTENDING

	Games	Min.	Goals	SO	Avg.
Rick Tabaracci	4	304	14	0	2.76
Don Beaupre	2	119	9	0	4.54

WINNIPEG JETS

(Lost Smythe Division semifinals to Vancouver, 4-2)

SCORING

	Games	G	A	Pts.	Pen.
Phil Housley	6	0	7	7	2
Teemu Selanne	6	4	2	6	2
Darrin Shannon	6	2	4	6	6
Keith Tkachuk	6	4	0	4	14
Thomas Steen	6	1	3	4	2
Stu Barnes	6	1	3	4	2
Andy Brickley	1	1	1	2	0
Kris King	6	1	1	2	4
Teppo Numminen	6	1	1	2	2
Mike Lalor	6	0	2	2	4
Fredrik Olausson	6	0	2	2	2
Alexei Zhamnov	6	0	2	2	2
Tie Domi	6	1	0	1	23
Luciano Borsato	6	1	0	1	4
Mike Eagles	5	0	1	1	6
Russ Romaniuk	1	0	0	0	0
John Druce	2	0	0	0	0
Bryan Erickson	3	0	0	0	0
Evgeny Davydov	4	0	0	0	0
Igor Ulanov	4	0	0	0	4
Sergei Bautin	6	0	0	0	2
Bob Essensa (goalie)	6	0	0	0	2
Dean Kennedy	6	0	0	0	2

GOALTENDING

	Games	Min.	Goals	SO	Avg.
Bob Essensa	6	367	20 (1)	0	3.27

MISCELLANEOUS

HAT TRICKS

(Players scoring three or more goals in a game)

Date	Player, Team	Opp.	Goals
4-18-93	Brian Noonan, Chicago	St.L.	3
4-20-93	Dale Hunter, Washington	NYI	3
4-23-93	Teemu Selanne, Winnipeg	Van.	3
4-26-93	Ray Ferraro, N.Y. Islanders	Was.	4
4-26-93	Al Iafrate, Washington	NYI	3

Date	Player, Team	Opp.	Goals
4-28-93	Paul DiPietro, Montreal	Que.	3
4-29-93	Dino Ciccarelli, Detroit	Tor.	3
5-27-93	Wendel Clark, Toronto	L.A.	3
5-29-93	Wayne Gretzky, Los Angeles	Tor.	3
6- 3-93	Eric Desjardins, Montreal	L.A.	3

OVERTIME GOALS

Date	Player, Team	Opponent	Time	Final score
4-18-93	—Bob Sweeney, Buffalo	Boston	11:03	Buffalo 5, Boston 4
4-18-93	—Scott Young, Quebec	Montreal	16:49	Quebec 3, Montreal 2
4-20-93	—Brian Mullen, N.Y. Islanders	Washington	*14:50	N.Y. Islanders 5, Washington 4
4-22-93	—Yuri Khmylev, Buffalo	Boston	1:05	Buffalo 4, Boston 3
4-22-93	—Vincent Damphousse, Montreal	Quebec	10:30	Montreal 2, Quebec 1
4-22-93	—Ray Ferraro, N.Y. Islanders	Washington	4:46	N.Y. Islanders 4, Washington 3
4-24-93	—Ray Ferraro, N.Y. Islanders	Washington	*5:40	N.Y. Islanders 4, Washington 3
4-24-93	—Brad May, Buffalo	Boston	4:48	Buffalo 6, Boston 5
4-25-93	—Craig Janney, St. Louis	Chicago	10:43	St. Louis 4, Chicago 3
4-26-93	—Kirk Muller, Montreal	Quebec	8:17	Montreal 5, Quebec 4
4-27-93	—Mike Foligno, Toronto	Detroit	2:05	Toronto 5, Detroit 4
4-27-93	—Teemu Selanne, Winnipeg	Vancouver	6:18	Winnipeg 4, Vancouver 3
4-29-93	—Greg Adams, Vancouver	Winnipeg	4:30	Vancouver 4, Winnipeg 3
5- 1-93	—Nikolai Borschevsky, Toronto	Detroit	2:35	Toronto 4, Detroit 3
5- 3-93	—Doug Gilmour, Toronto	St. Louis	*3:16	Toronto 2, St. Louis 1
5- 4-93	—Guy Carbonneau, Montreal	Buffalo	2:50	Montreal 4, Buffalo 3
5- 5-93	—Jeff Brown, St. Louis	Toronto	*3:03	St. Louis 2, Toronto 1
5- 6-93	—Gilbert Dionne, Montreal	Buffalo	8:28	Montreal 4, Buffalo 3
5- 8-93	—Kirk Muller, Montreal	Buffalo	11:37	Montreal 4, Buffalo 3
5-11-93	—Gary Shuchuk, Los Angeles	Vancouver	*6:31	Los Angeles 4, Vancouver 3
5-14-93	—David Volek, N.Y. Islanders	Pittsburgh	5:16	N.Y. Islanders 4, Pittsburgh 3
5-18-93	—Stephan Lebeau, Montreal	N.Y. Islanders	*6:21	Montreal 4, N.Y. Islanders 3
5-20-93	—Guy Carbonneau, Montreal	N.Y. Islanders	12:34	Montreal 2, N.Y. Islanders 1
5-25-93	—Glenn Anderson, Toronto	Los Angeles	19:20	Toronto 3, Los Angeles 2
5-27-93	—Wayne Gretzky, Los Angeles	Toronto	1:41	Los Angeles 5, Toronto 4
6- 3-93	—Eric Desjardins, Montreal	Los Angeles	0:51	Montreal 3, Los Angeles 2
6- 5-93	—John LeClair, Montreal	Los Angeles	0:34	Montreal 4, Los Angeles 3
6- 7-93	—John LeClair, Montreal	Los Angeles	14:37	Montreal 3, Los Angeles 2

*Double-overtime goal.

ALL - STAR GAME

ROSTERS

CAMPBELL CONFERENCE

Coach: Mike Keenan
Associate coaches: Tommy Ivan, Billy Reay

Forwards (Pos.)	Club
Brian Bradley (C)	Tampa Bay Lightning
Pavel Bure (RW)	Vancouver Canucks
Doug Gilmour (C)	Toronto Maple Leafs
Wayne Gretzky (C)	Los Angeles Kings
Brett Hull (RW)	St. Louis Blues
Kelly Kisio* (C)	San Jose Sharks
Jari Kurri (RW)	Los Angeles Kings
Mike Modano (RW)	Minnesota North Stars
Gary Roberts (LW)	Calgary Flames
Luc Robitaille (LW)	Los Angeles Kings
Jeremy Roenick (C)	Chicago Blackhawks
Teemu Selanne (RW)	Winnipeg Jets
Steve Yzerman (C)	Detroit Red Wings

Defensemen	
Garth Butcher*	St. Louis Blues
Randy Carlyle†	Winnipeg Jets
Steve Chiasson	Detroit Red Wings
Chris Chelios	Chicago Blackhawks
Paul Coffey	Detroit Red Wings
Phil Housley	Winnipeg Jets
Dave Manson	Edmonton Oilers

Goaltenders	
Ed Belfour	Chicago Blackhawks
Jon Casey	Minnesota North Stars
Mike Vernon	Calgary Flames

*Replacement for injured teammate (Butcher for Jeff Brown, Kisio for Pat Falloon).
†Senior category (in recognition of career accomplishments).

WALES CONFERENCE

Coach: Scotty Bowman
Assistant coaches: Rick Kehoe, Gilles Meloche, Rick Paterson, Barry Smith

Forwards (Pos.)	Club
Peter Bondra (RW)	Washington Capitals
Mike Gartner* (RW)	New York Rangers
Jaromir Jagr (RW)	Pittsburgh Penguins
Pat LaFontaine (C)	Buffalo Sabres
Alexander Mogilny (RW)	Buffalo Sabres
Kirk Muller (C)	Montreal Canadiens
Adam Oates (C)	Boston Bruins
Mark Recchi (RW)	Philadelphia Flyers
Joe Sakic (C)	Quebec Nordiques
Kevin Stevens (LW)	Pittsburgh Penguins
Rick Tocchet* (RW)	Pittsburgh Penguins
Pierre Turgeon (C)	New York Islanders

Defensemen	
Ray Bourque	Boston Bruins
Steve Duchesne	Quebec Nordiques
Al Iafrate	Washington Capitals
Kevin Lowe	New York Rangers
Brad Marsh†	Ottawa Senators
Scott Stevens	New Jersey Devils
Zarley Zalapski	Hartford Whalers

Goaltenders	
Craig Billington	New Jersey Devils
Patrick Roy	Montreal Canadiens
Peter Sidorkiewicz	Ottawa Senators

*Replacement for injured teammate (Gartner for Mark Messier, Tocchet for Mario Lemieux).
†Senior category (in recognition of career accomplishments).

GAME SUMMARY

Wales Conference 16, Campbell Conference 6

Campbell Conference	0	2	4— 6
Wales Conference	6	6	4—16

FIRST PERIOD—1. Wales, Gartner 1 (Lowe, Oates), 3:15. 2. Wales, Gartner 2 (Oates), 3:37. 3. Wales, Bondra 1 (Oates, Gartner), 4:24. 4. Wales, Mogilny 1 (Bourque), 11:40 (pp). 5. Wales, Turgeon 1 (Recchi), 13:05. 6. Wales, Gartner 3 (Oates, Bondra), 13:22. Penalty—Manson, Campbell (tripping), 11:12.

SECOND PERIOD—7. Wales, Tocchet 1 (K. Stevens, Recchi), 0:19. 8. Wales, Gartner 4 (Turgeon), 3:33. 9. Wales, Tocchet 2 (S. Stevens), 4:57. 10. Campbell, Roenick 1 (Selanne), 5:52. 11. Wales, Recchi 1 (Marsh), 9:25. 12. Campbell, Kisio 1 (Roenick, Modano), 10:15. 13. Wales, K. Stevens 1 (Recchi), 14:50. 14. Wales, Turgeon 2 (Sakic, Jagr), 17:56. Penalties—None.

THIRD PERIOD—15. Wales, LaFontaine 1 (Muller, Mogilny), 8:07. 16. Wales, Jagr 1 (Sakic, Turgeon), 9:08. 17. Wales, Marsh 1 (K. Stevens, Recchi), 12:52. 18. Campbell, Gilmour 1 (Coffey), 13:57. 19. Wales, Turgeon 3 (Sakic, S. Stevens), 15:51. 20. Campbell, Selanne 1 (Manson, Kurri), 17:03. 21. Campbell, Bure 1 (Kisio), 18:44. 22. Campbell, Bure 2 (unassisted), 19:32. Penalties—None.

Shots on goal—Campbell 11-16-14—41. Wales 22-15-12—49. Power-play opportunities—Campbell 0 of 0; Wales 1 of 1. Goalies—Campbell, Belfour (22 shots-16 saves); Vernon (0:00 second, 15-9); Casey (0:00 third, 12-8). Wales, Roy (11-11); Sidorkiewicz (0:00 second, 16-14); Billington (0:00 third, 14-10). A—17,137. Referee—Dan Marouelli. Linesmen—Ryan Bozak, Kevin Collins.

AWARDS

THE SPORTING NEWS

ALL-STAR TEAMS

Tom Barrasso, Pittsburgh	Goaltender	Ed Belfour, Chicago
Chris Chelios, Chicago	Defense	Larry Murphy, Pittsburgh
Ray Bourque, Boston	Defense	Al Iafrate, Washington
Luc Robitaille, Los Angeles	Left wing	Kevin Stevens, Pittsburgh
Mario Lemieux, Pittsburgh	Center	Doug Gilmour, Toronto
Teemu Selanne, Winnipeg	Right wing	Alexander Mogilny, Buffalo

Note: THE SPORTING NEWS All-Star Team is selected by the NHL players.

AWARD WINNERS

Player of the Year: Mario Lemieux, Pittsburgh
Rookie of the Year: Teemu Selanne, Winnipeg
Coach of the Year: Pat Burns, Toronto
Executive of the Year: Cliff Fletcher, Toronto

Note: THE SPORTING NEWS player and rookie awards are selected by the NHL players, the coaches award by the NHL coaches and the executive award by NHL executives.

NATIONAL HOCKEY LEAGUE

ALL-STAR TEAMS

Ed Belfour, Chicago	Goaltender	Tom Barrasso, Pittsburgh
Ray Bourque, Boston	Defense	Larry Murphy, Pittsburgh
Chris Chelios, Chicago	Defense	Al Iafrate, Washington
Luc Robitaille, Los Angeles	Left wing	Kevin Stevens, Pittsburgh
Mario Lemieux, Pittsburgh	Center	Pat LaFontaine, Buffalo
Teemu Selanne, Winnipeg	Right wing	Alexander Mogilny, Buffalo

AWARD WINNERS

Art Ross Trophy: Mario Lemieux, Pittsburgh
Hart Memorial Trophy: Mario Lemieux, Pittsburgh
James Norris Memorial Trophy: Chris Chelios, Chicago
Vezina Trophy: Ed Belfour, Chicago
Bill Jennings Trophy: Ed Belfour, Chicago
Calder Memorial Trophy: Teemu Selanne, Winnipeg

Lady Byng Memorial Trophy: Pierre Turgeon, N.Y. Islanders
Conn Smythe Trophy: Patrick Roy, Montreal
Bill Masterton Memorial Trophy: Mario Lemieux, Pittsburgh
Frank J. Selke Trophy: Doug Gilmour, Toronto
Jack Adams Award: Pat Burns, Toronto
King Clancy Trophy: Dave Poulin, Boston

PLAYER DRATS

EXPANSION DRAFT—JUNE 24, 1993

MIGHTY DUCKS OF ANAHEIM

GOALTENDERS

Name, Former team
Glenn Healy, N.Y. Islanders
Guy Hebert, St. Louis
Ron Tugnutt, Edmonton

DEFENSEMEN

Name, Former team
Bobby Dollas, Detroit
Mark Ferner, Ottawa
Sean Hill, Montreal
Bill Houlder, Buffalo
Alexei Kasatonov, New Jersey
Randy Ladouceur, Hartford
Dennis Vial, Tampa Bay
David Williams, San Jose

FORWARDS

Name, Former team
Robin Bawa, San Jose
Bob Corkum, Buffalo
Stu Grimson, Chicago
Trevor Halverson, Washington
Steven King, N.Y. Rangers
Lonnie Loach, Los Angeles
Troy Loney, Pittsburgh
Joe Sacco, Toronto
Anatoli Semenov, Vancouver
Jarrod Skalde, New Jersey
Tim Sweeney, Boston
Jim Thomson, Los Angeles
Terry Yake, Hartford

FLORIDA PANTHERS

GOALTENDERS

Name, Former team
Mark Fitzpatrick, Quebec
Daren Puppa, Toronto
John Vanbiesbrouck, Vancouver

DEFENSEMEN

Name, Former team
Steve Bancroft, Winnipeg
Joe Cirella, N.Y. Rangers
Alexander Godynyuk, Calgary
Gord Hynes, Philadelphia
Paul Laus, Pittsburgh
Gord Murphy, Dallas
Stephane Richer, Boston
Milan Tichy, Chicago

FORWARDS

Name, Former team
Doug Barrault, Dallas
Jesse Belanger, Montreal
Tom Fitzgerald, N.Y. Islanders
Randy Gilhen, Tampa Bay
Mike Hough, Washington
Marc Labelle, Ottawa
Scott Levins, Winnipeg
Bill Lindsay, Quebec
Andrei Lomakin, Philadelphia
Dave Lowry, St. Louis
Scott Mellanby, Edmonton
Brian Skrudland, Calgary
Pete Stauber, Detroit

PHASE II—JUNE 25, 1993

OTTAWA SENATORS

Name, Position, Former team
Dennis Vial, D, Anaheim

TAMPA BAY LIGHTNING

Name, Position, Former team
Glenn Healy, G, Anaheim
Daren Puppa, G, Florida

SUPPLEMENTAL DRAFT—JUNE 25, 1993

Pick	Team selecting	Name, Position, College
1.	Ottawa	Eric Flinton, LW, New Hampshire
2.	San Jose	Dean Sylvester, RW, Kent
3.	Tampa Bay	Brent Peterson, LW, Michigan Tech
4.	Florida	Chris Imes, D, Maine
5.	Anaheim	Pat Thompson, D, Brown
6.	Hartford	Kent Fearns, D, Colorado College
7.	Edmonton	Brett Able, G, New Hampshire
8.	N.Y. Rangers	Wayne Strachan, RW, Lake Superior St.
9.	Dallas	Jacques Joubert, C, Boston University
10.	Philadelphia	Shannon Finn, D, Illinois-Chicago

ENTRY DRAFT—JUNE 26, 1993

FIRST ROUND

No.—Selecting club	Player	Pos.	Previous team (league)
1—Ottawa	Alexandre Daigle	C	Victoriaville (QMJHL)
2—Hartford (from San Jose)	Chris Pronger	D	Peterborough (OHL)
3—Tampa Bay	Chris Gratton	F	Kingston (OHL)
4—Anaheim	Paul Kariya	F	University of Maine (H. East)
5—Florida	Rob Niedermayer	C	Medicine Hat (WHL)
6—San Jose (from Hartford)	Viktor Kozlov	F	Moscow, CIS
7—Edmonton	Jason Arnott	C	Oshawa (OHL)

No.—Selecting club	Player	Pos.	Previous team (league)
8—N.Y. Rangers	Niklas Sundstrom	C	Ornskoldsvik, Sweden
9—Dallas	Todd Harvey	C	Detroit (OHL)
10—Quebec (from Philadelphia)	Jocelyn Thibault	G	Sherbrooke (QMJHL)
11—Washington (from St. Louis)	Brendan Witt	D	Seattle (WHL)
12—Toronto (from Buffalo)	Kenny Jonsson	D	Rogle, Sweden
13—New Jersey	Denis Pederson	C	Prince Albert (WHL)
14—Quebec (from N.Y. Islanders)	Adam Deadmarsh	D	Portland (WHL)
15—Winnipeg	Mats Lindgren	C	Skelleftea, Sweden
16—Edmonton (from Los Angeles)	Nick Stajduhar	D	London (OHL)
17—Washington	Jason Allison	C	London (OHL)
18—Calgary	Jesper Mattsson	RW	Malmo, Sweden
19—Toronto	Landon Wilson	F	Dubuque, USHL (Jr. Tier II)
20—Vancouver	Mike Wilson	D	Sudbury (OHL)
21—Montreal	Saku Koivu	C	TPS Turku, Finland
22—Detroit	Anders Eriksson	D	MoDo, Sweden
23—N.Y. Islanders (from Quebec)	Todd Bertuzzi	C	Guelph (OHL)
24—Chicago	Eric Lecompte	F	Hull (QMJHL)
25—Boston	Kevyn Adams	C	Miami of Ohio (CCHA)
26—Pittsburgh	Stefan Bergqvist	D	Leksand, Sweden

SECOND ROUND

No.—Selecting club	Player	Pos.	Previous team (league)
27—Ottawa	Radim Bicanek	D	Duklajihlava, Czech.
28—San Jose	Shean Donovan	F	Ottawa (OHL)
29—Tampa Bay	Tyler Moss	G	Kingston (OHL)
30—Anaheim	Nikolai Tsulygin	D	Salavat Yulayev Ufa, CIS
31—Winnipeg (from Florida)	Scott Langkow	G	Portland (WHL)
32—New Jersey (from Hartford)	Jay Pandolfo	F	Boston University (H. East)
33—Edmonton	David Vyborny	C	Sparta Praha, Czech.
34—N.Y. Rangers	Lee Sorochan	D	Lethbridge (WHL)
35—Dallas	Jamie Langenbrunner	C	Cloquet H.S. (Minn.)
36—Philadelphia	Janne Niinimaa	D	Karpat, Finland
37—St. Louis	Maxim Bets	LW	Spokane (WHL)
38—Buffalo	Denis Tsygurov	D	Lada Togliatti, CIS
39—New Jersey	Brendan Morrison	C	Penticton (BCJHL, Jr. A, Tier II)
40—N.Y. Islanders	Bryan McCabe	D	Medicine Hat (WHL)
41—Florida (from Winnipeg)	Kevin Weekes	G	Owen Sound (OHL)
42—Los Angeles	Shayne Toporowski	F	Prince Albert (WHL)
43—Winnipeg (from Washington)	Alexander Budajev	F	Kristall Electrosal, CIS
44—Calgary	Jamie Allison	D	Detroit (OHL)
45—San Jose (from Toronto through Hartford)	Vlastimil Kroupa	D	Chemopetrol (Czech Jrs.)
46—Vancouver	Rick Girard	C	Swift Current (WHL)
47—Montreal	Rory Fitzpatrick	D	Sudbury (OHL)
48—Detroit	Jon Coleman	D	Phillips Andover Academy (Mass.)
49—Quebec	Ashley Buckberger	F	Swift Current (WHL)
50—Chicago	Eric Manlow	C	Kitchener (OHL)
51—Boston	Matt Alvey	F	Springfield Olympics (NEJHL)
52—Pittsburgh	Domenic Pittis	C	Lethbridge (WHL)

THIRD ROUND

No.—Selecting club	Player	Pos.	Previous team (league)
53—Ottawa	Patrick Charbonneau	G	Victoriaville (QMJHL)
54—Chicago (from San Jose)	Bogdan Savenko	F	Niagara Falls (OHL)
55—Tampa Bay	Allan Egeland	C	Tacoma (WHL)
56—Anaheim	Valeri Karpov	F	Chelyabinsk, CIS
57—Florida	Chris Armstrong	D	Moose Jaw (WHL)
58—San Jose (from Hartford)	Ville Peltonen	F	Helsinki IFK, Finland
59—Edmonton	Kevin Paden	C	Detroit (OHL)
60—Edmonton (from N.Y. Rangers)	Alexander Kerch	F	Dynamo Riga, CIS
61—N.Y. Rangers (from Dallas)	Maxim Galanov	D	Lada Togliatti, CIS
62—Pittsburgh (from Philadelphia)	Dave Roche	F	Peterborough (OHL)
63—St. Louis	Jamie Rivers	D	Sudbury (OHL)
64—Buffalo	Ethan Philpott	F	Phillips Andover Academy (Mass.)
65—New Jersey	Krzysztof Oliwa	F	Welland (JBR, Jr. B)
66—N.Y. Islanders	Vladim Cherbaturkin	D	Kristall Electrosal, CIS
67—Florida (from Winnipeg)	Mikael Tjallden	D	MoDo, Sweden
68—Los Angeles	Jeffrey Mitchell	C	Detroit (OHL)
69—Washington	Patrick Boileau	D	Laval (QMJHL)
70—Calgary	Dan Tomkins	F	Omaha (Jr. A, Tier II)
71—Philadelphia (from Toronto)	Vaclav Prospal	C	Budejovice, Czech.
72—Hartford (from Vancouver)	Marek Malik	D	Tj Vitkovice, Czech.
73—Montreal	Sebastien Bordeleau	C	Hull (QMJHL)
74—Detroit	Kevin Hilton	C	University of Michigan (CCHA)
75—Quebec	William Pierce	C	Lawrence Academy

No.—Selecting club	Player	Pos.	Previous team (league)
76—Chicago	Ryan Huska	F	Kamloops (WHL)
77—Philadelphia (from Boston)	Milos Holan	D	Tj Vitkovice, Czech.
78—Florida (from Pittsburgh through Tampa Bay)	Steve Washburn	C	Ottawa (OHL)

FOURTH ROUND

No.—Selecting club	Player	Pos.	Previous team (league)
79—Winnipeg (from Ottawa)	Ruslan Batyrshim	D	Dynamo Minsk, CIS
80—San Jose	Alenander Osadchy	D	CSKA Moscow, CIS
81—Tampa Bay	Marian Kacir	F	Owen Sound (OHL)
82—Anaheim	Joel Gagnon	G	Oshawa (OHL)
83—Florida	Bill McCauley	C	Detroit (OHL)
84—Hartford	Trevor Roenick	F	Boston Jr. Bruins
85—Montreal (from Edmonton)	Adam Wiesel	D	Springfield (USJ, Jr. B)
86—N.Y. Rangers	Sergei Olympijev	F	Dynamo Minsk, CIS
87—Dallas	Chad Lang	G	Peterborough (OHL)
88—Boston (from Philadelphia)	Charles Paquette	D	Sherbrooke (QMJHL)
89—St. Louis	Jamal Mayers	C	Western Michigan University
90—Chicago (from Buffalo)	Eric Daze	F	Beauport (QMJHL)
91—Ottawa (from New Jersey)	Cosmo Dupaul	C	Victoriaville (QMJHL)
92—N.Y. Islanders	Warren Luhning	F	Calgary Royals (AJHL, Tier II)
93—Winnipeg	Ravil Gusmanov	F	Chelyabinsk, CIS
94—Los Angeles	Bob Wren	F	Detroit (OHL)
95—Calgary (from Washington through Hartford)	Jason Smith	D	Princeton University
96—Calgary	Marty Murray	C	Brandon (WHL)
97—Detroit (from Tor. through Wash. and Win.)	John Jakopin	D	St. Michael's (Jr. B)
98—Vancouver	Dieter Kochan	G	Kelowna, B.C. (Jr. A)
99—Montreal	Jean-Francois Houle	F	Northwood Prep
100—Detroit	Benoit Larose	D	Laval (QMJHL)
101—Quebec	Ryan Tocher	D	Niagara Falls (OHL)
102—Chicago	Patrik Pysz	C	Augsburg, Germany
103—Boston	Shawn Bates	C	Medford
104—Pittsburgh	Jonas Andersson-Junkka	D	Kiruna, Sweden

FIFTH ROUND

No.—Selecting club	Player	Pos.	Previous team (league)
105—Los Angeles (from Ott. through NYR)	Frederick Baubien	G	St. Hyacinthe (QMJHL)
106—San Jose	Andrei Buschan	D	Sokol Kiev, CIS
107—Tampa Bay	Ryan Brown	D	Swift Current (WHL)
108—Anaheim	Mikhail Shtalenkov	G	Milwaukee (IHL)
109—Florida	Todd MacDonald	G	Tacoma (WHL)
110—New Jersey (from Hartford)	John Guirestante	F	London (OHL)
111—Edmonton	Miroslav Satan	C	Dukla Trencin, Czech.
112—N.Y. Rangers	Gary Roach	D	Sault Ste. Marie (OHL)
113—Montreal (from Dallas)	Jeff Lank	D	Prince Albert (WHL)
114—Philadelphia	Vladimir Krechin	F	Chelyabinsk, CIS
115—Hartford (from St. Louis)	Nolan Pratt	D	Portland (WHL)
116—Buffalo	Richard Safarik	F	Nitra, Czech.
117—Los Angeles (from New Jersey)	Jason Saal	G	Detroit (OHL)
118—N.Y. Islanders	Tommy Salo	G	Basteras, Europe
119—Winnipeg	Larry Courville	F	Newmarket (OHL)
120—Los Angeles	Tomas Vlasak	C	Slavia Praha, Czech.
121—Calgary (from Washington)	Darryl Lafrance	C	Oshawa (OHL)
122—Calgary	John Emmons	C	Yale University
123—Toronto	Zdenek Nedved	F	Sudbury (OHL)
124—Vancouver	Scott Walker	D	Owen Sound (OHL)
125—Montreal	Dion Darling	D	Spokane (WHL)
126—Detroit	Norm Maracle	G	Saskatoon (WHL)
127—Quebec	Anders Myrvold	D	Farjestad, Europe
128—Chicago	Jonni Vauhkonen	F	Keikki-Reipas Lahti, Finland
129—Boston	Andrei Sapozhnikov	D	Chelyabinsk, CIS
130—Pittsburgh	Chris Kelleher	D	St. Sebastian's H.S. (Mass.)

SIXTH ROUND

No.—Selecting club	Player	Pos.	Previous team (league)
131—Ottawa	Rick Bodkin	C	Sudbury (OHL)
132—San Jose	Petri Varis	F	Assat Pori, Finland
133—Tampa Bay	Kiley Hill	F	Sault Ste. Marie (OHL)
134—Anaheim	Antti Aalto	C	TPS Turku, Finland
135—Florida	Alain Nasreddine	D	Drummondville (QMJHL)
136—Dallas (from Hartford)	Rick Mrozik	D	Cloquet H.S. (Minn.)
137—Quebec (from Edmonton)	Nicholas Checco	C	Jefferson HS, Bloomington (Minn.)
138—N.Y. Rangers	Dave Trofimenkoff	G	Lethbridge (WHL)

No.—Selecting club	Player	Pos.	Previous team (league)
139—Dallas	Per Svartvadet	F	MoDo, Sweden
140—Philadelphia	Mike Crowley	D	Jefferson HS, Bloomington (Minn.)
141—St. Louis	Todd Kelman	D	Vernon (Jr. BC A)
142—Buffalo	Kevin Pozzo	D	Moose Jaw (WHL)
143—New Jersey	Steve Brule	C	St. Jean (QMJHL)
144—N.Y. Islanders	Peter Leboutillier	F	Red Deer (WHL)
145—Winnipeg	Michal Grosek	F	Zlin, Czech.
146—Los Angeles	Jere Karalanti	D	Helsinki IFK, Finland
147—Washington	Frank Banham	F	Saskatoon (WHL)
148—Calgary	Andreas Karlsson	F	Leksand, Sweden
149—Toronto	Paul Vincent	C	Cushing Academy (Conn.)
150—Vancouver	Troy Creurer	D	Notre Dame (SJHL, Jr. A)
151—Montreal	Darcy Tucker	C	Kamloops (WHL)
152—Detroit	Tim Spitzig	F	Kitchener (OHL)
153—Quebec	Christian Matte	F	Granby (QMJHL)
154—San Jose (from Chicago)	Fredrik Oduya	D	Ottawa (OHL)
155—Boston	Milt Mastad	D	Seattle (WHL)
156—Pittsburgh	Patrick Lalime	G	Shawinigan (QMJHL)

SEVENTH ROUND

No.—Selecting club	Player	Pos.	Previous team (league)
157—Ottawa	Sergei Polistchuk	D	Soviet Wings
158—San Jose	Anotoli Filatov	F	UST-Kamenogorsk, CIS
159—Tampa Bay	Mathieu Raby	D	Victoriaville (QMJHL)
160—Anaheim	Matt Peterson	D	OSSEO (Minn.) H.S.
161—Florida	Trevoe Doyle	D	Kingston (OHL)
162—N.Y. Rangers (from Hartford)	Sergei Kondrashkin	F	Cherepovets, Europe
163—Edmonton	Alexander Zhurik	D	Dynamo Minsk, CIS
164—N.Y. Rangers	Todd Marchant	C	University of Clarkson (ECAC)
165—Dallas	Jeremy Stasiuk	F	Spokane (WHL)
166—Philadelphia	Aaron Israel	G	Harvard University
167—St. Louis	Mike Buzak	G	Michigan State Univ. (CCHA)
168—Buffalo	Sergei Petrenko	F	Dynamo Minsk, CIS
169—New Jersey	Nikolai Zavarukhin	F	Salavat Yulayev Ufa, CIS
170—N.Y. Islanders	Darren Van Impe	D	Red Deer (WHL)
171—Winnipeg	Martin Woods	D	Victoriaville (QMJHL)
172—Los Angeles	Justin Martin	F	Essex Junction
173—Washington	Daniel Hendrickson	F	St. Paul (Jr. A, Tier II)
174—Washington (from Calgary)	Andrew Brunette	F	Owen Sound (OHL)
175—Toronto	Jeff Andrews	F	North Bay (OHL)
176—Vancouver	Jevgeni Babariko	C	Nizhni Novgorod, Europe
177—Montreal	David Ruhly	F	Culver Military Academy (Ind.)
178—Detroit	Yuri Yeresko	D	CSKA Moscow, CIS
179—Quebec	David Ling	F	Kingston (OHL)
180—Chicago	Tom White	C	Westminster
181—Boston	Ryan Golden	C	Reading
182—Pittsburgh	Sean Selmser	F	Red Deer (WHL)

EIGHTH ROUND

No.—Selecting club	Player	Pos.	Previous team (league)
183—Ottawa	Jason Disher	D	Kingston (OHL)
184—San Jose	Todd Holt	F	Swift Current (WHL)
185—Tampa Bay	Ryan Nauss	F	Peterborough (OHL)
186—Anaheim	Tom Askey	G	Ohio State University (CCHA)
187—Florida	Briane Thompson	D	Sault Ste. Marie (OHL)
188—Hartford	Emmanuel Legace	G	Niagara Falls (OHL)
189—Edmonton	Martin Bakula	D	Univ. of Alaska-Anchorage
190—N.Y. Rangers	Eddy Campbell	D	Omaha (Jr. A, Tier II)
191—Dallas	Rob Lurtsema	F	Burnsville H.S. (Minn.)
192—Philadelphia	Paul Healey	D/F	Prince Albert (WHL)
193—St. Louis	Eric Boguniecki	C	Westminster
194—Buffalo	Mike Barrie	C	Victoria (WHL)
195—New Jersey	Thomas Cullen	D	Toronto Wexford (Jr. B)
196—N.Y. Islanders	Rod Hinks	C	Sudbury (OHL)
197—Winnipeg	Adrian Murray	D	Newmarket (OHL)
198—Los Angeles	John-Tra Dillabough	C	Wexford (Jr. B)
199—Washington	Joel Poirier	F	Sudbury (OHL)
200—Calgary	Derek Sylvester	F	Niagara Falls (OHL)
201—Toronto	David Brumby	G	Tri-City (WHL)
202—Vancouver	Sean Tallaire	F	Lake Superior State (CCHA)
203—Montreal	Alan Letang	D	Newmarket (OHL)
204—Detroit	Viteslav Skuta	D	Tj Vitkovice, Czech.
205—Quebec	Petr Franek	G	Litvinov, Europe

No.—Selecting club	Player	Pos.	Previous team (league)
206—Chicago	Sergei Petrov	F	Cloquet H.S. (Minn.)
207—Boston	Hal Gill	D	Nashoba
208—Pittsburgh	Larry McMorran	C	Seattle (WHL)

NINTH ROUND

No.—Selecting club	Player	Pos.	Previous team (league)
209—Ottawa	Toby Kvalevog	G	Bemidji H.S. (Minn.)
210—San Jose	Jonas Forsberg	G	Djurgarden, Sweden
211—Tampa Bay	Alexandre Laporte	D	Victoriaville (QMJHL)
212—Anaheim	Vitaly Kozel	C	Novops, Europe
213—Florida	Chad Cabana	F	Tri-City (WHL)
214—Hartford	Dimitri Gorenko	F	CSKA Moscow, CIS
215—Edmonton	Brad Norton	D	Cushing Academy (Conn.)
216—N.Y. Rangers	Ken Shepard	G	Oshawa (OHL)
217—Winnipeg (from Dallas)	Vladimir Potatov	F	Kristall Electrosal, CIS
218—Philadelphia	Tripp Tracy	G	Harvard University
219—St. Louis	Michael Grier	F	St. Sebastian's H.S. (Mass.)
220—Buffalo	Barrie Moore	F	Sudbury (OHL)
221—New Jersey	Judd Lambert	G	Chilliwack, B.C. (Jr. A)
222—N.Y. Islanders	Daniel Johansson	D	Rogle, Sweden
223—Winnipeg	Ilja Stashenkov	D	Soviet Wings
224—Los Angeles	Martin Strebak	D	Presov, Europe
225—Washington	Jason Gladney	D	Kitchener (OHL)
226—Philadelphia (from Calgary)	E.J. Bradley	C	Tabor Academy
227—Ottawa (from Toronto)	Pavol Demitra	F	Dukla Trencin, Czech.
228—Winnipeg (from Vancouver)	Harijs Vitolinsh	C	Chur, Europe
229—Montreal	Alexandre Duchesne	F	Drummondville (QMJHL)
230—Detroit	Ryan Shanahan	F	Sudbury (OHL)
231—Quebec	Vincent Auger	C	Hawkesbury, Ont. (Jr. A)
232—Chicago	Mike Rusk	D	Guelph (OHL)
233—Boston	Joel Prpic	C	Waterloo, Ont. (Jr. B)
234—Pittsburgh	Timothy Harberts	C	Wayzata H.S. (Minn.)

10TH ROUND

No.—Selecting club	Player	Pos.	Previous team (league)
235—Ottawa	Rick Schuwerk	D	Canterbury Prep (Conn.)
236—San Jose	Jeff Salajko	G	Ottawa (OHL)
237—Tampa Bay	Brett Duncan	D	Seattle (WHL)
238—Anaheim	Anatoli Fedotov	D	Moncton (AHL)
239—Florida	John Demarco	D	Archbishop Williams H.S. (Mass.)
240—Hartford	Wes Swinson	D	Kitchener (OHL)
241—Edmonton	Oleg Maltsev	F	Chelyabinsk, CIS
242—N.Y. Rangers	Andrei Kudinov	F	Chelyabinsk, CIS
243—Dallas	Jordan Willis	G	London (OHL)
244—Philadelphia	Jeffrey Staples	D	Brandon (WHL)
245—St. Louis	Libor Prochazka	D	Poldi Kladno, Czech.
246—Buffalo	Chris Davis	G	Calgary Royals (AJHL, Tier II)
247—New Jersey	Jimmy Provencher	F	St. Jean (QMJHL)
248—N.Y. Islanders	Stephane Larocque	F	Sherbrooke (QMJHL)
249—Dallas (from Winnipeg)	Bill Lang	C	North Bay (OHL)
250—Los Angeles	Kimmo Timonen	D	Kalpa, Europe
251—Washington	Mark Seliger	G	Rosenheim, Germany
252—Calgary	German Titov	C	TPS Turku, Finland
253—Toronto	Kyle Ferguson	F	Michigan Tech (WCHA)
254—Vancouver	Bert Robertsson	D	Sodertalje, Europe
255—Montreal	Brian Larochelle	G	Phillips-Exeter
256—Detroit	James Kosecki	G	Berkshire H.S.
257—Quebec	Mark Pivetz	D	Saskatoon (Jr. A, Tier II)
258—Chicago	Mike McGhan	F	Prince Albert (WHL)
259—Boston	Joakim Persson	G	Hammarby, Europe
260—Pittsburgh	Leonid Toropchenko	C	Springfield (AHL)

11TH ROUND

No.—Selecting club	Player	Pos.	Previous team (league)
261—N.Y. Rangers (from Ottawa)	Pavel Komarov	D	Nizhni Novgorod, Europe
262—San Jose	Jamie Matthews	C	Sudbury (OHL)
263—Tampa Bay	Mark Szoke	F	Lethbridge (WHL)
264—Anaheim	David Penney	F	Worcester Academy
265—Florida	Eric Montreuil	C	Chicoutimi (QMJHL)
266—Hartford	Igor Chibiryev	F	Fort Wayne (IHL)
267—Edmonton	Ilya Byakin	D	Landshut, Europe
268—N.Y. Rangers	Maxim Smelnitski	C	Chelyabinsk, CIS
269—Dallas	Cory Peterson	D	Jefferson HS, Bloomington (Minn.)

No.—Selecting club	Player	Pos.	Previous team (league)
270—Philadelphia	Kenneth Hemmenway	D	Alaska All-Stars
271—St. Louis	Alexandre Vasilevskii	F	Victoria (WHL)
272—Buffalo	Scott Nichol	C	Portland (WHL)
273—New Jersey	Michael Legg	F	London (Jr. B)
274—N.Y. Islanders	Carl Charland	F	Hull (QMJHL)
275—St. Louis (from Winnipeg)	Christer Olsson	D	Brynas, Europe
276—Los Angeles	Patrick Howald	F	Lugano, Europe
277—Washington	Dany Bousquet	C	Penticton (BCJHL, Jr. A, Tier II)
278—Calgary	Burke Murphy	F	St. Lawrence University
279—Toronto	Mikhail Lapin	D	Western Michigan University
280—Vancouver	Sergei Tkachekko	G	Hamilton (AHL)
281—Montreal	Russell Guzior	C	Culver Military Academy (Ind.)
282—Detroit	Gordon Hunt	C	Detroit Compuware (Jr. A)
283—Quebec	John Hillman	C	St. Paul (Jr. A, Tier II)
284—Chicago	Tom Noble	G	Catholic Memorial H.S.
285—Winnipeg (from Boston through Chicago)	Russell Hewson	F	Swift Current (WHL)
286—Pittsburgh	Hans Jonsson	D	MoDo, Sweden

NHL HISTORY

Stanley Cup champions

All-Star Games

Records

Award winners

Team histories

STANLEY CUP CHAMPIONS

Season	Club	Coach
1917-18	Toronto Arenas	Dick Carroll
1919-20	Ottawa Senators	Pete Green
1920-21	Ottawa Senators	Pete Green
1921-22	Toronto St. Pats	Eddie Powers
1922-23	Ottawa Senators	Pete Green
1923-24	Montreal Canadiens	Leo Dandurand
1924-25	Victoria Cougars	Lester Patrick
1925-26	Montreal Maroons	Eddie Gerard
1926-27	Ottawa Senators	Dave Gill
1927-28	New York Rangers	Lester Patrick
1928-29	Boston Bruins	Cy Denneny
1929-30	Montreal Canadiens	Cecil Hart
1930-31	Montreal Canadiens	Cecil Hart
1931-32	Toronto Maple Leafs	Dick Irvin
1932-33	New York Rangers	Lester Patrick
1933-34	Chicago Black Hawks	Tommy Gorman
1934-35	Montreal Maroons	Tommy Gorman
1935-36	Detroit Red Wings	Jack Adams
1936-37	Detroit Red Wings	Jack Adams
1937-38	Chicago Black Hawks	Bill Stewart
1938-39	Boston Bruins	Art Ross
1939-40	New York Rangers	Frank Boucher
1940-41	Boston Bruins	Cooney Weiland
1941-42	Toronto Maple Leafs	Hap Day
1942-43	Detroit Red Wings	Jack Adams
1943-44	Montreal Canadiens	Dick Irvin
1944-45	Toronto Maple Leafs	Hap Day
1945-46	Montreal Canadiens	Dick Irvin
1946-47	Toronto Maple Leafs	Hap Day
1947-48	Toronto Maple Leafs	Hap Day
1948-49	Toronto Maple Leafs	Hap Day
1949-50	Detroit Red Wings	Tommy Ivan
1950-51	Toronto Maple Leafs	Joe Primeau
1951-52	Detroit Red Wings	Tommy Ivan
1952-53	Montreal Canadiens	Dick Irvin
1953-54	Detroit Red Wings	Tommy Ivan
1954-55	Detroit Red Wings	Jimmy Skinner
1955-56	Montreal Canadiens	Toe Blake
1956-57	Montreal Canadiens	Toe Blake
1957-58	Montreal Canadiens	Toe Blake
1958-59	Montreal Canadiens	Toe Blake
1959-60	Montreal Canadiens	Toe Blake
1960-61	Chicago Black Hawks	Rudy Pilous
1961-62	Toronto Maple Leafs	Punch Imlach
1962-63	Toronto Maple Leafs	Punch Imlach
1963-64	Toronto Maple Leafs	Punch Imlach
1964-65	Montreal Canadiens	Toe Blake
1965-66	Montreal Canadiens	Toe Blake
1966-67	Toronto Maple Leafs	Punch Imlach
1967-68	Montreal Canadiens	Toe Blake
1968-69	Montreal Canadiens	Claude Ruel
1969-70	Boston Bruins	Harry Sinden
1970-71	Montreal Canadiens	Al MacNeil
1971-72	Boston Bruins	Tom Johnson
1972-73	Montreal Canadiens	Scotty Bowman
1973-74	Philadelphia Flyers	Fred Shero
1974-75	Philadelphia Flyers	Fred Shero
1975-76	Montreal Canadiens	Scotty Bowman
1976-77	Montreal Canadiens	Scotty Bowman
1977-78	Montreal Canadiens	Scotty Bowman
1978-79	Montreal Canadiens	Scotty Bowman
1979-80	New York Islanders	Al Arbour
1980-81	New York Islanders	Al Arbour
1981-82	New York Islanders	Al Arbour
1982-83	New York Islanders	Al Arbour
1983-84	Edmonton Oilers	Glen Sather
1984-85	Edmonton Oilers	Glen Sather
1985-86	Montreal Canadiens	Jean Perron
1986-87	Edmonton Oilers	Glen Sather
1987-88	Edmonton Oilers	Glen Sather
1988-89	Calgary Flames	Terry Crisp
1989-90	Edmonton Oilers	John Muckler
1990-91	Pittsburgh Penguins	Bob Johnson
1991-92	Pittsburgh Penguins	Scotty Bowman
1992-93	Montreal Canadiens	Jacques Demers

NOTE: 1918-19 series between Montreal and Seattle cancelled after five games because of influenza epidemic.

ALL-STAR GAMES

RESULTS

Date	Site	Winning team, score	Losing team, score	Att.
2-14-34†	Maple Leaf Gardens, Toronto	Toronto Maple Leafs, 7	NHL All-Stars, 3	*14,000
11-3-37‡	Montreal Forum	NHL All-Stars, 6	Montreal All-Stars§, 5	8,683
10-29-39*	Montreal Forum	NHL All-Stars, 5	Montreal Canadiens, 2	*6,000
10-13-47	Maple Leaf Gardens, Toronto	NHL All-Stars, 4	Toronto Maple Leafs, 3	14,169
11-3-48	Chicago Stadium	NHL All-Stars, 3	Toronto Maple Leafs, 1	12,794
10-10-49	Maple Leaf Gardens, Toronto	NHL All-Stars, 3	Toronto Maple Leafs, 1	13,541
10-8-50	Olympia Stadium, Detroit	Detroit Red Wings, 7	NHL All-Stars, 1	9,166
10-9-51	Maple Leaf Gardens, Toronto	First Team•, 2	Second Team•, 2	11,469
10-5-52	Olympia Stadium, Detroit	First Team•, 1	Second Team•, 1	10,680
10-3-53	Montreal Forum	NHL All-Stars, 3	Montreal Canadiens, 1	14,153
10-2-54	Olympia Stadium, Detroit	NHL All-Stars, 2	Detroit Red Wings, 2	10,689
10-2-55	Olympia Stadium, Detroit	Detroit Red Wings, 3	NHL All-Stars, 1	10,111
10-9-56	Montreal Forum	NHL All-Stars, 1	Montreal Canadiens, 1	13,095
10-5-57	Montreal Forum	NHL All-Stars, 5	Montreal Canadiens, 3	13,095
10-4-58	Montreal Forum	Montreal Canadiens, 6	NHL All-Stars, 3	13,989
10-3-59	Montreal Forum	Montreal Canadiens, 6	NHL All-Stars, 1	13,818
10-1-60	Montreal Forum	NHL All-Stars, 2	Montreal Canadiens, 1	13,949
10-7-61	Chicago Stadium	NHL All-Stars, 3	Chicago Blackhawks, 1	14,534
10-6-62	Maple Leaf Gardens, Toronto	Toronto Maple Leafs, 4	NHL All-Stars, 1	14,236
10-5-63	Maple Leaf Gardens, Toronto	NHL All-Stars, 3	Toronto Maple Leafs, 3	14,034
10-10-64	Maple Leaf Gardens, Toronto	NHL All-Stars, 3	Toronto Maple Leafs, 2	14,232
10-20-65	Montreal Forum	NHL All-Stars, 5	Montreal Canadiens, 2	14,284
1-18-67	Montreal Forum	Montreal Canadiens, 3	NHL All-Stars, 0	14,284
1-16-68	Maple Leaf Gardens, Toronto	Toronto Maple Leafs, 4	NHL All-Stars, 3	15,753
1-21-69	Montreal Forum	West Division, 3	East Division, 3	16,260
1-20-70	St. Louis Arena	East Division, 4	West Division, 1	16,587
1-19-71	Boston Garden	West Division, 2	East Division, 1	14,790
1-25-72	Met Sports Center, Bloomington, Minn.	East Division, 3	West Division, 2	15,423
1-30-73	Madison Square Garden, New York	East Division, 5	West Division, 4	16,986
1-29-74	Chicago Stadium	West Division, 6	East Division, 4	16,426
1-21-75	Montreal Forum	Wales Conference, 7	Campbell Conference, 1	16,080
1-20-76	The Spectrum, Philadelphia	Wales Conference, 7	Campbell Conference, 5	16,436
1-25-77	Pacific Coliseum, Vancouver	Wales Conference, 4	Campbell Conference, 3	15,607
1-24-78	Buffalo Memorial Auditorium	Wales Conference, 3	Campbell Conference, 2 (OT)	16,433
	1979 All-Star Game replaced by Challenge Cup series between Team NHL and Soviet Union			
2-5-80	Joe Louis Arena, Detroit	Wales Conference, 6	Campbell Conference, 3	21,002
2-10-81	The Forum, Los Angeles	Campbell Conference, 4	Wales Conference, 1	15,761
2-9-82	Capital Centre, Landover, Md.	Wales Conference, 4	Campbell Conference, 2	18,130
2-8-83	Nassau Coliseum, Long Island, N.Y.	Campbell Conference, 9	Wales Conference, 3	15,230
1-31-84	Meadowlands Arena, East Rutherford, N.J.	Wales Conference, 7	Campbell Conference, 6	18,939
2-12-85	Olympic Saddledome, Calgary	Wales Conference, 6	Campbell Conference, 4	16,683
2-4-86	Hartford Civic Center	Wales Conference, 4	Campbell Conference, 3 (OT)	15,126
	1987 All-Star Game replaced by Rendez-Vous '87 between Team NHL and Soviet Union			
2-9-88	St. Louis Arena	Wales Conference, 6	Campbell Conference, 5 (OT)	17,878
2-7-89	Northlands Coliseum, Edmonton	Campbell Conference, 9	Wales Conference, 5	17,503
1-21-90	Pittsburgh Civic Arena	Wales Conference, 12	Campbell Conference, 7	17,503
1-19-91	Chicago Stadium	Campbell Conference, 11	Wales Conference, 5	18,472
1-18-92	The Spectrum, Philadelphia	Campbell Conference, 10	Wales Conference, 6	17,380
2-6-93	Montreal Forum	Wales Conference, 16	Campbell Conference, 6	17,137

*Estimated figure.
†Benefit game for Toronto Maple Leafs left wing Ace Bailey, who suffered a career-ending skull injury earlier in the season.
‡Benefit game for the family of Montreal Canadiens center Howie Morenz, who died of a heart attack earlier in the year.
§Montreal All-Star roster made up of players from Montreal Canadiens and Maroons.
*Benefit game for the family of Montreal Canadiens defenseman Babe Siebert, who drowned earlier in the year.
•First Team roster supplemented by players from the four American clubs and Second Team roster supplemented by players from the two Canadian clubs.

MOST VALUABLE PLAYERS

Date	Player, All-Star Game team (regular-season team)	Date	Player, All-Star Game team (regular-season team)
10-6-62	Eddie Shack, Toronto Maple Leafs	1-19-71	Bobby Hull, West Div. (Chicago Blackhawks)
10-5-63	Frank Mahovlich, Toronto Maple Leafs	1-25-72	Bobby Orr, East Division (Boston Bruins)
10-10-64	Jean Beliveau, All-Stars (Montreal Canadiens)	1-30-73	Greg Polis, West Div. (Pittsburgh Penguins)
10-20-65	Gordie Howe, All-Stars (Detroit Red Wings)	1-29-74	Garry Unger, West Division (St. Louis Blues)
1-18-67	Henri Richard, Montreal Canadiens	1-21-75	Syl Apps Jr., Wales Conf. (Pittsburgh Penguins)
1-16-68	Bruce Gamble, Toronto Maple Leafs	1-20-76	Peter Mahovlich, Wales Conf. (Mon. Canadiens)
1-21-69	Frank Mahovlich, East Div. (Detroit Red Wings)	1-25-77	Rick Martin, Wales Conference (Buffalo Sabres)
1-20-70	Bobby Hull, East Div. (Chicago Blackhawks)	1-24-78	Billy Smith, Campbell Conf. (New York Islanders)

Date	Player, All-Star Game team (regular-season team)
2-5-80	Reggie Leach, Campbell Conf. (Phila. Flyers)
2-10-81	Mike Liut, Campbell Conf. (St. Louis Blues)
2-9-82	Mike Bossy, Wales Conf. (New York Islanders)
2-8-83	Wayne Gretzky, Campbell Conf. (Edmonton Oilers)
1-31-84	Don Maloney, Wales Conf. (New York Rangers)
2-12-85	Mario Lemieux, Wales Conf. (Pittsburgh Penguins)
2-4-86	Grant Fuhr, Campbell Conf. (Edmonton Oilers)

Date	Player, All-Star Game team (regular-season team)
2-9-88	Mario Lemieux, Wales Conf. (Pittsburgh Penguins)
2-7-89	Wayne Gretzky, Campbell Conf. (L.A. Kings)
1-21-90	Mario Lemieux, Wales Conf. (Pittsburgh Penguins)
1-19-91	Vincent Damphousse, Camp. Conf. (T. Maple Leafs)
1-18-92	Brett Hull, Campbell Conf. (St. Louis Blues)
2-6-93	Mike Gartner, Wales Conf. (New York Rangers)

RECORDS

REGULAR SEASON

INDIVIDUAL—CAREER

Most seasons

NHL: 26—Gordie Howe, Detroit Red Wings and Hartford Whalers, 1946-47 through 1970-71 and 1979-80.
CHL: 9—Richie Hansen, Fort Worth Texans, Salt Lake Golden Eagles, Wichita Wind, 1975-76 through 1983-84.
AHL: 20—Fred Glover, Indianapolis Caps, St. Louis Flyers, Cleveland Barons.
        Willie Marshall, Pittsburgh Hornets, Rochester Americans, Hershey Bears, Providence Reds, Baltimore Clippers.
IHL: 18—Glenn Ramsay, Cincinnati Mohawks, Fort Wayne Komets, Troy Bruins, Toledo Blades, St. Paul Saints, Omaha
        Knights, Des Moines Oak Leafs, Toledo Hornets, Port Huron Flags, 1956-57 through 1973-74.

Most games played

NHL: 1,767—Gordie Howe, Detroit Red Wings and Hartford Whalers (26 seasons).
AHL: 1,205—Willie Marshall, Pittsburgh Hornets, Rochester Americans, Hershey Bears, Providence Reds, Baltimore Clip-
        pers (20 seasons).
IHL: 1,053—Glenn Ramsay, Cincinnati Mohawks, Fort Wayne Komets, Troy Bruins, Toledo Blades, St. Paul Saints, Omaha
        Knights, Des Moines Oak Leafs, Toledo Hornets, Port Huron Flags (18 seasons).
CHL: 575—Richie Hansen, Fort Worth Texans, Salt Lake Golden Eagles, Wichita Wind (9 seasons).
WHA: 551—Andre Lacroix, Philadelphia Blazers, New York Golden Blades, Jersey Knights, San Diego Mariners, Houston
        Aeros and New England Whalers (7 seasons).

Most goals

NHL: 801—Gordie Howe, Detroit Red Wings, Hartford Whalers (26 seasons).
IHL: 526—Joe Kastelic, Fort Wayne Komets, Troy Burins, Louisville Rebels, Muskegon Zephyrs, Muskegon Mohawks (15
        seasons).
AHL: 523—Willie Marshall, Pittsburgh Hornets, Rochester Americans, Hershey Bears, Providence Reds, Baltimore Clip-
        pers (20 seasons).
WHA: 316—Marc Tardif, Quebec Nordiques (6 seasons).
CHL: 204—Richie Hansen, Fort Worth Texans, Salt Lake Golden Eagles, Wichita Wind (9 seasons).

Most assists

NHL: 1,563—Wayne Gretzky, Edmonton Oilers, Los Angeles Kings (14 seasons).
AHL: 852—Willie Marshall, Pittsburgh Hornets, Hershey Bears, Rochester Americans, Providence Reds, Baltimore Clip-
        pers (20 seasons).
IHL: 826—Len Thornson, Huntington Hornets, Indianapolis Chiefs, Fort Wayne Komets (13 seasons).
WHA: 547—Andre Lacroix, Philadelphia Blazers, Jersey Knights, San Diego Mariners, Houston Aeros, New England Whal-
        ers (7 seasons).
CHL: 374—Richie Hansen, Fort Worth Texans, Salt Lake Golden Eagles, Wichita Wind (9 seasons).

Most points

NHL: 2,328—Wayne Gretzky, Edmonton Oilers, Los Angeles Kings (14 seasons).
AHL: 1,375—Willie Marshall, Pittsburgh Hornets, Hershey Bears, Rochester Americans, Providence Reds, Baltimore Clip-
        pers (20 seasons).
IHL: 1,252—Len Thornson, Huntington Hornets, Indianapolis Chiefs, Fort Wayne Komets (13 seasons).
WHA: 798—Andre Lacroix, Philadelphia Blazers, Jersey Knights, San Diego Mariners, Houston Aeros, New England Whal-
        ers (7 seasons).
CHL: 578—Richie Hansen, Fort Worth Texans, Salt Lake Golden Eagles, Wichita Wind (9 seasons).

Most penalty minutes

NHL: 3,966—Dave "Tiger" Williams, Toronto Maple Leafs, Vancouver Canucks, Detroit Red Wings, Los Angeles Kings,
        Hartford Whalers (13 seasons).
AHL: 2,402—Fred Glover, Indianapolis Caps, St. Louis Flyers, Cleveland Barons (20 seasons).
IHL: 2,175—Gord Malinoski, Dayton Gems, Saginaw Gears (9 seasons).
WHA: 962—Paul Baxter, Cleveland Crusaders, Quebec Nordiques (5 seasons).
CHL: 899—Brad Gassoff, Tulsa Oilers, Dallas Black Hawks (5 seasons).

Most shutouts

NHL: 103—Terry Sawchuk, Detroit Red Wings, Boston Bruins, Los Angeles Kings, New York Rangers, Toronto Maple Leafs
        (20 seasons).
AHL: 45—Johnny Bower, Cleveland Barons, Providence Reds (11 seasons).
IHL: 45—Glenn Ramsay, Cincinnati Mohawks, Fort Wayne Komets, Troy Bruins, Toledo Blades, St. Paul Saints, Omaha
        Knights, Des Moines Oak Leafs, Toledo Hornets, Port Huron Flags (18 seasons).
WHA: 16—Ernie Wakely, Winnipeg Jets, San Diego Mariners, Houston Aeros (6 seasons).
CHL: 12—Michel Dumas, Dallas Black Hawks (4 seasons).
        Mike Veisor, Dallas Black Hawks (5 seasons).

INDIVIDUAL—SEASON

Most goals

NHL: 92—Wayne Gretzky, Edmonton Oilers, 1981-82 season.
WHA: 77—Bobby Hull, Winnipeg Jets, 1974-75 season.

— 119 —

CHL: 77—Alain Caron, St. Louis Braves, 1963-64 season.
IHL: 75—Dan Lecours, Milwaukee Admirals, 1982-83 season.
AHL: 70—Stephan Lebeau, Sherbrooke Canadiens, 1988-89 season.

Most goals by a defenseman

NHL: 48—Paul Coffey, Edmonton Oilers, 1985-86 season.
IHL: 34—Roly McLenahan, Cincinnati Mohawks, 1955-56 season.
CHL: 29—Dan Poulin, Nashville South Stars, 1981-82 season.
AHL: 28—Greg Tebbutt, Baltimore Skipjacks, 1982-83 season.
WHA: 24—Kevin Morrison, Jersey Knights, 1973-74 season.

Most assists

NHL: 163—Wayne Gretzky, Edmonton Oilers, 1985-86 season.
IHL: 109—John Cullen, Flint Spirits, 1987-88 season.
WHA: 106—Andre Lacroix, San Diego Mariners, 1974-75 season.
AHL: 89—George "Red" Sullivan, Hershey Bears, 1953-54 season.
CHL: 81—Richie Hansen, Salt Lake Golden Eagles, 1981-82 season.

Most assists by a defenseman

NHL: 102—Bobby Orr, Boston Bruins, 1970-71 season.
IHL: 86—Gerry Glaude, Muskegon Zephyrs, 1962-63 season.
WHA: 77—J. C. Tremblay, Quebec Nordiques, 1975-76 season.
AHL: 62—Craig Levie, Nova Scotia Voyageurs, 1980-81 season.
         Shawn Evans, Nova Scotia Oilers, 1987-88 season.
CHL: 61—Barclay Plager, Omaha Knights, 1963-64 season.

Most points

NHL: 215—Wayne Gretzky, Edmonton Oilers, 1985-86 season.
IHL: 157—John Cullen, Flint Spirits, 1987-88 season.
WHA: 154—Marc Tardif, Quebec Nordiques, 1977-78 season.
AHL: 138—Don Biggs, Binghamton Rangers, 1992-93 season.
CHL: 125—Alain Caron, St. Louis Braves, 1963-64 season.

Most points by a defenseman

NHL: 139—Bobby Orr, Boston Bruins, 1970-71 season.
IHL: 101—Gerry Glaude, Muskegon Zephyrs, 1962-63 season.
WHA: 89—J. C. Tremblay, Quebec Nordiques, 1972-73 and 1975-76 seasons.
CHL: 85—Dan Poulin, Nashville South Stars, 1981-82 season.
AHL: 84—Greg Tebbutt, Baltimore Skipjacks, 1982-83 season.

Most penalty minutes

IHL: 648—Kevin Evans, Kalamazoo, 1986-87 season.
NHL: 472—Dave Schultz, Philadelphia Flyers, 1974-75 season.
AHL: 446—Robert Ray, Rochester Americans, 1988-89 season.
CHL: 411—Randy Holt, Dallas Black Hawks, 1974-75 season.
WHA: 365—Curt Brackenbury, Minnesota Fighting Saints and Quebec Nordiques, 1975-76 season.

Most shutouts

NHL: 22—George Hainsworth, Montreal Canadiens, 1928-29 season.
NHL: 15—(modern era) Tony Esposito, Chicago Black Hawks, 1969-70 season.
IHL: 10—Charlie Hodge, Cincinnati Mohawks, 1953-54 season.
         Joe Daley, Winnipeg Jets, 1975-76 season.
CHL: 9—Marcel Pelletier, St. Paul Rangers, 1963-64 season.
AHL: 9—Gordie Bell, Buffalo Bisons, 1942-43 season.
WHA: 5—Gerry Cheevers, Cleveland Crusaders, 1972-73 season.

Lowest goals against average

NHL: 0.98—George Hainsworth, Montreal Canadiens, 1928-29 season.
AHL: 1.79—Frank Brimsek, Providence Reds, 1937-38 season.
IHL: 1.88—Glenn Ramsay, Cincinnati Mohawks, 1956-57 season.
CHL: 2.16—Russ Gillow, Oklahoma City Blazers, 1967-68 season.
WHA: 2.57—Don McLeod, Houston Aeros, 1973-74 season.

INDIVIDUAL—GAME

Most goals

NHL: 7—Joe Malone, Quebec Bulldogs vs. Toronto St. Pats, January 31, 1920.
NHL: 6—(modern era) Syd Howe, Detroit Red Wings vs. N.Y. Rangers, Feb. 3, 1944.
         Gordon "Red" Berenson, St. Louis Blues vs. Philadelphia, Nov. 7, 1968.
         Darryl Sittler, Toronto Maple Leafs vs. Boston, Feb. 7, 1976.
CHL: 6—Jim Mayer, Dallas Black Hawks, February 23, 1979.
AHL: 6—Bob Heron, Pittsburgh Hornets, 1941-42.
         Harry Pidhirny, Springfield Indians, 1953-54.
         Camille Henry, Providence Reds, 1955-56.
         Patrick Lebeau, Fredericton Canadiens, Feb. 1, 1991.

IHL: 6—Pierre Brillant, Indianapolis Chiefs, Feb. 18, 1959.
      Bryan McLay, Muskegon Zephyrs, Mar. 8, 1961.
      Elliott Chorley, St. Paul Saints, Jan. 17, 1962.
      Joe Kastelic, Muskegon Zephyrs, Mar. 1, 1962.
      Tom St. James, Flint Generals, Mar. 15, 1985.
WHA: 5—Ron Ward, New York Raiders vs. Ottawa, January 4, 1973.
      Ron Climie, Edmonton Oilers vs. N.Y. Golden Blades, November 6, 1973.
      Andre Hinse, Houston Aeros vs. Edmonton, Jan. 16, 1975.
      Vaclav Nedomansky, Toronto Toros vs. Denver Spurs, Nov. 13, 1975.
      Wayne Connelly, Minnesota Fighting Saints vs. Cincinnati Stingers, Nov. 27, 1975.
      Ron Ward, Cleveland Crusaders vs. Toronto Toros, Nov. 30, 1975.
      Real Cloutier, Quebec Nordiques fs. Phoenix Roadrunners, Oct. 26, 1976.

Most assists
AHL: 9—Art Stratton, Buffalo Bisons vs. Pittsburgh, Mar. 17, 1963.
 IHL: 9—Jean-Paul Denis, St. Paul Saints, Jan. 17, 1962.
NHL: 7—Billy Taylor, Detroit Red Wings vs. Chicago, Mar. 16, 1947.
      Wayne Gretzky, Edmonton Oilers vs. Washington, Feb. 15, 1980.
WHA: 7—Jim Harrison, Alberta Oilers vs. New York, January 30, 1973.
      Jim Harrison, Cleveland Crusaders vs. Toronto, Nov. 30, 1975.
CHL: 6—Art Stratton, St. Louis Braves, 1966-67.
      Ron Ward, Tulsa Oilers, 1967-68.
      Bill Hogaboam, Omaha Knights, January 15, 1972.
      Jim Wiley, Tulsa Oilers, 1974-75.

Most points
 IHL: 11—Elliott Chorley, St. Paul Saints, Jan. 17, 1962.
       Jean-Paul Denis, St. Paul Saints, Jan. 17, 1962.
NHL: 10—Darryl Sittler, Toronto Maple Leafs vs. Boston, Feb. 7, 1976.
WHA: 10—Jim Harrison, Alberta Oilers vs. New York, January 30, 1973.
AHL: 9—Art Stratton, Buffalo Bisons vs Pittsburgh, Mar. 17, 1963.
CHL: 8—Steve Vickers, Omaha Knights vs. Kansas City, Jan. 15, 1972.

Most penalty minutes
NHL: 67—Randy Holt, Los Angeles Kings vs. Philadelphia, March 11, 1979.
 IHL: 63—Willie Trognitz, Dayton Gems, Oct. 29, 1977.
AHL: 54—Wally Weir, Rochester Americans vs. New Brunswick, Jan. 16, 1981.
CHL: 49—Gary Rissling, Birmingham Bulls vs. Salt Lake, Dec. 5, 1980.
WHA: 46—Dave Hanson, Birmingham Bulls vs. Indianapolis, Feb. 5, 1978.

STANLEY CUP PLAYOFFS

INDIVIDUAL—CAREER

Most years in playoffs: 20—Gordie Howe, Detroit, Hartford.
      Larry Robinson, Montreal, Los Angeles.
Most consecutive years in playoffs: 20—Larry Robinson, Montreal, Los Angeles.
Most games: 227—Larry Robinson, Montreal, Los Angeles.
Most games by goaltender: 131—Billy Smith, N.Y. Islanders.
Most goals: 110—Wayne Gretzky, Edmonton, Los Angeles.
Most assists: 236—Wayne Gretzky, Edmonton, Los Angeles.
Most points: 346—Wayne Gretzky, Edmonton, Los Angeles.
Most penalty minutes: 581—Dale Hunter, Quebec, Washington.
Most shutouts: 14—Jacques Plante, Montreal, St. Louis.

INDIVIDUAL—SEASON

Most goals: 19—Reggie Leach, Philadelphia (1975-76).
      Jari Kurri, Edmonton (1984-85).
Most goals by a defenseman: 12—Paul Coffey, Edmonton (1984-85).
Most assists: 31—Wayne Gretzky, Edmonton (1987-88).
Most assists by a defenseman: 25—Paul Coffey, Edmonton (1984-85).
Most points: 47—Wayne Gretzky, Edmonton (1984-85).
Most points by a defenseman: 37—Paul Coffey, Edmonton (1984-85).
Most penalty minutes: 141—Chris Nilan, Montreal (1985-86).
Most shutouts: 4—Clint Benedict, Montreal Maroons (1927-28).
      Dave Kerr, N.Y. Rangers (1936-37).
      Frank McCool, Toronto (1944-45).
      Terry Sawchuk, Detroit (1951-52).
      Bernie Parent, Philadelphia (1974-75).
      Ken Dryden, Montreal (1976-77).
Most consecutive shutouts: 3—Frank McCool, Toronto (1944-45).

INDIVIDUAL—GAME

Most goals: 5—Maurice Richard, Montreal vs. Toronto, March 23, 1944.
Darryl Sittler, Toronto vs. Philadelphia, April 22, 1976.
Reggie Leach, Philadelphia vs. Boston, May 6, 1976.
Mario Lemieux, Pittsburgh vs. Philadelphia, April 25, 1989.
Most assists: 6—Mikko Leinonen, N.Y. Rangers vs. Philadelphia, April 8, 1982.
Wayne Gretzky, Edmonton vs. Los Angeles, April 9, 1987.
Most points: 8—Patrik Sundstrom, New Jersey vs. Washington, April 22, 1988.
Mario Lemieux, Pittsburgh vs. Philadelphia, April 25, 1989.

CLUB

Most Stanley Cup championships: 24—Montreal Canadiens.
Most consecutive Stanley Cup championships: 5—Montreal Canadiens.
Most final series apperances: 32—Montreal Canadiens.
Most years in playoffs: 68—Montreal Canadiens.
Most consecutive playoff appearances: 26—Boston Bruins.
Most consecutive playoff game victories: 12—Edmonton Oilers.
Most goals, one team, one game: 13—Edmonton vs. Los Angeles, April 9, 1987.
Most goals, one team, one period: 7—Montreal Canadiens vs. Toronto, March 30, 1944, 3rd period.

AWARD WINNERS

ART ROSS TROPHY

(Leading scorer)

Season	Player, Team	Pts.
1917-18	Joe Malone, Montreal	44
1918-19	Newsy Lalonde, Montreal	32
1919-20	Joe Malone, Quebec Bulldogs	45
1920-21	Newsy Lalonde, Montreal	41
1921-22	Punch Broadbelt, Ottawa	46
1922-23	Babe Dye, Toronto	37
1923-24	Cy Denneny, Ottawa	23
1924-25	Babe Dye, Toronto	44
1925-26	Nels Stewart, Montreal Maroons	42
1926-27	Bill Cook, N.Y. Rangers	37
1927-28	Howie Morenz, Montreal	51
1928-29	Ace Bailey, Toronto	32
1929-30	Cooney Weiland, Boston	73
1930-31	Howie Morenz, Montreal	51
1931-32	Harvey Jackson, Toronto	53
1932-33	Bill Cook, N.Y. Rangers	50
1933-34	Charlie Conacher, Toronto	52
1934-35	Charlie Conacher, Toronto	57
1935-36	Dave Schriner, N.Y. Americans	45
1936-37	Dave Schriner, N.Y. Americans	46
1937-38	Gordie Drillion, Toronto	52
1938-39	Toe Blake, Montreal	47
1939-40	Milt Schmidt, Boston	52
1940-41	Bill Cowley, Boston	62
1941-42	Bryan Hextall, N.Y. Rangers	56
1942-43	Doug Bentley, Chicago	73
1943-44	Herbie Cain, Boston	82
1944-45	Elmer Lach, Montreal	80
1945-46	Max Bentley, Chicago	61
1946-47	Max Bentley, Chicago	72
1947-48	Elmer Lach, Montreal	61
1948-49	Roy Conacher, Chicago	68
1949-50	Ted Lindsay, Detroit	78
1950-51	Gordie Howe, Detroit	86
1951-52	Gordie Howe, Detroit	86
1952-53	Gordie Howe, Detroit	95
1953-54	Gordie Howe, Detroit	81
1954-55	Bernie Geoffrion, Montreal	75
1955-56	Jean Beliveau, Montreal	88
1956-57	Gordie Howe, Detroit	89
1957-58	Dickie Moore, Montreal	84
1958-59	Dickie Moore, Montreal	96
1959-60	Bobby Hull, Chicago	81
1960-61	Bernie Geoffrion, Montreal	95
1961-62	Bobby Hull, Chicago	84
1962-63	Gordie Howe, Detroit	86
1963-64	Stan Mikita, Chicago	89
1964-65	Stan Mikita, Chicago	87
1965-66	Bobby Hull, Chicago	97
1966-67	Stan Mikita, Chicago	97
1967-68	Stan Mikita, Chicago	87
1968-69	Phil Esposito, Boston	126
1969-70	Bobby Orr, Boston	120
1970-71	Phil Esposito, Boston	152
1971-72	Phil Esposito, Boston	133
1972-73	Phil Esposito, Boston	130
1973-74	Phil Esposito, Boston	145
1974-75	Bobby Orr, Boston	135
1975-76	Guy Lafleur, Montreal	125
1976-77	Guy Lafleur, Montreal	136
1977-78	Guy Lafleur, Montreal	132
1978-79	Bryan Trottier, N.Y. Islanders	134
1979-80	Marcel Dionne, Los Angeles	137
1980-81	Wayne Gretzky, Edmonton	164
1981-82	Wayne Gretzky, Edmonton	212
1982-83	Wayne Gretzky, Edmonton	196
1983-84	Wayne Gretzky, Edmonton	205
1984-85	Wayne Gretzky, Edmonton	208
1985-86	Wayne Gretzky, Edmonton	215

Season	Player, Team	Pts.
1986-87	Wayne Gretzky, Edmonton	183
1987-88	Mario Lemieux, Pittsburgh	168
1988-89	Mario Lemieux, Pittsburgh	199
1989-90	Wayne Gretzky, Los Angeles	142
1990-91	Wayne Gretzky, Los Angeles	163
1991-92	Mario Lemieux, Pittsburgh	131
1992-93	Mario Lemieux, Pittsburgh	160

The award was originally known as the Leading Scorer Trophy. The present trophy, first given in 1947, was presented to the NHL by Art Ross, former manager-coach of the Boston Bruins. In event of a tie, the player with the most goals receives the award.

HART MEMORIAL TROPHY

(Most Valuable Player)

Season	Player, Team
1923-24	Frank Nighbor, Ottawa
1924-25	Billy Burch, Hamilton
1925-26	Nels Stewart, Montreal Maroons
1926-27	Herb Gardiner, Montreal
1927-28	Howie Morenz, Montreal
1928-29	Roy Worters, N.Y. Americans
1929-30	Nels Stewart, Montreal Maroons
1930-31	Howie Morenz, Montreal
1931-32	Howie Morenz, Montreal
1932-33	Eddie Shore, Boston
1933-34	Aurel Joliat, Montreal
1934-35	Eddie Shore, Boston
1935-36	Eddie Shore, Boston
1936-37	Babe Siebert, Montreal
1937-38	Eddie Shore, Boston
1938-39	Toe Blake, Montreal
1939-40	Ebbie Goodfellow, Detroit
1940-41	Bill Cowley, Boston
1941-42	Tom Anderson, N.Y. Americans
1942-43	Bill Cowley, Boston
1943-44	Babe Pratt, Toronto
1944-45	Elmer Lach, Montreal
1945-46	Max Bentley, Chicago
1946-47	Maurice Richard, Montreal
1947-48	Buddy O'Connor, N.Y. Rangers
1948-49	Sid Abel, Detroit
1949-50	Chuck Rayner, N.Y. Rangers
1950-51	Milt Schmidt, Boston
1951-52	Gordie Howe, Detroit
1952-53	Gordie Howe, Detroit
1953-54	Al Rollins, Chicago
1954-55	Ted Kennedy, Toronto
1955-56	Jean Beliveau, Montreal
1956-57	Gordie Howe, Detroit
1957-58	Gordie Howe, Detroit
1958-59	Andy Bathgate, N.Y. Rangers
1959-60	Gordie Howe, Detroit
1960-61	Bernie Geoffrion, Montreal
1961-62	Jacques Plante, Montreal
1962-63	Gordie Howe, Detroit
1963-64	Jean Beliveau, Montreal
1964-65	Bobby Hull, Chicago
1965-66	Bobby Hull, Chicago
1966-67	Stan Mikita, Chicago
1967-68	Stan Mikita, Chicago
1968-69	Phil Esposito, Boston
1969-70	Bobby Orr, Boston
1970-71	Bobby Orr, Boston
1971-72	Bobby Orr, Boston
1972-73	Bobby Clarke, Philadelphia
1973-74	Phil Esposito, Boston
1974-75	Bobby Clarke, Philadelphia
1975-76	Bobby Clarke, Philadelphia
1976-77	Guy Lafleur, Montreal
1977-78	Guy Lafleur, Montreal

Season	Player, Team
1978-79	Bryan Trottier, N.Y. Islanders
1979-80	Wayne Gretzky, Edmonton
1980-81	Wayne Gretzky, Edmonton
1981-82	Wayne Gretzky, Edmonton
1982-83	Wayne Gretzky, Edmonton
1983-84	Wayne Gretzky, Edmonton
1984-85	Wayne Gretzky, Edmonton
1985-86	Wayne Gretzky, Edmonton
1986-87	Wayne Gretzky, Edmonton
1987-88	Mario Lemieux, Pittsburgh
1988-89	Wayne Gretzky, Los Angeles
1989-90	Mark Messier, Edmonton
1990-91	Brett Hull, St. Louis
1991-92	Mark Messier, N.Y. Rangers
1992-93	Mario Lemieux, Pittsburgh

JAMES NORRIS MEMORIAL TROPHY

(Outstanding defenseman)

Season	Player, Team
1953-54	Red Kelly, Detroit
1954-55	Doug Harvey, Montreal
1955-56	Doug Harvey, Montreal
1956-57	Doug Harvey, Montreal
1957-58	Doug Harvey, Montreal
1958-59	Tom Johnson, Montreal
1959-60	Doug Harvey, Montreal
1960-61	Doug Harvey, Montreal
1961-62	Doug Harvey, N.Y. Rangers
1962-63	Pierre Pilote, Chicago
1963-64	Pierre Pilote, Chicago
1964-65	Pierre Pilote, Chicago
1965-66	Jacques Laperriere, Montreal
1966-67	Harry Howell, N.Y. Rangers
1967-68	Bobby Orr, Boston
1968-69	Bobby Orr, Boston
1969-70	Bobby Orr, Boston
1970-71	Bobby Orr, Boston
1971-72	Bobby Orr, Boston
1972-73	Bobby Orr, Boston
1973-74	Bobby Orr, Boston
1974-75	Bobby Orr, Boston
1975-76	Denis Potvin, N.Y. Islanders
1976-77	Larry Robinson, Montreal
1977-78	Denis Potvin, N.Y. Islanders
1978-79	Denis Potvin, N.Y. Islanders
1979-80	Larry Robinson, Montreal
1980-81	Randy Carlyle, Pittsburgh
1981-82	Doug Wilson, Chicago
1982-83	Rod Langway, Washington
1983-84	Rod Langway, Washington
1984-85	Paul Coffey, Edmonton
1985-86	Paul Coffey, Edmonton
1986-87	Ray Bourque, Boston
1987-88	Ray Bourque, Boston
1988-89	Chris Chelios, Montreal
1989-90	Ray Bourque, Boston
1990-91	Ray Bourque, Boston
1991-92	Brian Leetch, N.Y. Rangers
1992-93	Chris Chelios, Chicago

VEZINA TROPHY

(Outstanding goaltender)

Season	Player, Team	GAA
1926-27	George Hainsworth, Montreal	1.52
1927-28	George Hainsworth, Montreal	1.09
1928-29	George Hainsworth, Montreal	0.98
1929-30	Tiny Thompson, Boston	2.23
1930-31	Roy Worters, N.Y. Americans	1.68
1931-32	Charlie Gardiner, Chicago	2.10
1932-33	Tiny Thompson, Boston	1.83
1933-34	Charlie Gardiner, Chicago	1.73
1934-35	Lorne Chabot, Chicago	1.83

Season	Player, Team	GAA
1935-36	Tiny Thompson, Boston	1.71
1936-37	Normie Smith, Detroit	2.13
1937-38	Tiny Thompson, Boston	1.85
1938-39	Frank Brimsek, Boston	1.60
1939-40	Dave Kerr, N.Y. Rangers	1.60
1940-41	Turk Broda, Toronto	2.60
1941-42	Frank Brimsek, Boston	2.38
1942-43	Johnny Mowers, Detroit	2.48
1943-44	Bill Durnan, Montreal	2.18
1944-45	Bill Durnan, Montreal	2.42
1945-46	Bill Durnan, Montreal	2.60
1946-47	Bill Durnan, Montreal	2.30
1947-48	Turk Broda, Toronto	2.38
1948-49	Bill Durnan, Montreal	2.10
1949-50	Bill Durnan, Montreal	2.20
1950-51	Al Rollins, Toronto	1.75
1951-52	Terry Sawchuk, Detroit	1.98
1952-53	Terry Sawchuk, Detroit	1.94
1953-54	Harry Lumley, Toronto	1.85
1954-55	Terry Sawchuk, Detroit	1.94
1955-56	Jacques Plante, Montreal	1.86
1956-57	Jacques Plante, Montreal	2.02
1957-58	Jacques Plante, Montreal	2.09
1958-59	Jacques Plante, Montreal	2.15
1959-60	Jacques Plante, Montreal	2.54
1960-61	Johnny Bower, Toronto	2.50
1961-62	Jacques Plante, Montreal	2.37
1962-63	Glenn Hall, Chicago	2.51
1963-64	Charlie Hodge, Montreal	2.26
1964-65	Terry Sawchuk, Toronto	2.56
	Johnny Bower, Toronto	2.38
1965-66	Lorne Worsley, Montreal	2.36
	Charlie Hodge, Montreal	2.58
1966-67	Glenn Hall, Chicago	2.38
	Denis DeJordy, Chicago	2.46
1967-68	Lorne Worsley, Montreal	1.98
	Rogatien Vachon, Montreal	2.48
1968-69	Glenn Hall, St. Louis	2.17
	Jacques Plante, St. Louis	1.96
1969-70	Tony Esposito, Chicago	2.17
1970-71	Ed Giacomin, N.Y. Rangers	2.15
	Gilles Villemure, N.Y. Rangers	2.29
1971-72	Tony Esposito, Chicago	1.76
	Gary Smith, Chicago	2.41
1972-73	Ken Dryden, Montreal	2.26
1973-74	Bernie Parent, Philadelphia	1.89
	Tony Esposito, Chicago	2.04
1974-75	Bernie Parent, Philadelphia	2.03
1975-76	Ken Dryden, Montreal	2.03
1976-77	Ken Dryden, Montreal	2.14
	Michel Larocque, Montreal	2.09
1977-78	Ken Dryden, Montreal	2.05
	Michel Larocque, Montreal	2.67
1978-79	Ken Dryden, Montreal	2.30
	Michel Larocque, Montreal	2.84
1979-80	Bob Sauve, Buffalo	2.36
	Don Edwards, Buffalo	2.57
1980-81	Richard Sevigny, Montreal	2.40
	Michel Larocque, Montreal	3.03
	Denis Herron, Montreal	3.50
1981-82	Billy Smith, N.Y. Islanders	2.97
1982-83	Pete Peeters, Boston	2.36
1983-84	Tom Barrasso, Buffalo	2.84
1984-85	Pelle Lindbergh, Philadelphia	3.02
1985-86	John Vanbiesbrouck, N.Y. Rangers	3.32
1986-87	Ron Hextall, Philadelphia	3.00
1987-88	Grant Fuhr, Edmonton	3.43
1988-89	Patrick Roy, Montreal	2.47
1989-90	Patrick Roy, Montreal	2.53
1990-91	Ed Belfour, Chicago	2.47
1991-92	Patrick Roy, Montreal	2.36
1992-93	Ed Belfour, Chicago	2.59

The award was formerly presented to the goaltender(s) having played a minimum of 25 games for the team with the fewest goals scored against. Beginning with the 1981-82 season, it was awarded to the outstanding goaltender.

BILL JENNINGS TROPHY

(Leading goaltender)

Season	Player, Team	GAA
1981-82	Denis Herron, Montreal	2.64
	Rick Wamsley, Montreal	2.75
1982-83	Roland Melanson, N.Y. Islanders	2.66
	Billy Smith, N.Y. Islanders	2.87
1983-84	Pat Riggin, Washington	2.66
	Al Jensen, Washington	2.91
1984-85	Tom Barrasso, Buffalo	2.66
	Bob Sauve, Buffalo	3.22
1985-86	Bob Froese, Philadelphia	2.55
	Darren Jensen, Philadelphia	3.68
1986-87	Brian Hayward, Montreal	2.81
	Patrick Roy, Montreal	2.93
1987-88	Brian Hayward, Montreal	2.86
	Patrick Roy, Montreal	2.90
1988-89	Patrick Roy, Montreal	2.47
	Brian Hayward, Montreal	2.90
1989-90	Rejean Lemelin, Boston	2.81
	Andy Moog, Boston	2.89
1990-91	Ed Belfour, Chicago	2.47
1991-92	Patrick Roy, Montreal	2.36
1992-93	Ed Belfour, Chicago	2.59

The award is presented to the goaltender(s) having played a minimum of 25 games for the team with the fewest goals scored against.

CALDER MEMORIAL TROPHY

(Rookie of the year)

Season	Player, Team
1932-33	Carl Voss, Detroit
1933-34	Russ Blinco, Montreal Maroons
1934-35	Dave Schriner, N.Y. Americans
1935-36	Mike Karakas, Chicago
1936-37	Syl Apps, Toronto
1937-38	Cully Dahlstrom, Chicago
1938-39	Frank Brimsek, Boston
1939-40	Kilby Macdonald, N.Y. Rangers
1940-41	John Quilty, Montreal
1941-42	Grant Warwick, N.Y. Rangers
1942-43	Gaye Stewart, Toronto
1943-44	Gus Bodnar, Toronto
1944-45	Frank McCool, Toronto
1945-46	Edgar Laprade, N.Y. Rangers
1946-47	Howie Meeker, Toronto
1947-48	Jim McFadden, Detroit
1948-49	Pentti Lund, N.Y. Rangers
1949-50	Jack Gelineau, Boston
1950-51	Terry Sawchuk, Detroit
1951-52	Bernie Geoffrion, Montreal
1952-53	Lorne Worsley, N.Y. Rangers
1953-54	Camille Henry, N.Y. Rangers
1954-55	Ed Litzenberger, Chicago
1955-56	Glenn Hall, Detroit
1956-57	Larry Regan, Boston
1957-58	Frank Mahovlich, Toronto
1958-59	Ralph Backstrom, Montreal
1959-60	Bill Hay, Chicago
1960-61	Dave Keon, Toronto
1961-62	Bobby Rousseau, Montreal
1962-63	Kent Douglas, Toronto
1963-64	Jacques Laperriere, Montreal
1964-65	Roger Crozier, Detroit
1965-66	Brit Selby, Toronto
1966-67	Bobby Orr, Boston
1967-68	Derek Sanderson, Boston
1968-69	Danny Grant, Minnesota
1969-70	Tony Esposito, Chicago
1970-71	Gilbert Perreault, Buffalo
1971-72	Ken Dryden, Montreal
1972-73	Steve Vickers, N.Y. Rangers
1973-74	Denis Potvin, N.Y. Islanders
1974-75	Eric Vail, Atlanta
1975-76	Bryan Trottier, N.Y. Islanders
1976-77	Willi Plett, Atlanta
1977-78	Mike Bossy, N.Y. Islanders
1978-79	Bobby Smith, Minnesota
1979-80	Ray Bourque, Boston
1980-81	Peter Stastny, Quebec
1981-82	Dale Hawerchuk, Winnipeg
1982-83	Steve Larmer, Chicago
1983-84	Tom Barrasso, Buffalo
1984-85	Mario Lemieux, Pittsburgh
1985-86	Gary Suter, Calgary
1986-87	Luc Robitaille, Los Angeles
1987-88	Joe Nieuwendyk, Calgary
1988-89	Brian Leetch, N.Y. Rangers
1989-90	Sergei Makarov, Calgary
1990-91	Ed Belfour, Chicago
1991-92	Pavel Bure, Vancouver
1992-93	Teemu Selanne, Winnipeg

The award was originally known as the Leading Rookie Award. It was renamed the Calder Trophy in 1936-37 and became the Calder Memorial Trophy in 1942-43, following the death of NHL President Frank Calder.

LADY BYNG MEMORIAL TROPHY

(Most gentlemanly player)

Season	Player, Team
1924-25	Frank Nighbor, Ottawa
1925-26	Frank Nighbor, Ottawa
1926-27	Billy Burch, N.Y. Americans
1927-28	Frank Boucher, N.Y. Rangers
1928-29	Frank Boucher, N.Y. Rangers
1929-30	Frank Boucher, N.Y. Rangers
1930-31	Frank Boucher, N.Y. Rangers
1931-32	Joe Primeau, Toronto
1932-33	Frank Boucher, N.Y. Rangers
1933-34	Frank Boucher, N.Y. Rangers
1934-35	Frank Boucher, N.Y. Rangers
1935-36	Doc Romnes, Chicago
1936-37	Marty Barry, Detroit
1937-38	Gordie Drillon, Toronto
1938-39	Clint Smith, N.Y. Rangers
1939-40	Bobby Bauer, Boston
1940-41	Bobby Bauer, Boston
1941-42	Syl Apps, Toronto
1942-43	Max Bentley, Chicago
1943-44	Clint Smith, Chicago
1944-45	Bill Mosienko, Chicago
1945-46	Toe Blake, Montreal
1946-47	Bobby Bauer, Boston
1947-48	Buddy O'Connor, N.Y. Rangers
1948-49	Bill Quackenbush, Detroit
1949-50	Edgar Laprade, N.Y. Rangers
1950-51	Red Kelly, Detroit
1951-52	Sid Smith, Toronto
1952-53	Red Kelly, Detroit
1953-54	Red Kelly, Detroit
1954-55	Sid Smith, Toronto
1955-56	Earl Reibel, Detroit
1956-57	Andy Hebenton, N.Y. Rangers
1957-58	Camille Henry, N.Y. Rangers
1958-59	Alex Delvecchio, Detroit
1959-60	Don McKenney, Boston
1960-61	Red Kelly, Toronto
1961-62	Dave Keon, Toronto
1962-63	Dave Keon, Toronto
1963-64	Ken Wharram, Chicago
1964-65	Bobby Hull, Chicago
1965-66	Alex Delvecchio, Detroit
1966-67	Stan Mikita, Chicago
1967-68	Stan Mikita, Chicago
1968-69	Alex Delvecchio, Detroit
1969-70	Phil Goyette, St. Louis
1970-71	John Bucyk, Boston
1971-72	Jean Ratelle, N.Y. Rangers
1972-73	Gilbert Perreault, Buffalo
1973-74	John Bucyk, Boston

Season	Player, Team
1974-75	Marcel Dionne, Detroit
1975-76	Jean Ratelle, N.Y.R.-Boston
1976-77	Marcel Dionne, Los Angeles
1977-78	Butch Goring, Los Angeles
1978-79	Bob MacMillan, Atlanta
1979-80	Wayne Gretzky, Edmonton
1980-81	Butch Goring, N.Y. Islanders
1981-82	Rick Middleton, Boston
1982-83	Mike Bossy, N.Y. Islanders
1983-84	Mike Bossy, N.Y. Islanders
1984-85	Jari Kurri, Edmonton
1985-86	Mike Bossy, N.Y. Islanders
1986-87	Joe Mullen, Calgary
1987-88	Mats Naslund, Montreal
1988-89	Joe Mullen, Calgary
1989-90	Brett Hull, St. Louis
1990-91	Wayne Gretzky, Los Angeles
1991-92	Wayne Gretzky, Los Angeles
1992-93	Pierre Turgeon, N.Y. Islanders

The award was originally known as the Lady Byng Trophy. After winning the award seven times, Frank Boucher received permanent possession and a new trophy was donated to the NHL in 1936. After Lady Byng's death in 1949, the NHL changed the name to Lady Byng Memorial Trophy.

CONN SMYTHE TROPHY

(Playoff MVP)

Season	Player, Team
1964-65	Jean Beliveau, Montreal
1965-66	Roger Crozier, Detroit
1966-67	Dave Keon, Toronto
1967-68	Glenn Hall, St. Louis
1968-69	Serge Savard, Montreal
1969-70	Bobby Orr, Boston
1970-71	Ken Dryden, Montreal
1971-72	Bobby Orr, Boston
1972-73	Yvan Cournoyer, Montreal
1973-74	Bernie Parent, Philadelphia
1974-75	Bernie Parent, Philadelphia
1975-76	Reggie Leach, Philadelphia
1976-77	Guy Lafleur, Montreal
1977-78	Larry Robinson, Montreal
1978-79	Bob Gainey, Montreal
1979-80	Bryan Trottier, N.Y. Islanders
1980-81	Butch Goring, N.Y. Islanders
1981-82	Mike Bossy, N.Y. Islanders
1982-83	Billy Smith, N.Y. Islanders
1983-84	Mark Messier, Edmonton
1984-85	Wayne Gretzky, Edmonton
1985-86	Patrick Roy, Montreal
1986-87	Ron Hextall, Philadelphia
1987-88	Wayne Gretzky, Edmonton
1988-89	Al MacInnis, Calgary
1989-90	Bill Ranford, Edmonton
1990-91	Mario Lemieux, Pittsburgh
1991-92	Mario Lemieux, Pittsburgh
1992-93	Patrick Roy, Montreal

BILL MASTERTON MEMORIAL TROPHY

(Sportsmanship—dedication to hockey)

Season	Player, Team
1967-68	Claude Provost, Montreal
1968-69	Ted Hampson, Oakland
1969-70	Pit Martin, Chicago
1970-71	Jean Ratelle, N.Y. Rangers
1971-72	Bobby Clarke, Philadelphia
1972-73	Lowell MacDonald, Pittsburgh
1973-74	Henri Richard, Montreal
1974-75	Don Luce, Buffalo
1975-76	Rod Gilbert, N.Y. Rangers
1976-77	Ed Westfall, N.Y. Islanders
1977-78	Butch Goring, Los Angeles
1978-79	Serge Savard, Montreal

Season	Player, Team
1979-80	Al MacAdam, Minnesota
1980-81	Blake Dunlop, St. Louis
1981-82	Glenn Resch, Colorado
1982-83	Lanny McDonald, Calgary
1983-84	Brad Park, Detroit
1984-85	Anders Hedberg, N.Y. Rangers
1985-86	Charlie Simmer, Boston
1986-87	Doug Jarvis, Hartford
1987-88	Bob Bourne, Los Angeles
1988-89	Tim Kerr, Philadelphia
1989-90	Gord Kluzak, Boston
1990-91	Dave Taylor, Los Angeles
1991-92	Mark Fitzpatrick, N.Y. Islanders
1992-93	Mario Lemieux, Pittsburgh

Presented by the Professional Hockey Writers' Association to the player who best exemplifies the qualities of perseverance, sportsmanship and dedication to hockey.

FRANK J. SELKE TROPHY

(Best defensive forward)

Season	Player, Team
1977-78	Bob Gainey, Montreal
1978-79	Bob Gainey, Montreal
1979-80	Bob Gainey, Montreal
1980-81	Bob Gainey, Montreal
1981-82	Steve Kasper, Boston
1982-83	Bobby Clarke, Philadelphia
1983-84	Doug Jarvis, Washington
1984-85	Craig Ramsay, Buffalo
1985-86	Troy Murray, Chicago
1986-87	Dave Poulin, Philadelphia
1987-88	Guy Carbonneau, Montreal
1988-89	Guy Carbonneau, Montreal
1989-90	Rick Meagher, St. Louis
1990-91	Dirk Graham, Chicago
1991-92	Guy Carbonneau, Montreal
1992-93	Doug Gilmour, Toronto

JACK ADAMS AWARD

(Coach of the year)

Season	Coach, Team
1973-74	Fred Shero, Philadelphia
1974-75	Bob Pulford, Los Angeles
1975-76	Don Cherry, Boston
1976-77	Scotty Bowman, Montreal
1977-78	Bobby Kromm, Detroit
1978-79	Al Arbour, N.Y. Islanders
1979-80	Pat Quinn, Philadelphia
1980-81	Red Berenson, St. Louis
1981-82	Tom Watt, Winnipeg
1982-83	Orval Tessier, Chicago
1983-84	Bryan Murray, Washington
1984-85	Mike Keenan, Philadelphia
1985-86	Glen Sather, Edmonton
1986-87	Jacques Demers, Detroit
1987-88	Jacques Demers, Detroit
1988-89	Pat Burns, Montreal
1989-90	Bob Murdoch, Winnipeg
1990-91	Brian Sutter, St. Louis
1991-92	Pat Quinn, Vancouver
1992-93	Pat Burns, Toronto

KING CLANCY TROPHY

(Humanitarian contributions)

Season	Player, Team
1987-88	Lanny McDonald, Calgary
1988-89	Bryan Trottier, N.Y. Islanders
1989-90	Kevin Lowe, Edmonton
1990-91	Dave Taylor, Los Angeles
1991-92	Ray Bourque, Boston
1992-93	Dave Poulin, Boston

TEAM HISTORIES

MIGHTY DUCKS OF ANAHEIM

FIRST-ROUND ENTRY DRAFT CHOICES

Year   Player, Overall, Last Amateur Team (League)
1993—Paul Kariya, 4, University of Maine

BOSTON BRUINS

YEAR-BY-YEAR RECORDS

Season	W	L	T	Pts.	Finish	W	L	Highest round	Coach
1924-25	6	24	0	12	6th	—	—		Art Ross
1925-26	17	15	4	38	4th	—	—		Art Ross
1926-27	21	20	3	45	2nd/American	*2	2	Stanley Cup finals	Art Ross
1927-28	20	13	11	51	1st/American	*0	1	Semifinals	Art Ross
1928-29	26	13	5	57	1st/American	5	0	Stanley Cup champ	Cy Denneny
1929-30	38	5	1	77	1st/American	3	3	Stanley Cup finals	Art Ross
1930-31	28	10	6	62	1st/American	2	3	Semifinals	Art Ross
1931-32	15	21	12	42	4th/American	—	—		Art Ross
1932-33	25	15	8	58	1st/American	2	3	Semifinals	Art Ross
1933-34	18	25	5	41	4th/American	—	—		Art Ross
1934-35	26	16	6	58	1st/American	1	3	Semifinals	Frank Patrick
1935-36	22	20	6	50	2nd/American	1	1	Quarterfinals	Frank Patrick
1936-37	23	18	7	53	2nd/American	1	2	Quarterfinals	Art Ross
1937-38	30	11	7	67	1st/American	0	3	Semifinals	Art Ross
1938-39	36	10	2	74	1st	8	4	Stanley Cup champ	Art Ross
1939-40	31	12	5	67	1st	2	4	Semifinals	Ralph (Cooney) Weiland
1940-41	27	8	13	67	1st	8	3	Stanley Cup champ	Ralph (Cooney) Weiland
1941-42	25	17	6	56	3rd	2	3	Semifinals	Art Ross
1942-43	24	17	9	57	2nd	4	5	Stanley Cup finals	Art Ross
1943-44	19	26	5	43	5th	—	—		Art Ross
1944-45	16	30	4	36	4th	3	4	League semifinals	Art Ross
1945-46	24	18	8	56	2nd	5	5	Stanley Cup finals	Dit Clapper
1946-47	26	23	11	63	3rd	1	4	League semifinals	Dit Clapper
1947-48	23	24	13	59	3rd	1	4	League semifinals	Dit Clapper
1948-49	29	23	8	66	2nd	1	4	League semifinals	Dit Clapper
1949-50	22	32	16	60	5th	—	—		George Boucher
1950-51	22	30	18	62	4th	†1	4	League semifinals	Lynn Patrick
1951-52	25	29	16	66	4th	3	4	League semifinals	Lynn Patrick
1952-53	28	29	13	69	3rd	5	6	League semifinals	Lynn Patrick
1953-54	32	28	10	74	4th	0	4	League semifinals	Lynn Patrick
1954-55	23	26	21	67	4th	1	4	League semifinals	Lynn Patrick, Milt Schmidt
1955-56	23	34	13	59	5th	—	—		Milt Schmidt
1956-57	34	24	12	80	3rd	5	5	Stanley Cup finals	Milt Schmidt
1957-58	27	28	15	69	4th	6	6	Stanley Cup finals	Milt Schmidt
1958-59	32	29	9	73	2nd	3	4	League semifinals	Milt Schmidt
1959-60	28	34	8	64	5th	—	—		Milt Schmidt
1960-61	15	42	13	43	6th	—	—		Milt Schmidt
1961-62	15	47	8	38	6th	—	—		Phil Watson
1962-63	14	39	17	45	6th	—	—		Phil Watson, Milt Schmidt
1963-64	18	40	12	48	6th	—	—		Milt Schmidt
1964-65	21	43	6	48	6th	—	—		Milt Schmidt
1965-66	21	43	6	48	5th	—	—		Milt Schmidt
1966-67	17	43	10	44	6th	—	—		Harry Sinden
1967-68	37	27	10	84	3rd/East	0	4	Division semifinals	Harry Sinden
1968-69	42	18	16	100	2nd/East	6	4	Division finals	Harry Sinden
1969-70	40	17	19	99	2nd/East	12	2	Stanley Cup champ	Harry Sinden
1970-71	57	14	7	121	1st/East	3	4	Division semifinals	Tom Johnson
1971-72	54	13	11	119	1st/East	12	3	Stanley Cup champ	Tom Johnson
1972-73	51	22	5	107	2nd/East	1	4	Division semifinals	Tom Johnson, Bep Guidolin
1973-74	52	17	9	113	1st/East	10	6	Stanley Cup finals	Bep Guidolin
1974-75	40	26	14	94	2nd/Adams	1	2	Preliminaries	Don Cherry
1975-76	48	15	17	113	1st/Adams	5	7	Semifinals	Don Cherry
1976-77	49	23	8	106	1st/Adams	8	6	Stanley Cup finals	Don Cherry
1977-78	51	18	11	113	1st/Adams	10	5	Stanley Cup finals	Don Cherry
1978-79	43	23	14	100	1st/Adams	7	4	Semifinals	Don Cherry
1979-80	46	21	13	105	2nd/Adams	4	6	Quarterfinals	Fred Creighton, Harry Sinden
1980-81	37	30	13	87	2nd/Adams	0	3	Preliminaries	Gerry Cheevers
1981-82	43	27	10	96	2nd/Adams	6	5	Division finals	Gerry Cheevers
1982-83	50	20	10	110	1st/Adams	9	8	Conference finals	Gerry Cheevers

Season	REGULAR SEASON					PLAYOFFS			
	W	L	T	Pts.	Finish	W	L	Highest round	Coach
1983-84	49	25	6	104	1st/Adams	0	3	Division semifinals	Gerry Cheevers
1984-85	36	34	10	82	4th/Adams	2	3	Division semifinals	Gerry Cheevers, Harry Sinden
1985-86	37	31	12	86	3rd/Adams	0	3	Division semifinals	Butch Goring
1986-87	39	34	7	85	3rd/Adams	0	4	Division semifinals	Butch Goring, Terry O'Reilly
1987-88	44	30	6	94	2nd/Adams	12	6	Conference finals	Terry O'Reilly
1988-89	37	29	14	88	2nd/Adams	5	5	Division finals	Terry O'Reilly
1989-90	46	25	9	101	1st/Adams	13	8	Stanley Cup finals	Mike Milbury
1990-91	44	24	12	100	1st/Adams	10	9	Conference finals	Mike Milbury
1991-92	36	32	12	84	2nd/Adams	8	7	Conference finals	Rick Bowness
1992-93	51	26	7	109	1st/Adams	0	4	Division semifinals	Brian Sutter

*Won-lost record does not indicate tie(s) resulting from two-game, total-goals series that year (two-game, total-goals series were played from 1917-18 through 1935-36).
†Tied after one overtime (curfew law).

FIRST-ROUND ENTRY DRAFT CHOICES

Year	Player, Overall, Last Amateur Team (League)
1969	Don Tannahill, 3, Niagara Falls (OHL)
	Frank Spring, 4, Edmonton (WCHL)
	Ivan Boldirev, 11, Oshawa (OHL)
1970	Reggie Leach, 3, Flin Flon (WCHL)
	Rick MacLeish, 4, Peterborough (OHL)
	Ron Plumb, 9, Peterborough (OHL)
	Bob Stewart, 13, Oshawa (OHL)
1971	Ron Jones, 6, Edmonton (WCHL)
	Terry O'Reilly, 14, Oshawa (OHL)
1972	Mike Bloom, 16, St. Catharines (OHL)
1973	Andre Savard, 6, Quebec (QMJHL)
1974	Don Laraway, 18, Swift Current (WCHL)
1975	Doug Halward, 14, Peterborough (OHL)
1976	Clayton Pachal, 16, New Westminster (WCHL)
1977	Dwight Foster, 16, Kitchener (OHL)
1978	Al Secord, 16, Hamilton (OHL)
1979	Ray Bourque, 8, Verdun (QMJHL)
	Brad McCrimmon, 15, Brandon (WHL)

Year	Player, Overall, Last Amateur Team (League)
1980	Barry Pederson, 18, Victoria (WHL)
1981	Norm Leveille, 14, Chicoutimi (QMJHL)
1982	*Gord Kluzak, 1, Billings (WHL)
1983	Nevin Markwart, 21, Regina (WHL)
1984	Dave Pasin, 19, Prince Albert (WHL)
1985	No first round selection
1986	Craig Janney, 13, Boston College
1987	Glen Wesley, 3, Portland (WHL)
	Stephane Quintal, 14, Granby (QMJHL)
1988	Robert Cimetta, 18, Toronto (OHL)
1989	Shayne Stevenson, 17, Kitchener (OHL)
1990	Bryan Smolinski, 21, Michigan State University
1991	Glen Murray, 18, Sudbury (OHL)
1992	Dmitri Kvartalnov, 16, San Diego (IHL)
1993	Kevyn Adams, 25, Miami of Ohio

*Designates first player chosen in draft.

FRANCHISE LEADERS

Current players in boldface

FORWARDS/DEFENSEMEN

Games

John Bucyk	1436
Ray Bourque	1028
Wayne Cashman	1027
Terry O'Reilly	891
Rick Middleton	881
Don Marcotte	868
Dallas Smith	861
Dit Clapper	833
Milt Schmidt	776
Woody Dumart	771

Goals

John Bucyk	545
Phil Esposito	459
Rick Middleton	402
Ray Bourque	291
Ken Hodge	289
Wayne Cashman	277
Bobby Orr	264
Peter McNab	263
Cam Neely	241
Don Marcotte	230

Assists

Ray Bourque	806
John Bucyk	794
Bobby Orr	624
Phil Esposito	553
Wayne Cashman	516
Rick Middleton	496
Terry O'Reilly	402
Ken Hodge	385
Bill Cowley	346
Milt Schmidt	346

Points

John Bucyk	1339
Ray Bourque	1097
Phil Esposito	1012
Rick Middleton	898
Bobby Orr	888
Wayne Cashman	793
Ken Hodge	674
Terry O'Reilly	606
Peter McNab	587
Milt Schmidt	575

Penalty minutes

Terry O'Reilly	2095
Mike Milbury	1552
Keith Crowder	1261
Wayne Cashman	1041
Eddie Shore	1038
Ted Green	1029

GOALTENDERS

Games

Cecil Thompson	468
Frankie Brimsek	444
Eddie Johnston	443
Gerry Cheevers	416
Gilles Gilbert	277
Jim Henry	236

Shutouts

Cecil Thompson	74
Frankie Brimsek	35
Eddie Johnston	27
Gerry Cheevers	26
Jim Henry	24
Hal Winkler	19
Gilles Gilbert	16
Don Simmons	15

Goals-against average
(2400 minutes minimum)

Hal Winkler	1.56
Cecil Thompson	1.99
Charles Stewart	2.46
John Henderson	2.52
Terry Sawchuk	2.57
Frankie Brimsek	2.58
Jim Henry	2.58

Wins

Cecil Thompson	252
Frankie Brimsek	230
Gerry Cheevers	229
Eddie Johnston	182
Gilles Gilbert	155

BUFFALO SABRES

YEAR-BY-YEAR RECORDS

Season	W	L	T	Pts.	Finish	W	L	Highest round	Coach
1970-71	24	39	15	63	5th/East	—	—		Punch Imlach
1971-72	16	43	19	51	6th/East	—	—		Punch Imlach, Joe Crozier
1972-73	37	27	14	88	4th/East	2	4	Division semifinals	Joe Crozier
1973-74	32	34	12	76	5th/East	—	—		Joe Crozier
1974-75	49	16	15	113	1st/Adams	10	7	Stanley Cup finals	Floyd Smith
1975-76	46	21	13	105	2nd/Adams	4	5	Quarterfinals	Floyd Smith
1976-77	48	24	8	104	2nd/Adams	2	4	Quarterfinals	Floyd Smith
1977-78	44	19	17	105	2nd/Adams	3	5	Quarterfinals	Marcel Pronovost
1978-79	36	28	16	88	2nd/Adams	1	2	Preliminaries	Marcel Pronovost, Bill Inglis
1979-80	47	17	16	110	1st/Adams	9	5	Semifinals	Scotty Bowman
1980-81	39	20	21	99	1st/Adams	4	4	Quarterfinals	Roger Neilson
1981-82	39	26	15	93	3rd/Adams	1	3	Division semifinals	Jim Roberts, Scotty Bowman
1982-83	38	29	13	89	3rd/Adams	6	4	Division finals	Scotty Bowman
1983-84	48	25	7	103	2nd/Adams	0	3	Division semifinals	Scotty Bowman
1984-85	38	28	14	90	3rd/Adams	2	3	Divison semifinals	Scotty Bowman
1985-86	37	37	6	80	5th/Adams	—	—		Jim Schoenfeld, Scotty Bowman
1986-87	28	44	8	64	5th/Adams	—	—		Scotty Bowman, Craig Ramsay Ted Sator
1987-88	37	32	11	85	3rd/Adams	2	4	Division semifinals	Ted Sator
1988-89	38	35	7	83	3rd/Adams	1	4	Division semifinals	Ted Sator
1989-90	45	27	8	98	2nd/Adams	2	4	Division semifinals	Rick Dudley
1990-91	31	30	19	81	3rd/Adams	2	4	Division semifinals	Rick Dudley
1991-92	31	37	12	74	3rd/Adams	3	4	Division semifinals	Rick Dudley, John Muckler
1992-93	38	36	10	86	4th/Adams	4	4	Division finals	John Muckler

FIRST-ROUND ENTRY DRAFT CHOICES

Year	Player, Overall, Last Amateur Team (League)
1970	*Gilbert Perreault, 1, Montreal (OHL)
1971	Rick Martin, 5, Montreal (OHL)
1972	Jim Schoenfeld, 5, Niagara Falls (OHL)
1973	Morris Titanic, 12, Sudbury (OHL)
1974	Lee Fogolin, 11, Oshawa (OHL)
1975	Robert Sauve, 17, Laval (QMJHL)
1976	No first round selection
1977	Ric Seiling, 14, St. Catharines (OHL)
1978	Larry Playfair, 13, Portland (WHL)
1979	Mike Ramsey, 11, University of Minnesota
1980	Steve Patrick, 20, Brandon (WHL)
1981	Jiri Dudacek, 17, Kladno (Czechoslovakia)
1982	Phil Housley, 6, South St. Paul H.S. (Minn.) Paul Cyr, 9, Victoria (WHL) Dave Andreychuk, 16, Oshawa (OHL)

Year	Player, Overall, Last Amateur Team (League)
1983	Tom Barrasso, 5, Acton Boxboro H.S. (Mass.) Norm Lacombe, 10, Univ. of New Hampshire Adam Creighton, 11, Ottawa (OHL)
1984	Bo Andersson, 18, Vastra Frolunda (Sweden)
1985	Carl Johansson, 14, Vastra Frolunda (Sweden)
1986	Shawn Anderson, 5, Team Canada
1987	*Pierre Turgeon, 1, Granby (QMJHL)
1988	Joel Savage, 13, Victoria (WHL)
1989	Kevin Haller, 14, Regina (WHL)
1990	Brad May, 14, Niagara Falls (OHL)
1991	Philippe Boucher, 13, Granby (QMJHL)
1992	David Cooper, 11, Medicine Hat (WHL)
1993	No first round selection

*Designates first player chosen in draft.

FRANCHISE LEADERS

Current players in boldface

FORWARDS/DEFENSEMEN

Games

Gilbert Perreault	1191
Craig Ramsay	1070
Mike Ramsey	911
Bill Hajt	854
Don Luce	766
Dave Andreychuk	763
Rick Martin	681
Ric Seiling	664
Mike Foligno	662
Lindy Ruff	608
Phil Housley	608

Goals

Gilbert Perreault	512
Rick Martin	382
Dave Andreychuk	348
Danny Gare	267
Craig Ramsay	252
Mike Foligno	247

Rene Robert	222
Don Luce	216
Phil Housley	178
Ric Seiling	176

Assists

Gilbert Perreault	814
Dave Andreychuk	423
Craig Ramsay	420
Phil Housley	380
Rene Robert	330
Rick Martin	313
Don Luce	310
Mike Foligno	264
Mike Ramsey	256
Danny Gare	233

Points

Gilbert Perreault	1326
Dave Andreychuk	710
Rick Martin	771
Criag Ramsay	672
Phil Housley	558

Rene Robert	552
Don Luce	526
Mike Foligno	511
Danny Gare	500
Ric Seiling	376

Penalty minutes

Mike Foligno	1447
Larry Playfair	1390
Lindy Ruff	1126
Jim Schoenfeld	1025
Rob Ray	1012

GOALTENDERS

Games

Don Edwards	307
Tom Barrasso	266
Bob Sauve	246
Daren Puppa	215
Roger Crozier	202
Jacques Cloutier	144
Dave Dryden	120
Gerry Desjardins	116

Shutouts	
Don Edwards	14
Tom Barrasso	13
Roger Crozier	10
Bob Sauve	7

Goals - against average
(2400 minutes minimum)
Gerry Desjardins 2.81

Don Edwards	2.90
Dave Dryden	3.06
Bob Sauve	3.20
Roger Crozier	3.23
Tom Barrasso	3.28
Clint Malarchuk	3.40
Daren Puppa	3.41
Jacques Cloutier	3.70

Wins	
Don Edwards	156
Tom Barrasso	124
Bob Sauve	119
Daren Puppa	96
Roger Crozier	74
Gerry Desjardins	66

CALGARY FLAMES

YEAR - BY - YEAR RECORDS

	REGULAR SEASON					PLAYOFFS			
Season	W	L	T	Pts.	Finish	W	L	Highest round	Coach
1972-73*	25	38	15	65	7th/West	—	—		Bernie Geoffrion
1973-74*	30	34	14	74	4th/West	0	4	Division semifinals	Bernie Geoffrion
1974-75*	34	31	15	83	4th/Patrick	—	—		Bernie Geoffrion, Fred Creighton
1975-76*	35	33	12	82	3rd/Patrick	0	2	Preliminaries	Fred Creighton
1976-77*	34	34	12	80	3rd/Patrick	1	2	Preliminaries	Fred Creighton
1977-78*	34	27	19	87	3rd/Patrick	0	2	Preliminaries	Fred Creighton
1978-79*	41	31	8	90	4th/Patrick	0	2	Preliminaries	Fred Creighton
1979-80*	35	32	13	83	4th/Patrick	1	3	Preliminaries	Al MacNeil
1980-81	39	27	14	92	3rd/Patrick	9	7	Semifinals	Al MacNeil
1981-82	29	34	17	75	3rd/Smythe	0	3	Division semifinals	Al MacNeil
1982-83	32	34	14	78	2nd/Smythe	4	5	Division finals	Bob Johnson
1983-84	34	32	14	82	2nd/Smythe	6	5	Division finals	Bob Johnson
1984-85	41	27	12	94	3rd/Smythe	1	3	Division semifinals	Bob Johnson
1985-86	40	31	9	89	2nd/Smythe	12	10	Stanley Cup finals	Bob Johnson
1986-87	46	31	3	95	2nd/Smythe	2	4	Division semifinals	Bob Johnson
1987-88	48	23	9	105	1st/Smythe	4	5	Division finals	Terry Crisp
1988-89	54	17	9	117	1st/Smythe	16	6	Stanley Cup champ	Terry Crisp
1989-90	42	23	15	99	1st/Smythe	2	4	Division semifinals	Terry Crisp
1990-91	46	26	8	100	2nd/Smythe	3	4	Division semifinals	Doug Risebrough
1991-92	31	37	12	74	5th/Smythe	—	—		Doug Risebrough, Guy Charron
1992-93	43	30	11	97	2nd/Smythe	2	4	Division semifinals	Dave King

*Atlanta Flames.

FIRST - ROUND ENTRY DRAFT CHOICES

Year   Player, Overall, Last Amateur Team (League)
1972—Jacques Richard, 2, Quebec (QMJHL)
1973—Tom Lysiak, 2, Medicine Hat (WCHL)
      Vic Mercredi, 16, New Westminster (WCHL)
1974—No first round selection
1975—Richcard Mulhern, 8, Sherbrooke (QMJHL)
1976—Dave Shand, 8, Peterborough (OHL)
      Harold Phillipoff, 10, New Westminster (WCHL)
1977—No first round selection
1978—Brad Marsh, 11, London (OHL)
1979—Paul Reinhart, 12, Kitchener (OHL)
1980—Denis Cyr, 13, Montreal (OHL)
1981—Al MacInnis, 15, Kitchener (OHL)

Year   Player, Overall, Last Amateur Team (League)
1982—No first round selection
1983—Dan Quinn, 13, Belleville (OHL)
1984—Gary Roberts, 12, Ottawa (OHL)
1985—Chris Biotti, 17, Belmont Hill H.S. (Mass.)
1986—George Pelawa, 16, Bemidji H.S. (Minn.)
1987—Bryan Deasley, 19, University of Michigan
1988—Jason Muzzatti, 21, Michigan State University
1989—No first round selection
1990—Trevor Kidd, 11, Brandon (WHL)
1991—Niklas Sundblad, 19, AIK (Sweden)
1992—Cory Stillman, 6, Windsor (OHL)
1993—Jesper Mattsson, 18, Malmo (Sweden)

FRANCHISE LEADERS

Current players in boldface

FORWARDS/DEFENSEMEN

Games
Al MacInnis	728
Jim Peplinski	705
Joel Otto	602
Gary Suter	592
Jamie Macoun	586
Tim Hunter	545
Eric Vail	539
Paul Reinhart	517
Guy Chouinard	514
Lanny McDonald	492

Goals
Joe Nieuwendyk	257
Kent Nilsson	229

Lanny McDonald	215
Eric Vail	206
Guy Chouinard	193
Hakan Loob	193
Joe Mullen	190
Al MacInnis	185
Jim Peplinski	161
Tom Lysiak	155

Assists
Al MacInnis	481
Gary Suter	427
Guy Chouinard	336
Paul Reinhart	335
Kent Nilsson	333
Tom Lysiak	276
Jim Peplinski	262
Eric Vail	246

Hakan Loob	236
Joel Otto	236

Points
Al MacInnis	740
Kent Nilsson	562
Gary Suter	551
Guy Chouinard	529
Joe Nieuwendyk	491
Eric Vail	452
Paul Reinhart	444
Tom Lysiak	431
Hakan Loob	429
Jim Peplinski	423

Penalty minutes
Tim Hunter	2405
Gary Roberts	1482
Jim Peplinski	1456

Joel Otto 1420
Willi Plett 1267
Al MacInnis 865
Gary Suter 854
Jamie Macoun 666

GOALTENDERS
Games
Mike Vernon 419
Dan Bouchard 398
Reggie Lemelin 324
Phil Myre 211
Pat Riggin 119
Don Edwards 114

Rick Wamsley 111
Shutouts
Dan Bouchard 20
Phil Myre 11
Reggie Lemelin 6
Mike Vernon 6
Pat Riggin 4
Rick Wamsley 4

Goals-against average
(2400 minutes minimum)
Dan Bouchard 3.03
Phil Myre 3.21
Rick Wamsley 3.21

Mike Vernon 3.34
Reggie Lemelin 3.67
Pat Riggin 3.88
Don Edwards 4.06
Wins
Mike Vernon 222
Dan Bouchard 170
Reggie Lemelin 144
Phil Myre 76
Rick Wamsley 53
Pat Riggin 50
Don Edwards 40

CHICAGO BLACKHAWKS

YEAR-BY-YEAR RECORDS

Season	W	L	T	Pts.	Finish	W	L	Highest round	Coach
1926-27	19	22	3	41	3rd/American	*0	1	Quarterfinals	Pete Muldoon
1927-28	7	34	3	17	5th/American	—	—		Barney Stanley, Hugh Lehman
1928-29	7	29	8	22	5th/American	—	—		Herb Gardiner
1929-30	21	18	5	47	2nd/American	*0	1	Quarterfinals	Tom Schaughnessy, Bill Tobin
1930-31	24	17	3	51	2nd/American	*5	3	Stanley Cup finals	Dick Irvin
1931-32	18	19	11	47	2nd/American	1	1	Quarterfinals	Dick Irvin, Bill Tobin
1932-33	16	20	12	44	4th/American	—	—		Godfrey Matheson, Emil Iverson
1933-34	20	17	11	51	2nd/American	6	2	Stanley Cup champ	Tom Gorman
1934-35	26	17	5	57	2nd/American	*0	1	Quarterfinals	Clem Loughlin
1935-36	21	19	8	50	3rd/American	1	1	Quarterfinals	Clem Loughlin
1936-37	14	27	7	35	4th/American	—	—		Clem Loughlin
1937-38	14	25	9	37	3rd/American	7	3	Stanley Cup champ	Bill Stewart
1938-39	12	28	8	32	7th	—	—		Bill Stewart, Paul Thompson
1939-40	23	19	6	52	4th	0	2	Quarterfinals	Paul Thompson
1940-41	16	25	7	39	5th	2	3	Semifinals	Paul Thompson
1941-42	22	23	3	47	4th	1	2	Quarterfinals	Paul Thompson
1942-43	17	18	15	49	5th	—	—		Paul Thompson
1943-44	22	23	5	49	4th	4	5	Stanley Cup finals	Paul Thompson
1944-45	13	30	7	33	5th	—	—		Paul Thompson, John Gottselig
1945-46	23	20	7	53	3rd	0	4	League semifinals	John Gottselig
1946-47	19	37	4	42	6th	—	—		John Gottselig
1947-48	20	34	6	46	6th	—	—		John Gottselig, Charlie Conacher
1948-49	21	31	8	50	5th	—	—		Charlie Conacher
1949-50	22	38	10	54	6th	—	—		Charlie Conacher
1950-51	13	47	10	36	6th	—	—		Ebbie Goodfellow
1951-52	17	44	9	43	6th	—	—		Ebbie Goodfellow
1952-53	27	28	15	69	4th	3	4	League semifinals	Sid Abel
1953-54	12	51	7	31	6th	—	—		Sid Abel
1954-55	13	40	17	43	6th	—	—		Frank Eddolls
1955-56	19	39	12	50	6th	—	—		Dick Irvin
1956-57	16	39	15	47	6th	—	—		Tommy Ivan
1957-58	24	39	7	55	5th	—	—		Tommy Ivan, Rudy Pilous
1958-59	28	29	13	69	3rd	2	4	League semifinals	Rudy Pilous
1959-60	28	29	13	69	3rd	0	4	League semifinals	Rudy Pilous
1960-61	29	24	17	75	3rd	8	4	Stanley Cup champ	Rudy Pilous
1961-62	31	26	13	75	3rd	6	6	Stanley Cup finals	Rudy Pilous
1962-63	32	21	17	81	2nd	2	4	League semifinals	Rudy Pilous
1963-64	36	22	12	84	2nd	3	4	League semifinals	Billy Reay
1964-65	34	28	8	76	3rd	7	7	Stanley Cup finals	Billy Reay
1965-66	37	25	8	82	2nd	2	4	League semifinals	Billy Reay
1966-67	41	17	12	94	1st	2	4	League semifinals	Billy Reay
1967-68	32	26	16	80	4th/East	5	6	Division finals	Billy Reay
1968-69	34	33	9	77	6th/East	—	—		Billy Reay
1969-70	45	22	9	99	1st/East	4	4	Division finals	Billy Reay
1970-71	49	20	9	107	1st/West	11	7	Stanley Cup finals	Billy Reay
1971-72	46	17	15	107	1st/West	4	4	Division finals	Billy Reay
1972-73	42	27	9	93	1st/West	10	6	Stanley Cup finals	Billy Reay
1973-74	41	14	23	105	2nd/West	6	5	Division finals	Billy Reay
1974-75	37	35	8	82	3rd/Smythe	3	5	Quarterfinals	Billy Reay
1975-76	32	30	18	82	1st/Smythe	0	4	Quarterfinals	Billy Reay
1976-77	26	43	11	63	3rd/Smythe	0	2	Preliminaries	Billy Reay, Bill White
1977-78	32	29	19	83	1st/Smythe	0	4	Quarterfinals	Bob Pulford
1978-79	29	36	15	73	1st/Smythe	0	4	Quarterfinals	Bob Pulford
1979-80	34	27	19	87	1st/Smythe	3	4	Quarterfinals	Eddie Johnston
1980-81	31	33	16	78	2nd/Smythe	0	3	Preliminaries	Keith Magnuson

Season	W	L	T	Pts.	Finish	W	L	Highest round	Coach
1981-82	30	38	12	72	4th/Norris	8	7	Conference finals	Keith Magnuson, Bob Pulford
1982-83	47	23	10	104	1st/Norris	7	6	Conference finals	Orval Tessier
1983-84	30	42	8	68	4th/Norris	2	3	Division semifinals	Orval Tessier
1984-85	38	35	7	83	2nd/Norris	9	6	Conference finals	Orval Tessier, Bob Pulford
1985-86	39	33	8	86	1st/Norris	0	3	Division semifinals	Bob Pulford
1986-87	29	37	14	72	3rd/Norris	0	4	Division semifinals	Bob Pulford
1987-88	30	41	9	69	3rd/Norris	1	4	Division semifinals	Bob Murdoch
1988-89	27	41	12	66	4th/Norris	9	7	Conference finals	Mike Keenan
1989-90	41	33	6	88	1st/Norris	10	10	Conference finals	Mike Keenan
1990-91	49	23	8	106	1st/Norris	2	4	Division semifinals	Mike Keenan
1991-92	36	29	15	87	2nd/Norris	12	6	Stanley Cup finals	Mike Keenan
1992-93	47	25	12	106	1st/Norris	0	4	Division semifinals	Darryl Sutter

*Won-lost record does not indicate tie(s) resulting from two-game, total-goals series that year (two-game, total-goals series were played from 1917-18 through 1935-36).

FIRST-ROUND ENTRY DRAFT CHOICES

Year	Player, Overall, Last Amateur Team (League)
1969	J.P. Bordeleau, 13, Montreal (OHL)
1970	Dan Maloney, 14, London (OHL)
1971	Dan Spring, 12, Edmonton (WCHL)
1972	Phil Russell, 13, Edmonton (WCHL)
1973	Darcy Rota, 13, Edmonton (WCHL)
1974	Grant Mulvey, 16, Calgary (WCHL)
1975	Greg Vaydik, 7, Medicine Hat (WCHL)
1976	Real Cloutier, 9, Quebec (WHA)
1977	Doug Wilson, 6, Ottawa (OHL)
1978	Tim Higgins, 10, Ottawa (OHL)
1979	Keith Brown, 7, Portland (WHL)
1980	Denis Savard, 3, Montreal (QMJHL)
	Jerome Dupont, 15, Toronto (OHL)

Year	Player, Overall, Last Amateur Team (League)
1981	Tony Tanti, 12, Oshawa (OHL)
1982	Ken Yaremchuk, 7, Portland (WHL)
1983	Bruce Cassidy, 18, Ottawa (OHL)
1984	Ed Olczyk, 3, U.S. Olympic Team
1985	Dave Manson, 11, Prince Albert (WHL)
1986	Everett Sanipass, 14, Verdun (QMJHL)
1987	Jimmy Waite, 8, Chicoutimi (QMJHL)
1988	Jeremy Roenick, 8, Thayer Academy (Mass.)
1989	Adam Bennett, 6, Sudbury (OHL)
1990	Karl Dykhuis, 16, Hull (QMJHL)
1991	Dean McAmmond, 22, Prince Albert (WHL)
1992	Sergei Krivokrasov, 12, Central Red Army (CIS)
1993	Eric Lecompte, 24, Hull (QMJHL)

FRANCHISE LEADERS

Current players in boldface

FORWARDS/DEFENSEMEN

Games

Stan Mikita	1394
Bobby Hull	1036
Eric Nesterenko	1013
Bob Murray	1008
Doug Wilson	938
Dennis Hull	904
Steve Larmer	**891**
Chico Maki	840
Pierre Pilote	821
Cliff Koroll	814
Keith Brown	**812**
Ken Wharram	766
Harold March	759
Pit Martin	740
Denis Savard	736

Goals

Bobby Hull	604
Stan Mikita	541
Steve Larmer	**406**
Denis Savard	351
Dennis Hull	298
Bill Mosienko	258
Ken Wharram	252

Pit Martin	243
Doug Wilson	225
Doug Bentley	217
Jim Pappin	216
Al Secord	213
Cliff Koroll	208
Eric Nesterenko	207
Troy Murray	**197**

Assists

Stan Mikita	926
Denis Savard	662
Doug Wilson	554
Bobby Hull	549
Steve Larmer	**517**
Pierre Pilote	400
Jeremy Roenick	**387**
Pit Martin	384
Bob Murray	382
Dennis Hull	342
Doug Bentley	313
Chico Maki	292
Troy Murray	**290**
Bill Mosienko	288
Eric Nesterenko	288

Points

Stan Mikita	1467
Bobby Hull	1153

Denis Savard	1013
Steve Larmer	**923**
Doug Wilson	779
Dennis Hull	640
Pit Martin	627
Bill Mosienko	550
Ken Wharram	533
Doug Bentley	531
Bob Murray	514
Eric Nesterenko	495
Troy Murray	**487**
Pierre Pilote	477
Cliff Koroll	462

GOALTENDERS

Shutouts

Tony Esposito	74
Glenn Hall	51
Chuck Gardiner	42
Mike Karakas	28
Al Rollins	17
Ed Belfour	**16**
Denis DeJordy	13
Murray Bannerman	8
Lorne Chabot	8
Paul Goodman	6
Hugh Lehman	6

CLEVELAND BARONS (DEFUNCT)

YEAR-BY-YEAR RECORDS

Season	W	L	T	Pts.	Finish	W	L	Highest round	Coach
1967-68†	15	42	17	42	6th/West	—	—		Bert Olmstead, Gordie Fashoway
1968-69†	29	36	11	69	2nd/West	3	4	Division semifinals	Fred Glover
1969-70†	22	40	14	58	4th/West	0	4	Division semifinals	Fred Glover

Season	W	L	T	Pts.	Finish	W	L	Highest round	Coach
					REGULAR SEASON			PLAYOFFS	
1970-71‡	20	53	5	45	7th/West	—	—		Fred Glover
1971-72‡	21	39	18	60	6th/West	—	—		Fred Glover, Vic Stasiuk
1972-73‡	16	46	16	48	8th/West	—	—		Garry Young, Fred Glover
1973-74‡	13	55	10	36	8th/West	—	—		Fred Glover, Marsh Johnston
1974-75‡	19	48	13	51	4th/Adams	—	—		Marsh Johnston
1975-76‡	27	42	11	65	4th/Adams	—	—		Jack Evans
1976-77	25	42	13	63	4th/Adams	—	—		Jack Evans
1977-78*	22	45	13	57	4th/Adams	—	—		Jack Evans

*Team disbanded after 1977-78 season. Owners bought Minnesota franchise and a number of Cleveland players were awarded to North Stars; remaining Cleveland players were dispersed to other clubs in draft.
†Oakland Seals.
‡California Golden Seals.

FIRST-ROUND ENTRY DRAFT CHOICES

Year	Player, Overall, Last Amateur Team (League)
1969	Tony Featherstone, 7, Peterborough (OHA)
1970	Chris Oddleifson, 10 Winnipeg (WCHL)
1971	No first-round selection
1972	No first-round selection
1973	No first-round selection
1974	Rick Hampton, 3, St. Catharines (OHA)
	Ron Chipperfield, 17, Brandon (WCHL)
1975	Ralph Klassen, 3, Saskatoon (WCHL)
1976	Bjorn Johansson, 5, Orebro IK (Sweden)
1977	Mike Crombeen, 5, Kingston (OHA)

DALLAS STARS

YEAR-BY-YEAR RECORDS

Season	W	L	T	Pts.	Finish	W	L	Highest round	Coach
					REGULAR SEASON			PLAYOFFS	
1967-68*	27	32	15	69	4th/West	7	7	Division finals	Wren Blair
1968-69*	18	43	15	51	6th/West	—	—		Wren Blair, John Muckler
1969-70*	19	35	22	60	3rd/West	2	4	Division semifinals	Wren Blair, Charlie Burns
1970-71*	28	34	16	72	4th/West	6	6	Division finals	Jack Gordon
1971-72*	37	29	12	86	2nd/West	3	4	Division semifinals	Jack Gordon
1972-73*	37	30	11	85	3rd/West	2	4	Division semifinals	Jack Gordon
1973-74*	23	38	17	63	7th/West	—	—		Jack Gordon, Parker MacDonald
1974-75*	23	50	7	53	4th/Smythe	—	—		Jack Gordon, Charlie Burns
1975-76*	20	53	7	47	4th/Smythe	—	—		Ted Harris
1976-77*	23	39	18	64	2nd/Smythe	0	2	Preliminaries	Ted Harris
1977-78*	18	53	9	45	5th/Smythe	—	—		Ted Harris, Andre Beaulieu, Lou Nanne
1978-79*	28	40	12	68	4th/Adams	—	—		Harry Howell, Glen Sonmor
1979-80*	36	28	16	88	3rd/Adams	8	7	Semifinals	Glen Sonmor
1980-81*	35	28	17	87	3rd/Adams	12	7	Stanley Cup finals	Glen Sonmor
1981-82*	37	23	20	94	1st/Norris	1	3	Division semifinals	Glen Sonmor, Murray Oliver
1982-83*	40	24	16	96	2nd/Norris	4	5	Division finals	Glen Sonmor, Murray Oliver
1983-84*	39	31	10	88	1st/Norris	7	9	Conference finals	Bill Maloney
1984-85*	25	43	12	62	4th/Norris	5	4	Division finals	Bill Maloney, Glen Sonmor
1985-86*	38	33	9	85	2nd/Norris	2	3	Division semifinals	Lorne Henning
1986-87*	30	40	10	70	5th/Norris	—	—		Lorne Henning, Glen Sonmor
1987-88*	19	48	13	51	5th/Norris	—	—		Herb Brooks
1988-89*	27	37	16	70	3rd/Norris	1	4	Division semifinals	Pierre Page
1989-90*	36	40	4	76	4th/Norris	3	4	Division semifinals	Pierre Page
1990-91*	27	39	14	68	4th/Norris	14	9	Stanley Cup finals	Bob Gainey
1991-92*	32	42	6	70	4th/Norris	3	4	Division semifinals	Bob Gainey
1992-93*	36	38	10	82	5th/Norris	—	—		Bob Gainey

*Minnesota North Stars.

FIRST-ROUND ENTRY DRAFT CHOICES

Year	Player, Overall, Last Amateur Team (League)
1969	Dick Redmond, 5, St. Catharines (OHL)
	Dennis O'Brien, 14, St. Catharines (OHL)
1970	No first-round selection
1971	No first-round selection
1972	Jerry Byers, 12, Kitchener (OHL)
1973	No first-round selection
1974	Doug Hicks, 6, Flin Flon (WCHL)
1975	Brian Maxwell, 4, Medicine Hat (WCHL)
1976	Glen Sharpley, 3, Hull (QMJHL)
1977	Brad Maxwell, 7, New Westminster (WCHL)
1978	*Bobby Smith, 1, Ottawa (OHL)
1979	Craig Hartsburg, 6, Birmingham (WHA)
	Tom McCarthy, 10, Oshawa (OHL)
1980	Brad Palmer, 16, Victoria (WHL)
1981	Ron Meighan, 13, Niagara Falls (OHL)
1982	Brian Bellows, 2, Kitchener (OHL)
1983	*Brian Lawton, 1, Mount St. Charles H.S. (R.I.)
1984	David Quinn, 13, Kent H.S. (Ct.)
1985	No first-round selection
1986	Warren Babe, 12, Lethbridge (WHL)
1987	Dave Archibald, 6, Portland (WHL)
1988	*Mike Modano, 1, Prince Albert (WHL)
1989	Doug Zmolek, 7, John Marshall H.S. (Minn.)
1990	Derian Hatcher, 8, North Bay (OHL)
1991	Richard Matvichuk, 8, Saskatoon (WHL)
1992	No first-round selection
1993	Todd Harvey, 9, Detroit (OHL)

*Designates first player chosen in draft.

FRANCHISE LEADERS

Current players in boldface

FORWARDS/DEFENSEMEN
Games

Neal Broten	876
Curt Giles	760
Brian Bellows	753
Fred Barrett	730
Bill Goldsworthy	670
Lou Nanne	635
Tom Reid	615
Steve Payne	613
Dino Ciccarelli	602
J.P. Parise	588

Goals

Brian Bellows	342
Dino Ciccarelli	332
Bill Goldsworthy	267
Neal Broten	249
Steve Payne	228
Dave Gagner	187
Bobby Smith	185
Tim Young	178
Danny Grant	176
J.P. Parise	154

Assists

Neal Broten	547
Brian Bellows	380
Bobby Smith	369
Dino Ciccarelli	319
Tim Young	316

Craig Hartsburg	315
J.P. Parise	242
Bill Goldsworthy	239
Steve Payne	238
Gordie Roberts	224

Points

Neal Broten	796
Brian Bellows	722
Dino Ciccarelli	651
Bobby Smith	554
Bill Goldsworthy	506
Tim Young	494
Steve Payne	466
Craig Hartsburg	413
Dave Gagner	405
J.P. Parise	396

Penalty minutes

Basil McRae	1567
Shane Churla	1194
Willi Plett	1137
Brad Maxwell	1031
Mark Tinordi	872
Dennis O'Brien	836
Gordie Roberts	832
Craig Hartsburg	818
Bob Rouse	735

GOALTENDERS
Games

Cesare Maniago	420

Gilles Meloche	328
Jon Casey	325
Don Beaupre	316
Pete LoPresti	173
Kari Takko	131
Gump Worsley	107

Shutouts

Cesare Maniago	29
Jon Casey	12
Gilles Meloche	9
Pete LoPresti	5

Goals-against average
(2400 minutes minimum)

Gump Worsley	2.62
Cesare Maniago	3.17
Jon Casey	3.28
Gilles Gilbert	3.39
Gary Edwards	3.44
Darcy Wakaluk	3.44
Gilles Meloche	3.51
Don Beaupre	3.74
Kari Takko	3.87
Gary Smith	3.92

Wins

Cesare Maniago	143
Gilles Meloche	141
Jon Casey	128
Don Beaupre	126
Pete LoPresti	43

DETROIT RED WINGS

YEAR-BY-YEAR RECORDS

	REGULAR SEASON					PLAYOFFS			
Season	W	L	T	Pts.	Finish	W	L	Highest round	Coach
1926-27†	12	28	4	28	5th/American	—	—		Art Duncan, Duke Keats
1927-28†	19	19	6	44	4th/American	—	—		Jack Adams
1928-29†	19	16	9	47	3rd/American	0	2	Quarterfinals	Jack Adams
1929-30†	14	24	6	34	4th/American	—	—		Jack Adams
1930-31‡	16	21	7	39	4th/American	—	—		Jack Adams
1931-32‡	18	20	10	46	3rd/American	*0	1	Quarterfinals	Jack Adams
1932-33	25	15	8	58	2nd/American	2	2	Semifinals	Jack Adams
1933-34	24	14	10	58	1st/American	4	5	Stanley Cup finals	Jack Adams
1934-35	19	22	7	45	4th/American	—	—		Jack Adams
1935-36	24	16	8	56	1st/American	6	1	Stanley Cup champ	Jack Adams
1936-37	25	14	9	59	1st/American	6	4	Stanley Cup champ	Jack Adams
1937-38	12	25	11	35	4th/American	—	—		Jack Adams
1938-39	18	24	6	42	5th	3	3	Semifinals	Jack Adams
1939-40	16	26	6	38	5th	2	3	Semifinals	Jack Adams
1940-41	21	16	11	53	3rd	4	5	Stanley Cup finals	Jack Adams
1941-42	19	25	4	42	5th	7	5	Stanley Cup finals	Jack Adams
1942-43	25	14	11	61	1st	8	2	Stanley Cup champ	Jack Adams
1943-44	26	18	6	58	2nd	1	4	League semifinals	Jack Adams
1944-45	31	14	5	67	2nd	7	7	Stanley Cup finals	Jack Adams
1945-46	20	20	10	50	4th	1	4	League semifinals	Jack Adams
1946-47	22	27	11	55	4th	1	4	League semifinals	Jack Adams
1947-48	30	18	12	72	2nd	4	6	Stanley Cup finals	Tommy Ivan
1948-49	34	19	7	75	1st	4	7	Stanley Cup finals	Tommy Ivan
1949-50	37	19	14	88	1st	8	6	Stanley Cup champ	Tommy Ivan
1950-51	44	13	13	101	1st	2	4	League semifinals	Tommy Ivan
1951-52	44	14	12	100	1st	8	0	Stanley Cup champ	Tommy Ivan
1952-53	36	16	18	90	1st	2	4	League semifinals	Tommy Ivan
1953-54	37	19	14	88	1st	8	4	Stanley Cup champ	Tommy Ivan
1954-55	42	17	11	95	1st	8	3	Stanley Cup champ	Jimmy Skinner
1955-56	30	24	16	76	2nd	5	5	Stanley Cup finals	Jimmy Skinner
1956-57	38	20	12	88	1st	1	4	League semifinals	Jimmy Skinner
1957-58	29	29	12	70	3rd	0	4	League semifinals	Jimmy Skinner, Sid Abel
1958-59	25	37	8	58	6th	—	—		Sid Abel
1959-60	26	29	15	67	4th	2	4	League semifinals	Sid Abel
1960-61	25	29	16	66	4th	6	5	Stanley Cup finals	Sid Abel

— 134 —

Season	W	L	T	Pts.	Finish	W	L	Highest round	Coach
					REGULAR SEASON			PLAYOFFS	
1961-62	23	33	14	60	5th	—	—		Sid Abel
1962-63	32	25	13	77	4th	5	6	Stanley Cup finals	Sid Abel
1963-64	30	29	11	71	4th	7	7	Stanley Cup finals	Sid Abel
1964-65	40	23	7	87	1st	3	4	League semifinals	Sid Abel
1965-66	31	27	12	74	4th	6	6	Stanley Cup finals	Sid Abel
1966-67	27	39	4	58	5th	—	—		Sid Abel
1967-68	27	35	12	66	6th/East	—	—		Sid Abel
1968-69	33	31	12	78	5th/East	—	—		Bill Gadsby
1969-70	40	21	15	95	3rd/East	0	4	Division semifinals	Bill Gadsby, Sid Abel
1970-71	22	45	11	55	7th/East	—	—		Ned Harkness, Doug Barkley
1971-72	33	35	10	76	5th/East	—	—		Doug Barkley, Johnny Wilson
1972-73	37	29	12	86	5th/East	—	—		Johnny Wilson
1973-74	29	39	10	68	6th/East	—	—		Ted Garvin, Alex Delvecchio
1974-75	23	45	12	58	4th/Norris	—	—		Alex Delvecchio
1975-76	26	44	10	62	4th/Norris	—	—		Ted Garvin, Alex Delvecchio
1976-77	16	55	9	41	5th/Norris	—	—		Alex Delvecchio, Larry Wilson
1977-78	32	34	14	78	2nd/Norris	3	4	Quarterfinals	Bobby Kromm
1978-79	23	41	16	62	5th/Norris	—	—		Bobby Kromm
1979-80	26	43	11	63	5th/Norris	—	—		Bobby Kromm, Ted Lindsay
1980-81	19	43	18	56	5th/Norris	—	—		Ted Lindsay, Wayne Maxner
1981-82	21	47	12	54	6th/Norris	—	—		Wayne Maxner, Billy Dea
1982-83	21	44	15	57	5th/Norris	—	—		Nick Polano
1983-84	31	42	7	69	3rd/Norris	1	3	Division semifinals	Nick Polano
1984-85	27	41	12	66	3rd/Norris	0	3	Division semifinals	Nick Polano
1985-86	17	57	6	40	5th/Norris	—	—		Harry Neale, Brad Park, Dan Belisle
1986-87	34	36	10	78	2nd/Norris	9	7	Conference finals	Jacques Demers
1987-88	41	28	11	93	1st/Norris	9	7	Conference finals	Jacques Demers
1988-89	34	34	12	80	1st/Norris	2	4	Division semifinals	Jacques Demers
1989-90	28	38	14	70	5th/Norris	—	—		Jacques Demers
1990-91	34	38	8	76	3rd/Norris	3	4	Division semifinals	Brian Murray
1991-92	43	25	12	98	1st/Norris	4	7	Division finals	Brian Murray
1992-93	47	28	9	103	2nd/Norris	3	4	Division semifinals	Brian Murray

*Won-lost record does not indicate tie(s) resulting from two-game, total-goals series that year (two-game, total-goals series were played from 1917-18 through 1935-36).
†Detroit Cougars.
‡Detroit Falcons.

FIRST-ROUND ENTRY DRAFT CHOICES

Year   Player, Overall, Last Amateur Team (League)
1969—Jim Rutherford, 10, Hamilton (OHL)
1970—Serge Lajeunesse, 12, Montreal (OHL)
1971—Marcel Dionne, 2, St. Catharines (OHL)
1972—No first-round selection
1973—Terry Richardson, 11, New Westminster (WCHL)
1974—Bill Lochead, 9, Oshawa (OHL)
1975—Rick Lapointe, 5, Victoria (WCHL)
1976—Fred Williams, 4, Saskatoon (WCHL)
1977—*Dale McCourt, 1, St. Catharines (OHL)
1978—Willie Huber, 9, Hamilton (OHL)
    Brent Peterson, 12, Portland (WCHL)
1979—Mike Foligno, 3, Sudbury (OHL)
1980—Mike Blaisdell, 11, Regina (WHL)
1981—No first-round selection

Year   Player, Overall, Last Amateur Team (League)
1982—Murray Craven, 17, Medicine Hat (WHL)
1983—Steve Yzerman, 4, Peterborough (OHL)
1984—Shawn Burr, 7, Kitchener (OHL)
1985—Brent Fedyk, 8, Regina (WHL)
1986—*Joe Murphy, 1, Michigan State University
1987—Yves Racine, 11, Longueuil (QMJHL)
1988—Kory Kocur, 17, Saskatoon (WHL)
1989—Mike Sillinger, 11, Regina (WHL)
1990—Keith Primeau, 3, Niagara Falls (OHL)
1991—Martin Lapointe, 10, Laval (QMJHL)
1992—Curtis Bowen, 22, Ottawa (OHL)
1993—Anders Eriksson, 22, MoDo (Sweden)

*Designates first player chosen in draft.

FRANCHISE LEADERS

Current players in boldface

FORWARDS/DEFENSEMEN

Games
Gordie Howe 1687
Alex Delvecchio 1549
Marcel Pronovost 983
Norm Ullman 875
Ted Lindsay 862
Nick Libett 861
Red Kelly 846
Syd Howe 793
Steve Yzerman 757
Reed Larson 708

Goals
Gordie Howe 786

Alex Delvecchio 456
Steve Yzerman 445
Ted Lindsay 335
Norm Ullman 324
John Ogrodnick 259
Nick Libett 217
Gerard Gallant 207
Syd Howe 202
Reed Larson 188

Assists
Gordie Howe 1023
Alex Delvecchio 825
Steve Yzerman 595
Norm Ullman 434
Ted Lindsay 393
Reed Larson 382

Red Kelly 297
Sid Abel 279
John Ogrodnick 275
Gerard Gallant 260

Points
Gordie Howe 1809
Alex Delvecchio 1281
Steve Yzerman 1040
Norm Ullman 758
Ted Lindsay 728
Reed Larson 570
John Ogrodnick 534
Gerard Gallant 467
Nick Libett 467
Sid Abel 463

GOALTENDERS

Games

Terry Sawchuk	734
Harry Lumley	324
Jim Rutherford	314
Roger Crozier	310
Greg Stefan	299
Tim Cheveldae	**234**
Roy Edwards	221
Glen Hanlon	186
Norm Smith	178
John Mowers	152

Shutouts

Terry Sawchuk	85

Harry Lumley	26
Roger Crozier	20
Clarence Dolson	17
Glenn Hall	17
Harry Holmes	17
Norm Smith	17

Goals-against average
(2400 minutes minimum)

Clarence Dolson	2.06
Harry Holmes	2.11
Glenn Hall	2.14
Alex Connell	2.25
John Ross Roach	2.26
Norm Smith	2.34

Terry Sawchuk	2.46
John Mowers	2.63
Cecil Thompson	2.65
Harry Lumley	2.73

Wins

Terry Sawchuk	352
Harry Lumley	163
Roger Crozier	130
Greg Stefan	115
Tim Cheveldae	**112**
Jim Rutherford	97
Roy Edwards	95
Norm Smith	76

EDMONTON OILERS

YEAR-BY-YEAR RECORDS

	REGULAR SEASON					PLAYOFFS			
Season	W	L	T	Pts.	Finish	W	L	Highest round	Coach
1972-73*	38	37	3	79	5th	—	—		Ray Kinasewich
1973-74†	38	37	3	79	3rd	1	4	League quarterfinals	Brian Shaw
1974-75†	36	38	4	76	5th	—	—		Brian Shaw, Bill Hunter
1975-76†	27	49	5	59	4th	0	4	League quarterfinals	Clare Drake, Bill Hunter
1976-77†	34	43	4	72	4th	1	4	League quarterfinals	Bep Guidolin, Glen Sather
1977-78†	38	39	3	79	5th	1	4	League quarterfinals	Glen Sather
1978-79†	48	30	2	98	1st	6	7	Avco World Cup finals	Glen Sather
1979-80	28	39	13	69	4th/Smythe	0	3	Preliminaries	Glen Sather
1980-81	29	35	16	74	4th/Smythe	5	4	Quarterfinals	Glen Sather
1981-82	48	17	15	111	1st/Smythe	2	3	Division semifinals	Glen Sather
1982-83	47	21	12	106	1st/Smythe	11	5	Stanley Cup finals	Glen Sather
1983-84	57	18	5	119	1st/Smythe	15	4	Stanley Cup champ	Glen Sather
1984-85	49	20	11	109	1st/Smythe	15	3	Stanley Cup champ	Glen Sather
1985-86	56	17	7	119	1st/Smythe	6	4	Division finals	Glen Sather
1986-87	50	24	6	106	1st/Smythe	16	5	Stanley Cup champ	Glen Sather
1987-88	44	25	11	99	2nd/Smythe	16	2	Stanley Cup champ	Glen Sather
1988-89	38	34	8	84	3rd/Smythe	3	4	Division semifinals	Glen Sather
1989-90	38	28	14	90	2nd/Smythe	16	6	Stanley Cup champ	John Muckler
1990-91	37	37	6	80	3rd/Smythe	9	9	Conference finals	John Muckler
1991-92	36	34	10	82	3rd/Smythe	8	8	Conference finals	Ted Green
1992-93	26	50	8	60	5th/Smythe	—	—		Ted Green

*Alberta Oilers, members of World Hockey Association.
†Members of World Hockey Association.

FIRST-ROUND ENTRY DRAFT CHOICES

Year	Player, Overall, Last Amateur Team (League)
1979	Kevin Lowe, 21, Quebec (QMJHL)
1980	Paul Coffey, 6, Kitchener (OHL)
1981	Grant Fuhr, 8, Victoria (WHL)
1982	Jim Playfair, 20, Portland (WHL)
1983	Jeff Beukeboom, 19, Sault Ste. Marie (OHL)
1984	Selmar Odelein, 21, Regina (WHL)
1985	Scott Metcalfe, 20, Kingston (OHL)
1986	Kim Issel, 21, Prince Albert (WHL)
1987	Peter Soberlak, 21, Swift Current (WHL)
1988	Francois Leroux, 19, St. Jean (QMJHL)

Year	Player, Overall, Last Amateur Team (League)
1989	Jason Soules, 15, Niagara Falls (OHL)
1990	Scott Allison, 17, Prince Albert (WHL)
1991	Tyler Wright, 12, Swift Current (WHL)
	Martin Rucinsky, 20, Litvinov (Czech.)
1992	Joe Hulbig, 13, St. Sebastian H.S. (Mass.)
1993	Jason Arnott, 7, Oshawa (OHL)
	Nick Stajduhar, 16, London (OHL)

NOTE: Edmonton chose Dave Dryden, Bengt Gustafsson and Ed Mio as priority selections before the 1979 expansion draft.

FRANCHISE LEADERS

Current players in boldface

FORWARDS/DEFENSEMEN

Games

Kevin Lowe	966
Mark Messier	851
Glenn Anderson	828
Jari Kurri	754
Wayne Gretzky	696
Charlie Huddy	694
Dave Hunter	653
Craig MacTavish	**635**

Lee Fogolin	586
Paul Coffey	532

Goals

Wayne Gretzky	583
Jari Kurri	474
Glenn Anderson	413
Mark Messier	392
Paul Coffey	209
Craig Simpson	185
Esa Tikkanen	178
Craig MacTavish	**139**
Dave Hunter	119

Petr Klima	118

Assists

Wayne Gretzky	1086
Mark Messier	642
Jari Kurri	569
Glenn Anderson	483
Paul Coffey	460
Kevin Lowe	295
Charlie Huddy	287
Esa Tikkanen	258
Craig Simpson	180
Steve Smith	172

Points		
Wayne Gretzky		1669
Jari Kurri		1043
Mark Messier		1034
Glenn Anderson		896
Paul Coffey		669
Esa Tikkanen		436
Charlie Huddy		368
Kevin Lowe		368
Craig Simpson		365
Craig MacTavish		**305**

Penalty minutes		
Kevin McClelland		1298
Kevin Lowe		1164
Mark Messier		1122
Steve Smith		1080
Dave Semenko		976
Kelly Buchberger		**933**

Lee Fogolin		886
Dave Hunter		776
Glenn Anderson		771
Esa Tikkanen		759

GOALTENDERS
Games

Grant Fuhr		423
Bill Ranford		**285**
Andy Moog		235
Eddie Mio		77
Ron Low		67
Ron Tugnutt		29
Jim Corsi		26
Gary Edwards		15
Dave Dryden		14
Pokey Reddick		13

Shutouts

Grant Fuhr		9

Andy Moog		4
Bill Ranford		**4**
Eddie Mio		1

Goals - against average
(2400 minutes minimum)

Bill Ranford		**3.46**
Andy Moog		3.61
Grant Fuhr		3.69
Eddie Mio		4.02
Ron Low		4.03

Wins

Grant Fuhr		226
Andy Moog		143
Bill Ranford		**113**
Ron Low		30
Eddie Mio		25
Ron Tugnutt		10
Jim Corsi		8

FLORIDA PANTHERS

FIRST - ROUND ENTRY DRAFT CHOICES

Year   Player, Overall, Last Amateur Team (League)
1993—Rob Niedermayer, 5, Medicine Hat (WHL)

HARTFORD WHALERS

YEAR - BY - YEAR RECORDS

	REGULAR SEASON					PLAYOFFS			
Season	W	L	T	Pts.	Finish	W	L	Highest round	Coach
1972-73*	46	30	2	94	1st	12	3	Avco World Cup champ	Jack Kelley
1973-74*	43	31	4	90	1st	3	4	League quarterfinals	Ron Ryan
1974-75*	43	30	5	91	1st	2	4	League quarterfinals	Ron Ryan, Jack Kelley
1975-76*	33	40	7	73	3rd	6	4	League semifinals	Jack Kelley, Don Blackburn, Harry Neale
1976-77*	35	40	6	76	4th	1	4	League quarterfinals	Harry Neale
1977-78*	44	31	5	93	2nd	8	6	Avco World Cup finals	Harry Neale
1978-79*	37	34	9	83	4th	5	5	League semifinals	Bill Dineen, Don Blackburn
1979-80	27	34	19	73	4th/Norris	0	3	Preliminaries	Don Blackburn
1980-81	21	41	18	60	4th/Norris	—	—		Don Blackburn, Larry Pleau
1981-82	21	41	18	60	5th/Adams	—	—		Larry Pleau
1982-83	19	54	7	45	5th/Adams	—	—		Larry Kish, Larry Pleau, John Cunniff
1983-84	28	42	10	66	5th/Adams	—	—		Jack Evans
1984-85	30	41	9	69	5th/Adams	—	—		Jack Evans
1985-86	40	36	4	84	4th/Adams	6	4	Division finals	Jack Evans
1986-87	43	30	7	93	1st/Adams	2	4	Division semifinals	Jack Evans
1987-88	35	38	7	77	4th/Adams	2	4	Division semifinals	Jack Evans, Larry Pleau
1988-89	37	38	5	79	4th/Adams	0	4	Division semifinals	Larry Pleau
1989-90	38	33	9	85	4th/Adams	3	4	Division semifinals	Rick Ley
1990-91	31	38	11	73	4th/Adams	2	4	Division semifinals	Rick Ley
1991-92	26	41	13	65	4th/Adams	3	4	Division semifinals	Jim Roberts
1992-93	26	52	6	58	5th/Adams	—	—		Paul Holmgren

*New England Whalers, members of World Hockey Association.

FIRST - ROUND ENTRY DRAFT CHOICES

Year   Player, Overall, Last Amateur Team (League)
1979—Ray Allison, 18, Brandon (WHL)
1980—Fred Arthur, 8, Cornwall (QMJHL)
1981—Ron Francis, 4, Sault Ste. Marie (OHL)
1982—Paul Lawless, 14, Windsor (OHL)
1983—Sylvain Turgeon, 2, Hull (QMJHL)
    David A. Jensen, 20, Lawrence Academy (Mass.)
1984—Sylvain Cote, 11, Quebec (QMJHL)
1985—Dana Murzyn, 5, Calgary (WHL)
1986—Scott Young, 11, Boston University
1987—Jody Hull, 18, Peterborough (OHL)

Year   Player, Overall, Last Amateur Team (League)
1988—Chris Govedaris, 11, Toronto (OHL)
1989—Robert Holik, 10, Jihlava (Czechoslovakia)
1990—Mark Greig, 15, Lethbridge (WHL)
1991—Patrick Poulin, 9, St. Hyacinthe (QMJHL)
1992—Robert Petrovicky, 9, Dukla Trencin (Czech.)
1993—Chris Pronger, 2, Peterborough (OHL)
  NOTE: Hartford chose Jordy Douglas, John Garrett and Mark Howe as priority selections before the 1979 expansion draft.

FRANCHISE LEADERS

Current players in boldface

FORWARDS/DEFENSEMEN
Games
Ron Francis	714
Kevin Dineen	489
Dave Tippett	483
Ulf Samuelsson	463
Joel Quenneville	457
Randy Ladouceur	452
Ray Ferraro	442
Dean Evason	434
Sylvain Cote	382
Paul MacDermid	373

Goals
Ron Francis	264
Blaine Stoughton	219
Kevin Dineen	214
Sylvain Turgeon	178
Ray Ferraro	157
Pat Verbeek	**148**
Ray Neufeld	106
Dean Evason	87
Mark Johnson	85
Mike Rogers	85

Assists
Ron Francis	557
Kevin Dineen	262
Dave Babych	196
Ray Ferraro	194

Pat Verbeek	**162**
Blaine Stoughton	158
Sylvain Turgeon	150
Dean Evason	148
Mark Howe	147
Ulf Samuelsson	144

Points
Ron Francis	821
Kevin Dineen	446
Blaine Stoughton	377
Ray Ferraro	351
Sylvain Turgeon	328
Pat Verbeek	**310**
Dave Babych	240
Dean Evason	235
Ray Neufeld	226
Mike Rogers	210
Mark Johnson	203

Penalty minutes
Torrie Robertson	1368
Ulf Samuelsson	1108
Kevin Dineen	1029
Pat Verbeek	**914**
Randy Ladouceur	717
Paul MacDermid	706
Dean Evason	617
Ron Francis	540
Ed Kastelic	485
Chris Kotsopoulos	443

GOALTENDERS
Games
Mike Liut	252
Greg Millen	219
Peter Sidorkiewicz	178
John Garrett	122
Steve Weeks	94
Kay Whitmore	75
Mike Veisor	69
Sean Burke	**50**

Shutouts
Mike Liut	13
Peter Sidorkiewicz	8
Greg Millen	4
Steve Weeks	4

Goals-against average
(2400 minutes minimum)
Peter Sidorkiewicz	3.33
Mike Liut	3.36
Kay Whitmore	3.61
Steve Weeks	3.68
Sean Burke	**4.16**
Greg Millen	4.25
John Garrett	4.28
Mike Veisor	4.87

Wins
Mike Liut	115
Peter Sidorkiewicz	71
Greg Millen	62
Steve Weeks	42
John Garrett	36

LOS ANGELES KINGS

YEAR-BY-YEAR RECORDS

Season	W	L	T	Pts.	Finish	W	L	Highest round	Coach
1967-68	31	33	10	72	2nd/West	3	4	Division semifinals	Red Kelly
1968-69	24	42	10	58	4th/West	4	7	Division finals	Red Kelly
1969-70	14	52	10	38	6th/West	—	—		Hal Laycoe, Johnny Wilson
1970-71	25	40	13	63	5th/West	—	—		Larry Regan
1971-72	20	49	9	49	7th/West	—	—		Larry Regan, Fred Glover
1972-73	31	36	11	73	6th/West	—	—		Bob Pulford
1973-74	33	33	12	78	3rd/West	1	4	Division semifinals	Bob Pulford
1974-75	42	17	21	105	2nd/Norris	1	2	Preliminaries	Bob Pulford
1975-76	38	33	9	85	2nd/Norris	5	4	Quarterfinals	Bob Pulford
1976-77	34	31	15	83	2nd/Norris	4	5	Quarterfinals	Bob Pulford
1977-78	31	34	15	77	3rd/Norris	0	2	Preliminaries	Ron Stewart
1978-79	34	34	12	80	3rd/Norris	0	2	Preliminaries	Bob Berry
1979-80	30	36	14	74	2nd/Norris	1	3	Preliminaries	Bob Berry
1980-81	43	24	13	99	2nd/Norris	1	3	Preliminaries	Bob Berry
1981-82	24	41	15	63	4th/Smythe	4	6	Division finals	Parker MacDonald, Don Perry
1982-83	27	41	12	66	5th/Smythe	—	—		Don Perry
1983-84	23	44	13	59	5th/Smythe	—	—		Don Perry, Rogie Vachon, Roger Neilson
1984-85	34	32	14	82	4th/Smythe	0	3	Division semifinals	Pat Quinn
1985-86	23	49	8	54	5th/Smythe	—	—		Pat Quinn
1986-87	31	41	8	70	4th/Smythe	1	4	Division semifinals	Pat Quinn, Mike Murphy
1987-88	30	42	8	68	4th/Smythe	1	4	Division semifinals	Mike Murphy, Rogie Vachon, Robbie Ftorek
1988-89	42	31	7	91	2nd/Norris	4	7	Division finals	Robbie Ftorek
1989-90	34	39	7	75	4th/Smythe	4	6	Division finals	Tom Webster
1990-91	46	24	10	102	1st/Smythe	6	6	Division finals	Tom Webster
1991-92	35	31	14	84	2nd/Smythe	2	4	Division semifinals	Tom Webster
1992-93	39	35	10	88	3rd/Smythe	13	11	Stanley Cup finals	Barry Melrose

FIRST-ROUND ENTRY DRAFT CHOICES

Year	Player, Overall, Last Amateur Team (League)
1969	No first-round selection
1970	No first-round selection
1971	No first-round selection
1972	No first-round selection
1973	No first-round selection
1974	No first-round selection
1975	Tim Young, 16, Ottawa (OHL)
1976	No first-round selection
1977	No first-round selection
1978	No first-round selection
1979	Jay Wells, 16, Kingston (OHL)
1980	Larry Murphy, 4, Peterborough (OHL)
	Jim Fox, 10, Ottawa (OHL)
1981	Doug Smith, 2, Ottawa (OHL)

Year	Player, Overall, Last Amateur Team (League)
1982	No first-round selection
1983	No first-round selection
1984	Craig Redmond, 6, Canadian Olympic Team
1985	Craig Duncanson, 9, Sudbury (OHL)
	Dan Gratton, 10, Oshawa (OHL)
1986	Jimmy Carson, 2, Verdun (QMJHL)
1987	Wayne McBean, 4, Medicine Hat (WHL)
1988	Martin Gelinas, 7, Hull (QMJHL)
1989	No first-round selection
1990	Darryl Sydor, 7, Kamloops (WHL)
1991	No first-round selection
1992	No first-round selection
1993	No first-round selection

FRANCHISE LEADERS

Current players in boldface

FORWARDS/DEFENSEMEN

Games

Dave Taylor	1078
Marcel Dionne	921
Butch Goring	736
Mike Murphy	673
Jay Wells	604
Bernie Nicholls	602
Mark Hardy	600
Jim Fox	578
Luc Robitaille	557
Bob Berry	539

Goals

Marcel Dionne	550
Dave Taylor	427
Luc Robitaille	348
Bernie Nicholls	327
Butch Goring	275
Charlie Simmer	222
Mike Murphy	194
Jim Fox	186
Wayne Gretzky	182
Bob Berry	159

Assists

Marcel Dionne	757
Dave Taylor	635
Wayne Gretzky	477

Bernie Nicholls	431
Butch Goring	384
Luc Robitaille	369
Jim Fox	292
Mike Murphy	262
Mark Hardy	247
Charlie Simmer	244

Points

Marcel Dionne	1307
Dave Taylor	1062
Bernie Nicholls	758
Luc Robitaille	717
Butch Goring	659
Wayne Gretzky	659
Jim Fox	478
Charlie Simmer	466
Mike Murphy	456
Bob Berry	350

Penalty minutes

Dave Taylor	1561
Marty McSorley	1560
Jay Wells	1446
Jay Miller	865
Mark Hardy	831

GOALTENDERS

Games

Rogie Vachon	389
Mario Lessard	240
Kelly Hrudey	225

Gary Edwards	155
Roland Melanson	119
Gerry Desjardins	103
Bob Janecyk	102
Dennis DeJordy	86

Shutouts

Rogie Vachon	32
Kelly Hrudey	9
Mario Lessard	9
Gerry Desjardins	7
Gary Edwards	7

Goals-against average
(2400 minutes minimum)

Rogie Vachon	2.86
Wayne Rutledge	3.34
Gary Edwards	3.39
Kelly Hrudey	3.49
Gerry Desjardins	3.52
Daniel Berthiaume	3.54
Dennis DeJordy	3.73
Mario Lessard	3.74
Doug Keans	4.08

Wins

Rogie Vachon	171
Kelly Hrudey	102
Mario Lessard	92
Gary Edwards	54
Bob Janecyk	41
Roland Melanson	40
Glenn Healy	37

MONTREAL CANADIENS

YEAR-BY-YEAR RECORDS

	REGULAR SEASON					PLAYOFFS			
Season	W	L	T	Pts.	Finish	W	L	Highest round	Coach
1917-18	13	9	0	26	1st/3rd	1	1	Semifinals	George Kennedy
1918-19	10	8	0	20	1st/2nd	†*6	3	Stanley Cup finals	George Kennedy
1919-20	13	11	0	26	2nd/3rd	—	—		George Kennedy
1920-21	13	11	0	26	3rd/2nd	—	—		George Kennedy
1921-22	12	11	1	25	3rd				Leo Dandurand
1922-23	13	9	2	28	2nd	1	1	Quarterfinals	Leo Dandurand
1923-24	13	11	0	26	2nd	6	0	Stanley Cup champ	Leo Dandurand
1924-25	17	11	2	36	3rd	3	3	Stanley Cup finals	Leo Dandurand
1925-26	11	24	1	23	7th	—	—		Cecil Hart
1926-27	28	14	2	58	2nd/Canadian	*1	1	Semifinals	Cecil Hart
1927-28	26	11	7	59	1st/Canadian	*0	1	Semifinals	Cecil Hart
1928-29	22	7	15	59	1st/Canadian	0	3	Semifinals	Cecil Hart
1929-30	21	14	9	51	2nd/Canadian	*5	0	Stanley Cup champ	Cecil Hart
1930-31	26	10	8	60	1st/Canadian	6	4	Stanley Cup champ	Cecil Hart
1931-32	25	16	7	57	1st/Canadian	1	3	Semifinals	Cecil Hart
1932-33	18	25	5	41	3rd/Canadian	*0	1	Quarterfinals	Newsy Lalonde

Season	W	L	T	Pts.	Finish	W	L	Highest round	Coach
					REGULAR SEASON			**PLAYOFFS**	
1933-34	22	20	6	50	2nd/Canadian	*0	1	Quarterfinals	Newsy Lalonde
1934-35	19	23	6	44	3rd/Canadian	*0	1	Quarterfinals	Newsy Lalonde, Leo Dandurand
1935-36	11	26	11	33	4th/Canadian	—	—		Sylvio Mantha
1936-37	24	18	6	54	1st/Canadian	2	3	Semifinals	Cecil Hart
1937-38	18	17	13	49	3rd/Canadian	1	2	Quarterfinals	Cecil Hart
1938-39	15	24	9	39	6th	1	2	Quarterfinals	Cecil Hart, Jules Dugal
1939-40	10	33	5	25	7th	—	—		Pit Lepine
1940-41	16	26	6	38	6th	1	2	Quarterfinals	Dick Irvin
1941-42	18	27	3	39	6th	1	2	Quarterfinals	Dick Irvin
1942-43	19	19	12	50	4th	1	4	League semifinals	Dick Irvin
1943-44	38	5	7	83	1st	8	1	Stanley Cup champ	Dick Irvin
1944-45	38	8	4	80	1st	2	4	League semifinals	Dick Irvin
1945-46	28	17	5	61	1st	8	1	Stanley Cup champ	Dick Irvin
1946-47	34	16	10	78	1st	6	5	Stanley Cup finals	Dick Irvin
1947-48	20	29	11	51	5th	—	—		Dick Irvin
1948-49	28	23	9	65	3rd	3	4	League semifinals	Dick Irvin
1949-50	29	22	19	77	2nd	1	4	League semifinals	Dick Irvin
1950-51	25	30	15	65	3rd	5	6	Stanley Cup finals	Dick Irvin
1951-52	34	26	10	78	2nd	4	7	Stanley Cup finals	Dick Irvin
1952-53	28	23	19	75	2nd	8	4	Stanley Cup champ	Dick Irvin
1953-54	35	24	11	81	2nd	7	4	Stanley Cup finals	Dick Irvin
1954-55	41	18	11	93	2nd	7	5	Stanley Cup finals	Dick Irvin
1955-56	45	15	10	100	1st	8	2	Stanley Cup champ	Toe Blake
1956-57	35	23	12	82	2nd	8	2	Stanley Cup champ	Toe Blake
1957-58	43	17	10	96	1st	8	2	Stanley Cup champ	Toe Blake
1958-59	39	18	13	91	1st	8	3	Stanley Cup champ	Toe Blake
1959-60	40	18	12	92	1st	8	0	Stanley Cup champ	Toe Blake
1960-61	41	19	10	92	1st	2	4	League semifinals	Toe Blake
1961-62	42	14	14	98	1st	2	4	League semifinals	Toe Blake
1962-63	28	19	23	79	3rd	1	4	League semifinals	Toe Blake
1963-64	36	21	13	85	1st	3	4	League semifinals	Toe Blake
1964-65	36	23	11	83	2nd	8	5	Stanley Cup champ	Toe Blake
1965-66	41	21	8	90	1st	8	2	Stanley Cup champ	Toe Blake
1966-67	32	25	13	77	2nd	6	4	Stanley Cup finals	Toe Blake
1967-68	42	22	10	54	1st/East	12	1	Stanley Cup champ	Toe Blake
1968-69	46	19	11	103	1st/East	12	2	Stanley Cup champ	Claude Ruel
1969-70	38	22	16	92	5th/East	—	—		Claude Ruel
1970-71	42	23	13	97	3rd/East	12	8	Stanley Cup champ	Claude Ruel, Al MacNeil
1971-72	46	16	16	108	3rd/East	2	4	Division semifinals	Scotty Bowman
1972-73	52	10	16	120	1st/East	12	5	Stanley Cup champ	Scotty Bowman
1973-74	45	42	9	99	2nd/East	2	4	Division semifinals	Scotty Bowman
1974-75	47	14	19	113	1st/Norris	6	5	Semifinals	Scotty Bowman
1975-76	58	11	11	127	1st/Norris	12	1	Stanley Cup champ	Scotty Bowman
1976-77	60	8	12	132	1st/Norris	12	2	Stanley Cup champ	Scotty Bowman
1977-78	59	10	11	129	1st/Norris	12	3	Stanley Cup champ	Scotty Bowman
1978-79	52	17	11	115	1st/Norris	12	4	Stanley Cup champ	Scotty Bowman
1979-80	47	20	13	107	1st/Norris	6	4	Quarterfinals	Bernie Geoffrion, Claude Ruel
1980-81	45	22	13	103	1st/Norris	0	3	Preliminaries	Claude Ruel
1981-82	46	17	17	109	1st/Adams	2	3	Division semifinals	Bob Berry
1982-83	42	24	14	98	2nd/Adams	0	3	Division semifinals	Bob Berry
1983-84	35	40	5	75	4th/Adams	9	6	Conference finals	Bob Berry, Jacques Lemaire
1984-85	41	27	12	94	1st/Adams	6	6	Division finals	Jacques Lemaire
1985-86	40	33	7	87	2nd/Adams	15	5	Stanley Cup champ	Jean Perron
1986-87	41	29	10	92	2nd/Adams	10	7	Conference finals	Jean Perron
1987-88	45	22	13	103	1st/Adams	5	6	Division finals	Jean Perron
1988-89	53	18	9	115	1st/Adams	14	7	Stanley Cup finals	Pat Burns
1989-90	41	28	11	93	3rd/Adams	5	6	Division finals	Pat Burns
1990-91	39	30	11	89	2nd/Adams	7	6	Division finals	Pat Burns
1991-92	41	28	11	93	1st/Adams	4	7	Division finals	Pat Burns
1992-93	48	30	6	102	3rd/Adams	16	4	Stanley Cup champ	Jacques Demers

*Won-lost record does not indicate tie(s) resulting from two-game, total-goals series that year (two-game, total-goals series were played from 1917-18 through 1935-36).
†1918-19 series abandoned with no Cup holder due to influenza epidemic.

FIRST-ROUND ENTRY DRAFT CHOICES

Year	Player, Overall, Last Amateur Team (League)
1969—	*Rejean Houle, 1, Montreal (OHL)
	Marc Tardif, 2, Montreal (OHL)
1970—	Ray Martiniuk, 5, Flin Flon (WCHL)
	Chuck Lefley, 6, Canadian Nationals
1971—	*Guy Lafleur, 1, Quebec (QMJHL)
	Chuck Arnason, 7, Flin Flon (WCHL)
	Murray Wilson, 11, Ottawa (OHL)

Year	Player, Overall, Last Amateur Team (League)
1972—	Steve Shutt, 4, Toronto (OHL)
	Michel Larocque, 6, Ottawa (OHL)
	Dave Gardner, 8, Toronto (OHL)
	John Van Boxmeer, 14, Guelph (SOJHL)
1973—	Bob Gainey, 8, Peterborough (OHL)
1974—	Cam Connor, 5, Flin Flon (WCHL)
	Doug Risebrough, 7, Kitchener (OHL)

Year	Player, Overall, Last Amateur Team (League)
	Rick Chartraw, 10, Kitchener (OHL)
	Mario Tremblay, 12, Montreal (OHL)
	Gord McTavish, 15, Sudbury (OHL)
1975—	Robin Sadler, 9, Edmonton (WCHL)
	Pierre Mondou, 15, Montreal (QMJHL)
1976—	Peter Lee, 12, Ottawa (OHL)
	Rod Schutt, 13, Sudbury (OHL)
	Bruce Baker, 18, Ottawa (OHL)
1977—	Mark Napier, 10, Birmingham (WHA)
	Normand Dupont, 18, Montreal (QMJHL)
1978—	Danny Geoffrion, 8, Cornwall (QMJHL)
	Dave Hunter, 17, Sudbury (OHL)
1979—	No first-round selection
1980—	*Doug Wickenheiser, 1, Regina (WHL)
1981—	Mark Hunter, 7, Brantford (OHL)
	Gilbert Delorme, 18, Chicoutimi (QMJHL)

Year	Player, Overall, Last Amateur Team (League)
	Jan Ingman, 19, Farjestads (Sweden)
1982—	Alain Heroux, 19, Chicoutimi (QMJHL)
1983—	Alfie Turcotte, 17, Portland (WHL)
1984—	Petr Svoboda, 5, Czechoslovakia
	Shayne Corson, 8, Brantford (OHL)
1985—	Jose Charbonneau, 12, Drummondville (QMJHL)
	Tom Chorske, 16, Minneapolis SW H.S. (Minn.)
1986—	Mark Pederson, 15, Medicine Hat (WHL)
1987—	Andrew Cassels, 17, Ottawa (OHL)
1988—	Eric Charron, 20, Trois-Rivieres (QMJHL)
1989—	Lindsay Vallis, 13, Seattle (WHL)
1990—	Turner Stevenson, 12, Seattle (WHL)
1991—	Brent Bilodeau, 17, Seattle (WHL)
1992—	David Wilkie, 20, Kamloops (WHL)
1993—	Saku Koivu, 21, TPS Turku (Finland)

*Designates first player chosen in draft.

FRANCHISE LEADERS

Current players in boldface

FORWARDS/DEFENSEMEN

Games
Henri Richard	1256
Larry Robinson	1202
Bob Gainey	1160
Jean Beliveau	1125
Claude Provost	1005
Maurice Richard	978
Yvan Cournoyer	968
Guy Lafleur	961
Serge Savard	917
Doug Harvey	890

Goals
Maurice Richard	544
Guy Lafleur	518
Jean Beliveau	507
Yvan Cournoyer	428
Steve Shutt	408
Bernie Geoffrion	371
Jacques Lemaire	366
Henri Richard	358
Aurele Joliat	270
Mario Tremblay	258

Assists
Guy Lafleur	728

Jean Beliveau	712
Henri Richard	688
Larry Robinson	686
Jacques Lemaire	469
Yvan Cournoyer	435
Maurice Richard	421
Elmer Lach	408
Guy Lapointe	406
Bernie Geoffrion	388

Points
Guy Lafleur	1246
Jean Beliveau	1219
Henri Richard	1046
Maurice Richard	965
Larry Robinson	883
Yvan Cournoyer	863
Jacques Lemaire	835
Steve Shutt	776
Bernie Geoffrion	759
Elmer Lach	623

Penalty minutes
Chris Nilan	2248
Maurice Richard	1285
John Ferguson	1214
Mario Tremblay	1043
Doug Harvey	1042
Jean Beliveau	1029

Doug Risebrough	959
Henri Richard	928
Tom Johnson	897
Shayne Corson	891

GOALTENDERS

Games
Jacques Plante	556
Patrick Roy	**418**
Ken Dryden	397
Bill Durnan	383
Georges Vezina	328
George Hainsworth	321
Gerry McNeil	276
Wilf Cude	249
Charlie Hodge	236
Michel Larocque	231

Shutouts
George Hainsworth	74
Jacques Plante	58
Ken Dryden	46
Bill Durnan	34
Gerry McNeil	28
Wilf Cude	22
Charlie Hodge	21
Patrick Roy	**20**
Michel Larocque	17
Gump Worsley	16

MONTREAL MAROONS (DEFUNCT)

YEAR-BY-YEAR RECORDS

	REGULAR SEASON					PLAYOFFS			
Season	W	L	T	Pts.	Finish	W	L	Highest round	Coach
1924-25	9	19	2	20	5th	—	—		Eddie Gerard
1925-26	20	11	5	45	2nd	3	1	Stanley Cup champ	Eddie Gerard
1926-27	20	20	4	44	3rd/Canadian	*0	1	Quarterfinals	Eddie Gerard
1927-28	24	14	6	54	2nd/Canadian	*5	3	Stanley Cup finals	Eddie Gerard
1928-29	15	20	9	39	5th/Canadian	—	—		Eddie Gerard
1929-30	23	16	5	51	1st/Canadian	1	3	Semifinals	Dunc Munro
1930-31	20	18	6	46	3rd/Canadian	*0	2	Quarterfinals	Dunc Munro, George Boucher
1931-32	19	22	7	45	3rd/Canadian	*1	1	Semifinals	Sprague Cleghorn
1932-33	22	20	6	50	2nd/Canadian	0	2	Quarterfinals	Eddie Gerard
1933-34	19	18	11	49	3rd/Canadian	*1	2	Semifinals	Eddie Gerard
1934-35	24	19	5	53	2nd/Canadian	*5	0	Stanley Cup champ	Tommy Gorman
1935-36	22	16	10	54	1st/Canadian	0	3	Semifinals	Tommy Gorman
1936-37	22	17	9	53	2nd/Canadian	2	3	Semifinals	Tommy Gorman
1937-38	12	30	6	30	4th/Canadian	—	—		King Clancy, Tommy Gorman

*Won-lost record does not indicate tie(s) resulting from two-game, total goals series that year (two-game, total-goals series were played from 1917-18 through 1935-36).

MONTREAL WANDERERS (DEFUNCT)

YEAR - BY - YEAR RECORDS

	REGULAR SEASON					PLAYOFFS			
Season	W	L	T	Pts.	Finish	W	L	Highest round	Coach
1917-18*	1	5	0	2	4th	—	—		Art Ross

*Franchise disbanded after Montreal Arena burned down. Montreal Canadiens and Toronto each counted one win for defaulted games with Wanderers.

NEW JERSEY DEVILS

YEAR - BY - YEAR RECORDS

	REGULAR SEASON					PLAYOFFS			
Season	W	L	T	Pts.	Finish	W	L	Highest round	Coach
1974-75*	15	54	11	41	5th/Smythe	—	—		Bep Guidolin
1975-76*	12	56	12	36	5th/Smythe	—	—		Bep Guidolin, Sid Abel, Eddie Bush
1976-77†	20	46	14	54	5th/Smythe	—	—		John Wilson
1977-78†	19	40	21	59	2nd/Smythe	0	2	Preliminaries	Pat Kelly
1978-79†	15	53	12	42	4th/Smythe	—	—		Pat Kelly, Bep Guidolin
1979-80†	19	48	13	51	6th/Smythe	—	—		Don Cherry
1980-81†	22	45	13	57	5th/Smythe	—	—		Billy MacMillan
1981-82†	18	49	13	49	5th/Smythe	—	—		Bert Marshall, Marshall Johnston
1982-83	17	49	14	48	5th/Patrick	—	—		Billy MacMillan
1983-84	17	56	7	41	5th/Patrick	—	—		Billy MacMillan, Tom McVie
1984-85	22	48	10	54	5th/Patrick	—	—		Doug Carpenter
1985-86	28	49	3	59	5th/Patrick	—	—		Doug Carpenter
1986-87	29	45	6	64	6th/Patrick	—	—		Doug Carpenter
1987-88	38	36	6	82	3rd/Patrick	11	9	Conference finals	Doug Carpenter, Jim Schoenfeld
1988-89	27	41	12	66	5th/Patrick	—	—		Jim Schoenfeld
1989-90	37	34	9	83	2nd/Patrick	2	4	Division semifinals	Jim Schoenfeld, John Cunniff
1990-91	32	33	15	79	4th/Patrick	3	4	Division semifinals	John Cunniff, Tom McVie
1991-92	38	31	11	87	4th/Patrick	3	4	Division semifinals	Tom McVie
1992-93	40	37	7	87	4th/Patrick	1	4	Division semifinals	Herb Brooks

*Kansas City Scouts.
†Colorado Rockies.

FIRST - ROUND ENTRY DRAFT CHOICES

Year	Player, Overall, Last Amateur Team (League)
1974	Wilf Paiement, 2, St. Catharines (OHL)
1975	Barry Dean, 2, Medicine Hat (WCHL)
1976	Paul Gardner, 11, Oshawa (OHL)
1977	Barry Beck, 2, New Westminster (WCHL)
1978	Mike Gillis, 5, Kingston (OHL)
1979	*Rob Ramage, 1, Birmingham (WHA)
1980	Paul Gagne, 19, Windsor (OHL)
1981	Joe Cirella, 5, Oshawa (OHL)
1982	Rocky Trottier, 8, Billings (WHL)
	Ken Daneyko, 18, Seattle (WHL)
1983	John MacLean, 6, Oshawa (OHL)
1984	Kirk Muller, 2, Guelph (OHL)
1985	Craig Wolanin, 3, Kitchener (OHL)

Year	Player, Overall, Last Amateur Team (League)
1986	Neil Brady, 3, Medicine Hat (WHL)
1987	Brendan Shanahan, 2, London (OHL)
1988	Corey Foster, 12, Peterborough (OHL)
1989	Bill Guerin, 5, Springfield (Mass.) Jr.
	Jason Miller, 18, Medicine Hat (WHL)
1990	Martin Brodeur, 20, St. Hyacinthe (QMJHL)
1991	Scott Niedermayer, 3, Kamloops (WHL)
	Brian Rolston, 11, Detroit Compuware Jr.
1992	Jason Smith, 18, Regina (WHL)
1993	Denis Pederson, 13, Prince Albert (WHL)

*Designates first player chosen in draft.

FRANCHISE LEADERS

Current players in boldface

FORWARDS/DEFENSEMEN
Games

Aaron Broten	641
John MacLean	626
Ken Daneyko	613
Bruce Driver	595
Kirk Muller	556
Joe Cirella	503
Mike Kitchen	474
Pat Verbeek	463
Wilf Paiement	392
Gary Croteau	390

Goals

John MacLean	241
Kirk Muller	185
Pat Verbeek	170
Aaron Broten	162
Wilf Paiement	153
Paul Gagne	106
Claude Lemieux	101
Brendan Shanahan	96
Gary Croteau	92
Mark Johnson	89

Assists

Kirk Muller	335
Aaron Broten	307
Bruce Driver	280
John MacLean	248
Wilf Paiement	183
Patrik Sundstrom	160
Joe Cirella	159
Pat Verbeek	151
Mel Bridgman	148
Mark Johnson	140

Points

Kirk Muller	520
John MacLean	489
Aaron Broten	469
Bruce Driver	351

Wilf Paiement	336	Rob Ramage	529	Bill McKenzie ... 1
Pat Verbeek	321	Brendan Shanahan	524	Bill Oleschuk ... 1
Patrik Sundstrom	246			Chico Resch ... 1
Mark Johnson	229			Sam St. Laurent ... 1
Mel Bridgman	224			
Brendan Shanahan	214			

GOALTENDERS

Games

Chico Resch	267
Chris Terreri	205
Sean Burke	162

Shutouts

Craig Billington	4
Sean Burke	4
Chris Terreri	4
Alain Chevrier	1
Doug Favell	1
Ron Low	1

Penalty minutes

Ken Daneyko	1706
Pat Verbeek	943
Joe Cirella	938
John MacLean	887
David Maley	683
Kirk Muller	572
Wilf Paiement	558
Perry Anderson	553

Goals-against average
(2400 minutes minimum)

Chris Terreri	3.21
Sean Burke	3.66
Hardy Astrom	3.76
Doug Favell	3.84

Wins

Chris Terreri	80
Chico Resch	67
Sean Burke	62

NEW YORK AMERICANS (DEFUNCT)

YEAR-BY-YEAR RECORDS

	REGULAR SEASON					PLAYOFFS			
Season	W	L	T	Pts.	Finish	W	L	Highest round	Coach
1919-20‡	4	20	0	8	4th	—	—		Mike Quinn
1920-21§	6	18	0	12	4th	—	—		Percy Thompson
1921-22§	7	17	0	14	4th	—	—		Percy Thompson
1922-23§	6	18	0	12	4th	—	—		Art Ross
1923-24§	9	15	0	18	4th	—	—		Percy Lesueur
1924-25§	19	10	1	39	1st	†—	—		Jimmy Gardner
1925-26	12	20	4	28	5th	—	—		Tommy Gorman
1926-27	17	25	2	36	4th/Canadian	—	—		Newsy Lalonde
1927-28	11	27	6	28	5th/Canadian	—	—		Wilf Green
1928-29	19	13	12	50	2nd/Canadian	*0	1	Semifinals	Tommy Gorman
1929-30	14	25	5	33	5th/Canadian	—	—		Lionel Conacher
1930-31	18	16	10	46	4th/Canadian	—	—		Eddie Gerard
1931-32	16	24	8	40	4th/Canadian	—	—		Eddie Gerard
1932-33	15	22	11	41	4th/Canadian	—	—		Joe Simpson
1933-34	15	23	10	40	4th/Canadian	—	—		Joe Simpson
1934-35	12	27	9	33	4th/Canadian	—	—		Joe Simpson
1935-36	16	25	7	39	3rd/Canadian	2	3	Semifinals	Red Dutton
1936-37	15	29	4	34	4th/Canadian	—	—		Red Dutton
1937-38	19	18	11	49	2nd/Canadian	3	3	Semifinals	Red Dutton
1938-39	17	21	10	44	4th	0	2	Quarterfinals	Red Dutton
1939-40	15	29	4	34	6th	1	2	Quarterfinals	Red Dutton
1940-41	8	29	11	27	7th	—	—		Red Dutton
1941-42*	16	29	3	35	7th	—	—		Red Dutton

*Won-lost record does not indicate tie(s) resulting from two-game, total goals series that year (two-game, total-goals series were played from 1917-18 through 1935-36).
†Refused to participate in playoffs—held out for more compensation.
‡Quebec Bulldogs.
§Hamilton Tigers.
*Brooklyn Americans.

NEW YORK ISLANDERS

YEAR-BY-YEAR RECORDS

	REGULAR SEASON					PLAYOFFS			
Season	W	L	T	Pts.	Finish	W	L	Highest round	Coach
1972-73	12	60	6	30	8th/East	—	—		Phil Goyette, Earl Ingarfield
1973-74	19	41	18	56	8th/East	—	—		Al Arbour
1974-75	33	25	22	88	3rd/Patrick	9	8	Semifinals	Al Arbour
1975-76	42	21	17	101	2nd/Patrick	7	6	Semifinals	Al Arbour
1976-77	47	21	12	106	2nd/Patrick	8	4	Semifinals	Al Arbour
1977-78	48	17	15	111	1st/Patrick	3	4	Quarterfinals	Al Arbour
1978-79	51	15	14	116	1st/Patrick	6	4	Semifinals	Al Arbour
1979-80	39	28	13	91	2nd/Patrick	15	6	Stanley Cup champ	Al Arbour
1980-81	48	18	14	110	1st/Patrick	15	3	Stanley Cup champ	Al Arbour
1981-82	54	16	10	118	1st/Patrick	15	4	Stanley Cup champ	Al Arbour
1982-83	42	26	12	96	2nd/Patrick	15	5	Stanley Cup champ	Al Arbour
1983-84	50	26	4	104	1st/Patrick	12	9	Stanley Cup finals	Al Arbour
1984-85	40	34	6	86	3rd/Patrick	4	6	Division finals	Al Arbour
1985-86	39	29	12	90	3rd/Patrick	0	3	Division semifinals	Al Arbour
1986-87	35	33	12	82	3rd/Patrick	7	7	Division finals	Terry Simpson
1987-88	39	31	10	88	1st/Patrick	2	4	Division semifinals	Terry Simpson

Season	W	L	T	Pts.	Finish	W	L	Highest round	Coach
			REGULAR SEASON				**PLAYOFFS**		
1988-89	28	47	5	61	6th/Patrick	—	—		Terry Simpson, Al Arbour
1989-90	31	38	11	73	4th/Patrick	1	4	Division semifinals	Al Arbour
1990-91	25	45	10	60	6th/Patrick	—	—		Al Arbour
1991-92	34	35	11	79	5th/Patrick	—	—		Al Arbour
1992-93	40	37	7	87	3rd/Patrick	9	9	Conference finals	Al Arbour

FIRST-ROUND ENTRY DRAFT CHOICES

Year   Player, Overall, Last Amateur Team (League)

1972—*Billy Harris, 1, Toronto (OHL)
1973—*Denis Potvin, 1, Ottawa (OHL)
1974—Clark Gillies, 4, Regina (WCHL)
1975—Pat Price, 11, Vancouver (WHA)
1976—Alex McKendry, 14, Sudbury (OHL)
1977—Mike Bossy, 15, Laval (QMJHL)
1978—Steve Tambellini, 15, Lethbridge (WCHL)
1979—Duane Sutter, 17, Lethbridge (WHL)
1980—Brent Sutter, 17, Red Deer (AJHL)
1981—Paul Boutilier, 21, Sherbrooke (QMJHL)
1982—Pat Flatley, 21, University of Wisconsin
1983—Pat LaFontaine, 3, Verdun (QMJHL)
      Gerald Diduck, 16, Lethbridge (WHL)

Year   Player, Overall, Last Amateur Team (League)

1984—Duncan MacPherson, 20, Saskatoon (WHL)
1985—Brad Dalgarno, 6, Hamilton (OHL)
      Derek King, 13, Sault Ste. Marie (OHL)
1986—Tom Fitzgerald, 17, Austin Prep (Mass.)
1987—Dean Chynoweth, 13, Medicine Hat (WHL)
1988—Kevin Cheveldayoff, 16, Brandon (WHL)
1989—Dave Chyzowski, 2, Kamloops (WHL)
1990—Scott Scissons, 6, Saskatoon (WHL)
1991—Scott Lachance, 4, Boston University
1992—Darius Kasparaitis, 5, Dynamo Moscow (CIS)
1993—Todd Bertuzzi, 23, Guelph (OHL)

*Designates first player chosen in draft.

FRANCHISE LEADERS

Current players in boldface

FORWARDS/DEFENSEMEN

Games

Bryan Trottier	1123
Denis Potvin	1080
Bob Nystrom	900
Clark Gillies	872
Bob Bourne	814
Mike Bossy	752
Brent Sutter	694
Billy Smith	675
Billy Harris	623
Stefan Persson	622

Goals

Mike Bossy	573
Bryan Trottier	500
Denis Potvin	310
Clark Gillies	304
Pat LaFontaine	287
Brent Sutter	287
Bob Bourne	238
Bob Nystrom	235
John Tonelli	206
Billy Harris	184

Assists

Bryan Trottier	853
Denis Potvin	742
Mike Bossy	553
Clark Gillies	359

John Tonelli	338
Brent Sutter	323
Stefan Persson	317
Bob Bourne	304
Pat LaFontaine	279
Bob Nystrom	278

Points

Bryan Trottier	1353
Mike Bossy	1126
Denis Potvin	1052
Clark Gillies	663
Brent Sutter	610
Pat LaFontaine	566
John Tonelli	544
Bob Bourne	542
Bob Nystrom	513
Billy Harris	443

Penalty minutes

Garry Howatt	1466
Mick Vukota	**1356**
Denis Potvin	1354
Bob Nystrom	1248
Clark Gillies	891
Duane Sutter	891
Bryan Trottier	798
Gerry Hart	783
Brent Sutter	761
Rich Pilon	**746**

GOALTENDERS

Games

Billy Smith	675
Chico Resch	282
Kelly Hrudey	241
Glenn Healy	176
Roland Melanson	136
Mark Fitzpatrick	129
Gerry Desjardins	80

Shutouts

Chico Resch	25
Billy Smith	22
Kelly Hrudey	6

Goals-against average
(2400 minutes minimum)

Chico Resch	2.56
Roland Melanson	3.14
Billy Smith	3.16
Mark Fitzpatrick	3.41
Glenn Healy	3.45
Kelly Hrudey	3.46

Wins

Billy Smith	304
Chico Resch	157
Kelly Hrudey	106
Roland Melanson	77
Glenn Healy	66
Mark Fitzpatrick	51
Gerry Desjardins	14

NEW YORK RANGERS

YEAR-BY-YEAR RECORDS

Season	W	L	T	Pts.	Finish	W	L	Highest round	Coach
			REGULAR SEASON				**PLAYOFFS**		
1926-27	25	13	6	56	1st/American	*0	1	Semifinals	Lester Patrick
1927-28	19	16	9	47	2nd/American	*5	3	Stanley Cup champ	Lester Patrick
1928-29	21	13	10	52	2nd/American	*3	2	Stanley Cup finals	Lester Patrick
1929-30	17	17	10	44	3rd/American	*1	2	Semifinals	Lester Patrick
1930-31	19	16	9	47	3rd/American	2	2	Semifinals	Lester Patrick
1931-32	23	17	8	54	1st/American	3	4	Stanley Cup finals	Lester Patrick
1932-33	23	17	8	54	3rd/American	*6	1	Stanley Cup champ	Lester Patrick
1933-34	21	19	8	50	3rd/American	*0	1	Quarterfinals	Lester Patrick
1934-35	22	20	6	50	3rd/American	*1	1	Semifinals	Lester Patrick

Season	W	L	T	Pts.	Finish	W	L	Highest round	Coach
1935-36	19	17	12	50	4th/American	—	—		Lester Patrick
1936-37	19	20	9	47	3rd/American	6	3	Stanley Cup finals	Lester Patrick
1937-38	27	15	6	60	2nd/American	1	2	Quarterfinals	Lester Patrick
1938-39	26	16	6	58	2nd	3	4	Semifinals	Lester Patrick
1939-40	27	11	10	64	2nd	8	4	Stanley Cup champ	Frank Boucher
1940-41	21	19	8	50	4th	1	2	Quarterfinals	Frank Boucher
1941-42	29	17	2	60	1st	2	4	Semifinals	Frank Boucher
1942-43	11	31	8	30	6th	—	—		Frank Boucher
1943-44	6	39	5	17	6th	—	—		Frank Boucher
1944-45	11	29	10	32	6th	—	—		Frank Boucher
1945-46	13	28	9	35	6th	—	—		Frank Boucher
1946-47	22	32	6	50	5th	—	—		Frank Boucher
1947-48	21	26	13	55	4th	2	4	League semifinals	Frank Boucher
1948-49	18	31	11	47	6th	—	—		Frank Boucher, Lynn Patrick
1949-50	28	31	11	67	4th	7	5	Stanley Cup finals	Lynn Patrick
1950-51	20	29	21	61	5th	—	—		Neil Colville
1951-52	23	34	13	59	5th	—	—		Neil Colville, Bill Cook
1952-53	17	37	16	50	6th	—	—		Bill Cook
1953-54	29	31	10	68	5th	—	—		Frank Boucher, Muzz Patrick
1954-55	17	35	18	52	5th	—	—		Muzz Patrick
1955-56	32	28	10	74	3rd	1	4	League semifinals	Phil Watson
1956-57	26	30	14	66	4th	1	4	League semifinals	Phil Watson
1957-58	32	25	13	77	2nd	2	4	League semifinals	Phil Watson
1958-59	26	32	12	64	5th	—	—		Phil Watson
1959-60	17	38	15	49	6th	—	—		Phil Watson, Alf Pike
1960-61	22	38	10	54	5th	—	—		Alf Pike
1961-62	26	32	12	64	4th	2	4	League semifinals	Doug Harvey
1962-63	22	36	12	56	5th	—	—		Muzz Patrick, Red Sullivan
1963-64	22	38	10	54	5th	—	—		Red Sullivan
1964-65	20	38	12	52	5th	—	—		Red Sullivan
1965-66	18	41	11	47	6th	—	—		Red Sullivan, Emile Francis
1966-67	30	28	12	72	4th	0	4	League semifinals	Emile Francis
1967-68	39	23	12	90	2nd/East	2	4	Division semifinals	Emile Francis
1968-69	41	26	9	91	3rd/East	0	4	Division semifinals	Bernie Geoffrion, Emile Francis
1969-70	38	22	16	92	4th/East	2	4	Division semifinals	Emile Francis
1970-71	49	18	11	109	2nd/East	7	6	Division finals	Emile Francis
1971-72	48	17	13	109	2nd/East	10	6	Stanley Cup finals	Emile Francis
1972-73	47	23	8	102	3rd/East	5	5	Division finals	Emile Francis
1973-74	40	24	14	94	3rd/East	7	6	Division finals	Larry Popein, Emile Francis
1974-75	37	29	14	88	2nd/Patrick	1	2	Preliminaries	Emile Francis
1975-76	29	42	9	67	4th/Patrick	—	—		Ron Stewart, John Ferguson
1976-77	29	37	14	72	4th/Patrick	—	—		John Ferguson
1977-78	30	37	13	73	4th/Patrick	1	2	Preliminaries	Jean-Guy Talbot
1978-79	40	29	11	91	3rd/Patrick	11	7	Stanley Cup finals	Fred Shero
1979-80	38	32	10	86	3rd/Patrick	4	5	Quarterfinals	Fred Shero
1980-81	30	36	14	74	4th/Patrick	7	7	Semifinals	Fred Shero, Craig Patrick
1981-82	39	27	14	92	2nd/Patrick	5	5	Division finals	Herb Brooks
1982-83	35	35	10	80	4th/Patrick	5	4	Division finals	Herb Brooks
1983-84	42	29	9	93	4th/Patrick	2	3	Division semifinals	Herb Brooks
1984-85	26	44	10	62	4th/Patrick	0	3	Division semifinals	Herb Brooks, Craig Patrick
1985-86	36	38	6	78	4th/Patrick	8	8	Conference finals	Ted Sator
1986-87	34	38	8	76	4th/Patrick	2	4	Division semifinals	Ted Sator, Tom Webster, Phil Esposito
1987-88	36	34	10	82	4th/Patrick	—	—		Michel Bergeron
1988-89	37	35	8	82	3rd/Patrick	0	4	Division semifinals	Michel Bergeron, Phil Esposito
1989-90	36	31	13	85	1st/Patrick	5	5	Division finals	Roger Neilson
1990-91	36	31	13	85	2nd/Patrick	2	4	Division semifinals	Roger Neilson
1991-92	50	25	5	105	1st/Patrick	6	7	Division finals	Roger Neilson
1992-93	34	39	11	79	6th/Patrick	—	—		Roger Neilson, Ron Smith

*Won-lost record does not indicate tie(s) resulting from two-game, total goals series that year (two-game, total-goals series were played from 1917-18 through 1935-36).

FIRST-ROUND ENTRY DRAFT CHOICES

Year Player, Overall, Last Amateur Team (League)

1969—Andre Dupont, 8, Montreal (OHL)
　　　Pierre Jarry, 12, Ottawa (OHL)
1970—Normand Gratton, 11, Montreal (OHL)
1971—Steve Vickers, 10, Toronto (OHL)
　　　Steve Durbano, 13, Toronto (OHL)
1972—Albert Blanchard, 10, Kitchener (OHL)
　　　Bobby MacMillan, 15, St. Catharines (OHL)
1973—Rick Middleton, 14, Oshawa (OHL)
1974—Dave Maloney, 14, Kitchener (OHL)
1975—Wayne Dillon, 12, Toronto (WHA)

Year Player, Overall, Last Amateur Team (League)

1976—Don Murdoch, 6, Medicine Hat (WCHL)
1977—Lucien DeBlois, 8, Sorel (QMJHL)
　　　Ron Duguay, 13, Sudbury (OHL)
1978—No first-round selection
1979—Doug Sulliman, 13, Kitchener (OHL)
1980—Jim Malone, 14, Toronto (OHL)
1981—James Patrick, 9, Prince Albert (AJHL)
1982—Chris Kontos, 15, Toronto (OHL)
1983—Dave Gagner, 12, Brantford (OHL)
1984—Terry Carkner, 14, Peterborough (OHL)

Year	Player, Overall, Last Amateur Team (League)
1985	Ulf Dahlen, 7, Ostersund (Sweden)
1986	Brian Leetch, 9, Avon Old Farms Prep (Ct.)
1987	Jayson More, 10, New Westminster (WCHL)
1988	No first-round selection
1989	Steven Rice, 20, Kitchener (OHL)

Year	Player, Overall, Last Amateur Team (League)
1990	Michael Stewart, 13, Michigan State University
1991	Alexei Kovalev, 15, Dynamo Moscow (USSR)
1992	Peter Ferraro, 24, Waterloo (USHL)
1993	Niklas Sundstrom, 8, Ornskoldsvik (Sweden)

FRANCHISE LEADERS

Current players in boldface

FORWARDS/DEFENSEMEN

Games
Harry Howell	1160
Rod Gilbert	1065
Ron Greschner	982
Walt Tkaczuk	945
Jean Ratelle	862
Vic Hadfield	838
Jim Neilson	810
Andy Bathgate	719
Steve Vickers	698
Dean Prentice	666

Goals
Rod Gilbert	406
Jean Ratelle	336
Andy Bathgate	272
Vic Hadfield	262
Camille Henry	256
Steve Vickers	246
Bill Cook	228
Walt Tkaczuk	227
Don Maloney	195
Bryan Hextall	187

Assists
Rod Gilbert	615
Jean Ratelle	481
Andy Bathgate	457
Walt Tkaczuk	451
Ron Greschner	431
James Patrick	**360**
Steve Vickers	340
Vic Hadfield	310
Don Maloney	307
Brad Park	283

Points
Rod Gilbert	1021
Jean Ratelle	817
Andy Bathgate	729
Walt Tkaczuk	678
Ron Greschner	610
Steve Vickers	586
Vic Hadfield	572
Don Maloney	502
Camille Henry	478
James Patrick	**464**

Penalty minutes
Ron Greschner	1226
Harry Howell	1147
Don Maloney	1113
Vic Hadfield	1036
Nick Fotiu	970

GOALTENDERS

Games
Gump Worsley	583
Ed Giacomin	539
John Vanbiesbrouck	449
Chuck Rayner	377
Dave Kerr	324
John Davidson	222
Gilles Villemure	184

Shutouts
Ed Giacomin	49
Dave Kerr	40
John Ross Roach	30
Chuck Rayner	24
Gump Worsley	24
Lorne Chabot	21

Goals-against average
(2400 minutes minimum)
Lorne Chabot	1.61
Dave Kerr	2.07
John Ross Roach	2.16
Andy Aitkenhead	2.42
Johnny Bower	2.62
Gilles Villemure	2.62
Ed Giacomin	2.73

Wins
Ed Giacomin	266
Gump Worsley	204
John Vanbiesbrouck	200
Dave Kerr	157
Chuck Rayner	123
Gilles Villemure	96
John Davidson	93

OTTAWA SENATORS (FIRST CLUB—DEFUNCT)

YEAR-BY-YEAR RECORDS

	REGULAR SEASON					PLAYOFFS			
Season	W	L	T	Pts.	Finish	W	L	Highest round	Coach
1917-18	9	13	0	18	3rd	—	—		Eddie Gerard
1918-19	12	6	0	24	1st	1	4	Semifinals	Alf Smith
1919-20	19	5	0	38	1st	3	2	Stanley Cup champ	Pete Green
1920-21	14	10	0	28	2nd	*4	2	Stanley Cup champ	Pete Green
1921-22	14	8	2	30	1st	*0	1	Semifinals	Pete Green
1922-23	14	9	1	29	1st	6	2	Stanley Cup champ	Pete Green
1923-24	16	8	0	32	1st	0	2	Semifinals	Pete Green
1924-25	17	12	1	35	4th	—	—		Pete Green
1925-26	24	8	4	52	1st	*0	1	Semifinals	Pete Green
1926-27	30	10	4	64	1st/Canadian	*3	0	Stanley Cup champ	Dave Gill
1927-28	20	14	10	50	3rd/Canadian	0	2	Quarterfinals	Dave Gill
1928-29	14	17	13	41	4th/Canadian	—	—		Dave Gill
1929-30	21	15	8	50	3rd/Canadian	*0	1	Semifinals	Newsy Lalonde
1930-31	10	30	4	24	5th/Canadian	—	—		Newsy Lalonde
1931-32					Club suspended operations for one season.				
1932-33	11	27	10	32	5th/Canadian	—	—		Cy Denneny
1933-34	13	29	6	32	5th/Canadian	—	—		George Boucher
1934-35†	11	31	6	28	5th/Canadian	—	—		Eddie Gerard, George Boucher

*Won-lost record does not indicate tie(s) resulting from two-game, total goals series that year (two-game, total-goals series were played from 1917-18 through 1935-36).

†St. Louis Eagles.

OTTAWA SENATORS (SECOND CLUB)

YEAR-BY-YEAR RECORDS

	REGULAR SEASON					PLAYOFFS			
Season	W	L	T	Pts.	Finish	W	L	Highest round	Coach
1992-93	10	70	4	24	6th/Adams	—	—		Rick Bowness

FIRST-ROUND ENTRY DRAFT CHOICES

Year   Player, Overall, Last Amateur Team (League)
1992—Alexei Yashin, 2, Dynamo Moscow (CIS)

Year   Player, Overall, Last Amateur Team (League)
1993—*Alexandre Daigle, 1, Victoriaville (QMJHL)
*Designates first player chosen in draft.

FRANCHISE LEADERS

Current players in boldface

FORWARDS/DEFENSEMEN
Games
Mike Peluso..81
Brad Shaw...81
Norm Maciver.....................................80
Darcy Loewen...79
Jamie Baker..76
Chris Luongo...76
Sylvain Turgeon.....................................72
Mark Lamb...71
Laurie Boschman.................................70
Jody Hull..69
Darren Rumble...................................69

Goals
Sylvain Turgeon....................................25
Bob Kudelski..21
Jamie Baker..19
Norm Maciver...17
Mike Peluso..15
Jody Hull..13
Mark Freer...10
Laurie Boschman....................................9
David Archibald..................................9

Assists
Norm Maciver.......................................46
Brad Shaw...34
Jamie Baker..29
Jody Hull..21
Mark Lamb..19
Sylvain Turgeon.....................................18
Neil Brady..17
Andrew McBain......................................16
Mark Freer...14
Bob Kudelski...14

Points
Norm Maciver.......................................63
Jamie Baker..48
Sylvain Turgeon.....................................43
Brad Shaw...41
Bob Kudelski..35
Jody Hull..34
Mark Lamb...26
Mike Peluso..25
Neil Brady..24
Mark Freer...24

Penalty minutes
Mike Peluso..318
Darcy Loewen.......................................145

Sylvain Turgeon 104
Ken Hammond 104
Laurie Boschman 101
Norm Maciver 84
Chris Luongo 68
Mark Lamb 64
Darren Rumble 61
Neil Brady 57

GOALTENDERS
Games
Peter Sidorkiewicz................................64
Daniel Berthiaume...............................25
Steve Weeks...7
Darrin Madeley.....................................2

Shutouts
Never accomplished

Goals-against average
(1200 minutes minimum)
Daniel Berthiaume 4.30
Peter Sidorkiewicz 4.43

Wins
Peter Sidorkiewicz 8
Daniel Berthiaume 2

PHILADELPHIA FLYERS

YEAR-BY-YEAR RECORDS

| | | REGULAR SEASON | | | | | PLAYOFFS | | |
Season	W	L	T	Pts.	Finish	W	L	Highest round	Coach
1967-68	31	32	11	73	1st/West	3	4	Division semifinals	Keith Allen
1968-69	20	35	21	61	3rd/West	0	4	Division semifinals	Keith Allen
1969-70	17	35	24	58	5th/West	—	—		Vic Stasiuk
1970-71	28	33	17	73	3rd/West	0	4	Division semifinals	Vic Stasiuk
1971-72	26	38	14	66	5th/West	—	—		Fred Shero
1972-73	37	30	11	85	2nd/West	5	6	Division finals	Fred Shero
1973-74	50	16	12	112	1st/West	12	5	Stanley Cup champ	Fred Shero
1974-75	51	18	11	113	1st/Patrick	12	5	Stanley Cup champ	Fred Shero
1975-76	51	13	16	118	1st/Patrick	8	8	Stanley Cup finals	Fred Shero
1976-77	48	16	16	112	1st/Patrick	4	6	Semifinals	Fred Shero
1977-78	45	20	15	105	2nd/Patrick	7	5	Semifinals	Fred Shero
1978-79	40	25	15	95	2nd/Patrick	3	5	Quarterfinals	Bob McCammon, Pat Quinn
1979-80	48	12	20	116	1st/Patrick	13	6	Stanley Cup finals	Pat Quinn
1980-81	41	24	15	97	2nd/Patrick	6	6	Quarterfinals	Pat Quinn
1981-82	38	31	11	87	3rd/Patrick	1	3	Division semifinals	Pat Quinn, Bob McCammon
1982-83	49	23	8	106	1st/Patrick	0	3	Division semifinals	Bob McCammon
1983-84	44	26	10	98	3rd/Patrick	0	3	Division semifinals	Bob McCammon
1984-85	53	20	7	113	1st/Patrick	12	7	Stanley Cup finals	Mike Keenan
1985-86	53	23	4	110	1st/Patrick	2	3	Division semifinals	Mike Keenan
1986-87	46	26	8	100	1st/Patrick	15	11	Stanley Cup finals	Mike Keenan
1987-88	38	33	9	85	2nd/Patrick	3	4	Division semifinals	Mike Keenan
1988-89	36	36	8	80	4th/Patrick	10	9	Conference finals	Paul Holmgren
1989-90	30	39	11	71	6th/Patrick	—	—		Paul Holmgren
1990-91	33	37	10	76	5th/Patrick	—	—		Paul Holmgren
1991-92	32	37	11	75	6th/Patrick	—	—		Paul Holmgren, Bill Dineen
1992-93	36	37	11	83	6th/Patrick	—	—		Bill Dineen

FIRST-ROUND ENTRY DRAFT CHOICES

Year Player, Overall, Last Amateur Team (League)
1969—Bob Currier, 6, Cornwall (QMJHL)
1970—No first-round selection
1971—Larry Wright, 8, Regina (WCHL)
      Pierre Plante, 9, Drummondville (QMJHL)
1972—Bill Barber, 7, Kitchener (OHL)
1973—No first-round selection
1974—No first-round selection
1975—*Mel Bridgeman, 1, Victoria (WCHL)
1976—Mark Suzor, 17, Kingston (OHL)
1977—Kevin McCarthy, 17, Winnipeg (WCHL)
1978—Behn Wilson, 6, Kingston (OHL)
      Ken Linseman, 7, Birmingham (WHA)
      Dan Lucas, 14, Sault Ste. Marie (OHL)
1979—Brian Propp, 14, Brandon (WHL)
1980—Mike Stothers, 21, Kingston (OHL)
1981—Steve Smith, 16, Sault Ste. Marie (OHL)

Year Player, Overall, Last Amateur Team (League)
1982—Ron Sutter, 4, Lethbridge (WHL)
1983—No first-round selection
1984—No first-round selection
1985—Glen Seabrooke, 21, Peterborough (OHL)
1986—Kerry Huffman, 20, Guelph (OHL)
1987—Darren Rumble, 20, Kitchener (OHL)
1988—Claude Boivin, 14, Drummondville (QMJHL)
1989—No first-round selection
1990—Mike Ricci, 4, Peterborough (OHL)
1991—Peter Forsberg, 6, Modo (Sweden)
1992—Ryan Sittler, 7, Nichols H.S. (N.Y.)
      Jason Bowen, 15, Tri-City (WHL)
1993—No first-round selection

*Designates first player chosen in draft.

FRANCHISE LEADERS

Current players in boldface

FORWARDS/DEFENSEMEN

Games
Bobby Clarke	1144
Bill Barber	903
Brian Propp	790
Joe Watson	746
Bob Kelly	741
Rick MacLeish	741
Gary Dornhoefer	725
Ed Van Impe	617
Jim Watson	613
Reggie Leach	606

Goals
Bill Barber	420
Brian Propp	369
Tim Kerr	363
Bobby Clarke	358
Rick MacLeish	328
Reggie Leach	306
Rick Tocchet	215
Gary Dornhoefer	202
Ilkka Sinisalo	199
Dave Poulin	161

Assists
Bobby Clarke	852
Brian Propp	480
Bill Barber	463

Rick MacLeish	369
Mark Howe	342
Pelle Eklund	**318**
Gary Dornhoefer	316
Tim Kerr	287
Murray Craven	272
Rick Tocchet	247

Points
Bobby Clarke	1210
Bill Barber	883
Brian Propp	849
Rick MacLeish	697
Tim Kerr	650
Gary Dornhoefer	518
Reggie Leach	514
Mark Howe	480
Rick Tocchet	462
Pelle Eklund	**435**

Penalty minutes
Rick Tocchet	1683
Paul Holmgren	1600
Andre Dupont	1505
Bobby Clarke	1453
Dave Schultz	1386
Bob Kelly	1285
Gary Dornhoefer	1256
Dave Brown	**1192**
Glen Cochrane	1110

GOALTENDERS

Games
Bernie Parent	486
Ron Hextall	281
Doug Favell	215
Pete Peeters	179
Wayne Stephenson	165
Pelle Lindbergh	157
Bob Froese	144

Shutouts
Bernie Parent	50
Doug Favell	16
Bob Froese	12
Wayne Stephenson	10

Goals-against average
(2400 minutes minimum)
Bernie Parent	2.42
Bob Froese	2.74
Wayne Stephenson	2.77
Doug Favell	2.78
Pete Peeters	3.19
Rick St. Croix	3.23
Ron Hextall	3.27
Pelle Lindbergh	3.30

Wins
Bernie Parent	232
Ron Hextall	130
Wayne Stephenson	93
Bob Froese	92
Pelle Lindbergh	87

PITTSBURGH PENGUINS

YEAR-BY-YEAR RECORDS

	REGULAR SEASON					PLAYOFFS			
Season	W	L	T	Pts.	Finish	W	L	Highest round	Coach
1967-68	27	34	13	67	5th/West	—	—		Red Sullivan
1968-69	20	45	11	51	5th/West	—	—		Red Sullivan
1969-70	26	38	12	64	2nd/West	6	4	Division finals	Red Kelly
1970-71	21	37	20	62	6th/West	—	—		Red Kelly
1971-72	26	38	14	66	4th/West	0	4	Division semifinals	Red Kelly
1972-73	32	37	9	73	5th/West	—	—		Red Kelly, Ken Schinkel
1973-74	28	41	9	65	5th/West	—	—		Ken Schinkel, Marc Boileau
1974-75	37	28	15	89	3rd/Norris	5	4	Quarterfinals	Marc Boileau
1975-76	35	33	12	82	3rd/Norris	1	2	Preliminaries	Marc Boileau, Ken Schinkel
1976-77	34	33	13	81	3rd/Norris	1	2	Preliminaries	Ken Schinkel
1977-78	25	37	18	68	4th/Norris	—	—		Johnny Wilson
1978-79	36	31	13	85	2nd/Norris	2	5	Quarterfinals	Johnny Wilson
1979-80	30	37	13	73	3rd/Norris	2	3	Preliminaries	Johnny Wilson
1980-81	30	37	13	73	3rd/Norris	2	3	Preliminaries	Eddie Johnston

Season	W	L	T	Pts.	Finish	W	L	Highest round	Coach
					REGULAR SEASON			PLAYOFFS	
1981-82	31	36	13	75	4th/Patrick	2	3	Division semifinals	Eddie Johnston
1982-83	18	53	9	45	6th/Patrick	—	—		Eddie Johnston
1983-84	16	58	6	38	6th/Patrick	—	—		Lou Angotti
1984-85	24	51	5	53	5th/Patrick	—	—		Bob Berry
1985-86	34	38	8	76	5th/Patrick	—	—		Bob Berry
1986-87	30	38	12	72	5th/Patrick	—	—		Bob Berry
1987-88	36	35	9	81	6th/Patrick	—	—		Pierre Creamer
1988-89	40	33	7	87	2nd/Patrick	7	4	Division finals	Gene Ubriaco
1989-90	32	40	8	72	5th/Patrick	—	—		Gene Ubriaco, Craig Patrick
1990-91	41	33	6	88	1st/Patrick	16	8	Stanley Cup champ	Bob Johnson
1991-92	39	32	9	87	3rd/Patrick	16	5	Stanley Cup champ	Scotty Bowman
1992-93	56	21	7	119	1st/Patrick	7	5	Division finals	Scotty Bowman

FIRST-ROUND ENTRY DRAFT CHOICES

Year Player, Overall, Last Amateur Team (League)

1969—No first-round selection
1970—Greg Polis, 7, Estevan (WCHL)
1971—No first-round selection
1972—No first-round selection
1973—Blaine Stoughton, 7, Flin Flon (WCHL)
1974—Pierre Larouche, 8, Sorel (QMJHL)
1975—Gord Laxton, 13, New Westminster (WCHL)
1976—Blair Chapman, 2, Saskatoon (WCHL)
1977—No first-round selection
1978—No first-round selection
1979—No first-round selection
1980—Mike Bullard, 9, Brantford (OHL)
1981—No first-round selection
1982—Rich Sutter, 10, Lethbridge (WHL)
1983—Bob Errey, 15, Peterborough (OHL)

Year Player, Overall, Last Amateur Team (League)

1984—*Mario Lemieux, 1, Laval (QMJHL)
  Doug Bodger, 9, Kamloops (WHL)
  Roger Belanger, 16, Kingston (OHL)
1985—Craig Simpson, 2, Michigan State University
1986—Zarley Zalapski, 4, Team Canada
1987—Chris Joseph, 5, Seattle (WHL)
1988—Darrin Shannon, 4, Windsor (OHL)
1989—Jamie Heward, 16, Regina (WHL)
1990—Jaromir Jagr, 5, Poldi Kladno (Czech.)
1991—Markus Naslund, 16, MoDo (Sweden)
1992—Martin Straka, 19, Skoda Plzen (Czech.)
1993—Stefan Bergqvist, 26, Leksand (Sweden)

*Designates first player chosen in draft.

FRANCHISE LEADERS

Current players in boldface

FORWARDS/DEFENSEMEN

Games

Jean Pronovost	753
Rick Kehoe	722
Ron Stackhouse	621
Ron Schock	619
Mario Lemieux	577
Dave Burrows	573
Bob Errey	518
Troy Loney	532
Syl Apps	495
Greg Malone	495

Goals

Mario Lemieux	477
Jean Pronovost	316
Rick Kehoe	312
Kevin Stevens	195
Mike Bullard	186
Syl Apps	151
Greg Malone	143
Lowell MacDonald	140
Bob Errey	132
Ron Schock	124

Assists

Mario Lemieux	697
Syl Apps	349
Paul Coffey	332
Rick Kehoe	324
Jean Pronovost	287
Ron Schock	280
Ron Stackhouse	277

Randy Carlyle	257
Greg Malone	221
Kevin Stevens	217

Points

Mario Lemieux	1174
Rick Kehoe	636
Jean Pronovost	603
Syl Apps	500
Paul Coffey	440
Kevin Stevens	412
Ron Schock	404
Greg Malone	364
Mike Bullard	361
Ron Stackhouse	343

Penalty minutes

Troy Loney	980
Rod Buskas	959
Bryan Watson	871
Paul Baxter	851
Gary Rissling	832
Kevin Stevens	760
Jay Caufield	714
Russ Anderson	684
Jim Johnson	658
Bob Errey	651

GOALTENDERS

Games

Denis Herron	290
Tom Barrasso	236
Les Binkley	196
Michel Dion	151

Greg Millen	135
Roberto Romano	123
Jim Rutherford	115
Gilles Meloche	104
Wendell Young	101
Gary Inness	100

Shutouts

Les Binkley	11
Tom Barrasso	6
Denis Herron	6
Dunc Wilson	5

Goals-against average
(2400 minutes minimum)

Al Smith	3.07
Les Binkley	3.12
Jim Rutherford	3.14
Gary Inness	3.34
Dunc Wilson	3.53
Michel Plasse	3.59
Tom Barrasso	3.60
Gilles Meloche	3.65
Andy Brown	3.78
Greg Millen	3.83

Wins

Tom Barrasso	77
Denis Herron	88
Les Binkley	58
Greg Millen	57
Roberto Romano	45
Jim Rutherford	44

PITTSBURGH PIRATES (DEFUNCT)

YEAR-BY-YEAR RECORDS

	REGULAR SEASON					PLAYOFFS			
Season	W	L	T	Pts.	Finish	W	L	Highest round	Coach
1925-26	19	16	1	39	3rd	—	—		Odie Cleghorn
1926-27	15	26	3	33	4th/American	—	—		Odie Cleghorn
1927-28	19	17	8	46	3rd/American	1	1	Quarterfinals	Odie Cleghorn
1928-29	9	27	8	26	4th/American	—	—		Odie Cleghorn
1929-30	5	36	3	13	5th/American	—	—		Frank Frederickson
1930-31*	4	36	4	12	5th/American	—	—		Cooper Smeaton

*Philadelphia Quakers.

QUEBEC NORDIQUES

YEAR-BY-YEAR RECORDS

	REGULAR SEASON					PLAYOFFS			
Season	W	L	T	Pts.	Finish	W	L	Highest round	Coach
1972-73*	33	40	5	71	5th	—	—		Maurice Richard, Maurice Filion
1973-74*	38	36	4	80	5th	—	—		Jacques Plante
1974-75*	46	32	0	92	1st	8	7	Avco World Cup finals	Jean-Guy Jendron
1975-76*	50	27	4	104	2nd	1	4	League quarterfinals	Jean-Guy Jendron
1976-77*	47	31	3	97	1st	12	5	Avco World Cup champ	Marc Boileau
1977-78*	40	37	3	83	4th	5	6	League semifinals	Marc Boileau
1978-79*	41	34	5	87	2nd	0	4	League semifinals	Jacques Demers
1979-80	25	44	11	61	5th/Adams	—	—		Jacques Demers
1980-81	30	32	18	78	4th/Adams	2	3	Preliminaries	Maurice Filion, Michel Bergeron
1981-82	33	31	16	82	4th/Adams	7	9	Conference finals	Michel Bergeron
1982-83	34	34	12	80	4th/Adams	1	3	Division semifinals	Michel Bergeron
1983-84	42	28	10	94	3rd/Adams	5	4	Division finals	Michel Bergeron
1984-85	41	30	9	91	2nd/Adams	9	9	Conference finals	Michel Bergeron
1985-86	43	31	6	92	1st/Adams	0	3	Division semifinals	Michel Bergeron
1986-87	31	39	10	72	4th/Adams	7	6	Division finals	Michel Bergeron
1987-88	32	43	5	69	5th/Adams	—	—		Andre Savard, Ron Lapointe
1988-89	27	46	7	61	5th/Adams	—	—		Ron Lapointe, Jean Perron
1989-90	12	61	7	31	5th/Adams	—	—		Michel Bergeron
1990-91	16	50	14	46	5th/Adams	—	—		Dave Chambers
1991-92	20	48	12	52	5th/Adams	—	—		Dave Chambers, Pierre Page
1992-93	47	27	10	104	2nd/Adams	2	4	Division semifinals	Pierre Page

*Members of World Hockey Association.

FIRST-ROUND ENTRY DRAFT CHOICES

Year Player, Overall, Last Amateur Team (League)
1979—Michel Goulet, 20, Birmingham (WHA)
1980—No first-round selection
1981—Randy Moller, 11, Lethbridge (WHL)
1982—David Shaw, 13, Kitchener (OHL)
1983—No first-round selection
1984—Trevor Steinburg, 15, Guelph (OHL)
1985—Dave Latta, 15, Kitchener (OHL)
1986—Ken McRae, 18, Sudbury (OHL)
1987—Bryan Fogarty, 9, Kingston (OHL)
      Joe Sakic, 15, Swift Current (WHL)
1988—Curtis Leschyshyn, 3, Saskatoon (WHL)
      Daniel Dore, 5, Drummondville (QMJHL)

Year Player, Overall, Last Amateur Team (League)
1989—*Mats Sundin, 1, Nacka (Sweden)
1990—*Owen Nolan, 1, Cornwall (OHL)
1991—*Eric Lindros, 1, Oshawa (OHL)
1992—Todd Warriner, 4, Windsor (OHL)
1993—Jocelyn Thibault, 10, Sherbrooke (QMJHL)
      Adam Deadmarsh, 14, Portland (WHL)

*Designates first player chosen in draft.
NOTE: Quebec chose Paul Baxter, Richard Brodeur and Garry Lariviere as priority selections before the 1979 expansion draft.

FRANCHISE LEADERS

Current players in boldface

FORWARDS/DEFENSEMEN

Games

Michel Goulet	813
Peter Stastny	737
Alain Cote	696
Anton Stastny	650
Paul Gillis	576
Dale Hunter	523
Randy Moller	508

Steven Finn	485
Normand Rochefort	480
Mario Marois	403

Goals

Michel Goulet	456
Peter Stastny	380
Anton Stastny	252
Joe Sakic	**187**
Dale Hunter	140
Real Cloutier	122
Marc Tardif	116

Alain Cote	103
Wilf Paiement	102
Marian Stastny	98

Assists

Peter Stastny	668
Michel Goulet	489
Anton Stastny	384
Dale Hunter	318
Joe Sakic	**284**
Alain Cote	190
Real Cloutier	162

Mario Marois	162
Paul Gillis	146
Marian Stastny	143

Points

Peter Stastny	1048
Michel Goulet	945
Anton Stastny	636
Joe Sakic	**471**
Dale Hunter	458
Alain Cote	293
Real Cloutier	284
Marc Tardif	244
Marian Stastny	241
Paul Gillis	233

Penalty minutes

Dale Hunter	1545
Paul Gillis	1351
Steven Finn	**1286**

Randy Moller	1002
Mario Marois	778
Peter Stastny	687
Gord Donnelly	668
Wilf Paiement	619
Michel Goulet	613
Wally Weir	535

GOALTENDERS

Games

Dan Bouchard	225
Mario Gosselin	192
Ron Tugnutt	150
Clint Malarchuk	140
Stephane Fiset	**69**
Michel Dion	62

Shutouts

Mario Gosselin	6

Dan Bouchard	5
Clint Malarchuk	5

Goals-against average
(2400 minutes minimum)

Ron Hextall	3.45
Dan Bouchard	3.59
Clint Malarchuk	3.63
Mario Gosselin	3.67
Stephane Fiset	**3.78**
Michel Dion	4.02
Ron Tugnutt	4.07

Wins

Dan Bouchard	107
Mario Gosselin	79
Clint Malarchuk	62
Ron Tugnutt	35
Ron Hextall	29
Stephane Fiset	**25**

ST. LOUIS BLUES

YEAR-BY-YEAR RECORDS

	REGULAR SEASON					PLAYOFFS			
Season	W	L	T	Pts.	Finish	W	L	Highest round	Coach
1967-68	27	31	16	70	3rd/West	8	10	Stanley Cup finals	Lynn Patrick, Scotty Bowman
1968-69	37	25	14	88	1st/West	8	4	Stanley Cup finals	Scotty Bowman
1969-70	37	27	12	86	1st/West	8	8	Stanley Cup finals	Scotty Bowman
1970-71	34	25	19	87	2nd/West	2	4	Division semifinals	Al Arbour, Scotty Bowman
1971-72	28	39	11	67	3rd/West	4	7	Division finals	Sid Abel, Bill McCreary, Al Arbour
1972-73	32	34	12	76	4th/West	1	4	Division semifinals	Al Arbour, Jean-Guy Talbot
1973-74	26	40	12	64	6th/West	—	—		Jean-Guy Talbot, Lou Angotti
1974-75	35	31	14	84	2nd/Smythe	0	2	Preliminaries	Lou Angotti, Lynn Patrick, Garry Young
1975-76	29	37	14	72	3rd/Smythe	1	2	Preliminaries	Garry Young, Lynn Patrick, Leo Boivin
1976-77	32	39	9	73	1st/Smythe	0	4	Quarterfinals	Emile Francis
1977-78	20	47	13	53	4th/Smythe	—	—		Leo Boivin, Barclay Plager
1978-79	18	50	12	48	3rd/Smythe	—	—		Barclay Plager
1979-80	34	34	12	80	2nd/Smythe	0	3	Preliminaries	Barclay Plager, Red Berenson
1980-81	45	18	17	107	1st/Smythe	5	6	Quarterfinals	Red Berenson
1981-82	32	40	8	72	3rd/Norris	5	5	Division finals	Red Berenson, Emile Francis
1982-83	25	40	15	65	4th/Norris	1	3	Division semifinals	Emile Francis, Barclay Plager
1983-84	32	41	7	71	2nd/Norris	6	5	Division finals	Jacques Demers
1984-85	37	31	12	86	1st/Norris	0	3	Division semifinals	Jacques Demers
1985-86	37	34	9	83	3rd/Norris	10	9	Conference finals	Jacques Demers
1986-87	32	33	15	79	1st/Norris	2	4	Division semifinals	Jacques Martin
1987-88	34	38	8	76	2nd/Norris	5	5	Division finals	Jacques Martin
1988-89	33	35	12	78	2nd/Norris	5	5	Division finals	Brian Sutter
1989-90	37	34	9	83	2nd/Norris	7	5	Division finals	Brian Sutter
1990-91	47	22	11	105	2nd/Norris	6	7	Division finals	Brian Sutter
1991-92	36	33	11	83	3rd/Norris	2	4	Division semifinals	Brian Sutter
1992-93	37	36	11	85	4th/Norris	7	4	Division finals	Bob Plager, Bob Berry

FIRST-ROUND ENTRY DRAFT CHOICES

Year Player, Overall, Last Amateur Team (League)
1969—No first-round selection
1970—No first-round selection
1971—Gene Carr, 4, Flin Flon (WCHL)
1972—Wayne Merrick, 9, Ottawa (OHL)
1973—John Davidson, 5, Calgary (WCHL)
1974—No first-round selection
1975—No first-round selection
1976—Bernie Federko, 7, Saskatoon (WCHL)
1977—Scott Campbell, 9, London (OHL)
1978—Wayne Babych, 3, Portland (WCHL)
1979—Perry Turnbull, 2, Portland (WHL)
1980—Rik Wilson, 12, Kingston (OHL)
1981—Marty Ruff, 20, Lethbridge (WHL)

Year Player, Overall, Last Amateur Team (League)
1982—No first-round selection
1983—No first-round selection
1984—No first-round selection
1985—No first-round selection
1986—Jocelyn Lemieux, 10, Laval (QMJHL)
1987—Keith Osborne, 12, North Bay (OHL)
1988—Rod Brind'Amour, 9, Notre Dame Academy (Sask.)
1989—Jason Marshall, 9, Vernon (B.C.) Tier II
1990—No first-round selection
1991—No first-round selection
1992—No first-round selection
1993—No first-round selection

FRANCHISE LEADERS

Current players in boldface

FORWARDS/DEFENSEMEN

Games

Bernie Federko	927
Brian Sutter	779
Garry Unger	662
Bob Plager	615
Barclay Plager	614
Larry Patey	603
Red Berenson	519
Gary Sabourin	463
Jack Brownschidle	455
Gino Cavillini	454

Goals

Bernie Federko	352
Brett Hull	329
Brian Sutter	303
Garry Unger	292
Red Berenson	172
Jorgen Pettersson	161
Wayne Babych	155
Joe Mullen	151
Doug Gilmour	149
Perry Turnbull	139

Assists

Bernie Federko	721
Brian Sutter	334
Garry Unger	283
Red Berenson	240
Rob Ramage	229
Adam Oates	228

Brett Hull	223
Doug Gilmour	205
Blake Dunlop	201
Wayne Babych	190

Points

Bernie Federko	1073
Brian Sutter	636
Garry Unger	575
Brett Hull	552
Red Berenson	412
Doug Gilmour	354
Wayne Babych	345
Joe Mullen	335
Jorgen Pettersson	332
Rob Ramage	296

Penalty minutes

Brian Sutter	1786
Barclay Plager	1115
Rob Ramage	998
Bob Gassoff	866
Perry Turnbull	829
Bob Plager	760
Garry Unger	744
Kelly Chase	727
Herb Raglan	571
Noel Picard	540

GOALTENDERS

Games

Mike Liut	347
Greg Millen	209
Curtis Joseph	173

Rick Wamsley	154
Glenn Hall	140
Ed Staniowski	137
Vincent Riendeau	122
Ernie Wakely	111
Eddie Johnston	108
Wayne Stephenson	87

Shutouts

Glenn Hall	16
Mike Liut	10
Jacques Plante	10
Ernie Wakely	8
Greg Millen	7

Goals-against average
(2400 minutes minimum)

Jacques Plante	2.07
Glenn Hall	2.43
Ernie Wakely	2.77
Jacques Caron	3.02
Curtis Joseph	3.06
Wayne Stephenson	3.12
Vincent Riendeau	3.34
Eddie Johnston	3.36
John Davidson	3.37
Rick Wamsley	3.41
Greg Millen	3.43

Wins

Mike Liut	151
Greg Millen	85
Curtis Joseph	81
Rick Wamsley	75
Glenn Hall	58
Vincent Riendeau	58

SAN JOSE SHARKS

YEAR-BY-YEAR RECORDS

		REGULAR SEASON					PLAYOFFS			
Season	W	L	T	Pts.	Finish	W	L	Highest round	Coach
1991-92	17	58	5	39	6th/Smythe	—	—		George Kingston
1992-93	11	71	2	24	6th/Smythe	—	—		George Kingston

FIRST-ROUND ENTRY DRAFT CHOICES

Year	Player, Overall, Last Amateur Team (League)
1991	Pat Falloon, 2, Spokane (WHL)
1992	Mike Rathje, 3, Medicine Hat (WHL)
	Andrei Nazarov, 10, Dynamo Moscow (CIS)

Year	Player, Overall, Last Amateur Team (League)
1993	Viktor Kozlov, 6, Moscow (CIS)

FRANCHISE LEADERS

Current players in boldface

FORWARDS/DEFENSEMEN

Games

Dean Evason	158
Rob Zettler	154
Mike Sullivan	145
Jeff Odgers	127
Kelly Kisio	126
Pat Falloon	120
Jay More	119
Neil Wilkinson	119
David Williams	96
Perry Berezan	94

Goals

Pat Falloon	39
Kelly Kisio	37

Johan Garpenlov	27
David Bruce	24
Dean Evason	23
Rob Gaudreau	23
Jeff Odgers	19
Brian Mullen	18
Brian Lawton	17
Perry Berezan	15

Assists

Kelly Kisio	78
Johan Garpenlov	50
Pat Falloon	48
David Williams	36
Doug Wilson	36
Dean Evason	34
Brian Lawton	30
Brian Mullen	28

Neil Wilkinson	22
Rob Gaudreau	20

Points

Kelly Kisio	115
Pat Falloon	87
Johan Garpenlov	77
Dean Evason	57
Doug Wilson	48
Brian Lawton	47
Brian Mullen	46
David Bruce	43
Rob Gaudreau	43
David Williams	40

Penalty minutes

Jeff Odgers	470
Link Gaetz	326
Jay More	264

Rob Zettler 249	Arturs Irbe 49
Dean Evason 231	Jarmo Myllys 27
Doug Zmolek 229	Brian Hayward 25
Neil Wilkinson 203	Wade Flaherty 4
Kelly Kisio 144	
Perry Anderson 143	**Shutouts**
David Maley 126	Arturs Irbe 1

GOALTENDERS
Games

Jeff Hackett 78

Goals-against average
(1200 minutes minimum)

Arturs Irbe 4.19

Jeff Hackett 4.51	
Jarmo Myllys 5.02	
Brian Hayward 5.39	

Wins

Jeff Hackett 13
Arturs Irbe 9
Jarmo Myllys 3
Brian Hayward 3

TAMPA BAY LIGHTNING

YEAR-BY-YEAR RECORDS

	REGULAR SEASON					PLAYOFFS			
Season	W	L	T	Pts.	Finish	W	L	Highest round	Coach
1992-93	23	54	7	53	6th/Norris	—	—		Terry Crisp

FIRST-ROUND ENTRY DRAFT CHOICES

Year   Player, Overall, Last Amateur Team (League)
1992—*Roman Hamrlik, 1, Zlin (Czech.)

Year   Player, Overall, Last Amateur Team (League)
1993—Chris Gratton, 3, Kingston (OHL)
*Designates first player chosen in draft.

FRANCHISE LEADERS

Current players in boldface

FORWARDS/DEFENSEMEN

Games

Rob Zamuner 84
Adam Creighton 83
Brian Bradley 80
Marc Bergevin 78
John Tucker 78
Mikael Andersson 77
Danton Cole 67
Roman Hamrlik 67
Chris Kontos 66
Rob Ramage 66

Goals

Brian Bradley 42
Chris Kontos 27
Adam Creighton 19
John Tucker 17
Mikael Andersson 16
Rob Zamuner 15
Bob Beers 12
Danton Cole 12
Marc Bureau 10

Shawn Chambers 10

Assists

Brian Bradley 44
John Tucker 39
Shawn Chambers 29
Rob Zamuner 28
Chris Kontos 24
Bob Beers 24
Marc Bureau 21
Doug Crossman 21
Adam Creighton 20

Points

Brian Bradley 86
John Tucker 56
Chris Kontos 51
Rob Zamuner 43
Shawn Chambers 39
Adam Creighton 39
Bob Beers 36
Marc Bureau 31
Doug Crossman 29

Penalty minutes

Mike Hartman 154
Peter Taglianetti 150

Rob Ramage 138
Marc Bureau 111
Adam Creighton 110
Brian Bradley 92
Rob Zamuner 74
Roman Hamrlik 71
Basil McRae 71
Bob Beers 70

GOALTENDERS
Games

Pat Jablonski 43
Wendell Young 31
J.C. Bergeron 21
Dave Littman 1

Shutouts

Pat Jablonski 1

Goals-against average
(1200 minutes minimum)

Wendell Young 3.66
Pat Jablonski 3.97

Wins

J.C. Bergeron 8
Pat Jablonski 8
Wendell Young 7

TORONTO MAPLE LEAFS

YEAR-BY-YEAR RECORDS

	REGULAR SEASON					PLAYOFFS			
Season	W	L	T	Pts.	Finish	W	L	Highest round	Coach
1917-18‡	13	9	0	26	2nd	4	3	Stanley Cup champ	Dick Carroll
1918-19‡	5	13	0	10	3rd	—	—		Dick Carroll
1919-20*	12	12	0	24	3rd	—	—		Frank Heffernan, Harry Sproule
1920-21*	15	9	0	30	1st	0	2	Semifinals	Dick Carroll
1921-22*	13	10	1	27	2nd	*4	2	Stanley Cup champ	Eddie Powers
1922-23*	13	10	1	27	3rd	—	—		Charlie Querrie, Jack Adams

— 153 —

Season	W	L	T	Pts.	Finish	W	L	Highest round	Coach
			REGULAR SEASON					**PLAYOFFS**	
1923-24*	10	14	0	20	3rd	—	—		Eddie Powers
1924-25*	19	11	0	38	2nd	0	2	Semifinals	Eddie Powers
1925-26*	12	21	3	27	6th	—	—		Eddie Powers
1926-27*	15	24	5	35	5th/Canadian	—	—		Conn Smythe
1927-28	18	18	8	44	4th/Canadian	—	—		Alex Roveril, Conn Smythe
1928-29	21	18	5	47	3rd/Canadian	2	2	Semifinals	Alex Roveril, Conn Smythe
1929-30	17	21	6	40	4th/Canadian	—	—		Alex Roveril, Conn Smythe
1930-31	22	13	9	53	2nd/Canadian	*0	1	Quarterfinals	Conn Smythe, Art Duncan
1931-32	23	18	7	53	2nd/Canadian	5	2	Stanley Cup champ	Art Duncan, Dick Irvin
1932-33	24	18	6	54	1st/Canadian	4	5	Stanley Cup finals	Dick Irvin
1933-34	26	13	9	61	1st/Canadian	2	3	Semifinals	Dick Irvin
1934-35	30	14	4	64	1st/Canadian	3	4	Stanley Cup finals	Dick Irvin
1935-36	23	19	6	52	2nd/Canadian	4	5	Stanley Cup finals	Dick Irvin
1936-37	22	21	5	49	3rd/Canadian	0	2	Quarterfinals	Dick Irvin
1937-38	24	15	9	57	1st/Canadian			Stanley Cup finals	Dick Irvin
1938-39	19	20	9	47	3rd	5	5	Stanley Cup finals	Dick Irvin
1939-40	25	17	6	56	3rd	6	4	Stanley Cup finals	Dick Irvin
1940-41	28	14	6	62	2nd	3	4	Semifinals	Hap Day
1941-42	27	18	3	57	2nd	8	5	Stanley Cup champ	Hap Day
1942-43	22	19	9	53	3rd	2	4	League semifinals	Hap Day
1943-44	23	23	4	50	3rd	1	4	League semifinals	Hap Day
1944-45	24	22	4	52	3rd	8	5	Stanley Cup champ	Hap Day
1945-46	19	24	7	45	5th	—	—		Hap Day
1946-47	31	19	10	72	2nd	8	3	Stanley Cup champ	Hap Day
1947-48	32	15	13	77	1st	8	1	Stanley Cup champ	Hap Day
1948-49	22	25	13	57	4th	8	1	Stanley Cup champ	Hap Day
1949-50	31	27	12	74	3rd	3	4	League semifinals	Hap Day
1950-51	41	16	13	95	2nd	†8	2	Stanley Cup champ	Joe Primeau
1951-52	29	25	16	74	3rd	0	4	League semifinals	Joe Primeau
1952-53	27	30	13	67	5th	—	—		Joe Primeau
1953-54	32	24	14	78	3rd	1	4	League semifinals	King Clancy
1954-55	24	24	22	70	3rd	0	4	League semifinals	King Clancy
1955-56	24	33	13	61	4th	1	4	League semifinals	King Clancy
1956-57	21	34	15	57	5th	—	—		Howie Meeker
1957-58	21	38	11	53	6th	—	—		Billy Reay
1958-59	27	32	11	65	4th	5	7	Stanley Cup finals	Billy Reay, Punch Imlach
1959-60	35	26	9	79	2nd	4	6	Stanley Cup finals	Punch Imlach
1960-61	39	19	12	90	2nd	1	4	League semifinals	Punch Imlach
1961-62	37	22	11	85	2nd	8	4	Stanely Cup champ	Punch Imlach
1962-63	35	23	12	82	1st	8	2	Stanely Cup champ	Punch Imlach
1963-64	33	25	12	78	3rd	8	6	Stanley Cup champ	Punch Imlach
1964-65	30	26	14	74	4th	2	4	League semifinals	Punch Imlach
1965-66	34	25	11	79	3rd	0	4	League semifinals	Punch Imlach
1966-67	32	27	11	75	3rd	8	4	Stanley Cup champ	Punch Imlach
1967-68	33	31	10	76	5th/East	—	—		Punch Imlach
1968-69	35	26	15	85	4th/East	0	4	Division semifinals	Punch Imlach
1969-70	29	34	13	71	6th/East	—	—		John McLellan
1970-71	37	33	8	82	4th/East	2	4	Division semifinals	John McLellan
1971-72	33	31	14	80	4th/East	1	4	Division semifinals	John McLellan
1972-73	27	41	10	64	6th/East	—	—		John McLellan
1973-74	35	27	16	86	4th/East	0	4	Division semifinals	Red Kelly
1974-75	31	33	16	78	3rd/Adams	2	5	Quarterfinals	Red Kelly
1975-76	34	31	15	83	3rd/Adams	5	5	Quarterfinals	Red Kelly
1976-77	33	32	15	81	3rd/Adams	4	5	Quarterfinals	Red Kelly
1977-78	41	29	10	92	3rd/Adams	4	2	Quarterfinals	Roger Neilson
1978-79	34	33	13	81	3rd/Adams	4	7	Quarterfinals	Roger Neilson
1979-80	35	40	5	75	4th/Adams	0	3	Preliminaries	Floyd Smith
1980-81	28	37	15	71	5th/Adams	0	3	Preliminaries	Punch Imlach, Joe Crozier
1981-82	20	44	16	56	5th/Norris	—	—		Mike Nykoluk
1982-83	28	40	12	68	3rd/Norris	1	3	Division semifinals	Mike Nykoluk
1983-84	26	45	9	61	5th/Norris	—	—		Mike Nykoluk
1984-85	20	52	8	48	5th/Norris	—	—		Dan Maloney
1985-86	25	48	7	57	4th/Norris	6	4	Division finals	Dan Maloney
1986-87	32	42	6	70	4th/Norris	7	6	Division finals	John Brophy
1987-88	21	49	10	52	4th/Norris	2	4	Division semifinals	John Brophy
1988-89	28	46	6	62	5th/Norris	—	—		John Brophy, George Armstrong
1989-90	38	38	4	80	3rd/Norris	1	4	Division semifinals	Doug Carpenter
1990-91	23	46	11	57	5th/Norris	—	—		Doug Carpenter, Tom Watt
1991-92	30	43	7	67	5th/Norris	—	—		Tom Watt
1992-93	44	29	11	99	3rd/Norris	11	10	Conference finals	Pat Burns

*Won-lost record does not indicate tie(s) resulting from two-game, total-goals series that year (two-game, total-goals series were played from 1917-18 through 1935-36).
†Tied after one overtime (curfew law).
‡Toronto Arenas.
*Toronto St. Patricks (until April 14, 1927).

FIRST-ROUND ENTRY DRAFT CHOICES

Year   Player, Overall, Last Amateur Team (League)
1969—Ernie Moser, 9, Esteven (WCHL)
1970—Darryl Sittler, 8, London (OHL)
1971—No first-round selection
1972—George Ferguson, 11, Toronto (OHL)
1973—Lanny McDonald, 4, Medicine Hat (WCHL)
      Bob Neely, 10, Peterborough (OHL)
      Ian Turnbull, 15, Ottawa (OHL)
1974—Jack Valiquette, 13, Sault Ste. Marie (OHL)
1975—Don Ashby, 6, Calgary (WCHL)
1976—No first-round selection
1977—John Anderson, 11, Toronto (OHA)
      Trevor Johansen, 12, Toronto (OHA)
1978—No first-round selection
1979—Laurie Boschman, 9, Brandon (WHL)
1980—No first-round selection
1981—Jim Benning, 6, Portland (WHL)
1982—Gary Nylund, 3, Portland (WHL)

Year   Player, Overall, Last Amateur Team (League)
1983—Russ Courtnall, 7, Victoria (WHL)
1984—Al Iafrate, 4, U.S. Olympics/Belleville (OHL)
1985—*Wendel Clark, 1, Saskatoon (WHL)
1986—Vincent Damphousse, 6, Laval (QMJHL)
1987—Luke Richardson, 7, Peterborough (OHL)
1988—Scott Pearson, 6, Kingston (OHL)
1989—Scott Thornton, 3, Belleville (OHL)
      Rob Pearson, 12, Belleville (OHL)
      Steve Bancroft, 21, Belleville (OHL)
1990—Drake Berehowsky, 10, Kingston (OHL)
1991—No first-round selection
1992—Brandon Convery, 8, Sudbury (OHL)
      Grant Marshall, 23, Ottawa (OHL)
1993—Kenny Jonsson, 12, Rogle (Sweden)
      Landon Wilson, 19, Dubuque (USHL)

*Designates first player chosen in draft.

FRANCHISE LEADERS

Current players in boldface

FORWARDS/DEFENSEMEN
Games
George Armstrong	1187
Tim Horton	1185
Borje Salming	1099
Dave Keon	1062
Ron Ellis	1034
Bob Pulford	947
Darryl Sittler	844
Ron Stewart	838
Bob Baun	739
Frank Mahovlich	720

Goals
Darryl Sittler	389
Dave Keon	365
Ron Ellis	332
Rick Vaive	299
George Armstrong	296
Frank Mahovlich	296
Bob Pulford	251
Ted Kennedy	231
Lanny McDonald	219
Syl Apps	201

Assists
Borje Salming	620
Darryl Sittler	527
Dave Keon	493
George Armstrong	417

Tim Horton	349
Ted Kennedy	329
Bob Pulford	312
Ron Ellis	308
Norm Ullman	305
Ian Turnbull	302

Points
Darryl Sittler	916
Dave Keon	858
Borje Salming	768
George Armstrong	713
Ron Ellis	640
Frank Mahovlich	597
Bob Pulford	563
Ted Kennedy	560
Rick Vaive	537
Norm Ullman	471

Penalty minutes
Dave Williams	1670
Tim Horton	1389
Borje Salming	1292
Red Horner	1264
Bob Baun	1155
Wendel Clark	**1228**

Goaltenders
Games
Turk Broda	629
Johnny Bower	472

Mike Palmateer	296
Harry Lumley	267
Lorne Chabot	214
Bruce Gamble	210
Ken Wregget	200

Shutouts
Turk Broda	62
Harry Lumley	34
Lorne Chabot	33
Johnny Bower	32
George Hainsworth	19

Goals-against average
(2400 minutes minimum)
John Ross Roach	2.00
Al Rollins	2.05
Lorne Chabot	2.20
Harry Lumley	2.21
George Hainsworth	2.26
Jacques Plante	2.46
Felix Potvin	**2.50**
Johnny Bower	2.51
Turk Broda	2.53
Bernie Parent	2.59

Wins
Turk Broda	302
Johnny Bower	220
Mike Palmateer	129
Lorne Chabot	108
Harry Lumley	104

VANCOUVER CANUCKS

YEAR-BY-YEAR RECORDS

	REGULAR SEASON					PLAYOFFS			
Season	W	L	T	Pts.	Finish	W	L	Highest round	Coach
1970-71	24	46	8	56	6th/East	—	—		Hal Laycoe
1971-72	20	50	8	48	7th/East	—	—		Hal Laycoe
1972-73	22	47	9	53	7th/East	—	—		Vic Stasiuk
1973-74	24	43	11	59	7th/East	—	—		Bill McCreary, Phil Maloney
1974-75	38	32	10	86	1st/Smythe	1	4	Quarterfinals	Phil Maloney
1975-76	33	32	15	81	2nd/Smythe	0	2	Preliminaries	Phil Maloney
1976-77	25	42	13	63	4th/Smythe	—	—		Phil Maloney, Orland Kurtenbach
1977-78	20	43	17	57	3rd/Smythe	—	—		Orland Kurtenbach
1978-79	25	42	13	63	2nd/Smythe	1	2	Preliminaries	Harry Neale
1979-80	27	37	16	70	3rd/Smythe	1	3	Preliminaries	Harry Neale
1980-81	28	32	20	76	3rd/Smythe	0	3	Preliminaries	Harry Neale
1981-82	30	33	17	77	2nd/Smythe	11	6	Stanley Cup finals	Harry Neale, Roger Neilson
1982-83	30	35	15	75	3rd/Smythe	1	3	Division semifinals	Roger Neilson

Season		REGULAR SEASON					PLAYOFFS			
	W	L	T	Pts.	Finish	W	L	Highest round		Coach
1983-84	32	39	9	73	3rd/Smythe	1	3	Division semifinals		Roger Neilson, Harry Neale
1984-85	25	46	9	59	5th/Smythe	—	—			Bill Laforge, Harry Neale
1985-86	23	44	13	59	4th/Smythe	0	3	Division semifinals		Tom Watt
1986-87	29	43	8	66	5th/Smythe	—	—			Tom Watt
1987-88	25	46	9	59	5th/Smythe	—	—			Bob McCammon
1988-89	33	39	8	74	4th/Smythe	3	4	Division semifinals		Bob McCammon
1989-90	25	41	14	64	5th/Smythe	—	—			Bob McCammon
1990-91	28	43	9	65	4th/Smythe	2	4	Division semifinals		Bob McCammon, Pat Quinn
1991-92	42	26	12	96	1st/Smythe	6	7	Division finals		Pat Quinn
1992-93	46	29	9	101	1st/Smythe	6	6	Division finals		Pat Quinn

FIRST-ROUND ENTRY DRAFT CHOICES

Year	Player, Overall, Last Amateur Team (League)
1970	Dale Tallon, 2, Toronto (OHL)
1971	Jocelyn Guevremont, 3, Montreal (OHL)
1972	Don Lever, 3, Niagara Falls (OHL)
1973	Dennis Ververgaert, 3, London (OHL)
	Bob Dailey, 9, Toronto (OHL)
1974	No first-round selection
1975	Rick Blight, 10, Brandon (WCHL)
1976	No first-round selection
1977	Jere Gillis, 4, Sherbrooke (QMJHL)
1978	Bill Derlago, 4, Brandon (WCHL)
1979	Rick Vaive, 5, Birmingham (WHA)
1980	Rick Lanz, 7, Oshawa (OHL)
1981	Garth Butcher, 10, Regina (WHL)

Year	Player, Overall, Last Amateur Team (League)
1982	Michel Petit, 11, Sherbrooke (QMJHL)
1983	Cam Neely, 9, Portland (WHL)
1984	J.J. Daigneault, 10, Can. Ol./Longueuil (QMJHL)
1985	Jim Sandlak, 4, London (OHL)
1986	Dan Woodley, 7, Portland (WHL)
1987	No first-round selection
1988	Trevor Linden, 2, Medicine Hat (WHL)
1989	Jason Herter, 8, University of North Dakota
1990	Petr Nedved, 2, Seattle (WHL)
	Shawn Antoski, 18, North Bay (OHL)
1991	Alex Stojanov, 7, Hamilton (OHL)
1992	Libor Polasek, 21, TJ Vikovice (Czech.)
1993	Mike Wilson, 20, Sudbury (OHL)

FRANCHISE LEADERS

Current players in boldface

FORWARDS/DEFENSEMEN

Games

Stan Smyl	896
Harold Snepsts	781
Dennis Kearns	677
Doug Lidster	666
Thomas Gradin	613

Goals

Stan Smyl	262
Tony Tanti	250
Thomas Gradin	197
Don Lever	186
Petri Skriko	171

Assists

Stan Smyl	411
Thomas Gradin	353
Dennis Kearns	290
Andre Boudrias	267
Doug Lidster	242

Points

Stan Smyl	673
Thomas Gradin	550
Tony Tanti	470

Don Lever	407
Andre Boudrias	388

Penalty minutes

Garth Butcher	1668
Stan Smyl	1556
Harold Snepsts	1446
Tiger Williams	1314
Gino Odjick	**1014**

GOALTENDERS

Games

Richard Brodeur	377
Kirk McLean	**306**
Gary Smith	208
Dunc Wilson	148
Glen Hanlon	137
Frank Caprice	102
Curt Ridley	96
Cesare Maniago	93
Gary Bromley	73
Steve Weeks	66

Shutouts

Gary Smith	11
Kirk McLean	**13**
Richard Brodeur	6
Glen Hanlon	5

Gary Bromley	3
Ken Lockett	2
Cesare Maniago	2
Dunc Wilson	2

Goals-against average
(2400 minutes minimum)

Kirk McLean	**3.33**
Gary Smith	3.33
Steve Weeks	3.44
Glen Hanlon	3.56
Gary Bromley	3.63
Cesare Maniago	3.68
Curt Ridley	3.80
Richard Brodeur	3.87
Dunc Wilson	3.93
John Garrett	4.11

Wins

Kirk McLean	**128**
Richard Brodeur	126
Gary Smith	72
Glen Hanlon	43
Frank Caprice	31
Cesare Maniago	27
Gary Bromley	25
Curt Ridley	25
Dunc Wilson	24
John Garrett	22

WASHINGTON CAPITALS

YEAR-BY-YEAR RECORDS

Season		REGULAR SEASON					PLAYOFFS		
	W	L	T	Pts.	Finish	W	L	Highest round	Coach
1974-75	8	67	5	21	5th/Norris	—	—		Jim Anderson, Red Sullivan
									Milt Schmidt
1975-76	11	59	10	32	5th/Norris	—	—		Milt Schmidt, Tom McVie
1976-77	24	42	14	62	4th/Norris	—	—		Tom McVie
1977-78	17	49	14	48	5th/Norris	—	—		Tom McVie
1978-79	24	41	15	63	4th/Norris	—	—		Dan Belisle
1979-80	27	40	13	67	5th/Patrick	—	—		Dan Belisle, Gary Green

	REGULAR SEASON					PLAYOFFS			
Season	W	L	T	Pts.	Finish	W	L	Highest round	Coach
1980-81	26	36	18	70	5th/Patrick	—	—		Gary Green
1981-82	26	41	13	65	5th/Patrick	—	—		Gary Green, Roger Crozier
									Bryan Murray
1982-83	39	25	16	94	3rd/Patrick	1	3	Division semifinals	Bryan Murray
1983-84	48	27	5	101	2nd/Patrick	4	4	Division finals	Bryan Murray
1984-85	46	25	9	101	2nd/Patrick	2	3	Division semifinals	Bryan Murray
1985-86	50	23	7	107	2nd/Patrick	5	4	Division finals	Bryan Murray
1986-87	38	32	10	86	2nd/Patrick	3	4	Division finals	Bryan Murray
1987-88	38	33	9	85	2nd/Patrick	7	7	Division finals	Bryan Murray
1988-89	41	29	10	92	1st/Patrick	2	4	Division semifinals	Bryan Murray
1989-90	36	38	6	78	3rd/Patrick	8	7	Conference finals	Bryan Murray, Terry Murray
1990-91	37	36	7	81	3rd/Patrick	5	6	Division finals	Terry Murray
1991-92	45	27	8	98	2nd/Patrick	3	4	Division finals	Terry Murray
1992-93	43	34	7	93	2nd/Patrick	2	4	Division semifinals	Terry Murray

FIRST-ROUND ENTRY DRAFT CHOICES

Year Player, Overall, Last Amateur Team (League)

1974—*Greg Joly, 1, Regina (WCHL)
1975—Alex Forsyth, 18, Kingston (OHA)
1976—*Rick Green, 1, London (OHL)
      Greg Carroll, 15, Medicine Hat (WCHL)
1977—Robert Picard, 3, Montreal (QMJHL)
1978—Ryan Walter, 2, Seattle (WCHL)
      Tim Coulis, 18, Hamilton (OHL)
1979—Mike Gartner, 4, Cincinnati (WHA)
1980—Darren Veitch, 5, Regina (WHL)
1981—Bobby Carpenter, 3, St. John's H.S. (Mass.)
1982—Scott Stevens, 5, Kitchener (OHL)
1983—No first-round selection
1984—Kevin Hatcher, 17, North Bay (OHL)

Year Player, Overall, Last Amateur Team (League)

1985—Yvon Corriveau, 19, Toronto (OHL)
1986—Jeff Greenlaw, 19, Team Canada
1987—No first-round selection
1988—Reggie Savage, 15, Victoriaville (QMJHL)
1989—Olaf Kolzig, 19, Tri-City (WHL)
1990—John Slaney, 9, Cornwall (OHL)
1991—Pat Peake, 14, Detroit (OHL)
      Trevor Halverson, 21, North Bay (OHL)
1992—Sergei Gonchar, 14, Dynamo Moscow (CIS)
1993—Brendan Witt, 11, Seattle (WHL)
      Jason Allison, 17, London (OHL)

*Designates first player chosen in draft.

FRANCHISE LEADERS

Current players in boldface

FORWARDS/DEFENSEMEN

Games

Mike Gartner	758
Rod Langway	726
Bengt Gustafsson	629
Kevin Hatcher	**613**
Scott Stevens	601
Bobby Gould	600
Kelly Miller	**519**
Mike Ridley	**507**
Dave Christian	504
Michal Pivonka	**501**

Goals

Mike Gartner	397
Bengt Gustafsson	196
Dave Christian	193
Mike Ridley	**192**
Bob Carpenter	**188**
Dennis Maruk	182
Bobby Gould	134
Kevin Hatcher	**133**
Alan Haworth	129
Dale Hunter	**252**

Assists

Mike Gartner	392
Bengt Gustafsson	359
Scott Stevens	331

Mike Ridley	285
Michal Pivonka	266
Larry Murphy	259
Kevin Hatcher	253
Dale Hunter	252
Dennis Maruk	249
Dave Christian	224

Points

Mike Gartner	789
Bengt Gustafsson	555
Mike Ridley	**477**
Dennis Maruk	431
Scott Stevens	429
Dave Christian	417
Bobby Carpenter	**395**
Michal Pivonka	**392**
Kevin Hatcher	**386**
Dale Hunter	381

Penalty minutes

Scott Stevens	1630
Dale Hunter	**1329**
Alan May	**1092**
Kevin Hatcher	**890**
Mike Gartner	770
Yvon Labre	756
Greg Adams	694
Gord Lane	614
Lou Franceschetti	562
Randy Holt	525

GOALTENDERS

Games

Don Beaupre	**216**
Al Jensen	173
Ron Low	145
Pat Riggin	143
Pete Peeters	139
Bernie Wolfe	120
Clint Malarchuk	96

Goals-against average
(2400 minutes minimum)

Pat Riggin	3.02
Pete Peeters	3.06
Don Beaupre	**3.10**
Bob Mason	3.16
Al Jensen	3.26

Wins

Don Beaupre	**104**
Al Jensen	94
Pete Peeters	70
Pat Riggin	67
Clint Malarchuk	40

Shutouts

Don Beaupre	**10**
Al Jensen	8
Pete Peeters	7
Pat Riggin	6
Clint Malarchuk	5

WINNIPEG JETS

YEAR-BY-YEAR RECORDS

	REGULAR SEASON					PLAYOFFS			
Season	W	L	T	Pts.	Finish	W	L	Highest round	Coach
1972-73*	43	31	4	90	1st	9	5	Avco World Cup finals	Nick Mickoski, Bobby Hull
1973-74*	34	39	5	73	4th	0	4	League quarterfinals	Nick Mickoski, Bobby Hull

Season	W	L	T	Pts.	Finish	W	L	Highest round	Coach
1974-75*	38	35	5	81	3rd	—	—		Rudy Pilous
1975-76*	52	27	2	106	1st	12	1	Avco World Cup champ	Bobby Kromm
1976-77*	46	32	2	94	2nd	11	9	Avco World Cup finals	Bobby Kromm
1977-78*	50	28	2	102	1st	8	1	Avco World Cup champ	Larry Hillman
1978-79*	39	35	6	84	3rd	8	2	Avco World Cup champ	Larry Hillman, Tom McVie
1979-80	20	49	11	51	5th/Smythe	—	—		Tom McVie
1980-81	9	57	14	32	6th/Smythe	—	—		Tom McVie, Bill Sutherland, Mike Smith
1981-82	33	33	14	80	2nd/Norris	1	3	Division semifinals	Tom Watt
1982-83	33	39	8	74	4th/Smythe	0	3	Division semifinals	Tom Watt
1983-84	31	38	11	73	3rd/Smythe	0	3	Division semifinals	Tom Watt, Barry Long
1984-85	43	27	10	96	2nd/Smythe	3	5	Division finals	Barry Long
1985-86	26	47	7	59	3rd/Smythe	0	3	Division semifinals	Barry Long, John Ferguson
1986-87	40	32	8	88	3rd/Smythe	4	6	Division finals	Dan Maloney
1987-88	33	36	11	77	3rd/Smythe	1	4	Division semifinals	Dan Maloney
1988-89	26	42	12	64	5th/Smythe	—	—		Dan Maloney, Rick Bowness
1989-90	37	32	11	85	3rd/Smythe	3	4	Division semifinals	Bob Murdoch
1990-91	26	43	11	63	5th/Smythe	—	—		Bob Murdoch
1991-92	33	32	15	81	4th/Smythe	3	4	Division semifinals	John Paddock
1992-93	40	37	7	87	4th/Smythe	2	4	Division semifinals	John Paddock

*Members of World Hockey Association.

FIRST-ROUND ENTRY DRAFT CHOICES

Year	Player, Overall, Last Amateur Team (League)
1979	Jimmy Mann, 19, Sherbrooke (QMJHL)
1980	David Babych, 2, Portland (WHL)
1981	*Dale Hawerchuk, 1, Cornwall (QMJHL)
1982	Jim Kyte, 12, Cornwall (OHL)
1983	Andrew McBain, 8, North Bay (OHL)
	Bobby Dollas, 14, Laval (QMJHL)
1984	No first-round selection
1985	Ryan Stewart, 18, Kamloops (WHL)
1986	Pat Elynuik, 8, Prince Albert (WHL)
1987	Bryan Marchment, 16, Belleville (OHL)
1988	Teemu Selanne, 10, Jokerit (Finland)

Year	Player, Overall, Last Amateur Team (League)
1989	Stu Barnes, 4, Tri-City (WHL)
1990	Keith Tkachuk, 19, Malden Cath. H.S. (Mass.)
1991	Aaron Ward, 5, University of Michigan
1992	Sergei Bautin, 17, Dynamo Moscow (CIS)
1993	Mats Lindgren, 15, Skelleftea (Sweden)

*Designates first player chosen in draft.
NOTE: Winnipeg chose Scott Campbell, Morris Lukowich and Markus Mattsson as priority selections before the 1979 expansion draft.

FRANCHISE LEADERS

Current players in boldface

FORWARDS/DEFENSEMEN

Games
Thomas Steen	843
Dale Hawerchuk	713
Doug Smail	691
Randy Carlyle	564
Ron Wilson	536

Goals
Dale Hawerchuk	379
Paul MacLean	248
Thomas Steen	240
Doug Smail	189
Morris Lukowich	168

Assists
Dale Hawerchuk	550
Thomas Steen	511
Paul MacLean	270
Dave Babych	248
Fredrik Olausson	244

Points
Dale Hawerchuk	929
Thomas Steen	751
Paul MacLean	518
Doug Smail	397
Laurie Boschman	379

Penalty minutes
Laurie Boschman	1338
Jim Kyte	772
Tim Watters	760

Randy Carlyle	736
Paul MacLean	726

GOALTENDERS

Shutouts
Bob Essensa	13
Daniel Berthiaume	4
Markus Mattsson	3
Stephane Beauregard	2
Dan Bouchard	2
Doug Soetaert	2
Ed Staniowski	2

Wins
Bob Essensa	97
Brian Hayward	63
Daniel Berthiaume	50
Eldon Reddick	41

MINOR LEAGUES

American Hockey League

International Hockey League

East Coast Hockey League

Central Hockey League

Colonial Hockey League

AMERICAN HOCKEY LEAGUE

LEAGUE OFFICE

Chairman of the board
Robert W. Clarke
President and treasurer
Jack A. Butterfield
Vice president and general counsel
Macgregor Kilpatrick
Vice president, secretary
Gordon C. Anziano

Asst. director of marketing
Maria D'Agostino
Statistician
Hellen Schoeder
Media relations
Steve Luce

Address
425 Union Street
West Springfield, MA 01089
Phone
413-781-2030
FAX
413-733-4767

TEAMS

ADIRONDACK RED WINGS

President
Doug MacLean
Head coach
Newell Brown
Home ice
Glens Falls Civic Center
Address
1 Civic Center Plaza
Glens Falls, NY 12801
Seating capacity
4,806
NHL affiliation
Detroit Red Wings
Phone
518-798-0366
FAX
518-798-0816

ALBANY RIVER RATS

General manager
Dave Hanson
Head coach
Robbie Ftorek
Home ice
Knickerbocker Arena
Address
51 South Pearl St.
Albany, NY 12207
Seating capacity
6,500
NHL affiliation
New Jersey Devils
Phone
518-487-2244
FAX
518-487-2248

BINGHAMTON RANGERS

Managing Partner
Tom Mitchell
Head coach
To be announced
Home ice
Broome County Veterans
Memorial Arena
Address
One Stuart Street
Binghamton, NY 13901
Seating capacity
4,803
NHL affiliation
New York Rangers
Phone
607-723-8937
FAX
607-724-6892

CAPE BRETON OILERS

General manager
Dave Andrews
Head coach
George Burnett
Home ice
Centre 200
Address
481 George Street
Sydney, Nova Scotia B1T 6R7
Seating capacity
4,850
NHL affiliation
Edmonton Oilers
Phone
902-562-0780
FAX
902-562-1806

CORNWALL ACES

General manager
Gilles Leger
Head coach
Doug Carpenter
Home ice
Cornwall Civic Complex
Address
100 Water Street
Cornwall, Ont. K6H 6G4
Seating capacity
3,991
NHL affiliation
Quebec Nordiques
Phone
613-937-2237
FAX
613-933-9632

FREDERICTON CANADIENS

Director of operations
Wayne Gamble
Head coach
Paulin Bordeleau
Home ice
Aitken University Centre
Address
P.O. Box HABS
Fredericton, N.B. E3B 4Y2
Seating capacity
3,583
NHL affiliation
Montreal Canadiens
Phone
506-459-4227
FAX
506-457-4250

HAMILTON CANUCKS

General manager
Pat Hickey
Head coach
Jack McIlhargey
Home ice
Copp Coliseum
Address
85 York St.
Hamilton, Ont. L8R 3L4
Seating capacity
17,500
NHL affiliation
Vancouver Canucks
Phone
416-546-1122
FAX
416-522-2138

HERSHEY BEARS

Asst. general manager
Doug Yingst
Head coach
To be announced
Home ice
Hersheypark Arena
Address
P.O. Box 866
Hershey, PA 17033
Seating capacity
7,256
NHL affiliation
Philadelphia Flyers
Phone
717-534-3380
FAX
717-534-3383

MONCTON HAWKS

General manager
Mike Smith
Head coach
Rob Laird
Home ice
Moncton Coliseum
Address
P.O. Box 25067
Moncton, N.B. E1C 9M9
Seating capacity
6,800
NHL affiliation
Winnipeg Jets
Phone
506-857-4000
FAX
506-859-8919

PORTLAND PIRATES

President
Godfrey Wood
Head coach
Barry Trotz
Home ice
Cumberland County Civic Center
Address
1 Civic Center Square
Portland, ME 04101
Seating capacity
6,746
NHL affiliation
Washington Capitals
Phone
207-828-4665
FAX
207-773-3278

PRINCE EDWARD ISLAND SENATORS

Director of operations
Gary Thompson
Head coach
Don MacAdam
Home ice
Charlottetown Civic Centre
Address
P.O. Box 22093
Charlottetown, PEI C1A 9J2
Seating capacity
3,600
NHL affiliation
Ottawa Senators
Phone
902-566-5450
FAX
902-566-5170

PROVIDENCE BRUINS

Chief executive officer
Ed Anderson
Head coach
Mike O'Connell
Home ice
Providence Civic Center
Address
1 LaSalle Square
Providence, RI 02903
Seating capacity
12,000
NHL affiliation
Boston Bruins
Phone
401-273-5000
FAX
401-273-5004

ROCHESTER AMERICANS

General manager
Joe Baumann
Head coach
John VanBoxmeer
Home ice
War Memorial Auditorium
Address
100 Exchange Street
Rochester, NY 14614
Seating capacity
6,973
NHL affiliation
Buffalo Sabres
Phone
716-454-5335
FAX
716-454-3954

SAINT JOHN FLAMES

General manager
Al Coates
Head coach
Bobby Francis
Home ice
Harbour Station
Address
P.O. Box 4040, Station "B"
Saint John, NB E2M 5E6
Seating capacity
5,400

NHL affiliation
Calgary Flames
Phone
506-635-2637
FAX
506-663-4625

ST. JOHN'S MAPLE LEAFS

General manager
Glenn Stanford
Head coach
Marc Crawford
Home ice
St. John's Memorial Stadium
Address
6 Logy Bay Road
St. John's, Newfoundland A1A 1J3
Seating capacity
3,910
NHL affiliation
Toronto Maple Leafs
Phone
709-726-1010
FAX
709-726-1511

SPRINGFIELD INDIANS

President
Peter R. Cooney
Head coach
Paul Gillis
Home ice
Springfield Civic Center
Address
P.O. Box 4896
Springfield, MA 01101
Seating capacity
7,452
NHL affiliation
Hartford Whalers
Phone
413-736-4546
FAX
413-788-6786

1992-93 REGULAR SEASON

FINAL STANDINGS

ATLANTIC DIVISION

Team	G	W	L	T	Pts.	GF	GA
St. John's	80	41	26	13	95	351	308
Fredericton	80	38	31	11	87	314	278
Cape Breton	80	36	32	12	84	356	336
Moncton	80	31	33	16	78	292	306
Halifax	80	33	37	10	76	312	348

NORTHERN DIVISION

Team	G	W	L	T	Pts.	GF	GA
Providence	80	46	32	2	94	384	348
Adirondack	80	36	35	9	81	331	308
Capital District	80	34	34	12	80	280	285
Springfield	80	25	41	14	64	282	336
New Haven	80	22	47	11	55	262	343

SOUTHERN DIVISION

Team	G	W	L	T	Pts.	GF	GA
Binghamton	80	57	13	10	124	392	246
Rochester	80	40	33	7	87	348	332
Utica	80	33	36	11	77	325	354
Baltimore	80	28	40	12	68	318	353
Hershey	80	27	41	12	66	316	339
Hamilton	80	29	45	6	64	284	327

INDIVIDUAL LEADERS

Goals: Chris Tancill, Adirondack (59)
Assists: Don Biggs, Binghamton (84)
Points: Don Biggs, Binghamton (138)
Penalty minutes: Kevin Kaminski, Halifax (345)
Goaltending average: Corey Hirsch, Binghamton (2.79)
Shutouts: Corey Schwab, Utica (2)

	Games	G	A	Pts.
Dan Currie, Cape Breton	75	57	41	98
Tim Sweeney, Providence	60	41	55	96
Yanic Perreault, St. John's	79	49	46	95
Craig Duncanson, Binghamton	69	35	59	94
Todd Simon, Rochester	68	27	66	93
Mike Stevens, Binghamton	68	31	61	92
Jozef Stumpel, Providence	56	31	61	92
Steve Larouche, Fredericton	77	27	65	92
John LeBlanc, Moncton	77	48	40	88
Bill McDougall, Cape Breton	71	42	46	88
Micah Aivazoff, Adirondack	79	32	53	85
Stephane Morin, Hamilton	70	31	54	85
Rob Cimetta, St. John's	76	28	57	85
Dave Tomlinson, St. John's	70	36	48	84

TOP SCORERS

	Games	G	A	Pts.
Don Biggs, Binghamton	78	54	84	138
Iain Fraser, Capital District	74	41	69	110
Tim Tookey, Hershey	80	38	70	108
Chris Tancill, Adirondack	68	59	43	102
Peter Ciavaglia, Rochester	64	35	67	102
Brian McReynolds, Binghamton	79	30	70	100

INDIVIDUAL STATISTICS

ADIRONDACK RED WINGS

SCORING

	Games	G	A	Pts.	Pen.
Chris Tancill	68	59	43	102	62
Micah Aivazoff	79	32	53	85	100
Gary Shuchuk	47	24	53	77	66
Ken Quinney	63	32	34	66	15
Viacheslav Kozlov	45	23	36	59	54
Jason York	77	15	40	55	86
Bobby Dollas	64	7	36	43	54
Darren McCarty	73	17	19	36	278
Sylvain Couturier	29	17	17	34	12
Mike Casselman	60	12	19	31	27
Mike Sillinger	15	10	20	30	31
Igor Malykhin	78	6	22	28	95
Petr Hrbek	37	10	12	22	6
Jeff Rohlicek	29	6	16	22	20
Jim Cummins	43	16	4	20	179
Marc Potvin	37	8	12	20	109
Kirk Tomlinson	50	8	12	20	224
Bob Boughner	69	1	16	17	190
Stewart Malgunas	45	3	12	15	39
Gord Kruppke	41	2	12	14	197
Dave Flanagan	30	6	7	13	17
Dennis Vial	30	2	11	13	177
Michael Maurice	25	4	7	11	4
Dmitri Motkov	41	3	7	10	30
Bob Wilkie	14	0	5	5	20
Pete Stauber	12	2	2	4	8
John Ogrodnick	4	2	2	4	0
Rick Judson	7	3	0	3	0
Martin Lapointe	8	1	2	3	9
Jim Bermingham	21	0	2	2	8
Joe Frederick	5	0	1	1	2
Derek Booth	8	0	1	1	25
Chris Osgood (goalie)	46	0	1	1	12
Iain Duncan	1	0	0	0	2
Guy Dupuis	1	0	0	0	0
Dave Gagnon (goalie)	1	0	0	0	0
Scott King (goalie)	1	0	0	0	0
Kelly Sorensen	1	0	0	0	4
Mark Woolf	1	0	0	0	0
Kory Kocur	2	0	0	0	0
Serge Anglehart	3	0	0	0	4
Alex Hicks	3	0	0	0	0
Allan Bester (goalie)	41	0	0	0	8

GOALTENDING

	Games	Min.	Goals	SO	Avg.
Scott King	1	60	1	0	1.00
Allan Bester	41	2268	133(6)	1	3.52
Chris Osgood	45	2438	159(4)	0	3.91
Dave Gagnon	1	60	5	0	5.00

BALTIMORE SKIPJACKS

SCORING

	Games	G	A	Pts.	Pen.
John Byce	62	35	44	79	26
Mike Boback	69	11	68	79	14
John Slaney	79	20	46	66	60
Reggie Savage	40	37	18	55	28
Jeff Nelson	72	14	38	52	12
Steve Konowalchuk	37	18	28	46	74
Martin Jiranek	64	18	26	44	39
Jason Woolley	29	14	27	41	22
Trevor Halverson	67	19	21	40	170
Tim Taylor	41	15	16	31	49
Mark Hunter	28	13	18	31	66
Eric Murano	32	16	14	30	10
Darren McAusland	61	14	14	28	16
Jeff Greenlaw	49	12	14	26	66
Chris Longo	74	7	18	25	52
Brad Schlegel	61	3	20	23	40
Ken Sabourin	30	5	14	19	68
Ken Klee	77	4	14	18	93
Randy Pearce	42	12	5	17	46
Rob Leask	68	4	8	12	76
Keith Jones	8	7	3	10	4
Jiri Vykoukal	13	3	7	10	12
Jim Mathieson	46	3	5	8	88
Rod Taylor	18	3	4	7	2
Victor Gervais	10	2	4	6	2
Shawn Anderson	10	1	5	6	8
Steve Martell	5	3	2	5	0
Terry Chitaroni	16	2	1	3	14
Martin Gendron	10	1	2	3	2
Al MacIsaac	13	1	2	3	20
Bob Babcock	26	0	2	2	93
Byron Dafoe (goalie)	48	0	2	2	14
Brian Martin	2	1	0	1	0
Mark Ouimet	1	0	1	1	0
Randy Burridge	2	0	1	1	2
Steve Poapst	7	0	1	1	4
Trevor Duhaime	1	0	0	0	0
Mark Bernard (goalie)	2	0	0	0	0
Darren Schwartz	2	0	0	0	4
John Blessman	6	0	0	0	4
Mike Parson (goalie)	16	0	0	0	0
Duane Derksen (goalie)	27	0	0	0	12

GOALTENDING

	Games	Min.	Goals	SO	Avg.
Mike Parson	16	916	58(4)	0	3.80
Duane Derksen	26	1247	86(3)	0	4.14
Byron Dafoe	48	2617	191(4)	1	4.38
Mark Bernard	2	64	7	0	6.56

BINGHAMTON RANGERS

SCORING

	Games	G	A	Pts.	Pen.
Don Biggs	78	54	84	138	112
Brian McReynolds	79	30	70	100	88
Craig Duncanson	69	35	59	94	126
Mike Stevens	68	31	61	92	230
Per Djoos	70	16	53	69	75
Steven King	53	35	33	68	100
Dave Thomlinson	54	25	35	60	61
Chris Cichocki	65	23	29	52	78
Daniel Lacroix	73	21	22	43	255
Rick Bennett	76	15	22	37	114
Mike Hurlbut	45	11	25	36	46
Sergei Zubov	30	7	29	36	14
Peter Andersson	27	11	22	33	16
Dave Marcinyshyn	67	5	25	30	184
Jean-Yves Roy	49	13	15	28	21
Alexei Kovalev	13	13	11	24	35
Rob Kenny	66	12	11	23	56
Joby Messier	60	5	16	21	63
Brad Tiley	26	6	10	16	19
Peter Fiorentino	64	9	5	14	286
Michael Stewart	68	2	10	12	71
Dave Archibald	8	6	3	9	10
Darren Langdon	18	3	4	7	115
Fredrik Jax	20	3	2	5	4
John Vary	12	0	2	2	8
Greg Capson	7	1	0	1	4
Mike Reier	3	0	1	1	0
Darcy Werenka	3	0	1	1	2
Boris Rousson (goalie)	31	0	1	1	0
Greg Spenrath	1	0	0	0	2
Sasha Lakovic	3	0	0	0	0
Mike Richter (goalie)	5	0	0	0	0
Corey Hirsch (goalie)	46	0	0	0	2

GOALTENDING

	Games	Min.	Goals	SO	Avg.
Mike Richter	5	305	6	0	1.18
Corey Hirsch	46	2692	125	1	2.79
Boris Rousson	31	1847	115	0	3.74

CAPE BRETON OILERS

SCORING

	Games	G	A	Pts.	Pen.
Dan Currie	75	57	41	98	73
Bill McDougall	71	42	46	88	161
David Haas	73	22	56	78	121
Shaun Van Allen	43	14	62	76	68
Steven Rice	51	34	28	62	63
Craig Fisher	75	32	29	61	74
Roman Oksiuta	43	26	25	51	22
Jeff Bloemberg	76	6	45	51	34
Scott Thornton	58	23	27	50	102
Kirk Maltby	73	22	23	45	130
Peter White	64	12	28	40	10
Shjon Podein	38	18	21	39	32
Francois Leroux	55	10	24	34	139
Brian Curran	61	2	24	26	223
Gord Mark	60	3	21	24	78
Ian Herbers	77	7	15	22	129
Richard Borgo	45	7	13	20	26
Vladimir Vujtek	20	10	9	19	14
Marc Laforge	77	1	12	13	208
Scott Allison	49	3	5	8	34
Darcy Martini	47	1	6	7	36
Al MacIsaac	13	1	3	4	4
Josef Beranek	6	1	2	3	8
Wayne Cowley (goalie)	42	0	3	3	8
Brad Werenka	4	1	1	2	4
Rhys Hollyman	7	1	1	2	6
Rob MacInnis	2	0	2	2	0
Andrew Verner (goalie)	36	0	1	1	0
Dean Antos	2	0	0	0	0
Shane Bogden	3	0	0	0	0

	Games	G	A	Pts.	Pen.
Scott Campbell	10	0	0	0	8
Norm Foster (goalie)	10	0	0	0	0

GOALTENDING

	Games	Min.	Goals	SO	Avg.
Andrew Verner	36	1974	126(1)	1	3.83
Wayne Cowley	42	2334	152(4)	1	3.91
Norm Foster	10	560	53	0	5.68

CAPITAL DISTRICT ISLANDERS

SCORING

	Games	G	A	Pts.	Pen.
Iain Fraser	74	41	69	110	16
Brent Grieve	79	34	28	62	122
Chris Taylor	77	19	43	62	32
Richard Kromm	79	20	34	54	28
Graeme Townshend	67	29	21	50	45
Steve Junker	79	16	31	47	20
Scott Scissons	43	14	30	44	33
Dave Chyzowski	66	15	21	36	177
Jeff Finley	61	6	29	35	34
Sean LeBrun	39	11	20	31	25
Wayne Doucet	72	11	16	27	155
Travis Green	20	12	11	23	39
Brad Turner	65	8	11	19	71
Dennis Vaske	42	4	15	19	70
Joni Lehto	57	4	13	17	33
Marty McInnis	10	4	12	16	2
Brad Dalgarno	19	10	4	14	16
Dean Chynoweth	52	3	10	13	197
Kevin Cheveldayoff	79	3	8	11	113
Wayne McBean	20	1	9	10	35
Tom Kurvers	7	3	4	7	8
Tom Searle	9	2	3	5	2
Dean Ewen	25	2	3	5	60
Martin LaCroix	20	1	4	5	21
Phil Huber	16	1	4	5	4
Jeff Kampersal	8	1	3	4	0
Vladimir Malakhov	3	2	1	3	11
Dan Marois	4	2	0	2	0
Ray Ferraro	1	0	2	2	2
Jamie McLennan (goalie)	38	0	2	2	16
Clayton Young	9	1	0	1	2
Steve Beadle	4	0	1	1	0
Richard Pilon	6	0	1	1	8
Dale Kushner	7	0	1	1	29
Rick Hayward	19	0	1	1	80
Danny Lorenz (goalie)	44	0	1	1	2
Trevor Dam	1	0	0	0	0
Gary Nylund	2	0	0	0	0
Chris Pryor	3	0	0	0	6
Jason Widmer	4	0	0	0	2
Mark Fitzpatrick (goalie)	5	0	0	0	2
Kord Cernich	6	0	0	0	4
Jeff Jablonski	6	0	0	0	2

GOALTENDING

	Games	Min.	Goals	SO	Avg.
Jamie McLennan	38	2171	117(2)	1	3.23
Danny Lorenz	44	2412	146(2)	1	3.63
Mark Fitzpatrick	5	284	18	0	3.80

FREDERICTON CANADIENS

SCORING

	Games	G	A	Pts.	Pen.
Steve Larouche	77	27	65	92	52
Pierre Sevigny	80	36	40	76	113
Turner Stevenson	79	25	34	59	102
Patrik Carnback	45	20	37	57	45
Oleg Petrov	55	26	29	55	36
Jesse Belanger	39	19	32	51	24
Luc Gauthier	78	9	33	42	167
Patric Kjellberg	41	10	27	37	14
Lindsay Vallis	65	18	16	34	38
Robert Guillet	42	16	15	31	38

	Games	G	A	Pts.	Pen.
Yves Sarault	59	14	17	31	41
Charles Poulin	58	12	19	31	99
Craig Ferguson	55	15	13	28	20
Alain Cote	61	10	17	27	83
Gerry Fleming	64	9	17	26	262
Paul Dipietro	26	8	16	24	16
Eric Charron	54	3	13	16	93
Ed Ronan	16	10	5	15	15
Donald Brashear	76	11	3	14	261
Steve Veilleux	63	3	11	14	94
Timothy Chase	25	4	8	12	16
Darcy Simon	57	2	7	9	257
Gilbert Dionne	3	4	3	7	0
Eric Brule	17	1	5	6	16
Eric Ricard	14	0	5	5	18
Sean Hill	6	1	3	4	10
Les Kuntar (goalie)	42	0	3	3	8
Ryan Kuwabara	10	0	2	2	4
Christian Proulx	2	1	0	1	2
Marc Laniel	7	0	1	1	6
Frederic Chabot (goalie)	45	0	0	0	16

GOALTENDING

	Games	Min.	Goals	SO	Avg.
Frederic Chabot	45	2544	141(3)	0	3.33
Les Kuntar	42	2315	130(4)	0	3.37

HALIFAX CITADELS

SCORING

	Games	G	A	Pts.	Pen.
Niklas Andersson	76	32	50	82	42
Mark Vermette	67	42	37	79	32
Denis Chasse	75	35	41	76	242
Kevin Kaminski	79	27	37	64	345
Dwayne Norris	50	25	28	53	62
Len Esau	75	11	31	42	79
Stephane Charbonneau	56	18	20	38	125
Mario Doyon	79	5	31	36	73
Ed Ward	70	13	19	32	56
Michel Mongeau	22	13	18	31	10
David Karpa	71	4	27	31	167
Steve Tuttle	22	11	17	28	2
Jim Sprott	77	6	21	27	180
Bill Lindsay	20	11	13	24	18
Jon Klemm	80	3	20	23	32
Ivan Matulik	56	7	15	22	36
Randy Velischek	49	6	16	22	18
Bryan Deasley	37	9	11	20	46
Chris Simon	36	12	6	18	131
Mike McKee	32	6	7	13	25
Herb Raglan	28	3	9	12	83
Andy Rymsha	43	4	6	10	62
Martin Simard	13	3	4	7	17
John Tanner (goalie)	51	0	5	5	14
Scott Pearson	5	3	1	4	25
Serge Roberge	16	2	2	4	34
Everett Sanipass	9	1	3	4	36
Roger Larche	3	0	1	1	2
Gerald Bzdel	5	0	1	1	16
Paul Krake (goalie)	17	0	1	1	2
Patrick LaBrecque (goalie)	20	0	1	1	14
Dean Zayonce	22	0	1	1	6
Darryl Noren	1	0	0	0	0
Stephane Fiset (goalie)	3	0	0	0	0
Marc Saumier	5	0	0	0	4

GOALTENDING

	Games	Min.	Goals	SO	Avg.
Stephane Fiset	3	180	11	0	3.67
Paul Krake	17	916	57(1)	1	3.73
John Tanner	51	2852	199(4)	0	4.19
Patrick LaBrecque	20	914	76	0	4.99

HAMILTON CANUCKS

SCORING

	Games	G	A	Pts.	Pen.
Stephane Morin	70	31	54	85	49
Neil Eisenhut	72	22	40	62	41
Eric Murano	42	25	24	49	10
Sandy Moger	78	23	26	49	57
Doug Torrel	75	16	28	44	24
Dane Jackson	68	23	20	43	59
Dan Kesa	62	16	24	40	76
Jay Mazur	59	21	17	38	30
Tim Taylor	36	15	22	37	37
Mario Marois	68	5	27	32	86
Rick Vaive	38	16	15	31	34
Phil Von Stefenelli	78	11	20	31	75
Jason Herter	70	7	16	23	68
Libor Polasek	60	7	12	19	34
Jiri Slegr	21	4	14	18	42
Rick Lessard	52	0	17	17	151
Troy Neumeier	79	3	11	14	73
Jassen Cullimore	56	5	7	12	60
Michael Maurice	13	3	7	10	6
Mark Cipriano	24	6	3	9	49
Mike Peca	9	6	3	9	11
Garry Valk	7	3	6	9	6
Robin Bawa	23	3	4	7	58
Shawn Antoski	41	3	4	7	172
Jeff Christian	11	2	5	7	35
Alain Deeks	18	0	6	6	6
Jason Christie	11	3	2	5	8
Alex Stojanov	4	4	0	4	0
Enrico Ciccone	6	1	3	4	44
Barry Dreger	13	0	3	3	50
Brian Loney	3	0	2	2	0
Dave Capuano	4	0	1	1	0
Mike Fountain (goalie)	12	0	1	1	0
Jason Fitzsimmons (goalie)	14	0	1	1	0
Troy Gamble (goalie)	14	0	1	1	15
Bob Mason (goalie)	44	0	1	1	2
Cam Brown	1	0	0	0	2
Serge Tkachenko (goalie)	1	0	0	0	2

GOALTENDING

	Games	Min.	Goals	SO	Avg.
Serge Tkachenko	1	60	3	0	3.00
Bob Mason	44	2601	159(2)	0	3.67
Jason Fitzsimmons	14	788	53(1)	0	4.04
Mike Fountain	12	618	46	0	4.47
Troy Gamble	14	769	62(1)	0	4.84

HERSHEY BEARS

SCORING

	Games	G	A	Pts.	Pen.
Tim Tookey	80	38	70	108	63
Wes Walz	78	35	45	80	106
Chris Jensen	74	33	47	80	95
Len Barrie	61	31	45	76	162
Al Conroy	60	28	32	60	130
Pat Murray	69	21	32	53	63
Andre Faust	62	26	25	51	71
Eric Dandenault	72	20	19	39	118
Yanick Dupre	63	13	24	37	22
Bob Wilkie	28	7	25	32	18
Corey Foster	80	9	25	34	102
Daniel Dore	65	12	10	22	192
Glenn Mulvenna	35	5	17	22	8
Toni Porkka	49	6	13	19	22
Jamie Cooke	36	11	7	18	12
Viacheslav Butsayev	24	8	10	18	51
Lance Pitlick	53	5	10	15	77
Dave Fenyves	42	3	11	14	14
Terran Sandwith	61	1	12	13	140
Bill C. Armstrong	80	2	10	12	205
Dale Kushner	26	1	7	8	98
Gord Hynes	9	1	3	4	4
Steve Morrow	38	0	4	4	59

	Games	G	A	Pts.	Pen.
Ryan McGill	4	0	2	2	26
Dan Kordic	14	0	2	2	17
Dominic Roussel (goalie)	6	0	1	1	0
Shawn Cronin	7	0	1	1	12
Yanick DeGrace (goalie)	30	0	1	1	4
Moe Mantha	1	0	0	0	0
Daryl Reaugh (goalie)	1	0	0	0	0
Perry Florio	3	0	0	0	0
Clayton Norris	4	0	0	0	5
Tommy Soderstrom (goalie)	7	0	0	0	0
Stephane Beauregard (goalie)	13	0	0	0	6
Scott LaGrand (goalie)	32	0	0	0	4

GOALTENDING

	Games	Min.	Goals	SO	Avg.
Tommy Soderstrom	7	373	15	0	2.41
Daryl Reaugh	1	22	1	0	2.73
Stephane Beauregard	13	794	48	0	3.63
Dominic Roussel	6	372	23(2)	0	3.71
Yanick DeGrace	30	1442	103(1)	1	4.29
Scott LaGrand	32	1854	145(1)	0	4.69

MONCTON HAWKS

SCORING

	Games	G	A	Pts.	Pen.
John LeBlanc	77	48	40	88	29
Bob Joyce	75	25	32	57	52
Stu Barnes	42	23	31	54	58
Andy Brickley	38	15	36	51	10
Scott Levins	54	22	26	48	158
Ken Gernander	71	18	29	47	20
Anatoli Fedotov	76	10	37	47	99
Dan Lambert	73	11	30	41	100
Rob Murray	56	16	21	37	147
Kris Draper	67	12	23	35	40
Pavel Kostichkin	65	16	18	34	51
Rob Cowie	67	12	20	32	91
Russ Romaniuk	28	18	8	26	40
Oleg Mikoulchik	75	6	20	26	159
Dave MacIntyre	50	5	17	22	37
Craig Martin	64	5	13	18	198
Andrei Raisky	35	7	10	17	14
Alan Kerr	36	6	10	16	85
Steve Bancroft	21	3	13	16	16
Al Stewart	45	3	8	11	118
Dallas Eakins	55	4	6	10	132
Tod Hartje	29	3	7	10	2
Todd Copeland	16	1	4	5	16
Igor Ulanov	9	1	3	4	26
Rick Hayward	47	1	3	4	231
Bryan Erickson	2	1	1	2	4
Charles Bourgeois	3	0	1	1	6
Rick Tabaracci (goalie)	5	0	1	1	4
Mark Richards (goalie)	13	0	1	1	2
Sean Gauthier (goalie)	38	0	1	1	10
Andy Bezeau	2	0	0	0	4
Mike O'Neill (goalie)	30	0	0	0	6

GOALTENDING

	Games	Min.	Goals	SO	Avg.
Mike O'Neill	30	1649	88(3)	1	3.20
Rick Tabaracci	5	290	18	0	3.72
Sean Gauthier	38	2196	145(3)	0	3.96
Mark Richards	13	736	49	0	3.99

NEW HAVEN SENATORS

SCORING

	Games	G	A	Pts.	Pen.
Martin St. Amour	71	21	39	60	78
Shawn McCosh	46	22	32	54	54
Scott White	80	10	44	54	72
Greg Pankewicz	62	23	20	43	163
Hugues Mongeon	73	14	27	41	26
Jake Grimes	76	18	20	38	30
Tony Cimellaro	76	18	16	34	73
Blair Atcheynum	51	16	18	34	47
Jeff Lazaro	27	12	13	25	49
Radek Hamr	59	4	21	25	18
Marc Fortier	16	9	15	24	42
Kent Paynter	48	7	17	24	81
Jim Kyte	63	6	18	24	163
John Ferguson	57	5	18	23	39
Paul Lawless	20	10	12	22	63
Rob Murphy	26	8	12	20	28
Vincent Faucher	36	7	8	15	22
Mark Ferner	34	5	7	12	69
Gerry St. Cyr	40	5	5	10	195
Lorne Knauft	59	4	6	10	107
Brad Miller	41	1	9	10	138
Harijs Vitolinsh	7	6	3	9	4
Neil Brady	8	6	3	9	2
Marc LaBelle	31	5	4	9	124
Dominic Lavoie	14	2	7	9	14
Chris Rowland	34	4	4	8	65
John Van Kessel	17	2	3	5	60
Andy Schneider	19	2	2	4	13
Brad Jones	4	2	1	3	6
Daniel Guerard	2	2	1	3	0
Trevor Jobe	3	1	2	3	0
Kent Hawley	6	1	1	2	2
Jerry Tarrant	15	1	1	2	8
Claude Savoie	2	1	1	2	0
Brian Downey	6	0	2	2	0
Chris Luongo	7	0	2	2	2
Trent McCleary	2	1	0	1	6
Darren Rumble	2	1	0	1	0
Andrew McBain	1	0	1	1	4
Steve Flomenhoft	2	0	1	1	0
Jason Firth	4	0	1	1	4
Ken Hammond	4	0	1	1	4
Mark Osiecki	4	0	1	1	4
Mark McCreary	6	0	1	1	2
Brad Treliving	8	0	1	1	6
Mark LaForest (goalie)	30	0	1	1	29
Alain Deeks	1	0	0	0	0
Stan Melanson	2	0	0	0	0
Kevin Patrick	2	0	0	0	2
Patrick Traverse	2	0	0	0	2
Scott Matusovich	3	0	0	0	0
Steve Weeks (goalie)	6	0	0	0	2
Mark Michaud (goalie)	12	0	0	0	0
Darrin Madeley (goalie)	41	0	0	0	4

GOALTENDING

	Games	Min.	Goals	SO	Avg.
Darrin Madeley	41	2295	127(6)	0	3.32
Mark LaForest	30	1688	121(4)	1	4.30
Mark Michaud	12	550	51(1)	0	5.56
Steve Weeks	6	323	32(1)	0	5.94

PROVIDENCE BRUINS

SCORING

	Games	G	A	Pts.	Pen.
Tim Sweeney	60	41	55	96	32
Jozef Stumpel	56	31	61	92	26
Jim Vesey	71	38	39	77	42
Andrew McKim	61	23	46	69	64
Sergei Zholtok	64	31	35	66	57
Chris Winnes	64	23	36	59	34
Glen Murray	48	30	26	56	42
Peter Douris	50	29	26	55	12
Peter Laviolette	74	13	42	55	64
Dominic Lavoie	53	16	27	43	62
Grigori Panteleyev	39	17	30	47	22
Bill Huard	72	18	19	37	302
Stephane Richer	53	8	29	37	60
Darryl Olsen	50	7	27	34	38
Clark Donatelli	57	12	14	26	40
Steve Jaques	51	3	21	24	187
Jamie Huscroft	69	2	15	17	257

	Games	G	A	Pts.	Pen.
Denis Chervyakov	48	4	12	16	99
Tod Hartje	29	2	14	16	32
Darren Banks	43	9	5	14	199
Brent Ashton	11	4	8	12	10
Mark Krys	34	1	10	11	36
Mark Kumpel	30	5	3	8	14
C.J. Young	7	4	3	7	26
Glen Featherstone	8	3	4	7	60
Darin Kimble	12	1	4	5	34
Matt Glennon	6	1	3	4	4
Gordon Murphy	2	1	3	4	2
Eugene Pavlov	9	2	1	3	8
Jim Wiemer	4	2	1	3	2
Bob Beers	6	1	2	3	10
Mike Walsh	5	2	0	2	8
Christian Lariviere	9	0	1	1	6
Mike Bales (goalie)	44	0	1	1	6
Sean Gorman	1	0	0	0	0
Rob Gribbin (goalie)	1	0	0	0	0
Bruce Coles	2	0	0	0	0
Paul Ohman	2	0	0	0	2
Kurt Seher	2	0	0	0	2
Jeff Ricciardi	3	0	0	0	0
Rick Lessard	6	0	0	0	6
Rick Allain	7	0	0	0	27
Matt DelGuidice (goalie)	9	0	0	0	4
Mike Parson (goalie)	16	0	0	0	0
John Blue (goalie)	19	0	0	0	18

GOALTENDING

	Games	Min.	Goals	SO	Avg.
Rob Gribbin	1	8	0	0	0.00
John Blue	19	1159	67(1)	0	3.47
Mike Parson	16	819	52(1)	0	3.81
Mike Bales	44	2363	166(2)	1	4.21
Matt DelGuidice	9	478	58(1)	0	7.28

ROCHESTER AMERICANS

SCORING

	Games	G	A	Pts.	Pen.
Peter Ciavaglia	64	35	67	102	32
Todd Simon	68	27	66	93	54
Jody Gage	71	40	40	80	76
Chris Snell	76	14	57	71	83
Scott Thomas	66	32	27	59	38
Doug MacDonald	64	25	33	58	58
Jozef Cierny	54	27	27	54	36
Mike McLaughlin	71	19	35	54	27
Greg Brown	61	11	38	49	46
Dan Frawley	75	17	27	44	216
Jason Young	59	20	20	40	60
Keith Carney	41	5	21	26	32
Viktor Gordijuk	35	11	14	25	8
Brad Rubachuk	61	10	15	25	218
Sean O'Donnell	74	3	18	21	203
Tony Iob	20	12	8	20	70
Peter Ambroziak	50	8	10	18	37
Jeff Sirkka	59	6	11	17	132
Jason Winch	31	1	13	14	29
Donald Audette	6	8	4	12	10
Bruce Shoebottom	65	7	5	12	253
Philippe Boucher	5	4	3	7	8
Andrei Iakovenko	16	2	2	4	20
Todd Flichel	15	1	3	4	4
Olaf Kolzig (goalie)	49	0	3	3	6
Dave DiVita	16	1	1	2	18
Joel Savage	6	1	1	2	6
Grant Ledyard	5	0	2	2	8
Bill Pye (goalie)	26	0	2	2	4
Randy Moller	3	1	0	1	10
Dan Blysma	2	0	1	1	0
Mike Smith	2	0	1	1	0
Dean Melanson	8	0	1	1	6
Brad Pascall	18	0	1	1	38
Mark Bernard (goalie)	1	0	0	0	0
Greg Menges (goalie)	2	0	0	0	0
Cam Brown	4	0	0	0	26

	Games	G	A	Pts.	Pen.
Kord Cernich	4	0	0	0	2
Tom Draper (goalie)	5	0	0	0	2
Bill Horn (goalie)	6	0	0	0	0

GOALTENDING

	Games	Min.	Goals	SO	Avg.
Mark Bernard	1	20	1	0	3.00
Olaf Kolzig	49	2737	168(3)	0	3.68
Bill Horn	6	304	22(1)	0	4.34
Tom Draper	5	303	22(1)	0	4.36
Bill Pye	26	1427	107(2)	0	4.50
Greg Menges	2	40	5	0	7.50

ST. JOHN'S MAPLE LEAFS

SCORING

	Games	G	A	Pts.	Pen.
Yanic Perreault	79	49	46	95	56
Rob Cimetta	76	28	57	85	125
Dave Tomlinson	70	36	48	84	115
Patrik Augusta	75	32	45	77	74
Ken McRae	64	30	44	74	135
Todd Hawkins	72	21	41	62	103
Mike Eastwood	60	24	35	59	32
Ted Crowley	79	19	38	57	41
Jeff Serowik	77	19	35	54	92
Kent Manderville	56	19	28	47	86
Eric Lacroix	76	15	19	34	59
Rudy Poeschek	78	7	24	31	189
Joe Sacco	37	14	16	30	45
Drake Berehowsky	28	10	17	27	38
Kevin McClelland	55	7	20	27	221
Curtis Hunt	48	4	19	23	148
Bob Halkidis	29	2	13	15	61
Terry Chitaroni	30	4	7	11	107
Greg Walters	27	4	5	9	82
Nick Wohlers	50	1	8	9	70
Guy Lehoux	42	3	2	5	72
Brad Miller	20	0	3	3	61
Scott Sharples (goalie)	25	0	3	3	2
Jeff Perry	13	1	1	2	22
Darryl Shannon	7	1	1	2	4
Guy Gadowsky	6	0	2	2	0
Frank Bialowas	7	1	0	1	28
Brad Aitken	4	0	1	1	2
Guy Larose	5	0	1	1	8
Felix Potvin (goalie)	5	0	1	1	0
Todd McCabe	1	0	0	0	0
Ryan VanderBusshe	1	0	0	0	0
Grant Marshall	2	0	0	0	0
Matt Martin	2	0	0	0	2
Rick Wamsley (goalie)	2	0	0	0	0
Brandon Convery	3	0	0	0	0
Jon Gustafson (goalie)	4	0	0	0	0
Damian Rhodes (goalie)	52	0	0	0	4

GOALTENDING

	Games	Min.	Goals	SO	Avg.
Jon Gustafson	4	202	10(1)	0	2.97
Felix Potvin	5	309	18	0	3.50
Damian Rhodes	52	3074	184(3)	1	3.59
Scott Sharples	25	1168	80(3)	0	4.11
Rick Wamsley	2	112	8(1)	0	4.29

SPRINGFIELD INDIANS

SCORING

	Games	G	A	Pts.	Pen.
Leonid Toropchenko	71	31	30	61	59
Mark Greig	55	20	38	58	86
Chris Govedaris	65	31	24	55	58
Todd Richards	78	13	42	55	53
Scott Morrow	70	22	29	51	80
Brian Chapman	72	17	34	51	212
Mike McHugh	67	19	27	46	111
Denis Chalifoux	64	17	27	44	22
Paul Guay	65	10	32	42	90
Mike Tomlak	38	16	21	37	56

	Games	G	A	Pts.	Pen.
Joe Day	33	15	20	35	118
Trevor Stienburg	65	14	20	34	244
Jamie Leach	29	13	15	28	33
Scott Daniels	60	11	12	23	181
Terry Yake	16	8	14	22	27
Paul Cyr	41	7	14	21	44
John Stevens	74	1	19	20	111
Dan Keczmer	37	1	13	14	38
Jukka Suomalainen	61	1	9	10	78
Robert Petrovicky	16	5	3	8	39
Karl Johnston	24	3	4	7	12
Barry Nieckar	21	2	4	6	65
Corey Beaulieu	68	1	5	6	201
Martin Hamrlik	8	1	3	4	16
Steve Yule	38	0	4	4	52
Scott Humeniuk	16	0	3	3	28
Nevin Markwart	7	2	0	2	24
Juri Krivokhizha	9	0	2	2	8
Mario Gosselin (goalie)	23	0	2	2	0
Kelly Ens	6	1	0	1	6
Jim Agnew	1	0	1	1	2
Pat McGarry (goalie)	3	0	0	0	0
Jim Powers	3	0	0	0	2
George Maneluk (goalie)	7	0	0	0	0
Corrie D'Alessio (goalie)	23	0	0	0	0
Mike Lenarduzzi (goalie)	36	0	0	0	4

GOALTENDING

	Games	Min.	Goals	SO	Avg.
Mario Gosselin	23	1345	75(2)	0	3.35
George Maneluk	7	343	23	0	4.02
Corrie D'Alessio	23	1120	77(1)	0	4.13
Mike Lenarduzzi	36	1945	142(3)	0	4.38
Pat McGarry	3	117	12(1)	0	6.15

UTICA DEVILS

SCORING

	Games	G	A	Pts.	Pen.
Jim Dowd	78	27	45	72	62
Jason Miller	72	28	42	70	43
Ben Hankinson	75	35	27	62	145
David Emma	61	21	40	61	47
Jarrod Skalde	59	21	39	60	76
Brian Sullivan	75	30	27	57	88
Brent Severyn	77	20	32	52	240
Jaroslav Modry	80	7	35	42	62
Jon Morris	31	16	24	40	28
Bill H. Armstrong	32	18	21	39	60
Scott Pellerin	27	15	18	33	33
Doug Brown	25	11	17	28	8
Frank Breault	32	8	20	28	56
Petr Kuchyna	76	3	24	27	56
Dean Malkoc	73	5	19	24	255
Donevan Hextall	51	11	11	22	12
Matt Ruchty	74	4	14	18	253
Kevin Dean	57	2	16	18	76
Bill Guerin	18	10	7	17	47
Mike Bodnarchuk	21	6	10	16	4
Claude Vilgrain	22	6	8	14	4
Curt Regnier	37	6	4	10	21
Jeff Christian	22	4	6	10	39
Troy Mallette	5	3	3	6	17
Myles O'Connor	9	1	5	6	10
Todd Copeland	16	3	2	5	10
Tom Chorske	6	1	4	5	2
Corey Schwab (goalie)	40	0	5	5	24
Martin Brodeur (goalie)	32	0	4	4	6
Kevin Todd	2	2	1	3	0
Serge Roberge	28	0	3	3	85
Chris Nelson	21	1	1	2	20
Bobby Holik	1	0	0	0	2
Robert Horyna (goalie)	1	0	0	0	0
Ralph Barahona	2	0	0	0	0
Kevin Riehl	3	0	0	0	2
Chad Erickson (goalie)	9	0	0	0	8

GOALTENDING

	Games	Min.	Goals	SO	Avg.
Robert Horyna	1	20	1	0	3.00
Martin Brodeur	32	1952	131(3)	0	4.03
Corey Schwab	40	2387	169(2)	2	4.25
Chad Erickson	9	505	47(1)	0	5.58

PLAYERS WITH TWO OR MORE TEAMS

SCORING

	Games	G	A	Pts.	Pen.
Mark Bernard (g), Rochester	1	0	0	0	0
Mark Bernard (g), Baltimore	2	0	0	0	0
Totals	3	0	0	0	0
Cam Brown, Hamilton	1	0	0	0	2
Cam Brown, Rochester	4	0	0	0	26
Totals	5	0	0	0	28
Kord Cernich, Rochester	4	0	0	0	2
Kord Cernich, Capital District	6	0	0	0	4
Totals	10	0	0	0	6
Terry Chitaroni, St. John's	30	4	7	11	107
Terry Chitaroni, Baltimore	16	2	1	3	14
Totals	46	6	8	14	121
Jeff Christian, Utica	22	4	6	10	39
Jeff Christian, Hamilton	11	2	5	7	35
Totals	33	6	11	17	74
Todd Copeland, Utica	16	3	2	5	10
Todd Copeland, Moncton	16	1	4	5	16
Totals	32	4	6	10	26
Alain Deeks, Hamilton	18	0	6	6	6
Alain Deeks, New Haven	1	0	0	0	0
Totals	19	0	6	6	6
Tod Hartje, Moncton	29	3	7	10	2
Tod Hartje, Providence	29	2	14	16	32
Totals	58	5	21	26	34
Rick Hayward, Moncton	47	1	3	4	231
Rick Hayward, Capital District	19	0	1	1	80
Totals	66	1	4	5	311
Dale Kushner, Hershey	26	1	7	8	98
Dale Kushner, Capital District	7	0	1	1	29
Totals	33	1	8	9	127
Dominic Lavoie, New Haven	14	2	7	9	14
Dominic Lavoie, Providence	53	16	27	43	62
Totals	67	18	34	52	76
Rick Lessard, Providence	6	0	0	0	6
Rick Lessard, Hamilton	52	0	17	17	151
Totals	58	0	17	17	157
Al MacIsaac, Cape Breton	13	1	3	4	4
Al MacIsaac, Baltimore	13	1	2	3	20
Totals	26	2	5	7	24
Michael Maurice, Hamilton	13	3	7	10	6
Michael Maurice, Adirondack	25	4	7	11	4
Totals	38	7	14	21	10
Brad Miller, New Haven	41	1	9	10	138
Brad Miller, St. John's	20	0	3	3	61
Totals	61	1	12	13	199
Mike Parson (g), Baltimore	16	0	0	0	0
Mike Parson (g), Providence	16	0	0	0	0
Totals	32	0	0	0	0
Serge Roberge, Halifax	16	2	2	4	34
Serge Roberge, Utica	28	0	3	3	85
Totals	44	2	5	7	119
Tim Taylor, Baltimore	41	15	16	31	49
Tim Taylor, Hamilton	36	15	22	37	37
Totals	77	30	38	68	86
Bob Wilkie, Adirondack	14	0	5	5	20
Bob Wilkie, Hershey	28	7	25	32	18
Totals	42	7	30	37	38

GOALTENDING

	Games	Min.	Goals	SO	Avg.
Mark Bernard, Roch.	1	20	1	0	3.00
Mark Bernard, Balt.	2	64	7	0	6.56
Totals	3	84	8	0	5.71
Mike Parson, Balt.	16	916	58(4)	0	3.80
Mike Parson, Prov.	16	819	52(1)	0	3.81
Totals	32	1735	110(5)	0	3.80

( )—Empty-net goals (do not count against a goaltender's average).

1993 CALDER CUP PLAYOFFS

RESULTS

FIRST ROUND

Series "A"

	W	L	Pts.	GF	GA
St. John's	4	1	8	25	16
Moncton	1	4	2	16	25

(St. John's won series, 4-1)

Series "B"

	W	L	Pts.	GF	GA
Cape Breton	4	1	8	23	16
Fredericton	1	4	2	16	23

(Cape Breton won series, 4-1)

Series "C"

	W	L	Pts.	GF	GA
Springfield	4	2	8	18	23
Providence	2	4	4	23	18

(Springfield won series, 4-2)

Series "D"

	W	L	Pts.	GF	GA
Adirondack	4	0	8	17	6
Capital District	0	4	0	6	17

(Adirondack won series, 4-0)

Series "E"

	W	L	Pts.	GF	GA
Binghamton	4	3	8	29	24
Baltimore	3	4	6	24	29

(Binghamton won series, 4-3)

Series "F"

	W	L	Pts.	GF	GA
Rochester	4	1	8	24	15
Utica	1	4	2	15	24

(Rochester won series, 4-1)

SECOND ROUND

Series "G"

	W	L	Pts.	GF	GA
Cape Breton	4	0	8	22	12
St. John's	0	4	0	12	22

(Cape Breton won series, 4-0)

Series "H"

	W	L	Pts.	GF	GA
Springfield	4	3	8	23	27
Adirondack	3	4	6	27	23

(Springfield won series, 4-3)

Series "J"

	W	L	Pts.	GF	GA
Rochester	4	3	8	26	21
Binghamton	3	4	6	21	26

(Rochester won series, 4-3)

DIVISION CHAMPIONS ROUND

Series "K"

	W	L	Pts.	GF	GA
Cape Breton	2	0	4	13	6
Springfield	0	2	0	6	13

(Cape Breton won series, 2-0)

FINALS—FOR THE CALDER CUP

Series "L"

	W	L	Pts.	GF	GA
Cape Breton	4	1	8	27	13
Rochester	1	4	2	13	27

(Cape Breton won series, 4-1)

INDIVIDUAL LEADERS

Goals: Bill McDougall, Cape Breton (26)
Assists: Bill McDougall, Cape Breton (26)
Points: Bill McDougall, Cape Breton (52)
Penalty minutes: Marc Laforge, Cape Breton (78)
Goaltending average: Mike Parson, Providence (2.231)
Shutouts: Allan Bester, Adirondack (1)
    Wayne Cowley, Cape Breton (1)
    Mike Parson, Providence (1)

TOP SCORERS

	Games	G	A	Pts.
Bill McDougall, Cape Breton	16	26	26	52
Roman Oksiuta, Cape Breton	16	9	19	28
Peter Ciavaglia, Rochester	17	9	16	25
David Haas, Cape Breton	16	11	13	24
Brad Werenka, Cape Breton	16	4	17	21
Viktor Gordiouk, Rochester	17	9	9	18
Mike Sillinger, Adirondack	11	5	13	18
Shaun Van Allen, Cape Breton	15	8	9	17
Todd Simon, Rochester	12	3	14	17
Steven King, Binghamton	14	7	9	16

INDIVIDUAL STATISTICS

ADIRONDACK RED WINGS

(Lost in second round to Springfield, 4-3)

SCORING

	Games	G	A	Pts.	Pen.
Mike Sillinger	11	5	13	18	10
Micah Aivazoff	11	8	6	14	10
Chris Tancill	10	7	7	14	10
Bobby Dollas	11	3	8	11	8
Ken Quinney	10	2	9	11	9
Jeff Rohlicek	11	4	5	9	10
Sylvain Couturier	11	3	5	8	10
Mike Casselman	8	3	3	6	0
Stewart Malgunas	11	3	3	6	8
Jim Cummins	9	3	1	4	4
Gord Kruppke	9	1	2	3	20
Jason York	11	0	3	3	18
Viacheslav Kozlov	4	1	1	2	4
Dennis Vial	11	1	1	2	14
Darren McCarty	11	0	1	1	33
Kirk Tomlinson	9	0	1	1	32

	Games	G	A	Pts.	Pen.
Dave Flanagan	1	0	0	0	0
Chris Osgood (goalie)	1	0	0	0	0
Michael Maurice	2	0	0	0	2
Igor Malykhin	6	0	0	0	4
Joe Frederick	8	0	0	0	6
Allan Bester (goalie)	10	0	0	0	0

GOALTENDING

	Games	Min.	Goals	SO	Avg.
Chris Osgood	1	59	2	0	2.03
Allan Bester	10	633	26 (1)	1	2.46

BALTIMORE SKIPJACKS

(Lost in first round to Binghamton, 4-3)

SCORING

	Games	G	A	Pts.	Pen.
Eric Murano	7	7	5	12	6
John Byce	7	4	5	9	4
John Slaney	7	0	7	7	8
Mike Boback	5	3	3	6	6
Brad Schlegel	7	0	5	5	6
Jeff Greenlaw	7	3	1	4	0
Mark Hunter	7	3	1	4	12
Jeff Nelson	7	1	3	4	2
Martin Jiranek	7	1	2	3	23
Steve Poapst	7	0	3	3	6
Victor Gervais	7	1	1	2	4
Jason Woolley	1	0	2	2	0
Trevor Halverson	2	1	0	1	0
Jim Mathieson	3	0	1	1	23
Chris Longo	7	0	1	1	0
Ken Klee	7	0	1	1	15
Rob Leask	7	0	1	1	14
Darwin McPherson	1	0	0	0	0
Martin Gendron	3	0	0	0	0
Duane Derksen (goalie)	4	0	0	0	0
Rod Taylor	4	0	0	0	10
Byron Dafoe (goalie)	5	0	0	0	0

GOALTENDING

	Games	Min.	Goals	SO	Avg.
Duane Derksen	4	188	7	0	2.23
Byron Dafoe	5	241	22	0	5.48

BINGHAMTON RANGERS

(Lost in second round to Rochester, 4-3)

SCORING

	Games	G	A	Pts.	Pen.
Steven King	14	7	9	16	26
Brian McReynolds	14	3	10	13	18
Craig Duncanson	14	7	5	12	9
Don Biggs	14	3	9	12	32
Mike Stevens	14	5	5	10	63
Sergei Zubov	11	5	5	10	2
Per Djoos	14	2	8	10	8
Alexei Kovalev	9	3	5	8	14
Jean-Yves Roy	14	5	2	7	4
Mike Hurlbut	14	2	5	7	12
Dave Thomlinson	12	2	5	7	8
Rob Kenny	8	2	4	6	8
Chris Cichocki	9	3	2	5	25
Dave Marcinyshyn	6	0	3	3	14
Peter Fiorentino	13	0	3	3	22
Joby Messier	14	1	1	2	6
Brad Tiley	8	0	1	1	2
Darren Langdon	8	0	1	1	14
Boris Rousson (goalie)	1	0	0	0	0
Michael Stewart	1	0	0	0	0
Darcy Werenka	3	0	0	0	0
Rick Bennett	10	0	0	0	30
Corey Hirsch (goalie)	14	0	0	0	2

GOALTENDING

	Games	Min.	Goals	SO	Avg.
Corey Hirsch	14	831	46 (2)	0	3.32
Boris Rousson	1	20	2		6.00

CAPE BRETON OILERS

(Winner of 1993 Calder Cup playoffs)

SCORING

	Games	G	A	Pts.	Pen.
Bill McDougall	16	26	26	52	30
Roman Oksiuta	16	9	19	28	12
David Haas	16	11	13	24	36
Brad Werenka	16	4	17	21	12
Shaun Van Allen	15	8	9	17	18
Jeff Bloemberg	16	5	10	15	10
Dan Currie	16	7	4	11	31
Steven Rice	14	4	6	10	22
Gord Mark	16	1	7	8	20
Kirk Maltby	16	3	3	6	45
Peter White	16	3	3	6	12
Francois Leroux	16	0	5	5	29
Shjon Podein	9	2	2	4	29
Scott Thornton	16	1	2	3	35
Marc Laforge	15	1	2	3	78
Brian Curran	12	0	3	3	12
Wayne Cowley (goalie)	16	0	3	3	2
Darcy Martini	2	0	1	1	0
Ian Herbers	10	0	1	1	16
Richard Borgo	1	0	0	0	2
Craig Fisher	1	0	0	0	2
Vladimir Vujtek	1	0	0	0	0

GOALTENDING

	Games	Min.	Goals	SO	Avg.
Wayne Cowley	16	1014	47	1	2.78

CAPITAL DISTRICT ISLANDERS

(Lost in first round to Adirondack, 4-0)

SCORING

	Games	G	A	Pts.	Pen.
Dave Chyzowski	3	2	0	2	0
Rick Hayward	4	1	1	2	27
Brent Grieve	4	1	1	2	10
Joni Lehto	3	1	1	2	2
Phil Huber	4	0	2	2	4
Dale Kushner	2	1	0	1	29
Dean Chynoweth	4	0	1	1	9
Kevin Cheveldayoff	4	0	1	1	8
Wayne McBean	3	0	1	1	9
Jeff Finley	4	0	1	1	0
Chris Taylor	4	0	1	1	2
Iain Fraser	4	0	1	1	0
Sean LeBrun	1	0	0	0	0
Jamie McLennan (goalie)	1	0	0	0	0
Graeme Townshend	2	0	0	0	0
Wayne Doucet	3	0	0	0	2
Richard Kromm	3	0	0	0	0
Brad Turner	3	0	0	0	2
Steve Junker	4	0	0	0	0
Danny Lorenz (goalie)	4	0	0	0	0
Scott Scissons	4	0	0	0	0

GOALTENDING

	Games	Min.	Goals	SO	Avg.
Danny Lorenz	4	219	12	0	3.29
Jamie McLennan	1	20	5	0	15.00

FREDERICTON CANADIENS

(Lost in first round to Cape Breton, 4-1)

SCORING

	Games	G	A	Pts.	Pen.
Steve Larouche	5	2	5	7	6
Ed Ronan	5	2	4	6	6
Oleg Petrov	5	4	1	5	0
Turner Stevenson	5	2	3	5	11
Patric Kjellberg	5	2	2	4	0
Luc Gauthier	5	2	1	3	20
Gerry Fleming	5	1	2	3	14
Patrik Carnback	5	0	3	3	14
Pierre Sevigny	5	1	1	2	2

— 169 —

	Games	G	A	Pts.	Pen.
Marc Laniel	5	0	2	2	23
Lindsay Vallis	5	0	2	2	10
Frederic Chabot (goalie)	4	0	1	1	4
Craig Ferguson	5	0	1	1	2
Yves Sarault	3	0	1	1	2
Robert Guillet	1	0	0	0	0
Les Kuntar (goalie)	1	0	0	0	0
Charles Poulin	1	0	0	0	0
Steve Veilleux	1	0	0	0	4
Darcy Simon	2	0	0	0	6
Timothy Chase	3	0	0	0	0
Christian Proulx	4	0	0	0	0
Donald Brashear	5	0	0	0	8

GOALTENDING

	Games	Min.	Goals	SO	Avg.
Frederic Chabot	4	261	16 (1)	0	3.68
Les Kuntar	1	64	6	0	5.63

MONCTON HAWKS

(Lost in first round to St. John's, 4-1)

SCORING

	Games	G	A	Pts.	Pen.
Rob Cowie	5	3	5	8	2
Andy Brickley	5	4	2	6	0
Ken Gernander	5	1	4	5	0
Kris Draper	5	2	2	4	18
Todd Copeland	5	1	3	4	2
Scott Levins	5	1	3	4	14
Russ Romaniuk	5	0	4	4	2
John LeBlanc	5	2	1	3	6
Dan Lambert	5	1	2	3	2
Alan Kerr	5	0	2	2	11
Al Stewart	2	1	0	1	20
Craig Martin	5	0	1	1	22
Andrei Raisky	1	0	0	0	0
Anatoli Fedotov	2	0	0	0	0
Sean Gauthier (goalie)	2	0	0	0	0
Dave MacIntyre	2	0	0	0	0
Rob Murray	3	0	0	0	6
Mark Richards (goalie)	4	0	0	0	4
Steve Bancroft	5	0	0	0	16
Bob Joyce	5	0	0	0	2
Oleg Mikoulchik	5	0	0	0	4

GOALTENDING

	Games	Min.	Goals	SO	Avg.
Sean Gauthier	2	75	6	0	4.80
Mark Richards	4	231	19	0	4.94

PROVIDENCE BRUINS

(Lost in first round to Springfield, 4-2)

SCORING

	Games	G	A	Pts.	Pen.
Jozef Stumpel	6	4	4	8	0
Sergei Zholtok	6	3	5	8	4
Steve Jaques	6	1	7	8	13
Jim Vesey	6	2	5	7	4
Glen Murray	6	1	4	5	4
Tim Sweeney	3	2	2	4	0
Andrew McKim	6	2	2	4	0
Peter Laviolette	6	0	4	4	10
Bill Huard	6	3	0	3	9
Clark Donatelli	4	2	1	3	2
Dominic Lavoie	6	1	2	3	24
Chris Winnes	4	0	2	2	5
C.J. Young	6	1	0	1	16
Tod Hartje	4	1	0	1	20
Jamie Huscroft	2	0	1	1	6
Darren Banks	1	0	0	0	0
Mike Bales (goalie)	4	0	0	0	0
Grigori Panteleyev	3	0	0	0	10
Kurt Seher	3	0	0	0	2

	Games	G	A	Pts.	Pen.
Mike Parson (goalie)	4	0	0	0	0
Rick Allain	6	0	0	0	8
Mark Krys	6	0	0	0	2

GOALTENDING

	Games	Min.	Goals	SO	Avg.
Mike Parson	2	242	9 (1)	1	2.23
Mike Bales	4	118	8	0	4.07

ROCHESTER AMERICANS

(Lost finals to Cape Breton, 4-1)

SCORING

	Games	G	A	Pts.	Pen.
Peter Ciavaglia	17	9	16	25	12
Viktor Gordijuk	17	9	9	18	4
Todd Simon	12	3	14	17	15
Scott Thomas	17	8	5	13	6
Jody Gage	9	5	8	13	2
Chris Snell	17	5	8	13	39
Greg Brown	16	3	8	11	14
Dan Frawley	17	1	7	8	70
Peter Ambroziak	12	4	3	7	6
Jason Young	14	3	4	7	31
Dean Melanson	14	1	6	7	18
Sean O'Donnell	17	1	6	7	38
Mike McLaughlin	16	4	2	6	8
Todd Flichel	16	2	4	6	22
Brad Rubachuk	12	3	1	4	63
Tony Iob	7	1	1	2	14
Doug MacDonald	7	0	2	2	4
Rod Hinks	7	0	2	2	0
Jason Dawe	3	1	0	1	0
Philippe Boucher	3	0	1	1	2
Olaf Kolzig (goalie)	17	0	1	1	8
Bill Horn (goalie)	1	0	0	0	2
David Cooper	2	0	0	0	2
Joel Savage	3	0	0	0	12
Jeff Sirkka	3	0	0	0	7
Bruce Shoebottom	14	0	0	0	19

GOALTENDING

	Games	Min.	Goals	SO	Avg.
Bill Horn	1	13	0	0	0.00
Olaf Kolzig	17	1040	61 (2)	0	3.52

ST. JOHN'S MAPLE LEAFS

(Lost second round to Cape Breton, 4-0)

SCORING

	Games	G	A	Pts.	Pen.
Ken McRae	9	6	6	12	27
Rob Cimetta	9	2	10	12	32
Joe Sacco	7	6	4	10	2
Yanic Perreault	9	4	5	9	2
Eric Lacroix	9	5	3	8	4
Guy Larose	9	5	2	7	6
Patrik Augusta	8	3	3	6	23
Jeff Serowik	9	1	5	6	8
Matt Martin	9	1	5	6	4
Dave Tomlinson	9	1	4	5	8
Ted Crowley	9	2	2	4	4
Todd Hawkins	9	1	3	4	10
Rudy Poeschek	9	0	4	4	13
Curtis Hunt	7	0	3	3	6
Kent Manderville	9	0	2	2	0
Brad Miller	8	0	2	2	10
Greg Walters	1	0	1	1	4
Brandon Convery	5	0	1	1	0
Frank Bialowas	1	0	0	0	0
Guy Gadowsky	1	0	0	0	0
Kevin McClelland	1	0	0	0	7
Scott Sharples (goalie)	1	0	0	0	0
Nathan Dempsey	2	0	0	0	0
Grant Marshall	2	0	0	0	2
Damian Rhodes (goalie)	9	0	0	0	4

GOALTENDING

	Games	Min.	Goals	SO	Avg.
Scott Sharples	1	7	0	0	0.00
Damian Rhodes	9	538	37 (1)	0	4.13

SPRINGFIELD INDIANS

(Lost semifinals to Cape Breton, 2-0)

SCORING

	Games	G	A	Pts.	Pen.
Scott Morrow	15	6	9	15	21
Denis Chalifoux	15	5	8	13	14
Chris Govedaris	15	7	4	11	18
Robert Petrovicky	15	5	6	11	14
Scott Daniels	12	2	7	9	12
Leonid Toropchenko..............	13	4	4	8	8
Joe Day	15	0	8	8	40
Mike McHugh	11	5	2	7	12
Brian Chapman	15	2	5	7	43
Mikael Nylander	3	3	3	6	2
Todd Richards	9	1	5	6	2
Paul Cyr	15	3	2	5	12
Scott Humeniuk	14	1	3	4	8
Dan Keczmer	12	0	4	4	14
Paul Guay	11	1	2	3	6
Mike Tomlak	5	1	1	2	2
Barry Nieckar	6	1	0	1	14
Corey Beaulieu	4	0	1	1	21
John Stevens	15	0	1	1	18
Mike Lenarduzzi (goalie)	2	0	0	0	0
Corrie D'Alessio (goalie)	4	0	0	0	0
Trevor Stienburg	10	0	0	0	31
Jukka Suomalainen	10	0	0	0	26
George Maneluk (goalie)	14	0	0	0	0

GOALTENDING

	Games	Min.	Goals	SO	Avg.
Corrie D'Alessio	4	75	3	0	2.40
Mike Lenarduzzi	2	100	5	0	3.00
George Maneluk.......	14	778	53 (2)	0	4.09

UTICA DEVILS

(Lost first round to Rochester, 4-1)

SCORING

	Games	G	A	Pts.	Pen.
Jason Miller	5	4	4	8	2
Jim Dowd	5	1	7	8	10
Ben Hankinson	5	2	2	4	6
David Emma	5	2	1	3	6
Mike Bodnarchuk	4	2	0	2	4
Frank Breault	4	2	0	2	0
Jaroslav Modry	5	0	2	2	2
Jarrod Skalde	5	0	2	2	19
Matt Ruchty	4	0	2	2	15
Donevan Hextall	2	1	0	1	0
Kevin Dean	5	1	0	1	8
Curt Regnier	2	0	1	1	0
Scott Pellerin	2	0	1	1	0
Claude Vilgrain	5	0	1	1	0
Dean Malkoc	5	0	1	1	8
Chris Nelson	1	0	0	0	2
Serge Roberge	1	0	0	0	0
Corey Schwab (goalie)	1	0	0	0	0
Jason Smith	1	0	0	0	2
Martin Brodeur (goalie)	4	0	0	0	2
Petr Kuchyna	4	0	0	0	4
Brent Severyn	5	0	0	0	35
Brian Sullivan	5	0	0	0	12

GOALTENDING

	Games	Min.	Goals	SO	Avg.
Martin Brodeur	4	258	18	0	4.19
Corey Schwab...........	1	59	6	0	6.10

1992-93 AWARD WINNERS

ALL-STAR TEAMS

First team	Pos.	Second team
Corey Hirsch, Binghamton	G	Darrin Madeley, New Haven
Brent Severyn, Utica	D	Per Djoos, Binghamton
Bobby Dollas, Adirondack	D	Jeff Serowik, St. John's
Don Biggs, Binghamton	C	Iain Fraser, Capital District
Dan Currie, Cape Breton	LW	Tim Sweeney, Providence
Chris Tancill, Adirondack	RW	Steven Rice, Cape Breton

TROPHY WINNERS

John B. Sollenberger Trophy: Don Biggs, Binghamton
Les Cunningham Plaque: Don Biggs, Binghamton
Harry (Hap) Holmes Memorial Trophy: Corey Hirsch, Binghamton
             Boris Rousson, Binghamton
Dudley (Red) Garrett Memorial Trophy: Corey Hirsch, Binghamton
Eddie Shore Plaque: Bobby Dollas, Adirondack
Fred Hunt Memorial Award: Tim Tookey, Hershey
Louis A.R. Pieri Memorial Award: Marc Crawford, St. John's
Baz Bastien Trophy: Corey Hirsch, Binghamton
Jack Butterfield Trophy: Bill McDougall, Cape Breton

ALL-TIME AWARD WINNERS

JOHN B. SOLLENBERGER TROPHY

(Leading scorer)

Season	Player, Team
1936-37—	Jack Markle, Syracuse
1937-38—	Jack Markle, Syracuse
1938-39—	Don Deacon, Pittsburgh
1939-40—	Norm Locking, Syracuse
1940-41—	Les Cunningham, Cleveland
1941-42—	Pete Kelly, Springfield
1942-43—	Wally Kilrea, Hershy
1943-44—	Tommy Burlington, Cleveland
1944-45—	Bob Gracie, Pittsburgh
	Bob Walton, Pittsburgh
1945-46—	Les Douglas, Indianapolis
1946-47—	Phil Hergesheimer, Philadelphia

Season	Player, Team
1947-48—	Carl Liscombe, Providence
1948-49—	Sid Smith, Pittsburgh
1949-50—	Les Douglas, Cleveland
1950-51—	Ab DeMarco, Buffalo
1951-52—	Ray Powell, Providence
1952-53—	Eddie Olson, Cleveland
1953-54—	George Sullivan, Hershey
1954-55—	Eddie Olson, Cleveland
1955-56—	Zellio Toppazzini, Providence
1956-57—	Fred Glover, Cleveland
1957-58—	Willie Marshall, Hershey
1958-59—	Bill Hicke, Rochester
1959-60—	Fred Glover, Cleveland
1960-61—	Bill Sweeney, Springfield
1961-62—	Bill Sweeney, Springfield

Season	Player, Team
1962-63	Bill Sweeney, Springfield
1963-64	Gerry Ehman, Rochester
1964-65	Art Stratton, Buffalo
1965-66	Dick Gamble, Rochester
1966-67	Gordon Labossiere, Quebec
1967-68	Simon Nolet, Quebec
1968-69	Jeannot Gilbert, Hershey
1969-70	Jude Drouin, Montreal
1970-71	Fred Speck, Baltimore
1971-72	Don Blackburn, Providence
1972-73	Yvon Lambert, Nova Scotia
1973-74	Steve West, New Haven
1974-75	Doug Gibson, Rochester
1975-76	Jean-Guy Gratton, Hershey
1976-77	Andre Peloffy, Springfield
1977-78	Gord Brooks, Philadelphia
	Rick Adduono, Rochester
1978-79	Bernie Johnston, Maine
1979-80	Norm Dube, Nova Scotia
1980-81	Mark Lofthouse, Hershey
1981-82	Mike Kasczyki, New Brunswick
1982-83	Ross Yates, Binghamton
1983-84	Claude Larose, Sherbrooke
1984-85	Paul Gardner, Binghamton
1985-86	Paul Gardner, Rochester
1986-87	Tim Tookey, Hershey
1987-88	Bruce Boudreau, Springfield
1988-89	Stephan Lebeau, Sherbrooke
1989-90	Paul Ysebaert, Utica
1990-91	Kevin Todd, Utica
1991-92	Shaun Van Allen, Cape Breton
1992-93	Don Biggs, Binghamton

LES CUNNINGHAM PLAQUE

(Most Valuable Player)

Season	Player, Team
1947-48	Carl Liscombe, Providence
1948-49	Carl Liscombe, Providence
1949-50	Les Douglas, Cleveland
1950-51	Ab DeMarco, Buffalo
1951-52	Ray Powell, Providence
1952-53	Eddie Olson, Cleveland
1953-54	George "Red" Sullivan, Hershey
1954-55	Ross Lowe, Springfield
1955-56	Johnny Bower, Providence
1956-57	Johnny Bower, Providence
1957-58	Johnny Bower, Cleveland
1958-59	Bill Hicke, Rochester
	Rudy Migay, Rochester
1959-60	Fred Glover, Cleveland
1960-61	Phil Maloney, Buffalo
1961-62	Fred Glover, Cleveland
1962-63	Denis DeJordy, Buffalo
1963-64	Fred Glover, Cleveland
1964-65	Art Stratton, Buffalo
1965-66	Dick Gamble, Rochester
1966-67	Mike Nykoluk, Hershey
1967-68	Dave Creighton, Providence
1968-69	Gilles Villemure, Buffalo
1969-70	Gilles Villemure, Buffalo
1970-71	Fred Speck, Baltimore
1971-72	Garry Peters, Boston
1972-73	Billy Inglis, Cincinnati
1973-74	Art Stratton, Rochester
1974-75	Doug Gibson, Rochester
1975-76	Ron Andruff, Nova Scotia
1976-77	Doug Gibson, Rochester
1977-78	Blake Dunlop, Maine
1978-79	Rocky Saganiuk, New Brunswick
1979-80	Norm Dube, Nova Scotia
1980-81	Pelle Lindbergh, Maine
1981-82	Mike Kasczyki, New Brunswick
1982-83	Ross Yates, Binghamton
1983-84	Mal Davis, Rochester
	Garry Lariviere, St. Catharines

Season	Player, Team
1984-85	Paul Gardner, Binghamton
1985-86	Paul Gardner, Rochester
1986-87	Tim Tookey, Hershey
1987-88	Jody Gage, Rochester
1988-89	Stephan Lebeau, Sherbrooke
1989-90	Paul Ysebaert, Utica
1990-91	Kevin Todd, Utica
1991-92	John Anderson, Hew Haven
1992-93	Don Biggs, Binghamton

HARRY (HAP) HOLMES MEMORIAL TROPHY

(Outstanding goaltender)

Season	Player, Team
1936-37	Bert Gardiner, Philadelphia
1937-38	Frank Brimsek, Providence
1938-39	Alfie Moore, Hershey
1939-40	Moe Roberts, Cleveland
1940-41	Chuck Rayner, Springfield
1941-42	Bill Beveridge, Cleveland
1942-43	Gordie Bell, Buffalo
1943-44	Nick Damore, Hershey
1944-45	Yves Nadon, Buffalo
1945-46	Connie Dion, St. Louis-Buffalo
1946-47	Baz Bastien, Pittsburgh
1947-48	Baz Bastien, Pittsburgh
1948-49	Baz Bastien, Pittsburgh
1949-50	Gil Mayer, Pittsburgh
1950-51	Gil Mayer, Pittsburgh
1951-52	Johnny Bower, Cleveland
1952-53	Gil Mayer, Pittsburgh
1953-54	Jacques Plante, Buffalo
1954-55	Gil Mayer, Pittsburgh
1955-56	Gil Mayer, Pittsburgh
1956-57	Johnny Bower, Providence
1957-58	Johnny Bower, Cleveland
1958-59	Bob Perreault, Hershey
1959-60	Ed Chadwick, Rochester
1960-61	Marcel Paille, Springfield
1961-62	Marcel Paille, Springfield
1962-63	Denis DeJordy, Buffalo
1963-64	Roger Crozier, Pittsburgh
1964-65	Gerry Cheevers, Rochester
1965-66	Les Binkley, Cleveland
1966-67	Andre Gill, Hershey
1967-68	Bob Perreault, Rochester
1968-69	Gilles Villemure, Buffalo
1969-70	Gilles Villemure, Buffalo
1970-71	Gary Kurt, Cleveland
1971-72	Dan Bouchard, Boston
	Ross Brooks, Boston
1972-73	Michel Larocque, Nova Scotia
1973-74	Jim Shaw, Nova Scotia
	Dave Elenbaas, Nova Scotia
1974-75	Ed Walsh, Nova Scotia
	Dave Elenbaas, Nova Scotia
1975-76	Dave Elenbaas, Nova Scotia
	Ed Walsh, Nova Scotia
1976-77	Ed Walsh, Nova Scotia
	Dave Elenbaas, Nova Scotia
1977-78	Bob Holland, Nova Scotia
	Maurice Barrette, Nova Scotia
1978-79	Pete Peeters, Maine
	Robbie Moore, Maine
1979-80	Rick St. Croix, Maine
	Robbie Moore, Maine
1980-81	Pelle Lindbergh, Maine
	Robbie Moore, Maine
1981-82	Bob Janecyk, New Brunswick
	Warren Skorodenski, New Brunswick
1982-83	Brian Ford, Fredericton
	Clint Malarchuk, Fredericton
1983-84	Brian Ford, Fredericton
1984-85	Jon Casey, Baltimore
1985-86	Sam St. Laurent, Maine
	Karl Friesen, Maine

Season	Player, Team
1986-87	Vincent Riendeau, Sherbrooke
1987-88	Vincent Riendeau, Sherbrooke
	Jocelyn Perreault, Sherbrooke
1988-89	Randy Exelby, Sherbrooke
	Francois Gravel, Sherbrooke
1989-90	Jean Claude Bergeron, Sherbrooke
	Andre Racicot, Sherbrooke
1990-91	David Littman, Rochester
	Darcy Wakaluk, Rochester
1991-92	David Littman, Rochester
1992-93	Corey Hirsch, Binghamton
	Boris Rousson, Binghamton

Beginning with the 1983-84 season, the award goes to the top goaltending team with each goaltender having played a minimum of 25 games for the team with the fewest goals against.

DUDLEY (RED) GARRETT MEMORIAL TROPHY

(Top rookie)

Season	Player, Team
1947-48	Bob Solinger, Cleveland
1948-49	Terry Sawchuk, Indianapolis
1949-50	Paul Meger, Buffalo
1950-51	Wally Hergesheimer, Cleveland
1951-52	Earl "Dutch" Reibel, Indianapolis
1952-53	Guyle Fielder, St. Louis
1953-54	Don Marshall, Buffalo
1954-55	Jimmy Anderson, Springfield
1955-56	Bruce Cline, Providence
1956-57	Boris "Bo" Elik, Cleveland
1957-58	Bill Sweeney, Providence
1958-59	Bill Hicke, Rochester
1959-60	Stan Baluik, Providence
1960-61	Ronald "Chico" Maki, Buffalo
1961-62	Les Binkley, Cleveland
1962-63	Doug Robinson, Buffalo
1963-64	Roger Crozier, Pittsburgh
1964-65	Ray Cullen, Buffalo
1965-66	Mike Walton, Rochester
1966-67	Bob Rivard, Quebec
1967-68	Gerry Desjardins, Cleveland
1968-69	Ron Ward, Rochester
1969-70	Jude Drouin, Montreal
1970-71	Fred Speck, Baltimore
1971-72	Terry Caffery, Cleveland
1972-73	Ron Anderson, Boston
1973-74	Rick Middleton, Providence
1974-75	Jerry Holland, Providence
1975-76	Greg Holst, Providence
	Pierre Mondou, Nova Scotia
1976-77	Rod Schutt, Nova Scotia
1977-78	Norm Dupont, Nova Scotia
1978-79	Mike Meeker, Binghamton
1979-80	Darryl Sutter, New Brunswick
1980-81	Pelle Lindbergh, Maine
1981-82	Bob Sullivan, Binghamton
1982-83	Mitch Lamoureux, Baltimore
1983-84	Claude Verret, Rochester
1984-85	Steve Thomas, St. Catharines
1985-86	Ron Hextall, Hershey
1986-87	Brett Hull, Moncton
1987-88	Mike Richard, Binghamton
1988-89	Stephan Lebeau, Sherbrooke
1989-90	Donald Audette, Sherbrooke
1990-91	Patrick Lebeau, Fredericton
1991-92	Felix Potvin, St. John's
1992-93	Corey Hirsch, Binghamton

EDDIE SHORE PLAQUE

(Outstanding defenseman)

Season	Player, Team
1958-59	Steve Kraftcheck, Rochester
1959-60	Larry Hillman, Providence

Season	Player, Team
1960-61	Bob McCord, Springfield
1961-62	Kent Douglas, Springfield
1962-63	Marc Reaume, Hershey
1963-64	Ted Harris, Cleveland
1964-65	Al Arbour, Rochester
1965-66	Jim Morrison, Quebec
1966-67	Bob McCord, Pittsburgh
1967-68	Bill Needham, Cleveland
1968-69	Bob Blackburn, Buffalo
1969-70	Noel Price, Springfield
1970-71	Marshall Johnston, Cleveland
1971-72	Noel Price, Nova Scotia
1972-73	Ray McKay, Cincinnati
1973-74	Gordon Smith, Springfield
1974-75	Joe Zanussi, Providence
1975-76	Noel Price, Nova Scotia
1976-77	Brian Engblom, Nova Scotia
1977-78	Terry Murray, Maine
1978-79	Terry Murray, Maine
1979-80	Rick Vasko, Adirondack
1980-81	Craig Levie, Nova Scotia
1981-82	Dave Farrish, New Brunswick
1982-83	Greg Tebbutt, Baltimore
1983-84	Garry Lariviere, St. Catharines
1984-85	Richie Dunn, Binghamton
1985-86	Jim Wiemer, New Haven
1986-87	Brad Shaw, Binghamton
1987-88	Dave Fenyves, Hershey
1988-89	Dave Fenyves, Hershey
1989-90	Eric Weinrich, Utica
1990-91	Norm Maciver, Cape Breton
1991-92	Greg Hawgood, Cape Breton
1992-93	Bobby Dollas, Adirondack

FRED HUNT MEMORIAL AWARD

(Sportsmanship, determination and dedication)

Season	Player, Team
1977-78	Blake Dunlop, Maine
1978-79	Bernie Johnston, Maine
1979-80	Norm Dube, Nova Scotia
1980-81	Tony Cassolato, Hershey
1981-82	Mike Kasczyki, New Brunswick
1982-83	Ross Yates, Binghamton
1983-84	Claude Larose, Sherbrooke
1984-85	Paul Gardner, Binghamton
1985-86	Steve Tsujiura, Maine
1986-87	Glenn Merkosky, Adirondack
1987-88	Bruce Boudreau, Springfield
1988-89	Murray Eaves, Adirondack
1989-90	Murray Eaves, Adirondack
1990-91	Glenn Merkosky, Adirondack
1991-92	John Anderson, New Haven
1992-93	Tim Tookey, Hershey

LOUIS A.R. PIERI MEMORIAL AWARD

(Top coach)

Season	Coach, Team
1967-68	Vic Stasiuk, Quebec
1968-69	Frank Mathers, Hershey
1969-70	Fred Shero, Buffalo
1970-71	Terry Reardon, Baltimore
1971-72	Al MacNeil, Nova Scotia
1972-73	Floyd Smith, Cincinnati
1973-74	Don Cherry, Rochester
1974-75	John Muckler, Providence
1975-76	Chuck Hamilton, Hershey
1976-77	Al MacNeil, Nova Scotia
1977-78	Bob McCammon, Maine
1978-79	Parker MacDonald, New Haven
1979-80	Doug Gibson, Hershey
1980-81	Bob McCammon, Maine
1981-82	Orval Tessier, New Brunswick
1982-83	Jacques Demers, Fredericton
1983-84	Gene Ubriaco, Baltimore

Season	Coach, Team
1984-85	Bill Dineen, Adirondack
1985-86	Bill Dineen, Adirondack
1986-87	Larry Pleau, Binghamton
1987-88	John Paddock, Hershey
	Mike Milbury, Maine
1988-89	Tom McVie, Utica
1989-90	Jimmy Roberts, Springfield
1990-91	Don Lever, Rochester
1991-92	Doug Carpenter, New Haven
1992-93	Marc Crawford, St. John's

BAZ BASTIEN TROPHY
(Coaches pick as top goaltender)

Season	Player, Team
1983-84	Brian Ford, Fredericton
1984-85	Jon Casey, Baltimore
1985-86	Sam St. Laurent, Maine
1986-87	Mark Laforest, Adirondack
1987-88	Wendell Young, Hershey

Season	Player, Team
1988-89	Randy Exelby, Sherbrooke
1989-90	Jean Claude Bergeron, Sherbrooke
1990-91	Mark Laforest, Binghamton
1991-92	Felix Potvin, St. John's
1992-93	Corey Hirsch, Binghamton

JACK BUTTERFIELD TROPHY
(Calder Cup playoff MVP)

Season	Player, Team
1983-84	Bud Stefanski, Maine
1984-85	Brian Skrudland, Sherbrooke
1985-86	Tim Tookey, Hershey
1986-87	Dave Fenyves, Rochester
1987-88	Wendell Young, Hershey
1988-89	Sam St. Laurent, Adirondack
1989-90	Jeff Hackett, Springfield
1990-91	Kay Whitmore, Springfield
1991-92	Allan Bester, Adirondack
1992-93	Bill McDougall, Cape Breton

ALL-TIME LEAGUE CHAMPIONS

	REGULAR-SEASON CHAMPION		PLAYOFF CHAMPION	
SEASON	Team	Coach	Team	Coach
1936-37	E—Philadelphia	Herb Gardiner	Syracuse	Eddie Powers
	W—Syracuse	Eddie Powers		
1937-38	E—Providence	Bun Cook	Providence	Bun Cook
	W—Cleveland	Bill Cook		
1938-39	E—Philadelphia	Herb Gardiner	Cleveland	Bill Cook
	W—Hershey	Herb Mitchell		
1939-40	E—Providence	Bun Cook	Providence	Bun Cook
	W—Indianapolis	Herb Lewis		
1940-41	E—Providence	Bun Cook	Cleveland	Bill Cook
	W—Cleveland	Bill Cook		
1941-42	E—Springfield	Johnny Mitchell	Indianapolis	Herb Lewis
	W—Indianapolis	Herb Lewis		
1942-43	—Hershey	Cooney Weiland	Buffalo	Art Chapman
1943-44	—Hershey	Cooney Weiland	Buffalo	Art Chapman
	W—Cleveland	Bun Cook		
1944-45	E—Buffalo	Art Chapman	Cleveland	Bun Cook
	W—Cleveland	Bun Cook		
1945-46	E—Buffalo	Frank Beisler	Buffalo	Frank Beisler
	W—Indianapolis	Earl Seibert		
1946-47	E—Hershey	Don Penniston	Hershey	Don Penniston
	W—Cleveland	Bun Cook		
1947-48	E—Providence	Terry Reardon	Cleveland	Bun Cook
	W—Cleveland	Bun Cook		
1948-49	E—Providence	Terry Reardon	Providence	Terry Reardon
	W—St. Louis	Ebbie Goodfellow		
1949-50	E—Buffalo	Roy Goldsworthy	Indianapolis	Ott Heller
	W—Cleveland	Bun Cook		
1950-51	E—Buffalo	Roy Goldsworthy	Cleveland	Bun Cook
	W—Cleveland	Bun Cook		
1951-52	E—Hershey	John Crawford	Pittsburgh	King Clancy
	W—Pittsburgh	King Clancy		
1952-53	—Cleveland	Bun Cook	Cleveland	Bun Cook
1953-54	—Buffalo	Frank Eddolls	Cleveland	Bun Cook
1954-55	—Pittsburgh	Howie Meeker	Pittsburgh	Howie Meeker
1955-56	—Providence	John Crawford	Providence	John Crawford
1956-57	—Providence	John Crawford	Cleveland	Jack Gordon
1957-58	—Hershey	Frank Mathers	Hershey	Frank Mathers
1958-59	—Buffalo	Bobby Kirk	Hershey	Frank Mathers
1959-60	—Springfield	Pat Egan	Springfield	Pat Egan
1960-61	—Springfield	Pat Egan	Springfield	Pat Egan
1961-62	E—Springfield	Pat Egan	Springfield	Pat Egan
	W—Cleveland	Jack Gordon		
1962-63	E—Providence	Fern Flaman	Buffalo	Billy Reay
	W—Buffalo	Billy Reay		
1963-64	E—Quebec	Floyd Curry	Cleveland	Fred Glover
	W—Pittsburgh	Vic Stasiuk		
1964-65	E—Quebec	Bernie Geoffrion	Rochester	Joe Crozier
	W—Rochester	Joe Crozier		
1965-66	E—Quebec	Bernie Geoffrion	Rochester	Joe Crozier
	W—Rochester	Joe Crozier		
1966-67	E—Hershey	Frank Mathers	Pittsburgh	Baz Bastien
	W—Pittsburgh	Baz Bastien		

	REGULAR-SEASON CHAMPION		PLAYOFF CHAMPION	
Season	**Team**	**Coach**	**Team**	**Coach**
1967-68	E—Hershey	Frank Mathers	Rochester	Joe Crozier
	W—Rochester	Joe Crozier		
1968-69	E—Hershey	Frank Mathers	Hershey	Frank Mathers
	W—Buffalo	Fred Shero		
1969-70	E—Montreal	Al MacNeil	Buffalo	Fred Shero
	W—Buffalo	Fred Shero		
1970-71	E—Providence	Larry Wilson	Springfield	John Wilson
	W—Baltimore	Terry Reardon		
1971-72	E—Boston	Armond Guidolin	Nova Scotia	Al MacNeil
	W—Baltimore	Terry Reardon		
1972-73	E—Nova Scotia	Al MacNeil	Cincinnati	Floyd Smith
	W—Cincinnati	Floyd Smith		
1973-74	N—Rochester	Don Cherry	Hershey	Chuck Hamilton
	S—Baltimore	Terry Reardon		
1974-75	N—Providence	John Muckler	Springfield	Ron Stewart
	S—Virginia	Doug Barkley		
1975-76	N—Nova Scotia	Al MacNeil	Nova Scotia	Al MacNeil
	S—Hershey	Chuck Hamilton		
1976-77	—Nova Scotia	Al MacNeil	Nova Scotia	Al MacNeil
1977-78	N—Maine	Bob McCammon	Maine	Bob McCammon
	S—Rochester	Duane Rupp		
1978-79	N—Maine	Bob McCammon	Maine	Bob McCammon
	S—New Haven	Parker MacDonald		
1979-80	N—New Brunswick	Joe Crozier-Lou Angotti	Hershey	Doug Gibson
	S—New Haven	Parker MacDonald		
1980-81	N—Maine	Bob McCammon	Adirondack	Tom Webster-J.P. LeBlanc
	S—Hershey	Bryan Murray		
1981-82	N—New Brunswick	Orval Tessier	New Brunswick	Orval Tessier
	S—Binghamton	Larry Kish		
1982-83	N—Fredericton	Jacques Demers	Rochester	Mike Keenan
	S—Rochester	Mike Keenan		
1983-84	N—Fredericton	Earl Jessiman	Maine	John Paddock
	S—Baltimore	Gene Ubriaco		
1984-85	N—Maine	Tom McVie-John Paddock	Sherbrooke	Pierre Creamer
	S—Binghamton	Larry Pleau		
1985-86	N—Adirondack	Bill Dineen	Adirondack	Bill Dineen
	S—Hershey	John Paddock		
1986-87	N—Sherbrooke	Pierre Creamer	Rochester	John Van Boxmeer
	S—Rochester	John Van Boxmeer*		
1987-88	N—Maine	Mike Milbury	Hershey	John Paddock
	S—Hershey	John Paddock		
1988-89	N—Sherbrooke	Jean Hamel	Adirondack	Bill Dineen
	S—Adirondack	Bill Dineen		
1989-90	N—Sherbrooke	Jean Hamel	Springfield	Jimmy Roberts
	S—Rochester	John Van Boxmeer		
1990-91	N—Springfield	Jimmy Roberts	Springfield	Jimmy Roberts
	S—Rochester	Don Lever		
1991-92	N—Springfield	Jay Leach	Adirondack	Barry Melrose
	S—Binghamton	Ron Smith		
	A—Fredericton	Paulin Bordeleau		
1992-93	N—Providence	Mike O'Connell	Cape Breton	George Burnett
	S—Binghamton	Ron Smith-Colin Campbell		
	A—St. John's	Marc Crawford		

*Rochester awarded division championship based on season-series record.

INTERNATIONAL HOCKEY LEAGUE

LEAGUE OFFICE

Commissioner
N. Thomas Berry Jr.
Chairman of the board of governors
Russell A. Parker
Vice chairman of the board of governors
Joseph E. Tierney Jr.
Consultants
N.R. (Bud) Poile
Jack Riley

Legal counsel
Robert P. Ufer
Director of marketing
Michael G. McCall
Director of operations
Michael A. Meyers
Public relations director
Andrew McGowan

Address
3850 Priority Way
South Drive
Suite 100
Indianapolis, IN 46240
Phone
317-573-3888
FAX
317-573-3880

TEAMS

ATLANTA KNIGHTS

General manager
Richard Adler
Coach
Gene Ubriaco
Home ice
Omni Coliseum
Address
100 Techwood Drive
Atlanta, GA 30303
Seating capacity
15,207
NHL affiliation
Tampa Bay Lightning
Phone
404-525-5800
FAX
404-525-0044

CINCINNATI CYCLONES

General manager
Doug Kirchhofer
Head coach
Dennis Desrosiers
Home ice
Cincinnati Gardens
Address
2250 Seymour Avenue
Cincinnati, OH 45212
Seating capacity
10,326
NHL affiliation
Florida Panthers
Phone
513-531-7825
FAX
513-531-0209

CLEVELAND LUMBERJACKS

General manager
Larry Gordon
Coach
Rick Paterson
Home ice
Richfield Coliseum
Address
504 Superior Avenue NE
Cleveland, OH 44114
Seating capacity
17,480

NHL affiliation
Pittsburgh Penguins
Phone
216-696-0909
FAX
616-696-3909

FORT WAYNE KOMETS

General manager
David Franke
Head coach
To be announced
Home ice
Allen County Memorial Coliseum
Address
4000 Parnell
Fort Wayne, IN 46805
Seating capacity
8,003
NHL affiliation
None
Phone
219-483-0011
FAX
219-483-3899

INDIANAPOLIS ICE

General manager
Ray Compton
Coach
Duane Sutter
Home ice
Pepsi Coliseum
Address
1202 East 38th Street
Indianapolis, IN 46205
Seating capacity
8,233
NHL affiliation
Chicago Blackhawks
Phone
317-924-1234
FAX
317-924-1248

KALAMAZOO WINGS

General manager
Bill Inglis
Coach
Ken Hitchcock

Home ice
Wings Stadium
Address
3620 Van Rick Drive,
Kalamazoo, MI 49002
Seating capacity
5,113
NHL affiliation
Dallas Stars
Phone
616-349-9772
FAX
616-345-6584

KANSAS CITY BLADES

Vice president and general manager
Doug Soetaert
Coach
To be announced
Home ice
Kemper Arena
Address
1800 Genessee
Kansas City, MO 64102
Seating capacity
15,771
NHL affiliation
San Jose Sharks
Phone
816-842-5233
FAX
816-842-5610

LAS VEGAS THUNDER

General manager
Bob Strumm
Head coach
Butch Goring
Home ice
Thomas & Mack Center
Address
P.O. Box 70065
Las Vegas, NV 89170
NHL affiliation
None
Phone
702-798-7825
FAX
702-798-9464

MILWAUKEE ADMIRALS

General manager
Phil Wittliff
Head coach
Curt Fraser
Home ice
Bradley Center
Address
1001 North Fourth Street
Milwaukee, WI 53203
Seating capacity
18,394
NHL affiliation
None
Phone
414-227-0550
FAX
414-227-0568

PEORIA RIVERMEN

General manager
Denis Cyr
Coach
Paul MacLean
Home ice
Peoria Civic Center
Address
201 S. W. Jefferson
Peoria, IL 61602
Seating capacity
9,438

NHL affiliation
St. Louis Blues
Phone
309-676-1040
FAX
309-676-2488

PHOENIX ROADRUNNERS

General manager
Adam Keller
Coach
Tim Bothwell
Home ice
Veterans Memorial Coliseum
Address
1826 West McDowell Road
Phoenix, AZ 85007
Seating capacity
13,739
NHL affiliation
Los Angeles Kings
Phone
602-340-0001
FAX
602-340-0041

SALT LAKE GOLDEN EAGLES

General manager
Mike Forbes
Coach
Dave Farrish

Home ice
Delta Center
Address
301 W. South Temple
Salt Lake City, UT 84101
Seating capacity
10,387
NHL affiliation
New York Islanders
Phone
801-325-2300
FAX
801-325-2314

SAN DIEGO GULLS

General manager
Don Waddell
Coach
Rick Dudley
Home ice
San Diego Sports Arena
Address
3780 Hancock Street
Suite "G"
San Diego, CA 92110
Seating capacity
13,200
NHL affiliation
Mighty Ducks of Anaheim
Phone
619-688-1800
FAX
619-688-1808

1992-93 REGULAR SEASON

FINAL STANDINGS

EASTERN CONFERENCE

ATLANTIC DIVISION

Team	G	W	L		Pts.	GF	GA
Atlanta	82	52	23	(7)	111	333	291
Cleveland	82	39	34	(9)	87	329	330
Cincinnati	82	27	48	(7)	61	305	364

CENTRAL DIVISION

Team	G	W	L		Pts.	GF	GA
Fort Wayne	82	49	27	(6)	104	339	294
Indianapolis	82	34	39	(9)	77	324	347
Kalamazoo	82	29	42	(11)	69	291	367

WESTERN CONFERENCE

MIDWEST DIVISION

Team	G	W	L		Pts.	GF	GA
Milwaukee	82	49	23	(10)	108	329	280
Kansas City	82	46	26	(10)	102	318	288
Peoria	82	41	33	(8)	90	297	307

PACIFIC DIVISION

Team	G	W	L		Pts.	GF	GA
San Diego	82	62	12	(8)	132	381	229
Salt Lake	82	38	39	(5)	81	269	305
Phoenix	82	26	50	(6)	58	248	361

( )—Indicates overtime losses and are worth one point.

INDIVIDUAL LEADERS

Goals: Brad Lauer, Indianapolis (50)
Assists: Tony Hrkac, Indianapolis (87)
Points: Tony Hrkac, Indianapolis (132)
Penalty minutes: Daniel Shank, San Diego (495)
Goaltending average: Rick Knickle, San Diego (2.17)
Shutouts: Rick Knickle, San Diego (4)

TOP SCORERS

	Games	G	A	Pts.
Tony Hrkac, Indianapolis	80	45	87	132
Dave Michayluk, Cleveland	82	47	65	112
Daniel Gauthier, Cleveland	80	40	66	106
Patrick Lebeau, Salt Lake	75	40	60	100
Daniel Shank, San Diego	77	39	53	92
Brad Lauer, Indianapolis	62	50	41	91

	Games	G	A	Pts.
Keith Osborne, Atlanta	72	40	49	89
Paul Willett, Fort Wayne	74	33	52	85
Brian Dobbin, Milwaukee	80	39	45	84
Jock Callander, Atlanta	69	34	50	84
Scott Arniel, San Diego	79	35	48	83
Dale DeGray, San Diego	79	18	64	82
Gary Emmons, Kansas City	80	37	44	81
Scott Gruhl, Fort Wayne	73	34	47	81
Colin Chin, Fort Wayne	69	30	51	81
John Anderson, San Diego	65	34	46	80
Shawn Evans, Milwaukee	79	13	65	78
Doug Wickenheiser, Peoria	80	30	45	75
Hubie McDonough, San Diego	48	26	49	75
Perry Ganchar, Cleveland	79	37	37	74
Rich Chernomaz, Salt Lake	76	26	48	74

ATLANTA KNIGHTS

SCORING

	Games	G	A	Pts.	Pen.
Keith Osborne	72	40	49	89	91
Jock Callander	69	34	50	84	172
Jason Lafreniere	63	23	47	70	34
Colin Miller	76	20	39	59	52
Dave Capuano	58	19	40	59	50
Stan Drulia	47	28	26	54	38
Brent Gretzky	77	20	34	54	84
Shawn Rivers	78	9	34	43	101
Tim Bergland	49	18	21	39	26
Shayne Stevenson	53	17	17	34	160
Matt Hervey	49	12	19	31	122
Ken Hodge	16	10	17	27	0
Jason Ruff	26	11	14	25	90
Steve Maltais	16	14	10	24	22
Jean Blouin	61	11	11	22	69
Jeff Buchanan	68	4	18	22	282
Scott Boston	76	2	17	19	75
Rick Lanz	25	6	12	18	30
Chris Lipuma	66	4	14	18	379
Herb Raglan	24	4	10	14	139
Eric DuBois	43	3	9	12	44
Martin Simard	19	5	5	10	77
Dan Vincelette	30	5	5	10	126
Christian Campeau	66	3	5	8	40
David Littman (goalie)	44	0	5	5	46
Stephane Richer	3	0	4	4	4
Don Burke	15	0	3	3	20
Roman Hamrlik	2	1	1	2	2
Shawn Chambers	6	0	2	2	18
Sergei Osipov	6	0	2	2	0
Eric Charron	11	0	2	2	12
Danton Cole	1	1	0	1	2
Alain Cote	8	1	0	1	0
Mark Green	5	0	1	1	0
Cory Cross	7	0	1	1	2
J.C. Bergeron (goalie)	31	0	1	1	0
Bob Beers	1	0	0	0	0
Denis Chervyakov	1	0	0	0	0
Manon Rheaume (goalie)	2	0	0	0	0
Wendell Young (goalie)	3	0	0	0	0
Mike Greenlay (goalie)	12	0	0	0	2

GOALTENDING

	Games	Min.	Goals	SO	Avg.
Wendell Young	3	183	8	0	2.62
J.C. Bergeron	31	1722	92(1)	1	3.21
David Littman	44	2390	134(2)	0	3.36
Mike Greenlay	12	637	40	0	3.77
Manon Rheaume	2	66	7(2)	0	6.36

CINCINNATI CYCLONES

SCORING

	Games	G	A	Pts.	Pen.
Dennis Holland	71	23	47	70	140
Darcy Norton	74	26	30	56	90
Paul Lawless	29	29	25	54	64
Jeff Madill	58	36	17	53	175
Mario Thyer	77	13	36	49	26
Claude Vilgrain	57	19	26	45	22
Kevin Kerr	39	18	23	41	93
Alan Hepple	70	7	31	38	201
Mike Dagenais	69	14	22	36	128
Mike Bodnarchuk	47	15	18	33	65
Sergei Kharin	60	13	18	31	25
Chris Nelson	58	4	26	30	69
Ian Kidd	23	6	23	29	10
Jon Morris	18	7	19	26	24
Bill H. Armstrong	42	14	11	25	99
Howie Rosenblatt	45	10	7	17	201
Jeff Christian	36	5	12	17	113

	Games	G	A	Pts.	Pen.
Brian Lawton	17	5	11	16	30
Todd Flichel	52	5	10	15	46
Ralph Barahona	30	8	6	14	4
Craig Charron	27	6	8	14	8
David Latta	13	4	7	11	26
Marc Laniel	13	1	9	10	2
Al Tuer	52	1	9	10	248
Scott Shaunessy	71	2	7	9	222
Janne Ojanen	7	1	8	9	0
Craig Coxe	20	5	3	8	34
Jim Larkin	11	1	3	4	2
Kevin Dean	13	2	1	3	15
Jarrod Skalde	4	1	2	3	4
David Craievich	21	0	3	3	33
Shaun Kane	22	0	3	3	10
Todd Copeland	37	0	3	3	47
Kevin Riehl	3	0	2	2	0
Troy Gamble (goalie)	33	0	2	2	22
Joe Flanagan	9	1	0	1	2
Mark Krys	3	0	1	1	2
Jerome Bechard	1	0	0	0	2
Jeff Hogden	1	0	0	0	0
Shaun Clouston	2	0	0	0	2
Kevin Grant	2	0	0	0	2
Sergei Khramtsov (goalie)	3	0	0	0	0
Corey Schwab (goalie)	3	0	0	0	0
Dean Morton	7	0	0	0	44
Chad Erickson (goalie)	10	0	0	0	2
Doug Dadswell (goalie)	17	0	0	0	6
Sandy Galuppo (goalie)	28	0	0	0	0

GOALTENDING

	Games	Min.	Goals	SO	Avg.
Sergei Khramtsov	3	120	7	0	3.50
Doug Dadswell	17	1006	63(2)	1	3.76
Sandy Galuppo	28	1356	93(2)	0	4.12
Troy Gamble	33	1762	134(1)	0	4.56
Chad Erickson	10	516	42(1)	0	4.88
Corey Schwab	3	185	17	0	5.51

CLEVELAND LUMBERJACKS

SCORING

	Games	G	A	Pts.	Pen.
Dave Michayluk	82	47	65	112	104
Daniel Gauthier	80	40	66	106	88
Perry Ganchar	79	37	37	74	156
Justin Duberman	77	29	42	71	69
Ken Priestlay	66	33	36	69	72
Sandy Smith	77	32	36	68	174
Jason Smart	78	12	36	48	151
Todd Nelson	76	7	35	42	115
George Zajankala	76	16	21	37	80
Mark Major	82	13	15	28	155
Jamie Heward	58	9	18	27	64
Paul Dyck	69	6	21	27	69
Paul Laus	76	8	18	26	427
Greg Andrusak	55	3	22	25	78
David Quinn	60	8	13	21	102
Ed Patterson	63	4	16	20	131
Travis Thiessen	64	3	7	10	69
Jamie Leach	9	5	3	8	2
Martin Straka	4	4	3	7	2
Bryan Fogarty	15	2	5	7	8
Grant Block	5	4	1	5	2
Al Tuer	13	1	4	5	29
Robert Melanson	27	0	5	5	123
Jeff Daniels	3	2	1	3	0
Rob Dopson (goalie)	50	0	3	3	2
Mike Needham	1	2	0	2	0
Peter Ahola	9	1	0	1	4
Jim Latos	1	0	0	0	0
Eric Raymond (goalie)	3	0	0	0	2
Bruce Racine (goalie)	35	0	0	0	10

GOALTENDING

	Games	Min.	Goals	SO	Avg.
Rob Dopson	50	2825	167(1)	1	3.55
Bruce Racine	35	1949	140(1)	1	4.31
Eric Raymond	3	180	16	0	5.33

FORT WAYNE KOMETS

SCORING

	Games	G	A	Pts.	Pen.
Paul Willett	74	33	52	85	109
Scott Gruhl	73	34	47	81	290
Colin Chin	69	30	51	81	44
Igor Chibirev	60	33	36	69	2
Kory Kocur	66	21	36	57	77
Kelly Hurd	71	23	31	54	81
Ian Boyce	69	19	34	53	63
Jean-Marc Richard	52	10	33	43	48
Lee Davidson	60	22	20	42	58
Bob Lakso	63	17	21	38	4
Joel Savage	46	21	16	37	60
Peter Hankinson	40	12	15	27	16
Bob Jay	78	5	21	26	100
Dan Ratushny	63	6	19	25	48
Grant Richison	52	5	18	23	73
Max Middendorf	24	9	13	22	58
Bob Wilkie	32	7	14	21	82
Carey Lucyk	72	4	16	20	75
Guy Dupuis	53	4	11	15	57
Dave Smith	25	7	6	13	77
Kevin MacDonald	65	4	9	13	283
Steve Fletcher	52	5	6	11	337
Phil Berger	8	2	5	7	14
Tod Hartje	5	1	2	3	6
Russ Romaniuk	4	2	0	2	7
Ralph Barahona	7	0	2	2	2
Pokey Reddick (goalie)	54	0	2	2	12
Jason Winch	2	0	1	1	0
Igor Ulanov	3	0	1	1	29
Steve Herniman	8	0	1	1	23
Serge Anglehart	2	0	0	0	2
Rik Wilson	2	0	0	0	4
Mark Richards (goalie)	3	0	0	0	0
Steve Wilson	12	0	0	0	4
Dave Gagnon (goalie)	31	0	0	0	12

GOALTENDING

	Games	Min.	Goals	SO	Avg.
Pokey Reddick	54	3043	156(3)	3	3.08
Dave Gagnon	31	1771	116(4)	0	3.93
Mark Richards	3	139	11	0	4.75

INDIANAPOLIS ICE

SCORING

	Games	G	A	Pts.	Pen.
Tony Hrkac	80	45	87	132	70
Brad Lauer	62	50	41	91	80
Sergei Krivokrasov	78	36	33	69	157
Sean Williams	81	28	37	65	66
Alexandr Andrievski	66	26	25	51	59
Steve Bancroft	53	10	35	45	138
Ivan Droppa	77	14	29	43	92
Milan Tichy	49	7	32	39	62
Rob Brown	19	14	19	33	32
Craig Woodcroft	65	12	19	31	80
Kevin St. Jacques	71	10	21	31	93
Rob Conn	75	13	14	27	81
Joe Cleary	63	10	17	27	110
Tracy Egeland	43	11	14	25	122
Adam Bennett	39	8	16	24	69
Karl Dykhuis	59	5	18	23	76
Zac Boyer	59	7	14	21	26
Shawn Byram	41	2	13	15	123
Vladimir Tsyplakov	11	6	7	13	4
Joe Crowley	55	2	3	5	111
Trevor Dam	11	1	3	4	27
Dave Hakstol	54	1	3	4	82

	Games	G	A	Pts.	Pen.
Rod Buskas	15	0	3	3	40
Tony Horacek	6	1	1	2	28
Mike Speer	38	1	1	2	109
Roch Belley (goalie)	7	0	2	2	0
Kevin Hodson (goalie)	14	0	2	2	0
Greg Spenrath	9	0	1	1	68
Stephan Tepper	12	0	1	1	40
Owen Lessard	1	0	0	0	2
Jason Muzzatti (goalie)	12	0	0	0	17
Kerry Toporowski	17	0	0	0	57
Ray LeBlanc (goalie)	56	0	0	0	12

GOALTENDING

	Games	Min.	Goals	SO	Avg.
Ray LeBlanc	56	3201	206(6)	0	3.86
Jason Muzzatti	12	707	48(1)	0	4.07
Kevin Hodson	14	777	53(2)	0	4.09
Roch Belley	7	289	25(1)	0	5.19

KALAMAZOO WINGS

SCORING

	Games	G	A	Pts.	Pen.
James Black	63	25	45	70	40
Yves Heroux	80	38	30	68	86
Doug Barrault	78	32	34	66	74
Cal McGowan	78	18	42	60	62
Kip Miller	61	17	39	56	59
Mike Kennedy	77	21	30	51	39
Derrick Smith	52	22	13	35	43
Mark Lawrence	57	22	13	35	47
Roy Mitchell	79	7	25	32	119
Kevin Evans	49	7	24	31	283
Tim Lenardon	60	12	18	30	56
Ross Wilson	58	15	14	29	49
Brian Straub	75	6	14	20	101
Dave Moylan	73	5	15	20	179
Paul Jerrard	80	8	11	19	187
Trent Klatt	31	8	11	19	18
Tom Nemeth	48	6	13	19	24
Mike Reier	31	4	14	18	12
Collin Bauer	32	4	14	18	31
Kevan Melrose	40	3	8	11	48
Reid Simpson	45	5	5	10	193
Jeff Bes	3	1	3	4	6
Enrico Ciccone	13	1	3	4	50
Derian Hatcher	2	1	2	3	21
Craig Coxe	12	1	1	2	8
Marc Savard	20	1	1	2	24
Shaun Kane	4	0	2	2	0
Jeff Levy (goalie)	28	0	2	2	6
Richard Matvichuk	3	0	1	1	6
Mike Torchia (goalie)	48	0	1	1	4
Shayne Green	1	0	0	0	0
Frank Kovacs	1	0	0	0	2
Jeff Stolp (goalie)	14	0	0	0	0

GOALTENDING

	Games	Min.	Goals	SO	Avg.
Mike Torchia	48	2729	173(1)	0	3.80
Jeff Levy	28	1512	115(2)	0	4.56
Jeff Stolp	14	733	62(4)	0	5.08

KANSAS CITY BLADES

SCORING

	Games	G	A	Pts.	Pen.
Gary Emmons	80	37	44	81	80
Mikhail Kravets	71	19	49	68	153
Mark Beaufait	66	19	40	59	22
Ray Whitney	46	20	33	53	14
Dale Craigwell	60	15	38	53	24
J.F. Quintin	64	20	29	49	169
Jeff McLean	60	21	23	44	45
Jaroslav Otevrel	62	17	27	44	58
Duane Joyce	75	15	25	40	30
Claudio Scremin	75	10	22	32	93

	Games	G	A	Pts.	Pen.
Dean Kolstad	63	9	21	30	79
Ed Courtenay	32	15	11	26	25
Jeff Sharples	39	5	21	26	43
Larry DePalma	30	11	11	22	83
Tom Pederson	26	6	15	21	10
Victor Ignatjev	64	5	16	21	68
Michel Picard	33	7	10	17	51
Pat MacLeod	18	8	8	16	14
Rob Gaudreau	19	8	6	14	6
Stephan Tepper	32	4	10	14	51
David Williams	31	1	11	12	28
Brian Lawton	9	6	4	10	10
Gord Frantti	21	3	6	9	47
John Weisbrod	16	6	2	8	6
Perry Berezan	9	4	4	8	31
John Carter	9	4	2	6	14
Mike Colman	80	1	5	6	191
Larry Olimb	11	0	6	6	4
Dody Wood	36	3	2	5	216
Don Barber	9	3	1	4	4
Tim Hanus	7	2	1	3	2
Robin Bawa	5	2	0	2	20
Lyndon Byers	4	1	1	2	22
Ron Handy	6	1	1	2	2
Norm Foster (goalie)	8	0	1	1	2
Troy Frederick	16	0	1	1	27
Wade Flaherty (goalie)	61	0	1	1	24
Rick Lessard	1	0	0	0	0
Link Gaetz	2	0	0	0	14
Vince Guidotti	2	0	0	0	0
Shaun Kane	2	0	0	0	2
Sean Gorman	3	0	0	0	0
Jeff Massey	3	0	0	0	0
Derry Menard	4	0	0	0	2
Arturs Irbe (goalie)	6	0	0	0	0
Chris Jensen	8	0	0	0	12
Dan Ryder (goalie)	10	0	0	0	0

GOALTENDING

	Games	Min.	Goals	SO	Avg.
Wade Flaherty	61	3642	195(4)	2	3.21
Arturs Irbe	6	364	20	0	3.30
Norm Foster	8	489	28(1)	0	3.44
Dan Ryder	10	514	35	0	4.09

MILWAUKEE ADMIRALS

SCORING

	Games	G	A	Pts.	Pen.
Brian Dobbin	80	39	45	84	50
Shawn Evans	79	13	65	78	83
Jeff Larmer	78	31	34	65	46
Michel Mongeau	45	24	41	65	69
Ladislav Tresl	67	28	35	63	30
Steve Tuttle	51	27	34	61	12
Alex Galchenyuk	44	13	33	46	22
Mitch Messier	62	18	23	41	84
Bruce Bell	70	10	28	38	120
Jergus Baca	73	9	29	38	108
Jim Johannson	71	14	22	36	72
Mike McNeill	75	17	17	34	34
Dennis Snedden	52	13	20	33	39
Lou Crawford	56	16	14	30	108
Scott Robinson	27	13	10	23	33
Carl Valimont	59	4	18	22	52
Jeff Madill	23	13	6	19	53
Don Gibson	68	3	14	17	381
Ian Kidd	32	3	10	13	36
Randy Skarda	54	3	9	12	104
Richard Zemlak	62	3	9	12	299
Steve Strunk	15	4	5	9	6
Bob Halkidis	26	0	9	9	79
Randy Boyd	8	1	4	5	8
Wayne Van Dorp	19	1	4	5	57
Jeff Rohlicek	11	1	1	2	8
Larry Dyck (goalie)	40	0	2	2	14

	Games	G	A	Pts.	Pen.
Mikhail Shtalenkov (goalie)	47	0	2	2	10
Rob Dumas	1	0	0	0	0
Shaun Kane	4	0	0	0	0

GOALTENDING

	Games	Min.	Goals	SO	Avg.
Mikhail Shtalenkov	47	2669	135(3)	2	3.03
Larry Dyck	40	2328	131(4)	0	3.38

PEORIA RIVERMEN

SCORING

	Games	G	A	Pts.	Pen.
Doug Wickenheiser	80	30	45	75	30
Richard Pion	74	20	35	55	119
Darren Veitch	79	12	37	49	16
Dave Mackey	42	24	22	46	112
Lee Leslie	72	22	24	46	46
Kevin Miehm	30	12	33	45	13
Brian McKee	63	14	30	44	78
Jason Ruff	40	22	21	43	81
Brian Pellerin	78	15	25	40	204
Derek Frenette	73	18	19	37	44
Denny Felsner	29	14	21	35	8
Kyle Reeves	50	17	14	31	83
Ron Hoover	58	17	13	30	28
Terry Hollinger	72	2	28	30	67
Daniel Laperriere	54	4	20	24	28
Joe Hawley	50	12	11	23	52
Jeff Batters	74	5	18	23	113
Vitali Karamnov	23	8	12	20	47
Jason Marshall	77	4	16	20	229
Peter Kasowski	22	5	5	10	24
Shawn Wheeler	45	6	3	9	185
Bret Hedican	19	0	8	8	10
Ron Handy	18	0	7	7	16
Mark Reeds	16	4	2	6	8
Philippe Bozon	4	3	2	5	2
Rob Robinson	34	0	4	4	38
Darren Colbourne	6	1	1	2	2
Geoff Sarjeant (goalie)	41	0	2	2	10
Parris Duffus (goalie)	38	0	1	1	18
Devin Edgerton	2	0	0	0	0
Nick Vitucci (goalie)	8	0	0	0	2
Brian Blad	12	0	0	0	14

GOALTENDING

	Games	Min.	Goals	SO	Avg.
Geoff Sarjeant	41	2356	130(2)	0	3.31
Nick Vitucci	8	479	27(2)	0	3.38
Parris Duffus	37	2149	142	0	3.96

PHOENIX ROADRUNNERS

SCORING

	Games	G	A	Pts.	Pen.
Guy Leveque	56	27	30	57	71
Sean Whyte	51	11	35	46	65
Tim Breslin	79	14	30	44	55
Mike Vukonich	70	25	15	40	27
Sylvain Couturier	38	23	16	39	63
Brad Tiley	46	11	27	38	35
Brad McCaughey	58	12	24	36	25
Robert Lang	38	9	21	30	20
Darryl Williams	61	18	7	25	314
Brandy Semchuk	56	13	12	25	58
Kevin Grant	49	4	17	21	119
Ed Kastelic	57	11	7	18	158
Jim Maher	47	5	13	18	72
Rene Chapdelaine	44	1	17	18	54
Shawn McCosh	22	9	8	17	36
Keith Redmond	53	6	10	16	285
Frank Breault	31	5	11	16	26
David Tretowicz	79	1	15	16	22
Marc Fortier	17	4	9	13	34
John Mokosak	46	4	9	13	169
Scott Bjugstad	7	5	4	9	4

	Games	G	A	Pts.	Pen.
Jim Thomson	14	4	5	9	44
Brett Seguin	16	2	7	9	8
Ted Kramer	31	3	4	7	4
Marc Saumier	6	3	3	6	17
Tim Watters	31	3	3	6	43
Mike Ruark	57	3	3	6	168
Phil Crowe	53	3	3	6	190
John Vary	9	0	6	6	10
Lonnie Loach	4	2	3	5	10
Brent Thompson	22	0	5	5	112
Dave Stewart	32	0	3	3	53
Jeff Chychrun	11	2	0	2	44
Jim Hiller	3	0	2	2	2
Kevin MacDonald	6	0	1	1	23
David Goverde (goalie)	46	0	1	1	30
Bob Berg	1	0	0	0	0
George Maneluk (goalie)	2	0	0	0	2
Paul Holden	3	0	0	0	6
Darryl Gilmour (goalie)	41	0	0	0	2

GOALTENDING

	Games	Min.	Goals	SO	Avg.
David Goverde	45	2569	173(2)	1	4.04
Darryl Gilmour	41	2281	168(3)	0	4.42
George Maneluk	2	120	10	0	5.00

SALT LAKE GOLDEN EAGLES

SCORING

	Games	G	A	Pts.	Pen.
Patrick Lebeau	75	40	60	100	65
Rich Chernomaz	76	26	48	74	172
Shawn Heaphy	78	29	36	65	63
Kevin Wortman	82	13	50	63	24
Tomas Forslund	63	31	23	54	68
David Struch	78	20	22	42	73
Sandy McCarthy	77	18	20	38	220
Todd Harkins	53	13	21	34	90
Todd Gillingham	75	12	21	33	267
Kerry Clark	64	14	15	29	255
Kris Miller	45	4	21	25	45
Todd Brost	82	5	17	22	42
David St. Pierre	35	7	8	15	18
Tim Harris	52	5	10	15	48
Paul Holden	63	5	8	13	86
Ken Sabourin	52	2	11	13	140
Alexander Yudin	16	3	7	10	85
Kevan Guy	33	1	9	10	50
Darren Stolk	64	4	5	9	65
Kevan Melrose	33	3	6	9	74
Alex Nikolic	37	4	4	8	133
Paul Kruse	35	1	4	5	206
Rod Buskas	31	0	2	2	52
Greg Smyth	5	0	1	1	31
Jason Muzzatti (goalie)	13	0	1	1	8
Trevor Kidd (goalie)	30	0	1	1	36
Kevin Grant	1	0	0	0	2
Mike Polano	2	0	0	0	0
Gary Socha	4	0	0	0	0
Andrei Trefilov (goalie)	44	0	0	0	44

GOALTENDING

	Games	Min.	Goals	SO	Avg.
Andrei Trefilov	44	2536	135(2)	0	3.19
Trevor Kidd	29	1696	111(2)	1	3.93
Jason Muzzatti	13	747	52(1)	0	4.18

SAN DIEGO GULLS

SCORING

	Games	G	A	Pts.	Pen.
Daniel Shank	77	39	53	92	495
Scott Arniel	79	35	48	83	116
Dale DeGray	79	18	64	82	181
John Anderson	65	34	46	80	18
Hubie McDonough	48	26	49	75	22

	Games	G	A	Pts.	Pen.
Bill Houlder	64	24	48	72	39
Mitch Lamoureux	71	28	39	67	130
Len Hachborn	59	23	36	59	49
Larry Floyd	80	27	31	58	28
Don McSween	80	15	40	55	85
Robbie Nichols	72	18	32	50	261
Lindy Ruff	81	10	32	42	100
Ken Hodge	30	11	24	35	16
Denny Lambert	56	18	12	30	277
Gord Dineen	41	6	23	29	36
Max Middendorf	30	15	11	26	25
Perry Anderson	51	8	13	21	217
Mark Ferner	26	0	15	15	34
Peter Hankinson	25	7	7	14	10
Tony McKegney	23	8	5	13	38
Darryl Olsen	21	2	8	10	26
Sergei Starikov	42	0	9	9	12
Keith Gretzky	20	1	7	8	2
Kord Cernich	17	1	5	6	4
Steve Martinson	10	0	4	4	55
Doug Smail	9	2	1	3	20
Lyndon Byers	9	0	3	3	35
Rene Chapdelaine	9	1	1	2	8
Marc LaBelle	5	0	2	2	5
Jean-Marc Richard	6	1	0	1	4
Alan Hepple	10	0	1	1	27
Clint Malarchuk (goalie)	27	0	1	1	8
Rick Knickle (goalie)	41	0	1	1	6
Matt DelGuidice (goalie)	1	0	0	0	0
Andrei Iakovenko	1	0	0	0	0
Bill Horn (goalie)	2	0	0	0	0
Dan Vincelette	6	0	0	0	6
Mitch Molloy	8	0	0	0	8
Peter Ing (goalie)	17	0	0	0	2

GOALTENDING

	Games	Min.	Goals	SO	Avg.
Rick Knickle	41	2437	88(1)	4	2.17
Bill Horn	2	120	5	0	2.50
Clint Malarchuk	27	1516	72(1)	3	2.85
Peter Ing	17	882	53	0	3.61
Matt DelGuidice	1	20	2	0	6.00

PLAYERS WITH TWO OR MORE TEAMS

SCORING

	Games	G	A	Pts.	Pen.
Ralph Barahona, Cincinnati	30	8	6	14	4
Ralph Barahona, Fort Wayne	7	0	2	2	2
Totals	37	8	8	16	6
Rod Buskas, Indianapolis	15	0	3	3	40
Rod Buskas, Salt Lake	31	0	2	2	52
Totals	46	0	5	5	92
Lyndon Byers, Kansas City	4	1	1	2	22
Lyndon Byers, San Diego	9	0	3	3	35
Totals	13	1	4	5	57
Rene Chapdelaine, Phoenix	44	1	17	18	54
Rene Chapdelaine, San Diego	9	1	1	2	8
Totals	53	2	18	20	62
Craig Coxe, Cincinnati	20	5	3	8	34
Craig Coxe, Kalamazoo	12	1	1	2	8
Totals	32	6	4	10	42
Kevin Grant, Salt Lake	1	0	0	0	2
Kevin Grant, Phoenix	49	4	17	21	119
Kevin Grant, Cincinnati	2	0	0	0	2
Totals	52	4	17	21	123
Ron Handy, Peoria	18	0	7	7	16
Ron Handy, Kansas City	6	1	1	2	2
Totals	24	1	8	9	18
Peter Hankinson, San Diego	25	7	7	14	10
Peter Hankinson, Fort Wayne	40	12	15	27	16
Totals	65	19	22	41	26
Alan Hepple, San Diego	10	0	1	1	27
Alan Hepple, Cincinnati	70	7	31	38	201
Totals	80	7	32	39	228

	Games	G	A	Pts.	Pen.
Ken Hodge, Atlanta	16	10	17	27	0
Ken Hodge, San Diego	30	11	24	35	16
Totals	46	21	41	62	16
Paul Holden, Phoenix	3	0	0	0	6
Paul Holden, Salt Lake	63	5	8	13	86
Totals	66	5	8	13	92
Shaun Kane, Kalamazoo	4	0	2	2	0
Shaun Kane, Milwaukee	4	0	0	0	0
Shaun Kane, Kansas City	2	0	0	0	2
Shaun Kane, Cincinnati	22	0	3	3	10
Totals	32	0	5	5	12
Ian Kidd, Milwaukee	32	3	10	13	36
Ian Kidd, Cincinnati	23	6	23	29	10
Totals	55	9	33	42	46
Brian Lawton, Kansas City	9	6	4	10	10
Brian Lawton, Cincinnati	17	5	11	16	30
Totals	26	11	15	26	40
Kevin MacDonald, Phoenix	6	0	1	1	23
Kevin MacDonald, Fort Wayne	65	4	9	13	283
Totals	71	4	10	14	306
Jeff Madill, Cincinnati	58	36	17	53	175
Jeff Madill, Milwaukee	23	13	6	19	53
Totals	81	49	23	72	228
Kevan Melrose, Salt Lake	33	3	6	9	74
Kevan Melrose, Kalamazoo	40	3	8	11	48
Totals	73	6	14	20	122

	Games	G	A	Pts.	Pen.
Jason Muzzatti, Ind. (g)	12	0	0	0	17
Jason Muzzatti, Salt Lake (g)	13	0	1	1	8
Totals	25	0	1	1	25
Jean-Marc Richard, S.D.	6	1	0	1	4
Jean-Marc Richard, F.W.	52	10	33	43	48
Totals	58	11	33	44	52
Jason Ruff, Peoria	40	22	21	43	81
Jason Ruff, Atlanta	26	11	14	25	90
Totals	66	33	35	68	171
Stephan Tepper, Ind.	12	0	1	1	40
Stephan Tepper, K.C.	32	4	10	14	51
Totals	44	4	11	15	91
Al Tuer, Cincinnati	52	1	9	10	248
Al Tuer, Cleveland	13	1	4	5	29
Totals	65	2	13	15	277
Dan Vincelette, Atlanta	30	5	5	10	126
Dan Vincelette, San Diego	6	0	0	0	6
Totals	36	5	5	10	132

GOALTENDING

	Games	Min.	Goals	SO	Avg.
Jason Muzzatti, Ind.	12	707	48(1)	0	4.07
Jason Muzzatti, S.L.	13	747	52(1)	0	4.18
Totals	25	1454	100(2)	0	4.13

1993 TURNER CUP PLAYOFFS

RESULTS

QUARTERFINALS

WESTERN CONFERENCE

Series "A"

	W	L	Pts.	GF	GA
San Diego	4	0	8	20	10
Peoria	0	4	0	10	20

(San Diego won series, 4-0)

Series "B"

	W	L	Pts.	GF	GA
Kansas City	4	2	8	22	18
Milwaukee	2	4	4	18	22

(Kansas City won series, 4-2)

EASTERN CONFERENCE

Series "C"

	W	L	Pts.	GF	GA
Atlanta	4	1	8	25	16
Indianapolis	1	4	2	16	25

(Atlanta won series, 4-1)

Series "D"

	W	L	Pts.	GF	GA
Fort Wayne	4	0	8	22	8
Cleveland	0	4	0	8	22

(Fort Wayne won series, 4-0)

SEMIFINALS

WESTERN CONFERENCE

Series "E"

	W	L	Pts.	GF	GA
San Diego	4	2	8	18	16
Kansas City	2	4	4	16	18

(San Diego won series, 4-2)

EASTERN CONFERENCE

Series "F"

	W	L	Pts.	GF	GA
Fort Wayne	4	0	8	11	5
Atlanta	0	4	0	5	11

(Fort Wayne won series, 4-0)

TURNER CUP FINALS

Series "G"

	W	L	Pts.	GF	GA
Fort Wayne	4	0	8	21	5
San Diego	0	4	0	5	21

(Fort Wayne won series, 4-0)

INDIVIDUAL LEADERS

Goals: Jock Callander, Atlanta (7)
 Igor Chibirev, Fort Wayne (7)
 Dale Craigwell, Kansas City (7)
 Gary Emmons, Kansas City (7)
 Paul Willett, Fort Wayne (7)
Assists: Igor Chibirev, Fort Wayne (13)
Points: Igor Chibirev, Fort Wayne (20)
Penalty minutes: Daniel Shank, San Diego (131)
Goaltending average: Pokey Reddick, Fort Wayne (1.49)
Shutouts: Wade Flaherty, Kansas City (1)

TOP SCORERS

	Games	G	A	Pts.
Igor Chibirev, Fort Wayne	12	7	13	20
Jean-Marc Richard, Fort Wayne	12	6	11	17
Daniel Shank, San Diego	14	5	10	15
Scott Gruhl, Fort Wayne	12	4	11	15
Dale DeGray, San Diego	14	3	11	14
Paul Willett, Fort Wayne	10	7	6	13
Gary Emmons, Kansas City	12	7	6	13
Jock Callander, Atlanta	9	7	5	12
Dale Craigwell, Kansas City	12	7	5	12
Ray Whitney, Kansas City	12	5	7	12

INDIVIDUAL STATISTICS

ATLANTA KNIGHTS

(Lost semifinals to Fort Wayne, 4-0)

SCORING

	Games	G	A	Pts.	Pen.
Jock Callander	9	7	5	12	25
Jason Lafreniere	9	3	4	7	22
Tim Bergland	9	3	3	6	10
Herb Raglan	9	3	3	6	32
Colin Miller	9	2	4	6	22
Keith Osborne	8	1	5	6	2
Brent Gretzky	9	3	2	5	8
Stan Drulia	3	2	3	5	4
Dave Capuano	8	2	2	4	9
Shawn Rivers	9	1	3	4	8
Matt Hervey	9	0	4	4	19
Jason Ruff	7	2	1	3	26
Chris Lipuma	9	1	1	2	35
Shayne Stevenson	6	0	2	2	21
Eric Charron	3	0	1	1	6
David Littman (goalie)	3	0	1	1	2
Alain Cote	1	0	0	0	0
Scott Boston	2	0	0	0	0
Christian Campeau	3	0	0	0	2
Cory Cross	4	0	0	0	6
J.C. Bergeron (goalie)	6	0	0	0	0
Jeff Buchanan	9	0	0	0	26
Eric DuBois	9	0	0	0	10

GOALTENDING

	Games	Min.	Goals	SO	Avg.
David Littman	3	178	8	0	2.70
J.C. Bergeron	6	368	19	0	3.10

CLEVELAND LUMBERJACKS

(Lost quarterfinals to Fort Wayne, 4-0)

SCORING

	Games	G	A	Pts.	Pen.
Daniel Gauthier	4	2	2	4	14
Ken Priestlay	4	2	1	3	4
Jamie Leach	4	1	2	3	0
Dave Michayluk	4	1	2	3	4
Ed Patterson	3	1	1	2	2
Todd Nelson	4	0	2	2	4
Paul Laus	4	1	0	1	27
Bruce Racine (goalie)	2	0	1	1	0
Bryan Fogarty	3	0	1	1	17
Paul Dyck	1	0	0	0	0
Robert Melanson	1	0	0	0	0
George Zajankala	1	0	0	0	0
Greg Andrusak	2	0	0	0	2
Al Tuer	2	0	0	0	4
Grant Block	3	0	0	0	0
Perry Ganchar	3	0	0	0	4
Mark Major	3	0	0	0	0
David Quinn	3	0	0	0	0
Jason Smart	3	0	0	0	6
Rob Dopson (goalie)	4	0	0	0	2
Justin Duberman	4	0	0	0	12
Sandy Smith	4	0	0	0	8
Travis Thiessen	4	0	0	0	16

GOALTENDING

	Games	Min.	Goals	SO	Avg.
Bruce Racine	2	37	2	0	3.24
Rob Dopson	4	203	20	0	5.91

FORT WAYNE KOMETS

(Winner of 1993 Turner Cup playoffs)

SCORING

	Games	G	A	Pts.	Pen.
Igor Chibirev	12	7	13	20	2
Jean-Marc Richard	12	6	11	17	6

	Games	G	A	Pts.	Pen.
Scott Gruhl	12	4	11	15	14
Paul Willett	10	7	6	13	22
Bob Wilkie	12	4	6	10	10
Kelly Hurd	10	4	5	9	12
Dave Smith	10	4	5	9	46
Joel Savage	10	3	5	8	22
Grant Richison	12	1	7	8	20
Colin Chin	8	5	2	7	10
Sylvain Couturier	4	2	3	5	2
Ian Boyce	12	3	1	4	6
Peter Hankinson	12	1	3	4	6
Lee Davidson	12	2	0	2	21
Kory Kocur	4	1	1	2	6
Bob Jay	8	0	2	2	14
Carey Lucyk	12	0	2	2	14
Bob Lakso	1	0	1	1	0
Guy Dupuis	4	0	1	1	6
Pokey Reddick (goalie)	12	0	1	1	10
Dave Gagnon (goalie)	1	0	0	0	0
Steve Wilson	1	0	0	0	0
Steve Fletcher	3	0	0	0	2
Kevin MacDonald	11	0	0	0	21

GOALTENDING

	Games	Min.	Goals	SO	Avg.
Dave Gagnon	1	6	0	0	0.00
Pokey Reddick	12	723	18	0	1.49

INDIANAPOLIS ICE

(Lost quarterfinals to Atlanta, 4-1)

SCORING

	Games	G	A	Pts.	Pen.
Tony Horacek	5	3	2	5	18
Alexandr Andrievski	4	2	3	5	10
Milan Tichy	4	0	5	5	14
Sergei Krivokrasov	5	3	1	4	2
Brad Lauer	5	3	1	4	6
Shawn Byram	5	1	2	3	8
Karl Dykhuis	5	1	1	2	8
Vladimir Tsiplakov	5	1	1	2	2
Tony Hrkac	5	0	2	2	2
Joe Cleary	3	1	0	1	4
Mike Speer	5	1	0	1	26
Rob Brown	2	0	1	1	2
Rob Conn	5	0	1	1	6
Ivan Droppa	5	0	1	1	2
Ray LeBlanc (goalie)	5	0	1	1	2
Sean Williams	5	0	1	1	4
Greg Spenrath	1	0	0	0	5
Roch Belley (goalie)	2	0	0	0	0
Adam Bennett	2	0	0	0	2
Dave Hakstol	4	0	0	0	7
Kevin St. Jacques	4	0	0	0	0

GOALTENDING

	Games	Min.	Goals	SO	Avg.
Roch Belley	2	33	2	0	3.64
Ray LeBlanc	5	276	23	0	5.00

KANSAS CITY BLADES

(Lost semifinals to San Diego, 4-2)

SCORING

	Games	G	A	Pts.	Pen.
Gary Emmons	12	7	6	13	8
Dale Craigwell	12	7	5	12	2
Ray Whitney	12	5	7	12	2
Mikhail Kravets	10	2	5	7	55
Tom Pederson	12	1	6	7	2

	Games	G	A	Pts.	Pen.
Pat MacLeod	10	2	4	6	7
Michel Picard	12	3	2	5	20
Jaroslav Otevrel	6	1	4	5	4
Larry DePalma	10	1	4	5	20
Claudio Scremin	12	0	5	5	18
Jeff McLean	10	3	1	4	2
J.F. Quintin	11	2	1	3	16
Victor Ignatjev	4	1	2	3	24
Duane Joyce	12	1	2	3	6
Mark Beaufait	9	1	1	2	8
Mike Colman	12	1	0	1	34
Stephan Tepper	4	0	1	1	6
Dody Wood	6	0	1	1	15
Wade Flaherty (goalie)	12	0	1	1	4
Norm Foster (goalie)	1	0	0	0	0
Dean Kolstad	3	0	0	0	2
Mike Rathje	5	0	0	0	12
Jeff Sharples	8	0	0	0	6

GOALTENDING

	Games	Min.	Goals	SO	Avg.
Norm Foster	1	16	0	0	0.00
Wade Flaherty	12	733	34(2)	1	2.78

MILWAUKEE ADMIRALS

(Lost quarterfinals to Kansas City, 4-2)

SCORING

	Games	G	A	Pts.	Pen.
Brian Dobbin	6	4	3	7	6
Michel Mongeau	4	1	4	5	4
Ladislav Tresl	5	3	1	4	2
Lou Crawford	6	2	2	4	8
Jeff Madill	4	3	0	3	9
Jergus Baca	6	0	3	3	2
Shawn Evans	6	0	3	3	6
Mike McNeill	6	2	0	2	0
Richard Zemlak	2	1	1	2	6
Steve Tuttle	4	0	2	2	2
Bruce Bell	6	0	2	2	6
Jeff Larmer	6	0	2	2	2
Steve Strunk	3	1	0	1	4
Jim Johannson	5	1	0	1	6
Dennis Snedden	2	0	1	1	6
Larry Dyck (goalie)	3	0	1	1	0
Mikhail Shtalenkov (goalie)	3	0	1	1	0
Carl Valimont	4	0	1	1	2
Bob Halkidis	5	0	1	1	27
Don Gibson	6	0	1	1	11
Mitch Messier	6	0	1	1	0
Alex Galchenyuk	1	0	0	0	0
Scott Robinson	3	0	0	0	0

GOALTENDING

	Games	Min.	Goals	SO	Avg.
Mikhail Shtalenkov	3	209	11	0	3.16
Larry Dyck	3	180	10(1)	0	3.33

PEORIA RIVERMEN

(Lost quarterfinals to San Diego, 4-0)

SCORING

	Games	G	A	Pts.	Pen.
Richard Pion	3	2	1	3	8
Derek Frenette	4	1	2	3	2
Lee Leslie	4	0	3	3	2
Darren Veitch	4	2	0	2	4
Mark Bassen	4	1	1	2	2
Terry Hollinger	4	1	1	2	0
Ron Hoover	4	1	1	2	2
Brian Pellerin	4	1	1	2	8
Kyle Reeves	3	0	2	2	2
Doug Wickenheiser	4	0	2	2	2
Dave Mackey	4	1	0	1	22
Kevin Miehm	4	0	1	1	2
Parris Duffus (goalie)	1	0	0	0	0
Mark Reeds	1	0	0	0	0
Geoff Sarjeant (goalie)	3	0	0	0	0
Jeff Batters	4	0	0	0	10
Brian Blad	4	0	0	0	17
Peter Kasowski	4	0	0	0	14
Jason Marshall	4	0	0	0	20

GOALTENDING

	Games	Min.	Goals	SO	Avg.
Geoff Sarjeant	3	179	13(2)	0	4.36
Parris Duffus	1	59	5	0	5.08

SAN DIEGO GULLS

(Lost finals to Fort Wayne, 4-0)

SCORING

	Games	G	A	Pts.	Pen.
Daniel Shank	14	5	10	15	131
Dale DeGray	14	3	11	14	77
Scott Arniel	14	6	5	11	16
John Anderson	11	5	6	11	4
Hubie McDonough	14	4	7	11	6
Ken Hodge	14	4	6	10	6
Robbie Nichols	10	2	5	7	34
Lindy Ruff	14	1	6	7	26
Doug Smail	9	3	2	5	20
Larry Floyd	14	3	1	4	4
Len Hachborn	10	2	2	4	2
Darryl Olsen	10	1	3	4	30
Max Middendorf	8	1	2	3	8
Mark Ferner	11	1	2	3	8
Don McSween	14	1	2	3	10
Denny Lambert	14	1	1	2	44
Tony McKegney	3	0	1	1	4
Rene Chapdelaine	14	0	1	1	27
Kord Cernich	3	0	0	0	2
Peter Ing (goalie)	4	0	0	0	0
Mitch Lamoureux	4	0	0	0	11
Perry Anderson	5	0	0	0	14
Clint Malarchuk (goalie)	12	0	0	0	4

GOALTENDING

	Games	Min.	Goals	SO	Avg.
Clint Malarchuk	12	668	34	0	3.05
Peter Ing	4	183	13	0	4.26

1992-93 AWARD WINNERS

ALL-STAR TEAMS

First team	Pos.	Second team
Rick Knickle, San Diego	G	Wade Flaherty, K.C.
Bill Houlder, San Diego	D	Dale DeGray, San Diego
Shawn Evans, Milwaukee	D	Kevin Wortman, Salt Lake
Brad Lauer, Indianapolis	LW	Dave Michayluk, Cleveland
Tony Hrkac, Indianapolis	C	Hubie McDonough, S.D.
Daniel Shank, San Diego	RW	Jeff Madill, Milwaukee

TROPHY WINNERS

James Gatschene Memorial Trophy: Tony Hrkac, Indianapolis
Leo P. Lamoureux Memorial Trophy: Tony Hrkac, Indianapolis
James Norris Memorial Trophy: Rick Knickle, San Diego
Clint Malarchuk, San Diego
Governors Trophy: Bill Houlder, San Diego
Garry F. Longman Memorial Trophy: Mikhail Shtalenkov, Mil.
Ken McKenzie Trophy: Mark Beaufait, Kansas City
Commissioner's Trophy: Al Sims, Fort Wayne
N.R. (Bud) Poile Trophy: Pokey Reddick, Fort Wayne
Fred A. Huber Trophy: San Diego Gulls
Joseph Turner Memorial Cup Winner: Fort Wayne Komets

MINOR LEAGUES

JAMES GATSCHENE MEMORIAL TROPHY

(Most Valuable Player)

Season	Player, Team
1946-47	Herb Jones, Detroit Auto Club
1947-48	Lyle Dowell, Det. Bright's Goodyears
1948-49	Bob McFadden, Det. Jerry Lynch
1949-50	Dick Kowcinak, Sarnia
1950-51	John McGrath, Toledo
1951-52	Ernie Dick, Chatham
1952-53	Donnie Marshall, Cincinnati
1953-54	No award given
1954-55	Phil Goyette, Cincinnati
1955-56	George Hayes, Grand Rapids
1956-57	Pierre Brillant, Indianapolis
1957-58	Pierre Brillant, Indianapolis
1958-59	Len Thornson, Fort Wayne
1959-60	Billy Reichart, Minneapolis
1960-61	Len Thornson, Fort Wayne
1961-62	Len Thornson, Fort Wayne
1962-63	Len Thornson, Fort Wayne
	Eddie Lang, Fort Wayne
1963-64	Len Thornson, Fort Wayne
1964-65	Chick Chalmers, Toledo
1965-66	Gary Schall, Muskegon
1966-67	Len Thornson, Fort Wayne
1967-68	Len Thornson, Fort Wayne
	Don Westbrooke, Dayton
1968-69	Don Westbrooke, Dayton
1969-70	Cliff Pennington, Des Moines
1970-71	Lyle Carter, Muskegon
1971-72	Len Fontaine, Port Huron
1972-73	Gary Ford, Muskegon
1973-74	Pete Mara, Des Moines
1974-75	Gary Ford, Muskegon
1975-76	Len Fontaine, Port Huron
1976-77	Tom Mellor, Toledo
1977-78	Dan Bonar, Fort Wayne
1978-79	Terry McDougall, Fort Wayne
1979-80	Al Dumba, Fort Wayne
1980-81	Marcel Comeau, Saginaw
1981-82	Brent Jarrett, Kalamazoo
1982-83	Claude Noel, Toledo
1983-84	Darren Jensen, Fort Wayne
1984-85	Scott Gruhl, Muskegon
1985-86	Darrell May, Peoria
1986-87	Jeff Pyle, Saginaw
	Jock Callander, Muskegon
1987-88	John Cullen, Flint
1988-89	Dave Michayluk, Muskegon
1989-90	Michel Mongeau, Peoria
1990-91	David Bruce, Peoria
1991-92	Dmitri Kvartalnov, San Diego
1992-93	Tony Hrkac, Indianapolis

LEO P. LAMOUREUX MEMORIAL TROPHY

(Leading scorer)

Season	Player, Team
1946-47	Harry Marchand, Windsor
1947-48	Dick Kowcinak, Det. Auto Club
1948-49	Leo Richard, Toledo
1949-50	Dick Kowcinak, Sarnia
1950-51	Herve Parent, Grand Rapids
1951-52	George Parker, Grand Rapids
1952-53	Alex Irving, Milwaukee
1953-54	Don Hall, Johnstown
1954-55	Phil Goyette, Cincinnati
1955-56	Max Mekilok, Cincinnati
1956-57	Pierre Brillant, Indianapolis
1957-58	Warren Hynes, Cincinnati
1958-59	George Ranieri, Louisville
1959-60	Chick Chalmers, Louisville
1960-61	Ken Yackel, Minneapolis

Season	Player, Team
1961-62	Len Thornson, Fort Wayne
1962-63	Moe Bartoli, Minneapolis
1963-64	Len Thornson, Fort Wayne
1964-65	Lloyd Maxfield, Port Huron
1965-66	Bob Rivard, Fort Wayne
1966-67	Len Thornson, Fort Wayne
1967-68	Gary Ford, Muskegon
1968-69	Don Westbrooke, Dayton
1969-70	Don Westbrooke, Dayton
1970-71	Darrel Knibbs, Muskegon
1971-72	Gary Ford, Muskegon
1972-73	Gary Ford, Muskegon
1973-74	Pete Mara, Des Moines
1974-75	Rick Bragnalo, Dayton
1975-76	Len Fontaine, Port Huron
1976-77	Jim Koleff, Flint
1977-78	Jim Johnston, Flint
1978-79	Terry McDougall, Fort Wayne
1979-80	Al Dumba, Fort Wayne
1980-81	Marcel Comeau, Saginaw
1981-82	Brent Jarrett, Kalamazoo
1982-83	Dale Yakiwchuk, Milwaukee
1983-84	Wally Schreiber, Fort Wayne
1984-85	Scott MacLeod, Salt Lake
1985-86	Scott MacLeod, Salt Lake
1986-87	Jock Callander, Muskegon
	Jeff Pyle, Saginaw
1987-88	John Cullen, Flint
1988-89	Dave Michayluk, Muskegon
1989-90	Michel Mongeau, Peoria
1990-91	Lonnie Loach, Fort Wayne
1991-92	Dmitri Kvartalnov, San Diego
1992-93	Tony Hrkac, Indianapolis

The award was originally known as the George H. Wilkinson Trophy from 1946-47 through 1959-60.

JAMES NORRIS MEMORIAL TROPHY

(Outstanding goaltenders)

Season	Player, Team
1955-56	Bill Tibbs, Troy
1956-57	Glenn Ramsey, Cincinnati
1957-58	Glenn Ramsey, Cincinnati
1958-59	Don Rigazio, Louisville
1959-60	Rene Zanier, Fort Wayne
1960-61	Ray Mikulan, Minneapolis
1961-62	Glenn Ramsey, Omaha
1962-63	Glenn Ramsey, Omaha
1963-64	Glenn Ramsey, Toledo
1964-65	Chuck Adamson, Fort Wayne
1965-66	Bob Sneddon, Port Huron
1966-67	Glenn Ramsey, Toledo
1967-68	Tim Tabor, Muskegon
	Bob Perani, Muskegon
1968-69	Pat Rupp, Dayton
	John Adams, Dayton
1969-70	Gaye Cooley, Des Moines
	Bob Perreault, Des Moines
1970-71	Lyle Carter, Muskegon
1971-72	Glenn Resch, Muskegon
1972-73	Robbie Irons, Fort Wayne
	Don Atchison, Fort Wayne
1973-74	Bill Hughes, Muskegon
1974-75	Bob Volpe, Flint
	Merlin Jenner, Flint
1975-76	Don Cutts, Muskegon
1976-77	Terry Richardson, Kalamazoo
1977-78	Lorne Molleken, Saginaw
	Pierre Chagnon, Saginaw
1978-79	Gord Laxton, Grand Rapids
1979-80	Larry Lozinski, Kalamazoo
1980-81	Claude Legris, Kalamazoo
	Georges Gagnon, Kalamazoo

Season	Player, Team
1981-82	Lorne Molleken, Toledo
	Dave Tardich, Toledo
1982-83	Lorne Molleken, Toledo
1983-84	Darren Jensen, Fort Wayne
1984-85	Rick Heinz, Peoria
1985-86	Rick St. Croix, Fort Wayne
	Pokey Reddick, Fort Wayne
1986-87	Alain Raymond, Fort Wayne
	Michel Dufour, Fort Wayne
1987-88	Steve Guenette, Muskegon
1988-89	Rick Knickle, Fort Wayne
1989-90	Jimmy Waite, Indianapolis
1990-91	Guy Hebert, Peoria
	Pat Jablonski, Peoria
1991-92	Arturs Irbe, Kansas City
	Wade Flaherty, Kansas City
1992-93	Rick Knickle, San Diego
	Clint Malarchuk, San Diego

GOVERNORS TROPHY

(Outstanding defenseman)

Season	Player, Team
1964-65	Lionel Repka, Fort Wayne
1965-66	Bob Lemieux, Muskegon
1966-67	Larry Mavety, Port Huron
1967-68	Carl Brewer, Muskegon
1968-69	Al Breaule, Dayton
	Moe Benoit, Dayton
1969-70	John Gravel, Toledo
1970-71	Bob LaPage, Des Moines
1971-72	Rick Pagnutti, Fort Wayne
1972-73	Bob McCammon, Port Huron
1973-74	Dave Simpson, Dayton
1974-75	Murry Flegel, Muskegon
1975-76	Murry Flegel, Muskegon
1976-77	Tom Mellor, Toledo
1977-78	Michel LaChance, Milwaukee
1978-79	Guido Tenesi, Grand Rapids
1979-80	John Gibson, Saginaw
1980-81	Larry Goodenough, Saginaw
1981-82	Don Waddell, Saginaw
1982-83	Jim Burton, Fort Wayne
	Kevin Willison, Milwaukee
1983-84	Kevin Willison, Milwaukee
1984-85	Lee Norwood, Peoria
1985-86	Jim Burton, Fort Wayne
1986-87	Jim Burton, Fort Wayne
1987-88	Phil Bourque, Muskegon
1988-89	Randy Boyd, Milwaukee
1989-90	Brian Glynn, Salt Lake
1990-91	Brian McKee, Fort Wayne
1991-92	Jean-Marc Richard, Fort Wayne
1992-93	Bill Houlder, San Diego

GARRY F. LONGMAN MEMORIAL TROPHY

(Outstanding rookie)

Season	Player, Team
1961-62	Dave Richardson, Fort Wayne
1962-63	John Gravel, Omaha
1963-64	Don Westbrooke, Toledo
1964-65	Bob Thomas, Toledo
1965-66	Frank Golembrowsky, Port Huron
1966-67	Kerry Bond, Columbus
1967-68	Gary Ford, Muskegon
1968-69	Doug Volmar, Columbus
1969-70	Wayne Zuk, Toledo
1970-71	Corky Agar, Flint
	Herb Howdle, Dayton
1971-72	Glenn Resch, Muskegon
1972-73	Danny Gloor, Des Moines
1973-74	Frank DeMarco, Des Moines
1974-75	Rick Bragnalo, Dayton
1975-76	Sid Veysey, Fort Wayne

Season	Player, Team
1976-77	Ron Zanussi, Fort Wayne
	Garth MacGuigan, Muskegon
1977-78	Dan Bonar, Fort Wayne
1978-79	Wes Jarvis, Port Huron
1979-80	Doug Robb, Milwaukee
1980-81	Scott Vanderburgh, Kalamazoo
1981-82	Scott Howson, Toledo
1982-83	Tony Fiore, Flint
1983-84	Darren Jensen, Fort Wayne
1984-85	Gilles Thibaudeau, Flint
1965-66	Guy Benoit, Muskegon
1986-87	Michel Mongeau, Saginaw
1987-88	Ed Belfour, Saginaw
	John Cullen, Flint
1988-89	Paul Ranheim, Salt Lake
1989-90	Rob Murphy, Milwaukee
1990-91	Nelson Emerson, Peoria
1991-92	Dmitri Kvartalnov, Kansas City
1992-93	Mikhail Shtalenkov, Milwaukee

KEN McKENZIE TROPHY

(Outstanding American-born rookie)

Season	Player, Team
1977-78	Mike Eruzione, Toledo
1978-79	Jon Fontas, Saginaw
1979-80	Bob Janecyk, Fort Wayne
1980-81	Mike Labianca, Toledo
	Steve Janaszak, Fort Wayne
1981-82	Steve Salvucci, Saginaw
1982-83	Paul Fenton, Peoria
1983-84	Mike Krensing, Muskegon
1984-85	Bill Schafhauser, Kalamazoo
1985-86	Brian Noonan, Saginaw
1986-87	Ray LeBlanc, Flint
1987-88	Dan Woodley, Flint
1988-89	Paul Ranheim, Salt Lake
1989-90	Tim Sweeney, Salt Lake
1990-91	C.J. Young, Salt Lake
1991-92	Kevin Wortman, Salt Lake
1992-93	Mark Beaufait, Kansas City

COMMISSIONER'S TROPHY

(Coach of the year)

Season	Coach, Team
1984-85	Rick Ley, Muskegon
	Pat Kelly, Peoria
1985-86	Rob Laird, Fort Wayne
1986-87	Wayne Thomas, Salt Lake
1987-88	Rick Dudley, Flint
1988-89	B. J. MacDonald, Muskegon
	Phil Russell, Muskegon
1989-90	Darryl Sutter, Indianapolis
1990-91	Bob Plager, Peoria
1991-92	Kevin Constantine, Kansas City
1992-93	Al Sims, Fort Wayne

N.R. (BUD) POILE TROPHY

(Playoff MVP)

Season	Player, Team
1984-85	Denis Cyr, Peoria
1985-86	Jock Callander, Muskegon
1986-87	Rick Heinz, Salt Lake
1987-88	Peter Lappin, Salt Lake
1988-89	Dave Michayluk, Muskegon
1989-90	Mike McNeill, Indianapolis
1990-91	Michel Mongeau, Peoria
1991-92	Ron Handy, Kansas City
1992-93	Pokey Reddick, Fort Wayne

The award was originally known as the Turner Cup Playoff MVP from 1984-85 through 1988-89.

REGULAR-SEASON CHAMPION

PLAYOFF CHAMPION

Season	Team	Coach	Team	Coach
1945-46	No trophy awarded		Detroit Auto Club	Jack Ward
1946-47	Windsor Staffords	Jack Ward	Windsor Spitfires	Ebbie Goodfellow
1947-48	Windsor Hettche Spitfires	Dent-Goodfellow	Toledo Mercurys	Andy Mulligan
1948-49	Toledo Mercurys	Andy Mulligan	Windsor Hettche Spitfires	Jimmy Skinner
1949-50	Sarnia Sailors	Dick Kowcinak	Catham Maroons	Bob Stoddart
1950-51	Grand Rapids Rockets	Lou Trudell	Toledo Mercurys	Alex Wood
1951-52	Grand Rapids Rockets	Lou Trudell	Toledo Mercurys	Alex Wood
1952-53	Cincinnati Mohawks	Buddy O'Conner	Cincinnati Mohawks	Buddy O'Conner
1953-54	Cincinnati Mohawks	Roly McLenahan	Cincinnati Mohawks	Roly McLenahan
1954-55	Cincinnati Mohawks	Roly McLenahan	Cincinnati Mohawks	Roly McLenahan
1955-56	Cincinnati Mohawks	Roly McLenahan	Cincinnati Mohawks	Roly McLenahan
1956-57	Cincinnati Mohawks	Roly McLenahan	Cincinnati Mohawks	Roly McLenahan
1957-58	Cincinnati Mohawks	Bill Gould	Indiana. Chiefs	Leo Lamoureux
1958-59	Louisville Rebels	Leo Gasparini	Louisville Rebels	Leo Gasparini
1959-60	Fort Wayne Komets	Ken Ullyot	St. Paul Saints	Fred Shero
1960-61	Minneapolis Millers	Ken Yachel	St. Paul Saints	Fred Shero
1961-62	Muskegon Zephrys	Moose Lallo	Muskegon Zephrys	Moose Lallo
1962-63	Fort Wayne Komets	Ken Ullyot	Fort Wayne Komets	Ken Ullyot
1963-64	Toledo Blades	Moe Benoit	Toledo Blades	Moe Benoit
1964-65	Port Huron Flags	Lloyd Maxfield	Fort Wayne Komets	Eddie Long
1965-66	Muskegon Mohawks	Moose Lallo	Port Huron Flags	Lloyd Maxfield
1966-67	Dayton Gems	Warren Back	Toledo Blades	Terry Slater
1967-68	Muskegon Mohawks	Moose Lallo	Muskegon Mohawks	Moose Lallo
1968-69	Dayton Gems	Larry Wilson	Dayton Gems	Larry Wilson
1969-70	Muskegon Mohawks	Moose Lallo	Dayton Gems	Larry Wilson
1970-71	Muskegon Mohawks	Moose Lallo	Port Huron Flags	Ted Garvin
1971-72	Muskegon Mohawks	Moose Lallo	Port Huron Flags	Ted Garvin
1972-73	Fort Wayne Komets	Marc Boileau	Fort Wayne Komets	Marc Boileau
1973-74	Des Moines Capitals	Dan Belisle	Des Moines Capitals	Dan Belisle
1974-75	Muskegon Mohawks	Moose Lallo	Toledo Goaldiggers	Ted Garvin
1975-76	Dayton Gems	Ivan Prediger	Dayton Gems	Ivan Prediger
1976-77	Saginaw Gears	Don Perry	Saginaw Gears	Don Perry
1977-78	Fort Wayne Komets	Gregg Pilling	Toledo Goaldiggers	Ted Garvin
1978-79	Grand Rapids Owls	Moe Bartoli	Kalamazoo Wings	Bill Purcell
1979-80	Kalamazoo Wings	Doug McKay	Kalamazoo Wings	Doug McKay
1980-81	Kalamazoo Wings	Doug McKay	Saginaw Gears	Don Perry
1981-82	Toledo Goaldiggers	Bill Inglis	Toledo Goaldiggers	Bill Inglis
1982-83	Toledo Goaldiggers	Bill Inglis	Toledo Goaldiggers	Bill Inglis
1983-84	Fort Wayne Komets	Ron Ullyot	Flint Generals	Dennis Desrosiers
1984-85	Peoria Rivermen	Pat Kelly	Peoria Rivermen	Pat Kelly
1985-86	Fort Wayne Komets	Rob Laird	Muskegon Lumberjacks	Rick Ley
1986-87	Fort Wayne Komets	Rob Laird	Salt Lake Golden Eagles	Wayne Thomas
1987-88	Muskegon Lumberjacks	Rick Ley	Salt Lake Golden Eagles	Paul Baxter
1988-89	Muskegon Lumberjacks	B.J. MacDonald	Muskegon Lumberjacks	B.J. MacDonald
1989-90	Muskegon Lumberjacks	B.J. MacDonald	Indianapolis Ice	Darryl Sutter
1990-91	Peoria Rivermen	Bob Plager	Peoria Rivermen	Bob Plager
1991-92	Kansas City Blades	Kevin Constantine	Kansas City Blades	Kevin Constantine
1992-93	San Diego Gulls	Rick Dudley	Fort Wayne Komets	Al Sims

The IHL regular-season champion is awarded the Fred A. Huber Trophy and the playoff champion is awarded the Joseph Turner Memorial Cup.

The regular-season championship award was originally called the J.P. McGuire Trophy from 1946-47 through 1953-54.

EAST COAST HOCKEY LEAGUE

LEAGUE OFFICE

President/commissioner
Patrick Kelly
Director of information
Doug Price
Director of marketing
Ted Cox

Administrative secretary
June Kelly
Address
AA 520
Mart Office Building
800 Briar Creek Road
Charlotte, NC 28205

Phone
704-358-3658
FAX
704-358-3560

TEAMS

BIRMINGHAM BULLS

General manager
Art Clarkson
Head coach
Phil Roberto
Home ice
Birmingham-Jefferson Civic Center
Coliseum
Address
P.O. Box 1506
Birmingham, AL 35201
Seating capacity
1,506
NHL affiliation
Florida Panthers
Phone
205-458-8833
FAX
205-458-8489

CHARLOTTE CHECKERS

General manager
Carl Scheer
Head coach
John Marks
Home ice
Independence Arena
Address
800 East Boulevard
Charlotte, NC 28203
Seating capacity
9,559
NHL affiliation
Boston Bruins
Phone
704-342-4423
FAX
704-377-4595

COLUMBUS CHILL

General manager
David Paitson
Head coach
Terry Ruskowski
Home ice
Fairgrounds Coliseum
Address
1460 West Lane Avenue
Columbus, OH 43221
Seating capacity
5,800

NHL affiliation
None
Phone
614-488-4455
FAX
614-488-4576

DAYTON BOMBERS

General manager
Arnold W. Johnson
Head coach
Claude Noel
Home ice
Hara Arena
Address
P.O. Box 5952
Dayton, OH 45405-5952
Seating capacity
5,543
NHL affiliation
To be announced
Phone
513-277-3765
FAX
513-278-3007

ERIE PANTHERS

General manager and head coach
Ron Hansis
Home ice
Erie Civic Center
Address
P.O. Box 6116
Erie, PA 16512
Seating capacity
5,374
NHL affiliation
To be announced
Phone
814-455-3936
FAX
814-456-8287

GREENSBORO MONARCHS

General manager and head coach
Jeff Brubaker
Home ice
Greensboro War Memorial Coliseum
Address
P.O. Box 5447
Greensboro, NC 27435-0447

Seating capacity
22,000
NHL affiliation
None
Phone
919-852-6170
FAX
919-852-6259

HAMPTON ROADS ADMIRALS

General manager
Blake Cullen
Head coach
John Brophy
Home ice
Norfolk Scope
Address
P.O. Box 299
Norfolk, VA 23501
Seating capacity
8,994
NHL affiliation
Washington Capitals
Phone
804-640-1212
FAX
804-640-8447

HUNTINGTON BLIZZARD

General manager
Bob Henry
Head coach
To be announced
Home ice
Huntington Civic Center
Address
763 Third Avenue
Huntington, WV 25701
Seating capacity
5,500
NHL affiliation
To be announced
Phone
304-697-7825
FAX
304-697-7832

HUNTSVILLE BLAST

General manager
Larry Revo

Head coach
Steve Gatzos
Home ice
Von Braun Civic Center
Address
700 Monroe Street
Huntsville, AL 35801
Seating capacity
6,852
NHL affiliation
To be announced
Phone
205-551-2356
FAX
205-551-2203

JOHNSTOWN CHIEFS

General manager
John Daley
Coach
Eddie Johnstone
Home ice
Cambria County War Memorial Arena
Address
326 Napoleon Street
Johnstown, PA 15901
Seating capacity
4,050
NHL affiliation
None
Phone
814-539-1799
FAX
814-536-1316

KNOXVILLE CHEROKEES

General manager
Tim Bernal
Head coach
Barry Smith
Home ice
Knoxville Civic Coliseum
Address
500 East Church St.
Knoxville, TN 37915
Seating capacity
5,668
NHL affiliation
None
Phone
615-546-6707
FAX
615-546-5521

LOUISVILLE ICEHAWKS

General manager
Dave Alcorta
Head coach
Warren Young
Home ice
Broadbent Arena
Address
P.O. Box 37130
Louisville, KY 40233
Seating capacity
6,618
NHL affiliation
To be announced

Phone
502-367-7797
FAX
502-367-7352

NASHVILLE KNIGHTS

General manager
W. Godfrey Wood
Head coach
Nick Fotiu
Home ice
Municipal Auditorium
Address
417 4th Avenue North
Nashville, TN 37201
Seating capacity
7,941
NHL affiliation
None
Phone
615-255-7825
FAX
615-255-0024

RALEIGH ICECAPS

President
Pete Bock
Head coach
Kurt Kleinendorst
Home ice
Dorton Arena
Address
P.O. Box 33219
Raleigh, NC 27636
Seating capacity
5,700
NHL affiliation
None
Phone
919-755-1427
FAX
919-755-0899

RICHMOND RENEGADES

General manager
Rich McArdle
Head coach
Roy Sommer
Home ice
Richmond Coliseum
Address
P.O. Box 10245
Richmond, VA 23240
Seating capacity
11,000
NHL affiliation
New York Islanders
Phone
804-643-7825
FAX
804-649-0651

ROANOKE EXPRESS

General manager
Pierre Paiemont
Head coach
Frank Anzalone

Home ice
Roanoke Civic Center
Address
P.O. Box 12145
Roanoke, VA 24023-2145
Seating capacity
8,372
NHL affiliation
To be announced
Phone
703-989-4625
FAX
703-989-8681

SOUTH CAROLINA STRINGRAYS

General manager
Frank Milne
Head coach
Rick Vaive
Home ice
North Charleston Coliseum
Address
5001 Coliseum Drive
N. Charleston, SC 29418
Seating capacity
10,500
NHL affiliation
Toronto Maple Leafs
Phone
803-744-2248
FAX
803-744-2898

TOLEDO STORM

General manager
Tim Houser
Head coach
Chris McSorley
Home ice
Toledo Sports Arena
Address
One Main Street
Toledo, OH 43605
Seating capacity
5,094
NHL affiliation
Detroit Red Wings
Phone
419-691-0200
FAX
419-698-8998

WHEELING THUNDERBIRDS

General manager
Larry Kish
Head coach
Doug Sauter
Home ice
Wheeling Civic Center
Address
P.O. Box 6563
Wheeling, WV 26003-0815
Seating capacity
5,406
NHL affiliation
None
Phone
304-234-4625
FAX
304-233-4846

1992-93 REGULAR SEASON

FINAL STANDINGS

EAST DIVISION

Team	G	W	L	Pts.	GF	GA
Wheeling	64	40	16 (8)	88	314	223
Hampton Roads	64	37	21 (6)	80	294	235
Raleigh	64	37	22 (5)	79	289	262
Johnstown	64	34	23 (7)	75	281	264
Richmond	64	34	28 (2)	70	292	292
Greensboro	64	33	29 (2)	68	256	261
Roanoke Valley	64	14	49 (1)	29	227	387

( )—Indicates overtime losses and are worth one point.

WEST DIVISION

Team	G	W	L	Pts.	GF	GA
Toledo	64	36	17 (11)	83	316	238
Dayton	64	35	23 (6)	76	282	270
Nashville	64	36	25 (3)	75	312	305
Erie	64	35	25 (4)	74	305	307
Louisville	64	30	27 (7)	67	302	293
Birmingham	64	30	29 (2)	65	290	313
Columbus	64	30	30 (4)	64	257	256
Knoxville	64	19	39 (6)	44	212	323

INDIVIDUAL LEADERS

Goals: Trevor Jobe, Nashville (85)
Assists: Victor Gervais, Hampton Roads (80)
Points: Trevor Jobe, Nashville (161)
Penalty minutes: Grant Chorney, Knoxville (443)
Goaltending average: Nick Vitucci, Hampton Roads (3.06)
Shutouts: Bill Horn, Greensboro (3)

	Games	G	A	Pts.
Sheldon Gorski, Louisville	63	51	47	98
Ed Zawatsky, Erie	61	35	62	97
Joe Flanagan, Birmingham	64	36	57	93
Peter Buckeridge, Erie	58	32	59	91
Iain Duncan, Toledo	50	40	50	90
Brent Sapergia, Nashville	56	37	50	87
Lyle Wildgoose, Raleigh	62	36	50	86
Darryl Noren, Greensboro	61	35	47	82
Darren Colbourne, Richmond	61	45	34	79
Mark Green, Louisville	61	48	29	77
Tim Tisdale, Wheeling	56	33	44	77
Jim Powers, Raleigh	55	28	49	77
Paul Marshall, Birmingham	62	21	56	77
Phil Berger, Greensboro	45	33	42	75
Brendan Flynn, Richmond	60	23	52	75

TOP SCORERS

	Games	G	A	Pts.
Trevor Jobe, Nashville	61	85	76	161
Victor Gervais, Hamton Roads	59	38	80	118
Devin Edgerton, Wheeling	57	46	71	117
Darren Schwartz, Wheeling	62	62	52	114
Brian Martin, Hampton Roads	49	50	52	102
Glen Goodall, Erie	60	38	62	100

INDIVIDUAL STATISTICS

BIRMINGHAM BULLS

SCORING

	Games	G	A	Pts.	Pen.
Joe Flanagan	64	36	57	93	42
Paul Marshall	62	21	56	77	109
Jim Larkin	60	25	47	72	18
Jerome Bechard	64	24	41	65	216
Kevin Kerr	39	30	34	64	217
David Craievich	56	10	35	45	139
Butch Kaebel	56	17	25	42	61
Kevin Riehl	34	23	18	41	36
Brett Barnett	48	16	24	40	125
Brett Strot	43	15	21	36	37
Bill Kovacs	36	16	13	29	40
Craig Charron	23	9	17	26	18
Greg Burke	33	9	16	25	57
Brad Belland	27	10	14	24	31
Murray Duval	41	5	15	20	154
Chris Marshall	21	6	13	19	86
Marc Laniel	21	5	9	14	26
J.A. Schneider	45	2	10	12	104
Jim Peters	21	1	9	10	55
Ray DeSouza	29	1	7	8	86
Howie Rosenblatt	6	4	3	7	23
Ray Edwards	16	0	7	7	60
Rob Krauss	45	1	5	6	231
Scott Matusovich	11	1	4	5	10
Sergei Kharin	2	0	3	3	0
Alexander Havanov	19	0	3	3	14
Matt Robbins	2	1	1	2	2
Chuck Hughes (goalie)	28	0	2	2	18
Jeff Hogden	4	1	0	1	2
Dan Poirier	7	1	0	1	41
Chris Stapleton	3	0	1	1	0
Sean Wallington	5	0	1	1	16
Chad Erickson (goalie)	14	0	1	1	0
Doug Dadswell (goalie)	8	0	0	0	40
Everett Cladwell	11	0	0	0	0
Mark Romaine (goalie)	24	0	0	0	6

GOALTENDING

	Games	Min.	Goals	SO	Avg.
Chad Erickson	14	856	54 (1)	0	3.79
Chuck Hughes	28	1494	121 (2)	0	4.86
Mark Romaine	24	1121	94 (2)	0	5.03
Doug Dadswell	8	401	36	0	5.39

COLUMBUS CHILL

SCORING

	Games	G	A	Pts.	Pen.
Jason Christie	63	20	41	61	190
Steven Strunk	62	32	28	60	61
Kurt Semandel	62	27	28	55	86
Jim Ballantine	62	18	34	52	42
Rob Schriner	64	26	24	50	64
Kevin Alexander	64	18	32	50	29
Don Granato	63	16	32	48	46
Frank Evans	64	11	28	39	201
Shaun Kane	41	7	25	32	68
Cam Brown	36	13	18	31	218
Frank LaScala	31	19	7	26	32
Randy Wong	50	7	16	23	80
Mark Woolf	26	8	10	18	45
Brad Treliving	56	3	14	17	234
Sasha Lakovic	27	7	9	16	162
Alain Deeks	23	5	11	16	34
Barry Dreger	37	4	12	16	301
Darren Perkins	20	9	4	13	44
Paul Dukovac	23	1	11	12	16
Mark Cipriano	18	4	4	8	64
Dennis Skapski	22	2	6	8	22

	Games	G	A	Pts.	Pen.
Sergei Khramtsov (goalie)	37	0	1	1	2
Dan Ryder (goalie)	1	0	0	0	0
Olie Sundstrom (goalie)	8	0	0	0	8
Jason Fitzsimmons (goalie)	23	0	0	0	10

GOALTENDING

	Games	Min.	Goals	SO	Avg.
Sergei Khramtsov	36	2039	117(7)	1	3.44
Olie Sundstrom	8	416	28	0	4.04
Jason Fitzsimmons	23	1340	91(3)	0	4.07
Dan Ryder	1	60	6(1)	0	6.00

DAYTON BOMBERS

SCORING

	Games	G	A	Pts.	Pen.
Frank Kovacs	61	31	36	67	177
Derek Donald	63	22	44	66	56
Mike Reier	40	20	43	63	60
Steve Bogoyevac	61	30	29	59	30
Peter Kasowski	51	17	40	57	81
Dave Smith	49	22	29	51	183
Darren Langdon	54	23	22	45	429
Shayne Green	55	17	24	41	117
Tom Nemeth	26	9	28	37	14
Darren Colbourne	32	19	11	30	41
Scott Drevitch	27	9	21	30	20
Steve Wilson	63	11	18	29	49
Doug Evans	58	5	18	23	71
Mark Lawrence	20	8	14	22	46
Ray Edwards	29	7	7	14	107
Darwin McPherson	47	4	10	14	214
Andrei Raisky	11	6	7	13	6
Derek Crawford	21	4	9	13	91
Darryl Mitchell	19	4	8	12	21
Marc Savard	25	1	11	12	36
Jim Peters	31	1	8	9	74
Wayne Muir	6	4	2	6	38
Dave MacIntyre	6	2	4	6	10
Brian Blad	19	1	5	6	90
Owen Lessard	8	2	2	4	4
Greg Carter	6	1	3	4	0
Jeff Stolp (goalie)	27	0	4	4	4
Mike Teeple	5	2	1	3	5
Tony Breslin (goalie)	1	0	0	0	0
Jeff Levy (goalie)	1	0	0	0	2
Rob Pallante	1	0	0	0	0
Mark Hilton	2	0	0	0	0
Dave Maksymiu	3	0	0	0	0
Denny Larocque	5	0	0	0	17
Rod Houk (goalie)	6	0	0	0	0
Eric Meloche	6	0	0	0	0
Sandy Galuppo (goalie)	17	0	0	0	2
Rob Laurie (goalie)	22	0	0	0	2

GOALTENDING

	Games	Min.	Goals	SO	Avg.
Jeff Levy	1	65	3	0	2.77
Tony Breslin	1	21	1	0	2.86
Sandy Galuppo	17	869	46(1)	2	3.18
Jeff Stolp	27	1550	99(4)	0	3.83
Rob Laurie	22	1197	90	0	4.51
Rod Houk	6	182	23	0	7.58

ERIE PANTHERS

SCORING

	Games	G	A	Pts.	Pen.
Glen Goodall	60	38	62	100	89
Ed Zawatsky	61	35	62	97	75
Peter Buckeridge	58	32	59	91	51
Bill Gall	64	24	47	71	54
Brian Sakic	51	18	33	51	22
John Vary	46	15	31	46	158
Greg Spenrath	55	17	28	45	344

	Games	G	A	Pts.	Pen.
Fredrik Jax	38	21	23	44	21
Brian Shantz	38	14	26	40	44
Tony Iob	25	14	13	27	194
Chris Panek	42	4	22	26	69
Jeff Whittle	45	9	16	25	133
Darren Perkins	28	7	17	24	40
Doug Marsden	25	13	10	23	61
Jim Lessard	48	6	17	23	214
Stu Kulak	21	13	8	21	23
Jason Winch	9	6	7	13	4
Jason Smith	22	3	8	11	2
Paul Flanagan	16	2	9	11	28
Marc DesChamps	42	1	9	10	52
Tom Sprague	31	2	6	8	72
Cam Brown	15	4	3	7	50
Brad Pascall	24	0	6	6	26
Dave Pergola	9	2	3	5	11
Rick Hillier	3	2	0	2	0
Jim McGroarty	3	1	1	2	2
Barry Potomski	5	1	1	2	31
Jack Carter	21	1	0	1	51
Mike Gilmore (goalie)	31	0	1	1	6
Jamie Loewen (goalie)	1	0	0	0	0
Chris Harvey (goalie)	2	0	0	0	0
Chris Lappin	4	0	0	0	21
Mike Parson (goalie)	8	0	0	0	0
Mike Millham (goalie)	29	0	0	0	2

GOALTENDING

	Games	Min.	Goals	SO	Avg.
Mike Millham	29	1636	115	0	4.22
Mike Gilmore	31	1762	134(1)	0	4.56
Mike Parson	8	350	33(1)	0	5.66
Jamie Loewen	1	55	7	0	7.64
Chris Harvey	2	67	13	0	11.64

GREENSBORO MONARCHS

SCORING

	Games	G	A	Pts.	Pen.
Darryl Noren	61	35	47	82	119
Phil Berger	45	33	42	75	135
Dan Bylsma	60	25	35	60	66
Wayne Muir	50	28	24	52	200
Davis Payne	57	15	20	35	178
Roger Larche	39	12	22	34	155
Brock Woods	63	8	25	33	295
Jamie Steer	35	16	14	30	8
Jamie Nicolls	30	9	18	27	45
Brent Fleetwood	36	9	18	27	57
Craig Herr	28	9	16	25	22
Chris Wolanin	40	6	18	24	166
David Burke	46	5	16	21	40
Chris Lappin	52	3	13	16	165
Andrei Yakovenko	14	3	12	15	35
Claude Maillet	26	5	9	14	78
Todd Gordon	29	3	11	14	76
Mike MacWilliam	12	5	5	10	137
Dean Zayonce	26	1	9	10	73
Vadim Slivtchenko	11	3	6	9	6
Greg Capson	54	1	8	9	258
Shawn Wheeler	5	3	4	7	25
Trevor Smith	15	2	4	6	4
Christian Bertrand	9	3	2	5	68
John Blessman	5	3	1	4	16
Jason Prosofsky	14	3	1	4	119
Andrei Kovalev	7	2	2	4	17
Scott McNair	8	2	2	4	4
Mike McKee	7	1	3	4	6
Rob Bateman	11	0	2	2	42
Bill Horn (goalie)	27	0	2	2	6
David Franzosa	1	1	0	1	0
Bill Harrington	6	1	0	1	6
Brian Vail	9	1	0	1	18
Alain Harvey (goalie)	5	0	1	1	2
Todd Drevitch	7	0	1	1	26

	Games	G	A	Pts.	Pen.
Peter Sentner	8	0	1	1	2
Patrick LaBrecque (goalie)	11	0	1	1	11
Dan Olson (goalie)	1	0	0	0	0
Ray Letourneau (goalie)	10	0	0	0	0
Greg Menges (goalie)	26	0	0	0	4

GOALTENDING

	Games	Min.	Goals	SO	Avg.
Dan Olson	1	6	0	0	0.00
Pat LaBrecque	11	650	31	0	2.86
Bill Horn	27	1465	81(4)	3	3.32
Greg Menges	26	1114	83(1)	0	4.47
Alain Harvey	5	268	20(1)	0	4.48
Ray Letourneau	10	366	38	0	6.23

HAMPTON ROADS ADMIRALS

SCORING

	Games	G	A	Pts.	Pen.
Victor Gervais	59	38	80	118	137
Brian Martin	49	50	52	102	85
Steve Martell	57	17	43	60	161
Rod Taylor	37	30	22	52	63
Steve Mirabile	37	24	24	48	66
Steve Poapst	63	10	35	45	57
Kevin Malgunas	27	14	18	32	94
Kurt Kabat	61	12	19	31	119
Shawn Snesar	53	7	24	31	251
Kelly Sorensen	58	14	12	26	127
Al MacIssac	39	4	22	26	128
Harry Mews	16	11	13	24	75
Randy Pearce	16	10	14	24	53
Dave Morissette	54	9	13	22	226
Paul Krepelka	52	8	14	22	157
Trevor Duhaime	31	8	13	21	46
Jason Rathbone	64	6	15	21	106
Bob Babcock	26	3	13	16	96
Trevor Halverson	9	7	5	12	6
Brent Fleetwood	13	5	2	7	4
Jiri Vykoukal	3	1	6	7	0
Brian Goudie	26	0	7	7	138
Keith Whitmore	7	1	3	4	10
Nick Vitucci (goalie)	29	0	3	3	10
Richie Walcott	14	1	1	2	116
Andrei Sidorov	3	0	2	2	0
Duane Derksen (goalie)	13	0	2	2	12
Jeff Whittle	5	1	0	1	19
Llew McWana	2	0	1	1	2
Chris McKenzie	3	0	1	1	0
Mark Bernard (goalie)	21	0	1	1	0
Tyler Davidson	1	0	0	0	0
Dan Bouchard (goalie)	1	0	0	0	0
Parris Duffus (goalie)	4	0	0	0	2

GOALTENDING

	Games	Min.	Goals	SO	Avg.
Nick Vitucci	29	1669	85	1	3.06
Parris Duffus	4	245	13	0	3.18
Duane Derksen	13	747	48(2)	0	3.86
Mark Bernard	21	1150	77	0	4.02
Dan Bouchard	1	60	7	0	7.00

JOHNSTOWN CHIEFS

SCORING

	Games	G	A	Pts.	Pen.
Chris Crombie	63	29	35	64	267
Matt Robbins	56	23	41	64	37
Tim Hanus	47	26	34	60	77
Bruce Coles	28	28	26	54	61
Rival Fullum	57	28	23	51	31
Bob Woods	61	11	36	47	72
Perry Florio	61	11	32	43	162
Mark Karpen	38	17	25	42	22
Jeff Ricciardi	61	7	29	36	248

	Games	G	A	Pts.	Pen.
Chuck Wiegand	37	15	15	30	10
Derry Menard	38	7	23	30	22
Jeff Massey	56	17	12	29	38
Christian Lariviere	51	4	20	24	93
Tommi Virkkunen	25	7	15	22	8
Brent Thurston	20	5	17	22	63
Scott Longstaff	19	6	14	20	0
Mark Krys	25	4	14	18	18
Dennis Purdy	17	10	7	17	38
Eugene Pavlov	24	8	9	17	40
Paul Ohman	42	3	10	13	31
Joey McTamney	27	3	8	11	26
Ted Miskolczi	6	6	3	9	27
Trevor Forsythe	25	2	6	8	92
David Earn	9	2	2	4	15
Shayne Antoski	8	1	3	4	2
John Bradley (goalie)	36	0	3	3	26
Phil Esposito	6	1	1	2	40
Scott Bailey (goalie)	36	0	2	2	6
Troy Frederick	8	0	1	1	0
Chic Pojar	1	0	0	0	0
Tyler Green	2	0	0	0	0
Dan Ryder (goalie)	4	0	0	0	26

GOALTENDING

	Games	Min.	Goals	SO	Avg.
Scott Bailey	36	1750	112(6)	1	3.84
John Bradley	36	1910	127	1	3.99
Dan Ryder	4	214	15	0	4.21

KNOXVILLE CHEROKEES

SCORING

	Games	G	A	Pts.	Pen.
Mike Murray	64	23	42	65	40
Jamie Adams	60	29	25	54	14
Kim Maier	55	31	19	50	45
John Vandale	63	18	26	44	112
Keith Whitmore	50	8	27	35	86
Trent Pankewicz	32	14	20	34	101
Chad Thompson	63	11	23	34	157
Michael Seaton	32	15	17	32	34
Doug Roberts	44	10	17	27	31
Grant Chorney	52	10	13	23	443
Carl LeBlanc	59	6	16	22	110
Vaclav Nedomansky	27	8	11	19	117
Hayden O'Rear	52	4	12	16	45
Pascal Vincent	57	4	7	11	33
Kyle Galloway	40	3	8	11	84
Bill Wagner	32	3	7	10	28
Claude Barthe	24	3	6	9	32
Chris Jensen	19	1	7	8	20
Chris Varga	19	3	3	6	12
Tim Kiriluk	10	3	1	4	56
Ron Aubrey	11	1	2	3	85
Brett Lawrence	10	0	3	3	8
Joey Simon	6	2	0	2	0
Jamie Dabanovich	12	1	1	2	37
Mike Williams (goalie)	21	0	2	2	0
Scott Phillips	4	1	0	1	0
Murray Caton (goalie)	4	0	1	1	2
Manny Hawkins	4	0	1	1	0
Cory Cadden (goalie)	42	0	1	1	52
Mike Millham (goalie)	2	0	0	0	0
Stephen LaPerriere	3	0	0	0	2
Phil Polomsky	4	0	0	0	0
Mike Polomsky	5	0	0	0	0
Carl Sasyn	9	0	0	0	40
Bill Harrington	12	0	0	0	9

GOALTENDING

	Games	Min.	Goals	SO	Avg.
Cory Cadden	42	2413	189(5)	0	4.70
Murray Caton	4	211	17	0	4.83
Mike Williams	21	1145	95	0	4.98
Mike Millham	2	100	15	0	9.00

LOUISVILLE ICEHAWKS

SCORING

	Games	G	A	Pts.	Pen.
Sheldon Gorski	63	51	47	98	103
Mark Green	61	48	29	77	57
Brian Cook	60	22	47	69	117
Chris Bright	63	30	38	68	159
Kelly Ens	52	22	46	68	80
Trevor Buchanan	64	23	38	61	270
Joe Spinelli	53	20	36	56	53
Scott Humeniuk	36	14	31	45	117
Jeff Sebastian	63	14	28	42	52
Mark Holick	54	10	21	31	299
Jamie Steer	30	13	16	29	14
Mark Sorensen	62	6	23	29	51
Karl Johnston	28	5	20	25	29
Rob Sumner	64	1	20	21	180
Terry Virtue	28	0	17	17	84
Rhys Hollyman	32	3	12	15	51
Paul Gherardi	18	4	10	14	26
Ken House	18	9	4	13	2
Chris Smith	17	0	10	10	8
Steve Shaunessy	38	2	5	7	200
Jean Blouin	2	3	1	4	0
David Ferguson	3	1	2	3	2
Kevin Koopman (goalie)	33	0	2	2	8
John Craighead	5	1	0	1	33
Pat McGarry (goalie)	18	0	1	1	10
Mike Greenlay (goalie)	27	0	1	1	10
Clint Thomas	1	0	0	0	0
Mark Hilton	2	0	0	0	0
Chris MacKensie	2	0	0	0	0
David Moore	2	0	0	0	0
Marc DesChamps	3	0	0	0	0
Mike Ross	5	0	0	0	2

GOALTENDING

	Games	Min.	Goals	SO	Avg.
Mike Greenlay	27	1437	96(1)	1	4.01
Kevin Koopman	33	1538	113	0	4.41
Pat McGarry	18	926	78	0	5.05

NASHVILLE KNIGHTS

SCORING

	Games	G	A	Pts.	Pen.
Trevor Jobe	61	85	76	161	222
Troy Mick	56	16	54	70	44
Brian Horan	61	28	38	66	348
Don Parsons	60	27	34	61	62
Rob Dumas	63	13	45	58	191
Brian Ferreira	36	22	28	50	47
Brent Sapergia	26	23	26	49	116
Mike DeCarle	29	18	27	45	76
Steve Sullivan	63	20	21	41	240
Bob Creamer	59	14	20	34	87
Stanislav Tkach	52	13	18	31	96
Bryan Krygier	36	11	18	29	73
Chris Grassie	46	3	22	25	66
Scott Matusovich	51	1	17	18	62
Michael Seaton	25	6	10	16	27
Andrei Dylevsky	59	3	13	16	52
Darcy Kaminski	42	3	6	9	133
Greg Burke	16	2	6	8	28
Ray DeSouza	26	0	6	6	115
Scott Gordon (goalie)	23	0	5	5	6
Brian Bellefeuille	19	1	3	4	21
Stan Panfilenkov	11	0	3	3	2
Olie Sundstrom (goalie)	21	0	2	2	28
Link Gaetz	3	1	0	1	10
Dan Poirier	5	1	0	1	7
Rob Pallante	15	1	0	1	75
Tom Cole (goalie)	27	0	1	1	2
Mel Angelstad	1	0	0	0	14

GOALTENDING

	Games	Min.	Goals	SO	Avg.
Scott Gordon	23	1380	99(2)	0	4.30
Tom Cole	27	1401	103	0	4.41
Olie Sundstrom	21	1087	99(1)	0	5.46

RALEIGH ICECAPS

SCORING

	Games	G	A	Pts.	Pen.
Lyle Wildgoose	62	36	50	86	51
Jim Powers	55	28	49	77	74
Joel Gardner	45	22	51	73	30
Kirby Lindal	52	27	28	55	47
Bruno Villeneuve	54	30	19	49	47
Rick Barkovich	27	22	25	47	41
Alan Leggett	64	16	30	46	79
Todd Person	64	19	25	44	37
Chris Marshall	36	11	25	36	78
Mike Lappin	49	11	21	32	24
Kris Miller	30	8	24	32	62
Derek Linnell	61	7	24	31	69
Brian Tulik	60	6	20	26	92
Jeff Tomlinson	20	8	17	25	19
Brad Aitken	25	11	12	23	129
Sean Cowan	60	5	18	23	88
Jeff Robison	44	7	9	16	74
Doug Bacon	31	6	10	16	151
Bill Kovacs	19	4	6	10	32
Chic Pojar	24	4	4	8	12
Alexander Havanov	17	0	6	6	8
Chris Venkus	9	1	2	3	8
Jim Mill (goalie)	29	0	3	3	2
Doug Roberts	11	0	2	2	6
Stan Reddick (goalie)	44	0	2	2	14
John Johnson	2	0	0	0	0
Joe Spinelli	5	0	0	0	0

GOALTENDING

	Games	Min.	Goals	SO	Avg.
Stan Reddick	44	2395	156(6)	0	3.91
Jim Mill	28	1466	97(1)	0	3.97

RICHMOND RENEGADES

SCORING

	Games	G	A	Pts.	Pen.
Brendan Flynn	60	23	52	75	38
Phil Huber	44	23	49	72	151
Darren Colbourne	29	26	23	49	12
Jeff Saterdalen	62	32	16	48	53
Jeffrey Torrey	54	22	26	48	29
Sean LeBrun	22	18	26	44	17
Jim McGeough	39	14	27	41	66
Guy Phillips	18	12	24	36	15
Will Averill	53	7	29	36	63
Alan Schuler	62	2	34	36	50
Guy Gadowsky	19	19	16	35	2
Martin Smith	40	15	17	32	39
Mark Hicks	29	15	15	30	38
Mark Kuntz	60	12	15	27	215
Steve Mirabile	27	11	15	26	42
Scott Drevitch	34	8	18	26	16
Jeffery Kampersal	56	6	18	24	45
Frank Bialowas	60	3	18	21	261
Martin LaCroix	17	5	13	18	40
Kevin Malgunas	29	7	5	12	106
Ben Wyzansky	34	2	9	11	51
Pat Bingham	10	5	4	9	35
Edward Sabo	19	2	4	6	17
Mike Heany	10	0	5	5	4
Brett Barnett	6	1	2	3	2
Dave Aiken	6	1	1	2	0
Dan Fowler	15	1	1	2	56
Chris Venkus	5	0	2	2	2
Mike James (goalie)	42	0	2	2	2

	Games	G	A	Pts.	Pen.
John Lorenzo (goalie)	6	0	1	1	0
Hayden O'Rear	1	0	0	0	2
Trevor Converse	2	0	0	0	4
Duane Rhinehart	2	0	0	0	0
Jon Gustafson (goalie)	24	0	0	0	2

GOALTENDING

	Games	Min.	Goals	SO	Avg.
Jon Gustafson	24	1316	88(2)	0	4.01
Mike James	42	2226	171(6)	0	4.61
John Lorenzo	6	258	23	1	5.35

ROANOKE VALLEY RAMPAGE

SCORING

	Games	G	A	Pts.	Pen.
Dean Dorchak	62	39	26	65	46
Scott Burfoot	48	28	32	60	22
Craig Endean	37	15	36	51	51
Trevor Smith	49	13	34	47	45
Jack Williams	43	19	26	45	28
Ken Blum	63	16	21	37	132
Ron Jones	42	16	14	30	123
Chris Smith	31	9	21	30	16
Joe Dragon	40	9	16	25	46
Chris MacKensie	22	8	14	22	4
Ken House	17	11	10	21	8
Andrei Kovalev	24	11	9	20	37
Darryl Mitchell	28	2	15	17	28
Mike Griffith	18	5	5	10	30
Roger Larche	11	3	7	10	41
Kent Anderson	37	3	7	10	39
Vaclav Nedomansky	22	5	4	9	31
Mike Manning	32	3	6	9	33
Devin Derksen	37	0	8	8	91
Paul Dukovac	20	2	5	7	26
Rob Bateman	39	2	5	7	51
Pete Speranza	14	2	3	5	8
Dennis Skapski	16	1	3	4	59
Chris Taylor	5	2	1	3	0
Claude Maillet	14	0	3	3	40
Mark Marinette	5	1	2	3	0
Doug Bacon	13	0	3	3	56
Mark Thompson	4	0	3	3	9
Steve Gatzos	1	1	1	2	0
Mike Kelly	4	0	2	2	4
Chris DePiero	1	1	0	1	0
Steve Ashe	1	0	0	0	0
Tom Benzio	1	0	0	0	0
Paul Caufield	1	0	0	0	0
Joe Currin	1	0	0	0	0
Ed Dearborn	1	0	0	0	0
Mario Mercier	1	0	0	0	0
Dave Silver	1	0	0	0	0
Bob Smith	1	0	0	0	0
Pete Fay	2	0	0	0	0
Brian Clark	3	0	0	0	0
Kyle Haviland	3	0	0	0	32
Bob Vermette	3	0	0	0	2
Bill Wagner	3	0	0	0	2
Clayton Norris	4	0	0	0	2
Dan Bouchard (goalie)	5	0	0	0	4
Jim McCarthy	5	0	0	0	2
Pete Fry (goalie)	6	0	0	0	0
Chris Puscian (goalie)	6	0	0	0	2
Tom Frye	7	0	0	0	17
Ray Letourneau (goalie)	7	0	0	0	0
Todd Drevitch	9	0	0	0	15
Don Burke	10	0	0	0	49
Rob Laurie (goalie)	14	0	0	0	2
Todd Chin (goalie)	39	0	0	0	10

GOALTENDING

	Games	Min.	Goals	SO	Avg.
Rob Laurie	14	716	55(1)	0	4.61
Pete Fry	6	293	28	0	5.73

	Games	Min.	Goals	SO	Avg.
Todd Chin	39	1869	197(2)	0	6.32
Chris Puscian	6	254	28	0	6.61
Dan Bouchard	5	253	29	0	6.88
Ray Letourneau	7	401	47	0	7.03

TOLEDO STORM

SCORING

	Games	G	A	Pts.	Pen.
Iain Duncan	50	40	50	90	190
Jeff Jablonski	61	26	46	72	93
Derek Booth	57	18	46	64	198
Alex Roberts	53	21	40	61	145
Alex Hicks	52	26	34	60	100
Rick Corriveau	63	11	44	55	113
Rick Judson	56	23	28	51	39
Greg Puhalski	27	19	29	48	73
Bruce MacDonald	55	20	27	47	80
Mark Deazeley	63	27	18	45	263
Brent Sapergia	30	14	24	38	98
Dan Wiebe	27	18	15	33	45
John Johnson	37	14	19	33	18
Barry Potomski	43	5	18	23	184
Andy Suhy	64	5	15	20	97
Jim Bermingham	18	8	9	17	21
Pat Pylypuik	42	1	15	16	168
Justin Morrison	13	6	8	14	47
Jeff Rohlicek	8	5	8	13	14
Wade Bartley	13	0	10	10	21
Jason Stos	29	1	8	9	57
Don Stone	10	3	5	8	4
Trent Pankewicz	7	1	6	7	6
Larry Olimb	5	3	2	5	2
Mark Hicks	6	1	4	5	14
Scott King (goalie)	45	0	2	2	18
Mike Casselman	3	0	1	1	2
Mike Williams (goalie)	8	0	1	1	2
Joe Decker	1	0	0	0	0
Tyler Ertel	1	0	0	0	0
Tom Xavier	1	0	0	0	2
Alain Harvey (goalie)	5	0	0	0	2
Dennis Purdy	6	0	0	0	17
Mark Richards (goalie)	11	0	0	0	4

GOALTENDING

	Games	Min.	Goals	SO	Avg.
Mark Richards	11	612	28	1	2.75
Alain Harvey	5	302	16	0	3.18
Scott King	45	2602	153(3)	2	3.53
Mike Williams	8	376	28	0	4.47

WHEELING THUNDERBIRDS

SCORING

	Games	G	A	Pts.	Pen.
Devin Edgerton	57	46	71	117	34
Darren Schwartz	62	62	52	114	212
Tim Tisdale	56	33	44	77	113
Dean Antos	61	25	42	67	76
Marc Rodgers	64	23	40	63	91
Tim Roberts	63	12	47	59	18
Trevor Senn	53	14	21	35	301
Robert Guillet	15	16	14	30	8
John Uniac	50	4	21	25	30
Cory Paterson	32	11	11	22	49
Tom Dion	60	5	17	22	76
Derek DeCosty	18	11	10	21	10
Ryan Kuwabara	18	7	13	20	22
Justin Lafayette	39	10	8	18	36
Terry Virtue	31	3	15	18	86
Marty Yewchuk	26	5	11	16	24
Alexander Legault	48	5	10	15	44
Joel Blain	29	5	9	14	29
Trevor Pochipinski	37	3	11	14	25
Craig Ferguson	9	6	5	11	24

	Games	G	A	Pts.	Pen.
Scott Allison	6	3	3	6	8
Eric Marcoux	26	1	4	5	91
Yves Sarault	2	1	3	4	0
Tony Burns	5	1	3	4	2
Claude Barthe	5	0	3	3	10
Rhys Hollyman	23	1	1	2	36
Joel Dyck	5	0	2	2	0
Darcy Martini	6	0	2	2	2
Kim Maier	5	1	0	1	2
Tom Holdeman	2	0	1	1	2
Darcy Simon	3	0	1	1	26
Rod Houk (goalie)	27	0	1	1	6
Wayne Cowley (goalie)	1	0	0	0	2
Eric Brule	4	0	0	0	2
Richie Walcott	8	0	0	0	46
Francis Ouellette (goalie)	43	0	0	0	4

GOALTENDING

	Games	Min.	Goals	SO	Avg.
Rod Houk	27	1453	72(4)	0	2.97
Wayne Cowley	1	60	3	0	3.00
Francis Ouellette	43	2376	138	2	3.48

PLAYERS WITH TWO OR MORE TEAMS

SCORING

	Games	G	A	Pts.	Pen.
Doug Bacon, Roanoke	13	0	3	3	56
Doug Bacon, Raleigh	31	6	10	16	151
Totals	44	6	13	19	207
Brett Barnett, Birmingham	48	16	24	40	125
Brett Barnett, Richmond	6	1	2	3	2
Totals	54	16	26	43	127
Claude Barthe, Wheeling	5	0	3	3	10
Claude Barthe, Knoxville	24	3	6	9	32
Totals	29	3	9	12	42
Rob Bateman, Greensboro	11	0	2	2	42
Rob Bateman, Roanoke	39	2	5	7	51
Totals	50	2	7	9	93
Dan Bouchard (g), Roanoke	5	0	0	0	4
Dan Bouchard (g), H.R.	1	0	0	0	0
Totals	6	0	0	0	4
Cam Brown, Columbus	36	13	18	31	218
Cam Brown, Erie	15	4	3	7	50
Totals	51	17	21	38	268
Greg Burke, Birmingham	33	9	16	25	57
Greg Burke, Nashville	16	2	6	8	28
Totals	49	11	22	33	85
Darren Colbourne, Dayton	32	19	11	30	41
Darren Colbourne, Richmond	29	26	23	49	12
Totals	61	45	34	79	53
Marc DesChamps, Erie	42	1	9	10	52
Marc DesChamps, Louisville	3	0	0	0	0
Totals	45	1	9	10	52
Ray DeSouza, Nashville	26	0	6	6	115
Ray DeSouza, Birmingham	29	1	7	8	86
Totals	55	1	13	14	201
Scott Drevitch, Richmond	34	8	18	26	16
Scott Drevitch, Dayton	27	9	21	30	20
Totals	61	17	39	56	36
Todd Drevitch, Roanoke	9	0	0	0	15
Todd Drevitch, Greensboro	7	0	1	1	26
Totals	16	0	1	1	41
Paul Dukovac, Columbus	23	1	11	12	16
Paul Dukovac, Roanoke	20	2	5	7	26
Totals	43	3	16	19	42
Ray Edwards, Dayton	29	7	7	14	107
Ray Edwards, Birmingham	16	0	7	7	60
Totals	45	7	14	21	167
Brent Fleetwood, Greensboro	36	9	18	27	57
Brent Fleetwood, H.R.	13	5	2	7	4
Totals	49	14	20	34	61
Bill Harrington, Greensboro	6	1	0	1	6
Bill Harrington, Knoxville	12	0	0	0	9
Totals	18	1	0	1	15

	Games	G	A	Pts.	Pen.
Alain Harvey (g), Toledo	5	0	0	0	2
Alain Harvey (g), Greensboro	5	0	1	1	2
Totals	10	0	1	1	4
Alexander Havanov, Birm.	19	0	3	3	14
Alexander Havanov, Raleigh	17	0	6	6	8
Totals	36	0	9	9	22
Mark Hicks, Toledo	6	1	4	5	14
Mark Hicks, Richmond	29	15	15	30	38
Totals	35	16	19	35	52
Mark Hilton, Louisville	2	0	0	0	0
Mark Hilton, Dayton	2	0	0	0	0
Totals	4	0	0	0	0
Rhys Hollyman, Wheeling	23	1	1	2	36
Rhys Hollyman, Louisville	32	3	12	15	51
Totals	55	4	13	17	87
Rod Houk (g), Dayton	6	0	0	0	2
Rod Houk (g), Wheeling	27	0	1	1	6
Totals	33	0	1	1	8
Ken House, Louisville	18	9	4	13	2
Ken House, Roanoke	17	11	10	21	8
Totals	35	20	14	34	10
John Johnson	37	14	19	33	18
John Johnson, Raleigh	2	0	0	0	0
Totals	39	14	19	33	18
Bill Kovacs, Raleigh	19	4	6	10	32
Bill Kovacs, Birmingham	36	16	13	29	40
Totals	55	20	19	39	72
Andrei Kovalev, Roanoke	24	11	9	20	37
Andrei Kovalev, Greensboro	7	2	2	4	17
Totals	31	13	11	24	54
Chris Lappin, Greensboro	52	3	13	16	165
Chris Lappin, Erie	4	0	0	0	21
Totals	56	3	13	16	186
Roger Larche, Greensboro	39	12	22	34	155
Roger Larche, Roanoke	11	3	7	10	41
Totals	50	15	29	44	196
Rob Laurie (g), Roanoke	14	0	0	0	2
Rob Laurie (g), Dayton	22	0	0	0	2
Totals	36	0	0	0	4
Ray Letourneau (g), Greens.	10	0	0	0	0
Ray Letourneau (g), Roanoke.	7	0	0	0	0
Totals	17	0	0	0	0
Chris MacKensie, Roanoke	22	8	14	22	4
Chris MacKensie, Louisville	2	0	0	0	0
Totals	24	8	14	22	4
Kim Maier, Wheeling	5	1	0	1	2
Kim Maier, Knoxville	55	31	19	50	45
Totals	60	32	19	51	47
Claude Maillet, Greensboro	26	5	9	14	78
Claude Maillet, Roanoke	14	0	3	3	40
Totals	40	5	12	17	118
Kevin Malgunas, Richmond	29	7	5	12	106
Kevin Malgunas, H.R.	27	14	18	32	94
Totals	56	21	23	44	200
Chris Marshall, Birmingham	21	6	13	19	86
Chris Marshall, Raleigh	36	11	25	36	78
Totals	57	17	38	55	164
Scott Matusovich, Birmingham	11	1	4	5	10
Scott Matusovich, Nashville	51	1	17	18	62
Totals	62	2	21	23	72
Mike Millham (g), Knoxville	2	0	0	0	0
Mike Millham (g), Erie	29	0	0	0	2
Totals	31	0	0	0	2
Steve Mirabile, Hampton Roads.	37	24	24	48	66
Steve Mirabile, Richmond	27	11	15	26	42
Totals	64	35	39	74	108
Darryl Mitchell, Dayton	19	4	8	12	21
Darryl Mitchell, Roanoke	28	2	15	17	28
Totals	47	6	23	29	49
Wayne Muir, Greensboro	50	28	24	52	200
Wayne Muir, Dayton	6	4	2	6	38
Totals	56	32	26	58	238
Vaclav Nedomansky, Knox.	27	8	11	19	117
Vaclav Nedomansky, Roanoke	22	5	4	9	31
Totals	49	13	15	28	148

	Games	G	A	Pts.	Pen.
Hayden O'Rear, Richmond	1	0	0	0	2
Hayden O'Rear, Knoxville	52	4	12	16	45
Totals	53	4	12	16	47
Rob Pallante, Dayton	1	0	0	0	0
Rob Pallante, Nashville	15	1	0	1	75
Totals	16	1	0	1	75
Trent Pankewicz, Toledo	7	1	6	7	6
Trent Pankewicz, Knox.	32	14	20	34	101
Totals	39	15	26	41	107
Darren Perkins, Erie	28	7	17	24	40
Darren Perkins, Columbus	20	9	4	13	44
Totals	48	16	21	37	84
Jim Peters, Birmingham	21	1	9	10	55
Jim Peters, Dayton	31	1	8	9	74
Totals	52	2	17	19	129
Dan Poirier, Nashville	5	1	0	1	7
Dan Poirier, Birmingham	7	1	0	1	41
Totals	12	2	0	2	48
Chic Pojar, Johnstown	1	0	0	0	0
Chic Pojar, Raleigh	24	4	4	8	12
Totals	25	4	4	8	12
Barry Potomski, Erie	5	1	1	2	31
Barry Potomski, Toledo	43	5	18	23	184
Totals	48	6	19	25	215
Dennis Purdy, Toledo	6	0	0	0	17
Dennis Purdy, Johnstown	17	10	7	17	38
Totals	23	10	7	17	55
Matt Robbins, Birmingham	2	1	1	2	2
Matt Robbins, Johnstown	56	23	41	64	37
Totals	58	24	42	66	39
Doug Roberts, Raleigh	11	0	2	2	6
Doug Roberts, Knoxville	44	10	17	27	31
Totals	55	10	19	29	37
Dan Ryder (g), Johnstown	4	0	0	0	26
Dan Ryder (g), Columbus	1	0	0	0	0
Totals	5	0	0	0	26
Brent Sapergia, Toledo	30	14	24	38	98
Brent Sapergia, Nash.	26	23	26	49	116
Totals	56	37	50	87	214
Michael Seaton, Nashville	25	6	10	16	27
Michael Seaton, Knoxville	32	15	17	32	34
Totals	57	21	27	48	61
Dennis Skapski, Columbus	22	2	6	8	22
Dennis Skapski, Roanoke	16	1	3	4	59
Totals	38	3	9	12	81
Chris Smith, Louisville	17	0	10	10	8
Chris Smith, Roanoke	31	9	21	30	16
Totals	48	9	31	40	24
Trevor Smith, Roanoke	49	13	34	47	45
Trevor Smith, Greensboro	15	2	4	6	4
Totals	64	15	38	53	49
Joe Spinelli, Raleigh	5	0	0	0	0
Joe Spinelli, Louisville	53	20	36	56	53
Totals	58	20	36	56	53
Jamie Steer, Greensboro	35	16	14	30	8
Jamie Steer, Louisville	30	13	16	29	14
Totals	65	29	30	59	22

	Games	G	A	Pts.	Pen.
Olie Sundstrom (g), Nash.	21	0	2	2	28
Olie Sundstrom (g), Columbus	8	0	0	0	8
Totals	29	0	2	2	36
Chris Venkus, Raleigh	9	1	2	3	8
Chris Venkus, Richmond	5	0	2	2	2
Totals	14	1	4	5	10
Terry Virtue, Louisville	28	0	17	17	84
Terry Virtue, Wheeling	31	3	15	18	86
Totals	59	3	32	35	170
Bill Wagner, Knoxville	32	3	7	10	28
Bill Wagner, Roanoke	3	0	0	0	2
Totals	35	3	7	10	30
Richie Walcott, Wheeling	8	0	0	0	46
Richie Walcott, H.R.	14	1	1	2	116
Totals	22	1	1	2	162
Keith Whitmore, H.R.	7	1	3	4	10
Keith Whitmore, Knoxville	50	8	27	35	86
Totals	57	9	30	39	96
Jeff Whittle, Hampton Roads	5	1	0	1	19
Jeff Whittle, Erie	45	9	16	25	133
Totals	50	10	16	26	152
Mike Williams (g), Toledo	8	0	1	1	2
Mike Williams (g), Knoxville	21	0	2	2	6
Totals	29	0	3	3	8

GOALTENDING

	Games	Min.	Goals	SO	Avg.
Dan Bouchard, Roa.	5	253	29	0	6.88
Dan Bouchard, H.R.	1	60	7	0	7.00
Totals	6	313	36	0	6.90
Alain Harvey, Toledo	5	302	16	0	3.18
Alain Harvey, Greens.	5	268	20(1)	0	4.48
Totals	10	570	36(1)	0	3.79
Rod Houk, Dayton	6	182	23	0	7.58
Rod Houk, Wheeling	27	1453	72(4)	0	2.97
Totals	33	1635	95(4)	0	3.49
Rob Laurie, Roanoke	14	716	55(1)	0	4.61
Rob Laurie, Dayton	22	1197	90	0	4.51
Totals	36	1913	145(1)	0	4.55
Ray Letourneau, Gre.	10	366	38	0	6.23
Ray Letourneau, Roa.	7	401	47	0	7.03
Totals	17	767	85	0	6.65
Mike Millham, Knox.	2	100	15	0	9.00
Mike Millham, Erie	29	1636	115	0	4.22
Totals	31	1736	130	0	4.49
Dan Ryder, Johns.	4	214	15	0	4.21
Dan Ryder, Columbus.	1	60	6(1)	0	6.00
Totals	5	274	21(1)	0	4.60
Olie Sundstrom, Nash.	21	1087	99(1)	0	5.46
Olie Sundstrom, Col.	8	416	28	0	4.04
Totals	29	1503	127(1)	0	5.07
Mike Williams, Toledo	8	376	28	0	4.47
Mike Williams, Knox.	21	1145	95	0	4.98
Totals	29	1521	123	0	4.85

1993 RILEY CUP PLAYOFFS

RESULTS

EAST DIVISION

WILD-CARD

Series "A"

	W	L	Pts.	GF	GA
Johnstown	1	0	2	5	4
Richmond	0	1	0	4	5

(Johnstown won series, 1-0)

SEMIFINALS

Series "B"

	W	L	Pts.	GF	GA
Wheeling	3	1	6	13	9
Johnstown	1	3	2	9	13

(Wheeling won series, 3-1)

Series "C"

	W	L	Pts.	GF	GA
Raleigh	3	1	6	13	11
Hampton Roads	1	3	2	11	13

(Raleigh won series, 3-1)

FINALS

Series "D"

	W	L	Pts.	GF	GA
Wheeling	4	2	8	24	19
Raleigh	2	4	4	19	24

(Wheeling won series, 4-2)

WEST DIVISION

WILD-CARD

Series "A"

	W	L	Pts.	GF	GA
Erie	1	0	2	6	2
Greensboro	0	1	0	2	6

(Erie won series, 1-0)

SEMIFINALS

Series "B"

	W	L	Pts.	GF	GA
Toledo	3	1	6	23	16
Erie	1	3	2	16	23

(Toledo won series, 3-1)

Series "C"

	W	L	Pts.	GF	GA
Nashville	3	0	6	13	9
Dayton	0	3	0	9	13

(Nashville won series, 3-0)

FINALS

Series "D"

	W	L	Pts.	GF	GA
Toledo	4	2	8	32	19
Nashville	2	4	4	19	32

(Toledo won series, 4-2)

RILEY CUP FINALS

Series "E"

	W	L	Pts.	GF	GA
Toledo	4	2	8	28	28
Wheeling	2	4	4	28	28

(Toledo won series, 4-2)

INDIVIDUAL LEADERS

Goals: Darren Schwartz, Wheeling (13)
Assists: Iain Duncan, Toledo (19)
Points: Darren Schwartz, Wheeling (31)
Penalty minutes: Trevor Senn, Wheeling (89)
Goaltending average: Nick Vitucci, Hampton Roads (2.33)
Shutouts: Rod Houk, Wheeling (2)

TOP SCORERS

	Games	G	A	Pts.
Darren Schwartz, Wheeling	16	13	18	31
Devin Edgerton, Wheeling	16	12	17	29
Iain Duncan, Toledo	16	9	19	28
Greg Puhalski, Toledo	16	12	12	24
Rick Judson, Toledo	16	7	16	23
Derek Booth, Toledo	16	7	14	21
Tim Roberts, Wheeling	16	2	16	18
Tim Tisdale, Wheeling	15	11	5	16
Alex Hicks, Toledo	16	5	10	15
Rick Corriveau, Toledo	12	4	11	15

INDIVIDUAL STATISTICS

DAYTON BOMBERS

(Lost West Division semifinals to Nashville, 3-0)

SCORING

	Games	G	A	Pts.	Pen.
Scott Drevitch	3	2	4	6	2
Frank Kovacs	3	3	1	4	2
Peter Kasowski	3	1	3	4	2
Derek Donald	3	1	2	3	0
Steve Bogoyevac	3	1	1	2	0
Wayne Muir	3	1	0	1	16
Marc Savard	3	0	1	1	6
Darwin McPherson	3	0	1	1	30
Shayne Green	3	0	1	1	0
Darren Langdon	3	0	1	1	40
Rob Laurie (goalie)	1	0	0	0	0
Brian Blad	1	0	0	0	0
Jeff Levy (goalie)	2	0	0	0	0
Doug Evans	3	0	0	0	0
Jim Peters	3	0	0	0	19
David Smith	3	0	0	0	26
Steve Wilson	3	0	0	0	7

GOALTENDING

	Games	Min.	Goals	SO	Avg.
Rob Laurie	1	68	4	0	3.53
Jeff Levy	2	139	9	0	3.88

ERIE PANTHERS

(Lost West Division semifinals to Toledo, 3-1)

SCORING

	Games	G	A	Pts.	Pen.
Glen Goodall	5	6	3	9	6
Ed Zawatsky	5	3	5	8	4
Jason Winch	5	2	5	7	4
Bill Gall	5	2	4	6	4
Brian Shantz	5	2	3	5	23
Tony Iob	5	2	2	4	45
Peter Buckeridge	5	1	3	4	4
John Vary	5	1	2	3	20
Fredric Jax	5	1	1	2	6
Jason Smith	5	1	1	2	2
Greg Spenrath	3	1	0	1	77
Cam Brown	5	0	1	1	62

	Games	G	A	Pts.	Pen.
Mike Gilmore (goalie)	5	0	1	1	0
Chris Panek	5	0	1	1	24
Brad Pascall	5	0	1	1	18

GOALTENDING

	Games	Min.	Goals	SO	Avg.
Mike Gilmore	5	300	24(1)	0	4.80

GREENSBORO MONARCHS

(Lost West Division wild-card round to Erie, 1-0)

SCORING

	Games	G	A	Pts.	Pen.
Phil Berger	1	1	1	2	26
Darryl Noren	1	1	0	1	0
David Burke	1	0	1	1	0
Dan Bylsma	1	0	1	1	10
Vadim Slivtchenko	1	0	1	1	0
Greg Capson	1	0	0	0	2
Todd Gordon	1	0	0	0	2
Craig Herr	1	0	0	0	2
Patrick LaBrecque (goalie)	1	0	0	0	2
Jamie Nicolls	1	0	0	0	2
Davis Payne	1	0	0	0	4
Jason Prosofsky	1	0	0	0	5
Trevor Smith	1	0	0	0	0
Chris Wolanin	1	0	0	0	2
Brock Woods	1	0	0	0	0
Dean Zayonce	1	0	0	0	0

GOALTENDING

	Games	Min.	Goals	SO	Avg.
Patrick LaBrecque	1	59	5(1)	0	5.08

HAMPTON ROADS ADMIRALS

(Lost East Division semifinals to Raleigh, 3-1)

SCORING

	Games	G	A	Pts.	Pen.
Brian Martin	4	2	4	6	8
Al MacIssac	4	1	3	4	20
Rod Taylor	2	3	0	3	10
Kevin Malgunas	4	2	1	3	4
Shawn Snesar	4	2	1	3	6
Victor Gervais	4	0	3	3	10
Steve Martell	4	0	2	2	26
Kelly Sorensen	4	0	2	2	0
Brent Fleetwood	4	1	0	1	0
Daniel Chaput	1	0	1	1	2
Steve Poapst	4	0	1	1	4
Bob Babcock	4	1	0	0	10
Mark Bernard (goalie)	1	0	0	0	0
Dave Morissette	2	0	0	0	2
Nick Vitucci (goalie)	3	0	0	0	0
Brian Goudie	4	0	0	0	6
Kurt Kabat	4	0	0	0	4
Jason Rathbone	4	0	0	0	4

GOALTENDING

	Games	Min.	Goals	SO	Avg.
Nick Vitucci	3	206	8	0	2.33
Mark Bernard	1	61	5	0	4.92

JOHNSTOWN CHIEFS

(Lost East Division semifinals to Wheeling, 3-1)

SCORING

	Games	G	A	Pts.	Pen.
Rival Fullum	5	5	0	5	2
Mark Karpen	5	1	4	5	4
Matt Robbins	5	0	5	5	2
Jeff Ricciardi	5	2	2	4	6
Bruce Coles	5	1	3	4	29
Christian Lariviere	5	1	3	4	4
Dennis Purdy	5	1	3	4	38
Chris Crombie	5	1	1	2	2

	Games	G	A	Pts.	Pen.
Bob Woods	5	1	1	2	8
Chuck Wiegand	5	0	2	2	0
Dusty McLellan	4	1	0	1	0
Steve Gibson	3	0	1	1	2
Derry Menard	3	0	1	1	2
Perry Florio	5	0	1	1	25
John Bradley (goalie)	5	0	0	0	2
Paul Ohman	5	0	0	0	14

GOALTENDING

	Games	Min.	Goals	SO	Avg.
John Bradley	5	307	17	0	3.32

NASHVILLE KNIGHTS

(Lost West Division finals to Toledo, 4-2)

SCORING

	Games	G	A	Pts.	Pen.
Trevor Jobe	9	7	7	14	38
Brian Ferreira	9	2	10	12	18
Troy Mick	9	2	7	9	8
Steve Sullivan	9	4	4	8	64
Brian Horan	7	2	4	6	20
Brent Sapergia	8	2	4	6	30
Don Parsons	9	3	2	5	12
Stanislav Tkach	8	2	1	3	15
Chris Grassie	8	1	2	3	35
Rob Dumas	9	2	0	2	37
Andrei Dylevsky	9	2	0	2	4
Scott Matusovich	8	1	1	2	8
Bob Creamer	9	0	2	2	2
Dean Gerald	4	1	0	1	0
Greg Burke	9	1	0	1	21
Tom Cole (goalie)	1	0	0	0	0
Darcy Kaminski	3	0	0	0	6
Scott Gordon (goalie)	9	0	0	0	4

GOALTENDING

	Games	Min.	Goals	SO	Avg.
Tom Cole	1	20	0	0	0.00
Scott Gordon	9	548	40(1)	0	4.38

RALEIGH ICECAPS

(Lost East Division finals to Wheeling, 4-2)

SCORING

	Games	G	A	Pts.	Pen.
Rick Barkovich	10	8	3	11	6
Lyle Wildgoose	10	3	8	11	2
Mike Lappin	10	8	2	10	4
Brad Aitken	10	1	9	10	12
Bruno Villeneuve	10	3	5	8	2
Jim Powers	10	2	4	6	8
Brian Tulik	10	1	5	6	14
Alan Leggett	10	1	4	5	10
Chris Marshall	10	1	3	4	28
Doug Bacon	10	1	1	2	20
Sean Cowan	10	1	1	2	16
John Johnson	10	0	2	2	6
Derek Linnell	10	0	2	2	28
Todd Person	10	1	0	1	2
Jeff Robison	10	1	0	1	18
Jim Mill (goalie)	2	0	0	0	0
Stan Reddick (goalie)	9	0	0	0	0

GOALTENDING

	Games	Min.	Goals	SO	Avg.
Stan Reddick	9	560	27(1)	0	2.89
Jim Mill	2	71	7	0	5.92

RICHMOND RENEGADES

(Lost East Division wild-card round to Johnstown, 1-0)

SCORING

	Games	G	A	Pts.	Pen.
Jeffrey Torrey	1	2	0	2	0
Phil Huber	1	1	1	2	6
Mark Hicks	1	0	2	2	0
Guy Phillips	1	0	2	2	0
Will Averill	1	1	0	1	0
Darren Colbourne	1	0	1	1	0
Jeff Saterdalen	1	0	1	1	0
Frank Bialowas	1	0	0	0	2
Brendan Flynn	1	0	0	0	0
Guy Gadowsky	1	0	0	0	0
Jon Gustafson (goalie)	1	0	0	0	0
Mike Heany	1	0	0	0	2
Mike James (goalie)	1	0	0	0	2
Jeffrey Kampersal	1	0	0	0	0
Mark Kuntz	1	0	0	0	0
Steve Mirabile	1	0	0	0	0
Alan Schuler	1	0	0	0	0

GOALTENDING

	Games	Min.	Goals	SO	Avg.
Jon Gustafson	1	52	2	0	2.31
Mike James	1	17	3	0	10.59

TOLEDO STORM

(Winner of Riley Cup playoffs)

SCORING

	Games	G	A	Pts.	Pen.
Iain Duncan	16	9	19	28	55
Greg Puhalski	16	12	12	24	30
Rick Judson	16	7	16	23	10
Derek Booth	16	7	14	21	65
Alex Hicks	16	5	10	15	79
Rick Corriveau	12	4	11	15	23
Mark Deazeley	15	8	6	14	66
Jeff Jablonski	16	3	11	14	20
Wade Bartley	16	5	8	13	22
Dan Wiebe	16	4	6	10	39
Dave Flanagan	12	6	3	9	10
Alex Roberts	8	1	8	9	12
Bruce MacDonald	14	5	3	8	16

	Games	G	A	Pts.	Pen.
Barry Potomski	14	5	2	7	73
Andy Suhy	15	1	4	5	60
Joe Cook	2	1	1	2	2
Scott Campbell	5	0	2	2	17
Scott King (goalie)	14	0	1	1	20
Jeff Jestadt	2	0	0	0	0
Alain Harvey (goalie)	4	0	0	0	4

GOALTENDING

	Games	Min.	Goals	SO	Avg.
Scott King	14	823	52	0	3.79
Alain Harvey	4	160	11	0	4.13

WHEELING THUNDERBIRDS

(Lost Riley Cup finals to Toledo, 4-2)

SCORING

	Games	G	A	Pts.	Pen.
Darren Schwartz	16	13	18	31	43
Devin Edgerton	16	12	17	29	12
Tim Roberts	16	2	16	18	14
Tim Tisdale	15	11	5	16	52
Ryan Kuwabara	16	5	8	13	40
Justin Lafayette	16	4	5	9	10
Terry Virtue	16	3	5	8	18
Dean Antos	16	2	5	7	30
Tom Dion	16	2	5	7	38
John Uniac	16	1	5	6	8
Joel Blain	14	3	2	5	18
Trevor Senn	14	3	2	5	89
Marty Yewchuk	16	2	3	5	16
Marc Rodgers	6	1	1	2	8
Alexander Legault	16	1	1	2	28
Darrin McKecknie	1	0	1	1	4
Brent Pope	2	0	0	0	6
Rod Houk (goalie)	7	0	0	0	10
Francis Ouellette (goalie)	9	0	0	0	6

GOALTENDING

	Games	Min.	Goals	SO	Avg.
Rod Houk	7	419	21(1)	2	3.01
Francis Ouellette	9	560	33(1)	0	3.54

1992-93 AWARD WINNERS

ALL-STAR TEAMS

First team	Pos.	Second team
Francis Ouellette, Wheeling	G	Scott King, Toledo
Derek Booth, Toledo	D	Paul Marshall, Birmingham
Steve Poapst, Hamp. Roads	D	Alan Leggett, Raleigh
Darren Schwartz, Wheeling	LW	Iain Duncan, Toledo
Trevor Jobe, Nashville	C	Devin Edgerton, Wheeling
Sheldon Gorski, Louisville	RW	Bruce Coles, Johnstown

Coach of the Year: Kurt Kleinendorst, Raleigh

TROPHY WINNERS

Most Valuable Player: Trevor Jobe, Nashville
Scoring leader: Trevor Jobe, Nashville
Outstanding defenseman: Derek Booth, Toledo
Rookie of the Year: Joe Flanagan, Birmingham
Playoff MVP: Rick Judson, Toledo
Coach of the Year: Kurt Kleinendorst, Raleigh

ALL-TIME AWARD WINNERS

MOST VALUABLE PLAYER

Season	Player, Team
1988-89	Daryl Harpe, Erie
1989-90	Bill McDougall, Erie
1990-91	Stan Drulia, Knoxville
1991-92	Phil Berger, Greensboro
1992-93	Trevor Jobe, Nashville

TOP SCORER

Season	Player, Team
1988-89	Daryl Harpe, Erie
1989-90	Bill McDougall, Erie
1990-91	Stan Drulia, Knoxville
1991-92	Phil Berger, Greensboro
1992-93	Trevor Jobe, Nashville

ROOKIE OF THE YEAR

Season	Player, Team
1988-89	Tom Sasso, Johnstown
1989-90	Bill McDougall, Erie
1990-91	Dan Gauthier, Knoxville
1991-92	Darren Colbourne, Dayton
1992-93	Joe Flanagan, Birmingham

TOP GOALTENDER

Season	Player, Team
1988-89	Scott Gordon, Johnstown
1989-90	Alain Raymond, Hampton Roads
1990-91	Dean Anderson, Knoxville
1991-92	Frederic Chabot, Winston-Salem
1992-93	Nick Vitucci, Hampton Roads

PLAYOFF MVP

Season	Player, Team
1988-89	Nick Vitucci, Carolina
1989-90	Wade Flaherty, Greensboro
1990-91	Dave Gagnon, Hampton Roads
	Dave Flanagan, Hampton Roads
1991-92	Mark Bernard, Hampton Roads
1992-93	Rick Judson, Toledo

COACH OF THE YEAR

Season	Coach, Team
1988-89	Ron Hansis, Erie
1989-90	Dave Allison, Virginia
1990-91	Don Jackson, Knoxville
1991-92	Doug Sauter, Winston-Salem
1992-93	Kurt Kleinendorst, Raleigh

TOP DEFENSEMAN

Season	Player, Team
1988-89	Kelly Szautner, Erie
1989-90	Bill Whitfield, Virginia
1990-91	Brett McDonald, Nashville
1991-92	Scott White, Greensboro
1992-93	Derek Booth, Toledo

ALL-TIME LEAGUE CHAMPIONS

REGULAR-SEASON CHAMPION

Season	Team	Coach
1988-89	Erie Panthers	Ron Hansis
1989-90	Winston-Salem Thunderbirds	C. McSorley, J. Fraser
1990-91	Knoxville Cherokees	Don Jackson
1991-92	Toledo Storm	Chris McSorley
1992-93	Wheeling Thunderbirds	Doug Sauter

PLAYOFF CHAMPION

Team	Coach
Carolina Thunderbirds	Brendon Watson
Greensboro Monarchs	Jeff Brubaker
Hampton Roads Admirals	John Brophy
Hampton Roads Admirals	John Brophy
Toledo Storm	Chris McSorley

The ECHL playoff champion is awarded the Bob Payne Trophy.

CENTRAL HOCKEY LEAGUE

LEAGUE OFFICE

President
Ray Miron
Commissioner
Monte Miron
Administrative director
Sheryl Kolb

Director of information
Eric Kolb
Address
5840 S. Memorial Drive
Suite 205
Tulsa, OK 74145

Phone
918-664-8881
FAX
918-664-2215

TEAMS

DALLAS FREEZE

General manager
Tom Koch
Head coach
Ron Flockhart
Home ice
Fair Park Coliseum
Address
2700 Stemmons Freeway
Suite 402 Tower East
Dallas, TX 75207
Seating Capacity
7,500
Phone
214-631-7825
FAX
214-631-8090

FORT WORTH FIRE

General manager
George A. Branum
Head coach
Peter Mahovlich
Home ice
Fort Worth/Tarrant County
Convention Center Arena
Address
910 Houston Street, Suite 400
Fort Worth, TX 76102
Seating capacity
11,400
Phone
817-336-1992
FAX
817-336-1997

MEMPHIS RIVERKINGS

General manager
Jim Riggs
Head coach
Randy Boyd
Home ice
Mid-South Coliseum
Address
The Fairgrounds
Memphis, TN 38104
Seating capacity
9,551
Phone
901-278-9009
FAX
901-274-3209

OKLAHOMA CITY BLAZERS

General manager
Brad Lund
Head coach
Michael McEwen
Home ice
Myriad Convention Center
and State Fair Arena
Address
Sheraton-Century Mall
100 W. Main, Suite 172
Oklahoma City, OK 73102-9201
Seating capacity
13,399 and 9,760
Phone
405-235-7825
FAX
405-272-9875

TULSA OILERS

General manager
Jeff D. Lund
Head coach
Garry Unger
Home ice
Tulsa Convention Center
Address
4528 S. Sheridan Road, Suite 212
Tulsa, OK 74145
Seating Capacity
6,847
Phone
918-663-5888
FAX
918-663-5977

WICHITA THUNDER

General manager
Bill Shuck
Head coach
Doug Shedden
Home ice
Kansas Coliseum
Address
410-A N. St. Francis
Wichita, KS 67202
Seating Capacity
9,682
Phone
316-264-4625
FAX
316-264-3037

1992-93 REGULAR SEASON

FINAL STANDINGS

Team	G	W	L		Pts.	GF	GA
Oklahoma City	60	39	18	(3)	81	291	232
Tulsa	60	35	22	(3)	73	270	230
Dallas	60	31	25	(4)	66	276	242
Memphis	60	26	27	(7)	59	253	272
Fort Worth	60	24	29	(7)	55	252	288
Wichita	60	25	33	(2)	52	242	320

( )—Indicates overtime losses and are worth one point.

INDIVIDUAL LEADERS

Goals: Sylvain Fleury, Oklahoma City (48)
Assists: Doug Lawrence, Tulsa (73)
Points: Sylvain Fleury, Oklahoma City (101)

Penalty minutes: Ron Aubrey, Fort Worth (237)
Goaltending average: Tony Martino, Tulsa (3.66)
Shutouts: Tony Martino, Tulsa (2)

TOP SCORERS

	Games	G	A	Pts.
Sylvain Fleury, Oklahoma City	59	48	53	101
Doug Lawrence, Tulsa	57	22	73	95
Sylvain Naud, Tulsa	58	39	48	87
Tom Mutch, Memphis	59	43	38	81
Taylor Hall, Tulsa	58	35	45	80
Ken Thibodeau, Memphis	54	40	35	75
Wayne Anchikoski, Dallas	57	35	37	72
Carl Boudreau, Oklahoma City	48	27	44	71
Daniel Larin, Oklahoma City	48	43	27	70
Jason Taylor, Dallas	60	38	32	70
Ted Dent, Wichita	60	25	44	69
Mike Sanderson, Fort Worth	60	37	31	68
Dave Gatti, Wichita	58	35	32	67
Mario Nobili, Tulsa	54	31	34	65
Keith Cyr, Wichita	58	21	44	65
Peter D'Amario, Memphis	60	28	35	63
Scot Johnston, Memphis	51	23	40	63
Joe Burton, Oklahoma City	55	35	26	61
Steve Simoni, Oklahoma City	56	33	28	61
Ernest Hornak, Fort Worth	52	22	37	59

INDIVIDUAL STATISTICS

DALLAS FREEZE

SCORING

	Games	G	A	Pts.	Pen.
Wayne Anchikoski	57	35	37	72	74
Jason Taylor	60	38	32	70	210
Dave Doucette	50	10	46	56	66
Gary Audette	60	24	26	50	42
Troy Binnie	43	22	28	50	44
Don Dwyer	41	15	21	36	79
Rico Rossi	39	18	17	35	128
Jeff Beaudin	52	15	20	35	120
Doug Sinclair	49	16	16	32	166
Frank LaScala	27	14	17	31	45
Derek Crawford	22	19	11	30	37
Pat Curcio	32	12	17	29	37
Joey Mittelsteadt	39	6	21	27	128
Richard Hajdu	21	10	14	24	57
Robert Lewis	45	5	19	24	34
Dean Shmyr	57	5	18	23	163
Steve Chelios	30	3	19	22	60
Brian Bruininks	23	4	16	20	27
Mike Paller	10	1	6	7	0
Craig Shepherd	9	3	3	6	6
Mike Zanier (goalie)	40	0	4	4	24
Joel Eagan	16	1	2	3	12
Brian Fleury	11	0	2	2	30
Greg Smith (goalie)	21	0	1	1	0
Martin Pavek	1	0	0	0	2
Roger Hunt	3	0	0	0	11

GOALTENDING

	Games	Min.	Goals	SO	Avg.
Mike Zanier	40	2384	150(3)	1	3.78
Greg Smith	21	1243	86	0	4.15

FORT WORTH FIRE

SCORING

	Games	G	A	Pts.	Pen.
Mike Sanderson	60	37	31	68	33
Ernest Hornak	52	22	37	59	58
Alex Kholomeyev	42	23	22	45	124
Steve Harrison	60	5	38	43	61
Pat Penner	60	12	28	40	77
Eric Brule	36	7	33	40	66
Ryan Leschasin	48	14	24	38	109
Jason Brousseau	38	19	16	35	36
Pete Speranza	37	16	19	35	81
Sean Curtin	36	12	21	33	39
Trevor Duhaime	26	20	12	32	48
Mike McCormick	49	14	16	30	91
Curt Krolak	39	15	10	25	84
Mike Paller	23	9	11	20	35
Andrei Sidorov	17	8	8	16	45
Dan Rolfe	35	0	12	12	77
Paolo Racicot	27	5	6	11	105
Ron Aubrey	28	2	6	8	237
Todd Drevitch	41	2	5	7	67
John Valo	17	3	3	6	18
Tyler Ertel	8	3	2	5	22
Steve Morrow	10	1	4	5	6

	Games	G	A	Pts.	Pen.
Ryan Schmidt	27	0	5	5	119
Frederic Boivin	9	3	1	4	21
Roch Belley (goalie)	33	0	3	3	37
Matt Ocello (goalie)	4	0	1	1	0
Michael O'Hara (goalie)	18	0	1	1	12
Paul Pachkevitch	2	0	0	0	0
Jake Linklater	6	0	0	0	2
Rocco Trentadue (goalie)	18	0	0	0	8

GOALTENDING

	Games	Min.	Goals	SO	Avg.
Matt Ocello	4	179	11(1)	0	3.69
Michael O'Hara	18	911	65	0	4.28
Roch Belley	33	1782	141(3)	0	4.75
Rocco Trentadue	17	746	62(3)	0	4.99

MEMPHIS RIVERKINGS

SCORING

	Games	G	A	Pts.	Pen.
Tom Mutch	59	43	38	81	100
Peter D'Amario	60	28	35	63	16
Scot Johnston	51	23	40	63	99
Mike Jackson	57	24	28	52	182
David Moore	60	18	30	48	114
Andy Ross	50	23	24	47	130
Doug Lawrence	19	8	26	34	47
Michael Martens	19	10	18	28	12
Paul Flaherty	58	13	14	27	133
Scott Phillips	60	5	22	27	52
John Batten	29	11	15	26	210
Mike Roberts	57	4	17	21	49
Keith Cyr	18	7	13	20	35
Ken Thibodeau	14	7	9	16	19
Ken Venis	40	6	10	16	27
Don Burke	28	3	13	16	58
John Mooney	15	3	10	13	16
Daniel Elsener	26	2	8	10	54
Angelo Russo	27	5	4	9	22
Mark McGinn	6	4	5	9	0
Tyler Davidson	32	3	2	5	35
Steve Shaunesey	13	1	3	4	79
Eric Daoust	3	2	1	3	0
Steve McKinley	12	0	3	3	58
Jerald Higgins	6	0	1	1	2
Mike Collins	5	0	0	0	11
Gary Cuesta	11	0	0	0	28
Steve Vasko (goalie)	16	0	0	0	2
Antonie Mindjimba (goalie)	57	0	0	0	52

GOALTENDING

	Games	Min.	Goals	SO	Avg.
Antoine Mindjimba	56	3097	214(4)	1	4.15
Steve Vasko	15	535	46(4)	0	5.16

OKLAHOMA CITY BLAZERS

SCORING

	Games	G	A	Pts.	Pen.
Sylvain Fleury	59	48	53	101	24
Carl Boudreau	48	27	44	71	109

	Games	G	A	Pts.	Pen.
Daniel Larin	48	43	27	70	188
Joe Burton	55	35	26	61	25
Steve Simoni	56	33	28	61	35
Guy Girouard	60	6	45	51	120
Jim Solly	60	22	18	40	53
Chris Laganas	57	18	22	40	193
Boyd Sutton	53	17	23	40	56
Jamie Hearn	59	10	28	38	161
Mark McGinn	42	16	17	33	18
Eric DuBois	25	5	20	25	70
Craig Johnson	50	8	11	19	219
Sean Gorman	51	1	15	16	94
Brendan Garvey	57	2	8	10	133
Alan Perry (goalie)	40	0	8	8	30
Kent Anderson	9	0	3	3	9
Marty Wells	3	0	2	2	0
Mark Berge	3	0	1	1	4
Martin Pavek	3	0	1	1	2
Yannick Gosselin (goalie)	1	0	0	0	0
Rocco Trentadue (goalie)	2	0	0	0	2
Paul Krake (goalie)	17	0	0	0	2

GOALTENDING

	Games	Min.	Goals	SO	Avg.
Paul Krake	17	1029	60	0	3.50
Alan Perry	40	2406	149(3)	0	3.72
Yannick Gosselin	1	60	5	0	5.00
Rocco Trentadue	2	120	13	0	6.50

TULSA OILERS

SCORING

	Games	G	A	Pts.	Pen.
Sylvain Naud	58	39	48	87	114
Taylor Hall	58	35	45	80	64
Mario Nobili	54	31	34	65	102
Doug Lawrence	38	14	47	61	114
Tony Fiore	37	23	35	58	67
Shaun Clouston	44	23	25	48	43
E.J. Sauer	60	13	31	44	82
Jody Praznik	55	11	33	44	50
Tom Karalis	56	11	33	44	235
Mike Berger	47	16	26	42	116
Scott Longstaff	18	10	11	21	12
Al Murphy	34	10	11	21	100
Aldo Iaquinta	35	2	15	17	26
Luc Beausoleil	16	7	9	16	6
Terry MacLean	16	2	12	14	12
Mark Bourgeois	12	5	3	8	6
Craig Shepherd	24	5	3	8	27
Greg MacEachern	56	4	3	7	107
Pat Cavanagh	16	3	3	6	33
Nick Beaulieu	3	2	2	4	2
Tyler Ertel	5	2	2	4	22
Michel Couvrette	3	0	4	4	9
Kevin Sullivan	17	0	4	4	14
Tony Martino (goalie)	39	0	3	3	46
Paul Caufield	4	2	0	2	0
Brian Flatt (goalie)	12	0	1	1	0
Michael Baker	3	0	0	0	0
Matt Ocello (goalie)	1	0	0	0	0
Dan McDonnell (goalie)	1	0	0	0	0
Matt Johnson	3	0	0	0	2
Eric Raymond (goalie)	3	0	0	0	0
Thomas Dobos	6	0	0	0	2
Jamie Loewen (goalie)	13	0	0	0	0

GOALTENDING

	Games	Min.	Goals	SO	Avg.
Brian Flatt	11	488	28(1)	1	3.44
Tony Martino	39	2182	133	2	3.66
Jamie Loewen	13	681	43(1)	0	3.79
Eric Raymond	3	181	12	0	3.98
Matt Ocello	1	34	3	0	5.29
Dan McDonnell	1	34	5	0	8.82
E.J. Sauer	1	12	2	0	10.00

WICHITA THUNDER

SCORING

	Games	G	A	Pts.	Pen.
Ted Dent	60	25	44	69	109
Dave Gatti	58	35	32	67	69
Ken Thibodeau	40	33	26	59	68
Dan Bates	48	21	31	52	12
Keith Cyr	40	14	31	45	71
Randy Boyd	22	10	26	36	92
Greg Neish	34	16	17	33	212
Otis Plageman	46	4	23	27	46
Mark Bourgeois	33	13	12	25	37
Peter Kravchuk	52	6	15	21	87
Paul Pachkevitch	22	10	10	20	21
Ron Handy	11	6	12	18	20
Steve Chelios	12	4	12	16	32
Stephane Venne	19	6	9	15	85
Eric Lindberg	47	6	9	15	127
Andrei Sidorov	11	6	7	13	14
Rob Weingartner	35	10	4	14	71
Pat Cavanagh	18	6	4	10	102
Pete Schure	28	4	5	9	108
Darin Srochenski	43	2	7	9	196
Rob Smith	19	1	5	6	17
Roger Hunt	35	2	3	5	102
John Valo	19	0	5	5	31
Daniel Elsener	8	0	4	4	15
Brian Fleury	13	0	4	4	26
Jeff Knight	14	0	4	4	4
Derek Kendall	20	0	3	3	44
Mike Tinkham	2	2	0	2	0
Robert Desjardins (goalie)	52	0	2	2	5
Joel Clark (goalie)	2	0	0	0	0
Murray Caton (goalie)	2	0	0	0	0
Steve Wachter (goalie)	2	0	0	0	0
Yancy Jones	4	0	0	0	0
Alain Harvey (goalie)	5	0	0	0	0
Kevin Sullivan	7	0	0	0	31
Yannick Gosselin (goalie)	11	0	0	0	2

GOALTENDING

	Games	Min.	Goals	SO	Avg.
Robert Desjardins	52	2849	220(6)	1	4.63
Alain Harvey	5	240	22(2)	0	5.50
Yannick Gosselin	10	345	37	0	6.43
Murray Caton	2	120	18	0	9.00
Joel Clark	2	48	8	0	10.00
Steve Wachter	2	24	5	0	12.50

PLAYERS WITH TWO OR MORE TEAMS

SCORING

	Games	G	A	Pts.	Pen.
Mark Bourgeois, Wichita	33	13	12	25	37
Mark Bourgeois, Tulsa	12	5	3	8	6
Totals	45	18	15	33	43
Pat Cavanagh, Tulsa	16	3	3	6	33
Pat Cavanagh, Wichita	18	6	4	10	102
Totals	34	9	7	16	135
Steve Chelios, Dallas	30	3	19	22	60
Steve Chelios, Wichita	12	4	12	16	32
Totals	42	7	31	38	92
Keith Cyr, Memphis	18	7	13	20	35
Keith Cyr, Wichita	40	14	31	45	71
Totals	58	21	44	65	106
Daniel Elsener, Memphis	26	2	8	10	54
Daniel Elsener, Wichita	8	0	4	4	15
Totals	34	2	12	14	69
Tyler Ertel, Tulsa	5	2	2	4	22
Tyler Ertel, Fort Worth	8	3	2	5	22
Totals	13	5	4	9	44
Brian Fleury, Dallas	11	0	2	2	30
Brian Fleury, Wichita	13	0	4	4	26
Totals	24	0	6	6	56
Yannick Gosselin (g), O.C.	1	0	0	0	0
Yannick Gosselin (g), Wichita	11	0	0	0	2
Totals	12	0	0	0	2

	Games	G	A	Pts.	Pen.
Roger Hunt, Dallas	3	0	0	0	11
Roger Hunt, Wichita	35	2	3	5	102
Totals	38	2	3	5	113
Doug Lawrence, Memphis	19	8	26	34	47
Doug Lawrence, Tulsa	38	14	47	61	114
Totals	57	22	73	95	161
Mark McGinn, Oklahoma City	42	16	17	33	18
Mark McGinn, Memphis	6	4	5	9	0
Totals	48	20	22	42	18
Matt Ocello (g), Tulsa	1	0	0	0	0
Matt Ocello (g), Fort Worth	4	0	1	1	0
Totals	5	0	1	1	0
Paul Pachkevitch, Fort Worth	2	0	0	0	0
Paul Pachkevitch, Wichita	22	10	10	20	21
Totals	24	10	10	20	21
Mike Paller, Fort Worth	23	9	11	20	35
Mike Paller, Dallas	10	1	6	7	0
Totals	33	10	17	27	35
Martin Pavek, Oklahoma City	3	0	1	1	2
Martin Pavek, Dallas	1	0	0	0	2
Totals	4	0	1	1	4
Craig Shepherd, Tulsa	24	5	3	8	27
Craig Shepherd, Dallas	9	3	3	6	6
Totals	33	8	6	14	33
Andrei Sidorov, Fort Worth	17	8	8	16	45

	Games	G	A	Pts.	Pen.
Andrei Sidorov, Wichita	11	6	7	13	14
Totals	28	14	15	29	59
Kevin Sullivan, Wichita	7	0	0	0	31
Kevin Sullivan, Tulsa	17	0	4	4	14
Totals	24	0	4	4	45
Ken Thibodeau, Wichita	40	33	26	59	68
Ken Thibodeau, Memphis	14	7	9	16	19
Totals	54	40	35	75	87
Rocco Trentadue (g), F.W.	18	0	0	0	8
Rocco Trentadue (g), O.C.	2	0	0	0	2
Totals	20	0	0	0	10
John Valo, Fort Worth	17	3	3	6	18
John Valo, Wichita	19	0	5	5	31
Totals	36	3	8	11	49

GOALTENDING

	Games	Min.	Goals	SO	Avg.
Yannick Gosselin, O.C.	1	60	5	0	5.00
Yannick Gosselin, Wic.	10	345	37	0	6.43
Totals	11	405	42	0	6.22
Matt Ocello, Tulsa	1	34	3	0	5.29
Matt Ocello, F.W.	4	179	11(1)	0	3.69
Totals	5	213	14(1)	0	3.94
Rocco Trentadue, F.W.	17	746	62(3)	0	4.99
Rocco Trentadue, O.C.	2	120	13	0	6.50
Totals	19	866	75(3)	0	5.20

1993 CALDER CUP PLAYOFFS

RESULTS

FIRST ROUND

Series "A"

	W	L	Pts.	GF	GA
St. John's	4	1	8	25	16
Moncton	1	4	2	16	25

(St. John's won series, 4-1)

Series "B"

	W	L	Pts.	GF	GA
Cape Breton	4	1	8	23	16
Fredericton	1	4	2	16	23

(Cape Breton won series, 4-1)

Series "C"

	W	L	Pts.	GF	GA
Springfield	4	2	8	18	23
Providence	2	4	4	23	18

(Springfield won series, 4-2)

Series "D"

	W	L	Pts.	GF	GA
Adirondack	4	0	8	17	6
Capital District	0	4	0	6	17

(Adirondack won series, 4-0)

Series "E"

	W	L	Pts.	GF	GA
Binghamton	4	3	8	29	24
Baltimore	3	4	6	24	29

(Binghamton won series, 4-3)

Series "F"

	W	L	Pts.	GF	GA
Rochester	4	1	8	24	15
Utica	1	4	2	15	24

(Rochester won series, 4-1)

SECOND ROUND

Series "G"

	W	L	Pts.	GF	GA
Cape Breton	4	0	8	22	12
St. John's	0	4	0	12	22

(Cape Breton won series, 4-0)

Series "H"

	W	L	Pts.	GF	GA
Springfield	4	3	8	23	27
Adirondack	3	4	6	27	23

(Springfield won series, 4-3)

Series "J"

	W	L	Pts.	GF	GA
Rochester	4	3	8	26	21
Binghamton	3	4	6	21	26

(Rochester won series, 4-3)

DIVISION CHAMPIONS ROUND

Series "K"

	W	L	Pts.	GF	GA
Cape Breton	2	0	4	13	6
Springfield	0	2	0	6	13

(Cape Breton won series, 2-0)

FINALS—FOR THE CALDER CUP

Series "L"

	W	L	Pts.	GF	GA
Cape Breton	4	1	8	27	13
Rochester	1	4	2	13	27

(Cape Breton won series, 4-1)

INDIVIDUAL LEADERS

Goals: Mario Nobili, Tulsa (11)
Tony Fiore, Tulsa (11)
Assists: Doug Lawrence, Tulsa (15)
Points: Tony Fiore, Tulsa (21)
Penalty minutes: Tom Karalis, Tulsa (87)
Goaltending average: Antoine Mindjimba, Memphis (2.97)
Shutouts: None

	Games	G	A	Pts.
Sylvain Naud, Tulsa	12	6	13	19
Mario Nobili, Tulsa	12	11	7	18
Doug Lawrence, Tulsa	12	3	15	18
Joe Burton, Oklahoma City	11	8	7	15
E.J. Sauer, Tulsa	12	6	9	15
Daniel Larin, Oklahoma City	11	6	9	15
Shaun Clouston, Tulsa	12	8	6	14
Carl Boudreau, Oklahoma City	11	8	5	13
Luc Beausoleil, Tulsa	11	5	8	13
Guy Girouard, Oklahoma City	11	4	9	13
Al Murphy, Tulsa	12	3	10	13

TOP SCORERS

	Games	G	A	Pts.
Tony Fiore, Tulsa	12	11	10	21
Jody Praznik, Tulsa	12	6	13	19

INDIVIDUAL STATISTICS

DALLAS FREEZE

(Lost semifinals to Tulsa, 4-3)

SCORING

	Games	G	A	Pts.	Pen.
Troy Binnie	7	7	3	10	6
Dave Doucette	7	0	10	10	10
Rico Rossi	7	4	4	8	30
Wayne Anchikoski	7	3	5	8	6
Derek Crawford	7	5	2	7	27
Frank LaScala	7	5	1	6	6
Jeff Beaudin	7	0	5	5	25
Joey Mittelsteadt	7	0	4	4	24
Gary Audette	7	2	1	3	30
Jason Taylor	7	1	2	3	23
Doug Sinclair	7	2	0	2	38
Brian Bruininks	3	1	1	2	4
Robert Lewis	7	0	2	2	16
Joel Eagan	4	0	1	1	2
Dean Shmyr	7	0	1	1	12
Greg Smith (goalie)	1	0	0	0	0
Mike Zanier (goalie)	7	0	0	0	20

GOALTENDING

	Games	Min.	Goals	SO	Avg.
Mike Zanier	7	424	33(1)	0	4.67
Greg Smith	1	8	2	0	15.00

MEMPHIS RIVERKINGS

(Lost semifinals to Oklahoma City, 4-2)

SCORING

	Games	G	A	Pts.	Pen.
Scot Johnston	6	7	1	8	2
Tom Mutch	6	1	5	6	4
Mark McGinn	6	3	2	5	2
Mike Jackson	6	1	4	5	15
Peter D'Amario	6	1	3	4	2
Scott Phillips	6	2	1	3	6
Michael Martens	6	1	2	3	8
Mike Roberts	6	0	3	3	2
Angelo Russo	4	1	1	2	2
Andy Ross	6	1	1	2	11
David Moore	6	0	2	2	10
Paul Flaherty	6	0	2	2	6
Steve Vasko (goalie)	1	0	0	0	0
Don Burke	2	0	0	0	4
Antoine Mindjimba (goalie)	6	0	0	0	2
Steve Shaunesey	6	0	0	0	14
Ken Venis	6	0	0	0	0

GOALTENDING

	Games	Min.	Goals	SO	Avg.
Steve Vasko	1	33	1	0	1.82
Antoine Mindjimba	6	323	16	0	2.97

OKLAHOMA CITY BLAZERS

(Lost finals to Tulsa, 4-1)

SCORING

	Games	G	A	Pts.	Pen.
Joe Burton	11	8	7	15	4
Daniel Larin	11	6	9	15	40
Carl Boudreau	11	8	5	13	20
Guy Girouard	11	4	9	13	6
Steve Simoni	11	4	5	9	12
Sylvain Fleury	6	5	3	8	8
Jamie Hearn	11	2	5	7	40
Kent Anderson	11	0	4	4	4
Boyd Sutton	11	0	4	4	0
Chris Laganas	11	1	2	3	16
Brendan Garvey	11	0	3	3	21
Jim Solly	11	1	1	2	2
Craig Johnson	11	0	2	2	67
Sean Gorman	11	0	1	1	11
Rocco Trentadue (goalie)	1	0	0	0	0
Sylvain Mayer	2	0	0	0	44
Alan Perry (goalie)	11	0	0	0	2

GOALTENDING

	Games	Min.	Goals	SO	Avg.
Alan Perry	11	630	46(3)	0	4.38
Rocco Trentadue	1	25	3	0	7.20

TULSA OILERS

(Winner of 1993 CHL playoffs)

SCORING

	Games	G	A	Pts.	Pen.
Tony Fiore	12	11	10	21	22
Sylvain Naud	12	6	13	19	35
Jody Praznik	12	6	13	19	22
Mario Nobili	12	11	7	18	21
Doug Lawrence	12	3	15	18	43
E.J. Sauer	12	6	9	15	24
Shaun Clouston	12	8	6	14	4
Luc Beausoleil	11	5	8	13	12
Al Murphy	12	3	10	13	48
Tom Karalis	12	3	7	10	87
Taylor Hall	9	3	5	8	16
Mike Berger	7	2	3	5	4
Kevin Sullivan	3	1	1	2	12
Greg MacEachern	12	1	1	2	32
Mark Bourgeois	7	0	2	2	16
Aldo Iaquinta	12	1	0	1	12
Jamie Loewen (goalie)	4	0	0	0	0
Tony Martino (goalie)	11	0	0	0	50

GOALTENDING

	Games	Min.	Goals	SO	Avg.
Tony Martino	11	622	42(1)	0	4.05
Jamie Loewen	4	107	8(1)	0	4.49

1992-93 AWARD WINNERS

ALL-STAR TEAMS

First team	Pos.	Second team
Tony Martino, Tulsa	G	Robert Desjardins, Wichita
		Alan Perry, Oklahoma City
Dave Doucette, Dallas	D	Mike Berger, Tulsa
Guy Girouard, Okla. City	D	Tom Karalis, Tulsa
Carl Boudreau, Okla. City	C	Joe Burton, Okla. City
Sylvain Fleury, Okla. City	LW	Doug Lawrence, Tulsa
Daniel Larin, Okla. City	RW	Tom Mutch, Memphis
		Sylvain Naud, Tulsa

TROPHY WINNERS

Most Valuable Player: Sylvain Fleury, Oklahoma City
Ken McKenzie Trophy: Sylvain Fleury, Oklahoma City
John Voss Trophy: Tony Martino, Tulsa
Defenseman of the Year: Dave Doucette, Dallas
Rookie of the Year: Robert Desjardins, Wichita
President's Trophy: Tony Fiore, Tulsa
Commissioner's Trophy: Garry Unger, Tulsa

ALL-TIME AWARD WINNERS

MOST VALUABLE PLAYER

Season	Player, Team
1992-93	Sylvain Fleury, Oklahoma City

KEN McKENZIE TROPHY

(Leading Scorer)

Season	Player, Team
1992-93	Sylvain Fleury, Oklahoma City

JOHN VOSS TROPHY

(Outstanding goaltender)

Season	Player, Team
1992-93	Tony Martino, Tulsa

DEFENSEMAN OF THE YEAR

Season	Player, Team
1992-93	Dave Doucette, Dallas

ROOKIE OF THE YEAR

Season	Player, Team
1992-93	Robert Desjardins, Wichita

PRESIDENT'S TROPHY

(Playoff MVP)

Season	Player, Team
1992-93	Tony Fiore, Tulsa

COMMISSIONER'S TROPHY

(Coach of the year)

Season	Coach, Team
1992-93	Garry Unger, Tulsa

ALL-TIME LEAGUE CHAMPIONS

REGULAR-SEASON CHAMPION

Season	Team	Coach
1992-93	Oklahoma City Blazers	Michael McEwen

PLAYOFF CHAMPION

Team	Coach
Tulsa Oilers	Garry Unger

COLONIAL HOCKEY LEAGUE

LEAGUE OFFICE

Commissioner
Bob Myers
Media director
Tony Fitzgerald
Secretary
Irene Puddester

Address
P.O. Box 45
Copetown, Ontario L0R 1J0

Phone
416-627-2096
FAX
416-627-2097

TEAMS

BRANTFORD SMOKE

President & general manager
Don Robertson
Head coach
Ken Gratton
Home ice
Brantford Civic Centre
Address
69-79 Market Street, South
Brantford, Ontario N3T 5R7
Seating Capacity
3,000
Phone
519-751-9467
FAX
519-751-2366

CHATHAM WHEELS

General manager/head coach
Tom Barrett
Home ice
Chatham Memorial Arena
Address
80 Tweedsmuir Avenue, West
P.O. Box 893
Chatham, Ontario N7M 5L3
Seating capacity
3,000
Phone
519-351-7025
FAX
519-351-1194

DETROIT FALCONS

President
Dr. Mostafa Afr
Head coach
To be announced
Home ice
Fraser Ice Arena

Address
34400 Utica Road
Fraser, MI 48026
Seating capacity
3,000
Phone
313-294-2488
FAX
313-294-2358

MUSKEGON FURY

Owner/president/general manager
Tony Lisman
Head coach
Bruce Boudreau
Home ice
L.C. Walker Arena
Address
470 W. Western Avenue
Muskegon, MI 49440
Seating capacity
5,034
Phone
616-726-5058
FAX
616-726-0428

ST. THOMAS WILDCATS

Owner/president
Doug Tarry
General manager/head coach
Peter Horachek
Home ice
St. Thomas Elgin Memorial Arena
Address
80 Wilson Avenue
P.O. Box 143
St. Thomas, Ontario N5R 3R2
Seating Capacity
2,400

Phone
519-631-1845
FAX
519-631-2992

THUNDER BAY THUNDER HAWKS

President
To be announced
Head coach
To be announced
Home ice
Fort William Gardens
Address
901 Myles Street, East
Thunder Bay, Ontario P7C 1J9
Seating Capacity
4,150
Phone
807-623-7121
FAX
807-622-3306

UTICA BULLDOGS

President/general manager
Skip Probst
Head coach
Marty Howe
Home ice
Utica Memorial Auditorium
Address
400 Oriskany Street West
Utica, NY 13502
Seating capacity
3,930
Phone
315-734-8483
FAX
315-734-8486

1992-93 REGULAR SEASON

FINAL STANDINGS

Team	G	W	L	Pts.	GF	GA
Brantford	60	39	18 (3)	81	308	264
Detroit	60	36	20 (4)	76	303	239
Thunder Bay	60	32	24 (4)	68	288	271
Muskegon	60	28	27 (5)	61	293	278
St. Thomas	60	27	27 (6)	60	306	322
Flint	60	27	29 (4)	58	256	296
Chatham	60	21	35 (4)	46	260	344

( )—Indicates overtime losses and are worth one point.

INDIVIDUAL LEADERS

Goals: Darin Smith, St. Thomas (57)
Assists: Len Soccio, St. Thomas (84)
Points: Len Soccio, St. Thomas (128)
Penalty minutes: Darren Miciak, Flint (396)
Goaltending average: Jamie Stewart, Detroit (3.59)
Shutouts: Mark LaForest, Brantford (1)
    Roland Melanson, Brantford (1)
    Jamie Stewart, Detroit (1)
    George Maneluk, Muskegon (1)
    Chris Clifford, Muskegon (1)
    Mark Michaud, Thunder Bay (1)

	Games	G	A	Pts.
Jason Firth, Thunder Bay	49	36	64	100
Paul Kelly, Muskegon	58	32	58	90
Todd Howarth, Thunder Bay	60	37	42	79
Marc Saumier, Muskegon	41	26	53	79
Mark Turner, Muskegon	52	34	43	77
Vladimir Tsiplakov, Detroit	44	33	43	76
Clayton Young, Detroit	42	30	46	76
Tom Searle, Brantford	49	25	48	73
Bob McKillop, Detroit	57	39	33	72
Sean Davidson, Flint	59	26	44	70
Kent Hawley, St. Thomas	45	24	46	70
Darcy Cahill, St. Thomas	54	25	44	69
Jason Simon, Detroit	55	24	45	69
Kelly Cain, Flint	54	24	44	68
Kerry Russell, Detroit	49	23	44	67
Ryan Kummu, Brantford	57	24	41	65
Brett Seguin, Muskegon	49	24	40	64

TOP SCORERS

	Games	G	A	Pts.
Len Soccio, St. Thomas	56	44	84	128
Paul Polillo, Brantford	59	33	79	112
Darin Smith, St. Thomas	57	57	50	107

INDIVIDUAL STATISTICS

BRANTFORD SMOKE

SCORING

	Games	G	A	Pts.	Pen.
Paul Polillo	59	33	79	112	18
Tom Searle	49	25	48	73	91
Ryan Kummu	57	24	41	65	99
Jamie Hicks	59	22	41	63	52
Terry McCutcheon	49	27	27	54	41
Cory Banika	56	24	26	50	318
Graeme Bonar	50	25	21	46	38
Mike Moes	45	14	20	34	10
Alex Kuzminski	45	14	20	34	10
Greg Walters	26	14	19	33	44
Andy Bezeau	38	18	13	31	278
Ed Ljubicic	32	12	17	29	44
Jeff Perry	23	11	13	24	30
Greg Bignell	57	2	22	24	201
Dean Morton	37	2	17	19	217
Michael Maurice	11	11	6	17	14
Danny Gratton	13	9	8	17	0
Ted Miskolczi	9	8	9	17	2
Wayne MacPhee	57	3	14	17	86
Wayne Gagne	21	1	12	13	6
Jason Hannigan	15	2	7	9	18
Rob Wilson	31	1	8	9	82
Kelly Cain	6	1	5	6	4
Guy Lehoux	13	0	5	5	28
Owen Lessard	5	1	3	4	2
Pat Bingham	14	0	4	4	26
Greg White	4	1	1	2	0
John East	17	0	2	2	25
Cory Lyons	4	0	1	1	0
Mark LaForest (goalie)	10	0	1	1	0
Roland Melanson (goalie)	15	0	1	1	8
Stephen Morden	16	0	1	1	51
Dean Smith (goalie)	1	0	0	0	0
John Johnson	2	0	0	0	0
Mike Tomlinson	3	0	0	0	2
Serge Tkachenko (goalie)	4	0	0	0	0
Scott Sharples (goalie)	7	0	0	0	2
Peter Richards (goalie)	9	0	0	0	6
Todd Bojcun (goalie)	22	0	0	0	6

GOALTENDING

	Games	Min.	Goals	SO	Avg.
Dean Smith	1	2	0	0	0.00
Mark LaForest	10	565	35	1	3.72
Roland Melanson	14	811	54	1	4.00
Scott Sharples	7	400	27	0	4.05
Todd Bojcun	22	1265	92(2)	0	4.36
Peter Richards	9	488	42(1)	0	5.16
Serge Tkachenko	4	96	11	0	6.88

CHATHAM WHEELS

SCORING

	Games	G	A	Pts.	Pen.
Vadim Slivtchenko	46	27	30	57	12
Jim Ritchie	60	18	39	57	108
Jason Hannigan	32	19	30	49	31
Rob Vanderydt	56	23	22	45	22
Tyler Ertel	42	19	25	44	58
Mike Tomlinson	48	14	27	41	58
Lee Giffin	29	14	26	40	65
Byron Lomow	54	6	28	34	77
Joel Dyck	48	8	23	31	48
Gary St. Pierre	18	8	21	29	81
John Johnson	22	10	16	26	22
Yvan Corbin	16	16	7	23	0
Joel Gardner	14	8	14	22	2
Mark Turner	15	9	10	19	30
Angelo Russo	32	9	9	18	12
Donny Martin	28	7	10	17	75
John East	31	2	13	15	26
Stan Pavelec	59	1	14	15	10
Mark Lindsay	25	7	6	13	2
Dave Shute	15	4	9	13	10
Sasha Lakovic	28	7	5	12	235
Jason Stos	22	2	8	10	12
Craig Chapman	11	1	9	10	12
Dan Poirier	22	6	3	9	64
Mike Siefker	16	3	6	9	41
Gary Miller	36	1	8	9	36
Kevin Doherty	17	1	7	8	2
Brad Hyatt	18	2	4	6	12
Serge Aumont	12	2	1	3	16
Tim Fingerhut	5	1	2	3	0
Roman Sykora	2	2	0	2	0
Jason Hueppelsheuser	11	1	1	2	4
Ron Bertrand (goalie)	18	0	2	2	8
Dave Schill (goalie)	26	0	2	2	20
Sean Burns	1	1	0	1	6
Blair McReynolds	1	0	1	1	0
Kevin MacKay	3	0	1	1	6
Peter Franta	1	0	0	0	0
Frank Gianfrido	1	0	0	0	0
Alan Gibson	1	0	0	0	0
Boyd Lomow	1	0	0	0	0
Dave Maksymiu	1	0	0	0	0
Archie Meridis	1	0	0	0	0
Burk Peters	1	0	0	0	0
Mark Reimer (goalie)	1	0	0	0	0
R. Roubos	1	0	0	0	2
Mike Torkoff	1	0	0	0	0
Carl Sasyn	2	0	0	0	0
Paul Cohen (goalie)	10	0	0	0	6
Jocelyn Provost (goalie)	17	0	0	0	4

GOALTENDING

	Games	Min.	Goals	SO	Avg.
Ron Bertrand	18	861	64(2)	0	4.46
Paul Cohen	9	496	46(1)	0	5.56
Dave Schill	26	1340	126(2)	0	5.64
Jocelyn Provost	17	876	94	0	6.44
Mark Reimer	1	44	6	0	8.18

DETROIT FALCONS

SCORING

	Games	G	A	Pts.	Pen.
Vladimir Tsiplakov	44	35	43	78	20
Clayton Young	42	30	46	76	91
Bob McKillop	57	39	33	72	18
Kerry Russell	49	21	44	65	29
Brent Bobyck	55	15	39	54	21
Steve Beadle	57	16	36	52	48
Savo Mitrovic	46	13	36	49	37
Vic Posa	39	15	26	41	188
Christian Lalonde	53	15	24	39	76
Jacques Mailhot	48	14	21	35	273
Tom O'Rourke	41	10	17	27	33
Trevor Dam	26	9	17	26	22
Greg Geldart	44	6	20	26	23
Luke Johnson	53	5	19	24	16
Frank Melone	26	11	11	22	15
Craig Herr	26	10	10	20	22
Jason Simon	11	7	13	20	38
Derek Clancy	11	4	13	17	6
Juri Krivokhizha	32	7	9	16	25
Clark Polglace	38	4	11	15	113
Murray Duval	16	5	9	14	60
Gary St. Pierre	23	3	9	12	43
Chris O'Rourke	51	0	10	10	165
Stephane Dugal	9	1	8	9	6
Dave DiVita	13	1	8	9	23
Mikael Zakharov	3	2	4	6	2
Brett Strot	7	3	2	5	6
David Burke	22	1	4	5	10
Mike Perodeau (goalie)	2	0	0	0	0
Peter Ing (goalie)	3	0	0	0	0
Shane Bogden	4	0	0	0	0
Pete Fry (goalie)	4	0	0	0	2
Bill Horn (goalie)	8	0	0	0	2
Jamie Stewart (goalie)	47	0	0	0	8

GOALTENDING

	Games	Min.	Goals	SO	Avg.
Peter Ing	3	136	6(1)	0	2.65
Jamie Stewart	47	2743	164(4)	1	3.59
Bill Horn	8	484	34(1)	0	4.21
Pete Fry	4	200	19	0	5.70
Mike Perodeau	2	61	6	0	5.90

FLINT BULLDOGS

SCORING

	Games	G	A	Pts.	Pen.
Mike Jorgensen	60	27	36	63	32
Kelly Cain	48	23	39	62	16
Dan Woodley	39	20	36	56	112
Brett MacDonald	60	12	39	51	60
Jason Simon	44	17	32	49	202
Larry Bernard	43	27	21	48	61
Sean Davidson	33	15	32	47	12
Brian Bellefeuille	33	16	22	38	71
Glen Mazurowski	39	16	19	35	17
Stephane Brochu	44	6	28	34	77
Scott Allen	44	15	11	26	66
Kord Cernich	31	5	12	17	18
John Heasty	38	5	11	16	42
Ken Spangler	41	3	13	16	128
John Messuri	18	6	9	15	6
Tom Sasso	17	5	9	14	0
Gary St. Pierre	13	4	8	12	38
Ange Guzzo	51	1	10	11	89
Roman Andrys	9	5	5	10	0

	Games	G	A	Pts.	Pen.
Carl Tetu	46	6	3	9	8
Jason Brousseau	19	2	7	9	15
Doug Garbarz	28	1	7	8	13
Steve McSwain	7	2	5	7	2
Darren Miciak	53	3	3	6	396
Paul Constantin	11	3	2	5	4
Frank Melone	6	2	1	3	2
Joe Musa	9	1	2	3	6
Paul Caufield	6	2	0	2	2
Dennis Miller	13	0	2	2	8
Mark Bourgeois	1	1	0	1	2
Marty Howe	3	0	1	1	4
Mike LaLonde	3	0	1	1	0
Mark Gowans (goalie)	34	0	1	1	2
Pat Szturm (goalie)	36	0	1	1	8
Cory Laylin	2	0	0	0	2
Don Stone	2	0	0	0	0

GOALTENDING

	Games	Min.	Goals	SO	Avg.
Mark Gowans	34	1718	125(3)	0	4.37
Pat Szturm	36	1919	166(1)	0	5.19

MUSKEGON FURY

SCORING

	Games	G	A	Pts.	Pen.
Paul Kelly	58	32	58	90	17
Marc Saumier	41	26	53	79	123
Brett Seguin	49	24	64	48	48
Mark Turner	37	25	33	58	33
Jeff Napierala	58	25	26	51	57
Grant Block	58	22	24	46	43
Todd Charlesworth	45	9	37	46	22
Bob Berg	49	19	24	43	87
Roman Hubalek	52	17	25	42	32
Doug Shedden	21	16	21	37	18
Jim Latos	59	10	34	34	163
Marc Vachon	55	12	20	32	60
Steve Herniman	49	9	22	31	173
Mark Brownschidle	60	5	26	31	20
Tim Fingerhut	44	13	7	20	35
Donny Martin	13	10	8	18	37
Darrel Newman	54	1	14	15	66
Dave Stewart	17	3	11	14	35
Phil Berger	4	4	7	11	2
Robert Melanson	23	0	7	7	108
Alexei Kovalev	7	3	3	6	0
Joe Dragon	15	2	2	4	10
Paul Constantin	9	1	3	4	4
Greg Andrusak	2	0	3	3	7
Daniel Elsener	4	0	3	3	10
Kevin Doherty	17	0	3	3	8
Brian Baldrica	4	0	2	2	2
George Maneluk (goalie)	27	0	2	2	10
Jim Maher	2	1	0	1	2
Keith Redmond	4	1	0	1	46
Grant Richison	2	0	1	1	0
Chris Clifford (goalie)	19	0	1	1	4
Eric Raymond (goalie)	19	0	1	1	0
Bob Jones	1	0	0	0	0
Mike Ruark	1	0	0	0	0
Keith Zbin	2	0	0	0	0
Glen Carvey	12	0	0	0	9

GOALTENDING

	Games	Min.	Goals	SO	Avg.
Eric Raymond	19	1098	77(1)	0	4.21
George Maneluk	27	1494	113(2)	1	4.54
Chris Clifford	19	1038	82	1	4.74

ST. THOMAS WILDCATS

SCORING

	Games	G	A	Pts.	Pen.
Len Soccio	56	44	84	128	90
Darin Smith	57	57	50	107	129

	Games	G	A	Pts.	Pen.
Darcy Cahill	54	25	44	69	53
Kent Hawley	40	22	38	60	47
Jamie Allan	46	15	35	50	108
Tim Bean	43	17	30	47	46
Todd Coopman	59	9	31	40	58
Conrade Thomas	55	16	21	37	32
Ted Mikolczi	32	13	17	30	42
Mark Karpen	29	9	21	30	32
Andrew Doxtater	40	13	12	25	38
Todd Humphrey	41	11	14	25	101
Sean Davidson	26	11	12	23	12
Hakan Falkenhall	51	1	18	19	22
Matt Hoffman	21	6	12	18	19
Mike Thomas	36	5	13	18	14
Mike Teeple	18	3	13	16	24
Mark Vichorek	12	5	10	15	14
Steve McCharles	49	3	10	13	35
Gary Miller	16	3	8	11	43
Tom Moulton	35	3	7	10	41
Denny Lambert	5	2	6	8	9
Mitch Malloy	9	2	6	8	14
Sean Burns	13	2	5	7	51
Roman Sykora	14	3	3	6	2
Brian Baldrica	33	1	5	6	4
Kevin Doherty	12	1	4	5	4
Denny Larocque	18	1	4	5	17
Dan Williams	10	1	4	5	63
Kevin Butt (goalie)	41	0	4	4	17
Dave Serraglio	10	0	2	2	8
Wayne Marion (goalie)	28	0	2	2	4
Ange Guzzo	2	0	0	0	0
Kevin Patrick	2	0	0	0	0
Dave Ritchie	3	0	0	0	0
Vince Oldford	4	0	0	0	16

GOALTENDING

	Games	Min.	Goals	SO	Avg.
Kevin Butt	41	2199	181(5)	0	4.94
Wayne Marion	28	1433	130(1)	0	5.44

THUNDER BAY THUNDER HAWKS

SCORING

	Games	G	A	Pts.	Pen.
Jason Firth	49	36	64	100	10
Todd Howarth	60	37	42	79	96
Barry McKinlay	55	17	39	56	47
Gary Callaghan	45	26	22	48	35
Brian Downey	43	17	31	48	14
Vincent Faucher	30	20	26	46	8
Tom Warden	59	19	26	45	263
Terry Menard	36	10	27	37	38
Mark Woolf	33	16	20	36	18
Brock Shyiak	60	7	29	36	17
Michael Martens	27	12	21	33	31
Brian Wells	34	17	12	29	163
Everton Blackwin	45	12	12	24	51
Marc Lyons	58	2	18	20	38
Bruce Ramsay	52	3	16	19	234
Harijs Vitolinsh	8	6	7	13	12
Bruce Rendall	17	6	5	11	12
Jamie Hayden	59	0	11	11	24
Gerry St. Cyr	11	6	4	10	70
Vern Ray	47	4	6	10	85
Kent Hawley	5	2	8	10	8
Chris Rowland	22	5	3	8	65
Mike Berger	8	3	5	8	20
Mel Andelstead	45	2	5	7	256
Trevor Converse	7	0	5	5	23
Marc LaBelle	9	0	5	5	17
D. Sheehan	2	0	2	2	0
Greg Hankkio	2	0	1	1	2
Jocelyn Provost (goalie)	13	0	1	1	17
Paul McLean	3	0	1	1	0
Mark Michaud (goalie)	22	0	1	1	4
Pierre Gagnon (goalie)	2	0	0	0	0
Lorne Knauft	3	0	0	0	2

	Games	G	A	Pts.	Pen.
Greg Shury	3	0	0	0	0
Llew McWana	9	0	0	0	0
Steve Hogg (goalie)	27	0	0	0	6

GOALTENDING

	Games	Min.	Goals	SO	Avg.
Mark Michaud	22	1280	82(3)	1	3.84
Jocelyn Provost	13	674	45(1)	0	4.01
Pierre Gagnon	2	124	9(1)	0	4.35
Steve Hogg	27	1550	123(5)	0	4.76

PLAYERS WITH TWO OR MORE TEAMS

SCORING

	Games	G	A	Pts.	Pen.
Brian Baldrica, Muskegon	4	0	2	2	4
Brian Baldrica, St. Thomas	33	1	5	6	4
Totals	37	1	7	8	6
Sean Burns, Chatham	1	1	0	1	6
Sean Burns, St. Thomas	13	2	5	7	51
Totals	14	3	5	8	57
Kelly Cain, Brantford	6	1	5	6	4
Kelly Cain, Flint	48	23	39	62	16
Totals	54	24	44	68	20
Paul Constantin, Muskegon	9	1	3	4	4
Paul Constantin, Flint	11	3	2	5	4
Totals	20	4	5	9	8
Sean Davidson, St. Thomas	26	11	12	23	12
Sean Davidson, Flint	33	15	32	47	12
Totals	59	26	44	70	24
Kevin Doherty, St. Thomas	12	1	4	5	4
Kevin Doherty, Muskegon	17	0	3	3	8
Kevin Doherty, Chatham	17	1	7	8	2
Totals	46	2	14	16	14
John East, Brantford	17	0	2	2	25
John East, Chatham	31	2	13	15	26
Totals	48	2	15	17	51
Tim Fingerhut, Muskegon	44	13	7	20	9
Tim Fingerhut, Chatham	5	1	2	3	0
Totals	49	14	9	23	9
Ange Guzzo, St. Thomas	2	0	0	0	0
Ange Guzzo, Flint	51	1	10	11	89
Totals	53	1	10	11	89
Jason Hannigan, Brantford	15	2	7	9	18
Jason Hannigan, Chatham	32	19	30	49	31
Totals	47	21	37	58	49
Kent Hawley, Thunder Bay	5	2	8	10	8
Kent Hawley, St. Thomas	40	22	38	60	47
Totals	45	24	46	70	55
John Johnson, Brantford	2	0	0	0	0
John Johnson, Chatham	22	10	16	26	22
Totals	24	10	16	26	22
Donny Martin, Chatham	28	7	10	17	75
Donny Martin, Muskegon	13	10	8	18	37
Totals	41	17	18	35	112
Frank Melone, Detroit	26	11	11	22	15
Frank Melone, Flint	6	2	1	3	2
Totals	32	13	12	25	17
Gary Miller, Chatham	36	1	8	9	36
Gary Miller, St. Thomas	16	3	8	11	43
Totals	52	4	16	20	79
Jocelyn Provost, T. Bay (g)	13	0	1	1	17
Jocelyn Provost, Chatham (g)	17	0	0	0	4
Totals	30	0	1	1	21
Jason Simon, Flint	44	17	32	49	202
Jason Simon, Detroit	11	7	13	20	38
Totals	55	24	45	69	240
Gary St. Pierre, Chatham	18	8	21	29	81
Gary St. Pierre, Detroit	23	3	9	12	43
Gary St. Pierre, Flint	13	4	8	12	38
Totals	54	15	38	53	162
Roman Sykora, St. Thomas	14	3	3	6	2
Roman Sykora, Chatham	2	2	0	2	0
Totals	16	5	3	8	2
Mike Tomlinson, Brantford	3	0	0	0	2
Mike Tomlinson, Chatham	48	14	27	41	58
Totals	51	14	27	41	60

	Games	G	A	Pts.	Pen.
Mark Turner, Chatham	15	9	10	19	30
Mark Turner, Muskegon	37	25	33	58	33
Totals	52	34	43	77	63

GOALTENDING

	Games	Min.	Goals	SO	Avg.
Jocelyn Provost, Chat.	17	876	94	0	6.44
Jocelyn Provost, T.B.	13	674	45(1)	0	4.01
Totals	30	1550	139(1)	0	5.38

1993 COLONIAL CUP PLAYOFFS

RESULTS

PRELIMINARY ROUND

Series "A"

	W	L	Pts.	GF	GA
Brantford	4	2	8	35	25
Flint	2	4	4	25	35

(Brantford won series, 4-2)

Series "B"

	W	L	Pts.	GF	GA
St. Thomas	4	2	8	27	25
Detroit	2	4	4	25	27

(St. Thomas won series, 4-2)

Series "C"

	W	L	Pts.	GF	GA
Thunder Bay	4	3	8	31	33
Muskegon	3	4	6	33	31

(Thunder Bay won series, 4-3)

SEMIFINALS

Series "D"

	W	L	Pts.	GF	GA
St. Thomas	3	1	6	17	12
Brantford	2	2	4	18	13
Thunder Bay	1	3	2	13	23

(Thunder Bay was eliminated in round-robin series, 1-3)

FINALS

Series "E"

	W	L	Pts.	GF	GA
Brantford	4	1	8	21	20
St. Thomas	1	4	2	20	21

(Brantford won series, 4-1)

INDIVIDUAL LEADERS

Goals: Terry McCutcheon, Brantford (14)
Assists: Len Soccio, St. Thomas (21)
Points: Len Soccio, St. Thomas (31)
Penalty minutes: Andy Bezeau, Brantford (132)
Goaltending average: Éric Raymond, Muskegon (3.04)
Shutouts: Kevin Butt, St. Thomas (1)
Eric Raymond, Muskegon (1)

	Games	G	A	Pts.
Tom Searle, Brantford	15	6	17	23
Kent Hawley, St. Thomas	15	4	18	22
Darin Smith, St. Thomas	14	4	17	21
Paul Polillo, Brantford	15	7	13	20
Tim Bean, St. Thomas	15	12	7	19
Greg Walters, Brantford	10	11	8	19
Jason Firth, Thunder Bay	11	8	9	17
Jeff Perry, Brantford	14	8	7	15
Todd Howarth, Thunder Bay	11	2	13	15

TOP SCORERS

	Games	G	A	Pts.
Len Soccio, St. Thomas	15	10	21	31
Terry McCutcheon, Brantford	15	14	12	26

INDIVIDUAL STATISTICS

BRANTFORD SMOKE

(Winner of 1993 Colonial Hockey League playoffs)

SCORING

	Games	G	A	Pts.	Pen.
Terry McCutcheon	15	14	12	26	49
Tom Searle	15	6	17	23	13
Paul Polillo	15	7	13	20	10
Greg Walters	10	11	8	19	20
Jeff Perry	14	8	7	15	27
Jamie Hicks	15	8	5	13	32
Danny Gratton	10	2	11	13	4
Wayne Gagne	12	2	10	12	2
Graeme Bonar	12	3	8	11	2
Ted Miskolczi	14	2	8	10	0
Cory Banika	15	4	5	9	79
Andy Bezeau	14	2	4	6	132
Greg Bignell	15	1	3	4	69
Dean Morton	15	1	3	4	38
Sasha Lakovic	5	2	1	3	62
Roland Melanson (goalie)	15	0	2	2	2
Ed Ljubicic	9	1	0	1	32
Guy Lehoux	4	0	1	1	15
Wayne MacPhee	15	0	1	1	32
Peter Richards (goalie)	3	0	0	0	15
Ryan Kummu	15	0	0	0	10

GOALTENDING

	Games	Min.	Goals	SO	Avg.
Roland Melanson	15	844	50(2)	0	3.55
Peter Richards	3	70	6	0	5.14

DETROIT FALCONS

(Lost preliminary round to St. Thomas, 4-2)

SCORING

	Games	G	A	Pts.	Pen.
Kerry Russell	6	2	10	12	4
Vladimir Tsiplakov	6	5	4	9	6
Steve Beadle	6	4	4	8	4
Jacques Mailhot	4	2	4	6	12
Savo Mitrovic	6	3	2	5	24
Juri Krivokhizha	5	1	4	5	6
Trevor Dam	6	3	1	4	17
Bob McKillop	5	2	1	3	0
Jason Simon	6	1	2	3	40
Clayton Young	3	0	3	3	12
Brent Bobyck	6	1	1	2	0
Christian Lalonde	6	1	0	1	8
Luke Johnson	1	0	1	1	0
Vic Posa	6	0	1	1	30
Pete Fry (goalie)	1	0	0	0	0
Derek Clancy	1	0	0	0	2

	Games	G	A	Pts.	Pen.
Tom O'Rourke	1	0	0	0	2
Greg Geldart	5	0	0	0	4
Dave DiVita	5	0	0	0	21
Chris O'Rourke	6	0	0	0	10
Clark Polglace	6	0	0	0	15
Jamie Stewart (goalie)	6	0	0	0	2

GOALTENDING

	Games	Min.	Goals	SO	Avg.
Jamie Stewart	6	343	24(1)	0	4.20
Pete Fry	1	23	2	0	5.22

FLINT BULLDOGS

(Lost preliminary round to Brantford, 4-2)

SCORING

	Games	G	A	Pts.	Pen.
Stephane Brochu	6	4	8	12	22
Dan Woodley	6	4	7	11	21
Tom Sasso	6	3	4	7	0
Sean Davidson	6	4	2	6	4
Kord Cernich	6	3	3	6	4
Mike Jorgensen	6	1	4	5	4
Brett MacDonald	6	0	5	5	21
Scott Allen	6	1	3	4	2
Glen Mazurowski	6	1	2	3	0
John Messuri	3	2	0	2	6
Cory Laylin	5	2	0	2	4
John Heasty	5	0	2	2	2
Ange Guzzo	3	0	1	1	2
Kelly Cain	5	0	1	1	5
Gary St. Pierre	5	0	1	1	23
Darren Miciak	3	0	0	0	14
Doug Garbarz	5	0	0	0	4
Mark Gowans (goalie)	6	0	0	0	0
Ken Spangler	6	0	0	0	39

GOALTENDING

	Games	Min.	Goals	SO	Avg.
Mark Gowans	6	362	35	0	5.80

MUSKEGON FURY

(Lost preliminary round to Thunder Bay, 4-3)

SCORING

	Games	G	A	Pts.	Pen.
Brett Seguin	7	6	8	14	20
Paul Kelly	7	4	8	12	9
Marc Saumier	7	4	7	11	21
Lee Giffin	5	6	3	9	0
Donny Martin	7	0	5	5	21
Todd Charlesworth	7	1	3	4	4
Grant Block	7	3	0	3	0
Mark Turner	2	2	1	3	4
Mark Brownschidle	7	0	3	3	4
Jim Latos	7	2	0	2	4
Bob Jones	5	1	1	2	4
Bob Berg	6	1	1	2	5
Steve Herniman	7	1	1	2	30
Jeff Napierala	7	1	1	2	6
Marc Vachon	7	1	0	1	0
Eric Raymond (goalie)	4	0	1	1	2
George Maneluk (goalie)	1	0	0	0	2
Chris Clifford (goalie)	2	0	0	0	2
Dave Stewart	2	0	0	0	0
Robert Melanson	7	0	0	0	11
Darrel Newman	7	0	0	0	6

GOALTENDING

	Games	Min.	Goals	SO	Avg.
Eric Raymond	4	257	13	1	3.04
Chris Clifford	2	117	11	0	5.64
George Maneluk	1	59	6(1)	0	6.10

ST. THOMAS WILDCATS

(Lost finals to Brantford, 4-1)

SCORING

	Games	G	A	Pts.	Pen.
Len Soccio	15	10	21	31	26
Kent Hawley	15	4	18	22	33
Darin Smith	14	4	17	21	55
Tim Bean	15	12	7	19	18
Jamie Allan	13	2	9	11	28
Matt Hoffman	13	7	3	10	44
Mitch Malloy	12	6	3	9	39
Dan Williams	13	4	5	9	25
Todd Coopman	15	4	5	9	34
Gary Miller	15	3	4	7	46
Conrade Thomas	15	0	6	6	23
Mark Vichorek	14	1	4	5	18
Tom Moulton	15	3	1	4	21
Denny Larocque	13	1	3	4	24
Darcy Cahill	5	2	1	3	0
Mike Teeple	15	0	3	3	27
Todd Humphrey	11	1	1	2	32
Andrew Doxtater	7	0	1	1	9
Kevin Butt (goalie)	14	0	1	1	19
Wayne Marion (goalie)	1	0	0	0	2
Hakan Falkenhall	2	0	0	0	6
Steve McCharles	3	0	0	0	9

GOALTENDING

	Games	Min.	Goals	SO	Avg.
Kevin Butt	14	854	49(3)	1	3.44
Wayne Marion	1	60	6	0	6.00

THUNDER BAY THUNDER HAWKS

(Lost round-robin semifinals to St. Thomas and Brantford, 1-3)

SCORING

	Games	G	A	Pts.	Pen.
Jason Firth	11	8	9	17	2
Todd Howarth	11	2	13	15	12
Terry Menard	11	4	6	10	36
Gary Callaghan	11	1	9	10	8
Gerry St. Cyr	11	5	4	9	44
Jamie Hayden	11	4	5	9	2
Brian Downey	11	4	5	9	14
Chris Rowland	11	3	4	7	44
Tom Warden	11	4	2	6	32
Barry McKinlay	11	2	3	5	11
Brian Wells	8	2	2	4	62
Marc Lyons	11	1	3	4	6
Brock Shyiak	9	1	3	4	6
Vern Ray	11	1	2	3	13
Everton Blackwin	7	2	0	2	12
Lorne Knauft	1	0	1	1	2
Marc LaBelle	7	0	1	1	11
Llew McWana	7	0	1	1	0
Steve Hogg (goalie)	1	0	0	0	0
Mel Andelstead	5	0	0	0	10
Mark Michaud (goalie)	10	0	0	0	12

GOALTENDING

	Games	Min.	Goals	SO	Avg.
Mark Michaud	10	617	50(1)	0	4.86
Steve Hogg	1	60	5	0	5.00

1992-93 AWARD WINNERS

ALL-STAR TEAMS

First team	Pos.	Second team
Jamie Stewart, Detroit	G	Kevin Butt, St. Thomas
Tom Searle, Brantford	D	Steve Beadle, Detroit
Brett MacDonald, Flint	D	Ryan Kummu, Brantford
Darin Smith, St. Thomas	LW	Paul Polillo, Brantford
Len Soccio, St. Thomas	C	Jason Firth, Thunder Bay
Vladimir Tsiplakov, Detroit	RW	Paul Kelly, Muskegon

Coach of the Year: Bill McDonald, Thunder Bay

TROPHY WINNERS

Most Valuable Player: Jason Firth, Thunder Bay
Scoring leader: Len Soccio, St. Thomas
Outstanding defenseman: Tom Searle, Brantford
Outstanding defensive forward: Todd Howarth, Thunder Bay
Rookie of the Year: Jason Firth, Thunder Bay
Most sportsmanlike player of the year: Paul Polillo, Brantford
Playoff MVP: Roland Melanson, Brantford
Coach of the Year: Bill McDonald, Thunder Bay

ALL-TIME AWARD WINNERS

MOST VALUABLE PLAYER

Season	Player, Team
1991-92	Terry McCutcheon, Brantford
1992-93	Jason Firth, Thunder Bay

SCORING LEADER

Season	Player, Team
1991-92	Tom Sasso, Flint
1992-93	Len Soccio, St. Thomas

ROOKIE OF THE YEAR

Season	Player, Team
1991-92	Kevin Butt, St. Thomas
1992-93	Jason Firth, Thunder Bay

DEFENSEMAN OF THE YEAR

Season	Player, Team
1991-92	Tom Searle, Brantford
1992-93	Tom Searle, Brantford

BEST DEFENSIVE FORWARD

Season	Player, Team
1991-92	Tim Bean, St. Thomas
1992-93	Todd Howarth, Thunder Bay

MOST SPORTSMANLIKE PLAYER

Season	Player, Team
1991-92	Tom Sasso, Flint
1992-93	Paul Polillo, Brantford

PLAYOFF MVP

Season	Player, Team
1991-92	Gary Callaghan, Thunder Bay
1992-93	Roland Melanson, Brantford

COACH OF THE YEAR

Season	Coach, Team
1991-92	Peter Horachek, St. Thomas
1992-93	Bill McDonald, Thunder Bay

ALL-TIME LEAGUE CHAMPIONS

REGULAR-SEASON CHAMPION

Season	Team	Coach
1991-92	Michigan Falcons	Terry Christensen
1992-93	Brantford Smoke	Ken Mann & Ken Gratton

PLAYOFF CHAMPION

Team	Coach
Thunder Bay Thunder Hawks	Bill McDonald
Brantford Smoke	Ken Gratton

MAJOR JUNIOR LEAGUES

Canadian Hockey League

Ontario Hockey League

Quebec Major Junior Hockey League

Western Hockey League

CANADIAN HOCKEY LEAGUE

GENERAL INFORMATION

The Canadian Hockey League is an alliance of the three Major Junior leagues—Ontario Hockey League, Quebec Major Junior Hockey League and Western Hockey League. After the regular season, the three leagues compete in a round-robin tournament to decide the Memorial Cup championship. Originally awarded to the national Junior champion, the Memorial Cup later signified Junior A supremacy (after Junior hockey in Canada was divided into ''A'' and ''B'' classes). Beginning in 1971, when Junior A hockey was split into Major Junior and Tier II Junior A, the Memorial Cup was awarded to the Major Junior champion.

LEAGUE OFFICE

Address
305 Milner Ave.
Scarborough, Ont. M1B 3V4
Phone
416-298-3523
FAX
416-298-3187
President
Ed Chynoweth

Vice presidents
David E. Branch
Gilles Courteau
Director of information
Jim Price
Directors
Jim Rutherford
Marcel Robert
Rick Brodsky

Director of officiating
Richard Doerksen
Member leagues
Ontario Hockey League
Quebec Major Junior Hockey League
Western Hockey League

1993 MEMORIAL CUP

FINAL STANDINGS

Team (League)	W	L	Pts.	GF	GA
Sault Ste. Marie (OHL)	3	1	6	17	12
Peterborough (OHL)	3	2	6	21	19
Laval (QMJHL)	2	3	4	15	18
Swift Current (WHL)	1	3	2	14	18

RESULTS

SATURDAY, MAY 15
Sault Ste. Marie 3, Laval 2

SUNDAY, MAY 16
Peterborough 6, Laval 4
Swift Current 5, Sault Ste. Marie 3

TUESDAY, MAY 18
Peterborough 7, Swift Current 3

WEDNESDAY, MAY 19
Laval 4, Swift Current 3

THURSDAY, MAY 20
Sault Ste. Marie 7, Peterborough 3

FRIDAY, MAY 21
Laval 4, Swift Current 3

SATURDAY, MAY 22
Peterborough 3, Laval 1

SUNDAY, MAY 23
Sault Ste. Marie 4, Peterborough 2

TOP TOURNAMENT SCORERS

	Games	G	A	Pts.
Mike Harding, Peterborough	5	4	9	*13
Jason Dawe, Peterborough	5	3	6	9
Martin Lapointe, Laval	5	1	8	9
Chad Penney, Sault Ste. Marie	4	*5	2	7
Ralph Intranuovo, Sault Ste. Marie	4	3	4	7
Andy Schneider, Swift Current	4	2	5	7
Todd Holt, Swift Current	4	*5	1	6
Chris Pronger, Peterborough	5	1	5	6
Dave Roche, Peterborough	5	4	1	5
Brent Tully, Peterborough	5	3	2	5
Aaron Gavey, Sault Ste. Marie	4	1	4	5
Jeff Toms, Sault Ste. Marie	4	1	4	5
Drew Bannister, Sault Ste. Marie	4	0	5	5
Marc Beaucage, Laval	5	0	5	5

*Indicates tournament leader.

1992-93 AWARD WINNERS

ALL-STAR TEAMS

First team	Pos.	Second team
Jocelyn Thibault, Sher.	G	Manny Legace, N. Falls
Chris Pronger, Peterborough	D	Mike Rathje, Medicine Hat
Jason Smith, Regina	D	Michal Sykora, Tacoma
Rene Corbet, Drummondville	LW	Andrew Brunette, O.S.
Pat Peake, Detroit	C	Jason Krywulak, Swift Cur.
Martin Gendron, St. Hy.	RW	Jason Dawe, Peterborough

Coach of the Year: Marcel Comeau, Tacoma

TROPHY WINNERS

Player of the year: Pat Peake, Detroit
Plus/minus award: Chris Pronger, Peterborough
Rookie of the year: Jeff Freisen, Regina
Defenseman of the year: Chris Pronger, Peterborough
Goaltender of the year: Jocelyn Thibault, Sherbrooke
Scholastic player of the year: David Trofimenkoff, Lethbridge
Coach of the year: Marcel Comeau, Tacoma
Executive of the year: Jim Rutherford, Detroit
Most sportsmanlike player of the year: Rick Girard, Swift Current
Top draft prospect award: Alexandre Daigle, Victoriaville
Humanitarian award: Keli Corpse, Kingston

ALL-TIME MEMORIAL CUP WINNERS

Season	Team
1918-19	Univ. of Toronto Schools
1919-20	Toronto Canoe Club
1920-21	Winnipeg Falcons
1921-22	Fort William War Veterans
1922-23	Univ. of Manitoba-Winnipeg
1923-24	Owen Sound Greys
1924-25	Regina Pats
1925-26	Calgary Canadians
1926-27	Owen Sound Greys
1927-28	Regina Monarchs
1928-29	Toronto Marlboros
1929-30	Regina Pats
1930-31	Winnipeg Elmwoods
1931-32	Sudbury Wolves
1932-33	Newmarket
1933-34	Toronto St. Michael's
1934-35	Winnipeg Monarchs
1935-36	West Toronto Redmen
1936-37	Winnipeg Monarchs
1937-38	St. Boniface Seals
1938-39	Oshawa Generals
1939-40	Oshawa Generals
1940-41	Winnipeg Rangers
1941-42	Portage la Prairie
1942-43	Winnipeg Rangers

Season	Team
1943-44	Oshawa Generals
1944-45	Toronto St. Michael's
1945-46	Winnipeg Monarchs
1946-47	Toronto St. Michael's
1947-48	Port Arthur W. End Bruins
1948-49	Montreal Royals
1949-50	Montreal Jr. Canadiens
1950-51	Barrie Flyers
1951-52	Guelph Biltmores
1952-53	Barrie Flyers
1953-54	St. Catharines Tee Pees
1954-55	Toronto Marlboros
1955-56	Toronto Marlboros
1956-57	Flin Flon Bombers
1957-58	Ottawa-Hull Jr. Canadiens
1958-59	Winnipeg Braves
1959-60	St. Catharines Tee Pees
1960-61	Tor. St. Michael's Majors
1961-62	Hamilton Red Wings
1962-63	Edmonton Oil Kings
1963-64	Toronto Marlboros
1964-65	Niagara Falls Flyers
1965-66	Edmonton Oil Kings
1966-67	Toronto Marlboros
1967-68	Niagara Falls Flyers

Season	Team
1968-69	Montreal Jr. Canadiens
1969-70	Montreal Jr. Canadiens
1970-71	Quebec Remparts
1971-72	Cornwall Royals
1972-73	Toronto Marlboros
1973-74	Regina Pats
1974-75	Toronto Marlboros
1975-76	Hamilton Fincups
1976-77	New Westminster Bruins
1977-78	New Westminster Bruins
1978-79	Peterborough Petes
1979-80	Cornwall Royals
1980-81	Cornwall Royals
1981-82	Kitchener Rangers
1982-83	Portland Winter Hawks
1983-84	Ottawa 67's
1984-85	Prince Albert Raiders
1985-86	Guelph Platers
1986-87	Medicine Hat Tigers
1987-88	Medicine Hat Tigers
1988-89	Swift Current Broncos
1989-90	Oshawa Generals
1990-91	Spokane Chiefs
1991-92	Kamloops Blazers
1992-93	Sault Ste. Marie Greyhounds

ALL-TIME AWARD WINNERS

PLAYER OF THE YEAR AWARD

Season	Player, Team
1974-75	Ed Staniowski, Regina
1975-76	Peter Lee, Ottawa
1976-77	Dale McCourt, Ste. Catharines
1977-78	Bobby Smith, Ottawa
1978-79	Pierre LaCroix, Trois-Rivieres
1979-80	Doug Wickenheiser, Regina
1980-81	Dale Hawerchuk, Cornwall
1981-82	Dave Simpson, London
1982-83	Pat LaFontaine, Verdun
1983-84	Mario Lemieux, Laval
1984-85	Dan Hodgson, Prince Albert
1985-86	Luc Robitaille, Hull
1986-87	Rob Brown, Kamloops
1987-88	Joe Sakic, Swift Current
1988-89	Bryan Fogarty, Niagara Falls
1989-90	Mike Ricci, Peterborough
1990-91	Eric Lindros, Oshawa
1991-92	Charles Poulin, St. Hyacinthe
1992-93	Pat Peake, Detroit

PLUS/MINUS AWARD

Season	Player, Team
1986-87	Rob Brown, Kamloops
1987-88	Marc Saumier, Hull
1988-89	Bryan Fogarty, Niagara Falls
1989-90	Len Barrie, Kamloops
1990-91	Eric Lindros, Oshawa
1991-92	Dean McAmmond, Prince Albert
1992-93	Chris Pronger, Peterborough

ROOKIE OF THE YEAR AWARD

Season	Player, Team
1987-88	Martin Gelinas, Hull
1988-89	Yanic Perreault, Trois-Rivieres
1989-90	Petr Nedved, Seattle
1990-91	Philippe Boucher, Granby
1991-92	Alexandre Daigle, Victoriaville
1992-93	Jeff Freisen, Regina

DEFENSEMAN OF THE YEAR AWARD

Season	Player, Team
1987-88	Greg Hawgood, Kamloops
1988-89	Bryan Fogarty, Niagara Falls
1989-90	John Slaney, Cornwall
1990-91	Patrice Brisebois, Drummondville
1991-92	Drake Berehowsky, North Bay
1992-93	Chris Pronger, Peterborough

GOALTENDER OF THE YEAR AWARD

Season	Player, Team
1987-88	Stephane Beauregard, St. Jean
1988-89	Stephane Fiset, Victoriaville
1989-90	Trevor Kidd, Brandon
1990-91	Felix Potvin, Chicoutimi
1991-92	Corey Hirsch, Kamloops
1992-93	Jocelyn Thibault, Sherbrooke

SCHOLASTIC PLAYER OF THE YEAR AWARD

Season	Player, Team
1987-88	Darrin Shannon, Windsor
1988-89	Jeff Nelson, Prince Albert
1989-90	Jeff Nelson, Prince Albert
1990-91	Scott Niedermayer, Kamloops
1991-92	Nathan LaFayette, Cornwall
1992-93	David Trofimenkoff, Lethbridge

COACH OF THE YEAR AWARD

Season	Coach, Team
1987-88	Alain Vigneault, Hull
1988-89	Joe McDonnell, Kitchener
1989-90	Ken Hitchcock, Kamloops
1990-91	Joe Canale, Chicoutimi
1991-92	Bryan Maxwell, Spokane
1992-93	Marcel Comeau, Tacoma

MAJOR JUNIOR LEAGUES

CHL

EXECUTIVE OF THE YEAR AWARD

Season	Executive, Team or League
1988-89	John Horman, QMJHL
1989-90	Russ Farwell, Seattle
1990-91	Sherwood Bassin, Sault Ste. Marie
1991-92	Bert Templeton, North Bay
1992-93	Jim Rutherford, Detroit

MOST SPORTSMANLIKE PLAYER OF THE YEAR AWARD

Season	Player, Team
1989-90	Andrew McKim, Hull
1990-91	Pat Falloon, Spokane
1991-92	Martin Gendron, St. Hyacinthe
1992-93	Rick Girard, Swift Current

TOP DRAFT PROSPECT AWARD

Season	Player, Team
1990-91	Eric Lindros, Oshawa
1991-92	Todd Warriner, Windsor
1992-93	Alexandre Daigle, Victoriaville

HUMANITARIAN AWARD

Season	Player, Team
1992-93	Keli Corpse, Kingston

ONTARIO HOCKEY LEAGUE

LEAGUE OFFICE

Commissioner
David E. Branch
Chairman of the board
Jim Rutherford
Director of administration
Herb Morell

Director of hockey operations
Ted Baker
Director of officiating
Ken Bodendistel
Director of central scouting
Jack Ferguson

Address
305 Milner Avenue
Suite 208
Scarborough, Ontario M1B 3V4
Phone
416-299-8700

1992-93 REGULAR SEASON

FINAL STANDINGS

MATT LEYDEN DIVISION

Team	G	W	L	T	Pts.	GF	GA
Peterborough	66	46	15	5	97	352	239
Kingston	66	36	19	11	83	314	265
Oshawa	66	33	28	5	71	270	268
Sudbury	66	31	30	5	67	291	300
Newmarket	66	29	28	9	67	310	301
Belleville	66	21	34	11	53	280	315
North Bay	66	22	38	6	50	251	299
Ottawa	66	16	42	8	40	220	310

HAP EMMS DIVISION

Team	G	W	L	T	Pts.	GF	GA
Sault Ste. Marie	66	38	23	5	81	334	260
Detroit	66	37	22	7	81	336	264
London	66	32	27	7	71	323	292
Owen Sound	66	29	29	8	66	330	324
Niagara Falls	66	29	30	7	65	299	274
Kitchener	66	26	31	9	61	280	314
Guelph	66	27	33	6	60	298	360
Windsor	66	19	42	5	43	240	343

INDIVIDUAL LEADERS

Goals: Andrew Brunette, Owen Sound (62)
Assists: Andrew Brunette, Owen Sound (100)
Points: Andrew Brunette, Owen Sound (162)
Penalty minutes: Dennis Bonvie, North Bay (316)
Goaltending average: Kevin Hodson, Sault Ste. Marie (3.10)
Shutouts: Eight tied with one each.

	Games	G	A	Pts.
Jim Brown, Owen Sound	60	53	66	119
Jason Allison, London	66	42	76	118
Jeff Bes, Guelph	59	48	67	115
Jeff Shevalier, North Bay	62	59	54	113
Chris Gratton, Kingston	58	55	54	109
Brad Smyth, London	66	54	55	109
Keli Corpse, Kingston	54	32	75	107
Derek Armstrong, Sudbury	66	44	62	106
Jeff Reid, Newmarket	64	36	70	106
Rod Hinks, Sudbury	64	47	57	104
Scott Hollis, Oshawa	62	49	53	102
Mike Peca, Ottawa	55	38	64	102
Todd Harvey, Detroit	55	50	50	100
Steve Gibson, Windsor	60	48	52	100
Kevin Brown, Niagara Falls	63	42	58	100
Dave Roche, Peterborough	56	40	60	100

TOP SCORERS

	Games	G	A	Pts.
Andrew Brunette, Owen Sound	66	62	100	162
Bob Wren, Detroit	63	57	88	145
Kevin Brown, Detroit	62	50	91	141
Pat Peake, Detroit	46	58	78	136
Mike Harding, Peterborough	66	54	82	136
Jason Dawe, Peterborough	59	58	68	126
Bill Bowler, Windsor	57	44	77	121

INDIVIDUAL STATISTICS

BELLEVILLE BULLS

SCORING

	Games	G	A	Pts.	Pen.
Mark Donahue	66	44	55	99	73
Chris Skoryna	66	39	49	88	31
Justin Morrison	37	25	48	73	65
Richard Park	66	23	38	61	38
Doug Doull	65	19	37	56	143
Paul McCallion	61	15	35	50	82
Dan Preston	63	4	42	46	52
Kyle Blacklock	65	14	28	42	23
Paul Rushforth	36	21	19	40	38
Brian Secord	66	16	18	34	57
Chris Clancy	62	10	21	31	76
Corey Isen	57	15	6	21	123
Jeff Kostuch	29	7	13	20	10
Daniel Godbout	65	2	17	19	66
Jason Weaver	15	8	10	18	28
Jeff Pawluk	24	4	9	13	20

	Games	G	A	Pts.	Pen.
Marc Dupuis	64	2	10	12	34
Steve Carter	57	1	11	12	58
Reuben Castella	51	1	8	9	98
Kevin Brown	6	2	5	7	4
Gord Dickie	15	2	4	6	5
Kelly Vipond	17	2	3	5	2
Ian Keiller	57	0	4	4	200
Derek Wilkinson (goalie)	59	0	3	3	4
Dominic Belanger	14	2	1	3	11
Jason Hughes	17	1	1	2	17
Sam Oliveira	5	0	2	2	0
Brian Stagg	9	1	0	1	2
Rick Marshall	1	0	1	1	0
Craig Binns	22	0	1	1	37
Brent Thombs (goalie)	2	0	0	0	0
Richard Gallace (goalie)	3	0	0	0	0
Charlie Lawson	4	0	0	0	0
Greg Bailey	5	0	0	0	21
Scott Hay (goalie)	14	0	0	0	2

GOALTENDING

	Games	Min.	Goals	SO	Avg.
Derek Wilkinson	59	3370	237(5)	0	4.22
Scott Hay	14	517	51(1)	0	5.92
Brent Thombs	2	69	10	0	8.70
Richard Gallace	3	68	11	0	9.71

( )—Empty-net goals (do not count against a goaltender's average).

DETROIT JR. RED WINGS

SCORING

	Games	G	A	Pts.	Pen.
Bob Wren	63	57	88	145	91
Pat Peake	46	58	78	136	64
Kevin Brown	56	48	86	134	76
Todd Harvey	55	50	50	100	83
Blair Scott	64	11	68	79	105
Bill McCauley	65	13	37	50	24
Pat Barton	59	20	20	40	59
Chris Varga	64	17	21	38	12
Tony McCabe	36	9	17	26	22
Jeff Mitchell	62	10	15	25	100
Kevin Paden	54	14	9	23	41
Mike Rucinski	66	6	13	19	54
J.D. Eaton	66	6	12	18	132
Darren Hurley	44	6	11	17	96
Eric Cairns	64	3	13	16	194
Jamie Allison	61	0	13	13	64
Richard Ujvary	64	0	13	13	55
Rob Boyko	59	5	7	12	53
John Pinches	35	2	10	12	13
Ryan Merritt	12	1	5	6	23
Chris Gignac	12	0	4	4	0
Fred Brathwaite (goalie)	37	0	3	3	10
Joe Harris	43	0	2	2	12
Derek Wilkinson (goalie)	4	0	1	1	0
Steve Carter	2	0	0	0	0
Sean McKegney	3	0	0	0	0
Steve Allen	4	0	0	0	0
Brian Kent (goalie)	5	0	0	0	7
Sam Oliveira	5	0	0	0	0
Greg Bailey	8	0	0	0	2
Jason Saal (goalie)	23	0	0	0	2

GOALTENDING

	Games	Min.	Goals	SO	Avg.
Fred Brathwaite	37	2192	134(2)	0	3.67
Jason Saal	23	1289	85(1)	0	3.96
Derek Wilkinson	4	245	18	0	4.41
Brian Kent	5	272	24	0	5.29

GUELPH STORM

SCORING

	Games	G	A	Pts.	Pen.
Jeff Bes	59	48	67	115	128
Wade Whitten	65	36	55	91	72
Jeff O'Neill	65	32	47	79	88
Todd Bertuzzi	60	27	31	58	168
Alek Stojanov	35	27	28	55	11
Sylvain Cloutier	44	26	29	55	78
Jean-Paul Davis	43	12	30	42	26
Grant Pritchett	56	6	23	29	56
Duane Harmer	62	4	25	29	67
Tony McCabe	28	14	14	28	4
Ken Belanger	29	10	14	24	84
Mike Prokopec	29	10	14	24	27
Brent Pope	33	10	14	24	40
Jeff Pawluk	38	3	20	23	33
Brent Watson	38	8	12	20	32
Mike Rusk	62	3	15	18	65
Ryan VandenBussche	29	3	14	17	99
Stephane Lefebvre	63	2	12	14	16
Gord Walsh	55	2	9	11	12
Chris McMurtry	57	1	10	11	38
Kelvin Solari	21	3	7	10	72
Regan Stocco	51	1	7	8	48

	Games	G	A	Pts.	Pen.
Aaron Downey	53	3	3	6	88
Fredrik Oduya	23	2	4	6	29
Murray Hogg	46	2	2	4	44
Phil Miaskowski	14	1	3	4	14
Rumun Ndur	22	1	3	4	30
Steve Pottie (goalie)	41	0	2	2	2
Dean Roberts	1	1	0	1	0
Shane Johnson	3	0	1	1	0
Mark McArthur (goalie)	35	0	1	1	0
Craig Crowe (goalie)	1	0	0	0	0

GOALTENDING

	Games	Min.	Goals	SO	Avg.
Steve Pottie	41	2126	174(1)	0	4.91
Mark McArthur	35	1853	180(1)	0	5.83
Craig Crowe	1	18	4	0	13.33

KINGSTON FRONTENACS

SCORING

	Games	G	A	Pts.	Pen.
Chris Gratton	58	55	54	109	125
Keli Corpse	54	32	75	107	45
Greg Clancy	65	37	49	86	27
Steve Parson	66	28	55	83	62
Craig Rivet	64	19	55	74	117
Jason Weaver	45	30	35	65	95
David Ling	64	17	46	63	275
Cory Johnson	64	22	37	59	41
Trent Cull	60	11	28	39	144
Bill Robinson	55	12	22	34	60
Richard Raymond	43	7	26	33	39
Brett Lindros	31	11	11	22	162
Joel Yates	46	7	12	19	173
Greg Kraemer	60	8	9	17	27
Duncan Fader	60	1	12	13	15
Bill Maranduik	58	4	6	10	29
Brian Stagg	20	4	5	9	17
Trevor Doyle	62	1	8	9	148
Jason Wadel	63	3	5	8	40
Jason Disher	46	2	4	6	100
Mike Dawson	11	0	5	5	17
John Drover	37	2	1	3	4
Steve Laforet	2	1	0	1	0
Brad Barton	12	0	1	1	15
Ed Rushlow (goalie)	1	0	0	0	0
Brian Sambirsky	3	0	0	0	7
Chris Gowan	8	0	0	0	14
Scott Thompson	21	0	0	0	18
Tyler Moss (goalie)	31	0	0	0	4
Marc Lamothe (goalie)	45	0	0	0	7

GOALTENDING

	Games	Min.	Goals	SO	Avg.
Ed Rushlow	1	1	0	0	0.00
Tyler Moss	31	1537	97(2)	0	3.79
Marc Lamothe	45	2489	162(4)	1	3.91

KITCHENER RANGERS

SCORING

	Games	G	A	Pts.	Pen.
Trevor Gallant	64	22	64	86	42
Tim Spitzig	66	39	39	78	127
Jason Gladney	64	16	55	71	86
Derek Gauthier	66	24	40	64	103
Chris Phelps	61	12	48	60	75
Norm Dezainde	66	27	24	51	100
Eric Manlow	53	26	21	47	31
Todd Warriner	32	19	24	43	35
Mike Polano	51	20	21	41	111
Joe Coombs	61	17	21	38	29
Shayne McCosh	32	7	25	32	43
Jamie Caruso	33	14	17	31	26
Gairin Smith	55	14	17	31	123
Ryan Pawluk	64	7	12	19	29
Wes Swinson	61	0	16	16	105

	Games	G	A	Pts.	Pen.
Mark Cardiff	30	0	14	14	36
Greg McLean	63	1	11	12	21
Marc Robillard	30	4	7	11	9
Peter Brearley	57	5	4	9	21
Grayden Reid	8	4	5	9	4
Justin Cullen	52	2	5	7	80
Jason Johnson	19	0	3	3	20
Dave Szabo	5	0	1	1	4
C.J. Denomme (goalie)	45	0	1	1	10
Todd Preston	3	0	0	0	5
Chris Shushack	3	0	0	0	0
Shamus Gregga (goalie)	11	0	0	0	0
Greg Scott (goalie)	20	0	0	0	8
Matt O'Dette	28	0	0	0	6
Rick Marshall	30	0	0	0	20

GOALTENDING

	Games	Min.	Goals	SO	Avg.
Greg Scott	20	1014	73(1)	0	4.32
C.J. Denomme	45	2514	189(4)	0	4.51
Shamus Gregga	11	490	46(1)	0	5.63

LONDON KNIGHTS

SCORING

	Games	G	A	Pts.	Pen.
Jason Allison	66	42	76	118	50
Brad Smyth	66	54	55	109	118
Scott McKay	63	38	57	95	49
Troy Sweet	66	30	50	80	69
Brett Marietti	57	31	43	74	76
Yvan Corbin	40	35	33	68	23
Nick Stajduhar	49	15	46	61	58
Mark Visheau	62	8	52	60	88
Dave Gilmore	65	22	21	43	48
Cory Evans	58	6	22	28	162
Chris Zanutto	66	4	22	26	30
John Guirestante	32	7	12	19	13
Don Margettie	61	5	13	18	29
Gord Ross	60	6	11	17	112
Derrick Crane	16	5	11	16	25
Brodie Coffin	49	4	10	14	37
Mike Shewan	31	2	12	14	26
Daryl Rivers	47	2	11	13	53
Chris Brassard	51	2	7	9	24
Chris Lizotte	35	3	2	5	13
Brian Stacey	38	2	2	4	45
Joel Sandie	29	0	4	4	24
Steve Smillie	2	0	2	2	4
Brent Holdsworth	59	0	2	2	18
Ilpo Kauhanen (goalie)	40	0	1	1	30
Gerry Arcella (goalie)	1	0	0	0	0
Mark Williams (goalie)	5	0	0	0	0
Robert Frid	8	0	0	0	7
Jordan Willis (goalie)	26	0	0	0	2

GOALTENDING

	Games	Min.	Goals	SO	Avg.
Gerry Arcella	1	63	4	0	3.81
Jordan Willis	26	1428	100(3)	1	4.20
Ilpo Kauhanen	40	2210	155(4)	0	4.21
Mark Williams	5	300	25(1)	0	5.00

NEWMARKET ROYALS

SCORING

	Games	G	A	Pts.	Pen.
Jeff Reid	64	36	70	106	90
Mark DeSantis	66	19	70	89	136
Nathan LaFayette	58	49	38	87	26
Shayne Gaffar	42	28	29	57	6
Jeremy Stevenson	54	28	28	56	144
Jason Bonsignore	66	22	20	42	6
Larry Courville	64	21	18	39	181
Matt Hogan	66	16	23	39	40

	Games	G	A	Pts.	Pen.
Grant Marshall	31	12	25	37	85
Derek Grant	60	11	24	35	14
Todd Walker	66	12	21	33	30
Mike Dawson	50	6	22	28	83
Ryan VandenBussche	30	15	12	27	161
Alain Letang	66	1	25	26	14
Dave Lemay	60	5	19	24	116
Mike Prokopec	40	6	14	20	70
Alek Stojanov	14	9	7	16	21
Paul Andrea	64	6	7	13	12
Jason Meloche	33	4	7	11	108
Gerry Skrypec	19	1	6	7	24
Richard Raymond	9	1	3	4	13
Rob Massa	45	2	1	3	41
Corey Bricknell	22	0	2	2	12
Greg Bailey	9	0	1	1	25
Richard Gallace (goalie)	17	0	1	1	2
Rob Dykeman (goalie)	23	0	1	1	10
Adrian Murray	51	0	1	1	34
Chris Selman (goalie)	1	0	0	0	0
Ilpo Kauhanen (goalie)	2	0	0	0	0
Kam White	8	0	0	0	8
Jason Fortier	24	0	0	0	35
Todd Laurin (goalie)	33	0	0	0	2

GOALTENDING

	Games	Min.	Goals	SO	Avg.
Todd Laurin	33	1698	116(1)	0	4.10
Richard Gallace	17	921	65(2)	0	4.23
Rob Dykeman	23	1256	97(1)	1	4.63
Ilpo Kauhanen	2	120	14(1)	0	7.00
Chris Selman	1	14	4	0	17.14

NIAGARA FALLS THUNDER

SCORING

	Games	G	A	Pts.	Pen.
Kevin Brown	63	42	58	100	47
Dale Junkin	65	29	49	78	50
Brandon Convery	51	38	39	77	24
Todd Wetzel	52	32	43	75	29
Ethan Moreau	65	32	41	73	69
Jason Clarke	64	13	41	54	313
Bogdan Savenko	51	29	19	48	15
Neil Fewster	66	7	34	41	81
Scott Campbell	31	4	26	30	65
Greg DeVries	62	3	23	26	86
Chris Baxter	60	4	21	25	31
Jeff Johnstone	55	10	13	23	12
Ryan Tocher	59	6	17	23	58
Darren Dougan	21	6	13	19	12
Mark Cardiff	30	5	13	18	32
Steve Staios	12	4	14	18	30
Tom Moores	17	6	11	17	32
Dale Greenwood	59	8	6	14	45
Dennis Maxwell	12	5	9	14	21
Jason Coles	33	4	6	10	75
Wyatt Buckland	30	5	4	9	45
Paul McInnes	53	2	5	7	23
Derek Sylvester	23	3	3	6	27
Jim Hibbert (goalie)	11	0	2	2	2
Tim Thompson	26	0	2	2	14
Kelly Wayling	52	0	2	2	33
Matt McGuffin	4	1	0	1	12
Dustin McArthur	33	1	0	1	11
Manny Legace (goalie)	48	0	1	1	15
Kade McAllister	1	0	0	0	0
Mike Majewski	4	0	0	0	27
Greg Scott (goalie)	16	0	0	0	4

GOALTENDING

	Games	Min.	Goals	SO	Avg.
Manny Legace	48	2630	170(2)	0	3.88
Jim Hibbert	11	503	36(1)	0	4.29
Greg Scott	16	876	64(1)	0	4.38

NORTH BAY CENTENNIALS

SCORING

	Games	G	A	Pts.	Pen.
Jeff Shevalier	62	59	54	113	46
Bill Lang	64	45	50	95	112
Paul Doherty	63	10	47	57	63
Robert Thorpe	62	20	27	47	52
Mike Burman	64	10	37	47	59
James Sheehan	56	15	23	38	88
Aaron Morrison	42	8	26	34	57
Brian Stagg	42	16	13	29	27
Shaun Imber	47	2	24	26	28
Jim Ensom	65	7	17	24	70
Dennis Bonvie	64	3	21	24	316
Stefan Rivard	62	13	10	23	174
Jason Campeau	28	9	13	22	18
Jeff Andrews	65	5	11	16	27
Chad Penney	18	8	7	15	19
Paul Rushforth	21	4	10	14	24
David Lylyk	45	3	11	14	22
Brad Brown	61	4	9	13	228
Wade Gibson	17	3	4	7	35
Jack Williams	7	2	4	6	19
Lucas Miller	24	1	5	6	0
Derek Lahnalampi	49	2	3	5	30
Ryan Gillis	50	1	2	3	15
Brad Shepard	10	0	3	3	6
Carl Halverson	18	0	3	3	20
Brent Rowley	5	1	1	2	14
Sandy Allan (goalie)	39	0	2	2	25
Mark Brooks	27	0	1	1	9
Ron Michaud	1	0	0	0	0
Perry Ohm	1	0	0	0	5
Bob Harrison (goalie)	4	0	0	0	0
Dave Szabo	4	0	0	0	12
Jud Richards	9	0	0	0	0
Domo Kovacevic (goalie)	10	0	0	0	0
Neil Iserhoff	12	0	0	0	0
Damien Bloye	19	0	0	0	4
Ron Bertrand (goalie)	31	0	0	0	12

GOALTENDING

	Games	Min.	Goals	SO	Avg.
Sandy Allan	39	1835	133	0	4.35
Ron Bertrand	31	1601	120(2)	0	4.50
Domo Kovacevic	10	342	26	0	4.56
Bob Harrison	4	221	18	0	4.89

OSHAWA GENERALS

SCORING

	Games	G	A	Pts.	Pen.
Scott Hollis	62	49	53	102	148
Jason Arnott	56	41	57	98	74
B.J. MacPherson	57	42	55	97	112
Darryl Lafrance	66	35	51	86	24
Stephane Yelle	66	24	50	74	20
Trevor Burgess	65	19	52	71	133
Sean Brown	64	12	27	39	168
Wade Simpson	63	4	17	21	123
Stephane Soulliere	65	11	7	18	77
Jason McQuat	54	9	4	13	95
Todd Bradley	48	5	8	13	89
Kelly Vipond	32	3	10	13	9
Rob McQuat	56	3	10	13	150
Chris Hall	49	3	5	8	28
Lucas Miller	25	2	5	7	6
Jason Julian	60	1	6	7	121
Kevin Spero	65	1	6	7	58
Joe Cook	66	1	6	7	133
Billy-Jay Johnston	52	2	4	6	2
Aaron Albright	20	2	2	4	8
Jason Campeau	15	0	3	3	23
Neil Iserhoff	21	0	3	3	8
Steven Haight	14	1	0	1	19
Jud Richards	13	0	1	1	7
Joel Gagnon (goalie)	48	0	1	1	4

	Games	G	A	Pts.	Pen.
Kevin Vaughan	1	0	0	0	2
Jason Weaver	2	0	0	0	11
Mark Brooks	4	0	0	0	2
Serge Dunphy	7	0	0	0	6
Brian Kent (goalie)	7	0	0	0	0
Jamie Kress	20	0	0	0	26
Ken Shepard (goalie)	31	0	0	0	15

GOALTENDING

	Games	Min.	Goals	SO	Avg.
Ken Shepard	31	1483	86(1)	0	3.48
Joel Gagnon	48	2248	159(2)	0	4.24
Brian Kent	7	257	20	1	4.67

OTTAWA 67's

SCORING

	Games	G	A	Pts.	Pen.
Mike Peca	55	38	64	102	80
Steve Washburn	66	20	38	58	54
Shean Donovan	66	29	23	52	33
Greg Ryan	60	12	35	47	93
Grant Marshall	30	14	28	42	83
Mark Edmundson	63	17	20	37	34
Curtis Bowen	21	9	19	28	51
Shawn Caplice	58	12	15	27	66
Mike Carr	46	7	15	22	51
Ken Belanger	34	6	12	18	139
Mike Johnson	66	7	10	17	139
Martin Hamrlik	26	4	11	15	41
Brent Pope	26	5	8	13	18
Mike Hartwick	31	5	8	13	20
Mark Yakabuski	65	7	5	12	56
Chris Coveny	57	5	7	12	86
Sean Gagnon	33	2	10	12	68
Cory Murphy	66	3	7	10	22
Brent Watson	24	4	5	9	26
Jonathan Hess	33	4	5	9	4
Rich Bronilla	54	2	5	7	29
Bill Hall	33	2	4	6	29
Derrick Crane	16	1	5	6	11
Gerry Skrypec	20	1	3	4	20
Mike Gamble	22	1	3	4	2
Fredrik Oduya	17	0	3	3	70
Mike Roberts	5	1	1	2	4
Jason Meloche	10	1	1	2	17
Grayson Lafoley	26	0	2	2	4
Jeff Salajko (goalie)	29	0	2	2	0
Corey Crane	6	1	0	1	2
Elio Malandra	3	0	1	1	0
Rob Dykeman (goalie)	25	0	1	1	11
Greg Lovell (goalie)	2	0	0	0	0
Olav Ebrahim	13	0	0	0	0
Mathew Burnett	17	0	0	0	0
Sean Spencer (goalie)	19	0	0	0	5

GOALTENDING

	Games	Min.	Goals	SO	Avg.
Rob Dykeman	25	1422	95(2)	1	4.01
Jeff Salajko	29	1435	108(1)	0	4.52
Sean Spencer	19	1095	94(3)	0	5.15
Greg Lovell	2	57	7	0	7.37

OWEN SOUND PLATERS

SCORING

	Games	G	A	Pts.	Pen.
Andrew Brunette	66	62	100	162	91
Jim Brown	60	53	66	119	66
Scott Walker	57	23	68	91	110
Jason MacDonald	56	46	43	89	197
Willie Skilliter	66	25	41	66	14
Marian Kacir	56	20	36	56	8
Jeff Kostuch	43	16	22	38	8
Luigi Calce	62	16	21	37	103
Wayne Primeau	66	10	27	37	110
Shayne Wright	62	9	21	30	101

	Games	G	A	Pts.	Pen.
Jeff Smith	57	7	23	30	82
Darren Dougan	28	7	21	28	10
Brian Medeiros	64	7	15	22	28
Rick Morton	58	2	19	21	161
Geordie Maynard	21	6	9	15	61
Mark Vilneff	52	3	9	12	37
Rob Schweyer	62	6	5	11	34
Bryan Gendron	9	5	4	9	45
Wyatt Buckland	18	3	5	8	21
Shawn Krueger	45	1	7	8	117
Craig Binns	36	0	8	8	34
David Benn	25	1	4	5	86
Gord Dickie	11	1	3	4	7
Tom Stewart	19	1	1	2	15
Brian Murphy	6	0	2	2	5
Jason Hughes	17	0	2	2	21
Kevin Weekes (goalie)	29	0	2	2	4
Jamie Storr (goalie)	41	0	1	1	0
Craig Minard	1	0	0	0	0
Scott Vader	2	0	0	0	0
Rob MacKenzie	7	0	0	0	0
Jason Campbell	28	0	0	0	6

GOALTENDING

	Games	Min.	Goals	SO	Avg.
Jamie Storr	41	2362	180	0	4.57
Kevin Weekes	29	1645	143(1)	0	5.22

PETERBOROUGH PETES

SCORING

	Games	G	A	Pts.	Pen.
Mike Harding	66	54	82	136	106
Jason Dawe	59	58	68	126	80
Dave Roche	56	40	60	100	105
Dale McTavish	66	31	50	81	98
Cory Stillman	61	25	55	80	55
Chris Pronger	61	15	62	77	108
Ryan Black	66	30	41	71	41
Brent Tully	59	15	45	60	81
Chad Grills	66	17	26	43	71
Matt St. Germain	66	17	14	31	59
Geordie Kinnear	58	6	22	28	161
Matt Johnson	66	8	17	25	211
Bill Weir	49	10	12	22	22
Rick Emmett	59	3	17	20	19
Darryl Moxam	53	6	9	15	32
Doug Searle	60	2	13	15	103
Jeff Walker	53	3	5	8	21
Steve Hogg	27	3	4	7	4
Kelly Vipond	5	4	2	6	0
Kelvin Solari	34	0	5	5	42
Ryan Nauss	27	2	2	4	15
Colin Wilson	4	2	0	2	0
Craig McGillivray	28	1	1	2	19
Ryan Douglas (goalie)	24	0	2	2	0
Chad Lang (goalie)	43	0	1	1	8
Jamie Josefik (goalie)	1	0	0	0	0
Brady Dillabough	2	0	0	0	2
Craig Johnson (goalie)	2	0	0	0	0
Shawn Heins	5	0	0	0	10
Quade Lightbody	21	0	0	0	2

GOALTENDING

	Games	Min.	Goals	SO	Avg.
Jamie Josefik	1	20	0	0	0.00
Craig Johnson	2	120	6	0	3.00
Chad Lang	43	2554	140(1)	1	3.29
Ryan Douglas	24	1302	92	1	4.24

SAULT STE. MARIE GREYHOUNDS

SCORING

	Games	G	A	Pts.	Pen.
Jarret Reid	64	36	60	96	28
Aaron Gavey	62	45	39	84	114
Ralph Intranuovo	54	31	47	78	61

	Games	G	A	Pts.	Pen.
Chad Penney	48	29	44	73	67
Rick Kowalsky	54	23	47	70	58
Steve Sullivan	62	36	27	63	44
David Matsos	55	31	28	59	27
Brad Baber	59	12	28	40	60
Jeff Toms	60	16	23	39	20
Wade Gibson	48	13	24	37	97
Tom MacDonald	50	13	24	37	134
Mark Matier	64	7	27	34	89
Drew Bannister	59	5	28	33	114
Perry Pappas	58	13	19	32	104
Gary Roach	65	4	27	31	31
Briane Thompson	63	2	21	23	57
Joe VanVolsen	47	5	11	16	72
Kiley Hill	49	6	8	14	76
Brian Goudie	29	2	6	8	89
Shaun Imber	15	0	8	8	6
Sean Gagnon	24	1	5	6	65
Jodi Murphy	38	3	1	4	51
Oliver Pastinsky	13	0	2	2	4
Kevin Hodson (goalie)	26	0	2	2	0
Dan Tanevski (goalie)	32	0	2	2	6
Jim Ratte	1	1	0	1	0
David Lylyk	8	0	1	1	0
Peter MacKellar	9	0	1	1	5
Dan Cloutier (goalie)	12	0	1	1	10
Joe Clarke	6	0	0	0	0
Bob Harrison (goalie)	6	0	0	0	2
Jud Richards	6	0	0	0	2
Neal Martin	17	0	0	0	5

GOALTENDING

	Games	Min.	Goals	SO	Avg.
Kevin Hodson	26	1470	76	1	3.10
Bob Harrison	6	302	20	0	3.97
Dan Tanevski	32	1650	118(2)	1	4.29
Dan Cloutier	12	572	44	0	4.62

SUDBURY WOLVES

SCORING

	Games	G	A	Pts.	Pen.
Derek Armstrong	66	44	62	106	56
Rod Hinks	64	47	57	104	100
Jamie Matthews	65	30	62	92	65
Steve Staios	53	13	44	57	67
Jamie Rivers	62	12	43	55	20
Bernie John	46	13	35	48	45
Dennis Maxwell	52	15	24	39	114
Barrie Moore	57	13	26	39	71
Joel Poirier	64	18	15	33	94
Jamie Caruso	26	17	16	33	32
Rory Fitzpatrick	58	4	20	24	68
Dominic Belanger	39	9	13	22	41
Ryan Shanahan	60	7	10	17	65
Steve Potvin	45	6	11	17	38
Brandon Convery	7	7	9	16	6
Matt Kiereck	42	6	9	15	68
Mike Yeo	24	8	5	13	47
Mike Wilson	53	6	7	13	58
Kayle Short	50	2	11	13	89
Gary Coupal	58	5	7	12	267
Zdenek Nedved	18	3	9	12	6
Rick Bodkin	50	4	4	8	17
Bob MacIsaac	59	0	7	7	139
Greg Dreveny (goalie)	36	0	4	4	11
Sean Gagnon	6	1	1	2	16
Joel Sandie	20	1	0	1	41
Dale Chokan	3	0	1	1	2
Chris Grenville	6	0	1	1	2
Jamie Spadafora	1	0	0	0	0
Don Landry (goalie)	6	0	0	0	2
Shawn Frappier	9	0	0	0	2
Mark Gowan (goalie)	11	0	0	0	0
Corey Crane	15	0	0	0	2
Shawn Silver (goalie)	27	0	0	0	0

GOALTENDING

	Games	Min.	Goals	SO	Avg.
Greg Dreveny	36	2014	139(2)	0	4.14
Shawn Silver	27	1403	101(2)	1	4.32
Don Landry	6	166	14(1)	0	5.06
Mark Gowan	11	407	41	0	6.04

WINDSOR SPITFIRES

SCORING

	Games	G	A	Pts.	Pen.
Bill Bowler	57	44	77	121	41
Steve Gibson	60	48	52	100	44
Craig Lutes	57	31	31	62	35
Dennis Purdie	37	20	29	49	62
Colin Wilson	52	19	22	41	35
Shayne McCosh	36	5	35	40	38
Stephen Webb	63	14	25	39	181
Todd Warriner	23	13	21	34	29
Brady Blain	66	8	20	28	18
Daryl Lavoie	60	5	17	22	54
Mike Hartwick	30	8	10	18	41
Shawn Heins	53	7	10	17	107
David Benn	30	1	15	16	133
Marc Robillard	36	2	12	14	6
Mike Martin	61	2	7	9	80
Rick Marshall	25	0	9	9	30
Kelly Vipond	11	2	6	8	4
Ryan O'Neill	42	3	3	6	64
Adam Young	62	3	3	6	65
Aaron Morrison	6	1	5	6	15
Jason Coles	28	0	6	6	87
Matt Mullin (goalie)	55	0	6	6	12
Andy Massa	9	1	2	3	2
Luke Clowes	61	0	3	3	114
David Pluck	54	1	1	2	42
Peter Allison	39	0	2	2	41
Craig Binns	3	1	0	1	14
Eric Stamp	3	1	0	1	9
Laine Schubert	11	0	1	1	4
Russell Wood	17	0	1	1	5
Mike Hurley	1	0	0	0	0
David Mitchell (goalie)	1	0	0	0	0
Reuben Castella	3	0	0	0	16
Mike Bogden	4	0	0	0	0
Jason Haelzle	4	0	0	0	0
Jason Joyal	4	0	0	0	0
Gerrard Masse	5	0	0	0	9
Joe McLean	5	0	0	0	2
Tim Bacik (goalie)	6	0	0	0	4
Ryan Stephenson	6	0	0	0	2
Derrick Crane	10	0	0	0	7
Craig Johnson (goalie)	12	0	0	0	6
Chris Peyton	15	0	0	0	0

GOALTENDING

	Games	Min.	Goals	SO	Avg.
Tim Bacik	6	347	24	0	4.15
Matt Mullin	55	3070	249(8)	0	4.87
David Mitchell	1	52	5	0	5.77
Craig Johnson	12	524	57	0	6.53

PLAYERS WITH TWO OR MORE TEAMS

SCORING

	Games	G	A	Pts.	Pen.
Greg Bailey, Belleville	5	0	0	0	21
Greg Bailey, Detroit	8	0	0	0	2
Greg Bailey, Newmarket	9	0	1	1	25
Totals	22	0	1	1	48
Dominic Belanger, Belleville	14	2	1	3	11
Dominic Belanger, Sudbury	39	9	13	22	41
Totals	53	11	14	25	52
Ken Belanger, Ottawa	34	6	12	18	139
Ken Belanger, Guelph	29	10	14	24	84
Totals	63	16	26	42	223
David Benn, Windsor	30	1	15	16	133

	Games	G	A	Pts.	Pen.
David Benn, Owen Sound	25	1	4	5	86
Totals	55	2	19	21	219
Craig Binns, Windsor	3	1	0	1	14
Craig Binns, Belleville	22	0	1	1	37
Craig Binns, Owen Sound	36	0	8	8	34
Totals	61	1	9	10	85
Mark Brooks, Oshawa	4	0	0	0	2
Mark Brooks, North Bay	27	0	1	1	9
Totals	31	0	1	1	11
Kevin Brown, Belleville	6	2	5	7	4
Kevin Brown, Detroit	56	48	86	134	76
Totals	62	50	91	141	80
Wyatt Buckland, Owen Sound	18	3	5	8	21
Wyatt Buckland, Niagara Falls	30	5	4	9	45
Totals	48	8	9	17	66
Jason Campeau, Oshawa	15	0	3	3	23
Jason Campeau, North Bay	28	9	13	22	18
Totals	43	9	16	25	41
Mark Cardiff, Niagara Falls	30	5	13	18	32
Mark Cardiff, Kitchener	30	0	14	14	36
Totals	60	5	27	32	68
Steve Carter, Detroit	2	0	0	0	0
Steve Carter, Belleville	57	1	11	12	58
Totals	59	1	11	12	58
Jamie Caruso, Kitchener	33	14	17	31	26
Jamie Caruso, Sudbury	26	17	16	33	32
Totals	59	31	33	64	58
Reuben Castella, Windsor	3	0	0	0	16
Reuben Castella, Belleville	51	1	8	9	98
Totals	54	1	8	9	114
Jason Coles, Niagara Falls	33	4	6	10	75
Jason Coles, Windsor	28	0	6	6	87
Totals	61	4	12	16	162
Brandon Convery, Sudbury	7	7	9	16	6
Brandon Convery, Niagara Falls	51	38	39	77	24
Totals	58	45	48	93	30
Corey Crane, Ottawa	6	1	0	1	2
Corey Crane, Sudbury	15	0	0	0	0
Totals	21	1	0	1	2
Derrick Crane, London	16	5	11	16	25
Derrick Crane, Ottawa	16	1	5	6	11
Derrick Crane, Windsor	10	0	0	0	7
Totals	42	6	16	22	43
Mike Dawson, Kingston	11	0	5	5	17
Mike Dawson, Newmarket	50	6	22	28	83
Totals	61	6	27	33	100
Gord Dickie, Owen Sound	11	1	3	4	7
Gord Dickie, Belleville	15	2	4	6	5
Totals	26	3	7	10	12
Darren Dougan, Niagara Falls	21	6	13	19	12
Darren Dougan, Owen Sound	28	7	21	28	10
Totals	49	13	34	47	22
Rob Dykeman (g), Newmarket	23	0	1	1	10
Rob Dykeman (g), Ottawa	25	0	1	1	11
Totals	48	0	2	2	21
Sean Gagnon, Sudbury	6	1	1	2	16
Sean Gagnon, Ottawa	33	2	10	12	68
Sean Gagnon, Sault Ste. Marie	24	1	5	6	65
Totals	63	4	16	20	149
Richard Gallace (g), Bel.	3	0	0	0	0
Richard Gallace (g), New.	17	0	1	1	2
Totals	20	0	1	1	2
Wade Gibson, North Bay	17	3	4	7	35
Wade Gibson, Sault Ste. Marie	48	13	24	37	97
Totals	65	16	28	44	132
Bob Harrison (g), S. Ste. Marie	6	0	0	0	2
Bob Harrison (g), North Bay	4	0	0	0	2
Totals	10	0	0	2	2
Mike Hartwick, Windsor	30	8	10	18	41
Mike Hartwick, Ottawa	31	5	8	13	20
Totals	61	13	18	31	61
Shawn Heins, Peterborough	5	0	0	0	10
Shawn Heins, Windsor	53	7	10	17	107
Totals	58	7	10	17	117
Jason Hughes, Owen Sound	17	0	2	2	21
Jason Hughes, Belleville	17	1	1	2	17
Totals	34	1	3	4	38

	Games	G	A	Pts.	Pen.
Shaun Imber, Sault Ste. Marie	15	0	8	8	6
Shaun Imber, North Bay	47	2	24	26	28
Totals	62	2	32	34	34
Neil Iserhoff, Oshawa	21	0	3	3	8
Neil Iserhoff, North Bay	12	0	0	0	0
Totals	33	0	3	3	8
Craig Johnson (g), Pet.	2	0	0	0	0
Craig Johnson (g), Windsor	12	0	0	0	6
Totals	14	0	0	0	6
Ilpo Kauhanen (g), Newmarket..	2	0	0	0	0
Ilpo Kauhanen (g), London	40	0	1	1	30
Totals	42	0	1	1	30
Brian Kent (g), Detroit	5	0	0	0	7
Brian Kent (g), Oshawa	7	0	0	0	0
Totals	12	0	0	0	7
Jeff Kostuch, Belleville	29	7	13	20	10
Jeff Kostuch, Owen Sound	43	16	22	38	8
Totals	72	23	35	58	18
David Lylyk, Sault Ste. Marie	8	0	1	1	0
David Lylyk, North Bay	45	3	11	14	22
Totals	53	3	12	15	22
Grant Marshall, Ottawa	30	14	28	42	83
Grant Marshall, Newmarket	31	12	25	37	85
Totals	61	26	53	79	168
Rick Marshall, Belleville............	1	0	1	1	0
Rick Marshall, Windsor	25	0	9	9	30
Rick Marshall, Kitchener	30	0	0	0	20
Totals	56	0	10	10	50
Dennis Maxwell, Niagara Falls...	12	5	9	14	21
Dennis Maxwell, Sudbury	52	15	24	39	114
Totals	64	20	33	53	135
Tony McCabe, Detroit	36	9	17	26	22
Tony McCabe, Guelph	28	14	14	28	4
Totals	64	23	31	54	26
Shayne McCosh, Kitchener........	32	7	25	32	43
Shayne McCosh, Windsor	36	5	35	40	38
Totals	68	12	60	72	81
Jason Meloche, Newmarket........	33	4	7	11	108
Jason Meloche, Ottawa	10	1	1	2	17
Totals	43	5	8	13	125
Lucas Miller, North Bay	24	1	5	6	0
Lucas Miller, Oshawa	25	2	5	7	6
Totals	49	3	10	13	6
Aaron Morrison, Windsor	6	1	5	6	15
Aaron Morrison, North Bay	42	8	26	34	57
Totals	48	9	31	40	72
Fredrik Oduya, Guelph	23	2	4	6	29
Fredrik Oduya, Ottawa	17	0	3	3	70
Totals	40	2	7	9	99
Sam Oliveira, Belleville............	5	0	2	2	0
Sam Oliveira, Detroit	5	0	0	0	0
Totals	10	0	2	2	0
Jeff Pawluk, Guelph	38	3	20	23	33
Jeff Pawluk, Belleville	24	4	9	13	20
Totals	62	7	29	36	53
Chad Penney, North Bay	18	8	7	15	19
Chad Penney, Sault Ste. Marie ..	48	29	44	73	67
Totals	66	37	51	88	86
Brent Pope, Guelph	33	10	14	24	40
Brent Pope, Ottawa	26	5	8	13	18
Totals	59	15	22	37	58
Mike Prokopec, Newmarket........	40	6	14	20	70
Mike Prokopec, Guelph	29	10	14	24	27
Totals	69	16	28	44	97
Richard Raymond, Newmarket.....	9	1	3	4	13
Richard Raymond, Kingston	43	7	26	33	39
Totals	52	8	29	37	52
Jud Richards, Sault Ste. Marie	6	0	0	0	2
Jud Richards, North Bay	9	0	0	0	0
Jud Richards, Oshawa	13	0	1	1	7
Totals	28	0	1	1	9
Marc Robillard, Kitchener	30	4	7	11	9
Marc Robillard, Windsor	36	2	12	14	6
Totals	66	6	19	25	15
Paul Rushforth, North Bay........	21	4	10	14	24
Paul Rushforth, Belleville..........	36	21	19	40	38
Totals	57	25	29	54	62

	Games	G	A	Pts.	Pen.
Joel Sandie, Sudbury................	20	1	0	1	41
Joel Sandie, London	29	0	4	4	24
Totals	49	1	4	5	65
Greg Scott (g), Niagara Falls.....	16	0	0	0	4
Greg Scott (g), Kitchener	20	0	0	0	8
Totals	36	0	0	0	12
Gerry Skrypec, Ottawa	20	1	3	4	20
Gerry Skrypec, Newmarket	19	1	6	7	24
Totals	39	2	9	11	44
Kelvin Solari, Guelph	21	3	7	10	72
Kelvin Solari, Peterborough	34	0	5	5	42
Totals	55	3	12	15	114
Brian Stagg, Kingston	20	4	5	9	17
Brian Stagg, Belleville	9	1	0	1	2
Brian Stagg, North Bay	42	16	13	29	27
Totals	71	21	18	39	46
Steve Staios, Niagara Falls........	12	4	14	18	30
Steve Staios, Sudbury	53	13	44	57	67
Totals	65	17	58	75	97
Alek Stojanov, Guelph	35	27	28	55	11
Alek Stojanov, Newmarket..........	14	9	7	16	21
Totals	49	36	35	71	79
Dave Szabo, North Bay	4	0	0	0	12
Dave Szabo, Kitchener	5	0	1	1	4
Totals	9	0	1	1	16
Ryan VandenBussche, New.	30	15	12	27	161
Ryan VandenBussche, Guelph..	29	3	14	17	99
Totals	59	18	26	44	260
Kelly Vipond, Peterborough	5	4	2	6	0
Kelly Vipond, Windsor	11	2	6	8	4
Kelly Vipond, Belleville	17	2	3	5	2
Kelly Vipond, Oshawa	32	3	10	13	9
Totals	65	11	21	32	15
Todd Warriner, Windsor	23	13	21	34	29
Todd Warriner, Kitchener	32	19	24	43	35
Totals	55	32	45	77	64
Brent Watson, Guelph	38	8	12	20	32
Brent Watson, Ottawa	24	4	5	9	26
Totals	62	12	17	29	58
Jason Weaver, Oshawa	2	0	0	0	0
Jason Weaver, Belleville	15	8	10	18	28
Jason Weaver, Kingston	45	30	35	65	95
Totals	62	38	45	83	134
Derek Wilkinson (g), Detroit	4	0	1	1	0
Derek Wilkinson (g), Belleville..	59	0	3	3	4
Totals	63	0	4	4	4
Colin Wilson, Peterborough	4	0	2	2	0
Colin Wilson, Windsor	52	19	22	41	35
Totals	56	21	22	43	35

GOALTENDING

	Games	Min.	Goals	SO	Avg.
Rob Dykeman, New. ..	23	1256	97(1)	1	4.63
Rob Dykeman, Ottawa	25	1422	95(2)	1	4.01
Totals....................	48	2678	182(3)	2	4.08
Richard Gallace, Bel.	3	68	11	0	9.71
Richard Gallace, New.	17	921	65(2)	0	4.23
Totals....................	20	989	76(2)	0	4.61
Bob Harrison, S.S.M.	6	302	20	0	3.97
Bob Harrison, N.B......	4	221	18	0	4.89
Totals....................	10	523	38	0	4.36
Craig Johnson, Pet. ...	2	120	6	0	3.00
Craig Johnson, Wind..	12	524	57	0	6.53
Totals....................	14	644	63	0	5.87
Ilpo Kauhanen, New. ..	2	120	14(1)	0	7.00
Ilpo Kauhanen, Lon...	40	2210	155(4)	1	4.21
Totals....................	42	2330	169(5)	1	4.35
Brian Kent, Detroit	5	272	24	0	5.29
Brian Kent, Oshawa...	7	257	20	1	4.67
Totals....................	12	529	44	1	4.99
Greg Scott, N.F.	16	876	64(1)	0	4.38
Greg Scott, Kitchener.	20	1014	73(1)	0	4.32
Totals....................	36	1890	137(2)	0	4.35
Derek Wilkinson, Det..	4	245	18	0	4.41
Derek Wilkinson, Bel..	59	3370	237(5)	0	4.22
Totals....................	63	3615	255(5)	0	4.23

OHL

MAJOR JUNIOR LEAGUES

SUPER SERIES

Series "A"

	W	L	Pts.	GF	GA
Sault Ste. Marie	4	0	8	18	10
Peterborough	0	4	0	10	18

(Sault Ste Marie won series, 4-0)

NOTE: The Super Series is played to determine the home-ice advantage during Memorial Cup play. Super Series participants receive quarterfinal-round byes during the playoffs.

LEYDEN DIVISION
QUARTERFINALS

Series "B"

	W	L	Pts.	GF	GA
Kingston	4	1	8	21	14
North Bay	1	4	2	14	21

(Kingston won series, 4-1)

Series "C"

	W	L	Pts.	GF	GA
Oshawa	4	3	8	30	27
Belleville	3	4	6	27	30

(Oshawa won series, 4-3)

Series "D"

	W	L	Pts.	GF	GA
Sudbury	4	3	8	24	33
Newmarket	3	4	6	33	24

(Sudbury won series, 4-3)

SEMIFINALS

Series "E"

	W	L	Pts.	GF	GA
Peterborough	4	3	8	35	26
Sudbury	3	4	6	26	35

(Peterborough won series, 4-3)

Series "F"

	W	L	Pts.	GF	GA
Kingston	4	2	8	29	20
Oshawa	2	4	4	20	29

(Kingston won series, 4-2)

FINALS

Series "G"

	W	L	Pts.	GF	GA
Peterborough	4	1	8	33	23
Kingston	1	4	2	23	33

(Peterborough won series, 4-1)

EMMS DIVISION
QUARTERFINALS

Series "B"

	W	L	Pts.	GF	GA
Detroit	4	1	8	21	16
Guelph	1	4	2	16	21

(Detroit won series, 4-1)

Series "C"

	W	L	Pts.	GF	GA
London	4	3	8	31	31
Kitchener	3	4	6	31	31

(London won series, 4-3)

Series "D"

	W	L	Pts.	GF	GA
Owen Sound	4	0	8	21	11
Niagara Falls	0	4	0	11	21

(Owen Sound won series, 4-0)

SEMIFINALS

Series "E"

	W	L	Pts.	GF	GA
Sault Ste. Marie	4	0	8	29	9
Owen Sound	0	4	0	9	29

(Sault Ste. Marie won series, 4-0)

Series "F"

	W	L	Pts.	GF	GA
Detroit	4	1	8	20	14
London	1	4	2	14	20

(Detroit won series, 4-1)

FINALS

Series "G"

	W	L	Pts.	GF	GA
Sault Ste. Marie	4	1	8	21	12
Detroit	1	4	2	12	21

(Sault Ste. Marie won series, 4-1)

J. ROSS ROBERTSON CUP FINALS

Series "H"

	W	L	Pts.	GF	GA
Peterborough	4	1	8	24	16
Sault Ste. Marie	1	4	2	16	24

(Peterborough won series, 4-1)

INDIVIDUAL LEADERS

Goals: Jarret Reid, Sault Ste. Marie (19)
Assists: Jason Dawe, Peterborough (33)
Points: Jason Dawe, Peterborough (51)
Penalty minutes: David Ling, Kingston (72)
Goaltending average: Kevin Hodson, Sault Ste. Marie (2.68)
Shutouts: Fred Braithwaite, Detroit (1)
Richard Gallace, Newmarket (1)
Marc Lamothe, Kingston (1)
Chad Lang, Peterborough (1)

TOP SCORERS

	Games	G	A	Pts.
Jason Dawe, Peterborough	21	18	33	51
Chris Pronger, Peterborough	21	15	25	40
Mike Harding, Peterborough	21	15	24	39
Jarrett Reid, Sault Ste. Marie	18	19	16	35
Brent Tully, Peterborough	21	8	24	32
Dave Roche, Peterborough	21	14	15	29
Chris Gratton, Kingston	16	11	18	29
Keli Corpse, Kingston	16	9	20	29
Kevin Brown, Detroit	15	10	18	28
Ralph Intranuovo, Sault Ste. Marie	18	10	16	26
Jamie Rivers, Sudbury	14	7	19	26

INDIVIDUAL STATISTICS

BELLEVILLE BULLS

(Lost Leyden Division quarterfinals to Oshawa, 4-3)

SCORING

	Games	G	A	Pts.	Pen.
Mark Donahue	7	7	9	16	13
Justin Morrison	7	3	11	14	11
Chris Skoryna	7	4	9	13	2
Paul Rushforth	7	7	2	9	4
Marc Dupuis	7	0	5	5	6
Kyle Blacklock	7	1	3	4	0
Paul McCallion	7	2	1	3	8
Chris Clancy	7	0	3	3	8
Dan Preston	7	0	3	3	0
Brian Secord	7	2	0	2	11
Jeff Pawluk	7	1	1	2	2
Doug Doull	7	0	2	2	17
Reuben Castella	6	0	1	1	9
Steve Carter	7	0	1	1	6
Daniel Godbout	7	0	1	1	8
Scott Hay (goalie)	1	0	0	0	0
Jason Hughes	3	0	0	0	0
Richard Park	5	0	0	0	14
Corey Isen	7	0	0	0	20
Ian Keiller	7	0	0	0	11
Derek Wilkinson (goalie)	7	0	0	0	0

GOALTENDING

	Games	Min.	Goals	SO	Avg.
Derek Wilkinson	7	434	29	0	4.01
Scott Hay	1	3	1	0	20.00

DETROIT JR. RED WINGS

(Lost Emms Division finals to Sault Ste. Marie, 4-1)

SCORING

	Games	G	A	Pts.	Pen.
Kevin Brown	15	10	18	28	18
Todd Harvey	15	9	12	21	39
Blair Scott	15	3	14	17	27
Bob Wren	15	4	11	15	20
Chris Varga	15	6	3	9	8
Darren Hurley	13	4	4	8	36
Jamie Allison	15	2	5	7	23
Pat Barton	15	2	5	7	17
Jeff Mitchell	15	3	3	6	16
Bill McCauley	15	1	4	5	6
J.D. Eaton	14	2	2	4	28
Pat Peake	2	1	3	4	2
Mike Rucinski	15	0	4	4	12
Eric Cairns	15	0	3	3	24
Richard Ujvary	12	2	0	2	6
John Pinches	12	1	1	2	6
Kevin Paden	15	1	1	2	2
Chris Gignac	8	1	0	1	2
Fred Brathwaite (goalie)	15	1	0	1	2

	Games	G	A	Pts.	Pen.
Steve Allen	2	0	0	0	0
Jason Saal (goalie)	3	0	0	0	0
Joe Harris	12	0	0	0	0
Rob Boyko	13	0	0	0	0

GOALTENDING

	Games	Min.	Goals	SO	Avg.
Jason Saal	3	42	2	0	2.86
Fred Brathwaite	15	858	48(1)	1	3.36

GUELPH STORM

(Lost Emms Division quarterfinals to Detroit, 4-1)

SCORING

	Games	G	A	Pts.	Pen.
Jeff Bes	5	3	5	8	4
Jean-Paul Davis	5	2	3	5	8
Sylvain Cloutier	5	0	5	5	14
Todd Bertuzzi	5	2	2	4	6
Jeff O'Neill	5	2	2	4	6
Ryan VandenBussche	5	1	3	4	13
Wade Whitten	5	1	3	4	4
Ken Belanger	5	2	1	3	16
Tony McCabe	5	1	1	2	2
Aaron Downey	5	1	0	1	0
Mike Prokopec	5	1	0	1	14
Rumun Ndur	4	0	1	1	4
Stephane Lefebvre	5	0	1	1	0
Mike Rusk	5	0	1	1	8
Regan Stocco	5	0	1	1	6
Chris McMurtry	1	0	0	0	2
Duane Harmer	5	0	0	0	2
Steve Pottie (goalie)	5	0	0	0	0
Grant Pritchett	5	0	0	0	2
Gord Walsh	5	0	0	0	2

GOALTENDING

	Games	Min.	Goals	SO	Avg.
Steve Pottie	5	300	19(2)	0	3.80

KINGSTON FRONTENACS

(Lost Leyden Division finals to Peterborough, 4-1)

SCORING

	Games	G	A	Pts.	Pen.
Chris Gratton	16	11	18	29	42
Keli Corpse	16	9	20	29	10
Steve Parson	16	11	11	22	18
Cory Johnson	16	10	10	20	11
Greg Clancy	16	4	12	16	16
Jason Weaver	14	7	8	15	27
David Ling	16	3	12	15	72
Craig Rivet	16	5	7	12	39
Trent Cull	16	2	8	10	37
Joel Yates	16	4	3	7	28

	Games	G	A	Pts.	Pen.
Bill Robinson	16	1	5	6	20
Trevor Doyle	16	2	3	5	23
Greg Kraemer	16	2	2	4	22
Bill Maranduik	15	1	3	4	8
Richard Raymond	8	0	4	4	0
Jason Wadel	16	1	1	2	2
Tyler Moss (goalie)	6	0	1	1	6
Brian Sambirsky	8	0	1	1	7
Jason Disher	14	0	1	1	18
Chris Gowan	6	0	0	0	20
Duncan Fader	14	0	0	0	2
Marc Lamothe (goalie)	15	0	0	0	4

GOALTENDING

	Games	Min.	Goals	SO	Avg.
Marc Lamothe	15	733	46(1)	1	3.77
Tyler Moss	6	228	19(1)	0	5.00

KITCHENER RANGERS

(Lost Emms Division quarterfinals to London, 4-3)

SCORING

	Games	G	A	Pts.	Pen.
Todd Warriner	7	5	14	19	14
Trevor Gallant	7	4	10	14	4
Jason Gladney	7	2	11	13	14
Tim Spitzig	7	5	4	9	14
Chris Phelps	7	3	5	8	16
Derek Gauthier	7	4	2	6	14
Mike Polano	7	2	3	5	29
Norm Dezainde	7	3	1	4	4
Gairin Smith	7	2	1	3	20
Wes Swinson	6	0	2	2	14
Jason Johnson	7	1	0	1	9
Eric Manlow	4	0	1	1	2
Peter Brearley	7	0	1	1	9
Joe Coombs	7	0	1	1	0
Ryan Pawluk	7	0	1	1	0
C.J. Denomme (goalie)	2	0	0	0	0
Rick Marshall	4	0	0	0	6
Mark Cardiff	6	0	0	0	11
Justin Cullen	7	0	0	0	4
Greg McLean	7	0	0	0	0
Greg Scott (goalie)	7	0	0	0	6

GOALTENDING

	Games	Min.	Goals	SO	Avg.
Greg Scott	7	376	24	0	3.83
C.J. Denomme	2	65	7	0	6.46

LONDON KNIGHTS

(Lost Emms Division semifinals to Detroit, 4-1)

SCORING

	Games	G	A	Pts.	Pen.
Jason Allison	12	7	13	20	8
Yvan Corbin	12	11	8	19	12
Dave Gilmore	12	9	9	18	10
Brad Smyth	12	7	8	15	25
Nick Stajduhar	12	4	11	15	10
Scott McKay	12	1	14	15	6
Mark Visheau	12	0	5	5	26
Chris Zanutto	12	2	2	4	14
Troy Sweet	12	1	3	4	17
Gord Ross	12	1	2	3	40
Brodie Coffin	12	2	0	2	17
Don Margettie	12	0	2	2	2
Brian Stacey	6	0	1	1	8
Chris Brassard	8	0	1	1	0
Brent Holdsworth	9	0	1	1	0
Cory Evans	11	0	1	1	18
Daryl Rivers	12	0	1	1	8
Chris Lizotte	1	0	0	0	0
John Guirestante	4	0	0	0	0
Brett Marietti	4	0	0	0	6
Robert Frid	5	0	0	0	2

	Games	G	A	Pts.	Pen.
Ilpo Kauhanen (goalie)	7	0	0	0	0
Jordan Willis (goalie)	7	0	0	0	4
Joel Sandie	12	0	0	0	9

GOALTENDING

	Games	Min.	Goals	SO	Avg.
Jordan Willis	7	355	19(1)	0	3.21
Ilpo Kauhanen	7	386	29(2)	0	4.51

NEWMARKET ROYALS

(Lost Leyden Division quarterfinals to Sudbury, 4-3)

SCORING

	Games	G	A	Pts.	Pen.
Jeff Reid	7	4	10	14	16
Mark DeSantis	7	3	11	14	14
Grant Marshall	7	4	7	11	20
Nathan LaFayette	7	4	6	10	19
Shayne Gaffar	7	4	4	8	0
Jeremy Stevenson	5	5	1	6	28
Larry Courville	7	0	6	6	14
Matt Hogan	7	4	0	4	6
Alek Stojanov	7	1	3	4	26
Alain Letang	6	0	3	3	2
Jason Bonsignore	7	0	3	3	0
Mike Dawson	7	1	1	2	14
Todd Walker	7	1	1	2	0
Derek Grant	7	0	2	2	2
Dave Lemay	7	1	0	1	18
Gerry Skrypec	7	1	0	1	20
Rob Massa	5	0	1	1	2
Corey Bricknell	1	0	0	0	2
Paul Andrea	4	0	0	0	0
Richard Gallace (goalie)	5	0	0	0	0
Todd Laurin (goalie)	5	0	0	0	2
Adrian Murray	7	0	0	0	0

GOALTENDING

	Games	Min.	Goals	SO	Avg.
Richard Gallace	5	219	7	1	1.92
Todd Laurin	5	216	16(1)	0	4.44

NIAGARA FALLS THUNDER

(Lost Emms Division quarterfinals to Owen Sound, 4-0)

SCORING

	Games	G	A	Pts.	Pen.
Todd Wetzel	4	4	4	8	2
Kevin Brown	4	3	2	5	2
Brandon Convery	4	1	3	4	4
Dale Junkin	4	1	3	4	0
Ethan Moreau	4	0	3	3	4
Jason Clarke	4	0	2	2	21
Bogdan Savenko	2	1	0	1	2
Neil Fewster	4	1	0	1	10
Scott Campbell	4	0	1	1	4
Greg DeVries	4	0	1	1	6
Mike Majewski	2	0	0	0	0
Derek Sylvester	2	0	0	0	4
Kelly Wayling	2	0	0	0	0
Chris Baxter	4	0	0	0	0
Wyatt Buckland	4	0	0	0	0
Jeff Johnstone	4	0	0	0	2
Manny Legace (goalie)	4	0	0	0	2
Dustin McArthur	4	0	0	0	0
Paul McInnes	4	0	0	0	0
Tim Thompson	4	0	0	0	0
Ryan Tocher	4	0	0	0	4

GOALTENDING

	Games	Min.	Goals	SO	Avg.
Manny Legace	4	240	18(3)	0	4.50

NORTH BAY CENTENNIALS

(Lost Leyden Division quarterfinals to Kingston, 4-1)

SCORING

	Games	G	A	Pts.	Pen.
Bill Lang	5	4	3	7	9
Mike Burman	5	1	3	4	2
Stefan Rivard	5	1	3	4	28
Paul Doherty	5	2	1	3	13
Jeff Shevalier	2	1	2	3	4
Jeff Andrews	5	1	2	3	6
Robert Thorpe	5	1	2	3	9
Jason Campeau	5	0	3	3	8
Brian Stagg	5	2	0	2	0
Brad Brown	2	0	2	2	13
Shaun Imber	5	0	2	2	2
Jim Ensom	5	1	0	1	7
Brent Dube	1	0	0	0	0
Brent Rowley	1	0	0	0	0
Rob Stark	2	0	0	0	0
Ron Bertrand (goalie)	3	0	0	0	2
Sandy Allan (goalie)	4	0	0	0	0
Dennis Bonvie	5	0	0	0	34
Mark Brooks	5	0	0	0	0
Ryan Gillis	5	0	0	0	0
Carl Halverson	5	0	0	0	5
Derek Lahnalampi	5	0	0	0	2
David Lylyk	5	0	0	0	4

GOALTENDING

	Games	Min.	Goals	SO	Avg.
Sandy Allan	4	180	10(1)	0	3.33
Ron Bertrand	3	120	10	0	5.00

OSHAWA GENERALS

(Lost Leyden Division semifinals to Kingston, 4-2)

SCORING

	Games	G	A	Pts.	Pen.
Scott Hollis	13	8	15	23	22
B.J. MacPherson	13	7	14	21	30
Jason Arnott	13	9	9	18	20
Darryl Lafrance	13	8	8	16	0
Trevor Burgess	13	5	8	13	13
Sean Brown	10	2	4	6	4
Stephane Yelle	13	0	5	5	58
Rob McQuat	13	1	3	4	27
Todd Bradley	13	2	1	3	18
Joe Cook	13	1	2	3	22
Jason McQuat	12	0	3	3	9
Wade Simpson	13	0	3	3	20
Chris Hall	13	0	2	2	12
Kelly Vipond	13	1	0	1	19
Stephane Soulliere	11	0	1	1	2
Billy-Jay Johnston	11	0	1	1	2
Ken Shepard (goalie)	12	0	1	1	12
Kevin Spero	0	0	0	0	0
Brian Kent (goalie)	1	0	0	0	0
Kevin Vaughan	2	0	0	0	0
Lucas Miller	4	0	0	0	6
Serge Dunphy	7	0	0	0	2
Joel Gagnon (goalie)	13	0	0	0	16
Jason Julian					

GOALTENDING

	Games	Min.	Goals	SO	Avg.
Ken Shepard	11	512	34(1)	0	3.98
Joel Gagnon	7	285	21	0	4.42

OWEN SOUND PLATERS

(Lost Emms Division semifinals to Sault Ste. Marie, 4-0)

SCORING

	Games	G	A	Pts.	Pen.
Andrew Brunette	8	8	6	14	16
Jason MacDonald	8	6	5	11	28
Jim Brown	8	1	10	11	18
Marian Kacir	8	3	5	8	4
Darren Dougan	6	1	6	7	8

	Games	G	A	Pts.	Pen.
Scott Walker	8	1	5	6	16
Luigi Calce	8	2	3	5	16
Wayne Primeau	8	1	4	5	0
Jeff Kostuch	8	2	2	4	6
Shayne Wright	8	2	0	2	5
Rick Morton	8	1	1	2	20
Willie Skilliter	8	1	1	2	6
David Benn	8	1	0	1	32
Craig Binns	7	0	1	1	2
Brian Medeiros	7	0	1	1	0
Jeff Smith	7	0	1	1	6
Shawn Krueger	8	0	1	1	2
Kevin Weekes (goalie)	1	0	0	0	0
Rob Schweyer	5	0	0	0	0
Jamie Storr (goalie)	8	0	0	0	0
Mark Vilneff	8	0	0	0	2

GOALTENDING

	Games	Min.	Goals	SO	Avg.
Jamie Storr	8	454	35	0	4.63
Kevin Weekes	1	26	5	0	11.54

PETERBOROUGH PETES

(Winner of 1993 J. Ross Robertson Cup playoffs)

SCORING

	Games	G	A	Pts.	Pen.
Jason Dawe	21	18	33	51	18
Chris Pronger	21	15	25	40	51
Mike Harding	21	15	24	39	30
Brent Tully	21	8	24	32	32
Dave Roche	21	14	15	29	42
Dale McTavish	21	9	8	17	22
Ryan Black	20	7	4	11	28
Cory Stillman	18	3	8	11	18
Steve Hogg	16	5	3	8	2
Geordie Kinnear	19	1	5	6	43
Chad Grills	21	1	5	6	26
Rick Emmett	21	1	3	4	4
Bill Weir	21	2	1	3	20
Matt St. Germain	21	1	2	3	17
Jeff Walker	20	0	3	3	14
Matt Johnson	16	1	1	2	54
Doug Searle	21	1	1	2	25
Darryl Moxam	14	0	1	1	11
Chad Lang (goalie)	21	0	1	1	7
Kelvin Solari	21	0	1	1	19
Ryan Nauss	1	0	0	0	0
Ryan Douglas (goalie)	2	0	0	0	2
Quade Lightbody	2	0	0	0	0

GOALTENDING

	Games	Min.	Goals	SO	Avg.
Chad Lang	21	1224	74	1	3.63
Ryan Douglas	2	50	9	0	10.8

SAULT STE. MARIE GREYHOUNDS

(Lost J. Ross Robertson Cup finals to Peterborough, 4-1)

SCORING

	Games	G	A	Pts.	Pen.
Jarret Reid	18	19	16	35	20
Ralph Intranuovo	18	10	16	26	30
David Matsos	18	9	8	17	16
Chad Penney	18	7	10	17	18
Tom MacDonald	18	5	10	15	62
Aaron Gavey	18	5	9	14	36
Rick Kowalsky	18	7	6	13	35
Steve Sullivan	16	3	8	11	18
Wade Gibson	18	1	9	10	41
Drew Bannister	18	2	7	9	12
Jeff Toms	16	4	4	8	7
Gary Roach	18	0	8	8	4
Brad Baber	17	4	2	6	29
Briane Thompson	18	0	6	6	37

	Games	G	A	Pts.	Pen.
Mark Matier	18	1	4	5	11
Perry Pappas	18	4	0	4	10
Sean Gagnon	15	2	2	4	25
Kevin Hodson (goalie)	14	0	2	2	6
Joe VanVolsen	3	1	0	1	0
Dan Tanevski (goalie)	4	0	1	1	0
Kiley Hill	1	0	0	0	2
Neal Martin	2	0	0	0	2
Oliver Pastinsky	2	0	0	0	2
Dan Cloutier (goalie)	4	0	0	0	0
Jodi Murphy	18	0	0	0	16

GOALTENDING

	Games	Min.	Goals	SO	Avg.
Kevin Hodson	14	760	34(1)	0	2.68
Dan Cloutier	4	231	12(2)	0	3.12
Dan Tanevski	4	102	6	0	3.53

SUDBURY WOLVES

(Lost Leyden Division semifinals to Peterborough, 4-3)

SCORING

	Games	G	A	Pts.	Pen.
Jamie Rivers	14	7	19	26	4
Jamie Matthews	14	7	17	24	22

	Games	G	A	Pts.	Pen.
Derek Armstrong	14	9	10	19	26
Rod Hinks	14	7	10	17	30
Steve Staios	11	5	6	11	22
Barrie Moore	14	4	3	7	19
Steve Potvin	14	4	3	7	11
Dennis Maxwell	14	3	4	7	42
Bernie John	13	0	6	6	5
Ryan Shanahan	14	2	2	4	12
Jamie Caruso	4	1	2	3	0
Joel Poirier	14	0	3	3	8
Mike Wilson	14	1	1	2	21
Dominic Belanger	6	0	1	1	9
Bob MacIsaac	12	0	1	1	31
Greg Dreveny (goalie)	14	0	1	1	19
Chris Grenville	2	0	0	0	0
Shawn Silver (goalie)	3	0	0	0	0
Mike Yeo	3	0	0	0	5
Matt Kiereck	9	0	0	0	12
Rick Bodkin	11	0	0	0	0
Gary Coupal	13	0	0	0	50
Rory Fitzpatrick	14	0	0	0	17
Kayle Short	14	0	0	0	26

GOALTENDING

	Games	Min.	Goals	SO	Avg.
Greg Dreveny	14	769	58(2)	0	4.53
Shawn Silver	3	86	8	0	5.58

1992-93 AWARD WINNERS

ALL-STAR TEAMS

First team	Pos.	Second team
Manny Legace, N.F.	G	Chad Lang, Peterborough
Chris Pronger, Peterborough	D	Brent Tully, Peterborough
Mark DeSantis, Newmarket	D	Scott Walker, Owen Sound
Andrew Brunette, O.S.	LW	Bob Wren, Detroit
Pat Peake, Detroit	C	Mike Harding, Peterborough
Jason Dawe, Peterborough	RW	Kevin Brown, Bel.-Det.

Coach of the Year: Gary Agnew, London

TROPHY WINNERS

Red Tilson Trophy: Pat Peake, Detroit
Eddie Powers Memorial Trophy: Andrew Brunette, Owen Sound
Dave Pinkney Trophy: Chad Lang, Peterborough
   Ryan Douglas, Peterborough
Max Kaminsky Trophy: Chris Pronger, Peterborough
William Hanley Trophy: Pat Peake, Detroit
Emms Family Award: Jeff O'Neill, Guelph
Matt Leyden Trophy: Gary Agnew, London
Jim Mahon Memorial Trophy: Kevin Brown, Belleville-Detroit
F.W. Dinty Moore Trophy: Ken Shepard, Oshawa
Leo Lalonde Memorial Trophy: Scott Hollis, Oshawa
Hamilton Spectator Trophy: Peterborough Petes
J. Ross Robertson Cup: Peterborough Petes

ALL-TIME AWARD WINNERS

RED TILSON TROPHY

(Outstanding player)

Season	Player, Team
1944-45	Doug McMurdy, St. Catharines
1945-46	Tod Sloan, St. Michael's
1946-47	Ed Sanford, St. Michael's
1947-48	George Armstrong, Stratford
1948-49	Gil Mayer, Barrie
1949-50	George Armstrong, Marlboros
1950-51	Glenn Hall, Windsor
1951-52	Bill Harrington, Kitchener
1952-53	Bob Attersley, Oshawa
1953-54	Brian Cullen, St. Catharines
1954-55	Hank Ciesla, St. Catharines
1955-56	Ron Howell, Guelph
1956-57	Frank Mahovlich, St. Michael's
1957-58	Murray Oliver, Hamilton
1958-59	Stan Mikita, St. Catharines
1959-60	Wayne Connelly, Peterborough
1960-61	Rod Gilbert, Guelph
1961-62	Pit Martin, Hamilton
1962-63	Wayne Maxner, Niagara Falls
1963-64	Yvan Cournoyer, Montreal
1964-65	Andre Lacroix, Peterborough
1965-66	Andre Lacroix, Peterborough

Season	Player, Team
1966-67	Mickey Redmond, Peterborough
1967-68	Walt Tkaczuk, Kitchener
1968-69	Rejean Houle, Montreal
1969-70	Gilbert Perreault, Montreal
1970-71	Dave Gardner, Marlboros
1971-72	Don Lever, Niagara Falls
1972-73	Rick Middleton, Oshawa
1973-74	Jack Valiquette, Sault Ste. Marie
1974-75	Dennis Maruk, London
1975-76	Peter Lee, Ottawa
1976-77	Dale McCourt, St. Catharines
1977-78	Bobby Smith, Ottawa
1978-79	Mike Foligno, Sudbury
1979-80	Jim Fox, Ottawa
1980-81	Ernie Godden, Windsor
1981-82	Dave Simpson, London
1982-83	Doug Gilmour, Cornwall
1983-84	John Tucker, Kitchener
1984-85	Wayne Groulx, Sault Ste. Marie
1985-86	Ray Sheppard, Cornwall
1986-87	Scott McCrory, Oshawa
1987-88	Andrew Cassels, Ottawa
1988-89	Bryan Fogarty, Niagara Falls
1989-90	Mike Ricci, Peterborough
1990-91	Eric Lindros, Oshawa

Season	Player, Team
1991-92	Todd Simon, Niagara Falls
1992-93	Pat Peake, Detroit

EDDIE POWERS MEMORIAL TROPHY

(Scoring champion)

Season	Player, Team
1933-34	J. Groboski, Oshawa
1934-35	J. Good, Toronto Lions
1935-36	John O'Flaherty, West Toronto
1936-37	Billy Taylor, Oshawa
1937-38	Hank Goldup, Tor. Marlboros
1938-39	Billy Taylor, Oshawa
1939-40	Jud McAtee, Oshawa
1940-41	Gaye Stewart, Tor. Marlboros
1941-42	Bob Wiest, Brantford
1942-43	Norman "Red" Tilson, Oshawa
1943-44	Ken Smith, Oshawa
1944-45	Leo Gravelle, St. Michael's
1945-46	Tod Sloan, St. Michael's
1946-47	Fleming Mackell, St. Michael's
1947-48	George Armstrong, Stratford
1948-49	Bert Giesebrecht, Windsor
1949-50	Earl Reibel, Windsor
1950-51	Lou Jankowski, Oshawa
1951-52	Ken Laufman, Guelph
1952-53	Jim McBurney, Galt
1953-54	Brian Cullen, St. Catharines
1954-55	Hank Ciesla, St. Catharines
1955-56	Stan Baliuk, Kitchener
1956-57	Bill Sweeney, Guelph
1957-58	John McKenzie, St. Catharines
1958-59	Stan Mikita, St. Catharines
1959-60	Chico Maki, St. Catharines
1960-61	Rod Gilbert, Guelph
1961-62	Andre Boudrias, Montreal
1962-63	Wayne Maxner, Niagara Falls
1963-64	Andre Boudrias, Montreal
1964-65	Ken Hodge, St. Catharines
1965-66	Andre Lacroix, Peterborough
1966-67	Derek Sanderson, Niagara Falls
1967-68	Tom Webster, Niagara Falls
1968-69	Rejean Houle, Montreal
1969-70	Marcel Dionne, St. Catharines
1970-71	Marcel Dionne, St. Catharines
1971-72	Bill Harris, Toronto
1972-73	Blake Dunlop, Ottawa
1973-74	Jack Valiquette, Sault Ste. Marie
	Rick Adduono, St. Catharines
1974-75	Bruce Boudreau, Toronto
1975-76	Mike Kaszycki, Sault Ste. Marie
1976-77	Dwight Foster, Kitchener
1977-78	Bobby Smith, Ottawa
1978-79	Mike Foligno, Sudbury
1979-80	Jim Fox, Ottawa
1980-81	John Goodwin, Sault Ste. Marie
1981-82	Dave Simpson, London
1982-83	Doug Gilmour, Cornwall
1983-84	Tim Salmon, Kingston
1984-85	Dave MacLean, Belleville
1985-86	Ray Sheppard, Cornwall
1986-87	Scott McCrory, Oshawa
1987-88	Andrew Cassels, Ottawa
1988-89	Bryan Fogarty, Niagara Falls
1989-90	Keith Primeau, Niagara Falls
1990-91	Eric Lindros, Oshawa
1991-92	Todd Simon, Niagara Falls
1992-93	Andrew Brunette, Owen Sound

DAVE PINKNEY TROPHY

(Top team goaltending)

Season	Player, Team
1948-49	Gil Mayer, Barrie
1949-50	Don Lockhart, Marlboros

Season	Player, Team
1950-51	Don Lockhart, Marlboros
	Lorne Howes, Barrie
1951-52	Don Head, Marlboros
1952-53	John Henderson, Marlboros
1953-54	Dennis Riggin, Hamilton
1954-55	John Albani, Marlboros
1955-56	Jim Crockett, Marlboros
1956-57	Len Broderick, Marlboros
1957-58	Len Broderick, Marlboros
1958-59	Jacques Caron, Peterborough
1959-60	Gerry Cheevers, St. Michael's
1960-61	Bud Blom, Hamilton
1961-62	George Holmes, Montreal
1962-63	Chuck Goddard, Peterborough
1963-64	Bernie Parent, Niagara Falls
1964-65	Bernie Parent, Niagara Falls
1965-66	Ted Quimet, Montreal
1966-67	Peter MacDuffe, St. Catharines
1967-68	Bruce Mullet, Montreal
1968-69	Wayne Wood, Montreal
1969-70	John Garrett, Peterborough
1970-71	John Garrett, Peterborough
1971-72	Michel Larocque, Ottawa
1972-73	Mike Palmateer, Toronto
1973-74	Don Edwards, Kitchener
1974-75	Greg Millen, Peterborough
1975-76	Jim Bedard, Sudbury
1976-77	Pat Riggin, London
1977-78	Al Jensen, Hamilton
1978-79	Nick Ricci, Niagara Falls
1979-80	Rick LaFerriere, Peterborough
1980-81	Jim Ralph, Ottawa
1981-82	Marc D'Amour, Sault Ste. Marie
1982-83	Peter Sidorkiewicz, Oshawa
	Jeff Hogg, Oshawa
1983-84	Darren Pang, Ottawa
	Greg Coram, Ottawa
1984-85	Scott Mosey, Sault Ste. Marie
	Marty Abrams, Sault Ste. Marie
1985-86	Kay Whitmore, Peterborough
	Ron Tugnutt, Peterborough
1986-87	Sean Evoy, Oshawa
	Jeff Hackett, Oshawa
1987-88	Todd Bojcun, Peterborough
	John Tanner, Peterborough
1988-89	Todd Bojcun, Peterborough
	John Tanner, Peterborough
1989-90	Jeff Wilson, Peterborough
	Sean Gauthier, Kingston
1990-91	Kevin Hodson, Sault Ste. Marie
	Mike Lenarduzzi, Sault Ste. Marie
1991-92	Kevin Hodson, Sault Ste. Marie
1991-92	Chad Lang, Peterborough
	Ryan Douglas, Peterborough

MAX KAMINSKY TROPHY

(Outstanding defenseman)

Season	Player, Team
1969-70	Ron Plumb, Peterborough
1970-71	Jocelyn Guevremont, Montreal
1971-72	Denis Potvin, Ottawa
1972-73	Denis Potvin, Ottawa
1973-74	Jim Turkiewicz, Peterborough
1974-75	Mike O'Connell, Kingston
1975-76	Rick Green, London
1976-77	Craig Hartsburg, S. Ste. Marie
1977-78	Brad Marsh, London
	Rob Ramage, London
1978-79	Greg Theberge, Peterborough
1979-80	Larry Murphy, Peterborough
1980-81	Steve Smith, Sault Ste. Marie
1981-82	Ron Meighan, Niagara Falls
1982-83	Allan MacInnis, Kitchener
1983-84	Brad Shaw, Ottawa
1984-85	Bob Halkidis, London

Season	Player, Team
1985-86	Terry Carkner, Peterborough
	Jeff Brown, Sudbury
1986-87	Kerry Huffman, Guelph
1987-88	Darryl Shannon, Windsor
1988-89	Bryan Fogarty, Niagara Falls
1989-90	John Slaney, Cornwall
1990-91	Chris Snell, Ottawa
1991-92	Drake Berehowsky, North Bay
1992-93	Chris Pronger, Peterborough

WILLIAM HANLEY TROPHY

(Most gentlemanly)

Season	Player, Team
1960-61	Bruce Draper, St. Michael's
1961-62	Lowell MacDonald, Hamilton
1962-63	Paul Henderson, Hamilton
1963-64	Fred Stanfield, St. Catharines
1964-65	Jimmy Peters, Hamilton
1965-66	Andre Lacroix, Peterborough
1966-67	Mickey Redmond, Peterborough
1967-68	Tom Webster, Niagara Falls
1968-69	Rejean Houle, Montreal
1969-74	No award presented
1974-75	Doug Jarvis, Peterborough
1975-76	Dale McCourt, Hamilton
1976-77	Dale McCourt, St. Catharines
1977-78	Waynbe Gretzky, S.S. Marie
1978-79	Sean Simpson, Ottawa
1979-80	Sean Simpson, Ottawa
1980-81	John Goodwin, Sault Ste. Marie
1981-82	Dave Simpson, London
1982-83	Kirk Muller, Guelph
1983-84	Kevin Conway, Kingston
1984-85	Scott Tottle, Peterborough
1985-86	Jason Lafreniere, Belleville
1986-87	Scott McCrory, Oshawa
	Keith Gretzky, Hamilton
1987-88	Andrew Cassels, Ottawa
1988-89	Kevin Miehm, Oshawa
1989-90	Mike Ricci, Peterborough
1990-91	Dale Craigwell, Oshawa
1991-92	John Spoltore, North Bay
1992-93	Pat Peake, Detroit

EMMS FAMILY AWARD

(Rookie of the year)

Season	Player, Team
1972-73	Dennis Maruk, London
1973-74	Jack Valiquette, Sault Ste. Marie
1974-75	Danny Shearer, Hamilton
1975-76	John Travella, Sault Ste. Marie
1976-77	Yvan Joly, Ottawa
1977-78	Wayne Gretzky, S.S. Marie
1978-79	John Goodwin, Sault Ste. Marie
1979-80	Bruce Dowie, Toronto
1980-81	Tony Tanti, Oshawa
1981-82	Pat Verbeek, Sudbury
1982-83	Bruce Cassidy, Ottawa
1983-84	Shawn Burr, Kitchener
1984-85	Derek King, Sault Ste. Marie
1985-86	Lonnie Loach, Guelph
1986-87	Andrew Cassels, Ottawa
1987-88	Rick Corriveau, London
1988-89	Owen Nolan, Cornwall
1989-90	Chris Longo, Peterborough
1990-91	Cory Stillman, Windsor
1991-92	Chris Gratton, Kingston
1992-93	Jeff O'Neill, Guelph

MATT LEYDEN TROPHY

(Coach of the year)

Season	Coach, Team
1971-72	Gus Bodnar, Oshawa
1972-73	George Armstrong, Toronto

Season	Player, Team
1973-74	Jack Bownass, Kingston
1974-75	Bert Templeton, Hamilton
1975-76	Jerry Toppazzini, Sudbury
1976-77	Bill Long, London
1977-78	Bill White, Oshawa
1978-79	Gary Green, Peterborough
1979-80	Dave Chambers, Toronto
1980-81	Brian Kilrea, Ottawa
1981-82	Brian Kilrea, Ottawa
1982-83	Terry Crisp, Sault Ste. Marie
1983-84	Tom Barrett, Kitchener
1984-85	Terry Crisp, Sault Ste. Marie
1985-86	Jacques Martin, Guelph
1986-87	Paul Theriault, Oshawa
1987-88	Dick Todd, Peterborough
1988-89	Joe McDonnell, Kitchener
1989-90	Larry Mavety, Kingston
1990-91	George Burnett, Niagara Falls
1991-92	George Burnett, Niagara Falls
1992-93	Gary Agnew, London

JIM MAHON MEMORIAL TROPHY

(Top scoring right wing)

Season	Player, Team
1971-72	Bill Harris, Toronto
1972-73	Dennis Ververgaert, London
1973-74	Dave Gorman, St. Catharines
1974-75	Mark Napier, Toronto
1975-76	Peter Lee, Ottawa
1976-77	John Anderson, Toronto
1977-78	Dino Ciccarelli, London
1978-79	Mike Foligno, Sudbury
1979-80	Jim Fox, Ottawa
1980-81	Tony Tanti, Oshawa
1981-82	Tony Tanti, Oshawa
1982-83	Ian MacInnis, Cornwall
1983-84	Wayne Presley, Kitchener
1984-85	Dave MacLean, Belleville
1985-86	Ray Sheppard, Cornwall
1986-87	Ron Goodall, Kitchener
1987-88	Sean Williams, Oshawa
1988-89	Stan Drulia, Niagara Falls
1989-90	Owen Nolan, Cornwall
1990-91	Rob Pearson, Oshawa
1991-92	Darren McCarty, Belleville
1992-93	Kevin Brown, Detroit

F.W. DINTY MOORE TROPHY

(Lowest average by a rookie goalie)

Season	Player, Team
1975-76	Mark Locken, Hamilton
1976-77	Barry Heard, London
1977-78	Ken Ellacott, Peterborough
1978-79	Nick Ricci, Niagara Falls
1979-80	Mike Vezina, Ottawa
1980-81	John Vanbiesbrouck, Sault Ste. Marie
1981-82	Shawn Kilroy, Peterborough
1982-83	Dan Burrows, Belleville
1983-84	Jerry Iuliano, Sault Ste. Marie
1984-85	Ron Tugnutt, Peterborough
1985-86	Paul Henriques, Belleville
1986-87	Jeff Hackett, Oshawa
1987-88	Todd Bojcun, Peterborough
1988-89	Jeff Wilson, Kingston
1989-90	Sean Basilio, London
1990-91	Kevin Hodson, Sault Ste. Marie
1991-92	Sandy Allan, North Bay
1992-93	Ken Shepard, Oshawa

LEO LALONDE MEMORIAL TROPHY

(Overage player of the year)

Season	Player, Team
1983-84	Don McLaren, Ottawa
1984-85	Dunc MacIntyre, Belleville

Season	Player, Team
1985-86	Steve Guenette, Guelph
1986-87	Mike Richard, Toronto
1987-88	Len Soccio, North Bay
1988-89	Stan Drulia, Niagara Falls

Season	Player, Team
1989-90	Iain Fraser, Oshawa
1990-91	Joey St. Aubin, Kitchener
1991-92	John Spoltore, North Bay
1992-93	Scott Hollis, Oshawa

ALL-TIME LEAGUE CHAMPIONS

REGULAR-SEASON CHAMPION / PLAYOFF CHAMPION

Season	Team (Regular-Season Champion)	Team (Playoff Champion)
1933-34	No trophy awarded	St. Michael's College
1934-35	No trophy awarded	Kitchener
1935-36	No trophy awarded	West Toronto Redmen
1936-37	No trophy awarded	St. Michael's College
1937-38	No trophy awarded	Oshawa Generals
1938-39	No trophy awarded	Oshawa Generals
1939-40	No trophy awarded	Oshawa Generals
1940-41	No trophy awarded	Oshawa Generals
1941-42	No trophy awarded	Oshawa Generals
1942-43	No trophy awarded	Oshawa Generals
1943-44	No trophy awarded	Oshawa Generals
1944-45	No trophy awarded	St. Michael's College
1945-46	No trophy awarded	St. Michael's College
1946-47	No trophy awarded	St. Michael's College
1947-48	No trophy awarded	Barrie Flyers
1948-49	No trophy awarded	Barrie Flyers
1949-50	No trophy awarded	Guelph Biltmores
1950-51	No trophy awarded	Barrie Flyers
1951-52	No trophy awarded	Guelph Biltmores
1952-53	No trophy awarded	Barrie Flyers
1953-54	No trophy awarded	St. Catharines Tee Pees
1954-55	No trophy awarded	Toronto Marlboros
1955-56	No trophy awarded	Toronto Marlboros
1956-57	No trophy awarded	Guelph Biltmores
1957-58	St. Catharines Tee Pees	Toronto Marlboros
1958-59	St. Catharines Tee Pees	Peterborough TPTs
1959-60	Toronto Marlboros	St. Catharines Tee Pees
1960-61	Guelph Royals	St. Michael's College
1961-62	Montreal Jr. Canadiens	Hamilton Red Wings
1962-63	Niagara Falls Flyers	Niagara Falls Flyers
1963-64	Toronto Marlboros	Toronto Marlboros
1964-65	Niagara Falls Flyers	Niagara Falls Flyers
1965-66	Peterborough Petes	Oshawa Generals
1966-67	Kitchener Rangers	Toronto Marlboros
1967-68	Kitchener Rangers	Niagara Falls Flyers
1968-69	Montreal Jr. Canadiens	Montreal Jr. Canadiens
1969-70	Montreal Jr. Canadiens	Montreal Jr. Canadiens
1970-71	Peterborough Petes	St. Catharines Black Hawks
1971-72	Toronto Marlboros	Peterborough Petes
1972-73	Toronto Marlboros	Toronto Marlboros
1973-74	Kitchener Rangers	St. Catharines Black Hawks
1974-75	Toronto Marlboros	Toronto Marlboros
1975-76	Sudbury Wolves	Hamilton Steelhawks
1976-77	St. Catharines Fincups	Ottawa 67's
1977-78	Ottawa 67's	Peterborough Petes
1978-79	Peterborough Petes	Peterborough Petes
1979-80	Peterborough Petes	Peterborough Petes
1980-81	Sault St. Marie Greyhounds	Kitchener Rangers
1981-82	Ottawa 67's	Kitchener Rangers
1982-83	Sault Ste. Marie Greyhounds	Oshawa Generals
1983-84	Kitchener Rangers	Ottawa 67's
1984-85	Sault Ste. Marie Greyhounds	Sault Ste. Marie Greyhounds
1985-86	Peterborough Petes	Guelph Platers
1986-87	Oshawa Generals	Oshawa Generals
1987-88	Windsor Compuware Spitfires	Windsor Compuware Spitfires
1988-89	Kitchener Rangers	Peterborough Petes
1989-90	Oshawa Generals	Oshawa Generals
1990-91	Oshawa Generals	Sault Ste. Marie Greyhounds
1991-92	Peterborough Petes	Sault Ste. Marie Greyhounds
1992-93	Peterborough Petes	Peterborough Petes

The OHL regular-season champion is awarded the Hamilton Spectator Trophy and the playoff champion is awarded the J. Ross Robertson Cup.

QUEBEC MAJOR JUNIOR HOCKEY LEAGUE

LEAGUE OFFICE

President and executive director
  Gilles Courteau
Statistician
  Richard Blouin

Communications assistant
  Manon Gagnon
Administrative assistant
  Claire Lussier

Address
  255 Roland-Therien Blvd.
  Suite 101
  Longueuil, Quebec
Phone
  514-442-3590

1992-93 REGULAR SEASON

FINAL STANDINGS

ROBERT LE BEL DIVISION

Team	G	W	L	T	Pts.	GF	GA
Laval	70	43	25	2	88	367	277
Hull	70	40	28	2	82	296	268
St. Jean	70	35	32	3	73	282	276
Verdun	70	34	34	2	70	286	279
St. Hyacinthe	70	29	37	4	62	312	320
Granby	70	23	46	1	47	288	414

FRANK DILIO DIVISION

Team	G	W	L	T	Pts.	GF	GA
Sherbrooke	70	44	20	6	94	302	241
Victoriaville	70	43	26	1	87	358	296
Drummondville	70	39	30	1	79	353	303
Chicoutimi	70	38	29	3	79	342	321
Shawinigan	70	19	46	5	43	262	357
Beauport	70	17	51	2	36	253	349

INDIVIDUAL LEADERS

Goals: Rene Corbet, Drummondville (79)
Assists: Ian Laperriere, Drummondville (96)
Points: Rene Corbet, Drummondville (148)
Penalty minutes: Matthew Barnaby, Victoriaville (448)
Goaltending average: Jocelyn Thibault, Sherbrooke (2.99)
Shutouts: Jocelyn Thibault, Sherbrooke (3)

	Games	G	A	Pts.
Martin Tanguay, St. Jean	72	53	58	111
Matthew Barnaby, Victoriaville	65	44	67	111
Stephane St. Amour, Chicoutimi	66	45	64	109
Jean-Francois Gregoire, St. Hy.	67	45	62	107
Danny Beauregard, Chicoutimi	66	47	59	106
Samuel Groleau, St. Jean	69	49	54	103
Daniel Paradis, Chicoutimi	69	43	59	102
Patrick Nadeau, Sherbrooke	64	37	65	102
Dominic Rheaume, Beauport	66	48	52	100
Patrick Carignan, St. Jean	65	36	59	95
Pierre Allard, Chicoutimi	70	39	55	94
Normand Paquet, St. Hyacinthe	68	40	53	93
Pierre-Francois Lalonde, Hull	62	41	50	91
Jean Imbeau, St. Jean	71	39	52	91
Jocelyn Langlois, Verdun	67	30	61	91

TOP SCORERS

	Games	G	A	Pts.
Rene Corbet, Drummondville	63	79	69	148
Ian Laperriere, Drummondville	60	44	96	140
Alexandre Daigle, Victoriaville	53	45	92	137
Martin Gendron, St. Hyacinthe	63	73	61	134
Claude Savoie, Victoriaville	67	70	61	131
Eric Veilleux, Laval	70	55	70	125
Michel St. Jacques, Chicoutimi	69	53	67	120

INDIVIDUAL STATISTICS

BEAUPORT HARFANGS

SCORING

	Games	G	A	Pts.	Pen.
Dominic Rheaume	66	48	52	100	93
Eric Daze	68	19	36	55	24
Simon Toupin	67	24	30	54	73
Jean-Yves Leroux	62	20	25	45	33
Charlie Boucher	65	15	30	45	22
Patrick Deraspe	66	19	25	44	109
Patrice Paquin	59	17	23	40	271
Ian McIntyre	44	14	18	32	115
Steve Searles	66	9	18	27	214
Herve Lapointe	59	7	17	24	200
Eric Moreau	69	4	17	21	43
Etienne Thibault	63	2	16	18	93
Claude St. Cyr	47	4	10	14	29
Francois Rivard	49	5	8	13	16
Jacques Blouin	29	4	5	9	44
Stephane Madore	60	1	8	9	159
Mario Cormier	67	2	5	7	197
Radoslav Balaz	63	4	2	6	13

	Games	G	A	Pts.	Pen.
Eric Joyal	44	1	4	5	94
Hugues Poirier	33	0	1	1	6
Martin Caron	6	0	0	0	2
Steve Vezina (goalie)	19	—	—	—	2
Stephane Menard (goalie)	44	—	—	—	6

GOALTENDING

	Games	Min.	Goals	SO	Avg.
Stephane Menard	44	2234	163	1	4.38
Steve Vezina	19	770	67	0	5.22

CHICOUTIMI SAGUENEENS

SCORING

	Games	G	A	Pts.	Pen.
Michel St. Jacques	69	53	67	120	51
Stephane St. Amour	66	45	64	109	48
Danny Beauregard	66	47	59	106	32
Daniel Paradis	69	43	59	102	176
Pierre Allard	70	39	55	94	64
Steve Gosselin	61	21	62	83	153

	Games	G	A	Pts.	Pen.
Dave Tremblay	56	30	47	77	22
Christian Caron	68	15	43	58	66
Raymond Delarosbil	71	8	39	47	119
Dave Boudreault	68	22	20	42	116
Eric Montreuil	70	19	13	32	98
Carl Lamothe	62	3	26	29	46
Steeve Leblanc	60	11	17	28	16
Allan Sirois	68	6	16	22	62
Patrick Lacombe	55	0	22	22	221
Jean-Alain Schneider	17	5	6	11	87
Dominic Savard	57	3	7	10	22
Sebastien Berube	63	2	5	7	71
Yanick Jean	50	2	2	4	40
Marc Thibeault	41	0	3	3	106
Jerome Boivin	13	1	0	1	6
Eric Fichaud (goalie)	43	—	—	—	0
Sylvain Rodrigue (goalie)	47	—	—	—	12

GOALTENDING

	Games	Min.	Goals	SO	Avg.
Eric Fichaud	43	2040	149	0	4.38
Sylvain Rodrigue	47	2227	170	0	4.58

DRUMMONDVILLE VOLTIGEURS

SCORING

	Games	G	A	Pts.	Pen.
Rene Corbet	63	79	69	148	143
Ian Laperriere	60	44	96	140	188
Eric Plante	70	35	48	83	70
Mario Therrien	63	31	38	69	137
Stephane Paradis	67	21	33	54	54
Serge Aubin	65	16	34	50	30
Vincent Tremblay	61	18	31	49	108
Louis Bernard	68	8	38	46	78
Sylvain Ducharme	62	7	38	45	121
Alexandre Duchesne	61	18	26	44	157
Luc Decelles	69	22	21	43	41
Joseph Napolitano	59	20	16	36	183
Eric Alarie	62	19	12	31	49
Sebastien Bety	70	1	21	22	126
Pascal Lebrasseur	65	4	15	19	54
Alain Nasreddine	64	0	14	14	137
Denis Gauthier	61	1	7	8	136
Patrice Charbonneau	35	2	5	7	10
Bruce McHugh	51	1	6	7	52
Maxime Peticlerc	38	2	4	6	6
Martin Latulippe	3	0	1	1	0
Jocelyn Lachance	1	0	0	0	0
Stephane Roughier (goalie)	42	—	—	—	10
Marcel Cousineau (goalie)	60	—	—	—	22

GOALTENDING

	Games	Min.	Goals	SO	Avg.
Marcel Cousineau	60	3298	225	0	4.09
Stephane Roughier	42	2171	153	1	4.23

GRANBY BISONS

SCORING

	Games	G	A	Pts.	Pen.
Martin Balleux	69	28	51	79	141
Christian Labonte	67	29	38	67	109
Nicolas Turmel	65	25	38	63	63
Martin Rozon	68	24	32	56	37
Alain Cote	68	25	29	54	42
Christian Matte	68	17	36	53	56
Maxime Blouin	67	15	30	45	29
Steve Dulac	67	16	23	39	49
David Lessard	65	15	21	36	83
Patrick Lamoureux	55	10	23	33	57
Jeremy Caissie	47	16	16	32	31
Daniel Laflamme	55	7	23	30	93
Eric Bertrand	64	10	15	25	82
Steve Ares	43	7	18	25	81
Francois Pilon	69	3	18	21	121

	Games	G	A	Pts.	Pen.
Martin Belanger	49	2	19	21	24
Dominic Grand'Maison	64	2	18	20	348
Martin Belair	56	1	17	18	44
Pascal Gagnon	45	2	11	13	95
Serge Labelle	25	1	3	4	206
Pascal Vincent (goalie)	2	—	—	—	0
Sebastien Dupuis (goalie)	12	—	—	—	6
Steve Plouffe (goalie)	52	—	—	—	16

GOALTENDING

	Games	Min.	Goals	SO	Avg.
Steve Plouffe	52	2679	240	0	5.38
Sebastien Dupuis	12	502	46	0	5.50
Pascal Vincent	2	60	13	0	12.98

HULL OLYMPIQUES

SCORING

	Games	G	A	Pts.	Pen.
Pierre-Francois Lalonde	62	41	50	91	26
Joey Deliva	69	35	47	82	64
Paul Brousseau	59	27	48	75	49
Jim Campbell	50	42	29	71	66
Eric Lecompte	66	33	38	71	149
Francois Bourdeau	68	24	41	65	118
Sebastien Bordeleau	60	18	39	57	95
Claude Jutras	64	21	33	54	338
Jamie Bird	70	9	44	53	98
Shane Doiron	70	12	34	46	69
Yannick Frechette	45	18	21	39	128
Eric Lavigne	59	7	20	27	221
Sylvain Lapointe	70	5	19	24	64
Carl Charland	70	8	12	20	122
Marty King	62	1	15	16	36
Thierry Mayer	64	2	9	11	172
Richard Lacasse	53	4	4	8	59
Harold Hersh	29	2	6	8	9
Paul MacDonald	32	0	6	6	34
Rocco Anoia	46	2	2	4	35
Christian Gosselin	49	1	3	4	24
Louis-Philippe Charbonneau	29	0	2	2	88
Dominic Letendre (goalie)	9	—	—	—	0
Martin Brochu (goalie)	29	—	—	—	20
Jean-Francois Labbe (goalie)	46	—	—	—	34

GOALTENDING

	Games	Min.	Goals	SO	Avg.
Jean-Francois Labbe	46	2701	156	2	3.46
Dominic Letendre	9	447	34	0	4.56
Martin Brochu	29	1453	137	0	5.66

LAVAL TITANS

SCORING

	Games	G	A	Pts.	Pen.
Eric Veilleux	70	55	70	125	100
Martin Lapointe	35	38	51	89	41
Dave Whittom	71	27	59	86	308
Yanick Dube	68	45	38	83	25
Robin Bouchard	67	44	37	81	270
Jean Roberge	67	29	49	78	133
Benoit Larose	63	16	62	78	218
Marc Beaucage	67	33	43	76	121
Michael Gaul	57	16	57	73	66
Brant Blackned	60	27	36	63	76
Stephane Desjardins	65	6	40	46	189
Daniel Goneau	62	16	25	41	44
Jason Boudrias	66	15	26	41	41
Frederic Chartier	62	10	18	28	59
Philippe Boucher	16	12	15	27	37
Patrick Boileau	69	4	19	23	73
Hugues Gervais	55	5	9	14	105
Dany Michaud	51	2	8	10	80
Sylvain Blouin	68	0	10	10	373
Francis Bouillon	46	0	7	7	45
Patrick Cassin	29	3	3	6	2

	Games	G	A	Pts.	Pen.
David Haynes	54	2	4	6	82
Francois Leblanc (goalie)	32	—	—	—	8
Emmanuel Fernandez (goalie)	43	—	—	—	4

GOALTENDING

	Games	Min.	Goals	SO	Avg.
Emmanuel Fernandez.	43	2348	141	1	3.60
Francois Leblanc	32	1737	127	0	4.39

ST. HYACINTHE LASERS

SCORING

	Games	G	A	Pts.	Pen.
Martin Gendron	63	73	61	134	44
Jean-Francois Gregoire	67	45	62	107	84
Normand Paquet	68	40	53	93	56
Hugo Proulx	41	30	57	87	38
Michal Longauer	69	20	39	59	68
Hugues Laliberte	55	13	39	52	30
Dean Melanson	57	13	29	42	253
Gregg Pineo	58	19	22	41	109
Martin Larochelle	69	9	23	32	53
Martin Gironne	50	9	14	23	26
Stan Melanson	48	4	16	20	107
Daniel Germain	61	2	16	18	55
Eric Gauvin	60	9	8	17	25
Nicolas Maheux	58	6	10	16	29
Martin Trudel	67	1	14	15	51
Patrick Lampron	64	0	15	15	108
Jean-Francois Tremblay	38	6	5	11	45
Paolo DeRubertis	58	5	3	8	153
David Desnoyers	70	0	8	8	179
Jonathan Dubois	8	0	2	2	6
Luc Bilodeau	7	0	1	1	0
Martin Barriault	2	0	0	0	2
Jimmy Dostie	3	0	0	0	0
Marc Fortin (goalie)	14	—	—	—	2
Frederick Beaubien (goalie)	33	—	—	—	4
Marc Legault (goalie)	39	—	—	—	29

GOALTENDING

	Games	Min.	Goals	SO	Avg.
Marc Fortin	14	592	46	0	4.66
Frederick Beaubien	33	1702	133	0	4.69
Marc Legault	39	2158	170	0	4.73

ST. JEAN LYNX

SCORING

	Games	G	A	Pts.	Pen.
Martin Tanguay	72	53	58	111	78
Samuel Groleau	69	49	54	103	62
Patrick Carignan	65	36	59	95	44
Jean Imbeau	71	39	52	91	151
Steve Brule	70	33	47	80	46
Dominic Maltais	61	34	41	75	164
Marquis Mathieu	70	31	36	67	115
Francois Groleau	48	7	38	45	66
Denis Beauchamp	70	9	29	38	100
Christian Proulx	70	3	34	37	147
Patrick Traverse	68	6	30	36	24
Brian Casey	58	1	28	29	41
Jimmy Provencher	45	7	12	19	16
Rony Valenti	53	8	7	15	174
Bruno Lajeunesse	63	7	7	14	41
Patrick Charbonneau	45	3	8	11	24
Jeff Mercer	52	3	5	8	135
Nathan Morin	23	1	7	8	181
Martin Lamarche	51	2	5	7	134
Frederic Barbeau	66	0	4	4	26
Jose Theodore (goalie)	34	—	—	—	12
Jean-Pascal Lemelin (goalie)	44	—	—	—	2

GOALTENDING

	Games	Min.	Goals	SO	Avg.
Jean-Pascal Lemelin .	44	2471	155	0	3.76
Jose Theodore	34	1776	112	0	3.78

SHAWINIGAN CATARACTES

SCORING

	Games	G	A	Pts.	Pen.
Stefan Simoes	69	26	41	67	82
Alain Savage	67	32	30	62	140
Simon Roy	68	5	34	39	56
Martin Lepage	61	7	26	33	133
Jean-Francois Laroche	64	10	18	28	37
Richard Aimonetto	47	8	15	23	41
Eric Ladouceur	61	3	17	20	67
Andre Alie	57	3	11	14	28
Jocelyn Charbonneau	65	2	12	14	57
Sylvain Brisson	70	3	10	13	104
David Brosseau	56	5	4	9	28
Steeve Finn	44	2	7	9	100
David Grenier	63	1	4	5	120
Luc Becotte	30	1	4	5	6
Simon Provencher	29	2	1	3	18
Eric Cloutier	36	1	2	3	112
Francois Cote	19	0	2	2	6
Mathieu Carpenter	10	1	0	1	14
Steve Santerre	2	0	1	1	0
Alexandre Chapdelaine	11	0	0	0	14
Patrick Dallaire (goalie)	7	—	—	—	0
Patrick Lalime (goalie)	44	—	—	—	6

GOALTENDING

	Games	Min.	Goals	SO	Avg.
Patrick Lalime	44	2467	192	0	4.67
Patrick Dallaire	7	235	29	0	7.41

SHERBROOKE FAUCONS

SCORING

	Games	G	A	Pts.	Pen.
Patrick Nadeau	64	37	65	102	60
Stephane Larocque	70	44	42	86	129
Jean-Francois Jomphe	60	43	43	86	86
Marc Tardif	63	21	46	67	249
Stephane Julien	69	20	44	64	121
Carl Fleury	64	25	38	63	124
Pascal Rheaume	65	28	34	62	88
Pascal Trepanier	59	15	33	48	130
Jean-Francois Robert	67	17	27	44	57
Eddy Gervais	68	7	29	36	39
Jason Downey	58	8	27	35	251
Dave Belliveau	65	14	20	34	51
Hugo Turcotte	46	14	20	34	24
Sebastien Fortier	38	10	20	30	23
Eric Messier	51	4	17	21	82
Dany Larochelle	52	4	11	15	34
Etienne Beaudry	26	3	7	10	23
Charles Paquette	54	2	5	7	104
Daniel Villaneuve	39	1	3	4	34
Christian Mathieu	42	1	1	2	101
Rock Isabel	27	0	1	1	74
Patrick Belisle	2	0	0	0	2
Hugo Hamelin (goalie)	17	—	—	—	0
Jocelyn Thibault (goalie)	56	—	—	—	0

GOALTENDING

	Games	Min.	Goals	SO	Avg.
Jocelyn Thibault	56	3190	159	3	2.99
Hugo Hamelin	17	817	55	0	4.04

VERDUN COLLEGE-FRANCAIS

SCORING

	Games	G	A	Pts.	Pen.
Jocelyn Langlois	67	30	61	91	16
Yan Arsenault	68	18	55	73	97
Martin Beauchamp	60	36	36	72	51
Eric Cool	70	22	49	71	95
Joel Bouchard	60	10	49	59	126
Daniel Guerard	58	31	26	57	131
Pierre Gendron	65	18	31	49	88

	Games	G	A	Pts.	Pen.
Nicolas Brousseau	65	16	32	48	46
Patrick Grise	70	18	25	43	56
Stacy Dallaire	62	6	30	36	90
Francois Gagnon	64	18	11	29	134
Guy Tremblay	70	10	18	28	30
Yannick Gaucher	55	9	11	20	43
Christian Laflamme	69	2	17	19	70
Claude Filion	67	7	10	17	180
Francois Leroux	17	7	9	16	39
Jean-Guy Trudel	45	6	7	13	20
Jeffrey Viitanen	62	0	11	11	27
Marian Lastiak	62	4	6	10	31
Simon Arial	53	3	3	6	38
Christian Desrochers	9	2	3	5	4
Michel Vincent	48	0	3	3	18
Jean-Sebastien Lefebvre	11	0	0	0	17
Mathieu Blanchet (goalie)	8	—	—	—	4
Christian Aubut (goalie)	10	—	—	—	4
Philippe DeRouville (goalie)	61	—	—	—	6

GOALTENDING

	Games	Min.	Goals	SO	Avg.
Philippe DeRouville	61	3491	210	1	3.61
Christian Aubut	10	421	33	0	4.70
Mathieu Blanchet	8	320	28	0	5.24

VICTORIAVILLE TIGRES

SCORING

	Games	G	A	Pts.	Pen.
Alexandre Daigle	53	45	92	137	85
Claude Savoie	67	70	61	131	113

	Games	G	A	Pts.	Pen.
Matthew Barnaby	65	44	67	111	448
Patrick Bisaillon	52	34	37	71	120
Nicolas Lefebvre	62	30	40	70	56
Pascal Chiasson	70	15	51	66	121
Cosmo DuPaul	67	23	35	58	16
Francois Paquette	70	12	35	47	53
Mario Dumoulin	69	4	39	43	85
Martin Woods	65	13	27	40	433
Jean-Martin Morin	52	16	21	37	96
Carl Poirier	67	10	15	25	61
Hughes Bouchard	67	2	22	24	121
Pascal Bernier	67	8	15	23	122
Bruno Gladu	55	10	12	22	12
Martin Laitre	53	8	13	21	315
Ian Laterreur	27	6	9	15	24
Philippe Gelineau	59	5	8	13	32
Carl Blondin	41	4	8	12	13
Mathieu Raby	53	2	2	4	103
Alexandre Laporte	56	1	3	4	30
Serge Leblanc	9	1	0	1	0
Jean-Francois Bessette	36	0	0	0	13
Sebastien Plouffe (goalie)	16	—	—	—	4
Danick Lepine (goalie)	25	—	—	—	18
Patrick Charbonneau (goalie)	59	—	—	—	30

GOALTENDING

	Games	Min.	Goals	SO	Avg.
Danick Lepine	25	1106	75	2	4.07
Patrick Charbonneau	59	3121	216	0	4.15
Sebastien Plouffe	16	793	68	0	5.15

1993 PRESIDENT CUP PLAYOFFS

RESULTS

QUARTERFINALS

Series "A"

	W	L	Pts.	GF	GA
Sherbrooke	4	0	8	17	11
Chicoutimi	0	4	0	11	17

(Sherbrooke won series, 4-0)

Series "B"

	W	L	Pts.	GF	GA
Drummondville	4	2	8	28	24
Victoriaville	2	4	4	24	28

(Drummondville won series, 4-2)

Series "C"

	W	L	Pts.	GF	GA
Laval	4	0	8	19	9
Verdun	0	4	0	9	19

(Laval won series, 4-0)

Series "D"

	W	L	Pts.	GF	GA
Hull	4	0	8	17	5
St. Jean	0	4	0	5	17

(Hull won series, 4-0)

SEMIFINALS

Series "E"

	W	L	Pts.	GF	GA
Sherbrooke	3	2	6	16	26
Hull	2	3	4	26	16

(Sherbrooke won series, 3-2)

Series "F"

	W	L	Pts.	GF	GA
Laval	4	0	8	22	15
Drummondville	0	4	0	15	22

(Laval won series, 4-0)

FINALS

Series "G"

	W	L	Pts.	GF	GA
Laval	4	1	8	24	18
Sherbrooke	1	4	2	18	24

(Laval won series, 4-1)

INDIVIDUAL LEADERS

Goals: Martin Lapointe, Laval (13)
Assists: Martin Lapointe, Laval (17)
Points: Martin Lapointe, Laval (30)
Penalty minutes: Sylvain Blouin, Laval (66)
Goaltending average: Jean-Francois Labbe, Hull (2.78)
Shutouts: Marcel Cousineau, Drummondville (1)
Jean-Francois Labbe, Hull (1)

TOP SCORERS

	Games	G	A	Pts.
Martin Lapointe, Laval	13	13	17	30
Jean-Francois Jomphe, Sherbrooke	15	10	13	23
Philippe Boucher, Laval	13	6	15	21
Eric Veilleux, Laval	13	9	11	20
Rene Corbet, Drummondville	10	7	13	20
Dave Whittom, Laval	13	8	11	19
Ian Laperriere, Drummondville	10	6	13	19
Marc Beaucage, Laval	13	6	10	16
Patrick Nadeau, Sherbrooke	14	5	11	16
Pierre-Francois Lalonde, Hull	10	5	11	16

INDIVIDUAL STATISTICS

CHICOUTIMI SAGUEENENS

(Lost quarterfinals to Sherbrooke, 4-0)

SCORING

	Games	G	A	Pts.	Pen.
Daniel Paradis	4	3	2	5	15
Stephane St. Amour	4	2	2	4	0
Dave Tremblay	4	1	3	4	0
Michel St. Jacques	4	2	1	3	6
Danny Beauregard	4	0	3	3	6
Raymond Delarosbil	4	0	3	3	7
Pierre Allard	4	1	1	2	4
Dave Boudreault	4	1	1	2	4
Carl Lamothe	4	0	2	2	0
Allan Sirois	4	1	0	1	0
Steve Gosselin	4	0	1	1	10
Christian Caron	4	0	1	1	0
Jean-Alain Schneider	4	0	1	1	16
Eric Montreuil	4	0	1	1	2
Steeve Leblanc	1	0	0	0	0
Yanick Jean	3	0	0	0	0
Sebastien Berube	4	0	0	0	4
Patrick Lacombe	4	0	0	0	20
Marc Thibeault	4	0	0	0	0
Sylvain Rodrigue (goalie)	4	—	—	—	0

GOALTENDING

	Games	Min.	Goals	SO	Avg.
Sylvain Rodrigue	4	210	16	0	4.57

DRUMMONDVILLE VOLTIGEURS

(Lost semifinals to Laval, 4-0)

SCORING

	Games	G	A	Pts.	Pen.
Rene Corbet	10	7	13	20	16
Ian Laperriere	10	6	13	19	20
Alexandre Duchesne	10	8	6	14	13
Vincent Tremblay	10	8	4	12	6
Eric Plante	10	3	5	8	6
Sylvain Ducharme	9	2	6	8	33
Mario Therrien	9	2	4	6	48
Stephane Paradis	6	3	2	5	2
Patrice Charbonneau	10	0	5	5	9
Denis Gauthier	10	0	5	5	40
Luc Decelles	6	1	3	4	5
Louis Bernard	10	0	4	4	14
Sebastien Bety	10	1	2	3	24
Joseph Napolitano	10	2	0	2	54
Eric Alarie	10	0	1	1	13
Alain Nasreddine	10	0	1	1	36
Serge Aubin	8	0	1	1	16
Patrick Livernoche	2	0	0	0	23
Bruce McHugh	2	0	0	0	2
Maxime Peticlerc	2	0	0	0	0
Pascal Lebrasseur	6	0	0	0	2
Martin Latulippe	10	0	0	0	2
Stephane Routhier (goalie)	3	—	—	—	2
Marcel Cousineau (goalie)	9	—	—	—	2

GOALTENDING

	Games	Min.	Goals	SO	Avg.
Marcel Cousineau	9	498	37	1	4.45
Stephane Routhier	3	101	9	0	5.35

HULL OLYMPIQUES

(Lost semifinals to Sherbrooke, 3-2)

SCORING

	Games	G	A	Pts.	Pen.
Pierre-Francois Lalonde	10	5	11	16	10
Jim Campbell	8	11	4	15	43
Paul Brousseau	10	7	8	15	6
Francois Bourdeau	10	2	11	13	8
Sebastien Bordeleau	10	3	8	11	20
Shane Doiron	10	3	6	9	13
Claude Jutras	10	5	3	8	54
Eric Lecompte	10	4	4	8	52
Eric Lavigne	10	2	4	6	47
Joey Deliva	10	1	5	6	10
Jamie Bird	9	0	4	4	33
Sylvain Lapointe	10	1	1	2	2
Carl Charland	10	1	1	2	36
Harold Hersh	10	0	1	1	17
Louis-Philippe Charbonneau	3	0	0	0	47
Christian Gosselin	4	0	0	0	0
Rocco Anoia	7	0	0	0	2
Thierry Mayer	9	0	0	0	21
Marty King	10	0	0	0	7
Richard Lacasse	10	0	0	0	8
Martin Brochu (goalie)	3	—	—	—	4
Jean-Francois Labbe (goalie)	10	—	—	—	2

GOALTENDING

	Games	Min.	Goals	SO	Avg.
Jean-Francois Labbe	10	518	24	1	2.78
Martin Brochu	3	80	8	0	5.97

LAVAL TITANS

(Winner of 1993 President Cup playoffs)

SCORING

	Games	G	A	Pts.	Pen.
Martin Lapointe	13	13	17	30	22
Philippe Boucher	13	6	15	21	12
Eric Veilleux	13	9	11	20	19
Dave Whittom	13	8	11	19	24
Marc Beaucage	13	6	10	16	10
Yanick Dube	13	6	7	13	6
Michael Gaul	13	3	10	13	10
Jean Roberge	12	4	4	8	40
Brant Blackned	10	3	4	7	4
Benoit Larose	8	1	6	7	10
Stephane Desjardins	13	1	4	5	32
Robin Bouchard	13	1	4	5	23
Daniel Goneau	13	0	4	4	4
Patrick Boileau	13	1	2	3	10
Frederic Chartier	12	1	2	3	10

	Games	G	A	Pts.	Pen.
Sylvain Blouin	13	1	0	1	66
Hugues Gervais	12	1	0	1	14
Dany Michaud	5	0	0	0	0
David Haynes	6	0	0	0	4
Jason Boudrias	13	0	0	0	2
Emmanuel Fernandez (goalie)	13	—	—	—	2

GOALTENDING

	Games	Min.	Goals	SO	Avg.
Emmanuel Fernandez	13	818	42	0	3.08

ST. JEAN LYNX

(Lost quarterfinals to Hull, 4-0)

SCORING

	Games	G	A	Pts.	Pen.
Martin Tanguay	4	1	2	3	21
Samuel Groleau	4	1	2	3	0
Patrick Carignan	4	1	1	2	4
Dominic Maltais	3	0	2	2	12
Marquis Mathieu	2	1	0	1	33
Jean Imbeau	2	1	0	1	9
Denis Beauchamp	4	0	1	1	26
Francois Groleau	4	0	1	1	14
Patrick Traverse	4	0	1	1	2
Georges Laraque	1	0	0	0	0
Martin Lamarche	2	0	0	0	0
Nathan Morin	2	0	0	0	19
Frederic Barbeau	3	0	0	0	0
Steve Brule	4	0	0	0	9
Brian Casey	4	0	0	0	8
Patrick Charbonneau	4	0	0	0	0
Girard Christian	1	0	0	0	2
Bruno Lajeunesse	4	0	0	0	10
Jeff Mercer	4	0	0	0	53
Christian Proulx	4	0	0	0	12
Jimmy Provencher	4	0	0	0	8
Rony Valenti	4	0	0	0	26
Jean-Pascal Lemelin (goalie)	2	—	—	—	2
Jose Theodore (goalie)	3	—	—	—	0

GOALTENDING

	Games	Min.	Goals	SO	Avg.
Jose Theodore	3	175	11	0	3.77
Jean-Pascal Lemelin	2	64	5	2	4.70

SHERBROOKE FAUCONS

(Lost finals to Laval, 4-1)

SCORING

	Games	G	A	Pts.	Pen.
Jean-Francois Jomphe	15	10	13	23	18
Patrick Nadeau	14	5	11	16	20
Carl Fleury	13	5	10	15	22
Stephane Larocque	14	5	9	14	35
Pascal Trepanier	15	5	7	12	36
Marc Tardif	14	4	8	12	55
Pascal Rheaume	14	6	5	11	31
Stephane Julien	15	4	5	9	12
Hugo Turcotte	14	4	5	9	0
Jason Downey	15	3	4	7	51
Sebastien Fortier	14	1	6	7	21
Eddy Gervais	15	3	3	6	8
Eric Messier	15	0	4	4	18
Dany Larochelle	15	0	4	4	8
Jean-Francois Robert	15	2	1	3	14
Rock Isabel	15	1	0	1	22
Dave Belliveau	4	0	1	1	0
Christian Mathieu	1	0	0	0	21
Patrick Belisle	3	0	0	0	0
Etienne Beaudry	5	0	0	0	0
Daniel Villeneuve	9	0	0	0	2
Charles Paquette	15	0	0	0	33
Hugo Hamelin (goalie)	2	—	—	—	0
Jocelyn Thibault (goalie)	15	—	—	—	2

GOALTENDING

	Games	Min.	Goals	SO	Avg.
Jocelyn Thibault	15	883	57	0	3.87
Hugo Hamelin	2	50	6	0	7.20

VERDUN COLLEGE-FRANCAIS

(Lost quarterfinals to Laval, 4-0)

SCORING

	Games	G	A	Pts.	Pen.
Eric Cool	4	2	4	6	2
Francois Leroux	4	3	0	3	10
Stacy Dallaire	4	1	1	2	10
Martin Beauchamp	4	1	1	2	7
Daniel Guerard	4	1	1	2	17
Yan Arsenault	4	0	2	2	4
Joel Bouchard	4	0	2	2	4
Christian Laflamme	3	0	2	2	6
Nicolas Brousseau	4	1	0	1	2
Jocelyn Langlois	4	0	1	1	2
Jeffrey Viitanen	4	0	1	1	2
Michel Vincent	1	0	0	0	0
Simon Arial	2	0	0	0	0
Marian Lastiak	2	0	0	0	0
Jean-Guy Trudel	2	0	0	0	5
Yannick Gaucher	3	0	0	0	2
Guy Tremblay	3	0	0	0	0
Claude Filion	4	0	0	0	0
Francois Gagnon	4	0	0	0	4
Pierre Gendron	4	0	0	0	2
Patrick Grise	4	0	0	0	15
Philippe DeRouville (goalie)	4	—	—	—	0

GOALTENDING

	Games	Min.	Goals	SO	Avg.
Philippe DeRouville	4	257	18	0	4.21

VICTORIAVILLE TIGRES

(Lost quarterfinals to Drummondville, 4-2)

SCORING

	Games	G	A	Pts.	Pen.
Alexandre Daigle	6	5	6	11	4
Claude Savoie	6	4	5	9	6
Patrick Bisaillon	6	4	3	7	8
Mario Dumoulin	6	1	6	7	17
Matthew Barnaby	6	2	4	6	44
Jean-Martin Morin	6	2	2	4	9
Pascal Chiasson	6	1	3	4	10
Cosmo DuPaul	6	1	3	4	2
Martin Woods	4	2	1	3	41
Hughes Bouchard	6	0	2	2	18
Nicolas Lefebvre	6	0	2	2	0
Carl Blondin	6	1	0	1	10
Bruno Gladu	5	1	0	1	2
Francois Paquette	6	0	1	1	12
Martin Laitre	5	0	1	1	35
Pascal Bernier	6	0	1	1	7
Philippe Gelineau	6	0	1	1	5
Serge Leblanc	1	0	0	0	0
Carl Poirier	1	0	0	0	0
Mathieu Raby	2	0	0	0	0
Alexandre Laporte	6	0	0	0	2
Patrick Charbonneau (goalie)	2	—	—	—	0
Danick Lepine (goalie)	3	—	—	—	0
Sebastien Plouffe (goalie)	3	—	—	—	2

GOALTENDING

	Games	Min.	Goals	SO	Avg.
Patrick Charbonneau	2	92	4	0	2.61
Sebastien Plouffe	3	154	11	0	4.30
Danick Lepine	3	113	13	0	6.88

1992-93 AWARD WINNERS

ALL-STAR TEAMS

First team	Pos.	Second team
Jocelyn Thibault, Sher.	G	Philippe DeRouville, Verdun
Benoit Larose, Laval	D	Steve Gosselin, Chicoutimi
Stephane Julien, Sherbrooke	D	Yan Arsenault, Verdun
Rene Corbet, Drummondville	LW	Michel St. Jacques, Chi.
Alexandre Daigle, Vic.	C	Ian Laperriere, Drum.
Martin Lapointe, Laval	RW	Martin Gendron, St. Hy.

Coach of the Year: Guy Chouinard, Sherbrooke

TROPHY WINNERS

Frank Selke Trophy: Martin Gendron, St. Hyacinthe
Michel Bergeron Trophy: Steve Brule, St. Jean
Raymond Lagace Trophy: Stephane Routhier, Drummondville
Jean Beliveau Trophy: Rene Corbet, Drummondville
Michel Briere Trophy: Jocelyn Thibault, Sherbrooke
Marcel Robert Trophy: Jocelyn Thibault, Sherbrooke
Mike Bossy Trophy: Alexandre Daigle, Victoriaville
Emile "Butch" Bouchard Trophy: Benoit Larose, Laval
Jacques Plante Trophy: Jocelyn Thibault, Sherbrooke
Guy Lafleur Trophy: Emmanuel Fernandez, Laval
Robert LeBel Trophy: Sherbrooke Faucons
John Rougeau Trophy: Sherbrooke Faucons
President Cup: Laval Titans

ALL-TIME AWARD WINNERS

FRANK SELKE TROPHY

(Most gentlemanly player)

Season	Player, Team
1970-71	Norm Dube, Sherbrooke
1971-72	Gerry Teeple, Cornwall
1972-73	Claude Larose, Drummondville
1973-74	Gary MacGregor, Cornwall
1974-75	Jean-Luc Phaneuf, Montreal
1975-76	Norm Dupont, Montreal
1976-77	Mike Bossy, Laval
1977-78	Kevin Reeves, Montreal
1978-79	Ray Bourque, Verdun
	Jean-Francois Sauve, Trois-Rivieres
1979-80	Jean-Francois Sauve, Trois-Rivieres
1980-81	Claude Verret, Trois-Rivieres
1981-82	Claude Verret, Trois-Rivieres
1982-83	Pat LaFontaine, Verdun
1983-84	Jerome Carrier, Verdun
1984-85	Patrick Emond, Chicoutimi
1985-86	Jimmy Carson, Verdun
1986-87	Luc Beausoleil, Laval
1987-88	Stephan Lebeau, Shawinigan
1988-89	Steve Cadieux, Shawinigan
1989-90	Andrew McKim, Hull
1990-91	Yanic Perreault, Trois-Rivieres
1991-92	Martin Gendron, St. Hyacinthe
1992-93	Martin Gendron, St. Hyacinthe

MICHEL BERGERON TROPHY

(Top rookie forward)

Season	Player, Team
1969-70	Serge Martel, Verdun
1970-71	Bob Murphy, Cornwall
1971-72	Bob Murray, Cornwall
1972-73	Pierre Larouche, Sorel
1973-74	Mike Bossy, Laval
1974-75	Dennis Pomerleau, Hull
1975-76	Jean-Marc Bonamie, Shawinigan
1976-77	Rick Vaive, Sherbrooke
1977-78	Norm Rochefort, Trois-Rivieres
	Denis Savard, Montreal
1978-79	Alan Grenier, Laval
1979-80	Dale Hawerchuk, Cornwall
1980-81	Claude Verret, Trois-Rivieres
1981-82	Sylvain Turgeon, Hull
1982-83	Pat LaFontaine, Verdun
1983-84	Stephane Richer, Granby
1984-85	Jimmy Carson, Verdun
1985-86	Pierre Turgeon, Granby
1986-87	Rob Murphy, Laval
1987-88	Martin Gelinas, Hull
1988-89	Yanic Perreault, Trois-Rivieres

Season	Player, Team
1989-90	Martin Lapointe, Laval
1990-91	Rene Corbet, Drummondville
1991-92	Alexandre Daigle, Victoriaville
1992-93	Steve Brule, St. Jean

Prior to 1980-81 season, award was given to QMJHL rookie of the year.

RAYMOND LAGACE TROPHY

(Top rookie defenseman or goaltender)

Season	Player, Team
1980-81	Billy Campbell, Montreal
1981-82	Michel Petit, Sherbrooke
1982-83	Bobby Dollas, Laval
1983-84	James Gasseau, Drummondville
1984-85	Robert Desjardins, Shawinigan
1985-86	Stephane Guerard, Shawinigan
1986-87	Jimmy Waite, Chicoutimi
1987-88	Stephane Beauregard, St. Jean
1988-89	Karl Dykhuis, Hull
1989-90	Francois Groleau, Shawinigan
1990-91	Philippe Boucher, Granby
1991-92	Philippe DeRouville, Longueuil
1992-93	Stephane Routhier, Drummondville

JEAN BELIVEAU TROPHY

(Scoring leader)

Season	Player, Team
1969-70	Luc Simard, Trois-Rivieres
1970-71	Guy Lafleur, Quebec
1971-72	Jacques Richard, Quebec
1972-73	Andre Savard, Quebec
1973-74	Pierre Larouche, Sorel
1974-75	Norm Dupont, Montreal
1975-76	Richard Dalpe, Trois-Rivieres
	Sylvain Locas, Chicoutimi
1976-77	Jean Savard, Quebec
1977-78	Ron Carter, Sherbooke
1978-79	Jean-Francois Sauve, Trois-Rivieres
1979-80	Jean-Francois Sauve, Trois-Rivieres
1980-81	Dale Hawerchuk, Cornwall
1981-82	Claude Verret, Trois-Rivieres
1982-83	Pat LaFontaine, Verdun
1983-84	Mario Lemieux, Laval
1984-85	Guy Rouleau, Longueuil
1985-86	Guy Rouleau, Hull
1986-87	Marc Fortier, Chicoutimi
1987-88	Patrice Lefebvre, Shawinigan
1988-89	Stephane Morin, Chicoutimi
1989-90	Patrick Lebeau, Victoriaville
1990-91	Yanic Perreault, Trois-Rivieres
1991-92	Patrick Poulin, St. Hyacinthe
1992-93	Rene Corbet, Drummondville

MICHEL BRIERE TROPHY

(Most Valuable Player)

Season	Player, Team
1972-73	Andre Savard, Quebec
1973-74	Gary MacGregor, Cornwall
1974-75	Mario Viens, Cornwall
1975-76	Peter Marsh, Sherbrooke
1976-77	Lucien DeBlois, Sorel
1977-78	Kevin Reeves, Montreal
1978-79	Pierre Lacroix, Trois-Rivieres
1979-80	Denis Savard, Montreal
1980-81	Dale Hawerchuk, Cornwall
1981-82	John Chabot, Sherbrooke
1982-83	Pat LaFontaine, Verdun
1983-84	Mario Lemieux, Laval
1984-85	Daniel Berthiaune, Chicoutimi
1985-86	Guy Rouleau, Hull
1986-87	Robert Desjardins, Longueuil
1987-88	Marc Saumier, Hull
1988-89	Stephane Morin, Chicoutimi
1989-90	Andrew McKim, Hull
1990-91	Yanic Perreault, Trois-Rivieres
1991-92	Charles Poulin, St. Hyacinthe
1992-93	Jocelyn Thibault, Sherbrooke

MARCEL ROBERT TROPHY

(Top scholastic/athletic performer)

Season	Player, Team
1981-82	Jacques Sylvestre, Granby
1982-83	Claude Gosselin, Quebec
1983-84	Gilbert Paiement, Chicoutimi
1984-85	Claude Gosselin, Longueuil
1985-86	Bernard Morin, Laval
1986-87	Patrice Tremblay, Chicoutimi
1987-88	Stephane Beauregard, St. Jean
1988-89	Daniel Lacroix, Granby
1989-90	Yanic Perreault, Trois-Rivieres
1990-91	Benoit Larose, Laval
1991-92	Simon Toupin, Beauport
1992-93	Jocelyn Thibault, Sherbrooke

MIKE BOSSY TROPHY

(Top pro prospect)

Season	Player, Team
1980-81	Dale Hawerchuk, Cornwall
1981-82	Michel Petit, Sherbrooke
1982-83	Pat LaFontaine, Verdun
	Sylvain Turgeon, Hull
1983-84	Mario Lemieux, Laval
1984-85	Jose Charbonneau, Drummondville
1985-86	Jimmy Carson, Verdun
1986-87	Pierre Turgeon, Granby
1987-88	Daniel Dore, Drummondville
1988-89	Patrice Brisebois, Laval
1989-90	Karl Dykhuis, Hull
1990-91	Philippe Boucher, Granby
1991-92	Paul Brousseau, Hull
1992-93	Alexandre Daigle, Victoriaville

Originally known as Association of Journalism of Hockey Trophy from 1980-81 through 1982-83.

EMILE "BUTCH" BOUCHARD TROPHY

(Top defenseman)

Season	Player, Team
1975-76	Jean Gagnon, Quebec
1976-77	Robert Picard, Montreal
1977-78	Mark Hardy, Montreal
1978-79	Ray Bourque, Verdun
1979-80	Gaston Therrien, Quebec
1980-81	Fred Boimistruck, Cornwall
1981-82	Paul Andre Boutilier, Sherbrooke
1982-83	J.J. Daigneault, Longueuil

Season	Player, Team
1983-84	Billy Campbell, Verdun
1984-85	Yves Beaudoin, Shawinigan
1985-86	Sylvain Cote, Hull
1986-87	Jean Marc Richard, Chicoutimi
1987-88	Eric Desjardins, Granby
1988-89	Yves Racine, Victoriaville
1989-90	Claude Barthe, Victoriaville
1990-91	Patrice Brisebois, Drummondville
1991-92	Francois Groleau, Shawinigan
1992-93	Benoit Larose, Laval

JACQUES PLANTE TROPHY

(Top goaltender)

Season	Player, Team
1969-70	Michael Deguise, Sorel
1970-71	Reynald Fortier, Quebec
1971-72	Richard Brodeur, Cornwall
1972-73	Pierre Perusee, Quebec
1973-74	Claude Legris, Sorel
1974-75	Nick Sanza, Sherbrooke
1975-76	Tim Bernhardt, Cornwall
1976-77	Tim Bernhardt, Cornwall
1977-78	Tim Bernhardt, Cornwall
1978-79	Jacques Cloutier, Trois-Rivieres
1979-80	Corrado Micalef, Sherbrooke
1980-81	Michel Dufour, Sorel
1981-82	Jeff Barratt, Montreal
1982-83	Tony Haladuick, Laval
1983-84	Tony Haladuick, Laval
1984-85	Daniel Berthiaume, Chicoutimi
1985-86	Robert Desjardins, Hull
1986-87	Robert Desjardins, Longueuil
1987-88	Stephane Beauregard, St. Jean
1988-89	Stephane Fiset, Victoriaville
1989-90	Pierre Gagnon, Victoriaville
1990-91	Felix Potvin, Chicoutimi
1991-92	Jean-Francois Labbe, Trois-Rivieres
1992-93	Jocelyn Thibault, Sherbrooke

GUY LAFLEUR TROPHY

(Playoff MVP)

Season	Player, Team
1977-78	Richard David, Trois-Rivieres
1978-79	Jean-Francois Sauve, Trois-Rivieres
1979-80	Dale Hawerchuk, Cornwall
1980-81	Alain Lemieux, Trois-Rivieres
1981-82	Michel Morissette, Sherbrooke
1982-83	Pat LaFontaine, Verdun
1983-84	Mario Lemieux, Laval
1984-85	Claude Lemieux, Verdun
1985-86	Sylvain Cote, Hull
	Luc Robitaille, Hull
1986-87	Marc Saumier, Longueuil
1987-88	Marc Saumier, Hull
1988-89	Donald Audette, Laval
1989-90	Denis Chalifoux, Laval
1990-91	Felix Potvin, Chicoutimi
1991-92	Robert Guillet, Longueuil
1992-93	Emmanuel Fernandez, Laval

ROBERT LeBEL TROPHY

(Best team defensive average)

Season	Team
1977-78	Trois-Rivieres Draveurs
1978-79	Trois-Rivieres Draveurs
1979-80	Sherbrooke Beavers
1980-81	Sorel Black Hawks
1981-82	Montreal Juniors
1982-83	Shawinigan Cataracts
1983-84	Shawinigan Cataracts
1984-85	Shawinigan Cataracts
1985-86	Hull Olympiques

Season	Team	Season	Team
1986-78	—Longueuil Chevaliers	1990-91	—Chicoutimi Sagueneens
1987-88	—St. Jean Castors	1991-92	—Trois-Rivieres Draveurs
1988-89	—Hull Olympiques	1992-93	—Sherbrooke Faucons
1989-90	—Victoriaville Tigres		

ALL-TIME LEAGUE CHAMPIONS

REGULAR-SEASON CHAMPION

PLAYOFF CHAMPION

Season	Team	Team
1969-70	—Quebec Remparts	Quebec Remparts
1970-71	—Quebec Remparts	Quebec Remparts
1971-72	—Cornwall Royals	Cornwall Royals
1972-73	—Quebec Remparts	Quebec Remparts
1973-74	—Sorel Black Hawks	Quebec Remparts
1974-75	—Sherbrooke Beavers	Sherbrooke Beavers
1975-76	—Sherbrooke Beavers	Quebec Remparts
1976-77	—Quebec Remparts	Sherbrooke Beavers
1977-78	—Trois-Rivieres Draveurs	Trois-Rivieres Draveurs
1978-79	—Trois-Rivieres Draveurs	Trois-Rivieres Draveurs
1979-80	—Sherbrooke Beavers	Cornwall Royals
1980-81	—Cornwall Royals	Cornwall Royals
1981-82	—Sherbrooke Beavers	Sherbrooke Beavers
1982-83	—Laval Voisins	Verdun Juniors
1983-84	—Laval Voisins	Laval Voisins
1984-85	—Shawinigan Cataracts	Verdun Junior Canadiens
1985-86	—Hull Olympiques	Hull Olympiques
1986-87	—Granby Bisons	Longueuil Chevaliers
1987-88	—Hull Olympiques	Hull Olympiques
1988-89	—Trois-Rivieres Draveurs	Laval Titans
1989-90	—Victoriaville Tigres	Laval Titans
1990-91	—Chicoutimi Sagueneens	Chicoutimi Sagueneens
1991-92	—Longueuil College Francais	Longueuil College Francais
1992-93	—Sherbrooke Faucons	Laval Titans

The QMJHL regular-season champion is awarded the John Rougeau Trophy and the playoff champion is awarded the Presidents Cup.

The John Rougeau Trophy was originally called the Governors Trophy from 1969-70 through 1982-83.

WESTERN HOCKEY LEAGUE

LEAGUE OFFICE

Note: League was known as Canadian Major Junior Hockey League in 1966-67 and Western Canadian Hockey League from 1967-68 through 1976-77.

Address
Suite 521, 10333 Southport Road SW
Calgary, Alberta T2W 3X6
Phone
403-253-8113

President
Ed Chynoweth
Vice president
Richard Doerksen

Executive assistant
Norman Dueck
Statistician
Stu Judge

1992-93 REGULAR SEASON

FINAL STANDINGS

EAST DIVISION

Team	G	W	L	T	Pts.	GF	GA
Swift Current	72	49	21	2	100	384	267
Brandon	72	43	25	4	90	347	258
Saskatoon	72	42	27	3	87	311	236
Regina	72	35	36	1	71	322	313
Lethbridge	72	33	36	3	69	317	328
Red Deer	72	31	39	2	64	284	329
Medicine Hat	72	29	38	5	63	285	343
Moose Jaw	72	27	42	3	57	277	326
Prince Albert	72	25	42	5	55	252	317

WEST DIVISION

Team	G	W	L	T	Pts.	GF	GA
Portland	72	45	24	3	93	343	277
Tacoma	72	45	27	0	90	324	259
Kamloops	72	42	28	2	86	302	253
Seattle	72	31	38	3	65	234	292
Spokane	72	28	40	4	60	311	319
Tri-City	72	28	41	3	59	245	312
Victoria	72	20	49	3	43	217	326

INDIVIDUAL LEADERS

Goals: Jason Krywulak, Swift Current (81)
Assists: Jason Krywulak, Swift Current (81)
Points: Jason Krywulak, Swift Current (162)
Penalty minutes: John Badduke, Portland (367)
Goaltending average: Mike Walker, Saskatoon (2.91)
Shutouts: Lance Leslie, Tri-City (3)

	Games	G	A	Pts.
Alan Egeland, Tacoma	71	56	57	113
Dean Tiltgen, Red Deer	72	50	61	111
Ryan Fujita, Saskatoon	72	56	54	110
Mike Mathers, Kamloops	69	52	56	108
Ivan Vologjaninov, Lethbridge	71	48	60	108
Maxim Bets, Spokane	54	49	57	106
Colin Foley, Portland	72	46	60	106
Craig Lyons, Kamloops	60	44	62	106
Stacy Roest, Medicine Hat	72	33	73	106
Jamie Black, Tacoma	69	42	61	103
Shane Peacock, Lethbridge	65	27	75	102
Mark Szoke, Lethbridge	71	55	44	99
Bobby House, Brandon	61	57	39	96
Marty Murray, Brandon	67	29	65	94

TOP SCORERS

	Games	G	A	Pts.
Jason Krywulak, Swift Current	72	81	81	162
Valerie Bure, Spokane	66	68	79	147
Rick Girard, Swift Current	72	71	70	141
Louis Dumont, Regina	72	62	59	121
Domenic Pittis, Lethbridge	66	46	73	119
Todd Holt, Swift Current	67	56	57	113

INDIVIDUAL STATISTICS

BRANDON WHEAT KINGS

SCORING

	Games	G	A	Pts.	Pen.
Bobby House	61	57	39	96	87
Marty Murray	67	29	65	94	50
Mike Maneluk	72	36	51	87	75
Jeff Hoad	70	28	32	60	158
Mark Kolesar	68	27	33	60	110
Darrin Ritchie	60	34	24	58	17
Aris Brimanis	71	8	50	58	110
Ryan Smith	71	9	38	47	103
Chris Johnston	57	24	21	45	144
Todd Dutiaume	66	17	28	45	57
Craig Geekie	72	7	29	36	169
Mike Dubinsky	64	10	25	35	44
Mark Franks	28	13	17	30	33
Darcy Werenka	36	4	25	29	19
Chris Dingman	50	10	17	27	64
Colin Cloutier	60	11	15	26	138
Chris Schmidt	24	7	10	17	4

	Games	G	A	Pts.	Pen.
Sean McFatridge	33	6	7	13	140
Dwayne Gylywoychuk	68	1	11	12	200
Jeff Jubenville	21	4	7	11	45
Scott Hlady	38	3	6	9	27
Jeff Staples	40	0	5	5	114
Trevor Robins (goalie)	59	0	4	4	53
Dan Kopek	7	1	2	3	27
Scott Laluk	42	0	3	3	21
Bobby Brown	5	1	1	2	0
Jason Bies	1	0	0	0	0
Brian Elder (goalie)	1	0	0	0	0
Paul Bailley	2	0	0	0	0
Stu Scantlebury	2	0	0	0	4
Adam Magarrell	8	0	0	0	0
Byron Penstock (goalie)	17	0	0	0	14

GOALTENDING

	Games	Min.	Goals	SO	Avg.
Brian Elder	1	30	1	0	2.00
Trevor Robins	59	3470	183(5)	2	3.16
Byron Penstock	17	882	68(1)	1	4.63

MAJOR JUNIOR LEAGUES

KAMLOOPS BLAZERS

SCORING

	Games	G	A	Pts.	Pen.
Mike Mathers	69	52	56	108	63
Craig Lyons	60	44	62	106	87
Darcy Tucker	67	31	58	89	155
Jarrett Deuling	68	31	32	63	93
Rod Stevens	68	26	28	54	42
Craig Bonner	72	8	43	51	143
Scott Loucks	71	21	29	50	128
Aaron Keller	70	4	34	38	34
David Wilkie	53	11	26	37	109
Ryan Huska	68	17	15	32	50
Tyson Nash	61	10	16	26	78
Scott Ferguson	71	4	19	23	206
Hnat Domenichelli	45	12	8	20	15
Shane Doan	51	7	12	19	55
Chris Murray	62	6	10	16	217
Mike Josephson	46	5	9	14	60
Jarrett Bousquet	58	3	11	14	142
Bob Westerby	45	3	6	9	192
Dustin Kelley	24	3	5	8	13
Bob Maudie	38	1	5	6	24
Nolan Baumgartner	43	0	5	5	30
Dale Masson (goalie)	36	0	4	4	8
Brad Hammerback	45	0	4	4	74
Shane Kuss	1	1	1	2	0
Dustin Green	5	1	0	1	0
Jason Becker	17	1	0	1	4
Lee Grant	3	0	1	1	0
Steve Passmore (goalie)	25	0	1	1	13
David Bernard	1	0	0	0	0
Brad Lukowich	1	0	0	0	0
Steve Parsons	1	0	0	0	0
David Pirnak (goalie)	1	0	0	0	0
Jason Holland	4	0	0	0	2
Fran Defrenza	6	0	0	0	4
Rod Branch (goalie)	17	0	0	0	8

GOALTENDING

	Games	Min.	Goals	SO	Avg.
Steve Passmore	25	1479	69	1	2.80
Rod Branch	17	847	51(4)	0	3.61
Dale Masson	36	2009	126(2)	1	3.76
David Pirnak	1	13	1	0	4.62

LETHBRIDGE HURRICANES

SCORING

	Games	G	A	Pts.	Pen.
Domenic Pittis	66	46	73	119	69
Ivan Vologjaninov	71	48	60	108	12
Shane Peacock	65	27	75	102	100
Mark Szoke	71	55	44	99	152
Cory Dosdall	53	22	45	67	139
Brantt Myhres	64	13	35	48	277
Lee Sorochan	69	8	32	40	208
Aaron Zarowny	71	13	18	31	62
Todd MacIsaac	58	14	16	30	147
Cadrin Smart	68	12	17	29	61
Jamie Pushor	72	6	22	28	200
Rob Hartnell	16	10	12	22	40
Darcy Werenka	19	4	17	21	12
Maurice Meagher	50	10	9	19	154
Jason Widmer	55	3	15	18	140
Brad Zimmer	13	4	8	12	7
Derek Wood	66	3	8	11	84
Garry Pearce	14	5	4	9	4
Slade Stephenson	43	5	3	8	120
Chris Catellier	37	1	6	7	55
Jay Bertsch	49	3	2	5	80
Randy Perry	59	1	4	5	27
Bryce Salvador	64	1	4	5	29
Darcy Austin (goalie)	51	0	5	5	11
Nick Polychronopoulos	24	2	2	4	72
Jason Sorochan	13	1	1	2	41
Rob Sawers	5	0	2	2	6

	Games	G	A	Pts.	Pen.
Keith Cassidy	5	0	1	1	8
Lee Grant	5	0	1	1	14
Derek Deiner	1	0	0	0	0
Chad Gans	1	0	0	0	0
Scott Grieco	2	0	0	0	0
David Trofimenkoff (goalie)	27	0	0	0	2

GOALTENDING

	Games	Min.	Goals	SO	Avg.
David Trofimenkoff	27	1419	103(6)	0	4.36
Darcy Austin	51	2924	216(3)	0	4.43

MEDICINE HAT TIGERS

SCORING

	Games	G	A	Pts.	Pen.
Stacy Roest	72	33	73	106	30
Rob Niedermayer	52	43	34	77	67
David Cooper	63	15	50	65	88
Olaf Kjenstad	44	26	28	54	56
Mike Rathje	57	12	37	49	103
Cam Danyluk	57	29	19	48	214
Mike Jickling	47	14	24	38	56
Clayton Norris	41	21	16	37	128
Ryan Petz	72	10	24	34	50
Mark Polak	68	11	20	31	50
Aaron Boh	58	6	21	27	173
Stacey Fritz	67	15	8	23	38
Lorne Toews	67	13	9	22	152
Jamie Linden	50	9	9	18	147
Scott Townsend	13	6	8	14	4
Bryan McCabe	14	0	13	13	83
Danny Faassen	71	1	11	12	112
Justin Hocking	54	1	9	10	119
Steve Cheredaryk	67	1	9	10	88
Brad Wilson	56	6	3	9	48
Sonny Mignacca (goalie)	50	0	9	9	43
Shawn Stone	33	3	5	8	6
Jared Bednar	9	1	4	5	20
Dana Rieder	14	1	4	5	14
Jon Duval	13	2	2	4	32
Scott Lindsay	4	2	1	3	4
Evan Anderson	3	0	3	3	2
Curtis Cardinal	21	2	0	2	28
Kyley Fyculak	26	1	0	1	15
Jeremy Schaefer	65	1	0	1	95
James Seney	4	0	1	1	9
Scott Bellefontaine (goalie)	28	0	1	1	6
Kent Baumbach (goalie)	1	0	0	0	0
Stacey Biever	1	0	0	0	2
Jeramie Heistad	2	0	0	0	18
Keith Cassidy	3	0	0	0	10
Rob McCaig	4	0	0	0	17
Mitch Walker (goalie)	6	0	0	0	0

GOALTENDING

	Games	Min.	Goals	SO	Avg.
Scott Bellefontaine	28	1426	105(2)	0	4.42
Sonny Mignacca	50	2724	210(4)	1	4.63
Kent Baumbach	1	60	5	0	5.00
Mitch Walker	6	185	17	0	5.51

MOOSE JAW WARRIORS

SCORING

	Games	G	A	Pts.	Pen.
Kevin Smyth	64	44	38	82	111
Grady Manson	72	15	44	59	84
Jarret Zukiwsky	44	29	27	56	113
Chris Schmidt	42	24	24	48	22
Chris Brandt	72	16	28	44	39
Chris Armstrong	67	9	35	44	104
Neil Johnston	56	14	28	42	107
Marc Hussey	68	12	28	40	121
Kevin Pozzo	72	10	29	39	95
Ryan Smyth	64	19	14	33	59
Trevor Couldwell	42	13	19	32	41

	Games	G	A	Pts.	Pen.
Mark Franks	23	18	13	31	24
Curtis Brown	71	13	16	29	30
Scott Ducharmie	64	11	12	23	46
Evan Marble	29	3	20	23	65
Dan O'Rourke	36	4	10	14	121
Lance Burns	24	6	6	12	36
Rob Trumbley	61	5	4	9	308
Mark McCoy	34	1	8	9	18
Brad Toporowski	51	2	6	8	59
David Jesiolowski	43	3	4	7	154
Jeff Budai	13	2	5	7	13
Jeff Petruic	8	1	5	6	10
Russ West	8	2	3	5	6
Travis Stevenson	70	0	5	5	128
Darren Stevenson	31	1	2	3	53
Fred Hettle	4	0	2	2	0
Ryan Dyck	4	0	1	1	4
Darcy Chartrand	5	0	1	1	11
Jarrod Daniel (goalie)	43	0	1	1	4
Ray Guze	1	0	0	0	2
Rob Wilson	1	0	0	0	0
Trevor Amundrud (goalie)	2	0	0	0	0
Blaine Hilbig	2	0	0	0	0
Dale Purington	2	0	0	0	2
Bill Hooson	5	0	0	0	29
Chad Reich	5	0	0	0	0
Rod Gorrill	7	0	0	0	7
Jeremy Riehl	8	0	0	0	0
Jason Carey (goalie)	10	0	0	0	0
Gary Lebsack	16	0	0	0	66
Jody Lehman (goalie)	28	0	0	0	13

GOALTENDING

	Games	Min.	Goals	SO	Avg.
Jarrod Daniel	43	2323	159(8)	0	4.11
Jason Carey	10	528	38(3)	1	4.32
Jody Lehman	28	1418	105(3)	0	4.44
Trevor Amundrud	2	75	10	0	8.00

PORTLAND WINTER HAWKS

SCORING

	Games	G	A	Pts.	Pen.
Colin Foley	72	46	60	106	123
Nick Vachon	66	33	58	91	100
Jiri Beranek	70	25	61	86	59
Layne Roland	69	41	36	77	99
Brandon Smith	72	20	54	74	38
Adam Deadmarsh	58	33	36	69	126
Scott Nichol	67	31	33	64	146
Jason Wiemer	68	18	34	52	159
Jason McBain	71	9	35	44	76
Lonnie Bohonos	27	20	17	37	16
Cale Hulse	72	10	26	36	284
John Badduke	71	12	14	26	367
Dave Cammock	70	11	14	25	154
Nolan Pratt	70	4	19	23	97
Shannon Briske	66	10	12	22	41
Mike Williamson	67	6	13	19	90
Brandon Coates	18	4	9	13	20
Shawn Collins	60	2	8	10	75
Brad Symes	68	4	2	6	107
Sheldon Szmata	47	3	3	6	14
Ryan Van Steinburg	45	1	1	2	97
Scott Langkow (goalie)	34	0	2	2	10
Joaquin Gage (goalie)	38	0	1	1	8

GOALTENDING

	Games	Min.	Goals	SO	Avg.
Scott Langkow	34	2064	119(1)	2	3.46
Joaquin Gage	38	2302	153(4)	2	3.99

PRINCE ALBERT RAIDERS

SCORING

	Games	G	A	Pts.	Pen.
Van Burgess	57	35	39	74	67

	Games	G	A	Pts.	Pen.
Denis Pederson	72	33	40	73	134
Shane Toporowski	72	25	32	57	235
Merv Haney	71	21	28	49	32
Duane Maruschak	45	22	26	48	20
Dean McAmmond	30	19	29	48	44
Jeff Gorman	69	21	23	44	79
Shane Zulyniak	72	8	27	35	144
Paul Healy	72	12	20	32	66
Jared Bednar	37	6	16	22	56
Steve Kelly	65	11	9	20	75
Mike McGhan	69	11	9	20	75
Cory Donaldson	62	8	8	16	53
Troy Hjertaas	61	2	13	15	226
Barkley Swenson	14	4	9	13	34
Darren Perkins	26	3	10	13	89
Shane Hnidy	27	2	10	12	43
Jeff Lank	63	1	11	12	60
Jay Fitzpatrick	42	1	7	8	111
Greg Lakovic	70	2	4	6	36
Nick Polychronopoulos	24	1	5	6	56
Darren Wright	53	0	4	4	131
Jason Klassen	24	1	2	3	15
Rob McCaig	13	0	2	2	32
Justin Borsato	1	1	0	1	0
Chris Mason	16	1	0	1	8
Greg Harvey	18	1	0	1	26
Jason Kwiatkowski	5	0	1	1	18
Pat Curcio	1	0	0	0	0
Charles Keshane	1	0	0	0	0
Brian Kostur	1	0	0	0	0
Kendall Sidoruk (goalie)	1	0	0	0	0
Brad Glassford (goalie)	2	0	0	0	0
Clarence Houle	3	0	0	0	2
Phillip LaVallee (goalie)	16	0	0	0	0
Jason Issel	20	0	0	0	0
Stan Matwijiw (goalie)	65	0	0	0	14

GOALTENDING

	Games	Min.	Goals	SO	Avg.
Kendall Sidoruk	1	4	0	0	0.00
Stan Matwijiw	65	3719	247(2)	1	3.98
Brad Glassford	2	120	10	0	5.00
Phillip LaVallee	16	546	57(1)	0	6.26

RED DEER REBELS

SCORING

	Games	G	A	Pts.	Pen.
Dean Tiltgen	72	50	61	111	33
Brian Loney	66	39	36	75	147
Todd Johnson	66	29	45	74	24
Darren Van Impe	54	23	47	70	118
Craig Reichert	66	32	33	65	62
Kevin Masters	71	9	40	49	107
Ken Richardson	63	23	20	43	140
Sean Selmser	70	13	27	40	216
Pete LeBoutillier	67	8	26	34	284
Vaclav Slansky	68	9	17	26	30
Eddy Marchant	51	12	11	23	110
Curtis Cardinal	42	10	13	23	16
Len MacAusland	67	2	20	22	162
Tony Vlastelic	56	8	5	13	27
Jeff Antonowich	34	5	7	12	17
Terry Lindgren	63	3	9	12	100
Cam MacGregor	65	2	8	10	35
Liam Weir	58	1	7	8	36
Shawn Stone	24	0	5	5	22
Mark Toljanich	53	0	5	5	110
Jason Becker	9	2	2	4	2
Scott Adair	22	1	3	4	94
Jeff Budai	8	1	2	3	0
Sean Halifax	28	1	2	3	27
Mark McCoy	20	0	3	3	19
Darby Walker	7	1	0	1	5
Rod Norquay	3	0	1	1	0
Fred Hettle	2	0	0	0	0

	Games	G	A	Pts.	Pen.
Peter Vandermeer	2	0	0	0	2
Derek Robertson (goalie)	4	0	0	0	0
Matt Young	4	0	0	0	0
Rob Herrington (goalie)	6	0	0	0	8
Jason Clague (goalie)	30	0	0	0	0
Mark Dawkins (goalie)	48	0	0	0	0

GOALTENDING

	Games	Min.	Goals	SO	Avg.
Rob Herrington	6	329	22(1)	0	4.01
Mark Dawkins	48	2439	166(4)	0	4.08
Jason Clague	30	1442	116(2)	0	4.83
Derek Robertson	4	154	18	0	7.01

REGINA PATS

SCORING

	Games	G	A	Pts.	Pen.
Louis Dumont	72	62	59	121	97
Kerry Biette	72	32	54	86	116
Jeff Friesen	70	45	38	83	23
Jeff Shantz	64	29	54	83	75
Jason Smith	64	14	52	66	175
Trevor Hanas	72	28	29	57	95
Derek Eberle	64	15	34	49	129
Nathan Dempsey	72	12	29	41	95
Brandon Coates	36	21	15	36	36
Russ Gronick	67	14	16	30	59
Grayden Reid	52	5	24	29	22
Randy Toye	69	5	17	22	49
Niklas Barklund	70	10	10	20	80
Mirsad Mujcin	33	6	13	19	67
Dion Zukiwsky	69	5	11	16	105
Steve Dowhy	22	4	12	16	10
Heath Weenk	48	2	12	14	82
Vernon Beardy	46	3	8	11	20
Garry Pearce	16	2	5	7	19
Russ West	21	4	2	6	8
Chris Zulyniak	61	2	2	4	138
Jeff Helperl	61	0	4	4	156
Rhett Gordon	2	1	0	1	2
Greg Story	33	1	0	1	16
Ryan Buttazzoni	2	0	1	1	7
Rob Herring	2	0	1	1	0
Frank Vogel	5	0	1	1	4
Chris Constant	8	0	1	1	13
Mike Risdale (goalie)	62	0	1	1	2
Jason Day	2	0	0	0	0
Don Dunnigan	2	0	0	0	0
Bobby Graham	3	0	0	0	2
Jodi Murphy	4	0	0	0	16
Jason Gibson	5	0	0	0	12
Barry Becker (goalie)	11	0	0	0	0
Chad Mercier (goalie)	14	0	0	0	0

GOALTENDING

	Games	Min.	Goals	SO	Avg.
Mike Risdale	62	3252	214(5)	2	3.95
Chad Mercier	14	595	46(1)	0	4.64
Barry Becker	11	509	47	0	5.54

SASKATOON BLADES

SCORING

	Games	G	A	Pts.	Pen.
Ryan Fujita	72	56	54	110	105
Shane Calder	72	40	45	85	209
Mark Wotton	71	15	51	66	90
Paul Buczkowski	72	22	43	65	57
Andy MacIntyre	72	35	29	64	82
Frank Banham	71	29	33	62	55
Derek Tibbatts	59	16	36	52	19
James Startup	48	18	32	50	73
Shawn Yakimishyn	71	18	24	42	234
Clarke Wilm	69	14	19	33	71
Peter Cox	69	16	9	25	102
Jason Duda	34	11	14	25	22

	Games	G	A	Pts.	Pen.
Rhett Warrener	68	2	17	19	100
Mike Gray	60	8	8	16	151
Mark Raiter	57	3	11	14	173
Chad Allan	69	2	10	12	67
Bryce Goebel	47	1	10	11	47
Stu Scantlebury	29	1	8	9	36
Norm Maracle (goalie)	53	0	8	8	4
Cory McKee	24	2	4	6	23
Marty Zdan	33	2	4	6	52
Andrew Kemper	24	0	3	3	41
David Hunchak	5	0	2	2	4
Mike Walker (goalie)	26	0	2	2	4
Trevor Ethier	1	0	0	0	0
Chris Hawes	2	0	0	0	12
Chris McAllister	4	0	0	0	2
Wade Belak	7	0	0	0	23
Chad Knippel	12	0	0	0	29
Rhett Trombley	27	0	0	0	47

GOALTENDING

	Games	Min.	Goals	SO	Avg.
Mike Walker	26	1443	70(4)	1	2.91
Norm Maracle	53	2939	160(2)	1	3.27

SEATTLE THUNDERBIRDS

SCORING

	Games	G	A	Pts.	Pen.
Blake Knox	70	23	60	83	200
Scott Lindsay	59	34	23	57	122
Chris Wells	63	18	37	55	111
John Lilley	45	22	28	50	55
Chris Herperger	46	20	11	31	30
Kurt Seher	69	9	20	29	125
Troy Hyatt	60	9	19	28	36
Brendan Witt	70	2	26	28	239
Tyler Quiring	55	15	11	26	54
Lonnie Bohonos	46	13	13	26	27
Kevin Mylander	55	10	12	22	61
Eric Bouchard	66	6	12	18	35
Duane Maruschak	25	4	13	17	18
Jeff Dewar	51	11	5	16	57
Jim Burcar	60	2	12	14	72
Chris Schmidt	61	6	7	13	17
Olaf Kjenstad	22	4	9	13	28
Brent Duncan	64	0	12	12	343
Darcy Mattersdorfer	45	8	3	11	13
Marko Elorinne	58	5	6	11	47
Larry McMorran	54	9	1	10	25
Andrew Kemper	30	1	3	4	34
Ryan Smith	7	1	2	3	2
Rob Tallas (goalie)	58	0	3	3	6
Milt Mastad	60	1	1	2	123
Wade Fennig	2	1	0	1	0
Ryan Brown	19	0	1	1	70
Doug Bonner (goalie)	30	0	1	1	0
Rob Derouin	2	0	0	0	0
Jeff Peddigrew	9	0	0	0	2
Shea Esselmont	19	0	0	0	13

GOALTENDING

	Games	Min.	Goals	SO	Avg.
Rob Tallas	58	3151	194(4)	2	3.69
Doug Bonner	30	1212	93(1)	1	4.60

SPOKANE CHIEFS

SCORING

	Games	G	A	Pts.	Pen.
Valeri Bure	66	68	79	147	49
Maxim Bets	54	49	57	106	130
Ryan Duthie	60	26	58	84	122
Paxton Schulte	45	38	35	73	142
Jason Podollan	72	36	33	69	108
Bryan McCabe	46	3	44	47	134
Jeremy Stasiuk	63	14	23	37	111
Sean Gillam	70	6	27	33	121

	Games	G	A	Pts.	Pen.
Tyler Romanchuk	71	8	23	31	141
Scott Townsend	39	12	18	30	4
Mike Jickling	15	8	15	23	41
Jared Bednar	16	2	14	16	62
Jon Duval	41	2	13	15	128
Lance Burns	38	5	9	14	34
Todd Harris	42	3	11	14	56
Aaron Boh	15	3	10	13	62
Derek Descouteau	62	7	5	12	44
Dana Rieder	38	4	6	10	41
Dean Kletzel	55	3	5	8	23
Randy Favaro	36	4	3	7	50
Kevin Sawyer	62	4	3	7	274
Dan Kopek	30	0	7	7	48
David Jesiolowski	27	1	5	6	135
Dion Darling	68	1	4	5	168
Jamie Linden	15	3	1	4	58
Shawn Byrne	50	0	3	3	180
Rennie McQueen	30	0	2	2	57
Barry Becker (goalie)	32	0	2	2	0
Richard Parent (goalie)	36	0	2	2	6
Brad Toporowski	12	1	0	1	28
Lance Barenz	2	0	1	1	0
Jeff Fancy	2	0	1	1	14
Trevor Shoaf	4	0	1	1	9
Justin Hocking	16	0	1	1	75
David Lemanowicz (goalie)	16	0	1	1	19
Darryl Onofrychuk (goalie)	3	0	0	0	0

GOALTENDING

	Games	Min.	Goals	SO	Avg.
Barry Becker	32	1718	118(1)	2	4.12
Richard Parent	36	1767	129	0	4.38
Darryl Onofrychuk	3	136	10	0	4.41
David Lemanowicz	16	738	61	1	4.96

SWIFT CURRENT BRONCOS

SCORING

	Games	G	A	Pts.	Pen.
Jason Krywulak	72	81	81	162	58
Rick Girard	72	71	70	141	25
Todd Holt	67	56	57	113	90
Andy Schneider	38	19	66	85	78
Brent Bilodeau	59	11	57	68	77
Ashley Buckberger	72	23	44	67	41
Tyler Wright	37	24	41	65	76
Trent McCleary	63	17	33	50	138
Regan Mueller	72	15	11	26	19
Russell Hewson	70	6	20	26	39
Steve Dowhy	45	14	9	23	11
Dean McAmmond	18	10	13	23	29
Jason Horvath	62	3	19	22	176
Shane Hnidy	45	5	12	17	62
Chris Herperger	20	9	7	16	31
Darren Perkins	26	5	9	14	48
Russ West	28	3	10	13	30
Fred Hettle	30	1	7	8	20
Darren McLean	32	4	3	7	34
Bill Hooson	47	2	5	7	98
Milan Hnilicka (goalie)	65	0	6	6	33
Keith McCambridge	70	0	6	6	87
Neil Johnston	14	2	3	5	10
Ryan Brown	47	1	4	5	104
Heath Weenk	26	0	4	4	22
Craig Millar	43	2	1	3	8
Trevor MacLean	19	0	3	3	7
Jason Sproul	23	0	3	3	4
Chris Low	51	0	3	3	6
Jamie Hayden	7	0	1	1	2
Ryan McConnell	1	0	0	0	0
Matt Young	1	0	0	0	0
Jason Renard	3	0	0	0	23
Kevin Felix	5	0	0	0	4
Jarrod Daniel (goalie)	6	0	0	0	0
Ian Gordon (goalie)	10	0	0	0	0

GOALTENDING

	Games	Min.	Goals	SO	Avg.
Milan Hnilicka	65	3679	206(6)	2	3.36
Jarrod Daniel	6	299	19(1)	0	3.81
Ian Gordon	10	365	31(4)	0	5.10

TACOMA ROCKETS

SCORING

	Games	G	A	Pts.	Pen.
Allan Egeland	71	56	57	113	119
Jamie Black	69	42	61	103	53
Michal Sykora	70	23	50	73	73
Kevin Powell	70	30	39	69	47
John Varga	61	32	32	64	63
Trever Fraser	71	28	36	64	207
Barkley Swenson	56	18	24	42	87
Marty Flichel	61	21	20	41	19
Jason Kwiatkowski	67	10	30	40	95
Alexander Alexeev	44	3	33	36	67
Mike Piersol	72	9	20	29	94
Cory McKee	37	9	15	24	53
Tyler Prosofsky	62	10	9	19	79
Drew Schoneck	71	7	11	18	125
Corey Stock	65	7	7	14	87
Adam Smith	67	0	12	12	43
Van Burgess	12	5	6	11	23
Jeff Calvert (goalie)	59	1	8	9	14
Dennis Pinfold	63	6	2	8	143
Dave McMillen	46	3	3	6	175
Dallas Thompson	68	2	3	5	161
Ryan Phillips	25	0	4	4	10
Jamie Butt	21	1	2	3	46
Toby Weishaar	23	1	2	3	15
Stu Scantlebury	16	0	2	2	13
Todd MacDonald (goalie)	19	0	1	1	6
Jason Knight	1	0	0	0	0
Scott Bellefontaine (goalie)	2	0	0	0	2
Ryan Pisiak	2	0	0	0	0

GOALTENDING

	Games	Min.	Goals	SO	Avg.
Jeff Calvert	59	3389	187(3)	1	3.31
Scott Bellefontaine	2	120	8	0	4.00
Todd MacDonald	19	823	59(2)	0	4.30

TRI-CITY AMERICANS

SCORING

	Games	G	A	Pts.	Pen.
Damon Langkow	65	22	42	64	96
Rob Hartnell	48	25	34	59	101
Todd Klassen	72	12	35	47	36
Brent Ashcroft	72	17	27	44	36
Chad Cabana	68	19	23	42	104
Tony Prpic	63	16	17	33	110
Jesse Wilson	32	13	20	33	47
Adam Rettschlag	57	16	12	28	70
Jason Smith	38	10	16	26	10
Todd Simpson	69	5	18	23	196
Jason Bowen	62	10	12	22	219
Jeff Petruic	38	12	9	21	35
Kimbi Daniels	9	9	12	21	12
Cory Dosdall	18	11	9	20	66
Jason Renard	40	10	10	20	178
Steve O'Rourke	61	3	17	20	104
Evan Marble	30	1	17	18	52
Geoff Lynch	67	7	5	12	21
Ryan Marsh	60	5	7	12	55
Kory Mullin	68	2	10	12	95
Marc Stephan	55	3	6	9	62
Todd Harris	14	6	2	8	14
Ivan Roulette	10	3	4	7	6
Gary Lebsack	46	1	6	7	249
A.J. Kelham	18	2	4	6	16
Mirsad Mujcin	22	2	4	6	42
Graham Harder	42	1	4	5	47
Darren Hastman	2	1	2	3	0

	Games	G	A	Pts.	Pen.
Lance Leslie (goalie)	49	0	3	3	4
Frank Esposito	6	0	2	2	24
Dan O'Rourke	18	0	2	2	83
Jamie Barnes	3	1	0	1	10
Ryan Mattersdorfer	2	0	1	1	28
Darcy Mattersdorfer	2	0	1	1	2
Kyuin Shim	2	0	1	1	6
Sean Matile (goalie)	7	0	1	1	2
Scott Adair	1	0	0	0	94
Terry Ryan	1	0	0	0	0
Jodi Murphy	2	0	0	0	10
Sheldon Souray	2	0	0	0	0
Dave Greenway	4	0	0	0	0
David Brumby (goalie)	30	0	0	0	6

GOALTENDING

	Games	Min.	Goals	SO	Avg.
Lance Leslie	49	2620	163(2)	3	3.73
David Brumby	30	1529	123(2)	0	4.83
Sean Matile	7	214	22	0	6.17

VICTORIA COUGARS

SCORING

	Games	G	A	Pts.	Pen.
Scott Fukami	70	38	38	76	28
Mike Barrie	70	31	39	70	244
Steve Lingren	72	10	43	53	148
Alex Vasilevskii	71	27	25	52	52
Brad Scott	68	22	26	48	170
Ross Harris	69	23	22	45	44
Jamie Burt	69	10	28	38	162
Travis Kelln	72	6	25	31	39
Shea Esselmont	43	7	15	22	72
Rob Butz	67	7	11	18	64
Ryan Pellaers	64	4	13	17	24
Randy Chadney	57	9	6	15	58
Mike Leclerc	70	4	11	15	118
Dorian Anneck	63	5	6	11	19
Byron Briske	66	1	10	11	110
Chris Petersen	58	5	3	8	26
Ryan Strain	64	4	4	8	96
Kelly Harris	63	3	3	6	308
Andrew Laming	42	0	3	3	50
Fran Defrenza	5	1	1	2	18
Dale Masson (goalie)	22	0	2	2	9
Steve Passmore (goalie)	43	0	2	2	26
Mark McCoy	5	0	1	1	4
Daryl Damini	6	0	1	1	0
Clayton Catellier	45	0	1	1	71
Jamie Morris (goalie)	1	0	0	0	0
Chris Hawes	2	0	0	0	10
Roland Monilaws	2	0	0	0	0
Rhett Trombley	12	0	0	0	66
Chad Anctil (goalie)	15	0	0	0	0

GOALTENDING

	Games	Min.	Goals	SO	Avg.
Steve Passmore	43	2402	150(3)	1	3.75
Dale Masson	22	1304	100(3)	0	4.60
Chad Anctil	15	624	64(1)	0	6.15
Jamie Morris	1	30	5	0	10.00

PLAYERS WITH TWO OR MORE TEAMS

SCORING

	Games	G	A	Pts.	Pen.
Scott Adair, Tri-City	1	0	0	0	94
Scott Adair, Red Deer	22	1	3	4	94
Totals	23	1	3	4	30
Barry Becker, Regina (goalie)	11	0	0	0	0
Barry Becker, Spokane (goalie)	32	0	2	2	0
Totals	43	0	2	2	0
Jason Becker, Red Deer	9	2	2	4	2
Jason Becker, Kamloops	17	1	0	1	4
Totals	26	3	2	5	6

	Games	G	A	Pts.	Pen.
Jared Bednar, Spokane	16	2	14	16	62
Jared Bednar, Medicine Hat	9	1	4	5	20
Jared Bednar, Prince Albert	37	6	16	22	56
Totals	62	9	34	43	138
Scott Bellefontaine, Tacoma (g)	2	0	0	0	2
Scott Bellefontaine, M.H. (g)	28	0	1	1	6
Totals	30	0	1	1	8
Aaron Boh, Spokane	15	3	10	13	62
Aaron Boh, Medicine Hat	58	6	21	27	173
Totals	73	9	31	40	235
Lonnie Bohonos, Seattle	46	13	13	26	27
Lonnie Bohonos, Portland	27	20	17	37	16
Totals	73	33	30	63	43
Ryan Brown, Seattle	19	0	1	1	70
Ryan Brown, Swift Current	47	1	4	5	104
Totals	66	1	5	6	174
Jeff Budai, Moose Jaw	13	2	5	7	13
Jeff Budai, Red Deer	8	1	2	3	0
Totals	21	3	7	10	13
Van Burgess, Tacoma	12	5	6	11	23
Van Burgess, Prince Albert	57	35	39	74	67
Totals	69	40	45	85	90
Lance Burns, Spokane	38	5	9	14	34
Lance Burns, Moose Jaw	24	6	6	12	36
Totals	62	11	15	26	70
Ryan Buttazzoni, Tri-City	2	0	1	1	28
Ryan Buttazzoni, Regina	2	0	1	1	7
Totals	4	0	2	2	35
Curtis Cardinal, Medicine Hat	21	2	0	2	28
Curtis Cardinal, Red Deer	42	10	13	23	16
Totals	63	12	13	25	44
Keith Cassidy, Lethbridge	5	0	1	1	8
Keith Cassidy, Medicine Hat	3	0	0	0	10
Totals	8	0	1	1	18
Brandon Coates, Portland	18	4	9	13	20
Brandon Coates, Regina	36	21	15	36	36
Totals	54	25	24	49	56
Jarrod Daniel, Swift Current (g)	6	0	0	0	0
Jarrod Daniel, Moose Jaw (g)	43	0	1	1	4
Totals	49	0	1	1	4
Fran Defrenza, Victoria	5	1	1	2	18
Fran Defrenza, Kamloops	6	0	0	0	4
Totals	11	1	1	2	22
Cory Dosdall, Tri-City	18	11	9	20	66
Cory Dosdall, Lethbridge	53	22	45	67	139
Totals	71	33	54	87	205
Steve Dowhy, Swift Current	45	14	9	23	11
Steve Dowhy, Regina	22	4	12	16	10
Totals	67	18	21	39	21
Jon Duval, Medicine Hat	13	2	2	4	32
Jon Duval, Spokane	41	2	13	15	128
Totals	54	4	15	19	160
Shea Esselmont, Victoria	43	7	15	22	72
Shea Esselmont, Seattle	19	0	0	0	13
Totals	62	7	15	22	85
Mark Franks, Brandon	28	13	17	30	33
Mark Franks, Moose Jaw	23	18	13	31	24
Totals	51	31	30	61	57
Lee Grant, Lethbridge	5	0	1	1	14
Lee Grant, Kamloops	3	0	1	1	0
Totals	8	0	2	2	14
Todd Harris, Tri-City	14	6	2	8	14
Todd Harris, Spokane	42	3	11	14	56
Totals	56	9	13	22	70
Rob Hartnell, Lethbridge	16	10	12	22	40
Rob Hartnell, Tri-City	48	25	34	59	101
Totals	64	35	46	81	141
Chris Hawes, Victoria	2	0	0	0	10
Chris Hawes, Saskatoon	2	0	0	0	12
Totals	4	0	0	0	22
Chris Herperger, Swift Current	20	9	7	16	31
Chris Herperger, Seattle	46	20	11	31	30
Totals	66	29	18	47	61
Fred Hettle, Moose Jaw	4	0	2	2	0
Fred Hettle, Swift Current	30	1	7	8	20
Fred Hettle, Red Deer	2	0	0	0	0
Totals	36	1	9	10	20

	Games	G	A	Pts.	Pen.
Shane Hnidy, Swift Current	45	5	12	17	62
Shane Hnidy, Prince Albert	27	2	10	12	43
Totals	72	7	22	29	105
Justin Hocking, Spokane	16	0	1	1	75
Justin Hocking, Medicine Hat	54	1	9	10	119
Totals	70	1	10	11	194
Bill Hooson, Moose Jaw	5	0	0	0	29
Bill Hooson, Swift Current	47	2	5	7	98
Totals	52	2	5	7	127
David Jesiolowski, Moose Jaw	43	3	4	7	154
David Jesiolowski, Spokane	27	1	5	6	135
Totals	70	4	9	13	289
Mike Jickling, Spokane	15	8	15	23	41
Mike Jickling, Medicine Hat	47	14	24	38	56
Totals	62	22	39	61	97
Neil Johnston, Swift Current	14	2	3	5	10
Neil Johnston, Moose Jaw	56	14	28	42	107
Totals	70	16	31	47	117
Andrew Kemper, Seattle	30	1	3	4	34
Andrew Kemper, Saskatoon	24	0	3	3	41
Totals	54	1	6	7	75
Olaf Kjenstad, Medicine Hat	44	26	28	54	56
Olaf Kjenstad, Seattle	22	4	9	13	28
Totals	66	30	37	67	84
Dan Kopek, Brandon	7	1	2	3	27
Dan Kopek, Spokane	30	0	7	7	48
Totals	37	1	9	10	75
Jason Kwiatkowski, P.A.	5	0	1	1	18
Jason Kwiatkowski, Tacoma	67	10	30	40	95
Totals	72	10	31	41	113
Gary Lebsack, Moose Jaw	16	0	0	0	66
Gary Lebsack, Tri-City	46	1	6	7	249
Totals	62	1	6	7	315
Jamie Linden, Spokane	15	3	1	4	58
Jamie Linden, Medicine Hat	50	9	9	18	147
Totals	65	12	10	22	205
Scott Lindsay, Medicine Hat	4	2	1	3	4
Scott Lindsay, Seattle	59	34	23	57	122
Totals	63	36	24	60	126
Evan Marble, Moose Jaw	29	3	20	23	65
Evan Marble, Tri-City	30	1	17	18	52
Totals	59	4	37	41	117
Duane Maruschak, Seattle	25	4	13	17	18
Duane Maruschak, P.A.	45	22	26	48	20
Totals	70	26	39	65	38
Dale Masson, Kamloops (g)	36	0	4	4	8
Dale Masson, Victoria (goalie)	22	0	2	2	9
Totals	58	0	6	6	17
Darcy Mattersdorfer, Tri-City	2	0	1	1	2
Darcy Mattersdorfer, Seattle	45	8	3	11	13
Totals	47	8	4	12	15
Dean McAmmond, Prince Albert	30	19	29	48	44
Dean McAmmond, Swift Current	18	10	13	23	29
Totals	48	29	42	71	73
Bryan McCabe, Medicine Hat	14	0	13	13	83
Bryan McCabe, Spokane	46	3	44	47	134
Totals	60	3	57	60	217
Rob McCaig, Medicine Hat	4	0	0	0	17
Rob McCaig, Prince Albert	13	0	2	2	32
Totals	17	0	2	2	49
Mark McCoy, Red Deer	20	0	3	3	19
Mark McCoy, Victoria	5	0	1	1	4
Mark McCoy, Moose Jaw	34	1	8	9	18
Totals	59	1	12	13	41
Cory McKee, Tacoma	37	9	15	24	53
Cory McKee, Saskatoon	24	2	4	6	23
Totals	61	11	19	30	76
Mirsad Mujcin, Tri-City	22	2	4	6	42
Mirsad Mujcin, Regina	33	6	13	19	67
Totals	55	8	17	25	109
Jodi Murphy, Tri-City	2	0	0	0	10
Jodi Murphy, Regina	4	0	0	0	16
Totals	6	0	0	0	26
Dan O'Rourke, Tri-City	18	0	2	2	83
Dan O'Rourke, Moose Jaw	36	4	10	14	121
Totals	54	4	12	16	204

	Games	G	A	Pts.	Pen.
Steve Passmore, Victoria (g)	43	0	2	2	26
Steve Passmore, Kamloops (g)	25	0	1	1	13
Totals	68	0	3	3	39
Garry Pearce, Regina	16	2	5	7	19
Garry Pearce, Lethbridge	14	5	4	9	4
Totals	30	7	9	16	23
Darren Perkins, Prince Albert	26	3	10	13	89
Darren Perkins, Swift Current	26	5	9	14	48
Totals	52	8	19	27	137
Jeff Petruic, Moose Jaw	8	1	5	6	10
Jeff Petruic, Tri-City	38	12	9	21	35
Totals	46	13	14	27	45
Nick Polychronopoulos, P.A.	24	1	5	6	56
Nick Polychronopoulos, Leth.	24	2	2	4	72
Totals	48	3	7	10	128
Jason Renard, Swift Current	3	0	0	0	23
Jason Renard, Tri-City	40	10	10	20	178
Totals	43	10	10	20	201
Dana Rieder, Medicine Hat	14	1	4	5	14
Dana Rieder, Spokane	38	4	6	10	41
Totals	52	5	10	15	55
Stu Scantlebury, Brandon	2	0	0	0	4
Stu Scantlebury, Saskatoon	29	1	8	9	36
Stu Scantlebury, Tacoma	16	0	2	2	13
Totals	47	1	10	11	53
Chris Schmidt, Moose Jaw	42	24	24	48	22
Chris Schmidt, Brandon	24	7	10	17	4
Totals	66	31	34	65	26
Shawn Stone, Red Deer	24	0	5	5	22
Shawn Stone, Medicine Hat	33	3	5	8	6
Totals	57	3	10	13	28
Barkley Swenson, Prince Albert	14	4	9	13	34
Barkley Swenson, Tacoma	56	18	24	42	87
Totals	70	22	33	55	121
Brad Toporowski, Spokane	12	1	0	1	28
Brad Toporowski, Moose Jaw	51	2	6	8	59
Totals	63	3	6	9	87
Scott Townsend, Medicine Hat	13	6	8	14	4
Scott Townsend, Spokane	39	12	18	30	4
Totals	52	18	26	44	8
Rhett Trombley, Saskatoon	27	0	0	0	47
Rhett Trombley, Victoria	12	0	0	0	66
Totals	39	0	0	0	113
Heath Weenk, Regina	48	2	12	14	82
Heath Weenk, Swift Current	26	0	4	4	22
Totals	74	2	16	18	104
Darcy Werenka, Lethbridge	19	4	17	21	12
Darcy Werenka, Brandon	36	4	25	29	19
Totals	55	8	42	50	31
Russ West, Moose Jaw	8	2	3	5	6
Russ West, Swift Current	28	3	10	13	30
Russ West, Regina	21	4	2	6	8
Totals	57	9	15	24	44
Matt Young, Swift Current	1	0	0	0	0
Matt Young, Red Deer	4	0	0	0	0
Totals	5	0	0	0	2

GOALTENDING

	Games	Min.	Goals	SO	Avg.
Barry Becker, Regina	11	509	47	0	5.54
Barry Becker, Spo.	32	1718	118(1)	2	4.12
Totals	43	2227	165	2	4.45
S. Bellefontaine, Tac.	2	120	8	0	4.00
S. Bellefontaine, M.H.	28	1426	105(2)	0	4.42
Totals	30	1546	113	0	4.39
Jarrod Daniel, S.C.	6	299	19(1)	0	3.81
Jarrod Daniel, M.J.	43	2323	159(8)	0	4.11
Totals	49	2622	178	0	4.07
Dale Masson, Kam.	36	2009	126(2)	1	3.76
Dale Masson, Vic.	22	1304	100(3)	0	4.60
Totals	58	3313	226	1	4.09
Steve Passmore, Vic.	43	2402	150(3)	1	3.75
Steve Passmore, Kam.	25	1479	69	1	2.80
Totals	68	3881	219	2	3.39

( )—Empty-net goals (do not count against a goaltender's average).

1993 PLAYOFFS

RESULTS

EAST DIVISION PRELIMINARY

Series "A"

	W	L	Pts.	GF	GA
Medicine Hat	3	1	6	12	8
Brandon	1	3	2	8	12

(Medicine Hat won series, 3-1)

Series "B"

	W	L	Pts.	GF	GA
Saskatoon	3	1	6	14	11
Red Deer	1	3	2	11	14

(Saskatoon won series, 3-1)

Series "C"

	W	L	Pts.	GF	GA
Regina	3	1	6	17	15
Lethbridge	1	3	2	15	17

(Regina won series, 3-1)

WEST DIVISION PRELIMINARY

Series "D"

	W	L	Pts.	GF	GA
Portland	4	0	8	20	9
Tri-City	0	4	0	9	20

(Portland won series, 4-0)

Series "E"

	W	L	Pts.	GF	GA
Spokane	4	3	8	30	31
Tacoma	3	4	6	31	30

(Spokane won series, 4-3)

Series "F"

	W	L	Pts.	GF	GA
Kamloops	4	1	8	19	14
Seattle	1	4	2	14	19

(Kamloops won series, 4-1)

EAST DIVISION SEMIFINALS

Series "G"

	W	L	Pts.	GF	GA
Swift Current	4	2	8	32	18
Medicine Hat	2	4	4	18	32

(Swift Current won series, 4-2)

Series "H"

	W	L	Pts.	GF	GA
Regina	4	1	8	24	16
Saskatoon	1	4	2	16	24

(Regina won series, 4-1)

WEST DIVISION SEMIFINALS

Series "I"

	W	L	Pts.	GF	GA
Kamloops	3	0	6	15	6
Spokane	0	3	0	6	15

(Kamloops won series, 3-0)

EAST DIVISION FINALS

Series "J"

	W	L	Pts.	GF	GA
Swift Current	4	0	8	27	13
Regina	0	4	0	13	27

(Swift Current won series, 4-0)

WEST DIVISION FINALS

Series "K"

	W	L	Pts.	GF	GA
Portland	4	1	8	28	19
Kamloops	1	4	2	19	28

(Portland won series, 4-1)

FINALS

Series "L"

	W	L	Pts.	GF	GA
Swift Current	4	3	8	34	27
Portland	3	4	6	27	34

(Swift Current won series, 4-3)

INDIVIDUAL LEADERS

Goals: Dean McAmmond, Swift Current (16)
Assists: Andy Schneider, Swift Current (26)
Points: Andy Schneider, Swift Current (39)
Penalty minutes: Cale Hulse, Portland (65)
Goaltending average: Trevor Robins, Brandon (2.56)
Shutouts: Milan Hnilicka, Swift Current (2)

TOP SCORERS

	Games	G	A	Pts.
Andy Schneider, Swift Current	17	13	26	39
Jason Krywulak, Swift Current	17	15	22	37
Dean McAmmond, Swift Current	17	16	19	35
Tyler Wright, Swift Current	17	9	17	26
Rick Girard, Swift Current	17	9	17	26
Todd Holt, Swift Current	16	10	12	22
Jamie Black, Tacoma	7	7	15	22
Lonny Bohonos, Portland	15	8	13	21
Colin Foley, Portland	16	6	13	19
Brent Bilodeau, Swift Current	17	5	14	19

BRANDON WHEAT KINGS

(Lost East Division preliminaries to Medicine Hat, 3-1)

SCORING

	Games	G	A	Pts.	Pen.
Bobby House	4	2	2	4	0
Marty Murray	4	1	3	4	0
Aris Brimanis	4	2	1	3	7
Mike Maneluk	4	2	1	3	2
Jeff Hoad	4	1	0	1	11
Chris Schmidt	4	0	1	1	4
Ryan Smith	4	0	1	1	4
Jeff Staples	4	0	1	1	4
Dwayne Gylywoychuk	1	0	0	0	2
Craig Geekie	2	0	0	0	2
Mike Dubinsky	3	0	0	0	0
Scott Hlady	3	0	0	0	2
Darcy Werenka	3	0	0	0	2
Colin Cloutier	4	0	0	0	18
Chris Dingman	4	0	0	0	0
Todd Dutiaume	4	0	0	0	0
Chris Johnston	4	0	0	0	8
Mark Kolesar	4	0	0	0	4
Sean McFatridge	4	0	0	0	13
Darrin Ritchie	4	0	0	0	0
Trevor Robins (goalie)	4	0	0	0	4

GOALTENDING

	Games	Min.	Goals	SO	Avg.
Trevor Robins	4	258	11(1)	0	2.56

KAMLOOPS BLAZERS

(Lost West Division finals to Portland, 4-1)

SCORING

	Games	G	A	Pts.	Pen.
Mike Mathers	13	5	12	17	15
Craig Lyons	12	6	10	16	8
Darcy Tucker	13	7	6	13	34
Jarrett Deuling	13	6	7	13	14
Rod Stevens	13	9	2	11	4
Scott Loucks	13	4	7	11	27
Ryan Huska	13	2	6	8	4
Aaron Keller	11	2	5	7	4
Craig Bonner	13	2	5	7	14
David Wilkie	6	4	2	6	2
Tyson Nash	13	3	2	5	32
Jason Becker	11	1	4	5	6
Chris Murray	13	0	4	4	34
Nolan Baumgartner	11	1	1	2	0
Hnat Domenichelli	11	1	1	2	2
Mike Josephson	10	0	2	2	4
Scott Ferguson	13	0	2	2	24
Steve Passmore (goalie)	7	0	1	1	4
Jarrett Bousquet	8	0	1	1	12
Rod Branch (goalie)	8	0	1	1	6
Shane Doan	13	0	1	1	8
Steve Parsons	2	0	0	0	9
Bob Maudie	3	0	0	0	0
Brad Hammerback	6	0	0	0	11

GOALTENDING

	Games	Min.	Goals	SO	Avg.
Steve Passmore	7	401	22	1	3.29
Rod Branch	8	412	25(1)	1	3.64

LETHBRIDGE HURRICANES

(Lost East Division preliminaries, 3-1)

SCORING

	Games	G	A	Pts.	Pen.
Shane Peacock	4	4	3	7	2
Domenic Pittis	4	3	3	6	8
Mark Szoke	4	3	1	4	8
Cory Dosdall	4	1	3	4	8

	Games	G	A	Pts.	Pen.
Ivan Vologjaninov	4	1	2	3	2
Jason Widmer	4	0	3	3	2
Todd MacIsaac	4	1	0	1	14
Nick Polychronopoulos	4	1	0	1	14
Brad Zimmer	4	1	0	1	0
Chris Catellier	4	0	1	1	7
Jamie Pushor	4	0	1	1	9
Lee Sorochan	4	0	1	1	12
Slade Stephenson	4	0	1	1	10
Aaron Zarowny	4	0	1	1	2
Jay Bertsch	1	0	0	0	0
Randy Perry	1	0	0	0	0
Brantt Myhres	3	0	0	0	11
Cadrin Smart	3	0	0	0	0
Darcy Austin (goalie)	4	0	0	0	2
Bryce Salvador	4	0	0	0	0
Derek Wood	4	0	0	0	6

GOALTENDING

	Games	Min.	Goals	SO	Avg.
Darcy Austin	4	266	17	0	3.83

MEDICINE HAT TIGERS

(Lost East Division semifinals to Swift Current, 4-2)

SCORING

	Games	G	A	Pts.	Pen.
Cam Danyluk	10	9	5	14	29
Stacy Roest	10	3	10	13	6
Jamie Linden	10	1	6	7	15
Mike Jickling	10	3	3	6	6
Mike Rathje	10	3	3	6	12
Clayton Norris	10	3	2	5	14
Lorne Toews	10	3	2	5	16
David Cooper	10	2	2	4	32
Aaron Boh	10	0	4	4	27
Mark Polak	10	1	2	3	2
Stacey Fritz	9	1	1	2	2
Jeremy Schaefer	9	0	2	2	32
Shawn Stone	10	1	0	1	6
Steve Cheredaryk	10	0	1	1	16
Justin Hocking	10	0	1	1	13
Scott Bellefontaine (goalie)	2	0	0	0	2
Danny Faassen	7	0	0	0	2
James Seney	7	0	0	0	2
Brad Wilson	7	0	0	0	0
Greg Cowie	10	0	0	0	0
Sonny Mignacca (goalie)	10	0	0	0	4

GOALTENDING

	Games	Min.	Goals	SO	Avg.
Sonny Mignacca	10	575	36	0	3.76
Scott Bellefontaine	2	43	4	0	5.58

PORTLAND WINTER HAWKS

(Lost WHL finals to Swift Current, 4-3)

SCORING

	Games	G	A	Pts.	Pen.
Lonnie Bohonos	15	8	13	21	19
Colin Foley	16	6	13	19	32
Nick Vachon	16	11	7	18	34
Scott Nichol	16	8	8	16	41
Adam Deadmarsh	16	7	8	15	29
Layne Roland	15	6	9	15	16
Jason McBain	16	2	12	14	14
Jiri Beranek	16	5	8	13	20
Brandon Smith	16	4	9	13	6
Jason Wiemer	16	7	3	10	27
Nolan Pratt	16	2	7	9	31
Cale Hulse	16	4	4	8	65
John Badduke	16	3	4	7	57
Mike Williamson	16	0	5	5	27
Shannon Briske	16	2	1	3	12

	Games	G	A	Pts.	Pen.
Dave Cammock	15	0	2	2	17
Brad Symes	16	0	1	1	7
Sheldon Szmata	2	0	0	0	0
Ryan Van Steinburg	5	0	0	0	2
Joaquin Gage (goalie)	8	0	0	0	2
Scott Langkow (goalie)	9	0	0	0	9
Shawn Collins	12	0	0	0	0

GOALTENDING

	Games	Min.	Goals	SO	Avg.
Scott Langkow	9	535	31(1)	0	3.48
Joaquin Gage	8	427	30	0	4.22

RED DEER REBELS

(Lost East Division preliminaries to Saskatoon, 3-1)

SCORING

	Games	G	A	Pts.	Pen.
Darren Van Impe	4	2	5	7	16
Craig Reichert	4	3	1	4	2
Dean Tiltgen	4	1	2	3	0
Tony Vlastelic	2	1	1	2	0
Curtis Cardinal	4	1	1	2	2
Brian Loney	4	1	1	2	19
Todd Johnson	4	0	2	2	0
Scott Adair	4	1	0	1	7
Ken Richardson	4	1	0	1	7
Pete LeBoutillier	2	0	1	1	5
Jeff Antonowich	4	0	1	1	2
Kevin Masters	4	0	1	1	4
Mark Dawkins (goalie)	4	0	0	0	0
Terry Lindgren	4	0	0	0	9
Len MacAusland	4	0	0	0	10
Cam MacGregor	4	0	0	0	0
Eddy Marchant	4	0	0	0	4
Sean Selmser	4	0	0	0	10
Vaclav Slansky	4	0	0	0	5
Mark Toljanich	4	0	0	0	0

GOALTENDING

	Games	Min.	Goals	SO	Avg.
Mark Dawkins	4	269	13(1)	0	2.90

REGINA PATS

(Lost East Division finals to Swift Current, 4-0)

SCORING

	Games	G	A	Pts.	Pen.
Jeff Friesen	13	7	10	17	8
Kerry Biette	13	7	7	14	28
Jeff Shantz	13	2	12	14	14
Louis Dumont	13	7	5	12	12
Jason Smith	13	4	8	12	39
Nathan Dempsey	13	3	8	11	14
Derek Eberle	13	2	8	10	19
Brandon Coates	12	7	2	9	6
Trevor Hanas	13	4	5	9	25
Grayden Reid	13	3	4	7	4
Russ Gronick	12	4	2	6	18
Niklas Barklund	13	2	3	5	22
Randy Toye	12	2	1	3	11
Russ West	13	0	3	3	22
Jeff Helperl	13	0	2	2	27
Steve Dowhy	11	0	1	1	6
Chad Mercier (goalie)	1	0	0	0	0
Rhett Gordon	4	0	0	0	0
Mirsad Mujcin	4	0	0	0	10
Chris Zulyniak	10	0	0	0	0
Mike Risdale (goalie)	13	0	0	0	4
Dion Zukiwsky	13	0	0	0	24

GOALTENDING

	Games	Min.	Goals	SO	Avg.
Mike Risdale	13	811	57	0	4.22
Chad Mercier	1	13	1	0	4.62

SASKATOON BLADES

(Lost East Division semifinals to Regina, 4-1)

SCORING

	Games	G	A	Pts.	Pen.
Mark Wotton	9	6	5	11	18
Frank Banham	9	2	7	9	8
Shawn Yakimishyn	9	3	4	7	29
Clarke Wilm	9	4	2	6	13
James Startup	9	2	4	6	8
Paul Buczkowski	9	1	5	6	8
Shane Calder	9	1	5	6	31
Jason Duda	9	1	5	6	8
Andy MacIntyre	9	3	2	5	2
Ryan Fujita	7	2	3	5	10
Derek Tibbatts	9	1	2	3	0
Peter Cox	9	1	1	2	11
Andrew Kemper	9	1	1	2	27
Mark Raiter	9	1	1	2	19
Mike Gray	6	1	0	1	9
Cory McKee	3	0	1	1	6
Marty Zdan	4	0	0	0	0
Wade Belak	7	0	0	0	0
Chad Allan	9	0	0	0	25
Norman Maracle (goalie)	9	0	0	0	0
Rhett Warrener	9	0	0	0	14

GOALTENDING

	Games	Min.	Goals	SO	Avg.
Norm Maracle	9	569	33(2)	0	3.48

SEATTLE THUNDERBIRDS

(Lost West Division preliminaries to Kamloops, 4-1)

SCORING

	Games	G	A	Pts.	Pen.
Scott Lindsay	5	2	3	5	4
Chris Wells	5	2	3	5	4
Troy Hyatt	5	1	4	5	5
Kevin Mylander	5	3	1	4	0
John Lilley	5	1	3	4	9
Blake Knox	5	2	1	3	17
Brendan Witt	5	1	2	3	30
Kurt Seher	5	0	3	3	10
Eric Bouchard	5	1	1	2	2
Chris Herperger	5	1	1	2	6
Jim Burcar	5	0	1	1	4
Brent Duncan	5	0	1	1	33
Milt Mastad	5	0	1	1	14
Chris Schmidt	5	0	1	1	0
Jeff Peddigrew	1	0	0	0	0
Marko Elorinne	2	0	0	0	0
Larry McMorran	3	0	0	0	0
Shea Esselmont	4	0	0	0	6
Jeff Dewar	5	0	0	0	4
Olaf Kjenstad	5	0	0	0	6
Rob Tallas (goalie)	5	0	0	0	2

GOALTENDING

	Games	Min.	Goals	SO	Avg.
Rob Tallas	5	333	18(1)	0	3.24

SPOKANE CHIEFS

(Lost West Division semifinals to Kamloops, 3-0)

SCORING

	Games	G	A	Pts.	Pen.
Valeri Bure	9	6	11	17	14
Maxim Bets	9	5	6	11	20
Paxton Schulte	10	5	6	11	12
Ryan Duthie	9	7	2	9	8
Jason Podollan	10	4	4	8	14
Jeremy Stasiuk	10	3	5	8	15
Bryan McCabe	10	1	5	6	28
Jon Duval	10	0	6	6	25
Scott Townsend	10	2	3	5	0
Tyler Romanchuk	9	1	3	4	16
Kevin Sawyer	8	1	1	2	13

	Games	G	A	Pts.	Pen.
Todd Harris	7	0	2	2	11
Dana Rieder	8	0	2	2	2
Sean Gillam	10	0	2	2	10
Dean Kletzel	8	1	0	1	0
Dion Darling	9	0	1	1	14
Randy Favaro	9	0	1	1	9
Trevor Shoaf	9	0	1	1	8
David Jesiolowski	10	0	1	1	15
Richard Parent (goalie)	1	0	0	0	0
Derek Descouteau	6	0	0	0	0
Barry Becker (goalie)	10	0	0	0	0

GOALTENDING

	Games	Min.	Goals	SO	Avg.
Richard Parent	1	5	0(1)	0	0.00
Barry Becker	10	614	45	0	4.40

SWIFT CURRENT

(Winner of 1993 playoffs)

SCORING

	Games	G	A	Pts.	Pen.
Andy Schneider	17	13	26	39	40
Jason Krywulak	17	15	22	37	24
Dean McAmmond	17	16	19	35	20
Tyler Wright	17	9	17	26	49
Rick Girard	17	9	17	26	10
Todd Holt	16	10	12	22	18
Brent Bilodeau	17	5	14	19	18
Ashley Buckberger	17	6	7	13	6
Trent McCleary	17	5	4	9	16
Russell Hewson	17	2	4	6	4
Darren Perkins	17	1	4	5	22
Jason Horvath	16	0	3	3	32
Regan Mueller	16	1	1	2	0
Heath Weenk	17	1	1	2	13
Ryan Brown	17	0	2	2	18
Keith McCambridge	17	0	1	1	27
Chris Szysky	1	0	0	0	0
Ian Gordon (goalie)	2	0	0	0	0
Paul Nicolls	2	0	0	0	0
Chris Low	6	0	0	0	0
Darren McLean	11	0	0	0	11
Milan Hnilicka (goalie)	17	0	0	0	0
Bill Hooson	17	0	0	0	13

GOALTENDING

	Games	Min.	Goals	SO	Avg.
Milan Hnilicka	17	1017	54(1)	2	3.19
Ian Gordon	2	53	3	0	3.40

TACOMA ROCKETS

(Lost West Division preliminaries to Spokane, 4-3)

SCORING

	Games	G	A	Pts.	Pen.
Allan Egeland	7	9	7	16	18
Michal Sykora	7	4	8	12	2
Alexander Alexeev	7	2	7	9	4
Trever Fraser	7	3	3	6	18
Kevin Powell	7	2	2	4	10
Barkley Swenson	7	0	4	4	4
Jason Kwiatkowski	7	1	1	2	2
Dallas Thompson	7	1	1	2	7
John Varga	7	1	1	2	8
Drew Schoneck	7	0	2	2	6
Jamie Butt	5	1	0	1	13
Adam Smith	7	0	1	1	4
Mike Piersol	2	0	0	0	0
Jeff Calvert (goalie)	7	0	0	0	0
Marty Flichel	7	0	0	0	8
Dave McMillen	7	0	0	0	17
Dennis Pinfold	7	0	0	0	5
Tyler Prosofsky	7	0	0	0	5
Corey Stock	7	0	0	0	4

GOALTENDING

	Games	Min.	Goals	SO	Avg.
Jeff Calvert	7	439	28(2)	0	3.83

TRI-CITY AMERICANS

(Lost West Division preliminaries to Portland, 4-0)

SCORING

	Games	G	A	Pts.	Pen.
Evan Marble	4	1	3	4	8
Todd Klassen	4	1	2	3	8
Adam Rettschlag	4	0	3	3	11
Jason Bowen	3	1	1	2	18
Brent Ashcroft	4	1	1	2	0
Steve O'Rourke	3	0	2	2	2
Rob Hartnell	4	0	2	2	23
Tony Prpic	3	1	0	1	0
Chad Cabana	4	1	0	1	10
Damon Langkow	4	1	0	1	4
Geoff Lynch	4	1	0	1	0
Jason Renard	4	1	0	1	16
Terry Ryan	1	0	1	1	5
Kimbi Daniels	3	0	1	1	8
Jeff Petruic	3	0	1	1	2
Graham Harder	1	0	0	0	9
Gary Lebsack	3	0	0	0	15
David Brumby (goalie)	4	0	0	0	11
Ryan Marsh	4	0	0	0	2
Kory Mullin	4	0	0	0	11
Todd Simpson	4	0	0	0	13
Marc Stephan	4	0	0	0	8

GOALTENDING

	Games	Min.	Goals	SO	Avg.
David Brumby	4	240	20	0	5.00

1992-93 AWARD WINNERS

ALL-STAR TEAMS

EAST DIVISION

First team	Pos.	Second team
Trevor Robins, Brandon	G	Norm Maracle, Saskatoon
Jason Smith, Regina	D	Brent Bilodeau, Swift Cur.
Darren Van Impe, Red Deer	D	Mike Rathje, Medicine Hat
Jeff Shantz, Regina	F	Andy Schneider, Swift Cur.
Jason Krywulak, Swift Cur.	F	Louis Dumont, Regina
Rick Girard, Swift Current	F	Bobby House, Brandon
Rob Niedermayer, Med. Hat		

WEST DIVISION

First team	Pos.	Second team
Steve Passmore, Kamloops	G	Jeff Calvert, Tacoma
Michal Sykora, Tacoma	D	Brandon Smith, Portland
Brendan Witt, Seattle	D	Bryan McCabe, Spokane
Allan Egeland, Tacoma	F	Jamie Black, Tacoma
Valeri Bure, Spokane	F	Craig Lyons, Kamloops
Mike Mathers, Kamloops	F	Colin Foley, Portland

TROPHY WINNERS

Four Broncos Memorial Trophy: Jason Krywulak, Swift Current
Bob Clarke Trophy: Jason Krywulak, Swift Current
Jim Piggott Memorial Trophy: Jeff Friesen, Regina
Brad Hornung Trophy: Rick Girard, Swift Current
Bill Hunter Trophy: Jason Smith, Regina
Del Wilson Trophy: Trevor Robins, Brandon
Player of the Year: Jason Krywulak, Swift Current
Dunc McCallum Memorial Trophy: Marcel Comeau, Tacoma
Scott Munro Memorial Trophy: Swift Current Broncos
President's Cup: Swift Current Broncos

ALL-TIME AWARD WINNERS

FOUR BRONCOS MEMORIAL TROPHY

(Most valuable player—selected by coaches)

Season	Player, Team
1966-67	Gerry Pinder, Saskatoon
1967-68	Jim Harrison, Estevan
1968-69	Bobby Clarke, Flin Flon
1969-70	Reggie Leach, Flin Flon
1970-71	Ed Dyck, Calgary
1971-72	John Davidson, Calgary
1972-73	Dennis Sobchuk, Regina
1973-74	Ron Chipperfield, Brandon
1974-75	Bryan Trottier, Lethbridge
1975-76	Bernie Federko, Saskatoon
1976-77	Barry Beck, New Westminster
1977-78	Ryan Walter, Seattle
1978-79	Perry Turnbull, Portland
1979-80	Doug Wickenheiser, Regina
1980-81	Steve Tsujiura, Medicine Hat
1981-82	Mike Vernon, Calgary
1982-83	Mike Vernon, Calgary
1983-84	Ray Ferraro, Brandon
1984-85	Cliff Ronning, New Westminster
1985-86	Emanuel Viveiros, Prince Albert (East Div.)
	Rob Brown, Kamloops (West Division)
1986-87	Joe Sakic, Swift Current (East Division)
	Rob Brown, Kamloops (West Division)
1987-88	Joe Sakic, Swift Current
1988-89	Stu Barnes, Tri-City
1989-90	Glen Goodall, Seattle
1990-91	Ray Whitney, Spokane
1991-92	Steve Konowalchuk, Portland
1992-93	Jason Krywulak, Swift Current

BOB CLARKE TROPHY

(Top scorer)

Season	Player, Team
1966-67	Gerry Pinder, Saskatoon
1967-68	Bobby Clarke, Flin Flon
1968-69	Bobby Clarke, Flin Flon
1969-70	Reggie Leach, Flin Flon
1970-71	Chuck Arnason, Flin Flon
1971-72	Tom Lysiak, Medicine Hat
1972-73	Tom Lysiak, Medicine Hat
1973-74	Ron Chipperfield, Brandon
1974-75	Mel Bridgman, Victoria
1975-76	Bernie Federko, Saskatoon
1976-77	Bill Derlago, Brandon
1977-78	Brian Propp, Brandon

Season	Player, Team
1978-79	Brian Propp, Brandon
1979-80	Doug Wickenheiser, Regina
1980-81	Brian Varga, Regina
1981-82	Jack Callander, Regina
1982-83	Dale Derkatch, Regina
1983-84	Ray Ferraro, Brandon
1984-85	Cliff Ronning, New Westminster
1985-86	Rob Brown, Kamloops
1986-87	Rob Brown, Kamloops
1987-88	Joe Sakic, Swift Current
	Theo Fleury, Moose Jaw
1988-89	Dennis Holland, Portland
1989-90	Len Barrie, Kamloops
1990-91	Ray Whitney, Spokane
1991-92	Kevin St. Jacques, Lethbridge
1992-93	Jason Krywulak, Swift Current

The award was originally known as the Bob Brownridge Memorial Trophy

JIM PIGGOTT MEMORIAL TROPHY

(Rookie of the year)

Season	Player, Team
1966-67	Ron Garwasiuk, Regina
1967-68	Ron Fairbrother, Saskatoon
1968-69	Ron Williams, Edmonton
1969-70	Gene Carr, Flin Flon
1970-71	Stan Weir, Medicine Hat
1971-72	Dennis Sobchuk, Regina
1972-73	Rick Blight, Brandon
1973-74	Cam Connor, Flin Flon
1974-75	Don Murdoch, Medicine Hat
1975-76	Steve Tambellini, Lethbridge
1976-77	Brian Propp, Brandon
1977-78	John Orgrodnick, New Westminster
	Keith Brown, Portland
1978-79	Kelly Kisio, Calgary
1979-80	Grant Fuhr, Victoria
1980-81	Dave Michayluk, Regina
1981-82	Dale Derkatch, Regina
1982-83	Dan Hodgson, Prince Albert
1983-84	Cliff Ronning, New Westminster
1984-85	Mark Mackay, Moose Jaw
1985-86	Neil Brady, Medicine Hat (East Division)
	Ron Shudra, Kamloops, (West Division)
	Dave Waldie, Portland (West Division)
1986-87	Joe Sakic, Swift Current (East Division)
	Dennis Holland, Portland (West Division)
1987-88	Stu Barnes, New Westminster

Season	Player, Team
1988-89	Wes Walz, Lethbridge
1989-90	Petr Nedved, Seattle
1990-91	Donevan Hextall, Prince Albert
1991-92	Ashley Buckberger, Swift Current
1992-93	Jeff Friesen, Regina

The award was originally known as the Stewart "Butch" Paul Memorial Trophy.

BRAD HORNUNG TROPHY

(Most sportsmanlike player)

Season	Player, Team
1966-67	Morris Stefaniw, Estevan
1967-68	Bernie Blanchette, Saskatoon
1968-69	Bob Liddington, Calgary
1969-70	Randy Rota, Calgary
1970-71	Lorne Henning, Estevan
1971-72	Ron Chipperfield, Brandon
1972-73	Ron Chipperfield, Brandon
1973-74	Mike Rogers, Calgary
1974-75	Danny Arndt, Saskatoon
1975-76	Blair Chapman, Saskatoon
1976-77	Steve Tambellini, Lethbridge
1977-78	Steve Tambellini, Lethbridge
1978-79	Errol Rausse, Seattle
1979-80	Steve Tsujiura, Medicine Hat
1980-81	Steve Tsujiura, Medicine Hat
1981-82	Mike Moller, Lethbridge
1982-83	Darren Boyko, Winnipeg
1983-84	Mark Lamb, Medicine Hat
1984-85	Cliff Ronning, New Westminster
1985-86	Randy Smith, Saskatoon (East Division)
	Ken Morrison, Kamloops (West Division)
1986-87	Len Nielsen, Regina (East Division)
	Dave Archibald, Portland (West Division)
1987-88	Craig Endean, Regina
1988-89	Blair Atcheynum, Moose Jaw
1989-90	Bryan Bosch, Lethbridge
1990-91	Pat Falloon, Spokane
1991-92	Steve Junker, Spokane
1992-93	Rick Girard, Swift Current

The award was originally known as the Frank Boucher Memorial Trophy for most gentlemanly player.

BILL HUNTER TROPHY

(Top defenseman)

Season	Player, Team
1966-67	Barry Gibbs, Estevan
1967-68	Gerry Hart, Flin Flon
1968-69	Dale Hoganson, Estevan
1969-70	Jim Hargreaves, Winnipeg
1970-71	Ron Jones, Edmonton
1971-72	Jim Watson, Calgary
1972-73	George Pesut, Saskatoon
1973-74	Pat Price, Saskatoon
1974-75	Rick LaPointe, Victoria
1975-76	Kevin McCarthy, Winnipeg
1976-77	Barry Beck, New Westminster
1977-78	Brad McCrimmon, Brandon
1978-79	Keith Brown, Portland
1979-80	David Babych, Portland
1980-81	Jim Benning, Portland
1981-82	Gary Nylund, Portland
1982-83	Gary Leeman, Regina
1983-84	Bob Rouse, Lethbridge
1984-85	Wendel Clark, Saskatoon
1985-86	Emanuel Viveiros, Prince Albert (East Division)
	Glen Wesley, Portland (West Division)
1986-87	Wayne McBean, Medicine Hat (East Division)
	Glen Wesley, Portland (West Division)
1987-88	Greg Hawgood, Kamloops
1988-89	Dan Lambert, Swift Current
1989-90	Kevin Haller, Regina
1990-91	Darryl Sydor, Kamloops

Season	Player, Team
1991-92	Richard Matvichuk, Saskatoon
1992-93	Jason Smith, Regina

DEL WILSON TROPHY

(Top goaltender)

Season	Player, Team
1966-67	Ken Brown, Moose Jaw
1967-68	Chris Worthy, Flin Flon
1968-69	Ray Martyniuk, Flin Flon
1969-70	Ray Martyniuk, Flin Flon
1970-71	Ed Dyck, Calgary
1971-72	John Davidson, Calgary
1972-73	Ed Humphreys, Saskatoon
1973-74	Garth Malarchuk, Calgary
1974-75	Bill Oleschuk, Saskatoon
1975-76	Carey Walker, New Westminster
1976-77	Glen Hanlon, Brandon
1977-78	Bart Hunter, Portland
1978-79	Rick Knickle, Brandon
1979-80	Kevin Eastman, Victoria
1980-81	Grant Fuhr, Victoria
1981-82	Mike Vernon, Calgary
1982-83	Mike Vernon, Calgary
1983-84	Ken Wregget, Lethbridge
1984-85	Troy Gamble, Medicine Hat
1985-86	Mark Fitzpatrick, Medicine Hat
1986-87	Kenton Rein, Prince Albert (East Division)
	Dean Cook, Kamloops (West Division)
1987-88	Troy Gamble, Spokane
1988-89	Danny Lorenz, Seattle
1989-90	Trevor Kidd, Brandon
1990-91	Jamie McLennan, Lethbridge
1991-92	Corey Hirsch, Kamloops
1992-93	Trevor Wilson, Brandon

PLAYER OF THE YEAR

(Selected by fans and media)

Season	Player, Team
1974-75	Ed Staniowski, Regina
1975-76	Bernie Federko, Saskatoon
1976-77	Kevin McCarthy, Winnipeg
1977-78	Ryan Walter, Seattle
1978-79	Brian Propp, Brandon
1979-80	Doug Wickenheiser, Regina
1980-81	Barry Pederson, Victoria
1981-82	Mike Vernon, Calgary
1982-83	Dean Evason, Kamloops
1983-84	Ray Ferraro, Brandon
1984-85	Dan Hodgson, Prince Albert
1985-86	Emanuel Viveiros, Prince Albert
1986-87	Rob Brown, Kamloops
1987-88	Joe Sakic, Swift Current
1988-89	Dennis Holland, Portland
1989-90	Wes Walz, Lethbridge
1990-91	Ray Whitney, Spokane
1991-92	Corey Hirsch, Kamloops
1992-93	Jason Krywulak, Swift Current

DUNC McCALLUM MEMORIAL TROPHY

(Coach of the year)

Season	Coach, Team
1968-69	Scotty Munro, Calgary
1969-70	Pat Ginnell, Flin Flon
1970-71	Pat Ginnell, Flin Flon
1971-72	Earl Ingarfield, Regina
1972-73	Pat Ginnell, Flin Flon
1973-74	Stan Dunn, Swift Current
1974-75	Pat Ginnell, Victoria
1975-76	Ernie McLean, New Westminster
1976-77	Dunc McCallum, Brandon
1977-78	Jack Shupe, Victoria
	Dave King, Billings
1978-79	Dunc McCallum, Brandon

Season	Coach, Team
1979-80	Doug Sauter, Calgary
1980-81	Ken Hodge, Portland
1981-82	Jack Sangster, Seattle
1982-83	Darryl Lubiniecki, Saskatoon
1983-84	Terry Simpson, Prince Albert
1984-85	Doug Sauter, Medicine Hat
1985-86	Terry Simpson, Prince Albert
1986-87	Ken Hitchcock, Kam. (W. Division)
	Graham James, S. Curr. (E. Div.)

Season	Coach, Team
1987-88	Marcel Comeau, Saskatoon
1988-89	Ron Kennedy, Medicine Hat
1989-90	Ken Hitchcock, Kamloops
1990-91	Tom Renney, Kamloops
1991-92	Bryan Maxwell, Spokane
1992-93	Marcel Comeau, Tacoma

ALL-TIME LEAGUE CHAMPIONS

	REGULAR-SEASON CHAMPION	PLAYOFF CHAMPION
Season	Team	Team
1966-67	Edmonton Oil Kings	Moose Jaw Canucks
1967-68	Flin Flon Bombers	Estevan Bruins
1968-69	Flin Flon Bombers	Flin Flon Bombers
1969-70	Flin Flon Bombers	Flin Flon Bombers
1970-71	Edmonton Oil Kings	Edmonton Oil Kings
1971-72	Calgary Centennials	Edmonton Oil Kings
1972-73	Saskatoon Blades	Medicine Hat Tigers
1973-74	Regina Pats	Regina Pats
1974-75	Victoria Cougars	New Westminster Bruins
1975-76	New Westminster Bruins	New Westminster Bruins
1976-77	New Westminster Bruins	New Westminster Bruins
1977-78	Brandon Wheat Kings	New Westminster Bruins
1978-79	Brandon Wheat Kings	Brandon Wheat Kings
1979-80	Portland Winter Hawks	Regina Pats
1980-81	Victoria Cougars	Victoria Cougars
1981-82	Lethbridge Broncos	Portland Winter Hawks
1982-83	Saskatoon Blades	Lethbridge Broncos
1983-84	Kamloops Junior Oilers	Kamloops Junior Oilers
1984-85	Prince Albert Raiders	Prince Albert Raiders
1985-86	Medicine Hat Tigers	Kamloops Blazers
1986-87	Kamloops Blazers	Medicine Hat Tigers
1987-88	Saskatoon Blades	Medicine Hat Tigers
1988-89	Swift Current Broncos	Swift Current Broncos
1989-90	Kamloops Blazers	Kamloops Blazers
1990-91	Kamloops Blazers	Spokane Chiefs
1991-92	Kamloops Blazers	Kamloops Blazers
1992-93	Swift Current Broncos	Swift Current Broncos

The WHL regular-season champion is awarded the Scott Munro Memorial Trophy and the playoff champion is awarded the President's Cup.

COLLEGE HOCKEY

NCAA Division I

Central Collegiate Hockey Association

Eastern College Athletic Conference

Hockey East

Western Collegiate Hockey Association

Independents

Canadian Interuniversity Athletic Union

Canadian Colleges

NCAA DIVISION I

1992-93 SEASON

NCAA TOURNAMENT

EAST REGIONAL
(Worcester, Mass.)

Minnesota 2, Clarkson 1
Northern Michigan 3, Harvard 2 (2 OT)
Maine 6, Minnesota 2
Boston University 4, Northern Michigan 1

WEST REGIONAL
(Detroit)

Wisconsin 3, Miami of Ohio 1
Minnesota-Duluth 7, Brown 3
Michigan 4, Wisconsin 3 (OT)
Lake Superior State 4, Minnesota-Duluth 3

SEMIFINAL SERIES
(Milwaukee)

Maine 4, Michigan 3 (OT)
Lake Superior State 6, Boston University 1

CHAMPIONSHIP GAME
(Milwaukee)

Maine 5, Lake Superior State 4

ALL-TOURNAMENT TEAM

Player	Pos.	College
Garth Snow	G	Maine
Chris Imes	D	Maine
Michael Smith	D	Lake Superior State
Paul Kariya	F	Maine
Jim Montgomery	F	Maine
Brian Rolston	F	Lake Superior State

NCAA Most Valuable Player: Jim Montgomery, Maine.

ALL-AMERICA TEAMS

EAST			WEST		
First team	Pos.	Second team	First team	Pos.	Second team
Mike Dunham, Maine	G	Neil Little, RPI	Jamie Ram, Mich. Tech	G	Steve Shields, Michigan
Chris Imes, Maine	D	Kaj Linna, Boston U.	Brett Hauer, Min.-Dul.	D	Bobby Marshall, Miami of O.
Jack Duffy, Yale	D	Aaron Miller, Vermont	Barry Richter, Wisconsin	D	Michael Smith, L. Superior
Ted Drury, Harvard	F	Cal Ingraham, Maine	Greg Johnson, N. Dakota	F	Fred Knipscheer, St. Cloud St.
Paul Kariya, Maine	F	Mark Kaufmann, Yale	Derek Plante, Min.-Dul.	F	Bryan Rolston, L. Superior
David Sacco, Boston U.	F	Jim Montgomery, Maine	Bryan Smolinski, Mich. St.	F	Brian Savage, Miami of O.

HISTORY

TOURNAMENT CHAMPIONS

Year	Champion	Coach	Score	Runner-up	Most outstanding player
1948	Michigan	Vic Heyliger	8-4	Dartmouth	Joe Riley, F, Dartmouth
1949	Boston College	John Kelley	4-3	Dartmouth	Dick Desmond, G, Dartmouth
1950	Colorado College	Cheddy Thompson	13-4	Boston University	Ralph Bevins, G, Boston University
1951	Michigan	Vic Heyliger	7-1	Brown	Ed Whiston, G, Brown
1952	Michigan	Vic Heyliger	4-1	Colorado College	Kenneth Kinsley, G, Colorado College
1953	Michigan	Vic Heyliger	7-3	Minnesota	John Matchefts, F, Michigan
1954	Rensselaer	Ned Harkness	5-4*	Minnesota	Abbie Moore, F, Rensselaer
1955	Michigan	Vic Heyliger	5-3	Colorado College	Philip Hilton, D, Colorado College
1956	Michigan	Vic Heyliger	7-5	Michigan Tech	Lorne Howes, G, Michigan
1957	Colorado College	Thomas Bedecki	13-6	Michigan	Bob McCusker, F, Colorado College
1958	Denver	Murray Armstrong	6-2	North Dakota	Murray Massier, F, Denver
1959	North Dakota	Bob May	4-3*	Michigan State	Reg Morelli, F, North Dakota
1960	Denver	Murray Armstrong	5-3	Michigan Tech	Bob Marquis, F, Boston University
					Barry Urbanski, G, Boston University
					Louis Angotti, F, Michigan Tech
1961	Denver	Murray Armstrong	12-2	St. Lawrence	Bill Masterton, F, Denver
1962	Michigan Tech	John MacInnes	7-1	Clarkson	Louis Angotti, F, Michigan Tech
1963	North Dakota	Barney Thorndycraft	6-5	Denver	Al McLean, F, North Dakota
1964	Michigan	Allen Renfrew	6-3	Denver	Bob Gray, G, Michigan
1965	Michigan Tech	John MacInnes	8-2	Boston College	Gary Milroy, F, Michigan Tech
1966	Michigan State	Amo Bessone	6-1	Clarkson	Gaye Cooley, G, Michigan State
1967	Cornell	Ned Harkness	4-1	Boston University	Walt Stanowski, D, Cornell
1968	Denver	Murray Armstrong	4-0	North Dakota	Gerry Powers, G, Denver
1969	Denver	Murray Armstrong	4-3	Cornell	Keith Magnuson, D, Denver
1970	Cornell	Ned Harkness	6-4	Clarkson	Daniel Lodboa, D, Cornell
1971	Boston University	Jack Kelley	4-2	Minnesota	Dan Brady, G, Boston University
1972	Boston University	Jack Kelley	4-0	Cornell	Tim Regan, G, Boston University
1973	Wisconsin	Bob Johnson	4-2	Vacated	Dean Talafous, F, Wisconsin
1974	Minnesota	Herb Brooks	4-2	Michigan Tech	Brad Shelstad, G, Minnesota
1975	Michigan Tech	John MacInnes	6-1	Minnesota	Jim Warden, G, Michigan Tech
1976	Minnesota	Herb Brooks	6-4	Michigan Tech	Tom Vanelli, F, Minnesota
1977	Wisconsin	Bob Johnson	6-5*	Michigan	Julian Baretta, G, Wisconsin
1978	Boston University	Jack Parker	5-3	Boston College	Jack O'Callahan, D, Boston University

Year	Champion	Coach	Score	Runner-up	Most outstanding player
1979	Minnesota	Herb Brooks	4-3	North Dakota	Steve Janaszak, G, Minnesota
1980	North Dakota	John Gasparini	5-2	Northern Michigan	Doug Smail, F, North Dakota
1981	Wisconsin	Bob Johnson	6-3	Minnesota	Marc Behrend, G, Wisconsin
1982	North Dakota	John Gasparini	5-2	Wisconsin	Phil Sykes, F, North Dakota
1983	Wisconsin	Jeff Sauer	6-2	Harvard	Marc Behrend, G, Wisconsin
1984	Bowling Green State	Jerry York	5-4*	Minnesota-Duluth	Gary Kruzich, G, Bowling Green State
1985	Rensselaer	Mike Addesa	2-1	Providence	Chris Terreri, G, Providence
1986	Michigan State	Ron Mason	6-5	Harvard	Mike Donnelly, F, Michigan State
1987	North Dakota	John Gasparini	5-3	Michigan State	Tony Hrkac, F, North Dakota
1988	Lake Superior State	Frank Anzalone	4-3*	St. Lawrence	Bruce Hoffort, G, Lake Superior State
1989	Harvard	Bill Cleary	4-3*	Minnesota	Ted Donato, F, Harvard
1990	Wisconsin	Jeff Sauer	7-3	Colgate	Chris Tancill, F, Wisconsin
1991	Northern Michigan	Rick Comley	8-7*	Boston University	Scott Beattie, F, Northern Michigan
1992	Lake Superior State	Jeff Jackson	5-3	Wisconsin	Paul Constantin, F, Lake Superior State
1993	Maine	Shawn Walsh	5-4	Lake Superior State	Jim Montgomery, F, Maine

*Overtime.

ALL-TIME TOURNAMENT RECORDS

	Visits	W	L	GF	GA	Pct.	Finished 1st	Finished 2nd
Colgate	1	3	1	10	11	.750	0	1
Michigan	16	25	11	210	132	.694	7	2
‡Wisconsin	14	27	12	164	117	.692	5	2
North Dakota	13	22	11	132	102	.667	5	3
Denver	11	17	9	121	73	.654	5	2
#Lake Superior State	7	14	9	107	77	.609	2	1
*Northeastern	2	3	2	25	24	.600	0	0
Michigan Tech	10	13	9	118	85	.591	3	4
†Michigan State	13	22	16	162	140	.579	2	2
Maine	6	12	9	89	86	.571	1	0
#Rensselaer Polytechnic Institute	6	8	6	52	50	.567	2	0
Minnesota	18	23	20	228	205	.535	3	6
Northern Michigan	6	8	7	65	65	.533	1	1
Boston University	19	24	24	201	206	.500	3	3
Merrimack	1	2	2	14	16	.500	0	0
Yale	1	1	1	7	5	.500	0	0
Cornell	9	9	10	66	71	.474	2	2
Minnesota-Duluth	4	5	6	43	41	.455	0	1
Providence	6	9	11	71	73	.450	0	1
Dartmouth	5	4	5	38	37	.444	0	2
Clarkson	12	11	15	84	111	.423	0	3
*Bowling Green State	9	8	12	66	88	.400	1	0
Colorado College	9	6	10	76	84	.375	2	2
†Harvard	15	13	23	134	162	.361	1	2
Boston College	18	13	27	141	105	.325	1	2
Alaska-Anchorage	3	2	5	22	39	.286	0	0
Brown	4	2	5	31	45	.286	0	1
St. Lawrence	12	5	21	76	123	.192	0	2
New Hampshire	5	2	9	37	60	.182	0	0
‡Lowell	1	0	1	5	11	.000	0	0
Miami of Ohio	1	0	1	1	3	.000	0	0
St. Cloud State	1	0	2	5	10	.000	0	0
Vermont	1	0	2	2	10	.000	0	0
Western Michigan	1	0	2	4	11	.000	0	0

(Denver also participated in 1973 tournament but its record was voided by the NCAA in 1977 upon discovery of violations by the University. The team had finished second in '73.)

*Bowling Green State and Northeastern played to a 2-2 tie in 1981-82.
†Harvard and Michigan State played to a 3-3 tie in 1982-83.
#Lake Superior State and RPI played to a 3-3 tie in 1984-85.
‡Wisconsin and Lowell played to a 4-4 tie in 1987-88.
Hobey Baker Memorial Trophy (Top college hockey player in U.S.): Paul Kariya, Maine.

HOBEY BAKER AWARD WINNERS

(Top college hockey player in United States)

Year	Player, College
1981	Neal Broten, Minnesota
1982	George McPhee, Bowling Green St.
1983	Mark Fusco, Harvard
1984	Tom Kurvers, Minnesota-Duluth
1985	Bill Watson, Minnesota-Duluth
1986	Scott Fusco, Harvard
1987	Tony Hrkac, North Dakota
1988	Robb Stauber, Minnesota
1989	Lane MacDonald, Harvard
1990	Kip Miller, Michigan State
1991	David Emma, Boston College
1992	Scott Pellerin, Maine
1993	Paul Kariya, Maine

CENTRAL COLLEGIATE HOCKEY ASSOCIATION

1992-93 SEASON

FINAL STANDINGS

Team	G	W	L	T	Pts.	GF	GA
Mia. of Ohio (26-7-5) .	30	22	3	5	49	150	88
Michigan (29-5-3)...	30	23	5	2	48	180	71
L. Sup. St. (25-7-5)...	30	20	5	5	45	147	91
Mich. St. (24-13-2) ..	30	18	10	2	38	128	98
W. Mich. (20-16-2)..	30	17	11	2	36	118	117
Ferris St. (20-15-4) ..	30	13	13	4	30	103	118
Bowl. Green (19-20-1)	30	12	17	1	25	121	132
Kent (13-22-3)	30	10	19	1	21	118	148
Ill.-Chi. (10-25-2).....	30	8	20	2	18	100	134
Notre Dame (7-27-2)	30	5	23	2	12	87	144
Ohio State (5-30-2) ..	30	3	25	2	8	74	185
A'ka F'banks (23-12-2)	Affiliate (7-6-0 vs. CCHA teams)						

Overall record in parentheses.

PLAYOFF RESULTS

FIRST ROUND

Miami of Ohio 8, Ohio State 2
Miami of Ohio 7, Ohio State 2
(Miami of Ohio won series, 2-0)

Michigan 13, Notre Dame 2
Michigan 8, Notre Dame 1
(Michigan won series, 2-0)

Lake Superior State 7, Illinois-Chicago 2
Lake Superior State 4, Illinois-Chicago 2
(Lake Superior State won series, 2-0)

Michigan State 6, Kent 5
Michigan State 5, Kent 2
(Michigan State won series, 2-0)

Bowling Green 5, Western Michigan 4
Bowling Green 6, Western Michigan 3
(Bowling Green won series, 2-0)

Ferris State 8, Alaska Fairbanks 6
Ferris State 7, Alaska Fairbanks 2
(Ferris State won series, 2-0)

QUARTERFINALS

Lake Superior State 7, Bowling Green 1
Ferris State 3, Michigan State 2

SEMIFINALS

Miami of Ohio 4, Ferris State 3 (OT)
Lake Superior State 5, Michigan 3

CHAMPIONSHIP GAME

Lake Superior State 7, Miami of Ohio 0

ALL-STAR TEAMS

First team	Pos.	Second team
Steve Shields, Michigan	G	Richard Shulmistra, Miami
Patrick Neaton, Michigan	D	Bobby Marshall, Miami
Joe Cook, Miami of Ohio	D	Michael Smith, L.S.S.
Brian Rolston, L.S.S.	F	Brian Holzinger, Bowl. Green
Brian Savage, Miami of Ohio	F	David Roberts, Michigan
Bryan Smolinski, Mich. St.	F	David Oliver, Michigan

AWARD WINNERS

Player of the year: Brian Savage, Miami of Ohio
Rookie of the year: Chris Brooks, Western Michigan
Coach of the year: George Gwozdecky, Miami of Ohio
Leading scorer: Bryan Smolinski, Michigan State
Playoff MVP: Blaine Lacher, Lake Superior State

INDIVIDUAL STATISTICS

ALASKA-FAIRBANKS (AFFILIATE)

SCORING

	Pos.	Class	Games	G	A	Pts.	Pen.
Dean Fedorchuk	F	Jr.	36	28	36	64	48
Tavis MacMillan....	F	Jr.	36	16	41	57	88
Shawn Ulrich	F	Sr.	35	26	29	55	32
Wade Klippenstein	F	Sr.	36	29	22	51	48
Don Lester	D	Jr.	37	12	39	51	28
Wayne Sawchuk ...	F	Sr.	35	19	22	41	64
Jason Eckel	F	So.	37	14	22	36	45
Derby Bognar.........	D	Sr.	36	6	26	32	32
Lorne Kanigan	F	So.	32	10	16	26	34
Doug Raycroft	F	Sr.	34	12	11	23	28
Dallas Ferguson ...	D	Fr.	35	3	15	18	8
Warren Carter.......	F	So.	29	6	11	17	22
Trent Schachle	F	Fr.	30	4	9	13	26
Greg Milles	F	Fr.	23	2	9	11	12
Corey Spring	F	So.	28	5	5	10	20
Scott Keyes...........	F	Jr.	23	3	7	10	16
Brian Sutton	D	Sr.	35	0	10	10	36
Fred Scott	F	Fr.	22	4	3	7	14
Kirk Patton............	D	So.	37	2	4	6	32
Glenn Odishaw	D	Jr.	19	1	5	6	14
Marcel Aubin	D	So.	23	2	2	4	42
Chris Carney	D	So.	2	1	0	1	0
Dima Kulmanovsky.	F	Fr.	7	0	1	1	0
Todd Henderson	G	Sr.	5	0	1	1	0
Brian Fish	G	So.	24	0	0	0	0

SCORING

	Pos.	Class	Games	G	A	Pts.	Pen.
Larry Moberg.........	G	Fr.	14	0	0	0	0
Kevin Oakenfold	F	Fr.	4	0	0	0	6
Bob Schwark	D	Fr.	2	0	0	0	6

GOALTENDING

	Games	W	L	T	Min.	GA	Avg.
Todd Henderson ...	5	1	1	0	179	10	3.34
Brian Fish	25	16	7	1	1418	79	3.34
Larry Moberg..........	14	6	4	1	631	37	3.52

BOWLING GREEN STATE

SCORING

	Pos.	Class	Games	G	A	Pts.	Pen.
Brian Holzinger......	F	So.	41	31	26	57	44
Brett Harkins	F	Sr.	35	19	28	47	28
Sean Pronger	F	Jr.	39	23	23	46	35
Jeff Wells	D	Jr.	41	11	27	38	22
Tom Glantz.............	F	So.	41	17	14	31	18
Jason Clark............	F	Fr.	40	10	19	29	42
Jason Helbing	F	Fr.	41	14	13	27	19
Brandon Carper	D	So.	41	7	20	27	72
Todd Reirdon	D	Jr.	41	8	17	25	48
Mike Hall	F	Fr.	37	6	8	14	8
Chad Ackerman	D	Fr.	41	4	10	14	28
Jeff Herman	F	Fr.	40	6	5	11	35
Mark Lindsay.........	F	Fr.	16	3	8	11	38

	Pos.	Class	Games	G	A	Pts.	Pen.
Kevin Lune	F	Fr.	35	3	6	9	72
Jamie Williams	F	Fr.	38	3	4	7	30
Glen Mears	D	Jr.	39	0	7	7	22
Ty Eigner	F	Sr.	41	0	6	6	24
Craig Mittleholt	F	Fr.	28	3	2	5	30
Paul Basic	F	Sr.	36	0	5	5	34
Aaron Ellis	G	Fr.	25	0	4	4	4
Rick Mullins	F	Sr.	8	1	1	2	4
Will Clarke	G	So.	15	0	1	1	0
Angelo Libertucci	G	Sr.	5	0	0	0	0
A.J. Plaskey	D	Jr.	3	0	0	0	0

GOALTENDING

	Games	W	L	T	Min.	GA	Avg.
Aaron Ellis	25	14	10	1	1479	94	3.81
Will Clarke	15	5	9	0	838	66	4.72
Angelo Libertucci	5	0	2	0	165	16	5.83

FERRIS STATE
SCORING

	Pos.	Class	Games	G	A	Pts.	Pen.
Kevin Moore	F	Sr.	41	14	24	38	6
Doug Smith	F	Jr.	41	20	12	32	26
Mike May	F	Sr.	38	14	17	31	30
John Gruden	D	Jr.	41	16	14	30	58
Tim Christian	F	So.	37	12	17	29	28
Jeff Jestadt	F	Sr.	40	19	9	28	55
Gary Kitching	F	So.	28	8	19	27	62
Daniel Chaput	D	Sr.	39	3	22	25	79
Daryl Filipek	D	Sr.	41	12	12	24	62
Valentino Passarelli	C	Fr.	41	6	17	23	38
Mike Kolenda	D	So.	39	9	12	21	52
Robb McIntyre	F	So.	32	10	9	19	76
Colin Dodunski	D	So.	41	6	12	18	96
Keith Sergott	D	Fr.	41	3	13	16	12
Brad Burnham	F	So.	40	5	9	14	32
Scot Bell	F	Fr.	36	2	10	12	18
Aaron Asp	F	Sr.	14	3	7	10	10
Dwight Parrish	D	Fr.	40	0	5	5	66
Luke Harvey	F	So.	31	0	5	5	18
Greg Paine	F	Fr.	22	0	2	2	6
Pat Mazzoli	G	Jr.	24	0	1	1	10
Craig Lisko	G	Jr.	22	0	0	0	2
J.J. Bamberger	F	Fr.	4	0	0	0	0
Seth Appert	G	Fr.	2	0	0	0	0

GOALTENDING

	Games	W	L	T	Min.	GA	Avg.
Seth Appert	2	1	0	0	73	4	3.30
Craig Lisko	22	10	7	2	1114	64	3.45
Pat Mazzoli	24	10	9	2	1297	79	3.65

ILLINOIS-CHICAGO
SCORING

	Pos.	Class	Games	G	A	Pts.	Pen.
Derek Knorr	F	So.	33	13	29	42	82
Rob Hutson	F	Fr.	37	26	11	37	94
Link Bessert	F	Sr.	37	18	14	32	38
Chris MacDonald	F	So.	35	12	17	29	38
Mark Zdan	F	So.	36	7	18	25	56
Mike Dennis	D	Jr.	36	8	16	24	45
Shannon Finn	D	So.	36	6	13	19	48
Matt Brenner	D	Fr.	37	2	13	15	48
Brian Thibodeau	F	Fr.	36	5	8	13	35
Marc Genest	F	Fr.	35	5	8	13	38
Trevor Mathias	F	Fr.	29	4	9	13	69
Cory Hextall	F	Sr.	36	5	6	11	31
Todd Finner	F	Jr.	33	4	7	11	59
Jeff Blum	D	So.	37	0	10	10	62
Justin O'Connor	F	So.	34	3	1	4	33
Rob LaChance	F	Fr.	27	2	2	4	47
Bob Gohde	D	So.	35	1	2	3	24
Rob Mottau	D	So.	31	0	3	3	38
Marty McMillan	D	Fr.	34	1	1	2	52

	Pos.	Class	Games	G	A	Pts.	Pen.
Jon Hillebrandt	G	So.	33	0	2	2	6
Jeff Featherstone	G	Jr.	10	0	0	0	0
Trent Levins	G	Fr.	3	0	0	0	0

GOALTENDING

	Games	W	L	T	Min.	GA	Avg.
Jeff Featherstone	10	1	2	0	336	22	3.93
Jon Hillebrandt	33	8	22	2	1783	134	4.51
Trent Levins	3	1	1	0	98	9	5.54

KENT
SCORING

	Pos.	Class	Games	G	A	Pts.	Pen.
Claude Morin	F	So.	38	25	34	59	27
Dean Sylvester	F	So.	38	33	20	53	28
David Dartsch	F	Fr.	37	11	15	26	42
Sam Thornbury	F	Jr.	37	7	19	26	32
Bob Krosky	F	Jr.	36	9	16	25	52
Kevin McPherson	F	Jr.	37	11	13	24	38
Jay Neal	D	Sr.	34	5	19	24	26
Steve McLean	F	Jr.	36	14	8	22	22
Brian Mulcahy	F	Sr.	37	5	11	16	30
Neal Purdon	F	Jr.	38	7	8	15	24
Roger Mischke	D	Jr.	35	3	10	13	110
Lane Gunderson	D	So.	25	0	13	13	18
Quinn Fair	D	Fr.	37	6	6	12	77
James Mitchell	F	Fr.	38	6	5	11	36
Marc Drouin	F	Fr.	31	4	6	10	40
Ross Antonini	F	Sr.	28	4	5	9	28
Jason Watt	D	So.	30	0	6	6	17
Matt Brait	D	Sr.	30	0	5	5	104
Scott Shaw	G	Jr.	34	0	3	3	30
Gregg Fesette	D	Sr.	27	0	3	3	48
Barry Cummins	D	So.	5	0	2	2	0
Dan Duffy	D	So.	12	0	1	1	12
Brad Baxter	F	Sr.	13	0	0	0	13
Paul Dixon	G	Jr.	9	0	0	0	0
Brent Mahoney	F	Sr.	3	0	0	0	2
Steve Chalupnik	F	Jr.	2	0	0	0	0

GOALTENDING

	Games	W	L	T	Min.	GA	Avg.
Scott Shaw	33	13	18	2	1932	140	4.35
Paul Dixon	9	0	4	1	363	38	6.28

LAKE SUPERIOR STATE
SCORING

	Pos.	Class	Games	G	A	Pts.	Pen.
Brian Rolston	F	So.	39	33	31	64	20
Clayton Beddoes	F	Jr.	43	18	40	58	30
Sean Tallaire	F	Fr.	43	26	26	52	26
Rob Valicevic	F	So.	43	21	20	41	28
Wayne Strachan	F	So.	38	20	21	41	44
Mike Morin	F	So.	43	16	25	41	68
Dean Hulett	F	Sr.	42	12	27	39	71
John Hendry	F	Sr.	37	13	20	33	46
Steven Barnes	D	Jr.	42	5	27	32	42
Michael Smith	D	Sr.	42	5	25	30	42
Kurt Miller	F	Jr.	26	9	14	23	24
Tim Hanley	D	Jr.	43	4	11	15	34
Mike Bachusz	F	Sr.	42	8	6	14	10
Keith Aldridge	D	Fr.	37	3	11	14	30
Darrin Wetherill	D	Jr.	43	2	10	12	64
Jay Ness	F	Jr.	39	2	10	12	14
Dan Angelelli	F	So.	27	4	4	8	29
Brad Willner	D	So.	37	2	4	6	28
Jason Trzcinski	F	Fr.	25	2	4	6	36
Mike Matteucci	D	Fr.	19	1	3	4	16
Jason Welch	F	Fr.	14	1	2	3	2
Blaine Lacher	G	So.	34	0	2	2	0
Adam Thompson	G	Fr.	13	0	2	2	0
Matt Hansen	F	Fr.	5	1	0	1	2
David Gartshore	F	So.	3	1	0	1	4
Paul Sass	G	Fr.	2	0	0	0	0

COLLEGE HOCKEY

GOALTENDING

	Games	W	L	T	Min.	GA	Avg.
Paul Sass	2	1	0	0	100	4	2.40
Adam Thompson	13	5	3	2	578	26	2.70
Blaine Lacher	34	24	5	3	1915	86	2.70

MIAMI OF OHIO
SCORING

	Pos.	Class	Games	G	A	Pts.	Pen.
Chris Bergeron	F	Sr.	41	21	40	61	54
Brian Savage	F	Jr.	38	37	21	58	44
Bobby Marshall	D	Jr.	40	2	43	45	40
Joe Cook	D	Sr.	38	11	32	43	82
Enrico Blasi	F	Jr.	41	17	21	38	16
Kevyn Adams	F	Fr.	41	17	16	33	18
Matt Oates	F	So.	38	11	14	25	82
Brendan Curley	F	Sr.	41	9	12	21	48
Dan Carter	F	So.	31	7	11	18	39
Stephen Rohr	F	Jr.	27	9	8	17	20
Jason Mallon	F	So.	41	8	8	16	60
Joey Saban	F	Sr.	21	6	10	16	8
Marc Boxer	F	So.	26	2	13	15	12
Rene Vonlanthen	F	Jr.	38	9	5	14	40
Trent Eigner	D	Jr.	39	1	12	13	30
Justin Krall	D	Fr.	39	5	6	11	26
Andrew Miller	F	So.	25	5	5	10	8
Andrew Backen	D	Fr.	41	2	7	9	46
Terry Ouimet	F	Sr.	26	5	3	8	8
Richard Shulmistra	G	Jr.	33	0	6	6	2
Pat Hanley	D	Fr.	31	2	3	5	66
Dan Daikawa	D	So.	20	1	4	5	12
Shawn Penn	F	So.	8	1	2	3	4
Brian Ensign	F	Fr.	5	1	1	2	2
K. Deschambeault	G	Fr.	12	0	0	0	10
Jason Crane	F	So.	2	0	0	0	2
Eustice King	G	Fr.	1	0	0	0	0

GOALTENDING

	Games	W	L	T	Min.	GA	Avg.
Eustice King	1	0	0	0	5	0	0.00
Richard Shulmistra	33	22	6	4	1949	88	2.71
Kevin Deschambeault	11	5	3	1	532	32	3.61

MICHIGAN
SCORING

	Pos.	Class	Games	G	A	Pts.	Pen.
David Roberts	F	Sr.	40	27	38	65	40
Mark Ouimet	F	Sr.	39	15	45	60	23
Cam Stewart	F	Jr.	39	20	39	59	69
David Oliver	F	Jr.	40	35	20	55	18
Brian Wiseman	F	Jr.	35	13	37	50	40
Dan Stiver	F	Sr.	36	23	20	43	22
Mike Knuble	F	So.	39	26	16	42	57
Ryan Sittler	F	Fr.	35	9	24	33	43
Kevin Hilton	F	Fr.	38	16	15	31	8
Patrick Neaton	D	Sr.	38	10	18	28	37
Mike Stone	F	Jr.	40	11	13	24	26
Chris Tamer	D	Sr.	39	5	18	23	113
Ron Sacka	F	So.	28	8	9	17	21
Aaron Ward	D	Jr.	30	5	8	13	73
Steven Halko	D	Fr.	39	1	12	13	12
David Harlock	D	Sr.	38	3	9	12	58
Rick Willis	F	So.	39	3	8	11	67
John Arnold	F	Fr.	22	3	4	7	22
Tim Hogan	D	So.	22	4	1	5	24
Mark Sakala	D	So.	18	1	4	5	4
Steve Shields	G	Jr.	39	0	4	4	10
Alan Sinclair	D	So.	20	0	3	3	26
Chris Gordon	G	Jr.	13	0	1	1	0
Al Loges	G	So.	5	0	1	1	0
Anton Fiodorov	F	So.	6	0	0	0	4

GOALTENDING

	Games	W	L	T	Min.	GA	Avg.
Chris Gordon	13	0	1	1	302	11	2.19
Steve Shields	39	30	6	2	2027	75	2.22
Al Loges	5	0	0	0	88	5	3.39

MICHIGAN STATE
SCORING

	Pos.	Class	Games	G	A	Pts.	Pen.
Bryan Smolinski	F	Sr.	40	31	37	68	93
Rem Murray	F	So.	40	22	35	57	24
Steve Guolla	F	So.	39	19	35	54	6
Steve Suk	F	So.	40	6	34	40	34
Kelly Harper	F	Jr.	39	11	20	31	20
Anson Carter	F	Fr.	36	19	11	30	20
Brian Clifford	F	Fr.	34	15	7	22	20
Rob Woodward	F	Sr.	36	12	9	21	90
Bart Turner	F	Jr.	39	5	9	14	53
Nicolas Perreault	D	Jr.	38	7	6	13	90
Ryan Fleming	D	Fr.	38	3	9	12	12
Michael Burkett	F	Jr.	39	2	10	12	28
Steve Norton	D	Jr.	40	2	9	11	58
Wes McCauley	D	Sr.	33	3	6	9	34
Chris Smith	D	Fr.	19	4	3	7	24
Scott Worden	F	Jr.	34	3	4	7	32
Bart Vanstaalduinen	D	Fr.	37	1	5	6	28
Chris Sullivan	D	Jr.	15	1	2	3	14
Scott Dean	F	So.	10	1	1	2	22
Ryan Folkening	F	Fr.	23	0	2	2	14
Mike Ware	F	Fr.	20	1	0	1	8
Matt Albers	F	So.	16	1	0	1	14
Mike Buzak	G	So.	38	0	1	1	6
Eric Kruse	G	So.	9	0	1	1	0
Bill Shalawylo	F	Sr.	9	0	1	1	4
Mike Mattis	F	Fr.	4	0	0	0	0

GOALTENDING

	Games	W	L	T	Min.	GA	Avg.
Mike Buzak	38	22	10	2	2090	102	2.93
Eric Kruse	9	2	4	0	315	24	4.57

NOTRE DAME
SCORING

	Pos.	Class	Games	G	A	Pts.	Pen.
Jamie Ling	F	Fr.	36	14	26	40	30
David Bankoske	F	Sr.	36	14	16	30	30
Curtis Janicke	F	Sr.	29	12	18	30	12
Jamie Morshead	F	Fr.	27	12	9	21	44
Brett Bruininks	F	Fr.	36	9	7	16	98
Matt Osiecki	D	Jr.	31	6	10	16	38
Eric Gregoire	D	Sr.	33	1	9	10	44
Jeff Hasselman	F	So.	34	7	1	8	8
Jeremy Coe	D	Fr.	30	4	4	8	66
Garry Gruber	D	Fr.	35	4	3	7	34
Sterling Black	F	Sr.	26	3	4	7	26
Chris Bales	F	Fr.	30	2	5	7	18
Dan Sawyer	D	Sr.	34	1	6	7	30
Brent Lamppa	F	So.	30	4	2	6	8
Jay Matushak	F	Fr.	35	2	4	6	22
Dan Marvin	F	Sr.	31	3	2	5	50
John Rushin	F	So.	36	1	4	5	46
Matt Bieck	D	Fr.	31	1	2	3	28
Davide DalGrande	D	Fr.	22	1	1	2	10
Troy Cusey	F	So.	15	0	2	2	12
Nate Rajala	D	Fr.	4	0	2	2	0
Carey Nemeth	F	So.	8	1	0	1	0
Greg Louder	G	Jr.	24	0	0	0	0
Tim Litchard	F	Jr.	15	0	0	0	12
Brent Lothrop	G	Jr.	14	0	0	0	0
Carl Picconatto	G	Sr.	10	0	0	0	14
Jason Konesco	D	Jr.	2	0	0	0	2
Tom Arkell	D	Jr.	2	0	0	0	0

GOALTENDING

	Games	W	L	T	Min.	GA	Avg.
Carl Picconato	10	1	4	1	381	29	4.57
Greg Louder	24	4	16	1	1177	95	4.84
Brent Lothrop	14	2	7	0	613	56	5.48

OHIO STATE
SCORING

	Pos.	Class	Games	G	A	Pts.	Pen.
Steve Richards	D	So.	37	7	23	30	46

SCORING

	Pos.	Class	Games	G	A	Pts.	Pen.
Ron White	F	Jr.	37	14	14	28	24
Glenn Painter	F	Sr.	36	3	20	23	24
Phil Cadman	F	Sr.	34	12	10	22	10
Sacha Guilbault	F	So.	37	10	11	21	24
Eddie Choi	F	Sr.	34	9	9	18	36
Randy Holmes	F	Fr.	33	6	9	15	6
Joe Sellers	F	Fr.	30	5	10	15	16
Craig Paterson	D	Fr.	37	4	11	15	196
Tim Green	D	Jr.	35	4	9	13	64
Rob Peters	F	Jr.	35	2	9	11	72
Adam Smith	F	So.	34	3	5	8	28
Sean Sutton	F	Fr.	16	4	3	7	6
Bryan Riedel	F	Fr.	28	2	5	7	42
Jeff Winter	D	Fr.	28	2	4	6	64
Mark Skogstad	D	Fr.	28	1	5	6	112
John B. Graham	F	Fr.	23	1	5	6	46
Bill Rathwell	F	Fr.	33	3	2	5	18
John E. Graham	F	Sr.	25	0	3	3	51
Sandy Fraser	D	So.	33	1	1	2	38
Gary Hirst	D	Fr.	27	1	0	1	16
Tom Askey	G	Fr.	25	0	0	0	2
Kurt Brown	G	Fr.	15	0	0	0	12
Jim Slazyk	G	Sr.	10	0	0	0	0
Brian Keller	D	Fr.	2	0	0	0	0

GOALTENDING

	Games	W	L	T	Min.	GA	Avg.
Kurt Brown	15	2	7	1	675	50	4.44
Tom Askey	25	2	19	0	1235	125	6.07
Jim Slazyk	10	1	4	1	318	42	7.91

WESTERN MICHIGAN

SCORING

	Pos.	Class	Games	G	A	Pts.	Pen.
Chris Brooks	F	Fr.	38	21	25	46	18
Pat Ferschweiler	F	Sr.	38	15	20	35	58
Colin Ward	F	Jr.	37	22	11	33	48
Scott Chartier	D	Fr.	38	6	23	29	84
Byron Witkowski	F	Sr.	38	14	12	26	44
Ryan D'Arcy	F	So.	37	7	19	26	30
Jamal Mayers	F	Fr.	38	8	17	25	26
Brian Gallentine	F	So.	38	9	15	24	20
Jason Jennings	F	Sr.	37	11	9	20	36
Chris Belanger	D	Jr.	27	3	16	19	23
Jeremy Brown	F	Fr.	38	8	10	18	26
Derek Schooley	D	Jr.	33	4	12	16	48
Joe Bonnett	F	Sr.	36	6	7	13	18
Mike Whitton	F	So.	33	6	5	11	78
Peter Wilkinson	F	Jr.	35	1	7	8	46
Brent Brekke	D	Jr.	38	3	2	5	42
Thomas Carriere	D	Fr.	38	2	3	5	20
Mikhail Lapin	D	Fr.	30	0	3	3	58
Francois Leroux	F	So.	14	1	1	2	18
Craig Brown	G	Jr.	21	0	2	2	12
Jim Holman	D	Fr.	12	0	1	1	4
Brian Renfrew	G	So.	20	0	0	0	2

GOALTENDING

	Games	W	L	T	Min.	GA	Avg.
Brian Renfrew	20	11	8	1	1155	74	3.84
Craig Brown	20	9	8	1	1125	72	3.84

EASTERN COLLEGE ATHLETIC CONFERENCE

1992-93 SEASON

FINAL STANDINGS

Team	G	W	L	T	Pts.	GF	GA
Harvard (22-5-3)	22	16	3	3	35	95	61
R.P.I. (20-11-4)	22	15	6	1	31	96	61
Clarkson (20-9-5)	22	12	6	4	28	103	64
Brown (16-11-3)	22	13	7	2	28	102	78
Yale (15-12-4)	22	12	7	3	27	97	86
St. Law. (17-12-3)....	22	12	8	2	26	89	77
Vermont (12-16-3) ..	22	10	11	1	21	71	68
Dartmouth (11-16-0)	22	9	13	0	18	82	96
Colgate (13-18-3) ...	22	9	13	0	18	81	101
Princeton (9-17-3) ...	22	6	13	3	15	70	98
Cornell (6-19-1)	22	5	16	1	11	61	94
Union (3-22-0)	22	3	19	0	6	44	107

Overall record in parentheses.

PLAYOFF RESULTS

PRELIMINARIES

Colgate 4, Dartmouth 3 (2 OT)
Princeton 3, Vermont 1

Harvard 6, Princeton 2
Harvard 8, Princeton 0
 (Harvard won series, 2-0)

QUARTERFINALS

Clarkson 3, St. Lawrence 1
Clarkson 5, St. Lawrence 3
 (Clarkson won series, 2-0)

Brown 3, Yale 3
Brown 5, Yale 3
 (Brown won series, 1-0-1)

Colgate 5, Rensselaer 2
Rensselaer 5, Colgate 4
Rensselaer 5, Colgate 1
 (Rensselaer won series, 2-1)

SEMIFINALS

Clarkson 5, Rensselaer 3
Brown 3, Harvard 1

CONSOLATION GAME

Harvard 6, Rensselaer 3

CHAMPIONSHIP GAME

Clarkson 3, Brown 1

ALL-STAR TEAMS

First team	Pos.	Second team
Neil Little, R.P.I.	G	Christian Soucy, Vermont
Jack Duffy, Yale	D	Ted Beattie, St. Lawrence
Aaron Miller, Vermont	D	Brad Layzell, R.P.I.
Ted Drury, Harvard	F	Scott Fraser, Dartmouth
Mark Kaufmann, Yale	F	Scott Hanley, Brown
Marko Tuomainen, Clarkson	F	Todd Marchant, Clarkson

AWARD WINNERS

Player of the year: Ted Drury, Harvard
Rookie of the year: Burke Murphy, St. Lawrence
Coach of the year: Roger Demment, Dartmouth
Leading scorer: Ted Drury, Harvard
　　　　　　　　　Mark Kaufmann, Yale
Playoff MVP: Chris Rogles, Clarkson

INDIVIDUAL STATISTICS

BROWN

SCORING

	Pos.	Class	Games	G	A	Pts.	Pen.
Scott Hanley	F	Sr.	31	19	23	42	26
Derek Chauvette....	F	Sr.	31	9	30	39	42
Kelly Jones.............	F	Jr.	31	18	19	37	48
Chris Kaban	F	Jr.	31	14	16	30	46
Mike Ross..............	F	Sr.	31	15	9	24	28
Ryan Mulhern	F	Fr.	31	15	9	24	46
Eric Trach	F	So.	31	5	15	20	27
Mark Fabbro	F	Jr.	23	5	14	19	24
Jim O'Brien	D	Sr.	26	5	10	15	60
Brian Jardine	F	Fr.	24	6	7	13	22
Tony Martino	F	So.	28	4	6	10	8
Mark Shaughnessy.	F	Jr.	26	1	9	10	10
Joe Beck...............	F	Sr.	28	4	4	8	16
Pat Thompson	D	So.	30	1	7	8	16
Tim Chase.............	F/D	Sr.	13	3	4	7	12
Mike Traggio..........	D	So.	19	2	5	7	48
Sean Murdoch	F	Sr.	17	1	6	7	14
Sascha Pogor	F	Sr.	12	2	3	5	22
Pasi Vanttinen	F	Jr.	11	2	3	5	8
Ron Smitko............	D	Fr.	29	1	4	5	32
Charlie Humber......	F	Fr.	7	1	2	3	8
Brendan Whittet	D	Jr.	26	0	2	2	42
Chris Schremp	F	Sr.	7	1	0	1	2
James Mooney	D	Fr.	4	0	1	1	6
Geoff Finch	G	Jr.	18	0	0	0	0
Brett Haywood.......	G	Jr.	2	0	0	0	2
Mike Parsons	G	Fr.	12	0	0	0	2
Jeff Reschny	D	So.	4	0	0	0	4
Kim Hannah	F	So.	5	0	0	0	0

GOALTENDING

	Games	W	L	T	Min.	GA	Avg.
Geoff Finch..............	18	11	5	1	1020	56	3.29
Mike Parsons..........	12	5	5	2	722	51	4.24
Brett Haywood..........	2	0	2	0	119	11	5.55

CLARKSON

SCORING

	Pos.	Class	Games	G	A	Pts.	Pen.
Marko Tuomainen .	F	So.	35	25	30	55	26
Todd Marchant......	F	So.	33	18	28	46	38
Steve Dubinsky	F	Sr.	35	18	26	44	58
Hugo Belanger	F	Sr.	31	17	23	40	36
Patrice Robitaille ...	F	So.	35	18	20	38	30
Craig Conroy	F	Jr.	35	10	23	33	26
Brian Mueller	D	So.	32	6	23	29	12
Guy Sanderson	D	Sr.	35	8	17	25	70
Steve Palmer	F	Sr.	35	10	11	21	20
Mikko Tavi	D	Sr.	34	4	13	17	20
David Seitz.............	F	Fr.	30	5	9	14	16
Martin d'Orsonnens.	D	Sr.	35	2	12	14	76
Ed Henrich	D	Jr.	35	0	11	11	30
Dave Green	F	Sr.	34	4	5	9	20
Kevin Murphy	F	Fr.	23	5	3	8	20
Chris DeRuiter	F	Fr.	32	2	5	7	40
S. Fotheringham	F	Jr.	17	2	3	5	22
Chris Lipsett	F	Fr.	19	1	3	4	16
Pat Theriault..........	F	Jr.	29	1	1	2	20
Jerry Rosenheck....	F	So.	13	0	2	2	4
Jason Currie	G	Jr.	12	0	2	2	6
Josh Bartell...........	D	Fr.	22	1	0	1	24
Chris Rogles..........	G	Sr.	27	0	1	1	2
Dave Ford	D	Fr.	2	0	0	0	2

GOALTENDING

	Games	W	L	T	Min.	GA	Avg.
Chris Rogles	27	16	4	4	1486	60	2.42
Jason Currie	12	4	6	1	642	34	3.18

COLGATE

SCORING

	Pos.	Class	Games	G	A	Pts.	Pen.
Andrew Dickson	F	Sr.	34	15	28	43	30
Bruce Gardiner	F	Jr.	33	17	12	29	64
Sam Raffoul	F	Jr.	33	10	19	29	66
Brent Wilde	F	Jr.	34	10	19	29	74
Marcel Richard	F	Jr.	27	12	16	28	53
Craig deBlois	F	Sr.	34	17	10	27	69
Dan Gardner	F	Jr.	32	7	18	25	8
Ron Fogarty	F	So.	34	5	14	19	16
Earl Cronan	F	Fr.	33	8	9	17	42
Clayton Fahey	F	Jr.	30	11	4	15	46
Bob Haddock	D	Sr.	32	6	9	15	20
Chris DeProfio	F	Fr.	34	5	8	13	16
Alan Brown	D	Sr.	32	4	9	13	38
Rod Pamenter	D	Fr.	33	1	9	10	38
Rob Metz	F	Jr.	22	3	6	9	6
Troy Mohns	D	Sr.	32	1	8	9	52
Jason Craig	D	So.	22	0	5	5	0
Dan Gibson	D	Jr.	25	0	5	5	42
Brad Dexter	D	So.	12	2	2	4	10
Nigel Creightney	D	So.	23	0	3	3	32
J.P. Paquin	D	Fr.	16	1	1	2	10
Jason Gates	G	So.	20	0	1	1	2
Shawn Murray	G	Jr.	15	0	0	0	0
Matt Weder	G	Fr.	6	0	0	0	2
Greg Lewis	F	Fr.	2	0	0	0	0
Clayt McCaffrey	F	So.	2	0	0	0	0

GOALTENDING

	Games	W	L	T	Min.	GA	Avg.
Jason Gates	20	8	9	2	1127	72	3.83
Shawn Murray	15	5	6	1	723	51	4.23
Matt Weder	6	0	3	0	221	20	5.43

CORNELL

SCORING

	Pos.	Class	Games	G	A	Pts.	Pen.
Ryan Hughes	F	Sr.	26	8	14	22	30
Geoff Bumstead	F	Jr.	23	5	14	19	18
Brad Chartrand	F	Fr.	26	10	6	16	16
Shaun Hannah	F	Jr.	25	5	11	16	30
Jason Vogel	F	Sr.	18	8	5	13	6
Jake Karam	F	So.	26	6	7	13	6
Russ Hammond	F	Sr.	22	6	5	11	18
Mark Scollan	F	Fr.	19	2	9	11	10
Tyler McManus	F	So.	17	6	3	9	20
P.C. Drouin	F	Fr.	23	3	6	9	30
Bill Holowatiuk	D	Fr.	26	2	7	9	44
Mike Sancimino	F	Fr.	14	3	5	8	18
Blair Ettles	D	So.	17	3	4	7	12
Geoff Lopatka	F	Fr.	22	3	3	6	8
Andre Doll	F	Fr.	17	1	4	5	14
Etienne Belzile	D	Sr.	26	2	2	4	24
John DeHart	F	Fr.	23	1	3	4	10
Christian Felli	D	So.	26	0	4	4	38
Alex Vershinin	F/D	Jr.	16	0	3	3	10
Jiri Kloboucek	F	So.	10	1	1	2	6
Tim Shean	D	Fr.	14	0	2	2	2
Andy Bandurski	G	So.	20	0	1	1	2
Dan Dufresne	D	Fr.	24	0	1	1	38
Joel McArter	F	Fr.	6	0	1	1	14
Rick Davis	F	Jr.	2	0	0	0	0
Eddy Skazyk	G	Fr.	9	0	0	0	0

GOALTENDING

	Games	W	L	T	Min.	GA	Avg.
Andy Bandurski	20	6	11	1	1109	72	3.90
Eddy Skazyk	9	0	8	0	468	39	5.00

DARTMOUTH

SCORING

	Pos.	Class	Games	G	A	Pts.	Pen.
Scott Fraser	F	Jr.	26	21	23	44	13
Bill Kelleher	F	Fr.	27	4	26	30	10
Tony DelCarmine	F	Jr.	24	11	17	28	60
Dion DelMonte	F	So.	27	8	18	26	32
Pat Turcotte	F	So.	27	12	7	19	20
Mike Stacchi	F	So.	27	4	12	16	58
Derek Geary	F	Jr.	27	7	8	15	4
Trevor Dodman	D	So.	27	4	8	12	14
Matt Collins	D	Jr.	21	7	3	10	12
Scott Dolesh	D	Fr.	27	2	8	10	28
Peter Clark	F	Sr.	26	5	4	9	8
Dax Burkhart	D	Fr.	27	4	4	8	36
Dan Bloom	D	Fr.	27	1	6	7	38
Greg Chapman	F	Sr.	27	3	2	5	12
Chris Clancy	F	Jr.	25	1	4	5	36
Mike Loga	D	Jr.	27	1	4	5	74
Rob Kerr	F	So.	6	2	2	4	5
Yanick Roussin	D	So.	26	1	2	3	26
Mike Bolf	F	Fr.	20	0	1	1	0
Shawn Burt	F	Sr.	11	0	0	0	4
Mike Bracco	G	Jr.	13	0	0	0	0
Vern Guetens	G	Sr.	17	0	0	0	0
Eric D'Orio	D	Jr.	1	0	0	0	0
Jon Hess	F	So.	1	0	0	0	2
Pavol Liska	F	So.	1	0	0	0	2

GOALTENDING

	Games	W	L	T	Min.	GA	Avg.
Vern Guetens	17	6	10	0	958	61	3.82
Mike Bracco	13	5	6	0	686	58	5.07

HARVARD

SCORING

	Pos.	Class	Games	G	A	Pts.	Pen.
Ted Drury	F	Jr.	31	22	41	63	26
Matt Mallgrave	F	Sr.	31	27	13	40	36
Steven Flomenhoft	F	Sr.	31	11	24	35	60
Brian Farrell	F	Fr.	31	10	23	33	33
Chris Baird	F	Jr.	31	12	17	29	41
Tom Holmes	F	Fr.	28	6	17	23	10
Lou Body	D	Jr.	31	3	17	20	10
Ben Coughlin	F	So.	31	10	8	18	30
Cory Gustafson	F	So.	31	7	10	17	28
Perry Cohagan	F	So.	31	5	10	15	34
Steve Martins	F	So.	18	6	8	14	40
Derek Maguire	D	Jr.	16	3	9	12	10
Bryan Lonsinger	D	So.	31	2	9	11	6
Sean McCann	D	Jr.	31	4	5	9	36
Jason Karmanos	F	Jr.	31	5	3	8	22
Pete McLaughlin	D	Fr.	31	2	6	8	30
Brad Konik	F	So.	7	0	6	6	4
Kirk Nielsen	F	Fr.	30	2	2	4	38
Michel Breistroff	F	Jr.	28	0	4	4	24
Geb Marett	D	Jr.	17	0	1	1	30
Tripp Tracy	G	Fr.	17	0	1	1	0
Aaron Israel	G	Fr.	14	0	0	0	0
Ian Kennish	F	Fr.	9	0	0	0	4
Eric Grahling	D	Fr.	1	0	0	0	0
Keith McLean	F	So.	1	0	0	0	0

GOALTENDING

	Games	W	L	T	Min.	GA	Avg.
Tripp Tracy	17	13	2	2	1055	40	2.27
Aaron Israel	14	9	4	1	842	43	3.06

PRINCETON

SCORING

	Pos.	Class	Games	G	A	Pts.	Pen.
Terry Morris	F	Sr.	26	15	16	31	14
Matt Zilinskas	F	Sr.	28	12	16	28	34
Sean O'Brien	D	Jr.	29	2	22	24	52
Brian Bigelow	F	Jr.	23	8	9	17	62
Scott Sinson	F	Sr.	28	6	11	17	54

	Pos.	Class	Games	G	A	Pts.	Pen.
Ian Sharp	F	So.	27	4	12	16	42
J.P. O'Connor	F	Fr.	27	8	5	13	20
Sverre Sears	D	Sr.	23	3	9	12	96
Troy Ewanchyna	F	Jr.	21	4	6	10	20
Jason Smith	D	Fr.	28	5	4	9	94
Mervin Kopeck	F	So.	29	3	6	9	14
Ethan Early	F	So.	28	2	6	8	20
Jonathan Kelley	F	Fr.	23	4	3	7	34
John Fust	F	Jr.	21	3	4	7	14
Dan Brown	D	Fr.	28	1	6	7	32
Keith Merkler	F	Sr.	15	3	2	5	6
Gavin Colquhoun	D	So.	25	1	4	5	48
Brent Flahr	D	Fr.	23	1	3	4	10
Miro Pasic	F	Jr.	17	2	1	3	12
Barrington Miller	D/F	Fr.	22	1	2	3	10
Corey Rhodes	F	So.	8	2	0	2	2
Tom Tucker	F	So.	2	0	1	1	0
David Scowby	D	So.	12	0	0	0	6
Rod Yorke	G	So.	10	0	0	0	0
Craig Fiander	G	Sr.	17	0	0	0	2
Scott Almon	D	So.	6	0	0	0	0
Chris Mitchell	F	Sr.	2	0	0	0	0
James Konte	G	Fr.	10	0	0	0	4

GOALTENDING

	Games	W	L	T	Min.	GA	Avg.
James Konte	10	2	3	2	456	25	3.29
Craig Fiander	17	5	9	1	916	66	4.32
Rod Yorke	10	2	5	0	391	32	4.91

RENSSELAER POLYTECHNIC INSTITUTE

SCORING

	Pos.	Class	Games	G	A	Pts.	Pen.
Xavier Majic	F	Jr.	35	16	26	42	18
Bryan Richardson	F	Jr.	35	14	24	38	26
Craig Hamelin	F	So.	35	10	27	37	28
Jeff Gabriel	F	Jr.	27	14	18	32	24
Kelly Askew	F	So.	34	14	16	30	101
Wayne Clarke	F	So.	32	13	16	29	23
Brad Layzell	D	Jr.	35	5	24	29	40
Ron Pasco	F	Jr.	35	14	12	26	96
Tim Regan	F	Fr.	35	13	12	25	28
Jeff Brick	F	So.	33	12	10	22	28
Adam Bartell	D	So.	32	2	17	19	46
Eric Perardi	F	So.	35	7	11	18	44
Allen Kummu	D	Sr.	35	4	8	12	72
Cam Cuthbert	D	Jr.	35	1	9	10	93
Jeff Matthews	F	So.	35	3	4	7	14
Pat Rochon	D	Fr.	35	0	6	6	32
Jeff O'Connor	F	Fr.	34	1	4	5	14
Jon Pirrong	D	Fr.	30	1	3	4	34
Chris Kiley	D	Fr.	22	1	2	3	6
Neil Little	G	Jr.	31	0	3	3	8
Tim Carvel	G	Jr.	2	0	0	0	0
Mike Tamburro	G	Fr.	7	0	0	0	0
Ken Kwasniewski	F	So.	2	0	0	0	0

GOALTENDING

	Games	W	L	T	Min.	GA	Avg.
Neil Little	31	19	9	3	1801	88	2.93
Mike Tamburro	7	1	2	1	279	15	3.23
Tim Carvel	2	0	0	0	45	3	4.00

ST. LAWRENCE

SCORING

	Pos.	Class	Games	G	A	Pts.	Pen.
Greg Carvel	F	Sr.	32	14	34	48	30
Lee Albert	F	So.	32	16	22	38	10
John Massoud	F	Sr.	31	12	18	30	28
Burke Murphy	F	Fr.	32	19	10	29	32
Gerard Verbeek	F	Sr.	32	9	16	25	35
Spencer Meany	F	Jr.	28	8	15	23	97
Mike Allain	F	Jr.	31	10	12	22	70
Ted Beattie	D	Sr.	32	5	15	20	74
Mike McCourt	D	Jr.	31	5	15	20	50
Mark McGeough	F	Jr.	32	8	11	19	32
Dan Skene	F	So.	32	7	10	17	34
Brian McCarthy	F	So.	18	7	5	12	44
Brian Kapeller	F	So.	32	3	9	12	56
Cade Blackburn	F	So.	32	3	6	9	16
Jeff Kungle	D	Fr.	32	2	5	7	28
Tom Perry	D	Fr.	31	1	6	7	50
John Roderick	D	Sr.	27	2	2	4	40
Chris Dashney	D	Fr.	15	1	3	4	10
Mike Terwilliger	D	Sr.	17	0	3	3	10
Jim Giacin	F	Jr.	19	1	1	2	14
Paul Spagnoletti	G	Jr.	15	0	2	2	4
Scott Celentano	D	Jr.	3	0	0	0	2
Brady Giroux	G	Sr.	20	0	0	0	0
Dave MacTavish	G	Sr.	2	0	0	0	0
Todd Oliver	F/D	Jr.	2	0	0	0	0

GOALTENDING

	Games	W	L	T	Min.	GA	Avg.
Dave MacTavish	2	0	0	0	14	0	0.00
Brady Giroux	20	11	4	2	1089	57	3.14
Paul Spagnoletti	15	6	8	1	831	57	4.12

UNION

SCORING

	Pos.	Class	Games	G	A	Pts.	Pen.
Chris Albert	F	So.	25	9	11	20	56
Ryan Alaspa	F	Fr.	25	4	13	17	16
Reid Simonton	D	Fr.	25	7	5	12	78
Brad Kukko	F	Fr.	22	5	5	10	10
Cory Holbrough	F	So.	18	3	6	9	12
Shane Holunga	D	Fr.	25	1	8	9	36
Jeff Jiampetti	F	Jr.	24	4	4	8	8
Kevin Darby	F	Sr.	24	4	3	7	22
Chris Sears	F	Fr.	15	3	3	6	6
Keith Darby	F	So.	19	1	5	6	8
Jayson Flowers	F	Jr.	21	3	2	5	6
Scott Boyd	D	Fr.	23	2	3	5	38
Dean Goulet	D	So.	25	0	4	4	28
Alex Vallee	F	Fr.	21	2	1	3	14
Chris Hancock	F	Fr.	20	2	1	3	39
Steve Battiston	F	Jr.	23	1	2	3	12
Jon MacDonald	F	Fr.	19	0	3	3	6
Alex MacLellan	D	So.	12	0	2	2	6
Greg Steele	D	Sr.	22	1	0	1	30
Craig Provancal	F	Fr.	5	1	0	1	6
Matt Kelley	D	So.	20	0	1	1	10
Mike Gallant	G	So.	10	0	1	1	0
Gary Edmands	F	So.	11	0	1	1	18
Bill McKenna	D	Jr.	2	0	0	0	2
Luigi Villa	G	So.	19	0	0	0	2
Jon Quint	F	Jr.	2	0	0	0	0
Mark Reid	F	Fr.	2	0	0	0	2

GOALTENDING

	Games	W	L	T	Min.	GA	Avg.
Luigi Villa	19	3	14	0	1018	81	4.77
Mike Gallant	10	0	8	0	475	38	4.80

VERMONT

SCORING

	Pos.	Class	Games	G	A	Pts.	Pen.
Dom Ducharme	F	So.	31	16	22	38	18
Nick Perreault	F	Jr.	31	18	19	37	30
Matt Johnson	F	Jr.	31	9	12	21	21
Brendan Creagh	D	Sr.	30	3	15	18	24
Aaron Miller	D	Sr.	30	4	13	17	16
Toby Kearney	F	Sr.	29	6	10	16	42
Bill Lincoln	F	So.	31	7	7	14	50
Phil Eboli	F	Fr.	29	5	8	13	34
Kevin Monty	F	Sr.	31	6	5	11	18
Brian Leddy	F	So.	31	7	2	9	56
Eric Lavoie	F	Fr.	29	3	4	7	4
Dale Patterson	F	Fr.	19	3	3	6	4

	Pos.	Class	Games	G	A	Pts.	Pen.
Bo Beckman	F	Sr.	29	1	5	6	14
Corey Machanic	D	Jr.	31	1	4	5	16
Jason Williams	D	So.	31	0	5	5	46
Steve McKell	D	Fr.	27	0	5	5	32
Tom Quinn	D	So.	19	3	1	4	8
Joe McCarthy	F	Sr.	17	1	2	3	31
Keith Festa	F	So.	15	1	1	2	2
Mike Larkin	D	So.	28	0	2	2	66
Dale Villeneuve	F	Fr.	8	1	0	1	12
Christian Soucy	G	So.	29	0	0	0	0
Tom Vukota	G	So.	4	0	0	0	0
Scott MacDonald	D	So.	1	0	0	0	0
Jim Beraldi	G	Jr.	1	0	0	0	0
Jon Miyamoto	G	So.	1	0	0	0	0

GOALTENDING

	Games	W	L	T	Min.	GA	Avg.
Tom Vukota	4	0	1	0	120	6	3.00
Jon Miyamoto	1	1	0	0	20	1	3.00
Christian Soucy	29	11	15	3	1708	90	3.16
Jim Beraldi	1	0	0	0	20	2	6.00

YALE
SCORING

	Pos.	Class	Games	G	A	Pts.	Pen.
Mark Kaufmann	F	Sr.	31	25	38	63	10
Martin Leroux	F	Jr.	31	25	23	48	47
Stephen Maltby	F	Sr.	31	17	21	38	52
James Lavish	F	Sr.	29	17	19	36	36
Andy Weidenbach	F	So.	30	13	13	26	36

	Pos.	Class	Games	G	A	Pts.	Pen.
Jack Duffy	D	Sr.	31	8	17	25	60
Peter Allen	D	Sr.	30	3	15	18	32
Jason Cipolla	F	So.	26	1	10	11	26
Yannick Chiasson	F	So.	30	5	5	10	22
John Emmons	F	Fr	28	3	5	8	66
Zoran Kozic	F	So.	29	3	4	7	16
Michael Yoshino	F	Fr.	27	3	4	7	6
Dave Cochran	D	Jr.	26	3	4	7	30
Steve Lombardi	F	So.	27	1	6	7	14
Dan Brierly	D	Fr.	29	0	7	7	32
Jeff Sorem	F	Fr.	25	3	3	6	2
Dan Nyberg	D	So.	29	1	5	6	38
James Mackey	D	Jr.	31	1	4	5	52
Dean Malish	D	Sr.	15	0	2	2	2
John Hockin	G	Sr.	7	0	1	1	2
Todd Sullivan	G	So.	22	0	0	0	0
Mike Kamatovic	G	Jr.	5	0	0	0	0
Todd Caricato	F	Jr.	12	0	0	0	13
Richard Giroux	D	So.	2	0	0	0	0
Jeff Williams	F	Sr.	3	0	0	0	0
Pelle Bildtsen	D	Jr.	2	0	0	0	2
Chris Barbanti	F	So.	1	0	0	0	0
Garrison Smith	D	So.	1	0	0	0	0
Brendan Doyle	F	Fr.	1	0	0	0	2

GOALTENDING

	Games	W	L	T	Min.	GA	Avg.
Todd Sullivan	22	10	10	2	1304	76	3.50
John Hockin	7	4	1	2	424	29	4.10
Mike Kamatovic	5	1	1	0	143	11	4.62

HOCKEY EAST

1992-93 SEASON

FINAL STANDINGS

Team	G	W	L	T	Pts.	GF	GA
Maine (42-1-2)	24	22	1	1	45	162	56
Boston U. (29-9-2)	24	18	5	1	37	126	84
New Hamp. (18-17-3)	24	11	11	2	24	102	99
Lowell (20-17-2)	24	10	13	1	21	100	100
Providence (16-16-4)	24	9	12	3	21	91	109
Merrimack (14-20-2)	24	8	16	0	16	85	141
Boston Col. (9-24-5)	24	6	15	3	15	80	120
N'eastern (10-24-1)	24	6	17	1	13	89	127

Overall record in parentheses.

PLAYOFF RESULTS

SEMIFINALS

Maine 7, Lowell 5
Boston University 2, New Hampshire 0

CONSOLATION GAME

Lowell 5, New Hampshire 4 (OT)

CHAMPIONSHIP GAME

Maine 5, Boston University 2

ALL-STAR TEAMS

First team	Pos.	Second team
Mike Dunham, Maine	G	Garth Snow, Maine
Chris Imes, Maine	D	Kaj Linna, Boston U.
Kevin O'Sullivan, Boston U.	D	Chris Therien, Providence
Paul Kariya, Maine	F	Rob Donovan, New Hamp.
Jim Montgomery, Maine	F	Shane Henry, Lowell
David Sacco, Boston U.	F	Mike Murray, Lowell

AWARD WINNERS

Player of the year: Paul Kariya, Maine
Rookie of the year: Paul Kariya, Maine
Coach of the year: Shawn Walsh, Maine
Leading scorer: Paul Kariya, Maine
Playoff MVP: Jim Montgomery, Maine

INDIVIDUAL STATISTICS

BOSTON COLLEGE

SCORING

	Pos.	Class	Games	G	A	Pts.	Pen.
John Joyce	F	Jr.	38	12	31	43	50
Marc Beran	F	Sr.	38	15	20	35	39
Jack Callahan	F	Jr.	38	19	15	34	56
Michael Spalla	D	Jr.	38	12	17	29	18
Ian Moran	D	So.	31	8	12	20	32
Rob Canavan	F	So.	30	8	8	16	30
Jerry Buckley	F	So.	31	3	11	14	44
David Hymovitz	F	Fr.	37	7	6	13	6
Don Chase	F	Fr.	38	7	5	12	48
Todd Hall	D	So.	34	2	10	12	22
Ryan Haggerty	F	So.	32	6	5	11	12
Rob Laferriere	F	So.	24	4	6	10	26
Ron Pascucci	D	Sr.	38	3	7	10	58
Brett Stickney	F	So.	21	2	4	6	10
Greg Callahan	D	Fr.	38	1	4	5	49
Sal Manganaro	F	So.	21	4	1	5	12
Jim Krayer	F	So.	24	1	3	4	8
Mike McCarthy	F	So.	35	0	4	4	6
Scott Zygulski	D	Sr.	35	2	2	4	14
Tom Ashe	D	Fr.	33	1	1	2	46
Clifton McHale	F	Fr.	20	0	1	1	17
Scott Caulfield	G	Fr.	1	0	0	0	0
Scott Haig	F	Fr.	1	0	0	0	2
Keith O'Connell	D	Fr.	8	0	0	0	4
Josh Singewald	G	So.	31	0	0	0	0
Mike Sparrow	G	So.	14	0	0	0	0

GOALTENDING

	Games	W	L	T	Min.	GA	Avg.
Scott Caulfield	1	0	0	0	15	1	4.11
Josh Singewald	31	8	15	5	1650	123	4.47
Mike Sparrow	14	1	9	0	642	62	5.80

BOSTON UNIVERSITY

SCORING

	Pos.	Class	Games	G	A	Pts.	Pen.
David Sacco	F	Sr.	40	25	37	62	86
Doug Friedman	F	Jr.	38	17	24	41	62
Jay Pandolfo	F	Fr.	39	17	23	40	16
Steve Thornton	F	So.	40	18	19	37	19
Jacques Joubert	F	So.	40	17	18	35	54
Mike Pomichter	F	So.	30	16	14	30	23
Kaj Linna	D	So.	36	2	27	29	71
Kevin O'Sullivan	D	Sr.	40	5	20	25	78
Mark Bavis	F	Sr.	40	14	10	24	58
Mike Bavis	F	Sr.	40	12	11	23	87
Rich Brennan	D	So.	40	9	11	20	68
Jon Pratt	F	Jr.	31	9	8	17	70
Mike Prendergast	F	So.	27	8	7	15	18
Bob Lachance	F	Fr.	33	4	10	14	24
Ken Rausch	F	So.	18	7	5	12	12
Dan Donato	D	Jr.	38	3	8	11	56
Jon Jenkins	F	So.	34	3	8	11	18
Petteri Koskimaki	F	Sr.	27	2	9	11	10
Stephen Foster	D	Jr.	34	2	6	8	42
Doug Wood	D	Fr.	37	3	5	8	38
Scott Cashman	G	Sr.	17	0	2	2	14
Derek Herlofsky	G	So.	19	0	2	2	0
Chris O'Sullivan	D	Fr.	5	0	2	2	4
Dave Dahlberg	F	Sr.	7	0	0	0	4
J.P. McKersie	G	So.	9	0	0	0	0

GOALTENDING

	Games	W	L	T	Min.	GA	Avg.
Derek Herlofsky	19	12	5	1	1060	50	2.83
Scott Cashman	17	11	4	0	888	44	2.97
J.P. McKersie	9	6	0	1	466	31	3.99

LOWELL

SCORING

	Pos.	Class	Games	G	A	Pts.	Pen.
Shane Henry	F	Jr.	39	23	35	58	12
Mike Murray	F	Jr.	39	23	33	56	78
Dan O'Connell	F	Sr.	37	21	14	35	77
Jeff Daw	D	Fr.	37	12	18	30	14
Dave Pensa	F	So.	38	18	11	29	62
Christian Sbrocca	F	Fr.	39	10	17	27	63
Ian Hebert	F	Jr.	26	10	16	26	29
Jon Mahoney	F	Sr.	34	11	9	20	63
David Mayes	D	Fr.	33	5	9	14	20
Keith Carney	D	Sr.	30	2	10	12	28
Gerry Daley	F	Sr.	30	5	7	12	22
Tim Smallwood	D	Sr.	34	3	8	11	32

	Pos.	Class	Games	G	A	Pts.	Pen.
Travis Tucker	D	Jr.	31	2	9	11	90
Normand Bazin	F	Jr.	31	4	5	9	28
Kerry Angus	D	So.	26	1	7	8	26
Aaron Kriss	D	So.	25	3	5	8	10
Scott Meehan	D	Sr.	39	3	5	8	46
Dave Stevens	F	Sr.	13	2	4	6	6
Scott Wenham	D	Jr.	14	0	5	5	12
Eric Brown	F	So.	33	2	2	4	12
Mark Carlson	F	Sr.	30	3	1	4	12
Brendan Concannon	F	Fr.	17	2	2	4	0
David Barozzino	D	Fr.	21	0	3	3	40
Bill Riga	F	Fr.	2	0	1	1	0
Dwayne Roloson	G	Jr.	39	0	1	1	12
Paul Botto	D	Fr.	4	0	0	0	2
Chris Hagan	G	Fr.	1	0	0	0	0

GOALTENDING

	Games	W	L	T	Min.	GA	Avg.
Chris Hagan	1	0	0	0	4	0	0.00
Dwayne Roloson	39	20	17	2	2342	150	3.84

	Pos.	Class	Games	G	A	Pts.	Pen.
Guy Ragault	F	Sr.	24	4	5	9	28
Tom Costa	D	Fr.	35	0	6	6	94
Alex Weinrich	D	Sr.	24	1	5	6	28
Matt Crowley	F	Sr.	17	3	2	5	12
Quentin Fendelet	F	Jr.	18	1	3	4	4
Matt Hayes	D	Sr.	23	0	4	4	12
Don MacLeod	D	Sr.	32	1	2	3	66
Chris Ross	D	So.	11	0	3	3	10
Mike Doneghey	G	Sr.	33	0	1	1	2
Mike Kelleher	D	So.	3	0	1	1	4
Jamie Brown	D	Fr.	1	0	0	0	0
Mike Cox	G	Sr.	2	0	0	0	0
Dan Millar	G	Fr.	11	0	0	0	0
Jason Pagni	D	Jr.	1	0	0	0	0
Matt Poska	G	Jr.	1	0	0	0	0

GOALTENDING

	Games	W	L	T	Min.	GA	Avg.
Matt Poska	1	0	0	0	6	0	0.00
Mike Cox	2	0	0	0	15	1	4.00
Mike Doneghey	33	13	15	1	1822	147	4.84
Dan Millar	10	1	5	1	324	33	6.11

MAINE
SCORING

	Pos.	Class	Games	G	A	Pts.	Pen.
Paul Kariya	F	Fr.	39	25	75	100	12
Jim Montgomery	F	Sr.	45	32	63	95	40
Cal Ingraham	F	Jr.	45	46	39	85	50
Chris Ferraro	F	Fr.	39	25	26	51	46
Mike Latendresse	F	So.	40	21	30	51	22
Peter Ferraro	F	Fr.	36	18	32	50	106
Patrice Tardif	F	Jr.	45	23	25	48	22
Dave MacIsaac	D	So.	35	5	32	37	14
Eric Fenton	F	Sr.	31	21	15	36	76
Chris Imes	D	Jr.	45	12	23	35	24
Matt Martin	D	Jr.	44	6	26	32	88
Kent Salfi	F	Sr.	33	10	13	23	24
Justin Tomberlin	F	Jr.	34	13	9	22	22
Martin Mercier	F	Sr.	39	11	8	19	23
Lee Saunders	D	Jr.	42	7	12	19	40
Dave LaCouture	F	Sr.	43	8	6	14	78
Dan Murphy	D	Sr.	44	0	11	11	56
Brad Purdie	F	Fr.	20	3	7	10	14
Jason Weinrich	D	Jr.	38	1	8	9	42
Andy Silverman	D	So.	37	1	7	8	56
Chuck Texiera	F	Jr.	13	1	3	4	16
Jamie Thompson	F	Fr.	16	3	1	4	10
Wayne Conlan	F	So.	3	0	3	3	0
Garth Snow	G	Sr.	23	0	3	3	6
Mike Dunham	G	Jr.	25	0	2	2	0
Jack Rodrigue	D	So.	2	0	2	2	2
Greg Hirsch	G	So.	11	0	0	0	0

GOALTENDING

	Games	W	L	T	Min.	GA	Avg.
Garth Snow	23	21	0	1	1210	42	2.08
Greg Hirsch	11	0	0	0	73	3	2.46
Mike Dunham	25	21	1	1	1429	63	2.65

MERRIMACK
SCORING

	Pos.	Class	Games	G	A	Pts.	Pen.
Dan Gravelle	F	Sr.	36	18	24	42	59
Jim Gibson	F	Jr.	35	12	24	36	50
Wayde McMillan	F	Sr.	36	18	18	36	58
Teal Fowler	F	Sr.	32	14	21	35	140
Mark Goble	F	Fr.	33	12	15	27	14
Mark Cornforth	D	So.	36	3	18	21	75
Rob Atkinson	F	Sr.	33	10	10	20	34
Dan Hodge	D	So.	36	3	17	20	30
Bryan Miller	D	Sr.	36	5	11	16	16
Cooper Naylor	F	Jr.	36	3	13	16	28
Matt Adams	F	Fr.	33	10	5	15	26
Martin Favreau	F	Fr.	21	6	6	12	7
John Barron	F	Sr.	32	7	4	11	38
Ryan Mailhiot	F	Fr.	23	4	6	10	12

NEW HAMPSHIRE
SCORING

	Pos.	Class	Games	G	A	Pts.	Pen.
Nick Poole	F	So.	38	15	26	41	16
Jason Dexter	F	Jr.	38	16	21	37	10
Rob Donovan	F	Jr.	38	18	19	37	56
Eric Flinton	F	So.	37	18	18	36	14
Greg Klym	F	Sr.	36	11	22	33	22
Glenn Stewart	F	Sr.	38	18	11	29	24
Kevin Thomson	F	Sr.	37	15	14	29	86
Jim McGrath	D	Sr.	36	6	20	26	42
Eric Royal	F	So.	27	8	18	26	20
Jesse Cooper	D	Sr.	38	4	15	19	20
Kent Schmidtke	F	Sr.	38	3	15	18	0
Bob Chebator	F	Jr.	38	3	10	13	68
Scott Malone	D	So.	36	5	6	11	96
Tom O'Brien	F	Fr.	32	5	5	10	14
Mike Sullivan	F	Fr.	36	5	5	10	12
Ted Russell	D	So.	33	1	7	8	56
Sean Perry	F	Fr.	30	4	3	7	28
Jeff Lenz	F	Fr.	13	1	3	4	4
Brian Muir	D	Fr.	26	1	2	3	24
Greg Blow	F	Jr.	17	1	1	2	10
Brett Abel	G	Sr.	32	0	0	0	6
Corey Cash	F	Fr.	2	0	0	0	0
Trent Cavicchi	G	Fr.	9	0	0	0	0
Eric Fitzgerald	D	Fr.	3	0	0	0	0
Mike Guilbert	D	Fr.	5	0	0	0	4
Pat Norton	F	Fr.	3	0	0	0	0
Steve Pleau	D	Fr.	11	0	0	0	2

GOALTENDING

	Games	W	L	T	Min.	GA	Avg.
Brett Abel	32	15	15	2	1903	109	3.44
Trent Cavicchi	9	3	2	1	391	32	4.91

NORTHEASTERN
SCORING

	Pos.	Class	Games	G	A	Pts.	Pen.
Jay Schiavo	F	Sr.	35	13	22	35	16
Dino Grossi	F	Sr.	35	18	16	34	69
Sebastien Laplante	F	Sr.	33	9	25	34	34
Mike Taylor	F	Jr.	35	10	24	34	76
Jordon Shields	F	Fr.	34	14	19	33	18
J.F. Aube	F	So.	33	15	9	24	6
Bob Kellogg	D	Jr.	35	5	15	20	44
Darryl MacNair	D	So.	34	7	12	19	63
Dan McGillis	D	Fr.	35	5	12	17	42
Tom O'Connor	F	Jr.	31	4	12	16	30
Chris Foy	D	Sr.	22	7	8	15	34
Jason Kelly	D	So.	33	4	11	15	57

	Pos.	Class	Games	G	A	Pts.	Pen.
Jason Melong	F	So.	31	7	6	13	12
Adam Hayes	F	Sr.	32	5	7	12	36
Dan Lupo	F	Fr.	32	5	7	12	19
Francois Bouchard	D	So.	26	4	6	10	20
Tom Parlon	F	So.	28	2	5	7	18
Mike Collett	F	Fr.	21	2	4	6	8
Tomas Persson	F	Fr.	26	2	1	3	16
Geoff Lucas	F	So.	20	0	1	1	4
Joe Eagan	D	Jr.	2	0	0	0	0
Todd Fisher	G	Fr.	3	0	0	0	0
Elijah Gold	G	Jr.	6	0	0	0	0
Steve Phillips	F	So.	5	0	0	0	0
Todd Reynolds	G	So.	5	0	0	0	0
Mike Veisor	G	Fr.	30	0	0	0	2

GOALTENDING

	Games	W	L	T	Min.	GA	Avg.
Elijah Gold	6	0	2	0	131	6	2.75
Mike Veisor	30	8	19	1	1699	151	5.33
Todd Reynolds	5	2	3	0	243	26	6.42
Todd Fisher	3	0	0	0	33	5	9.09

PROVIDENCE

SCORING

	Pos.	Class	Games	G	A	Pts.	Pen.
Brian Ridolfi	F	Jr.	36	24	25	49	38
Bob Cowan	F	Sr.	36	15	26	41	32
Chad Quenneville	F	So.	36	18	20	38	22

	Pos.	Class	Games	G	A	Pts.	Pen.
Craig Darby	F	So.	35	11	21	32	62
Brady Kramer	F	So.	32	14	14	28	52
Gary Socha	F	Sr.	33	13	15	28	22
Mark Devine	F	Sr.	36	6	20	26	36
Erik Peterson	F	Jr.	34	7	14	21	28
Chris Therien	D	Jr.	33	8	11	19	52
George Breen	F	So.	31	11	7	18	45
Joe Hulbig	F	Fr.	26	3	13	16	22
Scott Balboni	D	Fr.	35	3	10	13	32
Erik Sundquist	D	Fr.	21	4	7	11	24
Jay Kenney	D	Fr.	24	1	8	9	10
Dennis Burke	F	Fr.	25	2	6	8	14
Trevor Hanson	F	Fr.	23	3	4	7	14
Ian Paskowski	D	Jr.	35	1	4	5	22
John Charette	F	Jr.	24	2	2	4	2
Justin Gould	D	Fr.	25	0	4	4	28
Jon LaVarre	F	So.	12	2	2	4	0
Dennis Sousa	D	Fr.	17	0	4	4	10
Bob Bell	G	Fr.	21	0	2	2	4
Todd Huyber	D	Sr.	30	1	1	2	49
Brian Jeffries	F	Sr.	2	0	0	0	0
Chris Lamoriello	F	Jr.	7	0	0	0	2
Brad Mullahy	G	Sr.	25	0	0	0	6

GOALTENDING

	Games	W	L	T	Min.	GA	Avg.
Bob Bell	21	8	8	3	1035	65	3.65
Brad Mullahy	25	8	8	1	1169	82	4.16

WESTERN COLLEGIATE HOCKEY ASSOCIATION

1992-93 SEASON

FINAL STANDINGS

Team	G	W	L	T	Pts.	GF	GA
M.-Duluth (27-11-2) .	32	21	9	2	44	161	118
Wisconsin (24-15-3)	32	18	11	3	39	138	107
Minnesota (22-12-8)	32	16	9	7	39	128	123
Mich. Tech (17-15-5)	32	15	12	5	35	134	116
N. Mich. (21-18-4)	32	15	13	4	34	135	122
Denver (19-17-2)	32	15	15	2	32	122	138
St. Cloud St. (15-18-3)	32	14	16	2	30	121	123
N. Dakota (12-25-1) ..	32	11	20	1	23	118	146
Colorado C. (8-28-0)..	32	6	26	0	12	110	174
A'ka Anch. (18-13-5) .		Affiliate (4-7-1 vs. WCHA teams)						

Overall record in parentheses.

PLAYOFF RESULTS

FIRST ROUND

Minnesota-Duluth 7, Alaska Anchorage 2
Minnesota-Duluth 4, Alaska Anchorage 0
(Minnesota-Duluth won series, 2-0)

Wisconsin 6, Colorado College 3
Wisconsin 10, Colorado College 3
(Wisconsin won series, 2-0)

Northern Michigan 5, Denver 3
Northern Michigan 7, Denver 0
(Northern Michigan won series, 2-0)

Minnesota 6, North Dakota 4
Minnesota 5, North Dakota 4 (OT)
(Minnesota won series, 2-0)

Michigan Tech 3, St. Cloud State 1
Michigan Tech 6, St. Cloud State 5
(Michigan Tech won series, 2-0)

SECOND ROUND

Northern Michigan 4, Michigan Tech 3

SEMIFINALS

Minnesota 3, Wisconsin 2 (OT)
Northern Michigan 6, Minnesota-Duluth 2

CONSOLATION GAME

Minnesota-Duluth 7, Wisconsin 5

CHAMPIONSHIP GAME

Minnesota 5, Northern Michigan 3

ALL-STAR TEAMS

First team	Pos.	Second team
Jamie Ram, Mich. Tech	G	Jim Carey, Wisconsin
Brett Hauer, Min.-Dul.	D	Travis Richards, Min.
Barry Richter, Wisconsin	D	Jon Rohloff, Min.-Dul.
Derek Plante, Min.-Dul.	F	Chris Marinucci, Min.-Dul.
Greg Johnson, N. Dakota	F	John Young, Mich. Tech
Fred Knipscheer, S.C.S.	F	Joe Frederick, N. Michigan

AWARD WINNERS

Most Valuable Player: Derek Plante, Minnesota-Duluth
Rookie of the year: Jim Carey, Wisconsin
Coach of the year: Mike Sertich, Minnesota-Duluth
Leading scorer: Derek Plante, Minnesota-Duluth
Playoff MVP: Travis Richards, Minnesota

INDIVIDUAL STATISTICS

ALASKA-ANCHORAGE (AFFILIATE)

SCORING

	Pos.	Class	Games	G	A	Pts.	Pen.
Mitch Kean............	F	Jr.	35	20	19	39	34
Jack Kowal	F	Fr.	33	13	21	34	61
Kevin Brown	F	Sr.	35	16	16	32	40
Mark Stitt............	F	So.	35	9	22	31	58
Paul Williams........	F	So.	35	11	16	27	44
Petri Tuomisto	D	So.	34	5	21	26	91
Martin Bakula	D	Sr.	35	9	15	24	62
Randy Muise.........	F	So.	34	12	10	22	45
Brad Stewart.........	D	Jr.	36	3	11	14	14
Cotton Gore	F	So.	32	6	7	13	33
Troy Norcross........	F	So.	27	5	5	10	57
Darren Meek	D	Fr.	36	2	7	9	60
Brandon Carlson ...	F	Fr.	30	3	5	8	29
Trent Leggett	F	So.	24	1	7	8	26
Jason White..........	D	Fr.	33	1	7	8	54
Glen Thornborough.	F	Fr.	27	5	2	7	34
Jim Tobin	F	Sr.	31	2	5	7	138
Garnet Deschamps	F	Jr.	20	3	3	6	23
Jeremy Mylymok ...	D	Fr.	29	0	6	6	70
Andy Faulkner.......	F	So.	19	2	2	4	7
Kirk MacDonald.....	F	Fr.	6	1	0	1	4
Kelly Melton	D	Fr.	12	0	1	1	10
Todd Green	F	So.	1	0	0	0	0
Darren Holmes.......	D	Fr.	4	0	0	0	2
Jason Lowe...........	F	So.	5	0	0	0	21
Lee Schill	G	So.	10	0	0	0	0
Shaun Gravistin.....	G	Sr.	29	0	0	0	2

GOALTENDING

	Games	W	L	T	Min.	GA	Avg.
Shaun Gravistin........	29	16	9	4	1679	90	3.22
Lee Schill	10	2	4	1	499	34	4.09

COLORADO COLLEGE

SCORING

	Pos.	Class	Games	G	A	Pts.	Pen.
Jay McNeill	F	Fr.	36	18	21	39	80
Jody Jaraczewski..	F	Jr.	36	19	17	36	64
Chad Remackel......	F	Fr.	36	19	12	31	34
R.J. Enga	F	So.	36	12	19	31	16
Chris Hynnes	D	Sr.	36	8	18	26	71
Kent Fearns	D/F	So.	33	7	15	22	78
Colin Schmidt	F	Fr.	26	8	13	21	26
Brian Bethard	D	Sr.	36	7	10	17	60
Steve Nelson	F	Jr.	32	8	8	16	14
Peter Geronazzo	F	So.	24	7	7	14	26
Ryan Reynard	F	So.	29	6	8	14	102
Shawn Reid............	D/F	Jr.	31	3	11	14	54
David Paxton	D/F	So.	34	2	9	11	69
Chris McCafferty ...	F	Jr.	20	2	7	9	10
Jim Paradise	F	Jr.	30	2	5	7	26
Marcus Taeck.........	D/F	Jr.	30	2	5	7	43
Shawn Reddington ..	F	Sr.	20	0	6	6	0
J. Christopherson ...	F	Fr.	25	2	3	5	28
Rob Shypitka	F	So.	11	1	2	3	10
Dan Carney	F	Fr.	19	1	2	3	16
Mark Peterson	D	Sr.	28	0	3	3	28
Jon Steiner.............	D/F	So.	23	0	2	2	48

	Pos.	Class	Games	G	A	Pts.	Pen.
David Tucker	F	Jr.	1	0	0	0	2
Josh Hoekstra	F	Fr.	6	0	0	0	4
Tim Sweezo	F	Fr.	9	0	0	0	0
Paul Frank	G	So.	16	0	0	0	0
Paul Badalich	G	Sr.	24	0	0	0	0

GOALTENDING

	Games	W	L	T	Min.	GA	Avg.
Paul Badalich	24	5	17	0	1257	111	5.30
Paul Frank	16	2	8	0	658	65	5.93

DENVER
SCORING

	Pos.	Class	Games	G	A	Pts.	Pen.
Angelo Ricci	F	So.	38	21	30	51	26
Jason Elders	F	So.	38	19	20	39	10
Brian Konowalchuk	F	Jr.	37	12	20	32	59
Chris Kenady	F	So.	38	8	16	24	93
Warren Smith	F	So.	32	11	11	22	17
Maurice Hall	F	Fr.	36	9	13	22	38
Mike Naylor	F	So.	35	13	8	21	74
Ken MacArthur	D	Sr.	35	5	16	21	70
Craig McMillan	F	So.	34	8	11	19	34
Mark Luger	D	Jr.	38	5	12	17	58
Mike Markovich	D	Sr.	38	10	5	15	26
Ian DeCorby	F	Jr.	33	5	9	14	33
Ryan O'Leary	F	So.	37	5	7	12	37
Brent Cary	F	So.	6	3	6	9	6
Paul Koch	D	So.	37	0	9	9	111
John McLean	D	So.	37	2	6	8	57
Sean Ortiz	F	So.	38	3	3	6	24
Earl Rock	F	Fr.	24	2	3	5	16
Heath Sampson	F	So.	30	1	3	4	26
Jude Sandvall	F	Fr.	18	1	1	2	14
Bryan Schoen	G	Sr.	35	0	2	2	22
Kevin Oztekin	F	So.	2	0	0	0	0
Chris Burns	G	Fr.	12	0	0	0	0
Dave Klasnick	F	Fr.	21	0	0	0	0

GOALTENDING

	Games	W	L	T	Min.	GA	Avg.
Bryan Schoen	35	18	15	2	1860	121	3.90
Chris Burns	12	1	2	0	433	35	4.85

MICHIGAN TECH
SCORING

	Pos.	Class	Games	G	A	Pts.	Pen.
Jim Storm	F	Jr.	33	22	32	54	30
John Young	F	Sr.	37	13	38	51	38
Brent Peterson	F	So.	37	24	18	42	32
Pat Mikesch	F	Fr.	33	12	26	38	56
Layne LeBel	D/F	Jr.	37	9	21	30	45
Randy Stevens	F	So.	37	12	12	24	28
Jason Wright	D	Fr.	37	5	19	24	28
Justin Peca	F	So.	32	13	2	15	24
Don Osborne	D	Sr.	27	4	11	15	16
Kyle Ferguson	F	Fr.	31	9	5	14	74
Kirby Perrault	D	Jr.	37	4	9	13	68
Liam Garvey	D/F	So.	32	3	6	9	64
Martin Machacek	F	Fr.	31	4	3	7	53
Jeff Hill	D	Jr.	31	3	4	7	69
Jason Hanchuk	D	So.	34	2	5	7	38
Travis Seale	F	So.	37	2	5	7	12
Mitch Lane	F	Fr.	32	4	2	6	8
Hugh McEwen	F	Jr.	12	3	3	6	30
Mike Figliomeni	F	Fr.	31	2	4	6	12
Ken Plaquin	D	Sr.	26	1	4	5	12
Darren Brkic	F	Jr.	15	0	2	2	20
Jamie Ram	G	Jr.	36	0	1	1	10
Scott Vettraino	G	So.	4	0	0	0	0

GOALTENDING

	Games	W	L	T	Min.	GA	Avg.
Jamie Ram	36	16	14	5	2078	115	3.32
Scott Vettraino	4	1	1	0	160	11	4.12

MINNESOTA
SCORING

	Pos.	Class	Games	G	A	Pts.	Pen
Craig Johnson	F	Jr.	42	22	24	46	70
Jeff Nielsen	F	Jr.	42	21	20	41	80
Travis Richards	D	Sr.	42	12	26	38	52
Justin McHugh	F	So.	42	13	15	28	42
Brian Bonin	F	Fr.	38	10	18	28	10
Darby Hendrickson	F	So.	31	12	15	27	35
John Brill	F	Sr.	41	12	13	25	64
Joe Dziedzic	F	Jr.	41	11	14	25	62
Chris McAlpione	D	Jr.	41	14	9	23	82
Scott Bell	F	Jr.	37	5	11	16	64
Andy Brink	F	Fr.	20	5	9	14	2
Jed Fiebelkorn	F	So.	34	8	5	13	46
Dan Trebil	D	Fr.	36	2	11	13	16
Brandon Steege	F/D	So.	40	4	8	12	34
Steve Magnusson	F	So.	21	1	10	11	22
Tony Bianchi	F	Jr.	22	3	6	9	4
Dave Larson	F	Fr.	25	4	3	7	38
Bobby Dustin	F	Fr.	19	3	4	7	12
Charlie Wasley	F	Jr.	35	2	5	7	42
Eric Means	D	Jr.	22	2	2	4	35
Mike McAlpine	D	Fr.	26	0	3	3	30
Jesse Bertogliat	F	So.	16	1	0	1	12
Dan Woog	F	Fr.	3	0	1	1	4
Greg Zwakman	D	Fr.	36	0	1	1	30
Dave Norqual	D	Fr.	2	0	0	0	2
Todd Westlund	F	Jr.	2	0	0	0	6
Jeff Callinan	G	So.	21	0	0	0	0
Tom Newman	G	Sr.	22	0	0	0	0

GOALTENDING

	Games	W	L	T	Min.	GA	Avg.
Tom Newman	22	14	4	2	1172	61	3.13
Jeff Callinan	21	8	5	5	1113	72	3.88
Jeff Moen	6	0	3	1	303	20	3.96

MINNESOTA-DULUTH
SCORING

	Pos.	Class	Games	G	A	Pts.	Pen.
Derek Plante	F	Sr.	37	36	56	92	30
Chris Marinucci	F	Jr.	40	35	42	77	52
Brett Hauer	D	Sr.	40	10	46	56	54
Rusty Fitzgerald	F	So.	39	24	23	47	58
Jon Rohloff	D	Sr.	36	15	19	34	87
Joe Biondi	F	So.	40	15	18	33	14
Brian Caruso	F	Jr.	40	12	14	26	24
Corey Osmak	F	Jr.	39	11	15	26	96
Brad Penner	F	So.	40	10	10	20	22
Chris Sittlow	F	So.	40	9	10	19	56
Jeff Parrott	D	Sr.	39	4	13	17	116
Rod Aldhoff	D	So.	39	3	11	14	36
Marty Olson	F	Sr.	37	4	9	13	16
Joe Tamminen	F	So.	39	4	6	10	42
Jeff Romfo	F	Fr.	38	4	4	8	8
Brett Larson	D	So.	33	2	3	5	10
Joe Ciccarello	F	Fr.	39	2	3	5	12
Rod Miller	D	Jr.	36	1	2	3	63
Greg Hanson	D	Fr.	15	0	2	2	10
Jerome Butler	G	So.	21	0	1	1	0
Steve Cronkhite	D	Sr.	3	0	1	1	2
Taras Lendzyk	G	Fr.	22	0	1	1	4
Jeff Antonovich	F	Fr.	1	0	0	0	0
Marc Christian	F	So.	2	0	0	0	0
Brad Federenko	F	Fr.	2	0	0	0	0
Kraig Karakas	F	Jr.	7	0	0	0	0

GOALTENDING

	Games	W	L	T	Min.	GA	Avg.
Taras Lendzyk	22	15	5	0	1243	68	3.28
Jerome Butler	21	12	6	2	1183	74	3.75

NORTH DAKOTA
SCORING

	Pos.	Class	Games	G	A	Pts.	Pen.
Greg Johnson	F	Sr.	34	19	45	64	18
Kevin McKinnon	F	Jr.	38	20	18	38	38

	Pos.	Class	Games	G	A	Pts.	Pen.
Nick Naumenko	D	Fr.	38	10	24	34	26
Marty Schriner	F	Jr.	36	8	19	27	156
Darcy Mitani.........	F	Fr.	34	15	10	25	42
Brad Bombardir	D	Jr.	38	8	15	23	34
Chris Gotziaman	F	Jr.	35	10	10	20	50
Scott Kirton..........	F	So.	30	4	16	20	100
Donny Riendeau	F	Sr.	28	9	7	16	53
Brett Hryniuk........	F	So.	37	5	7	12	48
Dean Grillo	F	Fr.	29	7	4	11	14
Chad Johnson	F	Sr.	26	4	5	9	45
Sean Beswick	F	Fr.	32	4	5	9	18
Jon Larson...........	D	Sr.	30	2	6	8	28
Keith Murphy	F	Fr.	38	5	2	7	14
Darren Bear	D	So.	37	1	6	7	26
Jarrod Olson	D	So.	31	2	4	6	14
Corey Howe...........	D	So.	29	1	4	5	42
Corey Johnson......	F	Fr.	30	0	5	5	16
Teeder Wynne.......	F	Fr.	13	2	2	4	6
Lars Oxholm	D	So.	5	1	0	1	8
Joby Bond	F	Jr.	11	1	0	1	6
Todd Jones............	G	So.	21	0	1	1	0
Jeff Lembke	G	So.	4	0	0	0	0
Kevin Rappana	D	Fr.	12	0	0	0	0
Akil Adams	D	Fr.	14	0	0	0	49
Kevin Powell	G	Fr.	17	0	0	0	0

GOALTENDING

	Games	W	L	T	Min.	GA	Avg.
Kevin Powell	17	6	10	0	922	66	4.30
Todd Jones	21	6	13	1	1205	89	4.43
Jeff Lembke	4	0	2	0	160	16	5.99

NORTHERN MICHIGAN
SCORING

	Pos.	Class	Games	G	A	Pts.	Pen.
Greg Hadden	F	So.	42	26	24	50	125
Joe Frederick	F	Sr.	29	28	20	48	100
Mike Harding	F	So.	39	17	18	35	64
Jason Hehr	D/F	Jr.	43	8	27	35	40
Brent Riplinger.......	F	So.	39	21	11	32	14
Kory Karlander	F	Fr.	39	7	21	28	30
Bryan Ganz	F	Jr.	43	14	9	23	90
Geoff Simpson........	D	Sr.	43	8	14	22	18
Steve Carpenter	D	Jr.	38	2	20	22	123
Troy Johnson.........	F	So.	33	6	15	21	50
Scott Smith	F	Jr.	37	11	6	17	10
Garett MacDonald .	D	Jr.	39	4	12	16	68
Dan Ruoho	F/D	Sr.	37	7	8	15	53
Karson Kaebel	F	Fr.	31	2	13	15	34
Bill MacGillivray	F	So.	39	5	9	14	26
Steve Woog	F	Jr.	29	2	8	10	20
Dave Huettl	D	Sr.	42	2	8	10	99
Kyuin Shim	F	Fr.	20	4	2	6	6
Steve Hamilton	D	So.	37	0	6	6	46
Scott Green	F	Fr.	15	2	2	4	8
Don McCusker	F	Fr.	21	0	4	4	16
Chad Dameworth	D	So.	29	0	2	2	22
Corwin Saurdiff	G	So.	29	0	2	2	2
Justin George.........	F	So.	6	1	0	1	6
Brian Barker	F	Fr.	5	0	0	0	2
Rob Kruhlak	G	Sr.	5	0	0	0	0
Paul Taylor	G	Fr.	13	0	0	0	0

GOALTENDING

	Games	W	L	T	Min.	GA	Avg.
Paul Taylor	13	8	3	1	776	36	2.78
Corwin Saurdiff	29	13	12	3	1630	101	3.72
Rob Kruhlak	5	0	3	0	210	21	6.02

ST. CLOUD STATE
SCORING

	Pos.	Class	Games	G	A	Pts.	Pen.
Fred Knipscheer	F	Sr.	36	34	26	60	68
Tony Gruba	F	Jr.	35	15	27	42	81
Greg Hagen	F	Sr.	36	21	15	36	34
Kelly Hultgren........	D/F	So.	31	5	21	26	62
Dan O'Shea	F	So.	33	11	11	22	48
Bill Lund	F	So.	35	6	16	22	48
Gino Santerre........	D	So.	35	3	16	19	61
Steve Ross	D	Sr.	28	6	12	18	58
Mark Gagnon.........	F	So.	35	7	10	17	32
Sandy Gasseau......	F	So.	30	8	3	11	62
Jay Moser	D	So.	33	2	9	11	77
Eric Johnson..........	F	So.	33	3	7	10	6
Dave Holum	F	So.	33	5	4	9	43
Jeff Schmidt..........	F	So.	21	3	5	8	12
Dan Reimann	D	Fr.	36	5	2	7	58
P.J. Lepler	D/F	Fr.	27	2	4	6	20
Taj Melson	D	Fr.	36	2	4	6	20
Noel Rahn.............	F	Sr.	31	1	5	6	26
Jay Geisbaur.........	F	Fr.	14	2	3	5	4
Cory Fairchild........	F	So.	25	2	3	5	8
Kelly Rieder...........	F	Fr.	16	0	1	1	4
Neil Cooper...........	G	Fr.	2	0	0	0	0
Chris Ramberg........	F	So.	2	0	0	0	0
Chris Markstrom ...	F	So.	3	0	0	0	0
Dave Stone...........	G	Jr.	3	0	0	0	0
Grant Sjerven........	G	Jr.	34	0	0	0	22

GOALTENDING

	Games	W	L	T	Min.	GA	Avg.
Grant Sjerven............	34	14	16	2	1994	120	3.61
Neil Cooper...............	2	0	1	1	89	9	6.12
Dave Stone..............	3	1	1	0	96	10	6.29

WISCONSIN
SCORING

	Pos.	Class	Games	G	A	Pts.	Pen.
Andrew Shier	F	Jr.	42	22	36	58	87
Dan Plante	F	Jr.	42	26	31	57	142
Kelly Fairchild.......	F	So.	42	25	29	54	54
Barry Richter	D	Sr.	42	14	32	46	74
Blaine Moore	F	Jr.	37	16	28	44	95
Jason Zent	F	Jr.	40	26	12	38	88
Ulvis Katlaps	D	Jr.	41	4	31	35	20
Jamie Spencer	F	So.	39	13	18	31	48
Chris Tucker	F	Jr.	40	10	9	19	12
Jason Francisco	F	Sr.	41	8	11	19	26
Chris Tok	D	So.	41	3	12	15	68
Rob Granato...........	F	Jr.	42	8	5	13	16
Mark Strobel	D/F	So.	36	4	9	13	73
Brian Rafalski........	D	So.	32	0	13	13	10
Maco Balkovec	D	So.	16	1	9	10	16
Mike Doers	F	Jr.	40	4	5	9	30
Mickey Elick	D	Fr.	32	1	6	7	24
Max Williams	F	Fr.	26	5	1	6	20
Matt Buss	F	Jr.	22	0	3	3	24
Jim Carey	G	Fr.	26	0	3	3	0
Mike Strobel	F	So.	8	0	2	2	26
Shawn Carter	F	Fr.	5	1	0	1	4
Troy Howard	F	Fr.	17	1	0	1	2
Scott Sanderson ...	F	Fr.	12	0	1	1	0
Jon Michelizzi	G	Sr.	18	0	1	1	4
Todd Hedlund	F	So.	8	0	0	0	0
Jeff Sanderson.......	D	Jr.	11	0	0	0	2

GOALTENDING

	Games	W	L	T	Min.	GA	Avg.
Jim Carey	26	15	8	1	1525	78	3.07
Jon Michelizzi	18	9	7	2	1030	65	3.79
Jeff Althaus	1	0	0	0	6	1	11.11

INDEPENDENTS

1992-93 SEASON

FINAL STANDINGS

	W	L	T	GF	GA	Pct.
Army	16	11	1	133	86	.589
Air Force	8	20	2	93	150	.300

INDIVIDUAL STATISTICS

AIR FORCE

SCORING

	Pos.	Class	Games	G	A	Pts.	Pen.
Eric Rice	F	Sr.	30	12	15	27	44
Beau Bilek	D	So.	30	6	14	20	32
John Decker	C	So.	29	10	8	18	24
Andy Veneri	C	So.	30	9	9	18	44
T.J. Courtney	C	Sr.	28	6	10	16	118
Matt Tramonte	F	Sr.	26	4	12	16	57
Mark DeGironimo	F	Fr.	27	6	9	15	15
Anthony Retka	D	Jr.	29	5	8	13	54
Deron Christy	F	Sr.	27	8	4	12	18
Dan McAlister	F	So.	28	6	5	11	71
Jeff Barlow	F	Jr.	28	6	5	11	14
John Giusto	D	Fr.	27	4	4	8	131
Bob Ingraham	D	Sr.	20	2	6	8	24
George Kriz	F	So.	19	2	5	7	0
Erik Brown	F	So.	28	2	4	6	30
Scot Spann	D	Jr.	17	0	6	6	14
Daniel Leone	D	Fr.	21	2	2	4	10
John Sullivan	F	So.	20	2	0	2	12
Joe Javorski	F	So.	27	1	1	2	40
Patrick Ryan	D	Fr.	25	0	1	1	20
Steve Masiello	D	Sr.	4	0	0	0	4
Jim Tuomi	F	So.	6	0	0	0	4
Paul Northon	F	So.	10	0	0	0	12
Chris Mitchell	D	Fr.	3	0	0	0	0
David Michaud	D	Fr.	3	0	0	0	2
Mike Benson	G	So.	13	0	0	0	0
Derec Liebel	G	Sr.	22	0	0	0	2

GOALTENDING

	Games	W	L	T	Min.	GA	Avg.
Mike Benson	13	4	5	1	654	48	4.40
Derec Liebel	22	4	15	1	1154	102	5.30

ARMY

SCORING

	Pos.	Class	Games	G	A	Pts.	Pen.
Rick Berube	F	Sr.	28	34	18	52	16
Rick Randazzo	F	Sr.	28	15	25	40	29
Chad Sundem	F	Sr.	25	13	17	30	30
Bob Mansell	F	Sr.	25	11	17	28	12
Mark Stachelski	F	So.	24	9	18	27	84
Mike Mansell	D	Fr.	28	2	19	21	32
Mike Landers	D	Jr.	27	6	12	18	12
Kevin Backus	D	Sr.	28	4	14	18	36
Ian Winer	F	Fr.	14	3	13	16	4
Justin Lambert	F	So.	28	10	5	15	39
Roble MacLaughlin	F	So.	28	8	7	15	26
Brett Funck	D	Jr.	26	3	11	14	22
Sean Hennessy	D	So.	26	2	10	12	60
Eric Kindgren	F	Sr.	11	1	11	12	10
Scott Gardiner	F	Sr.	25	3	7	10	39
Milt Smith	F	Jr.	22	2	4	6	26
Jason Dickie	D	Fr.	18	0	6	6	29
Keith Tahtinen	F	Jr.	10	2	2	4	11
Marc Dorrer	F	Fr.	18	2	1	3	4
Tim Hocking	F	So.	18	1	2	3	0
Troy Eigner	F	So.	4	1	2	3	0
John Compton	D	Jr.	21	1	1	2	42
Ron Adimey	G	So.	11	0	2	2	4
Dave Pilarski	F	Jr.	12	0	1	1	8
Brian Bolio	G	So.	13	0	1	1	8
Scott Boyle	G	Sr.	7	0	0	0	4
Ethan Harding	D	Fr.	9	0	0	0	6
Derek Huffer	F	Jr.	1	0	0	0	0

GOALTENDING

	Games	W	L	T	Min.	GA	Avg.
Ron Adimey	6	3	1	0	308	12	2.34
Brian Bolio	11	6	4	1	637	31	2.92
Scott Boyle	13	7	6	0	737	40	3.26

CANADIAN INTERUNIVERSITY ATHLETIC UNION

GENERAL INFORMATION

The Canadian Interuniversity Athletic Union is an alliance of three Canadian college leagues—the Atlantic Universities Athletic Association, Canada West University Athletic Association and Ontario Universities Athletic Association. After the regular season, the three leagues compete in an elimination tournament to decide the CIAU national champion. The award and trophy winners are based on regular-season play.

1993 NATIONAL CHAMPIONSHIPS

PLAYOFF STANDINGS

Team (League)	W	L	Pts.	GF	GA
Acadia U. (AUAA)	2	0	4	21	5
U. of Toronto (OUAA)	1	1	2	4	14
U. of Guelph (OUAA)	0	1	0	2	3
Alberta (CWUAA)	0	1	0	4	9

RESULTS

SEMIFINALS

FRIDAY, MARCH 19

Acadia 9, Alberta 4
Toronto 3, Guelph 2

FINAL

SUNDAY, MARCH 21

Acadia 12, Toronto 1

1992-93 AWARD WINNERS

ALL-STAR TEAMS

First team	Pos.	Second team
Phil Comtois, Ottawa	G	Denis Sproxton, Acadia
Jaret Burgoyne, Calgary		
Vojtech Kucera, St. Thomas	D	Kevin Meisner, Dalhousie
Steve Perkovic, Guelph	D	Bart Cote, Regina
Serje Lajoie, Alberta		
Tom Diceman, Toronto		
Steve Kluczowski, St. Mary's	F	John Spoltore, Laurier
Mark McCreary, Laurier	F	Rob Arabski, Guelph
George Dupont, Acadia	F	Ryan Campbell, Manitoba
Todd Goodwin, Alberta		
Charles Loreto, Mt. Allison		
Wade Bucsis, Saskatchewan		

TROPHY WINNERS

Player of the year: Serje Lajoie, Alberta
Rookie of the year: John Spoltore, Laurier
Scholastic player of the year: Ryan Campbell, Manitoba
Coach of the year: Tom Coolen, Acadia

CANADIAN COLLEGES

COLLEGE HOCKEY

ATLANTIC UNIVERSITIES ATHLETIC ASSOCIATION. 1992-93 SEASON

FINAL STANDINGS

KELLY DIVISION

Team	G	W	L	T	Pts.	GF	GA
Acadia University......	26	22	2	2	46	160	73
Dalhousie University..	26	17	8	1	35	135	110
St. Mary's University .	26	12	13	1	25	120	132
U. Col. of Cape Breton.	26	10	15	1	21	117	131
St. Francis Xavier U. ...	26	7	19	0	14	107	148

MAC ADAM DIVISION

Team	G	W	L	T	Pts.	GF	GA
U. of New Brunswick ..	26	18	7	1	37	152	106
Univ. de Moncton.......	26	13	12	1	27	105	108
St. Thomas University	26	11	13	2	24	116	123
U. of P. Edward Island	26	7	15	4	18	99	133
Mount Allison Univ....	26	6	19	1	13	102	149

PLAYOFF RESULTS

KELLY DIVISION FINALS

Acadia 6, Dalhousie 2
Acadia 4, Dalhousie 0

MAC ADAM DIVISION FINALS

New Brunswick 9, Moncton 7
New Brunswick 5, Moncton 4 (OT)

LEAGUE FINALS

Acadia 3, New Brunswick 1
Acadia 6, New Brunswick 0

ALL-STAR TEAMS

Kelly Division	Pos.	MacAdam Division
Denis Sproxton, Acadia	G	Frantz Bergevin-Jean, Monc.
Kevin Knopp, Acadia	D	Vojtech Kuchera, St. Thomas
Kevin Meisner, Dalhousie	D	Serge Pepin, Moncton
George Dupont, Acadia	F	Chuck Loreto, Mt. Allison
Norm Batherson, Acadia	F	Mark Rupnow, St. Thomas
Steve Kluczkowski, St. M.	F	Ken Murchison, N.B.

AWARD WINNERS

Most Valuable Player: Steve Kluczkowski, St. Mary's
Rookie of the year: Derek Kletzel, Acadia
Coach of the year: Tom Coolen, Acadia
Leading scorer: George Dupont, Acadia

CANADA WEST UNIVERSITY ATHLETIC ASSOCIATION. 1992-93 SEASON

FINAL STANDINGS

Team	G	W	L	T	Pts.	GF	GA
Alberta (26-11-5)....	28	18	6	4	40	152	88
Regina (21-8-6).......	28	16	7	5	37	129	93
Calgary (21-16-4)....	28	17	8	3	37	127	110
Sask. (21-13-3).......	28	16	9	3	35	149	124
Manitoba (16-16-3) .	28	13	13	2	28	112	126
Leth. (15-18-5).......	28	9	16	3	21	108	135
Brit. Col. (14-22-2)..	28	7	19	2	16	97	128
Brandon (7-28-4)....	28	3	21	4	10	85	155

PLAYOFF RESULTS

SEMIFINALS

Alberta 4, Saskatchewan 3
Alberta 5, Saskatchewan 4

Calgary 4, Regina 2
Regina 6, Calgary 1
Regina 4, Calgary 1

FINALS

Alberta 5, Regina 1
Alberta 3, Regina 1

ALL-STAR TEAMS

First team	Pos.	Second team
Jaret Burgoyne, Calgary	G	Damon Kustra, Manitoba
Todd Hollinger, Regina		
Serje Lajoie, Alberta	D	Brad Woods, Manitoba
Bart Cote, Regina	D	Cory Cross, Alberta
Wayde Bucsis, Sask.	F	Len Nielsen, Regina
Todd Goodwin, Alberta	F	Darrin McKechnie, Regina
Ryan Campbell, Manitoba	F	Tracey Katelnikoff, Cal.

AWARD WINNERS

Most Valuable Player: Serge Lajoie, Alberta
Rookie of the year: Greg Gatto, Lethbridge
Most gentlemanly player: Ryan Campbell, Manitoba
Coach of the year: Bill Morres, Alberta
Leading scorer: Wade Bucsis, Saskatchewan

ONTARIO UNIVERSITIES ATHLETIC ASSOCIATION. 1992-93 SEASON

FINAL STANDINGS

EAST DIVISION

Team	G	W	L	T	Pts.	GF	GA
University of Ottawa ..	22	17	5	0	34	108	60
University of Toronto .	22	15	6	1	31	103	70
Que. at Trois-Rivieres .	22	11	7	4	26	107	77
McGill University.......	22	11	8	3	25	106	84
Concordia University .	22	10	10	2	22	93	98
Queen's University	22	8	11	3	19	80	97
York University..........	22	7	13	2	16	96	101
Ryerson Poly. Inst.	22	1	20	1	3	61	164

WEST DIVISION

Team	G	W	L	T	Pts.	GF	GA
University of Guelph..	22	16	5	1	33	131	74
Wilfrid Laurier Univ...	22	16	5	1	33	148	76
University of Waterloo.	22	14	5	3	31	158	90
U. of Western Ontario.	22	12	8	2	26	112	87
University of Windsor	22	9	12	1	19	106	139
Laurentian University	22	7	11	4	18	100	122
Brock University........	22	7	13	2	16	105	91
Royal Military College	22	0	22	0	0	39	218

PLAYOFF RESULTS

EAST DIVISION QUARTERFINALS

McGill 3, Concordia 2 (OT)
Queen's 4, Trois-Rivieres 3

WEST DIVISION QUARTERFINALS

Waterloo 10, Laurentian 4
Windsor 8, Western Ontario 4

EAST DIVISION SEMIFINALS

Ottawa 3, McGill 2 (OT)
Ottawa 3, McGill 2 (2 OT)

Toronto 4, Queen's 1
Queen's 5, Toronto 2
Toronto 11, Queen's 2

WEST DIVISION SEMIFINALS

Guelph 5, Windsor 4 (OT)
Guelph 4, Windsor 1

Laurier 4, Waterloo 2
Waterloo 7, Laurier 1
Waterloo 10, Laurier 4

EAST DIVISION FINALS

Toronto 6, Ottawa 4
Toronto 5, Ottawa 4

WEST DIVISION FINALS

Guelph 5, Waterloo 3
Waterloo 6, Guelph 1
Guelph 4, Waterloo 2

LEAGUE FINALS

Toronto 5, Guelph 4 (2 OT)

ALL-STAR TEAMS

EAST DIVISION

First team	Pos.	Second team
Phil Comtois, Ottawa	G	Paul Henriques, Toronto
Tom Diceman, Toronto	D	Martin Roy, Ottawa
Dan Brown, Queen's	D	Alexandre Fortin, UQTR
Mike Fiset, Ottawa	F	Chris Glover, Queen's
John Andersen, Toronto	F	Greg Van Sickle, Toronto
Alain Vogin, UQTR	F	Alain Tardif, Ottawa

WEST DIVISION

First team	Pos.	Second team
Jeff Wilson, Guelph	G	Rick Pracey, Laurier
Mark Strohack, Laurier	D	John Wynne, Waterloo
Steve Perkovic, Guelph	D	Craig Donaldson, Ontario
John Spoltore, Laurier	F	Pete DeBoer, Windsor
Mark McCreary, Laurier	F	Darren Snyder, Waterloo
Rob Arabski, Guelph	F	Steve Rucchin, Ontario

AWARD WINNERS

Most Valuable Player: Mark McCreary, Laurier
Rookie of the year: John Spoltore, Laurier
Most gentlemanly player: Tom Diceman, Toronto
Coach of the year: Mickey Goulet, Ottawa
Leading scorer: John Spoltore, Laurier

INDEX OF TEAMS

NHL, MINOR LEAGUES, MAJOR JUNIOR LEAGUES

Adirondack 160	Hull 234	Quebec 57
Anaheim 5	Indianapolis 176	Raleigh 188
Atlanta 176	Johnstown 188	Red Deer 243
Baltimore 160	Kalamazoo 176	Regina 243
Beauport 234	Kamloops 243	Richmond 188
Belleville 219	Kansas City 176	Roanoke Valley 188
Binghamton 160	Kingston 219	Rochester 160
Birmingham 188	Kitchener 219	St. Hyacinthe 234
Boston 7	Knoxville 188	St. Jean 234
Brandon 243	Laval 234	St. John's 160
Brantford 207	Lethbridge 243	St. Louis 60
Buffalo 10	London 219	St. Thomas 207
Calgary 13	Los Angeles 33	Salt Lake 176
Cape Breton 160	Louisville 188	San Diego 176
Capital District 160	Medicine Hat 243	San Jose 63
Chatham 207	Memphis 201	Saskatoon 243
Chicago 16	Miami 28	Sault Ste. Marie 219
Chicoutimi 234	Milwaukee 176	Seattle 243
Cincinnati 176	Moncton 160	Shawinigan 234
Cleveland 176	Montreal.............................36	Sherbrooke 234
Columbus 188	Moose Jaw 243	Spokane 243
Dallas (Cent.HL) 201	Muskegon 207	Springfield 160
Dallas (NHL) 19	Nashville 188	Sudbury 219
Dayton 188	New Haven 160	Swift Current 243
Detroit (Col.HL) 207	New Jersey 39	Tacoma 243
Detroit (NHL) 22	Newmarket 219	Tampa Bay 66
Detroit (OHL) 219	New York Islanders 42	Thunder Bay 207
Drummondville 234	New York Rangers 45	Toledo 188
Edmonton 25	Niagara Falls 219	Toronto 69
Erie 188	North Bay.........................219	Tri-City 243
Flint 207	Oklahoma City 201	Tulsa 201
Florida 28	Oshawa 219	Utica 160
Fort Wayne 176	Ottawa (NHL) 48	Vancouver 72
Fort Worth 201	Ottawa (OHL) 219	Verdun 234
Fredericton 160	Owen Sound.....................219	Victoria 243
Granby 234	Peoria 176	Victoriaville 234
Greensboro 188	Peterborough 219	Washington 75
Guelph 219	Philadelphia 51	Wheeling 188
Halifax 160	Phoenix 176	Wichita 201
Hamilton 160	Pittsburgh 54	Windsor 219
Hampton Roads 188	Portland 243	Winnipeg.............................78
Hartford 30	Prince Albert 243	
Hershey............................ 160	Providence 160	

COLLEGE TEAMS

Acadia 276	Illinois-Chicago 260	Prince Edward Island 276
Air Force 274	Kent 260	Princeton 264
Alaska-Anchorage 271	Lake Superior State........ 260	Providence 268
Alaska-Fairbanks 260	Laurentian 276	Quebec at Trois-Rivieres .276
Alberta 276	Lethbridge 276	Queen's 276
Army 274	Lowell 268	Regina 276
Boston College................ 268	Maine 268	Rensselaer Polytechnic Institute.....264
Boston University............ 268	Manitoba 276	Royal Military 276
Bowling Green State........ 260	McGill 276	Ryerson Polytechnic Institute 276
Brandon 276	Merrimack 268	St. Cloud State 271
British Columbia............. 276	Miami of Ohio 260	St. Francis Xavier 276
Brock................................ 276	Michigan 260	St. Lawrence 264
Brown............................... 264	Michigan State 260	St. Mary's 276
Calgary 276	Michigan Tech 271	St. Thomas 276
Cape Breton 276	Minnesota 271	Saskatchewan 276
Clarkson........................... 264	Minnesota-Duluth 271	Toronto 276
Colgate............................. 264	Moncton............................ 276	Union................................ 264
Colorado College............. 271	Mount Allison 276	Vermont 264
Concordia 276	New Brunswick................. 276	Waterloo 276
Cornell.............................. 264	New Hampshire 268	Western Michigan 260
Dalhousie......................... 276	North Dakota 271	Western Ontario 276
Dartmouth 264	Northeastern 268	Wilfrid Laurier 276
Denver 271	Northern Michigan 271	Windsor............................ 276
Ferris State 260	Notre Dame 260	Wisconsin 271
Guelph.............................. 276	Ohio State 260	Yale.................................. 264
Harvard............................. 264	Ottawa 276	York.................................. 276

HOCKEY REGISTER

Players

NHL head coaches

EXPLANATION OF FOOTNOTES AND ABBREVIATIONS

* Led league.
† Tied for league lead.
... Statistic unavailable, unofficial or mathematically impossible to calculate.
— Statistic inapplicable.

POSITIONS: C: center. **D:** defenseman. **G:** goaltender. **LW:** left winger. **RW:** right winger.

STATISTICS: A: assists. **Avg.:** goals-against average. **G:** goals. **GA:** goals against. **Gms.:** games. **L:** losses. **Min.:** minutes. **Pen.:** penalty minutes. **Pts:** points. **SO:** shutouts. **T:** ties. **W:** wins.

LEAGUES: AAHL: All American Hockey League. **ACHL:** Atlantic Coast Hockey League. **AHL:** American Hockey League. **AJHL:** Alberta Junior Hockey League. **AMHL:** Alberta Minor Hockey League. **AUAA:** Atlantic Universities Athletic Association. **BCJHL:** British Columbia Junior Hockey League. **CAHL:** Central Alberta Hockey League. **CAJHL:** Central Alberta Junior Hockey League. **Can. College:** Canadian College. **Can.HL:** Canadian Hockey League. **CCHA:** Central Collegiate Hockey Association. **CHL:** Central Hockey League. **CIS:** Commonwealth of Independent States. **CJHL:** Central Junior A Hockey League. **COJHL:** Central Ontario Junior Hockey League. **CPHL:** Central Professional Hockey League. **CWUAA:** Canada West University Athletic Association. **Conn. H.S.:** Connecticut High School. **Czech.:** Czechoslovakia. **ECAC:** Eastern College Athletic Conference. **ECAC-II:** Eastern College Athletic Conference, Division II. **ECHL:** East Coast Hockey League. **EHL:** Eastern Hockey League. **Fin.:** Finland. **Ger.:** Germany. **GWHC:** Great Western Hockey Conference. **Hoc. East:** Hockey East. **IHL:** International Hockey League. **Ill. H.S.:** Illinois High School. **Indiana H.S.:** Indiana High School. **Int'l:** International. **KIJHL:** Kootenay International Junior Hockey League. **Mass. H.S.:** Massachusetts High School. **Md. H.S.:** Maryland High School. **Met. Bos.:** Metro Boston. **Mich. H.S.:** Michigan High School. **Minn. H.S.:** Minnesota High School. **MJHL:** Manitoba Junior Hockey League. **MTHL:** Metro Toronto Hockey League. **NAHL:** North American Hockey League. **NAJHL:** North American Junior Hockey League. **N.B. H.S.:** New Brunswick High School. **NCAA-II:** National Collegiate Athletic Association, Division II. **N.D. H.S.:** North Dakota High School. **NEJHL:** New England Junior Hockey League. **NHL:** National Hockey League. **N.H. H.S.:** New Hampshire High School. **N.J. H.S.:** New Jersey High School. **Nia. D. Jr. C:** Niagara District Junior C. **NSJHL:** Nova Scotia Junior Hockey League. **N.S.Jr.A:** Nova Scotia Junior A. **N.Y. H.S.:** New York High School. **NYMJHL:** New York Major Junior Hockey League. **NYOHL:** North York Ontario Hockey League. **ODHA:** Ottawa & District Hockey Association. **OHA:** Ontario Hockey Association. **OHA Jr. A:** Ontario Hockey Association Junior A. **OHA Mjr. Jr. A:** Ontario Hockey Association Major Junior A. **OHA Senior:** Ontario Hockey Association Senior. **OHL:** Ontario Hockey League. **O. H.S.:** Ohio High School. **OJHA:** Ontario Junior Hockey Association. **OJHL:** Ontario Junior Hockey League. **OMJHL:** Ontario Major Junior Hockey League. **OPJHL:** Ontario Provincial Junior Hockey League. **OUAA:** Ontario Universities Athletic Association. **PCJHL:** Peace Caribou Junior Hockey League. **PEIHA:** Prince Edward Island Hockey Association. **PEIJHL:** Prince Edward Island Junior Hockey League. **QMJHL:** Quebec Major Junior Hockey League. **R.I. H.S.:** Rhode Island High School. **SAJHL:** Southern Alberta Junior Hockey League. **SJHL:** Saskatchewan Junior Hockey League. **Sask. H.S.:** Saskatchewan High School. **SOJHL:** Southern Ontario Junior Hockey League. **Swed. Jr.:** Sweden Junior. **Switz.:** Switzerland. **TBAHA:** Thunder Bay Amateur Hockey Association. **TBJHL:** Thunder Bay Junior Hockey League. **USHL:** United States Hockey League. **USSR:** Union of Soviet Socialist Republics. **Vt. H.S.:** Vermont High School. **W. Germany, W. Ger.:** West Germany. **WCHA:** Western Collegiate Hockey Association. **WCHL:** Western Canada Hockey League. **WHA:** World Hockey Association. **WHL:** Western Hockey League. **Wisc. H.S.:** Wisconsin High School. **Yukon Sr.:** Yukon Senior.

Included in the Hockey Register are every player who appeared in an NHL game in 1992-93, top prospects, other players listed on NHL rosters and the 26 NHL head coaches.

EXPLANATION OF AWARDS

NHL AWARDS: Alka-Seltzer Plus Award: plus/minus leader. **Art Ross Trophy:** leading scorer. **Bill Masterton Memorial Trophy:** perseverance, sportsmanship and dedication to hockey. **Bud Light/NHL Man of the Year:** service to community; called Budweiser/NHL Man of the Year prior to 1990-91. **Budweiser/NHL Man of the Year:** service to community; renamed Bud Light/NHL Man of the Year in 1990-91. **Calder Memorial Trophy:** rookie of the year. **Conn Smythe Trophy:** most valuable player in playoffs. **Dodge Performance of the Year Award:** most outstanding achievement or single-game performance. **Dodge Performer of the Year Award:** most outstanding performer in regular season. **Dodge Ram Tough Award:** highest combined total of power-play, shorthanded, game-winning and game-tying goals. **Emery Edge Award:** plus/minus leader; awarded from 1982-83 through 1987-88. **Frank J. Selke Trophy:** best defensive forward. **Hart Memorial Trophy:** most valuable player. **Jack Adams Award:** coach of the year. **James Norris Memorial Trophy:** outstanding defenseman. **King Clancy Memorial Trophy:** humanitarian contributions. **Lady Byng Memorial Trophy:** most gentlemanly player. **Lester B. Pearson Award:** outstanding player as selected by NHL Players' Association. **Lester Patrick Trophy:** outstanding service to hockey in U.S. **Trico Goaltender Award:** best save percentage. **Vezina Trophy:** best goaltender; awarded to goalkeeper(s) having played minimum of 25 games for team with fewest goals scored against prior to 1981-82. **William M. Jennings Trophy:** goalkeeper(s) having played minimum of 25 games for team with fewest goals scored against.

MINOR LEAGUE AWARDS: Baz Bastien Trophy: top goaltender (AHL). **Bobby Orr Trophy:** best defenseman (CHL); awarded prior to 1984-85. **Bob Gassoff Award:** most improved defenseman (CHL); awarded prior to 1984-85. **Commissioner's Trophy:** coach of the year (IHL). **Dudley (Red) Garrett Memorial Trophy:** rookie of the year (AHL). **Eddie Shore Plaque:** outstanding defenseman (AHL). **Fred Hunt Memorial Award:** sportsmanship, determination and dedication (AHL). **Garry F. Longman Memorial Trophy:** outstanding rookie (IHL). **Governors Trophy:** outstanding defenseman (IHL). **Harry (Hap) Holmes Memorial Trophy:** goaltender(s) having played minimum of 25 games for team with fewest goals scored against (AHL); awarded to outstanding goaltender prior to 1983-84. **Jack Butterfield Trophy:** Calder Cup playoffs MVP (AHL). **Jake Milford Trophy:** coach of the year (CHL); awarded prior to 1984-85. **James Gatschene Memorial Trophy:** most valuable player (IHL). **James Norris Memorial Trophy:** outstanding goaltender (IHL). **John B. Sollenberger Trophy:** leading scorer (AHL); originally called Wally Kilrea Trophy, later changed to Carl Liscombe Trophy until summer of 1955. **Ken McKenzie Trophy:** outstanding U.S.-born rookie (IHL). **Ken McKenzie Trophy:** top rookie (CHL); awarded to scoring leader from 1992-93. **Leo P. Lamoureux Memorial Trophy:** leading scorer (IHL); originally called George H. Wilkinson Trophy from 1946-47 through 1959-60. **Les Cunningham Plaque:** most valuable player (AHL). **Louis A.R. Pieri Memorial Award:** top coach (AHL). **Max McNab Trophy:** playoff MVP (CHL); awarded prior to 1984-85. **N.R. (Bud) Poile Trophy:** playoff MVP (IHL); originally called Turner Cup Playoff MVP from 1984-85 through 1988-89. **Phil Esposito Trophy:** leading scorer (CHL); awarded prior to 1984-85. **Terry Sawchuk Trophy:** top goaltenders (CHL); awarded prior to 1984-85. **Tommy Ivan Trophy:** most valuable player (CHL); awarded prior to 1984-85. **Turner Cup Playoff MVP:** playoff MVP (IHL); renamed N.R. (Bud) Poile Trophy in 1989-90.

MAJOR JUNIOR LEAGUE AWARDS: Association of Journalists for Major Junior League Hockey Trophy: top pro prospect (QMJHL); renamed Michael Bossy Trophy in 1983-84. **Bill Hunter Trophy:** top defenseman (WHL); called Top Defenseman Trophy prior to 1987-88 season. **Bob Brownridge Memorial Trophy:** top scorer (WHL); later renamed Bob Clarke Trophy. **Bobby Smith Trophy:** scholastic player of the year (OHL). **Bob Clarke Trophy:** top scorer (WHL); originally called Bob Brownridge Memorial Trophy. **Brad Hornung Trophy:** most sportsmanlike player (WHL); called Frank Boucher Memorial Trophy for most gentlemanly player prior to 1987-88 season. **Dave Pinkney Trophy:** top team goaltending (OHL). **Del Wilson Trophy:** top goaltender (WHL); called Top Goaltender Trophy prior to 1987-88 season. **Des Instructeurs Trophy:** rookie of the year (QMJHL); awarded to top rookie forward since 1981-82 season; renamed Michel Bergeron Trophy in 1985-86. **Dunc McCallum Memorial Trophy:** coach of the year (WHL). **Eddie Powers Memorial Trophy:** scoring champion (OHL). **Emile (Butch) Bouchard Trophy:** best defenseman (QMJHL). **Emms Family Award:** rookie of the year (OHL). **Four Broncos Memorial Trophy:** most valuable player as selected by coaches (WHL); called Most Valuable Player Trophy prior to 1987-88 season. **Frank Boucher Memorial Trophy:** most gentlemanly player (WHL); renamed Brad Hornung Trophy during 1987-88 season. **Frank J. Selke Trophy:** most gentlemanly player (QMJHL). **F.W. (Dinty) Moore Trophy:** rookie goalie with best goals-against average (OHL). **George Parsons Trophy:** sportsmanship in Memorial Cup (Can.HL). **Guy Lafleur Trophy:** most valuable player during playoffs (QMJHL). **Hap Emms Memorial Trophy:** outstanding goaltender in Memorial Cup (Can.HL). **Jacques Plante Trophy:** best goaltender (QMJHL). **Jean Beliveau Trophy:** leading point scorer (QMJHL). **Jim Mahon Memorial Trophy:** top-scoring right winger (OHL). **Jim Piggott Memorial Trophy:** rookie of the year (WHL); originally called Stewart (Butch) Paul Memorial Trophy. **Leo Lalonde Memorial Trophy:** overage player of the year (OHL). **Marcel Robert Trophy:** top scholastic/athletic performer (QMJHL). **Matt Leyden Trophy:** coach of the year (OHL). **Max Kaminsky Trophy:** outstanding defenseman (OHL); awarded to most gentlemanly player prior to 1969-70. **Michael Bossy Trophy:** top pro prospect (QMJHL); originally called Association of Journalists for Major Junior League Hockey Trophy from 1980-81 through 1982-83. **Michel Bergeron Trophy:** top rookie forward (QMJHL); awarded to rookie of the year prior to 1980-81 season. **Michel Briere Trophy:** most valuable player (QMJHL). **Most Valuable Player Trophy:** most valuable player (WHL); renamed Four Broncos Memorial Trophy during 1987-88 season. **Raymond Lagace Trophy:** top rookie defenseman or goaltender (QMJHL). **Red Tilson Trophy:** outstanding player (OHL). **Shell Cup:** awarded to offensive player of the year and defensive player of the year (QMJHL). **Stafford Smythe Memorial Trophy:** most valuable player of Memorial Cup (Can.HL). **Stewart (Butch) Paul Memorial Trophy:** rookie of the year (WHL); renamed Jim Piggott Memorial Trophy during 1987-88 season. **Top Defenseman Trophy:** top defenseman (WHL); renamed Bill Hunter Trophy during 1987-88 season. **Top Goaltender Trophy:** top goaltender (WHL); renamed Del Wilson Trophy during 1987-88 season. **William Hanley Trophy:** most gentlemanly player (OHL).

COLLEGE AWARDS: Hobey Baker Memorial Trophy: top college hockey player in U.S. **Senator Joseph A. Sullivan Trophy:** outstanding player in Canadian Interuniversity Athletic Union.

OTHER AWARDS: Golden Puck Award: Sweden's Player of the Year. **Golden Stick Award:** Europe's top player. **Izvestia Trophy:** leading scorer (Soviet Union).

A

AALTO, ANTTI
C, MIGHTY DUCKS

PERSONAL: Born April 8, 1975, at Lappeenranta, Finland.... 6-2/185.... Shoots left.
TRANSACTIONS/CAREER NOTES: Selected by Mighty Ducks of Anaheim in sixth round (sixth Mighty Ducks pick, 134th overall) of NHL entry draft (June 26, 1993).

			REGULAR SEASON					PLAYOFFS			
Season	Team	League	Gms.	G	A	Pts.	Pen.	Gms.	G	A	Pts.	Pen.
91-92	SaiPa Jr.	Finland	19	10	10	20	38	—	—	—	—	—
	SaiPa	Finland	20	6	6	12	20	—	—	—	—	—
92-93	SaiPa	Finland	23	6	8	14	14	—	—	—	—	—
	TPS Jr.	Finland	14	6	8	14	18	—	—	—	—	—
	TPS Turku	Finland	1	0	0	0	0	—	—	—	—	—

ACTON, KEITH
C, CAPITALS

PERSONAL: Born April 15, 1958, at Newmarket, Ont.... 5-8/170.... Shoots left.... Full name: Keith Edward Acton.
TRANSACTIONS/CAREER NOTES: Selected by Montreal Canadiens in sixth round (eighth Canadiens pick, 103rd overall) of NHL entry draft (June 15, 1978).... Traded by Canadiens with RW Mark Napier and third-round pick in 1984 draft previously acquired from Toronto Maple Leafs (C Ken Hodge) to Minnesota North Stars for C Bobby Smith (October 28, 1983).... Injured left wrist (April 20, 1984).... Traded by North Stars to Edmonton Oilers for D Moe Mantha (January 22, 1988).... Broke nose (December 14, 1988).... Traded by Oilers with sixth-round pick in 1991 draft (D Dimitri Yushkevich) to Philadelphia Flyers for RW Dave Brown (February 7, 1989).... Traded by Flyers with G Pete Peeters to Winnipeg Jets for future considerations (September 28, 1989).... Traded by Jets with G Pete Peeters to Flyers for fifth-round pick in 1991 draft previously acquired from Maple Leafs (C Juha Ylonen) (October 3, 1989); Jets did not have to surrender future considerations in a previous deal for Shawn Cronin (the NHL fined both Flyers and Jets $10,000 for violating a league by-law against loaning players to another team).... Underwent elbow surgery (September 1990).... Sprained knee (October 1990); missed three games.... Fractured wrist (November 27, 1991); missed 26 games.... Signed as free agent by Washington Capitals (July 27, 1993).
HONORS: Named to AHL All-Star second team (1979-80).... Played in NHL All-Star Game (1982).
MISCELLANEOUS: Member of Stanley Cup championship team (1988).

			REGULAR SEASON					PLAYOFFS			
Season	Team	League	Gms.	G	A	Pts.	Pen.	Gms.	G	A	Pts.	Pen.
74-75	Wexford Jr. B	MTHL	43	23	29	52	46	—	—	—	—	—
75-76	Peterborough	OHA Mj. Jr. A	35	9	17	26	30	—	—	—	—	—
76-77	Peterborough	OMJHL	65	52	69	121	93	4	1	4	5	6
77-78	Peterborough	OMJHL	68	42	86	128	52	21	10	8	18	16
78-79	Nova Scotia	AHL	79	15	26	41	22	10	4	2	6	4
79-80	Nova Scotia	AHL	75	45	53	98	38	6	1	2	3	8
	Montreal	NHL	2	0	1	1	0	—	—	—	—	—
80-81	Montreal	NHL	61	15	24	39	74	2	0	0	0	6
81-82	Montreal	NHL	78	36	52	88	88	5	0	4	4	16
82-83	Montreal	NHL	78	24	26	50	63	3	0	0	0	0
83-84	Montreal	NHL	9	3	7	10	4	—	—	—	—	—
	Minnesota	NHL	62	17	38	55	60	15	4	7	11	12
84-85	Minnesota	NHL	78	20	38	58	90	9	4	4	8	6
85-86	Minnesota	NHL	79	26	32	58	100	5	0	3	3	6
86-87	Minnesota	NHL	78	16	29	45	56	—	—	—	—	—
87-88	Minnesota	NHL	46	8	11	19	74	—	—	—	—	—
	Edmonton	NHL	26	3	6	9	21	7	2	0	2	16
88-89	Edmonton	NHL	46	11	15	26	47	—	—	—	—	—
	Philadelphia	NHL	25	3	10	13	64	16	2	3	5	18
89-90	Philadelphia	NHL	69	13	14	27	80	—	—	—	—	—
90-91	Philadelphia	NHL	76	14	23	37	131	—	—	—	—	—
91-92	Philadelphia	NHL	50	7	10	17	98	—	—	—	—	—
92-93	Philadelphia	NHL	83	8	15	23	51	—	—	—	—	—
	NHL totals		**946**	**224**	**351**	**575**	**1101**	**62**	**12**	**21**	**33**	**80**

ADAMS, GREG
C, CANUCKS

PERSONAL: Born August 1, 1963, at Nelson, B.C.... 6-3/198.... Shoots left.
COLLEGE: Northern Arizona.
TRANSACTIONS/CAREER NOTES: Signed as free agent by New Jersey Devils (June 25, 1984).... Tore tendon in right wrist (April 1986).... Traded by Devils with G Kirk McLean to Vancouver Canucks for C Patrik Sundstrom, fourth-round pick in 1988 draft (LW Matt Ruchty) and the option to flip second-round picks in 1988 draft; Devils exercised option and selected LW Jeff Christian and Canucks selected D Leif Rohlin (September 10, 1987).... Fractured ankle (February 1989).... Fractured cheekbone (January 4, 1990); missed 12 games.... Sprained left knee (October 17, 1990); missed 12 games.... Sprained forearm, wrist and abdomen (February 27, 1991).... Suffered concussion (October 8, 1991); missed one game.... Suffered charley horse (January 16, 1993); missed nine games.... Suffered charley horse (February 15, 1993); missed 22 games.
HONORS: Played in NHL All-Star Game (1988).

			REGULAR SEASON					PLAYOFFS			
Season	Team	League	Gms.	G	A	Pts.	Pen.	Gms.	G	A	Pts.	Pen.
80-81	Kelowna	BCJHL	47	40	50	90	16	—	—	—	—	—
81-82	Kelowna	BCJHL	45	31	42	73	24	—	—	—	—	—
82-83	Northern Arizona Univ.	Indep.	29	14	21	35	46	—	—	—	—	—
83-84	Northern Arizona Univ.	Indep.	47	40	50	90	16	—	—	—	—	—

| | | | REGULAR SEASON | | | | | PLAYOFFS | | | |
Season	Team	League	Gms.	G	A	Pts.	Pen.	Gms.	G	A	Pts.	Pen.
84-85—Maine		AHL	41	15	20	35	12	11	3	4	7	0
—New Jersey		NHL	36	12	9	21	14	—	—	—	—	—
85-86—New Jersey		NHL	78	35	42	77	30	—	—	—	—	—
86-87—New Jersey		NHL	72	20	27	47	19	—	—	—	—	—
87-88—Vancouver		NHL	80	36	40	76	30	—	—	—	—	—
88-89—Vancouver		NHL	61	19	14	33	24	7	2	3	5	2
89-90—Vancouver		NHL	65	30	20	50	18	—	—	—	—	—
90-91—Vancouver		NHL	55	21	24	45	10	5	0	0	0	2
91-92—Vancouver		NHL	76	30	27	57	26	6	0	2	2	4
92-93—Vancouver		NHL	53	25	31	56	14	12	7	6	13	6
NHL totals			576	228	234	462	185	30	9	11	20	14

ADAMS, KEVYN
C, BRUINS

PERSONAL: Born October 8, 1974, at Washington, D.C. . . . 6-1/182. . . . Shoots right.
COLLEGE: Miami of Ohio.
TRANSACTIONS/CAREER NOTES: Selected by Boston Bruins in first round (first Bruins pick, 25th overall) of NHL entry draft (June 26, 1993).

| | | | REGULAR SEASON | | | | | PLAYOFFS | | | |
Season	Team	League	Gms.	G	A	Pts.	Pen.	Gms.	G	A	Pts.	Pen.
90-91—Niagara Scenic		NAJHL	55	17	20	37	24	—	—	—	—	—
91-92—Niagara Scenic		NAJHL	40	25	33	58	51	—	—	—	—	—
92-93—Miami of Ohio		CCHA	41	17	16	33	18	—	—	—	—	—

AGNEW, JIM
D, WHALERS

PERSONAL: Born March 21, 1966, at Deloraine, Man. . . . 6-1/190. . . . Shoots left.
TRANSACTIONS/CAREER NOTES: Selected by Vancouver Canucks as underage junior in eighth round (10th Canucks pick, 157th overall) of NHL entry draft (June 9, 1984). . . . Tore knee ligaments (March 18, 1990). . . . Sprained left knee ligaments (November 19, 1990); missed 19 games. . . . Resprained left knee ligaments (January 6, 1991). . . . Signed as free agent by Hartford Whalers (June 29, 1992). . . . Pulled groin (November 15, 1992); missed eight games. . . . Sprained knee (December 9, 1992); missed 13 games. . . . Reinjured knee (January 21, 1993) and underwent knee surgery (January 25, 1993); missed remainder of season.
HONORS: Named to WHL (West) All-Star first team (1985-86). . . . Named to IHL All-Star second team (1989-90).

| | | | REGULAR SEASON | | | | | PLAYOFFS | | | |
Season	Team	League	Gms.	G	A	Pts.	Pen.	Gms.	G	A	Pts.	Pen.
82-83—Brandon		WHL	14	1	1	2	9	—	—	—	—	—
83-84—Brandon		WHL	71	6	17	23	107	12	0	1	1	39
84-85—Brandon		WHL	19	3	15	18	82	—	—	—	—	—
—Portland		WHL	44	5	24	29	223	6	0	2	2	44
85-86—Portland		WHL	70	6	30	36	386	9	0	1	1	48
86-87—Vancouver		NHL	4	0	0	0	0	—	—	—	—	—
—Fredericton		AHL	67	0	5	5	261	—	—	—	—	—
87-88—Vancouver		NHL	10	0	1	1	16	—	—	—	—	—
—Fredericton		AHL	63	2	8	10	188	14	0	2	2	43
88-89—Milwaukee		IHL	47	2	10	12	181	11	0	2	2	34
89-90—Milwaukee		IHL	51	4	10	14	238	—	—	—	—	—
—Vancouver		NHL	7	0	0	0	36	—	—	—	—	—
90-91—Vancouver		NHL	20	0	0	0	81	—	—	—	—	—
—Milwaukee		IHL	3	0	0	0	33	—	—	—	—	—
91-92—Vancouver		NHL	24	0	0	0	56	4	0	0	0	6
92-93—Hartford		NHL	16	0	0	0	68	—	—	—	—	—
—Springfield		AHL	1	0	1	1	2	—	—	—	—	—
NHL totals			81	0	1	1	257	4	0	0	0	6

AHOLA, PETER
D, LIGHTNING

PERSONAL: Born May 14, 1968, at Espoo, Finland. . . . 6-3/205. . . . Shoots left. . . . Full name: Peter Kristian Ahola. . . . Name pronounced AH-hoh-luh.
COLLEGE: Boston University.
TRANSACTIONS/CAREER NOTES: Signed as free agent by Los Angeles Kings (April 5, 1991). . . . Traded by Kings to Pittsburgh Penguins for D Jeff Chychrun (November 6, 1992). . . . Traded by Penguins to San Jose Sharks for future considerations (February 26, 1993). . . . Traded by Sharks to Tampa Bay Lightning for C Dave Capuano (June 19, 1993).
HONORS: Named to Hockey East All-Rookie team (1989-90). . . . Named to NCAA All-America East second team (1990-91).

| | | | REGULAR SEASON | | | | | PLAYOFFS | | | |
Season	Team	League	Gms.	G	A	Pts.	Pen.	Gms.	G	A	Pts.	Pen.
89-90—Boston University		Hockey East	43	3	20	23	65	—	—	—	—	—
90-91—Boston University		Hockey East	39	12	24	36	88	—	—	—	—	—
91-92—Los Angeles		NHL	71	7	12	19	101	6	0	0	0	2
—Phoenix		IHL	7	3	3	6	34	—	—	—	—	—
92-93—Los Angeles		NHL	8	1	1	2	6	—	—	—	—	—
—Pittsburgh		NHL	22	0	1	1	14	—	—	—	—	—
—Cleveland		IHL	9	1	0	1	4	—	—	—	—	—
—San Jose		NHL	20	2	3	5	16	—	—	—	—	—
NHL totals			121	10	17	27	137	6	0	0	0	2

AIVAZOFF, MICAH
C/LW, RED WINGS

PERSONAL: Born May 4, 1969, at Powell River, B.C. . . . 6-0/185. . . . Shoots left.
TRANSACTIONS/CAREER NOTES: Selected by Los Angeles Kings in sixth round (sixth Kings pick, 109th overall) of NHL entry draft (June 11, 1988). . . . Signed as free agent by Detroit Red Wings (July 2, 1991).

			REGULAR SEASON					PLAYOFFS			
Season Team	League	Gms.	G	A	Pts.	Pen.	Gms.	G	A	Pts.	Pen.
85-86—Victoria	WHL	27	3	4	7	25	—	—	—	—	—
86-87—Victoria	WHL	72	18	39	57	112	5	1	0	1	2
87-88—Victoria	WHL	69	26	57	83	79	8	3	4	7	14
88-89—Victoria	WHL	70	35	65	100	136	8	5	7	12	2
89-90—New Haven	AHL	77	20	39	59	71	—	—	—	—	—
90-91—New Haven	AHL	79	11	29	40	84	—	—	—	—	—
91-92—Adirondack	AHL	61	9	20	29	50	†19	2	8	10	25
92-93—Adirondack	AHL	79	32	53	85	100	11	8	6	14	10

ALBELIN, TOMMY
D, DEVILS

PERSONAL: Born May 21, 1964, at Stockholm, Sweden. . . . 6-1/190. . . . Shoots left. . . . Name pronounced AL-buh-LEEN.
TRANSACTIONS/CAREER NOTES: Selected by Quebec Nordiques in eighth round (seventh Nordiques pick, 152nd overall) of NHL entry draft (June 8, 1983). . . . Traded by Nordiques to New Jersey Devils for fourth-round pick in 1989 draft (LW Niclas Andersson) (December 12, 1988). . . . Injured right knee (March 2, 1990); missed four games. . . . Injured groin (November 21, 1992); missed two games.
HONORS: Named to Swedish League All-Star team (1986-87).

			REGULAR SEASON					PLAYOFFS			
Season Team	League	Gms.	G	A	Pts.	Pen.	Gms.	G	A	Pts.	Pen.
82-83—Djurgarden	Sweden	17	2	5	7	4	6	1	0	1	2
83-84—Djurgarden	Sweden	37	9	8	17	36	4	0	1	1	2
84-85—Djurgarden	Sweden	32	9	8	17	22	8	2	1	3	4
85-86—Djurgarden	Sweden	35	4	8	12	26	—	—	—	—	—
86-87—Djurgarden	Sweden	33	7	5	12	49	2	0	0	0	0
87-88—Quebec	NHL	60	3	23	26	47	—	—	—	—	—
88-89—Halifax	AHL	8	2	5	7	4	—	—	—	—	—
—Quebec	NHL	14	2	4	6	27	—	—	—	—	—
—New Jersey	NHL	46	7	24	31	40	—	—	—	—	—
89-90—New Jersey	NHL	68	6	23	29	63	—	—	—	—	—
90-91—Utica	AHL	14	4	2	6	10	—	—	—	—	—
—New Jersey	NHL	47	2	12	14	44	3	0	1	1	2
91-92—New Jersey	NHL	19	0	4	4	4	1	1	1	2	0
—Utica	AHL	11	4	6	10	4	—	—	—	—	—
92-93—New Jersey	NHL	36	1	5	6	14	5	2	0	2	0
NHL totals		290	21	95	116	239	9	3	2	5	2

ALEXEYEV, ALEXANDER
D, JETS

PERSONAL: Born March 23, 1974, at Kiev, U.S.S.R. . . . 5-11/198. . . . Shoots left.
TRANSACTIONS/CAREER NOTES: Selected by Winnipeg Jets in sixth round (fifth Jets pick, 132nd overall) of NHL entry draft (June 20, 1992).

			REGULAR SEASON					PLAYOFFS			
Season Team	League	Gms.	G	A	Pts.	Pen.	Gms.	G	A	Pts.	Pen.
90-91—Sokol Kiev	USSR	5	0	0	0	2	—	—	—	—	—
91-92—Sokol Kiev	CIS	25	1	5	6	22	—	—	—	—	—
92-93—Tacoma	WHL	44	3	33	36	67	7	2	7	9	4

ALLAN, SANDY
G, KINGS

PERSONAL: Born January 22, 1974, at Nassau, Bahamas. . . . 6-0/175. . . . Shoots left.
HIGH SCHOOL: Chippewa Secondary School (North Bay, Ont.).
TRANSACTIONS/CAREER NOTES: Selected by Los Angeles Kings in third round (second Kings pick, 63rd overall) of NHL entry draft (June 20, 1992).
HONORS: Won F.W. (Dinty) Moore Trophy (1991-92).

			REGULAR SEASON							PLAYOFFS					
Season Team	League	Gms.	Min.	W	L	T	GA	SO	Avg.	Gms.	Min.	W	L	GA	SO	Avg.
91-92—North Bay	OHL	34	1747	18	5	4	112	0	3.85	3	18	0	0	2	0	6.67
92-93—North Bay	OHL	39	1835	8	19	4	133	0	4.35	4	180	0	3	10	0	3.33

ALLISON, JAMIE
D, FLAMES

PERSONAL: Born May 13, 1975, at Lindsay, Ont. . . . 6-1/188. . . . Shoots left.
TRANSACTIONS/CAREER NOTES: Selected by Calgary Flames in second round (second Flames pick, 44th overall) of NHL entry draft (June 26, 1993).

			REGULAR SEASON					PLAYOFFS			
Season Team	League	Gms.	G	A	Pts.	Pen.	Gms.	G	A	Pts.	Pen.
90-91—Waterloo Jr. B	OHA	45	3	8	11	91	—	—	—	—	—
91-92—Windsor	OHL	59	4	8	12	52	4	1	1	2	2
92-93—Detroit	OHL	61	0	13	13	64	15	2	5	7	23

ALLISON, JASON
C, CAPITALS

PERSONAL: Born May 29, 1975, at Toronto.... 6-2/192.... Shoots right.
TRANSACTIONS/CAREER NOTES: Selected by Washington Capitals in first round (second Capitals pick, 17th overall) of NHL entry draft (June 26, 1993).

			REGULAR SEASON					PLAYOFFS				
Season	Team	League	Gms.	G	A	Pts.	Pen.	Gms.	G	A	Pts.	Pen.
91-92—London		OHL	65	11	18	29	15	7	0	0	0	0
92-93—London		OHL	66	42	76	118	50	12	7	13	20	8

ALLISON, SCOTT
LW, OILERS

PERSONAL: Born April 22, 1972, at St. Boniface, Man.... 6-4/194.... Shoots left.
TRANSACTIONS/CAREER NOTES: Selected by Edmonton Oilers in first round (first Oilers pick, 17th overall) of NHL entry draft (June 16, 1990).

			REGULAR SEASON					PLAYOFFS				
Season	Team	League	Gms.	G	A	Pts.	Pen.	Gms.	G	A	Pts.	Pen.
88-89—Prince Albert		WHL	51	6	9	15	37	3	0	0	0	0
89-90—Prince Albert		WHL	66	22	16	38	73	11	1	4	5	8
90-91—Prince Albert		WHL	37	0	6	6	44	—	—	—	—	—
—Portland		WHL	44	5	17	22	105	—	—	—	—	—
91-92—Moose Jaw		WHL	72	37	45	82	238	3	1	1	2	25
92-93—Cape Breton		AHL	49	3	5	8	34	—	—	—	—	—
—Wheeling		ECHL	6	3	3	6	8	—	—	—	—	—

ALVEY, MATT
C, BRUINS

PERSONAL: Born May 15, 1975, at Troy, N.Y.... 6-2/210.... Shoots right.
TRANSACTIONS/CAREER NOTES: Selected by Boston Bruins in second round (second Bruins pick, 51st overall) of NHL entry draft (June 26, 1993).

			REGULAR SEASON					PLAYOFFS				
Season	Team	League	Gms.	G	A	Pts.	Pen.	Gms.	G	A	Pts.	Pen.
90-91—Springfield Jr. B		NEJHL	...	12	20	32	...	—	—	—	—	—
91-92—Springfield Jr. B		NEJHL	32	22	35	57	34	—	—	—	—	—
92-93—Springfield Jr. B		NEJHL	38	22	37	59	85	—	—	—	—	—

AMBROZIAK, PETER
LW, SABRES

PERSONAL: Born September 15, 1971, at Toronto.... 6-0/191.... Shoots left.... Name pronounced am-BROH-zee-ak.
TRANSACTIONS/CAREER NOTES: Selected by Buffalo Sabres in fourth round (fourth Sabres pick, 72nd overall) of NHL entry draft (June 22, 1991).

			REGULAR SEASON					PLAYOFFS				
Season	Team	League	Gms.	G	A	Pts.	Pen.	Gms.	G	A	Pts.	Pen.
88-89—Ottawa		OHL	50	8	15	23	11	12	1	2	3	2
89-90—Ottawa		OHL	60	13	19	32	37	4	0	0	0	2
90-91—Ottawa		OHL	62	30	32	62	56	17	15	9	24	24
91-92—Rochester		AHL	2	0	1	1	0	—	—	—	—	—
—Ottawa		OHL	49	32	49	81	50	11	3	7	10	33
92-93—Rochester		AHL	50	8	10	18	37	12	4	3	7	16

AMONTE, TONY
RW, RANGERS

PERSONAL: Born August 2, 1970, at Weymouth, Mass.... 6-0/186.... Shoots left.... Full name: Anthony Lewis Amonte.... Name pronounced ah-MAHN-tee.
HIGH SCHOOL: Thayer Academy (Braintree, Mass.).
COLLEGE: Boston University.
TRANSACTIONS/CAREER NOTES: Selected by New York Rangers in fourth round (third Rangers pick, 68th overall) of NHL entry draft (June 11, 1988).... Separated shoulder (December 29, 1990).
HONORS: Named to Hockey East All-Rookie team (1989-90).... Named to NCAA All-Tournament team (1990-91).... Named to Hockey East All-Star second team (1990-91).... Named NHL Rookie of the Year by THE SPORTING NEWS (1991-92).... Named to NHL All-Rookie team (1991-92).

			REGULAR SEASON					PLAYOFFS				
Season	Team	League	Gms.	G	A	Pts.	Pen.	Gms.	G	A	Pts.	Pen.
86-87—Thayer Academy		Mass. H.S.	...	25	32	57	...	—	—	—	—	—
87-88—Thayer Academy		Mass. H.S.	...	30	38	68	...	—	—	—	—	—
88-89—Team USA Juniors		Int'l	7	1	3	4	...	—	—	—	—	—
89-90—Boston University		Hockey East	41	25	33	58	52	—	—	—	—	—
90-91—Boston University		Hockey East	38	31	37	68	82	—	—	—	—	—
—New York Rangers		NHL	—	—	—	—	—	2	0	2	2	2
91-92—New York Rangers		NHL	79	35	34	69	55	13	3	6	9	2
92-93—New York Rangers		NHL	83	33	43	76	49	—	—	—	—	—
NHL totals			162	68	77	145	104	15	3	8	11	4

ANDERSON, GLENN
RW, MAPLE LEAFS

PERSONAL: Born October 2, 1960, at Vancouver, B.C.... 6-1/190.... Shoots left.... Full name: Glenn Chris Anderson.
COLLEGE: Denver.
TRANSACTIONS/CAREER NOTES: Selected by Edmonton Oilers in fourth round (third Oilers pick, 69th overall) of NHL entry draft (August 9, 1979).... Underwent knee surgery to remove bone chips (November 1980).... Underwent nose surgery to correct breathing problem (spring 1982).... Suspended eight games by NHL for fighting (December 13, 1985).... Pulled side muscle (November 1988).... Fined $500 for deliberately breaking the cheekbone of RW

Tomas Sandstrom (February 28, 1990). . . . Missed first four games of 1990-91 season due to contract dispute (October 1990). . . . Injured thigh (March 5, 1991); missed two games. . . . Traded by Oilers with G Grant Fuhr and LW Craig Berube to Toronto Maple Leafs for LW Vincent Damphousse, D Luke Richardson, G Peter Ing, C Scott Thornton and future considerations (September 19, 1991). . . . Sprained knee (December 3, 1992); missed four games. . . . Injured knee (February 3, 1993); missed one game.
HONORS: Played in NHL All-Star Game (1984 through 1986 and 1988).
RECORDS: Shares NHL single-game playoff record for most points in one period—4 (April 6, 1988).
MISCELLANEOUS: Member of Stanley Cup championship teams (1984, 1985, 1987, 1988 and 1990).

			REGULAR SEASON					PLAYOFFS			
Season	Team	League	Gms.	G	A	Pts.	Pen.	Gms.	G	A	Pts.	Pen.
77-78	Bellingham Jr. A	BCJHL	58	61	64	125	96	—	—	—	—	—
	New Westminster	WCHL	1	0	1	1	2	—	—	—	—	—
78-79	Seattle	WHL	2	0	1	1	0	—	—	—	—	—
	University of Denver	WCHA	40	26	29	55	58	—	—	—	—	—
79-80	Canadian Olympic Team	Int'l	49	21	21	42	46	—	—	—	—	—
	Seattle	WHL	7	5	5	10	4	—	—	—	—	—
80-81	Edmonton	NHL	58	30	23	53	24	9	5	7	12	12
81-82	Edmonton	NHL	80	38	67	105	71	5	2	5	7	8
82-83	Edmonton	NHL	72	48	56	104	70	16	10	10	20	32
83-84	Edmonton	NHL	80	54	45	99	65	19	6	11	17	33
84-85	Edmonton	NHL	80	42	39	81	69	18	10	16	26	38
85-86	Edmonton	NHL	72	54	48	102	90	10	8	3	11	14
86-87	Edmonton	NHL	80	35	38	73	65	21	14	13	27	59
87-88	Edmonton	NHL	80	38	50	88	58	19	9	16	25	49
88-89	Edmonton	NHL	79	16	48	64	93	7	1	2	3	8
89-90	Edmonton	NHL	73	34	38	72	107	22	10	12	22	20
90-91	Edmonton	NHL	74	24	31	55	59	18	6	7	13	41
91-92	Toronto	NHL	72	24	33	57	100	—	—	—	—	—
92-93	Toronto	NHL	76	22	43	65	117	21	7	11	18	31
NHL totals			976	459	559	1018	988	185	88	113	201	345

ANDERSON, PERRY
LW

PERSONAL: Born October 14, 1961, at Barrie, Ont. . . . 6-1/230. . . . Shoots left. . . . Full name: Perry Lynn Anderson.
HIGH SCHOOL: North Park (Brantford, Ont.).
TRANSACTIONS/CAREER NOTES: Selected by St. Louis Blues as underage junior in sixth round (fifth Blues pick, 117th overall) of NHL entry draft (June 11, 1980). . . . Broke bone in foot (March 1984). . . . Traded by Blues to New Jersey Devils for C Rick Meagher and 12th-round pick in 1986 draft (LW Bill Butler) (August 29, 1985). . . . Strained abdominal muscle (January 13, 1986); missed eight games. . . . Suffered concussion (January 1988). . . . Strained rotator cuff (October 1988). . . . Sprained right knee (January 1989). . . . Separated left shoulder (March 1989). . . . Underwent surgery to left knee (August 1990). . . . Signed as free agent by San Jose Sharks (July 8, 1991). . . . Injured jaw (November 30, 1991); missed 18 games. . . . Signed as free agent by San Diego Gulls (September 1, 1992).
HONORS: Named to CHL All-Star team (1981-82).

			REGULAR SEASON					PLAYOFFS			
Season	Team	League	Gms.	G	A	Pts.	Pen.	Gms.	G	A	Pts.	Pen.
78-79	Kingston	OMJHL	60	6	13	19	85	5	2	1	3	6
79-80	Kingston	OMJHL	63	17	16	33	52	3	0	0	0	6
80-81	Kingston	OMJHL	38	9	13	22	118	—	—	—	—	—
	Brantford	OMJHL	31	8	27	35	43	6	4	2	6	15
81-82	Salt Lake City	IHL	71	32	32	64	117	2	1	0	1	2
	St. Louis	NHL	5	1	2	3	0	10	2	0	2	4
82-83	Salt Lake City	IHL	57	23	19	42	140	—	—	—	—	—
	St. Louis	NHL	18	5	2	7	14	—	—	—	—	—
83-84	Montana	CHL	8	7	3	10	34	—	—	—	—	—
	St. Louis	NHL	50	7	5	12	195	9	0	0	0	27
84-85	St. Louis	NHL	71	9	9	18	146	3	0	0	0	7
85-86	New Jersey	NHL	51	7	12	19	91	—	—	—	—	—
86-87	New Jersey	NHL	57	10	9	19	105	—	—	—	—	—
87-88	New Jersey	NHL	60	4	6	10	222	10	0	0	0	113
88-89	New Jersey	NHL	39	3	6	9	128	—	—	—	—	—
89-90	Utica	AHL	71	13	17	30	128	5	0	0	0	24
90-91	New Jersey	NHL	1	0	0	0	5	4	0	1	1	10
	Utica	AHL	68	19	14	33	245	—	—	—	—	—
91-92	San Jose	NHL	48	4	8	12	143	—	—	—	—	—
92-93	San Diego	IHL	51	8	13	21	217	5	0	0	0	14
NHL totals			400	50	59	109	1049	36	2	1	3	161

ANDERSON, SHAWN
D/LW, CAPITALS

PERSONAL: Born February 7, 1968, at Montreal. . . . 6-1/200. . . . Shoots left.
COLLEGE: Maine.
TRANSACTIONS/CAREER NOTES: Selected by Buffalo Sabres as underage player in first round (first Sabres pick, fifth overall) of NHL entry draft (June 21, 1986). . . . Sprained knee (October 1986). . . . Separated shoulder (March 3, 1987). . . . Reseparated shoulder (March 28, 1987). . . . Injured ankle (October 1987). . . . Injured ankle (December 1987). . . . Bruised knee (February 1988). . . . Traded by Sabres to Washington Capitals for D Bill Houlder (September 30, 1990). . . . Claimed by Quebec Nordiques in 1990 NHL waiver draft for $60,000 waiver price (October 2, 1990). . . . Traded by Nordiques to Winnipeg Jets for RW Sergei Kharin (October 22, 1991).

... Traded by Jets to Capitals for future considerations (October 23, 1991). ... Suffered back spasms (February 20, 1993); missed six games.

Season Team	League	REGULAR SEASON					PLAYOFFS				
		Gms.	G	A	Pts.	Pen.	Gms.	G	A	Pts.	Pen.
85-86—University of Maine	Hockey East	16	5	8	13	22	—	—	—	—	—
—Canadian national team	Int'l	33	2	6	8	16	—	—	—	—	—
86-87—Rochester	AHL	15	2	5	7	11	—	—	—	—	—
—Buffalo	NHL	41	2	11	13	23	—	—	—	—	—
87-88—Buffalo	NHL	23	1	2	3	17	—	—	—	—	—
—Rochester	AHL	22	5	16	21	19	6	0	0	0	0
88-89—Rochester	AHL	31	5	14	19	24	—	—	—	—	—
—Buffalo	NHL	33	2	10	12	18	5	0	1	1	4
89-90—Rochester	AHL	39	2	16	18	41	9	1	0	1	8
—Buffalo	NHL	16	1	3	4	8	—	—	—	—	—
90-91—Quebec	NHL	31	3	10	13	21	—	—	—	—	—
—Halifax	AHL	4	0	1	1	2	—	—	—	—	—
91-92—PEV Weiswasser	Germany	38	7	15	22	83	—	—	—	—	—
92-93—Baltimore	AHL	10	1	5	6	8	—	—	—	—	—
—Washington	NHL	60	2	6	8	18	6	0	0	0	0
NHL totals		204	11	42	53	105	11	0	1	1	4

ANDERSSON, MIKAEL
LW, LIGHTNING

PERSONAL: Born May 10, 1966, at Malmo, Sweden. ... 5-11/185. ... Shoots left. ... Full name: Bo Mikael Andersson.

TRANSACTIONS/CAREER NOTES: Selected by Buffalo Sabres in first round (first Sabres pick, 18th overall) of NHL entry draft (June 9, 1984). ... Sprained ankle (March 3, 1987); missed three weeks. ... Twisted ankle (March 1988). ... Sprained neck and shoulder (December 1988). ... Selected by Hartford Whalers in 1989 NHL waiver draft (October 2, 1989). ... Bruised left knee (December 13, 1989). ... Reinjured knee (February 9, 1990). ... Pulled right hamstring (March 8, 1990). ... Reinjured hamstring (March 17, 1990). ... Reinjured hamstring (April 1990). ... Underwent surgery to left knee (May 14, 1990). ... Suffered from the flu (October 4, 1990); missed two games. ... Pulled groin (January 1991). ... Injured toe (October 26, 1991); missed one game. ... Injured groin (December 17, 1991); missed three games. ... Suffered chip fracture to foot (April 12, 1992). ... Signed as free agent by Tampa Bay Lightning (July 8, 1992). ... Suffered back spasms (November 21, 1992); missed four games.

Season Team	League	REGULAR SEASON					PLAYOFFS				
		Gms.	G	A	Pts.	Pen.	Gms.	G	A	Pts.	Pen.
83-84—Vastra Frolunda	Sweden	12	0	2	2	6	—	—	—	—	—
84-85—Vastra Frolunda	Sweden	32	16	11	27	18	6	3	2	5	2
85-86—Rochester	AHL	20	10	4	14	6	—	—	—	—	—
—Buffalo	NHL	33	1	9	10	4	—	—	—	—	—
86-87—Rochester	AHL	42	6	20	26	14	9	1	2	3	2
—Buffalo	NHL	16	0	3	3	0	—	—	—	—	—
87-88—Rochester	AHL	35	12	24	36	16	—	—	—	—	—
—Buffalo	NHL	37	3	20	23	10	1	1	0	1	0
88-89—Buffalo	NHL	14	0	1	1	4	—	—	—	—	—
—Rochester	AHL	56	18	33	51	12	—	—	—	—	—
89-90—Hartford	NHL	50	13	24	37	6	5	0	3	3	2
90-91—Hartford	NHL	41	4	7	11	8	—	—	—	—	—
—Springfield	AHL	26	7	22	29	10	18	†10	8	18	12
91-92—Hartford	NHL	74	18	29	47	14	7	0	2	2	6
92-93—Tampa Bay	NHL	77	16	11	27	14	—	—	—	—	—
NHL totals		342	55	104	159	60	13	1	5	6	8

ANDERSSON, NIKLAS
LW, NORDIQUES

PERSONAL: Born May 20, 1971, at Kunglav, Sweden. ... 5-9/175. ... Shoots left.

TRANSACTIONS/CAREER NOTES: Selected by Quebec Nordiques in third round (fifth Nordiques pick, 68th overall) of NHL entry draft (June 17, 1989).

Season Team	League	REGULAR SEASON					PLAYOFFS				
		Gms.	G	A	Pts.	Pen.	Gms.	G	A	Pts.	Pen.
87-88—Frolunda	Sweden	15	5	5	10	...	—	—	—	—	—
88-89—Frolunda	Sweden	30	13	24	37	...	—	—	—	—	—
89-90—Frolunda	Sweden	38	10	21	31	14	—	—	—	—	—
90-91—Frolunda	Sweden	22	6	10	16	16	—	—	—	—	—
91-92—Halifax	AHL	57	8	26	34	41	—	—	—	—	—
92-93—Halifax	AHL	76	32	50	82	42	—	—	—	—	—
—Quebec	NHL	3	0	1	1	2	—	—	—	—	—
NHL totals		3	0	1	1	2	—	—	—	—	—

ANDERSSON, PETER
D, RANGERS

PERSONAL: Born August 29, 1965, at Orebro, Sweden. ... 6-0/187. ... Shoots left.

TRANSACTIONS/CAREER NOTES: Selected by New York Rangers in fourth round (fifth Rangers pick, 73rd overall) of NHL entry draft (June 8, 1983). ... Separated shoulder (October 24, 1992); missed five games.

HONORS: Named to Swedish League All-Star team (1991-92).

Season Team	League	REGULAR SEASON					PLAYOFFS				
		Gms.	G	A	Pts.	Pen.	Gms.	G	A	Pts.	Pen.
83-84—Farjestad	Sweden	36	4	7	11	22	—	—	—	—	—
84-85—Farjestad	Sweden	35	5	12	17	24	—	—	—	—	—
85-86—Farjestad	Sweden	34	6	10	16	18	—	—	—	—	—
86-87—Farjestad	Sweden	32	9	8	17	32	—	—	—	—	—
87-88—Farjestad	Sweden	38	14	20	34	44	—	—	—	—	—
88-89—Farjestad	Sweden	33	6	17	23	44	—	—	—	—	—
89-90—Malmo	Sweden-II	Statistics unavailable.									
90-91—Malmo	Sweden	34	9	17	26	26	—	—	—	—	—
91-92—Malmo	Sweden	40	12	20	32	18	—	—	—	—	—
92-93—New York Rangers	NHL	31	4	11	15	18	—	—	—	—	—
—Binghamton	AHL	27	11	22	33	16	—	—	—	—	—
NHL totals		31	4	11	15	18	—	—	—	—	—

ANDERSSON-JUNKKA, JONAS
D, PENGUINS

PERSONAL: Born May 4, 1975, at Kiruna, Sweden. . . . 6-2/165. . . . Shoots right.
TRANSACTIONS/CAREER NOTES: Selected by Pittsburgh Penguins in fourth round (fourth Penguins pick, 104th overall) of NHL entry draft (June 26, 1993).

Season Team	League	REGULAR SEASON					PLAYOFFS				
		Gms.	G	A	Pts.	Pen.	Gms.	G	A	Pts.	Pen.
91-92—Kiruna	Swed. Dv.II	1	0	0	0	0	—	—	—	—	—
92-93—Kiruna	Swed. Dv.II	30	3	7	10	32	—	—	—	—	—

ANDREYCHUK, DAVE
LW, MAPLE LEAFS

PERSONAL: Born September 29, 1963, at Hamilton, Ont. . . . 6-3/225. . . . Shoots right. . . . Name pronounced AN-druh-CHUCK.
TRANSACTIONS/CAREER NOTES: Selected by Buffalo Sabres as underage junior in first round (third Sabres pick, 16th overall) of NHL entry draft (June 9, 1982). . . . Sprained knee (March 1983). . . . Fractured collarbone (March 1985). . . . Twisted knee (September 1985). . . . Injured right knee (September 1986). . . . Strained medial collateral ligaments in left knee (November 27, 1988). . . . Broke left thumb (February 18, 1990). . . . Suspended two off-days and fined $500 by NHL for cross-checking (November 16, 1992). . . . Traded by Sabres with G Daren Puppa and first-round pick in 1993 draft (D Kenny Jonsson) to Toronto Maple Leafs for G Grant Fuhr and conditional pick in 1995 draft (February 2, 1993).
HONORS: Played in NHL All-Star Game (1990).
MISCELLANEOUS: Played with Team Canada in World Junior Championships (1982-83).

Season Team	League	REGULAR SEASON					PLAYOFFS				
		Gms.	G	A	Pts.	Pen.	Gms.	G	A	Pts.	Pen.
80-81—Oshawa	OMJHL	67	22	22	44	80	10	3	2	5	20
81-82—Oshawa	OHL	67	58	43	101	71	3	1	4	5	16
82-83—Oshawa	OHL	14	8	24	32	6	—	—	—	—	—
—Buffalo	NHL	43	14	23	37	16	4	1	0	1	4
83-84—Buffalo	NHL	78	38	42	80	42	2	0	1	1	2
84-85—Buffalo	NHL	64	31	30	61	54	5	4	2	6	4
85-86—Buffalo	NHL	80	36	51	87	61	—	—	—	—	—
86-87—Buffalo	NHL	77	25	48	73	46	—	—	—	—	—
87-88—Buffalo	NHL	80	30	48	78	112	6	2	4	6	0
88-89—Buffalo	NHL	56	28	24	52	40	5	0	3	3	0
89-90—Buffalo	NHL	73	40	42	82	42	6	2	5	7	2
90-91—Buffalo	NHL	80	36	33	69	32	6	2	2	4	8
91-92—Buffalo	NHL	80	41	50	91	71	7	1	3	4	12
92-93—Buffalo	NHL	52	29	32	61	48	—	—	—	—	—
—Toronto	NHL	31	25	13	38	8	21	12	7	19	35
NHL totals		794	373	436	809	572	62	24	27	51	67

ANDRIJEVSKI, ALEXANDER
RW, BLACKHAWKS

PERSONAL: Born August 10, 1968, at Minsk, U.S.S.R. . . . 6-5/211. . . . Shoots right. . . . Name pronounced ahn-dray-EHV-skee.
TRANSACTIONS/CAREER NOTES: Selected by Chicago Blackhawks in 10th round (13th Blackhawks pick, 220th overall) of NHL entry draft (June 22, 1991).

Season Team	League	REGULAR SEASON					PLAYOFFS				
		Gms.	G	A	Pts.	Pen.	Gms.	G	A	Pts.	Pen.
90-91—Dynamo Moscow	USSR	44	9	7	16	28	—	—	—	—	—
91-92—Dynamo Moscow	CIS	28	8	6	14	16	—	—	—	—	—
92-93—Indianapolis	IHL	66	26	25	51	59	4	2	3	5	10
—Chicago	NHL	1	0	0	0	0	—	—	—	—	—
NHL totals		1	0	0	0	0					

ANDRUSAK, GREG
D, PENGUINS

PERSONAL: Born November 14, 1969, at Cranbrook, B.C. . . . 6-1/195. . . . Shoots right. . . . Full name: Greg Frederick Andrusak.
COLLEGE: Minnesota-Duluth.
TRANSACTIONS/CAREER NOTES: Selected by Pittsburgh Penguins in fifth round (fifth Penguins pick, 88th overall) of NHL entry draft (June 11, 1988).
HONORS: Named to WCHA All-Star first team (1991-92).

Season Team	League	REGULAR SEASON					PLAYOFFS				
		Gms.	G	A	Pts.	Pen.	Gms.	G	A	Pts.	Pen.
86-87—Kelowna	BCJHL	45	10	24	34	95	—	—	—	—	—
87-88—Minnesota-Duluth	WCHA	37	4	5	9	42	—	—	—	—	—
88-89—Minnesota-Duluth	WCHA	35	4	8	12	74	—	—	—	—	—
—Canadian national team	Int'l	2	0	0	0	0	—	—	—	—	—
89-90—Minnesota-Duluth	WCHA	35	5	29	34	74	—	—	—	—	—
90-91—Canadian national team	Int'l	53	4	11	15	34	—	—	—	—	—
91-92—Minnesota-Duluth	WCHA	36	7	27	34	125	—	—	—	—	—
92-93—Cleveland	IHL	55	3	22	25	78	2	0	0	0	2
—Muskegon	Col.HL	2	0	3	3	7	—	—	—	—	—

ANGLEHART, SERGE

D, RED WINGS

PERSONAL: Born April 18, 1970, at Hull, Que. . . . 6-2/200. . . . Shoots right. . . . Name pronounced AN-guhl-HAHR.

TRANSACTIONS/CAREER NOTES: Selected by Detroit Red Wings as underage junior in second round (second Red Wings pick, 38th overall) of NHL entry draft (June 11, 1988). . . . Suspended one game by QMJHL for being aggressor in fight (March 26, 1989). . . . Traded by Drummondville Voltigeurs with LW Claude Boivin and fifth-round draft pick to Laval Titans for D Luc Doucet, D Brad MacIsaac and second- and third-round draft picks (February 15, 1990).

Season Team	League	REGULAR SEASON					PLAYOFFS				
		Gms.	G	A	Pts.	Pen.	Gms.	G	A	Pts.	Pen.
87-88—Drummondville	QMJHL	44	1	8	9	122	17	0	3	3	19
88-89—Drummondville	QMJHL	39	6	15	21	89	3	0	0	0	37
—Adirondack	AHL	—	—	—	—	—	2	0	0	0	0
89-90—Laval	QMJHL	48	2	19	21	131	10	1	6	7	69
90-91—Adirondack	AHL	52	3	8	11	113	—	—	—	—	—
91-92—Adirondack	AHL	16	0	1	1	43	—	—	—	—	—
92-93—Adirondack	AHL	3	0	0	0	4	—	—	—	—	—
—Fort Wayne	IHL	2	0	0	0	2	—	—	—	—	—

ANTOSKI, SHAWN

LW/RW, CANUCKS

PERSONAL: Born May 25, 1970, at Brantford, Ont. . . . 6-4/245. . . . Shoots left. . . . Name pronounced an-TAH-skee.

TRANSACTIONS/CAREER NOTES: Injured knee ligament (December 1988). . . . Separated shoulder (March 1989). . . . Selected by Vancouver Canucks in first round (second Canucks pick, 18th overall) of NHL entry draft (June 17, 1989). . . . Suffered sore back (December 1991).

Season Team	League	REGULAR SEASON					PLAYOFFS				
		Gms.	G	A	Pts.	Pen.	Gms.	G	A	Pts.	Pen.
87-88—North Bay	OHL	52	3	4	7	163	—	—	—	—	—
88-89—North Bay	OHL	57	6	21	27	201	9	5	3	8	24
89-90—North Bay	OHL	59	25	31	56	201	5	1	2	3	17
90-91—Milwaukee	IHL	62	17	7	24	330	5	1	2	3	10
—Vancouver	NHL	2	0	0	0	0	—	—	—	—	—
91-92—Milwaukee	IHL	52	17	16	33	346	5	2	0	2	20
—Vancouver	NHL	4	0	0	0	29	—	—	—	—	—
92-93—Hamilton	AHL	41	3	4	7	172	—	—	—	—	—
—Vancouver	NHL	2	0	0	0	0	—	—	—	—	—
NHL totals		8	0	0	0	29					

ARCHIBALD, DAVE

C/LW, SENATORS

PERSONAL: Born April 14, 1969, at Chilliwack, B.C. . . . 6-1/190. . . . Shoots left. . . . Full name: David John Archibald.

TRANSACTIONS/CAREER NOTES: Underwent shoulder surgery (January 1984). . . . Lacerated hand (October 1986). . . . Selected as underage junior by Minnesota North Stars in first round (first North Stars pick, sixth overall) of NHL entry draft (June 13, 1987). . . . Injured shoulder (September 1987). . . . Suffered sore back (February 1989). . . . Traded by North Stars to New York Rangers for D Jayson More (November 1, 1989). . . . Traded by Rangers to Ottawa Senators for fifth-round pick in 1993 draft (November 6, 1992). . . . Injured back (January 8, 1993); missed 26 games. . . . Injured groin (March 25, 1993); missed one game.

Season Team	League	REGULAR SEASON					PLAYOFFS				
		Gms.	G	A	Pts.	Pen.	Gms.	G	A	Pts.	Pen.
84-85—Portland	WHL	47	7	11	18	10	3	0	2	2	0
85-86—Portland	WHL	70	29	35	64	56	15	6	7	13	11
86-87—Portland	WHL	65	50	57	107	40	20	10	18	28	11
87-88—Minnesota	NHL	78	13	20	33	26	—	—	—	—	—
88-89—Minnesota	NHL	72	14	19	33	14	5	0	1	1	0
89-90—Minnesota	NHL	12	1	5	6	6	—	—	—	—	—
—New York Rangers	NHL	19	2	3	5	6	—	—	—	—	—
—Flint	IHL	41	14	38	52	16	4	3	2	5	0
90-91—Canadian national team	Int'l	29	19	12	31	20	—	—	—	—	—
91-92—Canadian national team	Int'l	58	20	43	63	62	—	—	—	—	—
—Canadian Olympic Team	Int'l	8	7	1	8	18	—	—	—	—	—
—Bolzano	Italy	12	12	12	24	16	—	—	—	—	—
92-93—Binghamton	AHL	8	6	3	9	10	—	—	—	—	—
—Ottawa	NHL	44	9	6	15	32	—	—	—	—	—
NHL totals		225	39	53	92	84	5	0	1	1	0

ARMSTRONG, BILL

D, FLYERS

PERSONAL: Born May 18, 1970, at Richmond Hill, Ont. . . . 6-5/220. . . . Shoots left.
TRANSACTIONS/CAREER NOTES: Selected by Philadelphia Flyers in third round (fifth Flyers pick, 46th overall) of NHL entry draft (June 16, 1990).

			REGULAR SEASON				PLAYOFFS				
Season Team	League	Gms.	G	A	Pts.	Pen.	Gms.	G	A	Pts.	Pen.
86-87—Barrie Jr. B	OHA	45	1	11	12	45	—	—	—	—	—
87-88—Toronto	OHL	64	1	10	11	99	—	—	—	—	—
88-89—Toronto	OHL	64	1	16	17	82	—	—	—	—	—
89-90—Dukes of Hamilton	OHL	18	0	2	2	38	—	—	—	—	—
—Niagara Falls	OHL	4	0	1	1	17	—	—	—	—	—
—Oshawa	OHL	41	2	8	10	115	17	0	7	7	39
90-91—Hershey	AHL	56	1	9	10	117	1	0	0	0	0
91-92—Hershey	AHL	†80	2	14	16	159	3	0	0	0	2
92-93—Hershey	AHL	80	2	10	12	205	—	—	—	—	—

ARMSTRONG, CHRIS

D, PANTHERS

PERSONAL: Born June 26, 1975, at Regina, Sask. . . . 6-0/184. . . . Shoots left.
HIGH SCHOOL: Vanier Collegiate (Moose Jaw, Sask.).
TRANSACTIONS/CAREER NOTES: Selected by Florida Panthers in third round (third Panthers pick, 57th overall) of NHL entry draft (June 26, 1993).

			REGULAR SEASON				PLAYOFFS				
Season Team	League	Gms.	G	A	Pts.	Pen.	Gms.	G	A	Pts.	Pen.
91-92—Moose Jaw	WHL	43	2	7	9	19	4	0	0	0	0
92-93—Moose Jaw	WHL	67	9	35	44	104	—	—	—	—	—

ARMSTRONG, DEREK

C, ISLANDERS

PERSONAL: Born April 23, 1973, at Ottawa. . . . 6-0/180. . . . Shoots right.
HIGH SCHOOL: Lo-Ellen Park Secondary School (Sudbury, Ont.).
TRANSACTIONS/CAREER NOTES: Selected by New York Islanders in sixth round (fifth Islanders pick, 128th overall) of NHL entry draft (June 20, 1992).

			REGULAR SEASON				PLAYOFFS				
Season Team	League	Gms.	G	A	Pts.	Pen.	Gms.	G	A	Pts.	Pen.
89-90—Hawkesbury	COJHL	48	8	10	18	30	—	—	—	—	—
90-91—Sudbury	OHL	2	0	2	2	0	—	—	—	—	—
—Hawkesbury	COJHL	54	27	45	72	49	—	—	—	—	—
91-92—Sudbury	OHL	66	31	54	85	22	9	2	2	4	2
92-93—Sudbury	OHL	66	44	62	106	56	14	9	10	19	26

ARNIEL, SCOTT

LW/C

PERSONAL: Born September 17, 1962, at Kingston, Ont. . . . 6-1/188. . . . Shoots left.
TRANSACTIONS/CAREER NOTES: Selected by Winnipeg Jets as underage junior in second round (second Jets pick, 22nd overall) of NHL entry draft (June 10, 1981). . . . Traded by Jets to Buffalo Sabres for LW Gilles Hamel (June 21, 1986). . . . Bruised abdominal muscle (March 1988). . . . Suffered concussion (April 9, 1990). . . . Traded by Sabres with D Phil Housley, RW Jeff Parker and first-round pick in 1990 draft (C Keith Tkachuk) to Jets for C Dale Hawerchuk, first-round pick in 1990 draft (LW Brad May) and future considerations (June 16, 1990); RW Greg Paslawski sent to Sabres to complete deal (February 5, 1991). . . . Traded by Jets to Boston Bruins for future considerations (November 22, 1991). . . . Strained shoulder (December 1, 1991); missed four games. . . . Fractured right thumb (January 1992). . . . Signed as free agent by San Diego Gulls (October 7, 1992).

			REGULAR SEASON				PLAYOFFS				
Season Team	League	Gms.	G	A	Pts.	Pen.	Gms.	G	A	Pts.	Pen.
79-80—Cornwall	QMJHL	61	22	28	50	51	—	—	—	—	—
80-81—Cornwall	QMJHL	68	52	71	123	102	19	14	19	33	24
81-82—Cornwall	OHL	24	18	26	44	43	—	—	—	—	—
—Winnipeg	NHL	17	1	8	9	14	3	0	0	0	0
82-83—Winnipeg	NHL	75	13	5	18	46	2	0	0	0	0
83-84—Winnipeg	NHL	80	21	35	56	68	2	0	0	0	5
84-85—Winnipeg	NHL	79	22	22	44	81	8	1	2	3	9
85-86—Winnipeg	NHL	80	18	25	43	40	3	0	0	0	12
86-87—Buffalo	NHL	63	11	14	25	59	—	—	—	—	—
87-88—Buffalo	NHL	73	17	23	40	61	6	0	1	1	5
88-89—Buffalo	NHL	80	18	23	41	46	5	1	0	1	4
89-90—Buffalo	NHL	79	18	14	32	77	5	1	0	1	4
90-91—Winnipeg	NHL	75	5	17	22	87	—	—	—	—	—
91-92—New Haven	AHL	11	3	3	6	10	—	—	—	—	—
—Boston	NHL	29	5	3	8	20	—	—	—	—	—
—Maine	AHL	14	4	4	8	8	—	—	—	—	—
92-93—San Diego	IHL	79	35	48	83	116	14	6	5	11	16
NHL totals		730	149	189	338	599	34	3	3	6	39

ARNOTT, JASON

C, OILERS

PERSONAL: Born October 11, 1974, at Collingworth, Ont. . . . 6-3/193. . . . Shoots right.
HIGH SCHOOL: Henry Street (Whitby, Ont.).
TRANSACTIONS/CAREER NOTES: Selected by Edmonton Oilers in first round (first Oilers pick, seventh overall) of NHL entry draft (June 26, 1993).

Season	Team	League	REGULAR SEASON Gms.	G	A	Pts.	Pen.	PLAYOFFS Gms.	G	A	Pts.	Pen.
90-91—Lindsay Jr. B		OHA	42	17	44	61	10	—	—	—	—	—
91-92—Oshawa		OHL	57	9	15	24	12	—	—	—	—	—
92-93—Oshawa		OHL	56	41	57	98	74	13	9	9	18	20

ASHTON, BRENT
LW/C, FLAMES

PERSONAL: Born May 18, 1960, at Saskatoon, Sask. . . . 6-1/200. . . . Shoots left. . . . Full name: Brent Kenneth Ashton.

TRANSACTIONS/CAREER NOTES: Selected by Vancouver Canucks as underage junior in second round (second Canucks pick, 26th overall) of NHL entry draft (August 9, 1979). . . . Injured knee ligament; missed parts of 1979-80 season. . . . Traded by Canucks with fourth-round pick in 1982 draft (LW Tom Martin) to Winnipeg Jets as compensation for Canucks signing of C Ivan Hlinka, a Czechoslovakian player drafted by Jets in a special draft on May 28, 1981 (July 15, 1981). . . . Traded by Jets with third-round pick in 1982 draft (C Dave Kasper) to Colorado Rockies for RW Lucien DeBlois (July 15, 1981). . . . Traded by New Jersey Devils to Minnesota North Stars for D Dave Lewis (October 3, 1983). . . . Traded by North Stars with D Brad Maxwell to Quebec Nordiques for LW Tony McKegney and RW Bo Berglund (December 14, 1984). . . . Injured hip (October 1985); missed three games. . . . Tore left knee ligaments (September 1986). . . . Traded by Nordiques with D Gilbert Delorme and RW Mark Kumpel to Detroit Red Wings for LW John Ogrodnick, C Doug Shedden and LW Basil McRae (January 17, 1987). . . . Traded by Red Wings to Jets for RW Paul MacLean (June 13, 1988). . . . Strained ligaments in right knee (March 15, 1989); missed two games. . . . Pulled groin (November 1, 1990); missed six games. . . . Broke nose and jaw (March 8, 1991). . . . Traded by Jets to Boston Bruins for RW Petri Skriko (October 29, 1991). . . . Underwent knee surgery (April 9, 1992). . . . Underwent arthroscopic knee surgery (September 28, 1992); missed first five games of season. . . . Traded by Bruins to Calgary Flames for RW C.J. Young (February 1, 1993).

Season	Team	League	REGULAR SEASON Gms.	G	A	Pts.	Pen.	PLAYOFFS Gms.	G	A	Pts.	Pen.
75-76—Saskatoon		WCHL	11	3	4	7	11	—	—	—	—	—
76-77—Saskatoon		WCHL	54	26	25	51	84	—	—	—	—	—
77-78—Saskatoon		WCHL	46	38	28	66	47	—	—	—	—	—
78-79—Saskatoon		WHL	62	64	55	119	80	11	14	4	18	5
79-80—Vancouver		NHL	47	5	14	19	11	4	1	0	1	6
80-81—Vancouver		NHL	77	18	11	29	57	3	0	0	0	0
81-82—Colorado		NHL	80	24	36	60	26	—	—	—	—	—
82-83—New Jersey		NHL	76	14	19	33	47	—	—	—	—	—
83-84—Minnesota		NHL	68	7	10	17	54	12	1	2	3	22
84-85—Minnesota		NHL	29	4	7	11	15	—	—	—	—	—
—Quebec		NHL	49	27	24	51	13	18	6	4	10	13
85-86—Quebec		NHL	77	26	32	58	64	3	2	1	3	9
86-87—Quebec		NHL	46	25	19	44	17	—	—	—	—	—
—Detroit		NHL	35	15	16	31	22	16	4	9	13	6
87-88—Detroit		NHL	73	26	27	53	50	16	7	5	12	10
88-89—Winnipeg		NHL	75	31	37	68	36	—	—	—	—	—
89-90—Winnipeg		NHL	79	22	34	56	37	7	3	1	4	2
90-91—Winnipeg		NHL	61	12	24	36	58	—	—	—	—	—
91-92—Winnipeg		NHL	7	1	0	1	4	—	—	—	—	—
—Boston		NHL	61	17	22	39	47	—	—	—	—	—
92-93—Boston		NHL	26	2	2	4	11	—	—	—	—	—
—Providence		AHL	11	4	8	12	10	—	—	—	—	—
—Calgary		NHL	32	8	11	19	41	6	0	3	3	2
NHL totals			998	284	345	629	635	85	24	25	49	70

ATCHEYNUM, BLAIR
RW, SENATORS

PERSONAL: Born April 20, 1969, at Estevan, Sask. . . . 6-2/190. . . . Shoots right. . . . Name pronounced ATCH-uh-num.

TRANSACTIONS/CAREER NOTES: Selected by Swift Current Broncos in special compensation draft to replace players injured and killed in a December 30, 1986 bus crash (February 1987). . . . Traded by Broncos to Moose Jaw Warriors for D Tim Logan (February 1987). . . . Selected by Hartford Whalers in third round (second Whalers pick, 52nd overall) of NHL entry draft (June 17, 1989). . . . Suffered concussion (January 12, 1991). . . . Selected by Ottawa Senators in NHL expansion draft (June 18, 1992).

HONORS: Won Brad Hornung Trophy (1988-89). . . . Named to WHL (East) All-Star first team (1988-89).

Season	Team	League	REGULAR SEASON Gms.	G	A	Pts.	Pen.	PLAYOFFS Gms.	G	A	Pts.	Pen.
85-86—North Battleford		SJHL	35	25	20	45	50	—	—	—	—	—
86-87—Saskatoon		WHL	21	0	4	4	4	—	—	—	—	—
—Swift Current		WHL	5	2	1	3	0	—	—	—	—	—
—Moose Jaw		WHL	12	3	0	3	2	—	—	—	—	—
87-88—Moose Jaw		WHL	60	32	16	48	52	—	—	—	—	—
88-89—Moose Jaw		WHL	71	70	68	138	70	7	2	5	7	13
89-90—Binghamton		AHL	78	20	21	41	45	—	—	—	—	—
90-91—Springfield		AHL	72	25	27	52	42	13	0	6	6	6
91-92—Springfield		AHL	62	16	21	37	64	6	1	1	2	2
92-93—New Haven		AHL	51	16	18	34	47	—	—	—	—	—
—Ottawa		NHL	4	0	1	1	0	—	—	—	—	—
NHL totals			4	0	1	1	0					

AUCOIN, ADRIAN
D, CANUCKS

PERSONAL: Born July 3, 1973, at London, Ont. . . . 6-1/194. . . . Shoots right.
COLLEGE: Boston University.
TRANSACTIONS/CAREER NOTES: Selected by Vancouver Canucks in fifth round (seventh Canucks pick, 117th overall) of NHL entry draft (June 20, 1992).

Season Team	League	REGULAR SEASON Gms.	G	A	Pts.	Pen.	PLAYOFFS Gms.	G	A	Pts.	Pen.
91-92—Boston University	Hockey East	33	2	10	12	62	—	—	—	—	—
92-93—Canadian national team ...	Int'l	42	8	10	18	71	—	—	—	—	—

AUDETTE, DONALD
RW, SABRES

PERSONAL: Born September 23, 1969, at Laval, Que.... 5-8/175.... Shoots right.... Name pronounced aw-DEHT.

TRANSACTIONS/CAREER NOTES: Selected by Buffalo Sabres in ninth round (eighth Sabres pick, 183rd overall) of NHL entry draft (June 17, 1989).... Broke left hand (February 11, 1990); missed seven games.... Bruised thigh (September 1990).... Bruised thigh (October 1990); missed five games.... Tore left knee ligaments (November 16, 1990).... Underwent surgery to left knee (December 10, 1990).... Sprained ankle (December 14, 1991); missed eight games.... Injured knee (March 31, 1992).... Underwent knee surgery prior to 1992-93 season; missed first 22 games of season.

HONORS: Won Guy Lafleur Trophy (1988-89).... Named to QMJHL All-Star first team (1988-89).... Won Dudley (Red) Garrett Memorial Trophy (1989-90).... Named to AHL All-Star first team (1989-90).

Season Team	League	REGULAR SEASON Gms.	G	A	Pts.	Pen.	PLAYOFFS Gms.	G	A	Pts.	Pen.
86-87—Laval	QMJHL	66	17	22	39	36	14	2	6	8	10
87-88—Laval	QMJHL	63	48	61	109	56	14	7	12	19	20
88-89—Laval	QMJHL	70	76	85	161	123	17	*17	12	29	43
89-90—Rochester	AHL	70	42	46	88	78	15	9	8	17	29
—Buffalo	NHL	—	—	—	—	—	2	0	0	0	0
90-91—Rochester	AHL	5	4	0	4	2	—	—	—	—	—
—Buffalo	NHL	8	4	3	7	4	—	—	—	—	—
91-92—Buffalo	NHL	63	31	17	48	75	—	—	—	—	—
92-93—Buffalo	NHL	44	12	7	19	51	8	2	2	4	6
—Rochester	AHL	6	8	4	12	10	—	—	—	—	—
NHL totals.................		115	47	27	74	130	10	2	2	4	6

AUGUSTA, PATRIK
RW, MAPLE LEAFS

PERSONAL: Born November 13, 1969, at Jihlava, Czech.... 5-10/169.... Shoots left.

TRANSACTIONS/CAREER NOTES: Selected by Toronto Maple Leafs in seventh round (eighth Maple Leafs pick, 149th overall) of NHL entry draft (June 20, 1992).

Season Team	League	REGULAR SEASON Gms.	G	A	Pts.	Pen.	PLAYOFFS Gms.	G	A	Pts.	Pen.
89-90—Dukla Jihlava	Czech.	46	12	12	24	...	—	—	—	—	—
90-91—Dukla Jihlava	Czech.	49	20	22	42	18	—	—	—	—	—
91-92—Dukla Jihlava	Czech.	34	15	11	26	...	—	—	—	—	—
—Czech. Olympic Team	Int'l	8	3	2	5	...	—	—	—	—	—
92-93—St. John's	AHL	75	32	45	77	74	8	3	3	6	23

BABCOCK, BOB
D, CAPITALS

PERSONAL: Born August 3, 1968, at Agincourt, Ont.... 6-1/220.... Shoots left.... Full name: Bob Frank Babcock.

TRANSACTIONS/CAREER NOTES: Selected by Washington Capitals as underage junior in 10th round (11th Capitals pick, 208th overall) of NHL entry draft (June 21, 1986).... Suspended 10 games by AHL for fighting (December 10, 1989).

Season Team	League	REGULAR SEASON Gms.	G	A	Pts.	Pen.	PLAYOFFS Gms.	G	A	Pts.	Pen.
85-86—Sault Ste. Marie	OHL	50	1	7	8	185	—	—	—	—	—
86-87—Sault Ste. Marie	OHL	62	7	8	15	243	4	0	0	0	11
87-88—Sault Ste. Marie	OHL	8	0	2	2	30	—	—	—	—	—
—Cornwall	OHL	42	0	16	16	120	—	—	—	—	—
88-89—Cornwall	OHL	42	0	9	9	163	18	1	3	4	29
89-90—Baltimore	AHL	67	0	4	4	249	6	0	0	0	23
90-91—Washington	NHL	1	0	0	0	0	—	—	—	—	—
—Baltimore	AHL	38	0	3	3	112	—	—	—	—	—
91-92—Baltimore	AHL	26	0	2	2	55	—	—	—	—	—
92-93—Baltimore	AHL	26	0	2	2	93	—	—	—	—	—
—Washington	NHL	1	0	0	0	2	—	—	—	—	—
—Hampton Roads	ECHL	26	3	13	16	96	1	0	0	0	10
NHL totals.........................		2	0	0	0	2					

BABYCH, DAVE
D, CANUCKS

PERSONAL: Born May 23, 1961, at Edmonton, Alta.... 6-2/215.... Shoots left.... Full name: David Michael Babych.... Name pronounced BA-bihch.... Brother of Wayne Babych, right winger for four NHL teams (1978-79 to 1986-87).

TRANSACTIONS/CAREER NOTES: Selected by Winnipeg Jets as underage junior in first round (first Jets pick, second overall) of NHL entry draft (June 11, 1980).... Separated shoulder (March 1984).... Suffered back spasms (December 1984).... Traded by Jets to Hartford Whalers for RW Ray Neufeld (November 21, 1985).... Injured hip (January 1987); missed 12 games.... Lacerated right hand (March 16, 1989); missed six games.... Bruised neck (March 1990).... Underwent surgery to right wrist (October 29, 1990); missed 44 games.... Broke right thumb (February 8, 1991); missed remainder of the season.... Selected by Minnesota North Stars in NHL expansion draft (May 30, 1991).... Traded by North Stars to Vancouver Canucks for D Craig Ludwig as part of a three-club deal in which Canucks sent D Tom Kurvers to Islanders for Ludwig (June 22, 1991).... Suffered sore back (November 3, 1991); missed one game.... Suffered hernia (September 22, 1992); missed 22 games.... Sprained knee (December 7, 1992); missed 12 games.... Suffered from the flu (March

20, 1993); missed one game. . . . Suffered facial lacerations (April 4, 1993); missed three games.
HONORS: Won AJHL Top Defenseman Trophy (1977-78). . . . Won AJHL Rookie of the Year Trophy (1977-78). . . . Named to AJHL All-Star first team (1977-78). . . . Won Top Defenseman Trophy (1979-80). . . . Named to WHL All-Star first team (1979-80). . . . Played in NHL All-Star Game (1983 and 1984).

			REGULAR SEASON					PLAYOFFS				
Season Team	League	Gms.	G	A	Pts.	Pen.	Gms.	G	A	Pts.	Pen.
77-78—Portland	WCHL	6	1	3	4	4	—	—	—	—	—
—Fort Saskatchewan	AJHL	56	31	69	100	37	—	—	—	—	—
78-79—Portland	WHL	67	20	59	79	63	25	7	22	29	22
79-80—Portland	WHL	50	22	60	82	71	8	1	10	11	2
80-81—Winnipeg	NHL	69	6	38	44	90	—	—	—	—	—
81-82—Winnipeg	NHL	79	19	49	68	92	4	1	2	3	29
82-83—Winnipeg	NHL	79	13	61	74	56	3	0	0	0	0
83-84—Winnipeg	NHL	66	18	39	57	62	3	1	1	2	0
84-85—Winnipeg	NHL	78	13	49	62	78	8	2	7	9	6
85-86—Winnipeg	NHL	19	4	12	16	14	—	—	—	—	—
—Hartford	NHL	62	10	43	53	36	8	1	3	4	14
86-87—Hartford	NHL	66	8	33	41	44	6	1	1	2	14
87-88—Hartford	NHL	71	14	36	50	54	6	3	2	5	2
88-89—Hartford	NHL	70	6	41	47	54	4	1	5	6	2
89-90—Hartford	NHL	72	6	37	43	62	7	1	2	3	0
90-91—Hartford	NHL	8	0	6	6	4	—	—	—	—	—
91-92—Vancouver	NHL	75	5	24	29	63	13	2	6	8	10
92-93—Vancouver	NHL	43	3	16	19	44	12	2	5	7	6
NHL totals		857	125	484	609	753	74	15	34	49	83

BACA, JERGUS
D, WHALERS

PERSONAL: Born April 1, 1965, at Liptovsky Mikulas, Czech. . . . 6-2/215. . . . Shoots left.
TRANSACTIONS/CAREER NOTES: Selected by Hartford Whalers in seventh round (sixth Whalers pick, 141st overall) of NHL entry draft (June 16, 1990). . . . Bruised shoulder (October 1990).
HONORS: Named Czechoslovakian League Rookie of the Year (1987-88). . . . Named to Czechoslovakian League All-Star team (1988-89 and 1989-90).

			REGULAR SEASON					PLAYOFFS				
Season Team	League	Gms.	G	A	Pts.	Pen.	Gms.	G	A	Pts.	Pen.
89-90—Kosice	Czech.	47	9	16	25	...	—	—	—	—	—
90-91—Hartford	NHL	9	0	2	2	14	—	—	—	—	—
—Springfield	AHL	57	6	23	29	89	18	3	13	16	18
91-92—Springfield	AHL	64	6	20	26	88	11	0	6	6	20
—Hartford	NHL	1	0	0	0	0	—	—	—	—	—
92-93—Milwaukee	IHL	73	9	29	38	108	6	0	3	3	2
NHL totals		10	0	2	2	14					

BAILEY, SCOTT
G, BRUINS

PERSONAL: Born May 2, 1972, at Calgary, Alta. . . . 5-11/185. . . . Shoots left.
TRANSACTIONS/CAREER NOTES: Selected by Boston Bruins in fifth round (Bruins third pick, 112th overall) of NHL entry draft (June 20, 1992).
HONORS: Won WHL (West) Rookie of the Year Award (1990-91). . . . Named to WHL (West) All-Star second team (1990-91 and 1991-92).

			REGULAR SEASON							PLAYOFFS					
Season Team	League	Gms.	Min.	W	L	T	GA	SO	Avg.	Gms.	Min.	W	L	GA	SO	Avg.
88-89—Moose Jaw	WHL	2	34	...	...	...	7	0	12.35	—	—	—	—	—	—	—
89-90—Calgary Flames	AMHL	17	991	...	...	...	55	1	3.33	—	—	—	—	—	—	—
90-91—Spokane Chiefs	WHL	46	2537	33	11	0	157	4	3.71	—	—	—	—	—	—	—
91-92—Spokane Chiefs	WHL	65	3748	34	23	5	206	1	3.30	10	605	5	5	43	0	4.26
92-93—Johnstown	ECHL	36	1750	...	...	...	112	1	3.84	—	—	—	—	—	—	—

BAKER, JAMIE
C, SENATORS

PERSONAL: Born August 31, 1966, at Nepean, Que. . . . 6-0/190. . . . Shoots left. . . . Full name: James Paul Baker.
HIGH SCHOOL: J.S. Woodsworth (Nepean, Ont.).
COLLEGE: St. Lawrence (N.Y.).
TRANSACTIONS/CAREER NOTES: Selected by Quebec Nordiques in NHL supplemental draft (June 10, 1988). . . . Broke left ankle (December 30, 1988). . . . Sprained ankle (January 9, 1992); missed two games. . . . Signed as free agent by Ottawa Senators (September 2, 1992). . . . Sprained ankle (December 15, 1992); missed six games. . . . Bruised foot (February 22, 1993); missed one game.

			REGULAR SEASON					PLAYOFFS				
Season Team	League	Gms.	G	A	Pts.	Pen.	Gms.	G	A	Pts.	Pen.
85-86—St. Lawrence University	ECAC	31	9	16	25	52	—	—	—	—	—
86-87—St. Lawrence University	ECAC	32	8	24	32	59	—	—	—	—	—
87-88—St. Lawrence University	ECAC	38	26	28	54	44	—	—	—	—	—
88-89—St. Lawrence University	ECAC	13	11	16	27	16	—	—	—	—	—
89-90—Quebec	NHL	1	0	0	0	0	—	—	—	—	—
—Halifax	AHL	74	17	43	60	47	6	0	0	0	7
90-91—Quebec	NHL	18	2	0	2	8	—	—	—	—	—
—Halifax	AHL	50	14	22	36	85	—	—	—	—	—

Season	Team	League	REGULAR SEASON					PLAYOFFS				
			Gms.	G	A	Pts.	Pen.	Gms.	G	A	Pts.	Pen.
91-92—Halifax	AHL	9	5	0	5	12	—	—	—	—	—
—Quebec	NHL	52	7	10	17	32	—	—	—	—	—
92-93—Ottawa	NHL	76	19	29	48	54	—	—	—	—	—
NHL totals		147	28	39	67	94	—	—	—	—	—

BALES, MIKE
G, BRUINS

PERSONAL: Born August 6, 1971, at Saskatoon, Sask. . . . 6-1/180. . . . Shoots left. . . . Full name: Michael Raymond Bales.
COLLEGE: Ohio State.
TRANSACTIONS/CAREER NOTES: Selected by Boston Bruins in fifth round (fourth Bruins pick, 105th overall) of NHL entry draft (June 16, 1990).

Season	Team	League	REGULAR SEASON							PLAYOFFS						
			Gms.	Min.	W	L	T	GA	SO	Avg.	Gms.	Min.	W	L	GA SO	Avg.
88-89—Estevan	SJHL	44	2412	...	...	...	197	1	4.90	—	—	—	—	— —	—
89-90—Ohio State	CCHA	21	1117	6	13	2	95	0	5.10	—	—	—	—	— —	—
90-91—Ohio State	CCHA	*39	*2180	11	24	3	*184	0	5.06	—	—	—	—	— —	—
91-92—Ohio State	CCHA	36	2061	11	20	5	*180	...	5.24	—	—	—	—	— —	—
92-93—Providence	AHL	44	2363	22	17	0	166	1	4.21	2	118	0	2	8 0	4.07
—Boston	NHL	1	25	0	0	0	1	0	2.40	—	—	—	—	— —	—
NHL totals		1	25	0	0	0	1	0	2.40	—	—	—	—	— —	—

BANCROFT, STEVE
D, PANTHERS

PERSONAL: Born October 6, 1970, at Toronto. . . . 6-1/214. . . . Shoots left.
TRANSACTIONS/CAREER NOTES: Underwent surgery to left shoulder (April 1989). . . . Selected by Toronto Maple Leafs in first round (third Maple Leafs pick, 21st overall) of NHL entry draft (June 17, 1989). . . . Traded by Maple Leafs to Boston Bruins for LW Rob Cimetta (November 9, 1990). . . . Traded by Bruins with 11th-round pick in 1993 draft to Chicago Blackhawks for 11th-round pick in 1992 draft (Eugene Pavlov) and 12th-round pick in 1993 draft (January 8, 1992). . . . Traded by Blackhawks with unspecified pick in 1993 draft to Winnipeg Jets for C Troy Murray (February 21, 1993); Jets later received 11th-round pick in 1993 draft (LW Russell Hewson) to complete deal. . . . Selected by Florida Panthers in NHL expansion draft (June 24, 1993).

Season	Team	League	REGULAR SEASON					PLAYOFFS				
			Gms.	G	A	Pts.	Pen.	Gms.	G	A	Pts.	Pen.
86-87—St. Catharines Jr. B	OHA	11	5	8	13	20	—	—	—	—	—
87-88—Belleville	OHL	56	1	8	9	42	—	—	—	—	—
88-89—Belleville	OHL	66	7	30	37	99	5	0	2	2	10
89-90—Belleville	OHL	53	10	33	43	135	11	3	9	12	38
90-91—Newmarket	AHL	9	0	3	3	22	—	—	—	—	—
—Maine	AHL	53	2	12	14	46	2	0	0	0	2
91-92—Maine	AHL	26	1	3	4	45	—	—	—	—	—
—Indianapolis	IHL	36	8	23	31	49	—	—	—	—	—
92-93—Indianapolis	IHL	53	10	35	45	138	—	—	—	—	—
—Chicago	NHL	1	0	0	0	0	—	—	—	—	—
—Moncton	AHL	21	3	13	16	16	5	0	0	0	16
NHL totals		1	0	0	0	0	—	—	—	—	—

BANHAM, FRANK
RW, CAPITALS

PERSONAL: Born April 14, 1975, at Calahoo, Alta. . . . 5-11/175. . . . Shoots right.
TRANSACTIONS/CAREER NOTES: Selected by Washington Capitals in sixth round (fourth Capitals pick, 147th overall) of NHL entry draft (June 26, 1993).

Season	Team	League	REGULAR SEASON					PLAYOFFS				
			Gms.	G	A	Pts.	Pen.	Gms.	G	A	Pts.	Pen.
91-92—Saskatoon	WHL	71	29	33	62	55	9	2	7	9	8
92-93—Saskatoon	WHL	71	29	33	62	55	9	2	7	9	8

BANKS, DARREN
LW, BRUINS

PERSONAL: Born March 18, 1966, at Toronto. . . . 6-2/215. . . . Shoots left. . . . Full name: Darren Alexander Banks.
COLLEGE: Brock University.
TRANSACTIONS/CAREER NOTES: Signed as free agent by Calgary Flames (December 12, 1990). . . . Signed as free agent by Boston Bruins (July 23, 1992).

Season	Team	League	REGULAR SEASON					PLAYOFFS				
			Gms.	G	A	Pts.	Pen.	Gms.	G	A	Pts.	Pen.
86-87—Brock University	OUAA	24	5	3	8	82	—	—	—	—	—
87-88—Brock University	OUAA	26	10	11	21	110	—	—	—	—	—
88-89—Brock University	OUAA	26	19	14	33	88	—	—	—	—	—
89-90—Salt Lake City	IHL	6	0	0	0	11	1	0	0	0	10
—Fort Wayne	IHL	2	0	1	1	0	—	—	—	—	—
—Knoxville	ECHL	52	25	22	47	258	—	—	—	—	—
90-91—Salt Lake City	IHL	56	9	7	16	286	3	0	1	1	6
91-92—Salt Lake City	IHL	55	5	5	10	303	—	—	—	—	—
92-93—Providence	AHL	43	9	5	14	199	1	0	0	0	0
—Boston	NHL	16	2	1	3	64	—	—	—	—	—
NHL totals		16	2	1	3	64	—	—	—	—	—

BANNISTER, DREW
D, LIGHTNING

PERSONAL: Born September 4, 1974, at Belleville, Ont. . . . 6-1/193. . . . Shoots right.
HIGH SCHOOL: Bawating Collegiate School (Sault Ste. Marie, Ont.).
TRANSACTIONS/CAREER NOTES: Selected by Tampa Bay Lightning in second round (second Lightning pick, 26th overall) of NHL entry draft (June 20, 1992).

HONORS: Named to Memorial Cup All-Star team (1991-92).

Season Team	League	Gms.	G	A	Pts.	Pen.	Gms.	G	A	Pts.	Pen.
		REGULAR SEASON					PLAYOFFS				
90-91—Sault Ste. Marie	OHL	41	2	8	10	51	4	0	0	0	0
91-92—Sault Ste. Marie	OHL	64	4	21	25	122	16	3	10	13	36
92-93—Sault Ste. Marie	OHL	59	5	28	33	114	18	2	7	9	12

BARNABY, MATTHEW
LW/RW, SABRES

PERSONAL: Born May 4, 1973, at Ottawa. . . . 6-0/170. . . . Shoots right.
TRANSACTIONS/CAREER NOTES: Selected by Buffalo Sabres in fourth round (fifth Sabres pick, 83rd overall) of NHL entry draft (June 20, 1992).

Season Team	League	Gms.	G	A	Pts.	Pen.	Gms.	G	A	Pts.	Pen.
		REGULAR SEASON					PLAYOFFS				
90-91—Beauport	QMJHL	52	9	5	14	262	—	—	—	—	—
91-92—Beauport	QMJHL	63	29	37	66	*476	—	—	—	—	—
92-93—Victoriaville	QMJHL	65	44	67	111	*448	6	2	4	6	44
—Buffalo	NHL	2	1	0	1	10	1	0	1	1	4
NHL totals		2	1	0	1	10	1	0	1	1	4

BARNES, STU
C, JETS

PERSONAL: Born December 25, 1970, at Edmonton, Alta. . . . 5-10/175. . . . Shoots right.
TRANSACTIONS/CAREER NOTES: Selected by Winnipeg Jets in first round (first Jets pick, fourth overall) of NHL entry draft (June 17, 1989).
HONORS: Won Jim Piggott Memorial Trophy (1987-88). . . . Named to WHL All-Star second team (1987-88). . . . Won Four Broncos Memorial Trophy (1988-89). . . . Named to WHL All-Star first team (1988-89).

Season Team	League	Gms.	G	A	Pts.	Pen.	Gms.	G	A	Pts.	Pen.
		REGULAR SEASON					PLAYOFFS				
86-87—St. Albert	AJHL	57	43	32	75	80	—	—	—	—	—
87-88—New Westminster	WHL	71	37	64	101	88	5	2	3	5	6
88-89—Tri-City	WHL	70	59	82	141	117	7	6	5	11	10
89-90—Tri-City	WHL	63	52	92	144	165	7	1	5	6	26
90-91—Canadian national team	Int'l	53	22	27	49	68	—	—	—	—	—
91-92—Winnipeg	NHL	46	8	9	17	26	—	—	—	—	—
—Moncton	AHL	30	13	19	32	10	11	3	9	12	6
92-93—Moncton	AHL	42	23	31	54	58	—	—	—	—	—
—Winnipeg	NHL	38	12	10	22	10	6	1	3	4	2
NHL totals		84	20	19	39	36	6	1	3	4	2

BARON, MURRAY
D, BLUES

PERSONAL: Born June 1, 1967, at Prince George, B.C. . . . 6-3/215. . . . Shoots left.
HIGH SCHOOL: Kamloops (B.C.).
COLLEGE: North Dakota.
TRANSACTIONS/CAREER NOTES: Selected by Philadelphia Flyers as underage player in eighth round (seventh Flyers pick, 167th overall) of NHL entry draft (June 21, 1986). . . . Separated left shoulder (October 5, 1989). . . . Underwent surgery to have bone spur removed from foot (April 1990). . . . Traded by Flyers with C Ron Sutter to St. Louis Blues for C Rod Brind'Amour and C Dan Quinn (September 22, 1991). . . . Injured shoulder (December 3, 1991); missed seven games. . . . Broke foot (March 22, 1993); missed remainder of regular season.

Season Team	League	Gms.	G	A	Pts.	Pen.	Gms.	G	A	Pts.	Pen.
		REGULAR SEASON					PLAYOFFS				
84-85—Vernon	BCJHL	37	5	9	14	93	—	—	—	—	—
85-86—Vernon	BCJHL	49	15	32	47	176	7	1	2	3	13
86-87—Univ. of North Dakota	WCHA	41	4	10	14	62	—	—	—	—	—
87-88—Univ. of North Dakota	WCHA	41	1	10	11	95	—	—	—	—	—
88-89—Univ. of North Dakota	WCHA	40	2	6	8	92	—	—	—	—	—
—Hershey	AHL	9	0	3	3	8	—	—	—	—	—
89-90—Hershey	AHL	50	0	10	10	101	—	—	—	—	—
—Philadelphia	NHL	16	2	2	4	12	—	—	—	—	—
90-91—Hershey	AHL	6	2	3	5	0	—	—	—	—	—
—Philadelphia	NHL	67	8	8	16	74	—	—	—	—	—
91-92—St. Louis	NHL	67	3	8	11	94	2	0	0	0	2
92-93—St. Louis	NHL	53	2	2	4	59	11	0	0	0	12
NHL totals		203	15	20	35	239	13	0	0	0	14

BARR, DAVE
RW, DEVILS

PERSONAL: Born November 30, 1960, at Edmonton, Alta. . . . 6-1/195. . . . Shoots right. . . . Full name: David Angus Barr.
TRANSACTIONS/CAREER NOTES: Signed as free agent by Boston Bruins (September 28, 1981). . . . Traded by Bruins to New York Rangers for C/RW Dave Silk (October 5, 1983). . . . Traded by Rangers with third-round pick in 1984 draft (G Alan Perry) and cash to St. Louis Blues for C Larry Patey and rights to RW Bob Brooke (March 5, 1984). . . . Sprained knee (March 19, 1986). . . . Traded by Blues to Hartford Whalers for D Tim Bothwell (October 21, 1986). . . . Traded by Whalers to Detroit Red Wings for D Randy Ladouceur (January 12, 1987). . . . Separated right shoulder (November 1987). . . . Broke right foot (December 1987). . . . Broke right ankle (March 14, 1991). . . . Sent to New Jersey Devils with RW Randy McKay as compensation for Red Wings signing free agent RW Troy Crowder (September 9,

1991).... Separated left shoulder (September 21, 1991); missed first nine games of season.... Lacerated tendon and artery in wrist (February 21, 1992); missed final 21 games of season.... Suffered from the flu (January 9, 1993); missed three games. ...Suffered sore foot (March 29, 1993); missed two games.

			REGULAR SEASON					PLAYOFFS				
Season	Team	League	Gms.	G	A	Pts.	Pen.	Gms.	G	A	Pts.	Pen.
77-78	Pincher Creek	AJHL	60	16	32	48	53	—	—	—	—	—
78-79	Edmonton	WHL	72	16	19	35	61	—	—	—	—	—
79-80	Lethbridge	WHL	60	16	38	54	47	—	—	—	—	—
80-81	Lethbridge	WHL	72	26	62	88	106	10	4	10	14	4
81-82	Erie	AHL	76	18	48	66	29	—	—	—	—	—
	Boston	NHL	2	0	0	0	0	5	1	0	1	0
82-83	Baltimore	AHL	72	27	51	78	67	—	—	—	—	—
	Boston	NHL	10	1	1	2	7	10	0	0	0	2
83-84	New York Rangers	NHL	6	0	0	0	2	—	—	—	—	—
	Tulsa	CHL	50	28	37	65	24	—	—	—	—	—
	St. Louis	NHL	1	0	0	0	0	5	0	1	1	15
84-85	St. Louis	NHL	75	16	18	34	32	2	0	0	0	2
85-86	St. Louis	NHL	75	13	38	51	70	11	1	1	2	14
86-87	St. Louis	NHL	2	0	0	0	0	—	—	—	—	—
	Hartford	NHL	30	2	4	6	19	—	—	—	—	—
	Detroit	NHL	37	13	13	26	49	13	1	0	1	14
87-88	Detroit	NHL	51	14	26	40	58	16	5	7	12	22
88-89	Detroit	NHL	73	27	32	59	69	6	3	1	4	6
89-90	Detroit	NHL	62	10	25	35	45	—	—	—	—	—
	Adirondack	AHL	9	1	14	15	17	—	—	—	—	—
90-91	Detroit	NHL	70	18	22	40	55	—	—	—	—	—
91-92	New Jersey	NHL	41	6	12	18	32	—	—	—	—	—
	Utica	AHL	1	0	0	0	7	—	—	—	—	—
92-93	New Jersey	NHL	62	6	8	14	61	5	1	0	1	6
	NHL totals		597	126	199	325	499	73	12	10	22	81

BARRASSO, TOM

G, PENGUINS

PERSONAL: Born March 31, 1965, at Boston.... 6-3/211.... Shoots right.... Name pronounced buh-RAH-soh.

HIGH SCHOOL: Acton-Boxborough (Mass.).

TRANSACTIONS/CAREER NOTES: Selected by Buffalo Sabres in first round (first Sabres pick, fifth overall) of NHL entry draft (June 8, 1983).... Suffered chip fracture of ankle (November 1987).... Pulled groin (April 9, 1988).... Traded by Sabres with third-round pick in 1990 draft to Pittsburgh Penguins for D Doug Bodger and LW Darrin Shannon (November 12, 1988).... Pulled groin muscle (Janurary 17, 1989).... Injured shoulder (March 1989).... Underwent surgery to right wrist (October 30, 1989); missed 21 games.... Pulled groin (February 1990).... Granted leave of absence to be with daughter as she underwent cancer treatment in Los Angeles (February 9, 1990).... Rejoined the Penguins (March 19, 1990).... Bruised right hand (October 29, 1991); missed two games.... Bruised right ankle (December 26, 1991); missed three games.... Suffered back spasms (March 1992); missed three games.... Suffered from chicken pox (January 14, 1993); missed nine games.

HONORS: Won Vezina Trophy (1983-84).... Won Calder Memorial Trophy (1983-84).... Named to THE SPORTING NEWS All-Star second team (1983-84, 1984-85 and 1987-88).... Named to NHL All-Star first team (1983-84).... Named to NHL All-Rookie team (1983-84).... Shared William M. Jennings Trophy with Bob Sauve (1984-85).... Named to NHL All-Star second team (1984-85 and 1992-93).... Played in NHL All-Star Game (1985).... Named to THE SPORTING NEWS All-Star first team (1992-93).

RECORDS: Shares NHL single-season playoff record for most wins by a goaltender—16 (1991-92).

MISCELLANEOUS: Member of U.S. National Junior Team (1983).... Member of Stanley Cup championship teams (1991 and 1992).

			REGULAR SEASON							PLAYOFFS						
Season	Team	League	Gms.	Min.	W	L	T	GA	SO	Avg.	Gms.	Min.	W	L	GA	SO	Avg.
81-82	Acton-Boxborough HS	Mass. HS	23	1035	...	...	...	32	7	1.86	—	—	—	—	—	—	—
82-83	Acton-Boxborough HS	Mass. HS	23	1035	...	...	...	17	10	0.99	—	—	—	—	—	—	—
83-84	Buffalo	NHL	42	2475	26	12	3	117	2	2.84	3	139	0	2	8	0	3.45
84-85	Rochester	AHL	5	267	3	1	1	6	1	1.35	—	—	—	—	—	—	—
	Buffalo	NHL	54	3248	25	18	10	144	*5	*2.66	5	300	2	3	22	0	4.40
85-86	Buffalo	NHL	60	*3561	29	24	5	214	2	3.61	—	—	—	—	—	—	—
86-87	Buffalo	NHL	46	2501	17	23	2	152	2	3.65	—	—	—	—	—	—	—
87-88	Buffalo	NHL	54	3133	25	18	8	173	2	3.31	4	224	1	3	16	0	4.29
88-89	Buffalo	NHL	10	545	2	7	0	45	0	4.95	—	—	—	—	—	—	—
	Pittsburgh	NHL	44	2406	18	15	7	162	0	4.04	11	631	7	4	40	0	3.80
89-90	Pittsburgh	NHL	24	1294	7	12	3	101	0	4.68	—	—	—	—	—	—	—
90-91	Pittsburgh	NHL	48	2754	27	16	3	165	1	3.59	20	1175	12	7	51	†1	*2.60
91-92	Pittsburgh	NHL	57	3329	25	22	9	196	1	3.53	*21	*1233	*16	5	*58	1	2.82
92-93	Pittsburgh	NHL	63	3702	43	14	5	186	4	3.01	12	722	7	5	35	2	2.91
	NHL totals		502	28948	244	181	55	1655	19	3.43	76	4424	45	29	230	4	3.12

BARRAULT, DOUGLAS

RW, PANTHERS

PERSONAL: Born April 21, 1970, at Golden, B.C.... 6-2/200.... Shoots right. ...Name pronounced buh-ROH.

TRANSACTIONS/CAREER NOTES: Selected by Minnesota North Stars in eighth round (eighth North Stars pick, 155th overall) of NHL entry draft (June 16, 1990).... Selected by Florida Panthers in NHL expansion draft (June 24, 1993).

HONORS: Named to WHL (West) All-Star second team (1990-91).

Season Team	League	REGULAR SEASON					PLAYOFFS				
		Gms.	G	A	Pts.	Pen.	Gms.	G	A	Pts.	Pen.
88-89—Lethbridge	WHL	57	14	13	27	34	—	—	—	—	—
89-90—Lethbridge	WHL	54	14	16	30	36	19	7	3	10	0
90-91—Lethbridge	WHL	4	2	2	4	16	—	—	—	—	—
—Seattle	WHL	61	42	42	84	69	6	5	3	8	4
91-92—Kalamazoo	IHL	60	5	14	19	26	—	—	—	—	—
92-93—Kalamazoo	IHL	78	32	34	66	74	—	—	—	—	—
—Minnesota	NHL	2	0	0	0	2	—	—	—	—	—
NHL totals		2	0	0	0	2	—	—	—	—	—

BARRIE, LEN
C, PANTHERS

PERSONAL: Born June 4, 1969, at Kimberly, B.C.... 6-0/190.... Shoots right. **TRANSACTIONS/CAREER NOTES:** Selected by Edmonton Oilers in sixth round (seventh Oilers pick, 124th overall) of NHL entry draft (June 11, 1988).... Broke finger (March 1989).... Traded by Victoria Cougars to Kamloops Blazers for RW Mark Cipriano (August 1989).... Signed as free agent by Philadelphia Flyers (February 8, 1990).... Signed as free agent by Florida Panthers (July 15, 1993). **HONORS:** Won CHL Plus/Minus Award (1989-90).... Won Bob Clarke Trophy (1989-90).... Named to WHL (West) All-Star first team (1989-90).

Season Team	League	REGULAR SEASON					PLAYOFFS				
		Gms.	G	A	Pts.	Pen.	Gms.	G	A	Pts.	Pen.
85-86—Calgary Spurs	AJHL	23	7	14	21	86	—	—	—	—	—
—Calgary	WHL	32	3	0	3	18	—	—	—	—	—
86-87—Calgary	WHL	34	13	13	26	81	—	—	—	—	—
—Victoria	WHL	34	7	6	13	92	5	0	1	1	15
87-88—Victoria	WHL	70	37	49	86	192	8	2	0	2	29
88-89—Victoria	WHL	67	39	48	87	157	7	5	2	7	23
89-90—Philadelphia	NHL	1	0	0	0	0	—	—	—	—	—
—Kamloops	WHL	70	*85	*100	*185	108	17	†14	23	†37	24
90-91—Hershey	AHL	63	26	32	58	60	7	4	0	4	12
91-92—Hershey	AHL	75	42	43	85	78	3	0	2	2	32
92-93—Hershey	AHL	61	31	45	76	162	—	—	—	—	—
—Philadelphia	NHL	8	2	2	4	9	—	—	—	—	—
NHL totals		9	2	2	4	9	—	—	—	—	—

BARTLEY, WADE
D, CAPITALS

PERSONAL: Born May 16, 1970, at Killarney, Man.... 6-0/190.... Shoots right. **COLLEGE:** North Dakota. **TRANSACTIONS/CAREER NOTES:** Tore knee cartilage (November 1986).... Selected by Washington Capitals in second round (third Capitals pick, 41st overall) of NHL entry draft (June 11, 1988).

Season Team	League	REGULAR SEASON					PLAYOFFS				
		Gms.	G	A	Pts.	Pen.	Gms.	G	A	Pts.	Pen.
86-87—Dauphin	MJHL	36	4	24	28	55	—	—	—	—	—
87-88—Dauphin	MJHL	47	10	64	74	104	—	—	—	—	—
88-89—Univ. of North Dakota	WCHA	32	1	1	2	8	—	—	—	—	—
89-90—Sudbury	OHL	60	23	36	59	53	7	1	4	5	10
90-91—Baltimore	AHL	2	0	0	0	0	—	—	—	—	—
—Sudbury	OHL	47	11	37	48	57	5	1	3	4	4
91-92—Hampton Roads	ECHL	43	8	26	34	75	14	4	8	12	38
—Baltimore	AHL	20	0	7	7	25	—	—	—	—	—
92-93—Toledo	ECHL	13	0	10	10	21	16	5	8	13	22

BASSEN, BOB
C, BLUES

PERSONAL: Born May 6, 1965, at Calgary, Alta.... 5-10/180.... Shoots left.... Name pronounced BA-suhn.... Son of Hank Bassen, goalie, Chicago Blackhawks, Detroit Red Wings and Pittsburgh Penguins (1954-55 through 1967-68). **HIGH SCHOOL:** Sir Winston Churchill (Calgary, Alta.).
TRANSACTIONS/CAREER NOTES: Signed as free agent by New York Islanders (October 19, 1984).... Injured knee (October 12, 1985).... Traded by Islanders with D Steve Konroyd to Chicago Blackhawks for D Gary Nylund and D Marc Bergevin (November 25, 1988).... Selected by St. Louis Blues in 1990 waiver draft for $25,000 (October 2, 1990).... Broke right foot (December 4, 1992); missed 22 games.... Broke finger (January 28, 1993); missed nine games. **HONORS:** Named to WHL (East) All-Star first team (1984-85).... Named to IHL All-Star first team (1989-90).

Season Team	League	REGULAR SEASON					PLAYOFFS				
		Gms.	G	A	Pts.	Pen.	Gms.	G	A	Pts.	Pen.
82-83—Medicine Hat	WHL	4	3	2	5	0	3	0	0	0	4
83-84—Medicine Hat	WHL	72	29	29	58	93	14	5	11	16	12
84-85—Medicine Hat	WHL	65	32	50	82	143	10	2	8	10	39
85-86—New York Islanders	NHL	11	2	1	3	6	3	0	1	1	0
—Springfield	AHL	54	13	21	34	111	—	—	—	—	—
86-87—New York Islanders	NHL	77	7	10	17	89	14	1	2	3	21
87-88—New York Islanders	NHL	77	6	16	22	99	6	0	1	1	23
88-89—New York Islanders	NHL	19	1	4	5	21	—	—	—	—	—
—Chicago	NHL	49	4	12	16	62	10	1	1	2	34
89-90—Indianapolis	IHL	73	22	32	54	179	12	3	8	11	33
—Chicago	NHL	6	1	1	2	8	—	—	—	—	—

B

Season Team	League	Gms.	G	A	Pts.	Pen.	Gms.	G	A	Pts.	Pen.
		REGULAR SEASON					PLAYOFFS				
90-91—St. Louis	NHL	79	16	18	34	183	13	1	3	4	24
91-92—St. Louis	NHL	79	7	25	32	167	6	0	2	2	4
92-93—St. Louis	NHL	53	9	10	19	63	11	0	0	0	10
NHL totals		450	53	97	150	698	63	3	10	13	116

BATES, SHAWN
C, BRUINS

PERSONAL: Born April 3, 1975, at Melrose, Mass. . . . 5-11/170. . . . Shoots right.
HIGH SCHOOL: Medford (Mass.).
TRANSACTIONS/CAREER NOTES: Selected by Boston Bruins in fourth round (fourth Bruins pick, 103rd overall) of NHL entry draft (June 26, 1993).

Season Team	League	Gms.	G	A	Pts.	Pen.	Gms.	G	A	Pts.	Pen.
		REGULAR SEASON					PLAYOFFS				
90-91—Medford H.S.	Mass. H.S.	22	18	43	61	6	—	—	—	—	—
91-92—Medford H.S.	Mass. H.S.	22	38	41	79	10	—	—	—	—	—
92-93—Medford H.S.	Mass. H.S.	25	49	46	95	20	—	—	—	—	—

BATTERS, JEFF
D, BLUES

PERSONAL: Born October 23, 1970, at Victoria, B.C. . . . 6-2/210. . . . Shoots right. . . . Full name: Jeffrey William Batters.
COLLEGE: Alaska-Anchorage.
TRANSACTIONS/CAREER NOTES: Selected by St. Louis Blues in seventh round (seventh Blues pick, 135th overall) of NHL entry draft (June 17, 1989).

Season Team	League	Gms.	G	A	Pts.	Pen.	Gms.	G	A	Pts.	Pen.
		REGULAR SEASON					PLAYOFFS				
88-89—Alaska-Anchorage	Indep.	33	8	14	22	123	—	—	—	—	—
89-90—Alaska-Anchorage	Indep.	34	6	9	15	102	—	—	—	—	—
90-91—Alaska-Anchorage	Indep.	39	16	14	30	90	—	—	—	—	—
91-92—Alaska-Anchorage	Indep.	34	6	17	23	86	—	—	—	—	—
92-93—Peoria	IHL	74	5	18	23	113	4	0	0	0	10

BATYRSHIN, RUSLAN
D, JETS

PERSONAL: Born February 19, 1975, at Moscow, U.S.S.R. . . . 6-1/180. . . . Shoots left.
TRANSACTIONS/CAREER NOTES: Selected by Winnipeg Jets in fourth round (fourth Jets pick, 79th overall) of NHL entry draft (June 26, 1993).

Season Team	League	Gms.	G	A	Pts.	Pen.	Gms.	G	A	Pts.	Pen.
		REGULAR SEASON					PLAYOFFS				
91-92—Dynamo Moscow	CIS Div. III	40	0	2	2	52	—	—	—	—	—
92-93—Dynamo Moscow	CIS Div. II			Statistics unavailable.							

BAUER, COLLIN
D, STARS

PERSONAL: Born September 6, 1970, at Edmonton, Alta. . . . 6-2/185. . . . Shoots left.
TRANSACTIONS/CAREER NOTES: Selected by Edmonton Oilers in third round (fourth Oilers pick, 61st overall) of NHL entry draft (June 11, 1988). . . . Fractured three vertebrae and a rib (November 11, 1990). . . . Traded by Oilers to Minnesota North Stars for future considerations (August 4, 1992). . . . North Stars franchise moved from Minnesota to Dallas and renamed Stars for 1993-94 season.
HONORS: Named to WHL (East) All-Star team (1988-89).

Season Team	League	Gms.	G	A	Pts.	Pen.	Gms.	G	A	Pts.	Pen.
		REGULAR SEASON					PLAYOFFS				
86-87—Saskatoon	WHL	61	1	25	26	37	11	0	6	6	10
87-88—Saskatoon	WHL	70	9	53	62	66	10	2	5	7	16
88-89—Saskatoon	WHL	61	17	62	79	71	8	1	8	9	8
89-90—Saskatoon	WHL	29	4	25	29	49	10	1	8	9	14
90-91—Cape Breton	AHL	40	4	14	18	18	4	1	1	2	4
91-92—Cape Breton	AHL	55	7	15	22	36	3	0	0	0	7
92-93—Kalamazoo	IHL	32	4	14	18	31	—	—	—	—	—

BAUMGARTNER, KEN
D/LW, MAPLE LEAFS

PERSONAL: Born March 11, 1966, at Flin Flon, Man. . . . 6-0/200. . . . Shoots left. . . . Full name: Ken James Baumgartner.
TRANSACTIONS/CAREER NOTES: Selected by Buffalo Sabres as underage junior in 12th round (12th Sabres pick, 245th overall) of NHL entry draft (June 15, 1985). . . . Traded by Sabres with D Larry Playfair and RW Sean McKenna to Los Angeles Kings for D Brian Engblom and C Doug Smith (January 29, 1986). . . . Traded by Kings with C Hubie McDonough to New York Islanders for RW Mikko Makela (November 29, 1989). . . . Suspended one game by NHL for fighting (April 5, 1990). . . . Fractured right orbital bone (December 19, 1991); missed 14 games. . . . Traded by Islanders with C Dave McLlwain to Toronto Maple Leafs for C Claude Loiselle and RW Daniel Marois (March 10, 1992).

Season Team	League	Gms.	G	A	Pts.	Pen.	Gms.	G	A	Pts.	Pen.
		REGULAR SEASON					PLAYOFFS				
83-84—Prince Albert	WHL	57	1	6	7	203	—	—	—	—	—
84-85—Prince Albert	WHL	60	3	9	12	252	13	1	3	4	*89
85-86—Prince Albert	WHL	70	4	23	27	277	20	3	9	12	112
86-87—Chur	Switzerland			Statistics unavailable.							
—New Haven	AHL	13	0	3	3	99	6	0	0	0	60

Season Team	League	REGULAR SEASON					PLAYOFFS				
		Gms.	G	A	Pts.	Pen.	Gms.	G	A	Pts.	Pen.
87-88—Los Angeles	NHL	30	2	3	5	189	5	0	1	1	28
—New Haven	AHL	48	1	5	6	181	—	—	—	—	—
88-89—Los Angeles	NHL	49	1	3	4	286	5	0	0	0	8
—New Haven	AHL	10	1	3	4	26	—	—	—	—	—
89-90—Los Angeles	NHL	12	1	0	1	28	—	—	—	—	—
—New York Islanders	NHL	53	0	5	5	194	4	0	0	0	27
90-91—New York Islanders	NHL	78	1	6	7	282	—	—	—	—	—
91-92—New York Islanders	NHL	44	0	1	1	202	—	—	—	—	—
—Toronto	NHL	11	0	0	0	23	—	—	—	—	—
92-93—Toronto	NHL	63	1	0	1	155	7	1	0	1	0
NHL totals		340	6	18	24	1359	21	1	1	2	63

BAUTIN, SERGEI
D, JETS

PERSONAL: Born March 11, 1967, at Murmansk, U.S.S.R. . . . 6-3/185. . . . Shoots left. . . . Name pronounced bigh-OO-tuhn.

TRANSACTIONS/CAREER NOTES: Selected by Winnipeg Jets in first round (first Jets pick, 17th overall) of NHL entry draft (June 20, 1992). . . . Injured hip (December 29, 1993); missed one game. . . . Re-injured hip (January 2, 1993); missed two games. . . . Fractured foot (February 28, 1993); missed nine games.

Season Team	League	REGULAR SEASON					PLAYOFFS				
		Gms.	G	A	Pts.	Pen.	Gms.	G	A	Pts.	Pen.
90-91—Dynamo Moscow	USSR	33	2	0	2	28	—	—	—	—	—
91-92—Dynamo Moscow	CIS	37	1	3	4	88	—	—	—	—	—
92-93—Winnipeg	NHL	71	5	18	23	96	6	0	0	0	2
NHL totals		71	5	18	23	96	6	0	0	0	2

BAVIS, MARK
C, RANGERS

PERSONAL: Born March 13, 1970, at Roslindale, Mass. . . . 6-0/175. . . . Shoots left. . . . Full name: Mark Lawrence Bavis.

HIGH SCHOOL: Catholic Memorial (Boston), then Cushing Academy (Ashburnham, Mass.).

COLLEGE: Boston University.

TRANSACTIONS/CAREER NOTES: Selected by New York Rangers in ninth round (10th Rangers pick, 181st overall) of NHL entry draft (June 17, 1989).

Season Team	League	REGULAR SEASON					PLAYOFFS				
		Gms.	G	A	Pts.	Pen.	Gms.	G	A	Pts.	Pen.
87-88—Catholic Memorial H.S.	Mass. H.S.	19	16	26	42	...	—	—	—	—	—
88-89—Cushing Academy	Mass. H.S.	29	27	31	58	18	—	—	—	—	—
89-90—Boston University	Hockey East	44	6	5	11	50	—	—	—	—	—
90-91—Boston University	Hockey East	40	5	18	23	47	—	—	—	—	—
91-92—Boston University	Hockey East	35	9	18	27	30	—	—	—	—	—
92-93—Boston University	Hockey East	40	14	10	24	58	—	—	—	—	—

BAWA, ROBIN
RW, MIGHTY DUCKS

PERSONAL: Born March 26, 1966, at Chemainus, B.C. . . . 6-2/215. . . . Shoots right. . . . Name pronounced BAH-WAH.

TRANSACTIONS/CAREER NOTES: Signed as free agent by Washington Capitals (May 22, 1987). . . . Traded by Capitals to Vancouver Canucks for future considerations (August 1, 1991). . . . Traded by Canucks to San Jose Sharks for D Rick Lessard (December 15, 1992). . . . Suffered from the flu (January 30, 1993); missed three games. . . . Injured ankle (April 9, 1993); missed one game. . . . Selected by Mighty Ducks of Anaheim in NHL expansion draft (June 24, 1993).

HONORS: Named to WHL (West) All-Star first team (1986-87).

Season Team	League	REGULAR SEASON					PLAYOFFS				
		Gms.	G	A	Pts.	Pen.	Gms.	G	A	Pts.	Pen.
82-83—Kamloops	WHL	66	10	24	34	17	7	1	2	3	0
83-84—Kamloops	WHL	64	16	28	44	40	13	4	2	6	4
84-85—New Westminster	WHL	26	4	6	10	20	—	—	—	—	—
—Kamloops	WHL	26	2	13	15	25	15	4	9	13	14
85-86—Kamloops	WHL	63	29	43	72	78	16	5	13	18	4
86-87—Kamloops	WHL	62	57	56	113	91	13	6	7	13	22
87-88—Fort Wayne	IHL	55	12	27	39	239	6	1	3	4	24
88-89—Baltimore	AHL	75	23	24	47	205	—	—	—	—	—
89-90—Baltimore	AHL	61	7	18	25	189	11	1	2	3	49
—Washington	NHL	5	1	0	1	6	—	—	—	—	—
90-91—Fort Wayne	IHL	72	21	26	47	381	18	4	4	8	87
91-92—Milwaukee	IHL	70	27	14	41	238	5	2	2	4	8
—Vancouver	NHL	2	0	0	0	0	1	0	0	0	0
92-93—Hamilton	AHL	23	3	4	7	58	—	—	—	—	—
—Kansas City	IHL	5	2	0	2	20	—	—	—	—	—
—San Jose	NHL	42	5	0	5	47	—	—	—	—	—
NHL totals		49	6	0	6	53	1	0	0	0	0

BEAUBIEN, FREDERICK
G, KINGS

PERSONAL: Born April 1, 1975, at Levis, Que. . . . 6-1/209. . . . Shoots left.

TRANSACTIONS/CAREER NOTES: Selected by Los Angeles Kings in fifth round (fourth Kings pick, 105th overall) of NHL entry draft (June 26, 1993).

Season Team	League	REGULAR SEASON Gms.	Min.	W	L	T	GA	SO	Avg.	PLAYOFFS Gms.	Min.	W	L	GA	SO	Avg.
92-93—St. Hyacinthe	QMJHL	33	1702	8	16	3	133	0	4.69	—	—	—	—	—	—	—

BEAUFAIT, MARK
C, SHARKS

PERSONAL: Born May 13, 1970, at Livonia, Mich. . . . 5-9/170. . . . Shoots right. . . . Name pronounced BOH-fay.
COLLEGE: Northern Michigan.
TRANSACTIONS/CAREER NOTES: Selected by San Jose Sharks in NHL supplemental draft (June 21, 1991).
HONORS: Won Ken McKenzie Trophy (1992-93).

Season Team	League	REGULAR SEASON Gms.	G	A	Pts.	Pen.	PLAYOFFS Gms.	G	A	Pts.	Pen.
88-89—Northern Michigan Univ...	WCHA	11	2	1	3	2	—	—	—	—	—
89-90—Northern Michigan Univ...	WCHA	34	10	14	24	12	—	—	—	—	—
90-91—Northern Michigan Univ...	WCHA	47	19	30	49	18	—	—	—	—	—
91-92—Northern Michigan Univ...	WCHA	41	31	50	81	47	—	—	—	—	—
92-93—Kansas City	IHL	66	19	40	59	22	9	1	1	2	8
—San Jose	NHL	5	1	0	1	0	—	—	—	—	—
NHL totals		5	1	0	1	0					

BEAUPRE, DON
G, CAPITALS

PERSONAL: Born September 19, 1961, at Kitchener, Ont. . . . 5-9/165. . . . Shoots left. . . . Full name: Donald William Beaupre. . . . Name pronounced boh-PRAY.
TRANSACTIONS/CAREER NOTES: Selected by Minnesota North Stars as underage junior in second round (second North Stars pick, 37th overall) of NHL entry draft (June 11, 1980). . . . Bruised ribs (October 1981). . . . Sprained knee (February 1985). . . . Pulled groin muscle (December 1987). . . . Traded by North Stars to Washington Capitals for rights to D Claudio Scremin (November 1, 1988). . . . Injured ligaments in right thumb (January 31, 1990); missed nine games. . . . Pulled left groin (October 30, 1990); missed 12 games. . . . Pulled muscle (November 5, 1992); missed three games. . . . Pulled groin (January 2, 1993); missed two games.
HONORS: Named to OMJHL All-Star first team (1979-80). . . . Played in NHL All-Star Game (1981 and 1992).

Season Team	League	REGULAR SEASON Gms.	Min.	W	L	T	GA	SO	Avg.	PLAYOFFS Gms.	Min.	W	L	GA	SO	Avg.
78-79—Sudbury	OMJHL	54	3248	...	...	...	*259	2	4.78	10	600	...	...	44	...	4.40
79-80—Sudbury	OMJHL	59	3447	28	29	2	248	0	4.32	9	552	5	4	38	0	4.13
80-81—Minnesota	NHL	44	2585	18	14	11	138	0	3.20	6	360	4	2	26	0	4.33
81-82—Nashville	CHL	5	299	2	3	0	25	0	5.02	—						
—Minnesota	NHL	29	1634	11	8	9	101	0	3.71	2	60	0	1	4	0	4.00
82-83—Birmingham	CHL	10	599	8	2	0	31	0	3.11	—						
—Minnesota	NHL	36	2011	19	10	5	120	0	3.58	4	245	2	2	20	0	4.90
83-84—Salt Lake City	CHL	7	419	2	5	0	30	0	4.30	—						
—Minnesota	NHL	33	1791	16	13	2	123	0	4.12	13	781	6	7	40	1	3.07
84-85—Minnesota	NHL	21	1770	10	17	3	109	1	3.69	4	184	1	1	12	0	3.91
85-86—Minnesota	NHL	52	3073	25	20	6	182	1	3.55	5	300	2	3	17	0	3.40
86-87—Minnesota	NHL	47	2622	17	20	6	174	1	3.98	—						
87-88—Minnesota	NHL	43	2288	10	22	3	161	0	4.22	—						
88-89—Minnesota	NHL	1	59	0	1	0	3	0	3.05	—						
—Kalamazoo	IHL	3	179	1	2	0	9	0	3.02	—						
—Baltimore	AHL	30	1715	14	12	2	102	0	3.57	—						
—Washington	NHL	11	578	5	4	0	28	1	2.91	—						
89-90—Washington	NHL	48	2793	23	18	5	150	2	3.22	8	401	4	3	18	0	2.69
90-91—Baltimore	AHL	2	120	2	0	0	3	0	1.50	—						
—Washington	NHL	45	2572	20	18	3	113	*5	2.64	11	624	5	5	29	†1	2.79
91-92—Baltimore	AHL	3	184	1	1	1	10	0	3.26	—						
—Washington	NHL	54	3108	29	17	6	166	1	3.20	7	419	3	4	22	0	3.15
92-93—Washington	NHL	58	3282	27	23	5	181	1	3.31	2	119	1	1	9	0	4.54
NHL totals		522	30166	230	205	64	1749	13	3.48	62	3493	28	29	197	2	3.38

BEAUREGARD, STEPHANE
G, JETS

PERSONAL: Born January 10, 1968, at Cowansville, Que. . . . 5-11/185. . . . Shoots right. . . . Name pronounced BOH-ree-gahrd.
TRANSACTIONS/CAREER NOTES: Selected by Winnipeg Jets in third round (third Jets pick, 52nd overall) of NHL entry draft (June 11, 1988). . . . Suffered hip flexor (October 29, 1991); missed four games. . . . Traded by Jets to Buffalo Sabres for C Christian Ruutu and future considerations (June 15, 1992). . . . Traded by Sabres with future considerations to Chicago Blackhawks for G Dominik Hasek (August 7, 1992). . . . Traded by Blackhawks to Jets for C Christian Ruutu and future considerations (August 10, 1992). . . . Traded by Jets to Philadelphia Flyers for third-round pick in 1993 draft and fifth-round pick in 1994 draft (October 1, 1992). . . . Traded by Flyers to Jets for third-round pick in 1993 draft and future considerations (February 8, 1993); trade nullified by NHL, citing league bylaw that prohibits trading player within month of waiver draft and reacquiring him later in season (February 9, 1993). . . . Traded by Flyers to Jets for fourth-round pick in 1993 draft and fifth-round pick in 1994 draft (June 11, 1993).
HONORS: Won Jacques Plante Trophy (1987-88). . . . Won Raymond Lagace Trophy (1987-88). . . . Won Marcel Robert Trophy (1987-88). . . . Named to QMJHL All-Star first team (1987-88).

Season Team	League	REGULAR SEASON Gms.	Min.	W	L	T	GA	SO	Avg.	PLAYOFFS Gms.	Min.	W	L	GA	SO	Avg.
86-87—St. Jean	QMJHL	13	785	6	7	0	58	0	4.43	5	260	1	3	26	0	6.00

Season Team	League	Gms.	Min.	W	L	T	GA	SO	Avg.	Gms.	Min.	W	L	GA	SO	Avg.
87-88—St. Jean	QMJHL	*66	*3766	38	20	3	229	2	*3.65	7	423	3	4	34	0	4.82
88-89—Moncton	AHL	15	824	4	8	2	62	0	4.51	—	—	—	—	—	—	—
—Fort Wayne	IHL	16	830	9	5	0	43	0	3.11	9	484	4	4	21	*1	*2.60
89-90—Fort Wayne	IHL	33	1949	20	8	3	115	1	3.54	—	—	—	—	—	—	—
—Winnipeg	NHL	19	1079	7	8	3	59	0	3.28	4	238	1	3	12	0	3.03
90-91—Winnipeg	NHL	16	836	3	10	1	55	0	3.95	—	—	—	—	—	—	—
—Moncton	AHL	9	504	3	4	1	20	1	2.38	1	60	1	0	1	0	1.00
—Fort Wayne	IHL	32	1761	14	13	2	109	0	3.71	*19	*1158	10	9	57	2	2.95
91-92—Winnipeg	NHL	26	1267	6	8	6	61	2	2.89	—	—	—	—	—	—	—
92-93—Philadelphia	NHL	16	802	3	9	0	59	0	4.41	—	—	—	—	—	—	—
—Hershey	AHL	13	794	5	5	3	48	0	3.63	—	—	—	—	—	—	—
NHL totals		77	3984	19	35	10	234	2	3.52	4	238	1	3	12	0	3.03

BEERS, BOB
D, LIGHTNING

PERSONAL: Born May 20, 1967, at Pittsburgh.... 6-2/200.... Shoots right. **COLLEGE:** Northern Arizona, then Maine.

TRANSACTIONS/CAREER NOTES: Selected by Boston Bruins in 11th round (10th Bruins pick, 220th overall) of NHL entry draft (June 15, 1985).... Broke right leg (May 9, 1990).... Underwent surgery to remove pin from right hip (December 10, 1990); missed four games.... Suffered tendinitis in right hip (January 6, 1991).... Traded by Bruins to Tampa Bay Lightning for D Stephane Richer (October 28, 1992).

HONORS: Named to NCAA All-America East second team (1988-89).... Named to Hockey East All-Star second team (1988-89).

Season Team	League	Gms.	G	A	Pts.	Pen.	Gms.	G	A	Pts.	Pen.
85-86—Northern Arizona Univ	Indep.	28	11	39	50	96	—	—	—	—	—
86-87—University of Maine	Hockey East	38	0	13	13	46	—	—	—	—	—
87-88—University of Maine	Hockey East	41	3	11	14	72	—	—	—	—	—
88-89—University of Maine	Hockey East	44	10	27	37	53	—	—	—	—	—
89-90—Maine	AHL	74	7	36	43	63	—	—	—	—	—
—Boston	NHL	3	0	1	1	6	14	1	1	2	18
90-91—Maine	AHL	36	2	16	18	21	—	—	—	—	—
—Boston	NHL	16	0	1	1	10	6	0	0	0	4
91-92—Boston	NHL	31	0	5	5	29	1	0	0	0	0
—Maine	AHL	33	6	23	29	24	—	—	—	—	—
92-93—Providence	AHL	6	1	2	3	10	—	—	—	—	—
—Tampa Bay	NHL	64	12	24	36	70	—	—	—	—	—
—Atlanta	IHL	1	0	0	0	0	—	—	—	—	—
NHL totals		114	12	31	43	115	21	1	1	2	22

BELANGER, JESSE
C, PANTHERS

PERSONAL: Born June 15, 1969, at St. Georges Beauce, Que.... 6-0/170.... Shoots right.

TRANSACTIONS/CAREER NOTES: Signed as free agent by Montreal Canadiens (October 3, 1990).... Selected by Florida Panthers in NHL expansion draft (June 24, 1993).

MISCELLANEOUS: Member of Stanley Cup championship team (1993).

Season Team	League	Gms.	G	A	Pts.	Pen.	Gms.	G	A	Pts.	Pen.
87-88—Granby	QMJHL	69	33	43	76	10	5	3	3	6	0
88-89—Granby	QMJHL	67	40	63	103	26	4	0	5	5	0
89-90—Granby	QMJHL	67	53	54	107	53	—	—	—	—	—
90-91—Fredericton	AHL	75	40	58	98	30	6	2	4	6	0
91-92—Fredericton	AHL	65	30	41	71	26	7	3	3	6	2
—Montreal	NHL	4	0	0	0	0	—	—	—	—	—
92-93—Fredericton	AHL	39	19	32	51	24	—	—	—	—	—
—Montreal	NHL	19	4	2	6	4	9	0	1	1	0
NHL totals		23	4	2	6	4	9	0	1	1	0

BELFOUR, ED
G, BLACKHAWKS

PERSONAL: Born April 21, 1965, at Carman, Man.... 5-11/182.... Shoots left. **COLLEGE:** North Dakota.

TRANSACTIONS/CAREER NOTES: Signed as free agent by Chicago Blackhawks (June 18, 1987).

HONORS: Named top goaltender in Manitoba Junior Hockey League (1985-86).... Named to NCAA All-America West second team (1986-87).... Named to NCAA All-Tournament team (1986-87).... Named to WCHA All-Star first team (1986-87).... Shared Garry F. Longman Memorial Trophy with John Cullen (1987-88).... Named to IHL All-Star first team (1987-88).... Named Rookie of the Year by THE SPORTING NEWS (1990-91).... Won the Vezina Trophy (1990-91 and 1992-93).... Won the Calder Memorial Trophy (1990-91).... Won the William M. Jennings Trophy (1990-91 and 1992-93).... Won Trico Goaltender Award (1990-91).... Named to THE SPORTING NEWS All-Star first team (1990-91).... Named to NHL All-Star first team (1990-91 and 1992-93).... Named to the NHL All-Rookie Team (1990-91).... Played in NHL All-Star Game (1992 and 1993).... Named to THE SPORTING NEWS All-Star second team (1992-93).

Season Team	League	Gms.	Min.	W	L	T	GA	SO	Avg.	Gms.	Min.	W	L	GA	SO	Avg.
85-86—Winkler	MJHL	48	2880	...	...	...	124	1	2.58	—	—	—	—	—	—	—
86-87—Univ. of North Dakota	WCHA	34	2049	29	4	0	81	3	2.37	—	—	—	—	—	—	—

Season Team	League	REGULAR SEASON								PLAYOFFS						
		Gms.	Min.	W	L	T	GA	SO	Avg.	Gms.	Min.	W	L	GA	SO	Avg.
87-88—Saginaw	IHL	61	*3446	32	25	0	183	3	3.19	9	561	4	5	33	0	3.53
88-89—Chicago	NHL	23	1148	4	12	3	74	0	3.87	—	—	—	—	—	—	—
—Saginaw	IHL	29	1760	12	10	0	92	0	3.14	5	298	2	3	14	0	2.82
89-90—Can. national team	Int'l	33	1808	...	...	...	93	...	3.09	—	—	—	—	—	—	—
—Chicago	NHL	—	—	—	—	—	—	—	—	9	409	4	2	17	0	2.49
90-91—Chicago	NHL	*74	*4127	*43	19	7	170	4	*2.47	6	295	2	4	20	0	4.07
91-92—Chicago	NHL	52	2928	21	18	10	132	†5	2.70	18	949	12	4	39	1	*2.47
92-93—Chicago	NHL	71	4106	41	18	11	177	7	2.59	4	249	0	4	13	0	3.13
NHL totals		220	12309	109	67	31	553	16	2.70	37	1902	18	14	89	1	2.81

BELL, BRUCE

D

PERSONAL: Born February 15, 1965, at Toronto.... 6-0/205.... Shoots left.
TRANSACTIONS/CAREER NOTES: Selected by Quebec Nordiques in third round (second Nordiques pick, 52nd overall) of NHL entry draft (June 8, 1983).... Traded by Nordiques to St. Louis Blues for D Gilbert Delorme (October 2, 1985).... Traded by Blues with fourth-round pick in 1988 draft and future considerations to New York Rangers for LW Tony McKegney and D Rob Whistle (May 28, 1987).... Traded by Rangers with C Walt Poddubny, D Jari Gronstrand and fourth-round pick in 1989 draft to Quebec Nordiques for D Normand Rochefort and C Jason Lafreniere (August 1, 1988).... Claimed on waivers by Detroit Red Wings (December 20, 1988).... Signed as free agent by Edmonton Oilers (February 1, 1990).... Traded by Oilers with future draft pick to Minnesota North Stars for G Kari Takko (November 23, 1990).... Signed as free agent by St. John's Maple Leafs (November 1991).
HONORS: Named to NHL All-Rookie team (1984-85).

Season Team	League	REGULAR SEASON					PLAYOFFS				
		Gms.	G	A	Pts.	Pen.	Gms.	G	A	Pts.	Pen.
81-82—Sault Ste. Marie	OHL	67	11	18	29	63	12	0	2	2	24
82-83—Sault Ste. Marie	OHL	5	0	2	2	2	—	—	—	—	—
—Windsor	OHL	61	10	35	45	39	3	0	4	4	0
83-84—Brantford	OHL	63	7	41	48	55	6	0	3	3	16
84-85—Quebec	NHL	75	6	31	37	44	16	2	2	4	21
85-86—St. Louis	NHL	75	2	18	20	43	14	0	2	2	13
86-87—St. Louis	NHL	45	3	13	16	18	4	1	1	2	7
87-88—Colorado	IHL	65	11	34	45	107	4	2	3	5	0
—New York Rangers	NHL	13	1	2	3	8	—	—	—	—	—
88-89—Rapperswill	Switzerland				Statistics unavailable.						
—Halifax	AHL	12	1	2	3	29	2	0	1	1	2
—Adirondack	AHL	9	1	4	5	4	—	—	—	—	—
89-90—Edmonton	NHL	1	0	0	0	0	—	—	—	—	—
—Cape Breton	AHL	52	8	26	34	64	6	3	4	7	2
90-91—Cape Breton	AHL	14	2	5	7	7	—	—	—	—	—
—Kalamazoo	IHL	48	5	21	26	32	3	0	0	0	8
91-92—St. John's	AHL	45	5	16	21	70	10	4	7	11	8
92-93—Milwaukee	IHL	70	10	28	38	120	6	0	2	2	6
NHL totals		209	12	64	76	113	34	3	5	8	41

BELLEY, ROCH

G, BLACKHAWKS

PERSONAL: Born August 12, 1971, at Hull, Que.... 5-9/171.... Shoots left.... Name pronounced ROCK BEHL-ee.
TRANSACTIONS/CAREER NOTES: Selected by Chicago Blackhawks in fourth round (11th Blackhawks pick, 176th overall) of NHL entry draft (June 22, 1991).

Season Team	League	REGULAR SEASON								PLAYOFFS						
		Gms.	Min.	W	L	T	GA	SO	Avg.	Gms.	Min.	W	L	GA	SO	Avg.
87-88—Gloucester	COJHL	34	1805	...	...	...	151	0	5.02	—	—	—	—	—	—	—
88-89—Gloucester	COJHL	36	1932	...	...	...	175	2	5.43	—	—	—	—	—	—	—
89-90—Niagara Falls	OHL	23	1029	...	...	...	114	0	6.65	—	—	—	—	—	—	—
90-91—Niagara Falls	OHL	45	2525	26	8	7	155	1	3.68	—	—	—	—	—	—	—
91-92—Indianapolis	IHL	25	1270	4	12	3	88	0	4.16	—	—	—	—	—	—	—
92-93—Indianapolis	IHL	7	289	1	2	0	25	0	5.19	2	33	0	0	2	0	3.64
—Fort Worth	CHL	33	1782	...	...	...	141	0	4.75	—	—	—	—	—	—	—

BELLOWS, BRIAN

LW, CANADIENS

PERSONAL: Born September 1, 1964, at St. Catharines, Ont.... 5-11/195.... Shoots right.
TRANSACTIONS/CAREER NOTES: Separated shoulder (November 1981); coached Kitchener Rangers for two games while recovering (became the youngest coach in OHL history at 17 years old).... Selected by Minnesota North Stars as underage junior in first round (first North Stars pick, second overall) of NHL entry draft (June 9, 1982).... Suffered tendinitis in elbow (October 1984).... Injured wrist (October 1986); missed 13 games.... Strained abdominal muscles (February 1989); missed 20 games.... Bruised left knee (September 1990). ...Strained hip and groin (December 18, 1990).... Traded by North Stars to Montreal Canadiens for RW Russ Courtnall (August 31, 1992).... Injured neck (December 3, 1992); missed two games.
HONORS: Named to Memorial Cup All-Star team (1980-81).... Won George Parsons Trophy (1981-82).... Named to OHL All-Star first team (1981-82).... Played in NHL All-Star Game (1984, 1988 and 1992).... Named to THE SPORTING NEWS All-Star second team (1989-90).... Named to NHL All-Star second team (1989-90).
MISCELLANEOUS: Member of Stanley Cup championship team (1993).

Season Team	League	REGULAR SEASON					PLAYOFFS				
		Gms.	G	A	Pts.	Pen.	Gms.	G	A	Pts.	Pen.
80-81—Kitchener	OMJHL	66	49	67	116	23	16	14	13	27	13

Season Team	League	REGULAR SEASON					PLAYOFFS				
		Gms.	G	A	Pts.	Pen.	Gms.	G	A	Pts.	Pen.
81-82—Kitchener	OHL	47	45	52	97	23	15	16	13	29	11
82-83—Minnesota	NHL	78	35	30	65	27	9	5	4	9	18
83-84—Minnesota	NHL	78	41	42	83	66	16	2	12	14	6
84-85—Minnesota	NHL	78	26	36	62	72	9	2	4	6	9
85-86—Minnesota	NHL	77	31	48	79	46	5	5	0	5	16
86-87—Minnesota	NHL	65	26	27	53	54	—	—	—	—	—
87-88—Minnesota	NHL	77	40	41	81	81	—	—	—	—	—
88-89—Minnesota	NHL	60	23	27	50	55	5	2	3	5	8
89-90—Minnesota	NHL	80	55	44	99	72	7	4	3	7	10
90-91—Minnesota	NHL	80	35	40	75	43	23	10	19	29	30
91-92—Minnesota	NHL	80	30	45	75	41	7	4	4	8	14
92-93—Montreal	NHL	82	40	48	88	44	18	6	9	15	18
NHL totals		835	382	428	810	601	99	40	58	98	129

BELZILE, ETIENNE
D, FLAMES

PERSONAL: Born May 2, 1972, at Quebec City. . . . 6-1/180. . . . Shoots left.
COLLEGE: Cornell.
TRANSACTIONS/CAREER NOTES: Selected by Calgary Flames in second round (fourth Flames pick, 41st overall) of NHL entry draft (June 16, 1989).

Season Team	League	REGULAR SEASON					PLAYOFFS				
		Gms.	G	A	Pts.	Pen.	Gms.	G	A	Pts.	Pen.
89-90—Cornell University	ECAC	28	1	4	5	18	—	—	—	—	—
90-91—Cornell University	ECAC	32	2	3	5	38	—	—	—	—	—
91-92—Cornell University	ECAC	29	1	1	2	20	—	—	—	—	—
92-93—Cornell University	ECAC	26	2	2	4	24	—	—	—	—	—

BENNETT, ADAM
D, BLACKHAWKS

PERSONAL: Born March 30, 1971, at Georgetown, Ont. . . . 6-4/206. . . . Shoots right.
TRANSACTIONS/CAREER NOTES: Separated both shoulders (1987-88). . . . Selected by Chicago Blackhawks in first round (first Blackhawks pick, sixth overall) of NHL entry draft (June 17, 1989).
HONORS: Named to OHL All-Star second team (1990-91).

Season Team	League	REGULAR SEASON					PLAYOFFS				
		Gms.	G	A	Pts.	Pen.	Gms.	G	A	Pts.	Pen.
86-87—Georgetown Jr. B	OHA	1	0	0	0	0	—	—	—	—	—
87-88—Georgetown Jr. B	OHA	32	9	31	40	63	—	—	—	—	—
88-89—Sudbury	OHL	66	7	22	29	133	—	—	—	—	—
89-90—Sudbury	OHL	65	18	43	61	116	7	1	2	3	23
90-91—Sudbury	OHL	54	21	29	50	123	5	1	2	3	11
—Indianapolis	IHL	3	0	1	1	12	2	0	0	0	0
91-92—Indianapolis	IHL	59	4	10	14	89	—	—	—	—	—
—Chicago	NHL	5	0	0	0	12	—	—	—	—	—
92-93—Indianapolis	IHL	39	8	16	24	69	2	0	0	0	2
—Chicago	NHL	16	0	2	2	8	—	—	—	—	—
NHL totals		21	0	2	2	20					

BENNETT, RIC
LW, RANGERS

PERSONAL: Born July 24, 1967, at Springfield, Mass. . . . 6-3/215. . . . Shoots left. . . . Full name: Eric John Bennett.
HIGH SCHOOL: Wilbraham and Monson Academy (Mass.).
COLLEGE: Providence.
TRANSACTIONS/CAREER NOTES: Selected by Minnesota North Stars in third round (fourth North Stars pick, 54th overall) of NHL entry draft (June 21, 1986). . . . Rights traded by North Stars with C Brian Lawton and LW Igor Liba to New York Rangers for D Mark Tinordi, D Paul Jerrard, C Mike Sullivan, RW Brett Barnett and the Los Angeles Kings third-round pick in 1989 draft (C Murray Garbutt) (October 11, 1988). . . . Underwent surgery to left knee (January 24, 1990).
HONORS: Named to Hockey East All-Freshman team (1986-87). . . . Named to NCAA All-America East second team (1988-89). . . . Named to Hockey East All-Star second team (1989-90).

Season Team	League	REGULAR SEASON					PLAYOFFS				
		Gms.	G	A	Pts.	Pen.	Gms.	G	A	Pts.	Pen.
85-86—Wilbraham Monson Acad.	Mass. H.S.	20	30	39	69	25	—	—	—	—	—
86-87—Providence College	Hockey East	32	15	12	27	34	—	—	—	—	—
87-88—Providence College	Hockey East	33	9	16	25	70	—	—	—	—	—
88-89—Providence College	Hockey East	32	14	32	46	74	—	—	—	—	—
89-90—Providence College	Hockey East	31	12	24	36	74	—	—	—	—	—
—New York Rangers	NHL	6	1	0	1	5	—	—	—	—	—
90-91—Binghamton	AHL	71	27	32	59	206	10	2	1	3	27
—New York Rangers	NHL	6	0	0	0	6	—	—	—	—	—
91-92—Binghamton	AHL	76	15	22	37	114	11	0	1	1	23
—New York Rangers	NHL	3	0	1	1	2	—	—	—	—	—
92-93—Binghamton	AHL	76	15	22	37	114	10	0	0	0	30
NHL totals		15	1	1	2	13					

BENNING, BRIAN

D, PANTHERS

PERSONAL: Born June 10, 1966, at Edmonton, Alta. . . . 6-0/195. . . . Shoots left. . . . Full name: Brian Anthony Benning. . . . Brother of Jim Benning, defenseman, Toronto Maple Leafs and Vancouver Canucks (1981-82 through 1989-90).
HIGH SCHOOL: St. Joseph (Edmonton, Alta.).

TRANSACTIONS/CAREER NOTES: Cracked bone in right wrist (December 1983); missed 38 games. . . . Selected by St.Louis Blues as underage junior in second round (first Blues pick, 26th overall) of NHL entry draft (June 9, 1984). . . . Broke right leg (December 28, 1984). . . . Traded by Blues to Los Angeles Kings for third-round pick in 1991 draft (November 10, 1989). . . . Underwent appendectomy (March 6, 1990); missed three weeks. . . . Suspended three games by NHL for cross-checking (September 28, 1990). . . . Suffered back spasms (December 1990). . . . Injured groin (October 22, 1991); missed three games. . . . Traded by Kings with D Jeff Chychrun and first-round pick in 1992 draft to Pittsburgh Penguins for D Paul Coffey (February 19, 1992). . . . Traded by Penguins with RW Mark Recchi and first-round pick in 1992 draft (LW Jason Bowen) previously acquired from Kings to Philadelphia Flyers for RW Rick Tocchet, D Kjell Samuelsson, G Ken Wregget and third-round pick in 1992 draft (February 19, 1992). . . . Strained back (October 26, 1992); missed three games. . . . Traded by Flyers to Edmonton Oilers for C Josef Beranek and D Greg Hawgood (January 16, 1993). . . . Strained groin (January 23, 1993); missed five games. . . . Strained wrist (February 23, 1993); missed three games. . . . Released by Oilers (July 1, 1993). . . . Signed by Florida Panthers (July 15, 1993).
HONORS: Named to NHL All-Rookie team (1986-87).

			REGULAR SEASON					PLAYOFFS			
Season Team	League	Gms.	G	A	Pts.	Pen.	Gms.	G	A	Pts.	Pen.
83-84—Portland	WHL	38	6	41	47	108	—	—	—	—	—
84-85—Kamloops	WHL	17	3	18	21	26	—	—	—	—	—
—St. Louis	NHL	4	0	2	2	0	—	—	—	—	—
85-86—Canadian national team	Int'l	60	6	13	19	43	—	—	—	—	—
—St. Louis	NHL	—	—	—	—	—	6	1	2	3	13
86-87—St. Louis	NHL	78	13	36	49	110	6	0	4	4	9
87-88—St. Louis	NHL	77	8	29	37	107	10	1	6	7	25
88-89—St. Louis	NHL	66	8	26	34	102	7	1	1	2	11
89-90—St. Louis	NHL	7	1	1	2	2	—	—	—	—	—
—Los Angeles	NHL	48	5	18	23	104	7	0	2	2	10
90-91—Los Angeles	NHL	61	7	24	31	127	12	0	5	5	6
91-92—Los Angeles	NHL	53	2	30	32	99	—	—	—	—	—
—Philadelphia	NHL	22	2	12	14	35	—	—	—	—	—
92-93—Philadelphia	NHL	37	9	17	26	93	—	—	—	—	—
—Edmonton	NHL	18	1	7	8	59	—	—	—	—	—
NHL totals		471	56	202	258	838	48	3	20	23	74

BERANEK, JOSEF

RW, FLYERS

PERSONAL: Born October 25, 1969, at Litvinov, Czechoslovakia. . . . 6-2/185. . . . Shoots left. . . . Name pronounced buh-RAH-nehk.
TRANSACTIONS/CAREER NOTES: Selected by Edmonton Oilers in fourth round (third Oilers pick, 78th overall) of NHL entry draft (June 17, 1989). . . . Traded by Oilers with D Greg Hawgood to Philadelphia Flyers for D Brian Benning (January 16, 1993).

			REGULAR SEASON					PLAYOFFS			
Season Team	League	Gms.	G	A	Pts.	Pen.	Gms.	G	A	Pts.	Pen.
87-88—CHZ Litvinov	Czech.	14	7	4	11	12	—	—	—	—	—
88-89—CHZ Litvinov	Czech.	32	18	10	28	47	—	—	—	—	—
—Czechoslovakia Jr.	Czech.	5	2	7	9	2	—	—	—	—	—
89-90—Dukla Trencin	Czech.	49	16	21	37	...	—	—	—	—	—
90-91—CHZ Litvinov	Czech.	50	27	27	54	98	—	—	—	—	—
91-92—Edmonton	NHL	58	12	16	28	18	12	2	1	3	0
92-93—Edmonton	NHL	26	2	6	8	28	—	—	—	—	—
—Cape Breton	AHL	6	1	2	3	8	—	—	—	—	—
—Philadelphia	NHL	40	13	12	25	50	—	—	—	—	—
NHL totals		124	27	34	61	96	12	2	1	3	0

BEREHOWSKY, DRAKE

D, MAPLE LEAFS

PERSONAL: Born January 3, 1972, at Toronto. . . . 6-1/211. . . . Shoots right. . . . Name pronounced BAIR-uh-HOW-skee.
TRANSACTIONS/CAREER NOTES: Injured knees and underwent reconstructive surgery (October 13, 1989); missed remainder of season. . . . Selected by Toronto Maple Leafs in first round (first Maple Leafs pick, 10th overall) of NHL entry draft (June 16, 1990). . . . Sprained knee (April 15, 1993); missed remainder of season.
HONORS: Won Can.HL Defenseman of the Year Award (1991-92). . . . Won Max Kaminsky Trophy (1991-92). . . . Named to Can.HL All-Star first team (1991-92). . . . Named to OHL All-Star first team (1991-92).

			REGULAR SEASON					PLAYOFFS			
Season Team	League	Gms.	G	A	Pts.	Pen.	Gms.	G	A	Pts.	Pen.
87-88—Barrie Jr. B	OHA	40	10	36	46	81	—	—	—	—	—
88-89—Kingston	OHL	63	7	39	46	85	—	—	—	—	—
89-90—Kingston	OHL	9	3	11	14	28	—	—	—	—	—
90-91—Toronto	NHL	8	0	1	1	25	—	—	—	—	—
—Kingston	OHL	13	5	13	18	28	—	—	—	—	—
—North Bay	OHL	26	7	23	30	51	10	2	7	9	21
91-92—North Bay	OHL	62	19	63	82	147	21	7	24	31	22
—Toronto	NHL	1	0	0	0	0	—	—	—	—	—
—St. John's	AHL	—	—	—	—	—	6	0	5	5	21

Season Team	League	REGULAR SEASON Gms.	G	A	Pts.	Pen.	PLAYOFFS Gms.	G	A	Pts.	Pen.
92-93—Toronto	NHL	41	4	15	19	61	—	—	—	—	—
—St. John's	AHL	28	10	17	27	38	—	—	—	—	—
NHL totals		50	4	16	20	86					

BEREZAN, PERRY

C, SHARKS

PERSONAL: Born December 5, 1964, at Edmonton, Alta. . . . 6-2/190. . . . Shoots right. . . . Full name: Perry Edmund Berezan. . . . Name pronounced BAIR-uh-zan.
COLLEGE: North Dakota.
TRANSACTIONS/CAREER NOTES: Selected by Calgary Flames as underage junior in third round (third Flames pick, 55th overall) of NHL entry draft (June 8, 1983). . . . Suffered from sinus problems (February 1986); missed eight games. . . . Broke ankle (March 19, 1986). . . . Injured groin (November 1986). . . . Underwent surgery for groin injury (March 1987). . . . Injured groin (November 1987). . . . Lacerated hand (February 1988). . . . Traded by Flames with RW Shane Churla to Minnesota North Stars for LW Brian MacLellan and fourth-round pick in 1989 draft (C Robert Reichel) (March 4, 1989). . . . Suffered concussion (October 1989). . . . Sprained ankle (December 18, 1989); missed eight games. . . . Broke nose (March 1990). . . . Signed as free agent by San Jose Sharks (October 10, 1991). . . . Sprained knee (October 23, 1991); missed five games. . . . Broke fibula prior to 1992-93 season; missed first seven games of season. . . . Injured groin (October 28, 1992); missed four games. . . . Sprained knee (February 10, 1993); missed remainder of season.
HONORS: Named to WCHA All-Star second team (1984-85).

Season Team	League	REGULAR SEASON Gms.	G	A	Pts.	Pen.	PLAYOFFS Gms.	G	A	Pts.	Pen.
81-82—St. Albert	AJHL	47	16	36	52	47	—	—	—	—	—
82-83—St. Albert	AJHL	57	37	40	77	110	—	—	—	—	—
83-84—Univ. of North Dakota	WCHA	44	28	24	52	29	—	—	—	—	—
84-85—Univ. of North Dakota	WCHA	42	23	35	58	32	—	—	—	—	—
—Calgary	NHL	9	3	2	5	4	2	1	0	1	4
85-86—Calgary	NHL	55	12	21	33	39	8	1	1	2	6
86-87—Calgary	NHL	24	5	3	8	24	2	0	2	2	7
87-88—Calgary	NHL	29	7	12	19	66	8	0	2	2	13
88-89—Calgary	NHL	35	4	4	8	21	—	—	—	—	—
—Minnesota	NHL	16	1	4	5	4	5	1	2	3	4
89-90—Minnesota	NHL	64	3	12	15	31	5	1	0	1	0
90-91—Kalamazoo	IHL	2	0	0	0	2	—	—	—	—	—
—Minnesota	NHL	52	11	6	17	30	1	0	0	0	0
91-92—San Jose	NHL	66	12	7	19	30	—	—	—	—	—
92-93—San Jose	NHL	28	3	4	7	28	—	—	—	—	—
—Kansas City	IHL	9	4	4	8	31	—	—	—	—	—
NHL totals		378	61	75	136	277	31	4	7	11	34

BERG, BILL

LW, MAPLE LEAFS

PERSONAL: Born October 21, 1967, at St. Catharines, Ont. . . . 6-1/198. . . . Shoots left. . . . Brother of Bob Berg, left winger in Los Angeles Kings system.
TRANSACTIONS/CAREER NOTES: Broke ankle (March 1985). . . . Selected by New York Islanders as underage junior in third round (third Islanders pick, 59th overall) of NHL entry draft (June 21, 1986). . . . Injured knee (October 1986). . . . Separated shoulder (May 1990). . . . Fractured left foot (November 9, 1991); missed 12 games. . . . Claimed on waivers by Toronto Maple Leafs (December 3, 1992).
MISCELLANEOUS: Moved from defense to left wing (1990).

Season Team	League	REGULAR SEASON Gms.	G	A	Pts.	Pen.	PLAYOFFS Gms.	G	A	Pts.	Pen.
84-85—Grimsby Jr. B	OHA	42	10	22	32	153	—	—	—	—	—
85-86—Toronto	OHL	64	3	35	38	143	4	0	0	0	19
86-87—Toronto	OHL	57	3	15	18	138	—	—	—	—	—
—Springfield	AHL	4	1	1	2	4	—	—	—	—	—
87-88—Springfield	AHL	76	6	26	32	148	—	—	—	—	—
—Peoria	IHL	5	0	1	1	8	7	0	3	3	31
88-89—New York Islanders	NHL	7	1	2	3	10	—	—	—	—	—
—Springfield	AHL	69	17	32	49	122	—	—	—	—	—
89-90—Springfield	AHL	74	12	42	54	74	15	5	12	17	35
90-91—New York Islanders	NHL	78	9	14	23	67	—	—	—	—	—
91-92—New York Islanders	NHL	47	5	9	14	28	—	—	—	—	—
—Capital District	AHL	3	0	2	2	16	—	—	—	—	—
92-93—New York Islanders	NHL	22	6	3	9	49	—	—	—	—	—
—Toronto	NHL	58	7	8	15	54	21	1	1	2	18
NHL totals		212	28	36	64	208	21	1	1	2	18

BERGERON, JEAN-CLAUDE

G, LIGHTNING

PERSONAL: Born October 14, 1968, at Hauterive, Que. . . . 6-2/192. . . . Shoots left.
TRANSACTIONS/CAREER NOTES: Selected by Montreal Canadiens in fifth round (sixth Canadiens pick, 104th overall of NHL entry draft (June 11, 1988). . . . Traded by Canadiens to Tampa Bay Lightning for G Frederic Chabot (June 18, 1992).
HONORS: Won Baz Bastien Trophy (1989-90). . . . Shared Harry (Hap) Holmes Memorial Trophy with Andre Racicot (1989-90). . . . Named to AHL All-Star first team (1989-90).

B

Season	Team	League	Gms.	Min.	W	L	T	GA	SO	Avg.	Gms.	Min.	W	L	GA	SO	Avg.
85-86—Shawinigan	QMJHL	33	1796	...	...	...	156	0	5.21	—	—	—	—	—	—	—
86-87—Verdun	QMJHL	52	2991	...	...	...	*306	0	6.14	—	—	—	—	—	—	—
87-88—Verdun	QMJHL	49	2715	13	31	3	*265	0	5.86	—	—	—	—	—	—	—
88-89—Verdun	QMJHL	44	2417	8	34	1	199	0	4.94	—	—	—	—	—	—	—
—Sherbrooke	AHL	5	302	4	1	0	18	0	3.58	—	—	—	—	—	—	—
89-90—Sherbrooke	AHL	40	2254	21	8	7	103	2	*2.74	9	497	6	2	28	0	3.38
90-91—Montreal	NHL	19	941	7	6	2	59	0	3.76	—	—	—	—	—	—	—
—Fredericton	AHL	18	1083	12	6	0	59	1	3.27	10	546	5	5	32	0	3.52
91-92—Fredericton	AHL	13	791	5	7	1	57	0	4.32	—	—	—	—	—	—	—
—Peoria	IHL	27	1632	14	9	3	96	1	3.53	6	352	3	3	24	0	4.09
92-93—Atlanta	IHL	31	1722	21	7	0	92	1	3.21	6	368	3	3	19	0	3.10
—Tampa Bay	NHL	21	1163	8	10	1	71	0	3.66	—	—	—	—	—	—	—
NHL totals		40	2104	15	16	3	130	0	3.71							

BERGEVIN, MARC

D, LIGHTNING

PERSONAL: Born August 11, 1965, at Montreal. . . . 6-1/197. . . . Shoots left. . . . Name pronounced BUHR-zhuh-van.

TRANSACTIONS/CAREER NOTES: Selected by Chicago Blackhawks as underage junior in third round (third Blackhawks pick, 59th overall) of NHL entry draft (June 8, 1983). . . . Sprained neck (March 18, 1987). . . . Traded by Blackhawks with D Gary Nylund to New York Islanders for D Steve Konroyd and C Bob Bassen (November 25, 1988). . . . Bruised ribs (November 25, 1989). . . . Broke hand (May 1990). . . . Traded by Islanders to Hartford Whalers for future considerations; Islanders later received fifth-round pick in 1992 draft (C Ryan Duthie) (October 31, 1990). . . . Signed as free agent by Tampa Bay Lightning (July 9, 1992). . . . Injured foot (March 18, 1993); missed one game.

Season	Team	League	Gms.	G	A	Pts.	Pen.	Gms.	G	A	Pts.	Pen.
82-83—Chicoutimi	QMJHL	64	3	27	30	113	—	—	—	—	—
83-84—Chicoutimi	QMJHL	70	10	35	45	125	—	—	—	—	—
—Springfield	AHL	7	0	1	1	2	—	—	—	—	—
84-85—Chicago	NHL	60	0	6	6	54	6	0	3	3	2
—Springfield	AHL	—	—	—	—	—	4	0	0	0	0
85-86—Chicago	NHL	71	7	7	14	60	3	0	0	0	0
86-87—Chicago	NHL	66	4	10	14	66	3	1	0	1	2
87-88—Chicago	NHL	58	1	6	7	85	—	—	—	—	—
—Saginaw	IHL	10	2	7	9	20	—	—	—	—	—
88-89—Chicago	NHL	11	0	0	0	18	—	—	—	—	—
—New York Islanders	NHL	58	2	13	15	62	—	—	—	—	—
89-90—New York Islanders	NHL	18	0	4	4	30	—	—	—	—	—
—Springfield	AHL	47	7	16	23	66	17	2	11	13	16
90-91—Hartford	NHL	4	0	0	0	4	—	—	—	—	—
—Capital District	AHL	7	0	5	5	6	—	—	—	—	—
—Springfield	AHL	58	4	23	27	85	18	0	7	7	26
91-92—Hartford	NHL	75	7	17	24	64	5	0	0	0	2
92-93—Tampa Bay	NHL	78	2	12	14	66	—	—	—	—	—
NHL totals		499	23	75	98	509	17	1	3	4	6

BERGLAND, TIM

RW, LIGHTNING

PERSONAL: Born January 11, 1965, at Crookston, Minn. . . . 6-3/194. . . . Shoots right. . . . Full name: Timothy Daniel Bergland.

HIGH SCHOOL: Lincoln (Thief River Falls, Minn.).

COLLEGE: Minnesota.

TRANSACTIONS/CAREER NOTES: Selected by Washington Capitals as underage junior in fourth round (first Capitals pick, 75th overall) of NHL entry draft (June 8, 1983). . . . Selected by Tampa Bay Lightning in NHL expansion draft (June 18, 1992).

Season	Team	League	Gms.	G	A	Pts.	Pen.	Gms.	G	A	Pts.	Pen.
82-83—Lincoln High School	Minn. H.S.	20	26	22	48	...	—	—	—	—	—
83-84—University of Minnesota	WCHA	24	4	11	15	4	—	—	—	—	—
84-85—University of Minnesota	WCHA	46	7	12	19	16	—	—	—	—	—
85-86—University of Minnesota	WCHA	48	11	16	27	26	—	—	—	—	—
86-87—University of Minnesota	WCHA	49	18	17	35	48	—	—	—	—	—
87-88—Fort Wayne	IHL	13	2	1	3	9	—	—	—	—	—
—Binghamton	AHL	63	21	26	47	31	4	0	0	0	0
88-89—Baltimore	AHL	78	24	29	53	39	—	—	—	—	—
89-90—Baltimore	AHL	47	12	19	31	55	—	—	—	—	—
—Washington	NHL	32	2	5	7	31	15	1	1	2	8
90-91—Washington	NHL	47	5	9	14	21	11	1	1	2	12
—Baltimore	AHL	15	8	9	17	16	—	—	—	—	—
91-92—Washington	NHL	22	1	4	5	2	—	—	—	—	—
—Baltimore	AHL	11	6	10	16	5	—	—	—	—	—
92-93—Atlanta	IHL	49	18	21	39	26	9	3	3	6	10
—Tampa Bay	NHL	27	3	3	6	11	—	—	—	—	—
NHL totals		128	11	21	32	65	26	2	2	4	20

BERGQVIST, STEFAN

D, PENGUINS

PERSONAL: Born March 10, 1975, at Leksand, Sweden. . . . 6-3/216. . . . Shoots left.

TRANSACTIONS/CAREER NOTES: Selected by Pittsburgh Penguins in first round (first Penguins pick, 26th overall) of NHL entry draft (June 26, 1993).

			REGULAR SEASON					PLAYOFFS				
Season	Team	League	Gms.	G	A	Pts.	Pen.	Gms.	G	A	Pts.	Pen.
92-93—Leksand		Sweden	15	0	0	0	6	—	—	—	—	—

BERNARD, LOUIS

D, CANADIENS

PERSONAL: Born July 10, 1974, at Victoriaville, Que. . . . 6-1/203. . . . Shoots right.

TRANSACTIONS/CAREER NOTES: Selected by Montreal Canadiens in fourth round (fifth Canadiens pick, 82nd overall) of NHL entry draft (June 20, 1992).

			REGULAR SEASON					PLAYOFFS				
Season	Team	League	Gms.	G	A	Pts.	Pen.	Gms.	G	A	Pts.	Pen.
91-92—Drummondville		QMJHL	70	8	24	32	59	4	0	1	1	4
92-93—Drummondville		QMJHL	68	8	38	46	78	10	0	4	4	14

B

BERRY, BRAD

D, STARS

PERSONAL: Born April 1, 1965, at Bashaw, Alta. . . . 6-2/190. . . . Shoots left. **COLLEGE:** North Dakota.

TRANSACTIONS/CAREER NOTES: Selected by Winnipeg Jets in second round (third Jets pick, 29th overall) of NHL entry draft (June 8, 1983). . . . Signed as free agent by Minnesota North Stars (October 14, 1991). . . . Strained lower back (December 31, 1992); missed two games. . . . Sprained knee (March 21, 1993); missed four games. . . . North Stars franchise moved from Minnesota to Dallas and renamed Stars for 1993-94 season.

			REGULAR SEASON					PLAYOFFS				
Season	Team	League	Gms.	G	A	Pts.	Pen.	Gms.	G	A	Pts.	Pen.
83-84—North Dakota		WCHA	32	2	7	9	8	—	—	—	—	—
84-85—North Dakota		WCHA	40	4	26	30	26	—	—	—	—	—
85-86—North Dakota		WCHA	40	6	29	35	26	—	—	—	—	—
—Winnipeg		NHL	13	1	0	1	10	3	0	0	0	0
86-87—Winnipeg		NHL	52	2	8	10	60	7	0	1	1	14
87-88—Winnipeg		NHL	48	0	6	6	75	—	—	—	—	—
—Moncton		AHL	10	1	3	4	14	—	—	—	—	—
88-89—Winnipeg		NHL	38	0	9	9	45	—	—	—	—	—
—Moncton		AHL	38	3	16	19	39	—	—	—	—	—
89-90—Winnipeg		NHL	12	1	2	3	6	1	0	0	0	0
—Moncton		AHL	38	1	9	10	58	—	—	—	—	—
90-91—Brynas		Sweden	38	3	1	4	38	—	—	—	—	—
91-92—Kalamazoo		IHL	65	5	18	23	90	5	2	0	2	6
—Minnesota		NHL	7	0	0	0	6	2	0	0	0	2
92-93—Minnesota		NHL	63	0	3	3	109	—	—	—	—	—
NHL totals			**233**	**4**	**28**	**32**	**311**	**13**	**0**	**1**	**1**	**16**

BERTHIAUME, DANIEL

G, SENATORS

PERSONAL: Born January 26, 1966, at Longueuil, Que. . . . 5-9/160. . . . Shoots left. . . . Name pronounced bahr-TAI-ohm.

TRANSACTIONS/CAREER NOTES: Traded by Drummondville Voltigeurs to Chicoutimi Sagueneens for RW Simon Massie (October 1984). . . . Selected by Winnipeg Jets as underage junior in third round (third Jets pick, 60th overall) of NHL entry draft (June 15, 1985). . . . Pulled chest muscle (March 1, 1988). . . . Suspended by Jets for failing to report to Moncton (October 4, 1988); suspension lifted (October 11, 1988). . . . Suspended by Moncton (November 4, 1988); suspension lifted (November 29, 1988). . . . Injured shoulder and suspended eight games by AHL for altercation (December 17, 1988). . . . Traded by Jets to Minnesota North Stars for future considerations (January 22, 1990). . . . Injured knee (February 13, 1990); missed 13 games. . . . Traded by North Stars to Los Angeles Kings for LW Craig Duncanson (September 6, 1990). . . . Suffered concussion (December 5, 1991); missed two games. . . . Traded by Kings to Boston Bruins for future considerations (January 20, 1992). . . . Traded by Bruins to Jets for LW Doug Evans (June 10, 1992). . . . Signed as free agent by Ottawa Senators (December 16, 1992).

HONORS: Won Michel Briere Trophy (1984-85). . . . Won Jacques Plante Trophy (1984-85).

			REGULAR SEASON							PLAYOFFS						
Season	Team	League	Gms.	Min.	W	L	T	GA	SO	Avg.	Gms.	Min.	W	L	GA	SO	Avg.
83-84—Drummondville		QMJHL	28	1562	...	...	...	131	0	5.03	—	—	—	—	—	—	—
84-85—Drummondville/Chicoutimi		QMJHL	*59	*3347	40	11	2	215	†2	3.85	†14	770	8	6	*51	0	3.97
85-86—Chicoutimi		QMJHL	*66	*3718	34	29	3	*286	1	4.62	9	580	4	5	36	0	3.72
—Winnipeg		NHL	—	—	—	—	—	—	—	—	1	68	0	1	4	0	3.53
86-87—Sherbrooke		AHL	7	420	4	3	0	23	0	3.29	—	—	—	—	—	—	—
—Winnipeg		NHL	31	1758	18	7	3	93	1	3.17	8	439	4	4	21	0	2.87
87-88—Winnipeg		NHL	56	3010	22	19	7	176	2	3.51	5	300	1	4	25	0	5.00
88-89—Winnipeg		NHL	9	443	0	8	0	44	0	5.96	—	—	—	—	—	—	—
—Moncton		AHL	21	1083	6	9	2	76	0	4.21	3	180	1	2	11	0	3.67
89-90—Winnipeg		NHL	24	1387	10	11	3	86	1	3.72	—	—	—	—	—	—	—
—Minnesota		NHL	5	240	1	3	0	14	0	3.50	—	—	—	—	—	—	—
90-91—Los Angeles		NHL	37	2119	20	11	4	117	1	3.31	—	—	—	—	—	—	—
91-92—Los Angeles		NHL	19	979	7	10	1	66	0	4.04	—	—	—	—	—	—	—
—Boston		NHL	8	399	1	4	2	21	0	3.16	—	—	—	—	—	—	—
92-93—Ottawa		NHL	25	1326	2	17	1	95	0	4.30	—	—	—	—	—	—	—
NHL totals			**214**	**11661**	**81**	**90**	**21**	**712**	**5**	**3.66**	**14**	**807**	**5**	**9**	**50**	**0**	**3.72**

BERTUZZI, TODD
C/RW, ISLANDERS

PERSONAL: Born February 2, 1975, at Sudbury, Ont. . . . 6-3/227. . . . Shoots left.
HIGH SCHOOL: Bishop MacDonnell (Guelph, Ont.).
TRANSACTIONS/CAREER NOTES: Selected by New York Islanders in first round (first Islanders pick, 23rd overall) of NHL entry draft (June 26, 1993).

Season Team	League	Gms.	G	A	Pts.	Pen.	Gms.	G	A	Pts.	Pen.
			REGULAR SEASON					PLAYOFFS			
91-92—Guelph	OHL	47	7	14	21	145	—	—	—	—	—
92-93—Guelph	OHL	60	27	31	58	168	5	2	2	4	6

BERUBE, CRAIG
LW, CAPITALS

PERSONAL: Born December 17, 1965, at Calihoo, Alta. . . . 6-2/195. . . . Shoots left. . . . Name pronounced buh-ROO-bee.
TRANSACTIONS/CAREER NOTES: Signed as free agent by Philadelphia Flyers (March 19, 1986). . . . Sprained left knee (March 1988). . . . Traded by Flyers with RW Scott Mellanby and C Craig Fisher to Edmonton Oilers for RW Dave Brown, D Corey Foster and the NHL rights to RW Jari Kurri (May 30, 1991). . . . Traded by Oilers with G Grant Fuhr and RW/LW Glenn Anderson to Toronto Maple Leafs for LW Vincent Damphousse, D Luke Richardson, G Peter Ing, C Scott Thornton and future considerations (September 19, 1991). . . . Traded by Maple Leafs with D Alexander Godynyuk, RW Gary Leeman, D Michel Petit and G Jeff Reese to Calgary Flames for C Doug Gilmour, D Jamie Macoun, LW Kent Manderville, D Ric Nattress and G Rick Wamsley (January 2, 1992). . . . Traded by Flames to Washington Capitals for fifth-round pick (C Darryl LaFrance) in 1993 draft (June 26, 1993).

Season Team	League	Gms.	G	A	Pts.	Pen.	Gms.	G	A	Pts.	Pen.
			REGULAR SEASON					PLAYOFFS			
82-83—Williams Lake	PCJHL	33	9	24	33	99	—	—	—	—	—
—Kamloops	WHL	4	0	0	0	0	—	—	—	—	—
83-84—New Westminster	WHL	70	11	20	31	104	8	1	2	3	5
84-85—New Westminster	WHL	70	25	44	69	191	10	3	2	5	4
85-86—Kamloops	WHL	32	17	14	31	119	—	—	—	—	—
—Medicine Hat	WHL	34	14	16	30	95	25	7	8	15	102
86-87—Hershey	AHL	63	7	17	24	325	—	—	—	—	—
—Philadelphia	NHL	7	0	0	0	57	5	0	0	0	17
87-88—Hershey	AHL	31	5	9	14	119	—	—	—	—	—
—Philadelphia	NHL	27	3	2	5	108	—	—	—	—	—
88-89—Hershey	AHL	7	0	2	2	19	—	—	—	—	—
—Philadelphia	NHL	53	1	1	2	199	16	0	0	0	56
89-90—Philadelphia	NHL	74	4	14	18	291	—	—	—	—	—
90-91—Philadelphia	NHL	74	8	9	17	293	—	—	—	—	—
91-92—Toronto	NHL	40	5	7	12	109	—	—	—	—	—
—Calgary	NHL	36	1	4	5	155	—	—	—	—	—
92-93—Calgary	NHL	77	4	8	12	209	6	0	1	1	21
NHL totals		388	26	45	71	1421	27	0	1	1	94

BES, JEFF
C, STARS

PERSONAL: Born July 31, 1973, at Tillsonburg, Ont. . . . 6-0/185. . . . Shoots left.
HIGH SCHOOL: Bishop MacDonnell (Guelph, Ont.).
TRANSACTIONS/CAREER NOTES: Selected by Minnesota North Stars in third round (second North Stars pick, 58th overall) of NHL entry draft (June 20, 1992). . . . North Stars franchise moved from Minnesota to Dallas and renamed Stars for 1993-94 season.

Season Team	League	Gms.	G	A	Pts.	Pen.	Gms.	G	A	Pts.	Pen.
			REGULAR SEASON					PLAYOFFS			
87-88—Woodstock Jr. C	OHA	33	19	10	29	16	—	—	—	—	—
88-89—St. Mary's Jr. B	OHA	37	8	22	30	37	—	—	—	—	—
89-90—St. Mary's Jr. B	OHA	39	25	37	62	127	—	—	—	—	—
90-91—Dukes of Hamilton	OHL	66	23	47	70	53	4	1	4	5	4
91-92—Guelph	OHL	62	40	62	102	123	—	—	—	—	—
92-93—Guelph	OHL	59	48	67	115	128	5	3	5	8	4
—Kalamazoo	IHL	3	1	3	4	6	—	—	—	—	—

BESTER, ALLAN
G, RED WINGS

PERSONAL: Born March 26, 1964, at Hamilton, Ont. . . . 5-7/155. . . . Shoots left.
TRANSACTIONS/CAREER NOTES: Selected by Toronto Maple Leafs as underage junior in third round (third Maple Leafs pick, 48th overall) of NHL entry draft (June 8, 1983). . . . Sprained left knee ligaments (February 1988); missed 14 games. . . . Suffered phlebitis in right leg (January 1989). . . . Stretched knee ligaments (April 1989). . . . Suffered from bone spurs in right heel (October 1989). . . . Underwent surgery for calcium deposits on his heels (October 1990). . . . Traded by Maple Leafs to Detroit Red Wings for sixth-round pick in 1991 draft (C Alexander Kuzminsky) (March 5, 1991).
HONORS: Named to OHL All-Star first team (1982-83). . . . Won Jack Butterfield Trophy (1991-92).

Season Team	League	Gms.	Min.	W	L	T	GA	SO	Avg.	Gms.	Min.	W	L	GA	SO	Avg.
			REGULAR SEASON								PLAYOFFS					
81-82—Brantford	OHL	19	970	4	11	0	68	0	4.21	—	—	—	—	—	—	—
82-83—Brantford	OHL	56	3210	29	21	3	188	0	3.51	8	480	3	3	20	†1	*2.50
83-84—Brantford	OHL	23	1271	12	9	1	71	1	3.35	1	60	0	1	5	0	5.00
—Toronto	NHL	32	1848	11	16	4	134	0	4.35	—	—	—	—	—	—	—
84-85—St. Catharines	AHL	30	1669	9	18	1	133	0	4.78	—	—	—	—	—	—	—
—Toronto	NHL	15	767	3	9	1	54	1	4.22	—	—	—	—	—	—	—
85-86—St. Catharines	AHL	50	2855	23	23	3	173	1	3.64	11	637	7	3	27	0	2.54
—Toronto	NHL	1	20	0	0	0	2	0	6.00	—	—	—	—	—	—	—

Season	Team	League	REGULAR SEASON								PLAYOFFS						
			Gms.	Min.	W	L	T	GA	SO	Avg.	Gms.	Min.	W	L	GA	SO	Avg.
86-87	—Newmarket	AHL	3	190	1	0	0	6	0	1.89	—	—	—	—	—	—	—
	—Toronto	NHL	36	1808	10	14	3	110	2	3.65	1	39	0	0	1	0	1.54
87-88	—Toronto	NHL	30	1607	8	12	5	102	2	3.81	5	253	2	3	21	0	4.98
88-89	—Toronto	NHL	43	2460	17	20	3	156	2	3.80	—	—	—	—	—	—	—
89-90	—Newmarket	AHL	5	264	2	1	1	18	0	4.09	—	—	—	—	—	—	—
	—Toronto	NHL	42	2206	20	16	0	165	0	4.49	—	—	—	—	—	—	—
90-91	—Toronto	NHL	6	247	0	4	0	18	0	4.37	—	—	—	—	—	—	—
	—Detroit	NHL	3	178	0	3	0	13	0	4.38	1	20	0	0	1	0	3.00
	—Newmarket	AHL	19	1157	7	8	4	58	1	3.01	—	—	—	—	—	—	—
91-92	—Detroit	NHL	1	31	0	0	0	2	0	3.87	—	—	—	—	—	—	—
	—Adirondack	AHL	22	1268	13	8	0	78	0	3.69	†19	1174	*14	5	50	1	2.56
92-93	—Adirondack	AHL	41	2268	16	15	5	133	1	3.52	10	633	7	3	26	†1	2.46
NHL totals			209	11172	69	94	16	756	7	4.06	7	312	2	3	23	0	4.42

BETS, MAXIM
LW, BLUES

PERSONAL: Born January 31, 1974, at Chelyabinsk, U.S.S.R. . . . 6-0/192. . . . Shoots left.
TRANSACTIONS/CAREER NOTES: Selected by St. Louis Blues in second round (first Blues pick, 37th overall) of NHL entry draft (June 26, 1993).
HONORS: Named to Can.HL All-Rookie team (1992-93).

Season	Team	League	REGULAR SEASON					PLAYOFFS				
			Gms.	G	A	Pts.	Pen.	Gms.	G	A	Pts.	Pen.
90-91	—Traktor Juniors	CIS	60	71	37	108	...	—	—	—	—	—
91-92	—Traktor Chelyabinsk	CIS	25	1	1	2	8	—	—	—	—	—
92-93	—Spokane	WHL	54	49	57	106	130	9	5	6	11	20

BEUKEBOOM, JEFF
D, RANGERS

PERSONAL: Born March 28, 1965, at Ajax, Ont. . . . 6-4/223. . . . Shoots right. . . . Name pronounced BOO-kuh-BOOM. . . . Nephew of Ed Kea, defenseman, Atlanta Flames and St. Louis Blues (1973-74 through 1982-83); cousin of Joe Nieuwendyk, center, Calgary Flames.
TRANSACTIONS/CAREER NOTES: Selected by Edmonton Oilers as underage junior in first round (first Oilers pick, 19th overall) of NHL entry draft (June 8,1983). . . . Injured knee (December 1984). . . . Lacerated knuckle (October 24, 1987). . . . Suspended 10 games by NHL for leaving the bench (October 2, 1988). . . . Sprained right knee (January 1989). . . . Suffered hairline fracture of ankle (February 22, 1991); missed two games. . . . Traded by Oilers to New York Rangers for D David Shaw (November 12, 1991), completing deal in which Oilers traded C Mark Messier with future considerations to Rangers for C Bernie Nicholls, LW Louie DeBrusk, RW Steven Rice and future considerations (October 4, 1991). . . . Strained back (March 16, 1992); missed one game. . . . Injured knee (December 21, 1992); missed one game. . . . Bruised ankle (February 1, 1993); missed one game.
HONORS: Named to OHL All-Star first team (1984-85).
MISCELLANEOUS: Member of Stanley Cup championship teams (1987, 1988 and 1990).

Season	Team	League	REGULAR SEASON					PLAYOFFS				
			Gms.	G	A	Pts.	Pen.	Gms.	G	A	Pts.	Pen.
81-82	—Newmarket	OPJHL	49	5	30	35	218	—	—	—	—	—
82-83	—Sault Ste. Marie	OHL	70	0	25	25	143	16	1	14	15	46
83-84	—Sault Ste. Marie	OHL	61	6	30	36	178	16	1	7	8	43
84-85	—Sault Ste. Marie	OHL	37	4	20	24	85	16	4	6	10	47
85-86	—Nova Scotia	AHL	77	9	20	29	175	—	—	—	—	—
	—Edmonton	NHL	—	—	—	—	—	1	0	0	0	4
86-87	—Nova Scotia	AHL	14	1	7	8	35	—	—	—	—	—
	—Edmonton	NHL	44	3	8	11	124	—	—	—	—	—
87-88	—Edmonton	NHL	73	5	20	25	201	7	0	0	0	16
88-89	—Cape Breton	AHL	8	0	4	4	36	—	—	—	—	—
	—Edmonton	NHL	36	0	5	5	94	1	0	0	0	2
89-90	—Edmonton	NHL	46	1	12	13	86	2	0	0	0	0
90-91	—Edmonton	NHL	67	3	7	10	150	18	1	3	4	28
91-92	—Edmonton	NHL	18	0	5	5	78	—	—	—	—	—
	—New York Rangers	NHL	56	1	10	11	122	13	2	3	5	*47
92-93	—New York Rangers	NHL	82	2	17	19	153	—	—	—	—	—
NHL totals			422	15	84	99	1008	42	3	6	9	97

BICANEK, RADIM
D, SENATORS

PERSONAL: Born January 18, 1975, at Uherske Hradiste, Czechoslovakia. . . . 6-1/178. . . . Shoots left.
TRANSACTIONS/CAREER NOTES: Selected by Ottawa Senators in second round (second Senators pick, 27th overall) of NHL entry draft (June 26, 1993).

Season	Team	League	REGULAR SEASON					PLAYOFFS				
			Gms.	G	A	Pts.	Pen.	Gms.	G	A	Pts.	Pen.
92-93	—Jihlava	Czech.	43	2	3	5	...	—	—	—	—	—

BIGGS, DON
C

PERSONAL: Born April 7, 1965, at Mississauga, Ont. . . . 5-8/180. . . . Shoots right.
TRANSACTIONS/CAREER NOTES: Injured knee ligaments (April 1982). . . . Selected by Minnesota North Stars as underage junior in eighth round (ninth North Stars pick, 156th overall) of NHL entry draft (June 8, 1983). . . . Traded by North Stars with RW Gord Sherven to Edmonton Oilers for C Marc Habscheid, D Emanuel Viveiros and LW Don Barber (December 20, 1985). . . . Signed as free agent by Philadelphia Flyers (July

B

17, 1987).... Suspended five games by AHL for biting (December 16, 1989).... Signed to play with Olten (Switzerland) (May 1990).... Claimed on waivers by Rochester Americans after signing contract with Hershey Bears upon returning from Switzerland (November 1, 1990).... Suspended three games by AHL for physically abusing linesman (February 1, 1991).... Traded by Flyers to New York Rangers for future considerations (August 8, 1991).... Signed as free agent by Cincinnati Cyclones (July 22, 1993).

HONORS: Won Les Cunningham Plaque (1992-93).... Won the John B. Sollenberger Trophy (1992-93).... Named to AHL All-Star first team (1992-93).

			REGULAR SEASON					PLAYOFFS				
Season	Team	League	Gms.	G	A	Pts.	Pen.	Gms.	G	A	Pts.	Pen.
82-83	—Oshawa	OHL	70	22	53	75	145	16	3	6	9	17
83-84	—Oshawa	OHL	58	31	60	91	149	7	4	4	8	18
84-85	—Oshawa	OHL	60	48	69	117	105	5	3	4	7	6
	—Springfield	AHL	6	0	3	3	0	2	1	0	1	0
	—Minnesota	NHL	1	0	0	0	0	—	—	—	—	—
85-86	—Springfield	AHL	28	15	16	31	46	—	—	—	—	—
	—Nova Scotia	AHL	47	6	23	29	36	—	—	—	—	—
86-87	—Nova Scotia	AHL	80	22	25	47	165	5	1	2	3	4
87-88	—Hershey	AHL	77	38	41	79	151	12	5	†11	†16	22
88-89	—Hershey	AHL	76	36	67	103	158	11	5	9	14	30
89-90	—Philadelphia	NHL	11	2	0	2	8	—	—	—	—	—
	—Hershey	AHL	66	39	53	92	125	—	—	—	—	—
90-91	—Olten	Switzerland				Statistics unavailable.						
	—Rochester	AHL	65	31	57	88	115	15	9	*14	*23	14
91-92	—Binghamton	AHL	74	32	50	82	122	11	3	7	10	8
92-93	—Binghamton	AHL	78	54	*84	*138	112	14	3	9	12	32
	NHL totals		12	2	0	2	8					

BILLINGTON, CRAIG
G, SENATORS

PERSONAL: Born September 11, 1966, at London, Ont.... 5-10/170.... Shoots left.
TRANSACTIONS/CAREER NOTES: Selected by New Jersey Devils as underage junior in second round (second Devils pick, 23rd overall) of NHL entry draft (June 9, 1984).... Suffered from mononucleosis (July 1984).... Injured hamstring (February 15, 1992); missed two games.... Strained knee (March 11, 1992); missed six games.... Underwent arthroscopic knee surgery (April 13, 1992).... Suffered from sore throat (March 27, 1993); missed one game.... Traded by Devils with C/LW Troy Mallette and fourth-round pick in 1993 draft (C Cosmo Dupaul) to Ottawa Senators for G Peter Sidorkiewicz and future considerations (June 20, 1993); Senators sent LW Mike Peluso to Devils to complete deal (June 26, 1993).

HONORS: Won Bobby Smith Trophy (1984-85).... Named to OHL All-Star first team (1984-85).... Played in NHL All-Star Game (1993).

			REGULAR SEASON							PLAYOFFS					
Season	Team	League	Gms.	Min.	W	L	T	GA	SO	Avg.	Gms.	Min.	W	L	GA	SO	Avg.
82-83	—London Diamonds	OPJHL	23	1338	...	...	...	76	0	3.41	—	—	—	—	—	—	—
83-84	—Belleville	OHL	44	2335	20	19	0	162	1	4.16	1	30	0	0	3	0	6.00
84-85	—Belleville	OHL	47	2544	26	19	0	180	1	4.25	14	761	7	5	47	†1	3.71
85-86	—Belleville	OHL	3	180	2	1	0	11	0	3.67	†20	1133	9	6	*68	0	3.60
	—New Jersey	NHL	18	902	4	9	1	77	0	5.12	—	—	—	—	—	—	—
86-87	—Maine	AHL	20	1151	9	8	2	70	0	3.65	—	—	—	—	—	—	—
	—New Jersey	NHL	22	1114	4	13	2	89	0	4.79	—	—	—	—	—	—	—
87-88	—Utica	AHL	*59	*3404	22	27	8	*208	1	3.67	—	—	—	—	—	—	—
88-89	—Utica	AHL	41	2432	17	18	6	150	2	3.70	4	219	1	3	18	0	4.93
89-90	—Utica	AHL	38	2087	20	13	1	138	0	3.97	—	—	—	—	—	—	—
90-91	—Can. national team	Int'l	34	1879	17	14	2	110	2	3.51	—	—	—	—	—	—	—
91-92	—New Jersey	NHL	26	1363	13	7	1	69	2	3.04	—	—	—	—	—	—	—
92-93	—New Jersey	NHL	42	2389	21	16	4	146	2	3.67	2	78	0	1	5	0	3.85
	NHL totals		108	5768	42	45	8	381	4	3.96	2	78	0	1	5	0	3.85

BILODEAU, BRENT
D, CANADIENS

PERSONAL: Born March 27, 1973, at Dallas.... 6-4/215.... Shoots left.... Name pronounced BIH-lih-DOH.
TRANSACTIONS/CAREER NOTES: Selected by Montreal Canadiens in first round (first Canadiens pick, 17th overall) of NHL entry draft (June 22, 1991).

HONORS: Named to WHL (East) All-Star second team (1991-92 and 1992-93).

			REGULAR SEASON					PLAYOFFS				
Season	Team	League	Gms.	G	A	Pts.	Pen.	Gms.	G	A	Pts.	Pen.
88-89	—St. Albert	AJHL	55	8	17	25	167	—	—	—	—	—
89-90	—Seattle	WHL	68	14	29	43	170	13	3	5	8	31
90-91	—Seattle	WHL	55	7	18	25	145	6	1	0	1	12
91-92	—Seattle	WHL	7	1	2	3	43	—	—	—	—	—
	—Swift Current	WHL	56	10	47	57	118	8	2	3	5	11
92-93	—Swift Current	WHL	59	11	57	68	77	17	5	14	19	18

BJUGSTAD, SCOTT
LW/C/RW, KINGS

PERSONAL: Born June 2, 1961, at St. Paul, Minn.... 6-1/185.... Shoots left.... Name pronounced BYOOG-stad.
HIGH SCHOOL: Irondale (St. Paul, Minn.).
COLLEGE: Minnesota.
TRANSACTIONS/CAREER NOTES: Selected by Minnesota North Stars in ninth round (13th North Stars pick, 181st overall) of NHL entry draft (June 10, 1981).... Pulled abdominal muscle (March 15, 1987).... Separated shoulder (October 31, 1987)....

Strained knee ligaments (December 1987).... Underwent knee surgery (February 1988).... Strained left knee ligaments (September 1988).... Traded by North Stars with D Gord Dineen to Pittsburgh Penguins for D Ville Siren and C Steve Gotaas (December 17, 1988).... Suspended by Penguins for refusing to report to Muskegon Lumberjacks (March 10, 1989).... Signed as free agent by Los Angeles Kings (August 21, 1989).... Injured groin (October 1989).... Sprained knee (April 1990).... Sprained left knee (December 20, 1990); missed five games.... Fractured nose (January 22, 1991); missed four games.... Suffered recurring abdominal strain (March 1992); missed remainder of season.
HONORS: Named to WCHL All-Star first team (1982-83).

			REGULAR SEASON					PLAYOFFS				
Season	Team	League	Gms.	G	A	Pts.	Pen.	Gms.	G	A	Pts.	Pen.
79-80—University of Minnesota ...		WCHA	18	2	2	4	2	—	—	—	—	—
80-81—University of Minnesota ...		WCHA	35	12	13	25	34	—	—	—	—	—
81-82—University of Minnesota ...		WCHA	36	29	14	43	24	—	—	—	—	—
82-83—University of Minnesota ...		WCHA	44	43	48	91	30	—	—	—	—	—
83-84—U.S. national team		Int'l	54	31	20	51	28	—	—	—	—	—
—U.S. Olympic Team		Int'l	6	3	1	4	6	—	—	—	—	—
—Minnesota		NHL	5	0	0	0	2	—	—	—	—	—
—Salt Lake City..................		IHL	15	10	8	18	6	5	3	4	7	0
84-85—Minnesota		NHL	72	11	4	15	32	—	—	—	—	—
—Springfield......................		AHL	5	2	3	5	2	—	—	—	—	—
85-86—Minnesota		NHL	80	43	33	76	24	5	0	1	1	0
86-87—Minnesota		NHL	39	4	9	13	43	—	—	—	—	—
—Springfield......................		AHL	11	6	4	10	7	—	—	—	—	—
87-88—Minnesota		NHL	33	10	12	22	15	—	—	—	—	—
88-89—Geneva		Switzerland			Statistics unavailable.							
—Pittsburgh		NHL	24	3	0	3	4	—	—	—	—	—
—Kalamazoo		IHL	4	5	0	5	4	—	—	—	—	—
89-90—New Haven		AHL	47	45	21	66	40	—	—	—	—	—
—Los Angeles....................		NHL	11	1	2	3	2	2	0	0	0	2
90-91—Phoenix		IHL	3	7	2	9	2	—	—	—	—	—
—Los Angeles....................		NHL	31	2	4	6	12	2	0	0	0	0
91-92—Los Angeles....................		NHL	22	2	4	6	10	—	—	—	—	—
—Phoenix		IHL	28	14	14	28	12	—	—	—	—	—
92-93—Phoenix		IHL	7	5	4	9	4	—	—	—	—	—
NHL totals..............			317	76	68	144	144	9	0	1	1	2

BLACK, JAMES
C, STARS

PERSONAL: Born August 15, 1969, at Regina, Sask.... 5-11/185.... Shoots left.
TRANSACTIONS/CAREER NOTES: Selected by Hartford Whalers in fifth round (fourth Whalers pick, 94th overall) of NHL entry draft (June 17, 1989).... Traded by Whalers to Minnesota North Stars for C Mark Janssens (September 3, 1992).... North Stars franchise moved from Minnesota to Dallas and renamed Stars for 1993-94 season.

			REGULAR SEASON					PLAYOFFS				
Season	Team	League	Gms.	G	A	Pts.	Pen.	Gms.	G	A	Pts.	Pen.
87-88—Portland		WHL	72	30	50	80	50	—	—	—	—	—
88-89—Portland		WHL	71	45	51	96	57	19	13	6	19	28
89-90—Hartford.........................		NHL	1	0	0	0	0	—	—	—	—	—
—Binghamton		AHL	80	37	35	72	34	—	—	—	—	—
90-91—Hartford.........................		NHL	1	0	0	0	0	—	—	—	—	—
—Springfield......................		AHL	79	35	61	96	34	18	9	9	18	6
91-92—Springfield......................		AHL	47	15	25	40	33	10	3	2	5	18
—Hartford.........................		NHL	30	4	6	10	10	—	—	—	—	—
92-93—Minnesota		NHL	10	2	1	3	4	—	—	—	—	—
—Kalamazoo		IHL	63	25	45	70	40	—	—	—	—	—
NHL totals..............			42	6	7	13	14	—	—	—	—	—

BLACK, RYAN
LW, DEVILS

PERSONAL: Born October 25, 1973, at Guelph, Ont.... 6-1/180.... Shoots left.
HIGH SCHOOL: Thomas A. Stewart (Peterborough, Ont.).
TRANSACTIONS/CAREER NOTES: Selected by New Jersey Devils in fifth round (sixth Devils pick, 114th overall) of NHL entry draft (June 20, 1992).

			REGULAR SEASON					PLAYOFFS				
Season	Team	League	Gms.	G	A	Pts.	Pen.	Gms.	G	A	Pts.	Pen.
88-89—New Hamburg Jr. C..........		OHA	23	3	3	6	24	—	—	—	—	—
89-90—Elmira Jr. B		OHA	33	19	21	40	94	—	—	—	—	—
—Waterloo Jr. B.................		OHA	15	5	4	9	37	—	—	—	—	—
90-91—Peterborough		OHL	59	7	16	23	41	4	0	1	1	0
91-92—Peterborough		OHL	66	18	33	51	57	7	1	1	2	11
92-93—Peterborough		OHL	66	30	41	71	41	20	7	4	11	28

BLAKE, ROB
D, KINGS

PERSONAL: Born December 10, 1969, at Simcoe, Ont.... 6-3/205.... Shoots right.... Full name: Robert Bowlby Blake.
COLLEGE: Bowling Green State.
TRANSACTIONS/CAREER NOTES: Dislocated shoulder (April 1987).... Selected by Los Angeles Kings in fourth round (fourth Kings pick, 70th overall) of NHL entry draft (June 11, 1988).... Sprained knee (April 1990).... Injured knee (February 12, 1991); missed two games.... Injured shoulder (October 8, 1991); missed 11 games.... Sprained

knee ligaments (November 28, 1991); missed six games. . . . Suffered from the flu (January 23, 1992); missed one game. . . . Suffered from the flu (February 13, 1992); missed one game. . . . Strained shoulder (March 14, 1992); missed four games. . . . Broke rib (December 19, 1992); missed three games. . . . Suffered lower back contusion (April 3, 1993); missed final five games of regular season and one playoff game.

HONORS: Named to CCHA All-Star second team (1988-89). . . . Named to NCAA All-America West first team (1989-90). . . . Named to CCHA All-Star first team (1989-90). . . . Named to NHL All-Rookie team (1990-91).

			REGULAR SEASON					PLAYOFFS				
Season	Team	League	Gms.	G	A	Pts.	Pen.	Gms.	G	A	Pts.	Pen.
86-87—	Stratford Jr. B	OHA	31	11	20	31	115	—	—	—	—	—
87-88—	Bowling Green State	CCHA	36	5	8	13	72	—	—	—	—	—
88-89—	Bowling Green State	CCHA	46	11	21	32	140	—	—	—	—	—
89-90—	Bowling Green State	CCHA	42	23	36	59	140	—	—	—	—	—
	—Los Angeles	NHL	4	0	0	0	4	8	1	3	4	4
90-91—	Los Angeles	NHL	75	12	34	46	125	12	1	4	5	26
91-92—	Los Angeles	NHL	57	7	13	20	102	6	2	1	3	12
92-93—	Los Angeles	NHL	76	16	43	59	152	23	4	6	10	46
	NHL totals		212	35	90	125	383	49	8	14	22	88

BLOEMBERG, JEFF
D, OILERS

PERSONAL: Born January 31, 1968, at Listowel, Ont. . . . 6-2/205. . . . Shoots right. . . . Name pronounced BLOOM-buhrg.
TRANSACTIONS/CAREER NOTES: Selected by New York Rangers as underage junior in fifth round (fifth Rangers pick, 93rd overall) of NHL entry draft (June 21, 1986). . . . Selected by Tampa Bay Lightning in NHL expansion draft (June 18, 1992). . . . Traded by Lightning to Edmonton Oilers for future considerations (September 25, 1992).
HONORS: Named to AHL All-Star second team (1990-91).

			REGULAR SEASON					PLAYOFFS				
Season	Team	League	Gms.	G	A	Pts.	Pen.	Gms.	G	A	Pts.	Pen.
84-85—	Listowel Jr. B	OHA	31	7	14	21	73	—	—	—	—	—
85-86—	North Bay	OHL	60	2	11	13	76	8	1	2	3	9
86-87—	North Bay	OHL	60	5	13	18	91	21	1	6	7	13
87-88—	North Bay	OHL	46	9	26	35	60	—	—	—	—	—
	—Colorado	IHL	5	0	0	0	0	11	1	0	1	8
88-89—	New York Rangers	NHL	9	0	0	0	0	—	—	—	—	—
	—Denver	IHL	64	7	22	29	55	1	0	0	0	0
89-90—	Flint	IHL	44	7	21	28	24	—	—	—	—	—
90-91—	Binghamton	AHL	77	16	46	62	28	10	0	6	6	10
91-92—	Binghamton	AHL	66	6	41	47	22	11	1	10	11	10
	—New York Rangers	NHL	3	0	1	1	0	—	—	—	—	—
92-93—	Cape Breton	AHL	76	6	45	51	34	16	5	10	15	10
	NHL totals		12	0	1	1	0					

BLUE, JOHN
G, BRUINS

PERSONAL: Born February 9, 1966, at Huntington Beach, Calif. . . . 5-10/185. . . . Shoots left.
COLLEGE: Minnesota.
TRANSACTIONS/CAREER NOTES: Selected by Winnipeg Jets in 10th round (ninth Jets pick, 197th overall) of NHL entry draft (June 21, 1986). . . . Traded by Jets to Minnesota North Stars for seventh-round pick in 1988 draft (C Markus Akerbloom) (March 7, 1988). . . . Signed as free agent by Boston Bruins (August 1, 1991).
HONORS: Named to WCHA All-Star second team (1984-85). . . . Named to WCHA All-Star first team (1985-86).

			REGULAR SEASON							PLAYOFFS						
Season	Team	League	Gms.	Min.	W	L	T	GA	SO	Avg.	Gms.	Min.	W	L	GA	SO	Avg.
83-84—	Des Moines	USHL	15	753	...	...	...	63	...	5.02	—	—	—	—	—	—	—
84-85—	Univ. of Minnesota	WCHA	34	1964	23	10	0	111	2	3.39	—	—	—	—	—	—	—
85-86—	Univ. of Minnesota	WCHA	29	1588	20	6	0	80	3	3.02	—	—	—	—	—	—	—
86-87—	Univ. of Minnesota	WCHA	33	1889	21	9	1	99	3	3.14	—	—	—	—	—	—	—
87-88—	U.S. national team	Int'l	13	588	3	4	1	33	0	3.37	—	—	—	—	—	—	—
	—Kalamazoo	IHL	15	847	3	8	4	65	0	4.60	1	40	0	1	6	0	9.00
88-89—	Kalamazoo	IHL	17	970	8	6	0	69	0	4.27	—	—	—	—	—	—	—
	—Virginia	ECHL	10	570	...	...	...	38	0	4.00	—	—	—	—	—	—	—
89-90—	Kalamazoo	IHL	4	232	2	1	1	18	0	4.66	—	—	—	—	—	—	—
	—Phoenix	IHL	19	986	5	10	3	93	0	5.66	—	—	—	—	—	—	—
	—Knoxville	ECHL	19	1000	6	10	1	85	...	5.10	—	—	—	—	—	—	—
90-91—	Maine	AHL	10	545	3	4	2	22	0	2.42	1	40	0	1	7	0	10.50
	—Kalamazoo	IHL	1	64	1	0	0	2	0	1.88	—	—	—	—	—	—	—
	—Albany	IHL	19	1077	11	6	0	71	0	3.96	—	—	—	—	—	—	—
	—Peoria	IHL	4	240	4	0	0	12	0	3.00	—	—	—	—	—	—	—
	—Knoxville	ECHL	3	149	1	1	0	13	0	5.23	—	—	—	—	—	—	—
91-92—	Maine	AHL	43	2168	11	*23	6	165	1	4.57	—	—	—	—	—	—	—
92-93—	Providence	AHL	19	1159	14	4	1	67	0	3.47	—	—	—	—	—	—	—
	—Boston	NHL	23	1322	9	8	4	64	1	2.90	2	96	0	1	5	0	3.13
	NHL totals		23	1322	9	8	4	64	1	2.90	2	96	0	1	5	0	3.13

BOBACK, MIKE
C, CAPITALS

PERSONAL: Born August 13, 1970, at Mt. Clemens, Mich. . . . 5-11/180. . . . Shoots right. . . . Name pronounced BOH-bak.
COLLEGE: Providence.
TRANSACTIONS/CAREER NOTES: Selected by Washington Capitals in 10th round (12th Capitals

pick, 198th overall) of NHL entry draft (June 16, 1990).
HONORS: Named to Hockey East All-Star first team (1989-90 and 1991-92).

Season	Team	League	REGULAR SEASON					PLAYOFFS				
			Gms.	G	A	Pts.	Pen.	Gms.	G	A	Pts.	Pen.
88-89—Providence College		Hockey East	29	19	19	38	24	—	—	—	—	—
89-90—Providence College		Hockey East	31	13	29	42	28	—	—	—	—	—
90-91—Providence College		Hockey East	26	15	24	39	6	—	—	—	—	—
91-92—Providence College		Hockey East	36	24	*48	*72	34	—	—	—	—	—
92-93—Baltimore		AHL	69	11	68	79	14	5	3	3	6	6

BODGER, DOUG
D, SABRES

PERSONAL: Born June 18, 1966, at Chemainus, B.C. . . . 6-2/213. . . . Shoots left. . . . Name pronounced BAH-juhr.
TRANSACTIONS/CAREER NOTES: Selected by Pittsburgh Penguins as underage junior in first round (second Penguins pick, ninth overall) of NHL entry draft (June 9, 1984). . . . Underwent surgery to remove bone chip on left foot (April 1985). . . . Sprained knee (December 1987). . . . Strained left knee (October 1988). . . . Traded by Penguins with LW Darrin Shannon to Buffalo Sabres for G Tom Barrasso and third-round pick in 1990 draft (November 12, 1988). . . . Sprained left knee (October 1989); missed eight games. . . . Injured shoulder (December 28, 1990); missed four games. . . . Separated left shoulder (February 17, 1991); missed 18 games. . . . Reinjured left shoulder (March 30, 1991). . . . Injured eye (February 11, 1992); missed seven games.
HONORS: Named to WHL All-Star second team (1982-83). . . . Named to WHL (West) All-Star first team (1983-84).

Season	Team	League	REGULAR SEASON					PLAYOFFS				
			Gms.	G	A	Pts.	Pen.	Gms.	G	A	Pts.	Pen.
82-83—Kamloops		WHL	72	26	66	92	98	7	0	5	5	2
83-84—Kamloops		WHL	70	21	77	98	90	17	2	15	17	12
84-85—Pittsburgh		NHL	65	5	26	31	67	—	—	—	—	—
85-86—Pittsburgh		NHL	79	4	33	37	63	—	—	—	—	—
86-87—Pittsburgh		NHL	76	11	38	49	52	—	—	—	—	—
87-88—Pittsburgh		NHL	69	14	31	45	103	—	—	—	—	—
88-89—Pittsburgh		NHL	10	1	4	5	7	—	—	—	—	—
—Buffalo		NHL	61	7	40	47	52	5	1	1	2	11
89-90—Buffalo		NHL	71	12	36	48	64	6	1	5	6	6
90-91—Buffalo		NHL	58	5	23	28	54	4	0	1	1	0
91-92—Buffalo		NHL	73	11	35	46	108	7	2	1	3	2
92-93—Buffalo		NHL	81	9	45	54	87	8	2	3	5	0
NHL totals			643	79	311	390	657	30	6	11	17	19

BODKIN, RICK
C, SENATORS

PERSONAL: Born March 30, 1975, at Hamilton, Ont. . . . 6-4/ 179. . . . Shoots left.
TRANSACTIONS/CAREER NOTES: Selected by Ottawa Senators in sixth round (fifth Senators pick, 131st overall) of NHL entry draft (June 26, 1993).

Season	Team	League	REGULAR SEASON					PLAYOFFS				
			Gms.	G	A	Pts.	Pen.	Gms.	G	A	Pts.	Pen.
91-92—Grimsby Jr. C		Nia. D. Jr.C	36	11	17	28	44	—	—	—	—	—
92-93—Sudbury		OHL	50	4	4	8	17	11	0	0	0	0

BODNARCHUK, MIKE
RW, DEVILS

PERSONAL: Born March 26, 1970, at Bramalea, Ont. . . . 6-1/ 185. . . . Shoots right. . . . Name pronounced bahd-NAHR-chuhk.
TRANSACTIONS/CAREER NOTES: Selected by New Jersey Devils in fourth round (sixth Devils pick, 64th overall) of NHL entry draft (June 16, 1990).
HONORS: Named to OHL All-Star second team (1989-90).

Season	Team	League	REGULAR SEASON					PLAYOFFS				
			Gms.	G	A	Pts.	Pen.	Gms.	G	A	Pts.	Pen.
86-87—Bramalea		MTHL	34	12	8	20	33	—	—	—	—	—
87-88—Kingston		OHL	63	12	20	32	12	—	—	—	—	—
88-89—Kingston		OHL	63	22	38	60	30	—	—	—	—	—
89-90—Kingston		OHL	66	40	59	99	31	7	2	4	6	4
90-91—Utica		AHL	69	23	32	55	28	—	—	—	—	—
91-92—Utica		AHL	76	21	19	40	36	4	0	2	2	0
92-93—Utica		AHL	21	6	10	16	4	4	2	0	2	4
—Cincinnati		IHL	47	15	18	33	65					

BOILEAU, PATRICK
D, CAPITALS

PERSONAL: Born February 22, 1975, at Montreal. . . . 6-0/ 184. . . . Shoots right.
TRANSACTIONS/CAREER NOTES: Selected by Washington Capitals in third round (third Capitals pick, 69th overall) of NHL entry draft (June 26, 1993).
HONORS: Named to Can.HL All-Rookie team (1992-93).

Season	Team	League	REGULAR SEASON					PLAYOFFS				
			Gms.	G	A	Pts.	Pen.	Gms.	G	A	Pts.	Pen.
92-93—Laval		QMJHL	69	4	19	23	73	13	1	2	3	10

BOIVIN, CLAUDE
LW, FLYERS

PERSONAL: Born March 1, 1970, at St. Foy, Que. . . . 6-2/200. . . . Shoots left.
TRANSACTIONS/CAREER NOTES: Selected by Philadelphia Flyers in first round (first Flyers pick, 14th overall) of NHL entry draft (June 11, 1988). . . . Traded by Drummondville Voltigeurs with D Serge Anglehart and fifth-round draft pick to Laval Titans for D Luc Doucet,

B

D Brad MacIsaac and second- and third-round draft picks (February 15, 1990). . . . Separated shoulder and bruised chest (October 6, 1992); missed first five games of season. . . . Tore ligaments in left knee (January 2, 1993) and underwent reconstructive knee surgery (January 18, 1993); missed remainder of season.

			REGULAR SEASON					PLAYOFFS			
Season Team	League	Gms.	G	A	Pts.	Pen.	Gms.	G	A	Pts.	Pen.
87-88—Drummondville................	QMJHL	63	23	26	49	233	17	5	3	8	74
88-89—Drummondville................	QMJHL	63	20	36	56	218	4	0	2	2	27
89-90—Laval................	QMJHL	59	24	51	75	309	13	7	13	20	59
90-91—Hershey....................	AHL	65	13	32	45	159	7	1	5	6	28
91-92—Hershey....................	AHL	20	4	5	9	96	—	—	—	—	—
—Philadelphia..................	NHL	58	5	13	18	187	—	—	—	—	—
92-93—Philadelphia..................	NHL	30	5	4	9	76	—	—	—	—	—
NHL totals........................		88	10	17	27	263					

BOMBARDIR, BRAD
D, DEVILS

PERSONAL: Born May 5, 1972, at Powell River, B.C. . . . 6-2/187. . . . Shoots left. . . . Full name: Luke Bradley Bombardir.
COLLEGE: North Dakota.
TRANSACTIONS/CAREER NOTES: Selected by New Jersey Devils in third round (fifth Devils pick, 56th overall) of NHL entry draft (June 16, 1990).

			REGULAR SEASON					PLAYOFFS			
Season Team	League	Gms.	G	A	Pts.	Pen.	Gms.	G	A	Pts.	Pen.
88-89—Powell River	BCJHL	30	6	5	11	24	6	0	0	0	0
89-90—Powell River	BCJHL	60	10	35	45	93	8	2	3	5	4
90-91—Univ. of North Dakota	WCHA	33	3	6	9	18	—	—	—	—	—
91-92—Univ. of North Dakota	WCHA	35	3	14	17	54	—	—	—	—	—
92-93—Univ. of North Dakota	WCHA	38	8	15	23	34	—	—	—	—	—

BONDRA, PETER
RW, CAPITALS

PERSONAL: Born February 7, 1968, at Luck, U.S.S.R. . . . 5-11/180. . . . Shoots left. . . . Name pronounced BAHN-druh.
TRANSACTIONS/CAREER NOTES: Selected by Washington Capitals in eighth round (ninth Capitals pick, 156th overall) of NHL entry draft (June 16, 1990). . . . Dislocated left shoulder (January 17, 1991). . . . Suffered recurring shoulder problems (February 13, 1991); missed 13 games. . . . Suffered throat injury (April 4, 1993); missed one game.
HONORS: Played in NHL All-Star Game (1993).

			REGULAR SEASON					PLAYOFFS			
Season Team	League	Gms.	G	A	Pts.	Pen.	Gms.	G	A	Pts.	Pen.
88-89—Kosice................	Czech.	40	30	10	40	20	—	—	—	—	—
89-90—Kosice................	Czech.	42	29	17	46	...	—	—	—	—	—
90-91—Washington	NHL	54	12	16	28	47	4	0	1	1	2
91-92—Washington	NHL	71	28	28	56	42	7	6	2	8	4
92-93—Washington	NHL	83	37	48	85	70	6	0	6	6	0
NHL totals........................		208	77	92	169	159	17	6	9	15	6

BORDELEAU, SEBASTIEN
C, CANADIENS

PERSONAL: Born February 15, 1975, at Vancouver, B.C. . . . 5-10/176. . . . Shoots right.
TRANSACTIONS/CAREER NOTES: Selected by Montreal Canadiens in third round (third Canadiens pick, 73rd overall) of NHL entry draft (June 26, 1993).

			REGULAR SEASON					PLAYOFFS			
Season Team	League	Gms.	G	A	Pts.	Pen.	Gms.	G	A	Pts.	Pen.
91-92—Hull	QMJHL	62	26	32	58	91	5	0	3	3	23
92-93—Hull	QMJHL	60	18	39	57	95	10	3	8	11	20

BORGO, RICHARD
RW, OILERS

PERSONAL: Born September 25, 1970, at Thunder Bay, Ont. . . . 5-11/190. . . . Shoots right.
TRANSACTIONS/CAREER NOTES: Selected by Edmonton Oilers in second round (second Oilers pick, 36th overall) of NHL entry draft (June 17, 1989).

			REGULAR SEASON					PLAYOFFS			
Season Team	League	Gms.	G	A	Pts.	Pen.	Gms.	G	A	Pts.	Pen.
85-86—Thunder Bay Twins	USHL	41	11	19	30	37	—	—	—	—	—
86-87—Kitchener...........................	OHL	62	5	10	15	29	—	—	—	—	—
87-88—Kitchener...........................	OHL	64	24	22	46	81	4	0	4	4	0
88-89—Kitchener...........................	OHL	66	23	23	46	75	5	0	1	1	4
89-90—Kitchener...........................	OHL	32	13	22	35	43	17	5	5	10	10
90-91—Kitchener...........................	OHL	60	43	56	99	50	6	1	0	1	12
91-92—Cape Breton	AHL	52	10	14	24	90	3	0	0	0	6
92-93—Cape Breton	AHL	45	7	13	20	26	1	0	0	0	2

BORSATO, LUCIANO
C, JETS

PERSONAL: Born January 7, 1966, at Richmond Hill, Ont. . . . 5-10/165. . . . Shoots right. . . . Name pronounced bohr-SAH-toh.
COLLEGE: Clarkson (N.Y.).
TRANSACTIONS/CAREER NOTES: Selected by Winnipeg Jets as underage junior in

seventh round (seventh Jets pick, 135th overall) of NHL entry draft (June 9, 1984).... Suffered back spasms (October 28, 1992); missed three games.... Fractured finger (November 19, 1992); missed eight games.... Suffered back spasms (January 17, 1993); missed six games.

HONORS: Named to NCAA All-America East second team (1987-88).... Named to ECAC All-Star second team (1987-88).

			REGULAR SEASON					PLAYOFFS			
Season Team	League	Gms.	G	A	Pts.	Pen.	Gms.	G	A	Pts.	Pen.
83-84—Bramalea	MTHL	37	20	36	56	59	—	—	—	—	—
84-85—Clarkson	ECAC	33	15	17	32	37	—	—	—	—	—
85-86—Clarkson	ECAC	32	17	20	37	50	—	—	—	—	—
86-87—Clarkson	ECAC	31	16	*41	57	55	—	—	—	—	—
87-88—Clarkson	ECAC	33	15	29	44	38	—	—	—	—	—
—Moncton	AHL	3	1	1	2	0	—	—	—	—	—
88-89—Tappara	Finland	44	31	36	67	69	7	0	3	3	4
—Moncton	AHL	6	2	5	7	4	—	—	—	—	—
89-90—Moncton	AHL	1	1	0	1	0	—	—	—	—	—
90-91—Moncton	AHL	41	14	24	38	40	9	3	7	10	22
—Winnipeg	NHL	1	0	1	1	2	—	—	—	—	—
91-92—Moncton	AHL	14	2	7	9	39	—	—	—	—	—
—Winnipeg	NHL	56	15	21	36	45	1	0	0	0	0
92-93—Winnipeg	NHL	67	15	20	35	38	6	1	0	1	4
NHL totals		124	30	42	72	85	7	1	0	1	4

BORSCHEVSKY, NIKOLAI
RW, MAPLE LEAFS

PERSONAL: Born January 12, 1965, at Tomsk, U.S.S.R.... 5-9/180.... Shoots left.... Name pronounced bohr-SHEHV-skee.

TRANSACTIONS/CAREER NOTES: Selected by Toronto Maple Leafs in fourth round (third Maple Leafs pick, 77th overall) of NHL entry draft (June 20, 1992).... Suffered bruised buttock (November 7, 1992); missed one game.... Strained neck (December 31, 1992); missed three games.... Strained back (March 9, 1993); missed one game.... Broke orbital bone (April 19, 1993); missed first five playoff games.

HONORS: Named CIS Player of the Year (1991-92).

			REGULAR SEASON					PLAYOFFS			
Season Team	League	Gms.	G	A	Pts.	Pen.	Gms.	G	A	Pts.	Pen.
83-84—Dynamo Moscow	USSR	34	4	5	9	4	—	—	—	—	—
84-85—Dynamo Moscow	USSR	34	5	9	14	6	—	—	—	—	—
85-86—Dynamo Moscow	USSR	31	6	4	10	4	—	—	—	—	—
86-87—Dynamo Moscow	USSR	28	1	4	5	8	—	—	—	—	—
87-88—Dynamo Moscow	USSR	37	11	7	18	6	—	—	—	—	—
88-89—Dynamo Moscow	USSR	43	7	8	15	18	—	—	—	—	—
89-90—Spartak Moscow	USSR	48	17	25	42	8	—	—	—	—	—
90-91—Spartak Moscow	USSR	45	19	16	35	16	—	—	—	—	—
91-92—Spartak Moscow	CIS	40	25	14	39	16	—	—	—	—	—
92-93—Toronto	NHL	78	34	40	74	28	16	2	7	9	0
NHL totals		78	34	40	74	28	16	2	7	9	0

BOSCHMAN, LAURIE
C

PERSONAL: Born June 4, 1960, at Major, Sask.... 6-0/185.... Shoots left.... Full name: Laurie Joseph Boschman.

HIGH SCHOOL: Neelin (Brandon, Man.).

TRANSACTIONS/CAREER NOTES: Selected by Toronto Maple Leafs in first round (first Maple Leafs pick, ninth overall) of NHL entry draft (August 9, 1979).... Injured finger tendon (December 7, 1980).... Suffered from mononucleosis (January 1981).... Traded by Maple Leafs to Edmonton Oilers for C Walt Poddubny and Phil Drouillard (March 8, 1982).... Traded by Oilers to Winnipeg Jets for RW Willy Lindstrom (March 7, 1983).... Dislocated shoulder (December 7, 1983).... Underwent surgery to reconstruct right shoulder (April 1988).... Lacerated ankle (October 16, 1988).... Suspended eight games by NHL for high-sticking (February 8, 1990).... Traded by Jets to New Jersey Devils for RW Bob Brooke (September 6, 1990); Brooke refused to report to Jets, announcing he would rather retire; Jets then received fifth-round pick in 1991 draft (LW Jan Kaminsky) as compensation.... Bruised shoulder (November 1990).... Selected by Ottawa Senators in NHL expansion draft (June 18, 1992).

HONORS: Named to WHL All-Star first team (1978-79).... Named to Memorial Cup All-Star team (1978-79).

			REGULAR SEASON					PLAYOFFS			
Season Team	League	Gms.	G	A	Pts.	Pen.	Gms.	G	A	Pts.	Pen.
76-77—Brandon	MJHL	47	17	40	57	139	—	—	—	—	—
—Brandon	WCHL	3	0	1	1	0	12	1	1	2	17
77-78—Brandon	WCHL	72	42	57	99	227	8	2	5	7	45
78-79—Brandon	WHL	65	66	83	149	215	22	11	23	34	56
79-80—Toronto	NHL	80	16	32	48	78	3	1	1	2	18
80-81—New Brunswick	AHL	4	4	1	5	47	—	—	—	—	—
—Toronto	NHL	53	14	19	33	178	3	0	0	0	7
81-82—Toronto	NHL	54	9	19	28	150	—	—	—	—	—
—Edmonton	NHL	11	2	3	5	37	3	0	1	1	4
82-83—Edmonton	NHL	62	8	12	20	183	—	—	—	—	—
—Winnipeg	NHL	12	3	5	8	33	3	0	1	1	12
83-84—Winnipeg	NHL	61	28	46	74	234	3	0	1	1	5
84-85—Winnipeg	NHL	80	32	44	76	180	8	2	1	3	21
85-86—Winnipeg	NHL	77	27	42	69	241	3	0	1	1	6
86-87—Winnipeg	NHL	80	17	24	41	152	10	2	3	5	32

Season Team	League	REGULAR SEASON					PLAYOFFS				
		Gms.	G	A	Pts.	Pen.	Gms.	G	A	Pts.	Pen.
87-88—Winnipeg	NHL	80	25	23	48	227	5	1	3	4	9
88-89—Winnipeg	NHL	70	10	26	36	163	—	—	—	—	—
89-90—Winnipeg	NHL	66	10	17	27	103	2	0	0	0	2
90-91—New Jersey	NHL	78	11	9	20	79	7	1	1	2	16
91-92—New Jersey	NHL	75	8	20	28	121	7	1	0	1	8
92-93—Ottawa	NHL	70	9	7	16	101	—	—	—	—	—
NHL totals		1009	229	348	577	2260	57	8	13	21	140

BOSTON, SCOTT
D, LIGHTNING

PERSONAL: Born July 13, 1971, at Ottawa.... 6-2/180.
TRANSACTIONS/CAREER NOTES: Signed as free agent by Tampa Bay Lightning (August 13, 1992).

Season Team	League	REGULAR SEASON					PLAYOFFS				
		Gms.	G	A	Pts.	Pen.	Gms.	G	A	Pts.	Pen.
88-89—Belleville	OHL	66	4	20	24	90	—	—	—	—	—
89-90—Belleville	OHL	58	2	26	28	99	11	1	0	1	13
90-91—Belleville	OHL	66	12	39	51	70	6	1	2	3	6
91-92—					Did not play.						
92-93—Atlanta	IHL	76	2	17	19	75	2	0	0	0	0

BOUCHARD, JOEL
D, FLAMES

PERSONAL: Born January 23, 1974, at Montreal.... 6-0/180.... Shoots left.
TRANSACTIONS/CAREER NOTES: Selected by Calgary Flames in sixth round (sixth Flames pick, 129th overall) of NHL entry draft (June 20, 1992).

Season Team	League	REGULAR SEASON					PLAYOFFS				
		Gms.	G	A	Pts.	Pen.	Gms.	G	A	Pts.	Pen.
90-91—Longueuil	QMJHL	53	3	19	22	34	8	0	1	1	11
91-92—Verdun	QMJHL	70	9	37	46	55	19	1	7	8	20
92-93—Verdun	QMJHL	60	10	49	59	126	4	0	2	2	4

BOUCHER, PHILIPPE
D, SABRES

PERSONAL: Born March 24, 1973, at St. Apollnaire, Que. ... 6-2/189.... Shoots right.... Name pronounced boo-SHAY.
TRANSACTIONS/CAREER NOTES: Selected by Buffalo Sabres in first round (first Sabres pick, 13th overall) of NHL entry draft (June 22, 1991).
HONORS: Won Can.HL Rookie of the Year Award (1990-91).... Won Raymond Lagace Trophy (1990-91).... Won Michael Bossy Trophy (1990-91).... Named to QMJHL All-Star second team (1990-91 and 1991-92).

Season Team	League	REGULAR SEASON					PLAYOFFS				
		Gms.	G	A	Pts.	Pen.	Gms.	G	A	Pts.	Pen.
90-91—Granby	QMJHL	69	21	46	67	92	—	—	—	—	—
91-92—Laval	QMJHL	65	29	48	77	83	10	5	6	11	8
92-93—Laval	QMJHL	16	12	15	27	37	13	6	15	21	12
—Rochester	AHL	5	4	3	7	8	3	0	1	1	2
—Buffalo	NHL	18	0	4	4	14	—	—	—	—	—
NHL totals		18	0	4	4	14					

BOUGHNER, BOB
D, RED WINGS

PERSONAL: Born March 8, 1971, at Windsor, Ont.... 5-11/201.... Shoots right.... Name pronounced BOOG-nuhr.
TRANSACTIONS/CAREER NOTES: Selected by Detroit Red Wings in second round (second Red Wings pick, 32nd overall) of NHL entry draft (June 17, 1989).

Season Team	League	REGULAR SEASON					PLAYOFFS				
		Gms.	G	A	Pts.	Pen.	Gms.	G	A	Pts.	Pen.
87-88—St. Mary's Jr. B	OHA	36	4	18	22	177	—	—	—	—	—
88-89—Sault Ste. Marie	OHL	64	6	15	21	182	—	—	—	—	—
89-90—Sault Ste. Marie	OHL	49	7	23	30	122	—	—	—	—	—
90-91—Sault Ste. Marie	OHL	64	13	33	46	156	14	2	9	11	35
91-92—Adirondack	AHL	1	0	0	0	7	—	—	—	—	—
—Toledo	ECHL	28	3	10	13	79	5	2	0	2	15
92-93—Adirondack	AHL	69	1	16	17	190	—	—	—	—	—

BOULIN, VLADISLAV
D, FLYERS

PERSONAL: Born May 18, 1972, at Penza, U.S.S.R.... 6-4/196.... Shoots right.
TRANSACTIONS/CAREER NOTES: Selected by Philadelphia Flyers in fifth round (fourth Flyers pick, 103rd overall) of NHL entry draft (June 20, 1992).

Season Team	League	REGULAR SEASON					PLAYOFFS				
		Gms.	G	A	Pts.	Pen.	Gms.	G	A	Pts.	Pen.
90-91—Dizelist Penza	USSR Div. II	68	...	...	...	...	—	—	—	—	—
91-92—Dizelist Penza	CIS Div. II				Statistics unavailable.						
92-93—Dynamo Moscow	CIS	32	2	1	3	55	4	0	0	0	2

BOURQUE, PHIL
LW, RANGERS

PERSONAL: Born June 8, 1962, at Chelmsford, Mass. ... 6-1/196. ... Shoots left.... Full name: Phillippe Richard Bourque.... Name pronounced BOHRK.
TRANSACTIONS/CAREER NOTES: Signed as free agent by Pittsburgh Penguins (October 4, 1982).... Suffered back spasms (November 1989).... Sprained wrist (December 1990).

... Suffered inflammation of left elbow (November 15, 1991); missed two games. . . . Strained back (December 18, 1991); missed three games. . . . Fractured left foot (January 10, 1992); missed nine games. . . . Reinjured foot (February 9, 1992); missed four games. . . . Signed as free agent by New York Rangers (August 31, 1992). . . . Suffered concussion (December 11, 1992); missed two games. . . . Sprained left knee (February 3, 1993); missed six games. . . . Bruised ankle (April 8, 1993); missed four games.

HONORS: Won Governors Trophy (1987-88). . . . Named to IHL All-Star first team (1987-88).
MISCELLANEOUS: Member of Stanley Cup championship teams (1991 and 1992).

Season Team	League	REGULAR SEASON Gms.	G	A	Pts.	Pen.	PLAYOFFS Gms.	G	A	Pts.	Pen.
80-81—Kingston	OMJHL	47	4	4	8	46	6	0	0	0	10
81-82—Kingston	OHL	67	11	40	51	111	4	0	0	0	0
82-83—Baltimore	AHL	65	1	15	16	93	—	—	—	—	—
83-84—Baltimore	AHL	58	5	17	22	96	—	—	—	—	—
—Pittsburgh	NHL	5	0	1	1	12	—	—	—	—	—
84-85—Baltimore	AHL	79	6	15	21	164	13	2	5	7	23
85-86—Pittsburgh	NHL	4	0	0	0	2	—	—	—	—	—
—Baltimore	AHL	74	8	18	26	226	—	—	—	—	—
86-87—Pittsburgh	NHL	22	2	3	5	32	—	—	—	—	—
—Baltimore	AHL	49	15	16	31	183	—	—	—	—	—
87-88—Muskegon	IHL	52	16	36	52	66	6	1	2	3	16
—Pittsburgh	NHL	21	4	12	16	20	—	—	—	—	—
88-89—Pittsburgh	NHL	80	17	26	43	97	11	4	1	5	66
89-90—Pittsburgh	NHL	76	22	17	39	108	—	—	—	—	—
90-91—Pittsburgh	NHL	78	20	14	34	106	24	6	7	13	16
91-92—Pittsburgh	NHL	58	10	16	26	58	†21	3	4	7	25
92-93—New York Rangers	NHL	55	6	14	20	39	—	—	—	—	—
NHL totals		399	81	103	184	474	56	13	12	25	107

BOURQUE, RAY
D, BRUINS

PERSONAL: Born December 28, 1960, at Montreal. . . . 5-11/210. . . . Shoots left. . . . Full name: Raymond Jean Bourque. . . . Name pronounced BOHRK.
TRANSACTIONS/CAREER NOTES: Selected by Boston Bruins in first round (first Bruins pick, eighth overall) of NHL entry draft (August 9, 1979). . . . Suffered broken jaw (November 11, 1980). . . . Injured left shoulder (October 1981). . . . Fractured left wrist (April 21, 1982). . . . Refractured left wrist and fractured left forearm (summer 1982). . . . Broke bone over left eye (October 1982). . . . Sprained left knee ligaments (December 10, 1988). . . . Bruised hip (April 7, 1990). . . . Bruised right shoulder (October 17, 1990); missed two games. . . . Fractured finger (May 5, 1992); missed remainder of playoffs. . . . Injured back (December 19, 1992); missed two games. . . . Injured ankle (January 21, 1993); missed three games.

HONORS: Named to QMJHL All-Star first team (1977-78 and 1978-79). . . . Won Frank J. Selke Trophy (1978-79). . . . Won Emile (Butch) Bouchard Trophy (1978-79). . . . Named NHL Rookie of the Year by THE SPORTING NEWS (1979-80). . . . Won Calder Memorial Trophy (1979-80). . . . Named to NHL All-Star first team (1979-80, 1981-82, 1983-84, 1984-85, 1986-87, 1987-88 and 1989-90 through 1992-93). . . . Named to THE SPORTING NEWS All-Star second team (1980-81, 1982-83, 1985-86 and 1988-89). . . . Named to NHL All-Star second team (1980-81, 1982-83, 1985-86 and 1988-89). . . . Played in NHL All-Star Game (1981 through 1986 and 1988 through 1993). . . . Named to THE SPORTING NEWS All-Star first team (1981-82, 1983-84, 1984-85, 1986-87, 1987-88 and 1989-90 through 1992-93). . . . Won James Norris Memorial Trophy (1986-87, 1987-88, 1989-90 and 1990-91). . . . Won King Clancy Memorial Trophy (1991-92).

Season Team	League	REGULAR SEASON Gms.	G	A	Pts.	Pen.	PLAYOFFS Gms.	G	A	Pts.	Pen.
76-77—Sorel	QMJHL	69	12	36	48	61	—	—	—	—	—
77-78—Verdun	QMJHL	72	22	57	79	90	4	2	1	3	0
78-79—Verdun	QMJHL	63	22	71	93	44	11	3	16	19	18
79-80—Boston	NHL	80	17	48	65	73	10	2	9	11	27
80-81—Boston	NHL	67	27	29	56	96	3	0	1	1	2
81-82—Boston	NHL	65	17	49	66	51	9	1	5	6	16
82-83—Boston	NHL	65	22	51	73	20	17	8	15	23	10
83-84—Boston	NHL	78	31	65	96	57	3	0	2	2	0
84-85—Boston	NHL	73	20	66	86	53	5	0	3	3	4
85-86—Boston	NHL	74	19	57	76	68	3	0	0	0	0
86-87—Boston	NHL	78	23	72	95	36	4	1	2	3	0
87-88—Boston	NHL	78	17	64	81	72	23	3	18	21	26
88-89—Boston	NHL	60	18	43	61	52	10	0	4	4	6
89-90—Boston	NHL	76	19	65	84	50	17	5	12	17	16
90-91—Boston	NHL	76	21	73	94	75	19	7	18	25	12
91-92—Boston	NHL	80	21	60	81	56	12	3	6	9	12
92-93—Boston	NHL	78	19	63	82	40	4	1	0	1	2
NHL totals		1028	291	805	1096	799	139	31	95	126	133

BOWEN, CURT
LW, RED WINGS

PERSONAL: Born March 24, 1974, at Kenora, Ont. . . . 6-1/189. . . . Shoots left.
HIGH SCHOOL: Ridgemont (Ottawa).
TRANSACTIONS/CAREER NOTES: Selected by Detroit Red Wings in first round (first Red Wings pick, 22nd overall) of NHL entry draft (June 20, 1992).

Season Team	League	REGULAR SEASON Gms.	G	A	Pts.	Pen.	PLAYOFFS Gms.	G	A	Pts.	Pen.
90-91—Ottawa	OHL	42	12	14	26	31	—	—	—	—	—
91-92—Ottawa	OHL	65	31	45	76	94	11	3	7	10	11
92-93—Ottawa	OHL	21	9	19	28	51	—	—	—	—	—

BOWEN, JASON
D, FLYERS

PERSONAL: Born November 11, 1973, at Courtenay, B.C. . . . 6-4/220. . . . Shoots left.
TRANSACTIONS/CAREER NOTES: Selected by Philadelphia Flyers in first round (second Flyers pick, 15th overall) of NHL entry draft (June 20, 1992).

Season Team	League	REGULAR SEASON					PLAYOFFS				
		Gms.	G	A	Pts.	Pen.	Gms.	G	A	Pts.	Pen.
89-90—Tri-City	WHL	61	8	5	13	129	7	0	3	3	4
90-91—Tri-City	WHL	60	7	13	20	252	6	2	2	4	18
91-92—Tri-City	WHL	19	5	3	8	135	5	0	1	1	42
92-93—Tri-City	WHL	62	10	12	22	219	3	1	1	2	18
—Philadelphia	NHL	7	1	0	1	2	—	—	—	—	—
NHL totals		7	1	0	1	2					

BOZON, PHILIPPE
LW, BLUES

PERSONAL: Born November 30, 1966, at Chamonix, France. . . . 5-10/175. . . . Shoots left. . . . Name pronounced BOH-zohn.
TRANSACTIONS/CAREER NOTES: Signed as free agent by St. Louis Blues (September 29, 1985). . . . On Blues inactive list while in France preparing for 1992 Olympics (1987-88 through 1990-91). . . . Returned to Blues (February 27, 1992). . . . Suffered from mononucleosis (January 30, 1993); missed 21 games.
HONORS: Named to QMJHL All-Star second team (1985-86).

Season Team	League	REGULAR SEASON					PLAYOFFS				
		Gms.	G	A	Pts.	Pen.	Gms.	G	A	Pts.	Pen.
84-85—St. Jean	QMJHL	67	32	50	82	82	3	1	0	1	0
85-86—St. Jean	QMJHL	65	59	52	111	72	10	10	6	16	16
—Peoria	IHL	—	—	—	—	—	5	1	0	1	0
86-87—Peoria	IHL	28	4	11	15	17	—	—	—	—	—
—St. Jean	QMJHL	25	20	21	41	75	8	5	5	10	30
87-88—Mont-Blanc	France	18	11	15	26	34	10	15	6	21	6
—French Olympic Team	Int'l	6	3	2	5	0	—	—	—	—	—
88-89—					Did not play.						
89-90—French national team	Int'l				Statistics unavailable.						
—Grenoble	France	36	45	38	83	34	—	—	—	—	—
90-91—Grenoble	France				Statistics unavailable.						
91-92—Chamonix	France	10	12	8	20	20	—	—	—	—	—
—French Olympic Team	Int'l	7	3	2	5	4	—	—	—	—	—
—St. Louis	NHL	9	1	3	4	4	6	1	0	1	27
92-93—St. Louis	NHL	54	6	6	12	55	9	1	0	1	0
—Peoria	IHL	4	3	2	5	2	—	—	—	—	—
NHL totals		63	7	9	16	59	15	2	0	2	27

BRADLEY, BRIAN
C, LIGHTNING

PERSONAL: Born January 21, 1965, at Kitchener, Ont. . . . 5-10/177. . . . Shoots right. . . . Full name: Brian Walter Richard Bradley.
TRANSACTIONS/CAREER NOTES: Selected by Calgary Flames as underage junior in third round (second Flames pick, 51st overall) of NHL entry draft (June 8, 1983). . . . Traded by Flames with RW Peter Bakovic and future considerations (D Kevan Guy) to Vancouver Canucks for C Craig Coxe (March 6, 1988). . . . Bruised knee (January 1989). . . . Broke thumb knuckle (February 1, 1990); missed seven games. . . . Traded by Canucks to Toronto Maple Leafs for D Tom Kurvers (January 12, 1991). . . . Sprained ankle (November 10, 1991); missed six games. . . . Suffered back spasms (December 10, 1991); missed two games. . . . Selected by Tampa Bay Lightning in NHL expansion draft (June 18, 1992).
HONORS: Played in NHL All-Star Game (1993).

Season Team	League	REGULAR SEASON					PLAYOFFS				
		Gms.	G	A	Pts.	Pen.	Gms.	G	A	Pts.	Pen.
81-82—London	OHL	62	34	44	78	34	—	—	—	—	—
82-83—London	OHL	67	37	82	119	37	3	1	0	1	0
83-84—London	OHL	49	40	60	100	24	4	2	4	6	0
84-85—London	OHL	32	27	49	76	22	8	5	10	15	4
85-86—Calgary	NHL	5	0	1	1	0	1	0	0	0	0
—Moncton	AHL	59	23	42	65	40	10	6	9	15	4
86-87—Moncton	AHL	20	12	16	28	8	—	—	—	—	—
—Calgary	NHL	40	10	18	28	16	—	—	—	—	—
87-88—Canadian national team	Int'l	47	18	19	37	42	—	—	—	—	—
—Canadian Olympic Team	Int'l	7	0	4	4	0	—	—	—	—	—
—Vancouver	NHL	11	3	5	8	6	—	—	—	—	—
88-89—Vancouver	NHL	71	18	27	45	42	7	3	4	7	10
89-90—Vancouver	NHL	67	19	29	48	65	—	—	—	—	—
90-91—Vancouver	NHL	44	11	20	31	42	—	—	—	—	—
—Toronto	NHL	26	0	11	11	20	—	—	—	—	—
91-92—Toronto	NHL	59	10	21	31	48	—	—	—	—	—
92-93—Tampa Bay	NHL	80	42	44	86	92	—	—	—	—	—
NHL totals		403	113	176	289	331	8	3	4	7	10

BRADY, NEIL
C

PERSONAL: Born April 12, 1968, at Montreal. . . . 6-2/200. . . . Shoots left. . . . Full name: Neil Patrick Brady.
HIGH SCHOOL: Medicine Hat (Alta.).
TRANSACTIONS/CAREER NOTES: Selected by New Jersey Devils as underage junior in first round

(first Devils pick, third overall) of NHL entry draft (June 21, 1986).... Traded by Devils to Ottawa Senators for future considerations (September 3, 1992).... Injured ankle (February 17, 1993); missed two games.... Suffered from the flu (February 23, 1993); missed two games.... Injured knee (March 4, 1993); missed one game.

HONORS: Won WHL (East) Stewart (Butch) Paul Memorial Trophy (1985-86).

			REGULAR SEASON					PLAYOFFS				
Season Team	League	Gms.	G	A	Pts.	Pen.	Gms.	G	A	Pts.	Pen.
84-85—Medicine Hat	WHL	—	—	—	—	—	3	0	0	0	2
85-86—Medicine Hat	WHL	72	21	60	81	104	21	9	11	20	23
86-87—Medicine Hat	WHL	57	19	64	83	126	18	1	4	5	25
87-88—Medicine Hat	WHL	61	16	35	51	110	15	0	3	3	19
88-89—Utica	AHL	75	16	21	37	56	4	0	3	3	0
89-90—New Jersey	NHL	19	1	4	5	13	—	—	—	—	—
—Utica	AHL	38	10	13	23	21	5	0	1	1	10
90-91—New Jersey	NHL	3	0	0	0	0	—	—	—	—	—
—Utica	AHL	77	33	63	96	91	—	—	—	—	—
91-92—Utica	AHL	33	12	30	42	28	—	—	—	—	—
—New Jersey	NHL	7	1	0	1	4	—	—	—	—	—
92-93—Ottawa	NHL	55	7	17	24	57	—	—	—	—	—
—New Haven	AHL	8	6	3	9	2	—	—	—	—	—
NHL totals		84	9	21	30	74					

BREAULT, FRANK
RW, KINGS

PERSONAL: Born May 11, 1967, at Acton Valley, Que.... 5-11/185.... Shoots left.... Name pronounced BROH.
TRANSACTIONS/CAREER NOTES: Traded by Trois Rivieres Draveurs to Granby Bisons for fifth-round draft pick (February 1987).... Signed as free agent by Los Angeles Kings (July 1988).... Injured cruciate ligament of right knee (December 13, 1990).... Bruised knee (October 28, 1991).

			REGULAR SEASON					PLAYOFFS				
Season Team	League	Gms.	G	A	Pts.	Pen.	Gms.	G	A	Pts.	Pen.
85-86—Trois-Rivieres	QMJHL	60	15	13	28	73	—	—	—	—	—
86-87—Granby	QMJHL	60	24	33	57	134	—	—	—	—	—
87-88—Trois-Rivieres	QMJHL	28	16	19	35	108	—	—	—	—	—
—Maine	AHL	11	0	1	1	37	—	—	—	—	—
88-89—New Haven	AHL	68	21	24	45	51	—	—	—	—	—
89-90—New Haven	AHL	37	17	21	38	33	—	—	—	—	—
90-91—Los Angeles	NHL	17	1	4	5	6	—	—	—	—	—
91-92—Los Angeles	NHL	6	1	0	1	30	—	—	—	—	—
—Phoenix	IHL	54	14	19	33	40	—	—	—	—	—
92-93—Phoenix	IHL	31	5	11	16	26	—	—	—	—	—
—Los Angeles	NHL	4	0	0	0	6	—	—	—	—	—
—Utica	AHL	32	8	20	28	56	4	2	0	2	0
NHL totals		27	2	4	6	42					

BRENNAN, RICH
D, NORDIQUES

PERSONAL: Born November 26, 1972, at Schenectady, N.Y.... 6-2/200.... Shoots right.
HIGH SCHOOL: Albany Academy (N.Y.), then Tabor Academy (Marion, Mass.).
COLLEGE: Boston University.
TRANSACTIONS/CAREER NOTES: Selected by Quebec Nordiques in third round (third Nordiques pick, 56th overall) of NHL entry draft (June 22, 1991).

			REGULAR SEASON					PLAYOFFS				
Season Team	League	Gms.	G	A	Pts.	Pen.	Gms.	G	A	Pts.	Pen.
88-89—Albany Academy	N.Y. H.S.	25	17	30	47	57	—	—	—	—	—
89-90—Tabor Academy	N.Y. H.S.	33	12	14	26	68	—	—	—	—	—
90-91—Tabor Academy	N.Y. H.S.	34	13	37	50	91	—	—	—	—	—
91-92—Boston University	Hockey East	31	4	13	17	54	—	—	—	—	—
92-93—Boston University	Hockey East	40	9	11	20	68	—	—	—	—	—

BRICKLEY, ANDY
LW, JETS

PERSONAL: Born August 9, 1961, at Melrose, Mass.... 5-11/200.... Shoots left.
COLLEGE: New Hampshire.
TRANSACTIONS/CAREER NOTES: Selected by Philadelphia Flyers in 10th round (10th Flyers pick, 210th overall) of NHL entry draft (June 11, 1980).... Traded by Flyers with C Ron Flockhart, C/LW Mark Taylor and first-round pick in 1984 draft (RW/C Roger Belanger) to Pittsburgh Penguins for RW Rich Sutter and second-round pick (D Greg Smyth) and third-round pick (LW David McLay) in 1984 draft (October 23, 1983).... Strained ankle (December 1983).... Released by Penguins (August 1985).... Signed as free agent by Maine Mariners (September 1985).... Suffered tendinitis in shoulder (December 1985).... Signed as free agent by New Jersey Devils (July 8, 1986).... Injured foot (September 1987).... Selected by Boston Bruins in 1988 waiver draft for $12,500 (October 3, 1988). ... Strained groin (December 1988).... Sprained right ankle (September 24, 1989); missed nine games.... Tore right groin muscle (January 27, 1990); missed eight games.... Underwent surgery to right thigh (July 17, 1990).... Separated shoulder (March 1991).... Injured shoulder (November 16, 1991); missed 38 games.... Signed as free agent by Winnipeg Jets (November 14, 1992).... Suffered quad contusion (January 2, 1993); missed one game.... Suffered back spasm (March 6, 1993); missed five games.
HONORS: Named to NCAA All-America East team (1981-82).... Named to ECAC All-Star first team (1981-82).... Named to AHL All-Star second team (1982-83).

Season Team	League	REGULAR SEASON					PLAYOFFS				
		Gms.	G	A	Pts.	Pen.	Gms.	G	A	Pts.	Pen.
79-80—Univ. of New Hampshire ...	ECAC	27	15	17	32	8	—	—	—	—	—
80-81—Univ. of New Hampshire ...	ECAC	31	27	25	52	16	—	—	—	—	—
81-82—Univ. of New Hampshire ...	ECAC	35	26	27	53	6	—	—	—	—	—
82-83—Philadelphia	NHL	3	1	1	2	0	—	—	—	—	—
—Maine................................	AHL	76	29	54	83	10	17	9	5	14	0
83-84—Springfield....................	AHL	7	1	5	6	2	—	—	—	—	—
—Pittsburgh	NHL	50	18	20	38	9	—	—	—	—	—
—Baltimore..........................	AHL	4	0	5	5	2	—	—	—	—	—
84-85—Baltimore......................	AHL	31	13	14	27	8	15	†10	8	18	0
—Pittsburgh	NHL	45	7	15	22	10	—	—	—	—	—
85-86—Maine...........................	AHL	60	26	34	60	20	5	0	4	4	0
86-87—New Jersey...................	NHL	51	11	12	23	8	—	—	—	—	—
87-88—Utica............................	AHL	9	5	8	13	4	—	—	—	—	—
—New Jersey.......................	NHL	45	8	14	22	14	4	0	1	1	4
88-89—Boston.........................	NHL	71	13	22	35	20	10	0	2	2	0
89-90—Boston.........................	NHL	43	12	28	40	8	2	0	0	0	0
90-91—Maine...........................	AHL	17	8	17	25	2	1	0	0	0	0
—Boston.............................	NHL	40	2	9	11	8	—	—	—	—	—
91-92—Maine...........................	AHL	14	5	15	20	2	—	—	—	—	—
—Boston.............................	NHL	23	10	17	27	2	—	—	—	—	—
92-93—Moncton.......................	AHL	38	15	36	51	10	5	4	2	6	0
—Winnipeg..........................	NHL	12	0	2	2	2	1	1	1	2	0
NHL totals...........................		383	82	140	222	81	17	1	4	5	4

BRIMANIS, ARIS
D, FLYERS

PERSONAL: Born March 14, 1972, at Cleveland. ... 6-3/195. ... Shoots right. ... Full name: Aris Aldis Brimanis. ... Name pronounced brih-MAN-ihz.
HIGH SCHOOL: Culver (Ind.) Military Academy.
COLLEGE: Bowling Green State.
TRANSACTIONS/CAREER NOTES: Selected by Philadelphia Flyers in fourth round (third Flyers pick, 86th overall) of NHL entry draft (June 22, 1991).

Season Team	League	REGULAR SEASON					PLAYOFFS				
		Gms.	G	A	Pts.	Pen.	Gms.	G	A	Pts.	Pen.
88-89—Culver Military Academy..	Indiana H.S.	38	10	13	23	...	—	—	—	—	—
89-90—Culver Military Academy..	Indiana H.S.	37	15	10	25	...	—	—	—	—	—
90-91—Bowling Green State	CCHA	38	3	6	9	42	—	—	—	—	—
91-92—Bowling Green State	CCHA	32	2	9	11	38	—	—	—	—	—
92-93—Brandon............................	WHL	71	8	50	58	110	4	2	1	3	12

BRIND'AMOUR, ROD
C/LW, FLYERS

PERSONAL: Born August 9, 1970, at Ottawa. ... 6-1/202. ... Shoots left. ... Full name: Rod Jean Brind'Amour. ... Name pronounced BRIHN-duh-mohr.
COLLEGE: Michigan State.
TRANSACTIONS/CAREER NOTES: Broke wrist (November 1985). ... Selected by St. Louis Blues in first round (first Blues pick, ninth overall) of NHL entry draft (June 11, 1988). ... Traded by Blues with C Dan Quinn to Philadelphia Flyers for C Ron Sutter and D Murray Baron (September 22, 1991). ... Lacerated elbow (November 19, 1992); missed two games. ... Bruised right hand (February 20, 1993); missed one game.
HONORS: Named to CCHA All-Rookie team (1988-89). ... Named CCHA Rookie of the Year (1988-89). ... Named to NHL All-Rookie team (1989-90). ... Played in NHL All-Star Game (1992).

Season Team	League	REGULAR SEASON					PLAYOFFS				
		Gms.	G	A	Pts.	Pen.	Gms.	G	A	Pts.	Pen.
87-88—Notre Dame	SJHL	56	46	61	107	136	—	—	—	—	—
88-89—Michigan State.................	CCHA	42	27	32	59	63	—	—	—	—	—
—St. Louis	NHL	—	—	—	—	—	5	2	0	2	4
89-90—St. Louis	NHL	79	26	35	61	46	12	5	8	13	6
90-91—St. Louis	NHL	78	17	32	49	93	13	2	5	7	10
91-92—Philadelphia	NHL	80	33	44	77	100	—	—	—	—	—
92-93—Philadelphia	NHL	81	37	49	86	89	—	—	—	—	—
NHL totals................................		318	113	160	273	328	30	9	13	22	20

BRISEBOIS, PATRICE
D, CANADIENS

PERSONAL: Born January 27, 1971, at Montreal. ... 6-2/175. ... Shoots right. ... Name pronounced BREES-bwah.
TRANSACTIONS/CAREER NOTES: Underwent surgery on fractured right thumb (February 1988). ... Tore ligaments in left knee (March 1988). ... Broke left thumb (August 1988). ... Selected by Montreal Canadiens in second round (second Canadiens pick, 30th overall) of NHL entry draft (June 17, 1989). ... Traded by Laval Titans with LW Allen Kerr to Drummondville Voltigeurs for second- and third-round picks in 1990 draft (May 26, 1990). ... Sprained right ankle (October 10, 1992); missed two games. ... Suffered charley horse (December 16, 1992); missed two games.
HONORS: Won Michael Bossy Trophy (1988-89). ... Named to QMJHL All-Star second team (1989-90). ... Won Can.HL Defenseman of the Year Award (1990-91). ... Won Emile (Butch) Bouchard Trophy (1990-91). ... Named to QMJHL All-Star first team (1990-91). ... Named to Memorial Cup All-Star team (1990-91).
MISCELLANEOUS: Member of Stanley Cup championship team (1993).

Season	Team	League	REGULAR SEASON					PLAYOFFS				
			Gms.	G	A	Pts.	Pen.	Gms.	G	A	Pts.	Pen.
87-88—Laval	QMJHL	48	10	34	44	95	6	0	2	2	2
88-89—Laval	QMJHL	50	20	45	65	95	17	8	14	22	45
89-90—Laval	QMJHL	56	18	70	88	108	13	7	9	16	26
90-91—Montreal	NHL	10	0	2	2	4	—	—	—	—	—
—Drummondville	QMJHL	54	17	44	61	72	14	6	18	24	49
91-92—Fredericton	AHL	53	12	27	39	51	—	—	—	—	—
—Montreal	NHL	26	2	8	10	20	11	2	4	6	6
92-93—Montreal	NHL	70	10	21	31	79	20	0	4	4	18
NHL totals			106	12	31	43	103	31	2	8	10	24

BRODEUR, MARTIN
G, DEVILS

PERSONAL: Born May 6, 1972, at Montreal. . . . 6-1/190. . . . Name pronounced broh-DOOR.
TRANSACTIONS/CAREER NOTES: Suffered pinched nerve in elbow and slight concussion (March 9, 1990). . . . Selected by New Jersey Devils in first round (first Devils pick, 20th overall) of NHL entry draft (June 16, 1990).
HONORS: Named to QMJHL All-Star second team (1991-92).

Season	Team	League	REGULAR SEASON							PLAYOFFS						
			Gms.	Min.	W	L	T	GA	SO	Avg.	Gms.	Min.	W	L	GA	SO	Avg.
89-90—St. Hyacinthe	QMJHL	42	2333	23	13	2	156	0	4.01	12	678	5	7	46	0	4.07
90-91—St. Hyacinthe	QMJHL	52	2946	22	24	4	162	2	3.30	4	232	0	4	16	0	4.14
91-92—St. Hyacinthe	QMJHL	48	2846	27	16	4	161	2	3.39	5	317	2	3	14	0	2.65
—New Jersey	NHL	4	179	2	1	0	10	0	3.35	1	32	0	1	3	0	5.63
92-93—Utica	AHL	32	1952	14	13	5	131	0	4.03	4	258	1	3	18	0	4.19
NHL totals			4	179	2	1	0	10	0	3.35	1	32	0	1	3	0	5.63

BROTEN, NEAL
C, STARS

PERSONAL: Born November 29, 1959, at Roseau, Minn. . . . 5-9/170. . . . Shoots left. . . . Full name: Neal LaMoy Broten. . . . Name pronounced BRAH-tuhn. . . . Brother of Aaron Broten, center/left winger for six NHL teams (1980-81 through 1991-92); and brother of Paul Broten, right winger, New York Rangers.
HIGH SCHOOL: Roseau (Minn.).
COLLEGE: Minnesota.
TRANSACTIONS/CAREER NOTES: Selected by Minnesota North Stars in second round (third North Stars pick, 42nd overall) of NHL entry draft (August 9, 1979). . . . Fractured ankle (December 26, 1981). . . . Dislocated shoulder (October 30, 1986). . . . Tore shoulder ligaments (March 1987). . . . Separated shoulder (November 1987). . . . Underwent reconstructive shoulder surgery (February 1988). . . . Suffered sterno-clavicular sprain (February 14, 1989). . . . Strained groin (December 18, 1990). . . . North Stars franchise moved from Minnesota to Dallas and renamed Stars for 1993-94 season.
HONORS: Won WCHA Rookie of the Year Award (1978-79). . . . Won Hobey Baker Memorial Trophy (1980-81). . . . Named to NCAA All-America West team (1980-81). . . . Named to WCHA All-Star first team (1980-81). . . . Named to NCAA All-Tournament team (1980-81). . . . Played in NHL All-Star Game (1983 and 1986).
MISCELLANEOUS: Member of gold-medal-winning U.S. Olympic team (1980).

Season	Team	League	REGULAR SEASON					PLAYOFFS				
			Gms.	G	A	Pts.	Pen.	Gms.	G	A	Pts.	Pen.
78-79—University of Minnesota	WCHA	40	21	50	71	18	—	—	—	—	—
79-80—U.S. national team	Int'l	55	25	30	55	20	—	—	—	—	—
—U.S. Olympic Team	Int'l	7	2	1	3	2	—	—	—	—	—
80-81—University of Minnesota	WCHA	36	17	54	71	56	—	—	—	—	—
—Minnesota	NHL	3	2	0	2	12	19	1	7	8	9
81-82—Minnesota	NHL	73	38	60	98	42	4	0	2	2	0
82-83—Minnesota	NHL	79	32	45	77	43	9	1	6	7	10
83-84—Minnesota	NHL	76	28	61	89	43	16	5	5	10	4
84-85—Minnesota	NHL	80	19	37	56	39	9	2	5	7	10
85-86—Minnesota	NHL	80	29	76	105	47	5	3	2	5	2
86-87—Minnesota	NHL	46	18	35	53	35	—	—	—	—	—
87-88—Minnesota	NHL	54	9	30	39	32	—	—	—	—	—
88-89—Minnesota	NHL	68	18	38	56	57	5	2	2	4	4
89-90—Minnesota	NHL	80	23	62	85	45	7	2	2	4	18
90-91—Minnesota	NHL	79	13	56	69	26	23	9	13	22	6
91-92—Minnesota	NHL	76	8	26	34	16	7	1	5	6	2
92-93—Minnesota	NHL	82	12	21	33	22	—	—	—	—	—
NHL totals			876	249	547	796	459	104	26	49	75	65

BROTEN, PAUL
RW, RANGERS

PERSONAL: Born October 27, 1965, at Roseau, Minn. . . . 5-11/183. . . . Shoots right. . . . Name pronounced BRAH-tuhn. . . . Brother of Aaron Broten, center/left winger for six NHL teams (1980-81 through 1991-92); and brother of Neal Broten, center, Dallas Stars.
HIGH SCHOOL: Roseau (Minn.).
COLLEGE: Minnesota.
TRANSACTIONS/CAREER NOTES: Selected by New York Rangers in fourth round (third Rangers pick, 77th overall) of NHL entry draft (June 9, 1984). . . . Pulled thigh muscle (September 1990).

Season Team	League	REGULAR SEASON					PLAYOFFS				
		Gms.	G	A	Pts.	Pen.	Gms.	G	A	Pts.	Pen.
83-84—Roseau H.S.	Minn. H.S.	26	26	29	55	4	—	—	—	—	—
84-85—University of Minnesota	WCHA	44	8	8	16	26	—	—	—	—	—
85-86—University of Minnesota	WCHA	38	6	16	22	24	—	—	—	—	—
86-87—University of Minnesota	WCHA	48	17	22	39	52	—	—	—	—	—
87-88—University of Minnesota	WCHA	62	19	26	45	54	—	—	—	—	—
88-89—Denver	IHL	77	28	31	59	133	4	0	2	2	6
89-90—Flint	IHL	28	17	9	26	55	—	—	—	—	—
—New York Rangers	NHL	32	5	3	8	26	6	1	1	2	2
90-91—New York Rangers	NHL	28	4	6	10	18	5	0	0	0	2
—Binghamton	AHL	8	2	2	4	4	—	—	—	—	—
91-92—New York Rangers	NHL	74	13	15	28	102	13	1	2	3	10
92-93—New York Rangers	NHL	60	5	9	14	48	—	—	—	—	—
NHL totals		194	27	33	60	194	24	2	3	5	14

BROUSSEAU, PAUL
RW, NORDIQUES

PERSONAL: Born September 18, 1973, at Montreal. . . . 6-2/212. . . . Shoots right. . . . Name pronounced broo-SOH.
COLLEGE: Heritage College (Fla.).
TRANSACTIONS/CAREER NOTES: Selected by Quebec Nordiques in second round (second Nordiques pick, 28th overall) of NHL entry draft (June 20, 1992).
HONORS: Won Mike Bossy Trophy (1991-92). . . . Won QMJHL Top Draft Prospect Award (1991-92).

Season Team	League	REGULAR SEASON					PLAYOFFS				
		Gms.	G	A	Pts.	Pen.	Gms.	G	A	Pts.	Pen.
89-90—Chicoutimi	QMJHL	57	17	24	41	32	7	0	3	3	0
90-91—Trois-Rivieres	QMJHL	67	30	66	96	48	6	3	2	5	2
91-92—Hull	QMJHL	57	35	61	96	54	6	3	5	8	10
92-93—Hull	QMJHL	59	27	48	75	49	10	7	8	15	6

BROWN, CAM
LW

PERSONAL: Born May 15, 1969, at Saskatoon, Sask. . . . 6-1/210. . . . Shoots left.
TRANSACTIONS/CAREER NOTES: Signed as free agent by Vancouver Canucks (April 6, 1990).

Season Team	League	REGULAR SEASON					PLAYOFFS				
		Gms.	G	A	Pts.	Pen.	Gms.	G	A	Pts.	Pen.
87-88—Brandon	WHL	69	2	13	15	185	4	1	1	2	15
88-89—Brandon	WHL	72	17	42	59	225	—	—	—	—	—
89-90—Brandon	WHL	68	34	41	75	182	—	—	—	—	—
90-91—Vancouver	NHL	1	0	0	0	7	—	—	—	—	—
—Milwaukee	IHL	74	11	13	24	218	3	0	0	0	0
91-92—Milwaukee	IHL	51	6	8	14	179	1	0	0	0	0
—Columbus	ECHL	10	11	6	17	64	—	—	—	—	—
92-93—Columbus	ECHL	36	13	18	31	218	—	—	—	—	—
—Erie	ECHL	15	4	3	7	50	5	0	1	1	62
—Rochester	AHL	4	0	0	0	26	—	—	—	—	—
—Hamilton	AHL	1	0	0	0	2	—	—	—	—	—
NHL totals		1	0	0	0	7					

BROWN, DAVE
RW, FLYERS

PERSONAL: Born October 12, 1962, at Saskatoon, Sask. . . . 6-5/205. . . . Shoots right.
TRANSACTIONS/CAREER NOTES: Selected by Philadelphia Flyers in seventh round (seventh Flyers pick, 140th overall) of NHL entry draft (June 9, 1982). . . . Bruised shoulder (March 1985). . . . Suspended five games by NHL for stick-swinging incident (March 1987). . . . Suspended 15 games by NHL for crosschecking (October 16, 1987). . . . Bruised left hand and wrist (January 1988). . . . Traded by Flyers to Edmonton Oilers for C Keith Acton and future considerations (February 7, 1989). . . . Lacerated face (March 3, 1989). . . . Sprained hand (March 1989). . . . Traded by Oilers with D Corey Foster and the NHL rights to RW Jari Kurri to Flyers for RW Scott Mellanby, LW Craig Berube and C Craig Fisher (May 30, 1991). . . . Injured shoulder (January 28, 1992); missed 10 games.
MISCELLANEOUS: Member of Stanley Cup championship team (1990).

Season Team	League	REGULAR SEASON					PLAYOFFS				
		Gms.	G	A	Pts.	Pen.	Gms.	G	A	Pts.	Pen.
80-81—Spokane Flyers	WHL	9	2	2	4	21	—	—	—	—	—
81-82—Saskatoon	WHL	62	11	33	44	344	5	1	0	1	4
82-83—Maine	AHL	71	8	6	14	*418	16	0	0	0	*107
—Philadelphia	NHL	2	0	0	0	5	—	—	—	—	—
83-84—Philadelphia	NHL	19	1	5	6	98	2	0	0	0	12
—Springfield	AHL	59	17	14	31	150	—	—	—	—	—
84-85—Philadelphia	NHL	57	3	6	9	165	11	0	0	0	59
85-86—Philadelphia	NHL	76	10	7	17	277	5	0	0	0	16
86-87—Philadelphia	NHL	62	7	3	10	274	26	1	2	3	59
87-88—Philadelphia	NHL	47	12	5	17	114	7	1	0	1	27
88-89—Philadelphia	NHL	50	0	3	3	100	—	—	—	—	—
—Edmonton	NHL	22	0	2	2	56	7	0	0	0	6
89-90—Edmonton	NHL	60	0	6	6	145	3	0	0	0	0
90-91—Edmonton	NHL	58	3	4	7	160	16	0	1	1	30

Season	Team	League	REGULAR SEASON					PLAYOFFS				
			Gms.	G	A	Pts.	Pen.	Gms.	G	A	Pts.	Pen.
91-92—Philadelphia	NHL		70	4	2	6	81	—	—	—	—	—
92-93—Philadelphia	NHL		70	0	2	2	78	—	—	—	—	—
NHL totals			593	40	45	85	1553	77	2	3	5	209

BROWN, DOUG
RW, DEVILS

PERSONAL: Born June 12, 1964, at Southborough, Mass.... 5-10/180.... Shoots right.... Full name: Douglas Allen Brown.... Brother of Greg Brown, defenseman, Buffalo Sabres.
COLLEGE: Boston College.
TRANSACTIONS/CAREER NOTES: Signed as free agent by New Jersey Devils (August 6, 1986). ... Broke nose (October 1988).... Injured back (November 25, 1989).... Bruised right foot (February 13, 1991).... Suspended by Devils for refusing to report to Utica (November 20, 1992).... Reinstated by Devils (November 30, 1992).
HONORS: Named to NCAA All-America East second team (1984-85 and 1985-86).... Named to Hockey East All-Star second team (1984-85 and 1985-86).

Season	Team	League	REGULAR SEASON					PLAYOFFS				
			Gms.	G	A	Pts.	Pen.	Gms.	G	A	Pts.	Pen.
82-83—Boston College	ECAC		22	9	8	17	0	—	—	—	—	—
83-84—Boston College	ECAC		38	11	10	21	6	—	—	—	—	—
84-85—Boston College	Hockey East		45	37	31	68	10	—	—	—	—	—
85-86—Boston College	Hockey East		38	16	40	56	16	—	—	—	—	—
86-87—Maine	AHL		73	24	34	58	15	—	—	—	—	—
—New Jersey	NHL		4	0	1	1	0	—	—	—	—	—
87-88—New Jersey	NHL		70	14	11	25	20	19	5	1	6	6
—Utica	AHL		2	0	2	2	2	—	—	—	—	—
88-89—New Jersey	NHL		63	15	10	25	15	—	—	—	—	—
—Utica	AHL		4	1	4	5	0	—	—	—	—	—
89-90—New Jersey	NHL		89	14	20	34	16	6	0	1	1	2
90-91—New Jersey	NHL		58	14	16	30	4	7	2	2	4	2
91-92—New Jersey	NHL		71	11	17	28	27	—	—	—	—	—
92-93—New Jersey	NHL		15	0	5	5	2	—	—	—	—	—
—Utica	AHL		25	11	17	28	8	—	—	—	—	—
NHL totals			370	68	80	148	84	32	7	4	11	10

BROWN, GREG
D, SABRES

PERSONAL: Born March 7, 1968, at Hartford, Conn.... 6-0/185.... Shoots right.... Full name: Gregory Curtis Brown.... Brother of Doug Brown, right winger, New Jersey Devils.
HIGH SCHOOL: St. Mark's (Southborough, Mass.).
COLLEGE: Boston College.
TRANSACTIONS/CAREER NOTES: Selected by Buffalo Sabres in second round (second Sabres pick, 26th overall) of NHL entry draft (June 21, 1986).
HONORS: Named to Hockey East All-Freshman team (1986-87).... Named Hockey East Player of the Year (1988-89 and 1989-90).... Named to NCAA All-America East first team (1988-89 and 1989-90).... Named to Hockey East All-Star first team (1988-89 and 1989-90).

Season	Team	League	REGULAR SEASON					PLAYOFFS				
			Gms.	G	A	Pts.	Pen.	Gms.	G	A	Pts.	Pen.
84-85—St. Marks H.S.	Mass. H.S.		24	16	24	40	12	—	—	—	—	—
85-86—St. Marks H.S.	Mass. H.S.		19	22	28	50	30	—	—	—	—	—
86-87—Boston College	Hockey East		37	10	27	37	22	—	—	—	—	—
87-88—U.S. Olympic Team	Int'l		6	0	4	4	2	—	—	—	—	—
88-89—Boston College	Hockey East		40	9	34	43	24	—	—	—	—	—
89-90—Boston College	Hockey East		42	5	35	40	42	—	—	—	—	—
90-91—Buffalo	NHL		39	1	2	3	35	—	—	—	—	—
—Rochester	AHL		31	6	17	23	16	14	1	4	5	8
91-92—Rochester	AHL		56	8	30	38	25	16	1	5	6	4
—U.S. national team	Int'l		8	0	0	0	5	—	—	—	—	—
—U.S. Olympic Team	Int'l		7	0	0	0	2	—	—	—	—	—
92-93—Rochester	AHL		61	11	38	49	46	16	3	8	11	14
—Buffalo	NHL		10	0	1	1	6	—	—	—	—	—
NHL totals			49	1	3	4	41	—	—	—	—	—

BROWN, JEFF
D, BLUES

PERSONAL: Born April 30, 1966, at Ottawa.... 6-1/204.... Shoots right.... Full name: Jeff Randall Brown.
HIGH SCHOOL: Sudbury (Ont.).
TRANSACTIONS/CAREER NOTES: Selected by Quebec Nordiques as underage junior in second round (second Nordiques pick, 36th overall) of NHL entry draft (June 9, 1984).... Traded by Nordiques to St. Louis Blues for G Greg Millen and C Tony Hrkac (December 13, 1989).... Broke left ankle (February 14, 1991); missed 13 games.... Broke foot (January 14, 1993); missed 11 games.... Suffered from sore foot (February 11, 1993); missed two games.
HONORS: Shared Max Kaminsky Trophy with Terry Carkner (1985-86).... Named to OHL All-Star first team (1985-86).

Season	Team	League	REGULAR SEASON					PLAYOFFS				
			Gms.	G	A	Pts.	Pen.	Gms.	G	A	Pts.	Pen.
81-82—Hawkesbury	COJHL		49	12	47	59	72	—	—	—	—	—
82-83—Sudbury	OHL		65	9	37	46	39	—	—	—	—	—
83-84—Sudbury	OHL		68	17	60	77	39	—	—	—	—	—
84-85—Sudbury	OHL		56	16	48	64	26	—	—	—	—	—

Season	Team	League	REGULAR SEASON					PLAYOFFS				
			Gms.	G	A	Pts.	Pen.	Gms.	G	A	Pts.	Pen.
85-86	—Sudbury	OHL	45	22	28	50	24	4	0	2	2	11
	—Quebec	NHL	8	3	2	5	6	1	0	0	0	0
	—Fredericton	AHL	—	—	—	—	—	1	0	1	1	0
86-87	—Fredericton	AHL	26	2	14	16	16	—	—	—	—	—
	—Quebec	NHL	44	7	22	29	16	13	3	3	6	2
87-88	—Quebec	NHL	78	16	37	53	64	—	—	—	—	—
88-89	—Quebec	NHL	78	21	47	68	62	—	—	—	—	—
89-90	—Quebec	NHL	29	6	10	16	18	—	—	—	—	—
	—St. Louis	NHL	48	10	28	38	37	12	2	10	12	4
90-91	—St. Louis	NHL	67	12	47	59	39	13	3	9	12	6
91-92	—St. Louis	NHL	80	20	39	59	38	6	2	1	3	2
92-93	—St. Louis	NHL	71	25	53	78	58	11	3	8	11	6
NHL totals			503	120	285	405	338	56	13	31	44	20

BROWN, KEITH

D, BLACKHAWKS

PERSONAL: Born May 6, 1960, at Corner Brook, Nfld. . . . 6-1/195. . . . Shoots right. . . . Full name: Keith Jeffrey Brown.

TRANSACTIONS/CAREER NOTES: Selected by Chicago Blackhawks as underage junior in first round (first Blackhawks pick, seventh overall) of NHL entry draft (August 9, 1979). . . . Tore ligaments in right knee (December 23, 1981). . . . Separated right shoulder (January 26, 1983). . . . Strained leg (January 1985). . . . Broke finger (October 1985); missed 10 games. . . . Tore ligaments and damaged cartilage in left knee (October 1987). . . . Bruised shoulder (January 1990). . . . Bruised ribs (February 25, 1990); missed 10 games. . . . Bruised elbow (April 1990). . . . Strained shoulder (September 1990). . . . Bruised ribs (November 1990). . . . Separated left shoulder (December 16, 1990); missed 30 games. . . . Strained chest muscle (March 1991). . . . Injured eye (October 10, 1991); missed one game. . . . Pulled groin (November 7, 1991); missed two games. . . . Reinjured groin (November 19, 1991); missed two games. . . . Reinjured groin (December 1991); missed three games. . . . Sprained right ankle (January 27, 1992); missed 14 games. . . . Underwent left shoulder surgery (September 27, 1992); missed first 47 games of 1992-93 season.. . . . Pulled groin (March 25, 1993); missed two games.

HONORS: Shared WCHL Rookie of the Year Award with John Ogrodnick (1977-78). . . . Named to WCHL All-Star second team (1977-78). . . . Won Top Defenseman Trophy (1978-79). . . . Named to WHL All-Star first team (1978-79).

Season	Team	League	REGULAR SEASON					PLAYOFFS				
			Gms.	G	A	Pts.	Pen.	Gms.	G	A	Pts.	Pen.
76-77	—Fort Saskatchewan	AJHL	59	14	61	75	14	—	—	—	—	—
	—Portland	WCHL	2	0	0	0	0	—	—	—	—	—
77-78	—Portland	WCHL	72	11	53	64	51	8	0	3	3	2
78-79	—Portland	WHL	70	11	85	96	75	25	3	*30	33	21
79-80	—Chicago	NHL	76	2	18	20	27	6	0	0	0	4
80-81	—Chicago	NHL	80	9	34	43	80	3	0	2	2	2
81-82	—Chicago	NHL	33	4	20	24	26	4	0	2	2	5
82-83	—Chicago	NHL	50	4	27	31	20	7	0	0	0	11
83-84	—Chicago	NHL	74	10	25	35	94	5	0	1	1	10
84-85	—Chicago	NHL	56	1	22	23	55	11	2	7	9	31
85-86	—Chicago	NHL	70	11	29	40	87	3	0	1	1	9
86-87	—Chicago	NHL	73	4	23	27	86	4	0	1	1	6
87-88	—Chicago	NHL	24	3	6	9	45	5	0	2	2	10
88-89	—Chicago	NHL	74	2	16	18	84	13	1	3	4	25
89-90	—Chicago	NHL	67	5	20	25	87	18	0	4	4	43
90-91	—Chicago	NHL	45	1	10	11	55	6	1	0	1	8
91-92	—Chicago	NHL	57	6	10	16	69	14	0	8	8	18
92-93	—Chicago	NHL	33	2	6	8	39	4	0	1	1	2
NHL totals			812	64	266	330	854	103	4	32	36	184

BROWN, KEVIN

RW, KINGS

PERSONAL: Born May 11, 1974, at Birmingham, England. . . . 6-2/211. . . . Shoots right. **HIGH SCHOOL:** Quinte Secondary School (Belleville, Ont.).

TRANSACTIONS/CAREER NOTES: Selected by Los Angeles Kings in fourth round (third Kings pick, 87th overall) of NHL entry draft (June 20, 1992).

HONORS: Won Jim Mahon Memorial Trophy (1992-93). . . . Named to OHL All-Star second team (1992-93).

Season	Team	League	REGULAR SEASON				PLAYOFFS			
			Gms.	G	A	Pts.	Pen.	Gms.	G	A	Pts.	Pen.
89-90	—Georgetown Jr. B	OHA	31	3	8	11	59	—	—	—	—	—
90-91	—Waterloo Jr. B	OHA	46	25	33	58	116	—	—	—	—	—
91-92	—Belleville	OHL	66	24	24	48	52	5	1	4	5	8
92-93	—Belleville	OHL	6	2	5	7	4	—	—	—	—	—
	—Detroit	OHL	56	48	86	134	76	15	10	18	28	18

BROWN, ROB

RW

PERSONAL: Born April 10, 1968, at Kingston, Ont. . . . 5-11/185. . . . Shoots left.

TRANSACTIONS/CAREER NOTES: Selected by Pittsburgh Penguins as underage junior in fourth round (fourth Penguins pick, 67th overall) of NHL entry draft (June 21, 1986). . . . Separated right shoulder (February 12, 1989); missed 12 games. . . . Traded by Penguins to Hartford Whalers for RW Scott Young (December 21, 1990). . . . Injured Adam's apple (April 5, 1991); missed one playoff game. . . . Traded by Whalers to Chicago Blackhawks for D Steve Konroyd (January 24, 1992). . . . Released by Blackhawks (July 22, 1993).

HONORS: Won WHL (West) Most Valuable Player Trophy (1985-86 and 1986-87). . . . Won Bob Brownridge Memorial Trophy (1985-86). . . . Named to WHL (West) All-Star first team (1985-86 and 1986-87). . . . Won Can.HL Player of the Year Award

(1986-87).... Won Can.HL Plus/Minus Award (1986-87).... Won WHL (West) Bob Brownridge Memorial Trophy (1986-87).... Won WHL Player of the Year Award (1986-87).... Played in NHL All-Star Game (1989).

			REGULAR SEASON					PLAYOFFS			
Season Team	League	Gms.	G	A	Pts.	Pen.	Gms.	G	A	Pts.	Pen.
83-84—Kamloops	WHL	50	16	42	58	80	15	1	2	3	17
84-85—Kamloops	WHL	60	29	50	79	95	15	8	8	16	28
85-86—Kamloops	WHL	69	58	*115	*173	171	16	*18	*28	*46	14
86-87—Kamloops	WHL	63	*76	*136	*212	101	5	6	5	11	6
87-88—Pittsburgh	NHL	51	24	20	44	56	—	—	—	—	—
88-89—Pittsburgh	NHL	68	49	66	115	118	11	5	3	8	22
89-90—Pittsburgh	NHL	80	33	47	80	102	—	—	—	—	—
90-91—Pittsburgh	NHL	25	6	10	16	31	—	—	—	—	—
—Hartford	NHL	44	18	24	42	101	5	1	0	1	7
91-92—Hartford	NHL	42	16	15	31	39	—	—	—	—	—
—Chicago	NHL	25	5	11	16	34	8	2	4	6	4
92-93—Chicago	NHL	15	1	6	7	33	—	—	—	—	—
—Indianapolis	IHL	19	14	19	33	32	2	0	1	1	2
NHL totals		350	152	199	351	514	24	8	7	15	33

BROWN, RYAN
D, LIGHTNING

PERSONAL: Born September 19, 1974, at Boyle, Alta.... 6-3/215.... Shoots right.
TRANSACTIONS/CAREER NOTES: Selected by Tampa Bay Lightning in fifth round (fifth Lightning pick, 107th overall) of NHL entry draft (June 26, 1993).

			REGULAR SEASON					PLAYOFFS			
Season Team	League	Gms.	G	A	Pts.	Pen.	Gms.	G	A	Pts.	Pen.
91-92—Seattle	WHL	60	1	1	2	230	14	0	2	2	38
92-93—Seattle	WHL	19	0	1	1	70	—	—	—	—	—
—Swift Current	WHL	47	1	4	5	104	17	0	2	2	18

BRUCE, DAVID
LW, SHARKS

PERSONAL: Born October 7, 1964, at Thunder Bay, Ont.... 5-11/190.... Shoots right.
TRANSACTIONS/CAREER NOTES: Selected by Vancouver Canucks as underage junior in second round (second Canucks pick, 30th overall) of NHL entry draft (June 8, 1983).... Suffered from mononucleosis (November 1987).... Bruised foot (March 1988).... Tore cartilage near thumb on left hand and underwent surgery (March 1989).... Signed as free agent by St. Louis Blues (July 23, 1990).... Selected by San Jose Sharks in NHL expansion draft (May 30, 1991).... Tore abdominal muscle (March 19, 1992).... Strained groin (November 7, 1992); missed 17 games.... Re-strained groin (December 23, 1992); missed 33 games.... Re-strained groin (March 11, 1993); missed remainder of season.
HONORS: Named to IHL All-Star first team (1989-90 and 1990-91).... Won James Gatschene Memorial Trophy (1990-91).

			REGULAR SEASON					PLAYOFFS			
Season Team	League	Gms.	G	A	Pts.	Pen.	Gms.	G	A	Pts.	Pen.
81-82—Thunder Bay	TBJHL	35	27	31	58	74	—	—	—	—	—
82-83—Kitchener	OHL	67	36	35	71	199	12	7	9	16	27
83-84—Kitchener	OHL	62	52	40	92	203	10	5	8	13	20
84-85—Fredericton	AHL	56	14	11	25	104	5	0	0	0	37
85-86—Fredericton	AHL	66	25	16	41	151	2	0	1	1	12
—Vancouver	NHL	12	0	1	1	14	1	0	0	0	0
86-87—Fredericton	AHL	17	7	6	13	73	—	—	—	—	—
—Vancouver	NHL	50	9	7	16	109	—	—	—	—	—
87-88—Fredericton	AHL	30	27	18	45	115	—	—	—	—	—
—Vancouver	NHL	28	7	3	10	57	—	—	—	—	—
88-89—Vancouver	NHL	53	7	7	14	65	—	—	—	—	—
89-90—Milwaukee	IHL	68	40	35	75	148	6	5	3	8	0
90-91—St. Louis	NHL	12	1	2	3	14	2	0	0	0	2
—Peoria	IHL	60	*64	52	116	78	18	*18	11	*29	40
91-92—Kansas City	IHL	7	5	5	10	6	—	—	—	—	—
—San Jose	NHL	60	22	16	38	46	—	—	—	—	—
92-93—San Jose	NHL	17	2	3	5	33	—	—	—	—	—
NHL totals		232	48	39	87	338	3	0	0	0	2

BRULE, STEVE
C, DEVILS

PERSONAL: Born January 15, 1975, at Montreal.... 5-11/184.... Shoots right.
TRANSACTIONS/CAREER NOTES: Selected by New Jersey Devils in sixth round (sixth Devils pick, 143rd overall) of NHL entry draft (June 26, 1993).
HONORS: Won Michel Bergeron Trophy (1992-93).... Named to QMJHL All-Rookie team (1992-93).

			REGULAR SEASON					PLAYOFFS			
Season Team	League	Gms.	G	A	Pts.	Pen.	Gms.	G	A	Pts.	Pen.
92-93—St. Jean	QMJHL	70	33	47	80	46	4	0	0	0	9

BRUNET, BENOIT
LW, CANADIENS

PERSONAL: Born August 24, 1968, at Montreal.... 5-11/184.... Shoots left.... Name pronounced behn-WAH broo-NAY.
TRANSACTIONS/CAREER NOTES: Selected by Montreal Canadiens as underage junior in second round (second Canadiens pick, 27th overall) of NHL entry draft (June 21, 1986)....
Injured ankle (September 1987).... Tore left knee ligaments (September 24, 1990); missed 24 games.... Fractured ankle

(December 4, 1991).... Sprained left knee (November 21, 1992); missed 10 games.... Fractured thumb (January 22, 1993); missed 14 games.
HONORS: Named to QMJHL All-Star second team (1986-87).... Named to AHL All-Star first team (1988-89).
MISCELLANEOUS: Member of Stanley Cup championship team (1993).

			REGULAR SEASON					PLAYOFFS			
Season Team	League	Gms.	G	A	Pts.	Pen.	Gms.	G	A	Pts.	Pen.
85-86—Hull	QMJHL	71	33	37	70	81	—	—	—	—	—
86-87—Hull	QMJHL	60	43	67	110	105	6	7	5	12	8
87-88—Hull	QMJHL	62	54	89	143	131	10	3	10	13	11
88-89—Montreal	NHL	2	0	1	1	0	—	—	—	—	—
—Sherbrooke	AHL	73	41	*76	117	95	6	2	0	2	4
89-90—Sherbrooke	AHL	72	32	35	67	82	12	8	7	15	20
90-91—Fredericton	AHL	24	13	18	31	16	6	5	6	11	2
—Montreal	NHL	17	1	3	4	0	—	—	—	—	—
91-92—Fredericton	AHL	6	7	9	16	27	—	—	—	—	—
—Montreal	NHL	18	4	6	10	14	—	—	—	—	—
92-93—Montreal	NHL	47	10	15	25	19	20	2	8	10	8
NHL totals		84	15	25	40	33	20	2	8	10	8

BRYLIN, SERGEI
C, DEVILS
PERSONAL: Born January 13, 1974, at Moscow, U.S.S.R.... 5-9/176.... Shoots left.
TRANSACTIONS/CAREER NOTES: Selected by New Jersey Devils in second round (second Devils pick, 42nd overall) of NHL entry draft (June 20, 1992).

			REGULAR SEASON					PLAYOFFS			
Season Team	League	Gms.	G	A	Pts.	Pen.	Gms.	G	A	Pts.	Pen.
91-92—CSKA Moscow	CIS	44	1	6	7	4	—	—	—	—	—
92-93—CSKA Moscow	CIS	42	5	4	9	36	—	—	—	—	—

BUCHANAN, JEFF
D, LIGHTNING
PERSONAL: Born May 23, 1971, at Swift Current, Sask.... 5-10/165.... Shoots right.
TRANSACTIONS/CAREER NOTES: Signed as free agent by Tampa Bay Lightning (August 13, 1992).

			REGULAR SEASON					PLAYOFFS			
Season Team	League	Gms.	G	A	Pts.	Pen.	Gms.	G	A	Pts.	Pen.
89-90—Saskatoon	WHL	66	7	12	19	96	9	0	2	2	2
90-91—Saskatoon	WHL	69	10	26	36	123	—	—	—	—	—
91-92—Saskatoon	WHL	72	17	37	54	143	—	—	—	—	—
92-93—Atlanta	IHL	68	4	18	22	282	9	0	0	0	26

BUCHBERGER, KELLY
RW/LW, OILERS
PERSONAL: Born December 12, 1966, at Langenburg, Sask.... 6-2/210.... Shoots left.... Full name: Kelly Michael Buchberger.... Name pronounced BUK-buhr-guhr.
HIGH SCHOOL: Langenburg (Sask.).
TRANSACTIONS/CAREER NOTES: Selected by Edmonton Oilers as underage junior in ninth round (eighth Oilers pick, 188th overall) of NHL entry draft (June 15, 1985).... Suspended six games by AHL for leaving bench to fight (March 30, 1988).... Fractured right ankle (March 1989).... Dislocated left shoulder (March 13, 1990).... Reinjured shoulder (May 4, 1990).... Strained shoulder (April 7, 1993); missed one game.
MISCELLANEOUS: Member of Stanley Cup championship teams (1987 and 1990).

			REGULAR SEASON					PLAYOFFS			
Season Team	League	Gms.	G	A	Pts.	Pen.	Gms.	G	A	Pts.	Pen.
83-84—Melville	SAJHL	60	14	11	25	139	—	—	—	—	—
84-85—Moose Jaw	WHL	51	12	17	29	114	—	—	—	—	—
85-86—Moose Jaw	WHL	72	14	22	36	206	13	11	4	15	37
86-87—Nova Scotia	AHL	70	12	20	32	257	5	0	1	1	23
—Edmonton	NHL	—	—	—	—	—	3	0	1	1	5
87-88—Edmonton	NHL	19	1	0	1	81	—	—	—	—	—
—Nova Scotia	AHL	49	21	23	44	206	2	0	0	0	11
88-89—Edmonton	NHL	66	5	9	14	234	—	—	—	—	—
89-90—Edmonton	NHL	55	2	6	8	168	19	0	5	5	13
90-91—Edmonton	NHL	64	3	1	4	160	12	2	1	3	25
91-92—Edmonton	NHL	79	20	24	44	157	16	1	4	5	32
92-93—Edmonton	NHL	83	12	18	30	133	—	—	—	—	—
NHL totals		366	43	58	101	933	50	3	11	14	75

BUCKBERGER, ASHLEY
RW, NORDIQUES
PERSONAL: Born February 19, 1975, at Esterhazy, Sask.... 6-2/200.... Shoots right.
HIGH SCHOOL: Swift Current (Sask.) Comprehensive.
TRANSACTIONS/CAREER NOTES: Selected by Quebec Nordiques in second round (third Nordiques pick, 49th overall) of NHL entry draft (June 26, 1993).
HONORS: Won Jim Piggot Memorial Trophy (1991-92).

			REGULAR SEASON					PLAYOFFS			
Season Team	League	Gms.	G	A	Pts.	Pen.	Gms.	G	A	Pts.	Pen.
90-91—Swift Current	WHL	10	2	3	5	0	3	0	0	0	0
91-92—Swift Current	WHL	67	23	22	45	38	8	2	1	3	2
92-93—Swift Current	WHL	72	23	44	67	41	17	6	7	13	6

BUDAYEV, ALEXEI
C, JETS

PERSONAL: Born April 24, 1975, at Elektrostal, U.S.S.R. . . . 6-2/183. . . . Shoots right.
TRANSACTIONS/CAREER NOTES: Selected by Winnipeg Jets in second round (third Jets pick, 43rd overall) of NHL entry draft (June 26, 1993).

			REGULAR SEASON					PLAYOFFS				
Season	Team	League	Gms.	G	A	Pts.	Pen.	Gms.	G	A	Pts.	Pen.
92-93—Kristall Elektrostal..........		CIS Div. II				Statistics unavailable.						

BURAKOVSKI, ROBERT
RW, SENATORS

PERSONAL: Born November 24, 1966, at Malmo, Sweden. . . . 5-10/178. . . . Shoots right. . . . Name pronounced boo-ruh-KAHV-skee.
TRANSACTIONS/CAREER NOTES: Selected by New York Rangers in 11th round (11th Rangers pick, 217th overall) of NHL entry draft (June 15, 1985). . . . Traded by Rangers to Ottawa Senators for future considerations (May 7, 1993).

			REGULAR SEASON					PLAYOFFS				
Season	Team	League	Gms.	G	A	Pts.	Pen.	Gms.	G	A	Pts.	Pen.
85-86—Leksand...........................		Sweden	19	4	3	7	4	—	—	—	—	—
86-87—Leksand...........................		Sweden	36	21	15	36	26	—	—	—	—	—
87-88—Leksand...........................		Sweden	36	10	11	21	10	—	—	—	—	—
88-89—Leksand...........................		Sweden	40	23	20	43	44	10	6	7	13	4
89-90—AIK.................................		Sweden	37	27	29	56	32	3	0	2	2	12
90-91—AIK.................................		Sweden	30	8	15	23	26	—	—	—	—	—
91-92—Malmo..............................		Sweden	40	19	22	41	42	9	5	0	5	4
92-93—Malmo..............................		Sweden	32	8	10	18	40	6	4	4	8	0

BURE, PAVEL
RW/LW, CANUCKS

PERSONAL: Born March 31, 1971, at Moscow, U.S.S.R. . . . 5-10/180. . . . Shoots left. . . . Name pronounced BUHR-ee. . . . Brother of Valeri Bure, left winger in Montreal Canadiens system.
TRANSACTIONS/CAREER NOTES: Selected by Vancouver Canucks in sixth round (Canucks fourth pick, 113th overall) of NHL entry draft (June 17, 1989).
HONORS: Named Soviet League Rookie of the Year (1988-89). . . . Won Calder Memorial Trophy (1991-92). . . . Played in NHL All-Star Game (1993).

			REGULAR SEASON					PLAYOFFS				
Season	Team	League	Gms.	G	A	Pts.	Pen.	Gms.	G	A	Pts.	Pen.
87-88—CSKA Moscow.................		USSR	5	1	1	2	0	—	—	—	—	—
88-89—CSKA Moscow.................		USSR	32	17	9	26	8	—	—	—	—	—
89-90—CSKA Moscow.................		USSR	46	14	11	25	22	—	—	—	—	—
90-91—CSKA Moscow.................		USSR	46	35	12	47	24	—	—	—	—	—
91-92—Vancouver......................		NHL	65	34	26	60	30	13	6	4	10	14
92-93—Vancouver......................		NHL	83	60	50	110	69	12	5	7	12	8
NHL totals................			**148**	**94**	**76**	**170**	**99**	**25**	**11**	**11**	**22**	**22**

BURE, VALERI
LW, CANADIENS

PERSONAL: Born June 13, 1974, at Moscow, U.S.S.R. . . . 5-10/160. . . . Shoots right. . . . Brother of Pavel Bure, right winger/left winger, Vancouver Canucks.
TRANSACTIONS/CAREER NOTES: Selected by Montreal Canadiens in second round (second Canadiens pick, 33rd overall) of NHL entry draft (June 20, 1992).
HONORS: Named to WHL (West) All-Star first team (1992-93).

			REGULAR SEASON					PLAYOFFS				
Season	Team	League	Gms.	G	A	Pts.	Pen.	Gms.	G	A	Pts.	Pen.
90-91—CSKA Moscow.................		USSR	3	0	0	0	0	—	—	—	—	—
91-92—Spokane		WHL	53	27	22	49	78	10	11	6	17	10
92-93—Spokane		WHL	66	68	79	147	49	9	6	11	17	14

BUREAU, MARC
C, LIGHTNING

PERSONAL: Born May 17, 1966, at Trois-Rivieres, Que. . . . 6-1/198. . . . Shoots right. . . . Name pronounced BYOOR-oh.
TRANSACTIONS/CAREER NOTES: Traded by Chicoutimi Sagueneens with C Stephane Roy, Lee Duhemee, Sylvain Demers and D Rene L'Ecuyer to Granby Bisons for LW Greg Choules and C Stephane Richer (January 1985). . . . Signed as free agent by Calgary Flames (May 16, 1987). . . . Suffered eye contusion (March 25, 1990); missed final two weeks of season. . . . Traded by Flames to Minnesota North Stars for third-round pick in 1991 draft (RW Sandy McCarthy) (March 5, 1991). . . . Injured shoulder (January 13, 1992); missed four games. . . . Separated shoulder (February 15, 1992); missed five games. . . . Separated shoulder (March 1, 1992); missed eight games. . . . Claimed on waivers by Tampa Bay Lightning (October 16, 1992). . . . Bruised shoulder (November 17, 1992); missed six games. . . . Bruised right knee (April 3, 1993); missed remainder of season.
HONORS: Named to IHL All-Star second team (1989-90 and 1990-91).

			REGULAR SEASON					PLAYOFFS				
Season	Team	League	Gms.	G	A	Pts.	Pen.	Gms.	G	A	Pts.	Pen.
83-84—Chicoutimi		QMJHL	56	6	16	22	14	—	—	—	—	—
84-85—Granby............................		QMJHL	68	50	70	120	29	—	—	—	—	—
85-86—Chicoutimi		QMJHL	63	36	62	98	69	9	3	7	10	10
86-87—Longueuil		QMJHL	66	54	58	112	68	20	17	20	37	12
87-88—Salt Lake City..................		IHL	69	7	20	27	86	7	0	3	3	8
88-89—Salt Lake City..................		IHL	76	28	36	64	119	14	7	5	12	31
89-90—Salt Lake City..................		IHL	67	43	48	91	173	11	4	8	12	0
—Calgary............................		NHL	5	0	0	0	4	—	—	—	—	—

B

Season	Team	League	REGULAR SEASON					PLAYOFFS				
			Gms.	G	A	Pts.	Pen.	Gms.	G	A	Pts.	Pen.
90-91—Calgary	NHL	5	0	0	0	2	—	—	—	—	—
—Salt Lake City	IHL	54	40	48	88	101	—	—	—	—	—
—Minnesota	NHL	9	0	6	6	4	23	3	2	5	20
91-92—Minnesota	NHL	46	6	4	10	50	5	0	0	0	14
—Kalamazoo	IHL	7	2	8	10	2	—	—	—	—	—
92-93—Tampa Bay	NHL	63	10	21	31	111	—	—	—	—	—
NHL totals			128	16	31	47	171	28	3	2	5	34

BURKE, SEAN
G, WHALERS

PERSONAL: Born January 29, 1967, at Windsor, Ont. . . . 6-4/210. . . . Shoots left.
TRANSACTIONS/CAREER NOTES: Selected by New Jersey Devils as underage junior in second round (second Devils pick, 24th overall) of NHL entry draft (June 15, 1985). . . . Injured groin (December 1988). . . . Underwent arthroscopic surgery to right knee (September 5, 1989). . . . Traded by Devils with D Eric Weinrich to Hartford Whalers for RW Bobby Holik, second-round pick in 1993 draft (LW Ray Pandolfo) and future considerations (August 28, 1992). . . . Sprained ankle (December 27, 1992); missed seven games. . . . Suffered back spasms (March 13, 1993); missed remainder of season.
HONORS: Played in NHL All-Star Game (1989).
MISCELLANEOUS: Member of silver-medal-winning Canadian Olympic team (1992).

Season	Team	League	REGULAR SEASON							PLAYOFFS						
			Gms.	Min.	W	L	T	GA	SO	Avg.	Gms.	Min.	W	L	GA	SO	Avg.
83-84—St. Michael's H.S.	MTHL	25	1482	. . .	. . .	. . .	120	0	4.86	—	—	—	—	—	—	—
84-85—Toronto	OHL	49	2987	25	21	3	211	0	4.24	5	266	1	3	25	0	5.64
85-86—Toronto	OHL	47	2840	16	27	3	†233	0	4.92	4	238	0	4	24	0	6.05
—Can. national team	Int'l	5	284	. . .	. . .	. . .	22	0	4.65	—	—	—	—	—	—	—
86-87—Can. national team	Int'l	46	2670	. . .	. . .	. . .	138	0	3.10	—	—	—	—	—	—	—
87-88—Can. national team	Int'l	37	1962	19	9	2	92	1	2.81	—	—	—	—	—	—	—
—Can. Olympic Team	Int'l	4	238	1	2	1	12	0	3.03	—	—	—	—	—	—	—
—New Jersey	NHL	13	689	10	1	0	35	1	3.05	17	1001	9	8	*57	†1	3.42
88-89—New Jersey	NHL	62	3590	22	31	9	†230	3	3.84	—	—	—	—	—	—	—
89-90—New Jersey	NHL	52	2914	22	22	6	175	0	3.60	2	125	0	2	8	0	3.84
90-91—New Jersey	NHL	35	1870	8	12	8	112	0	3.59	—	—	—	—	—	—	—
91-92—Can. national team	Int'l	31	1721	18	6	4	75	1	2.61	—	—	—	—	—	—	—
—Can. Olympic Team	Int'l	7	429	5	2	0	17	0	2.38	—	—	—	—	—	—	—
—San Diego	IHL	7	424	4	2	1	17	0	2.41	3	160	0	3	13	0	4.88
92-93—Hartford	NHL	50	2656	16	27	3	184	0	4.16	—	—	—	—	—	—	—
NHL totals			212	11719	78	93	26	736	4	3.77	19	1126	9	10	65	1	3.46

BURR, SHAWN
C/LW, RED WINGS

PERSONAL: Born July 1, 1966, at Sarnia, Ont. . . . 6-1/200. . . . Shoots left.
TRANSACTIONS/CAREER NOTES: Selected by Detroit Red Wings as underage junior in first round (first Red Wings Pick, seventh overall) of NHL entry draft (June 9, 1984). . . . Separated left shoulder (May 1988). . . . Suffered lower back spasms (October 20, 1992); missed three games.
HONORS: Won Emms Family Award (1983-84). . . . Named to OHL All-Star second team (1985-86).

Season	Team	League	REGULAR SEASON					PLAYOFFS				
			Gms.	G	A	Pts.	Pen.	Gms.	G	A	Pts.	Pen.
83-84—Kitchener	OHL	68	41	44	85	50	16	5	12	17	22
84-85—Kitchener	OHL	48	24	42	66	50	4	3	3	6	2
—Detroit	NHL	9	0	0	0	2	—	—	—	—	—
—Adirondack	AHL	4	0	0	0	2	—	—	—	—	—
85-86—Kitchener	OHL	59	60	67	127	83	5	2	3	5	8
—Adirondack	AHL	3	2	2	4	2	17	5	7	12	32
—Detroit	NHL	5	1	0	1	4	—	—	—	—	—
86-87—Detroit	NHL	80	22	25	47	107	16	7	2	9	20
87-88—Detroit	NHL	78	17	23	40	97	9	3	1	4	14
88-89—Detroit	NHL	79	19	27	46	78	6	1	2	3	6
89-90—Adirondack	AHL	3	4	2	6	2	—	—	—	—	—
—Detroit	NHL	76	24	32	56	82	—	—	—	—	—
90-91—Detroit	NHL	80	20	30	50	112	7	0	4	4	15
91-92—Detroit	NHL	79	19	32	51	118	11	1	5	6	10
92-93—Detroit	NHL	80	10	25	35	74	7	2	1	3	2
NHL totals			566	132	194	326	674	56	14	15	29	67

BURRIDGE, RANDY
LW, CAPITALS

PERSONAL: Born January 7, 1966, at Fort Erie, Ont. . . . 5-9/185. . . . Shoots left. . . . Name pronounced BUHR-ihdj.
TRANSACTIONS/CAREER NOTES: Selected by Boston Bruins in eighth round (seventh Bruins pick, 157th overall) of NHL entry draft (June 15, 1985). . . . Strained groin (March 1, 1986). . . . Suspended by AHL during playoffs (April 1987). . . . Sprained medial collateral ligament in left knee (February 6, 1990); missed 18 games. . . . Tore right knee ligaments (February 7, 1991). . . . Underwent surgery to right knee (February 13, 1991). . . . Traded by Bruins to Washington Capitals for RW Stephen Leach (June 21, 1991). . . . Partially tore left knee ligament (March 1, 1992); missed 14 games. . . . Underwent knee surgery (September 5, 1992); missed first 71 games of season.
HONORS: Played in NHL All-Star Game (1992).

Season	Team	League	REGULAR SEASON					PLAYOFFS				
			Gms.	G	A	Pts.	Pen.	Gms.	G	A	Pts.	Pen.
82-83—Fort Erie Jr. B		OHA	42	32	56	88	32	—	—	—	—	—
83-84—Peterborough		OHL	55	6	7	13	44	8	3	2	5	7
84-85—Peterborough		OHL	66	49	57	106	88	17	9	16	25	18
85-86—Peterborough		OHL	17	15	11	26	23	3	1	3	4	2
—Boston		NHL	52	17	25	42	28	3	0	4	4	12
—Moncton		AHL	—	—	—	—	—	3	0	2	2	2
86-87—Moncton		AHL	47	26	41	67	139	3	1	2	3	30
—Boston		NHL	23	1	4	5	16	2	1	0	1	2
87-88—Boston		NHL	79	27	28	55	105	23	2	10	12	16
88-89—Boston		NHL	80	31	30	61	39	10	5	2	7	8
89-90—Boston		NHL	63	17	15	32	47	21	4	11	15	14
90-91—Boston		NHL	62	15	13	28	40	19	0	3	3	39
91-92—Washington		NHL	66	23	44	67	50	2	0	1	1	0
92-93—Baltimore		AHL	2	0	1	1	2	—	—	—	—	—
—Washington		NHL	4	0	0	0	0	4	1	0	1	0
NHL totals			429	131	159	290	325	84	13	31	44	91

BURT, ADAM
D, WHALERS

PERSONAL: Born January 15, 1969, at Detroit.... 6-0/ 190.... Shoots left.
TRANSACTIONS/CAREER NOTES: Suffered broken jaw (December 1985).... Selected by Hartford Whalers as underage junior in second round (second Whalers pick, 39th overall) of NHL entry draft (June 13, 1987).... Separated left shoulder (September 13, 1988).... Bruised hip (December 1989).... Dislocated left shoulder (January 19, 1989).... Tore medial collateral ligaments in right knee (February 16, 1991); missed remainder of season.... Sprained left wrist (January 11, 1992); missed six games.... Broke bone in right foot (January 25, 1993); missed 13 games.
HONORS: Named to OHL All-Star second team (1987-88).

Season	Team	League	REGULAR SEASON					PLAYOFFS				
			Gms.	G	A	Pts.	Pen.	Gms.	G	A	Pts.	Pen.
85-86—North Bay		OHL	49	0	11	11	81	10	0	0	0	24
86-87—North Bay		OHL	57	4	27	31	138	24	1	6	7	68
87-88—North Bay		OHL	66	17	54	71	176	2	0	3	3	6
—Binghamton		AHL	—	—	—	—	—	2	1	1	2	0
88-89—North Bay		OHL	23	4	11	15	45	12	2	12	14	12
—Team USA Juniors		Int'l	7	1	6	7	...	—	—	—	—	—
—Binghamton		AHL	5	0	2	2	13	—	—	—	—	—
—Hartford		NHL	5	0	0	0	6	—	—	—	—	—
89-90—Hartford		NHL	63	4	8	12	105	2	0	0	0	0
90-91—Springfield		AHL	9	1	3	4	22	—	—	—	—	—
—Hartford		NHL	42	2	7	9	63	—	—	—	—	—
91-92—Hartford		NHL	66	9	15	24	93	2	0	0	0	0
92-93—Hartford		NHL	65	6	14	20	116	—	—	—	—	—
NHL totals			241	21	44	65	383	4	0	0	0	0

BUSCHAN, ANDREI
D, SHARKS

PERSONAL: Born August 21, 1970, at Kharkov, U.S.S.R.... 6-2/ 194.... Shoots left.
TRANSACTIONS/CAREER NOTES: Selected by San Jose Sharks in fifth round (sixth Sharks pick, 106th overall) of NHL entry draft (June 26, 1993).

Season	Team	League	REGULAR SEASON					PLAYOFFS				
			Gms.	G	A	Pts.	Pen.	Gms.	G	A	Pts.	Pen.
88-89—Dynamo Kharkov		USSR	2	0	0	0	0	—	—	—	—	—
89-90—Dynamo Kharkov		USSR	21	0	0	0	10	—	—	—	—	—
90-91—Dynamo Kharkov		USSR Div. II	62	0	3	3	14	—	—	—	—	—
91-92—Dynamo Kharkov		CIS Div. II	Statistics unavailable.									
92-93—Sokol-Eskulap Kiev		CIS	41	8	5	13	16	3	0	0	0	4

BUSKAS, ROD
D, BLACKHAWKS

PERSONAL: Born January 7, 1961, at Wetaskiwin, Alta.... 6-1/206.... Shoots right.... Full name: Rod Dale Buskas.... Name pronounced BUZ-kuhz.
TRANSACTIONS/CAREER NOTES: Selected by Pittsburgh Penguins in sixth round (fifth Penguins pick, 112th overall) of NHL entry draft (June 10, 1981).... Injured shoulder (February 1985). ...Injured shoulder (November 1986).... Traded by Penguins to Vancouver Canucks for sixth-round pick in 1990 draft (D Ian Moran) (October 24, 1989).... Broke ankle (December 13, 1989); missed 29 games.... Traded by Canucks to Penguins for RW Tony Tanti and C Barry Pederson to Penguins for C Dan Quinn, RW Andrew McBain and C Dave Capuano (January 8, 1990).... Selected by Los Angeles Kings in NHL waiver draft for $10,000 (October 1, 1990).... Strained chest muscle (December 20, 1990).... Injured foot (January 22, 1991).... Traded by Kings to Chicago Blackhawks for D Chris Norton (October 28, 1991). ...Bruised left foot (February 22, 1992); missed 14 games.... Loaned to Salt Lake City Golden Eagles (January 11, 1993).

Season	Team	League	REGULAR SEASON					PLAYOFFS				
			Gms.	G	A	Pts.	Pen.	Gms.	G	A	Pts.	Pen.
78-79—Red Deer		AJHL	37	13	22	35	63	—	—	—	—	—
—Billings		WHL	1	0	0	0	0	—	—	—	—	—
—Medicine Hat		WHL	35	1	12	13	60	—	—	—	—	—
79-80—Medicine Hat		WHL	72	7	40	47	284	—	—	—	—	—
80-81—Medicine Hat		WHL	72	14	46	60	164	5	1	1	2	8
81-82—Erie		AHL	69	1	18	19	78	—	—	—	—	—

B

Season Team	League	Gms.	G	A	Pts.	Pen.	Gms.	G	A	Pts.	Pen.
82-83—Muskegon	IHL	1	0	0	0	9	—	—	—	—	—
—Baltimore	AHL	31	2	8	10	45	—	—	—	—	—
—Pittsburgh	NHL	41	2	2	4	102	—	—	—	—	—
83-84—Baltimore	AHL	33	2	12	14	100	10	1	3	4	22
—Pittsburgh	NHL	47	2	4	6	60	—	—	—	—	—
84-85—Pittsburgh	NHL	69	2	7	9	191	—	—	—	—	—
85-86—Pittsburgh	NHL	72	2	7	9	159	—	—	—	—	—
86-87—Pittsburgh	NHL	68	3	15	18	123	—	—	—	—	—
87-88—Pittsburgh	NHL	76	4	8	12	206	—	—	—	—	—
88-89—Pittsburgh	NHL	52	1	5	6	105	10	0	0	0	23
89-90—Vancouver	NHL	17	0	3	3	36	—	—	—	—	—
—Pittsburgh	NHL	6	0	0	0	13	—	—	—	—	—
90-91—Los Angeles	NHL	57	3	8	11	182	2	0	2	2	22
91-92—Los Angeles	NHL	5	0	0	0	11	—	—	—	—	—
—Chicago	NHL	42	0	4	4	80	6	0	1	1	0
92-93—Chicago	NHL	4	0	0	0	26	—	—	—	—	—
—Indianapolis	IHL	15	0	3	3	40	—	—	—	—	—
—Salt Lake City	IHL	31	0	2	2	52	—	—	—	—	—
NHL totals		556	19	63	82	1294	18	0	3	3	45

BUTCHER, GARTH
D, BLUES

PERSONAL: Born January 8, 1963, at Regina, Sask.... 6-0/204.... Shoots right. **HIGH SCHOOL:** Thom (Regina, Sask.).
TRANSACTIONS/CAREER NOTES: Selected by Vancouver Canucks as underage junior in first round (first Canucks pick, 10th overall) of NHL entry draft (June 10, 1981)....
Separated shoulder (October 1984).... Traded by Canucks with C Dan Quinn to St. Louis Blues for LW Geoff Courtnall, D Robert Dirk, C Cliff Ronning, LW Sergio Momesso and fifth-round pick (RW Brian Loney) in 1992 draft (March 5, 1991).... Fractured bone in left foot (March 7, 1992); missed final 12 games of season.
HONORS: Named to WHL All-Star first team (1980-81 and 1981-82).... Played in NHL All-Star Game (1993).

Season Team	League	Gms.	G	A	Pts.	Pen.	Gms.	G	A	Pts.	Pen.
79-80—Regina Tier II	SJHL	51	15	31	46	236	—	—	—	—	—
—Regina	WHL	13	0	4	4	20	9	0	0	0	45
80-81—Regina	WHL	69	9	77	86	230	11	5	17	22	60
81-82—Regina	WHL	65	24	68	92	318	19	3	17	20	95
—Vancouver	NHL	5	0	0	0	9	1	0	0	0	0
82-83—Kamloops	WHL	5	4	2	6	4	6	4	8	12	16
—Vancouver	NHL	55	1	13	14	104	3	1	0	1	2
83-84—Fredericton	AHL	25	4	13	17	43	6	0	2	2	19
—Vancouver	NHL	28	2	0	2	34	—	—	—	—	—
84-85—Vancouver	NHL	75	3	9	12	152	—	—	—	—	—
—Fredericton	AHL	3	1	0	1	11	—	—	—	—	—
85-86—Vancouver	NHL	70	4	7	11	188	3	0	0	0	0
86-87—Vancouver	NHL	70	5	15	20	207	—	—	—	—	—
87-88—Vancouver	NHL	80	6	17	23	285	—	—	—	—	—
88-89—Vancouver	NHL	78	0	20	20	227	7	1	1	2	22
89-90—Vancouver	NHL	80	6	14	20	205	—	—	—	—	—
90-91—Vancouver	NHL	69	6	12	18	257	—	—	—	—	—
—St. Louis	NHL	13	0	4	4	32	13	2	1	3	54
91-92—St. Louis	NHL	68	5	15	20	189	5	1	2	3	16
92-93—St. Louis	NHL	84	5	10	15	211	11	1	1	2	20
NHL totals		775	43	136	179	2100	43	6	5	11	114

BUTSAYEV, VIACHESLAV
C, FLYERS

PERSONAL: Born June 13, 1970, at Tolyatti, U.S.S.R. ... 6-2/200. ... Shoots left.... Name pronounced boot-SIGH-yehf.
TRANSACTIONS/CAREER NOTES: Selected by Philadelphia Flyers in sixth round (10th Flyers pick, 109th overall) of NHL entry draft (June 16, 1990).

Season Team	League	Gms.	G	A	Pts.	Pen.	Gms.	G	A	Pts.	Pen.
89-90—CSKA Moscow	USSR	48	13	4	17	30	—	—	—	—	—
90-91—CSKA Moscow	USSR	46	14	9	23	32	—	—	—	—	—
91-92—CSKA Moscow	USSR	36	12	13	25	26	—	—	—	—	—
—Unified Olympic Team	Int'l	8	1	1	2	4	—	—	—	—	—
92-93—CSKA Moscow	CIS	5	3	4	7	6	—	—	—	—	—
—Philadelphia	NHL	52	2	14	16	61	—	—	—	—	—
—Hershey	AHL	24	8	10	18	51	—	—	—	—	—
NHL totals		52	2	14	16	61	—	—	—	—	—

BYAKIN, ILYA
D, OILERS

PERSONAL: Born February 2, 1963, at Sverdlovsk, U.S.S.R. ... 5-9/183. ... Shoots left.
TRANSACTIONS/CAREER NOTES: Selected by Edmonton Oilers in 11th round (11th Oilers pick, 267th overall) of NHL entry draft (June 26, 1993).

Season	Team	League	REGULAR SEASON					PLAYOFFS				
			Gms.	G	A	Pts.	Pen.	Gms.	G	A	Pts.	Pen.
83-84	Spartak Moscow	USSR	44	9	12	21	26	—	—	—	—	—
84-85	Spartak Moscow	USSR	46	7	11	18	56	—	—	—	—	—
85-86	Spartak Moscow	USSR	34	8	7	15	41	—	—	—	—	—
86-87	Automobilist Sverdlovsk	USSR					Did not play.					
87-88	Automobilist Sverdlovsk	USSR	30	10	10	20	37	—	—	—	—	—
88-89	Automobilist Sverdlovsk	USSR	40	11	9	20	53	—	—	—	—	—
89-90	Automobilist Sverdlovsk	USSR	27	14	7	21	20	—	—	—	—	—
90-91	CSKA Moscow	USSR	29	4	7	11	20	—	—	—	—	—
91-92	Rapperswill	Switzerland	36	27	40	67	36	—	—	—	—	—
92-93	Landshut	Germany	44	12	19	31	43	—	—	—	—	—

BYCE, JOHN

C, CAPITALS

B

PERSONAL: Born September 8, 1967, at Madison, Wis. . . . 6-0/175. . . . Shoots right. . . . Full name: John Arthur Byce.
HIGH SCHOOL: Madison (Wis.) Memorial.
COLLEGE: Wisconsin.
TRANSACTIONS/CAREER NOTES: Selected by Boston Bruins in 11th round (11th Bruins pick, 220th overall) of NHL entry draft (June 15, 1985). . . . Injured knee (November 18, 1988). . . . Dislocated left shoulder (September 22, 1990); missed first six games of season. . . . Broke bone in left foot (March 15, 1991). . . . Traded by Bruins with D Dennis Smith to Washington Capitals for LW Brent Hughes and future considerations (February 24, 1992).
HONORS: Named to WCHA All-Star second team (1988-89 and 1989-90). . . . Named to NCAA All-Tournament team (1989-90).

Season	Team	League	REGULAR SEASON					PLAYOFFS				
			Gms.	G	A	Pts.	Pen.	Gms.	G	A	Pts.	Pen.
84-85	Madison Memorial	Wisc. H.S.	24	39	47	86	32	—	—	—	—	—
85-86	—						Did not play.					
86-87	University of Wisconsin	WCHA	40	1	4	5	12	—	—	—	—	—
87-88	University of Wisconsin	WCHA	41	22	12	34	18	—	—	—	—	—
88-89	University of Wisconsin	WCHA	42	27	28	55	16	—	—	—	—	—
89-90	University of Wisconsin	WCHA	46	27	44	71	20	—	—	—	—	—
	—Boston	NHL	—	—	—	—	—	8	2	0	2	2
90-91	—Maine	AHL	53	19	29	48	20	—	—	—	—	—
	—Boston	NHL	18	1	3	4	6	—	—	—	—	—
91-92	—Maine	AHL	55	29	21	50	41	—	—	—	—	—
	—Boston	NHL	3	1	0	1	0	—	—	—	—	—
	—Baltimore	AHL	20	9	5	14	4	—	—	—	—	—
92-93	—Baltimore	AHL	62	35	44	79	26	7	4	5	9	4
NHL totals			**21**	**2**	**3**	**5**	**6**	**8**	**2**	**0**	**2**	**2**

BYERS, LYNDON

RW

PERSONAL: Born February 29, 1964, at Nipawin, Sask. . . . 6-2/195. . . . Shoots right. . . . Full name: Lyndon Svi Byers.
TRANSACTIONS/CAREER NOTES: Traded by Saskatoon Blades to Regina Pats for LW Todd Strueby (September 10, 1981). . . . Broke right wrist (April 1981). . . . Selected by Boston Bruins as underage junior in second round (third Bruins pick, 39th overall) of NHL entry draft (June 9, 1982). . . . Tore ligaments in right knee (September 1987). . . . Separated left shoulder (November 1987). . . . Bruised right hand (March 1988). . . . Bruised left thigh (April 1988). . . . Dislocated jaw (September 1988). . . . Separated right shoulder (December 1988). . . . Suffered inflammation of left elbow (February 1989). . . . Separated right shoulder (March 22, 1989). . . . Injured left knee (September 29, 1989); missed first seven games of season. . . . Tore tendon in left thumb (December 9, 1989); missed 14 games. . . . Broke left foot (February 1990); missed 14 games. . . . Strained quadricep (October 16, 1990); missed five games. . . . Bruised lower back (November 17, 1990); missed three games. . . . Suspended 10 games by NHL for leaving bench to fight (December 13, 1990). . . . Fractured left foot (December 16, 1990). . . . Underwent surgery to repair fractured navicular bone in left foot (February 8, 1991). . . . Refractured left foot (March 25, 1991). . . . Injured groin (October 27, 1991); missed seven games. . . . Signed as free agent by San Jose Sharks (November 5, 1992). . . . Bruised foot (November 19, 1992); missed three games. . . . Strained neck (December 9, 1992); missed three games. . . . Separated shoulder (January 21, 1993); missed six games. . . . Signed as free agent by San Diego Gulls (March 10, 1993).
HONORS: Named to SCMHL All-Star second team (1980-81).

Season	Team	League	REGULAR SEASON					PLAYOFFS				
			Gms.	G	A	Pts.	Pen.	Gms.	G	A	Pts.	Pen.
80-81	Notre Dame	SCMHL	37	35	42	77	106	—	—	—	—	—
81-82	Regina	WHL	57	18	25	43	169	20	5	6	11	48
82-83	Regina	WHL	70	32	38	70	153	5	1	1	2	16
83-84	Regina	WHL	58	32	57	89	154	23	17	18	35	78
	—Boston	NHL	10	2	4	6	32	—	—	—	—	—
84-85	Hershey	AHL	27	4	6	10	55	—	—	—	—	—
	—Boston	NHL	33	3	8	11	41	—	—	—	—	—
85-86	Boston	NHL	5	0	2	2	9	—	—	—	—	—
	—Moncton	AHL	14	2	4	6	26	—	—	—	—	—
	—Milwaukee	IHL	8	0	2	2	22	—	—	—	—	—
86-87	Moncton	AHL	27	5	5	10	63	—	—	—	—	—
	—Boston	NHL	18	2	3	5	53	1	0	0	0	0
87-88	Maine	AHL	2	0	1	1	18	—	—	—	—	—
	—Boston	NHL	53	10	14	24	236	11	1	2	3	62
88-89	Maine	AHL	4	1	3	4	2	—	—	—	—	—
	—Boston	NHL	49	0	4	4	218	2	0	0	0	0

Season Team	League	REGULAR SEASON					PLAYOFFS				
		Gms.	G	A	Pts.	Pen.	Gms.	G	A	Pts.	Pen.
89-90—Boston	NHL	43	4	4	8	159	17	1	0	1	12
90-91—Boston	NHL	19	2	2	4	82	1	0	0	0	10
91-92—Boston	NHL	31	1	1	2	129	5	0	0	0	12
—Maine	AHL	11	5	4	9	47	—	—	—	—	—
92-93—Kansas City	IHL	4	1	1	2	22	—	—	—	—	—
—San Jose	NHL	18	4	1	5	122	—	—	—	—	—
—San Diego	IHL	9	0	3	3	35	—	—	—	—	—
NHL totals		279	28	43	71	1081	37	2	2	4	96

CAIRNS, ERIC
D, RANGERS

PERSONAL: Born June 27, 1974, at Oakville, Ont. . . . 6-6/217. . . . Shoots left.
TRANSACTIONS/CAREER NOTES: Selected by New York Rangers in third round (third Rangers pick, 72nd overall) of NHL entry draft (June 20, 1992).

Season Team	League	REGULAR SEASON					PLAYOFFS				
		Gms.	G	A	Pts.	Pen.	Gms.	G	A	Pts.	Pen.
90-91—Burlington Jr. B	OHA	37	5	16	21	120	—	—	—	—	—
91-92—Detroit	OHL	64	1	11	12	237	7	0	0	0	31
92-93—Detroit	OHL	64	3	13	16	194	15	0	3	3	24

CALLANDER, JOCK
C/RW, LIGHTNING

PERSONAL: Born April 23, 1961, at Regina, Sask. . . . 6-1/188. . . . Shoots right. . . . Brother of Drew Callander, center, Philadelphia Flyers and Vancouver Canucks (1976-77 through 1979-80).
TRANSACTIONS/CAREER NOTES: Signed as free agent by St. Louis Blues (September 28, 1981). . . . Signed as free agent by Pittsburgh Penguins (July 31, 1987). . . . Underwent knee surgery (October 1990). . . . Tore knee ligaments (January 19, 1991). . . . Signed as free agent by Tampa Bay Lightning (July 29, 1992).
HONORS: Won Bob Brownridge Memorial Trophy (1981-82). . . . Named Turner Cup Playoff Most Valuable Player (1985-86). . . . Shared James Gatschene Memorial Trophy with Jeff Pyle (1986-87). . . . Shared Leo P. Lamoureux Memorial Trophy with Jeff Pyle (1986-87). . . . Named to IHL All-Star first team (1986-87 and 1991-92).
MISCELLANEOUS: Member of Stanley Cup championship team (1992).

Season Team	League	REGULAR SEASON					PLAYOFFS				
		Gms.	G	A	Pts.	Pen.	Gms.	G	A	Pts.	Pen.
78-79—Regina	WHL	19	3	2	5	0	—	—	—	—	—
—Regina Blues	SJHL	42	44	42	86	24	—	—	—	—	—
79-80—Regina	WHL	39	9	11	20	25	18	8	5	13	0
80-81—Regina	WHL	72	67	86	153	37	11	6	7	13	14
81-82—Regina	WHL	71	79	111	*190	59	20	13	*26	39	37
82-83—Salt Lake City	IHL	68	20	27	47	26	6	0	1	1	9
83-84—Montana	CHL	72	27	32	59	69	—	—	—	—	—
—Toledo	IHL	2	0	0	0	0	—	—	—	—	—
84-85—Muskegon	IHL	82	39	68	107	86	17	8	13	21	33
85-86—Muskegon	IHL	82	39	72	111	121	14	*12	11	*23	12
86-87—Muskegon	IHL	82	54	82	†136	110	15	13	7	20	23
87-88—Muskegon	IHL	31	20	36	56	49	6	2	3	5	25
—Pittsburgh	NHL	41	11	16	27	45	—	—	—	—	—
88-89—Muskegon	IHL	48	25	39	64	40	7	5	5	10	30
—Pittsburgh	NHL	30	6	5	11	20	10	2	5	7	10
89-90—Muskegon	IHL	46	29	49	78	118	15	6	†14	20	54
—Pittsburgh	NHL	30	4	7	11	49	—	—	—	—	—
90-91—Muskegon	IHL	30	14	20	34	102	—	—	—	—	—
91-92—Muskegon	IHL	81	42	70	112	160	10	4	10	14	13
—Pittsburgh	NHL	—	—	—	—	—	12	1	3	4	2
92-93—Atlanta	IHL	69	34	50	84	172	9	†7	5	12	25
—Tampa Bay	NHL	8	1	1	2	2	—	—	—	—	—
NHL totals		109	22	29	51	116	22	3	8	11	12

CAMPBELL, JIM
C, CANADIENS

PERSONAL: Born February 3, 1973, at Worcester, Mass. . . . 6-1/175. . . . Shoots right.
HIGH SCHOOL: Lawrence Academy (Groton, Mass.), then Northwood School (Lake Placid, N.Y.).
TRANSACTIONS/CAREER NOTES: Selected by Montreal Canadiens in second round (second Canadiens pick, 28th overall) of NHL entry draft (June 22, 1991).

Season Team	League	REGULAR SEASON					PLAYOFFS				
		Gms.	G	A	Pts.	Pen.	Gms.	G	A	Pts.	Pen.
88-89—Lawrence Academy	Mass. H.S.	12	12	8	20	6	—	—	—	—	—
89-90—Lawrence Academy	Mass. H.S.	8	14	7	21	8	—	—	—	—	—
90-91—Northwood School	N.Y. H.S.	26	36	47	83	36	—	—	—	—	—
91-92—Hull	QMJHL	64	41	44	85	51	6	7	3	10	8
92-93—Hull	QMJHL	50	42	29	71	66	8	11	4	15	43

CAPUANO, DAVE
LW/C, SHARKS

PERSONAL: Born July 27, 1968, at Warwick, R.I. . . . 6-2/190. . . . Shoots left. . . . Full name: David Alan Capuano. . . . Brother of Jack Capuano, defenseman, Toronto Maple Leafs, Vancouver Canucks and Boston Bruins (1989-90 through 1991-92).
HIGH SCHOOL: Mount St. Charles Academy (Woonsocket, R.I.).

BC

COLLEGE: Maine.
TRANSACTIONS/CAREER NOTES: Selected by Pittsburgh Penguins in second round (second Penguins pick, 25th overall) of NHL entry draft (June 21, 1986).... Broke hand (August 1986).... Traded by Penguins with C Dan Quinn and RW Andrew McBain to Vancouver Canucks for RW Tony Tanti, C Barry Pederson and D Rod Buskas (January 8, 1990).... Injured knee (November 27, 1990).... Underwent arthroscopic knee surgery (January 25, 1991); missed 14 games.... Traded by Canucks with fourth-round pick in 1994 draft to Tampa Bay Lightning for C Anatoli Semenov (November 3, 1992).... Traded by Lightning to San Jose Sharks for D Peter Ahola (June 19, 1993).
HONORS: Named to Hockey East All-Freshman team (1986-87).... Named to NCAA All-America East first team (1987-88 and 1988-89).... Named to NCAA All-Tournament team (1987-88).... Named to Hockey East All-Star first team (1987-88 and 1988-89).

			REGULAR SEASON					PLAYOFFS			
Season	Team	League	Gms.	G	A	Pts.	Pen.	Gms.	G	A	Pts.	Pen.
84-85—Mount St. Charles H.S.	R.I.H.S.	...	41	38	79	...	—	—	—	—	—
85-86—Mount St. Charles H.S.	R.I.H.S.	22	39	48	87	20	—	—	—	—	—
86-87—University of Maine	Hockey East	38	18	41	59	14	—	—	—	—	—
87-88—University of Maine	Hockey East	42	34	51	85	51	—	—	—	—	—
88-89—University of Maine	Hockey East	41	37	30	67	38	—	—	—	—	—
89-90—Muskegon	IHL	27	15	15	30	22	—	—	—	—	—
—Pittsburgh	NHL	6	0	0	0	2	—	—	—	—	—
—Vancouver	NHL	27	3	5	8	10	—	—	—	—	—
—Milwaukee	IHL	2	0	4	4	0	6	1	5	6	0
90-91—Vancouver	NHL	61	13	31	44	42	6	1	1	2	5
91-92—Milwaukee	IHL	9	2	6	8	8	—	—	—	—	—
92-93—Hamilton	AHL	4	0	1	1	0	—	—	—	—	—
—Atlanta	IHL	58	19	40	59	50	8	2	2	4	9
—Tampa Bay	NHL	6	1	1	2	2	—	—	—	—	—
NHL totals		100	17	37	54	56	6	1	1	2	5

CARBONNEAU, GUY
C, CANADIENS

PERSONAL: Born March 18, 1960, at Sept Iles, Que.... 5-11/184.... Shoots right. ...Name pronounced GEE KAHR-buh-NOH.
TRANSACTIONS/CAREER NOTES: Selected by Montreal Canadiens as underage junior in third round (fourth Canadiens pick, 44th overall) of NHL entry draft (August 9, 1979).... Strained right knee ligaments (October 7, 1989); missed nine games.... Broke nose (October 28, 1989).... Suffered concussion (October 8, 1990).... Fractured rib (January 13, 1992); missed six games.... Injured elbow (March 2, 1992); missed one game.... Suffered right knee tendinitis (October 1, 1992); missed five games.... Broke finger (November 14, 1992); missed three games.... Suffered knee tendinitis (February 4, 1993); missed 15 games.
HONORS: Named to QMJHL All-Star second team (1979-80).... Won Frank J. Selke Trophy (1987-88, 1988-89 and 1991-92).
MISCELLANEOUS: Member of Stanley Cup championship teams (1986 and 1993).

			REGULAR SEASON					PLAYOFFS			
Season	Team	League	Gms.	G	A	Pts.	Pen.	Gms.	G	A	Pts.	Pen.
76-77—Chicoutimi	QMJHL	59	9	20	29	8	4	1	0	1	0
77-78—Chicoutimi	QMJHL	70	28	55	83	60	—	—	—	—	—
78-79—Chicoutimi	QMJHL	72	62	79	141	47	4	2	1	3	4
79-80—Chicoutimi	QMJHL	72	72	110	182	66	12	9	15	24	28
—Nova Scotia	AHL	—	—	—	—	—	2	1	1	2	2
80-81—Montreal	NHL	2	0	1	1	0	—	—	—	—	—
—Nova Scotia	AHL	78	35	53	88	87	6	1	3	4	9
81-82—Nova Scotia	AHL	77	27	67	94	124	9	2	7	9	8
82-83—Montreal	NHL	77	18	29	47	68	3	0	0	0	2
83-84—Montreal	NHL	78	24	30	54	75	15	4	3	7	12
84-85—Montreal	NHL	79	23	34	57	43	12	4	3	7	8
85-86—Montreal	NHL	80	20	36	56	57	20	7	5	12	35
86-87—Montreal	NHL	79	18	27	45	68	17	3	8	11	20
87-88—Montreal	NHL	80	17	21	38	61	11	0	4	4	2
88-89—Montreal	NHL	79	26	30	56	44	21	4	5	9	10
89-90—Montreal	NHL	68	19	36	55	37	11	2	3	5	6
90-91—Montreal	NHL	78	20	24	44	63	13	1	5	6	10
91-92—Montreal	NHL	72	18	21	39	39	11	1	1	2	6
92-93—Montreal	NHL	61	4	13	17	20	20	3	3	6	10
NHL totals		833	207	302	509	575	154	29	40	69	121

CAREY, JIM
G, CAPITALS

PERSONAL: Born May 31, 1974, at Dorchester, Mass.... 6-2/190.... Shoots left.... Brother of Paul Carey, first baseman, Baltimore Orioles organization.
HIGH SCHOOL: Catholic Memorial (Boston).
COLLEGE: Wisconsin.
TRANSACTIONS/CAREER NOTES: Selected by Washington Capitals in second round (second Capitals pick, 32nd overall) of NHL entry draft (June 20, 1992).
HONORS: Won WCHA Rookie of the Year Award (1992-93).... Named to WCHA All-Star second team (1992-93).... Named to WCHA Rookie All-Star team (1992-93).

			REGULAR SEASON							PLAYOFFS					
Season	Team	League	Gms.	Min.	W	L	T	GA	SO	Avg.	Gms.	Min.	W	L	GA	SO	Avg.
89-90—Catholic Memorial H.S.	Mass. HS	12	...	12	0	0	...	...	...	—	—	—	—	—	—	—
90-91—Catholic Memorial H.S.	Mass. HS	14	...	13	0	0	...	6	...	—	—	—	—	—	—	—
91-92—Catholic Memorial H.S.	Mass. HS	21	1108	19	2	0	29	6	1.57	—	—	—	—	—	—	—
92-93—Univ. of Wisconsin	WCHA	26	1525	15	8	1	78	...	3.07	—	—	—	—	—	—	—

CARKNER, TERRY

D, FLYERS

PERSONAL: Born March 7, 1966, at Smith Falls, Ont.... 6-3/212.... Shoots left.
TRANSACTIONS/CAREER NOTES: Selected by New York Rangers as underage junior in first round (first Rangers pick, 14th overall) of NHL entry draft (June 9, 1984).... Traded by Rangers with LW Jeff Jackson to Quebec Nordiques for LW John Ogrodnick and D David Shaw (September 30, 1987).... Suspended 10 games by NHL for leaving the bench during fight (January 24, 1988).... Traded by Nordiques to Philadelphia Flyers for D Greg Smyth and third-round pick in 1989 draft (G John Tanner) (July 25, 1988). ... Underwent surgery to left knee (September 23, 1989); missed 15 games.... Bruised ankle (March 1990).... Bruised foot (November 23, 1991); missed two games.... Bruised wrist (November 19, 1992); missed one game.
HONORS: Named to OHL All-Star second team (1984-85).... Shared Max Kaminsky Trophy with Jeff Brown (1985-86).... Named to OHL All-Star first team (1985-86).

Season	Team	League	REGULAR SEASON					PLAYOFFS				
			Gms.	G	A	Pts.	Pen.	Gms.	G	A	Pts.	Pen.
82-83	Brockville	COJHL	47	8	32	40	94	—	—	—	—	—
83-84	Peterborough	OHL	66	4	21	25	91	8	0	6	6	13
84-85	Peterborough	OHL	64	14	47	61	125	17	2	10	12	11
85-86	Peterborough	OHL	54	12	32	44	106	16	1	7	8	17
86-87	New Haven	AHL	12	2	6	8	56	3	1	0	1	0
	New York Rangers	NHL	52	2	13	15	120	1	0	0	0	0
87-88	Quebec	NHL	63	3	24	27	159	—	—	—	—	—
88-89	Philadelphia	NHL	78	11	32	43	149	19	1	5	6	28
89-90	Philadelphia	NHL	63	4	18	22	167	—	—	—	—	—
90-91	Philadelphia	NHL	79	7	25	32	204	—	—	—	—	—
91-92	Philadelphia	NHL	73	4	12	16	195	—	—	—	—	—
92-93	Philadelphia	NHL	83	3	16	19	150	—	—	—	—	—
NHL totals			491	34	140	174	1144	20	1	5	6	28

CARLYLE, RANDY

D, JETS

PERSONAL: Born April 19, 1956, at Sudbury, Ont.... 5-10/200.... Shoots left.... Full name: Randolph Robert Carlyle.
TRANSACTIONS/CAREER NOTES: Selected by Toronto Maple Leafs from Sudbury Wolves in second round (first Maple Leafs pick, 30th overall) of NHL entry draft (June 1, 1976). ... Broke ankle; missed parts of 1978-79 season.... Traded by Maple Leafs with C George Ferguson to Pittsburgh Penguins for D Dave Burrows (June 14, 1978).... Injured back (October 1982).... Injured knee (January 1983).... Injured knee (March 1984).... Traded by Penguins to Winnipeg Jets for first-round pick in 1984 draft (D Doug Bodger) and player to be named after the 1983-84 season (D Moe Mantha) (March 5, 1984).... Injured thigh (November 12, 1985); missed eight games.... Suffered whiplash (November 1986); missed nine games.... Strained neck muscles (January 18, 1989).... Bruised left knee (November 5, 1989); missed nine games.... Missed 10 games due to death of parents (December 1989).... Tore ligaments in right knee (March 15, 1990).... Strained groin and bruised thigh (November 11, 1990); missed five games.... Strained triceps (February 20, 1991); missed seven games.... Bruised ribs (October 29, 1991); missed three games.... Strained abdomen (December 14, 1991); missed six games.... Suffered ankle contusion (January 4, 1992); missed two games.... Suffered quad strain (October 10, 1992); missed eight games.... Suffered quad strain (November 2, 1992); missed four games.... Strained shoulder (December 5, 1992); missed two games.... Strained groin (December 11, 1992); missed seven games.... Suffered quad strain (January 8, 1993); missed six games.... Pulled groin (February 28, 1993); missed three games.
HONORS: Named to OMJHL All-Star second team (1975-76).... Won James Norris Memorial Trophy (1980-81).... Named to NHL All-Star first team (1980-81).... Played in NHL All-Star Game (1981 through 1983, 1985 and 1993).
MISCELLANEOUS: Does not wear a helmet.

Season	Team	League	REGULAR SEASON					PLAYOFFS				
			Gms.	G	A	Pts.	Pen.	Gms.	G	A	Pts.	Pen.
73-74	Sudbury	OHA Mj. Jr. A	12	0	8	8	21	—	—	—	—	—
74-75	Sudbury	OHA Mj. Jr. A	67	17	47	64	118	15	3	6	9	21
75-76	Sudbury	OHA Mj. Jr. A	60	15	64	79	126	17	6	13	19	50
76-77	Dallas	CHL	26	2	7	9	63	—	—	—	—	—
	Toronto	NHL	45	0	5	5	51	9	0	1	1	20
77-78	Dallas	CHL	21	3	14	17	31	—	—	—	—	—
	Toronto	NHL	49	2	11	13	31	7	0	1	1	8
78-79	Pittsburgh	NHL	70	13	34	47	78	7	0	0	0	12
79-80	Pittsburgh	NHL	67	8	28	36	45	5	1	0	1	4
80-81	Pittsburgh	NHL	76	16	67	83	136	5	4	5	9	9
81-82	Pittsburgh	NHL	73	11	64	75	131	5	1	3	4	16
82-83	Pittsburgh	NHL	61	15	41	56	110	—	—	—	—	—
83-84	Pittsburgh	NHL	50	3	23	26	82	—	—	—	—	—
	Winnipeg	NHL	5	0	3	3	2	3	0	2	2	4
84-85	Winnipeg	NHL	71	13	38	51	98	8	1	5	6	13
85-86	Winnipeg	NHL	68	16	33	49	93	—	—	—	—	—
86-87	Winnipeg	NHL	71	16	26	42	93	10	1	5	6	18
87-88	Winnipeg	NHL	78	15	44	59	210	5	0	2	2	10
88-89	Winnipeg	NHL	78	6	38	44	78	—	—	—	—	—
89-90	Winnipeg	NHL	53	3	15	18	50	—	—	—	—	—
90-91	Winnipeg	NHL	52	9	19	28	44	—	—	—	—	—
91-92	Winnipeg	NHL	66	1	9	10	54	5	1	0	1	6
92-93	Winnipeg	NHL	22	1	1	2	14	—	—	—	—	—
NHL totals			1055	148	499	647	1400	69	9	24	33	120

CARNBACK, PATRIK

LW, CANADIENS

PERSONAL: Born February 1, 1968, at Goteborg, Sweden.... 6-0/187.... Shoots left.
TRANSACTIONS/CAREER NOTES: Selected by Montreal Canadiens in sixth round (seventh Canadiens pick, 125th overall) of NHL entry draft (June 11, 1988).

Season Team	League	REGULAR SEASON					PLAYOFFS				
		Gms.	G	A	Pts.	Pen.	Gms.	G	A	Pts.	Pen.
86-87—Vastra Frolunda...............	Sweden	28	3	1	4	4	—	—	—	—	—
87-88—Vastra Frolunda...............	Sweden	33	16	19	35	10	—	—	—	—	—
88-89—Vastra Frolunda...............	Sweden	53	39	36	75	52	—	—	—	—	—
89-90—Vastra Frolunda...............	Sweden	40	26	27	53	34	—	—	—	—	—
90-91—Vastra Frolunda...............	Sweden	22	10	9	19	46	—	—	—	—	—
91-92—Vastra Frolunda...............	Sweden	33	17	24	41	32	—	—	—	—	—
92-93—Fredericton	AHL	45	20	37	57	45	5	0	3	3	14
—Montreal...........................	NHL	6	0	0	0	2	—	—	—	—	—
NHL totals.......................		**6**	**0**	**0**	**0**	**2**					

CARNEY, KEITH
D, SABRES

PERSONAL: Born February 3, 1970, at Pawtucket, R.I. . . . . 6-2/205. . . . Shoots left. . . . Full name: Keith Edward Carney.
COLLEGE: Maine.
TRANSACTIONS/CAREER NOTES: Selected by Buffalo Sabres in fourth round (third Sabres pick, 76th overall) of NHL entry draft (June 11, 1988).
HONORS: Named to Hockey East All-Rookie team (1988-89). . . . Named to NCAA All-America East second team (1989-90). . . . Named to Hockey East All-Star second team (1989-90). . . . Named to NCAA All-America East first team (1990-91). . . . Named to Hockey East All-Star first team (1990-91).

Season Team	League	REGULAR SEASON					PLAYOFFS				
		Gms.	G	A	Pts.	Pen.	Gms.	G	A	Pts.	Pen.
88-89—University of Maine	Hockey East	40	4	22	26	24	—	—	—	—	—
89-90—University of Maine	Hockey East	41	3	41	44	43	—	—	—	—	—
90-91—University of Maine	Hockey East	40	7	49	56	38	—	—	—	—	—
91-92—U.S. national team	Int'l	49	2	17	19	16	—	—	—	—	—
—Rochester...........................	AHL	24	1	10	11	2	2	0	2	2	0
—Buffalo...............................	NHL	14	1	2	3	18	7	0	3	3	0
92-93—Buffalo.............................	NHL	30	2	4	6	55	8	0	3	3	6
—Rochester...........................	AHL	41	5	21	26	32	—	—	—	—	—
NHL totals.......................		**44**	**3**	**6**	**9**	**73**	**15**	**0**	**6**	**6**	**6**

CARPENTER, BOBBY
LW, CAPITALS

PERSONAL: Born July 13, 1963, at Beverly, Mass. . . . . 6-0/200. . . . Shoots left.
HIGH SCHOOL: St. John's Prep (Danvers, Mass.).
TRANSACTIONS/CAREER NOTES: Selected by Washington Capitals as underage junior in first round (first Capitals pick, third overall) of NHL entry draft (June 10, 1981). . . . Traded by Capitals with second-round pick in 1989 draft (RW Jason Prosofsky) to New York Rangers for C Mike Ridley, C Kelly Miller and RW Bobby Crawford (January 1, 1987). . . . Traded by Rangers with D Tom Laidlaw to Los Angeles Kings for C Marcel Dionne, C Jeff Crossman and third-round pick in 1989 draft (March 10, 1987). . . . Tore rotator cuff (January 1988). . . . Broke right thumb and wrist (December 31, 1988). . . . Traded by Kings to Boston Bruins for C Steve Kasper and LW Jay Miller (January 23, 1989). . . . Tore ligaments of right wrist (April 1989). . . . Injured left knee (October 1990). . . . Suffered multiple fracture of left kneecap (December 8, 1990); missed remainder of season. . . . Injured left wrist and suffered stiffness in knee (April 5, 1991). . . . Strained calf (March 19, 1992). . . . Signed as free agent by Capitals (June 30, 1992).
HONORS: Played in NHL All-Star Game (1985).

Season Team	League	REGULAR SEASON					PLAYOFFS				
		Gms.	G	A	Pts.	Pen.	Gms.	G	A	Pts.	Pen.
79-80—St. John's Prep School......	Mass. H.S.	...	28	37	65	...	—	—	—	—	—
80-81—St. John's Prep School......	Mass. H.S.	...	14	24	38	...	—	—	—	—	—
81-82—Washington	NHL	80	32	35	67	69	—	—	—	—	—
82-83—Washington	NHL	80	32	37	69	64	4	1	0	1	2
83-84—Washington	NHL	80	28	40	68	51	8	2	1	3	25
84-85—Washington	NHL	80	53	42	95	87	5	1	4	5	8
85-86—Washington	NHL	80	27	29	56	105	9	5	4	9	12
86-87—Washington	NHL	22	5	7	12	21	—	—	—	—	—
—New York Rangers..........	NHL	28	2	8	10	20	—	—	—	—	—
—Los Angeles.....................	NHL	10	2	3	5	6	5	1	2	3	2
87-88—Los Angeles.....................	NHL	71	19	33	52	84	5	1	1	2	0
88-89—Los Angeles.....................	NHL	39	11	15	26	16	—	—	—	—	—
—Boston	NHL	18	5	9	14	10	8	1	1	2	4
89-90—Boston	NHL	80	25	31	56	97	21	4	6	10	39
90-91—Boston	NHL	29	8	8	16	22	1	0	1	1	2
91-92—Boston	NHL	60	25	23	48	46	8	0	1	1	6
92-93—Washington	NHL	68	11	17	28	65	6	1	4	5	6
NHL totals.......................		**825**	**285**	**337**	**622**	**763**	**80**	**17**	**25**	**42**	**106**

CARSON, JIMMY
C, KINGS

PERSONAL: Born July 20, 1968, at Southfield, Mich. . . . . 6-1/200. . . . Shoots right.
TRANSACTIONS/CAREER NOTES: Selected by Los Angeles Kings as underage junior in first round (first Kings pick, second overall) of NHL entry draft (June 21, 1986). . . . Traded by Kings with LW Martin Gelinas and first-round picks in 1989 (traded to New Jersey), 1991 (LW Martin Rucinsky) and 1993 (D Nick Stajduhar) drafts and cash to Edmonton Oilers for C Wayne Gretzky, RW/D Marty McSorley and LW/C Mike Krushelnyski (August 9, 1988). . . . Bruised right knee (September 27, 1989). . . . Traded by Oilers with C Kevin McClelland and fifth-round pick in 1991 draft to Detroit Red Wings for C/RW Joe Murphy, C/LW Adam

Graves, LW Petr Klima and D Jeff Sharples (November 2, 1989).... Injured right knee ligaments (February 3, 1990); missed 14 games.... Suffered from tonsillitis and mononucleosis (March 1990).... Suffered sore left shoulder (November 1990).... Strained right knee (January 11, 1991); missed 15 games.... Underwent surgery to left shoulder ligaments (April 25, 1991). ... Traded by Red Wings with RW Marc Potvin and C Gary Shuchuk to Los Angeles Kings for D Paul Coffey, RW Jim Hiller and C/LW Sylvain Couturier (January 29, 1993).

HONORS: Won Frank J. Selke Trophy (1985-86).... Won Michael Bossy Trophy (1985-86).... Named to QMJHL All-Star second team (1985-86).... Named to NHL All-Rookie team (1986-87).... Played in NHL All-Star Game (1989).

			REGULAR SEASON					PLAYOFFS			
Season Team	League	Gms.	G	A	Pts.	Pen.	Gms.	G	A	Pts.	Pen.
84-85—Verdun	QMJHL	68	44	72	116	16	—	—	—	—	—
85-86—Verdun	QMJHL	69	70	83	153	46	5	2	6	8	0
86-87—Los Angeles	NHL	80	37	42	79	22	5	1	2	3	6
87-88—Los Angeles	NHL	80	55	52	107	45	5	5	3	8	4
88-89—Edmonton	NHL	80	49	51	100	36	7	2	1	3	6
89-90—Edmonton	NHL	4	1	2	3	0	—	—	—	—	—
—Detroit	NHL	44	20	16	36	8	—	—	—	—	—
90-91—Detroit	NHL	64	21	25	46	28	7	2	1	3	4
91-92—Detroit	NHL	80	34	35	69	30	11	2	3	5	0
92-93—Detroit	NHL	52	25	26	51	18	—	—	—	—	—
—Los Angeles	NHL	34	12	10	22	14	18	5	4	9	2
NHL totals		518	254	259	513	201	53	17	14	31	22

CARTER, JOHN
LW, SHARKS

PERSONAL: Born May 3, 1963, at Woburn, Mass.... 5-10/175.... Shoots left.
COLLEGE: Rensselaer Polytechnic Institute (N.Y.).
TRANSACTIONS/CAREER NOTES: Sprained knee (February 1986).... Signed as free agent by Boston Bruins (March 1986).... Bruised knee (March 1987).... Bruised knee (February 1988).... Suffered from the flu (October 31, 1990); missed two weeks.... Suffered concussion (December 1, 1990).... Signed as free agent by San Jose Sharks (August 22, 1991).

HONORS: Named to ECAC All-Star second team (1983-84).... Named to NCAA All-America East second team (1984-85).... Named to ECAC All-Star first team (1984-85).

			REGULAR SEASON					PLAYOFFS			
Season Team	League	Gms.	G	A	Pts.	Pen.	Gms.	G	A	Pts.	Pen.
82-83—R.P.I.	ECAC	29	16	22	38	33	—	—	—	—	—
83-84—R.P.I.	ECAC	38	35	39	74	52	—	—	—	—	—
84-85—R.P.I.	ECAC	37	43	29	72	52	—	—	—	—	—
85-86—R.P.I.	ECAC	27	23	18	41	68	—	—	—	—	—
—Boston	NHL	3	0	0	0	0	—	—	—	—	—
86-87—Moncton	AHL	58	25	30	55	60	6	2	3	5	5
—Boston	NHL	8	0	1	1	0	—	—	—	—	—
87-88—Boston	NHL	4	0	1	1	2	—	—	—	—	—
—Maine	AHL	76	38	38	76	145	10	4	4	8	44
88-89—Maine	AHL	24	13	6	19	12	—	—	—	—	—
—Boston	NHL	44	12	10	22	24	10	1	2	3	6
89-90—Maine	AHL	2	2	2	4	2	—	—	—	—	—
—Boston	NHL	76	17	22	39	26	21	6	3	9	45
90-91—Boston	NHL	50	4	7	11	68	—	—	—	—	—
—Maine	AHL	16	5	9	14	16	1	0	0	0	10
91-92—Kansas City	IHL	42	11	15	26	116	15	6	9	15	18
—San Jose	NHL	4	0	0	0	0	—	—	—	—	—
92-93—San Jose	NHL	55	7	9	16	81	—	—	—	—	—
—Kansas City	IHL	9	4	2	6	14	—	—	—	—	—
NHL totals		244	40	50	90	201	31	7	5	12	51

CASEY, JON
G, BRUINS

PERSONAL: Born August 29, 1962, at Grand Rapids, Minn.... 5-10/155.... Shoots left.
HIGH SCHOOL: Grand Rapids (Minn.).
COLLEGE: North Dakota.
TRANSACTIONS/CAREER NOTES: Signed as free agent by Minnesota North Stars (April 1, 1984).... North Stars franchise moved from Minnesota to Dallas and renamed Stars for 1993-94 season.... Traded by Stars to Boston Bruins for G Andy Moog (June 25, 1993) to complete deal in which Bruins sent D Gord Murphy to Stars for future considerations (June 20, 1993).

HONORS: Named to WCHL All-Star first team (1981-82 and 1983-84).... Won Harry (Hap) Holmes Memorial Trophy (1984-85).... Won Baz Bastien Trophy (1984-85).... Named to AHL All-Star first team (1984-85).... Played in NHL All-Star Game (1993).

			REGULAR SEASON							PLAYOFFS					
Season Team	League	Gms.	Min.	W	L	T	GA	SO	Avg.	Gms.	Min.	W	L	GA SO	Avg.
80-81—Univ. of North Dakota	WCHA	6	300	3	1	0	19	0	3.80	—	—	—	—	— —	—
81-82—Univ. of North Dakota	WCHA	18	1038	15	3	0	48	1	2.77	—	—	—	—	— —	—
82-83—Univ. of North Dakota	WCHA	17	1020	9	6	2	42	0	2.47	—	—	—	—	— —	—
83-84—Univ. of North Dakota	WCHA	37	2180	25	10	2	115	2	3.17	—	—	—	—	— —	—
—Minnesota	NHL	2	84	1	0	0	6	0	4.29	—	—	—	—	— —	—
84-85—Baltimore	AHL	46	2646	30	11	4	116	†4	*2.63	13	689	8	3	38 0	3.31
85-86—Springfield	AHL	9	464	4	3	1	30	0	3.88	—	—	—	—	— —	—
—Minnesota	NHL	26	1402	11	11	1	91	0	3.89	—	—	—	—	— —	—

— 336 —

Season Team	League	REGULAR SEASON								PLAYOFFS						
		Gms.	Min.	W	L	T	GA	SO	Avg.	Gms.	Min.	W	L	GA	SO	Avg.
86-87—Indianapolis	CHL	31	1794	14	15	0	133	0	4.45	—	—	—	—	—	—	—
—Springfield	AHL	13	770	1	8	0	56	0	4.36	—	—	—	—	—	—	—
87-88—Kalamazoo	IHL	42	2541	24	13	5	154	2	3.64	7	382	3	3	26	0	4.08
—Minnesota	NHL	14	663	1	7	4	41	0	3.71	—	—	—	—	—	—	—
88-89—Minnesota	NHL	55	2961	18	17	12	151	1	3.06	—	—	—	—	—	—	—
89-90—Minnesota	NHL	61	3407	*31	22	4	183	3	3.22	7	415	3	4	21	1	3.04
90-91—Minnesota	NHL	55	3185	21	20	11	158	3	2.98	*23	*1205	*14	7	*61	†1	3.04
91-92—Minnesota	NHL	52	2911	19	23	5	165	2	3.40	7	437	3	4	22	0	3.02
—Kalamazoo	IHL	4	250	2	1	1	11	0	2.64	—	—	—	—	—	—	—
92-93—Minnesota	NHL	60	3476	26	26	5	193	3	3.33	—	—	—	—	—	—	—
NHL totals		325	18089	128	126	42	988	12	3.28	37	2057	20	15	104	2	3.03

CASSELS, ANDREW
C, WHALERS

PERSONAL: Born July 23, 1969, at Mississauga, Ont.... 6-0/192.... Shoots left. **TRANSACTIONS/CAREER NOTES:** Broke wrist (January 1986).... Selected by Montreal Canadiens as underage junior in first round (first Canadiens pick, 17th overall) of NHL entry draft (June 13, 1987).... Sprained left knee ligaments (September 1988).... Separated right shoulder (November 22, 1989); missed 10 games.... Traded by Canadiens to Hartford Whalers for second-round pick in 1992 draft (RW Valeri Bure) (September 17, 1991).

HONORS: Won Emms Family Award (1986-87).... Won Red Tilson Trophy (1987-88).... Won Eddie Powers Memorial Trophy (1987-88).... Won William Hanley Trophy (1987-88).... Named to OHL All-Star first team (1987-88 and 1988-89).

Season Team	League	REGULAR SEASON					PLAYOFFS				
		Gms.	G	A	Pts.	Pen.	Gms.	G	A	Pts.	Pen.
85-86—Bramalea Jr. B	OHA	33	18	25	43	26	—	—	—	—	—
86-87—Ottawa	OHL	66	26	66	92	28	11	5	9	14	7
87-88—Ottawa	OHL	61	48	*103	*151	39	16	8	*24	†32	13
88-89—Ottawa	OHL	56	37	97	134	66	12	5	10	15	10
89-90—Sherbrooke	AHL	55	22	45	67	25	12	2	11	13	6
—Montreal	NHL	6	2	0	2	2	—	—	—	—	—
90-91—Montreal	NHL	54	6	19	25	20	8	0	2	2	2
91-92—Hartford	NHL	67	11	30	41	18	7	2	4	6	6
92-93—Hartford	NHL	84	21	64	85	62	—	—	—	—	—
NHL totals		211	40	113	153	102	15	2	6	8	8

CAUFIELD, JAY
RW, PENGUINS

PERSONAL: Born July 17, 1965, at Philadelphia.... 6-4/230.... Shoots right. **COLLEGE:** North Dakota. **TRANSACTIONS/CAREER NOTES:** Signed as free agent by New York Rangers (October 8, 1985).... Injured knee (October 1986).... Traded by Rangers with C Dave Gagner to Minnesota North Stars for D Jari Gronstrand and D Paul Boutilier (October 8, 1987).... Selected by Pittsburgh Penguins in NHL waiver draft for $40,000 (October 3, 1988).... Injured ankle and suffered blood poisoning (October 1988).... Pinched nerve in neck (December 1988).... Dislocated finger on right hand and underwent surgery (February 2, 1990); missed 18 games.... Suffered back spasms during preseason (September 1991); missed first eight games of season.... Suspended eight off-days and fined $500 by NHL for fighting (February 26, 1993).

MISCELLANEOUS: Member of Stanley Cup championship teams (1991 and 1992).

Season Team	League	REGULAR SEASON					PLAYOFFS				
		Gms.	G	A	Pts.	Pen.	Gms.	G	A	Pts.	Pen.
84-85—Univ. of North Dakota	WCHA	1	0	0	0	0	—	—	—	—	—
85-86—New Haven	AHL	42	2	3	5	40	1	0	0	0	0
—Toledo	IHL	30	5	3	8	54	—	—	—	—	—
86-87—New Haven	AHL	13	0	0	0	43	—	—	—	—	—
—Flint	IHL	14	4	3	7	59	—	—	—	—	—
—New York Rangers	NHL	13	2	1	3	45	3	0	0	0	12
87-88—Kalamazoo	IHL	65	5	10	15	273	6	0	1	1	47
—Minnesota	NHL	1	0	0	0	0	—	—	—	—	—
88-89—Pittsburgh	NHL	58	1	4	5	285	9	0	0	0	28
89-90—Pittsburgh	NHL	37	1	2	3	123	—	—	—	—	—
90-91—Muskegon	IHL	3	1	0	1	18	—	—	—	—	—
—Pittsburgh	NHL	23	1	1	2	71	5	0	0	0	2
91-92—Pittsburgh	NHL	50	0	0	0	175	—	—	—	—	—
92-93—Pittsburgh	NHL	26	0	0	0	60	—	—	—	—	—
NHL totals		208	5	8	13	759	17	0	0	0	42

CAVALLINI, GINO
LW, NORDIQUES

PERSONAL: Born November 24, 1962, at Toronto.... 6-2/215.... Shoots left.... Full name: Gino John Cavallini.... Name pronounced KAV-uh-LEE-nee.... Brother of Paul Cavallini, defenseman, Dallas Stars. **COLLEGE:** Bowling Green State.

TRANSACTIONS/CAREER NOTES: Signed as free agent by Calgary Flames (July 1984).... Traded by Flames with LW Eddy Beers and D Charles Bourgeois to St. Louis Blues for D Terry Johnson, RW Joe Mullen and D Rik Wilson (February 1, 1986).... Broke right hand (January 1988); missed 16 games.... Strained left knee (February 1989).... Claimed on waivers by Quebec Nordiques (February 27, 1992).... Sprained left knee (February 12, 1993); missed 13 games.

Season	Team	League	REGULAR SEASON					PLAYOFFS				
			Gms.	G	A	Pts.	Pen.	Gms.	G	A	Pts.	Pen.
81-82	Toronto St. Mikes	OJHL	37	27	56	83	...	—	—	—	—	—
82-83	Bowling Green State	CCHA	40	8	16	24	52	—	—	—	—	—
83-84	Bowling Green State	CCHA	43	25	23	48	16	—	—	—	—	—
84-85	Moncton	AHL	51	29	19	48	28	—	—	—	—	—
	Calgary	NHL	27	6	10	16	14	3	0	0	0	4
85-86	Moncton	AHL	4	3	2	5	7	—	—	—	—	—
	Calgary	NHL	27	7	7	14	26	—	—	—	—	—
	St. Louis	NHL	30	6	5	11	36	17	4	5	9	10
86-87	St. Louis	NHL	80	18	26	44	54	6	3	1	4	2
87-88	St. Louis	NHL	64	15	17	32	62	10	5	5	10	19
88-89	St. Louis	NHL	74	20	23	43	79	9	0	2	2	17
89-90	St. Louis	NHL	80	15	15	30	77	12	1	3	4	2
90-91	St. Louis	NHL	78	8	27	35	81	13	1	3	4	2
91-92	St. Louis	NHL	48	9	7	16	40	—	—	—	—	—
	Quebec	NHL	18	1	7	8	4	—	—	—	—	—
92-93	Quebec	NHL	67	9	15	24	34	4	0	0	0	0
NHL totals			593	114	159	273	507	74	14	19	33	56

CAVALLINI, PAUL
D, STARS

PERSONAL: Born October 13, 1965, at Toronto. . . . 6-1/210. . . . Shoots left. . . . Full name: Paul Edward Cavallini. . . . Name pronounced KAV-uh-LEE-nee. . . . Brother of Gino Cavallini, left winger, Quebec Nordiques.
HIGH SCHOOL: Henry Carr (Rexdale, Ont.).
COLLEGE: Providence.
TRANSACTIONS/CAREER NOTES: Selected by Washington Capitals as underage junior in 10th round (ninth Capitals pick, 205th overall) of NHL entry draft (June 9, 1984). . . . Traded by Capitals to St. Louis Blues for second-round pick in 1988 draft (D Wade Bartley) (December 1987). . . . Broke hand (December 11, 1987). . . . Injured neck (December 11, 1988). . . . Dislocated left shoulder (February 25, 1989). . . . Lost tip of left index finger (December 22, 1990); missed 13 games. . . . Strained knee ligament (October 20, 1991); missed 13 games. . . . Traded by Blues to Capitals for C Kevin Miller (November 1, 1992). . . . Missed one game due to personal reasons (March 16, 1993). . . . Traded by Capitals to Dallas Stars for future considerations (June 20, 1993); Stars sent D Enrico Ciccone to Capitals to complete deal (June 25, 1993).
HONORS: Named to Hockey East All-Freshman team (1984-85). . . . Won Alka-Seltzer Plus Award (1989-90). . . . Played in NHL All-Star Game (1990).

Season	Team	League	REGULAR SEASON					PLAYOFFS				
			Gms.	G	A	Pts.	Pen.	Gms.	G	A	Pts.	Pen.
83-84	Henry Carr H.S.	MTHL	54	20	41	61	190	—	—	—	—	—
84-85	Providence College	Hockey East	45	5	14	19	64	—	—	—	—	—
85-86	Canadian national team	Int'l	52	1	11	12	95	—	—	—	—	—
	Binghamton	AHL	15	3	4	7	20	6	0	2	2	56
86-87	Binghamton	AHL	66	12	24	36	188	13	2	7	9	35
	Washington	NHL	6	0	2	2	8	—	—	—	—	—
87-88	Washington	NHL	24	2	3	5	66	—	—	—	—	—
	St. Louis	NHL	48	4	7	11	86	10	1	6	7	26
88-89	St. Louis	NHL	65	4	20	24	128	10	2	2	4	14
89-90	St. Louis	NHL	80	8	39	47	106	12	2	3	5	20
90-91	St. Louis	NHL	67	10	25	35	89	13	2	3	5	20
91-92	St. Louis	NHL	66	10	25	35	95	4	0	1	1	6
92-93	St. Louis	NHL	11	1	4	5	10	—	—	—	—	—
	Washington	NHL	71	5	8	13	46	6	0	2	2	18
NHL totals			438	44	133	177	634	55	7	17	24	104

CHABOT, FREDERIC
G, CANADIENS

PERSONAL: Born February 12, 1968, at Hebertville, Que. . . . 5-11/175. . . . Shoots right. . . . Name pronounced shuh-BAHT.
TRANSACTIONS/CAREER NOTES: Selected by New Jersey Devils in 10th round (10th Devils pick, 192nd overall) of NHL entry draft (June 21, 1986). . . . Signed as free agent by Montreal Canadiens (January 16, 1990). . . . Selected by Tampa Bay Lightning in NHL expansion draft (June 18, 1992). . . . Traded by Lightning to Canadiens for G Jean-Claude Bergeron (June 18, 1992).
HONORS: Named to Memorial Cup All-Star team (1981-82). . . . Named to WHL (East) All-Star first team (1988-89).
STATISTICAL NOTES: Member of Stanley Cup championship team (1993).

Season	Team	League	REGULAR SEASON							PLAYOFFS						
			Gms.	Min.	W	L	T	GA	SO	Avg.	Gms.	Min.	W	L	GA	SO	Avg.
86-87	Drummondville	QMJHL	*62	*3508	31	29	0	293	1	5.01	8	481	2	6	40	0	4.99
87-88	Drummondville	QMJHL	58	3276	27	24	4	237	1	4.34	*16	1019	10	6	56	†1	*3.30
88-89	Moose Jaw	WHL	26	1385	...	...	...	114	1	4.94	—	—	—	—	—	—	—
	Prince Albert	WHL	28	1572	...	...	...	88	1	3.36	4	199	1	1	16	0	4.82
89-90	Fort Wayne	IHL	23	1208	6	13	3	87	1	4.32	—	—	—	—	—	—	—
	Sherbrooke	AHL	2	119	1	1	0	8	0	4.03	—	—	—	—	—	—	—
90-91	Montreal	NHL	3	108	0	0	1	6	0	3.33	—	—	—	—	—	—	—
	Fredericton	AHL	35	1800	9	15	5	122	0	4.07	—	—	—	—	—	—	—
91-92	Winston-Salem	ECHL	25	1449	15	7	2	71	0	*2.94	—	—	—	—	—	—	—
	Fredericton	AHL	30	1761	17	9	4	79	2	*2.69	7	457	3	4	20	0	2.63
92-93	Fredericton	AHL	45	2544	22	17	4	141	0	3.33	4	261	1	3	16	0	3.68
	Montreal	NHL	1	40	0	0	0	1	0	1.50	—	—	—	—	—	—	—
NHL totals			4	148	0	0	1	7	0	2.84							

CHAMBERS, SHAWN

D, LIGHTNING

PERSONAL: Born October 11, 1966, at Royal Oaks, Mich. . . . 6-2/200. . . . Shoots left. . . . Full name: Shawn Randall Chambers.
COLLEGE: Alaska-Fairbanks.
TRANSACTIONS/CAREER NOTES: Selected by Minnesota North Stars in NHL supplemental draft (June 13, 1987). . . . Dislocated shoulder (February 1988). . . . Separated right shoulder (September 1988). . . . Injured left knee (September 11, 1990); missed first 11 games of season. . . . Fractured left kneecap (December 5, 1990); missed three months. . . . Underwent surgery to left knee to remove piece of loose cartilage (May 1991). . . . Traded by North Stars to Washington Capitals for C Trent Klatt and LW Steve Maltais (June 21, 1991). . . . Suffered sore knee (October 1991); missed first 47 games of season. . . . Reinjured knee (January 26, 1992); missed final 31 games of season. . . . Underwent arthroscopic knee surgery (February 4, 1992). . . . Selected by Tampa Bay Lightning in NHL expansion draft (June 18, 1992). . . . Underwent knee surgery (October 9, 1992); missed first seven games of season.

Season Team	League	REGULAR SEASON Gms.	G	A	Pts.	Pen.	PLAYOFFS Gms.	G	A	Pts.	Pen.
85-86—Alaska-Fairbanks	GWHC	25	15	21	36	34	—	—	—	—	—
86-87—Alaska-Fairbanks	GWHC	17	11	19	30	. . .	—	—	—	—	—
—Seattle	WHL	28	8	25	33	58	—	—	—	—	—
—Fort Wayne	IHL	12	2	6	8	0	10	1	4	5	5
87-88—Minnesota	NHL	19	1	7	8	21	—	—	—	—	—
—Kalamazoo	IHL	19	1	6	7	22	—	—	—	—	—
88-89—Minnesota	NHL	72	5	19	24	80	3	0	2	2	0
89-90—Minnesota	NHL	78	8	18	26	81	7	2	1	3	0
90-91—Minnesota	NHL	29	1	3	4	24	23	0	7	7	16
—Kalamazoo	IHL	3	1	1	2	0	—	—	—	—	—
91-92—Baltimore	AHL	5	2	3	5	9	—	—	—	—	—
—Washington	NHL	2	0	0	0	2	—	—	—	—	—
92-93—Atlanta	IHL	6	0	2	2	18	—	—	—	—	—
—Tampa Bay	NHL	55	10	29	39	36	—	—	—	—	—
NHL totals		**255**	**25**	**76**	**101**	**244**	**33**	**2**	**10**	**12**	**16**

CHAPDELAINE, RENE

D, KINGS

PERSONAL: Born September 27, 1966, at Weyburn, Sask. . . . 6-1/195. . . . Shoots right. . . . Full name: Rene Ronald Chapdelaine. . . . Name pronounced SHAP-duh-LAYN.
COLLEGE: Lake Superior State (Mich.).
TRANSACTIONS/CAREER NOTES: Selected by Los Angeles Kings in eighth round (seventh Kings pick, 149th overall) of NHL entry draft (June 21, 1986).

Season Team	League	REGULAR SEASON Gms.	G	A	Pts.	Pen.	PLAYOFFS Gms.	G	A	Pts.	Pen.
84-85—Weyburn	SJHL	61	3	17	20	. . .	—	—	—	—	—
85-86—Lake Superior State	CCHA	40	2	7	9	24	—	—	—	—	—
86-87—Lake Superior State	CCHA	28	1	5	6	51	—	—	—	—	—
87-88—Lake Superior State	CCHA	35	1	9	10	44	—	—	—	—	—
88-89—Lake Superior State	CCHA	46	4	9	13	52	—	—	—	—	—
89-90—New Haven	AHL	41	0	1	1	35	—	—	—	—	—
90-91—Phoenix	IHL	17	0	2	2	10	11	0	0	0	8
—New Haven	AHL	65	3	11	14	49	—	—	—	—	—
—Los Angeles	NHL	3	0	1	1	10	—	—	—	—	—
91-92—Los Angeles	NHL	16	0	1	1	10	—	—	—	—	—
—Phoenix	IHL	62	4	22	26	87	—	—	—	—	—
—New Haven	AHL	—	—	—	—	—	4	0	2	2	0
92-93—Phoenix	IHL	44	1	17	18	54	—	—	—	—	—
—Los Angeles	NHL	13	0	0	0	12	—	—	—	—	—
—San Diego	IHL	9	1	1	2	8	14	0	1	1	27
NHL totals		**32**	**0**	**2**	**2**	**32**					

CHAPMAN, BRIAN

D

PERSONAL: Born February 10, 1968, at Brockville, Ont. . . . 6-0/195. . . . Shoots left.
TRANSACTIONS/CAREER NOTES: Selected by Hartford Whalers as underage junior in fourth round (third Whalers pick, 74th overall) of NHL entry draft (June 21, 1986). . . . Suspended 10 games by OHL (October 5, 1986). . . . Suspended six games by AHL for fighting (March 11, 1989). . . . Fractured left thumb (November 10, 1990). . . . Signed as free agent by Phoenix Roadrunners (July 16, 1993).

Season Team	League	REGULAR SEASON Gms.	G	A	Pts.	Pen.	PLAYOFFS Gms.	G	A	Pts.	Pen.
84-85—Brockville	COJHL	50	11	32	43	145	—	—	—	—	—
85-86—Belleville	OHL	66	6	31	37	168	24	2	6	8	54
86-87—Belleville	OHL	54	4	32	36	142	6	1	1	2	10
—Binghamton	AHL	—	—	—	—	—	1	0	0	0	0
87-88—Belleville	OHL	63	11	57	68	180	6	1	4	5	13
88-89—Binghamton	AHL	71	5	25	30	216	—	—	—	—	—
89-90—Binghamton	AHL	68	2	15	17	180	—	—	—	—	—
90-91—Hartford	NHL	3	0	0	0	29	—	—	—	—	—
—Springfield	AHL	60	4	23	27	200	18	1	4	5	62
91-92—Springfield	AHL	73	3	26	29	245	10	2	2	4	25
92-93—Springfield	AHL	72	17	34	51	212	15	2	5	7	43
NHL totals		**3**	**0**	**0**	**0**	**29**					

CHARBONNEAU, PATRICK
G, SENATORS

PERSONAL: Born July 22, 1975, at St. Jean-sur-Richelie, Que.... 5-11/217.... Shoots left.
TRANSACTIONS/CAREER NOTES: Selected by Ottawa Senators in third round (third Senators pick, 53rd overall) of NHL entry draft (June 26, 1993).

Season Team	League	Gms.	Min.	W	L	T	GA	SO	Avg.	Gms.	Min.	W	L	GA	SO	Avg.
				REGULAR SEASON								**PLAYOFFS**				
91-92—Victoriaville	QMJHL	37	1943	...	...	...	163	0	5.03	—	—	—	—	—	—	—
92-93—Victoriaville	QMJHL	59	3121	35	22	0	216	0	4.15	2	92	...	...	4	...	2.61

CHARBONNEAU, STEPHANE
RW, NORDIQUES

PERSONAL: Born June 27, 1970, at Ste.-Adele, Que.... 6-2/195. ... Shoots right.... Name pronounced SHAHR-buh-noh.
TRANSACTIONS/CAREER NOTES: Signed as free agent by Quebec Nordiques (April 25, 1991).

Season Team	League	Gms.	G	A	Pts.	Pen.	Gms.	G	A	Pts.	Pen.
			REGULAR SEASON					**PLAYOFFS**			
87-88—Hull	QMJHL	51	10	20	30	70	11	5	8	13	12
88-89—Hull	QMJHL	64	23	29	52	142	9	2	2	4	22
89-90—Shawinigan	QMJHL	62	37	58	95	154	6	4	2	6	11
90-91—Shawinigan	QMJHL	6	4	3	7	2	—	—	—	—	—
—Chicoutimi	QMJHL	55	37	30	67	109	17	†13	9	22	43
91-92—Halifax	AHL	64	22	25	47	183	—	—	—	—	—
—Quebec	NHL	2	0	0	0	0	—	—	—	—	—
92-93—Halifax	AHL	56	18	20	38	125	—	—	—	—	—
NHL totals		2	0	0	0	0					

CHARLESWORTH, TODD
D

PERSONAL: Born March 22, 1965, at Calgary, Alta.... 6-1/185.... Shoots left.
TRANSACTIONS/CAREER NOTES: Selected by Pittsburgh Penguins as under-age junior in second round (second Penguins pick, 22nd overall) of NHL entry draft (June 8, 1983).... Signed as free agent by Edmonton Oilers (June 21, 1989).... Traded by Oilers to New York Rangers for future considerations (January 18, 1990).... Sat out 1991-92 season due to thumb injury.... Signed as free agent by Muskegon Fury (October 1992).
HONORS: Named to IHL All-Star second team (1988-89).
MISCELLANEOUS: Served as player/assistant coach with Fury (1992-93).

Season Team	League	Gms.	G	A	Pts.	Pen.	Gms.	G	A	Pts.	Pen.
			REGULAR SEASON					**PLAYOFFS**			
81-82—Gloucester	COJHL	50	13	24	37	67	—	—	—	—	—
82-83—Oshawa	OHL	70	6	23	29	55	17	0	4	4	20
83-84—Oshawa	OHL	57	11	35	46	54	7	0	4	4	4
—Pittsburgh	NHL	10	0	0	0	8	—	—	—	—	—
84-85—Pittsburgh	NHL	67	1	8	9	31	—	—	—	—	—
85-86—Baltimore	AHL	19	1	3	4	10	—	—	—	—	—
—Muskegon	IHL	51	9	27	36	78	14	3	8	11	14
—Pittsburgh	NHL	2	0	1	1	0	—	—	—	—	—
86-87—Baltimore	AHL	75	5	21	26	64	—	—	—	—	—
—Pittsburgh	NHL	1	0	0	0	0	—	—	—	—	—
87-88—Pittsburgh	NHL	6	2	0	2	2	—	—	—	—	—
—Muskegon	IHL	64	9	31	40	49	5	0	0	0	18
88-89—Muskegon	IHL	74	10	53	63	85	14	2	13	15	8
89-90—Cape Breton	AHL	32	0	9	9	13	—	—	—	—	—
—Flint	IHL	26	3	6	9	12	—	—	—	—	—
—New York Rangers	NHL	7	0	0	0	6	—	—	—	—	—
90-91—Binghamton	AHL	11	0	3	3	2	—	—	—	—	—
—Muskegon	IHL	62	5	32	37	46	5	1	3	4	2
91-92—					Did not play.						
92-93—Muskegon	Col.HL	45	9	37	46	22	7	1	3	4	4
NHL totals		93	3	9	12	47					

CHARRON, ERIC
D, LIGHTNING

PERSONAL: Born January 14, 1970, at Verdun, Que.... 6-3/192.... Shoots left.
TRANSACTIONS/CAREER NOTES: Selected by Montreal Canadiens in first round (first Canadiens pick, 20th overall) of NHL entry draft (June 11, 1988).... Traded by Canadiens with D Alain Cote and future considerations to Tampa Bay Lightning for D Rob Ramage (March 20, 1993); Canadiens sent D Donald Dufresne to Lightning to complete deal (June 18, 1993).

Season Team	League	Gms.	G	A	Pts.	Pen.	Gms.	G	A	Pts.	Pen.
			REGULAR SEASON					**PLAYOFFS**			
87-88—Trois-Rivieres	QMJHL	67	3	13	16	135	—	—	—	—	—
88-89—Sherbrooke	AHL	1	0	0	0	0	—	—	—	—	—
—Verdun	QMJHL	67	4	31	35	177	—	—	—	—	—
89-90—St. Hyacinthe	QMJHL	68	13	38	51	152	11	3	4	7	67
—Sherbrooke	AHL	—	—	—	—	—	2	0	0	0	0
90-91—Fredericton	AHL	71	1	11	12	108	2	1	0	1	29

C

Season Team	League	REGULAR SEASON					PLAYOFFS				
		Gms.	G	A	Pts.	Pen.	Gms.	G	A	Pts.	Pen.
91-92—Fredericton	AHL	59	2	11	13	98	6	1	0	1	4
92-93—Fredericton	AHL	54	3	13	16	93	—	—	—	—	—
—Montreal	NHL	3	0	0	0	2	—	—	—	—	—
—Atlanta	IHL	11	0	2	2	12	3	0	1	1	6
NHL totals		3	0	0	0	2					

CHASE, KELLY
RW, BLUES

PERSONAL: Born October 25, 1967, at Porcupine Plain, Sask.... 5-11/195.... Shoots right.... Full name: Kelly Wayne Chase.

HIGH SCHOOL: Porcupine Plain (Sask.).

TRANSACTIONS/CAREER NOTES: Signed as free agent by St. Louis Blues (May 24, 1988).... Bruised right foot (January 1990).... Suffered back spasms (March 1990).... Suspended 10 games by NHL for fighting (March 18, 1991).... Injured knee (December 11, 1991); missed two games.... Sprained left wrist (January 14, 1992); missed three games.... Bruised thigh (February 2, 1992); missed five games.... Injured hand (February 23, 1992); missed four games.... Pulled groin (October 26, 1992); missed six games.... Injured wrist (January 9, 1993); missed five games.... Bruised lower leg (March 30, 1993); missed last six games of season.

Season Team	League	REGULAR SEASON					PLAYOFFS				
		Gms.	G	A	Pts.	Pen.	Gms.	G	A	Pts.	Pen.
85-86—Saskatoon	WHL	57	7	18	25	172	10	3	4	7	37
86-87—Saskatoon	WHL	68	17	29	46	285	11	2	8	10	37
87-88—Saskatoon	WHL	70	21	34	55	*343	9	3	5	8	32
88-89—Peoria	IHL	38	14	7	21	278	—	—	—	—	—
89-90—Peoria	IHL	10	1	2	3	76	—	—	—	—	—
—St. Louis	NHL	43	1	3	4	244	9	1	0	1	46
90-91—Peoria	IHL	61	20	34	54	406	10	4	3	7	61
—St. Louis	NHL	2	1	0	1	15	6	0	0	0	18
91-92—St. Louis	NHL	46	1	2	3	264	1	0	0	0	7
92-93—St. Louis	NHL	49	2	5	7	204	—	—	—	—	—
NHL totals		140	5	10	15	727	16	1	0	1	71

CHASSE, DENIS
RW, NORDIQUES

PERSONAL: Born February 7, 1970, at Montreal.... 6-2/190.... Shoots right.... Name pronounced shah-SAY.

TRANSACTIONS/CAREER NOTES: Signed as free agent by Quebec Nordiques (May 14, 1991).

Season Team	League	REGULAR SEASON					PLAYOFFS				
		Gms.	G	A	Pts.	Pen.	Gms.	G	A	Pts.	Pen.
87-88—St. Jean	QMJHL	13	0	1	1	2	1	0	0	0	0
88-89—Verdun	QMJHL	38	12	12	24	61	—	—	—	—	—
—Drummondville	QMJHL	30	15	16	31	77	3	0	2	2	28
89-90—Drummondville	QMJHL	34	14	29	43	85	—	—	—	—	—
—Chicoutimi	QMJHL	33	19	27	46	105	7	7	4	11	50
90-91—Drummondville	QMJHL	62	47	54	101	246	13	9	11	20	56
91-92—Halifax	AHL	73	26	35	61	254	—	—	—	—	—
92-93—Halifax	AHL	75	35	41	76	242	—	—	—	—	—

CHEBATURKIN, VLADIMIR
D, ISLANDERS

PERSONAL: Born April 23, 1975, at Tyumen, U.S.S.R.... 6-2/189.... Shoots left.... Name pronounced CHEH-buh-TURK-in.

TRANSACTIONS/CAREER NOTES: Selected by New York Islanders in third round (third Islanders pick, 66th overall) of NHL entry draft (June 26, 1993).

Season Team	League	REGULAR SEASON					PLAYOFFS				
		Gms.	G	A	Pts.	Pen.	Gms.	G	A	Pts.	Pen.
92-93—Kristall Elektrostal	CIS Div. II					Statistics unavailable.					

CHECCO, NICK
C, NORDIQUES

PERSONAL: Born November 18, 1974, at Minneapolis.... 5-11/185.... Shoots left.

HIGH SCHOOL: Thomas Jefferson (Bloomington, Minn.).

TRANSACTIONS/CAREER NOTES: Selected by Quebec Nordiques in sixth round (eighth Nordiques pick, 153rd overall) of NHL entry draft (June 26, 1993).

Season Team	League	REGULAR SEASON					PLAYOFFS				
		Gms.	G	A	Pts.	Pen.	Gms.	G	A	Pts.	Pen.
90-91—Jefferson HS	Minn. H.S.	25	2	10	12	18	—	—	—	—	—
91-92—Jefferson HS	Minn. H.S.	28	17	17	34	22	—	—	—	—	—
92-93—Jefferson HS	Minn. H.S.	26	22	23	45	18	—	—	—	—	—

CHELIOS, CHRIS
D, BLACKHAWKS

PERSONAL: Born January 25, 1962, at Chicago.... 6-1/192.... Shoots right.... Name pronounced CHEHL-ee-ohz.

COLLEGE: Wisconsin.

TRANSACTIONS/CAREER NOTES: Selected by Montreal Canadiens as underage junior in second round (fifth Canadiens pick, 40th overall) of NHL entry draft (June 10, 1981).... Sprained right ankle (January 1985).... Injured left knee (April 1985).... Sprained knee (December 19, 1985).... Reinjured knee (January 20, 1986).... Suffered back spasms (October 1986).... Broke finger of left hand (December 1987).... Bruised tailbone (February 7, 1988)....

Strained left knee ligaments (February 1990). . . . Underwent surgery to repair torn abdominal muscle (April 30, 1990). . . . Traded by Canadiens with second-round pick in 1991 draft (C Michael Pomichter) to Chicago Blackhawks for C Denis Savard (June 29, 1990). . . . Lacerated left temple (February 9, 1991).

HONORS: Named to WCHA All-Star second team (1982-83). . . . Named to NCAA All-Tournament team (1982-83). . . . Named to NHL All-Rookie team (1984-85). . . . Played in NHL All-Star Game (1985 and 1990 through 1993). . . . Won James Norris Memorial Trophy (1988-89 and 1992-93). . . . Named to THE SPORTING NEWS All-Star first team (1988-89 and 1992-93). . . . Named to NHL All-Star first team (1988-89 and 1992-93). . . . Named to THE SPORTING NEWS All-Star second team (1990-91 and 1991-92). . . . Named to NHL All-Star second team (1990-91).

MISCELLANEOUS: Member of Stanley Cup championship team (1986).

Season Team	League	REGULAR SEASON					PLAYOFFS				
		Gms.	G	A	Pts.	Pen.	Gms.	G	A	Pts.	Pen.
79-80—Moose Jaw	SJHL	53	12	31	43	118	—	—	—	—	—
80-81—Moose Jaw	SJHL	54	23	64	87	175	—	—	—	—	—
81-82—University of Wisconsin ...	WCHA	43	6	43	49	50	—	—	—	—	—
82-83—University of Wisconsin ...	WCHA	45	16	32	48	62	—	—	—	—	—
83-84—U.S. national team	Int'l	60	14	35	49	58	—	—	—	—	—
—U.S. Olympic Team	Int'l	6	0	3	3	8	—	—	—	—	—
—Montreal	NHL	12	0	2	2	12	15	1	9	10	17
84-85—Montreal	NHL	74	9	55	64	87	9	2	8	10	17
85-86—Montreal	NHL	41	8	26	34	67	20	2	9	11	49
86-87—Montreal	NHL	71	11	33	44	124	17	4	9	13	38
87-88—Montreal	NHL	71	20	41	61	172	11	3	1	4	29
88-89—Montreal	NHL	80	15	58	73	185	21	4	15	19	28
89-90—Montreal	NHL	53	9	22	31	136	5	0	1	1	8
90-91—Chicago	NHL	77	12	52	64	192	6	1	7	8	46
91-92—Chicago	NHL	80	9	47	56	245	18	6	15	21	37
92-93—Chicago	NHL	84	15	58	73	282	4	0	2	2	14
NHL totals		643	108	394	502	1502	126	23	76	99	283

CHERBAYEV, ALEXANDER
LW, SHARKS

PERSONAL: Born August 13, 1973, at Voskresensk, U.S.S.R. . . . 6-1/187. . . . Shoots left.

TRANSACTIONS/CAREER NOTES: Selected by San Jose Sharks in third round (third Sharks pick, 51st overall) of NHL entry draft (June 20, 1992).

Season Team	League	REGULAR SEASON					PLAYOFFS				
		Gms.	G	A	Pts.	Pen.	Gms.	G	A	Pts.	Pen.
90-91—Khimik Voskresensk	USSR	16	2	2	4	0	—	—	—	—	—
91-92—Khimik Voskresensk	CIS	38	3	3	6	14	—	—	—	—	—
92-93—Khimik Voskresensk	CIS	33	18	9	27	74	2	1	0	1	0

CHERNOMAZ, RICHARD
RW, FLAMES

PERSONAL: Born September 1, 1963, at Selkirk, Man. . . . 5-8/185. . . . Shoots right. . . . Name pronounced CHUHR-noh-maz.

TRANSACTIONS/CAREER NOTES: Selected by Colorado Rockies as underage junior in second round (third Rockies pick, 26th overall) of NHL entry draft (June 10, 1981). . . . Suffered recurring pain caused by separated shoulder; missed parts of 1981-82 season. . . . Injured knee ligaments (January 1983). . . . Sprained left knee and underwent arthroscopic surgery (November 27, 1984). . . . Signed as free agent by Calgary Flames (August 4, 1987). . . . Underwent surgery to remove ligament from right knee (November 1989); missed 13 games.

HONORS: Named to WHL All-Star first team (1982-83). . . . Named to IHL All-Star second team (1987-88 and 1990-91).

Season Team	League	REGULAR SEASON					PLAYOFFS				
		Gms.	G	A	Pts.	Pen.	Gms.	G	A	Pts.	Pen.
79-80—Saskatoon	SJHL	51	33	37	70	75	—	—	—	—	—
—Saskatoon	WHL	25	9	10	19	33	—	—	—	—	—
80-81—Victoria	WHL	72	49	64	113	92	15	11	15	26	38
81-82—Victoria	WHL	49	36	62	98	69	4	1	2	3	13
—Colorado	NHL	2	0	0	0	0	—	—	—	—	—
82-83—Victoria	WHL	64	71	53	124	113	12	10	5	15	18
83-84—Maine	AHL	69	17	29	46	39	2	0	1	1	0
—New Jersey	NHL	7	2	1	3	2	—	—	—	—	—
84-85—Maine	AHL	64	17	34	51	64	10	2	2	4	4
—New Jersey	NHL	3	0	2	2	2	—	—	—	—	—
85-86—Maine	AHL	78	21	28	49	82	5	0	0	0	2
86-87—Maine	AHL	58	35	27	62	65	—	—	—	—	—
—New Jersey	NHL	25	6	4	10	8	—	—	—	—	—
87-88—Calgary	NHL	2	1	0	1	0	—	—	—	—	—
—Salt Lake City	IHL	73	48	47	95	122	18	4	14	18	30
88-89—Calgary	NHL	1	0	0	0	0	—	—	—	—	—
—Salt Lake City	IHL	81	33	68	101	122	14	7	5	12	47
89-90—Salt Lake City	IHL	65	39	35	74	170	11	6	6	12	32
90-91—Salt Lake City	IHL	81	39	58	97	213	4	3	1	4	8
91-92—Salt Lake City	IHL	66	20	40	60	201	5	1	2	3	10
—Calgary	NHL	11	0	0	0	6	—	—	—	—	—
92-93—Salt Lake City	IHL	76	26	48	74	172	—	—	—	—	—
NHL totals		51	9	7	16	18					

CHERVYAKOV, DENIS

D, BRUINS

PERSONAL: Born April 20, 1970, at St. Petersburg, U.S.S.R. .... 6-0/185. .... Shoots left. ... Name pronounced chair-vuh-KAHF.
TRANSACTIONS/CAREER NOTES: Selected by Boston Bruins in 11th round (ninth Bruins pick, 256th overall) of NHL entry draft (June 20, 1992).... Loaned to Atlanta Knights (February 26, 1993).... Returned to Providence Bruins (March 2, 1993).

			REGULAR SEASON					PLAYOFFS			
Season Team	League	Gms.	G	A	Pts.	Pen.	Gms.	G	A	Pts.	Pen.
88-89—CSKA Moscow	USSR	4	1	2	3	...	—	—	—	—	—
89-90—CSKA Moscow	USSR	40	4	9	13	16	—	—	—	—	—
90-91—CSKA Moscow	USSR	60	5	14	19	34	—	—	—	—	—
91-92—Riga	CIS	48	4	6	10	46	—	—	—	—	—
92-93—Boston	NHL	2	0	0	0	2	—	—	—	—	—
—Providence	AHL	48	4	12	16	99	—	—	—	—	—
—Atlanta	IHL	1	0	0	0	0	—	—	—	—	—
NHL totals		2	0	0	0	2					

CHEVELDAE, TIM

G, RED WINGS

PERSONAL: Born February 15, 1968, at Melville, Sask. .... 5-11/180. .... Shoots left. .... Name pronounced SHEH-vehl-day.
TRANSACTIONS/CAREER NOTES: Selected by Detroit Red Wings as underage junior in fourth round (fourth Red Wings pick, 64th overall) of NHL entry draft (June 21, 1986).
HONORS: Named to WHL (East) All-Star first team (1987-88).... Played in NHL All-Star Game (1992).

			REGULAR SEASON								PLAYOFFS					
Season Team	League	Gms.	Min.	W	L	T	GA	SO	Avg.	Gms.	Min.	W	L	GA	SO	Avg.
84-85—Melville	SAJHL	23	1167	...	...	...	98	0	5.04	—	—	—	—	—	—	—
85-86—Saskatoon	WHL	36	2030	21	10	3	165	0	4.88	8	480	6	2	29	0	3.63
86-87—Saskatoon	WHL	33	1909	20	11	0	133	2	4.18	5	308	4	1	20	0	3.90
87-88—Saskatoon	WHL	66	3798	44	19	3	235	1	3.71	6	364	4	2	27	0	4.45
88-89—Detroit	NHL	2	122	0	2	0	9	0	4.43	—	—	—	—	—	—	—
—Adirondack	AHL	30	1694	20	8	0	98	1	3.47	2	99	1	0	9	0	5.45
89-90—Adirondack	AHL	31	1848	17	8	6	116	0	3.77	—	—	—	—	—	—	—
—Detroit	NHL	28	1600	10	9	8	101	0	3.79	—	—	—	—	—	—	—
90-91—Detroit	NHL	65	3615	30	26	5	*214	2	3.55	7	398	3	4	22	0	3.32
91-92—Detroit	NHL	*72	*4236	†38	23	9	226	2	3.20	11	597	3	7	25	†2	2.51
92-93—Detroit	NHL	67	3880	34	24	7	210	4	3.25	7	423	3	4	24	0	3.40
NHL totals		234	13453	112	84	29	760	8	3.39	25	1418	9	15	71	2	3.00

CHEVELDAYOFF, KEVIN

D, ISLANDERS

PERSONAL: Born February 4, 1970, at Saskatoon, Sask. .... 6-0/202. .... Shoots right.... Name pronounced sheh-vehl-DAY-ahf.
TRANSACTIONS/CAREER NOTES: Selected by New York Islanders in first round (first Islanders pick, 16th overall) of NHL entry draft (June 11, 1988).... Underwent reconstructive surgery to left knee (January 6, 1989).... missed remainder of season and part of 1989-90 season.

			REGULAR SEASON					PLAYOFFS			
Season Team	League	Gms.	G	A	Pts.	Pen.	Gms.	G	A	Pts.	Pen.
86-87—Brandon	WHL	70	0	16	16	259	—	—	—	—	—
87-88—Brandon	WHL	71	3	29	32	265	4	0	2	2	20
88-89—Brandon	WHL	40	4	12	16	135	—	—	—	—	—
89-90—Brandon	WHL	33	5	12	17	56	—	—	—	—	—
—Springfield	AHL	4	0	0	0	0	—	—	—	—	—
90-91—Capital District	AHL	76	0	14	14	203	—	—	—	—	—
91-92—Capital District	AHL	44	0	4	4	110	7	0	0	0	22
92-93—Capital District	AHL	79	3	8	11	113	4	0	1	1	8

CHIASSON, STEVE

D, RED WINGS

PERSONAL: Born April 14, 1967, at Barrie, Ont. .... 6-1/205. .... Shoots left. ... Name pronounced CHAY-sahn.
TRANSACTIONS/CAREER NOTES: Selected by Detroit Red Wings as underage junior in third round (third Red Wings pick, 50th overall) of NHL entry draft (June 15, 1985). ... Injured hand (October 1985).... Separated right shoulder (February 1988).... Injured foot (May 1988).... Injured groin (October 1988).... Bruised ribs (January 1989).... Injured ankle (February 1989).... Injured knee (November 29, 1990); missed three games.... Broke right ankle (January 2, 1991).... Reinjured right ankle (February 19, 1991); missed 26 games. ... Reinjured right ankle (March 9, 1991).... Injured ankle (October 22, 1991); missed 14 games.... Bruised thigh (October 25, 1992); missed three games.... Pulled hamstring (January 21, 1993); missed one game.
HONORS: Won Stafford Smythe Memorial Trophy (1985-86).... Named to Memorial Cup All-Star team (1985-86).... Played in NHL All-Star Game (1993).

			REGULAR SEASON					PLAYOFFS			
Season Team	League	Gms.	G	A	Pts.	Pen.	Gms.	G	A	Pts.	Pen.
83-84—Guelph	OHL	55	1	9	10	112	—	—	—	—	—
84-85—Guelph	OHL	61	8	22	30	139	—	—	—	—	—
85-86—Guelph	OHL	54	12	29	41	126	18	10	10	20	37
86-87—Detroit	NHL	45	1	4	5	73	2	0	0	0	19
87-88—Adirondack	AHL	23	6	11	17	58	—	—	—	—	—
—Detroit	NHL	29	2	9	11	57	9	2	2	4	31
88-89—Detroit	NHL	65	12	35	47	149	5	2	1	3	6
89-90—Detroit	NHL	67	14	28	42	114	—	—	—	—	—

— 343 —

Season	Team	League	REGULAR SEASON					PLAYOFFS				
			Gms.	G	A	Pts.	Pen.	Gms.	G	A	Pts.	Pen.
90-91—Detroit		NHL	42	3	17	20	80	5	3	1	4	19
91-92—Detroit		NHL	62	10	24	34	136	11	1	5	6	12
92-93—Detroit		NHL	79	12	50	62	155	7	2	2	4	19
NHL totals			389	54	167	221	764	39	10	11	21	106

CHORSKE, TOM
RW, DEVILS

PERSONAL: Born September 18, 1966, at Minneapolis.... 6-1/205.... Shoots right.... Name pronounced CHOR-skee.
HIGH SCHOOL: Southwest (Minneapolis).
COLLEGE: Minnesota.
TRANSACTIONS/CAREER NOTES: Selected by Montreal Canadiens in first round (second Canadiens pick, 16th overall) of NHL entry draft (June 15, 1985).... Separated shoulder (November 18, 1988); missed 11 games.... Suffered hip pointer (October 26, 1989).... Sprained right shoulder (March 14, 1991).... Traded by Canadiens with RW Stephane Richer to New Jersey Devils for LW Kirk Muller and G Roland Melanson (September 20, 1991).... Suffered charley horse (January 14, 1993); missed two games.
HONORS: Named to WCHA All-Star first team (1988-89).

Season	Team	League	REGULAR SEASON					PLAYOFFS				
			Gms.	G	A	Pts.	Pen.	Gms.	G	A	Pts.	Pen.
84-85—Minn. Southwest H.S.		Minn. H.S.	23	44	26	70	...	—	—	—	—	—
85-86—University of Minnesota		WCHA	39	6	4	10	6	—	—	—	—	—
86-87—University of Minnesota		WCHA	47	20	22	42	20	—	—	—	—	—
87-88—U.S. national team		Int'l	36	9	16	25	24	—	—	—	—	—
88-89—University of Minnesota		WCHA	37	25	24	49	28	—	—	—	—	—
89-90—Montreal		NHL	14	3	1	4	2	—	—	—	—	—
—Sherbrooke		AHL	59	22	24	46	54	12	4	4	8	8
90-91—Montreal		NHL	57	9	11	20	32	—	—	—	—	—
91-92—New Jersey		NHL	76	19	17	36	32	7	0	3	3	4
92-93—New Jersey		NHL	50	7	12	19	25	1	0	0	0	0
—Utica		AHL	6	1	4	5	2	—	—	—	—	—
NHL totals			197	38	41	79	91	8	0	3	3	4

CHRISTIAN, DAVE
RW, BLACKHAWKS

PERSONAL: Born May 12, 1959, at Warroad, Minn.... 6-0/195.... Shoots right.... Son of Bill Christian and nephew of Roger Christian, both members of 1960 gold-medal-winning U.S. Olympic team and 1964 U.S. Olympic team; and nephew of Gordon Christian, member of 1956 U.S. Olympic team.
COLLEGE: North Dakota.
TRANSACTIONS/CAREER NOTES: Selected by Winnipeg Jets in second round (second Jets pick, 40th overall) of NHL entry draft (August 9, 1979).... Tore shoulder muscles (December 1982); missed 25 games.... Traded by Jets to Washington Capitals for first-round pick in 1983 draft (D Bobby Dollas) (June 8, 1983).... Traded by Capitals to Boston Bruins for LW Bob Joyce (December 13, 1989).... Signed as free agent by St. Louis Blues; Bruins tried to block the signing, claiming Christian was not a free agent. Blues and Bruins later arranged trade in which Boston received D Glen Featherstone and LW Dave Thomlinson, whom they had previously signed as free agents, for Christian, third-round pick in 1992 draft (LW Vitali Prokhorov) and either seventh-round pick in 1992 draft or sixth-round pick in 1993 draft; Blues used seventh-round pick in 1992 draft to select C Lance Burns (July 30, 1991).... Bruised ribs (January 16, 1992); missed one game.... Selected by Chicago Blackhawks in NHL waiver draft (October 4, 1992).
HONORS: Played in NHL All-Star Game (1991).
MISCELLANEOUS: Member of gold-medal-winning U.S. Olympic team (1980).

Season	Team	League	REGULAR SEASON					PLAYOFFS				
			Gms.	G	A	Pts.	Pen.	Gms.	G	A	Pts.	Pen.
77-78—Univ. of North Dakota		WCHA	38	8	16	24	14	—	—	—	—	—
78-79—Univ. of North Dakota		WCHA	40	22	24	46	22	—	—	—	—	—
79-80—U.S. national team		Int'l	59	10	20	30	26	—	—	—	—	—
—U.S. Olympic Team		Int'l	7	0	8	8	6	—	—	—	—	—
—Winnipeg		NHL	15	8	10	18	2	—	—	—	—	—
80-81—Winnipeg		NHL	80	28	43	71	22	—	—	—	—	—
81-82—Winnipeg		NHL	80	25	51	76	28	4	0	1	1	2
82-83—Winnipeg		NHL	55	18	26	44	23	3	0	0	0	0
83-84—Washington		NHL	80	29	52	81	28	8	5	4	9	5
84-85—Washington		NHL	80	26	43	69	14	5	1	1	2	0
85-86—Washington		NHL	80	41	42	83	15	9	4	4	8	0
86-87—Washington		NHL	76	23	27	50	8	7	1	3	4	6
87-88—Washington		NHL	80	37	21	58	26	14	5	6	11	6
88-89—Washington		NHL	80	34	31	65	12	6	1	1	2	0
89-90—Washington		NHL	28	3	8	11	4	—	—	—	—	—
—Boston		NHL	50	12	17	29	8	21	4	1	5	4
90-91—Boston		NHL	78	32	21	53	41	19	8	4	12	4
91-92—St. Louis		NHL	78	20	24	44	41	4	3	0	3	0
92-93—Chicago		NHL	60	4	14	18	12	1	0	0	0	0
NHL totals			1000	340	430	770	284	101	32	25	57	27

CHRISTIAN, JEFF
LW, DEVILS

PERSONAL: Born July 30, 1970, at Burlington, Ont.... 6-2/205.... Shoots left.
TRANSACTIONS/CAREER NOTES: Selected by New Jersey Devils in second round (second Devils pick, 23rd overall) of NHL entry draft (June 11, 1988).... Traded by London Knights to Owen Sound Platers for C Todd Hlushko and D David Noseworthy (November

27, 1989).... Suspended three games by OHL for high-sticking (March 28, 1990).

Season	Team	League	REGULAR SEASON					PLAYOFFS				
			Gms.	G	A	Pts.	Pen.	Gms.	G	A	Pts.	Pen.
86-87—Dundas Jr. C	OHA	29	20	34	54	42	—	—	—	—	—
87-88—London	OHL	64	15	29	44	154	9	1	5	6	27
88-89—London	OHL	60	27	30	57	221	20	3	4	7	56
89-90—London	OHL	18	14	7	21	64	—	—	—	—	—
—Owen Sound	OHL	37	19	26	45	145	10	6	7	13	43
90-91—Utica	AHL	80	24	42	66	165	—	—	—	—	—
91-92—Utica	AHL	76	27	24	51	198	4	0	0	0	16
—New Jersey	NHL	2	0	0	0	2	—	—	—	—	—
92-93—Utica	AHL	22	4	6	10	39	—	—	—	—	—
—Cincinnati	IHL	36	5	12	17	113	—	—	—	—	—
—Hamilton	AHL	11	2	5	7	35	—	—	—	—	—
NHL totals		**2**	**0**	**0**	**0**	**2**					

CHURLA, SHANE
RW, STARS

PERSONAL: Born June 24, 1965, at Fernie, B.C. ... 6-1/200. ... Shoots right. ... Name pronounced CHUR-luh.

TRANSACTIONS/CAREER NOTES: Selected by Hartford Whalers in sixth round (fourth Whalers pick, 110th overall) of NHL entry draft (June 15, 1985). ... Suspended three games by AHL (October 5, 1986). ... Traded by Whalers with D Dana Murzyn to Calgary Flames for D Neil Sheehy, C Carey Wilson and the rights to LW Lane MacDonald (January 3, 1988). ... Traded by Flames with C Perry Berezan to Minnesota North Stars for LW Brian MacLellan and fourth-round pick in 1989 draft (C Robert Reichel) (March 4, 1989). ... Broke wrist (April 2, 1989). ... Bruised right hand (November 1989). ... Suspended 10 games by NHL for fighting (December 28, 1989). ... Underwent surgery to wrist (April 1990). ... Tore rib cartilage (November 17, 1990); missed five games. ... Separated shoulder (December 11, 1990); missed seven games. ... Separated right shoulder (January 17, 1991); missed 23 games. ... Selected by San Jose Sharks in dispersal draft of North Star roster (May 30, 1991). ... Traded by Sharks to North Stars for C Kelly Kisio (June 3, 1991). ... Suffered back spasms (January 30, 1992); missed five games. ... Injured shoulder (March 19, 1992); missed five games. ... Injured shoulder (December 1, 1992); missed one game. ... Injured shoulder (December 22, 1992); missed two games. ... Strained neck (February 28, 1993); missed two games. ... Suspended three games by NHL during 1992-93 season for game misconduct penalties. ... North Stars franchise moved from Minnesota to Dallas and renamed Stars for 1993-94 season.

Season	Team	League	REGULAR SEASON					PLAYOFFS				
			Gms.	G	A	Pts.	Pen.	Gms.	G	A	Pts.	Pen.
83-84—Medicine Hat	WHL	48	3	7	10	115	14	1	5	6	41
84-85—Medicine Hat	WHL	70	14	20	34	*370	9	1	0	1	55
85-86—Binghamton	AHL	52	4	10	14	306	3	0	0	0	22
86-87—Binghamton	AHL	24	1	5	6	249	—	—	—	—	—
—Hartford	NHL	20	0	1	1	78	2	0	0	0	42
87-88—Binghamton	AHL	25	5	8	13	168	—	—	—	—	—
—Hartford	NHL	2	0	0	0	14	—	—	—	—	—
—Calgary	NHL	29	1	5	6	132	7	0	1	1	17
88-89—Calgary	NHL	5	0	0	0	25	—	—	—	—	—
—Salt Lake City	IHL	32	3	13	16	278	—	—	—	—	—
—Minnesota	NHL	13	1	0	1	54	—	—	—	—	—
89-90—Minnesota	NHL	53	2	3	5	292	7	0	0	0	44
90-91—Minnesota	NHL	40	2	2	4	286	22	2	1	3	90
91-92—Minnesota	NHL	57	4	1	5	278	—	—	—	—	—
92-93—Minnesota	NHL	73	5	16	21	286	—	—	—	—	—
NHL totals		**292**	**15**	**28**	**43**	**1445**	**38**	**2**	**2**	**4**	**193**

CHYCHRUN, JEFF
D, KINGS

PERSONAL: Born May 3, 1966, at Lasalle, Que. ... 6-4/215. ... Shoots right. ... Name pronounced CHICK-ruhn.

TRANSACTIONS/CAREER NOTES: Selected by Philadelphia Flyers as underage junior in second round (second Flyers pick, 37th overall) of NHL entry draft (June 9, 1984). ... Suffered viral infection (November 1989). ... Suffered concussion (October 11, 1990); missed three games. ... Suffered concussion (October 23, 1990); missed three games. ... Fractured navicular bone in left wrist and underwent surgery (November 23, 1990); missed 41 games. ... Traded by Flyers with rights to RW Jari Kurri to Los Angeles Kings for D Steve Duchesne, C Steve Kasper and fourth-round pick in 1991 draft (D Aris Brimanis) (May 30, 1991). ... Underwent wrist surgery (summer 1991); missed 25 games. ... Traded by Kings with D Brian Benning and first-round pick in 1992 draft (LW Jason Bowen) to Pittsburgh Penguins for D Paul Coffey (February 19, 1992). ... Suspended by Penguins after he missed team flight (October 29, 1992). ... Reinstated by Penguins (November 3, 1992). ... Traded by Penguins to Kings for D Peter Ahola (November 6, 1992).

MISCELLANEOUS: Member of Stanley Cup championship team (1992).

Season	Team	League	REGULAR SEASON					PLAYOFFS				
			Gms.	G	A	Pts.	Pen.	Gms.	G	A	Pts.	Pen.
83-84—Kingston	OHL	83	1	13	14	137	—	—	—	—	—
84-85—Kingston	OHL	58	4	10	14	206	—	—	—	—	—
85-86—Kingston	OHL	61	4	21	25	127	10	2	1	3	17
—Kalamazoo	IHL	—	—	—	—	—	3	1	0	1	0
—Hershey	AHL	—	—	—	—	—	4	0	1	1	9
86-87—Hershey	AHL	74	1	17	18	239	4	0	0	0	10
—Philadelphia	NHL	1	0	0	0	4	—	—	—	—	—

C

Season Team	League	Gms.	G	A	Pts.	Pen.	Gms.	G	A	Pts.	Pen.
87-88—Philadelphia	NHL	3	0	0	0	4	—	—	—	—	—
—Hershey	AHL	55	0	5	5	210	12	0	2	2	44
88-89—Philadelphia	NHL	80	1	4	5	245	19	0	2	2	65
89-90—Philadelphia	NHL	79	2	7	9	250	—	—	—	—	—
90-91—Philadelphia	NHL	36	0	6	6	105	—	—	—	—	—
91-92—Phoenix	IHL	3	0	0	0	6	—	—	—	—	—
—Los Angeles	NHL	26	0	3	3	76	—	—	—	—	—
—Pittsburgh	NHL	17	0	1	1	35	—	—	—	—	—
92-93—Pittsburgh	NHL	1	0	0	0	2	—	—	—	—	—
—Los Angeles	NHL	17	0	1	1	23	—	—	—	—	—
—Phoenix	IHL	11	2	0	2	44	—	—	—	—	—
NHL totals		260	3	22	25	744	19	0	2	2	65

CHYNOWETH, DEAN
D, ISLANDERS

PERSONAL: Born October 30, 1968, at Saskatoon, Sask. . . . 6-2/190. . . . Shoots right. . . . Name pronounced shih-NOWTH. . . . Son of Ed Chynoweth, president of the Western Hockey League.

TRANSACTIONS/CAREER NOTES: Broke hand (September 1985). . . . Broke hand (April 1986). . . . Broke hand (October 1986). . . . Fractured rib and punctured lung (April 1987). . . . Selected by New York Islanders as underage junior in first round (first Islanders pick, 13th overall) of NHL entry draft (June 13, 1987). . . . Injured left eye (October 27, 1988); missed two months. . . . Developed Osgood-Schlatter disease, an abnormal relationship between the muscles and the growing bones (December 1988); missed remainder of season. . . . Injured ankle (October 31, 1989). . . . Sprained ligaments in right thumb (November 1989).

HONORS: Named to Memorial Cup All-Star team (1987-88).

		REGULAR SEASON					PLAYOFFS				
Season Team	League	Gms.	G	A	Pts.	Pen.	Gms.	G	A	Pts.	Pen.
85-86—Medicine Hat	WHL	69	3	12	15	208	17	3	2	5	52
86-87—Medicine Hat	WHL	67	3	18	21	285	13	4	2	6	28
87-88—Medicine Hat	WHL	64	1	21	22	274	16	0	6	6	*87
88-89—New York Islanders	NHL	6	0	0	0	48	—	—	—	—	—
89-90—New York Islanders	NHL	20	0	2	2	39	—	—	—	—	—
—Springfield	AHL	40	0	7	7	98	17	0	4	4	36
90-91—New York Islanders	NHL	25	1	1	2	59	—	—	—	—	—
—Capital District	AHL	44	1	5	6	176	—	—	—	—	—
91-92—Capital District	AHL	43	4	6	10	164	6	1	1	2	39
—New York Islanders	NHL	11	1	0	1	23	—	—	—	—	—
92-93—Capital District	AHL	52	3	10	13	197	4	0	1	1	9
NHL totals		62	2	3	5	169					

CHYZOWSKI, DAVE
LW, ISLANDERS

PERSONAL: Born July 11, 1971, at Edmonton, Alta. . . . 6-1/190. . . . Shoots left. . . . Name pronounced chih-ZOW-skee.

TRANSACTIONS/CAREER NOTES: Selected by New York Islanders in first round (first Islanders pick, second overall) of NHL entry draft (June 17, 1989).

HONORS: Named to WHL (West) All-Star first team (1988-89)

		REGULAR SEASON					PLAYOFFS				
Season Team	League	Gms.	G	A	Pts.	Pen.	Gms.	G	A	Pts.	Pen.
87-88—Kamloops	WHL	66	16	17	33	117	18	2	4	6	26
88-89—Kamloops	WHL	68	56	48	104	139	16	15	13	28	32
89-90—Kamloops	WHL	4	5	2	7	17	17	11	6	17	46
—Springfield	AHL	4	0	0	0	7	—	—	—	—	—
—New York Islanders	NHL	34	8	6	14	45	—	—	—	—	—
90-91—Capital District	AHL	7	3	6	9	22	—	—	—	—	—
—New York Islanders	NHL	56	5	9	14	61	—	—	—	—	—
91-92—New York Islanders	NHL	12	1	1	2	17	—	—	—	—	—
—Capital District	AHL	55	15	18	33	121	6	1	1	2	23
92-93—Capital District	AHL	66	15	21	36	177	3	2	0	2	0
NHL totals		102	14	16	30	123					

CIAVAGLIA, PETER
C, SABRES

PERSONAL: Born July 15, 1969, at Albany, N.Y. . . . 5-10/173. . . . Shoots left. . . . Full name: Peter Anthony Ciavaglia. . . . Name pronounced sa-VAG-lia.

COLLEGE: Harvard.

TRANSACTIONS/CAREER NOTES: Selected by Calgary Flames in seventh round (eighth Flames pick, 145th overall) of NHL entry draft (June 13, 1987). . . . Signed as free agent by Buffalo Sabres (August 1990). . . . Suffered stiff neck (February 14, 1993); missed two games.

HONORS: Named to ECAC All-Star second team (1988-89). . . . Named ECAC Player of the Year (1990-91). . . . Named to NCAA All-America East second team (1990-91). . . . Named to ECAC All-Star first team (1990-91).

		REGULAR SEASON					PLAYOFFS				
Season Team	League	Gms.	G	A	Pts.	Pen.	Gms.	G	A	Pts.	Pen.
86-87—Nichols/Wheatfield Jr. B.	NY Jr. B	...	53	84	137	...	—	—	—	—	—
87-88—Harvard University	ECAC	30	10	23	33	16	—	—	—	—	—
88-89—Harvard University	ECAC	34	15	48	63	36	—	—	—	—	—
89-90—Harvard University	ECAC	28	17	18	35	22	—	—	—	—	—

Season	Team	League	REGULAR SEASON Gms.	G	A	Pts.	Pen.	PLAYOFFS Gms.	G	A	Pts.	Pen.
90-91—Harvard University	ECAC	28	24	39	63	4	—	—	—	—	—
91-92—Rochester	AHL	77	37	61	98	16	6	2	5	7	6
—Buffalo	NHL	2	0	0	0	0	—	—	—	—	—
92-93—Rochester	AHL	64	35	67	102	32	17	9	16	25	12
—Buffalo	NHL	3	0	0	0	0	—	—	—	—	—
NHL totals			5	0	0	0	0					

CICCARELLI, DINO
RW, RED WINGS

PERSONAL: Born February 8, 1960, at Sarnia, Ont. . . . 5-10/175. . . . Shoots right. . . . Name pronounced SIH-sih-REHL-ee.
TRANSACTIONS/CAREER NOTES: Fractured midshaft of right femur (spring 1978). . . . Signed as free agent by Minnesota North Stars (September 1979). . . . Injured shoulder (November 1984). . . . Broke right wrist (December 1984). . . . Suspended three games by NHL for making contact with linesman (October 5, 1987). . . . Suspended 10 games by NHL for stick-swinging incident (January 6, 1988). . . . Suspended by North Stars for failure to report to training camp (September 10, 1988). . . . Traded by North Stars with D Bob Rouse to Washington Capitals for RW Mike Gartner and D Larry Murphy (March 7, 1989). . . . Suffered concussion (March 8, 1989). . . . Sprained left knee (April 23, 1990). . . . Fractured right hand (October 20, 1990); missed 21 games. . . . Injured groin (March 24, 1991); missed five games. . . . Injured eye (December 4, 1991); missed one game. . . . Traded by Capitals to Detroit Red Wings for RW Kevin Miller (June 20, 1992). . . . Suffered from the flu (January 30, 1993); missed two games.
HONORS: Won Jim Mahon Memorial Trophy (1977-78). . . . Named to OMJHL All-Star second team (1977-78). . . . Played in NHL All-Star Game (1982, 1983 and 1989).
RECORDS: Holds NHL single-season playoff record for most points as a rookie—21; and most goals as a rookie—14 (1981).

Season	Team	League	REGULAR SEASON Gms.	G	A	Pts.	Pen.	PLAYOFFS Gms.	G	A	Pts.	Pen.
76-77—London	OMJHL	66	39	43	82	45	—	—	—	—	—
77-78—London	OMJHL	68	*72	70	142	49	9	6	10	16	6
78-79—London	OMJHL	30	8	11	19	25	7	3	5	8	0
79-80—London	OMJHL	62	50	53	103	72	5	2	6	8	15
—Oklahoma City	CHL	6	3	2	5	0	—	—	—	—	—
80-81—Oklahoma City	CHL	48	32	25	57	45	—	—	—	—	—
—Minnesota	NHL	32	18	12	30	29	19	14	7	21	25
81-82—Minnesota	NHL	76	55	51	106	138	4	3	1	4	2
82-83—Minnesota	NHL	77	37	38	75	94	9	4	6	10	11
83-84—Minnesota	NHL	79	38	33	71	58	16	4	5	9	27
84-85—Minnesota	NHL	51	15	17	32	41	9	3	3	6	8
85-86—Minnesota	NHL	75	44	45	89	53	5	0	1	1	6
86-87—Minnesota	NHL	80	52	51	103	92	—	—	—	—	—
87-88—Minnesota	NHL	67	41	45	86	79	—	—	—	—	—
88-89—Minnesota	NHL	65	32	27	59	64	—	—	—	—	—
—Washington	NHL	11	12	3	15	12	6	3	3	6	12
89-90—Washington	NHL	80	41	38	79	122	8	8	3	11	6
90-91—Washington	NHL	54	21	18	39	66	11	5	4	9	22
91-92—Washington	NHL	78	38	38	76	78	7	5	4	9	14
92-93—Detroit	NHL	82	41	56	97	81	7	4	2	6	16
NHL totals			907	485	472	957	1007	101	53	39	92	149

CICCONE, ENRICO
D, CAPITALS

PERSONAL: Born April 10, 1970, at Montreal. . . . 6-4/200. . . . Shoots left.
TRANSACTIONS/CAREER NOTES: Selected by Minnesota North Stars in fifth round (fifth North Stars pick, 92nd overall) of NHL entry draft (June 16, 1990). . . . North Stars franchise moved from Minnesota to Dallas and renamed Stars for 1993-94 season. . . . Traded by Stars to Washington Capitals (June 25, 1993) to complete deal in which Capitals sent D Paul Cavallini to Stars for future considerations (June 20, 1993).

Season	Team	League	REGULAR SEASON Gms.	G	A	Pts.	Pen.	PLAYOFFS Gms.	G	A	Pts.	Pen.
87-88—Shawinigan	QMJHL	61	2	12	14	324	—	—	—	—	—
88-89—Shawinigan/T-Rivieres	QMJHL	58	7	19	26	289	—	—	—	—	—
89-90—Trois-Rivieres	QMJHL	40	4	24	28	227	3	0	0	0	15
90-91—Kalamazoo	IHL	57	4	9	13	384	4	0	1	1	32
91-92—Kalamazoo	IHL	53	4	16	20	406	10	0	1	1	58
—Minnesota	NHL	11	0	0	0	48	—	—	—	—	—
92-93—Minnesota	NHL	31	0	1	1	115	—	—	—	—	—
—Kalamazoo	IHL	13	1	3	4	50	—	—	—	—	—
—Hamilton	AHL	6	1	3	4	44	—	—	—	—	—
NHL totals			42	0	1	1	163					

CICHOCKI, CHRIS
RW, RANGERS

PERSONAL: Born September 17, 1963, at Detroit. . . . 5-11/185. . . . Shoots right.
COLLEGE: Michigan Tech.
TRANSACTIONS/CAREER NOTES: Signed as free agent by Detroit Red Wings (June 28, 1985). . . . Traded by Red wings with third-round pick in 1987 draft to New Jersey Devils for C Mel Bridgman (March 1987). . . . Separated shoulder (January 1989); missed 17 games. . . . Traded by Devils to Hartford Whalers for RW Jim Thomson (October 31, 1989). . . . Signed as free agent by New York Rangers (September 6, 1990).
MISCELLANEOUS: Member of 1983 U.S. Junior National Team.

Season Team	League	REGULAR SEASON					PLAYOFFS				
		Gms.	G	A	Pts.	Pen.	Gms.	G	A	Pts.	Pen.
82-83—Michigan Tech	WCHA	36	12	10	22	10	—	—	—	—	—
83-84—Michigan Tech	WCHA	40	25	20	45	36	—	—	—	—	—
84-85—Michigan Tech	WCHA	40	30	24	54	14	—	—	—	—	—
85-86—Adirondack	AHL	9	4	4	8	6	—	—	—	—	—
—Detroit	NHL	59	10	11	21	21	—	—	—	—	—
86-87—Adirondack	AHL	55	31	34	65	27	—	—	—	—	—
—Detroit	NHL	2	0	0	0	2	—	—	—	—	—
—Maine	AHL	7	2	2	4	0	—	—	—	—	—
87-88—New Jersey	NHL	5	1	0	1	2	—	—	—	—	—
—Utica	AHL	69	36	30	66	66	—	—	—	—	—
88-89—New Jersey	NHL	2	0	1	1	2	—	—	—	—	—
—Utica	AHL	59	32	31	63	50	5	0	1	1	2
89-90—Utica	AHL	11	3	1	4	10	—	—	—	—	—
—Binghamton	AHL	60	21	26	47	12	—	—	—	—	—
90-91—Binghamton	AHL	80	35	30	65	70	9	0	4	4	2
91-92—Binghamton	AHL	75	28	29	57	132	6	5	4	9	4
92-93—Binghamton	AHL	65	23	29	52	78	9	3	2	5	25
NHL totals		68	11	12	23	27					

CIERNY, JOZEF
LW, SABRES

PERSONAL: Born May 13, 1974, at Zvolen, Czechoslovakia. . . . 6-2/176. . . . Shoots left. . . . Name pronounced CHUR-nee.
TRANSACTIONS/CAREER NOTES: Selected by Buffalo Sabres in second round (second Sabres pick, 35th overall) of NHL entry draft (June 20, 1992).

Season Team	League	REGULAR SEASON					PLAYOFFS				
		Gms.	G	A	Pts.	Pen.	Gms.	G	A	Pts.	Pen.
91-92—Zvolen	Czech.	26	10	3	13	8	—	—	—	—	—
92-93—Rochester	AHL	54	27	27	54	36	—	—	—	—	—

CIGER, ZDENO
LW, OILERS

PERSONAL: Born October 19, 1969, at Martin, Czechoslovakia. . . . 6-1/190. . . . Shoots left. . . . Name pronounced SEE-guhr.
TRANSACTIONS/CAREER NOTES: Selected by New Jersey Devils in third round (third Devils pick, 54th overall) of NHL entry draft (June 11, 1988). . . . Bruised left shoulder (October 6, 1990). . . . Injured elbow (January 24, 1991). . . . Fractured right wrist (September 24, 1991); missed first 59 games of season. . . . Traded by Devils with C Kevin Todd to Edmonton Oilers for C Bernie Nicholls (January 13, 1993).
HONORS: Named Czechoslovakian League Rookie of the Year (1988-89).

Season Team	League	REGULAR SEASON					PLAYOFFS				
		Gms.	G	A	Pts.	Pen.	Gms.	G	A	Pts.	Pen.
88-89—Dukla Trencin	Czech.	32	15	21	36	18	—	—	—	—	—
89-90—Dukla Trencin	Czech.	53	18	28	46	...	—	—	—	—	—
90-91—New Jersey	NHL	45	8	17	25	8	6	0	2	2	4
—Utica	AHL	8	5	4	9	2	—	—	—	—	—
91-92—New Jersey	NHL	20	6	5	11	10	7	2	4	6	0
92-93—New Jersey	NHL	27	4	8	12	2	—	—	—	—	—
—Edmonton	NHL	37	9	15	24	6	—	—	—	—	—
NHL totals		129	27	45	72	26	13	2	6	8	4

CIMELLARO, TONY
C, SENATORS

PERSONAL: Born June 14, 1971, at Kingston, Ont. . . . 5-11/179. . . . Shoots left.
TRANSACTIONS/CAREER NOTES: Signed as free agent by Ottawa Senators (July 30, 1992).

Season Team	League	REGULAR SEASON					PLAYOFFS				
		Gms.	G	A	Pts.	Pen.	Gms.	G	A	Pts.	Pen.
91-92—Belleville	OHL	48	39	44	83	51	5	6	4	10	10
92-93—New Haven	AHL	76	18	16	34	73	—	—	—	—	—
—Ottawa	NHL	2	0	0	0	0	—	—	—	—	—
NHL totals		2	0	0	0	0					

CIMETTA, ROB
LW, MAPLE LEAFS

PERSONAL: Born February 15, 1970, at Toronto. . . . 6-0/190. . . . Shoots left. . . . Name pronounced sih-MEH-tuh.
TRANSACTIONS/CAREER NOTES: Fractured wrist (October 1986). . . . Selected by Boston Bruins in first round (first Bruins pick, 18th overall) of NHL entry draft (June 11, 1988). . . . Traded by Bruins to Toronto Maple Leafs for D Steve Bancroft (November 9, 1990). . . . Bruised bicep (March 16, 1991). . . . Pulled groin (December 11, 1991); missed eight games.
HONORS: Named to OHL All-Star first team (1988-89).

Season Team	League	REGULAR SEASON					PLAYOFFS				
		Gms.	G	A	Pts.	Pen.	Gms.	G	A	Pts.	Pen.
86-87—Toronto	OHL	66	21	35	56	65	—	—	—	—	—
87-88—Toronto	OHL	64	34	42	76	90	4	2	2	4	7
88-89—Toronto	OHL	50	*55	47	102	89	6	3	3	6	0
—Boston	NHL	7	2	0	2	0	1	0	0	0	15

Season Team	League	REGULAR SEASON					PLAYOFFS				
		Gms.	G	A	Pts.	Pen.	Gms.	G	A	Pts.	Pen.
89-90—Boston	NHL	47	8	9	17	33	—	—	—	—	—
—Maine	AHL	9	3	2	5	13	—	—	—	—	—
90-91—Toronto	NHL	25	2	4	6	21	—	—	—	—	—
—Newmarket	AHL	29	16	18	34	24	—	—	—	—	—
91-92—Toronto	NHL	24	4	3	7	12	—	—	—	—	—
—St. John's	AHL	19	4	13	17	23	10	3	7	10	24
92-93—St. John's	AHL	76	28	57	85	125	9	2	10	12	32
NHL totals		103	16	16	32	66	1	0	0	0	15

CIRELLA, JOE

D, PANTHERS

PERSONAL: Born May 9, 1963, at Hamilton, Ont. . . . 6-3/207. . . . Shoots right. . . . Name pronounced sih-REHL-uh.

TRANSACTIONS/CAREER NOTES: Selected by Colorado Rockies as underage junior in first round (first Rockies pick, fifth overall) of NHL entry draft (June 10, 1981). . . . Injured left knee (November 26, 1985). . . . Traded by New Jersey Devils to Quebec Nordiques for C Walt Poddubny (June 17, 1989). . . . Broke right foot (January 18, 1990). . . . Strained lower back (February 28, 1990). . . . Injured knee (October 21, 1990). . . . Traded by Nordiques to New York Rangers for C Aaron Broten and fifth-round pick in 1991 draft (LW Bill Lindsay) (January 17, 1991). . . . Strained lower back (October 4, 1991); missed 10 games. . . . Selected by Florida Panthers in NHL expansion draft (June 24, 1993).

HONORS: Named to OHL All-Star first team (1982-83). . . . Named to Memorial Cup All-Star team (1982-83). . . . Played in NHL All-Star Game (1984).

Season Team	League	REGULAR SEASON					PLAYOFFS				
		Gms.	G	A	Pts.	Pen.	Gms.	G	A	Pts.	Pen.
80-81—Oshawa	OMJHL	56	5	31	36	220	11	0	2	2	41
81-82—Oshawa	OHL	3	0	1	1	10	11	7	10	17	32
—Colorado	NHL	65	7	12	19	52	—	—	—	—	—
82-83—Oshawa	OHL	56	13	55	68	110	17	4	16	20	37
—New Jersey	NHL	2	0	1	1	4	—	—	—	—	—
83-84—New Jersey	NHL	79	11	33	44	137	—	—	—	—	—
84-85—New Jersey	NHL	66	6	18	24	143	—	—	—	—	—
85-86—New Jersey	NHL	66	6	23	29	147	—	—	—	—	—
86-87—New Jersey	NHL	65	9	22	31	111	—	—	—	—	—
87-88—New Jersey	NHL	80	8	31	39	191	19	0	7	7	49
88-89—New Jersey	NHL	80	3	19	22	155	—	—	—	—	—
89-90—Quebec	NHL	56	4	14	18	67	—	—	—	—	—
90-91—Quebec	NHL	39	2	10	12	59	—	—	—	—	—
—New York Rangers	NHL	19	1	0	1	52	6	0	2	2	26
91-92—New York Rangers	NHL	67	3	12	15	121	13	0	4	4	23
92-93—New York Rangers	NHL	55	3	6	9	85	—	—	—	—	—
NHL totals		739	63	201	264	1324	38	0	13	13	98

CLARK, JASON

C/LW, CANUCKS

PERSONAL: Born May 6, 1972, at London, Ont. . . . 6-1/180. . . . Shoots left.
COLLEGE: Bowling Green State.
TRANSACTIONS/CAREER NOTES: Selected by Vancouver Canucks in sixth round (eighth Canucks pick, 141st overall) of NHL entry draft (June 20, 1992).

Season Team	League	REGULAR SEASON					PLAYOFFS				
		Gms.	G	A	Pts.	Pen.	Gms.	G	A	Pts.	Pen.
91-92—St. Thomas Jr. B	OHA	47	25	52	77	66	—	—	—	—	—
92-93—Bowling Green State	CCHA	40	10	19	29	42	—	—	—	—	—

CLARK, KERRY

RW, FLAMES

PERSONAL: Born August 21, 1968, at Kelvington, Sask. . . . 6-1/205. . . . Shoots right. . . . Brother of Wendel Clark, left winger, Toronto Maple Leafs.
TRANSACTIONS/CAREER NOTES: Selected by New York Islanders as underage junior in 10th round (12th Islanders pick, 206th overall) of NHL entry draft (June 21, 1986). . . . Broke ankle (1986-87). . . . Suspended six games by AHL for fighting (October 15, 1988). . . . Signed as free agent by Calgary Flames (July 23, 1990).

Season Team	League	REGULAR SEASON					PLAYOFFS				
		Gms.	G	A	Pts.	Pen.	Gms.	G	A	Pts.	Pen.
84-85—Regina	WHL	36	1	1	2	66	—	—	—	—	—
85-86—Regina	WHL	23	4	4	8	58	—	—	—	—	—
—Saskatoon	WHL	39	5	8	13	104	13	2	2	4	33
86-87—Saskatoon	WHL	54	12	10	22	229	8	0	1	1	23
87-88—Saskatoon	WHL	67	15	11	26	241	10	2	2	4	16
88-89—Springfield	AHL	63	7	7	14	264	—	—	—	—	—
—Indianapolis	IHL	3	0	1	1	12	—	—	—	—	—
89-90—Phoenix	IHL	38	4	8	12	262	—	—	—	—	—
—Springfield	AHL	21	0	1	1	73	—	—	—	—	—
90-91—Salt Lake City	IHL	62	14	14	28	372	4	1	1	2	12
91-92—Salt Lake City	IHL	74	12	14	26	266	5	1	0	1	34
92-93—Salt Lake City	IHL	64	14	15	29	255	—	—	—	—	—

CLARK, WENDEL
LW, MAPLE LEAFS

PERSONAL: Born October 25, 1966, at Kelvington, Sask. . . . 5-11/194. . . . Shoots left. . . . Brother of Kerry Clark, right winger in Calgary Flames system.

TRANSACTIONS/CAREER NOTES: Selected by Toronto Maple Leafs as underage junior in first round (first Maple Leafs pick, first overall) of NHL entry draft (June 15, 1985). . . . Suffered from virus (November 1985). . . . Broke right foot (November 26, 1985); missed 14 games. . . . Suffered back spasms (November 1987); missed 23 games. . . . Suffered tendinitis in right shoulder (October 1987). . . . Reinjured back (February 1988); missed 90 regular season games before returning to lineup (March 1, 1989). . . . Suffered recurrance of back problems (October 1989). . . . Bruised muscle above left knee (November 4, 1989); missed seven games. . . . Tore ligament of right knee (January 26, 1990); missed 29 games. . . . Separated left shoulder (December 18, 1990). . . . Pulled rib cage muscle (February 6, 1991); missed 12 games. . . . Partially tore knee ligaments (October 7, 1991); missed 12 games. . . . Strained knee ligaments (November 6, 1991); missed 24 games. . . . Injured groin (October 24, 1992); missed four games. . . . Strained rib muscle (January 17, 1993); missed 13 games.

HONORS: Won Top Defenseman Trophy (1984-85). . . . Named to WHL (East) All-Star first team (1984-85). . . . Named NHL Rookie of the Year by THE SPORTING NEWS (1985-86). . . . Named to NHL All-Rookie team (1985-86). . . . Played in NHL All-Star Game (1986).

			REGULAR SEASON					PLAYOFFS			
Season Team	League	Gms.	G	A	Pts.	Pen.	Gms.	G	A	Pts.	Pen.
83-84—Saskatoon	WHL	72	23	45	68	225	—	—	—	—	—
84-85—Saskatoon	WHL	64	32	55	87	253	3	3	3	6	7
85-86—Toronto	NHL	66	34	11	45	227	10	5	1	6	47
86-87—Toronto	NHL	80	37	23	60	271	13	6	5	11	38
87-88—Toronto	NHL	28	12	11	23	80	—	—	—	—	—
88-89—Toronto	NHL	15	7	4	11	66	—	—	—	—	—
89-90—Toronto	NHL	38	18	8	26	116	5	1	1	2	19
90-91—Toronto	NHL	63	18	16	34	152	—	—	—	—	—
91-92—Toronto	NHL	43	19	21	40	123	—	—	—	—	—
92-93—Toronto	NHL	66	17	22	39	193	21	10	10	20	51
NHL totals		399	162	116	278	1228	49	22	17	39	155

CLEARY, JOSEPH
D, BLACKHAWKS

PERSONAL: Born January 17, 1970, at Buffalo, N.Y. . . . 6-0/204. . . . Shoots right. . . . Full name: Joseph Patrick Cleary.
HIGH SCHOOL: Cushing Academy (Ashburnham, Mass.).
COLLEGE: Boston College.

TRANSACTIONS/CAREER NOTES: Selected by Chicago Blackhawks in fifth round (fourth Blackhawks pick, 92nd overall) of NHL entry draft (June 11, 1988). . . . Suspended two games for fighting (December 8, 1990).

			REGULAR SEASON					PLAYOFFS			
Season Team	League	Gms.	G	A	Pts.	Pen.	Gms.	G	A	Pts.	Pen.
86-87—Cushing Academy	Mass. H.S.	...	15	30	45	...	—	—	—	—	—
87-88—Stratford Jr. B	OHA	41	20	37	57	160	—	—	—	—	—
88-89—Boston College	Hockey East	38	5	7	12	36	—	—	—	—	—
89-90—Boston College	Hockey East	42	5	21	26	56	—	—	—	—	—
90-91—Boston College	Hockey East	36	4	19	23	34	—	—	—	—	—
91-92—Boston College	Hockey East	29	5	20	25	66	—	—	—	—	—
92-93—Indianapolis	IHL	63	10	17	27	110	3	1	0	1	4

CLOUTIER, JACQUES
G, NORDIQUES

PERSONAL: Born January 3, 1960, at Noranda, Que. . . . 5-7/168. . . . Shoots left. . . . Name pronounced KLOO-chay.

TRANSACTIONS/CAREER NOTES: Selected by Buffalo Sabres as underage junior in third round (fourth Sabres pick, 55th overall) of NHL entry draft (August 9, 1979). . . . Suffered broken collarbone (January 1982). . . . Tore ligaments in knee (December 1984); missed remainder of season; spent the year as an assistant coach with Rochester. . . . Traded by Sabres to Chicago Blackhawks for future considerations; Steve Ludzik and draft pick later sent to Sabres to complete deal (September 1989). . . . Pulled groin (December 11, 1989); missed six games. . . . Strained left knee (March 25, 1990). . . . Traded by Blackhawks to Quebec Nordiques for LW Tony McKegney (January 29, 1991). . . . Sprained left ankle (December 16, 1992); missed 24 games.

HONORS: Won Jacques Plante Trophy (1978-79). . . . Named to QMJHL All-Star first team (1978-79).

			REGULAR SEASON						PLAYOFFS					
Season Team	League	Gms.	Min.	W	L	T	GA	SO	Avg.	Gms.	Min.	W	L	GA	SO	Avg.
76-77—Trois-Rivieres	QMJHL	24	1109	...	...	...	93	0	5.03	—	—	—	—	—	—	—
77-78—Trois-Rivieres	QMJHL	*71	*4134	...	...	...	240	*4	3.48	13	779	...	...	40	1	3.08
78-79—Trois-Rivieres	QMJHL	*72	*4168	...	...	...	218	†3	*3.14	13	780	...	...	36	0	2.77
79-80—Trois-Rivieres	QMJHL	55	3222	27	20	7	231	†2	4.30	7	420	3	4	33	0	4.71
80-81—Rochester	AHL	*61	*3478	27	27	6	*209	1	3.61	—	—	—	—	—	—	—
81-82—Rochester	AHL	23	1366	14	7	2	64	0	2.81	—	—	—	—	—	—	—
—Buffalo	NHL	7	311	5	1	0	13	0	2.51	—	—	—	—	—	—	—
82-83—Buffalo	NHL	25	1390	10	7	6	81	0	3.50	—	—	—	—	—	—	—
—Rochester	AHL	13	634	7	3	1	42	0	3.97	16	992	12	4	47	0	2.84
83-84—Rochester	AHL	*51	*2841	26	22	1	172	1	3.63	*18	*1145	9	9	*68	0	3.56
84-85—Rochester	AHL	14	803	10	2	1	36	0	2.69	—	—	—	—	—	—	—
—Buffalo	NHL	1	65	0	0	1	4	0	3.69	—	—	—	—	—	—	—
85-86—Rochester	AHL	14	835	10	2	2	38	1	2.73	—	—	—	—	—	—	—
—Buffalo	NHL	15	872	5	9	1	49	1	3.37	—	—	—	—	—	—	—
86-87—Buffalo	NHL	40	2167	11	19	5	137	0	3.79	—	—	—	—	—	—	—
87-88—Buffalo	NHL	20	851	4	8	2	67	0	4.72	—	—	—	—	—	—	—
88-89—Buffalo	NHL	36	1786	15	14	0	108	0	3.63	4	238	1	3	10	1	2.52
—Rochester	AHL	11	527	2	7	0	41	0	4.67	—	—	—	—	—	—	—

Season Team	League	REGULAR SEASON								PLAYOFFS						
		Gms.	Min.	W	L	T	GA	SO	Avg.	Gms.	Min.	W	L	GA	SO	Avg.
89-90—Chicago	NHL	43	2178	18	15	2	112	2	3.09	4	175	0	2	8	0	2.74
90-91—Chicago	NHL	10	403	2	3	0	24	0	3.57	—	—	—	—	—	—	—
—Quebec	NHL	15	829	3	8	2	61	0	4.41	—	—	—	—	—	—	—
91-92—Quebec	NHL	26	1345	6	14	3	88	0	3.93	—	—	—	—	—	—	—
92-93—Quebec	NHL	3	154	0	2	1	10	0	3.90	—	—	—	—	—	—	—
NHL totals		241	12351	79	100	23	754	3	3.66	8	413	1	5	18	1	2.62

CLOUTIER, SYLVAIN
C, RED WINGS

PERSONAL: Born February 13, 1974, at Mt. Laurier, Que. . . . 6-0/192. . . . Shoots left. . . . Name pronounced CLOO-chay.
HIGH SCHOOL: Bishop MacDonnell (Guelph, Ont.).
TRANSACTIONS/CAREER NOTES: Selected by Detroit Red Wings in third round (third Red Wings pick, 70th overall) of NHL entry draft (June 20, 1992).

Season Team	League	REGULAR SEASON					PLAYOFFS				
		Gms.	G	A	Pts.	Pen.	Gms.	G	A	Pts.	Pen.
91-92—Guelph	OHL	62	35	31	66	74	—	—	—	—	—
92-93—Guelph	OHL	44	26	29	55	78	5	0	5	5	14

COFFEY, PAUL
D, RED WINGS

PERSONAL: Born June 1, 1961, at Weston, Ont. . . . 6-0/200. . . . Shoots left. . . . Full name: Paul Douglas Coffey.
TRANSACTIONS/CAREER NOTES: Selected by Edmonton Oilers in first round (first Oilers pick, sixth overall) of NHL entry draft (June 11, 1980). . . . Suffered recurring back spasms (December 1986); missed 10 games. . . . Traded by Oilers with LW Dave Hunter and RW Wayne Van Dorp to Pittsburgh Penguins for C Craig Simpson, C Dave Hannan, D Moe Mantha and D Chris Joseph (November 24, 1987). . . . Tore knee cartilage (December 1987). . . . Bruised right shoulder (November 16, 1988). . . . Broke finger (May 1990). . . . Injured back (February 27, 1991). . . . Injured hip muscle (March 9, 1991). . . . Scratched left eye cornea (April 9, 1991). . . . Broke jaw (April 1991). . . . Pulled hip muscle (February 3, 1992); missed three games. . . . Traded by Penguins to Los Angeles Kings for D Brian Benning, D Jeff Chychrun and first-round pick in 1992 draft (LW Jason Bowen) (February 19, 1992). . . . Suffered back spasms (March 3, 1992); missed three games. . . . Fractured wrist (March 17, 1992); missed five games. . . . Traded by Kings with RW Jim Hiller and C/LW Sylain Couturier to Detroit Red Wings for C Jimmy Carson, RW Marc Potvin and C Gary Shuchuk (January 29, 1993). . . . Injured groin (March 18, 1993); missed one game.
HONORS: Named to OMJHL All-Star second team (1979-80). . . . Named to NHL All-Star second team (1980-81 through 1983-84 and 1989-90). . . . Named to THE SPORTING NEWS All-Star second team (1981-82 through 1983-84, 1986-87 and 1989-90). . . . Played in NHL All-Star Game (1982 through 1986 and 1988 through 1993). . . . Won James Norris Memorial Trophy (1984-85 and 1985-86). . . . Named to THE SPORTING NEWS All-Star first team (1984-85, 1985-86 and 1988-89). . . . Named to NHL All-Star first team (1984-85, 1985-86 and 1988-89).
RECORDS: Holds NHL career records for most goals by a defenseman—330; most assists by a defenseman—871; and most points by a defenseman—1,201. . . . Holds NHL single-season record for most goals by a defenseman—48 (1985-86). . . . Shares NHL single-game record for most points by a defenseman—8; and most assists by a defenseman—6 (March 14, 1986). . . . Holds NHL record for most consecutive games scoring points by a defenseman—28 (1985-86). . . . Holds NHL single-season playoff records for most goals by a defenseman—12; assists by a defenseman—25; and points by a defenseman—37 (1985). . . . Holds NHL single-game playoff record for most points by a defenseman—6 (May 14, 1985).
MISCELLANEOUS: Member of Stanley Cup championship teams (1984, 1985, 1987 and 1991).

Season Team	League	REGULAR SEASON					PLAYOFFS				
		Gms.	G	A	Pts.	Pen.	Gms.	G	A	Pts.	Pen.
77-78—Kingston	OMJHL	8	2	2	4	11	—	—	—	—	—
—North York	MTHL	50	14	33	47	64	—	—	—	—	—
78-79—Sault Ste. Marie	OMJHL	68	17	72	89	99	—	—	—	—	—
79-80—Sault Ste. Marie	OMJHL	23	10	21	31	63	—	—	—	—	—
—Kitchener	OMJHL	52	19	52	71	130	—	—	—	—	—
80-81—Edmonton	NHL	74	9	23	32	130	9	4	3	7	22
81-82—Edmonton	NHL	80	29	60	89	106	5	1	1	2	6
82-83—Edmonton	NHL	80	29	67	96	87	16	7	7	14	14
83-84—Edmonton	NHL	80	40	86	126	104	19	8	14	22	21
84-85—Edmonton	NHL	80	37	84	121	97	18	12	25	37	44
85-86—Edmonton	NHL	79	48	90	138	120	10	1	9	10	30
86-87—Edmonton	NHL	59	17	50	67	49	17	3	8	11	30
87-88—Pittsburgh	NHL	46	15	52	67	93	—	—	—	—	—
88-89—Pittsburgh	NHL	75	30	83	113	193	11	2	13	15	31
89-90—Pittsburgh	NHL	80	29	74	103	95	—	—	—	—	—
90-91—Pittsburgh	NHL	76	24	69	93	128	12	2	9	11	6
91-92—Pittsburgh	NHL	54	10	54	64	62	—	—	—	—	—
—Los Angeles	NHL	10	1	4	5	25	6	4	3	7	2
92-93—Los Angeles	NHL	50	8	49	57	50	—	—	—	—	—
—Detroit	NHL	30	4	26	30	27	7	2	9	11	2
NHL totals		953	330	871	1201	1366	130	46	101	147	208

COLE, DANTON
RW, LIGHTNING

PERSONAL: Born January 10, 1967, at Pontiac, Mich. . . . 5-11/185. . . . Shoots right. . . . Full name: Danton Edward Cole.
COLLEGE: Michigan State.
TRANSACTIONS/CAREER NOTES: Selected by Winnipeg Jets in sixth round (sixth Jets pick, 123rd overall) of NHL entry draft (June 15, 1985). . . . Strained knee (January 26, 1992); missed 11 games. . . . Traded by Jets

C

to Tampa Bay Lightning for future considerations (June 19, 1992).... Tore ligament in left knee (December 15, 1992); missed 10 games.

Season Team	League	REGULAR SEASON					PLAYOFFS				
		Gms.	G	A	Pts.	Pen.	Gms.	G	A	Pts.	Pen.
84-85—Aurora	OHA	41	51	44	95	91	—	—	—	—	—
85-86—Michigan State	CCHA	43	11	10	21	22	—	—	—	—	—
86-87—Michigan State	CCHA	44	9	15	24	16	—	—	—	—	—
87-88—Michigan State	CCHA	46	20	36	56	38	—	—	—	—	—
88-89—Michigan State	CCHA	47	29	33	62	46	—	—	—	—	—
89-90—Winnipeg	NHL	2	1	1	2	0	—	—	—	—	—
—Moncton	AHL	80	31	42	73	18	—	—	—	—	—
90-91—Winnipeg	NHL	66	13	11	24	24	—	—	—	—	—
—Moncton	AHL	3	1	1	2	0	—	—	—	—	—
91-92—Winnipeg	NHL	52	7	5	12	32	—	—	—	—	—
92-93—Tampa Bay	NHL	67	12	15	27	23	—	—	—	—	—
—Atlanta	IHL	1	1	0	1	2	—	—	—	—	—
NHL totals		187	33	32	65	79					

COLEMAN, JONATHAN

D, RED WINGS

PERSONAL: Born March 9, 1975, at Boston, Mass.... 6-2/195.... Shoots left.
HIGH SCHOOL: Phillips Academy (Andover, Mass.).
TRANSACTIONS/CAREER NOTES: Selected by Detroit Red Wings in second round (second Red Wings pick, 48th overall) of NHL entry draft (June 26, 1993).

Season Team	League	REGULAR SEASON					PLAYOFFS				
		Gms.	G	A	Pts.	Pen.	Gms.	G	A	Pts.	Pen.
89-90—Phillips Andover Acad.	Mass. H.S.	24	8	20	28	10	—	—	—	—	—
90-91—Phillips Andover Acad.	Mass. H.S.	24	11	25	36	18	—	—	—	—	—
91-92—Phillips Andover Acad.	Mass. H.S.	24	12	29	41	26	—	—	—	—	—
92-93—Phillips Andover Acad.	Mass. H.S.	23	14	33	47	72	—	—	—	—	—

COLMAN, MICHAEL

D, SHARKS

PERSONAL: Born August 4, 1968, at Stoneham, Mass.... 6-3/218.... Shoots right.
COLLEGE: Ferris State (Mich.).
TRANSACTIONS/CAREER NOTES: Signed as free agent by San Jose Sharks (September 3, 1991).

Season Team	League	REGULAR SEASON					PLAYOFFS				
		Gms.	G	A	Pts.	Pen.	Gms.	G	A	Pts.	Pen.
87-88—Humboldt	SJHL	55	3	7	10	188	—	—	—	—	—
88-89—Humboldt	SJHL	64	3	17	20	161	—	—	—	—	—
89-90—Ferris State	CCHA	23	0	4	4	62	—	—	—	—	—
90-91—Kansas City	IHL	66	1	6	7	115	—	—	—	—	—
91-92—Kansas City	IHL	59	0	4	4	130	3	0	0	0	4
—San Jose	NHL	15	0	1	1	32	—	—	—	—	—
92-93—Kansas City	IHL	80	1	5	6	191	12	1	0	1	34
NHL totals		15	0	1	1	32					

CONACHER, PAT

LW/C, KINGS

PERSONAL: Born May 1, 1959, at Edmonton, Alta.... 5-8/190.... Shoots left.... Full name: Patrick John Conacher.... Name pronounced KON-a-KER.
TRANSACTIONS/CAREER NOTES: Selected by New York Rangers in fourth round (third Rangers pick, 76th overall) of NHL entry draft (August 9, 1979).... Fractured left ankle (September 21, 1980).... Injured shoulder (November 1982).... Signed as free agent by Edmonton Oilers (October 4, 1983).... Injured groin (December 1984).... Signed as free agent by New Jersey Devils (August 14, 1985).... Sprained back (February 1988).... Bruised left shoulder (December 1988).... Underwent major reconstructive surgery to left shoulder (April 7, 1989). ... Lacerated face and lost two teeth (October 13, 1989).... Sprained left knee (April 9, 1990).... Strained left knee (September 22, 1990).... Suffered ulcer problems (February 1991).... Injured groin (October 24, 1991); missed two games. ... Injured groin (December 1991).... Underwent hernia surgery (January 9, 1992); missed 34 games.... Traded by Devils to Los Angeles Kings for future considerations (September 3, 1992).
MISCELLANEOUS: Member of Stanley Cup championship team (1984).

Season Team	League	REGULAR SEASON					PLAYOFFS				
		Gms.	G	A	Pts.	Pen.	Gms.	G	A	Pts.	Pen.
77-78—Billings	WCHL	72	31	44	75	105	20	15	14	29	22
78-79—Billings	WHL	39	25	37	62	50	—	—	—	—	—
—Saskatoon	WHL	33	15	32	47	37	—	—	—	—	—
79-80—New York Rangers	NHL	17	0	5	5	4	3	0	1	1	2
—New Haven	AHL	53	11	14	25	43	7	1	1	2	4
80-81—New York Rangers	NHL			Did not play—injured.							
81-82—Springfield	AHL	77	23	22	45	38	—	—	—	—	—
82-83—Tulsa	CHL	63	29	28	57	44	—	—	—	—	—
—New York Rangers	NHL	5	0	1	1	4	—	—	—	—	—
83-84—Moncton	AHL	28	7	16	23	30	—	—	—	—	—
—Edmonton	NHL	45	2	8	10	31	3	1	0	1	2
84-85—Nova Scotia	AHL	68	20	45	65	44	6	3	2	5	0
85-86—New Jersey	NHL	2	0	2	2	2	—	—	—	—	—
—Maine	AHL	69	15	30	45	83	5	1	1	2	11

Season Team	League	REGULAR SEASON					PLAYOFFS				
		Gms.	G	A	Pts.	Pen.	Gms.	G	A	Pts.	Pen.
86-87—Maine	AHL	56	12	14	26	47	—	—	—	—	—
87-88—Utica	AHL	47	14	33	47	32	—	—	—	—	—
—New Jersey	NHL	24	2	5	7	12	17	2	2	4	14
88-89—New Jersey	NHL	55	7	5	12	14	—	—	—	—	—
89-90—Utica	AHL	57	13	36	49	53	—	—	—	—	—
—New Jersey	NHL	19	3	3	6	4	5	1	0	1	10
90-91—Utica	AHL	4	0	1	1	6	—	—	—	—	—
—New Jersey	NHL	49	5	11	16	27	7	0	2	2	2
91-92—New Jersey	NHL	44	7	3	10	16	7	1	1	2	4
92-93—Los Angeles	NHL	81	9	8	17	20	24	6	4	10	6
NHL totals		341	35	51	86	134	66	11	10	21	40

CONN, ROB
LW/RW, 'HAWKS

PERSONAL: Born September 3, 1968, at Calgary, Alta. . . . 6-2/200. . . . Shoots right. . . . Full name: Robert Phillip Conn.
COLLEGE: Alaska-Anchorage.
TRANSACTIONS/CAREER NOTES: Signed as free agent by Chicago Blackhawks (July 31, 1991).

Season Team	League	REGULAR SEASON					PLAYOFFS				
		Gms.	G	A	Pts.	Pen.	Gms.	G	A	Pts.	Pen.
88-89—Alaska-Anchorage	Indep.	33	21	17	38	46	—	—	—	—	—
89-90—Alaska-Anchorage	Indep.	34	27	21	48	46	—	—	—	—	—
90-91—Alaska-Anchorage	Indep.	43	28	32	60	53	—	—	—	—	—
91-92—Indianapolis	IHL	72	19	16	35	100	—	—	—	—	—
—Chicago	NHL	2	0	0	0	2	—	—	—	—	—
92-93—Indianapolis	IHL	75	13	14	27	81	5	0	1	1	6
NHL totals		2	0	0	0	2					

CONNOLLY, JEFF
C, CANUCKS

PERSONAL: Born February 1, 1974, at Worcester, Mass. . . . 6-0/185. . . . Shoots right.
HIGH SCHOOL: Milton (Mass.) Academy, then St. Sebastian's Country Day School (Needham, Mass.).
TRANSACTIONS/CAREER NOTES: Selected by Vancouver Canucks in third round (fourth Canucks pick, 69th overall) of NHL entry draft (June 20, 1992).

Season Team	League	REGULAR SEASON					PLAYOFFS				
		Gms.	G	A	Pts.	Pen.	Gms.	G	A	Pts.	Pen.
89-90—Milton Academy	Mass. H.S.	21	14	18	32	...	—	—	—	—	—
90-91—Milton Academy	Mass. H.S.	23	28	19	47	...	—	—	—	—	—
91-92—St. Sebastian's	Mass. H.S.	28	31	35	66	...	—	—	—	—	—
92-93—St. Sebastian's	Mass. H.S.	24	17	34	51	...	—	—	—	—	—

CONROY, AL
LW, FLYERS

PERSONAL: Born January 17, 1966, at Calgary, Alta. . . . 5-8/170. . . . Shoots right.
TRANSACTIONS/CAREER NOTES: Signed as free agent by Detroit Red Wings (August 1989). . . . Signed as free agent by Philadelphia Flyers (August 21, 1991).
HONORS: Named to WHL (East) All-Star first team (1985-86).

Season Team	League	REGULAR SEASON					PLAYOFFS				
		Gms.	G	A	Pts.	Pen.	Gms.	G	A	Pts.	Pen.
86-87—Rapperswill	Switzerland	...	30	32	62	...	—	—	—	—	—
—Rochester	AHL	13	4	4	8	40	13	1	3	4	50
87-88—Varese	Italy	36	25	39	64	...	—	—	—	—	—
—Adirondack	AHL	13	5	8	13	20	11	1	3	4	41
88-89—Dortmund	Germany	46	53	78	131	...	—	—	—	—	—
89-90—Adirondack	AHL	77	23	33	56	147	5	0	0	0	20
90-91—Adirondack	AHL	80	26	39	65	172	2	1	1	2	0
91-92—Hershey	AHL	47	17	28	45	90	6	4	2	6	12
—Philadelphia	NHL	31	2	9	11	74	—	—	—	—	—
92-93—Hershey	AHL	60	28	32	60	130	—	—	—	—	—
—Philadelphia	NHL	21	3	2	5	17	—	—	—	—	—
NHL totals		52	5	11	16	91					

CONVERY, BRANDON
C, MAPLE LEAFS

PERSONAL: Born February 4, 1974, at Kingston, Ont. . . . 6-1/180. . . . Shoots right.
HIGH SCHOOL: Lasalle Secondary School (Sudbury, Ont.).
TRANSACTIONS/CAREER NOTES: Selected by Toronto Maple Leafs in first round (first Maple Leafs pick, eighth overall) of NHL entry draft (June 20, 1992).
HONORS: Won OHL Top Prospect Award (1991-92).

Season Team	League	REGULAR SEASON					PLAYOFFS				
		Gms.	G	A	Pts.	Pen.	Gms.	G	A	Pts.	Pen.
89-90—Kingston Jr. B	OHA	42	13	25	38	4	—	—	—	—	—
90-91—Sudbury	OHL	56	26	22	48	18	5	1	1	2	2
91-92—Sudbury	OHL	44	40	27	67	44	5	3	2	5	4
92-93—Niagara Falls	OHL	51	38	39	77	24	4	1	3	4	4
—Sudbury	OHL	7	7	9	16	6	—	—	—	—	—
—St. John's	AHL	3	0	0	0	0	5	0	1	1	0

C

COOKE, JAMIE
RW, FLYERS

PERSONAL: Born November 5, 1968, at Bramalea, Ont. . . . 6-2/206. . . . Shoots right. . . . Full name: Jamie William Cooke.
COLLEGE: Colgate.
TRANSACTIONS/CAREER NOTES: Selected by Philadelphia Flyers in seventh round (eighth Flyers pick, 140th overall) of NHL entry draft (June 11, 1988).

			REGULAR SEASON					PLAYOFFS				
Season	Team	League	Gms.	G	A	Pts.	Pen.	Gms.	G	A	Pts.	Pen.
86-87—Bramalea Jr. B		OHA	37	21	28	49	46	—	—	—	—	—
87-88—Bramalea Jr. B		OHA	37	26	44	70	56	—	—	—	—	—
88-89—Colgate University		ECAC	28	13	11	24	26	—	—	—	—	—
89-90—Colgate University		ECAC	38	16	20	36	24	—	—	—	—	—
90-91—Colgate University		ECAC	32	28	26	54	22	—	—	—	—	—
91-92—Hershey		AHL	66	15	26	41	49	—	—	—	—	—
92-93—Hershey		AHL	36	11	7	18	12	—	—	—	—	—

COOPER, DAVID
D, SABRES

PERSONAL: Born November 2, 1973, at Ottawa. . . . 6-1/190. . . . Shoots left.
HIGH SCHOOL: Medicine Hat (Alta.).
TRANSACTIONS/CAREER NOTES: Selected by Buffalo Sabres in first round (first Sabres pick, 11th overall) of NHL entry draft (June 20, 1992).
HONORS: Won WHL Top Prospect Award (1991-92). . . . Named to WHL (East) All-Star first team (1991-92).

			REGULAR SEASON					PLAYOFFS				
Season	Team	League	Gms.	G	A	Pts.	Pen.	Gms.	G	A	Pts.	Pen.
89-90—Medicine Hat		WHL	61	4	11	15	65	3	0	2	2	2
90-91—Medicine Hat		WHL	64	12	31	43	66	11	1	3	4	23
91-92—Medicine Hat		WHL	72	17	47	64	176	4	1	4	5	8
92-93—Medicine Hat		WHL	63	15	50	65	88	10	2	2	4	32

COPELAND, TODD
D, DEVILS

PERSONAL: Born May 18, 1968, at Ridgewood, N.J. . . . 6-2/210. . . . Shoots left. . . . Full name: John Todd Copeland.
HIGH SCHOOL: Belmont (Mass.) Hill.
COLLEGE: Michigan.
TRANSACTIONS/CAREER NOTES: Injured knee (February 1986). . . . Selected by New Jersey Devils in second round (second Devils pick, 24th overall) of NHL entry draft (June 21, 1986).

			REGULAR SEASON					PLAYOFFS				
Season	Team	League	Gms.	G	A	Pts.	Pen.	Gms.	G	A	Pts.	Pen.
84-85—Belmont Hill H.S.		Mass. H.S.	23	8	25	33	18	—	—	—	—	—
85-86—Belmont Hill H.S.		Mass. H.S.	19	4	19	23	19	—	—	—	—	—
86-87—University of Michigan		CCHA	34	2	10	12	57	—	—	—	—	—
87-88—University of Michigan		CCHA	41	3	10	13	58	—	—	—	—	—
88-89—University of Michigan		CCHA	39	5	14	19	102	—	—	—	—	—
89-90—University of Michigan		CCHA	34	6	16	22	62	—	—	—	—	—
90-91—Utica		AHL	79	6	24	30	53	—	—	—	—	—
91-92—Utica		AHL	80	4	23	27	96	4	2	2	4	2
92-93—Utica		AHL	16	3	2	5	10	—	—	—	—	—
—Cincinnati		IHL	37	0	3	3	47	—	—	—	—	—
—Moncton		AHL	16	1	4	5	16	5	1	3	4	2

CORBET, RENE
LW, NORDIQUES

PERSONAL: Born June 25, 1973, at Victoriaville, Que. . . . 6-0/176. . . . Shoots left.
TRANSACTIONS/CAREER NOTES: Selected by Quebec Nordiques in second round (second Nordiques pick, 24th overall) of NHL entry draft (June 22, 1991).
HONORS: Won Michel Bergeron Trophy (1990-91). . . . Named to QMJHL All-Rookie team (1990-91). . . . Won Jean Beliveau Trophy (1992-93). . . . Named to Can.HL All-Star first team (1992-93). . . . Named to QMJHL All-Star first team (1992-93).

			REGULAR SEASON					PLAYOFFS				
Season	Team	League	Gms.	G	A	Pts.	Pen.	Gms.	G	A	Pts.	Pen.
90-91—Drummondville		QMJHL	45	25	40	65	34	14	11	6	17	15
91-92—Drummondville		QMJHL	56	46	50	96	90	4	1	2	3	17
92-93—Drummondville		QMJHL	63	*79	69	*148	143	10	7	13	20	16

CORKUM, BOB
C/RW, MIGHTY DUCKS

PERSONAL: Born December 18, 1967, at Salisbury, Mass. . . . 6-2/212. . . . Shoots right. . . . Full name: Robert Freeman Corkum.
HIGH SCHOOL: Triton Regional (Byfield, Mass.).
COLLEGE: Maine.
TRANSACTIONS/CAREER NOTES: Selected by Buffalo Sabres in third round (third Sabres pick, 47th overall) of NHL entry draft (June 21, 1986). . . . Injured hip (March 19, 1992). . . . Selected by Mighty Ducks of Anaheim in NHL expansion draft (June 24, 1993).

			REGULAR SEASON					PLAYOFFS				
Season	Team	League	Gms.	G	A	Pts.	Pen.	Gms.	G	A	Pts.	Pen.
84-85—Triton Regional H.S.		Mass. H.S.	18	35	36	71	. . .	—	—	—	—	—
85-86—University of Maine		Hockey East	39	7	16	23	53	—	—	—	—	—
86-87—University of Maine		Hockey East	35	18	11	29	24	—	—	—	—	—
87-88—University of Maine		Hockey East	40	14	18	32	64	—	—	—	—	—

			REGULAR SEASON					PLAYOFFS				
88-89—University of Maine		Hockey East	45	17	31	48	64	—	—	—	—	—
89-90—Rochester		AHL	43	8	11	19	45	12	2	5	7	16
—Buffalo		NHL	8	2	0	2	4	5	1	0	1	4
90-91—Rochester		AHL	69	13	21	34	77	15	4	4	8	4
91-92—Rochester		AHL	52	16	12	28	47	8	0	6	6	8
—Buffalo		NHL	20	2	4	6	21	4	1	0	1	0
92-93—Buffalo		NHL	68	6	4	10	38	5	0	0	0	2
NHL totals			96	10	8	18	63	14	2	0	2	6

CORPSE, KELI

C, CANADIENS

PERSONAL: Born May 14, 1974, at London, Ont. . . . 5-11/174. . . . Shoots left.
HIGH SCHOOL: Loyalist Collegiate (Kingston, Ont.).
TRANSACTIONS/CAREER NOTES: Selected by Montreal Canadiens in second round (third Canadiens pick, 44th overall) of NHL entry draft (June 20, 1992).

Season	Team	League	REGULAR SEASON					PLAYOFFS				
			Gms.	G	A	Pts.	Pen.	Gms.	G	A	Pts.	Pen.
89-90—London Jr. B		OHA	39	26	31	57	10	—	—	—	—	—
90-91—Kingston		OHL	58	18	33	51	34	—	—	—	—	—
91-92—Kingston		OHL	65	31	52	83	20	—	—	—	—	—
92-93—Kingston		OHL	54	32	75	107	45	16	9	20	29	10
—Canadian national team		Int'l	1	0	0	0	2	—	—	—	—	—

CORRIVEAU, RICK

D, CAPITALS

PERSONAL: Born January 6, 1971, at Welland, Ont. . . . 6-0/208. . . . Shoots left. . . . Full name: Rick Claude Corriveau. . . . Brother of Yvon Corriveau, left winger, Hartford Whalers.
TRANSACTIONS/CAREER NOTES: Injured right knee ligaments (November 6, 1988). . . . Selected by St. Louis Blues in second round (second Blues pick, 31st overall) of NHL entry draft (June 17, 1989). . . . Returned to the draft pool by Blues and selected by Washington Capitals in eighth round (eighth Capitals pick, 168th overall) of entry draft (June 22, 1991).
HONORS: Won Emms Family Award (1987-88).

Season	Team	League	REGULAR SEASON					PLAYOFFS				
			Gms.	G	A	Pts.	Pen.	Gms.	G	A	Pts.	Pen.
86-87—Welland Jr. B		OHA	29	9	17	26	90	—	—	—	—	—
87-88—London		OHL	63	19	47	66	51	12	4	10	14	18
88-89—London		OHL	12	4	10	14	23	1	0	0	0	0
89-90—London		OHL	63	22	55	77	63	6	4	3	7	12
90-91—London		OHL	64	27	60	87	83	7	3	7	10	16
91-92—London		OHL	4	0	7	7	6	—	—	—	—	—
—Niagara Falls		OHL	54	21	57	78	72	17	5	16	21	36
92-93—Toledo		ECHL	63	11	44	55	113	12	4	11	15	23

CORRIVEAU, YVON

LW, WHALERS

PERSONAL: Born February 8, 1967, at Welland, Ont. . . . 6-1/195. . . . Shoots left. . . . Brother of Rick Corriveau, defenseman in Washington Capitals system.
TRANSACTIONS/CAREER NOTES: Injured shoulder (March 1985). . . . Selected by Washington Capitals as underage junior in first round (first Capitals pick, 19th overall) of NHL entry draft (June 15, 1985). . . . Bruised thigh (November 1988). . . . Traded by Capitals to Hartford Whalers for G Mike Liut (March 5, 1990). . . . Bruised foot (October 1990). . . . Traded by Whalers to Washington Capitals (August 20, 1992) to complete deal in which Whalers sent RW Mark Hunter to Capitals for LW Nick Kypreos (June 15, 1992). . . . Selected by San Jose Sharks in NHL waiver draft (October 4, 1992). . . . Suffered back strain (October 26, 1992); missed 11 games. . . . Suffered back strain (November 21, 1992); missed 16 games. . . . Traded by Sharks to Hartford Whalers (January 21, 1993) to complete deal in which Whalers sent LW Michel Picard to Sharks for future considerations (October 9, 1992).

Season	Team	League	REGULAR SEASON					PLAYOFFS				
			Gms.	G	A	Pts.	Pen.	Gms.	G	A	Pts.	Pen.
83-84—Welland Jr. B		OHA	36	16	21	37	51	—	—	—	—	—
84-85—Toronto		OHL	59	23	28	51	65	3	0	0	0	5
85-86—Toronto		OHL	59	54	36	90	75	4	1	1	2	0
—Washington		NHL	2	0	0	0	0	4	0	3	3	2
86-87—Toronto		OHL	23	14	19	33	23	—	—	—	—	—
—Binghamton		AHL	7	0	0	0	2	8	0	1	1	0
—Washington		NHL	17	1	1	2	24	—	—	—	—	—
87-88—Binghamton		AHL	35	15	14	29	64	—	—	—	—	—
—Washington		NHL	44	10	9	19	84	13	1	2	3	30
88-89—Baltimore		AHL	33	16	23	39	65	—	—	—	—	—
—Washington		NHL	33	3	2	5	62	1	0	0	0	0
89-90—Washington		NHL	50	9	6	15	50	—	—	—	—	—
—Hartford		NHL	13	4	1	5	22	4	1	0	1	0
90-91—Hartford		NHL	23	1	1	2	18	—	—	—	—	—
—Springfield		AHL	44	17	25	42	10	18	†10	6	16	31
91-92—Hartford		NHL	38	12	8	20	36	7	3	2	5	18
—Springfield		AHL	39	26	15	41	40	—	—	—	—	—
92-93—San Jose		NHL	20	3	7	10	40	—	—	—	—	—
—Hartford		NHL	37	5	5	10	14	—	—	—	—	—
NHL totals			277	48	40	88	310	29	5	7	12	50

CORSON, SHAYNE
LW/C, OILERS

PERSONAL: Born August 13, 1966, at Barrie, Ont.... 6-1/200.... Shoots left.
TRANSACTIONS/CAREER NOTES: Selected by Montreal Canadiens in first round (second Canadiens pick, eighth overall) of NHL entry draft (June 9, 1984).... Broke jaw (January 24, 1987).... Strained ligament in right knee (September 1987).... Injured groin (March 1988).... Injured knee (April 1988).... Injured knee (April 1989).... Bruised left shoulder (October 29, 1989).... Broke toe on right foot (December 1989).... Suffered hip pointer (November 10, 1990); missed seven games.... Pulled groin (February 11, 1991).... Traded by Canadiens with LW Vladimir Vujtek and C Brent Gilchrist to Edmonton Oilers for LW Vincent Damphousse and fourth-round pick (D Adam Wiesel) in 1993 draft (August 27, 1992).
HONORS: Played in NHL All-Star Game (1990).

			REGULAR SEASON					PLAYOFFS			
Season Team	League	Gms.	G	A	Pts.	Pen.	Gms.	G	A	Pts.	Pen.
82-83—Barrie	COJHL	23	13	29	42	87	—	—	—	—	—
83-84—Brantford	OHL	66	25	46	71	165	6	4	1	5	26
84-85—Hamilton	OHL	54	27	63	90	154	11	3	7	10	19
85-86—Hamilton	OHL	47	41	57	98	153	—	—	—	—	—
—Montreal	NHL	3	0	0	0	2	—	—	—	—	—
86-87—Montreal	NHL	55	12	11	23	144	17	6	5	11	30
87-88—Montreal	NHL	71	12	27	39	152	3	1	0	1	12
88-89—Montreal	NHL	80	26	24	50	193	21	4	5	9	65
89-90—Montreal	NHL	76	31	44	75	144	11	2	8	10	20
90-91—Montreal	NHL	71	23	24	47	138	13	9	6	15	36
91-92—Montreal	NHL	64	17	36	53	118	10	2	5	7	15
92-93—Edmonton	NHL	80	16	31	47	209	—	—	—	—	—
NHL totals		500	137	197	334	1100	75	24	29	53	178

COTE, ALAIN
D, LIGHTNING

PERSONAL: Born April 14, 1967, at Montmagny, Que.... 6-0/200.... Shoots right.... Full name: Alain Gabriel Cote.... Name pronounced al-LAI koh-TAY.... Brother of Sylvain Cote, defenseman, Washington Capitals.
TRANSACTIONS/CAREER NOTES: Selected by Boston Bruins as underage junior in second round (first Bruins pick, 31st overall) of NHL entry draft (June 15, 1985).... Traded by Bruins to Washington Capitals for RW Bobby Gould (September 27, 1989).... Traded by Capitals to Montreal Canadiens for D Marc Deschamps (June 23, 1990).... Injured eye (March 30, 1991).... Traded by Canadiens with D Eric Charron and future considerations to Tampa Bay Lightning for D Rob Ramage (March 20, 1993); Canadiens sent D Donald Dufresne to Lightning to complete deal (June 18, 1993).

			REGULAR SEASON					PLAYOFFS			
Season Team	League	Gms.	G	A	Pts.	Pen.	Gms.	G	A	Pts.	Pen.
83-84—Quebec	QMJHL	60	3	17	20	40	—	—	—	—	—
84-85—Quebec	QMJHL	68	9	25	34	173	—	—	—	—	—
85-86—Granby	QMJHL	22	4	12	16	48	—	—	—	—	—
—Moncton	AHL	3	0	0	0	0	—	—	—	—	—
—Boston	NHL	32	0	6	6	14	—	—	—	—	—
86-87—Granby	QMJHL	43	7	24	31	185	4	0	3	3	2
—Boston	NHL	3	0	0	0	0	—	—	—	—	—
87-88—Boston	NHL	2	0	0	0	0	—	—	—	—	—
—Maine	AHL	69	9	34	43	108	9	2	4	6	19
88-89—Maine	AHL	37	5	16	21	111	—	—	—	—	—
—Boston	NHL	31	2	3	5	51	—	—	—	—	—
89-90—Washington	NHL	2	0	0	0	7	—	—	—	—	—
—Baltimore	AHL	57	5	19	24	161	3	0	0	0	9
90-91—Montreal	NHL	28	0	6	6	26	11	0	2	2	26
—Fredericton	AHL	49	8	19	27	110	—	—	—	—	—
91-92—Montreal	NHL	13	0	3	3	22	—	—	—	—	—
—Fredericton	AHL	20	1	10	11	24	7	0	1	1	4
92-93—Fredericton	AHL	61	10	17	27	83	—	—	—	—	—
—Tampa Bay	NHL	2	0	0	0	0	—	—	—	—	—
—Atlanta	IHL	8	1	0	1	0	1	0	0	0	0
NHL totals		113	2	18	20	120	11	0	2	2	26

COTE, SYLVAIN
D, CAPITALS

PERSONAL: Born January 19, 1966, at Quebec City.... 6-0/190.... Shoots right.... Name pronounced KOH-tay.... Brother of Alain Cote, defenseman, Tampa Bay Lightning.
TRANSACTIONS/CAREER NOTES: Selected by Hartford Whalers as underage junior in first round (first Whalers pick, 11th overall) of NHL entry draft (June 9, 1984).... Broke toe on left foot (October 28, 1989).... Sprained left knee (December 1989).... Fractured right foot (January 22, 1990).... Traded by Whalers to Washington Capitals for second-round pick in 1992 draft (LW Andrei Nikolishin) (September 8, 1991).... Broke wrist (September 25, 1992); missed six games.... Suffered hip pointer (January 7, 1993); missed one game.
HONORS: Named to QMJHL All-Star second team (1983-84).... Won Emile (Butch) Bouchard Trophy (1985-86).... Shared Guy Lafleur Trophy with Luc Robitaille (1985-86).... Named to QMJHL All-Star first team (1985-86).

			REGULAR SEASON					PLAYOFFS			
Season Team	League	Gms.	G	A	Pts.	Pen.	Gms.	G	A	Pts.	Pen.
82-83—Quebec	QMJHL	66	10	24	34	50	—	—	—	—	—
83-84—Quebec	QMJHL	66	15	50	65	89	5	1	1	2	0
84-85—Hartford	NHL	67	3	9	12	17	—	—	—	—	—
85-86—Hartford	NHL	2	0	0	0	0	—	—	—	—	—
—Hull	QMJHL	26	10	33	43	14	13	6	*28	34	22

Season Team	League	REGULAR SEASON					PLAYOFFS				
		Gms.	G	A	Pts.	Pen.	Gms.	G	A	Pts.	Pen.
86-87—Binghamton	AHL	12	2	4	6	0	—	—	—	—	—
—Hartford	NHL	67	2	8	10	20	2	0	2	2	0
87-88—Hartford	NHL	67	7	21	28	30	6	1	1	2	4
88-89—Hartford	NHL	78	8	9	17	49	3	0	1	1	4
89-90—Hartford	NHL	28	4	2	6	14	5	0	0	0	0
90-91—Hartford	NHL	73	7	12	19	17	6	0	2	2	2
91-92—Washington	NHL	78	11	29	40	31	7	1	2	3	4
92-93—Washington	NHL	77	21	29	50	34	6	1	1	2	4
NHL totals		537	63	119	182	212	35	3	9	12	18

COURTENAY, ED
RW, SHARKS

PERSONAL: Born February 2, 1968, at Verdun, Que.... 6-4/200.... Shoots right.
TRANSACTIONS/CAREER NOTES: Signed as free agent by Minnesota North Stars (October 1, 1989).... Selected by San Jose Sharks in NHL dispersal draft (May 30, 1991).... Injured wrist (October 18, 1991); missed four games.... Injured back prior to 1992-93 season; missed first two games of season.... Sprained shoulder (October 23, 1992); missed four games.

Season Team	League	REGULAR SEASON					PLAYOFFS				
		Gms.	G	A	Pts.	Pen.	Gms.	G	A	Pts.	Pen.
87-88—Granby	QMJHL	54	37	34	71	19	5	1	1	2	2
88-89—Granby	QMJHL	68	59	55	114	68	4	1	1	2	22
—Kalamazoo	IHL	1	0	0	0	0	1	0	0	0	2
89-90—Kalamazoo	IHL	57	25	28	53	16	3	0	0	0	0
90-91—Kalamazoo	IHL	76	35	36	71	37	8	2	3	5	12
91-92—Kansas City	IHL	36	14	12	26	46	15	8	9	17	15
—San Jose	NHL	5	0	0	0	0	—	—	—	—	—
92-93—San Jose	NHL	39	7	13	20	10	—	—	—	—	—
—Kansas City	IHL	32	15	11	26	25	—	—	—	—	—
NHL totals		44	7	13	20	10					

COURTNALL, GEOFF
LW, CANUCKS

PERSONAL: Born August 18, 1962, at Victoria, B.C.... 6-1/190.... Shoots left.... Brother of Russ Courtnall, right winger, Dallas Stars.
TRANSACTIONS/CAREER NOTES: Signed as free agent by Boston Bruins (September 1983).... Traded by Bruins with G Bill Ranford to Edmonton Oilers for G Andy Moog (March 8, 1988).... Traded by Oilers to Washington Capitals for C Greg Adams (July 22, 1988).... Traded by Capitals to St. Louis Blues for C Peter Zezel and D Mike Lalor (July 13, 1990).... Traded by Blues with D Robert Dirk, C Cliff Ronning, LW Sergio Momesso and fifth-round pick (RW Brian Loney) in 1992 draft to Vancouver Canucks for C Dan Quinn and D Garth Butcher (March 5, 1991).... Lacerated foot (February 28, 1992) and suffered from chronic fatigue (March 1992); missed nine games.
MISCELLANEOUS: Member of Stanley Cup championship team (1988).

Season Team	League	REGULAR SEASON					PLAYOFFS				
		Gms.	G	A	Pts.	Pen.	Gms.	G	A	Pts.	Pen.
80-81—Victoria	WHL	11	3	5	8	6	15	2	1	3	7
81-82—Victoria	WHL	72	35	57	92	100	4	1	0	1	2
82-83—Victoria	WHL	71	41	73	114	186	12	6	7	13	42
83-84—Boston	NHL	5	0	0	0	0	—	—	—	—	—
—Hershey	AHL	74	14	12	26	51	—	—	—	—	—
84-85—Hershey	AHL	9	8	4	12	4	—	—	—	—	—
—Boston	NHL	64	12	16	28	82	5	0	2	2	7
85-86—Moncton	AHL	12	8	8	16	6	—	—	—	—	—
—Boston	NHL	64	21	17	38	61	3	0	0	0	2
86-87—Boston	NHL	65	13	23	36	117	1	0	0	0	0
87-88—Boston	NHL	62	32	26	58	108	—	—	—	—	—
—Edmonton	NHL	12	4	4	8	15	19	0	3	3	23
88-89—Washington	NHL	79	42	38	80	112	6	2	5	7	12
89-90—Washington	NHL	80	35	39	74	104	15	4	9	13	32
90-91—St. Louis	NHL	66	27	30	57	56	—	—	—	—	—
—Vancouver	NHL	11	6	2	8	8	6	3	5	8	4
91-92—Vancouver	NHL	70	23	34	57	116	12	6	8	14	20
92-93—Vancouver	NHL	84	31	46	77	167	12	4	10	14	12
NHL totals		662	246	275	521	946	79	19	42	61	112

COURTNALL, RUSS
RW, STARS

PERSONAL: Born June 3, 1965, at Victoria, B.C.... 5-11/183.... Shoots right.... Brother of Geoff Courtnall, left winger, Vancouver Canucks.
TRANSACTIONS/CAREER NOTES: Selected by Toronto Maple Leafs as underage junior in first round (first Maple Leafs pick, seventh overall) of NHL entry draft (June 8, 1983).... Bruised knee (November 1987).... Suffered from virus (February 1988).... Suffered back spasms (March 1988). ... Traded by Maple Leafs to Montreal Canadiens for RW John Kordic and sixth-round pick in 1989 draft (RW Michael Doers) (November 7, 1988).... Pulled muscle in right shoulder (October 8, 1991); missed 41 games.... Injured hand (January 15, 1992); missed 12 games.... Traded by Canadiens to Minnesota North Stars for LW Brian Bellows (August 31, 1992).... North Stars franchise moved from Minnesota to Dallas and renamed Stars for 1993-94 season.

Season Team	League	REGULAR SEASON					PLAYOFFS				
		Gms.	G	A	Pts.	Pen.	Gms.	G	A	Pts.	Pen.
82-83—Victoria	WHL	60	36	61	97	33	12	11	7	18	6
83-84—Victoria	WHL	32	29	37	66	63	—	—	—	—	—
—Canadian Olympic Team ..	Int'l	16	4	7	11	10	—	—	—	—	—
—Toronto	NHL	14	3	9	12	6	—	—	—	—	—

Season Team	League	REGULAR SEASON Gms.	G	A	Pts.	Pen.	PLAYOFFS Gms.	G	A	Pts.	Pen.
84-85—Toronto	NHL	69	12	10	22	44	—	—	—	—	—
85-86—Toronto	NHL	73	22	38	60	52	10	3	6	9	8
86-87—Toronto	NHL	79	29	44	73	90	13	3	4	7	11
87-88—Toronto	NHL	65	23	26	49	47	6	2	1	3	0
88-89—Toronto	NHL	9	1	1	2	4	—	—	—	—	—
—Montreal	NHL	64	22	17	39	15	21	8	5	13	18
89-90—Montreal	NHL	80	27	32	59	27	11	5	1	6	10
90-91—Montreal	NHL	79	26	50	76	29	13	8	3	11	7
91-92—Montreal	NHL	27	7	14	21	6	10	1	1	2	4
92-93—Minnesota	NHL	84	36	43	79	49	—	—	—	—	—
NHL totals		643	208	284	492	369	84	30	21	51	58

COURVILLE, LARRY
LW, JETS

PERSONAL: Born April 2, 1975, at Timmins, Ont. . . . 6-1/180. . . . Shoots left.
HIGH SCHOOL: Huron Heights Secondary School (Newmarket, Ont.).
TRANSACTIONS/CAREER NOTES: Selected by Winnipeg Jets in fifth round (sixth Jets pick, 119th overall) of NHL entry draft (June 26, 1993).

Season Team	League	REGULAR SEASON Gms.	G	A	Pts.	Pen.	PLAYOFFS Gms.	G	A	Pts.	Pen.
90-91—Waterloo	USHL	48	20	18	38	144	—	—	—	—	—
91-92—Cornwall	OHL	60	8	12	20	80	6	0	0	0	8
92-93—Newmarket	OHL	64	21	18	39	181	7	0	6	6	14

COUSINEAU, MARCEL
G, BRUINS

PERSONAL: Born April 30, 1973, at Delson, Que. . . . 5-10/175. . . . Shoots left. . . . Name pronounced KOO-sih-noh.
TRANSACTIONS/CAREER NOTES: Selected by Boston Bruins in third round (third Bruins pick, 62nd overall) of NHL entry draft (June 22, 1991).
HONORS: Named to QMJHL All-Rookie Team (1990-91).

Season Team	League	REGULAR SEASON Gms.	Min.	W	L	T	GA	SO	Avg.	PLAYOFFS Gms.	Min.	W	L	GA	SO	Avg.
90-91—Beauport	QMJHL	49	2739	13	29	3	196	1	4.29	—	—	—	—	—	—	—
91-92—Beauport	QMJHL	*67	*3673	26	*32	5	*241	0	3.94	—	—	—	—	—	—	—
92-93—Drummondville	QMJHL	60	3298	20	32	2	225	0	4.09	9	498	...	...	37	1	4.46

COUTURIER, SYLVAIN
C/LW, RED WINGS

PERSONAL: Born April 23, 1968, at Greenfield Park, Que. . . . 6-2/205. . . . Shoots left. . . . Name pronounced SIHL-vai koh-TOOR-ee-yay.
TRANSACTIONS/CAREER NOTES: Selected by Los Angeles Kings as underage junior in fourth round (third Kings pick, 65th overall) of NHL entry draft (June 21, 1986). . . . Broke jaw (October 1989). . . . Traded by Kings with D Paul Coffey and RW Jim Hiller to Detroit Red Wings for C Jimmy Carson, RW Marc Potvin and C Gary Shuchuk (January 29, 1993). . . . Loaned to Fort Wayne Komets (May 13, 1993).

Season Team	League	REGULAR SEASON Gms.	G	A	Pts.	Pen.	PLAYOFFS Gms.	G	A	Pts.	Pen.
85-86—Laval	QMJHL	68	21	37	58	64	14	1	7	8	28
86-87—Laval	QMJHL	67	39	51	90	77	13	12	14	26	19
87-88—Laval	QMJHL	67	70	67	137	115	—	—	—	—	—
88-89—Los Angeles	NHL	16	1	3	4	2	—	—	—	—	—
—New Haven	AHL	44	18	20	38	33	10	2	2	4	11
89-90—New Haven	AHL	50	9	8	17	47	—	—	—	—	—
90-91—Los Angeles	NHL	3	0	1	1	0	—	—	—	—	—
—Phoenix	IHL	66	50	37	87	49	10	8	2	10	10
91-92—Los Angeles	NHL	14	3	1	4	2	—	—	—	—	—
—Phoenix	IHL	39	19	20	39	68	—	—	—	—	—
92-93—Phoenix	IHL	38	23	16	39	63	—	—	—	—	—
—Adirondack	AHL	29	17	17	34	12	11	3	5	8	10
—Fort Wayne	IHL	—	—	—	—	—	4	2	3	5	2
NHL totals		33	4	5	9	4					

COWLEY, WAYNE
G, OILERS

PERSONAL: Born December 4, 1964, at Scarborough, Ont. . . . 6-0/185. . . . Shoots left. . . . Full name: Wayne Robert Cowley.
COLLEGE: Colgate.
TRANSACTIONS/CAREER NOTES: Dislocated left shoulder (December 19, 1987). . . . Signed as free agent by Calgary Flames (May 1, 1988). . . . Signed as free agent by Cape Breton Oilers (March 4, 1992).
HONORS: Named to ECAC All-Star second team (1986-87). . . . Named to ECHL All-Star second team (1990-91).

Season Team	League	REGULAR SEASON Gms.	Min.	W	L	T	GA	SO	Avg.	PLAYOFFS Gms.	Min.	W	L	GA	SO	Avg.
85-86—Colgate University	ECAC	7	313	2	2	0	23	1	4.41	—	—	—	—	—	—	—
86-87—Colgate University	ECAC	31	1805	21	8	1	106	0	3.52	—	—	—	—	—	—	—
87-88—Colgate University	ECAC	20	1162	11	7	1	58	1	2.99	—	—	—	—	—	—	—
88-89—Salt Lake City	IHL	29	1423	17	7	1	94	0	3.96	2	69	1	0	6	0	5.22
89-90—Salt Lake City	IHL	36	2009	15	12	5	124	1	3.70	3	118	0	0	6	0	3.05

Season Team	League	REGULAR SEASON								PLAYOFFS						
		Gms.	Min.	W	L	T	GA	SO	Avg.	Gms.	Min.	W	L	GA	SO	Avg.
90-91—Salt Lake City	IHL	7	377	3	4	0	23	1	3.66	—	—	—	—	—	—	—
—Cincinnati	ECHL	30	1680	19	9	2	108	1	3.86	4	249	...	...	13	*1	3.13
91-92—Raleigh	ECHL	38	2213	16	18	2	137	1	3.71	—	—	—	—	—	—	—
—Cape Breton	AHL	11	644	6	5	0	42	0	3.91	1	61	0	1	3	0	2.95
92-93—Cape Breton	AHL	42	2334	14	17	6	152	1	3.91	16	1014	*14	2	47	†1	2.78
—Wheeling	ECHL	1	60	1	0	0	3	0	3.00	—	—	—	—	—	—	—

CRAIG, MIKE
RW, STARS

PERSONAL: Born June 6, 1971, at London, Ont. . . . 6-1/180. . . . Shoots right.
TRANSACTIONS/CAREER NOTES: Selected by Minnesota North Stars in second round (second North Stars pick, 28th overall) of NHL entry draft (June 17, 1989). . . . Broke fibula (January 28, 1990). . . . Broke right wrist (February 4, 1991); missed 17 games. . . . Sprained knee (February 25, 1993); missed 12 games. . . . North Stars franchise moved from Minnesota to Dallas and renamed Stars for 1993-94 season.

Season Team	League	REGULAR SEASON					PLAYOFFS				
		Gms.	G	A	Pts.	Pen.	Gms.	G	A	Pts.	Pen.
86-87—Woodstock Jr. C.	OHA	32	29	19	48	64	—	—	—	—	—
87-88—Oshawa	OHL	61	6	10	16	39	7	7	0	7	11
88-89—Oshawa	OHL	63	36	36	72	34	6	3	1	4	6
89-90—Oshawa	OHL	43	36	40	76	85	17	10	16	26	46
90-91—Minnesota	NHL	39	8	4	12	32	10	1	1	2	20
91-92—Minnesota	NHL	67	15	16	31	155	4	1	0	1	7
92-93—Minnesota	NHL	70	15	23	38	106	—	—	—	—	—
NHL totals		176	38	43	81	293	14	2	1	3	27

CRAIGWELL, DALE
C, SHARKS

PERSONAL: Born April 24, 1971, at Toronto. . . . 5-10/180. . . . Shoots left.
COLLEGE: Toronto.
TRANSACTIONS/CAREER NOTES: Selected by San Jose Sharks in 10th round (11th Sharks pick, 199th overall) of NHL entry draft (June 22, 1991). . . . Strained back (October 1992); missed two games. . . . Strained back (November 1, 1992); missed 10 games.
HONORS: Won William Hanley Trophy (1990-91).

Season Team	League	REGULAR SEASON					PLAYOFFS				
		Gms.	G	A	Pts.	Pen.	Gms.	G	A	Pts.	Pen.
88-89—Oshawa	OHL	55	9	14	23	15	6	0	0	0	0
89-90—Oshawa	OHL	64	22	41	63	39	17	7	7	14	11
90-91—Oshawa	OHL	56	27	68	95	34	16	7	16	23	9
91-92—Kansas City	IHL	48	6	19	25	29	12	4	7	11	4
—San Jose	NHL	32	5	11	16	8	—	—	—	—	—
92-93—San Jose	NHL	8	3	1	4	4	—	—	—	—	—
—Kansas City	IHL	60	15	38	53	24	12	†7	5	12	2
NHL totals		40	8	12	20	12					

CRAVEN, MURRAY
C/LW, CANUCKS

PERSONAL: Born July 20, 1964, at Medicine Hat, Alta. . . . 6-2/185. . . . Shoots left.
TRANSACTIONS/CAREER NOTES: Selected by Detroit Red Wings as underage junior in first round (first Red Wings pick, 17th overall) of NHL entry draft (June 9, 1982). . . . Injured left knee cartilage (January 15, 1983). . . . Traded by Red Wings with LW/C Joe Paterson to Philadelphia Flyers for C Darryl Sittler (October 1984). . . . Broke foot (April 16, 1987). . . . Hyperextended right knee and lacerated eye (November 1988). . . . Bruised right foot (January 1989). . . . Fractured left wrist (February 24, 1989). . . . Fractured right wrist (April 5, 1989). . . . Suffered back spasms (February 1990). . . . Injured rotator cuff (March 24, 1990). . . . Traded by Flyers with fourth-round pick in 1992 draft (LW Kevin Smyth) to Hartford Whalers for RW Kevin Dineen (November 13, 1991). . . . Injured groin (January 21, 1992). . . . Traded by Whalers with fifth-round pick in 1993 draft to Vancouver Canucks for LW Robert Kron, third-round pick in 1993 draft (D Marek Malik) and future considerations (March 22, 1993); Canucks sent RW Jim Sandlak to complete deal (May 17, 1993).

Season Team	League	REGULAR SEASON					PLAYOFFS				
		Gms.	G	A	Pts.	Pen.	Gms.	G	A	Pts.	Pen.
80-81—Medicine Hat	WHL	69	5	10	15	18	5	0	0	0	2
81-82—Medicine Hat	WHL	72	35	46	81	49	—	—	—	—	—
82-83—Medicine Hat	WHL	28	17	29	46	35	—	—	—	—	—
—Detroit	NHL	31	4	7	11	6	—	—	—	—	—
83-84—Medicine Hat	WHL	48	38	56	94	53	4	5	3	8	4
—Detroit	NHL	15	0	4	4	6	—	—	—	—	—
84-85—Philadelphia	NHL	80	26	35	61	30	19	4	6	10	11
85-86—Philadelphia	NHL	78	21	33	54	34	5	0	3	3	4
86-87—Philadelphia	NHL	77	19	30	49	38	12	3	1	4	9
87-88—Philadelphia	NHL	72	30	46	76	58	7	2	5	7	4
88-89—Philadelphia	NHL	51	9	28	37	52	1	0	0	0	0
89-90—Philadelphia	NHL	76	25	50	75	42	—	—	—	—	—
90-91—Philadelphia	NHL	77	19	47	66	53	—	—	—	—	—
91-92—Philadelphia	NHL	12	3	3	6	8	—	—	—	—	—
—Hartford	NHL	61	24	30	54	38	7	3	3	6	6
92-93—Hartford	NHL	67	25	42	67	20	—	—	—	—	—
—Vancouver	NHL	10	0	10	10	12	12	4	6	10	4
NHL totals		707	205	365	570	397	63	16	24	40	38

C

CRAWFORD, LOU
LW, BRUINS

PERSONAL: Born November 5, 1962, at Belleville, Ont. . . . 6-0/185. . . . Shoots left.
TRANSACTIONS/CAREER NOTES: Signed as free agent by Buffalo Sabres (August 23, 1984). . . . Signed as free agent by Nova Scotia Oilers (October 1985). . . . Signed as free agent by Detroit Red Wings (August 11, 1988). . . . Signed as free agent by Boston Bruins (July 6, 1989).
HONORS: Named to Memorial Cup All-Star team (1980-81).

Season Team	League	REGULAR SEASON Gms.	G	A	Pts.	Pen.	PLAYOFFS Gms.	G	A	Pts.	Pen.
79-80—Belleville Jr. B	OHA	10	7	11	18	60	—	—	—	—	—
80-81—Kitchener	OMJHL	53	2	7	9	134	—	—	—	—	—
81-82—Kitchener	OHL	64	11	17	28	243	15	3	4	7	71
82-83—Rochester	AHL	64	5	11	16	142	13	1	1	2	7
83-84—Rochester	AHL	76	7	6	13	234	17	2	4	6	87
84-85—Rochester	AHL	70	8	7	15	213	1	0	0	0	10
85-86—Nova Scotia	AHL	78	8	11	19	214	—	—	—	—	—
86-87—Nova Scotia	AHL	35	3	4	7	48	—	—	—	—	—
87-88—Nova Scotia	AHL	65	15	15	30	170	4	1	2	3	9
88-89—Adirondack	AHL	74	23	23	46	179	9	0	6	6	32
89-90—Boston	NHL	7	0	0	0	20	1	0	0	0	0
—Maine	AHL	62	11	15	26	241	—	—	—	—	—
90-91—Maine	AHL	80	18	17	35	215	2	0	0	0	5
91-92—Maine	AHL	54	17	15	32	171	—	—	—	—	—
—Boston	NHL	19	2	1	3	9	—	—	—	—	—
92-93—Milwaukee	IHL	56	16	14	30	108	6	2	2	4	8
NHL totals		26	2	1	3	29	1	0	0	0	0

CREIGHTON, ADAM
C, LIGHTNING

PERSONAL: Born June 2, 1965, at Burlington, Ont. . . . 6-5/210. . . . Shoots left. . . . Son of Dave Creighton, center, four NHL teams (1948-49 through 1959-60).
TRANSACTIONS/CAREER NOTES: Selected by Buffalo Sabres in first round (third Sabres pick, 11th overall) of NHL entry draft (June 8, 1983). . . . Underwent knee surgery (January 1988). . . . Sprained knee (September 1988). . . . Traded by Sabres to Chicago Blackhawks for RW Rick Vaive (December 2, 1988). . . . Suspended five games by NHL for stick-swinging incident in preseason game (September 30, 1990). . . . Sprained right hand (February 10, 1991). . . . Traded by Blackhawks with LW Steve Thomas to New York Islanders for C Brent Sutter and RW Brad Lauer (October 25, 1991). . . . Selected by Tampa Bay Lightning in NHL waiver draft (October 4, 1992).
HONORS: Won Stafford Smythe Memorial Cup (May 1984). . . . Named to Memorial Cup All-Star team (1983-84).

Season Team	League	REGULAR SEASON Gms.	G	A	Pts.	Pen.	PLAYOFFS Gms.	G	A	Pts.	Pen.
81-82—Ottawa	OHL	60	14	27	41	73	17	7	1	8	40
82-83—Ottawa	OHL	68	44	46	90	88	9	0	2	2	12
83-84—Ottawa	OHL	56	42	49	91	79	13	16	11	27	28
—Buffalo	NHL	7	2	2	4	4	—	—	—	—	—
84-85—Ottawa	OHL	10	4	14	18	23	5	6	2	8	11
—Rochester	AHL	6	5	3	8	2	5	2	1	3	20
—Buffalo	NHL	30	2	8	10	33	—	—	—	—	—
85-86—Rochester	AHL	32	17	21	38	27	—	—	—	—	—
—Buffalo	NHL	20	1	1	2	2	—	—	—	—	—
86-87—Buffalo	NHL	56	18	22	40	26	—	—	—	—	—
87-88—Buffalo	NHL	36	10	17	27	87	—	—	—	—	—
88-89—Buffalo	NHL	24	7	10	17	44	—	—	—	—	—
—Chicago	NHL	43	15	14	29	92	15	5	6	11	44
89-90—Chicago	NHL	80	34	36	70	224	20	3	6	9	59
90-91—Chicago	NHL	72	22	29	51	135	6	0	1	1	10
91-92—Chicago	NHL	11	6	6	12	16	—	—	—	—	—
—New York Islanders	NHL	66	15	9	24	102	—	—	—	—	—
92-93—Tampa Bay	NHL	83	19	20	39	110	—	—	—	—	—
NHL totals		528	151	174	325	875	41	8	13	21	113

CREURER, TROY
D, CANUCKS

PERSONAL: Born May 2, 1975, at Regina, Sask. . . . 6-1/180. . . . Shoots left.
TRANSACTIONS/CAREER NOTES: Selected by Vancouver Canucks in sixth round (fifth Canucks pick, 150th overall) of NHL entry draft (June 26, 1993).

Season Team	League	REGULAR SEASON Gms.	G	A	Pts.	Pen.	PLAYOFFS Gms.	G	A	Pts.	Pen.
92-93—Notre Dame	SJHL	62	6	21	27	71	—	—	—	—	—

CRONIN, SHAWN
D, FLYERS

PERSONAL: Born August 20, 1963, at Flushing, Mich. . . . 6-2/210. . . . Shoots left. . . . Full name: Shawn Patrick Cronin.
COLLEGE: Illinois-Chicago.
TRANSACTIONS/CAREER NOTES: Signed as free agent by Hartford Whalers (March 1986). . . . Signed as free agent by Washington Capitals (June 6, 1988). . . . Signed as free agent by Philadelphia Flyers (June 13, 1989). . . . Traded by Flyers to Winnipeg Jets for future considerations (July 21, 1989); future considerations later cancelled. . . . Bruised hand (February 1990). . . . Bruised foot (October 27, 1991); missed three games. . . . Injured ribs (December 23, 1991). . . . Traded by Jets to Quebec Nordiques for D Danny Lambert (August 25, 1992). . . . Selected by Flyers in NHL waiver draft (October 4, 1992). . . . Sprained left knee (April 12, 1993); missed remainder of season.

Season Team	League	REGULAR SEASON Gms	G	A	Pts	Pen.	PLAYOFFS Gms	G	A	Pts	Pen.
82-83—Illinois-Chicago	CCHA	36	1	5	6	52	—	—	—	—	—
83-84—Illinois-Chicago	CCHA	32	0	4	4	41	—	—	—	—	—
84-85—Illinois-Chicago	CCHA	31	2	6	8	52	—	—	—	—	—
85-86—Illinois-Chicago	CCHA	38	3	8	11	70	—	—	—	—	—
86-87—Binghamton	AHL	12	0	1	1	60	10	0	0	0	41
—Salt Lake City	IHL	53	8	16	24	118	—	—	—	—	—
87-88—Binghamton	AHL	66	3	8	11	212	4	0	0	0	15
88-89—Washington	NHL	1	0	0	0	0	—	—	—	—	—
—Baltimore	AHL	75	3	9	12	267	—	—	—	—	—
89-90—Winnipeg	NHL	61	0	4	4	243	5	0	0	0	7
90-91—Winnipeg	NHL	67	1	5	6	189	—	—	—	—	—
91-92—Winnipeg	NHL	65	0	4	4	271	4	0	0	0	6
92-93—Philadelphia	NHL	35	2	1	3	37	—	—	—	—	—
—Hershey	AHL	7	0	1	1	12	—	—	—	—	—
NHL totals		229	3	14	17	740	9	0	0	0	13

CROSS, CORY
D, LIGHTNING

PERSONAL: Born January 3, 1971, at Prince Albert, Sask. . . . 6-5/212. . . . Shoots left. . . . Full name: Cory James Cross.
HIGH SCHOOL: Lloydminister (Alta.) Comprehensive.
COLLEGE: Alberta.
TRANSACTIONS/CAREER NOTES: Selected by Tampa Bay Lightning in NHL supplemental draft (June 19, 1992).

Season Team	League	REGULAR SEASON Gms	G	A	Pts	Pen.	PLAYOFFS Gms	G	A	Pts	Pen.
90-91—University of Alberta	CWUAA	20	2	5	7	16	—	—	—	—	—
91-92—University of Alberta	CWUAA	39	3	10	13	76	—	—	—	—	—
92-93—Atlanta	IHL	7	0	1	1	2	4	0	0	0	6

CROSSMAN, DOUG
D, BLUES

PERSONAL: Born June 30, 1960, at Peterborough, Ont. . . . 6-2/190. . . . Shoots left.
TRANSACTIONS/CAREER NOTES: Selected by Chicago Blackhawks as underage junior in sixth round (sixth Blackhawks pick, 112th overall) of NHL entry draft (August 9, 1979). . . . Injured thumb (February 1983). . . . Traded by Blackhawks with second-round pick in 1984 draft (RW Scott Mellanby) to Philadelphia Flyers for D Behn Wilson (June 8, 1983). . . . Traded by Flyers to Los Angeles Kings for D Jay Wells (September 29, 1988). . . . Traded by Kings to New York Islanders (May 23, 1989) to complete deal in which Islanders sent G Kelly Hrudey to Kings for G Mark Fitzpatrick, D Wayne McBean and future considerations (February 22, 1989). . . . Injured foot (November 6, 1990). . . . Traded by Islanders to Hartford Whalers for C Ray Ferraro (November 13, 1990). . . . Injured leg (February 12, 1991). . . . Traded by Whalers to Detroit Red Wings for D Doug Houda (February 20, 1991). . . . Traded by Red Wings with D Dennis Vial to Quebec Nordiques for cash (June 15, 1992). . . . Selected by Tampa Bay Lightning in NHL expansion draft (June 18, 1992). . . . Traded by Lightning with LW Basil McRae to St. Louis Blues for LW Jason Ruff, sixth-round pick in 1996 draft and either third-round pick in 1995 draft or fourth-round pick in 1994 draft (January 28, 1993).
HONORS: Named to OMJHL All-Star first team (1979-80).

Season Team	League	REGULAR SEASON Gms	G	A	Pts	Pen.	PLAYOFFS Gms	G	A	Pts	Pen.
76-77—London	OMJHL	1	0	0	0	0	—	—	—	—	—
77-78—Ottawa	OMJHL	65	4	17	21	17	—	—	—	—	—
78-79—Ottawa	OMJHL	67	12	51	63	63	4	1	3	4	0
79-80—Ottawa	OMJHL	66	20	96	116	48	11	7	6	13	19
80-81—Chicago	NHL	9	0	2	2	2	—	—	—	—	—
—New Brunswick	AHL	70	13	43	56	90	13	5	6	11	36
81-82—Chicago	NHL	70	12	28	40	24	11	0	3	3	4
82-83—Chicago	NHL	80	13	40	53	46	13	3	7	10	6
83-84—Philadelphia	NHL	78	7	28	35	63	3	0	0	0	0
84-85—Philadelphia	NHL	80	4	33	37	65	19	4	6	10	38
85-86—Philadelphia	NHL	80	6	37	43	55	5	0	1	1	4
86-87—Philadelphia	NHL	78	9	31	40	29	26	4	14	18	31
87-88—Philadelphia	NHL	76	9	29	38	43	7	1	1	2	8
88-89—New Haven	AHL	3	0	0	0	0	—	—	—	—	—
—Los Angeles	NHL	74	10	15	25	53	2	0	1	1	2
89-90—New York Islanders	NHL	80	15	44	59	54	5	0	1	1	6
90-91—New York Islanders	NHL	16	1	6	7	12	—	—	—	—	—
—Hartford	NHL	41	4	19	23	19	—	—	—	—	—
—Detroit	NHL	17	3	4	7	17	6	0	5	5	6
91-92—Detroit	NHL	26	0	8	8	14	—	—	—	—	—
92-93—Tampa Bay	NHL	40	8	21	29	18	—	—	—	—	—
—St. Louis	NHL	19	2	7	9	10	—	—	—	—	—
NHL totals		864	103	352	455	524	97	12	39	51	105

CROWLEY, MIKE
D, FLYERS

PERSONAL: Born July 4, 1975, at Bloomington, Minn. . . . 5-11/165. . . . Shoots left.
HIGH SCHOOL: Thomas Jefferson (Bloomington, Minn.).
TRANSACTIONS/CAREER NOTES: Selected by Philadelphia Flyers in sixth round (fifth Flyers pick, 140th overall) of NHL entry draft (June 26, 1993).

C

Season Team	League	REGULAR SEASON					PLAYOFFS				
		Gms.	G	A	Pts.	Pen.	Gms.	G	A	Pts.	Pen.
90-91—Jefferson HS	Minn. H.S.	20	3	9	12	2	—	—	—	—	—
91-92—Jefferson HS	Minn. H.S.	28	5	18	23	8	—	—	—	—	—
92-93—Jefferson HS	Minn. H.S.	22	10	32	42	18	—	—	—	—	—

CROWLEY, TED
D, MAPLE LEAFS

PERSONAL: Born May 3, 1970, at Concord, Mass.... 6-2/190.... Shoots right.
COLLEGE: Boston College.
TRANSACTIONS/CAREER NOTES: Selected by Toronto Maple Leafs in fourth round (fourth Maple Leafs pick, 69th overall) of NHL entry draft (June 11, 1988).

Season Team	League	REGULAR SEASON					PLAYOFFS				
		Gms.	G	A	Pts.	Pen.	Gms.	G	A	Pts.	Pen.
89-90—Boston College	Hockey East	39	7	24	31	34	—	—	—	—	—
90-91—Boston College	Hockey East	39	12	24	36	61	—	—	—	—	—
91-92—U.S. national team	Int'l	42	6	7	13	65	—	—	—	—	—
—St. John's	AHL	29	5	4	9	33	10	3	1	4	11
92-93—St. John's	AHL	79	19	38	57	41	9	2	2	4	4

CULLEN, JOHN
C, MAPLE LEAFS

PERSONAL: Born August 2, 1964, at Puslinch, Ont.... 5-10/187.... Shoots right.... Full name: Barry John Cullen.... Son of Barry Cullen, right winger, Toronto Maple Leafs and Detroit Red Wings (1955-56 through 1959-64).
COLLEGE: Boston University.
TRANSACTIONS/CAREER NOTES: Selected by Buffalo Sabres in NHL supplemental draft (September 17, 1986).... Signed as free agent by Pittsburgh Penguins (July 1988).... Suffered from hepatitis (October 1989); missed seven games.... Pulled stomach muscle (November 17, 1990).... Traded by Penguins with D Zarley Zalapski and RW Jeff Parker to Whalers for C Ron Francis, D Ulf Samuelsson and D Grant Jennings (March 4, 1991).... Missed first three games of 1991-92 season due to contract dispute.... Traded by Whalers to Toronto Maple Leafs for second-round pick in 1993 or 1994 draft (November 24, 1992). ... Suffered herniated disc in neck (March 2, 1993); missed 16 games.
HONORS: Named ECAC Rookie of the Year (1983-84).... Named to Hockey East All-Star first team (1984-85 and 1985-86). ... Named to NCAA All-America East second team (1985-86).... Named to Hockey East All-Star second team (1986-87).... Won James Gatschene Memorial Trophy (1987-88).... Won Leo P. Lamoureux Memorial Trophy (1987-88).... Shared Garry F. Longman Memorial Trophy with Ed Belfour (1987-88).... Named to IHL All-Star first team (1987-88).... Played in NHL All-Star Game (1991 and 1992).

Season Team	League	REGULAR SEASON					PLAYOFFS				
		Gms.	G	A	Pts.	Pen.	Gms.	G	A	Pts.	Pen.
83-84—Boston University	ECAC	40	23	33	56	28	—	—	—	—	—
84-85—Boston University	Hockey East	41	27	32	59	46	—	—	—	—	—
85-86—Boston University	Hockey East	43	25	49	74	54	—	—	—	—	—
86-87—Boston University	Hockey East	36	23	29	52	35	—	—	—	—	—
87-88—Flint	IHL	81	48	*109	*157	113	16	11	†15	26	16
88-89—Pittsburgh	NHL	79	12	37	49	112	11	3	6	9	28
89-90—Pittsburgh	NHL	72	32	60	92	138	—	—	—	—	—
90-91—Pittsburgh	NHL	65	31	63	94	83	—	—	—	—	—
—Hartford	NHL	13	8	8	16	18	6	2	7	9	10
91-92—Hartford	NHL	77	26	51	77	141	7	2	1	3	12
92-93—Hartford	NHL	19	5	4	9	58	—	—	—	—	—
—Toronto	NHL	47	13	28	41	53	12	2	3	5	0
NHL totals		372	127	251	378	603	36	9	17	26	50

CULLIMORE, JASSEN
D, CANUCKS

PERSONAL: Born December 4, 1972, at Simcoe, Ont.... 6-5/225.... Shoots left. ... Name pronounced KUHL-ih-MOHR.
TRANSACTIONS/CAREER NOTES: Selected by Vancouver Canucks in second round (second Canucks pick, 29th overall) of NHL entry draft (June 22, 1991).
HONORS: Named to OHL All-Star second team (1991-92).

Season Team	League	REGULAR SEASON					PLAYOFFS				
		Gms.	G	A	Pts.	Pen.	Gms.	G	A	Pts.	Pen.
88-89—Peterborough	OHL	20	2	1	3	6	—	—	—	—	—
89-90—Peterborough	OHL	59	2	6	8	61	11	0	2	2	8
90-91—Peterborough	OHL	62	8	16	24	74	4	1	0	1	7
91-92—Peterborough	OHL	54	9	37	46	65	10	3	6	9	8
92-93—Hamilton	AHL	56	5	7	12	60	—	—	—	—	—

CUMMINS, JIM
RW, FLYERS

PERSONAL: Born May 17, 1970, at Dearborn, Mich.... 6-2/200.... Shoots right.... Full name: James Stephen Cummins.
COLLEGE: Michigan State.
TRANSACTIONS/CAREER NOTES: Selected by New York Rangers in fourth round (fifth Rangers pick, 67th overall) of NHL entry draft (June 17, 1989).... Traded by Rangers with C Kevin Miller and D Dennis Vial to Detroit Red Wings for RW Joe Kocur and D Per Djoos (March 5, 1991).... Suspended 11 games by NHL for leaving penalty box to join fight (January 23, 1993).... Traded by Red Wings with fourth-round pick in 1993 draft to Philadelphia Flyers for rights to C Greg Johnson and future considerations (June 20, 1993).

Season	Team	League	REGULAR SEASON					PLAYOFFS				
			Gms.	G	A	Pts.	Pen.	Gms.	G	A	Pts.	Pen.
87-88	Detroit Compuware	NAJHL	31	11	15	26	146	—	—	—	—	—
88-89	Michigan State	CCHA	36	3	9	12	100	—	—	—	—	—
89-90	Michigan State	CCHA	41	8	7	15	94	—	—	—	—	—
90-91	Michigan State	CCHA	34	9	6	15	110	—	—	—	—	—
91-92	Adirondack	AHL	65	7	13	20	338	5	0	0	0	19
	Detroit	NHL	1	0	0	0	7	—	—	—	—	—
92-93	Adirondack	AHL	43	16	4	20	179	9	3	1	4	4
	Detroit	NHL	7	1	1	2	58	—	—	—	—	—
NHL totals			8	1	1	2	65					

CUNNEYWORTH, RANDY

LW, WHALERS

PERSONAL: Born May 10, 1961, at Etobicoke, Ont.... 6-0/180.... Shoots left.... Full name: Randolph William Cunneyworth.

TRANSACTIONS/CAREER NOTES: Selected by Buffalo Sabres as underage junior in eighth round (ninth Sabres pick, 167th overall) of NHL entry draft (June 11, 1980).... Attended Pittsburgh Penguins training camp as unsigned free agent (Summer 1985); Sabres then traded his equalization rights with RW Mike Moller to Penguins for future considerations (October 4, 1985); Penguins sent RW Pat Hughes to Sabres to complete deal (October 1985).... Suspended three games by NHL (January 1988).... Suspended five games by NHL (January 1988).... Fractured right foot (January 24, 1989).... Traded by Penguins with G Richard Tabaracci and RW Dave McIlwain to Winnipeg Jets for RW Andrew McBain, D Jim Kyte and LW Randy Gilhen (June 17, 1989). ... Broke bone in right foot (October 1989).... Traded by Jets to Hartford Whalers for C Paul MacDermid (December 13, 1989).... Broke tibia bone in left leg (November 28, 1990); missed 38 games.... Strained lower back (December 1991); missed one game.... Strained ankle (December 21, 1991); missed two games.... Strained left ankle (January 16, 1992); missed three games.... Reinjured ankle (February 1, 1992); missed six games.... Bruised ribs (November 15, 1992); missed four games.... Suffered neck spasms (December 31, 1992); missed three games.

Season	Team	League	REGULAR SEASON					PLAYOFFS				
			Gms.	G	A	Pts.	Pen.	Gms.	G	A	Pts.	Pen.
79-80	Ottawa	OMJHL	63	16	25	41	145	11	0	1	1	13
80-81	Ottawa	OMJHL	67	54	74	128	240	15	5	8	13	35
	Rochester	AHL	1	0	1	1	2	—	—	—	—	—
	Buffalo	NHL	1	0	0	0	2	—	—	—	—	—
81-82	Rochester	AHL	57	12	15	27	86	9	4	0	4	30
	Buffalo	NHL	20	2	4	6	47	—	—	—	—	—
82-83	Rochester	AHL	78	23	33	56	111	16	4	4	8	35
83-84	Rochester	AHL	54	18	17	35	85	17	5	5	10	55
84-85	Rochester	AHL	72	30	38	68	148	5	2	1	3	16
85-86	Pittsburgh	NHL	75	15	30	45	74	—	—	—	—	—
86-87	Pittsburgh	NHL	79	26	27	53	142	—	—	—	—	—
87-88	Pittsburgh	NHL	71	35	39	74	141	—	—	—	—	—
88-89	Pittsburgh	NHL	70	25	19	44	156	11	3	5	8	26
89-90	Winnipeg	NHL	28	5	6	11	34	—	—	—	—	—
	Hartford	NHL	43	9	9	18	41	4	0	0	0	2
90-91	Springfield	AHL	2	0	0	0	5	—	—	—	—	—
	Hartford	NHL	32	9	5	14	49	1	0	0	0	0
91-92	Hartford	NHL	39	7	10	17	71	7	3	0	3	9
92-93	Hartford	NHL	39	5	4	9	63	—	—	—	—	—
NHL totals			497	138	153	291	820	23	6	5	11	37

CURRAN, BRIAN

D, OILERS

PERSONAL: Born November 5, 1963, at Toronto.... 6-4/220.... Shoots left. **TRANSACTIONS/CAREER NOTES:** Underwent appendectomy (November 1981).... Selected by Boston Bruins as underage junior in second round (second Bruins pick, 22nd overall) of NHL entry draft (June 9, 1982).... Broke ankle (September 1982).... Bruised thigh (November 1984).... Broke leg (February 1, 1986).... Signed as free agent by New York Islanders (August 1986); Bruins awarded D Paul Boutilier as compensation.... Fractured jaw (January 12, 1988).... Traded by Islanders to Toronto Maple Leafs for sixth-round pick in 1988 draft (RW Pavel Gross) (March 1988).... Pulled pelvic muscle (November 1988).... Bruised spine (December 1, 1988).... Dislocated right wrist (February 25, 1989).... Bruised left wrist (November 1990).... Traded by Maple Leafs with LW Lou Franceschetti to Buffalo Sabres for RW Mike Foligno and eighth-round pick in 1991 draft (C Thomas Kucharcik) (December 17, 1990).... Injured shoulder (December 28, 1990); missed four games.... Signed as free agent by Edmonton Oilers (October 27, 1992)....

Season	Team	League	REGULAR SEASON					PLAYOFFS				
			Gms.	G	A	Pts.	Pen.	Gms.	G	A	Pts.	Pen.
80-81	Portland	WHL	51	2	16	18	132	14	1	7	8	63
81-82	Portland	WHL	59	2	28	30	275	7	0	1	1	13
82-83	Portland	WHL	56	1	30	31	187	14	1	3	4	57
83-84	Hershey	AHL	23	0	2	2	94	—	—	—	—	—
	Boston	NHL	16	1	1	2	57	3	0	0	0	7
84-85	Hershey	AHL	4	0	0	0	19	—	—	—	—	—
	Boston	NHL	56	0	1	1	158	—	—	—	—	—
85-86	Boston	NHL	43	2	5	7	192	2	0	0	0	4
86-87	New York Islanders	NHL	68	0	10	10	356	8	0	0	0	51
87-88	Springfield	AHL	8	1	0	1	43	—	—	—	—	—
	New York Islanders	NHL	22	0	1	1	68	—	—	—	—	—
	Toronto	NHL	7	0	1	1	19	6	0	0	0	41

Season Team	League	REGULAR SEASON					PLAYOFFS				
		Gms.	G	A	Pts.	Pen.	Gms.	G	A	Pts.	Pen.
88-89—Toronto	NHL	47	1	4	5	185	—	—	—	—	—
89-90—Toronto	NHL	72	2	9	11	301	5	0	1	1	19
90-91—Toronto	NHL	4	0	0	0	7	—	—	—	—	—
—Buffalo	NHL	17	0	1	1	43	—	—	—	—	—
—Newmarket	AHL	6	0	1	1	32	—	—	—	—	—
—Rochester	AHL	10	0	0	0	36	—	—	—	—	—
91-92—Buffalo	NHL	3	0	0	0	14	—	—	—	—	—
—Rochester	AHL	36	0	3	3	122	—	—	—	—	—
92-93—Cape Breton	AHL	61	2	24	26	223	12	0	3	3	12
NHL totals		355	6	33	39	1400	24	0	1	1	122

CURRIE, DAN
LW

PERSONAL: Born March 15, 1968, at Burlington, Ont. . . . 6-2/195. . . . Shoots left. . . . Full name: Daniel Robert Currie.
TRANSACTIONS/CAREER NOTES: Selected by Edmonton Oilers as underage junior in fourth round (fourth Oilers pick, 84th overall) of NHL entry draft (June 21, 1986). . . . Signed as free agent by Phoenix Roadrunners (July 16, 1993).
HONORS: Named to OHL All-Star first team (1987-88). . . . Named to AHL All-Star second team (1991-92). . . . Named to AHL All-Star first team (1992-93).

Season Team	League	REGULAR SEASON					PLAYOFFS				
		Gms.	G	A	Pts.	Pen.	Gms.	G	A	Pts.	Pen.
85-86—Sault Ste. Marie	OHL	66	21	22	43	37	—	—	—	—	—
86-87—Sault Ste. Marie	OHL	66	31	52	83	53	4	2	1	3	2
87-88—Sault Ste. Marie	OHL	57	50	59	109	53	6	3	9	12	4
—Nova Scotia	AHL	3	4	2	6	0	5	4	3	7	0
88-89—Cape Breton	AHL	77	29	36	65	29	—	—	—	—	—
89-90—Cape Breton	AHL	77	36	40	76	28	—	—	—	—	—
90-91—Cape Breton	AHL	71	47	45	92	51	4	3	1	4	8
—Edmonton	NHL	5	0	0	0	0	—	—	—	—	—
91-92—Cape Breton	AHL	66	*50	42	92	39	5	4	5	9	4
—Edmonton	NHL	7	1	0	1	0	—	—	—	—	—
92-93—Cape Breton	AHL	75	57	41	98	73	16	7	4	11	31
—Edmonton	NHL	5	0	0	0	4	—	—	—	—	—
NHL totals		17	1	0	1	4					

DAFOE, BYRON
G, CAPITALS

PERSONAL: Born February 25, 1971, at Duncan, B.C. . . . 5-11/175. . . . Shoots left. . . . Full name: Byron Jaromir Dafoe.
TRANSACTIONS/CAREER NOTES: Selected by Washington Capitals in second round (second Capitals pick, 35th overall) of NHL entry draft (June 17, 1989). . . . Underwent emergency appendectomy (December 1989).

Season Team	League	REGULAR SEASON							PLAYOFFS						
		Gms.	Min.	W	L	T	GA	SO	Avg.	Gms.	Min.	W	L	GA	SO	Avg.
87-88—Juan de Fuca	BCJHL	32	1716	. . .	. . .	. . .	129	0	4.51	—	—	—	—	—	—	—
88-89—Portland	WHL	59	3279	29	24	3	*291	1	5.32	*18	*1091	10	8	*81	*1	4.45
89-90—Portland	WHL	40	2265	14	21	3	193	0	5.11	—	—	—	—	—	—	—
90-91—Portland	WHL	8	414	1	5	1	41	0	5.94	—	—	—	—	—	—	—
—Prince Albert	WHL	32	1839	13	12	4	124	0	4.05	—	—	—	—	—	—	—
91-92—New Haven	AHL	7	364	3	2	1	22	0	3.63	—	—	—	—	—	—	—
—Baltimore	AHL	33	1847	12	16	4	119	0	3.87	—	—	—	—	—	—	—
—Hampton Roads	ECHL	10	562	6	4	0	26	1	2.78	—	—	—	—	—	—	—
92-93—Baltimore	AHL	48	2617	16	*20	7	191	1	4.38	5	241	2	3	22	0	5.48
—Washington	NHL	1	1	0	0	0	0	0	0.00	—	—	—	—	—	—	—
NHL totals		1	1	0	0	0	0	0	0.00							

DAGENAIS, MIKE
D

PERSONAL: Born July 22, 1969, at Ottawa. . . . 6-3/200. . . . Shoots left.
TRANSACTIONS/CAREER NOTES: Selected by Chicago Blackhawks in third round (fourth Blackhawks pick, 60th overall) of NHL entry draft (June 13, 1987). . . . Traded by Blackhawks to Quebec Nordiques for D Ryan McGill (September 26, 1991).

Season Team	League	REGULAR SEASON					PLAYOFFS				
		Gms.	G	A	Pts.	Pen.	Gms.	G	A	Pts.	Pen.
85-86—Peterborough	OHL	45	1	3	4	40	—	—	—	—	—
86-87—Peterborough	OHL	56	1	17	18	66	12	4	1	5	20
87-88—Peterborough	OHL	66	11	23	34	125	12	1	1	2	31
88-89—Peterborough	OHL	62	14	23	37	122	13	3	3	6	12
89-90—Peterborough	OHL	44	14	26	40	74	12	4	1	5	18
90-91—Indianapolis	IHL	76	13	14	27	115	4	0	0	0	4
91-92—Halifax	AHL	69	11	21	32	143	—	—	—	—	—
92-93—Cincinnati	IHL	69	14	22	36	128	—	—	—	—	—

DAHL, KEVIN
D, FLAMES

PERSONAL: Born December 30, 1968, at Regina, Sask. . . . 5-11/190. . . . Shoots right.
COLLEGE: Bowling Green.
TRANSACTIONS/CAREER NOTES: Selected by Montreal Canadiens in 11th round (12th Canadiens pick, 230th overall) of NHL entry draft (June 11, 1988). . . . Signed as free agent by Calgary

Flames (August 1, 1991).... Suffered charley horse (November 2, 1992); missed two games.... Injured heel (November 28, 1992); missed one game.... Strained left knee (December 15, 1992); missed 18 games.... Fractured left foot (April 9, 1993); missed one game.

			REGULAR SEASON					PLAYOFFS				
Season	Team	League	Gms.	G	A	Pts.	Pen.	Gms.	G	A	Pts.	Pen.
87-88	Bowling Green State	CCHA	44	2	23	25	78	—	—	—	—	—
88-89	Bowling Green State	CCHA	46	9	26	35	51	—	—	—	—	—
89-90	Bowling Green State	CCHA	43	8	22	30	74	—	—	—	—	—
90-91	Fredericton	AHL	32	1	15	16	45	9	0	1	1	11
	Winston-Salem	ECHL	36	7	17	24	58	—	—	—	—	—
91-92	Canadian national team	Int'l	45	2	15	17	44	—	—	—	—	—
	Canadian Olympic Team	Int'l	8	2	0	2	6	—	—	—	—	—
	Salt Lake City	IHL	13	0	2	2	12	5	0	0	0	13
92-93	Calgary	NHL	61	2	9	11	56	6	0	2	2	8
NHL totals			61	2	9	11	56	6	0	2	2	8

DAHLEN, ULF
RW, STARS

PERSONAL: Born January 12, 1967, at Ostersund, Sweden.... 6-2/195.... Shoots right.... Name pronounced DAH-luhn.
TRANSACTIONS/CAREER NOTES: Selected by New York Rangers in first round (first Rangers pick, seventh overall) of NHL entry draft (June 15, 1985).... Bruised shin (November 1987).... Bruised left shoulder (November 1988).... Separated right shoulder (January 1989).... Traded by Rangers with fourth-round pick in 1990 draft and future considerations to Minnesota North Stars for RW Mike Gartner (March 6, 1990).... North Stars franchise moved from Minnesota to Dallas and renamed Stars for 1993-94 season.

			REGULAR SEASON					PLAYOFFS				
Season	Team	League	Gms.	G	A	Pts.	Pen.	Gms.	G	A	Pts.	Pen.
83-84	Ostersund	Sweden	36	15	11	26	10	—	—	—	—	—
84-85	Ostersund	Sweden	36	33	26	59	20	—	—	—	—	—
85-86	Bjorkloven	Sweden	22	4	3	7	8	—	—	—	—	—
86-87	Bjorkloven	Sweden	31	9	12	21	20	6	6	2	8	4
87-88	New York Rangers	NHL	70	29	23	52	26	—	—	—	—	—
	Colorado	IHL	2	2	2	4	0	—	—	—	—	—
88-89	New York Rangers	NHL	56	24	19	43	50	4	0	0	0	0
89-90	New York Rangers	NHL	63	18	18	36	30	—	—	—	—	—
	Minnesota	NHL	13	2	4	6	0	7	1	4	5	2
90-91	Minnesota	NHL	66	21	18	39	6	15	2	6	8	4
91-92	Minnesota	NHL	79	36	30	66	10	7	0	3	3	2
92-93	Minnesota	NHL	83	35	39	74	6	—	—	—	—	—
NHL totals			430	165	151	316	128	33	3	13	16	8

DAHLQUIST, CHRIS
D, FLAMES

PERSONAL: Born December 14, 1962, at Fridley, Minn.... 6-1/190.... Shoots left.... Name pronounced DAHL-KWIHST.
COLLEGE: Lake Superior State (Mich.).
TRANSACTIONS/CAREER NOTES: Signed as free agent by Pittsburgh Penguins (May 1985).... Traded by Penguins with Jim Johnson to Minnesota North Stars for D Peter Taglianetti and D Larry Murphy (December 11, 1990).... Broke left wrist (January 1991).... Selected by Calgary Flames in NHL waiver draft (October 4, 1992). ... Suffered bruised ribs (November 11, 1992); missed five games.... Suffered charley horse (February 26, 1993); missed two games.

			REGULAR SEASON					PLAYOFFS				
Season	Team	League	Gms.	G	A	Pts.	Pen.	Gms.	G	A	Pts.	Pen.
81-82	Lake Superior State	CCHA	39	4	10	14	18	—	—	—	—	—
82-83	Lake Superior State	CCHA	35	0	12	12	63	—	—	—	—	—
83-84	Lake Superior State	CCHA	40	4	19	23	76	—	—	—	—	—
84-85	Lake Superior State	CCHA	44	4	15	19	112	—	—	—	—	—
85-86	Baltimore	AHL	65	4	21	25	64	—	—	—	—	—
	Pittsburgh	NHL	5	1	2	3	2	—	—	—	—	—
86-87	Baltimore	AHL	51	1	16	17	50	—	—	—	—	—
	Pittsburgh	NHL	19	0	1	1	20	—	—	—	—	—
87-88	Pittsburgh	NHL	44	3	6	9	69	—	—	—	—	—
88-89	Pittsburgh	NHL	43	1	5	6	42	2	0	0	0	0
	Muskegon	IHL	10	3	6	9	14	—	—	—	—	—
89-90	Muskegon	IHL	6	1	1	2	8	—	—	—	—	—
	Pittsburgh	NHL	62	4	10	14	56	—	—	—	—	—
90-91	Pittsburgh	NHL	22	1	2	3	30	—	—	—	—	—
	Minnesota	NHL	42	2	6	8	33	23	1	6	7	20
91-92	Minnesota	NHL	74	1	13	14	68	7	0	0	0	6
92-93	Calgary	NHL	74	3	7	10	66	6	3	1	4	4
NHL totals			385	16	52	68	386	38	4	7	11	30

DAIGLE, ALEXANDRE
C, SENATORS

PERSONAL: Born February 7, 1975, at Montreal.... 6-0/170.... Shoots left.
TRANSACTIONS/CAREER NOTES: Selected by Ottawa Senators in first round (first Senators pick, first overall) of NHL entry draft (June 26, 1993).
HONORS: Won Can.HL Rookie of the Year Award (1991-92).... Named to Can.HL

All-Rookie Team (1991-92).... Named QMJHL Rookie of the Year (1991-92).... Won Michel Bergeron Trophy (1991-92). ... Named to the QMJHL All-Star second team (1991-92).... Won Can.HL Top Draft Prospect Award (1992-93).... Won QMJHL Top Draft Prospect Award (1992-93).... Named to QMJHL All-Star first team (1992-93).

			REGULAR SEASON					PLAYOFFS				
Season	Team	League	Gms.	G	A	Pts.	Pen.	Gms.	G	A	Pts.	Pen.
91-92—Victoriaville		QMJHL	66	35	75	110	63	—	—	—	—	—
92-93—Victoriaville		QMJHL	53	45	92	137	85	6	5	6	11	4

DAIGNEAULT, J.J.
D, CANADIENS

PERSONAL: Born October 12, 1965, at Montreal.... 5-11/185.... Shoots left.... Name pronounced DAYN-yoh.

TRANSACTIONS/CAREER NOTES: Underwent knee surgery (March 1984).... Selected by Vancouver Canucks as underage junior in first round (first Canucks pick, 10th overall) of NHL entry draft (June 1984).... Broke finger (March 19, 1986).... Traded by Canucks with second-round pick in 1986 draft (C Kent Hawley) and fifth-round pick in 1987 draft to Philadelphia Flyers for RW Rich Sutter, D Dave Richter and third-round pick in 1986 draft (D Don Gibson) (June 1986).... Sprained ankle (April 12, 1987).... Traded by Flyers to Montreal Canadiens for D Scott Sandelin (November 1988).... Bruised shoulder (December 1990).... Suffered left hip pointer (March 16, 1991).... Injured knee (April 7, 1991).... Bruised left knee (November 28, 1992); missed one game.... Injured shoulder (December 23, 1992); missed two games.... Sprained right ankle (March 1, 1993); missed 11 games.

HONORS: Won Emile (Butch) Bouchard Trophy (1982-83).... Named to QMJHL All-Star first team (1982-83).

MISCELLANEOUS: Member of Stanley Cup championship team (1993).

			REGULAR SEASON					PLAYOFFS				
Season	Team	League	Gms.	G	A	Pts.	Pen.	Gms.	G	A	Pts.	Pen.
81-82—Laval		QMJHL	64	4	25	29	41	18	1	3	4	2
82-83—Longueuil		QMJHL	70	26	58	84	58	15	4	11	15	35
83-84—Canadian Olympic Team		Int'l	62	6	15	21	40	—	—	—	—	—
—Longueuil		QMJHL	10	2	11	13	6	14	3	13	16	30
84-85—Vancouver		NHL	67	4	23	27	69	—	—	—	—	—
85-86—Vancouver		NHL	64	5	23	28	45	3	0	2	2	0
86-87—Philadelphia		NHL	77	6	16	22	56	9	1	0	1	0
87-88—Philadelphia		NHL	28	2	2	4	12	—	—	—	—	—
—Hershey		AHL	10	1	5	6	8	—	—	—	—	—
88-89—Hershey		AHL	12	0	10	10	13	—	—	—	—	—
—Sherbrooke		AHL	63	10	33	43	48	6	1	3	4	2
89-90—Sherbrooke		AHL	28	8	19	27	18	—	—	—	—	—
—Montreal		NHL	36	2	10	12	14	9	0	0	0	2
90-91—Montreal		NHL	51	3	16	19	31	5	0	1	1	0
91-92—Montreal		NHL	79	4	14	18	36	11	0	3	3	4
92-93—Montreal		NHL	66	8	10	18	57	20	1	3	4	22
NHL totals			468	34	114	148	320	57	2	9	11	28

D'ALESSIO, CORRIE
G, WHALERS

PERSONAL: Born September 9, 1969, at Cornwall, Ont.... 5-11/155.... Shoots left. ... Full name: Corrie Vince D'Alessio.

COLLEGE: Cornell.

TRANSACTIONS/CAREER NOTES: Selected by Vancouver Canucks in sixth round (fourth Canucks pick, 107th overall) of NHL entry draft (June 11, 1988).... Traded by Canucks with conditional pick in 1993 draft to Hartford Whalers for G Kay Whitmore (October 1, 1992).

HONORS: Named to ECAC All-Rookie team (1987-88).

			REGULAR SEASON							PLAYOFFS						
Season	Team	League	Gms.	Min.	W	L	T	GA	SO	Avg.	Gms.	Min.	W	L	GA	SO	Avg.
86-87—Pembrooke		BCJHL	25	1327	...	...	...	95	0	4.30	—	—	—	—	—	—	—
87-88—Cornell University		ECAC	25	1457	17	8	0	67	0	2.76	—	—	—	—	—	—	—
88-89—Cornell University		ECAC	29	1684	15	13	1	96	1	3.42	—	—	—	—	—	—	—
89-90—Cornell University		ECAC	16	887	6	7	2	50	0	3.38	—	—	—	—	—	—	—
90-91—Cornell University		ECAC	24	1160	10	7	3	67	0	3.47	—	—	—	—	—	—	—
91-92—Milwaukee		IHL	27	1435	9	14	2	96	0	4.01	2	119	0	2	12	0	6.05
92-93—Springfield		AHL	23	1120	3	13	2	77	0	4.13	4	75	1	0	3	0	2.40
—Hartford		NHL	1	11	0	0	0	0	0	0.00	—	—	—	—	—	—	—
NHL totals			1	11	0	0	0	0	0	0.00							

DALGARNO, BRAD
RW, ISLANDERS

PERSONAL: Born August 8, 1967, at Vancouver, B.C.... 6-4/215.... Shoots right.

TRANSACTIONS/CAREER NOTES: Selected by New York Islanders as underage junior in first round (first Islanders pick, sixth overall) of NHL entry draft (June 15, 1985).... Suffered concussion (November 1988).... Fractured orbital bone of left eye (February 21, 1989).... Sat out season in retirement (1989-90).... Bruised kidney (December 9, 1990); missed four games.... Lacerated jaw (January 13, 1991); missed three games.... Sprained left shoulder (November 27, 1991); missed four games. ... Reinjured left shoulder (December 11, 1991); missed seven games.... Fractured left wrist (January 12, 1992); missed final 37 games of season.... Underwent shoulder surgery (April 1, 1992).... Bruised shoulder (February 3, 1993); missed one game.

			REGULAR SEASON					PLAYOFFS				
Season	Team	League	Gms.	G	A	Pts.	Pen.	Gms.	G	A	Pts.	Pen.
83-84—Markham		MTHL	40	17	11	28	59	—	—	—	—	—
84-85—Hamilton		OHL	66	23	30	53	86	—	—	—	—	—

Season	Team	League	Gms.	G	A	Pts.	Pen.	Gms.	G	A	Pts.	Pen.
			REGULAR SEASON					PLAYOFFS				
85-86—New York Islanders	NHL	2	1	0	1	0	—	—	—	—	—
—Hamilton	OHL	54	22	43	65	79	—	—	—	—	—
86-87—Hamilton	OHL	60	27	32	59	100	—	—	—	—	—
—New York Islanders	NHL	—	—	—	—	—	1	0	1	1	0
87-88—New York Islanders	NHL	38	2	8	10	58	4	0	0	0	19
—Springfield	AHL	39	13	11	24	76	—	—	—	—	—
88-89—New York Islanders	NHL	55	11	10	21	86	—	—	—	—	—
89-90—						Did not play—retired.					
90-91—New York Islanders	NHL	41	3	12	15	24	—	—	—	—	—
—Capital District	AHL	27	6	14	20	26	—	—	—	—	—
91-92—Capital District	AHL	14	7	8	15	34	—	—	—	—	—
—New York Islanders	NHL	15	2	1	3	12	—	—	—	—	—
92-93—Capital District	AHL	19	10	4	14	16	—	—	—	—	—
—New York Islanders	NHL	57	15	17	32	62	18	2	2	4	14
NHL totals		**208**	**34**	**48**	**82**	**242**	**23**	**2**	**3**	**5**	**33**

DAMPHOUSSE, VINCENT
LW, CANADIENS

PERSONAL: Born December 17, 1967, at Montreal.... 6-1/185.... Shoots left.... Name pronounced DAHM-FOOZ.

TRANSACTIONS/CAREER NOTES: Selected by Toronto Maple Leafs as underage junior in first round (first Maple Leafs pick, sixth overall) of NHL entry draft (June 21, 1986).... Traded by Maple Leafs with D Luke Richardson, G Peter Ing, C Scott Thornton and future considerations to Edmonton Oilers for G Grant Fuhr, LW/RW Glenn Anderson and LW Craig Berube (September 19, 1991).... Traded by Oilers with fourth-round pick in 1993 draft to Montreal Canadiens for LW Shayne Corson, LW Vladimir Vutek and C Brent Gilchrist (August 27, 1992).

HONORS: Named to QMJHL All-Star second team (1985-86).... Played in NHL All-Star Game (1991 and 1992).... Named All-Star Game Most Valuable Player (1991).

RECORDS: Shares NHL All-Star single-game record for most goals—4 (1991).

MISCELLANEOUS: Member of Stanley Cup championship team (1993).

Season	Team	League	Gms.	G	A	Pts.	Pen.	Gms.	G	A	Pts.	Pen.
			REGULAR SEASON					PLAYOFFS				
83-84—Laval	QMJHL	66	29	36	65	25	—	—	—	—	—
84-85—Laval	QMJHL	68	35	68	103	62	—	—	—	—	—
85-86—Laval	QMJHL	69	45	110	155	70	14	9	27	36	12
86-87—Toronto	NHL	80	21	25	46	26	12	1	5	6	8
87-88—Toronto	NHL	75	12	36	48	40	6	0	1	1	10
88-89—Toronto	NHL	80	26	42	68	75	—	—	—	—	—
89-90—Toronto	NHL	80	33	61	94	56	5	0	2	2	2
90-91—Toronto	NHL	79	26	47	73	65	—	—	—	—	—
91-92—Edmonton	NHL	80	38	51	89	53	16	6	8	14	8
92-93—Montreal	NHL	84	39	58	97	98	20	11	12	23	16
NHL totals		**558**	**195**	**320**	**515**	**413**	**59**	**18**	**28**	**46**	**44**

DANDENAULT, ERIC
D, FLYERS

PERSONAL: Born March 10, 1970, at Sherbrooke, Que.... 6-0/193.... Shoots right. ... Name pronounced DAN-duh-noh.

TRANSACTIONS/CAREER NOTES: Signed as free agent by Philadelphia Flyers (October 4, 1991).

Season	Team	League	Gms.	G	A	Pts.	Pen.	Gms.	G	A	Pts.	Pen.
			REGULAR SEASON					PLAYOFFS				
90-91—Drummondville	QMJHL	67	14	33	47	215	—	—	—	—	—
91-92—Hershey	AHL	69	6	13	19	149	3	0	0	0	4
92-93—Hershey	AHL	72	20	19	39	118	—	—	—	—	—

DANEYKO, KEN
D, DEVILS

PERSONAL: Born April 17, 1964, at Windsor, Ont.... 6-0/210.... Shoots left.... Name pronounced DAN-ee-KOH.

TRANSACTIONS/CAREER NOTES: Selected by Seattle Breakers from Spokane Flyers in WHL dispersal draft (December 1981).... Selected by New Jersey Devils as underage junior in first round (second Devils pick, 18th overall) of NHL entry draft (June 1982).... Fractured right fibula (November 2, 1983).... Suspended one game and fined $500 by NHL for playing in West Germany without permission (October 1985).... Injured wrist (February 25, 1987).... Broke nose (February 24, 1988).

Season	Team	League	Gms.	G	A	Pts.	Pen.	Gms.	G	A	Pts.	Pen.
			REGULAR SEASON					PLAYOFFS				
80-81—Spokane Flyers	WHL	62	6	13	19	140	4	0	0	0	6
81-82—Spokane Flyers	WHL	26	1	11	12	147	—	—	—	—	—
—Seattle	WHL	38	1	22	23	151	14	1	9	10	49
82-83—Seattle	WHL	69	17	43	60	150	4	1	3	4	14
83-84—Kamloops	WHL	19	6	28	34	52	17	4	9	13	28
—New Jersey	NHL	11	1	4	5	17	—	—	—	—	—
84-85—New Jersey	NHL	1	0	0	0	10	—	—	—	—	—
—Maine	AHL	80	4	9	13	206	11	1	3	4	36
85-86—Maine	AHL	21	3	2	5	75	—	—	—	—	—
—New Jersey	NHL	44	0	10	10	100	—	—	—	—	—

Season Team	League	REGULAR SEASON					PLAYOFFS				
		Gms.	G	A	Pts.	Pen.	Gms.	G	A	Pts.	Pen.
86-87—New Jersey	NHL	79	2	12	14	183	—	—	—	—	—
87-88—New Jersey	NHL	80	5	7	12	239	20	1	6	7	83
88-89—New Jersey	NHL	80	5	5	10	283	—	—	—	—	—
89-90—New Jersey	NHL	74	6	15	21	216	6	2	0	2	21
90-91—New Jersey	NHL	80	4	16	20	249	7	0	1	1	10
91-92—New Jersey	NHL	80	1	7	8	170	7	0	3	3	16
92-93—New Jersey	NHL	84	2	11	13	236	5	0	0	0	8
NHL totals		613	26	87	113	1703	45	3	10	13	138

DANIELS, JEFF
LW, PENGUINS

PERSONAL: Born June 24, 1968, at Oshawa, Ont. . . . 6-1/200. . . . Shoots left.
TRANSACTIONS/CAREER NOTES: Selected by Pittsburgh Penguins as underage junior in sixth round (sixth Penguins pick, 109th overall) of NHL entry draft (June 21, 1986).
MISCELLANEOUS: Member of Stanley Cup championship team (1992).

Season Team	League	REGULAR SEASON					PLAYOFFS				
		Gms.	G	A	Pts.	Pen.	Gms.	G	A	Pts.	Pen.
84-85—Oshawa	OHL	59	7	11	18	16	—	—	—	—	—
85-86—Oshawa	OHL	62	13	19	32	23	6	0	1	1	0
86-87—Oshawa	OHL	54	14	9	23	22	15	3	2	5	5
87-88—Oshawa	OHL	64	29	39	68	59	4	2	3	5	0
88-89—Muskegon	IHL	58	21	21	42	58	11	3	5	8	11
89-90—Muskegon	IHL	80	30	47	77	39	6	1	1	2	7
90-91—Pittsburgh	NHL	11	0	2	2	2	—	—	—	—	—
—Muskegon	IHL	62	23	29	52	18	5	1	3	4	2
91-92—Pittsburgh	NHL	2	0	0	0	0	—	—	—	—	—
—Muskegon	IHL	44	19	16	35	38	10	5	4	9	9
92-93—Pittsburgh	NHL	58	5	4	9	14	12	3	2	5	0
—Cleveland	IHL	3	2	1	3	0	—	—	—	—	—
NHL totals		71	5	6	11	16	12	3	2	5	0

DANIELS, SCOTT
LW, WHALERS

PERSONAL: Born September 19, 1969, at Prince Albert, Sask. . . . 6-3/200. . . . Shoots left.
TRANSACTIONS/CAREER NOTES: Selected by Hartford Whalers in seventh round (sixth Whalers pick, 136th overall) of NHL entry draft (June 17, 1989).

Season Team	League	REGULAR SEASON					PLAYOFFS				
		Gms.	G	A	Pts.	Pen.	Gms.	G	A	Pts.	Pen.
86-87—Kamloops	WHL	43	6	4	10	68	—	—	—	—	—
—New Westminster	WHL	19	4	7	11	30	—	—	—	—	—
87-88—New Westminster	WHL	37	6	11	17	157	—	—	—	—	—
—Regina	WHL	19	2	3	5	83	—	—	—	—	—
88-89—Regina	WHL	64	21	26	47	241	—	—	—	—	—
89-90—Regina	WHL	52	28	31	59	171	—	—	—	—	—
90-91—Springfield	AHL	40	2	6	8	121	—	—	—	—	—
—Louisville	ECHL	9	5	3	8	34	1	0	2	2	0
91-92—Springfield	AHL	54	7	15	22	213	10	0	0	0	32
92-93—Hartford	NHL	1	0	0	0	19	—	—	—	—	—
—Springfield	AHL	60	11	12	23	181	12	2	7	9	12
NHL totals		1	0	0	0	19					

DARBY, CRAIG
C, CANADIENS

PERSONAL: Born September 26, 1972, at Oneida, N.Y. . . . 6-3/180. . . . Shoots right.
HIGH SCHOOL: Albany (N.Y.) Academy.
COLLEGE: Providence.
TRANSACTIONS/CAREER NOTES: Selected by Montreal Canadiens in second round (third Canadiens pick, 43rd overall) of NHL entry draft (June 22, 1991).
HONORS: Named Hockey East co-Rookie of the Year with Ian Moran (1991-92). . . . Named to Hockey East All-Rookie team (1991-92).

Season Team	League	REGULAR SEASON					PLAYOFFS				
		Gms.	G	A	Pts.	Pen.	Gms.	G	A	Pts.	Pen.
89-90—Albany Academy	N.Y. H.S.	29	32	53	85	. . .	—	—	—	—	—
90-91—Albany Academy	N.Y. H.S.	. . .	33	61	94	. . .	—	—	—	—	—
91-92—Providence College	Hockey East	35	17	24	41	47	—	—	—	—	—
92-93—Providence College	Hockey East	35	11	21	32	62	—	—	—	—	—

DARLING, DION
D, CANADIENS

PERSONAL: Born October 22, 1974, at Edmonton, Alta. . . . 6-3/205. . . . Shoots left.
TRANSACTIONS/CAREER NOTES: Selected by Montreal Canadiens in fifth round (seventh Canadiens pick, 125th overall) of NHL entry draft (June 26, 1993).

Season Team	League	REGULAR SEASON					PLAYOFFS				
		Gms.	G	A	Pts.	Pen.	Gms.	G	A	Pts.	Pen.
91-92—St. Albert	AJHL	29	5	15	20	101	—	—	—	—	—
92-93—Spokane	WHL	68	1	4	5	168	9	0	1	1	14

DAVIDSON, LEE

C, JETS

PERSONAL: Born June 30, 1968, at Winnipeg, Man. . . . 5-10/180. . . . Shoots left.
COLLEGE: North Dakota.
TRANSACTIONS/CAREER NOTES: Selected by Washington Capitals in eighth round (ninth Capitals pick, 166th overall) of NHL entry draft (June 21, 1986). . . . Signed as free agent by Winnipeg Jets (September 4, 1990).
HONORS: Named to WCHA All-Star second team (1989-90). . . . Named to NCAA All-America West second team (1989-90).

		REGULAR SEASON					PLAYOFFS				
Season Team	League	Gms.	G	A	Pts.	Pen.	Gms.	G	A	Pts.	Pen.
85-86—Penticton	BCJHL	48	34	74	108	90	8	2	7	9	10
86-87—Univ. of North Dakota	WCHA	41	16	12	28	65	—	—	—	—	—
87-88—Univ. of North Dakota	WCHA	40	22	24	46	74	—	—	—	—	—
88-89—Univ. of North Dakota	WCHA	41	16	37	53	60	—	—	—	—	—
89-90—Univ. of North Dakota	WCHA	45	26	49	75	66	—	—	—	—	—
90-91—Moncton	AHL	69	15	17	32	24	—	—	—	—	—
91-92—Moncton	AHL	43	3	12	15	32	—	—	—	—	—
—Fort Wayne	IHL	22	4	10	14	30	7	2	5	7	8
92-93—Fort Wayne	IHL	60	22	20	42	58	12	2	0	2	21

DAVYDOV, EVGENY

LW/RW, JETS

PERSONAL: Born May 27, 1967, at Chelyabinsk, U.S.S.R. . . . 6-1/185. . . . Shoots right. . . . Name pronounced DAY-vih-dahf.
TRANSACTIONS/CAREER NOTES: Selected by Winnipeg Jets in 12th round (14th Jets pick, 235th overall) of NHL entry draft (June 17, 1989). . . . Suffered from the flu (December 27, 1993); missed one game.
MISCELLANEOUS: Member of gold-medal-winning Unified Olympic team (1992).

		REGULAR SEASON					PLAYOFFS				
Season Team	League	Gms.	G	A	Pts.	Pen.	Gms.	G	A	Pts.	Pen.
84-85—Chelyabinsk	USSR	5	1	0	1	2	—	—	—	—	—
85-86—Chelyabinsk	USSR	39	11	5	16	22	—	—	—	—	—
86-87—CSKA Moscow	USSR	32	11	2	13	8	—	—	—	—	—
87-88—CSKA Moscow	USSR	44	16	7	23	18	—	—	—	—	—
88-89—CSKA Moscow	USSR	35	9	7	16	4	—	—	—	—	—
89-90—CSKA Moscow	USSR	44	17	6	23	16	—	—	—	—	—
90-91—CSKA Moscow	USSR	44	10	10	20	26	—	—	—	—	—
91-92—CSKA Moscow	CIS	27	13	12	25	14	—	—	—	—	—
—Unified Olympic Team	Int'l	8	3	3	6	2	—	—	—	—	—
—Winnipeg	NHL	12	4	3	7	8	7	2	2	4	2
92-93—Winnipeg	NHL	79	28	21	49	66	4	0	0	0	0
NHL totals		91	32	24	56	74	11	2	2	4	2

DAWE, JASON

LW, SABRES

PERSONAL: Born May 29, 1973, at North York, Ont. . . . 5-10/195. . . . Shoots left. . . . Name pronounced DAW.
TRANSACTIONS/CAREER NOTES: Tore ankle ligaments (September 1989). . . . Selected by Buffalo Sabres in second round (second Sabres pick, 35th overall) of NHL entry draft (June 22, 1991).
HONORS: Named to Can. HL All-Star second team (1992-93). . . . Named to OHL All-Star first team (1992-93).

		REGULAR SEASON					PLAYOFFS				
Season Team	League	Gms.	G	A	Pts.	Pen.	Gms.	G	A	Pts.	Pen.
89-90—Peterborough	OHL	50	15	18	33	19	12	4	7	11	4
90-91—Peterborough	OHL	66	43	27	70	43	4	3	1	4	0
91-92—Peterborough	OHL	66	53	55	108	55	4	5	0	5	0
92-93—Peterborough	OHL	59	58	68	126	80	21	18	33	51	18

DAY, JOE

C, WHALERS

PERSONAL: Born May 11, 1968, at Chicago. . . . 5-11/180. . . . Shoots left. . . . Full name: Joseph Christopher Day.
COLLEGE: St. Lawrence (N.Y.).
TRANSACTIONS/CAREER NOTES: Selected by Hartford Whalers in ninth round (eighth Whalers pick, 186th overall) of NHL entry draft (June 13, 1987). . . . Fractured right foot (April 4, 1992); missed playoffs.
HONORS: Named to ECAC All-Star second team (1989-90).

		REGULAR SEASON					PLAYOFFS				
Season Team	League	Gms.	G	A	Pts.	Pen.	Gms.	G	A	Pts.	Pen.
85-86—Chicago Minor Hawks	Ill.	30	23	18	41	69	—	—	—	—	—
86-87—St. Lawrence University	ECAC	33	9	11	20	25	—	—	—	—	—
87-88—St. Lawrence University	ECAC	33	23	17	40	40	—	—	—	—	—
88-89—St. Lawrence University	ECAC	36	21	27	48	44	—	—	—	—	—
89-90—St. Lawrence University	ECAC	30	18	26	44	24	—	—	—	—	—
90-91—Springfield	AHL	75	24	29	53	82	18	5	5	10	27
91-92—Springfield	AHL	50	33	25	58	92	—	—	—	—	—
—Hartford	NHL	24	0	3	3	10	15	0	8	8	40
92-93—Springfield	AHL	33	15	20	35	118	—	—	—	—	—
—Hartford	NHL	24	1	7	8	47	—	—	—	—	—
NHL totals		48	1	10	11	57					

DAZE, ERIC

LW, BLACKHAWKS

PERSONAL: Born July 2, 1975, at Montreal. . . . 6-4/202. . . . Shoots left.
TRANSACTIONS/CAREER NOTES: Selected by Chicago Blackhawks in fourth round (fifth Blackhawks pick, 90th overall) of NHL entry draft (June 26, 1993).

Season Team	League	REGULAR SEASON					PLAYOFFS				
		Gms.	G	A	Pts.	Pen.	Gms.	G	A	Pts.	Pen.
92-93—Beauport	QMJHL	68	19	36	55	24	—	—	—	—	—

DEADMARSH, ADAM
RW, NORDIQUES

PERSONAL: Born May 10, 1975, at Trail, B.C. . . . . 5-11/200. . . . Shoots right.
HIGH SCHOOL: Lakeridge High School (Fruitvale, B.C.).
TRANSACTIONS/CAREER NOTES: Selected by Quebec Nordiques in first round (second Nordiques pick, 14th overall) of NHL entry draft (June 26, 1993).

Season Team	League	REGULAR SEASON					PLAYOFFS				
		Gms.	G	A	Pts.	Pen.	Gms.	G	A	Pts.	Pen.
91-92—Portland	WHL	68	30	30	60	81	6	3	3	6	13
92-93—Portland	WHL	58	33	36	69	126	16	7	8	15	29

DEAN, KEVIN
D, DEVILS

PERSONAL: Born April 1, 1969, at Madison, Wis. . . . 6-2/195. . . . Shoots left.
HIGH SCHOOL: Culver Military Academy (Ind.).
COLLEGE: New Hampshire.
TRANSACTIONS/CAREER NOTES: Selected by New Jersey Devils in fourth round (fourth Devils pick, 86th overall) of NHL entry draft (June 13, 1987).

Season Team	League	REGULAR SEASON					PLAYOFFS				
		Gms.	G	A	Pts.	Pen.	Gms.	G	A	Pts.	Pen.
85-86—Culver Military Academy..	Indiana H.S.	35	28	44	72	48	—	—	—	—	—
86-87—Culver Military Academy..	Indiana H.S.	25	19	25	44	30	—	—	—	—	—
87-88—Univ. of New Hampshire ...	Hockey East	27	1	6	7	34	—	—	—	—	—
88-89—Univ. of New Hampshire ...	Hockey East	34	1	12	13	28	—	—	—	—	—
89-90—Univ. of New Hampshire ...	Hockey East	39	2	6	8	42	—	—	—	—	—
90-91—Univ. of New Hampshire ...	Hockey East	31	10	12	22	22	—	—	—	—	—
—Utica	AHL	7	0	1	1	2	—	—	—	—	—
91-92—Utica	AHL	23	0	3	3	6	—	—	—	—	—
—Cincinnati	ECHL	30	3	22	25	43	9	1	6	7	8
92-93—Utica	AHL	57	2	16	18	76	5	1	0	1	8
—Cincinnati	IHL	13	2	1	3	15	—	—	—	—	—

DEASLEY, BRYAN
LW, NORDIQUES

PERSONAL: Born November 26, 1968, at Toronto. . . . 6-3/205. . . . Shoots left. . . . Full name: Bryan Thomas Deasley.
COLLEGE: Michigan.
TRANSACTIONS/CAREER NOTES: Broke ribs (February 1986). . . . Fractured wrist (January 1987). . . . Selected by Calgary Flames in first round (first Flames pick, 19th overall) of NHL entry draft (June 13, 1987). . . . Underwent ankle surgery (July 1987). . . . Traded by Flames to Quebec Nordiques for C Claude Loiselle (March 2, 1991); trade cancelled by NHL when Loiselle was claimed by Toronto Maple Leafs on waivers prior to the trade; Deasley returned to Flames. . . . Traded by Flames to Nordiques for future considerations (October 26, 1993).

Season Team	League	REGULAR SEASON					PLAYOFFS				
		Gms.	G	A	Pts.	Pen.	Gms.	G	A	Pts.	Pen.
85-86—St. Michael's Jr. B	ODHA	30	17	20	37	88	—	—	—	—	—
86-87—University of Michigan	CCHA	38	13	10	23	74	—	—	—	—	—
87-88—University of Michigan	CCHA	27	18	4	22	38	—	—	—	—	—
88-89—Canadian national team ...	Int'l	54	19	19	38	32	—	—	—	—	—
—Salt Lake City	IHL	—	—	—	—	—	7	3	3	6	25
89-90—Salt Lake City	IHL	71	16	11	27	46	11	4	0	4	8
90-91—Salt Lake City	IHL	75	24	21	45	63	1	0	0	0	0
91-92—Salt Lake City	IHL	65	12	23	35	67	2	0	0	0	4
92-93—Halifax	AHL	37	9	11	20	46	—	—	—	—	—

DeBRUSK, LOUIE
LW, OILERS

PERSONAL: Born March 19, 1971, at Cambridge, Ont. . . . 6-2/215. . . . Shoots left. . . . Full name: Dennis Louis DeBrusk. . . . Name pronounced duh-BRUHSK.
HIGH SCHOOL: Saugeen (Port Elgin, Ont.).
TRANSACTIONS/CAREER NOTES: Selected by New York Rangers in third round (fourth Rangers pick, 49th overall) of NHL entry draft (June 17, 1989). . . . Traded by Rangers with C Bernie Nicholls, RW Steven Rice and future considerations to Edmonton Oilers for C Mark Messier and future considerations (October 4, 1991); Rangers later traded D David Shaw to Oilers for D Jeff Beukeboom to complete the deal (November 12, 1991). . . . Separated shoulder (January 28, 1992); missed four games. . . . Strained groin (January 1993); missed five games. . . . Strained abdominal muscle (January 1993); missed 11 games.

Season Team	League	REGULAR SEASON					PLAYOFFS				
		Gms.	G	A	Pts.	Pen.	Gms.	G	A	Pts.	Pen.
87-88—Stratford Jr. B	OHA	43	13	14	27	205	—	—	—	—	—
88-89—London	OHL	59	11	11	22	149	19	1	1	2	43
89-90—London	OHL	61	21	19	40	198	6	2	2	4	24
90-91—London	OHL	61	31	33	64	*223	7	2	2	4	14
—Binghamton	AHL	2	0	0	0	7	2	0	0	0	9
91-92—Edmonton	NHL	25	2	1	3	124	—	—	—	—	—
—Cape Breton	AHL	28	2	2	4	73	—	—	—	—	—
92-93—Edmonton	NHL	51	8	2	10	205	—	—	—	—	—
NHL totals		76	10	3	13	329					

DEGRACE, YANICK
G, FLYERS

PERSONAL: Born April 16, 1971, at Lameque, N.B. . . . 5-11/175. . . . Shoots left. . . . Name pronounced deh-GRAHZ.
TRANSACTIONS/CAREER NOTES: Selected by Philadelphia Flyers in fifth round (fourth Flyers pick, 94th overall) of NHL entry draft (June 22, 1991).

			REGULAR SEASON								PLAYOFFS					
Season	Team	League	Gms.	Min.	W	L	T	GA	SO	Avg.	Gms.	Min.	W	L	GA	SO	Avg.
90-91	Trois-Rivieres	QMJHL	33	1726	13	11	2	97	1	3.37	—	—	—	—	—	—	—
91-92	Hull	QMJHL	35	1970	18	9	3	112	...	3.41	2	31	0	2	4	...	7.74
	—Hershey	AHL	2	125	0	1	1	6	0	2.88	—	—	—	—	—	—	—
92-93	Hershey	AHL	30	1442	10	15	2	103	1	4.29	—	—	—	—	—	—	—

DeGRAY, DALE
D

PERSONAL: Born September 3, 1963, at Oshawa, Ont. . . . 6-0/206. . . . Shoots right. . . . Full name: Dale Edward DeGray.
TRANSACTIONS/CAREER NOTES: Selected by Calgary Flames as underage junior in eighth round (seventh Flames pick, 162nd overall) of NHL entry draft (June 10, 1981). . . . Traded by Flames to Toronto Maple Leafs for future considerations (September 1987). . . . Separated left shoulder (January 1988); missed 15 games. . . . Selected by Los Angeles Kings in 1988 NHL waiver draft for $12,500 (October 3, 1988). . . . Sprained knee (October 1988). . . . Suffered concussion (December 1988). . . . Traded by Kings to Buffalo Sabres for D Bob Halkidis (November 24, 1989). . . . Signed as free agent by San Diego Gulls (August 27, 1992).
HONORS: Named to AHL All-Star second team (1984-85). . . . Named to IHL All-Star second team (1992-93).

			REGULAR SEASON					PLAYOFFS			
Season	Team	League	Gms.	G	A	Pts.	Pen.	Gms.	G	A	Pts.	Pen.
79-80	Oshawa Jr. B	ODHA	42	14	14	28	34	—	—	—	—	—
	—Oshawa	OMJHL	1	0	0	0	2	—	—	—	—	—
80-81	Oshawa	OMJHL	61	11	10	21	93	8	1	1	2	19
81-82	Oshawa	OHL	66	11	22	33	162	12	3	4	7	49
82-83	Oshawa	OHL	69	20	30	50	149	17	7	7	14	36
83-84	Colorado	CHL	67	16	14	30	67	6	1	1	2	2
84-85	Moncton	AHL	77	24	37	61	63	—	—	—	—	—
85-86	Moncton	AHL	76	10	31	41	128	6	0	1	1	0
	—Calgary	NHL	1	0	0	0	0	—	—	—	—	—
86-87	Moncton	AHL	45	10	22	32	57	5	2	1	3	19
	—Calgary	NHL	27	6	7	13	29	—	—	—	—	—
87-88	Toronto	NHL	56	6	18	24	63	5	0	1	1	16
	—Newmarket	AHL	8	2	10	12	8	—	—	—	—	—
88-89	Los Angeles	NHL	63	6	22	28	97	8	1	2	3	12
89-90	New Haven	AHL	16	2	10	12	38	—	—	—	—	—
	—Rochester	AHL	50	6	25	31	118	17	5	6	11	59
	—Buffalo	NHL	6	0	0	0	6	—	—	—	—	—
90-91	Rochester	AHL	64	9	25	34	121	15	3	4	7	*76
91-92	Alleghe	Italy	27	6	24	30	46	—	—	—	—	—
92-93	San Diego	IHL	79	18	64	82	181	14	3	11	14	77
	NHL totals		153	18	47	65	195	13	1	3	4	28

DelGUIDICE, MATT
G, BRUINS

PERSONAL: Born March 5, 1967, at West Haven, Conn. . . . 5-9/170. . . . Shoots right. . . . Name pronounced dehl-JOO-dihz.
COLLEGE: St. Anselm (N.H.), then Maine.
TRANSACTIONS/CAREER NOTES: Selected by Boston Bruins in fourth round (fourth Bruins pick, 77th overall) of NHL entry draft (June 13, 1987).

			REGULAR SEASON								PLAYOFFS					
Season	Team	League	Gms.	Min.	W	L	T	GA	SO	Avg.	Gms.	Min.	W	L	GA	SO	Avg.
86-87	St. Anselm College	ECAC-II	24	1437	11	13	0	76	...	3.17	—	—	—	—	—	—	—
87-88	University of Maine	Hoc. East					Did not play—transfer student.										
88-89	University of Maine	Hoc. East	20	1090	16	4	0	57	1	*3.14	—	—	—	—	—	—	—
89-90	University of Maine	Hoc. East	23	1257	16	4	0	68	0	3.25	—	—	—	—	—	—	—
90-91	Boston	NHL	1	10	0	0	0	0	0	0.00	—	—	—	—	—	—	—
	—Maine	AHL	52	2893	23	18	9	160	2	3.32	2	82	1	1	5	0	3.66
91-92	Maine	AHL	25	1369	5	15	0	101	0	4.43	—	—	—	—	—	—	—
	—Boston	NHL	10	424	2	5	1	28	0	3.96	—	—	—	—	—	—	—
92-93	Providence	AHL	9	478	0	7	1	58	0	7.28	—	—	—	—	—	—	—
	—San Diego	IHL	1	20	0	0	0	2	0	6.00	—	—	—	—	—	—	—
	NHL totals		11	434	2	5	1	28	0	3.87							

DePALMA, LARRY
LW, SHARKS

PERSONAL: Born October 27, 1965, at Trenton, Mich. . . . 5-11/200. . . . Shoots left.
TRANSACTIONS/CAREER NOTES: Signed as free agent by Minnesota North Stars (March 1986). . . . Injured wrist (October 1987). . . . Sprained ankle ligaments (February 1989). . . . Signed as free agent by San Jose Sharks (August 30, 1991). . . . Injured back (December 18, 1992); missed nine games.
HONORS: Named to WHL All-Star second team (1985-86).

			REGULAR SEASON					PLAYOFFS			
Season	Team	League	Gms.	G	A	Pts.	Pen.	Gms.	G	A	Pts.	Pen.
84-85	New Westminster	WHL	65	14	16	30	87	10	1	1	2	25
85-86	Saskatoon	WHL	65	61	51	112	232	13	7	9	16	58
	—Minnesota	NHL	1	0	0	0	0	—	—	—	—	—

D

Season Team	League	REGULAR SEASON					PLAYOFFS				
		Gms.	G	A	Pts.	Pen.	Gms.	G	A	Pts.	Pen.
86-87—Springfield	AHL	9	2	2	4	82	—	—	—	—	—
—Minnesota	NHL	56	9	6	15	219	—	—	—	—	—
87-88—Baltimore	AHL	16	8	10	18	121	—	—	—	—	—
—Kalamazoo	IHL	22	6	11	17	215	—	—	—	—	—
—Minnesota	NHL	7	1	1	2	15	—	—	—	—	—
88-89—Minnesota	NHL	43	5	7	12	102	2	0	0	0	6
89-90—Kalamazoo	IHL	36	7	14	21	218	4	1	1	2	32
90-91—Kalamazoo	IHL	55	27	32	59	160	11	5	4	9	25
—Minnesota	NHL	14	3	0	3	26	—	—	—	—	—
91-92—Kansas City	IHL	62	28	29	57	188	15	7	13	20	34
92-93—Kansas City	IHL	30	11	11	22	83	10	1	4	5	20
—San Jose	NHL	20	2	6	8	41	—	—	—	—	—
NHL totals		141	20	20	40	403	2	0	0	0	6

DERKSEN, DUANE
G, CAPITALS

PERSONAL: Born July 7, 1968, at St. Boniface, Man. . . . 6-1/180. . . . Shoots left. . . . Full name: Duane Edward Derksen.
COLLEGE: Wisconsin.
TRANSACTIONS/CAREER NOTES: Selected by Washington Capitals in third round (fourth Capitals choice, 57th overall) of NHL entry draft (June 11, 1988).
HONORS: Named NCAA Tournament Most Outstanding Goalie (1989-90). . . . Named to NCAA All-Tournament team (1989-90). . . . Named to WCHA All-Star second team (1989-90 and 1990-91). . . . Won WCHA Most Valuable Player Award (1991-92). . . . Named to NCAA All-America West second team (1991-92). . . . Named to WCHA All-Star first team (1991-92).

Season Team	League	REGULAR SEASON								PLAYOFFS						
		Gms.	Min.	W	L	T	GA	SO	Avg.	Gms.	Min.	W	L	GA	SO	Avg.
86-87—Winkler	SOJHL	48	2140	...	...	...	171	1	4.79	—	—	—	—	—	—	—
87-88—Winkler	SOJHL	38	2294	...	...	...	198	0	5.18	—	—	—	—	—	—	—
88-89—Univ. of Wisconsin	WCHA	11	561	4	5	0	37	0	3.96	—	—	—	—	—	—	—
89-90—Univ. of Wisconsin	WCHA	*41	*2345	*31	8	1	133	*2	*3.40	—	—	—	—	—	—	—
90-91—Univ. of Wisconsin	WCHA	*42	*2474	24	15	3	133	3	3.23	—	—	—	—	—	—	—
91-92—Univ. of Wisconsin	WCHA	35	*2064	21	12	†2	110	0	3.20	—	—	—	—	—	—	—
92-93—Baltimore	AHL	26	1247	6	13	3	86	0	4.14	4	188	1	1	7	0	2.23
—Hampton Roads	ECHL	13	747	...	...	...	48	0	3.86	—	—	—	—	—	—	—

DEROUVILLE, PHILLIPPE
G, PENGUINS

PERSONAL: Born August 7, 1974, at Arthabaska, Que. . . . 6-2/180. . . . Shoots left.
TRANSACTIONS/CAREER NOTES: Selected by Pittsburgh Penguins in fifth round (fifth Penguins pick, 115th overall) of NHL entry draft (June 20, 1992).
HONORS: Won Raymond Lagace Trophy (1991-92). . . . Named to QMJHL All-Star second team (1992-93).

Season Team	League	REGULAR SEASON								PLAYOFFS						
		Gms.	Min.	W	L	T	GA	SO	Avg.	Gms.	Min.	W	L	GA	SO	Avg.
90-91—Longueuil	QMJHL	20	1030	13	6	0	50	0	2.91	—	—	—	—	—	—	—
91-92—Longueuil	QMJHL	34	1854	20	6	3	99	2	3.20	11	593	†7	2	28	†1	2.83
92-93—Verdun	QMJHL	*61	*3491	30	27	2	210	1	3.61	4	257	...	...	18	0	4.20

DESJARDINS, ERIC
D, CANADIENS

PERSONAL: Born June 14, 1969, at Rouyn, Que. . . . 6-1/200. . . . Shoots right. . . . Name pronounced dez-zhar-DAI.
TRANSACTIONS/CAREER NOTES: Selected by Montreal Canadiens as underage junior in second round (third Canadiens pick, 38th overall) of NHL entry draft (June 13, 1987). . . . Suffered from the flu (January 1989). . . . Pulled groin (November 2, 1989); missed seven games. . . . Sprained left ankle (January 26, 1991); missed 16 games. . . . Fractured right thumb (December 8, 1991); missed two games.
HONORS: Named to QMJHL All-Star second team (1986-87). . . . Won Emile (Butch) Bouchard Trophy (1987-88). . . . Named to QMJHL All-Star first team (1987-88). . . . Played in NHL All-Star Game (1992).
MISCELLANEOUS: Member of Stanley Cup championship team (1993).

Season Team	League	REGULAR SEASON					PLAYOFFS				
		Gms.	G	A	Pts.	Pen.	Gms.	G	A	Pts.	Pen.
86-87—Granby	QMJHL	66	14	24	38	75	8	3	2	5	10
87-88—Granby	QMJHL	62	18	49	67	138	5	0	3	3	10
—Sherbrooke	AHL	3	0	0	0	6	4	0	2	2	2
88-89—Montreal	NHL	36	2	12	14	26	14	1	1	2	6
89-90—Montreal	NHL	55	3	13	16	51	6	0	0	0	10
90-91—Montreal	NHL	62	7	18	25	27	13	1	4	5	8
91-92—Montreal	NHL	77	6	32	38	50	11	3	3	6	4
92-93—Montreal	NHL	82	13	32	45	98	20	4	10	14	23
NHL totals		312	31	107	138	252	64	9	18	27	51

DIDUCK, GERALD
D, CANUCKS

PERSONAL: Born April 6, 1965, at Edmonton, Alta. . . . 6-2/207. . . . Shoots right. . . . Name pronounced DIH-duhk.
TRANSACTIONS/CAREER NOTES: Selected by New York Islanders as underage junior in first round (second Islanders pick, 16th overall) of NHL entry draft (June 8, 1983). . . . Frac-

tured left foot (November 1987).... Fractured right hand (November 1988).... Injured knee (January 1989).... Traded by Islanders to Montreal Canadiens for D Craig Ludwig (September 4, 1990).... Traded by Canadiens to Vancouver Canucks for fourth-round pick in 1991 draft (LW Vladimir Vujtek) (January 12, 1991).... Bruised knee (March 16, 1991).... Strained groin (January 4, 1993); missed three games.

| | | | REGULAR SEASON | | | | PLAYOFFS | | | |
Season	Team	League	Gms.	G	A	Pts.	Pen.	Gms.	G	A	Pts.	Pen.
81-82	—Lethbridge	WHL	71	1	15	16	81	12	0	3	3	27
82-83	—Lethbridge	WHL	67	8	16	24	151	20	3	12	15	49
83-84	—Lethbridge	WHL	65	10	24	34	133	5	1	4	5	27
	—Indianapolis	IHL	—	—	—	—	—	10	1	6	7	19
84-85	—New York Islanders	NHL	65	2	8	10	80	—	—	—	—	—
85-86	—New York Islanders	NHL	10	1	2	3	2	—	—	—	—	—
	—Springfield	AHL	61	6	14	20	175	—	—	—	—	—
86-87	—Springfield	AHL	45	6	8	14	120	—	—	—	—	—
	—New York Islanders	NHL	30	2	3	5	67	14	0	1	1	35
87-88	—New York Islanders	NHL	68	7	12	19	113	6	1	0	1	42
88-89	—New York Islanders	NHL	65	11	21	32	155	—	—	—	—	—
89-90	—New York Islanders	NHL	76	3	17	20	163	5	0	0	0	12
90-91	—Montreal	NHL	32	1	2	3	39	—	—	—	—	—
	—Vancouver	NHL	31	3	7	10	66	6	1	0	1	11
91-92	—Vancouver	NHL	77	6	21	27	229	5	0	0	0	10
92-93	—Vancouver	NHL	80	6	14	20	171	12	4	2	6	12
	NHL totals		534	42	107	149	1085	48	6	3	9	122

DiMAIO, ROB
C, LIGHTNING

PERSONAL: Born February 19, 1968, at Calgary, Alta.... 5-10/190.... Shoots right.... Name pronounced duh-MIGH-oh.

TRANSACTIONS/CAREER NOTES: Traded by Kamloops Blazers with LW Dave Mackey and C Kalvin Knibbs to Medicine Hat Tigers for LW Doug Pickel and LW Sean Pass (December 1985).... Selected by New York Islanders in sixth round (sixth Islanders pick, 118th overall) of NHL entry draft (June 13, 1987).... Suspended two games by WHL for leaving bench to fight (January 28, 1988).... Bruised left hand (February 1989).... Sprained clavicle (November 1989).... Sprained wrist (February 20, 1992); missed four games.... Reinjured wrist (February 29, 1992); missed final 17 games of season.... Underwent surgery to repair torn ligaments in wrist (March 11, 1992).... Selected by Tampa Bay Lightning in NHL expansion draft (June 18, 1992).... Bruised wrist (November 28, 1992); missed four games. ... Sprained ankle (February 14, 1993); missed nine games.... Reinjured right ankle (March 20, 1993); missed three games. ... Reinjured right ankle (April 1, 1993); missed remainder of season.

HONORS: Won Stafford Smythe Memorial Trophy (1987-88).... Named to Memorial Cup All-Star team (1987-88).

| | | | REGULAR SEASON | | | | PLAYOFFS | | | |
Season	Team	League	Gms.	G	A	Pts.	Pen.	Gms.	G	A	Pts.	Pen.
84-85	—Kamloops	WHL	55	9	18	27	29	—	—	—	—	—
85-86	—Kamloops	WHL	6	1	0	1	0	—	—	—	—	—
	—Medicine Hat	WHL	55	20	30	50	82	—	—	—	—	—
86-87	—Medicine Hat	WHL	70	27	43	70	130	20	7	11	18	46
87-88	—Medicine Hat	WHL	54	47	43	90	120	14	12	19	†31	59
88-89	—New York Islanders	NHL	16	1	0	1	30	—	—	—	—	—
	—Springfield	AHL	40	13	18	31	67	—	—	—	—	—
89-90	—New York Islanders	NHL	7	0	0	0	2	1	1	0	1	4
	—Springfield	AHL	54	25	27	52	69	16	4	7	11	45
90-91	—New York Islanders	NHL	1	0	0	0	0	—	—	—	—	—
	—Capital District	AHL	12	3	4	7	22	—	—	—	—	—
91-92	—New York Islanders	NHL	50	5	2	7	43	—	—	—	—	—
92-93	—Tampa Bay	NHL	54	9	15	24	62	—	—	—	—	—
	NHL totals		128	15	17	32	137	1	1	0	1	4

DINEEN, GORD
D, SENATORS

PERSONAL: Born September 21, 1962, at Quebec City.... 6-0/195.... Shoots right.... Son of Bill Dineen, right winger, Detroit Red Wings and Chicago Blackhawks (1953-54 through 1957-58) and former head coach, Philadelphia Flyers (1992-93); brother of Kevin Dineen, right winger, Flyers; and brother of Peter Dineen, defenseman, Los Angeles Kings and Red Wings (1986-87 and 1989-90).

HIGH SCHOOL: St. Micheal (Toronto).

TRANSACTIONS/CAREER NOTES: Selected by New York Islanders as underage junior in second round (second Islanders pick, 42nd overall) of NHL entry draft (June 10, 1981).... Bruised ribs (January 15, 1985).... Sprained left ankle (February 1988).... Traded by Islanders with future considerations to Minnesota North Stars for D Chris Pryor (March 1988).... Traded by North Stars with LW Scott Bjugstad to Pittsburgh Penguins for D Ville Siren and C Steve Gotaas (December 17, 1988).... Signed as free agent by Ottawa Senators (August 31, 1992).... Loaned to San Diego Gulls prior to 1992-93 season.... Returned to Senators (January 23, 1993).

HONORS: Won Bobby Orr Trophy (1982-83).... Won Bob Gassoff Award (1982-83).... Named to CHL All-Star first team (1982-83).... Named to IHL All-Star first team (1991-92).

| | | | REGULAR SEASON | | | | PLAYOFFS | | | |
Season	Team	League	Gms.	G	A	Pts.	Pen.	Gms.	G	A	Pts.	Pen.
79-80	—St. Michael's Jr. B	ODHA	42	15	35	50	103	—	—	—	—	—
80-81	—Sault Ste. Marie	OMJHL	68	4	26	30	158	19	1	7	8	58
81-82	—Sault Ste. Marie	OHL	68	9	45	54	185	13	1	2	3	52
82-83	—Indianapolis	CHL	73	10	47	57	78	13	2	10	12	29
	—New York Islanders	NHL	2	0	0	0	4	—	—	—	—	—

— 373 —

Season Team	League	REGULAR SEASON					PLAYOFFS				
		Gms.	G	A	Pts.	Pen.	Gms.	G	A	Pts.	Pen.
83-84—Indianapolis	CHL	26	4	13	17	63	—	—	—	—	—
—New York Islanders	NHL	43	1	11	12	32	9	1	1	2	28
84-85—Springfield	AHL	25	1	8	9	46	—	—	—	—	—
—New York Islanders	NHL	48	1	12	13	89	10	0	0	0	26
85-86—New York Islanders	NHL	57	1	8	9	81	3	0	0	0	2
—Springfield	AHL	11	2	3	5	20	—	—	—	—	—
86-87—New York Islanders	NHL	71	4	10	14	110	7	0	4	4	4
87-88—New York Islanders	NHL	57	4	12	16	62	—	—	—	—	—
—Minnesota	NHL	13	1	1	2	21	—	—	—	—	—
88-89—Kalamazoo	IHL	25	2	6	8	49	—	—	—	—	—
—Minnesota	NHL	2	0	1	1	2	—	—	—	—	—
—Pittsburgh	NHL	38	1	2	3	42	11	0	2	2	8
89-90—Pittsburgh	NHL	69	1	8	9	125	—	—	—	—	—
90-91—Muskegon	IHL	40	1	14	15	57	5	0	2	2	0
—Pittsburgh	NHL	9	0	0	0	6	—	—	—	—	—
91-92—Muskegon	IHL	79	8	37	45	83	14	2	4	6	33
—Pittsburgh	NHL	1	0	0	0	0	—	—	—	—	—
92-93—San Diego	IHL	41	6	23	29	36	—	—	—	—	—
—Ottawa	NHL	32	2	4	6	30	—	—	—	—	—
NHL totals		442	16	69	85	604	40	1	7	8	68

DINEEN, KEVIN

RW, FLYERS

PERSONAL: Born October 28, 1963, at Quebec City.... 5-11/190.... Shoots right.... Son of Bill Dineen, right winger with Detroit Red Wings and Chicago Blackhawks (1953-54 through 1957-58) and former head coach, Philadelphia Flyers (1992-93); brother of Gord Dineen, defenseman, Ottawa Senators; and brother of Peter Dineen, defenseman, Los Angeles Kings and Red Wings (1986-87 and 1989-90).

COLLEGE: Denver.

TRANSACTIONS/CAREER NOTES: Selected by Hartford Whalers as underage junior in third round (third Whalers pick, 56th overall) of NHL entry draft (June 9, 1982).... Sprained left shoulder (October 24, 1985); missed nine games.... Broke knuckle (January 12, 1986); missed seven games.... Sprained knee (February 14, 1986).... Suffered shoulder tendinitis (September 1988).... Underwent surgery to right knee cartilage (August 1, 1990).... Suffered hip pointer (November 28, 1990).... Hospitalized due to complications caused by Crohn's disease (January 1, 1991); missed eight games.... Injured groin (March 1991).... Traded by Whalers to Philadelphia Flyers for C/LW Murray Craven and fourth-round pick in 1992 draft (LW Kevin Smyth) (November 13, 1991).... Sprained wrist (February 4, 1992); missed one game.... Strained right rotator cuff (December 3, 1992); missed one game.

HONORS: Named to THE SPORTING NEWS All-Star second team (1986-87).... Played in NHL All-Star Game (1988 and 1989). ...Named Bud Light/NHL Man of the Year (1990-91).

Season Team	League	REGULAR SEASON					PLAYOFFS				
		Gms.	G	A	Pts.	Pen.	Gms.	G	A	Pts.	Pen.
80-81—St. Michael's Jr. B	ODHA	40	15	28	43	167	—	—	—	—	—
81-82—University of Denver	WCHA	38	12	22	34	105	—	—	—	—	—
82-83—University of Denver	WCHA	36	16	13	29	108	—	—	—	—	—
83-84—Canadian Olympic Team	Int'l					Statistics unavailable.					
84-85—Binghamton	AHL	25	15	8	23	41	—	—	—	—	—
—Hartford	NHL	57	25	16	41	120	—	—	—	—	—
85-86—Hartford	NHL	57	33	35	68	124	10	6	7	13	18
86-87—Hartford	NHL	78	40	69	109	110	6	2	1	3	31
87-88—Hartford	NHL	74	25	25	50	219	6	4	4	8	8
88-89—Hartford	NHL	79	45	44	89	167	4	1	0	1	10
89-90—Hartford	NHL	67	25	41	66	164	6	3	2	5	18
90-91—Hartford	NHL	61	17	30	47	104	6	1	0	1	16
91-92—Hartford	NHL	16	4	2	6	23	—	—	—	—	—
—Philadelphia	NHL	64	26	30	56	130	—	—	—	—	—
92-93—Philadelphia	NHL	83	35	28	63	201	—	—	—	—	—
NHL totals		636	275	320	595	1362	38	17	14	31	101

DIONNE, GILBERT

LW, CANADIENS

PERSONAL: Born September 19, 1970, at Drummondville, Que.... 6-0/194.... Shoots left.... Name pronounced ZHIHL-bair dee-AHN.... Brother of Marcel Dionne, Hall of Fame center, Detroit Red Wings, Los Angeles Kings and New York Rangers (1971-72 through 1988-89).

TRANSACTIONS/CAREER NOTES: Selected by Montreal Canadiens in fourth round (fifth Canadiens pick, 81st overall) of NHL entry draft (June 16, 1990).... Injured hand (December 3, 1992); missed one game.

HONORS: Named to NHL All-Rookie team (1991-92).

MISCELLANEOUS: Member of Stanley Cup championship team (1993).

Season Team	League	REGULAR SEASON					PLAYOFFS				
		Gms.	G	A	Pts.	Pen.	Gms.	G	A	Pts.	Pen.
87-88—Niagara Falls Jr. B	OHA	38	36	48	84	60	—	—	—	—	—
88-89—Kitchener	OHL	66	11	33	44	13	5	1	1	2	4
89-90—Kitchener	OHL	64	48	57	105	85	17	13	10	23	22
90-91—Fredericton	AHL	77	40	47	87	62	9	6	5	11	8
—Montreal	NHL	2	0	0	0	0	—	—	—	—	—
91-92—Fredericton	AHL	29	19	27	46	20	—	—	—	—	—
—Montreal	NHL	39	21	13	34	10	11	3	4	7	10

Season	Team	League	REGULAR SEASON					PLAYOFFS				
			Gms.	G	A	Pts.	Pen.	Gms.	G	A	Pts.	Pen.
92-93—Montreal		NHL	75	20	28	48	63	20	6	6	12	20
—Fredericton		AHL	3	4	3	7	0	—	—	—	—	—
NHL totals			116	41	41	82	73	31	9	10	19	30

DIPIETRO, PAUL
C, CANADIENS

PERSONAL: Born September 8, 1970, at Sault Ste. Marie, Ont. . . . 5-9/181. . . . Shoots right. . . . Name pronounced dee-pee-AY-troh. **TRANSACTIONS/CAREER NOTES:** Selected by Montreal Canadiens in fifth round (sixth Canadiens pick, 102nd overall) of NHL entry draft (June 16, 1990). . . . Strained hip flexor (February 12, 1992).
MISCELLANEOUS: Member of Stanley Cup championship team (1993).

Season	Team	League	REGULAR SEASON					PLAYOFFS				
			Gms.	G	A	Pts.	Pen.	Gms.	G	A	Pts.	Pen.
86-87—Sudbury		OHL	49	5	11	16	13	—	—	—	—	—
87-88—Sudbury		OHL	63	25	42	67	27	—	—	—	—	—
88-89—Sudbury		OHL	57	31	48	79	27	—	—	—	—	—
89-90—Sudbury		OHL	66	56	63	119	57	7	3	6	9	7
90-91—Fredericton		AHL	78	39	31	70	38	9	5	6	11	2
91-92—Fredericton		AHL	43	26	31	57	52	7	3	4	7	8
—Montreal		NHL	33	4	6	10	25	—	—	—	—	—
92-93—Fredericton		AHL	26	8	16	24	16	—	—	—	—	—
—Montreal		NHL	29	4	13	17	14	17	8	5	13	8
NHL totals			62	8	19	27	39	17	8	5	13	8

DIRK, ROBERT
D, CANUCKS

PERSONAL: Born August 20, 1966, at Regina, Sask. . . . 6-4/218. . . . Shoots left. **TRANSACTIONS/CAREER NOTES:** Selected by St. Louis Blues as underage junior in third round (fourth Blues pick, 53rd overall) of NHL entry draft (June 9, 1984). . . . Traded by Blues with LW Geoff Courtnall, C Cliff Ronning, LW Sergio Momesso and fifth-round pick in 1992 draft (RW Brian Loney) to Vancouver Canucks for C Dan Quinn and D Garth Butcher (March 5, 1991). . . . Sprained ankle (November 26, 1991); missed three games. . . . Sprained knee (February 1, 1992); missed four games. . . . Suffered bruised ribs (March 6, 1993); missed four games. . . . Suffered shoulder injury (September 22, 1992); missed two games. . . . Pulled groin (February 12, 1993); missed six games.
HONORS: Named to WHL All-Star second team (1985-86).

Season	Team	League	REGULAR SEASON					PLAYOFFS				
			Gms.	G	A	Pts.	Pen.	Gms.	G	A	Pts.	Pen.
82-83—Regina		WHL	1	0	0	0	0	—	—	—	—	—
—Kelowna		BCJHL	40	8	23	31	87	—	—	—	—	—
83-84—Regina		WHL	62	2	10	12	64	23	1	12	13	24
84-85—Regina		WHL	69	10	34	44	97	8	0	0	0	4
85-86—Regina		WHL	72	19	60	79	140	10	3	5	8	8
86-87—Peoria		IHL	76	5	17	22	155	—	—	—	—	—
87-88—St. Louis		NHL	7	0	1	1	16	6	0	1	1	2
—Peoria		IHL	54	4	21	25	126	—	—	—	—	—
88-89—St. Louis		NHL	9	0	1	1	11	—	—	—	—	—
—Peoria		IHL	22	0	2	2	54	—	—	—	—	—
89-90—Peoria		IHL	24	1	2	3	79	3	0	0	0	0
—St. Louis		NHL	37	1	1	2	128	9	0	1	1	2
90-91—Peoria		IHL	3	0	0	0	2	—	—	—	—	—
—St. Louis		NHL	41	1	3	4	100	—	—	—	—	—
—Vancouver		NHL	11	1	0	1	20	6	0	0	0	13
91-92—Vancouver		NHL	72	2	7	9	126	13	0	0	0	20
92-93—Vancouver		NHL	69	4	8	12	150	9	0	0	0	6
NHL totals			246	9	21	30	551	43	0	2	2	43

DJOOS, PER
D, RANGERS

PERSONAL: Born May 11, 1968, at Mora, Sweden. . . . 5-11/196. . . . Shoots left. . . . Name pronounced PAIR JOOZ. **TRANSACTIONS/CAREER NOTES:** Selected by Detroit Red Wings in seventh round (seventh Red Wings pick, 127th overall) of NHL entry draft (June 21, 1986). . . . Underwent surgery to repair right knee cartilage (October 19, 1990). . . . Traded by Red Wings with RW Joe Kocur to New York Rangers for C Kevin Miller, D Denis Vial and RW Jim Cummins (March 5, 1991).
HONORS: Named to AHL All-Star second team (1992-93).

Season	Team	League	REGULAR SEASON					PLAYOFFS				
			Gms.	G	A	Pts.	Pen.	Gms.	G	A	Pts.	Pen.
84-85—Mora		Sweden-II	20	2	3	5	2	—	—	—	—	—
85-86—Mora		Sweden-II	30	9	5	14	14	—	—	—	—	—
86-87—Brynas		Sweden	23	1	2	3	16	—	—	—	—	—
87-88—Brynas		Sweden	34	4	11	15	18	—	—	—	—	—
88-89—Brynas		Sweden	40	1	17	18	44	—	—	—	—	—
89-90—Brynas		Sweden	37	5	13	18	34	5	1	3	4	6
90-91—Adirondack		AHL	20	2	9	11	6	—	—	—	—	—
—Detroit		NHL	26	0	12	12	16	—	—	—	—	—
—Binghamton		AHL	14	1	8	9	10	9	2	2	4	4
91-92—New York Rangers		NHL	50	1	18	19	40					

Season Team	League	REGULAR SEASON					PLAYOFFS				
		Gms.	G	A	Pts.	Pen.	Gms.	G	A	Pts.	Pen.
92-93—Binghamton	AHL	70	16	53	69	75	14	2	8	10	8
—New York Rangers	NHL	6	1	1	2	2	—	—	—	—	—
NHL totals		82	2	31	33	58					

DOBBIN, BRIAN
RW, BRUINS

PERSONAL: Born August 18, 1966, at Petrolia, Ont.... 6-1/205.... Shoots right.
TRANSACTIONS/CAREER NOTES: Selected by Philadelphia Flyers as underage junior in fifth round (sixth Flyers pick, 100th overall) of NHL entry draft (June 9, 1984).... Damaged ligament in right knee (September 1986).... Traded by Flyers with D Gord Murphy and third-round pick in 1992 draft (LW Sergei Zholtok) to Boston Bruins for D Garry Galley, C Wes Walz and future considerations (January 2, 1992).... Strained lower back (February 1, 1992).
HONORS: Named to AHL All-Star first team (1988-89).... Named to AHL All-Star second team (1989-90).

Season Team	League	REGULAR SEASON					PLAYOFFS				
		Gms.	G	A	Pts.	Pen.	Gms.	G	A	Pts.	Pen.
81-82—Mooretown Jr. C	OHA	38	31	24	55	50	—	—	—	—	—
82-83—Kingston	OHL	69	16	39	55	35	—	—	—	—	—
83-84—London	OHL	70	30	40	70	70	—	—	—	—	—
84-85—London	OHL	53	42	57	99	63	8	7	4	11	2
85-86—London	OHL	59	38	55	93	113	5	2	1	3	9
—Hershey	AHL	2	1	0	1	0	18	5	5	10	21
86-87—Hershey	AHL	52	26	35	61	66	5	4	2	6	15
—Philadelphia	NHL	12	2	1	3	14	—	—	—	—	—
87-88—Hershey	AHL	54	36	47	83	58	12	7	8	15	15
—Philadelphia	NHL	21	3	5	8	6	—	—	—	—	—
88-89—Philadelphia	NHL	14	0	1	1	8	2	0	0	0	17
—Hershey	AHL	59	43	48	91	61	11	7	6	13	12
89-90—Hershey	AHL	68	38	47	85	58	—	—	—	—	—
—Philadelphia	NHL	9	1	1	2	11	—	—	—	—	—
90-91—Hershey	AHL	80	33	43	76	82	7	1	2	3	7
91-92—New Haven	AHL	33	16	21	37	20	—	—	—	—	—
—Maine	AHL	33	21	15	36	14	—	—	—	—	—
—Boston	NHL	7	1	0	1	22	—	—	—	—	—
92-93—Milwaukee	IHL	80	39	45	84	50	6	4	3	7	6
NHL totals		63	7	8	15	61	2	0	0	0	17

DOLLAS, BOBBY
D, MIGHTY DUCKS

PERSONAL: Born January 31, 1965, at Montreal.... 6-2/212.... Shoots left.
TRANSACTIONS/CAREER NOTES: Selected by Winnipeg Jets as underage junior in first round (second Jets pick, 14th overall) of NHL entry draft (June 8, 1983).... Traded by Jets to Quebec Nordiques for RW Stu Kulak (December 17, 1987).... Signed as free agent by Detroit Red Wings (October 18, 1990).... Suffered from the flu (December 15, 1990); missed two games.... Injured leg (January 9, 1991).... Strained abdomen (November 7, 1991); missed 15 games.... Selected by Mighty Ducks of Anaheim in NHL expansion draft (June 24, 1993).
HONORS: Won Raymond Lagace Trophy (1982-83).... Named to QMJHL All-Star second team (1982-83).... Won Eddie Shore Plaque (1992-93).... Named to AHL All-Star first team (1992-93).

Season Team	League	REGULAR SEASON					PLAYOFFS				
		Gms.	G	A	Pts.	Pen.	Gms.	G	A	Pts.	Pen.
82-83—Laval	QMJHL	63	16	45	61	144	11	5	5	10	23
83-84—Laval	QMJHL	54	12	33	45	80	14	1	8	9	23
—Winnipeg	NHL	1	0	0	0	0	—	—	—	—	—
84-85—Winnipeg	NHL	9	0	0	0	0	—	—	—	—	—
—Sherbrooke	AHL	8	1	3	4	4	17	3	6	9	17
85-86—Sherbrooke	AHL	25	4	7	11	29	—	—	—	—	—
—Winnipeg	NHL	46	0	5	5	66	3	0	0	0	2
86-87—Sherbrooke	AHL	75	6	18	24	87	16	2	4	6	13
87-88—Quebec	NHL	9	0	0	0	2	—	—	—	—	—
—Moncton	AHL	26	4	10	14	20	—	—	—	—	—
—Fredericton	AHL	33	4	8	12	27	15	2	2	4	24
88-89—Halifax	AHL	57	5	19	24	65	4	1	0	1	14
—Quebec	NHL	16	0	3	3	16	—	—	—	—	—
89-90—Canadian national team	Int'l	68	8	29	37	60	—	—	—	—	—
90-91—Detroit	NHL	56	3	5	8	20	7	1	0	1	13
91-92—Detroit	NHL	27	3	1	4	20	2	0	1	1	0
—Adirondack	AHL	19	1	6	7	33	18	7	4	11	22
92-93—Adirondack	AHL	64	7	36	43	54	11	3	8	11	8
—Detroit	NHL	6	0	0	0	2	—	—	—	—	—
NHL totals		170	6	14	20	126	12	1	1	2	15

DOMI, TIE
RW, JETS

PERSONAL: Born November 1, 1969, at Windsor, Ont.... 5-10/198.... Name pronounced DOH-MEE.
TRANSACTIONS/CAREER NOTES: Suspended indefinitely by OHL for leaving the bench during a fight (November 2, 1986).... Selected by Toronto Maple Leafs in second round (second Maple Leafs pick, 27th overall) of NHL entry draft (June 11, 1988).... Traded by Maple Leafs with G Mark Laforest to New York Rangers for RW Greg Johnston (June 28, 1990).... Suspended six games by AHL for pre-game fighting (November 25,

1990).... Sprained right knee (March 11, 1992); missed eight games.... Traded by Rangers with LW Kris King to Winnipeg Jets for C Ed Olczyk (December 28, 1992).... Fined $500 by NHL for premeditated fight (January 4, 1993).

	REGULAR SEASON					PLAYOFFS				
Season Team	League	Gms.	G	A	Pts.	Pen.	Gms.	G	A	Pts.	Pen.
85-86—Windsor Jr. B	OHA	32	8	17	25	346	—	—	—	—	—
86-87—Peterborough	OHL	18	1	1	2	79	—	—	—	—	—
87-88—Peterborough	OHL	60	22	21	43	*292	12	3	9	12	24
88-89—Peterborough	OHL	43	14	16	30	175	17	10	9	19	*70
89-90—Newmarket	AHL	57	14	11	25	285	—	—	—	—	—
—Toronto	NHL	2	0	0	0	42	—	—	—	—	—
90-91—New York Rangers	NHL	28	1	0	1	185	—	—	—	—	—
—Binghamton	AHL	25	11	6	17	219	7	3	2	5	16
91-92—New York Rangers	NHL	42	2	4	6	246	6	1	1	2	32
92-93—New York Rangers	NHL	12	2	0	2	95	—	—	—	—	—
—Winnipeg	NHL	49	3	10	13	249	6	1	0	1	23
NHL totals		133	8	14	22	817	12	2	1	3	55

DONATELLI, CLARK
LW, BRUINS

PERSONAL: Born November 22, 1967, at Providence, R.I.... 5-10/180.... Shoots left.... Full name: John Clark Donatelli.
COLLEGE: Boston University.
TRANSACTIONS/CAREER NOTES: Selected by New York Rangers in fifth round (fourth Rangers pick, 98th overall) of NHL entry draft (June 9, 1984).... Traded by Rangers with LW Ville Kentala, D Reijo Ruotsalainen and D Jim Wiemer to Edmonton Oilers for C Mike Golden, D Don Jackson and D Miloslav Horava (October 2, 1986).... Signed as free agent by Minnesota North Stars (June 20, 1989).... Signed as free agent by Boston Bruins (March 10, 1992).
HONORS: Named to Hockey East All-Freshman team (1984-85).... Named to NCAA All-America East second team (1985-86). ... Named to Hockey East All-Star second team (1985-86).

	REGULAR SEASON					PLAYOFFS				
Season Team	League	Gms.	G	A	Pts.	Pen.	Gms.	G	A	Pts.	Pen.
84-85—Boston University	Hockey East	40	17	18	35	46	—	—	—	—	—
85-86—Boston University	Hockey East	43	28	34	62	30	—	—	—	—	—
86-87—Boston University	Hockey East	37	15	23	38	46	—	—	—	—	—
87-88—U.S. national team	Int'l	50	11	27	38	26	—	—	—	—	—
—U.S. Olympic Team	Int'l	6	2	1	3	6	—	—	—	—	—
88-89—					Did not play.						
89-90—Minnesota	NHL	25	3	3	6	17	—	—	—	—	—
—Kalamazoo	IHL	27	8	9	17	47	4	0	2	2	12
90-91—San Diego	IHL	46	17	10	27	45	—	—	—	—	—
91-92—U.S. national team	Int'l	42	13	25	38	50	—	—	—	—	—
—U.S. Olympic Team	Int'l	8	2	1	3	6	—	—	—	—	—
—Boston	NHL	10	0	1	1	22	2	0	0	0	0
92-93—Providence	AHL	57	12	14	26	40	—	—	—	—	—
NHL totals		35	3	4	7	39	2	0	0	0	0

DONATO, TED
C, BRUINS

PERSONAL: Born April 28, 1968, at Dedham, Mass.... 5-10/170.... Shoots left.... Full name: Edward Paul Donato.... Name pronounced duh-NAH-toh.
HIGH SCHOOL: Catholic Memorial (Boston).
COLLEGE: Harvard.
TRANSACTIONS/CAREER NOTES: Selected by Boston Bruins in fifth round (fifth Bruins pick, 98th overall) of NHL entry draft (June 13, 1987).... Broke collarbone (November 18, 1989).
HONORS: Named NCAA Tournament Most Valuable Player (1988-89).... Named to NCAA All-Tournament team (1988-89). ... Named to ECAC All-Star first team (1990-91).

	REGULAR SEASON					PLAYOFFS				
Season Team	League	Gms.	G	A	Pts.	Pen.	Gms.	G	A	Pts.	Pen.
86-87—Catholic Memorial H.S.	Mass. H.S.	22	29	34	63	30	—	—	—	—	—
87-88—Harvard University	ECAC	28	12	14	26	24	—	—	—	—	—
88-89—Harvard University	ECAC	34	14	37	51	30	—	—	—	—	—
89-90—Harvard University	ECAC	16	5	6	11	34	—	—	—	—	—
90-91—Harvard University	ECAC	28	19	37	56	26	—	—	—	—	—
91-92—U.S. national team	Int'l	52	11	22	33	24	—	—	—	—	—
—U.S. Olympic Team	Int'l	8	4	3	7	8	—	—	—	—	—
—Boston	NHL	10	1	2	3	8	15	3	4	7	4
92-93—Boston	NHL	82	15	20	35	61	4	0	1	1	0
NHL totals		92	16	22	38	69	19	3	5	8	4

DONNELLY, GORD
D/RW, SABRES

PERSONAL: Born April 5, 1962, at Montreal.... 6-1/202.... Shoots right.
TRANSACTIONS/CAREER NOTES: Selected by St. Louis Blues in third round (third Blues pick, 62nd overall) of NHL entry draft (June 10, 1981).... Sent by Blues along with D Claude Julien to Quebec Nordiques as compensation for Blues signing coach Jacques Demers (August 1983).... Suspended five games by NHL for kneeing (October 29, 1987).... Suspended five games and fined $100 by NHL for pre-game fighting (February 26, 1988).... Suspended 10 games by NHL for hitting with stick (March 27, 1988); missed final four games of 1987-88 season and first six games of 1988-89 season.... Traded by Nordiques to Winnipeg Jets for D Mario Marois (December 6, 1988).... Fined $500 by NHL for kicking (April 12, 1990).... Traded by Jets with RW Dave McIlwain, fifth-round pick in 1992 draft (LW Yuri Khmylev) and future considerations to Buffalo Sabres for LW Darrin Shannon, LW Mike Hartman and D Dean Kennedy (October 11, 1991).

D

Season	Team	League	REGULAR SEASON					PLAYOFFS				
			Gms.	G	A	Pts.	Pen.	Gms.	G	A	Pts.	Pen.
78-79	Laval	QMJHL	71	1	14	15	79	—	—	—	—	—
79-80	Laval	QMJHL	44	5	10	15	47	—	—	—	—	—
—Chicoutimi		QMJHL	24	1	5	6	64	—	—	—	—	—
80-81	Sherbrooke	QMJHL	67	15	23	38	252	14	1	2	3	35
81-82	Sherbrooke	QMJHL	60	8	41	49	250	22	2	7	9	*106
82-83	Salt Lake City	IHL	67	3	12	15	222	6	1	1	2	8
83-84	Fredericton	AHL	30	2	3	5	146	7	1	1	2	43
—Quebec		NHL	38	0	5	5	60	—	—	—	—	—
84-85	Fredericton	AHL	42	1	5	6	134	6	0	1	1	25
—Quebec		NHL	22	0	0	0	33	—	—	—	—	—
85-86	Fredericton	AHL	37	3	5	8	103	5	0	0	0	33
—Quebec		NHL	36	2	2	4	85	1	0	0	0	0
86-87	Quebec	NHL	38	0	2	2	143	13	0	0	0	53
87-88	Quebec	NHL	63	4	3	7	301	—	—	—	—	—
88-89	Quebec	NHL	16	4	0	4	46	—	—	—	—	—
—Winnipeg		NHL	57	6	10	16	228	—	—	—	—	—
89-90	Winnipeg	NHL	55	3	3	6	222	6	0	1	1	8
90-91	Winnipeg	NHL	57	3	4	7	265	—	—	—	—	—
91-92	Winnipeg	NHL	4	0	0	0	11	—	—	—	—	—
—Buffalo		NHL	67	2	3	5	305	6	0	1	1	0
92-93	Buffalo	NHL	60	3	8	11	221	—	—	—	—	—
NHL totals			513	27	40	67	1920	26	0	2	2	61

DONNELLY, MIKE
LW, KINGS

PERSONAL: Born October 10, 1963, at Livonia, Mich.... 5-11/185.... Shoots left.... Full name: Michael Chene Donnelly.
HIGH SCHOOL: Franklin (Livonia, Mich.).
COLLEGE: Michigan State.
TRANSACTIONS/CAREER NOTES: Signed as free agent by New York Rangers (August 1986).... Dislocated and fractured right index finger (November 1987).... Traded by Rangers with fifth-round pick in 1988 draft (RW Alexander Mogilny) to Buffalo Sabres for LW Paul Cyr and 10th-round pick in 1988 draft (C Eric Fenton) (December 1987).... Traded by Sabres to Los Angeles Kings for LW Mikko Makela (October 1, 1990).
HONORS: Named NCAA Tournament Most Valuable Player (1985-86).... Named to NCAA All-America West first team (1985-86).... Named to NCAA All-Tournament team (1985-86).... Named to CCHA All-Star first team (1985-86).

Season	Team	League	REGULAR SEASON					PLAYOFFS				
			Gms.	G	A	Pts.	Pen.	Gms.	G	A	Pts.	Pen.
82-83	Michigan State	CCHA	24	7	13	20	8	—	—	—	—	—
83-84	Michigan State	CCHA	44	18	14	32	40	—	—	—	—	—
84-85	Michigan State	CCHA	44	26	21	47	48	—	—	—	—	—
85-86	Michigan State	CCHA	44	*59	38	97	65	—	—	—	—	—
86-87	New York Rangers	NHL	5	1	1	2	0	—	—	—	—	—
—New Haven		AHL	58	27	34	61	52	7	2	0	2	9
87-88	Colorado	IHL	8	7	11	18	15	—	—	—	—	—
—New York Rangers		NHL	17	2	2	4	8	—	—	—	—	—
—Buffalo		NHL	40	6	8	14	44	—	—	—	—	—
88-89	Buffalo	NHL	22	4	6	10	10	—	—	—	—	—
—Rochester		AHL	53	32	37	69	53	—	—	—	—	—
89-90	Rochester	AHL	68	43	55	98	71	16	*12	7	19	9
—Buffalo		NHL	12	1	2	3	8	—	—	—	—	—
90-91	Los Angeles	NHL	53	7	5	12	41	12	5	4	9	6
—New Haven		AHL	18	10	6	16	2	—	—	—	—	—
91-92	Los Angeles	NHL	80	29	16	45	20	6	1	0	1	4
92-93	Los Angeles	NHL	84	29	40	69	45	24	6	7	13	14
NHL totals			313	79	80	159	176	42	12	11	23	24

DONOVAN, SHEAN
RW, SHARKS

PERSONAL: Born January 22, 1975, at Timmins, Ont.... 6-1/172.... Shoots right.
TRANSACTIONS/CAREER NOTES: Selected by San Jose Sharks in second round (second Sharks pick, 28th overall) of NHL entry draft (June 26, 1993).

Season	Team	League	REGULAR SEASON					PLAYOFFS				
			Gms.	G	A	Pts.	Pen.	Gms.	G	A	Pts.	Pen.
91-92	Ottawa	OHL	58	11	8	19	14	11	1	0	1	5
92-93	Ottawa	OHL	66	29	23	52	33	—	—	—	—	—

DOPSON, ROB
G, PENGUINS

PERSONAL: Born August 21, 1967, at Smith Falls, Ont.... 6-0/200.... Shoots left.
COLLEGE: Wilfrid Laurier (Ont.).
TRANSACTIONS/CAREER NOTES: Signed as free agent by Pittsburgh Penguins (July 15, 1991).

Season	Team	League	REGULAR SEASON							PLAYOFFS						
			Gms.	Min.	W	L	T	GA	SO	Avg.	Gms.	Min.	W	L	GA	SO	Avg.
89-90	Wilfrid Laurier Univ.	OUAA	22	1319	...	...	...	57	0	2.59	—	—	—	—	—	—	—
90-91	Muskegon	IHL	24	1243	...	...	...	90	0	4.34	—	—	—	—	—	—	—
91-92	Muskegon	IHL	29	1655	13	12	2	90	4	3.26	12	697	8	4	40	0	3.44
92-93	Cleveland	IHL	50	2825	26	15	0	167	1	3.55	4	203	0	4	20	0	5.91

DORE, DANIEL
RW, NORDIQUES

PERSONAL: Born April 9, 1970, at St. Jerome, Que. . . . 6-3/202. . . . Shoots right. . . . Name pronounced dohr-AY.

TRANSACTIONS/CAREER NOTES: Selected by Quebec Nordiques in first round (second Nordiques pick, fifth overall) of NHL entry draft (June 11, 1988). . . . Underwent surgery to finger (April 1989). . . . Underwent surgery to nose (May 1989). . . . Traded by Drummondville Voltigeurs with RW Denis Chasse and D Pierre-Paul Landry to Chicoutimi Sagueneens for LW Yanic Dupre, D Guy Lehoux and RW Eric Meloche (December 19, 1989). . . . Suffered from recurring back pain (October 11, 1990).

HONORS: Won Michael Bossy Trophy (1987-88).

			REGULAR SEASON					PLAYOFFS				
Season	Team	League	Gms.	G	A	Pts.	Pen.	Gms.	G	A	Pts.	Pen.
86-87	—Drummondville	QMJHL	68	23	41	64	229	8	0	1	1	18
87-88	—Drummondville	QMJHL	64	24	39	63	218	17	7	11	18	42
88-89	—Drummondville	QMJHL	62	33	58	91	236	4	2	3	5	14
89-90	—Quebec	NHL	16	2	3	5	6	—	—	—	—	—
	—Chicoutimi	QMJHL	24	6	23	29	112	6	0	3	3	27
90-91	—Halifax	AHL	50	7	10	17	139	—	—	—	—	—
	—Quebec	NHL	1	0	0	0	0	—	—	—	—	—
91-92	—Halifax	AHL	29	4	1	5	45	—	—	—	—	—
	—Greensboro	ECHL	6	1	0	1	34	—	—	—	—	—
92-93	—Hershey	AHL	65	12	10	22	192	—	—	—	—	—
	NHL totals		17	2	3	5	6					

DOUCET, WAYNE
LW, ISLANDERS

PERSONAL: Born June 19, 1970, at Etobicoke, Ont. . . . 6-2/203. . . . Shoots left. . . . Name pronounced doo-SEHT.

TRANSACTIONS/CAREER NOTES: Separated shoulder (October 1986). . . . Selected by New York Islanders in second round (second Islanders pick, 29th overall) of NHL entry draft (June 11, 1988).

			REGULAR SEASON					PLAYOFFS				
Season	Team	League	Gms.	G	A	Pts.	Pen.	Gms.	G	A	Pts.	Pen.
86-87	—Sudbury	OHL	64	20	28	48	85	—	—	—	—	—
87-88	—Sudbury	OHL	23	9	4	13	53	—	—	—	—	—
	—Hamilton	OHL	37	11	14	25	74	1	0	0	0	8
88-89	—Kingston	OHL	59	26	43	69	89	—	—	—	—	—
	—Springfield	AHL	6	2	2	4	4	—	—	—	—	—
89-90	—Kingston	OHL	66	32	47	79	127	7	2	5	7	18
90-91	—Capital District	AHL	21	11	6	17	93	—	—	—	—	—
91-92	—Capital District	AHL	60	11	7	18	116	7	1	1	2	6
92-93	—Capital District	AHL	72	11	16	27	155	3	0	0	0	2

DOURIS, PETER
RW, MIGHTY DUCKS

PERSONAL: Born February 19, 1966, at Toronto. . . . 6-1/195. . . . Shoots right.

COLLEGE: New Hampshire.

TRANSACTIONS/CAREER NOTES: Selected by Winnipeg Jets in second round (first Jets pick, 30th overall) of NHL entry draft (June 9, 1984). . . . Traded by Jets to St. Louis Blues for LW/D Kent Carlson and 12th-round pick in 1989 draft (RW Sergei Kharin) (September 29, 1988). . . . Signed as free agent by Boston Bruins (September 1989). . . . Injured ankle (December 1990). . . . Strained hip flexor (November 1991); missed three games. . . . Signed as free agent by Mighty Ducks of Anaheim (July 22, 1993).

			REGULAR SEASON					PLAYOFFS				
Season	Team	League	Gms.	G	A	Pts.	Pen.	Gms.	G	A	Pts.	Pen.
83-84	—Univ. of New Hampshire	ECAC	38	19	15	34	14	—	—	—	—	—
84-85	—Univ. of New Hampshire	Hockey East	42	27	24	51	34	—	—	—	—	—
85-86	—Canadian national team	Int'l	33	16	7	23	18	—	—	—	—	—
	—Winnipeg	NHL	11	0	0	0	0	—	—	—	—	—
86-87	—Sherbrooke	AHL	62	14	28	42	24	17	7	*15	†22	16
	—Winnipeg	NHL	6	0	0	0	0	—	—	—	—	—
87-88	—Moncton	AHL	73	42	37	79	53	—	—	—	—	—
	—Winnipeg	NHL	4	0	2	2	0	1	0	0	0	0
88-89	—Peoria	IHL	81	28	41	69	32	4	1	2	3	0
89-90	—Maine	AHL	38	17	20	37	14	—	—	—	—	—
	—Boston	NHL	36	5	6	11	15	8	0	1	1	8
90-91	—Maine	AHL	35	16	15	31	9	7	0	1	1	6
	—Boston	NHL	39	5	2	7	9	2	3	0	3	2
91-92	—Boston	NHL	54	10	13	23	10	7	2	3	5	0
	—Maine	AHL	12	4	3	7	2	—	—	—	—	—
92-93	—Providence	AHL	50	29	26	55	12	—	—	—	—	—
	—Boston	NHL	19	4	4	8	4	4	1	0	1	0
	NHL totals		169	24	27	51	38	22	6	4	10	10

DOWD, JIM
C, DEVILS

PERSONAL: Born December 25, 1968, at Brick, N.J. . . . 6-1/185. . . . Shoots right.

HIGH SCHOOL: Brick Township (N.J.).

COLLEGE: Lake Superior State (Mich.).

TRANSACTIONS/CAREER NOTES: Selected by New Jersey Devils in eighth round (seventh Devils pick, 149th overall) of NHL entry draft (June 13, 1987).

HONORS: Named to NCAA All-America West second team (1989-90). . . . Named to CCHA All-Star second team (1989-90). . . .

Named CCHA Player of the Year (1990-91).... Named to NCAA All-America West first team (1990-91).... Named to CCHA All-Star first team (1990-91).

			REGULAR SEASON					PLAYOFFS			
Season	Team	League	Gms.	G	A	Pts.	Pen.	Gms.	G	A	Pts.	Pen.
85-86—Brick H.S.	N.J. H.S.	...	47	51	98	...	—	—	—	—	—
86-87—Brick H.S.	N.J. H.S.	24	22	33	55	...	—	—	—	—	—
87-88—Lake Superior State	CCHA	45	18	27	45	16	—	—	—	—	—
88-89—Lake Superior State	CCHA	46	24	35	59	40	—	—	—	—	—
89-90—Lake Superior State	CCHA	46	25	67	92	30	—	—	—	—	—
90-91—Lake Superior State	CCHA	44	24	54	78	53	—	—	—	—	—
91-92—Utica	AHL	78	17	42	59	47	4	2	2	4	4
—New Jersey	NHL	1	0	0	0	0	—	—	—	—	—
92-93—Utica	AHL	78	27	45	72	62	5	1	7	8	10
—New Jersey	NHL	1	0	0	0	0	—	—	—	—	—
NHL totals		2	0	0	0	0					

DOYLE, TREVOR
D, PANTHERS

PERSONAL: Born January 1, 1974, at Ottawa.... 6-3/204.... Shoots right.
TRANSACTIONS/CAREER NOTES: Selected by Florida Panthers in seventh round (ninth Panthers pick, 161st overall) of NHL entry draft (June 26, 1993).

			REGULAR SEASON					PLAYOFFS			
Season	Team	League	Gms.	G	A	Pts.	Pen.	Gms.	G	A	Pts.	Pen.
91-92—Kingston	OHL	26	0	1	1	19	—	—	—	—	—
92-93—Kingston	OHL	62	1	8	9	148	16	2	3	5	25

DOYON, MARIO
D, NORDIQUES

PERSONAL: Born August 27, 1968, at Quebec City.... 6-0/174.... Shoots right.... Name pronounced DOY-uhn.
TRANSACTIONS/CAREER NOTES: Selected by Chicago Blackhawks in sixth round (fifth Blackhawks pick, 119th overall) of NHL entry draft (June 21, 1986).... Traded by Blackhawks with LW Everett Sanipass and LW Dan Vincelette to Quebec Nordiques for LW Michel Goulet, G Greg Millen and sixth-round pick in 1991 draft (March 5, 1990).

			REGULAR SEASON					PLAYOFFS			
Season	Team	League	Gms.	G	A	Pts.	Pen.	Gms.	G	A	Pts.	Pen.
85-86—Drummondville	QMJHL	71	5	14	19	129	23	5	4	9	32
86-87—Drummondville	QMJHL	65	18	47	65	150	8	1	3	4	30
87-88—Drummondville	QMJHL	68	23	54	77	233	17	3	14	17	46
88-89—Saginaw	IHL	71	16	32	48	69	6	0	0	0	8
—Chicago	NHL	7	1	1	2	6	—	—	—	—	—
89-90—Indianapolis	IHL	66	9	25	34	50	—	—	—	—	—
—Halifax	AHL	5	1	2	3	0	6	1	3	4	2
—Quebec	NHL	9	2	3	5	6	—	—	—	—	—
90-91—Halifax	AHL	59	14	23	37	58	—	—	—	—	—
—Quebec	NHL	12	0	0	0	4	—	—	—	—	—
91-92—Halifax	AHL	9	0	0	0	22	—	—	—	—	—
—New Haven	AHL	64	11	29	40	44	5	1	1	2	2
92-93—Halifax	AHL	79	5	31	36	73	—	—	—	—	—
NHL totals		28	3	4	7	16					

DRAKE, DALLAS
LW, RED WINGS

PERSONAL: Born February 4, 1969, at Trail, B.C.... 6-0/170.... Shoots left.... Full name: Dallas James Drake.
COLLEGE: Northern Michigan.
TRANSACTIONS/CAREER NOTES: Selected by Detroit Red Wings in sixth round (sixth Red Wings pick, 116th overall) of NHL entry draft (June 17, 1989).... Suffered left leg contusion (November 27, 1992); missed three games.... Suffered back spasms (December 28, 1992); missed one game.... Bruised kneecap (January 23, 1993); missed three games.... Suffered concussion (February 13, 1993); missed one game.
HONORS: Won WCHA Player of the Year Award (1991-92).... Named to NCAA All-America West first team (1991-92).... Named to WCHA All-Star first team (1991-92).

			REGULAR SEASON					PLAYOFFS			
Season	Team	League	Gms.	G	A	Pts.	Pen.	Gms.	G	A	Pts.	Pen.
84-85—Rossland	KIJHL	30	13	37	50	...	—	—	—	—	—
85-86—Rossland	KIJHL	41	53	73	126	...	—	—	—	—	—
86-87—Rossland	KIJHL	40	55	80	135	...	—	—	—	—	—
87-88—Vernon	BCJHL	47	39	85	124	50	11	9	17	26	30
88-89—Northern Michigan Univ.	WCHA	45	18	24	42	26	—	—	—	—	—
89-90—Northern Michigan Univ.	WCHA	36	13	24	37	42	—	—	—	—	—
90-91—Northern Michigan Univ.	WCHA	44	22	36	58	89	—	—	—	—	—
91-92—Northern Michigan Univ.	WCHA	40	*39	44	83	58	—	—	—	—	—
92-93—Detroit	NHL	72	18	26	44	93	7	3	3	6	6
NHL totals		72	18	26	44	93	7	3	3	6	6

DRAPER, KRIS
C/LW, JETS

PERSONAL: Born May 24, 1971, at Toronto.... 5-11/190.... Shoots left.... Full name: Kris Bruce Draper.
TRANSACTIONS/CAREER NOTES: Selected by Winnipeg Jets in third round (fourth Jets pick, 62nd overall) of NHL entry draft (June 17, 1989).

Season	Team	League	REGULAR SEASON Gms.	G	A	Pts.	Pen.	PLAYOFFS Gms.	G	A	Pts.	Pen.
88-89—Canadian national team ...		Int'l	60	11	15	26	16	—	—	—	—	—
89-90—Canadian national team ...		Int'l	61	12	22	34	44	—	—	—	—	—
90-91—Winnipeg		NHL	3	1	0	1	5	—	—	—	—	—
—Moncton		AHL	7	2	1	3	2	—	—	—	—	—
—Ottawa		OHL	39	19	42	61	35	17	8	11	19	20
91-92—Moncton		AHL	61	11	18	29	113	4	0	1	1	6
—Winnipeg		NHL	10	2	0	2	2	2	0	0	0	0
92-93—Winnipeg		NHL	7	0	0	0	2	—	—	—	—	—
—Moncton		AHL	67	12	23	35	40	5	2	2	4	18
NHL totals			20	3	0	3	9	2	0	0	0	0

DRAPER, TOM

G, SABRES

PERSONAL: Born November 20, 1966, at Outremont, Que. ... 5-11/185. ... Shoots left. ... Full name: Thomas Edward Draper.
COLLEGE: Vermont.
TRANSACTIONS/CAREER NOTES: Selected by Winnipeg Jets in eight round (eighth Jets pick, 165th overall) of NHL entry draft (June 15, 1985). ... Traded by Jets to St. Louis Blues for future considerations (February 28, 1991); C Jim Vesey sent to Jets by Blues to complete deal (May 24, 1991). ... Traded by Blues to Jets for future considerations (May 24, 1991). ... Traded by Jets to Buffalo Sabres for future considerations; Jets later received seventh-round pick in 1992 draft (D Artur Oktyabrev) to complete deal (June 22, 1991).
HONORS: Named to ECAC All-Star first team (1985-86). ... Named to AHL All-Star second team (1988-89).

Season	Team	League	REGULAR SEASON Gms.	Min.	W	L	T	GA	SO	Avg.	PLAYOFFS Gms.	Min.	W	L	GA	SO	Avg.
83-84—University of Vermont ..		ECAC	20	1205	8	12	0	82	0	4.08	—	—	—	—	—	—	—
84-85—University of Vermont ..		ECAC	24	1316	5	17	0	90	0	4.10	—	—	—	—	—	—	—
85-86—University of Vermont ..		ECAC	29	1697	15	12	1	87	1	3.08	—	—	—	—	—	—	—
86-87—University of Vermont ..		ECAC	29	1662	16	13	0	96	2	3.47	—	—	—	—	—	—	—
87-88—Tappara		Finland	28	1619	16	3	9	87	0	3.22	—	—	—	—	—	—	—
88-89—Moncton		AHL	54	2962	27	17	5	171	2	3.46	7	419	5	2	24	0	3.44
—Winnipeg		NHL	2	120	1	1	0	12	0	6.00	—	—	—	—	—	—	—
89-90—Moncton		AHL	51	2844	20	24	3	167	1	3.52	—	—	—	—	—	—	—
—Winnipeg		NHL	6	359	2	4	0	26	0	4.35	—	—	—	—	—	—	—
90-91—Fort Wayne		IHL	10	564	5	3	1	32	0	3.40	—	—	—	—	—	—	—
—Moncton		AHL	30	1779	15	13	2	95	1	3.20	—	—	—	—	—	—	—
—Peoria		IHL	10	584	6	3	1	36	0	3.70	4	214	2	1	10	0	2.80
91-92—Rochester		AHL	9	531	4	3	2	28	0	3.16	—	—	—	—	—	—	—
—Buffalo		NHL	26	1403	10	9	5	75	1	3.21	7	433	3	4	19	1	2.63
92-93—Buffalo		NHL	11	664	5	6	0	41	0	3.70	—	—	—	—	—	—	—
—Rochester		AHL	5	303	3	2	0	22	0	4.36	—	—	—	—	—	—	—
NHL totals			45	2546	18	20	5	154	1	3.63	7	433	3	4	19	1	2.63

DRIVER, BRUCE

D, DEVILS

PERSONAL: Born April 29, 1962, at Toronto. ... 6-0/185. ... Shoots left. ... Full name: Bruce Douglas Driver.
COLLEGE: Wisconsin.
TRANSACTIONS/CAREER NOTES: Selected by Colorado Rockies as underage junior in sixth round (sixth Rockies pick, 108th overall) of NHL entry draft (June 10, 1981). ... Underwent surgery to left knee (February 1985). ... Reinjured knee (April 2, 1985). ... Bruised shoulder (March 9, 1986). ... Sprained ankle (February 1988). ... Broke right leg in three places (December 7, 1988). ... Broke rib (January 8, 1991); missed three games. ... Reinjured rib (January 22, 1991); missed four games.
HONORS: Named to NCAA All-America West team (1981-82). ... Named to WCHA All-Star first team (1981-82). ... Named to NCAA All-Tournament team (1981-82). ... Named to WCHA All-Star second team (1982-83).

Season	Team	League	REGULAR SEASON Gms.	G	A	Pts.	Pen.	PLAYOFFS Gms.	G	A	Pts.	Pen.
79-80—Royal York Royals		OPJHL	43	13	57	70	102	—	—	—	—	—
80-81—University of Wisconsin ...		WCHA	42	5	15	20	42	—	—	—	—	—
81-82—University of Wisconsin ...		WCHA	46	7	37	44	84	—	—	—	—	—
82-83—University of Wisconsin ...		WCHA	39	16	34	50	50	—	—	—	—	—
83-84—Canadian Olympic Team ..		Int'l	61	11	17	28	44	—	—	—	—	—
—Maine		AHL	12	2	6	8	15	16	0	10	10	8
—New Jersey		NHL	4	0	2	2	0	—	—	—	—	—
84-85—New Jersey		NHL	67	9	23	32	36	—	—	—	—	—
85-86—Maine		AHL	15	4	7	11	16	—	—	—	—	—
—New Jersey		NHL	40	3	15	18	32	—	—	—	—	—
86-87—New Jersey		NHL	74	6	28	34	36	—	—	—	—	—
87-88—New Jersey		NHL	74	15	40	55	68	20	3	7	10	14
88-89—New Jersey		NHL	27	1	15	16	24	—	—	—	—	—
89-90—New Jersey		NHL	75	7	46	53	63	6	1	5	6	6
90-91—New Jersey		NHL	73	9	36	45	62	7	1	2	3	12
91-92—New Jersey		NHL	78	7	35	42	66	7	0	4	4	2
92-93—New Jersey		NHL	83	14	40	54	66	5	1	3	4	4
NHL totals			595	71	280	351	453	45	6	21	27	38

DROPPA, IVAN

LW, BLACKHAWKS

PERSONAL: Born February 1, 1972, at Liptovsky Mikulas, Czechoslovakia. . . . 6-2/209. . . . Shoots left.

TRANSACTIONS/CAREER NOTES: Selected by Chicago Blackhawks in second round (second Blackhawks pick, 37th overall) of NHL entry draft (June 16, 1990).

Season Team	League		REGULAR SEASON					PLAYOFFS			
		Gms.	G	A	Pts.	Pen.	Gms.	G	A	Pts.	Pen.
89-90—Liptovsky Mikulas	Czech.				Statistics unavailable.						
90-91—VSZ Kosice	Czech.	49	1	7	8	12	—	—	—	—	—
91-92—VSZ Kosice	Czech.	43	4	9	13	...	—	—	—	—	—
92-93—Indianapolis	IHL	77	14	29	43	92	5	0	1	1	2

DRUCE, JOHN

RW, KINGS

PERSONAL: Born February 23, 1966, at Peterborough, Ont. . . . 6-1/200. . . . Shoots right. . . . Name pronounced DROOZ.

TRANSACTIONS/CAREER NOTES: Broke collarbone (October 1983). . . . Tore ligaments in ankle (December 1984). . . . Selected by Washington Capitals in second round (second Capitals pick, 40th overall) of NHL entry draft (June 15, 1985). . . . Tore thumb ligaments (October 1985). . . . Fractured wrist (October 18, 1992); missed 18 games. . . . Traded by Capitals to Winnipeg Jets with conditional pick in 1993 draft for RW Pat Elynuik (October 1, 1992). . . . Signed as free agent by Los Angeles Kings (August 2, 1993).

Season Team	League		REGULAR SEASON					PLAYOFFS			
		Gms.	G	A	Pts.	Pen.	Gms.	G	A	Pts.	Pen.
83-84—Peterborough Jr. B..........	OHA	40	15	18	33	69	—	—	—	—	—
84-85—Peterborough	OHL	54	12	14	26	90	17	6	2	8	21
85-86—Peterborough	OHL	49	22	24	46	84	16	0	5	5	34
86-87—Binghamton	AHL	7	13	9	22	131	12	0	3	3	28
87-88—Binghamton	AHL	68	32	29	61	82	1	0	0	0	0
88-89—Washington	NHL	48	8	7	15	62	1	0	0	0	0
—Baltimore	AHL	16	2	11	13	10	—	—	—	—	—
89-90—Washington	NHL	45	8	3	11	52	15	14	3	17	23
—Baltimore	AHL	26	15	16	31	38	—	—	—	—	—
90-91—Washington	NHL	80	22	36	58	46	11	1	1	2	7
91-92—Washington	NHL	67	19	18	37	39	7	1	0	1	2
92-93—Winnipeg	NHL	50	6	14	20	37	2	0	0	0	0
NHL totals.................		290	63	78	141	236	36	16	4	20	32

DRULIA, STAN

RW, LIGHTNING

PERSONAL: Born January 5, 1968, at Elmira, N.Y. . . . 5-11/190. . . . Shoots right. . . . Name pronounced DROOL-yuh.

TRANSACTIONS/CAREER NOTES: Selected by Pittsburgh Penguins as underage junior in 11th round (11th Penguins pick, 214th overall) of NHL entry draft (June 21, 1986). . . . Signed as free agent by Edmonton Oilers (May 1989). . . . Signed as free agent by Tampa Bay Lightning (September 1, 1992).

HONORS: Won Jim Mahon Memorial Trophy (1988-89). . . . Won Leo Lalonde Memorial Trophy (1988-89). . . . Named to OHL All-Star first team (1988-89). . . . Won ECHL Most Valuable Player Award (1990-91). . . . Won ECHL Top Scorer Award (1990-91). . . . Named to ECHL All-Star first team (1990-91). . . . Named to AHL All-Star second team (1991-92).

Season Team	League		REGULAR SEASON					PLAYOFFS			
		Gms.	G	A	Pts.	Pen.	Gms.	G	A	Pts.	Pen.
84-85—Belleville...........................	OHL	63	24	31	55	33	—	—	—	—	—
85-86—Belleville...........................	OHL	66	43	37	80	73	—	—	—	—	—
86-87—Hamilton..........................	OHL	55	27	51	78	26	—	—	—	—	—
87-88—Hamilton..........................	OHL	65	52	69	121	44	14	8	16	24	12
88-89—Niagara Falls	OHL	47	52	93	145	59	17	11	*26	37	18
—Maine	AHL	3	1	1	2	0	—	—	—	—	—
89-90—Cape Breton	AHL	31	5	7	12	2	—	—	—	—	—
—Phoenix	IHL	16	6	3	9	2	—	—	—	—	—
90-91—Knoxville	ECHL	64	*63	77	*140	39	3	3	2	5	4
91-92—New Haven	AHL	77	49	53	102	46	5	2	4	6	4
92-93—Tampa Bay.......................	NHL	24	2	1	3	10	—	—	—	—	—
—Atlanta	IHL	47	28	26	54	38	3	2	3	5	4
NHL totals.................		24	2	1	3	10					

DRURY, TED

C, FLAMES

PERSONAL: Born September 13, 1971, at Boston. . . . 6-0/185. . . . Shoots left. . . . Full name: Theodore Evans Drury.

HIGH SCHOOL: Fairfield (Conn.) College Prep School.

COLLEGE: Harvard.

TRANSACTIONS/CAREER NOTES: Broke ankle (January 1988). . . . Selected by Calgary Flames in second round (second Flames pick, 42nd overall) of NHL entry draft (June 17, 1989).

HONORS: Named ECAC Player of the Year (1992-93). . . . Named to NCAA All-America East first team (1992-93). . . . Named to ECAC All-Star first team (1992-93).

Season Team	League		REGULAR SEASON					PLAYOFFS			
		Gms.	G	A	Pts.	Pen.	Gms.	G	A	Pts.	Pen.
87-88—Fairfield College Prep	Conn. H.S.	...	21	28	49	...	—	—	—	—	—
88-89—Fairfield College Prep	Conn. H.S.	...	35	31	66	...	—	—	—	—	—
89-90—Harvard University..........	ECAC	17	9	13	22	10	—	—	—	—	—
90-91—Harvard University..........	ECAC	26	18	18	36	22	—	—	—	—	—

Season Team	League	REGULAR SEASON					PLAYOFFS				
		Gms.	G	A	Pts.	Pen.	Gms.	G	A	Pts.	Pen.
91-92—U.S. national team	Int'l	53	11	23	34	30	—	—	—	—	—
—U.S. Olympic Team	Int'l	7	1	1	2	0	—	—	—	—	—
92-93—Harvard University	ECAC	31	22	41	*63	26	—	—	—	—	—

DUBERMAN, JUSTIN
RW, PENGUINS

PERSONAL: Born March 23, 1970, at New Haven, Conn. . . . 6-1/185. . . . Shoots right.
COLLEGE: North Dakota.
TRANSACTIONS/CAREER NOTES: Selected by Montreal Canadiens in 11th round (11th Canadiens pick, 230th overall) of 1989 NHL entry draft (June 17, 1989). . . . Signed as free agent by Pittsburgh Penguins (October 1, 1992).

Season Team	League	REGULAR SEASON					PLAYOFFS				
		Gms.	G	A	Pts.	Pen.	Gms.	G	A	Pts.	Pen.
88-89—North Dakota	WCHA	33	3	1	4	30	—	—	—	—	—
89-90—North Dakota	WCHA	42	10	9	19	50	—	—	—	—	—
90-91—North Dakota	WCHA	42	19	18	37	68	—	—	—	—	—
91-92—North Dakota	WCHA	39	17	27	44	90	—	—	—	—	—
92-93—Cleveland	IHL	77	29	42	71	69	4	0	0	0	12

DUCHESNE, GAETAN
LW, SHARKS

PERSONAL: Born July 11, 1962, at Quebec City. . . . 5-11/200. . . . Shoots left. . . . Name pronounced gay-TAI doo-SHAYN.
TRANSACTIONS/CAREER NOTES: Selected by Washington Capitals in eighth round (eighth Capitals pick, 152nd overall) of NHL entry draft (June 10, 1981). . . . Bruised right ankle (December 30, 1981). . . . Broke finger (October 11, 1984). . . . Traded by Capitals with C Alan Haworth and first-round pick in 1987 draft (C Joe Sakic) to Quebec Nordiques for C Dale Hunter and G Clint Malarchuk (June 1987). . . . Sprained left knee (January 26, 1988). . . . Sprained left shoulder (November 1988). . . . Traded by Nordiques to Minnesota North Stars for C Kevin Kaminski (June 18, 1989). . . . Sprained right knee (November 11, 1989); missed eight games. . . . North Stars franchise moved from Minnesota to Dallas and renamed Stars for 1993-94 season. . . . Traded by Stars to San Jose Sharks for sixth-round pick in 1993 draft (June 20, 1993).

Season Team	League	REGULAR SEASON					PLAYOFFS				
		Gms.	G	A	Pts.	Pen.	Gms.	G	A	Pts.	Pen.
79-80—Quebec	QMJHL	46	9	28	37	22	5	0	2	2	9
80-81—Quebec	QMJHL	72	27	45	72	63	7	1	4	5	6
81-82—Washington	NHL	74	9	14	23	46	—	—	—	—	—
82-83—Hershey	AHL	1	1	0	1	0	—	—	—	—	—
—Washington	NHL	77	18	19	37	52	4	1	1	2	4
83-84—Washington	NHL	79	17	19	36	29	8	2	1	3	2
84-85—Washington	NHL	67	15	23	38	32	5	0	1	1	7
85-86—Washington	NHL	80	11	28	39	39	9	4	3	7	12
86-87—Washington	NHL	74	17	35	52	53	7	3	0	3	14
87-88—Quebec	NHL	80	24	23	47	83	—	—	—	—	—
88-89—Quebec	NHL	70	8	21	29	56	—	—	—	—	—
89-90—Minnesota	NHL	72	12	8	20	33	7	0	0	0	6
90-91—Minnesota	NHL	68	9	9	18	18	23	2	3	5	34
91-92—Minnesota	NHL	73	8	15	23	102	7	1	0	1	6
92-93—Minnesota	NHL	84	16	13	29	30	—	—	—	—	—
NHL totals................................		898	164	227	391	573	70	13	9	22	85

DUCHESNE, STEVE
D, NORDIQUES

PERSONAL: Born June 30, 1965, at Sept-Illes, Que. . . . 5-11/195. . . . Shoots left. . . . Name pronounced doo-SHAYN.
TRANSACTIONS/CAREER NOTES: Signed as free agent by Los Angeles Kings (October 1984). . . . Strained left knee (January 26, 1988). . . . Separated left shoulder (November 1988). . . . Traded by Kings with C Steve Kasper and fourth-round pick in 1991 draft (D Aris Brimanis) to Philadelphia Flyers for D Jeff Chychrun and rights to RW Jari Kurri (May 30, 1991). . . . Traded by Flyers with G Ron Hextall, C Mike Ricci, C Peter Forsberg, D Kerry Huffman, first-round pick in 1993 draft (G Jocelyn Thibault), cash and future considerations to Quebec Nordiques for C Eric Lindros (June 20, 1992). . . . Flyers sent LW Chris Simon and first-round pick in 1994 draft to Nordiques to complete deal (July 21, 1992). . . . Suffered a concussion (January 2, 1993); missed one game. . . . Suffered from the flu (March 20, 1993); missed one game.
HONORS: Named to QMJHL All-Star first team (1984-85). . . . Named to NHL All-Rookie team (1986-87). . . . Played in NHL All-Star Game (1989, 1990 and 1993).

Season Team	League	REGULAR SEASON					PLAYOFFS				
		Gms.	G	A	Pts.	Pen.	Gms.	G	A	Pts.	Pen.
83-84—Drummondville.................	QMJHL	67	1	34	35	79	—	—	—	—	—
84-85—Drummondville.................	QMJHL	65	22	54	76	94	5	4	7	11	8
85-86—New Haven	AHL	75	14	35	49	76	5	0	2	2	9
86-87—Los Angeles....................	NHL	75	13	25	38	74	5	2	2	4	4
87-88—Los Angeles....................	NHL	71	16	39	55	109	5	1	3	4	14
88-89—Los Angeles....................	NHL	79	25	50	75	92	11	4	4	8	12
89-90—Los Angeles....................	NHL	79	20	42	62	36	10	2	9	11	6
90-91—Los Angeles....................	NHL	78	21	41	62	66	12	4	8	12	8
91-92—Philadelphia	NHL	78	18	38	56	86	—	—	—	—	—
92-93—Quebec	NHL	82	20	62	82	57	6	0	5	5	6
NHL totals................................		542	133	297	430	520	49	13	31	44	50

DUFFUS, PARRIS
G, BLUES

PERSONAL: Born January 27, 1970, at Denver.... 6-2/192.... Shoots left.
COLLEGE: Cornell.
TRANSACTIONS/CAREER NOTES: Selected by St. Louis Blues in ninth round (sixth Blues pick, 180th overall) of NHL entry draft (June 16, 1990).
HONORS: Named to NCAA All-America East first team (1991-92).... Named to ECAC All-Star second team (1991-92).

			REGULAR SEASON								PLAYOFFS						
Season	Team	League	Gms.	Min.	W	L	T	GA	SO	Avg.	Gms.	Min.	W	L	GA	SO	Avg.
88-89	Melfort	SJHL	39	2207	5	28	3	227	1	6.17	—	—	—	—	—	—	—
89-90	Melfort	SJHL	51	2828	17	26	3	226	2	4.79	—	—	—	—	—	—	—
90-91	Cornell University	ECAC	4	37	0	0	0	3	0	4.86	—	—	—	—	—	—	—
91-92	Cornell University	ECAC	28	1677	14	11	3	74	1	2.65	—	—	—	—	—	—	—
92-93	Hampton Roads	ECHL	4	245	...	...	...	13	0	3.18	—	—	—	—	—	—	—
	—Peoria	IHL	37	2149	16	15	0	142	0	3.96	1	59	0	1	5	0	5.08

DUFRESNE, DONALD
D, LIGHTNING

PERSONAL: Born April 10, 1967, at Quebec City.... 6-1/206.... Shoots left.... Name pronounced DOH-nal doo-FRAYN.
TRANSACTIONS/CAREER NOTES: Suffered from pneumonia (November 1984).... Selected by Montreal Canadiens in sixth round (eighth Canadiens pick, 117th overall) of NHL entry draft (June 15, 1985).... Dislocated shoulder (January 8, 1988).... Sprained ankle (February 1989). ... Separated shoulder (October 5, 1989); missed 15 games.... Reinjured shoulder (December 9, 1989).... Tore ligaments in right knee (December 9, 1991); missed 15 games.... Sprained ankle (February 20, 1993); missed three games.... Strained rib cage muscles (March 3, 1993); missed three games.... Traded by Canadiens to Tampa Bay Lightning (June 18, 1993) to complete deal in which Canadiens sent D Eric Charron, D Alain Cote and future considerations to Lightning for D Rob Ramage (March 20, 1993).
HONORS: Named to QMJHL All-Star second team (1985-86 and 1986-87).
MISCELLANEOUS: Member of Stanley Cup championship team (1993).

			REGULAR SEASON					PLAYOFFS				
Season	Team	League	Gms.	G	A	Pts.	Pen.	Gms.	G	A	Pts.	Pen.
83-84	Trois-Rivieres	QMJHL	67	7	12	19	97	—	—	—	—	—
84-85	Trois-Rivieres	QMJHL	65	5	30	35	112	7	1	3	4	12
85-86	Trois-Rivieres	QMJHL	63	8	32	40	160	1	0	0	0	0
86-87	Longueuil	QMJHL	67	5	29	34	97	20	1	8	9	38
87-88	Sherbrooke	AHL	47	1	8	9	107	6	1	1	2	34
88-89	Montreal	NHL	13	0	1	1	43	6	1	1	2	4
	—Sherbrooke	AHL	47	0	12	12	170	—	—	—	—	—
89-90	Montreal	NHL	18	0	4	4	23	10	0	1	1	18
	—Sherbrooke	AHL	38	2	11	13	104	0	0	0	0	0
90-91	Fredericton	AHL	10	1	4	5	35	1	0	0	0	0
	—Montreal	NHL	53	2	13	15	55	10	0	1	1	21
91-92	Montreal	NHL	3	0	0	0	2	—	—	—	—	—
	—Fredericton	AHL	31	8	12	20	60	7	0	0	0	10
92-93	Montreal	NHL	32	1	2	3	32	2	0	0	0	0
	NHL totals		119	3	20	23	155	28	1	3	4	43

DUNCAN, BRETT
D, LIGHTNING

PERSONAL: Born August 12, 1974, at Kitchener, Ont.... 6-0/208.... Shoots right.
TRANSACTIONS/CAREER NOTES: Selected by Tampa Bay Lightning in 10th round (10th Lightning pick, 237th overall) of NHL entry draft (June 26, 1993).

			REGULAR SEASON					PLAYOFFS				
Season	Team	League	Gms.	G	A	Pts.	Pen.	Gms.	G	A	Pts.	Pen.
91-92	Bellingham Jr. A	BCJHL	57	3	11	14	354	—	—	—	—	—
	—Seattle	WHL	—	—	—	—	—	6	0	0	0	33
92-93	Seattle	WHL	64	0	12	12	343	5	0	1	1	33

DUNCANSON, CRAIG
LW, RANGERS

PERSONAL: Born March 17, 1967, at Sudbury, Ont.... 6-0/190.... Shoots left. ... Full name: Craig Murray Duncanson.
TRANSACTIONS/CAREER NOTES: Tore knee ligaments (September 1984).... Selected by Los Angeles Kings as underage junior in first round (first Kings pick, ninth overall) of NHL entry draft (June 15, 1985).... Suffered deep leg bruise (November 23, 1986).... Traded by Kings to Minnesota North Stars for G Daniel Berthiaume (September 6, 1990).... Traded by North Stars to Winnipeg Jets for C Brian Hunt (September 6, 1990).... Traded by Jets with LW Brent Hughes and C Simon Wheeldon to Washington Capitals for LW Bob Joyce, D Kent Paynter and C Tyler Larter (May 21, 1991).... Loaned to Jets organization (February 26, 1992).... Signed as free agent by New York Rangers (September 4, 1992).

			REGULAR SEASON					PLAYOFFS				
Season	Team	League	Gms.	G	A	Pts.	Pen.	Gms.	G	A	Pts.	Pen.
82-83	St. Michael's Jr. B	ODHA	32	14	19	33	68	—	—	—	—	—
83-84	Sudbury	OHL	62	38	38	76	178	—	—	—	—	—
84-85	Sudbury	OHL	53	35	28	63	129	—	—	—	—	—
85-86	Sudbury	OHL	21	12	17	29	55	—	—	—	—	—
	—Cornwall	OHL	40	31	50	81	135	6	4	7	11	2
	—Los Angeles	NHL	2	0	1	1	0	—	—	—	—	—
	—New Haven	AHL	—	—	—	—	—	2	0	0	0	5
86-87	Cornwall	OHL	52	22	45	67	88	5	4	3	7	20
	—Los Angeles	NHL	2	0	0	0	24	—	—	—	—	—

Season Team	League	REGULAR SEASON Gms.	G	A	Pts.	Pen.	PLAYOFFS Gms.	G	A	Pts.	Pen.
87-88—New Haven	AHL	57	15	25	40	170	—	—	—	—	—
—Los Angeles	NHL	9	0	0	0	12	—	—	—	—	—
88-89—New Haven	AHL	69	25	39	64	200	17	4	8	12	60
—Los Angeles	NHL	5	0	0	0	0	—	—	—	—	—
89-90—Los Angeles	NHL	10	3	2	5	9	—	—	—	—	—
—New Haven	AHL	51	17	30	47	152	—	—	—	—	—
90-91—Moncton	AHL	58	16	34	50	107	9	3	11	14	31
—Winnipeg	NHL	7	2	0	2	16	—	—	—	—	—
91-92—Baltimore	AHL	46	20	26	46	98	—	—	—	—	—
—Moncton	AHL	19	12	9	21	6	11	6	4	10	10
92-93—Binghamton	AHL	69	35	59	94	126	14	7	5	12	9
—New York Rangers	NHL	3	0	1	1	0	—	—	—	—	—
NHL totals		38	5	4	9	61					

DUNHAM, MIKE
G, DEVILS

PERSONAL: Born June 1, 1972, at Johnson City, N.Y. . . . 6-2/170. . . . Shoots left. . . . Full name: Michael Francis Dunham.
HIGH SCHOOL: Canterbury (New Milford, Conn.).
COLLEGE: Maine.
TRANSACTIONS/CAREER NOTES: Selected by New Jersey Devils in third round (fourth Devils pick, 53rd overall) of NHL entry draft (June 16, 1990).
HONORS: Named to NCAA All-America East first team (1992-93). . . . Named to Hockey East All-star first team (1992-93).

Season Team	League	REGULAR SEASON Gms.	Min.	W	L	T	GA	SO	Avg.	PLAYOFFS Gms.	Min.	W	L	GA	SO	Avg.
88-89—Canterbury School	Conn. HS	25	. . .	. . .	. . .	. . .	63	2	. . .	—	—	—	—	—	—	—
89-90—Canterbury School	Conn. HS	32	1558	. . .	. . .	. . .	55	. . .	2.12	—	—	—	—	—	—	—
90-91—University of Maine	Hoc. East	23	1275	14	5	2	63	2	*2.96	—	—	—	—	—	—	—
91-92—University of Maine	Hoc. East	7	382	6	0	0	14	1	2.20	—	—	—	—	—	—	—
—U.S. national team	Int'l	3	157	0	1	1	10	0	3.82	—	—	—	—	—	—	—
92-93—University of Maine	Hoc. East	25	1429	21	1	1	63	. . .	2.65	—	—	—	—	—	—	—

DUPAUL, COSMO
C, SENATORS

PERSONAL: Born April 11, 1975, at Pointe Claire, Que. . . . 6-0/186. . . . Shoots left.
TRANSACTIONS/CAREER NOTES: Selected by Ottawa Senators in fourth round (fourth Senators pick, 91st overall) of NHL entry draft (June 26, 1993).

Season Team	League	REGULAR SEASON Gms.	G	A	Pts.	Pen.	PLAYOFFS Gms.	G	A	Pts.	Pen.
92-93—Victoriaville	QMJHL	67	23	35	58	16	6	1	3	4	2

DUPRE, YANICK
LW, FLYERS

PERSONAL: Born November 20, 1972, at Montreal. . . . 6-0/195. . . . Shoots left. . . . Name pronounced YAHN-ihk doo-PRAY.
TRANSACTIONS/CAREER NOTES: Pulled ankle ligament (September 1989). . . . Traded by Chicoutimi Sagueneens with D Guy Lehoux and RW Eric Meloche to Drummondville Voltigeurs for RW Daniel Dore, RW Denis Chasse and D Pierre-Paul Landry (December 19, 1989). . . . Injured knee ligament (October 1990). . . . Selected by Philadelphia Flyers in third round (second Flyers pick, 50th overall) of NHL entry draft (June 1991).

Season Team	League	REGULAR SEASON Gms.	G	A	Pts.	Pen.	PLAYOFFS Gms.	G	A	Pts.	Pen.
89-90—Chicoutimi	QMJHL	24	5	9	14	27	—	—	—	—	—
—Drummondville	QMJHL	30	10	10	20	32	—	—	—	—	—
90-91—Drummondville	QMJHL	58	29	38	67	87	11	8	5	13	33
91-92—Philadelphia	NHL	1	0	0	0	0	—	—	—	—	—
—Drummondville	QMJHL	28	19	17	36	48	—	—	—	—	—
—Verdun	QMJHL	12	7	14	21	21	19	9	9	18	20
92-93—Hershey	AHL	63	13	24	37	22	—	—	—	—	—
NHL totals		1	0	0	0	0					

DUPUIS, GUY
D, RED WINGS

PERSONAL: Born May 10, 1970, at Moncton, N.B. . . . 6-2/205. . . . Shoots right. . . . Name pronounced GEE doo-PWEE.
TRANSACTIONS/CAREER NOTES: Selected by Detroit Red Wings in third round (third Red Wings pick, 47th overall) of NHL entry draft (June 11, 1988).
HONORS: Named to QMJHL All-Star second team (1988-89).

Season Team	League	REGULAR SEASON Gms.	G	A	Pts.	Pen.	PLAYOFFS Gms.	G	A	Pts.	Pen.
86-87—Hull	QMJHL	69	5	10	15	35	8	1	2	3	2
87-88—Hull	QMJHL	69	14	34	48	72	19	3	8	11	29
88-89—Hull	QMJHL	70	15	56	71	89	9	3	3	6	8
89-90—Hull	QMJHL	70	8	41	49	96	11	1	3	4	8
90-91—Adirondack	AHL	57	4	10	14	73	—	—	—	—	—
91-92—Adirondack	AHL	49	3	6	9	59	3	0	0	0	4
—Fort Wayne	IHL	10	2	7	9	0	—	—	—	—	—
92-93—Fort Wayne	IHL	53	4	11	15	57	4	0	1	1	6
—Adirondack	AHL	1	0	0	0	0	—	—	—	—	—

D

DYCK, LARRY
G, STARS

PERSONAL: Born December 15, 1965, at Winkler, Man.... 5-11/180.... Shoots left.
COLLEGE: Manitoba.
TRANSACTIONS/CAREER NOTES: Signed as free agent by Minnesota North Stars (August 1988).
HONORS: Named to WHL (West) All-Star first team (1985-86).... Named CWUAA Freshman of the Year (1986-87).... Named to CWUAA All-Star first team (1986-87).... Named to CWUAA All-Star second team (1987-88).

			REGULAR SEASON								PLAYOFFS						
Season Team	League	Gms.	Min.	W	L	T	GA	SO	Avg.	Gms.	Min.	W	L	GA	SO	Avg.
86-87—University of Manitoba.	CWUAA	18	1019	...	...	...	61	*3	3.59	—	—	—	—	—	—	—
87-88—University of Manitoba.	CWUAA	*19	*1118	...	...	...	87	0	4.67	—	—	—	—	—	—	—
88-89—Kalamazoo	IHL	42	2308	17	20	2	168	0	4.37	—	—	—	—	—	—	—
89-90—Kalamazoo	IHL	36	1959	20	12	2	116	0	3.55	7	353	2	3	22	0	3.74
—Knoxville	ECHL	3	184	1	1	1	12	0	3.91	—	—	—	—	—	—	—
90-91—Kalamazoo	IHL	38	2182	21	15	0	133	1	3.66	1	60	0	1	6	0	6.00
91-92—Kalamazoo	IHL	57	*3305	25	23	6	195	0	3.54	12	690	5	7	43	0	3.74
92-93—Milwaukee	IHL	40	2328	23	9	0	131	0	3.38	3	180	1	2	10	0	3.33

DYCK, PAUL
D, PENGUINS

PERSONAL: Born April 15, 1971, at Steinbach, Man.... 6-1/192.... Shoots left.
TRANSACTIONS/CAREER NOTES: Selected by Pittsburgh Penguins in 11th round (11th Penguins pick, 236th overall) of NHL entry draft (June 22, 1991).

		REGULAR SEASON					PLAYOFFS				
Season Team	League	Gms.	G	A	Pts.	Pen.	Gms.	G	A	Pts.	Pen.
89-90—Moose Jaw	WHL	72	5	10	15	86	—	—	—	—	—
90-91—Moose Jaw	WHL	72	12	41	53	63	8	0	7	7	17
91-92—Muskegon	IHL	73	6	21	27	40	14	1	3	4	4
92-93—Cleveland	IHL	69	6	21	27	69	1	0	0	0	0

DYKHUIS, KARL
D, BLACKHAWKS

PERSONAL: Born July 8, 1972, at Sept-Iles, Que.... 6-3/195.... Shoots left.... Name pronounced DIGH-kowz.
TRANSACTIONS/CAREER NOTES: Selected by Chicago Blackhawks in first round (first Blackhawks pick, 16th overall) of NHL entry draft (June 16, 1990).... QMJHL rights traded by Hull Olympiques to College Francais for first- and sixth-round draft picks (January 10, 1991).
HONORS: Won Raymond Lagace Trophy (1988-89).... Won Michael Bossy Trophy (1989-90).... Named to QMJHL All-Star first team (1989-90).

		REGULAR SEASON					PLAYOFFS				
Season Team	League	Gms.	G	A	Pts.	Pen.	Gms.	G	A	Pts.	Pen.
88-89—Hull	QMJHL	63	2	29	31	59	9	1	9	10	6
89-90—Hull	QMJHL	69	10	45	55	119	11	2	5	7	2
90-91—Longueuil	QMJHL	3	1	4	5	6					
—Canadian national team	Int'l			Statistics unavailable.							
91-92—Longueuil	QMJHL	29	5	19	24	55	17	0	12	12	14
—Chicago	NHL	6	1	3	4	4	—	—	—	—	—
92-93—Chicago	NHL	12	0	5	5	0	—	—	—	—	—
—Indianapolis	IHL	59	5	18	23	76	5	1	1	2	8
NHL totals		18	1	8	9	4					

DZIEDZIC, JOE
LW, PENGUINS

PERSONAL: Born December 18, 1971, at Minneapolis.... 6-3/200.... Shoots left.... Full name: Joseph Walter Dziedzic.
HIGH SCHOOL: Edison (Minneapolis).
COLLEGE: Minnesota.
TRANSACTIONS/CAREER NOTES: Selected by Pittsburgh Penguins in third round (second Penguins pick, 61st overall) of NHL entry draft (June 16, 1990).

		REGULAR SEASON					PLAYOFFS				
Season Team	League	Gms.	G	A	Pts.	Pen.	Gms.	G	A	Pts.	Pen.
88-89—Minneapolis Edison H.S.	Minn. H.S.	25	47	27	74	...	—	—	—	—	—
89-90—Minneapolis Edison H.S.	Minn. H.S.	17	29	19	48	...	—	—	—	—	—
90-91—University of Minnesota	WCHA	20	6	4	10	26	—	—	—	—	—
91-92—University of Minnesota	WCHA	37	9	10	19	68	—	—	—	—	—
92-93—University of Minnesota	WCHA	41	11	14	25	62	—	—	—	—	—

EAGLES, MIKE
C, JETS

PERSONAL: Born March 7, 1963, at Susex, N.B.... 5-10/180.... Shoots left.... Full name: Michael Bryant Eagles.
TRANSACTIONS/CAREER NOTES: Selected by Quebec Nordiques as underage junior in sixth round (fifth Nordiques pick, 116th overall) of NHL entry draft (June 10, 1981).... Broke hand (October 1984).... Injured ribs (February 21, 1986).... Traded by Nordiques to Chicago Blackhawks for G Bob Mason (July 1988).... Broke left hand (February 1989).... Bruised kidney (January 15, 1990); missed eight games.... Traded by Blackhawks to Winnipeg Jets for fourth-round pick in 1991 draft (D Igor Kravchuk) (December 14, 1990).... Fractured thumb (February 17, 1992); missed 14 games.

		REGULAR SEASON					PLAYOFFS				
Season Team	League	Gms.	G	A	Pts.	Pen.	Gms.	G	A	Pts.	Pen.
79-80—Melville	SJHL	55	46	30	76	77	—	—	—	—	—

Season	Team	League	Gms.	G	A	Pts.	Pen.	Gms.	G	A	Pts.	Pen.
					REGULAR SEASON					PLAYOFFS		
80-81—Kitchener		OMJHL	56	11	27	38	64	18	4	2	6	36
81-82—Kitchener		OHL	62	26	40	66	148	15	3	11	14	27
82-83—Kitchener		OHL	58	26	36	62	133	12	5	7	12	27
—Quebec		NHL	2	0	0	0	2	—	—	—	—	—
83-84—Fredericton		AHL	68	13	29	42	85	4	0	0	0	5
84-85—Fredericton		AHL	36	4	20	24	80	3	0	0	0	2
85-86—Quebec		NHL	73	11	12	23	49	3	0	0	0	2
86-87—Quebec		NHL	73	13	19	32	55	4	1	0	1	10
87-88—Quebec		NHL	76	10	10	20	74	—	—	—	—	—
88-89—Chicago		NHL	47	5	11	16	44	—	—	—	—	—
89-90—Indianapolis		IHL	24	11	13	24	47	13	*10	10	20	34
—Chicago		NHL	23	1	2	3	34	—	—	—	—	—
90-91—Indianapolis		IHL	25	15	14	29	47	—	—	—	—	—
—Winnipeg		NHL	44	0	9	9	79	—	—	—	—	—
91-92—Winnipeg		NHL	65	7	10	17	118	7	0	0	0	8
92-93—Winnipeg		NHL	84	8	18	26	131	5	0	1	1	6
NHL totals			487	55	91	146	586	19	1	1	2	26

EAKINS, DALLAS
D, PANTHERS

PERSONAL: Born January 20, 1967, at Dade City, Fla.... 6-2/195.... Shoots left.... Name pronounced EE-kihns.
TRANSACTIONS/CAREER NOTES: Selected by Washington Capitals as underage junior in 10th round (11th Capitals pick, 208th overall) of NHL entry draft (June 15, 1985).... Injured back (October 1988).... Signed as free agent by Winnipeg Jets (September 1989).... Signed as free agent by Florida Panthers (July 14, 1993).

Season	Team	League	Gms.	G	A	Pts.	Pen.	Gms.	G	A	Pts.	Pen.
					REGULAR SEASON					PLAYOFFS		
84-85—Peterborough		OHL	48	0	8	8	96	7	0	0	0	18
85-86—Peterborough		OHL	60	6	16	22	134	16	0	1	1	30
86-87—Peterborough		OHL	54	3	11	14	145	12	1	4	5	37
87-88—Peterborough		OHL	64	11	27	38	129	12	3	12	15	16
88-89—Baltimore		AHL	62	0	10	10	139	—	—	—	—	—
89-90—Moncton		AHL	75	2	11	13	189	—	—	—	—	—
90-91—Moncton		AHL	75	1	12	13	132	9	0	1	1	44
91-92—Moncton		AHL	67	3	13	16	136	11	2	1	3	16
92-93—Moncton		AHL	55	4	6	10	132	—	—	—	—	—
—Winnipeg		NHL	14	0	2	2	38	—	—	—	—	—
NHL totals			14	0	2	2	38					

EASTWOOD, MICHAEL
C/RW, MAPLE LEAFS

PERSONAL: Born July 1, 1967, at Cornwall, Ont.... 6-2/190.... Shoots right.
COLLEGE: Western Michigan.
TRANSACTIONS/CAREER NOTES: Selected by Toronto Maple Leafs in fifth round (fifth Maple Leafs pick, 91st overall) of NHL entry draft (June 13, 1987).

HONORS: Named to CCHA All-Star second team (1990-91).

Season	Team	League	Gms.	G	A	Pts.	Pen.	Gms.	G	A	Pts.	Pen.
					REGULAR SEASON					PLAYOFFS		
86-87—Pembroke		COJHL			Statistics unavailable.							
87-88—Western Michigan Univ.		CCHA	42	5	8	13	14	—	—	—	—	—
88-89—Western Michigan Univ.		CCHA	40	10	13	23	87	—	—	—	—	—
89-90—Western Michigan Univ.		CCHA	40	25	27	52	36	—	—	—	—	—
90-91—Western Michigan Univ.		CCHA	42	29	32	61	84	—	—	—	—	—
91-92—St. John's		AHL	61	18	25	43	28	16	9	10	19	16
—Toronto		NHL	9	0	2	2	4	—	—	—	—	—
92-93—St. John's		AHL	60	24	35	59	32	—	—	—	—	—
—Toronto		NHL	12	1	6	7	21	10	1	2	3	8
NHL totals			21	1	8	9	25	10	1	2	3	8

EGELAND, ALLAN
C, LIGHTNING

PERSONAL: Born January 31, 1973, at Lethbridge, Alta.... 6-0/184.... Shoots left.
TRANSACTIONS/CAREER NOTES: Selected by Tampa Bay Lightning in third round (third Lightning pick, 55th overall) of NHL entry draft (June 26, 1993).
HONORS: Named to WHL (West) All-Star first team (1992-93).

Season	Team	League	Gms.	G	A	Pts.	Pen.	Gms.	G	A	Pts.	Pen.
					REGULAR SEASON					PLAYOFFS		
90-91—Lethbridge		WHL	67	2	16	18	57	9	0	0	0	0
91-92—Tacoma		WHL	72	35	39	74	115	4	0	1	1	18
92-93—Tacoma		WHL	71	56	57	113	119	7	9	7	16	18

EGELAND, TRACY
RW, FLYERS

PERSONAL: Born August 20, 1970, at Lethbridge, Alta.... 6-1/180.... Shoots right.... Name pronounced EHG-uuh-luhnd.
TRANSACTIONS/CAREER NOTES: Injured elbow (November 1986); missed two weeks.... Traded by Swift Current Broncos to Medicine Hat Tigers for C Travis Kellin (August

E

1988).... Selected by Chicago Blackhawks in seventh round (fifth Blackhawks pick, 132nd overall) of NHL entry draft (June 17, 1989).... Signed as free agent by Philadelphia Flyers (August 4, 1993).

Season Team	League	REGULAR SEASON					PLAYOFFS				
		Gms.	G	A	Pts.	Pen.	Gms.	G	A	Pts.	Pen.
86-87—Swift Current	WHL	48	3	2	5	20	—	—	—	—	—
87-88—Swift Current	WHL	63	10	22	32	34	—	—	—	—	—
88-89—Medicine Hat	WHL	42	11	12	23	64	—	—	—	—	—
—Prince Albert	WHL	24	17	10	27	24	4	0	1	1	13
89-90—Prince Albert	WHL	61	39	26	65	160	13	7	10	17	26
90-91—Indianapolis	IHL	79	17	22	39	205	7	2	1	3	21
91-92—Indianapolis	IHL	66	20	11	31	214	—	—	—	—	—
92-93—Indianapolis	IHL	43	11	14	25	122	—	—	—	—	—

EISENHUT, NEIL
C, CANUCKS

PERSONAL: Born February 9, 1967, at Osoyoos, B.C.... 5-11/190.... Shoots left.
COLLEGE: North Dakota.
TRANSACTIONS/CAREER NOTES: Selected by Vancouver Canucks in 12th round (11th Canucks pick, 233rd overall) of NHL entry draft (June 13, 1987).

Season Team	League	REGULAR SEASON					PLAYOFFS				
		Gms.	G	A	Pts.	Pen.	Gms.	G	A	Pts.	Pen.
86-87—Langley Eagles	BCJHL	43	41	34	75	...	—	—	—	—	—
87-88—North Dakota	WCHA	42	12	20	32	14	—	—	—	—	—
88-89—North Dakota	WCHA	41	22	16	38	26	—	—	—	—	—
89-90—North Dakota	WCHA	45	22	32	54	46	—	—	—	—	—
90-91—North Dakota	WCHA	20	9	15	24	10	—	—	—	—	—
91-92—Milwaukee	IHL	76	13	23	36	26	2	1	2	3	0
92-93—Hamilton	AHL	72	22	40	62	41	—	—	—	—	—

EKLUND, PELLE
LW, FLYERS

PERSONAL: Born March 22, 1963, at Stockholm, Sweden.... 5-10/175.... Shoots left.
TRANSACTIONS/CAREER NOTES: Selected by Philadelphia Flyers in eighth round (seventh Flyers pick, 161st overall) of NHL entry draft (June 8, 1983).... Bruised hip (March 1988).... Strained left knee (October 1989).... Bruised right knee (November 24, 1989).... Strained hip flexor and stomach muscles (January 31, 1991); missed five games.... Bruised shoulder (November 20, 1991); missed one game.... Sprained knee (January 12, 1992); missed eight games.... Reinjured knee (February 6, 1992); missed five games.... Reinjured knee (February 27, 1992); missed three games.... Sprained knee (March 1992); missed final six games of season.... Underwent arthroscopic surgery to knee (April 14, 1992).... Broke right foot (October 1, 1992); missed first 22 games of season.... Suffered hip flexor (December 30, 1992); missed two games.... Suffered cut over left eye (February 18, 1993); missed one game.... Bruised thigh (March 30, 1993); missed three games.
HONORS: Won Golden Puck Award (1983-84).... Named to Swedish League All-Star team (1983-84).
RECORDS: Holds NHL playoff record for fastest goal from the start of a period—6 seconds (April 25, 1989).
MISCELLANEOUS: Member of bronze-medal-winning Swedish Olympic team (1984).... Named Sweden's Athlete of the Year for 1984.

Season Team	League	REGULAR SEASON					PLAYOFFS				
		Gms.	G	A	Pts.	Pen.	Gms.	G	A	Pts.	Pen.
81-82—Stockholm AIK	Sweden	23	2	3	5	2	—	—	—	—	—
82-83—Stockholm AIK	Sweden	34	13	17	30	14	3	1	4	5	2
83-84—Stockholm AIK	Sweden	35	9	18	27	24	6	6	7	13	2
—Swedish Olympic Team	Int'l	7	2	6	8	0	—	—	—	—	—
84-85—Stockholm AIK	Sweden	35	16	33	49	10	—	—	—	—	—
85-86—Philadelphia	NHL	70	15	51	66	12	5	0	2	2	0
86-87—Philadelphia	NHL	72	14	41	55	2	26	7	20	27	2
87-88—Philadelphia	NHL	71	10	32	42	12	7	0	3	3	0
88-89—Philadelphia	NHL	79	18	51	69	23	19	3	8	11	2
89-90—Philadelphia	NHL	70	23	39	62	16	—	—	—	—	—
90-91—Philadelphia	NHL	73	19	50	69	14	—	—	—	—	—
91-92—Philadelphia	NHL	51	7	16	23	4	—	—	—	—	—
92-93—Philadelphia	NHL	55	11	38	49	16	—	—	—	—	—
NHL totals		541	117	318	435	99	57	10	33	43	4

ELIK, TODD
C, OILERS

PERSONAL: Born April 15, 1966, at Brampton, Ont.... 6-2/190.... Shoots left.... Name pronounced EHL-ihk.
COLLEGE: Regina (Sask.).
TRANSACTIONS/CAREER NOTES: Signed as free agent by New York Rangers (February 26, 1988).... Traded by Rangers with LW Igor Liba, D Michael Boyce and future considerations to Los Angeles Kings for D Dean Kennedy and D Denis Larocque (December 12, 1988).... Suffered lacerations near right eye (January 1991).... Injured thigh (February 26, 1991); missed one game.... Traded by Kings to Minnesota North Stars for D Charlie Huddy, LW Randy Gilhen, RW Jim Thomson and fourth-round pick in 1991 draft (D Alexei Zhitnik) (June 22, 1991).... Broke foot (November 14, 1992); missed five games.... Suffered head injury (January 23, 1993); missed six games.... Traded by North Stars to Edmonton Oilers for C Brent Gilchrist (March 5, 1993).... Injured shoulder (April 6, 1993); missed remainder of season.

Season Team	League	REGULAR SEASON					PLAYOFFS				
		Gms.	G	A	Pts.	Pen.	Gms.	G	A	Pts.	Pen.
83-84—Kingston	OHL	64	5	16	21	17	—	—	—	—	—
84-85—Kingston	OHL	34	14	11	25	6	—	—	—	—	—
—North Bay	OHL	23	4	6	10	2	4	2	0	2	0

Season Team	League	REGULAR SEASON					PLAYOFFS				
		Gms.	G	A	Pts.	Pen.	Gms.	G	A	Pts.	Pen.
85-86—North Bay	OHL	40	12	34	46	20	10	7	6	13	0
86-87—University of Regina	CWUAA	27	26	34	60	137	—	—	—	—	—
87-88—Denver	IHL	81	44	56	100	83	12	8	12	20	9
88-89—Denver	IHL	28	20	15	35	22	—	—	—	—	—
—New Haven	AHL	43	11	25	36	31	17	10	12	22	44
89-90—Los Angeles	NHL	48	10	23	33	41	10	3	9	12	10
—New Haven	AHL	32	20	23	43	42	—	—	—	—	—
90-91—Los Angeles	NHL	74	21	37	58	58	12	2	7	9	6
91-92—Minnesota	NHL	62	14	32	46	125	5	1	1	2	2
92-93—Minnesota	NHL	46	13	18	31	48	—	—	—	—	—
—Edmonton	NHL	14	1	9	10	8	—	—	—	—	—
NHL totals		244	59	119	178	280	27	6	17	23	18

ELLETT, DAVE
D, MAPLE LEAFS

PERSONAL: Born March 30, 1964, at Cleveland. . . . 6-2/200. . . . Shoots left.
COLLEGE: Bowling Green State.
TRANSACTIONS/CAREER NOTES: Selected by Winnipeg Jets as underage junior in fourth round (third Jets pick, 75th overall) of NHL entry draft (June 9, 1982). . . . Bruised thigh (March 6, 1988); missed 10 games. . . . Sprained ankle (November 16, 1988). . . . Traded by Jets with C Paul Fenton to Toronto Maple Leafs for C Ed Olczyk and LW Mark Osborne (November 10, 1990). . . . Separated shoulder (March 2, 1993); missed 14 games.
HONORS: Named to CCHA All-Star second team (1983-84). . . . Named to NCAA All-Tournament team (1983-84). . . . Played in NHL All-Star Game (1989 and 1992).

Season Team	League	REGULAR SEASON					PLAYOFFS				
		Gms.	G	A	Pts.	Pen.	Gms.	G	A	Pts.	Pen.
81-82—Ottawa	COJHL	50	9	35	44	...	—	—	—	—	—
82-83—Bowling Green State	CCHA	40	4	13	17	34	—	—	—	—	—
83-84—Bowling Green State	CCHA	43	15	39	54	9	—	—	—	—	—
84-85—Winnipeg	NHL	80	11	27	38	85	8	1	5	6	4
85-86—Winnipeg	NHL	80	15	31	46	96	3	0	1	1	0
86-87—Winnipeg	NHL	78	13	31	44	53	10	0	8	8	2
87-88—Winnipeg	NHL	68	13	45	58	106	5	1	2	3	10
88-89—Winnipeg	NHL	75	22	34	56	62	—	—	—	—	—
89-90—Winnipeg	NHL	77	17	29	46	96	7	2	0	2	6
90-91—Winnipeg	NHL	17	4	7	11	6	—	—	—	—	—
—Toronto	NHL	60	8	30	38	69	—	—	—	—	—
91-92—Toronto	NHL	79	18	33	51	95	—	—	—	—	—
92-93—Toronto	NHL	70	6	34	40	46	21	4	8	12	8
NHL totals		684	127	301	428	714	54	8	24	32	30

ELYNUIK, PAT
RW, CAPITALS

PERSONAL: Born October 30, 1967, at Foam Lake, Sask. . . . 6-0/185. . . . Shoots right. . . . Full name: Pat Gerald Elynuik. . . . Name pronounced EHL-ih-nuhk.
TRANSACTIONS/CAREER NOTES: Selected by Winnipeg Jets as underage junior in first round (first Jets pick, eighth overall) of NHL entry draft (June 21, 1986). . . . Separated left shoulder (March 7, 1989). . . . Strained groin (December 14, 1991); missed six games. . . . Sprained knee (February 2, 1992); missed three games. . . . Injured eye (March 17, 1992); missed five games. . . . Traded by Jets to Washington Capitals for RW John Druce and conditional pick in 1993 draft (October 1, 1992).
HONORS: Named to WHL (East) All-Star first team (1985-86 and 1986-87).

Season Team	League	REGULAR SEASON					PLAYOFFS				
		Gms.	G	A	Pts.	Pen.	Gms.	G	A	Pts.	Pen.
84-85—Prince Albert	WHL	70	23	20	43	54	13	9	3	12	7
85-86—Prince Albert	WHL	68	53	53	106	62	20	7	9	16	17
86-87—Prince Albert	WHL	64	51	62	113	40	8	5	5	10	12
87-88—Moncton	AHL	30	11	18	29	35	—	—	—	—	—
—Winnipeg	NHL	13	1	3	4	12	—	—	—	—	—
88-89—Winnipeg	NHL	56	26	25	51	29	—	—	—	—	—
—Moncton	AHL	7	8	2	10	2	—	—	—	—	—
89-90—Winnipeg	NHL	80	32	42	74	83	7	2	4	6	2
90-91—Winnipeg	NHL	80	31	34	65	73	—	—	—	—	—
91-92—Winnipeg	NHL	60	25	25	50	65	7	2	2	4	4
92-93—Washington	NHL	80	22	35	57	66	6	2	3	5	19
NHL totals		369	137	164	301	328	20	6	9	15	25

EMERSON, NELSON
C, BLUES

PERSONAL: Born August 17, 1967, at Hamilton, Ont. . . . 5-11/178. . . . Shoots right. . . . Full name: Nelson Donald Emerson.
COLLEGE: Bowling Green State.
TRANSACTIONS/CAREER NOTES: Selected by St. Louis Blues in third round (second Blues pick, 44th overall) of NHL entry draft (June 15, 1985). . . . Fractured bone under his eye (December 28, 1991). . . . Injured leg (April 3, 1993); missed one game.
HONORS: Named CCHA Rookie of the Year (1986-87). . . . Named to NCAA All-America West second team (1987-88). . . . Named to CCHA All-Star first team (1987-88 and 1989-90). . . . Named to CCHA All-Star second team (1988-89). . . . Named to NCAA All-America West first team (1989-90). . . . Won Garry F. Longman Memorial Trophy (1990-91). . . . Named to IHL All-Star first team (1990-91).

E

Season Team	League	REGULAR SEASON Gms.	G	A	Pts.	Pen.	PLAYOFFS Gms.	G	A	Pts.	Pen.
84-85—Stratford Jr. B	OHA	40	23	38	61	70	—	—	—	—	—
85-86—Stratford Jr. B	OHA	39	54	58	112	91	—	—	—	—	—
86-87—Bowling Green State	CCHA	45	26	35	61	28	—	—	—	—	—
87-88—Bowling Green State	CCHA	45	34	49	83	54	—	—	—	—	—
88-89—Bowling Green State	CCHA	44	22	46	68	46	—	—	—	—	—
89-90—Bowling Green State	CCHA	44	30	52	82	42	—	—	—	—	—
—Peoria	IHL	3	1	1	2	0	—	—	—	—	—
90-91—St. Louis	NHL	4	0	3	3	2	—	—	—	—	—
—Peoria	IHL	73	36	79	115	91	17	9	12	21	16
91-92—St. Louis	NHL	79	23	36	59	66	6	3	3	6	21
92-93—St. Louis	NHL	82	22	51	73	62	11	1	6	7	6
NHL totals		165	45	90	135	130	17	4	9	13	27

EMMA, DAVID
C, DEVILS

PERSONAL: Born January 14, 1969, at Cranston, R.I. . . . 5-11/180. . . . Shoots left. . . . Full name: David Anaclethe Emma.
HIGH SCHOOL: Bishop Hendricken (Warwick, R.I.).
COLLEGE: Boston College.
TRANSACTIONS/CAREER NOTES: Selected by New Jersey Devils in sixth round (sixth Devils pick, 110th overall) of NHL entry draft (June 17, 1989)
HONORS: Named to Hockey East All-Freshman team (1987-88). . . . Named to Hockey East All-Star second team (1988-89). . . . Named to Hockey East All-Star first team (1989-90 and 1990-91). . . . Won Hobey Baker Memorial Trophy (1990-91). . . . Named Hockey East Player of the Year (1990-91). . . . Named to NCAA All-America East first team (1989-90 and 1990-91).

Season Team	League	REGULAR SEASON Gms.	G	A	Pts.	Pen.	PLAYOFFS Gms.	G	A	Pts.	Pen.
87-88—Boston College	Hockey East	30	19	16	35	30	—	—	—	—	—
88-89—Boston College	Hockey East	36	20	31	51	36	—	—	—	—	—
89-90—Boston College	Hockey East	42	38	34	*72	46	—	—	—	—	—
90-91—Boston College	Hockey East	39	35	46	81	44	—	—	—	—	—
91-92—U.S. national team	Int'l	55	15	16	31	32	—	—	—	—	—
—U.S. Olympic Team	Int'l	6	0	1	1	6	—	—	—	—	—
—Utica	AHL	15	4	7	11	12	4	1	1	2	2
92-93—Utica	AHL	61	21	40	61	47	5	2	1	3	6
—New Jersey	NHL	2	0	0	0	0	—	—	—	—	—
NHL totals		2	0	0	0	0					

EMMONS, GARY
C

PERSONAL: Born December 30, 1963, at Winnipeg, Man. . . . 5-9/170. . . . Shoots right.
COLLEGE: Northern Michigan.
TRANSACTIONS/CAREER NOTES: Selected by New York Rangers in NHL supplemental draft (September 17, 1986). . . . Signed as free agent by Edmonton Oilers (July 27, 1987). . . . Signed as free agent by Minnesota North Stars (July 11, 1989).
HONORS: Shared CCHA Rookie of the Year with Bill Shibicky (1983-84). . . . Named to WCHA All-Star first team (1985-86 and 1986-87). . . . Named to NCAA All-America West second team (1986-87). . . . Named to WCHA All-Star second team (1986-87).

Season Team	League	REGULAR SEASON Gms.	G	A	Pts.	Pen.	PLAYOFFS Gms.	G	A	Pts.	Pen.
83-84—Northern Michigan Univ.	CCHA	40	28	21	49	42	—	—	—	—	—
84-85—Northern Michigan Univ.	WCHA	40	25	28	53	22	—	—	—	—	—
85-86—Northern Michigan Univ.	WCHA	36	45	30	75	34	—	—	—	—	—
86-87—Northern Michigan Univ.	WCHA	35	32	34	66	59	—	—	—	—	—
87-88—Milwaukee	IHL	13	3	4	7	4	—	—	—	—	—
—Nova Scotia	AHL	59	18	27	45	22	—	—	—	—	—
88-89—Canadian national team	Int'l	49	16	26	42	42	—	—	—	—	—
89-90—Kalamazoo	IHL	81	41	59	100	38	—	—	—	—	—
90-91—Kalamazoo	IHL	62	25	33	58	26	11	5	8	13	6
91-92—Kansas City	IHL	80	29	54	83	60	15	6	13	19	8
92-93—Kansas City	IHL	80	37	44	81	80	12	†7	6	13	8

EMMONS, JOHN
C, FLAMES

PERSONAL: Born August 17, 1974, at San Jose, Calif. . . . 6-0/185. . . . Shoots left.
HIGH SCHOOL: New Canaan (Conn.).
COLLEGE: Yale.
TRANSACTIONS/CAREER NOTES: Selected by Calgary Flames in fifth round (seventh Flames pick, 122nd overall) of NHL entry draft (June 26, 1993).

Season Team	League	REGULAR SEASON Gms.	G	A	Pts.	Pen.	PLAYOFFS Gms.	G	A	Pts.	Pen.
90-91—New Canaan H.S.	Conn. H.S.	20	19	37	56	20	—	—	—	—	—
91-92—New Canaan H.S.	Conn. H.S.	22	24	49	73	24	—	—	—	—	—
92-93—Yale University	ECAC	28	3	5	8	66	—	—	—	—	—

ERICKSON, BRYAN
RW, JETS

PERSONAL: Born March 7, 1960, at Roseau, Minn. . . . 5-9/170. . . . Shoots right. . . . Full name: Bryan Lee Erickson.
COLLEGE: Minnesota.
TRANSACTIONS/CAREER NOTES: Fractured wrist (January 1983). . . . Signed as free

agent by Washington Capitals (April 5, 1983).... Broke thumb (October 1984).... Traded by Capitals to Los Angeles Kings for D Bruce Shoebottom (October 31, 1985).... Injured left knee cartilage (October 23, 1986).... Traded by Kings to Pittsburgh Penguins for C Chris Kontos and sixth-round pick in 1989 draft (C Micah Aivazoff) (February 5, 1988).... Separated shoulder (March 1988).... Signed as free agent by Winnipeg Jets (March 2, 1990).... Strained abdomen (October 12, 1991); missed 11 games.... Re-strained abdomen (December 1991); missed remainder of season.... Underwent off-season abdominal surgery (1992); missed 23 games.... Suffered back spasms (January 23, 1993); missed five games.
HONORS: Named to WCHA All-Star second team (1981-82).... Named to WCHA All-Star first team (1982-83).

			REGULAR SEASON					PLAYOFFS				
Season	Team	League	Gms.	G	A	Pts.	Pen.	Gms.	G	A	Pts.	Pen.
79-80—University of Minnesota ...		WCHA	23	10	15	25	14	—	—	—	—	—
80-81—University of Minnesota ...		WCHA	44	39	47	86	30	—	—	—	—	—
81-82—University of Minnesota ...		WCHA	35	25	20	45	20	—	—	—	—	—
82-83—University of Minnesota ...		WCHA	42	35	47	82	30	—	—	—	—	—
—Hershey		AHL	1	0	1	1	0	3	3	0	3	0
83-84—Hershey		AHL	31	16	12	28	11	—	—	—	—	—
—Washington		NHL	45	12	17	29	16	8	2	3	5	7
84-85—Binghamton		AHL	13	6	11	17	8	—	—	—	—	—
—Washington		NHL	57	15	13	28	23	—	—	—	—	—
85-86—Binghamton		AHL	7	5	3	8	2	—	—	—	—	—
—New Haven......................		AHL	14	8	3	11	11	—	—	—	—	—
—Los Angeles......................		NHL	55	20	23	43	36	—	—	—	—	—
86-87—Los Angeles......................		NHL	68	20	30	50	26	3	1	1	2	0
87-88—Los Angeles......................		NHL	42	6	15	21	20	—	—	—	—	—
—Pittsburgh		NHL	11	1	4	5	0	—	—	—	—	—
—New Haven		AHL	3	0	0	0	0	—	—	—	—	—
88-89—						Did not play.						
89-90—Moncton		AHL	13	4	7	11	4	—	—	—	—	—
90-91—Winnipeg		NHL	6	0	7	7	0	—	—	—	—	—
—Moncton		AHL	36	18	14	32	16	—	—	—	—	—
91-92—Winnipeg		NHL	10	2	4	6	0	—	—	—	—	—
92-93—Moncton		AHL	2	1	1	2	4	—	—	—	—	—
—Winnipeg		NHL	41	4	12	16	14	3	0	0	0	0
NHL totals...................			**335**	**80**	**125**	**205**	**135**	**14**	**3**	**4**	**7**	**7**

ERICKSON, CHAD

G, DEVILS

PERSONAL: Born August 21, 1970, at Warroad, Minn.... 5-9/175.... Shoots right.... Full name: Chad Carlyle Erickson.
HIGH SCHOOL: Warroad (Minn.).
COLLEGE: Minnesota-Duluth.
TRANSACTIONS/CAREER NOTES: Selected by New Jersey Devils in seventh round (eighth Devils pick, 138th overall) of NHL entry draft (June 11, 1988).
HONORS: Named to NCAA All-America West first team (1989-90).... Named to WCHA All-Star first team (1989-90).

			REGULAR SEASON						PLAYOFFS					
Season	Team	League	Gms.	Min.	W	L	T	GA	SO	Avg.	Gms.	Min.	W	L	GA	SO	Avg.
86-87—Warroad H.S.		Minn. HS	21	945	...	...	...	36	1	2.29	—	—	—	—	—	—	—
87-88—Warroad H.S.		Minn. HS	24	1080	...	...	...	33	7	1.83	—	—	—	—	—	—	—
88-89—Minnesota-Duluth		WCHA	15	821	5	7	1	49	0	3.58	—	—	—	—	—	—	—
89-90—Minnesota-Duluth		WCHA	39	2301	19	19	1	141	0	3.68	—	—	—	—	—	—	—
90-91—Minnesota-Duluth		WCHA	40	2393	14	19	7	*159	0	3.99	—	—	—	—	—	—	—
91-92—Utica..........................		AHL	44	2341	18	19	3	147	2	3.77	2	127	0	2	11	0	5.20
—New Jersey....................		NHL	2	120	1	1	0	9	0	4.50	—	—	—	—	—	—	—
92-93—Utica..........................		AHL	9	505	1	7	1	47	0	5.58	—	—	—	—	—	—	—
—Cincinnati....................		IHL	10	516	2	6	0	42	0	4.88	—	—	—	—	—	—	—
—Birmingham		ECHL	14	856	...	...	...	54	0	3.79	—	—	—	—	—	—	—
NHL totals...................			**2**	**120**	**1**	**1**	**0**	**9**	**0**	**4.50**							

ERIKSSON, ANDERS

D, RED WINGS

PERSONAL: Born January 9, 1975, at Bollnas, Sweden.... 6-3/218.... Shoots left.
TRANSACTIONS/CAREER NOTES: Selected by Detroit Red Wings in first round (first Red Wings pick, 22nd overall) of NHL entry draft (June 26, 1993).

			REGULAR SEASON					PLAYOFFS				
Season	Team	League	Gms.	G	A	Pts.	Pen.	Gms.	G	A	Pts.	Pen.
92-93—MoDo		Sweden	20	0	2	2	2	—	—	—	—	—

ERIXON, JAN

LW

PERSONAL: Born July 8, 1962, at Skelleftea, Sweden.... 6-0/192.... Shoots left.... Name pronounced AIR-ihk-suhn.
TRANSACTIONS/CAREER NOTES: Selected by New York Rangers in second round (second Rangers pick, 30th overall) of NHL entry draft (June 10, 1981).... Bruised foot (February 1985).... Bruised leg (December 8, 1985).... Fractured tibia (January 12, 1986).... Suffered hip injury (December 1986).... Sprained right knee (October 1988).... Sprained back (February 1989).... Suffered back spasms (December 2, 1989).... Underwent surgery to lower back to repair herniated disc (May 2, 1990).... Sprained right knee (November 26, 1990); missed 24 games. ... Reinjured knee (January 25, 1991); missed two games.... Injured back during preseason (September 1991); missed first nine games of season.... Injured ribs (January 6, 1992); missed five games.... Injured shoulder (February 12, 1992); missed eight games. ... Suffered lower back and hip stiffness (November 11, 1992); missed 18 games.... Suffered hip flexor strain (January 4, 1993); missed five games.... Strained neck (February 15, 1993); missed five games.... Announced plans to play in Sweden for 1992-93 season (July 20, 1993).

Season Team	League	REGULAR SEASON					PLAYOFFS				
		Gms.	G	A	Pts.	Pen.	Gms.	G	A	Pts.	Pen.
79-80—Skelleftea AIK	Sweden	32	9	3	12	22	—	—	—	—	—
80-81—Skelleftea AIK	Sweden	32	6	6	12	4	3	1	0	1	0
81-82—Skelleftea AIK	Sweden	30	7	7	14	26	—	—	—	—	—
82-83—Skelleftea AIK	Sweden	36	10	18	28	...	—	—	—	—	—
83-84—New York Rangers	NHL	75	5	25	30	16	5	2	0	2	4
84-85—New York Rangers	NHL	66	7	22	29	33	2	0	0	0	2
85-86—New York Rangers	NHL	31	2	17	19	4	12	0	1	1	4
86-87—New York Rangers	NHL	68	8	18	26	24	6	1	0	1	0
87-88—New York Rangers	NHL	70	7	19	26	33	—	—	—	—	—
88-89—New York Rangers	NHL	44	4	11	15	27	4	0	1	1	2
89-90—New York Rangers	NHL	58	4	9	13	8	10	1	0	1	2
90-91—New York Rangers	NHL	53	7	18	25	8	6	1	2	3	0
91-92—New York Rangers	NHL	46	8	9	17	4	13	2	3	5	2
92-93—New York Rangers	NHL	45	5	11	16	10	—	—	—	—	—
NHL totals		556	57	159	216	167	58	7	7	14	16

ERREY, BOB

LW, SABRES

PERSONAL: Born September 21, 1964, at Montreal. ... 5-10/183. ... Shoots left. ... Name pronounced AIR-ee.

TRANSACTIONS/CAREER NOTES: Selected by Pittsburgh Penguins as underage junior in first round (first Penguins pick, 15th overall) of NHL entry draft (June 8, 1983). ... Sprained right knee (March 18, 1987). ... Broke right wrist (October 1987). ... Injured shoulder (May 9, 1992). ... Sprained ankle (September 29, 1992); missed 14 games. ... Bruised tailbone (February 27, 1993); missed two games. ... Traded by Penguins to Buffalo Sabres for D Mike Ramsey (March 22, 1993). ... Sprained ankle (April 4, 1993); missed four games. ... Injured hip (April 18, 1993); missed two games.

HONORS: Named to OHL All-Star first team (1982-83).

MISCELLANEOUS: Member of Stanley Cup championship teams (1991 and 1992).

Season Team	League	REGULAR SEASON					PLAYOFFS				
		Gms.	G	A	Pts.	Pen.	Gms.	G	A	Pts.	Pen.
81-82—Peterborough	OHL	68	29	31	60	39	9	3	1	4	9
82-83—Peterborough	OHL	67	53	47	100	74	4	1	3	4	7
83-84—Pittsburgh	NHL	65	9	13	22	29	—	—	—	—	—
84-85—Baltimore	AHL	59	17	24	41	14	8	3	4	7	11
—Pittsburgh	NHL	16	0	2	2	7	—	—	—	—	—
85-86—Baltimore	AHL	18	8	7	15	28	—	—	—	—	—
—Pittsburgh	NHL	37	11	6	17	8	—	—	—	—	—
86-87—Pittsburgh	NHL	72	16	18	34	46	—	—	—	—	—
87-88—Pittsburgh	NHL	17	3	6	9	18	—	—	—	—	—
88-89—Pittsburgh	NHL	76	26	32	58	124	11	1	2	3	12
89-90—Pittsburgh	NHL	78	20	19	39	109	—	—	—	—	—
90-91—Pittsburgh	NHL	79	20	22	42	115	24	5	2	7	29
91-92—Pittsburgh	NHL	78	19	16	35	119	14	3	0	3	10
92-93—Pittsburgh	NHL	54	8	6	14	76	—	—	—	—	—
—Buffalo	NHL	8	1	3	4	4	4	0	1	1	10
NHL totals		580	133	143	276	655	53	9	5	14	61

ESAU, LEN

D, NORDIQUES

PERSONAL: Born March 16, 1968, at Meadow Lake, Sask. ... 6-3/195. ... Shoots right. ... Full name: Leonard Roy Esau. ... Name pronounced EE-saw.

COLLEGE: St. Cloud State (Minn.).

TRANSACTIONS/CAREER NOTES: Selected by Toronto Maple Leafs in fifth round (fifth Maple Leafs pick, 86th overall) of NHL entry draft (June 11, 1988). ... Traded by Maple Leafs to Quebec Nordiques for C Ken McRae (July 21, 1992).

Season Team	League	REGULAR SEASON					PLAYOFFS				
		Gms.	G	A	Pts.	Pen.	Gms.	G	A	Pts.	Pen.
86-87—Humboldt	SJHL	57	4	26	30	278	—	—	—	—	—
87-88—Humboldt	SJHL	57	16	37	53	229	—	—	—	—	—
88-89—St. Cloud State	WCHA	35	12	27	39	69	—	—	—	—	—
89-90—St. Cloud State	WCHA	29	8	11	19	83	—	—	—	—	—
90-91—Newmarket	AHL	75	4	14	18	28	—	—	—	—	—
91-92—St. John's	AHL	78	9	29	38	68	13	0	2	2	14
—Toronto	NHL	2	0	0	0	0	—	—	—	—	—
92-93—Halifax	AHL	75	11	31	42	19	—	—	—	—	—
—Quebec	NHL	4	0	1	1	2	—	—	—	—	—
NHL totals		6	0	1	1	2					

ESSENSA, BOB

G, JETS

PERSONAL: Born January 14, 1965, at Toronto. ... 6-0/160. ... Shoots left. ... Full name: Robert Earle Essensa. ... Name pronounced EH-sehn-suh.

HIGH SCHOOL: Henry Carr (Rexdale, Ont.).

COLLEGE: Michigan State.

TRANSACTIONS/CAREER NOTES: Selected by Winnipeg Jets in fourth round (fifth Jets pick, 69th overall) of NHL entry draft (June 8, 1983). ... Suffered severe lacerations to both hands and wrist (February 1985). ... Injured groin (September 1990); missed three weeks. ... Sprained knee (October 12, 1991); missed four games. ... Injured left hamstring (December 8, 1991); missed

E

four games. . . . Sprained knee (March 6, 1992); missed seven games.
HONORS: Named to CCHA All-Star first team (1984-85). . . . Named to CCHA All-Star second team (1985-86). . . . Named to NHL All-Rookie team (1989-90).

			REGULAR SEASON								PLAYOFFS						
Season	Team	League	Gms.	Min.	W	L	T	GA	SO	Avg.	Gms.	Min.	W	L	GA	SO	Avg.
81-82—Henry Carr H.S.	MTHL	17	948	...	...	...	79	...	5.00	—	—	—	—	—	—	—
82-83—Henry Carr H.S.	MTHL	31	1840	...	...	...	98		3.20	—	—	—	—	—	—	—
83-84—Michigan State	CCHA	17	947	11	4	0	44	2	2.79	—	—	—	—	—	—	—
84-85—Michigan State	CCHA	18	1059	15	2	0	29	2	1.64	—	—	—	—	—	—	—
85-86—Michigan State	CCHA	23	1333	17	4	1	74	1	3.33	—	—	—	—	—	—	—
86-87—Michigan State	CCHA	25	1383	19	3	1	64	*2	*2.78	—	—	—	—	—	—	—
87-88—Moncton	AHL	27	1287	7	11	1	100	1	4.66	—	—	—	—	—	—	—
88-89—Winnipeg	NHL	20	1102	6	8	3	68	1	3.70	—	—	—	—	—	—	—
—Fort Wayne	IHL	22	1287	14	7	0	70	0	3.26	—	—	—	—	—	—	—
89-90—Moncton	AHL	6	358	3	3	0	15	0	2.51	—	—	—	—	—	—	—
—Winnipeg	NHL	36	2035	18	9	5	107	1	3.15	4	206	2	1	12	0	3.50
90-91—Moncton	AHL	2	125	1	0	1	6	0	2.88	—	—	—	—	—	—	—
—Winnipeg	NHL	55	2916	19	24	6	153	4	3.15	—	—	—	—	—	—	—
91-92—Winnipeg	NHL	47	2627	21	17	6	126	†5	2.88	1	33	0	0	3	0	5.45
92-93—Winnipeg	NHL	67	3855	33	26	6	227	2	3.53	6	367	2	4	20	0	3.27
NHL totals		225	12535	97	84	26	681	13	3.26	11	606	4	5	35	0	3.47

EVANS, DOUG
LW

PERSONAL: Born June 2, 1963, at Peterborough, Ont. . . . 5-9/ 185. . . . Shoots left. . . . Full name: Doug Thomas Evans.
TRANSACTIONS/CAREER NOTES: Signed as free agent by St. Louis Blues (June 10, 1985). . . . Separated left shoulder (September 1987). . . . Traded by Blues to Winnipeg Jets for C Ron Wilson (January 22, 1990). . . . Loaned to Peoria Rivermen (November 9, 1991); returned (December 15, 1991). . . . Traded by Jets to Boston Bruins for G Daniel Berthiaume (June 10, 1992). . . . Selected by Philadelphia Flyers in NHL waiver draft (October 4, 1992). . . . Broke right foot (March 13, 1993); missed remainder of season. . . . Signed as free agent by Rivermen (August 2, 1993).
HONORS: Named to IHL All-Star first team (1985-86).

			REGULAR SEASON					PLAYOFFS				
Season	Team	League	Gms.	G	A	Pts.	Pen.	Gms.	G	A	Pts.	Pen.
80-81—Peterborough	OMJHL	51	9	24	33	139	—	—	—	—	—	
81-82—Peterborough	OHL	56	17	49	66	176	9	0	2	2	41
82-83—Peterborough	OHL	65	31	55	86	165	4	0	3	3	23
83-84—Peterborough	OHL	61	45	79	124	98	8	4	12	16	26
84-85—Peoria	IHL	81	36	61	97	189	20	18	14	32	†88
85-86—St. Louis	NHL	13	1	0	1	2	—	—	—	—	—
—Peoria	IHL	69	46	51	97	179	10	4	6	10	32
86-87—Peoria	IHL	18	10	15	25	39	—	—	—	—	—
—St. Louis	NHL	53	3	13	16	91	5	0	0	0	10
87-88—Peoria	IHL	11	4	16	20	64	—	—	—	—	—
—St. Louis	NHL	41	5	7	12	49	2	0	0	0	0
88-89—St. Louis	NHL	53	7	12	19	81	7	1	2	3	16
89-90—Peoria	IHL	42	19	28	47	128	—	—	—	—	—
—St. Louis	NHL	3	0	0	0	0	—	—	—	—	—
—Winnipeg	NHL	27	10	8	18	33	7	2	2	4	10
90-91—Winnipeg	NHL	70	7	27	34	108	—	—	—	—	—
91-92—Winnipeg	NHL	30	7	7	14	68	1	0	0	0	2
—Peoria	IHL	16	5	14	19	38	—	—	—	—	—
—Moncton	AHL	10	7	8	15	10	—	—	—	—	—
92-93—Philadelphia	NHL	65	8	13	21	70	—	—	—	—	—
NHL totals		355	48	87	135	502	22	3	4	7	38

EVANS, KEVIN
LW, STARS

PERSONAL: Born July 10, 1965, at Peterborough, Ont. . . . 5-11/ 185. . . . Shoots left. . . . Full name: Kevin Robert Evans.
TRANSACTIONS/CAREER NOTES: Signed as free agent by Minnesota North Stars (August 8, 1988). . . . Suspended three games and fined $100 by IHL for fighting (December 28, 1988). . . . Severed five tendons and an artery (February 24, 1989). . . . Suspended one game and fined $300 by IHL for fighting (November 25, 1989). . . . Underwent reconstructive knee surgery (December 1990). . . . Selected by San Jose Sharks in NHL dispersal draft (May 30, 1991). . . . Signed as free agent by North Stars (July 17, 1992). . . . North Stars franchise moved from Minnesota to Dallas and renamed Stars for 1993-94 season.

			REGULAR SEASON					PLAYOFFS				
Season	Team	League	Gms.	G	A	Pts.	Pen.	Gms.	G	A	Pts.	Pen.
83-84—Peterborough Jr. B	OHA	39	17	34	51	210	—	—	—	—	—	
84-85—London	OHL	52	3	7	10	148	—	—	—	—	—
85-86—Victoria	WHL	66	16	39	55	*441	—	—	—	—	—
—Kalamazoo	IHL	11	3	5	8	97	6	3	0	3	56
86-87—Kalamazoo	IHL	73	19	31	50	*648	—	—	—	—	—
87-88—Kalamazoo	IHL	54	9	28	37	404	5	1	1	2	46
88-89—Kalamazoo	IHL	54	22	32	54	328	—	—	—	—	—
89-90—Kalamazoo	IHL	76	30	54	84	346	—	—	—	—	—
90-91—Minnesota	NHL	4	0	0	0	19	—	—	—	—	—
—Kalamazoo	IHL	16	10	12	22	70	—	—	—	—	—

E

Season Team	League	REGULAR SEASON					PLAYOFFS				
		Gms.	G	A	Pts.	Pen.	Gms.	G	A	Pts.	Pen.
91-92—San Jose	NHL	5	0	1	1	25	—	—	—	—	—
—Kansas City	IHL	66	10	39	49	342	14	2	13	15	70
92-93—Kalamazoo	IHL	49	7	24	31	283	—	—	—	—	—
NHL totals		9	0	1	1	44					

EVANS, SHAWN
D, WHALERS

PERSONAL: Born September 7, 1965, at Kingston, Ont. . . . 6-3/190. . . . Shoots left. . . . Cousin of Dennis Kearns, defenseman, Vancouver Canucks (1971-72 through 1980-81).
TRANSACTIONS/CAREER NOTES: Selected by New Jersey Devils as underage junior in second round (second Devils pick, 24th overall) of NHL entry draft (June 8, 1983). . . . Traded by Devils with fifth-round (C Mike Wolak) pick in 1986 draft to St. Louis Blues for LW/C Mark Johnson (September 19, 1985). . . . Traded by Blues to Edmonton Oilers for RW Todd Ewen (October 15, 1986). . . . Signed as free agent by New York Islanders (June 20, 1988). . . . Signed to play with Olten, Switzerland (May 1990). . . . Signed as free agent by Hartford Whalers (August 14, 1991).
HONORS: Named to OHL All-Star second team (1983-84). . . . Named to AHL All-Star first team (1991-92). . . . Named to IHL All-Star first team (1992-93).

Season Team	League	REGULAR SEASON					PLAYOFFS				
		Gms.	G	A	Pts.	Pen.	Gms.	G	A	Pts.	Pen.
81-82—Kitchener Jr. B	OHA	21	9	13	22	55	—	—	—	—	—
82-83—Peterborough	OHL	58	7	41	48	116	4	2	0	2	12
83-84—Peterborough	OHL	67	21	88	109	116	8	1	16	17	8
84-85—Peterborough	OHL	66	16	83	99	78	16	6	18	24	6
85-86—Peoria	IHL	55	8	26	34	36	—	—	—	—	—
—St. Louis	NHL	7	0	0	0	2	—	—	—	—	—
86-87—Nova Scotia	AHL	55	7	28	35	29	5	0	4	4	6
87-88—Nova Scotia	AHL	79	8	62	70	109	5	1	1	2	40
88-89—Springfield	AHL	68	9	50	59	125	—	—	—	—	—
89-90—New York Islanders	NHL	2	1	0	1	0	—	—	—	—	—
—Springfield	AHL	63	6	35	41	102	18	6	11	17	35
90-91—Olten	Switzerland					Statistics unavailable.					
—Maine	AHL	51	9	37	46	44	2	0	1	1	0
91-92—Springfield	AHL	80	11	67	78	81	11	0	8	8	16
92-93—Milwaukee	IHL	79	13	65	78	83	6	0	3	3	6
NHL totals		9	1	0	1	2					

EVASON, DEAN
C, STARS

PERSONAL: Born August 22, 1964, at Flin Flon, Man. . . . 5-10/180. . . . Shoots left.
TRANSACTIONS/CAREER NOTES: Selected by Kamloops Junior Oilers in WHL disperal draft of players of Spokane Flyers (December 1981). . . . Selected by Washington Capitals as under-age junior in fifth round (third Capitals pick, 89th overall) of NHL entry draft (June 9, 1982). . . . Traded by Capitals with G Peter Sidorkiewicz to Hartford Whalers for LW David A. Jensen (March 1985). . . . Strained left ankle ligaments (December 14, 1988). . . . Traded by Whalers to San Jose Sharks for D Dan Keczmer (October 2, 1991). . . . Pulled abdominal muscles (January 27, 1992); missed two games. . . . Traded by Sharks to Dallas Stars for sixth-round pick in 1993 draft (June 26, 1993).
HONORS: Won WHL Player of the Year Award (1982-83). . . . Named to WHL (West) All-Star first team (1983-84).

Season Team	League	REGULAR SEASON					PLAYOFFS				
		Gms.	G	A	Pts.	Pen.	Gms.	G	A	Pts.	Pen.
80-81—Spokane Flyers	WHL	3	1	1	2	0	—	—	—	—	—
81-82—Kamloops	WHL	70	29	69	98	112	4	2	1	3	0
82-83—Kamloops	WHL	70	71	93	164	102	7	5	7	12	18
83-84—Kamloops	WHL	57	49	88	137	89	17	†21	20	41	33
—Washington	NHL	2	0	0	0	2	—	—	—	—	—
84-85—Binghamton	AHL	65	27	49	76	38	8	3	5	8	9
—Washington	NHL	15	3	4	7	2	—	—	—	—	—
—Hartford	NHL	2	0	0	0	0	—	—	—	—	—
85-86—Binghamton	AHL	26	9	17	26	29	—	—	—	—	—
—Hartford	NHL	55	20	28	48	65	10	1	4	5	10
86-87—Hartford	NHL	80	22	37	59	67	5	3	2	5	35
87-88—Hartford	NHL	77	10	18	28	117	6	1	1	2	2
88-89—Hartford	NHL	67	11	17	28	60	4	1	2	3	10
89-90—Hartford	NHL	78	18	25	43	138	7	2	2	4	22
90-91—Hartford	NHL	75	6	23	29	170	6	0	4	4	29
91-92—San Jose	NHL	74	11	15	26	99	—	—	—	—	—
92-93—San Jose	NHL	84	12	19	31	132	—	—	—	—	—
NHL totals		609	113	186	299	852	38	8	15	23	108

EWEN, TODD
RW, CANADIENS

PERSONAL: Born March 26, 1966, at Saskatoon, Sask. . . . 6-2/220. . . . Shoots right. . . . Name pro-nounced YOO-ihn.
TRANSACTIONS/CAREER NOTES: Selected by Edmonton Oilers as underage junior in eighth round (eighth Oilers pick, 168th overall) of NHL entry draft (June 9, 1984). . . . Traded by Oilers to St. Louis Blues for D Shawn Evans (October 15, 1986). . . . Sprained ankle (October 1987). . . . Suspended one game by NHL for third game misconduct of season (January 1988). . . . Pulled groin (October 1988). . . . Tore right eye muscle (December 1988). . . . Pulled left hamstring and bruised shoulder (February 1989). . . . Suspended 10 games by NHL for coming off bench

to instigate fight during playoff game (April 18, 1989); missed three playoff games and first seven games of 1989-90 season. ... Broke right hand (October 28, 1989).... Traded by Blues to Montreal Canadiens for the return of a draft pick dealt to Montreal for D Mike Lalor (December 12, 1989).... Strained knee ligaments and underwent surgery (November 19, 1990); missed 24 games.... Fractured right hand at home (February 14, 1991); missed remainder of season.... Separated shoulder (February 12, 1992); missed two games.... Injured hand (January 10, 1993); missed two games.... Pulled muscle in back (February 20, 1993); missed three games.

MISCELLANEOUS: Member of Stanley Cup championship team (1993).

			REGULAR SEASON					PLAYOFFS				
Season	Team	League	Gms.	G	A	Pts.	Pen.	Gms.	G	A	Pts.	Pen.
82-83	—Vernon	BCJHL	42	20	23	43	195	—	—	—	—	—
	—Kamloops	WHL	3	0	0	0	2	2	0	0	0	0
83-84	—New Westminster	WHL	68	11	13	24	176	7	2	1	3	15
84-85	—New Westminster	WHL	56	11	20	31	304	10	1	8	9	60
85-86	—New Westminster	WHL	60	28	24	52	289	—	—	—	—	—
	—Maine	AHL	—	—	—	—	—	3	0	0	0	7
86-87	—Peoria	IHL	16	3	3	6	110	—	—	—	—	—
	—St. Louis	NHL	23	2	0	2	84	4	0	0	0	23
87-88	—St. Louis	NHL	64	4	2	6	227	6	0	0	0	21
88-89	—St. Louis	NHL	34	4	5	9	171	2	0	0	0	21
89-90	—Peoria	IHL	2	0	0	0	12	—	—	—	—	—
	—St. Louis	NHL	3	0	0	0	11	—	—	—	—	—
	—Montreal	NHL	41	4	6	10	158	10	0	0	0	4
90-91	—Montreal	NHL	28	3	2	5	128	—	—	—	—	—
91-92	—Montreal	NHL	46	1	2	3	130	3	0	0	0	18
92-93	—Montreal	NHL	75	5	9	14	193	1	0	0	0	0
	NHL totals		314	23	26	49	1102	26	0	0	0	87

FALLOON, PAT
RW, SHARKS

PERSONAL: Born September 22, 1972, at Foxwarren, Man.... 5-11/192.... Shoots right.
TRANSACTIONS/CAREER NOTES: WHL rights traded with future considerations by Regina Pats to Spokane Chiefs for RW Jamie Heward (October 1987).... Tore right knee cartilage and underwent surgery (July 24, 1990).... Selected by San Jose Sharks in first round (first Sharks pick, second overall) of NHL entry draft (June 22, 1991).... Bruised shoulder (November 19, 1992); missed one game.... Dislocated right shoulder (January 10, 1993) and underwent arthroscopic surgery (January 15, 1993); missed remainder of season.

HONORS: Named WHL (West) Division Rookie of the Year (1988-89).... Named to WHL All-Star second team (1988-89).... Won WHL (West) Division Most Sportsmanlike Player Award (1989-90).... Named to WHL (West) All-Star first team (1989-90 and 1990-91).... Won Can.HL Most Sportsmanlike Player of the Year Award (1990-91).... Won Brad Hornung Trophy (1990-91).... Won Stafford Smythe Memorial Trophy (1990-91).... Named to Memorial Cup All-Star Team (1990-91).

			REGULAR SEASON					PLAYOFFS				
Season	Team	League	Gms.	G	A	Pts.	Pen.	Gms.	G	A	Pts.	Pen.
88-89	—Spokane Chiefs	WHL	72	22	56	78	41	5	5	8	13	4
89-90	—Spokane Chiefs	WHL	71	60	64	124	48	6	5	8	13	4
90-91	—Spokane Chiefs	WHL	61	64	74	138	33	15	10	14	24	10
91-92	—San Jose	NHL	79	25	34	59	16	—	—	—	—	—
92-93	—San Jose	NHL	41	14	14	28	12	—	—	—	—	—
	NHL totals		120	39	48	87	28					

FAUST, ANDRE
C, FLYERS

PERSONAL: Born October 7, 1969, at Joliette, Que.... 6-1/180.... Shoots left.
COLLEGE: Princeton.
TRANSACTIONS/CAREER NOTES: Selected by New Jersey Devils in ninth round (eighth Devils pick, 173rd overall) of NHL entry draft (June 17, 1989).... Signed as free agent by Philadelphia Flyers (October 14, 1992).

HONORS: Named to ECAC All-Star second team (1989-90 and 1991-92).

			REGULAR SEASON					PLAYOFFS				
Season	Team	League	Gms.	G	A	Pts.	Pen.	Gms.	G	A	Pts.	Pen.
88-89	—Princeton University	ECAC	27	15	24	39	28	—	—	—	—	—
89-90	—Princeton University	ECAC	22	9	28	37	20	—	—	—	—	—
90-91	—Princeton University	ECAC	26	15	22	37	51	—	—	—	—	—
91-92	—Princeton University	ECAC	27	14	21	35	38	—	—	—	—	—
92-93	—Hershey	AHL	62	26	25	51	71	—	—	—	—	—
	—Philadelphia	NHL	10	2	2	4	4	—	—	—	—	—
	NHL totals		10	2	2	4	4					

FEATHERSTONE, GLEN
D, BRUINS

PERSONAL: Born July 8, 1968, at Toronto.... 6-4/215.... Shoots left.
TRANSACTIONS/CAREER NOTES: Selected by St. Louis Blues as underage junior in fourth round (fourth Blues pick, 73rd overall) of NHL entry draft (June 21, 1986).... Suffered sore back (March 7, 1991); missed two games.... Signed as free agent by Boston Bruins (July 25, 1991); Bruins and Blues later arranged a trade in which Bruins received Featherstone and LW Dave Thomlinson, whom they had also previously signed as free agent, for RW Dave Christian, whom the Blues had previously signed as free agent, third-round pick in 1992 draft (LW Vitali Prokhorov) and either seventh-round pick in 1992 draft or sixth-round pick in 1993 draft; Blues used seventh-round pick in 1992 draft to select C Lance Burns.... Suffered hip pointer (October 5, 1991); missed three games.... Strained back (November 1991); missed remainder of season.... Un-

EF

derwent back surgery (November 15, 1991).... Injured groin (December 31, 1992); missed seven games.... Suffered knee/ thigh injury (March 1, 1993); missed remainder of season.

Season	Team	League	REGULAR SEASON					PLAYOFFS				
			Gms.	G	A	Pts.	Pen.	Gms.	G	A	Pts.	Pen.
85-86	Windsor	OHL	49	0	6	6	135	14	1	1	2	23
86-87	Windsor	OHL	47	6	11	17	154	14	2	6	8	19
87-88	Windsor	OHL	53	7	27	34	201	12	6	9	15	47
88-89	Peoria	IHL	37	5	19	24	97	—	—	—	—	—
	St. Louis	NHL	18	0	2	2	22	6	0	0	0	25
89-90	Peoria	IHL	15	1	4	5	43	—	—	—	—	—
	St. Louis	NHL	58	0	12	12	145	12	0	2	2	47
90-91	St. Louis	NHL	68	5	15	20	204	9	0	0	0	31
91-92	Boston	NHL	7	1	0	1	20	—	—	—	—	—
92-93	Providence	AHL	8	3	4	7	60	—	—	—	—	—
	Boston	NHL	34	5	5	10	102	—	—	—	—	—
NHL totals			185	11	34	45	493	27	0	2	2	103

FEDOROV, SERGEI
C, RED WINGS

PERSONAL: Born December 13, 1969, at Minsk, U.S.S.R.... 6-1/191.... Shoots left.... Name pronounced FEH-duh-rahf.
TRANSACTIONS/CAREER NOTES: Selected by Detroit Red Wings in fourth round (fourth Red Wings pick, 74th overall) of NHL entry draft (June 17, 1989).... Bruised left shoulder (October 1990).... Reinjured left shoulder (January 16, 1991).... Sprained left shoulder (November 27, 1992); missed seven games.... Suffered from the flu (January 30, 1993); missed two games.... Suffered charley horse (February 11, 1993); missed one game.
HONORS: Named to NHL All-Rookie team (1990-91).... Played in NHL All-Star Game (1992).

Season	Team	League	REGULAR SEASON					PLAYOFFS				
			Gms.	G	A	Pts.	Pen.	Gms.	G	A	Pts.	Pen.
85-86	Dynamo Minsk	USSR	15	6	1	7	10	—	—	—	—	—
86-87	CSKA Moscow	USSR	29	6	6	12	12	—	—	—	—	—
87-88	CSKA Moscow	USSR	48	7	9	16	20	—	—	—	—	—
88-89	CSKA Moscow	USSR	44	9	8	17	35	—	—	—	—	—
89-90	CSKA Moscow	USSR	48	19	10	29	20	—	—	—	—	—
90-91	Detroit	NHL	77	31	48	79	66	7	1	5	6	4
91-92	Detroit	NHL	80	32	54	86	72	11	5	5	10	8
92-93	Detroit	NHL	73	34	53	87	72	7	3	6	9	23
NHL totals			230	97	155	252	210	25	9	16	25	35

FEDOTOV, ANATOLI
D, MIGHTY DUCKS

PERSONAL: Born May 11, 1966, at Saratov, U.S.S.R.... 5-11/178.... Shoots left.... Name pronounced FEHD-uh-tahf.
TRANSACTIONS/CAREER NOTES: Signed as free agent by Winnipeg Jets (July 4, 1991).... Selected by Mighty Ducks of Anaheim in 10th round (10th Mighty Ducks pick, 238th overall) in NHL entry draft (June 26, 1993).

Season	Team	League	REGULAR SEASON					PLAYOFFS				
			Gms.	G	A	Pts.	Pen.	Gms.	G	A	Pts.	Pen.
85-86	Dynamo Moscow	USSR	35	0	2	2	10	—	—	—	—	—
86-87	Dynamo Moscow	USSR	18	3	2	5	12	—	—	—	—	—
87-88	Dynamo Moscow	USSR	48	2	3	5	38	—	—	—	—	—
88-89	Dynamo Moscow	USSR	40	2	1	3	24	—	—	—	—	—
89-90	Dynamo Moscow	USSR	41	2	4	6	22	—	—	—	—	—
90-91	Dynamo Moscow	USSR					Did not play.					
91-92	Dynamo Moscow	CIS	11	1	0	1	8	—	—	—	—	—
92-93	Moncton	AHL	76	10	37	47	99	2	0	0	0	0
	Winnipeg	NHL	1	0	2	2	0	—	—	—	—	—
NHL totals			1	0	2	2	0					

FEDYK, BRENT
LW, FLYERS

PERSONAL: Born March 8, 1967, at Yorkton, Sask.... 6-0/195.... Shoots right.... Name pronounced FEH-dihk.
TRANSACTIONS/CAREER NOTES: Selected by Detroit Red Wings as underage junior in first round (first Red Wings pick, eighth overall) of NHL entry draft (June 15, 1985).... Strained hip in Red Wings training camp (September 1985); missed three weeks.... Traded by Regina Pats with RW Ken McIntyre, LW Grant Kazuik, D Gerald Bzdel and WHL rights to LW Kevin Kowalchuk to Seattle Thunderbirds for RW Craig Endean, C Ray Savard, Grant Chorney, C Erin Ginnell and WHL rights to LW Frank Kovacs (November 1986).... Traded by Thunderbirds to Portland Winter Hawks for future considerations (February 1987).... Injured knee (December 22, 1990); missed one game.... Suffered deep shin bruise (January 26, 1991); missed five games.... Suffered concussion (March 1991).... Traded by Red Wings to Philadelphia Flyers for fourth-round pick in 1993 draft (October 1, 1992).... Strained right shoulder (December 11, 1992); missed three games.... Fractured thumb (January 31, 1993); missed one game.... Sprained left ankle (March 11, 1993); missed one game.... Fractured toe (April 6, 1993); missed remainder of season.
HONORS: Named to WHL All-Star second team (1985-86).

Season	Team	League	REGULAR SEASON					PLAYOFFS				
			Gms.	G	A	Pts.	Pen.	Gms.	G	A	Pts.	Pen.
82-83	Regina	WHL	1	0	0	0	0	—	—	—	—	—
83-84	Regina	WHL	63	15	28	43	30	23	8	7	15	6
84-85	Regina	WHL	66	35	35	70	48	8	5	4	9	0

F

Season	Team	League	REGULAR SEASON					PLAYOFFS				
			Gms.	G	A	Pts.	Pen.	Gms.	G	A	Pts.	Pen.
85-86—Regina	WHL	50	43	34	77	47	5	0	1	1	0
86-87—Regina	WHL	12	9	6	15	9	—	—	—	—	—
—Seattle	WHL	13	5	11	16	9	—	—	—	—	—
—Portland	WHL	11	5	4	9	6	14	5	6	11	0
87-88—Detroit	NHL	2	0	1	1	2	—	—	—	—	—
—Adirondack	AHL	34	9	11	20	22	5	0	2	2	6
88-89—Detroit	NHL	5	2	0	2	0	—	—	—	—	—
—Adirondack	AHL	66	40	28	68	33	15	7	8	15	23
89-90—Detroit	NHL	27	1	4	5	6	—	—	—	—	—
—Adirondack	AHL	33	14	15	29	24	6	2	1	3	4
90-91—Detroit	NHL	67	16	19	35	38	6	1	0	1	2
91-92—Adirondack	AHL	1	0	2	2	0	—	—	—	—	—
—Detroit	NHL	61	5	8	13	42	1	0	0	0	2
92-93—Philadelphia	NHL	74	21	38	59	48	—	—	—	—	—
NHL totals			236	45	70	115	136	7	1	0	1	4

FELSNER, DENNY

LW, BLUES

PERSONAL: Born April 29, 1970, at Warren, Mich. . . . 6-0/195. . . . Shoots left. . . . Full name: Denny Walter Felsner.
COLLEGE: Michigan.
TRANSACTIONS/CAREER NOTES: Selected by St. Louis Blues in third round (third Blues pick, 55th overall) of NHL entry draft (June 17, 1989). . . . Injured knee (December 29, 1989).
HONORS: Named to CCHA All-Rookie team (1988-89). . . . Named to NCAA All-America West second team (1990-91). . . . Named to CCHA All-Star first team (1990-91 and 1991-92). . . . Named to NCAA All-America West first team (1991-92).

Season	Team	League	REGULAR SEASON					PLAYOFFS				
			Gms.	G	A	Pts.	Pen.	Gms.	G	A	Pts.	Pen.
86-87—Detroit Falcons	NAJHL	37	22	33	55	18	—	—	—	—	—
87-88—Detroit Junior Red Wings	NAJHL	39	35	43	78	46	—	—	—	—	—
88-89—University of Michigan	CCHA	39	30	19	49	22	—	—	—	—	—
89-90—University of Michigan	CCHA	33	27	16	43	24	—	—	—	—	—
90-91—University of Michigan	CCHA	46	40	35	75	58	—	—	—	—	—
91-92—University of Michigan	CCHA	44	42	*52	*94	48	—	—	—	—	—
—St. Louis	NHL	3	0	1	1	0	1	0	0	0	0
92-93—Peoria	IHL	29	14	21	35	8	—	—	—	—	—
—St. Louis	NHL	6	0	3	3	2	9	2	3	5	2
NHL totals			9	0	4	4	2	10	2	3	5	2

FENYVES, DAVE

D, FLYERS

PERSONAL: Born April 29, 1960, at Dunnville, Ont. . . . 6-0/190. . . . Shoots left. . . . Full name: David Alan Fenyves. . . . Name pronounced FEHN-vehs.
TRANSACTIONS/CAREER NOTES: Separated shoulder (October 1977). . . . Signed as free agent by Buffalo Sabres (October 31, 1979). . . . Selected by Philadelphia Flyers during NHL waiver draft as compensation for Sabres drafting of D/RW Ed Hospodar (October 5, 1987).
HONORS: Named to OMJHL All-Star second team (1979-80). . . . Won Jack Butterfield Trophy (1986-87). . . . Named to AHL All-Star second team (1986-87). . . . Won Eddie Shore Plaque (1987-88 and 1988-89). . . . Named to AHL All-Star first team (1987-88 and 1988-89).

Season	Team	League	REGULAR SEASON					PLAYOFFS				
			Gms.	G	A	Pts.	Pen.	Gms.	G	A	Pts.	Pen.
77-78—Peterborough	OMJHL	59	3	12	15	36	—	—	—	—	—
78-79—Peterborough	OMJHL	66	2	23	25	122	19	0	5	5	18
79-80—Peterborough	OMJHL	66	9	36	45	92	14	0	3	3	14
80-81—Rochester	AHL	77	6	16	22	146	—	—	—	—	—
81-82—Rochester	AHL	73	3	14	17	68	5	0	1	1	4
82-83—Rochester	AHL	51	2	19	21	45	—	—	—	—	—
—Buffalo	NHL	24	0	8	8	14	4	0	0	0	0
83-84—Buffalo	NHL	10	0	4	4	9	2	0	0	0	7
—Rochester	AHL	70	3	16	19	55	16	1	4	5	22
84-85—Rochester	AHL	9	0	3	3	8	—	—	—	—	—
—Buffalo	NHL	60	1	8	9	27	5	0	0	0	2
85-86—Buffalo	NHL	47	0	7	7	37	—	—	—	—	—
86-87—Rochester	AHL	71	6	16	22	57	18	3	12	15	10
—Buffalo	NHL	7	1	0	1	0	—	—	—	—	—
87-88—Philadelphia	NHL	5	0	0	0	0	—	—	—	—	—
—Hershey	AHL	75	11	40	51	47	12	1	8	9	10
88-89—Philadelphia	NHL	1	0	1	1	0	—	—	—	—	—
—Hershey	AHL	79	15	51	66	41	12	2	6	8	6
89-90—Philadelphia	NHL	12	0	0	0	4	—	—	—	—	—
—Hershey	AHL	66	6	37	43	57	—	—	—	—	—
90-91—Philadelphia	NHL	40	1	4	5	28	—	—	—	—	—
—Hershey	AHL	29	4	11	15	13	7	0	3	3	6
91-92—Hershey	AHL	68	4	24	28	29	6	1	1	2	10
92-93—Hershey	AHL	42	3	11	14	14	—	—	—	—	—
NHL totals			206	3	32	35	119	11	0	0	0	9

F

FERGUS, TOM

C, CANUCKS

PERSONAL: Born June 16, 1962, at Chicago. . . . 6-3/210. . . . Shoots left. . . . Full name: Thomas Joseph Fergus.
TRANSACTIONS/CAREER NOTES: Selected by Boston Bruins as underage junior in third round (second Bruins pick, 60th overall) of NHL entry draft (June 11, 1980). . . . Tore ligaments in left knee (January 20, 1982). . . . Damaged knee ligaments (February 1984). . . . Traded by Bruins to Toronto Maple Leafs for C Bill Derlago (September 1985). . . . Suffered viral infection (March 1987); missed 23 games. . . . Pulled groin (November 1987). . . . Bruised ribs (March 1988). . . . Pulled groin and stomach muscle (February 6, 1990). . . . Underwent surgery to repair torn abdominal muscle (November 1990). . . . Injured back and chest (March 20, 1991). . . . Claimed on waivers by Vancouver Canucks for $5,000 (December 18, 1991).

Season Team	League	REGULAR SEASON Gms.	G	A	Pts.	Pen.	PLAYOFFS Gms.	G	A	Pts.	Pen.
79-80—Peterborough	OMJHL	63	8	6	14	14	14	1	5	6	6
80-81—Peterborough	OMJHL	63	43	45	88	33	5	1	4	5	2
81-82—Boston	NHL	61	15	24	39	12	6	3	0	3	0
82-83—Boston	NHL	80	28	35	63	39	15	2	2	4	15
83-84—Boston	NHL	69	25	36	61	12	3	2	0	2	9
84-85—Boston	NHL	79	30	43	73	75	5	0	0	0	4
85-86—Toronto	NHL	78	31	42	73	64	10	5	7	12	6
86-87—Newmarket	AHL	1	0	1	1	0	—	—	—	—	—
—Toronto	NHL	57	21	28	49	57	2	0	1	1	2
87-88—Toronto	NHL	63	19	31	50	81	6	2	3	5	2
88-89—Toronto	NHL	80	22	45	67	48	—	—	—	—	—
89-90—Toronto	NHL	54	19	26	45	62	5	2	1	3	4
90-91—Toronto	NHL	14	5	4	9	8	—	—	—	—	—
91-92—Toronto	NHL	11	1	3	4	4	—	—	—	—	—
—Vancouver	NHL	44	14	20	34	17	13	5	3	8	6
92-93—Vancouver	NHL	36	5	9	14	20	—	—	—	—	—
NHL totals		726	235	346	581	499	65	21	17	38	48

FERNANDEZ, EMMANUEL

G, NORDIQUES

PERSONAL: Born August 27, 1974, at Etobicoke, Ont. . . . 6-0/173. . . . Shoots left. . . . Nephew of Jacques Lemaire, center, Montreal Canadiens (1967-68 through 1978-79) and current head coach, New Jersey Devils.
TRANSACTIONS/CAREER NOTES: Selected by Quebec Nordiques in third round (fourth Nordiques pick, 52nd overall) of NHL entry draft (June 20, 1992).
HONORS: Won Guy Lafleur Trophy (1992-93).

Season Team	League	REGULAR SEASON Gms.	Min.	W	L	T	GA	SO	Avg.	PLAYOFFS Gms.	Min.	W	L	GA	SO	Avg.
91-92—Laval	QMJHL	31	1593	14	13	2	99	1	3.73	9	468	3	5	†39	0	5.00
92-93—Laval	QMJHL	43	2348	26	14	2	141	1	3.60	13	818	. .	. .	42	. .	3.08

FERNER, MARK

D, MIGHTY DUCKS

PERSONAL: Born September 5, 1965, at Regina, Sask. . . . 6-0/193. . . . Shoots left.
TRANSACTIONS/CAREER NOTES: Selected by Buffalo Sabres in 10th round (12th Sabres pick, 194th overall) of NHL entry draft (June 8, 1983). . . . Broke foot (March 1986). . . . Traded by Sabres to Washington Capitals for C Scott McCrory (June 1, 1989). . . . Traded by Capitals to Toronto Maple Leafs for 12th-round pick in 1992 draft (February 27, 1992). . . . Signed as free agent by Ottawa Senators (August 6, 1992). . . . Loaned to San Diego Gulls (February 17, 1993). . . . Selected by Mighty Ducks of Anaheim in NHL expansion draft (June 24, 1993).
HONORS: Named to WHL (West) All-Star first team (1984-85). . . . Named to AHL All-Star second team (1990-91).

Season Team	League	REGULAR SEASON Gms.	G	A	Pts.	Pen.	PLAYOFFS Gms.	G	A	Pts.	Pen.
82-83—Kamloops	WHL	69	6	15	21	81	7	0	0	0	7
83-84—Kamloops	WHL	72	9	30	39	162	14	1	8	9	20
84-85—Kamloops	WHL	69	15	39	54	91	15	4	9	13	21
85-86—Rochester	AHL	63	3	14	17	87	—	—	—	—	—
86-87—Buffalo	NHL	13	0	3	3	9	—	—	—	—	—
—Rochester	AHL	54	0	12	12	157	—	—	—	—	—
87-88—Rochester	AHL	69	1	25	26	165	7	1	4	5	31
88-89—Buffalo	NHL	2	0	0	0	2	—	—	—	—	—
—Rochester	AHL	55	0	18	18	97	—	—	—	—	—
89-90—Washington	NHL	2	0	0	0	0	—	—	—	—	—
—Baltimore	AHL	74	7	28	35	76	11	1	2	3	21
90-91—Baltimore	AHL	61	14	40	54	38	6	1	4	5	24
—Washington	NHL	7	0	1	1	4	—	—	—	—	—
91-92—Baltimore	AHL	57	7	38	45	67	—	—	—	—	—
—St. John's	AHL	15	1	8	9	6	14	2	14	16	39
92-93—New Haven	AHL	34	5	7	12	69	—	—	—	—	—
—San Diego	IHL	26	0	15	15	34	11	1	2	3	8
NHL totals		24	0	4	4	15					

FERRARO, CHRIS

RW, RANGERS

PERSONAL: Born January 24, 1973, at Port Jefferson, N.Y. . . . 5-10/175. . . . Shoots right. . . . Twin brother of Peter Ferraro, center in New York Rangers system.
COLLEGE: Maine.
TRANSACTIONS/CAREER NOTES: Selected by New York Rangers in fourth round (fourth

Rangers pick, 85th overall) of NHL entry draft (June 20, 1992).
HONORS: Named to Hockey East Rookie All-Star team (1992-93).

Season Team	League	Gms.	G	A	Pts.	Pen.	Gms.	G	A	Pts.	Pen.
			REGULAR SEASON					PLAYOFFS			
90-91—Dubuque	USHL	45	53	44	97	...	—	—	—	—	—
91-92—Waterloo	USHL	38	49	50	99	106	—	—	—	—	—
92-93—University of Maine	Hockey East	39	25	26	51	46	—	—	—	—	—

FERRARO, PETER
C, RANGERS

PERSONAL: Born January 24, 1973, at Port Jefferson, N.Y.... 5-10/175.... Shoots right. ... Twin brother of Chris Ferraro, right winger in New York Rangers system.
COLLEGE: Maine.
TRANSACTIONS/CAREER NOTES: Selected by New York Rangers in first round (first Rangers pick, 24th overall) of NHL entry draft (June 20, 1992).

Season Team	League	Gms.	G	A	Pts.	Pen.	Gms.	G	A	Pts.	Pen.
			REGULAR SEASON					PLAYOFFS			
90-91—Dubuque	USHL	29	21	31	52	83	—	—	—	—	—
91-92—Waterloo	USHL	42	48	53	101	168	—	—	—	—	—
92-93—University of Maine	Hockey East	36	18	32	50	106	—	—	—	—	—

FERRARO, RAY
C, ISLANDERS

PERSONAL: Born August 23, 1964, at Trail, B.C.... 5-10/185.... Shoots left.... Name pronounced fuh-RAH-roh.
TRANSACTIONS/CAREER NOTES: Selected by Hartford Whalers as underage junior in fifth round (fifth Whalers pick, 88th overall) of NHL entry draft (June 9, 1982).... Traded by Whalers to New York Islanders for D Doug Crossman (November 13, 1990).... Fractured right fibula (December 10, 1992); missed 36 games.... Suffered from the flu (March 25, 1993); missed one game.
HONORS: Won Most Valuable Player Trophy (1983-84).... Won Bob Brownridge Memorial Trophy (1983-84).... Won WHL Player of the Year Award (1983-84).... Named to WHL (East) All-Star first team (1983-84).... Played in NHL All-Star Game (1992).

Season Team	League	Gms.	G	A	Pts.	Pen.	Gms.	G	A	Pts.	Pen.
			REGULAR SEASON					PLAYOFFS			
81-82—Penticton	BCJHL	48	65	70	135	50	—	—	—	—	—
82-83—Portland	WHL	50	41	49	90	39	14	14	10	24	13
83-84—Brandon	WHL	72	*108	84	*192	84	11	13	15	28	20
84-85—Binghamton	AHL	37	20	13	33	29	—	—	—	—	—
—Hartford	NHL	44	11	17	28	40	—	—	—	—	—
85-86—Hartford	NHL	76	30	47	77	57	10	3	6	9	4
86-87—Hartford	NHL	80	27	32	59	42	6	1	1	2	8
87-88—Hartford	NHL	68	21	29	50	81	6	1	1	2	6
88-89—Hartford	NHL	80	41	35	76	86	4	2	0	2	4
89-90—Hartford	NHL	79	25	29	54	109	7	0	3	3	2
90-91—Hartford	NHL	15	2	5	7	18	—	—	—	—	—
—New York Islanders	NHL	61	19	16	35	52	—	—	—	—	—
91-92—New York Islanders	NHL	80	40	40	80	92	—	—	—	—	—
92-93—New York Islanders	NHL	46	14	13	27	40	18	13	7	20	18
—Capital District	AHL	1	0	2	2	2	—	—	—	—	—
NHL totals		629	230	263	493	617	51	20	18	38	42

FETISOV, VIACHESLAV
D, DEVILS

PERSONAL: Born May 20, 1958, at Moscow, U.S.S.R.... 6-1/220.... Shoots left.... Name pronounced vee-YACH-ih-SLAV feh-TEE-sahf.
TRANSACTIONS/CAREER NOTES: Selected by Montreal Canadiens in 12th round (14th Canadiens pick, 201st overall) of NHL entry draft (June 15, 1978).... Selected by New Jersey Devils in eighth round (sixth Devils pick, 150th overall) of NHL entry draft (June 8, 1983).... Tore cartilage in left knee (November 22, 1989); missed six games.... Suffered bronchial pneumonia and hospitalized twice (November 28, 1990); missed 10 games.... Suffered from the flu (October 14, 1992); missed one game.
HONORS: Named to Soviet League All-Star team (1977-78 and 1981-82 through 1987-88).... Won Soviet Player of the Year Award (1981-82 and 1985-86).... Won Golden Stick Award (1983-84, 1987-88 and 1988-89).
MISCELLANEOUS: Member of silver-medal-winning (1980) and gold-medal-winning U.S.S.R. Olympic teams (1984 and 1988).

Season Team	League	Gms.	G	A	Pts.	Pen.	Gms.	G	A	Pts.	Pen.
			REGULAR SEASON					PLAYOFFS			
76-77—CSKA Moscow	USSR	28	3	4	7	14	—	—	—	—	—
77-78—CSKA Moscow	USSR	35	9	18	27	46	—	—	—	—	—
78-79—CSKA Moscow	USSR	29	10	19	29	40	—	—	—	—	—
79-80—CSKA Moscow	USSR	37	10	14	24	46	—	—	—	—	—
—Soviet Olympic Team	Int'l	7	5	4	9	10	—	—	—	—	—
80-81—CSKA Moscow	USSR	48	13	16	29	44	—	—	—	—	—
81-82—CSKA Moscow	USSR	46	15	26	41	20	—	—	—	—	—
82-83—CSKA Moscow	USSR	43	6	17	23	46	—	—	—	—	—
83-84—CSKA Moscow	USSR	44	19	30	49	38	—	—	—	—	—
—Soviet Olympic Team	Int'l	7	3	8	11	8	—	—	—	—	—
84-85—CSKA Moscow	USSR	20	13	12	25	6	—	—	—	—	—
85-86—CSKA Moscow	USSR	40	15	19	34	12	—	—	—	—	—
86-87—CSKA Moscow	USSR	39	13	20	33	18	—	—	—	—	—
87-88—CSKA Moscow	USSR	46	18	17	35	26	—	—	—	—	—
—Soviet Olympic Team	Int'l	8	4	9	13	6	—	—	—	—	—

F

Season Team	League	Gms.	G	A	Pts.	Pen.	Gms.	G	A	Pts.	Pen.
88-89—CSKA Moscow	USSR	23	9	8	17	18	—	—	—	—	—
89-90—New Jersey	NHL	72	8	34	42	52	6	0	2	2	10
90-91—New Jersey	NHL	67	3	16	19	62	7	0	0	0	17
—Utica	AHL	1	1	1	2	0	—	—	—	—	—
91-92—New Jersey	NHL	70	3	23	26	108	6	0	3	3	8
92-93—New Jersey	NHL	76	4	23	27	158	5	0	2	2	4
NHL totals		285	18	96	114	380	24	0	7	7	39

FILIMONOV, DIMITRI
D, SENATORS

PERSONAL: Born October 14, 1971, at Perm, U.S.S.R. . . . . 6-4/207. . . . Shoots right.
TRANSACTIONS/CAREER NOTES: Selected by Winnipeg Jets in third round (second Jets pick, 49th overall) of NHL entry draft (June 22, 1991). . . . Traded by Jets to Ottawa Senators for fourth-round pick in 1993 draft (D Ruslan Batyrshin) and future considerations (March 15, 1993).

Season Team	League	Gms.	G	A	Pts.	Pen.	Gms.	G	A	Pts.	Pen.
90-91—Dynamo Moscow	USSR	45	4	6	10	12	—	—	—	—	—
91-92—Dynamo Moscow	CIS	38	3	2	5	12	—	—	—	—	—
92-93—Dynamo Moscow	CIS	42	2	3	5	30	—	—	—	—	—

FINLEY, JEFF
D, FLYERS

PERSONAL: Born April 14, 1967, at Edmonton, Alta. . . . 6-2/185. . . . Shoots left.
TRANSACTIONS/CAREER NOTES: Selected by New York Islanders as underage junior in third round (fourth Islanders pick, 55th overall) of NHL entry draft (June 15, 1985). . . . Suffered swollen left knee (September 1988). . . . Traded by Islanders to Ottawa Senators for D Chris Luongo (June 30, 1993). . . . Signed as free agent by Philadelphia Flyers (August 2, 1993).

Season Team	League	Gms.	G	A	Pts.	Pen.	Gms.	G	A	Pts.	Pen.
83-84—Portland	WHL	5	0	0	0	0	5	0	1	1	4
—Summerland	BCJHL	49	0	21	21	14	—	—	—	—	—
84-85—Portland	WHL	69	6	44	50	57	6	1	2	3	2
85-86—Portland	WHL	70	11	59	70	83	15	1	7	8	16
86-87—Portland	WHL	72	13	53	66	113	20	1	†21	22	27
87-88—Springfield	AHL	52	5	18	23	50	—	—	—	—	—
—New York Islanders	NHL	10	0	5	5	15	1	0	0	0	2
88-89—New York Islanders	NHL	4	0	0	0	6	—	—	—	—	—
—Springfield	AHL	65	3	16	19	55	—	—	—	—	—
89-90—New York Islanders	NHL	11	0	1	1	0	5	0	2	2	2
—Springfield	AHL	57	1	15	16	41	13	1	4	5	23
90-91—Capital District	AHL	67	10	34	44	34	—	—	—	—	—
—New York Islanders	NHL	11	0	0	0	4	—	—	—	—	—
91-92—Capital District	AHL	20	1	9	10	6	—	—	—	—	—
—New York Islanders	NHL	51	1	10	11	26	—	—	—	—	—
92-93—Capital District	AHL	61	6	29	35	34	4	0	1	1	0
NHL totals		87	1	16	17	51	6	0	2	2	4

F

FINN, STEVEN
D, NORDIQUES

PERSONAL: Born August 20, 1966, at Laval, Que. . . . 6-0/198. . . . Shoots left.
TRANSACTIONS/CAREER NOTES: Selected by Quebec Nordiques as underage junior in third round (third Nordiques pick, 57th overall) of NHL entry draft (June 9, 1984). . . . Separated left shoulder (January 31, 1990). . . . Lacerated right index finger (October 25, 1990); missed five games. . . . Sprained wrist (November 25, 1991); missed six games. . . . Sprained right wrist (February 15, 1992); missed seven games. . . . Injured eye (January 22, 1993); missed one game. . . . Bruised left arm (March 8, 1993); missed one game.
HONORS: Named to QMJHL All-Star first team (1983-84). . . . Named to QMJHL All-Star second team (1984-85).

Season Team	League	Gms.	G	A	Pts.	Pen.	Gms.	G	A	Pts.	Pen.
82-83—Laval	QMJHL	69	7	30	37	108	6	0	2	2	6
83-84—Laval	QMJHL	68	7	39	46	159	14	1	6	7	27
84-85—Laval	QMJHL	61	20	33	53	169	—	—	—	—	—
—Fredericton	AHL	4	0	0	0	14	6	1	1	2	4
85-86—Laval	QMJHL	29	4	15	19	111	14	6	16	22	57
—Quebec	NHL	17	0	1	1	28	—	—	—	—	—
86-87—Fredericton	AHL	38	7	19	26	73	—	—	—	—	—
—Quebec	NHL	36	2	5	7	40	13	0	2	2	29
87-88—Quebec	NHL	75	3	7	10	198	—	—	—	—	—
88-89—Quebec	NHL	77	2	6	8	235	—	—	—	—	—
89-90—Quebec	NHL	64	3	9	12	208	—	—	—	—	—
90-91—Quebec	NHL	71	6	13	19	228	—	—	—	—	—
91-92—Quebec	NHL	65	4	7	11	194	—	—	—	—	—
92-93—Quebec	NHL	80	5	9	14	160	6	0	1	1	8
NHL totals		485	25	57	82	1291	19	0	3	3	37

FIORENTINO, PETER

D, RANGERS

PERSONAL: Born December 22, 1968, at Niagara Falls, Ont. . . . 6-1/205. . . . Shoots right. . . . Name pronounced FYOOR-ihn-TEE-noh.
TRANSACTIONS/CAREER NOTES: Selected by New York Rangers in 11th round (11th Rangers pick, 215th overall) of NHL entry draft (June 11, 1988). . . . Suspended three games (October 19, 1990). . . . Tore tendon in left ring finger (March 1991).

			REGULAR SEASON					PLAYOFFS				
Season Team	League	Gms.	G	A	Pts.	Pen.	Gms.	G	A	Pts.	Pen.
84-85—Niagara Falls Jr. B..........	OHA	38	7	10	17	149	—	—	—	—	—
85-86—Sault Ste. Marie	OHL	58	1	6	7	87	—	—	—	—	—
86-87—Sault Ste. Marie	OHL	64	1	12	13	187	4	2	1	3	5
87-88—Sault Ste. Marie	OHL	65	5	27	32	252	6	2	2	4	21
88-89—Sault Ste. Marie	OHL	55	5	24	29	220	—	—	—	—	—
—Denver	IHL	10	0	0	0	39	4	0	0	0	24
89-90—Flint	IHL	64	2	7	9	302	—	—	—	—	—
90-91—Binghamton	AHL	55	2	11	13	361	1	0	0	0	0
91-92—Binghamton	AHL	70	2	11	13	340	5	0	1	1	24
—New York Rangers	NHL	1	0	0	0	0	—	—	—	—	—
92-93—Binghamton	AHL	64	9	5	14	286	13	0	3	3	22
NHL totals.................................		**1**	**0**	**0**	**0**	**0**					

FISET, STEPHANE

G, NORDIQUES

PERSONAL: Born June 17, 1970, at Montreal. . . . 6-0/175. . . . Shoots left.
TRANSACTIONS/CAREER NOTES: Selected by Quebec Nordiques in second round (third Nordiques pick, 24th overall) of NHL entry draft (June 13, 1987). . . . Underwent shoulder surgery (May 1989). . . . Twisted knee (December 9, 1990). . . . Sprained left knee (January 14, 1992); missed 12 games.
HONORS: Won Can.HL Goaltender of the Year Award (1988-89). . . . Won Jacques Plante Trophy (1988-89). . . . Named to QMJHL All-Star first team (1988-89).

			REGULAR SEASON							PLAYOFFS						
Season Team	League	Gms.	Min.	W	L	T	GA	SO	Avg.	Gms.	Min.	W	L	GA	SO	Avg.
87-88—Victoriaville..................	QMJHL	40	2221	14	17	4	146	1	3.94	2	163	0	2	10	0	3.68
88-89—Victoriaville..................	QMJHL	43	2401	25	14	0	138	1	*3.45	12	711	9	2	33	0	*2.78
89-90—Victoriaville..................	QMJHL	24	1383	14	6	3	63	1	2.73	*14	*790	7	6	*49	0	3.72
—Quebec	NHL	6	342	0	5	1	34	0	5.96	—	—	—	—	—	—	—
90-91—Quebec	NHL	3	186	0	2	1	12	0	3.87	—	—	—	—	—	—	—
—Halifax	AHL	36	1902	10	15	8	131	0	4.13	—	—	—	—	—	—	—
91-92—Halifax	AHL	29	1675	8	14	6	110	+3	3.94	—	—	—	—	—	—	—
—Quebec	NHL	23	1133	7	10	2	71	1	3.76	—	—	—	—	—	—	—
92-93—Quebec	NHL	37	1939	18	9	4	110	0	3.40	1	21	0	0	1	0	2.86
—Halifax	AHL	3	180	2	1	0	11	0	3.67	—	—	—	—	—	—	—
NHL totals.................................		**69**	**3600**	**25**	**26**	**8**	**227**	**1**	**3.78**	**1**	**21**	**0**	**0**	**1**	**0**	**2.86**

FISHER, CRAIG

C, OILERS

PERSONAL: Born June 30, 1970, at Oshawa, Ont. . . . 6-3/180. . . . Shoots left. . . . Full name: Craig Francis Fisher.
COLLEGE: Miami of Ohio.
TRANSACTIONS/CAREER NOTES: Suffered concussion (October 1987). . . . Selected by Philadelphia Flyers in third round (third Flyers pick, 56th overall) of NHL entry draft (June 11, 1988). . . . Traded by Flyers with RW Scott Mellanby and LW Craig Berube to Edmonton Oilers for RW Dave Brown, D Corey Foster and the NHL rights to RW Jari Kurri (May 30, 1991).
HONORS: Named to CCHA All-Rookie team (1988-89). . . . Named to CCHA All-Star first team (1989-90).

			REGULAR SEASON					PLAYOFFS				
Season Team	League	Gms.	G	A	Pts.	Pen.	Gms.	G	A	Pts.	Pen.
86-87—Oshawa Jr. B.....................	OHA	34	22	26	48	18	—	—	—	—	—
87-88—Oshawa Jr. B.....................	OHA	36	42	34	76	48	—	—	—	—	—
88-89—Miami of Ohio	CCHA	37	22	20	42	37	—	—	—	—	—
89-90—Miami of Ohio	CCHA	39	37	29	66	38	—	—	—	—	—
—Philadelphia	NHL	2	0	0	0	0	—	—	—	—	—
90-91—Hershey	AHL	77	43	36	79	46	7	5	3	8	2
—Philadelphia	NHL	2	0	0	0	0	—	—	—	—	—
91-92—Cape Breton	AHL	60	20	25	45	28	1	0	0	0	0
92-93—Cape Breton	AHL	75	32	29	61	74	1	0	0	0	2
NHL totals.................................		**4**	**0**	**0**	**0**	**0**					

FITZGERALD, RUSTY

C, PENGUINS

PERSONAL: Born October 4, 1972, at Minneapolis. . . . 6-1/185. . . . Shoots left.
HIGH SCHOOL: William M. Kelley (Silver Bay, Minn.), then East (Duluth, Minn.).
COLLEGE: Minnesota-Duluth.
TRANSACTIONS/CAREER NOTES: Selected by Pittsburgh Penguins in second round (second Penguins pick, 38th overall) of NHL entry draft (June 22, 1991).

			REGULAR SEASON					PLAYOFFS				
Season Team	League	Gms.	G	A	Pts.	Pen.	Gms.	G	A	Pts.	Pen.
87-88—William M. Kelley H.S........	Minn. H.S.	20	19	26	45	18	—	—	—	—	—
88-89—William M. Kelley H.S........	Minn. H.S.	22	24	25	49	26	—	—	—	—	—
89-90—William M. Kelley H.S........	Minn. H.S.	21	25	26	51	24	—	—	—	—	—
—Northland Jr. B..................	Minn.	20	11	5	16	12	—	—	—	—	—

F

Season Team	League	REGULAR SEASON					PLAYOFFS				
		Gms.	G	A	Pts.	Pen.	Gms.	G	A	Pts.	Pen.
90-91—Duluth East High School ..	Minn. H.S.	15	14	11	25	...	—	—	—	—	—
91-92—Minnesota-Duluth	WCHA	37	9	11	20	40	—	—	—	—	—
92-93—Minnesota-Duluth	WCHA	39	24	23	47	58	—	—	—	—	—

FITZGERALD, TOM
RW/C, PANTHERS

PERSONAL: Born August 28, 1968, at Melrose, Mass. . . . 6-1/197. . . . Shoots right. . . . Full name: Thomas James Fitzgerald.
HIGH SCHOOL: Austin Prep (Reading, Mass.).
COLLEGE: Providence.
TRANSACTIONS/CAREER NOTES: Selected by New York Islanders in first round (first Islanders pick, 17th overall) of NHL entry draft (June 21, 1986). . . . Bruised left knee (November 7, 1990). . . . Strained abdominal muscle (October 22, 1991); missed 16 games. . . . Tore rib cage muscle (October 24, 1992); missed four games. . . . Selected by Florida Panthers in NHL expansion draft (June 24, 1993).

Season Team	League	REGULAR SEASON					PLAYOFFS				
		Gms.	G	A	Pts.	Pen.	Gms.	G	A	Pts.	Pen.
84-85—Austin Prep.	Mass. H.S.	18	20	21	41	...	—	—	—	—	—
85-86—Austin Prep.	Mass. H.S.	24	35	38	73	...	—	—	—	—	—
86-87—Providence College	Hockey East	15	2	0	2	2	—	—	—	—	—
87-88—Providence College	Hockey East	36	19	15	34	50	—	—	—	—	—
88-89—Springfield	AHL	61	24	18	42	43	—	—	—	—	—
—New York Islanders	NHL	23	3	5	8	10	—	—	—	—	—
89-90—Springfield	AHL	53	30	23	53	32	14	2	9	11	13
—New York Islanders	NHL	19	2	5	7	4	4	1	0	1	4
90-91—New York Islanders	NHL	41	5	5	10	24	—	—	—	—	—
—Capital District	AHL	27	7	7	14	50	—	—	—	—	—
91-92—New York Islanders	NHL	45	6	11	17	28	—	—	—	—	—
—Capital District	AHL	4	1	1	2	4	—	—	—	—	—
92-93—New York Islanders	NHL	77	9	18	27	34	18	2	5	7	18
NHL totals		205	25	44	69	100	22	3	5	8	22

FITZPATRICK, MARK
G, PANTHERS

PERSONAL: Born November 13, 1968, at Toronto. . . . 6-2/190. . . . Shoots left.
TRANSACTIONS/CAREER NOTES: Injured knee (February 1987). . . . Selected by Los Angeles Kings as underage junior in second round (second Kings pick, 27th overall) of NHL entry draft (June 13, 1987). . . . Traded by Kings with D Wayne McBean and future considerations to New York Islanders for G Kelly Hrudey (February 22, 1989); Kings sent D Doug Crossman to the Islanders to complete the trade (May 23, 1989). . . . Developed Eosinophilic Myalgia Syndrome (EMS) after a reaction to L-Trytophan, an ingredient in a vitamin supplement (September 1990); returned to play (March 1991). . . . Suffered recurrence of EMS and underwent biopsy on right thigh (October 22, 1991); missed 10 games. . . . Strained abdominal muscle (December 15, 1992); missed five games. . . . Traded by Islanders with first-round pick in 1993 draft (C Adam Deadmarsh) to Quebec Nordiques for G Ron Hextall and first-round pick in 1993 draft (June 20, 1993). . . . Selected by Florida Panthers in NHL expansion draft (June 24, 1993).
HONORS: Won Top Goaltender Trophy (1985-86). . . . Named to WHL All-Star second team (1985-86 and 1987-88). . . . Named to Memorial Cup All-Star team (1986-87 and 1987-88). . . . Won Bill Masterton Memorial Trophy (1991-92).

Season Team	League	REGULAR SEASON							PLAYOFFS						
		Gms.	Min.	W	L	T	GA	SO	Avg.	Gms.	Min.	W	L	GA SO	Avg.
83-84—Revelstoke	BCJHL	21	1019	...	...	...	90	0	5.30	—	—			— —	—
84-85—Medicine Hat	WHL	3	180	...	...	...	9	0	3.00	—	—			— —	—
85-86—Medicine Hat	WHL	41	2074	26	6	1	99	1	*2.86	*19	986	12	5	*58 0	3.53
86-87—Medicine Hat	WHL	50	2844	31	11	4	159	*4	3.35	*20	*1224	12	8	71 †1	3.48
87-88—Medicine Hat	WHL	63	3600	36	15	6	194	†2	*3.23	16	959	12	4	52 †1	*3.25
88-89—New Haven	AHL	18	980	10	5	1	54	1	3.31	—	—			— —	—
—Los Angeles	NHL	17	957	6	7	3	64	0	4.01	—	—			— —	—
—New York Islanders	NHL	11	627	3	5	2	41	0	3.92	—	—			— —	—
89-90—New York Islanders	NHL	47	2653	19	19	5	150	3	3.39	4	152	0	2	13 0	5.13
90-91—Capital District	AHL	12	734	3	7	2	47	0	3.84	—	—			— —	—
—New York Islanders	NHL	2	120	1	1	0	6	0	3.00	—	—			— —	—
91-92—Capital District	AHL	14	782	6	5	1	39	0	2.99	—	—			— —	—
—New York Islanders	NHL	30	1743	11	13	5	93	0	3.20	—	—			— —	—
92-93—New York Islanders	NHL	39	2253	17	15	5	130	0	3.46	3	77	0	1	4 0	3.12
—Capital District	AHL	5	284	1	3	1	18	0	3.80	—	—			— —	—
NHL totals		146	8353	57	60	20	484	3	3.48	7	229	0	3	17 0	4.45

FITZPATRICK, RORY
D, CANADIENS

PERSONAL: Born January 11, 1975, at Rochester, N.Y. . . . 6-1/190. . . . Shoots right.
TRANSACTIONS/CAREER NOTES: Selected by Montreal Canadiens in second round (second Canadiens pick, 47th overall) of NHL entry draft (June 26, 1993).
HONORS: Named to OHL All-Rookie team (1992-93).

Season Team	League	REGULAR SEASON					PLAYOFFS				
		Gms.	G	A	Pts.	Pen.	Gms.	G	A	Pts.	Pen.
90-91—Rochester Jr. B	OHA	40	0	5	5	...	—	—	—	—	—
91-92—Rochester Jr. B	OHA	28	8	28	36	141	—	—	—	—	—
92-93—Sudbury	OHL	58	4	20	24	68	14	0	0	0	17

F

FLAHERTY, WADE
G, SHARKS

PERSONAL: Born January 11, 1968, at Terreace, B.C. . . . 6-0/175. . . . Shoots right.
TRANSACTIONS/CAREER NOTES: Selected by Buffalo Sabres in ninth round (tenth Sabres pick, 181st overall) of NHL entry draft (June 11, 1988). . . . Signed as free agent by San Jose Sharks (September 3, 1991).
HONORS: Named to WHL All-Star second team (1987-88). . . . Won ECHL Playoff Most Valuable Player Award (1989-90). . . . Shared James Norris Memorial Trophy with Arturs Irbe (1991-92). . . . Named to IHL All-Star second team (1992-93).

Season Team	League	REGULAR SEASON								PLAYOFFS						
		Gms.	Min.	W	L	T	GA	SO	Avg.	Gms.	Min.	W	L	GA	SO	Avg.
84-85—Kelowna Wings	WHL	1	55	0	0	0	5	0	5.45	—	—	—	—	—	—	—
85-86—Seattle	WHL	9	271	1	3	0	36	0	7.97	—	—	—	—	—	—	—
—Spokane	WHL	5	161	0	3	0	21	0	7.83	—	—	—	—	—	—	—
86-87—Nanaimo	BCJHL	15	830	...	...		53	0	3.83	—	—	—	—	—	—	—
—Victoria	WHL	3	127	0	2	0	16	0	7.56	—	—	—	—	—	—	—
87-88—Victoria	WHL	36	2052	20	15	0	135	0	3.95	5	300	2	3	18	0	3.60
88-89—Victoria	WHL	42	2408	21	19	0	180	0	4.49	8	480	3	5	35	0	4.38
89-90—Kalamazoo	IHL	1	13	0	0	0	0	0	0.00	—	—	—	—	—	—	—
—Greensboro	ECHL	27	1308	12	10	0	96	...	4.40	†9	567	8	1	21	0	*2.22
90-91—Kansas City	IHL	†56	2990	16	31	4	*224	0	4.49	—	—	—	—	—	—	—
91-92—Kansas City	IHL	43	2603	26	14	3	140	1	3.23	1	1	0	0	0	0	0.00
—San Jose	NHL	3	178	0	3	0	13	0	4.38	—	—	—	—	—	—	—
92-93—Kansas City	IHL	61	*3642	*34	19	0	*195	2	3.21	12	*733	6	*5	†34	*1	2.78
—San Jose	NHL	1	60	0	1	0	5	0	5.00	—	—	—	—	—	—	—
NHL totals		4	238	0	4	0	18	0	4.54							

FLATLEY, PATRICK
RW, ISLANDERS

PERSONAL: Born October 3, 1963, at Toronto. . . . 6-2/200. . . . Shoots right. . . . Full name: Patrick William Flatley.
HIGH SCHOOL: Henry Carr (Rexdale, Ont.).
COLLEGE: Wisconsin.
TRANSACTIONS/CAREER NOTES: Selected by New York Islanders as underage junior in first round (first Islanders pick, 21st overall) of NHL entry draft (June 9, 1982). . . . Broke bone in left hand (April 1985). . . . Strained left knee ligaments (February 4, 1987). . . . Separated left shoulder (November 1987). . . . Injured right knee (January 1988). . . . Underwent reconstructive knee surgery (February 1988). . . . Injured right knee (December 1988). . . . Suffered sore right ankle (February 1989). . . . Reinjured right knee (March 1989). . . . Bruised right ankle (October 1989). . . . Pulled groin muscle (February 13, 1990). . . . Reinjured groin (March 2, 1990); missed six games. . . . Sprained right knee (October 13, 1990). . . . Bruised left knee (November 30, 1990). . . . Fractured finger on left hand (February 16, 1991). . . . Fractured right thumb (December 19, 1991); missed 42 games. . . . Broke ribs (January 5, 1993); missed four games.
HONORS: Named to NCAA All-America West team (1982-83). . . . Named to NCAA All-Tournament team (1982-83). . . . Named to WCHA All-Star first team (1982-83).

Season Team	League	REGULAR SEASON					PLAYOFFS				
		Gms.	G	A	Pts.	Pen.	Gms.	G	A	Pts.	Pen.
80-81—Henry Carr H.S.	MTHL	42	30	61	91	122	—	—	—	—	—
81-82—University of Wisconsin	WCHA	33	17	20	37	65	—	—	—	—	—
82-83—University of Wisconsin	WCHA	43	25	44	69	76	—	—	—	—	—
83-84—Canadian Olympic Team	Int'l	57	33	17	50	136	—	—	—	—	—
—New York Islanders	NHL	16	2	7	9	6	21	9	6	15	14
84-85—New York Islanders	NHL	78	20	31	51	106	4	1	0	1	6
85-86—New York Islanders	NHL	73	18	34	52	66	3	0	0	0	21
86-87—New York Islanders	NHL	63	16	35	51	81	11	3	2	5	6
87-88—New York Islanders	NHL	40	9	15	24	28	—	—	—	—	—
88-89—New York Islanders	NHL	41	10	15	25	31	—	—	—	—	—
—Springfield	AHL	2	1	1	2	2	—	—	—	—	—
89-90—New York Islanders	NHL	62	17	32	49	101	5	3	0	3	2
90-91—New York Islanders	NHL	56	20	25	45	74	—	—	—	—	—
91-92—New York Islanders	NHL	38	8	28	36	31	—	—	—	—	—
92-93—New York Islanders	NHL	80	13	47	60	63	15	2	7	9	12
NHL totals		547	133	269	402	587	59	18	15	33	61

FLEURY, THEOREN
C/RW, FLAMES

PERSONAL: Born June 29, 1968, at Oxbow, Sask. . . . 5-6/155. . . . Shoots right. . . . Name pronounced FLUH-ree.
TRANSACTIONS/CAREER NOTES: Selected by Calgary Flames in eighth round (ninth Flames pick, 166th overall) of NHL entry draft (June 13, 1987).
HONORS: Named to WHL (East) All-Star first team (1986-87). . . . Shared Bob Clarke Trophy with Joe Sakic (1987-88). . . . Named to WHL All-Star second team (1987-88). . . . Shared Alka-Seltzer Plus Award with Marty McSorley (1990-91). . . . Played in NHL All-Star Game (1991 and 1992).
RECORDS: Holds NHL single-game record for highest plus-minus rating—9 (February 10, 1993).
MISCELLANEOUS: Member of Stanley Cup championship team (1989).

Season Team	League	REGULAR SEASON					PLAYOFFS				
		Gms.	G	A	Pts.	Pen.	Gms.	G	A	Pts.	Pen.
84-85—Moose Jaw	WHL	71	29	46	75	82	—	—	—	—	—
85-86—Moose Jaw	WHL	72	43	65	108	124	—	—	—	—	—
86-87—Moose Jaw	WHL	66	61	68	129	110	9	7	9	16	34
87-88—Moose Jaw	WHL	65	68	92	†160	235	—	—	—	—	—
—Salt Lake City	IHL	2	3	4	7	7	8	11	5	16	16

F

Season Team	League	REGULAR SEASON					PLAYOFFS				
		Gms.	G	A	Pts.	Pen.	Gms.	G	A	Pts.	Pen.
88-89—Salt Lake City	IHL	40	37	37	74	81	—	—	—	—	—
—Calgary	NHL	36	14	20	34	46	22	5	6	11	24
89-90—Calgary	NHL	80	31	35	66	157	6	2	3	5	10
90-91—Calgary	NHL	79	51	53	104	136	7	2	5	7	14
91-92—Calgary	NHL	80	33	40	73	133	—	—	—	—	—
92-93—Calgary	NHL	83	34	66	100	88	6	5	7	12	27
NHL totals		358	163	214	377	560	41	14	21	35	75

FLICHEL, TODD
D

PERSONAL: Born September 14, 1964, at Osgoode, Ont. . . . 6-3/195. . . . Shoots right.
COLLEGE: Bowling Green State.
TRANSACTIONS/CAREER NOTES: Selected by Winnipeg Jets in ninth round (10th Jets pick, 169th overall) of NHL entry draft (June 8, 1983).

Season Team	League	REGULAR SEASON					PLAYOFFS				
		Gms.	G	A	Pts.	Pen.	Gms.	G	A	Pts.	Pen.
83-84—Bowling Green State	CCHA	44	1	3	4	12	—	—	—	—	—
84-85—Bowling Green State	CCHA	42	5	7	12	62	—	—	—	—	—
85-86—Bowling Green State	CCHA	42	3	10	13	84	—	—	—	—	—
86-87—Bowling Green State	CCHA	42	4	15	19	75	—	—	—	—	—
87-88—Winnipeg	NHL	2	0	0	0	14	—	—	—	—	—
—Moncton	AHL	65	5	12	17	102	—	—	—	—	—
88-89—Moncton	AHL	74	2	29	31	81	10	1	4	5	25
—Winnipeg	NHL	1	0	0	0	0	—	—	—	—	—
89-90—Winnipeg	NHL	3	0	1	1	2	—	—	—	—	—
—Moncton	AHL	65	7	14	21	74	—	—	—	—	—
90-91—Moncton	AHL	75	8	21	29	44	9	0	0	0	8
91-92—Fort Wayne	IHL	64	3	10	13	79	7	0	0	0	2
92-93—Cincinnati	IHL	52	5	10	15	46	—	—	—	—	—
—Rochester	AHL	15	1	3	4	4	16	2	4	6	22
NHL totals		6	0	1	1	16					

FLOMENHOFT, STEVEN
C, SENATORS

PERSONAL: Born May 4, 1971, at Riverwoods, Ill. . . . 6-0/215. . . . Shoots right.
HIGH SCHOOL: Avon Old Farms School for Boys (Conn.).
COLLEGE: Harvard.
TRANSACTIONS/CAREER NOTES: Selected by Ottawa Senators in NHL supplemental draft (June 19, 1992).

Season Team	League	REGULAR SEASON					PLAYOFFS				
		Gms.	G	A	Pts.	Pen.	Gms.	G	A	Pts.	Pen.
89-90—Harvard University	ECAC	28	5	5	10	22	—	—	—	—	—
90-91—Harvard University	ECAC	29	12	14	26	48	—	—	—	—	—
91-92—Harvard University	ECAC	27	14	17	31	30	—	—	—	—	—
92-93—Harvard University	ECAC	31	11	24	35	60	—	—	—	—	—
—New Haven	AHL	2	0	1	1	0	—	—	—	—	—

FOGARTY, BRYAN
D, PENGUINS

PERSONAL: Born June 11, 1969, at Montreal. . . . 6-2/198. . . . Shoots left.
TRANSACTIONS/CAREER NOTES: Selected by Quebec Nordiques as underage junior in first round (first Nordiques pick, ninth overall) of NHL entry draft (June 13, 1987). . . . Traded by Kingston Raiders to Niagara Falls Thunder for D Garth Joy, LW Jason Simon, Kevin Lune and fourth-round pick in 1989 draft (August 1988). . . . Underwent appendectomy (September 1989). . . . Underwent substance-abuse treatment (February 1991); missed one month. . . . Left Nordiques to report to halfway house (March 28, 1991). . . . Suffered from the flu (November 30, 1991); missed five games. . . . Traded by Nordiques to Pittsburgh Penguins for rights to RW Scott Young (March 10, 1992). . . . Suspended by Penguins for leaving Cleveland Lumberjacks without approval (January 22, 1993). . . . Reinstated by Penguins (March 16, 1993).
HONORS: Named to OHL All-Star first team (1986-87 and 1988-89). . . . Won Can.HL Player of the Year Award (1988-89). . . . Won Can.HL Defenseman of the Year Award (1988-89). . . . Won Can.HL Plus/Minus Award (1988-89). . . . Won Red Tilson Trophy (1988-89). . . . Won Eddie Powers Memorial Trophy (1988-89). . . . Won Max Kaminsky Trophy (1988-89).

Season Team	League	REGULAR SEASON					PLAYOFFS				
		Gms.	G	A	Pts.	Pen.	Gms.	G	A	Pts.	Pen.
84-85—Aurora	OHA	66	18	39	57	180	—	—	—	—	—
85-86—Kingston	OHL	47	2	19	21	14	10	1	3	4	4
86-87—Kingston	OHL	56	20	50	70	46	12	2	3	5	5
87-88—Kingston	OHL	48	11	36	47	50	—	—	—	—	—
88-89—Niagara Falls	OHL	60	47	*108	*155	88	17	10	22	32	36
89-90—Quebec	NHL	45	4	10	14	31	—	—	—	—	—
—Halifax	AHL	22	5	14	19	6	6	4	2	6	0
90-91—Halifax	AHL	5	0	2	2	0	—	—	—	—	—
—Quebec	NHL	45	9	22	31	24	—	—	—	—	—
91-92—Quebec	NHL	20	3	12	15	16	—	—	—	—	—
—Halifax	AHL	2	0	0	0	2	—	—	—	—	—
—New Haven	AHL	4	0	1	1	6	—	—	—	—	—
—Muskegon	IHL	8	2	4	6	30	—	—	—	—	—
92-93—Pittsburgh	NHL	12	0	4	4	4	—	—	—	—	—
—Cleveland	IHL	15	2	5	7	8	3	0	1	1	17
NHL totals		122	16	48	64	75					

F

FOLIGNO, MIKE
RW, MAPLE LEAFS

PERSONAL: Born January 29, 1959, at Sudbury, Ont. . . . 6-2/200. . . . Shoots right. . . . Full name: Mike Anthony Foligno. . . . Name pronounced foh-LEE-noh.
TRANSACTIONS/CAREER NOTES: Selected by Detroit Red Wings in first round (first Red Wings pick, third overall) of NHL entry draft (August 9, 1979). . . . Traded by Red Wings with C Dale McCourt, C Brent Peterson and future considerations to Buffalo Sabres for G Bob Sauve, D Jim Schoenfeld and LW/C Derek Smith (December 2, 1981). . . . Injured tailbone (October 31, 1982). . . . Injured shoulder (February 12, 1983). . . . Bruised kidney (December 7, 1986). . . . Suffered back spasms (February 1988). . . . Pulled rib cartilage (January 14, 1989). . . . Fractured left thumb (February 18, 1990). . . . Traded by Sabres with eighth-round pick in 1991 draft (C Thomas Kucharcik) to Toronto Maple Leafs for D Brian Curran and LW Lou Franceschetti (December 17, 1990). . . . Tore medial collateral ligament in the left knee (December 18, 1990); missed seven games. . . . Fractured tibia (December 21, 1991); missed remainder of season.
HONORS: Won Red Tilson Trophy (1978-79). . . . Won Eddie Powers Memorial Trophy (1978-79). . . . Won Jim Mahon Memorial Trophy (1978-79). . . . Named to OMJHL All-Star first team (1978-79).

			REGULAR SEASON					PLAYOFFS			
Season Team	League	Gms.	G	A	Pts.	Pen.	Gms.	G	A	Pts.	Pen.
75-76—Sudbury	OHA Mj. Jr. A	57	22	14	36	45	—	—	—	—	—
76-77—Sudbury	OMJHL	66	31	44	75	62	—	—	—	—	—
77-78—Sudbury	OMJHL	67	47	39	86	112	—	—	—	—	—
78-79—Sudbury	OMJHL	68	65	85	*150	98	10	5	5	10	14
79-80—Detroit	NHL	80	36	35	71	109	—	—	—	—	—
80-81—Detroit	NHL	80	28	35	63	210	—	—	—	—	—
81-82—Detroit	NHL	26	13	13	26	28	—	—	—	—	—
—Buffalo	NHL	56	20	31	51	149	4	2	0	2	9
82-83—Buffalo	NHL	66	22	25	47	135	10	2	3	5	39
83-84—Buffalo	NHL	70	32	31	63	151	3	2	1	3	19
84-85—Buffalo	NHL	77	27	29	56	154	5	1	3	4	12
85-86—Buffalo	NHL	79	41	39	80	168	—	—	—	—	—
86-87—Buffalo	NHL	75	30	29	59	176	—	—	—	—	—
87-88—Buffalo	NHL	74	29	28	57	220	6	3	2	5	31
88-89—Buffalo	NHL	75	27	22	49	156	5	3	1	4	21
89-90—Buffalo	NHL	61	15	25	40	99	6	0	1	1	12
90-91—Buffalo	NHL	31	4	5	9	42	—	—	—	—	—
—Toronto	NHL	37	8	7	15	65	—	—	—	—	—
91-92—Toronto	NHL	33	6	8	14	50	—	—	—	—	—
92-93—Toronto	NHL	55	13	5	18	84	18	2	6	8	42
NHL totals		975	351	367	718	1996	57	15	17	32	185

FOOTE, ADAM
D, NORDIQUES

PERSONAL: Born July 10, 1971, at Toronto. . . . 6-1/180. . . . Shoots right. . . . Full name: Adam David Vernon Foote.
TRANSACTIONS/CAREER NOTES: Selected by Quebec Nordiques in second round (second Nordiques pick, 22nd overall) of NHL entry draft (June 17, 1989). . . . Fractured right thumb (February 1992); missed remainder of season. . . . Injured knee (October 21, 1992); missed one game. . . . Suffered from the flu (January 28, 1993); missed two games.
HONORS: Named to OHL All-Star first team (1990-91).

			REGULAR SEASON					PLAYOFFS			
Season Team	League	Gms.	G	A	Pts.	Pen.	Gms.	G	A	Pts.	Pen.
88-89—Sault Ste. Marie	OHL	66	7	32	39	120	—	—	—	—	—
89-90—Sault Ste. Marie	OHL	61	12	43	55	199	—	—	—	—	—
90-91—Sault Ste. Marie	OHL	59	18	51	69	93	14	5	12	17	28
91-92—Quebec	NHL	46	2	5	7	44	—	—	—	—	—
—Halifax	AHL	6	0	1	1	2	—	—	—	—	—
92-93—Quebec	NHL	81	4	12	16	168	6	0	1	1	2
NHL totals		127	6	17	23	212	6	0	1	1	2

FORSBERG, PETER
C, NORDIQUES

PERSONAL: Born July 20, 1973, at Ornskoldsvik, Sweden. . . . 6-0/181. . . . Shoots left.
TRANSACTIONS/CAREER NOTES: Selected by Philadelphia Flyers in first round (first Flyers pick, sixth overall) of NHL entry draft (June 22, 1991). . . . Traded by Flyers with G Ron Hextall, C Mike Ricci, D Steve Duchesne, D Kerry Huffman, first-round pick in 1993 draft (G Jocelyn Thibault), cash and future considerations to Quebec Nordiques for C Eric Lindros (June 20, 1992); Flyers sent LW Chris Simon and first-round pick in 1994 draft to Nordiques to complete deal (July 21, 1992).
HONORS: Named to Swedish League All-Star team (1991-92).

			REGULAR SEASON					PLAYOFFS			
Season Team	League	Gms.	G	A	Pts.	Pen.	Gms.	G	A	Pts.	Pen.
89-90—MoDo	Sweden Jr.	30	15	12	27	42	—	—	—	—	—
90-91—MoDo	Sweden	23	7	10	17	22	—	—	—	—	—
91-92—MoDo	Sweden	39	9	19	28	78	—	—	—	—	—
92-93—MoDo	Sweden	39	23	24	47	92	3	4	1	5	0

FORSLUND, TOMAS
RW, FLAMES

PERSONAL: Born November 24, 1968, at Falun, Sweden. . . . 5-11/200. . . . Shoots left.
TRANSACTIONS/CAREER NOTES: Selected by Calgary Flames in fourth round (Flames fourth pick, 85th overall) of NHL entry draft (June 11, 1988). . . . Strained right knee (November 16, 1991); missed 11 games. . . . Strained right knee (December 17, 1991). . . . Strained right knee (February 19, 1993); missed four games.

Season Team	League	REGULAR SEASON					PLAYOFFS				
		Gms.	G	A	Pts.	Pen.	Gms.	G	A	Pts.	Pen.
86-87—Leksand	Sweden	23	3	5	8	...	—	—	—	—	—
87-88—Leksand	Sweden	37	9	10	19	...	—	—	—	—	—
88-89—Leksand	Sweden	39	14	16	30	56	—	—	—	—	—
89-90—Leksand	Sweden	38	14	21	35	48	3	0	1	1	2
90-91—Swedish national team	Int'l	21	6	9	15	26	—	—	—	—	—
—Leksand	Sweden	39	15	19	34	54	4	2	3	5	0
91-92—Calgary	NHL	38	5	9	14	12	—	—	—	—	—
—Salt Lake City	IHL	22	10	6	16	25	5	2	2	4	2
92-93—Calgary	NHL	6	0	2	2	0	—	—	—	—	—
—Salt Lake City	IHL	63	31	23	54	68	—	—	—	—	—
NHL totals		44	5	11	16	12					

FORTIER, MARC

C, KINGS

PERSONAL: Born February 26, 1966, at Sherbrooke, Que. . . . 6-0/192. . . . Shoots right. . . . Name pronounced for-TEE-yay.
TRANSACTIONS/CAREER NOTES: Signed as free agent by Quebec Nordiques (February 3, 1987). . . . Injured groin (February 18, 1992). . . . Signed as free agent by Ottawa Senators (October 1, 1992). . . . Traded by Senators with RW Jim Thomson to Los Angeles Kings for RW Bob Kudelski and C Shawn McCosh (December 20, 1992).
HONORS: Won Jean Beliveau Trophy (1986-87). . . . Named to QMJHL All-Star first team (1986-87).

Season Team	League	REGULAR SEASON					PLAYOFFS				
		Gms.	G	A	Pts.	Pen.	Gms.	G	A	Pts.	Pen.
84-85—Chicoutimi	QMJHL	68	35	63	98	114	14	8	4	12	16
85-86—Chicoutimi	QMJHL	71	47	86	133	49	9	2	14	16	12
86-87—Chicoutimi	QMJHL	65	66	*135	*201	39	19	11	*40	*51	20
87-88—Quebec	NHL	27	4	10	14	12	—	—	—	—	—
—Fredericton	AHL	50	26	36	62	48	—	—	—	—	—
88-89—Quebec	NHL	57	20	19	39	45	—	—	—	—	—
—Halifax	AHL	16	11	11	22	14	—	—	—	—	—
89-90—Halifax	AHL	15	5	6	11	6	—	—	—	—	—
—Quebec	NHL	59	13	17	30	28	—	—	—	—	—
90-91—Halifax	AHL	58	24	32	56	85	—	—	—	—	—
—Quebec	NHL	14	0	4	4	6	—	—	—	—	—
91-92—Halifax	AHL	16	9	16	25	44	—	—	—	—	—
—Quebec	NHL	39	5	9	14	33	—	—	—	—	—
92-93—Ottawa	NHL	10	0	1	1	6	—	—	—	—	—
—New Haven	AHL	16	9	15	24	42	—	—	—	—	—
—Los Angeles	NHL	6	0	0	0	5	—	—	—	—	—
—Phoenix	IHL	17	4	9	13	34	—	—	—	—	—
NHL totals		212	42	60	102	135					

FOSTER, COREY

D, FLYERS

PERSONAL: Born October 27, 1969, at Ottawa. . . . 6-3/204. . . . Shoots left.
TRANSACTIONS/CAREER NOTES: Selected by New Jersey Devils in first round (first Devils pick, 12th overall) of NHL entry draft (June 11, 1988). . . . Traded by Devils to Edmonton Oilers for first-round pick in 1989 draft (C Jason Miller) (June 17, 1989). . . . Traded by Oilers with RW Dave Brown and rights to RW Jari Kurri to Philadelphia Flyers for RW Scott Mellanby, LW Craig Berube and C Craig Fisher (May 30, 1991). . . . Fractured collarbone during preseason (September 1991); missed 14 games.

Season Team	League	REGULAR SEASON					PLAYOFFS				
		Gms.	G	A	Pts.	Pen.	Gms.	G	A	Pts.	Pen.
86-87—Peterborough	OHL	30	3	4	7	4	1	0	0	0	0
87-88—Peterborough	OHL	66	13	31	44	58	11	5	9	14	13
88-89—Peterborough	OHL	55	14	42	56	42	17	1	17	18	12
—New Jersey	NHL	2	0	0	0	0	—	—	—	—	—
89-90—Cape Breton	AHL	54	7	17	24	32	1	0	0	0	0
90-91—Cape Breton	AHL	67	14	11	25	51	4	2	4	6	4
91-92—Philadelphia	NHL	25	3	4	7	20	—	—	—	—	—
—Hershey	AHL	19	5	9	14	26	6	1	1	2	5
92-93—Hershey	AHL	80	9	25	34	102	—	—	—	—	—
NHL totals		27	3	4	7	20					

FOSTER, NORM

G, OILERS

PERSONAL: Born February 10, 1965, at Vancouver, B.C. . . . 5-9/175. . . . Shoots left. . . . Full name: Norman Richard Foster.
COLLEGE: Michigan State.
TRANSACTIONS/CAREER NOTES: Selected by Boston Bruins in 11th round (11th Bruins pick, 222nd overall) of NHL entry draft (June 8, 1983). . . . Traded by Bruins to Edmonton Oilers for future considerations; Bruins received sixth-round pick in 1992 draft (C Jiri Dopita) to complete deal (September 10, 1991).
HONORS: Named to CCHA All-Star second team (1983-84). . . . Named to NCAA All-Tournament team (1985-86).

Season Team	League	REGULAR SEASON								PLAYOFFS						
		Gms.	Min.	W	L	T	GA	SO	Avg.	Gms.	Min.	W	L	GA	SO	Avg.
81-82—Penticton	BCJHL	21	1187	...	...	...	58	...	2.93	—	—	—	—	—	—	—
82-83—Penticton	BCJHL	33	1999	...	...	...	156	0	4.68	—	—	—	—	—	—	—

Season Team	League	REGULAR SEASON								PLAYOFFS						
		Gms.	Min.	W	L	T	GA	SO	Avg.	Gms.	Min.	W	L	GA	SO	Avg.
83-84—Michigan State	CCHA	32	1814	23	8	0	83	...	2.75	—	—	—	—	—	—	—
84-85—Michigan State	CCHA	26	1531	22	4	0	67	1	2.63	—	—	—	—	—	—	—
85-86—Michigan State	CCHA	24	1414	17	5	1	87	1	3.69	—	—	—	—	—	—	—
86-87—Michigan State	CCHA	24	1383	14	7	1	90	1	3.90	—	—	—	—	—	—	—
87-88—Milwaukee	IHL	38	2001	10	22	1	170	1	5.10	—	—	—	—	—	—	—
88-89—Maine	AHL	47	2411	16	17	6	156	1	3.88	—	—	—	—	—	—	—
89-90—Maine	AHL	*64	*3664	23	28	10	*217	3	3.55	—	—	—	—	—	—	—
90-91—Maine	AHL	2	122	1	1	0	7	0	3.44	—	—	—	—	—	—	—
—Cape Breton	AHL	40	2207	15	14	7	135	1	3.67	2	128	0	2	8	0	3.75
—Boston	NHL	3	184	2	1	0	14	0	4.57	—	—	—	—	—	—	—
91-92—Cape Breton	AHL	29	1699	15	13	1	119	0	4.20	3	193	1	2	14	0	4.35
—Edmonton	NHL	10	439	5	3	0	20	0	2.73	—	—	—	—	—	—	—
92-93—Cape Breton	AHL	10	560	5	5	0	53	0	5.68	—	—	—	—	—	—	—
—Kansas City	IHL	8	489	6	1	0	28	0	3.44	1	16	0	0	0	0	0.00
NHL totals		13	623	7	4	0	34	0	3.27							

FOUNTAIN, MIKE
G, CANUCKS

PERSONAL: Born January 26, 1972, at Gravenhurst, Ont. . . . 6-0/176. . . . Shoots left.
COLLEGE: Trent (Ont.).
TRANSACTIONS/CAREER NOTES: Selected by Vancouver Canucks in second round (third Canucks pick, 45th overall) of NHL entry draft (June 20, 1992).
HONORS: Named to Can.HL All-Star second team (1991-92). . . . Named to OHL All-Star first team (1991-92).

Season Team	League	REGULAR SEASON								PLAYOFFS						
		Gms.	Min.	W	L	T	GA	SO	Avg.	Gms.	Min.	W	L	GA	SO	Avg.
88-89—Huntsville Jr. C	OHA	22	1306	...	...	...	82	0	3.77	—	—	—	—	—	—	—
89-90—Chatham Jr. B	OHA	21	1249	...	...	...	76	0	3.65	—	—	—	—	—	—	—
90-91—Sault Ste. Marie	OHL	7	380	5	2	0	19	0	3.00	—	—	—	—	—	—	—
—Oshawa	OHL	30	1483	17	5	1	84	0	3.40	8	292	1	4	26	0	5.34
91-92—Oshawa	OHL	40	2260	18	13	6	149	1	3.96	7	428	3	4	26	0	3.64
92-93—Hamilton	AHL	12	618	2	8	0	46	0	4.47	—	—	—	—	—	—	—
—Can. national team	Int'l	13	45	7	5	1	37	1	2.98	—	—	—	—	—	—	—

FRANCIS, RON
C, PENGUINS

PERSONAL: Born March 1, 1963, at Sault Ste. Marie, Ont. . . . 6-2/200. . . . Shoots left. . . . Cousin of Mike Liut, goaltender, St. Louis Blues, Hartford Whalers and Washington Capitals (1979-80 through 1991-92) and Cincinnati Stingers of WHA (1977-78 and 1978-79).
TRANSACTIONS/CAREER NOTES: Selected by Hartford Whalers as underage junior in first round (first Whalers pick, fourth overall) of NHL entry draft (June 10, 1981). . . . Injured eye (January 27, 1982); missed three weeks. . . . Strained ligaments in right knee (November 30, 1983). . . . Broke left ankle (January 18, 1986); missed 27 games. . . . Broke left index finger (January 28, 1989); missed 11 games. . . . Broke nose (November 24, 1990). . . . Traded by Whalers with D Ulf Samuelsson and D Grant Jennings to Pittsburgh Penguins for C John Cullen, D Zarley Zalapski and RW Jeff Parker (March 4, 1991).
HONORS: Played in NHL All-Star Game (1983, 1985 and 1990).
MISCELLANEOUS: Member of Stanley Cup championship teams (1991 and 1992).

Season Team	League	REGULAR SEASON					PLAYOFFS				
		Gms.	G	A	Pts.	Pen.	Gms.	G	A	Pts.	Pen.
80-81—Sault Ste. Marie	OMJHL	64	26	43	69	33	19	7	8	15	34
81-82—Sault Ste. Marie	OHL	25	18	30	48	46	—	—	—	—	—
—Hartford	NHL	59	25	43	68	51	—	—	—	—	—
82-83—Hartford	NHL	79	31	59	90	60	—	—	—	—	—
83-84—Hartford	NHL	72	23	60	83	45	—	—	—	—	—
84-85—Hartford	NHL	80	24	57	81	66	—	—	—	—	—
85-86—Hartford	NHL	53	24	53	77	24	10	1	2	3	4
86-87—Hartford	NHL	75	30	63	93	45	6	2	2	4	6
87-88—Hartford	NHL	80	25	50	75	89	6	2	5	7	2
88-89—Hartford	NHL	69	29	48	77	36	4	0	2	2	0
89-90—Hartford	NHL	80	32	69	101	73	7	3	3	6	8
90-91—Hartford	NHL	67	21	55	76	51	—	—	—	—	—
—Pittsburgh	NHL	14	2	9	11	21	24	7	10	17	24
91-92—Pittsburgh	NHL	70	21	33	54	30	21	8	*19	27	6
92-93—Pittsburgh	NHL	84	24	76	100	68	12	6	11	17	19
NHL totals		882	311	675	986	659	90	29	54	83	69

FRASER, IAIN
C, ISLANDERS

PERSONAL: Born August 10, 1969, at Scarborough, Ont. . . . 5-10/184. . . . Shoots left.
TRANSACTIONS/CAREER NOTES: Selected by New York Islanders in 12th round (fourteenth Islanders pick, 233rd overall) of NHL entry draft (June 17, 1989).
HONORS: Won Leo LaLonde Memorial Trophy (1989-90). . . . Won Stafford Smythe Memorial Trophy (1989-90). . . . Named to Memorial Cup All-Star team (1989-90). . . . Named to AHL All-Star second team (1992-93).

Season Team	League	REGULAR SEASON					PLAYOFFS				
		Gms.	G	A	Pts.	Pen.	Gms.	G	A	Pts.	Pen.
86-87—Oshawa Jr. B	OHA	31	18	22	40	119	—	—	—	—	—
87-88—Oshawa	OHL	16	4	4	8	22	6	2	3	5	2
88-89—Oshawa	OHL	62	33	57	90	87	6	2	8	10	12

Season Team	League	REGULAR SEASON					PLAYOFFS				
		Gms.	G	A	Pts.	Pen.	Gms.	G	A	Pts.	Pen.
89-90—Oshawa	OHL	56	40	65	105	75	17	10	*22	32	8
90-91—Richmond	ECHL	3	1	1	2	0	—	—	—	—	—
—Capital District	AHL	32	5	13	18	16	—	—	—	—	—
91-92—Capital District	AHL	45	9	11	20	24	—	—	—	—	—
92-93—Capital District	AHL	74	41	69	110	16	4	0	1	1	0
—New York Islanders	NHL	7	2	2	4	2	—	—	—	—	—
NHL totals		7	2	2	4	2					

FRAWLEY, DANNY
RW, SABRES

PERSONAL: Born June 2, 1962, at Sturgeon Falls, Ont.... 6-0/193.... Shoots right.... Full name: William Daniel Frawley.
TRANSACTIONS/CAREER NOTES: Selected by Chicago Blackhawks as underage junior in 10th round (15th Blackhawks pick, 204th overall) of NHL entry draft (June 11, 1980). ... Selected by Pittsburgh Penguins in NHL waiver draft (October 7, 1985).... Underwent knee surgery (December 1987).... Signed as free agent by Buffalo Sabres (September 1990).

Season Team	League	REGULAR SEASON					PLAYOFFS				
		Gms.	G	A	Pts.	Pen.	Gms.	G	A	Pts.	Pen.
79-80—Sudbury	OMJHL	63	21	26	47	67	8	0	1	1	2
80-81—Cornwall	QMJHL	28	10	14	24	76	18	5	12	17	37
81-82—Cornwall	OHL	64	27	50	77	239	5	3	8	11	19
82-83—Springfield	AHL	80	30	27	57	107	—	—	—	—	—
83-84—Chicago	NHL	3	0	0	0	0	—	—	—	—	—
—Springfield	AHL	69	22	34	56	137	4	0	1	1	12
84-85—Milwaukee	IHL	26	11	12	23	125	—	—	—	—	—
—Chicago	NHL	30	4	3	7	64	1	0	0	0	0
85-86—Pittsburgh	NHL	69	10	11	21	174	—	—	—	—	—
86-87—Pittsburgh	NHL	78	14	14	28	218	—	—	—	—	—
87-88—Pittsburgh	NHL	47	6	8	14	152	—	—	—	—	—
88-89—Muskegon	IHL	24	12	16	28	35	14	6	4	10	31
—Pittsburgh	NHL	46	3	4	7	66	—	—	—	—	—
89-90—Muskegon	IHL	82	31	47	78	165	15	9	12	21	51
90-91—Rochester	AHL	74	15	31	46	152	14	4	7	11	34
91-92—Rochester	AHL	78	28	23	51	208	16	7	5	12	35
92-93—Rochester	AHL	75	17	27	44	216	17	1	7	8	70
NHL totals		273	37	40	77	674	1	0	0	0	0

FREER, MARK
C

PERSONAL: Born July 14, 1968, at Peterborough, Ont.... 5-10/180.... Shoots left.
HIGH SCHOOL: Crestwood (Peterborough, Ont.).
TRANSACTIONS/CAREER NOTES: Signed as free agent by Philadelphia Flyers (September 1986).... Selected by Ottawa Senators in NHL expansion draft (June 18, 1992).... Suffered charley horse (October 24, 1992); missed 14 games.

Season Team	League	REGULAR SEASON					PLAYOFFS				
		Gms.	G	A	Pts.	Pen.	Gms.	G	A	Pts.	Pen.
85-86—Peterborough	OHL	65	16	28	44	24	14	3	4	7	13
86-87—Peterborough	OHL	65	39	43	82	44	12	2	6	8	5
—Philadelphia	NHL	1	0	1	1	0	—	—	—	—	—
87-88—Philadelphia	NHL	1	0	0	0	0	—	—	—	—	—
—Peterborough	OHL	63	38	71	109	63	12	5	12	17	4
88-89—Philadelphia	NHL	5	0	1	1	0	—	—	—	—	—
—Hershey	AHL	75	30	49	79	77	12	4	6	10	2
89-90—Hershey	AHL	65	28	36	64	31	—	—	—	—	—
90-91—Hershey	AHL	77	18	44	62	45	7	1	3	4	17
91-92—Hershey	AHL	31	13	11	24	38	6	0	3	3	2
—Philadelphia	NHL	50	6	7	13	18	—	—	—	—	—
92-93—Ottawa	NHL	63	10	14	24	39	—	—	—	—	—
NHL totals		120	16	23	39	57					

FRENETTE, DEREK
LW, BLUES

PERSONAL: Born July 13, 1971, at Montreal.... 6-1/205.... Shoots left.
COLLEGE: Ferris State (Mich.).
TRANSACTIONS/CAREER NOTES: Selected by St. Louis Blues in sixth round (sixth Blues pick, 124th overall) of NHL entry draft (June 17, 1989).

Season Team	League	REGULAR SEASON					PLAYOFFS				
		Gms.	G	A	Pts.	Pen.	Gms.	G	A	Pts.	Pen.
88-89—Ferris State	CCHA	27	3	4	7	17	—	—	—	—	—
89-90—Ferris State	CCHA	29	1	4	5	48	—	—	—	—	—
90-91—Hull	QMJHL	66	27	42	69	72	6	4	3	7	12
—Peoria	IHL	—	—	—	—	—	6	0	0	0	0
91-92—Peoria	IHL	46	2	11	13	51	10	0	3	3	4
92-93—Peoria	IHL	73	18	19	37	44	4	1	2	3	2

FUHR, GRANT

G, SABRES

PERSONAL: Born September 28, 1962, at Spruce Grove, Alta. . . . 5-9/190. . . . Shoots right. . . . Name pronounced FYOOR.

TRANSACTIONS/CAREER NOTES: Selected by Edmonton Oilers in first round (first Oilers pick, eighth overall) of NHL entry draft (June 10, 1981). . . . Suffered partial separation of right shoulder (December 1981). . . . Strained left knee ligaments and underwent surgery (December 13, 1983). . . . Separated shoulder (February 1985). . . . Bruised left shoulder (November 3, 1985); missed 10 games. . . . Bruised left shoulder (November 1987). . . . Injured right knee (November 1987). . . . Suffered cervical neck strain (January 18, 1989). . . . Underwent appendectomy (September 14, 1989); missed first six games of season. . . . Underwent reconstructive surgery to left shoulder (December 27, 1989). . . . Tore adhesions in left shoulder (March 13, 1990). . . . Suspended six months by the NHL for admitting to using drugs earlier in career (September 27, 1990). . . . Traded by Oilers with RW/LW Glenn Anderson and LW Craig Berube to Toronto Maple Leafs for LW Vincent Damphousse, D Luke Richardson, G Peter Ing, C Scott Thornton and future considerations (September 19, 1991). . . . Sprained thumb (October 17, 1991); missed two games. . . . Pulled groin (November 12, 1991); missed three games. . . . Sprained knee (February 11, 1992); missed four games. . . . Sprained knee (October 20, 1992); missed 10 games. . . . Strained shoulder (December 5, 1992); missed three games. . . . Bruised shoulder muscle (January 17, 1993); missed four games. . . . Traded by Maple Leafs with conditional pick in 1995 draft to Buffalo Sabres for LW Dave Andreychuk, G Daren Puppa and first-round pick in 1993 draft (D Kenny Jonsson) (February 2, 1993).

HONORS: Won Stewart (Butch) Paul Memorial Trophy (1979-80). . . . Named to WHL All-Star first team (1979-80 and 1980-81). . . . Won Top Goaltender Trophy (1980-81). . . . Named to THE SPORTING NEWS All-Star second team (1981-82 and 1985-86). . . . Named to NHL All-Star second team (1981-82). . . . Played in NHL All-Star Game (1982, 1984 through 1986, 1988 and 1989). . . . Named All-Star Game Most Valuable Player (1986). . . . Won Vezina Trophy (1987-88). . . . Named to THE SPORTING NEWS All-Star first team (1987-88). . . . Named to NHL All-Star first team (1987-88).

RECORDS: Holds NHL single-season record for most points by a goaltender—14 (1983-84); and most games by a goaltender—75 (1987-88). . . . Shares NHL single-season playoff record for most wins by a goaltender—16 (1987-88).

MISCELLANEOUS: Member of Stanley Cup championship teams (1984, 1985, 1987, 1988 and 1990).

				REGULAR SEASON								**PLAYOFFS**					
Season	Team	League	Gms.	Min.	W	L	T	GA	SO	Avg.	Gms.	Min.	W	L	GA	SO	Avg.
79-80—Victoria		WHL	43	2488	30	12	0	130	2	3.14	8	465	5	3	22	0	2.84
80-81—Victoria		WHL	59	*3448	48	9	1	160	†4	*2.78	15	899	12	3	45	1	3.00
81-82—Edmonton		NHL	48	2847	28	5	14	157	0	3.31	5	309	2	3	26	0	5.05
82-83—Moncton		AHL	10	604	4	5	1	40	0	3.97	—	—	—	—	—	—	...
—Edmonton		NHL	32	1803	13	12	5	129	0	4.29	1	11	0	0	0	0	...
83-84—Edmonton		NHL	45	2625	30	10	4	171	1	3.91	16	883	11	4	44	1	2.99
84-85—Edmonton		NHL	46	2559	26	8	7	165	1	3.87	†18	*1064	*15	3	55	0	3.10
85-86—Edmonton		NHL	40	2184	29	8	0	143	0	3.93	9	541	5	4	28	0	3.11
86-87—Edmonton		NHL	44	2388	22	13	3	137	0	3.44	19	1148	14	5	47	0	2.46
87-88—Edmonton		NHL	*75	*4304	40	24	9	*246	†4	3.43	*19	*1136	*16	2	55	0	2.90
88-89—Edmonton		NHL	59	3341	23	26	6	213	1	3.83	7	417	3	4	24	1	3.45
89-90—Cape Breton		AHL	2	120	2	0	0	6	0	3.00	—	—	—	—	—	—	—
—Edmonton		NHL	21	1081	9	7	3	70	1	3.89	—	—	—	—	—	—	—
90-91—Cape Breton		AHL	4	240	2	2	0	17	0	4.25	—	—	—	—	—	—	—
—Edmonton		NHL	13	778	6	4	3	39	1	3.01	17	1019	8	7	51	0	3.00
91-92—Toronto		NHL	65	3774	25	*33	5	*230	2	3.66	—	—	—	—	—	—	—
92-93—Toronto		NHL	29	1665	13	9	4	87	1	3.14	—	—	—	—	—	—	—
—Buffalo		NHL	29	1694	11	15	2	98	0	3.47	8	474	3	4	27	1	3.42
NHL totals			546	31043	275	174	65	1885	12	3.64	119	7002	77	36	357	3	3.06

GAETZ, LINK

LW, SHARKS

PERSONAL: Born October 2, 1968, at Vancouver, B.C. . . . 6-2/223. . . . Shoots left. . . . Name pronounced GAYTZ.

TRANSACTIONS/CAREER NOTES: Suspended indefinitely by Spokane Chiefs (April 12, 1988). . . . Selected by Minnesota North Stars in second round (second North Stars pick, 40th overall) of NHL entry draft (June 11, 1988). . . . Suspended four games by IHL for high-sticking (January 23, 1989). . . . Suspended by North Stars for not reporting to Kansas City Blades (November 9, 1990). . . . Suspended by Blades for off-ice incident (February 5, 1991). . . . Entered in-patient alcohol abuse program (February 19, 1991). . . . Selected by San Jose Sharks in NHL dispersal draft (May 30, 1991). . . . Injured hand (October 5, 1991); missed four games. . . . Sprained knee (November 2, 1991); missed four games. . . . Suffered injuries from auto accident (April 2, 1992); missed first 62 games of 1992-93 season.

				REGULAR SEASON					**PLAYOFFS**			
Season	Team	League	Gms.	G	A	Pts.	Pen.	Gms.	G	A	Pts.	Pen.
85-86—Quesnel		PCJHL	15	0	7	7	4	—	—	—	—	—
86-87—New Westminster		WHL	44	2	7	9	52	—	—	—	—	—
—Merritt		BCJHL	7	4	2	6	27	—	—	—	—	—
—Delta		BCJHL	23	9	12	21	53	—	—	—	—	—
87-88—Spokane		WHL	59	9	20	29	313	10	2	2	4	70
88-89—Minnesota		NHL	12	0	2	2	53	—	—	—	—	—
—Kalamazoo		IHL	37	3	4	7	192	5	0	0	0	56
89-90—Kalamazoo		IHL	61	5	16	21	318	9	2	2	4	59
—Minnesota		NHL	5	0	0	0	33	—	—	—	—	—
90-91—Kalamazoo		IHL	9	0	1	1	44	—	—	—	—	—
—Kansas City		IHL	18	1	10	11	178	—	—	—	—	—
91-92—San Jose		NHL	48	6	6	12	326	—	—	—	—	—
92-93—Nashville		ECHL	3	1	0	1	10	—	—	—	—	—
—Kansas City		IHL	2	0	0	0	14	—	—	—	—	—
NHL totals			65	6	8	14	412					

FG

GAGE, JOAQUIN
G, OILERS

PERSONAL: Born October 19, 1973, at Vancouver, B.C.... 6-0/200.... Shoots left.... Name pronounced WOK-een.
COLLEGE: Portland (Ore.) Community College.
TRANSACTIONS/CAREER NOTES: Selected by Edmonton Oilers in fifth round (sixth Oilers pick, 109th overall) of NHL entry draft (June 20, 1992).

											REGULAR SEASON							PLAYOFFS	
Season	Team	League	Gms.	Min.	W	L	T	GA	SO	Avg.	Gms.	Min.	W	L	GA	SO	Avg.
90-91—Bellingham Jr. A		BCJHL	16	751	...	...	...	64	0	5.11	—	—	—	—	—	—	—
—Portland		WHL	3	180	0	3	0	17	0	5.67	—	—	—	—	—	—	—
91-92—Portland		WHL	63	3635	27	30	4	269	2	4.44	6	366	2	4	28	0	4.59
92-93—Portland		WHL	38	2302	21	16	1	153	2	3.99	8	427	5	2	30	0	4.22

GAGE, JODY
RW, SABRES

PERSONAL: Born November 29, 1959, at Toronto.... 6-0/190.... Shoots right.... Full name: Joseph William Gage.
TRANSACTIONS/CAREER NOTES: Selected by Detroit Red Wings in third round (second Detroit pick, 46th overall) of NHL entry draft (August 9, 1979).... Signed as free agent by Buffalo Sabres (August 1985).... Strained ankle and knee ligaments in preseason game (September 27, 1988); missed two months.
HONORS: Named to AHL All-Star first team (1985-86, 1987-88 and 1990-91).... Won Les Cunningham Plaque (1987-88).

			REGULAR SEASON					PLAYOFFS			
Season	Team	League	Gms.	G	A	Pts.	Pen.	Gms.	G	A	Pts.	Pen.
76-77—St. Catharines	OMJHL	47	13	20	33	2	—	—	—	—	—
77-78—Hamilton Fincups	OMJHL	32	15	18	33	19	—	—	—	—	—
—Kitchener	OMJHL	36	17	27	44	21	9	4	3	7	4
78-79—Kitchener	OMJHL	59	46	43	89	40	10	1	2	3	6
79-80—Adirondack	AHL	63	25	21	46	15	5	2	1	3	0
—Kalamazoo	IHL	14	17	12	29	0	—	—	—	—	—
80-81—Detroit	NHL	16	2	2	4	22	—	—	—	—	—
—Adirondack	AHL	59	17	31	48	44	17	9	6	15	12
81-82—Adirondack	AHL	47	21	20	41	21	—	—	—	—	—
—Detroit	NHL	31	9	10	19	2	—	—	—	—	—
82-83—Adirondack	AHL	65	23	30	53	33	6	1	5	6	8
83-84—Detroit	NHL	3	0	0	0	0	—	—	—	—	—
—Adirondack	AHL	73	40	32	72	32	6	3	4	7	2
84-85—Adirondack	AHL	78	27	33	60	55	—	—	—	—	—
85-86—Buffalo	NHL	7	3	2	5	0	—	—	—	—	—
—Rochester	AHL	73	42	57	99	56	—	—	—	—	—
86-87—Rochester	AHL	70	26	39	65	60	17	*14	5	19	24
87-88—Rochester	AHL	76	*60	44	104	46	5	2	5	7	10
—Buffalo	NHL	2	0	0	0	0	—	—	—	—	—
88-89—Rochester	AHL	65	31	38	69	50	—	—	—	—	—
89-90—Rochester	AHL	75	45	38	83	42	17	4	6	10	12
90-91—Rochester	AHL	73	42	43	85	34	15	6	10	16	14
91-92—Rochester	AHL	67	40	40	80	54	16	5	9	14	10
—Buffalo	NHL	9	0	1	1	2	—	—	—	—	—
92-93—Rochester	AHL	71	40	40	80	76	9	5	8	13	2
NHL totals		**68**	**14**	**15**	**29**	**26**					

GAGNER, DAVE
C, STARS

PERSONAL: Born December 11, 1964, at Chatham, Ont.... 5-10/188.... Shoots left.... Name pronounced GAN-yay.
TRANSACTIONS/CAREER NOTES: Selected by New York Rangers as underage junior in first round (first Rangers pick, 12th overall) of NHL entry draft (June 8, 1983).... Fractured ankle (February 5, 1986).... Underwent emergency appendectomy (December 1986).... Traded by Rangers with RW Jay Caufield to Minnesota North Stars for D Jari Gronstrad and D Paul Boutilier (October 8, 1987).... Broke kneecap (March 31, 1989).... Underwent surgery to left knee cartilage (November 11, 1990).... Underwent arthroscopic knee surgery (December 18, 1991); missed one game.... Hyperextended knee (March 17, 1992); missed one game.... North Stars franchise moved from Minnesota to Dallas and renamed Stars for 1993-94 season.
HONORS: Won Bobby Smith Trophy (1982-83).... Named to OHL All-Star second team (1982-83).... Played in NHL All-Star Game (1991).
RECORDS: Shares NHL single-game playoff record for most points in one period—4 (April 8, 1991, first period.).

			REGULAR SEASON					PLAYOFFS			
Season	Team	League	Gms.	G	A	Pts.	Pen.	Gms.	G	A	Pts.	Pen.
81-82—Brantford	OHL	68	30	46	76	31	11	3	6	9	6
82-83—Brantford	OHL	70	55	66	121	57	8	5	5	10	4
83-84—Canadian Olympic Team	Int'l	50	19	18	37	26	—	—	—	—	—
—Brantford	OHL	12	7	13	20	4	6	0	4	4	6
84-85—New Haven	AHL	38	13	20	33	23	—	—	—	—	—
—New York Rangers	NHL	38	6	6	12	16	—	—	—	—	—
85-86—New York Rangers	NHL	32	4	6	10	19	—	—	—	—	—
—New Haven	AHL	16	10	11	21	11	4	1	2	3	2
86-87—New York Rangers	NHL	10	1	4	5	12	—	—	—	—	—
—New Haven	AHL	56	22	41	63	50	7	1	5	6	18
87-88—Kalamazoo	IHL	14	16	10	26	26	—	—	—	—	—
—Minnesota	NHL	51	8	11	19	55	—	—	—	—	—
88-89—Minnesota	NHL	75	35	43	78	104	—	—	—	—	—
—Kalamazoo	IHL	1	0	1	1	4					

G

Season Team	League	REGULAR SEASON Gms.	G	A	Pts.	Pen.	PLAYOFFS Gms.	G	A	Pts.	Pen.
89-90—Minnesota	NHL	79	40	38	78	54	7	2	3	5	16
90-91—Minnesota	NHL	73	40	42	82	114	23	12	15	27	28
91-92—Minnesota	NHL	78	31	40	71	107	7	2	4	6	8
92-93—Minnesota	NHL	84	33	43	76	143	—	—	—	—	—
NHL totals		520	198	233	431	624	37	16	22	38	52

GAGNON, DAVE
G, RED WINGS

PERSONAL: Born October 31, 1967, at Windsor, Ont. . . . 6-0/185. . . . Shoots left. . . . Full name: David Anthony Gagnon.
COLLEGE: Colgate.
TRANSACTIONS/CAREER NOTES: Signed as free agent by Detroit Red Wings (June 11, 1990). . . . Injured hamstring (December 1, 1991).
HONORS: Named ECAC Player of the Year (1989-90). . . . Named to NCAA All-America East first team (1989-90). . . . Named to ECAC All-Star first team (1989-90). . . . Named to ECAC All-Tournament team (1989-90). . . . Won ECHL Playoff Most Valuable Player Award (1990-91).

Season Team	League	REGULAR SEASON Gms.	Min.	W	L	T	GA	SO	Avg.	PLAYOFFS Gms.	Min.	W	L	GA	SO	Avg.
87-88—Colgate University	ECAC	13	743	6	4	2	43	1	3.47	—	—	—	—	—	—	—
88-89—Colgate University	ECAC	28	1622	17	9	2	102	0	3.77	—	—	—	—	—	—	—
89-90—Colgate University	ECAC	33	1986	28	3	1	93	0	2.81	—	—	—	—	—	—	—
90-91—Detroit	NHL	2	35	0	1	0	6	0	10.29	—	—	—	—	—	—	—
—Adirondack	AHL	24	1356	7	8	5	94	0	4.16	—	—	—	—	—	—	—
—Hampton Roads	ECHL	10	606	7	1	2	26	2	2.57	11	696	*10	1	27	0	*2.33
91-92—Toledo	ECHL	7	354	4	2	0	18	0	3.05	—	—	—	—	—	—	—
—Fort Wayne	IHL	2	125	2	0	0	7	0	3.36	—	—	—	—	—	—	—
92-93—Fort Wayne	IHL	31	1771	15	11	0	116	0	3.93	1	60	0	0	0	0	...
—Adirondack	AHL	1	60	0	1	0	5	0	5.00	—	—	—	—	—	—	—
NHL totals		2	35	0	1	0	6	0	10.29							

GAGNON, JOEL
G, MIGHTY DUCKS

PERSONAL: Born March 14, 1975, at Hearst, Ont. . . . 6-0/194. . . . Shoots left.
TRANSACTIONS/CAREER NOTES: Selected by Mighty Ducks of Anaheim in fourth round (fourth Mighty Ducks pick, 82nd overall) of NHL entry draft (June 26, 1993).

Season Team	League	REGULAR SEASON Gms.	Min.	W	L	T	GA	SO	Avg.	PLAYOFFS Gms.	Min.	W	L	GA	SO	Avg.
92-93—Oshawa	OHL	48	2248	...	...	...	159	0	4.24	7	285	...	...	21	0	4.42

GALANOV, MAXIM
D, RANGERS

PERSONAL: Born March 13, 1974, at Krasnoyarsk, U.S.S.R. . . . 6-1/167. . . . Shoots left.
TRANSACTIONS/CAREER NOTES: Selected by New York Rangers in third round (third Rangers pick, 61st overall) of NHL entry draft (June 26, 1993).

Season Team	League	REGULAR SEASON Gms.	G	A	Pts.	Pen.	PLAYOFFS Gms.	G	A	Pts.	Pen.
92-93—Lada Togliatti	CIS	41	4	2	6	12	10	1	1	2	12

GALLANT, GERARD
LW, LIGHTNING

PERSONAL: Born September 2, 1963, at Summerside, P.E.I. . . . 5-10/190. . . . Shoots left.
TRANSACTIONS/CAREER NOTES: Selected by Detroit Red Wings in sixth round (fourth Red Wings pick, 107th overall) of NHL entry draft (June 10, 1981). . . . Broke jaw (December 11, 1985); missed 25 games. . . . Fined $500 by NHL for stick-swinging incident (April 8, 1989). . . . Suspended five games by NHL for slashing (October 7, 1989). . . . Suspended three games by NHL for hitting linesman (January 13, 1990). . . . Suffered sore back (November 1990); missed eight games. . . . Suffered back spasms (December 1990); missed 18 games. . . . Underwent surgery to remove bone spur in back (March 14, 1991); missed remainder of season. . . . Injured hand (February 1992); missed five games. . . . Strained back (March 20, 1992); missed five games. . . . Injured hip (December 15, 1992); missed three games. . . . Suffered from the flu (January 17, 1993); missed one game. . . . Signed as free agent by Tampa Bay Lightning (July 21, 1993).
HONORS: Named to NHL All-Star second team (1988-89).

Season Team	League	REGULAR SEASON Gms.	G	A	Pts.	Pen.	PLAYOFFS Gms.	G	A	Pts.	Pen.
79-80—Summerside	PEIHA	45	60	55	115	90	—	—	—	—	—
80-81—Sherbrooke	QMJHL	68	41	60	101	220	14	6	13	19	46
81-82—Sherbrooke	QMJHL	58	34	58	92	260	22	14	24	38	84
82-83—St. Jean	QMJHL	33	28	25	53	139	—	—	—	—	—
—Verdun	QMJHL	29	26	49	75	105	15	†14	19	33	*84
83-84—Adirondack	AHL	77	31	33	64	195	7	1	3	4	34
84-85—Adirondack	AHL	46	18	29	47	131	—	—	—	—	—
—Detroit	NHL	32	6	12	18	66	3	0	0	0	11
85-86—Detroit	NHL	52	20	19	39	106	—	—	—	—	—
86-87—Detroit	NHL	80	38	34	72	216	16	8	6	14	43
87-88—Detroit	NHL	73	34	39	73	242	16	6	9	15	55
88-89—Detroit	NHL	76	39	54	93	230	6	1	2	3	40
89-90—Detroit	NHL	69	36	44	80	254	—	—	—	—	—
90-91—Detroit	NHL	45	10	16	26	111					

G

Season	Team	League	REGULAR SEASON					PLAYOFFS				
			Gms.	G	A	Pts.	Pen.	Gms.	G	A	Pts.	Pen.
91-92—Detroit		NHL	69	14	22	36	187	11	2	2	4	25
92-93—Detroit		NHL	67	10	20	30	188	6	1	2	3	4
NHL totals			563	207	260	467	1600	58	18	21	39	178

GALLEY, GARRY
D, FLYERS

PERSONAL: Born April 16, 1963, at Ottawa.... 6-0/190.... Shoots left.
COLLEGE: Bowling Green State.
TRANSACTIONS/CAREER NOTES: Selected by Los Angeles Kings in fifth round (fourth Kings pick, 100th overall) of NHL entry draft (June 8, 1983).... Injured knee (December 8, 1985).... Traded by Kings to Washington Capitals for G Al Jensen (February 14, 1987).... Signed as free agent by Boston Bruins with Capitals getting third-round pick in 1989 draft as compensation (July 8, 1988).... Sprained left shoulder (September 30, 1989); missed first nine games of season.... Suffered lacerations to cheek, both lips and part of his neck (October 6, 1990).... Dislocated right shoulder (December 22, 1990).... Bruised left kneecap (March 23, 1991); missed two games. ... Pulled hamstring (April 17, 1991); missed three playoff games.... Traded by Bruins with C Wes Walz and future considerations to Philadelphia Flyers for D Gord Murphy, RW Brian Dobbin and third-round pick in 1992 draft (LW Sergei Zholtok) (January 2, 1992).... Bruised ribs (January 9, 1992); missed one game.... Fractured foot (March 3, 1992); missed two games.... Bruised jaw (February 24, 1993); missed one game.
HONORS: Named to CCHA All-Star first team (1982-83 and 1983-84).... Named to NCAA All-Tournament team (1983-84). ... Played in NHL All-Star Game (1991).

Season	Team	League	REGULAR SEASON					PLAYOFFS				
			Gms.	G	A	Pts.	Pen.	Gms.	G	A	Pts.	Pen.
81-82—Bowling Green State		CCHA	42	3	36	39	48	—	—	—	—	—
82-83—Bowling Green State		CCHA	40	17	29	46	40	—	—	—	—	—
83-84—Bowling Green State		CCHA	44	15	52	67	61	—	—	—	—	—
84-85—Los Angeles		NHL	78	8	30	38	82	3	1	0	1	2
85-86—Los Angeles		NHL	49	9	13	22	46	—	—	—	—	—
—New Haven		AHL	4	2	6	8	6	—	—	—	—	—
86-87—Los Angeles		NHL	30	5	11	16	57	—	—	—	—	—
—Washington		NHL	18	1	10	11	10	2	0	0	0	0
87-88—Washington		NHL	58	7	23	30	44	13	2	4	6	13
88-89—Boston		NHL	78	8	21	29	80	9	0	1	1	33
89-90—Boston		NHL	71	8	27	35	75	21	3	3	6	34
90-91—Boston		NHL	70	6	21	27	84	16	1	5	6	17
91-92—Boston		NHL	38	2	12	14	83	—	—	—	—	—
—Philadelphia		NHL	39	3	15	18	34	—	—	—	—	—
92-93—Philadelphia		NHL	83	13	49	62	115	—	—	—	—	—
NHL totals			612	70	232	302	710	64	7	13	20	99

GAMBLE, TROY
G, CANUCKS

PERSONAL: Born April 7, 1967, at New Glasgow, N.S.... 5-11/195.... Shoots left.
TRANSACTIONS/CAREER NOTES: Selected by Vancouver Canucks as underage junior in second round (second Canucks pick, 25th overall) of NHL entry draft (June 15, 1985).... Traded by Medicine Hat Tigers with D Kevin Ekdahl to Spokane Chiefs for D Keith Van Rooyen, RW Kirby Lindal and RW Rocky Dundas (December 1986).
HONORS: Won Top Goaltender Trophy (1984-85).... Named to WHL All-Star first team (1984-85 and 1987-88).... Won Del Wilson Trophy (1987-88).

Season	Team	League	REGULAR SEASON							PLAYOFFS						
			Gms.	Min.	W	L	T	GA	SO	Avg.	Gms.	Min.	W	L	GA	SO	Avg.
83-84—Hobbema		AJHL	22	1102	...	...	...	90	0	4.90	—						
84-85—Medicine Hat		WHL	37	2095	27	6	2	100	*3	*2.86	2	120	1	1	9	0	4.50
85-86—Medicine Hat		WHL	45	2264	28	11	0	142	0	3.76	11	530	5	4	31	0	3.51
86-87—Medicine Hat		WHL	11	646	7	3	0	46	0	4.27	—						
—Spokane		WHL	38	2157	17	17	1	163	0	4.53	5	298	0	5	35	0	7.05
—Vancouver		NHL	1	60	0	1	0	4	0	4.00	—						
87-88—Spokane		WHL	*67	*3824	35	26	1	235	0	3.69	15	875	7	8	56	†1	3.84
88-89—Vancouver		NHL	5	302	2	3	0	12	0	2.38	—						
—Milwaukee		IHL	42	2198	23	9	0	138	0	3.77	11	640	5	5	35	0	3.28
89-90—Milwaukee		IHL	*56	3033	22	21	4	*213	2	4.21	—						
90-91—Vancouver		NHL	47	2433	16	16	6	140	1	3.45	4	249	1	3	16	0	3.86
91-92—Vancouver		NHL	19	1009	4	9	3	73	0	4.34	—						
—Milwaukee		IHL	9	521	2	4	2	31	0	3.57	—						
92-93—Hamilton		AHL	14	769	1	10	2	62	0	4.84	—						
—Cincinnati		IHL	33	1762	11	18	0	134	0	4.56	—						
NHL totals			72	3804	22	29	9	229	1	3.61	4	249	1	3	16	0	3.86

GANCHAR, PERRY
RW, PENGUINS

PERSONAL: Born October 28, 1963, at Saskatoon, Sask.... 5-9/188.... Shoots right.
TRANSACTIONS/CAREER NOTES: Selected by St. Louis Blues as underage junior in sixth round (third Blues pick, 113th overall) of NHL entry draft (June 9, 1982).... Traded by Blues to Montreal Canadiens for C/LW Ron Flockhart (August 26, 1985).... Traded by Canadiens to Pittsburgh Penguins for future considerations (December 17, 1987).... Injured knee (January 1988).
HONORS: Named to IHL All-Star second team (1984-85).

Season	Team	League	Gms.	G	A	Pts.	Pen.	Gms.	G	A	Pts.	Pen.
77-78—Saskatoon		WCHL	4	2	0	2	2	—	—	—	—	—
78-79—Saskatoon		WHL	14	5	3	8	15	—	—	—	—	—
—Saskatoon		SJHL	50	21	33	54	72	—	—	—	—	—
79-80—Saskatoon		WHL	70	41	24	65	116	—	—	—	—	—
80-81—Saskatoon		WHL	68	36	20	56	195	—	—	—	—	—
81-82—Saskatoon		WHL	53	38	52	90	82	5	3	3	6	17
82-83—Saskatoon		WHL	68	68	48	116	105	6	1	4	5	24
—Salt Lake City		IHL	—	—	—	—	—	1	0	1	1	0
83-84—Montana		CHL	59	23	22	45	77	—	—	—	—	—
—St. Louis		NHL	1	0	0	0	0	7	3	1	4	0
84-85—Peoria		IHL	63	41	29	70	114	20	4	11	15	49
—St. Louis		NHL	7	0	2	2	0	—	—	—	—	—
85-86—Sherbrooke		AHL	75	25	29	54	42	—	—	—	—	—
86-87—Sherbrooke		AHL	68	22	29	51	64	17	9	8	17	37
87-88—Sherbrooke		AHL	28	12	18	30	61	—	—	—	—	—
—Montreal		NHL	1	1	0	1	0	—	—	—	—	—
—Pittsburgh		NHL	30	2	5	7	36	—	—	—	—	—
88-89—Pittsburgh		NHL	3	0	0	0	0	—	—	—	—	—
—Muskegon		IHL	70	39	34	73	114	14	7	8	15	6
89-90—Muskegon		IHL	70	40	45	85	111	14	3	5	8	27
90-91—Muskegon		IHL	80	37	38	75	87	5	2	1	3	0
91-92—Muskegon		IHL	65	29	20	49	65	14	9	9	18	18
92-93—Cleveland		IHL	79	37	37	74	156	3	0	0	0	4
NHL totals			42	3	7	10	36	7	3	1	4	0

GARBUTT, MURRAY
C/LW, NORDIQUES

PERSONAL: Born July 29, 1971, at Hanna, Alta. . . . 6-1/205. . . . Shoots left.
TRANSACTIONS/CAREER NOTES: Selected by Minnesota North Stars in third round (third North Stars pick, 60th overall) of NHL entry draft (June 17, 1989). . . . Became property of San Jose Sharks as part of ownership change with Minnesota North Stars (September 1990). . . . Traded by Sharks to Quebec Nordiques for LW Don Barber (March 7, 1992). . . . Suspended by Nordiques prior to 1992-93 season for personal problems.

Season	Team	League	Gms.	G	A	Pts.	Pen.	Gms.	G	A	Pts.	Pen.
87-88—Medicine Hat		WHL	9	2	1	3	15	16	0	1	1	15
88-89—Medicine Hat		WHL	64	14	24	38	145	3	1	0	1	6
89-90—Medicine Hat		WHL	72	38	27	65	221	3	1	0	1	21
90-91—Medicine Hat		WHL	30	15	26	41	97	—	—	—	—	—
—Spokane		WHL	31	17	19	36	90	15	4	8	12	44
91-92—Kansas City		IHL	25	2	6	8	19	—	—	—	—	—
92-93—Quebec		NHL						Did not play.				

GARPENLOV, JOHAN
LW, SHARKS

PERSONAL: Born March 21, 1968, at Stockholm, Sweden. . . . 5-11/185. . . . Shoots left. . . . Name pronounced YOH-hahn GAHR-puhn-lahf.
TRANSACTIONS/CAREER NOTES: Selected by Detroit Red Wings in fifth round (fifth Red Wings pick, 85th overall) of NHL entry draft (June 9, 1984). . . . Traded by Red Wings to San Jose Sharks for D Bob McGill and eighth-round pick in 1992 draft (G C.J. Denomme) previously acquired from Vancouver Canucks (March 10, 1992). . . . Strained back (October 20, 1992); missed three games. . . . Suffered from the flu (March 25, 1993); missed one game.

Season	Team	League	Gms.	G	A	Pts.	Pen.	Gms.	G	A	Pts.	Pen.
86-87—Djurgarden		Sweden	29	5	8	13	20	—	—	—	—	—
87-88—Djurgarden		Sweden	30	7	10	17	12	—	—	—	—	—
88-89—Djurgarden		Sweden	36	12	19	31	20	—	—	—	—	—
89-90—Djurgarden		Sweden	39	20	13	33	36	8	2	4	6	4
90-91—Detroit		NHL	71	18	22	40	18	6	0	1	1	4
91-92—Detroit		NHL	16	1	1	2	4	—	—	—	—	—
—Adirondack		AHL	9	3	3	6	6	—	—	—	—	—
—San Jose		NHL	12	5	6	11	4	—	—	—	—	—
92-93—San Jose		NHL	79	22	44	66	56	—	—	—	—	—
NHL totals			178	46	73	119	82	6	0	1	1	4

G

GARTNER, MIKE
RW, RANGERS

PERSONAL: Born October 29, 1959, at Ottawa. . . . 6-0/188. . . . Shoots right. . . . Full name: Michael Alfred Gartner.
TRANSACTIONS/CAREER NOTES: Signed as underage junior by Cincinnati Stingers (August 1978). . . . Selected by Washington Capitals in first round (first Capitals pick, fourth overall) of NHL entry draft (August 9, 1979). . . . Injured eye (February 1983). . . . Underwent arthroscopic surgery to repair torn cartilage in left knee (March 1986). . . . Sprained right knee (November 1988). . . . Traded by Capitals with D Larry Murphy to Minnesota North Stars for RW Dino Ciccarelli and D Bob Rouse (March 7, 1989). . . . Underwent surgery to repair cartilage in left knee (April 14, 1989). . . . Traded by North Stars to New York Rangers for C Ulf Dahlen, fourth-round pick in 1990 draft and future considerations (March 6, 1990).
HONORS: Won Emms Family Award (1976-77). . . . Named to OMJHL All-Star first team (1977-78). . . . Played in NHL All-Star Game (1980, 1985, 1986, 1988, 1990 and 1993). . . . Named All-Star Game Most Valuable Player (1993).
RECORDS: Holds NHL career record for most consecutive 30-goal seasons—14 (1979-80 through 1992-93).

Season	Team	League	Gms.	G	A	Pts.	Pen.	Gms.	G	A	Pts.	Pen.
75-76—St. Catharines	OHA Mj. Jr. A	3	1	3	4	0	—	—	—	—	—
76-77—Niagara Falls	OMJHL	62	33	42	75	125	—	—	—	—	—
77-78—Niagara Falls	OMJHL	64	41	49	90	56	—	—	—	—	—
78-79—Cincinnati	WHA	78	27	25	52	123	3	0	2	2	2
79-80—Washington	NHL	77	36	32	68	66	—	—	—	—	—
80-81—Washington	NHL	80	48	46	94	100	—	—	—	—	—
81-82—Washington	NHL	80	35	45	80	121	—	—	—	—	—
82-83—Washington	NHL	73	38	38	76	54	4	0	0	0	4
83-84—Washington	NHL	80	40	45	85	90	8	3	7	10	16
84-85—Washington	NHL	80	50	52	102	71	5	4	3	7	9
85-86—Washington	NHL	74	35	40	75	63	9	2	10	12	4
86-87—Washington	NHL	78	41	32	73	61	7	4	3	7	14
87-88—Washington	NHL	80	48	33	81	73	14	3	4	7	14
88-89—Washington	NHL	56	26	29	55	71	—	—	—	—	—
—Minnesota	NHL	13	7	7	14	2	5	0	0	0	0
89-90—Minnesota	NHL	67	34	36	70	32	—	—	—	—	—
—New York Rangers	NHL	12	11	5	16	6	10	5	3	8	12
90-91—New York Rangers	NHL	79	49	20	69	53	6	1	1	2	0
91-92—New York Rangers	NHL	76	40	41	81	55	13	8	8	16	4
92-93—New York Rangers	NHL	84	45	23	68	59	—	—	—	—	—
WHA totals			78	27	25	52	123	3	0	2	2	2
NHL totals			1089	583	524	1107	977	81	30	39	69	77

GAUDREAU, ROB
RW, SHARKS

PERSONAL: Born January 20, 1970, at Cranston, R.I. . . . . 5-11/185. . . . Shoots right. . . . Full name: Robert Rene Gaudreau. . . . Name pronounced GUD-roh.
HIGH SCHOOL: Bishop Hendricken (Warwick, R.I.).
COLLEGE: Providence.
TRANSACTIONS/CAREER NOTES: Separated shoulder (February 1987). . . . Selected by Pittsburgh Penguins in ninth round (eighth Penguins pick, 127th overall) of NHL entry draft (June 11, 1988). . . . Traded by Penguins to Minnesota North Stars for C Richard Zemlak (November 1, 1988). . . . Selected by San Jose Sharks in NHL dispersal draft (May 30, 1991). . . . Bruised hand (March 21, 1993); missed one game.
HONORS: Named Hockey East co-Rookie of the Year with Scott Pellerin (1988-89). . . . Named to Hockey East All-Rookie team (1988-89). . . . Named to Hockey East All-Star second team (1990-91). . . . Named to NCAA All-America East second team (1991-92). . . . Named to Hockey East All-Star first team (1991-92).

Season	Team	League	Gms.	G	A	Pts.	Pen.	Gms.	G	A	Pts.	Pen.
86-87—Bishop Hendricken	R.I.H.S.	33	41	39	80	. . .	—	—	—	—	—
87-88—Bishop Hendricken	R.I.H.S.	. . .	52	60	112	. . .	—	—	—	—	—
88-89—Providence College	Hockey East	42	28	29	57	32	—	—	—	—	—
89-90—Providence College	Hockey East	32	20	18	38	12	—	—	—	—	—
90-91—Providence College	Hockey East	36	34	27	61	20	—	—	—	—	—
91-92—Providence College	Hockey East	36	21	34	55	22	—	—	—	—	—
92-93—Kansas City	IHL	19	8	6	14	6	—	—	—	—	—
—San Jose	NHL	59	23	20	43	18	—	—	—	—	—
NHL totals			59	23	20	43	18	—	—	—	—	—

GAUTHIER, DANIEL
C, PANTHERS

PERSONAL: Born May 17, 1970, at Charlemagne, Que. . . . 6-2/192. . . . Shoots left.
TRANSACTIONS/CAREER NOTES: Selected by Pittsburgh Penguins in third round (third Penguins pick, 62nd overall) of NHL entry draft (June 11, 1988). . . . Left Victoriaville (January 2, 1990); returned (January 16, 1990). . . . Signed as free agent by Florida Panthers (July 27, 1993).
HONORS: Won ECHL Rookie of the Year Award (1990-91). . . . Named to ECHL All-Star first team (1990-91).

Season	Team	League	Gms.	G	A	Pts.	Pen.	Gms.	G	A	Pts.	Pen.
86-87—Longueuil	QMJHL	64	23	22	45	23	18	4	5	9	15
87-88—Victoriaville	QMJHL	66	43	47	90	53	5	2	1	3	0
88-89—Victoriaville	QMJHL	64	41	75	116	84	16	12	17	29	30
89-90—Victoriaville	QMJHL	62	45	69	114	32	16	8	*19	27	16
90-91—Albany	IHL	1	1	0	1	0	—	—	—	—	—
—Knoxville	ECHL	61	41	*93	134	40	2	0	4	4	4
91-92—Muskegon	IHL	68	19	18	37	28	9	3	6	9	8
92-93—Cleveland	IHL	80	40	66	106	88	4	2	2	4	14

GAUTHIER, LUC
D, CANADIENS

PERSONAL: Born April 19, 1964, at Longueuil, Que. . . . 5-9/195. . . . Shoots left.
TRANSACTIONS/CAREER NOTES: Signed as free agent by Montreal Canadiens (October 7, 1986). . . . Broke ankle (October 1987).

Season	Team	League	Gms.	G	A	Pts.	Pen.	Gms.	G	A	Pts.	Pen.
82-83—Longueuil	QMJHL	67	3	18	21	132	—	—	—	—	—
83-84—Longueuil	QMJHL	70	8	54	62	207	—	—	—	—	—
84-85—Longueuil	QMJHL	60	13	47	60	111	—	—	—	—	—
—Flint	IHL	21	1	0	1	20	—	—	—	—	—

G

			REGULAR SEASON					PLAYOFFS				
Season	Team	League	Gms.	G	A	Pts.	Pen.	Gms.	G	A	Pts.	Pen.
85-86—Saginaw		IHL	66	9	29	38	165	—	—	—	—	—
86-87—Sherbrooke		AHL	78	5	17	22	81	17	2	4	6	31
87-88—Sherbrooke		AHL	61	4	10	14	105	6	0	0	0	18
88-89—Sherbrooke		AHL	77	8	20	28	178	6	0	0	0	10
89-90—Sherbrooke		AHL	79	3	23	26	139	12	0	4	4	35
90-91—Fredericton		AHL	69	7	20	27	238	9	1	1	2	10
—Montreal		NHL	3	0	0	0	2	—	—	—	—	—
91-92—Fredericton		AHL	80	4	14	18	252	7	1	1	2	26
92-93—Fredericton		AHL	78	9	33	42	167	5	2	1	3	20
NHL totals			3	0	0	0	2					

GAUTHIER, SEAN
G, JETS

PERSONAL: Born March 28, 1971, at Sudbury, Ont. . . . 5-11/194. . . . Name pronounced GO-chay.
TRANSACTIONS/CAREER NOTES: Selected by Winnipeg Jets in ninth round (seventh Jets pick, 181st overall) of NHL entry draft (June 22, 1991).
HONORS: Shared Dave Pinkney Trophy with Jeff Wilson (1992-93).

			REGULAR SEASON							PLAYOFFS				
Season	Team	League	Gms.	Min.	W	L	T	GA	SO	Avg.	Gms.	Min.	W	L	GA	SO	Avg.
91-92—Fort Wayne	IHL	18	978	10	4	2	59	1	3.62	2	48	. . .	. . .	7	0	8.75
—Moncton	AHL	25	1415	8	10	5	88	1	3.73	2	26	. . .	. . .	2	0	4.62
92-93—Moncton	AHL	38	2196	10	16	9	145	0	3.96	2	75	0	1	6	0	4.80

GAVEY, AARON
C, LIGHTNING

PERSONAL: Born February 22, 1974, at Sudbury, Ont. . . . 6-1/169. . . . Shoots left.
TRANSACTIONS/CAREER NOTES: Selected by Tampa Bay Lightning in fourth round (fourth Lightning pick, 74th overall) of NHL entry draft (June 20, 1992).

			REGULAR SEASON					PLAYOFFS				
Season	Team	League	Gms.	G	A	Pts.	Pen.	Gms.	G	A	Pts.	Pen.
90-91—Peterborough Jr. B	OHA	42	26	30	56	68	—	—	—	—	—
91-92—Sault Ste. Marie	OHL	48	7	11	18	27	19	5	1	6	10
92-93—Sault Ste. Marie	OHL	62	45	39	84	114	18	5	9	14	36

GAVIN, STEWART
RW, STARS

PERSONAL: Born March 15, 1960, at Ottawa. . . . 6-0/190. . . . Shoots left. . . . Full name: Robert Stewart Gavin.
TRANSACTIONS/CAREER NOTES: Selected by Toronto Maple Leafs in fourth round (fourth Maple Leafs pick, 74th overall) of NHL entry draft (June 11, 1980). . . . Separated shoulder (October 1981). . . . Reinjured shoulder (December 1981). . . . Sprained ankle (October 1982). . . . Traded by Maple Leafs to Hartford Whalers for D Chris Kotsopoulos (October 7, 1985). . . . Strained ligaments in right ankle (December 8, 1987); missed 22 games. . . . Selected by Minnesota North Stars in NHL waiver draft for $7,500 (October 3, 1988). . . . Broke cheekbone (December 13, 1988). . . . Tore medial collateral ligament in left knee (November 4, 1990); missed 19 games. . . . Strained lower back (December 1990). . . . Resprained left knee ligament (January 13, 1991); missed 13 games. . . . Reaggravated left knee ligament injury (February 14, 1991); missed six games. . . . Injured groin (November 23, 1991); missed 44 games. . . . Pulled groin (October 18, 1992); missed five games. . . . Suffered from the flu (February 4, 1993); missed two games. . . . Sprained knee (April 4, 1993); missed remainder of season. . . . North Stars franchise moved from Minnesota to Dallas and renamed Stars for 1993-94 season.

			REGULAR SEASON					PLAYOFFS				
Season	Team	League	Gms.	G	A	Pts.	Pen.	Gms.	G	A	Pts.	Pen.
76-77—Ottawa	OMJHL	1	0	0	0	0	—	—	—	—	—
77-78—Toronto	OMJHL	67	16	24	40	19	—	—	—	—	—
78-79—Toronto	OMJHL	61	24	25	49	83	3	1	0	1	0
79-80—Toronto	OMJHL	66	27	30	57	52	4	1	1	2	2
80-81—Toronto	NHL	14	1	2	3	13	—	—	—	—	—
—New Brunswick	AHL	46	7	12	19	42	13	1	0	1	2
81-82—Toronto	NHL	38	5	6	11	29	—	—	—	—	—
82-83—St. Catharines	AHL	6	2	4	6	17	—	—	—	—	—
—Toronto	NHL	63	6	5	11	44	4	0	0	0	0
83-84—Toronto	NHL	80	10	22	32	90	—	—	—	—	—
84-85—Toronto	NHL	73	12	13	25	38	—	—	—	—	—
85-86—Hartford	NHL	76	26	29	55	51	10	4	1	5	13
86-87—Hartford	NHL	79	20	22	42	28	6	2	4	6	10
87-88—Hartford	NHL	56	11	10	21	59	6	2	2	4	4
88-89—Minnesota	NHL	73	8	18	26	34	5	3	1	4	10
89-90—Minnesota	NHL	80	12	13	25	76	7	0	2	2	12
90-91—Minnesota	NHL	38	4	4	8	36	21	3	10	13	20
91-92—Minnesota	NHL	35	5	4	9	27	7	0	0	0	6
92-93—Minnesota	NHL	63	10	8	18	59	—	—	—	—	—
NHL totals			768	130	156	286	584	66	14	20	34	75

GELINAS, MARTIN
LW, NORDIQUES

PERSONAL: Born June 5, 1970, at Shawinigan, Que. . . . 5-11/195. . . . Shoots left. . . . Name pronounced mahr-TAI JEL-in-uh.
HIGH SCHOOL: Polyvalente Val-Maurice (Shawinigan, Que.).
TRANSACTIONS/CAREER NOTES: Broke left clavicle (November 1983). . . . Suffered hair-

G

line fracture of clavicle (July 1986).... Selected by Los Angeles Kings in first round (first Kings pick, seventh overall) of NHL entry draft (June 11, 1988).... Traded by Kings with C Jimmy Carson, first-round picks in 1989 (traded to New Jersey), 1991 (LW Martin Rucinsky) and 1993 (D Nick Stajduhar) drafts and cash to Edmonton Oilers for C Wayne Gretzky, RW/D Marty McSorley and LW/C Mike Krushelnyski (August 9, 1988).... Suspended five games (March 9, 1990).... Underwent shoulder surgery (June 1990).... Traded by Oilers with sixth-round pick in 1993 draft (C Nicholas Checco) to Quebec Nordiques for LW Scott Pearson (June 20, 1993).
HONORS: Won Can.HL Rookie of the Year Award (1987-88).... Won Michel Bergeron Trophy (1987-88).... Named to QMJHL All-Star first team (1987-88).
MISCELLANEOUS: Member of Stanley Cup championship team (1990).

			REGULAR SEASON					PLAYOFFS			
Season	Team	League	Gms.	G	A	Pts.	Pen.	Gms.	G	A	Pts.	Pen.
87-88—Hull		QMJHL	65	63	68	131	74	17	15	18	33	32
88-89—Edmonton		NHL	6	1	2	3	0	—	—	—	—	—
—Hull		QMJHL	41	38	39	77	31	9	5	4	9	14
89-90—Edmonton		NHL	46	17	8	25	30	20	2	3	5	6
90-91—Edmonton		NHL	73	20	20	40	34	18	3	6	9	25
91-92—Edmonton		NHL	68	11	18	29	62	15	1	3	4	10
92-93—Edmonton		NHL	65	11	12	23	30	—	—	—	—	—
NHL totals			258	60	60	120	156	53	6	12	18	41

GENDRON, MARTIN
RW, CAPITALS

PERSONAL: Born February 15, 1974, at Valleyfield, Que.... 5-8/180.... Shoots right.
TRANSACTIONS/CAREER NOTES: Selected by Washington Capitals in third round (fourth Capitals pick, 71st overall) of NHL entry draft (June 20, 1992).
HONORS: Named to QMJHL All-Rookie team (1990-91).... Won Can.HL Most Sportsmanlike Player of the Year Award (1991-92).... Won Shell Cup (1991-92).... Won Frank J. Selke Trophy (1991-92 and 1992-93).... Named to QMJHL All-Star first team (1991-92).... Named to Can.HL All-Star first team (1992-93).... Named to QMJHL All-Star second team (1992-93).

			REGULAR SEASON					PLAYOFFS			
Season	Team	League	Gms.	G	A	Pts.	Pen.	Gms.	G	A	Pts.	Pen.
90-91—St. Hyacinthe		QMJHL	55	34	23	57	33	4	1	2	3	0
91-92—St. Hyacinthe		QMJHL	69	*71	66	137	45	6	7	4	11	14
92-93—St. Hyacinthe		QMJHL	63	73	61	134	44	—	—	—	—	—
—Baltimore		AHL	10	1	2	3	2	3	0	0	0	0

GERNANDER, KEN
LW, JETS

PERSONAL: Born June 30, 1969, at Grand Rapids, Minn.... 5-10/175.... Shoots left.... Full name: Kenneth Robert Gernander.... Name pronounced juhr-NAN-duhr.
HIGH SCHOOL: Greenway (Coleraine, Minn.).
COLLEGE: Minnesota.
TRANSACTIONS/CAREER NOTES: Selected by Winnipeg Jets in fifth round (fourth Jets pick, 96th overall) of NHL entry draft (June 13, 1987).

			REGULAR SEASON					PLAYOFFS			
Season	Team	League	Gms.	G	A	Pts.	Pen.	Gms.	G	A	Pts.	Pen.
85-86—Greenway H.S.		Minn. H.S.	23	14	23	37	...	—	—	—	—	—
86-87—Greenway H.S.		Minn. H.S.	26	35	34	69	...	—	—	—	—	—
87-88—University of Minnesota		WCHA	44	14	14	28	14	—	—	—	—	—
88-89—University of Minnesota		WCHA	44	9	11	20	2	—	—	—	—	—
89-90—University of Minnesota		WCHA	44	32	17	49	24	—	—	—	—	—
90-91—University of Minnesota		WCHA	44	23	20	43	24	—	—	—	—	—
91-92—Moncton		AHL	43	8	18	26	9	8	1	1	2	2
—Fort Wayne		IHL	13	7	6	13	2	—	—	—	—	—
92-93—Moncton		AHL	71	18	29	47	20	5	1	4	5	0

GIBSON, STEVE
LW, OILERS

PERSONAL: Born September 10, 1972, at Listowel, Ont.... 6-0/204.... Shoots left.
TRANSACTIONS/CAREER NOTES: Selected by Edmonton Oilers in seventh round (seventh Oilers pick, 157th overall) in NHL entry draft (June 20, 1992).

			REGULAR SEASON					PLAYOFFS			
Season	Team	League	Gms.	G	A	Pts.	Pen.	Gms.	G	A	Pts.	Pen.
89-90—Windsor		OHL	35	6	8	14	24	—	—	—	—	—
90-91—Windsor		OHL	62	15	18	33	37	—	—	—	—	—
91-92—Windsor		OHL	63	49	40	89	41	—	—	—	—	—
92-93—Windsor		OHL	60	48	52	100	44	—	—	—	—	—
—Johnstown		ECHL	—	—	—	—	—	3	0	1	1	2

GILBERT, GREG
LW, RANGERS

PERSONAL: Born January 22, 1962, at Mississauga, Ont.... 6-1/191.... Shoots left.... Full name: Gregory Scott Gilbert.
TRANSACTIONS/CAREER NOTES: Sprained ankle (December 1979).... Selected by New York Islanders as underage junior in fourth round (fifth Islanders pick, 80th overall) of NHL entry draft (June 11, 1980).... Stretched ligaments in left ankle (September 1984).... Injured ligaments in knee and underwent arthroscopic surgery then major reconstructive surgery (February 27, 1985).... Broke jaw (October 11, 1986); missed 10 games.... Bruised thigh (December 7, 1986).... Bruised hip (February 1987).... Separated right shoulder (March 1987). ... Bruised right knee (February 20, 1988).... Injured left foot (April 1988).... Suffered back spasms and injured left shoulder (February 1989).... Traded by Islanders to Chicago Blackhawks for fifth-round pick in 1989 draft (RW Steve Young)

(March 7, 1989).... Broke foot (March 1989).... Strained abdominal muscle during practice (March 8, 1990).... Bruised left shoulder (September 28 ,1990); missed first eight games of season.... Hyperextended left knee (April 1991).... Pulled lateral muscle (November 13, 1991); missed two games.... Fractured ankle (February 16, 1992).... Suffered slight strain of left knee (April 4, 1992).... Suspended three off-days and fined $500 by NHL for fighting (February 26, 1993).... Suffered from the flu (March 5, 1993); missed two games.... Signed as free agent by New York Rangers (July 29, 1993).
MISCELLANEOUS: Member of Stanley Cup championship teams (1982 and 1983).

			REGULAR SEASON					PLAYOFFS				
Season Team	League	Gms.	G	A	Pts.	Pen.	Gms.	G	A	Pts.	Pen.
79-80—Toronto	OMJHL	68	10	11	21	35	—	—	—	—	—
80-81—Toronto	OMJHL	64	30	37	67	73	5	2	6	8	16
81-82—Toronto	OHL	65	41	67	108	119	10	4	12	16	23
—New York Islanders	NHL	1	1	0	1	0	4	1	1	2	2
82-83—Indianapolis	CHL	24	11	16	27	23	—	—	—	—	—
—New York Islanders	NHL	45	8	11	19	30	10	1	0	1	14
83-84—New York Islanders	NHL	79	31	35	66	59	21	5	7	12	39
84-85—New York Islanders	NHL	58	13	25	38	36	—	—	—	—	—
85-86—Springfield	AHL	2	0	0	0	2	—	—	—	—	—
—New York Islanders	NHL	60	9	19	28	82	2	0	0	0	9
86-87—New York Islanders	NHL	51	6	7	13	26	10	2	2	4	6
87-88—New York Islanders	NHL	76	17	28	45	46	4	0	0	0	6
88-89—New York Islanders	NHL	55	8	13	21	45	—	—	—	—	—
—Chicago	NHL	4	0	0	0	0	15	1	5	6	20
89-90—Chicago	NHL	70	12	25	37	54	19	5	8	13	34
90-91—Chicago	NHL	72	10	15	25	58	5	0	1	1	2
91-92—Chicago	NHL	50	7	5	12	35	10	1	3	4	16
92-93—Chicago	NHL	77	13	19	32	57	3	0	0	0	0
NHL totals		698	135	202	337	528	103	16	27	43	148

GILCHRIST, BRENT
C, STARS

PERSONAL: Born April 3, 1967, at Moose Jaw, Sask.... 5-11/181.... Shoots left.
TRANSACTIONS/CAREER NOTES: Strained medial collateral ligament (January 1985). ... Selected by Montreal Canadiens as underage junior in sixth round (sixth Canadiens pick, 79th overall) of NHL entry draft (June 15, 1985).... Injured knee (January 1987).... Broke right index finger (November 17, 1990); missed 19 games.... Separated left shoulder (February 6, 1991); missed two games.... Reinjured left shoulder (February 13, 1991); missed five games.... Traded by Canadiens with LW Shayne Corson and LW Vladimir Vujtek to Edmonton Oilers for LW Vincent Damphousse and fourth-round pick in 1993 draft (August 27, 1992).... Suffered concussion (October 1992); missed two games.... Fractured nose (December 21, 1992); missed two games.... Traded by Oilers to Minnesota North Stars for C Todd Elik (March 5, 1993).... Separated shoulder (March 18, 1993); missed remainder of season.... North Stars franchise moved from Minnesota to Dallas and renamed Stars for 1993-94 season.

			REGULAR SEASON					PLAYOFFS				
Season Team	League	Gms.	G	A	Pts.	Pen.	Gms.	G	A	Pts.	Pen.
83-84—Kelowna Wings	WHL	69	16	11	27	16	—	—	—	—	—
84-85—Kelowna Wings	WHL	51	35	38	73	58	6	5	2	7	8
85-86—Spokane	WHL	52	45	45	90	57	9	6	7	13	19
86-87—Spokane	WHL	46	45	55	100	71	5	2	7	9	6
—Sherbrooke	AHL	—	—	—	—	—	10	2	7	9	2
87-88—Sherbrooke	AHL	77	26	48	74	83	6	1	3	4	6
88-89—Montreal	NHL	49	8	16	24	16	9	1	1	2	10
—Sherbrooke	AHL	7	6	5	11	7	—	—	—	—	—
89-90—Montreal	NHL	57	9	15	24	28	8	2	0	2	2
90-91—Montreal	NHL	51	6	9	15	10	13	5	3	8	6
91-92—Montreal	NHL	79	23	27	50	57	11	2	4	6	6
92-93—Edmonton	NHL	60	10	10	20	47	—	—	—	—	—
—Minnesota	NHL	8	0	1	1	2	—	—	—	—	—
NHL totals		304	56	78	134	160	41	10	8	18	24

GILES, CURT
D

PERSONAL: Born October 30, 1958, at The Pas, Man.... 5-8/175.... Shoots left.... Full name: Curtis Jon Giles.
COLLEGE: Minnesota-Duluth.
TRANSACTIONS/CAREER NOTES: Selected by Minnesota North Stars in fourth round (fourth North Stars pick, 54th overall) of NHL entry draft (June 15, 1978).... Suffered right knee strain (February 1981).... Injured knee (January 1984).... Underwent surgery to amputate left ring finger due to a tumor that had grown into the bone (March 24, 1986).... Traded by North Stars with LW Tony McKegney and second-round pick in 1988 draft (C Troy Mallette) to New York Rangers for RW/C/D Bob Brooke and fourth-round pick in 1988 draft (Jeffrey Stolp) (November 13, 1986).... Fractured elbow (April 14, 1987).... Traded by Rangers to North Stars for C Byron Lomow and future considerations (November 20, 1987).... Injured groin (November 6, 1989).... Strained lower back (March 1990).... Sprained left knee ligament (January 25, 1991).... Announced retirement (October 4, 1991).... Signed as free agent by St. Louis Blues (February 29, 1992).... Injured knee (November 21, 1992); missed eight games.... Sprained shoulder (March 30, 1993); missed six games.... Released by Blues (June 30, 1993).
HONORS: Named to NCAA All-America team (1977-78 and 1978-79).... Named to WCHA All-Star first team (1977-78 and 1978-79).
MISCELLANEOUS: Member of silver-medal-winning Canadian Olympic team (1992).

G

Season Team	League	REGULAR SEASON					PLAYOFFS				
		Gms.	G	A	Pts.	Pen.	Gms.	G	A	Pts.	Pen.
75-76—Minnesota-Duluth	WCHA	34	5	17	22	76	—	—	—	—	—
76-77—Minnesota-Duluth	WCHA	37	12	37	49	64	—	—	—	—	—
77-78—Minnesota-Duluth	WCHA	34	11	36	47	62	—	—	—	—	—
78-79—Minnesota-Duluth	WCHA	30	3	38	41	38	—	—	—	—	—
79-80—Oklahoma City	CHL	42	4	24	28	35	—	—	—	—	—
—Minnesota	NHL	37	2	7	9	31	12	2	4	6	10
80-81—Minnesota	NHL	67	5	22	27	56	19	1	4	5	14
81-82—Minnesota	NHL	74	3	12	15	87	4	0	0	0	2
82-83—Minnesota	NHL	76	2	21	23	70	5	0	2	2	6
83-84—Minnesota	NHL	70	6	22	28	59	16	1	3	4	25
84-85—Minnesota	NHL	77	5	25	30	49	9	0	0	0	17
85-86—Minnesota	NHL	69	6	21	27	30	5	0	1	1	10
86-87—Minnesota	NHL	11	0	3	3	4	—	—	—	—	—
—New York Rangers	NHL	61	2	17	19	50	5	0	0	0	6
87-88—New York Rangers	NHL	13	0	0	0	10	—	—	—	—	—
—Minnesota	NHL	59	1	12	13	66	—	—	—	—	—
88-89—Minnesota	NHL	76	5	10	15	77	5	0	0	0	4
89-90—Minnesota	NHL	74	1	12	13	48	7	0	1	1	6
90-91—Minnesota	NHL	70	4	10	14	48	10	1	0	1	16
91-92—Canadian national team ...	Int'l	31	3	6	9	37	—	—	—	—	—
—Canadian Olympic Team ..	Int'l	8	1	0	1	6	—	—	—	—	—
—St. Louis	NHL	13	1	1	2	8	3	1	1	2	0
92-93—St. Louis	NHL	48	0	4	4	40	3	0	0	0	2
NHL totals................................		895	43	199	242	733	103	6	16	22	118

GILHEN, RANDY

C, PANTHERS

PERSONAL: Born June 13, 1963, at Zweibrucken, West Germany. . . . 6-0/192. . . . Shoots left. . . . Name pronounced GIHL-ihn.

TRANSACTIONS/CAREER NOTES: Selected by Hartford Whalers as underage junior in sixth round (sixth Whalers pick, 109th overall) of NHL entry draft (June 9, 1982). . . . Signed as free agent by Winnipeg Jets (August 1985). . . . Separated shoulder (November 16, 1988). . . . Traded by Jets with RW Andrew McBain and D Jim Kyte to Pittsburgh Penguins for C/LW Randy Cunneyworth, G Richard Tabaracci and RW Dave McLlwain (June 17, 1989). . . . Sprained knee (November 2, 1989). . . . Selected by Minnesota North Stars in NHL expansion draft (May 30, 1991). . . . Traded by North Stars with D Charlie Huddy, RW Jim Thomson and fourth-round pick in 1991 draft (D Alexei Zhitnik) to Los Angeles Kings for C Todd Elik (June 22, 1991). . . . Traded by Kings to New York Rangers for C Corey Millen (December 23, 1991). . . . Sprained right knee (January 30, 1993); missed seven games. . . . Traded by Rangers to Tampa Bay Lightning for LW Mike Hartman (March 22, 1993). . . . Selected by Florida Panthers in NHL expansion draft (June 24, 1993).
MISCELLANEOUS: Member of Stanley Cup championship team (1991).

Season Team	League	REGULAR SEASON					PLAYOFFS				
		Gms.	G	A	Pts.	Pen.	Gms.	G	A	Pts.	Pen.
79-80—Saskatoon	SJHL	55	18	34	52	112	—	—	—	—	—
—Saskatoon	WHL	9	2	2	4	20	—	—	—	—	—
80-81—Saskatoon	WHL	68	10	5	15	154	—	—	—	—	—
81-82—Winnipeg	WHL	61	41	37	78	87	—	—	—	—	—
82-83—Winnipeg	WHL	71	57	44	101	84	3	2	2	4	0
—Hartford	NHL	2	0	1	1	0	—	—	—	—	—
—Binghamton	AHL	—	—	—	—	—	5	2	0	2	2
83-84—Binghamton	AHL	73	8	12	20	72	—	—	—	—	—
84-85—Salt Lake City	IHL	57	20	20	40	28	—	—	—	—	—
—Binghamton	AHL	18	3	3	6	9	8	4	1	5	16
85-86—Fort Wayne	IHL	82	44	40	84	48	15	10	8	18	6
86-87—Winnipeg	NHL	2	0	0	0	0	—	—	—	—	—
—Sherbrooke	AHL	75	36	29	65	44	17	7	13	20	10
87-88—Winnipeg	NHL	13	3	2	5	15	4	1	0	1	10
—Moncton	AHL	68	40	47	87	51	—	—	—	—	—
88-89—Winnipeg	NHL	64	5	3	8	38	—	—	—	—	—
89-90—Pittsburgh	NHL	61	5	11	16	54	—	—	—	—	—
90-91—Pittsburgh	NHL	72	15	10	25	51	16	1	0	1	14
91-92—Los Angeles..................	NHL	33	3	6	9	14	—	—	—	—	—
—New York Rangers	NHL	40	7	7	14	14	13	1	2	3	2
92-93—New York Rangers	NHL	33	3	2	5	8	—	—	—	—	—
—Tampa Bay	NHL	11	0	2	2	6	—	—	—	—	—
NHL totals................................		331	41	44	85	200	33	3	2	5	26

GILL, TODD

D, MAPLE LEAFS

PERSONAL: Born November 9, 1965, at Brockville, Ont. . . . 6-0/185. . . . Shoots left.
TRANSACTIONS/CAREER NOTES: Selected by Toronto Maple Leafs as underage junior in second round (second Maple Leafs pick, 25th overall) of NHL entry draft (June 9, 1984). . . . Broke bone in right foot (October 1987). . . . Bruised shoulder (March 1989). . . . Fractured finger (October 15, 1991); missed three games. . . . Strained back (February 8, 1992); missed three games. . . . Injured back prior to 1992-93 season; missed first two games of season. . . . Suffered foot contusion (November 14, 1992); missed 11 games.

Season Team	League	REGULAR SEASON					PLAYOFFS				
		Gms.	G	A	Pts.	Pen.	Gms.	G	A	Pts.	Pen.
82-83—Windsor..............................	OHL	70	12	24	36	108	3	0	0	0	11
83-84—Windsor..............................	OHL	68	9	48	57	184	3	1	1	2	10

Season Team	League	REGULAR SEASON					PLAYOFFS				
		Gms.	G	A	Pts.	Pen.	Gms.	G	A	Pts.	Pen.
84-85—Toronto	NHL	10	1	0	1	13	—	—	—	—	—
—Windsor	OHL	53	17	40	57	148	4	0	1	1	14
85-86—St. Catharines	AHL	58	8	25	33	90	10	1	6	7	17
—Toronto	NHL	15	1	2	3	28	1	0	0	0	0
86-87—Newmarket	AHL	11	1	8	9	33	—	—	—	—	—
—Toronto	NHL	61	4	27	31	92	13	2	2	4	42
87-88—Newmarket	AHL	2	0	1	1	2	—	—	—	—	—
—Toronto	NHL	65	8	17	25	131	6	1	3	4	20
88-89—Toronto	NHL	59	11	14	25	72	—	—	—	—	—
89-90—Toronto	NHL	48	1	14	15	92	5	0	3	3	16
90-91—Toronto	NHL	72	2	22	24	113	—	—	—	—	—
91-92—Toronto	NHL	74	2	15	17	91	—	—	—	—	—
92-93—Toronto	NHL	69	11	32	43	66	21	1	10	11	26
NHL totals		473	41	143	184	698	46	4	18	22	104

GILLIS, PAUL
RW

PERSONAL: Born December 31, 1963, at Toronto. . . . 5-11/198. . . . Shoots left.
TRANSACTIONS/CAREER NOTES: Selected by Quebec Nordiques as underage junior in second round (second Nordiques pick, 34th overall) of NHL entry draft (June 9, 1982). . . . Suspended three games by NHL for scratching during a fight (November 2, 1986). . . . Developed Guillain-Barre Syndrome, a neurological disorder brought on by a virus (summer 1989); missed first eight games of season. . . . Sprained knee (November 1989). . . . Separated right shoulder (September 1990); missed first 13 games of season. . . . Traded by Nordiques with LW Dan Vincelette to Chicago Blackhawks for C Mike McNeil and D Ryan McGill (March 5, 1991). . . . Traded by Blackhawks to Hartford Whalers for future considerations (January 27, 1992). . . . Fractured left foot (February 4, 1992); missed 22 games. . . . Named assistant coach of Springfield Indians (July 22, 1993).

Season Team	League	REGULAR SEASON					PLAYOFFS				
		Gms.	G	A	Pts.	Pen.	Gms.	G	A	Pts.	Pen.
80-81—Niagara Falls	OMJHL	59	14	19	33	165	—	—	—	—	—
81-82—Niagara Falls	OHL	66	27	62	89	247	5	1	5	6	26
82-83—North Bay	OHL	61	34	52	86	151	6	1	3	4	26
—Quebec	NHL	7	0	2	2	2	—	—	—	—	—
83-84—Fredericton	AHL	18	7	8	15	47	—	—	—	—	—
—Quebec	NHL	57	8	9	17	59	1	0	0	0	2
84-85—Quebec	NHL	77	14	28	42	168	18	1	7	8	73
85-86—Quebec	NHL	80	19	24	43	203	3	0	2	2	16
86-87—Quebec	NHL	76	13	26	39	267	13	2	4	6	65
87-88—Quebec	NHL	80	7	10	17	164	—	—	—	—	—
88-89—Quebec	NHL	79	15	25	40	163	—	—	—	—	—
89-90—Quebec	NHL	71	8	14	22	234	—	—	—	—	—
90-91—Quebec	NHL	49	3	8	11	91	—	—	—	—	—
—Chicago	NHL	13	0	5	5	53	2	0	0	0	2
91-92—Chicago	NHL	2	0	0	0	6	—	—	—	—	—
—Indianapolis	IHL	42	10	15	25	170	—	—	—	—	—
—Hartford	NHL	12	0	2	2	48	5	0	1	1	0
92-93—Hartford	NHL	21	1	1	2	40	—	—	—	—	—
NHL totals		624	88	154	242	1498	42	3	14	17	158

GILMOUR, DARRYL
G, KINGS

PERSONAL: Born February 13, 1967, at Winnipeg, Man. . . . 6-0/171. . . . Shoots left. . . . Full name: Darryl Robert Gilmour.
TRANSACTIONS/CAREER NOTES: Selected by Philadelphia Flyers as underage junior in third round (third Flyers pick, 48th overall) of NHL entry draft (June 15, 1985). . . . Signed as free agent by Los Angeles Kings (December 15, 1989).
HONORS: Named to WHL (East) All-Star first team (1985-86).

Season Team	League	REGULAR SEASON								PLAYOFFS						
		Gms.	Min.	W	L	T	GA	SO	Avg.	Gms.	Min.	W	L	GA	SO	Avg.
83-84—St. James	MJHL	15	900	...	...	...	45	...	3.00	—	—	—	—	—	—	—
84-85—Moose Jaw	WHL	*58	3004	15	35	0	*297	0	5.93	—	—	—	—	—	—	—
85-86—Moose Jaw	WHL	*62	*3482	19	34	3	*276	1	4.76	9	490	4	4	48	0	5.88
86-87—Moose Jaw	WHL	31	1776	14	13	2	123	2	4.16	—	—	—	—	—	—	—
—Portland	WHL	24	1460	15	7	1	111	0	4.56	19	1167	12	7	83	1	4.27
87-88—Hershey	AHL	25	1273	14	7	0	78	1	3.68	—	—	—	—	—	—	—
88-89—Hershey	AHL	38	2093	16	14	5	144	0	4.13	—	—	—	—	—	—	—
89-90—Nashville	ECHL	10	529	6	3	0	43	0	4.88	—	—	—	—	—	—	—
—New Haven	AHL	23	1356	10	11	2	85	0	3.76	—	—	—	—	—	—	—
90-91—Phoenix	IHL	4	180	2	0	0	13	0	4.33	—	—	—	—	—	—	—
—New Haven	AHL	26	1375	5	14	3	90	1	3.93	—	—	—	—	—	—	—
91-92—Phoenix	IHL	30	1774	10	15	3	120	0	4.06	—	—	—	—	—	—	—
92-93—Phoenix	IHL	41	2281	7	*28	0	168	0	4.42	—	—	—	—	—	—	—

G

GILMOUR, DOUG
C, MAPLE LEAFS

PERSONAL: Born June 25, 1963, at Kingston, Ont. . . . 5-11/164. . . . Shoots left.
TRANSACTIONS/CAREER NOTES: Selected by St. Louis Blues as underage junior in seventh round (fourth Blues pick, 134th overall) of NHL entry draft (June 9, 1982). . . . Sprained ankle (October 7, 1985); missed four games. . . . Suffered concussion (January 1988). . . .

Bruised shoulder (March 1988).... Traded by Blues with RW Mark Hunter, LW Steve Bozek and D/RW Michael Dark to Calgary Flames for C Mike Bullard, C Craig Coxe and D Tim Corkery (September 5, 1988).... Suffered abscessed jaw (March 1989); missed six games.... Broke bone in right foot (August 12, 1989).... Traded by Flames with D Ric Nattress, D Jamie Macoun, LW Kent Manderville and G Rick Wamsley to Toronto Maple Leafs for LW Craig Berube, D Alexander Godynyuk, LW Gary Leeman, D Michel Petit and G Jeff Reese (January 2, 1992).... Suspended eight off-days and fined $500 by NHL for slashing (November 27, 1992).

HONORS: Won Red Tilson Trophy (1982-83).... Won Eddie Powers Memorial Trophy (1982-83).... Named to OHL All-Star first team (1982-83).... Named to THE SPORTING NEWS All-Star second team (1992-93).... Won Frank J. Selke Trophy (1992-93).... Played in NHL All-Star Game (1993).

MISCELLANEOUS: Member of Stanley Cup championship team (1989).

			REGULAR SEASON					PLAYOFFS				
Season	Team	League	Gms.	G	A	Pts.	Pen.	Gms.	G	A	Pts.	Pen.
80-81	Cornwall	QMJHL	51	12	23	35	35	—	—	—	—	—
81-82	Cornwall	OHL	67	46	73	119	42	5	6	9	15	2
82-83	Cornwall	OHL	68	*70	*107	*177	62	8	8	10	18	16
83-84	St. Louis	NHL	80	25	28	53	57	11	2	9	11	10
84-85	St. Louis	NHL	78	21	36	57	49	3	1	1	2	2
85-86	St. Louis	NHL	74	25	28	53	41	19	9	12	†21	25
86-87	St. Louis	NHL	80	42	63	105	58	6	2	2	4	16
87-88	St. Louis	NHL	72	36	50	86	59	10	3	14	17	18
88-89	Calgary	NHL	72	26	59	85	44	22	11	11	22	20
89-90	Calgary	NHL	78	24	67	91	54	6	3	1	4	8
90-91	Calgary	NHL	78	20	61	81	144	7	1	1	2	0
91-92	Calgary	NHL	38	11	27	38	46	—	—	—	—	—
	Toronto	NHL	40	15	34	49	32	—	—	—	—	—
92-93	Toronto	NHL	83	32	95	127	100	21	10	25	35	30
NHL totals			773	277	548	825	684	105	42	76	118	129

GIRARD, RICK
C, CANUCKS

PERSONAL: Born May 1, 1974, at Edmonton, Alta.... 5-11/180.... Shoots left.
TRANSACTIONS/CAREER NOTES: Selected by Vancouver Canucks in second round (second Canucks pick, 20th overall) of NHL entry draft (June 26, 1993).
HONORS: Won Brad Hornung Trophy (1992-93).... Won the Can.HL Most Sportsmanlike Player of the Year Award (1992-93).... Named to WHL (East) All-Star first team (1992-93).

			REGULAR SEASON					PLAYOFFS				
Season	Team	League	Gms.	G	A	Pts.	Pen.	Gms.	G	A	Pts.	Pen.
91-92	Swift Current	WHL	45	14	17	31	6	8	2	0	2	2
92-93	Swift Current	WHL	72	71	70	141	25	17	9	17	26	10

GLYNN, BRIAN
D, OILERS

PERSONAL: Born November 23, 1967, at Iserlohn, West Germany.... 6-4/220.... Shoots left.... Full name: Brian Thomas Glynn.
TRANSACTIONS/CAREER NOTES: Selected by Calgary Flames in second round (second Flames pick, 37th overall) of NHL entry draft (June 21, 1986).... Traded by Flames to Minnesota North Stars for D Frantisek Musil (October 26, 1990).... Traded by North Stars to Edmonton Oilers for D David Shaw (January 21, 1992).... Injured knee (March 15, 1992); missed seven games.... Injured knee (November 4, 1992); missed two games.
HONORS: Won Governors Trophy (1989-90).... Named to IHL All-Star first team (1989-90).

			REGULAR SEASON					PLAYOFFS				
Season	Team	League	Gms.	G	A	Pts.	Pen.	Gms.	G	A	Pts.	Pen.
84-85	Saskatoon	SJHL	12	1	0	1	2	3	0	0	0	0
85-86	Saskatoon	WHL	66	7	25	32	131	13	0	3	3	30
86-87	Saskatoon	WHL	44	2	26	28	163	11	1	3	4	19
87-88	Calgary	NHL	67	5	14	19	87	1	0	0	0	0
88-89	Salt Lake City	IHL	31	3	10	13	105	14	3	7	10	31
	Calgary	NHL	9	0	1	1	19	—	—	—	—	—
89-90	Calgary	NHL	1	0	0	0	0	—	—	—	—	—
	Salt Lake City	IHL	80	17	44	61	164	—	—	—	—	—
90-91	Salt Lake City	IHL	8	1	3	4	18	—	—	—	—	—
	Minnesota	NHL	66	8	11	19	83	23	2	6	8	18
91-92	Minnesota	NHL	37	2	12	14	24	—	—	—	—	—
	Edmonton	NHL	25	2	6	8	6	16	4	1	5	12
92-93	Edmonton	NHL	64	4	12	16	60	—	—	—	—	—
NHL totals			269	21	56	77	279	40	6	7	13	30

GODYNYUK, ALEXANDER
D, PANTHERS

PERSONAL: Born January 27, 1970, at Kiev, U.S.S.R. ... 6-0/207. ... Shoots left. ... Name pronounced goh-DIHN-yuhk.
TRANSACTIONS/CAREER NOTES: Selected by Toronto Maple Leafs in sixth round (fifth Maple Leafs pick, 115th overall) of NHL entry draft (June 16, 1990).... Traded by Maple Leafs with LW Craig Berube, RW Gary Leeman, D Michel Petit and G Jeff Reese to Calgary Flames for C Doug Gilmour, D Jamie Macoun, LW Kent Manderville, D Ric Nattress and G Rick Wamsley (January 2, 1992).... Injured shoulder (February 23, 1993); missed one game.... Selected by Florida Panthers in NHL expansion draft (June 24, 1993).

G

Season Team	League	Gms.	G	A	Pts.	Pen.	Gms.	G	A	Pts.	Pen.
89-90—Sokol Kiev	USSR	38	3	2	5	31	—	—	—	—	—
90-91—Sokol Kiev	USSR	19	3	1	4	20	—	—	—	—	—
—Toronto	NHL	18	0	3	3	16	—	—	—	—	—
—Newmarket	AHL	11	0	1	1	29	—	—	—	—	—
91-92—Toronto	NHL	31	3	6	9	59	—	—	—	—	—
—Calgary	NHL	6	0	1	1	4	—	—	—	—	—
—Salt Lake City	IHL	17	2	1	3	24	—	—	—	—	—
92-93—Calgary	NHL	27	3	4	7	19	—	—	—	—	—
NHL totals		82	6	14	20	98					

GONCHAR, SERGEI
D, CAPITALS

PERSONAL: Born April 13, 1974, at Chelyabinsk, U.S.S.R. . . . . 6-0/178. . . . Shoots left.
TRANSACTIONS/CAREER NOTES: Selected by Washington Capitals in first round (first Capitals pick, 14th overall) of NHL entry draft (June 20, 1992).

Season Team	League	Gms.	G	A	Pts.	Pen.	Gms.	G	A	Pts.	Pen.
90-91—Mechel Chelyabinsk	USSR	2	0	0	0	0	—	—	—	—	—
91-92—Traktor Chelyabinsk	CIS	31	1	0	1	6	—	—	—	—	—
92-93—Dynamo Moscow	CIS	31	1	3	4	70	10	0	0	0	12

GORDIOUK, VIKTOR
RW, SABRES

PERSONAL: Born April 11, 1970, at Moscow, U.S.S.R. . . . . 5-10/176. . . . Shoots right. . . . Name pronounced gohr-dee-YOOK.
TRANSACTIONS/CAREER NOTES: Selected by Buffalo Sabres in seventh round (sixth Sabres pick, 142nd overall) of NHL entry draft (June 16, 1990).

Season Team	League	Gms.	G	A	Pts.	Pen.	Gms.	G	A	Pts.	Pen.
89-90—Soviet Wings	USSR	48	11	4	15	24	—	—	—	—	—
90-91—Soviet Wings	USSR	46	12	10	22	22	—	—	—	—	—
91-92—Soviet Wings	CIS	42	16	7	23	24	—	—	—	—	—
92-93—Buffalo	NHL	16	3	6	9	0	—	—	—	—	—
—Rochester	AHL	35	11	14	25	8	17	9	9	18	4
NHL totals		16	3	6	9	0					

GOSSELIN, MARIO
G, WHALERS

PERSONAL: Born June 15, 1963, at Thetford Mines, Que. . . . 5-8/160. . . . Shoots left. . . . Name pronounced GAHZ-uh-lai.
TRANSACTIONS/CAREER NOTES: Selected by Quebec Nordiques as underage junior in third round (third Nordiques pick, 55th overall) of NHL entry draft (June 9, 1982). . . . Injured knee (March 8, 1984); missed remainder of season. . . . Suffered from the flu (January 16, 1986); missed one game. . . . Signed as free agent by Los Angeles Kings (June 1989). . . . Suffered from the flu (October 1989). . . . Signed as free agent by Hartford Whalers (September 4, 1991). . . . Injured back (April 13, 1993); missed final two games of regular season.
HONORS: Named to QMJHL All-Star second team (1981-82). . . . Named to QMJHL All-Star first team (1982-83). . . . Played in NHL All-Star Game (1986).

Season Team	League	Gms.	Min.	W	L	T	GA	SO	Avg.	Gms.	Min.	W	L	GA	SO	Avg.
80-81—Shawinigan	QMJHL	21	907	4	9	0	75	0	4.96	1	20	0	0	2	0	6.00
81-82—Shawinigan	QMJHL	*60	*3404	...	...	...	230	0	4.05	14	788	...	...	58	0	4.42
82-83—Shawinigan	QMJHL	46	2556	32	9	1	133	*3	*3.12	8	457	5	3	29	0	3.81
83-84—Can. Olympic Team	Int'l	36	2007	...	...	...	126	0	3.77	—	—	—	—	—	—	—
—Quebec	NHL	3	148	2	0	0	3	1	1.22	—	—	—	—	—	—	—
84-85—Quebec	NHL	35	1960	19	10	3	109	1	3.34	17	1059	9	8	54	0	3.06
85-86—Fredericton	AHL	5	304	2	2	1	15	0	2.96	—	—	—	—	—	—	—
—Quebec	NHL	31	1726	14	14	1	111	2	3.86	1	40	0	1	5	0	7.50
86-87—Quebec	NHL	30	1625	13	11	1	86	0	3.18	11	654	7	4	37	0	3.39
87-88—Quebec	NHL	54	3002	20	28	4	189	2	3.78	—	—	—	—	—	—	—
88-89—Quebec	NHL	39	2064	11	19	3	146	0	4.24	—	—	—	—	—	—	—
—Halifax	AHL	3	183	3	0	0	9	0	2.95	—	—	—	—	—	—	—
89-90—Los Angeles	NHL	26	1226	7	11	1	79	0	3.87	3	63	0	2	3	0	2.86
90-91—Phoenix	IHL	46	2673	24	15	4	172	1	3.86	11	670	7	4	*43	0	3.85
91-92—Springfield	AHL	47	2606	28	11	5	142	0	3.27	6	319	1	4	18	0	3.39
92-93—Springfield	AHL	23	1345	8	7	7	75	0	3.35	—	—	—	—	—	—	—
—Hartford	NHL	16	867	5	9	1	57	0	3.94	—	—	—	—	—	—	—
NHL totals		234	12618	91	102	14	780	6	3.71	32	1816	16	15	99	0	3.27

GOTZIAMAN, CHRIS
RW, DEVILS

PERSONAL: Born November 29, 1971, at Roseau, Minn. . . . 6-2/190. . . . Shoots right.
HIGH SCHOOL: Roseau (Minn.).
COLLEGE: North Dakota.
TRANSACTIONS/CAREER NOTES: Underwent surgery to knee cartilage (February 1988). . . . Selected by New Jersey Devils in second round (third Devils pick, 29th overall) of NHL entry draft (June 16, 1990). . . . Broke right wrist (December 1990).

G

Season Team	League	REGULAR SEASON					PLAYOFFS				
		Gms.	G	A	Pts.	Pen.	Gms.	G	A	Pts.	Pen.
88-89—Roseau H.S.	Minn. H.S.	25	13	18	31	...	—	—	—	—	—
89-90—Roseau H.S.	Minn. H.S.	28	34	31	65	...	—	—	—	—	—
90-91—Univ. of North Dakota	WCHA	40	11	8	19	26	—	—	—	—	—
91-92—Univ. of North Dakota	WCHA	38	9	6	15	47	—	—	—	—	—
92-93—Univ. of North Dakota	WCHA	35	10	10	20	50	—	—	—	—	—

GOULET, MICHEL

LW, BLACKHAWKS

PERSONAL: Born April 21, 1960, at Peribonqua, Que. . . . 6-1/195. . . . Shoots left. . . . Name pronounced goo-LAY.

TRANSACTIONS/CAREER NOTES: Signed as underage junior by Birmingham Bulls (July 1978). . . . Selected by Quebec Nordiques in first round (first Nordiques pick, 20th overall) of NHL entry draft (August 9, 1979). . . . Fractured thumb (January 2, 1985). . . . Suspended by Nordiques after leaving training camp to renegotiate contract (September 1985). . . . Broke finger on right hand (October 13, 1986). . . . Strained ligaments in left knee (October 6, 1988). . . . Underwent surgery to finger (May 1989). . . . Sprained right ankle (October 28, 1989); missed nine games. . . . Traded by Nordiques with G Greg Millen and sixth-round pick in 1991 draft to Chicago Blackhawks for LW Everett Sanipass, LW Dan Vincelette and D Mario Doyon (March 5, 1990). . . . Bruised ribs and stretched rib cartilage (March 11, 1990). . . . Bruised right ankle (November 1990). . . . Sprained right knee (March 30, 1991); missed playoffs. . . . Pulled groin (March 31, 1992). . . . Pulled groin (December 8, 1992); missed nine games.

HONORS: Named to QMJHL All-Star second team (1977-78). . . . Named to THE SPORTING NEWS All-Star second team (1982-83 and 1987-88). . . . Named to NHL All-Star second team (1982-83 and 1987-88). . . . Named to THE SPORTING NEWS All-Star first team (1983-84 through 1986-87). . . . Named to NHL All-Star first team (1983-84, 1985-86, and 1986-87). . . . Played in NHL All-Star Game (1983 through 1986 and 1988).

Season Team	League	REGULAR SEASON					PLAYOFFS				
		Gms.	G	A	Pts.	Pen.	Gms.	G	A	Pts.	Pen.
76-77—Quebec	QMJHL	37	17	18	35	9	14	3	8	11	19
77-78—Quebec	QMJHL	72	73	62	135	109	1	0	1	1	0
78-79—Birmingham	WHA	78	28	30	58	64	—	—	—	—	—
79-80—Quebec	NHL	77	22	32	54	48	—	—	—	—	—
80-81—Quebec	NHL	76	32	39	71	45	4	3	4	7	7
81-82—Quebec	NHL	80	42	42	84	48	16	8	5	13	6
82-83—Quebec	NHL	80	57	48	105	51	4	0	0	0	6
83-84—Quebec	NHL	75	56	65	121	76	9	2	4	6	17
84-85—Quebec	NHL	69	55	40	95	55	17	11	10	21	17
85-86—Quebec	NHL	75	53	50	103	64	3	1	2	3	10
86-87—Quebec	NHL	75	49	47	96	61	13	9	5	14	35
87-88—Quebec	NHL	80	48	58	106	56	—	—	—	—	—
88-89—Quebec	NHL	69	26	38	64	67	—	—	—	—	—
89-90—Quebec	NHL	57	16	29	45	42	—	—	—	—	—
—Chicago	NHL	8	4	1	5	9	14	4	2	6	6
90-91—Chicago	NHL	74	27	38	65	65	—	—	—	—	—
91-92—Chicago	NHL	75	22	41	63	69	9	3	4	7	6
92-93—Chicago	NHL	63	23	21	44	43	3	0	1	1	0
WHA totals		78	28	30	58	64					
NHL totals		1033	532	589	1121	799	92	41	37	78	110

GOVEDARIS, CHRIS

LW, WHALERS

PERSONAL: Born February 2, 1970, at Toronto. . . . 6-0/200. . . . Shoots left. . . . Name pronounced goh-vih-DAIR-ihz.

TRANSACTIONS/CAREER NOTES: Suspended two games by OHL (October 1986). . . . Selected by Hartford Whalers in first round (first Whalers pick, 11th overall) of NHL entry draft (June 11, 1988). . . . Suspended 15 games by OHL for shattering stick across another player's hip (January 22, 1989). . . . Bruised right leg (January 23, 1991); missed five games. . . . Suspended by Whalers for failure to report to AHL game (October 31, 1991); reinstated (January 3, 1992).

Season Team	League	REGULAR SEASON					PLAYOFFS				
		Gms.	G	A	Pts.	Pen.	Gms.	G	A	Pts.	Pen.
85-86—Toronto Young Nationals	MTHL	38	35	50	85	...	—	—	—	—	—
86-87—Toronto	OHL	64	36	28	64	148	—	—	—	—	—
87-88—Toronto	OHL	62	42	38	80	118	4	2	1	3	10
88-89—Toronto	OHL	49	41	38	79	117	6	2	3	5	0
89-90—Hartford	NHL	12	0	1	1	6	2	0	0	0	2
—Binghamton	AHL	14	3	3	6	4	—	—	—	—	—
—Dukes of Hamilton	OHL	23	11	21	32	53	—	—	—	—	—
90-91—Hartford	NHL	14	1	3	4	4	—	—	—	—	—
—Springfield	AHL	56	26	36	62	133	9	2	5	7	36
91-92—Springfield	AHL	43	14	25	39	55	11	3	2	5	25
92-93—Springfield	AHL	65	31	24	55	58	15	7	4	11	18
—Hartford	NHL	7	1	0	1	0	—	—	—	—	—
NHL totals		33	2	4	6	10	2	0	0	0	2

GOVERDE, DAVID

G, KINGS

PERSONAL: Born April 9, 1970, at Toronto. . . . 6-0/210. . . . Shoots left. . . . Name pronounced go-VUHR-dee.

TRANSACTIONS/CAREER NOTES: Selected by Los Angeles Kings in fifth round (fifth Kings pick, 91st overall) of NHL entry draft (June 16, 1990).

G

Season	Team	League	REGULAR SEASON Gms.	Min.	W	L	T	GA	SO	Avg.	PLAYOFFS Gms.	Min.	W	L	GA	SO	Avg.
87-88—Windsor	OHL	10	471	...	...	...	28	0	3.57	—	—	—	—	—	—	—
88-89—Windsor	OHL	5	221	...	...	...	24	0	6.52	—	—	—	—	—	—	—
—Sudbury	OHL	39	2189	...	...	...	156	0	4.28	—	—	—	—	—	—	—
89-90—Sudbury	OHL	52	2941	28	12	7	182	0	3.71	7	394	3	3	25	0	3.81
90-91—Phoenix	IHL	40	2007	11	19	5	137	1	4.10	—	—	—	—	—	—	—
91-92—Phoenix	IHL	35	1951	11	19	3	129	1	3.97	—	—	—	—	—	—	—
—Los Angeles	NHL	2	120	1	1	0	9	0	4.50	—	—	—	—	—	—	—
—New Haven	AHL	5	248	1	3	0	17	0	4.11	—	—	—	—	—	—	—
92-93—Phoenix	IHL	46	2569	18	21	0	173	1	4.04	—	—	—	—	—	—	—
—Los Angeles	NHL	2	98	0	2	0	13	0	7.96	—	—	—	—	—	—	—
NHL totals		4	218	1	3	0	22	0	6.06							

GRAHAM, DIRK
LW/RW, BLACKHAWKS

PERSONAL: Born July 29, 1959, at Regina, Sask. . . . 5-11/190. . . . Shoots right. . . . Full name: Dirk Milton Graham.

TRANSACTIONS/CAREER NOTES: Selected by Vancouver Canucks in fifth round (fifth Canucks pick, 89th overall) of NHL entry draft (August 9, 1979). . . . Signed as free agent by Minnesota North Stars (August 17, 1983). . . . Sprained wrist (November 1987); missed seven games. . . . Traded by North Stars to Chicago Blackhawks for LW Curt Fraser (January 4, 1988). . . . Fined $500 by NHL for fighting (December 28, 1989). . . . Fractured left kneecap (March 17, 1990); missed six weeks. . . . Underwent surgery to left knee (May 1990).

HONORS: Named to WHL All-Star second team (1978-79). . . . Named to IHL All-Star second team (1980-81). . . . Named to IHL All-Star first team (1982-83). . . . Named to CHL All-Star first team (1983-84). . . . Won Frank J. Selke Trophy (1990-91).

Season	Team	League	REGULAR SEASON Gms.	G	A	Pts.	Pen.	PLAYOFFS Gms.	G	A	Pts.	Pen.
75-76—Regina Blues	SJHL	54	36	32	68	82	—	—	—	—	—
—Regina	WCHL	2	0	0	0	0	6	1	1	2	5
76-77—Regina	WCHL	65	37	28	65	66	—	—	—	—	—
77-78—Regina	WCHL	72	49	61	110	87	13	15	19	34	37
78-79—Regina	WHL	71	48	60	108	252	—	—	—	—	—
79-80—Dallas	CHL	62	17	15	32	96	—	—	—	—	—
80-81—Fort Wayne	IHL	6	1	2	3	12	—	—	—	—	—
—Toledo	IHL	61	40	45	85	88	—	—	—	—	—
81-82—Toledo	IHL	72	49	56	105	68	13	10	11	21	8
82-83—Toledo	IHL	78	70	55	125	86	11	13	7	†20	30
83-84—Minnesota	NHL	6	1	1	2	0	1	0	0	0	2
—Salt Lake City	CHL	57	37	57	94	72	5	3	8	11	2
84-85—Springfield	AHL	37	20	28	48	41	—	—	—	—	—
—Minnesota	NHL	36	12	11	23	23	9	0	4	4	7
85-86—Minnesota	NHL	80	22	33	55	87	5	3	1	4	2
86-87—Minnesota	NHL	76	25	29	54	142	—	—	—	—	—
87-88—Minnesota	NHL	28	7	5	12	39	—	—	—	—	—
—Chicago	NHL	42	17	19	36	32	4	1	2	3	4
88-89—Chicago	NHL	80	33	45	78	89	16	2	4	6	38
89-90—Chicago	NHL	73	22	32	54	102	5	1	5	6	2
90-91—Chicago	NHL	80	24	21	45	88	6	1	2	3	17
91-92—Chicago	NHL	80	17	30	47	89	18	7	5	12	8
92-93—Chicago	NHL	84	20	17	37	139	4	0	0	0	0
NHL totals		665	200	243	443	830	68	15	23	38	80

GRANATO, TONY
LW, KINGS

PERSONAL: Born July 25, 1964, at Downers Grove, Ill. . . . 5-10/185. . . . Shoots right. . . . Full name: Anthony Lewis Granato.

HIGH SCHOOL: Northwood School (Lake Placid, N.Y.).

COLLEGE: Wisconsin.

TRANSACTIONS/CAREER NOTES: Selected by New York Rangers in sixth round (fifth Rangers pick, 120th overall) of NHL entry draft (June 9, 1982). . . . Bruised foot (February 1989). . . . Traded by Rangers with RW Tomas Sandstrom to Los Angeles Kings for C Bernie Nicholls (January 20, 1990). . . . Pulled groin (January 25, 1990); missed 12 games. . . . Injured knee (March 20, 1990). . . . Tore rib cartilage (December 18, 1990); missed 10 games. . . . Strained back (October 6, 1992); missed three games.

HONORS: Named to NCAA All-America West second team (1984-85 and 1986-87). . . . Named to WCHA All-Star second team (1986-87). . . . Named to NHL All-Rookie team (1988-89).

Season	Team	League	REGULAR SEASON Gms.	G	A	Pts.	Pen.	PLAYOFFS Gms.	G	A	Pts.	Pen.
81-82—Northwood School	N.Y. H.S.				Statistics unavailable.						
82-83—Northwood School	N.Y. H.S.				Statistics unavailable.						
83-84—University of Wisconsin	WCHA	35	14	17	31	48	—	—	—	—	—
84-85—University of Wisconsin	WCHA	42	33	34	67	94	—	—	—	—	—
85-86—University of Wisconsin	WCHA	32	25	24	49	36	—	—	—	—	—
86-87—University of Wisconsin	WCHA	42	28	45	73	64	—	—	—	—	—
87-88—U.S. national team	Int'l	49	40	31	71	55	—	—	—	—	—
—U.S. Olympic Team	Int'l	6	1	7	8	4	—	—	—	—	—
—Denver	IHL	22	13	14	27	36	8	9	4	13	16
88-89—New York Rangers	NHL	78	36	27	63	140	4	1	1	2	21

G

Season Team	League	REGULAR SEASON					PLAYOFFS				
		Gms.	G	A	Pts.	Pen.	Gms.	G	A	Pts.	Pen.
89-90—New York Rangers	NHL	37	7	18	25	77	—	—	—	—	—
—Los Angeles	NHL	19	5	6	11	45	10	5	4	9	12
90-91—Los Angeles	NHL	68	30	34	64	154	12	1	4	5	28
91-92—Los Angeles	NHL	80	39	29	68	187	6	1	5	6	10
92-93—Los Angeles	NHL	81	37	45	82	171	24	6	11	17	50
NHL totals		363	154	159	313	774	56	14	25	39	121

GRANT, KEVIN
D, FLAMES

PERSONAL: Born January 9, 1969, at Toronto. . . . 6-3/210. . . . Shoots right. **TRANSACTIONS/CAREER NOTES:** Injured knee ligaments (February 1, 1987). . . . Selected by Calgary Flames as underage junior in second round (third Flames pick, 40th overall) of NHL entry draft (June 13, 1987). . . . Traded by Kitchener Rangers with C Sean Stansfield and fourth-round pick in 1989 draft (traded to Sault Ste. Marie Greyhounds) and fourth-round pick in 1990 draft to Sudbury Wolves for RW Pierre Gagnon, D John Uniac and seventh-round pick in 1989 draft (Jamie Israel) (November 1988). . . . Traded by Salt Lake City Golden Eagles to Phoenix Roadrunners for D Paul Holden (October 16, 1992).

Season Team	League	REGULAR SEASON					PLAYOFFS				
		Gms.	G	A	Pts.	Pen.	Gms.	G	A	Pts.	Pen.
85-86—Kitchener	OHL	63	2	15	17	204	5	0	1	1	11
86-87—Kitchener	OHL	52	5	18	23	125	4	0	1	1	16
87-88—Kitchener	OHL	48	3	20	23	138	4	0	1	1	4
88-89—Sudbury	OHL	60	9	41	50	186	—	—	—	—	—
—Salt Lake City	IHL	3	0	1	1	5	3	0	0	0	12
89-90—Salt Lake City	IHL	78	7	17	24	117	11	0	2	2	22
90-91—Salt Lake City	IHL	63	6	19	25	200	3	0	0	0	8
91-92—Salt Lake City	IHL	73	7	16	23	181	—	—	—	—	—
92-93—Salt Lake City	IHL	1	0	0	0	2	—	—	—	—	—
—Phoenix	IHL	49	4	17	21	119	—	—	—	—	—
—Cincinnati	IHL	2	0	0	0	2	—	—	—	—	—

GRATTON, CHRIS
C, LIGHTNING

PERSONAL: Born July 5, 1975, at Brantford, Ont. . . . 6-3/202. . . . Shoots left. **HIGH SCHOOL:** Loyalist Collegiate (Brantford, Ont.). **TRANSACTIONS/CAREER NOTES:** Selected by Tampa Bay Lightning in first round (first Lightning pick, third overall) of NHL entry draft (June 26, 1993). **HONORS:** Won Emms Family Award (1991-92). . . . Named to OHL Rookie All-Star Team (1991-92). . . . Won OHL Top Draft Prospect Award (1992-93).

Season Team	League	REGULAR SEASON					PLAYOFFS				
		Gms.	G	A	Pts.	Pen.	Gms.	G	A	Pts.	Pen.
90-91—Brantford Jr. B	OHA	31	30	30	60	28	—	—	—	—	—
91-92—Kingston	OHL	62	27	39	66	35	—	—	—	—	—
92-93—Kingston	OHL	58	55	54	109	125	16	11	18	29	42

GRAVES, ADAM
LW, RANGERS

PERSONAL: Born April 12, 1968, at Toronto. . . . 6-0/203. . . . Shoots left. **TRANSACTIONS/CAREER NOTES:** Bruised shoulder (February 1986). . . . Selected by Detroit Red Wings as underage junior in second round (second Red Wings pick, 22nd overall) of NHL entry draft (June 21, 1986). . . . Traded by Red Wings with C/RW Joe Murphy, LW Petr Klima and D Jeff Sharples to Edmonton Oilers for C Jimmy Carson, C Kevin McClelland and fifth-round pick in 1991 draft (later traded to Montreal Canadiens) (November 2, 1989). . . . Signed as free agent by New York Rangers (September 2, 1991); Oilers received C/LW Troy Mallette as compensation (September 9, 1991). **MISCELLANEOUS:** Member of Stanley Cup championship team (1990).

Season Team	League	REGULAR SEASON					PLAYOFFS				
		Gms.	G	A	Pts.	Pen.	Gms.	G	A	Pts.	Pen.
84-85—King City Jr. B	OHA	25	23	33	56	29	—	—	—	—	—
85-86—Windsor	OHL	62	27	37	64	35	16	5	11	16	10
86-87—Windsor	OHL	66	45	55	100	70	14	9	8	17	32
—Adirondack	AHL	—	—	—	—	—	5	0	1	1	0
87-88—Detroit	NHL	9	0	1	1	8	—	—	—	—	—
—Windsor	OHL	37	28	†32	60	107	12	14	18	32	16
88-89—Detroit	NHL	56	7	5	12	60	5	0	0	0	4
—Adirondack	AHL	14	10	11	21	28	14	11	7	18	17
89-90—Detroit	NHL	13	0	1	1	13	—	—	—	—	—
—Edmonton	NHL	63	9	12	21	123	22	5	6	11	17
90-91—Edmonton	NHL	76	7	18	25	127	18	2	4	6	22
91-92—New York Rangers	NHL	80	26	33	59	139	10	5	3	8	22
92-93—New York Rangers	NHL	84	36	29	65	148	—	—	—	—	—
NHL totals		381	85	99	184	618	55	12	13	25	65

GREEN, MARK
C/LW, LIGHTNING

PERSONAL: Born December 26, 1967, at Massensa, N.Y. . . . 6-3/200. . . . Shoots right. **COLLEGE:** Clarkson (N.Y.). **TRANSACTIONS/CAREER NOTES:** Selected by Winnipeg Jets in ninth round (eighth Jets pick, 176th overall) of NHL entry draft (June 21, 1986). . . . Signed as free agent by Tampa Bay Lightning (August 18, 1992). **HONORS:** Named to ECHL ALL-Star first team (1991-92).

G

Season	Team	League	REGULAR SEASON Gms.	G	A	Pts.	Pen.	PLAYOFFS Gms.	G	A	Pts.	Pen.
85-86—New Hampton Prep.	N.Y. H.S.		26	26	28	54	20	—	—	—	—	—
86-87—New Hampton Prep.	N.Y. H.S.				Statistics unavailable.							
87-88—Clarkson..........	ECAC		18	3	6	9	18	—	—	—	—	—
88-89—Clarkson..........	ECAC		30	16	11	27	42	—	—	—	—	—
89-90—Clarkson..........	ECAC		32	18	17	35	42	—	—	—	—	—
90-91—Clarkson..........	ECAC		38	21	24	45	30	—	—	—	—	—
91-92—Johnstown..........	ECHL		64	68	49	117	44	6	2	3	5	4
92-93—Louisville..........	ECHL		61	48	29	77	57	—	—	—	—	—
—Atlanta..........	IHL		5	0	1	1	0	—	—	—	—	—

GREEN, TRAVIS
C, ISLANDERS

PERSONAL: Born December 20, 1970, at Creston, B.C. . . . 6-0/195. . . . Shoots right.
TRANSACTIONS/CAREER NOTES: Selected by New York Islanders in second round (second Islanders pick, 23rd overall) of NHL entry draft (June 17, 1989). . . . Traded by Spokane Chiefs to Medicine Hat Tigers for RW Mark Woolf, D/LW Chris Lafreniere and C Frank Esposito (January 26, 1990).

Season	Team	League	REGULAR SEASON Gms.	G	A	Pts.	Pen.	PLAYOFFS Gms.	G	A	Pts.	Pen.
85-86—Castlegar..........	KIJHL		35	30	40	70	41	—	—	—	—	—
86-87—Spokane	WHL		64	8	17	25	27	3	0	0	0	0
87-88—Spokane	WHL		72	33	53	86	42	15	10	10	20	13
88-89—Spokane	WHL		72	51	51	102	79	—	—	—	—	—
89-90—Spokane	WHL		50	45	44	89	80	—	—	—	—	—
—Medicine Hat	WHL		25	15	24	39	19	3	0	0	0	2
90-91—Capital District..........	AHL		73	21	34	55	26	—	—	—	—	—
91-92—Capital District..........	AHL		71	23	27	50	10	7	0	4	4	21
92-93—Capital District..........	AHL		20	12	11	23	39	—	—	—	—	—
—New York Islanders..........	NHL		61	7	18	25	43	12	3	1	4	6
NHL totals..........			61	7	18	25	43	12	3	1	4	6

GREENLAW, JEFF
RW, PANTHERS

PERSONAL: Born February 28, 1968, at Toronto. . . . 6-1/230. . . . Shoots left. . . . Full name: Jeff Carl Greenlaw.
TRANSACTIONS/CAREER NOTES: Selected by Washington Capitals in first round (first Capitals pick, 19th overall) of NHL entry draft (June 21, 1986). . . . Suffered stress fracture of vertebrae (April 1987). . . . Suffered deep bruise in right leg (September 1989); missed 65 games. . . . Signed as free agent by Florida Panthers (July 14, 1993).

Season	Team	League	REGULAR SEASON Gms.	G	A	Pts.	Pen.	PLAYOFFS Gms.	G	A	Pts.	Pen.
84-85—St. Catharines Jr. B..........	OHA		33	21	29	50	141	—	—	—	—	—
85-86—Canadian national team ...	Int'l		57	3	16	19	81	—	—	—	—	—
86-87—Washington	NHL		22	0	3	3	44	—	—	—	—	—
—Binghamton	AHL		4	0	2	2	0	—	—	—	—	—
87-88—Binghamton	AHL		56	8	7	15	142	1	0	0	0	2
—Washington	NHL		—	—	—	—	—	1	0	0	0	19
88-89—Baltimore..........	AHL		55	12	15	27	115	—	—	—	—	—
89-90—Baltimore..........	AHL		10	3	2	5	26	7	1	0	1	13
90-91—Baltimore..........	AHL		50	17	17	34	93	3	1	1	2	2
—Washington	NHL		10	2	0	2	10	1	0	0	0	2
91-92—Baltimore..........	AHL		37	6	8	14	57	—	—	—	—	—
—Washington	NHL		5	0	1	1	34	—	—	—	—	—
92-93—Baltimore..........	AHL		49	12	14	26	66	7	3	1	4	0
—Washington	NHL		16	1	1	2	18	—	—	—	—	—
NHL totals..........			53	3	5	8	106	2	0	0	0	21

GREENLAY, MIKE
G, LIGHTNING

PERSONAL: Born September 15, 1968, at Calgary, Alta. . . . 6-3/210. . . . Shoots left. . . . Full name: Michael Ronald Greenlay.
COLLEGE: Lake Superior State (Mich.).
TRANSACTIONS/CAREER NOTES: Selected by Edmonton Oilers in ninth round (ninth Oilers pick, 189th overall) of NHL entry draft (June 21, 1986). . . . Loaned to Knoxville Cherokees (December 2, 1991); returned (January 6, 1992). . . . Loaned to Cherokees (January 1992); returned (February 13, 1992). . . . Signed as free agent by Tampa Bay Lightning (July 29, 1992).
HONORS: Named to Memorial Cup All-Star team (1988-89).

Season	Team	League	REGULAR SEASON Gms.	Min.	W	L	T	GA	SO	Avg.	PLAYOFFS Gms.	Min.	W	L	GA	SO	Avg.
86-87—Lake Superior State	CCHA		17	744	...	...	...	44	...	3.55	—	—	—	—	—	—	—
87-88—Lake Superior State	CCHA		19	1023	...	...	...	57	...	3.34	—	—	—	—	—	—	—
88-89—Lake Superior State	CCHA		2	85	...	...	...	6	0	4.24	—	—	—	—	—	—	—
—Saskatoon..........	WHL		20	1128	...	...	...	86	0	4.57	—	—	—	—	—	—	—
89-90—Cape Breton	AHL		46	2595	...	...	...	146	2	3.38	—	—	—	—	—	—	—
—Edmonton..........	NHL		2	20	0	0	0	4	0	12.00	—	—	—	—	—	—	—
90-91—Knoxville	ECHL		29	1725	...	...	...	108	0	3.76	—	—	—	—	—	—	—
—Cape Breton	AHL		11	493	...	...	...	33	0	4.02	—	—	—	—	—	—	—

G

Season	Team	League	Gms.	Min.	W	L	T	GA	SO	Avg.	Gms.	Min.	W	L	GA	SO	Avg.
91-92—Cape Breton		AHL	3	144	1	1	1	12	0	5.00	—	—	—	—	—	—	—
—Knoxville		ECHL	27	1415	8	12	2	113	1	4.79	—	—	—	—	—	—	—
92-93—Louisville		ECHL	27	1437	...	...	...	96	1	4.01	—	—	—	—	—	—	—
—Atlanta		IHL	12	637	5	3	0	40	0	3.77	—	—	—	—	—	—	—
NHL totals			2	20	0	0	0	4	0	12.00							

GREGG, RANDY

D

PERSONAL: Born February 19, 1956, at Edmonton, Alta. . . . 6-4/215. . . . Shoots left. . . . Full name: Randall John Gregg.
COLLEGE: Alberta (degree in medicine).
TRANSACTIONS/CAREER NOTES: Signed as free agent by Edmonton Oilers (March 1981). . . . Bruised left shoulder (December 1984). . . . Sprained left knee (January 1985). . . . Separated ribs (October 28, 1985); missed 16 games. . . . Announced retirement (September 1986). . . . Returned to Oilers (November 1986). . . . Dislocated left shoulder (March 17, 1987). . . . Pulled leg muscle (December 1988). . . . Pulled leg muscle (September 1989); missed first 21 games of season. . . . Bruised thigh (May 10, 1990). . . . Claimed by Vancouver Canucks in NHL waiver draft (October 2, 1990). . . . Injured groin (October 27, 1991); missed three games.
HONORS: Won Senator Joseph A. Sullivan Award (1978-79).
MISCELLANEOUS: Is a medical doctor. . . . Member of Stanley Cup championship teams (1984, 1985, 1987, 1988 and 1990).

Season	Team	League	Gms.	G	A	Pts.	Pen.	Gms.	G	A	Pts.	Pen.
75-76—University of Alberta		CWUAA	20	3	14	17	27	—	—	—	—	—
76-77—University of Alberta		CWUAA	24	9	17	26	34	—	—	—	—	—
77-78—University of Alberta		CWUAA	24	7	23	30	37	—	—	—	—	—
78-79—University of Alberta		CWUAA	24	5	16	21	47	—	—	—	—	—
79-80—Canadian national team		Int'l	56	7	17	24	36	—	—	—	—	—
—Canadian Olympic Team		Int'l	6	1	1	2	2	—	—	—	—	—
80-81—Kokudo		Japan	35	12	18	30	30	—	—	—	—	—
81-82—Kokudo		Japan	36	12	20	32	25	—	—	—	—	—
—Edmonton		NHL	—	—	—	—	—	4	0	0	0	0
82-83—Edmonton		NHL	80	6	22	28	54	16	2	4	6	13
83-84—Edmonton		NHL	80	13	27	40	56	19	3	7	10	21
84-85—Edmonton		NHL	57	3	20	23	32	17	0	6	6	12
85-86—Edmonton		NHL	64	2	26	28	47	10	1	0	1	12
86-87—Edmonton		NHL	52	8	16	24	42	18	3	6	9	17
87-88—Canadian national team		Int'l	37	2	6	8	37	—	—	—	—	—
—Canadian Olympic Team		Int'l	8	1	2	3	8	—	—	—	—	—
—Edmonton		NHL	15	1	2	3	8	19	1	8	9	24
88-89—Edmonton		NHL	57	3	15	18	28	7	1	0	1	4
89-90—Edmonton		NHL	48	4	20	24	42	20	2	6	8	16
90-91—Vancouver		NHL			Did not play.							
91-92—Vancouver		NHL	21	1	4	5	24	7	0	1	1	8
NHL totals			474	41	152	193	333	137	13	38	51	127

GREIG, MARK

RW, WHALERS

PERSONAL: Born January 25, 1970, at High River, Alta. . . . 5-11/190. . . . Shoots right. . . . Name pronounced GRAYG.
TRANSACTIONS/CAREER NOTES: Selected by Hartford Whalers in first round (first Whalers pick, 15th overall) of NHL entry draft (June 16, 1990). . . . Injured right knee (April 11, 1993); missed final three games of regular season.
HONORS: Named to WHL (East) All-Star first team (1989-90).

Season	Team	League	Gms.	G	A	Pts.	Pen.	Gms.	G	A	Pts.	Pen.
86-87—Calgary		WHL	5	0	0	0	0	—	—	—	—	—
87-88—Lethbridge		WHL	65	9	18	27	38	—	—	—	—	—
88-89—Lethbridge		WHL	71	36	72	108	113	8	5	5	10	16
89-90—Lethbridge		WHL	65	55	80	135	149	18	11	21	32	35
90-91—Hartford		NHL	4	0	0	0	0	—	—	—	—	—
—Springfield		AHL	73	32	55	87	73	17	2	6	8	22
91-92—Hartford		NHL	17	0	5	5	6	—	—	—	—	—
—Springfield		AHL	50	20	27	47	38	9	1	1	2	20
92-93—Hartford		NHL	22	1	7	8	27	—	—	—	—	—
—Springfield		AHL	55	20	38	58	86	—	—	—	—	—
NHL totals			43	1	12	13	33					

GRETZKY, BRENT

C, LIGHTNING

PERSONAL: Born February 20, 1972, at Brantford, Ont. . . . 5-10/160. . . . Shoots left. . . . Brother of Wayne Gretzky, center, Los Angeles Kings.
HIGH SCHOOL: Quinte Secondary School (Belleville, Ont.).
TRANSACTIONS/CAREER NOTES: Selected by Tampa Bay Lightning in third round (third Lightning pick, 49th overall) of NHL entry draft (June 20, 1992).

G

			REGULAR SEASON					PLAYOFFS			
Season	Team	League	Gms.	G	A	Pts.	Pen.	Gms.	G	A	Pts.	Pen.
87-88—Brantford Jr. B		OHA	14	4	11	15	2	—	—	—	—	—
88-89—Brantford Jr. B		OHA	40	29	47	76	57	—	—	—	—	—
89-90—Belleville		OHL	40	29	47	76	57	11	0	0	0	2
90-91—Belleville		OHL	66	26	56	82	25	6	3	3	6	2
91-92—Belleville		OHL	62	43	78	121	37	—	—	—	—	—
92-93—Atlanta		IHL	77	20	34	54	84	9	3	2	5	8

GRETZKY, WAYNE

C, KINGS

PERSONAL: Born January 26, 1961, at Brantford, Ont. . . . 6-0/170. . . . Shoots left. . . . Full name: Wayne Douglas Gretzky. . . . Brother of Brent Gretzky, center in Tampa Bay Lightning system.

TRANSACTIONS/CAREER NOTES: Signed as underage junior by Indianapolis Racers to multi-year contract (May 1978). . . . Traded by Racers with LW Peter Driscoll and G Ed Mio to Edmonton Oilers for cash and future considerations (November 1978). . . . Bruised right shoulder (January 28, 1984). . . . Underwent surgery on left ankle to remove benign growth (June 1984). . . . Twisted right knee (December 30, 1987). . . . Suffered corneal abrasion to left eye (February 19, 1988); missed three games. . . . Traded by Oilers with RW/D Marty McSorley and LW/C Mike Krushelnyski to Los Angeles Kings for C Jimmy Carson, LW Martin Gelinas, first-round picks in 1989 (traded to New Jersey), 1991 (LW Martin Rucinsky) and 1993 (D Nick Stajduhar) drafts and cash (August 9, 1988). . . . Injured groin (March 17, 1990). . . . Strained lower back (March 22, 1990); missed five regular-season games and two playoff games. . . . Missed five games due to personal reasons (October 1991). . . . Sprained knee (February 25, 1992); missed one game. . . . Suffered herniated thoracic disc prior to 1992-93 season; missed first 39 games of season.

HONORS: Won William Hanley Trophy (1977-78). . . . Won Emms Family Award (1977-78). . . . Named to OMJHL All-Star second team (1977-78). . . . Named WHA Rookie of the Year by THE SPORTING NEWS (1978-79). . . . Won WHA Rookie of the Year Award (1978-79). . . . Named to WHA All-Star second team (1978-79). . . . Won Hart Memorial Trophy (1979-80 through 1986-87 and 1988-89). . . . Won Lady Byng Memorial Trophy (1979-80, 1990-91 and 1991-92). . . . Named to THE SPORTING NEWS All-Star second team (1979-80, 1987-88, 1988-89 and 1991-92). . . . Named to NHL All-Star second team (1979-80 and 1987-88 through 1989-90). . . . Named NHL Player of Year by THE SPORTING NEWS (1980-81 through 1986-87). . . . Won Art Ross Memorial Trophy (1980-81 through 1986-87, 1989-90 and 1990-91). . . . Named to THE SPORTING NEWS All-Star first team (1980-81 through 1986-87 and 1990-91) . . . Named to NHL All-Star first team (1980-81 through 1986-87 and 1990-91). . . . Played in NHL All-Star Game (1980 through 1986 and 1988 through 1993). . . . Named Man of the Year by THE SPORTING NEWS (1981). . . . Won Lester B. Pearson Award (1981-82 through 1984-85 and 1986-87). . . . Won Emery Edge Award (1983-84, 1984-85 and 1986-87). . . . Named All-Star Game Most Valuable Player (1983 and 1989). . . . Named Canadian Athlete of the Year (1985). . . . Won Conn Smythe Trophy (1984-85 and 1987-88). . . . Won Dodge Performer of the Year Award (1984-85 through 1986-87). . . . Won Dodge Performance of the Year Award (1988-89).

RECORDS: Holds NHL career records for points—2,328; assists—1,563; overtime assists—10; most games with three or more goals—48; most 40-or-more goal seasons—12; most consecutive 40-or-more goal seasons—12 (1979-80 through 1990-91); most consecutive 60-or-more goal seasons—4 (1981-82 through 1984-85); most 100-or-more point seasons—13; most consecutive 100-or-more point seasons—13 (1979-80 through 1991-92); highest assist-per-game average—1.497; and highest points-per-game average—2.230. . . . Shares NHL career records for most 50-or-more goal seasons—9; and most 60-or-more goal seasons—5. . . . Holds NHL single-season records for most goals—92 (1981-82); assists—163 (1985-86); points—215 (1985-86); games with three or more goals—10 (1981-82 and 1983-84); highest goals-per-game average—1.18 (1983-84); highest assists-per-game average—2.04 (1985-86); and highest points-per-game average—2.77 (1983-84). . . . Shares NHL single-game records for most assists—7 (February 15, 1980; December 11, 1985; and February 14, 1986); and most goals in one period—4 (February 18, 1981). . . . Holds NHL records for most consecutive games scoring points—51 (October 5, 1983 through January 28, 1984); and most consecutive games with an assist—23 (1990-91). . . . Holds NHL career playoff records for most points—346; most goals—110; most assists—236; and most games with three-or-more goals—7. . . . Shares NHL career playoff record for most game-winning goals—18. . . . Holds NHL single-season playoff records for most assists—31 (1988); and most points—47 (1985). . . . Shares NHL single-season playoff record for most shorthanded goals—3 (1983). . . . Holds NHL final-series playoff records for most assists—10 (1988); and most points—13 (1988). . . . Shares NHL single-series playoff record for most assists—14 (1985). . . . Shares NHL single-game playoff records for most assists—6 (April 9, 1987); most shorthanded goals—2 (April 6, 1983); most assists in one period—3 (done five times); and most points in one period—4 (April 12, 1987). . . . Holds NHL career All-Star Game record for most goals—11. . . . Holds NHL All-Star Game records for most goals in one period—4 (1983); and most points in one period—4 (1983). . . . Shares NHL All-Star Game record for most goals—4 (February 8, 1983).

MISCELLANEOUS: Member of Stanley Cup championship teams (1984, 1985, 1987 and 1988).

			REGULAR SEASON					PLAYOFFS			
Season	Team	League	Gms.	G	A	Pts.	Pen.	Gms.	G	A	Pts.	Pen.
76-77—Peterborough		OMJHL	3	0	3	3	0	—	—	—	—	—
77-78—Sault Ste. Marie		OMJHL	64	70	112	182	14	13	6	20	26	0
78-79—Indianapolis		WHA	8	3	3	6	0	—	—	—	—	—
—Edmonton		WHA	72	43	61	104	19	13	†10	10	*20	2
79-80—Edmonton		NHL	79	51	*86	†137	21	3	2	1	3	0
80-81—Edmonton		NHL	80	55	*109	*164	28	9	7	14	21	4
81-82—Edmonton		NHL	80	*92	*120	*212	26	5	5	7	12	8
82-83—Edmonton		NHL	80	*71	*125	*196	59	16	12	*26	*38	4
83-84—Edmonton		NHL	74	*87	*118	*205	39	19	13	*22	*35	12
84-85—Edmonton		NHL	80	*73	*135	*208	52	18	17	*30	*47	4
85-86—Edmonton		NHL	80	52	*163	*215	46	10	8	11	19	2
86-87—Edmonton		NHL	79	*62	*121	*183	28	21	5	*29	*34	6
87-88—Edmonton		NHL	64	40	*109	149	24	19	12	*31	*43	16
88-89—Los Angeles		NHL	78	54	†114	168	26	11	5	17	22	0
89-90—Los Angeles		NHL	73	40	*102	*142	42	7	3	7	10	0
90-91—Los Angeles		NHL	78	41	*122	*163	16	12	4	11	15	2
91-92—Los Angeles		NHL	74	31	*90	121	34	6	2	5	7	2

G

Season Team	League	REGULAR SEASON					PLAYOFFS				
		Gms.	G	A	Pts.	Pen.	Gms.	G	A	Pts.	Pen.
92-93—Los Angeles	NHL	45	16	49	65	6	24	15	25	40	4
WHA totals		80	46	64	110	19	13	10	10	20	2
NHL totals		1044	765	1563	2328	447	180	110	236	346	64

GRIEVE, BRENT
LW, ISLANDERS

PERSONAL: Born May 9, 1969, at Oshawa, Ont. . . . 6-1/205. . . . Shoots left. . . . Name pronounced GREEV.
TRANSACTIONS/CAREER NOTES: Selected by New York Islanders in fourth round (fourth Islanders pick, 65th overall) of NHL entry draft (June 17, 1989).

Season Team	League	REGULAR SEASON					PLAYOFFS				
		Gms.	G	A	Pts.	Pen.	Gms.	G	A	Pts.	Pen.
86-87—Oshawa	OHL	60	9	19	28	102	24	3	8	11	22
87-88—Oshawa	OHL	56	19	20	39	122	7	0	1	1	8
88-89—Oshawa	OHL	49	34	33	67	105	6	4	3	7	4
89-90—Oshawa	OHL	62	46	47	93	125	17	10	10	20	26
90-91—Kansas City	IHL	5	2	2	4	2	—	—	—	—	—
—Capital District	AHL	61	14	13	27	80	—	—	—	—	—
91-92—Capital District	AHL	74	34	32	66	84	7	3	1	4	16
92-93—Capital District	AHL	79	34	28	62	122	4	1	1	2	10

GRIMES, JAKE
C, SENATORS

PERSONAL: Born September 13, 1972, at Montreal. . . . 6-1/196. . . . Shoots left. . . . Full name: Jake Stephen Grimes.
TRANSACTIONS/CAREER NOTES: Selected by Ottawa Senators in 10th round (10th Senators pick, 217th overall) of NHL entry draft (June 20, 1992).

Season Team	League	REGULAR SEASON					PLAYOFFS				
		Gms.	G	A	Pts.	Pen.	Gms.	G	A	Pts.	Pen.
89-90—Belleville	OHA	66	9	12	21	11	—	—	—	—	—
90-91—Belleville	OHA	66	31	41	72	16	—	—	—	—	—
91-92—Belleville	OHA	66	44	69	113	18	—	—	—	—	—
92-93—New Haven	AHL	76	18	20	38	30	—	—	—	—	—

GRIMSON, STU
LW, MIGHTY DUCKS

PERSONAL: Born May 20, 1965, at Kamloops, B.C. . . . 6-5/227. . . . Shoots left.
COLLEGE: Manitoba.
TRANSACTIONS/CAREER NOTES: Fractured forearm (February 1983). . . . Selected by Detroit Red Wings in 10th round (11th Red Wings pick, 186th overall) of NHL entry draft (June 8, 1983). . . . Did not sign with Detroit and returned to entry draft pool (May 1985). . . . Selected by Calgary Flames in seventh round (eighth Flames pick, 143rd overall) of NHL entry draft (June 15, 1985). . . . Broke cheekbone (January 9, 1990). . . . Claimed on waivers by Chicago Blackhawks (October 1, 1990). . . . Injured eye (February 3, 1993). . . . Selected by Mighty Ducks of Anaheim in NHL expansion draft (June 24, 1993).

Season Team	League	REGULAR SEASON					PLAYOFFS				
		Gms.	G	A	Pts.	Pen.	Gms.	G	A	Pts.	Pen.
82-83—Regina	WHL	48	0	1	1	144	5	0	0	0	14
83-84—Regina	WHL	63	8	8	16	131	21	0	1	1	29
84-85—Regina	WHL	71	24	32	56	248	8	1	2	3	14
85-86—University of Manitoba	CWUAA	12	7	4	11	113	3	1	1	2	20
86-87—University of Manitoba	CWUAA	29	8	8	16	67	14	4	2	6	28
87-88—Salt Lake City	IHL	38	9	5	14	268	—	—	—	—	—
88-89—Calgary	NHL	1	0	0	0	5	—	—	—	—	—
—Salt Lake City	IHL	72	9	18	27	*397	15	2	3	5	*86
89-90—Salt Lake City	IHL	62	8	8	16	319	4	0	0	0	8
—Calgary	NHL	3	0	0	0	17	—	—	—	—	—
90-91—Chicago	NHL	35	0	1	1	183	5	0	0	0	46
91-92—Chicago	NHL	54	2	2	4	234	14	0	1	1	10
—Indianapolis	IHL	5	1	1	2	17	—	—	—	—	—
92-93—Chicago	NHL	78	1	1	2	193	2	0	0	0	4
NHL totals		171	3	4	7	632	21	0	1	1	60

GROLEAU, FRANCOIS
D, FLAMES

PERSONAL: Born January 23, 1973, at Longueuil, Que. . . . 6-0/193. . . . Shoots left. . . . Name pronounced GROH-loh.
TRANSACTIONS/CAREER NOTES: Selected by Calgary Flames in second round (second Flames pick, 41st overall) of NHL entry draft (June 22, 1991).
HONORS: Won Raymond Lagace Trophy (1989-90). . . . Named to QMJHL All-Star second team (1989-90). . . . Won Emile (Butch) Bouchard Trophy (1991-92). . . . Named to QMJHL All-Star first team (1991-92).

Season Team	League	REGULAR SEASON					PLAYOFFS				
		Gms.	G	A	Pts.	Pen.	Gms.	G	A	Pts.	Pen.
89-90—Shawinigan	QMJHL	60	11	54	65	80	6	0	1	1	12
90-91—Shawinigan	QMJHL	70	9	60	69	70	6	0	3	3	2
91-92—Shawinigan	QMJHL	65	8	70	78	74	10	5	15	20	8
92-93—St. Jean	QMJHL	48	7	38	45	66	4	0	1	1	14

G

GRONMAN, TUOMAS
D, NORDIQUES

PERSONAL: Born March 22, 1974, at Vitasaari, Finland. . . . 6-2/193. . . . Shoots left.
TRANSACTIONS/CAREER NOTES: Selected by Quebec Nordiques in second round (third Nordiques pick, 29th overall) of NHL entry draft (June 20, 1992).

			REGULAR SEASON					PLAYOFFS				
Season Team	League	Gms.	G	A	Pts.	Pen.	Gms.	G	A	Pts.	Pen.
90-91—Rauman Lukko	Finland	40	15	20	35	60	—	—	—	—	—
91-92—Tacoma	WHL	61	5	18	23	102	4	0	1	1	2
—Finland national Jr. team	Int'l	7	1	0	1	10	—	—	—	—	—
92-93—Rauman Lukko	Finland	45	2	11	13	46	—	—	—	—	—

GROSEK, MICHAL
LW, JETS

PERSONAL: Born June 1, 1975, at Gottwaldov, Czechoslovakia. . . . 6-1/183. . . . Shoots right.
TRANSACTIONS/CAREER NOTES: Selected by Winnipeg Jets in sixth round (seventh Jets pick, 145th overall) of NHL entry draft (June 26, 1993).

			REGULAR SEASON					PLAYOFFS				
Season Team	League	Gms.	G	A	Pts.	Pen.	Gms.	G	A	Pts.	Pen.
92-93—ZPS Zlin	Czech.	17	1	3	4	0	—	—	—	—	—

GRUHL, SCOTT
LW/D

PERSONAL: Born September 13, 1959, at Port Colborne, Ont. . . . 6-0/200. . . . Shoots left. . . . Full name: Scott Kenneth Gruhl.
COLLEGE: Northeastern.
TRANSACTIONS/CAREER NOTES: Signed as free agent by Los Angeles Kings (September 1980). . . . Signed as free agent by Pittsburgh Penguins (December 14, 1987). . . . Fractured left hand (March 1988). . . . Broke two bones in wrist (September 1990). . . . Claimed by Fort Wayne Komets on IHL waivers from Muskegon Lumberjacks (December 3, 1990).
HONORS: Named to IHL All-Star second team (1979-80, 1985-86 and 1991-92). . . . Named to IHL All-Star first team (1983-84 and 1984-85). . . . Won James Gatschene Memorial Trophy (1984-85).

			REGULAR SEASON					PLAYOFFS				
Season Team	League	Gms.	G	A	Pts.	Pen.	Gms.	G	A	Pts.	Pen.
76-77—Northeastern University	Hockey East	17	6	4	10	. . .	—	—	—	—	—
77-78—Northeastern University	Hockey East	28	21	38	59	46	—	—	—	—	—
78-79—Sudbury	OMJHL	68	35	49	84	78	10	5	7	12	15
79-80—Binghamton	AHL	4	1	0	1	6	—	—	—	—	—
—Saginaw	IHL	75	53	40	93	100	7	2	6	8	16
80-81—Houston	CHL	4	0	0	0	0	—	—	—	—	—
—Saginaw	IHL	77	56	34	90	87	13	*11	8	*19	12
81-82—New Haven	AHL	73	28	41	69	107	4	0	4	4	2
—Los Angeles	NHL	7	2	1	3	2	—	—	—	—	—
82-83—New Haven	AHL	68	25	38	63	114	12	3	3	6	22
—Los Angeles	NHL	7	0	2	2	4	—	—	—	—	—
83-84—Muskegon	IHL	56	40	56	96	49	—	—	—	—	—
84-85—Muskegon	IHL	82	62	64	126	102	17	7	*16	23	25
85-86—Muskegon	IHL	82	*59	50	109	178	14	7	†13	20	22
86-87—Muskegon	IHL	67	34	39	73	157	15	5	7	12	54
87-88—Pittsburgh	NHL	6	1	0	1	0	—	—	—	—	—
—Muskegon	IHL	55	28	47	75	115	6	5	1	6	12
88-89—Muskegon	IHL	79	37	55	92	163	14	8	11	19	37
89-90—Muskegon	IHL	80	41	51	92	206	15	8	6	14	26
90-91—Fort Wayne	IHL	59	23	47	70	109	19	4	6	10	39
91-92—Fort Wayne	IHL	78	44	61	105	196	6	2	2	4	48
92-93—Fort Wayne	IHL	73	34	47	81	290	12	4	11	15	14
NHL totals		20	3	3	6	6					

GUAY, PAUL
RW, WHALERS

PERSONAL: Born September 2, 1963, at Providence, R.I. . . . 6-0/185. . . . Shoots right. . . . Name pronounced GAY.
HIGH SCHOOL: Mount St. Charles Academy (Woonsocket, R.I.).
COLLEGE: Providence.
TRANSACTIONS/CAREER NOTES: Selected by Minnesota North Stars as underage junior in sixth round (10th North Stars pick, 118th overall) of NHL entry draft (June 10, 1981). . . . Traded by North Stars with third-round pick in 1985 draft to Philadelphia Flyers for RW Paul Holmgren (February 23, 1984). . . . Traded by Flyers to Los Angeles Kings for RW Steve Seguin (October 11, 1985). . . . Traded by Kings to Boston Bruins for RW Dave Pasin (November 3, 1988). . . . Signed as free agent by New Jersey Devils (August 14, 1989). . . . Signed as free agent by New York Islanders (August 13, 1990). . . . Signed as free agent by Vancouver Canucks (August 22, 1991). . . . Signed as free agent by Hartford Whalers (August 1992).
HONORS: Named to ECAC All-Star second team (1982-83).

			REGULAR SEASON					PLAYOFFS				
Season Team	League	Gms.	G	A	Pts.	Pen.	Gms.	G	A	Pts.	Pen.
79-80—Mount St. Charles H.S.	R.I.H.S.	23	18	19	37	. . .	—	—	—	—	—
80-81—Mount St. Charles H.S.	R.I.H.S.	23	28	38	66	. . .	—	—	—	—	—
81-82—Providence College	ECAC	33	23	17	40	38	—	—	—	—	—
82-83—Providence College	ECAC	42	34	31	65	83	—	—	—	—	—
83-84—U.S. national team	Int'l	62	20	18	38	44	—	—	—	—	—
—U.S. Olympic Team	Int'l	6	1	0	1	8	—	—	—	—	—
—Philadelphia	NHL	14	2	6	8	14	3	0	0	0	4

G

Season	Team	League	REGULAR SEASON Gms.	G	A	Pts.	Pen.	PLAYOFFS Gms.	G	A	Pts.	Pen.
84-85—Hershey		AHL	74	23	30	53	123	—	—	—	—	—
—Philadelphia		NHL	2	0	1	1	0	—	—	—	—	—
85-86—Los Angeles		NHL	23	3	3	6	18	—	—	—	—	—
—New Haven		AHL	57	15	36	51	101	5	3	0	3	11
86-87—Los Angeles		NHL	35	2	5	7	16	2	0	0	0	0
—New Haven		AHL	6	1	3	4	11	—	—	—	—	—
87-88—New Haven		AHL	42	21	26	47	53	—	—	—	—	—
—Los Angeles		NHL	33	4	4	8	40	4	0	1	1	8
88-89—New Haven		AHL	4	4	6	10	20	—	—	—	—	—
—Los Angeles		NHL	2	0	0	0	2	—	—	—	—	—
—Boston		NHL	5	0	2	2	0	—	—	—	—	—
—Maine		AHL	61	15	29	44	77	—	—	—	—	—
89-90—Utica		AHL	75	25	30	55	103	5	2	2	4	13
90-91—New York Islanders		NHL	3	0	2	2	2	—	—	—	—	—
—Capital District		AHL	74	26	35	61	81	—	—	—	—	—
91-92—Milwaukee		IHL	81	24	33	57	93	3	2	1	3	7
92-93—Springfield		AHL	65	10	32	42	90	11	1	2	3	6
NHL totals			117	11	23	34	92	9	0	1	1	12

GUERARD, DANIEL
C/RW, SENATORS

PERSONAL: Born April 9, 1974, at Lasalle, Que. . . . 6-4/211. . . . Shoots right. . . . Name pronounced gair-AHR.

TRANSACTIONS/CAREER NOTES: Selected by Ottawa Senators in fifth round (fifth Senators pick, 98th overall) of NHL entry draft (June 20, 1992).

Season	Team	League	REGULAR SEASON Gms.	G	A	Pts.	Pen.	PLAYOFFS Gms.	G	A	Pts.	Pen.
91-92—Victoriaville		QMJHL	31	5	16	21	66	—	—	—	—	—
92-93—Verdun		QMJHL	58	31	26	57	131	4	1	1	2	17
—New Haven		AHL	2	2	1	3	0	—	—	—	—	—

GUERIN, BILL
C/RW, DEVILS

PERSONAL: Born November 9, 1970, at Wilbraham, Mass. . . . 6-2/190. . . . Shoots right. . . . Full name: William Robert Guerin. . . . Name pronounced GAIR-ihn.

COLLEGE: Boston College.

TRANSACTIONS/CAREER NOTES: Selected by New Jersey Devils in first round (first Devils pick, fifth overall) of NHL entry draft (June 17, 1989). . . . Suffered from the flu (February 1992); missed three games.

Season	Team	League	REGULAR SEASON Gms.	G	A	Pts.	Pen.	PLAYOFFS Gms.	G	A	Pts.	Pen.
85-86—Springfield Jr. B		NEJHL	48	26	19	45	71	—	—	—	—	—
86-87—Springfield Jr. B		NEJHL	32	34	20	54	40	—	—	—	—	—
87-88—Springfield Jr. B		NEJHL	38	31	44	75	146	—	—	—	—	—
88-89—Springfield Jr. B		NEJHL	31	32	37	69	90	—	—	—	—	—
89-90—Boston College		Hockey East	39	14	11	25	64	—	—	—	—	—
90-91—Boston College		Hockey East	38	26	19	45	102	—	—	—	—	—
91-92—U.S. national team		Int'l	46	12	15	27	67	—	—	—	—	—
—Utica		AHL	22	13	10	23	6	4	1	3	4	14
—New Jersey		NHL	5	0	1	1	9	6	3	0	3	4
92-93—New Jersey		NHL	65	14	20	34	63	5	1	1	2	4
—Utica		AHL	18	10	7	17	47	—	—	—	—	—
NHL totals			70	14	21	35	72	11	4	1	5	8

GUILLET, ROBERT
RW, CANADIENS

PERSONAL: Born February 22, 1972, at Montreal. . . . 5-11/189. . . . Shoots right.

TRANSACTIONS/CAREER NOTES: Selected by Montreal Canadiens in third round (fourth Canadiens pick, 60th overall) of NHL entry draft (June 16, 1990).

HONORS: Named to QMJHL All-Star first team (1990-91). . . . Won Guy Lafleur Trophy (1991-92). . . . Named to QMJHL All-Star second team (1991-92).

Season	Team	League	REGULAR SEASON Gms.	G	A	Pts.	Pen.	PLAYOFFS Gms.	G	A	Pts.	Pen.
89-90—Longueuil		QMJHL	69	32	40	72	132	7	2	1	3	16
90-91—Longueuil		QMJHL	69	55	32	87	96	8	4	7	11	27
91-92—Longueuil		QMJHL	67	56	62	118	104	19	†14	11	*25	26
92-93—Fredericton		AHL	42	16	15	31	38	1	0	0	0	0
—Wheeling		ECHL	15	16	14	30	8	—	—	—	—	—

GUIRESTANTE, JOHN
RW, DEVILS

PERSONAL: Born May 11, 1975, at Toronto. . . . 6-2/172. . . . Shoots right.

TRANSACTIONS/CAREER NOTES: Selected by New Jersey Devils in fifth round (fifth Devils pick, 110th overall) of NHL entry draft (June 26, 1993).

Season	Team	League	REGULAR SEASON Gms.	G	A	Pts.	Pen.	PLAYOFFS Gms.	G	A	Pts.	Pen.
91-92—Streetsville Jr. B		OHA	2	1	0	1	2	—	—	—	—	—
92-93—London		OHL	32	7	12	19	13	4	0	0	0	0

G

GUSAROV, ALEXEI

D, NORDIQUES

PERSONAL: Born July 8, 1964, at Leningrad, U.S.S.R. . . . 6-2/170. . . . Shoots left. . . . Name pronounced goo-SAH-rahf.

TRANSACTIONS/CAREER NOTES: Selected by Quebec Nordiques in 11th round (11th Nordiques pick, 213th overall) in the NHL entry draft (June 11, 1988). . . . Suffered hairline fracture of left ankle (December 15, 1990); missed seven games. . . . Hyperextended right knee (February 28, 1991). . . . Fractured finger (October 13, 1991); missed four games. . . . Suffered from the flu (February 9, 1993); missed two games. . . . Suffered concussion (March 31, 1993); missed two games.

MISCELLANEOUS: Member of gold-medal-winning U.S.S.R. Olympic team (1988).

Season Team	League	REGULAR SEASON					PLAYOFFS				
		Gms.	G	A	Pts.	Pen.	Gms.	G	A	Pts.	Pen.
81-82—Leningrad SKA	USSR	20	1	2	3	16	—	—	—	—	—
82-83—Leningrad SKA	USSR	42	2	1	3	32	—	—	—	—	—
83-84—Leningrad SKA	USSR	43	2	3	5	32	—	—	—	—	—
84-85—CSKA Moscow	USSR	36	3	2	5	26	—	—	—	—	—
85-86—CSKA Moscow	USSR	40	3	5	8	30	—	—	—	—	—
86-87—CSKA Moscow	USSR	38	4	7	11	24	—	—	—	—	—
87-88—CSKA Moscow	USSR	39	3	2	5	28	—	—	—	—	—
88-89—CSKA Moscow	USSR	42	5	4	9	37	—	—	—	—	—
89-90—CSKA Moscow	USSR	42	4	7	11	42	—	—	—	—	—
90-91—CSKA Moscow	USSR	15	0	0	0	12	—	—	—	—	—
—Quebec	NHL	36	3	9	12	12	—	—	—	—	—
—Halifax	AHL	2	0	3	3	2	—	—	—	—	—
91-92—Quebec	NHL	68	5	18	23	22	—	—	—	—	—
—Halifax	AHL	3	0	0	0	0	—	—	—	—	—
92-93—Quebec	NHL	79	8	22	30	57	5	0	1	1	0
NHL totals		183	16	49	65	91	5	0	1	1	0

GUSMANOV, RAVIL

RW, JETS

PERSONAL: Born July 22, 1972, at Naberezhnye Chelny, U.S.S.R. . . . 6-3/185. . . . Shoots left.

TRANSACTIONS/CAREER NOTES: Selected by Winnipeg Jets in fourth round (fifth Jets pick, 93rd overall) of NHL entry draft (June 26, 1993).

Season Team	League	REGULAR SEASON					PLAYOFFS				
		Gms.	G	A	Pts.	Pen.	Gms.	G	A	Pts.	Pen.
90-91—Traktor Chelyabinsk	USSR	15	0	0	0	10	—	—	—	—	—
91-92—Traktor Chelyabinsk	CIS	38	4	4	8	20	—	—	—	—	—
92-93—Traktor Chelyabinsk	CIS	39	15	8	23	30	8	4	0	4	2

GUY, KEVAN

D, FLAMES

PERSONAL: Born July 16, 1965, at Edmonton, Alta. . . . 6-3/205. . . . Shoots right.

TRANSACTIONS/CAREER NOTES: Selected by Calgary Flames as underage junior in fourth round (fifth Flames pick, 71st overall) of NHL entry draft (June 8, 1983). . . . Traded by Flames to Vancouver Canucks to complete March 1988 deal in which Flames sent C Brian Bradley and RW Peter Bakovic to Canucks for C Craig Coxe (June 1988). . . . Fractured bone in right foot (February 18, 1990); missed 10 games. . . . Traded by Canucks with RW Ronnie Stern and fourth-round pick in 1992 draft to Flames for D Dana Murzyn and option to switch fourth-round picks in 1992 draft; Calgary did not exercise option (March 5, 1991). . . . Pulled hamstring (December 2, 1991).

Season Team	League	REGULAR SEASON					PLAYOFFS				
		Gms.	G	A	Pts.	Pen.	Gms.	G	A	Pts.	Pen.
82-83—Medicine Hat	WHL	69	7	20	27	89	5	0	3	3	16
83-84—Medicine Hat	WHL	72	15	42	57	117	14	3	4	7	14
84-85—Medicine Hat	WHL	31	7	17	24	46	10	1	2	3	2
85-86—Moncton	AHL	73	4	20	24	56	10	0	2	2	6
86-87—Moncton	AHL	46	2	10	12	38	—	—	—	—	—
—Calgary	NHL	24	0	4	4	19	4	0	1	1	23
87-88—Calgary	NHL	11	0	3	3	8	—	—	—	—	—
—Salt Lake City	IHL	61	6	30	36	49	19	1	6	7	26
88-89—Vancouver	NHL	45	2	2	4	34	1	0	0	0	0
89-90—Milwaukee	IHL	29	2	11	13	33	—	—	—	—	—
—Vancouver	NHL	30	2	5	7	32	—	—	—	—	—
90-91—Vancouver	NHL	39	1	6	7	39	—	—	—	—	—
—Calgary	NHL	4	0	0	0	4	—	—	—	—	—
91-92—Salt Lake City	IHL	60	3	14	17	89	5	0	1	1	4
—Calgary	NHL	3	0	0	0	2	—	—	—	—	—
92-93—Salt Lake City	IHL	33	1	9	10	50	—	—	—	—	—
NHL totals		156	5	20	25	138	5	0	1	1	23

HAAS, DAVID

LW, OILERS

PERSONAL: Born July 23, 1968, at Toronto. . . . 6-2/196. . . . Shoots left. . . . Full name: David John Haas.

TRANSACTIONS/CAREER NOTES: Selected by Edmonton Oilers as underage junior in fifth round (fifth Oilers pick, 105th overall) of NHL entry draft (June 21, 1986). . . . Traded by London Knights with C Kelly Cain and D Ed Kister to Kitchener Rangers for RW Peter Lisy, D Ian Pound, D Steve Marcolini and C Greg Hankkio (October 1986). . . . Loaned to New Haven Nighthawks (December 4, 1991).

HONORS: Named to OHL All-Star second team (1987-88).

GH

Season	Team	League	REGULAR SEASON					PLAYOFFS				
			Gms.	G	A	Pts.	Pen.	Gms.	G	A	Pts.	Pen.
85-86	London	OHL	62	4	13	17	91	5	0	1	1	0
86-87	London	OHL	5	1	0	1	5	—	—	—	—	—
	Kitchener	OHL	4	0	1	1	4	—	—	—	—	—
	Belleville	OHL	55	10	13	23	86	6	3	0	3	13
87-88	Belleville	OHL	5	1	1	2	9	—	—	—	—	—
	Windsor	OHL	58	59	46	105	237	11	9	11	20	50
88-89	Cape Breton	AHL	61	9	9	18	325	—	—	—	—	—
89-90	Cape Breton	AHL	53	6	12	18	230	4	2	2	4	15
90-91	Cape Breton	AHL	60	24	23	47	137	3	0	2	2	12
	Edmonton	NHL	5	1	0	1	0	—	—	—	—	—
91-92	Cape Breton	AHL	16	3	7	10	32	—	—	—	—	—
	New Haven	AHL	50	13	23	36	97	5	3	0	3	13
92-93	Cape Breton	AHL	73	22	56	78	121	16	11	13	24	36
	NHL totals		5	1	0	1	0					

HACKETT, JEFF
G, BLACKHAWKS

PERSONAL: Born June 1, 1968, at London, Ont. . . . 6-1/180. . . . Shoots left.
TRANSACTIONS/CAREER NOTES: Selected by New York Islanders as underage junior in second round (second Islanders pick, 34th overall) of NHL entry draft (June 13, 1987). . . . Strained groin (May 13, 1990). . . . Selected by San Jose Sharks in NHL expansion draft (May 30, 1991). . . . Injured groin and hamstring (December 3, 1991); missed nine games. . . . Injured knee (March 23, 1992). . . . Injured groin (October 30, 1992); missed 12 games. . . . Suffered from the flu (February 20, 1993); missed five games. . . . Traded by Sharks to Chicago Blackhawks for conditional pick in 1994 draft (July 13, 1993).
HONORS: Won F.W. (Dinty) Moore Trophy (1986-87). . . . Shared Dave Pinkney Trophy with Sean Evoy (1986-87). . . . Won Jack Butterfield Trophy (1989-90).

Season	Team	League	REGULAR SEASON								PLAYOFFS						
			Gms.	Min.	W	L	T	GA	SO	Avg.	Gms.	Min.	W	L	GA	SO	Avg.
85-86	London Jr. B	OHA	19	1150	...	...	...	66	0	3.44	—	—					
86-87	Oshawa	OHL	31	1672	18	9	2	85	2	3.05	15	895	8	7	40	0	2.68
87-88	Oshawa	OHL	53	3165	30	21	2	205	0	3.89	7	438	3	4	31	0	4.25
88-89	New York Islanders	NHL	13	662	4	7	0	39	0	3.53	—	—					
	Springfield	AHL	29	1677	12	14	2	116	0	4.15	—	—					
89-90	Springfield	AHL	54	3045	24	25	3	187	1	3.68	†17	934	10	5	*60	0	3.85
90-91	New York Islanders	NHL	30	1508	5	18	1	91	0	3.62	—	—					
91-92	San Jose	NHL	42	2314	11	27	1	148	0	3.84	—	—					
92-93	San Jose	NHL	36	2000	2	30	1	176	0	5.28	—	—					
	NHL totals		121	6484	22	82	3	454	0	4.20							

HALKIDIS, BOB
D, MAPLE LEAFS

PERSONAL: Born March 5, 1966, at Toronto. . . . 6-0/200. . . . Shoots left. . . . Name pronounced hal-KEE-dihz.
TRANSACTIONS/CAREER NOTES: Broke ankle (September 1982). . . . Reinjured ankle (November 1982); missed two weeks. . . . Selected by Buffalo Sabres as underage junior in fourth round (fourth Sabres pick, 81st overall) of NHL entry draft (June 9, 1984). . . . Dislocated right shoulder (December 4, 1985); missed 15 games. . . . Suspended six games by AHL for fighting (October 23, 1987). . . . Injured ankle (December 1987). . . . Injured shoulder (December 1988). . . . Traded by Sabres to Los Angeles Kings for D Dale DeGray (November 24, 1989). . . . Underwent surgery to left shoulder (May 1990). . . . Underwent surgery to left shoulder (October 16, 1990). . . . Signed as free agent by Toronto Maple Leafs (July 24, 1991). . . . Pulled groin (November 21, 1991); missed three games.
HONORS: Won Max Kaminsky Trophy (1984-85). . . . Named to OHL All-Star first team (1984-85).

Season	Team	League	REGULAR SEASON					PLAYOFFS				
			Gms.	G	A	Pts.	Pen.	Gms.	G	A	Pts.	Pen.
82-83	London	OHL	37	3	12	15	52	—	—	—	—	—
83-84	London	OHL	51	9	22	31	123	8	0	2	2	27
84-85	London	OHL	62	14	50	64	154	8	3	6	9	22
	Buffalo	NHL	—					4	0	0	0	19
85-86	Buffalo	NHL	37	1	9	10	115	—	—	—	—	—
86-87	Buffalo	NHL	6	1	1	2	19	—	—	—	—	—
	Rochester	AHL	59	1	8	9	144	8	0	0	0	43
87-88	Rochester	AHL	15	2	5	7	50	—	—	—	—	—
	Buffalo	NHL	30	0	3	3	115	4	0	0	0	22
88-89	Buffalo	NHL	16	0	1	1	66	—	—	—	—	—
	Rochester	AHL	16	0	6	6	64	—	—	—	—	—
89-90	Rochester	AHL	18	1	13	14	70	—	—	—	—	—
	Los Angeles	NHL	20	0	4	4	56	—	—	—	—	—
	New Haven	AHL	30	3	17	20	67	—	—	—	—	—
90-91	Phoenix	IHL	4	1	5	6	6	—	—	—	—	—
	New Haven	AHL	7	1	3	4	10	—	—	—	—	—
	Los Angeles	NHL	34	1	3	4	133	3	0	0	0	0
91-92	Toronto	NHL	46	3	3	6	145	—	—	—	—	—
92-93	St. John's	AHL	29	2	13	15	61	—	—	—	—	—
	Milwaukee	IHL	26	0	9	9	79	5	0	1	1	27
	NHL totals		189	6	24	30	649	11	0	0	0	41

H

HALL, TODD
D, WHALERS

PERSONAL: Born January 22, 1973, at Columbia, S.C. . . . 6-1/212. . . . Shoots left.
HIGH SCHOOL: Hamden (Conn.).
COLLEGE: Boston College.
TRANSACTIONS/CAREER NOTES: Selected by Hartford Whalers in third round (third Whalers pick, 53rd overall) of NHL entry draft (June 12, 1991).

			REGULAR SEASON					PLAYOFFS				
Season	Team	League	Gms.	G	A	Pts.	Pen.	Gms.	G	A	Pts.	Pen.
88-89—Hamden H.S.		Conn. H.S.	24	12	21	33	6	—	—	—	—	—
89-90—Hamden H.S.		Conn. H.S.	17	10	22	32	6	—	—	—	—	—
90-91—Hamden H.S.		Conn. H.S.	23	10	15	25	12	—	—	—	—	—
91-92—Boston College		Hockey East	33	2	10	12	14	—	—	—	—	—
92-93—Boston College		Hockey East	34	2	10	12	22	—	—	—	—	—

HALLER, KEVIN
D, CANADIENS

PERSONAL: Born December 5, 1970, at Trochu, Alta. . . . 6-2/183. . . . Shoots left.
TRANSACTIONS/CAREER NOTES: Broke leg (October 1986). . . . Broke leg (May 1987). . . . Selected by Buffalo Sabres in first round (first Sabres pick, 14th overall) of NHL entry draft (June 17, 1989). . . . Separated shoulder (May 7, 1991); missed seven games. . . . Traded by Sabres to Montreal Canadiens for D Petr Svoboda (March 10, 1992).
HONORS: Won Bill Hunter Trophy (1989-90). . . . Named to WHL (East) All-Star first team (1989-90).
MISCELLANEOUS: Member of Stanley Cup championship team (1993).

			REGULAR SEASON					PLAYOFFS				
Season	Team	League	Gms.	G	A	Pts.	Pen.	Gms.	G	A	Pts.	Pen.
87-88—Olds		AJHL	54	13	31	44	58	—	—	—	—	—
88-89—Regina		WHL	72	10	31	41	99	—	—	—	—	—
89-90—Regina		WHL	58	16	37	53	93	11	2	9	11	16
—Buffalo		NHL	2	0	0	0	0	—	—	—	—	—
90-91—Rochester		AHL	52	2	8	10	53	10	2	1	3	6
—Buffalo		NHL	21	1	8	9	20	6	1	4	5	10
91-92—Buffalo		NHL	58	6	15	21	75	—	—	—	—	—
—Rochester		AHL	4	0	0	0	18	—	—	—	—	—
—Montreal		NHL	8	2	2	4	17	9	0	0	0	6
92-93—Montreal		NHL	73	11	14	25	117	17	1	6	7	16
NHL totals			162	20	39	59	229	32	2	10	12	32

HALVERSON, TREVOR
LW, MIGHTY DUCKS

PERSONAL: Born April 6, 1971, at White River, Ont. . . . 6-1/195. . . . Shoots left. . . . Full name: Trevor Lloyd Halverson.
TRANSACTIONS/CAREER NOTES: Selected by Washington Capitals in first round (second Capitals pick, 21st overall) of NHL entry draft (June 22, 1991). . . . Selected by Mighty Ducks of Anaheim in NHL expansion draft (June 24, 1993).
HONORS: Named to OHL All-Star first team (1990-91).

			REGULAR SEASON					PLAYOFFS				
Season	Team	League	Gms.	G	A	Pts.	Pen.	Gms.	G	A	Pts.	Pen.
88-89—North Bay		OHL	52	8	10	18	77	—	—	—	—	—
89-90—North Bay		OHL	54	22	20	42	162	2	2	1	3	2
90-91—North Bay		OHL	64	59	36	95	128	10	3	6	9	4
91-92—Baltimore		AHL	74	10	11	21	181	—	—	—	—	—
92-93—Baltimore		AHL	67	19	21	40	170	2	1	0	1	0
—Hampton Roads		ECHL	9	7	5	12	6	—	—	—	—	—

HAMMOND, KEN
D, SENATORS

PERSONAL: Born August 23, 1963, at London, Ont. . . . 6-1/190. . . . Shoots left. . . . Full name: Kenneth Paul Hammond.
HIGH SCHOOL: Saunders (London, Ont.).
COLLEGE: Rensselaer Polytechnic Institute (N.Y.).
TRANSACTIONS/CAREER NOTES: Selected by Los Angeles Kings in eighth round (eighth Kings pick, 147th overall) of NHL entry draft (June 8, 1983). . . . Sprained knee (March 13, 1988). . . . Selected by Edmonton Oilers in NHL waiver draft for $30,000 (October 3, 1988). . . . Claimed on waivers by New York Rangers when the Oilers attempted to assign him to Cape Breton (November 1, 1988). . . . Traded by Rangers to Toronto Maple Leafs for LW Chris McRae (February 19, 1989). . . . Suffered back spasms (March 1989). . . . Sold by Maple Leafs to Boston Bruins (August 20, 1990). . . . Signed as free agent by San Jose Sharks (August 9, 1991). . . . Pulled groin (January 23, 1992); missed five games. . . . Fractured hand (February 21, 1992); missed seven games. . . . Traded by Sharks to Vancouver Canucks for eighth-round pick in 1992 draft, later traded to Detroit (March 9, 1992). . . . Underwent surgery to hand (March 1992). . . . Selected by Ottawa Senators in NHL expansion draft (June 18, 1992).
HONORS: Named to NCAA All-America East first team (1984-85). . . . Named to NCAA All-Tournament team (1984-85). . . . Named to ECAC All-Star first team (1984-85).

			REGULAR SEASON					PLAYOFFS				
Season	Team	League	Gms.	G	A	Pts.	Pen.	Gms.	G	A	Pts.	Pen.
81-82—R.P.I.		ECAC	29	2	3	5	54	—	—	—	—	—
82-83—R.P.I.		ECAC	28	4	13	17	54	—	—	—	—	—
83-84—R.P.I.		ECAC	34	5	11	16	72	—	—	—	—	—
84-85—R.P.I.		ECAC	38	11	28	39	90	—	—	—	—	—
—Los Angeles		NHL	3	1	0	1	0	3	0	0	0	4
85-86—New Haven		AHL	67	4	12	16	96	4	0	0	0	7
—Los Angeles		NHL	3	0	1	1	2	—	—	—	—	—

H

Season Team	League	REGULAR SEASON Gms.	G	A	Pts.	Pen.	PLAYOFFS Gms.	G	A	Pts.	Pen.
86-87—New Haven	AHL	66	1	15	16	76	6	0	1	1	21
—Los Angeles	NHL	10	0	2	2	11	—	—	—	—	—
87-88—New Haven	AHL	26	3	8	11	27	—	—	—	—	—
—Los Angeles	NHL	46	7	9	16	69	2	0	0	0	4
88-89—Edmonton	NHL	5	0	1	1	8	—	—	—	—	—
—New York Rangers	NHL	3	0	0	0	0	—	—	—	—	—
—Toronto	NHL	14	0	2	2	12	—	—	—	—	—
—Denver	IHL	38	5	18	23	24	—	—	—	—	—
89-90—Newmarket	AHL	75	9	45	54	106	—	—	—	—	—
90-91—Boston	NHL	1	1	0	1	2	8	0	0	0	10
—Maine	AHL	80	10	41	51	159	2	0	1	1	16
91-92—San Jose	NHL	46	5	10	15	82	—	—	—	—	—
—Vancouver	NHL	—	—	—	—	—	2	0	0	0	6
92-93—Ottawa	NHL	62	4	4	8	104	—	—	—	—	—
—New Haven	AHL	4	0	1	1	4	—	—	—	—	—
NHL totals		193	18	29	47	290	15	0	0	0	24

HAMR, RADEK
D, SENATORS

PERSONAL: Born June 15, 1974, at Prague, Czechoslovakia. . . . 5-11/167. . . . Shoots left.
TRANSACTIONS/CAREER NOTES: Selected by Ottawa Senators in fourth round (fourth Senators pick, 73rd overall) of NHL entry draft (June 20, 1992).

Season Team	League	REGULAR SEASON Gms.	G	A	Pts.	Pen.	PLAYOFFS Gms.	G	A	Pts.	Pen.
91-92—Sparta Prague	Czech.	3	0	0	0	0	—	—	—	—	—
92-93—New Haven	AHL	59	4	21	25	18	—	—	—	—	—
—Ottawa	NHL	4	0	0	0	0	—	—	—	—	—
NHL totals		4	0	0	0	0					

HAMRLIK, MARTIN
D, WHALERS

PERSONAL: Born May 6, 1973, at Zlin, Czechoslovakia. . . . 5-11/176. . . . Shoots right. . . . Name pronounced HAM-uhr-lihk. . . . Brother of Roman Hamrlik, defenseman, Tampa Bay Lightning.
TRANSACTIONS/CAREER NOTES: Selected by Hartford Whalers in second round (second Whalers pick, 31st overall) of NHL entry draft (June 22, 1991). . . . Suffered from Lyme disease (October 1991); missed remainder of season.

Season Team	League	REGULAR SEASON Gms.	G	A	Pts.	Pen.	PLAYOFFS Gms.	G	A	Pts.	Pen.
89-90—TJ Zlin	Czech.	12	2	0	2	. . .	—	—	—	—	—
90-91—TJ Zlin	Czech.	50	8	14	22	44	—	—	—	—	—
91-92—ZPS Zlin	Czech.	4	0	2	2	. . .	—	—	—	—	—
92-93—Ottawa	OHL	26	4	11	15	41	—	—	—	—	—
—Springfield	AHL	8	1	3	4	16	—	—	—	—	—

HAMRLIK, ROMAN
D, LIGHTNING

PERSONAL: Born April 12, 1974, at Gottwaldov, Czechoslovakia. . . . 6-2/189. . . . Shoots left. . . . Name pronounced ROH-muhn HAM-uhr-lihk. . . . Brother of Martin Hamrlik, defenseman in Hartford Whalers system.
TRANSACTIONS/CAREER NOTES: Selected by Tampa Bay Lightning in first round (first Lightning pick, first overall) of NHL entry draft (June 20, 1992).

Season Team	League	REGULAR SEASON Gms.	G	A	Pts.	Pen.	PLAYOFFS Gms.	G	A	Pts.	Pen.
90-91—TJ Zlin	Czech.	14	2	2	4	18	—	—	—	—	—
91-92—ZPS Zlin	Czech.	34	5	5	10	34	—	—	—	—	—
92-93—Tampa Bay	NHL	67	6	15	21	71	—	—	—	—	—
—Atlanta	IHL	2	1	1	2	2	—	—	—	—	—
NHL totals		67	6	15	21	71					

HANKINSON, BEN
RW, DEVILS

PERSONAL: Born January 5, 1969, at Edina, Minn. . . . 6-2/180. . . . Shoots right. . . . Full name: Benjamin John Hankinson.
HIGH SCHOOL: Edina (Minn.).
COLLEGE: Minnesota.
TRANSACTIONS/CAREER NOTES: Selected by New Jersey Devils in sixth round (fifth Devils pick, 107th overall) of NHL entry draft (June 13, 1987).
HONORS: Named to WCHA All-Star first team (1989-90).

Season Team	League	REGULAR SEASON Gms.	G	A	Pts.	Pen.	PLAYOFFS Gms.	G	A	Pts.	Pen.
85-86—Edina High School	Minn. H.S.	. . .	9	21	30	. . .	—	—	—	—	—
86-87—Edina High School	Minn. H.S.	26	14	20	34	. . .	—	—	—	—	—
87-88—University of Minnesota	WCHA	24	4	7	11	36	—	—	—	—	—
88-89—University of Minnesota	WCHA	43	7	11	18	115	—	—	—	—	—
89-90—University of Minnesota	WCHA	46	25	41	66	34	—	—	—	—	—
90-91—University of Minnesota	WCHA	43	19	21	40	133	—	—	—	—	—

H

Season Team	League	REGULAR SEASON					PLAYOFFS				
		Gms.	G	A	Pts.	Pen.	Gms.	G	A	Pts.	Pen.
91-92—Utica	AHL	77	17	16	33	186	4	3	1	4	2
92-93—Utica	AHL	75	35	27	62	145	5	2	2	4	6
—New Jersey	NHL	4	2	1	3	9	—	—	—	—	—
NHL totals		4	2	1	3	9					

HANKINSON, PETER
C

PERSONAL: Born November 24, 1967, at Edina, Minn. . . . 5-9/175. . . . Shoots right. . . . Brother of Ben Hankinson, right winger in New Jersey Devils system.
HIGH SCHOOL: Edina (Minn.).
COLLEGE: Minnesota.
TRANSACTIONS/CAREER NOTES: Selected by Winnipeg Jets in NHL supplemental draft (June 16, 1989). . . . Signed as free agent by San Diego Gulls (July 22, 1992). . . . Traded by Gulls to Fort Wayne Komets for future considerations (December 17, 1992); Komets sent RW Max Middendorf to Gulls to complete deal (January 4, 1993).

Season Team	League	REGULAR SEASON					PLAYOFFS				
		Gms.	G	A	Pts.	Pen.	Gms.	G	A	Pts.	Pen.
86-87—University of Minnesota	WCHA	43	16	12	28	10	—	—	—	—	—
87-88—University of Minnesota	WCHA	39	25	20	45	32	—	—	—	—	—
88-89—University of Minnesota	WCHA	48	16	27	43	42	—	—	—	—	—
89-90—University of Minnesota	WCHA	45	19	12	31	116	—	—	—	—	—
90-91—Moncton	AHL	47	2	14	16	10	4	0	0	0	0
—Fort Wayne	IHL	10	1	2	3	4	—	—	—	—	—
91-92—Fort Wayne	IHL	75	25	38	63	44	7	1	3	4	2
92-93—San Diego	IHL	25	7	7	14	10	—	—	—	—	—
—Fort Wayne	IHL	40	12	15	27	16	12	1	3	4	6

HANNAN, DAVE
C, SABRES

PERSONAL: Born November 26, 1961, at Sudbury, Ont. . . . 5-10/185. . . . Shoots left.
TRANSACTIONS/CAREER NOTES: Bruised shoulder; missed part of 1980-81 season. . . . Selected by Pittsburgh Penguins in 10th round (ninth Penguins pick, 196th overall) of NHL entry draft (June 10, 1981). . . . Injured knee and underwent surgery (January 9, 1987). . . . Traded by Penguins with C Craig Simpson, D Chris Joseph and D Moe Mantha to Edmonton Oilers for D Paul Coffey, LW Dave Hunter and RW Wayne Van Dorp (November 24, 1987). . . . Selected by Penguins in NHL waiver draft (October 3, 1988); LW Dave Hunter was taken by Oilers as compensation. . . . Suffered hip pointer (October 1988). . . . Sprained knee (March 1989). . . . Selected by Toronto Maple Leafs in NHL waiver draft for $7,500 (October 2, 1989). . . . Injured left knee ligaments (November 22, 1989). . . . Underwent surgery to left knee (December 18, 1989); missed 23 games. . . . Traded by Maple Leafs to Buffalo Sabres for fifth-round pick in 1992 draft (RW Chris Deruiter) (March 10, 1992). . . . Injured shoulder (April 12, 1992). . . . Broke toe (January 19, 1993); missed three games.
MISCELLANEOUS: Member of Stanley Cup championship team (1988). . . . Member of silver-medal-winning Canadian Olympic team (1992).

Season Team	League	REGULAR SEASON					PLAYOFFS				
		Gms.	G	A	Pts.	Pen.	Gms.	G	A	Pts.	Pen.
77-78—Windsor	OMJHL	68	14	16	30	43	—	—	—	—	—
78-79—Sault Ste. Marie	OMJHL	26	7	8	15	13	—	—	—	—	—
79-80—Sault Ste. Marie	OMJHL	28	11	10	21	31	—	—	—	—	—
—Brantford	OMJHL	25	5	10	15	26	—	—	—	—	—
80-81—Brantford	OMJHL	56	46	35	81	155	6	2	4	6	20
81-82—Erie	AHL	76	33	37	70	129	—	—	—	—	—
—Pittsburgh	NHL	1	0	0	0	0	—	—	—	—	—
82-83—Baltimore	AHL	5	2	2	4	13	—	—	—	—	—
—Pittsburgh	NHL	74	11	22	33	127	—	—	—	—	—
83-84—Baltimore	AHL	47	18	24	42	98	10	2	6	8	27
—Pittsburgh	NHL	24	2	3	5	33	—	—	—	—	—
84-85—Baltimore	AHL	49	20	25	45	91	—	—	—	—	—
—Pittsburgh	NHL	30	6	7	13	43	—	—	—	—	—
85-86—Pittsburgh	NHL	75	17	18	35	91	—	—	—	—	—
86-87—Pittsburgh	NHL	58	10	15	25	56	—	—	—	—	—
87-88—Pittsburgh	NHL	21	4	3	7	23	—	—	—	—	—
—Edmonton	NHL	51	9	11	20	43	12	1	1	2	8
88-89—Pittsburgh	NHL	72	10	20	30	157	8	0	1	1	4
89-90—Toronto	NHL	39	6	9	15	55	3	1	0	1	4
90-91—Toronto	NHL	74	11	23	34	82	—	—	—	—	—
91-92—Toronto	NHL	35	2	2	4	16	—	—	—	—	—
—Canadian national team	Int'l	3	0	0	0	2	—	—	—	—	—
—Canadian Olympic Team	Int'l	8	3	5	8	8	—	—	—	—	—
—Buffalo	NHL	12	2	4	6	48	7	2	0	2	2
92-93—Buffalo	NHL	55	5	15	20	43	8	1	1	2	18
NHL totals		621	95	152	247	817	38	5	3	8	36

HARDY, MARK
D, KINGS

PERSONAL: Born February 1, 1959, at Semaden, Switzerland. . . . 5-11/195. . . . Shoots left. . . . Full name: Mark Lea Hardy.
TRANSACTIONS/CAREER NOTES: Selected by Los Angeles Kings in second round (third Kings pick, 30th overall) of NHL entry draft (August 9, 1979). . . . Underwent surgery to sublexation tendon in left wrist (October 1985); missed 25 games. . . . Suffered viral infection (January 1988). . . . Traded by Kings to New

H

York Rangers for RW Ron Duguay (February 23, 1988).... Traded by Rangers to Minnesota North Stars for future draft considerations (LW Louie DeBrusk) (June 13, 1988).... Injured wrist (October 19, 1988).... Traded by North Stars to Rangers for LW Larry Bernard and fifth-round pick in 1989 draft (D Rhys Hollyman) (December 10, 1988).... Sprained wrist (March 1989).... Sprained right ankle (March 3, 1990); missed 13 regular-season games and two playoff games.... Reinjured ankle (April 9, 1990); missed remainder of playoffs.... Suspended five games by NHL for stick-swinging (November 16, 1990).... Strained back (November 4, 1991); missed four games.... Separated shoulder (December 31, 1991); missed 24 games.... Traded by Rangers with fifth-round pick in 1993 draft (G Frederick Beaubien) to Los Angeles Kings for C John McIntyre (March 22, 1993).

HONORS: Won Emile (Butch) Bouchard Trophy (1977-78).... Named to QMJHL All-Star first team (1977-78).

Season	Team	League	REGULAR SEASON					PLAYOFFS				
			Gms.	G	A	Pts.	Pen.	Gms.	G	A	Pts.	Pen.
75-76—Montreal		QMJHL	64	6	17	23	44	—	—	—	—	—
76-77—Montreal		QMJHL	72	20	40	60	137	12	4	8	12	14
77-78—Montreal		QMJHL	72	25	57	82	150	13	3	10	13	22
78-79—Montreal		QMJHL	67	18	52	70	117	11	5	8	13	40
79-80—Binghamton		AHL	56	3	13	16	32	—	—	—	—	—
—Los Angeles		NHL	15	0	1	1	10	4	1	1	2	9
80-81—Los Angeles		NHL	77	5	20	25	77	4	1	2	3	4
81-82—Los Angeles		NHL	77	6	39	45	130	10	1	2	3	9
82-83—Los Angeles		NHL	74	5	34	39	101	—	—	—	—	—
83-84—Los Angeles		NHL	79	8	41	49	122	—	—	—	—	—
84-85—Los Angeles		NHL	78	14	39	53	97	3	0	1	1	2
85-86—Los Angeles		NHL	55	6	21	27	71	—	—	—	—	—
86-87—Los Angeles		NHL	73	3	27	30	120	5	1	2	3	10
87-88—Los Angeles		NHL	61	6	22	28	99	—	—	—	—	—
—New York Rangers		NHL	19	2	2	4	31	—	—	—	—	—
88-89—Minnesota		NHL	15	2	4	6	26	—	—	—	—	—
—New York Rangers		NHL	45	2	12	14	45	4	0	1	1	31
89-90—New York Rangers		NHL	54	0	15	15	94	3	0	1	1	2
90-91—New York Rangers		NHL	70	1	5	6	89	6	0	1	1	30
91-92—New York Rangers		NHL	52	1	8	9	65	13	0	3	3	31
92-93—New York Rangers		NHL	44	1	10	11	85	—	—	—	—	—
—Los Angeles		NHL	11	0	3	3	4	15	1	2	3	30
NHL totals			899	62	303	365	1266	67	5	16	21	158

HARKINS, BRETT
LW/C, ISLANDERS

PERSONAL: Born July 2, 1970, at North Ridgefield, O.... 6-1/170.... Shoots left.... Full name: Brett Alan Harkins.... Brother of Todd Harkins, center, Calgary Flames.
COLLEGE: Bowling Green State.
TRANSACTIONS/CAREER NOTES: Selected by New York Islanders in seventh round (ninth Islanders pick, 133rd overall) of NHL entry draft (June 17, 1989).
HONORS: Named to CCHA All-Rookie team (1989-90).

Season	Team	League	REGULAR SEASON					PLAYOFFS				
			Gms.	G	A	Pts.	Pen.	Gms.	G	A	Pts.	Pen.
87-88—Brockville		COJHL	55	21	55	76	36	—	—	—	—	—
88-89—Detroit Compuware		NAJHL	38	23	46	69	94	—	—	—	—	—
89-90—Bowling Green State		CCHA	41	11	43	54	45	—	—	—	—	—
90-91—Bowling Green State		CCHA	40	22	38	60	30	—	—	—	—	—
91-92—Bowling Green State		CCHA	34	8	39	47	32	—	—	—	—	—
92-93—Bowling Green State		CCHA	35	19	28	47	28	—	—	—	—	—

HARKINS, TODD
C, FLAMES

PERSONAL: Born October 8, 1968, at Cleveland.... 6-3/210.... Shoots right.... Full name: Todd Michael Harkins.... Brother of Brett Harkins, left winger/center in New York Islanders system.
COLLEGE: Miami of Ohio.
TRANSACTIONS/CAREER NOTES: Selected by Calgary Flames in second round (second Flames pick, 42nd overall) of NHL entry draft (June 11, 1988).

Season	Team	League	REGULAR SEASON					PLAYOFFS				
			Gms.	G	A	Pts.	Pen.	Gms.	G	A	Pts.	Pen.
86-87—Aurora Jr. B		OHA	40	19	29	48	102	—	—	—	—	—
87-88—Miami of Ohio		CCHA	34	9	7	16	133	—	—	—	—	—
88-89—Miami of Ohio		CCHA	36	8	7	15	77	—	—	—	—	—
89-90—Miami of Ohio		CCHA	40	27	17	44	78	—	—	—	—	—
90-91—Salt Lake City		IHL	79	15	27	42	113	3	0	0	0	2
91-92—Salt Lake City		IHL	72	32	30	62	67	5	1	1	2	6
—Calgary		NHL	5	0	0	0	7	—	—	—	—	—
92-93—Salt Lake City		IHL	53	13	21	34	90	—	—	—	—	—
—Calgary		NHL	15	2	3	5	22	—	—	—	—	—
NHL totals			20	2	3	5	29					

HARLOCK, DAVID
D, DEVILS

PERSONAL: Born March 16, 1971, at Toronto.... 6-2/195.... Shoots left.... Full name: David Alan Harlock.
COLLEGE: Michigan.
TRANSACTIONS/CAREER NOTES: Injured knee (October 1988).... Selected by New Jersey Devils in second round (second Devils pick, 24th overall) of NHL entry draft (June 16, 1990).

Season Team	League	REGULAR SEASON					PLAYOFFS				
		Gms.	G	A	Pts.	Pen.	Gms.	G	A	Pts.	Pen.
86-87—Toronto Red Wings	MTHL	86	17	55	72	60	—	—	—	—	—
87-88—Toronto Red Wings	MTHL	70	16	56	72	100	—	—	—	—	—
88-89—St. Michael's Jr. B	ODHA	25	4	15	19	34	—	—	—	—	—
89-90—University of Michigan	CCHA	42	2	13	15	44	—	—	—	—	—
90-91—University of Michigan	CCHA	39	2	8	10	70	—	—	—	—	—
91-92—University of Michigan	CCHA	44	1	6	7	80	—	—	—	—	—
92-93—University of Michigan	CCHA	38	3	9	12	58	—	—	—	—	—
—Canadian national team	Int'l	4	0	0	0	2	—	—	—	—	—

HARTJE, TOD
RW, JETS

PERSONAL: Born February 27, 1968, at Anoka, Minn. . . . 6-1/200. . . . Shoots left. . . . Full name: Tod Dale Hartje. . . . Name pronounced HAHRT-jee.
HIGH SCHOOL: Anoka (Minn.).
COLLEGE: Harvard.
TRANSACTIONS/CAREER NOTES: Selected by Winnipeg Jets in seventh round (seventh Jets pick, 142nd overall) of NHL entry draft (June 13, 1987). . . . Assigned to Sokol Kiev for 1990-91 season (April 9, 1990).

Season Team	League	REGULAR SEASON					PLAYOFFS				
		Gms.	G	A	Pts.	Pen.	Gms.	G	A	Pts.	Pen.
85-86—Anoka H.S.	Minn. H.S.	22	25	34	59	. . .	—	—	—	—	—
86-87—Harvard University	ECAC	34	3	9	12	36	—	—	—	—	—
87-88—Harvard University	ECAC	32	5	17	22	40	—	—	—	—	—
88-89—Harvard University	ECAC	33	4	17	21	40	—	—	—	—	—
89-90—Harvard University	ECAC	28	6	10	16	29	—	—	—	—	—
90-91—Sokol Kiev	USSR	32	2	4	6	18	—	—	—	—	—
—Fort Wayne	IHL	1	1	0	1	2	—	—	—	—	—
91-92—Moncton	AHL	38	9	9	18	35	—	—	—	—	—
92-93—Moncton	AHL	29	3	7	10	2	—	—	—	—	—
—Fort Wayne	IHL	5	1	2	3	6	—	—	—	—	—
—Providence	AHL	29	2	14	16	32	4	1	0	1	20

HARTMAN, MIKE
LW/RW, RANGERS

PERSONAL: Born February 7, 1967, at West Bloomfield, Mich. . . . 6-0/192. . . . Shoots left. . . . Full name: Michael Jay Hartman.
TRANSACTIONS/CAREER NOTES: Selected by Buffalo Sabres in seventh round (eighth Sabres pick, 131th overall) of NHL entry draft (June 21, 1986). . . . Suffered sore back (January 1989). . . . Sprained right ankle (December 1, 1989); missed five games. . . . Reinjured right ankle (December 29, 1989); missed five games. . . . Injured ankle (March 10, 1990). . . . Injured elbow (Novembr 3, 1990); missed seven games. . . . Traded by Sabres with LW Darrin Shannon and D Dean Kennedy to Winnipeg Jets for RW Dave McIlwain, D Gordon Donnelly, fifth-round pick in 1992 draft (LW Yuri Khmylev) and future considerations (October 11, 1991). . . . Suffered from the flu (December 1991); missed one game. . . . Selected by Tampa Bay Lightning in NHL expansion draft (June 18, 1992). . . . Suffered forearm cut (October 20, 1992); missed four games. . . . Bruised ribs (December 5, 1992); missed three games. . . . Traded by Lightning to New York Rangers for C Randy Gilhen (March 22, 1993).

Season Team	League	REGULAR SEASON					PLAYOFFS				
		Gms.	G	A	Pts.	Pen.	Gms.	G	A	Pts.	Pen.
84-85—Belleville	OHL	49	13	12	25	119	—	—	—	—	—
85-86—Belleville	OHL	4	2	1	3	5	—	—	—	—	—
—North Bay	OHL	53	19	16	35	205	10	2	4	6	34
86-87—North Bay	OHL	32	15	24	39	144	19	7	8	15	88
—Buffalo	NHL	17	3	3	6	69	—	—	—	—	—
87-88—Rochester	AHL	57	13	14	27	283	4	1	0	1	22
—Buffalo	NHL	18	3	1	4	90	6	0	0	0	35
88-89—Buffalo	NHL	70	8	9	17	316	5	0	0	0	34
89-90—Buffalo	NHL	60	11	10	21	211	6	0	0	0	18
90-91—Buffalo	NHL	60	9	3	12	204	2	0	0	0	17
91-92—Winnipeg	NHL	75	4	4	8	264	2	0	0	0	2
92-93—Tampa Bay	NHL	58	4	4	8	154	—	—	—	—	—
—New York Rangers	NHL	3	0	0	0	6	—	—	—	—	—
NHL totals		361	42	34	76	1314	21	0	0	0	106

HARVEY, TODD
C, STARS

PERSONAL: Born February 17, 1975, at Hamilton, Ont. . . . 5-11/190. . . . Shoots right.
TRANSACTIONS/CAREER NOTES: Selected by Dallas Stars in first round (first Stars pick, ninth overall) of NHL entry draft (June 26, 1993).
HONORS: Named to Can.HL All-Rookie Team (1991-92). . . . Named to OHL Rookie All-Star Team (1991-92).

Season Team	League	REGULAR SEASON					PLAYOFFS				
		Gms.	G	A	Pts.	Pen.	Gms.	G	A	Pts.	Pen.
89-90—Cambridge Jr. B	OHA	41	35	27	62	213	—	—	—	—	—
90-91—Cambridge Jr. B	OHA	35	32	39	71	174	—	—	—	—	—
91-92—Detroit	OHL	58	21	43	64	141	7	3	5	8	32
92-93—Detroit	OHL	55	50	50	100	83	15	9	12	21	39

H

HASEK, DOMINIK
G, SABRES

PERSONAL: Born January 29, 1965, at Pardubice, Czechoslovakia. .... 5-11/168. .... Name pronounced HA-sheek.
TRANSACTIONS/CAREER NOTES: Selected by Chicago Blackhawks in 10th round (11th Blackhawks pick, 199th overall) of NHL entry draft (June 8, 1983).... Traded by Blackhawks to Buffalo Sabres for G Stephane Beauregard and future considerations (August 7, 1992).... Injured groin (November 25, 1992); missed three games.... Pulled stomach muscle (January 6, 1993); missed six games.
HONORS: Named Czechoslovakian League Player of the Year (1986-87, 1988-89 and 1989-90).... Named to Czechoslovakian League All-Star team (1988-89 and 1989-90).... Named to IHL All-Star first team (1990-91).... Named to NHL All-Rookie team (1991-92).

Season	Team	League	Gms.	Min.	W	L	T	GA	SO	Avg.	Gms.	Min.	W	L	GA	SO	Avg.
81-82	Pardubice	Czech.	12	661	...	...	...	34	0	3.09	—	—	—	—	—	—	—
82-83	Pardubice	Czech.	42	2358	...	...	...	105	0	2.67	—	—	—	—	—	—	—
83-84	Pardubice	Czech.	40	2304	...	...	...	108	0	2.81	—	—	—	—	—	—	—
84-85	Pardubice	Czech.	42	2419	...	...	...	131	0	3.25	—	—	—	—	—	—	—
85-86	Pardubice	Czech.	45	2689	...	...	...	138	0	3.08	—	—	—	—	—	—	—
86-87	Pardubice	Czech.	23	2515	...	...	...	103	0	2.46	—	—	—	—	—	—	—
87-88	Pardubice	Czech.	31	2265	...	...	...	98	0	2.60	—	—	—	—	—	—	—
88-89	Pardubice	Czech.	42	2507	...	...	...	114	0	2.73	—	—	—	—	—	—	—
89-90	Dukla Jihlava	Czech.	40	2251	...	...	...	80	0	2.13	—	—	—	—	—	—	—
90-91	Chicago	NHL	5	195	3	0	1	8	0	2.46	3	69	0	0	3	0	2.61
	Indianapolis	IHL	33	1903	20	11	4	80	*5	*2.52	1	60	1	0	3	0	3.00
91-92	Indianapolis	IHL	20	1162	7	10	3	69	1	3.56	—	—	—	—	—	—	—
	Chicago	NHL	20	1014	10	4	1	44	1	2.60	3	158	0	2	8	0	3.04
92-93	Buffalo	NHL	28	1429	11	10	4	75	0	3.15	1	45	1	0	1	0	1.33
NHL totals			53	2638	24	14	6	127	1	2.89	7	272	1	2	12	0	2.65

HATCHER, DERIAN
D, STARS

PERSONAL: Born June 4, 1972, at Sterling Heights, Mich. .... 6-5/205. .... Shoots left. ... Brother of Kevin Hatcher, defenseman, Washington Capitals.
TRANSACTIONS/CAREER NOTES: Underwent knee surgery (January 1989).... Selected by Minnesota North Stars in first round (first North Stars pick, eighth overall) of NHL entry draft (June 16, 1990).... Suspended 10 games by NHL (December 1991).... Fractured ankle in off-ice incident (January 19, 1992); missed 21 games.... Sprained knee (January 6, 1993); missed 14 games.... Suspended one game by NHL for game misconduct penalties (March 9, 1993).... North Stars franchise moved from Minnesota to Dallas and renamed Stars for 1993-94 season.

Season	Team	League	Gms.	G	A	Pts.	Pen.	Gms.	G	A	Pts.	Pen.
88-89	Detroit G.P.D.	MNHL	51	19	35	54	100	—	—	—	—	—
89-90	North Bay	OHL	64	14	38	52	81	5	2	3	5	8
90-91	North Bay	OHL	64	13	50	63	163	10	2	10	12	28
91-92	Minnesota	NHL	43	8	4	12	88	5	0	2	2	8
92-93	Minnesota	NHL	67	4	15	19	178	—	—	—	—	—
	Kalamazoo	IHL	2	1	2	3	21	—	—	—	—	—
NHL totals			110	12	19	31	266	5	0	2	2	8

HATCHER, KEVIN
D, CAPITALS

PERSONAL: Born September 9, 1966, at Detroit. .... 6-4/225. .... Shoots right. ... Full name: Kevin John Hatcher. ... Brother of Derian Hatcher, defenseman, Dallas Stars.
TRANSACTIONS/CAREER NOTES: Selected by Washington Capitals as underage junior in first round (first Capitals pick, 17th overall) of NHL entry draft (June 9, 1984).... Tore cartilage in left knee (October 1987).... Pulled groin (January 1989).... Fractured two metatarsal bones in left foot (February 5, 1989); missed 15 games.... Sprained left knee (April 27, 1990).... Did not attend Capitals training camp due to contract dispute (September 1990).... Injured right knee (November 10, 1990).... Suspended one game by NHL for game misconduct penalties (February 2, 1993).
HONORS: Named to OHL All-Star second team (1984-85).... Played in NHL All-Star Game (1990 through 1992).

Season	Team	League	Gms.	G	A	Pts.	Pen.	Gms.	G	A	Pts.	Pen.
83-84	North Bay	OHL	67	10	39	49	61	4	2	2	4	11
84-85	North Bay	OHL	58	26	37	63	75	8	5	8	13	9
	Washington	NHL	2	1	0	1	0	1	0	0	0	0
85-86	Washington	NHL	79	9	10	19	119	9	1	1	2	19
86-87	Washington	NHL	78	8	16	24	144	7	1	0	1	20
87-88	Washington	NHL	71	14	27	41	137	14	5	7	12	55
88-89	Washington	NHL	62	13	27	40	101	6	1	4	5	20
89-90	Washington	NHL	80	13	41	54	102	11	0	8	8	32
90-91	Washington	NHL	79	24	50	74	69	11	3	3	6	8
91-92	Washington	NHL	79	17	37	54	105	7	2	4	6	19
92-93	Washington	NHL	83	34	45	79	114	6	0	1	1	14
NHL totals			613	133	253	386	891	72	13	28	41	187

HAUER, BRETT
D, CANUCKS

PERSONAL: Born July 11, 1971, at Edina, Minn. .... 6-2/180. .... Shoots right. ... Full name: Brett Timothy Hauer.... Cousin of Don Jackson, defenseman, Minnesota North Stars, Edmonton Oilers and New York Rangers (1977-78 through 1986-87).
HIGH SCHOOL: Richfield (Minn.).

COLLEGE: Minnesota-Duluth.
TRANSACTIONS/CAREER NOTES: Selected by Vancouver Canucks in fourth round (third Canucks pick, 71st overall) of NHL entry draft (June 17, 1989).... Separated shoulder (December 1990).
HONORS: Named WCHA Student-Athlete of the Year (1992-93).... Named to NCAA All-America West first team (1992-1993). ... Named to WCHA All-Star first team (1992-93).

			REGULAR SEASON					PLAYOFFS				
Season	Team	League	Gms.	G	A	Pts.	Pen.	Gms.	G	A	Pts.	Pen.
87-88	Richfield H.S.	Minn. H.S.	24	3	3	6	...	—	—	—	—	—
88-89	Richfield H.S.	Minn. H.S.	24	8	15	23	70	—	—	—	—	—
89-90	Minnesota-Duluth	WCHA	37	2	6	8	44	—	—	—	—	—
90-91	Minnesota-Duluth	WCHA	30	1	7	8	54	—	—	—	—	—
91-92	Minnesota-Duluth	WCHA	33	8	14	22	40	—	—	—	—	—
92-93	Minnesota-Duluth	WCHA	40	10	46	56	54	—	—	—	—	—

HAWERCHUK, DALE
C, SABRES

PERSONAL: Born April 4, 1963, at Toronto.... 5-11/190.... Name pronounced HOW-uhr-CHUHK.
TRANSACTIONS/CAREER NOTES: Selected by Winnipeg Jets as underage junior in first round (first Jets pick, first overall) of NHL entry draft (June 10, 1981).... Broke rib (April 13, 1985).... Fractured cheekbone (February 1, 1989).... Traded by Jets with first-round pick in 1990 draft (LW Brad May) to Buffalo Sabres for D Phil Housley, LW Scott Arniel, RW Jeff Parker and first-round pick in 1990 draft (C Keith Tkachuk) (June 16, 1990).... Injured hip (March 8, 1992); missed one game.... Sprained right knee (February 12, 1993); missed three games.
HONORS: Won the Instructeurs Trophy (1979-80).... Won the Guy Lafleur Trophy (1979-80).... Named to Memorial Cup All-Star team (1979-80 and 1980-81).... Won the Can.HL Player of the Year Award (1980-81).... Won the Michel Briere Trophy (1980-81).... Won the Jean Beliveau Trophy (1980-81).... Won Association of Journalists for Major Junior League Hockey Trophy (1980-81).... Won the CCM Trophy (1980-81).... Named to QMJHL All-Star first team (1980-81).... Named NHL Rookie of the Year by THE SPORTING NEWS (1981-82).... Won the Calder Memorial Trophy (1981-82).... Played in NHL All-Star Game (1982, 1985, 1986 and 1988).... Named to THE SPORTING NEWS All-Star second team (1984-85).... Named to NHL All-Star second team (1984-85).
RECORDS: Holds NHL single-game record for most assists in one period—5 (March 6, 1984).
STATISTICAL NOTES: Youngest player in NHL history to have 100-point season (18 years 351 days).

			REGULAR SEASON					PLAYOFFS				
Season	Team	League	Gms.	G	A	Pts.	Pen.	Gms.	G	A	Pts.	Pen.
79-80	Cornwall	QMJHL	72	37	66	103	21	18	20	25	45	0
80-81	Cornwall	QMJHL	72	*81	*102	*183	69	19	15	20	35	8
81-82	Winnipeg	NHL	80	45	58	103	47	4	1	7	8	5
82-83	Winnipeg	NHL	79	40	51	91	31	3	1	4	5	8
83-84	Winnipeg	NHL	80	37	65	102	73	3	1	1	2	0
84-85	Winnipeg	NHL	80	53	77	130	74	3	2	1	3	4
85-86	Winnipeg	NHL	80	46	59	105	44	3	0	3	3	0
86-87	Winnipeg	NHL	80	47	53	100	54	10	5	8	13	4
87-88	Winnipeg	NHL	80	44	77	121	59	5	3	4	7	16
88-89	Winnipeg	NHL	75	41	55	96	28	—	—	—	—	—
89-90	Winnipeg	NHL	79	26	55	81	60	7	3	5	8	2
90-91	Buffalo	NHL	80	31	58	89	32	6	2	4	6	10
91-92	Buffalo	NHL	77	23	75	98	27	7	2	5	7	0
92-93	Buffalo	NHL	81	16	80	96	52	8	5	9	14	2
NHL totals			951	449	763	1212	581	59	25	51	76	51

HAWGOOD, GREG
D, FLYERS

PERSONAL: Born August 10, 1968, at St. Albert, Alta.... 5-10/190.... Shoots left.... Full name: Gregory William Hawgood.
TRANSACTIONS/CAREER NOTES: Selected by Boston Bruins as underage junior in 10th round (ninth Bruins pick, 202nd overall) of NHL entry draft (June 21, 1986).... Announced that he would play in Italy for 1990-91 season (July 1990).... Traded by Bruins to Edmonton Oilers for C Vladimir Ruzicka (October 22, 1990).... Traded by Oilers with C Josef Beranek to Philadelphia Flyers for D Brian Benning (January 16, 1993).
HONORS: Named to WHL (West) All-Star first team (1985-86 through 1987-88).... Won Can.HL Defenseman of the Year Award (1987-88).... Won Bill Hunter Trophy (1987-88).... Won Eddie Shore Plaque (1991-92).... Named to AHL All-Star first team (1991-92).

			REGULAR SEASON					PLAYOFFS				
Season	Team	League	Gms.	G	A	Pts.	Pen.	Gms.	G	A	Pts.	Pen.
83-84	Kamloops	WHL	49	10	23	33	39	—	—	—	—	—
84-85	Kamloops	WHL	66	25	40	65	72	—	—	—	—	—
85-86	Kamloops	WHL	71	34	85	119	86	16	9	22	31	16
86-87	Kamloops	WHL	61	30	93	123	139	—	—	—	—	—
87-88	Boston	NHL	1	0	0	0	0	3	1	0	1	0
	Kamloops	WHL	63	48	85	133	142	16	10	16	26	33
88-89	Boston	NHL	56	16	24	40	84	10	0	2	2	2
	Maine	AHL	21	2	9	11	41	—	—	—	—	—
89-90	Boston	NHL	77	11	27	38	76	15	1	3	4	12
90-91	Asiago	Italy	2	...	...	...	...	—	—	—	—	—
	Maine	AHL	5	0	1	1	13	—	—	—	—	—
	Cape Breton	AHL	55	10	32	42	73	4	0	3	3	23
	Edmonton	NHL	6	0	1	1	6	—	—	—	—	—

H

Season	Team	League	Gms.	G	A	Pts.	Pen.	Gms.	G	A	Pts.	Pen.
			REGULAR SEASON					**PLAYOFFS**				
91-92	—Cape Breton	AHL	56	20	55	75	26	3	2	2	4	0
	—Edmonton	NHL	20	2	11	13	22	13	0	3	3	23
92-93	—Edmonton	NHL	29	5	13	18	35	—	—	—	—	—
	—Philadelphia	NHL	40	6	22	28	39	—	—	—	—	—
	NHL totals		229	40	98	138	262	41	2	8	10	37

HAWKINS, TODD
RW, MAPLE LEAFS

PERSONAL: Born August 2, 1966, at Kingston, Ont. . . . 6-1/195. . . . Shoots right.
TRANSACTIONS/CAREER NOTES: Selected by Vancouver Canucks in 11th round (10th Canucks pick, 217th overall) of NHL entry draft (June 21, 1986). . . . Suspended two games by OHL (October 1, 1986). . . . Bruised hand (September 1988). . . . Traded by Canucks to Toronto Maple Leafs for D Brian Blad (January 22, 1991).
HONORS: Named to OHL All-Star second team (1986-87).

Season	Team	League	Gms.	G	A	Pts.	Pen.	Gms.	G	A	Pts.	Pen.
			REGULAR SEASON					**PLAYOFFS**				
84-85	—Belleville	OHL	58	7	16	23	117	12	1	0	1	10
85-86	—Belleville	OHL	60	14	13	27	172	24	9	7	16	60
86-87	—Belleville	OHL	60	47	40	87	187	6	3	5	8	16
87-88	—Flint	IHL	50	13	13	26	337	16	3	5	8	*174
	—Fredericton	AHL	2	0	0	0	11	—	—	—	—	—
88-89	—Vancouver	NHL	4	0	0	0	9	—	—	—	—	—
	—Milwaukee	IHL	63	12	14	26	307	9	1	0	1	33
89-90	—Vancouver	NHL	4	0	0	0	6	—	—	—	—	—
	—Milwaukee	IHL	61	23	17	40	273	5	4	1	5	19
90-91	—Milwaukee	IHL	39	9	11	20	134	—	—	—	—	—
	—Newmarket	AHL	22	2	5	7	66	—	—	—	—	—
91-92	—St. John's	AHL	66	30	27	57	139	7	1	0	1	10
	—Toronto	NHL	2	0	0	0	0	—	—	—	—	—
92-93	—St. John's	AHL	72	21	41	62	103	9	1	3	4	10
	NHL totals		10	0	0	0	15					

HAYWARD, BRIAN
G, SHARKS

PERSONAL: Born June 25, 1960, at Georgetown, Ont. . . . 5-10/180. . . . Shoots left. . . . Full name: Brian George Hayward.
COLLEGE: Cornell.
TRANSACTIONS/CAREER NOTES: Signed as free agent by Winnipeg Jets (September 1982). . . . Traded by Jets to Montreal Canadiens for G Steve Penney and LW Jan Ingman (August 1986). . . . Suffered back spasms (November 1987). . . . Pulled thigh muscle (December 26, 1987). . . . Injured back (February 23, 1988). . . . Suffered back spasms (November 1988). . . . Sprained left wrist (February 1990). . . . Suspended by Canadiens after missing team practice (October 8, 1990); missed a month. . . . Traded by Canadiens to Minnesota North Stars for D Jayson More (November 7, 1990). . . . Selected by San Jose Sharks in NHL dispersal draft (May 30, 1991). . . . Injured back (October 21, 1991); missed 19 games. . . . Injured back (January 27, 1992). . . . Suffered hip flexor strain (January 10, 1993); missed two games. . . . Injured back (January 15, 1993); missed remainder of season.
HONORS: Named to NCAA All-America team (1981-82). . . . Named to ECAC All-Star first team (1981-82). . . . Shared William M. Jennings Trophy with Patrick Roy (1988-89).

Season	Team	League	Gms.	Min.	W	L	T	GA	SO	Avg.	Gms.	Min.	W	L	GA	SO	Avg.
			REGULAR SEASON								**PLAYOFFS**						
78-79	—Cornell University	ECAC	25	1469	18	6	0	95	0	3.88	3	179	2	1	14	0	4.69
79-80	—Cornell University	ECAC	12	508	2	7	0	52	0	6.14	—	—	—	—	—	—	—
80-81	—Cornell University	ECAC	19	967	11	4	1	58	1	3.60	4	181	2	1	18	0	5.97
81-82	—Cornell University	ECAC	22	1320	11	10	1	68	0	3.09	—	—	—	—	—	—	—
82-83	—Sherbrooke	AHL	22	1208	6	11	3	89	1	4.42	—	—	—	—	—	—	—
	—Winnipeg	NHL	24	1440	10	12	2	89	1	3.71	3	160	0	3	14	0	5.25
83-84	—Sherbrooke	AHL	15	781	4	8	0	69	0	5.30	—	—	—	—	—	—	—
	—Winnipeg	NHL	28	1530	7	18	2	124	0	4.86	—	—	—	—	—	—	—
84-85	—Winnipeg	NHL	61	3436	33	17	7	220	0	3.84	6	309	2	4	23	0	4.47
85-86	—Sherbrooke	AHL	3	185	2	0	1	5	0	1.62	—	—	—	—	—	—	—
	—Winnipeg	NHL	52	2721	13	28	5	217	0	4.79	2	68	0	1	6	0	5.29
86-87	—Montreal	NHL	37	2178	19	13	4	102	1	2.81	13	708	6	5	32	0	2.71
87-88	—Montreal	NHL	39	2247	22	10	4	107	2	2.86	4	230	2	2	9	0	2.35
88-89	—Montreal	NHL	36	2091	20	13	3	101	1	2.90	2	124	1	1	7	0	3.39
89-90	—Montreal	NHL	29	1674	10	12	6	94	1	3.37	1	33	0	0	2	0	3.64
90-91	—Minnesota	NHL	26	1473	6	15	3	77	2	3.14	6	171	0	2	11	0	3.86
	—Kalamazoo	IHL	2	120	...	...	...	5	0	2.50	—	—	—	—	—	—	—
91-92	—San Jose	NHL	7	305	1	4	0	25	0	4.92	—	—	—	—	—	—	—
	—Kansas City	IHL	2	119	1	1	0	3	1	1.51	—	—	—	—	—	—	—
92-93	—San Jose	NHL	18	930	2	14	1	86	0	5.55	—	—	—	—	—	—	—
	NHL totals		357	20025	143	156	37	1242	8	3.72	37	1803	11	18	104	0	3.46

HAYWARD, RICK
D, ISLANDERS

PERSONAL: Born February 25, 1966, at Toledo, O. . . . 6-0/200. . . . Shoots left.
TRANSACTIONS/CAREER NOTES: Selected by Montreal Canadiens in eighth round (ninth Canadiens pick, 162nd overall) of NHL entry draft (June 21, 1986). . . . Traded by Canadiens to Calgary Flames for RW Martin Nicoletti (February 20, 1988). . . . Suspended six games

by IHL for abusing an official (October 12, 1988).... Signed as free agent by Los Angeles Kings (August 1990).... Signed as free agent by New York Islanders (July 25, 1991).... Signed as free agent by Winnipeg Jets (July 30, 1992).... Traded by Jets to New York Islanders for future considerations (February 22, 1993).

		REGULAR SEASON					PLAYOFFS				
Season Team	League	Gms.	G	A	Pts.	Pen.	Gms.	G	A	Pts.	Pen.
84-85—Hull	QMJHL	56	7	27	34	367	—	—	—	—	—
85-86—Hull	QMJHL	59	3	40	43	354	15	2	11	13	*98
86-87—Sherbrooke	AHL	43	2	3	5	153	3	0	1	1	15
87-88—Sherbrooke	AHL	22	1	5	6	91	—	—	—	—	—
—Saginaw	IHL	24	3	4	7	129	—	—	—	—	—
—Salt Lake City	IHL	17	1	3	4	124	13	0	1	1	120
88-89—Salt Lake City	IHL	72	4	20	24	313	10	4	3	7	42
89-90—Salt Lake City	IHL	58	5	13	18	*419	—	—	—	—	—
90-91—Los Angeles	NHL	4	0	0	0	5	—	—	—	—	—
—Phoenix	IHL	60	9	13	22	369	7	1	2	3	44
91-92—Capital District	AHL	27	3	8	11	139	7	0	0	0	58
92-93—Moncton	AHL	47	1	3	4	231	4	1	1	2	27
—Capital District	AHL	19	0	1	1	80	—	—	—	—	—
NHL totals		4	0	0	0	5					

HEALY, GLENN
G, RANGERS

PERSONAL: Born August 23, 1962, at Pickering, Ont.... 5-10/185.... Shoots left.
COLLEGE: Western Michigan.
TRANSACTIONS/CAREER NOTES: Signed as free agent by Los Angeles Kings (June 13, 1985).... Signed as free agent by New York Islanders (August 16, 1989); Kings received fourth-round pick in 1990 draft, later traded to Minnesota.... Strained left ankle ligaments (October 13, 1990); missed eight games.... Fractured right index finger (November 10, 1991); missed five games.... Fractured right thumb (January 3, 1992); missed 10 games.... Severed tip of finger in practice and underwent reconstructive surgery (March 2, 1992); missed 13 games.... Suffered from tendinitis in right wrist (January 9, 1993); missed four games.... Selected by Mighty Ducks of Anaheim in NHL expansion draft (June 24, 1993).... Selected by Tampa Bay Lightning in Phase II of NHL expansion draft (June 25, 1993).... Traded by Lightning to New York Rangers for third-round pick in 1993 draft; Lighting reacquired their original pick which they had traded away earlier (June 25, 1993).
HONORS: Named to NCAA All-America West second team (1984-85).... Named to CCHA All-Star second team (1984-85).

		REGULAR SEASON							PLAYOFFS						
Season Team	League	Gms.	Min.	W	L	T	GA	SO	Avg.	Gms.	Min.	W	L	GA	SO	Avg.
81-82—Western Michigan U.	CCHA	27	1569	7	19	1	116	0	4.44	—	—	—	—	—	—	—
82-83—Western Michigan U.	CCHA	30	1733	8	19	2	116	0	4.02	—	—	—	—	—	—	—
83-84—Western Michigan U.	CCHA	38	2242	19	16	3	146	0	3.91	—	—	—	—	—	—	—
84-85—Western Michigan U.	CCHA	37	2172	21	14	2	118	...	3.26	—	—	—	—	—	—	—
85-86—Toledo	IHL	7	402	...	...	...	28	0	4.18	—	—	—	—	—	—	—
—New Haven	AHL	43	2410	21	15	4	160	0	3.98	2	119	0	2	11	0	5.55
—Los Angeles	NHL	1	51	0	0	0	6	0	7.06	—	—	—	—	—	—	—
86-87—New Haven	AHL	47	2828	21	15	0	173	0	3.67	7	427	3	4	19	0	2.67
87-88—Los Angeles	NHL	34	1869	12	18	1	135	1	4.33	4	240	1	3	20	0	5.00
88-89—Los Angeles	NHL	48	2699	25	19	2	192	0	4.27	3	97	0	1	6	0	3.71
89-90—New York Islanders	NHL	39	2197	12	19	6	128	2	3.50	4	166	1	2	9	0	3.25
90-91—New York Islanders	NHL	53	2999	18	24	9	166	0	3.32	—	—	—	—	—	—	—
91-92—New York Islanders	NHL	37	1960	14	16	4	124	1	3.80	—	—	—	—	—	—	—
92-93—New York Islanders	NHL	47	2655	22	20	2	146	1	3.30	18	1109	9	8	59	0	3.19
NHL totals		259	14430	103	116	24	897	5	3.73	29	1612	11	14	94	0	3.50

HEAPHY, SHAWN
C, FLAMES

PERSONAL: Born November 27, 1968, at Sudbury, Ont. ... 5-8/175. ... Shoots left. ... Name pronounced HEE-FEE.
COLLEGE: Michigan State.
TRANSACTIONS/CAREER NOTES: Selected by Calgary Flames in NHL supplemental draft (June 10, 1989).

		REGULAR SEASON					PLAYOFFS				
Season Team	League	Gms.	G	A	Pts.	Pen.	Gms.	G	A	Pts.	Pen.
87-88—Michigan State	CCHA	44	19	24	43	48	—	—	—	—	—
88-89—Michigan State	CCHA	47	26	17	43	80	—	—	—	—	—
89-90—Michigan State	CCHA	45	28	31	59	54	—	—	—	—	—
90-91—Michigan State	CCHA	39	30	19	49	57	—	—	—	—	—
—Salt Lake City	IHL	—	—	—	—	—	1	0	0	0	0
91-92—Salt Lake City	IHL	76	41	36	77	85	5	2	2	4	2
92-93—Salt Lake City	IHL	78	29	36	65	63	—	—	—	—	—
—Calgary	NHL	1	0	0	0	0	—	—	—	—	—
NHL totals		1	0	0	0	0					

HEBERT, GUY
G, MIGHTY DUCKS

PERSONAL: Born January 7, 1967, at Troy, N.Y. ... 5-11/180. ... Shoots left. ... Full name: Guy Andrew Hebert. ... Name pronounced GEE hee-BAIR.
HIGH SCHOOL: LaSalle Institute (Troy, N.Y.).
COLLEGE: Hamilton (N.Y.).
TRANSACTIONS/CAREER NOTES: Selected by St. Louis Blues in eighth round (eighth Blues choice, 159th overall) of NHL entry draft (June 13, 1987).... Selected by Mighty Ducks of Anaheim in NHL expansion draft (June 24, 1993).

H

HONORS: Shared James Norris Memorial Trophy with Pat Jablonski (1990-91). . . . Named to IHL All-Star second team (1990-91).

			REGULAR SEASON								PLAYOFFS						
Season Team	League	Gms.	Min.	W	L	T	GA	SO	Avg.	Gms.	Min.	W	L	GA	SO	Avg.
86-87—Hamilton College	Div. II	18	1070	12	5	0	40	0	2.24	—	—	—	—	—	—	—
87-88—Hamilton College	Div. II	8	450	5	3	0	19	0	2.53	—	—	—	—	—	—	—
88-89—Hamilton College	Div. II	25	1453	18	7	0	62	0	2.56	—	—	—	—	—	—	—
89-90—Peoria	IHL	30	1706	7	13	7	124	1	4.36	2	76	0	1	5	0	3.95
90-91—Peoria	IHL	36	2093	24	10	1	100	2	*2.87	8	458	3	4	32	0	4.19
91-92—Peoria	IHL	29	1731	20	9	0	98	0	3.40	4	239	3	1	9	0	*2.26
—St. Louis	NHL	13	738	5	5	1	36	0	2.93	—	—	—	—	—	—	—
92-93—St. Louis	NHL	24	1210	8	8	2	74	1	3.67	1	2	0	0	0	0	0.00
NHL totals		37	1948	13	13	3	110	1	3.39	1	2	0	0	0	0	0.00

HEDICAN, BRET
D, BLUES

PERSONAL: Born August 10, 1970, at St. Paul, Minn. . . . 6-2/195. . . . Shoots left. . . . Full name: Bret Michael Hedican. . . . Name pronounced HEH-dih-kihn.
HIGH SCHOOL: North St. Paul (Minn.).
COLLEGE: St. Cloud State (Minn.).
TRANSACTIONS/CAREER NOTES: Selected by St. Louis Blues in 10th round (10th Blues pick, 198th overall) of NHL entry draft (June 11, 1988). . . . Sprained knee ligaments (September 27, 1992); missed first 15 games of season.
HONORS: Named to WCHA All-Star first team (1990-91).

		REGULAR SEASON					PLAYOFFS				
Season Team	League	Gms.	G	A	Pts.	Pen.	Gms.	G	A	Pts.	Pen.
88-89—St. Cloud State	WCHA	28	5	3	8	28	—	—	—	—	—
89-90—St. Cloud State	WCHA	36	4	17	21	37	—	—	—	—	—
90-91—St. Cloud State	WCHA	41	18	30	48	52	—	—	—	—	—
91-92—U.S. national team	Int'l	54	1	8	9	59	—	—	—	—	—
—U.S. Olympic Team	Int'l	8	0	0	0	4	—	—	—	—	—
—St. Louis	NHL	4	1	0	1	0	5	0	0	0	0
92-93—Peoria	IHL	19	0	8	8	10	—	—	—	—	—
—St. Louis	NHL	42	0	8	8	30	10	0	0	0	14
NHL totals		46	1	8	9	30	15	0	0	0	14

HEINZE, STEVE
RW, BRUINS

PERSONAL: Born January 30, 1970, at Lawrence, Mass. . . . 5-11/180. . . . Shoots right. . . . Full name: Stephen Herbert Heinze. . . . Name pronounced HINZ.
HIGH SCHOOL: Lawrence Academy (Groton, Mass.).
COLLEGE: Boston College.
TRANSACTIONS/CAREER NOTES: Selected by Boston Bruins in second round (second Bruins pick, 60th overall) of NHL entry draft (June 11, 1988). . . . Injured shoulder (May 1, 1992). . . . Injured shoulder (March 20, 1993); missed 11 games.
HONORS: Named to Hockey East All-Rookie Team (1988-89). . . . Named to NCAA All-America East first team (1989-90). . . . Named to Hockey East All-Star first team (1989-90).

		REGULAR SEASON					PLAYOFFS				
Season Team	League	Gms.	G	A	Pts.	Pen.	Gms.	G	A	Pts.	Pen.
86-87—Lawrence Academy	Mass. H.S.	23	26	24	50	...	—	—	—	—	—
87-88—Lawrence Academy	Mass. H.S.	23	30	25	55	...	—	—	—	—	—
88-89—Boston College	Hockey East	36	26	23	49	26	—	—	—	—	—
89-90—Boston College	Hockey East	40	27	36	63	41	—	—	—	—	—
90-91—Boston College	Hockey East	35	21	26	47	35	—	—	—	—	—
91-92—U.S. national team	Int'l	49	18	15	33	38	—	—	—	—	—
—U.S. Olympic Team	Int'l	8	1	3	4	8	—	—	—	—	—
—Boston	NHL	14	3	4	7	6	7	0	3	3	17
92-93—Boston	NHL	73	18	13	31	24	4	1	1	2	2
NHL totals		87	21	17	38	30	11	1	4	5	19

HELENIUS, SAMI
D, FLAMES

PERSONAL: Born January 22, 1974, at Helsinki, Finland. . . . 6-5/200. . . . Shoots left.
TRANSACTIONS/CAREER NOTES: Selected by Calgary Flames in fifth round (fifth Flames pick, 102nd overall) of NHL entry draft (June 20, 1992).

		REGULAR SEASON					PLAYOFFS				
Season Team	League	Gms.	G	A	Pts.	Pen.	Gms.	G	A	Pts.	Pen.
91-92—Jokerit Helsinki Jrs.	Finland				Statistics unavailable.		—	—	—	—	—
92-93—Vantaa HT	Finland Dv.II	21	3	2	5	60	—	—	—	—	—
—Jokerit Helsinki Jrs.	Finland	1	0	0	0	0	—	—	—	—	—

HENDRICKSON, DARBY
C, MAPLE LEAFS

PERSONAL: Born August 28, 1972, at Richfield, Minn. . . . 6-0/175. . . . Shoots left.
HIGH SCHOOL: Richfield (Minn.).
COLLEGE: Minnesota.
TRANSACTIONS/CAREER NOTES: Selected by Toronto Maple Leafs in fourth round (third Maple Leafs pick, 73rd overall) of NHL entry draft (June 16, 1990).
HONORS: Won WCHA Rookie of the Year Award (1991-92). . . . Named to WCHA All-Rookie team (1991-92).

Season	Team	League	REGULAR SEASON					PLAYOFFS				
			Gms.	G	A	Pts.	Pen.	Gms.	G	A	Pts.	Pen.
87-88—Richfield H.S.	Minn. H.S.	22	12	9	21	10	—	—	—	—	—
88-89—Richfield H.S.	Minn. H.S.	22	22	20	42	12	—	—	—	—	—
89-90—Richfield H.S.	Minn. H.S.	24	23	27	50	49	—	—	—	—	—
90-91—Richfield H.S.	Minn. H.S.	27	32	29	61	...	—	—	—	—	—
91-92—University of Minnesota	WCHA	44	25	30	55	63	—	—	—	—	—
92-93—University of Minnesota	WCHA	31	12	15	27	35	—	—	—	—	—

HERBERS, IAN
D, OILERS

PERSONAL: Born July 18, 1967, at Jasper, Alta. . . . 6-4/225. . . . Shoots left.
COLLEGE: Alberta.
TRANSACTIONS/CAREER NOTES: Signed as free agent by Edmonton Oilers (September 9, 1992).

Season	Team	League	REGULAR SEASON					PLAYOFFS				
			Gms.	G	A	Pts.	Pen.	Gms.	G	A	Pts.	Pen.
88-89—University of Alberta	CWUAA	47	4	22	26	137	—	—	—	—	—
89-90—University of Alberta	CWUAA	45	5	31	36	83	—	—	—	—	—
90-91—University of Alberta	CWUAA	45	6	24	30	87	—	—	—	—	—
91-92—University of Alberta	CWUAA	43	14	34	48	86	—	—	—	—	—
92-93—Cape Breton	AHL	77	7	15	22	129	10	0	1	1	16

HEROUX, YVES
RW, STARS

PERSONAL: Born April 27, 1965, at Terrebonne, Que. . . . 6-0/200. . . . Shoots right. . . . Name pronounced EEV air-OO.
TRANSACTIONS/CAREER NOTES: Suffered foot infection (December 1981). . . . Selected by Quebec Nordiques in second round (first Nordiques pick, 32nd overall) of NHL entry draft (June 8, 1983). . . . Signed as free agent by St. Louis Blues (March 13, 1990). . . . Signed as free agent by Minnesota North Stars (August 5, 1992).

Season	Team	League	REGULAR SEASON					PLAYOFFS				
			Gms.	G	A	Pts.	Pen.	Gms.	G	A	Pts.	Pen.
82-83—Chicoutimi	QMJHL	70	41	40	81	44	5	0	4	4	8
83-84—Chicoutimi	QMJHL	56	28	25	53	67	—	—	—	—	—
—Fredericton	AHL	4	0	0	0	0	—	—	—	—	—
84-85—Chicoutimi	QMJHL	66	42	54	96	123	14	5	8	13	16
85-86—Fredericton	AHL	31	12	10	22	42	2	0	1	1	7
—Muskegon	IHL	42	14	8	22	41	—	—	—	—	—
86-87—Fredericton	AHL	37	8	6	14	13	—	—	—	—	—
—Quebec	NHL	1	0	0	0	0	—	—	—	—	—
—Muskegon	IHL	25	6	8	14	31	2	0	0	0	0
87-88—Baltimore	AHL	5	0	2	2	2	—	—	—	—	—
88-89—Flint	IHL	82	43	42	85	98	—	—	—	—	—
89-90—Peoria	IHL	14	3	2	5	4	5	2	2	4	0
90-91—Albany	IHL	45	22	18	40	46	—	—	—	—	—
—Peoria	IHL	33	16	8	24	26	17	4	4	8	16
91-92—Peoria	IHL	80	41	36	77	72	8	5	1	6	6
92-93—Kalamazoo	IHL	80	38	30	68	86	—	—	—	—	—
NHL totals			1	0	0	0	0					

HERTER, JASON
D, CANUCKS

PERSONAL: Born October 2, 1970, at Hafford, Sask. . . . 6-1/190. . . . Shoots right.
COLLEGE: North Dakota.
TRANSACTIONS/CAREER NOTES: Strained shoulder (September 1988). . . . Selected by Vancouver Canucks in first round (first Canucks pick, eighth overall) of NHL entry draft (June 17, 1989).
HONORS: Named to WCHA All-Star second team (1989-90 and 1990-91).

Season	Team	League	REGULAR SEASON					PLAYOFFS				
			Gms.	G	A	Pts.	Pen.	Gms.	G	A	Pts.	Pen.
87-88—Notre Dame	SJHL	54	5	33	38	152	—	—	—	—	—
88-89—Univ. of North Dakota	WCHA	41	8	24	32	62	—	—	—	—	—
89-90—Univ. of North Dakota	WCHA	38	11	39	50	40	—	—	—	—	—
90-91—Univ. of North Dakota	WCHA	39	11	26	37	52	—	—	—	—	—
91-92—Milwaukee	IHL	56	7	18	25	34	1	0	0	0	2
92-93—Hamilton	AHL	70	7	16	23	68	—	—	—	—	—

HERVEY, MATT
D, LIGHTNING

PERSONAL: Born May 16, 1966, at Whittier, Calif. . . . 5-11/205. . . . Shoots right.
TRANSACTIONS/CAREER NOTES: Suspended six games by WHL for stick-swinging incident (November 1986). . . . Signed as free agent by Winnipeg Jets (October 1987). . . . Signed as free agent by Boston Bruins (August 15, 1991). . . . Suffered sore back (March 23, 1992). . . . Traded by Bruins with C Ken Hodge to Tampa Bay Lightning for RW Darin Kimble and future considerations (September 4, 1992).

Season	Team	League	REGULAR SEASON					PLAYOFFS				
			Gms.	G	A	Pts.	Pen.	Gms.	G	A	Pts.	Pen.
83-84—Victoria	WHL	67	4	19	23	89	—	—	—	—	—
84-85—Victoria	WHL	14	1	3	4	17	—	—	—	—	—
—Lethbridge	WHL	54	3	9	12	88	—	—	—	—	—

H

Season Team	League	REGULAR SEASON					PLAYOFFS				
		Gms.	G	A	Pts.	Pen.	Gms.	G	A	Pts.	Pen.
85-86—Lethbridge	WHL	60	9	17	26	110	—	—	—	—	—
86-87—Seattle	WHL	9	4	5	9	59	—	—	—	—	—
—Richmond	BCJHL	17	4	21	25	99	11	3	10	13	22
87-88—Moncton	AHL	69	9	20	29	265	—	—	—	—	—
88-89—Moncton	AHL	73	8	28	36	295	10	1	2	3	42
—Winnipeg	NHL	2	0	0	0	4	—	—	—	—	—
89-90—Moncton	AHL	47	3	13	16	168	—	—	—	—	—
90-91—Moncton	AHL	71	4	28	32	132	7	0	1	1	23
91-92—Boston	NHL	16	0	1	1	55	5	0	0	0	6
—Maine	AHL	36	1	7	8	47	—	—	—	—	—
92-93—Atlanta	IHL	49	12	19	31	122	9	0	4	4	19
—Tampa Bay	NHL	17	0	4	4	38	—	—	—	—	—
NHL totals		35	0	5	5	97	5	0	0	0	6

HEWARD, JAMIE
D, PENGUINS

PERSONAL: Born March 30, 1971, at Regina, Sask.... 6-2/198.... Shoots right. **TRANSACTIONS/CAREER NOTES:** Traded by Spokane Chiefs to Regina Pats for RW Pat Falloon and future considerations (October 1987).... Broke jaw (November 1988).... Selected by Pittsburgh Penguins in first round (first Penguins pick, 16th overall) of NHL entry draft (June 17, 1989).... Suffered from mononucleosis (September 1989). **HONORS:** Named to WHL (East) All-Star first team (1990-91).

Season Team	League	REGULAR SEASON					PLAYOFFS				
		Gms.	G	A	Pts.	Pen.	Gms.	G	A	Pts.	Pen.
87-88—Regina	WHL	68	10	17	27	17	4	1	1	2	2
88-89—Regina	WHL	52	31	28	59	29	—	—	—	—	—
89-90—Regina	WHL	72	14	44	58	42	11	2	2	4	10
90-91—Regina	WHL	71	23	61	84	41	8	2	9	11	6
91-92—Muskegon	IHL	54	6	21	27	37	14	1	4	5	4
92-93—Cleveland	IHL	58	9	18	27	64					

HEXTALL, DONEVAN
LW, DEVILS

PERSONAL: Born February 24, 1972, at Wolseley, Sask.... 6-3/190.... Shoots left. **TRANSACTIONS/CAREER NOTES:** Selected by New Jersey Devils in second round (third Devils pick, 33rd overall) of NHL entry draft (June 22, 1991). **HONORS:** Won Jim Piggott Memorial Trophy (1990-91).... Named to WHL (East) All-Star second team (1991-92).

Season Team	League	REGULAR SEASON					PLAYOFFS				
		Gms.	G	A	Pts.	Pen.	Gms.	G	A	Pts.	Pen.
89-90—Prince Albert	WHL	7	1	2	3	4	—	—	—	—	—
—Weyburn	SJHL	63	23	45	68	127	—	—	—	—	—
90-91—Prince Albert	WHL	70	30	59	89	55	3	1	3	4	0
91-92—Prince Albert	WHL	71	33	71	104	105	10	3	6	9	10
92-93—Utica	AHL	51	11	11	22	12	2	1	0	1	0
—Canadian national team	Int'l	6	0	1	1	4	—	—	—	—	—

HEXTALL, RON
G, ISLANDERS

PERSONAL: Born May 3, 1964, at Winnipeg, Man.... 6-3/192.... Shoots left. **TRANSACTIONS/CAREER NOTES:** Selected by Philadelphia Flyers as underage junior in sixth round (sixth Flyers pick, 119th overall) of NHL entry draft (June 9, 1982).... Suspended eight games by NHL for slashing (May 1987).... Pulled hamstring (March 7, 1989).... Suspended for first 12 games of 1989-90 season by NHL for attacking opposing player in final playoff game (May 11, 1989).... Did not attend training camp due to a contract dispute (September 1989).... Pulled groin (November 4, 1989).... Pulled hamstring (November 15, 1989).... Tore right groin muscle (December 13, 1989); missed 29 games.... Injured left groin (March 8, 1990).... Pulled groin (October 11, 1990); missed five games.... Sprained left knee medial collateral ligament (October 27, 1990); missed five weeks.... Tore groin muscle (March 12, 1991); missed nine games.... Suffered from the flu (November 14, 1991); missed one game.... Developed shoulder tendinitis (November 27, 1991); missed nine games.... Traded by Flyers with C Mike Ricci, C Peter Forsberg, D Steve Duchesne, D Kerry Huffman, first-round pick in 1993 draft (G Jocelyn Thibault), cash and future considerations to Quebec Nordiques for C Eric Lindros (June 20, 1992).... Flyers sent LW Chris Simon and first-round pick in 1994 draft to Nordiques to complete deal (July 21, 1992).... Strained muscle in left thigh (February 20, 1993); missed 14 games.... Traded by Nordiques with first-round pick in 1993 draft to New York Islanders for G Mark Fitzpatrick and first-round pick in 1993 draft (C Adam Deadmarsh) (June 20, 1993). **HONORS:** Won Dudley (Red) Garrett Memorial Trophy (1985-86).... Named to AHL All-Star first team (1985-86).... Named NHL Rookie of the Year by THE SPORTING NEWS (1986-87).... Won Vezina Trophy (1986-87).... Won Conn Smythe Trophy (1986-87).... Named to THE SPORTING NEWS All-Star second team (1986-87).... Named to NHL All-Star first team (1986-87).... Named to NHL All-Rookie team (1986-87).... Played in NHL All-Star Game (1988). **RECORDS:** Holds NHL single-season playoff record for most minutes played by a goaltender—1,540 (1987). **STATISTICAL NOTES:** Scored a goal into a Washington empty net, becoming the first goalie to score a goal in Stanley Cup play (April 11, 1989).

Season Team	League	REGULAR SEASON							PLAYOFFS						
		Gms.	Min.	W	L	T	GA	SO	Avg.	Gms.	Min.	W	L	GA	SO	Avg.
80-81—Melville	SJHL	42	2127	...	...	...	254	0	7.17	—	—	—	—	—	—	—
81-82—Brandon	WHL	30	1398	12	11	0	133	0	5.71	3	103	0	2	16	0	9.32
82-83—Brandon	WHL	44	2589	13	30	0	249	0	5.77	—	—	—	—	—	—	—
83-84—Brandon	WHL	46	2670	29	13	2	190	0	4.27	10	592	5	5	37	0	3.75

H

Season Team	League		REGULAR SEASON								PLAYOFFS					
		Gms.	Min.	W	L	T	GA	SO	Avg.	Gms.	Min.	W	L	GA	SO	Avg.
84-85—Kalamazoo	IHL	19	1103	6	11	1	80	0	4.35	—	—	—	—	—	—	—
—Hershey	AHL	11	555	4	6	0	34	0	3.68	—	—	—	—	—	—	—
85-86—Hershey	AHL	*53	*3061	30	19	2	174	*5	3.41	13	780	5	7	42	*1	3.23
86-87—Philadelphia	NHL	*66	*3799	37	21	6	190	1	3.00	*26	*1540	15	11	*71	†2	2.77
87-88—Philadelphia	NHL	62	3561	30	22	7	208	0	3.50	7	379	2	4	30	0	4.75
88-89—Philadelphia	NHL	64	3756	30	28	6	202	0	3.23	15	886	8	7	49	0	3.32
89-90—Philadelphia	NHL	8	419	4	2	1	29	0	4.15	—	—	—	—	—	—	—
—Hershey	AHL	1	49	1	0	0	3	0	3.67	—	—	—	—	—	—	—
90-91—Philadelphia	NHL	36	2035	13	16	5	106	0	3.13	—	—	—	—	—	—	—
91-92—Philadelphia	NHL	45	2668	16	21	6	151	3	3.40	—	—	—	—	—	—	—
92-93—Quebec	NHL	54	2988	29	16	5	172	0	3.45	6	372	2	4	18	0	2.90
NHL totals		335	19226	159	126	36	1058	4	3.30	54	3177	27	26	168	2	3.17

HILL, KILEY
LW, LIGHTNING

PERSONAL: Born January 2, 1975, at Sudbury, Ont. . . . 6-3/205. . . . Shoots left.
TRANSACTIONS/CAREER NOTES: Selected by Tampa Bay Lightning in sixth round (sixth Lightning pick, 133rd overall) of NHL entry draft (June 26, 1993).

Season Team	League		REGULAR SEASON					PLAYOFFS				
		Gms.	G	A	Pts.	Pen.		Gms.	G	A	Pts.	Pen.
91-92—Sault Ste. Marie	OHL	32	4	3	7	28		5	1	0	1	0
92-93—Sault Ste. Marie	OHL	49	6	8	14	76		1	0	0	0	2

HILL, SEAN
D, MIGHTY DUCKS

PERSONAL: Born February 14, 1970, at Duluth, Minn. . . . 6-0/195. . . . Shoots right. . . . Full name: Sean Ronald Hill.
COLLEGE: Wisconsin.
TRANSACTIONS/CAREER NOTES: Selected by Montreal Canadiens in eighth round (ninth Canadiens pick, 167th overall) of NHL entry draft (June 11, 1988). . . . Injured knee (December 29, 1990). . . . Suspended two games by WCHA for elbowing (January 18, 1991). . . . Suffered abdominal strain (October 13, 1992); missed 14 games. . . . Selected by Mighty Ducks of Anaheim in NHL expansion draft (June 24, 1993).
HONORS: Named to WCHA All-Star second team (1989-90 and 1990-91). . . . Named to NCAA All-America West second team (1990-91).
MISCELLANEOUS: Member of Stanley Cup championship team (1993).

Season Team	League		REGULAR SEASON					PLAYOFFS				
		Gms.	G	A	Pts.	Pen.		Gms.	G	A	Pts.	Pen.
88-89—University of Wisconsin	WCHA	45	2	23	25	69		—	—	—	—	—
89-90—University of Wisconsin	WCHA	42	14	39	53	78		—	—	—	—	—
90-91—University of Wisconsin	WCHA	37	19	32	51	122		—	—	—	—	—
—Fredericton	AHL	—	—	—	—	—		3	0	2	2	2
—Montreal	NHL	—	—	—	—	—		1	0	0	0	0
91-92—Fredericton	AHL	42	7	20	27	65		7	1	3	4	6
—U.S. national team	Int'l	12	4	3	7	16		—	—	—	—	—
—U.S. Olympic Team	Int'l	8	2	0	2	6		—	—	—	—	—
—Montreal	NHL	—	—	—	—	—		4	1	0	1	2
92-93—Montreal	NHL	31	2	6	8	54		3	0	0	0	4
—Fredericton	AHL	6	1	3	4	10		—	—	—	—	—
NHL totals		31	2	6	8	54		8	1	0	1	6

HILLER, JIM
RW, RED WINGS

PERSONAL: Born May 15, 1969, at Port Alberni, B.C. . . . 6-0/190. . . . Shoots right.
COLLEGE: Northern Michigan.
TRANSACTIONS/CAREER NOTES: Selected by Los Angeles Kings in 10th round (10th Kings pick, 207th overall) of NHL entry draft (June 10, 1989). . . . Strained back (November 21, 1992); missed four games. . . . Traded by Kings with D Paul Coffey and C/LW Sylvain Couturier to Deroit Red Wings for C Jimmy Carson, RW Marc Potvin and C Gary Shuchuk (January 29, 1993). . . . Separated shoulder (March 18, 1993); missed four games.
HONORS: Named to NCAA All-America West second team (1991-92). . . . Named WCHA All-Star second team (1991-92).

Season Team	League		REGULAR SEASON					PLAYOFFS				
		Gms.	G	A	Pts.	Pen.		Gms.	G	A	Pts.	Pen.
89-90—Northern Michigan Univ.	WCHA	39	23	33	56	52		—	—	—	—	—
90-91—Northern Michigan Univ.	WCHA	43	22	41	63	59		—	—	—	—	—
91-92—Northern Michigan Univ.	WCHA	39	28	52	80	115		—	—	—	—	—
92-93—Los Angeles	NHL	40	6	6	12	90		—	—	—	—	—
—Phoenix	IHL	3	0	2	2	2		—	—	—	—	—
—Detroit	NHL	21	2	6	8	19		2	0	0	0	4
NHL totals		61	8	12	20	109		2	0	0	0	4

HILTON, KEVIN
C, RED WINGS

PERSONAL: Born January 12, 1975, at Trenton, Mich. . . . 5-11/170. . . . Shoots left.
COLLEGE: Michigan.
TRANSACTIONS/CAREER NOTES: Selected by Detroit Red Wings in third round (third Red Wings pick, 74th overall) of NHL entry draft (June 26, 1993).

Season Team	League	REGULAR SEASON Gms.	G	A	Pts.	Pen.	PLAYOFFS Gms.	G	A	Pts.	Pen.
91-92—Detroit Compuware..........	NAJHL	39	35	42	77	42	—	—	—	—	—
92-93—University of Michigan	CCHA	38	16	15	31	8	—	—	—	—	—

HIRSCH, COREY
G, RANGERS

PERSONAL: Born July 1, 1972, at Medicine Hat, Alta.... 5-10/170.... Shoots left.
TRANSACTIONS/CAREER NOTES: Selected by New York Rangers in eighth round (seventh Rangers pick, 169th overall) in NHL entry draft (June 22, 1991).
HONORS: Named to WHL (West) All-Star second team (1989-90).... Won Can.HL Goaltender of the Year Award (1991-92).... Won Hap Emms Memorial Trophy (1991-92)... Won Del Wilson Trophy (1991-92). ...Won WHL Player of the Year Award (1991-92).... Named to Can.HL All-Star first team (1991-92).... Named to Memorial Cup All-Star team (1991-92).... Named to WHL (West) All-Star first team (1991-92).... Won Baz Bastien Trophy (1992-93).... Won Dudley (Red) Garrett Memorial Trophy (1992-93).... Shared Harry (Hap) Holmes Memorial Trophy with Boris Rouson (1992-93).... Named to AHL All-Star first team (1992-93).

Season Team	League	REGULAR SEASON Gms.	Min.	W	L	T	GA	SO	Avg.	PLAYOFFS Gms.	Min.	W	L	GA	SO	Avg.
88-89—Kamloops	WHL	32	1516	11	12	2	106	2	4.20	5	245	3	2	19	0	4.65
89-90—Kamloops	WHL	63	3608	48	13	0	230	3	3.82	17	1043	14	3	60	0	3.45
90-91—Kamloops	WHL	38	1970	26	7	1	100	3	3.05	11	623	5	6	42	0	4.04
91-92—Kamloops	WHL	48	2732	35	10	2	124	*5	*2.72	*16	*954	*11	5	35	*2	*2.20
92-93—Binghamton	AHL	46	2692	*35	4	5	125	1	*2.79	14	831	7	7	46	0	3.32
—New York Rangers	NHL	4	224	1	2	1	14	0	3.75	—	—	—	—	—	—	—
NHL totals.................		4	224	1	2	1	14	0	3.75							

HNILICKA, MILAN
G, ISLANDERS

PERSONAL: Born June 24, 1973, at Kladno, Czech.... 6-0/180.... Shoots left.
TRANSACTIONS/CAREER NOTES: Selected by New York Islanders in fourth round (fourth Islanders pick, 70th overall) of NHL entry draft (June 22, 1991).

Season Team	League	REGULAR SEASON Gms.	Min.	W	L	T	GA	SO	Avg.	PLAYOFFS Gms.	Min.	W	L	GA	SO	Avg.
90-91—Poldi Kladno	Czech.	35	2122	...	...	...	98	...	2.77	—	—	—	—	—	—	—
91-92—Poldi Kladno	Czech.	30	1788	...	...	...	107	...	3.59	—	—	—	—	—	—	—
92-93—Swift Current	WHL	65	3679	46	12	2	206	2	3.36	17	1017	12	5	54	*2	3.19

HOCKING, JUSTIN
D, KINGS

PERSONAL: Born January 9, 1974, at Stettler, Alta.... 6-4/210.... Shoots right.
COLLEGE: Spokane Falls Community College (Wash.).
TRANSACTIONS/CAREER NOTES: Selected by Los Angeles Kings in second round (first Kings pick, 39th overall) of NHL entry draft (June 20, 1992).

Season Team	League	REGULAR SEASON Gms.	G	A	Pts.	Pen.	PLAYOFFS Gms.	G	A	Pts.	Pen.
90-91—Fort Saskatchewan	AJHL	38	4	6	10	84	—	—	—	—	—
91-92—Spokane	WHL	71	4	6	10	309	10	0	3	3	28
92-93—Spokane	WHL	16	0	1	1	75	—	—	—	—	—
—Medicine Hat	WHL	54	1	9	10	119	10	0	1	1	75

HODGE, KEN
C

PERSONAL: Born April 13, 1966, at Windsor, Ont.... 6-1/200.... Shoots left.... Full name: Kenneth David Hodge Jr.... Son of Ken Hodge, right winger, Chicago Blackhawks, Boston Bruins and New York Rangers (1965-66 through 1977-78).
HIGH SCHOOL: St. John's Prep School (Danvers, Mass.).
COLLEGE: Boston College.
TRANSACTIONS/CAREER NOTES: Selected by Minnesota North Stars in third round (second North Stars pick, 46th overall) of NHL entry draft (June 9, 1984).... Injured shoulders (November 1987).... Reinjured shoulders (November 1987).... Traded by North Stars to Boston Bruins for future considerations; North Stars later received fourth-round pick in 1992 draft (RW Jere Lehtinen) to complete deal (August 21, 1990).... Sprained knee (October 27, 1991); missed nine games.... Traded by Bruins with D Matt Hervey to Tampa Bay Lightning for RW Darin Kimble and future considerations (September 4, 1992).... Cut upper lip (October 24, 1992); missed three games.... Signed as free agent by San Diego Gulls (February 9, 1993).
HONORS: Named Hockey East Freshman of the Year (1984-85).... Named to Hockey East All-Freshman team (1984-85).... Named to NHL All-Rookie team (1990-91).

Season Team	League	REGULAR SEASON Gms.	G	A	Pts.	Pen.	PLAYOFFS Gms.	G	A	Pts.	Pen.
83-84—St. John's Prep School......	Mass. H.S.	22	25	38	63	...	—	—	—	—	—
84-85—Boston College	Hockey East	41	20	44	64	28	—	—	—	—	—
85-86—Boston College	Hockey East	21	11	17	28	16	—	—	—	—	—
86-87—Boston College	Hockey East	37	29	33	62	30	—	—	—	—	—
87-88—Kalamazoo	IHL	70	15	35	50	24	—	—	—	—	—
88-89—Minnesota	NHL	5	1	1	2	0	—	—	—	—	—
—Kalamazoo	IHL	72	26	45	71	34	6	1	5	6	16
89-90—Kalamazoo	IHL	68	33	53	86	19	10	5	13	18	2
90-91—Maine	AHL	8	7	10	17	2	—	—	—	—	—
—Boston	NHL	70	30	29	59	20	15	4	6	10	6
91-92—Boston	NHL	42	6	11	17	10	—	—	—	—	—
—Maine	AHL	19	6	11	17	4	—	—	—	—	—

Season Team	League	REGULAR SEASON					PLAYOFFS				
		Gms.	G	A	Pts.	Pen.	Gms.	G	A	Pts.	Pen.
92-93—Tampa Bay	NHL	25	2	7	9	2	—	—	—	—	—
—Atlanta	IHL	16	10	17	27	0	—	—	—	—	—
—San Diego	IHL	30	11	24	35	16	14	4	6	10	6
NHL totals		142	39	48	87	32	15	4	6	10	6

HOGUE, BENOIT
LW, ISLANDERS

PERSONAL: Born October 28, 1966, at Repentigny, Que. . . . 5-10/190. . . . Shoots left. . . . Name pronounced BEHN-wah HOHG.

TRANSACTIONS/CAREER NOTES: Selected by Buffalo Sabres as underage junior in second round (second Sabres pick, 35th overall) of NHL entry draft (June 15, 1985). . . . Suspended six games by AHL for fighting (October 1987). . . . Suffered sore back (March 1988). . . . Broke left cheekbone (October 11, 1989); missed 20 games. . . . Sprained left ankle (March 14, 1990). . . . Traded by Sabres with C Pierre Turgeon, D Uwe Krupp and C Dave McLlwain to New York Islanders for C Pat LaFontaine, LW Randy Wood, D Randy Hillier and future considerations; Sabres later received fourth-round pick in 1992 draft (D Dean Melanson) (October 25, 1991). . . . Suffered stiff neck (December 7, 1992); missed five games. . . . Suffered sore hand and foot (January 14, 1993); missed three games. . . . Sprained knee ligament (March 14, 1993); missed six games.

Season Team	League	REGULAR SEASON					PLAYOFFS				
		Gms.	G	A	Pts.	Pen.	Gms.	G	A	Pts.	Pen.
83-84—St. Jean	QMJHL	59	14	11	25	42	—	—	—	—	—
84-85—St. Jean	QMJHL	63	46	44	90	92	—	—	—	—	—
85-86—St. Jean	QMJHL	65	54	54	108	115	9	6	4	10	26
86-87—Rochester	AHL	52	14	20	34	52	12	5	4	9	8
87-88—Buffalo	NHL	3	1	1	2	0	—	—	—	—	—
—Rochester	AHL	62	24	31	55	141	7	6	1	7	46
88-89—Buffalo	NHL	69	14	30	44	120	5	0	0	0	17
89-90—Buffalo	NHL	45	11	7	18	79	3	0	0	0	10
90-91—Buffalo	NHL	76	19	28	47	76	5	3	1	4	10
91-92—Buffalo	NHL	3	0	1	1	0	—	—	—	—	—
—New York Islanders	NHL	72	30	45	75	67	—	—	—	—	—
92-93—New York Islanders	NHL	70	33	42	75	108	18	6	6	12	31
NHL totals		338	108	154	262	450	31	9	7	16	68

HOLAN, MILOS
D, FLYERS

PERSONAL: Born April 22, 1971, at Bilovec, Czechoslovakia. . . . 5-11/183. . . . Shoots left. . . . Name pronounced HO-lahn.

TRANSACTIONS/CAREER NOTES: Selected by Philadelphia Flyers in third round (third Flyers pick, 77th overall) of NHL entry draft (June 26, 1993).

Season Team	League	REGULAR SEASON					PLAYOFFS				
		Gms.	G	A	Pts.	Pen.	Gms.	G	A	Pts.	Pen.
88-89—TJ Vitkovice	Czech.	7	0	0	0	0	—	—	—	—	—
89-90—TJ Vitkovice	Czech.	50	8	8	16	...	—	—	—	—	—
90-91—Dukla Trencin	Czech.	53	6	13	19	...	—	—	—	—	—
91-92—Dukla Trencin	Czech.	51	13	22	35	32	—	—	—	—	—
92-93—TJ Vitkovice	Czech.	53	35	33	68	...	—	—	—	—	—

HOLDEN, PAUL
D, KINGS

PERSONAL: Born March 15, 1970, at Kitchener, Ont. . . . 6-3/210. . . . Shoots left.

TRANSACTIONS/CAREER NOTES: Selected by Los Angeles Kings in second round (second Kings pick, 28th overall) of NHL entry draft (June 11, 1988). . . . Traded by Phoenix Roadrunners to Salt Lake City Golden Eagles for D Kevin Grant (October 16, 1992).

HONORS: Named to OHL All-Star second team (1989-90).

Season Team	League	REGULAR SEASON					PLAYOFFS				
		Gms.	G	A	Pts.	Pen.	Gms.	G	A	Pts.	Pen.
86-87—St. Thomas Jr. B	OHA	23	5	11	16	112	—	—	—	—	—
87-88—London	OHL	65	8	12	20	87	12	1	1	2	10
88-89—London	OHL	54	11	21	32	90	20	1	3	4	17
89-90—London	OHL	61	11	31	42	78	6	1	1	2	7
—New Haven	AHL	2	1	1	2	2	—	—	—	—	—
90-91—New Haven	AHL	59	2	8	10	23	—	—	—	—	—
91-92—Phoenix	IHL	47	3	3	6	63	—	—	—	—	—
92-93—Phoenix	IHL	3	0	0	0	6	—	—	—	—	—
—Salt Lake City	IHL	63	5	8	13	86	—	—	—	—	—

HOLIK, BOBBY
RW, DEVILS

PERSONAL: Born January 1, 1971, at Jihlava, Czechoslovakia. . . . 6-3/210. . . . Shoots right. . . . Name pronounced hoh-LEEK.

TRANSACTIONS/CAREER NOTES: Selected by Hartford Whalers in first round (first Whalers pick, 10th overall) of NHL entry draft (June 17, 1989). . . . Broke right thumb (February 1990). . . . Traded by Whalers with second-round pick in 1993 draft (LW Jay Pandolfo) and future considerations to New Jersey Devils for G Sean Burke and D Eric Weinrich (August 28, 1992). . . . Fractured right thumb (January 22, 1993); missed 22 games.

Season Team	League	REGULAR SEASON					PLAYOFFS				
		Gms.	G	A	Pts.	Pen.	Gms.	G	A	Pts.	Pen.
87-88—Dukla Jihlava	Czech.	31	5	9	14	...	—	—	—	—	—
88-89—Dukla Jihlava	Czech.	24	7	10	17	...	—	—	—	—	—

H

Season Team	League	REGULAR SEASON					PLAYOFFS				
		Gms.	G	A	Pts.	Pen.	Gms.	G	A	Pts.	Pen.
89-90—Dukla Jihlava	Czech.	31	12	18	30	...	—	—	—	—	—
90-91—Hartford	NHL	78	21	22	43	113	6	0	0	0	7
91-92—Hartford	NHL	76	21	24	45	44	7	0	1	1	6
92-93—Utica	AHL	1	0	0	0	2	—	—	—	—	—
—New Jersey	NHL	61	20	19	39	76	5	1	1	2	6
NHL totals		215	62	65	127	233	18	1	2	3	19

HOLLAND, DENNIS
C, FLAMES

PERSONAL: Born January 30, 1969, at Vernon, B.C. . . . 5-10/175. . . . Shoots left.
TRANSACTIONS/CAREER NOTES: Selected by Detroit Red Wings as underage junior in third round (fourth Red Wings pick, 52nd overall) of NHL entry draft (June 10, 1987). . . . Traded by Red Wings to Calgary Flames for future considerations (October 1991).
HONORS: Won Stewart (Butch) Paul Memorial Trophy West (1986-87). . . . Named to WHL (West) All-Star first team (1987-88 and 1988-89). . . . Won Bob Clarke Trophy (1988-89). . . . Won WHL Player of the Year Award (1988-89).

Season Team	League	REGULAR SEASON					PLAYOFFS				
		Gms.	G	A	Pts.	Pen.	Gms.	G	A	Pts.	Pen.
85-86—Vernon	BCJHL	51	43	62	105	40	7	4	6	10	14
—Portland	WHL	1	3	2	5	0	—	—	—	—	—
86-87—Portland	WHL	72	36	77	113	96	20	7	14	21	20
87-88—Portland	WHL	67	58	86	144	115	—	—	—	—	—
88-89—Portland	WHL	69	*82	85	*167	120	19	15	*22	*37	18
89-90—Adirondack	AHL	78	19	34	53	53	6	1	1	2	10
90-91—Adirondack	AHL	28	8	7	15	31	2	0	0	0	4
—San Diego	IHL	45	25	30	55	129	—	—	—	—	—
91-92—Fort Wayne	IHL	6	2	4	6	21	—	—	—	—	—
—Salt Lake City	IHL	72	20	25	45	102	4	0	2	2	2
92-93—Cincinnati	IHL	71	23	47	70	140	—	—	—	—	—

HOOVER, RON
C, BLUES

PERSONAL: Born October 28, 1966, at Oakville, Ont. . . . 6-1/190. . . . Shoots left. . . . Full name: Ronald Kenneth Hoover.
COLLEGE: Western Michigan.
TRANSACTIONS/CAREER NOTES: Selected by Hartford Whalers in eighth round (seventh Whalers pick, 158th overall) of NHL entry draft (June 21, 1986). . . . Signed as free agent by Boston Bruins (September 1, 1989). . . . Injured right eye (February 2, 1991); missed two weeks. . . . Signed as free agent by St. Louis Blues (July 23, 1991).
HONORS: Named to CCHA All-Star second team (1987-88).

Season Team	League	REGULAR SEASON					PLAYOFFS				
		Gms.	G	A	Pts.	Pen.	Gms.	G	A	Pts.	Pen.
85-86—Western Michigan Univ.	CCHA	43	10	23	33	36	—	—	—	—	—
86-87—Western Michigan Univ.	CCHA	34	7	10	17	22	—	—	—	—	—
87-88—Western Michigan Univ.	CCHA	42	39	23	62	40	—	—	—	—	—
88-89—Western Michigan Univ.	CCHA	42	32	27	59	66	—	—	—	—	—
89-90—Boston	NHL	2	0	0	0	0	—	—	—	—	—
—Maine	AHL	75	28	26	54	57	—	—	—	—	—
90-91—Maine	AHL	62	28	16	44	40	—	—	—	—	—
—Boston	NHL	15	4	0	4	31	8	0	0	0	18
91-92—St. Louis	NHL	1	0	0	0	0	—	—	—	—	—
—Peoria	IHL	71	27	34	61	30	10	4	4	8	4
92-93—Peoria	IHL	58	17	13	30	28	4	1	1	2	2
NHL totals		18	4	0	4	31	8	0	0	0	18

HORACEK, TONY
LW, BLACKHAWKS

PERSONAL: Born February 3, 1967, at Vancouver, B.C. . . . 6-4/215. . . . Shoots left. . . . Name pronounced HOHR-uh-CHECK.
TRANSACTIONS/CAREER NOTES: Selected by Philadelphia Flyers as underage junior in seventh round (eighth eighth pick, 147th overall) of NHL entry draft (June 15, 1985). . . . Suspended one game by WHL for swinging stick at fans (November 1, 1987). . . . Suspended eight games by WHL for fighting (November 27, 1987). . . . Suffered broken knuckle (December 1989). . . . Injured left eye (March 19, 1991); missed six games. . . . Traded by Flyers to Chicago Blackhawks for D Ryan McGill (February 7, 1992). . . . Suffered hip pointer (February 25, 1992); missed nine games.

Season Team	League	REGULAR SEASON					PLAYOFFS				
		Gms.	G	A	Pts.	Pen.	Gms.	G	A	Pts.	Pen.
84-85—Kelowna Wings	WHL	67	9	18	27	114	6	0	1	1	11
85-86—Spokane	WHL	64	19	28	47	129	9	4	5	9	29
86-87—Spokane	WHL	64	23	37	60	177	5	1	3	4	18
—Hershey	AHL	1	0	0	0	0	1	0	0	0	0
87-88—Hershey	AHL	1	0	0	0	0	—	—	—	—	—
—Spokane	WHL	24	17	23	40	63	—	—	—	—	—
—Kamloops	WHL	26	14	17	31	51	18	6	4	10	73
88-89—Hershey	AHL	10	0	0	0	38	—	—	—	—	—
—Indianapolis	IHL	43	11	13	24	138	—	—	—	—	—
89-90—Philadelphia	NHL	48	5	5	10	117	—	—	—	—	—
—Hershey	AHL	12	0	5	5	25	—	—	—	—	—

Season Team	League	REGULAR SEASON					PLAYOFFS				
		Gms.	G	A	Pts.	Pen.	Gms.	G	A	Pts.	Pen.
90-91—Hershey	AHL	19	5	3	8	35	4	2	0	2	14
—Philadelphia	NHL	34	3	6	9	49	—	—	—	—	—
91-92—Philadelphia	NHL	34	1	3	4	51	—	—	—	—	—
—Chicago	NHL	12	1	4	5	21	2	1	0	1	2
92-93—Indianapolis	IHL	6	1	1	2	28	5	3	2	5	18
NHL totals		128	10	18	28	238	2	1	0	1	2

HOUDA, DOUG
D, WHALERS

PERSONAL: Born June 3, 1966, at Blairmore, Alta.... 6-2/200.... Shoots right.... Name pronounced HOO-DUH.
TRANSACTIONS/CAREER NOTES: Selected by Detroit Red Wings as underage junior in second round (second Red Wings pick, 28th overall) of NHL entry draft (June 9, 1984).... Fractured left cheekbone (September 23, 1988).... Injured knee and underwent surgery (November 21, 1989).... Traded by Red Wings to Hartford Whalers for D Doug Crossman (February 20, 1991).
HONORS: Named to WHL All-Star second team (1984-85).... Named to AHL All-Star first team (1987-88).

Season Team	League	REGULAR SEASON					PLAYOFFS				
		Gms.	G	A	Pts.	Pen.	Gms.	G	A	Pts.	Pen.
81-82—Calgary	WHL	3	0	0	0	0	—	—	—	—	—
82-83—Calgary	WHL	71	5	23	28	99	16	1	3	4	44
83-84—Calgary	WHL	69	6	30	36	195	4	0	0	0	7
84-85—Calgary	WHL	65	20	54	74	182	8	3	4	7	29
—Kalamazoo	IHL	—	—	—	—	—	7	0	2	2	10
85-86—Calgary	WHL	16	4	10	14	60	—	—	—	—	—
—Medicine Hat	WHL	35	9	23	32	80	25	4	19	23	64
—Detroit	NHL	6	0	0	0	4	—	—	—	—	—
86-87—Adirondack	AHL	77	6	23	29	142	11	1	8	9	50
87-88—Detroit	NHL	11	1	1	2	10	—	—	—	—	—
—Adirondack	AHL	71	10	32	42	169	11	0	3	3	44
88-89—Adirondack	AHL	7	0	3	3	8	—	—	—	—	—
—Detroit	NHL	57	2	11	13	67	6	0	1	1	0
89-90—Detroit	NHL	73	2	9	11	127	—	—	—	—	—
90-91—Adirondack	AHL	38	9	17	26	67	—	—	—	—	—
—Detroit	NHL	22	0	4	4	43	—	—	—	—	—
—Hartford	NHL	19	1	2	3	41	6	0	0	0	8
91-92—Hartford	NHL	56	3	6	9	125	6	0	2	2	13
92-93—Hartford	NHL	60	2	6	8	167	—	—	—	—	—
NHL totals		304	11	39	50	584	18	0	3	3	21

HOUGH, MIKE
LW, PANTHERS

PERSONAL: Born February 6, 1963, at Montreal.... 6-1/192.... Shoots left.... Name pronounced HUHF.
TRANSACTIONS/CAREER NOTES: Selected by Quebec Nordiques as underage junior in ninth round (seventh Nordiques pick, 181st overall) of NHL entry draft (June 9, 1982).... Sprained left shoulder and developed tendinitis (November 5, 1989); missed 14 games.... Broke right thumb (January 23, 1990); missed 12 games.... Injured back (November 8, 1990); missed nine games.... Separated left shoulder (January 15, 1991); missed three games.... Suffered concussion (February 10, 1991).... Injured knee (December 28, 1991); missed three games.... Fractured left thumb (February 15, 1992); missed 14 games.... Suffered concussion in preseason (October 1992); missed first two games of season.... Sprained right shoulder (April 6, 1993); missed four games.... Traded by Nordiques to Washington Capitals for RW Paul MacDermid and RW Reggie Savage (June 20, 1993).... Selected by Florida Panthers in NHL expansion draft (June 24, 1993).

Season Team	League	REGULAR SEASON					PLAYOFFS				
		Gms.	G	A	Pts.	Pen.	Gms.	G	A	Pts.	Pen.
80-81—Dixie	OPJHL	24	15	20	35	84	—	—	—	—	—
81-82—Kitchener	OHL	58	14	34	48	172	14	1	5	6	16
82-83—Kitchener	OHL	61	17	27	44	156	12	5	4	9	30
83-84—Fredericton	AHL	69	11	16	27	142	1	0	0	0	7
84-85—Fredericton	AHL	76	21	27	48	49	6	1	1	2	2
85-86—Fredericton	AHL	74	21	33	54	68	6	0	3	3	8
86-87—Quebec	NHL	56	6	8	14	79	9	0	3	3	26
—Fredericton	AHL	10	1	3	4	20	—	—	—	—	—
87-88—Quebec	NHL	17	3	2	5	2	—	—	—	—	—
—Fredericton	AHL	46	16	25	41	133	15	4	8	12	55
88-89—Halifax	AHL	22	11	10	21	87	—	—	—	—	—
—Quebec	NHL	46	9	10	19	39	—	—	—	—	—
89-90—Quebec	NHL	43	13	13	26	84	—	—	—	—	—
90-91—Quebec	NHL	63	13	20	33	111	—	—	—	—	—
91-92—Quebec	NHL	61	16	22	38	77	—	—	—	—	—
92-93—Quebec	NHL	77	8	22	30	69	6	0	1	1	2
NHL totals		363	68	97	165	461	15	0	4	4	28

HOULDER, BILL
D, MIGHTY DUCKS

PERSONAL: Born March 11, 1967, at Thunder Bay, Ont.... 6-3/218.... Shoots left.
TRANSACTIONS/CAREER NOTES: Selected by Washington Capitals as underage junior in fourth round (fourth Capitals pick, 82nd overall) of NHL entry draft (June 15, 1985).... Pulled groin (January 1989).... Traded by Capitals to Buffalo Sabres for D Shawn Anderson

H

(September 30, 1990). . . . Selected by Mighty Ducks of Anaheim in NHL expansion draft (June 24, 1993).
HONORS: Named to AHL All-Star first team (1990-91). . . . Won Governors Trophy (1992-93). . . . Named to IHL All-Star first team (1992-93).

Season Team	League	REGULAR SEASON					PLAYOFFS				
		Gms.	G	A	Pts.	Pen.	Gms.	G	A	Pts.	Pen.
83-84—Thunder Bay Beavers	TBAHA	23	4	18	22	37	—	—	—	—	—
84-85—North Bay	OHL	66	4	20	24	37	8	0	0	0	2
85-86—North Bay	OHL	59	5	30	35	97	10	1	6	7	12
86-87—North Bay	OHL	62	17	51	68	68	22	4	19	23	20
87-88—Washington	NHL	30	1	2	3	10	—	—	—	—	—
—Fort Wayne	IHL	43	10	14	24	32	—	—	—	—	—
88-89—Baltimore	AHL	65	10	36	46	50	—	—	—	—	—
—Washington	NHL	8	0	3	3	4	—	—	—	—	—
89-90—Baltimore	AHL	26	3	7	10	12	7	0	2	2	2
—Washington	NHL	41	1	11	12	28	—	—	—	—	—
90-91—Rochester	AHL	69	13	53	66	28	15	5	13	18	4
—Buffalo	NHL	7	0	2	2	4	—	—	—	—	—
91-92—Rochester	AHL	42	8	26	34	16	16	5	6	11	4
—Buffalo	NHL	10	1	0	1	8	—	—	—	—	—
92-93—San Diego	IHL	64	24	48	72	39	—	—	—	—	—
—Buffalo	NHL	15	3	5	8	6	8	0	2	2	4
NHL totals		111	6	23	29	60	8	0	2	2	4

HOULE, JEAN-FRANCOIS
LW, CANADIENS

PERSONAL: Born January 14, 1975, at LaSalle, Que. . . . 5-8/145. . . . Shoots left.
HIGH SCHOOL: Northwood (Lake Placid, N.Y.).
TRANSACTIONS/CAREER NOTES: Selected by Montreal Canadiens in fourth round (fifth Canadiens pick, 99th overall) of NHL entry draft (June 26, 1993).

Season Team	League	REGULAR SEASON					PLAYOFFS				
		Gms.	G	A	Pts.	Pen.	Gms.	G	A	Pts.	Pen.
92-93—Northwood School	N.Y. H.S.	28	37	45	82	0	—	—	—	—	—

HOUSE, BOBBY
RW, BLACKHAWKS

PERSONAL: Born January 7, 1973, at Whitehorse, Yukon. . . . 6-1/200. . . . Shoots right.
TRANSACTIONS/CAREER NOTES: Traded by Spokane Chiefs with Marty Murray and G Don Blishen to Brandon Wheat Kings for G Trevor Kidd and Bart Cote (January 21, 1991). . . . Selected by Chicago Blackhawks in third round (fourth Blackhawks pick, 66th overall) of NHL entry draft (June 22, 1991).
HONORS: Named to WHL (East) All-Star second team (1992-93).

Season Team	League	REGULAR SEASON					PLAYOFFS				
		Gms.	G	A	Pts.	Pen.	Gms.	G	A	Pts.	Pen.
88-89—Houjens	Yukon Sr.	28	36	27	63	28	—	—	—	—	—
89-90—Spokane	WHL	64	18	16	34	74	5	0	0	0	6
90-91—Spokane	WHL	38	11	19	30	63	—	—	—	—	—
—Brandon	WHL	23	18	7	25	14	—	—	—	—	—
91-92—Brandon	WHL	71	35	42	77	133	—	—	—	—	—
92-93—Brandon	WHL	61	57	39	96	87	4	2	2	4	0

HOUSLEY, PHIL
D, JETS

PERSONAL: Born March 9, 1964, at St. Paul, Minn. . . . 5-10/179. . . . Shoots left.
HIGH SCHOOL: South St. Paul (Minn.).
TRANSACTIONS/CAREER NOTES: Selected by Buffalo Sabres as underage player in first round (first Sabres pick, sixth overall) of NHL entry draft (June 9, 1982). . . . Bruised shoulder (January 1984). . . . Suspended three games by NHL (October 1984). . . . Injured back (November 1987). . . . Bruised back (January 12, 1989). . . . Suffered hip pointer and bruised back (March 18, 1989). . . . Pulled shoulder ligaments while playing at World Cup Tournament (April 1989). . . . Traded by Sabres with LW Scott Arniel, RW Jeff Parker and first-round pick in 1990 draft (C Keith Tkachuk) to Winnipeg Jets for C Dale Hawerchuk and first-round pick in 1990 draft (LW Brad May) (June 16, 1990). . . . Strained abdomen (February 26, 1992); missed five games. . . . Strained groin (October 31, 1992); missed two games. . . . Sprained wrist (January 19, 1993); missed two games.
HONORS: Named to NHL All-Rookie team (1982-83). . . . Played in NHL All-Star Game (1984 and 1989 through 1993). . . . Named to THE SPORTING NEWS All-Star second team (1991-92). . . . Named to NHL All-Star second team (1991-92).
MISCELLANEOUS: Member of Team U.S.A. at World Junior Championships (1982). . . . Member of Team U.S.A. at World Cup Tournament (1982).

Season Team	League	REGULAR SEASON					PLAYOFFS				
		Gms.	G	A	Pts.	Pen.	Gms.	G	A	Pts.	Pen.
80-81—St. Paul	USHL	6	7	7	14	6	—	—	—	—	—
81-82—South St. Paul H.S.	Minn. H.S.	22	31	34	65	18	—	—	—	—	—
82-83—Buffalo	NHL	77	19	47	66	39	10	3	4	7	2
83-84—Buffalo	NHL	75	31	46	77	33	3	0	0	0	6
84-85—Buffalo	NHL	73	16	53	69	28	5	3	2	5	2
85-86—Buffalo	NHL	79	15	47	62	54	—	—	—	—	—
86-87—Buffalo	NHL	78	21	46	67	57	—	—	—	—	—
87-88—Buffalo	NHL	74	29	37	66	96	6	2	4	6	6
88-89—Buffalo	NHL	72	26	44	70	47	5	1	3	4	2
89-90—Buffalo	NHL	80	21	60	81	32	6	1	4	5	4

H

Season Team	League	REGULAR SEASON					PLAYOFFS				
		Gms.	G	A	Pts.	Pen.	Gms.	G	A	Pts.	Pen.
90-91—Winnipeg	NHL	78	23	53	76	24	—	—	—	—	—
91-92—Winnipeg	NHL	74	23	63	86	92	7	1	4	5	0
92-93—Winnipeg	NHL	80	18	79	97	52	6	0	7	7	2
NHL totals		840	242	575	817	554	48	11	28	39	24

HOWE, MARK
D, RED WINGS

PERSONAL: Born May 28, 1955, at Detroit. . . . 5-11/185. . . . Shoots left. . . . Full name: Mark Steven Howe. . . . Son of Gordie Howe, Hall of Fame right winger, Detroit Red Wings and Hartford Whalers (1946-47 through 1970-71 and 1979-80) and Houston Aeros and New England Whalers of WHA (1973-74 through 1978-79); and brother of Marty Howe, defenseman, Hartford Whalers and Boston Bruins (1979-80 through 1984-85) and Houston Aeros and New England Whalers of WHA (1973-74 through 1978-79).

TRANSACTIONS/CAREER NOTES: Signed by Houston Aeros (June 1972). . . . Traded by London Knights to Toronto Marlboros for D Larry Goodenough and C Dennis Maruk (August 1972). . . . Underwent corrective knee surgery; missed most of 1971-72 season. . . . Selected by Boston Bruins from Marlboros in second round (second Bruins pick, 25th overall) of amateur draft (May 28, 1974). . . . Suffered shoulder separation; missed part of 1976-77 season. . . . Signed as free agent by New England Whalers (June 1977). . . . Injured ribs; missed part of 1977-78 season. . . . Selected by Boston Bruins in NHL reclaim draft, but remained Hartford Whalers property as a priority selection for the expansion draft (June 9, 1979). . . . Suffered five-inch puncture wound to upper thigh (December 27, 1980). . . . Traded by Whalers to Philadelphia Flyers for C Ken Linseman, C Greg Adams and first-round pick in 1983 draft (LW David A. Jensen) and exchange of third-round picks in 1983 draft (August 19, 1982). . . . Injured shoulder (February 1984). . . . Bruised collarbone (January 1985). . . . Suffered back spasms (January 1987). . . . Broke rib and vertebrae (September 1987). . . . Strained back (March 1988). . . . Bruised right foot (October 1988). . . . Pulled groin muscle (December 1988). . . . Sprained left knee cruciate ligament (February 1989); missed eight games. . . . Reinjured left knee (February 27, 1989). . . . Injured groin (December 22, 1989). . . . Injured back (January 27, 1990). . . . Injured back (November 3, 1990); missed four games. . . . Reinjured back (November 25, 1990). . . . Underwent surgery for herniated disk (January 18, 1991); missed 54 games. . . . Aggravated back injury (October 4, 1991); missed seven games. . . . Fractured thumb (November 23, 1991); missed 24 games. . . . Signed as free agent by Detroit Red Wings (July 8, 1992). . . . Injured back (November 28, 1992); missed three games. . . . Injured rib (December 28, 1992); missed three games. . . . Injured back (January 17, 1993); missed two games. . . . Sprained neck (March 18, 1993); missed eight games.

HONORS: Won Most Valuable Player and Outstanding Forward Awards (1970-71). . . . Named to SOJHL All-Star first team (1970-71). . . . Won WHA Rookie of the Year Award (1973-74). . . . Named to WHA All-Star second team (1973-74 and 1976-77). . . . Named to WHA All-Star first team (1978-79). . . . Named to THE SPORTING NEWS All-Star second team (1979-80). . . . Played in NHL All-Star Game (1981, 1983, 1986 and 1988). . . . Named to THE SPORTING NEWS All-Star first team (1982-83, 1985-86 and 1986-87). . . . Named to NHL All-Star first team (1982-83, 1985-86 and 1986-87). . . . Won Emery Edge Award (1985-86).

Season Team	League	REGULAR SEASON					PLAYOFFS				
		Gms.	G	A	Pts.	Pen.	Gms.	G	A	Pts.	Pen.
70-71—Detroit Junior Red Wings	SOJHL	44	37	*70	*107	...	—	—	—	—	—
71-72—Detroit Junior Red Wings	SOJHL	9	5	9	14	...	—	—	—	—	—
—U.S. Olympic Team	Int'l				Statistics unavailable.						
72-73—Toronto	OHA Mj. Jr. A	60	38	66	104	27	—	—	—	—	—
73-74—Houston	WHA	76	38	41	79	20	14	9	10	19	4
74-75—Houston	WHA	74	36	40	76	30	13	†10	12	*22	0
75-76—Houston	WHA	72	39	37	76	38	†17	6	10	16	18
76-77—Houston	WHA	57	23	52	75	46	10	4	10	14	2
77-78—New England	WHA	70	30	61	91	32	14	8	7	15	18
78-79—New England	WHA	77	42	65	107	32	6	4	2	6	6
79-80—Hartford	NHL	74	24	56	80	20	3	1	2	3	2
80-81—Hartford	NHL	63	19	46	65	54	—	—	—	—	—
81-82—Hartford	NHL	76	8	45	53	18	—	—	—	—	—
82-83—Philadelphia	NHL	76	20	47	67	18	3	0	2	2	4
83-84—Philadelphia	NHL	71	19	34	53	44	3	0	0	0	2
84-85—Philadelphia	NHL	73	18	39	57	31	19	3	8	11	6
85-86—Philadelphia	NHL	77	24	58	82	36	5	0	4	4	0
86-87—Philadelphia	NHL	69	15	43	58	37	26	2	10	12	4
87-88—Philadelphia	NHL	75	19	43	62	62	7	3	6	9	4
88-89—Philadelphia	NHL	52	9	29	38	45	19	0	15	15	10
89-90—Philadelphia	NHL	40	7	21	28	24	—	—	—	—	—
90-91—Philadelphia	NHL	19	0	10	10	8	—	—	—	—	—
91-92—Philadelphia	NHL	42	7	18	25	18	—	—	—	—	—
92-93—Detroit	NHL	60	3	31	34	22	7	1	3	4	2
WHA totals		426	208	296	504	198	74	41	51	92	48
NHL totals		867	192	520	712	437	92	10	50	60	34

HRIVNAK, JIM
G, BLUES

PERSONAL: Born May 28, 1968, at Montreal. . . . 6-2/185. . . . Shoots left. . . . Full name: James Richard Hrivnak. . . . Name pronounced RIHV-nak.

COLLEGE: Merrimack (Mass.).

TRANSACTIONS/CAREER NOTES: Selected by Washington Capitals in third round (fourth Capitals pick, 61st overall) of NHL entry draft (June 21, 1986). . . . Traded by Capitals with future considerations to Winnipeg Jets for G Rick Tabaracci (March 22, 1993). . . . Traded by Jets to St. Louis Blues for seventh-round pick in 1994 draft (July 29, 1993).

HONORS: Named to AHL All-Star second team (1989-90).

H

Season	Team	League	REGULAR SEASON							PLAYOFFS						
			Gms.	Min.	W	L	T	GA	SO	Avg.	Gms.	Min.	W	L	GA	SO	Avg.
85-86—Merrimack College	ECAC-II	21	1230	12	6	2	75	0	3.66	—	—	—	—	—	—	—
86-87—Merrimack College	ECAC-II	34	1618	27	7	0	58	3	2.15	—	—	—	—	—	—	—
87-88—Merrimack College	ECAC-II	37	2119	31	6	0	84	4	2.38	—	—	—	—	—	—	—
88-89—Merrimack College	ECAC-II	22	1295	...	...	...	52	4	2.41	—	—	—	—	—	—	—
—Baltimore	AHL	10	502	1	8	0	55	0	6.57	—	—	—	—	—	—	—
89-90—Washington	NHL	11	609	5	5	0	36	0	3.55	—	—	—	—	—	—	—
—Baltimore	AHL	47	2722	24	19	2	139	*4	3.06	6	360	4	2	19	*1	3.17
90-91—Washington	NHL	9	432	4	2	1	26	0	3.61	—	—	—	—	—	—	—
—Baltimore	AHL	42	2481	20	16	6	134	1	3.24	6	324	2	3	21	0	3.89
91-92—Washington	NHL	12	605	6	3	0	35	0	3.47	—	—	—	—	—	—	—
—Baltimore	AHL	22	1303	10	8	3	73	0	3.36	—	—	—	—	—	—	—
92-93—Washington	NHL	27	1421	13	9	2	83	0	3.50	—	—	—	—	—	—	—
—Winnipeg	NHL	3	180	2	1	0	13	0	4.33	—	—	—	—	—	—	—
NHL totals		62	3247	30	20	3	193	0	3.57							

HRKAC, TONY

C, BLUES

PERSONAL: Born July 7, 1966, at Thunder Bay, Ont. . . . 5-11/170. . . . Shoots left. . . . Name pronounced HUHR-kuhz.

COLLEGE: North Dakota.

TRANSACTIONS/CAREER NOTES: Selected by St. Louis Blues as underage junior in second round (second Blues pick, 32nd overall) of NHL entry draft (June 9, 1984). . . . Suspended six games by coach for disciplinary reasons (January 1985). . . . Bruised left leg (January 1987). . . . Sprained shoulder (January 12, 1988). . . . Lacerated ankle (March 1988). . . . Bruised left shoulder (November 28, 1989). . . . Traded by Blues with G Greg Millen to Quebec Nordiques for D Jeff Brown (December 13, 1989). . . . Traded by Nordiques to San Jose Sharks for RW Greg Paslawski (May 30, 1991). . . . Injured wrist during preseason (September 1991); missed first 27 games of season. . . . Traded to Chicago Blackhawks for conditional pick in 1993 draft (February 7, 1992). . . . Signed as free agent by Blues (July 30, 1993).

HONORS: Won Hobey Baker Memorial Trophy (1986-87). . . . Won WCHA Most Valuable Player Award (1986-87). . . . Named NCAA Tournament Most Valuable Player (1986-87). . . . Named to NCAA All-America West first team (1986-87). . . . Named to WCHA All-Star first team (1986-87). . . . Named to NCAA All-Tournament team (1986-87). . . . Won James Gatschene Memorial Trophy (1992-93). . . . Won Leo P. Lamoureux Memorial Trophy (1992-93). . . . Named to IHL All-Star first team (1992-93).

Season	Team	League	REGULAR SEASON					PLAYOFFS				
			Gms.	G	A	Pts.	Pen.	Gms.	G	A	Pts.	Pen.
83-84—Orillia	OHA	42	*52	54	*106	20	—	—	—	—	—
84-85—Univ. of North Dakota	WCHA	36	18	36	54	16	—	—	—	—	—
85-86—Canadian national team	Int'l	62	19	30	49	36	—	—	—	—	—
86-87—Univ. of North Dakota	WCHA	48	46	*70	*116	48	—	—	—	—	—
—St. Louis	NHL	—	—	—	—	—	3	0	0	0	0
87-88—St. Louis	NHL	67	11	37	48	22	10	6	1	7	4
88-89—St. Louis	NHL	70	17	28	45	8	4	1	1	2	0
89-90—St. Louis	NHL	28	5	12	17	8	—	—	—	—	—
—Quebec	NHL	22	4	8	12	2	—	—	—	—	—
—Halifax	AHL	20	12	21	33	4	6	5	9	14	4
90-91—Halifax	AHL	3	4	1	5	2	—	—	—	—	—
—Quebec	NHL	70	16	32	48	16	—	—	—	—	—
91-92—San Jose	NHL	22	2	10	12	4	—	—	—	—	—
—Chicago	NHL	18	1	2	3	6	3	0	0	0	2
92-93—Indianapolis	IHL	80	45	*87	*132	70	5	0	2	2	2
NHL totals		297	56	129	185	66	20	7	2	9	6

HRUDEY, KELLY

G, KINGS

PERSONAL: Born January 13, 1961, at Edmonton, Alta. . . . 5-10/189. . . . Shoots left. . . . Full name: Kelly Stephen Hrudey. . . . Name pronounced ROO-dee.

TRANSACTIONS/CAREER NOTES: Selected by New York Islanders as underage junior in second round (second Islanders pick, 38th overall) of NHL entry draft (June 11, 1980). . . . Traded by Islanders to Los Angeles Kings for D Wayne McBean, G Mark Fitzpatrick and future considerations (February 27, 1989); Kings sent D Doug Crossman to the Islanders to complete the deal (May 23, 1989). . . . Suffered from the flu (April 1989). . . . Suffered from mononucleosis (February 1990); missed 14 games. . . . Bruised ribs (April 20, 1990). . . . Suffered from the flu (March 11, 1993); missed one game. . . . Suffered from the flu (March 26, 1993); missed one game.

HONORS: Named to WHL All-Star second team (1980-81). . . . Shared Terry Sawchuk Trophy with Robert Holland (1981-82 and 1982-83). . . . Won Max McNab Trophy (1981-82). . . . Named to CHL All-Star first team (1981-82 and 1982-83). . . . Won Tommy Ivan Trophy (1982-83).

Season	Team	League	REGULAR SEASON							PLAYOFFS						
			Gms.	Min.	W	L	T	GA	SO	Avg.	Gms.	Min.	W	L	GA	SO	Avg.
78-79—Medicine Hat	WHL	57	3093	12	34	7	*318	0	6.17	—	—	—	—	—	—	—
79-80—Medicine Hat	WHL	57	3049	25	23	4	212	1	4.17	13	638	6	6	48	0	4.51
80-81—Medicine Hat	WHL	55	3023	32	19	1	200	†4	3.97	4	244	...	...	17	0	4.18
—Indianapolis	CHL	—	—	—	—	—	—	—	—	2	135	...	...	8	0	3.56
81-82—Indianapolis	CHL	51	3033	27	19	4	149	1	*2.95	13	842	11	2	34	*1	*2.42
82-83—Indianapolis	CHL	47	2744	26	17	1	139	2	3.04	10	†637	*7	3	28	0	*2.64
83-84—Indianapolis	CHL	6	370	3	2	1	21	0	3.41	—	—	—	—	—	—	—
—New York Islanders	NHL	12	535	7	2	0	28	0	3.14	—	—	—	—	—	—	—
84-85—New York Islanders	NHL	41	2335	19	17	3	141	2	3.62	5	281	1	3	8	0	1.71
85-86—New York Islanders	NHL	45	2563	19	15	8	137	1	3.21	2	120	0	2	6	0	3.00

H

Season Team	League	REGULAR SEASON								PLAYOFFS						
		Gms.	Min.	W	L	T	GA	SO	Avg.	Gms.	Min.	W	L	GA	SO	Avg.
86-87—New York Islanders......	NHL	46	2634	21	15	7	145	0	3.30	14	842	7	7	38	0	2.71
87-88—New York Islanders......	NHL	47	2751	22	17	5	153	3	3.34	6	381	2	4	23	0	3.62
88-89—New York Islanders......	NHL	50	2800	18	24	3	183	0	3.92	—	—	—	—	—	—	—
—Los Angeles.................	NHL	16	974	10	4	2	47	1	2.90	10	566	4	6	35	0	3.71
89-90—Los Angeles.................	NHL	52	2860	22	21	6	194	2	4.07	9	539	4	4	39	0	4.34
90-91—Los Angeles.................	NHL	47	2730	26	13	6	132	3	2.90	12	798	6	6	37	0	2.78
91-92—Los Angeles.................	NHL	60	3509	26	17	*13	197	1	3.37	6	355	2	4	22	0	3.72
92-93—Los Angeles.................	NHL	50	2718	18	21	6	175	2	3.86	20	1261	10	10	74	0	3.52
NHL totals...............................		466	26409	208	166	59	1532	15	3.48	84	5143	36	46	282	0	3.29

HUARD, BILL
LW, SENATORS

PERSONAL: Born June 24, 1967, at Alland, Ont.... 6-1/200.... Shoots left.... Name pronounced HYOO-erd.

TRANSACTIONS/CAREER NOTES: Signed as free agent by Boston Bruins (December 4, 1992).... Signed as free agent by Ottawa Senators (July 20, 1993).

Season Team	League	REGULAR SEASON					PLAYOFFS				
		Gms.	G	A	Pts.	Pen.	Gms.	G	A	Pts.	Pen.
92-93—Providence	AHL	72	18	19	37	302	6	3	0	3	9
—Boston	NHL	2	0	0	0	0	—	—	—	—	—
NHL totals....................................		2	0	0	0	0					

HUBER, PHIL
C, ISLANDERS

PERSONAL: Born January 10, 1969, at Calgary, Alta.... 5-11/187.... Shoots left.

TRANSACTIONS/CAREER NOTES: Selected by New York Islanders in eighth round (10th Islanders pick, 149th overall) of NHL entry draft (June 17, 1989).

HONORS: Named to WHL (West) All-Star first team (1989-90).

Season Team	League	REGULAR SEASON					PLAYOFFS				
		Gms.	G	A	Pts.	Pen.	Gms.	G	A	Pts.	Pen.
87-88—Kamloops	WHL	63	19	30	49	54	18	3	9	12	23
88-89—Kamloops	WHL	72	54	68	122	103	16	*18	13	31	48
89-90—Kamloops	WHL	72	63	89	152	176	17	12	11	23	44
90-91—Capital District..............	AHL	5	1	1	2	0	—	—	—	—	—
—Richmond	ECHL	56	32	40	72	87	4	1	3	4	4
91-92—Capital District..............	AHL	71	26	32	58	85	7	0	2	2	10
92-93—Capital District..............	AHL	16	1	4	5	4	4	0	2	2	4
—Richmond	ECHL	44	23	49	72	151	1	1	1	2	6

HUDDY, CHARLIE
D, KINGS

PERSONAL: Born June 2, 1959, at Oshawa, Ont.... 6-0/210.... Shoots left.... Full name: Charles William Huddy.

TRANSACTIONS/CAREER NOTES: Signed as free agent by Edmonton Oilers (September 14, 1979).... Injured shoulder (November 10, 1980).... Suffered back spasms (February 1986); missed three games.... Broke finger (April 1986).... Suffered hematoma of left thigh and underwent surgery (May 7, 1988); missed six playoff games.... Strained hamstring (January 2, 1989).... Sprained right ankle (December 22, 1990); missed 17 games.... Broke left toe (February 16, 1991); missed nine games.... Twisted back (March 1991).... Selected by Minnesota North Stars in NHL expansion draft (May 30, 1991).... Traded by North Stars with LW Randy Gilhen, RW Jim Thomson and fourth-round pick in 1991 draft (D Alexei Zhitnik) to Los Angeles Kings for C Todd Elik (June 22, 1991).... Injured groin (October 10, 1991); missed seven games.... Strained groin (November 7, 1991); missed five games.... Suffered chest contusion (February 1, 1992); missed seven games.... Suffered chest contusion (March 3, 1992); missed five games. ... Suffered from the flu (January 14, 1993); missed one game.

HONORS: Won Emery Edge Award (1982-83).

MISCELLANEOUS: Member of Stanley Cup championship teams (1984, 1985, 1987, 1988 and 1990).

Season Team	League	REGULAR SEASON					PLAYOFFS				
		Gms.	G	A	Pts.	Pen.	Gms.	G	A	Pts.	Pen.
77-78—Oshawa	OMJHL	59	17	18	35	81	6	2	1	3	10
78-79—Oshawa	OMJHL	64	20	38	58	108	5	3	4	7	12
79-80—Houston	CHL	79	14	34	48	46	6	1	0	1	2
80-81—Edmonton.......................	NHL	12	2	5	7	6	—	—	—	—	—
—Wichita..........................	CHL	47	8	36	44	71	17	3	11	14	10
81-82—Wichita	CHL	32	7	19	26	51	—	—	—	—	—
—Edmonton......................	NHL	41	4	11	15	46	5	1	2	3	14
82-83—Edmonton.......................	NHL	76	20	37	57	58	15	1	6	7	10
83-84—Edmonton.......................	NHL	75	8	34	42	43	12	1	9	10	8
84-85—Edmonton.......................	NHL	80	7	44	51	46	18	3	17	20	17
85-86—Edmonton.......................	NHL	76	6	35	41	55	7	0	2	2	0
86-87—Edmonton.......................	NHL	58	4	15	19	35	21	1	7	8	21
87-88—Edmonton.......................	NHL	77	13	28	41	71	13	4	5	9	10
88-89—Edmonton.......................	NHL	76	11	33	44	52	7	2	0	2	4
89-90—Edmonton.......................	NHL	70	1	23	24	56	22	0	6	6	11
90-91—Edmonton.......................	NHL	53	5	22	27	32	18	3	7	10	10
91-92—Los Angeles....................	NHL	56	4	19	23	43	6	1	1	2	10
92-93—Los Angeles....................	NHL	82	2	25	27	64	23	1	4	5	12
NHL totals....................................		832	87	331	418	607	167	18	66	84	127

— 453 —

HUDSON, MIKE
C/LW, OILERS

PERSONAL: Born February 6, 1967, at Guelph, Ont.... 6-1/205.... Shoots left.
TRANSACTIONS/CAREER NOTES: Traded by Hamilton Steelhawks with D Keith Vanrooyen to Sudbury Wolves for C Brad Belland (October 1985).... Selected by Chicago Blackhawks as underage junior in seventh round (sixth Blackhawks pick, 140th overall) of NHL entry draft (June 21, 1986).... Lacerated right hand (December 21, 1989); missed 12 games.... Suffered elbow tendinitis (September 1990).... Underwent elbow surgery (May 1991).... Suffered viral infection (December 20, 1992); missed 21 games.... Traded by Blackhawks to Edmonton Oilers for D Craig Muni (March 22, 1993).... Suffered nerve disorder in left shoulder (March 1993); missed two games.

			REGULAR SEASON					PLAYOFFS			
Season Team	League	Gms.	G	A	Pts.	Pen.	Gms.	G	A	Pts.	Pen.
84-85—Hamilton............	OHL	50	10	12	22	13	—	—	—	—	—
85-86—Hamilton............	OHL	7	3	2	5	4	—	—	—	—	—
—Sudbury..............	OHL	59	35	42	77	20	4	2	5	7	7
86-87—Sudbury.............	OHL	63	40	57	97	18	—	—	—	—	—
87-88—Saginaw	IHL	75	18	30	48	44	10	2	3	5	20
88-89—Chicago	NHL	41	7	16	23	20	10	1	2	3	18
—Saginaw	IHL	30	15	17	32	10	—	—	—	—	—
89-90—Chicago	NHL	49	9	12	21	56	4	0	0	0	2
90-91—Chicago	NHL	55	7	9	16	62	6	0	2	2	8
—Indianapolis	IHL	3	1	2	3	0	—	—	—	—	—
91-92—Chicago	NHL	76	14	15	29	92	16	3	5	8	26
92-93—Chicago	NHL	36	1	6	7	44	—	—	—	—	—
—Edmonton.........	NHL	5	0	1	1	2	—	—	—	—	—
NHL totals.............		262	38	59	97	276	36	4	9	13	54

HUFFMAN, KERRY
D, NORDIQUES

PERSONAL: Born January 3, 1968, at Peterborough, Ont.... 6-3/205.... Shoots left.... Brother-in-law of Mike Posavad, defenseman, St. Louis Blues (1985-86 through 1986-87).
TRANSACTIONS/CAREER NOTES: Selected by Philadelphia Flyers as underage junior in first round (first Flyers pick, 20th overall) of NHL entry draft (June 21, 1986).... Sprained ankle (November 1987).... Suffered calcium deposits in thigh (January 1988); missed 22 games.... Bruised right knee (March 15, 1990).... Suspended by Flyers after leaving team in dispute over ice time (November 16, 1990).... Returned to Flyers (December 10, 1990).... Suffered from tonsilitis (October 1991); missed one game.... Traded by Flyers with G Ron Hextall, C Mike Ricci, C Peter Forsberg, D Steve Duchesne, first-round pick in 1993 draft (G Jocelyn Thibault), cash and future considerations to Quebec Nordiques for C Eric Lindros (June 20, 1992); Flyers sent LW Chris Simon and first-round pick in 1994 draft to Nordiques to complete deal (July 21, 1992).... Broke ribs (October 17, 1992); missed three games.... Injured shoulder (November 28, 1992); missed 14 games.... Fractured finger (March 8, 1993); missed 10 games.
HONORS: Won Max Kaminsky Trophy (1986-87).... Named to OHL All-Star first team (1986-87).

			REGULAR SEASON					PLAYOFFS			
Season Team	League	Gms.	G	A	Pts.	Pen.	Gms.	G	A	Pts.	Pen.
84-85—Peterborough Jr. B..........	OHA	24	2	5	7	53	—	—	—	—	—
85-86—Guelph	OHL	56	3	24	27	35	20	1	10	11	10
86-87—Guelph	OHL	44	4	31	35	20	5	0	2	2	8
—Hershey	AHL	3	0	1	1	0	4	0	0	0	0
—Philadelphia	NHL	9	0	0	0	2	—	—	—	—	—
87-88—Philadelphia	NHL	52	6	17	23	34	2	0	0	0	0
88-89—Hershey	AHL	29	2	13	15	16	—	—	—	—	—
—Philadelphia	NHL	29	0	11	11	31	—	—	—	—	—
89-90—Philadelphia	NHL	43	1	12	13	34	—	—	—	—	—
90-91—Hershey	AHL	45	5	29	34	20	7	1	2	3	0
—Philadelphia	NHL	10	1	2	3	10	—	—	—	—	—
91-92—Philadelphia	NHL	60	14	18	32	41	—	—	—	—	—
92-93—Quebec	NHL	52	4	18	22	54	3	0	0	0	0
NHL totals.............		255	26	78	104	206	5	0	0	0	0

HUGHES, BRENT
LW, BRUINS

PERSONAL: Born April 5, 1966, at New Westminster, B.C.... 5-11/180.... Shoots left.... Full name: Brent Allen Hughes.
TRANSACTIONS/CAREER NOTES: Traded by New Westminster Bruins to Victoria Cougars for future considerations (October 1986).... Signed as free agent by Winnipeg Jets (July 1987).... Traded by Jets with LW Craig Duncanson and C Simon Wheeldon to Washington Capitals for LW Bob Joyce, D Kent Paynter and C Tyler Larter (May 21, 1991).... Traded by Capitals with future considerations to Boston Bruins for RW John Byce and D Dennis Smith (February 24, 1992).... Separated shoulder (November 28, 1992); missed 11 games.
HONORS: Named to WHL (West) All-Star first team (1986-87).

			REGULAR SEASON					PLAYOFFS			
Season Team	League	Gms.	G	A	Pts.	Pen.	Gms.	G	A	Pts.	Pen.
83-84—New Westminster	WHL	67	21	18	39	133	9	2	2	4	27
84-85—New Westminster	WHL	64	25	32	57	135	11	2	1	3	37
85-86—New Westminster	WHL	71	28	52	80	180	—	—	—	—	—
86-87—New Westminster	WHL	8	5	4	9	22	—	—	—	—	—
—Victoria..............	WHL	61	38	61	99	146	5	4	1	5	8
87-88—Moncton	AHL	77	13	19	32	206	—	—	—	—	—
88-89—Winnipeg	NHL	28	3	2	5	82	—	—	—	—	—
—Moncton	AHL	54	34	34	68	286	10	9	4	13	40

H

			REGULAR SEASON					PLAYOFFS			
Season Team	League	Gms.	G	A	Pts.	Pen.	Gms.	G	A	Pts.	Pen.
89-90—Moncton	AHL	65	31	29	60	277	—	—	—	—	—
—Winnipeg	NHL	11	1	2	3	33	—	—	—	—	—
90-91—Moncton	AHL	63	21	22	43	144	3	0	0	0	7
91-92—Baltimore	AHL	55	25	29	54	190	—	—	—	—	—
—Maine	AHL	12	6	4	10	34	—	—	—	—	—
—Boston	NHL	8	1	1	2	38	10	2	0	2	20
92-93—Boston	NHL	62	5	4	9	191	1	0	0	0	2
NHL totals		109	10	9	19	344	11	2	0	2	22

HUGHES, RYAN
C, NORDIQUES

PERSONAL: Born January 17, 1972, at Montreal. . . . 6-1/180. . . . Shoots left. . . . Full name: Ryan Laine Hughes.
COLLEGE: Cornell.
TRANSACTIONS/CAREER NOTES: Selected by Quebec Nordiques in second round (second Nordiques pick, 22nd overall) of NHL entry draft (June 16, 1990).

			REGULAR SEASON					PLAYOFFS			
Season Team	League	Gms.	G	A	Pts.	Pen.	Gms.	G	A	Pts.	Pen.
89-90—Cornell University	ECAC	28	7	16	23	35	—	—	—	—	—
90-91—Cornell University	ECAC	32	18	34	52	28	—	—	—	—	—
—Victoria	WHL	1	0	1	1	2	—	—	—	—	—
91-92—Cornell University	ECAC	27	8	13	21	36	—	—	—	—	—
92-93—Cornell University	ECAC	26	8	14	22	30	—	—	—	—	—

HULBIG, JOE
LW, OILERS

PERSONAL: Born September 29, 1973, at Wrentham, Mass. . . . 6-3/215. . . . Shoots left.
HIGH SCHOOL: St. Sebastian's Country Day School (Needham, Mass.).
COLLEGE: Providence.
TRANSACTIONS/CAREER NOTES: Selected by Edmonton Oilers in first round (first Oilers pick, 13th overall) of NHL entry draft (June 20, 1992).

			REGULAR SEASON					PLAYOFFS			
Season Team	League	Gms.	G	A	Pts.	Pen.	Gms.	G	A	Pts.	Pen.
90-91—St. Sebastian's	Mass. H.S.	...	23	19	42	...	—	—	—	—	—
91-92—St. Sebastian's	Mass. H.S.	17	19	24	43	30	—	—	—	—	—
92-93—Providence College	Hockey East	26	3	13	16	22	—	—	—	—	—

HULL, BRETT
RW, BLUES

PERSONAL: Born August 9, 1964, at Belleville, Ont. . . . 5-10/203. . . . Shoots right. . . . Son of Bobby Hull, Hall of Fame left winger, Chicago Blackhawks, Winnipeg Jets and Hartford Whalers (1957-58 through 1971-72 and 1979-80) and Winnipeg Jets of WHA (1972-73 through 1978-79); and nephew of Dennis Hull, left winger, Blackhawks and Detroit Red Wings (1964-65 through 1977-78).
COLLEGE: Minnesota-Duluth.
TRANSACTIONS/CAREER NOTES: Selected by Calgary Flames in sixth round (sixth Flames pick, 117th overall) of NHL entry draft (June 9, 1984). . . . Traded by Flames with LW Steve Bozek to St. Louis Blues for D Rob Ramage and G Rick Wamsley (March 7, 1988). . . . Sprained left ankle (January 15, 1991); missed two regular-season games and All-Star Game. . . . Suffered back spasms (March 12, 1992); missed seven games. . . . Suffered sore wrist (March 20, 1993); missed four games.
HONORS: Won WCHA Freshman of the Year Award (1984-85). . . . Named to WCHA All-Star first team (1985-86). . . . Won Dudley (Red) Garrett Memorial Trophy (1986-87). . . . Named to AHL All-Star first team (1986-87). . . . Won Lady Byng Memorial Trophy (1989-90). . . . Won Dodge Ram Tough Award (1989-90 and 1990-91). . . . Named to THE SPORTING NEWS All-Star first team (1989-90 through 1991-92). . . . Named to NHL All-Star first team (1989-90 through 1991-92). . . . Played in NHL All-Star Game (1989, 1990, 1992 and 1993). . . . Named NHL Player of the Year by THE SPORTING NEWS (1990-91). . . . Won Hart Memorial Trophy (1990-91). . . . Won Lester B. Pearson Award (1990-91). . . . Won Pro Set NHL Player of the Year Award (1990-91). . . . Named All-Star Game Most Valuable Player (1992).
RECORDS: Holds NHL single-season record for most goals by a right winger—86 (1990-91).
MISCELLANEOUS: Shares distinction with Bobby Hull of being the first father-son duo to win the same NHL trophy (both the Lady Byng Memorial and Hart Memorial trophies). . . . Became the first son of an NHL 50-goal scorer to score 50 goals in one season (1989-90).

			REGULAR SEASON					PLAYOFFS			
Season Team	League	Gms.	G	A	Pts.	Pen.	Gms.	G	A	Pts.	Pen.
82-83—Penticton	BCJHL	50	48	56	104	27	—	—	—	—	—
83-84—Penticton	BCJHL	56	*105	83	*188	20	—	—	—	—	—
84-85—Minnesota-Duluth	WCHA	48	32	28	60	24	—	—	—	—	—
85-86—Minnesota-Duluth	WCHA	42	*52	32	84	46	—	—	—	—	—
—Calgary	NHL	—	—	—	—	—	2	0	0	0	0
86-87—Moncton	AHL	67	50	42	92	16	3	2	2	4	2
—Calgary	NHL	5	1	0	1	0	4	2	1	3	0
87-88—Calgary	NHL	52	26	24	50	12	—	—	—	—	—
—St. Louis	NHL	13	6	8	14	4	10	7	2	9	4
88-89—St. Louis	NHL	78	41	43	84	33	10	5	5	10	6
89-90—St. Louis	NHL	80	*72	41	113	24	12	13	8	21	17
90-91—St. Louis	NHL	78	*86	45	131	22	13	11	8	19	4
91-92—St. Louis	NHL	73	*70	39	109	48	6	4	4	8	4
92-93—St. Louis	NHL	80	54	47	101	41	11	8	5	13	2
NHL totals		459	356	247	603	184	68	50	33	83	37

H

HULL, JODY

RW, PANTHERS

PERSONAL: Born February 2, 1969, at Petrolia, Ont.... 6-2/200.... Shoots right.
HIGH SCHOOL: Thomas A. Stewart (Peterborough, Ont.).
TRANSACTIONS/CAREER NOTES: Strained ankle ligaments (September 1986).... Pulled groin (February 1987).... Selected by Hartford Whalers as underage junior in first round (first Whalers pick, 18th overall) of NHL entry draft (June 13, 1987).... Pulled hamstring (March 1989).... Traded by Whalers to New York Rangers for C Carey Wilson and third-round pick in 1991 draft (C Mikael Nylander) (July 9, 1990).... Sprained muscle in right hand (October 6, 1990).... Bruised left big toe (November 19, 1990); missed six games.... Injured knee (March 13, 1991).... Traded by Rangers to Ottawa Senators for future considerations (July 28, 1992).... Injured groin (December 7, 1992); missed three games.... Suffered concussion (January 10, 1993); missed one game.... Sprained ankle (January 19, 1993); missed eight games.... Sprained left ankle (April 1, 1993); missed two games.... Signed as free agent by Florida Panthers (August 2, 1993).
HONORS: Named to OHL All-Star second team (1987-88).

| | | | —REGULAR SEASON— | | | | —PLAYOFFS— | | | |
Season Team	League	Gms.	G	A	Pts.	Pen.	Gms.	G	A	Pts.	Pen.
84-85—Cambridge Jr. B	OHA	38	13	17	30	39	—	—	—	—	—
85-86—Peterborough	OHL	61	20	22	42	29	16	1	5	6	4
86-87—Peterborough	OHL	49	18	34	52	22	12	4	9	13	14
87-88—Peterborough	OHL	60	50	44	94	33	12	10	8	18	8
88-89—Hartford	NHL	60	16	18	34	10	1	0	0	0	2
89-90—Binghamton	AHL	21	7	10	17	6	—	—	—	—	—
—Hartford	NHL	38	7	10	17	21	5	0	1	1	2
90-91—New York Rangers	NHL	47	5	8	13	10	—	—	—	—	—
91-92—New York Rangers	NHL	3	0	0	0	2	—	—	—	—	—
—Binghamton	AHL	69	34	31	65	28	11	5	2	7	4
92-93—Ottawa	NHL	69	13	21	34	14	—	—	—	—	—
NHL totals
NHL totals	217	41	57	98	57	6	0	1	1	4

HULSE, CALE

D, DEVILS

PERSONAL: Born November 10, 1973, at Edmonton, Alta.... 6-3/210.... Shoots right.... Name pronounced HUHLS.
COLLEGE: Portland.
TRANSACTIONS/CAREER NOTES: Selected by New Jersey Devils in third round (third Devils pick, 66th overall) of NHL entry draft (June 20, 1992).

| | | | —REGULAR SEASON— | | | | —PLAYOFFS— | | | |
Season Team	League	Gms.	G	A	Pts.	Pen.	Gms.	G	A	Pts.	Pen.
90-91—Calgary Royals	AJHL	49	3	23	26	220	—	—	—	—	—
91-92—Portland	WHL	70	4	18	22	250	6	0	2	2	27
92-93—Portland	WHL	72	10	26	36	284	16	4	4	8	*65

HUNTER, DALE

C, CAPITALS

PERSONAL: Born July 31, 1960, at Petrolia, Ont.... 5-10/198.... Shoots left.... Full name: Dale Robert Hunter.... Brother of Mark Hunter, right winger, Washington Capitals; and brother of Dave Hunter, left winger, Edmonton Oilers of WHA (1978-79); and Edmonton Oilers, Pittsburgh Penguins and Winnipeg Jets (1979-80 through 1988-89).
TRANSACTIONS/CAREER NOTES: Selected by Quebec Nordiques as underage junior in second round (second Nordiques pick, 41st overall) of NHL entry draft (August 9, 1979).... Suspended three games by NHL (March 1984).... Suffered hand infection (April 21, 1985).... Broke lower left leg (November 25, 1986).... Traded by Nordiques with G Clint Malarchuk to Washington Capitals for C Alan Haworth, LW Gaeten Duchesne and first-round pick in 1987 draft (C Joe Sakic) (June 13, 1987).... Broke thumb (September 1988).... Suspended four games by NHL for elbowing D Gord Murphy (February 10, 1991).... Suspended for first 21 games of 1993-94 by NHL for blindside check on player (May 4, 1993).
RECORDS: Holds NHL career playoff record for most penalty minutes—581.

| | | | —REGULAR SEASON— | | | | —PLAYOFFS— | | | |
Season Team	League	Gms.	G	A	Pts.	Pen.	Gms.	G	A	Pts.	Pen.
77-78—Kitchener	OMJHL	68	22	42	64	115	—	—	—	—	—
78-79—Sudbury	OMJHL	59	42	68	110	188	10	4	12	16	47
79-80—Sudbury	OMJHL	61	34	51	85	189	9	6	9	15	45
80-81—Quebec	NHL	80	19	44	63	226	5	4	2	6	34
81-82—Quebec	NHL	80	22	50	72	272	16	3	7	10	52
82-83—Quebec	NHL	80	17	46	63	206	4	2	1	3	24
83-84—Quebec	NHL	77	24	55	79	232	9	2	3	5	41
84-85—Quebec	NHL	80	20	52	72	209	17	4	6	10	*97
85-86—Quebec	NHL	80	28	42	70	265	3	0	0	0	15
86-87—Quebec	NHL	46	10	29	39	135	13	1	7	8	56
87-88—Washington	NHL	79	22	37	59	238	14	7	5	12	88
88-89—Washington	NHL	80	20	37	57	219	6	0	4	4	29
89-90—Washington	NHL	80	23	39	62	233	15	4	8	12	61
90-91—Washington	NHL	76	16	30	46	234	11	1	9	10	41
91-92—Washington	NHL	80	28	50	78	205	7	1	4	5	16
92-93—Washington	NHL	84	20	59	79	198	6	7	1	8	35
NHL totals
NHL totals	1002	269	570	839	2872	126	36	57	93	589

HUNTER, MARK

RW, CAPITALS

PERSONAL: Born November 12, 1962, at Petrolia, Ont.... 6-0/205.... Shoots right.... Brother of Dale Hunter, center, Washington Capitals; and brother of Dave Hunter, left winger, Edmonton Oilers of WHA (1978-79); and Edmonton Oilers, Pittsburgh Penguins and Winnipeg Jets (1979-80 through 1988-89).
TRANSACTIONS/CAREER NOTES: Selected by Montreal Canadiens as underage junior in first round (first Canadiens pick, seventh overall) of NHL entry draft (June 10, 1981).... Pulled tendon in right knee (November 13, 1982).... Suffered laceration under right arm (November 29, 1982).... Tore medial ligaments in right knee and underwent surgery (December 26, 1982); missed

42 games. . . . Injured right knee and underwent surgery (October 1983). . . . Injured knee (February 21, 1984). . . . Reinjured knee (February 1985). . . . Traded by Canadiens with rights to D Michael Dark and second-round (RW Herb Raglan), third-round (C Nelson Emerson), fifth-round (D Dan Brooks) and sixth-round (G Rich Burchill) picks in 1985 draft to St. Louis Blues for first-round (RW Jose Charbonneau), second-round (D Todd Richards), fourth-round (C Martin Desjardins), fifth-round (RW Tom Sagissor) and sixth-round (D Donald Dufresne) picks in 1985 draft (June 15, 1985). . . . Strained shoulder (March 1987). . . . Bruised thigh (November 3, 1987). . . . Strained left knee (March 22, 1988). . . . Traded by Blues with C Doug Gilmour, LW Steve Bozek and D/RW Michael Dark to Calgary Flames for C Mike Bullard, C Craig Coxe and D Tim Corkery (September 5, 1988). . . . Dislocated right shoulder (November 1988). . . . Suffered concussion (December 26, 1988). . . . Suspended three games by NHL for striking another player with stick (March 13, 1989). . . . Broke hand (April 13, 1989). . . . Strained anterior cruciate ligament of right knee (October 11, 1989); missed 11 games. . . . Reinjured knee (November 18, 1989). . . . Reinjured knee (December 1989). . . . Underwent surgery to right knee (December 15, 1989). . . . Bruised shoulder (October 30, 1990); missed seven games. . . . Traded by Flames to Hartford Whalers for C Carey Wilson (March 5, 1991). . . . Suffered thigh contusion (December 4, 1991); missed one game. . . . Injured shoulder (February 4, 1992); missed one game. . . . Traded by Whalers with future considerations to Washington Capitals for LW Nick Kypreos (June 15, 1992); Whalers sent LW Yvon Corriveau to Capitals to complete deal (August 20, 1992). . . . Suffered concussion (October 28, 1992); missed four games.
HONORS: Played in NHL All-Star Game (1986).
MISCELLANEOUS: Member of Stanley Cup championship team (1989).

			REGULAR SEASON					PLAYOFFS			
Season Team	League	Gms.	G	A	Pts.	Pen.	Gms.	G	A	Pts.	Pen.
79-80—Brantford	OMJHL	66	34	55	89	171	11	2	8	10	27
80-81—Brantford	OMJHL	53	39	40	79	157	6	3	3	6	27
81-82—Montreal	NHL	71	18	11	29	143	5	0	0	0	20
82-83—Montreal	NHL	31	8	8	16	73	—	—	—	—	—
83-84—Montreal	NHL	22	6	4	10	42	14	2	1	3	69
84-85—Montreal	NHL	72	21	12	33	123	11	0	3	3	13
85-86—St. Louis	NHL	78	44	30	74	171	19	7	7	14	48
86-87—St. Louis	NHL	74	36	33	69	169	5	0	3	3	10
87-88—St. Louis	NHL	66	32	31	63	136	5	2	3	5	24
88-89—Calgary	NHL	66	22	8	30	194	10	2	2	4	23
89-90—Calgary	NHL	10	2	3	5	39	—	—	—	—	—
90-91—Calgary	NHL	57	10	15	25	125	—	—	—	—	—
—Hartford	NHL	11	4	3	7	40	6	5	1	6	17
91-92—Hartford	NHL	63	10	13	23	159	4	0	0	0	6
92-93—Washington	NHL	7	0	0	0	14	—	—	—	—	—
—Baltimore	AHL	28	13	18	31	66	7	3	1	4	12
NHL totals		628	213	171	384	1428	79	18	20	38	230

HUNTER, TIM
LW/RW, CANUCKS

PERSONAL: Born September 10, 1960, at Calgary, Alta. . . . 6-2/205. . . . Shoots right. . . . Full name: Timothy Robert Hunter.
TRANSACTIONS/CAREER NOTES: Selected by Atlanta Flames in third round (fourth Flames pick, 54th overall) of NHL entry draft (August 9, 1979). . . . Flames franchise moved to Calgary (May 21, 1980). . . . Bruised hand (October 1987). . . . Injured right eye (October 17, 1988). . . . Suspended 10 games and fined $500 by NHL for leaving bench to fight (November 1, 1989). . . . Tore shoulder muscles (October 6, 1990); missed four games. . . . Reinjured shoulder (October 18, 1990); missed 21 games. . . . Reinjured shoulder (December 2, 1990); missed one game. . . . Suffered back spasms (October 1991); missed one game. . . . Fractured left ankle (December 8, 1991); missed 39 games. . . . Selected by Tampa Bay Lightning in NHL expansion draft (June 18, 1992). . . . Traded by Lightning to Quebec Nordiques for future considerations (June 22, 1992); Nordiques sent RW Martin Simard to Lightning to complete deal (September 14, 1992). . . . Bruised knee (December 29, 1992); missed one game. . . . Suffered back spasms (January 28, 1993); missed three games. . . . Claimed on waivers by Vancouver Canucks (February 12, 1993).
MISCELLANEOUS: Member of Stanley Cup championship team (1989).

			REGULAR SEASON					PLAYOFFS			
Season Team	League	Gms.	G	A	Pts.	Pen.	Gms.	G	A	Pts.	Pen.
77-78—Kamloops	BCJHL	51	9	28	37	266	—	—	—	—	—
—Seattle	WCHL	3	1	2	3	4	—	—	—	—	—
78-79—Seattle	WHL	70	8	41	49	300	—	—	—	—	—
79-80—Seattle	WHL	72	14	53	67	311	12	1	2	3	41
80-81—Birmingham	CHL	58	3	5	8	*236	—	—	—	—	—
—Nova Scotia	AHL	17	0	0	0	62	6	0	1	1	45
81-82—Oklahoma City	CHL	55	4	12	16	222	—	—	—	—	—
—Calgary	NHL	2	0	0	0	9	—	—	—	—	—
82-83—Calgary	NHL	16	1	0	1	54	9	1	0	1	*70
—Colorado	CHL	46	5	12	17	225	—	—	—	—	—
83-84—Calgary	NHL	43	4	4	8	130	7	0	0	0	21
84-85—Calgary	NHL	71	11	11	22	259	4	0	0	0	24
85-86—Calgary	NHL	66	8	7	15	291	19	0	3	3	108
86-87—Calgary	NHL	73	6	15	21	361	6	0	0	0	51
87-88—Calgary	NHL	68	8	5	13	337	9	4	0	4	32
88-89—Calgary	NHL	75	3	9	12	*375	19	0	4	4	32
89-90—Calgary	NHL	67	2	3	5	279	6	0	0	0	4
90-91—Calgary	NHL	34	5	2	7	143	7	0	0	0	10
91-92—Calgary	NHL	30	1	3	4	167	—	—	—	—	—
92-93—Quebec	NHL	48	5	3	8	94	—	—	—	—	—
—Vancouver	NHL	26	0	4	4	99	11	0	0	0	26
NHL totals		619	54	66	120	2598	97	5	7	12	378

H

HURD, KELLY
RW, RED WINGS

PERSONAL: Born May 13, 1968, at Castlegar, B.C. . . . 5-11/185. . . . Shoots right.
TRANSACTIONS/CAREER NOTES: Selected by Detroit Red Wings in seventh round (sixth Red Wings pick, 143rd overall) of NHL entry draft (June 11, 1988).
HONORS: Named to WCHA All-Star second team (1990-91).

			REGULAR SEASON					PLAYOFFS			
Season Team	League	Gms.	G	A	Pts.	Pen.	Gms.	G	A	Pts.	Pen.
86-87—Kelowna	BCJHL	50	40	53	93	121	—	—	—	—	—
87-88—Michigan Tech	WCHA	41	18	22	40	34	—	—	—	—	—
88-89—Michigan Tech	WCHA	42	18	14	32	36	—	—	—	—	—
89-90—Michigan Tech	WCHA	37	12	13	25	50	—	—	—	—	—
90-91—Michigan Tech	WCHA	35	29	22	51	44	—	—	—	—	—
91-92—Adirondack	AHL	35	9	7	16	16	8	1	4	5	2
—Fort Wayne	IHL	30	13	9	22	12	3	3	0	3	9
92-93—Fort Wayne	IHL	71	23	31	54	81	10	4	5	9	12

HURLBUT, MIKE
D, RANGERS

PERSONAL: Born July 10, 1966, at Massenna, N.Y. . . . 6-2/200. . . . Shoots left. . . . Full name: Michael Ray Hurlbut.
COLLEGE: St. Lawrence (N.Y.).
TRANSACTIONS/CAREER NOTES: Selected by New York Rangers in NHL supplemental draft (June 10, 1988). . . . Sprained left knee (January 25, 1993); missed 13 games.
HONORS: Named to NCAA All-America East first team (1988-89). . . . Named to ECAC All-Star first team (1988-89).

			REGULAR SEASON					PLAYOFFS			
Season Team	League	Gms.	G	A	Pts.	Pen.	Gms.	G	A	Pts.	Pen.
85-86—St. Lawrence University	ECAC	25	2	10	12	40	—	—	—	—	—
86-87—St. Lawrence University	ECAC	35	8	15	23	44	—	—	—	—	—
87-88—St. Lawrence University	ECAC	38	6	12	18	18	—	—	—	—	—
88-89—St. Lawrence University	ECAC	36	8	25	33	30	—	—	—	—	—
—Flint	IHL	8	0	2	2	13	4	1	2	3	2
89-90—Flint	IHL	74	3	34	37	38	3	0	1	1	2
90-91—Binghamton	AHL	33	2	11	13	27	3	0	1	1	0
—San Diego	IHL	2	1	0	1	0	—	—	—	—	—
91-92—Binghamton	AHL	79	16	39	55	64	11	2	7	9	8
92-93—Binghamton	AHL	45	11	25	36	46	14	2	5	7	12
—New York Rangers	NHL	23	1	8	9	16	—	—	—	—	—
NHL totals		23	1	8	9	16					

HUSCROFT, JAMIE
D, DEVILS

PERSONAL: Born January 9, 1967, at Creston, B.C. . . . 6-2/200. . . . Shoots right.
TRANSACTIONS/CAREER NOTES: Selected by New Jersey Devils as underage junior in ninth round (ninth Devils pick, 171st overall) of NHL entry draft (June 15, 1985). . . . Fractured arm (October 1986); missed eight weeks. . . . Traded by Seattle Thunderbirds to Medicine Hat Tigers for C Mike Schwengler (February 1987). . . . Fractured right wrist (October 1988). . . . Injured groin (December 1988). . . . Broke foot (January 1989); missed 19 games.

			REGULAR SEASON					PLAYOFFS			
Season Team	League	Gms.	G	A	Pts.	Pen.	Gms.	G	A	Pts.	Pen.
83-84—Portland	WHL	63	0	12	12	77	5	0	0	0	15
84-85—Seattle	WHL	69	3	13	16	273	—	—	—	—	—
85-86—Seattle	WHL	66	6	20	26	394	5	0	1	1	18
86-87—Seattle	WHL	21	1	18	19	99	20	0	3	3	0
—Medicine Hat	WHL	35	4	21	25	170	20	0	3	3	*125
87-88—Flint	IHL	3	1	0	1	2	16	0	1	1	110
—Utica	AHL	71	5	7	12	316	—	—	—	—	—
88-89—Utica	AHL	41	2	10	12	215	5	0	0	0	40
—New Jersey	NHL	15	0	2	2	51	—	—	—	—	—
89-90—New Jersey	NHL	42	2	3	5	149	5	0	0	0	16
—Utica	AHL	22	3	6	9	122	—	—	—	—	—
90-91—New Jersey	NHL	8	0	1	1	27	3	0	0	0	6
—Utica	AHL	59	3	15	18	339	—	—	—	—	—
91-92—Utica	AHL	50	4	7	11	224	—	—	—	—	—
92-93—Providence	AHL	69	2	15	17	257	2	0	1	1	6
NHL totals		65	2	6	8	227	8	0	0	0	22

HUSKA, RYAN
LW, BLACKHAWKS

PERSONAL: Born July 2, 1975, at Cranbrook, B.C. . . . 6-2/194. . . . Shoots left.
HIGH SCHOOL: Norkam Secondary School (Kamloops, B.C.).
TRANSACTIONS/CAREER NOTES: Selected by Chicago Blackhawks in third round (fourth Blackhawks pick, 76th overall) of NHL entry draft (June 26, 1993).

			REGULAR SEASON					PLAYOFFS			
Season Team	League	Gms.	G	A	Pts.	Pen.	Gms.	G	A	Pts.	Pen.
91-92—Kamloops	WHL	44	4	5	9	23	6	0	1	1	0
92-93—Kamloops	WHL	68	17	15	32	50	13	2	6	8	4

HUSSEY, MARC
D, PENGUINS

PERSONAL: Born January 22, 1974, at Chatham, N.B. . . . 6-4/185. . . . Shoots right.
HIGH SCHOOL: Vanier Collegiate (Moose Jaw, Sask.).
TRANSACTIONS/CAREER NOTES: Selected by Pittsburgh Penguins in second round (second Penguins pick, 43rd overall) of NHL entry draft (June 20, 1992).

H

Season Team	League	REGULAR SEASON					PLAYOFFS				
		Gms.	G	A	Pts.	Pen.	Gms.	G	A	Pts.	Pen.
90-91—Moose Jaw	WHL	68	5	8	13	67	8	2	2	4	7
91-92—Moose Jaw	WHL	72	7	27	34	203	4	1	1	2	0
92-93—Moose Jaw	WHL	68	12	28	40	121	—	—	—	—	—

HYNES, GORD
D, PANTHERS

PERSONAL: Born July 22, 1966, at Montreal.... 6-1/170.... Shoots left.
TRANSACTIONS/CAREER NOTES: Selected by Boston Bruins in sixth round (fifth Bruins pick, 115th overall) of NHL entry draft (June 15, 1985).... Signed as free agent by Philadelphia Flyers (August 25, 1992).... Selected by Florida Panthers in NHL expansion draft (June 24, 1993).
MISCELLANEOUS: Member of silver-medal-winning Canadian Olympic team (1992).

Season Team	League	REGULAR SEASON					PLAYOFFS				
		Gms.	G	A	Pts.	Pen.	Gms.	G	A	Pts.	Pen.
83-84—Medicine Hat	WHL	72	5	14	19	39	14	0	0	0	0
84-85—Medicine Hat	WHL	70	18	45	63	61	10	6	9	15	17
85-86—Medicine Hat	WHL	58	22	39	61	45	25	8	15	23	32
86-87—Moncton	AHL	69	2	19	21	21	4	0	0	0	2
87-88—Maine.............................	AHL	69	5	30	35	65	7	1	3	4	4
88-89—Canadian national team ...	Int'l	61	8	38	46	44	—	—	—	—	—
89-90—Varese	Italy	29	13	36	49	16	3	3	3	6	0
—Canadian national team ...	Int'l	12	3	1	4	4	—	—	—	—	—
90-91—Canadian national team ...	Int'l	57	12	30	42	62	—	—	—	—	—
91-92—Canadian national team ...	Int'l	48	12	22	34	50	—	—	—	—	—
—Canadian Olympic Team ..	Int'l	8	3	3	6	6	—	—	—	—	—
—Boston	NHL	15	0	5	5	6	12	1	2	3	6
92-93—Philadelphia	NHL	37	3	4	7	16	—	—	—	—	—
—Hershey.........................	AHL	9	1	3	4	4	—	—	—	—	—
NHL totals................................		52	3	9	12	22	12	1	2	3	6

IAFRATE, AL
D, CAPITALS

PERSONAL: Born March 21, 1966, at Dearborn, Mich.... 6-3/220.... Shoots left.... Full name: Al Anthony Iafrate.... Name pronounced EYE-uh-FRAY-tee.
TRANSACTIONS/CAREER NOTES: Selected by Toronto Maple Leafs as underage junior in first round (first Maple Leafs pick, fourth overall) of NHL entry draft (June 9, 1984).... Bruised knee (February 1985).... Broke nose (October 2, 1985); missed five games.... Strained neck (January 29, 1986); missed six games. ...Suffered stiff back (January 1988).... Broke back (October 22, 1988).... Lacerated hand (December 9, 1988).... Tore right knee ligament (March 24, 1990).... Underwent knee surgery (April 9, 1990).... Traded by Maple Leafs to Washington Capitals for D Bob Rouse and C Peter Zezel (January 16, 1991).... Took a leave of absence due to mental exhaustion (March 30, 1991).... Injured eye (February 19, 1992); missed one game.... Pulled hamstring (April 10, 1993); missed three games.
HONORS: Played in NHL All-Star Game (1988, 1990 and 1993).... Named to THE SPORTING NEWS All-Star second team (1992-93).... Named to NHL All-Star second team (1992-93).

Season Team	League	REGULAR SEASON					PLAYOFFS				
		Gms.	G	A	Pts.	Pen.	Gms.	G	A	Pts.	Pen.
83-84—U.S. national team	Int'l	55	4	17	21	26	—	—	—	—	—
—U.S. Olympic Team	Int'l	6	0	0	0	2	—	—	—	—	—
—Belleville...........................	OHL	10	2	4	6	2	3	0	1	1	2
84-85—Toronto..........................	NHL	68	5	16	21	51	—	—	—	—	—
85-86—Toronto..........................	NHL	65	8	25	33	40	10	0	3	3	4
86-87—Toronto..........................	NHL	80	9	21	30	55	13	1	3	4	11
87-88—Toronto..........................	NHL	77	22	30	52	80	6	3	4	7	6
88-89—Toronto..........................	NHL	65	13	20	33	72	—	—	—	—	—
89-90—Toronto..........................	NHL	75	21	42	63	135	—	—	—	—	—
90-91—Toronto..........................	NHL	42	3	15	18	113	—	—	—	—	—
—Washington	NHL	30	6	8	14	124	10	1	3	4	22
91-92—Washington	NHL	78	17	34	51	180	7	4	2	6	14
92-93—Washington	NHL	81	25	41	66	169	6	6	0	6	4
NHL totals................................		661	129	252	381	1019	52	15	15	30	61

ING, PETER
G, OILERS

PERSONAL: Born April 28, 1969, at Toronto.... 6-2/165.... Shoots left.
TRANSACTIONS/CAREER NOTES: Selected by Toronto Maple Leafs in third round (third Maple Leafs pick, 48th overall) of NHL entry draft (June 11, 1988).... Traded by Maple Leafs with LW Vincent Damphousse, D Luke Richardson, C Scott Thornton and future considerations to Edmonton Oilers for G Grant Fuhr, RW/LW Glenn Anderson and LW Craig Berube (September 19, 1991).... Signed as free agent by Detroit Falcons (January 8, 1993).... Signed as free agent by San Diego Gulls (January 9, 1993).

Season Team	League	REGULAR SEASON							PLAYOFFS						
		Gms.	Min.	W	L	T	GA	SO	Avg.	Gms.	Min.	W	L	GA	SO	Avg.
86-87—Windsor........................	OHL	28	1615	13	11	3	105	0	3.90	5	161	4	0	9	0	3.35
87-88—Windsor........................	OHL	43	2422	30	7	1	125	2	3.10	3	225	2	0	7	0	1.87
88-89—Windsor........................	OHL	19	1043	7	7	3	76	1	4.37	—	—	—	—	—	—	—
—London........................	OHL	32	1848	18	11	2	104	†2	3.38	*21	*1093	11	9	*82	0	4.50
89-90—Toronto........................	NHL	3	182	0	2	1	18	0	5.93	—	—	—	—	—	—	—
—Newmarket..................	AHL	48	2829	16	19	2	184	1	3.90	—	—	—	—	—	—	—
90-91—Toronto........................	NHL	56	3126	16	†29	8	200	1	3.84	—	—	—	—	—	—	—

Season	Team	League	Gms.	Min.	W	L	T	GA	SO	Avg.	Gms.	Min.	W	L	GA	SO	Avg.
91-92	—Edmonton	NHL	12	463	3	4	0	33	0	4.28	—	—	—	—	—	—	—
	—Cape Breton	AHL	24	1411	9	10	4	92	0	3.91	1	60	0	1	9	0	9.00
92-93	—Detroit	Col.HL	3	136	...	...	...	6	...	2.65	—	—	—	—	—	—	—
	—San Diego	IHL	17	882	11	4	0	53	0	3.61	4	183	2	2	13	0	4.26
	NHL totals		71	3771	19	35	9	251	1	3.99							

INTRANUOVO, RALPH
C, OILERS

PERSONAL: Born December 11, 1973, at Scarborough, Ont. . . . 5-8/180. . . . Shoots left. . . . Name pronounced ihn-trah-NWOH-voh.
TRANSACTIONS/CAREER NOTES: Selected by Edmonton Oilers in fourth round (fifth Oilers pick, 96th overall) of NHL entry draft (June 20, 1992).

Season	Team	League	Gms.	G	A	Pts.	Pen.	Gms.	G	A	Pts.	Pen.
90-91	—Sault Ste. Marie	OHL	63	25	42	67	22	14	7	13	20	17
91-92	—Sault Ste. Marie	OHL	65	50	63	113	44	18	10	14	24	12
92-93	—Sault Ste. Marie	OHL	54	31	47	78	61	18	10	16	26	30

IRBE, ARTURS
G, SHARKS

PERSONAL: Born February 2, 1967, at Riga, U.S.S.R. . . . 5-7/180. . . . Shoots left. . . . Name pronounced AHR-tuhrs UHR-bay.
TRANSACTIONS/CAREER NOTES: Selected by Minnesota North Stars in 10th round (11th North Stars pick, 196th overall) of NHL entry draft (June 17, 1989). . . . Selected by San Jose Sharks in NHL dispersal draft (May 30, 1991). . . . Sprained knee (November 27, 1992); missed 19 games.
HONORS: Named Soviet League Rookie of the Year (1987-88). . . . Shared James Norris Memorial Trophy with Wade Flaherty (1991-92). . . . Named to IHL All-Star first team (1991-92).

Season	Team	League	Gms.	Min.	W	L	T	GA	SO	Avg.	Gms.	Min.	W	L	GA	SO	Avg.
86-87	—Dynamo Riga	USSR	2	27	...	...	...	1	0	2.22	—	—	—	—	—	—	—
87-88	—Dynamo Riga	USSR	34	1870	...	...	...	84	0	2.70	—	—	—	—	—	—	—
88-89	—Dynamo Riga	USSR	41	2460	...	...	...	117	0	2.85	—	—	—	—	—	—	—
89-90	—Dynamo Riga	USSR	48	2880	...	...	...	116	0	2.42	—	—	—	—	—	—	—
90-91	—Dynamo Riga	USSR	46	2713	...	...	...	133	0	2.94	—	—	—	—	—	—	—
91-92	—Kansas City	IHL	32	1955	24	7	1	80	0	*2.46	15	914	12	3	44	0	2.89
	—San Jose	NHL	13	645	2	6	3	48	0	4.47	—	—	—	—	—	—	—
92-93	—Kansas City	IHL	6	364	3	3	0	20	0	3.30	—	—	—	—	—	—	—
	—San Jose	NHL	36	2074	7	26	0	142	1	4.11	—	—	—	—	—	—	—
	NHL totals		49	2719	9	32	3	190	1	4.19							

JABLONSKI, JEFF
LW, ISLANDERS

PERSONAL: Born June 20, 1967, at Toledo, O. . . . 6-1/185. . . . Shoots left. . . . Full name: Jeffrey Scott Jablonski. . . . Brother of Pat Jablonski, goaltender, Tampa Bay Lightning.
COLLEGE: Lake Superior State (Mich.).
TRANSACTIONS/CAREER NOTES: Selected by New York Islanders in ninth round (11th Islanders pick, 185th overall) of NHL entry draft (June 21, 1986).

Season	Team	League	Gms.	G	A	Pts.	Pen.	Gms.	G	A	Pts.	Pen.
85-86	—London Jr. B	OHA	42	28	32	60	47	—	—	—	—	—
86-87	—Lake Superior State	CCHA	40	17	10	27	42	—	—	—	—	—
87-88	—Lake Superior State	CCHA	45	13	12	25	54	—	—	—	—	—
88-89	—Lake Superior State	CCHA	45	11	12	23	50	—	—	—	—	—
89-90	—Lake Superior State	CCHA	46	38	33	71	82	—	—	—	—	—
90-91	—Capital District	AHL	44	6	6	12	4	—	—	—	—	—
	—Kansas City	IHL	10	3	4	7	4	—	—	—	—	—
91-92	—New Haven	AHL	1	0	0	0	0	—	—	—	—	—
	—Capital District	AHL	4	1	1	2	0	—	—	—	—	—
	—Nashville	ECHL	63	36	39	75	74	—	—	—	—	—
92-93	—Toledo	ECHL	61	26	46	72	93	16	3	11	14	20
	—Capital District	AHL	6	0	0	0	2	—	—	—	—	—

JABLONSKI, PAT
G, LIGHTNING

PERSONAL: Born June 20, 1967, at Toledo, O. . . . 6-0/178. . . . Shoots right. . . . Brother of Jeff Jablonski, left winger in New York Islanders system.
TRANSACTIONS/CAREER NOTES: Selected by St. Louis Blues in seventh round (sixth Blues pick, 138th overall) of NHL entry draft (June 15, 1985). . . . Pulled groin (December 7, 1991); missed 26 games. . . . Traded by Blues with D Rob Robinson, RW Darin Kimble and RW Steve Tuttle to Tampa Bay Lightning for future considerations (June 19, 1992).
HONORS: Shared James Norris Memorial Trophy with Guy Hebert (1990-91).

Season	Team	League	Gms.	Min.	W	L	T	GA	SO	Avg.	Gms.	Min.	W	L	GA	SO	Avg.
84-85	—Detroit Compuware	NAJHL	29	1483	...	...	...	95	0	3.84	—	—	—	—	—	—	—
85-86	—Windsor	OHL	29	1600	6	16	4	119	1	4.46	6	263	0	3	20	0	4.56
86-87	—Windsor	OHL	41	2328	22	14	2	128	†3	3.30	12	710	8	4	38	0	3.21
87-88	—Windsor	OHL	18	994	14	3	0	48	2	*2.90	9	537	8	0	28	0	3.13
	—Peoria	IHL	5	285	2	2	1	17	0	3.58	—	—	—	—	—	—	—

			REGULAR SEASON								PLAYOFFS						
Season Team	League	Gms.	Min.	W	L	T	GA	SO	Avg.	Gms.	Min.	W	L	GA	SO	Avg.
88-89—Peoria	IHL	35	2051	11	20	3	163	1	4.77	3	130	0	2	13	0	6.00
89-90—St. Louis	NHL	4	208	0	3	0	17	0	4.90	—	—	—	—	—	—	—
—Peoria	IHL	36	2043	14	17	4	165	0	4.85	4	223	1	3	19	0	5.11
90-91—St. Louis	NHL	8	492	2	3	3	25	0	3.05	3	90	0	0	5	0	3.33
—Peoria	IHL	29	1738	23	3	2	87	0	3.00	10	532	7	2	23	0	*2.59
91-92—St. Louis	NHL	10	468	3	6	0	38	0	4.87	—	—	—	—	—	—	—
—Peoria	IHL	8	493	6	1	1	29	1	3.53	—	—	—	—	—	—	—
92-93—Tampa Bay	NHL	43	2268	8	24	4	150	1	3.97	—	—	—	—	—	—	—
NHL totals		65	3436	13	36	7	230	1	4.02	3	90	0	0	5	0	3.33

JACKSON, DANE
RW, CANUCKS

PERSONAL: Born May 17, 1970, at Winnipeg, Man. . . . 6-1/190. . . . Shoots right.
COLLEGE: North Dakota.
TRANSACTIONS/CAREER NOTES: Selected by Vancouver Canucks in third round (third Canucks pick, 44th overall) of NHL entry draft (June 11, 1988).

		REGULAR SEASON					PLAYOFFS				
Season Team	League	Gms.	G	A	Pts.	Pen.	Gms.	G	A	Pts.	Pen.
87-88—Vernon	BCJHL	50	28	32	60	99	13	7	10	17	49
88-89—Univ. of North Dakota	WCHA	30	4	5	9	33	—	—	—	—	—
89-90—Univ. of North Dakota	WCHA	44	15	11	26	56	—	—	—	—	—
90-91—Univ. of North Dakota	WCHA	37	17	9	26	79	—	—	—	—	—
91-92—Univ. of North Dakota	WCHA	39	23	19	42	81	—	—	—	—	—
92-93—Hamilton	AHL	68	23	20	43	59	—	—	—	—	—

JAGR, JAROMIR
RW, PENGUINS

PERSONAL: Born February 15, 1972, at Kladno, Czechoslovakia. . . . 6-2/208. . . . Shoots left. . . . Name pronounced YAH-guhr.
TRANSACTIONS/CAREER NOTES: Selected by Pittsburgh Penguins in first round (first Penguins pick, fifth overall) of NHL entry draft (June 16, 1990). . . . Separated shoulder (February 23, 1993); missed three games.
HONORS: Named to Czechoslovakian League All-Star team (1989-90). . . . Named to NHL All-Rookie team (1990-91). . . . Played in NHL All-Star Game (1992 and 1993).
MISCELLANEOUS: Member of Stanley Cup championship teams (1991 and 1992).

		REGULAR SEASON					PLAYOFFS				
Season Team	League	Gms.	G	A	Pts.	Pen.	Gms.	G	A	Pts.	Pen.
88-89—Poldi Kladno	Czech.	39	8	10	18	...	—	—	—	—	—
89-90—Poldi Kladno	Czech.	51	30	30	60	...	—	—	—	—	—
90-91—Pittsburgh	NHL	80	27	30	57	42	24	3	10	13	6
91-92—Pittsburgh	NHL	70	32	37	69	34	†21	11	13	24	6
92-93—Pittsburgh	NHL	81	34	60	94	61	12	5	4	9	23
NHL totals		231	93	127	220	137	57	19	27	46	35

JAKOPIN, JOHN
LW, RED WINGS

PERSONAL: Born July 2, 1975, at Cranbrook, B.C. . . . 6-2/194. . . . Shoots left.
HIGH SCHOOL: St. Michael's (Victoria, B.C.).
TRANSACTIONS/CAREER NOTES: Selected by Detroit Red Wings in fourth round (fourth Red Wings pick, 97th overall) of NHL entry draft (June 26, 1993).

		REGULAR SEASON					PLAYOFFS				
Season Team	League	Gms.	G	A	Pts.	Pen.	Gms.	G	A	Pts.	Pen.
92-93—St. Michael's H.S.	Jr. A	45	9	21	30	42	—	—	—	—	—

JANNEY, CRAIG
C, BLUES

PERSONAL: Born September 26, 1967, at Hartford, Conn. . . . 6-1/190. . . . Shoots left. . . . Full name: Craig Harlan Janney.
HIGH SCHOOL: Deerfield Academy (Mass.).
COLLEGE: Boston College.
TRANSACTIONS/CAREER NOTES: Broke collarbone (December 1985). . . . Selected by Boston Bruins in first round (first Bruins pick, 13th overall) of NHL entry draft (June 21, 1986). . . . Suffered from mononucleosis (December 1986). . . . Pulled right groin (December 1988); missed seven games. . . . Tore right groin muscle (October 26, 1989); missed 21 games. . . . Strained left shoulder (April 5, 1990). . . . Sprained left shoulder (December 13, 1990). . . . Sprained right ankle (March 30, 1991). . . . Traded by Bruins with D Stephane Quintal to St. Louis Blues for C Adam Oates (February 7, 1992).
HONORS: Named to NCAA All-America East first team (1986-87). . . . Named to Hockey East All-Star first team (1986-87).

		REGULAR SEASON					PLAYOFFS				
Season Team	League	Gms.	G	A	Pts.	Pen.	Gms.	G	A	Pts.	Pen.
84-85—Deerfield Academy	Mass. H.S.	17	33	35	68	6	—	—	—	—	—
85-86—Boston College	Hockey East	34	13	14	27	8	—	—	—	—	—
86-87—Boston College	Hockey East	37	28	*55	*83	6	—	—	—	—	—
87-88—U.S. national team	Int'l	52	26	44	70	6	—	—	—	—	—
—U.S. Olympic Team	Int'l	5	3	1	4	2	—	—	—	—	—
—Boston	NHL	15	7	9	16	0	23	6	10	16	11
88-89—Boston	NHL	62	16	46	62	12	10	4	9	13	21
89-90—Boston	NHL	55	24	38	62	4	18	3	19	22	2
90-91—Boston	NHL	77	26	66	92	8	18	4	18	22	11

Season	Team	League	Gms.	G	A	Pts.	Pen.	Gms.	G	A	Pts.	Pen.
					REGULAR SEASON					PLAYOFFS		
91-92—Boston		NHL	53	12	39	51	20	—	—	—	—	—
—St. Louis		NHL	25	6	30	36	2	6	0	6	6	0
92-93—St. Louis		NHL	84	24	82	106	12	11	2	9	11	0
NHL totals			371	115	310	425	58	86	19	71	90	45

JANSSENS, MARK
C/LW, WHALERS

PERSONAL: Born May 19, 1968, at Surrey, B.C.... 6-3/216.... Shoots left. **TRANSACTIONS/CAREER NOTES:** Selected by New York Rangers as underage junior in fourth round (fourth Rangers pick, 72nd overall) of NHL entry draft (June 21, 1986).... Fractured skull and suffered cerebral concussion (December 10, 1988).... Traded by Rangers to Minnesota North Stars for C Mario Thyer and third-round pick in 1993 draft (March 10, 1992).... Traded by North Stars to Hartford Whalers for C James Black (September 3, 1992).... Separated shoulder (December 26, 1992); missed five games.

Season	Team	League	Gms.	G	A	Pts.	Pen.	Gms.	G	A	Pts.	Pen.
					REGULAR SEASON					PLAYOFFS		
84-85—Regina		WHL	70	8	22	30	51	5	1	1	2	0
85-86—Regina		WHL	71	25	38	63	146	9	0	2	2	17
86-87—Regina		WHL	68	24	38	62	209	3	0	1	1	14
87-88—Regina		WHL	71	39	51	90	202	4	3	4	7	6
—New York Rangers		NHL	1	0	0	0	0	—	—	—	—	—
—Colorado		IHL	6	2	2	4	24	12	3	2	5	20
88-89—New York Rangers		NHL	5	0	0	0	0	—	—	—	—	—
—Denver		IHL	38	19	19	38	104	4	3	0	3	18
89-90—New York Rangers		NHL	80	5	8	13	161	9	2	1	3	10
90-91—New York Rangers		NHL	67	9	7	16	172	6	3	0	3	6
91-92—New York Rangers		NHL	4	0	0	0	5	—	—	—	—	—
—Binghamton		AHL	55	10	23	33	109	—	—	—	—	—
—Minnesota		NHL	3	0	0	0	0	—	—	—	—	—
—Kalamazoo		IHL	2	0	0	0	2	11	1	2	3	22
92-93—Hartford		NHL	76	12	17	29	237	—	—	—	—	—
NHL totals			236	26	32	58	575	15	5	1	6	16

JELINEK, TOMAS
RW, SENATORS

PERSONAL: Born April 29, 1962, at Prague, Czechoslovakia.... 5-10/189.... Shoots left. ... Name pronounced JEHL-ih-nehk. **TRANSACTIONS/CAREER NOTES:** Selected by Ottawa Senators in 11th round (11th Senators pick, 242nd overall) of NHL entry draft (June 20, 1992).... Injured knee (December 21, 1992) and underwent arthroscopic knee surgery (December 23, 1992); missed nine games.... Reinjured knee (February 27, 1993) and underwent reconstructive knee surgery (March 2, 1993); missed remainder of season.

Season	Team	League	Gms.	G	A	Pts.	Pen.	Gms.	G	A	Pts.	Pen.
					REGULAR SEASON					PLAYOFFS		
79-80—Sparta Prague		Czech.	7	0	1	1	...	—	—	—	—	—
80-81—Dukla Trencin		Czech.	34	5	6	11	...	—	—	—	—	—
81-82—Dukla Trencin		Czech.	36	9	3	12	...	—	—	—	—	—
82-83—Sparta Prague		Czech.	40	20	25	45	...	—	—	—	—	—
83-84—Sparta Prague		Czech.	43	13	5	18	...	—	—	—	—	—
84-85—Sparta Prague		Czech.	44	15	4	19	...	—	—	—	—	—
85-86—Sparta Prague		Czech.	40	7	2	9	...	—	—	—	—	—
86-87—Sparta Prague		Czech.	36	7	5	12	...	—	—	—	—	—
87-88—Sparta Prague		Czech.	45	14	11	25	...	—	—	—	—	—
88-89—Sparta Prague		Czech.	45	15	17	32	...	—	—	—	—	—
89-90—Motor Ceske-Budejovice		Czech.	48	23	20	43	...	—	—	—	—	—
90-91—Motor Ceske-Budejovice		Czech.	51	24	23	47	...	—	—	—	—	—
91-92—HPK Hameenlinna		Finland	41	24	23	47	98	—	—	—	—	—
92-93—Ottawa		NHL	49	7	6	13	52	—	—	—	—	—
NHL totals			49	7	6	13	52					

JENNINGS, GRANT
D, PENGUINS

PERSONAL: Born May 5, 1965, at Hudson Bay, Sask.... 6-3/200.... Shoots left. **TRANSACTIONS/CAREER NOTES:** Injured shoulder (1984-85) ... Signed as free agent by Washington Capitals (June 25, 1985).... Injured knee (October 1986).... Traded by Capitals with RW Ed Kastelic to Hartford Whalers for D Neil Sheehy and RW Mike Millar (July 6, 1988).... Broke left hand (October 6, 1988).... Bruised right foot (October 1988).... Sprained left shoulder (December 1988).... Underwent surgery to left shoulder (April 14, 1989).... Sprained left knee (February 7, 1990).... Twisted knee (March 14, 1990).... Strained left ankle (September 1990).... Bruised shoulder (December 1, 1990); missed six games.... Injured shoulder (February 13, 1991).... Traded by Whalers with C Ron Francis and D Ulf Samuelsson to Pittsburgh Penguins for C John Cullen, D Zarley Zalapski and RW Jeff Parker (March 4, 1991).... Separated left shoulder (March 1991).... Bruised hand (February 15, 1992); missed seven games.... Bruised right hand (March 15, 1992); missed one game.... Bruised left foot (March 11, 1993); missed one game. **MISCELLANEOUS:** Member of Stanley Cup championship teams (1991 and 1992).

Season	Team	League	Gms.	G	A	Pts.	Pen.	Gms.	G	A	Pts.	Pen.
					REGULAR SEASON					PLAYOFFS		
83-84—Saskatoon		WHL	64	5	13	18	102	—	—	—	—	—
84-85—Saskatoon		WHL	47	10	24	34	134	2	1	0	1	2

Season Team	League	REGULAR SEASON					PLAYOFFS				
		Gms.	G	A	Pts.	Pen.	Gms.	G	A	Pts.	Pen.
85-86—Binghamton	AHL	51	0	4	4	109	—	—	—	—	—
86-87—Fort Wayne	IHL	3	0	0	0	0	—	—	—	—	—
—Binghamton	AHL	47	1	5	6	125	13	0	2	2	17
87-88—Binghamton	AHL	56	2	12	14	195	3	1	0	1	15
—Washington	NHL	—	—	—	—	—	1	0	0	0	0
88-89—Hartford	NHL	55	3	10	13	159	4	1	0	1	17
—Binghamton	AHL	2	0	0	0	2	—	—	—	—	—
89-90—Hartford	NHL	64	3	6	9	171	7	0	0	0	13
90-91—Hartford	NHL	44	1	4	5	82	—	—	—	—	—
—Pittsburgh	NHL	13	1	3	4	26	13	1	1	2	16
91-92—Pittsburgh	NHL	53	4	5	9	104	10	0	0	0	12
92-93—Pittsburgh	NHL	58	0	5	5	65	12	0	0	0	8
NHL totals		287	12	33	45	607	47	2	1	3	66

JENSEN, CHRIS
RW, FLYERS

PERSONAL: Born October 28, 1963, at Fort St. John, B.C. . . . 5-11/180. . . . Shoots right.
COLLEGE: North Dakota.
TRANSACTIONS/CAREER NOTES: Selected by New York Rangers as underage player in fourth round (fourth Rangers pick, 78th overall) of NHL entry draft (June 9, 1982). . . . Injured knee (October 1985). . . . Strained shoulder (October 1986). . . . Underwent shoulder surgery (April 1987). . . . Traded by Rangers to Philadelphia Flyers for D Michael Boyce (September 28, 1988). . . . Underwent surgery to knee (February 1989); missed five weeks. . . . Injured hand (October 1989).

Season Team	League	REGULAR SEASON					PLAYOFFS				
		Gms.	G	A	Pts.	Pen.	Gms.	G	A	Pts.	Pen.
80-81—Kelowna	BCJHL	53	51	45	96	120	—	—	—	—	—
81-82—Kelowna	BCJHL	48	46	46	92	212	—	—	—	—	—
82-83—Univ. of North Dakota	WCHA	13	3	3	6	28	—	—	—	—	—
83-84—Univ. of North Dakota	WCHA	44	24	25	49	100	—	—	—	—	—
84-85—Univ. of North Dakota	WCHA	40	25	27	52	80	—	—	—	—	—
85-86—Univ. of North Dakota	WCHA	34	25	40	65	53	—	—	—	—	—
—New York Rangers	NHL	9	1	3	4	0	—	—	—	—	—
86-87—New York Rangers	NHL	37	6	7	13	21	—	—	—	—	—
—New Haven	AHL	14	4	9	13	41	—	—	—	—	—
87-88—New York Rangers	NHL	7	0	1	1	2	—	—	—	—	—
—Colorado	IHL	43	10	23	33	68	10	3	7	10	8
88-89—Hershey	AHL	45	27	31	58	66	10	4	5	9	29
89-90—Philadelphia	NHL	1	0	0	0	2	—	—	—	—	—
—Hershey	AHL	43	16	26	42	101	—	—	—	—	—
90-91—Philadelphia	NHL	18	2	1	3	2	—	—	—	—	—
—Hershey	AHL	50	26	20	46	83	6	2	2	4	10
91-92—Hershey	AHL	71	38	33	71	134	6	0	1	1	2
—Philadelphia	NHL	2	0	0	0	0	—	—	—	—	—
92-93—Hershey	AHL	74	33	47	80	95	—	—	—	—	—
—Knoxville	ECHL	19	1	7	8	20	—	—	—	—	—
NHL totals		74	9	12	21	27					

JIRANEK, MARTIN
C, CAPITALS

PERSONAL: Born October 3, 1969, at Bashaw, Alta. . . . 5-11/170. . . . Shoots left. . . . Name pronounced JEER-uh-nehk.
COLLEGE: Bowling Green State.
TRANSACTIONS/CAREER NOTES: Selected by Washington Capitals in NHL supplemental draft (June 15, 1990).
HONORS: Named to CCHA All-Star second team (1991-92).

Season Team	League	REGULAR SEASON					PLAYOFFS				
		Gms.	G	A	Pts.	Pen.	Gms.	G	A	Pts.	Pen.
88-89—Bowling Green State	CCHA	41	9	18	27	36	—	—	—	—	—
89-90—Bowling Green State	CCHA	41	13	21	34	38	—	—	—	—	—
90-91—Bowling Green State	CCHA	39	31	23	54	33	—	—	—	—	—
91-92—Bowling Green State	CCHA	34	25	28	53	46	—	—	—	—	—
—Baltimore	AHL	8	2	8	10	0	—	—	—	—	—
92-93—Baltimore	AHL	64	18	26	44	39	7	1	2	3	23

JOHANNSON, JIM
C, BLACKHAWKS

PERSONAL: Born March 10, 1965, at Rochester, Minn. . . . 6-1/195. . . . Shoots right.
COLLEGE: Wisconsin.
TRANSACTIONS/CAREER NOTES: Signed as free agent by Calgary Flames (February 1988). . . . Signed as free agent by Chicago Blackhawks (July 6, 1989).
HONORS: Won Iron Man Award (June 1991).

Season Team	League	REGULAR SEASON					PLAYOFFS				
		Gms.	G	A	Pts.	Pen.	Gms.	G	A	Pts.	Pen.
82-83—University of Wisconsin	WCHA	43	12	9	21	16	—	—	—	—	—
83-84—University of Wisconsin	WCHA	35	17	21	38	52	—	—	—	—	—
84-85—University of Wisconsin	WCHA	40	16	24	40	54	—	—	—	—	—

Season Team	League	REGULAR SEASON Gms.	G	A	Pts.	Pen.	PLAYOFFS Gms.	G	A	Pts.	Pen.
85-86—University of Wisconsin ...	WCHA	30	18	13	31	44	—	—	—	—	—
86-87—Landsberg	W. Germany	57	46	56	102	90	—	—	—	—	—
87-88—U.S. national team	Int'l	47	16	14	30	64	—	—	—	—	—
—U.S. Olympic Team	Int'l	5	0	1	1	4	—	—	—	—	—
—Salt Lake City	IHL	18	14	7	21	50	19	8	†15	23	55
88-89—Salt Lake City	IHL	82	35	40	75	87	13	2	5	7	13
89-90—Indianapolis	IHL	82	22	41	63	74	14	1	4	5	6
90-91—Indianapolis	IHL	82	28	41	69	116	7	1	2	3	8
91-92—U.S. national team	Int'l	50	9	8	17	79	—	—	—	—	—
—U.S. Olympic Team	Int'l	8	1	0	1	2	—	—	—	—	—
—Indianapolis	IHL	11	2	2	4	4	—	—	—	—	—
92-93—Milwaukee	IHL	71	14	22	36	72	5	1	0	1	6

JOHANSSON, CALLE

D, CAPITALS

PERSONAL: Born February 14, 1967, at Goteborg, Sweden. ... 5-11/205. ... Shoots left. ... Name pronounced KAH-lee jo-HAHN-suhn.
TRANSACTIONS/CAREER NOTES: Selected by Buffalo Sabres in first round (first Sabres pick, 14th overall) of NHL entry draft (June 15, 1985). ... Dislocated thumb (October 9, 1988). ... Traded by Sabres with second-round pick in 1989 draft (G Byron Dafoe) to Washington Capitals for D Grant Ledyard, G Clint Malarchuk and sixth-round pick in 1991 draft (March 6, 1989). ... Injured back (October 7, 1989); missed 10 games. ... Bruised ribs (January 9, 1993); missed seven games.
HONORS: Named to NHL All-Rookie team (1987-88).

Season Team	League	REGULAR SEASON Gms.	G	A	Pts.	Pen.	PLAYOFFS Gms.	G	A	Pts.	Pen.
83-84—Vastra Frolunda	Sweden	34	5	10	15	20	—	—	—	—	—
84-85—Vastra Frolunda	Sweden	36	14	15	29	20	6	1	2	3	4
85-86—Bjorkloven	Sweden	17	1	1	2	14	—	—	—	—	—
86-87—Bjorkloven	Sweden	30	2	13	15	18	6	1	3	4	6
87-88—Buffalo	NHL	71	4	38	42	37	6	0	1	1	0
88-89—Buffalo	NHL	47	2	11	13	33	—	—	—	—	—
—Washington	NHL	12	1	7	8	4	6	1	2	3	0
89-90—Washington	NHL	70	8	31	39	25	15	1	6	7	4
90-91—Washington	NHL	80	11	41	52	23	10	2	7	9	8
91-92—Washington	NHL	80	14	42	56	49	7	0	5	5	4
92-93—Washington	NHL	77	7	38	45	56	6	0	5	5	4
NHL totals		**437**	**47**	**208**	**255**	**227**	**50**	**4**	**26**	**30**	**20**

JOHANSSON, ROGER

D, FLAMES

PERSONAL: Born April 17, 1967, at Ljungby, Sweden. ... 6-4/190. ... Shoots left. ... Name pronounced joh-HAN-suhn.
TRANSACTIONS/CAREER NOTES: Selected by Calgary Flames in fourth round (fifth Flames pick, 80th overall) of NHL entry draft (June 15, 1985). ... Suffered intestinal infection (November 24, 1990); missed 11 games. ... Suffered infected elbow (December 12, 1992); missed two games.

Season Team	League	REGULAR SEASON Gms.	G	A	Pts.	Pen.	PLAYOFFS Gms.	G	A	Pts.	Pen.
83-84—Troja Sr.	Sweden	8	2	1	3	8	—	—	—	—	—
84-85—Troja Sr.	Sweden	30	1	10	11	28	—	—	—	—	—
85-86—Troja Sr.	Sweden	32	5	16	21	42	—	—	—	—	—
86-87—Farjestad	Sweden	31	6	11	17	22	7	1	1	2	8
87-88—Farjestad	Sweden	24	3	11	14	20	—	—	—	—	—
88-89—Farjestad	Sweden	40	5	15	20	36	—	—	—	—	—
89-90—Calgary	NHL	35	0	5	5	48	—	—	—	—	—
90-91—Calgary	NHL	38	4	13	17	47	—	—	—	—	—
91-92—Leksand	Sweden	22	3	9	12	42	—	—	—	—	—
92-93—Calgary	NHL	77	4	16	20	62	5	0	1	1	2
NHL totals		**150**	**8**	**34**	**42**	**157**	**5**	**0**	**1**	**1**	**2**

JOHNSON, CRAIG

LW, BLUES

PERSONAL: Born March 18, 1972, at St. Paul, Minn. ... 6-2/185. ... Shoots left.
HIGH SCHOOL: Hill-Murray (St. Paul, Minn.).
COLLEGE: Minnesota.
TRANSACTIONS/CAREER NOTES: Suffered stress fracture of vertebrae (February 1987). ... Selected by St. Louis Blues in second round (first Blues pick, 33rd overall) of NHL entry draft (June 16, 1990). ... Separated shoulder (December 1990).
HONORS: Named to WCHA All-Rookie Team (1990-91).

Season Team	League	REGULAR SEASON Gms.	G	A	Pts.	Pen.	PLAYOFFS Gms.	G	A	Pts.	Pen.
87-88—Hill Murray H.S.	Minn. H.S.	28	14	20	34	4	—	—	—	—	—
88-89—Hill Murray H.S.	Minn. H.S.	24	22	30	52	10	—	—	—	—	—
89-90—Hill Murray H.S.	Minn. H.S.	23	15	36	51	...	—	—	—	—	—
90-91—University of Minnesota ...	WCHA	33	13	18	31	34	—	—	—	—	—
91-92—University of Minnesota ...	WCHA	44	19	39	58	70	—	—	—	—	—
92-93—University of Minnesota ...	WCHA	42	22	24	46	70	—	—	—	—	—

JOHNSON, GREG
C, RED WINGS

PERSONAL: Born March 16, 1971, at Thunder Bay, Ont. . . . 5-11/180. . . . Shoots left.
COLLEGE: North Dakota.
TRANSACTIONS/CAREER NOTES: Selected by Philadelphia Flyers in second round (first Flyers first pick, 33rd overall) of NHL entry draft (June 17, 1989). . . . Separated right shoulder (November 24, 1990). . . . Rights traded by Flyers with future considerations to Detroit Red Wings for RW Jim Cummins and fourth-round pick in 1993 draft (June 20, 1993).
HONORS: Named to USHL All-Star first team (1988-89). . . . Named Canadian Junior A Player of the Year (1989). . . . Named to Centennial Cup All-Star first team (1989). . . . Named to NCAA All-America West first team (1990-91 and 1992-93). . . . Named to WCHA All-Star first team (1990-91 through 1992-93). . . . Named to NCAA All-America West second team (1991-92).

			REGULAR SEASON					PLAYOFFS				
Season	Team	League	Gms.	G	A	Pts.	Pen.	Gms.	G	A	Pts.	Pen.
88-89	Thunder Bay Jrs.	USHL	47	32	64	96	4	12	5	13	18	0
89-90	Univ. of North Dakota	WCHA	44	17	38	55	11	—	—	—	—	—
90-91	Univ. of North Dakota	WCHA	38	18	*61	79	6	—	—	—	—	—
91-92	Univ. of North Dakota	WCHA	39	20	54	74	8	—	—	—	—	—
92-93	Canadian national team	Int'l	23	6	14	20	2	—	—	—	—	—
	Univ. of North Dakota	WCHA	34	19	45	64	18	—	—	—	—	—

JOHNSON, JIM
D, STARS

PERSONAL: Born August 9, 1962, at New Hope, Minn. . . . 6-1/190. . . . Shoots left. . . . Full name: James Erik Johnson.
HIGH SCHOOL: Cooper (New Hope, Minn.).
COLLEGE: Minnesota-Duluth.
TRANSACTIONS/CAREER NOTES: Signed as free agent by Pittsburgh Penguins (June 9, 1985). . . . Tore cartilage in right knee (January 1988). . . . Suffered back pain (October 1990). . . . Injured neck (November 12, 1990); missed three games. . . . Traded by Penguins with D Chris Dahlquist to Minnesota North Stars for D Peter Taglianetti and D Larry Murphy (December 11, 1990). . . . Sprained back (February 12, 1991); missed two games. . . . Bruised hip (April 1991). . . . Injured groin (December 7, 1991); missed five games. . . . Strained hamstring (March 10, 1992); missed two games. . . . Suffered face laceration (November 14, 1992); missed two games. . . . Broke finger (January 3, 1993); missed one game. . . . Sprained knee (April 14, 1993); missed final two games of season. . . . North Stars franchise moved from Minnesota to Dallas and renamed Stars for 1993-94 season.

			REGULAR SEASON					PLAYOFFS				
Season	Team	League	Gms.	G	A	Pts.	Pen.	Gms.	G	A	Pts.	Pen.
81-82	Minnesota-Duluth	WCHA	40	0	10	10	62	—	—	—	—	—
82-83	Minnesota-Duluth	WCHA	44	3	18	21	118	—	—	—	—	—
83-84	Minnesota-Duluth	WCHA	43	3	13	16	116	—	—	—	—	—
84-85	Minnesota-Duluth	WCHA	47	7	29	36	49	—	—	—	—	—
85-86	Pittsburgh	NHL	80	3	26	29	115	—	—	—	—	—
86-87	Pittsburgh	NHL	80	5	25	30	116	—	—	—	—	—
87-88	Pittsburgh	NHL	55	1	12	13	87	—	—	—	—	—
88-89	Pittsburgh	NHL	76	2	14	16	163	11	0	5	5	44
89-90	Pittsburgh	NHL	75	3	13	16	154	—	—	—	—	—
90-91	Pittsburgh	NHL	24	0	5	5	23	—	—	—	—	—
	Minnesota	NHL	44	1	9	10	100	14	0	1	1	52
91-92	Minnesota	NHL	71	4	10	14	102	7	1	3	4	18
92-93	Minnesota	NHL	79	3	20	23	105	—	—	—	—	—
NHL totals			584	22	134	156	965	32	1	9	10	114

JONES, BRAD
RW, SENATORS

PERSONAL: Born June 26, 1965, at Sterling Heights, Mich. . . . 6-0/195. . . . Shoots left. . . . Full name: Brad Scott Jones.
COLLEGE: Michigan.
TRANSACTIONS/CAREER NOTES: Selected by Winnipeg Jets in eighth round (eighth Jets pick, 156th overall) of NHL entry draft (June 9, 1984). . . . Injured knee (November 1984). . . . Traded by Jets to Los Angeles Kings for LW Phil Sykes (November 1989). . . . Injured shoulder (February 1991). . . . Signed as free agent by Philadelphia Flyers (August 6, 1991). . . . Tore ligament and chipped bone in ankle (January 28, 1991); missed 29 games. . . . Signed as free agent by Ottawa Senators (September 28, 1992).
HONORS: Named to CCHA All-Star second team (1985-86). . . . Named to NCAA All-America West second team (1986-87). . . . Named to CCHA All-Star first team (1986-87).

			REGULAR SEASON					PLAYOFFS				
Season	Team	League	Gms.	G	A	Pts.	Pen.	Gms.	G	A	Pts.	Pen.
83-84	University of Michigan	CCHA	37	8	26	34	32	—	—	—	—	—
84-85	University of Michigan	CCHA	34	21	27	48	69	—	—	—	—	—
85-86	University of Michigan	CCHA	36	28	39	67	40	—	—	—	—	—
86-87	University of Michigan	CCHA	40	32	46	78	64	—	—	—	—	—
	Winnipeg	NHL	4	1	0	1	0	—	—	—	—	—
87-88	Winnipeg	NHL	19	2	5	7	15	1	0	0	0	0
	U.S. national team	Int'l	50	27	23	50	59	—	—	—	—	—
88-89	Winnipeg	NHL	22	6	5	11	6	—	—	—	—	—
	Moncton	AHL	44	20	19	39	62	7	0	1	1	22
89-90	Winnipeg	NHL	2	0	0	0	0	—	—	—	—	—
	Moncton	AHL	15	5	6	11	47	—	—	—	—	—
	New Haven	AHL	36	8	11	19	71	—	—	—	—	—
90-91	Los Angeles	NHL	53	9	11	20	57	8	1	1	2	2

Season Team	League	REGULAR SEASON					PLAYOFFS				
		Gms.	G	A	Pts.	Pen.	Gms.	G	A	Pts.	Pen.
91-92—Philadelphia	NHL	48	7	10	17	44	—	—	—	—	—
92-93—New Haven	AHL	4	2	1	3	6	—	—	—	—	—
NHL totals		148	25	31	56	122	9	1	1	2	2

JONES, KEITH
RW, CAPITALS

PERSONAL: Born November 8, 1968, at Brantford, Ont. . . . 6-2/190. . . . Shoots left. **COLLEGE:** Western Michigan. **TRANSACTIONS/CAREER NOTES:** Selected by Washington Capitals in seventh round (seventh Capitals pick, 141st overall) of NHL entry draft (June 11, 1988). . . . Suffered from the flu (January 21, 1993); missed two games. **HONORS:** Named to CCHL All-Star first team (1991-92).

Season Team	League	REGULAR SEASON					PLAYOFFS				
		Gms.	G	A	Pts.	Pen.	Gms.	G	A	Pts.	Pen.
87-88—Niagara Falls	OHA	40	50	80	130	. . .	—	—	—	—	—
88-89—Western Michigan Univ.	CCHA	37	9	12	21	51	—	—	—	—	—
89-90—Western Michigan Univ.	CCHA	40	19	18	37	82	—	—	—	—	—
90-91—Western Michigan Univ.	CCHA	41	30	19	49	106	—	—	—	—	—
91-92—Western Michigan Univ.	CCHA	35	25	31	56	77	—	—	—	—	—
—Baltimore	AHL	6	2	4	6	0	—	—	—	—	—
92-93—Baltimore	AHL	8	7	3	10	4	—	—	—	—	—
—Washington	NHL	71	12	14	26	124	6	0	0	0	10
NHL totals		71	12	14	26	124	6	0	0	0	10

JONSSON, KENNY
D, MAPLE LEAFS

PERSONAL: Born October 5, 1974, at Angelholm, Sweden. . . . 6-3/187. . . . Shoots left. **TRANSACTIONS/CAREER NOTES:** Selected by Toronto Maple Leafs in first round (first Leafs pick, 12th overall) of NHL entry draft (June 26, 1993). **HONORS:** Named Swedish League Rookie of the Year (1992-93).

Season Team	League	REGULAR SEASON					PLAYOFFS				
		Gms.	G	A	Pts.	Pen.	Gms.	G	A	Pts.	Pen.
91-92—Rogle	Sweden	30	4	11	15	24	—	—	—	—	—
92-93—Rogle	Sweden	39	3	10	13	42	—	—	—	—	—

JOSEPH, CHRIS
D, OILERS

PERSONAL: Born September 10, 1969, at Burnaby, B.C. . . . 6-2/210. . . . Shoots right. . . . Full name: Robin Christopher Joseph. **HIGH SCHOOL:** Alpha (Burnaby, B.C.). **TRANSACTIONS/CAREER NOTES:** Selected by Pittsburgh Penguins in first round (first Penguins pick, fifth overall) of NHL entry draft (June 13, 1987). . . . Traded by Penguins with C Craig Simpson, C Dave Hannan and D Moe Mantha to Edmonton Oilers for D Paul Coffey, LW Dave Hunter and RW Wayne Van Dorp (November 24, 1987). . . . Strained knee ligaments (January 1989).

Season Team	League	REGULAR SEASON					PLAYOFFS				
		Gms.	G	A	Pts.	Pen.	Gms.	G	A	Pts.	Pen.
85-86—Seattle	WHL	72	4	8	12	50	5	0	3	3	12
86-87—Seattle	WHL	67	13	45	58	155	—	—	—	—	—
87-88—Pittsburgh	NHL	17	0	4	4	12	—	—	—	—	—
—Edmonton	NHL	7	0	4	4	6	—	—	—	—	—
—Nova Scotia	AHL	8	0	2	2	8	4	0	0	0	9
—Seattle	WHL	23	5	14	19	49	—	—	—	—	—
88-89—Cape Breton	AHL	5	1	1	2	18	—	—	—	—	—
—Edmonton	NHL	44	4	5	9	54	—	—	—	—	—
89-90—Edmonton	NHL	4	0	2	2	2	—	—	—	—	—
—Cape Breton	AHL	61	10	20	30	69	6	2	1	3	4
90-91—Edmonton	NHL	49	5	17	22	59	—	—	—	—	—
91-92—Edmonton	NHL	7	0	0	0	8	5	1	3	4	2
—Cape Breton	AHL	63	14	29	43	72	5	0	2	2	8
92-93—Edmonton	NHL	33	2	10	12	48	—	—	—	—	—
NHL totals		161	11	42	53	189	5	1	3	4	2

JOSEPH, CURTIS
G, BLUES

PERSONAL: Born April 29, 1967, at Keswick, Ont. . . . 5-11/182. . . . Shoots left. . . . Full name: Curtis Shayne Joseph. **HIGH SCHOOL:** Huron Heights (Newmarket, Ont.). **COLLEGE:** Wisconsin.
TRANSACTIONS/CAREER NOTES: Signed as free agent by St. Louis Blues (June 16, 1989). . . . Dislocated left shoulder (April 11, 1990). . . . Underwent surgery to left shoulder (May 10, 1990). . . . Sprained right knee (February 26, 1991); missed remainder of season. . . . Injured ankle (March 12, 1992); missed seven games. . . . Suffered sore knee (January 2, 1993); missed three games. . . . Suffered from the flu (February 9, 1993); missed one game.
HONORS: Named OHA Most Valuable Player (1986-87). . . . Won WCHA Most Valuable Player Award (1988-89). . . . Won WCHA Rookie of the Year Award (1988-89). . . . Named to NCAA All-America West second team (1988-89). . . . Named to WCHA All-Star first team (1988-89).

Season Team	League	REGULAR SEASON								PLAYOFFS					
		Gms.	Min.	W	L	T	GA	SO	Avg.	Gms.	Min.	W	L	GA SO	Avg.
86-87—Richmond Hill	OHA						Statistics unavailable.								
87-88—Notre Dame	SCMHL	36	2174	25	4	7	94	1	2.59	—	—	—	—	— —	—

— 466 —

Season	Team	League	REGULAR SEASON Gms.	Min.	W	L	T	GA	SO	Avg.	PLAYOFFS Gms.	Min.	W	L	GA	SO	Avg.
88-89	Univ. of Wisconsin	WCHA	38	2267	21	11	5	94	1	2.49	—	—	—	—	—	—	—
89-90	Peoria	IHL	23	1241	10	8	2	80	0	3.87	—	—	—	—	—	—	—
	St. Louis	NHL	15	852	9	5	1	48	0	3.38	6	327	4	1	18	0	3.30
90-91	St. Louis	NHL	30	1710	16	10	2	89	0	3.12	—	—	—	—	—	—	—
91-92	St. Louis	NHL	60	3494	27	20	10	175	2	3.01	6	379	2	4	23	0	3.64
92-93	St. Louis	NHL	68	3890	29	28	9	196	1	3.02	11	715	7	4	27	2	2.27
	NHL totals		173	9946	81	63	22	508	3	3.06	23	1421	13	9	68	2	2.87

JOYCE, BOB
LW

PERSONAL: Born July 11, 1966, at St. Johns, N.B. . . . 6-1/195. . . . Shoots left. . . . Full name: Robert Thomas Joyce.
HIGH SCHOOL: Atholol Murray College of Notre Dame (Wilcox, Sask.).
COLLEGE: North Dakota.
TRANSACTIONS/CAREER NOTES: Selected by Boston Bruins in fourth round (fourth Bruins pick, 82nd overall) of NHL entry draft (June 9, 1984). . . . Sprained right knee in training camp (September 1988). . . . Suffered concussion and laceration to lip (October 6, 1988). . . . Pulled groin muscle (March 1989). . . . Dislocated shoulder (November 23, 1989). . . . Traded by Bruins to Washington Capitals for RW/C Dave Christian (December 13, 1989). . . . Sprained right knee and underwent surgery (January 3, 1990); missed 17 games. . . . Sprained left ankle (October 1990). . . . Traded by Capitals with D Kent Paynter and C Tyler Larter to Winnipeg Jets for LW Brent Hughes, LW Craig Duncanson and C Simon Wheeldon (May 21, 1991). . . . Signed as free agent by Las Vegas Thunder (July 8, 1993).
HONORS: Named to NCAA All-America West first team (1986-87). . . . Named to NCAA All-Tournament team (1986-87). . . . Named to WCHA All-Star first team (1986-87).

Season	Team	League	REGULAR SEASON Gms.	G	A	Pts.	Pen.	PLAYOFFS Gms.	G	A	Pts.	Pen.
83-84	Wilcox Notre Dame H.S.	Sask. H.S.	30	33	37	70	...	—	—	—	—	—
84-85	Univ. of North Dakota	WCHA	41	18	16	34	10	—	—	—	—	—
85-86	Univ. of North Dakota	WCHA	38	31	28	59	40	—	—	—	—	—
86-87	Univ. of North Dakota	WCHA	48	*52	37	89	42	—	—	—	—	—
87-88	Canadian national team	Int'l	46	12	10	22	28	—	—	—	—	—
	Canadian Olympic Team	Int'l	4	1	0	1	0	—	—	—	—	—
	Boston	NHL	15	7	5	12	10	23	8	6	14	18
88-89	Boston	NHL	77	18	31	49	46	9	5	2	7	2
89-90	Boston	NHL	23	1	2	3	22	—	—	—	—	—
	Washington	NHL	24	5	8	13	4	14	2	1	3	9
90-91	Baltimore	AHL	36	10	8	18	14	6	1	0	1	4
	Washington	NHL	17	3	3	6	8	—	—	—	—	—
91-92	Moncton	AHL	66	19	29	48	51	10	0	5	5	9
	Winnipeg	NHL	1	0	0	0	0	—	—	—	—	—
92-93	Moncton	AHL	75	25	32	57	52	5	0	0	0	2
	Winnipeg	NHL	1	0	0	0	0	—	—	—	—	—
	NHL totals		158	34	49	83	90	46	15	9	24	29

JUNEAU, JOE
C, BRUINS

PERSONAL: Born January 5, 1968, at Pont-Rouge, Que. . . . 6-0/175. . . . Shoots right. . . . Name pronounced ZHOH-ee ZHOO-noh.
COLLEGE: Rensselaer Polytechnic Institute (N.Y.).
TRANSACTIONS/CAREER NOTES: Selected by Boston Bruins in fourth round (third Bruins pick, 81st overall) of NHL entry draft (June 11, 1988). . . . Suffered ligament problem in back (November 1990).
HONORS: Named to NCAA All-America East first team (1989-90). . . . Named to ECAC All-Star first team (1989-90). . . . Named to NCAA All-America East second team (1990-91). . . . Named to ECAC All-Star second team (1990-91). . . . Named to NHL All-Rookie team (1992-93).
RECORDS: Shares NHL single-season record for most assists by a rookie—70 (1992-93).
MISCELLANEOUS: Member of silver-medal-winning Canadian Olympic team (1992).

Season	Team	League	REGULAR SEASON Gms.	G	A	Pts.	Pen.	PLAYOFFS Gms.	G	A	Pts.	Pen.
87-88	R.P.I.	ECAC	31	16	29	45	18	—	—	—	—	—
88-89	R.P.I.	ECAC	30	12	23	35	40	—	—	—	—	—
89-90	R.P.I.	ECAC	34	18	*52	*70	31	—	—	—	—	—
90-91	R.P.I.	ECAC	29	23	40	63	70	—	—	—	—	—
91-92	Canadian national team	Int'l	60	20	49	69	35	—	—	—	—	—
	Canadian Olympic Team	Int'l	8	6	9	15	4	—	—	—	—	—
	Boston	NHL	14	5	14	19	4	15	4	8	12	21
92-93	Boston	NHL	84	32	70	102	33	4	2	4	6	6
	NHL totals		98	37	84	121	37	19	6	12	18	27

JUNKER, STEVE
LW, ISLANDERS

PERSONAL: Born June 26, 1972, at Castlegar, B.C. . . . 6-0/184. . . . Shoots left.
TRANSACTIONS/CAREER NOTES: Selected by New York Islanders in fifth round (fifth Islanders pick, 92nd overall) of NHL entry draft (June 22, 1991).

Season	Team	League	REGULAR SEASON Gms.	G	A	Pts.	Pen.	PLAYOFFS Gms.	G	A	Pts.	Pen.
90-91	Spokane	WHL	71	39	38	77	86	15	5	13	18	6
91-92	Spokane	WHL	58	28	32	60	110	10	6	7	13	18
92-93	Capital District	AHL	79	16	31	47	20	4	0	0	0	0
	New York Islanders	NHL	—	—	—	—	—	3	0	1	1	0
	NHL totals							3	0	1	1	0

KACIR, MARIAN
RW, LIGHTNING

PERSONAL: Born September 29, 1974, at Hodonin, Czechoslovakia.... 6-1/183.... Shoots left.

TRANSACTIONS/CAREER NOTES: Selected by Tampa Bay Lightning in fourth round (fourth Lightning pick, 81st overall) of NHL entry draft (June 26, 1993).

Season Team	League	REGULAR SEASON					PLAYOFFS				
		Gms.	G	A	Pts.	Pen.	Gms.	G	A	Pts.	Pen.
91-92—Czechoslovakia Jr.	Czech.	6	6	4	10	2	8	3	5	8	4
92-93—Owen Sound	OHL	56	20	36	56	8	8	3	5	8	4

KAMENSKY, VALERI
LW, NORDIQUES

PERSONAL: Born April 18, 1966, at Voskresensk, U.S.S.R.... 6-2/198.... Shoots right.... Name pronounced kuh-MEHN-skee.

TRANSACTIONS/CAREER NOTES: Selected by Quebec Nordiques in seventh round (eighth Nordiques pick, 129th overall) of NHL entry draft (June 11, 1988).... Fractured leg (October 1991); missed 57 games.... Broke left thumb (October 17, 1992); missed three games.... Broke right ankle (October 27, 1992); missed 47 games.

HONORS: Won Soviet Player of the Year Award (1990-91).

MISCELLANEOUS: Member of gold-medal-winning U.S.S.R. Olympic team (1988).

Season Team	League	REGULAR SEASON					PLAYOFFS				
		Gms.	G	A	Pts.	Pen.	Gms.	G	A	Pts.	Pen.
82-83—Khimik	USSR	5	0	0	0	0	—	—	—	—	—
83-84—Khimik	USSR	20	2	2	4	6	—	—	—	—	—
84-85—Khimik	USSR	45	9	3	12	24	—	—	—	—	—
85-86—CSKA Moscow	USSR	40	15	9	24	8	—	—	—	—	—
86-87—CSKA Moscow	USSR	37	13	8	21	16	—	—	—	—	—
87-88—CSKA Moscow	USSR	51	26	20	46	40	—	—	—	—	—
—Soviet Olympic Team	Int'l	8	4	2	6	4	—	—	—	—	—
88-89—CSKA Moscow	USSR	40	18	10	28	30	—	—	—	—	—
89-90—CSKA Moscow	USSR	45	19	18	37	38	—	—	—	—	—
90-91—CSKA Moscow	USSR	46	20	26	46	66	—	—	—	—	—
91-92—Quebec	NHL	23	7	14	21	14	—	—	—	—	—
92-93—Quebec	NHL	32	15	22	37	14	6	0	1	1	6
NHL totals		55	22	36	58	28	6	0	1	1	6

KAMINSKI, KEVIN
C, NORDIQUES

PERSONAL: Born March 13, 1969, at Churchbridge, Sask.... 5-9/170.... Shoots left.

TRANSACTIONS/CAREER NOTES: Selected by Minnesota North Stars as underage junior in third round (third North Stars pick, 48th overall) of NHL entry draft (June 13, 1987). ... Suspended 12 games by WHL for cross-checking (November 4, 1987).... Traded by North Stars to Quebec Nordiques for LW Gaetan Duchesne (June 18, 1989).... Separated shoulder in training camp (September 1989).... Suspended two games by AHL for head-butting (January 26, 1990).

Season Team	League	REGULAR SEASON					PLAYOFFS				
		Gms.	G	A	Pts.	Pen.	Gms.	G	A	Pts.	Pen.
84-85—Saskatoon	WHL	5	0	1	1	17	—	—	—	—	—
85-86—Saskatoon	WHL	4	1	1	2	35	—	—	—	—	—
86-87—Saskatoon	WHL	67	26	44	70	235	11	5	6	11	45
87-88—Saskatoon	WHL	55	38	61	99	247	10	5	7	12	37
88-89—Saskatoon	WHL	52	25	43	68	199	8	4	9	13	25
—Minnesota	NHL	1	0	0	0	0	—	—	—	—	—
89-90—Quebec	NHL	1	0	0	0	0	—	—	—	—	—
—Halifax	AHL	19	3	4	7	128	2	0	0	0	5
90-91—Halifax	AHL	7	1	0	1	44	—	—	—	—	—
—Fort Wayne	IHL	56	9	15	24	*455	19	4	2	6	*169
91-92—Halifax	AHL	63	18	27	45	329	—	—	—	—	—
—Quebec	NHL	5	0	0	0	45	—	—	—	—	—
92-93—Halifax	AHL	79	27	37	64	*345	—	—	—	—	—
NHL totals		7	0	0	0	45					

KAMINSKY, JAN
LW, JETS

PERSONAL: Born July 28, 1971, at Penza, U.S.S.R.... 6-2/176.... Shoots left.

TRANSACTIONS/CAREER NOTES: Selected by Winnipeg Jets in fifth round (fourth Jets pick, 99th overall) of NHL entry draft (June 22, 1991).

Season Team	League	REGULAR SEASON					PLAYOFFS				
		Gms.	G	A	Pts.	Pen.	Gms.	G	A	Pts.	Pen.
89-90—Dynamo Moscow	USSR	6	1	0	1	4	—	—	—	—	—
90-91—Dynamo Moscow	USSR	25	10	5	15	2	—	—	—	—	—
91-92—Dynamo Moscow	CIS	42	9	7	16	22	—	—	—	—	—
92-93—Dynamo Moscow	CIS	39	15	14	29	12	10	2	5	7	8

KARALAHTI, JERE
D, KINGS

PERSONAL: Born March 25, 1975, at Helsinki, Finland.... 6-1/180.... Shoots right.

TRANSACTIONS/CAREER NOTES: Selected by Los Angeles Kings in sixth round (seventh Kings pick, 146th overall) of NHL entry draft (June 26, 1993).

Season Team	League	REGULAR SEASON					PLAYOFFS				
		Gms.	G	A	Pts.	Pen.	Gms.	G	A	Pts.	Pen.
91-92—HIFK Juniors	Finland Jrs	30	12	5	17	36	—	—	—	—	—
92-93—HIFK Juniors	Finland Jrs	30	2	13	15	49	—	—	—	—	—

K

KARAMNOV, VITALI
LW, BLUES

PERSONAL: Born July 6, 1968, at Moscow, U.S.S.R. . . . . 6-2/185. . . . Shoots left. . . . Name pronounced kuh-RAHM-nahf.
TRANSACTIONS/CAREER NOTES: Selected by St. Louis Blues in third round (second Blues pick, 62nd overall) of NHL entry draft (June 20, 1992). . . . Pulled groin (October 15, 1992); missed 14 games.

			REGULAR SEASON					PLAYOFFS				
Season Team	League	Gms.	G	A	Pts.	Pen.	Gms.	G	A	Pts.	Pen.
86-87—Dynamo Moscow	USSR	4	0	0	0	0	—	—	—	—	—
87-88—Dynamo Moscow	USSR	2	0	1	1	0	—	—	—	—	—
88-89—Dynamo Kharkov	USSR	23	4	1	5	19	—	—	—	—	—
89-90—Torpedo Yaroslavl	USSR	47	6	7	13	32	—	—	—	—	—
90-91—Torpedo Yaroslavl	USSR	45	14	7	21	30	—	—	—	—	—
91-92—Dynamo Moscow	CIS	40	13	19	32	25	—	—	—	—	—
92-93—St. Louis	NHL	7	0	1	1	0	—	—	—	—	—
—Peoria	IHL	23	8	12	20	47	—	—	—	—	—
NHL totals...................................		7	0	1	1	0					

KARIYA, PAUL
LW, MIGHTY DUCKS

PERSONAL: Born October 16, 1974, at Vancouver, B.C. . . . 5-11/157. . . . Shoots left.
COLLEGE: Maine.
TRANSACTIONS/CAREER NOTES: Selected by Mighty Ducks of Anaheim in first round (first Mighty Ducks pick, fourth overall) of NHL entry draft (June 26, 1993).
HONORS: Won Hobey Baker Memorial Trophy (1992-93). . . . Named Hockey East Player of the Year (1992-93). . . . Named Hockey East Rookie of the Year (1992-93). . . . Named to NCAA All-America East first team (1992-93). . . . Named to NCAA All-Tournament team (1992-93). . . . Named to Hockey East All-Star first team (1992-93). . . . Named to Hockey East Rookie All-Star team (1992-93).

			REGULAR SEASON					PLAYOFFS				
Season Team	League	Gms.	G	A	Pts.	Pen.	Gms.	G	A	Pts.	Pen.
90-91—Penticton	BCJHL	54	45	67	112	8	—	—	—	—	—
91-92—Penticton	BCJHL	40	46	86	132	16	—	—	—	—	—
92-93—University of Maine	Hockey East	39	25	*75	*100	12	—	—	—	—	—

KARLSSON, ANDREAS
C, FLAMES

PERSONAL: Born August 19, 1975, at Leksand, Sweden. . . . 6-2/180. . . . Shoots left.
TRANSACTIONS/CAREER NOTES: Selected by Calgary Flames in sixth round (eighth Flames pick, 148th overall) of NHL entry draft (June 26, 1993).

			REGULAR SEASON					PLAYOFFS				
Season Team	League	Gms.	G	A	Pts.	Pen.	Gms.	G	A	Pts.	Pen.
92-93—Leksand	Sweden	13	0	0	0	6	—	—	—	—	—

KARPA, DAVID
D, NORDIQUES

PERSONAL: Born May 7, 1971, at Regina, Sask. . . . 6-1/193. . . . Shoots right. . . . Full name: David James Karpa.
COLLEGE: Ferris State (Mich.).
TRANSACTIONS/CAREER NOTES: Selected by Quebec Nordiques in fourth round (fourth Nordiques pick, 68th overall) of NHL entry draft (June 22, 1991).

			REGULAR SEASON					PLAYOFFS				
Season Team	League	Gms.	G	A	Pts.	Pen.	Gms.	G	A	Pts.	Pen.
88-89—Notre Dame	SCMHL	...	16	37	53	...	—	—	—	—	—
89-90—Notre Dame	SCMHL	43	9	19	28	271	—	—	—	—	—
90-91—Ferris State	CCHA	41	6	19	25	109	—	—	—	—	—
91-92—Ferris State	CCHA	34	7	12	19	124	—	—	—	—	—
—Halifax	AHL	2	0	0	0	4	—	—	—	—	—
—Quebec	NHL	4	0	0	0	14	—	—	—	—	—
92-93—Halifax	AHL	71	4	27	31	167	—	—	—	—	—
—Quebec	NHL	12	0	1	1	13	3	0	0	0	0
NHL totals...................................		16	0	1	1	27	3	0	0	0	0

KARPOV, VALERI
LW/RW, MIGHTY DUCKS

PERSONAL: Born August 5, 1971, at Chelyabinsk, U.S.S.R. . . . 5-10/176. . . . Shoots left.
TRANSACTIONS/CAREER NOTES: Selected by Mighty Ducks of Anaheim in third round (third Mighty Ducks pick, 56th overall) of NHL entry draft (June 26, 1993).
HONORS: Named to CIS All-Star team (1992-93).

			REGULAR SEASON					PLAYOFFS				
Season Team	League	Gms.	G	A	Pts.	Pen.	Gms.	G	A	Pts.	Pen.
88-89—Traktor Chelyabinsk........	USSR	5	0	0	0	0	—	—	—	—	—
89-90—Traktor Chelyabinsk........	USSR	24	1	2	3	6	—	—	—	—	—
90-91—Traktor Chelyabinsk........	USSR	25	8	4	12	15	—	—	—	—	—
91-92—Traktor Chelyabinsk........	CIS	44	16	10	26	34	—	—	—	—	—
92-93—CSKA Moscow.................	CIS	9	2	6	8	0	—	—	—	—	—
—Traktor Chelyabinsk........	CIS	38	12	21	33	6	8	0	1	1	10

K

KARPOVTSEV, ALEXANDER
D, NORDIQUES

PERSONAL: Born April 7, 1970, at Moscow. . . . 5-11/180. . . . Shoots left. . . . Name pronounced kar-POV-tzev.
TRANSACTIONS/CAREER NOTES: Selected by Quebec Nordiques in seventh round (seventh Nordiques pick, 158th overall) of NHL entry draft (June 16, 1990).

			REGULAR SEASON					PLAYOFFS			
Season Team	League	Gms.	G	A	Pts.	Pen.	Gms.	G	A	Pts.	Pen.
88-89—					Statistics unavailable.						
89-90—Dynamo Moscow	USSR	35	1	1	2	27	—	—	—	—	—
90-91—Dynamo Moscow	USSR	40	0	5	5	15	—	—	—	—	—
91-92—Dynamo Moscow	CIS	28	3	2	5	22	—	—	—	—	—
92-93—Dynamo Moscow	CIS	40	3	11	14	...	—	—	—	—	—

KASATONOV, ALEXEI
D, MIGHTY DUCKS

PERSONAL: Born October 14, 1959, at Leningrad, U.S.S.R. . . . 6-1/215. . . . Shoots left. . . . Name pronounced KA-sa-TAHN-ahf.
TRANSACTIONS/CAREER NOTES: Selected by New Jersey Devils in 12th round (ninth Devils pick, 225th overall) of NHL entry draft (June 8, 1983). . . . Broke toe on right foot (February 1990). . . . Suffered from hemorrhoids (December 1991); missed three games. . . . Injured left hand (October 6, 1992); missed three games. . . . Suffered from the flu (December 27, 1992); missed two games. . . . Selected by Mighty Ducks of Anaheim in NHL expansion draft (June 24, 1993).
HONORS: Named to Soviet League All-Star first team (1979-80 through 1987-88).
MISCELLANEOUS: Member of silver-medal-winning U.S.S.R. Olympic team (1980) and gold-medal-winning U.S.S.R. Olympic team (1984 and 1988).

			REGULAR SEASON					PLAYOFFS			
Season Team	League	Gms.	G	A	Pts.	Pen.	Gms.	G	A	Pts.	Pen.
76-77—Leningrad SKA	USSR	7	0	0	0	0	—	—	—	—	—
77-78—Leningrad SKA	USSR	35	4	7	11	15	—	—	—	—	—
78-79—CSKA Moscow	USSR	40	5	14	19	30	—	—	—	—	—
79-80—CSKA Moscow	USSR	37	5	8	13	26	—	—	—	—	—
—Soviet Olympic Team	Int'l	7	2	5	7	8	—	—	—	—	—
80-81—CSKA Moscow	USSR	47	10	12	22	38	—	—	—	—	—
81-82—CSKA Moscow	USSR	46	12	27	39	45	—	—	—	—	—
82-83—CSKA Moscow	USSR	44	12	19	31	37	—	—	—	—	—
83-84—CSKA Moscow	USSR	39	12	24	36	20	—	—	—	—	—
—Soviet Olympic Team	Int'l	7	3	2	5	0	—	—	—	—	—
84-85—CSKA Moscow	USSR	40	18	18	36	26	—	—	—	—	—
85-86—CSKA Moscow	USSR	40	6	17	23	27	—	—	—	—	—
86-87—CSKA Moscow	USSR	40	13	17	30	16	—	—	—	—	—
87-88—CSKA Moscow	USSR	43	8	12	20	8	—	—	—	—	—
—Soviet Olympic Team	Int'l	7	2	6	8	0	—	—	—	—	—
88-89—CSKA Moscow	USSR	41	8	14	22	8	—	—	—	—	—
89-90—New Jersey	NHL	39	6	15	21	16	6	0	3	3	14
—Utica	AHL	3	0	2	2	7	—	—	—	—	—
90-91—New Jersey	NHL	78	10	31	41	76	7	1	3	4	8
91-92—New Jersey	NHL	76	12	28	40	70	7	1	1	2	12
92-93—New Jersey	NHL	64	3	14	17	57	4	0	0	0	0
NHL totals		**257**	**31**	**88**	**119**	**219**	**24**	**2**	**7**	**9**	**34**

KASPARAITIS, DARIUS
D, ISLANDERS

PERSONAL: Born October 16, 1972, at Elektrenai, U.S.S.R. . . . 5-11/190. . . . Shoots left. . . . Name pronounced KAS-puh-RIGH-tihz.
TRANSACTIONS/CAREER NOTES: Selected by New York Islanders in first round (first Islanders pick, fifth overall) of NHL entry draft (June 20, 1992). . . . Suffered back spasms (February 12, 1993); missed two games. . . . Strained back (April 15, 1993); missed one game.
MISCELLANEOUS: Member of gold-medal-winning Unified Olympic team (1992).

			REGULAR SEASON					PLAYOFFS			
Season Team	League	Gms.	G	A	Pts.	Pen.	Gms.	G	A	Pts.	Pen.
89-90—Dynamo Moscow	USSR	1	0	0	0	0	—	—	—	—	—
90-91—Dynamo Moscow	USSR	17	0	1	1	10	—	—	—	—	—
91-92—Dynamo Moscow	CIS	31	2	10	12	14	—	—	—	—	—
—Unified Olympic Team	Int'l	8	0	2	2	2	—	—	—	—	—
92-93—Dynamo Moscow	CIS	7	1	3	4	8	—	—	—	—	—
—New York Islanders	NHL	79	4	17	21	166	18	0	5	5	31
NHL totals		**79**	**4**	**17**	**21**	**166**	**18**	**0**	**5**	**5**	**31**

KASPER, STEVE
C, LIGHTNING

PERSONAL: Born September 28, 1961, at Montreal. . . . 5-8/175. . . . Shoots left. . . . Full name: Stephen Neil Kasper.
TRANSACTIONS/CAREER NOTES: Selected by Boston Bruins in fourth round (third Bruins pick, 81st overall) of NHL entry draft (June 11, 1980). . . . Suffered hip pointer (October 17, 1981). . . . Underwent surgery to remove torn shoulder cartilage (November 9, 1982). . . . Underwent surgery to left shoulder for torn capsule (December 7, 1982). . . . Suffered concussion (April 1983). . . . Separated left shoulder (November 1983). . . . Underwent surgery to shoulder (January 7, 1984). . . . Reinjured shoulder (February 1984). . . . Traded by Bruins with LW Jay Miller to Los Angeles Kings for C Bobby Carpenter (January 23, 1989). . . . Ruptured sinus cavity and fractured eye socket (January 2, 1991); missed 10 games. . . . Traded by Kings with D Steve Duchesne and fourth-round pick in 1991 draft (D Aris

Brimanis) to Philadelphia Flyers for D Jeff Chychrun and rights to RW Jari Kurri (May 30, 1991).... Tore knee ligaments (November 20, 1991); missed remainder of season.... Traded by Flyers to Tampa Bay Lightning for LW Dan Vincelette (December 8, 1992).... Bruised shoulder (January 30, 1993); missed two games.
HONORS: Won Frank J. Selke Trophy (1981-82).

			REGULAR SEASON					PLAYOFFS			
Season	Team	League	Gms.	G	A	Pts.	Pen.	Gms.	G	A	Pts.	Pen.
77-78—Verdun		QMJHL	63	26	45	71	16	—	—	—	—	—
78-79—Verdun		QMJHL	67	37	67	104	53	11	7	6	13	22
79-80—Sorel		QMJHL	70	57	65	122	117	—	—	—	—	—
80-81—Sorel		QMJHL	2	5	2	7	0	—	—	—	—	—
—Boston		NHL	76	21	35	56	94	3	0	1	1	0
81-82—Boston		NHL	73	20	31	51	72	11	3	6	9	22
82-83—Boston		NHL	24	2	6	8	24	12	2	1	3	10
83-84—Boston		NHL	27	3	11	14	19	3	0	0	0	7
84-85—Boston		NHL	77	16	24	40	33	5	1	0	1	9
85-86—Boston		NHL	80	17	23	40	73	3	1	0	1	4
86-87—Boston		NHL	79	20	30	50	51	3	0	2	2	0
87-88—Boston		NHL	79	26	44	70	35	23	7	6	13	10
88-89—Boston		NHL	49	10	16	26	49	—	—	—	—	—
—Los Angeles		NHL	29	9	15	24	14	11	1	5	6	10
89-90—Los Angeles		NHL	77	17	28	45	27	10	1	1	2	2
90-91—Los Angeles		NHL	67	9	19	28	33	10	4	6	10	8
91-92—Philadelphia		NHL	16	3	2	5	10	—	—	—	—	—
92-93—Philadelphia		NHL	21	1	3	4	2	—	—	—	—	—
—Tampa Bay		NHL	47	3	4	7	18	—	—	—	—	—
NHL totals			821	177	291	468	554	94	20	28	48	82

KASTELIC, ED
RW, KINGS

PERSONAL: Born January 29, 1964, at Toronto.... 6-4/215.... Shoots right.... Name pronounced KAS-tuh-lihk.

TRANSACTIONS/CAREER NOTES: Selected by Washington Capitals as an underage junior in sixth round (fourth Capitals pick, 110th overall) of NHL entry draft (June 9, 1982).... Fractured left cheekbone in preseason game (September 30, 1985).... Suspended by Capitals (January 20, 1986).... Traded by Capitals with D Grant Jennings to Hartford Whalers for D Neil Sheehy and RW Mike Millar (July 1988).... Suspended 20 games by AHL for biting linesman during a fight (December 30, 1988).... Cracked rib (October 1990); missed seven games.... Injured rotator cuff of right shoulder (February 3, 1991).... Suspended 10 games by NHL for fighting (February 10, 1991).... Signed as free agent by Los Angeles Kings (August 1992).... Sprained knee prior to 1992-93 season; missed first six games of season.
MISCELLANEOUS: Played defense prior to 1981-82 season.

			REGULAR SEASON					PLAYOFFS			
Season	Team	League	Gms.	G	A	Pts.	Pen.	Gms.	G	A	Pts.	Pen.
81-82—London		OHL	68	5	18	23	63	4	0	1	1	4
82-83—London		OHL	68	12	11	23	96	3	0	0	0	5
83-84—London		OHL	68	17	16	33	218	8	0	2	2	41
84-85—Fort Wayne		IHL	5	1	0	1	37	—	—	—	—	—
—Binghamton		AHL	4	0	0	0	7	—	—	—	—	—
—Moncton		AHL	62	5	11	16	187	—	—	—	—	—
85-86—Washington		NHL	15	0	0	0	73	—	—	—	—	—
—Binghamton		AHL	23	7	9	16	76	—	—	—	—	—
86-87—Binghamton		AHL	48	17	11	28	124	—	—	—	—	—
—Washington		NHL	23	1	1	2	83	5	1	0	1	13
87-88—Binghamton		AHL	6	4	1	5	6	—	—	—	—	—
—Washington		NHL	35	1	0	1	78	1	0	0	0	19
88-89—Hartford		NHL	10	0	2	2	15	—	—	—	—	—
—Binghamton		AHL	35	9	6	15	124	—	—	—	—	—
89-90—Hartford		NHL	67	6	2	8	198	2	0	0	0	0
90-91—Hartford		NHL	45	2	2	4	211	—	—	—	—	—
91-92—Hartford		NHL	25	1	3	4	61	—	—	—	—	—
92-93—Phoenix		IHL	57	11	7	18	158	—	—	—	—	—
NHL totals			220	11	10	21	719	8	1	0	1	32

KEANE, MIKE
RW, CANADIENS

PERSONAL: Born May 29, 1967, at Winnipeg, Man.... 5-10/178.... Shoots right.
TRANSACTIONS/CAREER NOTES: Signed as free agent by Montreal Canadiens (March 1987).... Separated right shoulder (December 21, 1988).... Suffered laceration of left kneecap (October 31, 1990); missed seven games.... Injured neck (March 1991).... Sprained ankle (January 16, 1992); missed four games.... Resprained ankle (February 1, 1992); missed 10 games.... Bruised ankle (March 11, 1992); missed one game.... Suspended four off-days and fined $500 by NHL for swinging stick in preseason game (October 13, 1992).... Suffered wrist tendinitis (January 26, 1993); missed three games.... Suffered back spasms (February 12, 1993); missed two games.... Fractured toe (February 27, 1993); missed two games.
MISCELLANEOUS: Member of Stanley Cup championship team (1993).

			REGULAR SEASON					PLAYOFFS			
Season	Team	League	Gms.	G	A	Pts.	Pen.	Gms.	G	A	Pts.	Pen.
83-84—Winnipeg		WHL	1	0	0	0	0	—	—	—	—	—
84-85—Moose Jaw		WHL	65	17	26	43	141	—	—	—	—	—
85-86—Moose Jaw		WHL	67	34	49	83	162	13	6	8	14	9

K

Season	Team	League	REGULAR SEASON Gms.	G	A	Pts.	Pen.	PLAYOFFS Gms.	G	A	Pts.	Pen.
86-87	Moose Jaw	WHL	53	25	45	70	107	9	3	9	12	11
	Sherbrooke	AHL	—	—	—	—	—	9	2	2	4	16
87-88	Sherbrooke	AHL	78	25	43	68	70	6	1	1	2	18
88-89	Montreal	NHL	69	16	19	35	69	21	4	3	7	17
89-90	Montreal	NHL	74	9	15	24	78	11	0	1	1	8
90-91	Montreal	NHL	73	13	23	36	50	12	3	2	5	6
91-92	Montreal	NHL	67	11	30	41	64	8	1	1	2	16
92-93	Montreal	NHL	77	15	45	60	95	19	2	13	15	6
	NHL totals		360	64	132	196	356	71	10	20	30	53

KECZMER, DAN
D, WHALERS

PERSONAL: Born May 25, 1968, at Mt. Clemens, Mich.... 6-1/190.... Shoots left.... Full name: Daniel Leonard Keczmer.... Name pronounced KEHZ-muhr.
COLLEGE: Lake Superior State (Mich.).
TRANSACTIONS/CAREER NOTES: Selected by Minnesota North Stars in 10th round (11th North Stars pick, 201st overall) of NHL entry draft (June 21, 1986).... Injured shoulder (February 2, 1990).... Claimed by San Jose Sharks as part of ownership change with North Stars (October 1990).... Traded by Sharks to Hartford Whalers for C Dean Evason (October 2, 1991).... Released by U.S. National team prior to Olympics (January 1992).... Suffered right leg contusion (February 8, 1993); missed three games.
HONORS: Named to CCHA All-Star second team (1989-90).

Season	Team	League	REGULAR SEASON Gms.	G	A	Pts.	Pen.	PLAYOFFS Gms.	G	A	Pts.	Pen.
86-87	Lake Superior State	CCHA	38	3	5	8	28	—	—	—	—	—
87-88	Lake Superior State	CCHA	41	2	15	17	34	—	—	—	—	—
88-89	Lake Superior State	CCHA	46	3	26	29	70	—	—	—	—	—
89-90	Lake Superior State	CCHA	43	13	23	36	48	—	—	—	—	—
90-91	Minnesota	NHL	9	0	1	1	6	—	—	—	—	—
	Kalamazoo	IHL	60	4	20	24	60	9	1	2	3	10
91-92	U.S. national team	Int'l	51	3	11	14	56	—	—	—	—	—
	Springfield	AHL	18	3	4	7	10	4	0	0	0	6
	Hartford	NHL	1	0	0	0	0	—	—	—	—	—
92-93	Springfield	AHL	37	1	13	14	38	12	0	4	4	14
	Hartford	NHL	23	4	4	8	28	—	—	—	—	—
	NHL totals		33	4	5	9	34					

KELLEHER, CHRIS
D, PENGUINS

PERSONAL: Born March 23, 1975, at Cambridge, Mass.... 6-1/215.... Shoots left.
HIGH SCHOOL: Belmont (Mass.) Hill, then St. Sebastian's (Needham, Mass.).
TRANSACTIONS/CAREER NOTES: Selected by Pittsburgh Penguins in fifth round (fifth Penguins pick, 130th overall) of NHL entry draft (June 26, 1993).

Season	Team	League	REGULAR SEASON Gms.	G	A	Pts.	Pen.	PLAYOFFS Gms.	G	A	Pts.	Pen.
90-91	Belmont Hill H.S.	Mass. H.S.	20	4	23	27	14	—	—	—	—	—
91-92	St. Sebastian's	Mass. H.S.	28	7	27	34	12	—	—	—	—	—
92-93	St. Sebastian's	Mass. H.S.	25	8	30	38	16	—	—	—	—	—

KELLOGG, ROBERT
D, BLACKHAWKS

PERSONAL: Born February 16, 1971, at Springfield, Mass.... 6-4/210.... Shoots left. ... Full name: Robert Edward Kellogg.
HIGH SCHOOL: Cathedral (Springfield, Mass.).
COLLEGE: Northeastern.
TRANSACTIONS/CAREER NOTES: Selected by Chicago Blackhawks in third round (third Blackhawks pick, 48th overall) of NHL entry draft (June 17, 1989).... Suffered from mononucleosis (November 1990); missed 30 games.

Season	Team	League	REGULAR SEASON Gms.	G	A	Pts.	Pen.	PLAYOFFS Gms.	G	A	Pts.	Pen.
87-88	Springfield Jr. B	NEJHL	38	8	36	44	54	—	—	—	—	—
88-89	Springfield Jr. B	NEJHL	...	13	34	47	...	—	—	—	—	—
89-90	Northeastern University	Hockey East	36	3	12	15	30	—	—	—	—	—
90-91	Northeastern University	Hockey East	2	0	0	0	6	—	—	—	—	—
91-92	Northeastern University	Hockey East	27	2	3	5	34	—	—	—	—	—
92-93	Northeastern University	Hockey East	35	5	15	20	44	—	—	—	—	—

KELMAN, TODD
D, BLUES

PERSONAL: Born January 5, 1975, at Calgary, Alta.... 6-1/190.... Shoots left.
TRANSACTIONS/CAREER NOTES: Selected by St. Louis Blues in sixth round (fourth Blues pick, 141st overall) of NHL entry draft (June 26, 1993).

Season	Team	League	REGULAR SEASON Gms.	G	A	Pts.	Pen.	PLAYOFFS Gms.	G	A	Pts.	Pen.
92-93	Vernon	BCJHL	48	16	30	46	54	—	—	—	—	—

KENNEDY, DEAN
D, JETS

PERSONAL: Born January 18, 1963, at Redvers, Sask.... 6-2/200.... Shoots right.... Full name: Edward Dean Kennedy.
TRANSACTIONS/CAREER NOTES: Selected by Los Angeles Kings as underage junior in second round (second Kings pick, 39th overall) of NHL entry draft (June 10, 1981).... Sus-

pended four games by NHL for off-ice altercation (February 18, 1983)... . Injured knee; missed part of 1981-82 season.... Suffered hip pointer (March 1987)... . Broke finger (November 1987)... . Injured groin (March 1988)... . Suffered concussion (November 10, 1988)... . Traded by Kings with D Denis Larocque to New York Rangers for LW Igor Liba, C Todd Elik, D Michael Boyce and future considerations (December 12, 1988)... . Traded by Rangers to Los Angeles Kings for fifth-round pick in 1990 draft (February 3, 1989)... . Traded by Kings to Buffalo Sabres for fourth-round pick in 1990 draft (October 4, 1989)... . Suffered hip pointer (January 31, 1991); missed nine games.... Broke jaw (April 5, 1991)... . Traded by Sabres with LW Darrin Shannon and D Mike Hartman to Winnipeg Jets for RW Dave McLlwain, D Gordon Donnelly, fifth-round pick in 1992 draft (LW Yuri Khmylev) and future considerations (October 11, 1991)... . Injured knee (November 20, 1991)... . Suffered back spasms (December 21, 1992); missed two games.

			REGULAR SEASON					PLAYOFFS			
Season Team	League	Gms.	G	A	Pts.	Pen.	Gms.	G	A	Pts.	Pen.
79-80—Weyburn	SJHL	57	12	20	32	64	—	—	—	—	—
—Brandon	WHL	1	0	0	0	0	—	—	—	—	—
80-81—Brandon	WHL	71	3	29	32	157	5	0	2	2	7
81-82—Brandon	WHL	49	5	38	43	103	—	—	—	—	—
82-83—Brandon	WHL	14	2	15	17	22	—	—	—	—	—
—Los Angeles	NHL	55	0	12	12	97	—	—	—	—	—
—Saskatoon	WHL	—	—	—	—	—	4	0	3	3	0
83-84—New Haven	AHL	26	1	7	8	23	—	—	—	—	—
—Los Angeles	NHL	37	1	5	6	50	—	—	—	—	—
84-85—New Haven	AHL	76	3	14	17	104	—	—	—	—	—
85-86—Los Angeles	NHL	78	2	10	12	132	—	—	—	—	—
86-87—Los Angeles	NHL	66	6	14	20	91	5	0	2	2	10
87-88—Los Angeles	NHL	58	1	11	12	158	4	0	1	1	10
88-89—New York Rangers	NHL	16	0	1	1	40	—	—	—	—	—
—Los Angeles	NHL	51	3	10	13	63	11	0	2	2	8
89-90—Buffalo	NHL	80	2	12	14	53	6	1	1	2	12
90-91—Buffalo	NHL	64	4	8	12	119	2	0	1	1	17
91-92—Winnipeg	NHL	18	2	4	6	21	2	0	0	0	0
92-93—Winnipeg	NHL	78	1	7	8	105	6	0	0	0	2
NHL totals		601	22	94	116	929	36	1	7	8	59

KENNEDY, SHELDON
RW, RED WINGS

PERSONAL: Born June 15, 1969, at Brandon, Man.... 5-11/175.... Shoots right.
TRANSACTIONS/CAREER NOTES: Broke ankle (January 18, 1987); missed six weeks.... Selected by Detroit Red Wings in fourth round (fifth Red Wings pick, 80th overall) of NHL entry draft (June 11, 1988)... . Separated shoulder (December 5, 1989)... . Injured thumb (March 2, 1990)... . Took leave of absence to attend alcohol treatment program (March 21, 1990). ... Injured left arm in automobile accident (summer 1990); missed 48 games.... Suffered from tonsilitis (February 8, 1991); missed two games.... Suffered from food poisoning (February 19, 1991)... . Sent to alchohol treatment center for evaluation (March 27, 1991).
HONORS: Named to Memorial Cup All-Star team (1988-89).

			REGULAR SEASON					PLAYOFFS			
Season Team	League	Gms.	G	A	Pts.	Pen.	Gms.	G	A	Pts.	Pen.
86-87—Swift Current	WHL	49	23	41	64	64	4	0	3	3	4
87-88—Swift Current	WHL	59	53	64	117	45	10	8	9	17	12
88-89—Swift Current	WHL	51	58	48	106	92	—	—	—	—	—
89-90—Detroit	NHL	20	2	7	9	10	—	—	—	—	—
—Adirondack	AHL	26	11	15	26	35	—	—	—	—	—
90-91—Adirondack	AHL	11	1	3	4	8	—	—	—	—	—
—Detroit	NHL	7	1	0	1	12	—	—	—	—	—
91-92—Adirondack	AHL	46	25	24	49	56	16	5	9	14	12
—Detroit	NHL	27	3	8	11	24	—	—	—	—	—
92-93—Detroit	NHL	68	19	11	30	46	7	1	1	2	2
NHL totals		122	25	26	51	92	7	1	1	2	2

KERCH, ALEXANDER
LW, OILERS

PERSONAL: Born March 16, 1967, at Arkhangelsk, U.S.S.R. ... 5-10/187. ... Shoots right.
TRANSACTIONS/CAREER NOTES: Selected by Edmonton Oilers in third round (fifth Oilers pick, 60th overall) of NHL entry draft (June 26, 1993).

			REGULAR SEASON					PLAYOFFS			
Season Team	League	Gms.	G	A	Pts.	Pen.	Gms.	G	A	Pts.	Pen.
84-85—Dynamo Riga	USSR	8	0	0	0	6	—	—	—	—	—
85-86—Dynamo Riga	USSR	23	5	2	7	16	—	—	—	—	—
86-87—Dynamo Riga	USSR	26	5	4	9	10	—	—	—	—	—
87-88—Dynamo Riga	USSR	50	14	4	18	28	—	—	—	—	—
88-89—Dynamo Riga	USSR	39	6	7	13	41	—	—	—	—	—
89-90—Dynamo Riga	USSR	46	9	11	20	22	—	—	—	—	—
90-91—Dynamo Riga	USSR	46	16	17	33	46	—	—	—	—	—
91-92—Riga	CIS	42	23	14	37	28	—	—	—	—	—
92-93—Pardaugava Riga	CIS	42	23	14	37	28	2	1	2	3	12

KERR, ALAN

RW, JETS

PERSONAL: Born March 28, 1964, at Hazelton, B.C. . . . 5-11/195. . . . Shoots right. . . . Cousin of Reg Kerr, left winger, Cleveland Barons, Chicago Blackhawks and Edmonton Oilers (1977-78 through 1983-84).

TRANSACTIONS/CAREER NOTES: Selected by New York Islanders as underage junior in fourth round (fourth Islanders pick, 84th overall) of NHL entry draft (June 9, 1982). . . . Lacerated face (April 1988). . . . Sprained left knee (December 1988). . . . Bruised left knee (April 1990). . . . Bruised kidney (September 23, 1990). . . . Lacerated eyelid (October 15, 1990). . . . Underwent surgery to left eye (October 31, 1990). . . . Traded by Islanders to Detroit Red Wings for D Rick Green and future considerations (May 28, 1991). . . . Injured ankle (February 1992); missed 10 games. . . . Signed as free agent by Winnipeg Jets (August 6, 1992).

HONORS: Named to WHL (West) All-Star first team (1983-84).

			REGULAR SEASON					PLAYOFFS			
Season Team	League	Gms.	G	A	Pts.	Pen.	Gms.	G	A	Pts.	Pen.
81-82—Seattle	WHL	68	15	18	33	107	10	6	6	12	32
82-83—Seattle	WHL	71	38	53	91	183	4	2	3	5	0
83-84—Seattle	WHL	66	46	66	112	141	5	1	4	5	12
84-85—Springfield	AHL	62	32	27	59	140	4	1	2	3	2
—New York Islanders	NHL	19	3	1	4	24	4	1	0	1	4
85-86—Springfield	AHL	71	35	36	71	127	—	—	—	—	—
—New York Islanders	NHL	7	0	1	1	16	1	0	0	0	0
86-87—New York Islanders	NHL	72	7	10	17	175	14	1	4	5	25
87-88—New York Islanders	NHL	80	24	34	58	198	6	1	0	1	14
88-89—New York Islanders	NHL	71	20	18	38	144	—	—	—	—	—
89-90—New York Islanders	NHL	75	15	20	35	129	4	0	0	0	10
90-91—Capital District	AHL	43	11	21	32	131	—	—	—	—	—
—New York Islanders	NHL	2	0	0	0	5	—	—	—	—	—
91-92—Detroit	NHL	58	3	8	11	133	9	2	0	2	17
92-93—Winnipeg	NHL	7	0	1	1	2	—	—	—	—	—
—Moncton	AHL	36	6	10	16	85	5	0	2	2	11
NHL totals		391	72	93	165	826	38	5	4	9	70

KERR, TIM

RW

PERSONAL: Born January 5, 1960, at Windsor, Ont. . . . 6-3/228. . . . Shoots right.

TRANSACTIONS/CAREER NOTES: Signed as free agent by Philadelphia Flyers (January 1980). . . . Injured shoulder (November 1, 1980). . . . Injured knee cartilage (October 1981). . . . Underwent hernia surgery (September 1982). . . . Stretched knee ligaments and underwent surgery (November 10, 1982). . . . Broke fibula of left leg (March 1983). . . . Strained knee ligaments (March 1985). . . . Strained right knee (May 5, 1985). . . . Suffered viral infection of the brain lining (September 1985). . . . Pulled hamstring (November 29, 1986); missed three games. . . . Tore ligaments and damaged cartilage in left shoulder (May 1987); missed six playoff games. . . . Underwent five operations to repair left shoulder (June-November 1987); missed 66 games. . . . Served as assistant coach behind Flyer's bench during rehabilitation (December 1987). . . . Pulled muscle in left shoulder (December 27, 1988). . . . Bruised left shoulder (October 6, 1989); missed four games. . . . Tore rotator cuff in left shoulder and underwent surgery to remove bone chips and scar tissue (November 12, 1989); missed 33 games. . . . Separated left shoulder and underwent surgery (March 18, 1990). . . . Missed four games after death of wife (October 17, 1990). . . . Tore cartilage in right knee (November 11, 1990); missed 22 games. . . . Reinjured right knee (January 7, 1991); missed eight games. . . . Injured groin (February 5, 1991); missed 16 games. . . . Selected by San Jose Sharks in NHL expansion draft (May 30, 1991). . . . Traded by Sharks to New York Rangers for LW Brian Mullen and future considerations (May 30, 1991). . . . Injured shoulder (October 11, 1991); missed 39 games. . . . Underwent shoulder surgery (November 13, 1991). . . . Irritated right knee (February 17, 1992); missed four games. . . . Strained back (March 14, 1992); missed three games. . . . Traded by Rangers to Hartford Whalers for conditional pick in 1993 draft (July 8, 1992). . . . Underwent knee surgery (November 23, 1992); missed 18 games. . . . Announced retirement to become assistant coach of Springfield Indians (January 21, 1993).

HONORS: Played in NHL All-Star Game (1984 through 1986). . . . Named to THE SPORTING NEWS All-Star first team (1986-87). . . . Named to NHL All-Star second team (1986-87). . . . Won Bill Masterton Memorial Trophy (1988-89).

RECORDS: Holds NHL single-season record for most power-play goals—34 (1985-86). . . . Holds NHL single-game playoff record for most power-play goals in one period—3 (April 13, 1985). . . . Shares NHL single-game playoff records for most power-play goals—3; most goals in one period—4; and most points in one period—4 (April 13, 1985).

			REGULAR SEASON					PLAYOFFS			
Season Team	League	Gms.	G	A	Pts.	Pen.	Gms.	G	A	Pts.	Pen.
76-77—Windsor	OMJHL	9	2	4	6	7	—	—	—	—	—
77-78—Kingston	OMJHL	67	14	25	39	33	—	—	—	—	—
78-79—Kingston	OMJHL	57	17	25	42	27	6	1	1	2	2
79-80—Kingston	OMJHL	63	40	33	73	39	3	0	1	1	16
—Maine	AHL	7	2	4	6	2	—	—	—	—	—
80-81—Philadelphia	NHL	68	22	23	45	84	10	1	3	4	2
81-82—Philadelphia	NHL	61	21	30	51	138	4	0	2	2	2
82-83—Philadelphia	NHL	24	11	8	19	6	2	2	0	2	0
83-84—Philadelphia	NHL	79	54	39	93	29	3	0	0	0	0
84-85—Philadelphia	NHL	74	54	44	98	57	12	10	4	14	13
85-86—Philadelphia	NHL	76	58	26	84	79	5	3	3	6	8
86-87—Philadelphia	NHL	75	58	37	95	57	12	8	5	13	2
87-88—Philadelphia	NHL	8	3	2	5	12	6	1	3	4	4
88-89—Philadelphia	NHL	69	48	40	88	73	19	14	11	25	27
89-90—Philadelphia	NHL	40	24	24	48	34	—	—	—	—	—
90-91—Philadelphia	NHL	27	10	14	24	8	—	—	—	—	—
91-92—New York Rangers	NHL	32	7	11	18	12	8	1	0	1	0
92-93—Hartford	NHL	22	0	6	6	7	—	—	—	—	—
NHL totals		655	370	304	674	596	81	40	31	71	58

KHMYLEV, YURI
LW, SABRES

PERSONAL: Born August 9, 1964, at Moscow, U.S.S.R. . . . 6-1/189. . . . Shoots right.
TRANSACTIONS/CAREER NOTES: Selected by Buffalo Sabres in fifth round (seventh Sabres pick, 108th overall) of NHL entry draft (June 20, 1992). . . . Strained right shoulder (November 2, 1992); missed two games.
MISCELLANEOUS: Member of gold-medal-winning Unified Olympic team (1992).

Season Team	League	Gms.	G	A	Pts.	Pen.	Gms.	G	A	Pts.	Pen.
81-82—Soviet Wings	USSR	8	2	2	4	2	—	—	—	—	—
82-83—Soviet Wings	USSR	51	9	7	16	14	—	—	—	—	—
83-84—Soviet Wings	USSR	43	7	8	15	10	—	—	—	—	—
84-85—Soviet Wings	USSR	30	11	4	15	24	—	—	—	—	—
85-86—Soviet Wings	USSR	40	24	9	33	22	—	—	—	—	—
86-87—Soviet Wings	USSR	40	15	15	30	48	—	—	—	—	—
87-88—Soviet Wings	USSR	48	21	8	29	46	—	—	—	—	—
88-89—Soviet Wings	USSR	44	16	18	34	38	—	—	—	—	—
89-90—Soviet Wings	USSR	44	14	13	27	30	—	—	—	—	—
90-91—Soviet Wings	USSR	45	25	14	39	26	—	—	—	—	—
91-92—Soviet Wings	CIS	42	19	17	36	20	—	—	—	—	—
—Unified Olympic Team	Int'l	8	4	6	10	. . .	—	—	—	—	—
92-93—Buffalo	NHL	68	20	19	39	28	8	4	3	7	4
NHL totals		68	20	19	39	28	8	4	3	7	4

KHRISTICH, DIMITRI
LW, CAPITALS

PERSONAL: Born July 23, 1969, at Kiev, U.S.S.R. . . . 6-2/190. . . . Shoots right.
TRANSACTIONS/CAREER NOTES: Selected by Washington Capitals in sixth round (sixth Capitals pick, 120th overall) of NHL entry draft (June 11, 1988). . . . Injured hip (February 16, 1990); missed six games. . . . Broke foot (October 3, 1992); missed 20 games.

Season Team	League	Gms.	G	A	Pts.	Pen.	Gms.	G	A	Pts.	Pen.
88-89—Sokol Kiev	USSR	42	17	8	25	15	—	—	—	—	—
89-90—Sokol Kiev	USSR	47	14	22	36	32	—	—	—	—	—
90-91—Sokol Kiev	USSR	28	10	12	22	20	—	—	—	—	—
—Baltimore	AHL	3	0	0	0	0	—	—	—	—	—
—Washington	NHL	40	13	14	27	21	11	1	3	4	6
91-92—Washington	NHL	80	36	37	73	35	7	3	2	5	15
92-93—Washington	NHL	64	31	35	66	28	6	2	5	7	2
NHL totals		184	80	86	166	84	24	6	10	16	23

KIDD, IAN
D

PERSONAL: Born May 11, 1964, at Gresham, Ore. . . . 6-0/200. . . . Shoots right.
COLLEGE: North Dakota.
TRANSACTIONS/CAREER NOTES: Selected by Detroit Red Wings first overall in NHL supplemental draft (September 17, 1986); choice was later voided by NHL. . . . Signed as free agent by Vancouver Canucks (August 1987). . . . Signed as free agent by Milwaukee Admirals (June 1992). . . . Traded by Admirals with D Shaun Kane to Cincinnati Cyclones for RW Jeff Madill (February 25, 1993).
HONORS: Named to NCAA All-America West first team (1986-87). . . . Named to NCAA All-Tournament team (1986-87). . . . Named to WCHA All-Star first team (1986-87).

Season Team	League	Gms.	G	A	Pts.	Pen.	Gms.	G	A	Pts.	Pen.
85-86—Univ. of North Dakota	WCHA	37	6	16	22	65	—	—	—	—	—
86-87—Univ. of North Dakota	WCHA	47	13	47	60	58	—	—	—	—	—
87-88—Fredericton	AHL	53	1	21	22	70	12	0	4	4	22
—Vancouver	NHL	19	4	7	11	25	—	—	—	—	—
88-89—Vancouver	NHL	1	0	0	0	0	—	—	—	—	—
—Milwaukee	IHL	76	13	40	53	124	4	0	2	2	7
89-90—Milwaukee	IHL	65	11	36	47	86	6	2	5	7	0
90-91—Milwaukee	IHL	72	5	26	31	41	6	0	1	1	2
91-92—Milwaukee	IHL	80	9	24	33	75	5	0	1	1	11
92-93—Milwaukee	IHL	32	3	10	13	36	—	—	—	—	—
—Cincinnati	IHL	23	6	23	29	10	—	—	—	—	—
NHL totals		20	4	7	11	25					

KIDD, TREVOR
G, FLAMES

PERSONAL: Born March 29, 1972, at St. Boniface, Man. . . . 6-2/190. . . . Shoots left.
TRANSACTIONS/CAREER NOTES: Selected by Calgary Flames in first round (first Flames pick, 11th overall) of NHL entry draft (June 16, 1990). . . . Traded by Brandon Wheat Kings with D Bart Cote to Spokane Chiefs for RW Bobby House, C Marty Murray and G Don Blishen (January 21, 1991).
HONORS: Won Del Wilson Trophy (1989-90). . . . Named to WHL (West) All-Star first team (1989-90).
MISCELLANEOUS: Member of silver-medal-winning Canadian Olympic team (1992).

Season Team	League	Gms.	Min.	W	L	T	GA	SO	Avg.	Gms.	Min.	W	L	GA	SO	Avg.
88-89—Brandon	WHL	32	1509	. . .	. . .	. . .	102	0	4.06	—	—	—	—	—	—	—
89-90—Brandon	WHL	*63	*3676	24	32	2	254	2	4.15	—	—	—	—	—	—	—

Season Team	League	REGULAR SEASON								PLAYOFFS						
		Gms.	Min.	W	L	T	GA	SO	Avg.	Gms.	Min.	W	L	GA	SO	Avg.
90-91—Brandon	WHL	30	1730	10	19	1	117	0	4.06	—	—	—	—	—	—	—
—Spokane	WHL	14	749	8	3	0	44	0	3.52	15	926	*14	1	32	*2	*2.07
91-92—Can. national team	Int'l	28	1349	18	4	4	79	2	3.51	—	—	—	—	—	—	—
—Can. Olympic Team	Int'l	1	60	1	0	0	0	1	0.00	—	—	—	—	—	—	—
—Calgary	NHL	2	120	1	1	0	8	0	4.00	—	—	—	—	—	—	—
92-93—Salt Lake City	IHL	30	1696	10	16	0	111	1	3.93	—	—	—	—	—	—	—
NHL totals		2	120	1	1	0	8	0	4.00							

KIMBLE, DARIN
RW, PANTHERS

PERSONAL: Born November 22, 1968, at Lucky Lake, Sask. . . . 6-2/205. . . . Shoots right.
TRANSACTIONS/CAREER NOTES: Traded by Brandon Wheat Kings with Kerry Angus to Prince Albert Raiders for C Graham Garden, C Ryan Stewart and Kim Rasmuessen (September 1986). . . . Selected by Quebec Nordiques in fourth round (fifth Nordiques pick, 66th overall) of NHL entry draft (June 11, 1988). . . . Suspended eight games by NHL for slashing (March 23, 1989); missed final four games of 1988-89 season and first four games of 1989-90. . . . Sprained right wrist (September 1989). . . . Bruised ribs (November 5, 1989). . . . Pulled abdominal muscle (December 1990). . . . Bruised right hand (January 24, 1991). . . . Traded by Nordiques to St. Louis Blues for RW Herb Raglan, D Tony Twist and LW Andy Rymsha (February 4, 1991). . . . Broke nose (February 1992). . . . Traded by Blues with D Rob Robinson, G Pat Jablonski and RW Steve Tuttle to Tampa Bay Lightning for future considerations (June 19, 1992). . . . Traded by Lightning with future considerations to Boston Bruins for C Ken Hodge and D Matt Hervey (September 4, 1992). . . . Signed as free agent by Florida Panthers (July 14, 1993).

Season Team	League	REGULAR SEASON					PLAYOFFS				
		Gms.	G	A	Pts.	Pen.	Gms.	G	A	Pts.	Pen.
84-85—Swift Current Jr. A	SAJHL	59	28	32	60	264	—	—	—	—	—
—Calgary	WHL	—	—	—	—	—	1	0	0	0	0
85-86—Calgary	WHL	37	14	8	22	93	—	—	—	—	—
—New Westminster	WHL	11	1	1	2	22	—	—	—	—	—
—Brandon	WHL	15	1	6	7	39	—	—	—	—	—
86-87—Prince Albert	WHL	68	17	13	30	190	—	—	—	—	—
87-88—Prince Albert	WHL	67	35	36	71	307	10	3	2	5	4
88-89—Halifax	AHL	39	8	6	14	188	—	—	—	—	—
—Quebec	NHL	26	3	1	4	149	—	—	—	—	—
89-90—Quebec	NHL	44	5	5	10	185	—	—	—	—	—
—Halifax	AHL	18	6	6	12	37	6	1	1	2	61
90-91—Halifax	AHL	7	1	4	5	20	—	—	—	—	—
—Quebec	NHL	35	2	5	7	114	—	—	—	—	—
—St. Louis	NHL	26	1	1	2	128	13	0	0	0	38
91-92—St. Louis	NHL	46	4	3	7	166	5	0	0	0	7
92-93—Providence	AHL	12	1	4	5	34	—	—	—	—	—
—Boston	NHL	55	7	3	10	177	4	0	0	0	2
NHL totals		232	19	18	37	919	22	0	0	0	47

KING, DEREK
LW, ISLANDERS

PERSONAL: Born February 11, 1967, at Hamilton, Ont. . . . 6-1/210. . . . Shoots left.
TRANSACTIONS/CAREER NOTES: Selected by New York Islanders as underage junior in first round (second Islanders pick, 13th overall) of NHL entry draft (June 15, 1985). . . . Sprained right knee (September 1985). . . . Fractured left wrist (December 12, 1987). . . . Separated shoulder (November 23, 1988). . . . Suffered concussion (November 2, 1990). . . . Separated right shoulder (February 14, 1991). . . . Bruised hip (November 27, 1992); missed two games. . . . Suffered hip pointer (December 26, 1992); missed four games. . . . Broke finger on left hand (April 3, 1993); missed one game.
HONORS: Won Emms Family Award (1984-85). . . . Named to OHL All-Star first team (1986-87).

Season Team	League	REGULAR SEASON					PLAYOFFS				
		Gms.	G	A	Pts.	Pen.	Gms.	G	A	Pts.	Pen.
83-84—Hamilton Jr. A	OHA	37	10	14	24	142	—	—	—	—	—
84-85—Sault Ste. Marie	OHL	63	35	38	73	106	16	3	13	16	11
85-86—Sault Ste. Marie	OHL	25	12	17	29	33	—	—	—	—	—
—Oshawa	OHL	19	8	13	21	15	6	3	2	5	13
86-87—Oshawa	OHL	57	53	53	106	74	17	14	10	24	40
—New York Islanders	NHL	2	0	0	0	0	—	—	—	—	—
87-88—New York Islanders	NHL	55	12	24	36	30	5	0	2	2	2
—Springfield	AHL	10	7	6	13	6	—	—	—	—	—
88-89—Springfield	AHL	4	4	0	4	0	—	—	—	—	—
—New York Islanders	NHL	60	14	29	43	14	—	—	—	—	—
89-90—Springfield	AHL	21	11	12	23	33	—	—	—	—	—
—New York Islanders	NHL	46	13	27	40	20	4	0	0	0	4
90-91—New York Islanders	NHL	66	19	26	45	44	—	—	—	—	—
91-92—New York Islanders	NHL	80	40	38	78	46	—	—	—	—	—
92-93—New York Islanders	NHL	77	38	38	76	47	18	3	11	14	14
NHL totals		386	136	182	318	201	27	3	13	16	20

KING, KRIS
LW/C, JETS

PERSONAL: Born February 18, 1966, at Bracebridge, Ont. . . . 5-11/208. . . . Shoots left.
TRANSACTIONS/CAREER NOTES: Selected by Washington Capitals as underage junior in fourth round (fourth pick, 80th overall) of NHL entry draft (June 9, 1984). . . . Signed as free agent by Detroit Red Wings (June 1987). . . . Traded by Red Wings to New York Rangers for LW Chris McRae and fifth-

round pick in 1990 draft (September 7, 1989).... Sprained knee (January 7, 1991); missed six games.... Traded by Rangers with RW Tie Domi to Winnipeg Jets for C Ed Olczyk (December 28, 1992).

Season Team	League	REGULAR SEASON					PLAYOFFS				
		Gms.	G	A	Pts.	Pen.	Gms.	G	A	Pts.	Pen.
82-83—Gravenhurst	SOJHL	32	72	53	125	115	—	—	—	—	—
83-84—Peterborough	OHL	62	13	18	31	168	8	3	3	6	14
84-85—Peterborough	OHL	61	18	35	53	222	16	2	8	10	28
85-86—Peterborough	OHL	58	19	40	59	254	8	4	0	4	21
86-87—Peterborough	OHL	46	23	33	56	160	12	5	8	13	41
—Binghamton	AHL	7	0	0	0	18	—	—	—	—	—
87-88—Adirondack	AHL	78	21	32	53	337	10	4	4	8	53
—Detroit	NHL	3	1	0	1	2	—	—	—	—	—
88-89—Detroit	NHL	55	2	3	5	168	2	0	0	0	2
89-90—New York Rangers	NHL	68	6	7	13	286	10	0	1	1	38
90-91—New York Rangers	NHL	72	11	14	25	154	6	2	0	2	36
91-92—New York Rangers	NHL	79	10	9	19	224	13	4	1	5	14
92-93—New York Rangers	NHL	30	0	3	3	67	—	—	—	—	—
—Winnipeg	NHL	48	8	8	16	136	6	1	1	2	4
NHL totals		355	38	44	82	1037	37	7	3	10	94

KING, SCOTT
G, RED WINGS

PERSONAL: Born June 25, 1967, at Thunder Bay, Ont.... 6-1/170.... Shoots left.... Full name: Scott Glenndale Martin King.
COLLEGE: Maine.
TRANSACTIONS/CAREER NOTES: Selected by Detroit Red Wings in 10th round (10th Red Wings pick, 190th overall) of NHL entry draft (June 21, 1986).
HONORS: Named to Hockey East All-Star first team (1987-88 and 1989-90).... Named to Hockey East All-Star second team (1988-89).... Named to ECHL All-Star second team (1992-93).

Season Team	League	REGULAR SEASON								PLAYOFFS						
		Gms.	Min.	W	L	T	GA	SO	Avg.	Gms.	Min.	W	L	GA	SO	Avg.
85-86—Vernon	BCJHL	29	1718	17	9	0	134	0	4.68	—	—	—	—	—	—	—
86-87—University of Maine	Hoc. East	21	1111	11	6	1	58	0	3.13	—	—	—	—	—	—	—
87-88—University of Maine	Hoc. East	33	1762	25	5	1	91	0	3.10	—	—	—	—	—	—	—
88-89—University of Maine	Hoc. East	27	1394	13	8	1	83	...	3.57	—	—	—	—	—	—	—
89-90—University of Maine	Hoc. East	29	1526	17	7	2	67	1	2.63	—	—	—	—	—	—	—
90-91—Adirondack	AHL	24	1287	8	10	2	91	0	4.24	1	32	0	0	4	0	7.50
—Hampton Roads	ECHL	15	819	8	4	1	57	0	4.18	—	—	—	—	—	—	—
—Detroit	NHL	1	45	0	0	0	2	0	2.67	—	—	—	—	—	—	—
91-92—Toledo	ECHL	7	424	4	2	1	25	0	3.54	—	—	—	—	—	—	—
—Detroit	NHL	1	16	0	0	0	1	0	3.75	—	—	—	—	—	—	—
—Adirondack	AHL	33	1904	14	14	3	112	0	3.53	—	—	—	—	—	—	—
92-93—Toledo	ECHL	45	2602	...	...	...	153	0	3.53	14	823	...	...	52	0	3.79
—Adirondack	AHL	1	60	1	0	0	1	0	1.00	—	—	—	—	—	—	—
NHL totals		2	61	0	0	0	3	0	2.95							

KING, STEVEN
RW, MIGHTY DUCKS

PERSONAL: Born July 22, 1969, at East Greenwich, R.I.... 6-0/195.... Shoots right.
COLLEGE: Brown.
TRANSACTIONS/CAREER NOTES: Selected by New York Rangers in NHL supplemental draft (June 21, 1991).... Selected by Mighty Ducks of Anaheim in NHL expansion draft (June 24, 1993).

Season Team	League	REGULAR SEASON					PLAYOFFS				
		Gms.	G	A	Pts.	Pen.	Gms.	G	A	Pts.	Pen.
87-88—Brown University	ECAC	24	10	5	15	30	—	—	—	—	—
88-89—Brown University	ECAC	26	8	5	13	73	—	—	—	—	—
89-90—Brown University	ECAC	27	19	8	27	53	—	—	—	—	—
90-91—Brown University	ECAC	27	19	15	34	76	—	—	—	—	—
91-92—Binghamton	AHL	66	27	15	42	56	10	2	0	2	14
92-93—Binghamton	AHL	53	35	33	68	100	14	7	9	16	26
—New York Rangers	NHL	24	7	5	12	16	—	—	—	—	—
NHL totals		24	7	5	12	16					

KISIO, KELLY
C, SHARKS

PERSONAL: Born September 18, 1959, at Peace River, Alta.... 5-9/183.... Shoots right.... Name pronounced KIHZ-ee-oh.
HIGH SCHOOL: Lindsay Thurber (Red Deer, Alta.).
TRANSACTIONS/CAREER NOTES: Traded by Toledo Goaldiggers to Kalamazoo Wings for LW/C Jean Chouinard (February 1981).... Signed as free agent by Detroit Red Wings (February 1983).... Suspended five games by NHL for stick-swinging incident (February 1985).... Traded by Red Wings with RW Lane Lambert, D Jim Leavins and fifth-round pick in 1988 draft to New York Rangers for G Glen Hanlon, third-round picks in 1987 (C Dennis Holland) and 1988 drafts and future considerations (July 1986).... Dislocated left shoulder (October 1986).... Underwent surgery on shoulder (April 1987).... Bruised and twisted left knee (February 1988).... Fractured left hand (October 1988); missed five games.... Suffered back spasms (November 1988).... Bruised left thigh and suffered back spasms (November 9, 1989); missed 11 games. ... Tore ligaments and suffered chip fracture of right ankle (October 6, 1990); missed 18 games.... Suffered bruised thigh (December 7, 1990).... Injured groin (January 17, 1991).... Selected by Minnesota North Stars in NHL expansion draft (May 30, 1991).... Traded by North Stars to San Jose Sharks for RW Shane Churla (June 3, 1991).... Injured ankle (October 17, 1991); missed 18 games.... Strained abdominal muscle (February 4, 1992); missed two games.... Injured shoulder (March

19, 1992). . . . Suffered sore body (January 1993); missed one game. . . . Strained groin (February 22, 1993); missed four games.
HONORS: Named to AJHL All-Star first team (1977-78). . . . Played in NHL All-Star Game (1993).

			REGULAR SEASON					PLAYOFFS			
Season Team	League	Gms.	G	A	Pts.	Pen.	Gms.	G	A	Pts.	Pen.
76-77—Red Deer	AJHL	60	53	48	101	101	—	—	—	—	—
77-78—Red Deer	AJHL	58	74	68	142	66	—	—	—	—	—
78-79—Calgary	WHL	70	60	61	121	73	—	—	—	—	—
79-80—Calgary	WHL	71	65	73	138	64	—	—	—	—	—
80-81—Adirondack	AHL	41	10	14	24	43	—	—	—	—	—
—Kalamazoo	IHL	31	27	16	43	48	8	7	7	14	13
81-82—Dallas	CHL	78	*62	39	101	59	16	*12	†17	*29	38
82-83—Davos HC	Switzerland	. . .	49	38	87	. . .	—	—	—	—	—
—Detroit	NHL	15	4	3	7	0	—	—	—	—	—
83-84—Detroit	NHL	70	23	37	60	34	4	1	0	1	4
84-85—Detroit	NHL	75	20	41	61	56	3	0	2	2	2
85-86—Detroit	NHL	76	21	48	69	85	—	—	—	—	—
86-87—New York Rangers	NHL	70	24	40	64	73	4	0	1	1	2
87-88—New York Rangers	NHL	77	23	55	78	88	—	—	—	—	—
88-89—New York Rangers	NHL	70	26	36	62	91	4	0	0	0	9
89-90—New York Rangers	NHL	68	22	44	66	105	10	2	8	10	8
90-91—New York Rangers	NHL	51	15	20	35	58	—	—	—	—	—
91-92—San Jose	NHL	48	11	26	37	54	—	—	—	—	—
92-93—San Jose	NHL	78	26	52	78	90	—	—	—	—	—
NHL totals		698	215	402	617	734	25	3	11	14	25

KJELLBERG, PATRIK
LW, CANADIENS

PERSONAL: Born June 17, 1969, at Falun, Sweden. . . . 6-2/196. . . . Shoots left.
TRANSACTIONS/CAREER NOTES: Selected by Montreal Canadiens in fourth round (fourth Canadiens pick, 83rd overall) of NHL entry draft (June 11, 1988).

			REGULAR SEASON					PLAYOFFS			
Season Team	League	Gms.	G	A	Pts.	Pen.	Gms.	G	A	Pts.	Pen.
86-87—Falun	Sweden	27	11	13	24	14	—	—	—	—	—
87-88—Falun	Sweden	29	15	10	25	18	—	—	—	—	—
88-89—AIK Solna	Sweden	25	7	9	16	8	—	—	—	—	—
89-90—AIK Solna	Sweden	33	8	16	24	6	3	1	0	1	0
90-91—AIK Solna	Sweden	38	4	11	15	18	—	—	—	—	—
91-92—AIK Solna	Sweden	40	20	13	33	16	—	—	—	—	—
92-93—Montreal	NHL	7	0	0	0	2	—	—	—	—	—
—Fredericton	AHL	41	10	27	37	14	5	2	2	4	0
NHL totals		7	0	0	0	2					

IN MEMORIAM

KLASSEN, TODD
D/RW, PENGUINS

PERSONAL: Born April 17, 1974, at Saskatoon, Sask. . . . Died July 22, 1993. . . . 6-0/205. . . . Shoots right.
HIGH SCHOOL: Kamiakin (Kennewick, Wash.).
TRANSACTIONS/CAREER NOTES: Selected by Pittsburgh Penguins in fourth round (fourth Penguins pick, 91st overall) of NHL entry draft (June 20, 1992).
HONORS: Named to WHL (West) All-Star second team (1991-92).

			REGULAR SEASON					PLAYOFFS			
Season Team	League	Gms.	G	A	Pts.	Pen.	Gms.	G	A	Pts.	Pen.
90-91—Tri-City	WHL	67	6	27	33	72	7	0	1	1	2
91-92—Tri-City	WHL	69	23	42	65	60	5	0	0	0	2
92-93—Tri-City	WHL	72	12	35	47	51	4	1	2	3	8

KLATT, TRENT
RW, STARS

PERSONAL: Born January 30, 1971, at Robbinsdale, Minn. . . . 6-1/210. . . . Shoots right. . . . Full name: Trent Thomas Klatt.
HIGH SCHOOL: Osseo (Minn.).
COLLEGE: Minnesota.
TRANSACTIONS/CAREER NOTES: Selected by Washington Capitals in fourth round (fifth Capitals pick, 82nd overall) of NHL entry draft (June 17, 1989). . . . Rights traded by Capitals with LW Steve Maltais to Minnesota North Stars for D Sean Chambers (June 21, 1991). . . . Injured finger (January 7, 1993); missed three games. . . . North Stars franchise moved from Minnesota to Dallas and renamed Stars for 1993-94 season.

			REGULAR SEASON					PLAYOFFS			
Season Team	League	Gms.	G	A	Pts.	Pen.	Gms.	G	A	Pts.	Pen.
87-88—Ossea H.S.	Minn. H.S.	22	19	17	36	. . .	—	—	—	—	—
88-89—Ossea H.S.	Minn. H.S.	22	24	39	63	. . .	—	—	—	—	—
89-90—University of Minnesota	WCHA	38	22	14	36	16	—	—	—	—	—
90-91—University of Minnesota	WCHA	39	16	28	44	58	—	—	—	—	—
91-92—University of Minnesota	WCHA	44	30	36	66	78	—	—	—	—	—
—Minnesota	NHL	1	0	0	0	0	6	0	0	0	2
92-93—Kalamazoo	IHL	31	8	11	19	18	—	—	—	—	—
—Minnesota	NHL	47	4	19	23	38	—	—	—	—	—
NHL totals		48	4	19	23	38	6	0	0	0	2

KLEE, KEN
D, CAPITALS

PERSONAL: Born April 24, 1971, at Indianapolis. . . . 6-1/200. . . . Shoots right. . . . Full name: Kenneth William Klee.
HIGH SCHOOL: Rockhurst (Kansas City, Mo.).
COLLEGE: St. Michael's College (Vt.), then Bowling Green State.
TRANSACTIONS/CAREER NOTES: Selected by Washington Capitals in ninth round (11th Capitals pick, 177th overall) of NHL entry draft (June 16, 1990).

			REGULAR SEASON					PLAYOFFS			
Season Team	League	Gms.	G	A	Pts.	Pen.	Gms.	G	A	Pts.	Pen.
89-90—Bowling Green State	CCHA	39	0	5	5	52	—	—	—	—	—
90-91—Bowling Green State	CCHA	37	7	28	35	50	—	—	—	—	—
91-92—Bowling Green State	CCHA	10	0	1	1	14	—	—	—	—	—
92-93—Baltimore..........................	AHL	77	4	14	18	68	7	0	1	1	15

KLEMM, JON
D, NORDIQUES

PERSONAL: Born January 6, 1970, at Cranbrook, B.C. . . . 6-3/200. . . . Shoots right. . . . Full name: Jonathan Darryl Klemm.
TRANSACTIONS/CAREER NOTES: Signed as free agent by Quebec Nordiques (May 1991).
HONORS: Named to WHL (West) All-Star second team (1990-91).

			REGULAR SEASON					PLAYOFFS			
Season Team	League	Gms.	G	A	Pts.	Pen.	Gms.	G	A	Pts.	Pen.
87-88—Seattle	WHL	68	6	7	13	24	—	—	—	—	—
88-89—Seattle	WHL	2	1	1	2	0	—	—	—	—	—
—Spokane	WHL	66	6	34	40	42	—	—	—	—	—
89-90—Spokane	WHL	66	3	28	31	100	6	1	1	2	5
90-91—Spokane	WHL	72	7	58	65	65	15	3	6	9	8
91-92—Halifax.............................	AHL	70	6	13	19	40	—	—	—	—	—
—Quebec..........................	NHL	4	0	1	1	0	—	—	—	—	—
92-93—Halifax.............................	AHL	80	3	20	23	32	—	—	—	—	—
NHL totals...................................		4	0	1	1	0					

KLIMA, PETR
LW/RW, LIGHTNING

PERSONAL: Born December 23, 1964, at Chaomutov, Czechoslovakia. . . . 6-0/190. . . . Shoots right. . . . Name pronounced KLEE-muh.
TRANSACTIONS/CAREER NOTES: Selected by Detroit Red Wings in fifth round (fifth Red Wings pick, 88th overall) of NHL entry draft (June 8, 1983). . . . Broke right thumb (May 1988). . . . Sprained right ankle (November 12, 1988). . . . Pulled groin (December 1988). . . . Injured back (February 1989). . . . Traded by Red Wings with C/RW Joe Murphy, C/LW Adam Graves and D Jeff Sharples to Edmonton Oilers for C Jimmy Carson, C Kevin McClelland and fifth-round pick in 1991 draft (November 2, 1989). . . . Suspended four games by NHL for butt-ending player (October 25, 1990). . . . Pulled groin (March 15, 1991). . . . Scratched cornea in right eye (November 18, 1991); missed one game. . . . Strained groin (February 2, 1992); missed six games. . . . Strained left knee ligaments (October 14, 1992); missed six games. . . . Strained groin (January 7, 1993); missed eight games. . . . Traded by Oilers to Tampa Bay Lightning for future considerations (June 16, 1993).
MISCELLANEOUS: Member of Stanley Cup championship team (1990).

			REGULAR SEASON					PLAYOFFS			
Season Team	League	Gms.	G	A	Pts.	Pen.	Gms.	G	A	Pts.	Pen.
82-83—Czech. national team	Int'l	44	19	17	36	74	—	—	—	—	—
83-84—Dukla Jihlava	Czech.	41	20	16	36	46	—	—	—	—	—
—Czech. national team	Int'l	7	6	5	11	...	—	—	—	—	—
84-85—Dukla Jihlava	Czech.	35	23	22	45	...	—	—	—	—	—
85-86—Detroit	NHL	74	32	24	56	16	—	—	—	—	—
86-87—Detroit	NHL	77	30	23	53	42	13	1	2	3	4
87-88—Detroit	NHL	78	37	25	62	46	12	10	8	18	10
88-89—Adirondack	AHL	5	5	1	6	4	—	—	—	—	—
—Detroit	NHL	51	25	16	41	44	6	2	4	6	19
89-90—Detroit	NHL	13	5	5	10	6	—	—	—	—	—
—Edmonton........................	NHL	63	25	28	53	66	21	5	0	5	8
90-91—Edmonton........................	NHL	70	40	28	68	113	18	7	6	13	16
91-92—Edmonton........................	NHL	57	21	13	34	52	15	1	4	5	8
92-93—Edmonton........................	NHL	68	32	16	48	100	—	—	—	—	—
NHL totals....................................		551	247	178	425	485	85	26	24	50	65

KNICKLE, RICK
G, KINGS

PERSONAL: Born February 26, 1960, at Chatham, N.B. . . . 5-11/170. . . . Shoots left.
TRANSACTIONS/CAREER NOTES: Selected by Buffalo Sabres as underage junior in sixth round (seventh Buffalo pick, 116th overall) of NHL entry draft (August 9, 1979). . . . Sprained thumb (February 1981). . . . Signed as free agent by Montreal Canadiens (February 8, 1985). . . . Signed as free agent by Springfield Indians (1991). . . . Signed as free agent by Los Angeles Kings (February 15, 1993).
HONORS: Won Top Goaltender Trophy (1978-79). . . . Named to WHL All-Star first team (1978-79). . . . Named to EHL All-Star first team (1980-81). . . . Named to IHL All-Star second team (1983-84 and 1991-92). . . . Won James Norris Memorial Trophy (1988-89). . . . Named to IHL All-Star first team (1988-89). . . . Shared James Norris Memorial Trophy with Clint Malarchuk (1992-93). . . . Named to IHL All-Star first team (1992-93).

			REGULAR SEASON						PLAYOFFS					
Season Team	League	Gms.	Min.	W	L	T	GA	SO	Avg.	Gms.	Min.	W	L	GA	SO	Avg.
77-78—Brandon......................	WCHL	49	2806	34	5	7	182	0	3.89	8	450			36	0	4.80
78-79—Brandon......................	WHL	38	2240	26	3	8	118	1	*3.16	16	886	12	3	41	*1	*2.78

Season	Team	League	Gms.	Min.	W	L	T	GA	SO	Avg.	Gms.	Min.	W	L	GA	SO	Avg.
79-80—Brandon	WHL	33	1604	11	14	1	125	0	4.68	—						
—Muskegon	IHL	16	829	...	...	...	51	0	3.69	3	156	...	...	17	0	6.54
80-81—Erie	AHL	43	2347	...	...	...	125	1	*3.20	*8	*446	...	...	14	0	*1.88
81-82—Rochester	AHL	31	1753	10	12	5	108	1	3.70	3	125	0	2	7	0	3.36
82-83—Flint	IHL	27	1638	...	...	...	92	†2	3.37	3	193	...	...	10	0	3.11
—Rochester	AHL	4	143	...	...	...	11	0	4.62	—						
83-84—Flint	IHL	60	3518	32	21	5	203	3	3.46	8	480	8	0	24	0	*3.00
84-85—Sherbrooke	AHL	14	780	7	6	0	53	0	4.08	—						
—Flint	IHL	36	2018	18	11	3	115	2	3.42	7	401	3	4	27	0	4.04
85-86—Saginaw	IHL	39	2235	16	15	0	135	2	3.62	3	193	2	1	12	0	3.73
86-87—Saginaw	IHL	26	1413	9	13	0	113	0	4.80	5	329	1	4	21	0	3.83
87-88—Flint	IHL	1	60	0	1	0	4	0	4.00	—						
—Peoria	IHL	13	705	2	8	1	58	0	4.94	6	294	3	3	20	0	4.08
88-89—Fort Wayne	IHL	47	2719	22	16	0	141	1	3.11	4	173	1	2	15	0	5.20
89-90—Flint	IHL	55	2998	25	24	1	210	1	4.20	2	101	0	2	13	0	7.72
90-91—Springfield	AHL	9	509	6	0	2	28	0	3.30	—						
91-92—San Diego	IHL	46	2686	*28	13	4	155	0	3.46	2	78	0	1	3	0	2.31
92-93—San Diego	IHL	41	2437	33	4	0	88	*4	*2.17	—						
—Los Angeles	NHL	10	532	6	4	0	35	0	3.95	—						
NHL totals		10	532	6	4	0	35	0	3.95							

KOCHAN, DIETER
G, CANUCKS

PERSONAL: Born November 5, 1974, at Saskatoon, Sask.... 6-1/165.... Shoots left.
TRANSACTIONS/CAREER NOTES: Selected by Vancouver Canucks in fourth round (third Canucks pick, 98th overall) of NHL entry draft (June 26, 1993).

Season	Team	League	Gms.	Min.	W	L	T	GA	SO	Avg.	Gms.	Min.	W	L	GA	SO	Avg.
91-92—Sioux City	USHL	23	1131	7	10	0	100	...	5.31	—	—	—	—	—	—	—
92-93—Kelowna	BCJHL	44	2582	34	8	0	137	1	*3.18	—	—	—	—	—	—	—

KOCUR, JOEY
RW, RANGERS

PERSONAL: Born December 21, 1964, at Calgary, Alta.... 6-0/209.... Shoots right.... Name pronounced KOH-suhr.... Cousin of Kory Kocur, right winger in Detroit Red Wings system.
TRANSACTIONS/CAREER NOTES: Stretched knee ligaments (December 1981).... Selected by Detroit Red Wings as underage junior in fifth round (sixth Red Wings pick, 88th overall) of NHL entry draft (June 8, 1983).... Lacerated right hand (January 1985).... Sprained thumb (December 11, 1985).... Strained ligaments (March 26, 1986).... Suffered sore right elbow (October 1987).... Strained sternum and collarbone (November 1987).... Injured shoulder (December 1987).... Separated shoulder (May 1988).... Injured knee (November 1988).... Injured back (February 1989).... Bruised right foot (February 16, 1990).... Strained right knee ligaments (March 1990).... Injured right hand and arm (December 1, 1990); missed three weeks.... Traded by Red Wings with D Per Djoos to New York Rangers for C Kevin Miller, D Dennis Vial and RW Jim Cummins (March 5, 1991).... Suspended four games by NHL for high-sticking (March 10, 1991).... Suspended additional four games by NHL for high-sticking during appeal of March 10 incident (March 14, 1991); missed final eight games of 1990-91 season and first game of 1991-92 season.... Underwent surgery to middle knuckle of right hand (May 10, 1991).... Injured hip flexor (October 1991); missed first five games of season.... Separated shoulder (January 28, 1992); missed 13 games.... Slightly sprained right knee (March 5, 1992); missed six games.... Sprained leg (November 21, 1992); missed one game.... Injured back (February 10, 1993); missed two games.... Injured back (February 20, 1993); missed two games.... Pulled groin (April 9, 1993); missed three games.

Season	Team	League	Gms.	G	A	Pts.	Pen.	Gms.	G	A	Pts.	Pen.
80-81—Yorkton	SJHL	48	6	9	15	307	—	—	—	—	—
81-82—Yorkton	SJHL	47	20	21	41	199	—	—	—	—	—
82-83—Saskatoon	WHL	62	23	17	40	289	6	2	3	5	25
83-84—Saskatoon	WHL	69	40	41	81	258	—	—	—	—	—
84-85—Detroit	NHL	17	1	0	1	64	3	1	0	1	5
—Adirondack	AHL	47	12	7	19	171	—	—	—	—	—
85-86—Adirondack	AHL	9	6	2	8	34	—	—	—	—	—
—Detroit	NHL	59	9	6	15	*377	—	—	—	—	—
86-87—Detroit	NHL	77	9	9	18	276	16	2	3	5	71
87-88—Detroit	NHL	64	7	7	14	263	10	0	1	1	13
88-89—Detroit	NHL	60	9	9	18	213	3	0	1	1	6
89-90—Detroit	NHL	71	16	20	36	268	—	—	—	—	—
90-91—Detroit	NHL	52	5	4	9	253	—	—	—	—	—
—New York Rangers	NHL	5	0	0	0	36	6	0	2	2	21
91-92—New York Rangers	NHL	51	7	4	11	121	12	1	1	2	38
92-93—New York Rangers	NHL	65	3	6	9	131	—	—	—	—	—
NHL totals		521	66	65	131	2002	50	4	8	12	154

KOCUR, KORY
RW, RED WINGS

PERSONAL: Born March 6, 1969, at Kelvington, Sask.... 6-0/190.... Shoots right.... Cousin of Joey Kocur, right winger, New York Rangers.
TRANSACTIONS/CAREER NOTES: Selected by Detroit Red Wings in first round (first Red Wings pick, 17th overall) of NHL entry draft (June 11, 1988).

Season Team	League	REGULAR SEASON Gms.	G	A	Pts.	Pen.	PLAYOFFS Gms.	G	A	Pts.	Pen.
86-87—Saskatoon	WHL	62	13	17	30	98	4	0	0	0	7
87-88—Saskatoon	WHL	69	34	37	71	95	10	5	4	9	18
88-89—Saskatoon	WHL	66	45	57	102	111	8	7	11	18	15
89-90—Adirondack	AHL	79	18	37	55	36	6	2	1	3	2
90-91—Adirondack	AHL	65	8	13	21	83	2	0	0	0	12
91-92—Fort Wayne	IHL	69	25	40	65	68	7	3	3	6	49
92-93—Fort Wayne	IHL	66	21	36	57	77	4	1	1	2	6
—Adirondack	AHL	2	0	0	0	0	—	—	—	—	—

KOIVU, SAKU
C, CANADIENS

PERSONAL: Born November 23, 1974, at Turku, Finland. . . . 5-9/163. . . . Shoots left.
TRANSACTIONS/CAREER NOTES: Selected by Montreal Canadiens in first round (first Canadiens pick, 21st overall) of NHL entry draft (June 26, 1993).

Season Team	League	REGULAR SEASON Gms.	G	A	Pts.	Pen.	PLAYOFFS Gms.	G	A	Pts.	Pen.
91-92—TPS Jr.	Finland	42	30	37	67	63	—	—	—	—	—
92-93—TPS	Finland	46	3	7	10	28	—	—	—	—	—

KOLSTAD, DEAN
D, SHARKS

PERSONAL: Born June 16, 1968, at Edmonton, Alta. . . . 6-6/228. . . . Shoots left.
TRANSACTIONS/CAREER NOTES: Selected by Minnesota North Stars as underage junior in second round (third North Stars pick, 33rd overall) of NHL entry draft (June 21, 1986). . . . Selected by San Jose Sharks in NHL dispersal draft (May 30, 1991).
HONORS: Named to WHL All-Star first team (1986-87). . . . Named to IHL All-Star second team (1989-90).

Season Team	League	REGULAR SEASON Gms.	G	A	Pts.	Pen.	PLAYOFFS Gms.	G	A	Pts.	Pen.
84-85—Langley Eagles	BCJHL	25	3	11	14	61	—	—	—	—	—
—New Westminster	WHL	13	0	0	0	16	—	—	—	—	—
85-86—New Westminster	WHL	16	0	5	5	19	—	—	—	—	—
—Prince Albert	WHL	54	2	15	17	80	20	5	3	8	26
86-87—Prince Albert	WHL	72	17	37	54	112	8	1	5	6	8
87-88—Prince Albert	WHL	72	14	37	51	121	10	0	9	9	20
88-89—Minnesota	NHL	25	1	5	6	42	—	—	—	—	—
—Kalamazoo	IHL	51	10	23	33	91	6	1	0	1	23
89-90—Kalamazoo	IHL	77	10	40	50	172	10	3	4	7	14
90-91—Minnesota	NHL	5	0	0	0	15	—	—	—	—	—
—Kalamazoo	IHL	33	4	8	12	50	9	1	6	7	4
91-92—Kansas City	IHL	74	9	20	29	83	15	3	6	9	8
92-93—Kansas City	IHL	63	9	21	30	79	3	0	0	0	2
—San Jose	NHL	10	0	2	2	12	—	—	—	—	—
NHL totals		40	1	7	8	69					

KOLZIG, OLAF
G, CAPITALS

PERSONAL: Born April 6, 1970, at Johannesburg, South Africa. . . . 6-3/205. . . . Shoots left. . . . Name pronounced KOHLT zihg.
TRANSACTIONS/CAREER NOTES: Underwent surgery to right knee (November 1988). . . . Selected by Washington Capitals in first round (first Capitals pick, 19th overall) of NHL entry draft (June 17, 1989). . . . Loaned to Rochester Americans (October 2, 1992).

Season Team	League	REGULAR SEASON Gms.	Min.	W	L	T	GA	SO	Avg.	PLAYOFFS Gms.	Min.	W	L	GA	SO	Avg.
87-88—New Westminster	WHL	15	650	6	5	0	48	1	4.43	—	—	—	—	—	—	—
88-89—Tri-City	WHL	30	1671	16	10	2	97	1	*3.48	—	—	—	—	—	—	—
89-90—Washington	NHL	2	120	0	2	0	12	0	6.00	—	—	—	—	—	—	—
—Tri-City	WHL	48	2504	27	27	3	187	1	4.48	6	318	4	0	27	0	5.09
90-91—Baltimore	AHL	26	1367	10	12	1	72	0	3.16	—	—	—	—	—	—	—
—Hampton Roads	ECHL	21	1248	11	9	1	71	2	3.41	3	180	1	2	14	0	4.67
91-92—Baltimore	AHL	28	1503	5	17	2	105	1	4.19	—	—	—	—	—	—	—
—Hampton Roads	ECHL	14	847	11	3	0	41	0	2.90	—	—	—	—	—	—	—
92-93—Rochester	AHL	49	2737	25	16	4	168	0	3.68	17	*1040	9	*8	61	0	3.52
—Washington	NHL	1	20	0	0	0	2	0	6.00	—	—	—	—	—	—	—
NHL totals		3	140	0	2	0	14	0	6.00							

KONOWALCHUK, BRIAN
C, SHARKS

PERSONAL: Born October 14, 1971, at Prince Albert, Sask. . . . 5-11/180. . . . Shoots left.
COLLEGE: Denver.
TRANSACTIONS/CAREER NOTES: Selected by San Jose Sharks in NHL supplemental draft (June 19, 1992).

Season Team	League	REGULAR SEASON Gms.	G	A	Pts.	Pen.	PLAYOFFS Gms.	G	A	Pts.	Pen.
90-91—University of Denver	WCHA	38	8	19	27	. . .	—	—	—	—	—
91-92—University of Denver	WCHA	33	8	17	25	53	—	—	—	—	—
92-93—University of Denver	WCHA	37	12	20	32	59	—	—	—	—	—

K

KONOWALCHUK, STEVE

C, CAPITALS

PERSONAL: Born November 11, 1972, at Salt Lake City. . . . 6-0/180. . . . Shoots left. . . . Full name: Steven Reed Konowalchuk. . . . Name pronounced KAH-nuh-WAHL-chuhk.

TRANSACTIONS/CAREER NOTES: Selected by Washington Capitals in third round (fifth Capitals pick, 58th overall) of NHL entry draft (June 22, 1991).

HONORS: Won Four Broncos Memorial Trophy (1991-92). . . . Named to Can.HL All-Star second team (1991-92). . . . Named to WHL (West) All-Star first team (1991-92).

Season Team	League	REGULAR SEASON					PLAYOFFS				
		Gms.	G	A	Pts.	Pen.	Gms.	G	A	Pts.	Pen.
90-91—Portland	WHL	72	43	49	92	78	—	—	—	—	—
91-92—Portland	WHL	64	51	53	104	95	6	3	6	9	12
—Baltimore	AHL	3	1	1	2	0	—	—	—	—	—
—Washington	NHL	1	0	0	0	0	—	—	—	—	—
92-93—Baltimore	AHL	37	18	28	46	74	—	—	—	—	—
—Washington	NHL	36	4	7	11	16	2	0	1	1	0
NHL totals		37	4	7	11	16	2	0	1	1	0

KONROYD, STEVE

D, RED WINGS

PERSONAL: Born February 10, 1961, at Scarborough, Ont. . . . 6-1/195. . . . Shoots left. . . . Full name: Stephen Mark Konroyd.

TRANSACTIONS/CAREER NOTES: Selected by Calgary Flames as underage junior in second round (fourth Flames pick, 39th overall) of NHL entry draft (June 11, 1980). . . . Dislocated elbow (December 1984). . . . Pulled chest muscle (February 1986). . . . Traded by Flames with LW Richard Kromm to New York Islanders for LW/C John Tonelli (March 1986). . . . Bruised collarbone (December 1986). . . . Suspended four games by NHL for stick-swinging incident (January 1988). . . . Traded by Islanders with C Bob Bassen to Chicago Blackhawks for D Gary Nylund and D Marc Bergevin (November 25, 1988). . . . Bruised thigh (January 1990). . . . Suffered back spasms (February 10, 1991). . . . Broke knuckle on little finger of right hand (March 10, 1991); missed 18 days. . . . Traded by Blackhawks to Hartford Whalers for RW Rob Brown (January 24, 1992). . . . Traded by Whalers to Detroit Red Wings for sixth-round pick in 1993 draft (March 22, 1993).

HONORS: Won Bobby Smith Trophy (1979-80). . . . Named to OMJHL All-Star second team (1980-81).

Season Team	League	REGULAR SEASON					PLAYOFFS				
		Gms.	G	A	Pts.	Pen.	Gms.	G	A	Pts.	Pen.
78-79—Oshawa	OMJHL	65	4	19	23	63	—	—	—	—	—
79-80—Oshawa	OMJHL	62	11	23	34	133	7	0	2	2	14
80-81—Calgary	NHL	4	0	0	0	4	—	—	—	—	—
—Oshawa	OMJHL	59	19	49	68	232	11	3	11	14	35
81-82—Oklahoma City	CHL	14	2	3	5	15	—	—	—	—	—
—Calgary	NHL	63	3	14	17	78	3	0	0	0	12
82-83—Calgary	NHL	79	4	13	17	73	9	2	1	3	18
83-84—Calgary	NHL	80	1	13	14	94	8	1	2	3	8
84-85—Calgary	NHL	64	3	23	26	73	4	1	4	5	2
85-86—Calgary	NHL	59	7	20	27	64	—	—	—	—	—
—New York Islanders	NHL	14	0	5	5	16	3	0	0	0	6
86-87—New York Islanders	NHL	72	5	16	21	70	14	1	4	5	10
87-88—New York Islanders	NHL	62	2	15	17	99	6	1	0	1	4
88-89—New York Islanders	NHL	21	1	5	6	2	—	—	—	—	—
—Chicago	NHL	57	5	7	12	40	16	2	0	2	10
89-90—Chicago	NHL	75	3	14	17	34	20	1	3	4	19
90-91—Chicago	NHL	70	0	12	12	40	6	1	0	1	8
91-92—Chicago	NHL	49	2	14	16	65	—	—	—	—	—
—Hartford	NHL	33	2	10	12	32	7	0	1	1	2
92-93—Hartford	NHL	59	3	11	14	63	—	—	—	—	—
—Detroit	NHL	6	0	1	1	4	1	0	0	0	0
NHL totals		867	41	193	234	851	97	10	15	25	99

KONSTANTINOV, VLADIMIR

D, RED WINGS

PERSONAL: Born March 19, 1967, at Murmansk, U.S.S.R. . . . 5-11/185. . . . Shoots right. . . . Name pronounced KAHN-stan-TEE-nahf.

TRANSACTIONS/CAREER NOTES: Selected by Detroit Red Wings in 11th round (12th Red Wings pick, 221st overall) of NHL entry draft (June 17, 1989). . . . Injured groin (December 3, 1992); missed two games.

HONORS: Named to NHL All-Rookie team (1991-92).

Season Team	League	REGULAR SEASON					PLAYOFFS				
		Gms.	G	A	Pts.	Pen.	Gms.	G	A	Pts.	Pen.
84-85—CSKA Moscow	USSR	40	1	4	5	10	—	—	—	—	—
85-86—CSKA Moscow	USSR	26	4	3	7	12	—	—	—	—	—
86-87—CSKA Moscow	USSR	35	2	2	4	19	—	—	—	—	—
87-88—CSKA Moscow	USSR	50	3	6	9	32	—	—	—	—	—
88-89—CSKA Moscow	USSR	37	7	8	15	20	—	—	—	—	—
89-90—CSKA Moscow	USSR	47	14	13	27	44	—	—	—	—	—
90-91—CSKA Moscow	USSR	45	5	12	17	42	—	—	—	—	—
91-92—Detroit	NHL	79	8	26	34	172	11	0	1	1	16
92-93—Detroit	NHL	82	5	17	22	137	7	0	1	1	8
NHL totals		161	13	43	56	309	18	0	2	2	24

KONTOS, CHRIS
C/LW, LIGHTNING

PERSONAL: Born December 10, 1963, at Toronto. . . . 6-1/195. . . . Shoots left.
TRANSACTIONS/CAREER NOTES: Traded by Sudbury Wolves to Toronto Marlboros for C Keith Knight (October 1981). . . . Selected by New York Rangers as underage junior in first round (first Rangers pick, 15th overall) of NHL entry draft (June 1982). . . . Suspended by Rangers after refusing to report to Tulsa Oilers (November 1983). . . . Reinstated by Rangers (January 1984). . . . Traded by Rangers to Pittsburgh Penguins for RW Ron Duguay (January 1987). . . . Traded by Penguins with sixth-round pick in 1988 draft (C Micah Aivazoff) to Los Angeles Kings for RW Bryan Erickson (February 5, 1988). . . . Signed as free agent by Tampa Bay Lightning (July 21, 1992). . . . Strained knee (March 12, 1993); missed remainder of season.
RECORDS: Holds NHL single-series playoff record for most power-play goals—6 (1989).

			REGULAR SEASON					PLAYOFFS			
Season Team	League	Gms.	G	A	Pts.	Pen.	Gms.	G	A	Pts.	Pen.
79-80—North York Flames	OPJHL	42	39	55	94	37	—	—	—	—	—
80-81—Sudbury	OMJHL	56	17	27	44	36	—	—	—	—	—
81-82—Sudbury	OHL	12	6	6	12	18	—	—	—	—	—
—Toronto	OHL	59	36	56	92	68	10	7	9	16	2
82-83—Toronto	OHL	28	21	33	54	23	—	—	—	—	—
—New York Rangers	NHL	44	8	7	15	33	—	—	—	—	—
83-84—New York Rangers	NHL	6	0	1	1	8	—	—	—	—	—
—Tulsa	CHL	21	5	13	18	8	—	—	—	—	—
84-85—New Haven	AHL	48	19	24	43	30	—	—	—	—	—
—New York Rangers	NHL	28	4	8	12	24	—	—	—	—	—
85-86—New Haven	AHL	21	8	15	23	12	5	4	2	6	4
86-87—New Haven	AHL	36	14	17	31	29	—	—	—	—	—
—Pittsburgh	NHL	31	8	9	17	6	—	—	—	—	—
87-88—Pittsburgh	NHL	36	1	7	8	12	—	—	—	—	—
—Los Angeles	NHL	6	2	10	12	2	4	1	0	1	4
—New Haven	AHL	16	8	16	24	4	—	—	—	—	—
—Muskegon	IHL	10	3	6	9	8	—	—	—	—	—
88-89—Kloten	Switzerland				Statistics unavailable.						
—Los Angeles	NHL	7	2	1	3	2	11	9	0	9	8
89-90—New Haven	AHL	42	10	20	30	25	—	—	—	—	—
—Los Angeles	NHL	6	2	2	4	4	5	1	0	1	0
90-91—Phoenix	IHL	69	26	36	62	19	11	9	12	21	0
91-92—Canadian national team	Int'l	25	10	10	20	16	—	—	—	—	—
92-93—Tampa Bay	NHL	66	27	24	51	12	—	—	—	—	—
NHL totals		230	54	69	123	103	20	11	0	11	12

KORDIC, DAN
D, FLYERS

PERSONAL: Born April 18, 1971, at Edmonton, Alta. . . . 6-5/220. . . . Shoots left. . . . Name pronounced KOHR-dihk. . . . Brother of John Kordic, right winger for four NHL teams (1985-86 through 1991-92).
TRANSACTIONS/CAREER NOTES: Selected by Philadelphia Flyers in fifth round (eighth Flyers pick, 88th overall) of NHL entry draft (June 16, 1990). . . . Suffered from the flu (January 1992); missed five games.

			REGULAR SEASON					PLAYOFFS			
Season Team	League	Gms.	G	A	Pts.	Pen.	Gms.	G	A	Pts.	Pen.
87-88—Medicine Hat	WHL	63	1	5	6	75	—	—	—	—	—
88-89—Medicine Hat	WHL	70	1	13	14	190	—	—	—	—	—
89-90—Medicine Hat	WHL	59	4	12	16	182	3	0	0	0	9
90-91—Medicine Hat	WHL	67	8	15	23	150	12	2	6	8	42
91-92—Philadelphia	NHL	46	1	3	4	126	—	—	—	—	—
92-93—Hershey	AHL	14	0	2	2	17	—	—	—	—	—
NHL totals		46	1	3	4	126					

KOROLEV, IGOR
RW, BLUES

PERSONAL: Born September 6, 1970, at Moscow, U.S.S.R. . . . 6-1/176. . . . Shoots left. . . . Name pronounced KOHR-oh-lehf.
TRANSACTIONS/CAREER NOTES: Selected by St. Louis Blues in second round (first Blues pick, 38th overall) of NHL entry draft (June 20, 1992).

			REGULAR SEASON					PLAYOFFS			
Season Team	League	Gms.	G	A	Pts.	Pen.	Gms.	G	A	Pts.	Pen.
88-89—Dynamo Moscow	USSR	1	0	0	0	2	—	—	—	—	—
89-90—Dynamo Moscow	USSR	17	3	2	5	2	—	—	—	—	—
90-91—Dynamo Moscow	USSR	38	12	4	16	12	—	—	—	—	—
91-92—Dynamo Moscow	CIS	39	15	12	27	16	—	—	—	—	—
92-93—Dynamo Moscow	CIS	5	1	2	3	4	—	—	—	—	—
—St. Louis	NHL	74	4	23	27	20	3	0	0	0	0
NHL totals		74	4	23	27	20	3	0	0	0	0

KOVALENKO, ANDREI
RW, NORDIQUES

PERSONAL: Born July 7, 1970, at Gorky, U.S.S.R. . . . 5-9/161. . . . Shoots left. . . . Name pronounced koh-vuh-LEHN-koh.
TRANSACTIONS/CAREER NOTES: Selected by Quebec Nordiques in eighth round (sixth Nordiques pick, 148th overall) of NHL entry draft (June 16, 1990). . . . Suffered tonsilitis (December 22, 1992); missed two games. . . . Suffered from the flu (March 15, 1993); missed one game.

Season Team	League	REGULAR SEASON					PLAYOFFS				
		Gms.	G	A	Pts.	Pen.	Gms.	G	A	Pts.	Pen.
89-90—CSKA Moscow	USSR	48	8	5	13	18	—	—	—	—	—
90-91—CSKA Moscow	USSR	45	13	8	21	26	—	—	—	—	—
91-92—CSKA Moscow	CIS	44	19	13	32	32	—	—	—	—	—
92-93—CSKA Moscow	CIS	3	3	1	4	4	—	—	—	—	—
—Quebec	NHL	81	27	41	68	57	4	1	0	1	2
NHL totals		81	27	41	68	57	4	1	0	1	2

KOVALEV, ALEXEI
RW, RANGERS

PERSONAL: Born February 24, 1973, at Moscow, U.S.S.R. . . . 6-1/189. . . . Shoots left. . . . Name pronounced KOH-vuh-lehv.
TRANSACTIONS/CAREER NOTES: Selected by New York Rangers in first round (first Rangers pick, 15th overall) of NHL entry draft (June 22, 1991). . . . Suffered back spasms (January 16, 1993); missed one game.

Season Team	League	REGULAR SEASON					PLAYOFFS				
		Gms.	G	A	Pts.	Pen.	Gms.	G	A	Pts.	Pen.
89-90—Dynamo Moscow	USSR	1	0	0	0	0	—	—	—	—	—
90-91—Dynamo Moscow	USSR	18	1	2	3	4	—	—	—	—	—
91-92—Dynamo Moscow	CIS	33	16	9	25	20	—	—	—	—	—
92-93—New York Rangers	NHL	65	20	18	38	79	—	—	—	—	—
—Binghamton	AHL	13	13	11	24	35	9	3	5	8	14
NHL totals		65	20	18	38	79					

K

KOZLOV, VIKTOR
RW, SHARKS

PERSONAL: Born February 14, 1975, at Togliatti, U.S.S.R. . . . 6-5/209. . . . Shoots right.
TRANSACTIONS/CAREER NOTES: Selected by San Jose Sharks in first round (first Sharks pick, sixth overall) of NHL entry draft (June 26, 1993).

Season Team	League	REGULAR SEASON					PLAYOFFS				
		Gms.	G	A	Pts.	Pen.	Gms.	G	A	Pts.	Pen.
90-91—Lada Togliatti	USSR Div. II	2	2	0	2	0	—	—	—	—	—
91-92—Lada Togliatti	CIS	3	0	0	0	0	—	—	—	—	—
92-93—Dynamo Moscow	CIS	30	6	5	11	4	10	3	0	3	0

KOZLOV, VYACHESLAV
LW, RED WINGS

PERSONAL: Born May 3, 1972, at Voskresensk, U.S.S.R. . . . 5-10/172. . . . Shoots left. . . . Name pronounced KAS-lahf.
TRANSACTIONS/CAREER NOTES: Selected by Detroit Red Wings in third round (second Red Wings pick, 45th overall) of NHL entry draft (June 16, 1990).
HONORS: Named Soviet League Rookie of the Year (1989-90).

Season Team	League	REGULAR SEASON					PLAYOFFS				
		Gms.	G	A	Pts.	Pen.	Gms.	G	A	Pts.	Pen.
89-90—Khimik	USSR	45	14	12	26	38	—	—	—	—	—
90-91—Khimik	USSR	45	11	13	24	46	—	—	—	—	—
91-92—CSKA Moscow	CIS	11	6	5	11	12	—	—	—	—	—
—Detroit	NHL	7	0	2	2	2	—	—	—	—	—
92-93—Detroit	NHL	17	4	1	5	14	4	0	2	2	2
—Adirondack	AHL	45	23	36	59	54	4	1	1	2	4
NHL totals		24	4	3	7	16	4	0	2	2	2

KRAKE, PAUL
G, NORDIQUES

PERSONAL: Born March 25, 1969, at Lloydminster, Alta. . . . 6-0/175.
COLLEGE: Alaska-Anchorage.
TRANSACTIONS/CAREER NOTES: Selected by Quebec Nordiques in 10th round (10th Nordiques pick, 148th overall) of NHL entry draft (June 17, 1989).

Season Team	League	REGULAR SEASON							PLAYOFFS						
		Gms.	Min.	W	L	T	GA	SO	Avg.	Gms.	Min.	W	L	GA SO	Avg.
88-89—Alaska-Anchorage	Indep.	19	1111	...	...	...	75	0	4.05	—	—	—	—	—	—
89-90—Alaska-Anchorage	Indep.	18	937	8	6	2	58	0	3.71	—	—	—	—	—	—
90-91—Alaska-Anchorage	Indep.	37	2183	18	15	3	123	4	3.38	—	—	—	—	—	—
91-92—Alaska-Anchorage	Indep.	28	1647	19	8	0	94	0	3.42	—	—	—	—	—	—
92-93—Halifax	AHL	17	916	8	6	1	57	1	3.73	—	—	—	—	—	—
—Oklahoma City	CHL	17	1029	13	4	0	60	0	3.50	—	—	—	—	—	—

KRAVCHUK, IGOR
D, OILERS

PERSONAL: Born September 13, 1966, at Ufa, U.S.S.R. . . . 6-1/200. . . . Shoots left.
TRANSACTIONS/CAREER NOTES: Selected by Chicago Blackhawks in fourth round (fifth Blackhawks pick, 71st overall) of NHL entry draft (June 22, 1991). . . . Sprained knee (October 25, 1992); missed four games. . . . Sprained left ankle (December 29, 1992); missed 18 games. . . . Traded by Blackhawks with C Dean McAmmond to Edmonton Oilers for RW Joe Murphy (February 25, 1993). . . . Sprained left knee (April 6, 1993); missed remainder of season.
MISCELLANEOUS: Member of gold-medal-winning U.S.S.R. Olympic team (1988) and gold-medal-winning Unified Olympic team (1992).

Season Team	League	REGULAR SEASON					PLAYOFFS				
		Gms.	G	A	Pts.	Pen.	Gms.	G	A	Pts.	Pen.
90-91—CSKA Moscow	USSR	41	6	5	11	16	—	—	—	—	—

Season	Team	League	Gms.	G	A	Pts.	Pen.	Gms.	G	A	Pts.	Pen.
					REGULAR SEASON					PLAYOFFS		
91-92	CSKA Moscow	CIS	30	3	7	10	2	—	—	—	—	—
	Unified Olympic Team	Int'l	8	3	2	5	...	—	—	—	—	—
	Chicago	NHL	18	1	8	9	4	18	2	6	8	8
92-93	Chicago	NHL	38	6	9	15	30	—	—	—	—	—
	Edmonton	NHL	17	4	8	12	2	—	—	—	—	—
NHL totals			73	11	25	36	36	18	2	6	8	8

KRAVETS, MIKHAIL
LW, SHARKS

PERSONAL: Born November 12, 1963, at Leningrad, U.S.S.R. ... 5-10/182. ... Shoots left.... Name pronounced mih-KAYL KRA-vihts.
TRANSACTIONS/CAREER NOTES: Selected by San Jose Sharks in 12th round (13th Sharks pick, 243rd overall) of NHL entry draft (June 22, 1991).

Season	Team	League	Gms.	G	A	Pts.	Pen.	Gms.	G	A	Pts.	Pen.
					REGULAR SEASON					PLAYOFFS		
88-89	SKA Leningrad	USSR	44	9	5	14	36	—	—	—	—	—
89-90	SKA Leningrad	USSR	43	8	18	26	20	—	—	—	—	—
90-91	SKA Leningrad	USSR	25	8	6	14	28	—	—	—	—	—
91-92	Kansas City	IHL	74	10	32	42	172	15	6	8	14	12
	San Jose	NHL	1	0	0	0	0	—	—	—	—	—
92-93	San Jose	NHL	1	0	0	0	0	—	—	—	—	—
	Kansas City	IHL	71	19	49	68	153	10	2	5	7	55
NHL totals			2	0	0	0	0					

KRECHIN, VLADIMIR
LW/RW, FLYERS

PERSONAL: Born March 23, 1975, at Chelyabinsk, U.S.S.R. ... 5-11/180. ... Shoots left.
TRANSACTIONS/CAREER NOTES: Selected by Philadelphia Flyers in fifth round (fourth Flyers pick, 114th overall) of NHL entry draft (June 26, 1993).

Season	Team	League	Gms.	G	A	Pts.	Pen.	Gms.	G	A	Pts.	Pen.
					REGULAR SEASON					PLAYOFFS		
92-93	Traktor Chelyabinsk	CIS	1	0	0	0	0	—	—	—	—	—

KRIVOKRASOV, SERGEI
RW, BLACKHAWKS

PERSONAL: Born April 15, 1974, at Angarsk, U.S.S.R. ... 5-11/175. ... Shoots left.... Name pronounced KREE-voh-KRAS-ahf.
TRANSACTIONS/CAREER NOTES: Selected by Chicago Blackhawks in first round (first Blackhawks pick, 12th overall) of NHL entry draft (June 20, 1992).

Season	Team	League	Gms.	G	A	Pts.	Pen.	Gms.	G	A	Pts.	Pen.
					REGULAR SEASON					PLAYOFFS		
90-91	CSKA Moscow	USSR	41	4	0	4	8	—	—	—	—	—
91-92	CSKA Moscow	CIS	42	10	8	18	35	—	—	—	—	—
92-93	Chicago	NHL	4	0	0	0	2	—	—	—	—	—
	Indianapolis	IHL	78	36	33	69	157	5	3	1	4	2
NHL totals			4	0	0	0	2					

KROMM, RICH
LW, ISLANDERS

PERSONAL: Born March 29, 1964, at Trail, B.C. ... 5-11/190. ... Shoots left. ... Full name: Richard Gordon Kromm. ... Son of Bobby Kromm, coach, Winnipeg Jets of WHA (1975-76 through 1976-77) and Detroit Red Wings (1977-78 through 1979-80).
TRANSACTIONS/CAREER NOTES: Broke ankle (October 1981).... Selected by Calgary Flames as underage junior in second round (second Flames pick, 37th overall) of NHL entry draft (June 9, 1982).... Pinched nerve (February 1985).... Traded by Flames with LW Steve Konroyd to New York Islanders for LW/C John Tonelli (March 1986). ... Sprained left knee (December 2, 1986); missed seven games.... Reinjured knee (March 1987).... Fractured rib (February 1988).

Season	Team	League	Gms.	G	A	Pts.	Pen.	Gms.	G	A	Pts.	Pen.
					REGULAR SEASON					PLAYOFFS		
80-81	Windsor Jr. B	OHA	39	22	31	53	40	—	—	—	—	—
81-82	Portland	WHL	60	16	38	54	30	14	0	3	3	17
82-83	Portland	WHL	72	35	68	103	64	14	7	13	20	12
83-84	Portland	WHL	10	10	4	14	13	—	—	—	—	—
	Calgary	NHL	53	11	12	23	27	11	1	1	2	9
84-85	Calgary	NHL	73	20	32	52	32	3	0	1	1	4
85-86	Calgary	NHL	63	12	17	29	31	—	—	—	—	—
	New York Islanders	NHL	14	7	7	14	4	3	0	1	1	0
86-87	New York Islanders	NHL	70	12	17	29	20	14	1	3	4	4
87-88	New York Islanders	NHL	71	5	10	15	20	5	0	0	0	5
88-89	New York Islanders	NHL	20	1	6	7	4	—	—	—	—	—
	Springfield	AHL	48	21	26	47	15	—	—	—	—	—
89-90	Leksand	Sweden	40	8	16	24	28	3	3	1	4	0
	Springfield	AHL	9	3	4	7	4	16	1	5	6	4
90-91	Capital District	AHL	76	19	36	55	18	—	—	—	—	—
	New York Islanders	NHL	6	1	0	1	0	—	—	—	—	—
91-92	Capital District	AHL	76	16	39	55	36	7	2	3	5	6
	New York Islanders	NHL	1	0	0	0	0	—	—	—	—	—

K

Season Team	League	REGULAR SEASON Gms.	G	A	Pts.	Pen.	PLAYOFFS Gms.	G	A	Pts.	Pen.
92-93—Capital District................	AHL	79	20	34	54	28	3	0	0	0	0
—New York Islanders..........	NHL	1	1	2	3	0	—	—	—	—	—
NHL totals....................................		372	70	103	173	138	36	2	6	8	22

KRON, ROBERT
LW, WHALERS

PERSONAL: Born February 27, 1967, at Brno, Czechoslovakia.... 5-10/180.... Shoots right. ... Name pronounced KRAHN.

TRANSACTIONS/CAREER NOTES: Selected by Vancouver Canucks in fourth round (fifth Canucks pick, 88th overall) of NHL entry draft (June 15, 1985).... Played entire season with a broken bone in his left wrist (1990-91).... Underwent surgery to repair torn knee ligaments and wrist fracture (March 22, 1991).... Fractured ankle (January 28, 1992); missed 22 games.... Traded by Canucks with third-round pick in 1993 draft and future considerations to Hartford Whalers for C/LW Murray Craven and fifth-round pick in 1993 draft (March 22, 1993); Canucks sent RW Jim Sandlak to Whalers to complete deal (May 17, 1993).

Season Team	League	REGULAR SEASON Gms.	G	A	Pts.	Pen.	PLAYOFFS Gms.	G	A	Pts.	Pen.
86-87—Zetor Brno	Czech.	28	14	11	25	...	—	—	—	—	—
87-88—Zetor Brno	Czech.	32	12	6	18	...	—	—	—	—	—
88-89—Zetor Brno	Czech.	43	28	19	47	...	—	—	—	—	—
89-90—Dukla Trencin	Czech.	39	22	22	44	...	—	—	—	—	—
90-91—Vancouver	NHL	76	12	20	32	21	—	—	—	—	—
91-92—Vancouver	NHL	36	2	2	4	2	11	1	2	3	2
92-93—Vancouver	NHL	32	10	11	21	14	—	—	—	—	—
—Hartford............................	NHL	13	4	2	6	4	—	—	—	—	—
NHL totals....................................		157	28	35	63	41	11	1	2	3	2

KROUPA, VLASTIMIL
D, SHARKS

PERSONAL: Born April 27, 1975, at Most, Czechoslovakia.... 6-3/176.... Shoots left.

TRANSACTIONS/CAREER NOTES: Selected by San Jose Sharks in second round (third Sharks pick, 45th overall) of NHL entry draft (June 26, 1993).

Season Team	League	REGULAR SEASON Gms.	G	A	Pts.	Pen.	PLAYOFFS Gms.	G	A	Pts.	Pen.
92-93—Chemopetrol Litvinov	Czech.	9	0	1	1	...	—	—	—	—	—

KRUPP, UWE
D, ISLANDERS

PERSONAL: Born June 24, 1965, at Cologne, West Germany.... 6-6/236.... Shoots right.... Name pronounced OO-vay KROOP.

TRANSACTIONS/CAREER NOTES: Selected by Buffalo Sabres in 11th round (13th Sabres pick, 214th overall) of NHL entry draft (June 8, 1983).... Bruised hip (November 1987).... Injured head (April 1988).... Broke rib (January 6, 1989).... Banned from international competition for 18 months by IIHF after failing random substance test (April 20, 1990).... Suffered from cyst on foot (January 2, 1991).... Traded by Sabres with C Pierre Turgeon, RW Benoit Hogue and C Dave McLlwain to New York Islanders for C Pat LaFontaine, LW Randy Wood, D Randy Hillier and future considerations; Sabres later received fourth-round pick in 1992 draft (D Dean Melanson) (October 25, 1991).... Sprained left knee (December 28, 1991); missed five games.... Bruised thigh (February 7, 1992).... Suffered from the flu (March 2, 1993); missed one game.... Suffered sore shoulder (April 10, 1993); missed three games.

HONORS: Played in NHL All-Star Game (1991).

Season Team	League	REGULAR SEASON Gms.	G	A	Pts.	Pen.	PLAYOFFS Gms.	G	A	Pts.	Pen.
83-84—KEC..................................	W. Germany	40	0	4	4	22	—	—	—	—	—
84-85—KEC..................................	W. Germany	39	11	8	19	36	—	—	—	—	—
85-86—KEC..................................	W. Germany	45	10	21	31	83	—	—	—	—	—
86-87—Rochester	AHL	42	3	19	22	50	17	1	11	12	16
—Buffalo............................	NHL	26	1	4	5	23	—	—	—	—	—
87-88—Buffalo............................	NHL	75	2	9	11	151	6	0	0	0	15
88-89—Buffalo............................	NHL	70	5	13	18	55	5	0	1	1	4
89-90—Buffalo............................	NHL	74	3	20	23	85	6	0	0	0	4
90-91—Buffalo............................	NHL	74	12	32	44	66	6	1	1	2	6
91-92—Buffalo............................	NHL	8	2	0	2	6	—	—	—	—	—
—New York Islanders..........	NHL	59	6	29	35	43	—	—	—	—	—
92-93—New York Islanders..........	NHL	80	9	29	38	67	18	1	5	6	12
NHL totals....................................		466	40	136	176	496	41	2	7	9	41

KRUPPKE, GORD
D, RED WINGS

PERSONAL: Born April 2, 1969, at Edmonton, Alta.... 6-1/200.... Shoots right.

TRANSACTIONS/CAREER NOTES: Underwent surgery to have spleen removed (December 1986).... Selected by Detroit Red Wings as underage junior in second round (second Red Wings pick, 32nd overall) of NHL entry draft (June 13, 1987).... Injured left knee ligaments (October 1987).... Suffered elbow contusion (December 2, 1992); missed one game.

HONORS: Named to WHL All-Star second team (1988-89).

Season Team	League	REGULAR SEASON Gms.	G	A	Pts.	Pen.	PLAYOFFS Gms.	G	A	Pts.	Pen.
85-86—Prince Albert	WHL	62	1	8	9	81	20	4	4	8	22
86-87—Prince Albert	WHL	49	2	10	12	129	8	0	0	0	9

			REGULAR SEASON					PLAYOFFS			
Season Team	League	Gms.	G	A	Pts.	Pen.	Gms.	G	A	Pts.	Pen.
87-88—Prince Albert	WHL	54	8	8	16	113	10	0	0	0	46
88-89—Prince Albert	WHL	62	6	26	32	254	3	0	0	0	11
89-90—Adirondack	AHL	59	2	12	14	103	—	—	—	—	—
90-91—Adirondack	AHL	45	1	8	9	153	—	—	—	—	—
—Detroit	NHL	4	0	0	0	0	—	—	—	—	—
91-92—Adirondack	AHL	65	3	9	12	208	16	0	1	1	52
92-93—Adirondack	AHL	41	2	12	14	197	9	1	2	3	20
—Detroit	NHL	10	0	0	0	20	—	—	—	—	—
NHL totals		14	0	0	0	20					

KRUSE, PAUL
LW, FLAMES

PERSONAL: Born March 15, 1970, at Merritt, B.C. . . . 6-0/200. . . . Shoots left. . . . Name pronounced KROOS.

TRANSACTIONS/CAREER NOTES: Selected by Calgary Flames in fourth round (sixth Flames pick, 83rd overall) of NHL entry draft (June 16, 1990). . . . Injured eye (March 8, 1992); missed four games. . . . Suffered hip pointer (March 21, 1993); missed one game.

			REGULAR SEASON					PLAYOFFS			
Season Team	League	Gms.	G	A	Pts.	Pen.	Gms.	G	A	Pts.	Pen.
86-87—Merritt	BCJHL	35	8	15	23	120	—	—	—	—	—
87-88—Merritt	BCJHL	44	12	32	44	227	4	1	4	5	18
—Moose Jaw	WHL	1	0	0	0	0	—	—	—	—	—
88-89—Kamloops	WHL	68	8	15	23	209	—	—	—	—	—
89-90—Kamloops	WHL	67	22	23	45	291	17	3	5	8	†79
90-91—Salt Lake City	IHL	83	24	20	44	313	4	1	1	2	4
—Calgary	NHL	1	0	0	0	7	—	—	—	—	—
91-92—Salt Lake City	IHL	57	14	15	29	267	5	1	2	3	19
—Calgary	NHL	16	3	1	4	65	—	—	—	—	—
92-93—Salt Lake City	IHL	35	1	4	5	206	—	—	—	—	—
—Calgary	NHL	27	2	3	5	41	—	—	—	—	—
NHL totals		44	5	4	9	113					

KRUSHELNYSKI, MIKE
C/LW, MAPLE LEAFS

PERSONAL: Born April 27, 1960, at Montreal. . . . 6-2/200. . . . Shoots left. . . . Name pronounced kroo-shihl-NIH-skee.

TRANSACTIONS/CAREER NOTES: Started 1978-79 season at St. Louis University then left to return to junior hockey. . . . Selected by Boston Bruins as underage junior in sixth round (seventh Bruins pick, 120th overall) of NHL entry draft (August 9, 1979). . . . Separated right shoulder (January 1984). . . . Traded by Bruins to Edmonton Oilers for C Ken Linseman (June 1984). . . . Sprained right knee (December 10, 1985); missed 17 games. . . . Twisted knee (February 14, 1986); missed nine games. . . . Suspended by Oilers for not reporting to training camp (September 1987). . . . Traded by Oilers with C Wayne Gretzky and RW/D Marty McSorley to Los Angeles Kings for C Jimmy Carson, LW Martin Gelinas, first-round picks in 1989 (traded to New Jersey), 1991 (LW Martin Rucinsky) and 1993 (D Nick Stajduhar) drafts and cash (August 9, 1988). . . . Fractured left wrist (October 5, 1989); missed 17 games. . . . Traded by Kings to Toronto Maple Leafs for C John McIntyre (November 9, 1990).

HONORS: Played in NHL All-Star Game (1985).

MISCELLANEOUS: Member of Stanley Cup championship teams (1985, 1987 and 1988).

			REGULAR SEASON					PLAYOFFS			
Season Team	League	Gms.	G	A	Pts.	Pen.	Gms.	G	A	Pts.	Pen.
78-79—Montreal	QMJHL	46	15	29	44	42	11	3	4	7	8
79-80—Montreal	QMJHL	72	39	61	100	78	6	2	3	5	2
80-81—Springfield	AHL	80	25	38	63	47	7	1	1	2	29
81-82—Erie	AHL	62	31	52	83	44	—	—	—	—	—
—Boston	NHL	17	3	3	6	2	1	0	0	0	2
82-83—Boston	NHL	79	23	42	65	43	17	8	6	14	12
83-84—Boston	NHL	66	25	20	45	55	2	0	0	0	0
84-85—Edmonton	NHL	80	43	45	88	60	18	5	8	13	22
85-86—Edmonton	NHL	54	16	24	40	22	10	4	5	9	16
86-87—Edmonton	NHL	80	16	35	51	67	21	3	4	7	18
87-88—Edmonton	NHL	76	20	27	47	64	19	4	6	10	12
88-89—Los Angeles	NHL	78	26	36	62	110	11	1	4	5	4
89-90—Los Angeles	NHL	63	16	25	41	50	10	1	3	4	12
90-91—Los Angeles	NHL	15	1	5	6	10	—	—	—	—	—
—Toronto	NHL	59	17	22	39	48	—	—	—	—	—
91-92—Toronto	NHL	72	9	15	24	72	—	—	—	—	—
92-93—Toronto	NHL	84	19	20	39	62	16	3	7	10	8
NHL totals		823	234	319	553	665	125	29	43	72	106

KRYGIER, TODD
LW, CAPITALS

PERSONAL: Born October 12, 1965, at Northville, Mich. . . . 5-11/180. . . . Shoots left. . . . Full name: Todd Andrew Krygier.

COLLEGE: Connecticut.

TRANSACTIONS/CAREER NOTES: Selected by Hartford Whalers in NHL supplemental draft (June 10, 1988). . . . Bruised heel (March 13, 1990). . . . Traded by Whalers to Washington Capitals for fourth-round pick in 1993 draft (October 3, 1991).

Season Team	League	REGULAR SEASON					PLAYOFFS				
		Gms.	G	A	Pts.	Pen.	Gms.	G	A	Pts.	Pen.
84-85—University of Connecticut.	ECAC-II	14	14	11	25	12	—	—	—	—	—
85-86—University of Connecticut.	ECAC-II	32	29	27	56	46	—	—	—	—	—
86-87—University of Connecticut.	ECAC-II	28	24	24	48	44	—	—	—	—	—
87-88—University of Connecticut.	ECAC-II	27	32	39	71	38	—	—	—	—	—
—New Haven	AHL	13	1	5	6	34	—	—	—	—	—
88-89—Binghamton	AHL	76	26	42	68	77	—	—	—	—	—
89-90—Binghamton	AHL	12	1	9	10	16	—	—	—	—	—
—Hartford	NHL	58	18	12	30	52	7	2	1	3	4
90-91—Hartford	NHL	72	13	17	30	95	6	0	2	2	0
91-92—Washington	NHL	67	13	17	30	107	5	2	1	3	4
92-93—Washington	NHL	77	11	12	23	60	6	1	1	2	4
NHL totals		274	55	58	113	314	24	5	5	10	12

KUCERA, FRANTISEK
D, BLACKHAWKS

PERSONAL: Born February 3, 1968, at Prague, Czechoslovakia. . . . 6-2/205. . . . Shoots right. . . . Name pronounced koo-CHAIR-uh.

TRANSACTIONS/CAREER NOTES: Selected by Chicago Blackhawks in fourth round (third Blackhawks pick, 77th overall) of NHL entry draft (June 21, 1986). . . . Pulled groin (March 20, 1993); missed 11 games.

Season Team	League	REGULAR SEASON					PLAYOFFS				
		Gms.	G	A	Pts.	Pen.	Gms.	G	A	Pts.	Pen.
85-86—Sparta Prague	Czech.	15	0	0	0	...	—	—	—	—	—
86-87—Sparta Prague	Czech.	33	7	2	9	...	—	—	—	—	—
87-88—Sparta Prague	Czech.	34	4	2	6	...	—	—	—	—	—
88-89—Dukla Jihlava	Czech.	45	10	9	19	...	—	—	—	—	—
89-90—Dukla Jihlava	Czech.	43	9	10	19	...	—	—	—	—	—
90-91—Indianapolis	IHL	35	8	19	27	23	7	0	1	1	15
—Chicago	NHL	40	2	12	14	32	—	—	—	—	—
91-92—Chicago	NHL	61	3	10	13	36	6	0	0	0	0
—Indianapolis	IHL	7	1	2	3	4	—	—	—	—	—
92-93—Chicago	NHL	71	5	14	19	59	—	—	—	—	—
NHL totals		172	10	36	46	127	6	0	0	0	0

KUDASHOV, ALEXEI
C, MAPLE LEAFS

PERSONAL: Born July 21, 1971, at Elekhrostal, U.S.S.R. . . . 6-0/180. . . . Shoots right.

TRANSACTIONS/CAREER NOTES: Selected by Toronto Maple Leafs in fifth round (third Maple Leafs pick, 102nd overall) of NHL entry draft (June 22, 1991).

Season Team	League	REGULAR SEASON					PLAYOFFS				
		Gms.	G	A	Pts.	Pen.	Gms.	G	A	Pts.	Pen.
90-91—Soviet Wings	USSR	45	9	5	14	10	—	—	—	—	—
91-92—Soviet Wings	CIS	36	8	16	24	12	—	—	—	—	—
92-93—Soviet Wings	CIS	41	8	20	28	24	7	1	3	4	4

KUDELSKI, BOB
RW, SENATORS

PERSONAL: Born March 3, 1964, at Springfield, Mass. . . . 6-1/200. . . . Shoots right. . . . Name pronounced kuh-DEHL-skee.

HIGH SCHOOL: Cathedral (Springfield, Mass.).

COLLEGE: Yale.

TRANSACTIONS/CAREER NOTES: Selected by Los Angeles Kings in NHL supplemental draft (September 17, 1986). . . . Broke knuckle on left hand (November 22, 1989); missed 15 games. . . . Strained medial collateral knee ligament (April 24, 1991). . . . Traded by Kings with C Shawn McCosh to Ottawa Senators for RW Jim Thomson and C Marc Fortier (December 20, 1992).

HONORS: Named to ECAC All-Star first team (1986-87).

Season Team	League	REGULAR SEASON					PLAYOFFS				
		Gms.	G	A	Pts.	Pen.	Gms.	G	A	Pts.	Pen.
83-84—Yale University	ECAC	21	14	12	26	12	—	—	—	—	—
84-85—Yale University	ECAC	32	21	23	44	38	—	—	—	—	—
85-86—Yale University	ECAC	31	18	23	41	48	—	—	—	—	—
86-87—Yale University	ECAC	30	25	22	47	34	—	—	—	—	—
87-88—New Haven	AHL	50	15	19	34	41	—	—	—	—	—
—Los Angeles	NHL	26	0	1	1	8	—	—	—	—	—
88-89—New Haven	AHL	60	32	19	51	43	17	8	5	13	12
—Los Angeles	NHL	14	1	3	4	17	—	—	—	—	—
89-90—Los Angeles	NHL	62	23	13	36	49	8	1	2	3	2
90-91—Los Angeles	NHL	72	23	13	36	46	8	3	2	5	2
91-92—Los Angeles	NHL	80	22	21	43	42	6	0	0	0	0
92-93—Los Angeles	NHL	15	3	3	6	8	—	—	—	—	—
—Ottawa	NHL	48	21	14	35	22	—	—	—	—	—
NHL totals		317	93	68	161	192	22	4	4	8	4

KUMMU, AL
D, FLYERS

PERSONAL: Born January 21, 1969, at Kitchener, Ont. . . . 6-4/195. . . . Shoots right. . . . Full name: Allen Arnold Kummu.

COLLEGE: Rensselaer Polytechnic Institute (N.Y.).

TRANSACTIONS/CAREER NOTES: Selected by Philadelphia Flyers in 10th round (eighth Flyers pick, 201st overall) of NHL entry draft (June 17, 1989).

HONORS: Named to ECAC All-Rookie team (1989-90).

Season	Team	League	Gms.	G	A	Pts.	Pen.	Gms.	G	A	Pts.	Pen.
88-89—Humboldt Jr. A		OPJHL	35	7	22	29	115	—	—	—	—	—
89-90—R.P.I.		ECAC	33	9	13	22	50	—	—	—	—	—
90-91—R.P.I.		ECAC	29	6	8	14	86	—	—	—	—	—
91-92—R.P.I.		ECAC	31	6	14	20	54	—	—	—	—	—
92-93—R.P.I.		ECAC	35	4	8	12	72	—	—	—	—	—

KUNTAR, LES
G, CANADIENS

PERSONAL: Born July 28, 1969, at Buffalo, N.Y. . . . 6-2/195. . . . Shoots left. . . . Full name: Leslie Steven Kuntar.
HIGH SCHOOL: Nichols School (Buffalo, N.Y.).
COLLEGE: St. Lawrence (N.Y.).
TRANSACTIONS/CAREER NOTES: Selected by Montreal Canadiens in sixth round (sixth Canadiens pick, 122nd overall) of NHL entry draft (June 13, 1987).
HONORS: Named to NCAA All-America East first team (1990-91). . . . Named to ECAC All-Star first team (1990-91).

					REGULAR SEASON						PLAYOFFS				
Season	Team	League	Gms.	Min.	W	L	T	GA	SO	Avg.	Gms.	Min.	W	L	GA	SO	Avg.
86-87—Nichols School	N.Y.H.S.	22	1585	...	......		56	3	2.12	—	—	—	—	—	—	—
87-88—St. Lawrence Univ.	ECAC	10	488	6	1	0	27	0	3.32	—	—	—	—	—	—
88-89—St. Lawrence Univ.	ECAC	14	786	11	2	0	31	0	2.37	—	—	—	—	—	—
89-90—St. Lawrence Univ.	ECAC	19	1076	7	11	1	76	1	4.24	—	—	—	—	—	—
90-91—St. Lawrence Univ.	ECAC	*33	*1794	*19	11	1	97	2	*3.24	—	—	—	—	—	—
91-92—Fredericton	AHL	11	638	7	3	0	26	0	2.45	—	—	—	—	—	—
—U.S. national team	Int'l	2	100	...	......		4	0	2.40	—	—	—	—	—	—
92-93—Fredericton	AHL	42	2315	16	14	7	130	0	3.37	1	64	0	1	6	0	5.63

KURRI, JARI
C/RW, KINGS

PERSONAL: Born May 18, 1960, at Helsinki, Finland. . . . 6-1/195. . . . Shoots right. . . . Name pronounced YAR-ee KUHR-ee.
TRANSACTIONS/CAREER NOTES: Selected by Edmonton Oilers in fourth round (third Oilers pick, 69th overall) of NHL entry draft (June 11, 1980). . . . Pulled groin (November 24, 1981). . . . Pulled groin muscle (January 1984); missed 16 games. . . . Sprained medial collateral ligament in left knee (February 12, 1989). . . . Signed two-year contract with Milan Devils of Italian Hockey League (July 30, 1990). . . . Injured knee (January 1991). . . . Rights traded by Oilers with RW Dave Brown and D Corey Foster to Philadelphia Flyers for RW Scott Mellanby, LW Craig Berube and C Craig Fisher (May 30, 1991). . . . Rights traded by Flyers to Los Angeles Kings for D Steve Duchesne, C Steve Kasper and fourth-round pick in 1991 draft (D Aris Brimanis) (May 30, 1991). . . . Sprained shoulder (November 12, 1991); missed three games. . . . Suffered from the flu (January 1992); missed two games.
HONORS: Named to NHL All-Star second team (1983-84, 1985-86 and 1988-89). . . . Played in NHL All-Star Game (1983, 1985, 1986, 1988 through 1990 and 1993). . . . Won Lady Byng Memorial Trophy (1984-85). . . . Named to THE SPORTING NEWS All-Star first team (1984-85). . . . Named to NHL All-Star first team (1984-85 and 1986-87). . . . Named to THE SPORTING NEWS All-Star second team (1985-86 and 1988-89).
RECORDS: Shares NHL career record for most overtime goals—7. . . . Shares NHL career playoff record for most three-or-more-goal games—7. . . . Holds NHL single-season playoff record for most three-or-more-goal games—4 (1985). . . . Shares NHL single-series playoff records for most goals—19 (1985); and most game-winning goals—5 (1987). . . . Holds NHL single-game playoff records for most goals—12 (1985); and most three-or-more-goal games—3 (1985). . . . Shares NHL single-game playoff records for most shorthanded goals—2 (April 24, 1983); most shorthanded goals in one period—2 (April 24, 1983); and most power-play goals—3 (April 9, 1987).
MISCELLANEOUS: Member of Stanley Cup championship teams (1984, 1985, 1987, 1988 and 1990).

					REGULAR SEASON						PLAYOFFS			
Season	Team	League	Gms.	G	A	Pts.	Pen.	Gms.	G	A	Pts.	Pen.
77-78—Jokerit	Finland	29	2	9	11	12	—	—	—	—	—
78-79—Jokerit	Finland	33	16	14	30	12	—	—	—	—	—
79-80—Jokerit	Finland	33	23	16	39	22	6	7	2	9	13
—Finland Olympic Team	Int'l	7	2	1	3	6	—	—	—	—	—
80-81—Edmonton	NHL	75	32	43	75	40	9	5	7	12	4
81-82—Edmonton	NHL	71	32	54	86	32	5	2	5	7	10
82-83—Edmonton	NHL	80	45	59	104	22	16	8	15	23	8
83-84—Edmonton	NHL	64	52	61	113	14	19	*14	14	28	13
84-85—Edmonton	NHL	73	71	64	135	30	18	*19	12	31	6
85-86—Edmonton	NHL	78	*68	63	131	22	10	2	10	12	4
86-87—Edmonton	NHL	79	54	54	108	41	21	*15	10	25	20
87-88—Edmonton	NHL	80	43	53	96	30	19	*14	17	31	12
88-89—Edmonton	NHL	76	44	58	102	69	7	3	5	8	6
89-90—Edmonton	NHL	78	33	60	93	48	22	10	15	25	18
90-91—Milan	Italy	40	37	60	97	8	10	10	12	22	2
91-92—Los Angeles	NHL	73	23	37	60	24	4	1	2	3	4
92-93—Los Angeles	NHL	82	27	60	87	38	24	9	8	17	12
NHL totals			909	524	666	1190	410	174	102	120	222	117

KURVERS, TOM
D, ISLANDERS

PERSONAL: Born September 14, 1962, at Minneapolis. . . . 6-1/197. . . . Shoots left. . . . Full name: Thomas James Kurvers.
COLLEGE: Minnesota-Duluth.
TRANSACTIONS/CAREER NOTES: Selected by Montreal Canadiens as underage player in seventh round (10th Canadiens pick, 145th overall) of NHL entry draft (June 10, 1981). . . . Suffered facial injuries (October 23, 1984); missed five games. . . . Traded by Canadiens to Buffalo Sabres for second-round pick in 1988 draft (LW Martin St. Amour) (November 18, 1986). . . . Traded by Sabres to New Jersey Devils for third-round pick in 1988 draft (LW Andrew MacVicar)

K

(June 13, 1987).... Fractured left index finger (November 1987).... Pulled groin (February 1988).... Injured right thumb (May 1988).... Pulled groin (November 17, 1988).... Traded by Devils to Toronto Maple Leafs for first-round pick in 1991 draft (D Scott Niedermayer) (October 16, 1989).... Injured knee (March 8, 1990).... Underwent arthroscopic knee surgery (November 15, 1990).... Traded by Maple Leafs to Canucks for C Brian Bradley (January 12, 1991).... Traded by Canucks to New York Islanders as part of three-way deal in which Minnesota North Stars sent D Dave Babych to Canucks and Islanders sent D Craig Ludwig to North Stars (June 22, 1991).

HONORS: Won Hobey Baker Memorial Trophy (1983-84).... Named to NCAA All-America West team (1983-84).... Named to WCHA All-Star first team (1983-84).

MISCELLANEOUS: Member of Stanley Cup championship team (1986).

			REGULAR SEASON					PLAYOFFS			
Season Team	League	Gms.	G	A	Pts.	Pen.	Gms.	G	A	Pts.	Pen.
80-81—Minnesota-Duluth..........	WCHA	39	6	24	30	48	—	—	—	—	—
81-82—Minnesota-Duluth..........	WCHA	37	11	31	42	18	—	—	—	—	—
82-83—Minnesota-Duluth..........	WCHA	45	8	36	44	42	—	—	—	—	—
83-84—Minnesota-Duluth..........	WCHA	43	18	58	76	46	—	—	—	—	—
84-85—Montreal........................	NHL	75	10	35	45	30	12	0	6	6	6
85-86—Montreal........................	NHL	62	7	23	30	36	—	—	—	—	—
86-87—Montreal........................	NHL	1	0	0	0	0	—	—	—	—	—
—Buffalo........................	NHL	55	6	17	23	24	—	—	—	—	—
87-88—New Jersey....................	NHL	56	5	29	34	46	19	6	9	15	38
88-89—New Jersey....................	NHL	74	16	50	66	38	—	—	—	—	—
89-90—New Jersey....................	NHL	1	0	0	0	0	—	—	—	—	—
—Toronto........................	NHL	70	15	37	52	29	5	0	3	3	4
90-91—Toronto........................	NHL	19	0	3	3	8	—	—	—	—	—
—Vancouver....................	NHL	32	4	23	27	20	6	2	2	4	12
91-92—New York Islanders..........	NHL	74	9	47	56	30	—	—	—	—	—
92-93—New York Islanders..........	NHL	52	8	30	38	38	12	0	2	2	6
—Capital District................	AHL	7	3	4	7	8	—	—	—	—	—
NHL totals.............................		**571**	**80**	**294**	**374**	**299**	**54**	**8**	**22**	**30**	**66**

KUSHNER, DALE

RW, FLYERS

PERSONAL: Born June 13, 1966, at Terrace, B.C.... 6-1/195.... Shoots left.... Name pronounced KUSH-nuhr.

TRANSACTIONS/CAREER NOTES: Signed as free agent by New York Islanders (March 1987). ... Suspended six games by AHL for leaving penalty box to fight (December 30, 1988).... Suspended eight games by AHL for leaving penalty box to fight (November 24, 1989).... Signed as free agent by Philadelphia Flyers (August 1, 1990).

HONORS: Named to Memorial Cup All-Star team (1986-87).

			REGULAR SEASON					PLAYOFFS			
Season Team	League	Gms.	G	A	Pts.	Pen.	Gms.	G	A	Pts.	Pen.
83-84—Fort McMurray................	AJHL	44	15	6	21	139	—	—	—	—	—
—Prince Albert..................	WHL	1	0	0	0	5	—	—	—	—	—
84-85—Prince Albert..................	WHL	2	0	0	0	2	—	—	—	—	—
—Moose Jaw....................	WHL	17	5	2	7	23	—	—	—	—	—
—Medicine Hat..................	WHL	48	23	17	40	173	10	3	3	6	18
85-86—Medicine Hat..................	WHL	66	25	19	44	218	25	0	5	5	*114
86-87—Medicine Hat..................	WHL	65	34	34	68	250	20	8	13	21	57
87-88—Springfield....................	AHL	68	13	23	36	201	—	—	—	—	—
88-89—Springfield....................	AHL	45	5	8	13	132	—	—	—	—	—
89-90—New York Islanders..........	NHL	2	0	0	0	2	—	—	—	—	—
—Springfield....................	AHL	45	14	11	25	163	7	2	3	5	61
90-91—Philadelphia..................	NHL	63	7	11	18	195	—	—	—	—	—
—Hershey........................	AHL	5	3	4	7	14	—	—	—	—	—
91-92—Hershey........................	AHL	46	9	7	16	98	6	0	2	2	23
—Philadelphia..................	NHL	19	3	2	5	18	—	—	—	—	—
92-93—Hershey........................	AHL	26	1	7	8	98	—	—	—	—	—
—Capital District................	AHL	7	0	1	1	29	2	1	0	1	29
NHL totals.............................		**84**	**10**	**13**	**23**	**215**					

KUWABARA, RYAN

RW/D, CANADIENS

PERSONAL: Born March 23, 1972, at Hamilton, Ont.... 6-0/205.... Shoots right.

TRANSACTIONS/CAREER NOTES: Selected by Montreal Canadiens in second round (second Canadiens pick, 39th overall) of NHL entry draft (June 16, 1990).

HONORS: Won Bobby Smith Trophy (1989-90).

			REGULAR SEASON					PLAYOFFS			
Season Team	League	Gms.	G	A	Pts.	Pen.	Gms.	G	A	Pts.	Pen.
88-89—Hamilton Jr. B	OHA	39	13	23	36	128	—	—	—	—	—
89-90—Ottawa...........................	OHL	66	30	38	68	62	4	0	0	0	0
90-91—Ottawa...........................	OHL	64	34	38	72	67	17	12	15	27	25
91-92—Ottawa...........................	OHL	66	43	57	100	84	10	6	5	11	9
92-93—Fredericton	AHL	10	0	2	2	4	—	—	—	—	—

KVARTALNOV, DMITRI

LW/RW, BRUINS

PERSONAL: Born March 25, 1966, at Voskresensk, U.S.S.R.... 5-11/180.... Shoots left.... Name pronounced kwahr-TAHL-nahf.

TRANSACTIONS/CAREER NOTES: Selected by Boston Bruins in first round (first Bruins pick, 16th overall) of NHL entry draft (June 20, 1992).... Suffered from strep throat (November 1992); missed three games. . . . Injured knee (February 1993); missed four games. . . . Injured wrist (March 1993); missed one game. . . . Suffered asthma attack (April 1993); missed one game.

HONORS: Won James Gatschene Memorial Trophy (1991-92). . . . Won Leo P. Lamoureux Memorial Trophy (1991-92). . . . Won Garry F. Longman Memorial Trophy (1991-92). . . . Named to IHL All-Star first team (1991-92).

			REGULAR SEASON					PLAYOFFS				
Season	Team	League	Gms.	G	A	Pts.	Pen.	Gms.	G	A	Pts.	Pen.
82-83	Khimik Voskresensk	USSR	7	0	0	0	0	—	—	—	—	—
83-84	Khimik Voskresensk	USSR	2	0	0	0	0	—	—	—	—	—
84-85	SKA MVO Kalinin	USSR				Statistics unavailable.						
85-86	SKA MVO Kalinin	USSR				Statistics unavailable.						
86-87	Khimik Voskresensk	USSR	40	11	6	17	28	—	—	—	—	—
87-88	Khimik Voskresensk	USSR	43	16	11	27	16	—	—	—	—	—
88-89	Khimik Voskresensk	USSR	44	20	12	32	18	—	—	—	—	—
89-90	Khimik Voskresensk	USSR	46	25	28	*53	33	—	—	—	—	—
90-91	Khimik Voskresensk	USSR	42	12	10	22	18	—	—	—	—	—
91-92	San Diego	IHL	77	*60	58	*118	16	4	2	0	2	2
92-93	Khimik Voskresensk	CIS	3	0	0	0	0	—	—	—	—	—
	Boston	NHL	73	30	42	72	16	4	0	0	0	0
	NHL totals		73	30	42	72	16	4	0	0	0	0

KYPREOS, NICK
RW, WHALERS

PERSONAL: Born June 4, 1966, at Toronto. . . . 6-0/195. . . . Shoots left. . . . Full name: Nicholas George Kypreos. . . . Name pronounced KIHP-ree-ohz.

TRANSACTIONS/CAREER NOTES: Signed as free agent by Philadelphia Flyers (September 30, 1984). . . . Underwent surgery to right knee (summer 1988); missed first 52 games of 1988-89 season. . . . Selected by Washington Capitals in NHL waiver draft for $20,000 (October 2, 1989). . . . Underwent surgery to right knee (February 8, 1990). . . . Traded by Capitals to Hartford Whalers for RW Mark Hunter and future considerations (June 15, 1992); Whalers sent LW Yvon Corriveau to Capitals to complete deal (August 20, 1992). . . . Suspended two games by NHL for game misconduct penalties (February 3, 1993). . . . Injured abdominal muscle (April 3, 1993); missed remainder of season.

HONORS: Named to OHL All-Star first team (1985-86). . . . Named to OHL All-Star second team (1986-87).

			REGULAR SEASON					PLAYOFFS				
Season	Team	League	Gms.	G	A	Pts.	Pen.	Gms.	G	A	Pts.	Pen.
83-84	North Bay	OHL	51	12	11	23	36	4	3	2	5	9
84-85	North Bay	OHL	64	41	36	77	71	8	2	2	4	15
85-86	North Bay	OHL	64	62	35	97	112	—	—	—	—	—
86-87	North Bay	OHL	46	49	41	90	54	24	11	5	16	78
	Hershey	AHL	10	0	1	1	4	—	—	—	—	—
87-88	Hershey	AHL	71	24	20	44	101	12	0	2	2	17
88-89	Hershey	AHL	28	12	15	27	19	12	4	5	9	11
89-90	Washington	NHL	31	5	4	9	82	7	1	0	1	15
	Baltimore	AHL	14	6	5	11	6	7	4	1	5	17
90-91	Washington	NHL	79	9	9	18	196	9	0	1	1	38
91-92	Washington	NHL	65	4	6	10	206	—	—	—	—	—
92-93	Hartford	NHL	75	17	10	27	325	—	—	—	—	—
	NHL totals		250	35	29	64	809	16	1	1	2	53

KYTE, JIM
D, SENATORS

PERSONAL: Born March 21, 1964, at Ottawa. . . . 6-5/220. . . . Shoots left.

TRANSACTIONS/CAREER NOTES: Broke left wrist (March 1980). . . . Selected by Winnipeg Jets as underage junior in first round (first Jets pick, 12th overall) of NHL entry draft (June 9, 1982). . . . Suffered stress fracture in lower back (February 1988). . . . Sprained shoulder (March 1989). . . . Traded by Jets with RW Andrew McBain and LW Randy Gilhen to Pittsburgh Penguins for C/LW Randy Cunneyworth, G Richard Tabaracci and RW Dave McLlwain (June 17, 1989). . . . Traded by Penguins to Calgary Flames for C Jiri Hrdina (December 13, 1990). . . . Fractured bone in left hand during preseason (September 1991). . . . Fractured right ankle (January 27, 1991); missed remainder of season. . . . Signed as free agent by Ottawa Senators (September 10, 1992).

			REGULAR SEASON					PLAYOFFS				
Season	Team	League	Gms.	G	A	Pts.	Pen.	Gms.	G	A	Pts.	Pen.
80-81	Hawkesbury	COJHL	42	2	24	26	133	—	—	—	—	—
81-82	Cornwall	OHL	52	4	13	17	148	5	0	0	0	10
82-83	Cornwall	OHL	65	6	30	36	195	8	0	2	2	24
	Winnipeg	NHL	2	0	0	0	0	—	—	—	—	—
83-84	Winnipeg	NHL	58	1	2	3	55	3	0	0	0	11
84-85	Winnipeg	NHL	71	0	3	3	111	8	0	0	0	14
85-86	Winnipeg	NHL	71	1	3	4	126	3	0	0	0	12
86-87	Winnipeg	NHL	72	5	5	10	162	10	0	4	4	36
87-88	Winnipeg	NHL	51	1	3	4	128	—	—	—	—	—
88-89	Winnipeg	NHL	74	3	9	12	190	—	—	—	—	—
89-90	Pittsburgh	NHL	56	3	1	4	125	—	—	—	—	—
90-91	Muskegon	IHL	25	2	5	7	157	—	—	—	—	—
	Pittsburgh	NHL	1	0	0	0	2	—	—	—	—	—
	Calgary	NHL	42	0	9	9	153	7	0	0	0	7
91-92	Calgary	NHL	21	0	1	1	107	—	—	—	—	—
	Salt Lake City	IHL	6	0	1	1	9	—	—	—	—	—
92-93	New Haven	AHL	63	6	18	24	163	—	—	—	—	—
	Ottawa	NHL	4	0	1	1	4	—	—	—	—	—
	NHL totals		523	14	37	51	1163	31	0	4	4	80

LABELLE, MARC
LW, PANTHERS

PERSONAL: Born December 20, 1969, at Maniwaki, Que. . . . 6-1/215. . . . Shoots left.
TRANSACTIONS/CAREER NOTES: Signed as free agent by Montreal Canadiens (January 21, 1991). . . . Signed as free agent by Ottawa Senators (August 6, 1992). . . . Selected by Florida Panthers in NHL expansion draft (June 24, 1993).

			REGULAR SEASON					PLAYOFFS				
Season	Team	League	Gms.	G	A	Pts.	Pen.	Gms.	G	A	Pts.	Pen.
87-88	Victoriaville	QMJHL	63	11	14	25	236	5	2	4	6	20
88-89	Victoriaville	QMJHL	62	9	26	35	202	5	6	3	9	30
89-90	Victoriaville	QMJHL	56	18	21	39	192	6	4	8	12	42
90-91	Fredericton	AHL	25	1	4	5	95	4	0	2	2	25
	Richmond	ECHL	5	1	1	2	37	—	—	—	—	—
91-92	Fredericton	AHL	62	7	10	17	238	3	0	0	0	6
92-93	New Haven	AHL	31	5	4	9	124	—	—	—	—	—
	San Diego	IHL	5	0	2	2	5	—	—	—	—	—
	Thunder Bay	Col.HL	9	0	5	5	17	7	0	1	1	11

LABRECQUE, PATRICK
G, NORDIQUES

PERSONAL: Born March 6, 1971, at Laval, Que. . . . 6-0/187.
TRANSACTIONS/CAREER NOTES: Selected by Quebec Nordiques in fifth round (fifth Nordiques pick, 90th overall) of NHL entry draft (June 22, 1991).

			REGULAR SEASON							PLAYOFFS						
Season	Team	League	Gms.	Min.	W	L	T	GA	SO	Avg.	Gms.	Min.	W	L	GA	SO	Avg.
89-90	St. Jean	QMJHL	48	2630	...	...	...	196	0	4.47	—	—	—	—	—	—	—
90-91	St. Jean	QMJHL	59	3375	...	...	...	216	1	3.84	—	—	—	—	—	—	—
91-92	Halifax	AHL	29	1570	5	12	8	114	0	4.36	—	—	—	—	—	—	—
92-93	Halifax	AHL	20	914	3	12	2	76	0	4.99	—	—	—	—	—	—	—
	Greensboro	ECHL	11	650	6	3	2	31	0	2.86	1	59	...	...	5	0	5.08

LACHANCE, BOB
RW, BLUES

PERSONAL: Born February 1, 1974, at North Hampton, Mass. . . . 5-11/175. . . . Shoots right.
COLLEGE: Boston University.
TRANSACTIONS/CAREER NOTES: Selected by St. Louis Blues in sixth round (fifth Blues pick, 134th overall) of NHL entry draft (June 20, 1992).

			REGULAR SEASON					PLAYOFFS				
Season	Team	League	Gms.	G	A	Pts.	Pen.	Gms.	G	A	Pts.	Pen.
91-92	Springfield Jr. B	NEJHL	46	40	98	138	87	—	—	—	—	—
92-93	Boston University	Hockey East	33	4	10	14	24	—	—	—	—	—

LACHANCE, SCOTT
D, ISLANDERS

PERSONAL: Born October 22, 1972, at Charlottesville, Va. . . . 6-2/197. . . . Shoots left. . . . Full name: Scott Joseph Lachance.
COLLEGE: Boston University.
TRANSACTIONS/CAREER NOTES: Selected by New York Islanders in first round (first Islanders pick, fourth overall) of NHL entry draft (June 22, 1991). . . . Sprained wrist (April 13, 1993); missed remainder of season. . . . Underwent wrist surgery (April 30, 1993).
HONORS: Named to Hockey East All-Rookie team (1990-91).

			REGULAR SEASON					PLAYOFFS				
Season	Team	League	Gms.	G	A	Pts.	Pen.	Gms.	G	A	Pts.	Pen.
88-89	Springfield Jr. B	NEJHL	36	8	28	36	20	—	—	—	—	—
89-90	Springfield Jr. B	NEJHL	34	25	41	66	62	—	—	—	—	—
90-91	Boston University	Hockey East	31	5	19	24	48	—	—	—	—	—
91-92	U.S. national team	Int'l	36	1	10	11	34	—	—	—	—	—
	U.S. Olympic Team	Int'l	8	0	1	1	6	—	—	—	—	—
	New York Islanders	NHL	17	1	4	5	9	—	—	—	—	—
92-93	New York Islanders	NHL	75	7	17	24	67	—	—	—	—	—
	NHL totals		92	8	21	29	76					

LACROIX, DANIEL
LW, RANGERS

PERSONAL: Born March 11, 1969, at Montreal. . . . 6-2/188. . . . Shoots left. . . . Name pronounced luh-KWAH.
TRANSACTIONS/CAREER NOTES: Selected as underage junior by New York Rangers in second round (second Rangers pick, 31st overall) of NHL entry draft (June 13, 1987).
HONORS: Won Marcel Robert Trophy (1988-89).

			REGULAR SEASON					PLAYOFFS				
Season	Team	League	Gms.	G	A	Pts.	Pen.	Gms.	G	A	Pts.	Pen.
86-87	Granby	QMJHL	54	9	16	25	311	8	1	2	3	22
87-88	Granby	QMJHL	58	24	50	74	468	5	0	4	4	12
88-89	Granby	QMJHL	70	45	49	94	320	4	1	1	2	57
	Denver	IHL	2	0	1	1	0	2	0	1	1	0
89-90	Flint	IHL	61	12	16	28	128	4	2	0	2	24
90-91	Binghamton	AHL	54	7	12	19	237	5	1	0	1	24
91-92	Binghamton	AHL	52	12	20	32	149	11	2	4	6	28
92-93	Binghamton	AHL	73	21	22	43	255	—	—	—	—	—

LADOUCEUR, RANDY

D, MIGHTY DUCKS

PERSONAL: Born June 30, 1960, at Brockville, Ont. . . . 6-2/220. . . . Shoots left. . . . Name pronounced LAD-uh-SOOR.
TRANSACTIONS/CAREER NOTES: Signed as free agent by Detroit Red Wings (November 1, 1979). . . . Suffered back spasms (March 1986). . . . Traded by Red Wings to Hartford Whalers for C Dave Barr (January 12, 1987). . . . Sprained right knee (March 1990). . . . Sprained knee (January 10, 1991); missed 10 games. . . . Bruised knee (October 28, 1992); missed one game. . . . Suffered right elbow infection (December 8, 1992); missed three games. . . . Suffered right foot contusion (March 3, 1993); missed two games. . . . Selected by Mighty Ducks of Anaheim in NHL expansion draft (June 24, 1993).

			REGULAR SEASON					PLAYOFFS				
Season Team	League	Gms.	G	A	Pts.	Pen.	Gms.	G	A	Pts.	Pen.
78-79—Brantford	OMJHL	64	3	17	20	141	—	—	—	—	—
79-80—Brantford	OMJHL	37	6	15	21	125	8	0	5	5	18
80-81—Kalamazoo	IHL	80	7	30	37	52	8	1	3	4	10
81-82—Adirondack	AHL	78	4	28	32	78	5	1	1	2	6
82-83—Adirondack	AHL	48	11	21	32	54	—	—	—	—	—
—Detroit	NHL	27	0	4	4	16	—	—	—	—	—
83-84—Adirondack	AHL	11	3	5	8	12	—	—	—	—	—
—Detroit	NHL	71	3	17	20	58	4	1	0	1	6
84-85—Detroit	NHL	80	3	27	30	108	3	1	0	1	0
85-86—Detroit	NHL	78	5	13	18	196	—	—	—	—	—
86-87—Detroit	NHL	34	3	6	9	70	—	—	—	—	—
—Hartford	NHL	36	2	3	5	51	6	0	2	2	12
87-88—Hartford	NHL	68	1	7	8	91	6	1	1	2	4
88-89—Hartford	NHL	75	2	5	7	95	1	0	0	0	10
89-90—Hartford	NHL	71	3	12	15	126	7	1	0	1	10
90-91—Hartford	NHL	67	1	3	4	118	6	1	4	5	6
91-92—Hartford	NHL	74	1	9	10	127	7	0	1	1	11
92-93—Hartford	NHL	62	2	4	6	109	—	—	—	—	—
NHL totals		743	26	110	136	1165	40	5	8	13	59

LAFAYETTE, NATHAN

C, BLUES

PERSONAL: Born February 17, 1973, at New Westminster, B.C. . . . 6-1/194. . . . Shoots right. . . . Name pronounced LAH-FAY-EHT.
TRANSACTIONS/CAREER NOTES: Traded by Kingston Fronenacs with Joel Sandie to Cornwall Royals for D Rod Pasma and Shawn Caplice (January 6, 1991). . . . Selected by St. Louis Blues in third round (third Blues pick, 65th overall) of NHL entry draft (June 22, 1991).
HONORS: Won Can.HL Scholastic Player of the Year Award (1991-92). . . . Won Bobby Smith Trophy (1990-91 and 1991-92).

			REGULAR SEASON					PLAYOFFS				
Season Team	League	Gms.	G	A	Pts.	Pen.	Gms.	G	A	Pts.	Pen.
89-90—Kingston	OHL	53	6	8	14	14	7	0	1	1	0
90-91—Kingston	OHL	35	13	13	26	10	—	—	—	—	—
—Cornwall	OHL	28	16	22	38	25	—	—	—	—	—
91-92—Cornwall	OHL	66	28	45	73	26	6	2	5	7	16
92-93—Newmarket	OHL	58	49	38	87	26	7	4	6	10	19

LaFONTAINE, PAT

C, SABRES

PERSONAL: Born February 22, 1965, at St. Louis. . . . 5-10/177. . . . Shoots right. . . . Name pronounced luh-FAHN-tayn.
TRANSACTIONS/CAREER NOTES: Selected by New York Islanders as underage junior in first round (first Islanders pick, third overall) of NHL entry draft (June 8, 1983). . . . Damaged ligaments in left knee (August 16, 1984). . . . Suffered from mononucleosis (January 1985). . . . Separated right shoulder (January 25, 1986). . . . Bruised knee (March 1988). . . . Broke nose (October 7, 1988); played entire season with injury. . . . Sprained ligaments in right wrist (November 5, 1988). . . . Strained left hamstring (October 13, 1990); missed three games. . . . Traded by Islanders with LW Randy Wood, D Randy Hillier and future considerations to Buffalo Sabres for C Pierre Turgeon, RW Benoit Hogue, D Uwe Krupp and C Dave McLlwain; Sabres later received fourth-round pick in 1992 draft (D Dean Melanson) (October 25, 1991). . . . Fractured jaw (November 16, 1991); missed 13 games.
HONORS: Won Can.HL Player of the Year Award (1982-83). . . . Won Michel Briere Trophy (1982-83). . . . Won Jean Beliveau Trophy (1982-83). . . . Won Frank J. Selke Trophy (1982-83). . . . Won Des Instructeurs Trophy (1982-83). . . . Won Guy Lafleur Trophy (1982-83). . . . Named to QMJHL All-Star first team (1982-83). . . . Played in NHL All-Star Game (1988 through 1991 and 1993). . . . Won Dodge Performer of the Year Award (1989-90). . . . Named to THE SPORTING NEWS All-Star second team (1989-90). . . . Named to NHL All-Star second team (1992-93).
RECORDS: Holds NHL playoff record for fastest two goals from the start of a period—35 seconds (May 19, 1984).

			REGULAR SEASON					PLAYOFFS				
Season Team	League	Gms.	G	A	Pts.	Pen.	Gms.	G	A	Pts.	Pen.
82-83—Verdun	QMJHL	70	*104	*130	*234	10	15	11	*24	*35	4
83-84—U.S. national team	Int'l	58	56	55	111	22	—	—	—	—	—
—U.S. Olympic Team	Int'l	6	5	3	8	0	—	—	—	—	—
—New York Islanders	NHL	15	13	6	19	6	16	3	6	9	8
84-85—New York Islanders	NHL	67	19	35	54	32	9	1	2	3	4
85-86—New York Islanders	NHL	65	30	23	53	43	3	1	0	1	0
86-87—New York Islanders	NHL	80	38	32	70	70	14	5	7	12	10
87-88—New York Islanders	NHL	75	47	45	92	52	6	4	5	9	8
88-89—New York Islanders	NHL	79	45	43	88	26	—	—	—	—	—
89-90—New York Islanders	NHL	74	54	51	105	38	2	0	1	1	0
90-91—New York Islanders	NHL	75	41	44	85	42	—	—	—	—	—
91-92—Buffalo	NHL	57	46	47	93	98	7	8	3	11	4
92-93—Buffalo	NHL	84	53	95	148	63	7	2	10	12	0
NHL totals		671	386	421	807	470	64	24	34	58	34

LAFORGE, MARC
RW/D, OILERS

PERSONAL: Born January 3, 1968, at Sudbury, Ont. . . . 6-2/210. . . . Shoots left.
TRANSACTIONS/CAREER NOTES: Selected by Hartford Whalers as underage junior in second round (second Whalers pick, 32nd overall) of NHL entry draft (June 21, 1986). . . . Suspended nine games by OHL (October 1986). . . . Suspended two years by OHL for attacking several members of opposing team in game-ending fight (November 6, 1987). . . . Suspended three games by AHL for head-butting (November 26, 1988). . . . Suspended six games for leaving bench to start fight (December 8, 1988). . . . Suspended by Whalers for refusing to report to Indianapolis (December 28, 1988). . . . Whalers lifted suspension when he reported to Indianapolis (January 19, 1989). . . . Suffered sore back (November 1989). . . . Suspended five games by AHL for head-butting (February 5, 1990). . . . Traded by Whalers to Edmonton Oilers for rights to D Cam Brauer (March 6, 1990). . . . Suspended 10 games by AHL for cross-checking and kneeing (December 3, 1990). . . . Suspended 10 games by AHL for cross-checking (January 13, 1991). . . . Suspended six games by AHL for leaving the bench to start fight (February 1991). . . . Suspended 10 games by NHL (September 26, 1991).

			REGULAR SEASON					PLAYOFFS				
Season	Team	League	Gms.	G	A	Pts.	Pen.	Gms.	G	A	Pts.	Pen.
84-85—Kingston		OHL	57	1	5	6	214	—	—	—	—	—
85-86—Kingston		OHL	60	1	13	14	248	10	0	1	1	30
86-87—Kingston		OHL	53	2	10	12	224	12	1	0	1	79
—Binghamton		AHL	—	—	—	—	—	4	0	0	0	7
87-88—Sudbury		OHL	14	0	2	2	68	—	—	—	—	—
88-89—Indianapolis		IHL	14	0	2	2	138	—	—	—	—	—
—Binghamton		AHL	38	2	2	4	179	—	—	—	—	—
89-90—Hartford		NHL	9	0	0	0	43	—	—	—	—	—
—Binghamton		AHL	25	2	6	8	111	—	—	—	—	—
—Cape Breton		AHL	3	0	1	1	24	3	0	0	0	27
90-91—Cape Breton		AHL	49	1	7	8	217	—	—	—	—	—
91-92—Cape Breton		AHL	59	0	14	14	341	4	0	0	0	24
92-93—Cape Breton		AHL	77	1	12	13	208	15	1	2	3	*78
NHL totals			9	0	0	0	43					

LaFRANCE, DARRYL
C, FLAMES

PERSONAL: Born March 20, 1974, at Sudbury, Ont. . . . 5-11/175. . . . Shoots right.
HIGH SCHOOL: Henry Street (Whitby, Ont.).
TRANSACTIONS/CAREER NOTES: Selected by Calgary Flames in fifth round (sixth Flames pick, 121st overall) of NHL entry draft (June 26, 1993).

			REGULAR SEASON					PLAYOFFS				
Season	Team	League	Gms.	G	A	Pts.	Pen.	Gms.	G	A	Pts.	Pen.
91-92—Oshawa		OHL	48	12	20	32	24	7	0	1	1	2
92-93—Oshawa		OHL	66	35	51	86	24	13	8	8	16	0

LAFRENIERE, JASON
C, LIGHTNING

PERSONAL: Born December 6, 1966, at St. Catharines, Ont. . . . 5-11/185. . . . Shoots right. . . . Name pronounced la-FREHN-yair.
TRANSACTIONS/CAREER NOTES: Selected by Quebec Nordiques as underage junior in second round (second Nordiques pick, 36th overall) of NHL entry draft (June 15, 1985). . . . Traded by Hamilton Steelhawks with RW Peter Choma, G Steve Norkaitis and D Lawrence Hinch to Belleville Bulls for D Shane Doyle, RW John Purves, LW Niels Jensen and D Brian Hoard (November 1985). . . . Traded by Nordiques with D Norman Rochefort to New York Rangers for C Walt Poddubny, D Bruce Bell, D Jari Gronstrand and fourth-round pick in 1989 draft (D Eric DuBois) (August 1, 1988). . . . Signed as free agent by Tampa Bay Lightning (July 29, 1992).
HONORS: Won William Hanley Trophy (1985-86). . . . Named to OHL All-Star first team (1985-86).

			REGULAR SEASON					PLAYOFFS				
Season	Team	League	Gms.	G	A	Pts.	Pen.	Gms.	G	A	Pts.	Pen.
83-84—Brantford		OHL	70	24	57	81	4	6	2	4	6	2
84-85—Hamilton		OHL	59	26	69	95	10	17	12	16	28	0
85-86—Hamilton		OHL	14	12	10	22	2	—	—	—	—	—
—Belleville		OHL	48	37	73	110	2	23	10	22	32	6
86-87—Quebec		NHL	56	13	15	28	8	12	1	5	6	2
—Fredericton		AHL	11	3	11	14	0	—	—	—	—	—
87-88—Quebec		NHL	40	10	19	29	4	—	—	—	—	—
—Fredericton		AHL	32	12	19	31	38	—	—	—	—	—
88-89—New York Rangers		NHL	38	8	16	24	6	3	0	0	0	17
—Denver		IHL	24	10	19	29	17	—	—	—	—	—
89-90—Flint		IHL	41	9	25	34	34	—	—	—	—	—
—Phoenix		IHL	14	4	9	13	0	—	—	—	—	—
90-91—Canadian national team		Int'l	59	26	33	59	50	—	—	—	—	—
91-92—San Diego		IHL	5	1	2	3	2	—	—	—	—	—
—Landshut		Germany	23	7	22	29	16	—	—	—	—	—
92-93—Atlanta		IHL	63	23	47	70	34	9	3	4	7	22
—Tampa Bay		NHL	11	3	3	6	4	—	—	—	—	—
NHL totals			145	34	53	87	22	15	1	5	6	19

LaGRAND, SCOTT
G, FLYERS

PERSONAL: Born February 11, 1970, at Potsdam, N.Y. . . . 6-1/170. . . . Shoots right.
HIGH SCHOOL: Hotchkiss (Lakeville, Conn.).
COLLEGE: Boston College.
TRANSACTIONS/CAREER NOTES: Selected by Philadelphia Flyers in fourth round (fifth Flyers pick, 77th overall) of NHL entry draft (June 11, 1988).
HONORS: Named to Hockey East All-Star first team (1990-91). . . . Named to NCAA All-America East second team (1991-92).

Season	Team	League	Gms.	Min.	W	L	T	GA	SO	Avg.	Gms.	Min.	W	L	GA	SO	Avg.
86-87—Hotchkiss	N.Y. H.S.	17	1020	...	...	...	36	0	2.12	—	—	—	—	—	—	—
87-88—Hotchkiss	N.Y. H.S.			Statistics unavailable.													
88-89—Hotchkiss	N.Y. H.S.			Statistics unavailable.													
89-90—Boston College	Hoc. East	24	1268	17	4	0	57	0	2.70	7	377	5	1	17	0	2.71
90-91—Boston College	Hoc. East	12	557	7	2	0	39	0	4.20	—	—	—	—	—	—	—
91-92—Boston College	Hoc. East	30	1750	11	16	2	108	1	3.70	—	—	—	—	—	—	—
92-93—Hershey	AHL	32	1854	8	17	4	145	0	4.69	—	—	—	—	—	—	—

LALIME, PATRICK
G, PENGUINS

PERSONAL: Born July 7, 1974, at St. Bonaventure, Que.... 6-2/165.... Shoots left.
TRANSACTIONS/CAREER NOTES: Selected by Pittsburgh Penguins in sixth round (sixth Penguins pick, 156th overall) of NHL entry draft (June 26, 1993).

Season	Team	League	Gms.	Min.	W	L	T	GA	SO	Avg.	Gms.	Min.	W	L	GA	SO	Avg.
92-93—Shawinigan	QMJHL	44	2467	10	24	4	192	0	4.67	—	—	—	—	—	—	—

LALOR, MIKE
D, JETS

PERSONAL: Born March 8, 1963, at Fort Erie, Ont.... 6-0/190.... Shoots left.... Full name: John Michael Lalor.... Name pronounced LAH-luhr.
TRANSACTIONS/CAREER NOTES: Signed as free agent by Montreal Canadiens (September 1983). ... Suffered from bursitis in right ankle (September 1987).... Suffered stress fracture of left ankle (November 1, 1988).... Traded by Canadiens to St. Louis Blues for the option to flip first-round picks in 1990 draft and second- or third-round picks in 1991 draft (January 16, 1989).... Traded by Blues with C Peter Zezel to Washington Capitals for LW Geoff Courtnall (July 13, 1990).... Traded by Capitals to Winnipeg Jets for RW Paul MacDermid (March 2, 1992).... Broke finger (November 12, 1992); missed 13 games.... Strained neck (January 8, 1993); missed one game.... Suffered rib contusion (March 23, 1993); missed two games.
MISCELLANEOUS: Member of Stanley Cup championship team (1986).

Season	Team	League	Gms.	G	A	Pts.	Pen.	Gms.	G	A	Pts.	Pen.
81-82—Brantford	OHL	64	3	13	16	114	11	0	6	6	11
82-83—Brantford	OHL	65	10	30	40	113	6	1	3	4	20
83-84—Nova Scotia	AHL	67	5	11	16	80	12	0	2	2	13
84-85—Sherbrooke	AHL	79	9	23	32	114	17	3	5	8	36
85-86—Montreal	NHL	62	3	5	8	56	17	1	2	3	29
86-87—Montreal	NHL	57	0	10	10	47	13	2	1	3	29
87-88—Montreal	NHL	66	1	10	11	113	11	0	0	0	11
88-89—Montreal	NHL	12	1	4	5	15	—	—	—	—	—
—St. Louis	NHL	36	1	14	15	54	10	1	1	2	14
89-90—St. Louis	NHL	78	0	16	16	81	12	0	2	2	31
90-91—Washington	NHL	68	1	5	6	61	10	1	2	3	22
91-92—Washington	NHL	64	5	7	12	64	—	—	—	—	—
—Winnipeg	NHL	15	2	3	5	14	7	0	0	0	19
92-93—Winnipeg	NHL	64	1	8	9	76	4	0	2	2	4
NHL totals		522	15	82	97	581	84	5	10	15	159

LAMB, MARK
C, SENATORS

PERSONAL: Born August 3, 1964, at Swift Current, Sask.... 5-9/180.... Shoots left.
HIGH SCHOOL: Swift Current (Sask.).
TRANSACTIONS/CAREER NOTES: Selected by Calgary Flames as underage junior in fourth round (fifth Flames pick, 72nd overall) of NHL entry draft (June 9, 1982).... Refused to dress for a game after Nanaimo Islanders released coach Les Calder; asked to be traded (December 1982).... Traded by Islanders to Medicine Hat Tigers for Glen Kulka and G Daryl Reaugh (December 1982).... Signed as free agent by Detroit Red Wings (July 1, 1986).... Selected by Edmonton Oilers in NHL waiver draft (October 5, 1987).... Pinched nerve in neck (October 21, 1990). ... Selected by Ottawa Senators in NHL expansion draft (June 18, 1992).... Suffered sore foot (October 24, 1992); missed two games.... Injured neck (December 17, 1992); missed 10 games.
HONORS: Won Frank Boucher Memorial Trophy (1983-84).... Named to WHL (East) All-Star first team (1983-84).
MISCELLANEOUS: Member of Stanley Cup championship team (1990).

Season	Team	League	Gms.	G	A	Pts.	Pen.	Gms.	G	A	Pts.	Pen.
80-81—Billings	WHL	24	1	8	9	12	—	—	—	—	—
81-82—Billings	WHL	72	45	56	101	46	5	4	6	10	4
82-83—Nanaimo	WHL	30	14	37	51	16	—	—	—	—	—
—Medicine Hat	WHL	46	22	43	65	33	5	3	2	5	4
—Colorado	CHL	—	—	—	—	—	6	0	2	2	0
83-84—Medicine Hat	WHL	72	59	77	136	30	14	12	11	23	6
84-85—Moncton	AHL	80	23	49	72	53	—	—	—	—	—
—Medicine Hat	WHL	—	—	—	—	—	6	3	2	5	2
85-86—Calgary	NHL	1	0	0	0	0	—	—	—	—	—
—Moncton	AHL	79	26	50	76	51	10	2	6	8	17
86-87—Detroit	NHL	22	2	1	3	8	11	0	0	0	11
—Adirondack	AHL	49	14	36	50	45	—	—	—	—	—
87-88—Nova Scotia	AHL	69	27	61	88	45	5	0	5	5	6
—Edmonton	NHL	2	0	0	0	0	—	—	—	—	—
88-89—Cape Breton	AHL	54	33	49	82	29	—	—	—	—	—
—Edmonton	NHL	20	2	8	10	14	6	0	2	2	8

Season Team	League	REGULAR SEASON					PLAYOFFS				
		Gms.	G	A	Pts.	Pen.	Gms.	G	A	Pts.	Pen.
89-90—Edmonton	NHL	58	12	16	28	42	22	6	11	17	2
90-91—Edmonton	NHL	37	4	8	12	25	15	0	5	5	20
91-92—Edmonton	NHL	59	6	22	28	46	16	1	1	2	10
92-93—Ottawa	NHL	71	7	19	26	64	—	—	—	—	—
NHL totals		270	33	74	107	199	70	7	19	26	51

LAMBERT, DAN
D, JETS

PERSONAL: Born January 12, 1970, at St. Boniface, Man. . . . 5-8/177. . . . Shoots left. . . . Name pronounced lam-BAIR.
TRANSACTIONS/CAREER NOTES: Selected by Quebec Nordiques in sixth round (eighth Nordiques pick, 106th overall) of NHL entry draft (June 17, 1989). . . . Suffered facial paralysis (December 4, 1991); missed two games. . . . Traded by Nordiques to Winnipeg Jets for D Shawn Cronin (August 25, 1992).
HONORS: Won Bill Hunter Trophy (1988-89). . . . Named to WHL (East) All-Star first team (1988-89 and 1989-90). . . . Named to Memorial Cup All-Star team (1988-89).

Season Team	League	REGULAR SEASON					PLAYOFFS				
		Gms.	G	A	Pts.	Pen.	Gms.	G	A	Pts.	Pen.
86-87—Swift Current	WHL	68	13	53	66	95	4	1	1	2	9
87-88—Swift Current	WHL	69	20	63	83	120	10	2	10	12	45
88-89—Swift Current	WHL	57	25	77	102	158	12	9	19	28	12
89-90—Swift Current	WHL	50	17	51	68	119	4	2	3	5	12
90-91—Fort Wayne	IHL	49	10	27	37	65	19	4	10	14	20
—Halifax	AHL	30	7	13	20	20	—	—	—	—	—
—Quebec	NHL	1	0	0	0	0	—	—	—	—	—
91-92—Halifax	AHL	47	3	28	31	33	—	—	—	—	—
—Quebec	NHL	28	6	9	15	22	—	—	—	—	—
92-93—Moncton	AHL	73	11	30	41	100	5	1	2	3	2
NHL totals		29	6	9	15	22					

LAMOTHE, MARC
G, CANADIENS

PERSONAL: Born February 27, 1974, at New Liskeard, Ont. . . . 6-2/186. . . . Shoots left.
TRANSACTIONS/CAREER NOTES: Selected by Montreal Canadiens in fourth round (sixth Canadiens pick, 92nd overall) of NHL entry draft (June 20, 1992).

Season Team	League	REGULAR SEASON							PLAYOFFS					
		Gms.	Min.	W	L	T	GA	SO	Avg.	Gms.	Min.	W	L	GA SO	Avg.
90-91—Ottawa	OHA Mj Jr.A	25	1220	...	...	...	82	1	4.03	—	—	—	—	— —	—
91-92—Kingston	OHL	42	2378	10	25	2	189	1	4.77	—	—	—	—	— —	—
92-93—Kingston	OHL	45	2489	...	...	...	162	†1	3.91	15	733	...	...	46 †1	3.77

LANG, CHAD
G, STARS

PERSONAL: Born February 11, 1975, at Newmarket, Ont. . . . 5-10/188. . . . Shoots left. . . . Cousin of Gerard Gallant, left winger, Detroit Red Wings.
TRANSACTIONS/CAREER NOTES: Selected by Dallas Stars in fourth round (third Stars pick, 87th overall) of NHL entry draft (June 26, 1993).
HONORS: Shared Dave Pinkney Trophy with Ryan Douglas (1992-93). . . . Named to OHL All-Star second team (1992-93).

Season Team	League	REGULAR SEASON							PLAYOFFS					
		Gms.	Min.	W	L	T	GA	SO	Avg.	Gms.	Min.	W	L	GA SO	Avg.
90-91—Newmarket	Jr. B	34	1733	...	...	...	149	1	5.16	—	—	—	—	— —	—
91-92—Peterborough	OHL	16	886	...	...	...	63	0	4.27	2	65	...	...	9 0	8.31
92-93—Peterborough	OHL	43	2554	...	...	...	140	1	3.29	21	1224	...	...	74 1	3.63

LANG, ROBERT
C, KINGS

PERSONAL: Born December 19, 1970, at Teplice, Czechoslovakia. . . . 6-2/180. . . . Shoots right.
TRANSACTIONS/CAREER NOTES: Selected by Los Angeles Kings in seventh round (sixth Kings pick, 133rd overall) of NHL entry draft (June 16, 1990).

Season Team	League	REGULAR SEASON					PLAYOFFS				
		Gms.	G	A	Pts.	Pen.	Gms.	G	A	Pts.	Pen.
89-90—Litvinov	Czech.	39	11	10	21	20	—	—	—	—	—
90-91—Litvinov	Czech.	48	24	22	46	38	—	—	—	—	—
91-92—Litvinov	Czech.	43	12	31	43	34	—	—	—	—	—
—Czech. national team	Int'l	8	5	8	13	8	—	—	—	—	—
92-93—Los Angeles	NHL	11	0	5	5	2	—	—	—	—	—
—Phoenix	IHL	38	9	21	30	20	—	—	—	—	—
NHL totals		11	0	5	5	2					

LANGENBRUNNER, JAMIE
C, STARS

PERSONAL: Born April 21, 1975, at Edmonton, Alta. . . . 5-11/170. . . . Shoots right.
HIGH SCHOOL: Cloquet (Minn.).
TRANSACTIONS/CAREER NOTES: Selected by Dallas Stars in second round (second Stars pick, 35th overall) of NHL entry draft (June 26, 1993).

Season Team	League	REGULAR SEASON					PLAYOFFS				
		Gms.	G	A	Pts.	Pen.	Gms.	G	A	Pts.	Pen.
90-91—Cloquet H.S.	Minn. H.S.	20	6	16	22	8	—	—	—	—	—
91-92—Cloquet H.S.	Minn. H.S.	23	16	23	39	24	—	—	—	—	—
92-93—Cloquet H.S.	Minn. H.S.	27	27	62	89	18	—	—	—	—	—

LANGKOW, SCOTT
G, JETS

PERSONAL: Born April 21, 1975, at Edmonton, Alta.... 5-11/180.... Shoots left.
HIGH SCHOOL: Aloha (Beaverton, Oregon).
TRANSACTIONS/CAREER NOTES: Selected by Winnipeg Jets in second round (second Jets pick, 31st overall) of NHL entry draft (June 26, 1993).

			REGULAR SEASON								PLAYOFFS						
Season Team	League	Gms.	Min.	W	L	T	GA	SO	Avg.	Gms.	Min.	W	L	GA	SO	Avg.
91-92—Portland	WHL	1	33	...	... ...	...	2	...	3.64	—	—	—	—	—	—	—
92-93—Portland	WHL	34	2064	...	... ...	...	119	...	3.46	9	535	...	...	31	0	3.48

LANGWAY, ROD
D

PERSONAL: Born May 3, 1957, at Maag, Formosa.... 6-3/225.... Shoots left.... Full name: Rod Corry Langway.
COLLEGE: New Hampshire.
TRANSACTIONS/CAREER NOTES: Bruised left foot (January 5, 1982).... Selected by Montreal Canadiens from University of New Hampshire in second round (third Canadiens pick, 36th overall) of NHL amateur draft (June 14, 1977).... Selected by Birmingham Bulls in WHA amateur draft (May 1977).... Signed as free agent by Canadiens (October 1978).... Injured left knee (February 9, 1982).... Traded by Canadiens with D Brian Engblom, C Doug Jarvis and RW Craig Laughlin to Washington Capitals for LW Ryan Walter and D Rick Green (September 9, 1982).... Bruised right knee (October 23, 1985); missed eight games.... Ruptured disc in back (November 1987).... Pulled thigh muscle (February 1988). ... Bruised thigh (April 1988).... Bruised left knee (November 1988).... Strained left knee ligaments (October 7, 1989); missed six games.... Underwent surgery to both knees (December 23, 1989); missed 10 games.... Suffered back spasms (January 11, 1991); missed 18 games.... Suffered slight concussion (November 13, 1991); missed two games.... Fractured two toes on left foot (December 5, 1991); missed eight games.... Injured groin (March 20, 1992); missed five games.... Underwent knee and shoulder surgery (November 20, 1992); missed 30 games.... Announced he would not play for remainder of 1992-93 season (March 12, 1993).... Released by Capitals (June 28, 1993).
HONORS: Played in NHL All-Star Game (1981 through 1986).... Won James Norris Memorial Trophy (1982-83 and 1983-84). ... Named to THE SPORTING NEWS All-Star first team (1982-83 and 1983-84).... Named to NHL All-Star first team (1982-83 and 1983-84).... Named to THE SPORTING NEWS All-Star second team (1984-85).... Named to NHL All-Star second team (1984-85).
MISCELLANEOUS: Does not wear a helmet.... Member of Stanley Cup championship team (1979).

		REGULAR SEASON					PLAYOFFS				
Season Team	League	Gms.	G	A	Pts.	Pen.	Gms.	G	A	Pts.	Pen.
75-76—Univ. of New Hampshire	ECAC				Statistics unavailable.						
76-77—Univ. of New Hampshire	ECAC	34	10	43	53	52	—	—	—	—	—
77-78—Hampton	AHL	30	6	16	22	50	—	—	—	—	—
—Birmingham	WHA	52	3	18	21	52	4	0	0	0	9
78-79—Montreal	NHL	45	3	4	7	30	8	0	0	0	16
—Nova Scotia	AHL	18	6	13	19	29	—	—	—	—	—
79-80—Montreal	NHL	77	7	29	36	81	10	3	3	6	2
80-81—Montreal	NHL	80	11	34	45	120	3	0	0	0	6
81-82—Montreal	NHL	66	5	34	39	116	5	0	3	3	18
82-83—Washington	NHL	80	3	29	32	75	4	0	0	0	0
83-84—Washington	NHL	80	9	24	33	61	8	0	5	5	7
84-85—Washington	NHL	79	4	22	26	54	5	0	1	1	6
85-86—Washington	NHL	71	1	17	18	61	9	1	2	3	6
86-87—Washington	NHL	78	2	25	27	53	7	0	1	1	2
87-88—Washington	NHL	63	3	13	16	28	6	0	0	0	8
88-89—Washington	NHL	76	2	19	21	67	6	0	0	0	6
89-90—Washington	NHL	58	0	8	8	39	15	1	4	5	12
90-91—Washington	NHL	56	1	7	8	24	11	0	2	2	6
91-92—Washington	NHL	64	0	13	13	22	7	0	1	1	2
92-93—Washington	NHL	21	0	0	0	20	—	—	—	—	—
WHA totals		52	3	18	21	52	4	0	0	0	9
NHL totals		994	51	278	329	851	104	5	22	27	97

L

LANK, JEFF
D, CANADIENS

PERSONAL: Born March 1, 1975, at Indianhead, Sask.... 6-3/185.... Shoots left.
HIGH SCHOOL: Carlton Comprehensive (Prince Albert, Sask.).
TRANSACTIONS/CAREER NOTES: Selected by Montreal Canadiens in fifth round (sixth Canadiens pick, 113th overall) of NHL entry draft (June 26, 1993).

		REGULAR SEASON					PLAYOFFS				
Season Team	League	Gms.	G	A	Pts.	Pen.	Gms.	G	A	Pts.	Pen.
90-91—Columbia Valley	KIJHL	36	4	28	32	40	—	—	—	—	—
91-92—Prince Albert	WHL	56	2	8	10	26	9	0	0	0	2
92-93—Prince Albert	WHL	63	1	11	12	60	—	—	—	—	—

LAPERRIERE, DAN
D, BLUES

PERSONAL: Born March 28, 1969, at Laval, Que.... 6-1/180.... Shoots left.... Full name: Daniel Jacques Laperriere.... Name pronounced luh-PAIR-ee-YAIR.... Son of Jacques Laperriere, Hall of Fame defenseman, Montreal Canadiens (1962-63 through 1973-74).
COLLEGE: St. Lawrence (N.Y.).
TRANSACTIONS/CAREER NOTES: Selected by St. Louis Blues in fifth round (fourth Blues pick, 93rd overall) of NHL entry draft (June 17, 1989).... Suffered from the flu (October 9, 1992); missed two games.
HONORS: Named to ECAC All-Star second team (1990-91).... Named ECAC Player of the Year (1991-92).... Named ECAC Playoff Most Valuable Player (1991-92).... Named to NCAA All-America East first team (1991-92).... Named to ECAC All-Star first team (1991-92).

Season Team	League	REGULAR SEASON					PLAYOFFS				
		Gms.	G	A	Pts.	Pen.	Gms.	G	A	Pts.	Pen.
88-89—St. Lawrence University...	ECAC	34	1	11	12	14	—	—	—	—	—
89-90—St. Lawrence University...	ECAC	29	6	19	25	16	—	—	—	—	—
90-91—St. Lawrence University...	ECAC	34	7	32	39	18	—	—	—	—	—
91-92—St. Lawrence University...	ECAC	32	8	*45	53	36	—	—	—	—	—
92-93—St. Louis	NHL	5	0	1	1	0	—	—	—	—	—
—Peoria	IHL	54	4	20	24	28	—	—	—	—	—
NHL totals		5	0	1	1	0					

LAPERRIERE, IAN
C, BLUES

PERSONAL: Born January 19, 1974, at Montreal.... 6-1/195.... Shoots right.
TRANSACTIONS/CAREER NOTES: Selected by St. Louis Blues in seventh round (sixth Blues pick, 158th overall) of NHL entry draft (June 20, 1992).
HONORS: Named to QMJHL All-Star second team (1992-93).

Season Team	League	REGULAR SEASON					PLAYOFFS				
		Gms.	G	A	Pts.	Pen.	Gms.	G	A	Pts.	Pen.
90-91—Drummondville	QMJHL	65	19	29	48	117	—	—	—	—	—
91-92—Drummondville	QMJHL	70	28	49	77	160	—	—	—	—	—
92-93—Drummondville	QMJHL	60	44	†96	140	188	10	6	13	19	20

LAPOINTE, CLAUDE
C, NORDIQUES

PERSONAL: Born October 11, 1968, at Ville Emard, Que.... 5-9/173.... Shoots left. ... Name pronounced luh-PWAH.
TRANSACTIONS/CAREER NOTES: Traded by Trois-Rivieres Draveurs with G Alain Dubeau and third-round draft pick (D Patrice Brisebois) to Laval Titans for D Raymond Saumier, LW Mike Gober, D Eric Gobeil and second-round draft pick (D Eric Charron) (May 1987).... Selected by Quebec Nordiques in 12th round (12th Nordiques pick, 234th overall) of NHL entry draft (June 11, 1988).... Tore groin muscle (February 9, 1991).... Injured groin (October 23, 1991); missed one game.... Suffered back injury in training camp (September 1992); missed five games.... Bruised hip (April 6, 1993); missed two games.

Season Team	League	REGULAR SEASON					PLAYOFFS				
		Gms.	G	A	Pts.	Pen.	Gms.	G	A	Pts.	Pen.
85-86—Trois-Rivieres	QMJHL	72	19	38	57	74	—	—	—	—	—
86-87—Trois-Rivieres	QMJHL	70	47	57	104	123	—	—	—	—	—
87-88—Laval	QMJHL	69	37	83	120	143	13	2	17	19	53
88-89—Laval	QMJHL	63	32	72	104	158	17	5	14	19	66
89-90—Halifax	AHL	63	18	19	37	51	6	1	1	2	34
90-91—Quebec	NHL	13	2	2	4	4	—	—	—	—	—
—Halifax	AHL	43	17	17	34	46	—	—	—	—	—
91-92—Quebec	NHL	78	13	20	33	86	—	—	—	—	—
92-93—Quebec	NHL	74	10	26	36	98	6	2	4	6	8
NHL totals		165	25	48	73	188	6	2	4	6	8

LAPOINTE, MARTIN
RW, RED WINGS

PERSONAL: Born September 12, 1973, at Lachine, Que. ... 5-11/197. ... Shoots right.
TRANSACTIONS/CAREER NOTES: Selected by Detroit Red Wings in first round (first Red Wings pick, 10th overall) of NHL entry draft (June 22, 1991).... Fractured wrist (October 9, 1991); missed 22 games.
HONORS: Won Michel Bergeron Trophy (1989-90).... Named to QMJHL All-Star first team (1989-90 and 1992-93).... Named to QMJHL All-Star second team (1990-91).

Season Team	League	REGULAR SEASON					PLAYOFFS				
		Gms.	G	A	Pts.	Pen.	Gms.	G	A	Pts.	Pen.
89-90—Laval	QMJHL	65	42	54	96	77	14	8	17	25	54
90-91—Laval	QMJHL	64	44	54	98	66	13	7	14	21	26
91-92—Detroit	NHL	4	0	1	1	5	3	0	1	1	4
—Laval	QMJHL	31	25	30	55	84	10	4	10	14	32
—Adirondack	AHL	—	—	—	—	—	8	2	2	4	4
92-93—Adirondack	AHL	8	1	2	3	9	—	—	—	—	—
—Detroit	NHL	3	0	0	0	0	—	—	—	—	—
—Laval	QMJHL	35	38	51	89	41	13	*13	*17	*30	22
NHL totals		7	0	1	1	5	3	0	1	1	4

LAPOINTE, SYLVAIN
D, CANADIENS

PERSONAL: Born March 14, 1973, at Anjou, Que.... 6-0/190.... Shoots left. ... Name pronounced sihl-VAI la-PWAH.
COLLEGE: Clarkson (N.Y.).
TRANSACTIONS/CAREER NOTES: Selected by Montreal Canadiens in fourth round (sixth Canadiens pick, 83rd overall) of NHL entry draft (June 22, 1991).

Season Team	League	REGULAR SEASON					PLAYOFFS				
		Gms.	G	A	Pts.	Pen.	Gms.	G	A	Pts.	Pen.
90-91—Clarkson	ECAC	40	2	12	14	30	—	—	—	—	—
91-92—Hull	QMJHL	67	0	11	11	65	6	1	1	2	10
92-93—Hull	QMJHL	70	5	19	24	64	10	1	1	2	2

LARIONOV, IGOR
C, SHARKS

PERSONAL: Born December 3, 1960, at Voskresensk, U.S.S.R.... 5-9/165.... Shoots left.
TRANSACTIONS/CAREER NOTES: Selected by Vancouver Canucks in 11th round (11th Canucks pick, 214th overall) of NHL entry draft (June 15, 1985).... Suffered groin injury (October 25, 1990); missed four games.... Sprained ankle (January 8, 1991).... Reinjured ankle (January 30, 1991); missed seven games.... Signed to play with Lugano of Switzerland (July 14, 1992).... Selected by San Jose Sharks in NHL waiver draft (October 4, 1992).
HONORS: Named to Soviet League All-Star team (1982-83 and 1985-86 through 1987-88).... Won Soviet Player of the Year Award (1987-88).
MISCELLANEOUS: Member of gold-medal-winning U.S.S.R. Olympic teams (1984 and 1988).

			REGULAR SEASON					PLAYOFFS				
Season	Team	League	Gms.	G	A	Pts.	Pen.	Gms.	G	A	Pts.	Pen.
77-78	Khimik Voskresensk	USSR	6	3	0	3	4	—	—	—	—	—
78-79	Khimik Voskresensk	USSR	25	3	4	7	12	—	—	—	—	—
79-80	Khimik Voskresensk	USSR	42	11	7	18	24	—	—	—	—	—
80-81	Khimik Voskresensk	USSR	56	22	23	45	36	—	—	—	—	—
81-82	CSKA Moscow	USSR	46	31	22	53	6	—	—	—	—	—
82-83	CSKA Moscow	USSR	44	20	19	39	20	—	—	—	—	—
83-84	CSKA Moscow	USSR	43	15	26	41	30	—	—	—	—	—
	Soviet Olympic Team	Int'l	7	1	4	5	6	—	—	—	—	—
84-85	CSKA Moscow	USSR	40	18	28	46	20	—	—	—	—	—
85-86	CSKA Moscow	USSR	40	21	31	52	33	—	—	—	—	—
86-87	CSKA Moscow	USSR	39	20	26	46	34	—	—	—	—	—
87-88	CSKA Moscow	USSR	51	25	32	57	54	—	—	—	—	—
	Soviet Olympic Team	Int'l	8	4	9	13	4	—	—	—	—	—
88-89	CSKA Moscow	USSR	31	15	12	27	22	—	—	—	—	—
89-90	Vancouver	NHL	74	17	27	44	20	—	—	—	—	—
90-91	Vancouver	NHL	64	13	21	34	14	6	1	0	1	6
91-92	Vancouver	NHL	72	21	44	65	54	13	3	7	10	4
92-93	Lugano	Switzerland	24	10	19	29	44	—	—	—	—	—
NHL totals			210	51	92	143	88	19	4	7	11	10

LARMER, STEVE
RW, BLACKHAWKS

PERSONAL: Born June 16, 1961, at Peterborough, Ont.... 5-10/189.... Shoots left.... Full name: Steve Donald Larmer.... Brother of Jeff Larmer, left winger, Colorado Rockies, New Jersey Devils and Chicago Blackhawks (1981-82 through 1985-86).
TRANSACTIONS/CAREER NOTES: Selected by Chicago Blackhawks as underage junior in sixth round (11th Blackhawks pick, 120th overall) of NHL entry draft (June 11, 1980).
HONORS: Named to OMJHL All-Star second team (1980-81).... Named to AHL All-Star second team (1981-82).... Named NHL Rookie of the Year by THE SPORTING NEWS (1982-83).... Won Calder Memorial Trophy (1982-83).... Named to NHL All-Rookie team (1982-83).... Played in NHL All-Star Game (1990 and 1991).

			REGULAR SEASON					PLAYOFFS				
Season	Team	League	Gms.	G	A	Pts.	Pen.	Gms.	G	A	Pts.	Pen.
77-78	Peterborough	OMJHL	62	24	17	41	51	18	5	7	12	27
78-79	Niagara Falls	OMJHL	66	37	47	84	108	—	—	—	—	—
79-80	Niagara Falls	OMJHL	67	45	69	114	71	10	5	9	14	15
80-81	Niagara Falls	OMJHL	61	55	78	133	73	12	13	8	21	24
	Chicago	NHL	4	0	1	1	0	—	—	—	—	—
81-82	New Brunswick	AHL	74	38	44	82	46	15	6	6	12	0
	Chicago	NHL	3	0	0	0	0	—	—	—	—	—
82-83	Chicago	NHL	80	43	47	90	28	11	5	7	12	8
83-84	Chicago	NHL	80	35	40	75	34	5	2	2	4	7
84-85	Chicago	NHL	80	46	40	86	16	15	9	13	22	14
85-86	Chicago	NHL	80	31	45	76	47	3	0	3	3	4
86-87	Chicago	NHL	80	28	56	84	22	4	0	0	0	2
87-88	Chicago	NHL	80	41	48	89	42	5	1	6	7	0
88-89	Chicago	NHL	80	43	44	87	54	16	8	9	17	22
89-90	Chicago	NHL	80	31	59	90	40	20	7	15	22	8
90-91	Chicago	NHL	80	44	57	101	79	6	5	1	6	4
91-92	Chicago	NHL	80	29	45	74	65	18	8	7	15	6
92-93	Chicago	NHL	84	35	35	70	48	4	0	3	3	0
NHL totals			891	406	517	923	475	107	45	66	111	75

LAROSE, BENOIT
D, RED WINGS

PERSONAL: Born May 31, 1973, at Ottawa, Ont.... 6-0/200.... Shoots left.
TRANSACTIONS/CAREER NOTES: Selected by Detroit Red Wings in fourth round (fifth Red Wings pick, 100th overall) of NHL entry draft (June 26, 1993).
HONORS: Named to QMJHL All-Star first team (1992-93).

			REGULAR SEASON					PLAYOFFS				
Season	Team	League	Gms.	G	A	Pts.	Pen.	Gms.	G	A	Pts.	Pen.
92-93	Laval	QMJHL	63	16	62	78	218	8	1	6	7	10

LAROSE, GUY
C/LW, MAPLE LEAFS

PERSONAL: Born July 31, 1967, at Hull, Que.... 5-10/175.... Shoots left.... Name pronounced GEE luh-ROHS.... Son of Claude Larose, right winger, Montreal Canadiens, Minnesota North Stars and St. Louis Blues (1962-63 through 1977-78).
TRANSACTIONS/CAREER NOTES: Fractured third left metacarpal (February 22, 1985).... Selected by Buffalo Sabres as underage junior in 11th round (11th Sabres pick, 224th overall) of NHL entry draft (June 15, 1985)....

Signed as free agent by Winnipeg Jets (July 21, 1987).... Traded by Jets to New York Rangers for D Rudy Poeschek (January 22, 1991).... Traded by Rangers to Toronto Maple Leafs for C/LW Mike Stevens (December 26, 1991).... Injured stomach before season (1992); missed first two games of season.

Season	Team	League	REGULAR SEASON					PLAYOFFS				
			Gms.	G	A	Pts.	Pen.	Gms.	G	A	Pts.	Pen.
83-84—	Ottawa	COJHL	54	37	66	103	66	—	—	—	—	—
84-85—	Guelph	OHL	58	30	30	60	63	—	—	—	—	—
85-86—	Guelph	OHL	37	12	36	48	55	—	—	—	—	—
	—Ottawa	OHL	28	19	25	44	63	—	—	—	—	—
86-87—	Ottawa	OHL	66	28	49	77	77	11	2	8	10	27
87-88—	Moncton	AHL	77	22	31	53	127	—	—	—	—	—
88-89—	Winnipeg	NHL	3	0	1	1	6	—	—	—	—	—
	—Moncton	AHL	72	32	27	59	176	10	4	4	8	37
89-90—	Moncton	AHL	79	44	26	70	232	—	—	—	—	—
90-91—	Moncton	AHL	35	14	10	24	60	—	—	—	—	—
	—Binghamton	AHL	34	21	15	36	48	10	8	5	13	37
	—Winnipeg	NHL	7	0	0	0	8	—	—	—	—	—
91-92—	Binghamton	AHL	30	10	11	21	36	—	—	—	—	—
	—St. John's	AHL	15	7	7	14	26	—	—	—	—	—
	—Toronto	NHL	34	9	5	14	27	—	—	—	—	—
92-93—	Toronto	NHL	9	0	0	0	8	—	—	—	—	—
	—St. John's	AHL	5	0	1	1	8	9	5	2	7	6
NHL totals			53	9	6	15	49					

LAROUCHE, STEVE
C, CANADIENS

PERSONAL: Born April 14, 1971, at Rouyn, Que.... 5-11/180.... Shoots right.
TRANSACTIONS/CAREER NOTES: Selected by Montreal Canadiens in second round (third Canadiens pick, 41st overall) of NHL entry draft (June 17, 1989).... Injured shoulder (October 8, 1989).... QMJHL rights traded by Trois-Rivieres Draveurs with C Sabastien Parent and sixth-round pick in 1990 draft to Chicoutimi Sagueneens for Paul Brosseau and Jasmin Ouellet (May 26, 1990). ... Tore left knee ligaments (October 5, 1990); missed two months.... Sent home by Chicoutimi coach Joe Canale for indifferent play (January 1991).
HONORS: Named to QMJHL All-Star second team (1989-90).

Season	Team	League	REGULAR SEASON					PLAYOFFS				
			Gms.	G	A	Pts.	Pen.	Gms.	G	A	Pts.	Pen.
87-88—	Trois-Rivieres	QMJHL	66	11	29	40	25	—	—	—	—	—
88-89—	Trois-Rivieres	QMJHL	70	51	102	153	53	4	4	2	6	6
89-90—	Trois-Rivieres	QMJHL	60	55	90	145	40	7	3	5	8	8
90-91—	Chicoutimi	QMJHL	45	35	41	76	64	17	†13	*20	*33	20
91-92—	Fredericton	AHL	74	21	35	56	41	7	1	0	1	0
92-93—	Fredericton	AHL	77	27	65	92	52	5	2	5	7	6

LAUER, BRAD
LW

PERSONAL: Born October 27, 1966, at Humboldt, Sask.... 6-0/195.... Shoots left.
TRANSACTIONS/CAREER NOTES: Selected by New York Islanders as underage junior in second round (third Islanders pick, 34th overall) of NHL entry draft (June 15, 1985).... Fractured left kneecap (October 1988).... Reinjured left knee (March 1989).... Suffered abdominal strain (February 1990).... Bruised right quadricep (April 1990).... Traded by Islanders with C Brent Sutter to Chicago Blackhawks for C Adam Creighton and LW Steve Thomas (October 25, 1991).... Signed as free agent by Las Vegas Thunder (July 19, 1993).
HONORS: Named to IHL All-Star first team (1992-93).

Season	Team	League	REGULAR SEASON					PLAYOFFS				
			Gms.	G	A	Pts.	Pen.	Gms.	G	A	Pts.	Pen.
83-84—	Regina	WHL	60	5	7	12	51	16	0	1	1	24
84-85—	Regina	WHL	72	33	46	79	57	8	6	6	12	9
85-86—	Regina	WHL	57	36	38	74	69	10	4	5	9	2
86-87—	New York Islanders	NHL	61	7	14	21	65	6	2	0	2	4
87-88—	New York Islanders	NHL	69	17	18	35	67	5	3	1	4	4
88-89—	Springfield	AHL	8	1	5	6	0	—	—	—	—	—
	—New York Islanders	NHL	14	3	2	5	2	—	—	—	—	—
89-90—	New York Islanders	NHL	63	6	18	24	19	4	0	2	2	10
	—Springfield	AHL	7	4	2	6	0	—	—	—	—	—
90-91—	New York Islanders	NHL	44	4	8	12	45	—	—	—	—	—
	—Capital District	AHL	11	5	11	16	14	—	—	—	—	—
91-92—	New York Islanders	NHL	8	1	0	1	2	—	—	—	—	—
	—Indianapolis	IHL	57	24	30	54	46	—	—	—	—	—
	—Chicago	NHL	6	0	0	0	4	7	1	1	2	2
92-93—	Indianapolis	IHL	62	*50	41	91	80	5	3	1	4	6
	—Chicago	NHL	7	0	1	1	2	—	—	—	—	—
NHL totals			272	38	61	99	206	22	6	4	10	20

LAUS, PAUL
D, PANTHERS

PERSONAL: Born September 26, 1970, at Beamsville, Ont.... 6-2/205.... Shoots right.
TRANSACTIONS/CAREER NOTES: Suffered inflamed knuckles (September 1988).... Suspended three playoff games by OHL for spearing (April 28, 1989).... Selected by Pittsburgh Penguins in second round (second Penguins pick, 37th overall) of NHL entry draft (June 17, 1989).... Selected by Florida Panthers in NHL expansion draft (June 24, 1993).

Season	Team	League	Gms.	G	A	Pts.	Pen.	Gms.	G	A	Pts.	Pen.
86-87	St. Catharines Jr. B	OHA	40	1	8	9	56					
87-88	Hamilton	OHL	56	1	9	10	171	14	0	0	0	28
88-89	Niagara Falls	OHL	49	1	10	11	225	15	0	5	5	56
89-90	Niagara Falls	OHL	60	13	35	48	231	16	6	16	22	71
90-91	Muskegon	IHL	35	3	4	7	103	4	0	0	0	13
	Albany	IHL	7	0	0	0	7	—	—	—	—	—
	Knoxville	ECHL	20	6	12	18	83	—	—	—	—	—
91-92	Muskegon	IHL	75	0	21	21	248	14	2	5	7	70
92-93	Cleveland	IHL	76	8	18	26	427	4	1	0	1	27

LAVIGNE, ERIC
D, CAPITALS

PERSONAL: Born November 14, 1972, at Victoriaville, Que. . . . 6-3/194. . . . Shoots left. . . . Name pronounced luh-VEEN.
TRANSACTIONS/CAREER NOTES: Selected by Washington Capitals in second round (third Capitals pick, 25th overall) of NHL entry draft (June 22, 1991).

Season	Team	League	Gms.	G	A	Pts.	Pen.	Gms.	G	A	Pts.	Pen.
89-90	Hull	QMJHL	69	7	11	18	203	11	0	0	0	32
90-91	Hull	QMJHL	66	11	11	22	153	4	0	1	1	16
91-92	Hull	QMJHL	46	4	17	21	101	6	0	0	0	32
92-93	Hull	QMJHL	59	7	20	27	221	10	2	4	6	47

LAVISH, JAMES
RW, BRUINS

PERSONAL: Born October 13, 1970, at Albany, N.Y. . . . 5-11/175. . . . Shoots right. . . . Full name: James Alexander Lavish.
HIGH SCHOOL: Deerfield (Mass.) Academy.
COLLEGE: Yale.
TRANSACTIONS/CAREER NOTES: Selected by Boston Bruins in ninth round (ninth Bruins pick, 185th overall) of NHL entry draft (June 17, 1989).

Season	Team	League	Gms.	G	A	Pts.	Pen.	Gms.	G	A	Pts.	Pen.
88-89	Deerfield Academy	Mass. H.S.	...	16	18	34	...	—	—	—	—	—
89-90	Yale University	ECAC	27	6	11	17	40	—	—	—	—	—
90-91	Yale University	ECAC	29	13	6	19	42	—	—	—	—	—
91-92	Yale University	ECAC	26	16	13	29	44	—	—	—	—	—
92-93	Yale University	ECAC	29	17	19	36	36	—	—	—	—	—

LAVOIE, DOMINIC
D

PERSONAL: Born November 21, 1967, at Montreal. . . . 6-2/205. . . . Shoots right. . . . Name pronounced luh-VWAH.
TRANSACTIONS/CAREER NOTES: Signed as free agent by St. Louis Blues (September 22, 1986). . . . Dislocated shoulder (January 1991). . . . Suffered hairline fracture to foot during preseason (September 1991); missed first seven games of season. . . . Selected by Ottawa Senators in NHL expansion draft (June 18, 1992). . . . Claimed on waivers by Boston Bruins (November 20, 1992). . . . Signed as free agent by Phoenix Roadrunners (July 16, 1993).
HONORS: Named to IHL All-Star first team (1990-91). . . . Named to IHL All-Star second team (1991-92).

Season	Team	League	Gms.	G	A	Pts.	Pen.	Gms.	G	A	Pts.	Pen.
84-85	St. Jean	QMJHL	30	1	1	2	10	—	—	—	—	—
85-86	St. Jean	QMJHL	70	12	37	49	99	10	2	3	5	20
86-87	St. Jean	QMJHL	64	12	42	54	97	8	2	7	9	2
87-88	Peoria	IHL	65	7	26	33	54	7	2	2	4	8
88-89	St. Louis	NHL	1	0	0	0	0	—	—	—	—	—
	Peoria	IHL	69	11	31	42	98	4	0	0	0	4
89-90	St. Louis	NHL	13	1	1	2	16	—	—	—	—	—
	Peoria	IHL	58	19	23	42	32	5	2	2	4	16
90-91	St. Louis	NHL	6	1	2	3	2	—	—	—	—	—
	Peoria	IHL	46	15	25	40	72	16	5	7	12	22
91-92	Peoria	IHL	58	20	32	52	87	10	3	4	7	12
	St. Louis	NHL	6	0	1	1	10	—	—	—	—	—
92-93	New Haven	AHL	14	2	7	9	14	—	—	—	—	—
	Ottawa	NHL	2	0	1	1	0	—	—	—	—	—
	Boston	NHL	2	0	0	0	2	—	—	—	—	—
	Providence	AHL	53	16	27	43	62	6	1	2	3	24
NHL totals			30	2	5	7	30					

LAWTON, BRIAN
LW, DEVILS

PERSONAL: Born June 29, 1965, at New Brunswick, N.J. . . . 6-0/180. . . . Shoots left.
HIGH SCHOOL: Mount St. Charles Academy (Woonsocket, R.I.).
TRANSACTIONS/CAREER NOTES: Selected by Minnesota North Stars in first round (first North Stars pick, first overall) of NHL entry draft (June 8, 1983). . . . Separated shoulder (November 1983). . . . Injured shoulder (October 1984). . . . Broke thumb (October 1987). . . . Bruised ribs (February 1988). . . . Suspended by North Stars for refusing to report to Kalamazoo Wings (October 8, 1988). . . . Traded by North Stars with LW Igor Liba and rights to LW Eric Bennett to New York Rangers for D Mark Tinordi and D Paul Jerrard and the rights to C Mike Sullivan and RW Brett Barnett and the Los Angeles Kings' third-round draft pick (C Murray Garbutt) in 1989 (acquired March

10, 1987, by North Stars) (October 11, 1988).... Traded by Rangers with D Norm Maciver and LW Don Maloney to Hartford Whalers for C Carey Wilson and fifth-round pick in 1990 draft (Rob Lubos) (December 26, 1988).... Suffered facial and jaw injuries (January 27, 1989).... Broke left wrist (January 28, 1989).... Sprained ankle (March 25, 1989).... Fractured bone in left foot (September 1989).... Acquired by Quebec Nordiques from Whalers for $12,500 (December 1, 1989).... Released by Nordiques (February 1, 1990).... Signed as free agent by Boston Bruins (February 6, 1990).... Signed as free agent by Kings (July 27, 1990).... Signed as free agent by San Jose Sharks (August 9, 1991).... Injured foot (October 4, 1991); missed three games.... Injured knee (November 27, 1991); missed eight games.... Traded to New Jersey Devils for future considerations (January 26, 1993).

			REGULAR SEASON					PLAYOFFS				
Season	Team	League	Gms.	G	A	Pts.	Pen.	Gms.	G	A	Pts.	Pen.
81-82—Mount St. Charles H.S.		R.I.H.S.	26	45	43	88	...	—	—	—	—	—
82-83—Mount St. Charles H.S.		R.I.H.S.	23	40	43	83	...	—	—	—	—	—
—U.S. national team		Int'l	7	3	2	5	6	—	—	—	—	—
83-84—Minnesota		NHL	58	10	21	31	33	5	0	0	0	10
84-85—Springfield		AHL	42	14	28	42	37	4	1	1	2	2
—Minnesota		NHL	40	5	6	11	24	—	—	—	—	—
85-86—Minnesota		NHL	65	18	17	35	36	3	0	1	1	2
86-87—Minnesota		NHL	66	21	23	44	86	—	—	—	—	—
87-88—Minnesota		NHL	74	17	24	41	71	—	—	—	—	—
88-89—New York Rangers		NHL	30	7	10	17	39	—	—	—	—	—
—Hartford.....................		NHL	35	10	16	26	28	3	1	0	1	0
89-90—Hartford..................		NHL	13	2	1	3	6	—	—	—	—	—
—Quebec		NHL	14	5	6	11	10	—	—	—	—	—
—Boston		NHL	8	0	0	0	14	—	—	—	—	—
—Maine		AHL	5	0	0	0	14	—	—	—	—	—
90-91—Phoenix		IHL	63	26	40	66	108	11	4	9	13	40
91-92—San Jose		NHL	59	15	22	37	42	—	—	—	—	—
92-93—San Jose		NHL	21	2	8	10	12	—	—	—	—	—
—Kansas City.................		IHL	9	6	4	10	10	—	—	—	—	—
—Cincinnati..................		IHL	17	5	11	16	30	—	—	—	—	—
NHL totals..................			**483**	**112**	**154**	**266**	**401**	**11**	**1**	**1**	**2**	**12**

LAZARO, JEFF

LW, SENATORS

PERSONAL: Born March 21, 1968, at Waltham, Mass. ... 5-10/180. ... Shoots left. ... Full name: Jeffrey Adam Lazaro.
HIGH SCHOOL: Waltham (Mass.).
COLLEGE: New Hampshire.
TRANSACTIONS/CAREER NOTES: Signed as free agent by Boston Bruins (September 26, 1990). ... Bruised back (February 9, 1991). ... Suffered concussion (February 23, 1991). ... Sprained knee (January 23, 1992); missed 14 games. ... Sprained knee (March 11, 1992). ... Selected by Ottawa Senators in NHL expansion draft (June 18, 1992). ... Suffered right leg contusion (January 10, 1993); missed 14 games.
MISCELLANEOUS: Played defense prior to 1989-90 season.

			REGULAR SEASON					PLAYOFFS				
Season	Team	League	Gms.	G	A	Pts.	Pen.	Gms.	G	A	Pts.	Pen.
86-87—Univ. of New Hampshire ...		Hockey East	38	7	14	21	38	—	—	—	—	—
87-88—Univ. of New Hampshire ...		Hockey East	30	4	13	17	48	—	—	—	—	—
88-89—Univ. of New Hampshire ...		Hockey East	31	8	14	22	38	—	—	—	—	—
89-90—Univ. of New Hampshire ...		Hockey East	39	16	19	35	34	—	—	—	—	—
90-91—Maine.....................		AHL	26	8	11	19	18	—	—	—	—	—
—Boston		NHL	49	5	13	18	67	19	3	2	5	30
91-92—Boston		NHL	27	3	6	9	31	9	0	1	1	2
—Maine		AHL	21	8	4	12	32	—	—	—	—	—
92-93—Ottawa....................		NHL	26	6	4	10	16	—	—	—	—	—
—New Haven		AHL	27	12	13	25	49	—	—	—	—	—
NHL totals..................			**102**	**14**	**23**	**37**	**114**	**28**	**3**	**3**	**6**	**32**

LEACH, JAMIE

RW, WHALERS

PERSONAL: Born August 25, 1969, at Winnipeg, Man. ... 6-1/205. ... Shoots right. ... Son of Reggie Leach, right winger, four NHL teams (1970-71 through 1982-83).
HIGH SCHOOL: Cherry Hill (N.J.) East.
TRANSACTIONS/CAREER NOTES: Suffered hip injury (February 1986). ... Selected by Pittsburgh Penguins as underage junior in third round (third Penguins pick, 47th overall) of NHL entry draft (June 13, 1987). ... Tore left knee ligaments (September 30, 1990). ... Claimed on waivers by Hartford Whalers (November 21, 1992).
MISCELLANEOUS: Member of Stanley Cup championship team (1992).

			REGULAR SEASON					PLAYOFFS				
Season	Team	League	Gms.	G	A	Pts.	Pen.	Gms.	G	A	Pts.	Pen.
84-85—Cherry Hill East H.S.		N.J. H.S.	60	48	51	99	68	—	—	—	—	—
85-86—New Westminster		WHL	58	8	7	15	20	—	—	—	—	—
86-87—Hamilton..................		OHL	64	12	19	31	67	—	—	—	—	—
87-88—Hamilton..................		OHL	64	24	19	43	79	14	6	7	13	12
88-89—Niagara Falls		OHL	58	45	62	107	47	17	9	11	20	25
89-90—Muskegon..................		IHL	72	22	36	58	39	15	9	4	13	14
—Pittsburgh..................		NHL	10	0	3	3	0	—	—	—	—	—
90-91—Pittsburgh................		NHL	7	2	0	2	0	—	—	—	—	—
—Muskegon..................		IHL	43	33	22	55	26	—	—	—	—	—

Season	Team	League	REGULAR SEASON					PLAYOFFS				
			Gms.	G	A	Pts.	Pen.	Gms.	G	A	Pts.	Pen.
91-92—Pittsburgh	NHL	38	5	4	9	8	—	—	—	—	—
—Muskegon	IHL	3	1	1	2	2	—	—	—	—	—
92-93—Pittsburgh	NHL	5	0	0	0	2	—	—	—	—	—
—Hartford	NHL	19	3	2	5	2	—	—	—	—	—
—Springfield	AHL	29	13	15	28	33	—	—	—	—	—
—Cleveland	IHL	9	5	3	8	2	4	1	2	3	0
NHL totals		**79**	**10**	**9**	**19**	**12**					

LEACH, STEVE
RW, BRUINS

PERSONAL: Born January 16, 1966, at Cambridge, Mass. . . . 5-11/200. . . . Shoots right. **HIGH SCHOOL:** Matignon (Cambridge, Mass.). **COLLEGE:** New Hampshire.
TRANSACTIONS/CAREER NOTES: Selected by Washington Capitals in second round (second Capitals pick, 34th overall) of NHL entry draft (June 9, 1984). . . . Strained left knee (February 1989). . . . Injured thumb (March 1990). . . . Suffered concussion (October 10, 1990). . . . Separated right shoulder (February 2, 1991); missed four games. . . . Traded by Capitals to Boston Bruins for LW Randy Burridge (June 21, 1991). . . . Injured thigh (October 1992); missed one game. . . . Injured ribs (January 1993); missed four games.
HONORS: Named to Hockey East All-Freshman team (1984-85).

Season	Team	League	REGULAR SEASON					PLAYOFFS				
			Gms.	G	A	Pts.	Pen.	Gms.	G	A	Pts.	Pen.
83-84—Matignon H.S.	Mass. H.S.	21	27	22	49	49	—	—	—	—	—
84-85—Univ. of New Hampshire	Hockey East	41	12	25	37	53	—	—	—	—	—
85-86—Univ. of New Hampshire	Hockey East	25	22	6	28	30	—	—	—	—	—
—Washington	NHL	11	1	1	2	2	6	0	1	1	0
86-87—Binghamton	AHL	54	18	21	39	39	13	3	1	4	6
—Washington	NHL	15	1	0	1	6	—	—	—	—	—
87-88—U.S. national team	Int'l	53	26	20	46	. . .	—	—	—	—	—
—U.S. Olympic Team	Int'l	6	1	2	3	0	—	—	—	—	—
—Washington	NHL	8	1	1	2	17	9	2	1	3	0
88-89—Washington	NHL	74	11	19	30	94	6	1	0	1	12
89-90—Washington	NHL	70	18	14	32	104	14	2	2	4	6
90-91—Washington	NHL	68	11	19	30	99	9	1	2	3	8
91-92—Boston	NHL	78	31	29	60	147	15	4	0	4	10
92-93—Boston	NHL	79	26	25	51	126	4	1	1	2	2
NHL totals		**403**	**100**	**108**	**208**	**595**	**63**	**11**	**7**	**18**	**38**

LEBEAU, PATRICK
LW, FLAMES

PERSONAL: Born March 17, 1970, at St. Jerome, Que. . . . 5-10/173. . . . Shoots left. . . . Name pronounced leh-BOH. . . . Brother of Stephan Lebeau, center, Montreal Canadiens.
TRANSACTIONS/CAREER NOTES: Traded by Shawinigan Cataractes with QMJHL rights to G Eric Metivier to St. Jean Castors for LW Steve Cadieux and D Pierre Cote (November 5, 1988). . . . Selected by Montreal Canadiens in eighth round (eighth Canadiens pick, 147th overall) of NHL entry draft (June 17, 1989). . . . Traded by St. Jean Lynx with D Francois Leroux and LW Jean Blouin to Victoriaville Tigres for RW Trevor Duhaime, second- and third-round draft picks and future considerations (February 15, 1990). . . . Traded by Canadiens to Calgary Flames for future considerations (October 6, 1992).
HONORS: Won Jean Beliveau Trophy (1989-90). . . . Named to QMJHL All-Star first team (1989-90). . . . Won Dudley (Red) Garrett Memorial Trophy (1990-91). . . . Named to AHL All-Star second team (1990-91).
MISCELLANEOUS: Member of silver-medal-winning Canadian Olympic team (1992).

Season	Team	League	REGULAR SEASON					PLAYOFFS				
			Gms.	G	A	Pts.	Pen.	Gms.	G	A	Pts.	Pen.
86-87—Shawinigan	QMJHL	66	26	52	78	90	13	2	6	8	17
87-88—Shawinigan	QMJHL	53	43	56	99	116	11	3	9	12	16
88-89—Shawinigan/St. Jean	QMJHL	66	62	87	149	89	4	4	3	7	6
89-90—St. Jean/Victoriaville	QMJHL	72	68	*106	*174	109	16	7	15	22	12
90-91—Montreal	NHL	2	1	1	2	0	—	—	—	—	—
—Fredericton	AHL	69	50	51	101	32	9	4	7	11	8
91-92—Fredericton	AHL	55	33	38	71	48	7	4	5	9	10
—Canadian national team	Int'l	7	4	1	5	6	—	—	—	—	—
—Canadian Olympic Team	Int'l	8	1	3	4	4	—	—	—	—	—
92-93—Salt Lake City	IHL	75	40	60	100	65	—	—	—	—	—
—Calgary	NHL	1	0	0	0	0	—	—	—	—	—
NHL totals		**3**	**1**	**1**	**2**	**0**					

LEBEAU, STEPHAN
C, CANADIENS

PERSONAL: Born February 28, 1968, at Sherbrooke, Que. . . . 5-10/172. . . . Shoots right. . . . Name pronounced leh-BOH. . . . Brother of Patrick Lebeau, left winger in Calgary Flames system.
TRANSACTIONS/CAREER NOTES: Signed as free agent by Montreal Canadiens (September 27, 1986). . . . Injured thigh (January 25, 1992); missed one game. . . . Injured ankle (February 26, 1993); missed four games. . . . Reinjured ankle (March 17, 1993); missed nine games.
HONORS: Named to QMJHL All-Star second team (1986-87 and 1987-88). . . . Won Frank J. Selke Trophy (1987-88). . . . Won Les Cunningham Plaque (1988-89). . . . Won John B. Sollenberger Trophy (1988-89). . . . Won Dudley (Red) Garrett Memorial Trophy (1988-89). . . . Named to AHL All-Star first team (1988-89).
MISCELLANEOUS: Member of Stanley cup championship team (1993).

Season	Team	League	REGULAR SEASON					PLAYOFFS				
			Gms.	G	A	Pts.	Pen.	Gms.	G	A	Pts.	Pen.
84-85—Shawinigan	QMJHL	66	41	38	79	18	9	4	5	9	4
85-86—Shawinigan	QMJHL	72	69	77	146	22	5	4	2	6	4
86-87—Shawinigan	QMJHL	65	*77	90	167	60	14	9	20	29	20
87-88—Shawinigan	QMJHL	67	*94	94	188	66	11	†17	9	26	10
—Sherbrooke	AHL	—	—	—	—	—	1	0	1	1	0
88-89—Sherbrooke	AHL	78	*70	64	*134	47	6	1	4	5	8
—Montreal	NHL	1	0	1	1	2	—	—	—	—	—
89-90—Montreal	NHL	57	15	20	35	11	2	3	0	3	0
90-91—Montreal	NHL	73	22	31	53	24	7	2	1	3	2
91-92—Montreal	NHL	77	27	31	58	14	8	1	3	4	4
92-93—Montreal	NHL	71	31	49	80	20	13	3	3	6	6
NHL totals		279	95	132	227	71	30	9	7	16	12

LeBLANC, JOHN
LW/RW, JETS

PERSONAL: Born January 21, 1964, at Campbellton, N.B. . . . 6-1/195. . . . Shoots left. . . . Full name: John Glenn LeBlanc.
TRANSACTIONS/CAREER NOTES: Suffered ankle contusion (February 1992); missed three games. . . . Signed by Vancouver Canucks as free agent (April 12, 1986). . . . Traded by Canucks with fifth-round pick in 1989 draft (LW Peter White) to Edmonton Oilers for C Doug Smith and LW Greg C. Adams (March 7, 1989). . . . Traded by Oilers with 10th-round pick in 1992 draft (C Teemu Numminen) to Winnipeg Jets for fifth-round pick (C Ryan Haggerty) in 1991 draft (June 12, 1991).
HONORS: Won Senator Joseph A. Sullivan Trophy (1985-86).

Season	Team	League	REGULAR SEASON					PLAYOFFS				
			Gms.	G	A	Pts.	Pen.	Gms.	G	A	Pts.	Pen.
83-84—Hull	QMJHL	69	39	35	74	32	—	—	—	—	—
84-85—New Brunswick	AHL	24	25	34	59	32	—	—	—	—	—
85-86—New Brunswick	AHL	24	38	28	66	35	—	—	—	—	—
86-87—Vancouver	NHL	2	1	0	1	0	—	—	—	—	—
—Fredericton	AHL	75	40	30	70	27	—	—	—	—	—
87-88—Vancouver	NHL	41	12	10	22	18	—	—	—	—	—
—Fredericton	AHL	35	26	25	51	54	15	6	7	13	34
88-89—Milwaukee	IHL	61	39	31	70	42	—	—	—	—	—
—Edmonton	NHL	2	1	0	1	0	1	0	0	0	0
—Cape Breton	AHL	3	4	0	4	0	—	—	—	—	—
89-90—Cape Breton	AHL	77	*54	34	88	50	6	4	0	4	4
90-91—Cape Breton	AHL				Did not play.						
91-92—Moncton	AHL	56	31	22	53	24	10	3	2	5	8
—Winnipeg	NHL	16	6	1	7	6	—	—	—	—	—
92-93—Winnipeg	NHL	3	0	0	0	2	—	—	—	—	—
—Moncton	AHL	77	48	40	88	29	5	2	1	3	6
NHL totals		64	20	11	31	26	1	0	0	0	0

LeBLANC, RAY
G, BLACKHAWKS

PERSONAL: Born October 24, 1964, at Fitchburg, Mass. . . . 5-10/170. . . . Shoots left.
TRANSACTIONS/CAREER NOTES: Signed as free agent by Chicago Blackhawks (September 1989).
HONORS: Named to ACHL All-Star second team (1984-85). . . . Won ECHL Top Goaltender Award (1985-86). . . . Named to ACHL All-Star first team (1985-86). . . . Won Ken McKenzie Trophy (1986-87). . . . Named to IHL All-Star second team (1986-87).

Season	Team	League	REGULAR SEASON								PLAYOFFS						
			Gms.	Min.	W	L	T	GA	SO	Avg.	Gms.	Min.	W	L	GA	SO	Avg.
82-83—Dixie Flyers	OPJHL	30	1705	...	...	...	111	0	3.91	—	—			—	—	—
83-84—Kitchener	OHL	*54	2965	...	...	...	185	1	3.74	†16	914	...	...	*79	0	5.19
84-85—Pinebridge	ACHL	40	2178	...	...	...	150	0	4.13	—	—			—	—	—
85-86—Carolina	ECHL	*42	*2505	...	...	...	133	*3	*3.19	*11	*669	...	...	42	0	*3.77
86-87—Flint	IHL	64	3417	...	...	...	222	1	3.90	—	—			—	—	—
87-88—Flint	IHL	60	3269	27	19	8	*239	1	4.39	16	925	10	6	55	†1	3.57
88-89—Flint	IHL	15	852	5	9	0	67	0	4.72	—	—			—	—	—
—Saginaw	IHL	29	1655	19	7	2	99	0	3.59	1	59	0	1	3	0	3.05
—New Haven	AHL	1	20	0	0	0	3	0	9.00	—	—			—	—	—
89-90—Fort Wayne	IHL	15	680	3	3	3	44	0	3.88	3	139	0	2	11	0	4.75
—Indianapolis	IHL	23	1334	15	6	2	71	2	3.19	—	—			—	—	—
90-91—Fort Wayne	IHL	21	1072	10	8	0	69	0	3.86	—	—			—	—	—
—Indianapolis	IHL	3	145	2	0	0	8	0	3.31	—	—			—	—	—
91-92—Indianapolis	IHL	25	1468	14	9	2	84	2	3.43	—	—			—	—	—
—U.S. national team	Int'l	17	891	5	10	1	54	0	3.64	—	—			—	—	—
—U.S. Olympic Team	Int'l	8	463	5	2	1	17	2	2.20	—	—			—	—	—
—Chicago	NHL	1	60	1	0	0	1	0	1.00	—	—			—	—	—
92-93—Indianapolis	IHL	56	3201	23	22	0	206	0	3.86	5	276	1	3	23	0	5.00
NHL totals		1	60	1	0	0	1	0	1.00							

LeBOUTILLIER, PETER
RW, ISLANDERS

PERSONAL: Born January 11, 1975, at Neepawa, Man. . . . 6-1/198. . . . Shoots right.
HIGH SCHOOL: Lindsay Thurber (Red Deer, Alta.).
TRANSACTIONS/CAREER NOTES: Selected by New York Islanders in sixth round

(sixth Islanders pick, 144th overall) of NHL entry draft (June 26, 1993).

Season Team	League	REGULAR SEASON					PLAYOFFS				
		Gms.	G	A	Pts.	Pen.	Gms.	G	A	Pts.	Pen.
91-92—Neepawa	Jr. A	35	11	14	25	99	—	—	—	—	—
92-93—Red Deer	WHL	67	8	26	34	284	2	0	1	1	5

LeBRUN, SEAN
LW, ISLANDERS

PERSONAL: Born May 2, 1969, at Prince George, B.C. . . . 6-2/205. . . . Shoots left. . . . Name pronounced leh-BRUHN.
TRANSACTIONS/CAREER NOTES: Selected by New York Islanders in third round (third Islanders pick, 37th overall) of NHL entry draft (June 11, 1988). . . . Broke wrist (March 26, 1989).
HONORS: Named to WHL West All-Star second team (1987-88).

Season Team	League	REGULAR SEASON					PLAYOFFS				
		Gms.	G	A	Pts.	Pen.	Gms.	G	A	Pts.	Pen.
85-86—Spokane	WHL	70	6	11	17	41	—	—	—	—	—
86-87—Spokane	WHL	6	2	5	7	9	—	—	—	—	—
—New Westminster	WHL	55	21	32	53	47	—	—	—	—	—
87-88—New Westminster	WHL	72	36	53	89	59	5	1	3	4	2
88-89—Tri-City	WHL	71	52	73	125	92	5	0	4	4	13
89-90—Springfield	AHL	63	9	33	42	20	—	—	—	—	—
90-91—Capital District	AHL	56	14	26	40	35	—	—	—	—	—
91-92—Capital District	AHL	14	0	2	2	15	—	—	—	—	—
—Richmond	ECHL	2	0	0	0	2	—	—	—	—	—
92-93—Capital District	AHL	39	11	20	31	25	1	0	0	0	0

LeCLAIR, JOHN
C, CANADIENS

PERSONAL: Born July 5, 1969, at St. Albans, Vt. . . . 6-2/205. . . . Shoots left. . . . Full name: John Clark LeClair.
HIGH SCHOOL: Bellows Free Academy (St. Albans, Vt.).
COLLEGE: Vermont.
TRANSACTIONS/CAREER NOTES: Selected by Montreal Canadiens in second round (second Canadiens pick, 33rd overall) of NHL entry draft (June 13, 1987). . . . Injured thigh; missed 16 games during 1988-89 season. . . . Injured knee and underwent surgery (January 20, 1990); missed remainder of season. . . . Injured shoulder (January 15, 1992); missed four games. . . . Suffered charley horse (January 20, 1993); missed four games.
HONORS: Named to ECAC All-Star second team (1990-91).
MISCELLANEOUS: Member of Stanley Cup championship team (1993).

Season Team	League	REGULAR SEASON					PLAYOFFS				
		Gms.	G	A	Pts.	Pen.	Gms.	G	A	Pts.	Pen.
85-86—Bellows Free Academy	Vt. H.S.	22	41	28	69	14	—	—	—	—	—
86-87—Bellows Free Academy	Vt. H.S.	23	44	40	84	25	—	—	—	—	—
87-88—University of Vermont	ECAC	31	12	22	34	62	—	—	—	—	—
88-89—University of Vermont	ECAC	19	9	12	21	40	—	—	—	—	—
89-90—University of Vermont	ECAC	10	10	6	16	38	—	—	—	—	—
90-91—University of Vermont	ECAC	33	25	20	45	58	—	—	—	—	—
—Montreal	NHL	10	2	5	7	2	3	0	0	0	0
91-92—Montreal	NHL	59	8	11	19	14	8	1	1	2	4
—Fredericton	AHL	8	7	7	14	10	2	0	0	0	4
92-93—Montreal	NHL	72	19	25	44	33	20	4	6	10	14
NHL totals		141	29	41	70	49	31	5	7	12	18

LECOMPTE, ERIC
LW, BLACKHAWKS

PERSONAL: Born April 4, 1975, at Montreal. . . . 6-4/190. . . . Shoots left.
TRANSACTIONS/CAREER NOTES: Selected by Chicago Blackhawks in first round (first Blackhawks pick, 24th overall) of NHL entry draft (June 26, 1993).

Season Team	League	REGULAR SEASON					PLAYOFFS				
		Gms.	G	A	Pts.	Pen.	Gms.	G	A	Pts.	Pen.
91-92—Hull	QMJHL	60	16	17	33	138	6	1	0	1	4
92-93—Hull	QMJHL	66	33	38	71	149	10	4	4	8	52

LEDYARD, GRANT
D, SABRES

PERSONAL: Born November 19, 1961, at Winnipeg, Man. . . . 6-2/195. . . . Shoots left.
TRANSACTIONS/CAREER NOTES: Signed as free agent by New York Rangers (July 7, 1982). . . . Suffered hip injury (October 1984). . . . Traded by Rangers to Los Angeles Kings for LW Brian MacLellan and fourth-round pick in 1987 draft (C Michael Sullivan); Rangers also sent second-round pick in 1986 draft (D Neil Wilkinson) and fourth-round pick in 1987 draft (RW John Weisbrod) to Minnesota and the North Stars sent G Roland Melanson to the Kings as part of the same deal (December 1986). . . . Sprained ankle (October 1987). . . . Traded by Kings to Washington Capitals for RW Craig Laughlin (February 9, 1988). . . . Traded by Capitals with G Clint Malarchuk and sixth-round pick in 1991 draft to Buffalo Sabres for D Calle Johansson and second-round pick in 1989 draft (G Byron Dafoe) (March 6, 1989). . . . Injured knee (February 12, 1991). . . . Injured shoulder (March 2, 1991). . . . Bruised ankle (March 14, 1992); missed four games. . . . Broke finger (October 28, 1992); missed 25 games. . . . Injured eye (March 7, 1993); missed three games.
HONORS: Named Manitoba Junior Hockey League Most Valuable Player (1981-82). . . . Named to MJHL All-Star first team (1981-82). . . . Won Bob Gassoff Award (1983-84). . . . Won Max McNab Trophy (1983-84).

Season Team	League	REGULAR SEASON					PLAYOFFS				
		Gms.	G	A	Pts.	Pen.	Gms.	G	A	Pts.	Pen.
79-80—Fort Garry	MJHL	49	13	24	37	90	—	—	—	—	—
80-81—Saskatoon	WHL	71	9	28	37	148	—	—	—	—	—

Season	Team	League	REGULAR SEASON					PLAYOFFS				
			Gms.	G	A	Pts.	Pen.	Gms.	G	A	Pts.	Pen.
81-82—Fort Garry	MJHL	63	25	45	70	150	—	—	—	—	—	
82-83—Tulsa	CHL	80	13	29	42	115	—	—	—	—	—	
83-84—Tulsa	CHL	58	9	17	26	71	9	5	4	9	10	
84-85—New Haven	AHL	36	6	20	26	18	—	—	—	—	—	
—New York Rangers	NHL	42	8	12	20	53	3	0	2	2	4	
85-86—New York Rangers	NHL	27	2	9	11	20	—	—	—	—	—	
—Los Angeles	NHL	52	7	18	25	78	—	—	—	—	—	
86-87—Los Angeles	NHL	67	14	23	37	93	5	0	0	0	10	
87-88—New Haven	AHL	3	2	1	3	4	—	—	—	—	—	
—Los Angeles	NHL	23	1	7	8	52	—	—	—	—	—	
—Washington	NHL	21	4	3	7	14	14	1	0	1	30	
88-89—Washington	NHL	61	3	11	14	43	—	—	—	—	—	
—Buffalo	NHL	13	1	5	6	8	5	1	2	3	2	
89-90—Buffalo	NHL	67	2	13	15	37	—	—	—	—	—	
90-91—Buffalo	NHL	60	8	23	31	46	6	3	3	6	10	
91-92—Buffalo	NHL	50	5	16	21	45	—	—	—	—	—	
92-93—Buffalo	NHL	50	2	14	16	45	8	0	0	0	8	
—Rochester	AHL	5	0	2	2	8	—	—	—	—	—	
NHL totals			533	57	154	211	534	41	5	7	12	64

LEEMAN, GARY

RW, CANADIENS

PERSONAL: Born February 19, 1964, at Toronto.... 5-11/180.... Shoots right.
TRANSACTIONS/CAREER NOTES: Selected by Toronto Maple Leafs as underage junior in second round (second Maple Leafs pick, 24th overall) of NHL entry draft (June 9, 1982).... Broke finger (January 1984).... Broke wrist (March 1984). ... Separated shoulder (March 1985).... Cracked kneecap (April 14, 1987).... Cracked bone in right hand (April 1988).... Fractured bone behind left ear (October 22, 1988).... Injured back (January 1988).... Separated right shoulder (November 10, 1990); missed 21 games. ... Suffered back spasms (November 18, 1991); missed one game.... Traded by Maple Leafs with D Alexander Godynyuk, LW Craig Berube, D Michel Petit and G Jeff Reese to Calgary Flames for C Doug Gilmour, D Jamie Macoun, LW Kent Manderville, D Ric Nattress and G Rick Wamsley (January 2, 1992).... Bruised thigh (February 1992).... Sprained ankle (February 21, 1992); missed eight games.... Traded by Flames to Montreal Canadiens for C Brian Skrudland (January 28, 1993).... Bruised lower back (February 3, 1993); missed four games.... Injured ankle (April 2, 1993); missed five games.
HONORS: Won Top Defenseman Trophy (1982-83).... Named to WHL All-Star first team (1982-83).... Played in NHL All-Star Game (1989).
MISCELLANEOUS: Member of Stanley Cup championship team (1993).

Season	Team	League	REGULAR SEASON					PLAYOFFS				
			Gms.	G	A	Pts.	Pen.	Gms.	G	A	Pts.	Pen.
81-82—Regina	WHL	72	19	41	60	112	3	2	2	4	0	
82-83—Regina	WHL	63	24	62	86	88	5	1	5	6	4	
—Toronto	NHL	—	—	—	—	—	2	0	0	0	0	
83-84—Toronto	NHL	52	4	8	12	31	—	—	—	—	—	
84-85—St. Catharines	AHL	7	2	2	4	11	—	—	—	—	—	
—Toronto	NHL	53	5	26	31	72	—	—	—	—	—	
85-86—St. Catharines	AHL	25	15	13	28	6	—	—	—	—	—	
—Toronto	NHL	53	9	23	32	20	10	2	10	12	2	
86-87—Toronto	NHL	80	21	31	52	66	5	0	1	1	14	
87-88—Toronto	NHL	80	30	31	61	62	2	2	0	2	2	
88-89—Toronto	NHL	61	32	43	75	66	—	—	—	—	—	
89-90—Toronto	NHL	80	51	44	95	63	5	3	3	6	16	
90-91—Toronto	NHL	52	17	12	29	39	—	—	—	—	—	
91-92—Toronto	NHL	34	7	13	20	44	—	—	—	—	—	
—Calgary	NHL	29	2	7	9	27	—	—	—	—	—	
92-93—Calgary	NHL	30	9	5	14	10	—	—	—	—	—	
—Montreal	NHL	20	6	12	18	14	11	1	2	3	2	
NHL totals			624	193	255	448	514	35	8	16	24	36

LEETCH, BRIAN

D, RANGERS

PERSONAL: Born March 3, 1968, at Corpus Christi, Tex.... 5-11/190.... Shoots left.... Full name: Brian Joseph Leetch.
HIGH SCHOOL: Avon (Conn.) Old Farms School For Boys.
COLLEGE: Boston College.
TRANSACTIONS/CAREER NOTES: Selected by New York Rangers in first round (first Rangers pick, ninth overall) of NHL entry draft (June 21, 1986).... Suffered sprained ligaments in left knee at U.S. Olympic Festival (July 1987).... Fractured bone in left foot (December 1988).... Suffered hip pointer (March 15, 1989).... Fractured left ankle (March 14, 1990).... Injured ankle (November 21, 1992); missed one game.... Suffered stretched nerve in neck (December 17, 1992); missed 34 games.... Broke ankle (March 19, 1993) and underwent ankle surgery (March 31, 1993); missed remainder of season.
HONORS: Named Hockey East Player of the Year (1986-87).... Named Hockey East Rookie of the Year (1986-87).... Named to NCAA All-America East first team (1986-87).... Named to Hockey East All-Star first team (1986-87).... Named to Hockey East All-Freshman team (1986-87).... Named NHL Rookie of the Year by THE SPORTING NEWS (1988-89).... Won Calder Memorial Trophy (1988-89).... Named to NHL All-Rookie team (1988-89).... Named to THE SPORTING NEWS All-Star second team (1990-91).... Named to NHL All-Star second team (1990-91).... Played in NHL All-Star Game (1990 through 1992).... Won James Norris Memorial Trophy (1991-92).... Named to THE SPORTING NEWS All-Star first team (1991-92).... Named to NHL All-Star first team (1991-92).
RECORDS: Holds NHL single-season record for most goals by a rookie defenseman—23 (1988-89).

Season	Team	League	REGULAR SEASON					PLAYOFFS				
			Gms.	G	A	Pts.	Pen.	Gms.	G	A	Pts.	Pen.
84-85—Avon Old Farms H.S.	Conn. H.S.	26	30	46	76	15	—	—	—	—	—	
85-86—Avon Old Farms H.S.	Conn. H.S.	28	40	44	84	18	—	—	—	—	—	
86-87—Boston College	Hockey East	37	9	38	47	10	—	—	—	—	—	
87-88—U.S. national team	Int'l	60	13	61	74	38	—	—	—	—	—	
—U.S. Olympic Team	Int'l	6	1	5	6	4	—	—	—	—	—	
—New York Rangers	NHL	17	2	12	14	0	—	—	—	—	—	
88-89—New York Rangers	NHL	68	23	48	71	50	4	3	2	5	2	
89-90—New York Rangers	NHL	72	11	45	56	26	—	—	—	—	—	
90-91—New York Rangers	NHL	80	16	72	88	42	6	1	3	4	0	
91-92—New York Rangers	NHL	80	22	80	102	26	13	4	11	15	4	
92-93—New York Rangers	NHL	36	6	30	36	26	—	—	—	—	—	
NHL totals			353	80	287	367	170	23	8	16	24	6

LEFEBVRE, SYLVAIN
D, MAPLE LEAFS

PERSONAL: Born October 14, 1967, at Richmond, Que. . . . 6-2/204. . . . Shoots left. . . . Name pronounced luh-FAYV.
TRANSACTIONS/CAREER NOTES: Signed as free agent by Montreal Canadiens (September 24, 1986). . . . Traded by Canadiens to Toronto Maple Leafs for third-round pick in 1994 draft (August 20, 1992).
HONORS: Named to AHL All-Star second team (1988-89).

Season	Team	League	REGULAR SEASON					PLAYOFFS				
			Gms.	G	A	Pts.	Pen.	Gms.	G	A	Pts.	Pen.
84-85—Laval	QMJHL	66	7	5	12	31	—	—	—	—	—	
85-86—Laval	QMJHL	71	8	17	25	48	14	1	0	1	25	
86-87—Laval	QMJHL	70	10	36	46	44	15	1	6	7	12	
87-88—Sherbrooke	AHL	79	3	24	27	73	6	2	3	5	4	
88-89—Sherbrooke	AHL	77	15	32	47	119	6	1	3	4	4	
89-90—Montreal	NHL	68	3	10	13	61	6	0	0	0	2	
90-91—Montreal	NHL	63	5	18	23	30	11	0	1	1	6	
91-92—Montreal	NHL	69	3	14	17	91	2	0	0	0	2	
92-93—Toronto	NHL	81	2	12	14	90	21	3	3	6	20	
NHL totals			281	13	54	67	272	40	4	3	7	30

LEGACE, MANNY
G, WHALERS

PERSONAL: Born February 4, 1973, at Toronto. . . . 5-9/162. . . . Shoots left.
HIGH SCHOOL: Stamford Collegiate (Niagara Falls, Ont.).
TRANSACTIONS/CAREER NOTES: Selected by Hartford Whalers in eighth round (fifth Whalers pick, 188th overall) of NHL entry draft (June 26, 1993).
HONORS: Named to Can.HL All-Star second team (1992-93). . . . Named to OHL All-Star first team (1992-93).

Season	Team	League	REGULAR SEASON							PLAYOFFS					
			Gms.	Min.	W	L	T	GA	SO	Avg.	Gms.	Min.	W	L	GA	SO	Avg.
90-91—Niagara Falls	OHL	30	1515	...	...	...	107	0	4.24	4	119	...	...	10	0	5.04
91-92—Niagara Falls	OHL	43	2384	...	...	...	143	0	3.60	14	791	...	...	56	0	4.25
92-93—Niagara Falls	OHL	48	2630	...	...	...	170	0	3.88	4	240	...	...	18	0	4.50

LEHTINEN, JERE
RW, STARS

PERSONAL: Born June 24, 1973, at Espoo, Finland. . . . 6-0/180. . . . Shoots right.
TRANSACTIONS/CAREER NOTES: Selected by Minnesota North Stars in fourth round (third North Stars pick, 88th overall) of NHL entry draft (June 20, 1992). . . . North Stars franchise moved from Minnesota to Dallas and renamed Stars for 1993-94 season.

Season	Team	League	REGULAR SEASON					PLAYOFFS				
			Gms.	G	A	Pts.	Pen.	Gms.	G	A	Pts.	Pen.
90-91—Kiekko-Espoo	Finland	32	15	9	24	12	—	—	—	—	—	
91-92—Kiekko-Espoo	Finland	43	32	17	49	6	—	—	—	—	—	
92-93—Kiekko-Espoo	Finland	45	13	14	27	6	—	—	—	—	—	

LEHTO, JONI
D, ISLANDERS

PERSONAL: Born July 15, 1970, at Turku, Finland. . . . 6-0/205. . . . Shoots left. . . . Name pronounced YAH-nee LAY-toh.
TRANSACTIONS/CAREER NOTES: Selected by New York Islanders in sixth round (fifth Islanders pick, 111th overall) of NHL entry draft (June 16, 1990). . . . Damaged ligaments in left knee (December 1990); while sidelined, served as an assistant coach for Ottawa 67's; became acting head coach on December 2 when head coach Brian Kilrea was ejected and suspended for the following two games; coached the team to a 2-1 record as head coach.
HONORS: Named to OHL All-Star second team (1989-90).

Season	Team	League	REGULAR SEASON					PLAYOFFS				
			Gms.	G	A	Pts.	Pen.	Gms.	G	A	Pts.	Pen.
87-88—TPS Turku	Finland	30	9	14	23	42	—	—	—	—	—	
88-89—Ottawa	OHL	63	9	25	34	26	—	—	—	—	—	
91-92—Richmond	ECHL	18	2	9	11	10	—	—	—	—	—	
—Capital District	AHL	26	2	5	7	6	—	—	—	—	—	
92-93—Capital District	AHL	57	4	13	17	33	3	1	1	2	0	

LEMELIN, REGGIE
G

PERSONAL: Born November 19, 1954, at Sherbrooke, Que. . . . 5-11/170. . . . Shoots left. . . . Name pronounced LEM-uh-lin.
TRANSACTIONS/CAREER NOTES: Selected by Philadelphia Flyers from Sherbrooke Beavers in sixth round (sixth Flyers pick, 125th overall) of NHL entry draft (May 28, 1974). . . .

Signed as free agent by Atlanta Flames (August 1978).... Broke thumb on right hand (February 8, 1981).... Flames franchise moved to Calgary (May 21, 1980).... Injured back (January 1984).... Signed as free agent by Boston Bruins (August 1987).... Strained hamstring (January 2, 1992); missed 29 games. ... Reinjured hamstring (March 23, 1992).... Announced retirement (January 11, 1993).
HONORS: Named to AHL All-Star first team (1977-78).... Shared William M. Jennings Trophy with Andy Moog (1989-90).... Played in NHL All-Star Game (1989).

			REGULAR SEASON								PLAYOFFS						
Season	Team	League	Gms.	Min.	W	L	T	GA	SO	Avg.	Gms.	Min.	W	L	GA	SO	Avg.
72-73	Sherbrooke	QMJHL	28	1681	...	...	...	146	0	5.21	2	120	...	...	12	0	6.00
73-74	Sherbrooke	QMJHL	35	2061	...	...	...	158	0	4.60	1	60	...	...	3	0	3.00
74-75	Philadelphia	NAHL	43	2277	...	...	...	131	3	3.45	—	—	—	—	—	—	—
75-76	Richmond	AHL	7	402	...	...	...	30	0	4.48	—						
	—Philadelphia	NAHL	29	1601	...	...	...	97	1	3.64	3	171	...	...	15	0	5.26
76-77	Philadelphia	NAHL	51	2763	26	19	1	170	1	3.69	3	191	...	...	14	0	4.40
	—Springfield	AHL	3	180	2	1	0	10	0	3.33	—						
77-78	Philadelphia	AHL	*60	*3585	31	21	7	177	4	2.96	2	119	0	2	12	0	6.05
78-79	Atlanta	NHL	18	994	8	8	1	55	0	3.32	1	20	0	0	0	0	0.00
	—Philadelphia	AHL	13	780	3	9	1	36	0	2.77	—						
79-80	Birmingham	CHL	38	2188	13	21	2	137	0	3.76	2	79	0	1	5	0	3.80
	—Atlanta	NHL	3	150	0	2	0	15	0	6.00	—						
80-81	Birmingham	CHL	13	757	3	8	2	56	0	4.44	—						
	—Calgary	NHL	29	1629	14	6	7	88	2	3.24	6	366	3	3	22	0	3.61
81-82	Calgary	NHL	34	1866	10	5	6	135	0	4.34	—						
82-83	Calgary	NHL	39	2211	16	12	8	133	0	3.61	7	327	3	3	27	0	4.95
83-84	Calgary	NHL	51	2568	21	12	9	150	0	3.50	8	448	4	4	32	0	4.29
84-85	Calgary	NHL	56	3176	30	12	10	183	1	3.46	4	248	1	3	15	1	3.63
85-86	Calgary	NHL	60	3369	29	24	4	229	1	4.08	3	109	0	1	7	0	3.85
86-87	Calgary	NHL	34	1735	16	9	1	94	2	3.25	2	101	0	1	6	0	3.56
87-88	Boston	NHL	49	2828	24	17	6	138	3	2.93	17	1027	11	6	45	†1	*2.63
88-89	Boston	NHL	40	2392	19	15	6	120	0	3.01	4	252	1	3	16	0	3.81
89-90	Boston	NHL	43	2310	22	15	2	108	2	2.81	3	135	0	1	13	0	5.78
90-91	Boston	NHL	33	1829	17	10	3	111	1	3.64	2	32	0	0	0	0	0.00
91-92	Boston	NHL	8	407	5	1	0	23	0	3.39	2	54	0	0	3	0	3.33
92-93	Boston	NHL	10	542	5	4	0	31	0	3.43	—	—	—	—	—	—	—
NHL totals			507	28006	236	152	63	1613	12	3.46	59	3119	23	25	186	2	3.58

LEMIEUX, CLAUDE
RW, DEVILS

PERSONAL: Born July 16, 1965, at Buckingham, Que.... 6-1/215.... Shoots right.... Name pronounced luh-MYOO.... Brother of Jocelyn Lemieux, right winger, Chicago Blackhawks.
TRANSACTIONS/CAREER NOTES: Selected by Montreal Canadiens as underage junior in second round (second Canadiens pick, 26th overall) of NHL entry draft (June 8, 1983).... Tore ankle ligaments (October 1987).... Fractured orbital bone above right eye (January 14, 1988).... Pulled groin (March 1989).... Underwent surgery to repair torn stomach muscle (November 1, 1989); missed 41 games.... Traded by Canadiens to New Jersey Devils for LW Sylvain Turgeon (September 4, 1990).... Suffered contusion of right eye retina (February 25, 1991).... Suffered sore back (November 27, 1991); missed four games.... Injured ankle (March 11, 1992).... Suffered back spasms (October 24, 1992); missed three games.... Injured right elbow (March 21, 1993); missed one game.
HONORS: Named to QMJHL All-Star second team (1983-84).... Won Guy Lafleur Trophy (1984-85).... Named to QMJHL All-Star first team (1984-85).
MISCELLANEOUS: Member of Stanley Cup championship team (1986).

			REGULAR SEASON					PLAYOFFS				
Season	Team	League	Gms.	G	A	Pts.	Pen.	Gms.	G	A	Pts.	Pen.
82-83	Trois-Rivieres	QMJHL	62	28	38	66	187	4	1	0	1	30
83-84	Verdun	QMJHL	51	41	45	86	225	9	8	12	20	63
	—Montreal	NHL	8	1	1	2	12	—				
	—Nova Scotia	AHL	—	—	—	—	—	2	1	0	1	0
84-85	Verdun	QMJHL	52	58	66	124	152	14	*23	17	*40	38
	—Montreal	NHL	1	0	1	1	7	—				
85-86	Sherbrooke	AHL	58	21	32	53	145	—				
	—Montreal	NHL	10	1	2	3	22	20	10	6	16	68
86-87	Montreal	NHL	76	27	26	53	156	17	4	9	13	41
87-88	Montreal	NHL	80	31	30	61	137	11	3	2	5	20
88-89	Montreal	NHL	69	29	22	51	136	18	4	3	7	58
89-90	Montreal	NHL	39	8	10	18	106	11	1	3	4	38
90-91	New Jersey	NHL	78	30	17	47	105	7	4	0	4	34
91-92	New Jersey	NHL	74	41	27	68	109	7	4	3	7	26
92-93	New Jersey	NHL	77	30	51	81	155	5	2	0	2	19
NHL totals			512	198	187	385	945	96	32	26	58	304

LEMIEUX, JOCELYN
RW, BLACKHAWKS

PERSONAL: Born November 18, 1967, at Mont Laurier, Que.... 5-10/200.... Shoots left.... Brother of Claude Lemieux, right winger, New Jersey Devils.
TRANSACTIONS/CAREER NOTES: Selected by St. Louis Blues as underage junior in first round (first Blues pick, 10th overall) of NHL entry draft (June 21, 1986).... Severed tendon in little finger of left hand (December 1986).... Broke left leg and tore ligaments (January 1988).... Traded by Blues with G Darrell May and second-round pick in 1989 draft (D Patrice Brisebois) to Montreal Canadiens for LW Sergio Mo-

messo and G Vincent Riendeau (August 9, 1988).... Traded by Canadiens to Chicago Blackhawks for third-round pick in 1990 draft (D Charles Poulin) (January 5, 1990).... Suffered concussion and cracked orbital bone above right eye (February 26, 1991); missed a month.
HONORS: Named to QMJHL All-Star first team (1985-86).

			REGULAR SEASON					PLAYOFFS			
Season Team	League	Gms.	G	A	Pts.	Pen.	Gms.	G	A	Pts.	Pen.
84-85—Laval	QMJHL	68	13	19	32	92	—	—	—	—	—
85-86—Laval	QMJHL	71	57	68	125	131	14	9	15	24	37
86-87—St. Louis	NHL	53	10	8	18	94	5	0	1	1	6
87-88—Peoria	IHL	8	0	5	5	35	—	—	—	—	—
—St. Louis	NHL	23	1	0	1	42	5	0	0	0	0
88-89—Montreal	NHL	1	0	1	1	0	—	—	—	—	—
—Sherbrooke	AHL	73	25	28	53	134	4	3	1	4	6
89-90—Montreal	NHL	34	4	2	6	61	—	—	—	—	—
—Chicago	NHL	39	10	11	21	47	18	1	8	9	28
90-91—Chicago	NHL	67	6	7	13	119	4	0	0	0	0
91-92—Chicago	NHL	78	6	10	16	80	18	3	1	4	33
92-93—Chicago	NHL	81	10	21	31	111	4	1	0	1	2
NHL totals		376	47	60	107	554	54	5	10	15	69

LEMIEUX, MARIO
C, PENGUINS

PERSONAL: Born October 5, 1965, at Montreal.... 6-4/210.... Shoots right.... Name pronounced luh-MYOO.... Brother of Alain Lemieux, center, St. Louis Blues, Quebec Nordiques and Pittsburgh Penguins (1981-82 through 1986-87).
TRANSACTIONS/CAREER NOTES: Selected by Pittsburgh Penguins as underage junior in first round (first Penguins pick, first overall) of NHL entry draft (June 9, 1984).... Sprained left knee (September 1984).... Reinjured knee (December 2, 1984).... Sprained right knee (December 20, 1986).... Bruised right shoulder (November 1987).... Sprained right wrist (November 3, 1988).... Suffered herniated disk (February 14, 1990); missed 21 games.... Underwent surgery to remove part of herniated disk (July 11, 1990); missed first 50 games of season.... Suffered back spasms (October 1991); missed three games.... Suffered back spasms (January 4, 1992); missed three games.... Injured back (January 29, 1992); missed six games.... Suffered from the flu (February 1992); missed one game.... Fractured bone in hand (May 5, 1992).... Injured heel (December 1992); missed one game.... Injured back (January 5, 1993); missed three games.... Diagnosed with Hodgkin's Disease (January 12, 1993) and underwent radiation treatment (February 1-March 2); missed 20 games.
HONORS: Named to QMJHL All-Star second team (1982-83).... Won Can.HL Player of the Year Award (1983-84).... Won Michel Briere Trophy (1983-84).... Won Jean Beliveau Trophy (1983-84).... Won Michael Bossy Trophy (1983-84).... Won Guy Lafleur Trophy (1983-84).... Named to QMJHL All-Star first team (1983-84).... Named NHL Rookie of the Year by THE SPORTING NEWS (1984-85).... Won Calder Memorial Trophy (1984-85).... Named to NHL All-Rookie team (1984-85).... Won Lester B. Pearson Award (1985-86 and 1987-88).... Named to THE SPORTING NEWS All-Star second team (1985-86).... Named to NHL All-Star second team (1985-86, 1986-87 and 1991-92).... Played in NHL All-Star Game (1985, 1986, 1988 through 1990 and 1992).... Named All-Star Game Most Valuable Player (1985, 1988 and 1990).... Named NHL Player of the Year by THE SPORTING NEWS (1987-88, 1988-89 and 1992-93).... Won Hart Memorial Trophy (1987-88 and 1992-93).... Won Art Ross Memorial Trophy (1987-88, 1988-89, 1991-92 and 1992-93).... Won Dodge Performance of the Year Award (1987-88 and 1988-89).... Won Dodge Performer of the Year Award (1987-88 and 1988-89).... Named to THE SPORTING NEWS All-Star first team (1987-88, 1988-89 and 1992-93).... Named to NHL All-Star first team (1987-88, 1988-89 and 1992-93).... Won Dodge Ram Tough Award (1988-89).... Won the Conn Smythe Trophy (1990-91 and 1991-92).... Won Pro Set NHL Player of the Year Award (1991-92).... Won Bill Masterton Memorial Trophy (1992-93).
RECORDS: Holds NHL career records for highest goals-per-game average—.827; most overtime points—14.... Shares NHL career record for most overtime goals—7.... Holds NHL single-season record for most shorthanded goals—13 (1988-89).... Shares NHL single-game playoff records for most goals—5 (April 25, 1989); most points—8 (April 25, 1989); most goals in one period—4 (April 25, 1989); and most points in one period—4 (April 25, 1989).... Holds NHL All-Star single-game record for most points—6 (1988).... Shares NHL All-Star single-game record for most goals—4 (1990).
MISCELLANEOUS: Member of Stanley Cup championship teams (1991 and 1992).

			REGULAR SEASON					PLAYOFFS			
Season Team	League	Gms.	G	A	Pts.	Pen.	Gms.	G	A	Pts.	Pen.
81-82—Laval	QMJHL	64	30	66	96	22	18	5	9	14	31
82-83—Laval	QMJHL	66	84	100	184	76	12	†14	18	32	18
83-84—Laval	QMJHL	70	*133	*149	*282	92	14	*29	*23	*52	29
84-85—Pittsburgh	NHL	73	43	57	100	54	—	—	—	—	—
85-86—Pittsburgh	NHL	79	48	93	141	43	—	—	—	—	—
86-87—Pittsburgh	NHL	63	54	53	107	57	—	—	—	—	—
87-88—Pittsburgh	NHL	77	*70	98	*168	92	—	—	—	—	—
88-89—Pittsburgh	NHL	76	*85	†114	*199	100	11	12	7	19	16
89-90—Pittsburgh	NHL	59	45	78	123	78	—	—	—	—	—
90-91—Pittsburgh	NHL	26	19	26	45	30	23	16	*28	*44	16
91-92—Pittsburgh	NHL	64	44	87	*131	94	15	*16	18	*34	2
92-93—Pittsburgh	NHL	60	69	91	*160	38	11	8	10	18	10
NHL totals		577	477	697	1174	586	60	52	63	115	44

LENARDUZZI, MIKE
G, WHALERS

PERSONAL: Born September 14, 1972, at Mississauga, Ont.... 6-1/168.... Shoots left.... Name pronounced leh-nuhr-DOO-zee.
TRANSACTIONS/CAREER NOTES: Traded by Oshawa 67's with RW Mike DeCoff, RW Jason Denomme, second-round picks in 1990 (D Drew Bannister) and 1991 drafts and cash to Sault Ste. Marie Greyhounds for C Eric Lindros (December 17, 1989).... Selected by Hartford Whalers in third round (third Whalers pick, 57th overall) of NHL entry draft (June 16, 1990).
HONORS: Shared Dave Pinkney Trophy with Kevin Hodson (1990-91).

Season	Team	League	REGULAR SEASON								PLAYOFFS						
			Gms.	Min.	W	L	T	GA	SO	Avg.	Gms.	Min.	W	L	GA	SO	Avg.
88-89	—Markham Jr. B	OHA	20	1149	...	...	...	111	0	5.80	—	—	—	—	—	—	—
	—Oshawa	OHL	6	166	...	...	...	9	0	3.25	—	—	—	—	—	—	—
89-90	—Oshawa	OHL	12	444	6	3	1	32	0	4.32	—	—	—	—	—	—	—
	—Sault Ste. Marie	OHL	20	1117	...	...	...	66	0	3.55	—	—	—	—	—	—	—
90-91	—Sault Ste. Marie	OHL	35	1966	19	8	3	107	0	3.27	5	268	3	1	13	*1	2.91
91-92	—Sault Ste. Marie	OHL	9	486	5	3	0	33	0	4.07	—	—	—	—	—	—	—
	—Ottawa	OHL	18	986	5	12	1	60	1	3.65	—	—	—	—	—	—	—
	—Sudbury	OHL	22	1201	11	5	4	84	2	4.20	11	651	4	7	38	0	3.50
	—Springfield	AHL	—	—	—	—	—	—	—	—	1	39	0	0	2	0	3.08
92-93	—Springfield	AHL	36	1945	10	17	5	142	0	4.38	2	100	1	0	5	0	3.00
	—Hartford	NHL	3	168	1	1	1	9	0	3.21	—	—	—	—	—	—	—
NHL totals			3	168	1	1	1	9	0	3.21							

LEROUX, FRANCOIS
D, OILERS

PERSONAL: Born April 18, 1970, at St. Adele, Que. . . . 6-6/221. . . . Shoots left. . . . Name pronounced fran-SWAH-luh-ROO.
TRANSACTIONS/CAREER NOTES: Selected by Edmonton Oilers in first round (first Oilers pick, 19th overall) of NHL entry draft (June 11, 1988). . . . Separated shoulder (March 20, 1989). . . . Traded by St. Jean Lynx with LW Patrick Lebeau and LW Jean Blouin to Victoriaville Tigres for RW Trevor Duhaime, second- and third-round draft picks and future considerations (February 15, 1990). . . . Tore left knee ligaments (March 18, 1990). . . . Underwent surgery to left knee (March 22, 1990).

Season	Team	League	REGULAR SEASON					PLAYOFFS				
			Gms.	G	A	Pts.	Pen.	Gms.	G	A	Pts.	Pen.
87-88	—St. Jean	QMJHL	58	3	8	11	143	7	2	0	2	21
88-89	—Edmonton	NHL	2	0	0	0	0	—	—	—	—	—
	—St. Jean	QMJHL	57	8	34	42	185	—	—	—	—	—
89-90	—Edmonton	NHL	3	0	1	1	0	—	—	—	—	—
	—St. Jean/Victoriaville	QMJHL	54	4	33	37	160	—	—	—	—	—
90-91	—Cape Breton	AHL	71	2	7	9	124	4	0	1	1	19
	—Edmonton	NHL	1	0	2	2	0	—	—	—	—	—
91-92	—Cape Breton	AHL	61	7	22	29	114	5	0	0	0	8
	—Edmonton	NHL	4	0	0	0	7	—	—	—	—	—
92-93	—Cape Breton	AHL	55	10	24	34	139	16	0	5	5	29
	—Edmonton	NHL	1	0	0	0	4	—	—	—	—	—
NHL totals			11	0	3	3	11					

LESCHYSHYN, CURTIS
D, NORDIQUES

PERSONAL: Born September 21, 1969, at Thompson, Man. . . . 6-1/205. . . . Shoots left. . . . Full name: Curtis Michael Leschyshyn. . . . Name pronounced luh-SIH-shuhn.
TRANSACTIONS/CAREER NOTES: Selected by Quebec Nordiques in first round (first Nordiques pick, third overall) of NHL entry draft (June 11, 1988). . . . Separated shoulder (January 10, 1989). . . . Sprained left knee (November 1989). . . . Damaged knee ligaments (February 18, 1991) and underwent surgery (February 20, 1991); missed final 19 games of 1990-91 season and first 30 games of 1991-92 season. . . . Suffered back strain (October 13, 1992); missed two games.
HONORS: Named to WHL (East) All-Star first team (1987-88).

Season	Team	League	REGULAR SEASON					PLAYOFFS				
			Gms.	G	A	Pts.	Pen.	Gms.	G	A	Pts.	Pen.
85-86	—Saskatoon	WHL	1	0	0	0	0	—	—	—	—	—
86-87	—Saskatoon	WHL	70	14	26	40	107	11	1	5	6	14
87-88	—Saskatoon	WHL	56	14	41	55	86	10	2	5	7	16
88-89	—Quebec	NHL	71	4	9	13	71	—	—	—	—	—
89-90	—Quebec	NHL	68	2	6	8	44	—	—	—	—	—
90-91	—Quebec	NHL	55	3	7	10	49	—	—	—	—	—
91-92	—Quebec	NHL	42	5	12	17	42	—	—	—	—	—
	—Halifax	AHL	6	0	2	2	4	—	—	—	—	—
92-93	—Quebec	NHL	82	9	23	32	61	6	1	1	2	6
NHL totals			318	23	57	80	267	6	1	1	2	6

LESLIE, LEE
LW, SHARKS

PERSONAL: Born August 15, 1972, at Prince George, B.C. . . . 6-4/203. . . . Shoots left.
HIGH SCHOOL: Carlton Comprensive (Prince Albert, Sask.).
TRANSACTIONS/CAREER NOTES: Selected by St. Louis Blues in fourth round (fourth Blues pick, 86th overall) of NHL entry draft (June 20, 1992). . . . Signed as free agent by San Jose Sharks (June 21, 1993).

Season	Team	League	REGULAR SEASON					PLAYOFFS				
			Gms.	G	A	Pts.	Pen.	Gms.	G	A	Pts.	Pen.
88-89	—Prince George	BCJHL	50	19	23	42	62	—	—	—	—	—
89-90	—Prince Albert	WHL	62	14	16	30	13	14	2	3	5	4
90-91	—Prince Albert	WHL	72	29	42	71	68	3	0	0	0	5
91-92	—Prince Albert	WHL	72	52	48	100	70	10	6	6	12	12
92-93	—Peoria	IHL	72	22	24	46	46	4	0	3	3	2

LESSARD, RICK
D, CANUCKS

PERSONAL: Born January 9, 1968, at Timmons, Ont. . . . 6-2/215. . . . Shoots left. . . . Name pronounced luh-SAHRD.
TRANSACTIONS/CAREER NOTES: Selected by Calgary Flames as underage junior in seventh round (sixth Flames pick, 142nd overall) of NHL entry draft (June 21, 1986). . . . Selected by San Jose Sharks in NHL expansion draft (May 30, 1991). . . . Punctured ear drum (October 23, 1991). . . . Traded by Sharks to Vancouver Canucks for RW Robin Bawa (December 15, 1992).
HONORS: Named to IHL All-Star first team (1988-89).

			—REGULAR SEASON—					—PLAYOFFS—				
Season Team	League	Gms.	G	A	Pts.	Pen.	Gms.	G	A	Pts.	Pen.
84-85—Ottawa	OHL	60	2	13	15	128	—	—	—	—	—
85-86—Ottawa	OHL	64	1	20	21	231	—	—	—	—	—
86-87—Ottawa	OHL	66	5	36	41	188	11	1	7	8	30
87-88—Ottawa	OHL	58	5	34	39	210	16	1	0	1	31
88-89—Calgary	NHL	6	0	1	1	2	—	—	—	—	—
—Salt Lake City	IHL	76	10	42	52	239	14	1	6	7	35
89-90—Salt Lake City	IHL	66	3	18	21	169	10	1	2	3	64
90-91—Calgary	NHL	1	0	1	1	0	—	—	—	—	—
—Salt Lake City	IHL	80	8	27	35	272	4	0	1	1	12
91-92—San Jose	NHL	8	0	2	2	16	—	—	—	—	—
—Kansas City	IHL	46	3	16	19	117	3	0	0	0	2
92-93—Kansas City	IHL	1	0	0	0	0	—	—	—	—	—
—Providence	AHL	6	0	0	0	6	—	—	—	—	—
—Hamilton	AHL	52	0	17	17	151	—	—	—	—	—
NHL totals		15	0	4	4	18					

LEVEQUE, GUY
C, KINGS

PERSONAL: Born December 28, 1972, at Kingston, Ont. . . . 5-11/180. . . . Shoots right. . . . Full name: Guy Scott Leveque. . . . Name pronounced luh-VECK. . . . Cousin of Mike Murray, center, Philadelphia Flyers (1987-88).
TRANSACTIONS/CAREER NOTES: Selected by Los Angeles Kings in second round (first Kings pick, 42nd overall) of NHL entry draft (June 22, 1991).

			—REGULAR SEASON—					—PLAYOFFS—				
Season Team	League	Gms.	G	A	Pts.	Pen.	Gms.	G	A	Pts.	Pen.
89-90—Cornwall	OHL	62	10	15	25	30	3	0	0	0	4
90-91—Cornwall	OHL	66	41	56	97	34	—	—	—	—	—
91-92—Cornwall	OHL	37	23	36	59	40	6	3	5	8	2
92-93—Phoenix	IHL	56	27	30	57	71	—	—	—	—	—
—Los Angeles	NHL	12	2	1	3	19	—	—	—	—	—
NHL totals		12	2	1	3	19					

LEVINS, SCOTT
RW, PANTHERS

PERSONAL: Born January 30, 1970, at Portland, Ore. . . . 6-3/200. . . . Shoots right. . . . Name pronounced LEH-vihns.
TRANSACTIONS/CAREER NOTES: Selected by Winnipeg Jets in fourth round (fourth Jets pick, 75th overall) of NHL entry draft (June 16, 1990). . . . Bruised shoulder (November 17, 1992); missed four games. . . . Selected by Florida Panthers in NHL expansion draft (June 24, 1993).
HONORS: Named to WHL All-Star second team (1989-90).

			—REGULAR SEASON—					—PLAYOFFS—				
Season Team	League	Gms.	G	A	Pts.	Pen.	Gms.	G	A	Pts.	Pen.
88-89—Penticton	BCJHL	50	27	58	85	154	—	—	—	—	—
89-90—Tri-City	WHL	71	25	37	62	132	6	2	3	5	18
90-91—Moncton	AHL	74	12	26	38	133	4	0	0	0	4
91-92—Moncton	AHL	69	15	18	33	271	11	3	4	7	30
92-93—Moncton	AHL	54	22	26	48	158	5	1	3	4	14
—Winnipeg	NHL	9	0	1	1	18	—	—	—	—	—
NHL totals		9	0	1	1	18					

LEVY, JEFF
G, STARS

PERSONAL: Born December 9, 1970, at Omaha, Neb. . . . 6-0/180. . . . Shoots left.
COLLEGE: New Hampshire.
TRANSACTIONS/CAREER NOTES: Selected by Minnesota North Stars in seventh round (seventh North Stars pick, 134th overall) of NHL entry draft (June 16, 1990). . . . North Stars franchise moved from Minnesota to Dallas and renamed Stars for 1993-94 season.
HONORS: Named Hockey East Rookie of the Year (1990-91). . . . Named to NCAA All-America East second team (1990-91). . . . Named to Hockey East All-Star second team (1990-91).

			—REGULAR SEASON—							—PLAYOFFS—					
Season Team	League	Gms.	Min.	W	L	T	GA	SO	Avg.	Gms.	Min.	W	L	GA	SO	Avg.
89-90—Rochester	USHL	32	1823	24	7	0	97	3	3.19	—	—	—	—	—	—	—
90-91—U. of New Hampshire	Hoc. East	24	1490	15	7	2	80	0	3.22	—	—	—	—	—	—	—
91-92—U. of New Hampshire	Hoc. East	35	2030	20	13	2	111	...	3.28	—	—	—	—	—	—	—
92-93—Kalamazoo	IHL	28	1512	8	14	0	115	0	4.56	—	—	—	—	—	—	—
—Dayton	ECHL	1	65	...	...	...	3	0	2.77	2	139	...	...	9	0	3.88

LIDSTER, DOUG
D, RANGERS

PERSONAL: Born October 18, 1960, at Kamloops, B.C. . . . 6-1/200. . . . Shoots right. . . . Full name: John Douglas Andrew Lidster.
COLLEGE: Colorado College.
TRANSACTIONS/CAREER NOTES: Selected by Vancouver Canucks in seventh round (sixth

Canucks pick, 133rd overall) of NHL entry draft (June 11, 1980).... Strained left knee (January 1988).... Hyperextended elbow (October 1988).... Broke hand (November 13, 1988).... Fractured cheekbone (March 1989).... Separated shoulder (March 1, 1992); missed 13 games.... Sprained knee (December 13, 1992); missed nine games.... Suffered from the flu (February 24, 1993); missed one game.... Traded by Canucks to New York Rangers (June 25, 1993) to complete deal in which Rangers sent G John Vanbiesbrouck to Canucks for future considerations (June 20, 1993).
HONORS: Named to WCHA All-Star first team (1981-82 and 1982-83).... Named to NCAA All-America West team (1982-83).

Season Team	League	REGULAR SEASON					PLAYOFFS				
		Gms.	G	A	Pts.	Pen.	Gms.	G	A	Pts.	Pen.
78-79—Kamloops	BCJHL	59	36	47	83	50	—	—	—	—	—
79-80—Colorado College	WCHA	39	18	25	43	52	—	—	—	—	—
80-81—Colorado College	WCHA	36	10	30	40	54	—	—	—	—	—
81-82—Colorado College	WCHA	36	13	22	35	32	—	—	—	—	—
82-83—Colorado College	WCHA	34	15	41	56	30	—	—	—	—	—
83-84—Canadian Olympic Team	Int'l	59	6	20	26	28	—	—	—	—	—
—Vancouver	NHL	8	0	0	0	4	2	0	1	1	0
84-85—Vancouver	NHL	78	6	24	30	55	—	—	—	—	—
85-86—Vancouver	NHL	78	12	16	28	56	3	0	1	1	2
86-87—Vancouver	NHL	80	12	51	63	40	—	—	—	—	—
87-88—Vancouver	NHL	64	4	32	36	105	—	—	—	—	—
88-89—Vancouver	NHL	63	5	17	22	78	7	1	1	2	9
89-90—Vancouver	NHL	80	8	28	36	36	—	—	—	—	—
90-91—Vancouver	NHL	78	6	32	38	77	6	0	2	2	6
91-92—Vancouver	NHL	66	6	23	29	39	11	1	2	3	11
92-93—Vancouver	NHL	71	6	19	25	36	12	0	3	3	8
NHL totals		666	65	242	307	526	41	2	10	12	36

LIDSTROM, NICKLAS
D, RED WINGS

PERSONAL: Born April 28, 1970, at Vasteras, Sweden.... 6-2/180.... Shoots left.... Name pronounced LIHD-struhm.
TRANSACTIONS/CAREER NOTES: Selected by Detroit Red Wings in third round (third Red Wings pick, 53rd overall) of NHL entry draft (June 17, 1989).
HONORS: Named to Swedish League All-Star team (1990-91).... Named to NHL All-Rookie team (1991-92).

Season Team	League	REGULAR SEASON					PLAYOFFS				
		Gms.	G	A	Pts.	Pen.	Gms.	G	A	Pts.	Pen.
88-89—Vasteras	Sweden	19	0	2	2	4	—	—	—	—	—
89-90—Vasteras	Sweden	39	8	8	16	14	—	—	—	—	—
90-91—Vasteras	Sweden	20	2	12	14	14	—	—	—	—	—
91-92—Detroit	NHL	80	11	49	60	22	11	1	2	3	0
92-93—Detroit	NHL	84	7	34	41	28	7	1	0	1	0
NHL totals		164	18	83	101	50	18	2	2	4	0

LINDBERG, CHRIS
LW, FLAMES

PERSONAL: Born April 16, 1967, at Fort Francis, Ont.... 6-1/185.... Shoots left.
COLLEGE: Minnesota-Duluth.
TRANSACTIONS/CAREER NOTES: Signed as free agent by Hartford Whalers (March 17, 1989).... Signed as free agent by Calgary Flames (August 1991).... Selected by Ottawa Senators in NHL expansion draft (June 18, 1992).... Traded by Senators to Calgary Flames for D Mark Osiecki (June 23, 1992).... Injured knee (January 19, 1993); missed two games.
MISCELLANEOUS: Member of silver-medal-winning Canadian Olympic team (1992).

Season Team	League	REGULAR SEASON					PLAYOFFS				
		Gms.	G	A	Pts.	Pen.	Gms.	G	A	Pts.	Pen.
87-88—Minnesota-Duluth	WCHA	35	12	10	22	36	—	—	—	—	—
88-89—Minnesota-Duluth	WCHA	36	15	18	33	51	—	—	—	—	—
89-90—Binghamton	AHL	32	4	4	8	36	—	—	—	—	—
90-91—Canadian national team	Int'l	55	25	31	56	53	—	—	—	—	—
—Springfield	AHL	1	0	0	0	2	1	0	0	0	0
91-92—Canadian national team	Int'l	56	33	35	68	63	—	—	—	—	—
—Canadian Olympic Team	Int'l	8	1	4	5	4	—	—	—	—	—
—Calgary	NHL	17	2	5	7	17	—	—	—	—	—
92-93—Calgary	NHL	62	9	12	21	18	2	0	1	1	2
NHL totals		79	11	17	28	35	2	0	1	1	2

LINDEN, TREVOR
C, CANUCKS

PERSONAL: Born April 11, 1970, at Medicine Hat, Alta.... 6-4/205.... Shoots right.
TRANSACTIONS/CAREER NOTES: Selected by Vancouver Canucks in first round (first Canucks pick, second overall) of NHL entry draft (June 11, 1988).... Hyperextended elbow (October 1989).... Separated shoulder (March 17, 1990).
HONORS: Named to WHL All-Star second team (1987-88).... Named to Memorial Cup All-Star team (1987-88).... Named to NHL All-Rookie team (1988-89).... Played in NHL All-Star Game (1991 and 1992).

Season Team	League	REGULAR SEASON					PLAYOFFS				
		Gms.	G	A	Pts.	Pen.	Gms.	G	A	Pts.	Pen.
85-86—Medicine Hat	WHL	5	2	0	2	0	—	—	—	—	—
86-87—Medicine Hat	WHL	72	14	22	36	59	20	5	4	9	17
87-88—Medicine Hat	WHL	67	46	64	110	76	16	†13	12	25	19
88-89—Vancouver	NHL	80	30	29	59	41	7	3	4	7	8
89-90—Vancouver	NHL	73	21	30	51	43	—	—	—	—	—

Season Team	League	REGULAR SEASON					PLAYOFFS				
		Gms.	G	A	Pts.	Pen.	Gms.	G	A	Pts.	Pen.
90-91—Vancouver	NHL	80	33	37	70	65	6	0	7	7	2
91-92—Vancouver	NHL	80	31	44	75	101	13	4	8	12	6
92-93—Vancouver	NHL	84	33	39	72	64	12	5	8	13	16
NHL totals		397	148	179	327	314	38	12	27	39	32

LINDGREN, MATS
C, JETS

PERSONAL: Born October 1, 1974, at Skelleftea, Sweden.... 6-1/187.... Shoots left.
TRANSACTIONS/CAREER NOTES: Selected by Winnipeg Jets in first round (first Jets pick, 15th overall) of NHL entry draft (June 26, 1993).

Season Team	League	REGULAR SEASON					PLAYOFFS				
		Gms.	G	A	Pts.	Pen.	Gms.	G	A	Pts.	Pen.
90-91—Skelleftea	Swed. Dv.II	1	0	0	0	0	—	—	—	—	—
91-92—Skelleftea	Swed. Dv.II	29	14	8	22	14	—	—	—	—	—
92-93—Skelleftea	Swed. Dv.II	32	20	14	34	18	—	—	—	—	—

LINDROS, ERIC
C, FLYERS

PERSONAL: Born February 28, 1973, at London, Ont.... 6-5/235.... Shoots right.... Name pronounced LIHND-rahz.
TRANSACTIONS/CAREER NOTES: Selected by Sault Ste. Marie Greyhounds in OHL priority draft; refused to report (August 30, 1989); played for Detroit Compuware.... Rights traded by Greyhounds to Oshawa Generals for RW Mike DeCoff, RW Jason Denomme, G Mike Lenarduzzi, second-round picks in 1991 and 1992 drafts and cash (December 17, 1989).... Suspended two games by OHL for fighting (February 7, 1990).... Selected by Quebec Nordiques in first round (first Nordiques pick, first overall) of NHL entry draft (June 22, 1991); refused to report.... Traded by Nordiques to Philadelphia Flyers for G Ron Hextall, C Mike Ricci, C Peter Forsberg, D Steve Duchesne, D Kerry Huffman, first-round pick in 1993 draft (G Jocelyn Thibault), cash and future considerations (June 20, 1992); Flyers sent LW Chris Simon and first-round pick in 1994 draft to Nordiques to complete deal (July 21, 1992).... Sprained medial collateral ligament (November 22, 1992); missed nine games.... Injured knee (December 29, 1992); missed two games.... Reinjured knee (January 10, 1993); missed 12 games.
HONORS: Named to Memorial Cup All-Star Team (1989-90).... Won Can.HL Player of the Year Award (1990-91).... Won Can.HL Plus/Minus Award (1990-91).... Won Can.HL Top Draft Prospect Award (1990-91).... Won Red Tilson Trophy (1990-91).... Won Eddie Powers Memorial Trophy (1990-91).... Named to OHL All-Star first team (1990-91).
MISCELLANEOUS: Member of silver-medal-winning Canadian Olympic team (1992).... Named to NHL All-Rookie team (1992-93).

Season Team	League	REGULAR SEASON					PLAYOFFS				
		Gms.	G	A	Pts.	Pen.	Gms.	G	A	Pts.	Pen.
88-89—St. Michaels	MTHL	36	25	42	67	...	—	—	—	—	—
89-90—Detroit Compuware	NAJHL	14	25	27	52	...	—	—	—	—	—
—Oshawa	OHL	25	17	19	36	61	17	*18	18	36	*76
90-91—Oshawa	OHL	57	*71	78	*149	189	16	*18	20	*38	*93
91-92—Oshawa	OHL	13	9	22	31	54	—	—	—	—	—
—Canadian national team	Int'l	24	19	16	35	34	—	—	—	—	—
—Canadian Olympic Team	Int'l	8	5	6	11	6	—	—	—	—	—
92-93—Philadelphia	NHL	61	41	34	75	147	—	—	—	—	—
NHL totals		61	41	34	75	147					

LINDSAY, BILL
LW, PANTHERS

PERSONAL: Born May 17, 1971, at Big Fork, Mont.... 5-11/185.... Shoots left.... Full name: William Hamilton Lindsay.
TRANSACTIONS/CAREER NOTES: Selected by Quebec Nordiques in fifth round (sixth Nordiques pick, 103rd overall) of NHL entry draft (June 22, 1991).... Separated right shoulder (December 26, 1992); missed four games.... Selected by Florida Panthers in NHL expansion draft (June 24, 1993).
HONORS: Named to WHL (West) All-Star second team (1991-92).

Season Team	League	REGULAR SEASON					PLAYOFFS				
		Gms.	G	A	Pts.	Pen.	Gms.	G	A	Pts.	Pen.
89-90—Tri-City	WHL	72	40	45	85	84	—	—	—	—	—
90-91—Tri-City	WHL	63	46	47	93	151	—	—	—	—	—
91-92—Tri-City	WHL	42	34	59	93	111	3	2	3	5	16
—Quebec	NHL	23	2	4	6	14	—	—	—	—	—
92-93—Quebec	NHL	44	4	9	13	16	—	—	—	—	—
—Halifax	AHL	20	11	13	24	18	—	—	—	—	—
NHL totals		67	6	13	19	30					

LiPUMA, CHRIS
D, LIGHTNING

PERSONAL: Born March 23, 1971, at Chicago.... 6-0/183.... Shoots left.
TRANSACTIONS/CAREER NOTES: Signed as free agent by Tampa Bay Lightning (August 24, 1992).

Season Team	League	REGULAR SEASON					PLAYOFFS				
		Gms.	G	A	Pts.	Pen.	Gms.	G	A	Pts.	Pen.
88-89—Kitchener	OHL	59	7	13	20	101	—	—	—	—	—
89-90—Kitchener	OHL	63	11	26	37	125	17	1	4	5	6
90-91—Kitchener	OHL	61	6	30	36	145	4	0	1	1	4
91-92—Kitchener	OHL	61	13	59	72	115	14	4	9	13	34
92-93—Atlanta	IHL	66	4	14	18	379	9	1	1	2	35
—Tampa Bay	NHL	15	0	5	5	34	—	—	—	—	—
NHL totals		15	0	5	5	34					

LITTMAN, DAVID

G, LIGHTNING

PERSONAL: Born June 13, 1967, at Cranston, R.I. . . . 6-0/183. . . . Shoots left. **COLLEGE:** Boston College.

TRANSACTIONS/CAREER NOTES: Selected by Buffalo Sabres in 11th round (12th Sabres pick, 211th overall) of NHL entry draft (June 13, 1987). . . . Separated shoulder (December 1989); missed six games. . . . Signed as free agent by Tampa Bay Lightning (August 27, 1992).

HONORS: Named to Hockey East All-Star second team (1987-88). . . . Named to NCAA All-America East second team (1988-89). . . . Named to Hockey East All-Star first team (1988-89). . . . Shared Harry (Hap) Holmes Memorial Trophy with Darcy Wakaluk (1990-91). . . . Named to AHL All-Star first team (1990-91). . . . Won Harry (Hap) Holmes Memorial Trophy (1991-92). . . . Named to AHL All-Star second team (1991-92).

Season Team	League	Gms.	Min.	W	L	T	GA	SO	Avg.	Gms.	Min.	W	L	GA	SO	Avg.
85-86—Boston College	Hoc. East	9	442	4	0	1	22	1	2.99	—	—	—	—	—	—	—
86-87—Boston College	Hoc. East	21	1182	15	5	0	68	0	3.45	—	—	—	—	—	—	—
87-88—Boston College	Hoc. East	30	1726	11	16	2	116	0	4.03	—	—	—	—	—	—	—
88-89—Boston College	Hoc. East	32	1945	19	9	4	107	0	3.30	—	—	—	—	—	—	—
89-90—Rochester	AHL	14	681	5	6	1	37	0	3.26	1	33	. . .	. . .	4	0	7.27
—Phoenix	IHL	18	1047	8	7	2	64	0	3.67	—	—	—	—	—	—	—
90-91—Buffalo	NHL	1	36	0	0	0	3	0	5.00	—	—	—	—	—	—	—
—Rochester	AHL	*56	*3155	*33	13	5	160	3	3.04	8	378	4	2	16	0	2.54
91-92—Rochester	AHL	*61	*3558	*29	20	9	174	†3	2.93	15	879	8	†7	43	1	2.94
—Buffalo	NHL	1	60	0	1	0	4	0	4.00	—	—	—	—	—	—	—
92-93—Atlanta	IHL	44	2390	23	12	0	134	0	3.36	3	178	1	2	8	0	2.70
—Tampa Bay	NHL	1	45	0	1	0	7	0	9.33	—	—	—	—	—	—	—
NHL totals		3	141	0	2	0	14	0	5.96							

LOACH, LONNIE

LW, MIGHTY DUCKS

PERSONAL: Born April 14, 1968, at New Liskeard, Ont. . . . 5-10/181. . . . Shoots left. **TRANSACTIONS/CAREER NOTES:** Selected by Chicago Blackhawks as underage junior in fifth round (fourth Blackhawks pick, 98th overall) of NHL entry draft (June 21, 1986). . . . Signed as free agent by Fort Wayne Komets after being released by Blackhawks (August 1990). . . . Signed as free agent by Detroit Red Wings (April 20, 1991). . . . Selected by Ottawa Senators in NHL expansion draft (June 18, 1992). . . . Claimed on waivers by Los Angeles Kings (October 21, 1992). . . . Fractured thumb (December 13, 1992); missed 11 games. . . . Selected by Mighty Ducks of Anaheim in NHL expansion draft (June 24, 1993).

HONORS: Won Emms Family Award (1985-86). . . . Won Leo P. Lamoureux Memorial Trophy (1990-91). . . . Named to IHL All-Star second team (1990-91).

Season Team	League	Gms.	G	A	Pts.	Pen.	Gms.	G	A	Pts.	Pen.
84-85—St. Mary's Jr. B	OHA	44	26	36	62	113	—	—	—	—	—
85-86—Guelph	OHL	65	41	42	83	63	20	7	8	15	16
86-87—Guelph	OHL	56	31	24	55	42	5	2	1	3	2
87-88—Guelph	OHL	66	43	49	92	75	—	—	—	—	—
88-89—Saginaw	IHL	32	7	6	13	27	—	—	—	—	—
—Flint	IHL	41	22	26	48	30	—	—	—	—	—
89-90—Indianapolis	IHL	3	0	1	1	0	—	—	—	—	—
—Fort Wayne	IHL	54	15	33	48	40	5	4	2	6	15
90-91—Fort Wayne	IHL	81	55	76	*131	45	19	5	11	16	13
91-92—Adirondack	AHL	67	37	49	86	69	†19	*13	4	17	10
92-93—Ottawa	NHL	3	0	0	0	0	—	—	—	—	—
—Los Angeles	NHL	50	10	13	23	27	1	0	0	0	0
—Phoenix	IHL	4	2	3	5	10	—	—	—	—	—
NHL totals		53	10	13	23	27	1	0	0	0	0

LOEWEN, DARCY

LW, SENATORS

PERSONAL: Born February 26, 1969, at Calgary, Alta. . . . 5-10/185. . . . Shoots left. . . . Full name: Darcy Alan Loewen. . . . Name pronounced LOH-wuhn. **HIGH SCHOOL:** H.J. Cody (Sylvan Lake, Alta.).

TRANSACTIONS/CAREER NOTES: Selected by Buffalo Sabres in third round (second Sabres pick, 55th overall) of NHL entry draft (June 11, 1988). . . . Selected by Ottawa Senators in NHL expansion draft (June 18, 1992). . . . Lacerated forearm (April 3, 1993); missed one game.

Season Team	League	Gms.	G	A	Pts.	Pen.	Gms.	G	A	Pts.	Pen.
85-86—Spokane	WHL	8	2	1	3	19	—	—	—	—	—
86-87—Spokane	WHL	68	15	25	40	129	5	0	0	0	0
87-88—Spokane	WHL	72	30	44	74	231	15	7	5	12	54
88-89—Spokane	WHL	60	31	27	58	194	—	—	—	—	—
—Canadian national team	Int'l	2	0	0	0	0	—	—	—	—	—
89-90—Rochester	AHL	50	7	11	18	193	5	1	0	1	6
—Buffalo	NHL	4	0	0	0	4	—	—	—	—	—
90-91—Buffalo	NHL	6	0	0	0	8	—	—	—	—	—
—Rochester	AHL	71	13	15	28	130	15	1	5	6	14
91-92—Buffalo	NHL	2	0	0	0	2	—	—	—	—	—
—Rochester	AHL	73	11	20	31	193	4	0	1	1	8
92-93—Ottawa	NHL	79	4	5	9	145	—	—	—	—	—
NHL totals		91	4	5	9	159					

LOISELLE, CLAUDE

C, ISLANDERS

PERSONAL: Born May 29, 1963, at Ottawa. . . . 5-11/195. . . . Shoots left.
TRANSACTIONS/CAREER NOTES: Selected as underage junior by Detroit Red Wings in second round (first Red Wings pick, 23rd overall) of NHL entry draft (June 10, 1981). . . . Suspended six games by NHL for stick-swinging incident (January 7, 1984). . . . Injured knee (December 17, 1985); missed 11 games. . . . Traded by Red Wings to New Jersey Devils for RW Tim Higgins (June 25, 1986). . . . Separated right shoulder (February 1988). . . . Traded by Devils with D Joe Cirella and eighth-round pick in 1990 draft (D Alexander Karpovtsev) to Quebec Nordiques for C Walt Poddubny and fourth-round pick (RW Mike Bodnarchuk) in 1990 draft (June 17, 1989). . . . Broke finger on left hand (February 1990). . . . Traded by Nordiques to Calgary Flames for LW Bryan Deasley (March 2, 1991); trade voided when Loiselle claimed on waivers by Toronto Maple Leafs (March 4, 1991). . . . Traded by Maple Leafs with RW Daniel Marois to New York Islanders for LW Ken Baumgartner and C Dave McLIwain (March 10, 1992). . . . Suffered sore shoulder (December 12, 1992); missed seven games. . . . Suffered concussion (January 9, 1993); missed one game. . . . Suffered back spasms (April 2, 1993); missed two games.

			REGULAR SEASON					PLAYOFFS				
Season	Team	League	Gms.	G	A	Pts.	Pen.	Gms.	G	A	Pts.	Pen.
79-80—	Gloucester	OPJHL	50	21	38	59	26	—	—	—	—	—
80-81—	Windsor	OMJHL	68	38	56	94	103	11	3	3	6	40
81-82—	Windsor	OHL	68	36	73	109	192	9	2	10	12	42
	—Detroit	NHL	4	1	0	1	2	—	—	—	—	—
82-83—	Detroit	NHL	18	2	0	2	15	—	—	—	—	—
	—Windsor	OHL	46	39	49	88	75	—	—	—	—	—
	—Adirondack	AHL	6	1	7	8	0	6	2	4	6	0
83-84—	Adirondack	AHL	29	13	16	29	59	—	—	—	—	—
	—Detroit	NHL	28	4	6	10	32	—	—	—	—	—
84-85—	Adirondack	AHL	47	22	29	51	24	—	—	—	—	—
	—Detroit	NHL	30	8	1	9	45	3	0	2	2	0
85-86—	Adirondack	AHL	21	15	11	26	32	16	5	10	15	38
	—Detroit	NHL	48	7	15	22	142	—	—	—	—	—
86-87—	New Jersey	NHL	75	16	24	40	137	—	—	—	—	—
87-88—	New Jersey	NHL	68	17	18	35	121	20	4	6	10	50
88-89—	New Jersey	NHL	74	7	14	21	209	—	—	—	—	—
89-90—	Quebec	NHL	72	11	14	25	104	—	—	—	—	—
90-91—	Quebec	NHL	59	5	10	15	86	—	—	—	—	—
	—Toronto	NHL	7	1	1	2	2	—	—	—	—	—
91-92—	Toronto	NHL	64	6	9	15	102	—	—	—	—	—
	—New York Islanders	NHL	11	1	1	2	13	—	—	—	—	—
92-93—	New York Islanders	NHL	41	5	3	8	90	18	0	3	3	10
NHL totals			599	91	116	207	1100	41	4	11	15	60

LOMAKIN, ANDREI

LW, PANTHERS

PERSONAL: Born April 3, 1964, at Voskresensk, U.S.S.R. . . . 5-10/176. . . . Shoots left. . . . Name pronounced loh-MAH-kihn.
TRANSACTIONS/CAREER NOTES: Selected by Philadelphia Flyers in seventh round (sixth Flyers pick, 107th overall) of NHL entry draft (June 22, 1991). . . . Fractured thumb (January 23, 1992); missed 15 games. . . . Bruised ribs prior to 1992-93 season; missed first game of season. . . . Bruised right foot (November 27, 1992); missed one game. . . . Separated shoulder (February 14, 1993); missed 10 games. . . . Selected by Florida Panthers in NHL expansion draft (June 24, 1993).
MISCELLANEOUS: Member of gold-medal-winning U.S.S.R. Olympic team (1988).

			REGULAR SEASON					PLAYOFFS				
Season	Team	League	Gms.	G	A	Pts.	Pen.	Gms.	G	A	Pts.	Pen.
81-82—	Khimik Voskresensk	USSR	8	1	1	2	2	—	—	—	—	—
82-83—	Khimik Voskresensk	USSR	56	15	8	23	32	—	—	—	—	—
83-84—	Khimik Voskresensk	USSR	44	10	8	18	26	—	—	—	—	—
84-85—	Khimik Voskresensk	USSR	52	13	10	23	24	—	—	—	—	—
86-87—	Dynamo Moscow	USSR	40	15	14	29	30	—	—	—	—	—
87-88—	Dynamo Moscow	USSR	45	10	15	25	24	—	—	—	—	—
88-89—	Dynamo Moscow	USSR	44	9	16	25	22	—	—	—	—	—
89-90—	Dynamo Moscow	USSR	48	11	15	26	36	—	—	—	—	—
90-91—	Dynamo Moscow	USSR	45	16	17	33	22	—	—	—	—	—
91-92—	Philadelphia	NHL	57	14	16	30	26	—	—	—	—	—
92-93—	Philadelphia	NHL	51	8	12	20	34	—	—	—	—	—
NHL totals			108	22	28	50	60	—	—	—	—	—

LONEY, BRIAN

RW, CANUCKS

PERSONAL: Born August 9, 1972, at Winnipeg, Man. . . . 6-2/195. . . . Shoots right.
COLLEGE: Ohio State.
TRANSACTIONS/CAREER NOTES: Selected by Vancouver Canucks in fifth round (sixth Canucks pick, 110th overall) of NHL entry draft (June 20, 1992).
HONORS: Named CCHA Rookie of the Year (1991-92).

			REGULAR SEASON					PLAYOFFS				
Season	Team	League	Gms.	G	A	Pts.	Pen.	Gms.	G	A	Pts.	Pen.
91-92—	Ohio State	CCHA	37	21	34	55	109	—	—	—	—	—
92-93—	Red Deer	WHL	66	39	36	75	147	4	1	1	2	19
	—Canadian national team	Int'l	1	0	1	1	0	—	—	—	—	—
	—Hamilton	AHL	3	0	2	2	0	—	—	—	—	—

LONEY, TROY

PERSONAL: Born September 21, 1963, at Bow Island, Alta.... 6-3/209.... Shoots left.... Name pronounced LOH-nee.

TRANSACTIONS/CAREER NOTES: Selected by Pittsburgh Penguins as underage junior in third round (third Penguins pick, 52nd overall) of NHL entry draft (June 9, 1982).... Suspended by AHL (December 1986).... Sprained right shoulder (January 17, 1987).... Underwent knee surgery (October 1987).... Suspended 10 games by NHL for leaving bench to fight (November 13, 1988).... Broke right hand (November 24, 1989); missed 12 games.... Underwent surgery to right knee (June 1990); missed first two months of season.... Bruised neck (November 8, 1992); missed two games.... Selected by Mighty Ducks of Anaheim in NHL expansion draft (June 24, 1993).

MISCELLANEOUS: Member of Stanley Cup championship teams (1991 and 1992).

				REGULAR SEASON					PLAYOFFS			
Season	Team	League	Gms.	G	A	Pts.	Pen.	Gms.	G	A	Pts.	Pen.
80-81	Lethbridge	WHL	71	18	13	31	100	9	2	3	5	14
81-82	Lethbridge	WHL	71	26	31	57	152	12	3	3	6	10
82-83	Lethbridge	WHL	72	33	34	67	156	20	10	7	17	43
83-84	Baltimore	AHL	63	18	13	31	147	10	0	2	2	19
	Pittsburgh	NHL	13	0	0	0	9	—	—	—	—	—
84-85	Baltimore	AHL	15	4	2	6	25	—	—	—	—	—
	Pittsburgh	NHL	46	10	8	18	59	—	—	—	—	—
85-86	Baltimore	AHL	33	12	11	23	84	—	—	—	—	—
	Pittsburgh	NHL	47	3	9	12	95	—	—	—	—	—
86-87	Baltimore	AHL	40	13	14	27	134	—	—	—	—	—
	Pittsburgh	NHL	23	8	7	15	22	—	—	—	—	—
87-88	Pittsburgh	NHL	65	5	13	18	151	—	—	—	—	—
88-89	Pittsburgh	NHL	69	10	6	16	165	11	1	3	4	24
89-90	Pittsburgh	NHL	67	11	16	27	168	—	—	—	—	—
90-91	Muskegon	IHL	2	0	0	0	5	—	—	—	—	—
	Pittsburgh	NHL	44	7	9	16	85	24	2	2	4	41
91-92	Pittsburgh	NHL	76	10	16	26	127	†21	4	5	9	32
92-93	Pittsburgh	NHL	82	5	16	21	99	10	1	4	5	0
	NHL totals		532	69	100	169	980	66	8	14	22	97

LONGO, CHRIS

PERSONAL: Born January 5, 1972, at Belleville, Ont.... 5-10/180.... Shoots right.... Full name: Chris Anthony Longo.

TRANSACTIONS/CAREER NOTES: Selected by Washington Capitals in third round (third Capitals pick, 51st overall) of NHL entry draft (June 16, 1990).

HONORS: Won Emms Family Award (1989-90).

				REGULAR SEASON					PLAYOFFS			
Season	Team	League	Gms.	G	A	Pts.	Pen.	Gms.	G	A	Pts.	Pen.
87-88	Kingston Jr. A	MTHL	37	15	16	31	...	—	—	—	—	—
88-89	Kingston Jr. A	MTHL	40	28	29	57	54	—	—	—	—	—
89-90	Peterborough	OHL	66	33	42	75	48	11	2	3	5	14
90-91	Peterborough	OHL	64	30	38	68	68	4	1	0	1	9
91-92	Peterborough	OHL	25	5	14	19	16	10	5	6	11	16
92-93	Baltimore	AHL	74	7	18	25	52	7	0	1	1	0

LORENZ, DANNY

PERSONAL: Born December 12, 1969, at Murrayville, B.C.... 5-10/183.... Shoots left.... Name pronounced luh-REHNS.

TRANSACTIONS/CAREER NOTES: Selected by New York Islanders in third round (fourth Islanders pick, 58th overall) of NHL entry draft (June 11, 1988).

HONORS: Won Del Wilson Trophy (1988-89).... Named to WHL (West) All-Star first team (1988-89 and 1989-90).

				REGULAR SEASON							PLAYOFFS					
Season	Team	League	Gms.	Min.	W	L	T	GA	SO	Avg.	Gms.	Min.	W	L	GA	SO	Avg.
86-87	Seattle	WHL	38	2103	12	21	2	199	0	5.68	—	—	—	—	—	—	—
87-88	Seattle	WHL	62	3302	20	37	2	*314	0	5.71	—	—	—	—	—	—	—
88-89	Seattle	WHL	*68	*4003	31	33	4	240	*3	3.60	—	—	—	—	—	—	—
	Springfield	AHL	4	210	2	1	0	12	0	3.43	—	—	—	—	—	—	—
89-90	Seattle	WHL	56	3226	37	15	2	221	0	4.11	13	751	6	7	40	0	*3.20
90-91	New York Islanders	NHL	2	80	0	1	0	5	0	3.75	—	—	—	—	—	—	—
	Capital District	AHL	17	940	5	9	2	70	0	4.47	—	—	—	—	—	—	—
	Richmond	ECHL	20	1020	6	9	2	75	0	4.41	—	—	—	—	—	—	—
91-92	Capital District	AHL	53	3050	22	22	7	*181	2	3.56	7	442	3	4	25	0	3.39
	New York Islanders	NHL	2	120	0	2	0	10	0	5.00	—	—	—	—	—	—	—
92-93	Capital District	AHL	44	2412	16	17	5	146	1	3.63	4	219	0	3	12	0	3.29
	New York Islanders	NHL	4	157	1	2	0	10	0	3.82	—	—	—	—	—	—	—
	NHL totals		8	357	1	5	0	25	0	4.20							

LOWE, KEVIN

PERSONAL: Born April 15, 1959, at Lachute, Que.... 6-2/195.... Shoots left.... Full name: Kevin Hugh Lowe.... Husband of Karen Percy, Canadian Olympic bronze-medal-winning downhill skier (1988).

TRANSACTIONS/CAREER NOTES: Selected by Edmonton Oilers in first round (first Oilers pick, 21st overall) of NHL entry draft (August 9, 1979).... Broke index finger (March 7, 1986); missed six games.... Broke left wrist (March 9, 1988).... Pulled rib muscle (September 1988).... Suffered concussion (October 14, 1988).... Suffered back spasms (April 8, 1990).... Bruised back (December 28, 1991); missed one game.... Strained rotator cuff (January 28,

1992); missed three games. . . . Re-strained rotator cuff (February 5, 1992); missed 21 games. . . . Strained groin (April 12, 1992); missed playoffs. . . . Did not report to Oilers in 1992-93 season because of contract dispute; missed 30 games. . . . Traded by Oilers to New York Rangers for RW Roman Oksyuta and third-round pick in 1993 draft (December 11, 1992). . . . Suffered stiff neck (December 19, 1992); missed one game. . . . Suffered from the flu (December 23, 1992); missed one game. . . . Injured back (February 15, 1993); missed one game. . . . Injured back (February 24, 1993); missed one game.
HONORS: Named to QMJHL All-Star second team (1977-78 and 1978-79). . . . Played in NHL All-Star Game (1984 through 1986, 1988 through 1990 and 1993). . . . Won King Clancy Memorial Trophy (1989-90). . . . Named Budweiser/NHL Man of the Year (1989-90).
MISCELLANEOUS: Member of Stanley Cup championship teams (1984, 1985, 1987, 1988 and 1990).

			REGULAR SEASON					PLAYOFFS			
Season Team	League	Gms.	G	A	Pts.	Pen.	Gms.	G	A	Pts.	Pen.
76-77—Quebec	QMJHL	69	3	19	22	39	—	—	—	—	—
77-78—Quebec	QMJHL	64	13	52	65	86	4	1	2	3	6
78-79—Quebec	QMJHL	68	26	60	86	120	6	1	7	8	36
79-80—Edmonton	NHL	64	2	19	21	70	3	0	1	1	0
80-81—Edmonton	NHL	79	10	24	34	94	9	0	2	2	11
81-82—Edmonton	NHL	80	9	31	40	63	5	0	3	3	0
82-83—Edmonton	NHL	80	6	34	40	43	16	1	8	9	10
83-84—Edmonton	NHL	80	4	42	46	59	19	3	7	10	16
84-85—Edmonton	NHL	80	4	22	26	104	16	0	5	5	8
85-86—Edmonton	NHL	74	2	16	18	90	10	1	3	4	15
86-87—Edmonton	NHL	77	8	29	37	94	21	2	4	6	22
87-88—Edmonton	NHL	70	9	15	24	89	19	0	2	2	26
88-89—Edmonton	NHL	76	7	18	25	98	7	1	2	3	4
89-90—Edmonton	NHL	78	7	26	33	140	20	0	2	2	10
90-91—Edmonton	NHL	73	3	13	16	113	14	1	1	2	14
91-92—Edmonton	NHL	55	2	8	10	107	11	0	3	3	16
92-93—New York Rangers	NHL	49	3	12	15	58	—	—	—	—	—
NHL totals		1015	76	309	385	1222	170	9	43	52	152

LOWRY, DAVE
LW, PANTHERS

PERSONAL: Born January 14, 1965, at Sudbury, Ont. . . . 6-1/195. . . . Shoots left.
HIGH SCHOOL: Sir Wilfrid Laurier (London, Ont.).
TRANSACTIONS/CAREER NOTES: Underwent arthroscopic knee surgery (December 1982). . . . Selected as underage junior by Vancouver Canucks in sixth round (fourth Canucks pick, 110th overall) of NHL entry draft (June 8, 1983). . . . Traded by Canucks to St. Louis Blues for C Ernie Vargas (September 29, 1988). . . . Suffered groin injury (March 1990). . . . Sprained shoulder (October 1991); missed two games. . . . Injured knee (October 26, 1992); missed 26 games. . . . Selected by Florida Panthers in NHL expansion draft (June 24, 1993).
HONORS: Named to OHL All-Star first team (1984-85).

			REGULAR SEASON					PLAYOFFS			
Season Team	League	Gms.	G	A	Pts.	Pen.	Gms.	G	A	Pts.	Pen.
82-83—London	OHL	42	11	16	27	48	3	0	0	0	14
83-84—London	OHL	66	29	47	76	125	8	6	6	12	41
84-85—London	OHL	61	60	60	120	94	8	6	5	11	10
85-86—Vancouver	NHL	73	10	8	18	143	3	0	0	0	0
86-87—Vancouver	NHL	70	8	10	18	176	—	—	—	—	—
87-88—Fredericton	AHL	46	18	27	45	59	14	7	3	10	72
—Vancouver	NHL	22	1	3	4	38	—	—	—	—	—
88-89—Peoria	IHL	58	31	35	66	45	—	—	—	—	—
—St. Louis	NHL	21	3	3	6	11	10	0	5	5	4
89-90—St. Louis	NHL	78	19	6	25	75	12	2	1	3	39
90-91—St. Louis	NHL	79	19	21	40	168	13	1	4	5	35
91-92—St. Louis	NHL	75	7	13	20	77	6	0	1	1	20
92-93—St. Louis	NHL	58	5	8	13	101	11	2	0	2	14
NHL totals		476	72	72	144	789	55	5	11	16	112

LUDWIG, CRAIG
D, STARS

PERSONAL: Born March 15, 1961, at Rhinelander, Wis. . . . 6-3/217. . . . Shoots left. . . . Full name: Craig Lee Ludwig.
COLLEGE: North Dakota.
TRANSACTIONS/CAREER NOTES: Selected by Montreal Canadiens in third round (fifth Canadiens pick, 61st overall) of NHL entry draft (June 11, 1980). . . . Fractured knuckle in left hand (October 1984). . . . Broke hand (December 2, 1985); missed nine games. . . . Broke right facial bone (January 1988); missed five games. . . . Suspended five games by NHL for elbowing (November 19, 1988). . . . Separated right shoulder (March 21, 1990). . . . Traded by Canadiens to New York Islanders for D Gerald Diduck (September 4, 1990). . . . Traded by Islanders to Minnesota North Stars as part of a three-way trade in which North Stars sent D Dave Babych to Vancouver Canucks and Canucks sent D Tom Kurvers to Islanders (June 22, 1991). . . . Injured foot (December 8, 1991); missed six games. . . . Injured foot (January 30, 1993); missed two games. . . . Suffered pinched nerve in neck (March 18, 1993); missed two games. . . . North Stars franchise moved from Minnesota to Dallas and renamed Stars for 1993-94 season.
HONORS: Named to WCHA All-Star second team (1981-82).
MISCELLANEOUS: Member of Stanley Cup championship team (1986).

			REGULAR SEASON					PLAYOFFS			
Season Team	League	Gms.	G	A	Pts.	Pen.	Gms.	G	A	Pts.	Pen.
79-80—Univ. of North Dakota	WCHA	33	1	8	9	32	—	—	—	—	—
80-81—Univ. of North Dakota	WCHA	34	4	8	12	48	—	—	—	—	—
81-82—Univ. of North Dakota	WCHA	47	5	26	31	70	—	—	—	—	—

Season Team	League	REGULAR SEASON					PLAYOFFS				
		Gms.	G	A	Pts.	Pen.	Gms.	G	A	Pts.	Pen.
82-83—Montreal	NHL	80	0	25	25	59	3	0	0	0	2
83-84—Montreal	NHL	80	7	18	25	52	15	0	3	3	23
84-85—Montreal	NHL	72	5	14	19	90	12	0	2	2	6
85-86—Montreal	NHL	69	2	4	6	63	20	0	1	1	48
86-87—Montreal	NHL	75	4	12	16	105	17	2	3	5	30
87-88—Montreal	NHL	74	4	10	14	69	11	1	1	2	6
88-89—Montreal	NHL	74	3	13	16	73	21	0	2	2	24
89-90—Montreal	NHL	73	1	15	16	108	11	0	1	1	16
90-91—New York Islanders	NHL	75	1	8	9	77	—	—	—	—	—
91-92—Minnesota	NHL	73	2	9	11	54	7	0	1	1	19
92-93—Minnesota	NHL	78	1	10	11	153	—	—	—	—	—
NHL totals		823	30	138	168	903	117	3	14	17	174

LUHNING, WARREN
RW, ISLANDERS

PERSONAL: Born July 3, 1975, at Edmonton, Alta.... 6-2/185.... Shoots right. **TRANSACTIONS/CAREER NOTES:** Selected by New York Islanders in fourth round (fourth Islanders pick, 92nd overall) of NHL entry draft (June 26, 1993).

Season Team	League	REGULAR SEASON					PLAYOFFS				
		Gms.	G	A	Pts.	Pen.	Gms.	G	A	Pts.	Pen.
92-93—Calgary Royals	AJHL	46	18	25	43	287	—	—	—	—	—

LUMME, JYRKI
D, CANUCKS

PERSONAL: Born July 16, 1966, at Tampere, Finland.... 6-1/207.... Shoots left.... Name pronounced LOO-MEE.
TRANSACTIONS/CAREER NOTES: Selected by Montreal Canadiens in third round (third Canadiens pick, 57th overall) of NHL entry draft (June 21, 1986).... Strained left knee ligaments (December 1988).... Stretched knee ligaments (February 21, 1989).... Bruised right foot (November 1989).... Traded by Canadiens to Vancouver Canucks for second-round pick in 1991 draft (C Craig Darby) (March 6, 1990).... Lacerated eye (November 19, 1991); missed three games.... Sprained knee (January 19, 1993); missed nine games.
MISCELLANEOUS: Member of silver-medal-winning Finnish Olympic team (1988).

Season Team	League	REGULAR SEASON					PLAYOFFS				
		Gms.	G	A	Pts.	Pen.	Gms.	G	A	Pts.	Pen.
84-85—Koo Vee	Finland	30	6	4	10	44	—	—	—	—	—
85-86—Ilves Tampere	Finland	31	1	5	6	4	—	—	—	—	—
86-87—Ilves Tampere	Finland	43	12	12	24	52	4	0	1	1	0
87-88—Ilves Tampere	Finland	43	8	22	30	75	—	—	—	—	—
88-89—Montreal	NHL	21	1	3	4	10	—	—	—	—	—
—Sherbrooke	AHL	26	4	11	15	10	6	1	3	4	4
89-90—Montreal	NHL	54	1	19	20	41	—	—	—	—	—
—Vancouver	NHL	11	3	7	10	8	—	—	—	—	—
90-91—Vancouver	NHL	80	5	27	32	59	6	2	3	5	0
91-92—Vancouver	NHL	75	12	32	44	65	13	2	3	5	4
92-93—Vancouver	NHL	74	8	36	44	55	12	0	5	5	6
NHL totals		315	30	124	154	238	31	4	11	15	10

LUONGO, CHRISTOPHER
D, ISLANDERS

PERSONAL: Born March 17, 1967, at Detroit.... 6-0/180.... Shoots right.... Full name: Christopher John Luongo.... Name pronounced luh-WAHN-goh.
HIGH SCHOOL: Notre Dame (Harper Woods, Mich.).
COLLEGE: Michigan State.
TRANSACTIONS/CAREER NOTES: Selected by Detroit Red Wings in fifth round (fifth Red Wings pick, 92nd overall) of NHL entry draft (June 15, 1985).... Signed by Ottawa Senators as free agent (September 9, 1992).... Traded by Senators to New York Islanders for D Jeff Finley (June 30, 1993).
HONORS: Named to NCAA All-Tournament team (1986-87).... Named to CCHA All-Star second team (1988-89).

Season Team	League	REGULAR SEASON					PLAYOFFS				
		Gms.	G	A	Pts.	Pen.	Gms.	G	A	Pts.	Pen.
84-85—St. Clair Shores	NAJHL	41	2	25	27	...	—	—	—	—	—
85-86—Michigan State	CCHA	38	1	5	6	29	—	—	—	—	—
86-87—Michigan State	CCHA	27	4	16	20	38	—	—	—	—	—
87-88—Michigan State	CCHA	45	3	15	18	49	—	—	—	—	—
88-89—Michigan State	CCHA	47	4	21	25	42	—	—	—	—	—
89-90—Adirondack	AHL	53	9	14	23	37	3	0	0	0	0
—Phoenix	IHL	23	5	9	14	41	—	—	—	—	—
90-91—Detroit	NHL	4	0	1	1	4	—	—	—	—	—
—Adirondack	AHL	76	14	25	39	71	2	0	0	0	7
91-92—Adirondack	AHL	80	6	20	26	60	19	3	5	8	10
92-93—Ottawa	NHL	76	3	9	12	68	—	—	—	—	—
—New Haven	AHL	7	0	2	2	2	—	—	—	—	—
NHL totals		80	3	10	13	72					

MacDERMID, PAUL
RW, NORDIQUES

PERSONAL: Born April 14, 1963, at Chesley, Ont. . . . 6-1/205. . . . Shoots right.
TRANSACTIONS/CAREER NOTES: Selected by Hartford Whalers as underage junior in third round (second Whalers pick, 61st overall) of NHL entry draft (June 10, 1981). . . . Injured knee (December 1982). . . . Injured neck and shoulder (December 6, 1988). . . . Sprained right knee ligament (February 4, 1989). . . . Traded by Whalers to Winnipeg Jets for C/LW Randy Cunneyworth (December 13, 1989). . . . Suffered back spasms (November 3, 1990); missed six games. . . . Strained knee (December 1990). . . . Traded by Jets to Washington Capitals for D Mike Lalor (March 2, 1992). . . . Traded by Capitals with RW Reggie Savage to Quebec Nordiques for LW Mike Hough (June 20, 1993).

			REGULAR SEASON					PLAYOFFS			
Season Team	League	Gms.	G	A	Pts.	Pen.	Gms.	G	A	Pts.	Pen.
79-80—Port Elgin Jr. C	OHA	30	23	20	43	87	—	—	—	—	—
80-81—Windsor	OMJHL	68	15	17	32	106	—	—	—	—	—
81-82—Windsor	OHL	65	26	45	71	179	9	6	4	10	17
—Hartford	NHL	3	1	0	1	2	—	—	—	—	—
82-83—Windsor	OHL	42	35	45	80	90	—	—	—	—	—
—Hartford	NHL	7	0	0	0	2	—	—	—	—	—
83-84—Hartford	NHL	3	0	1	1	0	—	—	—	—	—
—Binghamton	AHL	70	31	30	61	130	—	—	—	—	—
84-85—Binghamton	AHL	48	9	31	40	87	—	—	—	—	—
—Hartford	NHL	31	4	7	11	299	—	—	—	—	—
85-86—Hartford	NHL	74	13	10	23	160	10	2	1	3	20
86-87—Hartford	NHL	72	7	11	18	202	6	2	1	3	34
87-88—Hartford	NHL	80	20	15	35	139	6	0	5	5	14
88-89—Hartford	NHL	74	17	27	44	141	4	1	1	2	16
89-90—Hartford	NHL	29	6	12	18	69	—	—	—	—	—
—Winnipeg	NHL	44	7	10	17	100	7	0	2	2	8
90-91—Winnipeg	NHL	69	15	21	36	128	—	—	—	—	—
91-92—Winnipeg	NHL	59	10	11	21	151	—	—	—	—	—
—Washington	NHL	15	2	5	7	43	7	0	1	1	22
92-93—Washington	NHL	72	9	8	17	80	—	—	—	—	—
NHL totals		**632**	**111**	**138**	**249**	**1516**	**40**	**5**	**11**	**16**	**114**

MacDONALD, DOUG
LW, SABRES

PERSONAL: Born February 8, 1969, at Point Moody, B.C. . . . 6-0/192. . . . Shoots left. . . . Full name: Douglas Bruce MacDonald.
COLLEGE: Wisconsin.
TRANSACTIONS/CAREER NOTES: Selected by Buffalo Sabres in fourth round (third Sabres pick, 77th overall) of NHL entry draft (June 17, 1989). . . . Injured knee (December 29, 1990).

			REGULAR SEASON					PLAYOFFS			
Season Team	League	Gms.	G	A	Pts.	Pen.	Gms.	G	A	Pts.	Pen.
85-86—Langley Eagles	BCJHL	42	19	37	56	16	—	—	—	—	—
86-87—Delta	BCJHL	51	28	49	77	61	—	—	—	—	—
87-88—Delta	BCJHL	51	50	54	104	70	9	5	9	14	16
88-89—University of Wisconsin	WCHA	44	23	25	48	50	—	—	—	—	—
89-90—University of Wisconsin	WCHA	44	16	35	51	52	—	—	—	—	—
90-91—University of Wisconsin	WCHA	31	20	26	46	50	—	—	—	—	—
91-92—University of Wisconsin	WCHA	33	16	28	44	76	—	—	—	—	—
92-93—Rochester	AHL	64	25	33	58	58	7	0	2	2	4
—Buffalo	NHL	5	1	0	1	2	—	—	—	—	—
NHL totals		**5**	**1**	**0**	**1**	**2**					

MacDONALD, GARRETT
D, FLYERS

PERSONAL: Born January 12, 1971, at Burnaby, B.C. . . . 6-0/183. . . . Shoots right. . . . Full name: Garrett Robert MacDonald.
HIGH SCHOOL: Burnaby (B.C.) North Secondary School.
COLLEGE: Northern Michigan.
TRANSACTIONS/CAREER NOTES: Selected by Philadelphia Flyers in NHL supplemental draft (June 19, 1992).

			REGULAR SEASON					PLAYOFFS			
Season Team	League	Gms.	G	A	Pts.	Pen.	Gms.	G	A	Pts.	Pen.
90-91—Northern Michigan Univ.	WCHA	41	2	8	10	56	—	—	—	—	—
91-92—Northern Michigan Univ.	WCHA	36	0	6	6	86	—	—	—	—	—
92-93—Northern Michigan Univ.	WCHA	39	4	12	16	68	—	—	—	—	—

MacDONALD, JASON
RW, RED WINGS

PERSONAL: Born April 1, 1974, at Charlettetown, P.E.I. . . . 6-0/195. . . . Shoots right.
HIGH SCHOOL: St. Mary's (Owen Sound, Ont.).
TRANSACTIONS/CAREER NOTES: Selected by Detroit Red Wings in sixth round (fifth Red Wings pick, 142nd overall) of NHL entry draft (June 20, 1992).

			REGULAR SEASON					PLAYOFFS			
Season Team	League	Gms.	G	A	Pts.	Pen.	Gms.	G	A	Pts.	Pen.
89-90—Charlottetown	PEIJHL	25	11	29	40	206	—	—	—	—	—
90-91—North Bay	OHL	57	12	15	27	126	10	3	3	6	15
91-92—North Bay	OHL	17	5	8	13	50	—	—	—	—	—
—Owen Sound	OHL	42	17	19	36	129	5	0	2	2	8
92-93—Owen Sound	OHL	55	46	43	89	197	8	6	5	11	28

M

MacDONALD, TODD
G, PANTHERS

PERSONAL: Born July 5, 1975, at Charlottetown, P.E.I. . . . 6-0/155. . . . Shoots left.
TRANSACTIONS/CAREER NOTES: Selected by Florida Panthers in fifth round (seventh Panthers pick, 109th overall) of NHL entry draft (June 26, 1993).

			—————REGULAR SEASON—————							—————PLAYOFFS—————						
Season Team	League	Gms.	Min.	W	L	T	GA	SO	Avg.	Gms.	Min.	W	L	GA	SO	Avg.
91-92—Kingston	OHA Mj Jr.A	28	1680	. . .	. . .	. . .	84	0	3.00	—	—	—	—	—	—	—
92-93—Tacoma	WHL	19	823	6	6	0	59	0	4.30	—	—	—	—	—	—	—

MacINNIS, AL
D, FLAMES

PERSONAL: Born July 11, 1963, at Inverness, N.S. . . . 6-2/196. . . . Shoots right. . . . Name pronounced muh-KIHN-ihz.
TRANSACTIONS/CAREER NOTES: Selected by Calgary Flames as underage junior in first round (first Flames pick, 15th overall) of NHL entry draft (June 10, 1981). . . . Twisted knee (February 1985). . . . Lacerated hand (March 23, 1986). . . . Stretched ligaments of knee (April 8, 1990). . . . Separated shoulder (November 22, 1991); missed eight games. . . . Dislocated left hip (November 12, 1992); missed 34 games.
HONORS: Named to OHL All-Star first team (1981-82 and 1982-83). . . . Named to Memorial Cup All-Star team (1981-82). . . . Won Max Kaminsky Trophy (1982-83). . . . Played in NHL All-Star Game (1985, 1988 and 1990 through 1992). . . . Named to NHL All-Star second team (1986-87 and 1988-89). . . . Won Conn Smythe Trophy (1988-89). . . . Named to THE SPORTING NEWS All-Star first team (1989-90 and 1990-91). . . . Named to NHL All-Star first team (1989-90 and 1990-91).
MISCELLANEOUS: Member of Stanley Cup championship team (1989).

		—————REGULAR SEASON—————					—————PLAYOFFS—————				
Season Team	League	Gms.	G	A	Pts.	Pen.	Gms.	G	A	Pts.	Pen.
79-80—Regina Blues	SJHL	59	20	28	48	110	—	—	—	—	—
80-81—Kitchener	OMJHL	47	11	28	39	59	18	4	12	16	20
81-82—Kitchener	OHL	59	25	50	75	145	15	5	10	15	44
—Calgary	NHL	2	0	0	0	0	—	—	—	—	—
82-83—Kitchener	OHL	51	38	46	84	67	8	3	8	11	9
—Calgary	NHL	14	1	3	4	9	—	—	—	—	—
83-84—Colorado	CHL	19	5	14	19	22	—	—	—	—	—
—Calgary	NHL	51	11	34	45	42	11	2	12	14	13
84-85—Calgary	NHL	67	14	52	66	75	4	1	2	3	8
85-86—Calgary	NHL	77	11	57	68	76	21	4	*15	19	30
86-87—Calgary	NHL	79	20	56	76	97	4	1	0	1	0
87-88—Calgary	NHL	80	25	58	83	114	7	3	6	9	18
88-89—Calgary	NHL	79	16	58	74	126	22	7	*24	*31	46
89-90—Calgary	NHL	79	28	62	90	82	6	2	3	5	8
90-91—Calgary	NHL	78	28	75	103	90	7	2	3	5	8
91-92—Calgary	NHL	72	20	57	77	83	—	—	—	—	—
92-93—Calgary	NHL	50	11	43	54	61	6	1	6	7	10
NHL totals		**728**	**185**	**555**	**740**	**855**	**88**	**23**	**71**	**94**	**141**

M

MacINTYRE, ANDY
LW, BLACKHAWKS

PERSONAL: Born April 16, 1974, at Thunder Bay, Ont. . . . 6-2/195. . . . Shoots left.
HIGH SCHOOL: Marion Graham (Saskatoon, Sask.).
TRANSACTIONS/CAREER NOTES: Selected by Chicago Blackhawks in fourth round (fourth Blackhawks pick, 89th overall) of NHL entry draft (June 20, 1992).

		—————REGULAR SEASON—————					—————PLAYOFFS—————				
Season Team	League	Gms.	G	A	Pts.	Pen.	Gms.	G	A	Pts.	Pen.
89-90—Elk Valley	BCJHL	40	24	22	46	14	—	—	—	—	—
90-91—Seattle	WHL	71	16	13	29	52	6	0	0	0	2
91-92—Seattle	WHL	12	6	2	8	18	—	—	—	—	—
—Saskatoon	WHL	55	22	13	35	66	22	10	2	12	17
92-93—Saskatoon	WHL	72	35	29	64	82	9	3	2	5	2

MACIVER, NORM
D, SENATORS

PERSONAL: Born September 8, 1964, at Thunder Bay, Ont. . . . 5-11/180. . . . Shoots left. . . . Full name: Norman Steven Maciver.
HIGH SCHOOL: Sir Winston Churchill (Thunder Bay, Ont.).
COLLEGE: Minnesota-Duluth.
TRANSACTIONS/CAREER NOTES: Signed as free agent by New York Rangers (September 8, 1986). . . . Dislocated right shoulder (March 1988). . . . Suffered hip pointer (November 1988). . . . Traded by Rangers with LW Don Maloney and C Brian Lawton to Hartford Whalers for C Carey Wilson and fifth-round pick in 1990 draft (December 26, 1988). . . . Traded by Whalers to Edmonton Oilers for D Jim Ennis (October 9, 1989). . . . Selected by Ottawa Senators in NHL waiver draft (October 4, 1992). . . . Suffered sore back (December 9, 1992); missed one game. . . . Injured back (January 19, 1993); missed one game. . . . Injured wrist (January 28, 1993); missed two games.
HONORS: Named to WCHA All-Star second team (1983-84). . . . Named to WCHA All-Star first team (1984-85 and 1985-86). . . . Named to NCAA All-America West first team (1984-85 and 1985-86). . . . Won Eddie Shore Plaque (1990-91). . . . Named to AHL All-Star first team (1990-91).

		—————REGULAR SEASON—————					—————PLAYOFFS—————				
Season Team	League	Gms.	G	A	Pts.	Pen.	Gms.	G	A	Pts.	Pen.
82-83—Minnesota-Duluth	WCHA	45	1	26	27	40	6	0	2	2	2
83-84—Minnesota-Duluth	WCHA	31	13	28	41	28	8	1	10	11	8
84-85—Minnesota-Duluth	WCHA	47	14	47	61	63	10	3	3	6	6
85-86—Minnesota-Duluth	WCHA	42	11	51	62	36	4	2	3	5	2
86-87—New Haven	AHL	71	6	30	36	73	7	0	0	0	9
—New York Rangers	NHL	3	0	1	1	0	—	—	—	—	—

Season	Team	League	REGULAR SEASON					PLAYOFFS				
			Gms.	G	A	Pts.	Pen.	Gms.	G	A	Pts.	Pen.
87-88	Colorado	IHL	27	6	20	26	22	—	—	—	—	—
	New York Rangers	NHL	37	9	15	24	14	—	—	—	—	—
88-89	New York Rangers	NHL	26	0	10	10	14	—	—	—	—	—
	Hartford	NHL	37	1	22	23	24	1	0	0	0	2
89-90	Binghamton	AHL	2	0	0	0	0	—	—	—	—	—
	Cape Breton	AHL	68	13	37	50	55	6	0	7	7	10
	Edmonton	NHL	1	0	0	0	0	—	—	—	—	—
90-91	Cape Breton	AHL	56	13	46	59	60	—	—	—	—	—
	Edmonton	NHL	21	2	5	7	14	18	0	4	4	8
91-92	Edmonton	NHL	57	6	34	40	38	13	1	2	3	10
92-93	Ottawa	NHL	80	17	46	63	84	—	—	—	—	—
	NHL totals		262	35	133	168	188	32	1	6	7	20

MACKEY, DAVE
LW, BLUES

PERSONAL: Born July 24, 1966, at New Westminster, B.C. . . . . 6-3/205. . . . Shoots left. . . . Name pronounced MAK-ee.

TRANSACTIONS/CAREER NOTES: Selected by Chicago Blackhawks as underage junior in 11th round (12th Blackhawks pick, 224th overall) of NHL entry draft (June 9, 1984). . . . Traded by Kamloops Blazers with C Rob DiMaio and C Kalvin Knibbs to Medicine Hat Tigers for LW Doug Pickel and LW Sean Pass (December 1986). . . . Selected by Minnesota North Stars in NHL waiver draft for $40,000 (October 2, 1989). . . . Tore right thumb ligaments (November 6, 1989); missed 10 games. . . . Suspended five games and fined $500 by NHL for fighting (December 28, 1989). . . . Sprained knee and ankle (January 24, 1990); missed 15 games. . . . Traded by North Stars to Vancouver Canucks for future considerations (September 6, 1990). . . . Signed as free agent by St. Louis Blues (July 1991).

Season	Team	League	REGULAR SEASON					PLAYOFFS				
			Gms.	G	A	Pts.	Pen.	Gms.	G	A	Pts.	Pen.
82-83	Victoria	WHL	69	16	16	32	53	12	1	1	2	4
83-84	Victoria	WHL	69	15	15	30	97	—	—	—	—	—
84-85	Victoria	WHL	16	5	6	11	45	—	—	—	—	—
	Portland	WHL	56	28	32	60	122	6	2	1	3	13
85-86	Kamloops	WHL	9	3	4	7	13	—	—	—	—	—
	Medicine Hat	WHL	60	25	32	57	167	25	6	3	9	72
86-87	Saginaw	IHL	81	26	49	75	173	10	5	6	11	22
87-88	Saginaw	IHL	62	29	22	51	211	10	3	7	10	44
	Chicago	NHL	23	1	3	4	71	—	—	—	—	—
88-89	Chicago	NHL	23	1	2	3	78	—	—	—	—	—
	Saginaw	IHL	57	22	23	45	223	—	—	—	—	—
89-90	Minnesota	NHL	16	2	0	2	28	—	—	—	—	—
90-91	Milwaukee	IHL	82	28	30	58	226	6	7	2	9	6
91-92	Peoria	IHL	35	20	17	37	90	—	—	—	—	—
	St. Louis	NHL	19	1	0	1	49	1	0	0	0	0
92-93	Peoria	IHL	42	24	22	46	112	4	1	0	1	22
	St. Louis	NHL	15	1	4	5	23	—	—	—	—	—
	NHL totals		96	6	9	15	249	1	0	0	0	0

MacLEAN, JOHN
RW, DEVILS

PERSONAL: Born November 20, 1964, at Oshawa, Ont. . . . 6-0/200. . . . Shoots right.

TRANSACTIONS/CAREER NOTES: Selected by New Jersey Devils as underage junior in first round (first Devils pick, sixth overall) of NHL entry draft (June 8, 1983). . . . Bruised shoulder (November 1984). . . . Injured right knee (January 25, 1985). . . . Reinjured knee and underwent arthroscopic surgery (January 31, 1985). . . . Bruised ankle (November 2, 1986). . . . Sprained right elbow (December 1988). . . . Bruised ribs (March 1, 1989). . . . Suffered concussion and stomach contusions (October 1990). . . . Suffered concussion (December 11, 1990). . . . Tore ligament in right knee (September 30, 1991); missed entire 1991-92 season. . . . Underwent surgery to right knee (November 23, 1991).

HONORS: Named to Memorial Cup All-Star team (1982-83). . . . Played in NHL All-Star Game (1989 and 1991).

Season	Team	League	REGULAR SEASON					PLAYOFFS				
			Gms.	G	A	Pts.	Pen.	Gms.	G	A	Pts.	Pen.
81-82	Oshawa	OHL	67	17	22	39	197	12	3	6	9	63
82-83	Oshawa	OHL	66	47	51	98	138	17	*18	20	†38	35
83-84	New Jersey	NHL	23	1	0	1	10	—	—	—	—	—
	Oshawa	OHL	30	23	36	59	58	7	2	5	7	18
84-85	New Jersey	NHL	61	13	20	33	44	—	—	—	—	—
85-86	New Jersey	NHL	74	21	37	58	112	—	—	—	—	—
86-87	New Jersey	NHL	80	31	36	67	120	—	—	—	—	—
87-88	New Jersey	NHL	76	23	16	39	145	20	7	11	18	60
88-89	New Jersey	NHL	74	42	45	87	127	—	—	—	—	—
89-90	New Jersey	NHL	80	41	38	79	80	6	4	1	5	12
90-91	New Jersey	NHL	78	45	33	78	150	7	5	3	8	20
91-92	New Jersey	NHL			Did not play—injured.							
92-93	New Jersey	NHL	80	24	24	48	102	5	0	1	1	10
	NHL totals		626	241	249	490	890	38	16	16	32	102

MacLEOD, PAT
D, SHARKS

PERSONAL: Born June 15, 1969, at Melfort, Sask. . . . 5-11/190. . . . Shoots left. . . . Name pronounced muh-KLOWD.

TRANSACTIONS/CAREER NOTES: Injured knee (March 1989). . . . Selected by Minnesota North Stars in fifth round (fifth North Stars pick, 87th overall) of NHL entry draft (June 17, 1989).

M

... Selected by San Jose Sharks in NHL dispersal draft (May 30, 1991).... Sprained shoulder (December 30, 1992); missed 21 games.
HONORS: Named to WHL All-Star first team (1988-89).... Named to IHL All-Star second team (1991-92).

			REGULAR SEASON					PLAYOFFS			
Season Team	League	Gms.	G	A	Pts.	Pen.	Gms.	G	A	Pts.	Pen.
87-88—Kamloops	WHL	50	13	33	46	27	18	2	7	9	6
88-89—Kamloops	WHL	37	11	34	45	14	15	7	18	25	24
89-90—Kalamazoo	IHL	82	9	38	47	27	10	1	6	7	2
90-91—Kalamazoo	IHL	59	10	30	40	16	11	1	2	3	5
—Minnesota	NHL	1	0	1	1	0	—	—	—	—	—
91-92—San Jose	NHL	37	5	11	16	4	—	—	—	—	—
—Kansas City	IHL	45	9	21	30	19	11	1	4	5	4
92-93—San Jose	NHL	13	0	1	1	10	—	—	—	—	—
—Kansas City	IHL	18	8	8	16	14	10	2	4	6	7
NHL totals		51	5	13	18	14					

MACOUN, JAMIE
D, MAPLE LEAFS

PERSONAL: Born August 17, 1961, at Newmarket, Ont.... 6-2/200.... Shoots left.... Name pronounced muh-KOW-ihn.
COLLEGE: Ohio State.
TRANSACTIONS/CAREER NOTES: Signed as free agent by Calgary Flames (January 30, 1983).... Fractured cheekbone (December 26, 1984).... Suffered nerve damage to left arm in automobile accident (May 1987).... Suffered concussion (January 23, 1989).... Traded by Flames with C Doug Gilmour, LW Kent Manderville, D Ric Nattress and G Rick Wamsley to Toronto Maple Leafs for LW Craig Berube, D Alexander Godynyuk, LW Gary Leeman, D Michel Petit and G Jeff Reese (January 2, 1992).... Pulled groin (February 27, 1993); missed four games.
HONORS: Named to NHL All-Rookie team (1983-84).
MISCELLANEOUS: Member of Stanley Cup championship team (1989).

			REGULAR SEASON					PLAYOFFS			
Season Team	League	Gms.	G	A	Pts.	Pen.	Gms.	G	A	Pts.	Pen.
80-81—Ohio State	CCHA	38	9	20	29	83	—	—	—	—	—
81-82—Ohio State	CCHA	25	2	18	20	89	—	—	—	—	—
82-83—Ohio State	CCHA	19	6	21	27	54	—	—	—	—	—
—Calgary	NHL	22	1	4	5	25	9	0	2	2	8
83-84—Calgary	NHL	72	9	23	32	97	11	1	0	1	0
84-85—Calgary	NHL	70	9	30	39	67	4	1	0	1	4
85-86—Calgary	NHL	77	11	21	32	81	22	1	6	7	23
86-87—Calgary	NHL	79	7	33	40	111	3	0	1	1	8
87-88—Calgary	NHL			Did not play—injured.							
88-89—Calgary	NHL	72	8	19	27	78	22	3	6	9	30
89-90—Calgary	NHL	78	8	27	35	70	6	0	3	3	10
90-91—Calgary	NHL	79	7	15	22	84	7	0	1	1	4
91-92—Calgary	NHL	37	2	12	14	53	—	—	—	—	—
—Toronto	NHL	39	3	13	16	18	—	—	—	—	—
92-93—Toronto	NHL	77	4	15	19	55	21	0	6	6	36
NHL totals		702	69	212	281	739	105	6	25	31	123

MacTAVISH, CRAIG
C, OILERS

PERSONAL: Born August 15, 1958, at London, Ont.... 6-1/195.... Shoots left.
HIGH SCHOOL: Westminster (London, Ont.).
COLLEGE: Lowell (Mass.).
TRANSACTIONS/CAREER NOTES: Selected by Boston Bruins in ninth round (ninth Bruins pick, 153rd overall) of NHL amateur draft (June 15, 1978).... Involved in automobile accident in which another driver was killed (January 25, 1984); pleaded guilty to vehicular homicide, driving while under the influence of alcohol and reckless driving and sentenced to a year in prison (May 1984); missed 1984-85 season.... Signed as free agent by Edmonton Oilers (February 1, 1985).... Strained lower back (January 1993); missed one game.... Suffered concussion (March 10, 1993); missed one game.
HONORS: Named ECAC Division II Rookie of the Year (1977-78).... Named to ECAC-II All-Star second team (1977-78).... Named ECAC Division II Player of the Year (1978-79).... Named to NCAA All-America East (College Division) first team (1978-79).... Named to ECAC-II All-Star first team (1978-79).
MISCELLANEOUS: Does not wear a helmet.... Member of Stanley Cup championship teams (1987, 1988 and 1990).

			REGULAR SEASON					PLAYOFFS			
Season Team	League	Gms.	G	A	Pts.	Pen.	Gms.	G	A	Pts.	Pen.
77-78—University of Lowell	ECAC-II	24	26	19	45	...	—	—	—	—	—
78-79—University of Lowell	ECAC-II	31	36	52	*88	...	—	—	—	—	—
79-80—Binghamton	AHL	34	17	15	32	20	—	—	—	—	—
—Boston	NHL	46	11	17	28	8	10	2	3	5	7
80-81—Boston	NHL	24	3	5	8	13	—	—	—	—	—
—Springfield	AHL	53	19	24	43	89	7	5	4	9	8
81-82—Erie	AHL	72	23	32	55	37	—	—	—	—	—
—Boston	NHL	2	0	1	1	0	—	—	—	—	—
82-83—Boston	NHL	75	10	20	30	18	17	3	1	4	18
83-84—Boston	NHL	70	20	23	43	35	1	0	0	0	0
84-85—Boston	NHL			Did not play.							
85-86—Edmonton	NHL	74	23	24	47	70	10	4	4	8	11
86-87—Edmonton	NHL	79	20	19	39	55	21	1	9	10	16
87-88—Edmonton	NHL	80	15	17	32	47	19	0	1	1	31

M

Season Team	League	REGULAR SEASON					PLAYOFFS				
		Gms.	G	A	Pts.	Pen.	Gms.	G	A	Pts.	Pen.
88-89—Edmonton	NHL	80	21	31	52	55	7	0	1	1	8
89-90—Edmonton	NHL	80	21	22	43	89	22	2	6	8	29
90-91—Edmonton	NHL	80	17	15	32	76	18	3	3	6	20
91-92—Edmonton	NHL	80	12	18	30	98	16	3	0	3	28
92-93—Edmonton	NHL	82	10	20	30	110	—	—	—	—	—
NHL totals		852	183	232	415	674	141	18	28	46	168

MADELEY, DARRIN
G, SENATORS

PERSONAL: Born February 25, 1968, at Holland Landing, Ont. . . . 5-11/165. . . . Shoots right.
HIGH SCHOOL: Aurora (Ont.).
COLLEGE: Lake Superior State (Mich.).
TRANSACTIONS/CAREER NOTES: Signed as free agent by Ottawa Senators (June 20, 1992).
HONORS: Named to CCHA All-Star second team (1989-90). . . . Named to NCAA All-America West first team (1990-91). . . . Named to CCHA All-Star first team (1990-91 and 1991-92). . . . Named NCAA Tournament Most Valuable Player (1991-92). . . . Named CCHA Playoff Most Valuable Player (1991-92). . . . Named to NCAA All-Tournament team (1991-92). . . . Named to AHL All-Star second team (1992-93).

Season Team	League	REGULAR SEASON							PLAYOFFS						
		Gms.	Min.	W	L	T	GA	SO	Avg.	Gms.	Min.	W	L	GA	SO	Avg.
89-90—Lake Superior State	CCHA	30	1683	21	7	1	68	...	2.42	—	—	—	—	—	—	—
90-91—Lake Superior State	CCHA	36	2137	29	3	3	93	...	2.61	—	—	—	—	—	—	—
91-92—Lake Superior State	CCHA	35	2144	25	6	4	74	...	2.07	—	—	—	—	—	—	—
92-93—New Haven	AHL	41	2295	10	16	9	127	0	3.32	—	—	—	—	—	—	—
—Ottawa	NHL	2	90	0	2	0	10	0	6.67	—	—	—	—	—	—	—
NHL totals		2	90	0	2	0	10	0	6.67							

MAHER, JIM
D, KINGS

PERSONAL: Born June 10, 1970, at Warren, Mich. . . . 6-1/205. . . . Shoots left.
COLLEGE: Illinois-Chicago.
TRANSACTIONS/CAREER NOTES: Selected by Los Angeles Kings in fourth round (second Kings pick, 81st overall) of NHL entry draft (June 17, 1989).

Season Team	League	REGULAR SEASON					PLAYOFFS				
		Gms.	G	A	Pts.	Pen.	Gms.	G	A	Pts.	Pen.
87-88—Detroit Junior Red Wings	NAJHL	24	6	11	17	26	—	—	—	—	—
88-89—Illinois-Chicago	CCHA	41	1	5	6	40	—	—	—	—	—
89-90—Illinois-Chicago	CCHA	38	4	12	16	64	—	—	—	—	—
90-91—Illinois-Chicago	CCHA	37	6	8	14	49	—	—	—	—	—
91-92—Illinois-Chicago	CCHA	34	5	9	14	52	—	—	—	—	—
—Phoenix	IHL	9	0	3	3	21	—	—	—	—	—
92-93—Phoenix	IHL	47	5	13	18	72	—	—	—	—	—
—Muskegon	Col.HL	2	1	0	1	2	—	—	—	—	—

MAJOR, MARK
LW, PENGUINS

PERSONAL: Born March 20, 1970, at Toronto. . . . 6-4/216. . . . Shoots left.
TRANSACTIONS/CAREER NOTES: Selected by Pittsburgh Penguins in second round (second Penguins pick, 25th overall) of NHL entry draft (June 11, 1988). . . . Broke hand (September 1989); missed training camp.

Season Team	League	REGULAR SEASON					PLAYOFFS				
		Gms.	G	A	Pts.	Pen.	Gms.	G	A	Pts.	Pen.
87-88—North Bay	OHL	57	16	17	33	272	4	0	2	2	8
88-89—North Bay	OHL	11	3	2	5	58	—	—	—	—	—
—Kingston	OHL	53	22	29	51	193	—	—	—	—	—
89-90—Kingston	OHL	62	29	32	61	168	6	3	3	6	12
90-91—Muskegon	IHL	60	8	10	18	160	5	0	0	0	0
91-92—Muskegon	IHL	80	13	18	31	302	12	1	3	4	29
92-93—Cleveland	IHL	82	13	15	28	155	3	0	0	0	0

MAKAROV, SERGEI
RW, SHARKS

PERSONAL: Born June 19, 1958, at Chelyabinsk, U.S.S.R. . . . 5-11/185. . . . Shoots left. . . . Name pronounced SIHR-ghay muh-KAH-rahf.
TRANSACTIONS/CAREER NOTES: Selected by Calgary Flames in 12th round (14th Flames pick, 231st overall) of NHL entry draft (June 8, 1983). . . . Traded by Flames to Hartford Whalers for future considerations (June 20, 1993). . . . Traded by Whalers with first-round (RW Victor Kozlov), second-round (D Vlastimil Kroupa) picks in 1993 draft to San Jose Sharks for first-round and third-round (LW Ville Peltonen) picks in 1993 draft to San Jose Sharks for first-round pick (D Chris Pronger) in 1993 draft (June 26, 1993).
HONORS: Won Golden Stick Award (1979-80 and 1985-86). . . . Won Soviet Player of the Year Award (1979-80, 1984-85 and 1988-89). . . . Won Izvestia Trophy (1979-80 through 1981-82 and 1983-84 through 1988-89). . . . Named to Soviet League All-Star team (1978-79 and 1980-81 through 1987-88). . . . Won Calder Memorial Trophy (1989-90). . . . Named to NHL All-Rookie team (1989-90).
MISCELLANEOUS: Member of silver-medal-winning U.S.S.R. Olympic team (1980) and gold-medal-winning U.S.S.R. Olympic team (1984 and 1988).

Season Team	League	REGULAR SEASON					PLAYOFFS				
		Gms.	G	A	Pts.	Pen.	Gms.	G	A	Pts.	Pen.
76-77—Traktor Chelyabinsk	USSR	11	1	0	1	4	—	—	—	—	—
77-78—Traktor Chelyabinsk	USSR	36	18	13	31	10	—	—	—	—	—

M

Season Team	League	REGULAR SEASON					PLAYOFFS				
		Gms.	G	A	Pts.	Pen.	Gms.	G	A	Pts.	Pen.
78-79—CSKA Moscow	USSR	44	18	21	39	12	—	—	—	—	—
79-80—CSKA Moscow	USSR	44	29	39	*68	16	—	—	—	—	—
—Soviet Olympic Team	Int'l	7	5	6	11	2	—	—	—	—	—
80-81—CSKA Moscow	USSR	49	42	37	*79	22	—	—	—	—	—
81-82—CSKA Moscow	USSR	46	32	43	*75	18	—	—	—	—	—
82-83—CSKA Moscow	USSR	30	25	17	42	6	—	—	—	—	—
83-84—CSKA Moscow	USSR	44	36	37	*73	28	—	—	—	—	—
—Soviet Olympic Team	Int'l	7	3	3	6	6	—	—	—	—	—
84-85—CSKA Moscow	USSR	40	26	39	*65	28	—	—	—	—	—
85-86—CSKA Moscow	USSR	40	30	32	*62	28	—	—	—	—	—
86-87—CSKA Moscow	USSR	40	21	32	*53	26	—	—	—	—	—
87-88—CSKA Moscow	USSR	51	23	45	*68	50	—	—	—	—	—
—Soviet Olympic Team	Int'l	8	3	8	11	10	—	—	—	—	—
88-89—CSKA Moscow	USSR	44	21	33	*54	42	—	—	—	—	—
89-90—Calgary	NHL	80	24	62	86	55	6	0	6	6	0
90-91—Calgary	NHL	78	30	49	79	44	3	1	0	1	0
91-92—Calgary	NHL	68	22	48	70	60	—	—	—	—	—
92-93—Calgary	NHL	71	18	39	57	40	—	—	—	—	—
NHL totals		297	94	198	292	199	9	1	6	7	0

MALAKHOV, VLADIMIR
D, ISLANDERS

PERSONAL: Born August 30, 1968, at Sverdlovsk, U.S.S.R. . . . . 6-3/220. . . . Name pronounced MAL-ih-kahf.

TRANSACTIONS/CAREER NOTES: Selected by New York Islanders in 10th round (12th Islanders pick, 191st overall) of NHL entry draft (June 17, 1989). . . . Suffered sore groin prior to 1992-93 season; missed first two games of season. . . . Injured right shoulder (January 16, 1993); missed eight games. . . . Sprained shoulder (March 14, 1993); missed five games.

HONORS: Named to NHL All-Rookie team (1992-93).

MISCELLANEOUS: Member of gold-medal-winning Unified Olympic team (1992).

Season Team	League	REGULAR SEASON					PLAYOFFS				
		Gms.	G	A	Pts.	Pen.	Gms.	G	A	Pts.	Pen.
86-87—Spartak Moscow	USSR	22	0	1	1	12	—	—	—	—	—
87-88—Spartak Moscow	USSR	28	2	2	4	26	—	—	—	—	—
88-89—CSKA Moscow	USSR	34	6	2	8	16	—	—	—	—	—
89-90—CSKA Moscow	USSR	48	2	10	12	34	—	—	—	—	—
90-91—CSKA Moscow	USSR	46	5	13	18	22	—	—	—	—	—
91-92—CSKA Moscow	USSR	40	1	9	10	12	—	—	—	—	—
—Unified Olympic Team	Int'l	8	3	0	3	4	—	—	—	—	—
92-93—Capital District	AHL	3	2	1	3	11	—	—	—	—	—
—New York Islanders	NHL	64	14	38	52	59	17	3	6	9	12
NHL totals		64	14	38	52	59	17	3	6	9	12

MALARCHUK, CLINT
G, SABRES

PERSONAL: Born May 1, 1961, at Grande Prarie, Alta. . . . 6-0/185. . . . Shoots left. . . . Name pronounced muh-LAHR-chuhk.

TRANSACTIONS/CAREER NOTES: Selected by Quebec Nordiques in fourth round (third Nordiques pick, 74th overall) of NHL entry draft (June 11, 1981). . . . Traded by Nordiques with C Dale Hunter to Washington Capitals for C Alan Haworth, LW Gaeten Duchesne and first-round pick in 1987 draft (C Joe Sakic) (June 1987). . . . Traded by Capitals with D Grant Ledyard and sixth-round pick in 1991 draft to Buffalo Sabres for D Calle Johansson and second-round pick in 1989 draft (G Byron Dafoe) (March 6, 1989). . . . Suffered severed jugular vein (March 22, 1989). . . . Strained neck and shoulder (January 23, 1991); missed 14 games. . . . Suffered from strep throat (November 2, 1991); missed three games. . . . Suffered from medicine reaction (January 27, 1992); missed six games. . . . Loaned to San Diego Gulls (October 12, 1992).

HONORS: Shared Harry (Hap) Holmes Memorial Trophy with Brian Ford (1982-83). . . . Shared James Norris Memorial Trophy with Rick Knickle (1992-93).

Season Team	League	REGULAR SEASON							PLAYOFFS					
		Gms.	Min.	W	L	T	GA	SO	Avg.	Gms.	Min.	W	L	GA	SO	Avg.
78-79—Portland	WHL	2	120	...	...	...	4	0	2.00	—	—	—	—	—	—	—
79-80—Portland	WHL	37	1948	21	10	0	147	0	4.53	1	40	0	0	3	0	4.50
80-81—Portland	WHL	38	2235	28	8	0	142	3	3.81	4	307	0	0	21	0	4.10
81-82—Quebec	NHL	2	120	0	1	1	14	0	7.00	—	—	—	—	—	—	—
—Fredericton	AHL	51	2962	15	34	2	*253	0	5.12	—	—	—	—	—	—	—
82-83—Quebec	NHL	15	900	8	5	2	71	0	4.73	—	—	—	—	—	—	—
—Fredericton	AHL	25	1506	0	0	0	78	1	*3.11	—	—	—	—	—	—	—
83-84—Fredericton	AHL	11	663	5	5	1	40	0	3.62	—	—	—	—	—	—	—
—Quebec	NHL	23	1215	10	9	2	80	0	3.95	—	—	—	—	—	—	—
84-85—Fredericton	AHL	*56	*3347	26	25	4	*198	2	3.55	6	379	2	4	20	0	3.17
85-86—Quebec	NHL	46	2657	26	12	4	142	4	3.21	3	143	0	2	11	0	4.62
86-87—Quebec	NHL	54	3092	18	26	9	175	1	3.40	3	140	0	2	8	0	3.43
87-88—Washington	NHL	54	2926	24	20	4	154	†4	3.16	4	193	0	2	15	0	4.66
88-89—Washington	NHL	42	2428	16	18	7	141	1	3.48	1	59	0	1	5	0	5.08
—Buffalo	NHL	7	326	3	1	1	13	1	2.39	—	—	—	—	—	—	—
89-90—Buffalo	NHL	29	1596	14	11	2	89	0	3.35	—	—	—	—	—	—	—
90-91—Buffalo	NHL	37	2131	12	14	10	119	1	3.35	4	246	2	2	17	0	4.15

M

Season	Team	League	Gms.	Min.	W	L	T	GA	SO	Avg.	Gms.	Min.	W	L	GA	SO	Avg.
91-92	Buffalo	NHL	29	1639	10	13	3	102	0	3.73	—	—	—	—	—	—	—
	—Rochester	AHL	2	120	2	0	0	3	1	1.50	—	—	—	—	—	—	—
92-93	San Diego	IHL	27	1516	17	3	0	72	3	2.85	†12	668	6	3	†34	0	3.05
	NHL totals		338	19030	141	130	45	1100	12	3.47	15	781	2	9	56	0	4.30

MALEY, DAVID
C, SHARKS

PERSONAL: Born April 24, 1963, at Beaver Dam, Wis. ... 6-3/200. ... Shoots left. ... Full name: David Joseph Maley.
HIGH SCHOOL: Edina (Minn.).
COLLEGE: Wisconsin.
TRANSACTIONS/CAREER NOTES: Selected by Montreal Canadiens as underage player in second round (fourth Canadiens pick, 33rd overall) of NHL entry draft (June 9, 1982). ... Suspended by AHL (May 1987). ... Traded by Canadiens to New Jersey Devils for third-round pick in 1987 draft (D Mathieu Schneider) (June 13, 1987). ... Injured back (December 1988). ... Tore right knee cartilage (January 16, 1990). ... Underwent surgery to right knee (January 24, 1990); missed eight games. ... Injured knee (February 22, 1990). ... Injured left hand ligaments (September 22, 1990). ... Sprained left ankle (November 28, 1990); missed 11 games. ... Fractured left wrist (March 27, 1991). ... Traded by Devils to Edmonton Oilers for LW Troy Mallette (January 12, 1991). ... Twisted knee (March 4, 1992); missed 12 games. ... Claimed on waivers by San Jose Sharks (Janaury 1, 1993). ... Suspended three games by NHL for physically abusing an official (April 4, 1993).
MISCELLANEOUS: Member of Stanley Cup championship team (1986).

Season	Team	League	Gms.	G	A	Pts.	Pen.	Gms.	G	A	Pts.	Pen.
81-82	Edina High School	Minn. H.S.	26	22	28	50	26	—	—	—	—	—
82-83	University of Wisconsin	WCHA	47	17	23	40	24	—	—	—	—	—
83-84	University of Wisconsin	WCHA	38	10	28	38	56	—	—	—	—	—
84-85	University of Wisconsin	WCHA	35	19	9	28	86	—	—	—	—	—
85-86	University of Wisconsin	WCHA	42	20	40	60	*135	—	—	—	—	—
	—Montreal	NHL	3	0	0	0	0	7	1	3	4	2
86-87	Sherbrooke	AHL	11	1	5	6	25	12	7	7	14	10
	—Montreal	NHL	48	6	12	18	55	—	—	—	—	—
87-88	Utica	AHL	9	5	3	8	40	—	—	—	—	—
	—New Jersey	NHL	44	4	2	6	65	20	3	1	4	80
88-89	New Jersey	NHL	68	5	6	11	249	—	—	—	—	—
89-90	New Jersey	NHL	67	8	17	25	160	6	0	0	0	25
90-91	New Jersey	NHL	64	8	14	22	151	—	—	—	—	—
91-92	New Jersey	NHL	37	7	11	18	58	—	—	—	—	—
	—Edmonton	NHL	23	3	6	9	46	10	1	1	2	4
92-93	Edmonton	NHL	13	1	1	2	29	—	—	—	—	—
	—San Jose	NHL	43	1	6	7	126	—	—	—	—	—
	NHL totals		410	43	75	118	939	43	5	5	10	111

MALGUNAS, STEWART
D, RED WINGS

PERSONAL: Born April 21, 1970, at Prince George, B.C. ... 5-11/190. ... Shoots left.
TRANSACTIONS/CAREER NOTES: Selected by Detroit Red Wings in fourth round (third Red Wings pick, 66th overall) of NHL entry draft (June 16, 1990). ... Injured knee (September 26, 1992); missed first ten games of season.
HONORS: Named to WHL (West) All-Star first team (1989-90).

Season	Team	League	Gms.	G	A	Pts.	Pen.	Gms.	G	A	Pts.	Pen.
87-88	Prince George	BCJHL	54	12	34	46	99	—	—	—	—	—
	—New Westminster	WHL	6	0	0	0	0	—	—	—	—	—
88-89	Seattle	WHL	72	11	41	52	51	—	—	—	—	—
89-90	Seattle	WHL	63	15	48	63	116	13	2	9	11	32
90-91	Adirondack	AHL	78	5	19	24	70	2	0	0	0	4
91-92	Adirondack	AHL	69	4	28	32	82	18	2	6	8	28
92-93	Adirondack	AHL	45	3	12	15	39	11	3	3	6	8

MALIK, MAREK
D, WHALERS

PERSONAL: Born June 24, 1975, at Ostrava, Czechoslovakia. ... 6-5/185. ... Shoots left.
TRANSACTIONS/CAREER NOTES: Selected by Hartford Whalers in third round (second Whalers pick, 72nd overall) of NHL entry draft (June 26, 1993).

Season	Team	League	Gms.	G	A	Pts.	Pen.	Gms.	G	A	Pts.	Pen.
91-92	TJ Vitkovice Jrs	Czech. Jrs.				Statistics unavailable.						
92-93	TJ Vitkovice	Czech.				Did not play.						

MALKOC, DEAN
D, DEVILS

PERSONAL: Born January 26, 1970, at Vancouver, B.C. ... 6-3/200. ... Shoots left. ... Name pronounced MAL-KAHK.
TRANSACTIONS/CAREER NOTES: Selected by New Jersey Devils in fifth round (seventh Devils pick, 95th overall) of NHL entry draft (June 16, 1990). ... Traded by Kamloops Blazers with LW Todd Esselmont to Swift Current Broncos for RW Eddie Patterson (October 17, 1990).

M

Season Team	League	REGULAR SEASON Gms.	G	A	Pts.	Pen.	PLAYOFFS Gms.	G	A	Pts.	Pen.
87-88—Williams Lake	PCJHL	...	6	32	38	215	—	—	—	—	—
88-89—Powell River	BCJHL	55	10	32	42	370	—	—	—	—	—
89-90—Kamloops	WHL	48	3	18	21	209	17	0	3	3	56
90-91—Kamloops	WHL	8	1	4	5	47	—	—	—	—	—
—Swift Current	WHL	56	10	23	33	248	3	0	2	2	5
—Utica	AHL	1	0	0	0	0	—	—	—	—	—
91-92—Utica	AHL	66	1	11	12	274	4	0	2	2	6
92-93—Utica	AHL	73	5	19	24	255	5	0	1	1	8

MALLETTE, TROY
C/LW, SENATORS

PERSONAL: Born February 25, 1970, at Sudbury, Ont. ... 6-2/190. ... Shoots left. ... Full name: Troy Matthew Mallette. ... Name pronounced muh-LEHT.

TRANSACTIONS/CAREER NOTES: Selected by New York Rangers in second round (first Rangers pick, 22nd overall) of NHL entry draft (June 11, 1988). ... Fined $500 by NHL for head-butting (March 19, 1990). ... Sprained left knee ligaments (September 1990). ... Fined $500 by NHL for attempting to injure another player (October 28, 1990). ... Reinjured knee (October 29, 1990). ... Injured shoulder (January 13, 1991). ... Awarded to Edmonton Oilers as compensation for Rangers signing free agent C/LW Adam Graves (September 9, 1991). ... Strained knee ligament (November 1991); missed two games. ... Traded by Oilers to New Jersey Devils for LW David Maley (January 12, 1992). ... Sprained right ankle (January 24, 1992); missed four games. ... Suffered pinched nerve in neck (January 2, 1993); missed one game. ... Traded by Devils with G Craig Billington and fourth-round pick in 1993 draft to Ottawa Senators for G Peter Sidorkiewicz and future considerations (June 20, 1993); Senators sent LW Mike Peluso to Devils to complete deal (June 26, 1993).

Season Team	League	REGULAR SEASON Gms.	G	A	Pts.	Pen.	PLAYOFFS Gms.	G	A	Pts.	Pen.
86-87—Sault Ste. Marie	OHL	65	20	25	45	157	4	0	2	2	2
87-88—Sault Ste. Marie	OHL	62	18	30	48	186	6	1	3	4	12
88-89—Sault Ste. Marie	OHL	64	39	37	76	172	—	—	—	—	—
89-90—New York Rangers	NHL	79	13	16	29	305	10	2	2	4	81
90-91—New York Rangers	NHL	71	12	10	22	252	5	0	0	0	18
91-92—Edmonton	NHL	15	1	3	4	36	—	—	—	—	—
—New Jersey	NHL	17	3	4	7	43	—	—	—	—	—
92-93—New Jersey	NHL	34	4	3	7	56	—	—	—	—	—
—Utica	AHL	5	3	3	6	17	—	—	—	—	—
NHL totals		216	33	36	69	692	15	2	2	4	99

MALLGRAVE, MATTHEW
RW, MAPLE LEAFS

PERSONAL: Born May 3, 1970, at Washington, D.C. ... 6-0/180. ... Shoots right. ... Full name: Matthew Francis X. Mallgrave.
HIGH SCHOOL: St. Paul's School For Boys (Brooklandville, Md.).
COLLEGE: Harvard.

TRANSACTIONS/CAREER NOTES: Selected by Toronto Maple Leafs in seventh round (sixth Maple Leafs pick, 132nd overall) of NHL entry draft (June 11, 1988).

Season Team	League	REGULAR SEASON Gms.	G	A	Pts.	Pen.	PLAYOFFS Gms.	G	A	Pts.	Pen.
87-88—St. Paul's H.S.	Md. H.S.	...	21	22	43	...	—	—	—	—	—
88-89—St. Paul's H.S.	Md. H.S.	...	24	14	38	...	—	—	—	—	—
89-90—Harvard University	ECAC	26	3	3	6	33	—	—	—	—	—
90-91—Harvard University	ECAC	27	5	13	18	14	—	—	—	—	—
91-92—Harvard University	ECAC	27	12	15	27	20	—	—	—	—	—
92-93—Harvard University	ECAC	31	27	13	40	36	—	—	—	—	—

MALTAIS, STEVE
LW, RED WINGS

PERSONAL: Born January 25, 1969, at Arvida, Ont. ... 6-2/210. ... Shoots left. ... Name pronounced MAHL-TEH.

TRANSACTIONS/CAREER NOTES: Selected by Washington Capitals as underage junior in third round (second Capitals pick, 57th overall) of NHL entry draft (June 13, 1987). ... Traded by Capitals with C Trent Klatt to Minnesota North Stars for D Shawn Chambers (June 21, 1991). ... Traded by North Stars to Quebec Nordiques for C Kip Miller (March 8, 1992). ... Selected by Tampa Bay Lightning in NHL expansion draft (June 18, 1992). ... Traded by Lightning to Detroit Red Wings for D Dennis Vial (June 8, 1993).
HONORS: Name to OHL All-Star second team (1988-89).

Season Team	League	REGULAR SEASON Gms.	G	A	Pts.	Pen.	PLAYOFFS Gms.	G	A	Pts.	Pen.
85-86—Wexford Jr. B	MTHL	33	35	19	54	38	—	—	—	—	—
86-87—Cornwall	OHL	65	32	12	44	29	5	0	0	0	2
87-88—Cornwall	OHL	59	39	46	85	30	11	9	6	15	33
88-89—Cornwall	OHL	58	53	70	123	67	18	14	16	30	16
—Fort Wayne	IHL	—	—	—	—	—	4	2	1	3	0
89-90—Washington	NHL	8	0	0	0	2	1	0	0	0	0
—Baltimore	AHL	67	29	37	66	54	12	6	10	16	6
90-91—Baltimore	AHL	73	36	43	79	97	6	1	4	5	10
—Washington	NHL	7	0	0	0	2	—	—	—	—	—
91-92—Kalamazoo	IHL	48	25	31	56	51	—	—	—	—	—
—Minnesota	NHL	12	2	1	3	2	—	—	—	—	—
—Halifax	AHL	10	3	3	6	0	—	—	—	—	—
92-93—Atlanta	IHL	16	14	10	24	22	—	—	—	—	—
—Tampa Bay	NHL	63	7	13	20	35	—	—	—	—	—
NHL totals		90	9	14	23	41	1	0	0	0	0

M

MALTBY, KIRK
RW, OILERS

PERSONAL: Born December 22, 1972, at Guelph, Ont.... 6-0/180.... Shoots right.
COLLEGE: Georgian (Ont.).
TRANSACTIONS/CAREER NOTES: Selected by Edmonton Oilers in third round (fourth Oilers pick, 65th overall) of NHL entry draft (June 20, 1992).

			REGULAR SEASON					PLAYOFFS			
Season Team	League	Gms.	G	A	Pts.	Pen.	Gms.	G	A	Pts.	Pen.
88-89—Cambridge Jr. B	OHA	48	28	18	46	138	—	—	—	—	—
89-90—Owen Sound	OHL	61	12	15	27	90	12	1	6	7	15
90-91—Owen Sound	OHL	66	34	32	66	100	—	—	—	—	—
91-92—Owen Sound	OHL	64	50	41	91	99	5	3	3	6	18
92-93—Cape Breton	AHL	73	22	23	45	130	16	3	3	6	45

MANDERVILLE, KENT
LW, MAPLE LEAFS

PERSONAL: Born April 12, 1971, at Edmonton, Alta.... 6-3/195.... Shoots left. ... Full name: Kent Stephen Manderville.
COLLEGE: Cornell.
TRANSACTIONS/CAREER NOTES: Selected by Calgary Flames in second round (first Flames pick, 24th overall) of NHL entry draft (June 17, 1989).... Traded by Flames with C Doug Gilmour, D Jamie Macoun, D Ric Nattress and G Rick Wamsley to Toronto Maple Leafs for LW Craig Berube, D Alexander Godynyuk, RW Gary Leeman, D Michel Petit and G Jeff Reese (Janaury 2, 1992).
HONORS: Named ECAC Rookie of the Year (1989-90).... Named to ECAC All-Rookie team (1989-90).
MISCELLANEOUS: Member of silver-medal-winning Canadian Olympic team (1992).

			REGULAR SEASON					PLAYOFFS			
Season Team	League	Gms.	G	A	Pts.	Pen.	Gms.	G	A	Pts.	Pen.
88-89—Notre Dame	SJHL	58	39	36	75	165	—	—	—	—	—
89-90—Cornell University	ECAC	26	11	15	26	28	—	—	—	—	—
90-91—Cornell University	ECAC	28	17	14	31	60	—	—	—	—	—
—Canadian national team	Int'l	3	1	2	3	0	—	—	—	—	—
91-92—Canadian national team	Int'l	63	16	23	39	75	—	—	—	—	—
—Canadian Olympic Team	Int'l	8	1	2	3	0	—	—	—	—	—
—Toronto	NHL	15	0	4	4	0	—	—	—	—	—
—St. John's	AHL	—	—	—	—	—	12	5	9	14	14
92-93—Toronto	NHL	18	1	1	2	17	18	1	0	1	8
—St. John's	AHL	56	19	28	47	86	2	0	2	2	0
NHL totals		33	1	5	6	17	18	1	0	1	8

MANLOW, ERIC
C, BLACKHAWKS

PERSONAL: Born April 7, 1975, at Belleville, Ont.... 6-0/190.... Shoots left.
TRANSACTIONS/CAREER NOTES: Selected by Chicago Blackhawks in second round (second Blackhawks pick, 50th overall) of NHL entry draft (June 26, 1993).

			REGULAR SEASON					PLAYOFFS			
Season Team	League	Gms.	G	A	Pts.	Pen.	Gms.	G	A	Pts.	Pen.
91-92—Kitchener	OHL	59	12	20	32	17	14	2	5	7	8
92-93—Kitchener	OHL	53	26	21	47	31	4	0	1	1	2

M

MANSON, DAVE
D, OILERS

PERSONAL: Born January 27, 1967, at Prince Albert, Sask.... 6-2/210.... Shoots left.
HIGH SCHOOL: Carleton (Prince Albert, Sask.).
TRANSACTIONS/CAREER NOTES: Selected by Chicago Blackhawks as underage junior in first round (first Blackhawks pick, 11th overall) of NHL entry draft (June 15, 1985).... Suspended three games by NHL for pushing linesman (October 8, 1989).... Bruised right thigh (December 8, 1989).... Suspended 13 games by NHL for abusing linesman and returning to the ice to fight (December 23, 1989).... Suspended three games by NHL for biting (February 27, 1990).... Suspended four games by NHL for attempting to injure another player (October 20, 1990).... Traded by Blackhawks with third-round pick in either 1992 or 1993 draft to Edmonton Oilers for D Steve Smith (October 2, 1991); Oilers used third-round pick in 1992 draft to select RW Kirk Maltby.... Suspended five off-days and fined $500 by NHL for spearing (October 19, 1992).... Strained ligaments in left knee (December 7, 1992); missed one game.
HONORS: Named to WHL All-Star second team (1985-86).... Played in NHL All-Star Game (1989 and 1993).

			REGULAR SEASON					PLAYOFFS			
Season Team	League	Gms.	G	A	Pts.	Pen.	Gms.	G	A	Pts.	Pen.
83-84—Prince Albert	WHL	70	2	7	9	233	5	0	0	0	4
84-85—Prince Albert	WHL	72	8	30	38	247	13	1	0	1	34
85-86—Prince Albert	WHL	70	14	34	48	177	20	1	8	9	63
86-87—Chicago	NHL	63	1	8	9	146	3	0	0	0	10
87-88—Saginaw	IHL	6	0	3	3	37	—	—	—	—	—
—Chicago	NHL	54	1	6	7	185	5	0	0	0	27
88-89—Chicago	NHL	79	18	36	54	352	16	0	8	8	*84
89-90—Chicago	NHL	59	5	23	28	301	20	2	4	6	46
90-91—Chicago	NHL	75	14	15	29	191	6	0	1	1	36
91-92—Edmonton	NHL	79	15	32	47	220	16	3	9	12	44
92-93—Edmonton	NHL	83	15	30	45	210	—	—	—	—	—
NHL totals		492	69	150	219	1605	66	5	22	27	247

MARACLE, NORM
G, RED WINGS

PERSONAL: Born October 2, 1974, at Belleville, Ont.... 5-9/175.... Shoots left.
HIGH SCHOOL: Marion Graham (Regina, Sask.).
TRANSACTIONS/CAREER NOTES: Selected by Detroit Red Wings in fifth round (sixth Red Wings pick, 126th overall) of NHL entry draft (June 26, 1993).
HONORS: Named to Can.HL All-Rookie team (1991-92).... Named to WHL (East) All-Star second team (1992-93).

Season Team	League	Gms.	Min.	W	L	T	GA	SO	Avg.	Gms.	Min.	W	L	GA	SO	Avg.
91-92—Saskatoon	WHL	29	1529	13	6	3	87	1	3.41	15	860	9	5	37	0	2.58
92-93—Saskatoon	WHL	53	2939	27	18	3	160	1	3.27	9	569	4	5	33	0	3.48

MARCHMENT, BRYAN
D, BLACKHAWKS

PERSONAL: Born May 1, 1969, at Scarborough, Ont. . . . 6-1/198. . . . Shoots left.
TRANSACTIONS/CAREER NOTES: Suspended three games by OHL (October 1, 1986). . . . Selected by Winnipeg Jets as underage junior in first round (first Jets pick, 16th overall) of NHL entry draft (June 13, 1987). . . . Suspended six games by AHL for fighting (December 10, 1989). . . . Sprained shoulder (March 1990). . . . Suffered back spasms (March 13, 1991). . . . Traded by Jets with D Chris Norton to Chicago Blackhawks for C Troy Murray and LW Warren Rychel (July 22, 1991). . . . Fractured cheekbone (December 12, 1991); missed 12 games.
HONORS: Named to OHL All-Star second team (1988-89).

Season Team	League	Gms.	G	A	Pts.	Pen.	Gms.	G	A	Pts.	Pen.
84-85—Toronto Nationals	MTHL	. . .	14	35	49	229	—	—	—	—	—
85-86—Belleville	OHL	57	5	15	20	225	21	0	7	7	*83
86-87—Belleville	OHL	52	6	38	44	238	6	0	4	4	17
87-88—Belleville	OHL	56	7	51	58	200	6	1	3	4	19
88-89—Belleville	OHL	43	14	36	50	198	5	0	1	1	12
—Winnipeg	NHL	2	0	0	0	2	—	—	—	—	—
89-90—Winnipeg	NHL	7	0	2	2	28	—	—	—	—	—
—Moncton	AHL	56	4	19	23	217	—	—	—	—	—
90-91—Winnipeg	NHL	28	2	2	4	91	—	—	—	—	—
—Moncton	AHL	33	2	11	13	101	—	—	—	—	—
91-92—Chicago	NHL	58	5	10	15	168	16	1	0	1	36
92-93—Chicago	NHL	78	5	15	20	313	4	0	0	0	12
NHL totals		173	12	29	41	602	20	1	0	1	48

MARCINYSHYN, DAVID
D, RANGERS

PERSONAL: Born February 4, 1967, at Edmonton, Alta. . . . 6-3/210. . . . Shoots left. . . . Name pronounced MAHR-sih-NIH-shuhn.
TRANSACTIONS/CAREER NOTES: Signed as free agent by New Jersey Devils (September 26, 1986). . . . Traded by Devils to Quebec Nordiques for D Brent Severyn (June 3, 1991). . . . Signed as free agent by New York Rangers (August 26, 1992).

Season Team	League	Gms.	G	A	Pts.	Pen.	Gms.	G	A	Pts.	Pen.
84-85—Fort Saskatchewan	AJHL	55	11	41	52	311	—	—	—	—	—
85-86—Kamloops	WHL	57	2	7	9	111	16	1	3	4	12
86-87—Kamloops	WHL	68	5	27	32	106	13	0	3	3	35
87-88—Utica	AHL	73	2	7	9	179	—	—	—	—	—
—Flint	IHL	3	0	0	0	4	16	0	2	2	31
88-89—Utica	AHL	74	4	14	18	101	5	0	0	0	13
89-90—Utica	AHL	74	6	18	24	164	5	0	2	2	21
90-91—Utica	AHL	52	4	9	13	81	—	—	—	—	—
—New Jersey	NHL	9	0	1	1	21	—	—	—	—	—
91-92—Halifax	AHL	74	10	42	52	138	—	—	—	—	—
—Quebec	NHL	5	0	0	0	26	—	—	—	—	—
92-93—Binghamton	AHL	67	5	25	30	184	6	0	3	3	14
—New York Rangers	NHL	2	0	0	0	2	—	—	—	—	—
NHL totals		16	0	1	1	49	—	—	—	—	—

MARINUCCI, CHRIS
C, ISLANDERS

PERSONAL: Born December 29, 1971, at Grand Rapids, Minn. . . . 6-0/175. . . . Shoots left. . . . Full name: Christopher Jon Marinucci.
HIGH SCHOOL: Grand Rapids (Minn.).
COLLEGE: Minnesota-Duluth.
TRANSACTIONS/CAREER NOTES: Selected by New York Islanders in fifth round (fourth Islanders pick, 90th overall) of NHL entry draft (June 16, 1990).
HONORS: Named to WCHA All-Star second team (1992-93).

Season Team	League	Gms.	G	A	Pts.	Pen.	Gms.	G	A	Pts.	Pen.
88-89—Grand Rapids H.S.	Minn. H.S.	25	24	18	42	. . .	—	—	—	—	—
89-90—Grand Rapids H.S.	Minn. H.S.	28	24	39	63	0	—	—	—	—	—
90-91—Minnesota-Duluth	WCHA	36	6	10	16	20	—	—	—	—	—
91-92—Minnesota-Duluth	WCHA	37	6	13	19	41	—	—	—	—	—
92-93—Minnesota-Duluth	WCHA	40	35	42	77	52	—	—	—	—	—

MARK, GORD
D, OILERS

PERSONAL: Born September 10, 1964, at Edmonton, Alta. . . . 6-4/210. . . . Shoots right.
TRANSACTIONS/CAREER NOTES: Selected by New Jersey Devils in sixth round (fourth Devils pick, 108th overall) of NHL entry draft (June 8, 1983). . . . Retired from 1988-89 to 1991-92 seasons. . . . Broke knee cap (September 1992). . . . Signed as free agent by Edmonton Oilers (November 10, 1992).

Season Team	League	REGULAR SEASON					PLAYOFFS				
		Gms.	G	A	Pts.	Pen.	Gms.	G	A	Pts.	Pen.
82-83—Kamloops	WHL	71	12	20	32	135	7	1	1	2	8
83-84—Kamloops	WHL	67	12	30	42	202	17	2	6	8	27
84-85—Kamloops	WHL	32	11	23	34	68	7	1	2	3	10
85-86—Maine	AHL	77	9	13	22	134	5	0	1	1	9
86-87—New Jersey	NHL	36	3	5	8	82	—	—	—	—	—
—Maine	AHL	29	4	10	14	66	—	—	—	—	—
87-88—New Jersey	NHL	19	0	2	2	27	—	—	—	—	—
—Utica	AHL	50	5	21	26	96	—	—	—	—	—
88-89—					Did not play—retired.						
89-90—					Did not play—retired.						
90-91—					Did not play—retired.						
91-92—					Did not play—retired.						
92-93—Cape Breton	AHL	60	3	21	24	78	16	1	7	8	20
NHL totals		55	3	7	10	109					

MARKOVICH, MIKE

D, PENGUINS

PERSONAL: Born April 25, 1969, at Grand Forks, N.D.... 6-3/200.... Shoots left.
HIGH SCHOOL: Central (Devils Lake, N.D.).
COLLEGE: Denver.
TRANSACTIONS/CAREER NOTES: Suffered subflexation of left shoulder (September 1988).... Selected by Pittsburgh Penguins in sixth round (sixth Penguins pick, 121st overall) of NHL entry draft (June 17, 1989).

Season Team	League	REGULAR SEASON					PLAYOFFS				
		Gms.	G	A	Pts.	Pen.	Gms.	G	A	Pts.	Pen.
84-85—Central High School	N.D. H.S.	23	8	11	19	12	—	—	—	—	—
85-86—Central High School	N.D. H.S.	23	19	18	37	20	—	—	—	—	—
86-87—Central High School	N.D. H.S.	23	26	25	51	24	—	—	—	—	—
87-88—Rochester	USHL	48	13	41	54	38	—	—	—	—	—
88-89—University of Denver	WCHA	43	5	13	18	38	—	—	—	—	—
89-90—University of Denver	WCHA	42	4	17	21	34	—	—	—	—	—
90-91—University of Denver	WCHA	37	5	15	20	41	—	—	—	—	—
91-92—University of Denver	WCHA	3	0	1	1	10	—	—	—	—	—
92-93—University of Denver	WCHA	38	10	5	15	26	—	—	—	—	—

MAROIS, DANIEL

RW, ISLANDERS

PERSONAL: Born October 3, 1968, at Montreal.... 6-0/190.... Shoots right.
TRANSACTIONS/CAREER NOTES: Selected by Toronto Maple Leafs as underage junior in second round (second Maple Leafs pick, 28th overall) of NHL entry draft (June 13, 1987).... Suffered from the flu (January 1989).... Damaged ligaments in right knee and underwent surgery (April 2, 1989).... Bruised left shoulder (November 12, 1989); missed 11 games.... Injured wrist (October 25, 1991); missed two games.... Traded by Maple Leafs with C Claude Loiselle to New York Islanders for LW Ken Baumgartner and C Dave McLlwain (March 10, 1992).... Strained lower back (December 23, 1992); missed three games.... Strained lower back (March 7, 1993); missed five games.... Traded by Islanders to Boston Bruins for conditional pick in 1994 draft (March 18, 1993).... Underwent back surgery (April 1, 1993).

Season Team	League	REGULAR SEASON					PLAYOFFS				
		Gms.	G	A	Pts.	Pen.	Gms.	G	A	Pts.	Pen.
85-86—Verdun	QMJHL	58	42	35	77	110	5	4	2	6	6
86-87—Chicoutimi	QMJHL	40	22	26	48	143	16	7	14	21	25
87-88—Verdun	QMJHL	67	52	36	88	153	—	—	—	—	—
—Newmarket	AHL	8	4	4	8	4	3	1	0	1	0
—Toronto	NHL	—	—	—	—	—	—	—	—	—	—
88-89—Toronto	NHL	76	31	23	54	76	—	—	—	—	—
89-90—Toronto	NHL	68	39	37	76	82	5	2	2	4	12
90-91—Toronto	NHL	78	21	9	30	112	—	—	—	—	—
91-92—Toronto	NHL	63	15	11	26	76	—	—	—	—	—
—New York Islanders	NHL	12	2	5	7	18	—	—	—	—	—
92-93—New York Islanders	NHL	28	2	5	7	35	—	—	—	—	—
—Capital District	AHL	4	2	0	2	0	—	—	—	—	—
NHL totals		325	110	90	200	399	8	3	2	5	12

MAROIS, MARIO

D

PERSONAL: Born December 15, 1957, at Ancienne Lorette, Que.... 5-11/197.... Shoots right.... Full name: Mario Joseph Marois.
TRANSACTIONS/CAREER NOTES: Selected by New York Rangers from Quebec Remparts in fourth round (sixth Rangers pick, 62nd overall) of NHL amateur draft (June 14, 1977).... Broke ankle; missed part of 1977-78 season.... Traded by Rangers with RW Jim Mayer to Vancouver Canucks for LW Jere Gillis and D Jeff Bandura (November 11, 1980).... Traded by Canucks to Quebec Nordiques for D Garry Lariviere (March 10, 1981).... Broke right wrist (March 27, 1982).... Broke right leg (December 30, 1982).... Traded by Nordiques to Winnipeg Jets for D Robert Picard (November 27, 1985).... Traded by Jets to Nordiques for D Gord Donnelly (December 6, 1988).... Fractured collarbone (January 28, 1989).... Sprained right shoulder (November 9, 1989); missed 12 games.... Claimed by St. Louis Blues in NHL waiver draft (October 1, 1990).... Traded by Blues to Jets for future considerations; Blues later received eighth-round pick in 1992 draft (C Igor Boldin) to complete deal (November 26, 1991).... Released by Jets (July 28, 1992).... Signed as free agent by Hamilton Canucks (September 29, 1992).
HONORS: Named to QMJHL All-Star second team (1976-77).
MISCELLANEOUS: Served as player/assistant coach with Hamilton (1992-93).

M

Season	Team	League	REGULAR SEASON					PLAYOFFS				
			Gms.	G	A	Pts.	Pen.	Gms.	G	A	Pts.	Pen.
75-76	Quebec	QMJHL	67	11	42	53	270	15	2	3	5	86
76-77	Quebec	QMJHL	72	17	67	84	249	14	1	17	18	75
77-78	New Haven	AHL	52	8	23	31	147	12	5	3	8	31
	New York Rangers	NHL	8	1	1	2	15	1	0	0	0	0
78-79	New York Rangers	NHL	71	5	26	31	153	18	0	6	6	29
79-80	New York Rangers	NHL	79	8	23	31	142	9	0	2	2	8
80-81	New York Rangers	NHL	8	1	2	3	46	—	—	—	—	—
	Vancouver	NHL	50	4	12	16	115	—	—	—	—	—
	Quebec	NHL	11	0	7	7	20	5	0	1	1	6
81-82	Quebec	NHL	71	11	32	43	161	13	1	2	3	44
82-83	Quebec	NHL	36	2	12	14	108	—	—	—	—	—
83-84	Quebec	NHL	80	13	36	49	151	9	1	4	5	6
84-85	Quebec	NHL	76	6	37	43	91	18	0	8	8	12
85-86	Quebec	NHL	20	1	12	13	42	—	—	—	—	—
	Winnipeg	NHL	56	4	28	32	110	3	1	4	5	6
86-87	Winnipeg	NHL	79	4	40	44	106	10	1	3	4	23
87-88	Winnipeg	NHL	79	7	44	51	111	5	0	4	4	6
88-89	Winnipeg	NHL	7	1	1	2	17	—	—	—	—	—
	Quebec	NHL	42	2	11	13	101	—	—	—	—	—
89-90	Quebec	NHL	67	3	15	18	104	—	—	—	—	—
90-91	St. Louis	NHL	64	2	14	16	81	0	0	0	0	37
91-92	St. Louis	NHL	17	0	1	1	38	—	—	—	—	—
	Winnipeg	NHL	34	1	3	4	34	—	—	—	—	—
92-93	Hamilton	AHL	68	5	27	32	86	—	—	—	—	—
NHL totals			955	76	357	433	1746	100	4	34	38	177

MARSH, BRAD

D, SENATORS

PERSONAL: Born March 31, 1958, at London, Ont. . . . 6-3/220. . . . Shoots left. . . . Full name: Charles Bradley Marsh.
HIGH SCHOOL: Westminster (London, Ont.).
TRANSACTIONS/CAREER NOTES: Selected by Atlanta Flames from London Knights in first round (first Flames pick, 11th overall) of NHL amateur draft (June 15, 1978). . . . Flames franchise moved to Calgary (May 21, 1980). . . . Traded by Flames to Philadelphia Flyers for C Mel Bridgman (November 11, 1981). . . . Bruised knee tendon (January 2, 1983). . . . Broke fibula (March 24, 1983). . . . Suffered concussion (December 1987). . . . Bruised knee (February 1988). . . . Selected by Toronto Maple Leafs in NHL waiver draft for $2,500 (October 3, 1988). . . . Injured groin (October 31, 1989). . . . Suffered back spasms (December 27, 1990); missed 19 games. . . . Traded by Maple Leafs to Detroit Red Wings for eighth-round pick in 1991 draft (LW Robb McIntyre) (February 4, 1991). . . . Traded by Red Wings to Maple Leafs for future considerations (June 15, 1992). . . . Traded by Maple Leafs to Ottawa Senators for future considerations (July 20, 1992). . . . Suffered back spasms (February 27, 1993); missed two games.
HONORS: Shared Max Kaminsky Memorial Trophy with D Rob Ramage (1977-78). . . . Named to OMJHL All-Star first team (1977-78). . . . Played in NHL All-Star Game (1993).
MISCELLANEOUS: Does not wear a helmet.

Season	Team	League	REGULAR SEASON					PLAYOFFS				
			Gms.	G	A	Pts.	Pen.	Gms.	G	A	Pts.	Pen.
74-75	London	OHA Mj. Jr. A	70	4	17	21	160	—	—	—	—	—
75-76	London	OHA Mj. Jr. A	61	3	26	29	184	—	—	—	—	—
76-77	London	OMJHL	63	7	33	40	121	20	3	5	8	47
77-78	London	OMJHL	62	8	55	63	192	11	2	10	12	21
78-79	Atlanta	NHL	80	0	19	19	101	2	0	0	0	17
79-80	Atlanta	NHL	80	2	9	11	119	4	0	1	1	2
80-81	Calgary	NHL	80	1	12	13	87	16	0	5	5	8
81-82	Calgary	NHL	17	0	1	1	10	—	—	—	—	—
	Philadelphia	NHL	66	2	22	24	106	4	0	0	0	2
82-83	Philadelphia	NHL	68	2	11	13	52	2	0	1	1	0
83-84	Philadelphia	NHL	77	3	14	17	83	3	1	1	2	2
84-85	Philadelphia	NHL	77	2	18	20	91	19	0	6	6	65
85-86	Philadelphia	NHL	79	0	13	13	123	5	0	0	0	2
86-87	Philadelphia	NHL	77	2	9	11	124	26	3	4	7	16
87-88	Philadelphia	NHL	70	3	9	12	57	7	1	0	1	8
88-89	Toronto	NHL	80	1	15	16	79	—	—	—	—	—
89-90	Toronto	NHL	79	1	13	14	95	5	1	0	1	2
90-91	Toronto	NHL	22	0	0	0	15	—	—	—	—	—
	Detroit	NHL	20	1	3	4	16	1	0	0	0	0
91-92	Detroit	NHL	55	3	4	7	53	3	0	0	0	0
92-93	Ottawa	NHL	59	0	3	3	30	—	—	—	—	—
NHL totals			1086	23	175	198	1241	97	6	18	24	124

MARSHALL, GRANT

LW/RW/D, MAPLE LEAFS

PERSONAL: Born June 9, 1973, at Toronto. . . . 6-1/185. . . . Shoots right.
HIGH SCHOOL: Hillcrest (Thunder Bay, Ont.).
TRANSACTIONS/CAREER NOTES: Selected by Toronto Maple Leafs in first round (second Maple Leafs pick, 23rd overall) of NHL entry draft (June 20, 1992).

Season	Team	League	REGULAR SEASON					PLAYOFFS				
			Gms.	G	A	Pts.	Pen.	Gms.	G	A	Pts.	Pen.
90-91	Ottawa	OHL	26	6	11	17	25	1	0	0	0	0

Season Team	League	REGULAR SEASON					PLAYOFFS				
		Gms.	G	A	Pts.	Pen.	Gms.	G	A	Pts.	Pen.
91-92—Ottawa	OHL	61	32	51	83	132	11	6	11	17	11
92-93—Newmarket	OHL	31	12	25	37	85	7	4	7	11	20
—Ottawa	OHL	30	14	28	42	83	—	—	—	—	—
—St. John's	AHL	2	0	0	0	0	2	0	0	0	2

MARSHALL, JASON
D, BLUES

PERSONAL: Born February 22, 1971, at Cranbrook, B.C. . . . . 6-2/195. . . . Shoots right.
TRANSACTIONS/CAREER NOTES: WHL rights traded by Regina Pats with RW Devin Derksen to Tri-City Americans for RW Mark Cipriano (August 1988). . . . Selected by St. Louis Blues in first round (first Blues pick, ninth overall) of NHL entry draft (June 17, 1989).

Season Team	League	REGULAR SEASON					PLAYOFFS				
		Gms.	G	A	Pts.	Pen.	Gms.	G	A	Pts.	Pen.
87-88—Columbia Valley	KIJHL	40	4	28	32	150	—	—	—	—	—
88-89—Vernon	BCJHL	48	10	30	40	197	31	6	6	12	141
—Canadian national team	Int'l	2	0	1	1	0	—	—	—	—	—
89-90—Canadian national team	Int'l	72	1	11	12	57	—	—	—	—	—
90-91—Tri-City	WHL	59	10	34	44	236	7	1	2	3	20
—Peoria	IHL	—	—	—	—	—	18	0	1	1	48
91-92—Peoria	IHL	78	4	18	22	178	10	0	1	1	16
—St. Louis	NHL	2	1	0	1	4	—	—	—	—	—
92-93—Peoria	IHL	77	4	16	20	229	4	0	0	0	20
NHL totals		2	1	0	1	4					

MARTIN, CRAIG
RW, JETS

PERSONAL: Born January 21, 1971, at Amherst, N.S. . . . 6-2/219. . . . Shoots right.
TRANSACTIONS/CAREER NOTES: Suspended by QMJHL for opening game of 1990-91 season for fighting in a playoff game (April 14, 1990). . . . Selected by Winnipeg Jets in fifth round (sixth Jets pick, 98th overall) of NHL entry draft (June 16, 1990). . . . Suspended by QMJHL for striking referee with stick (December 9, 1990).

Season Team	League	REGULAR SEASON					PLAYOFFS				
		Gms.	G	A	Pts.	Pen.	Gms.	G	A	Pts.	Pen.
87-88—Hull	QMJHL	66	5	5	10	137	—	—	—	—	—
88-89—Hull	QMJHL	70	14	29	43	260	—	—	—	—	—
89-90—Hull	QMJHL	66	14	31	45	299	11	2	1	3	65
90-91—St. Hyacinthe	QMJHL	54	13	16	29	257	—	—	—	—	—
91-92—Fort Wayne	IHL	24	0	0	0	115	—	—	—	—	—
—Moncton	AHL	11	1	1	2	70	—	—	—	—	—
92-93—Moncton	AHL	64	5	13	18	198	5	0	1	1	22

MARTIN, MATT
D, MAPLE LEAFS

PERSONAL: Born April 30, 1971, at Hamden, Conn. . . . . 6-3/190. . . . Shoots left.
HIGH SCHOOL: Avon (Conn.) Old Farms School For Boys.
COLLEGE: Maine.
TRANSACTIONS/CAREER NOTES: Selected by Toronto Maple Leafs in fourth round (fourth Maple Leaf pick, 66th overall) of 1989 NHL entry draft (June 17, 1989).

Season Team	League	REGULAR SEASON					PLAYOFFS				
		Gms.	G	A	Pts.	Pen.	Gms.	G	A	Pts.	Pen.
88-89—Avon Old Farms H.S.	Conn. H.S.	. . .	9	23	32	. . .	—	—	—	—	—
89-90—					Statistics unavailable.						
90-91—University of Maine	Hockey East	35	3	12	15	48	—	—	—	—	—
91-92—University of Maine	Hockey East	30	4	14	18	46	—	—	—	—	—
92-93—University of Maine	Hockey East	44	6	26	32	88	—	—	—	—	—
—St. John's	AHL	2	0	0	0	2	9	1	5	6	4

MARTTILA, JUKKA
D, JETS

PERSONAL: Born April 15, 1968, at Tampere, Finland. . . . 6-0/185. . . . Shoots left.
TRANSACTIONS/CAREER NOTES: Selected by Winnipeg Jets in seventh round (ninth Jets pick, 136th overall) of NHL entry draft (June 11, 1988).

Season Team	League	REGULAR SEASON					PLAYOFFS				
		Gms.	G	A	Pts.	Pen.	Gms.	G	A	Pts.	Pen.
86-87—Tappara	Finland	33	4	1	5	18	—	—	—	—	—
87-88—Tappara	Finland	39	5	7	12	16	—	—	—	—	—
88-89—Tappara	Finland	43	11	20	31	32	—	—	—	—	—
89-90—Tappara	Finland	44	12	14	26	14	—	—	—	—	—
90-91—Tappara	Finland	42	10	21	31	32	—	—	—	—	—
91-92—Tappara	Finland	17	2	4	6	14	—	—	—	—	—
92-93—Tappara	Finland	32	1	3	4	36	—	—	—	—	—

MASTAD, MILT
D, BRUINS

PERSONAL: Born March 5, 1975, at Regina, Sask. . . . 6-3/205. . . . Shoots left.
HIGH SCHOOL: Meadowdale (Lynwood, Wash.).
TRANSACTIONS/CAREER NOTES: Selected by Boston Bruins in sixth round (sixth Bruins pick, 155th overall) of NHL entry draft (June 26, 1993).

Season Team	League	REGULAR SEASON					PLAYOFFS				
		Gms.	G	A	Pts.	Pen.	Gms.	G	A	Pts.	Pen.
91-92—Surrey Jr. A	BCJHL	55	1	13	14	122	—	—	—	—	—
92-93—Seattle	WHL	60	1	1	2	123	5	0	1	1	14

MATHIESON, JIM
D, CAPITALS

PERSONAL: Born January 24, 1970, at Kindersley, Sask.... 6-1/209.... Shoots left.... Full name: James Johnson Mathieson.
TRANSACTIONS/CAREER NOTES: Selected by Washington Capitals in third round (third Capitals pick, 59th overall) of NHL entry draft (June 17, 1989).

Season Team	League	REGULAR SEASON					PLAYOFFS				
		Gms.	G	A	Pts.	Pen.	Gms.	G	A	Pts.	Pen.
86-87—Regina	WHL	40	0	9	9	40	3	0	1	1	2
87-88—Regina	WHL	72	3	12	15	115	4	0	2	2	4
88-89—Regina	WHL	62	5	22	27	151	—	—	—	—	—
89-90—Regina	WHL	67	1	26	27	158	11	0	7	7	16
—Baltimore	AHL	—	—	—	—	—	3	0	0	0	4
—Washington	NHL	2	0	0	0	4	—	—	—	—	—
90-91—Baltimore	AHL	65	3	5	8	168	4	1	0	1	6
91-92—Baltimore	AHL	74	2	9	11	206	—	—	—	—	—
92-93—Baltimore	AHL	46	3	5	8	88	3	0	1	1	23
NHL totals		2	0	0	0	4					

MATTE, CHRISTIAN
RW, NORDIQUES

PERSONAL: Born January 20, 1975, at Hull, Que.... 5-11/164.... Shoots right.
TRANSACTIONS/CAREER NOTES: Selected by Quebec Nordiques in sixth round (eighth Nordiques pick, 153rd overall) of NHL entry draft (June 26, 1993).

Season Team	League	REGULAR SEASON					PLAYOFFS				
		Gms.	G	A	Pts.	Pen.	Gms.	G	A	Pts.	Pen.
92-93—Granby	QMJHL	68	17	36	53	56	—	—	—	—	—

MATTEAU, STEPHANE
LW, BLACKHAWKS

PERSONAL: Born September 2, 1969, at Rouyn, Que.... 6-3/195.... Shoots left.... Name pronounced ma-TOH.
TRANSACTIONS/CAREER NOTES: Selected by Calgary Flames as underage junior in second round (second Flames pick, 25th overall) of NHL entry draft (June 13, 1987).... Bruised thigh (October 10, 1991); missed 43 games.... Traded by Flames to Chicago Blackhawks for D Trent Yawney (December 16, 1991).... Fractured left foot (January 27, 1992); missed 12 games.... Suffered tonsilitis (September 1992); missed first three games of 1992-93 season.

Season Team	League	REGULAR SEASON					PLAYOFFS				
		Gms.	G	A	Pts.	Pen.	Gms.	G	A	Pts.	Pen.
85-86—Hull	QMJHL	60	6	8	14	19	4	0	0	0	0
86-87—Hull	QMJHL	69	27	48	75	113	8	3	7	10	8
87-88—Hull	QMJHL	57	17	40	57	179	18	5	14	19	84
88-89—Hull	QMJHL	59	44	45	89	202	9	8	6	14	30
—Salt Lake City	IHL	—	—	—	—	—	9	0	4	4	13
89-90—Salt Lake City	IHL	81	23	35	58	130	10	6	3	9	38
90-91—Calgary	NHL	78	15	19	34	93	5	0	1	1	0
91-92—Calgary	NHL	4	1	0	1	19	—	—	—	—	—
—Chicago	NHL	20	5	8	13	45	18	4	6	10	24
92-93—Chicago	NHL	79	15	18	33	98	3	0	1	1	2
NHL totals		181	36	45	81	255	26	4	8	12	26

MATTSSON, JESPER
C, FLAMES

PERSONAL: Born May 13, 1975, at Malmo, Sweden.... 6-0/173.... Shoots right.
TRANSACTIONS/CAREER NOTES: Selected by Calgary Flames in first round (first Flames pick, 18th overall) of NHL entry draft (June 26, 1993).

Season Team	League	REGULAR SEASON					PLAYOFFS				
		Gms.	G	A	Pts.	Pen.	Gms.	G	A	Pts.	Pen.
91-92—Malmo	Sweden	24	0	1	1	2	—	—	—	—	—
92-93—Malmo	Sweden	40	9	8	17	14	—	—	—	—	—

MATVICHUK, RICHARD
D, STARS

PERSONAL: Born February 5, 1973, at Edmonton, Alta. ... 6-2/190. ... Shoots left.... Name pronounced MAT-vih-CHUHK.
TRANSACTIONS/CAREER NOTES: Selected by Minnesota North Stars in first round (first North Stars pick, eighth overall) of 1991 NHL entry draft (June 22, 1991).... Strained lower back (November 9, 1992); missed two games.... Sprained ankle (December 27, 1992); missed ten games.... North Stars franchise moved from Minnesota to Dallas and renamed Stars for 1993-94 season.
HONORS: Won Bill Hunter Trophy (1991-92).... Named to Can.HL All-Star second team (1991-92).... Named to WHL (East) All-Star first team (1991-92).

Season Team	League	REGULAR SEASON					PLAYOFFS				
		Gms.	G	A	Pts.	Pen.	Gms.	G	A	Pts.	Pen.
88-89—Fort Saskatchewan	AJHL	58	7	36	43	147	—	—	—	—	—
89-90—Saskatoon	WHL	56	8	24	32	126	10	2	8	10	16
90-91—Saskatoon	WHL	68	13	36	49	117	—	—	—	—	—

M

Season	Team	League	Gms.	G	A	Pts.	Pen.	Gms.	G	A	Pts.	Pen.
91-92—Saskatoon		WHL	58	14	40	54	126	22	1	9	10	61
92-93—Minnesota		NHL	53	2	3	5	26	—	—	—	—	—
—Kalamazoo		IHL	3	0	1	1	6	—	—	—	—	—
NHL totals			53	2	3	5	26					

MAY, ALAN
RW, CAPITALS

PERSONAL: Born January 14, 1965, at Swan Hills, Alta. . . . 6-1/200. . . . Shoots right. . . . Full name: Alan Randy May.

TRANSACTIONS/CAREER NOTES: Signed as free agent by Boston Bruins (September 1987). . . . Traded by Bruins to Edmonton Oilers for LW Moe Lemay (March 8, 1988). . . . Traded by Oilers with D Jim Wiemer to Los Angeles Kings for C Brian Wilks and D John English (March 7, 1989). . . . Traded by Kings to Washington Capitals for fifth-round pick in 1989 draft (G Tom Newman) (June 17, 1989). . . . Fractured knuckle on left hand (October 20, 1990). . . . Strained shoulder (December 8, 1990). . . . Underwent surgery to nose (March 1992); missed two games.
HONORS: Named to ACHL All-Star second team (1986-87).

			—REGULAR SEASON—					—PLAYOFFS—				
Season	Team	League	Gms.	G	A	Pts.	Pen.	Gms.	G	A	Pts.	Pen.
84-85—Estevan		SAJHL	64	51	47	98	409	—	—	—	—	—
85-86—Medicine Hat		WHL	6	1	0	1	25	—	—	—	—	—
86-87—New Westminster		WHL	32	8	9	17	81	—	—	—	—	—
—Springfield		AHL	4	0	2	2	11	—	—	—	—	—
—Carolina		ECHL	42	23	14	37	310	5	2	2	4	57
87-88—Maine		AHL	61	14	11	25	357	—	—	—	—	—
—Boston		NHL	3	0	0	0	15	—	—	—	—	—
—Nova Scotia		AHL	12	4	1	5	54	4	0	0	0	51
88-89—Edmonton		NHL	3	1	0	1	7	—	—	—	—	—
—Cape Breton		AHL	50	12	13	25	214	—	—	—	—	—
—New Haven		AHL	12	2	8	10	99	16	6	3	9	*105
89-90—Washington		NHL	77	7	10	17	339	15	0	0	0	37
90-91—Washington		NHL	67	4	6	10	264	11	1	1	2	37
91-92—Washington		NHL	75	6	9	15	221	7	0	0	0	0
92-93—Washington		NHL	83	6	10	16	268	6	0	1	1	6
NHL totals			308	24	35	59	1114	39	1	2	3	80

MAY, BRAD
LW, SABRES

PERSONAL: Born November 29, 1971, at Toronto. . . . 6-0/200. . . . Shoots left.
TRANSACTIONS/CAREER NOTES: Selected by Buffalo Sabres in first round (first Sabres pick, 14th overall) of NHL entry draft (June 16, 1990). . . . Injured knee (August 1990). . . . Injured left knee ligaments (November 1990).
HONORS: Named to OHL All-Star second team (1989-90 and 1990-91).

			—REGULAR SEASON—					—PLAYOFFS—				
Season	Team	League	Gms.	G	A	Pts.	Pen.	Gms.	G	A	Pts.	Pen.
87-88—Markham Jr. B		OHA	6	1	1	2	21	—	—	—	—	—
88-89—Niagara Falls		OHL	65	8	14	22	304	17	0	1	1	55
89-90—Niagara Falls		OHL	61	33	58	91	223	16	9	13	22	64
90-91—Niagara Falls		OHL	34	37	32	69	93	14	11	14	25	53
91-92—Buffalo		NHL	69	11	6	17	309	7	1	4	5	2
92-93—Buffalo		NHL	82	13	13	26	242	8	1	1	2	14
NHL totals			151	24	19	43	551	15	2	5	7	16

M

MAYERS, JAMAL
C, BLUES

PERSONAL: Born October 24, 1974, at Toronto. . . . 6-0/190. . . . Shoots right. . . . Name pronounced MAY-ohrs.
COLLEGE: Western Michigan.
TRANSACTIONS/CAREER NOTES: Selected by St. Louis Blues in fourth round (third Blues pick, 89th overall) of NHL entry draft (June 26, 1993).

			—REGULAR SEASON—					—PLAYOFFS—				
Season	Team	League	Gms.	G	A	Pts.	Pen.	Gms.	G	A	Pts.	Pen.
90-91—Thornhill		Jr. A	44	12	24	36	78	—	—	—	—	—
91-92—Thornhill		Jr. A	56	38	69	107	36	—	—	—	—	—
92-93—Western Michigan Univ.		CCHA	38	8	17	25	26	—	—	—	—	—

MAZUR, JAY
C, CANUCKS

PERSONAL: Born January 22, 1965, at Hamilton, Ont. . . . 6-2/205. . . . Shoots right. . . . Full name: Jay John Mazur. . . . Name pronounced MAY-zuhr.
HIGH SCHOOL: Breck (Minneapolis).
COLLEGE: Maine.

TRANSACTIONS/CAREER NOTES: Selected by Vancouver Canucks in 12th round (12th Canucks pick, 230th overall) of NHL entry draft (June 8, 1983). . . . Strained rib cartilage (October 12, 1990). . . . Injured right calf and underwent emergency surgery to relieve circulatory problem (February 21, 1991); missed 11 games.

			—REGULAR SEASON—					—PLAYOFFS—				
Season	Team	League	Gms.	G	A	Pts.	Pen.	Gms.	G	A	Pts.	Pen.
82-83—Breck H.S.		Minn. H.S.				Statistics unavailable.						
83-84—University of Maine		ECAC	34	14	9	23	14	—	—	—	—	—
84-85—University of Maine		Hockey East	31	0	6	6	20					

Season Team	League	REGULAR SEASON					PLAYOFFS				
		Gms.	G	A	Pts.	Pen.	Gms.	G	A	Pts.	Pen.
85-86—University of Maine	Hockey East	35	5	7	12	18	—	—	—	—	—
86-87—University of Maine	Hockey East	39	16	10	26	61	—	—	—	—	—
87-88—Flint	IHL	43	17	11	28	36	—	—	—	—	—
—Fredericton	AHL	31	14	6	20	28	15	4	2	6	38
88-89—Milwaukee	IHL	73	33	31	64	86	11	6	5	11	2
—Vancouver	NHL	1	0	0	0	0	—	—	—	—	—
89-90—Milwaukee	IHL	70	20	27	47	63	6	3	0	3	6
—Vancouver	NHL	5	0	0	0	4	—	—	—	—	—
90-91—Milwaukee	IHL	7	2	3	5	21	—	—	—	—	—
—Vancouver	NHL	36	11	7	18	14	6	0	1	1	8
91-92—Milwaukee	IHL	56	17	20	37	49	5	2	3	5	0
—Vancouver	NHL	5	0	0	0	2	—	—	—	—	—
92-93—Hamilton	AHL	59	21	17	38	30	—	—	—	—	—
NHL totals		47	11	7	18	20	6	0	1	1	8

McAMMOND, DEAN
C, OILERS

PERSONAL: Born June 15, 1973, at Grand Cache, Alta.... 5-11/185.... Shoots left.
TRANSACTIONS/CAREER NOTES: Selected by Chicago Blackhawks in first round (first Blackhawks pick, 22nd overall) of NHL entry draft (June 22, 1991).... Traded by Blackhawks with D Igor Kravchuk to Edmonton Oilers for RW Joe Murphy (February 25, 1993).
HONORS: Won Can.HL Plus/Minus Award (1991-92).

Season Team	League	REGULAR SEASON					PLAYOFFS				
		Gms.	G	A	Pts.	Pen.	Gms.	G	A	Pts.	Pen.
89-90—Prince Albert	WHL	53	11	11	22	49	14	2	3	5	18
90-91—Prince Albert	WHL	71	33	35	68	108	2	0	1	1	6
91-92—Prince Albert	WHL	63	37	54	91	189	10	12	11	23	26
—Chicago	NHL	5	0	2	2	0	3	0	0	0	2
92-93—Prince Albert	WHL	30	19	29	48	44	—	—	—	—	—
—Swift Current	WHL	18	10	13	23	29	17	*16	19	35	20
NHL totals		5	0	2	2	0	3	0	0	0	2

McBAIN, ANDREW
RW, SENATORS

PERSONAL: Born January 18, 1965, at Toronto.... 6-1/205.... Shoots right.... Full name: Andrew Burton McBain.
HIGH SCHOOL: David and Mary Thomson (Scarborough, Ont.).
TRANSACTIONS/CAREER NOTES: Fractured cheekbone (November 1982).... Separated sterno clavicular joint (March 1983).... Selected by Winnipeg Jets as underage junior in first round (first Jets pick, eighth overall) of NHL entry draft (June 8, 1983).... Suffered from mononucleosis (April 25, 1985).... Injured knee (December 8, 1985).... Suspended four games by NHL for stick-swinging incident (March 1987).... Traded by Jets with D Jim Kyte and LW Randy Gilhen to Pittsburgh Penguins for C/LW Randy Cunneyworth, G Richard Tabaracci and RW Dave McLlwain (June 17, 1989).... Traded by Penguins with C Dan Quinn and C Dave Capuano to Vancouver Canucks for RW Tony Tanti, C Barry Pederson and D Rod Buskas (January 8, 1990).... Suffered sore ribs (February 1990).... Signed as free agent by Ottawa Senators (June 23, 1992).... Injured knee (December 17, 1992); missed 18 games.
HONORS: Named to OHL All-Star second team (1982-83).

Season Team	League	REGULAR SEASON					PLAYOFFS				
		Gms.	G	A	Pts.	Pen.	Gms.	G	A	Pts.	Pen.
81-82—Niagara Falls	OHL	68	19	25	44	35	5	0	3	3	4
82-83—North Bay	OHL	67	33	87	120	61	8	2	6	8	17
83-84—Winnipeg	NHL	78	11	19	30	37	3	2	0	2	0
84-85—Winnipeg	NHL	77	7	15	22	45	7	1	0	1	0
85-86—Winnipeg	NHL	28	3	3	6	17	—	—	—	—	—
86-87—Winnipeg	NHL	71	11	21	32	106	9	0	2	2	10
87-88—Winnipeg	NHL	74	32	31	63	145	5	2	5	7	29
88-89—Winnipeg	NHL	80	37	40	77	71	—	—	—	—	—
89-90—Pittsburgh	NHL	41	5	9	14	51	—	—	—	—	—
—Vancouver	NHL	26	4	5	9	22	—	—	—	—	—
90-91—Vancouver	NHL	13	0	5	5	32	—	—	—	—	—
—Milwaukee	IHL	47	27	24	51	69	6	2	5	7	12
91-92—Milwaukee	IHL	65	24	54	78	132	5	1	2	3	10
—Vancouver	NHL	6	1	0	1	0	—	—	—	—	—
92-93—Ottawa	NHL	59	7	16	23	43	—	—	—	—	—
—New Haven	AHL	1	0	1	1	4	—	—	—	—	—
NHL totals		553	118	164	282	569	24	5	7	12	39

McBAIN, JASON
D, WHALERS

PERSONAL: Born April 12, 1974, at Ilion, N.Y.... 6-2/178.... Shoots right.
TRANSACTIONS/CAREER NOTES: Selected by Hartford Whalers in fourth round (fifth Whalers pick, 81st overall) of NHL entry draft (June 20, 1992).

Season Team	League	REGULAR SEASON					PLAYOFFS				
		Gms.	G	A	Pts.	Pen.	Gms.	G	A	Pts.	Pen.
90-91—Lethbridge	WHL	52	2	7	9	39	1	0	0	0	0
91-92—Lethbridge	WHL	13	0	1	1	12	—	—	—	—	—
—Portland	WHL	54	9	23	32	95	6	1	0	1	13
92-93—Portland	WHL	71	9	35	44	76	16	2	12	14	14

M

McBEAN, WAYNE
D, ISLANDERS

PERSONAL: Born February 21, 1969, at Calgary, Alta.... 6-2/185.... Shoots left.
TRANSACTIONS/CAREER NOTES: Selected by Los Angeles Kings as underage junior in first round (first Kings pick, fourth overall) of NHL entry draft (June 13, 1987).... Traded by Kings with G Mark Fitzpatrick and future considerations to New York Islanders for G Kelly Hrudey (February 22, 1989); D Doug Crossman was sent to Islanders to complete the deal.... Injured left knee (December 23, 1991); missed final 47 games of season.... Underwent arthroscopic surgery to left knee (December 31, 1991).
HONORS: Won Top Defenseman Trophy East (1986-87).... Named to WHL (East) All-Star first team (1986-87).... Named to Memorial Cup All-Star team (1986-87).

			REGULAR SEASON					PLAYOFFS				
Season	Team	League	Gms.	G	A	Pts.	Pen.	Gms.	G	A	Pts.	Pen.
85-86—	Medicine Hat	WHL	67	1	14	15	73	25	1	5	6	36
86-87—	Medicine Hat	WHL	71	12	41	53	163	20	2	8	10	40
87-88—	Los Angeles	NHL	27	0	1	1	26	—	—	—	—	—
	Medicine Hat	WHL	30	15	30	45	48	16	6	17	23	50
88-89—	New Haven	AHL	7	1	1	2	2	—	—	—	—	—
	Los Angeles	NHL	33	0	5	5	23	—	—	—	—	—
	New York Islanders	NHL	19	0	1	1	12	—	—	—	—	—
89-90—	Springfield	AHL	68	6	33	39	48	17	4	11	15	31
	New York Islanders	NHL	5	0	1	1	2	2	1	1	2	0
90-91—	Capital District	AHL	22	9	9	18	19	—	—	—	—	—
	New York Islanders	NHL	52	5	14	19	47	—	—	—	—	—
91-92—	New York Islanders	NHL	25	2	4	6	18	—	—	—	—	—
92-93—	Capital District	AHL	20	1	9	10	35	3	0	1	1	9
NHL totals			161	7	26	33	128	2	1	1	2	0

McCABE, BRYAN
D, ISLANDERS

PERSONAL: Born June 8, 1975, at St. Catherine's, Ont.... 6-1/200.... Shoots left.
HIGH SCHOOL: Ferris (Calgary, Alta.).
TRANSACTIONS/CAREER NOTES: Selected by New York Islanders in second round (second Islanders pick, 40th overall) of NHL entry draft (June 26, 1993).
HONORS: Named to WHL (West) All-Star second team (1992-93).

			REGULAR SEASON					PLAYOFFS				
Season	Team	League	Gms.	G	A	Pts.	Pen.	Gms.	G	A	Pts.	Pen.
91-92—	Medicine Hat	WHL	66	6	24	30	157	4	0	0	0	6
92-93—	Medicine Hat	WHL	14	0	13	13	83	—	—	—	—	—
	Spokane	WHL	46	3	44	47	134	10	1	5	6	28

McCARTHY, SANDY
RW, FLAMES

PERSONAL: Born June 15, 1972, at Toronto.... 6-3/225.... Shoots right.
TRANSACTIONS/CAREER NOTES: Suspended one game by QMJHL for attempting to injure another player (October 2, 1989).... Suspended one playoff game by QMJHL for a pre-game fight (March 19, 1990).... Selected by Calgary Flames in third round (third Flames pick, 52nd overall) of NHL entry draft (June 22, 1991).

			REGULAR SEASON					PLAYOFFS				
Season	Team	League	Gms.	G	A	Pts.	Pen.	Gms.	G	A	Pts.	Pen.
89-90—	Laval	QMJHL	65	10	11	21	269	—	—	—	—	—
90-91—	Laval	QMJHL	68	21	19	40	297	—	—	—	—	—
91-92—	Laval	QMJHL	62	39	51	90	326	8	4	5	9	81
92-93—	Salt Lake City	IHL	77	18	20	38	220	—	—	—	—	—

McCARTY, DARREN
RW, RED WINGS

PERSONAL: Born April 1, 1972, at Burnaby, B.C.... 6-1/211.... Shoots right.
HIGH SCHOOL: Quinte Secondary School (Belleville, Ont.).
TRANSACTIONS/CAREER NOTES: Selected by Detroit Red Wings in second round (second Red Wings pick, 46th overall) of NHL entry draft (June 20, 1992).
HONORS: Won Jim Mahon Memorial Trophy (1991-92).... Named to Can.HL All-Star first team (1991-92).... Named to OHL All-Star first team (1991-92).

			REGULAR SEASON					PLAYOFFS				
Season	Team	League	Gms.	G	A	Pts.	Pen.	Gms.	G	A	Pts.	Pen.
88-89—	Peterborough Jr. B	OHA	34	18	17	35	135	—	—	—	—	—
89-90—	Belleville	OHL	63	12	15	27	142	11	1	1	2	21
90-91—	Belleville	OHL	60	30	37	67	151	6	2	2	4	13
91-92—	Belleville	OHL	65	*55	72	127	177	5	1	4	5	13
92-93—	Adirondack	AHL	73	17	19	36	278	11	0	1	1	33

McCAULEY, BILL
C, PANTHERS

PERSONAL: Born April 20, 1975, at Detroit.... 6-0/173.... Shoots left.
TRANSACTIONS/CAREER NOTES: Selected by Florida Panthers in fourth round (sixth Panthers pick, 83rd overall) of NHL entry draft (June 26, 1993).

			REGULAR SEASON					PLAYOFFS				
Season	Team	League	Gms.	G	A	Pts.	Pen.	Gms.	G	A	Pts.	Pen.
91-92—	Detroit Junior Red Wings	NAJHL	38	25	35	60	64	—	—	—	—	—
92-93—	Detroit	OHL	65	13	37	50	24	15	1	4	5	6

M

McCLELLAND, KEVIN

RW, MAPLE LEAFS

PERSONAL: Born July 4, 1962, at Oshawa, Ont. . . . 6-2/205. . . . Shoots right. . . . Full name: Kevin William McClelland.

TRANSACTIONS/CAREER NOTES: Selected by Hartford Whalers as underage junior in fourth round (fourth Whalers pick, 71st overall) of NHL entry draft (June 11, 1980). . . . Acquired by Pittsburgh Penguins with C/LW Pat Boutette as compensation from Whalers for Whalers signing free agent G Greg Millen. Decision required by NHL Arbitrator Judge Joseph Kane when Hartford and Pittsburgh were unable to agree on compensation (July 1981). . . . Dislocated shoulder (September 21, 1981). . . . Dislocated shoulder and underwent surgery (January 24, 1983); missed remainder of season. . . . Traded by Penguins with sixth-round pick in 1984 draft (D Emanuel Viveiros) to Edmonton Oilers for C Tom Roulston (December 5, 1983). . . . Sprained left knee (January 1985). . . . Suspended three games by NHL for being first off the bench during a fight (December 10, 1986). . . . Sprained knee (November 1987). . . . Bruised right knee (February 1988). . . . Traded by Oilers with C Jimmy Carson and fifth-round pick in 1991 draft to Detroit Red Wings for C/RW Joe Murphy, C/LW Adam Graves, LW Petr Klima and D Jeff Sharples (November 2, 1989). . . . Suffered sore left shoulder (September 1990). . . . Released by Red Wings (April 21, 1991). . . . Signed as free agent by Toronto Maple Leafs (September 2, 1991).

MISCELLANEOUS: Member of Stanley Cup championship team (1984, 1985, 1987 and 1988).

			REGULAR SEASON					PLAYOFFS			
Season Team	League	Gms.	G	A	Pts.	Pen.	Gms.	G	A	Pts.	Pen.
79-80—Niagara Falls	OMJHL	67	14	14	28	71	—	—	—	—	—
80-81—Niagara Falls	OMJHL	68	36	72	108	184	12	8	13	21	42
81-82—Niagara Falls	OHL	46	36	47	83	184	—	—	—	—	—
—Pittsburgh	NHL	10	1	4	5	4	5	1	1	2	5
82-83—Pittsburgh	NHL	38	5	4	9	73	—	—	—	—	—
83-84—Baltimore	AHL	3	1	1	2	0	—	—	—	—	—
—Pittsburgh	NHL	24	2	4	6	62	—	—	—	—	—
—Edmonton	NHL	52	8	20	28	127	18	4	6	10	42
84-85—Edmonton	NHL	62	8	15	23	205	18	1	3	4	75
85-86—Edmonton	NHL	79	11	25	36	266	10	1	0	1	32
86-87—Edmonton	NHL	72	12	13	25	238	21	2	3	5	43
87-88—Edmonton	NHL	74	10	6	16	281	19	2	3	5	68
88-89—Edmonton	NHL	79	6	14	20	161	7	0	2	2	16
89-90—Edmonton	NHL	10	1	1	2	13	—	—	—	—	—
—Detroit	NHL	61	4	5	9	183	—	—	—	—	—
90-91—Adirondack	AHL	27	5	14	19	125	—	—	—	—	—
—Detroit	NHL	3	0	0	0	7	—	—	—	—	—
91-92—St. John's	AHL	34	7	15	22	199	5	0	1	1	9
—Toronto	NHL	18	0	1	1	33	—	—	—	—	—
92-93—St. John's	AHL	55	7	20	27	221	1	0	0	0	7
NHL totals		582	68	112	180	1653	98	11	18	29	281

McCOSH, SHAWN

C, SENATORS

PERSONAL: Born June 5, 1969, at Oshawa, Ont. . . . 6-0/188. . . . Shoots right.

TRANSACTIONS/CAREER NOTES: Selected by Detroit Red Wings in fifth round (fifth Red Wings pick, 95th overall) of NHL entry draft (June 17, 1989). . . . Traded by Red Wings to Los Angeles Kings for eighth-round pick in 1992 draft (D Justin Krall) (August 15, 1990). . . . Traded by Kings with RW Bob Kudelski to Ottawa Senators for RW Jim Thomson and C Marc Fortier (December 20, 1992).

			REGULAR SEASON					PLAYOFFS			
Season Team	League	Gms.	G	A	Pts.	Pen.	Gms.	G	A	Pts.	Pen.
86-87—Hamilton	OHL	50	11	17	28	49	6	1	0	1	2
87-88—Hamilton	OHL	64	17	36	53	96	14	6	8	14	14
88-89—Niagara Falls	OHL	56	41	62	103	75	14	4	13	17	23
89-90—Niagara Falls	OHL	9	6	10	16	24	—	—	—	—	—
—Dukes of Hamilton	OHL	39	24	28	52	65	—	—	—	—	—
90-91—New Haven	AHL	66	16	21	37	104	—	—	—	—	—
91-92—Los Angeles	NHL	4	0	0	0	4	—	—	—	—	—
—Phoenix	IHL	71	21	32	53	118	—	—	—	—	—
—New Haven	AHL	—	—	—	—	—	5	0	1	1	0
92-93—Phoenix	IHL	22	9	8	17	36	—	—	—	—	—
—New Haven	AHL	46	22	32	54	54	—	—	—	—	—
NHL totals		4	0	0	0	4					

McCRIMMON, BRAD

D, WHALERS

PERSONAL: Born March 29, 1959, at Dodsland, Sask. . . . 5-11/197. . . . Shoots left. . . . Full name: Byron Brad McCrimmon.

TRANSACTIONS/CAREER NOTES: Selected by Boston Bruins in first round (second Bruins pick, 15th overall) of NHL entry draft (August 9, 1979). . . . Traded by Bruins to Philadelphia Flyers for G Pete Peeters (June 1982). . . . Broke bone in right hand (February 2, 1985); missed 13 games. . . . Separated left shoulder and underwent surgery (May 9, 1985). . . . Missed start of 1986-87 season due to contract dispute. . . . Traded by Flyers to Calgary Flames for first-round pick in 1989 draft and third-round pick in 1988 draft (G Dominic Roussel) (August 1987). . . . Suffered from skin rash (February 1989). . . . Fractured ankle (March 1989). . . . Traded by Flames to Detroit Red Wings for second-round pick in 1990 draft (later traded to New Jersey Devils) (June 16, 1990). . . . Fractured right ankle (January 12, 1991); missed 16 games. . . . Suffered from the flu (October 24, 1992); missed one game. . . . Traded by Red Wings to Hartford Whalers for sixth-round pick in 1993 draft (June 1, 1993).

HONORS: Named to WCHL All-Star second team (1976-77). . . . Won Top Defenseman Trophy (1977-78). . . . Named to WCHL All-Star first team (1977-78). . . . Named to WHL All-Star first team (1978-79). . . . Named to Memorial Cup All-Star team (1978-79). . . . Won Emery Edge Award (1987-88). . . . Named to THE SPORTING NEWS All-Star second team (1987-88). . . .

Named to NHL All-Star second team (1987-88).... Played in NHL All-Star Game (1988).
MISCELLANEOUS: Member of Stanley Cup championship team (1989).

			REGULAR SEASON					PLAYOFFS				
Season	Team	League	Gms.	G	A	Pts.	Pen.	Gms.	G	A	Pts.	Pen.
76-77—Brandon		WCHL	72	18	66	84	96	—	—	—	—	—
77-78—Brandon		WCHL	65	19	78	97	245	8	2	11	13	20
78-79—Brandon		WHL	66	24	74	98	139	22	9	19	28	34
79-80—Boston		NHL	72	5	11	16	94	10	1	1	2	28
80-81—Boston		NHL	78	11	18	29	148	3	0	1	1	2
81-82—Boston		NHL	78	1	8	9	83	2	0	0	0	2
82-83—Philadelphia		NHL	79	4	21	25	61	3	0	0	0	4
84-85—Philadelphia		NHL	66	8	25	33	81	11	2	1	3	15
85-86—Philadelphia		NHL	80	13	42	55	85	5	2	0	2	2
86-87—Philadelphia		NHL	71	10	29	39	52	26	3	5	8	30
87-88—Calgary		NHL	80	7	35	42	98	9	2	3	5	22
88-89—Calgary		NHL	72	5	17	22	96	22	0	3	3	30
89-90—Calgary		NHL	79	4	15	19	78	6	0	2	2	8
90-91—Detroit		NHL	64	0	13	13	81	7	1	1	2	21
91-92—Detroit		NHL	79	7	22	29	118	11	0	1	1	8
92-93—Detroit		NHL	60	1	14	15	71	—	—	—	—	—
NHL totals			958	76	270	346	1146	115	11	18	29	172

McDONOUGH, HUBIE
C, SHARKS

PERSONAL: Born July 8, 1963, at Manchester, N.H.... 5-9/180.... Shoots left. HIGH SCHOOL: Memorial (Manchester, N.H.). COLLEGE: St. Anselm (N.H.). TRANSACTIONS/CAREER NOTES: Signed as free agent by Los Angeles Kings (October 1987).... Traded by Kings with D Ken Baumgartner to New York Islanders for RW Mikko Makela (November 29, 1989).... Injured knee (September 1990).... Fractured left thumb (October 22, 1991).... Traded by Islanders to San Jose Sharks for cash (August 31, 1992).... Loaned to San Diego Gulls (September 29, 1992).... Returned to Sharks (January 6, 1993).... Loaned to Gulls (March 20, 1993).
HONORS: Named to IHL All-Star second team (1992-93).

			REGULAR SEASON					PLAYOFFS				
Season	Team	League	Gms.	G	A	Pts.	Pen.	Gms.	G	A	Pts.	Pen.
82-83—St. Anselm College		ECAC-II	27	24	21	45	12	—	—	—	—	—
83-84—St. Anselm College		ECAC-II	26	37	15	52	20	—	—	—	—	—
84-85—St. Anselm College		ECAC-II	26	41	30	71	48	—	—	—	—	—
85-86—St. Anselm College		ECAC-II	25	22	20	42	16	—	—	—	—	—
86-87—Flint		IHL	82	27	52	79	59	6	3	2	5	0
87-88—New Haven		AHL	78	30	29	59	43	—	—	—	—	—
88-89—New Haven		AHL	74	37	55	92	41	17	10	*21	*31	6
—Los Angeles		NHL	4	0	1	1	0	—	—	—	—	—
89-90—Los Angeles		NHL	22	3	4	7	10	—	—	—	—	—
—New York Islanders		NHL	54	18	11	29	26	5	1	0	1	4
90-91—Capital District		AHL	17	9	9	18	4	—	—	—	—	—
—New York Islanders		NHL	52	6	6	12	10	—	—	—	—	—
91-92—Capital District		AHL	21	11	18	29	14	—	—	—	—	—
—New York Islanders		NHL	33	7	2	9	15	—	—	—	—	—
92-93—San Diego		IHL	48	26	49	75	26	14	4	7	11	6
—San Jose		NHL	30	6	2	8	6	—	—	—	—	—
NHL totals			195	40	26	66	67	5	1	0	1	4

McDOUGALL, BILL
C, OILERS

PERSONAL: Born August 10, 1966, at Mississauga, Ont.... 6-0/180.... Shoots right. ... Full name: William Henry McDougall.
TRANSACTIONS/CAREER NOTES: Signed as free agent by Detroit Red Wings (March 1990).... Traded by Red Wings to Edmonton Oilers for C Max Middendorf (February 22, 1992).
HONORS: Won ECHL Most Valuable Player Award (1989-90).... Won ECHL Top Scorer Award (1989-90).... Won ECHL Rookie of the Year Award (1989-90).... Named to ECHL All-Star first team (1989-90).... Won Jack Butterfield Trophy (1992-93).

			REGULAR SEASON					PLAYOFFS				
Season	Team	League	Gms.	G	A	Pts.	Pen.	Gms.	G	A	Pts.	Pen.
89-90—Erie		ECHL	57	*80	68	*148	226	7	5	5	10	20
—Adirondack		AHL	11	10	7	17	4	2	1	1	2	2
90-91—Detroit		NHL	2	0	1	1	0	1	0	0	0	0
—Adirondack		AHL	71	47	53	100	192	2	1	2	3	2
91-92—Adirondack		AHL	45	28	24	52	112	—	—	—	—	—
—Cape Breton		AHL	22	8	18	26	36	4	0	1	1	8
92-93—Cape Breton		AHL	71	42	46	88	161	16	*26	*26	*52	30
—Edmonton		NHL	4	2	1	3	4	—	—	—	—	—
NHL totals			6	2	2	4	4	1	0	0	0	0

McEACHERN, SHAWN
C/LW, PENGUINS

PERSONAL: Born February 28, 1969, at Waltham, Mass. ... 5-11/195. ... Shoots left.... Name pronounced muh-KEHK-ruhn.
HIGH SCHOOL: Matignon (Cambridge, Mass.).
COLLEGE: Boston University.

Season Team	League	REGULAR SEASON					PLAYOFFS				
		Gms.	G	A	Pts.	Pen.	Gms.	G	A	Pts.	Pen.
85-86—Matignon H.S.	Mass. H.S.	20	32	20	52	...	—	—	—	—	—
86-87—Matignon H.S.	Mass. H.S.	16	29	28	57	...	—	—	—	—	—
87-88—Matignon H.S.	Mass. H.S.	...	52	40	92	...	—	—	—	—	—
88-89—Boston University	Hockey East	36	20	28	48	32	—	—	—	—	—
89-90—Boston University	Hockey East	43	25	31	56	78	—	—	—	—	—
90-91—Boston University	Hockey East	41	34	48	82	43	—	—	—	—	—
91-92—U.S. national team	Int'l	57	26	23	49	38	—	—	—	—	—
—U.S. Olympic Team	Int'l	8	1	0	1	10	—	—	—	—	—
—Pittsburgh	NHL	15	0	4	4	0	19	2	7	9	4
92-93—Pittsburgh	NHL	84	28	33	61	46	12	3	2	5	10
NHL totals		99	28	37	65	46	31	5	9	14	14

McGILL, BOB
D, MAPLE LEAFS

PERSONAL: Born April 27, 1962, at Edmonton, Alta.... 6-1/193.... Shoots right.... Full name: Robert Paul McGill.
TRANSACTIONS/CAREER NOTES: Selected by Toronto Maple Leafs as underage junior in second round (second Maple Leafs pick, 26th overall) of NHL entry draft (June 11, 1980).... Suspended three games by NHL (January 1985).... Suspended seven games by NHL (March 1, 1986).... Injured ankle (October 1986). ... Traded by Maple Leafs with RW Rick Vaive and LW Steve Thomas to Chicago Blackhawks for LW Al Secord and RW Ed Olczyk (September 3, 1987).... Broke cheekbone (November 4, 1989).... Fined $500 by NHL for fighting (December 28, 1989). ... Bruised left foot (May 1990).... Broke right foot in preparation for training camp (August 30, 1990); missed six weeks.... Selected by San Jose Sharks in NHL expansion draft (May 30, 1991).... Traded by Sharks with eighth-round pick in 1992 draft (G C.J. Denomme) previously acquired form Vancouver Canucks to Detroit Red Wings for LW Johan Garpenlov (March 10, 1992).... Selected by Tampa Bay Lightning in NHL expansion draft (June 18, 1992).... Claimed on waivers by Toronto Maple Leafs (September 7, 1992).... Sprained knee (November 19, 1992); missed 13 games.... Broke jaw (March 27, 1993); missed final nine regular season games and first eight playoff games.

Season Team	League	REGULAR SEASON					PLAYOFFS				
		Gms.	G	A	Pts.	Pen.	Gms.	G	A	Pts.	Pen.
78-79—Abbotsford	BCJHL	46	3	20	23	242	—	—	—	—	—
79-80—Victoria	WHL	70	3	18	21	230	15	0	5	5	64
80-81—Victoria	WHL	66	5	36	41	295	11	1	5	6	67
81-82—Toronto	NHL	68	1	10	11	263	—	—	—	—	—
82-83—Toronto	NHL	30	0	0	0	146	—	—	—	—	—
—St. Catharines	AHL	32	2	5	7	95	—	—	—	—	—
83-84—Toronto	NHL	11	0	2	2	51	—	—	—	—	—
—St. Catharines	AHL	55	1	15	16	217	6	0	0	0	26
84-85—Toronto	NHL	72	0	5	5	250	—	—	—	—	—
85-86—Toronto	NHL	61	1	4	5	141	9	0	0	0	35
86-87—Toronto	NHL	56	1	4	5	103	3	0	0	0	0
87-88—Chicago	NHL	67	4	7	11	131	3	0	0	0	2
88-89—Chicago	NHL	68	0	4	4	155	16	0	0	0	33
89-90—Chicago	NHL	69	2	10	12	204	5	0	0	0	2
90-91—Chicago	NHL	77	4	5	9	151	5	0	0	0	2
91-92—San Jose	NHL	62	3	1	4	70	—	—	—	—	—
—Detroit	NHL	12	0	0	0	21	8	0	0	0	14
92-93—Toronto	NHL	19	1	0	1	34	—	—	—	—	—
NHL totals		672	17	52	69	1720	49	0	0	0	88

McGILL, RYAN
D, FLYERS

PERSONAL: Born February 28, 1969, at Prince Albert, Sask.... 6-2/195.... Shoots right.
TRANSACTIONS/CAREER NOTES: Sprained ankle (January 1986).... Underwent knee surgery (July 1986).... Selected by Chicago Blackhawks as underage junior in second round (second Blackhawks pick, 29th overall) of NHL entry draft (June 13, 1987).... Traded by Swift Current Broncos to Medicine Hat Tigers for G Kelly Hitching (September 1987).... Traded by Blackhawks with C Mike McNeil to Quebec Nordiques for LW Dan Vincelette and C Paul Gillis (March 5, 1991).... Traded by Nordiques to Blackhawks for C Mike Dagenais (September 26, 1991).... Traded by Blackhawks to Philadelphia Flyers for LW Tony Horacek (February 7, 1992).
HONORS: Named to IHL All-Star second team (1990-91).

Season Team	League	REGULAR SEASON					PLAYOFFS				
		Gms.	G	A	Pts.	Pen.	Gms.	G	A	Pts.	Pen.
85-86—Lethbridge	WHL	64	5	10	15	171	10	0	1	1	9
86-87—Swift Current	WHL	71	12	36	48	226	4	1	0	1	9
87-88—Medicine Hat	WHL	67	5	30	35	224	15	7	3	10	47
88-89—Medicine Hat	WHL	57	26	45	71	172	3	0	2	2	15
—Saginaw	IHL	8	2	0	2	12	6	0	0	0	42
89-90—Indianapolis	IHL	77	11	17	28	215	14	2	2	4	29
90-91—Indianapolis	IHL	63	11	40	51	200	—	—	—	—	—
—Halifax	AHL	7	0	4	4	6	—	—	—	—	—
91-92—Indianapolis	IHL	40	7	19	26	170	—	—	—	—	—
—Chicago	NHL	9	0	2	2	20	—	—	—	—	—
—Hershey	AHL	17	3	5	8	67	6	1	1	2	4

Season Team	League	Gms.	G	A	Pts.	Pen.	Gms.	G	A	Pts.	Pen.
92-93—Hershey	AHL	4	0	2	2	26	—	—	—	—	—
—Philadelphia	NHL	72	3	10	13	238	—	—	—	—	—
NHL totals		81	3	12	15	258					

McGOWAN, CAL
C, STARS

PERSONAL: Born June 19, 1970, at Sidney, Neb.... 6-1/185.... Shoots left.... Name pronounced muh-GOW-uhn.
TRANSACTIONS/CAREER NOTES: Selected by Minnesota North Stars in fourth round (third North Stars pick, 70th overall) of NHL entry draft (June 16, 1990).... North Stars franchise moved from Minnesota to Dallas and renamed Stars for 1993-94 season.
HONORS: Named to WHL (West) All-Star first team (1990-91).

			REGULAR SEASON					PLAYOFFS			
Season Team	League	Gms.	G	A	Pts.	Pen.	Gms.	G	A	Pts.	Pen.
86-87—Merritt	BCJHL	50	18	30	48	60	—	—	—	—	—
87-88—Merritt	BCJHL	50	24	62	86	40	4	2	7	9	14
88-89—Kamloops	WHL	72	21	31	52	44	—	—	—	—	—
89-90—Kamloops	WHL	71	33	44	77	78	17	4	5	9	42
90-91—Kamloops	WHL	71	58	81	139	147	12	7	7	14	24
91-92—Kalamazoo	IHL	77	13	30	43	62	1	0	0	0	2
92-93—Kalamazoo	IHL	78	18	42	60	62	—	—	—	—	—

McINNIS, MARTY
C/LW, ISLANDERS

PERSONAL: Born June 2, 1970, at Weymouth, Mass.... 6-0/185.... Shoots right.... Full name: Martin Edward McInnis.... Name pronounced muh-KIH-nihz.
HIGH SCHOOL: Milton (Mass.) Academy.
COLLEGE: Boston College.
TRANSACTIONS/CAREER NOTES: Selected by New York Islanders in eighth round (10th Islanders pick, 163rd overall) of NHL entry draft (June 11, 1988).... Injured eye (March 9, 1993); missed two games.... Fractured patella (March 27, 1993); missed remainder of regular season and 14 playoff games.

			REGULAR SEASON					PLAYOFFS			
Season Team	League	Gms.	G	A	Pts.	Pen.	Gms.	G	A	Pts.	Pen.
86-87—Milton Academy	Mass. H.S.	...	21	19	40	...	—	—	—	—	—
87-88—Milton Academy	Mass. H.S.	...	26	25	51	...	—	—	—	—	—
88-89—Boston College	Hockey East	39	13	19	32	8	—	—	—	—	—
89-90—Boston College	Hockey East	41	24	29	53	43	—	—	—	—	—
90-91—Boston College	Hockey East	38	21	36	57	40	—	—	—	—	—
91-92—U.S. national team	Int'l	54	15	19	34	20	—	—	—	—	—
—U.S. Olympic Team	Int'l	8	5	2	7	4	—	—	—	—	—
—New York Islanders	NHL	15	3	5	8	0	—	—	—	—	—
92-93—New York Islanders	NHL	56	10	20	30	24	3	0	1	1	0
—Capital District	AHL	10	4	12	16	2	—	—	—	—	—
NHL totals		71	13	25	38	24	3	0	1	1	0

McINTYRE, IAN
LW, NORDIQUES

PERSONAL: Born February 12, 1974, at Montreal.... 6-0/184.... Shoots left.
TRANSACTIONS/CAREER NOTES: Selected by Quebec Nordiques in fourth round (fifth Nordiques pick, 76th overall) of NHL entry draft (June 20, 1992).
HONORS: Named to Can.HL All-Rookie team (1991-92).... Named to QMJHL All-Rookie team (1991-92).

			REGULAR SEASON					PLAYOFFS			
Season Team	League	Gms.	G	A	Pts.	Pen.	Gms.	G	A	Pts.	Pen.
91-92—Beauport	QMJHL	63	29	32	61	250	—	—	—	—	—
92-93—Beauport	QMJHL	44	14	18	32	115	—	—	—	—	—

McINTYRE, JOHN
C/LW, RANGERS

PERSONAL: Born April 29, 1969, at Ravenswood, Ont.... 6-1/175.... Shoots left.
TRANSACTIONS/CAREER NOTES: Broke ankle (November 1985).... Severed nerve in right leg (February 1987).... Selected by Toronto Maple Leafs as underage junior in third round (third Maple Leafs pick, 49th overall) of NHL entry draft (June 13, 1987).... Traded by Maple Leafs to Los Angeles Kings for LW/C Mike Krushelnyski (November 9, 1990).... Sprained left thumb (October 22, 1991); missed two games.... Broke nose (March 9, 1992); missed five games.... Traded by Kings to New York Rangers for D Mike Hardy and fifth-round pick in 1993 draft (G Frederick Beaubien) (March 22, 1993).
HONORS: Won Bobby Smith Trophy (1986-87).

			REGULAR SEASON					PLAYOFFS			
Season Team	League	Gms.	G	A	Pts.	Pen.	Gms.	G	A	Pts.	Pen.
84-85—Strathroy Jr. B	OHA	48	21	23	44	49	—	—	—	—	—
85-86—Guelph	OHL	30	4	6	10	25	20	1	5	6	31
86-87—Guelph	OHL	47	8	22	30	95	—	—	—	—	—
87-88—Guelph	OHL	39	24	18	42	109	—	—	—	—	—
88-89—Guelph	OHL	52	30	26	56	129	7	5	4	9	25
—Newmarket	AHL	3	0	2	2	7	5	1	1	2	20
89-90—Newmarket	AHL	6	2	2	4	12	—	—	—	—	—
—Toronto	NHL	59	5	12	17	117	2	0	0	0	2
90-91—Toronto	NHL	13	0	3	3	25	—	—	—	—	—
—Los Angeles	NHL	56	8	5	13	115	12	0	1	1	24

M

Season Team	League	REGULAR SEASON					PLAYOFFS				
		Gms.	G	A	Pts.	Pen.	Gms.	G	A	Pts.	Pen.
91-92—Los Angeles	NHL	73	5	19	24	100	6	0	4	4	12
92-93—Los Angeles	NHL	49	2	5	7	80	—	—	—	—	—
—New York Rangers	NHL	11	1	0	1	4	—	—	—	—	—
NHL totals		261	21	44	65	441	20	0	5	5	38

McKAY, RANDY

PERSONAL: Born January 25, 1967, at Montreal.... 6-1/185.... Shoots right.... Full name: Hugh Randall McKay.
COLLEGE: Michigan Tech.
TRANSACTIONS/CAREER NOTES: Selected by Detroit Red Wings in sixth round (sixth Red Wings pick, 113th overall) of NHL entry draft (June 15, 1985).... Injured knee (February 1989).... Lacerated forearm (February 23, 1991).... Sent by Red Wings with C Dave Barr to New Jersey Devils as compensation for Red Wings signing free agent RW Troy Crowder (September 1991).... Sprained knee (January 16, 1993); missed nine games.

Season Team	League	REGULAR SEASON					PLAYOFFS				
		Gms.	G	A	Pts.	Pen.	Gms.	G	A	Pts.	Pen.
84-85—Michigan Tech	WCHA	25	4	5	9	32	—	—	—	—	—
85-86—Michigan Tech	WCHA	40	12	22	34	46	—	—	—	—	—
86-87—Michigan Tech	WCHA	39	5	11	16	46	—	—	—	—	—
87-88—Michigan Tech	WCHA	41	17	24	41	70	—	—	—	—	—
—Adirondack	AHL	10	0	3	3	12	6	0	4	4	0
88-89—Adirondack	AHL	58	29	34	63	170	14	4	7	11	60
—Detroit	NHL	3	0	0	0	0	2	0	0	0	2
89-90—Detroit	NHL	33	3	6	9	51	—	—	—	—	—
—Adirondack	AHL	36	16	23	39	99	6	3	0	3	35
90-91—Detroit	NHL	47	1	7	8	183	5	0	1	1	41
91-92—New Jersey	NHL	80	17	16	33	246	7	1	3	4	10
92-93—New Jersey	NHL	73	11	11	22	206	5	0	0	0	16
NHL totals		236	32	40	72	686	19	1	4	5	69

McKENZIE, JIM

PERSONAL: Born November 3, 1969, at Gull Lake, Sask.... 6-3/210.... Shoots left.
TRANSACTIONS/CAREER NOTES: Selected by Hartford Whalers in fourth round (third Whalers pick, 73rd overall) of NHL entry draft (June 17, 1989).... Injured elbow (January 31, 1992); missed two games.... Suffered hip flexor (November 11, 1992); missed three games. ...Suffered hip flexor (December 5, 1992); missed four games.... Suffered back spasms (January 24, 1993); missed three games.... Suspended two games by NHL for game misconduct penalties (April 3, 1993).... Suspended three games by NHL for game misconduct penalties (April 10, 1993).

Season Team	League	REGULAR SEASON					PLAYOFFS				
		Gms.	G	A	Pts.	Pen.	Gms.	G	A	Pts.	Pen.
85-86—Moose Jaw	WHL	3	0	2	2	0	—	—	—	—	—
86-87—Moose Jaw	WHL	65	5	3	8	125	9	0	0	0	7
87-88—Moose Jaw	WHL	62	1	17	18	134	—	—	—	—	—
88-89—Victoria	WHL	67	15	27	42	176	8	1	4	5	30
89-90—Binghamton	AHL	56	4	12	16	149	—	—	—	—	—
—Hartford	NHL	5	0	0	0	4	—	—	—	—	—
90-91—Springfield	AHL	24	3	4	7	102	—	—	—	—	—
—Hartford	NHL	41	4	3	7	108	6	0	0	0	8
91-92—Hartford	NHL	67	5	1	6	87	—	—	—	—	—
92-93—Hartford	NHL	64	3	6	9	202	—	—	—	—	—
NHL totals		177	12	10	22	401	6	0	0	0	8

McKIM, ANDREW

PERSONAL: Born July 6, 1970, at St. Johns, N.B.... 5-7/170.... Shoots right.... Full name: Andrew Harry McKim.
TRANSACTIONS/CAREER NOTES: Traded by Verdun Jr. Canadiens with C Trevor Boland to Hull Olympiques for third-round pick in 1989 draft (G Martin Brodeur) (May 26, 1989). ... Signed as free agent by Calgary Flames (October 5, 1990).... Signed as free agent by Boston Bruins (July 23, 1992).... Broke jaw (January 2, 1993); missed 17 games.
HONORS: Won Can.HL Most Sportsmanlike Player of the Year Award (1989-90).... Won Frank J. Selke Trophy (1989-90).... Won Michel Briere Trophy (1989-90).... Named to QMJHL All-Star first team (1989-90).

Season Team	League	REGULAR SEASON					PLAYOFFS				
		Gms.	G	A	Pts.	Pen.	Gms.	G	A	Pts.	Pen.
86-87—Verdun	QMJHL	70	28	59	87	12	—	—	—	—	—
87-88—Verdun	QMJHL	62	27	32	59	27	—	—	—	—	—
88-89—Verdun	QMJHL	68	50	56	106	36	—	—	—	—	—
89-90—Hull	QMJHL	70	66	64	130	44	11	8	10	18	8
90-91—Salt Lake City	IHL	74	30	30	60	48	4	0	2	2	6
91-92—St. John's	AHL	79	43	50	93	79	16	11	12	23	4
92-93—Providence	AHL	61	23	46	69	64	6	2	2	4	0
—Boston	NHL	7	1	3	4	0	—	—	—	—	—
NHL totals		7	1	3	4	0	—	—	—	—	—

McLAUGHLIN, MIKE
LW, SABRES

PERSONAL: Born March 29, 1970, at Springfield, Mass.... 6-1/175.... Shoots left. ... Full name: Michael Sean McLaughlin.
HIGH SCHOOL: Choate Rosemary Hall (Wallingford, Conn.).
COLLEGE: Vermont.
TRANSACTIONS/CAREER NOTES: Selected by Buffalo Sabres in sixth round (seventh Sabres pick, 118th overall) of NHL entry draft (June 11, 1988).

			REGULAR SEASON					PLAYOFFS				
Season Team	League	Gms.	G	A	Pts.	Pen.	Gms.	G	A	Pts.	Pen.
86-87—Choate Rosemary Hall	Conn. H.S.	...	19	18	37	...	—	—	—	—	—
87-88—Choate Rosemary Hall	Conn. H.S.	...	17	18	35	...	—	—	—	—	—
88-89—University of Vermont	ECAC	32	5	6	11	12	—	—	—	—	—
89-90—University of Vermont	ECAC	29	11	12	23	37	—	—	—	—	—
90-91—University of Vermont	ECAC	32	12	14	26	26	—	—	—	—	—
91-92—University of Vermont	ECAC	30	9	9	18	34	—	—	—	—	—
92-93—Rochester	AHL	71	19	35	54	27	16	4	2	6	8

McLEAN, KIRK
G, CANUCKS

PERSONAL: Born June 26, 1966, at Willowdale, Ont.... 6-0/185.... Shoots left.
TRANSACTIONS/CAREER NOTES: Selected by New Jersey Devils as underage junior in sixth round (sixth Devils pick, 107th overall) of NHL entry draft (June 9, 1984).... Traded by Devils with C Greg Adams to Vancouver Canucks for C Patrik Sundstrom, a fourth-round pick in 1988 draft (LW Matt Ruchty) and a switch of second-round picks in 1988 NHL entry draft (September 1987).... Suffered tendinitis in left wrist (February 25, 1991).
HONORS: Played in NHL All-Star Game (1990 and 1992).... Named to THE SPORTING NEWS All-Star second team (1991-92). ... Named to NHL All-Star second team (1991-92).

			REGULAR SEASON							PLAYOFFS					
Season Team	League	Gms.	Min.	W	L	T	GA	SO	Avg.	Gms.	Min.	W	L	GA	SO	Avg.
83-84—Oshawa	OHL	17	940	5	9	0	67	0	4.28	—	—	—	—	—	—	—
84-85—Oshawa	OHL	47	2581	23	17	2	143	1	*3.32	5	271	1	3	21	0	4.65
85-86—Oshawa	OHL	51	2830	24	21	2	169	1	3.58	4	201	1	2	18	0	5.37
—New Jersey	NHL	2	111	1	1	0	11	0	5.95	—	—	—	—	—	—	—
86-87—New Jersey	NHL	4	160	1	1	0	10	0	3.75	—	—	—	—	—	—	—
—Maine	AHL	45	2606	15	23	4	140	1	3.22	—	—	—	—	—	—	—
87-88—Vancouver	NHL	41	2380	11	27	3	147	1	3.71	—	—	—	—	—	—	—
88-89—Vancouver	NHL	42	2477	20	17	3	127	4	3.08	5	302	2	3	18	0	3.58
89-90—Vancouver	NHL	*63	*3739	21	30	10	*216	0	3.47	—	—	—	—	—	—	—
90-91—Vancouver	NHL	41	1969	10	22	3	131	0	3.99	2	123	1	1	7	0	3.41
91-92—Vancouver	NHL	65	3852	†38	17	9	176	†5	2.74	13	785	6	7	33	†2	2.52
92-93—Vancouver	NHL	54	3261	28	21	5	184	3	3.39	12	754	6	6	42	0	3.34
NHL totals		312	17949	130	136	33	1002	13	3.35	32	1964	15	17	100	2	3.05

McLENNAN, JAMIE
G, ISLANDERS

PERSONAL: Born June 30, 1971, at Edmonton, Alta.... 6-0/190.... Shoots left.
TRANSACTIONS/CAREER NOTES: Selected by New York Islanders in third round (third Islanders pick, 48th overall) of NHL entry draft (June 22, 1991).
HONORS: Won Del Wilson Trophy (1990-91).... Named to WHL (East) All-Star first team (1990-91).

			REGULAR SEASON							PLAYOFFS					
Season Team	League	Gms.	Min.	W	L	T	GA	SO	Avg.	Gms.	Min.	W	L	GA	SO	Avg.
88-89—Spokane	WHL	11	578	...	...	...	63	0	6.54	—	—	—	—	—	—	—
—Lethbridge	WHL	7	368	...	...	...	22	0	3.59	—	—	—	—	—	—	—
89-90—Lethbridge	WHL	34	1690	20	4	2	110	1	3.91	13	677	6	5	44	0	3.90
90-91—Lethbridge	WHL	56	3230	32	18	4	205	0	3.81	*16	*970	8	8	*56	0	3.46
91-92—Capital District	AHL	18	952	4	10	2	60	1	3.78	—	—	—	—	—	—	—
—Richmond	ECHL	32	1837	16	12	2	114	0	3.72	—	—	—	—	—	—	—
92-93—Capital District	AHL	38	2171	17	14	6	117	1	3.23	1	20	0	1	5	0	15.00

McLLWAIN, DAVID
RW/C, MAPLE LEAFS

PERSONAL: Born January 9, 1967, at Seaforth, Ont.... 6-0/190.... Shoots right.... Name pronounced MAK-uhl-WAIN.
TRANSACTIONS/CAREER NOTES: Traded by Kitchener Rangers with D John Keller and RW Todd Strombeck to North Bay Centennials for RW Ron Sanko, RW Peter Lisy, Richard Hawkins and D Brett MacDonald (November 1985).... Selected by Pittsburgh Penguins as underage junior in ninth round (ninth Penguins pick, 172nd overall) of NHL entry draft (June 21, 1986).... Traded by Penguins with C/LW Randy Cunneyworth and G Richard Tabaracci to Winnipeg Jets for RW Andrew McBain, D Jim Kyte and LW Randy Gilhen (June 17, 1989).... Injured wrist (October 28, 1990).... Tore medial collateral ligament of right knee (December 3, 1990); missed 16 games.... Traded by Jets with D Gord Donnelly, fifth-round pick in 1992 draft (LW Yuri Khmylev) and future considerations to Buffalo Sabres for LW Darrin Shannon, LW Mike Hartman and D Dean Kennedy (October 11, 1991).... Traded by Sabres with C Pierre Turgeon, RW Benoit Hogue and D Uwe Krupp to New York Islanders for C Pat LaFontaine, LW Randy Wood, D Randy Hillier and future considerations; Sabres later received fourth-round pick in 1992 draft (D Dean Melanson) (October 25, 1991). ... Traded by Islanders with LW Ken Baumgartner to Toronto Maple Leafs for C Claude Loiselle and RW Daniel Marois (March 10, 1992).
HONORS: Named to OHL All-Star second team (1986-87).

			REGULAR SEASON					PLAYOFFS				
Season Team	League	Gms.	G	A	Pts.	Pen.	Gms.	G	A	Pts.	Pen.
84-85—Kitchener	OHL	61	13	21	34	29	—	—	—	—	—
85-86—Kitchener	OHL	13	7	7	14	12	—	—	—	—	—
—North Bay	OHL	51	30	28	58	25	10	4	4	8	2

Season	Team	League	Gms.	G	A	Pts.	Pen.	Gms.	G	A	Pts.	Pen.
86-87—North Bay	OHL	60	46	73	119	35	24	7	18	25	40
87-88—Muskegon	IHL	9	4	6	10	23	6	2	3	5	8
—Pittsburgh	NHL	66	11	8	19	40	—	—	—	—	—
88-89—Muskegon	IHL	46	37	35	72	51	7	8	2	10	6
—Pittsburgh	NHL	24	1	2	3	4	3	0	1	1	0
89-90—Winnipeg	NHL	80	25	26	51	60	7	0	1	1	2
90-91—Winnipeg	NHL	60	14	11	25	46	—	—	—	—	—
91-92—Winnipeg	NHL	3	1	1	2	2	—	—	—	—	—
—Buffalo	NHL	5	0	0	0	2	—	—	—	—	—
—New York Islanders	NHL	54	8	15	23	28	—	—	—	—	—
—Toronto	NHL	11	1	2	3	4	—	—	—	—	—
92-93—Toronto	NHL	66	14	4	18	30	4	0	0	0	0
NHL totals			369	75	69	144	216	14	0	2	2	2

McNEILL, MIKE
RW, NORDIQUES

PERSONAL: Born July 22, 1966, at Winona, Minn. . . . 6-1/ 175. . . . Shoots right.
TRANSACTIONS/CAREER NOTES: Selected by St. Louis Blues in NHL supplemental draft (June 10, 1988). . . . Signed as free agent by Chicago Blackhawks (September 1989). . . . Traded by Blackhawks with D Ryan McGill to Quebec Nordiques for LW Dan Vincelette and C Paul Gillis (March 5, 1991). . . . Separated shoulder (February 15, 1992).
HONORS: Won N.R. (Bud) Poile Trophy (1989-90).

Season	Team	League	Gms.	G	A	Pts.	Pen.	Gms.	G	A	Pts.	Pen.
84-85—University of Notre Dame	Indep.	28	16	26	42	12	—	—	—	—	—
85-86—University of Notre Dame	Indep.	34	18	29	47	32	—	—	—	—	—
86-87—University of Notre Dame	Indep.	30	21	16	37	24	—	—	—	—	—
87-88—University of Notre Dame	Indep.	32	28	44	72	12	—	—	—	—	—
88-89—Fort Wayne	IHL	75	27	35	62	12	11	1	5	6	2
—Moncton	AHL	1	0	0	0	0	—	—	—	—	—
89-90—Indianapolis	IHL	74	17	24	41	15	14	6	4	10	21
90-91—Indianapolis	IHL	33	16	9	25	19	—	—	—	—	—
—Chicago	NHL	23	2	2	4	6	—	—	—	—	—
—Quebec	NHL	14	2	5	7	4	—	—	—	—	—
91-92—Quebec	NHL	26	1	4	5	8	—	—	—	—	—
—Halifax	AHL	30	10	8	18	20	—	—	—	—	—
92-93—Milwaukee	IHL	75	17	17	34	34	6	2	0	2	0
NHL totals			63	5	11	16	18					

McPHEE, MIKE
LW, STARS

PERSONAL: Born February 14, 1960, at Sydney, N.S. . . . 6-1/203. . . . Shoots left. . . . Full name: Michael Joseph McPhee.
COLLEGE: Rensselaer Polytechnic Institute (N.Y.).
TRANSACTIONS/CAREER NOTES: Selected by Montreal Canadiens in sixth round (eighth Canadiens pick, 124th overall) of NHL entry draft (June 11, 1980). . . . Broke hand (September 1982). . . . Injured ankle (January 10, 1986); missed 10 games. . . . Broke little toe on left foot (February 1989). . . . Pulled muscle in rib cage (April 8, 1989). . . . Tore abdominal muscle (October 7, 1989); missed 13 games. . . . Injured groin, knee and thumb (November 13, 1990); missed 16 games. . . . Bruised thigh (February 26, 1992); missed one game. . . . Traded by Canadiens to Minnesota North Stars for fifth-round pick (D Jeff Lank) in 1993 draft (August 17, 1992). . . . North Stars franchise moved from Minnesota to Dallas and renamed Stars for 1993-94 season.
HONORS: Played in NHL All-Star Game (1989).
MISCELLANEOUS: Member of Stanley Cup championship team (1986).

Season	Team	League	Gms.	G	A	Pts.	Pen.	Gms.	G	A	Pts.	Pen.
78-79—R.P.I.	ECAC	26	14	19	33	16	—	—	—	—	—
79-80—R.P.I.	ECAC	27	15	21	36	22	—	—	—	—	—
80-81—R.P.I.	ECAC	29	28	18	46	22	—	—	—	—	—
81-82—R.P.I.	ECAC	6	0	3	3	4	—	—	—	—	—
82-83—Nova Scotia	AHL	42	10	15	25	29	7	1	1	2	14
83-84—Nova Scotia	AHL	67	22	33	55	101	—	—	—	—	—
—Montreal	NHL	14	5	2	7	41	15	1	0	1	31
84-85—Montreal	NHL	70	17	22	39	120	12	4	1	5	32
85-86—Montreal	NHL	70	19	21	40	69	20	3	4	7	45
86-87—Montreal	NHL	79	18	21	39	58	17	7	2	9	13
87-88—Montreal	NHL	77	23	20	43	53	11	4	3	7	8
88-89—Montreal	NHL	73	19	22	41	74	20	4	7	11	30
89-90—Montreal	NHL	56	23	18	41	47	9	1	1	2	16
90-91—Montreal	NHL	64	22	21	43	56	13	1	7	8	12
91-92—Montreal	NHL	78	16	15	31	63	8	1	1	2	4
92-93—Minnesota	NHL	84	18	22	40	44	—	—	—	—	—
NHL totals			665	180	184	364	625	125	26	26	52	191

M

McRAE, BASIL
LW, BLUES

PERSONAL: Born January 5, 1961, at Beaverton, Ont. . . . 6-2/205. . . . Shoots left. . . . Full name: Basil Paul McRae. . . . Brother of Chris McRae, left winger, Toronto Maple Leafs and Detroit Red Wings (1987-88 through 1989-90).
TRANSACTIONS/CAREER NOTES: Selected by Quebec Nordiques as underage junior in fifth round (third Nordiques pick, 87th overall) of NHL entry draft (June 11, 1980). . . . Traded by Nordiques to Toronto Maple Leafs for D Richard Turmel (August 12, 1983). . . . Signed as free agent by Detroit Red Wings (August 1985). . . . Traded by Red Wings with LW John Ogrodnick and RW Doug Shedden to Nordiques for LW Brent Ashton, RW Mark Kumpel and D Gilbert Delorme (January 17, 1987). . . . Signed as free agent by Minnesota North Stars (July 1987). . . . Strained right knee ligaments (October 10, 1989); missed nine games. . . . Suspended five games and fined $500 by NHL for fighting (December 28, 1989). . . . Strained abdominal muscle (October 1990). . . . Underwent abdominal surgery (November 29, 1990); missed 35 games. . . . Severed tendon (February 29, 1992); missed final 17 games of regular season. . . . Selected by Tampa Bay Lightning in NHL expansion draft (June 18, 1992). . . . Fractured bone in lower leg (October 11, 1992); missed 35 games. . . . Traded by Lightning with D Doug Crossman to St. Louis Blues for LW Jason Ruff, sixth-round pick in 1996 draft and either third-round pick in 1995 draft or fourth-round pick in 1994 draft (January 28, 1993).

			REGULAR SEASON					PLAYOFFS			
Season Team	League	Gms.	G	A	Pts.	Pen.	Gms.	G	A	Pts.	Pen.
77-78—Seneca Jr. B	OHA	36	21	38	59	80	—	—	—	—	—
78-79—London	OMJHL	66	13	28	41	79	—	—	—	—	—
79-80—London	OMJHL	67	23	35	58	116	5	0	0	0	18
80-81—London	OMJHL	65	29	23	52	266	—	—	—	—	—
81-82—Fredericton	AHL	47	11	15	26	175	—	—	—	—	—
—Quebec	NHL	20	4	3	7	69	9	1	0	1	34
82-83—Fredericton	AHL	53	22	19	41	146	12	1	5	6	75
—Quebec	NHL	22	1	1	2	59	—	—	—	—	—
83-84—Toronto	NHL	3	0	0	0	19	—	—	—	—	—
—St. Catharines	AHL	78	14	25	39	187	6	0	0	0	40
84-85—St. Catharines	AHL	72	30	25	55	186	—	—	—	—	—
—Toronto	NHL	1	0	0	0	0	—	—	—	—	—
85-86—Detroit	NHL	4	0	0	0	5	—	—	—	—	—
—Adirondack	AHL	69	22	30	52	259	17	5	4	9	101
86-87—Detroit	NHL	36	2	2	4	193	—	—	—	—	—
—Quebec	NHL	33	9	5	14	149	13	3	1	4	*99
87-88—Minnesota	NHL	80	5	11	16	378	—	—	—	—	—
88-89—Minnesota	NHL	78	12	19	31	365	5	0	0	0	58
89-90—Minnesota	NHL	66	9	17	26	*351	7	1	0	1	22
90-91—Minnesota	NHL	40	1	3	4	224	22	1	1	2	*94
91-92—Minnesota	NHL	59	5	8	13	245	—	—	—	—	—
92-93—Tampa Bay	NHL	14	2	3	5	71	—	—	—	—	—
—St. Louis	NHL	33	1	3	4	98	11	0	1	1	24
NHL totals		489	51	75	126	2226	67	6	3	9	331

McRAE, KEN
C, MAPLE LEAFS

PERSONAL: Born April 23, 1968, at Finch, Ont. . . . 6-1/195. . . . Shoots right. . . . Full name: Kenneth Duncan McRae.
TRANSACTIONS/CAREER NOTES: Selected by Quebec Nordiques as underage junior in first round (first Nordiques pick, 18th overall) of NHL entry draft (June 21, 1986). . . . Traded by Sudbury Wolves with C Andy Paquette and D Ken Alexander to Hamilton Steelhawks for C Dan Hie, C Joe Simon, RW Steve Locke, C Shawn Heaphy and D Jordan Fois (December 1986). . . . Lacerated right elbow (December 26, 1989); missed seven games. . . . Bruised shoulder (March 10, 1990). . . . Traded by Nordiques to Toronto Maple Leafs for D Leonard Esau (July 21, 1992).

			REGULAR SEASON					PLAYOFFS			
Season Team	League	Gms.	G	A	Pts.	Pen.	Gms.	G	A	Pts.	Pen.
84-85—Hawkesbury	COJHL	51	38	50	88	77	—	—	—	—	—
85-86—Sudbury	OHL	66	25	40	65	127	4	2	1	3	12
86-87—Sudbury	OHL	21	12	15	27	40	—	—	—	—	—
—Hamilton	OHL	20	7	12	19	25	7	1	1	2	12
87-88—Fredericton	AHL	—	—	—	—	—	3	0	0	0	8
—Quebec	NHL	1	0	0	0	0	—	—	—	—	—
—Hamilton	OHL	62	30	55	85	158	14	13	9	22	35
88-89—Halifax	AHL	41	20	21	41	87	—	—	—	—	—
—Quebec	NHL	37	6	11	17	68	—	—	—	—	—
89-90—Quebec	NHL	66	7	8	15	191	—	—	—	—	—
90-91—Quebec	NHL	12	0	0	0	36	—	—	—	—	—
—Halifax	AHL	60	10	36	46	193	—	—	—	—	—
91-92—Halifax	AHL	52	30	41	71	184	—	—	—	—	—
—Quebec	NHL	10	0	1	1	31	—	—	—	—	—
92-93—St. John's	AHL	64	30	44	74	135	9	6	6	12	27
—Toronto	NHL	2	0	0	0	2	—	—	—	—	—
NHL totals		128	13	20	33	328					

McREYNOLDS, BRIAN
C, RANGERS

PERSONAL: Born January 5, 1965, at Penetanguishene, Ont. . . . 6-1/180. . . . Shoots left.
COLLEGE: Michigan State.
TRANSACTIONS/CAREER NOTES: Selected by New York Rangers as underage junior in sixth round (sixth Rangers pick, 112th overall) of NHL entry draft (June 15, 1985). . . . Signed as free agent by Winnipeg Jets (July 1989). . . . Traded by Jets to Rangers for C Simon Wheeldon (July 10, 1990).

Season Team	League	REGULAR SEASON					PLAYOFFS				
		Gms.	G	A	Pts.	Pen.	Gms.	G	A	Pts.	Pen.
84-85—Orillia	OHA	48	40	54	94	...	—	—	—	—	—
85-86—Michigan State	CCHA	45	14	24	38	78	—	—	—	—	—
86-87—Michigan State	CCHA	45	16	24	40	68	—	—	—	—	—
87-88—Michigan State	CCHA	43	10	24	34	50	—	—	—	—	—
88-89—Canadian national team	Int'l	58	5	25	30	59	—	—	—	—	—
89-90—Winnipeg	NHL	9	0	2	2	4	—	—	—	—	—
—Moncton	AHL	72	18	41	59	87	—	—	—	—	—
90-91—Binghamton	AHL	77	30	42	72	74	10	0	4	4	6
—New York Rangers	NHL	1	0	0	0	0	—	—	—	—	—
91-92—Binghamton	AHL	48	19	28	47	22	7	2	2	4	12
92-93—Binghamton	AHL	79	30	70	100	88	14	3	10	13	18
NHL totals		10	0	2	2	4					

McSORLEY, MARTY

D/RW, KINGS

PERSONAL: Born May 18, 1963, at Hamilton, Ont. ... 6-1/225. ... Shoots right. ... Full name: Martin James McSorley.

TRANSACTIONS/CAREER NOTES: Signed as free agent by Pittsburgh Penguins (April 1983). ... Traded by Penguins with C Tim Hrynewich to Edmonton Oilers for G Gilles Meloche (August 1985). ... Suspended by NHL for an AHL incident (March 1987). ... Sprained knee (November 1987). ... Suspended three playoff games by NHL for spearing (April 23, 1988). ... Traded by Oilers with C Wayne Gretzky and LW/C Mike Krushelnyski to Los Angeles Kings for C Jimmy Carson, LW Martin Gelinas, first-round picks in 1989 (traded to New Jersey), 1991 (LW Martin Rucinsky) and 1993 (D Nick Stajduhar) drafts and cash (August 9, 1988). ... Injured shoulder (December 31, 1988). ... Sprained knee (February 1989). ... Suspended four games by NHL for game-misconduct penalties (1989-90). ... Twisted right knee (October 14, 1990); missed four games. ... Twisted ankle (February 9, 1991). ... Suspended three games by NHL for striking another player with a gloved hand (March 2, 1991). ... Suffered from throat virus (November 23, 1991); missed six games. ... Sprained shoulder (February 19, 1992); missed three games. ... Suspended six off-days and fined $500 by NHL for cross-checking (October 31, 1992). ... Suspended one game by NHL for game misconduct penalties (November 27, 1992).

HONORS: Shared Alka-Seltzer Plus Award with Theoren Fleury (1990-91).

MISCELLANEOUS: Member of Stanley Cup championship teams (1987 and 1988).

Season Team	League	REGULAR SEASON					PLAYOFFS				
		Gms.	G	A	Pts.	Pen.	Gms.	G	A	Pts.	Pen.
81-82—Belleville	OHL	58	6	13	19	234	—	—	—	—	—
82-83—Belleville	OHL	70	10	41	51	183	4	0	0	0	7
—Baltimore	AHL	2	0	0	0	22	—	—	—	—	—
83-84—Pittsburgh	NHL	72	2	7	9	224	—	—	—	—	—
84-85—Baltimore	AHL	58	6	24	30	154	14	0	7	7	47
—Pittsburgh	NHL	15	0	0	0	15	—	—	—	—	—
85-86—Edmonton	NHL	59	11	12	23	265	8	0	2	2	50
—Nova Scotia	AHL	9	2	4	6	34	—	—	—	—	—
86-87—Edmonton	NHL	41	2	4	6	159	21	4	3	7	65
—Nova Scotia	AHL	7	2	2	4	48	—	—	—	—	—
87-88—Edmonton	NHL	60	9	17	26	223	16	0	3	3	67
88-89—Los Angeles	NHL	66	10	17	27	350	11	0	2	2	33
89-90—Los Angeles	NHL	75	15	21	36	322	10	1	3	4	18
90-91—Los Angeles	NHL	61	7	32	39	221	12	0	0	0	58
91-92—Los Angeles	NHL	71	7	22	29	268	6	1	0	1	21
92-93—Los Angeles	NHL	81	15	26	41	*399	24	4	6	10	60
NHL totals		601	78	158	236	2446	108	10	19	29	372

McSWEEN, DON

D, RED WINGS

PERSONAL: Born June 9, 1964, at Detroit. ... 5-11/197. ... Shoots left. ... Full name: Donald Kennedy McSween.

COLLEGE: Michigan State.

TRANSACTIONS/CAREER NOTES: Selected by Buffalo Sabres in eighth round (10th Sabres pick, 154th overall) of NHL entry draft (June 8, 1983). ... Signed as free agent by Detroit Red Wings (August 29, 1992). ... Loaned to San Diego Gulls (October 6, 1992).

HONORS: Named to CCHA All-Star first team (1985-86 and 1986-87). ... Named to NCAA All-America West second team (1985-86 and 1986-87). ... Named to NCAA All-Tournament team (1986-87). ... Named to AHL All-Star first team (1989-90).

Season Team	League	REGULAR SEASON					PLAYOFFS				
		Gms.	G	A	Pts.	Pen.	Gms.	G	A	Pts.	Pen.
83-84—Michigan State	CCHA	46	10	26	36	30	—	—	—	—	—
84-85—Michigan State	CCHA	44	2	23	25	52	—	—	—	—	—
85-86—Michigan State	CCHA	45	9	29	38	18	—	—	—	—	—
86-87—Michigan State	CCHA	45	7	23	30	34	—	—	—	—	—
87-88—Rochester	AHL	63	9	29	38	108	6	0	1	1	15
—Buffalo	NHL	5	0	1	1	4	—	—	—	—	—
88-89—Rochester	AHL	66	7	22	29	45	—	—	—	—	—
89-90—Buffalo	NHL	4	0	0	0	6	—	—	—	—	—
—Rochester	AHL	70	16	43	59	43	17	3	10	13	12
90-91—Rochester	AHL	74	7	44	51	57	15	2	5	7	8
91-92—Rochester	AHL	75	6	32	38	60	16	5	6	11	18
92-93—San Diego	IHL	80	15	40	55	85	14	1	2	3	10
NHL totals		9	0	1	1	10					

M

MEARS, GLEN
D, FLAMES

PERSONAL: Born July 14, 1972, at Anchorage, Alaska. . . . 6-3/215. . . . Shoots right. . . . Full name: Glen Anthony Mears.
COLLEGE: Bowling Green State.
TRANSACTIONS/CAREER NOTES: Selected by Calgary Flames in third round (fifth Flames pick, 62nd overall) of NHL entry draft (June 16, 1990).

			REGULAR SEASON						PLAYOFFS			
Season Team	League	Gms.	G	A	Pts.	Pen.	Gms.	G	A	Pts.	Pen.
88-89—Rochester	USHL	39	2	7	9	56	—	—	—	—	—
89-90—Rochester	USHL	46	5	20	25	95	—	—	—	—	—
90-91—Bowling Green State	CCHA	40	0	7	7	54	—	—	—	—	—
91-92—Bowling Green State	CCHA	32	1	2	3	38	—	—	—	—	—
92-93—Bowling Green State	CCHA	39	0	7	7	22	—	—	—	—	—

MELANSON, DEAN
D, SABRES

PERSONAL: Born November 19, 1973, at Antigonish, N.S. . . . 6-0/213. . . . Shoots right. . . . Name pronounced muh-LAHN-suhn.
TRANSACTIONS/CAREER NOTES: Selected by Buffalo Sabres in fourth round (fourth Sabres pick, 80th overall) of NHL entry draft (June 20, 1992).

			REGULAR SEASON						PLAYOFFS			
Season Team	League	Gms.	G	A	Pts.	Pen.	Gms.	G	A	Pts.	Pen.
90-91—St. Hyacinthe	QMJHL	69	10	17	27	110	4	0	1	1	2
91-92—St. Hyacinthe	QMJHL	42	8	19	27	158	6	1	2	3	25
92-93—St. Hyacinthe	QMJHL	57	13	29	42	253	—	—	—	—	—
—Rochester	AHL	8	0	1	1	6	14	1	6	7	18

MELLANBY, SCOTT
RW, PANTHERS

PERSONAL: Born June 11, 1966, at Montreal. . . . 6-1/205. . . . Shoots right. . . . Full name: Scott Edgar Mellanby.
HIGH SCHOOL: Henry Carr (Rexdale, Ont.).
COLLEGE: Wisconsin.
TRANSACTIONS/CAREER NOTES: Selected by Philadelphia Flyers as underage junior in second round (first Flyers pick, 27th overall) of NHL entry draft (June 9, 1984). . . . Lacerated index finger on right hand (October 1987). . . . Severed nerve and damaged tendon in left forearm (August 1989); missed first 20 games of season. . . . Suffered viral infection (November 1989). . . . Traded by Flyers with LW Craig Berube and C Craig Fisher to Edmonton Oilers for RW Dave Brown, D Corey Foster and rights to RW Jari Kurri (May 30, 1991). . . . Injured shoulder (February 14, 1993); missed 15 games. . . . Selected by Florida Panthers in NHL expansion draft (June 24, 1993).

			REGULAR SEASON						PLAYOFFS			
Season Team	League	Gms.	G	A	Pts.	Pen.	Gms.	G	A	Pts.	Pen.
83-84—Henry Carr H.S.	MTHL	39	37	37	74	97	—	—	—	—	—
84-85—University of Wisconsin	WCHA	40	14	24	38	60	—	—	—	—	—
85-86—University of Wisconsin	WCHA	32	21	23	44	89	—	—	—	—	—
—Philadelphia	NHL	2	0	0	0	0	—	—	—	—	—
86-87—Philadelphia	NHL	71	11	21	32	94	24	5	5	10	46
87-88—Philadelphia	NHL	75	25	26	51	185	7	0	1	1	16
88-89—Philadelphia	NHL	76	21	29	50	183	19	4	5	9	28
89-90—Philadelphia	NHL	57	6	17	23	77	—	—	—	—	—
90-91—Philadelphia	NHL	74	20	21	41	155	—	—	—	—	—
91-92—Edmonton	NHL	80	23	27	50	197	16	2	1	3	29
92-93—Edmonton	NHL	69	15	17	32	147	—	—	—	—	—
NHL totals		**504**	**121**	**158**	**279**	**1038**	**66**	**11**	**12**	**23**	**119**

MESSIER, JOBY
D, RANGERS

PERSONAL: Born March 2, 1970, at Regina, Sask. . . . 6-0/193. . . . Shoots right. . . . Full name: Marcus Cyril Messier. . . . Name pronounced MEHZ-yay. . . . Brother of Mitch Messier, center/right winger in Dallas Stars system; and cousin of Mark Messier, center, New York Rangers.
COLLEGE: Michigan State.
TRANSACTIONS/CAREER NOTES: Broke right arm (December 1984). . . . Broke right arm (September 1987). . . . Selected by New York Rangers in sixth round (seventh Rangers seventh pick, 118th overall) of NHL entry draft (June 17, 1989).
HONORS: Named to NCAA All-America West first team (1991-92). . . . Named to CCHA All-Star first team (1991-92).

			REGULAR SEASON						PLAYOFFS			
Season Team	League	Gms.	G	A	Pts.	Pen.	Gms.	G	A	Pts.	Pen.
87-88—Notre Dame	SJHL	53	9	22	31	208	—	—	—	—	—
88-89—Michigan State	CCHA	46	2	10	12	70	—	—	—	—	—
89-90—Michigan State	CCHA	42	1	11	12	58	—	—	—	—	—
90-91—Michigan State	CCHA	39	5	11	16	71	—	—	—	—	—
91-92—Michigan State	CCHA	44	13	16	29	85	—	—	—	—	—
92-93—Binghamton	AHL	60	5	16	21	63	14	1	1	2	6
—New York Rangers	NHL	11	0	0	0	6	—	—	—	—	—
NHL totals		**11**	**0**	**0**	**0**	**6**					

MESSIER, MARK
C, RANGERS

PERSONAL: Born January 18, 1961, at Edmonton, Alta. . . . 6-1/202. . . . Shoots left. . . . Full name: Mark Douglas Messier. . . . Name pronounced MEHZ-yay. . . . Brother of Paul Messier, center, Colorado Rockies (1978-79); cousin of Mitch Messier, center/right winger in Dallas Stars system; cousin of Joby Messier, defenseman in New York Rangers system;

and brother-in-law of John Blum, defenseman for four NHL teams (1982-83 through 1989-90).

TRANSACTIONS/CAREER NOTES: Given five-game trial by Indianapolis Racers (November 1978).... Signed as free agent by Cincinnati Stingers (January 1979).... Selected by Edmonton Oilers in third round (second Oilers pick, 48th overall) of NHL entry draft (August 9, 1979).... Injured ankle (November 7, 1981).... Chipped bone in wrist (March 1983).... Suspended six games by NHL for hitting another player with his stick (January 18, 1984).... Sprained knee ligaments (November 1984).... Suspended 10 games by NHL for injuring another player (December 26, 1984).... Bruised left foot (December 3, 1985); missed 17 games.... Suspended and fined by Oilers after refusing to report to training camp (October 1987); missed three weeks of camp.... Suspended six games by NHL for injuring another player with his stick (October 23, 1988).... Twisted left knee (January 28, 1989).... Strained right knee (February 3, 1989).... Bruised left knee (February 12, 1989).... Sprained left knee ligaments (October 16, 1990); missed 10 games.... Reinjured left knee (December 12, 1990); missed three games.... Reinjured knee (December 22, 1990); missed nine games.... Broke left thumb (February 11, 1991); missed eight games.... Missed one game due to contract dispute (October 1991).... Traded by Oilers with future considerations to New York Rangers for C Bernie Nicholls, LW Louie DeBrusk, RW Steven Rice and future considerations (October 4, 1991); Oilers traded D Jeff Beukeboom to Rangers for D David Shaw to complete deal (November 12, 1991).... Sprained ligament in wrist (January 19, 1993); missed six games.... Strained rib cage muscle (February 27, 1993); missed two games.... Strained rib cage muscle (March 11, 1993); missed one game.... Suspended three off-days and fined $500 by NHL for stick-swinging incident (March 18, 1993).

HONORS: Named to THE SPORTING NEWS All-Star first team (1981-82, 1982-83, 1989-90 and 1991-92).... Named to NHL All-Star first team (1981-82, 1982-83, 1989-90 and 1991-92).... Played in NHL All-Star Game (1982 through 1984, 1986 and 1988 through 1992).... Won Conn Smythe Trophy (1983-84).... Named to NHL All-Star second team (1983-84).... Named to THE SPORTING NEWS All-Star second team (1986-87).... Named NHL Player of the Year by THE SPORTING NEWS (1989-90 and 1991-92).... Won Hart Memorial Trophy (1989-90 and 1991-92).... Won Lester B. Pearson Award (1989-90 and 1991-92).

RECORDS: Holds NHL career playoff record for most shorthanded goals—11.... Holds NHL All-Star single-game record for most assists in one period—3 (1983).

MISCELLANEOUS: Member of Stanley Cup championship teams (1984, 1985, 1987, 1988 and 1990).

Season Team	League	REGULAR SEASON					PLAYOFFS				
		Gms.	G	A	Pts.	Pen.	Gms.	G	A	Pts.	Pen.
76-77—Spruce Grove	AJHL	57	27	39	66	91	—	—	—	—	—
77-78—St. Albert	AJHL			Statistics unavailable.			—	—	—	—	—
—Portland	WHL	—	—	—	—	—	7	4	1	5	2
78-79—Indianapolis	WHA	5	0	0	0	0	—	—	—	—	—
—Cincinnati	WHA	47	1	10	11	58	—	—	—	—	—
79-80—Houston	CHL	4	0	3	3	4	—	—	—	—	—
—Edmonton	NHL	75	12	21	33	120	3	1	2	3	2
80-81—Edmonton	NHL	72	23	40	63	102	9	2	5	7	13
81-82—Edmonton	NHL	78	50	38	88	119	5	1	2	3	8
82-83—Edmonton	NHL	77	48	58	106	72	15	15	6	21	14
83-84—Edmonton	NHL	73	37	64	101	165	19	8	18	26	19
84-85—Edmonton	NHL	55	23	31	54	57	18	12	13	25	12
85-86—Edmonton	NHL	63	35	49	84	68	10	4	6	10	18
86-87—Edmonton	NHL	77	37	70	107	73	21	12	16	28	16
87-88—Edmonton	NHL	77	37	74	111	103	19	11	23	34	29
88-89—Edmonton	NHL	72	33	61	94	130	7	1	11	12	8
89-90—Edmonton	NHL	79	45	84	129	79	22	9	*22	†31	20
90-91—Edmonton	NHL	53	12	52	64	34	18	4	11	15	16
91-92—New York Rangers	NHL	79	35	72	107	76	11	7	7	14	6
92-93—New York Rangers	NHL	75	25	66	91	72	—	—	—	—	—
WHA totals		52	1	10	11	58					
NHL totals		1005	452	780	1232	1270	177	87	142	229	181

MICHAYLUK, DAVE
LW, PENGUINS

PERSONAL: Born May 18, 1962, at Wakaw, Sask.... 5-10/185.... Shoots left.
TRANSACTIONS/CAREER NOTES: Selected by Philadelphia Flyers as underage junior in fourth round (fifth Flyers pick, 65th overall) of NHL entry draft (June 10, 1981).... Lacerated right arm (May 1989).... Signed as free agent by Pittsburgh Penguins (May 24, 1989).

HONORS: Won Stewart (Butch) Paul Memorial Trophy (1980-81).... Named to WHL All-Star second team (1980-81 and 1981-82).... Named to IHL All-Star second team (1984-85, 1991-92 and 1992-93).... Named to IHL All-Star first team (1986-87 through 1989-90).... Won James Gatschene Memorial Trophy (1988-89).... Won Leo P. Lamoureux Memorial Trophy (1988-89).... Named Turner Cup Playoff Most Valuable Player (1988-89).

MISCELLANEOUS: Member of Stanley Cup championship team (1992).

Season Team	League	REGULAR SEASON					PLAYOFFS				
		Gms.	G	A	Pts.	Pen.	Gms.	G	A	Pts.	Pen.
79-80—Prince Albert	AJHL	60	46	67	113	49	—	—	—	—	—
80-81—Regina	WHL	72	62	71	133	39	11	5	12	17	8
81-82—Regina	WHL	72	62	111	173	128	12	16	24	*40	23
—Philadelphia	NHL	1	0	0	0	0	—	—	—	—	—
82-83—Philadelphia	NHL	13	2	6	8	8	—	—	—	—	—
—Maine	AHL	69	32	40	72	16	8	0	2	2	0
83-84—Springfield	AHL	79	18	44	62	37	4	0	0	0	2
84-85—Hershey	AHL	3	0	2	2	2	—	—	—	—	—
—Kalamazoo	IHL	82	*66	33	99	49	11	7	7	14	0
85-86—Nova Scotia	AHL	3	0	1	1	0	—	—	—	—	—
—Muskegon	IHL	77	52	52	104	73	14	6	9	15	12
86-87—Muskegon	IHL	82	47	53	100	69	15	2	14	16	8

Season	Team	League	REGULAR SEASON					PLAYOFFS				
			Gms.	G	A	Pts.	Pen.	Gms.	G	A	Pts.	Pen.
87-88—Muskegon	IHL	81	*56	81	137	46	6	2	0	2	18	
88-89—Muskegon	IHL	80	50	72	*122	84	13	†9	12	†21	24	
89-90—Muskegon	IHL	79	*51	51	102	80	15	8	†14	*22	10	
90-91—Muskegon	IHL	83	40	62	102	116	5	2	2	4	4	
91-92—Muskegon	IHL	82	39	63	102	154	13	9	8	17	4	
—Pittsburgh	NHL	—	—	—	—	—	7	1	1	2	0	
92-93—Cleveland	IHL	82	47	65	112	104	4	1	2	3	4	
NHL totals		14	2	6	8	8	7	1	1	2	0	

MIEHM, KEVIN
C, BLUES

PERSONAL: Born September 10, 1969, at Kitchener, Ont. . . . 6-2/195. . . . Shoots left. . . . Name pronounced MEE-yuhm.

TRANSACTIONS/CAREER NOTES: Selected by St. Louis Blues as underage junior in third round (second Blues pick, 54th overall) of NHL entry draft (June 13, 1987).

HONORS: Won William Hanley Trophy (1988-89).

Season	Team	League	REGULAR SEASON					PLAYOFFS				
			Gms.	G	A	Pts.	Pen.	Gms.	G	A	Pts.	Pen.
85-86—Kitchener Jr. B	OHA	1	0	0	0	0	—	—	—	—	—	
86-87—Oshawa	OHL	61	12	27	39	19	26	1	8	9	12	
87-88—Oshawa	OHL	52	16	36	52	30	7	2	5	7	0	
88-89—Oshawa	OHL	63	43	79	122	19	6	6	6	12	0	
—Peoria	IHL	3	1	1	2	0	4	0	2	2	0	
89-90—Peoria	IHL	76	23	38	61	20	3	0	0	0	4	
90-91—Peoria	IHL	73	25	39	64	14	16	5	7	12	2	
91-92—Peoria	IHL	66	21	53	74	22	10	3	4	7	2	
92-93—Peoria	IHL	30	12	33	45	13	4	0	1	1	2	
—St. Louis	NHL	8	1	3	4	4	2	0	1	1	0	
NHL totals		8	1	3	4	4	2	0	1	1	0	

MILLEN, COREY
C, DEVILS

PERSONAL: Born April 29, 1964, at Cloquet, Minn. . . . 5-7/168. . . . Shoots right.

HIGH SCHOOL: Cloquet (Minn.).

COLLEGE: Minnesota.

TRANSACTIONS/CAREER NOTES: Selected by New York Rangers as underage player in third round (third Rangers pick, 57th overall) of NHL entry draft (June 9, 1982). . . . Injured knee and underwent surgery (November 1982). . . . Injured shoulder (October 1984). . . . Tested positive for a non-anabolic steroid in a random test at World Cup Tournament and was banned from play (April 1989). . . . Sprained left knee ligaments and underwent surgery (September 18, 1989); missed four months. . . . Underwent surgery to left knee (August 1990); missed four months. . . . Traded by Rangers to Los Angeles Kings for C Randy Gilhen (December 23, 1991). . . . Suffered shoulder contusion (February 29, 1992); missed one game. . . . Strained back (October 13, 1992); missed four games. . . . Strained groin (December 22, 1992); missed 38 games . . . Traded by Kings to New Jersey Devils for fifth-round pick (G Jason Saal) in 1993 draft (June 26, 1993).

HONORS: Named to WCHA All-Star second team (1984-85 through 1986-87). . . . Named to NCAA All-America West second team (1985-86). . . . Named to NCAA All-Tournament team (1986-87).

Season	Team	League	REGULAR SEASON					PLAYOFFS				
			Gms.	G	A	Pts.	Pen.	Gms.	G	A	Pts.	Pen.
81-82—Cloquet H.S.	Minn. H.S.	18	46	35	81	. . .	—	—	—	—	—	
82-83—University of Minnesota	WCHA	21	14	15	29	18	—	—	—	—	—	
83-84—U.S. national team	Int'l	45	15	11	26	10	—	—	—	—	—	
—U.S. Olympic Team	Int'l	6	0	0	0	2	—	—	—	—	—	
84-85—University of Minnesota	WCHA	38	28	36	64	60	—	—	—	—	—	
85-86—University of Minnesota	WCHA	48	41	42	83	64	—	—	—	—	—	
86-87—University of Minnesota	WCHA	42	36	29	65	62	—	—	—	—	—	
87-88—U.S. Olympic Team	Int'l	51	46	45	91	. . .	—	—	—	—	—	
88-89—Ambri Piotta	Switzerland	36	32	22	54	18	6	4	3	7	0	
89-90—New York Rangers	NHL	4	0	0	0	2	—	—	—	—	—	
—Flint	IHL	11	4	5	9	2	—	—	—	—	—	
90-91—Binghamton	AHL	40	19	37	56	68	6	0	7	7	8	
—New York Rangers	NHL	4	3	1	4	0	6	1	2	3	0	
91-92—New York Rangers	NHL	11	1	4	5	10	—	—	—	—	—	
—Binghamton	AHL	15	8	7	15	44	—	—	—	—	—	
—Los Angeles	NHL	46	20	21	41	44	6	0	1	1	6	
92-93—Los Angeles	NHL	42	23	16	39	42	23	2	4	6	12	
NHL totals		107	47	42	89	98	35	3	7	10	18	

MILLER, AARON
D, NORDIQUES

PERSONAL: Born August 11, 1971, at Buffalo, N.Y. . . . 6-3/197. . . . Shoots right. . . . Full name: Aaron Michael Miller.

COLLEGE: Vermont.

TRANSACTIONS/CAREER NOTES: Selected by New York Rangers in fifth round (sixth Rangers pick, 88th overall) of NHL entry draft (June 17, 1989). . . . Traded by Rangers with fifth-round pick in 1991 draft (LW Bill Lindsay) to Quebec Nordiques for D Joe Cirella (January 17, 1991).

HONORS: Named to ECAC All-Rookie team (1989-90). . . . Named to NCAA All-America East second team (1992-93). . . . Named to ECAC All-Star first team (1992-93).

M

			REGULAR SEASON					PLAYOFFS				
Season	Team	League	Gms.	G	A	Pts.	Pen.	Gms.	G	A	Pts.	Pen.
87-88—Niagara Scenic		NAJHL	30	4	9	13	2	—	—	—	—	—
88-89—Niagara Scenic		NAJHL	59	24	38	62	60	—	—	—	—	—
89-90—University of Vermont		ECAC	31	1	15	16	24	—	—	—	—	—
90-91—University of Vermont		ECAC	30	3	7	10	22	—	—	—	—	—
91-92—University of Vermont		ECAC	31	3	16	19	36	—	—	—	—	—
92-93—University of Vermont		ECAC	30	4	13	17	16	—	—	—	—	—

MILLER, BRAD
D, MAPLE LEAFS

PERSONAL: Born July 23, 1969, at Edmonton, Alta.... 6-4/226.... Shoots left.
TRANSACTIONS/CAREER NOTES: Selected by Buffalo Sabres as underage junior in second round (second Sabres pick, 22nd overall) of NHL entry draft (June 13, 1987).... Suspended three games by AHL for abusing an official (February 23, 1990).... Suspended nine games by AHL for abuse of officials and continuing to fight (April 11, 1990).... Selected by Ottawa Senators in NHL expansion draft (June 18, 1992).... Traded by Senators to Toronto Maple Leafs for ninth-round pick in 1993 draft.

			REGULAR SEASON					PLAYOFFS				
Season	Team	League	Gms.	G	A	Pts.	Pen.	Gms.	G	A	Pts.	Pen.
85-86—Regina		WHL	71	2	14	16	99	10	1	1	2	4
86-87—Regina		WHL	67	10	38	48	154	3	0	0	0	6
87-88—Regina		WHL	61	9	34	43	148	4	1	1	2	12
—Rochester		AHL	3	0	0	0	4	2	0	0	0	2
88-89—Buffalo		NHL	7	0	0	0	6	—	—	—	—	—
—Rochester		AHL	3	0	0	0	4	—	—	—	—	—
—Regina		WHL	34	8	18	26	95	—	—	—	—	—
89-90—Buffalo		NHL	1	0	0	0	0	—	—	—	—	—
—Rochester		AHL	60	2	10	12	273	8	1	0	1	52
90-91—Buffalo		NHL	13	0	0	0	67	—	—	—	—	—
—Rochester		AHL	49	0	9	9	248	12	0	4	4	67
91-92—Buffalo		NHL	42	1	4	5	192	—	—	—	—	—
—Rochester		AHL	27	0	4	4	113	11	0	0	0	61
92-93—Ottawa		NHL	11	0	0	0	42	—	—	—	—	—
—New Haven		AHL	41	1	9	10	138	—	—	—	—	—
—St. John's		AHL	20	0	3	3	61	8	0	2	2	10
NHL totals			**74**	**1**	**4**	**5**	**307**					

MILLER, JASON
C, DEVILS

PERSONAL: Born March 1, 1971, at Edmonton, Alta.... 6-1/190.... Shoots left.
TRANSACTIONS/CAREER NOTES: Separated shoulder (May 1986).... Selected by New Jersey Devils in first round (second Devils pick, 18th overall) of NHL entry draft (June 17, 1989). ... Suffered sore back (January 23, 1993); missed two games.
HONORS: Named to WHL (East) All-Star second team (1990-91).

			REGULAR SEASON					PLAYOFFS				
Season	Team	League	Gms.	G	A	Pts.	Pen.	Gms.	G	A	Pts.	Pen.
87-88—Medicine Hat		WHL	71	11	18	29	28	15	0	1	1	2
88-89—Medicine Hat		WHL	72	51	55	106	44	3	1	2	3	2
89-90—Medicine Hat		WHL	66	43	56	99	40	3	3	2	5	0
90-91—New Jersey		NHL	1	0	0	0	0	—	—	—	—	—
—Medicine Hat		WHL	66	60	76	136	31	12	9	10	19	8
91-92—Utica		AHL	71	23	32	55	31	4	1	3	4	0
—New Jersey		NHL	3	0	0	0	0	—	—	—	—	—
92-93—Utica		AHL	72	28	42	70	43	5	4	4	8	2
—New Jersey		NHL	2	0	0	0	0	—	—	—	—	—
NHL totals			**6**	**0**	**0**	**0**	**0**					

MILLER, KELLY
LW, CAPITALS

PERSONAL: Born March 3, 1963, at Lansing, Mich. ... 5-11/195. ... Shoots left. ... Full name: Kelly David Miller.... Brother of Kevin Miller, right winger, St. Louis Blues; and brother of Kip Miller, center in Dallas Stars system.
COLLEGE: Michigan State.
TRANSACTIONS/CAREER NOTES: Selected by New York Rangers in ninth round (ninth Rangers pick, 183rd overall) of NHL entry draft (June 9, 1982).... Injured ankle (September 1985).... Sprained knee (January 27, 1986); missed five games.... Traded by Rangers with C Mike Ridley and RW Bobby Crawford to Washington Capitals for C Bobby Carpenter and second-round pick in 1989 draft (RW Jason Prosofsky) (January 1, 1987).... Pulled groin (November 1988).... Sprained knee (September 22, 1990).
HONORS: Named to NCAA All-America West first team (1984-85).... Named to CCHA All-Star first team (1984-85).

			REGULAR SEASON					PLAYOFFS				
Season	Team	League	Gms.	G	A	Pts.	Pen.	Gms.	G	A	Pts.	Pen.
81-82—Michigan State		CCHA	40	11	19	30	21	—	—	—	—	—
82-83—Michigan State		CCHA	36	16	19	35	12	—	—	—	—	—
83-84—Michigan State		CCHA	46	28	21	49	12	—	—	—	—	—
84-85—Michigan State		CCHA	43	27	23	50	21	—	—	—	—	—
—New York Rangers		NHL	5	0	2	2	2	3	0	0	0	2
85-86—New York Rangers		NHL	74	13	20	33	52	16	3	4	7	4
86-87—New York Rangers		NHL	38	6	14	20	22	—	—	—	—	—
—Washington		NHL	39	10	12	22	26	7	2	2	4	0

			REGULAR SEASON					PLAYOFFS			
Season Team	League	Gms.	G	A	Pts.	Pen.	Gms.	G	A	Pts.	Pen.
87-88—Washington	NHL	80	9	23	32	35	14	4	4	8	10
88-89—Washington	NHL	78	19	21	40	45	6	1	0	1	2
89-90—Washington	NHL	80	18	22	40	49	15	3	5	8	23
90-91—Washington	NHL	80	24	26	50	29	11	4	2	6	6
91-92—Washington	NHL	78	14	38	52	49	7	1	2	3	4
92-93—Washington	NHL	84	18	27	45	32	6	0	3	3	2
NHL totals		636	131	205	336	341	85	18	22	40	53

MILLER, KEVIN
RW, BLUES

PERSONAL: Born August 9, 1965, at Lansing, Mich. . . . 5-9/170. . . . Shoots right. . . . Full name: Kevin Bradley Miller. . . . Brother of Kelly Miller, left winger, Washington Capitals; and brother of Kip Miller, center in Dallas Stars system.
HIGH SCHOOL: Eastern (Lansing, Mich.).

COLLEGE: Michigan State.
TRANSACTIONS/CAREER NOTES: Selected by New York Rangers in 10th round (10th Rangers pick, 202nd overall) of NHL entry draft (June 9, 1984). . . . Pulled groin (September 1990). . . . Sprained shoulder (December 1990). . . . Traded by Rangers with D Dennis Vial and RW Jim Cummings to Detroit Red Wings for RW Joe Kocur and D Per Djoos (March 5, 1991). . . . Traded by Red Wings to Washington Capitals for RW Dino Ciccarelli (June 20, 1992). . . . Traded by Capitals to St. Louis Blues for D Paul Cavallini (November 1, 1992).

			REGULAR SEASON					PLAYOFFS			
Season Team	League	Gms.	G	A	Pts.	Pen.	Gms.	G	A	Pts.	Pen.
84-85—Michigan State	CCHA	44	11	29	40	84	—	—	—	—	—
85-86—Michigan State	CCHA	45	19	52	71	112	—	—	—	—	—
86-87—Michigan State	CCHA	42	25	56	81	63	—	—	—	—	—
87-88—Michigan State	CCHA	9	6	3	9	18	—	—	—	—	—
—U.S. Olympic Team	Int'l	50	32	34	66	...	—	—	—	—	—
88-89—New York Rangers	NHL	24	3	5	8	2	—	—	—	—	—
—Denver	IHL	55	29	47	76	19	4	2	1	3	2
89-90—New York Rangers	NHL	16	0	5	5	2	1	0	0	0	0
—Flint	IHL	48	19	23	42	41	—	—	—	—	—
90-91—New York Rangers	NHL	63	17	27	44	63	—	—	—	—	—
—Detroit	NHL	11	5	2	7	4	7	3	2	5	20
91-92—Detroit	NHL	80	20	26	46	53	9	0	2	2	4
92-93—Washington	NHL	10	0	3	3	35	—	—	—	—	—
—St. Louis	NHL	72	24	22	46	65	10	0	3	3	11
NHL totals		276	69	90	159	224	27	3	7	10	35

MILLER, KIP
C, STARS

PERSONAL: Born June 11, 1969, at Lansing, Mich. . . . 5-11/190. . . . Shoots left. . . . Full name: Kip Charles Miller. . . . Brother of Kelly Miller, left winger, Washington Capitals; and brother of Kevin Miller, right winger, St. Louis Blues.
COLLEGE: Michigan State.

TRANSACTIONS/CAREER NOTES: Selected by Quebec Nordiques in fourth round (fourth Nordiques pick, 72nd overall) of NHL entry draft (June 13, 1987). . . . Suffered hand and forearm injuries in off-ice accident (November 1987). . . . Traded by Nordiques to Minnesota North Stars for LW Steve Maltais (March 8, 1992). . . . North Stars franchise moved from Minnesota to Dallas and renamed Stars for 1993-94 season.
HONORS: Named to NCAA All-America West first team (1988-89 and 1989-90). . . . Named to CCHA All-Star first team (1988-89 and 1989-90). . . . Won Hobey Baker Memorial Trophy (1989-90). . . . Named CCHA Player of the Year (1989-90).

			REGULAR SEASON					PLAYOFFS			
Season Team	League	Gms.	G	A	Pts.	Pen.	Gms.	G	A	Pts.	Pen.
86-87—Michigan State	CCHA	45	22	19	41	96	—	—	—	—	—
87-88—Michigan State	CCHA	39	16	25	41	51	—	—	—	—	—
88-89—Michigan State	CCHA	47	32	45	77	94	—	—	—	—	—
89-90—Michigan State	CCHA	45	*48	53	*101	60	—	—	—	—	—
90-91—Quebec	NHL	15	4	3	7	7	—	—	—	—	—
—Halifax	AHL	· 66	36	33	69	40	—	—	—	—	—
91-92—Quebec	NHL	36	5	10	15	12	—	—	—	—	—
—Halifax	AHL	24	9	17	26	8	—	—	—	—	—
—Minnesota	NHL	3	1	2	3	2	—	—	—	—	—
—Kalamazoo	IHL	6	1	8	9	4	12	3	9	12	12
92-93—Kalamazoo	IHL	61	17	39	56	59	—	—	—	—	—
NHL totals		54	10	15	25	21					

MIRONOV, BORIS
D, JETS

PERSONAL: Born March 21, 1972, at Moscow, U.S.S.R. . . . 6-3/196. . . . Shoots right. . . . Name pronounced MIH-rih-nahf. . . . Brother of Dimitri Mironov, defenseman, Toronto Maple Leafs.
TRANSACTIONS/CAREER NOTES: Selected by Winnipeg Jets in second round (second Jets pick, 27th overall) of NHL entry draft (June 20, 1992).

			REGULAR SEASON					PLAYOFFS			
Season Team	League	Gms.	G	A	Pts.	Pen.	Gms.	G	A	Pts.	Pen.
88-89—CSKA Moscow	USSR	1	0	0	0	0	—	—	—	—	—
89-90—CSKA Moscow	USSR	7	0	0	0	0	—	—	—	—	—
90-91—CSKA Moscow	USSR	36	1	5	6	16	—	—	—	—	—

M

Season	Team	League	Gms.	G	A	Pts.	Pen.	Gms.	G	A	Pts.	Pen.
			REGULAR SEASON					PLAYOFFS				
91-92—CSKA Moscow		CIS	36	2	1	3	22	—	—	—	—	—
92-93—CSKA Moscow		CIS	19	0	5	5	20	—	—	—	—	—

MIRONOV, DMITRI
D, MAPLE LEAFS

PERSONAL: Born December 25, 1965, at Moscow, U.S.S.R. . . . 6-2/191. . . . Shoots right. . . . Name pronounced MIH-rih-nahf. . . . Brother of Boris Mironov, defenseman in Winnipeg Jets system.
TRANSACTIONS/CAREER NOTES: Selected by Toronto Maple Leafs in eighth round (seventh Maple Leafs pick, 160th overall) of NHL entry draft (June 22, 1991). . . . Broke nose (March 23, 1992). . . . Suffered infected tooth (March 18, 1993); missed 10 games.
MISCELLANEOUS: Member of gold-medal-winning Unified Olympic team (1992).

Season	Team	League	Gms.	G	A	Pts.	Pen.	Gms.	G	A	Pts.	Pen.
			REGULAR SEASON					PLAYOFFS				
90-91—Soviet Wings		USSR	44	16	12	28	22	—	—	—	—	—
91-92—Soviet Wings		USSR	30	11	16	27	44	—	—	—	—	—
—Unified Olympic Team		Int'l	8	3	1	4	4	—	—	—	—	—
—Toronto		NHL	7	1	0	1	0	—	—	—	—	—
92-93—Toronto		NHL	59	7	24	31	40	14	1	2	3	2
NHL totals			66	8	24	32	40	14	1	2	3	2

MITCHELL, JEFFREY
C/RW, KINGS

PERSONAL: Born May 16, 1975, at Wayne, Mich. . . . 6-1/175. . . . Shoots right.
TRANSACTIONS/CAREER NOTES: Selected by Los Angeles Kings in third round (second Kings pick, 68th overall) of NHL entry draft (June 26, 1993).

Season	Team	League	Gms.	G	A	Pts.	Pen.	Gms.	G	A	Pts.	Pen.
			REGULAR SEASON					PLAYOFFS				
92-93—Detroit		OHL	62	10	15	25	100	15	3	3	6	16

MITCHELL, ROY
D, STARS

PERSONAL: Born March 14, 1969, at Edmonton, Alta. . . . 6-1/200. . . . Shoots right.
TRANSACTIONS/CAREER NOTES: Selected by Montreal Canadiens in ninth round (ninth Canadiens pick, 188th overall) of 1989 NHL entry draft (June 17, 1989). . . . Signed as free agent by Minnesota North Stars (July 25, 1991). . . . North Stars franchise moved from Minnesota to Dallas and renamed Stars for 1993-94 season.

Season	Team	League	Gms.	G	A	Pts.	Pen.	Gms.	G	A	Pts.	Pen.
			REGULAR SEASON					PLAYOFFS				
85-86—St. Albert		AJHL	39	2	18	20	32	—	—	—	—	—
86-87—Portland		WHL	68	7	32	39	103	20	0	3	3	23
87-88—Portland		WHL	72	5	42	47	219	—	—	—	—	—
88-89—Portland		WHL	72	9	34	43	177	19	1	8	9	38
89-90—Sherbrooke		AHL	77	5	12	17	98	12	0	2	2	31
90-91—Fredericton		AHL	71	2	15	17	137	9	0	1	1	11
91-92—Kalamazoo		IHL	69	3	26	29	102	11	1	4	5	18
92-93—Kalamazoo		IHL	79	7	25	32	119	—	—	—	—	—
—Minnesota		NHL	3	0	0	0	0	—	—	—	—	—
NHL totals			3	0	0	0	0					

MODANO, MIKE
RW/C, STARS

PERSONAL: Born June 7, 1970, at Livonia, Mich. . . . 6-3/190. . . . Shoots left. . . . Name pronounced muh-DAH-noh.
TRANSACTIONS/CAREER NOTES: Selected by Minnesota North Stars in first round (first North Stars pick, first overall) of NHL entry draft (June 11, 1988). . . . Fractured scaphoid bone in left wrist (January 24, 1989). . . . Broke nose (March 4, 1990). . . . Pulled groin (November 30, 1992); missed two games. . . . North Stars franchise moved from Minnesota to Dallas and renamed Stars for 1993-94 season.
HONORS: Named to WHL (East) All-Star first team (1988-89). . . . Named to NHL All-Rookie team (1989-90). . . . Played in NHL All-Star Game (1993).

Season	Team	League	Gms.	G	A	Pts.	Pen.	Gms.	G	A	Pts.	Pen.
			REGULAR SEASON					PLAYOFFS				
86-87—Prince Albert		WHL	70	32	30	62	96	8	1	4	5	4
87-88—Prince Albert		WHL	65	47	80	127	80	9	7	11	18	18
88-89—Prince Albert		WHL	41	39	66	105	74	—	—	—	—	—
—Minnesota		NHL	—	—	—	—	—	2	0	0	0	0
89-90—Minnesota		NHL	80	29	46	75	63	7	1	1	2	12
90-91—Minnesota		NHL	79	28	36	64	61	23	8	12	20	16
91-92—Minnesota		NHL	76	33	44	77	46	7	3	2	5	4
92-93—Minnesota		NHL	82	33	60	93	83	—	—	—	—	—
NHL totals			317	123	186	309	253	39	12	15	27	32

MOGER, SANDY
RW, CANUCKS

PERSONAL: Born March 21, 1969, at 100 Mile House, B.C. . . . 6-2/190. . . . Shoots right. . . . Full name: Alexander Sandy Moger.
COLLEGE: Lake Superior State (Mich.).
TRANSACTIONS/CAREER NOTES: Broke wrist (September 1988). . . . Selected by Vancouver Canucks in ninth round (seventh Canucks pick, 176th overall) of NHL entry draft (June 17, 1989).
HONORS: Named to CCHA All-Star second team (1991-92).

Season Team	League	REGULAR SEASON					PLAYOFFS				
		Gms.	G	A	Pts.	Pen.	Gms.	G	A	Pts.	Pen.
86-87—Vernon	BCJHL	13	5	4	9	10	—	—	—	—	—
87-88—Yorkton	SJHL	60	39	41	80	144	—	—	—	—	—
88-89—Lake Superior State	CCHA	31	4	6	10	28	—	—	—	—	—
89-90—Lake Superior State	CCHA	46	17	15	32	76	—	—	—	—	—
90-91—Lake Superior State	CCHA	45	27	21	48	*172	—	—	—	—	—
91-92—Lake Superior State	CCHA	42	26	25	51	111	—	—	—	—	—
92-93—Hamilton	AHL	78	23	26	49	57	—	—	—	—	—

MOGILNY, ALEXANDER
RW, SABRES

PERSONAL: Born February 18, 1969, at Khabarovsk, U.S.S.R. . . . . 5-11/187. . . . Shoots left. . . . Name pronounced moh-GIHL-nee.

TRANSACTIONS/CAREER NOTES: Selected by Buffalo Sabres in fifth round (fourth Sabres pick, 89th overall) of NHL entry draft (June 11, 1988). . . . Suffered from the flu (November 26, 1989). . . . Missed games due to fear of flying (January 22, 1990); spent remainder of season traveling on ground. . . . Separated shoulder (February 8, 1991); missed six games. . . . Suffered from the flu (November 1991); missed two games. . . . Suffered from the flu (December 18, 1991); missed one game. . . . Bruised shoulder (October 10, 1992); missed six games. . . . Broke fibula and tore ankle ligaments (May 6, 1993); missed remainder of playoffs.

HONORS: Played in NHL All-Star Game (1992 and 1993). . . . Named to THE SPORTING NEWS All-Star second team (1992-93). . . . Named to NHL All-Star second team (1992-93).

MISCELLANEOUS: Member of gold-medal-winning U.S.S.R. Olympic team (1988).

Season Team	League	REGULAR SEASON					PLAYOFFS				
		Gms.	G	A	Pts.	Pen.	Gms.	G	A	Pts.	Pen.
86-87—CSKA Moscow	USSR	28	15	1	16	4	—	—	—	—	—
87-88—CSKA Moscow	USSR	39	12	8	20	20	—	—	—	—	—
88-89—CSKA Moscow	USSR	31	11	11	22	24	—	—	—	—	—
89-90—Buffalo	NHL	65	15	28	43	16	4	0	1	1	2
90-91—Buffalo	NHL	62	30	34	64	16	6	0	6	6	2
91-92—Buffalo	NHL	67	39	45	84	73	2	0	2	2	0
92-93—Buffalo	NHL	77	†76	51	127	40	7	7	3	10	6
NHL totals		271	160	158	318	145	19	7	12	19	10

MOLLER, RANDY
D, SABRES

PERSONAL: Born August 23, 1963, at Red Deer, Alta. . . . 6-2/207. . . . Shoots right. . . . Name pronounced MOH-luhr. . . . Brother of Mike Moller, right winger, Buffalo Sabres and Edmonton Oilers (1980-81 through 1986-87).

TRANSACTIONS/CAREER NOTES: Tore knee ligaments and underwent surgery (December 1980). . . . Selected by Quebec Nordiques in first round (first Nordiques pick, 11th overall) of NHL entry draft (June 10, 1981). . . . Broke hand (October 28, 1986). . . . Suffered lingering neck problem (November 1987). . . . Injured knee (January 1988). . . . Suffered back spasms (March 1988). . . . Separated shoulder (October 29, 1988). . . . Broke toe (September 1989). . . . Traded by Nordiques to New York Rangers for D Michel Petit (October 5, 1989). . . . Dislocated right shoulder (December 13, 1989). . . . Suffered back spasms (March 21, 1990); missed six games. . . . Dislocated left shoulder (November 7, 1990); missed 15 games. . . . Separated shoulder (January 22, 1992); missed four games. . . . Traded by Rangers to Buffalo Sabres for D Jay Wells (March 9, 1992). . . . Suffered knee ligament damage (November 11, 1992); missed 25 games. . . . Strained back muscle (January 17, 1993); missed 21 games.

HONORS: Named to WHL All-Star second team (1981-82).

Season Team	League	REGULAR SEASON					PLAYOFFS				
		Gms.	G	A	Pts.	Pen.	Gms.	G	A	Pts.	Pen.
79-80—Red Deer	AJHL	56	3	34	37	253	—	—	—	—	—
80-81—Lethbridge	WHL	46	4	21	25	176	9	0	4	4	24
81-82—Lethbridge	WHL	60	20	55	75	249	12	4	6	10	65
—Quebec	NHL	—	—	—	—	—	1	0	0	0	2
82-83—Quebec	NHL	75	2	12	14	145	4	1	0	1	4
83-84—Quebec	NHL	74	4	14	18	147	9	1	0	1	45
84-85—Quebec	NHL	79	7	22	29	120	18	2	2	4	40
85-86—Quebec	NHL	69	5	18	23	141	3	0	0	0	26
86-87—Quebec	NHL	71	5	9	14	144	13	1	4	5	23
87-88—Quebec	NHL	66	3	22	25	169	—	—	—	—	—
88-89—Quebec	NHL	74	7	22	29	136	—	—	—	—	—
89-90—New York Rangers	NHL	60	1	12	13	139	10	1	6	7	32
90-91—New York Rangers	NHL	61	4	19	23	161	6	0	2	2	11
91-92—New York Rangers	NHL	43	2	7	9	78	—	—	—	—	—
—Binghamton	AHL	3	0	1	1	0	—	—	—	—	—
—Buffalo	NHL	13	1	2	3	59	7	0	0	0	8
92-93—Buffalo	NHL	35	2	7	9	83	—	—	—	—	—
—Rochester	AHL	3	1	0	1	10	—	—	—	—	—
NHL totals		720	43	166	209	1522	71	6	14	20	191

MOMESSO, SERGIO
LW, CANUCKS

PERSONAL: Born September 4, 1965, at Montreal. . . . 6-3/215. . . . Shoots left. . . . Name pronounced moh-MEH-soh.

TRANSACTIONS/CAREER NOTES: Selected by Montreal Canadiens as underage junior in second round (third Canadiens pick, 27th overall) of NHL entry draft (June 8, 1983). . . . Tore cruciate ligament in left knee and underwent surgery (December 5, 1985); missed remainder of season. . . . Tore ligaments, injured cartilage and fractured left knee (December 5, 1986). . . . Lacerated leg (February 1988). . . . Traded by Cana-

M

diens with G Vincent Riendeau to St. Louis Blues for LW Jocelyn Lemieux, G Darrell May and second-round pick in 1989 draft (D Patrice Brisebois) (August 9, 1988).... Fractured right ankle (November 12, 1988).... Traded by Blues with LW Geoff Courtnall, D Robert Dirk, C Cliff Ronning and fifth-round pick in 1992 draft (RW Brian Loney) to Vancouver Canucks for C Dan Quinn and D Garth Butcher (March 5, 1991).... Separated shoulder (December 3, 1991); missed 22 games.
HONORS: Named to QMJHL All-Star first team (1984-85).

			REGULAR SEASON					PLAYOFFS			
Season Team	League	Gms.	G	A	Pts.	Pen.	Gms.	G	A	Pts.	Pen.
82-83—Shawinigan	QMJHL	70	27	42	69	93	10	5	4	9	55
83-84—Nova Scotia	AHL	—	—	—	—	—	8	0	2	2	4
—Shawinigan	QMJHL	68	42	88	130	235	6	4	4	8	13
—Montreal	NHL	1	0	0	0	0	—	—	—	—	—
84-85—Shawinigan	QMJHL	64	56	90	146	216	8	7	8	15	17
85-86—Montreal	NHL	24	8	7	15	46	—	—	—	—	—
86-87—Montreal	NHL	59	14	17	31	96	11	1	3	4	31
—Sherbrooke	AHL	6	1	6	7	10	—	—	—	—	—
87-88—Montreal	NHL	53	7	14	21	101	6	0	2	2	16
88-89—St. Louis	NHL	53	9	17	26	139	10	2	5	7	24
89-90—St. Louis	NHL	79	24	32	56	199	12	3	2	5	63
90-91—St. Louis	NHL	59	10	18	28	131	—	—	—	—	—
—Vancouver	NHL	11	6	2	8	43	6	0	3	3	25
91-92—Vancouver	NHL	58	20	23	43	198	13	0	5	5	30
92-93—Vancouver	NHL	84	18	20	38	200	12	3	0	3	30
NHL totals		481	116	150	266	1153	70	9	20	29	219

MONGEAU, MICHEL
C, NORDIQUES

PERSONAL: Born February 9, 1965, at Nun's Island, Que.... 5-9/180.... Shoots left. ... Name pronounced mahn-ZHOH.
TRANSACTIONS/CAREER NOTES: Signed as free agent by St. Louis Blues (August 21, 1989).... Selected by Tampa Bay Lightning in NHL expansion draft (June 18, 1992).... Loaned to Milwaukee Admirals at beginning of 1992-93 season.... Traded by Lightning with RW Martin Simard and RW Steve Tuttle to Quebec Nordiques for RW Herb Raglan (February 12, 1993).
HONORS: Named to QMJHL All-Star second team (1985-86).... Won Garry F. Longman Memorial Trophy (1986-87).... Won James Gatschene Memorial Trophy (1989-90).... Won Leo P. Lamoureux Memorial Trophy (1989-90).... Named to IHL All-Star first team (1989-90).... Won N.R. (Bud) Poile Trophy (1990-91).... Named to IHL All-Star second team (1990-91).

			REGULAR SEASON					PLAYOFFS			
Season Team	League	Gms.	G	A	Pts.	Pen.	Gms.	G	A	Pts.	Pen.
83-84—Laval	QMJHL	60	45	49	94	30	—	—	—	—	—
84-85—Laval	QMJHL	67	60	84	144	56	—	—	—	—	—
85-86—Laval	QMJHL	72	71	109	180	45	—	—	—	—	—
86-87—Saginaw	IHL	76	42	53	95	34	10	3	6	9	10
87-88—Played in France	France	30	31	21	52	...	—	—	—	—	—
88-89—Flint	IHL	82	41	*76	117	57	—	—	—	—	—
89-90—St. Louis	NHL	7	1	5	6	2	2	0	1	1	0
—Peoria	IHL	73	39	*78	*117	53	5	3	4	7	6
90-91—St. Louis	NHL	7	1	1	2	0	—	—	—	—	—
—Peoria	IHL	73	41	65	106	114	19	10	*16	26	32
91-92—Peoria	IHL	32	21	34	55	77	10	5	14	19	8
—St. Louis	NHL	36	3	12	15	6	—	—	—	—	—
92-93—Milwaukee	IHL	45	24	41	65	69	4	1	4	5	4
—Tampa Bay	NHL	4	1	1	2	2	—	—	—	—	—
—Halifax	AHL	22	13	18	31	10	—	—	—	—	—
NHL totals		54	6	19	25	10	2	0	1	1	0

MONTGOMERY, JIM
C, BLUES

PERSONAL: Born June 30, 1969, at Montreal.... 5-10/185.... Shoots right.
TRANSACTIONS/CAREER NOTES: Signed as free agent by St. Louis Blues (June 2, 1993).
HONORS: Named to NCAA All-America East second team (1990-91 and 1992-93). ... Named to Hockey East All-Star second team (1990-91 and 1991-92).... Named NCAA Tournament Most Valuable Player (1992-93).... Named Hockey East Playoff Most Valuable Player (1992-93).... Named to NCAA All-Tournament team (1992-93).... Named to Hockey East All-Star first team (1992-93).

			REGULAR SEASON					PLAYOFFS			
Season Team	League	Gms.	G	A	Pts.	Pen.	Gms.	G	A	Pts.	Pen.
89-90—University of Maine	Hockey East	45	26	34	60	35	—	—	—	—	—
90-91—University of Maine	Hockey East	43	24	57	81	44	—	—	—	—	—
91-92—University of Maine	Hockey East	37	21	44	65	46	—	—	—	—	—
92-93—University of Maine	Hockey East	45	32	63	95	40	—	—	—	—	—

MOOG, ANDY
G, STARS

PERSONAL: Born February 18, 1960, at Penticton, B.C.... 5-8/170.... Shoots left.... Full name: Donald Andrew Moog.... Name pronounced MOHG.
TRANSACTIONS/CAREER NOTES: Selected by Edmonton Oilers in seventh round (sixth Oilers pick, 132nd overall) of NHL entry draft (June 11, 1980).... Suffered viral infection (December 1983). ... Injured ligaments in both knees (March 1, 1985).... Traded by Oilers to Boston Bruins for LW Geoff Courtnall and G Bill Ranford (March 1988).... Hyperextended right knee (January 31, 1991); missed three weeks.... Injured back (January 1993); missed three games.... Injured hamstring (February 1993); missed four games.... Traded by Bruins to Dallas Stars

for G Jon Casey (June 25, 1993) to complete deal in which Bruins sent D Gord Murphy to Stars for future considerations (June 20, 1993).
HONORS: Named to WHL All-Star second team (1979-80).... Named to CHL All-Star second team (1981-82).... Named to THE SPORTING NEWS All-Star second team (1982-83).... Played in NHL All-Star Game (1985, 1986 and 1991).... Shared William M. Jennings Trophy with Rejean Lemelin (1989-90).
MISCELLANEOUS: Member of Stanley Cup championship teams (1984, 1985 and 1987).

| | | | REGULAR SEASON | | | | | | | PLAYOFFS | | | | | | |
Season Team	League	Gms.	Min.	W	L	T	GA	SO	Avg.	Gms.	Min.	W	L	GA	SO	Avg.
76-77—Kamloops	BCJHL	44	2735	...	...	...	173	0	*3.80	—	—	—	—	—	—	—
—Kamloops	WCHL	1	35	...	...	...	6	0	10.29	—	—	—	—	—	—	—
77-78—Penticton	BCJHL	39	2243	...	...	...	191	0	5.11	—	—	—	—	—	—	—
78-79—Billings	WHL	26	1306	13	5	4	90	*3	4.13	5	229	1	3	21	0	5.50
79-80—Billings	WHL	46	2435	23	14	1	149	1	3.67	3	190	2	1	10	0	3.16
80-81—Wichita	CHL	29	1602	14	13	1	89	0	3.33	5	300	3	2	16	0	3.20
—Edmonton	NHL	7	313	3	3	0	20	0	3.83	9	526	5	4	32	0	3.65
81-82—Edmonton	NHL	8	399	3	5	0	32	0	4.81	—	—	—	—	—	—	—
—Wichita	CHL	40	2391	23	13	3	119	1	2.99	7	434	3	4	23	0	3.18
82-83—Edmonton	NHL	50	2833	33	8	7	167	1	3.54	16	949	11	5	48	0	3.03
83-84—Edmonton	NHL	38	2212	27	8	1	139	1	3.77	7	263	4	0	12	0	2.74
84-85—Edmonton	NHL	39	2019	22	9	3	111	1	3.30	2	20	0	0	0	0	...
85-86—Edmonton	NHL	47	2664	27	9	7	164	1	3.69	1	60	1	0	1	0	1.00
86-87—Edmonton	NHL	46	2461	28	11	3	144	0	3.51	2	120	2	0	8	0	4.00
87-88—Can. national team	Int'l	27	1438	10	7	5	86	0	3.59	—	—	—	—	—	—	—
—Can. Olympic Team	Int'l	4	240	4	0	0	9	1	2.25	—	—	—	—	—	—	—
—Boston	NHL	6	360	4	2	0	17	1	2.83	7	354	1	4	25	0	4.24
88-89—Boston	NHL	41	2482	18	14	8	133	1	3.22	6	359	4	2	14	0	2.34
89-90—Boston	NHL	46	2536	24	10	7	122	3	2.89	20	1195	13	7	44	*2	*2.21
90-91—Boston	NHL	51	2844	25	13	9	136	4	2.87	19	1133	10	9	60	0	3.18
91-92—Boston	NHL	62	3640	28	22	9	196	1	3.23	15	866	8	7	46	1	3.19
92-93—Boston	NHL	55	3194	37	14	3	168	3	3.16	3	161	0	3	14	0	5.22
NHL totals		496	27957	279	128	57	1549	17	3.32	107	6006	59	41	304	3	3.04

MORAN, IAN
D, PENGUINS

PERSONAL: Born August 24, 1972, at Cleveland.... 5-11/170.... Shoots right.
HIGH SCHOOL: Belmont Hill (Mass.).
COLLEGE: Boston College.
TRANSACTIONS/CAREER NOTES: Underwent knee surgery (June 1988).... Separated shoulder (March 1989).... Selected by Pittsburgh Penguins in sixth round (fifth Penguins pick, 107th overall) of NHL entry draft (June 16, 1990).
HONORS: Named Hockey East co-Rookie of the Year with Craig Darby (1991-92).... Named to Hockey East All-Rookie team (1991-92).

| | | REGULAR SEASON | | | | | PLAYOFFS | | | | |
Season Team	League	Gms.	G	A	Pts.	Pen.	Gms.	G	A	Pts.	Pen.
87-88—Belmont Hill H.S.	Mass. H.S.	25	3	13	16	15	—	—	—	—	—
88-89—Belmont Hill H.S.	Mass. H.S.	23	7	25	32	8	—	—	—	—	—
89-90—Belmont Hill H.S.	Mass. H.S.	...	10	36	46	0	—	—	—	—	—
90-91—Belmont Hill H.S.	Mass. H.S.	23	7	44	51	12	—	—	—	—	—
91-92—Boston College	Hockey East	30	2	16	18	44	—	—	—	—	—
92-93—Boston College	Hockey East	31	8	12	20	32	—	—	—	—	—

MORE, JAY
D, SHARKS

PERSONAL: Born January 12, 1969, at Souris, Man.... 6-1/190.... Shoots right.
TRANSACTIONS/CAREER NOTES: Selected by New York Rangers as underage junior in first round (first Rangers pick, 10th overall) of NHL entry draft (June 13, 1987).... Traded by Rangers to Minnesota North Stars for C Dave Archibald (November 1, 1989).... Traded by North Stars to Montreal Canadiens for G Brian Hayward (November 7, 1990).... Selected by San Jose Sharks in NHL expansion draft (May 30, 1991).... Injured foot during preseason (September 1991); missed 16 games.... Injured knee (March 1992).... Pulled groin (December 9, 1992); missed four games.... Reaggravated groin injury (December 23, 1992); missed four games.... Suspended one game by NHL for accumulating three game misconduct penalties (January 27, 1993).... Strained hip (March 7, 1993); missed one game.... Suspended for last game of season and first game of 1993-94 season for accumulating four game misconduct penalties (April 11, 1993).
HONORS: Named to WHL (West) All-Star first team (1987-88).

| | | REGULAR SEASON | | | | | PLAYOFFS | | | | |
Season Team	League	Gms.	G	A	Pts.	Pen.	Gms.	G	A	Pts.	Pen.
84-85—Lethbridge	WHL	71	3	9	12	101	4	1	0	1	7
85-86—Lethbridge	WHL	61	7	18	25	155	9	0	2	2	36
86-87—New Westminster	WHL	64	8	29	37	217	—	—	—	—	—
87-88—New Westminster	WHL	70	13	47	60	270	5	0	2	2	26
88-89—Denver	IHL	62	7	15	22	138	3	0	1	1	26
—New York Rangers	NHL	1	0	0	0	0	—	—	—	—	—
89-90—Flint	IHL	9	1	5	6	41	—	—	—	—	—
—Kalamazoo	IHL	64	9	25	34	216	10	0	3	3	13
—Minnesota	NHL	5	0	0	0	16	—	—	—	—	—
90-91—Kalamazoo	IHL	10	0	5	5	46	—	—	—	—	—
—Fredericton	AHL	57	7	17	24	152	9	1	1	2	34

M

Season Team	League	REGULAR SEASON					PLAYOFFS				
		Gms.	G	A	Pts.	Pen.	Gms.	G	A	Pts.	Pen.
91-92—San Jose	NHL	46	4	13	17	85	—	—	—	—	—
—Kansas City	IHL	2	0	2	2	4	—	—	—	—	—
92-93—San Jose	NHL	73	5	6	11	179	—	—	—	—	—
NHL totals		125	9	19	28	280					

MORIN, STEPHANE
C, CANUCKS

PERSONAL: Born March 27, 1969, at Montreal. . . . 6-0/175. . . . Shoots left. . . . Name pronounced MOHR-ay.
TRANSACTIONS/CAREER NOTES: Traded by Shawinigan Cataractes with second-round draft pick to Chicoutimi Sagueneens for D Daniel Bock (December 1987). . . . Selected by Quebec Nordiques in third round (third Nordiques pick, 43rd overall) of NHL entry draft (June 17, 1989). . . . Stretched right knee ligaments (January 8, 1991); missed six games. . . . Broke finger on right hand (February 20, 1991); missed eight games. . . . Sprained knee (October 12, 1991); missed nine games. . . . Signed as free agent by Vancouver Canucks (October 5, 1992).
HONORS: Won Michel Briere Trophy (1988-89). . . . Won Jean Beliveau Trophy (1988-89). . . . Named to QMJHL All-Star first team (1988-89).

Season Team	League	REGULAR SEASON					PLAYOFFS				
		Gms.	G	A	Pts.	Pen.	Gms.	G	A	Pts.	Pen.
86-87—Shawinigan	QMJHL	65	9	14	23	28	14	1	3	4	27
87-88—Shawinigan/Chicoutimi	QMJHL	68	38	45	83	18	6	3	8	11	2
88-89—Chicoutimi	QMJHL	70	77	*109	*186	71	—	—	—	—	—
89-90—Quebec	NHL	6	0	2	2	2	—	—	—	—	—
—Halifax	AHL	65	28	32	60	60	6	3	4	7	6
90-91—Halifax	AHL	17	8	14	22	18	—	—	—	—	—
—Quebec	NHL	48	13	27	40	30	—	—	—	—	—
91-92—Quebec	NHL	30	2	8	10	14	—	—	—	—	—
—Halifax	AHL	30	17	13	30	29	—	—	—	—	—
92-93—Hamilton	AHL	70	31	54	85	49	—	—	—	—	—
—Vancouver	NHL	1	0	1	1	0	—	—	—	—	—
NHL totals		85	15	38	53	46					

MORRIS, JON
C, SHARKS

PERSONAL: Born May 6, 1966, at Lowell, Mass. . . . 6-0/175. . . . Shoots right.
HIGH SCHOOL: Chelmsford (North Chelmsford, Mass.).
COLLEGE: Lowell (Mass.).
TRANSACTIONS/CAREER NOTES: Selected by New Jersey Devils in fifth round (fifth Devils pick, 86th overall) of NHL entry draft (June 9, 1984). . . . Missed most of 1988-89 season while attending school. . . . Strained rib cage (October 7, 1990). . . . Claimed on waivers by San Jose Sharks (March 13, 1993).
HONORS: Named to Hockey East All-Freshman team (1984-85). . . . Named to NCAA All-America East second team (1986-87). . . . Named to Hockey East All-Star first team (1986-87).

Season Team	League	REGULAR SEASON					PLAYOFFS				
		Gms.	G	A	Pts.	Pen.	Gms.	G	A	Pts.	Pen.
83-84—Chelmsford H.S.	Mass. H.S.	24	31	50	81	...	—	—	—	—	—
84-85—University of Lowell	Hockey East	42	29	31	60	16	—	—	—	—	—
85-86—University of Lowell	Hockey East	39	25	31	56	52	—	—	—	—	—
86-87—University of Lowell	Hockey East	36	28	33	61	48	—	—	—	—	—
87-88—University of Lowell	Hockey East	37	15	39	54	39	—	—	—	—	—
88-89—New Jersey	NHL	4	0	2	2	0	—	—	—	—	—
89-90—Utica	AHL	49	27	37	64	6	—	—	—	—	—
—New Jersey	NHL	20	6	7	13	8	6	1	3	4	23
90-91—New Jersey	NHL	53	9	19	28	27	5	0	4	4	2
—Utica	AHL	6	4	2	6	5	—	—	—	—	—
91-92—New Jersey	NHL	7	1	2	3	6	—	—	—	—	—
—Utica	AHL	7	1	4	5	0	—	—	—	—	—
92-93—Utica	AHL	31	16	24	40	28	—	—	—	—	—
—Cincinnati	IHL	18	7	19	26	24	—	—	—	—	—
—New Jersey	NHL	2	0	0	0	0	—	—	—	—	—
—San Jose	NHL	13	0	3	3	6	—	—	—	—	—
NHL totals		99	16	33	49	47	11	1	7	8	25

MORRISON, BRENDAN
C, DEVILS

PERSONAL: Born August 12, 1975, at North Vancouver, B.C. . . . 5-11/170. . . . Shoots left.
TRANSACTIONS/CAREER NOTES: Selected by New Jersey Devils in second round (third Devils pick, 39th overall) of NHL entry draft (June 26, 1993).

Season Team	League	REGULAR SEASON					PLAYOFFS				
		Gms.	G	A	Pts.	Pen.	Gms.	G	A	Pts.	Pen.
92-93—Penticton	BCJHL	56	35	59	94	45	—	—	—	—	—

MORRISON, JUSTIN
C, CAPITALS

PERSONAL: Born February 9, 1972, at Newmarket, Ont. . . . 5-10/180. . . . Shoots right. . . . Full name: Justin George Morrison.
TRANSACTIONS/CAREER NOTES: Selected by Washington Capitals in fourth round (sixth Capitals pick, 80th overall) of NHL entry draft (June 22, 1991).

M

Season Team	League	REGULAR SEASON					PLAYOFFS				
		Gms.	G	A	Pts.	Pen.	Gms.	G	A	Pts.	Pen.
86-87—King City Jr. B.	OHA	34	15	20	35	95	—	—	—	—	—
87-88—Richmond Hill Jr. B	OHA	36	16	33	49	155	—	—	—	—	—
88-89—Kingston	OHL	44	13	13	26	101	—	—	—	—	—
89-90—Kingston	OHL	65	27	40	67	201	—	—	—	—	—
90-91—Kingston	OHL	61	44	57	101	222	—	—	—	—	—
91-92—Kingston	OHL	23	18	21	39	63	—	—	—	—	—
—Owen Sound	OHL	36	9	43	52	106	5	3	2	5	11
92-93—Toledo	ECHL	13	6	8	14	47	—	—	—	—	—
—Belleville	OHL	37	25	48	73	65	7	3	11	14	11

MORROW, SCOTT
LW, WHALERS

PERSONAL: Born June 18, 1969, at Chicago.... 6-1/181.... Shoots left.... Brother of Steve Morrow, defenseman in Philadelphia Flyers system.
HIGH SCHOOL: Northwood School (Lake Placid, N.Y.).
COLLEGE: New Hampshire.
TRANSACTIONS/CAREER NOTES: Selected by Hartford Whalers in fifth round (fourth Whalers pick, 95th overall) of NHL entry draft (June 11, 1988).... Broke ankle (November 18, 1988).
HONORS: Named to Hockey East All-Star second team (1991-92).

Season Team	League	REGULAR SEASON					PLAYOFFS				
		Gms.	G	A	Pts.	Pen.	Gms.	G	A	Pts.	Pen.
87-88—Northwood School	N.Y. H.S.	24	10	13	23	...	—	—	—	—	—
88-89—Univ. of New Hampshire	Hockey East	19	6	7	13	14	—	—	—	—	—
89-90—Univ. of New Hampshire	Hockey East	29	10	11	21	35	—	—	—	—	—
90-91—Univ. of New Hampshire	Hockey East	31	11	11	22	52	—	—	—	—	—
91-92—Univ. of New Hampshire	Hockey East	35	30	23	53	65	—	—	—	—	—
—Springfield	AHL	2	0	1	1	0	5	0	0	0	9
92-93—Springfield	AHL	70	22	29	51	80	15	6	9	15	21

MOSS, TYLER
G, LIGHTNING

PERSONAL: Born June 29, 1975, at Ottawa.... 6-0/168.... Shoots right.
TRANSACTIONS/CAREER NOTES: Selected by Tampa Bay Lightning in second round (second Lightning pick, 29th overall) of NHL entry draft (June 26, 1993).
HONORS: Named to OHL All-Rookie team (1992-93).

Season Team	League	REGULAR SEASON							PLAYOFFS						
		Gms.	Min.	W	L	T	GA	SO	Avg.	Gms.	Min.	W	L	GA	SO	Avg.
91-92—Nepean	COJHL	26	1335	...	...	...	109	...	4.90	—	—	—	—	—	—	—
92-93—Kingston	OHL	31	1537	13	7	5	97	0	3.79	6	228	1	2	19	0	5.00

MROZIK, RICK
D, STARS

PERSONAL: Born January 2, 1975, at Duluth, Minn.... 6-2/185.... Shoots left.
HIGH SCHOOL: Cloquet (Minn.).
TRANSACTIONS/CAREER NOTES: Selected by Dallas Stars in sixth round (fourth Stars pick, 136th overall) of NHL entry draft (June 26, 1993).

Season Team	League	REGULAR SEASON					PLAYOFFS				
		Gms.	G	A	Pts.	Pen.	Gms.	G	A	Pts.	Pen.
92-93—Cloquet H.S.	Minn. H.S.	28	9	38	47	12	—	—	—	—	—

MULLEN, BRIAN
RW, ISLANDERS

PERSONAL: Born March 16, 1962, at New York.... 5-10/185.... Shoots left.... Full name: Brian Patrick Mullen.... Brother of Joe Mullen, right winger, Pittsburgh Penguins.
COLLEGE: Wisconsin.
TRANSACTIONS/CAREER NOTES: Selected by Winnipeg Jets in seventh round (seventh Jets pick, 128th overall) of NHL entry draft (June 11, 1980).... Traded by Jets with 10th-round pick in 1987 draft (LW Brett Barnett) to New York Rangers for fifth-round pick in 1988 draft (LW Benoit Lebeau) and third-round pick in 1989 draft (later traded to St. Louis Blues) (June 8, 1987).... Bruised left knee (January 1988).... Traded by Rangers with future considerations to San Jose Sharks for RW/C Tim Kerr (May 30, 1991).... Sprained knee (January 3, 1992); missed six games.... Traded by Sharks to New York Islanders for rights to C Markus Thuresson (August 24, 1992).
HONORS: Played in NHL All-Star Game (1989).

Season Team	League	REGULAR SEASON					PLAYOFFS				
		Gms.	G	A	Pts.	Pen.	Gms.	G	A	Pts.	Pen.
77-78—New York Westsiders	NYMJHL	33	21	36	57	38	—	—	—	—	—
78-79—New York Westsiders	NYMJHL				Statistics unavailable.						
79-80—New York Westsiders	NYMJHL				Statistics unavailable.						
80-81—University of Wisconsin	WCHA	38	11	13	24	28	—	—	—	—	—
81-82—University of Wisconsin	WCHA	33	20	17	37	10	—	—	—	—	—
82-83—Winnipeg	NHL	80	24	26	50	14	3	1	0	1	0
83-84—Winnipeg	NHL	75	21	41	62	28	3	0	3	3	6
84-85—Winnipeg	NHL	69	32	39	71	32	8	1	2	3	4
85-86—Winnipeg	NHL	79	28	34	62	38	3	1	2	3	6
86-87—Winnipeg	NHL	69	19	32	51	20	9	4	2	6	0
87-88—New York Rangers	NHL	74	25	29	54	42	—	—	—	—	—
88-89—New York Rangers	NHL	78	29	35	64	60	3	0	1	1	4
89-90—New York Rangers	NHL	76	27	41	68	42	10	2	2	4	8
90-91—New York Rangers	NHL	79	19	43	62	44	6	0	2	2	0
91-92—San Jose	NHL	72	18	28	46	66	—	—	—	—	—
92-93—New York Islanders	NHL	81	18	14	32	28	18	3	4	7	2
NHL totals		832	260	362	622	414	63	12	18	30	30

MULLEN, JOE
RW, PENGUINS

PERSONAL: Born February 26, 1957, at New York.... 5-9/180.... Shoots right.... Full name: Joseph Patrick Mullen.... Brother of Brian Mullen, right winger, New York Islanders.
COLLEGE: Boston College.
TRANSACTIONS/CAREER NOTES: Signed as free agent by St. Louis Blues (August 16, 1979).... Suffered leg injury (October 18, 1982).... Tore ligaments in left knee and underwent surgery (January 29, 1983); missed remainder of season.... Traded by Blues with D Terry Johnson and D Rik Wilson to Calgary Flames for LW Eddy Beers, LW Gino Cavallini and D Charles Bourgeois (February 1, 1986).... Bruised knee (April 1988).... Suffered from the flu (April 1989). ... Traded by Flames to Pittsburgh Penguins for second-round pick in 1990 draft (D Nicolas Perreault) (June 16, 1990).... Injured neck (January 22, 1991).... Underwent neck surgery for herniated disk (February 6, 1991).... missed remainder of season.... Damaged ligament in knee (May 5, 1992); missed remainder of playoffs and first 11 games of 1992-93 season.
HONORS: Named Most Valuable Player (1974-75).... Named to NCAA All-America East (University Division) first team (1977-78).... Named to ECAC All-Star first team (1977-78 and 1978-79).... Named to NCAA All-America East (University Division) first team (1978-79).... Won Ken McKenzie Trophy (1979-80).... Named to CHL All-Star second team (1979-80).... Won Tommy Ivan Trophy (1980-81).... Won Phil Esposito Trophy (1980-81).... Named to CHL All-Star first team (1980-81).... Won Lady Byng Memorial Trophy (1986-87 and 1988-89).... Named to THE SPORTING NEWS All-Star first team (1988-89).... Named to NHL All-Star first team (1988-89).... Played in NHL All-Star Game (1989 and 1990).... Named to THE SPORTING NEWS All-Star second team (1991-92).
MISCELLANEOUS: Member of Stanley Cup championship teams (1989, 1991 and 1992).

Season Team	League	REGULAR SEASON Gms.	G	A	Pts.	Pen.	PLAYOFFS Gms.	G	A	Pts.	Pen.
71-72—New York 14th Precinct....	NYMJHL	30	13	11	24	2	—	—	—	—	—
72-73—New York Westsiders	NYMJHL	40	14	28	42	8	—	—	—	—	—
73-74—New York Westsiders	NYMJHL	†42	71	49	120	41	7	9	9	18	0
74-75—New York Westsiders	NYMJHL	40	*110	72	*182	20	13	*24	13	*37	2
75-76—Boston College	ECAC	24	16	18	34	4	—	—	—	—	—
76-77—Boston College	ECAC	28	28	26	54	8	—	—	—	—	—
77-78—Boston College	ECAC	34	34	34	68	12	—	—	—	—	—
78-79—Boston College	ECAC	25	32	24	56	8	—	—	—	—	—
79-80—Salt Lake City	IHL	75	40	32	72	21	13	†9	11	20	0
—St. Louis	NHL	—	—	—	—	—	1	0	0	0	0
80-81—Salt Lake City	IHL	80	59	58	*117	8	17	11	9	20	0
81-82—Salt Lake City	IHL	27	21	27	48	12	—	—	—	—	—
—St. Louis	NHL	45	25	34	59	4	10	7	11	18	4
82-83—St. Louis	NHL	49	17	30	47	6	—	—	—	—	—
83-84—St. Louis	NHL	80	41	44	85	19	6	2	0	2	0
84-85—St. Louis	NHL	79	40	52	92	6	3	0	0	0	0
85-86—St. Louis	NHL	48	28	24	52	10	—	—	—	—	—
—Calgary	NHL	29	16	22	38	11	21	*12	7	19	4
86-87—Calgary	NHL	79	47	40	87	14	6	2	1	3	0
87-88—Calgary	NHL	80	40	44	84	30	7	2	4	6	10
88-89—Calgary	NHL	79	51	59	110	16	21	*16	8	24	4
89-90—Calgary	NHL	78	36	33	69	24	6	3	0	3	0
90-91—Pittsburgh	NHL	47	17	22	39	6	22	8	9	17	4
91-92—Pittsburgh	NHL	77	42	45	87	30	9	3	1	4	4
92-93—Pittsburgh	NHL	72	33	37	70	14	12	4	2	6	6
NHL totals.........		**842**	**433**	**486**	**919**	**190**	**124**	**59**	**43**	**102**	**36**

MULLER, KIRK
LW, CANADIENS

PERSONAL: Born February 8, 1966, at Kingston, Ont.... 6-0/205.... Shoots left.
TRANSACTIONS/CAREER NOTES: Selected by New Jersey Devils as underage junior in first round (first Devils pick, second overall) of NHL entry draft (June 9, 1984).... Strained knee (January 13, 1986).... Fractured ribs (April 1986).... Traded by Devils with G Roland Melanson to Montreal Canadiens for RW Stephane Richer and RW Tom Chorske (September 1991).... Injured eye (January 21, 1992); missed one game.... Bruised ribs (November 7, 1992); missed one game.... Sprained wrist (March 6, 1993); missed two games.
HONORS: Won William Hanley Trophy (1982-83).... Played in NHL All-Star Game (1985, 1986, 1988, 1990, 1992 and 1993).
MISCELLANEOUS: Member of Stanley Cup championship team (1993).

Season Team	League	REGULAR SEASON Gms.	G	A	Pts.	Pen.	PLAYOFFS Gms.	G	A	Pts.	Pen.
80-81—Kingston...........................	OMJHL	2	0	0	0	0	—	—	—	—	—
81-82—Kingston...........................	OHL	67	12	39	51	27	4	5	1	6	4
82-83—Guelph..............................	OHL	66	52	60	112	41	—	—	—	—	—
83-84—Canadian Olympic Team ..	Int'l	15	2	2	4	6	—	—	—	—	—
—Guelph..............................	OHL	49	31	63	94	27	—	—	—	—	—
84-85—New Jersey.....................	NHL	80	17	37	54	69	—	—	—	—	—
85-86—New Jersey.....................	NHL	77	25	42	67	45	—	—	—	—	—
86-87—New Jersey.....................	NHL	79	26	50	76	75	—	—	—	—	—
87-88—New Jersey.....................	NHL	80	37	57	94	114	20	4	8	12	37
88-89—New Jersey.....................	NHL	80	31	43	74	119	—	—	—	—	—
89-90—New Jersey.....................	NHL	80	30	56	86	74	6	1	3	4	11
90-91—New Jersey.....................	NHL	80	19	51	70	76	7	0	2	2	10
91-92—Montreal..........................	NHL	78	36	41	77	86	11	4	3	7	31
92-93—Montreal..........................	NHL	80	37	57	94	77	20	10	7	17	18
NHL totals.........		**714**	**258**	**434**	**692**	**735**	**64**	**19**	**23**	**42**	**107**

MULLER, MIKE
D, JETS

PERSONAL: Born September 18, 1971, at Minneapolis. . . . 6-2/205. . . . Shoots left. . . . Full name: Mike Todd Muller.
HIGH SCHOOL: Wayzata (Plymouth, Minn.).
COLLEGE: Minnesota.
TRANSACTIONS/CAREER NOTES: Selected by Winnipeg Jets in second round (second Jets pick, 35th overall) of NHL entry draft (June 16, 1990).

Season Team	League	REGULAR SEASON					PLAYOFFS				
		Gms.	G	A	Pts.	Pen.	Gms.	G	A	Pts.	Pen.
88-89—Wayzata H.S.	Minn. H.S.	24	10	11	21	56	—	—	—	—	—
89-90—Wayzata H.S.	Minn. H.S.	23	11	15	26	45	—	—	—	—	—
90-91—University of Minnesota	WCHA	33	4	4	8	44	—	—	—	—	—
91-92—University of Minnesota	WCHA	44	4	12	16	60	—	—	—	—	—
92-93—Dynamo Moscow	CIS	18	1	0	1	...	—	—	—	—	—

MULVENNA, GLENN
C, FLYERS

PERSONAL: Born February 18, 1967, at Calgary, Alta. . . . 5-11/187. . . . Shoots left.
TRANSACTIONS/CAREER NOTES: Signed as free agent by Pittsburgh Penguins (December 3, 1987). . . . Signed as free agent by Philadelphia Flyers (July 7, 1992).

Season Team	League	REGULAR SEASON					PLAYOFFS				
		Gms.	G	A	Pts.	Pen.	Gms.	G	A	Pts.	Pen.
86-87—New Westminster	WHL	53	24	44	68	43	—	—	—	—	—
—Kamloops	WHL	18	13	8	21	18	13	4	6	10	10
87-88—Kamloops	WHL	38	21	38	59	35	—	—	—	—	—
88-89—Flint	IHL	32	9	14	23	12	—	—	—	—	—
—Muskegon	IHL	11	3	2	5	0	—	—	—	—	—
—Knoxville	ECHL	2	0	0	0	5	—	—	—	—	—
89-90—Muskegon	IHL	52	14	21	35	17	11	2	3	5	0
—Fort Wayne	IHL	6	2	5	7	2	—	—	—	—	—
90-91—Muskegon	IHL	48	9	27	36	25	5	1	1	2	0
91-92—Pittsburgh	NHL	1	0	0	0	2	—	—	—	—	—
—Muskegon	IHL	70	15	27	42	24	14	5	6	11	11
92-93—Philadelphia	NHL	1	0	0	0	2	—	—	—	—	—
—Hershey	AHL	35	5	17	22	8	—	—	—	—	—
NHL totals		2	0	0	0	4					

MUNI, CRAIG
D, BLACKHAWKS

PERSONAL: Born July 19, 1962, at Toronto. . . . 6-3/200. . . . Shoots left. . . . Full name: Craig Douglas Muni. . . . Name pronounced MYOO-nee.
TRANSACTIONS/CAREER NOTES: Selected by Toronto Maple Leafs as underage junior in second round (first Maple Leafs pick, 25th overall) of NHL entry draft (June 11, 1980). . . . Tore left knee ligaments (September 1981). . . . Broke ankle (January 1983). . . . Signed as free agent by Edmonton Oilers (August 18, 1986). . . . Traded by Oilers to Buffalo Sabres for cash (October 2, 1986). . . . Traded by Sabres to Pittsburgh Penguins for future considerations (October 3, 1986). . . . Traded by Penguins to Oilers to complete earlier trade for G Gilles Meloche (October 6, 1986). . . . Bruised kidney (May 1987). . . . Bruised ankle (January 1988). . . . Bruised ankle (December 17, 1988). . . . Strained right shoulder (January 1989). . . . Broke little finger of right hand (January 27, 1990); missed eight games. . . . Suffered pinched nerve (January 15, 1992); missed 17 games. . . . Injured knee (March 19, 1992); missed eight games. . . . Suspended two games by NHL during playoffs for kneeing (May 22, 1992); missed final 1992 playoff game and first game of 1992-93 regular season. . . . Suffered from the flu (December 1992); missed one game. . . . Suffered eye injury (February 18, 1993); missed two games. . . . Traded by Oilers to Chicago Blackhawks for C Mike Hudson (March 22, 1993).
MISCELLANEOUS: Member of Stanley Cup championship teams (1987, 1988 and 1990).

M

Season Team	League	REGULAR SEASON					PLAYOFFS				
		Gms.	G	A	Pts.	Pen.	Gms.	G	A	Pts.	Pen.
79-80—Kingston	OMJHL	66	6	28	34	114	—	—	—	—	—
80-81—Kingston	OMJHL	38	2	14	16	65	—	—	—	—	—
—Windsor	OMJHL	25	5	11	16	41	11	1	4	5	14
—New Brunswick	AHL	—	—	—	—	—	2	0	1	1	10
81-82—Toronto	NHL	3	0	0	0	2	—	—	—	—	—
—Windsor	OHL	49	5	32	37	92	9	2	3	5	16
—Cincinnati	CHL	—	—	—	—	—	3	0	2	2	2
82-83—Toronto	NHL	2	0	1	1	0	—	—	—	—	—
—St. Catharines	AHL	64	6	32	38	52	—	—	—	—	—
83-84—St. Catharines	AHL	64	4	16	20	79	7	0	1	1	0
84-85—St. Catharines	AHL	68	7	17	24	54	—	—	—	—	—
—Toronto	NHL	8	0	0	0	0	—	—	—	—	—
85-86—Toronto	NHL	6	0	1	1	4	—	—	—	—	—
—St. Catharines	AHL	73	3	34	37	91	13	0	5	5	16
86-87—Edmonton	NHL	79	7	22	29	85	14	0	2	2	17
87-88—Edmonton	NHL	72	4	15	19	77	19	0	4	4	31
88-89—Edmonton	NHL	69	5	13	18	71	7	0	3	3	8
89-90—Edmonton	NHL	71	5	12	17	81	22	0	3	3	16
90-91—Edmonton	NHL	76	1	9	10	77	18	0	3	3	20
91-92—Edmonton	NHL	54	2	5	7	34	3	0	0	0	2
92-93—Edmonton	NHL	72	0	11	11	67	—	—	—	—	—
—Chicago	NHL	9	0	0	0	8	4	0	0	0	2
NHL totals		521	24	89	113	506	87	0	15	15	96

MURANO, ERIC
C, CAPITALS

PERSONAL: Born May 4, 1967, at LaSalle, Que.... 6-0/200.... Shoots right.... Name pronounced muh-RAH-noh.
COLLEGE: Denver.
TRANSACTIONS/CAREER NOTES: Selected by Vancouver Canucks in fifth round (fourth Canucks pick, 91st overall) of NHL entry draft (June 21, 1986).... Traded by Canucks to Washington Capitals for C Tim Taylor (January 29, 1993).
HONORS: Named to WCHA All-Star second team (1989-90).

| | | | REGULAR SEASON | | | | PLAYOFFS | | | |
Season Team	League	Gms.	G	A	Pts.	Pen.	Gms.	G	A	Pts.	Pen.
85-86—Calgary Canucks	AJHL	52	34	47	81	32	—	—	—	—	—
86-87—University of Denver	WCHA	31	5	7	12	12	—	—	—	—	—
87-88—University of Denver	WCHA	37	8	13	21	26	—	—	—	—	—
88-89—University of Denver	WCHA	42	13	16	29	52	—	—	—	—	—
89-90—University of Denver	WCHA	42	33	35	68	52	—	—	—	—	—
—Canadian national team	Int'l	6	1	0	1	4	—	—	—	—	—
90-91—Milwaukee	IHL	63	32	35	67	63	3	0	1	1	4
91-92—Milwaukee	IHL	80	35	48	83	61	5	3	4	7	0
92-93—Hamilton	AHL	42	25	24	49	10	—	—	—	—	—
—Baltimore	AHL	32	16	14	30	10	7	7	5	12	6

MURPHY, GORD
D, PANTHERS

PERSONAL: Born February 23, 1967, at Willowdale, Ont.... 6-1/180.... Shoots right.
TRANSACTIONS/CAREER NOTES: Injured clavicle (January 1985).... Selected by Philadelphia Flyers as underage junior in ninth round (10th Flyers pick, 189th overall) of NHL entry draft (June 15, 1985).... Suffered foot injury and hip pointer (March 24, 1990).... Traded by Flyers with RW Brian Dobbin and third-round pick in 1992 draft (LW Sergei Zholtok) to Boston Bruins for D Garry Galley, C Wes Walz and future considerations (January 2, 1992).... Injured ankle (January 1993); missed 16 games.... Traded by Bruins to Dallas Stars for future considerations (June 20, 1993); Bruins sent G Andy Moog to Stars for G Jon Casey to complete deal (June 25, 1993).... Selected by Florida Panthers in NHL expansion draft (June 24, 1993).
HONORS: Named to Memorial Cup All-Star team (1986-87).

| | | | REGULAR SEASON | | | | PLAYOFFS | | | |
Season Team	League	Gms.	G	A	Pts.	Pen.	Gms.	G	A	Pts.	Pen.
83-84—Don Mills Flyers	MTHL	65	24	42	66	130	—	—	—	—	—
84-85—Oshawa	OHL	59	3	12	15	25	—	—	—	—	—
85-86—Oshawa	OHL	64	7	15	22	56	6	1	1	2	6
86-87—Oshawa	OHL	56	7	30	37	95	24	6	16	22	22
87-88—Hershey	AHL	62	8	20	28	44	12	0	8	8	12
88-89—Philadelphia	NHL	75	4	31	35	68	19	2	7	9	13
89-90—Philadelphia	NHL	75	14	27	41	95	—	—	—	—	—
90-91—Philadelphia	NHL	80	11	31	42	58	—	—	—	—	—
91-92—Philadelphia	NHL	31	2	8	10	33	—	—	—	—	—
—Boston	NHL	42	3	6	9	51	15	1	0	1	12
92-93—Boston	NHL	49	5	12	17	62	—	—	—	—	—
—Providence	AHL	2	1	3	4	2	—	—	—	—	—
NHL totals		352	39	115	154	367	34	3	7	10	25

MURPHY, JOE
RW, BLACKHAWKS

PERSONAL: Born October 16, 1967, at London, Ont.... 6-1/190.... Shoots left.... Full name: Joseph Patrick Murphy.
COLLEGE: Michigan State.
TRANSACTIONS/CAREER NOTES: Selected by Detroit Red Wings in first round (first Red Wings pick, first overall) of NHL entry draft (June 21, 1986).... Sprained right ankle (January 1988).... Traded by Red Wings with C/LW Adam Graves, LW Petr Klima and D Jeff Sharples to Edmonton Oilers for C Jimmy Carson, C Kevin McClelland and fifth-round pick in 1991 draft (November 2, 1989).... Bruised both thighs (March 1990).... Did not report to Oilers in 1992-93 season because of contract dispute; missed 63 games.... Traded by Oilers to Chicago Blackhawks for D Igor Kravchuk and C Dean McAmmond (February 25, 1993).
HONORS: Named BCJHL Rookie of the Year (1984-85).... Named CCHA Rookie of the Year (1985-86).
MISCELLANEOUS: Member of Stanley Cup championship team (1990).

| | | | REGULAR SEASON | | | | PLAYOFFS | | | |
Season Team	League	Gms.	G	A	Pts.	Pen.	Gms.	G	A	Pts.	Pen.
84-85—Penticton	BCJHL	51	68	84	*152	92	—	—	—	—	—
85-86—Michigan State	CCHA	35	24	37	61	50	—	—	—	—	—
—Canadian national team	Int'l	8	3	3	6	2	—	—	—	—	—
86-87—Adirondack	AHL	71	21	38	59	61	10	2	1	3	33
—Detroit	NHL	5	0	1	1	2	—	—	—	—	—
87-88—Adirondack	AHL	6	5	6	11	4	—	—	—	—	—
—Detroit	NHL	50	10	9	19	37	8	0	1	1	6
88-89—Detroit	NHL	26	1	7	8	28	—	—	—	—	—
—Adirondack	AHL	47	31	35	66	66	16	6	11	17	17
89-90—Detroit	NHL	9	3	1	4	4	—	—	—	—	—
—Edmonton	NHL	62	7	18	25	56	22	6	8	14	16
90-91—Edmonton	NHL	80	27	35	62	35	15	2	5	7	14
91-92—Edmonton	NHL	80	35	47	82	52	16	8	16	24	12
92-93—Chicago	NHL	19	7	10	17	18	4	0	0	0	8
NHL totals		331	90	128	218	232	65	16	30	46	56

M

MURPHY, LARRY

D, PENGUINS

PERSONAL: Born March 8, 1961, at Scarborough, Ont. . . . 6-2/210. . . . Shoots right. . . . Full name: Lawrence Thomas Murphy.

TRANSACTIONS/CAREER NOTES: Selected by Los Angeles Kings as underage junior in first round (first Kings pick, fourth overall) of NHL entry draft (June 11, 1980). . . . Traded by Kings to Washington Capitals for D Brian Engblom and RW Ken Houston (October 18, 1983). . . . Injured foot (October 29, 1985). . . . Broke ankle (May 1988). . . . Traded by Capitals with RW Mike Gartner to Minnesota North Stars for RW Dino Ciccarelli and D Bob Rouse (March 7, 1989). . . . Traded by North Stars with D Peter Taglianetti to Pittsburgh Penguins for D Jim Johnson and D Chris Dahlquist (December 11, 1990). . . . Fractured right foot (February 22, 1991); played until March 5 then missed five games. . . . Suffered back spasms (March 28, 1993); missed one game.

HONORS: Won Max Kaminsky Trophy (1979-80). . . . Named to OMJHL All-Star first team (1979-80). . . . Named to Memorial Cup All-Star team (1979-80). . . . Named to THE SPORTING NEWS All-Star second team (1986-87 and 1992-93). . . . Named to NHL All-Star second team (1986-87 and 1992-93).

RECORDS: Holds NHL single-season record for most points by a rookie defenseman—76; and most assists by a rookie defenseman—60 (1980-81).

MISCELLANEOUS: Member of Stanley Cup championship teams (1991 and 1992).

			REGULAR SEASON					PLAYOFFS				
Season	Team	League	Gms.	G	A	Pts.	Pen.	Gms.	G	A	Pts.	Pen.
78-79—Peterborough		OMJHL	66	6	21	27	82	19	1	9	10	42
79-80—Peterborough		OMJHL	68	21	68	89	88	14	4	13	17	20
80-81—Los Angeles		NHL	80	16	60	76	79	4	3	0	3	2
81-82—Los Angeles		NHL	79	22	44	66	95	10	2	8	10	12
82-83—Los Angeles		NHL	77	14	48	62	81	—	—	—	—	—
83-84—Los Angeles		NHL	6	0	3	3	0	—	—	—	—	—
—Washington		NHL	72	13	33	46	50	8	0	3	3	6
84-85—Washington		NHL	79	13	42	55	51	5	2	3	5	0
85-86—Washington		NHL	78	21	44	65	50	9	1	5	6	6
86-87—Washington		NHL	80	23	58	81	39	7	2	2	4	6
87-88—Washington		NHL	79	8	53	61	72	13	4	4	8	33
88-89—Washington		NHL	65	7	29	36	70	—	—	—	—	—
—Minnesota		NHL	13	4	6	10	12	5	0	2	2	8
89-90—Minnesota		NHL	77	10	58	68	44	7	1	2	3	31
90-91—Minnesota		NHL	31	4	11	15	38	—	—	—	—	—
—Pittsburgh		NHL	44	5	23	28	30	23	5	18	23	44
91-92—Pittsburgh		NHL	77	21	56	77	48	†21	6	10	16	19
92-93—Pittsburgh		NHL	83	22	63	85	73	12	2	11	13	10
NHL totals			1020	203	631	834	832	124	28	68	96	177

MURPHY, ROB

C, KINGS

PERSONAL: Born April 7, 1969, at Hull, Que. . . . 6-3/205. . . . Shoots left.

HIGH SCHOOL: Philemon Wright (Hull, Que.).

TRANSACTIONS/CAREER NOTES: Selected by Vancouver Canucks as underage junior in second round (first Canucks pick, 24th overall) of NHL entry draft (June 13, 1987). . . . Separated shoulder (November 13, 1988). . . . Sprained right knee (November 3, 1990). . . . Selected by Ottawa Senators in NHL expansion draft (June 18, 1992). . . . Signed as free agent by Los Angeles Kings (August 2, 1993).

HONORS: Won Michel Bergeron Trophy (1986-87). . . . Won Garry F. Longman Memorial Trophy (1989-90).

			REGULAR SEASON					PLAYOFFS				
Season	Team	League	Gms.	G	A	Pts.	Pen.	Gms.	G	A	Pts.	Pen.
86-87—Laval		QMJHL	70	35	54	89	86	14	3	4	7	15
87-88—Vancouver		NHL	5	0	0	0	2	—	—	—	—	—
—Laval		QMJHL	26	11	25	36	82	—	—	—	—	—
—Drummondville		QMJHL	33	16	28	44	41	17	4	15	19	45
88-89—Drummondville		QMJHL	26	13	25	38	16	4	1	3	4	20
—Vancouver		NHL	8	0	1	1	2	—	—	—	—	—
—Milwaukee		IHL	8	4	2	6	4	11	3	5	8	34
89-90—Milwaukee		IHL	64	24	47	71	87	6	2	6	8	12
—Vancouver		NHL	12	1	1	2	0	—	—	—	—	—
90-91—Vancouver		NHL	42	5	1	6	90	4	0	0	0	2
—Milwaukee		IHL	23	1	7	8	48	—	—	—	—	—
91-92—Milwaukee		IHL	73	26	38	64	141	5	0	3	3	2
—Vancouver		NHL	6	0	1	1	6	—	—	—	—	—
92-93—Ottawa		NHL	44	3	7	10	30	—	—	—	—	—
—New Haven		AHL	26	8	12	20	28	—	—	—	—	—
NHL totals			117	9	11	20	130	4	0	0	0	2

MURRAY, GLEN

RW, BRUINS

PERSONAL: Born November 1, 1972, at Halifax, N.S. . . . 6-2/200. . . . Shoots right.

TRANSACTIONS/CAREER NOTES: Selected by Boston Bruins in first round (first Bruins pick, 18th overall) of NHL entry draft (June 22, 1991).

			REGULAR SEASON					PLAYOFFS				
Season	Team	League	Gms.	G	A	Pts.	Pen.	Gms.	G	A	Pts.	Pen.
89-90—Sudbury		OHL	62	8	28	36	17	7	0	0	0	4
90-91—Sudbury		OHL	66	27	38	65	82	5	8	4	12	10
91-92—Sudbury		OHL	54	37	47	84	93	11	7	4	11	18
—Boston		NHL	5	3	1	4	0	15	4	2	6	10
92-93—Providence		AHL	48	30	26	56	42	6	1	4	5	4
—Boston		NHL	27	3	4	7	8	—	—	—	—	—
NHL totals			32	6	5	11	8	15	4	2	6	10

M

MURRAY, MARTY
C, FLAMES

PERSONAL: Born February 16, 1975, at Deloraine, Man. . . . 5-8/164. . . . Shoots left.
TRANSACTIONS/CAREER NOTES: Selected by Calgary Flames in fourth round (fifth Flames pick, 96th overall) of NHL entry draft (June 26, 1993).

			REGULAR SEASON					PLAYOFFS				
Season	Team	League	Gms.	G	A	Pts.	Pen.	Gms.	G	A	Pts.	Pen.
91-92—Brandon		WHL	68	20	36	56	12	—	—	—	—	—
92-93—Brandon		WHL	67	29	65	94	50	4	1	3	4	0

MURRAY, PAT
RW, FLYERS

PERSONAL: Born August 20, 1969, at Stratford, Ont. . . . 6-3/195. . . . Shoots left. . . . Full name: Patrick Edward Murray.
COLLEGE: Michigan State.
TRANSACTIONS/CAREER NOTES: Selected by Philadelphia Flyers in second round (second Flyers pick, 35th overall) of NHL entry draft (June 11, 1988).
HONORS: Named to CCHA All-Star second team (1989-90).

			REGULAR SEASON					PLAYOFFS				
Season	Team	League	Gms.	G	A	Pts.	Pen.	Gms.	G	A	Pts.	Pen.
86-87—Stratford Jr. B		OHA	42	34	75	109	38	—	—	—	—	—
87-88—Michigan State		CCHA	44	14	23	37	26	—	—	—	—	—
88-89—Michigan State		CCHA	46	21	41	62	65	—	—	—	—	—
89-90—Michigan State		CCHA	45	24	60	84	36	—	—	—	—	—
90-91—Philadelphia		NHL	16	2	1	3	15	—	—	—	—	—
—Hershey		AHL	57	15	38	53	8	7	5	2	7	0
91-92—Hershey		AHL	69	19	43	62	25	6	1	2	3	0
—Philadelphia		NHL	9	1	0	1	0	—	—	—	—	—
92-93—Hershey		AHL	69	21	32	53	63	—	—	—	—	—
NHL totals			**25**	**3**	**1**	**4**	**15**					

MURRAY, ROB
C, JETS

PERSONAL: Born April 4, 1967, at Toronto. . . . 6-1/185. . . . Shoots right.
TRANSACTIONS/CAREER NOTES: Selected by Washington Capitals as underage junior in third round (third Capitals pick, 61st overall) of NHL entry draft (June 15, 1985). . . . Suspended two games by OHL (November 2, 1986). . . . Injured right hip (December 21, 1989); missed 10 games. . . . Selected by Minnesota North Stars in NHL expansion draft (May 30, 1991). . . . Traded by North Stars with future considerations to Winnipeg Jets for seventh-round pick in 1991 draft (G Geoff Finch) and future considerations (May 30, 1991). . . . Strained groin (November 2, 1992); missed three games. . . . Suffered back spasms (December 15, 1992); missed six games.

			REGULAR SEASON					PLAYOFFS				
Season	Team	League	Gms.	G	A	Pts.	Pen.	Gms.	G	A	Pts.	Pen.
83-84—Mississauga		OHA	35	18	36	54	32	—	—	—	—	—
84-85—Peterborough		OHL	63	12	9	21	155	17	2	7	9	45
85-86—Peterborough		OHL	52	14	18	32	125	16	1	2	3	50
86-87—Peterborough		OHL	62	17	37	54	204	3	1	4	5	8
87-88—Fort Wayne		IHL	80	12	21	33	139	6	0	2	2	16
88-89—Baltimore		AHL	80	11	23	34	235	—	—	—	—	—
89-90—Baltimore		AHL	23	5	4	9	63	—	—	—	—	—
—Washington		NHL	41	2	7	9	58	9	0	0	0	18
90-91—Baltimore		AHL	48	6	20	26	177	4	0	0	0	12
—Washington		NHL	17	0	3	3	19	—	—	—	—	—
91-92—Moncton		AHL	60	16	15	31	247	8	0	1	1	56
—Winnipeg		NHL	9	0	1	1	18	—	—	—	—	—
92-93—Moncton		AHL	56	16	21	37	147	3	0	0	0	6
—Winnipeg		NHL	10	1	0	1	6	—	—	—	—	—
NHL totals			**77**	**3**	**11**	**14**	**101**	**9**	**0**	**0**	**0**	**18**

MURRAY, TROY
C, BLACKHAWKS

PERSONAL: Born July 31, 1962, at Winnipeg, Man. . . . 6-1/195. . . . Shoots right. . . . Full name: Troy Norman Murray.
COLLEGE: North Dakota.
TRANSACTIONS/CAREER NOTES: Selected by Chicago Blackhawks in third round (sixth Blackhawks pick, 57th overall) of NHL entry draft (June 11, 1980). . . . Injured knee ligaments (November 1983). . . . Lacerated face (December 1988). . . . Injured right elbow and underwent surgery (December 26, 1989). . . . Developed bursitis on right elbow and hospitalized (February 8, 1990). . . . Traded by Blackhawks with LW Warren Rychel to Winnipeg Jets for D Bryan Marchment and D Chris Norton (July 22, 1991). . . . Separated shoulder (October 23, 1991); missed four games. . . . Lacerated knee (December 14, 1991); missed three games. . . . Separated shoulder (October 7, 1992); missed five games. . . . Suffered hip pointer (November 10, 1992); missed two games. . . . Fractured foot (December 19, 1992); missed 22 games. . . . Traded by Jets to Chicago Blackhawks for D Steve Bancroft and unspecified pick in 1993 draft (February 21, 1993).
HONORS: Won WCHA Freshman of the Year Award (1980-81). . . . Named to WCHA All-Star second team (1980-81 and 1981-82). . . . Won Frank J. Selke Trophy (1985-86).

			REGULAR SEASON					PLAYOFFS				
Season	Team	League	Gms.	G	A	Pts.	Pen.	Gms.	G	A	Pts.	Pen.
79-80—St. Albert		AJHL	60	53	47	100	101	—	—	—	—	—
80-81—Univ. of North Dakota		WCHA	38	33	45	78	28	—	—	—	—	—
81-82—Univ. of North Dakota		WCHA	42	22	29	51	62	—	—	—	—	—
—Chicago		NHL	1	0	0	0	0	7	1	0	1	5

Season Team	League	REGULAR SEASON					PLAYOFFS				
		Gms.	G	A	Pts.	Pen.	Gms.	G	A	Pts.	Pen.
82-83—Chicago	NHL	54	8	8	16	27	2	0	0	0	0
83-84—Chicago	NHL	61	15	15	30	45	5	1	0	1	7
84-85—Chicago	NHL	80	26	40	66	82	15	5	14	19	24
85-86—Chicago	NHL	80	45	54	99	94	2	0	0	0	2
86-87—Chicago	NHL	77	28	43	71	59	4	0	0	0	5
87-88—Chicago	NHL	79	22	36	58	96	5	1	0	1	8
88-89—Chicago	NHL	79	21	30	51	113	16	3	6	9	25
89-90—Chicago	NHL	68	17	38	55	86	20	4	4	8	22
90-91—Chicago	NHL	75	14	23	37	74	6	0	1	1	12
91-92—Winnipeg	NHL	74	17	30	47	69	7	0	0	0	2
92-93—Winnipeg	NHL	29	3	4	7	34	—	—	—	—	—
—Chicago	NHL	22	1	3	4	25	4	0	0	0	2
NHL totals		779	217	324	541	804	93	15	25	40	114

MURZYN, DANA
D, CANUCKS

PERSONAL: Born December 9, 1966, at Regina, Sask.... 6-2/200.... Shoots left.... Name pronounced MUHR-zihn. **TRANSACTIONS/CAREER NOTES:** Selected by Hartford Whalers as underage junior in first round (first Whalers pick, fifth overall) of NHL entry draft (June 15, 1985).... Traded by Whalers with RW Shane Churla to Calgary Flames for C Carey Wilson, D Neil Sheehy and LW Lane MacDonald (January 3, 1988).... Strained knee (March 13, 1989).... Pulled groin (February 4, 1990).... Bruised hip (October 25, 1990); missed 11 games.... Separated shoulder (December 1, 1990); missed 34 games.... Traded by Flames to Vancouver Canucks for RW Ron Stern, D Kevan Guy and option to switch fourth-round picks in 1992 draft; Flames did not exercise option (March 5, 1991).... Suffered from the flu (February 26, 1993); missed two games.
HONORS: Named to WHL (East) All-Star first team (1984-85).... Named to NHL All-Rookie team (1985-86).
MISCELLANEOUS: Member of Stanley Cup championship team (1989).

Season Team	League	REGULAR SEASON					PLAYOFFS				
		Gms.	G	A	Pts.	Pen.	Gms.	G	A	Pts.	Pen.
83-84—Calgary	WHL	65	11	20	31	135	2	0	0	0	0
84-85—Calgary	WHL	72	32	60	92	233	8	1	11	12	16
85-86—Hartford	NHL	78	3	23	26	125	4	0	0	0	10
86-87—Hartford	NHL	74	9	19	28	95	6	2	1	3	29
87-88—Hartford	NHL	33	1	6	7	45	—	—	—	—	—
—Calgary	NHL	41	6	5	11	94	5	2	0	2	13
88-89—Calgary	NHL	63	3	19	22	142	21	0	3	3	20
89-90—Calgary	NHL	78	7	13	20	140	6	2	2	4	2
90-91—Calgary	NHL	19	0	2	2	30	—	—	—	—	—
—Vancouver	NHL	10	1	0	1	8	6	0	1	1	8
91-92—Vancouver	NHL	70	3	11	14	147	1	0	0	0	15
92-93—Vancouver	NHL	79	5	11	16	196	12	3	2	5	18
NHL totals		545	38	109	147	1022	61	9	9	18	115

MUSIL, FRANTISEK
D, FLAMES

PERSONAL: Born December 17, 1964, at Pardubice, Czechoslovakia.... 6-3/215.... Shoots left.... Name pronounced moo-SIHL. **TRANSACTIONS/CAREER NOTES:** Selected by Minnesota North Stars in second round (third North Stars pick, 38th overall) of NHL entry draft (June 8, 1983).... Separated shoulder (December 9, 1986).... Fractured foot (December 17, 1988).... Suffered concussion (February 9, 1989).... Strained lower back muscles (February 18, 1989).... Suffered back spasms (November 2, 1989); missed 10 games.... Separated right shoulder (April 1990).... Traded by North Stars to Calgary Flames for D Brian Glynn (October 26, 1990).... Suffered back spasms (November 8, 1993); missed one game.

Season Team	League	REGULAR SEASON					PLAYOFFS				
		Gms.	G	A	Pts.	Pen.	Gms.	G	A	Pts.	Pen.
85-86—Dukla Jihlava	Czech.	35	3	7	10	85	—	—	—	—	—
86-87—Minnesota	NHL	72	2	9	11	148	—	—	—	—	—
87-88—Minnesota	NHL	80	9	8	17	213	—	—	—	—	—
88-89—Minnesota	NHL	55	1	19	20	54	5	1	1	2	4
89-90—Minnesota	NHL	56	2	8	10	109	4	0	0	0	14
90-91—Minnesota	NHL	8	0	2	2	23	—	—	—	—	—
—Calgary	NHL	67	7	14	21	160	7	0	0	0	10
91-92—Calgary	NHL	78	4	8	12	103	—	—	—	—	—
92-93—Calgary	NHL	80	6	10	16	131	6	1	1	2	7
NHL totals		496	31	78	109	941	22	2	2	4	35

MUZZATTI, JASON
G, FLAMES

PERSONAL: Born February 3, 1970, at Toronto.... 6-1/190.... Shoots left.... Full name: Jason Mark Muzzatti.... Name pronounced muh-ZAH-tee.
COLLEGE: Michigan State.
TRANSACTIONS/CAREER NOTES: Selected by Calgary Flames in first round (first Flames pick, 21st overall) of NHL entry draft (June 11, 1988).... Loaned to Indianapolis Ice (January 11, 1993).
HONORS: Named to CCHA All-Star second team (1987-88).... Named to NCAA All-America West second team (1989-90).... Named to CCHA All-Star first team (1989-90).... Named to CCHA All-Tournament team (1989-90).

M

			REGULAR SEASON								PLAYOFFS					
Season	Team	League	Gms.	Min.	W	L	T	GA	SO	Avg.	Gms.	Min.	W	L	GA	SO	Avg.
86-87—St. Mikes Jr. B	MTHL	20	1054	...	...	...	69	1	3.93	—	—	—	—	—	—	—
87-88—Michigan State	CCHA	33	1916	19	9	3	109	1	3.41	—	—	—	—	—	—	—
88-89—Michigan State	CCHA	42	2515	32	9	1	127	3	3.03	—	—	—	—	—	—	—
89-90—Michigan State	CCHA	33	1976	24	6	0	99	0	3.01	—	—	—	—	—	—	—
90-91—Michigan State	CCHA	22	1204	8	10	2	75	0	3.74	—	—	—	—	—	—	—
91-92—Salt Lake City	IHL	52	3033	24	22	5	167	2	3.30	4	247	1	3	18	0	4.37
92-93—Salt Lake City	IHL	13	747	5	6	0	52	0	4.18	—	—	—	—	—	—	—
—Can. national team	Int'l	16	880	6	9	0	53	0	3.64	—	—	—	—	—	—	—
—Indianapolis	IHL	12	707	5	6	0	48	0	4.07	—	—	—	—	—	—	—

MYHRES, BRANTT
LW, LIGHTNING

PERSONAL: Born March 18, 1974, at Edmonton, Alta. . . . 6-3/195. . . . Shoots right. . . . Name pronounced MY-ers.
HIGH SCHOOL: Sir Winston Churchill (Calgary, Alta.).
TRANSACTIONS/CAREER NOTES: Selected by Tampa Bay Lightning in fifth round (fifth Lightning pick, 97th overall) of NHL entry draft (June 20, 1992).

			REGULAR SEASON				PLAYOFFS			
Season	Team	League	Gms.	G	A	Pts.	Pen.	Gms.	G	A	Pts.	Pen.
90-91—Portland	WHL	59	2	7	9	125	—	—	—	—	—
91-92—Portland	WHL	4	0	2	2	22	—	—	—	—	—
—Lethbridge	WHL	53	4	11	15	359	5	0	0	0	36
92-93—Lethbridge	WHL	64	13	35	48	277	3	0	0	0	11

MYRVOLD, ANDERS
D, NORDIQUES

PERSONAL: Born August 12, 1975, at Lorenskog, Norway. . . . 6-1/178. . . . Shoots left.
TRANSACTIONS/CAREER NOTES: Selected by Quebec Nordiques in fifth round (sixth Nordiques pick, 127th overall) of NHL entry draft (June 26, 1993).

			REGULAR SEASON				PLAYOFFS			
Season	Team	League	Gms.	G	A	Pts.	Pen.	Gms.	G	A	Pts.	Pen.
92-93—Farjestad	Sweden	2	0	0	0	0	—	—	—	—	—

NASLUND, MARKUS
LW, PENGUINS

PERSONAL: Born July 30, 1973, at Harnosand, Sweden. . . . 5-11/174. . . . Shoots left.
TRANSACTIONS/CAREER NOTES: Selected by Pittsburgh Penguins in first round (first Penguins pick, 16th overall) of NHL entry draft (June 22, 1991).

			REGULAR SEASON				PLAYOFFS			
Season	Team	League	Gms.	G	A	Pts.	Pen.	Gms.	G	A	Pts.	Pen.
89-90—MoDo	Sweden Jr.	33	43	35	78	20	—	—	—	—	—
90-91—MoDo	Sweden	32	10	9	19	14	—	—	—	—	—
91-92—MoDo	Sweden	39	22	17	39	52	—	—	—	—	—
92-93—MoDo	Sweden	39	22	17	39	67	3	3	2	5	0

NASREDDINE, ALAIN
D, PANTHERS

PERSONAL: Born July 10, 1975, at Montreal. . . . 6-1/201. . . . Shoots left.
TRANSACTIONS/CAREER NOTES: Selected by Florida Panthers in sixth round (eighth Panthers pick, 135th overall) of NHL entry draft (June 26, 1993).

			REGULAR SEASON				PLAYOFFS			
Season	Team	League	Gms.	G	A	Pts.	Pen.	Gms.	G	A	Pts.	Pen.
91-92—Drummondville	QMJHL	61	1	9	10	78	4	0	0	0	17
92-93—Drummondville	QMJHL	64	0	14	14	137	10	0	1	1	36

NATTRESS, RIC
D, FLYERS

PERSONAL: Born May 25, 1962, at Hamilton, Ont. . . . 6-2/210. . . . Shoots right. . . . Full name: Eric Ric Nattress.
TRANSACTIONS/CAREER NOTES: Selected by Montreal Canadiens as underage junior in second round (second Canadiens pick, 27th overall) of NHL entry draft (June 11, 1980). . . . Suspended 40 games by NHL following his conviction in Ontario court for drug possession (September 1983). . . . Fractured finger (March 1984). . . . Traded by Canadiens to St. Louis Blues to complete June deal for RW Mark Hunter (September 1985). . . . Injured shoulder (March 17, 1986). . . . Strained knee (February 1987). . . . Traded by Blues to Calgary Flames for fourth-round pick in 1987 draft (LW Andy Rymsha) and fifth-round pick in 1988 draft (RW Dave Lacouture) (June 13, 1987). . . . Bruised right shoulder (March 1988). . . . Underwent knee surgery (March 1988). . . . Pulled hamstring (November 1988). . . . Injured groin (February 1989). . . . Bruised hand (December 10, 1989); missed six games. . . . Broke right ankle (February 7, 1990); in cast until March 16. . . . Underwent surgery for torn knee cartilage (September 27, 1990). . . . Twisted knee (October 22, 1991); missed 16 games. . . . Underwent arthroscopic knee surgery (November 4, 1991). . . . Bruised left foot (December 21, 1991); missed four games. . . . Traded by Flames with C Doug Gilmour, LW Kent Manderville, D Jamie Macoun and G Rick Wamsley to Toronto Maple Leafs for LW Craig Berube, D Alexander Godynyuk, LW Gary Leeman, D Michel Petit and G Jeff Reese (January 2, 1992). . . . Signed as free agent by Philadelphia Flyers (August 21, 1992). . . . Strained lower back prior to 1992-93 season; missed first 23 games of season. . . . Suffered sinus infection (March 2, 1993); missed one game. . . . Bruised left leg (March 11, 1993); missed one game. . . . Bruised left knee (March 21, 1993); missed remainder of season.
MISCELLANEOUS: Member of Stanley Cup championship team (1989).

Season	Team	League	REGULAR SEASON					PLAYOFFS				
			Gms.	G	A	Pts.	Pen.	Gms.	G	A	Pts.	Pen.
79-80	Brantford	OMJHL	65	3	21	24	94	11	1	6	7	38
80-81	Brantford	OMJHL	51	8	34	42	106	6	1	4	5	19
81-82	Brantford	OHL	59	11	50	61	126	11	3	7	10	17
	Nova Scotia	AHL	—	—	—	—	—	5	0	1	1	7
82-83	Nova Scotia	AHL	9	0	4	4	16	—	—	—	—	—
	Montreal	NHL	40	1	3	4	19	3	0	0	0	10
83-84	Montreal	NHL	34	0	12	12	15	—	—	—	—	—
84-85	Sherbrooke	AHL	72	8	40	48	37	16	4	13	17	20
	Montreal	NHL	5	0	1	1	2	2	0	0	0	2
85-86	St. Louis	NHL	78	4	20	24	52	18	1	4	5	24
86-87	St. Louis	NHL	73	6	22	28	24	6	0	0	0	2
87-88	Calgary	NHL	63	2	13	15	37	6	1	3	4	0
88-89	Calgary	NHL	38	1	8	9	47	19	0	3	3	20
89-90	Calgary	NHL	49	1	14	15	26	6	2	0	2	8
90-91	Calgary	NHL	58	5	13	18	63	7	1	0	1	2
91-92	Calgary	NHL	18	0	5	5	31	—	—	—	—	—
	Toronto	NHL	36	2	14	16	32	—	—	—	—	—
92-93	Philadelphia	NHL	44	7	10	17	29	—	—	—	—	—
NHL totals			536	29	135	164	377	67	5	10	15	68

NAZAROV, ANDREI
LW, SHARKS

PERSONAL: Born March 21, 1972, at Chelyabinsk, U.S.S.R. . . . 6-4/209. . . . Shoots right.
TRANSACTIONS/CAREER NOTES: Selected by San Jose Sharks in first round (second Sharks pick, 10th overall) of NHL entry draft (June 20, 1992).

Season	Team	League	REGULAR SEASON					PLAYOFFS				
			Gms.	G	A	Pts.	Pen.	Gms.	G	A	Pts.	Pen.
90-91	Mechel Chelyabinsk	USSR	2	0	0	0	0	—	—	—	—	—
91-92	Dynamo Moscow	CIS	2	1	0	1	2	—	—	—	—	—
92-93	Dynamo Moscow	CIS	42	8	2	10	79	10	1	1	2	8

NEATON, PATRICK
D, PENGUINS

PERSONAL: Born May 21, 1971, at Redford, Mich. . . . 6-0/180. . . . Shoots left.
COLLEGE: Michigan.
TRANSACTIONS/CAREER NOTES: Selected by Pittsburgh Penguins in seventh round (ninth Penguins pick, 145th overall) of NHL entry draft (June 16, 1990).
HONORS: Named to CCHA All-Star second team (1990-91). . . . Named to CCHA All-Star first team (1992-93).

Season	Team	League	REGULAR SEASON					PLAYOFFS				
			Gms.	G	A	Pts.	Pen.	Gms.	G	A	Pts.	Pen.
89-90	University of Michigan	CCHA	42	3	23	26	36	—	—	—	—	—
90-91	University of Michigan	CCHA	44	15	28	43	78	—	—	—	—	—
91-92	University of Michigan	CCHA	43	10	20	30	62	—	—	—	—	—
92-93	University of Michigan	CCHA	38	10	18	28	37	—	—	—	—	—

NEDVED, PETR
C, CANUCKS

PERSONAL: Born December 9, 1971, at Liberec, Czechoslovakia. . . . 6-3/185. . . . Shoots left. . . . Name pronounced NEHD-VEHD.
TRANSACTIONS/CAREER NOTES: Defected from Czechoslovakia to Canada when Czechoslovakian midget team was playing in Calgary, Alberta (January 1989). . . . WHL rights traded by Moose Jaw Warriors with D Brian Ilkuf to Seattle Thunderbirds for D Corey Beaulieu (February 3, 1989). . . . Selected by Vancouver Canucks in first round (first Canucks pick, second overall) of NHL entry draft (June 16, 1990).
HONORS: Won Can.HL Rookie of the Year Award (1989-90). . . . Won Jim Piggott Memorial Trophy (1989-90).

Season	Team	League	REGULAR SEASON					PLAYOFFS				
			Gms.	G	A	Pts.	Pen.	Gms.	G	A	Pts.	Pen.
89-90	Seattle	WHL	71	65	80	145	80	11	4	9	13	2
90-91	Vancouver	NHL	61	10	6	16	20	6	0	1	1	0
91-92	Vancouver	NHL	77	15	22	37	36	10	1	4	5	16
92-93	Vancouver	NHL	84	38	33	71	96	12	2	3	5	2
NHL totals			222	63	61	124	152	28	3	8	11	18

NEDVED, ZDENEK
RW, MAPLE LEAFS

PERSONAL: Born March 3, 1975, at Lany, Czechoslovakia. . . . 6-0/179. . . . Shoots left.
TRANSACTIONS/CAREER NOTES: Selected by Toronto Maple Leafs in fifth round (third Leafs pick, 123rd overall) of NHL entry draft (June 26, 1993).

Season	Team	League	REGULAR SEASON					PLAYOFFS				
			Gms.	G	A	Pts.	Pen.	Gms.	G	A	Pts.	Pen.
91-92	PZ Kladno	Czech.	19	15	12	27	22	—	—	—	—	—
92-93	Sudbury	OHL	18	3	9	12	6	—	—	—	—	—

NEEDHAM, MIKE
RW, PENGUINS

PERSONAL: Born April 4, 1970, at Calgary, Alta. . . . 5-10/185. . . . Shoots right.
TRANSACTIONS/CAREER NOTES: Selected by Pittsburgh Penguins in sixth round (seventh Penguins pick, 126th overall) of NHL entry draft (June 17, 1989). . . . Sprained left knee (October 8, 1992); missed one game. . . . Suffered back spasms (December 11, 1992);

missed eight games.... Bruised left foot (February 25, 1993); missed one game.
HONORS: Shared Most Dedicated Player Trophy with Bob Calhoon (1985-86).... Named to WHL (West) All-Star first team (1989-90).
MISCELLANEOUS: Member of Stanley Cup championship team (1992).

Season	Team	League	REGULAR SEASON					PLAYOFFS				
			Gms.	G	A	Pts.	Pen.	Gms.	G	A	Pts.	Pen.
85-86	Fort Saskatchewan	AJHL	49	19	26	45	97	—	—	—	—	—
86-87	Fort Saskatchewan	AJHL				Statistics unavailable.						
	Kamloops	WHL	3	1	2	3	0	11	2	1	3	5
87-88	Kamloops	WHL	64	31	33	64	93	5	0	1	1	5
88-89	Kamloops	WHL	49	24	27	51	55	16	2	9	11	13
89-90	Kamloops	WHL	60	59	66	125	75	17	11	13	24	10
90-91	Muskegon	IHL	65	14	32	46	17	5	2	2	4	5
91-92	Muskegon	IHL	80	41	37	78	83	8	4	4	8	6
	Pittsburgh	NHL	—	—	—	—	—	5	1	0	1	2
92-93	Pittsburgh	NHL	56	8	5	13	14	9	1	0	1	2
	Cleveland	IHL	1	2	0	2	0	—	—	—	—	—
NHL totals			**56**	**8**	**5**	**13**	**14**	**14**	**2**	**0**	**2**	**4**

NEELY, CAM
RW, BRUINS

PERSONAL: Born June 6, 1965, at Comox, B.C.... 6-1/210.... Shoots right.... Full name: Cameron Michael Neely.
TRANSACTIONS/CAREER NOTES: Selected by Vancouver Canucks as underage junior in first round (first Canucks pick, ninth overall) of NHL entry draft (June 8, 1983).... Dislocated kneecap (October 1984).... Traded by Canucks with first-round pick in 1987 draft (D Glen Wesley) to Boston Bruins for C Barry Pederson (June 6, 1986).... Slipped right kneecap (March 1988).... Fractured right thumb and inflamed right knee (December 1988). ... Suffered recurrance of right knee inflammation (March 1989).... Hyperextended knee (October 1989).... Pulled groin (March 1990).... Suspended five games by NHL for high-sticking (November 23, 1990).... Suffered thigh injury (May 11, 1991); missed first 38 games of 1991-92 season.... Suffered knee inflammation (January 1992).... Underwent knee surgery (February 3, 1992); missed remainder of season.... Underwent arthroscopic knee surgery (September 17, 1992); missed first 60 games of season.... Injured knee (March 1993); missed eight games.... Injured knee (April 1993); missed three games.
HONORS: Named to THE SPORTING NEWS All-Star first team (1987-88).... Named to NHL All-Star second team (1987-88, 1989-90 and 1990-91).... Played in NHL All-Star Game (1988 through 1991).... Named to THE SPORTING NEWS All-Star second team (1989-90 and 1990-91).
RECORDS: Shares NHL single-season playoff record for most power-play goals—9 (1991).

Season	Team	League	REGULAR SEASON					PLAYOFFS				
			Gms.	G	A	Pts.	Pen.	Gms.	G	A	Pts.	Pen.
82-83	Portland	WHL	72	56	64	120	130	14	9	11	20	17
83-84	Portland	WHL	19	8	18	26	29	—	—	—	—	—
	Vancouver	NHL	56	16	15	31	57	4	2	0	2	2
84-85	Vancouver	NHL	72	21	18	39	137	—	—	—	—	—
85-86	Vancouver	NHL	73	14	20	34	126	3	0	0	0	6
86-87	Boston	NHL	75	36	36	72	143	4	5	1	6	8
87-88	Boston	NHL	69	42	27	69	175	23	9	8	17	51
88-89	Boston	NHL	74	37	38	75	190	10	7	2	9	8
89-90	Boston	NHL	76	55	37	92	117	21	12	16	28	51
90-91	Boston	NHL	69	51	40	91	98	19	16	4	20	36
91-92	Boston	NHL	9	9	3	12	16	—	—	—	—	—
92-93	Boston	NHL	13	11	7	18	25	4	4	1	5	4
NHL totals			**586**	**292**	**241**	**533**	**1084**	**88**	**55**	**32**	**87**	**166**

NELSON, CHRISTOPHER
D, DEVILS

PERSONAL: Born February 12, 1969, at Philadelphia. ... 6-2/190. ... Shoots right.... Full name: Christopher Viscount Nelson.
COLLEGE: Wisconsin.
TRANSACTIONS/CAREER NOTES: Selected by New Jersey Devils in fifth round (sixth Devils pick, 96th overall) of NHL entry draft (June 11, 1988).

Season	Team	League	REGULAR SEASON					PLAYOFFS				
			Gms.	G	A	Pts.	Pen.	Gms.	G	A	Pts.	Pen.
87-88	Rochester	USHL	48	6	29	35	82	—	—	—	—	—
88-89	University of Wisconsin	WCHA	21	1	4	5	24	—	—	—	—	—
89-90	University of Wisconsin	WCHA	38	1	3	4	38	—	—	—	—	—
90-91	University of Wisconsin	WCHA	42	5	12	17	48	—	—	—	—	—
91-92	University of Wisconsin	WCHA	43	4	12	16	96	—	—	—	—	—
92-93	Utica	AHL	21	1	1	2	20	1	0	0	0	2
	Cincinnati	IHL	58	4	26	30	69	—	—	—	—	—

NELSON, JEFF
C, CAPITALS

PERSONAL: Born December 18, 1972, at Prince Albert, Sask.... 6-0/180.... Shoots left.... Full name: Jeffrey Arthur Nelson.... Brother of Todd Nelson, defenseman in Pittsburgh Penguins system.
TRANSACTIONS/CAREER NOTES: Selected by Washington Capitals in second round (fourth Capitals pick, 36th overall) of NHL entry draft (June 22, 1991).
HONORS: Won Can.HL Scholastic Player of the Year Award (1988-89 and 1989-90).... Named WHL Scholastic Player of the Year (1988-89 and 1989-90).... Named WHL (East) Player of the Year (1990-91).... Named to WHL All-Star second team (1990-91).... Named to WHL (East) All-Star second team (1991-92).

Season Team	League	REGULAR SEASON					PLAYOFFS				
		Gms.	G	A	Pts.	Pen.	Gms.	G	A	Pts.	Pen.
88-89—Prince Albert	WHL	71	30	57	87	74	4	0	3	3	4
89-90—Prince Albert	WHL	72	28	69	97	79	14	2	11	13	10
90-91—Prince Albert	WHL	72	46	74	120	58	3	1	1	2	4
91-92—Prince Albert	WHL	64	48	65	113	84	9	7	14	21	18
92-93—Baltimore	AHL	72	14	38	52	12	7	1	3	4	2

NELSON, TODD

D, PENGUINS

PERSONAL: Born May 15, 1969, at Prince Albert, Sask.... 6-0/200.... Shoots left.... Brother of Jeff Nelson, center in Washington Capitals system.
TRANSACTIONS/CAREER NOTES: Dislocated right shoulder (October 1986).... Dislocated left shoulder (May 1987).... Selected by Pittsburgh Penguins in fourth round (fourth Penguins pick, 79th overall) of NHL entry draft (June 17, 1989).
HONORS: Named to WHL All-Star second team (1988-89 and 1989-90).

Season Team	League	REGULAR SEASON					PLAYOFFS				
		Gms.	G	A	Pts.	Pen.	Gms.	G	A	Pts.	Pen.
85-86—Prince Albert	WHL	4	0	0	0	0	—	—	—	—	—
86-87—Prince Albert	WHL	35	1	6	7	10	4	0	0	0	0
87-88—Prince Albert	WHL	72	3	21	24	59	10	3	2	5	4
88-89—Prince Albert	WHL	72	14	45	59	72	4	1	3	4	4
89-90—Prince Albert	WHL	69	13	42	55	88	14	3	12	15	12
90-91—Muskegon	IHL	79	4	20	24	32	3	0	0	0	4
91-92—Muskegon	IHL	80	6	35	41	46	14	1	11	12	4
—Pittsburgh	NHL	1	0	0	0	0	—	—	—	—	—
92-93—Cleveland	IHL	76	7	35	42	115	4	0	2	2	4
NHL totals		1	0	0	0	0					

NEMCHINOV, SERGEI

C, RANGERS

PERSONAL: Born January 14, 1964, at Moscow, U.S.S.R. ... 6-0/199. ... Shoots left.... Name pronounced SUHR-gay nehm-CHEE-nahf.
TRANSACTIONS/CAREER NOTES: Selected by New York Rangers in 12th round (14th Rangers pick, 244th overall) of NHL entry draft (June 16, 1990).... Sprained knee (November 4, 1991); missed seven games.... Strained buttock (April 4, 1993); missed three games.

Season Team	League	REGULAR SEASON					PLAYOFFS				
		Gms.	G	A	Pts.	Pen.	Gms.	G	A	Pts.	Pen.
81-82—Soviet Wings	USSR	15	1	0	1	0	—	—	—	—	—
82-83—CSKA Moscow	USSR	11	0	0	0	2	—	—	—	—	—
83-84—CSKA Moscow	USSR	20	6	5	11	4	—	—	—	—	—
84-85—CSKA Moscow	USSR	31	2	4	6	4	—	—	—	—	—
85-86—Soviet Wings	USSR	39	7	12	19	28	—	—	—	—	—
86-87—Soviet Wings	USSR	40	13	9	22	24	—	—	—	—	—
87-88—Soviet Wings	USSR	48	17	11	28	26	—	—	—	—	—
88-89—Soviet Wings	USSR	43	15	14	29	28	—	—	—	—	—
89-90—Soviet Wings	USSR	48	17	16	33	34	—	—	—	—	—
90-91—Soviet Wings	USSR	46	21	24	45	30	—	—	—	—	—
91-92—New York Rangers	NHL	73	30	28	58	15	13	1	4	5	8
92-93—New York Rangers	NHL	81	23	31	54	34	—	—	—	—	—
NHL totals		154	53	59	112	49	13	1	4	5	8

NEWMAN, THOMAS

G, KINGS

PERSONAL: Born February 23, 1971, at Golden Valley, Minn.... 6-1/185.... Shoots left.... Full name: Thomas Dean Newman.
HIGH SCHOOL: Blaine (Minn.).
COLLEGE: Minnesota.
TRANSACTIONS/CAREER NOTES: Broke foot (April 1987).... Selected by Los Angeles Kings in fifth round (fourth Kings pick, 103rd overall) of NHL entry draft (June 17, 1989).

Season Team	League	REGULAR SEASON							PLAYOFFS					
		Gms.	Min.	W	L	T	GA	SO	Avg.	Gms.	Min.	W	L	GA	SO	Avg.
87-88—Blaine H.S.	Minn. HS	16	960	...	...	...	32	...	2.00	—	—	—	—	—	—	—
88-89—Blaine H.S.	Minn. HS	18	810	...	...	...	43	3	3.19	—	—	—	—	—	—	—
89-90—Univ. of Minnesota	WCHA	35	1982	19	13	2	127	0	3.84	—	—	—	—	—	—	—
90-91—Univ. of Minnesota	WCHA	22	942	12	2	2	54	2	3.44	—	—	—	—	—	—	—
91-92—Univ. of Minnesota	WCHA	12	418	5	1	0	17	0	2.44	—	—	—	—	—	—	—
92-93—Univ. of Minnesota	WCHA	22	1172	14	4	2	61	2	3.12	—	—	—	—	—	—	—

NICHOLLS, BERNIE

C, DEVILS

PERSONAL: Born June 24, 1961, at Haliburton, Ont.... 6-0/185.... Shoots right.... Full name: Bernard Irvine Nicholls.
TRANSACTIONS/CAREER NOTES: Selected by Los Angeles Kings as underage junior in fourth round (fourth Kings pick, 73rd overall) of NHL entry draft (June 11, 1980).... Suffered partial tear of medial colateral ligament in right knee (November 18, 1982).... Suffered broken jaw (February 1984); missed two games.... Fractured left index finger in three places (October 8, 1987).... Traded by Kings to New York Rangers for RW Tomas Sandstrom and LW Tony Granato (January 20, 1990).... Separated left shoulder (January 22, 1991); missed five games.... Suspended three games by NHL for stick-swinging incident (February 14, 1991).... Traded by Rangers with LW Louie DeBrusk, RW Steven Rice and future considerations to Edmonton Oilers for C Mark Messier and future considerations (October 4, 1991); Rangers traded D David Shaw to Oilers for D Jeff Beukeboom to complete the deal (November 12, 1991)....

N

Did not report to Oilers to be with his wife for the birth of their child (October 4, 1991); missed 27 games. . . . Reported to Oilers (December 6, 1991). . . . Strained abdominal muscle (February 16, 1992); missed two games. . . . Suspended seven off-days and fined $500 by NHL for swinging stick in preseason game (October 13, 1992). . . . Traded by Oilers to New Jersey Devils for C Kevin Todd and LW Zdeno Ciger (January 13, 1993). . . . Fractured left foot (February 27, 1993); missed 13 games.
HONORS: Played in NHL All-Star Game (1984, 1989 and 1990).

			REGULAR SEASON					PLAYOFFS			
Season Team	League	Gms.	G	A	Pts.	Pen.	Gms.	G	A	Pts.	Pen.
78-79—Kingston	OMJHL	2	0	1	1	0	—	—	—	—	—
79-80—Kingston	OMJHL	68	36	43	79	85	3	1	0	1	10
80-81—Kingston	OMJHL	65	63	89	152	109	14	8	10	18	17
81-82—New Haven	AHL	55	41	30	71	31	—	—	—	—	—
—Los Angeles	NHL	22	14	18	32	27	10	4	0	4	23
82-83—Los Angeles	NHL	71	28	22	50	124	—	—	—	—	—
83-84—Los Angeles	NHL	78	41	54	95	83	—	—	—	—	—
84-85—Los Angeles	NHL	80	46	54	100	76	3	1	1	2	9
85-86—Los Angeles	NHL	80	36	61	97	78	—	—	—	—	—
86-87—Los Angeles	NHL	80	33	48	81	101	5	2	5	7	6
87-88—Los Angeles	NHL	65	32	46	78	114	5	2	6	8	11
88-89—Los Angeles	NHL	79	70	80	150	96	11	7	9	16	12
89-90—Los Angeles	NHL	47	27	48	75	66	—	—	—	—	—
—New York Rangers	NHL	32	12	25	37	20	10	7	5	12	16
90-91—New York Rangers	NHL	71	25	48	73	96	5	4	3	7	8
91-92—New York Rangers	NHL	1	0	0	0	0	—	—	—	—	—
—Edmonton	NHL	49	20	29	49	60	16	8	11	19	25
92-93—Edmonton	NHL	46	8	32	40	40	—	—	—	—	—
—New Jersey	NHL	23	5	15	20	40	5	0	0	0	6
NHL totals		824	397	580	977	1021	70	35	40	75	116

NIECKAR, BARRY
LW, WHALERS

PERSONAL: Born December 16, 1967, at Rama, Sask. . . . 6-3/200. . . . Shoots left.
TRANSACTIONS/CAREER NOTES: Signed as free agent by Hartford Whalers (September 1992).

			REGULAR SEASON					PLAYOFFS			
Season Team	League	Gms.	G	A	Pts.	Pen.	Gms.	G	A	Pts.	Pen.
91-92—Phoenix	IHL	5	0	0	0	9	—	—	—	—	—
—Raleigh	ECHL	46	10	18	28	229	4	4	0	4	22
92-93—Springfield	AHL	21	2	4	6	65	6	1	0	1	14
—Hartford	NHL	2	0	0	0	2	—	—	—	—	—
NHL totals		2	0	0	0	2	—	—	—	—	—

NIEDERMAYER, ROB
C, PANTHERS

PERSONAL: Born December 28, 1974, at Cassiar, B.C. . . . 6-2/200. . . . Shoots left. . . . Brother of Scott Niedermayer, defenseman, New Jersey Devils.
COLLEGE: Medicine Hat.
TRANSACTIONS/CAREER NOTES: Selected by Florida Panthers in first round (first Panthers pick, fifth overall) of NHL entry draft (June 26, 1993).
HONORS: Won the WHL Top Draft Prospect Award (1992-93). . . . Named to WHL (East) All-Star first team (1992-93).

			REGULAR SEASON					PLAYOFFS			
Season Team	League	Gms.	G	A	Pts.	Pen.	Gms.	G	A	Pts.	Pen.
90-91—Medicine Hat	WHL	71	24	26	50	8	12	3	7	10	2
91-92—Medicine Hat	WHL	71	32	46	78	77	4	2	3	5	2
92-93—Medicine Hat	WHL	52	43	34	77	67	—	—	—	—	—

NIEDERMAYER, SCOTT
D, DEVILS

PERSONAL: Born August 31, 1973, at Edmonton, Alta. . . . 6-0/200. . . . Shoots left. . . . Brother of Rob Niedermayer, Center, Florida Panthers. . . . Name pronounced NEE-duhr-MIGH-uhr.
TRANSACTIONS/CAREER NOTES: Stretched left knee ligaments (March 12, 1991); missed nine games. . . . Selected by New Jersey Devils in first round (first Devils pick, third overall) of NHL entry draft (June 22, 1991). . . . Suffered sore back (December 9, 1992); missed four games.
HONORS: Won Can.HL Scholastic Player of the Year Award (1990-91). . . . Named WHL Scholastic Player of the Year (1990-91). . . . Named to WHL (West) All-Star first team (1990-91 and 1991-92). . . . Won Stafford Smythe Memorial Trophy (1991-92). . . . Named to Can.HL All-Star first team (1991-92). . . . Named to Memorial Cup All-Star team (1991-92). . . . Named to NHL All-Rookie team (1992-93).

			REGULAR SEASON					PLAYOFFS			
Season Team	League	Gms.	G	A	Pts.	Pen.	Gms.	G	A	Pts.	Pen.
89-90—Kamloops	WHL	64	14	55	69	64	17	2	14	16	35
90-91—Kamloops	WHL	57	26	56	82	52	—	—	—	—	—
91-92—New Jersey	NHL	4	0	1	1	2	—	—	—	—	—
—Kamloops	WHL	35	7	32	39	61	17	9	14	23	28
92-93—New Jersey	NHL	80	11	29	40	47	5	0	3	3	2
NHL totals		84	11	30	41	49	5	0	3	3	2

NIELSEN, JEFFREY
RW, RANGERS

PERSONAL: Born September 20, 1971, at Grand Rapids, Minn. . . . 6-0/170. . . . Shoots right. . . . Full name: Jeffrey Michael Nielsen.
HIGH SCHOOL: Grand Rapids (Minn.).
COLLEGE: Minnesota.
TRANSACTIONS/CAREER NOTES: Selected by New York Rangers in fourth round (fourth Rangers pick, 69th overall) of NHL entry draft (June 16, 1990).

Season Team	League	REGULAR SEASON					PLAYOFFS				
		Gms.	G	A	Pts.	Pen.	Gms.	G	A	Pts.	Pen.
87-88—Grand Rapids H.S............	Minn. H.S.	21	9	11	20	14	—	—	—	—	—
88-89—Grand Rapids H.S............	Minn. H.S.	25	13	17	30	26	—	—	—	—	—
89-90—Grand Rapids H.S............	Minn. H.S.	28	32	25	57	...	—	—	—	—	—
90-91—University of Minnesota ...	WCHA	45	11	14	25	50	—	—	—	—	—
91-92—University of Minnesota ...	WCHA	44	15	15	30	74	—	—	—	—	—
92-93—University of Minnesota ...	WCHA	42	21	20	41	80	—	—	—	—	—

NIEUWENDYK, JOE
C, FLAMES

PERSONAL: Born September 10, 1966, at Oshawa, Ont. . . . 6-1/175. . . . Shoots left. . . . Name pronounced NOO-ihn-DIGHK. . . . Cousin of Jeff Beukeboom, defenseman, New York Rangers.
COLLEGE: Cornell.
TRANSACTIONS/CAREER NOTES: Selected by Calgary Flames in second round (second Flames pick, 27th overall) of NHL entry draft (June 15, 1985). . . . Suffered concussion (November 1987). . . . Bruised ribs (May 25, 1989). . . . Tore anterior cruciate ligament of left knee (April 17, 1990). . . . Underwent arthroscopic surgery to knee (September 28, 1991); missed 12 games. . . . Suffered from the flu (November 19, 1992); missed one game. . . . Strained right knee (March 26, 1993); missed four games.
HONORS: Won Ivy League Rookie of the Year Trophy (1984-85). . . . Named to NCAA All-America East first team (1985-86 and 1986-87). . . . Named to ECAC All-Star first team (1985-86 and 1986-87). . . . Named ECAC Player of the Year (1986-87). . . . Named NHL Rookie of the Year by THE SPORTING NEWS (1987-88). . . . Won Calder Memorial Trophy (1987-88). . . . Won Dodge Ram Tough Award (1987-88). . . . Named to NHL All-Rookie team (1987-88). . . . Played in NHL All-Star Game (1988 through 1990).
RECORDS: Shares NHL single-game record for most goals in one period—4 (January 11, 1989).
MISCELLANEOUS: Member of Stanley Cup championship team (1989).
STATISTICAL NOTES: Only the third player in NHL history to score 50 goals in each of his first two seasons.

Season Team	League	REGULAR SEASON					PLAYOFFS				
		Gms.	G	A	Pts.	Pen.	Gms.	G	A	Pts.	Pen.
83-84—Pickering Jr. B	MTHL	38	30	28	58	35	—	—	—	—	—
84-85—Cornell University	ECAC	29	21	24	45	30	—	—	—	—	—
85-86—Cornell University	ECAC	29	26	28	54	67	—	—	—	—	—
86-87—Cornell University	ECAC	23	26	26	52	26	—	—	—	—	—
—Calgary............................	NHL	9	5	1	6	0	6	2	2	4	0
87-88—Calgary............................	NHL	75	51	41	92	23	8	3	4	7	2
88-89—Calgary............................	NHL	77	51	31	82	40	22	10	4	14	10
89-90—Calgary............................	NHL	79	45	50	95	40	6	4	6	10	4
90-91—Calgary............................	NHL	79	45	40	85	36	7	4	1	5	10
91-92—Calgary............................	NHL	69	22	34	56	55	—	—	—	—	—
92-93—Calgary............................	NHL	79	38	37	75	52	6	3	6	9	10
NHL totals..		**467**	**257**	**234**	**491**	**246**	**55**	**26**	**23**	**49**	**36**

NIINIMAA, JANNE
D, FLYERS

PERSONAL: Born May 22, 1975, at Raahe, Finland. . . . 6-1/196. . . . Shoots left.
TRANSACTIONS/CAREER NOTES: Selected by Philadelphia Flyers in second round (first Flyers pick, 36th overall) of NHL entry draft (June 26, 1993).

Season Team	League	REGULAR SEASON					PLAYOFFS				
		Gms.	G	A	Pts.	Pen.	Gms.	G	A	Pts.	Pen.
91-92—Karpat Oulu.....................	Finland Dv.II	41	2	11	13	49	—	—	—	—	—
92-93—Karpat Oulu.....................	Finland Dv.II	29	2	3	5	14	—	—	—	—	—
—Karpat Jr.........................	Finland	10	3	9	12	16	—	—	—	—	—

NILSSON, FREDRICK
C, SHARKS

PERSONAL: Born April 16, 1971, at Vasteras, Sweden. . . . 6-1/198. . . . Shoots left. . . . Name pronounced NEEL-son.
TRANSACTIONS/CAREER NOTES: Selected by San Jose Sharks in sixth round (seventh Sharks pick, 111th overall) of NHL entry draft (June 22, 1991).

Season Team	League	REGULAR SEASON					PLAYOFFS				
		Gms.	G	A	Pts.	Pen.	Gms.	G	A	Pts.	Pen.
89-90—Vasteras..........................	Sweden	23	1	1	2	4	1	0	0	0	0
90-91—Vasteras..........................	Sweden	35	13	7	20	20	—	—	—	—	—
91-92—Vasteras..........................	Sweden	40	5	14	19	40	—	—	—	—	—
92-93—Vasteras..........................	Sweden	40	14	15	29	69	1	1	1	2	0

NOBILI, MARIO
LW, OILERS

PERSONAL: Born February 16, 1971, at Montreal. . . . 6-1/185. . . . Shoots left. . . . Name pronounced NOH-bih-lee.
TRANSACTIONS/CAREER NOTES: Selected by Edmonton Oilers in fourth round (fourth Oilers pick, 78th overall) of NHL entry draft (June 22, 1991).

N

Season	Team	League	Gms.	G	A	Pts.	Pen.	Gms.	G	A	Pts.	Pen.
88-89—Longueuil	QMJHL	61	8	6	14	32	—	—	—	—	—	
89-90—Longueuil	QMJHL	67	11	34	45	64	—	—	—	—	—	
90-91—Longueuil	QMJHL	70	33	52	85	115	—	—	—	—	—	
91-92—Longueuil	QMJHL	52	27	48	75	184	18	6	9	15	10	
92-93—Tulsa	CHL	54	31	34	65	102	12	†11	7	18	21	

NOLAN, OWEN
RW, NORDIQUES

PERSONAL: Born February 12, 1972, at Belfast, Northern Ireland. . . . 6-1/194. . . . Shoots right. **TRANSACTIONS/CAREER NOTES:** Separated shoulder (February 22, 1990); missed eight games. . . . Selected by Quebec Nordiques in first round (first Nordiques pick, first overall) of NHL entry draft (June 16, 1990). . . . Suffered concussion, sore knee and sore back (October 1990). . . . Suspended four off-days by NHL for cross-checking (December 7, 1992). . . . Bruised hand (March 2, 1993); missed three games. . . . Suffered shoulder contusion (March 15, 1993); eight games.
HONORS: Won Emms Family Award (1988-89). . . . Won Jim Mahon Memorial Trophy (1989-90). . . . Named to OHL All-Star first team (1989-90). . . . Played in NHL All-Star Game (1992).

Season	Team	League	Gms.	G	A	Pts.	Pen.	Gms.	G	A	Pts.	Pen.
88-89—Cornwall	OHL	62	34	25	59	213	18	5	11	16	41	
89-90—Cornwall	OHL	58	51	59	110	240	6	7	5	12	26	
90-91—Quebec	NHL	59	3	10	13	109	—	—	—	—	—	
—Halifax	AHL	6	4	4	8	11	—	—	—	—	—	
91-92—Quebec	NHL	75	42	31	73	183	—	—	—	—	—	
92-93—Quebec	NHL	73	36	41	77	185	5	1	0	1	2	
NHL totals		207	81	82	163	477	5	1	0	1	2	

NOONAN, BRIAN
C/RW, BLACKHAWKS

PERSONAL: Born May 29, 1965, at Boston. . . . 6-1/180. . . . Shoots right. **HIGH SCHOOL:** Archbishop Williams (Braintree, Mass.). **TRANSACTIONS/CAREER NOTES:** Selected by Chicago Blackhawks in ninth round (10th Blackhawks pick, 179th overall) of NHL entry draft (June 8, 1983). . . . Separated shoulder (April 3, 1988). . . . Refused to report to Indianapolis (October 18, 1990); returned home and suspended without pay by Blackhawks. . . . Suffered death in family (February 28, 1991); missed six games. . . . Damaged left knee ligaments (January 30, 1992); missed 12 games. . . . Bruised shoulder (October 31, 1992); missed four games. . . . Suspended one game by NHL for accumulating three game misconduct penalties (January 21, 1993). . . . Suffered from the flu (February 25, 1993); missed three games.
HONORS: Won Ken McKenzie Trophy (1985-86). . . . Named to IHL All-Star second team (1989-90). . . . Named to IHL All-Star first team (1990-91).

Season	Team	League	Gms.	G	A	Pts.	Pen.	Gms.	G	A	Pts.	Pen.
82-83—Archbishop Williams H.S..	Mass. H.S.	21	26	17	43	. . .	—	—	—	—	—	
83-84—Archbishop Williams H.S..	Mass. H.S.	17	14	23	37	. . .	—	—	—	—	—	
84-85—New Westminster	WHL	72	50	66	116	76	11	8	7	15	4	
85-86—Saginaw	IHL	76	39	39	78	69	11	6	3	9	6	
—Nova Scotia	AHL	2	0	0	0	0	—	—	—	—	—	
86-87—Nova Scotia	AHL	70	25	26	51	30	5	3	1	4	4	
87-88—Chicago	NHL	77	10	20	30	44	3	0	0	0	4	
88-89—Chicago	NHL	45	4	12	16	28	1	0	0	0	0	
—Saginaw	IHL	19	18	13	31	36	1	0	0	0	0	
89-90—Chicago	NHL	8	0	2	2	6	—	—	—	—	—	
—Indianapolis	IHL	56	40	36	76	85	14	6	9	15	20	
90-91—Indianapolis	IHL	59	38	53	91	67	7	6	4	10	18	
—Chicago	NHL	7	0	4	4	2	—	—	—	—	—	
91-92—Chicago	NHL	65	19	12	31	81	18	6	9	15	30	
92-93—Chicago	NHL	63	16	14	30	82	4	3	0	3	4	
NHL totals		265	49	64	113	243	26	9	9	18	38	

NORRIS, DWAYNE
RW, NORDIQUES

PERSONAL: Born January 8, 1970, at St. John's, Nfld. . . . 5-10/175. . . . Shoots right. . . . Full name: Dwayne Carl Norris.
COLLEGE: Michigan State.
TRANSACTIONS/CAREER NOTES: Selected by Quebec Nordiques in seventh round (fifth Nordiques pick, 127th overall) of NHL entry draft (June 16, 1990).
HONORS: Named CCHA Player of the Year (1991-92). . . . Named to NCAA All-America West first team (1991-92). . . . Named to CCHA All-Star first team (1991-92).

Season	Team	League	Gms.	G	A	Pts.	Pen.	Gms.	G	A	Pts.	Pen.
88-89—Michigan State	CCHA	47	16	23	39	40	—	—	—	—	—	
89-90—Michigan State	CCHA	36	19	26	45	30	—	—	—	—	—	
90-91—Michigan State	CCHA	40	26	25	51	60	—	—	—	—	—	
91-92—Michigan State	CCHA	44	*44	39	83	62	—	—	—	—	—	
92-93—Halifax	AHL	50	25	28	53	62	—	—	—	—	—	

NORSTROM, MATTIAS

D, RANGERS

PERSONAL: Born January 2, 1972, at Mora, Sweden. . . . 6-1/196. . . . Name pronounced NOHR-struhm.
TRANSACTIONS/CAREER NOTES: Selected by New York Rangers in second round (second Rangers pick, 48th overall) of NHL entry draft (June 20, 1992).

			REGULAR SEASON					PLAYOFFS			
Season Team	League	Gms.	G	A	Pts.	Pen.	Gms.	G	A	Pts.	Pen.
91-92—AIK Solna	Sweden	39	4	4	8	28	—	—	—	—	—
92-93—AIK Solna	Sweden	22	0	1	1	16	—	—	—	—	—

NORTON, JEFF

D, SHARKS

PERSONAL: Born November 25, 1965, at Cambridge, Mass. . . . 6-2/195. . . . Shoots left. . . . Full name: Jeffrey Zaccari Norton.
HIGH SCHOOL: Cushing Academy (Ashburnham, Mass.).
COLLEGE: Michigan.
TRANSACTIONS/CAREER NOTES: Selected by New York Islanders in third round (third Islanders pick, 62nd overall) of NHL entry draft (June 9, 1984). . . . Bruised ribs (November 16, 1988). . . . Injured groin (February 1990). . . . Strained groin and abdominal muscles (March 2, 1990); missed games. . . . Suffered concussion (April 9, 1990). . . . Suspended eight games by NHL for intentionally injuring another player in preseason game (September 30, 1990). . . . Dislocated right shoulder (November 3, 1990); missed four games. . . . Reinjured shoulder (December 27, 1990); missed five games. . . . Reinjured shoulder and underwent surgery (February 23, 1991); missed remainder of season. . . . Suffered concussion (October 26, 1991); missed one game. . . . Tore ligaments in left wrist (January 3, 1992); missed final 42 games of season. . . . Underwent surgery to left wrist (January 8, 1992). . . . Suffered hip flexor (October 23, 1992); missed five games. . . . Suffered sore shoulder (December 31, 1992); missed one game. . . . Pulled groin (February 25, 1993); missed two games. . . . Traded by Islanders to San Jose Sharks for conditional pick in 1994 draft (June 20, 1993).
HONORS: Named to CCHA All-Star second team (1986-87).

			REGULAR SEASON					PLAYOFFS			
Season Team	League	Gms.	G	A	Pts.	Pen.	Gms.	G	A	Pts.	Pen.
83-84—Cushing Academy	Mass. H.S.	21	22	33	55	. . .	—	—	—	—	—
84-85—University of Michigan	CCHA	37	8	16	24	103	—	—	—	—	—
85-86—University of Michigan	CCHA	37	15	30	45	99	—	—	—	—	—
86-87—University of Michigan	CCHA	39	12	37	49	92	—	—	—	—	—
87-88—U.S. national team	Int'l	57	7	25	32	. . .	—	—	—	—	—
—U.S. Olympic Team	Int'l	6	0	4	4	4	—	—	—	—	—
—New York Islanders	NHL	15	1	6	7	14	3	0	2	2	13
88-89—New York Islanders	NHL	69	1	30	31	74	—	—	—	—	—
89-90—New York Islanders	NHL	60	4	49	53	65	4	1	3	4	17
90-91—New York Islanders	NHL	44	3	25	28	16	—	—	—	—	—
91-92—New York Islanders	NHL	28	1	18	19	18	—	—	—	—	—
92-93—New York Islanders	NHL	66	12	38	50	45	10	1	1	2	4
NHL totals		**282**	**22**	**166**	**188**	**232**	**17**	**2**	**6**	**8**	**34**

NORWOOD, LEE

D

PERSONAL: Born February 2, 1960, at Oakland, Calif. . . . 6-0/190. . . . Shoots left. . . . Full name: Lee Charles Norwood.
HIGH SCHOOL: Trenton (Mich.).
TRANSACTIONS/CAREER NOTES: Selected by Quebec Nordiques as underage junior in third round (third Nordiques pick, 62nd overall) of NHL entry draft (August 9, 1979). . . . Traded by Nordiques to Washington Capitals for C Tim Tookey and seventh-round pick in 1982 draft (D Daniel Poudrier) (January 1982). . . . Traded by Capitals to Toronto Maple Leafs for D Dave Shand (October 6, 1983). . . . Signed as free agent by St. Louis Blues (August 13, 1985). . . . Traded by Blues to Detroit Red Wings for D Larry Trader (August 7, 1986). . . . Pulled stomach muscle (February 1987). . . . Injured groin (October 1987). . . . Injured knee (December 1987). . . . Sprained ankle (November 1988). . . . Pulled hamstring (February 1989). . . . Suffered hip pointer (November 6, 1989); missed six games. . . . Sprained right wrist (March 15, 1990). . . . Traded by Red Wings with future considerations to New Jersey Devils for C Paul Ysebaert; Devils later received fourth-round pick in 1992 draft (D Scott McCabe) to complete deal (November 27, 1990). . . . Separated left shoulder (January 3, 1991); missed six games. . . . Fractured cheekbone and underwent surgery (February 16, 1991); missed 19 games. . . . Underwent surgery to left shoulder (summer 1991). . . . Traded by Devils to Hartford Whalers for future considerations (October 3, 1991). . . . Traded by Whalers to Blues for future considerations (November 13, 1991). . . . Injured ankle (January 28, 1992); missed one game. . . . Broke ankle (January 22, 1993); missed remainder of regular season. . . . Released by Blues (June 30, 1993).
HONORS: Won Governors Trophy (1984-85). . . . Named to IHL All-Star first team (1984-85).

			REGULAR SEASON					PLAYOFFS			
Season Team	League	Gms.	G	A	Pts.	Pen.	Gms.	G	A	Pts.	Pen.
77-78—Hull	QMJHL	51	3	17	20	83	—	—	—	—	—
78-79—Oshawa	OMJHL	61	23	38	61	171	5	2	2	4	17
79-80—Oshawa	OMJHL	60	13	39	52	143	6	2	7	9	15
80-81—Hershey	AHL	52	11	32	43	78	8	0	4	4	14
—Quebec	NHL	11	1	1	2	9	3	0	0	0	2
81-82—Fredericton	AHL	29	6	13	19	74	—	—	—	—	—
—Quebec	NHL	2	0	0	0	2	—	—	—	—	—
—Washington	NHL	26	7	10	17	125	—	—	—	—	—
82-83—Washington	NHL	8	0	1	1	14	—	—	—	—	—
—Hershey	AHL	67	12	36	48	90	5	0	1	1	2
83-84—St. Catharines	AHL	75	13	46	59	91	7	0	5	5	31
84-85—Peoria	IHL	80	17	60	77	229	18	1	11	12	62
85-86—St. Louis	NHL	71	5	24	29	134	19	2	7	9	64
86-87—Adirondack	AHL	3	0	3	3	0	—	—	—	—	—

N

Season	Team	League	REGULAR SEASON					PLAYOFFS				
			Gms.	G	A	Pts.	Pen.	Gms.	G	A	Pts.	Pen.
	—Detroit	NHL	57	6	21	27	163	16	1	6	7	31
87-88	—Detroit	NHL	51	9	22	31	131	16	2	6	8	40
88-89	—Detroit	NHL	66	10	32	42	100	6	1	2	3	16
89-90	—Detroit	NHL	64	8	14	22	95	—	—	—	—	—
90-91	—Detroit	NHL	21	3	7	10	50	—	—	—	—	—
	—New Jersey	NHL	28	3	2	5	87	4	0	0	0	18
91-92	—Hartford	NHL	6	0	0	0	16	—	—	—	—	—
	—St. Louis	NHL	44	3	11	14	94	1	0	1	1	0
92-93	—St. Louis	NHL	32	3	7	10	63	—	—	—	—	—
	NHL totals		487	58	152	210	1083	65	6	22	28	171

NUMMINEN, TEPPO
D, JETS

PERSONAL: Born July 3, 1968, at Tampere, Finland.... 6-1/190.... Shoots right.... Full name: Teppo Kalevi Numminen.... Name pronounced TEH-poh NOO-mih-nehn.
TRANSACTIONS/CAREER NOTES: Selected by Winnipeg Jets in second round (second Jets pick, 29th overall) of NHL entry draft (June 21, 1986).... Separated shoulder (March 5, 1989).... Broke thumb (April 14, 1990).... Fractured foot (January 28, 1993); missed 17 games.
MISCELLANEOUS: Member of silver-medal-winning Finnish Olympic team (1988).

Season	Team	League	REGULAR SEASON					PLAYOFFS				
			Gms.	G	A	Pts.	Pen.	Gms.	G	A	Pts.	Pen.
84-85	—Tappara	Finland	30	14	17	31	10	—	—	—	—	—
85-86	—Tappara	Finland	39	2	4	6	6	8	0	0	0	0
86-87	—Tappara	Finland	44	9	9	18	16	9	4	1	5	4
87-88	—Tappara	Finland	44	10	10	20	29	10	6	6	12	6
88-89	—Winnipeg	NHL	69	1	14	15	36	—	—	—	—	—
89-90	—Winnipeg	NHL	79	11	32	43	20	7	1	2	3	10
90-91	—Winnipeg	NHL	80	8	25	33	28	—	—	—	—	—
91-92	—Winnipeg	NHL	80	5	34	39	32	7	0	0	0	0
92-93	—Winnipeg	NHL	66	7	30	37	33	6	1	1	2	2
	NHL totals		374	32	135	167	149	20	2	3	5	12

NYLANDER, MIKAEL
C, WHALERS

PERSONAL: Born October 3, 1972, at Stockholm, Sweden.... 5-11/176.... Shoots left.... Name pronounced NEE-lan-duhr.
TRANSACTIONS/CAREER NOTES: Selected by Hartford Whalers in third round (fourth Whalers pick, 59th overall) of NHL entry draft (June 22, 1991).... Broke jaw (January 23, 1993); missed 15 games.
HONORS: Named Swedish League Rookie of the Year (1991-92).

Season	Team	League	REGULAR SEASON					PLAYOFFS				
			Gms.	G	A	Pts.	Pen.	Gms.	G	A	Pts.	Pen.
89-90	—Huddinge	Sweden	31	7	15	22	4	—	—	—	—	—
90-91	—Huddinge	Sweden	33	14	20	34	10	—	—	—	—	—
91-92	—AIK Solna	Sweden	40	11	17	28	30	—	—	—	—	—
	—Swedish national Jr. team...	Sweden	7	8	9	17	...	—	—	—	—	—
	—Swedish national team	Int'l	6	0	1	1	0	—	—	—	—	—
92-93	—Hartford	NHL	59	11	22	33	36	—	—	—	—	—
	NHL totals		59	11	22	33	36	—	—	—	—	—

N

NYLUND, GARY
D, ISLANDERS

PERSONAL: Born October 28, 1963, at Surrey, B.C.... 6-4/192.... Shoots left.
TRANSACTIONS/CAREER NOTES: Selected by Toronto Maple Leafs as underage junior in first round (first Maple Leafs pick, third overall) of NHL entry draft (June 9, 1982).... Injured left knee and underwent surgery (September 1982).... Underwent knee surgery (October 1983).... Suffered concussion (November 5, 1984).... Signed as free agent by Chicago Blackhawks (August 27, 1986); Blackhawks sent C Ken Yaremchuk, D Jerome Dupont and fourth-round pick in 1987 draft (LW Joe Sacco) to compensate Maple Leafs.... Bruised elbow (October 1987).... Broke bone in right forearm (September 1988).... Traded by Blackhawks with D Marc Bergevin to New York Islanders for D Steve Konroyd and C Bob Bassen (January 11, 1989).... Underwent arthroscopic surgery to right knee (January 11, 1989); missed 10 games.... Bruised ribs and lung (March 1989).... Irritated right knee ligament (March 8, 1990).... Dislocated right shoulder (December 29, 1990); missed five games.... Fractured left heel (March 25, 1991).... Underwent surgery to heel (March 28, 1991); missed final three games of 1990-91 season and first 52 games of 1991-92 season.... Pulled groin (February 29, 1992); missed 11 games.... Pulled groin (November 14, 1992); missed six games.... Strained right knee ligaments (January 12, 1993); missed remainder of season.
HONORS: Named to WHL All-Star second team (1980-81).... Won Top Defenseman Trophy (1981-82).... Named to WHL All-Star first team (1981-82).... Named to Memorial Cup All-Star team (1981-82).

Season	Team	League	REGULAR SEASON					PLAYOFFS				
			Gms.	G	A	Pts.	Pen.	Gms.	G	A	Pts.	Pen.
78-79	—Delta	BCJHL	57	6	29	35	107	—	—	—	—	—
	—Portland	WHL	2	0	0	0	0	—	—	—	—	—
79-80	—Portland	WHL	72	5	21	26	59	8	0	1	1	2
80-81	—Portland	WHL	70	6	40	46	186	9	1	7	8	17
81-82	—Portland	WHL	65	7	59	66	267	15	3	16	19	74
82-83	—Toronto	NHL	16	0	3	3	16	—	—	—	—	—
83-84	—Toronto	NHL	47	2	14	16	103	—	—	—	—	—
84-85	—Toronto	NHL	76	3	17	20	99	—	—	—	—	—

Season Team	League	REGULAR SEASON					PLAYOFFS				
		Gms.	G	A	Pts.	Pen.	Gms.	G	A	Pts.	Pen.
85-86—Toronto	NHL	79	2	16	18	180	10	0	2	2	25
86-87—Chicago	NHL	80	7	20	27	190	4	0	2	2	11
87-88—Chicago	NHL	76	4	15	19	208	5	0	0	0	10
88-89—Chicago	NHL	23	3	2	5	63	—	—	—	—	—
—New York Islanders	NHL	46	4	8	12	74	—	—	—	—	—
89-90—New York Islanders	NHL	64	4	21	25	144	5	0	2	2	17
90-91—New York Islanders	NHL	72	2	21	23	105	—	—	—	—	—
91-92—New York Islanders	NHL	7	0	1	1	10	—	—	—	—	—
—Capital District	AHL	4	0	0	0	0	—	—	—	—	—
92-93—Capital District	AHL	2	0	0	0	0	—	—	—	—	—
—New York Islanders	NHL	22	1	1	2	43	—	—	—	—	—
NHL totals		608	32	139	171	1235	24	0	6	6	63

OATES, ADAM
C, BRUINS

PERSONAL: Born August 27, 1962, at Weston, Ont. . . . 5-11/190. . . . Shoots right. . . . Name pronounced OHTZ.
COLLEGE: Rensselaer Polytechnic Institute (N.Y.).
TRANSACTIONS/CAREER NOTES: Signed as free agent by Detroit Red Wings (June 28, 1985). . . . Pulled abdominal muscle (October 1987). . . . Suffered from chicken pox (November 1988). . . . Bruised thigh (December 1988). . . . Traded by Red Wings with RW Paul MacLean to St. Louis Blues for LW Tony McKegney and C Bernie Federko (June 15, 1989). . . . Tore rib and abdominal muscles (November 5, 1990); missed 18 games. . . . Traded by Blues to Boston Bruins for C Craig Janney and D Stephane Quintal (February 7, 1992).
HONORS: Named to ECAC All-Star second team (1983-84). . . . Named to NCAA All-America East first team (1984-85). . . . Named to NCAA All-Tournament team (1984-85). . . . Named to ECAC All-Star first team (1984-85). . . . Named to THE SPORTING NEWS All-Star second team (1990-91). . . . Named to NHL All-Star second team (1990-91). . . . Played in NHL All-Star Game (1991 through 1993).

Season Team	League	REGULAR SEASON					PLAYOFFS				
		Gms.	G	A	Pts.	Pen.	Gms.	G	A	Pts.	Pen.
82-83—R.P.I.	ECAC	22	9	33	42	8	—	—	—	—	—
83-84—R.P.I.	ECAC	38	26	57	83	15	—	—	—	—	—
84-85—R.P.I.	ECAC	38	31	60	91	29	—	—	—	—	—
85-86—Adirondack	AHL	34	18	28	46	4	17	7	14	21	4
—Detroit	NHL	38	9	11	20	10	—	—	—	—	—
86-87—Detroit	NHL	76	15	32	47	21	16	4	7	11	6
87-88—Detroit	NHL	63	14	40	54	20	16	8	12	20	6
88-89—Detroit	NHL	69	16	62	78	14	6	0	8	8	2
89-90—St. Louis	NHL	80	23	79	102	30	12	2	12	14	4
90-91—St. Louis	NHL	61	25	90	115	29	13	7	13	20	10
91-92—St. Louis	NHL	54	10	59	69	12	—	—	—	—	—
—Boston	NHL	26	10	20	30	10	15	5	14	19	4
92-93—Boston	NHL	84	45	*97	142	32	4	0	9	9	4
NHL totals		551	167	490	657	178	82	26	75	101	36

O'CONNOR, MYLES
D, MIGHTY DUCKS

PERSONAL: Born April 2, 1967, at Calgary, Alta. . . . 5-11/165. . . . Shoots left. . . . Full name: Myles Alexander O'Connor.
COLLEGE: Michigan.
TRANSACTIONS/CAREER NOTES: Selected by New Jersey Devils in third round (fourth Devils pick, 45th overall) of NHL entry draft (June 15, 1985). . . . Fractured ankle (February 18, 1991). . . . Signed as free agent by Mighty Ducks of Anaheim (July 22, 1993).
HONORS: Named to NCAA All-America West first team (1988-89). . . . Named to CCHA All-Star first team (1988-89).

Season Team	League	REGULAR SEASON					PLAYOFFS				
		Gms.	G	A	Pts.	Pen.	Gms.	G	A	Pts.	Pen.
84-85—Notre Dame H.S.	Sask. H.S.	40	20	35	55	40	—	—	—	—	—
85-86—University of Michigan	CCHA	37	6	19	25	73	—	—	—	—	—
—Canadian national team	Int'l	8	0	0	0	0	—	—	—	—	—
86-87—University of Michigan	CCHA	39	15	30	45	111	—	—	—	—	—
87-88—University of Michigan	CCHA	40	9	25	34	78	—	—	—	—	—
88-89—University of Michigan	CCHA	40	3	31	34	91	—	—	—	—	—
—Utica	AHL	1	0	0	0	0	—	—	—	—	—
89-90—Utica	AHL	76	14	33	47	124	5	1	2	3	26
90-91—New Jersey	NHL	22	3	1	4	41	—	—	—	—	—
—Utica	AHL	33	6	17	23	62	—	—	—	—	—
91-92—Utica	AHL	66	9	39	48	184	—	—	—	—	—
—New Jersey	NHL	9	0	2	2	13	—	—	—	—	—
92-93—Utica	AHL	9	1	5	6	10	—	—	—	—	—
—New Jersey	NHL	7	0	0	0	9	—	—	—	—	—
NHL totals		38	3	3	6	63	—	—	—	—	—

ODELEIN, LYLE
D, CANADIENS

PERSONAL: Born July 21, 1968, at Quill Lake, Sask. . . . 5-10/206. . . . Shoots right. . . . Name pronounced OH-duh-LIGHN.
TRANSACTIONS/CAREER NOTES: Selected by Montreal Canadiens as underage junior in seventh round (eighth Canadiens pick, 141st overall) of NHL entry draft (June 21, 1986). . . . Bruised

right ankle (January 22, 1991); missed five games.... Twisted right ankle (February 9, 1991).... Suspended one game by NHL for game misconduct penalties (March 1, 1993).
MISCELLANEOUS: Member of Stanley Cup championship team (1993).

Season	Team	League	REGULAR SEASON					PLAYOFFS				
			Gms.	G	A	Pts.	Pen.	Gms.	G	A	Pts.	Pen.
85-86	Moose Jaw	WHL	67	9	37	46	117	13	1	6	7	34
86-87	Moose Jaw	WHL	59	9	50	59	70	9	2	5	7	26
87-88	Moose Jaw	WHL	63	15	43	58	166	—	—	—	—	—
88-89	Sherbrooke	AHL	33	3	4	7	120	3	0	2	2	5
	Peoria	IHL	36	2	8	10	116	—	—	—	—	—
89-90	Sherbrooke	AHL	68	7	24	31	265	12	6	5	11	79
	Montreal	NHL	8	0	2	2	33	—	—	—	—	—
90-91	Montreal	NHL	52	0	2	2	259	12	0	0	0	54
91-92	Montreal	NHL	71	1	7	8	212	7	0	0	0	11
92-93	Montreal	NHL	83	2	14	16	205	20	1	5	6	30
NHL totals			214	3	25	28	709	39	1	5	6	95

ODGERS, JEFF
LW, SHARKS

PERSONAL: Born May 31, 1969, at Spy Hill, Sask.... 6-0/195.... Shoots right.... Name pronounced AHD-juhrs.
TRANSACTIONS/CAREER NOTES: Signed as free agent by San Jose Sharks (September 3, 1991). ... Injured hand (December 21, 1991); missed four games.... Broke hand (November 5, 1992); missed 15 games.... Suspended one game by NHL for accumulating three game misconduct penalties (January 29, 1993).... Suspended two games by NHL for accumulating four game misconduct penalties (February 19, 1993).

Season	Team	League	REGULAR SEASON					PLAYOFFS				
			Gms.	G	A	Pts.	Pen.	Gms.	G	A	Pts.	Pen.
86-87	Brandon	WHL	70	7	14	21	150	—	—	—	—	—
87-88	Brandon	WHL	70	17	18	35	202	4	1	1	2	14
88-89	Brandon	WHL	71	31	29	60	277	—	—	—	—	—
89-90	Brandon	WHL	64	37	28	65	209	—	—	—	—	—
90-91	Kansas City	IHL	77	12	19	31	*318	—	—	—	—	—
91-92	Kansas City	IHL	12	2	2	4	56	9	3	0	3	13
	San Jose	NHL	61	7	4	11	217	—	—	—	—	—
92-93	San Jose	NHL	66	12	15	27	253	—	—	—	—	—
NHL totals			127	19	19	38	470					

ODJICK, GINO
LW, CANUCKS

PERSONAL: Born September 7, 1970, at Maniwaki, Que.... 6-3/220.... Shoots left.
TRANSACTIONS/CAREER NOTES: Suspended five games by QMJHL for attempting to attack another player (May 1, 1989).... Suspended one game by QMJHL for fighting (March 19, 1990). ... Suspended one game by QMJHL for fighting (April 14, 1990).... Selected by Vancouver Canucks in fifth round (fifth Canucks pick, 86th overall) of NHL entry draft (June 16, 1990).... Suspended six games by NHL for stick foul (November 26, 1991).... Underwent arthroscopic knee surgery (February 11, 1993); missed five games.... Suspended one game by NHL for accumulating three game misconduct penalties (January 27, 1993).... Suspended one game by NHL for accumulating four game misconduct penalties (March 26, 1993).... Suspended two games by NHL for stick incident (April 8, 1993).

Season	Team	League	REGULAR SEASON					PLAYOFFS				
			Gms.	G	A	Pts.	Pen.	Gms.	G	A	Pts.	Pen.
88-89	Laval	QMJHL	50	9	15	24	278	16	0	9	9	*129
89-90	Laval	QMJHL	51	12	26	38	280	13	6	5	11	*110
90-91	Milwaukee	IHL	17	7	3	10	102	—	—	—	—	—
	Vancouver	NHL	45	7	1	8	296	6	0	0	0	18
91-92	Vancouver	NHL	65	4	6	10	348	4	0	0	0	6
92-93	Vancouver	NHL	75	4	13	17	370	1	0	0	0	0
NHL totals			185	15	20	35	1014	11	0	0	0	24

ODUYA, FREDRIK
D, SHARKS

PERSONAL: Born May 31, 1975, at Stockholm, Sweden.... 6-2/184.... Shoots left.
TRANSACTIONS/CAREER NOTES: Selected by San Jose Sharks in sixth round (eighth Sharks pick, 154th overall) of NHL entry draft (June 26, 1993).

Season	Team	League	REGULAR SEASON					PLAYOFFS				
			Gms.	G	A	Pts.	Pen.	Gms.	G	A	Pts.	Pen.
91-92	Windsor	OHL Jr. B	43	2	8	10	24	—	—	—	—	—
92-93	Guelph	OHL	23	2	4	6	29	—	—	—	—	—
	Ottawa	OHL	17	0	3	3	70	—	—	—	—	—

OGRODNICK, JOHN
LW, RED WINGS

PERSONAL: Born June 20, 1959, at Ottawa.... 6-0/208.... Shoots left.... Full name: John Alexander Ogrodnick.
TRANSACTIONS/CAREER NOTES: Selected by Detroit Red Wings in fourth round (fourth Red Wings pick, 66th overall) of NHL entry draft (August 9, 1979).... Fractured left wrist (February 26, 1984).... Sprained ankle (October 1986).... Traded by Red Wings with RW Doug Shedden and LW Basil McRae to Quebec Nordiques for LW Brent Ashton, RW Mark Kumpel and D Gilbert Delorme (January 17, 1987).... Traded by Nordiques with D David Shaw to New York Rangers for LW Jeff Jackson and D Terry Carkner (September 30, 1987).... Suffered ligament damage and cracked bone in left instep (December 1987).... Bruised ribs (February 1988).... Suffered back spasms (February 12, 1992); missed four games.... Bruised wrist (March 4, 1992); missed one game.... Suffered from the

flu (March 7, 1993); missed two games.... Signed as free agent by Red Wings (September 29, 1992).
HONORS: Shared WCHL Rookie of the Year Award with Keith Brown (1977-78).... Played in NHL All-Star Game (1981, 1982 and 1984 through 1986).... Named to NHL All-Star first team (1984-85).

Season Team	League	REGULAR SEASON					PLAYOFFS				
		Gms.	G	A	Pts.	Pen.	Gms.	G	A	Pts.	Pen.
76-77—Maple Ridge Bruins..........	BCJHL	67	54	56	110	63	—	—	—	—	—
—New Westminster	WCHL	14	2	4	6	0	14	3	3	6	2
77-78—New Westminster	WCHL	72	59	29	88	47	21	14	7	21	14
78-79—New Westminster	WHL	72	48	36	84	38	6	2	0	2	4
79-80—Adirondack	AHL	39	13	20	33	21	—	—	—	—	—
—Detroit	NHL	41	8	24	32	8	—	—	—	—	—
80-81—Detroit	NHL	80	35	35	70	14	—	—	—	—	—
81-82—Detroit	NHL	80	28	26	54	28	—	—	—	—	—
82-83—Detroit	NHL	80	41	44	85	30	—	—	—	—	—
83-84—Detroit	NHL	64	42	36	78	14	4	0	0	0	0
84-85—Detroit	NHL	79	55	50	105	30	3	1	1	2	0
85-86—Detroit	NHL	76	38	32	70	18	—	—	—	—	—
86-87—Detroit	NHL	39	12	28	40	6	—	—	—	—	—
—Quebec	NHL	32	11	16	27	4	13	9	4	13	6
87-88—New York Rangers	NHL	64	22	32	54	16	—	—	—	—	—
88-89—Denver	IHL	3	2	0	2	0	—	—	—	—	—
—New York Rangers	NHL	60	13	29	42	14	3	2	0	2	0
89-90—New York Rangers	NHL	80	43	31	74	44	10	6	3	9	0
90-91—New York Rangers	NHL	79	31	23	54	10	4	0	0	0	0
91-92—New York Rangers	NHL	55	17	13	30	22	3	0	0	0	0
92-93—Detroit	NHL	19	6	6	12	2	1	0	0	0	0
—Adirondack	AHL	4	2	2	4	0	—	—	—	—	—
NHL totals.................		928	402	425	827	260	41	18	8	26	6

OJANEN, JANNE
C, DEVILS

PERSONAL: Born April 9, 1968, at Tampere, Finland.... 6-2/200.... Shoots left.... Full name: Janne Juhani Ojanen.... Name pronounced oh-YAHN-ihn.
TRANSACTIONS/CAREER NOTES: Selected by New Jersey Devils in third round (third Devils pick, 45th overall) of NHL entry draft (June 1986).... Sprained right knee (November 5, 1992); missed eight games.... Injured back (March 7, 1993); missed one game.
HONORS: Named Finland Rookie of the Year (1986-87).
MISCELLANEOUS: Member of silver-medal-winning Finnish Olympic team (1988).

Season Team	League	REGULAR SEASON					PLAYOFFS				
		Gms.	G	A	Pts.	Pen.	Gms.	G	A	Pts.	Pen.
84-85—Tappara...........................	Finland				Statistics	unavailable.	—	—	—	—	—
85-86—Tappara...........................	Finland	14	5	17	22	14	—	—	—	—	—
86-87—Tappara...........................	Finland	49	22	19	41	28	—	—	—	—	—
87-88—Tappara...........................	Finland	54	25	35	60	42	—	—	—	—	—
88-89—Utica...............................	AHL	72	23	37	60	10	5	0	3	3	0
—New Jersey......................	NHL	3	0	1	1	2	—	—	—	—	—
89-90—New Jersey......................	NHL	64	17	13	30	12	—	—	—	—	—
90-91—Tappara...........................	Finland	44	15	23	38	...	—	—	—	—	—
91-92—Tappara...........................	Finland	44	21	27	48	24	—	—	—	—	—
—New Jersey......................	NHL	—	—	—	—	—	3	0	2	2	0
92-93—New Jersey......................	NHL	31	4	9	13	14	—	—	—	—	—
—Cincinnati.......................	IHL	7	1	8	9	0	—	—	—	—	—
NHL totals.................		98	21	23	44	28	3	0	2	2	0

OKSIUTA, ROMAN
RW, OILERS

PERSONAL: Born August 21, 1970, at Murmansk, U.S.S.R.... 6-3/229.... Shoots left. ... Name pronounced ohk-SEW-tah.
TRANSACTIONS/CAREER NOTES: Selected by New York Rangers in 10th round (11th Rangers pick, 202nd overall) of NHL entry draft (June 17, 1989).... Traded by Rangers with third-round draft pick in 1993 NHL entry draft (RW Alexander Kerch) to Edmonton Oilers for D Kevin Lowe (December 5, 1992).

Season Team	League	REGULAR SEASON					PLAYOFFS				
		Gms.	G	A	Pts.	Pen.	Gms.	G	A	Pts.	Pen.
87-88—Khimik Voskresensk........	USSR	11	1	0	1	4	—	—	—	—	—
88-89—Khimik Voskresensk........	USSR	34	13	3	16	14	—	—	—	—	—
89-90—Khimik Voskresensk........	USSR	37	13	6	19	16	—	—	—	—	—
90-91—Khimik Voskresensk........	USSR	41	12	8	20	24	—	—	—	—	—
91-92—Khimik Voskresensk........	CIS	42	24	20	*44	28	—	—	—	—	—
92-93—Cape Breton	AHL	43	26	25	51	22	16	9	19	28	12

OLAUSSON, FREDRIK
D, JETS

PERSONAL: Born October 5, 1966, at Vaxsjo, Sweden.... 6-2/200.... Shoots right.... Name pronounced OHL-uh-suhn.
TRANSACTIONS/CAREER NOTES: Selected by Winnipeg Jets in fourth round (fourth Jets pick, 81st overall) of NHL entry draft (June 15, 1985).... Dislocated shoulder (August 1987).... Underwent shoulder surgery (November 1987).... Signed five-year contract with Farjestads, Sweden (June 19, 1989); Farjestads agreed to allow Olausson to remain in Winnipeg.... Sprained knee (January 22, 1993); missed 11

games. . . . Suffered ankle laceration (November 8, 1993); missed two games. . . . Suffered from the flu (January 18, 1993); missed one game. . . . Sprained knee (January 23, 1993); missed 11 games. . . . Suffered from the flu (March 4, 1993); missed one game.

HONORS: Named to Swedish League All-Star team (1985-86).

			REGULAR SEASON					PLAYOFFS			
Season Team	League	Gms.	G	A	Pts.	Pen.	Gms.	G	A	Pts.	Pen.
83-84—Nybro	Sweden	28	8	14	22	32	—	—	—	—	—
84-85—Farjestad	Sweden	34	6	12	18	24	3	1	0	1	0
85-86—Farjestad	Sweden	33	5	12	17	14	8	3	2	5	6
86-87—Winnipeg	NHL	72	7	29	36	24	10	2	3	5	4
87-88—Winnipeg	NHL	38	5	10	15	18	5	1	1	2	0
88-89—Winnipeg	NHL	75	15	47	62	32	—	—	—	—	—
89-90—Winnipeg	NHL	77	9	46	55	32	7	0	2	2	2
90-91—Winnipeg	NHL	71	12	29	41	24	—	—	—	—	—
91-92—Winnipeg	NHL	77	20	42	62	34	7	1	5	6	4
92-93—Winnipeg	NHL	68	16	41	57	22	6	0	2	2	2
NHL totals		478	84	244	328	186	35	4	13	17	12

OLCZYK, ED
C/RW/LW, RANGERS

PERSONAL: Born August 16, 1966, at Chicago. . . . 6-1/200. . . . Shoots left. . . . Name pronounced OHL-chehk.

TRANSACTIONS/CAREER NOTES: Selected by Chicago Blackhawks in first round (first Blackhawks pick, third overall) of NHL entry draft (June 9, 1984). . . . Hyperextended knee (September 3, 1984). . . . Broke bone in left foot (December 16, 1984). . . . Traded by Blackhawks with LW Al Secord to Toronto Maple Leafs for RW Rick Vaive, LW Steve Thomas and D Bob McGill (September 1987). . . . Pinched nerve in left knee (January 3, 1990). . . . Traded by Maple Leafs with LW Mark Osborne to Winnipeg Jets for D Dave Ellett and LW Paul Fenton (November 10, 1990). . . . Dislocated elbow and sprained ankle (January 8, 1992); missed 15 games. . . . Sprained knee (November 24, 1992); missed nine games. . . . Traded by Jets to New York Rangers for LW Kris King and RW Tie Domi (December 28, 1992).

			REGULAR SEASON					PLAYOFFS			
Season Team	League	Gms.	G	A	Pts.	Pen.	Gms.	G	A	Pts.	Pen.
83-84—U.S. national team	Int'l	56	19	40	59	36	—	—	—	—	—
—U.S. Olympic Team	Int'l	6	2	6	8	0	—	—	—	—	—
84-85—Chicago	NHL	70	20	30	50	67	15	6	5	11	11
85-86—Chicago	NHL	79	29	50	79	47	3	0	0	0	0
86-87—Chicago	NHL	79	16	35	51	119	4	1	1	2	4
87-88—Toronto	NHL	80	42	33	75	55	6	5	4	9	2
88-89—Toronto	NHL	80	38	52	90	75	—	—	—	—	—
89-90—Toronto	NHL	79	32	56	88	78	5	1	2	3	14
90-91—Toronto	NHL	18	4	10	14	13	—	—	—	—	—
—Winnipeg	NHL	61	26	31	57	69	—	—	—	—	—
91-92—Winnipeg	NHL	64	32	33	65	67	6	2	1	3	4
92-93—Winnipeg	NHL	25	8	12	20	26	—	—	—	—	—
—New York Rangers	NHL	46	13	16	29	26	—	—	—	—	—
NHL totals		681	260	358	618	642	39	15	13	28	35

OLIMPIYEV, SERGEI
LW, RANGERS

PERSONAL: Born January 12, 1975, at Minsk, U.S.S.R. . . . 5-10/172.
TRANSACTIONS/CAREER NOTES: Selected by New York Rangers in fourth round (fourth Rangers pick, 86th overall) of NHL entry draft (June 26, 1993).

			REGULAR SEASON					PLAYOFFS			
Season Team	League	Gms.	G	A	Pts.	Pen.	Gms.	G	A	Pts.	Pen.
91-92—Traktor Lipetsk	CIS Div. III	20	0	0	0	2	—	—	—	—	—
92-93—Dynamo Minsk	CIS	6	1	0	1	2	—	—	—	—	—

OLIWA, KRZYSZTOF
LW, DEVILS

PERSONAL: Born April 12, 1973, at Tychy, Poland. . . . 6-5/220. . . . Shoots left.
TRANSACTIONS/CAREER NOTES: Selected by New Jersey Devils in third round (fourth Devils pick, 65th overall) of NHL entry draft (June 26, 1993).

			REGULAR SEASON					PLAYOFFS			
Season Team	League	Gms.	G	A	Pts.	Pen.	Gms.	G	A	Pts.	Pen.
90-91—GKS Katowice	Poland Jrs.	5	4	4	8	10	—	—	—	—	—
91-92—GKS Tychy	Poland	10	3	7	10	6	—	—	—	—	—
92-93—Welland Jr. B	OHA	30	13	21	34	127	—	—	—	—	—

OLSEN, DARRYL
D

PERSONAL: Born October 7, 1966, at Calgary, Alta. . . . 6-0/180. . . . Shoots left.
COLLEGE: Northern Michigan.
TRANSACTIONS/CAREER NOTES: Selected by Calgary Flames in ninth round (10th Flames pick, 185th overall) of NHL entry draft (June 15, 1985). . . . Signed as free agent by Boston Bruins (July 16, 1992). . . . Signed as free agent by San Diego Gulls (February 26, 1993).
HONORS: Named to NCAA All-America West second team (1988-89). . . . Named to WCHA All-Star first team (1988-89).

			REGULAR SEASON					PLAYOFFS			
Season Team	League	Gms.	G	A	Pts.	Pen.	Gms.	G	A	Pts.	Pen.
84-85—St. Albert	AJHL	57	19	48	67	77	—	—	—	—	—
85-86—Northern Michigan Univ.	WCHA	37	5	20	25	46	—	—	—	—	—

Season Team	League	REGULAR SEASON					PLAYOFFS				
		Gms.	G	A	Pts.	Pen.	Gms.	G	A	Pts.	Pen.
86-87—Northern Michigan Univ...	WCHA	37	5	20	25	96	—	—	—	—	—
87-88—Northern Michigan Univ...	WCHA	35	11	20	31	59	—	—	—	—	—
88-89—Northern Michigan Univ...	WCHA	45	16	26	42	88	—	—	—	—	—
—Canadian national team ...	Int'l	3	1	0	1	4	—	—	—	—	—
89-90—Salt Lake City..............	IHL	72	16	50	66	90	11	3	6	9	2
90-91—Salt Lake City..............	IHL	76	15	40	55	89	4	1	5	6	2
91-92—Salt Lake City..............	IHL	59	7	33	40	80	5	2	1	3	4
—Calgary............................	NHL	1	0	0	0	0	—	—	—	—	—
92-93—Providence	AHL	50	7	27	34	38	—	—	—	—	—
—San Diego	IHL	21	2	8	10	26	10	1	3	4	30
NHL totals..		1	0	0	0	0					

O'NEILL, MIKE
G, JETS

PERSONAL: Born November 3, 1967, at Montreal. ... 5-7/155. ... Shoots left. ... Full name: Michael Anthony O'Neill Jr.
COLLEGE: Yale.
TRANSACTIONS/CAREER NOTES: Selected by Winnipeg Jets in NHL supplemental draft (June 10, 1988). ... Dislocated shoulder (April 8, 1991); missed remainder of playoffs. ... Dislocated shoulder (February 1, 1993); missed two games. ... Underwent shoulder surgery (February 12, 1993); missed remainder of season.
HONORS: Named to ECAC All-Star first team (1986-87 and 1988-89). ... Named to NCAA All-America East first team (1988-89). ... Won Emms Family Award (1992-93).

Season Team	League	REGULAR SEASON							PLAYOFFS						
		Gms.	Min.	W	L	T	GA	SO	Avg.	Gms.	Min.	W	L	GA	SO	Avg.
85-86—Yale University	ECAC	6	389	3	1	0	17	0	2.62	—	—	—	—	—	—	—
86-87—Yale University	ECAC	16	964	9	6	1	55	2	3.42	—	—	—	—	—	—	—
87-88—Yale University	ECAC	24	1385	6	17	0	101	0	4.38	—	—	—	—	—	—	—
88-89—Yale University	ECAC	25	1490	10	14	1	93	0	3.74	—	—	—	—	—	—	—
89-90—Tappara......................	Finland	41	2369	23	13	5	127	2	3.22	—	—	—	—	—	—	—
90-91—Fort Wayne	IHL	8	490	5	2	1	31	0	3.80	—	—	—	—	—	—	—
—Moncton	AHL	30	1613	13	7	6	84	0	3.12	8	435	3	4	29	0	4.00
91-92—Fort Wayne	IHL	33	1858	22	6	3	97	†4	3.13	—	—	—	—	—	—	—
—Moncton	AHL	32	1902	14	16	2	108	1	3.41	11	670	4	†7	43	1	3.85
—Winnipeg	NHL	1	13	0	0	0	1	0	4.62	—	—	—	—	—	—	—
92-93—Moncton	AHL	30	1649	13	10	4	88	1	3.20	—	—	—	—	—	—	—
—Winnipeg	NHL	2	73	0	0	1	6	0	4.93	—	—	—	—	—	—	—
NHL totals..		3	86	0	0	1	7	0	4.88							

OSADCHY, ALEXANDER
D, SHARKS

PERSONAL: Born July 19, 1975, at Kharkov, U.S.S.R. ... 5-11/191. ... Shoots right.
TRANSACTIONS/CAREER NOTES: Selected by San Jose Sharks in fourth round (fifth Sharks pick, 80th overall) of NHL entry draft (June 26, 1993).

Season Team	League	REGULAR SEASON					PLAYOFFS				
		Gms.	G	A	Pts.	Pen.	Gms.	G	A	Pts.	Pen.
92-93—CSKA Moscow..................	CIS	37	0	1	1	60	—	—	—	—	—

OSBORNE, KEITH
RW, LIGHTNING

PERSONAL: Born April 2, 1969, at Toronto. ... 6-1/180. ... Shoots right.
TRANSACTIONS/CAREER NOTES: Selected by St. Louis Blues as underage junior in first round (first Blues pick, 12th overall) of NHL entry draft (June 13, 1987). ... Broke wrist (September 1987). ... Broke ankle (October 1987). ... Traded by Blues to Toronto Maple Leafs for D Darren Veitch (March 5, 1991). ... Selected by Tampa Bay Lightning in NHL expansion draft (June 18, 1992).

Season Team	League	REGULAR SEASON					PLAYOFFS				
		Gms.	G	A	Pts.	Pen.	Gms.	G	A	Pts.	Pen.
86-87—North Bay	OHL	61	34	55	89	31	24	11	11	22	25
87-88—North Bay	OHL	30	14	22	36	20	4	1	5	6	8
88-89—North Bay	OHL	15	11	15	26	12	—	—	—	—	—
—Niagara Falls	OHL	50	34	49	83	45	17	12	12	24	36
89-90—St. Louis	NHL	5	0	2	2	8	—	—	—	—	—
—Peoria	IHL	56	23	24	47	58	—	—	—	—	—
90-91—Peoria	IHL	54	10	20	30	79	—	—	—	—	—
—Newmarket.....................	AHL	12	0	3	3	6	—	—	—	—	—
91-92—St. John's	AHL	53	11	16	27	21	4	0	1	1	2
92-93—Atlanta	IHL	72	40	49	89	91	8	1	5	6	2
—Tampa Bay	NHL	11	1	1	2	8	—	—	—	—	—
NHL totals..		16	1	3	4	16					

OSBORNE, MARK
LW, MAPLE LEAFS

PERSONAL: Born August 13, 1961, at Toronto. ... 6-2/200. ... Shoots left. ... Full name: Mark Anatole Osborne.
TRANSACTIONS/CAREER NOTES: Selected by Detroit Red Wings as underage junior in third round (second Red Wings pick, 46th overall) of NHL entry draft (June 11, 1980). ... Traded by Red Wings with D Willie Huber and RW Mike Blaisdell to New York Rangers for RW Ron Duguay, G Eddie Mio and RW Ed Johnstone (June 13, 1983). ... Injured hip (October 1984). ... Sprained ankle (February 12, 1986); missed 12 games. ...

Suffered laceration behind left knee (February 1987).... Traded by Rangers to Toronto Maple Leafs for third-round pick in 1989 draft (C Rob Zamuner) (March 5, 1987).... Separated left shoulder (April 1988).... Traded by Maple Leafs with C/RW Ed Olczyk to Winnipeg Jets for D Dave Ellett and C Paul Fenton (November 10, 1990).... Fractured left thumb and injured ligaments (December 3, 1990); missed 21 games.... Separated shoulder (October 29, 1991); missed three games.... Fractured ankle (January 1992); missed 14 games.... Traded by Jets to Maple Leafs for RW Lucien Deblois (March 10, 1992).... Sprained knee (March 28, 1993); missed seven games.

			REGULAR SEASON					PLAYOFFS			
Season Team	League	Gms.	G	A	Pts.	Pen.	Gms.	G	A	Pts.	Pen.
78-79—Niagara Falls	OMJHL	62	17	25	42	53	—	—	—	—	—
79-80—Niagara Falls	OMJHL	52	10	33	43	104	10	2	1	3	23
80-81—Niagara Falls	OMJHL	54	39	41	80	140	12	11	10	21	20
—Adirondack	AHL	—	—	—	—	—	13	2	3	5	2
81-82—Detroit	NHL	80	26	41	67	61	—	—	—	—	—
82-83—Detroit	NHL	80	19	24	43	83	—	—	—	—	—
83-84—New York Rangers	NHL	73	23	28	51	88	5	0	1	1	7
84-85—New York Rangers	NHL	23	4	4	8	33	3	0	0	0	4
85-86—New York Rangers	NHL	62	16	24	40	80	15	2	3	5	26
86-87—New York Rangers	NHL	58	17	15	32	101	—	—	—	—	—
—Toronto	NHL	16	5	10	15	12	9	1	3	4	6
87-88—Toronto	NHL	79	23	37	60	102	6	1	3	4	16
88-89—Toronto	NHL	75	16	30	46	112	—	—	—	—	—
89-90—Toronto	NHL	78	23	50	73	91	5	2	3	5	12
90-91—Toronto	NHL	18	3	3	6	4	—	—	—	—	—
—Winnipeg	NHL	37	8	8	16	59	—	—	—	—	—
91-92—Winnipeg	NHL	43	4	12	16	65	—	—	—	—	—
—Toronto	NHL	11	3	1	4	8	—	—	—	—	—
92-93—Toronto	NHL	76	12	14	26	89	19	1	1	2	16
NHL totals		809	202	301	503	988	62	7	14	21	87

OSGOOD, CHRIS
G, RED WINGS

PERSONAL: Born November 26, 1972, at Peace River, Alta.... 5-10/156.... Shoots left.
TRANSACTIONS/CAREER NOTES: Selected by Detroit Red Wings in third round (third Red Wings pick, 54th overall) of NHL entry draft (June 22, 1991).
HONORS: Named to WHL (East) All-Star second team (1990-91).

			REGULAR SEASON								PLAYOFFS					
Season Team	League	Gms.	Min.	W	L	T	GA	SO	Avg.	Gms.	Min.	W	L	GA	SO	Avg.
89-90—Medicine Hat	WHL	57	3094	24	28	2	228	0	4.42	3	173	3	4	17	0	5.90
90-91—Medicine Hat	WHL	46	2630	23	18	3	173	2	3.95	12	714	7	5	42	0	3.53
91-92—Medicine Hat	WHL	15	819	10	3	0	44	0	3.22	—	—	—	—	—	—	—
—Brandon	WHL	16	890	3	10	1	60	1	4.04	—	—	—	—	—	—	—
—Seattle	WHL	21	1217	12	7	1	65	1	3.20	15	904	9	6	51	0	3.38
92-93—Adirondack	AHL	45	2438	19	19	4	159	0	3.91	1	59	0	1	2	0	2.03

OSIECKI, MARK
D, STARS

PERSONAL: Born July 23, 1968, at St. Paul, Minn.... 6-2/200.... Shoots right.... Full name: Mark Anthony Osiecki.... Name pronounced oh-SEE-kee.
COLLEGE: Wisconsin.
TRANSACTIONS/CAREER NOTES: Selected by Calgary Flames in ninth round (10th Flames pick, 187th overall) of NHL entry draft (June 13, 1987).... Traded by Flames to Ottawa Senators for LW Chris Lindberg (June 23, 1992).... Claimed on waivers by Winnipeg Jets (February 20, 1993).... Traded by Jets to Minnesota North Stars for ninth and 10th-round picks in 1993 draft (March 20, 1993).... North Stars franchise moved from Minnesota to Dallas and renamed Stars for 1993-94 season.
HONORS: Named to NCAA All-Tournament team (1989-90).

			REGULAR SEASON					PLAYOFFS			
Season Team	League	Gms.	G	A	Pts.	Pen.	Gms.	G	A	Pts.	Pen.
86-87—University of Wisconsin	WCHA	8	0	1	1	4	—	—	—	—	—
87-88—University of Wisconsin	WCHA	18	0	1	1	22	—	—	—	—	—
88-89—University of Wisconsin	WCHA	44	1	3	4	56	—	—	—	—	—
89-90—University of Wisconsin	WCHA	46	5	38	43	78	—	—	—	—	—
90-91—Salt Lake City	IHL	75	1	24	25	36	4	2	0	2	2
91-92—Calgary	NHL	50	2	7	9	24	—	—	—	—	—
—Salt Lake City	IHL	1	0	0	0	0	—	—	—	—	—
92-93—Ottawa	NHL	34	0	4	4	12	—	—	—	—	—
—New Haven	AHL	4	0	1	1	0	—	—	—	—	—
—Winnipeg	NHL	4	1	0	1	2	—	—	—	—	—
—Minnesota	NHL	5	0	0	0	5	—	—	—	—	—
NHL totals		93	3	11	14	43	—	—	—	—	—

O'SULLIVAN, CHRIS
D, FLAMES

PERSONAL: Born May 15, 1974, at Dorchester, Mass.... 6-2/180.... Shoots left.
HIGH SCHOOL: Catholic Memorial (Boston).
TRANSACTIONS/CAREER NOTES: Selected by Calgary Flames in second round (second Flames pick, 30th overall) of NHL entry draft (June 20, 1992).

			REGULAR SEASON					PLAYOFFS			
Season Team	League	Gms.	G	A	Pts.	Pen.	Gms.	G	A	Pts.	Pen.
91-92—Catholic Memorial H.S.	Mass. H.S.	26	26	23	49	65	—	—	—	—	—
92-93—Boston University	Hockey East	5	0	2	2	4	—	—	—	—	—

O'SULLIVAN, KEVIN

D, ISLANDERS

PERSONAL: Born November 13, 1970, at Dorchester, Mass. . . . 6-0/180. . . . Shoots left. . . . Full name: Kevin Patrick O'Sullivan.
HIGH SCHOOL: Catholic Memorial (Boston).
COLLEGE: Boston University.
TRANSACTIONS/CAREER NOTES: Selected by New York Islanders in fifth round (seventh Islanders pick, 99th overall) of NHL entry draft (June 17, 1989).
HONORS: Named to Hockey East All-Star second team (1991-92). . . . Named to Hockey East All-Star first team (1992-93).

Season Team	League	REGULAR SEASON					PLAYOFFS				
		Gms.	G	A	Pts.	Pen.	Gms.	G	A	Pts.	Pen.
87-88—Catholic Memorial H.S.	Mass. H.S.	. . .	8	24	32	. . .	—	—	—	—	—
88-89—Catholic Memorial H.S.	Mass. H.S.	19	6	14	20	. . .	—	—	—	—	—
89-90—Boston University	Hockey East	43	0	6	6	42	—	—	—	—	—
90-91—Boston University	Hockey East	37	4	7	11	50	—	—	—	—	—
91-92—Boston University	Hockey East	33	3	18	21	62	—	—	—	—	—
92-93—Boston University	Hockey East	40	5	20	25	78	—	—	—	—	—

OTEVREL, JAROSLAV

C, SHARKS

PERSONAL: Born September 16, 1968, at Gottwaldov, Czechoslovakia. . . . 6-2/185. . . . Shoots left.
TRANSACTIONS/CAREER NOTES: Selected by San Jose Sharks in seventh round (eighth Sharks pick, 133rd overall) of NHL entry draft (June 22, 1991). . . . Bruised thigh (January 26, 1993); missed four games.

Season Team	League	REGULAR SEASON					PLAYOFFS				
		Gms.	G	A	Pts.	Pen.	Gms.	G	A	Pts.	Pen.
87-88—TJ Gottwaldov	Czech.	32	4	7	11	18	—	—	—	—	—
88-89—TJ Zlin	Czech.	40	14	6	20	37	—	—	—	—	—
89-90—Dukla Trencin	Czech.	43	7	10	17	20	—	—	—	—	—
90-91—TJ Zlin	Czech.	49	24	26	50	105	—	—	—	—	—
91-92—ZPS Zlin	Czech.	40	14	15	29	. . .	—	—	—	—	—
92-93—Kansas City	IHL	62	17	27	44	58	6	1	4	5	4
—San Jose	NHL	7	0	2	2	0	—	—	—	—	—
NHL totals		7	0	2	2	0	—	—	—	—	—

OTTO, JOEL

C, FLAMES

PERSONAL: Born October 29, 1961, at Elk River, Minn. . . . 6-4/220. . . . Shoots right. . . . Full name: Joel Stuart Otto.
COLLEGE: Bemidji State (Minn.).
TRANSACTIONS/CAREER NOTES: Signed as free agent by Calgary Flames (September 11, 1984). . . . Tore cartilage in right knee (March 10, 1987). . . . Strained right knee ligaments (October 8, 1987). . . . Bruised ribs (November 1989). . . . Hospitalized after being crosschecked from behind (January 13, 1990). . . . Injured ankle (March 10, 1992); missed two games. . . . Suffered rib injury (January 5, 1993); missed eight games.
MISCELLANEOUS: Member of Stanley Cup championship team (1989).

Season Team	League	REGULAR SEASON					PLAYOFFS				
		Gms.	G	A	Pts.	Pen.	Gms.	G	A	Pts.	Pen.
80-81—Bemidji State	NCAA-II	23	5	11	16	10	—	—	—	—	—
81-82—Bemidji State	NCAA-II	31	19	33	52	24	—	—	—	—	—
82-83—Bemidji State	NCAA-II	37	33	28	61	68	—	—	—	—	—
83-84—Bemidji State	NCAA-II	31	32	43	75	32	—	—	—	—	—
84-85—Moncton	AHL	56	27	36	63	89	—	—	—	—	—
—Calgary	NHL	17	4	8	12	30	3	2	1	3	10
85-86—Calgary	NHL	79	25	34	59	188	22	5	10	15	80
86-87—Calgary	NHL	68	19	31	50	185	2	0	2	2	6
87-88—Calgary	NHL	62	13	39	52	194	9	3	2	5	26
88-89—Calgary	NHL	72	23	30	53	213	22	6	13	19	46
89-90—Calgary	NHL	75	13	20	33	116	6	2	2	4	2
90-91—Calgary	NHL	76	19	20	39	183	7	1	2	3	8
91-92—Calgary	NHL	78	13	21	34	161	—	—	—	—	—
92-93—Calgary	NHL	75	19	33	52	150	6	4	2	6	4
NHL totals		602	148	236	384	1420	77	23	34	57	182

OUIMET, MARK

C, CAPITALS

PERSONAL: Born October 2, 1971, at London, Ont. . . . 5-10/165. . . . Shoots left. . . . Full name: Mark Edward Ouimet.
COLLEGE: Michigan.
TRANSACTIONS/CAREER NOTES: Pulled groin (August 1989). . . . Selected by Washington Capitals in fifth round (fifth Capitals pick, 94th overall) of NHL entry draft (June 16, 1990).

Season Team	League	REGULAR SEASON					PLAYOFFS				
		Gms.	G	A	Pts.	Pen.	Gms.	G	A	Pts.	Pen.
87-88—Strathroy Jr. B	OHA	47	28	36	64	12	—	—	—	—	—
88-89—Strathroy Jr. B	OHA	42	43	50	93	20	—	—	—	—	—
89-90—University of Michigan	CCHA	38	15	32	47	14	—	—	—	—	—
90-91—University of Michigan	CCHA	46	18	32	50	22	—	—	—	—	—
91-92—University of Michigan	CCHA	40	10	19	29	30	—	—	—	—	—
92-93—University of Michigan	CCHA	39	15	45	60	23	—	—	—	—	—
—Baltimore	AHL	1	0	1	1	0	—	—	—	—	—

O

OZOLINSH, SANDIS
D, SHARKS

PERSONAL: Born August 3, 1972, at Riga, U.S.S.R. . . . . 6-1/189. . . . Shoots left. . . . Name pronounced SAN-diz OH-zoh-lihnch.

TRANSACTIONS/CAREER NOTES: Selected by San Jose Sharks in second round (third Sharks pick, 30th overall) of NHL entry draft (June 22, 1991). . . . Strained back (November 7, 1992); missed one game. . . . Tore knee ligaments (December 30, 1992) and underwent surgery to repair anterior cruciate ligament; missed remainder of season.

Season Team	League	REGULAR SEASON					PLAYOFFS				
		Gms.	G	A	Pts.	Pen.	Gms.	G	A	Pts.	Pen.
90-91—Dynamo Riga	USSR	44	0	3	3	49	—	—	—	—	—
91-92—Riga	CIS	30	5	0	5	42	—	—	—	—	—
—Kansas City	IHL	34	6	9	15	20	15	2	5	7	22
92-93—San Jose	NHL	37	7	16	23	40	—	—	—	—	—
NHL totals		37	7	16	23	40					

PADEN, KEVIN
C/LW, OILERS

PERSONAL: Born February 12, 1975, at Woodhaven, Mich. . . . 6-3/175. . . . Shoots left.
TRANSACTIONS/CAREER NOTES: Selected by Edmonton Oilers in third round (fourth Oilers pick, 59th overall) of NHL entry draft (June 26, 1993).

Season Team	League	REGULAR SEASON					PLAYOFFS				
		Gms.	G	A	Pts.	Pen.	Gms.	G	A	Pts.	Pen.
92-93—Detroit	OHL	54	14	9	23	41	15	1	1	2	2

PAEK, JIM
D, PENGUINS

PERSONAL: Born April 7, 1967, at Seoul, South Korea. . . . 6-1/195. . . . Shoots left. . . . Name pronounced PAK.
TRANSACTIONS/CAREER NOTES: Selected by Pittsburgh Penguins as underage junior in ninth round (ninth Penguins pick, 170th overall) of NHL entry draft (June 15, 1985). . . . Suspended two games by OHL for being involved in bench-clearing incident (November 2, 1986). . . . Dislocated finger on left hand (January 10, 1992); missed 14 games. . . . Suspended three off-days and fined $500 by NHL for fighting (February 26, 1993).
MISCELLANEOUS: Member of Stanley Cup championship teams (1991 and 1992).

Season Team	League	REGULAR SEASON					PLAYOFFS				
		Gms.	G	A	Pts.	Pen.	Gms.	G	A	Pts.	Pen.
84-85—Oshawa	OHL	54	2	13	15	57	5	1	0	1	9
85-86—Oshawa	OHL	64	5	21	26	122	6	0	1	1	9
86-87—Oshawa	OHL	57	5	17	22	75	26	1	14	15	43
87-88—Muskegon	IHL	82	7	52	59	141	6	0	0	0	29
88-89—Muskegon	IHL	80	3	54	57	96	14	1	10	11	24
89-90—Muskegon	IHL	81	9	41	50	115	15	1	10	11	41
90-91—Canadian national team	Int'l	48	2	12	14	24	—	—	—	—	—
—Pittsburgh	NHL	3	0	0	0	9	8	1	0	1	2
91-92—Pittsburgh	NHL	49	1	7	8	36	19	0	4	4	6
92-93—Pittsburgh	NHL	77	3	15	18	64	—	—	—	—	—
NHL totals		129	4	22	26	109	27	1	4	5	8

PALFFY, ZIGMUND
LW, ISLANDERS

PERSONAL: Born May 5, 1972, at Skalica, Czechoslovakia. . . . 5-10/169. . . . Shoots left. . . . Name pronounced PAHL-fee.
TRANSACTIONS/CAREER NOTES: Selected by New York Islanders in second round (second Islanders pick, 26th overall) of NHL entry draft (June 22, 1991).
HONORS: Named Czechoslovakian League Rookie of the Year (1990-91). . . . Named to Czechoslovakian League All-Star team (1991-92).

Season Team	League	REGULAR SEASON					PLAYOFFS				
		Gms.	G	A	Pts.	Pen.	Gms.	G	A	Pts.	Pen.
90-91—Nitra	Czech.	50	34	16	50	18	—	—	—	—	—
91-92—Dukla Trencin	Czech.	32	23	25	*48	. . .	—	—	—	—	—
92-93—Dukla Trencin	Czech.	43	38	41	79	. . .	—	—	—	—	—

PANDOLFO, JAY
LW, DEVILS

PERSONAL: Born December 27, 1974, at Winchester, Mass. . . . 6-1/195. . . . Shoots left.
HIGH SCHOOL: Burlington (Mass.).
COLLEGE: Boston University.
TRANSACTIONS/CAREER NOTES: Selected by New Jersey Devils in second round (second Devils pick, 32nd overall) of NHL entry draft (June 26, 1993).

Season Team	League	REGULAR SEASON					PLAYOFFS				
		Gms.	G	A	Pts.	Pen.	Gms.	G	A	Pts.	Pen.
90-91—Burlington H.S.	Mass. H.S.	20	19	27	46	10	—	—	—	—	—
91-92—Burlington H.S.	Mass. H.S.	20	35	34	69	14	—	—	—	—	—
92-93—Boston University	Hockey East	39	17	23	40	16	—	—	—	—	—

PANTELEYEV, GRIGORI
LW/RW, BRUINS

PERSONAL: Born November 13, 1972, at Riga, U.S.S.R. . . . 5-9/194. . . . Shoots left. . . . Name pronounced pant-uh-LAY-eff.
TRANSACTIONS/CAREER NOTES: Selected by Boston Bruins in sixth round (fifth Bruins pick, 136th overall) of NHL entry draft (June 20, 1992).

OP

Season Team	League	REGULAR SEASON					PLAYOFFS				
		Gms.	G	A	Pts.	Pen.	Gms.	G	A	Pts.	Pen.
90-91—Dynamo Riga	USSR	23	4	1	5	4	—	—	—	—	—
91-92—Riga	CIS	26	4	8	12	4	—	—	—	—	—
92-93—Providence	AHL	39	17	30	47	22	3	0	0	0	10
—Boston	NHL	39	8	6	14	12	—	—	—	—	—
NHL totals		39	8	6	14	12					

PAQUETTE, CHARLES
D, BRUINS

PERSONAL: Born June 17, 1975, at Lachute, Que.... 6-1/193.... Shoots left.
TRANSACTIONS/CAREER NOTES: Selected by Boston Bruins in fourth round (third Bruins pick, 88th overall) of NHL entry draft (June 26, 1993).

Season Team	League	REGULAR SEASON					PLAYOFFS				
		Gms.	G	A	Pts.	Pen.	Gms.	G	A	Pts.	Pen.
91-92—Trois-Rivieres	QMJHL	60	1	7	8	101	6	0	0	0	2
92-93—Sherbrooke	QMJHL	54	2	5	7	104	15	0	0	0	33

PARKS, GREG
C, ISLANDERS

PERSONAL: Born March 25, 1967, at Edmonton, Alta.... 5-9/180.... Shoots right.... Full name: Gregory Roy Parks.
COLLEGE: Bowling Green State.
TRANSACTIONS/CAREER NOTES: Signed as free agent by Springfield Indians (September 1989).... Signed as free agent by New York Islanders (August 13, 1990).
HONORS: Named to NCAA All-America West first team (1988-89).... Named to CCHA All-Star first team (1988-89).

Season Team	League	REGULAR SEASON					PLAYOFFS				
		Gms.	G	A	Pts.	Pen.	Gms.	G	A	Pts.	Pen.
84-85—St. Albert	AJHL	48	36	74	110	...	—	—	—	—	—
85-86—Bowling Green State	CCHA	41	16	26	42	43	—	—	—	—	—
86-87—Bowling Green State	CCHA	45	23	27	50	52	—	—	—	—	—
87-88—Bowling Green State	CCHA	45	30	44	74	86	—	—	—	—	—
88-89—Bowling Green State	CCHA	47	32	42	74	96	—	—	—	—	—
89-90—Springfield	AHL	49	22	32	54	30	18	9	†13	*22	22
—Johnstown	ECHL	8	5	9	14	7	—	—	—	—	—
90-91—Capital District	AHL	48	32	43	75	67	—	—	—	—	—
—New York Islanders	NHL	20	1	2	3	4	—	—	—	—	—
91-92—New York Islanders	NHL	1	0	0	0	2	—	—	—	—	—
—Capital District	AHL	70	36	57	93	84	7	5	8	13	4
92-93—Leksand	Sweden	39	21	19	40	66	1	0	0	0	4
—Canadian national team	Int'l	9	2	2	4	4	—	—	—	—	—
—New York Islanders	NHL	2	0	0	0	0	2	0	0	0	0
NHL totals		23	1	2	3	6	2	0	0	0	0

PARROTT, JEFF
D, NORDIQUES

PERSONAL: Born April 6, 1971, at The Pas, Man.... 6-1/195.... Shoots right.
COLLEGE: Minnesota-Duluth.
TRANSACTIONS/CAREER NOTES: Strained knee ligaments (November 1988).... Selected by Quebec Nordiques in sixth round (fourth Nordiques pick, 106th overall) of NHL entry draft (June 16, 1990).

Season Team	League	REGULAR SEASON					PLAYOFFS				
		Gms.	G	A	Pts.	Pen.	Gms.	G	A	Pts.	Pen.
88-89—Notre Dame	SJHL	51	6	18	24	143	—	—	—	—	—
89-90—Minnesota-Duluth	WCHA	35	1	6	7	64	—	—	—	—	—
90-91—Minnesota-Duluth	WCHA	39	2	8	10	65	—	—	—	—	—
91-92—Minnesota-Duluth	WCHA	33	1	8	9	78	—	—	—	—	—
92-93—Minnesota-Duluth	WCHA	39	4	13	17	116	—	—	—	—	—

PASLAWSKI, GREG
RW, FLAMES

PERSONAL: Born August 25, 1961, at Kindersley, Sask. ... 5-11/190. ... Shoots right.... Full name: Gregory Stephen Paslawski.
TRANSACTIONS/CAREER NOTES: Signed as free agent by Montreal Canadiens (October 5, 1981).... Traded by Canadiens with C Doug Wickenheiser and D Gilbert Delorme to St. Louis Blues for LW Perry Turnbull (December 21, 1983).... Injured knee (February 20, 1986).... Injured knee (December 1986).... Pinched nerve in left leg (October 1987).... Underwent disk surgery (November 1987).... Traded by Blues with third-round pick in 1989 draft (C Kris Draper) to Winnipeg Jets for second-round pick in 1989 draft (LW Denny Felsner) (June 17, 1989).... Ruptured bicep muscle in right shoulder (December 13, 1990).... Pulled groin (January 21, 1991).... Traded by Jets to Buffalo Sabres as future considerations to complete the C Dale Hawerchuk trade of June 1990 (February 4, 1991).... Selected by San Jose Sharks in NHL expansion draft (May 30, 1991).... Traded by Sharks to Quebec Nordiques for C Tony Hrkac (May 30, 1991).... Signed as free agent by Philadelphia Flyers (August 25, 1992).... Traded by Flyers to Calgary Flames for future considerations (March 18, 1993).

Season Team	League	REGULAR SEASON					PLAYOFFS				
		Gms.	G	A	Pts.	Pen.	Gms.	G	A	Pts.	Pen.
80-81—Prince Albert	SJHL	59	55	60	115	106	—	—	—	—	—
81-82—Nova Scotia	AHL	43	15	11	26	31	—	—	—	—	—
82-83—Nova Scotia	AHL	75	46	42	88	32	6	1	3	4	8
83-84—Montreal	NHL	26	1	4	5	4	—	—	—	—	—
—St. Louis	NHL	34	8	6	14	17	9	1	0	1	2
84-85—St. Louis	NHL	72	22	20	42	21	3	0	0	0	2

Season	Team	League	REGULAR SEASON					PLAYOFFS				
			Gms.	G	A	Pts.	Pen.	Gms.	G	A	Pts.	Pen.
85-86	St. Louis	NHL	56	22	11	33	18	17	10	7	17	13
86-87	St. Louis	NHL	76	29	35	64	27	6	1	1	2	4
87-88	St. Louis	NHL	17	2	1	3	4	3	1	1	2	2
88-89	St. Louis	NHL	75	26	26	52	18	9	2	1	3	2
89-90	Winnipeg	NHL	71	18	30	48	14	7	1	3	4	0
90-91	Winnipeg	NHL	43	9	10	19	10	—	—	—	—	—
	Buffalo	NHL	12	2	1	3	4	—	—	—	—	—
91-92	Quebec	NHL	80	28	17	45	18	—	—	—	—	—
92-93	Philadelphia	NHL	60	14	19	33	12	—	—	—	—	—
	Calgary	NHL	13	4	5	9	0	6	3	0	3	0
NHL totals			635	185	185	370	167	60	19	13	32	25

PATRICK, JAMES
D, RANGERS

PERSONAL: Born June 14, 1963, at Winnipeg, Man. . . . 6-2/192. . . . Shoots right. . . . Brother of Steve Patrick, right winger, Buffalo Sabres, New York Rangers and Quebec Nordiques (1980-81 through 1985-86).
COLLEGE: North Dakota.
TRANSACTIONS/CAREER NOTES: Selected by New York Rangers as underage junior in first round (first Rangers pick, ninth overall) of NHL entry draft (June 10, 1981). . . . Injured groin (October 1984). . . . Pinched nerve (December 15, 1985). . . . Strained left knee ligaments (March 1988). . . . Bruised shoulder and chest (December 1988). . . . Pulled groin (March 13, 1989). . . . Sprained shoulder (November 4, 1992); missed three games. . . . Bruised right shoulder (November 27, 1992); missed three games. . . . Sprained left knee (January 27, 1993); missed four games. . . . Suffered herniated disc (February 24, 1993); missed two games. . . . Suffered herniated disc (March 28, 1993); missed remainder of season.
HONORS: Named Player of the Year (1980-81). . . . Named to SJHL All-Star first team (1980-81). . . . Won WCHA Rookie of the Year Award (1981-82). . . . Named to WCHA All-Star second team (1981-82). . . . Named to NCAA All-Tournament team (1981-82). . . . Named to NCAA All-America West team (1982-83). . . . Named to WCHA All-Star first team (1982-83).

Season	Team	League	REGULAR SEASON					PLAYOFFS				
			Gms.	G	A	Pts.	Pen.	Gms.	G	A	Pts.	Pen.
80-81	Prince Albert	SJHL	59	21	61	82	162	4	1	6	7	0
81-82	Univ. of North Dakota	WCHA	42	5	24	29	26	—	—	—	—	—
82-83	Univ. of North Dakota	WCHA	36	12	36	48	29	—	—	—	—	—
83-84	Canadian Olympic Team	Int'l	63	7	24	31	52	—	—	—	—	—
	New York Rangers	NHL	12	1	7	8	2	5	0	3	3	2
84-85	New York Rangers	NHL	75	8	28	36	71	3	0	0	0	4
85-86	New York Rangers	NHL	75	14	29	43	88	16	1	5	6	34
86-87	New York Rangers	NHL	78	10	45	55	62	6	1	2	3	2
87-88	New York Rangers	NHL	70	17	45	62	52	—	—	—	—	—
88-89	New York Rangers	NHL	68	11	36	47	41	4	0	1	1	2
89-90	New York Rangers	NHL	73	14	43	57	50	10	3	8	11	0
90-91	New York Rangers	NHL	74	10	49	59	58	6	0	0	0	6
91-92	New York Rangers	NHL	80	14	57	71	54	13	0	7	7	12
92-93	New York Rangers	NHL	60	5	21	26	61	—	—	—	—	—
NHL totals			665	104	360	464	539	63	5	26	31	62

PATTERSON, COLIN
RW/C, SABRES

PERSONAL: Born May 11, 1960, at Rexdale, Ont. . . . 6-2/195. . . . Shoots right.
COLLEGE: Clarkson (N.Y.).
TRANSACTIONS/CAREER NOTES: Signed as free agent by Calgary Flames (March 24, 1983). . . . Injured shoulder (March 14, 1984). . . . Tore knee ligaments (January 1985). . . . Pulled hamstring (October 1987). . . . Sprained ankle (December 1987). . . . Suffered concussion (November 1988). . . . Bruised foot (January 11, 1989). . . . Broke nose (April 24, 1989). . . . Broke right ankle (March 24, 1990). . . . Tore anterior cruciate ligament of right knee (September 18, 1990). . . . Underwent knee surgery (October 12, 1990). . . . Underwent additional surgery (December 7, 1990); missed remainder of regular season. . . . Traded by Flames to Buffalo Sabres for future considerations (October 24, 1991). . . . Suffered sore left knee (February 7, 1992); missed six games. . . . Injured left knee (February 29, 1992); missed seven games. . . . Suffered lacerated knee (March 7, 1993); missed three games.
HONORS: Named to ECAC All-Star second team (1982-83).
MISCELLANEOUS: Member of Stanley Cup championship team (1989).

Season	Team	League	REGULAR SEASON					PLAYOFFS				
			Gms.	G	A	Pts.	Pen.	Gms.	G	A	Pts.	Pen.
80-81	Clarkson	ECAC	34	20	31	51	8	—	—	—	—	—
81-82	Clarkson	ECAC	35	21	31	52	32	—	—	—	—	—
82-83	Clarkson	ECAC	31	23	29	52	30	—	—	—	—	—
	Colorado	CHL	7	1	1	2	0	3	0	0	0	15
83-84	Colorado	CHL	6	2	3	5	9	—	—	—	—	—
	Calgary	NHL	56	13	14	27	15	11	1	1	2	6
84-85	Calgary	NHL	57	22	21	43	5	4	0	0	0	5
85-86	Calgary	NHL	61	14	13	27	22	19	6	3	9	10
86-87	Calgary	NHL	68	13	13	26	41	6	0	2	2	2
87-88	Calgary	NHL	39	7	11	18	28	9	1	0	1	8
88-89	Calgary	NHL	74	14	24	38	56	22	3	10	13	24
89-90	Calgary	NHL	61	5	3	8	20	—	—	—	—	—
90-91	Calgary	NHL	—	—	—	—	—	1	0	0	0	0
91-92	Buffalo	NHL	52	4	8	12	30	5	1	0	1	0
92-93	Buffalo	NHL	36	4	2	6	22	8	0	1	1	57
NHL totals			504	96	109	205	239	85	12	17	29	57

P

PAYNTER, KENT
D, SENATORS

PERSONAL: Born April 27, 1965, at Summerside, P.E.I. . . . 6-0/185. . . . Shoots left. . . . Full name: Kent Douglas Paynter. **HIGH SCHOOL:** Three Oaks (Summerside, P.E.I.).
TRANSACTIONS/CAREER NOTES: Selected by Chicago Blackhawks as underage junior in eighth round (ninth Blackhawks pick, 159th overall) of NHL entry draft (June 8, 1983). . . . Signed as free agent by Washington Capitals (August 21, 1989). . . . Traded by Capitals with LW Bob Joyce and C Tyler Larter to Winnipeg Jets for LW Brent Hughes, LW Craig Duncanson and C Simon Wheeldon (May 21, 1991). . . . Selected by Ottawa Senators in NHL expansion draft (June 18, 1992). . . . Suffered charley horse (January 30, 1993); missed four games.

			REGULAR SEASON					PLAYOFFS			
Season Team	League	Gms.	G	A	Pts.	Pen.	Gms.	G	A	Pts.	Pen.
81-82—Western Capitals	PEIJHL	35	7	23	30	66	—	—	—	—	—
82-83—Kitchener	OHL	65	4	11	15	97	12	1	0	1	20
83-84—Kitchener	OHL	65	9	27	36	94	16	4	9	13	18
84-85—Kitchener	OHL	58	7	28	35	93	4	2	1	3	4
85-86—Nova Scotia	AHL	23	1	2	3	36	—	—	—	—	—
—Saginaw	IHL	4	0	1	1	2	—	—	—	—	—
86-87—Nova Scotia	AHL	66	2	6	8	57	2	0	0	0	0
87-88—Saginaw	IHL	74	8	20	28	141	10	0	1	1	30
—Chicago	NHL	2	0	0	0	2	—	—	—	—	—
88-89—Chicago	NHL	1	0	0	0	2	—	—	—	—	—
—Saginaw	IHL	69	12	14	26	148	6	2	2	4	17
89-90—Washington	NHL	13	1	2	3	18	3	0	0	0	10
—Baltimore	AHL	60	7	20	27	110	11	5	6	11	34
90-91—Baltimore	AHL	43	10	17	27	64	6	2	1	3	8
—Washington	NHL	1	0	0	0	15	1	0	0	0	0
91-92—Moncton	AHL	62	3	30	33	71	11	2	6	8	25
—Winnipeg	NHL	5	0	0	0	4	—	—	—	—	—
92-93—New Haven	AHL	48	7	17	24	81	—	—	—	—	—
—Ottawa	NHL	6	0	0	0	20	—	—	—	—	—
NHL totals		28	1	2	3	61	4	0	0	0	10

PEACOCK, SHANE
D, PENGUINS

PERSONAL: Born July 7, 1973, at Edmonton, Alta. . . . 5-9/198. . . . Shoots right.
TRANSACTIONS/CAREER NOTES: Selected by Pittsburgh Penguins in third round (third Penguins pick, 60th overall) of NHL entry draft (June 22, 1991).

			REGULAR SEASON					PLAYOFFS			
Season Team	League	Gms.	G	A	Pts.	Pen.	Gms.	G	A	Pts.	Pen.
88-89—Notre Dame	SCMHL	28	8	12	20	160	—	—	—	—	—
89-90—Lethbridge	WHL	65	7	23	30	60	19	2	8	10	42
90-91—Lethbridge	WHL	69	12	50	62	102	16	1	14	15	26
91-92—Lethbridge	WHL	67	35	45	80	217	5	2	5	7	2
92-93—Lethbridge	WHL	65	27	75	102	100	4	4	3	7	2

PEAKE, PAT
C, CAPITALS

PERSONAL: Born May 28, 1973, at Detroit. . . . 6-0/195. . . . Shoots right. . . . Full name: Patrick Michael Peake.
TRANSACTIONS/CAREER NOTES: Injured wrist (August 31, 1990). . . . Selected by Washington Capitals in first round (Capitals first pick, 14th overall) of NHL entry draft (June 22, 1991).
HONORS: Can.HL Player of the Year (1992-93). . . . Won Red Tilson Trophy (1992-93). . . . Won William Hanley Trophy (1992-93). . . . Named to Can.HL All-Star first team (1992-93). . . . Named to OHL All-Star first team (1992-93).

			REGULAR SEASON					PLAYOFFS			
Season Team	League	Gms.	G	A	Pts.	Pen.	Gms.	G	A	Pts.	Pen.
89-90—Detroit Compuware	NAJHL	40	36	37	73	57	—	—	—	—	—
90-91—Detroit	OHL	63	39	51	90	54	—	—	—	—	—
91-92—Detroit	OHL	53	41	52	93	44	7	8	9	17	10
—Baltimore	AHL	3	1	0	1	4	—	—	—	—	—
92-93—Detroit	OHL	46	58	78	136	64	2	1	3	4	2

PEARSON, ROB
RW, MAPLE LEAFS

PERSONAL: Born August 3, 1971, at Oshawa, Ont. . . . 6-1/180. . . . Shoots right.
TRANSACTIONS/CAREER NOTES: Broke wrist (November 13, 1988). . . . Selected by Toronto Maple Leafs in first round (second Maple Leafs pick, 12th overall) of NHL entry draft (June 17, 1989). . . . Dislocated right knee (August 15, 1989). . . . Suspended five games by OHL for checking from behind (February 7, 1990). . . . Broke collarbone (August 1990). . . . Traded by Belleville Bulls to Oshawa Generals for C Jarrod Skalde (November 18, 1990).
HONORS: Won Jim Mahon Memorial Trophy (1990-91). . . . Named to OHL All-Star first team (1990-91).

			REGULAR SEASON					PLAYOFFS			
Season Team	League	Gms.	G	A	Pts.	Pen.	Gms.	G	A	Pts.	Pen.
88-89—Belleville	OHL	26	8	12	20	51	—	—	—	—	—
89-90—Belleville	OHL	58	48	40	88	174	11	5	5	10	26
90-91—Belleville	OHL	10	6	3	9	27	—	—	—	—	—
—Oshawa	OHL	41	57	52	109	76	16	16	17	33	39
—Newmarket	AHL	3	0	0	0	29	—	—	—	—	—
91-92—Toronto	NHL	47	14	10	24	58	—	—	—	—	—
—St. John's	AHL	27	15	14	29	107	13	5	4	9	40
92-93—Toronto	NHL	78	23	14	37	211	14	2	2	4	31
NHL totals		125	37	24	61	269	14	2	2	4	31

P

PEARSON, SCOTT
LW, OILERS

PERSONAL: Born December 19, 1969, at Cornwall, Ont.... 6-1/205.... Shoots left.
TRANSACTIONS/CAREER NOTES: Underwent surgery to left wrist (May 1988).... Selected by Toronto Maple Leafs in first round (first Maple Leafs pick, sixth overall) of NHL entry draft (June 11, 1988).... Traded by Maple Leafs with second-round picks in 1991 draft (D Eric Lavigne) and 1992 draft (D Tuomas Gronman) to Quebec Nordiques for C/LW Aaron Broten, D Michel Petit and RW Lucien Deblois (November 17, 1990).... Sprained left knee (September 27, 1992); missed first 22 games of season.... Traded by Nordiques to Edmonton Oilers for LW Martin Gelinas and sixth-round pick (C Nicholas Checco) in 1993 draft (June 20, 1993).

			REGULAR SEASON					PLAYOFFS			
Season	Team	League	Gms.	G	A	Pts.	Pen.	Gms.	G	A	Pts.	Pen.
85-86—Kingston		OHL	63	16	23	39	56	—	—	—	—	—
86-87—Kingston		OHL	62	30	24	54	101	9	3	3	6	42
87-88—Kingston		OHL	46	26	32	58	118	—	—	—	—	—
88-89—Kingston		OHL	13	9	8	17	34	—	—	—	—	—
—Niagara Falls		OHL	32	26	34	60	90	17	14	10	24	53
—Toronto		NHL	9	0	1	1	2	—	—	—	—	—
89-90—Newmarket		AHL	18	12	11	23	64	—	—	—	—	—
—Toronto		NHL	41	5	10	15	90	2	2	0	2	10
90-91—Toronto		NHL	12	0	0	0	20	—	—	—	—	—
—Quebec		NHL	35	11	4	15	86	—	—	—	—	—
—Halifax		AHL	24	12	15	27	44	—	—	—	—	—
91-92—Quebec		NHL	10	1	2	3	14	—	—	—	—	—
—Halifax		AHL	5	2	1	3	4	—	—	—	—	—
92-93—Halifax		AHL	5	3	1	4	25	—	—	—	—	—
—Quebec		NHL	41	13	1	14	95	3	0	0	0	0
NHL totals			148	30	18	48	307	5	2	0	2	10

PECA, MIKE
RW/C, CANUCKS

PERSONAL: Born March 26, 1974, at Toronto.... 5-11/165.... Shoots right.
HIGH SCHOOL: LaSalle Secondary School (Kinston, Ont.).
TRANSACTIONS/CAREER NOTES: Selected by Vancouver Canucks in second round (second Canucks pick, 40th overall) of NHL entry draft (June 20, 1992).

			REGULAR SEASON					PLAYOFFS			
Season	Team	League	Gms.	G	A	Pts.	Pen.	Gms.	G	A	Pts.	Pen.
90-91—Sudbury		OHL	62	14	27	41	24	5	1	0	1	7
91-92—Sudbury		OHL	39	16	34	50	61	—	—	—	—	—
—Ottawa		OHL	27	8	17	25	32	11	6	10	16	6
92-93—Ottawa		OHL	55	38	64	102	80	—	—	—	—	—
—Hamilton		AHL	9	6	3	9	11	—	—	—	—	—

PEDERSEN, ALLEN
D, WHALERS

PERSONAL: Born January 13, 1965, at Edmonton, Alta.... 6-3/210.... Shoots left....
Name pronounced PEE-duhr-suhn.
TRANSACTIONS/CAREER NOTES: Selected by Boston Bruins as underage junior in fifth round (fifth Bruins pick, 102nd overall) of NHL entry draft (June 8, 1983).... Separated right shoulder (November 3, 1988).... Pulled abdominal muscle (December 1988).... Bruised hip (January 1990).... Selected by Minnesota North Stars in NHL expansion draft (May 30, 1991).... Suffered back spasms (October 28, 1991); missed nine games.... Tore abdominal muscles (February 17, 1992); missed 23 games.... Traded by North Stars to Hartford Whalers for future considerations (June 15, 1992).... Injured groin (February 17, 1993); missed six games.

			REGULAR SEASON					PLAYOFFS			
Season	Team	League	Gms.	G	A	Pts.	Pen.	Gms.	G	A	Pts.	Pen.
82-83—Medicine Hat		WHL	63	3	10	13	49	5	0	0	0	7
83-84—Medicine Hat		WHL	44	0	11	11	47	14	0	2	2	24
84-85—Medicine Hat		WHL	72	6	16	22	66	10	0	0	0	9
85-86—Moncton		AHL	59	1	8	9	39	3	0	0	0	0
86-87—Boston		NHL	79	1	11	12	71	4	0	0	0	4
87-88—Boston		NHL	78	0	6	6	90	21	0	0	0	34
88-89—Boston		NHL	51	0	6	6	69	10	0	0	0	2
89-90—Boston		NHL	68	1	2	3	71	21	0	0	0	41
90-91—Maine		AHL	15	0	6	6	18	2	0	1	1	2
—Boston		NHL	57	2	6	8	107	8	0	0	0	10
91-92—Minnesota		NHL	29	0	1	1	10	—	—	—	—	—
92-93—Hartford		NHL	59	1	4	5	60	—	—	—	—	—
NHL totals			421	5	36	41	478	64	0	0	0	91

PEDERSON, DENIS
C, DEVILS

PERSONAL: Born September 10, 1975, at Prince Albert, Sask.... 6-2/189.... Shoots right.
HIGH SCHOOL: Carlton Comprehensive (Prince Albert, Sask.).
TRANSACTIONS/CAREER NOTES: Selected by New Jersey Devils in first round (first Devils pick, 13th overall) of NHL entry draft (June 26, 1993).
HONORS: Named to WHL All-Rookie team (1992-93).

			REGULAR SEASON					PLAYOFFS			
Season	Team	League	Gms.	G	A	Pts.	Pen.	Gms.	G	A	Pts.	Pen.
91-92—Prince Albert		WHL	10	0	0	0	6	7	0	1	1	13
92-93—Prince Albert		WHL	72	33	40	73	134	—	—	—	—	—

P

PEDERSON, MARK
LW, SHARKS

PERSONAL: Born January 14, 1968, at Prelate, Sask. . . . 6-2/196. . . . Shoots left. . . . Name pronounced PEE-duhr-suhn.

TRANSACTIONS/CAREER NOTES: Injured shoulder (March 1985). . . . Selected by Montreal Canadiens as underage junior in first round (first Canadiens pick, 15th overall) of NHL entry draft (June 21, 1986). . . . Traded by Canadiens to Philadelphia Flyers for second-round pick in 1991 draft (C Jim Campbell) and future considerations (March 5, 1991). . . . Dislocated shoulder (November 23, 1991); missed 10 games. . . . Traded by Flyers to San Jose Sharks for RW Dave Snuggerud (December 19, 1992). . . . Separated shoulder (January 5, 1993); missed 13 games. . . . Sprained knee (February 14, 1993); missed nine games.

HONORS: Named to WHL (East) All-Star first team (1986-87). . . . Named to WHL All-Star second team (1987-88). . . . Named to AHL All-Star first team (1989-90).

Season	Team	League	REGULAR SEASON Gms.	G	A	Pts.	Pen.	PLAYOFFS Gms.	G	A	Pts.	Pen.
84-85	Medicine Hat	WHL	71	42	40	82	63	10	3	2	5	0
85-86	Medicine Hat	WHL	72	46	60	106	46	25	12	6	18	25
86-87	Medicine Hat	WHL	69	56	46	102	58	20	†19	7	26	14
87-88	Medicine Hat	WHL	62	53	58	111	55	16	†13	6	19	16
88-89	Sherbrooke	AHL	75	43	38	81	53	6	7	5	12	4
89-90	Montreal	NHL	9	0	2	2	2	2	0	0	0	0
	Sherbrooke	AHL	72	53	42	95	60	11	10	8	18	19
90-91	Montreal	NHL	47	8	15	23	18	—	—	—	—	—
	Philadelphia	NHL	12	2	1	3	5	—	—	—	—	—
91-92	Philadelphia	NHL	58	15	25	40	22	—	—	—	—	—
92-93	Philadelphia	NHL	14	3	4	7	6	—	—	—	—	—
	San Jose	NHL	27	7	3	10	22	—	—	—	—	—
NHL totals			167	35	50	85	75	2	0	0	0	0

PEDERSON, TOM
D, SHARKS

PERSONAL: Born January 14, 1970, at Bloomington, Minn. . . . 5-9/180. . . . Shoots right. . . . Full name: Thomas Stuart Pederson.

HIGH SCHOOL: Thomas Jefferson (Bloomington, Minn.).

COLLEGE: Minnesota.

TRANSACTIONS/CAREER NOTES: Selected by Minnesota North Stars in 11th round (12th North Stars pick, 217th overall) of NHL entry draft (June 17, 1989). . . . Selected by San Jose Sharks in NHL dispersal draft (May 30, 1991). . . . Strained back (January 8, 1993); missed one game. . . . Injured shoulder (January 30, 1993); missed four games. . . . Strained groin (February 22, 1993); missed five games.

Season	Team	League	REGULAR SEASON Gms.	G	A	Pts.	Pen.	PLAYOFFS Gms.	G	A	Pts.	Pen.
87-88	Jefferson HS	Minn. H.S.	22	16	27	43	...	—	—	—	—	—
88-89	University of Minnesota	WCHA	42	5	24	29	46	—	—	—	—	—
89-90	University of Minnesota	WCHA	43	8	30	38	58	—	—	—	—	—
90-91	University of Minnesota	WCHA	36	12	20	32	46	—	—	—	—	—
91-92	U.S. national team	Int'l	44	3	11	14	41	—	—	—	—	—
	Kansas City	IHL	20	6	9	15	16	13	1	6	7	14
92-93	Kansas City	IHL	26	6	15	21	10	12	1	6	7	2
	San Jose	NHL	44	7	13	20	31	—	—	—	—	—
NHL totals			44	7	13	20	31					

PELLERIN, SCOTT
LW, DEVILS

PERSONAL: Born January 9, 1970, at Shediac, N.B. . . . 5-10/185. . . . Shoots left. . . . Full name: Jaque-Frederick Scott Pellerin.

COLLEGE: Maine.

TRANSACTIONS/CAREER NOTES: Selected by New Jersey Devils in third round (fourth Devils pick, 47th overall) of NHL entry draft (June 17, 1989).

HONORS: Named Hockey East co-Rookie of the Year with Rob Gaudreau (1988-89). . . . Named to Hockey East All-Rookie team (1988-89). . . . Won Hobey Baker Memorial Trophy (1991-92). . . . Named Hockey East Player of the Year (1991-92). . . . Named Hockey East Playoff Most Valuable Player (1991-92). . . . Named to NCAA All-America East first team (1991-92). . . . Named to Hockey East All-Star first team (1991-92).

Season	Team	League	REGULAR SEASON Gms.	G	A	Pts.	Pen.	PLAYOFFS Gms.	G	A	Pts.	Pen.
87-88	Notre Dame	SJHL	57	37	49	86	139	—	—	—	—	—
88-89	University of Maine	Hockey East	45	29	33	62	92	—	—	—	—	—
89-90	University of Maine	Hockey East	42	22	34	56	68	—	—	—	—	—
90-91	University of Maine	Hockey East	43	23	25	48	60	—	—	—	—	—
91-92	University of Maine	Hockey East	37	†32	25	57	54	—	—	—	—	—
	Utica	AHL	—	—	—	—	—	3	1	0	1	0
92-93	Utica	AHL	27	15	18	33	33	2	0	1	1	0
	New Jersey	NHL	45	10	11	21	41	—	—	—	—	—
NHL totals			45	10	11	21	41					

PELTOLA, PEKKA
C/RW, JETS

PERSONAL: Born June 24, 1965, at Helsinki, Finland. . . . 6-2/196. . . . Shoots right.

TRANSACTIONS/CAREER NOTES: Selected by Winnipeg Jets in seventh round (eighth Jets pick, 130th overall) of NHL entry draft (June 17, 1989).

HONORS: Named Finland Rookie of the Year (1988-89).

P

Season Team	League	REGULAR SEASON					PLAYOFFS				
		Gms.	G	A	Pts.	Pen.	Gms.	G	A	Pts.	Pen.
88-89—Helsinki HPK	Finland	43	28	30	58	62	—	—	—	—	—
89-90—Helsinki HPK	Finland	44	25	24	49	42	—	—	—	—	—
90-91—Helsinki HPK	Finland	41	23	18	41	66	8	3	2	5	10
91-92—Helsinki HPK	Finland	37	22	20	42	91	—	—	—	—	—
92-93—Lukko	Finland	48	26	24	50	42	3	0	0	0	4

PELTONEN, VILLE
LW/RW, SHARKS

PERSONAL: Born May 24, 1973, at Vantaa, Finland. . . . 5-11/172. . . . Shoots left.
TRANSACTIONS/CAREER NOTES: Selected by San Jose Sharks in third round (fourth Sharks pick, 58th overall) of NHL entry draft (June 26, 1993).

Season Team	League	REGULAR SEASON					PLAYOFFS				
		Gms.	G	A	Pts.	Pen.	Gms.	G	A	Pts.	Pen.
91-92—HIFK Helsinki	Finland	6	0	0	0	0	—	—	—	—	—
92-93—HIFK Helsinki	Finland	46	13	24	37	16	4	0	2	2	2

PELUSO, MIKE
LW, DEVILS

PERSONAL: Born November 8, 1965, at Hibbing, Minn. . . . 6-4/200. . . . Shoots left. . . . Full name: Michael David Peluso. . . . Name pronounced puh-LOO-soh.
HIGH SCHOOL: Greenway (Coleraine, Minn.).
COLLEGE: Alaska-Anchorage.
TRANSACTIONS/CAREER NOTES: Selected by New Jersey Devils in 10th round (10th Devils pick, 190th overall) of NHL entry draft (June 15, 1985). . . . Signed as free agent by Chicago Blackhawks (September 7, 1989). . . . Bruised jaw and cheek (November 8, 1990); missed five games. . . . Suspended 10 games by NHL for fighting (March 17, 1991). . . . Selected by Ottawa Senators in NHL expansion draft (June 18, 1992). . . . Suspended one game by NHL for accumulating three game misconduct penalties (February 1, 1993). . . . Suffered pinched nerve in neck (March 27, 1993); missed two games. . . . Traded by Senators to Devils (June 26, 1993) to complete deal in which Devils sent G Craig Billington, C/LW Troy Mallette and fourth-round pick in 1993 draft to Senators for G Peter Sidorkiewicz and future considerations (June 20, 1993).

Season Team	League	REGULAR SEASON					PLAYOFFS				
		Gms.	G	A	Pts.	Pen.	Gms.	G	A	Pts.	Pen.
84-85—Stratford	OPJHL	52	11	45	56	114	—	—	—	—	—
85-86—Alaska-Anchorage	Indep.	32	2	11	13	59	—	—	—	—	—
86-87—Alaska-Anchorage	Indep.	30	5	21	26	68	—	—	—	—	—
87-88—Alaska-Anchorage	Indep.	35	4	33	37	76	—	—	—	—	—
88-89—Alaska-Anchorage	Indep.	33	10	27	37	75	—	—	—	—	—
89-90—Indianapolis	IHL	75	7	10	17	279	14	0	1	1	58
—Chicago	NHL	2	0	0	0	15	—	—	—	—	—
90-91—Indianapolis	IHL	6	2	1	3	21	5	0	2	2	40
—Chicago	NHL	53	6	1	7	320	3	0	0	0	2
91-92—Chicago	NHL	63	6	3	9	*408	17	1	2	3	8
—Indianapolis	IHL	4	0	1	1	15	—	—	—	—	—
92-93—Ottawa	NHL	81	15	10	25	318	—	—	—	—	—
NHL totals		199	27	14	41	1061	20	1	2	3	10

PENNEY, CHAD
LW, SENATORS

PERSONAL: Born September 18, 1973, at Labrador City, Nfld. . . . 6-0/195. . . . Shoots left. . . . Full name: Chadwick Paul Penney.
HIGH SCHOOL: Chippewa Secondary School (North Bay, Ont.).
TRANSACTIONS/CAREER NOTES: Selected by Ottawa Senators in second round (second Senators pick, 25th overall) of NHL entry draft (June 20 1992).

Season Team	League	REGULAR SEASON					PLAYOFFS				
		Gms.	G	A	Pts.	Pen.	Gms.	G	A	Pts.	Pen.
90-91—North Bay	OHL	66	33	34	67	56	10	2	6	8	12
91-92—North Bay	OHL	57	25	27	52	93	21	13	17	30	9
—Can. national Jr. team	Int'l	7	0	0	0	2	—	—	—	—	—
92-93—North Bay	OHL	18	8	7	15	19	—	—	—	—	—
—Sault Ste. Marie	OHL	48	29	44	73	67	18	7	10	17	18

PERREAULT, NICOLAS
D, FLAMES

PERSONAL: Born April 24, 1972, at Loretteville, Que. . . . 6-3/200. . . . Shoots left.
COLLEGE: Michigan State.
TRANSACTIONS/CAREER NOTES: Separated shoulder (April 1988). . . . Selected by Calgary Flames in second round (second Flames pick, 26th overall) of NHL entry draft (June 16, 1990).

Season Team	League	REGULAR SEASON					PLAYOFFS				
		Gms.	G	A	Pts.	Pen.	Gms.	G	A	Pts.	Pen.
89-90—Hawksbury Hawks	QJHL	46	22	34	56	188	—	—	—	—	—
90-91—Michigan State	CCHA	34	1	7	8	32	—	—	—	—	—
91-92—Michigan State	CCHA	44	12	11	23	77	—	—	—	—	—
92-93—Michigan State	CCHA	38	7	6	13	90	—	—	—	—	—

PERREAULT, YANIC
C, MAPLE LEAFS

PERSONAL: Born April 4, 1971, at Sherbrooke, Que. . . . 5-11/182. . . . Shoots left. . . . Name pronounced puh-ROH.
TRANSACTIONS/CAREER NOTES: Selected by Toronto Maple Leafs in third round (first Maple Leafs pick, 47th overall) of NHL entry draft (June 22, 1991).

P

HONORS: Won Can.HL Rookie of the Year Award (1988-89).... Won Michel Bergeron Trophy (1988-89).... Won Marcel Robert Trophy (1989-90).... Won Michel Briere Trophy (1990-91).... Won Jean Beliveau Trophy (1990-91).... Won Frank J. Selke Trophy (1990-91).... Won Shell Cup (1990-91).... Named to QMJHL All-Star first team (1990-91).

			REGULAR SEASON					PLAYOFFS			
Season Team	League	Gms.	G	A	Pts.	Pen.	Gms.	G	A	Pts.	Pen.
88-89—Trois-Rivieres	QMJHL	70	53	55	108	48	—	—	—	—	—
89-90—Trois-Rivieres	QMJHL	63	51	63	114	75	7	6	5	11	19
90-91—Trois-Rivieres	QMJHL	67	*87	98	*185	103	6	4	7	11	6
91-92—St. John's	AHL	62	38	38	76	19	16	7	8	15	4
92-93—St. John's	AHL	79	49	46	95	56	9	4	5	9	2

PERSSON, JOAKIM
G, BRUINS

PERSONAL: Born May 4, 1970, at Stockholm, Sweden.... 5-11/168.... Shoots left.
TRANSACTIONS/CAREER NOTES: Selected by Boston Bruins in 10th round (10th Bruins pick, 259th overall) of NHL entry draft (June 26, 1993).

			REGULAR SEASON							PLAYOFFS						
Season Team	League	Gms.	Min.	W	L	T	GA	SO	Avg.	Gms.	Min.	W	L	GA	SO	Avg.
91-92—Hemmarby Stockholm	Sweden						Statistics unavailable.									
92-93—Hemmarby Stockholm	Sweden						Statistics unavailable.									

PETIT, MICHEL
D, FLAMES

PERSONAL: Born February 12, 1964, at St. Malo, Que.... 6-1/185.... Shoots right.... Name pronounced puh-TEE.
TRANSACTIONS/CAREER NOTES: Selected by Vancouver Canucks as underage junior in first round (first Canucks pick, 11th overall) of NHL entry draft (June 9, 1982).... Separated shoulder (March 1984).... Injured knee (February 1987).... Traded by Canucks to New York Rangers for D Willie Huber and D Larry Melnyk (November 1987).... Pulled groin (December 1987).... Fractured right collarbone (December 27, 1988); missed 11 games.... Traded by Rangers to Quebec Nordiques for D Randy Moller (October 5, 1989).... Traded by Nordiques with C/LW Aaron Broten and RW Lucien DeBlois to Toronto Maple Leafs for LW Scott Pearson and second-round picks in 1991 draft (D Eric Lavigne) and 1992 draft (D Tuomas Gronman) (November 17, 1990).... Sprained knee (February 4, 1991); missed five games.... Sprained thumb (November 9, 1991); missed six games.... Traded by Maple Leafs with D Alexander Godynyuk, RW Gary Leeman, LW Craig Berube and G Jeff Reese to Calgary Flames for C Doug Gilmour, D Jamie Macoun, LW Kent Manderville, D Ric Nattress and G Rick Wamsley (January 2, 1992).... Suffered back spasms (March 3, 1992); missed four games.... Pulled groin prior to 1992-93 season; missed first four games of season.... Dislocated right shoulder (October 22, 1992); missed 29 games.
HONORS: Won Raymond Lagace Trophy (1981-82).... Won Association of Journalists of Hockey Trophy (1981-82).... Named to QMJHL All-Star first team (1981-82 and 1982-83).

			REGULAR SEASON					PLAYOFFS			
Season Team	League	Gms.	G	A	Pts.	Pen.	Gms.	G	A	Pts.	Pen.
81-82—Sherbrooke	QMJHL	63	10	39	49	106	22	5	20	25	24
82-83—St. Jean	QMJHL	62	19	67	86	196	3	0	0	0	35
—Vancouver	NHL	2	0	0	0	0	—	—	—	—	—
83-84—Canadian Olympic Team	Int'l	19	3	10	13	58	—	—	—	—	—
—Vancouver	NHL	44	6	9	15	53	1	0	0	0	0
84-85—Vancouver	NHL	69	5	26	31	127	—	—	—	—	—
85-86—Fredericton	AHL	25	0	13	13	79	—	—	—	—	—
—Vancouver	NHL	32	1	6	7	27	—	—	—	—	—
86-87—Vancouver	NHL	69	12	13	25	131	—	—	—	—	—
87-88—Vancouver	NHL	10	0	3	3	35	—	—	—	—	—
—New York Rangers	NHL	64	9	24	33	223	—	—	—	—	—
88-89—New York Rangers	NHL	69	8	25	33	156	4	0	2	2	27
89-90—Quebec	NHL	63	12	24	36	215	—	—	—	—	—
90-91—Quebec	NHL	19	4	7	11	47	—	—	—	—	—
—Toronto	NHL	54	9	19	28	132	—	—	—	—	—
91-92—Toronto	NHL	34	1	13	14	85	—	—	—	—	—
—Calgary	NHL	36	3	10	13	79	—	—	—	—	—
92-93—Calgary	NHL	35	3	9	12	54	—	—	—	—	—
NHL totals		600	73	188	261	1364	5	0	2	2	27

PETROV, OLEG
RW, CANADIENS

PERSONAL: Born April 18, 1971, at Moscow, U.S.S.R.... 5-9/161.... Shoots left.
TRANSACTIONS/CAREER NOTES: Selected by Montreal Canadiens in sixth round (ninth Canadiens pick, 127th overall) of NHL entry draft (June 22, 1991).

			REGULAR SEASON					PLAYOFFS			
Season Team	League	Gms.	G	A	Pts.	Pen.	Gms.	G	A	Pts.	Pen.
90-91—CSKA Moscow	USSR	43	7	4	11	8	—	—	—	—	—
91-92—CSKA Moscow	CIS	34	8	13	21	6	—	—	—	—	—
92-93—Montreal	NHL	9	2	1	3	10	1	0	0	0	0
—Fredericton	AHL	55	26	29	55	36	5	4	1	5	0
NHL totals		9	2	1	3	10	1	0	0	0	0

PETROVICKY, ROBERT
C, WHALERS

PERSONAL: Born October 26, 1973, at Kosice, Czechoslovakia.... 5-11/172.... Shoots left.... Name pronounced PEH-troh-VEET-skee.
TRANSACTIONS/CAREER NOTES: Selected by Hartford Whalers in first round (first Whalers pick, ninth overall) of NHL entry draft (June 20, 1992)....

P

Sprained left ankle (February 28, 1993); missed five games.
HONORS: Named to Czechoslovakian League All-Star team (1991-92).

			REGULAR SEASON					PLAYOFFS				
Season	Team	League	Gms.	G	A	Pts.	Pen.	Gms.	G	A	Pts.	Pen.
90-91—Dukla Trencin		Czech.	33	9	14	23	12	—	—	—	—	—
91-92—Dukla Trencin		Czech.	46	25	36	61	...	—	—	—	—	—
92-93—Hartford		NHL	42	3	6	9	45	—	—	—	—	—
—Springfield		AHL	16	5	3	8	39	15	5	6	11	14
NHL totals			42	3	6	9	45					

PHILPOTT, ETHAN
RW, SABRES

PERSONAL: Born February 11, 1975, at Rochester, Minn. . . . 6-4/230. . . . Shoots right. **HIGH SCHOOL:** Phillips Academy (Andover, Mass.). **TRANSACTIONS/CAREER NOTES:** Selected by Buffalo Sabres in third round (second Sabres pick, 64th overall) of NHL entry draft (June 26, 1993).

			REGULAR SEASON					PLAYOFFS				
Season	Team	League	Gms.	G	A	Pts.	Pen.	Gms.	G	A	Pts.	Pen.
90-91—Phillips Andover Acad.		Mass. H.S.	20	13	7	20	0	—	—	—	—	—
91-92—Phillips Andover Acad.		Mass. H.S.	22	7	20	27	16	—	—	—	—	—
92-93—Phillips Andover Acad.		Mass. H.S.	18	17	19	36	22	—	—	—	—	—

PICARD, MICHEL
LW, SHARKS

PERSONAL: Born November 7, 1969, at Beauport, Que. . . . 5-11/190. . . . Shoots left. **TRANSACTIONS/CAREER NOTES:** Selected by Hartford Whalers in ninth round (eighth Whalers pick, 178th overall) of NHL entry draft (June 17, 1989). . . . Separated shoulder (November 14, 1991); missed seven games. . . . Traded by Whalers to San Jose Sharks for future considerations (October 9, 1992); Sharks sent LW Yvon Corriveau to complete deal (January 21, 1993).
HONORS: Named to QMJHL All-Star second team (1988-89). . . . Named to AHL All-Star first team (1990-91).

			REGULAR SEASON					PLAYOFFS				
Season	Team	League	Gms.	G	A	Pts.	Pen.	Gms.	G	A	Pts.	Pen.
86-87—Trois-Rivieres		QMJHL	66	33	35	68	53	—	—	—	—	—
87-88—Trois-Rivieres		QMJHL	69	40	55	95	71	—	—	—	—	—
88-89—Trois-Rivieres		QMJHL	66	59	81	140	107	4	1	3	4	2
89-90—Binghamton		AHL	67	16	24	40	98	—	—	—	—	—
90-91—Hartford		NHL	5	1	0	1	2	—	—	—	—	—
—Springfield		AHL	77	*56	40	96	61	18	8	13	21	18
91-92—Hartford		NHL	25	3	5	8	6	—	—	—	—	—
—Springfield		AHL	40	21	17	38	44	11	2	0	2	34
92-93—Kansas City		IHL	33	7	10	17	51	12	3	2	5	20
—San Jose		NHL	25	4	0	4	24	—	—	—	—	—
NHL totals			55	8	5	13	32					

PIERCE, BILL
C, NORDIQUES

PERSONAL: Born October 6, 1974, at Woburn, Mass. . . . 6-1/190. . . . Shoots left. **HIGH SCHOOL:** Lawrence Academy (Groton, Mass.). **TRANSACTIONS/CAREER NOTES:** Selected by Quebec Nordiques in third round (fourth Nordiques pick, 75th overall) of NHL entry draft (June 26, 1993).

			REGULAR SEASON					PLAYOFFS				
Season	Team	League	Gms.	G	A	Pts.	Pen.	Gms.	G	A	Pts.	Pen.
90-91—Lawrence Academy		Mass. H.S.	20	10	25	35	...	—	—	—	—	—
91-92—Lawrence Academy		Mass. H.S.	20	20	26	46	26	—	—	—	—	—
92-93—Lawrence Academy		Mass. H.S.	20	12	26	38	22	—	—	—	—	—

PIETRANGELO, FRANK
G, WHALERS

PERSONAL: Born December 17, 1964, at Niagara Falls, Ont. . . . 5-10/185. . . . Shoots left. . . . Name pronounced PEE-tuhr-AN-juh-loh. **COLLEGE:** Minnesota. **TRANSACTIONS/CAREER NOTES:** Selected by Pittsburgh Penguins in fourth round (fourth Penguins pick, 63rd overall) of NHL entry draft (June 8, 1983). . . . Pulled groin (February 1989). . . . Pulled groin (February 3, 1991); missed eight games. . . . Injured back (November 9, 1991); missed four games. . . . Traded by Penguins to Hartford Whalers for conditional draft pick (March 10, 1992); arbitrator later ruled that Penguins would receive third- and seventh-round picks in 1994 draft from Whalers (September 14, 1992). . . . Suffered groin injury (October 17, 1992); missed one game. . . . Fractured kneecap (December 5, 1992); missed six games. . . . Suffered from the flu (February 15, 1993); missed one game. . . . Bruised ribs (March 3, 1993); missed nine games. . . . Reinjured bruised ribs (April 1, 1993); missed remainder of season.
MISCELLANEOUS: Member of Stanley Cup championship team (1991).

			REGULAR SEASON							PLAYOFFS						
Season	Team	League	Gms.	Min.	W	L	T	GA	SO	Avg.	Gms.	Min.	W	L	GA	SO	Avg.
82-83—Univ. of Minnesota		WCHA	25	1348	15	6	1	80	1	3.56	—	—	—	—	—	—	—
83-84—Univ. of Minnesota		WCHA	20	1141	13	7	0	66	0	3.47	—	—	—	—	—	—	—
84-85—Univ. of Minnesota		WCHA	17	912	8	3	3	52	0	3.42	—	—	—	—	—	—	—
85-86—Univ. of Minnesota		WCHA	23	1284	15	7	0	76	0	3.55	—	—	—	—	—	—	—
86-87—Muskegon		IHL	35	2090	23	11	0	119	2	3.42	15	923	10	4	46	0	*2.99
87-88—Pittsburgh		NHL	21	1207	9	11	0	80	1	3.98	—	—	—	—	—	—	—
—Muskegon		IHL	15	868	11	3	1	43	2	2.97	—	—	—	—	—	—	—
88-89—Pittsburgh		NHL	15	669	5	3	0	45	0	4.04	—	—	—	—	—	—	—

Season Team	League	Gms.	Min.	W	L	T	GA	SO	Avg.	Gms.	Min.	W	L	GA	SO	Avg.
—Muskegon	IHL	13	760	10	1	0	38	1	3.00	9	566	8	1	29	0	3.07
89-90—Muskegon	IHL	12	691	9	2	1	38	0	3.30	—	—	—	—	—	—	—
—Pittsburgh	NHL	21	1066	8	6	2	77	0	4.33	—	—	—	—	—	—	—
90-91—Pittsburgh	NHL	25	1311	10	11	1	86	0	3.94	5	288	4	1	15	†1	3.13
91-92—Pittsburgh	NHL	5	225	2	1	0	20	0	5.33	—	—	—	—	—	—	—
—Hartford	NHL	5	306	3	1	1	12	0	2.35	7	425	3	4	19	0	2.68
92-93—Hartford	NHL	30	1373	4	15	1	111	0	4.85	—	—	—	—	—	—	—
NHL totals		122	6157	41	48	5	431	1	4.20	12	713	7	5	34	1	2.86

PILON, RICH
D, ISLANDERS

PERSONAL: Born April 30, 1968, at Saskatoon, Sask. . . . 6-0/211. . . . Shoots left. . . . Name pronounced PEE-lahn.

TRANSACTIONS/CAREER NOTES: Selected by New York Islanders as underage junior in seventh round (ninth Islanders pick, 143rd overall) of NHL entry draft (June 21, 1986). . . . Injured right leg (December 1988). . . . Injured right eye (November 4, 1989); missed remainder of season. . . . Injured medial collateral ligament in left knee (February 23, 1991). . . . Suffered sore left shoulder (January 9, 1992); missed three games. . . . Lacerated finger (January 30, 1992); missed four games. . . . Bruised hand (October 31, 1992); missed two games. . . . Bruised hand (November 22, 1992); missed four games. . . . Sprained left knee (December 10, 1992); missed eight games. . . . Injured lower back (January 10, 1993); missed 11 games.

HONORS: Named to WHL All-Star second team (1987-88).

Season Team	League	Gms.	G	A	Pts.	Pen.	Gms.	G	A	Pts.	Pen.
85-86—Prince Albert	WHL	6	0	0	0	0	—	—	—	—	—
86-87—Prince Albert	WHL	68	4	21	25	192	7	1	6	7	17
87-88—Prince Albert	WHL	65	13	34	47	177	9	0	6	6	38
88-89—New York Islanders	NHL	62	0	14	14	242	—	—	—	—	—
89-90—New York Islanders	NHL	14	0	2	2	31	—	—	—	—	—
90-91—New York Islanders	NHL	60	1	4	5	126	—	—	—	—	—
91-92—New York Islanders	NHL	65	1	6	7	183	—	—	—	—	—
92-93—New York Islanders	NHL	44	1	3	4	164	15	0	0	0	50
—Capital District	AHL	6	0	1	1	8	—	—	—	—	—
NHL totals		245	3	29	32	746	15	0	0	0	50

PITTIS, DOMENIC
C, PENGUINS

PERSONAL: Born October 1, 1974, at Calgary, Alta. . . . 5-11/180. . . . Shoots left.
HIGH SCHOOL: Catholic Central (Lethbridge, Alta.).
TRANSACTIONS/CAREER NOTES: Selected by Pittsburgh Penguins in second round (second Penguins pick, 52nd overall) of NHL entry draft (June 26, 1993).

Season Team	League	Gms.	G	A	Pts.	Pen.	Gms.	G	A	Pts.	Pen.
91-92—Lethbridge	WHL	65	6	17	23	48	5	0	2	2	4
92-93—Lethbridge	WHL	66	46	73	119	69	4	3	3	6	8

PIVONKA, MICHAL
C, CAPITALS

PERSONAL: Born January 28, 1966, at Kladno, Czechoslovakia. . . . 6-2/196. . . . Shoots left. . . . Name pronounced puh-VAHN-kuh.
TRANSACTIONS/CAREER NOTES: Selected by Washington Capitals in third round (third Capitals pick, 59th overall) of NHL entry draft (June 9, 1984). . . . Strained ankle ligaments (March 1987). . . . Sprained right wrist (October 1987). . . . Sprained left ankle (March 1988). . . . Sprained left knee (March 9, 1990). . . . Pulled groin (October 10, 1992); missed three games. . . . Pulled groin (October 21, 1992); missed 12 games.

Season Team	League	Gms.	G	A	Pts.	Pen.	Gms.	G	A	Pts.	Pen.
85-86—Dukla Jihlava	Czech.				Statistics unavailable.						
86-87—Washington	NHL	73	18	25	43	41	7	1	1	2	2
87-88—Washington	NHL	71	11	23	34	28	14	4	9	13	4
88-89—Baltimore	AHL	31	12	24	36	19	—	—	—	—	—
—Washington	NHL	52	8	19	27	30	6	3	1	4	10
89-90—Washington	NHL	77	25	39	64	54	11	0	2	2	6
90-91—Washington	NHL	79	20	50	70	34	11	2	3	5	8
91-92—Washington	NHL	80	23	57	80	47	7	1	5	6	13
92-93—Washington	NHL	69	21	53	74	66	6	0	2	2	0
NHL totals		501	126	266	392	300	62	11	23	34	43

PLANTE, DAN
RW, ISLANDERS

PERSONAL: Born October 5, 1971, at St. Louis. . . . 5-11/190. . . . Shoots right. . . . Full name: Daniel Leon Plante.
HIGH SCHOOL: Edina (Minn.).
COLLEGE: Wisconsin.
TRANSACTIONS/CAREER NOTES: Selected by New York Islanders in third round (third Islanders pick, 48th overall) of NHL entry draft (June 16, 1990).

Season Team	League	Gms.	G	A	Pts.	Pen.	Gms.	G	A	Pts.	Pen.
88-89—Edina High School	Minn. H.S.	27	10	26	36	12	—	—	—	—	—
89-90—Edina High School	Minn. H.S.	24	8	18	26	. . .	—	—	—	—	—

P

Season	Team	League	Gms.	G	A	Pts.	Pen.	Gms.	G	A	Pts.	Pen.
			REGULAR SEASON					**PLAYOFFS**				
90-91—University of Wisconsin ...		WCHA	33	1	2	3	54	—	—	—	—	—
91-92—University of Wisconsin ...		WCHA	40	15	16	31	113	—	—	—	—	—
92-93—University of Wisconsin ...		WCHA	42	26	31	57	142	—	—	—	—	—

PLANTE, DEREK
C, SABRES

PERSONAL: Born January 17, 1971, at Cloquet, Minn. ... 5-11/160. ... Shoots left. ... Full name: Derek John Plante.
HIGH SCHOOL: Cloquet (Minn.).
COLLEGE: Minnesota-Duluth.
TRANSACTIONS/CAREER NOTES: Broke arm (March 1988). ... Selected by Buffalo Sabres in eighth round (seventh Sabres pick, 161st overall) of NHL entry draft (June 17, 1989). ... Injured collarbone (December 15, 1989). ... Reinjured collarbone (January 20, 1990).
HONORS: Named WCHA Player of the Year (1992-93). ... Named WCHA Leading Scorer (1992-93). ... Named to NCAA All-America West first team (1992-93). ... Named to WCHA All-Star first team (1992-93).

Season	Team	League	Gms.	G	A	Pts.	Pen.	Gms.	G	A	Pts.	Pen.
			REGULAR SEASON					**PLAYOFFS**				
87-88—Cloquet H.S.		Minn. H.S.	23	16	25	41	...	—	—	—	—	—
88-89—Cloquet H.S.		Minn. H.S.	24	30	33	63	...	—	—	—	—	—
89-90—Minnesota-Duluth		WCHA	28	10	11	21	12	—	—	—	—	—
90-91—Minnesota-Duluth		WCHA	36	23	20	43	6	—	—	—	—	—
91-92—Minnesota-Duluth		WCHA	37	27	36	63	28	—	—	—	—	—
92-93—Minnesota-Duluth		WCHA	37	*36	*56	*92	30	—	—	—	—	—

PLAVSIC, ADRIEN
D, CANUCKS

PERSONAL: Born January 13, 1970, at Montreal. ... 6-1/205. ... Shoots left. ... Name pronounced PLAV-sihk.
COLLEGE: New Hampshire.
TRANSACTIONS/CAREER NOTES: Selected by St. Louis Blues in second round (second Blues pick, 30th overall) of NHL entry draft (June 11, 1988). ... Suffered concussion (September 25, 1989). ... Traded by Blues with first-round pick in 1990 draft (Shawn Antoski) and second-round pick in 1991 draft to Vancouver Canucks for RW Rich Sutter, D Harold Snepsts and second-round pick in 1990 draft (Craig Johnson) that had been traded to Canucks in an earlier deal (March 6, 1990). ... Sprained knee (November 9, 1990); missed 15 games. ... Suffered from the flu (February 22, 1993); missed one game.
MISCELLANEOUS: Member of silver-medal-winning Canadian Olympic team (1992).

Season	Team	League	Gms.	G	A	Pts.	Pen.	Gms.	G	A	Pts.	Pen.
			REGULAR SEASON					**PLAYOFFS**				
87-88—Univ. of New Hampshire ...		Hockey East	30	5	6	11	45	—	—	—	—	—
88-89—Canadian national team ...		Int'l	62	5	10	15	25	—	—	—	—	—
89-90—Peoria		IHL	51	7	14	21	87	—	—	—	—	—
—St. Louis		NHL	4	0	1	1	2	—	—	—	—	—
—Vancouver		NHL	11	3	2	5	8	—	—	—	—	—
—Milwaukee		IHL	3	1	2	3	14	6	1	3	4	6
90-91—Vancouver		NHL	48	2	10	12	62	—	—	—	—	—
91-92—Canadian national team ...		Int'l	38	6	9	15	29	—	—	—	—	—
—Canadian Olympic Team ..		Int'l	8	0	2	2	0	—	—	—	—	—
—Vancouver		NHL	16	1	9	10	14	13	1	7	8	4
92-93—Vancouver		NHL	57	6	21	27	53	—	—	—	—	—
NHL totals			136	12	43	55	139	13	1	7	8	4

PODEIN, SHJON
LW, OILERS

PERSONAL: Born March 5, 1968, at Rochester, Minn. ... 6-2/200. ... Shoots left. ... Name pronounced SHAWN poh-DEEN.
COLLEGE: Minnesota-Duluth.
TRANSACTIONS/CAREER NOTES: Selected by Edmonton Oilers in eighth round (ninth Oilers pick, 166th overall) of NHL entry draft (June 11, 1988).

Season	Team	League	Gms.	G	A	Pts.	Pen.	Gms.	G	A	Pts.	Pen.
			REGULAR SEASON					**PLAYOFFS**				
87-88—Minnesota-Duluth		WCHA	30	4	4	8	48	—	—	—	—	—
88-89—Minnesota-Duluth		WCHA	36	7	5	12	46	—	—	—	—	—
89-90—Minnesota-Duluth		WCHA	35	21	18	39	36	—	—	—	—	—
90-91—Cape Breton		AHL	63	14	15	29	65	4	0	0	0	5
91-92—Cape Breton		AHL	80	30	24	54	46	5	3	1	4	2
92-93—Cape Breton		AHL	38	18	21	39	32	9	2	2	4	29
—Edmonton		NHL	40	13	6	19	25	—	—	—	—	—
NHL totals			40	13	6	19	25	—	—	—	—	—

POLASEK, LIBOR
C, CANUCKS

PERSONAL: Born April 22, 1974, at Vitkovice, Czechoslovakia. ... 6-3/198. ... Shoots right.
TRANSACTIONS/CAREER NOTES: Selected by Vancouver Canucks in first round (first Canucks pick, 21st overall) of NHL entry draft (June 20, 1992).

Season	Team	League	Gms.	G	A	Pts.	Pen.	Gms.	G	A	Pts.	Pen.
			REGULAR SEASON					**PLAYOFFS**				
91-92—TJ Vitkovice		Czech.	17	2	2	4	2	—	—	—	—	—
92-93—Hamilton		AHL	60	7	12	19	34	—	—	—	—	—

P

POMICHTER, MIKE
C, BLACKHAWKS

PERSONAL: Born September 10, 1973, at New Haven, Conn. . . . 6-1/200. . . . Shoots left. **HIGH SCHOOL:** North Haven (Conn.).

TRANSACTIONS/CAREER NOTES: Selected by Chicago Blackhawks in second round (second Blackhawks pick, 39th overall) of NHL entry draft (June 22, 1991).

			REGULAR SEASON					PLAYOFFS				
Season Team	League	Gms.	G	A	Pts.	Pen.	Gms.	G	A	Pts.	Pen.
88-89—North Haven H.S.	Conn. H.S.	22	52	22	74	...	—	—	—	—	—
89-90—Springfield Jr. B	NEJHL	39	37	31	68	8	—	—	—	—	—
90-91—Springfield Jr. B	NEJHL	38	61	64	125	22	—	—	—	—	—
91-92—Boston University	Hockey East	35	11	27	38	14	—	—	—	—	—
92-93—Boston University	Hockey East	30	16	14	30	23	—	—	—	—	—

PORKKA, TONI
D, FLYERS

PERSONAL: Born February 4, 1970, at Rauma, Finland. . . . 6-2/190. . . . Shoots right. . . . Name pronounced POHR-kuh.

TRANSACTIONS/CAREER NOTES: Selected by Philadelphia Flyers in ninth round (12th Flyers pick, 172nd overall) of NHL entry draft (June 16, 1990).

			REGULAR SEASON					PLAYOFFS				
Season Team	League	Gms.	G	A	Pts.	Pen.	Gms.	G	A	Pts.	Pen.
89-90—Lukko	Finland	41	0	3	3	18	—	—	—	—	—
90-91—Lukko	Finland	34	2	2	4	8	—	—	—	—	—
91-92—Hershey	AHL	64	3	5	8	34	—	—	—	—	—
92-93—Hershey	AHL	49	6	13	19	22	—	—	—	—	—

POTVIN, FELIX
G, MAPLE LEAFS

PERSONAL: Born June 23, 1971, at Anjou, Que. . . . 6-0/185. . . . Shoots left. . . . Name pronounced PAHT-vihn.

TRANSACTIONS/CAREER NOTES: Selected by Toronto Maple Leafs in second round (second Maple Leafs pick, 31st overall) of NHL entry draft (June 16, 1990).

HONORS: Named to QMJHL All-Star second team (1989-90). . . . Won Can.HL Goaltender of the Year Award (1990-91). . . . Won Hap Emms Memorial Trophy (1990-91). . . . Won Jacques Plante Trophy (1990-91). . . . Won Shell Cup (1990-91). . . . Won Guy Lafleur Trophy (1990-91). . . . Named to Memorial Cup All-Star team (1990-91). . . . Named to QMJHL All-Star first team (1990-91). . . . Won Baz Bastien Trophy (1991-92). . . . Won Dudley (Red) Garrett Memorial Trophy (1991-92). . . . Named to AHL All-Star first team (1991-92). . . . Named to NHL All-Rookie team (1992-93).

			REGULAR SEASON							PLAYOFFS						
Season Team	League	Gms.	Min.	W	L	T	GA	SO	Avg.	Gms.	Min.	W	L	GA	SO	Avg.
88-89—Chicoutimi	QMJHL	*65	*3489	25	31	1	*271	†2	4.66	—	—	—	—	—	—	—
89-90—Chicoutimi	QMJHL	*62	*3478	31	26	2	231	†2	3.99	—	—	—	—	—	—	—
90-91—Chicoutimi	QMJHL	54	3216	33	15	4	145	*6	†2.71	*16	*992	*11	5	46	0	*2.78
91-92—St. John's	AHL	35	2070	18	10	6	101	2	2.93	11	642	7	4	41	0	3.83
—Toronto	NHL	4	210	0	2	1	8	0	2.29	—	—	—	—	—	—	—
92-93—Toronto	NHL	48	2781	25	15	7	116	2	*2.50	21	1308	11	10	62	1	2.84
—St. John's	AHL	5	309	3	0	2	18	0	3.50	—	—	—	—	—	—	—
NHL totals		52	2991	25	17	8	124	2	2.49	21	1308	11	10	62	1	2.84

POTVIN, MARC
RW, KINGS

PERSONAL: Born January 29, 1967, at Ottawa. . . . 6-1/215. . . . Shoots right. . . . Full name: Marc Richard Potvin. . . . Name pronounced PAHT-vihn.

COLLEGE: Bowling Green State.

TRANSACTIONS/CAREER NOTES: Selected by Detroit Red Wings in ninth round (ninth Red Wings pick, 169th overall) of NHL entry draft (June 21, 1986). . . . Traded by Red Wings with C Jimmy Carson and C Gary Shuchuk to Los Angeles Kings for D Paul Coffey, RW Jim Hiller and C/LW Sylvain Couturier (January 29, 1993). . . . Broke nose (February 18, 1993); missed one game.

			REGULAR SEASON					PLAYOFFS				
Season Team	League	Gms.	G	A	Pts.	Pen.	Gms.	G	A	Pts.	Pen.
85-86—Stratford	OPJHL	63	5	6	11	117	—	—	—	—	—
86-87—Bowling Green State	CCHA	43	5	15	20	74	—	—	—	—	—
87-88—Bowling Green State	CCHA	45	15	21	36	80	—	—	—	—	—
88-89—Bowling Green State	CCHA	46	23	12	35	63	—	—	—	—	—
89-90—Bowling Green State	CCHA	40	19	17	36	72	—	—	—	—	—
—Adirondack	AHL	5	2	1	3	9	4	0	1	1	23
90-91—Adirondack	AHL	63	9	13	22	†365	—	—	—	—	—
—Detroit	NHL	9	0	0	0	55	6	0	0	0	32
91-92—Adirondack	AHL	51	13	16	29	314	†19	5	4	9	57
—Detroit	NHL	5	1	0	1	52	1	0	0	0	0
92-93—Adirondack	AHL	37	8	12	20	109	—	—	—	—	—
—Los Angeles	NHL	20	0	1	1	61	1	0	0	0	0
NHL totals		34	1	1	2	168	8	0	0	0	32

POULIN, DAVE
C, CAPITALS

PERSONAL: Born December 17, 1958, at Mississauga, Ont. . . . 5-11/190. . . . Shoots left. . . . Full name: David James Poulin. . . . Name pronounced POO-lihn.

COLLEGE: Notre Dame.

TRANSACTIONS/CAREER NOTES: Signed as free agent by Philadelphia Flyers (February 1983). . . . Pulled hamstring and groin muscle (November 1986). . . . Fractured rib (April 16, 1987). . . . Pulled groin (February 1988). . . . Separated shoulder (November 1988). . . . Sent home due to irregular heartbeat (December 15, 1988). . . . Bruised right

P

hand (January 1989).... Fractured ring finger of right hand (April 8, 1989).... Suffered multiple fracture of left thumb (May 1989).... Bruised abdomen (October 1989).... Broke left thumb (October 28, 1989).... Traded by Flyers to Boston Bruins for C Ken Linseman (January 16, 1990).... Stretched nerve in neck and left arm (April 21, 1990).... Pulled groin (October 15, 1990); missed 17 games.... Broke jaw (December 28, 1990); missed 14 games.... Broke right shoulder blade (February 2, 1991); missed 15 games.... Strained groin and abdomen during preseason (September 1991); missed first 61 games of season.... Underwent surgery to groin and abdomen (December 6, 1991).... Signed as free agent by Washington Capitals (August 3, 1993).

HONORS: Named to CCHA All-Star second team (1981-82).... Won Frank J. Selke Trophy (1986-87).... Played in NHL All-Star Game (1986 and 1988).... Won King Clancy Memorial Trophy (1992-93).

Season Team	League	REGULAR SEASON					PLAYOFFS				
		Gms.	G	A	Pts.	Pen.	Gms.	G	A	Pts.	Pen.
78-79—University of Notre Dame	WCHA	37	28	31	59	32	—	—	—	—	—
79-80—University of Notre Dame	WCHA	24	19	24	43	46	—	—	—	—	—
80-81—University of Notre Dame	WCHA	35	13	22	35	53	—	—	—	—	—
81-82—University of Notre Dame	WCHA	39	29	30	59	44	—	—	—	—	—
82-83—Rogle	Sweden	33	35	18	53	...	—	—	—	—	—
—Maine	AHL	16	7	9	16	2	—	—	—	—	—
—Philadelphia	NHL	2	2	0	2	2	3	1	3	4	9
83-84—Philadelphia	NHL	73	31	45	76	47	3	0	0	0	2
84-85—Philadelphia	NHL	73	30	44	74	59	11	3	5	8	6
85-86—Philadelphia	NHL	79	27	42	69	49	5	2	0	2	2
86-87—Philadelphia	NHL	75	25	45	70	53	15	3	3	6	14
87-88—Philadelphia	NHL	68	19	32	51	32	7	2	6	8	4
88-89—Philadelphia	NHL	69	18	17	35	49	19	6	5	11	16
89-90—Philadelphia	NHL	28	9	8	17	12	—	—	—	—	—
—Boston	NHL	32	6	19	25	12	18	8	5	13	8
90-91—Boston	NHL	31	8	12	20	25	16	0	9	9	20
91-92—Boston	NHL	18	4	4	8	18	15	3	3	6	22
92-93—Boston	NHL	84	16	33	49	62	4	1	1	2	10
NHL totals		632	195	301	496	420	116	29	40	69	113

POULIN, PATRICK
LW, WHALERS

PERSONAL: Born April 23, 1973, at Vanier, Que.... 6-1/208.... Shoots left.... Name pronounced POO-lai.

TRANSACTIONS/CAREER NOTES: Broke wrist (January 15, 1991).... Selected by Hartford Whalers in first round (first Whalers pick, ninth overall) of NHL entry draft (June 22, 1991).

HONORS: Won Jean Beliveau Trophy (1991-92).... Named to Can.HL All-Star first team (1991-92).... Named to QMJHL All-Star first team (1991-92).

Season Team	League	REGULAR SEASON					PLAYOFFS				
		Gms.	G	A	Pts.	Pen.	Gms.	G	A	Pts.	Pen.
89-90—St. Hyacinthe	QMJHL	60	25	26	51	55	12	1	9	10	5
90-91—St. Hyacinthe	QMJHL	56	32	38	70	.82	4	0	2	2	23
91-92—St. Hyacinthe	QMJHL	56	52	86	*138	58	5	2	2	4	4
—Springfield	AHL	—	—	—	—	—	1	0	0	0	0
—Hartford	NHL	1	0	0	0	2	7	2	1	3	0
92-93—Hartford	NHL	81	20	31	51	37	—	—	—	—	—
NHL totals		82	20	31	51	39	7	2	1	3	0

POZZO, KEVIN
D, SABRES

PERSONAL: Born October 10, 1974, at Calgary, Alta.... 6-1/176.... Shoots right.
HIGH SCHOOL: Vanier Collegiate (Moose Jaw, Sask.).
TRANSACTIONS/CAREER NOTES: Selected by Buffalo Sabres in sixth round (fourth Sabres pick, 142nd overall) of NHL entry draft (June 26, 1993).

Season Team	League	REGULAR SEASON					PLAYOFFS				
		Gms.	G	A	Pts.	Pen.	Gms.	G	A	Pts.	Pen.
92-93—Moose Jaw	WHL	72	10	29	39	95	—	—	—	—	—

PRATT, NOLAN
D, WHALERS

PERSONAL: Born August 14, 1975, at Fort McMurray, Alta.... 6-2/190.... Shoots left.
HIGH SCHOOL: Sunset (Beaverton, Ore.).
TRANSACTIONS/CAREER NOTES: Selected by Hartford Whalers in fifth round (fourth Whalers pick, 115th overall) of NHL entry draft (June 26, 1993).

Season Team	League	REGULAR SEASON					PLAYOFFS				
		Gms.	G	A	Pts.	Pen.	Gms.	G	A	Pts.	Pen.
91-92—Portland	WHL	22	2	9	11	13	6	1	3	4	12
92-93—Portland	WHL	70	4	19	23	97	16	2	7	9	31

PRESLEY, WAYNE
RW, SABRES

PERSONAL: Born March 23, 1965, at Dearborn, Mich.... 5-11/180.... Shoots right.
TRANSACTIONS/CAREER NOTES: Selected by Chicago Blackhawks as an underage junior in second round (second Blackhawks pick, 39th overall) of NHL entry draft (June 8, 1983).... Traded by Kitchener Rangers to Sault Ste. Marie Greyhounds for RW Shawn Tyers (January 1985).... Underwent surgery to repair ligaments and cartilage in right knee (November 1987); missed 36 games.... Dislocated shoulder (May 6, 1989).... Traded by Blackhawks to San Jose Sharks for third-round pick in 1993 draft (September 20, 1991).... Injured knee (November 17, 1991).... Injured hand (December 3, 1991); missed eight games.... Traded by Sharks to Buffalo Sabres for C Dave Snuggerud (March 9, 1992).... Bruised foot (October 8, 1992); missed one game.

P

HONORS: Won Jim Mahon Memorial Trophy (1983-84).... Named to OHL All-Star first team (1983-84).
RECORDS: Shares NHL single-season and single-series playoff records for most shorthanded goals—3 (1989).

			REGULAR SEASON					PLAYOFFS			
Season Team	League	Gms.	G	A	Pts.	Pen.	Gms.	G	A	Pts.	Pen.
82-83—Kitchener	OHL	70	39	48	87	99	12	1	4	5	9
83-84—Kitchener	OHL	70	63	76	139	156	16	12	16	28	38
84-85—Kitchener	OHL	31	25	21	46	77	—	—	—	—	—
—Sault Ste. Marie	OHL	11	5	9	14	14	16	13	9	22	13
—Chicago	NHL	3	0	1	1	0	—	—	—	—	—
85-86—Nova Scotia	AHL	29	6	9	15	22	—	—	—	—	—
—Chicago	NHL	38	7	8	15	38	3	0	0	0	0
86-87—Chicago	NHL	80	32	29	61	114	4	1	0	1	9
87-88—Chicago	NHL	42	12	10	22	52	5	0	0	0	4
88-89—Chicago	NHL	72	21	19	40	100	14	7	5	12	18
89-90—Chicago	NHL	49	6	7	13	67	19	9	6	15	29
90-91—Chicago	NHL	71	15	19	34	122	6	0	1	1	38
91-92—San Jose	NHL	47	8	14	22	76	—	—	—	—	—
—Buffalo	NHL	12	2	2	4	57	7	3	3	6	14
92-93—Buffalo	NHL	79	15	17	32	96	8	1	0	1	6
NHL totals		493	118	126	244	722	66	21	15	36	118

PRIESTLAY, KEN
C, PENGUINS

PERSONAL: Born August 24, 1967, at Vancouver, B.C.... 5-11/190.... Shoots left.
TRANSACTIONS/CAREER NOTES: Separated shoulder (November 1984).... Selected by Buffalo Sabres as underage junior in fifth round (fifth Sabres pick, 98th overall) of NHL entry draft (June 15, 1985).... Traded by Sabres to Pittsburgh Penguins for RW Tony Tanti (March 5, 1991).
HONORS: Named to WHL All-Star second team (1985-86 and 1986-87).
MISCELLANEOUS: Member of Stanley Cup championship team (1992).

			REGULAR SEASON					PLAYOFFS			
Season Team	League	Gms.	G	A	Pts.	Pen.	Gms.	G	A	Pts.	Pen.
83-84—Victoria	WHL	55	10	18	28	31	—	—	—	—	—
84-85—Victoria	WHL	50	25	37	62	48	—	—	—	—	—
85-86—Victoria	WHL	72	73	72	145	45	—	—	—	—	—
—Rochester	AHL	4	0	2	2	0	—	—	—	—	—
86-87—Victoria	WHL	33	43	39	82	37	—	—	—	—	—
—Buffalo	NHL	34	11	6	17	8	—	—	—	—	—
—Rochester	AHL	—	—	—	—	—	8	3	2	5	4
87-88—Buffalo	NHL	33	5	12	17	35	6	0	0	0	11
—Rochester	AHL	43	27	24	51	47	—	—	—	—	—
88-89—Rochester	AHL	64	56	37	93	60	—	—	—	—	—
—Buffalo	NHL	15	2	0	2	2	3	0	0	0	2
89-90—Rochester	AHL	40	19	39	58	46	—	—	—	—	—
—Buffalo	NHL	35	7	7	14	14	5	0	0	0	8
90-91—Canadian national team	Int'l	40	20	26	46	34	—	—	—	—	—
—Pittsburgh	NHL	2	0	1	1	0	—	—	—	—	—
91-92—Pittsburgh	NHL	49	2	8	10	4	—	—	—	—	—
—Muskegon	IHL	13	4	11	15	6	13	5	11	16	10
92-93—Cleveland	IHL	66	33	36	69	72	4	2	1	3	4
NHL totals		168	27	34	61	63	14	0	0	0	21

PRIMEAU, KEITH
C/LW, RED WINGS

PERSONAL: Born November 24, 1971, at Toronto.... 6-4/225.... Shoots left.... Name pronounced PREE-moh.
TRANSACTIONS/CAREER NOTES: Selected by Detroit Red Wings in first round (first Red Wings pick, third overall) of NHL entry draft (June 16, 1990).... Suffered from the flu (January 13, 1993); missed two games.... Sprained right shoulder (February 9, 1993); missed one game.... Sprained right knee (March 2, 1993); missed two games.... Sprained right knee (April 1, 1993); missed four games.
HONORS: Won Eddie Powers Memorial Trophy (1989-90).... Named to OHL All-Star second team (1989-90).

			REGULAR SEASON					PLAYOFFS			
Season Team	League	Gms.	G	A	Pts.	Pen.	Gms.	G	A	Pts.	Pen
87-88—Hamilton	OHL	47	6	6	12	69	11	0	2	2	2
88-89—Niagara Falls	OHL	48	20	35	55	56	17	9	6	15	12
89-90—Niagara Falls	OHL	65	*57	70	*127	97	16	*16	17	*33	49
90-91—Detroit	NHL	58	3	12	15	106	5	1	1	2	25
—Adirondack	AHL	6	3	5	8	8	—	—	—	—	—
91-92—Detroit	NHL	35	6	10	16	83	11	0	0	0	14
—Adirondack	AHL	42	21	24	45	89	9	1	7	8	27
92-93—Detroit	NHL	73	15	17	32	152	7	0	2	2	26
NHL totals		166	24	39	63	341	23	1	3	4	65

PROBERT, BOB
LW, RED WINGS

PERSONAL: Born June 5, 1965, at Windsor, Ont.... 6-3/225.... Shoots left.... Name pronounced PROH-burt.
TRANSACTIONS/CAREER NOTES: Selected by Detroit Red Wings as underage junior in third round (third Red Wings pick, 46th overall) of NHL entry draft (June 8, 1983).... Entered in-patient

P

alchohol abuse treatment center (July 22, 1986).... Suspended six games by NHL during the 1987-88 season for game misconduct penalties.... Suspended without pay by Red Wings for skipping practice and missing team buses, flights and curfews (September 23, 1988).... Reactivated by Red Wings (November 23, 1988).... Suspended three games by NHL for hitting another player (December 10, 1988).... Removed from team after showing up late for a game (January 26, 1989).... Reactivated by Red Wings (February 15, 1989).... Charged with smuggling cocaine into the U.S (March 2, 1989).... Expelled from the NHL (March 4, 1989).... Reinstated by NHL (March 14, 1990).... Unable to play any games in Canada while appealing deportation order by U.S. Immigration Department during 1990-91 and 1991-92 seasons.... Fractured left wrist (December 1, 1990); missed 12 games.... Suspended one game by NHL for game misconduct penalties (February 9, 1993).
HONORS: Played in NHL All-Star Game (1988).

			REGULAR SEASON					PLAYOFFS				
Season	Team	League	Gms.	G	A	Pts.	Pen.	Gms.	G	A	Pts.	Pen.
82-83—Brantford	OHL	51	12	16	28	133	8	2	2	4	23
83-84—Brantford	OHL	65	35	38	73	189	6	0	3	3	16
84-85—Hamilton	OHL	4	0	1	1	21	—	—	—	—	—
—Sault Ste. Marie	OHL	44	20	52	72	172	15	6	11	17	*60
85-86—Adirondack	AHL	32	12	15	27	152	10	2	3	5	68
—Detroit	NHL	44	8	13	21	186	—	—	—	—	—
86-87—Detroit	NHL	63	13	11	24	221	16	3	4	7	63
—Adirondack	AHL	7	1	4	5	15	—	—	—	—	—
87-88—Detroit	NHL	74	29	33	62	*398	16	8	13	21	51
88-89—Detroit	NHL	25	4	2	6	106	—	—	—	—	—
89-90—Detroit	NHL	4	3	0	3	21	—	—	—	—	—
90-91—Detroit	NHL	55	16	23	39	315	6	1	2	3	50
91-92—Detroit	NHL	63	20	24	44	276	11	1	6	7	28
92-93—Detroit	NHL	80	14	29	43	292	7	0	3	3	10
NHL totals		408	107	135	242	1815	56	13	28	41	202

PROKHOROV, VITALI
LW, BLUES

PERSONAL: Born December 25, 1966, at Moscow, U.S.S.R.... 5-9/185.... Shoots left.... Name pronounced vih-TAL-ee PRO-kuhr-ahf.
TRANSACTIONS/CAREER NOTES: Selected by St. Louis Blues in third round (third Blues pick, 64th overall) of NHL entry draft (June 20, 1992).... Injured shoulder (November 10, 1992); missed two games.... Injured shoulder (December 17, 1992); missed 14 games.... Reinjured shoulder (February 10, 1993); missed remainder of season.
MISCELLANEOUS: Member of gold-medal-winning Unified Olympic team (1992).

			REGULAR SEASON					PLAYOFFS				
Season	Team	League	Gms.	G	A	Pts.	Pen.	Gms.	G	A	Pts.	Pen.
83-84—Spartak Moscow	USSR	5	0	0	0	0	—	—	—	—	—
84-85—Spartak Moscow	USSR	31	1	1	2	10	—	—	—	—	—
85-86—Spartak Moscow	USSR	29	3	9	12	4	—	—	—	—	—
86-87—Spartak Moscow	USSR	27	1	6	7	2	—	—	—	—	—
87-88—Spartak Moscow	USSR	19	5	0	5	4	—	—	—	—	—
88-89—Spartak Moscow	USSR	37	11	5	16	10	—	—	—	—	—
89-90—Spartak Moscow	USSR	43	13	8	21	35	—	—	—	—	—
90-91—Spartak Moscow	USSR	43	21	10	31	29	—	—	—	—	—
91-92—Spartak Moscow	CIS	38	13	19	32	68	—	—	—	—	—
—Unified Olympic Team	Int'l	8	2	4	6	6	—	—	—	—	—
92-93—St. Louis	NHL	26	4	1	5	15	—	—	—	—	—
NHL totals		26	4	1	5	15	—	—	—	—	—

PRONGER, CHRIS
D, WHALERS

PERSONAL: Born October 10, 1974, at Dryden, Ont.... 6-5/190.... Shoots left.
COLLEGE: Trent University (Ont.).
TRANSACTIONS/CAREER NOTES: Selected by Hartford Whalers in first round (first Whalers pick, second overall) of NHL entry draft (June 26, 1993).
HONORS: Named to Can.HL All-Rookie team (1991-92).... Named to OHL Rookie All-Star team (1991-92).... Won the Can.HL Plus/Minus Award (1992-93).... Won the Can.HL Top Defenseman Award (1992-93).... Won the OHL Most Outstanding Defenseman Award (1992-93).... Named to Can.HL All-Star first team (1992-93).... Named to OHL All-Star first team (1992-93).

			REGULAR SEASON					PLAYOFFS				
Season	Team	League	Gms.	G	A	Pts.	Pen.	Gms.	G	A	Pts.	Pen.
90-91—Stratford	OPJHL	48	15	37	52	132	—	—	—	—	—
91-92—Peterborough	OHL	63	17	45	62	90	10	1	8	9	28
92-93—Peterborough	OHL	61	15	62	77	108	21	15	25	40	51

PRONGER, SEAN
C, CANUCKS

PERSONAL: Born November 30, 1972, at Thunder Bay, Ont.... 6-3/195.... Shoots left.... Full name: Sean James Pronger.
COLLEGE: Bowling Green State.
TRANSACTIONS/CAREER NOTES: Selected by Vancouver Canucks in third round (third Canucks pick, 51st overall) of NHL entry draft (June 22, 1991).

			REGULAR SEASON					PLAYOFFS				
Season	Team	League	Gms.	G	A	Pts.	Pen.	Gms.	G	A	Pts.	Pen.
89-90—Thunder Bay Flyers	USHL	48	18	34	52	61	—	—	—	—	—
90-91—Bowling Green State	CCHA	40	3	7	10	30	—	—	—	—	—

P

Season Team	League	Gms.	G	A	Pts.	Pen.	Gms.	G	A	Pts.	Pen.
91-92—Bowling Green State	CCHA	34	9	7	16	28	—	—	—	—	—
92-93—Bowling Green State	CCHA	39	23	23	46	35	—	—	—	—	—

PROPP, BRIAN

LW, STARS

PERSONAL: Born February 15, 1959, at Lanigan, Sask. ... 5-10/195. ... Shoots left. ... Full name: Brian Philip Propp.

TRANSACTIONS/CAREER NOTES: Selected by Philadelphia Flyers in first round (first Flyers pick, 14th overall) of NHL entry draft (August 9, 1979). ... Suspended four games by NHL (January 1985). ... Injured eye (March 4, 1986); missed eight games. ... Fractured left knee (December 7, 1986). ... Sprained left knee (December 1987). ... Traded by Flyers to Boston Bruins for second-round pick in 1990 draft (D Terran Sandwith) (March 2, 1990). ... Signed as free agent by Minnesota North Stars (July 25, 1990). ... Injured groin (November 29, 1991); missed eight games. ... Dislocated shoulder (February 9, 1992); missed 13 games. ... Sprained knee (March 14, 1992); missed two games. ... Injured shoulder (April 14, 1992). ... Assigned to Lugano of Swiss League (November 14, 1992).

HONORS: Named WCHL Rookie of the Year (1976-77). ... Named to WCHL All-Star second team (1976-77). ... Named to WCHL All-Star first team (1977-78). ... Won WHL Player of the Year Award (1978-79). ... Named to WHL All-Star first team (1978-79). ... Played in NHL All-Star Game (1980, 1982, 1984, 1986 and 1990).

			REGULAR SEASON					PLAYOFFS			
Season Team	League	Gms.	G	A	Pts.	Pen.	Gms.	G	A	Pts.	Pen.
75-76—Melville	SAJHL	57	76	92	168	36	—	—	—	—	—
76-77—Brandon	WCHL	72	55	80	135	47	16	†14	12	26	5
77-78—Brandon	WCHL	70	70	*112	*182	200	8	7	6	13	12
78-79—Brandon	WHL	71	*94	*100	*194	127	22	15	23	*38	40
79-80—Philadelphia	NHL	80	34	41	75	54	19	5	10	15	29
80-81—Philadelphia	NHL	79	26	40	66	110	12	6	6	12	32
81-82—Philadelphia	NHL	80	44	47	91	117	4	2	2	4	4
82-83—Philadelphia	NHL	80	40	42	82	72	3	1	2	3	8
83-84—Philadelphia	NHL	79	39	53	92	37	3	0	1	1	6
84-85—Philadelphia	NHL	76	43	53	96	43	19	8	10	18	6
85-86—Philadelphia	NHL	72	40	57	97	47	5	0	2	2	4
86-87—Philadelphia	NHL	53	31	36	67	45	26	12	16	28	10
87-88—Philadelphia	NHL	74	27	49	76	76	7	4	2	6	8
88-89—Philadelphia	NHL	77	32	46	78	37	18	14	9	23	14
89-90—Philadelphia	NHL	40	13	15	28	31	—	—	—	—	—
—Boston	NHL	14	3	9	12	10	20	4	9	13	2
90-91—Minnesota	NHL	79	26	47	73	58	23	8	15	23	28
91-92—Minnesota	NHL	51	12	23	35	49	1	0	0	0	0
92-93—Minnesota	NHL	17	3	3	6	0	—	—	—	—	—
—Lugano	Switzerland	24	21	6	27	32	—	—	—	—	—
—Canadian national team ...	Int'l	3	3	1	4	2	—	—	—	—	—
NHL totals................................		951	413	561	974	786	160	64	84	148	151

PROSPAL, VACLAV

C, FLYERS

PERSONAL: Born February 17, 1975, at Ceske-Budejovice, Czechoslovakia. ... 6-2/167. ... Shoots left.

TRANSACTIONS/CAREER NOTES: Selected by Philadelphia Flyers in third round (second Flyers pick, 71st overall) of NHL entry draft (June 26, 1993).

			REGULAR SEASON					PLAYOFFS			
Season Team	League	Gms.	G	A	Pts.	Pen.	Gms.	G	A	Pts.	Pen.
91-92—Motor Ceske-Budejovice..	Czech. Jrs.	36	16	16	32	12	—	—	—	—	—
92-93—Motor Ceske-Budejovice..	Czech. Jrs.				Did not play.						

PUPPA, DAREN

G, LIGHTNING

PERSONAL: Born March 23, 1965, at Kirkland Lake, Ont. ... 6-3/205. ... Shoots right. ... Full name: Daren James Puppa. ... Name pronounced POO-pah.

COLLEGE: Rensselaer Polytechnic Institute (N.Y.).

TRANSACTIONS/CAREER NOTES: Selected by Buffalo Sabres in fourth round (sixth Sabres pick, 74th overall) of NHL entry draft (June 8, 1983). ... Injured knee (February 1986). ... Fractured left index finger (October 1987). ... Sprained right wrist (January 14, 1989). ... Broke right arm (January 27, 1989). ... Injured back (November 21, 1990); missed nine games. ... Pulled groin and stomach muscles (February 19, 1991). ... Fractured arm (November 12, 1991); missed 16 games. ... Suffered sore knee (January 21, 1993); missed seven games. ... Traded by Sabres with LW Dave Andreychuk and first-round pick in 1993 draft to (D Kenny Jonsson) Toronto Maple Leafs for G Grant Fuhr and conditional pick in 1995 draft (February 2, 1993). ... Selected by Florida Panthers in NHL expansion draft (June 24, 1993). ... Selected by Tampa Bay Lightning in Phase II of NHL expansion draft (June 25, 1993).

HONORS: Named to AHL All-Star first team (1986-87). ... Named to THE SPORTING NEWS All-Star second team (1989-90). ... Named to NHL All-Star second team (1989-90). ... Played in NHL All-Star Game (1990).

			REGULAR SEASON						PLAYOFFS					
Season Team	League	Gms.	Min.	W	L	T	GA	SO	Avg.	Gms.	Min.	W	L	GA	SO	Avg.
83-84—R.P.I.	ECAC	32	1816	24	6	0	89	...	2.94	—	—	—	—	—	—	—
84-85—R.P.I.	ECAC	32	1830	31	1	0	78	0	2.56	—	—	—	—	—	—	—
85-86—Buffalo...........................	NHL	7	401	3	4	0	21	1	3.14	—	—	—	—	—	—	—
—Rochester........................	AHL	20	1092	8	11	0	79	0	4.34	—	—	—	—	—	—	—
86-87—Buffalo...........................	NHL	3	185	0	2	1	13	0	4.22	—	—	—	—	—	—	—
—Rochester........................	AHL	57	3129	33	14	0	146	1	*2.80	*16	*944	10	6	*48	*1	3.05
87-88—Rochester.....................	AHL	26	1415	14	8	2	65	2	2.76	2	108	0	1	5	0	2.78

P

Season	Team	League	Gms.	Min.	W	L	T	GA	SO	Avg.	Gms.	Min.	W	L	GA	SO	Avg.
	—Buffalo	NHL	17	874	8	6	1	61	0	4.19	3	142	1	1	11	0	4.65
88-89	—Buffalo	NHL	37	1908	17	10	6	107	1	3.36	—	—	—	—	—	—	—
89-90	—Buffalo	NHL	56	3241	31	16	6	156	1	2.89	6	370	2	4	15	0	2.43
90-91	—Buffalo	NHL	38	2092	15	11	6	118	2	3.38	2	81	0	1	10	0	7.41
91-92	—Buffalo	NHL	33	1757	11	14	4	114	0	3.89	—	—	—	—	—	—	—
	—Rochester	AHL	2	119	0	2	0	9	0	4.54	—	—	—	—	—	—	—
92-93	—Buffalo	NHL	24	1306	11	5	4	78	0	3.58	—	—	—	—	—	—	—
	—Toronto	NHL	8	479	6	2	0	18	2	2.25	1	20	0	0	1	0	3.00
NHL totals			223	12243	102	70	28	686	7	3.36	12	613	3	6	37	0	3.62

PYE, BILL

G, SABRES

PERSONAL: Born April 4, 1969, at Royal Oak, Mich. . . . 5-9/170. . . . Shoots right. . . . Full name: William Francis Pye III.
COLLEGE: Northern Michigan.
TRANSACTIONS/CAREER NOTES: Selected by Buffalo Sabres in sixth round (fifth Sabres pick, 107th overall) of NHL entry draft (June 17, 1989).
HONORS: Won WCHA Playoff Most Valuable Player Award (1990-91). . . . Named to NCAA All-America West second team (1990-91). . . . Named to NCAA All-Tournament team (1990-91). . . . Named to WCHA All-Star first team (1990-91).

Season	Team	League	Gms.	Min.	W	L	T	GA	SO	Avg.	Gms.	Min.	W	L	GA	SO	Avg.
87-88	—N. Michigan U.	WCHA	13	654	3	7	0	49	0	4.50	—	—	—	—	—	—	—
88-89	—N. Michigan U.	WCHA	43	2533	26	15	2	133	1	3.15	—	—	—	—	—	—	—
89-90	—N. Michigan U.	WCHA	36	2035	20	14	1	149	1	4.39	—	—	—	—	—	—	—
90-91	—N. Michigan U.	WCHA	39	2300	32	3	4	109	*4	2.84	—	—	—	—	—	—	—
91-92	—Rochester	AHL	7	272	0	4	0	13	0	2.87	1	60	1	0	2	0	2.00
	—New Haven	AHL	4	200	0	3	1	19	0	5.70	—	—	—	—	—	—	—
	—Fort Wayne	IHL	8	451	5	2	1	29	0	3.86	—	—	—	—	—	—	—
	—Erie	ECHL	5	310	5	0	0	22	0	4.26	4	220	1	3	15	0	4.09
92-93	—Rochester	AHL	26	1427	9	14	2	107	0	4.50	—	—	—	—	—	—	—

PYSZ, PATRIK

C, BLACKHAWKS

PERSONAL: Born January 15, 1975, at Zakopane, Poland. . . . 5-11/187. . . . Shoots left.
TRANSACTIONS/CAREER NOTES: Selected by Chicago Blackhawks in fourth round (sixth Blackhawks pick, 102nd overall) of NHL entry draft (June 26, 1993).

Season	Team	League	Gms.	G	A	Pts.	Pen.	Gms.	G	A	Pts.	Pen.
91-92	—Podhale Nowy Targ	Poland					Statistics unavailable.					
92-93	—Augsburg	Ger. Div. II	36	7	5	12	12	8	2	1	3	0

QUINN, DAN

C/RW

PERSONAL: Born June 1, 1965, at Ottawa. . . . 5-11/182. . . . Shoots left.
TRANSACTIONS/CAREER NOTES: Selected by Calgary Flames as underage junior in first round (first Flames pick, 13th overall) of NHL entry draft (June 8, 1983). . . . Traded by Flames to Pittsburgh Penguins for C Mike Bullard (November 1986). . . . Broke left wrist (October 1987). . . . Traded by Penguins with RW Andrew McBain and C Dave Capuano to Vancouver Canucks for RW Tony Tanti, C Barry Pederson and D Rod Buskas (January 8, 1990). . . . Bruised shoulder (January 1991). . . . Traded by Canucks with D Garth Butcher to St. Louis Blues for LW Geoff Courtnall, D Robert Dirk, C Cliff Ronning, LW Sergio Mommesso and undisclosed pick in 1992 draft; Canucks later received fifth-round pick in 1992 draft (RW Brian Loney) (March 5, 1991). . . . Traded by Blues with C Rod Brind'Amour to Philadelphia Flyers for C Ron Sutter and D Murray Baron (September 22, 1991). . . . Signed as free agent by Minnesota North Stars (October 5, 1992).

Season	Team	League	Gms.	G	A	Pts.	Pen.	Gms.	G	A	Pts.	Pen.
81-82	—Belleville	OHL	67	19	32	51	41	—	—	—	—	—
82-83	—Belleville	OHL	70	59	88	147	27	4	2	6	8	2
83-84	—Belleville	OHL	24	23	36	59	12	—	—	—	—	—
	—Calgary	NHL	54	19	33	52	20	8	3	5	8	4
84-85	—Calgary	NHL	74	20	38	58	22	3	0	0	0	0
85-86	—Calgary	NHL	78	30	42	72	44	18	8	7	15	10
86-87	—Calgary	NHL	16	3	6	9	14	—	—	—	—	—
	—Pittsburgh	NHL	64	28	43	71	40	—	—	—	—	—
87-88	—Pittsburgh	NHL	70	40	39	79	50	—	—	—	—	—
88-89	—Pittsburgh	NHL	79	34	60	94	102	11	6	3	9	10
89-90	—Pittsburgh	NHL	41	9	20	29	22	—	—	—	—	—
	—Vancouver	NHL	37	16	18	34	27	—	—	—	—	—
90-91	—Vancouver	NHL	64	18	31	49	46	—	—	—	—	—
	—St. Louis	NHL	14	4	7	11	20	13	4	7	11	32
91-92	—Philadelphia	NHL	67	11	26	37	26	—	—	—	—	—
92-93	—Minnesota	NHL	11	0	4	4	6	—	—	—	—	—
NHL totals			669	232	367	599	439	53	21	22	43	56

QUINTAL, STEPHANE

D, BLUES

PERSONAL: Born October 22, 1968, at Boucherville, Que. . . . 6-3/220. . . . Shoots right. . . . Name pronounced KAYN-TAHL.
HIGH SCHOOL: Polyvalente de Mortagne (Boucherville, Que.).
TRANSACTIONS/CAREER NOTES: Broke wrist (December 1985). . . . Selected by

Boston Bruins as underage junior in first round (second Bruins pick, 14th overall) of NHL entry draft (June 13, 1987).... Broke bone near eye (October 1988).... Injured knee (January 1989).... Sprained right knee (October 17, 1989); missed eight games.... Fractured left ankle (April 9, 1991); missed remainder of playoffs.... Traded by Bruins with C Craig Janney to St. Louis Blues for C Adam Oates (February 7, 1992).
HONORS: Named to QMJHL All-Star first team (1986-87).

			REGULAR SEASON					PLAYOFFS				
Season Team	League	Gms.	G	A	Pts.	Pen.	Gms.	G	A	Pts.	Pen.
85-86—Granby	QMJHL	67	2	17	19	144	—	—	—	—	—
86-87—Granby	QMJHL	67	13	41	54	178	8	0	9	9	10
87-88—Hull	QMJHL	38	13	23	36	138	19	7	12	19	30
88-89—Maine	AHL	16	4	10	14	28	—	—	—	—	—
—Boston	NHL	26	0	1	1	29	—	—	—	—	—
89-90—Boston	NHL	38	2	2	4	22	—	—	—	—	—
—Maine	AHL	37	4	16	20	27	—	—	—	—	—
90-91—Maine	AHL	23	1	5	6	30	—	—	—	—	—
—Boston	NHL	45	2	6	8	89	3	0	1	1	7
91-92—Boston	NHL	49	4	10	14	77	—	—	—	—	—
—St. Louis	NHL	26	0	6	6	32	4	1	2	3	6
92-93—St. Louis	NHL	75	1	10	11	100	9	0	0	0	8
NHL totals		259	9	35	44	349	16	1	3	4	21

QUINTIN, J.F.
LW, SHARKS

PERSONAL: Born May 28, 1969, at St. Jean, Que.... 6-1/180.... Shoots left. **TRANSACTIONS/CAREER NOTES:** Fractured knee (October 1985).... Selected by Minnesota North Stars in fourth round (fourth North Stars pick, 75th overall) of NHL entry draft (June 17, 1989). ...Selected by San Jose Sharks in NHL dispersal draft (May 30, 1991).
HONORS: Named to QMJHL All-Star second team (1988-89).

			REGULAR SEASON					PLAYOFFS				
Season Team	League	Gms.	G	A	Pts.	Pen.	Gms.	G	A	Pts.	Pen.
86-87—Shawinigan	QMJHL	43	1	9	10	17	—	—	—	—	—
87-88—Shawinigan	QMJHL	70	28	70	98	143	11	5	8	13	26
88-89—Shawinigan	QMJHL	69	52	100	152	105	10	9	15	24	16
89-90—Kalamazoo	IHL	68	20	18	38	38	10	8	4	12	14
90-91—Kalamazoo	IHL	78	31	43	74	64	9	1	5	6	11
91-92—Kansas City	IHL	21	4	6	10	29	13	2	10	12	29
—San Jose	NHL	8	3	0	3	0	—	—	—	—	—
92-93—San Jose	NHL	14	2	5	7	4	—	—	—	—	—
—Kansas City	IHL	64	20	29	49	169	11	2	1	3	16
NHL totals		22	5	5	10	4					

RABY, MATHIEU
D, LIGHTNING

PERSONAL: Born January 19, 1975, at Hull, Que.... 6-2/204.... Shoots right.
TRANSACTIONS/CAREER NOTES: Selected by Tampa Bay Lightning in seventh round (seventh Lightning pick, 159th overall) of NHL entry draft (June 26, 1993).

			REGULAR SEASON					PLAYOFFS				
Season Team	League	Gms.	G	A	Pts.	Pen.	Gms.	G	A	Pts.	Pen.
92-93—Victoriaville	QMJHL	53	2	2	4	103	2	0	0	0	0

RACICOT, ANDRE
G, CANADIENS

PERSONAL: Born June 9, 1969, at Rouyn-Noranda, Que.... 5-11/165.... Shoots left.... Name pronounced RAH-sih-koh.
TRANSACTIONS/CAREER NOTES: Selected by Montreal Canadiens in fourth round (fifth Canadiens pick, 83rd overall) of NHL draft (June 17, 1989).
HONORS: Shared Harry (Hap) Holmes Memorial Trophy with Jean-Claude Bergeron (1989-90).... Named to QMJHL All-Star second team (1988-89).
MISCELLANEOUS: Member of Stanley Cup championship team (1993).

			REGULAR SEASON							PLAYOFFS					
Season Team	League	Gms.	Min.	W	L	T	GA	SO	Avg.	Gms.	Min.	W	L	GA	SO	Avg.
86-87—Longueuil	QMJHL	3	180	1	2	0	19	0	6.33	—						
87-88—Hull/Granby	QMJHL	30	1547	15	11	1	105	1	4.07	5	298	1	4	23	0	4.63
88-89—Granby	QMJHL	54	2944	22	24	3	198	0	4.04	4	218	0	4	18	0	4.95
89-90—Sherbrooke	AHL	33	1948	19	11	2	97	1	2.99	5	227	0	4	18	0	4.76
—Montreal	NHL	1	13	0	0	0	3	0	13.85	—						
90-91—Fredericton	AHL	22	1252	13	8	1	60	1	2.88	—						
—Montreal	NHL	21	975	7	9	2	52	1	3.20	2	12	0	1	2	0	10.00
91-92—Fredericton	AHL	28	1666	14	8	5	86	0	3.10	—						
—Montreal	NHL	9	436	0	3	3	23	0	3.17	1	1	0	0	0	0	0.00
92-93—Montreal	NHL	26	1433	17	5	1	81	1	3.39	1	18	0	0	2	0	6.67
NHL totals		57	2857	24	17	6	159	2	3.34	4	31	0	1	4	0	7.74

RACINE, BRUCE
G, PENGUINS

PERSONAL: Born August 9, 1966, at Cornwall, Ont.... 6-0/178.... Shoots left.... Full name: Bruce Michael Racine.
HIGH SCHOOL: St. Pius X (Ottawa).
COLLEGE: Northeastern.

TRANSACTIONS/CAREER NOTES: Selected by Pittsburgh Penguins in third round (third Penguins pick, 58th overall) of NHL entry draft (June 15, 1985).
HONORS: Named to Hockey East All-Star second team (1984-85).... Named to Hockey East All-Freshman team (1984-85). ... Named to NCAA All-America East first team (1986-87 and 1987-88).... Named to Hockey East All-Star first team (1986-87).

Season Team	League	Gms.	Min.	W	L	T	GA	SO	Avg.	Gms.	Min.	W	L	GA	SO	Avg.
84-85—Northeastern Univ.	Hoc. East	26	1615	11	14	1	103	1	3.83	—	—	—	—	—	—	—
85-86—Northeastern Univ.	Hoc. East	37	2212	17	14	1	171	0	4.64	—	—	—	—	—	—	—
86-87—Northeastern Univ.	Hoc. East	33	1966	12	18	3	133	0	4.06	—	—	—	—	—	—	—
87-88—Northeastern Univ.	Hoc. East	30	1809	15	11	4	108	1	3.58	—	—	—	—	—	—	—
88-89—Muskegon..................	IHL	51	*3039	37	11	0	184	*3	3.63	5	300	4	1	15	0	3.00
89-90—Muskegon..................	IHL	49	2911	29	15	4	182	1	3.75	—	—	—	—	—	—	—
90-91—Albany	IHL	29	1567	7	18	1	104	0	3.98	—	—	—	—	—	—	—
—Muskegon..................	IHL	9	516	4	4	1	40	0	4.65	—	—	—	—	—	—	—
91-92—Muskegon..................	IHL	27	1559	13	10	3	91	1	3.50	1	60	0	1	6	0	6.00
92-93—Cleveland	IHL	35	1949	13	16	0	140	1	4.31	2	37	0	0	2	0	3.24

RACINE, YVES

D, RED WINGS

PERSONAL: Born February 7, 1969, at Matane, Que.... 6-0/200.... Shoots left.... Name pronounced EEV ruh-SEEN.
TRANSACTIONS/CAREER NOTES: Selected by Detroit Red Wings as underage junior in first round (first Red Wings pick, 11th overall) of NHL entry draft (June 13, 1987).... Injured shoulder (March 22, 1991); missed four games.... Sprained left shoulder (November 11, 1992); missed four games.
HONORS: Named to QMJHL All-Star first team (1987-88 and 1988-89).... Won Emile (Butch) Bouchard Trophy (1988-89).

Season Team	League	Gms.	G	A	Pts.	Pen.	Gms.	G	A	Pts.	Pen.
86-87—Longueuil	QMJHL	70	7	43	50	50	20	3	11	14	14
87-88—Victoriaville....................	QMJHL	69	10	84	94	150	5	0	0	0	13
—Adirondack	AHL	—	—	—	—	—	9	4	2	6	2
88-89—Victoriaville....................	QMJHL	63	23	85	108	95	18	3	*30	*33	41
—Adirondack	AHL	—	—	—	—	—	2	1	1	2	0
89-90—Detroit	NHL	28	4	9	13	23	—	—	—	—	—
—Adirondack	AHL	46	8	27	35	31	—	—	—	—	—
90-91—Adirondack	AHL	16	3	9	12	10	—	—	—	—	—
—Detroit	NHL	62	7	40	47	33	7	2	0	2	0
91-92—Detroit	NHL	61	2	22	24	94	11	2	1	3	10
92-93—Detroit	NHL	80	9	31	40	80	7	1	3	4	27
NHL totals..............		231	22	102	124	230	25	5	4	9	37

RAGLAN, HERB

RW, LIGHTNING

PERSONAL: Born August 5, 1967, at Peterborough, Ont.... 6-0/205.... Shoots right.... Son of Clare Raglan, defenseman, Detroit Red Wings and Chicago Blackhawks (1950-51 through 1952-53).
TRANSACTIONS/CAREER NOTES: Selected by St. Louis Blues as underage junior in second round (first Blues pick, 37th overall) of NHL entry draft (June 15, 1985).... Suffered severe ankle sprain (December 1985).... Strained right knee ligaments (November 1987).... Sprained right wrist (October 1988).... Separated left shoulder (November 1988).... Pulled right groin (February 1989).... Broke right wrist and underwent surgery (November 4, 1989).... Bruised ribs (October 27, 1990).... Pulled left groin (December 1990).... Sprained left knee (February 2, 1991); missed 11 games.... Traded by Blues with D Tony Twist and LW Andy Rymsha to Quebec Nordiques for RW Darin Kimble (February 4, 1991).... Broke nose (November 2, 1991); missed 12 games.... Traded by Nordiques to Tampa Bay Lightning for RW Martin Simard, C Michel Mongeau and RW Steve Tuttle (February 12, 1993).

Season Team	League	Gms.	G	A	Pts.	Pen.	Gms.	G	A	Pts.	Pen.
84-85—Kingston...........................	OHL	58	20	22	42	166	—	—	—	—	—
85-86—Kingston...........................	OHL	28	10	9	19	88	10	5	2	7	30
—St. Louis.........................	NHL	7	0	0	0	5	10	1	1	2	24
86-87—St. Louis.........................	NHL	62	6	10	16	159	4	0	0	0	2
87-88—St. Louis.........................	NHL	73	10	15	25	190	10	1	3	4	11
88-89—St. Louis.........................	NHL	50	7	10	17	144	8	1	2	3	13
89-90—St. Louis.........................	NHL	11	0	1	1	21	—	—	—	—	—
90-91—St. Louis.........................	NHL	32	3	3	6	52	—	—	—	—	—
—Quebec...........................	NHL	15	1	3	4	30	—	—	—	—	—
91-92—Quebec...........................	NHL	62	6	14	20	120	—	—	—	—	—
92-93—Halifax...........................	AHL	28	3	9	12	83	—	—	—	—	—
—Tampa Bay.....................	NHL	2	0	0	0	2	—	—	—	—	—
—Atlanta...........................	IHL	24	4	10	14	139	9	3	3	6	32
NHL totals...............................		314	33	56	89	723	32	3	6	9	50

RAITER, MARK

D, MAPLE LEAFS

PERSONAL: Born January 27, 1973, at Calgary, Alta.... 6-4/220.... Shoots right.
HIGH SCHOOL: Marion Graham (Saskatoon, Sask.).
TRANSACTIONS/CAREER NOTES: Selected by Toronto Maple Leafs in fourth round (fourth Maple Leafs pick, 95th overall) of NHL entry draft (June 20, 1992).

			REGULAR SEASON					PLAYOFFS			
Season Team	League	Gms.	G	A	Pts.	Pen.	Gms.	G	A	Pts.	Pen.
89-90—Saskatoon	WHL	14	1	1	2	51	—	—	—	—	—
90-91—Saskatoon	WHL	35	2	3	5	73	22	0	7	7	45
91-92—Saskatoon	WHL	72	2	12	14	354	22	0	7	7	45
92-93—Saskatoon	WHL	57	3	11	14	173	9	1	1	2	19

RAMAGE, ROB
D, CANADIENS

PERSONAL: Born January 11, 1959, at Byron, Ont.... 6-2/200.... Shoots right.... Full name: George Robert Ramage.... Name pronounced RAM-ij.
TRANSACTIONS/CAREER NOTES: Signed as underage junior by Birmingham Bulls (July 1978).... Selected by Colorado Rockies in first round (first Rockies pick, first overall) of NHL entry draft (August 9, 1979).... Traded by Rockies to St. Louis Blues for first-round picks in 1982 draft (C Rocky Trottier) and 1983 draft (RW John MacLean) (June 9, 1982).... Sprained knee (March 22, 1986).... Suffered tendinitis around left kneecap (November 24, 1986); missed 21 games.... Traded by Blues with G Rick Wamsley to Calgary Flames for RW Brett Hull and LW Steve Bozek (March 7, 1988).... Suspended eight games by NHL for high-sticking (February 3, 1989).... Traded by Flames to Toronto Maple Leafs for second-round pick in 1989 draft (LW Kent Manderville) (June 16, 1989).... Selected by Minnesota North Stars in NHL expansion draft (May 30, 1991).... Underwent knee surgery (January 23, 1992); missed 38 games.... Selected by Tampa Bay Lightning in NHL expansion draft (June 18, 1992).... Traded by Lightning to Montreal Canadiens for D Eric Charron, D Alain Cote and future considerations (March 20, 1993); Canadiens sent D Donald Dufresne to Lightning to complete deal (June 18, 1993).... Sprained knee (April 7, 1993); missed final three games of regular season.
HONORS: Shared Max Kaminsky Trophy with Brad Marsh (1977-78).... Named to OMJHL All-Star first team (1977-78).... Named to WHA All-Star first team (1978-79).... Played in NHL All-Star Game (1981, 1984, 1986 and 1988).
MISCELLANEOUS: Member of Stanley Cup championship teams (1989 and 1993).

			REGULAR SEASON					PLAYOFFS			
Season Team	League	Gms.	G	A	Pts.	Pen.	Gms.	G	A	Pts.	Pen.
75-76—London	OHA Mj. Jr. A	65	12	31	43	113	5	0	1	1	11
76-77—London	OMJHL	65	15	58	73	177	20	3	11	14	55
77-78—London	OMJHL	59	17	47	64	162	11	4	5	9	29
78-79—Birmingham	WHA	80	12	36	48	165	—	—	—	—	—
79-80—Colorado	NHL	75	8	20	28	135	—	—	—	—	—
80-81—Colorado	NHL	79	20	42	62	193	—	—	—	—	—
81-82—Colorado	NHL	80	13	29	42	201	—	—	—	—	—
82-83—St. Louis	NHL	78	16	35	51	193	4	0	3	3	22
83-84—St. Louis	NHL	80	15	45	60	121	11	1	8	9	32
84-85—St. Louis	NHL	80	7	31	38	178	3	1	3	4	6
85-86—St. Louis	NHL	77	10	56	66	171	19	1	10	11	66
86-87—St. Louis	NHL	59	11	28	39	106	6	2	2	4	21
87-88—St. Louis	NHL	67	8	34	42	127	—	—	—	—	—
—Calgary	NHL	12	1	6	7	37	9	1	3	4	21
88-89—Calgary	NHL	68	3	13	16	156	20	1	11	12	26
89-90—Toronto	NHL	80	8	41	49	202	5	1	2	3	20
90-91—Toronto	NHL	80	10	25	35	173	—	—	—	—	—
91-92—Minnesota	NHL	34	4	5	9	69	—	—	—	—	—
92-93—Tampa Bay	NHL	66	5	12	17	138	—	—	—	—	—
—Montreal	NHL	8	0	1	1	8	7	0	0	0	4
WHA totals		80	12	36	48	165					
NHL totals		1023	139	423	562	2208	84	8	42	50	218

RAMSEY, MIKE
D, PENGUINS

PERSONAL: Born December 3, 1960, at Minneapolis.... 6-3/195.... Shoots left.... Full name: Michael Allen Ramsey.
COLLEGE: Minnesota.
TRANSACTIONS/CAREER NOTES: Selected by Buffalo Sabres in first round (first Sabres pick, 11th round) of NHL entry draft (August 9, 1979).... Dislocated thumb (December 4, 1983).... Injured groin (October 1987).... Fractured bone in right hand (November 2, 1988).... Pulled groin (January 12, 1989).... Pulled rib cage muscle (November 26, 1990); missed seven games.... Injured groin (November 22, 1991); missed five games.... Injured groin (January 31, 1992); missed three games.... Injured groin (March 8, 1992); missed three games.... Injured leg (April 12, 1992).... Underwent shoulder surgery (August 8, 1992); missed first nine games of season.... Strained groin (November 7, 1992); missed four games.... Bruised hand (November 18, 1992); missed six games.... Sprained knee (January 29, 1993); missed four games.... Traded by Sabres to Pittsburgh Penguins for LW Bob Errey (March 22, 1993).
HONORS: Played in NHL All-Star Game (1982, 1983, 1985 and 1986).
MISCELLANEOUS: Member of gold-medal-winning U.S. Olympic team (1980).

			REGULAR SEASON					PLAYOFFS			
Season Team	League	Gms.	G	A	Pts.	Pen.	Gms.	G	A	Pts.	Pen.
78-79—University of Minnesota	WCHA	26	6	11	17	30	—	—	—	—	—
79-80—U.S. national team	Int'l	56	11	22	33	55	—	—	—	—	—
—U.S. Olympic Team	Int'l	7	0	2	2	8	—	—	—	—	—
—Buffalo	NHL	13	1	6	7	6	13	1	2	3	12
80-81—Buffalo	NHL	72	3	14	17	56	8	0	3	3	20
81-82—Buffalo	NHL	80	7	23	30	56	4	1	1	2	14
82-83—Buffalo	NHL	77	8	30	38	55	10	4	4	8	15
83-84—Buffalo	NHL	72	9	22	31	82	3	0	1	1	6
84-85—Buffalo	NHL	79	8	22	30	102	5	0	1	1	23
85-86—Buffalo	NHL	76	7	21	28	117	—	—	—	—	—
86-87—Buffalo	NHL	80	8	31	39	109	—	—	—	—	—

R

Season Team	League	REGULAR SEASON					PLAYOFFS				
		Gms.	G	A	Pts.	Pen.	Gms.	G	A	Pts.	Pen.
87-88—Buffalo	NHL	63	5	16	21	77	6	0	3	3	29
88-89—Buffalo	NHL	56	2	14	16	84	5	1	0	1	11
89-90—Buffalo	NHL	73	4	21	25	47	6	0	1	1	8
90-91—Buffalo	NHL	71	6	14	20	46	5	1	0	1	12
91-92—Buffalo	NHL	66	3	14	17	67	7	0	2	2	8
92-93—Buffalo	NHL	33	2	8	10	20	—	—	—	—	—
—Pittsburgh	NHL	12	1	2	3	8	12	0	6	6	4
NHL totals		923	74	258	332	932	84	8	24	32	162

RANFORD, BILL
G, OILERS

PERSONAL: Born December 14, 1966, at Brandon, Man. . . . 5-11/185. . . . Shoots left.
HIGH SCHOOL: New Westminster (B.C.).
TRANSACTIONS/CAREER NOTES: Selected by Boston Bruins as underage junior in third round (second Bruins pick, 52nd overall) of NHL entry draft (June 15, 1985). . . . Traded by Bruins with LW Geoff Courtnall and second-round pick in 1988 draft (C Petro Koivunen) to Edmonton Oilers for G Andy Moog (March 1988). . . . Sprained ankle (February 14, 1990); missed six games. . . . Strained groin (January 4, 1992); missed two games. . . . Strained hamstring (January 29, 1992); missed five games. . . . Strained right quadriceps (November 12, 1992); missed two games. . . . Strained left hamstring (April 7, 1993); missed two games.
HONORS: Named to WHL All-Star second team (1985-86). . . . Won Conn Smythe Trophy (1989-90). . . . Played in NHL All-Star Game (1991).
RECORDS: Shares NHL single-season playoff record for most wins by a goaltender—16 (1990).
MISCELLANEOUS: Member of Stanley Cup championship teams (1988 and 1990).

Season Team	League	REGULAR SEASON							PLAYOFFS						
		Gms.	Min.	W	L	T	GA	SO	Avg.	Gms.	Min.	W	L	GA	SO	Avg.
83-84—New Westminster	WHL	27	1450	10	14	0	130	0	5.38	1	27	0	0	2	0	4.44
84-85—New Westminster	WHL	38	2034	19	17	0	142	0	4.19	7	309	2	3	26	0	5.05
85-86—New Westminster	WHL	53	2791	17	29	1	225	1	4.84	—	—	—	—	—	—	—
—Boston	NHL	4	240	3	1	0	10	0	2.50	2	120	0	2	7	0	3.50
86-87—Moncton	AHL	3	180	3	0	0	6	0	2.00	—	—	—	—	—	—	—
—Boston	NHL	41	2234	16	20	2	124	3	3.33	2	123	0	2	8	0	3.90
87-88—Maine	AHL	51	2856	27	16	6	165	1	3.47	—	—	—	—	—	—	—
—Edmonton	NHL	6	325	3	0	2	16	0	2.95	—	—	—	—	—	—	—
88-89—Edmonton	NHL	29	1509	15	8	2	88	1	3.50	—	—	—	—	—	—	—
89-90—Edmonton	NHL	56	3107	24	16	9	165	1	3.19	*22	*1401	*16	6	*59	0	2.53
90-91—Edmonton	NHL	60	3415	27	27	3	182	0	3.20	3	135	1	2	8	0	3.56
91-92—Edmonton	NHL	67	3822	27	26	10	228	1	3.58	16	909	8	*8	51	†2	3.37
92-93—Edmonton	NHL	67	3753	17	38	6	240	1	3.84	—	—	—	—	—	—	—
NHL totals		330	18405	132	136	34	1053	7	3.43	45	2688	25	20	133	2	2.97

RANHEIM, PAUL
LW, FLAMES

PERSONAL: Born January 25, 1966, at St. Louis. . . . 6-0/195. . . . Shoots right. . . . Full name: Paul Stephen Ranheim. . . . Name pronounced RAN-HIGHM.
HIGH SCHOOL: Edina (Minn.).
COLLEGE: Wisconsin.
TRANSACTIONS/CAREER NOTES: Selected by Calgary Flames in second round (third Flames pick, 38th overall) of NHL entry draft (June 8, 1983). . . . Broke right ankle (December 11, 1990); missed 41 games.
HONORS: Named to WCHA All-Star second team (1986-87). . . . Named to NCAA All-America West first team (1987-88). . . . Named to WCHA All-Star first team (1987-88). . . . Won Garry F. Longman Memorial Trophy (1988-89). . . . Won Ken McKenzie Trophy (1988-89). . . . Named to IHL All-Star second team (1988-89).

Season Team	League	REGULAR SEASON					PLAYOFFS				
		Gms.	G	A	Pts.	Pen.	Gms.	G	A	Pts.	Pen.
82-83—Edina High School	Minn. H.S.	26	12	25	37	4	—	—	—	—	—
83-84—Edina High School	Minn. H.S.	26	16	24	40	6	—	—	—	—	—
84-85—University of Wisconsin	WCHA	42	11	11	22	40	—	—	—	—	—
85-86—University of Wisconsin	WCHA	33	17	17	34	34	—	—	—	—	—
86-87—University of Wisconsin	WCHA	42	24	35	59	54	—	—	—	—	—
87-88—University of Wisconsin	WCHA	44	36	26	62	63	—	—	—	—	—
88-89—Calgary	NHL	5	0	0	0	0	—	—	—	—	—
—Salt Lake City	IHL	75	*68	29	97	16	14	5	5	10	8
89-90—Calgary	NHL	80	26	28	54	23	6	1	3	4	2
90-91—Calgary	NHL	39	14	16	30	4	7	2	2	4	0
91-92—Calgary	NHL	80	23	20	43	32	—	—	—	—	—
92-93—Calgary	NHL	83	21	22	43	26	6	0	1	1	0
NHL totals		287	84	86	170	85	19	3	6	9	2

RATHJE, MIKE
D, SHARKS

PERSONAL: Born May 11, 1974, at Manville, Alta. . . . 6-5/195. . . . Shoots left. . . . Name pronounced RATH-jee.
HIGH SCHOOL: Medicine Hat (Alta.).
TRANSACTIONS/CAREER NOTES: Selected by San Jose Sharks in first round (first Sharks pick, third overall) of NHL entry draft (June 20, 1992).
HONORS: Named to Can.HL All-Star second team (1992-93). . . . Named to WHL (East) All-Star second team (1991-92 and 1992-93).

Season Team	League	REGULAR SEASON					PLAYOFFS				
		Gms.	G	A	Pts.	Pen.	Gms.	G	A	Pts.	Pen.
90-91—Medicine Hat	WHL	64	1	16	17	28	12	0	4	4	2
91-92—Medicine Hat	WHL	67	11	23	34	109	4	0	1	1	2
92-93—Medicine Hat	WHL	57	12	37	49	103	10	3	3	6	12
—Kansas City	IHL	—	—	—	—	—	5	0	0	0	12

RATUSHNY, DAN
D, CANUCKS

PERSONAL: Born October 29, 1970, at Windsor, Ont.... 6-1/210.... Shoots right.... Full name: Daniel Paul Ratushny.
COLLEGE: Cornell.
TRANSACTIONS/CAREER NOTES: Selected by Winnipeg Jets in second round (second Jets pick, 25th overall) of NHL entry draft (June 17, 1989).... Traded by Jets to Vancouver Canucks for ninth-round pick in 1993 draft (March 22, 1993).
HONORS: Named to NCAA All-America East second team (1989-90).... Named to NCAA All-America East first team (1989-90 and 1990-91).... Named to ECAC All-Star first team (1990-91).
MISCELLANEOUS: Member of silver-medal-winning Canadian Olympic team (1992).

Season Team	League	REGULAR SEASON					PLAYOFFS				
		Gms.	G	A	Pts.	Pen.	Gms.	G	A	Pts.	Pen.
87-88—Napean	COJHL	54	8	20	28	116	—	—	—	—	—
88-89—Cornell University	ECAC	28	2	13	15	50	—	—	—	—	—
—Canadian national team	Int'l	2	0	0	0	2	—	—	—	—	—
89-90—Cornell University	ECAC	26	5	14	19	54	—	—	—	—	—
90-91—Cornell University	ECAC	26	7	24	31	52	—	—	—	—	—
—Canadian national team	Int'l	12	0	1	1	6	—	—	—	—	—
91-92—Canadian national team	Int'l	58	5	13	18	50	—	—	—	—	—
—Canadian Olympic Team	Int'l	8	0	0	0	4	—	—	—	—	—
92-93—Fort Wayne	IHL	63	6	19	25	48	—	—	—	—	—
—Vancouver	NHL	1	0	1	1	2	—	—	—	—	—
NHL totals		1	0	1	1	2					

RAY, ROB
LW, SABRES

PERSONAL: Born June 8, 1968, at Stirling, Ont.... 6-0/203.... Shoots left.
TRANSACTIONS/CAREER NOTES: Broke jaw (January 1987).... Selected by Buffalo Sabres in fifth round (fifth Sabres pick, 97th overall) of NHL entry draft (June 11, 1988).... Tore ligament in right knee (April 11, 1993); missed remainder of season.

Season Team	League	REGULAR SEASON					PLAYOFFS				
		Gms.	G	A	Pts.	Pen.	Gms.	G	A	Pts.	Pen.
84-85—Whitby Lawmen	OPJHL	35	5	10	15	318	—	—	—	—	—
85-86—Cornwall	OHL	53	6	13	19	253	6	0	0	0	26
86-87—Cornwall	OHL	46	17	20	37	158	5	1	1	2	16
87-88—Cornwall	OHL	61	11	41	52	179	11	2	3	5	33
88-89—Rochester	AHL	74	11	18	29	*446	—	—	—	—	—
89-90—Buffalo	NHL	27	2	1	3	99	—	—	—	—	—
—Rochester	AHL	43	2	13	15	335	17	1	3	4	*115
90-91—Rochester	AHL	8	1	1	2	15	—	—	—	—	—
—Buffalo	NHL	66	8	8	16	*350	6	1	1	2	56
91-92—Buffalo	NHL	63	5	3	8	354	7	0	0	0	2
92-93—Buffalo	NHL	68	3	2	5	211	—	—	—	—	—
NHL totals		224	18	14	32	1014	13	1	1	2	58

RECCHI, MARK
RW, FLYERS

PERSONAL: Born February 1, 1968, at Kamloops, B.C.... 5-10/185.... Shoots left.... Name pronounced REH-kee.
TRANSACTIONS/CAREER NOTES: Broke ankle (January 1987).... Selected by Pittsburgh Penguins in fourth round (fourth Penguins pick, 67th overall) of NHL entry draft (June 11, 1988). ... Injured left shoulder (December 23, 1990).... Sprained right knee (March 30, 1991).... Traded by Penguins with D Brian Benning and first-round pick in 1992 draft (LW Jason Bowen) (previously acquired from Los Angeles Kings) to Philadelphia Flyers for RW Rick Tocchet, D Kjell Samuelsson, G Ken Wregget and third-round pick in 1992 draft (February 19, 1992).
HONORS: Named to WHL (West) All-Star team (1987-88).... Named to IHL All-Star second team (1988-89).... Named to NHL All-Star second team (1991-92).... Played in NHL All-Star Game (1991 and 1993).
MISCELLANEOUS: Member of Stanley Cup championship team (1991).

Season Team	League	REGULAR SEASON					PLAYOFFS				
		Gms.	G	A	Pts.	Pen.	Gms.	G	A	Pts.	Pen.
84-85—Langley Eagles	BCJHL	51	26	39	65	39	—	—	—	—	—
85-86—New Westminster	WHL	72	21	40	61	55	—	—	—	—	—
86-87—Kamloops	WHL	40	26	50	76	63	13	3	16	19	17
87-88—Kamloops	WHL	62	61	*93	154	75	17	10	*21	†31	18
88-89—Pittsburgh	NHL	15	1	1	2	0	—	—	—	—	—
—Muskegon	IHL	63	50	49	99	86	14	7	*14	†21	28
89-90—Muskegon	IHL	4	7	4	11	2	—	—	—	—	—
—Pittsburgh	NHL	74	30	37	67	44	—	—	—	—	—
90-91—Pittsburgh	NHL	78	40	73	113	48	24	10	24	34	33
91-92—Pittsburgh	NHL	58	33	37	70	78	—	—	—	—	—
—Philadelphia	NHL	22	10	17	27	18	—	—	—	—	—
92-93—Philadelphia	NHL	84	53	70	123	95	—	—	—	—	—
NHL totals		331	167	235	402	283	24	10	24	34	33

REDDICK, ELDON
G, PANTHERS

PERSONAL: Born October 6, 1964, at Halifax, N.S. . . . 5-8/170. . . . Shoots left.
TRANSACTIONS/CAREER NOTES: Traded by New Westminster Bruins to Brandon Wheat Kings for D Jayson Meyer and D Lee Trim (October 1984). . . . Signed as free agent by Winnipeg Jets (September 1985). . . . Traded by Jets to Edmonton Oilers for future considerations (September 28, 1989). . . . Signed as free agent by Florida Panthers (July 14, 1993).
HONORS: Named to WHL All-Star second team (1983-84). . . . Shared James Norris Memorial Trophy with Rick St. Croix (1985-86). . . . Won N.R. (Bud) Poile Trophy (1992-93).
MISCELLANEOUS: Member of Stanley Cup championship team (1990).

Season	Team	League	Gms.	Min.	W	L	T	GA	SO	Avg.	Gms.	Min.	W	L	GA	SO	Avg.
81-82	Billings	WHL	1	60	...	...	...	7	0	7.00	—	—	—	—	—	—	—
82-83	Nanaimo	WHL	*66	*3549	19	38	1	*383	0	6.48	—	—	—	—	—	—	—
83-84	New Westminster	WHL	50	2930	24	22	2	215	0	4.40	9	542	4	5	53	0	5.87
84-85	Brandon	WHL	47	2585	14	30	1	243	0	5.64	—	—	—	—	—	—	—
	—Fort Wayne	IHL	10	491	...	...	...	32	2	3.91	4	246	...	...	17	0	4.15
85-86	Fort Wayne	IHL	32	1811	15	11	0	92	†3	3.05	—	—	—	—	—	—	—
86-87	Winnipeg	NHL	48	2762	21	21	4	149	0	3.24	3	166	0	2	10	0	3.61
87-88	Winnipeg	NHL	28	1487	9	13	3	102	0	4.12	—	—	—	—	—	—	—
	—Moncton	AHL	9	545	2	6	1	26	0	2.86	—	—	—	—	—	—	—
88-89	Winnipeg	NHL	41	2109	11	17	7	144	0	4.10	—	—	—	—	—	—	—
89-90	Edmonton	NHL	11	604	5	4	2	31	0	3.08	1	2	0	0	0	0	0.00
	—Cape Breton	AHL	15	821	9	4	1	54	0	3.95	—	—	—	—	—	—	—
	—Phoenix	IHL	3	185	2	1	0	7	0	2.27	—	—	—	—	—	—	—
90-91	Edmonton	NHL	2	120	0	2	0	9	0	4.50	—	—	—	—	—	—	—
	—Cape Breton	AHL	31	1673	19	10	0	97	2	3.48	2	124	0	2	10	0	4.84
91-92	Cape Breton	AHL	16	765	5	3	3	45	0	3.53	—	—	—	—	—	—	—
	—Fort Wayne	IHL	14	787	6	5	2	40	1	3.05	7	369	3	4	18	0	2.93
92-93	Fort Wayne	IHL	54	3043	33	16	0	156	3	3.08	12	723	*12	0	18	0	*1.49
NHL totals			130	7082	46	57	16	435	0	3.69	4	168	0	2	10	0	3.57

REDMOND, KEITH
LW, KINGS

PERSONAL: Born October 25, 1972, at Richmond Hill, Ont. . . . 6-3/208. . . . Shoots left. . . . Full name: Keith Christopher Redmond.
COLLEGE: Bowling Green State.
TRANSACTIONS/CAREER NOTES: Selected by Los Angeles Kings in fourth round (second Kings pick, 79th overall) of NHL entry draft (June 22, 1991).

Season	Team	League	Gms.	G	A	Pts.	Pen.	Gms.	G	A	Pts.	Pen.
88-89	—Nepean	COJHL	59	3	12	15	110	—	—	—	—	—
89-90	—Nepean	COJHL	40	14	10	24	169	—	—	—	—	—
90-91	—Bowling Green State	CCHA	35	1	3	4	72	—	—	—	—	—
91-92	—Bowling Green State	CCHA	8	0	0	0	14	—	—	—	—	—
	—Belleville	OHL	16	1	7	8	52	—	—	—	—	—
	—Detroit	OHL	25	6	12	18	61	7	1	3	4	49
92-93	—Muskegon	Col.HL	4	1	0	1	46	—	—	—	—	—
	—Phoenix	IHL	53	6	10	16	285	—	—	—	—	—

REEKIE, JOE
D, LIGHTNING

PERSONAL: Born February 22, 1965, at Victoria, B.C. . . . 6-3/215. . . . Shoots left. . . . Full name: Joseph James Reekie.
TRANSACTIONS/CAREER NOTES: Selected by Hartford Whalers as underage junior in seventh round (eighth Whalers pick, 124th overall) of NHL entry draft (June 8, 1983). . . . Released by Whalers (June 1984). . . . Selected by Buffalo Sabres in sixth round (sixth Sabres pick, 119th overall) of NHL entry draft (June 15, 1985). . . . Injured ankle (March 14, 1987). . . . Injured shoulder (October 1987). . . . Broke kneecap (November 15, 1987). . . . Underwent surgery to left knee (September 1988). . . . Traded by Sabres to New York Islanders for sixth-round pick in 1989 draft (G Bill Pye) (June 17, 1989). . . . Sprained right knee (November 1989). . . . Broke two bones in left hand and suffered facial cuts in automobile accident and underwent surgery (December 7, 1989). . . . Broke left middle finger (March 21, 1990). . . . Injured eye (January 12, 1991); missed six games. . . . Fractured knuckle on left hand (January 3, 1992); missed 22 games. . . . Selected by Tampa Bay Lightning in NHL expansion draft (June 18, 1992). . . . Broke left leg (January 16, 1993); missed remainder of season.

Season	Team	League	Gms.	G	A	Pts.	Pen.	Gms.	G	A	Pts.	Pen.
81-82	—Nepean	COJHL	16	2	5	7	4	—	—	—	—	—
82-83	—North Bay	OHL	59	2	9	11	49	8	0	1	1	11
83-84	—North Bay	OHL	9	1	0	1	18	—	—	—	—	—
	—Cornwall	OHL	53	6	27	33	166	3	0	0	0	4
84-85	—Cornwall	OHL	65	19	63	82	134	9	4	13	17	18
85-86	—Rochester	AHL	77	3	25	28	178	—	—	—	—	—
	—Buffalo	NHL	3	0	0	0	14	—	—	—	—	—
86-87	—Buffalo	NHL	56	1	8	9	82	—	—	—	—	—
	—Rochester	AHL	22	0	6	6	52	—	—	—	—	—
87-88	—Buffalo	NHL	30	1	4	5	68	2	0	0	0	4
88-89	—Rochester	AHL	21	1	2	3	56	—	—	—	—	—
	—Buffalo	NHL	15	1	3	4	26	—	—	—	—	—
89-90	—New York Islanders	NHL	31	1	8	9	43	—	—	—	—	—
	—Springfield	AHL	15	1	4	5	24	—	—	—	—	—

Season Team	League	REGULAR SEASON					PLAYOFFS				
		Gms.	G	A	Pts.	Pen.	Gms.	G	A	Pts.	Pen.
90-91—Capital District................	AHL	2	1	0	1	0	—	—	—	—	—
—New York Islanders..........	NHL	66	3	16	19	96	—	—	—	—	—
91-92—New York Islanders..........	NHL	54	4	12	16	85	—	—	—	—	—
—Capital District................	AHL	3	2	2	4	2	—	—	—	—	—
92-93—Tampa Bay.......................	NHL	42	2	11	13	69	—	—	—	—	—
NHL totals...............		297	13	62	75	483	2	0	0	0	4

REESE, JEFF
G, FLAMES

PERSONAL: Born March 24, 1966, at Brantford, Ont. . . . 5-9/155. . . . Shoots left.
TRANSACTIONS/CAREER NOTES: Selected by Toronto Maple Leafs as underage junior in fourth round (third Maple Leafs pick, 67th overall) of NHL entry draft (June 9, 1984). . . . Broke left kneecap (October 23, 1989); missed two months. . . . Suffered contusion to left kneecap (April 12, 1990). . . . Broke transverse processes (March 23, 1991); missed remainder of season. . . . Traded by Maple Leafs with D Alexander Godynyuk, RW Gary Leeman, D Michel Petit and LW Craig Berube to Calgary Flames for C Doug Gilmour, D Jamie Macoun, LW Kent Manderville, D Ric Nattress and G Rick Wamsley (January 2, 1992). . . . Lacerated hand prior to 1992-93 season; missed first three games of season.

Season Team	League	REGULAR SEASON							PLAYOFFS						
		Gms.	Min.	W	L	T	GA	SO	Avg.	Gms.	Min.	W	L	GA	SO	Avg.
82-83—Hamilton A's	OJHL	40	2380	...	...	...	176	0	4.44	—						
83-84—London	OHL	43	2308	18	19	0	173	0	4.50	6	327	3	3	27	0	4.95
84-85—London	OHL	50	2878	31	15	1	186	1	3.88	8	440	5	2	20	†1	*2.73
85-86—London	OHL	*57	*3281	25	26	3	215	0	3.93	5	299	0	4	25	0	5.02
86-87—Newmarket....................	AHL	50	2822	11	29	0	193	1	4.10	—						
87-88—Newmarket....................	AHL	28	1587	10	14	3	103	0	3.89	—						
—Toronto............................	NHL	5	249	1	2	1	17	0	4.10	—						
88-89—Toronto.........................	NHL	10	486	2	6	1	40	0	4.94	—						
—Newmarket.....................	AHL	37	2072	17	14	3	132	0	3.82	—						
89-90—Newmarket....................	AHL	7	431	3	2	2	29	0	4.04	—						
—Toronto............................	NHL	21	1101	9	6	3	81	0	4.41	2	108	1	1	6	0	3.33
90-91—Toronto.........................	NHL	30	1430	6	13	3	92	1	3.86	—						
—Newmarket.....................	AHL	3	180	2	1	0	7	0	2.33	—						
91-92—Toronto.........................	NHL	8	413	1	5	1	20	1	2.91	—						
—Calgary............................	NHL	12	587	3	2	2	37	0	3.78	—						
92-93—Calgary.........................	NHL	26	1311	14	4	1	70	1	3.20	4	209	1	3	17	0	4.88
NHL totals.................................		112	5577	36	38	12	357	3	3.84	6	317	2	4	23	0	4.35

REEVES, KYLE
RW, BLUES

PERSONAL: Born May 12, 1971, at Swan River, Man. . . . 5-11/200. . . . Shoots right.
TRANSACTIONS/CAREER NOTES: Traded by Swift Current Broncos with G Don Blishen to Tri-City Americans for D Kelly Chotowetz (October 4, 1989). . . . Selected by St. Louis Blues in third round (second Blues pick, 64th overall) of NHL entry draft (June 22, 1991).
HONORS: Named to WHL (West) All-Star second team (1990-91).

Season Team	League	REGULAR SEASON					PLAYOFFS				
		Gms.	G	A	Pts.	Pen.	Gms.	G	A	Pts.	Pen.
88-89—Swift Current...................	WHL	68	19	21	40	49	—	—	—	—	—
89-90—Swift Current...................	WHL	2	1	1	2	2	—	—	—	—	—
—Tri-City	WHL	67	67	36	103	94	7	2	1	3	8
90-91—Tri-City	WHL	63	*89	40	129	146	3	1	3	4	10
91-92—Peoria	IHL	60	12	7	19	92	—	—	—	—	—
92-93—Peoria	IHL	50	17	14	31	83	3	0	2	2	2

REICHEL, ROBERT
C, FLAMES

PERSONAL: Born June 25, 1971, at Litvinov, Czechoslovakia. . . . 5-10/185. . . . Shoots right. . . . Name pronounced RIGH-kuhl. . . . Brother of Martin Reichel, right winger/center in Edmonton Oilers system.
TRANSACTIONS/CAREER NOTES: Selected by Calgary Flames in fourth round (fifth Flames pick, 70th overall) of NHL entry draft (June 17, 1989). . . . Strained right knee (March 16, 1993); missed three games.
HONORS: Named to Czechoslovakian League All-Star team (1989-90).

Season Team	League	REGULAR SEASON					PLAYOFFS				
		Gms.	G	A	Pts.	Pen.	Gms.	G	A	Pts.	Pen.
88-89—Litvinov	Czech.	...	20	31	51	...	—	—	—	—	—
89-90—Litvinov	Czech.	52	49	34	*83	...	—	—	—	—	—
90-91—Calgary.............................	NHL	66	19	22	41	22	6	1	1	2	0
91-92—Calgary.............................	NHL	77	20	34	54	32	—	—	—	—	—
92-93—Calgary.............................	NHL	80	40	48	88	54	6	2	4	6	2
NHL totals.................................		223	79	104	183	108	12	3	5	8	2

REID, DAVID
LW, BRUINS

PERSONAL: Born May 15, 1964, at Toronto. . . . 6-1/205. . . . Shoots left.
TRANSACTIONS/CAREER NOTES: Selected by Boston Bruins as underage junior in third round (fourth Bruins pick, 60th overall) of NHL entry draft (June 9, 1982). . . . Underwent knee surgery (December 1986). . . . Separated shoulder (November 1987); missed 10 games. . . . Signed as free agent by Toronto Maple Leafs (August 1988). . . . Suffered from pneumonia (March 1992); missed 10 games. . . . Injured knee (March 25, 1993); missed remainder of season.

R

Season Team	League	REGULAR SEASON					PLAYOFFS				
		Gms.	G	A	Pts.	Pen.	Gms.	G	A	Pts.	Pen.
81-82—Peterborough	OHL	68	10	32	42	41	9	2	3	5	11
82-83—Peterborough	OHL	70	23	34	57	33	4	3	1	4	0
83-84—Peterborough	OHL	60	33	64	97	12	—	—	—	—	—
—Boston	NHL	8	1	0	1	2	—	—	—	—	—
84-85—Hershey	AHL	43	10	14	24	6	—	—	—	—	—
—Boston	NHL	35	14	13	27	27	5	1	0	1	0
85-86—Moncton	AHL	26	14	18	32	4	—	—	—	—	—
—Boston	NHL	37	10	10	20	10	—	—	—	—	—
86-87—Boston	NHL	12	3	3	6	0	2	0	0	0	0
—Moncton	AHL	40	12	22	34	23	5	0	1	1	0
87-88—Maine	AHL	63	21	37	58	40	10	6	7	13	0
—Boston	NHL	3	0	0	0	0	—	—	—	—	—
88-89—Toronto	NHL	77	9	21	30	22	—	—	—	—	—
89-90—Toronto	NHL	70	9	19	28	9	3	0	0	0	0
90-91—Toronto	NHL	69	15	13	28	18	—	—	—	—	—
91-92—Maine	AHL	12	1	5	6	4	—	—	—	—	—
—Boston	NHL	43	7	7	14	27	15	2	5	7	4
92-93—Boston	NHL	65	20	16	36	10	—	—	—	—	—
NHL totals		419	88	102	190	125	25	3	5	8	4

REID, JARRET
C, WHALERS

PERSONAL: Born March 10, 1973, at Sault Ste. Marie, Ont. . . . 5-10/180. . . . Shoots right.
HIGH SCHOOL: St. Mary's College (Sault Ste. Marie, Ont.).
TRANSACTIONS/CAREER NOTES: Selected by Hartford Whalers in sixth round (sixth Whalers pick, 143rd overall) of NHL entry draft (June 20, 1992).

Season Team	League	REGULAR SEASON					PLAYOFFS				
		Gms.	G	A	Pts.	Pen.	Gms.	G	A	Pts.	Pen.
90-91—Sault Ste. Marie	OHL	63	37	29	66	18	14	5	12	17	14
91-92—Sault Ste. Marie	OHL	61	53	40	93	67	19	5	13	18	17
92-93—Sault Ste. Marie	OHL	64	36	60	96	28	18	19	16	35	20

RENBERG, MIKAEL
RW, FLYERS

PERSONAL: Born May 5, 1972, at Pitea, Sweden. . . . 6-2/183. . . . Shoots left.
TRANSACTIONS/CAREER NOTES: Selected by Philadelphia Flyers in second round (third Flyers pick, 40th overall) of NHL entry draft (June 16, 1990).

Season Team	League	REGULAR SEASON					PLAYOFFS				
		Gms.	G	A	Pts.	Pen.	Gms.	G	A	Pts.	Pen.
88-89—Pitea	Sweden	12	6	3	9	. . .	—	—	—	—	—
89-90—Pitea	Sweden	29	15	19	34	. . .	—	—	—	—	—
90-91—Lulea	Sweden	29	11	6	17	12	—	—	—	—	—
91-92—Lulea	Sweden	38	8	15	23	20	—	—	—	—	—
92-93—Lulea	Sweden	39	19	13	32	61	11	4	4	8	0

RHEAUME, MANON
G, LIGHTNING

PERSONAL: Born February 24, 1972, at Lac Beauport, Que. . . . 5-6/136. . . . Shoots left. . . . Name pronounced MA-noh ray-OHM.
TRANSACTIONS/CAREER NOTES: Signed as free agent by Tampa Bay Lightning (August 8, 1992).

Season Team	League	REGULAR SEASON							PLAYOFFS						
		Gms.	Min.	W	L	T	GA	SO	Avg.	Gms.	Min.	W	L	GA SO	Avg.
91-92—Trois-Rivieres	QMJHL	1	17	0	1	0	3	0	10.59	—	—	—	—	— —	—
—Can. nat'l women's team	Int'l	3	. . .	3	0	0	. . .	2	0.67	—	—	—	—	— —	—
92-93—Atlanta	IHL	2	66	0	1	0	7	0	6.36	—	—	—	—	— —	—

RHODES, DAMIAN
G, MAPLE LEAFS

PERSONAL: Born May 28, 1969, at St. Paul, Minn. . . . 6-0/170. . . . Shoots right.
HIGH SCHOOL: Richfield (Minn.).
COLLEGE: Michigan Tech.
TRANSACTIONS/CAREER NOTES: Selected by Toronto Maple Leafs in sixth round (sixth Maple Leafs pick, 112th overall) of NHL entry draft (June 13, 1987).

Season Team	League	REGULAR SEASON							PLAYOFFS						
		Gms.	Min.	W	L	T	GA	SO	Avg.	Gms.	Min.	W	L	GA SO	Avg.
85-86—Richfield H.S.	Minn. HS	16	720	. . .	. . .	. . .	56	0	4.67	—	—	—	—	— —	—
86-87—Richfield H.S.	Minn. HS	19	673	. . .	. . .	. . .	51	1	4.55	—	—	—	—	— —	—
87-88—Michigan Tech	WCHA	29	1623	16	10	1	114	0	4.21	—	—	—	—	— —	—
88-89—Michigan Tech	WCHA	37	2216	15	22	0	163	0	4.41	—	—	—	—	— —	—
89-90—Michigan Tech	WCHA	25	1358	6	17	0	119	0	5.26	—	—	—	—	— —	—
90-91—Toronto	NHL	1	60	1	0	0	1	0	1.00	—	—	—	—	— —	—
—Newmarket	AHL	38	2154	8	24	3	144	1	4.01	—	—	—	—	— —	—
91-92—St. John's	AHL	43	2454	20	16	5	148	0	3.62	6	331	4	1	16 0	2.90
92-93—St. John's	AHL	52	*3074	27	16	8	184	1	3.59	9	538	4	5	37 0	4.13
NHL totals		1	60	1	0	0	1	0	1.00						

RICCI, MIKE
C, NORDIQUES

PERSONAL: Born October 27, 1971, at Scarborough, Ont. . . . 6-0/190. . . . Shoots left. . . . Name pronounced REE-CHEE.
TRANSACTIONS/CAREER NOTES: Separated right shoulder (December 1989). . . . Selected by Philadelphia Flyers in first round (first Flyers pick, fourth overall) of NHL entry draft (June 16, 1990). . . . Broke right index finger and thumb (October 4, 1990); missed nine games. . . . Traded by Flyers with G Ron Hextall, C Peter Forsberg, D Steve Duchesne, D Kerry Huffman, first-round pick in 1993 draft (G Jocelyn Thibault), cash and future considerations to Quebec Nordiques for C Eric Lindros (June 20, 1992); Flyers sent LW Chris Simon and first-round pick in 1994 draft to Nordiques to complete deal (July 21, 1992). . . . Sprained left wrist (November 3, 1992); missed four games. . . . Suffered from the flu (January 5, 1993); missed two games.
HONORS: Named to OHL All-Star second team (1988-89). . . . Won Can.HL Player of the Year Award (1989-90). . . . Won Red Tilson Trophy (1989-90). . . . Won William Hanley Trophy (1989-90). . . . Named to OHL All-Star first team (1989-90).

			REGULAR SEASON					PLAYOFFS			
Season	Team	League	Gms.	G	A	Pts.	Pen.	Gms.	G	A	Pts.	Pen.
87-88—Peterborough		OHL	41	24	37	61	20	8	5	5	10	4
88-89—Peterborough		OHL	60	54	52	106	43	17	19	16	35	18
89-90—Peterborough		OHL	60	52	64	116	39	12	5	7	12	26
90-91—Philadelphia		NHL	68	21	20	41	64	—	—	—	—	—
91-92—Philadelphia		NHL	78	20	36	56	93	—	—	—	—	—
92-93—Quebec		NHL	77	27	51	78	123	6	0	6	6	8
NHL totals			223	68	107	175	280	6	0	6	6	8

RICE, STEVE
RW, OILERS

PERSONAL: Born May 26, 1971, at Waterloo, Ont. . . . 6-0/215. . . . Shoots right.
TRANSACTIONS/CAREER NOTES: Underwent knee surgery (October 1986). . . . Selected by New York Rangers in first round (first Rangers pick, 20th overall) of NHL entry draft (June 17, 1989). . . . Suffered back spasms (September 14, 1989). . . . Injured left shoulder (October 1990). . . . Traded by Rangers with C Bernie Nicholls, LW Louie DeBrusk and future considerations to Edmonton Oilers for C Mark Messier and future considerations (October 4, 1991); Rangers later traded D David Shaw to Oilers for D Jeff Beukeboom to complete the deal (November 12, 1991). . . . Suffered right hip contusion (March 1993); missed two games.
HONORS: Named to Memorial Cup All-Star team (1989-90). . . . Named to OHL All-Star second team (1990-91). . . . Named to AHL All-Star second team (1992-93).

			REGULAR SEASON					PLAYOFFS			
Season	Team	League	Gms.	G	A	Pts.	Pen.	Gms.	G	A	Pts.	Pen.
87-88—Kitchener		OHL	59	11	14	25	43	4	0	1	1	0
88-89—Kitchener		OHL	64	36	31	67	42	5	2	1	3	8
89-90—Kitchener		OHL	58	39	37	76	102	16	4	8	12	24
90-91—New York Rangers		NHL	11	1	1	2	4	2	2	1	3	6
—Binghamton		AHL	8	4	1	5	12	5	2	0	2	2
—Kitchener		OHL	29	30	30	60	43	6	5	6	11	2
91-92—Edmonton		NHL	3	0	0	0	2	—	—	—	—	—
—Cape Breton		AHL	45	32	20	52	38	5	4	4	8	10
92-93—Cape Breton		AHL	51	34	28	62	63	14	4	6	10	22
—Edmonton		NHL	28	2	5	7	28	—	—	—	—	—
NHL totals			42	3	6	9	34	2	2	1	3	6

RICHARDSON, LUKE
D, OILERS

PERSONAL: Born March 26, 1969, at Ottawa. . . . 6-4/210. . . . Shoots left. . . . Full name: Luke Glen Richardson.
TRANSACTIONS/CAREER NOTES: Selected by Toronto Maple Leafs as underage junior in first round (first Maple Leafs pick, seventh overall) of NHL entry draft (June 13, 1987). . . . Traded by Maple Leafs with LW Vincent Damphousse, G Peter Ing, C Scott Thornton and future considerations to Edmonton Oilers for G Grant Fuhr, LW Glenn Anderson and LW Craig Berube (September 19, 1991). . . . Strained clavicular joint (February 11, 1992); missed three games. . . . Suffered from the flu (March 1993); missed one game.

			REGULAR SEASON					PLAYOFFS			
Season	Team	League	Gms.	G	A	Pts.	Pen.	Gms.	G	A	Pts.	Pen.
84-85—Ottawa Jr. B		ODHA	35	5	26	31	72	—	—	—	—	—
85-86—Peterborough		OHL	63	6	18	24	57	16	2	1	3	50
86-87—Peterborough		OHL	59	13	32	45	70	12	0	5	5	24
87-88—Toronto		NHL	78	4	6	10	90	2	0	0	0	0
88-89—Toronto		NHL	55	2	7	9	106	—	—	—	—	—
89-90—Toronto		NHL	67	4	14	18	122	5	0	0	0	22
90-91—Toronto		NHL	78	1	9	10	238	—	—	—	—	—
91-92—Edmonton		NHL	75	2	19	21	118	16	0	5	5	45
92-93—Edmonton		NHL	82	3	10	13	142	—	—	—	—	—
NHL totals			435	16	65	81	816	23	0	5	5	67

RICHER, STEPHANE
D, PANTHERS

PERSONAL: Born April 28, 1966, at Hull, Que. . . . 5-11/190. . . . Shoots right.
TRANSACTIONS/CAREER NOTES: Signed as free agent by Montreal Canadiens (January 9, 1988). . . . Signed as free agent by Los Angeles Kings (July 11, 1990). . . . Signed as free agent by Canadiens (September 1, 1991). . . . Signed as free agent by Tampa Bay Lightning (July 29, 1992). . . . Traded by Lightning to Boston Bruins for D Bob Beers (October 28, 1992). . . . Selected by Florida Panthers in NHL expansion draft (June 24, 1993).
HONORS: Named to AHL All-Star second team (1991-92).

R

Season	Team	League	Gms.	G	A	Pts.	Pen.	Gms.	G	A	Pts.	Pen.
			REGULAR SEASON					PLAYOFFS				
83-84—Hull		QMJHL	70	8	38	46	42	—	—	—	—	—
84-85—Hull		QMJHL	67	21	56	77	98	—	—	—	—	—
85-86—Hull		QMJHL	71	14	52	66	166	—	—	—	—	—
86-87—Hull		QMJHL	33	6	22	28	74	8	3	4	7	17
87-88—Baltimore		AHL	22	0	3	3	6	—	—	—	—	—
—Sherbrooke		AHL	41	4	7	11	46	5	1	0	1	10
88-89—Sherbrooke		AHL	70	7	26	33	158	6	1	2	3	18
89-90—Sherbrooke		AHL	60	10	12	22	85	12	4	9	13	16
90-91—Phoenix		IHL	67	11	38	49	48	11	4	6	10	6
—New Haven		AHL	3	0	1	1	0	—	—	—	—	—
91-92—Fredericton		AHL	80	17	47	64	74	7	0	5	5	18
92-93—Tampa Bay		NHL	3	0	0	0	0	—	—	—	—	—
—Providence		AHL	53	8	29	37	60	—	—	—	—	—
—Boston		NHL	21	1	4	5	18	3	0	0	0	0
NHL totals			24	1	4	5	18	3	0	0	0	0

RICHER, STEPHANE

RW, DEVILS

PERSONAL: Born June 7, 1966, at Buckingham, Que. . . . 6-2/200. . . . Shoots right. . . . Full name: Stephane Joseph Jean Richer. . . . Name pronounced REE-shay.
TRANSACTIONS/CAREER NOTES: Selected by Montreal Canadiens as underage junior in second round (third Canadiens pick, 29th overall) of NHL entry draft (June 9, 1984). . . . Traded by Granby Bisons with LW Greg Choules to Chicoutimi Sagueneens for C Stephane Roy, RW Marc Bureau, Lee Duhemee, Sylvain Demers and D Rene L'Ecuyer (January 1985). . . . Sprained ankle (November 18, 1985); missed 13 games. . . . Bruised right hand (March 12, 1988). . . . Broke right thumb (April 1988). . . . Sprained right thumb (September 1988). . . . Suspended 10 games by NHL for slashing (November 16, 1988). . . . Suffered from the flu (March 15, 1989). . . . Bruised right shoulder (September 1989). . . . Bruised left foot (February 1990). . . . Injured left ankle (April 21, 1990). . . . Injured knee (December 12, 1990). . . . Traded by Canadiens with RW Tom Chorske to New Jersey Devils for LW Kirk Muller and G Roland Melanson (September 20, 1991). . . . Injured groin (October 22, 1991); missed two games. . . . Injured left knee (March 24, 1992); missed three games. . . . Injured back (December 6, 1992); missed two games.
HONORS: Named QMJHL Rookie of the Year (1983-84). . . . Named to QMJHL All-Star second team (1984-85). . . . Played in NHL All-Star Game (1990).
MISCELLANEOUS: Member of Stanley Cup championship team (1986).

Season	Team	League	Gms.	G	A	Pts.	Pen.	Gms.	G	A	Pts.	Pen.
			REGULAR SEASON					PLAYOFFS				
83-84—Granby		QMJHL	67	39	37	76	58	3	1	1	2	4
84-85—Granby/Chicoutimi		QMJHL	57	61	59	120	71	12	13	13	26	25
—Montreal		NHL	1	0	0	0	0	—	—	—	—	—
—Sherbrooke		AHL	—	—	—	—	—	9	6	3	9	10
85-86—Montreal		NHL	65	21	16	37	50	16	4	1	5	23
86-87—Sherbrooke		AHL	12	10	4	14	11	—	—	—	—	—
—Montreal		NHL	57	20	19	39	80	5	3	2	5	0
87-88—Montreal		NHL	72	50	28	78	72	8	7	5	12	6
88-89—Montreal		NHL	68	25	35	60	61	21	6	5	11	14
89-90—Montreal		NHL	75	51	40	91	46	9	7	3	10	2
90-91—Montreal		NHL	75	31	30	61	53	13	9	5	14	6
91-92—New Jersey		NHL	74	29	35	64	25	7	1	2	3	0
92-93—New Jersey		NHL	78	38	35	73	44	5	2	2	4	2
NHL totals			565	265	238	503	431	84	39	25	64	53

RICHTER, BARRY

D/RW, WHALERS

PERSONAL: Born September 11, 1970, at Madison, Wis. . . . 6-2/205. . . . Shoots left. . . . Full name: Barron Patrick Richter. . . . Son of Pat Richter, tight end, Washington Redskins of National Football League (1963-70).
HIGH SCHOOL: Culver (Ind.) Military Academy.
COLLEGE: Wisconsin.
TRANSACTIONS/CAREER NOTES: Selected by Hartford Whalers in second round (second Whalers pick, 32nd overall) of NHL entry draft (June 11, 1988).
HONORS: Named to NCAA All-Tournament team (1991-92). . . . Named to NCAA All-America West first team (1992-93). . . . Named to WCHA All-Star first team (1992-93).

Season	Team	League	Gms.	G	A	Pts.	Pen.	Gms.	G	A	Pts.	Pen.
			REGULAR SEASON					PLAYOFFS				
86-87—Culver Military Academy		Indiana H.S.	35	19	26	45	. . .	—	—	—	—	—
87-88—Culver Military Academy		Indiana H.S.	35	24	29	53	18	—	—	—	—	—
88-89—Culver Military Academy		Indiana H.S.	19	21	29	50	16	—	—	—	—	—
89-90—University of Wisconsin		WCHA	42	13	23	36	26	—	—	—	—	—
90-91—University of Wisconsin		WCHA	43	15	20	35	42	—	—	—	—	—
91-92—University of Wisconsin		WCHA	43	10	29	39	62	—	—	—	—	—
92-93—University of Wisconsin		WCHA	42	14	32	46	74	—	—	—	—	—

RICHTER, MIKE

G, RANGERS

PERSONAL: Born September 22, 1966, at Philadelphia. . . . 5-11/182. . . . Shoots left. . . . Full name: Michael Thomas Richter. . . . Name pronounced RIHK-tuhr.
HIGH SCHOOL: Northwood School (Lake Placid, N.Y.).
COLLEGE: Wisconsin.

TRANSACTIONS/CAREER NOTES: Selected by New York Rangers in second round (second Rangers pick, 28th overall) of NHL entry draft (June 15, 1985).... Bruised thigh (January 30, 1992); missed 12 games.
HONORS: Won WCHA Rookie of the Year Award (1985-86).... Named to WCHA All-Star second team (1985-86 and 1986-87). ... Played in NHL All-Star Game (1992).

Season Team	League	REGULAR SEASON								PLAYOFFS						
		Gms.	Min.	W	L	T	GA	SO	Avg.	Gms.	Min.	W	L	GA	SO	Avg.
84-85—Northwood School	N.Y. H.S.	24	1374	...	...	...	52	2	2.27	—	—	—	—	—	—	—
85-86—Univ. of Wisconsin	WCHA	24	1394	14	9	0	92	1	3.96	—	—	—	—	—	—	—
86-87—Univ. of Wisconsin	WCHA	36	2136	19	16	1	126	0	3.54	—	—	—	—	—	—	—
87-88—U.S. national team	Int'l	29	1559	17	7	2	86	0	3.31	—	—	—	—	—	—	—
—U.S. Olympic Team	Int'l	4	230	2	2	0	15	0	3.91	—	—	—	—	—	—	—
—Colorado	IHL	22	1298	16	5	0	68	1	3.14	10	536	5	3	35	0	3.92
88-89—Denver	IHL	*57	3031	23	26	0	*217	1	4.30	4	210	0	4	21	0	6.00
89-90—New York Rangers	NHL	23	1320	12	5	5	66	0	3.00	6	330	3	2	19	0	3.45
—Flint	IHL	13	782	7	4	2	49	0	3.76	—	—	—	—	—	—	—
90-91—New York Rangers	NHL	45	2596	21	13	7	135	0	3.12	6	313	2	4	14	†1	2.68
91-92—New York Rangers	NHL	41	2298	23	12	2	119	3	3.11	7	412	4	2	24	1	3.50
92-93—New York Rangers	NHL	38	2105	13	19	3	134	1	3.82	—	—	—	—	—	—	—
—Binghamton	AHL	5	305	4	0	1	6	0	1.18	—	—	—	—	—	—	—
NHL totals		147	8319	69	49	17	454	4	3.27	19	1055	9	8	57	2	3.24

RIDLEY, MIKE

C, CAPITALS

PERSONAL: Born July 8, 1963, at Winnipeg, Man.... 6-1/200.... Shoots left.
COLLEGE: Manitoba.
TRANSACTIONS/CAREER NOTES: Signed as free agent by New York Rangers (September 1985).... Traded by Rangers with LW Kelly Miller and RW Bobby Crawford to Washington Capitals for C Bobby Carpenter and second-round pick in 1989 draft (RW Jason Prosofsky) (January 1987).... Suffered collapsed left lung (March 9, 1990); missed six games.... Bruised ribs (April 5, 1990).
HONORS: Won Senator Joseph A. Sullivan Trophy (1983-84).... Named to NHL All-Rookie team (1985-86).... Played in NHL All-Star Game (1989).

Season Team	League	REGULAR SEASON					PLAYOFFS				
		Gms.	G	A	Pts.	Pen.	Gms.	G	A	Pts.	Pen.
83-84—University of Manitoba	CWUAA	46	39	41	80	...	—	—	—	—	—
84-85—University of Manitoba	CWUAA	30	29	38	67	48	—	—	—	—	—
85-86—New York Rangers	NHL	80	22	43	65	69	16	6	8	14	26
86-87—New York Rangers	NHL	38	16	20	36	20	—	—	—	—	—
—Washington	NHL	40	15	19	34	20	7	2	1	3	6
87-88—Washington	NHL	70	28	31	59	22	14	6	5	11	10
88-89—Washington	NHL	80	41	48	89	49	6	0	5	5	2
89-90—Washington	NHL	74	30	43	73	27	14	3	4	7	8
90-91—Washington	NHL	79	23	48	71	26	11	3	4	7	8
91-92—Washington	NHL	80	29	40	69	38	7	0	11	11	0
92-93—Washington	NHL	84	26	56	82	44	6	1	5	6	0
NHL totals		625	230	348	578	315	81	21	43	64	60

RIENDEAU, VINCE

G, RED WINGS

PERSONAL: Born April 20, 1966, at St. Hyacinthe, Que.... 5-10/185.... Shoots left.... Name pronounced ree-EHN-doh.
COLLEGE: Sherbrooke (Que.).
TRANSACTIONS/CAREER NOTES: Signed as free agent by Montreal Canadiens (October 1985).... Suffered skin rash (November 1987).... Broke leg (April 10, 1988).... Traded by Canadiens with LW Sergio Momesso to St. Louis Blues for LW Jocelyn Lemieux, G Darrell May and second-round pick in 1989 draft (D Patrice Brisebois) (August 1988).... Suffered compound fracture of little finger of left hand (October 4, 1989); missed 10 games.... Pulled groin (February 17, 1991); missed seven games.... Traded by Blues to Detroit Red Wings for D Rick Zombo (October 18, 1991).... Sprained knee (October 25, 1991); missed 59 games.... Strained hip (January 2, 1993); missed six games.
HONORS: Named to QMJHL All-Star second team (1985-86).... Won Harry (Hap) Holmes Memorial Trophy (1986-87).... Shared Harry (Hap) Holmes Memorial Trophy with Jocelyn Perreault (1987-88).... Named to AHL All-Star second team (1987-88).

Season Team	League	REGULAR SEASON								PLAYOFFS						
		Gms.	Min.	W	L	T	GA	SO	Avg.	Gms.	Min.	W	L	GA	SO	Avg.
83-84—Verdun	QMJHL	41	2133	...	...	...	147	†2	4.14	—	—	—	—	—	—	—
84-85—Univ. of Sherbrooke	Can. Coll.					Statistics unavailable.										
85-86—Drummondville	QMJHL	57	3336	33	20	3	215	†2	3.87	*23	*1271	10	13	*106	1	5.00
86-87—Sherbrooke	AHL	41	2363	25	14	0	114	2	2.89	13	742	8	5	47	0	3.80
87-88—Sherbrooke	AHL	44	2521	27	13	3	112	*4	*2.67	2	127	0	2	7	0	3.31
—Montreal	NHL	1	36	0	0	0	5	0	8.33	—	—	—	—	—	—	—
88-89—St. Louis	NHL	32	1842	11	15	5	108	0	3.52	—	—	—	—	—	—	—
89-90—St. Louis	NHL	43	2551	17	19	5	149	1	3.50	8	397	3	4	24	0	3.63
90-91—St. Louis	NHL	44	2671	29	9	6	134	3	3.01	13	687	6	7	35	†1	3.06
91-92—St. Louis	NHL	3	157	1	2	0	11	0	4.20	—	—	—	—	—	—	—
—Detroit	NHL	2	87	2	0	0	2	0	1.38	2	73	1	0	4	0	3.29
—Adirondack	AHL	3	179	2	1	0	8	0	2.68	—	—	—	—	—	—	—
92-93—Detroit	NHL	22	1193	13	4	2	64	0	3.22	—	—	—	—	—	—	—
NHL totals		147	8537	73	49	18	473	4	3.32	23	1157	10	11	63	1	3.27

RIIHIJARVI, JUHA
RW, OILERS

PERSONAL: Born December 15, 1969, at Salla, Finland. . . . 6-3/205. . . . Shoots right. . . . Name pronounced ree-HEE-yahr-vee.

TRANSACTIONS/CAREER NOTES: Selected by Edmonton Oilers in 12th round (11th Oilers pick, 254th overall) of NHL entry draft (June 22, 1991).

Season Team	League		REGULAR SEASON					PLAYOFFS			
		Gms.	G	A	Pts.	Pen.	Gms.	G	A	Pts.	Pen.
90-91—Karpat Oulu	Finland Dv.II	42	29	41	70	34	—	—	—	—	—
91-92—JyP HT	Finland	38	29	33	62	37	10	4	4	8	10
92-93—JyP HT	Finland	41	25	31	56	38	9	4	2	6	2

RIVERS, JAMIE
D, BLUES

PERSONAL: Born March 16, 1975, at Ottawa, Ont. . . . 6-0/180. . . . Shoots left.

HIGH SCHOOL: Lasalle Secondary School (Sudbury, Ont.).

TRANSACTIONS/CAREER NOTES: Selected by St. Louis Blues in third round (second Blues pick, 63rd overall) of NHL entry draft (June 26, 1993).

Season Team	League		REGULAR SEASON					PLAYOFFS			
		Gms.	G	A	Pts.	Pen.	Gms.	G	A	Pts.	Pen.
90-91—Ottawa	OHA Jr. A	55	4	30	34	74	—	—	—	—	—
91-92—Sudbury	OHL	55	3	13	16	20	8	0	0	0	0
92-93—Sudbury	OHL	62	12	43	55	20	14	7	19	26	4

RIVERS, SHAWN
D, LIGHTNING

PERSONAL: Born January 30, 1971, at Ottawa. . . . 5-10/185. . . . Shoots left.

COLLEGE: St. Lawrence (N.Y.).

TRANSACTIONS/CAREER NOTES: Signed as free agent by Tampa Bay Lightning (August 13, 1992).

Season Team	League		REGULAR SEASON					PLAYOFFS			
		Gms.	G	A	Pts.	Pen.	Gms.	G	A	Pts.	Pen.
88-89—St. Lawrence University	ECAC	36	3	23	26	20	—	—	—	—	—
89-90—St. Lawrence University	ECAC	28	3	15	18	31	—	—	—	—	—
90-91—Sudbury	OHL	66	18	33	51	43	5	2	7	9	0
92-93—Atlanta	IHL	78	9	34	43	101	9	1	3	4	8
—Tampa Bay	NHL	4	0	2	2	2	—	—	—	—	—
NHL totals		4	0	2	2	2					

RIVET, CRAIG
D, CANADIENS

PERSONAL: Born September 13, 1974, at North Bay, Ont. . . . 6-2/172. . . . Shoots right.

TRANSACTIONS/CAREER NOTES: Selected by Montreal Canadiens in third round (fourth Canadiens pick, 68th overall) of NHL entry draft (June 20, 1992).

Season Team	League		REGULAR SEASON					PLAYOFFS			
		Gms.	G	A	Pts.	Pen.	Gms.	G	A	Pts.	Pen.
90-91—Barrie Jr. B	OHA	42	9	17	26	55	—	—	—	—	—
91-92—Kingston	OHL	66	5	21	26	97	—	—	—	—	—
92-93—Kingston	OHL	64	19	55	74	117	16	5	7	12	39

ROACH, GARY
D, RANGERS

PERSONAL: Born February 4, 1975, at Sault Ste. Marie, Ont. . . . 6-1/180. . . . Shoots left.

HIGH SCHOOL: White Pines Collegiate (Sault Ste Marie, Ont.).

TRANSACTIONS/CAREER NOTES: Selected by New York Rangers in fifth round (fifth Rangers pick, 112th overall) of NHL entry draft (June 26, 1993).

Season Team	League		REGULAR SEASON					PLAYOFFS			
		Gms.	G	A	Pts.	Pen.	Gms.	G	A	Pts.	Pen.
91-92—Sault Ste. Marie	OHL	41	2	9	11	6	9	0	0	0	0
92-93—Sault Ste. Marie	OHL	65	4	27	31	31	18	0	8	8	4

ROBERGE, MARIO
LW, CANADIENS

PERSONAL: Born January 31, 1964, at Quebec City. . . . 5-11/185. . . . Shoots left. . . . Name pronounced roh-BAIRZH. . . . Brother of Serge Roberge, right winger in Quebec Nordiques system.

TRANSACTIONS/CAREER NOTES: Signed as free agent by Sherbrooke Canadiens (January 1988). . . . Signed as free agent by Montreal Canadiens (October 5, 1988). . . . Injured thigh (December 22, 1991). . . . Suspended one off-day and fined $500 by NHL for fighting with taped hand (March 3, 1993).

MISCELLANEOUS: Member of Stanley Cup championship team (1993).

Season Team	League		REGULAR SEASON					PLAYOFFS			
		Gms.	G	A	Pts.	Pen.	Gms.	G	A	Pts.	Pen.
81-82—Quebec	QMJHL	8	0	3	3	2	—	—	—	—	—
82-83—Quebec	QMJHL	69	3	27	30	153	—	—	—	—	—
83-84—Quebec	QMJHL	60	12	28	40	253	—	—	—	—	—
84-85—					Did not play.						
85-86—					Did not play.						
86-87—					Did not play.						
87-88—Port Aux Basques	Nova Scotia	35	25	64	89	152	—	—	—	—	—
88-89—Sherbrooke	AHL	58	4	9	13	249	6	0	2	2	8
89-90—Sherbrooke	AHL	73	13	27	40	247	12	5	2	7	53
90-91—Fredericton	AHL	68	12	27	39	†365	2	0	2	2	5
—Montreal	NHL	5	0	0	0	21	12	0	0	0	24

Season Team	League	REGULAR SEASON Gms.	G	A	Pts.	Pen.	PLAYOFFS Gms.	G	A	Pts.	Pen.
91-92—Montreal	NHL	20	2	1	3	62	—	—	—	—	—
—Fredericton	AHL	6	1	2	3	20	7	0	2	2	20
92-93—Montreal	NHL	50	4	4	8	142	3	0	0	0	0
NHL totals		75	6	5	11	225	15	0	0	0	24

ROBERGE, SERGE
RW, NORDIQUES

PERSONAL: Born March 31, 1965, at Quebec City.... 6-1/195.... Shoots right.... Brother of Mario Roberge, left winger, Montreal Canadiens.

TRANSACTIONS/CAREER NOTES: Signed as free agent by Montreal Canadiens (January 25, 1988).... Signed as free agent by Quebec Nordiques (December 28, 1990).

Season Team	League	REGULAR SEASON Gms.	G	A	Pts.	Pen.	PLAYOFFS Gms.	G	A	Pts.	Pen.
82-83—Quebec	QMJHL	9	0	0	0	30	—	—	—	—	—
—Hull	QMJHL	22	0	4	4	115	—	—	—	—	—
83-84—Drummondville	QMJHL	58	1	7	8	287	10	0	2	2	*105
84-85—Drummondville	QMJHL	45	8	19	27	299	—	—	—	—	—
85-86—					Did not play.						
86-87—Virginia	ACHL	49	9	16	25	*353	12	4	2	6	*104
87-88—Sherbrooke	AHL	30	0	1	1	130	5	0	0	0	21
88-89—Sherbrooke	AHL	65	5	7	12	352	6	0	1	1	10
89-90—Sherbrooke	AHL	66	8	5	13	*343	12	2	0	2	44
90-91—Halifax	AHL	52	0	5	5	152	—	—	—	—	—
—Quebec	NHL	9	0	0	0	24	—	—	—	—	—
91-92—Halifax	AHL	66	2	8	10	319	—	—	—	—	—
92-93—Halifax	AHL	16	2	2	4	34	—	—	—	—	—
—Utica	AHL	28	0	3	3	85	1	0	0	0	0
NHL totals		9	0	0	0	24					

ROBERTS, DAVID
LW, BLUES

PERSONAL: Born May 28, 1970, at Alameda, Calif.... 6-0/185.... Shoots left.... Full name: David Lance Roberts.... Son of Doug Roberts, defenseman, four NHL teams (1965-66 through 1974-75) and New England Whalers of WHA (1975-76 through 1976-77); and nephew of Gord Roberts, defenseman, Boston Bruins.

HIGH SCHOOL: Avon (Conn.) Old Farms School For Boys.

COLLEGE: Michigan.

TRANSACTIONS/CAREER NOTES: Selected by St. Louis Blues in sixth round (fifth Blues pick, 114th overall) of NHL entry draft (June 17, 1989).

HONORS: Named CCHA Rookie of the Year (1989-90).... Named to CCHA All-Rookie team (1989-90).... Named to NCAA All-America West second team (1990-91).... Named to CCHA All-Star second team (1990-91 and 1992-93).

Season Team	League	REGULAR SEASON Gms.	G	A	Pts.	Pen.	PLAYOFFS Gms.	G	A	Pts.	Pen.
87-88—Avon Old Farms H.S.	Conn. H.S.	...	18	39	57	...	—	—	—	—	—
88-89—Avon Old Farms H.S.	Conn. H.S.	...	28	48	76	...	—	—	—	—	—
89-90—University of Michigan	CCHA	42	21	32	53	46	—	—	—	—	—
90-91—University of Michigan	CCHA	43	26	45	71	44	—	—	—	—	—
91-92—University of Michigan	CCHA	44	16	42	58	68	—	—	—	—	—
92-93—University of Michigan	CCHA	40	27	38	65	40	—	—	—	—	—

ROBERTS, GARY
LW, FLAMES

PERSONAL: Born May 23, 1966, at North York, Ont.... 6-1/190.... Shoots left.

TRANSACTIONS/CAREER NOTES: Selected by Calgary Flames as underage junior in first round (first Flames pick, 12th overall) of NHL entry draft (June 9, 1984).... Injured back (January 1989).... Suffered whiplash (November 9, 1991); missed one game.... Suffered from the flu (January 19, 1993); missed one game.... Suffered left quadricep hematoma (February 16, 1993); missed 25 games.

HONORS: Named to OHL All-Star second team (1984-85 and 1985-86).... Played in NHL All-Star Game (1992 and 1993).

MISCELLANEOUS: Member of Stanley Cup championship team (1989).

Season Team	League	REGULAR SEASON Gms.	G	A	Pts.	Pen.	PLAYOFFS Gms.	G	A	Pts.	Pen.
82-83—Ottawa	OHL	53	12	8	20	83	5	1	0	1	19
83-84—Ottawa	OHL	48	27	30	57	144	13	10	7	17	*62
84-85—Ottawa	OHL	59	44	62	106	186	5	2	8	10	10
—Moncton	AHL	7	4	2	6	7	—	—	—	—	—
85-86—Ottawa	OHL	24	26	25	51	83	—	—	—	—	—
—Guelph	OHL	23	18	15	33	65	20	18	13	31	43
86-87—Moncton	AHL	38	20	18	38	72	—	—	—	—	—
—Calgary	NHL	32	5	10	15	85	2	0	0	0	4
87-88—Calgary	NHL	74	13	15	28	282	9	2	3	5	29
88-89—Calgary	NHL	71	22	16	38	250	22	5	7	12	57
89-90—Calgary	NHL	78	39	33	72	222	6	2	5	7	41
90-91—Calgary	NHL	80	22	31	53	252	7	1	3	4	18
91-92—Calgary	NHL	76	53	37	90	207	—	—	—	—	—
92-93—Calgary	NHL	58	38	41	79	172	5	1	6	7	43
NHL totals		469	192	183	375	1470	51	11	24	35	192

R

ROBERTS, GORD
D, BRUINS

PERSONAL: Born October 2, 1957, at Detroit. . . . 6-1/195. . . . Shoots left. . . . Brother of Doug Roberts, defenseman, four NHL teams (1965-66 through 1974-75) and New England Whalers of WHA (1975-76 through 1976-77); and uncle of David Roberts, left winger in St. Louis Blues system.

TRANSACTIONS/CAREER NOTES: Signed by New England Whalers (September 1975). . . . Selected by Montreal Canadiens from Whalers in third round (seventh Canadiens pick, 54th overall) of NHL amateur draft (June 14, 1977). . . . Selected by Hartford Whalers from Canadiens in NHL expansion draft (June 22, 1979). . . . Traded by Whalers to Minnesota North Stars for LW Mike Fidler (December 16, 1980). . . . Bruised hip (April 1984). . . . Injured foot (November 13, 1985); missed four games. . . . Dislocated shoulder (October 1986). . . . Bruised shoulder (January 1988). . . . Traded by North Stars to Philadelphia Flyers for fourth-round pick in 1989 draft (C Jean-Francois Quintin) (February 8, 1988). . . . Traded by Flyers to St. Louis Blues for fourth-round pick in 1989 draft (LW Reid Simpson) (March 1988). . . . Traded by Blues to Pittsburgh Penguins for future considerations; Blues later received 11th-round pick in 1992 draft (G Wade Salzman) to complete deal (October 27, 1990). . . . Signed as free agent by Boston Bruins (June 19, 1992). . . . Suffered from the flu (December 1992); missed two games. . . . Injured shoulder (December 1992); missed 11 games. . . . Injured arm (January 1993); missed three games. . . . Injured hip (March 1993); missed one game.

MISCELLANEOUS: Member of Stanley Cup championship teams (1991 and 1992).

			REGULAR SEASON					PLAYOFFS				
Season	Team	League	Gms.	G	A	Pts.	Pen.	Gms.	G	A	Pts.	Pen.
73-74	Detroit Junior Red Wings	SOJHL	70	25	55	80	340	—	—	—	—	—
74-75	Victoria	WCHL	53	19	45	64	145	12	1	9	10	42
75-76	New England	WHA	77	3	19	22	102	17	2	9	11	36
76-77	New England	WHA	77	13	33	46	169	5	2	2	4	6
77-78	New England	WHA	78	15	46	61	118	14	0	5	5	29
78-79	New England	WHA	79	11	46	57	113	10	0	4	4	10
79-80	Hartford	NHL	80	8	28	36	89	3	1	1	2	2
80-81	Hartford	NHL	27	2	11	13	81	—	—	—	—	—
	Minnesota	NHL	50	6	31	37	94	19	1	5	6	17
81-82	Minnesota	NHL	79	4	30	34	119	4	0	3	3	27
82-83	Minnesota	NHL	80	3	41	44	103	9	1	5	6	14
83-84	Minnesota	NHL	77	8	45	53	132	15	3	7	10	23
84-85	Minnesota	NHL	78	6	36	42	112	9	1	6	7	6
85-86	Minnesota	NHL	76	2	21	23	101	5	0	4	4	8
86-87	Minnesota	NHL	67	3	10	13	68	—	—	—	—	—
87-88	Minnesota	NHL	48	1	10	11	103	—	—	—	—	—
	Philadelphia	NHL	11	1	2	3	15	—	—	—	—	—
	St. Louis	NHL	11	1	3	4	25	10	1	2	3	33
88-89	St. Louis	NHL	77	2	24	26	90	10	1	7	8	8
89-90	St. Louis	NHL	75	3	14	17	140	10	0	2	2	26
90-91	Peoria	IHL	6	0	8	8	4	—	—	—	—	—
	St. Louis	NHL	3	0	1	1	8	—	—	—	—	—
	Pittsburgh	NHL	61	3	12	15	70	24	1	2	3	63
91-92	Pittsburgh	NHL	73	2	22	24	87	19	0	2	2	32
92-93	Boston	NHL	65	5	12	17	105	4	0	0	0	6
	WHA totals		311	42	144	186	502	46	4	20	24	81
	NHL totals		1038	60	353	413	1542	141	10	46	56	265

ROBINSON, ROB
D, LIGHTNING

PERSONAL: Born April 19, 1967, at St. Catharines, Ont. . . . 6-1/214. . . . Shoots left. . . . Full name: Robert Douglas Robinson. . . . Son of Doug Robinson, left winger, Chicago Blackhawks, New York Rangers and Los Angeles Kings (1964-65 through 1970-71).

COLLEGE: Miami of Ohio.

TRANSACTIONS/CAREER NOTES: Selected by St. Louis Blues in sixth round (sixth Blues pick, 117th overall) of NHL entry draft (June 13, 1987). . . . Traded by Blues with G Pat Jablonski, RW Darin Kimble and RW Steve Tuttle to Tampa Bay Lightning for future considerations (June 19, 1992).

HONORS: Named to IHL All-Star second team (1990-91).

			REGULAR SEASON					PLAYOFFS				
Season	Team	League	Gms.	G	A	Pts.	Pen.	Gms.	G	A	Pts.	Pen.
85-86	Miami of Ohio	CCHA	38	1	9	10	24	—	—	—	—	—
86-87	Miami of Ohio	CCHA	33	3	5	8	32	—	—	—	—	—
87-88	Miami of Ohio	CCHA	35	1	3	4	56	—	—	—	—	—
88-89	Miami of Ohio	CCHA	30	3	4	7	42	—	—	—	—	—
	Peoria	IHL	11	2	0	2	6	—	—	—	—	—
89-90	Peoria	IHL	60	2	11	13	72	5	0	1	1	10
90-91	Peoria	IHL	79	2	21	23	42	19	0	6	6	8
91-92	St. Louis	NHL	22	0	1	1	8	—	—	—	—	—
	Peoria	IHL	35	1	10	11	29	10	0	2	2	12
92-93	Peoria	IHL	34	0	4	4	38	—	—	—	—	—
	NHL totals		22	0	1	1	8					

ROBITAILLE, LUC
LW, KINGS

PERSONAL: Born February 17, 1966, at Montreal. . . . 6-1/195. . . . Shoots left. . . . Name pronounced ROH-buh-tigh.

TRANSACTIONS/CAREER NOTES: Selected by Los Angeles Kings as underage junior in ninth round (ninth Kings pick, 171st overall) of NHL entry draft (June 9, 1984). . . . Suspended four games by NHL games for cross-checking from behind (November 10, 1990).

HONORS: Named to QMJHL All-Star second team (1984-85). . . . Won Can.HL Player of the Year Award (1985-86). . . . Shared

Guy Lafleur Trophy with Sylvain Cote (1985-86).... Named to QMJHL All-Star first team (1985-86).... Named to Memorial Cup All-Star team (1985-86).... Won Calder Memorial Trophy (1986-87).... Named to THE SPORTING NEWS All-Star second team (1986-87 and 1991-92).... Named to NHL All-Star second team (1986-87 and 1991-92).... Named to NHL All-Rookie team (1986-87).... Named to THE SPORTING NEWS All-Star first team (1987-88 through 1990-91 and 1992-93).... Played in NHL All-Star Game (1988 through 1993).... Named to NHL All-Star first team (1987-88 through 1990-91 and 1992-93).
RECORDS: Holds NHL single-season records for most points by a left-winger—125 (1992-93); and most goals by a left-winger—63 (1992-93).

		REGULAR SEASON					PLAYOFFS				
Season Team	League	Gms.	G	A	Pts.	Pen.	Gms.	G	A	Pts.	Pen.
83-84—Hull	QMJHL	70	32	53	85	48	—	—	—	—	—
84-85—Hull	QMJHL	64	55	94	149	115	5	4	2	6	27
85-86—Hull	QMJHL	63	68	*123	†191	93	15	17	27	*44	28
86-87—Los Angeles	NHL	79	45	39	84	28	5	1	4	5	2
87-88—Los Angeles	NHL	80	53	58	111	82	5	2	5	7	18
88-89—Los Angeles	NHL	78	46	52	98	65	11	2	6	8	10
89-90—Los Angeles	NHL	80	52	49	101	38	10	5	5	10	10
90-91—Los Angeles	NHL	76	45	46	91	68	12	12	4	16	22
91-92—Los Angeles	NHL	80	44	63	107	95	6	3	4	7	12
92-93—Los Angeles	NHL	84	63	62	125	100	24	9	13	22	28
NHL totals		557	348	369	717	476	73	34	41	75	102

ROCHE, DAVE
LW, PENGUINS

PERSONAL: Born June 13, 1975, at Lindsay, Ont.... 6-4/224.... Shoots left.
TRANSACTIONS/CAREER NOTES: Selected by Pittsburgh Penguins in third round (third Penguins pick, 62nd overall) of NHL entry draft (June 26, 1993).

		REGULAR SEASON					PLAYOFFS				
Season Team	League	Gms.	G	A	Pts.	Pen.	Gms.	G	A	Pts.	Pen.
90-91—Peterborough Jr. B	OHA	40	22	17	39	85	—	—	—	—	—
91-92—Peterborough	OHL	62	10	17	27	105	10	0	0	0	34
92-93—Peterborough	OHL	56	40	60	100	105	21	14	15	29	42

ROENICK, JEREMY
C, BLACKHAWKS

PERSONAL: Born January 17, 1970, at Boston.... 6-0/170.... Shoots right.... Name pronounced ROH-nihk.... Brother of Trevor Roenick, right winger in Hartford Whalers system.
HIGH SCHOOL: Thayer Academy (Braintree, Mass.).
TRANSACTIONS/CAREER NOTES: Selected by Chicago Blackhawks in first round (first Blackhawks pick, eighth overall) of NHL entry draft (June 11, 1988).... Sprained knee ligaments (January 9, 1989); missed one month.
HONORS: Named to QMJHL All-Star second team (1988-89).... Named NHL Rookie of the Year by THE SPORTING NEWS (1989-90).... Played in NHL All-Star Game (1991 through 1993).

		REGULAR SEASON					PLAYOFFS				
Season Team	League	Gms.	G	A	Pts.	Pen.	Gms.	G	A	Pts.	Pen.
86-87—Thayer Academy	Mass. H.S.	24	31	34	65	...	—	—	—	—	—
87-88—Thayer Academy	Mass. H.S.	...	34	50	84	...	—	—	—	—	—
88-89—Chicago	NHL	20	9	9	18	4	10	1	3	4	7
—Hull	QMJHL	28	34	36	70	14	—	—	—	—	—
89-90—Chicago	NHL	78	26	40	66	54	20	11	7	18	8
90-91—Chicago	NHL	79	41	53	94	80	6	3	5	8	4
91-92—Chicago	NHL	80	53	50	103	98	18	12	10	22	12
92-93—Chicago	NHL	84	50	57	107	86	4	1	2	3	2
NHL totals		341	179	209	388	322	58	28	27	55	33

ROENICK, TREVOR
RW, WHALERS

PERSONAL: Born October 7, 1974, at Derby, Conn.... 6-1/200.... Shoots right.... Brother of Jeremy Roenick, center, Chicago Blackhawks.
HIGH SCHOOL: Thayer Academy (Braintree, Mass.).
TRANSACTIONS/CAREER NOTES: Selected by Hartford Whalers in fourth round (third Whalers pick, 84th overall) of NHL entry draft (June 26, 1993).

		REGULAR SEASON					PLAYOFFS				
Season Team	League	Gms.	G	A	Pts.	Pen.	Gms.	G	A	Pts.	Pen.
90-91—Thayer Academy	Mass. H.S.	17	10	7	17	0	—	—	—	—	—
91-92—Thayer Academy	Mass. H.S.	26	16	16	32	8	—	—	—	—	—
92-93—Boston	NEJHL	58	61	48	109	94	—	—	—	—	—

ROGLES, CHRIS
G, BLACKHAWKS

PERSONAL: Born January 22, 1969, at St. Louis, Mo.... 5-11/175.... Shoots right.
COLLEGE: Clarkson (N.Y.).
TRANSACTIONS/CAREER NOTES: Signed as free agent by Chicago Blackhawks (June 21, 1993).

		REGULAR SEASON							PLAYOFFS						
Season Team	League	Gms.	Min.	W	L	T	GA	SO	Avg.	Gms.	Min.	W	L	GA SO	Avg.
89-90—Clarkson	ECAC	7	142	1	0	0	7	0	2.96	—	—	—	—	— —	—
90-91—Clarkson	ECAC	28	1359	16	6	0	76	3	3.36	—	—	—	—	— —	—
91-92—Clarkson	ECAC	19	998	11	3	0	51	0	3.07	—	—	—	—	— —	—
92-93—Clarkson	ECAC	27	1482	16	4	4	60	3	2.43	—	—	—	—	— —	—

ROHLOFF, JON
D, BRUINS

PERSONAL: Born October 3, 1969, at Mankato, Minn. . . . 6-0/200. . . . Shoots right. . . . Full name: Jon Richard Rohloff.
HIGH SCHOOL: Grand Rapids (Minn.).
COLLEGE: Minnesota-Duluth.
TRANSACTIONS/CAREER NOTES: Selected by Boston Bruins in ninth round (seventh Bruins pick, 186th overall) of NHL entry draft (June 11, 1988).
HONORS: Named to WCHA All-Star second team (1992-93).

			REGULAR SEASON					PLAYOFFS				
Season	Team	League	Gms.	G	A	Pts.	Pen.	Gms.	G	A	Pts.	Pen.
86-87—Grand Rapids H.S.	Minn. H.S.	21	12	23	35	16	—	—	—	—	—
87-88—Grand Rapids H.S.	Minn. H.S.	23	10	13	23	. . .	—	—	—	—	—
88-89—Minnesota-Duluth	WCHA	39	1	2	3	44	—	—	—	—	—
89-90—Minnesota-Duluth	WCHA	5	0	1	1	6	2	0	0	0	2
90-91—Minnesota-Duluth	WCHA	32	6	11	17	38	—	—	—	—	—
91-92—Minnesota-Duluth	WCHA	27	9	9	18	48	—	—	—	—	—
92-93—Minnesota-Duluth	WCHA	36	15	19	34	87	—	—	—	—	—

ROLSTON, BRIAN
C, DEVILS

PERSONAL: Born February 21, 1973, at Flint, Mich. . . . 6-1/175. . . . Shoots left.
TRANSACTIONS/CAREER NOTES: Selected by New Jersey Devils in first round (second Devils pick, 11th overall) of NHL entry draft (June 22, 1991).
HONORS: Named to NCAA All-Tournament team (1991-92 and 1992-93). . . . Named to NCAA All-America West second team (1992-93). . . . Named to CCHA All-Star first team (1992-93).

			REGULAR SEASON					PLAYOFFS				
Season	Team	League	Gms.	G	A	Pts.	Pen.	Gms.	G	A	Pts.	Pen.
89-90—Detroit Compuware	NAJHL	40	36	37	73	57	—	—	—	—	—
90-91—Detroit Compuware	NAJHL	36	49	46	95	14	—	—	—	—	—
91-92—Lake Superior State	CCHA	41	18	28	46	16	—	—	—	—	—
92-93—Lake Superior State	CCHA	39	33	31	64	20	—	—	—	—	—

ROMANIUK, RUSS
LW, JETS

PERSONAL: Born May 9, 1970, at Winnipeg, Man. . . . 6-0/185. . . . Shoots left. . . . Full name: Russell James Romaniuk. . . . Name pronounced ROH-muh-nuhk.
COLLEGE: North Dakota.
TRANSACTIONS/CAREER NOTES: Suffered chip fracture of left knee (December 1987). . . . Sprained right shoulder (February 1988). . . . Selected by Winnipeg Jets in second round (second Jets pick, 31st overall) of NHL entry draft (June 11, 1988). . . . Fractured knuckle (October 27, 1991); missed six games. . . . Sprained wrist (December 10, 1991); missed one game. . . . Sprained knee (November 17, 1992); missed one game. . . . Sprained ankle (December 17, 1992); missed 10 games.
HONORS: Named to WCHA All-Tournament team (1989-90). . . . Named to WCHA All-Star first team (1990-91).

			REGULAR SEASON					PLAYOFFS				
Season	Team	League	Gms.	G	A	Pts.	Pen.	Gms.	G	A	Pts.	Pen.
87-88—St. Boniface	MJHL				Statistics unavailable.						
88-89—Univ. of North Dakota	WCHA	39	17	14	31	32	—	—	—	—	—
89-90—Canadian national team	Int'l	3	1	0	1	0	—	—	—	—	—
—Univ. of North Dakota	WCHA	45	36	15	51	54	—	—	—	—	—
90-91—Univ. of North Dakota	WCHA	39	40	28	68	30	—	—	—	—	—
91-92—Winnipeg	NHL	27	3	5	8	18	—	—	—	—	—
—Moncton	AHL	45	16	15	31	25	10	5	4	9	19
92-93—Winnipeg	NHL	28	3	1	4	22	1	0	0	0	0
—Fort Wayne	IHL	4	2	0	2	7	—	—	—	—	—
—Moncton	AHL	28	18	8	26	40	5	0	4	4	2
NHL totals		55	6	6	12	40	1	0	0	0	0

RONAN, ED
RW, CANADIENS

PERSONAL: Born March 21, 1968, at Quincy, Mass. . . . 6-0/197. . . . Shoots right.
TRANSACTIONS/CAREER NOTES: Selected by Montreal Canadiens in 11th round (13th Canadiens pick, 227th overall) of NHL entry draft (June 13, 1987).
MISCELLANEOUS: Member of Stanley Cup championship team (1993).

			REGULAR SEASON					PLAYOFFS				
Season	Team	League	Gms.	G	A	Pts.	Pen.	Gms.	G	A	Pts.	Pen.
87-88—Boston University	Hockey East	31	2	5	7	20	—	—	—	—	—
88-89—Boston University	Hockey East	36	4	11	15	34	—	—	—	—	—
89-90—Boston University	Hockey East	44	17	23	40	50	—	—	—	—	—
90-91—Boston University	Hockey East	41	16	19	35	38	—	—	—	—	—
91-92—Fredericton	AHL	78	25	34	59	82	7	5	1	6	6
—Montreal	NHL	3	0	0	0	0	—	—	—	—	—
92-93—Montreal	NHL	53	5	7	12	20	14	2	3	5	10
—Fredericton	AHL	16	10	5	15	15	5	2	4	6	6
NHL totals		56	5	7	12	20	14	2	3	5	10

RONNING, CLIFF
C, CANUCKS

PERSONAL: Born October 1, 1965, at Vancouver, B.C. . . . 5-8/175. . . . Shoots left.
HIGH SCHOOL: Burnaby North (B.C.).
TRANSACTIONS/CAREER NOTES: Selected by St. Louis Blues as underage junior in seventh round (ninth Blues pick, 134th overall) of NHL entry draft (June 9, 1984). . . . Injured groin

(November 1988).... Agreed to play in Italy for 1989-90 season (August 1989).... Fractured right index finger (November 12, 1990); missed 12 games.... Traded by Blues with LW Geoff Courtnall, D Robert Dirk, LW Sergio Momesso and fifth-round pick in 1992 draft (RW Brian Loney) to Vancouver Canucks for C Dan Quinn and D Garth Butcher (March 5, 1991).... Sprained hand (January 4, 1993); missed five games.
HONORS: Won Stewart (Butch) Paul Memorial Trophy (1983-84).... Named to WHL All-Star second team (1983-84).... Won Most Valuable Player Trophy (1984-85).... Won Bob Brownridge Memorial Trophy (1984-85).... Won Frank Boucher Memorial Trophy (1984-85).... Named to WHL (West) All-Star first team (1984-85).

			REGULAR SEASON					PLAYOFFS			
Season Team	League	Gms.	G	A	Pts.	Pen.	Gms.	G	A	Pts.	Pen.
82-83—New Westminster	BCJHL	52	82	68	150	42	—	—	—	—	—
83-84—New Westminster	WHL	71	69	67	136	10	9	8	13	21	10
84-85—New Westminster	WHL	70	*89	108	*197	20	11	10	14	24	4
85-86—Canadian national team ...	Int'l	71	55	63	118	53	—	—	—	—	—
—St. Louis	NHL	—	—	—	—	—	5	1	1	2	2
86-87—Canadian national team ...	Int'l	26	16	16	32	12	—	—	—	—	—
—St. Louis	NHL	42	11	14	25	6	4	0	1	1	0
87-88—St. Louis	NHL	26	5	8	13	12	—	—	—	—	—
88-89—St. Louis	NHL	64	24	31	55	18	7	1	3	4	0
—Peoria	IHL	12	11	20	31	8	—	—	—	—	—
89-90—Asiago	Italy	42	76	60	136	30	6	7	12	19	4
90-91—St. Louis	NHL	48	14	18	32	10	—	—	—	—	—
—Vancouver.........................	NHL	11	6	6	12	0	6	6	3	9	12
91-92—Vancouver.....................	NHL	80	24	47	71	42	13	8	5	13	6
92-93—Vancouver.....................	NHL	79	29	56	85	30	12	2	9	11	6
NHL totals.................................		350	113	180	293	118	47	18	22	40	26

ROUSE, BOB

D, MAPLE LEAFS

PERSONAL: Born June 18, 1964, at Surrey, B.C.... 6-2/210.... Shoots right.... Name pronounced ROWZ.
TRANSACTIONS/CAREER NOTES: Selected by Minnesota North Stars as underage junior in fourth round (third North Stars pick, 80th overall) of NHL entry draft (June 9, 1982).... Suffered hip contusions (January 1988).... Traded by North Stars with RW Dino Ciccarelli to Washington Capitals for RW Mike Gartner and D Larry Murphy (March 7, 1989).... Sprained right knee (December 12, 1989); missed eight games.... Traded by Capitals with C Peter Zezel to Toronto Maple Leafs for D Al Iafrate (January 16, 1991).... Broke collarbone (February 16, 1991).
HONORS: Won Top Defenseman Trophy (1983-84).... Named to WHL (East) All-Star first team (1983-84).

			REGULAR SEASON					PLAYOFFS			
Season Team	League	Gms.	G	A	Pts.	Pen.	Gms.	G	A	Pts.	Pen.
80-81—Billings	WHL	70	0	13	13	116	5	0	0	0	2
81-82—Billings	WHL	71	7	22	29	209	5	0	2	2	10
82-83—Nanaimo.......................	WHL	29	7	20	27	86	—	—	—	—	—
—Lethbridge.........................	WHL	42	8	30	38	82	20	2	13	15	55
83-84—Lethbridge.....................	WHL	71	18	42	60	101	5	0	1	1	28
—Minnesota	NHL	1	0	0	0	0	—	—	—	—	—
84-85—Springfield.....................	AHL	8	0	3	3	6	—	—	—	—	—
—Minnesota	NHL	63	2	9	11	113	—	—	—	—	—
85-86—Minnesota	NHL	75	1	14	15	151	3	0	0	0	2
86-87—Minnesota	NHL	72	2	10	12	179	—	—	—	—	—
87-88—Minnesota	NHL	74	0	12	12	168	—	—	—	—	—
88-89—Minnesota	NHL	66	4	13	17	124	—	—	—	—	—
—Washington	NHL	13	0	2	2	36	6	2	0	2	4
89-90—Washington	NHL	70	4	16	20	123	15	2	3	5	47
90-91—Washington	NHL	47	5	15	20	65	—	—	—	—	—
—Toronto............................	NHL	13	2	4	6	10	—	—	—	—	—
91-92—Toronto........................	NHL	79	3	19	22	97	—	—	—	—	—
92-93—Toronto........................	NHL	82	3	11	14	130	21	3	8	11	29
NHL totals.................................		655	26	125	151	1196	45	7	11	18	82

ROUSSEL, DOMINIC

G, FLYERS

PERSONAL: Born February 22, 1970, at Hull, Que.... 6-1/185.... Shoots left.... Name pronounced roo-SEHL.
TRANSACTIONS/CAREER NOTES: Selected by Philadelphia Flyers as underage junior in third round (fourth Flyers pick, 63rd overall) of NHL entry draft (June 11, 1988). ... Pulled groin (November 29, 1992); missed three games.... Reinjured groin (December 11, 1992); missed 11 games.

			REGULAR SEASON						PLAYOFFS					
Season Team	League	Gms.	Min.	W	L	T	GA	SO	Avg.	Gms.	Min.	W	L	GA	SO	Avg.
87-88—Trois-Rivieres..............	QMJHL	51	2905	18	25	4	251	0	5.18	—	—	—	—	—	—	—
88-89—Shawinigan	QMJHL	46	2555	24	15	2	171	0	4.02	10	638	6	4	36	0	3.39
89-90—Shawinigan	QMJHL	37	1985	20	14	1	133	0	4.02	2	120	1	1	12	0	6.00
90-91—Hershey	AHL	45	2507	20	14	7	151	1	3.61	7	366	3	4	21	0	3.44
91-92—Hershey	AHL	35	2040	15	11	6	121	1	3.56	—	—	—	—	—	—	—
—Philadelphia	NHL	17	922	7	8	2	40	1	2.60	—	—	—	—	—	—	—
92-93—Philadelphia	NHL	34	1769	13	11	5	111	1	3.76	—	—	—	—	—	—	—
—Hershey	AHL	6	372	0	3	3	23	0	3.71	—	—	—	—	—	—	—
NHL totals.................................		51	2691	20	19	7	151	2	3.37							

ROUSSON, BORIS
G, RANGERS

PERSONAL: Born June 14, 1970, at Val d'Or, Que.... 6-2/195.
TRANSACTIONS/CAREER NOTES: Signed as free agent by New York Rangers (March 31, 1991).
HONORS: Named to QMJHL All-Star second team (1990-91).... Shared Harry (Hap) Holmes Memorial Trophy with Corey Hirsch (1992-93).

									REGULAR SEASON				PLAYOFFS				
Season	Team	League	Gms.	Min.	W	L	T	GA	SO	Avg.	Gms.	Min.	W	L	GA	SO	Avg.
87-88	Laval	QMJHL	2	104	0	1	0	14	0	8.08	—	—	—	—	—	—	—
88-89	Laval	QMJHL	22	1187	12	7	0	88	0	4.45	6	295	4	1	15	0	3.05
89-90	Granby	QMJHL	39	2076	10	26	0	158	0	4.57	—	—	—	—	—	—	—
90-91	Granby	QMJHL	*63	*3693	28	25	6	190	2	3.09	—	—	—	—	—	—	—
91-92	Binghamton	AHL	38	2261	16	15	6	123	1	3.26	—	—	—	—	—	—	—
92-93	Binghamton	AHL	31	1847	18	9	4	115	0	3.74	1	20	0	0	2	0	6.00

ROY, ALLAIN
G, JETS

PERSONAL: Born February 6, 1970, at Campbelltown, N.B.... 5-10/165.... Shoots left.... Full name: Allain Roland Roy.
COLLEGE: Harvard.
TRANSACTIONS/CAREER NOTES: Selected by Winnipeg Jets in fourth round (sixth Jets pick, 69th overall) of NHL entry draft (June 17, 1989).
HONORS: Named to NCAA All-Tournament team (1988-89).

									REGULAR SEASON				PLAYOFFS				
Season	Team	League	Gms.	Min.	W	L	T	GA	SO	Avg.	Gms.	Min.	W	L	GA	SO	Avg.
88-89	Harvard University	ECAC	16	952	14	2	0	40	0	2.52	—	—	—	—	—	—	—
89-90	Harvard University	ECAC	15	867	7	8	0	54	1	3.74	—	—	—	—	—	—	—
	Can. national team	Int'l	3	180	...	...	...	11	...	3.67	—	—	—	—	—	—	—
90-91	Harvard University	ECAC	14	821	7	5	2	45	*1	3.29	—	—	—	—	—	—	—
91-92	Harvard University	ECAC	15	919	9	4	2	39	1	2.55	—	—	—	—	—	—	—
92-93	Can. national team	Int'l	36	2055	16	15	2	120	1	3.50	—	—	—	—	—	—	—

ROY, JEAN-YVES
RW, RANGERS

PERSONAL: Born February 17, 1969, at Rosemere, Que.... 5-10/185.... Shoots left.
COLLEGE: Maine.
TRANSACTIONS/CAREER NOTES: Signed as free agent by New York Rangers (July 20, 1992).
HONORS: Named to NCAA All-America East second team (1989-90).... Named to Hockey East All-Rookie team (1989-90).... Named to NCAA All-America East first team (1990-91 and 1991-92).... Named to NCAA All-Tournament team (1990-91). ... Named to Hockey East All-Star first team (1990-91).... Named to Hockey East All-Star second team (1991-92).

					REGULAR SEASON				PLAYOFFS			
Season	Team	League	Gms.	G	A	Pts.	Pen.	Gms.	G	A	Pts.	Pen.
89-90	University of Maine	Hockey East	46	39	26	65	52	—	—	—	—	—
90-91	University of Maine	Hockey East	43	37	45	82	26	—	—	—	—	—
91-92	University of Maine	Hockey East	35	32	24	56	62	—	—	—	—	—
92-93	Canadian national team	Int'l	23	9	6	15	35	—	—	—	—	—
	Binghamton	AHL	49	13	15	28	21	14	5	2	7	4

ROY, PATRICK
G, CANADIENS

PERSONAL: Born October 5, 1965, at Quebec City.... 6-0/182.... Shoots left.... Name pronounced WAH.
TRANSACTIONS/CAREER NOTES: Selected by Monteral Canadiens as underage junior in third round (fourth Canadiens pick, 51st overall) of NHL entry draft (June 9, 1984).... Suspended eight games by NHL for slashing (October 19, 1987).... Sprained medial collateral ligaments in left knee (December 12, 1990); missed nine games.... Tore left ankle ligaments (January 27, 1991); missed 14 games.... Reinjured left ankle (March 16, 1991).... Strained hip flexor (March 6, 1993); missed two games.
HONORS: Won Conn Smythe Trophy (1985-86 and 1992-93).... Named to NHL All-Rookie team (1985-86).... Shared William M. Jennings Trophy with Brian Hayward (1986-87 through 1988-89).... Named to NHL All-Star second team (1987-88 and 1990-91).... Named to THE SPORTING NEWS All-Star first team (1988-89, 1989-90, and 1991-92).... Won Trico Goaltender Award (1988-89 and 1989-90).... Named to NHL All-Star first team (1988-89, 1989-90 and 1991-92).... Won Vezina Trophy (1988-89, 1989-90 and 1991-92).... Played in NHL All-Star Game (1988 and 1990 through 1993).... Named to THE SPORTING NEWS All-Star second team (1990-91).... Won William M. Jennings Trophy (1991-92).
MISCELLANEOUS: Member of Stanley Cup championship teams (1986 and 1993).

									REGULAR SEASON				PLAYOFFS				
Season	Team	League	Gms.	Min.	W	L	T	GA	SO	Avg.	Gms.	Min.	W	L	GA	SO	Avg.
82-83	Granby	QMJHL	54	2808	...	...	...	293	0	6.26	—	—	—	—	—	—	—
83-84	Granby	QMJHL	61	3585	29	29	1	265	0	4.44	4	244	0	4	22	0	5.41
84-85	Granby	QMJHL	44	2463	16	25	1	228	0	5.55	—	—	—	—	—	—	—
	Montreal	NHL	1	20	1	0	0	0	0	0.00	—	—	—	—	—	—	—
	Sherbrooke	AHL	1	60	1	0	0	4	0	4.00	*13	*769	10	3	37	0	*2.89
85-86	Montreal	NHL	47	2651	23	18	3	148	1	3.35	20	1218	*15	5	39	†1	1.92
86-87	Montreal	NHL	46	2686	22	16	6	131	1	2.93	6	330	4	2	22	0	4.00
87-88	Montreal	NHL	45	2586	23	12	9	125	3	2.90	8	430	3	4	24	0	3.35
88-89	Montreal	NHL	48	2744	33	5	6	113	4	*2.47	19	1206	13	6	42	2	*2.09
89-90	Montreal	NHL	54	3173	31	16	5	134	3	2.53	11	641	5	6	26	1	2.43
90-91	Montreal	NHL	48	2835	25	15	6	128	1	2.71	13	785	7	5	40	0	3.06
91-92	Montreal	NHL	67	3935	36	22	8	155	†5	*2.36	11	686	4	7	30	1	2.62
92-93	Montreal	NHL	62	3595	31	25	5	192	2	3.20	20	1293	16	4	46	0	2.13
NHL totals			418	24225	225	129	48	1126	20	2.79	108	6589	67	39	269	5	2.45

ROY, SIMON
D, OILERS

PERSONAL: Born June 14, 1974, at Montreal. ... 6-1/180. ... Shoots left. ... Name pronounced WAH.
TRANSACTIONS/CAREER NOTES: Selected by Edmonton Oilers in third round (third Oilers pick, 61st overall) of NHL entry draft (June 20, 1992).

Season Team	League	REGULAR SEASON					PLAYOFFS				
		Gms.	G	A	Pts.	Pen.	Gms.	G	A	Pts.	Pen.
91-92—Shawinigan	QMJHL	63	3	24	27	24	10	1	4	5	9
92-93—Shawinigan	QMJHL	68	5	34	39	56	—	—	—	—	—

RUCHTY, MATT
LW, DEVILS

PERSONAL: Born November 27, 1969, at Kitchener, Ont. ... 6-1/210. ... Shoots left. ... Full name: Matthew Kerry Ruchty. ... Name pronounced RUHK-tee.
COLLEGE: Bowling Green State.
TRANSACTIONS/CAREER NOTES: Selected by New Jersey Devils in fourth round (fourth Devils pick, 65th overall) of NHL entry draft (June 11, 1988).

Season Team	League	REGULAR SEASON					PLAYOFFS				
		Gms.	G	A	Pts.	Pen.	Gms.	G	A	Pts.	Pen.
87-88—Bowling Green State	CCHA	41	6	15	21	78	—	—	—	—	—
88-89—Bowling Green State	CCHA	43	11	21	32	110	—	—	—	—	—
89-90—Bowling Green State	CCHA	42	28	21	49	135	—	—	—	—	—
90-91—Bowling Green State	CCHA	38	13	18	31	147	—	—	—	—	—
91-92—Utica	AHL	73	9	14	23	250	4	0	0	0	25
92-93—Utica	AHL	74	4	14	18	253	4	0	2	2	15

RUCINSKY, MARTIN
LW, NORDIQUES

PERSONAL: Born March 11, 1971, at Most, Czechoslovakia. ... 5-11/178. ... Shoots left. ... Name pronounced roo-SHIHN-skee.
TRANSACTIONS/CAREER NOTES: Selected by Edmonton Oilers in first round (second Oilers pick, 20th overall) of NHL entry draft (June 22, 1991). ... Traded by Oilers to Quebec Nordiques for G Ron Tugnutt and LW Brad Zavisha (March 10, 1992). ... Suffered from the flu (February 28, 1993); missed one game.

Season Team	League	REGULAR SEASON					PLAYOFFS				
		Gms.	G	A	Pts.	Pen.	Gms.	G	A	Pts.	Pen.
88-89—CHZ Litvinov	Czech.	3	1	0	1	2	—	—	—	—	—
89-90—CHZ Litvinov	Czech.	47	12	6	18	...	—	—	—	—	—
90-91—CHZ Litvinov	Czech.	49	23	18	41	79	—	—	—	—	—
—Czechoslovakia Jr.	Czech.	7	9	5	14	2	—	—	—	—	—
91-92—Cape Breton	AHL	35	11	12	23	34	—	—	—	—	—
—Edmonton	NHL	2	0	0	0	0	—	—	—	—	—
—Halifax	AHL	7	1	1	2	6	—	—	—	—	—
—Quebec	NHL	4	1	1	2	2	—	—	—	—	—
92-93—Quebec	NHL	77	18	30	48	51	6	1	1	2	4
NHL totals		83	19	31	50	53	6	1	1	2	4

RUFF, JASON
LW, LIGHTNING

PERSONAL: Born January 27, 1970, at Kelowna, B.C. ... 6-2/192. ... Shoots left.
TRANSACTIONS/CAREER NOTES: Underwent heel surgery (May 1988). ... Selected by St. Louis Blues in fifth round (third Blues pick, 96th overall) of NHL entry draft (June 16, 1990). ... Traded by Blues with sixth-round pick in 1996 draft and either third-round pick in 1995 draft or fourth-round pick in 1994 draft to Tampa Bay Lightning for LW Basil McRae and D Doug Crossman (January 28, 1993).
HONORS: Named to WHL (East) All-Star first team (1990-91).

Season Team	League	REGULAR SEASON					PLAYOFFS				
		Gms.	G	A	Pts.	Pen.	Gms.	G	A	Pts.	Pen.
86-87—Kelowna	BCJHL	45	25	20	45	70	—	—	—	—	—
87-88—Lethbridge	WHL	69	25	22	47	109	—	—	—	—	—
88-89—Lethbridge	WHL	69	42	38	80	127	—	—	—	—	—
89-90—Lethbridge	WHL	72	55	64	119	114	19	9	10	19	18
90-91—Lethbridge	WHL	66	61	75	136	154	16	12	17	29	18
—Peoria	IHL	—	—	—	—	—	5	0	0	0	2
91-92—Peoria	IHL	67	27	45	72	148	10	7	7	14	19
92-93—Peoria	IHL	40	22	21	43	81	—	—	—	—	—
—St. Louis	NHL	7	2	1	3	8	—	—	—	—	—
—Tampa Bay	NHL	1	0	0	0	0	—	—	—	—	—
—Atlanta	IHL	26	11	14	25	90	7	2	1	3	26
NHL totals		8	2	1	3	8					

RUFF, LINDY
D

PERSONAL: Born February 17, 1960, at Warburg, Alta. ... 6-2/202. ... Shoots left. ... Full name: Lindy Cameron Ruff.
TRANSACTIONS/CAREER NOTES: Selected by Buffalo Sabres as underage junior in second round (second Sabres pick, 32nd overall) of NHL entry draft (August 9, 1979). ... Fractured ankle (December 1980). ... Broke hand (March 1983). ... Injured shoulder (January 14, 1984). ... Separated shoulder (October 26, 1984). ... Broke left clavicle (March 5, 1986). ... Sprained shoulder (November 1988). ... Traded by Sabres to New York Rangers for fifth-round pick in 1990 draft (D Richard Smehlik) (March 7, 1989). ... Fractured rib (January 23, 1990); missed seven games. ... Broke nose (March 21, 1990). ... Bruised left thigh (April 1990). ... Signed as free agent by Sabres (Sep-

tember 1991).... Signed as free agent by San Diego Gulls (August 24, 1992).
HONORS: Named to IHL All-Star team (1992-93).

Season Team	League	REGULAR SEASON					PLAYOFFS				
		Gms.	G	A	Pts.	Pen.	Gms.	G	A	Pts.	Pen.
76-77—Taber	AJHL	60	13	33	46	112	—	—	—	—	—
—Lethbridge	WCHL	2	0	2	2	0	—	—	—	—	—
77-78—Lethbridge	WCHL	66	9	24	33	219	8	2	8	10	4
78-79—Lethbridge	WHL	24	9	18	27	108	6	0	1	1	0
79-80—Buffalo	NHL	63	5	14	19	38	8	1	1	2	19
80-81—Buffalo	NHL	65	8	18	26	121	6	3	1	4	23
81-82—Buffalo	NHL	79	16	32	48	194	4	0	0	0	28
82-83—Buffalo	NHL	60	12	17	29	130	10	4	2	6	47
83-84—Buffalo	NHL	58	14	31	45	101	3	1	0	1	9
84-85—Buffalo	NHL	39	13	11	24	45	5	2	4	6	15
85-86—Buffalo	NHL	54	20	12	32	158	—	—	—	—	—
86-87—Buffalo	NHL	50	6	14	20	74	—	—	—	—	—
87-88—Buffalo	NHL	77	2	23	25	179	6	0	2	2	23
88-89—Buffalo	NHL	63	6	11	17	86	—	—	—	—	—
—New York Rangers	NHL	13	0	5	5	31	2	0	0	0	17
89-90—New York Rangers	NHL	56	3	6	9	80	8	0	3	3	12
90-91—New York Rangers	NHL	14	0	1	1	27	—	—	—	—	—
91-92—Rochester	AHL	62	10	24	34	110	13	0	4	4	16
92-93—San Diego	IHL	81	10	32	42	100	14	1	6	7	26
NHL totals		691	105	195	300	1264	52	11	13	24	193

RUMBLE, DARREN
D, SENATORS

PERSONAL: Born January 23, 1969, at Barrie, Ont.... 6-1/200.... Shoots left.... Full name: Darren William Rumble.
HIGH SCHOOL: Eastview (Barrie, Ont.).
TRANSACTIONS/CAREER NOTES: Selected by Philadelphia Flyers as underage junior in first round (first Flyers pick, 20th overall) of NHL entry draft (June 13, 1987).... Stretched knee ligaments (November 27, 1988).... Selected by Ottawa Senators in NHL expansion draft (June 18, 1992).

Season Team	League	REGULAR SEASON					PLAYOFFS				
		Gms.	G	A	Pts.	Pen.	Gms.	G	A	Pts.	Pen.
85-86—Barrie Jr. B	OHA	46	14	32	46	91	—	—	—	—	—
86-87—Kitchener	OHL	64	11	32	43	44	4	0	1	1	9
87-88—Kitchener	OHL	55	15	50	65	64	—	—	—	—	—
88-89—Kitchener	OHL	46	11	29	40	25	5	1	0	1	2
89-90—Hershey	AHL	57	2	13	15	31	—	—	—	—	—
90-91—Philadelphia	NHL	3	1	0	1	0	—	—	—	—	—
—Hershey	AHL	73	6	35	41	48	3	0	5	5	2
91-92—Hershey	AHL	79	12	54	66	118	6	0	3	3	2
92-93—Ottawa	NHL	69	3	13	16	61	—	—	—	—	—
—New Haven	AHL	2	1	0	1	0	—	—	—	—	—
NHL totals		72	4	13	17	61					

RUSSELL, CAM
D, BLACKHAWKS

PERSONAL: Born January 12, 1969, at Halifax, N.S.... 6-4/175.... Shoots left.
TRANSACTIONS/CAREER NOTES: Selected by Chicago Blackhawks as underage junior in third round (third Blackhawks pick, 50th overall) of NHL entry draft (June 13, 1987).... Suffered from the flu (December 26, 1992); missed one game.... Suspended one game by NHL for accumulating three game misconduct penalties (February 11, 1993).

Season Team	League	REGULAR SEASON					PLAYOFFS				
		Gms.	G	A	Pts.	Pen.	Gms.	G	A	Pts.	Pen.
85-86—Hull	QMJHL	56	3	4	7	24	15	0	2	2	4
86-87—Hull	QMJHL	66	3	16	19	119	8	0	1	1	16
87-88—Hull	QMJHL	53	9	18	27	141	19	2	5	7	39
88-89—Hull	QMJHL	66	8	32	40	109	9	2	6	8	6
89-90—Indianapolis	IHL	46	3	15	18	114	9	0	1	1	24
—Chicago	NHL	19	0	1	1	27	1	0	0	0	0
90-91—Indianapolis	IHL	53	5	9	14	125	6	0	2	2	30
—Chicago	NHL	3	0	0	0	5	1	0	0	0	0
91-92—Indianapolis	IHL	41	4	9	13	78	—	—	—	—	—
—Chicago	NHL	19	0	0	0	34	12	0	2	2	2
92-93—Chicago	NHL	67	2	4	6	151	4	0	0	0	0
NHL totals		108	2	5	7	217	18	0	2	2	2

RUUTTU, CHRISTIAN
C, BLACKHAWKS

PERSONAL: Born February 20, 1964, at Lappeenranta, Finland.... 5-11/192.... Shoots left.... Name pronounced ROO-TOO.
TRANSACTIONS/CAREER NOTES: Selected by Buffalo Sabres in seventh round (ninth Sabres pick, 134th overall) of NHL entry draft (June 8, 1983).... Injured knee (February 1988).... Sprained knee (September 1988).... Tore pectoral muscle (October 22, 1988).... Separated left shoulder (April 5, 1989).... Injured leg (January 21, 1992); missed four games.... Suffered from the flu (March 16, 1992); missed three games.... Traded by Sabres with future considerations to Winnipeg Jets for G Stephane Beauregard (June 15, 1992).... Traded by Jets with future considerations to Chicago Blackhawks for G Stephane Beauregard (August 10, 1992).
HONORS: Named to Finland All-Star team (1985-86).... Played in NHL All-Star Game (1988).

Season	Team	League	REGULAR SEASON					PLAYOFFS				
			Gms.	G	A	Pts.	Pen.	Gms.	G	A	Pts.	Pen.
82-83—Pori Assat		Finland	36	15	18	33	34	—	—	—	—	—
83-84—Pori Assat		Finland	37	18	42	60	72	9	2	5	7	12
84-85—Pori Assat		Finland	32	14	32	46	34	8	1	6	7	8
85-86—Helsinki IFK		Finland	36	14	42	56	41	10	3	6	9	8
86-87—Buffalo		NHL	76	22	43	65	62	—	—	—	—	—
87-88—Buffalo		NHL	73	26	45	71	85	6	2	5	7	4
88-89—Buffalo		NHL	67	14	46	60	98	2	0	0	0	0
89-90—Buffalo		NHL	75	19	41	60	66	6	0	0	0	4
90-91—Buffalo		NHL	77	16	34	50	96	6	1	3	4	29
91-92—Buffalo		NHL	70	4	21	25	76	3	0	0	0	6
92-93—Chicago		NHL	84	17	37	54	134	4	0	0	0	2
NHL totals			522	118	267	385	617	27	3	8	11	45

RUZICKA, VLADIMIR
C, BRUINS

PERSONAL: Born June 6, 1963, at Most, Czechoslovakia. . . . 6-3/212. . . . Shoots left. . . . Name pronounced roo-ZEECH-kuh.

TRANSACTIONS/CAREER NOTES: Selected by Toronto Maple Leafs in fourth round (fifth Maple Leafs pick, 73rd overall) of NHL entry draft (June 9, 1982). . . . Rights traded by Maple Leafs to Edmonton Oilers for fourth-round pick in 1990 draft (C Greg Walters) (December 21, 1989). . . . Traded by Oilers to Boston Bruins for D Greg Hawgood (October 22, 1990). . . . Injured left ankle and developed tendinitis (December 29, 1990). . . . Underwent surgery to left ankle tendon (February 12, 1991). . . . Strained groin (December 1992); missed 15 games. . . . Injured ankle (March 1993); missed three games. . . . Injured groin (April 1993); missed six games.

HONORS: Named Czechoslovakian League Player of the Year (1985-86 and 1987-88). . . . Named to Czechoslovakian League All-Star team (1987-88 and 1989-90).

Season	Team	League	REGULAR SEASON					PLAYOFFS				
			Gms.	G	A	Pts.	Pen.	Gms.	G	A	Pts.	Pen.
83-84—Czech. Olympic Team		Int'l	7	4	6	10	0	—	—	—	—	—
84-85—						Statistics unavailable.						
85-86—						Statistics unavailable.						
86-87—CHZ Litvinov		Czech.	32	24	15	39	. . .	—	—	—	—	—
87-88—Dukla Trencin		Czech.	34	32	21	53	. . .	—	—	—	—	—
—Czech. Olympic Team		Int'l	8	4	3	7	12	—	—	—	—	—
88-89—Dukla Trencin		Czech.	45	46	38	*84	. . .	—	—	—	—	—
89-90—CHZ Litvinov		Czech.	32	21	23	44	. . .	—	—	—	—	—
—Edmonton		NHL	25	11	6	17	10	—	—	—	—	—
90-91—Boston		NHL	29	8	8	16	19	17	2	11	13	0
91-92—Boston		NHL	77	39	36	75	48	13	2	3	5	2
92-93—Boston		NHL	60	19	22	41	38	—	—	—	—	—
NHL totals			191	77	72	149	115	30	4	14	18	2

RYCHEL, WARREN
LW, KINGS

PERSONAL: Born May 12, 1967, at Tecumseh, Ont. . . . 6-0/202. . . . Shoots left. . . . Full name: Warren Stanley Rychel. . . . Name pronounced RYE-kel.

TRANSACTIONS/CAREER NOTES: Signed as free agent by Chicago Blackhawks (September 19, 1986). . . . Hyperextended left knee (February 1989). . . . Traded by Blackhawks with C Troy Murray to Winnipeg Jets for D Bryan Marchment and D Chris Norton (July 22, 1991). . . . Traded by Jets to Minnesota North Stars for RW Tony Joseph and future considerations (December 30, 1991). . . . Signed as free agent by San Diego Gulls (August 11, 1992). . . . Signed as free agent by Los Angeles Kings (October 3, 1992). . . . Suffered ankle contusion (December 1, 1992); missed 14 games.

Season	Team	League	REGULAR SEASON					PLAYOFFS				
			Gms.	G	A	Pts.	Pen.	Gms.	G	A	Pts.	Pen.
83-84—Essex Jr. C		OHA	24	11	16	27	86	—	—	—	—	—
84-85—Sudbury		OHL	35	5	8	13	74	—	—	—	—	—
—Guelph		OHL	29	1	3	4	48	—	—	—	—	—
85-86—Guelph		OHL	38	14	5	19	119	—	—	—	—	—
—Ottawa		OHL	29	11	18	29	54	—	—	—	—	—
86-87—Ottawa		OHL	28	11	7	18	57	—	—	—	—	—
—Kitchener		OHL	21	5	5	10	39	4	0	0	0	9
87-88—Saginaw		IHL	51	2	7	9	113	1	0	0	0	0
—Peoria		IHL	7	2	1	3	7	—	—	—	—	—
88-89—Saginaw		IHL	50	15	14	29	226	6	0	0	0	51
—Chicago		NHL	2	0	0	0	17	—	—	—	—	—
89-90—Indianapolis		IHL	77	23	16	39	374	14	1	3	4	64
90-91—Indianapolis		IHL	68	33	30	63	338	5	2	1	3	30
—Chicago		NHL	—	—	—	—	—	3	1	3	4	2
91-92—Moncton		AHL	36	14	15	29	211	—	—	—	—	—
—Kalamazoo		IHL	45	15	20	35	165	8	0	3	3	51
92-93—Los Angeles		NHL	70	6	7	13	314	23	6	7	13	39
NHL totals			72	6	7	13	331	26	7	10	17	41

RYMSHA, ANDY
D, NORDIQUES

PERSONAL: Born December 10, 1968, at St. Catharines, Ont. . . . 6-3/210. . . . Shoots left. . . . Full name: Andrew Anthony Rymsha.

COLLEGE: Western Michigan.

TRANSACTIONS/CAREER NOTES: Selected by St. Louis Blues in fourth round (fifth Blues pick,

82nd overall) of NHL entry draft (June 13, 1987).... Traded by Blues with RW Herb Raglan and D Tony Twist to Quebec Nordiques for RW Darin Kimble (February 4, 1991).

Season Team	League	REGULAR SEASON Gms.	G	A	Pts.	Pen.	PLAYOFFS Gms.	G	A	Pts.	Pen.
85-86—St. Catharines Jr. B	OHA	39	6	13	19	170	—	—	—	—	—
86-87—Western Michigan Univ.	CCHA	42	7	10	17	122	—	—	—	—	—
87-88—Western Michigan Univ.	CCHA	42	5	6	11	114	—	—	—	—	—
88-89—Western Michigan Univ.	CCHA	35	3	4	7	139	—	—	—	—	—
89-90—Western Michigan Univ.	CCHA	37	1	10	11	108	—	—	—	—	—
90-91—Peoria	IHL	45	2	9	11	64	—	—	—	—	—
—Halifax	AHL	12	1	2	3	22	—	—	—	—	—
91-92—Halifax	AHL	44	4	7	11	54	—	—	—	—	—
—New Haven	AHL	16	0	5	5	20	—	—	—	—	—
—Quebec	NHL	6	0	0	0	23	—	—	—	—	—
92-93—Halifax	AHL	43	4	6	10	62	—	—	—	—	—
—Canadian national team	Int'l	6	8	2	10	16	—	—	—	—	—
NHL totals		6	0	0	0	23					

SAAL, JASON
G, KINGS

PERSONAL: Born February 1, 1975, at Detroit.... 5-9/165.... Shoots left.
TRANSACTIONS/CAREER NOTES: Selected by Los Angeles Kings in fifth round (fifth Kings pick, 117th overall) of NHL entry draft (June 26, 1993).

Season Team	League	REGULAR SEASON Gms.	Min.	W	L	T	GA	SO	Avg.	PLAYOFFS Gms.	Min.	W	L	GA	SO	Avg.
92-93—Detroit	OHL	23	1289	11	8	1	85	0	3.96	3	42	0	0	2	0	2.86

SABOURIN, KEN
D, FLAMES

PERSONAL: Born April 28, 1966, at Scarborough, Ont.... 6-3/210.... Shoots left.... Name pronounced SAB-uhr-ihn.
TRANSACTIONS/CAREER NOTES: Selected by Calgary Flames as underage junior in second round (second Flames pick, 33rd overall) of NHL entry draft (June 9, 1984).... Traded by Sault Ste. Marie Greyhounds to Cornwall Royals for Kent Trolley and fifth-round pick in 1986 OHL priority draft (March 1986). ... Traded by Flames to Washington Capitals for C Paul Fenton (January 24, 1991).... Traded by Capitals to Flames for future considerations (December 15, 1992).

Season Team	League	REGULAR SEASON Gms.	G	A	Pts.	Pen.	PLAYOFFS Gms.	G	A	Pts.	Pen.
82-83—Sault Ste. Marie	OHL	58	0	8	8	90	10	0	0	0	14
83-84—Sault Ste. Marie	OHL	63	7	13	20	157	9	0	1	1	25
84-85—Sault Ste. Marie	OHL	63	5	19	24	139	16	1	4	5	10
85-86—Sault Ste. Marie	OHL	25	1	5	6	77	—	—	—	—	—
—Cornwall	OHL	37	3	12	15	94	6	1	2	3	6
—Moncton	AHL	3	0	0	0	0	6	0	1	1	2
86-87—Moncton	AHL	75	1	10	11	166	6	0	1	1	27
87-88—Salt Lake City	IHL	71	2	8	10	186	16	1	6	7	57
88-89—Calgary	NHL	6	0	1	1	26	1	0	0	0	0
—Salt Lake City	IHL	74	2	18	20	197	11	0	1	1	26
89-90—Calgary	NHL	5	0	0	0	10	—	—	—	—	—
—Salt Lake City	IHL	76	5	19	24	336	11	0	2	2	40
90-91—Salt Lake City	IHL	28	2	15	17	77	—	—	—	—	—
—Calgary	NHL	16	1	3	4	36	—	—	—	—	—
—Washington	NHL	28	1	4	5	81	11	0	0	0	34
91-92—Baltimore	AHL	30	3	8	11	106	—	—	—	—	—
—Washington	NHL	19	0	0	0	48	—	—	—	—	—
92-93—Baltimore	AHL	30	5	14	19	68	—	—	—	—	—
—Salt Lake City	IHL	52	2	11	13	140	—	—	—	—	—
NHL totals		74	2	8	10	201	12	0	0	0	34

SACCO, DAVID
C, MAPLE LEAFS

PERSONAL: Born July 31, 1970, at Medford, Mass.... 6-0/190.... Shoots right.... Full name: David Anthony Sacco.... Brother of Joe Sacco, left winger, Mighty Ducks of Anaheim.
HIGH SCHOOL: Medford (Mass.).
COLLEGE: Boston University.
TRANSACTIONS/CAREER NOTES: Selected by Toronto Maple Leafs in 10th round (ninth Maple Leafs pick, 195th overall) of NHL entry draft (June 11, 1988).
HONORS: Named to NCAA All-America East first team (1991-92 and 1992-93).... Named to Hockey East All-Star first team (1991-92 and 1992-93).

Season Team	League	REGULAR SEASON Gms.	G	A	Pts.	Pen.	PLAYOFFS Gms.	G	A	Pts.	Pen.
88-89—Boston University	Hockey East	35	14	29	43	40	—	—	—	—	—
89-90—Boston University	Hockey East	3	0	4	4	2	—	—	—	—	—
90-91—Boston University	Hockey East	40	21	40	61	24	—	—	—	—	—
91-92—Boston University	Hockey East	35	14	33	47	30	—	—	—	—	—
92-93—Boston University	Hockey East	40	25	37	62	86	—	—	—	—	—

SACCO, JOE

LW, MIGHTY DUCKS

PERSONAL: Born February 4, 1969, at Medford, Mass. . . . 6-1/195. . . . Shoots left. . . . Full name: Joseph William Sacco. . . . Name pronounced SAK-oh. . . . Brother of David Sacco, center in Toronto Maple Leafs system.
HIGH SCHOOL: Medford (Mass.).
COLLEGE: Boston University.
TRANSACTIONS/CAREER NOTES: Selected by Toronto Maple Leafs in fourth round (fourth Maple Leafs pick, 71st overall) of NHL entry draft (June 13, 1987). . . . Selected by Mighty Ducks of Anaheim in NHL expansion draft (June 24, 1993).

			REGULAR SEASON					PLAYOFFS				
Season Team	League	Gms.	G	A	Pts.	Pen.	Gms.	G	A	Pts.	Pen.
85-86—Medford H.S.	Mass. H.S.	20	30	30	60	...	—	—	—	—	—
86-87—Medford H.S.	Mass. H.S.	21	22	32	54	...	—	—	—	—	—
87-88—Boston University	Hockey East	34	14	22	36	38	—	—	—	—	—
88-89—Boston University	Hockey East	33	21	19	40	66	—	—	—	—	—
89-90—Boston University	Hockey East	44	28	24	52	70	—	—	—	—	—
90-91—Newmarket	AHL	49	18	17	35	24	—	—	—	—	—
—Toronto	NHL	20	0	5	5	2	—	—	—	—	—
91-92—U.S. national team	Int'l	50	11	26	37	51	—	—	—	—	—
—U.S. Olympic Team	Int'l	8	0	2	2	0	—	—	—	—	—
—Toronto	NHL	17	7	4	11	4	—	—	—	—	—
—St. John's	AHL	—	—	—	—	—	1	1	1	2	0
92-93—Toronto	NHL	23	4	4	8	8	—	—	—	—	—
—St. John's	AHL	37	14	16	30	45	7	6	4	10	2
NHL totals		60	11	13	24	14					

SAFARIK, RICHARD

LW/RW, SABRES

PERSONAL: Born February 26, 1975, at Nova Zausky, Czechoslovakia. . . . 6-3/194. . . . Shoots left.
TRANSACTIONS/CAREER NOTES: Selected by Buffalo Sabres in fifth round (third Sabres pick, 116th overall) of NHL entry draft (June 26, 1993).

			REGULAR SEASON					PLAYOFFS				
Season Team	League	Gms.	G	A	Pts.	Pen.	Gms.	G	A	Pts.	Pen.
91-92—Nitra	Czech Dv.II	2	0	0	0	0	—	—	—	—	—
92-93—Nitra	Czech Dv.II	16	0	0	0	2	—	—	—	—	—

SAKIC, JOE

C, NORDIQUES

PERSONAL: Born July 7, 1969, at Burnaby, B.C. . . . 5-11/185. . . . Shoots left. . . . Full name: Joseph Steve Sakic. . . . Name pronounced SA-kihk. . . . Brother of Brian Sakic, left winger in New York Rangers system.
TRANSACTIONS/CAREER NOTES: Selected by Quebec Nordiques as underage junior in first round (second Nordiques pick, 15th overall) of NHL entry draft (June 13, 1987). . . . Sprained right ankle (November 28, 1988). . . . Developed bursitis in left ankle (January 21, 1992); missed three games. . . . Suffered recurrence of bursitis in left ankle (January 30, 1992); missed eight games. . . . Injured eye (January 2, 1993); missed six games.
HONORS: Won WHL (East) Most Valuable Player Trophy (1986-87). . . . Won WHL (East) Stewart (Butch) Paul Memorial Trophy (1986-87). . . . Named to WHL All-Star second team (1986-87). . . . Won Can.HL Player of the Year Award (1987-88). . . . Won Four Broncos Memorial Trophy (1987-88). . . . Shared Bob Clarke Trophy with Theoren Fleury (1987-88). . . . Won WHL Player of the Year Award (1987-88). . . . Named to WHL (East) All-Star first team (1987-88). . . . Played in NHL All-Star Game (1990 through 1993).

			REGULAR SEASON					PLAYOFFS				
Season Team	League	Gms.	G	A	Pts.	Pen.	Gms.	G	A	Pts.	Pen.
86-87—Swift Current	WHL	72	60	73	133	31	4	0	1	1	0
87-88—Swift Current	WHL	64	†78	82	†160	64	10	11	13	24	12
88-89—Quebec	NHL	70	23	39	62	24	—	—	—	—	—
89-90—Quebec	NHL	80	39	63	102	27	—	—	—	—	—
90-91—Quebec	NHL	80	48	61	109	24	—	—	—	—	—
91-92—Quebec	NHL	69	29	65	94	20	—	—	—	—	—
92-93—Quebec	NHL	78	48	57	105	40	6	3	3	6	2
NHL totals		377	187	285	472	135	6	3	3	6	2

SALO, TOMMY

G, ISLANDERS

PERSONAL: Born February 1, 1971, at Surahammar, Sweden. . . . 5-11/161. . . . Shoots left.
TRANSACTIONS/CAREER NOTES: Selected by New York Islanders in fifth round (fifth Islanders pick, 118th overall) of NHL entry draft (June 26, 1993).

			REGULAR SEASON						PLAYOFFS					
Season Team	League	Gms.	Min.	W	L	T	GA	SO	Avg.	Gms.	Min.	W	L	GA	SO	Avg.
90-91—Vasteras	Sweden	2	100	...	...	...	11	0	6.60	—	—	—	—	—	—	—
91-92—Vasteras	Sweden				Did not play.										
92-93—Vasteras	Sweden	24	1431	...	...	...	59	2	2.47	—	—	—	—	—	—	—

SAMUELSSON, KJELL

D, PENGUINS

PERSONAL: Born October 18, 1958, at Tyngsryd, Sweden. . . . 6-6/235. . . . Shoots right.
TRANSACTIONS/CAREER NOTES: Selected by New York Rangers in sixth round (fifth Rangers pick, 119th overall) of NHL entry draft (June 9, 1984). . . . Traded by Rangers with second-round pick in 1989 draft (LW Patrik Juhlin) to Philadelphia Flyers for G Bob Froese (December 18, 1986). . . . Pulled groin (February 1988). . . . Suffered herniated disc (October 1988). . . . Bruised hand (March 1989). . . . Bruised right shoulder (November 22, 1989); missed 13 games. . . . Underwent shoulder surgery (March 1990). . . . Traded by

Flyers with RW Rick Tocchet, G Ken Wregget and third-round pick in 1992 draft to Pittsburgh Penguins for RW Mark Recchi, D Brian Benning and first-round pick in 1992 draft (LW Jason Bowen) previously acquired from Los Angeles Kings (February 19, 1992).... Bruised knee (November 27, 1992); missed one game.... Broke bone in foot (December 1, 1992); missed nine games.... Fractured cheekbone (December 27, 1992); missed nine games.... Suffered from the flu (March 18, 1993); missed one game.
HONORS: Played in NHL All-Star Game (1988).
MISCELLANEOUS: Member of Stanley Cup championship team (1992).

Season Team	League	REGULAR SEASON					PLAYOFFS				
		Gms.	G	A	Pts.	Pen.	Gms.	G	A	Pts.	Pen.
82-83—Tyngsryd	Sweden	32	11	6	17	57	—	—	—	—	—
83-84—Leksand	Sweden	36	6	7	13	59	—	—	—	—	—
84-85—Leksand	Sweden	35	9	5	14	34	—	—	—	—	—
85-86—New York Rangers	NHL	9	0	0	0	10	9	0	1	1	8
—New Haven	AHL	56	6	21	27	87	3	0	0	0	10
86-87—New York Rangers	NHL	30	2	6	8	50	—	—	—	—	—
—Philadelphia	NHL	46	1	6	7	86	26	0	4	4	25
87-88—Philadelphia	NHL	74	6	24	30	184	7	2	5	7	23
88-89—Philadelphia	NHL	69	3	14	17	140	19	1	3	4	24
89-90—Philadelphia	NHL	66	5	17	22	91	—	—	—	—	—
90-91—Philadelphia	NHL	78	9	19	28	82	—	—	—	—	—
91-92—Philadelphia	NHL	54	4	9	13	76	—	—	—	—	—
—Pittsburgh	NHL	20	1	2	3	34	15	0	3	3	12
92-93—Pittsburgh	NHL	63	3	6	9	106	12	0	3	3	2
NHL totals		509	34	103	137	859	88	3	19	22	94

SAMUELSSON, ULF
D, PENGUINS

PERSONAL: Born March 26, 1964, at Fagersta, Sweden.... 6-1/195.... Shoots left. **TRANSACTIONS/CAREER NOTES:** Selected by Hartford Whalers in fourth round (fourth Whalers pick, 67th overall) of NHL entry draft (June 9, 1982).... Suffered from the flu (December 1988); missed nine games.... Tore ligaments in right knee and underwent surgery (August 1989); missed part of 1989-90 season.... Traded by Whalers with C Ron Francis and D Grant Jennings to Pittsburgh Penguins for C John Cullen, D Zarley Zalapski and RW Jeff Parker (March 4, 1991).... Injured hip flexor (October 29, 1991); missed six games.... Underwent surgery to right elbow (December 1991); missed four games.... Bruised left hand (February 8, 1992); missed one game.... Suffered from the flu (February 1992); missed one game.... Strained shoulder (November 10, 1992); missed two games.... Broke cheekbone (November 27, 1992); missed two games.... Bruised knee (January 1993); missed one game.... Suspended one game by NHL (February 1993).... Suspended three off-days by NHL for stick-swinging incident (March 18, 1993).... Suffered back spasms (April 4, 1993); missed one game.
MISCELLANEOUS: Member of Stanley Cup championship teams (1991 and 1992).

Season Team	League	REGULAR SEASON					PLAYOFFS				
		Gms.	G	A	Pts.	Pen.	Gms.	G	A	Pts.	Pen.
83-84—Leksand	Sweden	36	5	10	15	53	—	—	—	—	—
84-85—Binghamton	AHL	36	5	11	16	92	—	—	—	—	—
—Hartford	NHL	41	2	6	8	83	—	—	—	—	—
85-86—Hartford	NHL	80	5	19	24	174	10	1	2	3	38
86-87—Hartford	NHL	78	2	31	33	162	5	0	1	1	41
87-88—Hartford	NHL	76	8	33	41	159	5	0	0	0	8
88-89—Hartford	NHL	71	9	26	35	181	4	0	2	2	4
89-90—Hartford	NHL	55	2	11	13	167	7	1	0	1	2
90-91—Hartford	NHL	62	3	18	21	174	—	—	—	—	—
—Pittsburgh	NHL	14	1	4	5	37	20	3	2	5	34
91-92—Pittsburgh	NHL	62	1	14	15	206	21	0	2	2	39
92-93—Pittsburgh	NHL	77	3	26	29	249	12	1	5	6	24
NHL totals		616	36	188	224	1592	84	6	14	20	190

SANDERSON, GEOFF
LW, WHALERS

PERSONAL: Born February 1, 1972, at Hay River, N.W.T.... 6-0/185.... Shoots left. **TRANSACTIONS/CAREER NOTES:** Selected by Hartford Whalers in second round (second Whalers pick, 36th overall) of NHL entry draft (June 16, 1990).... Bruised shoulder (October 14, 1991); missed one game.... Injured groin (November 13, 1991); missed three games.... Bruised knee (December 7, 1991); missed five games.

Season Team	League	REGULAR SEASON					PLAYOFFS				
		Gms.	G	A	Pts.	Pen.	Gms.	G	A	Pts.	Pen.
88-89—Swift Current	WHL	58	17	11	28	16	12	3	5	8	6
89-90—Swift Current	WHL	70	32	62	94	56	4	1	4	5	8
90-91—Swift Current	WHL	70	62	50	112	57	3	1	2	3	4
—Hartford	NHL	2	1	0	1	0	3	0	0	0	0
—Springfield	AHL	—	—	—	—	—	1	0	0	0	2
91-92—Hartford	NHL	64	13	18	31	18	7	1	0	1	2
92-93—Hartford	NHL	82	46	43	89	28	—	—	—	—	—
NHL totals		148	60	61	121	46	10	1	0	1	2

SANDLAK, JIM
RW, WHALERS

PERSONAL: Born December 12, 1966, at Kitchener, Ont.... 6-4/219.... Shoots right. **TRANSACTIONS/CAREER NOTES:** Selected by Vancouver Canucks as underage junior in first round (first Canucks pick, fourth overall) of NHL entry draft (June 15, 1985).... Ruptured ligaments in right thumb (January 1986).... Bruised shoulder (October 1988).... Suffered

sore back (November 5, 1991).... Sprained hand (December 1, 1991); missed seven games.... Strained groin (December 31, 1991).... Sprained knee (March 1992); missed seven games.... Strained back and suffered bulging disc (November 18, 1992); missed 17 games.... Sprained hand (April 1, 1993); missed remainder of season.... Traded by Canucks to Hartford Whalers (May 17, 1993); to complete deal in which Canucks sent LW Robert Kron, third-round pick in 1993 draft (D Marek Malik) and future considerations to Whalers for LW Murray Craven and fifth-round pick in 1993 draft (March 22, 1993).
HONORS: Named to NHL All-Rookie team (1986-87).

			REGULAR SEASON					PLAYOFFS			
Season	Team	League	Gms.	G	A	Pts.	Pen.	Gms.	G	A	Pts.	Pen.
82-83—	Kitchener	OHL	38	26	25	51	100	—	—	—	—	—
83-84—	London	OHL	68	23	18	41	143	8	1	11	12	13
84-85—	London	OHL	58	40	24	64	128	8	3	2	5	14
85-86—	London	OHL	16	7	13	20	36	5	2	3	5	24
—	Vancouver	NHL	23	1	3	4	10	3	0	1	1	0
86-87—	Vancouver	NHL	78	15	21	36	66	—	—	—	—	—
87-88—	Vancouver	NHL	49	16	15	31	81	—	—	—	—	—
—	Fredericton	AHL	24	10	15	25	47	—	—	—	—	—
88-89—	Vancouver	NHL	72	20	20	40	99	6	1	1	2	2
89-90—	Vancouver	NHL	70	15	8	23	104	—	—	—	—	—
90-91—	Vancouver	NHL	59	7	6	13	125	—	—	—	—	—
91-92—	Vancouver	NHL	66	16	24	40	176	13	4	6	10	22
92-93—	Vancouver	NHL	59	10	18	28	122	6	2	2	4	4
NHL totals			476	100	115	215	783	28	7	10	17	28

SANDSTROM, TOMAS
RW, KINGS

PERSONAL: Born September 4, 1964, at Jakobstad, Finland.... 6-2/200.... Shoots left.
TRANSACTIONS/CAREER NOTES: Selected by New York Rangers in second round (second Rangers pick, 36th overall) of NHL entry draft (June 9, 1982).... Suffered concussion (February 24, 1986).... Fractured right ankle (February 11, 1987).... Fractured right index finger (November 1987).... Traded by Rangers with LW Tony Granato to Los Angeles Kings for C Bernie Nicholls (January 20, 1990).... Fractured vertebrae (November 29, 1990); missed 10 games.... Partially dislocated shoulder (December 28, 1991); missed 26 games.... Fractured left forearm (November 21, 1992); missed 24 games.... Fractured jaw (February 28, 1993); missed 21 games.
HONORS: Named to NHL All-Rookie team (1984-85).... Played in NHL All-Star Game (1988 and 1991).

			REGULAR SEASON					PLAYOFFS			
Season	Team	League	Gms.	G	A	Pts.	Pen.	Gms.	G	A	Pts.	Pen.
82-83—	Brynas	Sweden	36	22	14	36	36	—	—	—	—	—
83-84—	Brynas	Sweden	...	20	10	30	...	—	—	—	—	—
—	Swedish Olympic Team	Int'l	7	2	1	3	6	—	—	—	—	—
84-85—	New York Rangers	NHL	74	29	29	58	51	3	0	2	2	0
85-86—	New York Rangers	NHL	73	25	29	54	109	16	4	6	10	20
86-87—	New York Rangers	NHL	64	40	34	74	60	6	1	2	3	20
87-88—	New York Rangers	NHL	69	28	40	68	95	—	—	—	—	—
88-89—	New York Rangers	NHL	79	32	56	88	148	4	3	2	5	12
89-90—	New York Rangers	NHL	48	19	19	38	100	—	—	—	—	—
—	Los Angeles	NHL	28	13	20	33	28	10	5	4	9	19
90-91—	Los Angeles	NHL	68	45	44	89	106	10	4	4	8	14
91-92—	Los Angeles	NHL	49	17	22	39	70	6	0	3	3	8
92-93—	Los Angeles	NHL	39	25	27	52	57	24	8	17	25	12
NHL totals			591	273	320	593	824	79	25	40	65	105

SANDWITH, TERRAN
D, FLYERS

PERSONAL: Born April 17, 1972, at Edmonton, Alta.... 6-4/210.... Shoots left.
TRANSACTIONS/CAREER NOTES: Selected by Philadelphia Flyers in second round (fourth Flyers pick, 42nd overall) of NHL entry draft (June 16, 1990).... Suffered blood disorder (September 1990).

			REGULAR SEASON					PLAYOFFS			
Season	Team	League	Gms.	G	A	Pts.	Pen.	Gms.	G	A	Pts.	Pen.
87-88—	Hobbema	AJHL	58	5	8	13	106	—	—	—	—	—
88-89—	Tri-City	WHL	31	0	0	0	29	6	0	0	0	4
89-90—	Tri-City	WHL	70	4	14	18	92	7	0	2	2	14
90-91—	Tri-City	WHL	46	5	17	22	132	7	1	0	1	14
91-92—	Brandon	WHL	41	6	14	20	145	—	—	—	—	—
—	Saskatoon	WHL	18	2	5	7	53	18	2	1	3	28
92-93—	Hershey	AHL	61	1	12	13	140	—	—	—	—	—

SAPOZHNIKOV, ANDREI
D, BRUINS

PERSONAL: Born June 15, 1971, at Chelyabinsk, U.S.S.R.... 6-1/185.... Shoots left.
TRANSACTIONS/CAREER NOTES: Selected by Boston Bruins in fifth round (fifth Bruins pick, 129th overall) of NHL entry draft (June 26, 1993).

			REGULAR SEASON					PLAYOFFS			
Season	Team	League	Gms.	G	A	Pts.	Pen.	Gms.	G	A	Pts.	Pen.
90-91—	Traktor Chelyabinsk	USSR	28	0	0	0	14	—	—	—	—	—
91-92—	Traktor Chelyabinsk	CIS	43	3	4	7	22	—	—	—	—	—
92-93—	Traktor Chelyabinsk	CIS	40	2	7	9	30	8	0	1	1	6

SARAULT, YVES
LW, CANADIENS

PERSONAL: Born December 23, 1972, at Valleyfield, Que. . . . 6-1/170. . . . Shoots left.
TRANSACTIONS/CAREER NOTES: Traded by Victoriaville Tigers with D Jason Downey to St. Jean Lynx for D Sylvain Bourgeois (May 26, 1990). . . . Selected by Montreal Canadiens in third round (fourth Canadiens pick, 61st overall) of NHL entry draft (June 22, 1991).
HONORS: Named to QMJHL All-Star second team (1991-92).

			REGULAR SEASON					PLAYOFFS				
Season Team	League	Gms.	G	A	Pts.	Pen.	Gms.	G	A	Pts.	Pen.
89-90—Victoriaville	QMJHL	70	12	28	40	140	16	0	3	3	26
90-91—St. Jean	QMJHL	56	22	24	46	113	—	—	—	—	—
91-92—St. Jean	QMJHL	50	28	38	66	96	—	—	—	—	—
—Trois-Rivieres	QMJHL	18	16	14	30	10	15	10	10	20	18
92-93—Fredericton	AHL	59	14	17	31	41	3	0	1	1	2
—Wheeling	ECHL	2	1	3	4	0	—	—	—	—	—

SARJEANT, GEOFF
G, BLUES

PERSONAL: Born November 30, 1969, at Orillia, Ont. . . . 5-9/180. . . . Shoots left. . . . Full name: Geoff Ian Sarjeant. . . . Name pronounced SAHR-jehnt.
HIGH SCHOOL: Newmarket (Ont.).
COLLEGE: Michigan Tech.
TRANSACTIONS/CAREER NOTES: Selected by St. Louis Blues in NHL supplemental draft (June 15, 1990).

			REGULAR SEASON							PLAYOFFS						
Season Team	League	Gms.	Min.	W	L	T	GA	SO	Avg.	Gms.	Min.	W	L	GA	SO	Avg.
88-89—Michigan Tech	WCHA	6	329	0	3	2	22	0	4.01	—	—	—	—	—	—	—
89-90—Michigan Tech	WCHA	19	1043	4	13	0	94	0	5.41	—	—	—	—	—	—	—
90-91—Michigan Tech	WCHA	28	1540	6	16	3	97	1	3.78	—	—	—	—	—	—	—
91-92—Michigan Tech	WCHA	23	1246	7	13	0	90	1	4.33	—	—	—	—	—	—	—
92-93—Peoria	IHL	41	2356	22	14	0	130	0	3.31	3	179	0	3	13	0	4.36

SATAN, MIROSLAV
C, OILERS

PERSONAL: Born October 22, 1974, at Topolcany, Czechoslovakia. . . . 6-1/176. . . . Shoots left. . . . Name pronounced SHAH-tahn.
TRANSACTIONS/CAREER NOTES: Selected by Edmonton Oilers in fifth round (sixth Oilers pick, 111th overall) of NHL entry draft (June 26, 1993).

			REGULAR SEASON					PLAYOFFS				
Season Team	League	Gms.	G	A	Pts.	Pen.	Gms.	G	A	Pts.	Pen.
91-92—VTJ Topolcany	Czech Dv.II	9	2	1	3	6	—	—	—	—	—
—VTJ Topolcany Jrs	Czech. Jrs.	31	30	22	52	. . .	—	—	—	—	—
92-93—Dukla Trencin	Czech.	38	11	6	17	. . .	—	—	—	—	—

SAVAGE, BRIAN
C, CANADIENS

PERSONAL: Born February 24, 1971, at Sudbury, Ont. . . . 6-1/195. . . . Shoots left.
HIGH SCHOOL: Lo-Ellen Park Secondary (Sudbury, Ont.).
COLLEGE: Miami of Ohio.
TRANSACTIONS/CAREER NOTES: Selected by Montreal Canadiens in eighth round (11th Canadiens pick, 171st overall) of NHL entry draft (June 22, 1991).
HONORS: Named to NCAA All-America West second team (1992-93). . . . Named CCHA Player of the Year (1992-93). . . . Named to CCHA All-Star first team (1992-93).

			REGULAR SEASON					PLAYOFFS				
Season Team	League	Gms.	G	A	Pts.	Pen.	Gms.	G	A	Pts.	Pen.
90-91—Miami of Ohio	CCHA	28	5	6	11	26	—	—	—	—	—
91-92—Miami of Ohio	CCHA	40	24	16	40	43	—	—	—	—	—
92-93—Miami of Ohio	CCHA	38	37	21	58	44	—	—	—	—	—
—Canadian national team	Int'l	9	3	0	3	12	—	—	—	—	—

SAVAGE, JOEL
RW, SABRES

PERSONAL: Born December 25, 1969, at Surrey, B.C. . . . 5-11/205. . . . Shoots right.
TRANSACTIONS/CAREER NOTES: Suffered concussion (October 1985). . . . Selected by Buffalo Sabres in first round (first Sabres pick, 13th overall) of NHL entry draft (June 11, 1988).
HONORS: Named to WHL All-Star second team (1987-88).

			REGULAR SEASON					PLAYOFFS				
Season Team	League	Gms.	G	A	Pts.	Pen.	Gms.	G	A	Pts.	Pen.
85-86—Kelowna	BCJHL	43	10	12	22	76	11	2	1	3	6
86-87—Victoria	WHL	68	14	13	27	48	5	2	0	2	0
87-88—Victoria	WHL	69	37	32	69	73	—	—	—	—	—
88-89—Victoria	WHL	60	17	30	47	95	6	1	1	2	8
89-90—Rochester	AHL	43	6	7	13	39	5	0	1	1	4
90-91—Rochester	AHL	61	25	19	44	45	15	3	3	6	8
—Buffalo	NHL	3	0	1	1	0	—	—	—	—	—
91-92—Rochester	AHL	59	8	14	22	39	9	2	0	2	8
92-93—Rochester	AHL	6	1	1	2	6	3	0	0	0	12
—Fort Wayne	IHL	46	21	16	37	60	10	3	5	8	22
NHL totals		3	0	1	1	0					

SAVAGE, REGGIE
RW, NORDIQUES

PERSONAL: Born May 1, 1970, at Montreal. . . . 5-10/187. . . . Shoots left. . . . Full name: Reginald David Savage.
TRANSACTIONS/CAREER NOTES: Selected by Washington Capitals in first round (first Capitals pick, 15th overall) of NHL entry draft (June 11, 1988). . . . Suspended six games by

QMJHL for stick-swinging incident (February 19, 1989)....Traded by Capitals with RW Paul MacDermid to Quebec Nordiques for LW Mike Hough (June 20, 1993).

			REGULAR SEASON					PLAYOFFS				
Season	Team	League	Gms.	G	A	Pts.	Pen.	Gms.	G	A	Pts.	Pen.
87-88—Victoriaville		QMJHL	68	68	54	122	77	5	2	3	5	8
88-89—Victoriaville		QMJHL	54	58	55	113	178	16	15	13	28	52
89-90—Victoriaville		QMJHL	63	51	43	94	79	16	13	10	23	40
90-91—Baltimore		AHL	62	32	29	61	10	6	1	1	2	6
—Washington		NHL	1	0	0	0	0	—	—	—	—	—
91-92—Baltimore		AHL	77	42	28	70	51	—	—	—	—	—
92-93—Baltimore		AHL	40	37	18	55	28	—	—	—	—	—
—Washington		NHL	16	2	3	5	12	—	—	—	—	—
NHL totals			17	2	3	5	12					

SAVARD, DENIS
C, LIGHTNING

PERSONAL: Born February 4, 1961, at Pointe Gatineau, Que....5-10/175....Shoots right. ...Full name: Denis Joseph Savard....Name pronounced suh-VAHRD.
TRANSACTIONS/CAREER NOTES: Selected by Chicago Blackhawks as underage junior in first round (first Blackhawks pick, third overall) of NHL entry draft (June 11, 1980)....Strained knee (October 15, 1980)....Broke nose (January 7, 1984)....Injured ankle (October 13, 1984)....Bruised ribs (March 22, 1987)....Broke right ankle (January 21, 1989); missed 19 games....Sprained left ankle (January 17, 1990)....Broke left index finger (January 26, 1990); missed 17 games....Traded by Blackhawks to Montreal Canadiens for D Chris Chelios and second-round pick in 1991 draft (C Michael Pomichter) (June 29, 1990)....Suffered sinus infection (January 17, 1991); missed five games....Injured right thumb (March 16, 1991)....Injured eye (October 30, 1991); missed two games. ...Suffered from the flu (November 22, 1992); missed two games....Sprained knee (January 2, 1993); missed four games. ...Suspended one game by NHL for game misconduct penalties (January 23, 1993)....Separated shoulder (February 17, 1993); missed 10 games....Signed as free agent by Tampa Bay Lightning (July 30, 1993).
HONORS: Won Michel Briere Trophy (1979-80)....Named to QMJHL All-Star first team (1979-80)....Named to THE SPORTING NEWS All-Star second team (1982-83)....Named to NHL All-Star second team (1982-83)....Played in NHL All-Star Game (1982 through 1984, 1986, 1988 and 1991).
RECORDS: Shares NHL record for fastest goal from the start of a period—4 seconds (January 12, 1986).
MISCELLANEOUS: Member of Stanley Cup championship team (1993).

			REGULAR SEASON					PLAYOFFS				
Season	Team	League	Gms.	G	A	Pts.	Pen.	Gms.	G	A	Pts.	Pen.
77-78—Montreal		QMJHL	72	37	79	116	22	—	—	—	—	—
78-79—Montreal		QMJHL	70	46	*112	158	88	11	5	6	11	46
79-80—Montreal		QMJHL	72	63	118	181	93	10	7	16	23	8
80-81—Chicago		NHL	76	28	47	75	47	3	0	0	0	0
81-82—Chicago		NHL	80	32	87	119	82	15	11	7	18	52
82-83—Chicago		NHL	78	35	86	121	99	13	8	9	17	22
83-84—Chicago		NHL	75	37	57	94	71	5	1	3	4	9
84-85—Chicago		NHL	79	38	67	105	56	15	9	20	29	20
85-86—Chicago		NHL	80	47	69	116	111	3	4	1	5	6
86-87—Chicago		NHL	70	40	50	90	108	4	1	0	1	12
87-88—Chicago		NHL	80	44	87	131	95	5	4	3	7	17
88-89—Chicago		NHL	58	23	59	82	110	16	8	11	19	10
89-90—Chicago		NHL	60	27	53	80	56	20	7	15	22	41
90-91—Montreal		NHL	70	28	31	59	52	13	2	11	13	35
91-92—Montreal		NHL	77	28	42	70	73	11	3	9	12	8
92-93—Montreal		NHL	63	16	34	50	90	14	0	5	5	4
NHL totals			946	423	769	1192	1050	137	58	94	152	236

SAVENKO, BOGDAN
RW, BLACKHAWKS

PERSONAL: Born November 20, 1974, at Kiev, U.S.S.R....6-1/192....Shoots right.
HIGH SCHOOL: Niagara Falls (Ont.).
TRANSACTIONS/CAREER NOTES: Selected by Chicago Blackhawks in third round (third Blackhawks pick, 54th overall) of NHL entry draft (June 26, 1993).

			REGULAR SEASON					PLAYOFFS				
Season	Team	League	Gms.	G	A	Pts.	Pen.	Gms.	G	A	Pts.	Pen.
90-91—SVSM Kiev		USSR Div. II	40	30	18	48	24	—	—	—	—	—
91-92—Sokol Kiev		CIS	25	3	1	4	4	—	—	—	—	—
92-93—Niagara Falls		OHL	51	29	19	48	15	2	1	0	1	2

SAVOIE, CLAUDE
RW, SENATORS

PERSONAL: Born March 12, 1973, at Montreal....5-11/182....Shoots right.
TRANSACTIONS/CAREER NOTES: Selected by Ottawa Senators in ninth round (ninth Senators pick, 194th overall) of NHL entry draft (June 20, 1992).

			REGULAR SEASON					PLAYOFFS				
Season	Team	League	Gms.	G	A	Pts.	Pen.	Gms.	G	A	Pts.	Pen.
91-92—Victoriaville		QMJHL	69	39	40	79	140	—	—	—	—	—
92-93—Victoriaville		QMJHL	67	70	61	131	113	6	4	5	9	6
—New Haven		AHL	2	1	1	2	0	—	—	—	—	—

SCHLEGEL, BRAD
D, FLAMES

PERSONAL: Born July 22, 1968, at Kitchener, Ont....5-10/190....Shoots right....Full name: Bradley Wilfred Schlegel....Name pronounced SHLAY-guhl.
TRANSACTIONS/CAREER NOTES: Selected by Washington Capitals in seventh round (eighth Capitals pick, 144th overall) of NHL entry draft (June 17, 1989)....Traded by

Capitals to Calgary Flames for seventh-round (LW Andrew Brunette) pick in 1993 draft (June 26, 1993).
HONORS: Named to OHL All-Star second team (1987-88).
MISCELLANEOUS: Member of silver-medal-winning Canadian Olympic team (1992).

			REGULAR SEASON					PLAYOFFS				
Season Team	League	Gms.	G	A	Pts.	Pen.		Gms.	G	A	Pts.	Pen.
86-87—London	OHL	65	4	23	27	24		—	—	—	—	—
87-88—London	OHL	66	13	63	76	49		12	8	17	25	6
88-89—Canadian national team	Int'l	60	2	22	24	30		—	—	—	—	—
89-90—Canadian national team	Int'l	61	7	25	32	38		—	—	—	—	—
90-91—Canadian national team	Int'l	53	8	18	26	62		—	—	—	—	—
91-92—Canadian national team	Int'l	61	3	18	21	84		—	—	—	—	—
—Canadian Olympic Team	Int'l	8	1	2	3	4		—	—	—	—	—
—Baltimore	AHL	2	0	1	1	0		—	—	—	—	—
—Washington	NHL	15	0	1	1	0		7	0	1	1	2
92-93—Baltimore	AHL	61	3	20	23	40		7	0	5	5	6
—Washington	NHL	7	0	1	1	6		—	—	—	—	—
NHL totals		22	0	2	2	6		7	0	1	1	2

SCHNEIDER, MATHIEU
D, CANADIENS

PERSONAL: Born June 12, 1969, at New York. . . . 5-11/189. . . . Shoots left.
HIGH SCHOOL: Mount St. Charles Academy (Woonsocket, R.I.).
TRANSACTIONS/CAREER NOTES: Selected by Montreal Canadiens in third round (fourth Canadiens pick, 44th overall) of NHL entry draft (June 13, 1987). . . . Bruised left shoulder (February 1990). . . . Sprained left ankle (January 26, 1991); missed nine games. . . . Sprained ankle (January 27, 1993); missed 24 games. . . . Separated shoulder (April 18, 1993); missed seven playoff games.
HONORS: Named to OHL All-Star first team (1987-88 and 1988-89).
MISCELLANEOUS: Member of Stanley Cup championship team (1993).

			REGULAR SEASON					PLAYOFFS				
Season Team	League	Gms.	G	A	Pts.	Pen.		Gms.	G	A	Pts.	Pen.
85-86—Mount St. Charles H.S.	R.I.H.S.	19	3	27	30	. . .		—	—	—	—	—
86-87—Cornwall	OHL	63	7	29	36	75		5	0	0	0	22
87-88—Montreal	NHL	4	0	0	0	2		—	—	—	—	—
—Cornwall	OHL	48	21	40	61	85		11	2	6	8	14
—Sherbrooke	AHL	—	—	—	—	—		3	0	3	3	12
88-89—Cornwall	OHL	59	16	57	73	96		18	7	20	27	30
89-90—Sherbrooke	AHL	28	6	13	19	20		—	—	—	—	—
—Montreal	NHL	44	7	14	21	25		9	1	3	4	31
90-91—Montreal	NHL	69	10	20	30	63		13	2	7	9	18
91-92—Montreal	NHL	78	8	24	32	72		10	1	4	5	6
92-93—Montreal	NHL	60	13	31	44	91		11	1	2	3	16
NHL totals		255	38	89	127	253		43	5	16	21	71

SCHULTE, PAXTON
LW, NORDIQUES

PERSONAL: Born July 16, 1972, at Edmonton, Alta. . . . 6-2/210. . . . Shoots left.
COLLEGE: North Dakota, then Spokane Falls (Wash.).
TRANSACTIONS/CAREER NOTES: Selected by Quebec Nordiques in sixth round (seventh Nordiques pick, 124th overall) of NHL entry draft (June 20, 1992).

			REGULAR SEASON					PLAYOFFS				
Season Team	League	Gms.	G	A	Pts.	Pen.		Gms.	G	A	Pts.	Pen.
89-90—Sherwood Park	AJHL	56	28	38	66	151		—	—	—	—	—
90-91—North Dakota	WCHA	38	2	4	6	32		—	—	—	—	—
91-92—Spokane	WHL	70	42	42	84	222		10	2	8	10	48
92-93—Spokane	WHL	45	38	35	73	142		10	5	6	11	12

SCISSONS, SCOTT
C, ISLANDERS

PERSONAL: Born October 29, 1971, at Saskatoon, Sask. . . . 6-1/201. . . . Shoots left. . . . Name pronounced SIH-suhns.
TRANSACTIONS/CAREER NOTES: Selected by New York Islanders in first round (first Islanders pick, sixth overall) of NHL entry draft (June 16, 1990). . . . Injured right arm in preseason game (October 29, 1990); missed 11 games.

			REGULAR SEASON					PLAYOFFS				
Season Team	League	Gms.	G	A	Pts.	Pen.		Gms.	G	A	Pts.	Pen.
88-89—Saskatoon	WHL	71	30	56	86	65		7	0	4	4	16
89-90—Saskatoon	WHL	61	40	47	87	81		10	3	8	11	6
90-91—Saskatoon	WHL	57	24	53	77	61		—	—	—	—	—
—New York Islanders	NHL	1	0	0	0	0		—	—	—	—	—
91-92—Canadian national team	Int'l	27	4	8	12	23		—	—	—	—	—
92-93—Capital District	AHL	43	14	30	44	33		4	0	0	0	0
—New York Islanders	NHL	—	—	—	—	—		1	0	0	0	0
NHL totals		1	0	0	0	0		1	0	0	0	0

SCREMIN, CLAUDIO
D, SHARKS

PERSONAL: Born May 28, 1968, at Burnaby, B.C. . . . 6-2/205. . . . Shoots right. . . . Full name: Claudio Francesco Scremin. . . . Name pronounced SKREH-mihn.
COLLEGE: Maine.
TRANSACTIONS/CAREER NOTES: Selected by Washington Capitals in 12th round

(12th Capitals pick, 204th overall) in NHL entry draft (June 11, 1988).... Traded by Capitals to Minnesota North Stars for G Don Beaupre (November 1, 1988).... Signed as free agent by San Jose Sharks (September 3, 1991).

			REGULAR SEASON					PLAYOFFS			
Season Team	League	Gms.	G	A	Pts.	Pen.	Gms.	G	A	Pts.	Pen.
86-87—University of Maine	Hockey East	15	0	1	1	2	—	—	—	—	—
87-88—University of Maine	Hockey East	44	6	18	24	22	—	—	—	—	—
88-89—University of Maine	Hockey East	45	5	24	29	42	—	—	—	—	—
89-90—University of Maine	Hockey East	45	4	26	30	14	—	—	—	—	—
90-91—Kansas City	IHL	77	7	14	21	60	—	—	—	—	—
91-92—Kansas City	IHL	70	5	23	28	44	15	1	6	7	14
—San Jose	NHL	13	0	0	0	25	—	—	—	—	—
92-93—Kansas City	IHL	75	10	22	32	93	12	0	5	5	18
—San Jose	NHL	4	0	1	1	4	—	—	—	—	—
NHL totals		17	0	1	1	29					

SEHER, KURT
D, BRUINS

PERSONAL: Born April 15, 1973, at Lethbridge, Alta.... 6-2/170.... Shoots left.
TRANSACTIONS/CAREER NOTES: Selected by Boston Bruins in eighth round (sixth Bruins pick, 184th overall) of NHL entry draft (June 20, 1993).

			REGULAR SEASON					PLAYOFFS			
Season Team	League	Gms.	G	A	Pts.	Pen.	Gms.	G	A	Pts.	Pen.
89-90—Swift Current	WHL	55	2	3	5	28	4	0	0	0	2
90-91—Swift Current	WHL	59	4	26	30	63	2	0	0	0	0
91-92—Swift Current	WHL	5	0	0	0	25	—	—	—	—	—
—Seattle	WHL	55	15	23	38	103	15	3	12	15	32
92-93—Seattle	WHL	69	9	20	29	125	5	0	3	3	10
—Providence	AHL	2	0	0	0	2	3	0	0	0	2

SELANNE, TEEMU
RW, JETS

PERSONAL: Born July 3, 1970, at Helsinki, Finland. ... 6-0/180. ... Shoots right. ... Name pronounced TAY-moo suh-LAH-nee.
TRANSACTIONS/CAREER NOTES: Selected by Winnipeg Jets in first round (first Jets pick, 10th overall) of NHL entry draft (June 11, 1988).... Broke left leg (October 19, 1989).
HONORS: Named to Finland All-Star team (1990-91 and 1991-92).... Named NHL Rookie of the Year by THE SPORTING NEWS (1992-93).... Won Calder Memorial Trophy (1992-93).... Named to THE SPORTING NEWS All-Star first team (1992-93). ... Named to NHL All-Star first team (1992-93).... Named to NHL All-Rookie team (1992-93).... Played in NHL All-Star Game (1993).
RECORDS: Holds NHL rookie-season record for most points—132 (1992); goals—76 (1992).

			REGULAR SEASON					PLAYOFFS			
Season Team	League	Gms.	G	A	Pts.	Pen.	Gms.	G	A	Pts.	Pen.
87-88—Jokerit	Finland	33	42	23	65	18	5	4	3	7	2
88-89—Jokerit	Finland	34	35	33	68	12	5	7	3	10	4
89-90—Jokerit	Finland	11	4	8	12	0	—	—	—	—	—
90-91—Jokerit	Finland	42	*33	25	58	12	—	—	—	—	—
91-92—Finland Olympic Team	Int'l	8	7	4	11	...	—	—	—	—	—
—Jokerit	Finland	44	39	23	62	20	—	—	—	—	—
92-93—Winnipeg	NHL	84	†76	56	132	45	6	4	2	6	2
NHL totals		84	76	56	132	45	6	4	2	6	2

SEMAK, ALEXANDER
C, DEVILS

PERSONAL: Born February 11, 1966, at Ufa, U.S.S.R.... 5-9/190.... Shoots left. ... Name pronounced SEE-mak.
TRANSACTIONS/CAREER NOTES: Selected by New Jersey Devils in 10th round (12 Devils pick, 207th overall) of NHL entry draft (June 11, 1988).... Injured shoulder (February 8, 1992); missed seven games.

			REGULAR SEASON					PLAYOFFS			
Season Team	League	Gms.	G	A	Pts.	Pen.	Gms.	G	A	Pts.	Pen.
87-88—Dynamo Moscow	USSR	47	21	14	35	40	—	—	—	—	—
88-89—Dynamo Moscow	USSR	44	18	10	28	22	—	—	—	—	—
89-90—Dynamo Moscow	USSR	43	23	11	34	33	—	—	—	—	—
90-91—Dynamo Moscow	USSR	46	17	21	38	48	—	—	—	—	—
91-92—Dynamo Moscow	CIS	18	6	11	17	18	—	—	—	—	—
—Utica	AHL	7	3	2	5	0	—	—	—	—	—
—New Jersey	NHL	25	5	6	11	0	1	0	0	0	0
92-93—New Jersey	NHL	82	37	42	79	70	5	1	1	2	0
NHL totals		107	42	48	90	70	6	1	1	2	0

SEMCHUK, BRANDY
RW/LW, KINGS

PERSONAL: Born September 22, 1971, at Calgary, Alta. ... 6-1/190. ... Shoots right.
TRANSACTIONS/CAREER NOTES: Selected by Los Angeles Kings in second round (second Kings pick, 28th overall) of NHL entry draft (June 16, 1990).... Bruised thigh (December 1989).... Strained hip flexor (March 1990).

Season	Team	League	REGULAR SEASON					PLAYOFFS				
			Gms.	G	A	Pts.	Pen.	Gms.	G	A	Pts.	Pen.
87-88—Calgary Canucks	AJHL		90	44	42	86	120	—	—	—	—	—
88-89—Canadian national team ...	Int'l		42	11	11	22	60	—	—	—	—	—
89-90—Canadian national team ...	Int'l		60	9	14	23	14	—	—	—	—	—
90-91—Lethbridge......................	WHL		14	9	8	17	10	15	8	5	13	18
—New Haven	AHL		21	1	4	5	6	—	—	—	—	—
91-92—Phoenix	IHL		15	1	5	6	6	—	—	—	—	—
—Raleigh	ECHL		5	1	2	3	16	2	1	0	1	4
92-93—Phoenix	IHL		56	13	12	25	58	—	—	—	—	—
—Los Angeles......................	NHL		1	0	0	0	2	—	—	—	—	—
NHL totals................................			1	0	0	0	2					

SEMENOV, ANATOLI
C/LW, MIGHTY DUCKS

PERSONAL: Born March 5, 1962, at Moscow, U.S.S.R.... 6-2/190.... Shoots left. ... Name pronounced AN-uh-TOH-lee SEHM-ih-nahf.

TRANSACTIONS/CAREER NOTES: Selected by Edmonton Oilers in sixth round (fifth Oilers pick, 120th overall) of 1989 NHL entry draft (June 17, 1989).... Bruised ribs (March 1, 1991); missed five games.... Suffered hairline fracture in left foot (October 1991); missed four games.... Suffered concussion (November 1991); missed two games. ... Injured shoulder (January 4, 1992); missed six games. ... Sprained ankle (February 28, 1992); missed one game.... Selected by Tampa Bay Lightning in NHL expansion draft (June 18, 1992).... Traded by Lightning to Vancouver Canucks for C Dave Capuano and fourth-round pick in 1994 draft (November 3, 1992).... Strained knee (January 9, 1993); missed six games. ... Selected by Mighty Ducks of Anaheim in NHL expansion draft (June 24, 1993).

HONORS: Named to Soviet League All-Star team (1984-85).

MISCELLANEOUS: Member of gold-medal-winning U.S.S.R. Olympic team (1988).

Season	Team	League	REGULAR SEASON					PLAYOFFS				
			Gms.	G	A	Pts.	Pen.	Gms.	G	A	Pts.	Pen.
79-80—Dynamo Moscow	USSR		8	3	0	3	2	—	—	—	—	—
80-81—Dynamo Moscow	USSR		47	18	14	32	18	—	—	—	—	—
81-82—Dynamo Moscow	USSR		44	12	14	26	28	—	—	—	—	—
82-83—Dynamo Moscow	USSR		44	22	18	40	26	—	—	—	—	—
83-84—Dynamo Moscow	USSR		19	10	5	15	14	—	—	—	—	—
84-85—Dynamo Moscow	USSR		30	17	12	29	32	—	—	—	—	—
85-86—Dynamo Moscow	USSR		32	18	17	35	19	—	—	—	—	—
86-87—Dynamo Moscow	USSR		40	15	29	44	32	—	—	—	—	—
87-88—Dynamo Moscow	USSR		32	17	8	25	22	—	—	—	—	—
88-89—Dynamo Moscow	USSR		31	9	12	21	24	—	—	—	—	—
89-90—Dynamo Moscow	USSR		48	13	20	33	16	—	—	—	—	—
—Edmonton........................	NHL		—	—	—	—	—	2	0	0	0	0
90-91—Edmonton........................	NHL		57	15	16	31	26	12	5	5	10	6
91-92—Edmonton........................	NHL		59	20	22	42	16	8	1	1	2	6
92-93—Tampa Bay	NHL		13	2	3	5	4	—	—	—	—	—
—Vancouver......................	NHL		62	10	34	44	28	12	1	3	4	0
NHL totals.................................			191	47	75	122	74	34	7	9	16	12

SEROWIK, JEFF
D, PANTHERS

PERSONAL: Born October 1, 1967, at Manchester, N.H.... 6-0/190.... Shoots right.... Full name: Jeff Michael Serowik.... Name pronounced SAIR-oh-wihk.

HIGH SCHOOL: West (Manchester, N.H.), then Lawrence Academy (Groton, Mass.).

COLLEGE: Providence.

TRANSACTIONS/CAREER NOTES: Broke left ankle (April 1982).... Broke right ankle (March 1983).... Selected by Toronto Maple Leafs in fifth round (fifth Maple Leafs pick, 85th overall) of NHL entry draft (June 15, 1985).... Signed as free agent by Florida Panthers (July 15, 1993).

HONORS: Named to Hockey East All-Star second team (1989-90).... Named to AHL All-Star second team (1992-93).

Season	Team	League	REGULAR SEASON					PLAYOFFS				
			Gms.	G	A	Pts.	Pen.	Gms.	G	A	Pts.	Pen.
83-84—Manchester West H.S......	N.H. H.S.		21	12	12	24	...	—	—	—	—	—
84-85—Lawrence Academy	Mass. H.S.		24	8	25	33	...	—	—	—	—	—
85-86—Lawrence Academy	Mass. H.S.				Statistics unavailable.							
86-87—Providence College	Hockey East		33	3	8	11	22	—	—	—	—	—
87-88—Providence College	Hockey East		33	3	9	12	44	—	—	—	—	—
88-89—Providence College	Hockey East		35	3	14	17	48	—	—	—	—	—
89-90—Providence College	Hockey East		35	6	19	25	34	—	—	—	—	—
90-91—Toronto.............................	NHL		1	0	0	0	0	—	—	—	—	—
—Newmarket......................	AHL		60	8	15	23	45	—	—	—	—	—
91-92—St. John's	AHL		78	11	34	45	60	16	4	9	13	22
92-93—St. John's	AHL		77	19	35	54	92	9	1	5	6	8
NHL totals.................................			1	0	0	0	0					

SEVERYN, BRENT
D, DEVILS

PERSONAL: Born February 22, 1966, at Vegreville, Alta.... 6-2/210.... Shoots left.... Full name: Brent Leonard Severyn.

COLLEGE: Alberta.

TRANSACTIONS/CAREER NOTES: Selected by Winnipeg Jets in fifth round (fifth Jets pick, 99th overall) of NHL entry draft (June 9, 1984).... Injured knee (October 1985).... Signed as free agent by Quebec Nordiques

(July 15, 1988).... Traded by Nordiques to New Jersey Devils for D Dave Marcinyshyn (June 3, 1991).
HONORS: Named to AHL All-Star first team (1992-93).

			REGULAR SEASON					PLAYOFFS				
Season	Team	League	Gms.	G	A	Pts.	Pen.	Gms.	G	A	Pts.	Pen.
82-83	Vegreville	CAJHL	21	20	22	42	10	—	—	—	—	—
83-84	Seattle	WHL	72	14	22	36	49	5	2	1	3	2
84-85	Seattle	WHL	38	8	32	40	54	—	—	—	—	—
	Brandon	WHL	26	7	16	23	57	—	—	—	—	—
85-86	Seattle	WHL	33	11	20	31	164	5	0	4	4	4
	Saskatoon	WHL	9	1	4	5	38	—	—	—	—	—
86-87	University of Alberta	CWUAA	43	7	19	26	171	—	—	—	—	—
87-88	University of Alberta	CWUAA	46	21	29	50	178	—	—	—	—	—
88-89	Halifax	AHL	47	2	12	14	141	—	—	—	—	—
89-90	Quebec	NHL	35	0	2	2	42	—	—	—	—	—
	Halifax	AHL	43	6	9	15	105	6	1	2	3	49
90-91	Halifax	AHL	50	7	26	33	202	—	—	—	—	—
91-92	Utica	AHL	80	11	33	44	211	4	0	1	1	4
92-93	Utica	AHL	77	20	32	52	240	5	0	0	0	35
NHL totals			35	0	2	2	42					

SEVIGNY, PIERRE
LW, CANADIENS

PERSONAL: Born September 8, 1971, at Trois-Rivieres, Que.... 6-0/189.... Shoots left. ... Name pronounced SEH-vihn-yee.
TRANSACTIONS/CAREER NOTES: Selected by Montreal Canadiens in third round (fourth Canadiens pick, 51st overall) of NHL entry draft (June 17, 1989).... Severed knee ligament in off-ice accident (March 25, 1991).
HONORS: Named to QMJHL All-Star first team (1980-81).... Named to QMJHL All-Star second team (1989-90 and 1990-91).

			REGULAR SEASON					PLAYOFFS				
Season	Team	League	Gms.	G	A	Pts.	Pen.	Gms.	G	A	Pts.	Pen.
88-89	Verdun	QMJHL	67	27	43	70	88	—	—	—	—	—
89-90	St. Hyacinthe	QMJHL	67	47	72	119	205	12	8	8	16	42
90-91	St. Hyacinthe	QMJHL	60	36	46	82	203	—	—	—	—	—
91-92	Fredericton	AHL	74	22	37	59	145	7	1	1	2	26
92-93	Fredericton	AHL	80	36	40	76	113	5	1	1	2	2

SHANAHAN, BRENDAN
RW/LW, BLUES

PERSONAL: Born January 23, 1969, at Mimico, Ont.... 6-3/210.... Shoots right.... Full name: Brendan Frederick Shanahan.
HIGH SCHOOL: Michael Power/St. Joseph's (Islington, Ont.).
TRANSACTIONS/CAREER NOTES: Bruised tendons in shoulder (January 1987). ... Selected by New Jersey Devils as underage junior in first round (first Devils pick, second overall) of NHL entry draft (June 13, 1987).... Broke nose (December 1987).... Suffered back spasms (March 1989).... Suspended five games by NHL for stick-fighting (January 13, 1990).... Suffered lower abdominal strain (February 1990).... Suffered lacerations to lower right side of face and underwent surgery (January 8, 1991); missed five games.... Signed as free agent by St. Louis Blues (July 25, 1991); D Scott Stevens awarded to New Jersey Devils as compensation (September 3, 1991).... Pulled groin (October 24, 1992); missed 12 games.... Suspended six off-days and fined $500 by NHL for hitting another player in face with his stick (January 7, 1993).... Suspended one game by NHL for high-sticking incident (February 23, 1993).

			REGULAR SEASON					PLAYOFFS				
Season	Team	League	Gms.	G	A	Pts.	Pen.	Gms.	G	A	Pts.	Pen.
84-85	Mississauga	MTHL	36	20	21	41	26	—	—	—	—	—
85-86	London	OHL	59	28	34	62	70	5	5	5	10	5
86-87	London	OHL	56	39	53	92	128	—	—	—	—	—
87-88	New Jersey	NHL	65	7	19	26	131	12	2	1	3	44
88-89	New Jersey	NHL	68	22	28	50	115	—	—	—	—	—
89-90	New Jersey	NHL	73	30	42	72	137	6	3	3	6	20
90-91	New Jersey	NHL	75	29	37	66	141	7	3	5	8	12
91-92	St. Louis	NHL	80	33	36	69	171	6	2	3	5	14
92-93	St. Louis	NHL	71	51	43	94	174	11	4	3	7	18
NHL totals			432	172	205	377	869	42	14	15	29	108

SHANK, DANIEL
RW, WHALERS

PERSONAL: Born May 12, 1967, at Montreal.... 5-11/200.... Shoots right.
TRANSACTIONS/CAREER NOTES: Signed as free agent by Detroit Red Wings (July 13, 1988). ... Traded by Red Wings to Hartford Whalers for C/LW Chris Tancill (December 18, 1991).
HONORS: Named to IHL All-Star first team (1992-93).

			REGULAR SEASON					PLAYOFFS				
Season	Team	League	Gms.	G	A	Pts.	Pen.	Gms.	G	A	Pts.	Pen.
85-86	Shawinigan	QMJHL	51	34	38	72	184	—	—	—	—	—
86-87	Hull	QMJHL	46	26	43	69	325	—	—	—	—	—
87-88	Hull	QMJHL	52	31	42	73	343	19	10	19	29	*106
88-89	Adirondack	AHL	42	5	20	25	113	17	11	8	19	102
89-90	Detroit	NHL	57	11	13	24	143	—	—	—	—	—
	Adirondack	AHL	14	8	8	16	36	—	—	—	—	—
90-91	Detroit	NHL	7	0	1	1	14	—	—	—	—	—
	Adirondack	AHL	60	26	49	75	278	—	—	—	—	—

Season Team	League	REGULAR SEASON					PLAYOFFS				
		Gms.	G	A	Pts.	Pen.	Gms.	G	A	Pts.	Pen.
91-92—Adirondack	AHL	27	13	21	34	112	—	—	—	—	—
—Hartford	NHL	13	2	0	2	18	5	0	0	0	22
—Springfield	AHL	31	9	19	28	83	8	8	0	8	48
92-93—San Diego	IHL	77	39	53	92	*495	14	5	10	15	*131
NHL totals		77	13	14	27	175	5	0	0	0	22

SHANNON, DARRIN
LW, JETS

PERSONAL: Born December 8, 1969, at Barrie, Ont.... 6-2/200.... Shoots left.... Brother of Darryl Shannon, defenseman, Toronto Maple Leafs. **TRANSACTIONS/CAREER NOTES:** Separated right shoulder (November 1986).... Dislocated left elbow (November 1987).... Separated left shoulder (January 1988). ...Selected by Pittsburgh Penguins in first round (first Penguins pick, fourth overall) of NHL entry draft (June 11, 1988).... Traded by Penguins with D Doug Bodger to Buffalo Sabres for G Tom Barrasso and third-round pick in 1990 draft (LW Joe Dziedzic) (November 12, 1988).... Strained knee ligaments (May 1990).... Injured jaw (January 8, 1991); missed five games.... Traded by Sabres with LW Mike Hartman and D Dean Kennedy to Winnipeg Jets for RW Dave McLlwain, D Gordon Donnelly, fifth-round pick in 1992 draft (LW Yuri Khmylev) and future considerations (October 11, 1991).... Injured knee (November 20, 1991).... Injured eye (November 25, 1991); missed one game.... Sprained leg (December 31, 1991); missed seven games. **HONORS:** Named to OHL All-Scholastic team (1986-87).... Won Bobby Smith Trophy (1987-88).... Named to Memorial Cup All-Star team (1987-88).

Season Team	League	REGULAR SEASON					PLAYOFFS				
		Gms.	G	A	Pts.	Pen.	Gms.	G	A	Pts.	Pen.
85-86—Barrie Jr. B	OHA	40	13	22	35	21	—	—	—	—	—
86-87—Windsor	OHL	60	16	67	83	116	14	4	6	10	8
87-88—Windsor	OHL	43	33	41	74	49	12	6	12	18	9
88-89—Windsor	OHL	54	33	48	81	47	4	1	6	7	2
—Buffalo	NHL	3	0	0	0	0	2	0	0	0	0
89-90—Buffalo	NHL	17	2	7	9	4	6	0	1	1	4
—Rochester	AHL	50	20	23	43	25	9	4	1	5	2
90-91—Rochester	AHL	49	26	34	60	56	10	3	5	8	22
—Buffalo	NHL	34	8	6	14	12	6	1	2	3	4
91-92—Buffalo	NHL	1	0	1	1	0	—	—	—	—	—
—Winnipeg	NHL	68	13	26	39	41	7	0	1	1	10
92-93—Winnipeg	NHL	84	20	40	60	91	6	2	4	6	6
NHL totals		207	43	80	123	148	27	3	8	11	24

SHANNON, DARRYL
D, MAPLE LEAFS

PERSONAL: Born June 21, 1968, at Barrie, Ont.... 6-2/195.... Shoots left.... Brother of Darrin Shannon, left winger, Winnipeg Jets. **TRANSACTIONS/CAREER NOTES:** Selected by Toronto Maple Leafs in second round (second Maple Leafs pick, 36th overall) of NHL entry draft (June 21, 1986).... Broke right leg and right thumb, bruised chest and suffered slipped disk in automobile accident (June 20, 1990). **HONORS:** Named to OHL All-Star second team (1986-87).... Won Max Kaminsky Trophy (1987-88).... Named to OHL All-Star first team (1987-88).... Named to Memorial Cup All-Star team (1987-88).

Season Team	League	REGULAR SEASON					PLAYOFFS				
		Gms.	G	A	Pts.	Pen.	Gms.	G	A	Pts.	Pen.
84-85—Barrie Jr. B	OHA	39	5	23	28	50	—	—	—	—	—
85-86—Windsor	OHL	57	6	21	27	52	16	5	6	11	22
86-87—Windsor	OHL	64	23	27	50	83	14	4	8	12	18
87-88—Windsor	OHL	60	16	70	86	116	12	3	8	11	17
88-89—Toronto	NHL	14	1	3	4	6	—	—	—	—	—
—Newmarket	AHL	61	5	24	29	37	5	0	3	3	10
89-90—Newmarket	AHL	47	4	15	19	58	—	—	—	—	—
—Toronto	NHL	10	0	1	1	12	—	—	—	—	—
90-91—Toronto	NHL	10	0	1	1	0	—	—	—	—	—
—Newmarket	AHL	47	2	14	16	51	—	—	—	—	—
91-92—Toronto	NHL	48	2	8	10	23	—	—	—	—	—
92-93—Toronto	NHL	16	0	0	0	11	—	—	—	—	—
—St. John's	AHL	7	1	1	2	4	—	—	—	—	—
NHL totals		98	3	13	16	52					

SHANTZ, JEFF
C, BLACKHAWKS

PERSONAL: Born October 10, 1973, at Edmonton, Alta.... 6-0/185.... Shoots right. **HIGH SCHOOL:** R. Usher Collegiate (Regina, Sask.). **TRANSACTIONS/CAREER NOTES:** Selected by Chicago Blackhawks in second round (second Blackhawks pick, 36th overall) of NHL entry draft (June 20, 1992). **HONORS:** Named to WHL (East) All-Star first team (1992-93).

Season Team	League	REGULAR SEASON					PLAYOFFS				
		Gms.	G	A	Pts.	Pen.	Gms.	G	A	Pts.	Pen.
89-90—Regina	WHL	1	0	0	0	0	—	—	—	—	—
90-91—Regina	WHL	69	16	21	37	22	8	2	2	4	2
91-92—Regina	WHL	72	39	50	89	75	—	—	—	—	—
92-93—Regina	WHL	64	29	54	83	75	13	2	12	14	14

SHAW, BRAD
D, SENATORS

PERSONAL: Born April 28, 1964, at Cambridge, Ont. . . . 6-0/190. . . . Shoots right. . . . Full name: Bradley William Shaw.
HIGH SCHOOL: Canterbury (Ottawa), then Eastwood (Kitchner, Ont.).
TRANSACTIONS/CAREER NOTES: Selected by Detroit Red Wings as underage junior in fifth round (fifth Red Wings pick, 86th overall) of NHL entry draft (June 9, 1982). . . . Traded by Red Wings to Hartford Whalers for eighth-round pick in 1984 draft (LW Lars Karlsson) (May 29, 1984). . . . Fractured finger on left hand (February 1988). . . . Broke nose (October 21, 1989). . . . Suffered back spasms (November 12, 1989). . . . Bruised right foot (February 28, 1990). . . . Injured groin (October 28, 1991); missed two games. . . . Injured knee (January 31, 1992); missed four games. . . . Bruised knee (February 29, 1992); missed four games. . . . Injured groin (March 14, 1992); missed three games. . . . Traded by Whalers to New Jersey Devils for future considerations (June 15, 1992). . . . Selected by Ottawa Senators in NHL expansion draft (June 18, 1992). . . . Suffered slight concussion (October 8, 1992); missed two games.
HONORS: Won Max Kaminsky Trophy (1983-84). . . . Named to OHL All-Star first team (1983-84). . . . Won Eddie Shore Plaque (1986-87). . . . Named to AHL All-Star first team (1986-88 and 1987-88). . . . Named to NHL All-Rookie team (1989-90).

			REGULAR SEASON					PLAYOFFS				
Season	Team	League	Gms.	G	A	Pts.	Pen.	Gms.	G	A	Pts.	Pen.
81-82—Ottawa		OHL	68	13	59	72	24	15	1	13	14	4
82-83—Ottawa		OHL	63	12	66	78	24	9	2	9	11	4
83-84—Ottawa		OHL	68	11	71	82	75	13	2	*27	29	9
84-85—Salt Lake City		IHL	44	3	29	32	25	—	—	—	—	—
—Binghamton		AHL	24	1	10	11	4	8	1	8	9	6
85-86—Hartford		NHL	8	0	2	2	4	—	—	—	—	—
—Binghamton		AHL	64	10	44	54	33	5	0	2	2	6
86-87—Hartford		NHL	2	0	0	0	0	—	—	—	—	—
—Binghamton		AHL	77	9	30	39	43	12	1	8	9	2
87-88—Binghamton		AHL	73	12	50	62	50	4	0	5	5	4
—Hartford		NHL	1	0	0	0	0	—	—	—	—	—
88-89—Verice		Italy	35	10	30	40	44	11	4	8	12	13
—Hartford		NHL	3	1	0	1	0	3	1	0	1	0
—Canadian national team		Int'l	4	1	0	1	2	—	—	—	—	—
89-90—Hartford		NHL	64	3	32	35	40	7	2	5	7	0
90-91—Hartford		NHL	72	4	28	32	29	6	1	2	3	2
91-92—Hartford		NHL	62	3	22	25	44	3	0	1	1	4
92-93—Ottawa		NHL	81	7	34	41	34	—	—	—	—	—
NHL totals			293	18	118	136	151	19	4	8	12	6

SHAW, DAVID
D, BRUINS

PERSONAL: Born May 25, 1964, at St. Thomas, Ont. . . . 6-2/204. . . . Shoots right.
TRANSACTIONS/CAREER NOTES: Selected by Quebec Nordiques as underage junior in first round (first Nordiques pick, 13th overall) of NHL entry draft (June 9, 1982). . . . Sprained wrist (December 18, 1985). . . . Traded by Nordiques with LW John Ogrodnick to New York Rangers for LW Jeff Jackson and D Terry Carkner (September 30, 1987). . . . Separated shoulder (October 1987). . . . Suspended 12 games by NHL for slashing (October 27, 1988). . . . Bruised shoulder (March 15, 1989). . . . Dislocated right shoulder (November 2, 1989). . . . Reinjured right shoulder (November 22, 1989); missed 10 games. . . . Underwent surgery to right shoulder (February 7, 1990). . . . Bruised finger (September 1990). . . . Bruised left big toe (October 31, 1990). . . . Sprained knee (October 20, 1991). . . . Traded by Rangers to Edmonton Oilers for D Jeff Beukeboom (November 12, 1991) to complete deal in which Rangers traded C Bernie Nicholls, LW Louie DeBrusk, RW Steven Rice and future considerations to Oilers for C Mark Messier and future considerations (October 4, 1991). . . . Traded by Oilers to Minnesota North Stars for D Brian Glynn (January 21, 1992). . . . Traded by North Stars to Boston Bruins for future considerations (September 2, 1992). . . . Injured thigh (October 1992); missed one game. . . . Injured foot (December 1992); missed one game. . . . Injured ribs (March 1993); missed five games.
HONORS: Named to OHL All-Star first team (1983-84). . . . Named to Memorial Cup All-Star team (1983-84).

			REGULAR SEASON					PLAYOFFS				
Season	Team	League	Gms.	G	A	Pts.	Pen.	Gms.	G	A	Pts.	Pen.
80-81—Stratford Jr. B		OHA	41	12	19	31	30	—	—	—	—	—
81-82—Kitchener		OHL	68	6	25	31	99	15	2	2	4	51
82-83—Kitchener		OHL	57	18	56	74	78	12	2	10	12	18
—Quebec		NHL	2	0	0	0	0	—	—	—	—	—
83-84—Kitchener		OHL	58	14	34	48	73	16	4	9	13	12
—Quebec		NHL	3	0	0	0	0	—	—	—	—	—
84-85—Guelph		OHL	2	0	0	0	0	—	—	—	—	—
—Fredericton		AHL	48	7	6	13	73	2	0	0	0	7
—Quebec		NHL	14	0	0	0	11	—	—	—	—	—
85-86—Quebec		NHL	73	7	19	26	78	—	—	—	—	—
86-87—Quebec		NHL	75	0	19	19	69	—	—	—	—	—
87-88—New York Rangers		NHL	68	7	25	32	100	—	—	—	—	—
88-89—New York Rangers		NHL	63	6	11	17	88	4	0	2	2	30
89-90—New York Rangers		NHL	22	2	10	12	22	—	—	—	—	—
90-91—New York Rangers		NHL	77	2	10	12	89	6	0	0	0	11
91-92—New York Rangers		NHL	10	0	1	1	15	—	—	—	—	—
—Edmonton		NHL	12	1	1	2	8	—	—	—	—	—
—Minnesota		NHL	37	0	7	7	49	7	2	2	4	10
92-93—Boston		NHL	77	10	14	24	108	4	0	1	1	6
NHL totals			533	35	117	152	637	21	2	5	7	57

SHEPPARD, RAY
RW, RED WINGS

PERSONAL: Born May 27, 1966, at Pembroke, Ont. . . . 6-1/190. . . . Shoots right.
TRANSACTIONS/CAREER NOTES: Selected by Buffalo Sabres as underage junior in third round (third Sabres pick, 60th overall) of NHL entry draft (June 9, 1984). . . . Injured left knee (September 1986); missed Sabres training camp. . . . Bruised back during training camp

S

(September 1988).... Suffered facial lacerations (November 25, 1988).... Suffered facial lacerations (November 27, 1988). ... Suffered from the flu (December 1988).... Sprained ankle (January 30, 1989).... Injured left knee (March 16, 1990).... Traded by Sabres to New York Rangers for future considerations and cash (July 10, 1990).... Sprained medial collateral ligaments of right knee (February 18, 1991); missed 13 games.... Dislocated left shoulder (March 24, 1991).... Signed as free agent by Detroit Red Wings (August 5, 1991).... Strained lower abdomen (March 20, 1992); missed five games.... Injured knee (October 8, 1992); missed five games.... Reinjured knee (October 28, 1992); missed two games.... Suffered back spasms (February 13, 1993); missed three games.... Strained back (March 2, 1993); missed two games.

HONORS: Won Red Tilson Trophy (1985-86).... Won Eddie Powers Memorial Trophy (1985-86).... Won Jim Mahon Memorial Trophy (1985-86).... Named to OHL All-Star first team (1985-86).... Named to NHL All-Rookie team (1987-88).

Season	Team	League	REGULAR SEASON					PLAYOFFS				
			Gms.	G	A	Pts.	Pen.	Gms.	G	A	Pts.	Pen.
82-83—	Brockville	COJHL	48	27	36	63	81	—	—	—	—	—
83-84—	Cornwall	OHL	68	44	36	80	69	—	—	—	—	—
84-85—	Cornwall	OHL	49	25	33	58	51	9	2	12	14	4
85-86—	Cornwall	OHL	63	*81	61	*142	25	6	7	4	11	0
86-87—	Rochester	AHL	55	18	13	31	11	15	12	3	15	2
87-88—	Buffalo	NHL	74	38	27	65	14	6	1	1	2	2
88-89—	Buffalo	NHL	67	22	21	43	15	1	0	1	1	0
89-90—	Buffalo	NHL	18	4	2	6	0	—	—	—	—	—
	—Rochester	AHL	5	3	5	8	2	17	8	7	15	9
90-91—	New York Rangers	NHL	59	24	23	47	21	—	—	—	—	—
91-92—	Detroit	NHL	74	36	26	62	27	11	6	2	8	4
92-93—	Detroit	NHL	70	32	34	66	29	7	2	3	5	0
NHL totals			362	156	133	289	106	25	9	7	16	6

SHEVALIER, JEFF
LW/C, KINGS

PERSONAL: Born March 14, 1974, at Mississauga, Ont.... 5-11/178.... Shoots left.
HIGH SCHOOL: Chippewa Secondary School (North Bay, Ont.).
TRANSACTIONS/CAREER NOTES: Selected by Los Angeles Kings in fifth round (fourth Kings pick, 111th overall) of NHL entry draft (June 20, 1992).

Season	Team	League	REGULAR SEASON					PLAYOFFS				
			Gms.	G	A	Pts.	Pen.	Gms.	G	A	Pts.	Pen.
90-91—	Oakville Jr.B	OHA	5	1	4	5	0	—	—	—	—	—
	—Georgetown Jr. B	OHA	12	11	11	22	8	—	—	—	—	—
	—Acton Jr. C	OHA	28	29	31	60	62	—	—	—	—	—
91-92—	North Bay	OHL	64	28	29	57	26	21	5	11	16	25
92-93—	North Bay	OHL	62	59	54	113	46	2	1	2	3	4

SHOEBOTTOM, BRUCE
D

PERSONAL: Born August 20, 1965, at Windsor, Ont.... 6-2/200.... Shoots left.
TRANSACTIONS/CAREER NOTES: Broke leg (December 1982).... Selected by Los Angeles Kings as underage junior in third round (first Kings pick, 47th overall) of NHL entry draft (June 8, 1983).... Traded by Kings to Washington Capitals for RW Bryan Erickson (October 31, 1985).... Suspended by IHL for going into stands (January 24, 1987).... Signed as free agent by Boston Bruins (July 20, 1987).... Broke collarbone (April 1988).... Suffered facial lacerations (November 29, 1989).... Suspended 10 games by AHL for physically abusing linesman (November 17, 1990); suspension later reduced to five games.

Season	Team	League	REGULAR SEASON					PLAYOFFS				
			Gms.	G	A	Pts.	Pen.	Gms.	G	A	Pts.	Pen.
81-82—	Peterborough	OHL	51	0	4	4	67	—	—	—	—	—
82-83—	Peterborough	OHL	34	2	10	12	106	—	—	—	—	—
83-84—	Peterborough	OHL	16	0	5	5	73	—	—	—	—	—
84-85—	Peterborough	OHL	60	2	15	17	143	17	0	4	4	26
85-86—	New Haven	AHL	6	2	0	2	12	—	—	—	—	—
	—Binghamton	AHL	62	7	5	12	249	—	—	—	—	—
86-87—	Fort Wayne	IHL	75	2	10	12	309	10	0	0	0	31
87-88—	Maine	AHL	70	2	12	14	138	—	—	—	—	—
	—Boston	NHL	3	0	1	1	0	4	1	0	1	42
88-89—	Maine	AHL	44	0	8	8	265	—	—	—	—	—
	—Boston	NHL	29	1	3	4	44	10	0	2	2	35
89-90—	Maine	AHL	66	3	11	14	228	—	—	—	—	—
	—Boston	NHL	2	0	0	0	4	—	—	—	—	—
90-91—	Maine	AHL	71	2	8	10	238	1	0	0	0	14
	—Boston	NHL	1	0	0	0	5	—	—	—	—	—
91-92—	Peoria	IHL	79	4	12	16	234	10	0	0	0	33
92-93—	Rochester	AHL	65	7	5	12	253	14	0	0	0	19
NHL totals			35	1	4	5	53	14	1	2	3	77

SHTALENKOV, MIKHAIL
G, MIGHTY DUCKS

PERSONAL: Born October 20, 1965, at Moscow, U.S.S.R.... 6-2/180.... Shoots left.
TRANSACTIONS/CAREER NOTES: Selected by Mighty Ducks of Anaheim in fifth round (fifth Mighty Ducks pick, 108th overall) of NHL entry draft (June 26, 1993).
HONORS: Named Soviet League Rookie of the Year (1986-87).... Won Garry F. Longman Memorial Trophy (1992-93).

Season	Team	League	Gms.	Min.	W	L	T	GA	SO	Avg.	Gms.	Min.	W	L	GA	SO	Avg.
					REGULAR SEASON								**PLAYOFFS**				
86-87—Dynamo Moscow	USSR	17	893	...	... ...		36	1	2.42	—	—	—	—	—	—	—
87-88—Dynamo Moscow	USSR	25	1302	...	... ...		72	1	3.32	—	—	—	—	—	—	—
88-89—Dynamo Moscow	USSR	4	80	...	... ...		3	0	2.25	—	—	—	—	—	—	—
89-90—Dynamo Moscow	USSR	6	20	...	... ...		1	0	3.00	—	—	—	—	—	—	—
90-91—Dynamo Moscow	USSR	31	1568	...	... ...		56	2	2.14	—	—	—	—	—	—	—
91-92—Dynamo Moscow	CIS	27	1268	...	... ...		45	1	2.13	—	—	—	—	—	—	—
92-93—Milwaukee	IHL	47	2669	26	14	5	135	2	3.03	3	209	1	1	11	0	3.16

SHUCHUK, GARY

RW/C, KINGS

PERSONAL: Born February 17, 1967, at Edmonton, Alta.... 5-11/191.... Shoots right.... Full name: Gary Robert Shuchuk.
COLLEGE: Wisconsin.
TRANSACTIONS/CAREER NOTES: Selected by Detroit Red Wings in NHL supplemental draft (June 10, 1988).... Traded by Red Wings with C Jimmy Carson and RW Marc Potvin to Los Angeles Kings for D Paul Coffey, RW Jim Hiller and C/LW Sylvain Couturier (January 29, 1993).... Hyperextended right elbow (February 20, 1993); missed four games.
HONORS: Named to NCAA All-America West first team (1989-90).... Won WCHA Most Valuable Player Award (1989-90).... Named to WCHA All-Star first team (1989-90).

Season	Team	League	Gms.	G	A	Pts.	Pen.	Gms.	G	A	Pts.	Pen.
				REGULAR SEASON					**PLAYOFFS**			
86-87—University of Wisconsin	WCHA	42	19	11	30	72	—	—	—	—	—
87-88—University of Wisconsin	WCHA	44	7	22	29	70	—	—	—	—	—
88-89—University of Wisconsin	WCHA	46	18	19	37	102	—	—	—	—	—
89-90—University of Wisconsin	WCHA	45	*41	39	*80	70	—	—	—	—	—
90-91—Detroit	NHL	6	1	2	3	6	3	0	0	0	0
—Adirondack	AHL	59	23	24	47	32	—	—	—	—	—
91-92—Adirondack	AHL	79	32	48	80	48	†19	4	9	13	18
92-93—Adirondack	AHL	47	24	53	77	66	—	—	—	—	—
—Los Angeles	NHL	25	2	4	6	16	17	2	2	4	12
NHL totals		31	3	6	9	22	20	2	2	4	12

SHULMISTRA, RICH

G, NORDIQUES

PERSONAL: Born April 1, 1971, at Sudbury, Ont.... 6-2/186.
HIGH SCHOOL: LaSalle Secondary School (Kingston, Ont.).
COLLEGE: Miami of Ohio.
TRANSACTIONS/CAREER NOTES: Selected by Quebec Nordiques in NHL supplemental draft (June 19, 1992).
HONORS: Named to CCHA All-Star second team (1992-93).

Season	Team	League	Gms.	Min.	W	L	T	GA	SO	Avg.	Gms.	Min.	W	L	GA	SO	Avg.
					REGULAR SEASON								**PLAYOFFS**				
90-91—Miami of Ohio	CCHA	15	920	2	12	2	80	0	5.22	—	—	—	—	—	—	—
91-92—Miami of Ohio	CCHA	19	850	3	5	2	67	0	4.73	—	—	—	—	—	—	—
92-93—Miami of Ohio	CCHA	33	1949	22	6	4	88	...	2.71	—	—	—	—	—	—	—

SIDORKIEWICZ, PETER

G, DEVILS

PERSONAL: Born June 29, 1963, at Dabrown Bialostocka, Poland.... 5-9/180.... Shoots left.... Full name: Peter Paul Sidorkiewicz.... Name pronounced sih-DOHR-kih-VIHCH.
HIGH SCHOOL: O'Neill (Oshawa, Ont.).
TRANSACTIONS/CAREER NOTES: Selected by Washington Capitals as underage junior in fifth round (fifth Capitals pick, 91st overall) of NHL entry draft (June 10, 1981).... Sprained right ankle (March 3, 1991).... Traded by Capitals with C Dean Evason to Hartford Whalers for LW David Jensen (March 1985).... Selected by Ottawa Senators in NHL expansion draft (June 18, 1992).... Traded by Senators with future considerations to New Jersey Devils for G Craig Billington and C/LW Troy Mallette and fourth-round pick in 1993 draft (June 20, 1993); Senators sent LW Mike Peluso to Devils to complete deal (June 26, 1993).
HONORS: Shared Dave Pinkney Trophy with Jeff Hogg (1982-83).... Named to Memorial Cup All-Star team (1982-83).... Named to AHL All-Star second team (1986-87).... Named to NHL All-Rookie team (1988-89).... Played in NHL All-Star Game (1993).

Season	Team	League	Gms.	Min.	W	L	T	GA	SO	Avg.	Gms.	Min.	W	L	GA	SO	Avg.
					REGULAR SEASON								**PLAYOFFS**				
80-81—Oshawa	OMJHL	7	308	3	3	0	24	0	4.68	5	266	2	2	20	0	4.51
81-82—Oshawa	OHL	29	1553	14	11	1	123	*2	4.75	1	13	0	0	1	0	4.62
82-83—Oshawa	OHL	60	3536	36	20	3	213	0	3.61	*17	*1020	15	1	*60	0	3.53
83-84—Oshawa	OHL	52	2966	28	21	1	205	1	4.15	7	420	3	4	27	†1	3.86
84-85—Fort Wayne	IHL	10	590	4	4	2	43	0	4.37	—	—	—	—	—	—	—
—Binghamton	AHL	45	2691	31	9	5	137	3	3.05	8	481	4	4	31	0	3.87
85-86—Binghamton	AHL	49	2819	21	22	3	150	2	*3.19	4	235	1	3	12	0	3.06
86-87—Binghamton	AHL	57	3304	23	16	0	161	4	2.92	13	794	6	7	36	0	*2.72
87-88—Hartford	NHL	1	60	0	1	0	6	0	6.00	—	—	—	—	—	—	—
—Binghamton	AHL	42	2346	19	17	3	144	0	3.68	3	147	0	2	8	0	3.27
88-89—Hartford	NHL	44	2635	22	18	4	133	4	3.03	2	124	0	2	8	0	3.87
89-90—Hartford	NHL	46	2703	19	19	7	161	1	3.57	7	429	3	4	23	0	3.22
90-91—Hartford	NHL	52	2953	21	22	7	164	1	3.33	6	359	2	4	24	0	4.01
91-92—Hartford	NHL	35	1995	9	19	6	111	2	3.34	—	—	—	—	—	—	—

Season Team	League	REGULAR SEASON							PLAYOFFS						
		Gms.	Min.	W	L	T	GA	SO	Avg.	Gms.	Min.	W	L	GA	SO	Avg.
92-93—Ottawa	NHL	64	3388	8	*46	3	*250	0	4.43	—	—	—	—	—	—	—
NHL totals		242	13734	79	125	27	825	8	3.60	15	912	5	10	55	0	3.62

SILLINGER, MIKE
C, RED WINGS

PERSONAL: Born June 29, 1971, at Regina, Sask. . . . 5-10/191. . . . Shoots right. . . . Name pronounced SIHL-ihn-juhr.
TRANSACTIONS/CAREER NOTES: Selected by Detroit Red Wings in first round (first Red Wings pick, 11th overall) of NHL entry draft (June 17, 1989). . . . Fractured rib in training camp (September 1990). . . . Suffered from the flu (March 5, 1993); missed three games.
HONORS: Named to WHL All-Star second team (1989-90). . . . Named to WHL (East) All-Star first team (1990-91).

Season Team	League	REGULAR SEASON					PLAYOFFS				
		Gms.	G	A	Pts.	Pen.	Gms.	G	A	Pts.	Pen.
87-88—Regina	WHL	67	18	25	43	17	4	2	2	4	0
88-89—Regina	WHL	72	53	78	131	52	—	—	—	—	—
89-90—Regina	WHL	70	57	72	129	41	11	12	10	22	2
—Adirondack	AHL	—	—	—	—	—	1	0	0	0	0
90-91—Regina	WHL	57	50	66	116	42	8	6	9	15	4
—Detroit	NHL	3	0	1	1	0	3	0	1	1	0
91-92—Adirondack	AHL	64	25	41	66	26	15	9	*19	*28	12
—Detroit	NHL	—	—	—	—	—	8	2	2	4	2
92-93—Detroit	NHL	51	4	17	21	16	—	—	—	—	—
—Adirondack	AHL	15	10	20	30	31	11	5	13	18	10
NHL totals		54	4	18	22	16	11	2	3	5	2

SIMARD, MARTIN
RW, NORDIQUES

PERSONAL: Born June 25, 1966, at Montreal. . . . 6-3/215. . . . Shoots right.
TRANSACTIONS/CAREER NOTES: Signed as free agent by Calgary Flames (May 19, 1987). . . . Underwent surgery to right knee (September 26, 1988). . . . Suspended 10 games by IHL for fighting (December 11, 1988). . . . Underwent appendectomy (November 28, 1989). . . . Strained right knee (November 21, 1991). . . . Traded by Flames to Quebec Nordiques for D Greg Smyth (March 10, 1992). . . . Traded by Nordiques to Tampa Bay Lightning (September 14, 1992) to complete deal in which Lightning sent RW Tim Hunter to Nordiques (June 22, 1992). . . . Injured knee (November 3, 1992); missed 12 games. . . . Traded by Lightning with C Michel Mongeau and RW Steve Tuttle to Nordiques for RW Herb Raglan (February 12, 1993).

Season Team	League	REGULAR SEASON					PLAYOFFS				
		Gms.	G	A	Pts.	Pen.	Gms.	G	A	Pts.	Pen.
83-84—Quebec	QMJHL	59	6	10	16	26	—	—	—	—	—
84-85—Granby	QMJHL	58	22	31	53	78	—	—	—	—	—
85-86—Granby	QMJHL	54	32	28	60	129	—	—	—	—	—
—Hull	QMJHL	14	8	8	16	55	14	8	19	27	19
86-87—Granby	QMJHL	41	30	47	77	105	8	3	7	10	21
87-88—Salt Lake City	IHL	82	8	23	31	281	19	6	3	9	100
88-89—Salt Lake City	IHL	71	13	15	28	221	14	4	0	4	45
89-90—Salt Lake City	IHL	59	22	23	45	151	11	5	8	13	10
90-91—Calgary	NHL	16	0	2	2	53	—	—	—	—	—
—Salt Lake City	IHL	54	24	25	49	113	4	3	0	3	20
91-92—Salt Lake City	IHL	11	3	7	10	51	—	—	—	—	—
—Calgary	NHL	21	1	3	4	119	—	—	—	—	—
—Halifax	AHL	10	5	3	8	26	—	—	—	—	—
92-93—Tampa Bay	NHL	7	0	0	0	11	—	—	—	—	—
—Atlanta	IHL	19	5	5	10	77	—	—	—	—	—
—Halifax	AHL	13	3	4	7	17	—	—	—	—	—
NHL totals		44	1	5	6	183	—	—	—	—	—

SIMON, CHRIS
LW, NORDIQUES

PERSONAL: Born January 30, 1972, at Wawa, Ont. . . . 6-3/230. . . . Shoots left.
TRANSACTIONS/CAREER NOTES: Suspended six games by OHL for shooting the puck in frustration and striking another player (January 20, 1990). . . . Selected by Philadelphia Flyers in second round (second Flyers pick, 25th overall) of NHL entry draft (June 16, 1990). . . . Underwent surgery to repair left rotator cuff and a torn muscle (September 1990). . . . Traded by Flyers with first-round pick in 1994 draft to Quebec Nordiques (July 21, 1992) to complete deal in which Flyers sent G Ron Hextall, C Mike Ricci, C Peter Forsberg, D Steve Duchesne, first-round pick in 1993 draft (G Jocelyn Thibault) and cash to Nordiques for C Eric Lindros (June 20, 1992). . . . Suffered from the flu (March 13, 1993); missed one game.

Season Team	League	REGULAR SEASON					PLAYOFFS				
		Gms.	G	A	Pts.	Pen.	Gms.	G	A	Pts.	Pen.
87-88—Sault Ste. Marie	OHA	55	42	36	78	172	—	—	—	—	—
88-89—Ottawa	OHL	36	4	2	6	31	—	—	—	—	—
89-90—Ottawa	OHL	57	36	38	74	146	3	2	1	3	4
90-91—Ottawa	OHL	20	16	6	22	69	17	5	9	14	59
91-92—Ottawa	OHL	2	1	1	2	24	—	—	—	—	—
—Sault Ste. Marie	OHL	31	19	25	44	143	11	5	8	13	49
92-93—Halifax	AHL	36	12	6	18	131	—	—	—	—	—
—Quebec	NHL	16	1	1	2	67	5	0	0	0	26
NHL totals		16	1	1	2	67	5	0	0	0	26

SIMPSON, CRAIG
LW

PERSONAL: Born February 15, 1967, at London, Ont. . . . 6-2/195. . . . Shoots right. . . . Full name: Craig Andrew Simpson.
COLLEGE: Michigan State.
TRANSACTIONS/CAREER NOTES: Selected by Pittsburgh Penguins in first round (first Penguins pick, second overall) of NHL entry draft (June 15, 1985). . . . Pulled muscle in right hip (March 1987). . . . Sprained right wrist (March 14, 1987). . . . Traded by Penguins with C Dave Hannan, D Chris Joseph and D Moe Mantha to Edmonton Oilers for D Paul Coffey, LW Dave Hunter and RW Wayne Van Dorp (November 24, 1987). . . . Broke right ankle (December 4, 1988). . . . Suspended three games by NHL for injuring an opposing player (January 23, 1991). . . . Bruised chest (November 1991); missed one game. . . . Bruised shoulder (April 18, 1992). . . . Strained lower back (January 5, 1993); missed four games. . . . Strained lower back (February 23, 1993); missed three games. . . . Suffered protruded disk (March 1993); missed remainder of season. . . . Signed as free agent by San Jose Sharks (July 17, 1993). . . . Deal with Sharks invalidated by NHL (July 26, 1993).
HONORS: Named to NCAA All-America West first team (1984-85). . . . Named to CCHA All-Star first team (1984-85).
MISCELLANEOUS: Member of Stanley Cup championship teams (1988 and 1990).

Season Team	League	REGULAR SEASON					PLAYOFFS				
		Gms.	G	A	Pts.	Pen.	Gms.	G	A	Pts.	Pen.
82-83—London Jr. B	OHA	...	48	63	*111	...	—	—	—	—	—
83-84—Michigan State	CCHA	30	8	28	36	22	—	—	—	—	—
84-85—Michigan State	CCHA	42	31	53	84	33	—	—	—	—	—
85-86—Pittsburgh	NHL	76	11	17	28	49	—	—	—	—	—
86-87—Pittsburgh	NHL	72	26	25	51	57	—	—	—	—	—
87-88—Pittsburgh	NHL	21	13	13	26	34	—	—	—	—	—
—Edmonton	NHL	59	43	21	64	43	19	13	6	19	26
88-89—Edmonton	NHL	66	35	41	76	80	7	2	0	2	10
89-90—Edmonton	NHL	80	29	32	61	180	22	*16	15	†31	8
90-91—Edmonton	NHL	75	30	27	57	66	18	5	11	16	12
91-92—Edmonton	NHL	79	24	37	61	80	1	0	0	0	0
92-93—Edmonton	NHL	60	24	22	46	36	—	—	—	—	—
NHL totals		588	235	235	470	625	67	36	32	68	56

SIMPSON, GEOFF
D, BRUINS

PERSONAL: Born March 6, 1969, at Victoria, B.C. . . . 6-1/180. . . . Shoots right. . . . Full name: Geoffrey Ronald Simpson.
COLLEGE: Northern Michigan.
TRANSACTIONS/CAREER NOTES: Broke ankle (February 1988). . . . Selected by Boston Bruins in 10th round (10th Bruins pick, 206th overall) of NHL entry draft (June 17, 1989).

Season Team	League	REGULAR SEASON					PLAYOFFS				
		Gms.	G	A	Pts.	Pen.	Gms.	G	A	Pts.	Pen.
86-87—Estevan	SJHL	62	5	16	21	145	—	—	—	—	—
87-88—Estevan	SJHL	58	9	28	37	151	—	—	—	—	—
88-89—Estevan	SJHL	63	20	53	73	57	—	—	—	—	—
89-90—Northern Michigan Univ.	WCHA	39	4	9	13	40	—	—	—	—	—
90-91—Northern Michigan Univ.	WCHA	44	2	15	17	27	—	—	—	—	—
91-92—Northern Michigan Univ.	WCHA	25	1	3	4	20	—	—	—	—	—
92-93—Northern Michigan Univ.	WCHA	43	8	14	22	18	—	—	—	—	—

SIMPSON, REID
LW, STARS

PERSONAL: Born May 21, 1969, at Flin Flon, Man. . . . 6-1/210. . . . Shoots left.
TRANSACTIONS/CAREER NOTES: Selected by Philadelphia Flyers in fourth round (third Flyers pick, 72nd overall) of NHL entry draft (June 17, 1989). . . . Signed as free agent by Minnesota North Stars (December 13, 1992). . . . North Stars franchise moved from Minnesota to Dallas and renamed Stars for 1993-94 season.

Season Team	League	REGULAR SEASON					PLAYOFFS				
		Gms.	G	A	Pts.	Pen.	Gms.	G	A	Pts.	Pen.
85-86—Flin Flon	MJHL	40	20	21	41	200	—	—	—	—	—
—New Westminster	WHL	2	0	0	0	0	—	—	—	—	—
86-87—Prince Albert	WHL	47	3	8	11	105	—	—	—	—	—
87-88—Prince Albert	WHL	72	13	14	27	164	10	1	0	1	43
88-89—Prince Albert	WHL	59	26	29	55	264	4	2	1	3	30
89-90—Prince Albert	WHL	29	15	17	32	121	14	4	7	11	34
—Hershey	AHL	28	2	2	4	175	—	—	—	—	—
90-91—Hershey	AHL	54	9	15	24	183	1	0	0	0	0
91-92—Hershey	AHL	60	11	7	18	145	—	—	—	—	—
—Philadelphia	NHL	1	0	0	0	0	—	—	—	—	—
92-93—Kalamazoo	IHL	45	5	5	10	193	—	—	—	—	—
—Minnesota	NHL	1	0	0	0	5	—	—	—	—	—
NHL totals		2	0	0	0	5					

SITTLER, RYAN
LW/C, FLYERS

PERSONAL: Born January 28, 1974, at London, Ont. . . . 6-2/185. . . . Shoots left. . . . Son of Darryl Sittler, Hall of Fame center, Toronto Maple Leafs, Philadelphia Flyers and Detroit Red Wings (1970-71 through 1984-85).
HIGH SCHOOL: Nichols School (Buffalo, N.Y.).
TRANSACTIONS/CAREER NOTES: Selected by Philadelphia Flyers in first round (first Flyers pick, seventh overall) of NHL entry draft (June 20, 1992).

Season	Team	League	REGULAR SEASON					PLAYOFFS				
			Gms.	G	A	Pts.	Pen.	Gms.	G	A	Pts.	Pen.
90-91—Nichols School		N.Y. H.S.	7	8	9	17	8	—	—	—	—	—
—Buffalo		AHAUS	20	25	34	59	26	—	—	—	—	—
91-92—Nichols School		N.Y. H.S.	21	19	29	48	38	—	—	—	—	—
—Buffalo		AHAUS	30	39	54	93	...	—	—	—	—	—
92-93—University of Michigan		CCHA	35	9	24	33	43	—	—	—	—	—

SJODIN, TOMMY
D, STARS

PERSONAL: Born August 13, 1965, at Sundsvall, Sweden. . . . 5-11/185. . . . Shoots right. . . . Name pronounced shoh-DEEN.
TRANSACTIONS/CAREER NOTES: Selected by Minnesota North Stars in 12th round (10th North Stars pick, 237th overall) of NHL entry draft (June 15, 1985). . . . Injured hand (December 19, 1992); missed one game. . . . Suffered chest contusion (March 14, 1993); missed one game. . . . North Stars franchise moved from Minnesota to Dallas and renamed Stars for 1993-94 season.
HONORS: Won Golden Puck Award (1991-92). . . . Named to Swedish League All-Star team (1991-92).

Season	Team	League	REGULAR SEASON					PLAYOFFS				
			Gms.	G	A	Pts.	Pen.	Gms.	G	A	Pts.	Pen.
87-88—Brynas		Sweden	40	6	9	15	28	—	—	—	—	—
88-89—Brynas		Sweden	40	8	11	19	54	—	—	—	—	—
89-90—Brynas		Sweden	40	14	14	28	46	5	0	0	0	2
90-91—Brynas		Sweden	38	12	17	29	79	—	—	—	—	—
91-92—Brynas		Sweden	40	6	16	22	46	—	—	—	—	—
—Swedish national team		Int'l	8	0	1	1	6	—	—	—	—	—
—Swedish Olympic Team		Int'l	8	4	1	5	2	—	—	—	—	—
92-93—Minnesota		NHL	77	7	29	36	30	—	—	—	—	—
NHL totals			**77**	**7**	**29**	**36**	**30**					

SKALDE, JARROD
C, MIGHTY DUCKS

PERSONAL: Born February 26, 1971, at Niagara Falls, Ont. . . . 6-0/170. . . . Shoots left. . . . Name pronounced SKAHL-dee.
TRANSACTIONS/CAREER NOTES: Selected by New Jersey Devils in second round (third Devils pick, 26th overall) of NHL entry draft (June 17, 1989). . . . Traded by Oshawa Generals to Belleville Bulls for RW Rob Pearson (November 18, 1990). . . . Selected by Mighty Ducks of Anaheim in NHL expansion draft (June 24, 1993).
HONORS: Named to OHL All-Star second team (1990-91).

Season	Team	League	REGULAR SEASON					PLAYOFFS				
			Gms.	G	A	Pts.	Pen.	Gms.	G	A	Pts.	Pen.
86-87—Fort Erie Jr. B		OHA	41	27	34	61	36	—	—	—	—	—
87-88—Oshawa		OHL	60	12	16	28	24	7	2	1	3	2
88-89—Oshawa		OHL	65	38	38	76	36	6	1	5	6	2
89-90—Oshawa		OHL	62	40	52	92	66	17	10	7	17	6
90-91—New Jersey		NHL	1	0	1	1	0	—	—	—	—	—
—Utica		AHL	3	3	2	5	0	—	—	—	—	—
—Oshawa		OHL	15	8	14	22	14	—	—	—	—	—
—Belleville		OHL	40	30	52	82	21	6	9	6	15	10
91-92—Utica		AHL	62	20	20	40	56	4	3	1	4	8
—New Jersey		NHL	15	2	4	6	4	—	—	—	—	—
92-93—Cincinnati		IHL	4	1	2	3	4	—	—	—	—	—
—Utica		AHL	59	21	39	60	76	5	0	2	2	19
—New Jersey		NHL	11	0	2	2	4	—	—	—	—	—
NHL totals			**27**	**2**	**7**	**9**	**8**					

SKRIKO, PETRI
RW

PERSONAL: Born March 12, 1962, at Laapeenranta, Finland. . . . 5-10/172. . . . Shoots left. . . . Name pronounced SKREE-koh.
TRANSACTIONS/CAREER NOTES: Selected by Vancouver Canucks in seventh round (seventh Canucks pick, 157th overall) of NHL entry draft (June 10, 1981). . . . Broke thumb (October 1984). . . . Bruised knee (October 1987). . . . Sprained ankle (January 1988). . . . Strained knee (December 1988). . . . Twisted knee (February 12, 1989). . . . Suffered from the flu (March 1990). . . . Traded by Canucks to Boston Bruins for second-round pick (C Mike Peca) in 1992 draft (January 16, 1991). . . . Traded by Bruins to Winnipeg Jets for LW Brent Ashton (October 29, 1991). . . . Signed as free agent by San Jose Sharks (August 27, 1992). . . . Pulled groin (October 28, 1992); missed three games. . . . Injured groin (November 12, 1992); missed three games. . . . Released by Sharks (November 30, 1992).
HONORS: Named Finland Rookie of the Year (1980-81). . . . Named to Finland All-Star team (1983-84).

Season	Team	League	REGULAR SEASON					PLAYOFFS				
			Gms.	G	A	Pts.	Pen.	Gms.	G	A	Pts.	Pen.
80-81—SaiPa		Finland	36	20	13	33	14	—	—	—	—	—
81-82—SaiPa		Finland	33	19	27	46	24	—	—	—	—	—
82-83—SaiPa		Finland	36	23	12	35	12	—	—	—	—	—
83-84—SaiPa		Finland	32	25	26	51	13	—	—	—	—	—
—Finland Olympic Team		Int'l	6	8	5	13	8	—	—	—	—	—
84-85—Vancouver		NHL	72	21	14	35	10	—	—	—	—	—
85-86—Vancouver		NHL	80	38	40	78	34	3	0	0	0	0
86-87—Vancouver		NHL	76	33	41	74	44	—	—	—	—	—
87-88—Vancouver		NHL	73	30	34	64	32	—	—	—	—	—
88-89—Vancouver		NHL	74	30	36	66	57	7	1	5	6	0

Season	Team	League	REGULAR SEASON Gms.	G	A	Pts.	Pen.	PLAYOFFS Gms.	G	A	Pts.	Pen.
89-90—Vancouver	NHL	77	15	33	48	36	—	—	—	—	—	
90-91—Vancouver	NHL	20	4	4	8	8	—	—	—	—	—	
—Boston	NHL	28	5	14	19	9	18	4	4	8	4	
91-92—Finland Olympic Team	Int'l	8	1	4	5	...	—	—	—	—	—	
—Boston	NHL	9	1	0	1	6	—	—	—	—	—	
—Winnipeg	NHL	15	2	3	5	4	—	—	—	—	—	
92-93—San Jose	NHL	17	4	3	7	6	—	—	—	—	—	
—Kiekko-Espoo	Finland	18	5	4	9	8	—	—	—	—	—	
NHL totals		541	183	222	405	246	28	5	9	14	4	

SKRUDLAND, BRIAN
C, PANTHERS

PERSONAL: Born July 31, 1963, at Peace River, Alta. . . . 6-0/196. . . . Shoots left. . . . Name pronounced SKROOD-luhnd. . . . Cousin of Barry Pederson, center, four NHL teams (1980-81 through 1991-92).

TRANSACTIONS/CAREER NOTES: Signed as free agent by Montreal Canadiens (August 1983). . . . Injured groin (February 1988). . . . Strained left knee ligaments (December 27, 1988). . . . Bruised right foot (January 1989). . . . Sprained right ankle (October 7, 1989); missed 21 games. . . . Pulled hip muscle (November 4, 1990); missed six games. . . . Broke foot (January 17, 1991); missed 14 games including All-Star game. . . . Broke left thumb (October 5, 1991); missed five games. . . . Sprained knee (October 26, 1991); missed 25 games. . . . Broke nose (January 25, 1992); missed eight games. . . . Tore right knee ligaments (October 6, 1992); missed 27 games. . . . Injured shoulder (January 14, 1993); missed one game. . . . Traded by Canadiens to Calgary Flames for RW Gary Leeman (January 28, 1993). . . . Sprained ankle (February 16, 1993); missed four games. . . . Broke thumb (March 2, 1993); missed 12 games. . . . Lacerated right ear (April 11, 1993); missed one game. . . . Selected by Florida Panthers in NHL expansion draft (June 24, 1993).

HONORS: Won Jack Butterfield Trophy (1984-85).

MISCELLANEOUS: Member of Stanley Cup championship team (1986).

Season	Team	League	REGULAR SEASON Gms.	G	A	Pts.	Pen.	PLAYOFFS Gms.	G	A	Pts.	Pen.
80-81—Saskatoon	WHL	66	15	27	42	97	—	—	—	—	—	
81-82—Saskatoon	WHL	71	27	29	56	135	5	0	1	1	2	
82-83—Saskatoon	WHL	71	35	59	94	42	6	1	3	4	19	
83-84—Nova Scotia	AHL	56	13	12	25	55	12	2	8	10	14	
84-85—Sherbrooke	AHL	70	22	28	50	109	17	9	8	17	23	
85-86—Montreal	NHL	65	9	13	22	57	20	2	4	6	76	
86-87—Montreal	NHL	79	11	17	28	107	14	1	5	6	29	
87-88—Montreal	NHL	79	12	24	36	112	11	1	5	6	24	
88-89—Montreal	NHL	71	12	29	41	84	21	3	7	10	40	
89-90—Montreal	NHL	59	11	31	42	56	11	3	5	8	30	
90-91—Montreal	NHL	57	15	19	34	85	13	3	10	13	42	
91-92—Montreal	NHL	42	3	3	6	36	11	1	1	2	20	
92-93—Montreal	NHL	23	5	3	8	55	—	—	—	—	—	
—Calgary	NHL	16	2	4	6	10	6	0	3	3	12	
NHL totals		491	80	143	223	602	107	14	40	54	273	

SLANEY, JOHN
D, CAPITALS

PERSONAL: Born February 7, 1972, at St. John's, Nfld. . . . 5-11/180. . . . Shoots left.

TRANSACTIONS/CAREER NOTES: Selected by Washington Capitals in first round (first Capitals pick, ninth overall) of NHL entry draft (June 16, 1990).

HONORS: Won Max Kaminsky Trophy (1989-90). . . . Named to OHL All-Star first team (1989-90). . . . Named to OHL All-Star second team (1990-91).

Season	Team	League	REGULAR SEASON Gms.	G	A	Pts.	Pen.	PLAYOFFS Gms.	G	A	Pts.	Pen.
88-89—Cornwall	OHL	66	16	43	59	23	18	8	16	24	10	
89-90—Cornwall	OHL	64	38	59	97	60	6	0	8	8	11	
90-91—Cornwall	OHL	34	21	25	46	28	—	—	—	—	—	
91-92—Cornwall	OHL	34	19	41	60	43	6	3	8	11	0	
—Baltimore	AHL	6	2	4	6	0	—	—	—	—	—	
92-93—Baltimore	AHL	79	20	46	66	60	7	0	7	7	8	

SLEGR, JIRI
D, CANUCKS

PERSONAL: Born May 30, 1971, at Litvinov, Czechoslovakia. . . . 5-11/190. . . . Shoots left. . . . Name pronounced SLAY-guhr. . . . Son of Jiri Bubla, defenseman, Vancouver Canucks (1981-82 through 1985-86).

TRANSACTIONS/CAREER NOTES: Selected by Vancouver Canucks in second round (third Canucks pick, 23rd overall) of NHL entry draft (June 16, 1990).

HONORS: Named to Czechoslovakian League All-Star team (1990-91).

Season	Team	League	REGULAR SEASON Gms.	G	A	Pts.	Pen.	PLAYOFFS Gms.	G	A	Pts.	Pen.
88-89—Litvinov	Czech.	8	0	0	0	...	—	—	—	—	—	
89-90—Litvinov	Czech.	51	4	15	19	...	—	—	—	—	—	
90-91—Litvinov	Czech.	39	10	33	43	26	—	—	—	—	—	
91-92—Litvinov	Czech.	38	7	22	29	30	—	—	—	—	—	
—Czech. Olympic Team	Int'l	8	1	1	2	...	—	—	—	—	—	

S

Season Team	League	REGULAR SEASON					PLAYOFFS				
		Gms.	G	A	Pts.	Pen.	Gms.	G	A	Pts.	Pen.
92-93—Vancouver	NHL	41	4	22	26	109	5	0	3	3	4
—Hamilton	AHL	21	4	14	18	42	—	—	—	—	—
NHL totals		41	4	22	26	109	5	0	3	3	4

SMAIL, DOUG
LW, SENATORS

PERSONAL: Born September 2, 1957, at Moose Jaw, Sask. . . . 5-9/175. . . . Shoots left.
COLLEGE: North Dakota.
TRANSACTIONS/CAREER NOTES: Signed as free agent by Winnipeg Jets (May 22, 1980). . . . Fractured jaw in practice (November 1980). . . . Fractured jaw (January 10, 1981). . . . Stretched knee ligaments (December 1983). . . . Pulled leg muscle (October 25, 1985); missed seven games. . . . Underwent arthroscopic knee surgery (September 1987). . . . Lacerated left calf (December 1988). . . . Fractured orbital bone near eye (February 13, 1989). . . . Traded by Jets to Minnesota North Stars for LW Don Barber and future draft considerations (November 7, 1990). . . . Signed as free agent by Quebec Nordiques (September 1991). . . . Pulled ligaments during preseason (September 1991); missed first 10 games of season. . . . Injured knee (February 22, 1992). . . . Signed as free agent by Ottawa Senators (August 29, 1992). . . . Injured groin (November 14, 1992); missed six games. . . . Loaned to San Diego Gulls (March 10, 1993).
HONORS: Named NCAA Tournament Most Valuable Player (1979-80). . . . Named to NCAA Tournament All-Team (1979-80). . . . Named to WCHA All-Star second team (1979-80). . . . Played in NHL All-Star Game (1990).
RECORDS: Shares NHL record for fastest goal at the start of a game—5 seconds (December 20, 1981).

Season Team	League	REGULAR SEASON					PLAYOFFS				
		Gms.	G	A	Pts.	Pen.	Gms.	G	A	Pts.	Pen.
77-78—Univ. of North Dakota	WCHA	38	22	28	50	52	—	—	—	—	—
78-79—Univ. of North Dakota	WCHA	35	24	34	58	46	—	—	—	—	—
79-80—Univ. of North Dakota	WCHA	40	43	44	87	70	—	—	—	—	—
80-81—Winnipeg	NHL	30	10	8	18	45	—	—	—	—	—
81-82—Winnipeg	NHL	72	17	18	35	55	4	0	0	0	0
82-83—Winnipeg	NHL	80	15	29	44	32	3	0	0	0	6
83-84—Winnipeg	NHL	66	20	17	37	62	3	0	1	1	7
84-85—Winnipeg	NHL	80	31	35	66	45	8	2	1	3	4
85-86—Winnipeg	NHL	73	16	26	42	32	3	1	0	1	0
86-87—Winnipeg	NHL	78	25	18	43	36	10	4	0	4	10
87-88—Winnipeg	NHL	71	15	16	31	34	5	1	0	1	22
88-89—Winnipeg	NHL	47	14	15	29	52	—	—	—	—	—
89-90—Winnipeg	NHL	79	25	24	49	63	5	1	0	1	0
90-91—Winnipeg	NHL	15	1	2	3	10	—	—	—	—	—
—Minnesota	NHL	57	7	13	20	38	1	0	0	0	0
91-92—Quebec	NHL	46	10	18	28	47	—	—	—	—	—
92-93—Ottawa	NHL	51	4	10	14	51	—	—	—	—	—
—San Diego	IHL	9	2	1	3	20	9	3	2	5	20
NHL totals		845	210	249	459	602	42	9	2	11	49

SMART, JASON
C, PENGUINS

PERSONAL: Born January 23, 1970, at Red Deer, B.C. . . . 6-4/215. . . . Shoots left.
TRANSACTIONS/CAREER NOTES: Injured shoulder (November 1986); missed 10 days. . . . Underwent shoulder surgery (May 1987). . . . Traded by Prince Albert Raiders to Brandon Wheat Kings for Graham Garden (December 1, 1988); refused to report to Wheat Kings and later dealt to Saskatoon Blades. . . . Selected by Pittsburgh Penguins in 12th round (13th Penguins pick, 247th overall) of NHL entry draft (June 17, 1989).

Season Team	League	REGULAR SEASON					PLAYOFFS				
		Gms.	G	A	Pts.	Pen.	Gms.	G	A	Pts.	Pen.
86-87—Prince Albert	WHL	57	9	22	31	62	8	3	3	6	8
87-88—Prince Albert	WHL	72	16	29	45	79	10	1	2	3	11
88-89—Prince Albert	WHL	12	1	3	4	31	—	—	—	—	—
—Saskatoon	WHL	36	6	17	23	33	8	1	6	7	16
89-90—Saskatoon	WHL	66	27	48	75	187	10	1	5	6	19
90-91—Albany	IHL	15	4	2	6	28	—	—	—	—	—
—Muskegon	IHL	36	12	27	39	55	5	0	3	3	11
91-92—Muskegon	IHL	45	10	14	24	49	—	—	—	—	—
92-93—Cleveland	IHL	78	12	36	48	151	3	0	0	0	0

SMEHLIK, RICHARD
D, SABRES

PERSONAL: Born January 23, 1970, at Ostrava, Czechoslovakia. . . . 6-3/208. . . . Shoots left.
TRANSACTIONS/CAREER NOTES: Selected by Buffalo Sabres in fifth round (third Sabres pick, 97th overall) of NHL entry draft (June 16, 1990). . . . Injured hip (October 30, 1992); missed two games.

Season Team	League	REGULAR SEASON					PLAYOFFS				
		Gms.	G	A	Pts.	Pen.	Gms.	G	A	Pts.	Pen.
89-90—Vitkovice	Czech.	43	4	3	7	. . .	—	—	—	—	—
90-91—Dukla Jihlava	Czech.	51	4	2	6	22	—	—	—	—	—
91-92—Vitkovice	Czech.	47	9	10	19	. . .	—	—	—	—	—
92-93—Buffalo	NHL	80	4	27	31	59	8	0	4	4	2
NHL totals		80	4	27	31	59	8	0	4	4	2

SMITH, BOBBY
C

PERSONAL: Born February 12, 1958, at North Sydney, N.S. . . . 6-4/210. . . . Shoots left. . . . Full name: Robert David Smith.
TRANSACTIONS/CAREER NOTES: Selected by Minnesota North Stars from Ottawa 67's in first round (first North Stars pick, first overall) of NHL amateur draft (June 15, 1978). . . . Fractured ankle; missed part of 1979-80 season. . . . Traded by North Stars to Montreal Canadiens for RW Mark Napier, C Keith Acton and third-round pick (C Kenneth Hodge) in 1984 draft (October 28, 1983). . . . Fractured jaw (December 1984). . . . Lost tooth (December 1, 1988). . . . Separated right shoulder (January 6, 1990); missed seven games. . . . Fractured jaw (February 4, 1990); missed 18 games. . . . Traded by Canadiens to North Stars for fourth-round pick in 1992 draft (D Louis Bernard) (August 7, 1990). . . . Suffered mouth injury (January 21, 1993); missed seven games. . . . Announced retirement (April 20, 1993).
HONORS: Won George Parsons Trophy (1976-77). . . . Named to OMJHL All-Star second team (1976-77). . . . Named to Memorial Cup All-Star team (1976-77). . . . Won Can.HL Player of the Year Award (1977-78). . . . Won Albert (Red) Tilson Memorial Trophy (1977-78). . . . Won Eddie Powers Memorial Trophy (1977-78). . . . Named to OMJHL All-Star first team (1977-78). . . . Won Calder Memorial Trophy (1978-79). . . . Named NHL Rookie of the Year by THE SPORTING NEWS (1978-79). . . . Played in NHL All-Star Game (1981, 1982, 1989 and 1991).
RECORDS: Shares NHL single-season playoff record for most game-winning goals—5 (1991).
MISCELLANEOUS: Member of Stanley Cup championship team (1986).

			REGULAR SEASON					PLAYOFFS			
Season Team	League	Gms.	G	A	Pts.	Pen.	Gms.	G	A	Pts.	Pen.
75-76—Ottawa	OHA Mj. Jr. A	62	24	34	58	21	—	—	—	—	—
76-77—Ottawa	OMJHL	64	*65	70	135	52	19	16	16	32	29
77-78—Ottawa	OMJHL	61	69	*123	*192	44	16	15	15	30	10
78-79—Minnesota	NHL	80	30	44	74	39	—	—	—	—	—
79-80—Minnesota	NHL	61	27	56	83	24	15	1	13	14	9
80-81—Minnesota	NHL	78	29	64	93	73	19	8	17	25	13
81-82—Minnesota	NHL	80	43	71	114	82	4	2	4	6	5
82-83—Minnesota	NHL	77	24	53	77	81	9	6	4	10	17
83-84—Minnesota	NHL	10	3	6	9	9	—	—	—	—	—
—Montreal	NHL	70	26	37	63	62	15	2	7	9	8
84-85—Montreal	NHL	65	16	40	56	59	12	5	6	11	30
85-86—Montreal	NHL	79	31	55	86	55	20	7	8	15	22
86-87—Montreal	NHL	80	28	47	75	72	17	9	9	18	19
87-88—Montreal	NHL	78	27	66	93	78	11	3	4	7	8
88-89—Montreal	NHL	80	32	51	83	69	21	11	8	19	46
89-90—Montreal	NHL	53	12	14	26	35	11	1	4	5	6
90-91—Minnesota	NHL	73	15	31	46	60	23	8	8	16	56
91-92—Minnesota	NHL	68	9	37	46	109	7	1	4	5	6
92-93—Minnesota	NHL	45	5	7	12	10	—	—	—	—	—
NHL totals		1077	357	679	1036	917	184	64	96	160	245

SMITH, DERRICK
LW, STARS

PERSONAL: Born January 22, 1965, at Scarborough, Ont. . . . 6-2/215. . . . Shoots left.
TRANSACTIONS/CAREER NOTES: Selected by Philadelphia Flyers as underage junior in third round (second Flyers pick, 44th overall) of NHL entry draft (June 8, 1983). . . . Bruised back (November 1987). . . . Bruised left shoulder (February 1989). . . . Fractured left foot during training camp (September 1989). . . . Sprained right ankle and developed an infected toe (October 30, 1989). . . . Injured ribs (February 20, 1990); missed six games. . . . Claimed by Minnesota North Stars on waivers (October 26, 1991). . . . Injured ankle (December 8, 1991); missed 20 games. . . . Separated shoulder (March 19, 1992); missed five games. . . . North Stars franchise moved from Minnesota to Dallas and renamed Stars for 1993-94 season.

			REGULAR SEASON					PLAYOFFS			
Season Team	League	Gms.	G	A	Pts.	Pen.	Gms.	G	A	Pts.	Pen.
82-83—Peterborough	OHL	70	16	19	35	47	—	—	—	—	—
83-84—Peterborough	OHL	70	30	36	66	31	8	4	4	8	7
84-85—Philadelphia	NHL	77	17	22	39	31	19	2	5	7	16
85-86—Philadelphia	NHL	69	6	6	12	57	4	0	0	0	10
86-87—Philadelphia	NHL	71	11	21	32	34	26	6	4	10	26
87-88—Philadelphia	NHL	76	16	8	24	104	7	0	0	0	6
88-89—Philadelphia	NHL	74	16	14	30	43	19	5	2	7	12
89-90—Philadelphia	NHL	55	3	6	9	32	—	—	—	—	—
90-91—Philadelphia	NHL	72	11	10	21	37	—	—	—	—	—
91-92—Minnesota	NHL	33	2	4	6	33	7	1	0	1	9
—Kalamazoo	IHL	6	1	5	6	4	—	—	—	—	—
92-93—Kalamazoo	IHL	52	22	13	35	43	—	—	—	—	—
—Minnesota	NHL	9	0	1	1	2	—	—	—	—	—
NHL totals		536	82	92	174	373	82	14	11	25	79

SMITH, GEOFF
D, OILERS

PERSONAL: Born March 7, 1969, at Edmonton, Alta. . . . 6-3/200. . . . Shoots left. . . . Full name: Geoff Arthur Smith.
HIGH SCHOOL: Harry Ainlay (Edmonton, Alta.).
COLLEGE: North Dakota.
TRANSACTIONS/CAREER NOTES: Selected by Edmonton Oilers in third round (third Oilers pick, 63rd overall) of NHL entry draft (June 13, 1987). . . . Fractured ankle (October 1988); missed first 10 games. . . . Left University of North Dakota and signed to play with Kamloops Blazers (January 1989). . . . Broke jaw (March 1989). . . . Pulled back muscle (February 8, 1991); missed eight games. . . . Bruised shoulder (April 26, 1992).
HONORS: Named to WHL All-Star first team (1988-89). . . . Named to NHL All-Rookie team (1989-90).
MISCELLANEOUS: Member of Stanley Cup championship team (1990).

Season Team	League	REGULAR SEASON Gms.	G	A	Pts.	Pen.	PLAYOFFS Gms.	G	A	Pts.	Pen.
86-87—St. Albert	AJHL	57	7	28	35	101	—	—	—	—	—
87-88—Univ. of North Dakota	WCHA	42	4	12	16	34	—	—	—	—	—
88-89—Kamloops	WHL	32	4	31	35	29	6	1	3	4	12
89-90—Edmonton	NHL	74	4	11	15	52	3	0	0	0	0
90-91—Edmonton	NHL	59	1	12	13	55	4	0	0	0	0
91-92—Edmonton	NHL	74	2	16	18	43	5	0	1	1	6
92-93—Edmonton	NHL	78	4	14	18	30	—	—	—	—	—
NHL totals		285	11	53	64	180	12	0	1	1	6

SMITH, JASON
D, DEVILS

PERSONAL: Born November 2, 1973, at Calgary, Alta.... 6-3/185.... Shoots right.
TRANSACTIONS/CAREER NOTES: Selected by New Jersey Devils in first round (first Devils pick, 18th overall) of NHL entry draft (June 20, 1992).
HONORS: Named to Can.HL All-Rookie team (1991-92).... Won Bill Hunter Trophy (1992-93).... Named to Can.HL All-Star first team (1992-93).... Named to WHL (East) All-Star first team (1992-93).

Season Team	League	REGULAR SEASON Gms.	G	A	Pts.	Pen.	PLAYOFFS Gms.	G	A	Pts.	Pen.
90-91—Calgary Canucks	AJHL	45	3	15	18	69	—	—	—	—	—
—Regina	WHL	2	0	0	0	7	—	—	—	—	—
91-92—Regina	WHL	62	9	29	38	168	—	—	—	—	—
92-93—Regina	WHL	64	14	52	66	175	13	4	8	12	39

SMITH, JASON
D, FLAMES

PERSONAL: Born November 19, 1974, at Calgary, Alta.... 6-4/218.... Shoots left.
COLLEGE: Princeton.
TRANSACTIONS/CAREER NOTES: Selected by Calgary Flames in fourth round (fourth Flames pick, 95th overall) of NHL entry draft (June 26, 1993).
HONORS: Named to ECAC Rookie All-Star team (1992-93).

Season Team	League	REGULAR SEASON Gms.	G	A	Pts.	Pen.	PLAYOFFS Gms.	G	A	Pts.	Pen.
91-92—Calgary Royals	AJHL	58	4	28	32	203	—	—	—	—	—
92-93—Princeton University	ECAC	28	5	4	9	94	—	—	—	—	—

SMITH, SANDY
RW, PENGUINS

PERSONAL: Born October 23, 1967, at Brainerd, Minn.... 5-11/200.... Shoots right.... Full name: James Sanford Smith.
HIGH SCHOOL: Brainerd (Minn.).
COLLEGE: Minnesota-Duluth.
TRANSACTIONS/CAREER NOTES: Tore knee ligaments (September 1985).... Selected by Pittsburgh Penguins in fifth round (fifth Penguins pick, 88th overall) of NHL entry draft (June 21, 1986).

Season Team	League	REGULAR SEASON Gms.	G	A	Pts.	Pen.	PLAYOFFS Gms.	G	A	Pts.	Pen.
84-85—Brainerd H.S.	Minn. H.S.	21	30	20	50	...	—	—	—	—	—
85-86—Brainerd H.S.	Minn. H.S.	17	28	22	50	...	—	—	—	—	—
86-87—Minnesota-Duluth	WCHA	35	3	3	6	26	—	—	—	—	—
87-88—Minnesota-Duluth	WCHA	41	22	9	31	47	—	—	—	—	—
88-89—Minnesota-Duluth	WCHA	40	6	16	22	75	—	—	—	—	—
89-90—Minnesota-Duluth	WCHA	39	15	16	31	53	—	—	—	—	—
—Muskegon	IHL	3	1	0	1	0	—	—	—	—	—
90-91—Muskegon	IHL	82	25	29	54	51	5	1	1	2	6
91-92—Muskegon	IHL	64	15	18	33	109	14	7	2	9	4
92-93—Cleveland	IHL	77	32	36	68	174	4	0	0	0	8

SMITH, STEVE
D, BLACKHAWKS

PERSONAL: Born April 30, 1963, at Glasgow, Scotland.... 6-4/215.... Shoots left.... Full name: James Stephen Smith.
TRANSACTIONS/CAREER NOTES: Selected by Edmonton Oilers as underage junior in sixth round (fifth Oilers pick, 111th overall) of NHL entry draft (June 10, 1981).... Strained right shoulder (November 1, 1985).... Pulled stomach muscle (February 1986).... Separated left shoulder (September 20, 1988).... Aggravated shoulder injury (October 1988).... Dislocated left shoulder and tore cartilage (January 2, 1989).... Underwent surgery to left shoulder (January 23, 1989); missed 45 games.... Traded by Oilers to Chicago Blackhawks for D Dave Manson and third-round pick in either 1992 or 1993 draft; Oilers used third-round pick in 1992 draft to select RW Kirk Maltby (September 26, 1991).... Pulled rib-cage muscle (December 31, 1991); missed three games.... Suffered strained back muscle (December 27, 1992); missed four games.
HONORS: Played in NHL All-Star Game (1991).
MISCELLANEOUS: Member of Stanley Cup championship teams (1987, 1988 and 1990).

Season Team	League	REGULAR SEASON Gms.	G	A	Pts.	Pen.	PLAYOFFS Gms.	G	A	Pts.	Pen.
80-81—London	OMJHL	62	4	12	16	141	—	—	—	—	—
81-82—London	OHL	58	10	36	46	207	4	1	2	3	13
82-83—London	OHL	50	6	35	41	133	3	1	0	1	10
—Moncton	AHL	2	0	0	0	0	—	—	—	—	—
83-84—Moncton	AHL	64	1	8	9	176	—	—	—	—	—
84-85—Nova Scotia	AHL	68	2	28	30	161	5	0	3	3	40
—Edmonton	NHL	2	0	0	0	2	—	—	—	—	—

Season Team	League	REGULAR SEASON					PLAYOFFS				
		Gms.	G	A	Pts.	Pen.	Gms.	G	A	Pts.	Pen.
85-86—Nova Scotia	AHL	4	0	2	2	11	—	—	—	—	—
—Edmonton	NHL	55	4	20	24	166	6	0	1	1	14
86-87—Edmonton	NHL	62	7	15	22	165	15	1	3	4	45
87-88—Edmonton	NHL	79	12	43	55	286	19	1	11	12	55
88-89—Edmonton	NHL	35	3	19	22	97	7	2	2	4	20
89-90—Edmonton	NHL	75	7	34	41	171	22	5	10	15	37
90-91—Edmonton	NHL	77	13	41	54	193	18	1	2	3	45
91-92—Chicago	NHL	76	9	21	30	304	18	1	11	12	16
92-93—Chicago	NHL	78	10	47	57	214	4	0	0	0	10
NHL totals		539	65	240	305	1598	109	11	40	51	242

SMOLINSKI, BRYAN
C, BRUINS

PERSONAL: Born December 27, 1971, at Toledo, O. . . . 6-0/185. . . . Shoots right. . . . Full name: Bryan Anthony Smolinski.
COLLEGE: Michigan State.
TRANSACTIONS/CAREER NOTES: Selected by Boston Bruins in first round (first Bruins pick, 21st overall) of NHL entry draft (June 16, 1990).
HONORS: Named to CCHA All-Rookie team (1989-90). . . . Named to NCAA All-America West first team (1992-93). . . . Named to CCHA All-Star first team (1992-93).

Season Team	League	REGULAR SEASON					PLAYOFFS				
		Gms.	G	A	Pts.	Pen.	Gms.	G	A	Pts.	Pen.
87-88—Detroit Little Caesars	MNHL	80	43	77	120	. . .	—	—	—	—	—
88-89—Stratford Jr. B	OHA	46	32	62	94	132	—	—	—	—	—
89-90—Michigan State	CCHA	39	10	17	27	45	—	—	—	—	—
90-91—Michigan State	CCHA	35	9	12	21	24	—	—	—	—	—
91-92—Michigan State	CCHA	44	30	35	65	59	—	—	—	—	—
92-93—Michigan State	CCHA	40	31	37	*68	93	—	—	—	—	—
—Boston	NHL	9	1	3	4	0	4	1	0	1	2
NHL totals		9	1	3	4	0	4	1	0	1	2

SMYTH, GREG
D, PANTHERS

PERSONAL: Born April 23, 1966, at Oakville, Ont. . . . 6-3/212. . . . Shoots right.
TRANSACTIONS/CAREER NOTES: Selected by Philadelphia Flyers as underage junior in second round (first Flyers pick, 22nd overall) of NHL entry draft (June 9, 1984). . . . Suspended 10 games by OHL for fighting with fans (December 1984). . . . Suspended by London Knights (October 1985). . . . Suspended eight games by OHL (November 7, 1985). . . . Traded by Flyers with third-round pick in 1989 draft (G John Tanner) to Quebec Nordiques for D Terry Carkner (July 25, 1988). . . . Broke two bones in right hand during training camp (September 1988). . . . Suspended eight games by AHL for fighting (December 17, 1988). . . . Injured back (February 15, 1990). . . . Recalled from Halifax by Quebec and refused to report (February 10, 1991). . . . Traded by Nordiques to Calgary Flames for RW Martin Simard (March 10, 1992). . . . Strained stomach (October 6, 1992); missed first four games of season. . . . Injured ribs (December 4, 1992); missed four games. . . . Signed as free agent by Florida Panthers (July 14, 1993).
HONORS: Named to OHL All-Star second team (1985-86).

Season Team	League	REGULAR SEASON					PLAYOFFS				
		Gms.	G	A	Pts.	Pen.	Gms.	G	A	Pts.	Pen.
83-84—London	OHL	64	4	21	25	*252	6	1	0	1	24
84-85—London	OHL	47	7	16	23	188	8	2	2	4	27
85-86—London	OHL	46	12	42	54	197	4	1	2	3	28
—Hershey	AHL	2	0	1	1	5	8	0	0	0	60
86-87—Hershey	AHL	35	0	2	2	158	2	0	0	0	19
—Philadelphia	NHL	1	0	0	0	0	1	0	0	0	2
87-88—Hershey	AHL	21	0	10	10	102	—	—	—	—	—
—Philadelphia	NHL	48	1	6	7	192	5	0	0	0	38
88-89—Halifax	AHL	43	3	9	12	310	4	0	1	1	35
—Quebec	NHL	10	0	1	1	70	—	—	—	—	—
89-90—Quebec	NHL	13	0	0	0	57	—	—	—	—	—
—Halifax	AHL	49	5	14	19	235	6	1	0	1	52
90-91—Quebec	NHL	1	0	0	0	0	—	—	—	—	—
—Halifax	AHL	56	6	23	29	340	—	—	—	—	—
91-92—Quebec	NHL	29	0	2	2	138	—	—	—	—	—
—Halifax	AHL	9	1	3	4	35	—	—	—	—	—
—Calgary	NHL	7	1	1	2	15	—	—	—	—	—
92-93—Calgary	NHL	35	1	2	3	95	—	—	—	—	—
—Salt Lake City	IHL	5	0	1	1	31	—	—	—	—	—
NHL totals		144	3	12	15	567	6	0	0	0	40

SMYTH, KEVIN
LW, WHALERS

PERSONAL: Born November 22, 1973, at Banff, Alta. . . . 6-2/210. . . . Shoots left.
TRANSACTIONS/CAREER NOTES: Selected by Hartford Whalers in fourth round (fourth Whalers pick, 79th overall) of NHL entry draft (June 20, 1992).

Season Team	League	REGULAR SEASON					PLAYOFFS				
		Gms.	G	A	Pts.	Pen.	Gms.	G	A	Pts.	Pen.
90-91—Moose Jaw	WHL	66	30	45	75	96	6	1	1	2	0
91-92—Moose Jaw	WHL	71	30	55	85	114	4	1	3	4	6
92-93—Moose Jaw	WHL	64	44	38	82	111	—	—	—	—	—

SNOW, GARTH
G, NORDIQUES

PERSONAL: Born July 28, 1969, at Wrentham, Mass. . . . 6-3/200.
HIGH SCHOOL: Mount St. Charles Academy (Woonsocket, R.I.).
COLLEGE: Maine.
TRANSACTIONS/CAREER NOTES: Selected by Quebec Nordiques in sixth round (sixth Nordiques pick, 114th overall) of NHL entry draft (June 13, 1987).
HONORS: Named to NCAA All-Tournament team (1992-93). . . . Named to Hockey East All-Star second team (1992-93).

						REGULAR SEASON							PLAYOFFS				
Season	Team	League	Gms.	Min.	W	L	T	GA	SO	Avg.	Gms.	Min.	W	L	GA	SO	Avg.
88-89—University of Maine		Hoc. East	5	241	2	2	0	14	1	3.49	—	—	—	—	—	—	—
89-90—University of Maine		Hoc. East							Did not play.			—	—	—	—	—	—	—
90-91—University of Maine		Hoc. East	25	1290	18	4	0	64	0	2.98	—	—	—	—	—	—	—
91-92—University of Maine		Hoc. East	31	1792	25	4	2	73	2	2.44	—	—	—	—	—	—	—
92-93—University of Maine		Hoc. East	23	1210	21	0	1	42	1	2.08	—	—	—	—	—	—	—

SNUGGERUD, DAVE
LW

PERSONAL: Born June 20, 1966, at Minnetonka, Minn. . . . 6-0/170. . . . Shoots left. . . . Name pronounced SNUHG-uhr-ROOD.
COLLEGE: Minnesota.
TRANSACTIONS/CAREER NOTES: Selected by Buffalo Sabres in NHL supplemental draft (June 13, 1987). . . . Injured knee (January 3, 1992); missed eight games. . . . Traded by Sabres to San Jose Sharks for RW Wayne Presley (March 9, 1992). . . . Bruised foot (December 5, 1992); missed two games. . . . Traded by Sharks to Philadelphia Flyers for LW Mark Pederson (December 19, 1992).
HONORS: Named to USHL All-Star second team (1984-85). . . . Named to NCAA All-America West second team (1988-89). . . . Named to WCHA All-Star second team (1988-89).

				REGULAR SEASON					PLAYOFFS			
Season	Team	League	Gms.	G	A	Pts.	Pen.	Gms.	G	A	Pts.	Pen.
84-85—Minneapolis		USHL	48	38	35	73	26	—	—	—	—	—
85-86—University of Minnesota ...		WCHA	42	14	18	32	47	—	—	—	—	—
86-87—University of Minnesota ...		WCHA	39	30	29	59	38	—	—	—	—	—
87-88—U.S. national team		Int'l	51	14	21	35	26	—	—	—	—	—
—U.S. Olympic Team		Int'l	6	3	2	5	4	—	—	—	—	—
88-89—University of Minnesota ...		WCHA	45	29	20	49	39	—	—	—	—	—
89-90—Buffalo		NHL	80	14	16	30	41	6	0	0	0	2
90-91—Buffalo		NHL	80	9	15	24	32	6	1	3	4	4
91-92—Buffalo		NHL	55	3	15	18	36	—	—	—	—	—
—San Jose		NHL	11	0	1	1	4	—	—	—	—	—
92-93—San Jose		NHL	25	4	5	9	14	—	—	—	—	—
—Philadelphia		NHL	14	0	2	2	0	—	—	—	—	—
NHL totals			265	30	54	84	127	12	1	3	4	6

SODERSTROM, TOMMY
G, FLYERS

PERSONAL: Born July 17, 1969, at Stockholm, Swe. . . . 5-9/163. . . . Name pronounced SAH-duhr-STRUHM.
TRANSACTIONS/CAREER NOTES: Selected by Philadelphia Flyers in 11th round (14th Flyers pick, 214th overall) of NHL entry draft (June 16, 1990).
HONORS: Named Swedish League Rookie of the Year (1990-91). . . . Named to Swedish League All-Star team (1991-92).

						REGULAR SEASON							PLAYOFFS			
Season	Team	League	Gms.	Min.	W	L	T	GA	SO	Avg.	Gms.	Min.	W	L	GA	SO	Avg.
89-90—Djurgarden		Sweden	4	240	...	...	...	14	0	3.50	—	—	—	—	—	—	—
90-91—Djurgarden		Sweden	39	2340	22	12	6	104	3	2.67	7	423	...	...	...	10	2	1.42
91-92—Djurgarden		Sweden	31	2357	15	8	11	112	...	2.85	—	—	—	—	—	—	—
—Swedish Olympic Team		Int'l	5	296	...	...	...	13	0	2.64	—	—	—	—	—	—	—
92-93—Hershey		AHL	7	373	4	1	0	15	0	2.41	—	—	—	—	—	—	—
—Philadelphia		NHL	44	2512	20	17	6	143	5	3.42	—	—	—	—	—	—	—
NHL totals			44	2512	20	17	6	143	5	3.42							

SOROCHAN, LEE
D, RANGERS

PERSONAL: Born September 9, 1975, at Edmonton, Alta. . . . 5-11/208. . . . Shoots left.
HIGH SCHOOL: Gibbons (Alta.).
TRANSACTIONS/CAREER NOTES: Selected by New York Rangers in second round (second Rangers pick, 34th overall) of NHL entry draft (June 26, 1993).

				REGULAR SEASON					PLAYOFFS			
Season	Team	League	Gms.	G	A	Pts.	Pen.	Gms.	G	A	Pts.	Pen.
91-92—Lethbridge		WHL	67	2	9	11	105	5	0	2	2	6
92-93—Lethbridge		WHL	69	8	32	40	208	4	0	1	1	12

SOUCY, CHRISTIAN
G, BLACKHAWKS

PERSONAL: Born September 14, 1970, at Gatineau, Que. . . . 5-11/160. . . . Shoots left.
COLLEGE: Vermont.
TRANSACTIONS/CAREER NOTES: Signed as free agent by Chicago Blackhawks (June 21, 1993).
HONORS: Named to NCAA All-America East second team (1991-92). . . . Named to ECAC All-Star second team (1992-93).

						REGULAR SEASON							PLAYOFFS			
Season	Team	League	Gms.	Min.	W	L	T	GA	SO	Avg.	Gms.	Min.	W	L	GA	SO	Avg.
89-90—Pembroke		CJHL	47	2721	16	24	4	212	1	4.67	—	—	—	—	—	—	—

Season Team	League	Gms.	Min.	W	L	T	GA	SO	Avg.	Gms.	Min.	W	L	GA	SO	Avg.
90-91—Pembroke	CJHL	54	3109	27	24	1	198	2	3.82	—	—	—	—	—	—	—
91-92—University of Vermont ..	ECAC	30	1783	15	11	3	84	1	2.83	—	—	—	—	—	—	—
92-93—University of Vermont ..	ECAC	29	1711	11	15	3	90	2	3.16	—	—	—	—	—	—	—

SPEER, MIKE
D, BLACKHAWKS

PERSONAL: Born March 26, 1971, at Toronto.... 6-2/202.... Shoots left.
TRANSACTIONS/CAREER NOTES: Selected by Chicago Blackhawks in second round (second Black-hawks pick, 27th overall) of NHL entry draft (June 17, 1989).... Traded by Owen Sound Platers to Windsor Spitfires for D Rick Morton (January 10, 1991).

Season Team	League	Gms.	G	A	Pts.	Pen.	Gms.	G	A	Pts.	Pen.
87-88—Guelph	OHL	53	4	10	14	60	—	—	—	—	—
88-89—Guelph	OHL	65	9	31	40	185	7	2	4	6	23
89-90—Owen Sound	OHL	61	18	39	57	176	12	3	7	10	21
90-91—Owen Sound	OHL	32	13	19	32	86	—	—	—	—	—
—Windsor...........................	OHL	25	8	28	36	40	11	2	7	9	15
—Indianapolis	IHL	1	0	1	1	0	1	0	0	0	5
91-92—Indianapolis	IHL	54	0	6	6	67	—	—	—	—	—
92-93—Indianapolis	IHL	38	1	1	2	109	5	1	0	1	26

SPENRATH, GREG
LW

PERSONAL: Born September 27, 1969, at Edmonton, Alta.... 6-1/212.... Shoots left.
TRANSACTIONS/CAREER NOTES: Selected by New York Rangers in eighth round (ninth Rangers pick, 160th overall) of NHL entry draft (June 17, 1989).... Signed as free agent by Minnesota North Stars (July 25, 1991).... North Stars franchise moved from Minnesota to Dallas and renamed Stars for 1993-94 season.

Season Team	League	Gms.	G	A	Pts.	Pen.	Gms.	G	A	Pts.	Pen.
87-88—New Westminster	WHL	72	18	24	42	210	5	0	4	4	16
88-89—Tri-City	WHL	64	26	35	61	213	7	4	2	6	23
89-90—Tri-City	WHL	67	36	32	68	256	7	1	0	1	15
90-91—Binghamton	AHL	2	0	0	0	14	—	—	—	—	—
—Erie	ECHL	61	29	36	65	*407	4	1	2	3	46
91-92—Kalamazoo	IHL	69	4	7	11	237	—	—	—	—	—
92-93—Erie	ECHL	55	17	28	45	344	3	1	0	1	77
—Indianapolis	IHL	9	0	1	1	68	1	0	0	0	5
—Binghamton	AHL	1	0	0	0	2	—	—	—	—	—

SPITZIG, TIM
RW, RED WINGS

PERSONAL: Born April 15, 1974, at Goderich, Ont.... 6-0/195.... Shoots right.
TRANSACTIONS/CAREER NOTES: Selected by Detroit Red Wings in sixth round (seventh Red Wings pick, 152nd overall) of NHL entry draft (June 26, 1993).

Season Team	League	Gms.	G	A	Pts.	Pen.	Gms.	G	A	Pts.	Pen.
91-92—Kitchener..........................	OHL	62	8	13	21	87	4	0	0	0	2
92-93—Kitchener..........................	OHL	66	39	39	78	127	—	—	—	—	—

STAIOS, STEVE
D, BLUES

PERSONAL: Born July 28, 1973, at Hamilton, Ont.... 6-0/183.... Shoots right.... Name pronounced STAY-ohz.
TRANSACTIONS/CAREER NOTES: Selected by St. Louis Blues in second round (first Blues pick, 27th overall) of NHL entry draft (June 22, 1991).

Season Team	League	Gms.	G	A	Pts.	Pen.	Gms.	G	A	Pts.	Pen.
89-90—Hamilton Jr. B	OHA	40	9	27	36	66	—	—	—	—	—
90-91—Niagara Falls	OHL	66	17	29	46	115	12	2	3	5	10
91-92—Niagara Falls	OHL	65	11	42	53	122	17	7	8	15	27
92-93—Niagara Falls	OHL	12	4	14	18	30	—	—	—	—	—
—Sudbury...........................	OHL	53	13	44	57	67	11	5	6	11	22

STAJDUHAR, NICK
D, OILERS

PERSONAL: Born December 6, 1974, at Kitchener, Ont.... 6-2/194.... Shoots left.
TRANSACTIONS/CAREER NOTES: Selected by Edmonton Oilers in first round (second Oilers pick, 16th overall) of NHL entry draft (June 26, 1993).

Season Team	League	Gms.	G	A	Pts.	Pen.	Gms.	G	A	Pts.	Pen.
90-91—London	OHL	66	3	12	15	39	7	0	0	0	2
91-92—London	OHL	66	6	15	21	62	10	1	4	5	10
92-93—London	OHL	49	15	46	61	58	12	4	11	15	10

ST. AMOUR, MARTIN
LW, SENATORS

PERSONAL: Born January 30, 1970, at Montreal.... 6-2/195.... Shoots left.
TRANSACTIONS/CAREER NOTES: Selected by Montreal Canadiens in second round (second Canadiens pick, 34th overall) of NHL entry draft (June 11, 1988)....
Signed as free agent by Ottawa Senators (July 16, 1992).

Season	Team	League	REGULAR SEASON					PLAYOFFS				
			Gms.	G	A	Pts.	Pen.	Gms.	G	A	Pts.	Pen.
87-88—Verdun	QMJHL	61	20	50	70	111	—	—	—	—	—
88-89—Verdun	QMJHL	28	19	17	36	87	—	—	—	—	—
—Trois-Rivieres	QMJHL	26	8	21	29	69	4	1	2	3	0
89-90—Trois-Rivieres	QMJHL	60	57	79	136	162	7	7	9	16	19
—Sherbrooke	AHL	—	—	—	—	—	1	0	0	0	0
90-91—Fredericton	AHL	45	13	16	29	51	1	0	0	0	0
91-92—Cincinnati	ECHL	60	44	44	88	183	9	4	9	13	18
92-93—New Haven	AHL	71	21	39	60	78	—	—	—	—	—
—Ottawa	NHL	1	0	0	0	2	—	—	—	—	—
NHL totals		1	0	0	0	2					

STANTON, PAUL
D, PENGUINS

PERSONAL: Born June 22, 1967, at Boston. . . . 6-1/200. . . . Shoots right. . . . Full name: Paul Fredrick Stanton.
HIGH SCHOOL: Catholic Memorial (Boston).
COLLEGE: Wisconsin.
TRANSACTIONS/CAREER NOTES: Selected by Pittsburgh Penguins in eighth round (eighth Penguins pick, 149th overall) of NHL entry draft (June 15, 1985). . . . Injured knee ligament (October 31, 1991); missed 16 games.
HONORS: Named to NCAA All-America West first team (1987-88). . . . Named to WCHA All-Star first team (1988-89).
MISCELLANEOUS: Member of Stanley Cup championship teams (1991 and 1992).

Season	Team	League	REGULAR SEASON					PLAYOFFS				
			Gms.	G	A	Pts.	Pen.	Gms.	G	A	Pts.	Pen.
83-84—Catholic Memorial H.S.	Mass. H.S.	...	15	20	35	...	—	—	—	—	—
84-85—Catholic Memorial H.S.	Mass. H.S.	20	16	21	37	17	—	—	—	—	—
85-86—University of Wisconsin	WCHA	36	4	6	10	16	—	—	—	—	—
86-87—University of Wisconsin	WCHA	41	5	17	22	70	—	—	—	—	—
87-88—University of Wisconsin	WCHA	45	9	38	47	98	—	—	—	—	—
88-89—University of Wisconsin	WCHA	45	7	29	36	126	—	—	—	—	—
89-90—Muskegon	IHL	77	5	27	32	61	15	2	4	6	21
90-91—Pittsburgh	NHL	75	5	18	23	40	22	1	2	3	24
91-92—Pittsburgh	NHL	54	2	8	10	62	†21	1	7	8	42
92-93—Pittsburgh	NHL	77	4	12	16	97	1	0	1	1	0
NHL totals		206	11	38	49	199	44	2	10	12	66

STAPLETON, MIKE
C, PENGUINS

PERSONAL: Born May 5, 1966, at Sarnia, Ont. . . . 5-10/183. . . . Shoots right. . . . Son of Pat Stapleton, defenseman, Boston Bruins and Chicago Blackhawks (1961-62 through 1972-73); and Chicago Cougars, Indianapolis Racers and Cincinnati Stingers of WHA (1973-74 through 1977-78).
TRANSACTIONS/CAREER NOTES: Selected by Chicago Blackhawks in seventh round (seventh Blackhawks pick, 132nd overall) of NHL entry draft (June 9, 1984). . . . Signed as free agent by Pittsburgh Penguins (September 4, 1992).

Season	Team	League	REGULAR SEASON					PLAYOFFS				
			Gms.	G	A	Pts.	Pen.	Gms.	G	A	Pts.	Pen.
82-83—Strathroy Jr. B	OHA	40	39	38	77	99	—	—	—	—	—
83-84—Cornwall	OHL	70	24	45	69	94	3	1	2	3	4
84-85—Cornwall	OHL	56	41	44	85	68	9	2	4	6	23
85-86—Cornwall	OHL	56	39	65	104	74	6	2	3	5	2
86-87—Canadian national team	Int'l	21	2	4	6	4	—	—	—	—	—
—Chicago	NHL	39	3	6	9	6	4	0	0	0	2
87-88—Saginaw	IHL	31	11	19	30	52	10	5	6	11	10
—Chicago	NHL	53	2	9	11	59	—	—	—	—	—
88-89—Chicago	NHL	7	0	1	1	7	—	—	—	—	—
—Saginaw	IHL	69	21	47	68	162	6	1	3	4	4
89-90—Arvika	Sweden	30	15	18	33	...	—	—	—	—	—
—Indianapolis	IHL	16	5	10	15	6	13	9	10	19	38
90-91—Chicago	NHL	7	0	1	1	2	—	—	—	—	—
—Indianapolis	IHL	75	29	52	81	76	7	1	4	5	0
91-92—Indianapolis	IHL	59	18	40	58	65	—	—	—	—	—
—Chicago	NHL	19	4	4	8	8	—	—	—	—	—
92-93—Pittsburgh	NHL	78	4	9	13	10	4	0	0	0	0
NHL totals		203	13	30	43	92	8	0	0	0	2

STARIKOV, SERGEI
D

PERSONAL: Born December 4, 1958, at Chelyabinsk, U.S.S.R. . . . 5-11/215. . . . Shoots left.
TRANSACTIONS/CAREER NOTES: Selected by New Jersey Devils in eighth round (seventh Devils pick, 152nd overall) of NHL entry draft (June 17, 1989). . . . Signed as free agent by San Diego Gulls (July 17, 1992).
MISCELLANEOUS: Member of silver-medal-winning U.S.S.R. Olympic team (1980) and gold-medal-winning U.S.S.R. Olympic team (1984 and 1988).

Season	Team	League	REGULAR SEASON					PLAYOFFS				
			Gms.	G	A	Pts.	Pen.	Gms.	G	A	Pts.	Pen.
76-77—Traktor Chelyabinsk	USSR	35	2	4	6	28	—	—	—	—	—
77-78—Traktor Chelyabinsk	USSR	36	3	5	8	26	—	—	—	—	—

Season Team	League	REGULAR SEASON					PLAYOFFS				
		Gms.	G	A	Pts.	Pen.	Gms.	G	A	Pts.	Pen.
78-79—Traktor Chelyabinsk........	USSR	44	6	8	14	34	—	—	—	—	—
79-80—CSKA Moscow..................	USSR	39	10	8	18	14	—	—	—	—	—
—Soviet Olympic Team........	Int'l	7	1	6	7	0	—	—	—	—	—
80-81—CSKA Moscow..................	USSR	49	4	8	12	26	—	—	—	—	—
81-82—CSKA Moscow..................	USSR	40	1	4	5	14	—	—	—	—	—
82-83—CSKA Moscow..................	USSR	44	6	14	20	14	—	—	—	—	—
83-84—CSKA Moscow..................	USSR	44	11	7	18	20	—	—	—	—	—
—Soviet Olympic Team........	Int'l	7	1	1	2	2	—	—	—	—	—
84-85—CSKA Moscow..................	USSR	40	3	10	13	12	—	—	—	—	—
85-86—CSKA Moscow..................	USSR	37	3	2	5	6	—	—	—	—	—
86-87—CSKA Moscow..................	USSR	34	4	2	6	8	—	—	—	—	—
87-88—CSKA Moscow..................	USSR	38	2	11	13	12	—	—	—	—	—
88-89—CSKA Moscow..................	USSR	30	3	3	6	4	—	—	—	—	—
89-90—Utica..........................	AHL	43	8	11	19	14	4	0	3	3	0
—New Jersey......................	NHL	16	0	1	1	8	—	—	—	—	—
90-91—Utica..........................	AHL	51	2	7	9	26	—	—	—	—	—
91-92—San Diego	IHL	70	7	31	38	42	4	0	0	0	0
92-93—San Diego	IHL	42	0	9	9	12	—	—	—	—	—
NHL totals................................		16	0	1	1	8					

STASTNY, PETER

C

PERSONAL: Born September 18, 1956, at Bratislava, Czechoslovakia. . . . 6-1/200. . . . Shoots left. . . . Name pronounced STAST-nee. . . . Brother of Anton Stastny, left winger, Quebec Nordiques (1980-81 through 1988-89); and brother of Marian Stastny, right winger, Quebec Nordiques and Toronto Maple Leafs (1981-82 through 1985-86).

TRANSACTIONS/CAREER NOTES: Signed as free agent by Quebec Nordiques (August 26, 1980). . . . Injured knee (December 18, 1982). . . . Suspended five games by NHL (October 1984). . . . Injured lower back (November 1987). . . . Sprained left shoulder (December 1988). . . . Suffered sore left knee (December 1989). . . . Traded by Nordiques to New Jersey Devils for D Craig Wolanin and future considerations (D Randy Velischek was sent to Quebec in August 1990) (March 6, 1990). . . . Suffered from digestive virus (February 29, 1992); missed eight games. . . . Suffered from minor knee sprain and the flu (March 21, 1992); missed five games. . . . Missed first five games of regular season due to contract dispute (October 1992). . . . Suffered from the flu (January 22, 1993); missed two games. . . . Bruised shoulder (March 7, 1993); missed one game.

HONORS: Named to Czechoslovakian League All-Star second team (1977-78). . . . Named to Czechoslovakian League All-Star first team (1978-79). . . . Named Czechoslovakian League Player of the Year (1979-80). . . . Named NHL Rookie of the Year by THE SPORTING NEWS (1980-81). . . . Won Calder Memorial Trophy (1980-81). . . . Played in NHL All-Star Game (1981, 1982 through 1986 and 1988).

RECORDS: Shares NHL single-season record for most assists by a rookie—70 (1980-81). . . . Shares NHL single-game record for most points by a rookie—8 (February 22, 1981).

STATISTICAL NOTES: One of only three players to score 100 points in each of their first six NHL seasons (Wayne Gretzky and Mario Lemieux).

Season Team	League	REGULAR SEASON					PLAYOFFS				
		Gms.	G	A	Pts.	Pen.	Gms.	G	A	Pts.	Pen.
77-78—Slovan Bratislava	Czech.	44	29	24	53	...	—	—	—	—	—
—Czech. national team........	Int'l	16	5	2	7	...	—	—	—	—	—
78-79—Slovan Bratislava	Czech.	44	32	23	55	...	—	—	—	—	—
—Czech. national team........	Int'l	18	12	9	21	...	—	—	—	—	—
79-80—Slovan Bratislava	Czech.	40	28	30	58	...	—	—	—	—	—
—Czech. Olympic Team	Int'l	6	7	7	14	6	—	—	—	—	—
80-81—Quebec	NHL	77	39	70	109	37	5	2	8	10	7
81-82—Quebec	NHL	80	46	93	139	91	12	7	11	18	10
82-83—Quebec	NHL	75	47	77	124	78	4	3	2	5	10
83-84—Quebec	NHL	80	46	73	119	73	9	2	7	9	31
84-85—Quebec	NHL	75	32	68	100	95	18	4	19	23	24
85-86—Quebec	NHL	76	41	81	122	60	3	0	1	1	2
86-87—Quebec	NHL	64	24	53	77	43	13	6	9	15	12
87-88—Quebec	NHL	76	46	65	111	69	—	—	—	—	—
88-89—Quebec	NHL	72	35	50	85	117	—	—	—	—	—
89-90—Quebec	NHL	62	24	38	62	24	—	—	—	—	—
—New Jersey......................	NHL	12	5	6	11	16	6	3	2	5	4
90-91—New Jersey......................	NHL	77	18	42	60	53	7	3	4	7	2
91-92—New Jersey......................	NHL	66	24	38	62	42	7	3	7	10	19
92-93—New Jersey......................	NHL	62	17	23	40	22	5	0	2	2	2
NHL totals..................		954	444	777	1221	820	89	33	72	105	123

STAUBER, PETE

LW, PANTHERS

PERSONAL: Born May 10, 1966, at Duluth, Minn. . . . 5-11/185. . . . Shoots left. . . . Brother of Robb Stauber, goaltender, Los Angeles Kings.

COLLEGE: Lake Superior State (Mich.).

TRANSACTIONS/CAREER NOTES: Signed as free agent by Detroit Red Wings (June 21, 1990). . . . Selected by Florida Panthers in NHL expansion draft (June 24, 1993).

Season Team	League	REGULAR SEASON					PLAYOFFS				
		Gms.	G	A	Pts.	Pen.	Gms.	G	A	Pts.	Pen.
86-87—Lake Superior State	CCHA	40	22	13	35	80	—	—	—	—	—
87-88—Lake Superior State	CCHA	45	25	33	58	103	—	—	—	—	—

Season Team	League	REGULAR SEASON					PLAYOFFS				
		Gms.	G	A	Pts.	Pen.	Gms.	G	A	Pts.	Pen.
88-89—Lake Superior State	CCHA	46	25	13	38	115	—	—	—	—	—
89-90—Lake Superior State	CCHA	46	25	31	56	90	—	—	—	—	—
90-91—Adirondack	AHL	26	7	11	18	2	—	—	—	—	—
91-92—Adirondack	AHL	25	2	5	7	14	—	—	—	—	—
—Toledo.............................	ECHL	25	7	21	28	46	5	2	3	5	46
92-93—Adirondack	AHL	12	2	2	4	8	—	—	—	—	—

STAUBER, ROBB
G, KINGS

PERSONAL: Born November 25, 1967, at Duluth, Minn. . . . 5-11/170. . . . Shoots left. . . . Brother of Pete Stauber, left winger, Florida Panthers.
HIGH SCHOOL: Denfeld (Duluth, Minn.).
COLLEGE: Minnesota.
TRANSACTIONS/CAREER NOTES: Selected by Los Angeles Kings in fifth round (fifth Kings pick, 107th overall) of NHL entry draft (June 21, 1986). . . . Twisted left knee and ankle (December 3, 1988); missed 14 games. . . . Injured groin and back (October 1989). . . . Underwent knee surgery (March 1991).
HONORS: Won Hobey Baker Memorial Trophy (1987-88). . . . Named to NCAA All-America West first team (1987-88). . . . Won WCHA Most Valuable Player Award (1987-88). . . . Named to WCHA All-Star first team (1987-88). . . . Won WCHA Goaltender of the Year Award (1987-88 and 1988-89). . . . Named to WCHA All-Star second team (1988-89).

Season Team	League	REGULAR SEASON							PLAYOFFS						
		Gms.	Min.	W	L	T	GA	SO	Avg.	Gms.	Min.	W	L	GA	SO	Avg.
84-85—Duluth Denfeld H.S.	Minn. HS	22	990	...	...	...	37	0	2.24	—	—	—	—	—	—	—
85-86—Duluth Denfeld H.S.	Minn. HS	27	1215	...	...	...	66	0	3.26	—	—	—	—	—	—	—
86-87—Univ. of Minnesota.......	WCHA	20	1072	13	5	0	63	0	3.53	—	—	—	—	—	—	—
87-88—Univ. of Minnesota.......	WCHA	44	2621	34	10	0	119	5	2.72	—	—	—	—	—	—	—
88-89—Univ. of Minnesota.......	WCHA	34	2024	26	8	0	82	0	2.43	—	—	—	—	—	—	—
89-90—New Haven	AHL	14	851	6	6	2	43	0	3.03	5	302	2	3	24	0	4.77
—Los Angeles................	NHL	2	83	0	1	0	11	0	7.95	—	—	—	—	—	—	—
90-91—Phoenix	IHL	4	160	1	2	0	11	0	4.13	—	—	—	—	—	—	—
—New Haven	AHL	33	1882	13	16	4	115	1	3.67	—	—	—	—	—	—	—
91-92—Phoenix	IHL	22	1242	8	12	1	80	0	3.86	—	—	—	—	—	—	—
92-93—Los Angeles................	NHL	31	1735	15	8	4	111	0	3.84	4	240	3	1	16	0	4.00
NHL totals................................		**33**	**1818**	**15**	**9**	**4**	**122**	**0**	**4.03**	**4**	**240**	**3**	**1**	**16**	**0**	**4.00**

STEEN, THOMAS
C, JETS

PERSONAL: Born June 8, 1960, at Tocksmark, Sweden. . . . 5-10/195. . . . Shoots left.
TRANSACTIONS/CAREER NOTES: Selected by Winnipeg Jets in fifth round (fifth Jets pick, 103rd overall) of NHL entry draft (June 11, 1979). . . . Lacerated elbow during Canada Cup (September 1981). . . . Injured knee in training camp (October 1981). . . . Suffered protruding disk (December 1989); missed 22 games. . . . Fractured right ankle (November 28, 1990); missed 20 games. . . . Suffered lower back spasms during preseason (September 1991); missed first 24 games of season. . . . Suffered ankle contusion (December 1991); missed 10 games. . . . Suffered recurrance of back spasms (January 1992); missed six games. . . . Suffered hip pointer (October 31, 1992); missed one game. . . . Suffered from the flu (February 12, 1993); missed three games.
HONORS: Named Swedish League Player of the Year (1980-81).

Season Team	League	REGULAR SEASON					PLAYOFFS				
		Gms.	G	A	Pts.	Pen.	Gms.	G	A	Pts.	Pen.
76-77—Leksand............................	Sweden	2	1	1	2	2	—	—	—	—	—
77-78—Leksand............................	Sweden	35	5	6	11	30	—	—	—	—	—
78-79—Leksand............................	Sweden	25	13	4	17	35	2	0	0	0	0
—Swedish national team	Int'l	2	0	0	0	0	—	—	—	—	—
79-80—Leksand............................	Sweden	18	7	7	14	14	2	0	0	0	6
80-81—Farjestad..........................	Sweden	32	16	23	39	30	7	4	2	6	8
—Swedish national team	Int'l	19	2	5	7	12	—	—	—	—	—
81-82—Winnipeg	NHL	73	15	29	44	42	4	0	4	4	2
82-83—Winnipeg	NHL	75	26	33	59	60	3	0	2	2	0
83-84—Winnipeg	NHL	78	20	45	65	69	3	0	1	1	9
84-85—Winnipeg	NHL	79	30	54	84	80	8	2	3	5	17
85-86—Winnipeg	NHL	78	17	47	64	76	3	1	1	2	4
86-87—Winnipeg	NHL	75	17	33	50	59	10	3	4	7	8
87-88—Winnipeg	NHL	76	16	38	54	53	5	1	5	6	2
88-89—Winnipeg	NHL	80	27	61	88	80	—	—	—	—	—
89-90—Winnipeg	NHL	53	18	48	66	35	7	2	5	7	16
90-91—Winnipeg	NHL	58	19	48	67	49	—	—	—	—	—
91-92—Winnipeg	NHL	38	13	25	38	29	7	2	4	6	2
92-93—Winnipeg	NHL	80	22	50	72	75	6	1	3	4	2
NHL totals.................................		**843**	**240**	**511**	**751**	**707**	**56**	**12**	**32**	**44**	**62**

STERN, RONNIE
RW, FLAMES

PERSONAL: Born January 11, 1967, at Ste. Agatha Des Mont, Que. . . . 6-0/195. . . . Shoots right.
TRANSACTIONS/CAREER NOTES: Selected by Vancouver Canucks as underage junior in fourth round (third Canucks pick, 70th overall) of NHL entry draft (June 21, 1986). . . . Bruised shoulder (April 1989). . . . Suffered laceration near eye and dislocated shoulder (March 19, 1990). . . . Fractured wrist (October 30, 1990); missed 10 weeks. . . . Traded by Canucks with D Kevan Guy and option to switch fourth-round picks in 1992 draft to Calgary Flames for D Dana Murzyn; Flames did not exercise option (March 5, 1991). . . . Suffered back spasms (October 15, 1992); missed 11 games.

Season	Team	League	Gms.	G	A	Pts.	Pen.	Gms.	G	A	Pts.	Pen.
84-85—Longueuil	QMJHL		67	6	14	20	176	—	—	—	—	—
85-86—Longueuil	QMJHL		70	39	33	72	317	—	—	—	—	—
86-87—Longueuil	QMJHL		56	32	39	71	266	19	11	9	20	55
87-88—Fredericton	AHL		2	1	0	1	4	—	—	—	—	—
—Flint	IHL		55	14	19	33	294	16	8	8	16	94
—Vancouver	NHL		15	0	0	0	52	—	—	—	—	—
88-89—Milwaukee	IHL		45	19	23	42	280	5	1	0	1	11
—Vancouver	NHL		17	1	0	1	49	3	0	1	1	17
89-90—Milwaukee	IHL		26	8	9	17	165	—	—	—	—	—
—Vancouver	NHL		34	2	3	5	208	—	—	—	—	—
90-91—Milwaukee	IHL		7	2	2	4	81	—	—	—	—	—
—Vancouver	NHL		31	2	3	5	171	—	—	—	—	—
—Calgary	NHL		13	1	3	4	69	7	1	3	4	14
91-92—Calgary	NHL		72	13	9	22	338	—	—	—	—	—
92-93—Calgary	NHL		70	10	15	25	207	6	0	0	0	43
NHL totals			252	29	33	62	1094	16	1	4	5	74

STEVENS, JOHN
D, WHALERS

PERSONAL: Born May 4, 1966, at Completon, N.B. . . . 6-1/195. . . . Shoots left.
TRANSACTIONS/CAREER NOTES: Selected by Philadelphia Flyers as underage junior in third round (fifth Flyers pick, 47th overall) of NHL entry draft (June 9, 1984). . . . Underwent knee surgery (September 1984). . . . Signed as free agent by Hartford Whalers (July 16, 1990).

			REGULAR SEASON					PLAYOFFS				
Season	Team	League	Gms.	G	A	Pts.	Pen.	Gms.	G	A	Pts.	Pen.
82-83—Newmarket	OHA		48	2	9	11	111	—	—	—	—	—
83-84—Oshawa	OHL		70	1	10	11	71	7	0	1	1	6
84-85—Oshawa	OHL		45	2	10	12	61	5	0	2	2	4
—Hershey	AHL		3	0	0	0	2	—	—	—	—	—
85-86—Oshawa	OHL		65	1	7	8	146	6	0	2	2	14
—Kalamazoo	IHL		6	0	1	1	8	6	0	3	3	9
86-87—Hershey	AHL		63	1	15	16	131	3	0	0	0	7
—Philadelphia	NHL		6	0	2	2	14	—	—	—	—	—
87-88—Philadelphia	NHL		3	0	0	0	0	—	—	—	—	—
—Hershey	AHL		59	1	15	16	108	—	—	—	—	—
88-89—Hershey	AHL		78	3	13	16	129	12	1	1	2	29
89-90—Hershey	AHL		79	3	10	13	193	—	—	—	—	—
90-91—Hartford	NHL		14	0	1	1	11	—	—	—	—	—
—Springfield	AHL		65	0	12	12	139	18	0	6	6	35
91-92—Springfield	AHL		45	1	12	13	73	11	1	3	4	27
—Hartford	NHL		21	0	4	4	19	—	—	—	—	—
92-93—Springfield	AHL		74	1	19	20	111	15	0	1	1	18
NHL totals			44	0	7	7	44					

STEVENS, KEVIN
LW, PENGUINS

PERSONAL: Born April 15, 1965, at Brockton, Mass. . . . 6-3/217. . . . Shoots left. . . . Full name: Kevin Michael Stevens.
HIGH SCHOOL: Silver Lake (Mass.).
COLLEGE: Boston College.
TRANSACTIONS/CAREER NOTES: Selected by Los Angeles Kings in sixth round (sixth Kings pick, 108th overall) of NHL entry draft (June 8, 1983). . . . Traded by Kings to Pittsburgh Penguins for LW Anders Hakansson (September 9, 1983). . . . Suffered cartilage damage in left knee (November 5, 1992) and underwent arthroscopic surgery (November 6, 1992); missed nine games. . . . Suspended one game by NHL (March 1993). . . . Suffered from bronchitis (April 3, 1993); missed two games.
HONORS: Named to NCAA All-America East second team (1986-87). . . . Named to Hockey East All-Star first team (1986-87). . . . Named to THE SPORTING NEWS All-Star second team (1990-91 and 1992-93). . . . Named to NHL All-Star second team (1990-91 and 1992-93). . . . Named to THE SPORTING NEWS All-Star first team (1991-92). . . . Named to NHL All-Star first team (1991-92). . . . Played in NHL All-Star Game (1991 through 1993).
RECORDS: Holds NHL single-season records for most assists by a left winger—69 (1991-92).
MISCELLANEOUS: Member of Stanley Cup championship teams (1991 and 1992).

			REGULAR SEASON					PLAYOFFS				
Season	Team	League	Gms.	G	A	Pts.	Pen.	Gms.	G	A	Pts.	Pen.
82-83—Silver Lake H.S.	Minn. H.S.		18	24	27	51	...	—	—	—	—	—
83-84—Boston College	ECAC		37	6	14	20	36	—	—	—	—	—
84-85—Boston College	Hockey East		40	13	23	36	36	—	—	—	—	—
85-86—Boston College	Hockey East		42	17	27	44	56	—	—	—	—	—
86-87—Boston College	Hockey East		39	*35	35	70	54	—	—	—	—	—
87-88—U.S. national team	Int'l		44	22	23	45	52	—	—	—	—	—
—U.S. Olympic Team	Int'l		5	1	3	4	2	—	—	—	—	—
—Pittsburgh	NHL		16	5	2	7	8	—	—	—	—	—
88-89—Pittsburgh	NHL		24	12	3	15	19	11	3	7	10	16
—Muskegon	IHL		45	24	41	65	113	—	—	—	—	—
89-90—Pittsburgh	NHL		76	29	41	70	171	—	—	—	..	—
90-91—Pittsburgh	NHL		80	40	46	86	133	24	*17	16	33	53

			REGULAR SEASON					PLAYOFFS			
Season Team	League	Gms.	G	A	Pts.	Pen.	Gms.	G	A	Pts.	Pen.
91-92—Pittsburgh	NHL	80	54	69	123	254	†21	13	15	28	28
92-93—Pittsburgh	NHL	72	55	56	111	177	12	5	11	16	22
NHL totals		348	195	217	412	762	68	38	49	87	119

STEVENS, MIKE
C/LW, RANGERS

PERSONAL: Born December 30, 1965, at Kitchener, Ont. . . . 5-11/195. . . . Shoots left. . . . Brother of Scott Stevens, defenseman, New Jersey Devils.

TRANSACTIONS/CAREER NOTES: Selected by Vancouver Canucks as underage junior in third round (fourth Canucks pick, 58th overall) of NHL entry draft (June 9, 1984). . . . Underwent arthroscopic knee surgery (October 1984). . . . Traded by Canucks to Boston Bruins for future considerations (October 1987). . . . Signed as free agent by New York Islanders (August 1988). . . . Traded by Islanders with C Gilles Thibaudeau to Toronto Maple Leafs for LW Paul Gagne, RW Derek Laxdal and D Jack Capuano (December 20, 1989). . . . Traded by Maple Leafs to New York Rangers for C Guy Larose (December 26, 1991).

			REGULAR SEASON					PLAYOFFS			
Season Team	League	Gms.	G	A	Pts.	Pen.	Gms.	G	A	Pts.	Pen.
82-83—Kitchener Jr. B	OHA	29	5	18	23	86	—	—	—	—	—
—Kitchener	OHL	13	0	4	4	16	12	0	1	1	9
83-84—Kitchener	OHL	66	19	21	40	109	16	10	7	17	40
84-85—Kitchener	OHL	37	17	18	35	121	4	1	1	2	8
—Vancouver	NHL	6	0	3	3	6	—	—	—	—	—
85-86—Fredericton	AHL	79	12	19	31	208	6	1	1	2	35
86-87—Fredericton	AHL	71	7	18	25	258	—	—	—	—	—
87-88—Maine	AHL	63	30	25	55	265	7	1	2	3	37
—Boston	NHL	7	0	1	1	9	—	—	—	—	—
88-89—Springfield	AHL	42	17	13	30	120	—	—	—	—	—
—New York Islanders	NHL	9	1	0	1	14	—	—	—	—	—
89-90—Springfield	AHL	28	12	10	22	75	—	—	—	—	—
—Toronto	NHL	1	0	0	0	0	—	—	—	—	—
—Newmarket	AHL	46	16	28	44	86	—	—	—	—	—
90-91—Newmarket	AHL	68	24	23	47	229	—	—	—	—	—
91-92—St. John's	AHL	30	13	11	24	65	—	—	—	—	—
—Binghamton	AHL	44	15	15	30	87	11	7	6	13	45
92-93—Binghamton	AHL	68	31	61	92	230	14	5	5	10	63
NHL totals		23	1	4	5	29					

STEVENS, SCOTT
D, DEVILS

PERSONAL: Born April 1, 1964, at Kitchener, Ont. . . . 6-2/215. . . . Shoots left. . . . Brother of Mike Stevens, center/left winger in New York Rangers system.

TRANSACTIONS/CAREER NOTES: Selected by Washington Capitals as underage junior in first round (fifth Capitals pick, first overall) of NHL entry draft (June 9, 1982). . . . Bruised right knee (November 6, 1985); missed seven games. . . . Broke right index finger (December 14, 1986). . . . Bruised shoulder (April 1988). . . . Suffered from poison oak (November 1988). . . . Suffered facial lacerations during World Cup (April 21, 1989). . . . Broke left foot (December 29, 1989); missed 17 games. . . . Suspended three games by NHL for scratching (February 27, 1990). . . . Bruised left shoulder (March 27, 1990). . . . Dislocated left shoulder (May 3, 1990). . . . Signed as free agent by St. Louis Blues (July 9, 1990); Blues owed Capitals two first-round draft picks among the top seven over next two years and $100,000 cash; upon failing to get a pick in the top seven in 1991, Blues forfeited their first-round pick in 1991 (LW Trevor Halverson), 1992 (D Sergei Gonchar), 1993 (D Brendan Witt), 1994 and 1995 drafts to Capitals (July 9, 1990). . . . Awarded to New Jersey Devils as compensation for Blues signing free agent RW/LW Brendan Shanahan (September 1, 1991). . . . Strained right knee (February 20, 1992); missed 12 games. . . . Suffered concussion (December 27, 1992); missed three games.

HONORS: Named to NHL All-Rookie team (1982-83). . . . Named to NHL All-Star first team (1987-88). . . . Named to NHL All-Star second team (1991-92). . . . Played in NHL All-Star Game (1985, 1989, 1991 through 1993).

			REGULAR SEASON					PLAYOFFS			
Season Team	League	Gms.	G	A	Pts.	Pen.	Gms.	G	A	Pts.	Pen.
80-81—Kitchener Jr. B	OHA	39	7	33	40	82	—	—	—	—	—
—Kitchener	OHL	1	0	0	0	0	—	—	—	—	—
81-82—Kitchener	OHL	68	6	36	42	158	15	1	10	11	71
82-83—Washington	NHL	77	9	16	25	195	4	1	0	1	26
83-84—Washington	NHL	78	13	32	45	201	8	1	8	9	21
84-85—Washington	NHL	80	21	44	65	221	5	0	1	1	20
85-86—Washington	NHL	73	15	38	53	165	9	3	8	11	12
86-87—Washington	NHL	77	10	51	61	283	7	0	5	5	19
87-88—Washington	NHL	80	12	60	72	184	13	1	11	12	46
88-89—Washington	NHL	80	7	61	68	225	6	1	4	5	11
89-90—Washington	NHL	56	11	29	40	154	15	2	7	9	25
90-91—St. Louis	NHL	78	5	44	49	150	13	0	3	3	36
91-92—New Jersey	NHL	68	17	42	59	124	7	2	1	3	29
92-93—New Jersey	NHL	81	12	45	57	120	5	2	2	4	10
NHL totals		828	132	462	594	2022	92	13	50	63	255

STEVENSON, JEREMY
LW/C, JETS

PERSONAL: Born July 28, 1974, at San Bernardino, Calif. . . . 6-1/212. . . . Shoots left. . . . Full name: Jeremy Joseph Stevenson.

HIGH SCHOOL: St. Lawrence (Cornwall, Ont.).

TRANSACTIONS/CAREER NOTES: Selected by Winnipeg Jets in third round (third

Jets pick, 60th overall) of NHL entry draft (June 20, 1992).

Season Team	League	REGULAR SEASON					PLAYOFFS				
		Gms.	G	A	Pts.	Pen.	Gms.	G	A	Pts.	Pen.
90-91—Cornwall	OHL	58	13	20	33	124	—	—	—	—	—
91-92—Cornwall	OHL	63	15	23	38	176	6	3	1	4	4
92-93—Newmarket	OHL	54	28	28	56	144	5	5	1	6	28

STEVENSON, SHAYNE
RW, LIGHTNING

PERSONAL: Born October 26, 1970, at Aurora, Ont. . . . 6-1/190. . . . Shoots right.

TRANSACTIONS/CAREER NOTES: Selected by Boston Bruins in first round (first Bruins pick, 17th overall) of NHL entry draft (June 17, 1989). . . . Selected by Tampa Bay Lightning in NHL expansion draft (June 18, 1992).

Season Team	League	REGULAR SEASON					PLAYOFFS				
		Gms.	G	A	Pts.	Pen.	Gms.	G	A	Pts.	Pen.
85-86—Barrie Jr. B	OHA	38	14	23	37	75	—	—	—	—	—
86-87—London	OHL	61	7	15	22	56	—	—	—	—	—
87-88—London	OHL	36	14	25	39	56	—	—	—	—	—
—Kitchener	OHL	30	10	25	35	48	4	1	1	2	4
88-89—Kitchener	OHL	56	25	51	76	86	5	2	3	5	4
89-90—Kitchener	OHL	56	28	62	90	115	17	16	21	*37	31
90-91—Maine	AHL	58	22	28	50	112	—	—	—	—	—
—Boston	NHL	14	0	0	0	26	—	—	—	—	—
91-92—Maine	AHL	54	10	23	33	150	—	—	—	—	—
—Boston	NHL	5	0	1	1	2	—	—	—	—	—
92-93—Tampa Bay	NHL	8	0	1	1	7	—	—	—	—	—
—Atlanta	IHL	53	17	17	34	160	6	0	2	2	2
NHL totals		27	0	2	2	35					

STEVENSON, TURNER
RW, CANADIENS

PERSONAL: Born May 18, 1972, at Port Alberni, B.C. . . . 6-3/200. . . . Shoots right.

TRANSACTIONS/CAREER NOTES: Underwent surgery to remove growth in chest (August 1987). . . . Injured shoulder (December 1987). . . . Selected by Montreal Canadiens in first round (first Canadiens pick, 12th overall) of NHL entry draft (June 16, 1990).

HONORS: Named to Can.HL All-Star second team (1991-92). . . . Named to Memorial Cup All-Star team (1991-92). . . . Named to WHL (West) All-Star first team (1991-92).

Season Team	League	REGULAR SEASON					PLAYOFFS				
		Gms.	G	A	Pts.	Pen.	Gms.	G	A	Pts.	Pen.
88-89—Seattle	WHL	69	15	12	27	84	—	—	—	—	—
89-90—Seattle	WHL	62	29	32	61	276	13	3	2	5	35
90-91—Seattle	WHL	57	36	27	63	222	6	1	5	6	15
—Fredericton	AHL	—	—	—	—	—	4	0	0	0	5
91-92—Seattle	WHL	58	20	32	52	304	15	9	3	12	55
92-93—Fredericton	AHL	79	25	34	59	102	5	2	3	5	11
—Montreal	NHL	1	0	0	0	0	—	—	—	—	—
NHL totals		1	0	0	0	0					

STEWART, CAMERON
C, BRUINS

PERSONAL: Born September 18, 1971, at Kitchener, Ont. . . . 5-10/188. . . . Shoots left.

COLLEGE: Michigan.

TRANSACTIONS/CAREER NOTES: Strained knee ligaments (June 1989). . . . Selected by Boston Bruins in third round (second Bruins pick, 63rd overall) of NHL entry draft (June 16, 1990).

Season Team	League	REGULAR SEASON					PLAYOFFS				
		Gms.	G	A	Pts.	Pen.	Gms.	G	A	Pts.	Pen.
88-89—Elmira Jr. B	OHA	43	38	50	88	138	—	—	—	—	—
89-90—Elmira Jr. B	OHA	46	44	95	139	172	—	—	—	—	—
90-91—University of Michigan	CCHA	44	8	24	32	122	—	—	—	—	—
91-92—University of Michigan	CCHA	44	13	15	28	106	—	—	—	—	—
92-93—University of Michigan	CCHA	39	20	39	59	69	—	—	—	—	—

STEWART, MICHAEL
D, RANGERS

PERSONAL: Born March 30, 1972, at Calgary, Alta. . . . 6-2/197. . . . Shoots left. . . . Full name: Michael Donald Stewart.

COLLEGE: Michigan State.

TRANSACTIONS/CAREER NOTES: Selected by New York Rangers in first round (first Rangers pick, 13th overall) of NHL entry draft (June 16, 1990).

HONORS: Named to CCHA All-Rookie team (1989-90).

Season Team	League	REGULAR SEASON					PLAYOFFS				
		Gms.	G	A	Pts.	Pen.	Gms.	G	A	Pts.	Pen.
89-90—Michigan State	CCHA	45	2	6	8	45	—	—	—	—	—
90-91—Michigan State	CCHA	37	3	12	15	58	—	—	—	—	—
91-92—Michigan State	CCHA	8	1	3	4	6	—	—	—	—	—
92-93—Binghamton	AHL	68	2	10	12	71	1	0	0	0	0

STIENBURG, TREVOR
RW

PERSONAL: Born May 13, 1966, at Kingston, Ont. . . . 6-1/200. . . . Shoots right. . . . Full name: Trevor Malcolm Stienburg.

TRANSACTIONS/CAREER NOTES: Selected by Quebec Nordiques as underage junior in first round (first Nordiques pick, 15th overall) of NHL entry draft (June 9, 1984). . . . Traded by Guelph Platers to London Knights for C Mike Murray and Ron Coutts (January 1985). . . . Tore knee ligaments in training camp (September 1985). . . . Sprained left ankle (October 1988). . . . Sprained right shoulder (November 1988). . . . Signed as free agent by Hartford Whalers (July 1992).

			REGULAR SEASON					PLAYOFFS				
Season	Team	League	Gms.	G	A	Pts.	Pen.	Gms.	G	A	Pts.	Pen.
82-83—Brockville		COJHL	47	39	30	69	182	—	—	—	—	—
83-84—Guelph		OHL	65	33	18	51	104	—	—	—	—	—
84-85—Guelph		OHL	18	7	12	19	38	—	—	—	—	—
—London		OHL	22	9	11	20	45	8	1	3	4	22
85-86—Quebec		NHL	2	1	0	1	0	1	0	0	0	0
—London		OHL	31	12	18	30	88	5	0	0	0	20
86-87—Fredericton		AHL	48	14	12	26	123	—	—	—	—	—
—Quebec		NHL	6	1	0	1	12	—	—	—	—	—
87-88—Quebec		NHL	8	0	1	1	24	—	—	—	—	—
88-89—Quebec		NHL	55	6	3	9	125	—	—	—	—	—
89-90—Halifax		AHL	11	3	3	6	36	—	—	—	—	—
90-91—Halifax		AHL	41	16	7	23	190	—	—	—	—	—
91-92—New Haven		AHL	66	17	22	39	201	1	0	0	0	2
92-93—Springfield		AHL	65	14	20	34	244	10	0	0	0	31
NHL totals			**71**	**8**	**4**	**12**	**161**	**1**	**0**	**0**	**0**	**0**

STILLMAN, CORY
C, FLAMES

PERSONAL: Born December 20, 1973, at Peterborough, Ont. . . . 6-0/174. . . . Shoots left.
HIGH SCHOOL: Herman E. Fawcett (Brantford, Ont.).
TRANSACTIONS/CAREER NOTES: Selected by Calgary Flames in first round (first Flames pick, sixth overall) of NHL entry draft (June 20, 1992).
HONORS: Won Emms Family Award (1990-91).

			REGULAR SEASON					PLAYOFFS				
Season	Team	League	Gms.	G	A	Pts.	Pen.	Gms.	G	A	Pts.	Pen.
89-90—Peterborough Jr. B		OHA	41	30	54	84	76	—	—	—	—	—
90-91—Windsor		OHL	64	31	70	101	31	11	3	6	9	8
91-92—Windsor		OHL	53	29	61	90	59	7	2	4	6	8
92-93—Peterborough		OHL	61	25	55	80	55	18	3	8	11	18
—Canadian national team		Int'l	1	0	0	0	0	—	—	—	—	—

STOJANOV, ALEX
LW, CANUCKS

PERSONAL: Born April 25, 1973, at Windsor, Ont. . . . 6-4/225. . . . Shoots left. . . . Name pronounced STOY-uh-nahf.
TRANSACTIONS/CAREER NOTES: Dislocated shoulder (July 1989). . . . Selected by Vancouver Canucks in first round (first Canucks pick, seventh overall) of NHL entry draft (June 22, 1991).

			REGULAR SEASON					PLAYOFFS				
Season	Team	League	Gms.	G	A	Pts.	Pen.	Gms.	G	A	Pts.	Pen.
89-90—Dukes of Hamilton		OHL	37	4	4	8	91	—	—	—	—	—
90-91—Dukes of Hamilton		OHL	62	25	20	45	179	4	1	1	2	14
91-92—Guelph		OHL	33	12	15	27	91	—	—	—	—	—
92-93—Guelph		OHL	35	27	28	55	11	—	—	—	—	—
—Newmarket		OHL	14	9	7	16	21	7	1	3	4	26
—Hamilton		AHL	4	4	0	4	0	—	—	—	—	—

STOLP, JEFF
G, STARS

PERSONAL: Born June 20, 1970, at Hibbing, Minn. . . . 6-0/195. . . . Shoots left.
HIGH SCHOOL: Greenway (Coleraine, Minn.).
COLLEGE: Minnesota.
TRANSACTIONS/CAREER NOTES: Selected by Minnesota North Stars in fourth round (fourth North Stars pick, 64th overall) of NHL entry draft (June 11, 1988). . . . North Stars franchise moved from Minnesota to Dallas and renamed Stars for 1993-94 season.
HONORS: Named to WCHA All-Tournament team (1990-91). . . . Named to WCHA All-Star second team (1991-92).

			REGULAR SEASON							PLAYOFFS						
Season	Team	League	Gms.	Min.	W	L	T	GA	SO	Avg.	Gms.	Min.	W	L	GA SO	Avg.
86-87—Greenway H.S.		Minn. HS	24	1080	. . .	. . .	. . .	39	1	2.17	—	—	—	—	— —	—
87-88—Greenway H.S.		Minn. HS	23	1035	. . .	. . .	. . .	57	1	3.30	—	—	—	—	— —	—
88-89—Univ. of Minnesota		WCHA	16	742	7	2	3	45	0	3.64	—	—	—	—	— —	—
89-90—Univ. of Minnesota		WCHA	10	417	5	1	0	33	1	4.75	—	—	—	—	— —	—
90-91—Univ. of Minnesota		WCHA	32	1766	18	8	3	82	2	*2.79	—	—	—	—	— —	—
91-92—Univ. of Minnesota		WCHA	†36	2017	*26	9	0	98	*2	*2.92	—	—	—	—	— —	—
92-93—Kalamazoo		IHL	14	733	2	11	0	62	0	5.08	—	—	—	—	— —	—
—Dayton		ECHL	27	1550	12	13	2	99	0	3.83	—	—	—	—	— —	—

STORM, JIM
LW, WHALERS

PERSONAL: Born February 5, 1971, at Detroit. . . . 6-2/200. . . . Shoots left. . . . Full name: James David Storm.
COLLEGE: Michigan Tech.
TRANSACTIONS/CAREER NOTES: Selected by Hartford Whalers in fourth round (fifth Whalers pick,

75th overall) of NHL entry draft (June 22, 1991).

Season Team	League	REGULAR SEASON					PLAYOFFS				
		Gms.	G	A	Pts.	Pen.	Gms.	G	A	Pts.	Pen.
88-89—Detroit Compuware	NAJHL	60	30	45	75	50	—	—	—	—	—
89-90—Detroit Compuware	NAJHL	55	38	73	111	58	—	—	—	—	—
90-91—Michigan Tech	WCHA	36	16	17	33	46	—	—	—	—	—
91-92—Michigan Tech	WCHA	39	25	33	58	12	—	—	—	—	—
92-93—Michigan Tech	WCHA	33	22	32	54	30	—	—	—	—	—

STRAKA, MARTIN
C, PENGUINS

PERSONAL: Born September 3, 1972, at Plzen, Czechoslovakia. . . . 5-10/178. . . . Shoots left. . . . Name pronounced STRAH-kuh.
TRANSACTIONS/CAREER NOTES: Selected by Pittsburgh Penguins in first round (first Penguins pick, 19th overall) of NHL entry draft (June 20, 1992).
HONORS: Named to Czechoslovakian League All-Star team (1991-92).

Season Team	League	REGULAR SEASON					PLAYOFFS				
		Gms.	G	A	Pts.	Pen.	Gms.	G	A	Pts.	Pen.
89-90—Skoda Plzen	Czech.	1	0	3	3	...	—	—	—	—	—
90-91—Skoda Plzen	Czech.	47	7	24	31	6	—	—	—	—	—
91-92—Skoda Plzen	Czech.	50	27	28	55	...	—	—	—	—	—
92-93—Pittsburgh	NHL	42	3	13	16	29	11	2	1	3	2
—Cleveland	IHL	4	4	3	7	0	—	—	—	—	—
NHL totals		42	3	13	16	29	11	2	1	3	2

STUMPEL, JOZEF
RW, BRUINS

PERSONAL: Born June 20, 1972, at Nitra, Czechoslovakia. . . . 6-1/190. . . . Shoots right. . . . Name pronounced STUHM-puhl.
TRANSACTIONS/CAREER NOTES: Selected by Boston Bruins in second round (second Bruins pick, 40th overall) of NHL entry draft (June 22, 1991). . . . Injured shoulder (December 1992); missed nine games.

Season Team	League	REGULAR SEASON					PLAYOFFS				
		Gms.	G	A	Pts.	Pen.	Gms.	G	A	Pts.	Pen.
89-90—Nitra	Czech.	38	12	11	23	0	—	—	—	—	—
90-91—Nitra	Czech.	49	23	22	45	14	—	—	—	—	—
91-92—Boston	NHL	4	1	0	1	0	—	—	—	—	—
—Koln	Germany	33	19	18	37	35	—	—	—	—	—
92-93—Providence	AHL	56	31	61	92	26	6	4	4	8	0
—Boston	NHL	13	1	3	4	4	—	—	—	—	—
NHL totals		17	2	3	5	4					

SULLIVAN, BRIAN
LW, DEVILS

PERSONAL: Born April 23, 1969, at South Windsor, Conn. . . . 6-4/195. . . . Shoots right. . . . Full name: Brian Scott Sullivan.
HIGH SCHOOL: South Windsor (Conn.).
COLLEGE: Northeastern.
TRANSACTIONS/CAREER NOTES: Selected by New Jersey Devils in fourth round (third Devils pick, 65th overall) of NHL entry draft (June 13, 1987). . . . Bruised shoulder (November 1989).

Season Team	League	REGULAR SEASON					PLAYOFFS				
		Gms.	G	A	Pts.	Pen.	Gms.	G	A	Pts.	Pen.
85-86—South Windsor H.S.	Conn. H.S.	...	39	50	89	...	—	—	—	—	—
86-87—Springfield Jr. B	NEJHL	...	30	35	65	...	—	—	—	—	—
87-88—Northeastern University	Hockey East	37	20	12	32	18	—	—	—	—	—
88-89—Northeastern University	Hockey East	34	13	14	27	65	—	—	—	—	—
89-90—Northeastern University	Hockey East	34	24	21	45	72	—	—	—	—	—
90-91—Northeastern University	Hockey East	32	17	23	40	75	—	—	—	—	—
91-92—Utica	AHL	70	23	24	47	58	4	0	4	4	6
92-93—Utica	AHL	75	30	27	57	88	5	0	0	0	12
—New Jersey	NHL	2	0	1	1	0	—	—	—	—	—
NHL totals		2	0	1	1	0					

SULLIVAN, MIKE
C, SHARKS

PERSONAL: Born February 28, 1968, at Marshfield, Mass. . . . 6-2/193. . . . Shoots left. . . . Full name: Michael Barry Sullivan.
HIGH SCHOOL: Boston College.
COLLEGE: Boston University.
TRANSACTIONS/CAREER NOTES: Selected by New York Rangers in fourth round (fourth Rangers pick, 69th overall) of NHL entry draft (June 13, 1987). . . . Traded by Rangers with D Mark Tinordi, D Paul Jerrard, RW Brett Barnett and third-round pick in 1989 draft (C Murray Garbutt) to Minnesota North Stars for LW Igor Liba, C Brian Lawton and NHL rights to LW Eric Bennett (October 11, 1988). . . . Signed as free agent by San Jose Sharks (August 9, 1991). . . . Sprained left knee (April 6, 1993); missed remainder of season.

Season Team	League	REGULAR SEASON					PLAYOFFS				
		Gms.	G	A	Pts.	Pen.	Gms.	G	A	Pts.	Pen.
85-86—Boston College H.S.	Mass. H.S.	22	26	33	59	...	—	—	—	—	—
86-87—Boston College H.S.	Mass. H.S.	37	13	18	31	18	—	—	—	—	—
87-88—Boston College H.S.	Mass. H.S.	30	18	22	40	30	—	—	—	—	—

Season Team	League	REGULAR SEASON					PLAYOFFS				
		Gms.	G	A	Pts.	Pen.	Gms.	G	A	Pts.	Pen.
88-89—Boston College H.S...........	Mass. H.S.	36	19	17	36	30	—	—	—	—	—
—Virginia.............................	ECHL	2	0	0	0	0	—	—	—	—	—
89-90—Boston University	Hockey East	38	11	20	31	26	—	—	—	—	—
90-91—San Diego	IHL	74	12	23	35	27	—	—	—	—	—
91-92—Kansas City....................	IHL	10	2	8	10	8	—	—	—	—	—
—San Jose.........................	NHL	64	8	11	19	15	—	—	—	—	—
92-93—San Jose	NHL	81	6	8	14	30	—	—	—	—	—
NHL totals.................................		145	14	19	33	45					

SULLIVAN, MIKE
C, RED WINGS

PERSONAL: Born October 16, 1973, at Woburn, Mass.... 6-1/190.... Shoots left.
HIGH SCHOOL: Reading (Mass.) Memorial.
COLLEGE: New Hampshire.
TRANSACTIONS/CAREER NOTES: Selected by Detroit Red Wings in fifth round (fourth Red Wings pick, 118th overall) of NHL entry draft (June 20, 1992).

Season Team	League	REGULAR SEASON					PLAYOFFS				
		Gms.	G	A	Pts.	Pen.	Gms.	G	A	Pts.	Pen.
91-92—Reading H.S.....................	Mass. H.S.	24	39	41	80	0	—	—	—	—	—
92-93—Univ. of New Hampshire ...	Hockey East	36	5	5	10	12	—	—	—	—	—

SUNDBLAD, NIKLAS
RW, FLAMES

PERSONAL: Born January 3, 1973, at Stockholm, Sweden.... 6-1/196.... Shoots right.
TRANSACTIONS/CAREER NOTES: Selected by Calgary Flames in first round (first Flames pick, 19th overall) of NHL entry draft (June 22, 1991).

Season Team	League	REGULAR SEASON					PLAYOFFS				
		Gms.	G	A	Pts.	Pen.	Gms.	G	A	Pts.	Pen.
90-91—AIK...................................	Sweden	39	1	3	4	14	—	—	—	—	—
91-92—AIK...................................	Sweden	33	9	2	11	24	3	3	1	4	0
92-93—AIK...................................	Sweden	22	5	4	9	56	—	—	—	—	—

SUNDIN, MATS
RW, NORDIQUES

PERSONAL: Born February 13, 1971, at Sollentuna, Sweden.... 6-2/190.... Shoots right.... Full name: Mats Johan Sundin.... Name pronounced suhn-DEEN.
TRANSACTIONS/CAREER NOTES: Selected by Quebec Nordiques in first round (first Nordiques pick, first overall) of NHL entry draft (June 17, 1989).... Separated right shoulder (January 2, 1993); missed three games. ... Suspended one game by NHL for second stick-related game misconduct (March 2, 1993).
HONORS: Named to Swedish League All-Star team (1990-91 and 1991-92).

Season Team	League	REGULAR SEASON					PLAYOFFS				
		Gms.	G	A	Pts.	Pen.	Gms.	G	A	Pts.	Pen.
88-89—Nacka	Sweden	25	10	8	18	18	—	—	—	—	—
89-90—Djurgarden	Sweden	34	10	8	18	16	8	7	0	7	4
90-91—Quebec	NHL	80	23	36	59	58	—	—	—	—	—
91-92—Quebec	NHL	80	33	43	76	103	—	—	—	—	—
92-93—Quebec	NHL	80	47	67	114	96	6	3	1	4	6
NHL totals.................................		240	103	146	249	257	6	3	1	4	6

SUNDSTROM, NIKLAS
LW, RANGERS

PERSONAL: Born June 6, 1975, at Ornskoldsvik, Sweden.... 5-11/183.... Shoots left.
TRANSACTIONS/CAREER NOTES: Selected by New York Rangers in first round (first Rangers pick, 8th overall) of NHL entry draft (June 26, 1993).

Season Team	League	REGULAR SEASON					PLAYOFFS				
		Gms.	G	A	Pts.	Pen.	Gms.	G	A	Pts.	Pen.
91-92—MoDo	Sweden	9	1	3	4	0	—	—	—	—	—
92-93—MoDo	Sweden	40	7	11	18	18	—	—	—	—	—

SUTER, GARY
D, FLAMES

PERSONAL: Born June 24, 1964, at Madison, Wis.... 6-0/190.... Shoots left.... Full name: Gary Lee Suter.
COLLEGE: Wisconsin.
TRANSACTIONS/CAREER NOTES: Selected by Calgary Flames in ninth round (ninth Flames pick, 180th overall) of NHL entry draft (June 9, 1984).... Stretched ligament in knee (December 1986).... Suspended first four games of regular season and next six international games in which NHL participates for high-sticking during Canada Cup (September 4, 1987).... Injured left knee (February 1988).... Pulled hamstring (February 1989).... Ruptured appendix (February 22, 1989); missed 16 games.... Broke jaw (April 11, 1989).... Bruised knee (December 12, 1991); missed 10 games.... Injured ribs (March 16, 1993); missed one game.... Suffered from the flu (March 30, 1993); missed one game.
HONORS: Named USHL Top Defenseman (1982-83).... Named to USHL All-Star first team (1982-83).... Won Calder Memorial Trophy (1985-86).... Named to NHL All-Rookie team (1985-86).... Played in NHL All-Star Game (1986, 1988, 1989 and 1991).... Named to THE SPORTING NEWS All-Star first team (1987-88).... Named to NHL All-Star second team (1987-88). ...Named to THE SPORTING NEWS All-Star second team (1988-89).
RECORDS: Shares NHL single-game record for most assists by a defenseman—6 (April 4, 1986).
MISCELLANEOUS: Member of Stanley Cup championship team (1989).

Season Team	League	REGULAR SEASON					PLAYOFFS				
		Gms.	G	A	Pts.	Pen.	Gms.	G	A	Pts.	Pen.
81-82—Dubuque	USHL	18	3	4	7	32	—	—	—	—	—
82-83—Dubuque	USHL	41	9	10	19	112	—	—	—	—	—
83-84—University of Wisconsin	WCHA	35	4	18	22	68	—	—	—	—	—
84-85—University of Wisconsin	WCHA	39	12	39	51	110	—	—	—	—	—
85-86—Calgary	NHL	80	18	50	68	141	10	2	8	10	8
86-87—Calgary	NHL	68	9	40	49	70	6	0	3	3	10
87-88—Calgary	NHL	75	21	70	91	124	9	1	9	10	6
88-89—Calgary	NHL	63	13	49	62	78	5	0	3	3	10
89-90—Calgary	NHL	76	16	60	76	97	6	0	1	1	14
90-91—Calgary	NHL	79	12	58	70	102	7	1	6	7	12
91-92—Calgary	NHL	70	12	43	55	128	—	—	—	—	—
92-93—Calgary	NHL	81	23	58	81	112	6	2	3	5	8
NHL totals		592	124	428	552	852	49	6	33	39	68

SUTTER, BRENT
C, BLACKHAWKS

PERSONAL: Born June 10, 1962, at Viking, Alta. . . . 5-11/180. . . . Shoots right. . . . Full name: Brent Colin Sutter. . . . Brother of Brian Sutter, left winger, St. Louis Blues (1976-77 through 1987-88) and current head coach, Boston Bruins; brother of Darryl Sutter, left winger, Chicago Blackhawks (1979-80 through 1986-87) and current head coach, Blackhawks; brother of Duane Sutter, right winger, New York Islanders and Blackhawks (1979-80 through 1989-90) and current head coach, Indianapolis Ice of IHL; brother of Rich Sutter, right winger, Blues; and brother of Ron Sutter, center, Blues.

TRANSACTIONS/CAREER NOTES: Selected by New York Islanders as underage junior in first round (first Islanders pick, 17th overall) of NHL entry draft (June 11, 1980). . . . Damaged tendon and developed infection in right hand (January 1984); missed 11 games. . . . Separated shoulder (March 1985). . . . Bruised left shoulder (October 19, 1985); missed 12 games. . . . Bruised shoulder (December 21, 1985); missed seven games. . . . Strained abductor muscle in right leg (March 1987). . . . Suffered non-displaced fracture of right thumb (December 1987). . . . Lacerated right leg (January 19, 1990). . . . Hospitalized upon developing an infection in right leg after stitches were removed (January 28, 1990); missed seven games. . . . Traded by Islanders with RW Brad Lauer to Chicago Blackhawks for C Adam Creighton and LW Steve Thomas (October 25, 1991). . . . Injured abdomen (March 11, 1992). . . . Broke foot (September 25, 1992); missed 14 games. . . . Bruised index finger (January 19, 1993); missed three games. . . . Suffered eye injury (March 9, 1993); missed two games.

HONORS: Played in NHL All-Star Game (1985).

MISCELLANEOUS: Member of Stanley Cup championship teams (1982 and 1983).

Season Team	League	REGULAR SEASON					PLAYOFFS				
		Gms.	G	A	Pts.	Pen.	Gms.	G	A	Pts.	Pen.
77-78—Red Deer	AJHL	60	12	18	30	33	—	—	—	—	—
78-79—Red Deer	AJHL	60	42	42	84	79	—	—	—	—	—
79-80—Red Deer	AJHL	59	70	101	171	131	—	—	—	—	—
—Lethbridge	WHL	5	1	0	1	2	—	—	—	—	—
80-81—New York Islanders	NHL	3	2	2	4	0	—	—	—	—	—
—Lethbridge	WHL	68	54	54	108	116	9	6	4	10	51
81-82—Lethbridge	WHL	34	46	34	80	162	—	—	—	—	—
—New York Islanders	NHL	43	21	22	43	114	19	2	6	8	36
82-83—New York Islanders	NHL	80	21	19	40	128	20	10	11	21	26
83-84—New York Islanders	NHL	69	34	15	49	69	20	4	10	14	18
84-85—New York Islanders	NHL	72	42	60	102	51	10	3	3	6	14
85-86—New York Islanders	NHL	61	24	31	55	74	3	0	1	1	2
86-87—New York Islanders	NHL	69	27	36	63	73	5	1	0	1	4
87-88—New York Islanders	NHL	70	29	31	60	55	6	2	1	3	18
88-89—New York Islanders	NHL	77	29	34	63	77	—	—	—	—	—
89-90—New York Islanders	NHL	67	33	35	68	65	5	2	3	5	2
90-91—New York Islanders	NHL	75	21	32	53	49	—	—	—	—	—
91-92—New York Islanders	NHL	8	4	6	10	6	—	—	—	—	—
—Chicago	NHL	61	18	32	50	30	18	3	5	8	22
92-93—Chicago	NHL	65	20	34	54	67	4	1	1	2	4
NHL totals		820	325	389	714	858	110	28	41	69	146

SUTTER, RICH
RW, BLUES

PERSONAL: Born December 2, 1963, at Viking, Alta. . . . 5-11/188. . . . Shoots right. . . . Brother of Brian Sutter, left winger, St. Louis Blues (1976-77 through 1987-88) and current head coach, Boston Bruins; brother of Brent Sutter, center, Chicago Blackhawks; brother of Darryl Sutter, left winger, Blackhawks (1979-80 through 1986-87) and current head coach, Blackhawks; brother of Duane Sutter, right winger, New York Islanders and Blackhawks (1979-80 through 1989-90) and current head coach, Indianapolis Ice of IHL; and twin brother of Ron Sutter, center, Blues.

HIGH SCHOOL: Winston Churchill (Lethbridge, Alta.).

TRANSACTIONS/CAREER NOTES: Selected as underage junior by Pittsburgh Penguins in first round (first Penguins pick, 10th overall) of NHL entry draft (June 9, 1982). . . . Traded by Penguins with second-round pick (D Greg Smyth) and third-round pick (LW David McLay) in 1984 draft to Philadelphia Flyers for C Ron Flockhart, C/LW Mark Taylor, LW Andy Brickley, first-round pick (RW/C Roger Belanger) and third-round pick in 1984 draft (October 1983). . . . Traded by Flyers with D Dave Richter and third-round pick in 1986 draft to Vancouver Canucks for D J.J. Daigneault, second-round pick in 1986 draft (C Kent Hawley) and fifth-round pick in 1987 draft (June 1986). . . . Lost four teeth (October 23, 1988). . . . Injured lower back (January 17, 1989). . . . Broke nose (March 24, 1989). . . . Suspended five games by NHL for slashing (January 27, 1990). . . . Traded by Canucks with D Harold Snepsts and second-round pick in 1990 draft (previously acquired from St. Louis Blues) to Blues for D Adrien Plavsic, first-round pick in 1990 draft (later traded to Montreal Canadiens) and second-round pick in 1991 draft (March 6, 1990). . . . Suffered concussion (November 1, 1991); missed two games.

Season Team	League	REGULAR SEASON					PLAYOFFS				
		Gms.	G	A	Pts.	Pen.	Gms.	G	A	Pts.	Pen.
79-80—Red Deer	AJHL	60	13	19	32	157	—	—	—	—	—
80-81—Lethbridge	WHL	72	23	18	41	255	9	3	1	4	35
81-82—Lethbridge	WHL	57	38	31	69	263	12	3	3	6	55
82-83—Lethbridge	WHL	64	37	30	67	200	17	14	9	23	43
—Pittsburgh	NHL	4	0	0	0	0	—	—	—	—	—
83-84—Baltimore	AHL	2	0	1	1	0	—	—	—	—	—
—Pittsburgh	NHL	5	0	0	0	0	—	—	—	—	—
—Philadelphia	NHL	70	16	12	28	93	3	0	0	0	15
84-85—Hershey	AHL	13	3	7	10	14	—	—	—	—	—
—Philadelphia	NHL	56	6	10	16	89	11	3	0	3	10
85-86—Philadelphia	NHL	78	14	25	39	199	5	2	0	2	19
86-87—Vancouver	NHL	74	20	22	42	113	—	—	—	—	—
87-88—Vancouver	NHL	80	15	15	30	165	—	—	—	—	—
88-89—Vancouver	NHL	75	17	15	32	122	7	2	1	3	12
89-90—Vancouver	NHL	62	9	9	18	133	—	—	—	—	—
—St. Louis	NHL	12	2	0	2	22	12	2	1	3	39
90-91—St. Louis	NHL	77	16	11	27	122	13	4	2	6	16
91-92—St. Louis	NHL	77	9	16	25	107	6	0	0	0	8
92-93—St. Louis	NHL	84	13	14	27	100	11	0	1	1	10
NHL totals		754	137	149	286	1265	68	13	5	18	129

SUTTER, RON
C, BLUES

PERSONAL: Born December 2, 1963, at Viking, Alta. . . . 6-0/180. . . . Shoots right. . . . Brother of Brian Sutter, left winger, St. Louis Blues (1976-77 through 1987-88) and current head coach, Boston Bruins; brother of Brent Sutter, center, Chicago Blackhawks; brother of Darryl Sutter, left winger, Blackhawks (1979-80 through 1986-87) and current head coach, Blackhawks; brother of Duane Sutter, right winger, New York Islanders and Blackhawks (1979-80 through 1989-90) and current head coach, Indianapolis Ice of WHL; and twin brother of Rich Sutter, right winger, Blues.
HIGH SCHOOL: Winston Churchill (Lethbridge, Ont.).
TRANSACTIONS/CAREER NOTES: Selected by Philadelphia Flyers as underage junior in first round (first Flyers pick, fourth overall) of NHL entry draft (June 9, 1982). . . . Broke ankle (November 27, 1981). . . . Bruised ribs (March 1985). . . . Suffered stress fracture in lower back (January 1987). . . . Tore rib cartilage (March 1988). . . . Fractured jaw (October 29, 1988). . . . Pulled groin (March 1989). . . . Traded by Flyers with D Murray Baron to St. Louis Blues for C Rod Brind'Amour and C Dan Quinn (September 22, 1991). . . . Strained ligament in right knee (February 1, 1992); missed 10 games. . . . Suffered abdominal pull (September 1992); missed first 18 games of season. . . . Separated shoulder (March 30, 1993); missed remainder of season.

Season Team	League	REGULAR SEASON					PLAYOFFS				
		Gms.	G	A	Pts.	Pen.	Gms.	G	A	Pts.	Pen.
79-80—Red Deer	AJHL	60	12	33	45	44	—	—	—	—	—
80-81—Lethbridge	WHL	72	13	32	45	152	9	2	5	7	29
81-82—Lethbridge	WHL	59	38	54	92	207	12	6	5	11	28
82-83—Lethbridge	WHL	58	35	48	83	98	20	*22	†19	*41	45
—Philadelphia	NHL	10	1	1	2	9	—	—	—	—	—
83-84—Philadelphia	NHL	79	19	32	51	101	3	0	0	0	22
84-85—Philadelphia	NHL	73	16	29	45	94	19	4	8	12	28
85-86—Philadelphia	NHL	75	18	42	60	159	5	0	2	2	10
86-87—Philadelphia	NHL	39	10	17	27	69	16	1	7	8	12
87-88—Philadelphia	NHL	69	8	25	33	146	7	0	1	1	26
88-89—Philadelphia	NHL	55	26	22	48	80	19	1	9	10	51
89-90—Philadelphia	NHL	75	22	26	48	104	—	—	—	—	—
90-91—Philadelphia	NHL	80	17	28	45	92	—	—	—	—	—
91-92—St. Louis	NHL	68	19	27	46	91	6	1	3	4	8
92-93—St. Louis	NHL	59	12	15	27	99	—	—	—	—	—
NHL totals		682	168	264	432	1044	75	7	30	37	157

SUTTON, KEN
D, SABRES

PERSONAL: Born May 11, 1969, at Edmonton, Alta. . . . 6-0/198. . . . Shoots left.
TRANSACTIONS/CAREER NOTES: Selected by Buffalo Sabres in fifth round (fourth Sabres pick, 98th overall) of NHL entry draft (June 17, 1989). . . . Separated shoulder (March 3, 1992); missed six games. . . . Broke ankle (September 15, 1992); missed first 19 games of season.
HONORS: Named to Memorial Cup All-Star team (1988-89).

Season Team	League	REGULAR SEASON					PLAYOFFS				
		Gms.	G	A	Pts.	Pen.	Gms.	G	A	Pts.	Pen.
87-88—Calgary Canucks	AJHL	53	13	43	56	228	—	—	—	—	—
88-89—Saskatoon	WHL	71	22	31	53	104	8	2	5	7	12
89-90—Rochester	AHL	57	5	14	19	83	11	1	6	7	15
90-91—Buffalo	NHL	15	3	6	9	13	6	0	1	1	2
—Rochester	AHL	62	7	24	31	65	3	1	1	2	14
91-92—Buffalo	NHL	64	2	18	20	71	7	0	2	2	4
92-93—Buffalo	NHL	63	8	14	22	30	8	3	1	4	8
NHL totals		142	13	38	51	114	21	3	4	7	14

SVARTVADET, PER
C, STARS

PERSONAL: Born May 17, 1975, at Ornskoldsvik, Sweden. . . . 6-1/180. . . . Shoots left.
TRANSACTIONS/CAREER NOTES: Selected by Dallas Stars in sixth round (fifth Stars pick, 139th overall) of NHL entry draft (June 26, 1993).

Season Team	League	REGULAR SEASON Gms.	G	A	Pts.	Pen.	PLAYOFFS Gms.	G	A	Pts.	Pen.
91-92—MoDo	Sweden Jr.	30	17	19	36	36	—	—	—	—	—
92-93—MoDo	Sweden	2	0	0	0	0	—	—	—	—	—
—MoDo	Sweden Jr.	22	19	27	46	38	—	—	—	—	—

SVOBODA, PETR
D, SABRES

PERSONAL: Born February 14, 1966, at Most, Czechoslovakia.... 6-1/175.... Shoots left.
TRANSACTIONS/CAREER NOTES: Selected by Montreal Canadiens in first round (first Canadiens pick, fifth overall) of NHL entry draft (June 9, 1984).... Suffered back spasms (January 1988).... Suffered hip pointer (March 1988).... Sprained right wrist (November 21, 1988); missed five games.... Injured back (March 1989).... Separated shoulder (November 1989).... Pulled groin (November 22, 1989).... Aggravated groin injury (December 11, 1989); missed 15 games.... Bruised left foot (March 11, 1990).... Suffered stomach disorder (November 28, 1990); missed five games.... Suffered broken left foot (January 15, 1991); missed 15 games.... Injured mouth (December 14, 1991).... Sprained ankle (February 17, 1992); missed seven games.... Traded by Canadiens to Buffalo Sabres for D Kevin Haller (March 10, 1992).... Bruised knee (October 28, 1992); missed four games.... Tore ligament in right knee (January 17, 1993); missed remainder of season.
MISCELLANEOUS: Member of Stanley Cup championship team (1986).

Season Team	League	REGULAR SEASON Gms.	G	A	Pts.	Pen.	PLAYOFFS Gms.	G	A	Pts.	Pen.
83-84—Czechoslovakia Jr.	Czech.	40	15	21	36	14	—	—	—	—	—
84-85—Montreal	NHL	73	4	27	31	65	7	1	1	2	12
85-86—Montreal	NHL	73	1	18	19	93	8	0	0	0	21
86-87—Montreal	NHL	70	5	17	22	63	14	0	5	5	10
87-88—Montreal	NHL	69	7	22	29	149	10	0	5	5	12
88-89—Montreal	NHL	71	8	37	45	147	21	1	11	12	16
89-90—Montreal	NHL	60	5	31	36	98	10	0	5	5	2
90-91—Montreal	NHL	60	4	22	26	52	2	0	1	1	2
91-92—Montreal	NHL	58	5	16	21	94	—	—	—	—	—
—Buffalo	NHL	13	1	6	7	52	7	1	4	5	6
92-93—Buffalo	NHL	40	2	24	26	59	—	—	—	—	—
NHL totals		587	42	220	262	872	79	3	32	35	81

SWEENEY, BOB
C/RW, SABRES

PERSONAL: Born January 25, 1964, at Boxborough, Mass.... 6-3/200.... Shoots right.... Full name: Robert Emmett Sweeney.... Brother of Tim Sweeney, center, Mighty Ducks of Anaheim.
HIGH SCHOOL: Acton-Boxborough (Mass.).
COLLEGE: Boston College.
TRANSACTIONS/CAREER NOTES: Selected by Boston Bruins in sixth round (sixth Bruins pick, 123rd overall) of NHL entry draft (June 9, 1982).... Pulled rib muscle (November 1989); missed six games.... Injured left shoulder (April 23, 1991).... Sprained knee (February 4, 1992); missed 11 games.... Claimed on waivers by both Buffalo Sabres and Calgary Flames; NHL awarded rights to Sabres (October 9, 1992).
HONORS: Named to NCAA All-America East second team (1984-85).... Named to Hockey East All-Star second team (1984-85).

Season Team	League	REGULAR SEASON Gms.	G	A	Pts.	Pen.	PLAYOFFS Gms.	G	A	Pts.	Pen.
82-83—Boston College	ECAC	30	17	11	28	10	—	—	—	—	—
83-84—Boston College	ECAC	23	14	7	21	10	—	—	—	—	—
84-85—Boston College	Hockey East	44	32	32	64	43	—	—	—	—	—
85-86—Boston College	Hockey East	41	15	24	39	52	—	—	—	—	—
86-87—Boston	NHL	14	2	4	6	21	3	0	0	0	0
—Moncton	AHL	58	29	26	55	81	4	0	2	2	13
87-88—Boston	NHL	80	22	23	45	73	23	6	8	14	66
88-89—Boston	NHL	75	14	14	28	99	10	2	4	6	19
89-90—Boston	NHL	70	22	24	46	93	20	0	2	2	30
90-91—Boston	NHL	80	15	33	48	115	17	4	2	6	45
91-92—Boston	NHL	63	6	14	20	103	14	1	0	1	25
—Maine	AHL	1	1	0	1	0	—	—	—	—	—
92-93—Buffalo	NHL	80	21	26	47	118	8	2	2	4	8
NHL totals		462	102	138	240	622	95	15	18	33	193

SWEENEY, DON
D, BRUINS

PERSONAL: Born August 17, 1966, at St. Stephen, N.B.... 5-11/170.... Shoots left.... Full name: Donald Clark Sweeney.
COLLEGE: Harvard.
TRANSACTIONS/CAREER NOTES: Selected by Boston Bruins in eighth round (eighth Bruins pick, 166th overall) of NHL entry draft (June 9, 1984).... Bruised left heel (February 22, 1990).... Injured knee (October 12, 1991); missed four games.
HONORS: Named to NCAA All-America East second team (1987-88).... Named to ECAC All-Star first team (1987-88).

Season Team	League	REGULAR SEASON Gms.	G	A	Pts.	Pen.	PLAYOFFS Gms.	G	A	Pts.	Pen.
83-84—St. Paul N.B. H.S.	N.B. H.S.	22	33	26	59	...	—	—	—	—	—
84-85—Harvard University	ECAC	29	3	7	10	30	—	—	—	—	—
85-86—Harvard University	ECAC	31	4	5	9	29	—	—	—	—	—
86-87—Harvard University	ECAC	34	7	14	21	22	—	—	—	—	—

S

Season Team	League	REGULAR SEASON					PLAYOFFS				
		Gms.	G	A	Pts.	Pen.	Gms.	G	A	Pts.	Pen.
87-88—Harvard University	ECAC	30	6	23	29	37	—	—	—	—	—
—Maine	AHL	—	—	—	—	—	6	1	3	4	0
88-89—Maine	AHL	42	8	17	25	24	—	—	—	—	—
—Boston	NHL	36	3	5	8	20	—	—	—	—	—
89-90—Boston	NHL	58	3	5	8	58	21	1	5	6	18
—Maine	AHL	11	0	8	8	8	—	—	—	—	—
90-91—Boston	NHL	77	8	13	21	67	19	3	0	3	25
91-92—Boston	NHL	75	3	11	14	74	15	0	0	0	10
92-93—Boston	NHL	84	7	27	34	68	4	0	0	0	4
NHL totals		330	24	61	85	287	59	4	5	9	57

SWEENEY, TIM
C, MIGHTY DUCKS

PERSONAL: Born April 12, 1967, at Boston.... 5-11/185.... Shoots left.... Full name: Timothy Paul Sweeney.... Brother of Bob Sweeney, center/right winger, Buffalo Sabres.
HIGH SCHOOL: Weymouth (East Weymouth, Mass.).
COLLEGE: Boston College.
TRANSACTIONS/CAREER NOTES: Selected by Calgary Flames in sixth round (seventh Flames pick, 122nd overall) of NHL entry draft (June 15, 1985).... Fractured index finger (January 26, 1988).... Bruised ankle (May 1990).... Signed as free agent by Boston Bruins (September 1992).... Selected by Mighty Ducks of Anaheim in NHL expansion draft (June 24, 1993).
HONORS: Named to NCAA All-America East second team (1988-89).... Named to Hockey East All-Star first team (1988-89). ... Won Ken McKenzie Trophy (1989-90).... Named to IHL All-Star second team (1989-90).... Named to AHL All-Star second team (1992-93).

Season Team	League	REGULAR SEASON					PLAYOFFS				
		Gms.	G	A	Pts.	Pen.	Gms.	G	A	Pts.	Pen.
83-84—Weymouth North H.S.	Mass. H.S.	23	33	26	59	...	—	—	—	—	—
84-85—Weymouth North H.S.	Mass. H.S.	22	32	56	88	...	—	—	—	—	—
85-86—Boston College	Hockey East	32	8	4	12	8	—	—	—	—	—
86-87—Boston College	Hockey East	38	31	16	47	28	—	—	—	—	—
87-88—Boston College	Hockey East	18	9	11	20	18	—	—	—	—	—
88-89—Boston College	Hockey East	39	29	44	73	26	—	—	—	—	—
89-90—Salt Lake City	IHL	81	46	51	97	32	11	5	4	9	4
90-91—Calgary	NHL	42	7	9	16	8	—	—	—	—	—
—Salt Lake City	IHL	31	19	16	35	8	4	3	3	6	0
91-92—Calgary	NHL	11	1	2	3	4	—	—	—	—	—
—U.S. national team	Int'l	21	9	11	20	10	—	—	—	—	—
—U.S. Olympic Team	Int'l	8	3	4	7	6	—	—	—	—	—
92-93—Providence	AHL	60	41	55	96	32	3	2	2	4	0
—Boston	NHL	14	1	7	8	6	3	0	0	0	0
NHL totals		67	9	18	27	18	3	0	0	0	0

SYDOR, DARRYL
D, KINGS

PERSONAL: Born May 13, 1972, at Edmonton, Alta.... 6-0/200.... Shoots left.... Full name: Darryl Marion Sydor.
TRANSACTIONS/CAREER NOTES: Selected by Los Angeles Kings in first round (first Kings pick, seventh overall) of NHL entry draft (June 16, 1990).... Bruised hip (November 27, 1992); missed two games.... Sprained right shoulder (March 15, 1993); missed two games.
HONORS: Named to WHL (West) All-Star first team (1989-90 through 1991-92).... Won Bill Hunter Trophy (1990-91).... Named to Can.HL All-Star second team (1991-92)

Season Team	League	REGULAR SEASON					PLAYOFFS				
		Gms.	G	A	Pts.	Pen.	Gms.	G	A	Pts.	Pen.
88-89—Kamloops	WHL	65	12	14	26	86	15	1	4	5	19
89-90—Kamloops	WHL	67	29	66	95	129	17	2	9	11	28
90-91—Kamloops	WHL	66	27	78	105	88	12	3	*22	25	10
91-92—Kamloops	WHL	29	9	39	48	43	17	3	15	18	18
—Los Angeles	NHL	18	1	5	6	22	—	—	—	—	—
92-93—Los Angeles	NHL	80	6	23	29	63	24	3	8	11	16
NHL totals		98	7	28	35	85	24	3	8	11	16

SYKORA, MICHAL
D, SHARKS

PERSONAL: Born July 5, 1973, at Pardubice, Czechoslovakia.... 6-3/195.... Shoots left.
TRANSACTIONS/CAREER NOTES: Selected by San Jose Sharks in sixth round (sixth Sharks pick, 123rd overall) of NHL entry draft (June 20, 1992).
HONORS: Named to Can.HL All-Star second team (1992-93).... Named to WHL (West) All-Star first team (1992-93).

Season Team	League	REGULAR SEASON					PLAYOFFS				
		Gms.	G	A	Pts.	Pen.	Gms.	G	A	Pts.	Pen.
90-91—Pardubice	Czech.	2	0	0	0	0	—	—	—	—	—
91-92—Tacoma	WHL	61	13	23	36	66	4	0	2	2	2
92-93—Tacoma	WHL	70	23	50	73	73	7	4	8	12	2

TABARACCI, RICK
G, CAPITALS

PERSONAL: Born January 2, 1969, at Toronto.... 5-11/179.... Shoots left.... Full name: Richard Stephen Tabaracci.... Name pronounced TA-buh-RA-chee.
TRANSACTIONS/CAREER NOTES: Selected by Pittsburgh Penguins as underage junior in second round (second Penguins pick, 26th overall) of NHL entry draft (June 13, 1987).

... Traded by Penguins with C/LW Randy Cunneyworth and RW Dave McLlwain to Winnipeg Jets for RW Andrew McBain, D Jim Kyte and LW Randy Gilhen (June 17, 1989).... Pulled right hamstring (December 11, 1990); missed seven games.... Strained back (October 10, 1992); missed one game.... Suffered back spasms (December 1, 1992); missed one game.... Suffered back spasms (January 19, 1993); missed seven games.... Traded by Jets to Washington Capitals for G Jim Hrivnak and future considerations (March 22, 1993).

HONORS: Named to OHL All-Star first team (1987-88).... Named to OHL All-Star second team (1988-89).

					REGULAR SEASON							PLAYOFFS					
Season	Team	League	Gms.	Min.	W	L	T	GA	SO	Avg.	Gms.	Min.	W	L	GA	SO	Avg.
85-86	Markham Jr. B	OHA	40	2176	...	...	...	188	1	5.18	—	—	—	—	—	—	—
86-87	Cornwall	OHL	*59	*3347	23	32	3	*290	1	5.20	5	303	1	4	26	0	5.15
87-88	Cornwall	OHL	58	3448	33	18	6	200	†3	3.48	11	642	5	6	37	0	3.46
	Muskegon	IHL	—	—	—	—	—	—	—	—	1	13	0	0	1	0	4.62
88-89	Cornwall	OHL	50	2974	24	20	5	*210	1	4.24	18	1080	10	8	65	†1	3.61
	Pittsburgh	NHL	1	33	0	0	0	4	0	7.27	—	—	—	—	—	—	—
89-90	Moncton	AHL	27	1580	10	15	2	107	2	4.06	—	—	—	—	—	—	—
	Fort Wayne	IHL	22	1064	8	9	1	73	0	4.12	3	159	1	2	19	0	7.17
90-91	Moncton	AHL	11	645	4	5	2	41	0	3.81	—	—	—	—	—	—	—
	Winnipeg	NHL	24	1093	4	9	4	71	1	3.90	—	—	—	—	—	—	—
91-92	Moncton	AHL	23	1313	10	11	1	80	0	3.66	—	—	—	—	—	—	—
	Winnipeg	NHL	18	966	6	7	3	52	0	3.23	7	387	3	4	26	0	4.03
92-93	Winnipeg	NHL	19	959	5	10	0	70	0	4.38	—	—	—	—	—	—	—
	Moncton	AHL	5	290	2	1	2	18	0	3.72	—	—	—	—	—	—	—
	Washington	NHL	6	343	3	2	0	10	2	1.75	4	304	1	3	14	0	2.76
NHL totals			68	3394	18	28	7	207	3	3.66	11	691	4	7	40	0	3.47

TAGLIANETTI, PETER
D, PENGUINS

PERSONAL: Born August 15, 1963, at Framingham, Mass. ... 6-2/200. ... Shoots left. ... Full name: Peter Anthony Taglianetti. ... Name pronounced TAG-lee-uh-NEH-tee.
COLLEGE: Providence.

TRANSACTIONS/CAREER NOTES: Selected by Winnipeg Jets in third round (fourth Jets pick, 43rd overall) of NHL entry draft (June 8, 1983).... Dislocated shoulder during training camp (October 1985).... Dislocated shoulder (February 20, 1986). ... Underwent surgery to correct recurring shoulder dislocations (March 1986).... Damaged right knee cartilage during training camp and underwent surgery (September 1988).... Injured knee and underwent surgery (October 6, 1989).... Suspended five games by NHL for attempting to injure opposing player (February 20, 1990).... Bruised ribs (April 1990).... Traded by Jets to Minnesota North Stars for future considerations (September 23, 1990).... Traded by North Stars with D Larry Murphy to Pittsburgh Penguins for D Jim Johnson and D Chris Dahlquist (December 11, 1990).... Suffered collapsed lung (February 11, 1991); missed nine games.... Injured back (December 21, 1991); missed two games.... Injured back (March 7, 1992); missed final 15 games of season.... Underwent back surgery (April 5, 1992); missed entire playoffs.... Selected by Tampa Bay Lightning in NHL expansion draft (June 18, 1992).... Suffered concussion (March 20, 1993); missed one game.... Traded by Lightning to Penguins for third-round pick in 1993 draft (March 22, 1993).

HONORS: Named to ECAC All-Star second team (1983-84).... Named to NCAA All-America East second team (1984-85).... Named to Hockey East All-Star first team (1984-85).

MISCELLANEOUS: Member of Stanley Cup championship teams (1991 and 1992).

					REGULAR SEASON				PLAYOFFS			
Season	Team	League	Gms.	G	A	Pts.	Pen.	Gms.	G	A	Pts.	Pen.
81-82	Providence College	ECAC	2	0	0	0	2	—	—	—	—	—
82-83	Providence College	ECAC	43	4	17	21	68	—	—	—	—	—
83-84	Providence College	ECAC	30	4	25	29	68	—	—	—	—	—
84-85	Providence College	Hockey East	43	8	21	29	114	—	—	—	—	—
	Winnipeg	NHL	1	0	0	0	0	1	0	0	0	0
85-86	Sherbrooke	AHL	24	1	8	9	75	—	—	—	—	—
	Winnipeg	NHL	18	0	0	0	48	3	0	0	0	2
86-87	Winnipeg	NHL	3	0	0	0	12	—	—	—	—	—
	Sherbrooke	AHL	54	5	14	19	104	10	2	5	7	25
87-88	Winnipeg	NHL	70	6	17	23	182	5	1	1	2	12
88-89	Winnipeg	NHL	66	1	14	15	226	—	—	—	—	—
89-90	Moncton	AHL	3	0	2	2	2	—	—	—	—	—
	Winnipeg	NHL	49	3	6	9	136	5	0	0	0	6
90-91	Minnesota	NHL	16	0	1	1	14	—	—	—	—	—
	Pittsburgh	NHL	39	3	8	11	93	19	0	3	3	49
91-92	Pittsburgh	NHL	44	1	3	4	57	—	—	—	—	—
92-93	Tampa Bay	NHL	61	1	8	9	150	—	—	—	—	—
	Pittsburgh	NHL	11	1	4	5	34	11	1	2	3	16
NHL totals			378	16	61	77	952	44	2	6	8	85

TAMER, CHRIS
D, PENGUINS

PERSONAL: Born November 17, 1970, at Dearborn, Mich. ... 6-2/185. ... Shoots left. ... Full name: Chris Thomas Tamer.
COLLEGE: Michigan.
TRANSACTIONS/CAREER NOTES: Selected by Pittsburgh Penguins in fourth round (third Penguins pick, 68th overall) of NHL entry draft (June 16, 1990).

					REGULAR SEASON				PLAYOFFS			
Season	Team	League	Gms.	G	A	Pts.	Pen.	Gms.	G	A	Pts.	Pen.
87-88	Redford	NAJHL	40	10	20	30	217	—	—	—	—	—

Season	Team	League	REGULAR SEASON					PLAYOFFS				
			Gms.	G	A	Pts.	Pen.	Gms.	G	A	Pts.	Pen.
88-89	Redford	NAJHL	31	6	13	19	79	—	—	—	—	—
89-90	University of Michigan	CCHA	42	2	7	9	147	—	—	—	—	—
90-91	University of Michigan	CCHA	45	8	19	27	130	—	—	—	—	—
91-92	University of Michigan	CCHA	43	4	15	19	*125	—	—	—	—	—
92-93	University of Michigan	CCHA	39	5	18	23	113	—	—	—	—	—

TANCILL, CHRIS
C, RED WINGS

PERSONAL: Born February 7, 1968, at Livonia, Mich. . . . 5- 10/ 185. . . . Shoots left. . . . Full name: Christopher William Tancill.
COLLEGE: Wisconsin.
TRANSACTIONS/CAREER NOTES: Selected by Hartford Whalers in NHL supplemental draft (June 16, 1989). . . . Traded by Whalers to Detroit Red Wings for RW Daniel Shank (December 18, 1991).
HONORS: Named NCAA Tournament Most Valuable Player (1990- 91). . . . Named to NCAA All-Tournament team (1990- 91). . . . Named to AHL All-Star first team (1991-92 and 1992- 93).

Season	Team	League	REGULAR SEASON					PLAYOFFS				
			Gms.	G	A	Pts.	Pen.	Gms.	G	A	Pts.	Pen.
87-88	University of Wisconsin	WCHA	44	13	14	27	48	—	—	—	—	—
88-89	University of Wisconsin	WCHA	44	20	23	43	50	—	—	—	—	—
89-90	University of Wisconsin	WCHA	45	39	32	71	44	—	—	—	—	—
90-91	Hartford	NHL	9	1	1	2	4	—	—	—	—	—
	Springfield	AHL	72	37	35	72	46	17	8	4	12	32
91-92	Springfield	AHL	17	12	7	19	20	—	—	—	—	—
	Hartford	NHL	10	0	0	0	2	—	—	—	—	—
	Adirondack	AHL	50	36	34	70	42	19	7	9	16	31
	Detroit	NHL	1	0	0	0	0	—	—	—	—	—
92-93	Adirondack	AHL	68	*59	43	102	62	10	7	7	14	10
	Detroit	NHL	4	1	0	1	2	—	—	—	—	—
NHL totals			24	2	1	3	8					

TANGUAY, MARTIN
C, LIGHTNING

PERSONAL: Born January 12, 1973, at Ste.- Julie, Que. . . . 5- 11/ 185. . . . Shoots left.
TRANSACTIONS/CAREER NOTES: Selected by Tampa Bay Lightning in sixth round (sixth Lightning pick, 122nd overall) of NHL entry draft (June 20, 1992).

Season	Team	League	REGULAR SEASON					PLAYOFFS				
			Gms.	G	A	Pts.	Pen.	Gms.	G	A	Pts.	Pen.
89-90	Longueuil	QMJHL	61	11	16	27	35	7	1	4	5	9
90-91	Longueuil	QMJHL	69	27	34	61	14	8	3	4	7	6
91-92	Verdun	QMJHL	67	41	50	91	117	19	8	13	21	32
92-93	Verdun	QMJHL	72	53	58	111	78	4	1	2	3	21

TANNER, JOHN
G, NORDIQUES

PERSONAL: Born March 17, 1971, at Cambridge, Ont. . . . 6-3/ 182. . . . Shoots left.
TRANSACTIONS/CAREER NOTES: Selected by Quebec Nordiques in third round (fourth Nordiques pick, 54th overall) of NHL entry draft (June 17, 1989). . . . Traded by Peterborough Petes to London Knights for second-round pick in 1990 draft they had acquired earlier from Windsor, and second- and third-round picks in 1991 draft (January 1990). . . . Traded by Knights to Sudbury Wolves for fourth-round pick in 1991 draft (December 1990).
HONORS: Shared Dave Pinkney Trophy with G Todd Bojcun (1987-88 and 1988-89).

Season	Team	League	REGULAR SEASON							PLAYOFFS					
			Gms.	Min.	W	L	T	GA	SO	Avg.	Gms.	Min.	W	L	GA	SO	Avg.
86-87	New Hamburg Jr. C	OHA	15	889	. . .	. . .	. . .	83	0	5.60	—	—	—	—	—	—	—
87-88	Peterborough	OHL	26	1532	18	4	3	88	0	3.45	2	98	1	0	3	0	1.84
88-89	Peterborough	OHL	34	1923	22	10	0	107	†2	*3.34	8	369	4	3	23	0	3.74
89-90	Quebec	NHL	1	60	0	1	0	3	0	3.00	—	—	—	—	—	—	—
	Peterborough	OHL	18	1037	6	8	2	70	0	4.05	—	—	—	—	—	—	—
	London	OHL	19	1097	12	5	1	53	1	2.90	6	341	2	4	24	0	4.22
90-91	Quebec	NHL	6	228	1	3	1	16	0	4.21	—	—	—	—	—	—	—
	London	OHL	7	427	3	3	1	29	0	4.07	—	—	—	—	—	—	—
	Sudbury	OHL	19	1043	10	8	0	60	0	3.45	5	274	1	4	21	0	4.60
91-92	Halifax	AHL	12	672	6	5	1	29	2	2.59	—	—	—	—	—	—	—
	New Haven	AHL	16	908	7	6	2	57	0	3.77	—	—	—	—	—	—	—
	Quebec	NHL	14	796	1	7	4	46	1	3.47	—	—	—	—	—	—	—
92-93	Halifax	AHL	51	2852	20	18	7	199	0	4.19	—	—	—	—	—	—	—
NHL totals			21	1084	2	11	5	65	1	3.60							

TARDIF, PATRICE
C, BLUES

PERSONAL: Born October 30, 1970, at Thetford Mines, Que. . . . 6-2/ 175. . . . Shoots left. . . . Name pronounced TAHR-dihf.
COLLEGE: Champlain Regional (Que.), then Maine.
TRANSACTIONS/CAREER NOTES: Selected by St. Louis Blues in third round (second Blues pick, 54th overall) of NHL entry draft (June 16, 1990).
HONORS: Named to Hockey East All-Rookie team (1990-91).

Season Team	League	REGULAR SEASON Gms.	G	A	Pts.	Pen.	PLAYOFFS Gms.	G	A	Pts.	Pen.
89-90—Champlain Junior College	Can. Coll.	27	58	36	94	36	—	—	—	—	—
90-91—University of Maine	Hockey East	36	13	12	25	18	—	—	—	—	—
91-92—University of Maine	Hockey East	31	18	20	38	14	—	—	—	—	—
92-93—University of Maine	Hockey East	45	23	25	48	22	—	—	—	—	—

TATARINOV, MIKHAIL
D, BRUINS

PERSONAL: Born July 16, 1966, at Penza, U.S.S.R. . . . 5-10/194. . . . Shoots left. . . . Name pronounced mih-KAYL tah-TAH-rih-nahf.
TRANSACTIONS/CAREER NOTES: Selected by Washington Capitals in 11th round (10th Capitals pick, 225th overall) of NHL entry draft (June 9, 1984). . . . Traded by Capitals to Quebec Nordiques for second-round pick in 1991 draft (D Eric Lavigne) (June 22, 1991). . . . Injured ribs (November 16, 1991); missed six games. . . . Bruised ribs (February 18, 1992); missed five games. . . . Sprained right thumb (November 11, 1992); missed 15 games. . . . Suffered back injury (March 15, 1993); missed remainder of season. . . . Signed as free agent by Boston Bruins (July 30, 1993).

Season Team	League	REGULAR SEASON Gms.	G	A	Pts.	Pen.	PLAYOFFS Gms.	G	A	Pts.	Pen.
83-84—Sokol Kiev	USSR	38	7	3	10	46	—	—	—	—	—
84-85—Sokol Kiev	USSR	34	3	6	9	54	—	—	—	—	—
85-86—Sokol Kiev	USSR	37	7	5	12	41	—	—	—	—	—
86-87—Dynamo Moscow	USSR	40	10	8	18	43	—	—	—	—	—
87-88—Dynamo Moscow	USSR	30	2	2	4	8	—	—	—	—	—
88-89—Dynamo Moscow	USSR	4	1	0	1	2	—	—	—	—	—
89-90—Dynamo Moscow	USSR	44	11	10	21	34	—	—	—	—	—
90-91—Dynamo Moscow	USSR	11	5	4	9	. . .	—	—	—	—	—
—Washington	NHL	65	8	15	23	82	—	—	—	—	—
91-92—Quebec	NHL	66	11	27	38	72	—	—	—	—	—
92-93—Quebec	NHL	28	2	6	8	28	—	—	—	—	—
NHL totals		159	21	48	69	182					

TAYLOR, CHRIS
C, ISLANDERS

PERSONAL: Born March 6, 1972, at Stratford, Ont. . . . 6-1/190. . . . Shoots left. . . . Brother of Tim Taylor, center in Vancouver Canucks system.
TRANSACTIONS/CAREER NOTES: Tore knee ligaments when checked by Scott Pearson vs. Niagara Falls (March 1989). . . . Selected by New York Islanders in second round (second Islanders pick, 27th overall) of NHL entry draft (June 16, 1990).

Season Team	League	REGULAR SEASON Gms.	G	A	Pts.	Pen.	PLAYOFFS Gms.	G	A	Pts.	Pen.
88-89—London	OHL	62	7	16	23	52	15	0	2	2	15
89-90—London	OHL	66	45	60	105	60	6	3	2	5	6
90-91—London	OHL	65	50	78	128	50	7	4	8	12	6
91-92—London	OHL	66	48	74	122	57	10	8	16	24	9
92-93—Capital District	AHL	77	19	43	62	32	4	0	1	1	2

TAYLOR, DAVE
RW, KINGS

PERSONAL: Born December 4, 1955, at Levack, Ont. . . . 6-0/195. . . . Shoots right. . . . Full name: David Andrew Taylor.
HIGH SCHOOL: Levack District (Ont.).
COLLEGE: Clarkson (N.Y.).
TRANSACTIONS/CAREER NOTES: Selected by Los Angeles Kings in 15th round (14th Kings pick, 210th overall) of NHL amateur draft (June 3, 1975). . . . Pulled back muscle and sprained left knee; missed parts of 1979-80 season. . . . Sprained shoulder (November 5, 1980). . . . Broke right wrist (October 29, 1982); missed 33 games. . . . Injured right knee (January 1983). . . . Broke wrist at World Championships and underwent surgery (May 28, 1983); missed games. . . . Sprained knee (November 1986). . . . Injured groin (December 1987). . . . Tore knee cartilage (January 1989). . . . Pulled groin (December 13, 1989); missed 15 games. . . . Suffered knee inflamation (January 1990). . . . Strained shoulder (April 1990). . . . Suffered concussion (Novmeber 14, 1992); missed 18 games. . . . Suffered recurring symptoms of previous concussion (February 9, 1993); missed 16 games.
HONORS: Named ECAC Player of the Year (1976-77). . . . Named to NCAA All-America East team (1976-77). . . . Named to THE SPORTING NEWS All-Star second team (1980-81). . . . Named to NHL All-Star second team (1980-81). . . . Played in NHL All-Star Game (1981, 1982 and 1986). . . . Won King Clancy Memorial Trophy (1990-91). . . . Won Bill Masterton Trophy (1990-91).

Season Team	League	REGULAR SEASON Gms.	G	A	Pts.	Pen.	PLAYOFFS Gms.	G	A	Pts.	Pen.
74-75—Clarkson	ECAC	. . .	20	34	54	. . .	—	—	—	—	—
75-76—Clarkson	ECAC	. . .	26	33	59	. . .	—	—	—	—	—
76-77—Clarkson	ECAC	34	41	67	108	. . .	—	—	—	—	—
—Fort Worth	CHL	7	2	4	6	6	—	—	—	—	—
77-78—Los Angeles	NHL	64	22	21	43	47	2	0	0	0	5
78-79—Los Angeles	NHL	78	43	48	91	124	2	0	0	0	2
79-80—Los Angeles	NHL	61	37	53	90	72	4	2	1	3	4
80-81—Los Angeles	NHL	72	47	65	112	130	4	2	2	4	10
81-82—Los Angeles	NHL	78	39	67	106	130	10	4	6	10	20
82-83—Los Angeles	NHL	46	21	37	58	76	—	—	—	—	—
83-84—Los Angeles	NHL	63	20	49	69	91	—	—	—	—	—
84-85—Los Angeles	NHL	79	41	51	92	132	3	2	2	4	8
85-86—Los Angeles	NHL	76	33	38	71	110	—	—	—	—	—

Season Team	League	REGULAR SEASON Gms.	G	A	Pts.	Pen.	PLAYOFFS Gms.	G	A	Pts.	Pen.
86-87—Los Angeles	NHL	67	18	44	62	84	5	2	3	5	6
87-88—Los Angeles	NHL	68	26	41	67	129	5	3	3	6	6
88-89—Los Angeles	NHL	70	26	37	63	80	11	1	5	6	19
89-90—Los Angeles	NHL	58	15	26	41	96	6	4	4	8	2
90-91—Los Angeles	NHL	73	23	30	53	148	12	2	1	3	12
91-92—Los Angeles	NHL	77	10	19	29	63	6	1	1	2	20
92-93—Los Angeles	NHL	48	6	9	15	49	22	3	5	8	31
NHL totals		1078	427	635	1062	1561	92	26	33	59	145

TAYLOR, TIM
C, CANUCKS

PERSONAL: Born February 6, 1969, at Stratford, Ont. . . . 6-1/180. . . . Shoots left. . . . Full name: Tim Robertson Taylor. . . . Brother of Chris Taylor, center in New York Islanders system.
TRANSACTIONS/CAREER NOTES: Suffered from mononucleosis (October 1986). . . . Selected by Washington Capitals in second round (second Capitals pick, 36th overall) of NHL entry draft (June 11, 1988). . . . Traded by Capitals to Vancouver Canucks for C Eric Murano (January 29, 1993).

Season Team	League	REGULAR SEASON Gms.	G	A	Pts.	Pen.	PLAYOFFS Gms.	G	A	Pts.	Pen.
86-87—London	OHL	34	7	9	16	11	—	—	—	—	—
87-88—London	OHL	64	46	50	96	66	12	9	9	18	26
88-89—London	OHL	61	34	80	114	93	21	*21	25	*46	58
89-90—Baltimore	AHL	74	22	21	43	63	9	2	2	4	13
90-91—Baltimore	AHL	79	25	42	67	75	5	0	1	1	4
91-92—Baltimore	AHL	65	9	18	27	131	—	—	—	—	—
92-93—Baltimore	AHL	41	15	16	31	49	—	—	—	—	—
—Hamilton	AHL	36	15	22	37	37	—	—	—	—	—

TEPPER, STEPHEN
RW, BLACKHAWKS

PERSONAL: Born March 10, 1969, at Santa Ana, Calif. . . . 6-4/211. . . . Shoots left. . . . Full name: Stephen Christopher Tepper.
HIGH SCHOOL: Westborough (Mass.).
COLLEGE: Maine.
TRANSACTIONS/CAREER NOTES: Selected by Chicago Blackhawks in seventh round (seventh Blackhawks pick, 134th overall) of NHL entry draft (June 13, 1987).

Season Team	League	REGULAR SEASON Gms.	G	A	Pts.	Pen.	PLAYOFFS Gms.	G	A	Pts.	Pen.
85-86—Westborough H.S.	Mass. H.S.	...	18	26	44	...	—	—	—	—	—
86-87—Westborough H.S.	Mass. H.S.	...	34	18	52	...	—	—	—	—	—
87-88—Westborough H.S.	Mass. H.S.	24	39	24	63	...	—	—	—	—	—
88-89—University of Maine	Hockey East	26	3	9	12	32	—	—	—	—	—
89-90—University of Maine	Hockey East	41	10	6	16	68	—	—	—	—	—
90-91—University of Maine	Hockey East	38	6	11	17	58	—	—	—	—	—
91-92—University of Maine	Hockey East	16	0	3	3	20	—	—	—	—	—
92-93—Indianapolis	IHL	12	0	1	1	40	—	—	—	—	—
—Chicago	NHL	1	0	0	0	0	—	—	—	—	—
—Kansas City	IHL	32	4	10	14	51	4	0	1	1	6
NHL totals		1	0	0	0	0					

TERRERI, CHRIS
G, DEVILS

PERSONAL: Born November 15, 1964, at Warwick, R.I. . . . 5-8/155. . . . Shoots left. . . . Full name: Christopher Arnold Terreri. . . . Name pronounced tuh-RAIR-ee.
COLLEGE: Providence.
TRANSACTIONS/CAREER NOTES: Selected by New Jersey Devils in fifth round (third Devils pick, 87th overall) of NHL entry draft (June 8, 1983). . . . Strained knee (October 1986). . . . Strained lower back (March 21, 1992); missed five games.
HONORS: Named NCAA Tournament Most Valuable Player (1984-85). . . . Named to NCAA All-Tournament team (1984-85). . . . Named to NCAA All-America East first team (1984-85). . . . Named Hockey East Player of the Year (1984-85). . . . Named Hockey East Most Valuable Player (1984-85). . . . Named to Hockey East All-Star first team (1984-85). . . . Named to NCAA All-America East second team (1985-86).

Season Team	League	REGULAR SEASON Gms.	Min.	W	L	T	GA	SO	Avg.	PLAYOFFS Gms.	Min.	W	L	GA	SO	Avg.
82-83—Providence College	ECAC	11	529	7	1	0	17	2	1.93	—	—	—	—	—	—	—
83-84—Providence College	ECAC	10	391	4	2	0	20	0	3.07	—	—	—	—	—	—	—
84-85—Providence College	Hoc. East	41	2515	15	13	5	131	1	3.13	—	—	—	—	—	—	—
85-86—Providence College	Hoc. East	27	1540	6	16	0	96	0	3.74	—	—	—	—	—	—	—
86-87—Maine	AHL	14	765	4	9	1	57	0	4.47	—	—	—	—	—	—	—
—New Jersey	NHL	7	286	0	3	1	21	0	4.41	—	—	—	—	—	—	—
87-88—U.S. national team	Int'l	26	1430	17	7	2	81	0	3.40	—	—	—	—	—	—	—
—U.S. Olympic Team	Int'l	3	128	1	1	0	14	0	6.56	—	—	—	—	—	—	—
—Utica	AHL	7	399	5	1	0	18	0	2.71	—	—	—	—	—	—	—
88-89—New Jersey	NHL	8	402	0	4	2	18	0	2.69	—	—	—	—	—	—	—
—Utica	AHL	39	2314	20	15	3	132	0	3.42	2	80	0	1	6	0	4.50
89-90—New Jersey	NHL	35	1931	15	12	3	110	0	3.42	4	238	2	2	13	0	3.28
90-91—New Jersey	NHL	53	2970	24	21	7	144	1	2.91	7	428	3	4	21	0	2.94

Season Team	League	REGULAR SEASON								PLAYOFFS					
		Gms.	Min.	W	L	T	GA	SO	Avg.	Gms.	Min.	W	L	GA SO	Avg.
91-92—New Jersey	NHL	54	3186	22	22	10	169	1	3.18	7	386	3	3	23 0	3.58
92-93—New Jersey	NHL	48	2672	19	21	3	151	2	3.39	4	219	1	3	17 0	4.66
NHL totals		205	11447	80	83	26	613	4	3.21	22	1271	9	12	74 0	3.49

THIBAULT, JOCELYN
G, NORDIQUES

PERSONAL: Born January 12, 1975, at Montreal. . . . 5-11/170. . . . Shoots left.
TRANSACTIONS/CAREER NOTES: Selected by Quebec Nordiques in first round (first Nordiques pick, 10th overall) of NHL entry draft (June 26, 1993).
HONORS: Named to QMJHL All-Rookie team (1991-92). . . . Won Can.HL Goal-tender-of-the-Year Award (1992-93). . . . Named to Can.HL All-Star first team (1992-93). . . . Won Jacques Plante Trophy (1992-93). . . . Won Michel Briere Trophy (1992-93). . . . Won Marcel Robert Trophy (1992-93). . . . Named to QMJHL All-Star first team (1992-93).

Season Team	League	REGULAR SEASON								PLAYOFFS					
		Gms.	Min.	W	L	T	GA	SO	Avg.	Gms.	Min.	W	L	GA SO	Avg.
91-92—Trois-Rivieres	QMJHL	30	1497	...	...	...	77	...	3.09	3	300	...	...	20 0	4.00
92-93—Sherbrooke	QMJHL	56	3190	34	14	5	159	*3	*2.99	15	883	9	6	57 0	3.87

THIESSEN, TRAVIS
D, PENGUINS

PERSONAL: Born November 7, 1972, at North Battleford, Sask. . . . 6-3/202. . . . Shoots left.
TRANSACTIONS/CAREER NOTES: Selected by Pittsburgh Penguins in third round (third Penguins pick, 67th overall) of NHL entry draft (June 20, 1992).

Season Team	League	REGULAR SEASON					PLAYOFFS				
		Gms.	G	A	Pts.	Pen.	Gms.	G	A	Pts.	Pen.
90-91—Moose Jaw	WHL	69	4	14	18	80	8	0	0	0	10
91-92—Moose Jaw	WHL	72	9	50	59	112	4	0	2	2	8
92-93—Cleveland	IHL	64	3	7	10	69	4	0	0	0	16

THOMAS, SCOTT
RW, SABRES

PERSONAL: Born January 18, 1970, at Buffalo, N.Y. . . . 6-2/195. . . . Shoots right. . . . Full name: John Scott Thomas.
HIGH SCHOOL: Nichols School (Buffalo, N.Y.).
COLLEGE: Clarkson (N.Y.).
TRANSACTIONS/CAREER NOTES: Selected by Buffalo Sabres in third round (second Sabres pick, 56th overall) of NHL entry draft (June 17, 1989). . . . Broke left thumb (December 1990).
HONORS: Named to ECAC All-Rookie team (1989-90).

Season Team	League	REGULAR SEASON					PLAYOFFS				
		Gms.	G	A	Pts.	Pen.	Gms.	G	A	Pts.	Pen.
87-88—Nichols School	N.Y. H.S.	16	23	39	62	82	—	—	—	—	—
88-89—Nichols School	N.Y. H.S.	...	38	52	90	...	—	—	—	—	—
89-90—Clarkson	ECAC	34	19	13	32	95	—	—	—	—	—
90-91—Clarkson	ECAC	40	28	14	42	90	—	—	—	—	—
91-92—Clarkson	ECAC	30	†25	21	46	62	—	—	—	—	—
—Rochester	AHL	—	—	—	—	—	9	0	1	1	17
92-93—Rochester	AHL	66	32	27	59	38	17	8	5	13	6
—Buffalo	NHL	7	1	1	2	15	—	—	—	—	—
NHL totals		7	1	1	2	15					

THOMAS, STEVE
LW/RW, ISLANDERS

PERSONAL: Born July 15, 1963, at Stockport, England. . . . 5-11/185. . . . Shoots left.
TRANSACTIONS/CAREER NOTES: Signed as free agent by Toronto Maple Leafs (June 1984). . . . Broke wrist during training camp (September 1984). . . . Traded by Maple Leafs with RW Rick Vaive and D Bob McGill to Chicago Blackhawks for LW Al Secord and RW Ed Olczyk (September 1987). . . . Pulled stomach muscle (October 1987). . . . Separated left shoulder (February 20, 1988); underwent surgery (May 1988). . . . Pulled back muscle (October 18, 1988). . . . Separated right shoulder (December 21, 1988). . . . Underwent surgery to repair chronic shoulder separation problem (January 25, 1989). . . . Strained knee ligaments during training camp (September 1990); missed first 11 games of season. . . . Traded by Blackhawks with C Adam Creighton to New York Islanders for C Brent Sutter and RW Brad Lauer (October 25, 1991). . . . Bruised ribs (March 10, 1992); missed one game. . . . Bruised ribs (November 21, 1992); missed three games.
HONORS: Won Dudley (Red) Garrett Memorial Trophy (1984-85). . . . Named to AHL All-Star first team (1984-85).

Season Team	League	REGULAR SEASON					PLAYOFFS				
		Gms.	G	A	Pts.	Pen.	Gms.	G	A	Pts.	Pen.
81-82—Markham Tier II Jr. A	OHA	48	68	57	125	113	—	—	—	—	—
82-83—Toronto	OHL	61	18	20	38	42	—	—	—	—	—
83-84—Toronto	OHL	70	51	54	105	77	—	—	—	—	—
84-85—Toronto	NHL	18	1	1	2	2	—	—	—	—	—
—St. Catharines	AHL	64	42	48	90	56	—	—	—	—	—
85-86—St. Catharines	AHL	19	18	14	32	35	—	—	—	—	—
—Toronto	NHL	65	20	37	57	36	10	6	8	14	9
86-87—Toronto	NHL	78	35	27	62	114	13	2	3	5	13
87-88—Chicago	NHL	30	13	13	26	40	3	1	2	3	6
88-89—Chicago	NHL	45	21	19	40	69	12	3	5	8	10
89-90—Chicago	NHL	76	40	30	70	91	20	7	6	13	33

Season Team	League	REGULAR SEASON Gms.	G	A	Pts.	Pen.	PLAYOFFS Gms.	G	A	Pts.	Pen.
90-91—Chicago	NHL	69	19	35	54	129	6	1	2	3	15
91-92—Chicago	NHL	11	2	6	8	26	—	—	—	—	—
—New York Islanders	NHL	71	28	42	70	71	—	—	—	—	—
92-93—New York Islanders	NHL	79	37	50	87	111	18	9	8	17	37
NHL totals		542	216	260	476	689	82	29	34	63	123

THOMLINSON, DAVE
LW, KINGS

PERSONAL: Born October 22, 1966, at Edmonton, Alta.... 6-1/195.... Shoots left. **TRANSACTIONS/CAREER NOTES:** Separated shoulder (November 1983).... Separated shoulder (November 1984).... Selected by Toronto Maple Leafs as underage junior in third round (third Maple Leafs pick, 43rd overall) of NHL entry draft (June 15, 1985).... Signed as free agent by St. Louis Blues (July 1987).... Bruised foot (February 1990).... Signed as free agent by Boston Bruins; Bruins and Blues later arranged trade in which Bruins received Thomlinson and D Glen Featherstone, whom they had also previously signed as free agent, for RW Dave Christian, whom the Blues had previously signed as free agent, third-round pick in 1992 draft (LW Vitali Prokhorov) and either seventh-round pick in 1992 draft or sixth-round pick in 1993 draft; Blues used seventh-round pick in 1992 draft to select C Lance Burns (July 1991).... Suffered sore back (December 1991).... Signed as free agent by New York Rangers (September 4, 1992).... Signed as free agent by Los Angeles Kings (July 22, 1993).

Season Team	League	REGULAR SEASON Gms.	G	A	Pts.	Pen.	PLAYOFFS Gms.	G	A	Pts.	Pen.
83-84—Brandon	WHL	41	17	12	29	62	—	—	—	—	—
84-85—Brandon	WHL	26	13	14	27	70	—	—	—	—	—
85-86—Brandon	WHL	53	25	20	45	116	—	—	—	—	—
86-87—Brandon	WHL	2	0	1	1	9	—	—	—	—	—
—Moose Jaw	WHL	69	44	36	80	126	9	7	3	10	19
87-88—Peoria	IHL	74	27	30	57	56	7	4	3	7	11
88-89—Peoria	IHL	64	27	29	56	154	3	0	1	1	8
89-90—St. Louis	NHL	19	1	2	3	12	—	—	—	—	—
—Peoria	IHL	59	27	40	67	87	5	1	1	2	15
90-91—Peoria	IHL	80	53	54	107	107	11	6	7	13	28
—St. Louis	NHL	3	0	0	0	0	9	3	1	4	4
91-92—Boston	NHL	12	0	1	1	17	—	—	—	—	—
—Maine	AHL	25	9	11	20	36	—	—	—	—	—
92-93—Binghamton	AHL	54	25	35	60	61	12	2	5	7	8
NHL totals		34	1	3	4	29	9	3	1	4	4

THOMPSON, BRENT
D, KINGS

PERSONAL: Born January 9, 1971, at Calgary, Alta.... 6-2/200.... Shoots left.... Full name: Brenton Keith Thompson. **TRANSACTIONS/CAREER NOTES:** Stretched knee ligaments and separated shoulder (September 1987).... Selected by Los Angeles Kings in second round (first Kings pick, 39th overall) of NHL entry draft (June 17, 1989).... Suffered hip flexor prior to 1992-93 season; missed first six games of season.... Suffered abdominal strain (January 23, 1992); missed 17 games. **HONORS:** Named to WHL (East) All-Star second team (1990-91).

Season Team	League	REGULAR SEASON Gms.	G	A	Pts.	Pen.	PLAYOFFS Gms.	G	A	Pts.	Pen.
88-89—Medicine Hat	WHL	72	3	10	13	160	3	0	0	0	2
89-90—Medicine Hat	WHL	68	10	35	45	167	3	0	1	1	14
90-91—Medicine Hat	WHL	51	5	40	45	87	12	1	7	8	16
—Phoenix	IHL	—	—	—	—	—	4	0	1	1	6
91-92—Phoenix	IHL	42	4	13	17	139	—	—	—	—	—
—Los Angeles	NHL	27	0	5	5	89	4	0	0	0	4
92-93—Phoenix	IHL	22	0	5	5	112	—	—	—	—	—
—Los Angeles	NHL	30	0	4	4	76	—	—	—	—	—
NHL totals		57	0	9	9	165	4	0	0	0	4

THOMPSON, BRIANE
D, PANTHERS

PERSONAL: Born April 17, 1974, at Peterborough, Ont.... 6-3/205.... Shoots left. **TRANSACTIONS/CAREER NOTES:** Selected by Florida Panthers in eighth round (10th Panthers pick, 187th overall) of NHL entry draft (June 26, 1993).

Season Team	League	REGULAR SEASON Gms.	G	A	Pts.	Pen.	PLAYOFFS Gms.	G	A	Pts.	Pen.
90-91—Lindsay Jr. B	OHA	42	5	15	20	40	—	—	—	—	—
91-92—Sault Ste. Marie	OHL	42	0	4	4	17	6	0	0	0	4
92-93—Sault Ste. Marie	OHL	63	2	21	23	57	18	0	6	6	35

THOMSON, JIM
RW, MIGHTY DUCKS

PERSONAL: Born December 30, 1965, at Edmonton, Alta.... 6-1/205.... Shoots right. **TRANSACTIONS/CAREER NOTES:** Selected by Washington Capitals as underage junior in ninth round (eighth Capitals pick, 185th overall) of NHL entry draft (June 9, 1984).... Traded by Capitals to Hartford Whalers for D Scot Kleinendorst (March 6, 1989).... Traded by Whalers to New Jersey Devils for RW Chris Cichocki (October 31, 1989).... Signed as free agent by Los Angeles Kings (July 11, 1990).... Fractured foot (January 19, 1991).... Selected by Minnesota North Stars in NHL expansion draft (May 30, 1991).... Traded by North Stars with D Charlie Huddy, LW Randy Gilhen and fourth-round pick in 1991 draft (D Alexei Zhitnik) to

Kings for C Todd Elik (June 22, 1991). . . . Hyperextended elbow (November 11, 1991); missed four games. . . . Selected by Ottawa Senators in NHL expansion draft (June 18, 1992). . . . Traded by Senators with C Marc Fortier to Kings for RW Bob Kudelski and C Shawn McCosh (December 20, 1992). . . . Selected by Mighty Ducks of Anaheim in NHL expansion draft (June 24, 1993).

Season Team	League	REGULAR SEASON					PLAYOFFS				
		Gms.	G	A	Pts.	Pen.	Gms.	G	A	Pts.	Pen.
82-83—Markham Waxers............	OPJHL	35	6	7	13	81	—	—	—	—	—
83-84—Toronto...........................	OHL	60	10	18	28	68	9	1	0	1	26
84-85—Toronto...........................	OHL	63	23	28	51	122	5	3	1	4	25
—Binghamton	AHL	4	0	0	0	2	—	—	—	—	—
85-86—Binghamton	AHL	59	15	9	24	195	—	—	—	—	—
86-87—Binghamton	AHL	57	13	10	23	*360	10	0	1	1	40
—Washington	NHL	10	0	0	0	35	—	—	—	—	—
87-88—Binghamton	AHL	25	8	9	17	64	4	1	2	3	7
88-89—Baltimore.......................	AHL	41	25	16	41	129	—	—	—	—	—
—Washington	NHL	14	2	0	2	53	—	—	—	—	—
—Hartford...........................	NHL	5	0	0	0	14	—	—	—	—	—
89-90—Binghamton	AHL	8	1	2	3	30	—	—	—	—	—
—Utica................................	AHL	60	20	23	43	124	4	1	0	1	19
—New Jersey.....................	NHL	3	0	0	0	31	—	—	—	—	—
90-91—New Haven.....................	AHL	27	5	8	13	121	—	—	—	—	—
—Los Angeles....................	NHL	8	1	0	1	19	—	—	—	—	—
91-92—Los Angeles....................	NHL	45	1	2	3	162	—	—	—	—	—
—Phoenix	IHL	2	1	0	1	0	—	—	—	—	—
92-93—Ottawa...........................	NHL	15	0	1	1	41	—	—	—	—	—
—Los Angeles....................	NHL	9	0	0	0	56	1	0	0	0	0
—Phoenix	IHL	14	4	5	9	44	—	—	—	—	—
NHL totals................		109	4	3	7	411	1	0	0	0	0

THORNTON, SCOTT
C, OILERS

PERSONAL: Born January 9, 1971, at London, Ont. . . . 6-2/200. . . . Shoots left.
TRANSACTIONS/CAREER NOTES: Selected by Toronto Maple Leafs in first round (first Maple Leafs pick, third overall) of NHL entry draft (June 17, 1989). . . . Suspended 12 games by OHL for refusing to leave ice following penalty (February 7, 1990). . . . Separated shoulder (January 24, 1991); missed eight games. . . . Traded by Maple Leafs with LW Vincent Damphousse, D Luke Richardson, G Peter Ing and future considerations to Edmonton Oilers for G Grant Fuhr, RW/LW Glenn Anderson and LW Craig Berube (September 19, 1991). . . . Suffered concussion (November 23, 1991); missed one game.

Season Team	League	REGULAR SEASON					PLAYOFFS				
		Gms.	G	A	Pts.	Pen.	Gms.	G	A	Pts.	Pen.
86-87—London Diamonds............	OPJHL	31	10	7	17	10	—	—	—	—	—
87-88—Belleville.........................	OHL	62	11	19	30	54	6	0	1	1	2
88-89—Belleville.........................	OHL	59	28	34	62	103	5	1	1	2	6
89-90—Belleville.........................	OHL	47	21	28	49	91	11	2	10	12	15
90-91—Belleville.........................	OHL	3	2	1	3	2	6	0	7	7	14
—Newmarket.....................	AHL	5	1	0	1	4	—	—	—	—	—
—Toronto...........................	NHL	33	1	3	4	30	—	—	—	—	—
91-92—Edmonton	NHL	15	0	1	1	43	1	0	0	0	0
—Cape Breton	AHL	49	9	14	23	40	5	1	0	1	8
92-93—Cape Breton	AHL	58	23	27	50	102	16	1	2	3	35
—Edmonton	NHL	9	0	1	1	0	—	—	—	—	—
NHL totals................		57	1	5	6	73	1	0	0	0	0

THYER, MARIO
C, STARS

PERSONAL: Born September 29, 1966, at Montreal. . . . 5-11/170. . . . Shoots left.
COLLEGE: St. Lawrence College St. Laurent (Ont.), then Maine.
TRANSACTIONS/CAREER NOTES: Broke leg (November 1988). . . . Signed as free agent by Minnesota North Stars (July 12, 1989). . . . Traded by North Stars with third-round pick in 1993 draft to New York Rangers for C Mark Janssens (March 10, 1992). . . . Traded by Rangers to North Stars for future considerations (July 16, 1992). . . . North Stars franchise moved from Minnesota to Dallas and renamed Stars for 1993-94 season.
HONORS: Named Hockey East Rookie of the Year (1987-88). . . . Named to Hockey East All-Freshman team (1987-88).

Season Team	League	REGULAR SEASON					PLAYOFFS				
		Gms.	G	A	Pts.	Pen.	Gms.	G	A	Pts.	Pen.
86-87—St. Laurent College	QCAAA					Statistics unavailable.					
87-88—University of Maine	Hockey East	44	24	42	66	4	—	—	—	—	—
88-89—University of Maine	Hockey East	9	9	7	16	0	—	—	—	—	—
89-90—Minnesota	NHL	5	0	0	0	0	1	0	0	0	2
—Kalamazoo	IHL	68	19	42	61	12	10	2	6	8	4
90-91—Kalamazoo	IHL	75	15	51	66	15	10	4	5	9	2
91-92—Kalamazoo	IHL	46	17	28	45	0	—	—	—	—	—
—Binghamton	AHL	9	2	7	9	0	3	0	0	0	0
92-93—Cincinnati.......................	IHL	77	13	36	49	26	—	—	—	—	—
NHL totals................		5	0	0	0	0	1	0	0	0	2

TICHY, MILAN

D, PANTHERS

PERSONAL: Born September 22, 1969, at Plzen, Czechoslovakia.... 6-0/200.... Shoots left.... Name pronounced TEE-kee.

TRANSACTIONS/CAREER NOTES: Selected by Chicago Blackhawks in eighth round (sixth Blackhawks pick, 153rd overall) of NHL entry draft (June 17, 1989).... Selected by Florida Panthers in NHL expansion draft (June 24, 1993).

			REGULAR SEASON					PLAYOFFS				
Season Team	League	Gms.	G	A	Pts.	Pen.	Gms.	G	A	Pts.	Pen.
87-88—Skoda Plzen	Czech.	30	1	3	4	20	—	—	—	—	—
88-89—Skoda Plzen	Czech.	36	1	12	13	44	—	—	—	—	—
89-90—Dukla Trencin	Czech.	51	14	8	22	87	—	—	—	—	—
90-91—Dukla Trencin	Czech.	39	9	11	20	72	—	—	—	—	—
91-92—Indianapolis	IHL	49	6	23	29	28	—	—	—	—	—
92-93—Indianapolis	IHL	49	7	32	39	62	4	0	5	5	14
—Chicago	NHL	13	0	1	1	30	—	—	—	—	—
NHL totals		13	0	1	1	30	—	—	—	—	—

TIKKANEN, ESA

LW, RANGERS

PERSONAL: Born January 25, 1965, at Helsinki, Finland.... 6-1/200.... Shoots left.... Full name: Esa Kalervo Tikkanen.... Name pronounced EH-suh TEE-kuh-nehn.

TRANSACTIONS/CAREER NOTES: Selected by Edmonton Oilers in fourth round (fourth Oilers pick, 82nd overall) of NHL entry draft (August 8, 1983).... Broke foot (December 10, 1985).... Lacerated elbow, developed bursitis and underwent surgery (December 9, 1986).... Fractured left wrist (January 1989).... Injured right knee (October 28, 1989).... Underwent left knee surgery (August 1990); missed first 10 days of training camp.... Sprained wrist (December 1, 1991); missed one game.... Sprained wrist (December 20, 1991); missed two games.... Fractured shoulder (January 4, 1992); missed 37 games.... Suffered from the flu (December 1992); missed one game.... Suffered elbow infection (February 1993); missed two games.... Traded by Oilers to Rangers for C Doug Weight (March 17, 1993).

MISCELLANEOUS: Member of Stanley Cup championship team (1985, 1987, 1988 and 1990).

			REGULAR SEASON					PLAYOFFS				
Season Team	League	Gms.	G	A	Pts.	Pen.	Gms.	G	A	Pts.	Pen.
81-82—Regina	WHL	2	0	0	0	0	—	—	—	—	—
82-83—Helsinki Junior IFK	Finland	30	34	31	65	104	4	4	3	7	10
—Helsinki IFK	Finland	—	—	—	—	—	1	0	0	0	2
83-84—Helsinki IFK	Finland	36	19	11	30	30	2	0	0	0	0
—Helsinki Junior IFK	Finland	6	5	9	14	13	4	4	3	7	8
84-85—Helsinki IFK	Finland	36	21	33	54	42	—	—	—	—	—
—Edmonton	NHL	—	—	—	—	—	3	0	0	0	2
85-86—Nova Scotia	AHL	15	4	8	12	17	—	—	—	—	—
—Edmonton	NHL	35	7	6	13	28	8	3	2	5	7
86-87—Edmonton	NHL	76	34	44	78	120	21	7	2	9	22
87-88—Edmonton	NHL	80	23	51	74	153	19	10	17	27	72
88-89—Edmonton	NHL	67	31	47	78	92	7	1	3	4	12
89-90—Edmonton	NHL	79	30	33	63	161	22	13	11	24	26
90-91—Edmonton	NHL	79	27	42	69	85	18	12	8	20	24
91-92—Edmonton	NHL	40	12	16	28	44	16	5	3	8	8
92-93—Edmonton	NHL	66	14	19	33	76	—	—	—	—	—
—New York Rangers	NHL	15	2	5	7	18	—	—	—	—	—
NHL totals		537	180	263	443	777	114	51	46	97	173

TILEY, BRAD

D, RANGERS

PERSONAL: Born July 5, 1971, at Markdale, Ont.... 6-1/190.... Shoots left.... Name pronounced TIGH-lee.

TRANSACTIONS/CAREER NOTES: Selected by Boston Bruins in fourth round (fourth Bruins pick, 84th overall) of NHL entry draft (June 22, 1991).... Signed as free agent by New York Rangers (September 4, 1992).

HONORS: Named to Memorial Cup All-Star team (1990-91).

			REGULAR SEASON					PLAYOFFS				
Season Team	League	Gms.	G	A	Pts.	Pen.	Gms.	G	A	Pts.	Pen.
87-88—Owen Sound Jr. B	OHA	40	19	25	44	68	—	—	—	—	—
88-89—Sault Ste. Marie	OHL	50	4	11	15	31	—	—	—	—	—
89-90—Sault Ste. Marie	OHL	66	9	32	41	47	—	—	—	—	—
90-91—Sault Ste. Marie	OHL	66	11	55	66	29	—	—	—	—	—
91-92—Maine	AHL	62	7	22	29	36	—	—	—	—	—
92-93—Binghamton	AHL	26	6	10	16	19	8	0	1	1	2
—Phoenix	IHL	46	11	27	38	35	—	—	—	—	—

TILLEY, TOM

D, BLUES

PERSONAL: Born March 28, 1965, at Trenton, Ont.... 6-0/189.... Shoots right.... Full name: Thomas Robert Tilley.

COLLEGE: Michigan State.

TRANSACTIONS/CAREER NOTES: Selected by St. Louis Blues as underage junior in 10th round (13th Blues pick, 196th overall) of NHL entry draft (June 9, 1984).... Collapsed on bench during game due to the flu (January 28, 1989).... Bruised left shoulder (March 1989).... Strained lower back (October 14, 1989); missed eight games.... Signed as free agent by Blues (July 30, 1993).

HONORS: Named to CCHA All-Star first team (1988).... Named to IHL All-Star second team (1990-91).

			REGULAR SEASON					PLAYOFFS			
Season Team	League	Gms.	G	A	Pts.	Pen.	Gms.	G	A	Pts.	Pen.
83-84—Orillia	OHA	38	16	35	51	113	—	—	—	—	—
84-85—Michigan State	CCHA	37	1	5	6	58	—	—	—	—	—
85-86—Michigan State	CCHA	42	9	25	34	48	—	—	—	—	—
86-87—Michigan State	CCHA	42	7	14	21	46	—	—	—	—	—
87-88—Michigan State	CCHA	46	8	18	26	44	—	—	—	—	—
88-89—St. Louis	NHL	70	1	22	23	47	10	1	2	3	17
89-90—St. Louis	NHL	34	0	5	5	6	—	—	—	—	—
—Salt Lake City	IHL	22	1	8	9	13	—	—	—	—	—
90-91—Peoria	IHL	48	7	38	45	53	13	2	9	11	25
—St. Louis	NHL	22	2	4	6	4	—	—	—	—	—
91-92—Milan	Italy	18	7	13	20	12	12	5	12	17	10
92-93—Milan	Italy	32	5	17	22	21	—	—	—	—	—
NHL totals		126	3	31	34	57	10	1	2	3	17

TINORDI, MARK
D, STARS

PERSONAL: Born May 9, 1966, at Red Deer, Alta. . . . 6-4/205. . . . Shoots left. . . . Name pronounced tuh-NOHR-dee.

TRANSACTIONS/CAREER NOTES: Signed as free agent by New York Rangers (January 4, 1987). . . . Suffered abdominal pains (January 1988). . . . Underwent left knee surgery (October 6, 1988). . . . Traded by Rangers with D Paul Jerrard, C Mike Sullivan, RW Brett Barnett and Los Angeles Kings third-round pick in 1989 draft (C Murray Garbutt) to Minnesota North Stars for LW Igor Liba, C Brian Lawton and rights to LW Eric Bennett (October 11, 1988). . . . Bruised ribs (December 1988). . . . Underwent knee surgery (April 1989). . . . Suspended four games by NHL for cross-checking in a preseason game (September 27, 1989). . . . Bruised shoulder (December 1989). . . . Fined $500 by NHL for fighting (December 28, 1989). . . . Suffered concussion (January 17, 1990); missed six games. . . . Suspended 10 games by NHL for leaving the penalty box to fight during a pre-season game (September 26, 1990). . . . Suffered from foot palsy (October 15, 1991); missed 17 games. . . . Sprained knee (January 19, 1993); missed four games. . . . Broke collarbone (March 16, 1993); missed remainder of season. . . . North Stars franchise moved from Minnesota to Dallas and renamed Stars for 1993-94 season.

HONORS: Named to WHL (East) All-Star first team (1986-87). . . . Played in NHL All-Star Game (1992).

			REGULAR SEASON					PLAYOFFS			
Season Team	League	Gms.	G	A	Pts.	Pen.	Gms.	G	A	Pts.	Pen.
82-83—Lethbridge	WHL	64	0	4	4	50	20	1	1	2	6
83-84—Lethbridge	WHL	72	5	14	19	53	5	0	1	1	7
84-85—Lethbridge	WHL	58	10	15	25	134	4	0	2	2	12
85-86—Lethbridge	WHL	58	8	30	38	139	8	1	3	4	15
86-87—Calgary	WHL	61	29	37	66	148	—	—	—	—	—
—New Haven	AHL	2	0	0	0	2	2	0	0	0	0
87-88—New York Rangers	NHL	24	1	2	3	50	—	—	—	—	—
—Colorado	IHL	41	8	19	27	150	11	1	5	6	31
88-89—Minnesota	NHL	47	2	3	5	107	5	0	0	0	0
—Kalamazoo	IHL	10	0	0	0	35	—	—	—	—	—
89-90—Minnesota	NHL	66	3	7	10	240	7	0	1	1	16
90-91—Minnesota	NHL	69	5	27	32	189	23	5	6	11	78
91-92—Minnesota	NHL	63	4	24	28	179	7	1	2	3	11
92-93—Minnesota	NHL	69	15	27	42	157	—	—	—	—	—
NHL totals		338	30	90	120	922	42	6	9	15	105

TIPPETT, DAVE
C/LW, FLYERS

PERSONAL: Born August 25, 1961, at Moosomin, Sask. . . . 5-10/180. . . . Shoots left. **COLLEGE:** North Dakota.

TRANSACTIONS/CAREER NOTES: Signed as free agent by Hartford Whalers (February 1984). . . . Injured right thumb tendons (October 8, 1989). . . . Traded by Whalers to Washington Capitals for sixth-round pick in 1992 draft (C Jarret Reid) (September 30, 1990). . . . Separated shoulder (November 28, 1990); missed 11 games. . . . Signed as free agent by Pittsburgh Penguins (August 28, 1992). . . . Fractured thumb (November 20, 1992); missed six games. . . . Signed as free agent by Philadelphia Flyers (August 2, 1993).

MISCELLANEOUS: Member of silver-medal-winning Canadian Olympic team (1992).

			REGULAR SEASON					PLAYOFFS			
Season Team	League	Gms.	G	A	Pts.	Pen.	Gms.	G	A	Pts.	Pen.
79-80—Prince Albert	SJHL	85	72	95	167	. . .	—	—	—	—	—
80-81—Prince Albert	SJHL	84	62	93	155	. . .	—	—	—	—	—
81-82—Univ. of North Dakota	WCHA	43	13	28	41	24	—	—	—	—	—
82-83—Univ. of North Dakota	WCHA	36	15	31	46	44	—	—	—	—	—
83-84—Canadian Olympic Team	Int'l	66	14	19	33	24	—	—	—	—	—
—Hartford	NHL	17	4	2	6	2	—	—	—	—	—
84-85—Hartford	NHL	80	7	12	19	12	—	—	—	—	—
85-86—Hartford	NHL	80	14	20	34	18	10	2	2	4	4
86-87—Hartford	NHL	80	9	22	31	42	6	0	2	2	4
87-88—Hartford	NHL	80	16	21	37	32	6	0	0	0	2
88-89—Hartford	NHL	80	17	24	41	45	4	0	1	1	0
89-90—Hartford	NHL	66	8	19	27	32	7	1	3	4	2
90-91—Washington	NHL	61	6	9	15	24	10	2	3	5	8
91-92—Washington	NHL	30	2	10	12	16	7	0	1	1	0
—Canadian national team	Int'l	1	0	0	0	4	—	—	—	—	—
—Canadian Olympic Team	Int'l	6	1	2	3	10	—	—	—	—	—

Season Team	League	REGULAR SEASON					PLAYOFFS				
		Gms.	G	A	Pts.	Pen.	Gms.	G	A	Pts.	Pen.
92-93—Pittsburgh	NHL	74	6	19	25	56	12	1	4	5	14
NHL totals		648	89	158	247	279	62	6	16	22	34

TJALLDEN, MIKAEL
D, PANTHERS

PERSONAL: Born February 16, 1975, at Ornskoldsvik, Sweden. . . . 6-2/194. . . . Shoots left.

TRANSACTIONS/CAREER NOTES: Selected by Florida Panthers in third round (fourth Panthers pick, 67th overall) of NHL entry draft (June 26, 1993).

Season Team	League	REGULAR SEASON					PLAYOFFS			
		Gms.	G	A	Pts.	Pen.	Gms.	G	A	Pts.	Pen.
91-92—MoDo	Sweden Jr.				Did not play.					
92-93—MoDo	Sweden Jr.				Statistics unavailable.					

TKACHUK, KEITH
C/LW, JETS

PERSONAL: Born March 28, 1972, at Melrose, Mass. . . . 6-2/200. . . . Shoots left. . . . Full name: Keith Matthew Tkachuk. . . . Name pronounced kuh-CHUHK.

HIGH SCHOOL: Malden (Mass.) Catholic.

COLLEGE: Boston University.

TRANSACTIONS/CAREER NOTES: Selected by Winnipeg Jets in first round (first Jets pick, 19th overall) of NHL entry draft (June 16, 1990). . . . Suffered laceration to forearm (November 12, 1993); missed one game.

HONORS: Named to Hockey East All-Rookie team (1990-91).

Season Team	League	REGULAR SEASON					PLAYOFFS				
		Gms.	G	A	Pts.	Pen.	Gms.	G	A	Pts.	Pen.
88-89—Malden Catholic H.S.	Mass. H.S.	21	30	16	46	...	—	—	—	—	—
89-90—Malden Catholic H.S.	Mass. H.S.	6	12	14	26	...	—	—	—	—	—
90-91—Boston University	Hockey East	36	17	23	40	70	—	—	—	—	—
91-92—U.S. national team	Int'l	45	10	10	20	141	—	—	—	—	—
—U.S. Olympic Team	Int'l	8	1	1	2	12	—	—	—	—	—
—Winnipeg	NHL	17	3	5	8	28	7	3	0	3	30
92-93—Winnipeg	NHL	83	28	23	51	201	6	4	0	4	14
NHL totals		100	31	28	59	229	13	7	0	7	44

TOCCHET, RICK
RW, PENGUINS

PERSONAL: Born April 9, 1964, at Scarborough, Ont. . . . 6-0/205. . . . Shoots right. . . . Name pronounced TAH-keht.

TRANSACTIONS/CAREER NOTES: Selected by Philadelphia Flyers as underage junior in sixth round (fifth Flyers pick, 121st overall) of NHL entry draft (June 8, 1983). . . . Bruised right knee (November 23, 1985); missed seven games. . . . Separated left shoulder (February 1988). . . . Suspended 10 games by NHL for injuring an opposing player during a fight (October 27, 1988). . . . Hyperextended right knee (April 21, 1989). . . . Suffered viral infection (November 1989). . . . Tore tendon in left groin area (January 26, 1991); missed five games. . . . Reinjured groin (March 1991); missed five games. . . . Sprained knee (November 29, 1991); missed five games. . . . Bruised heel (January 18, 1991); missed 10 games. . . . Traded by Flyers with G Ken Wregget, D Kjell Samuelsson and third-round pick in 1992 draft to Pittsburgh Penguins for RW Mark Recchi, D Brian Benning and first-round pick in 1992 draft (LW Jason Bowen) previously acquired from Los Angeles Kings (February 19, 1992). . . . Fractured jaw (March 15, 1992); missed three games. . . . Bruised left foot (October 10, 1992); missed two games. . . . Bruised foot (February 8, 1993); missed one game.

HONORS: Played in NHL All-Star Game (1989 through 1991 and 1993).

MISCELLANEOUS: Member of Stanley Cup championship team (1992).

Season Team	League	REGULAR SEASON					PLAYOFFS				
		Gms.	G	A	Pts.	Pen.	Gms.	G	A	Pts.	Pen.
81-82—Sault Ste. Marie	OHL	59	7	15	22	184	11	1	1	2	28
82-83—Sault Ste. Marie	OHL	66	32	34	66	146	16	4	13	17	*67
83-84—Sault Ste. Marie	OHL	64	44	64	108	209	16	*22	14	†36	41
84-85—Philadelphia	NHL	75	14	25	39	181	19	3	4	7	72
85-86—Philadelphia	NHL	69	14	21	35	284	5	1	2	3	26
86-87—Philadelphia	NHL	69	21	26	47	288	26	11	10	21	72
87-88—Philadelphia	NHL	65	31	33	64	301	5	1	4	5	55
88-89—Philadelphia	NHL	66	45	36	81	183	16	6	6	12	69
89-90—Philadelphia	NHL	75	37	59	96	196	—	—	—	—	—
90-91—Philadelphia	NHL	70	40	31	71	150	—	—	—	—	—
91-92—Philadelphia	NHL	42	13	16	29	102	—	—	—	—	—
—Pittsburgh	NHL	19	14	16	30	49	14	6	13	19	24
92-93—Pittsburgh	NHL	80	48	61	109	252	12	7	6	13	24
NHL totals		630	277	324	601	1986	97	35	45	80	342

TOCHER, RYAN
D, NORDIQUES

PERSONAL: Born June 14, 1975, at Hamilton, Ont. . . . 6-1/194. . . . Shoots right.

HIGH SCHOOL: St. Paul (Nepean, Ont.).

TRANSACTIONS/CAREER NOTES: Selected by Quebec Nordiques in fourth round (fifth Nordiques pick, 101st overall) of NHL entry draft (June 26, 1993).

Season Team	League	REGULAR SEASON					PLAYOFFS				
		Gms.	G	A	Pts.	Pen.	Gms.	G	A	Pts.	Pen.
90-91—Hamilton Jr. B	OHA	38	2	11	13	90	—	—	—	—	—
91-92—Niagara Falls	OHL	58	4	8	12	53	16	0	0	0	2
92-93—Niagara Falls	OHL	59	6	17	23	58	4	0	0	0	4

TODD, KEVIN
C, OILERS

PERSONAL: Born May 4, 1968, at Winnipeg, Man. . . . 5-10/180. . . . Shoots left. . . . Full name: Kevin Lee Todd.
HIGH SCHOOL: Tec Voc (Winnipeg, Man.).
TRANSACTIONS/CAREER NOTES: Stretched knee ligaments (December 1985). . . . Selected by New Jersey Devils as underage junior in seventh round (seventh Devils pick, 129th overall) of NHL entry draft (June 21, 1986). . . . Injured thigh (October 31, 1992); missed one game. . . . Reinjured thigh (November 13, 1992); missed three games. . . . Bruised shoulder (December 15, 1992); missed five games. . . . Traded by Devils with LW Zdeno Ciger to Edmonton Oilers for C Bernie Nicholls (January 13, 1993). . . . Separated left shoulder (March 14, 1993); missed remainder of season.
HONORS: Won Les Cunningham Plaque (1990-91). . . . Won the John B. Sollenberger Trophy (1990-91). . . . Named to AHL All-Star first team (1990-91). . . . Named to NHL All-Rookie team (1991-92).

			REGULAR SEASON					PLAYOFFS			
Season Team	League	Gms.	G	A	Pts.	Pen.	Gms.	G	A	Pts.	Pen.
85-86—Prince Albert	WHL	55	14	25	39	19	20	7	6	13	29
86-87—Prince Albert	WHL	71	39	46	85	92	8	2	5	7	17
87-88—Prince Albert	WHL	72	49	72	121	83	10	8	11	19	27
88-89—New Jersey	NHL	1	0	0	0	0	—	—	—	—	—
—Utica	AHL	78	26	45	71	62	4	2	0	2	6
89-90—Utica	AHL	71	18	36	54	72	5	2	4	6	2
90-91—Utica	AHL	75	37	*81	*118	75	—	—	—	—	—
—New Jersey	NHL	1	0	0	0	0	1	0	0	0	6
91-92—New Jersey	NHL	80	21	42	63	69	7	3	2	5	8
92-93—New Jersey	NHL	30	5	5	10	16	—	—	—	—	—
—Utica	AHL	2	2	1	3	0	—	—	—	—	—
—Edmonton	NHL	25	4	9	13	10	—	—	—	—	—
NHL totals		137	30	56	86	95	8	3	2	5	14

TOMLAK, MIKE
LW, WHALERS

PERSONAL: Born October 17, 1964, at Thunder Bay, Ont. . . . 6-3/205. . . . Shoots left. . . . Full name: Michael Ronald Tomlak.
COLLEGE: Western Ontario.
TRANSACTIONS/CAREER NOTES: Selected by Toronto Maple Leafs in 11th round (10th Maple Leafs pick, 208th overall) of NHL entry draft (June 8, 1983). . . . Signed as free agent by Hartford Whalers (May 28, 1989). . . . Sprained right wrist (February 9, 1990). . . . Bruised left foot (January 26, 1992); missed 15 games. . . . Fractured left leg (March 6, 1992); missed remainder of season and playoffs.
HONORS: Named to CIAU All-Canada team (1986-87). . . . Named to OUAA All-Star first team (1988-89).

			REGULAR SEASON					PLAYOFFS			
Season Team	League	Gms.	G	A	Pts.	Pen.	Gms.	G	A	Pts.	Pen.
81-82—Thunder Bay	TBJHL	25	19	26	45	30	—	—	—	—	—
82-83—Cornwall	OHL	70	18	49	67	26	—	—	—	—	—
83-84—Cornwall	OHL	64	24	64	88	21	—	—	—	—	—
84-85—Cornwall	OHL	66	30	70	100	9	—	—	—	—	—
85-86—Univ. of Western Ontario	OUAA	38	28	20	48	45	—	—	—	—	—
86-87—Univ. of Western Ontario	OUAA	38	16	30	46	10	—	—	—	—	—
87-88—Univ. of Western Ontario	OUAA	39	24	52	76	. . .	—	—	—	—	—
88-89—Univ. of Western Ontario	OUAA	35	16	34	50	. . .	—	—	—	—	—
89-90—Hartford	NHL	70	7	14	21	48	7	0	1	1	2
90-91—Springfield	AHL	15	4	9	13	15	—	—	—	—	—
—Hartford	NHL	64	8	8	16	55	3	0	0	0	2
91-92—Springfield	AHL	39	16	21	37	24	—	—	—	—	—
—Hartford	NHL	6	0	0	0	0	—	—	—	—	—
92-93—Springfield	AHL	38	16	21	37	56	5	1	1	2	2
NHL totals		140	15	22	37	103	10	0	1	1	4

TOMLINSON, DAVE
C, JETS

PERSONAL: Born May 8, 1968, at North Vancouver, B.C. . . . 5-11/190. . . . Shoots left.
COLLEGE: Boston University.
TRANSACTIONS/CAREER NOTES: Selected by Toronto Maple Leafs in NHL supplemental draft (June 16, 1989). . . . Traded by Leafs to Florida Panthers for future considerations (August 3, 1993). . . . Traded by Panthers to Winnipeg Jets for C Jason Cirone (August 3, 1993).

			REGULAR SEASON					PLAYOFFS			
Season Team	League	Gms.	G	A	Pts.	Pen.	Gms.	G	A	Pts.	Pen.
87-88—Boston University	Hockey East	34	16	20	36	28	—	—	—	—	—
88-89—Boston University	Hockey East	34	16	30	46	40	—	—	—	—	—
89-90—Boston University	Hockey East	43	15	22	37	53	—	—	—	—	—
90-91—Boston University	Hockey East	41	30	30	60	55	—	—	—	—	—
91-92—St. John's	AHL	75	23	34	57	75	12	4	5	9	6
—Toronto	NHL	3	0	0	0	2	—	—	—	—	—
92-93—St. John's	AHL	70	36	48	84	115	9	1	4	5	8
—Toronto	NHL	3	0	0	0	2	—	—	—	—	—
NHL totals		6	0	0	0	4					

TOMPKINS, DAN
LW, FLAMES

PERSONAL: Born January 31, 1975, at Minnesota. . . . 6-2/205. . . . Shoots left.
HIGH SCHOOL: Hopkins (Minnetonka, Minn.).
TRANSACTIONS/CAREER NOTES: Selected by Calgary Flames in third round (third Flames pick, 70th overall) of NHL entry draft (June 26, 1993).

Season Team	League	Gms.	G	A	Pts.	Pen.	Gms.	G	A	Pts.	Pen.
90-91—Hopkins H.S.	Minn. H.S.	25	17	12	29	26	—	—	—	—	—
91-92—Hopkins H.S.	Minn. H.S.	17	10	12	22	20	—	—	—	—	—
92-93—Omaha	Jr. A	43	16	34	50	48	—	—	—	—	—

TOOKEY, TIM
C

PERSONAL: Born August 29, 1960, at Edmonton, Alta.... 5-11/190.... Shoots left.... Full name: Timothy Raymond Tookey.... Name pronounced TOO-kee.
TRANSACTIONS/CAREER NOTES: Selected by Washington Capitals as underage junior in fifth round (fourth Capitals pick, 88th overall) of 1979 NHL entry draft (August 9, 1979).... Sprained left ankle (December 30, 1981).... Traded by Capitals to Quebec Nordiques for D Lee Norwood (January 1982).... Suffered concussion (February 1983).... Injured shoulder (April 1983).... Signed as free agent by Pittsburgh Penguins (August 1983).... Signed as free agent by Philadelphia Flyers (August 1985).... Selected by Los Angeles Kings in 1987 NHL waiver draft (October 1987).... Placed on recallable waivers by Kings in an attempt to designate him for assignment; claimed by Philadelphia; recalled by Kings and assigned to New Haven (October 1987).... Underwent knee surgery (December 1987).... Traded by Kings to Pittsburgh Penguins for D Patrick Mayer (March 7, 1989).... Signed as free agent by Flyers (July 12, 1989).... Underwent knee surgery (October 1989).... Broke ankle (October 1990); out two months.
HONORS: Won Jack Butterfield Trophy (1985-86).... Named to AHL All-Star second team (1985-86 and 1991-92).... Won Les Cunningham Plaque (1986-87).... Won John B. Sollenberger Trophy (1986-87).... Named to AHL All-Star first team (1986-87).... Won Fred Hunt Memorial Award (1992-93).

Season Team	League	Gms.	G	A	Pts.	Pen.	Gms.	G	A	Pts.	Pen.
77-78—Portland	WCHL	72	16	15	31	55	8	2	2	4	5
78-79—Portland	WHL	56	33	47	80	55	25	6	14	20	6
79-80—Portland	WHL	70	58	83	141	55	8	2	5	7	4
80-81—Hershey	AHL	47	20	38	58	129	—	—	—	—	—
—Washington	NHL	29	10	13	23	18	—	—	—	—	—
81-82—Washington	NHL	28	8	8	16	35	—	—	—	—	—
—Hershey	AHL	14	4	9	13	10	—	—	—	—	—
—Fredericton	AHL	16	6	10	16	16	—	—	—	—	—
82-83—Quebec	NHL	12	1	6	7	4	—	—	—	—	—
—Fredericton	AHL	53	24	43	67	24	9	5	4	9	0
83-84—Pittsburgh	NHL	8	0	2	2	2	—	—	—	—	—
—Baltimore	AHL	58	16	28	44	25	8	1	1	2	2
84-85—Baltimore	AHL	74	25	43	68	74	15	8	10	18	13
85-86—Hershey	AHL	69	35	*62	97	*66	18	†11	8	19	10
86-87—Hershey	AHL	80	51	*73	*124	45	5	5	4	9	0
—Philadelphia	NHL	2	0	0	0	0	10	1	3	4	2
87-88—Los Angeles	NHL	20	1	6	7	8	—	—	—	—	—
—New Haven	AHL	11	6	7	13	2	—	—	—	—	—
88-89—Muskegon	IHL	18	7	14	21	7	8	2	9	11	4
—New Haven	AHL	33	11	18	29	30	—	—	—	—	—
—Los Angeles	NHL	7	2	1	3	4	—	—	—	—	—
89-90—Hershey	AHL	42	18	22	40	28	—	—	—	—	—
90-91—Hershey	AHL	51	17	42	59	43	5	0	5	5	0
91-92—Hershey	AHL	†80	36	69	105	63	6	4	2	6	4
92-93—Hershey	AHL	80	38	70	108	63	—	—	—	—	—
NHL totals		106	22	36	58	71	10	1	3	4	2

TOPOROWSKI, KERRY
RW, BLACKHAWKS

PERSONAL: Born April 9, 1971, at Prince Albert, Sask.... 6-2/212.... Shoots right.
TRANSACTIONS/CAREER NOTES: Selected by San Jose Sharks in fourth round (fourth Sharks pick, 67th overall) of NHL entry draft (June 22, 1991).... Traded by Sharks with second-round pick in 1992 draft to Chicago Blackhawks for D Doug Wilson (September 6, 1991).

Season Team	League	Gms.	G	A	Pts.	Pen.	Gms.	G	A	Pts.	Pen.
89-90—Spokane	WHL	65	1	13	14	*384	6	0	0	0	37
90-91—Spokane	WHL	65	11	16	27	*505	15	2	2	4	*108
91-92—Indianapolis	IHL	18	1	2	3	206	—	—	—	—	—
92-93—Indianapolis	IHL	17	0	0	0	57	—	—	—	—	—

TOPOROWSKI, SHAYNE
RW, KINGS

PERSONAL: Born August 6, 1975, at Prince Albert, Sask.... 6-2/204.... Shoots right.
HIGH SCHOOL: Carlton Comprehensive (Paddockwood, Sask.).
TRANSACTIONS/CAREER NOTES: Selected by Los Angeles Kings in second round (first Kings pick, 42nd overall) of NHL entry draft (June 26, 1993).

Season Team	League	Gms.	G	A	Pts.	Pen.	Gms.	G	A	Pts.	Pen.
91-92—Prince Albert	WHL	6	2	0	2	2	7	2	1	3	6
92-93—Prince Albert	WHL	72	25	32	57	235	—	—	—	—	—

TORCHIA, MIKE
G, STARS

PERSONAL: Born February 23, 1972, at Toronto.... 5-11/215.... Shoots left.
TRANSACTIONS/CAREER NOTES: Broke ankle (July 1989).... Selected by Minnesota North Stars in fourth round (second North Stars pick, 74th overall) of NHL entry draft (June 22, 1991).... North Stars franchise moved from Minnesota to Dallas and renamed Stars for

1993-94 season.
HONORS: Won Hap Emms Memorial Trophy (1989-90).... Named to OHL All-Star first team (1990-91).... Named to Memorial Cup All-Star team (1989-90).

					REGULAR SEASON							PLAYOFFS					
Season	Team	League	Gms.	Min.	W	L	T	GA	SO	Avg.	Gms.	Min.	W	L	GA	SO	Avg.
88-89—Kitchener		OHL	30	1672	14	9	4	112	0	4.02	2	126	0	2	8	0	3.81
89-90—Kitchener		OHL	40	2280	25	11	2	136	1	3.58	*17	*1023	*11	6	60	0	3.52
90-91—Kitchener		OHL	57	*3317	25	24	7	219	0	3.96	6	382	2	4	30	0	4.71
91-92—Kitchener		OHL	55	3042	25	24	3	203	1	4.00	14	900	7	7	47	0	3.13
92-93—Can. national team		Int'l	5	300	5	0	0	11	1	2.20	—	—	—	—	—	—	—
—Kalamazoo		IHL	48	2729	19	17	0	173	0	3.80	—	—	—	—	—	—	—

TORREL, DOUGLAS
LW, CANUCKS

PERSONAL: Born April 29, 1969, at Hibbing, Minn.... 6-2/180.... Shoots right.... Full name: Douglas James Torrel.... Name pronounced toh-REHL.
HIGH SCHOOL: Hibbing (Minn.).
COLLEGE: Minnesota-Duluth.
TRANSACTIONS/CAREER NOTES: Broke hand (January 1987).... Selected by Vancouver Canucks in fourth round (third Canucks pick, 66th overall) of NHL entry draft (June 13, 1987).

				REGULAR SEASON					PLAYOFFS			
Season	Team	League	Gms.	G	A	Pts.	Pen.	Gms.	G	A	Pts.	Pen.
85-86—Hibbing H.S.		Minn. H.S.	26	13	18	31	...	—	—	—	—	—
86-87—Hibbing H.S.		Minn. H.S.	20	22	21	43	...	—	—	—	—	—
87-88—Hibbing H.S.		Minn. H.S.	20	22	16	38	38	—	—	—	—	—
88-89—Minnesota-Duluth		WCHA	40	4	6	10	36	—	—	—	—	—
89-90—Minnesota-Duluth		WCHA	39	11	11	22	48	—	—	—	—	—
90-91—Minnesota-Duluth		WCHA	40	17	18	35	78	—	—	—	—	—
91-92—Minnesota-Duluth		WCHA	37	22	22	44	84	—	—	—	—	—
92-93—Hamilton		AHL	75	16	28	44	24	—	—	—	—	—

TOWNSHEND, GRAEME
RW, ISLANDERS

PERSONAL: Born October 2, 1965, at Kingston, Jamaica.... 6-2/225.... Shoots right.... Full name: Graeme Scott Townshend.
COLLEGE: Rensselaer Polytechnic Institute (N.Y.).
TRANSACTIONS/CAREER NOTES: Signed as free agent by Boston Bruins (May 12, 1989).... Suspended six games by AHL for a pre-game fight (December 15, 1990).... Signed as free agent by New York Islanders (September 3, 1991).

				REGULAR SEASON					PLAYOFFS			
Season	Team	League	Gms.	G	A	Pts.	Pen.	Gms.	G	A	Pts.	Pen.
85-86—R.P.I.		ECAC	29	1	7	8	52	—	—	—	—	—
86-87—R.P.I.		ECAC	31	7	1	8	56	—	—	—	—	—
87-88—R.P.I.		ECAC	32	6	14	20	64	—	—	—	—	—
88-89—R.P.I.		ECAC	31	6	16	22	50	—	—	—	—	—
—Maine		AHL	5	2	1	3	11	—	—	—	—	—
89-90—Boston		NHL	4	0	0	0	7	—	—	—	—	—
—Maine		AHL	64	15	13	28	162	—	—	—	—	—
90-91—Maine		AHL	46	16	10	26	119	2	2	0	2	4
—Boston		NHL	18	2	5	7	12	—	—	—	—	—
91-92—Capital District		AHL	61	14	23	37	94	4	0	2	2	0
—New York Islanders		NHL	7	1	2	3	0	—	—	—	—	—
92-93—Capital District		AHL	67	29	21	50	45	2	0	0	0	0
—New York Islanders		NHL	2	0	0	0	0	—	—	—	—	—
NHL totals			**31**	**3**	**7**	**10**	**19**					

TRAVERSE, PATRICK
D, SENATORS

PERSONAL: Born March 14, 1974, at Montreal.... 6-3/173.... Shoots left.
TRANSACTIONS/CAREER NOTES: Selected by Ottawa Senators in third round (third Senators pick, 50th overall) of NHL entry draft (June 20, 1992).

				REGULAR SEASON					PLAYOFFS			
Season	Team	League	Gms.	G	A	Pts.	Pen.	Gms.	G	A	Pts.	Pen.
91-92—Shawinigan		QMJHL	59	3	11	14	12	10	0	0	0	4
92-93—St. Jean		QMJHL	68	6	30	36	24	4	0	1	1	2
—New Haven		AHL	2	0	0	0	2	—	—	—	—	—

TREBIL, DANIEL
D, DEVILS

PERSONAL: Born April 10, 1974, at Edina, Minn.... 6-3/185.... Shoots right.
HIGH SCHOOL: Thomas Jefferson (Bloomington, Minn.).
COLLEGE: Minnesota.
TRANSACTIONS/CAREER NOTES: Selected by New Jersey Devils in sixth round (seventh Devils pick, 138th overall) of NHL entry draft (June 20, 1992).

				REGULAR SEASON					PLAYOFFS			
Season	Team	League	Gms.	G	A	Pts.	Pen.	Gms.	G	A	Pts.	Pen.
89-90—Jefferson HS		Minn. H.S.	22	3	6	9	10	—	—	—	—	—
90-91—Jefferson HS		Minn. H.S.	23	4	12	16	8	—	—	—	—	—
91-92—Jefferson HS		Minn. H.S.	28	7	26	33	6	—	—	—	—	—
92-93—University of Minnesota		WCHA	36	2	11	13	16	—	—	—	—	—

TREFILOV, ANDREI
G, FLAMES

PERSONAL: Born August 31, 1969, at Moscow, U.S.S.R. . . . 6-0/180. . . . Shoots left. . . . Name pronounced treh-FEE-lohv.
TRANSACTIONS/CAREER NOTES: Selected by Calgary Flames in 12th round (14th Flames pick, 261st overall) of NHL entry draft (June 22, 1991).

			REGULAR SEASON							PLAYOFFS					
Season Team	League	Gms.	Min.	W	L	T	GA	SO	Avg.	Gms.	Min.	W	L	GA SO	Avg.
90-91—Dynamo Moscow	USSR	20	1070	...	...	...	36	0	2.02	—	—	—	—	— —	—
91-92—Dynamo Moscow	CIS	28	1326	...	...	◆	35	0	1.58	—	—	—	—	— —	—
92-93—Salt Lake City	IHL	44	2536	23	17	0	135	0	3.19	—	—	—	—	— —	—
—Calgary	NHL	1	65	0	0	1	5	0	4.62	—	—	—	—	— —	—
NHL totals		1	65	0	0	1	5	0	4.62						

TRETOWICZ, DAVE
D, KINGS

PERSONAL: Born March 15, 1969, at Liverpool, N.Y. . . . 5-11/195. . . . Shoots left. . . . Name pronounced TREH-toh-wihtz.
COLLEGE: Clarkson (N.Y.).
TRANSACTIONS/CAREER NOTES: Selected by Calgary Flames in 11th round (11th Flames pick, 231st overall) of NHL entry draft (June 11, 1988). . . . Signed as free agent by Los Angeles Kings (March 2, 1992).
HONORS: Named to ECAC All-Star second team (1989-90). . . . Named to ECAC All-Star first team (1990-91).

			REGULAR SEASON				PLAYOFFS			
Season Team	League	Gms.	G	A	Pts.	Pen.	Gms.	G	A	Pts.	Pen.
87-88—Clarkson	ECAC	35	8	14	22	28	—	—	—	—	—
88-89—Clarkson	ECAC	32	6	17	23	22	—	—	—	—	—
89-90—Clarkson	ECAC	35	2	27	29	12	—	—	—	—	—
90-91—Clarkson	ECAC	40	4	31	35	18	—	—	—	—	—
91-92—Phoenix	IHL	16	3	2	5	14	—	—	—	—	—
—U.S. national team	Int'l	57	1	7	8	4	—	—	—	—	—
—U.S. Olympic Team	Int'l	8	0	0	0	0	—	—	—	—	—
92-93—Phoenix	IHL	79	1	15	16	22	—	—	—	—	—

TROFIMENKOFF, DAVE
G, RANGERS

PERSONAL: Born January 20, 1975, at Calgary, Alta. . . . 6-0/177. . . . Shoots right.
TRANSACTIONS/CAREER NOTES: Selected by New York Rangers in sixth round (sixth Rangers pick, 138th overall) of NHL entry draft (June 26, 1993).

			REGULAR SEASON							PLAYOFFS					
Season Team	League	Gms.	Min.	W	L	T	GA	SO	Avg.	Gms.	Min.	W	L	GA SO	Avg.
91-92—Lethbridge	WHL	21	1080	...	...	...	67	0	3.72	—	—	—	—	— —	—
92-93—Lethbridge	WHL	27	1419	14	9	...	103	0	4.36	—	—	—	—	— —	—

TROTTIER, BRYAN
C, PENGUINS

PERSONAL: Born July 17, 1956, at Val Marie, Sask. . . . 5-11/195. . . . Shoots left. . . . Full name: Bryan John Trottier.
TRANSACTIONS/CAREER NOTES: Selected by New York Islanders from Swift Current Broncos in second round (second Islanders pick, 22nd overall) of NHL amateur draft (May 28, 1974). . . . Sprained left knee (April 1983). . . . Injured left knee (January 1984). . . . Injured knee (October 1984). . . . Fined $1,000 by NHL for being critical of officiating (March 1987). . . . Suffered back spasms (March 1989); missed seven games. . . . Broke little toe on left foot (September 23, 1989). . . . Broke rib at New Jersey (December 13, 1989); missed 12 games. . . . Released by Islanders (July 3, 1990). . . . Signed as free agent by Pittsburgh Penguins (July 20, 1990). . . . Suffered lower back pain (September 1990); missed five preseason games (September 1990); missed 13 games (November 1990); missed 13 games (January 1991). . . . Sprained right knee (November 30, 1991); missed 14 games. . . . Bruised lower back (March 15, 1992); missed two games. . . . Named assistant coach of Pittsburgh Penguins (June 22, 1993).
HONORS: Won WCHL Most Valuable Player Award (1974-75). . . . Named to WCHL All-Star first team (1974-75). . . . Named NHL Rookie of the Year by THE SPORTING NEWS (1975-76). . . . Won Calder Memorial Trophy (1975-76). . . . Played in NHL All-Star Game (1976, 1978, 1980, 1982, 1983, 1985, 1986 and 1992). . . . Named to THE SPORTING NEWS All-Star first team (1977-78 and 1978-79). . . . Named to NHL All-Star first team (1977-78 and 1978-79). . . . Named NHL Player of the Year by THE SPORTING NEWS (1978-79). . . . Won Hart Memorial Trophy (1978-79). . . . Won Art Ross Trophy (1978-79). . . . Won Conn Smythe Trophy (1979-80). . . . Named to THE SPORTING NEWS All-Star second team (1981-82 and 1983-84). . . . Named to NHL All-Star second team (1981-82 and 1983-84). . . . Won Budweiser/NHL Man of the Year (1987-88). . . . Won King Clancy Memorial Trophy (1988-89).
RECORDS: Holds NHL record for most points in one period—6 (December 23, 1978). . . . Shares NHL record for most goals in one period—4 (February 13, 1982). . . . Holds NHL playoff record for scoring points in most consecutive games—27 (1980-82). . . . Shares NHL record for fastest goal from the start of a game—5 seconds (March 22, 1984). . . . Holds NHL single-season playoff record for scoring points in most consecutive games—18 (1981). . . . Shares NHL single-game playoff records for most shorthanded goals in one period—2; and most shorthanded goals—2 (April 8, 1980).
MISCELLANEOUS: Member of Stanley Cup championship teams (1980 through 1983, 1991 and 1992).

			REGULAR SEASON				PLAYOFFS			
Season Team	League	Gms.	G	A	Pts.	Pen.	Gms.	G	A	Pts.	Pen.
72-73—Swift Current	WCHL	67	16	29	45	10	—	—	—	—	—
73-74—Swift Current	WCHL	68	41	71	112	76	13	7	8	15	8
74-75—Lethbridge	WCHL	67	46	*98	144	103	6	2	5	7	14
75-76—New York Islanders	NHL	80	32	63	95	21	13	1	7	8	8
76-77—New York Islanders	NHL	76	30	42	72	34	12	2	8	10	2
77-78—New York Islanders	NHL	77	46	*77	123	46	7	0	3	3	4
78-79—New York Islanders	NHL	76	47	*87	*134	50	10	2	4	6	13

Season	Team	League	Gms.	G	A	Pts.	Pen.	Gms.	G	A	Pts.	Pen.
79-80—New York Islanders..........	NHL	78	42	62	104	68	21	†12	17	*29	16
80-81—New York Islanders..........	NHL	73	31	72	103	74	18	11	†18	29	34
81-82—New York Islanders..........	NHL	80	50	79	129	88	19	6	*23	*29	40
82-83—New York Islanders..........	NHL	80	34	55	89	68	17	8	12	20	18
83-84—New York Islanders..........	NHL	68	40	71	111	59	21	8	6	14	49
84-85—New York Islanders..........	NHL	68	28	31	59	47	10	4	2	6	8
85-86—New York Islanders..........	NHL	78	37	59	96	72	3	1	1	2	2
86-87—New York Islanders..........	NHL	80	23	64	87	50	14	8	5	13	12
87-88—New York Islanders..........	NHL	77	30	52	82	48	6	0	0	0	10
88-89—New York Islanders..........	NHL	73	17	28	45	44	—	—	—	—	—
89-90—New York Islanders..........	NHL	59	13	11	24	29	4	1	0	1	4
90-91—Pittsburgh	NHL	52	9	19	28	24	23	3	4	7	49
91-92—Pittsburgh	NHL	63	11	18	29	54	21	4	3	7	8
92-93—					Did not play—retired.						
NHL totals................................		1238	520	890	1410	876	219	71	113	184	277

TSULYGAN, NIKOLAI
D, MIGHTY DUCKS

PERSONAL: Born May 29, 1975, at Ufa, U.S.S.R. . . . 6-3/196. . . . Shoots right.
TRANSACTIONS/CAREER NOTES: Selected by Mighty Ducks of Anaheim in second round (second Mighty Ducks pick, 30th overall) of NHL entry draft (June 26, 1993).

			—REGULAR SEASON—					—PLAYOFFS—				
Season	Team	League	Gms.	G	A	Pts.	Pen.	Gms.	G	A	Pts.	Pen.
92-93—Salavat..............	CIS	42	5	4	9	21	2	0	0	0	0

TSYGUROV, DENIS
D, SABRES

PERSONAL: Born February 26, 1971, at Chelyabinsk, U.S.S.R. . . . 6-3/198. . . . Shoots left.
TRANSACTIONS/CAREER NOTES: Selected by Buffalo Sabres in second round (first Sabres pick, 38th overall) of NHL entry draft (June 26, 1993).
HONORS: Named to CIS All-Star team (1992-93).

			—REGULAR SEASON—					—PLAYOFFS—				
Season	Team	League	Gms.	G	A	Pts.	Pen.	Gms.	G	A	Pts.	Pen.
88-89—Traktor Chelyabinsk.......	USSR	8	0	0	0	2	—	—	—	—	—
89-90—Traktor Chelyabinsk.......	USSR	27	0	1	1	18	—	—	—	—	—
90-91—Traktor Chelyabinsk.......	USSR	26	0	1	1	16	—	—	—	—	—
91-92—Lada Togliatti	CIS	29	3	2	5	6	—	—	—	—	—
92-93—Lada Togliatti	CIS	37	7	13	20	29	10	1	1	2	6

TUCKER, DARCY
C, CANADIENS

PERSONAL: Born March 15, 1975, at Castor, Alta. . . . 5-10/163. . . . Shoots left.
TRANSACTIONS/CAREER NOTES: Selected by Montreal Canadiens in sixth round (eighth Canadiens pick, 151st overall) of NHL entry draft (June 26, 1993).

			—REGULAR SEASON—					—PLAYOFFS—				
Season	Team	League	Gms.	G	A	Pts.	Pen.	Gms.	G	A	Pts.	Pen.
91-92—Kamloops	WHL	26	3	10	13	42	9	0	1	1	16
92-93—Kamloops	WHL	67	31	58	89	155	13	7	6	13	34

TUCKER, JOHN
C, LIGHTNING

PERSONAL: Born September 29, 1964, at Windsor, Ont. . . . 6-0/200. . . . Shoots right.
TRANSACTIONS/CAREER NOTES: Selected by Buffalo Sabres as underage junior in second round (fourth Sabres pick, 31st overall) of NHL entry draft (June 8, 1983). . . . Broke bone in foot (November 7, 1984). . . . Injured disk (January 28, 1987); underwent surgery following end of season. . . . Tore knee ligaments (November 7, 1987). . . . Suffered shoulder injury (December 1987). . . . Injured shoulder (February 25, 1988). . . . Injured back (January 1989); missed 16 games. . . . Traded by Sabres to Washington Capitals for conditional pick in 1990 draft (January 4, 1990). . . . Sold by Capitals to Sabres (July 3, 1990). . . . Traded by Sabres to New York Islanders for future considerations (January 21, 1991). . . . Signed as a free agent by Tampa Bay Lightning (July 21, 1992). . . . Injured knee (March 16, 1993); missed six games.
HONORS: Won Red Tilson Trophy (1983-84). . . . Named to OHL All-Star first team (1983-84).

			—REGULAR SEASON—					—PLAYOFFS—				
Season	Team	League	Gms.	G	A	Pts.	Pen.	Gms.	G	A	Pts.	Pen.
81-82—Kitchener...........................	OHL	67	16	32	48	32	15	2	3	5	2
82-83—Kitchener...........................	OHL	70	60	80	140	33	11	5	9	14	10
83-84—Kitchener...........................	OHL	39	40	60	100	25	12	12	18	30	8
—Buffalo................................	NHL	21	12	4	16	4	3	1	0	1	0
84-85—Buffalo...............................	NHL	64	22	27	49	21	5	1	5	6	0
85-86—Buffalo...............................	NHL	75	31	34	65	39	—	—	—	—	—
86-87—Buffalo...............................	NHL	54	17	34	51	21	—	—	—	—	—
87-88—Buffalo...............................	NHL	45	19	19	38	20	6	7	3	10	18
88-89—Buffalo...............................	NHL	60	13	31	44	31	3	0	3	3	0
89-90—Buffalo...............................	NHL	8	1	2	3	2	—	—	—	—	—
—Washington	NHL	38	9	19	28	10	12	1	7	8	4
90-91—Buffalo...............................	NHL	18	1	3	4	4	—	—	—	—	—
—New York Islanders..........	NHL	20	3	4	7	4	—	—	—	—	—
91-92—Asiago...............................	Italy				Statistics unavailable.		—	—	—	—	—
92-93—Tampa Bay	NHL	78	17	39	56	69	—	—	—	—	—
NHL totals................................		481	145	216	361	225	29	10	18	28	22

TUER, AL

D

PERSONAL: Born July 19, 1963, at North Battleford, Sask. . . . 6-0/190. . . . Shoots left.
TRANSACTIONS/CAREER NOTES: Selected by Los Angles Kings as underage junior in ninth round (eighth Kings pick, 186th overall) of NHL entry draft (June 11, 1980). . . . Signed as free agent by Edmonton Oilers (August 1986). . . . Selected by Minnesota North Stars in 1987 NHL waiver draft (October 1987). . . . Signed as free agent by Hartford Whalers (August 1988). . . . Suspended five games by AHL for returning from dressing room to enter a fight (March 11, 1989). . . . Named assistant coach of Cincinnati Cyclones (September 14, 1992).

			REGULAR SEASON					PLAYOFFS				
Season Team	League	Gms.	G	A	Pts.	Pen.	Gms.	G	A	Pts.	Pen.
80-81—Regina	WHL	31	0	7	7	58	8	0	1	1	37
81-82—Regina	WHL	63	2	18	20	*486	13	0	3	3	117
82-83—Regina	WHL	71	3	27	30	229	5	0	0	0	37
83-84—New Haven	AHL	78	0	20	20	195	—	—	—	—	—
84-85—New Haven	AHL	56	0	7	7	241	—	—	—	—	—
85-86—New Haven	AHL	8	1	0	1	53	—	—	—	—	—
—Los Angeles	NHL	45	0	1	1	150	—	—	—	—	—
86-87—Nova Scotia	AHL	31	0	1	1	4	5	0	1	1	48
87-88—Minnesota	NHL	6	1	0	1	29	—	—	—	—	—
—Kalamazoo	IHL	68	2	15	17	303	7	0	0	0	34
88-89—Hartford	NHL	4	0	0	0	23	—	—	—	—	—
—Binghamton	AHL	43	1	7	8	234	—	—	—	—	—
89-90—Hartford	NHL	2	0	0	0	6	—	—	—	—	—
—Binghamton	AHL	58	3	7	10	176	—	—	—	—	—
90-91—San Diego	IHL	60	0	5	5	305	—	—	—	—	—
91-92—New Haven	AHL	68	2	10	12	199	4	0	1	1	12
92-93—Cincinnati	IHL	52	1	9	10	248	—	—	—	—	—
—Cleveland	IHL	13	1	4	5	29	2	0	0	0	4
NHL totals		57	1	1	2	208					

TUGNUTT, RON

G, MIGHTY DUCKS

PERSONAL: Born October 22, 1967, at Scarborough, Ont. . . . 5-11/155. . . . Shoots left. . . . Full name: Ronald Frederick Bradley Tugnutt.
TRANSACTIONS/CAREER NOTES: Selected by Quebec Nordiques as underage junior in fourth round (fourth Nordiques pick, 81st overall) of NHL entry draft (June 21, 1986). . . . Sprained ankle (March 1989). . . . Sprained knee (January 13, 1990). . . . Injured hamstring (January 29, 1991); missed 11 games. . . . Traded by Nordiques with LW Brad Zavisha to Edmonton Oilers for LW Martin Rucinsky (March 10, 1992). . . . Selected by Mighty Ducks of Anaheim in NHL expansion draft (June 24, 1993).
HONORS: Won F.W. (Dinty) Moore Trophy (1984-85). . . . Shared Dave Pinkney Trophy with Kay Whitmore (1985-86). . . . Named to OHL All-Star first team (1986-87).

			REGULAR SEASON							PLAYOFFS					
Season Team	League	Gms.	Min.	W	L	T	GA	SO	Avg.	Gms.	Min.	W	L	GA	SO	Avg.
84-85—Peterborough	OHL	18	938	7	4	2	59	0	3.77	—	—	—	—	—	—	—
85-86—Peterborough	OHL	26	1543	18	7	0	74	1	2.88	3	133	2	0	6	0	2.71
86-87—Peterborough	OHL	31	1891	21	7	2	88	2	*2.79	6	374	3	3	21	1	3.37
87-88—Quebec	NHL	6	284	2	3	0	16	0	3.38	—	—	—	—	—	—	—
—Fredericton	AHL	34	1962	20	9	4	118	1	3.61	4	204	1	2	11	0	3.24
88-89—Quebec	NHL	26	1367	10	10	3	82	0	3.60	—	—	—	—	—	—	—
—Halifax	AHL	24	1368	14	7	2	79	1	3.46	—	—	—	—	—	—	—
89-90—Quebec	NHL	35	1978	5	24	3	152	0	4.61	—	—	—	—	—	—	—
—Halifax	AHL	6	366	1	5	0	23	0	3.77	—	—	—	—	—	—	—
90-91—Halifax	AHL	2	100	0	1	0	8	0	4.80	—	—	—	—	—	—	—
—Quebec	NHL	56	3144	12	†29	10	212	0	4.05	—	—	—	—	—	—	—
91-92—Quebec	NHL	30	1583	6	17	3	106	1	4.02	—	—	—	—	—	—	—
—Halifax	AHL	8	447	3	3	1	30	0	4.03	—	—	—	—	—	—	—
—Edmonton	NHL	3	124	1	1	0	10	0	4.84	2	60	0	0	3	0	3.00
92-93—Edmonton	NHL	26	1338	9	12	2	93	0	4.17	—	—	—	—	—	—	—
NHL totals		182	9818	45	96	21	671	1	4.10	2	60	0	0	3	0	3.00

TULLY, BRENT

D, CANUCKS

PERSONAL: Born March 26, 1974, at Peterborough, Ont. . . . 6-3/185. . . . Shoots right.
HIGH SCHOOL: Thomas A. Stewart (Peterborough, Ont.).
TRANSACTIONS/CAREER NOTES: Selected by Vancouver Canucks in fourth round (fifth Canucks pick, 93rd overall) of NHL entry draft (June 20, 1992).
HONORS: Named to OHL All-Star second team (1992-93).

			REGULAR SEASON					PLAYOFFS				
Season Team	League	Gms.	G	A	Pts.	Pen.	Gms.	G	A	Pts.	Pen.
90-91—Peterborough Jr. B	OHA	9	3	0	3	23	—	—	—	—	—
—Peterborough	OHL	45	3	5	8	35	2	0	0	0	0
91-92—Peterborough	OHL	65	9	23	32	65	10	0	0	0	2
92-93—Peterborough	OHL	59	15	45	60	81	21	8	24	32	32

TURCOTTE, DARREN

C, RANGERS

PERSONAL: Born March 2, 1968, at Boston. . . . 6-0/178. . . . Shoots left. . . . Name pronounced TUHR-kaht.
TRANSACTIONS/CAREER NOTES: Selected by New York Rangers as underage junior in sixth round (sixth Rangers pick, 114th overall) of NHL entry draft (June 21, 1986). . . . Separated shoulder (October 1987); missed 34 games. . . . Suffered concussion (March 1989). . . . Sprained left

ankle (October 1989).... Injured knee (April 11, 1990).... Broke left foot (April 27, 1990).... Suffered contusion above left ankle (November 13, 1991); missed two games.... Bruised right foot (March 4, 1992); missed one game.... Reinjured right foot (March 9, 1992); missed two games.... Sprained ankle (January 2, 1993); missed one game.... Suffered hairline fracture in foot (February 10, 1993); missed 11 games.
HONORS: Played in NHL All-Star Game (1991).

Season Team	League	REGULAR SEASON					PLAYOFFS				
		Gms.	G	A	Pts.	Pen.	Gms.	G	A	Pts.	Pen.
84-85—North Bay	OHL	62	33	32	65	28	8	0	2	2	0
85-86—North Bay	OHL	62	35	37	72	35	10	3	4	7	8
86-87—North Bay	OHL	55	30	48	78	20	18	12	8	20	6
87-88—Colorado	IHL	8	4	3	7	9	6	2	6	8	8
—North Bay	OHL	32	30	33	63	16	4	3	0	3	4
88-89—Denver	IHL	40	21	28	49	32	—	—	—	—	—
—New York Rangers	NHL	20	7	3	10	4	1	0	0	0	0
89-90—New York Rangers	NHL	76	32	34	66	32	10	1	6	7	4
90-91—New York Rangers	NHL	74	26	41	67	37	6	1	2	3	0
91-92—New York Rangers	NHL	71	30	23	53	57	8	4	0	4	6
92-93—New York Rangers	NHL	71	25	28	53	40	—	—	—	—	—
NHL totals		312	120	129	249	170	25	6	8	14	10

TURGEON, PIERRE
C, ISLANDERS

PERSONAL: Born August 29, 1969, at Rouyn, Que.... 6-1/203.... Shoots left.... Name pronounced TUHR-zhaw.... Brother of Sylvain Turgeon, left winger/center, Ottawa Senators.
TRANSACTIONS/CAREER NOTES: Underwent knee surgery (June 1985).... Selected by Buffalo Sabres as underage junior in first round (first Sabres pick, first overall) of NHL entry draft (June 13, 1987).... Traded by Sabres with RW Benoit Hogue, D Uwe Krupp and C Dave McLlwain to New York Islanders for C Pat LaFontaine, LW Randy Wood, D Randy Hillier and future considerations; Sabres later received fourth-round pick in 1992 draft (D Dean Melanson) (October 25, 1991).... Injured right knee (January 3, 1992); missed three games.... Separated shoulder (April 28, 1993); missed six playoff games.
HONORS: Won Michel Bergeron Trophy (1985-86).... Won Michael Bossy Trophy (1986-87).... Played in NHL All-Star Game (1990 and 1993).... Won Lady Bing Memorial Trophy (1992-93).

Season Team	League	REGULAR SEASON					PLAYOFFS				
		Gms.	G	A	Pts.	Pen.	Gms.	G	A	Pts.	Pen.
85-86—Granby	QMJHL	69	47	67	114	31	—	—	—	—	—
86-87—Granby	QMJHL	58	69	85	154	8	7	9	6	15	15
87-88—Buffalo	NHL	76	14	28	42	34	6	4	3	7	4
88-89—Buffalo	NHL	80	34	54	88	26	5	3	5	8	2
89-90—Buffalo	NHL	80	40	66	106	29	6	2	4	6	2
90-91—Buffalo	NHL	78	32	47	79	26	6	3	1	4	6
91-92—Buffalo	NHL	8	2	6	8	4	—	—	—	—	—
—New York Islanders	NHL	69	38	49	87	16	—	—	—	—	—
92-93—New York Islanders	NHL	83	58	74	132	26	11	6	7	13	0
NHL totals		474	218	324	542	161	34	18	20	38	14

TURGEON, SYLVAIN
LW/C, SENATORS

PERSONAL: Born January 17, 1965, at Noranda, Que.... 6-0/200.... Shoots left.... Full name: Sylvain Dorila Turgeon.... Name pronounced TUHR-zhaw.... Brother of Pierre Turgeon, center, New York Islanders.
TRANSACTIONS/CAREER NOTES: Selected by Hartford Whalers as underage junior in first round (first Whalers pick, second overall) of NHL entry draft (June 8, 1983).... Pulled abdominal muscles (October 1984).... Underwent surgery to repair torn abdominal muscle (November 14, 1986); missed 39 games.... Broke left arm during Team Canada practice (August 11, 1987).... Sprained right knee during training camp (September 1988).... Separated left shoulder (December 21, 1988); missed 36 games.... Burned both eyes from ultra-violet light produced by welder's torch while working on car (February 28, 1989).... Traded by Whalers to New Jersey Devils for RW/LW Pat Verbeek (June 17, 1989).... Aggravated groin injury (March 20, 1990).... Underwent hernia surgery (August 23, 1990); missed first 33 games of season.... Traded by Devils to Montreal Canadiens for RW Claude Lemieux (September 4, 1990).... Broke right kneecap (February 6, 1991); missed remainder of regular season and returned during playoffs.... Selected by Ottawa Senators in NHL expansion draft (June 18, 1992).... Suspended one game by NHL for receiving two major stick fouls in one game (October 23, 1992).... Injured groin (February 8, 1993); missed 11 games.
HONORS: Won Des Instructeurs Trophy (1981-82).... Won Association of Journalists of Hockey Trophy (1982-83).... Named to QMJHL All-Star first team (1982-83).... Named to NHL All-Rookie team (1983-84).... Played in NHL All-Star Game (1986).

Season Team	League	REGULAR SEASON					PLAYOFFS				
		Gms.	G	A	Pts.	Pen.	Gms.	G	A	Pts.	Pen.
81-82—Hull	QMJHL	57	33	40	73	78	14	11	11	22	16
82-83—Hull	QMJHL	67	54	109	163	103	7	8	7	15	10
83-84—Hartford	NHL	76	40	32	72	55	—	—	—	—	—
84-85—Hartford	NHL	64	31	31	62	67	—	—	—	—	—
85-86—Hartford	NHL	76	45	34	79	88	9	2	3	5	4
86-87—Hartford	NHL	41	23	13	36	45	6	1	2	3	4
87-88—Hartford	NHL	71	23	26	49	71	6	0	0	0	4
88-89—Hartford	NHL	42	16	14	30	40	4	0	2	2	4
89-90—New Jersey	NHL	72	30	17	47	81	1	0	0	0	0
90-91—Montreal	NHL	19	5	7	12	20	5	0	0	0	2

Season Team	League	REGULAR SEASON					PLAYOFFS				
		Gms.	G	A	Pts.	Pen.	Gms.	G	A	Pts.	Pen.
91-92—Montreal	NHL	56	9	11	20	39	5	1	0	1	4
92-93—Ottawa	NHL	72	25	18	43	104	—	—	—	—	—
NHL totals		589	247	203	450	610	36	4	7	11	22

TURNER, BRAD
D, ISLANDERS

PERSONAL: Born May 25, 1968, at Winnipeg, Man.... 6-2/205.... Shoots right.
COLLEGE: Michigan.
TRANSACTIONS/CAREER NOTES: Selected by Minnesota North Stars in third round (sixth North Stars pick, 58th overall) of NHL entry draft (June 21, 1986).... Signed as free agent by New York Islanders (September 1990).

Season Team	League	REGULAR SEASON					PLAYOFFS				
		Gms.	G	A	Pts.	Pen.	Gms.	G	A	Pts.	Pen.
86-87—University of Michigan	CCHA	40	3	10	13	40	—	—	—	—	—
87-88—University of Michigan	CCHA	39	3	11	14	52	—	—	—	—	—
88-89—University of Michigan	CCHA	33	3	8	11	38	—	—	—	—	—
89-90—University of Michigan	CCHA	32	8	9	17	34	—	—	—	—	—
90-91—Capital District	AHL	31	1	2	3	8	—	—	—	—	—
—Richmond	ECHL	40	16	25	41	31	—	—	—	—	—
91-92—New Haven	AHL	32	6	11	17	58	—	—	—	—	—
—Capital District	AHL	35	3	6	9	17	—	—	—	—	—
—New York Islanders	NHL	3	0	0	0	0	—	—	—	—	—
92-93—Capital District	AHL	65	8	11	19	71	3	0	0	0	2
NHL totals		3	0	0	0	0					

T

TUTTLE, STEVE
RW, NORDIQUES

PERSONAL: Born January 5, 1966, at Vancouver, B.C.... 6-1/180.... Shoots right.... Full name: Steven Walter Tuttle.
COLLEGE: Wisconsin.
TRANSACTIONS/CAREER NOTES: Selected by St. Louis Blues in sixth round (eighth Blues pick, 113th overall) of NHL entry draft (June 9, 1984).... Sprained left knee (December 1988); missed 15 games.... Sprained shoulder (February 1989).... Traded by Blues with D Rob Robinson, RW Darin Kimble and G Pat Jablonski to Tampa Bay Lightning for future considerations (June 19, 1992).... Loaned to Milwaukee Admirals at beginning of 1992-93 season.... Traded by Lightning with RW Martin Simard and C Michel Mongeau to Quebec Nordiques for RW Herb Raglan (February 12, 1993).
HONORS: Named to NCAA All-America West second team (1987-88).... Named to IHL All-Star first team (1991-92).

Season Team	League	REGULAR SEASON					PLAYOFFS				
		Gms.	G	A	Pts.	Pen.	Gms.	G	A	Pts.	Pen.
83-84—Richmond	BCJHL	46	46	34	80	22	—	—	—	—	—
84-85—University of Wisconsin	WCHA	28	3	4	7	0	—	—	—	—	—
85-86—University of Wisconsin	WCHA	32	2	10	12	2	—	—	—	—	—
86-87—University of Wisconsin	WCHA	42	31	21	52	14	—	—	—	—	—
87-88—University of Wisconsin	WCHA	45	27	39	66	18	—	—	—	—	—
88-89—St. Louis	NHL	53	13	12	25	6	6	1	2	3	0
89-90—St. Louis	NHL	71	12	10	22	4	5	0	1	1	2
90-91—St. Louis	NHL	20	3	6	9	2	6	0	3	3	0
—Peoria	IHL	42	24	32	56	8	—	—	—	—	—
91-92—Peoria	IHL	71	43	46	89	22	10	4	8	12	4
92-93—Milwaukee	IHL	51	27	34	61	12	4	0	2	2	2
—Halifax	AHL	22	11	17	28	2	—	—	—	—	—
NHL totals		144	28	28	56	12	17	1	6	7	2

TWIST, TONY
LW, NORDIQUES

PERSONAL: Born May 9, 1968, at Sherwood Park, Alta.... 6-1/212.... Shoots left.... Full name: Anthony Rory Twist.
TRANSACTIONS/CAREER NOTES: Suspended three games and fined $250 by WHL for leaving the penalty box to fight (January 28, 1988).... Selected by St. Louis Blues in ninth round (ninth Blues pick, 177th overall) of NHL entry draft (June 11, 1988).... Suspended 13 games by IHL for checking goaltender after play had been blown dead (December 15, 1990).... Traded by Blues with RW Herb Raglan and LW Andy Rymsha to Quebec Nordiques for RW Darin Kimble (February 4, 1991).

Season Team	League	REGULAR SEASON					PLAYOFFS				
		Gms.	G	A	Pts.	Pen.	Gms.	G	A	Pts.	Pen.
86-87—Saskatoon	WHL	64	0	8	8	181	—	—	—	—	—
87-88—Saskatoon	WHL	55	1	8	9	226	10	1	1	2	6
88-89—Peoria	IHL	67	3	8	11	312	—	—	—	—	—
89-90—St. Louis	NHL	28	0	0	0	124	—	—	—	—	—
—Peoria	IHL	36	1	5	6	200	5	0	1	1	8
90-91—Peoria	IHL	38	2	10	12	244	—	—	—	—	—
—Quebec	NHL	24	0	0	0	104	—	—	—	—	—
91-92—Quebec	NHL	44	0	1	1	164	—	—	—	—	—
92-93—Quebec	NHL	34	0	2	2	64	—	—	—	—	—
NHL totals		130	0	3	3	456					

ULANOV, IGOR
D, JETS

PERSONAL: Born October 1, 1969, at Kraskokamsk, U.S.S.R. . . . 6-2/202. . . . Shoots right. . . . Name pronounced yoo-LAH-naf.
TRANSACTIONS/CAREER NOTES: Selected by Winnipeg Jets in 10th round (eighth Jets pick, 203rd overall) in NHL entry draft (June 22, 1991). . . . Suffered back spasms (March 7, 1992); missed five games.

					REGULAR SEASON					PLAYOFFS		
Season	Team	League	Gms.	G	A	Pts.	Pen.	Gms.	G	A	Pts.	Pen.
90-91—Khimik		USSR	41	2	2	4	52	—	—	—	—	—
91-92—Khimik		CIS	27	1	4	5	24	—	—	—	—	—
—Winnipeg		NHL	27	2	9	11	67	7	0	0	0	39
—Moncton		AHL	3	0	1	1	16	—	—	—	—	—
92-93—Moncton		AHL	9	1	3	4	26	—	—	—	—	—
—Fort Wayne		IHL	3	0	1	1	29	—	—	—	—	—
—Winnipeg		NHL	56	2	14	16	124	4	0	0	0	4
NHL totals			83	4	23	27	191	11	0	0	0	43

USTORF, STEFAN
C, CAPITALS

PERSONAL: Born January 3, 1974, at Kaufbeuren, West Germany. . . . 5-11/172. . . . Shoots left.
TRANSACTIONS/CAREER NOTES: Selected by Washington Capitals in third round (third Capitals pick, 53rd overall) of NHL entry draft (June 20, 1992).

					REGULAR SEASON					PLAYOFFS		
Season	Team	League	Gms.	G	A	Pts.	Pen.	Gms.	G	A	Pts.	Pen.
91-92—Kaufbeuren		Germany	41	2	22	24	46	—	—	—	—	—
92-93—Kaufbeuren		Germany	37	14	18	32	32	3	1	0	1	10

VALK, GARRY
LW/RW, CANUCKS

PERSONAL: Born November 27, 1967, at Edmonton, Alta. . . . 6-1/195. . . . Shoots left. . . . Name pronounced VAHLK.
COLLEGE: North Dakota.
TRANSACTIONS/CAREER NOTES: Selected by Vancouver Canucks in sixth round (fifth Canucks pick, 108th overall) of NHL entry draft (June 13, 1987). . . . Sprained thumb (November 24, 1991); missed one game. . . . Sprained shoulder (January 21, 1992); missed eight games. . . . Sprained knee (February 26, 1993); missed 12 games.

					REGULAR SEASON					PLAYOFFS		
Season	Team	League	Gms.	G	A	Pts.	Pen.	Gms.	G	A	Pts.	Pen.
85-86—Sherwood Park		AJHL	40	20	26	46	116	—	—	—	—	—
86-87—Sherwood Park		AJHL	59	42	44	86	204	—	—	—	—	—
87-88—Univ. of North Dakota		WCHA	38	23	12	35	64	—	—	—	—	—
88-89—Univ. of North Dakota		WCHA	40	14	17	31	71	—	—	—	—	—
89-90—Univ. of North Dakota		WCHA	43	22	17	39	92	—	—	—	—	—
90-91—Vancouver		NHL	59	10	11	21	67	5	0	0	0	20
—Milwaukee		IHL	10	12	4	16	13	3	0	0	0	2
91-92—Vancouver		NHL	65	8	17	25	56	4	0	0	0	5
92-93—Vancouver		NHL	48	6	7	13	77	7	0	1	1	12
—Hamilton		AHL	7	3	6	9	6	—	—	—	—	—
NHL totals			172	24	35	59	200	16	0	1	1	37

VALLIS, LINDSAY
RW, CANADIENS

PERSONAL: Born January 12, 1971, at Winnipeg, Man. . . . 6-3/207. . . . Shoots right.
TRANSACTIONS/CAREER NOTES: Selected by Montreal Canadiens in first round (first Canadiens pick, 13th overall) of NHL entry draft (June 17, 1989).

					REGULAR SEASON					PLAYOFFS		
Season	Team	League	Gms.	G	A	Pts.	Pen.	Gms.	G	A	Pts.	Pen.
87-88—Seattle		WHL	68	31	45	76	65	—	—	—	—	—
88-89—Seattle		WHL	63	21	32	53	48	13	6	5	11	14
89-90—Seattle		WHL	65	34	43	77	68	13	6	5	11	14
90-91—Seattle		WHL	72	41	38	79	119	6	1	3	4	17
—Fredericton		AHL	—	—	—	—	—	7	0	0	0	6
91-92—Fredericton		AHL	71	10	19	29	84	4	0	1	1	7
92-93—Fredericton		AHL	65	18	16	34	38	5	0	2	2	10

VAN ALLEN, SHAUN
C, MIGHTY DUCKS

PERSONAL: Born August 29, 1967, at Shaunavon, Sask. . . . 6-1/200. . . . Shoots left. . . . Full name: Shaun Kelly Van Allen.
HIGH SCHOOL: Walter Murray (Saskatoon, Sask.).
TRANSACTIONS/CAREER NOTES: Selected by Edmonton Oilers in fifth round (fifth Oilers pick, 105th overall) of NHL entry draft (June 13, 1987). . . . Suffered concussion (January 9, 1993); missed 11 games. . . . Signed as free agent by Mighty Ducks of Anaheim (July 22, 1993).
HONORS: Named to AHL All-Star second team (1990-91). . . . Won John B. Sollenberger Trophy (1991-92). . . . Named to AHL All-Star first team (1991-92).

					REGULAR SEASON					PLAYOFFS		
Season	Team	League	Gms.	G	A	Pts.	Pen.	Gms.	G	A	Pts.	Pen.
84-85—Swift Current		SAJHL	61	12	20	32	136	—	—	—	—	—
85-86—Saskatoon		WHL	55	12	11	23	43	13	4	8	12	28
86-87—Saskatoon		WHL	72	38	59	97	116	11	4	6	10	24

UV

Season Team	League	REGULAR SEASON					PLAYOFFS				
		Gms.	G	A	Pts.	Pen.	Gms.	G	A	Pts.	Pen.
87-88—Nova Scotia	AHL	19	4	10	14	17	4	1	1	2	4
—Milwaukee	IHL	40	14	28	42	34	—	—	—	—	—
88-89—Cape Breton	AHL	76	32	42	74	81	—	—	—	—	—
89-90—Cape Breton	AHL	61	25	44	69	83	4	0	2	2	8
90-91—Edmonton	NHL	2	0	0	0	0	—	—	—	—	—
—Cape Breton	AHL	76	25	75	100	182	4	0	1	1	8
91-92—Cape Breton	AHL	77	29	*84	*113	80	5	3	7	10	14
92-93—Cape Breton	AHL	43	14	62	76	68	15	8	9	17	18
—Edmonton	NHL	21	1	4	5	6	—	—	—	—	—
NHL totals		23	1	4	5	6					

VANBIESBROUCK, JOHN
G, PANTHERS

PERSONAL: Born September 4, 1963, at Detroit. . . . 5-8/172. . . . Shoots left. . . . Name pronounced van-BEES-bruhk.

TRANSACTIONS/CAREER NOTES: Selected by New York Rangers in fourth round (fifth Rangers pick, 72nd overall) of NHL entry draft (June 10, 1981). . . . Fractured jaw (October 1987). . . . Severely lacerated wrist (June 1988). . . . Underwent knee surgery (May 11, 1990). . . . Suffered lower back spasms (February 25, 1992); missed 11 games. . . . Pulled groin (November 2, 1992); missed four games. . . . Traded by Rangers to Vancouver Canucks for future considerations (June 20, 1993); Canucks sent D Doug Lidster to Rangers to complete deal (June 25, 1993). . . . Selected by Florida Panthers in NHL expansion draft (June 24, 1993).

HONORS: Won F.W. (Dinty) Moore Trophy (1980-81). . . . Shared Dave Pinkney Trophy with Marc D'Amour (1981-82). . . . Named to OHL All-Star second team (1982-83). . . . Shared Tommy Ivan Trophy with D Bruce Affleck (1983-84). . . . Shared Terry Sawchuk Trophy with Ron Scott (1983-84). . . . Named to CHL All-Star first team (1983-84). . . . Won Vezina Trophy (1985-86). . . . Named to THE SPORTING NEWS All-Star first team (1985-86). . . . Named to NHL All-Star first team (1985-86).

Season Team	League	REGULAR SEASON							PLAYOFFS					
		Gms.	Min.	W	L	T	GA	SO	Avg.	Gms.	Min.	W	L	GA	SO	Avg.
80-81—Sault Ste. Marie	OMJHL	56	2941	31	16	1	203	0	4.14	11	457	3	3	24	1	3.15
81-82—Sault Ste. Marie	OHL	31	1686	12	12	2	102	0	3.63	7	276	1	4	20	0	4.35
—New York Rangers	NHL	1	60	1	0	0	1	0	1.00	—	—	—	—	—	—	...
82-83—Sault Ste. Marie	OHL	*62	3471	39	21	1	209	0	3.61	16	944	7	6	56	†1	3.56
83-84—New York Rangers	NHL	3	180	2	1	0	10	0	3.33	1	1	0	0	0	0	...
—Tulsa	CHL	37	2153	20	13	2	124	*3	3.46	4	240	4	0	10	0	*2.50
84-85—New York Rangers	NHL	42	2358	12	24	3	166	1	4.22	1	20	0	0	0	0	...
85-86—New York Rangers	NHL	61	3326	31	21	5	184	3	3.32	16	899	8	8	49	†1	3.27
86-87—New York Rangers	NHL	50	2656	18	20	5	161	0	3.64	4	195	1	3	11	1	3.38
87-88—New York Rangers	NHL	56	3319	27	22	7	187	2	3.38	—	—	—	—	—	—	...
88-89—New York Rangers	NHL	56	3207	28	21	4	197	0	3.69	2	107	0	1	6	0	3.36
89-90—New York Rangers	NHL	47	2734	19	19	7	154	1	3.38	6	298	2	3	15	0	3.02
90-91—New York Rangers	NHL	40	2257	15	18	6	126	3	3.35	1	52	0	1	0	1	1.15
91-92—New York Rangers	NHL	45	2526	27	13	3	120	2	2.85	7	368	2	5	23	0	3.75
92-93—New York Rangers	NHL	48	2757	20	18	7	152	4	3.31	—	—	—	—	—	—	...
NHL totals		449	25380	200	177	47	1458	16	3.45	38	1940	13	20	105	2	3.25

VAN DORP, WAYNE
LW

PERSONAL: Born May 19, 1961, at Vancouver, B.C. . . . 6-4/225. . . . Shoots right.

TRANSACTIONS/CAREER NOTES: Traded by Buffalo Sabres with RW Norm Lacombe and future considerations to Edmonton Oilers for D Lee Fogolin and RW Mark Napier (March 1987). . . . Traded by Oilers with D Paul Coffey and LW Dave Hunter to Pittsburgh Penguins for D Chris Joseph, C Craig Simpson, C Dave Hannan and D Moe Mantha (November 1987). . . . Injured right knee during team practice (February 1988). . . . Traded by Penguins to Buffalo Sabres for future considerations (October 3, 1988). . . . Suspended two games by AHL (December 2, 1988). . . . Traded by Sabres to Chicago Blackhawks for future considerations (February 16, 1989). . . . Suspended 10 games and fined $500 by NHL for fighting (December 28, 1989). . . . Tore right shoulder muscle during training camp (September 1990); missed first 21 games of season. . . . Selected by Quebec Nordiques in NHL waiver draft for $50,000 (October 1, 1990). . . . Reinjured shoulder and underwent surgery (November 24, 1990); missed remainder of season. . . . Separated shoulder (October 23, 1991); missed seven games. . . . Injured groin (November 22, 1991); missed 10 games. . . . Bruised ankle (February 13, 1992); missed four games.

HONORS: Named Playoff Most Valuable Player (1985-86).

Season Team	League	REGULAR SEASON					PLAYOFFS				
		Gms.	G	A	Pts.	Pen.	Gms.	G	A	Pts.	Pen.
78-79—Billington	BCJHL	61	18	30	48	66	—	—	—	—	—
79-80—Seattle	WHL	68	8	13	21	195	12	3	1	4	33
80-81—Seattle	WHL	63	22	30	52	242	5	1	0	1	10
81-82—						Did not play.					
82-83—						Did not play.					
83-84—Erie	AHL	45	19	18	37	131	—	—	—	—	—
84-85—Gronigen	Holland	29	38	46	84	112	6	6	2	8	23
—Erie	AHL	7	9	8	17	21	10	0	2	2	2
85-86—Gronigen	Holland	29	19	24	43	81	8	9	*12	21	6
86-87—Rochester	AHL	47	7	3	10	192	—	—	—	—	—
—Nova Scotia	AHL	11	2	3	5	37	5	0	0	0	56
—Edmonton	NHL	3	0	0	0	25	3	0	0	0	2
87-88—Pittsburgh	NHL	25	1	3	4	75	—	—	—	—	—
—Nova Scotia	AHL	12	2	2	4	87	—	—	—	—	—

Season Team	League	REGULAR SEASON Gms.	G	A	Pts.	Pen.	PLAYOFFS Gms.	G	A	Pts.	Pen.
88-89—Rochester	AHL	28	3	6	9	202	—	—	—	—	—
—Chicago	NHL	8	0	0	0	23	16	0	1	1	17
—Saginaw	IHL	11	4	3	7	60	—	—	—	—	—
89-90—Chicago	NHL	61	7	4	11	303	8	0	0	0	23
90-91—Quebec	NHL	4	1	0	1	30	—	—	—	—	—
91-92—Quebec	NHL	24	3	5	8	109	—	—	—	—	—
—Halifax	AHL	15	5	5	10	54	—	—	—	—	—
92-93—Milwaukee	IHL	19	1	4	5	57	—	—	—	—	—
NHL totals		125	12	12	24	565	27	0	1	1	42

VAN KESSEL, JOHN
RW, SENATORS

PERSONAL: Born December 19, 1969, at Bridgewater, Ont. . . . 6-4/193. . . . Shoots right.
TRANSACTIONS/CAREER NOTES: Selected by Los Angeles Kings in third round (third Kings pick, 49th overall) of NHL entry draft (June 11, 1988). . . . Selected by Ottawa Senators in NHL expansion draft (June 18, 1992).

Season Team	League	REGULAR SEASON Gms.	G	A	Pts.	Pen.	PLAYOFFS Gms.	G	A	Pts.	Pen.
86-87—Belleville	OHL	61	1	10	11	58	—	—	—	—	—
87-88—North Bay	OHL	50	13	16	29	214	4	1	1	2	16
88-89—North Bay	OHL	50	7	13	20	218	11	2	4	6	31
89-90—North Bay	OHL	40	7	21	28	127	5	0	3	3	16
—New Haven	AHL	6	1	1	2	9	—	—	—	—	—
90-91—Phoenix	IHL	65	15	15	30	246	3	1	1	2	16
91-92—Phoenix	IHL	44	2	6	8	247	—	—	—	—	—
92-93—New Haven	AHL	17	2	3	5	60	—	—	—	—	—

VARGA, JOHN
LW, CAPITALS

PERSONAL: Born January 31, 1974, at Chicago. . . . 5-10/170. . . . Shoots left.
HIGH SCHOOL: Clover Park (Tacoma, Wash.).
TRANSACTIONS/CAREER NOTES: Selected by Washington Capitals in fifth round (fifth Capitals pick, 119th overall) of NHL entry draft (June 20, 1992).

Season Team	League	REGULAR SEASON Gms.	G	A	Pts.	Pen.	PLAYOFFS Gms.	G	A	Pts.	Pen.
91-92—Tacoma	WHL	72	25	34	59	93	4	1	2	3	0
92-93—Tacoma	WHL	61	32	32	64	63	7	1	1	2	8

VARIS, PETRI
LW, SHARKS

PERSONAL: Born May 13, 1969, at Varkaus, Finland. . . . 6-1/200. . . . Shoots left.
TRANSACTIONS/CAREER NOTES: Selected by San Jose Sharks in sixth round (seventh Sharks pick, 132nd overall) of NHL entry draft (June 26, 1993).
HONORS: Named Finland Rookie of the Year (1991-92).

Season Team	League	REGULAR SEASON Gms.	G	A	Pts.	Pen.	PLAYOFFS Gms.	G	A	Pts.	Pen.
90-91—KooKoo Kouvola	Finland Dv.II	44	20	31	51	42	—	—	—	—	—
91-92—Assat Pori	Finland	36	13	23	36	24	—	—	—	—	—
92-93—Assat Pori	Finland	46	14	35	49	42	8	2	2	4	12

VARVIO, JARKKO
RW, STARS

PERSONAL: Born April 28, 1972, at Tampere, Finland. . . . 5-9/172. . . . Shoots right.
TRANSACTIONS/CAREER NOTES: Selected by Minnesota North Stars in second round (first North Stars pick, 34th overall) of NHL entry draft (June 20, 1992). . . . North Stars franchise moved from Minnesota to Dallas and renamed Stars for 1993-94 season.

Season Team	League	REGULAR SEASON Gms.	G	A	Pts.	Pen.	PLAYOFFS Gms.	G	A	Pts.	Pen.
89-90—Ilves Tampere	Finland	1	0	0	0	0	—	—	—	—	—
90-91—Ilves Tampere	Finland	37	10	7	17	6	—	—	—	—	—
91-92—HPK Hameenlinna	Finland	41	25	9	34	6	—	—	—	—	—
92-93—HPK Hameenlinna	Finland	40	29	19	48	16	12	3	2	5	8

VASKE, DENNIS
D, ISLANDERS

PERSONAL: Born October 11, 1967, at Rockford, Ill. . . . 6-2/211. . . . Shoots left. . . . Full name: Dennis James Vaske. . . . Name pronounced VAS-kee.
HIGH SCHOOL: Armstrong (Plymouth, Minn.).
COLLEGE: Minnesota-Duluth.
TRANSACTIONS/CAREER NOTES: Selected by New York Islanders in second round (second Islanders pick, 38th overall) of NHL entry draft (June 21, 1986). . . . Suffered lacerated forehead (April 8, 1993); missed three games.

Season Team	League	REGULAR SEASON Gms.	G	A	Pts.	Pen.	PLAYOFFS Gms.	G	A	Pts.	Pen.
84-85—Armstrong H.S.	Minn. H.S.	22	5	18	23	...	—	—	—	—	—
85-86—Armstrong H.S.	Minn. H.S.	20	9	13	22	...	—	—	—	—	—
86-87—Minnesota-Duluth	WCHA	33	0	2	2	40	—	—	—	—	—
87-88—Minnesota-Duluth	WCHA	39	1	6	7	90	—	—	—	—	—
88-89—Minnesota-Duluth	WCHA	37	9	19	28	86	—	—	—	—	—

V

Season Team	League	REGULAR SEASON					PLAYOFFS				
		Gms.	G	A	Pts.	Pen.	Gms.	G	A	Pts.	Pen.
89-90—Minnesota-Duluth	WCHA	37	5	24	29	72	—	—	—	—	—
90-91—New York Islanders	NHL	5	0	0	0	2	—	—	—	—	—
—Capital District	AHL	67	10	10	20	65	—	—	—	—	—
91-92—Capital District	AHL	31	1	11	12	59	—	—	—	—	—
—New York Islanders	NHL	39	0	1	1	39	—	—	—	—	—
92-93—Capital District	AHL	42	4	15	19	70	—	—	—	—	—
—New York Islanders	NHL	27	1	5	6	32	18	0	6	6	14
NHL totals		71	1	6	7	73	18	0	6	6	14

VAUHKONEN, JONNI
RW, BLACKHAWKS

PERSONAL: Born January 1, 1975, at Sounenjoki, Finland. . . . 6-2/189. . . . Shoots left.

TRANSACTIONS/CAREER NOTES: Selected by Chicago Blackhawks in fifth round (seventh Blackhawks pick, 128th overall) of NHL entry draft (June 26, 1993).

Season Team	League	REGULAR SEASON					PLAYOFFS				
		Gms.	G	A	Pts.	Pen.	Gms.	G	A	Pts.	Pen.
92-93—Reipas Lahti	Finland	41	8	5	13	63	—	—	—	—	—

VEILLEUX, STEVE
D, CANADIENS

PERSONAL: Born March 9, 1969, at Montreal. . . . 6-0/190. . . . Shoots right. . . . Name pronounced vay-YOO.

TRANSACTIONS/CAREER NOTES: Selected by Vancouver Canucks as underage junior in third round (second Canucks pick, 45th overall) of NHL entry draft (June 13, 1987). . . . Signed as free agent by Montreal Canadiens (August 6, 1991).

HONORS: Named to QMJHL All-Star second team (1987-88 and 1988-89).

Season Team	League	REGULAR SEASON					PLAYOFFS				
		Gms.	G	A	Pts.	Pen.	Gms.	G	A	Pts.	Pen.
85-86—Trois-Rivieres..................	QMJHL	67	1	20	21	132	5	0	0	0	13
86-87—Trois-Rivieres..................	QMJHL	62	6	22	28	227	—	—	—	—	—
87-88—Trois-Rivieres..................	QMJHL	63	7	25	32	150	—	—	—	—	—
88-89—Trois-Rivieres..................	QMJHL	49	5	28	33	149	4	0	0	0	10
—Milwaukee	IHL	1	0	0	0	0	4	0	0	0	13
89-90—Milwaukee	IHL	76	4	12	16	195	2	0	0	0	2
90-91—Milwaukee	IHL	58	0	9	9	152	—	—	—	—	—
—Indianapolis	IHL	11	1	3	4	30	7	0	3	3	13
91-92—Fredericton	AHL	53	3	7	10	122	—	—	—	—	—
92-93—Fredericton	AHL	63	3	11	14	94	1	0	0	0	4

VEITCH, DARREN
D

PERSONAL: Born April 24, 1960, at Saskatoon, Sask. . . . 6-0/200. . . . Shoots right. . . . Full name: Darren William Veitch. . . . Name pronounced VEECH.

TRANSACTIONS/CAREER NOTES: Selected by Washington Capitals in first round (first Capitals pick, fifth overall) of NHL entry draft (June 11, 1980). . . . Fractured collarbone in three places (October 27, 1982). . . . Refractured collarbone (February 19, 1983). . . . Fractured ribs (February 11, 1984). . . . Bruised ribs (January 1985). . . . Traded by Capitals to Detroit Red Wings for D John Barrett and D Greg Smith (March 1986). . . . Injured ankle (March 1988). . . . Traded by Red Wings to Toronto Maple Leafs for RW Miroslav Frycer (June 1988). . . . Traded by Maple Leafs to St. Louis Blues for Keith Osborne (March 5, 1991). . . . Signed as free agent by Moncton Hawks (November 8, 1991). . . . Signed as free agent by Peoria Rivermen (July 27, 1992).

HONORS: Named to WHL All-Star first team (1979-80). . . . Named to Memorial Cup All-Star team (1979-80). . . . Named to AHL All-Star second team (1989-90).

Season Team	League	REGULAR SEASON					PLAYOFFS				
		Gms.	G	A	Pts.	Pen.	Gms.	G	A	Pts.	Pen.
76-77—Regina Blues	SJHL	60	15	21	36	121	—	—	—	—	—
—Regina	WCHL	1	0	0	0	0	—	—	—	—	—
77-78—Regina	WCHL	71	13	32	45	135	9	0	2	2	4
78-79—Regina	WHL	51	11	36	47	80	—	—	—	—	—
79-80—Regina	WHL	71	29	*93	122	118	18	13	18	31	13
80-81—Hershey	AHL	26	6	22	28	12	10	6	3	9	15
—Washington	NHL	59	4	21	25	46	—	—	—	—	—
81-82—Hershey	AHL	10	5	10	15	16	—	—	—	—	—
—Washington	NHL	67	9	44	53	54	—	—	—	—	—
82-83—Hershey	AHL	5	0	1	1	2	—	—	—	—	—
—Washington	NHL	10	0	8	8	0	—	—	—	—	—
83-84—Washington	NHL	46	6	18	24	17	5	0	1	1	15
—Hershey	AHL	11	1	6	7	4	—	—	—	—	—
84-85—Washington	NHL	75	3	18	21	37	5	0	1	1	4
85-86—Washington	NHL	62	3	9	12	27	—	—	—	—	—
—Detroit	NHL	13	0	5	5	2	—	—	—	—	—
86-87—Detroit	NHL	77	13	45	58	52	12	3	4	7	8
87-88—Detroit	NHL	63	7	33	40	45	11	1	5	6	6
88-89—Newmarket	AHL	33	5	19	24	29	5	0	4	4	4
—Toronto...........................	NHL	37	3	7	10	16	—	—	—	—	—
89-90—Newmarket	AHL	78	13	54	67	30	—	—	—	—	—
90-91—Newmarket	AHL	56	7	28	35	26	—	—	—	—	—

Season	Team	League	Gms.	G	A	Pts.	Pen.	Gms.	G	A	Pts.	Pen.
	—Toronto	NHL	2	0	1	1	0	—	—	—	—	—
	—Peoria	IHL	18	2	14	16	10	19	4	12	16	10
91-92	—Moncton	AHL	61	6	23	29	47	11	0	6	6	2
92-93	—Peoria	IHL	79	12	37	49	16	4	2	0	2	4
NHL totals			**511**	**48**	**209**	**257**	**296**	**33**	**4**	**11**	**15**	**33**

VELISCHEK, RANDY
D, NORDIQUES

PERSONAL: Born February 10, 1962, at Montreal. . . . 6-0/200. . . . Shoots left. . . . Full name: Randolph John Velischek. . . . Name pronounced VEHL-ih-SHEHK.
COLLEGE: Providence.
TRANSACTIONS/CAREER NOTES: Selected by Minnesota North Stars as underage player in third round (third North Stars pick, 53rd overall) of NHL entry draft (June 11, 1980). . . . Selected by New Jersey Devils in NHL waiver draft (October 7, 1985). . . . Sprained left knee during training camp (September 1988). . . . Suffered concussion (March 20, 1990). . . . Traded by Devils to Quebec Nordiques to complete trade of C Peter Stastny from Nordiques to Devils for D Craig Wolanin and future considerations on March 6, 1990 (August 1990). . . . Fractured foot (October 24, 1991); missed 13 games. . . . Suffered from the flu (December 1991); missed two games.
HONORS: Named to ECAC All-Star second team (1981-82). . . . Named ECAC Player of the Year (1982-83). . . . Named to NCAA All-America East team (1982-83). . . . Named to ECAC All-Star first team (1982-83).

Season	Team	League	Gms.	G	A	Pts.	Pen.	Gms.	G	A	Pts.	Pen.
79-80	—Providence College	ECAC	31	5	5	10	20	—	—	—	—	—
80-81	—Providence College	ECAC	33	3	12	15	26	—	—	—	—	—
81-82	—Providence College	ECAC	33	1	14	15	34	—	—	—	—	—
82-83	—Providence College	ECAC	41	18	34	52	50	—	—	—	—	—
	—Minnesota	NHL	3	0	0	0	2	9	0	0	0	0
83-84	—Salt Lake City	IHL	43	7	21	28	54	5	0	3	3	2
	—Minnesota	NHL	33	2	2	4	10	1	0	0	0	0
84-85	—Springfield	AHL	26	2	7	9	22	—	—	—	—	—
	—Minnesota	NHL	52	4	9	13	26	9	2	3	5	8
85-86	—New Jersey	NHL	47	2	7	9	39	—	—	—	—	—
	—Maine	AHL	21	0	4	4	4	—	—	—	—	—
86-87	—New Jersey	NHL	64	2	16	18	52	—	—	—	—	—
87-88	—New Jersey	NHL	51	3	9	12	66	19	0	2	2	20
88-89	—New Jersey	NHL	80	4	14	18	70	—	—	—	—	—
89-90	—New Jersey	NHL	62	0	6	6	72	6	0	0	0	4
90-91	—Quebec	NHL	79	2	10	12	42	—	—	—	—	—
91-92	—Quebec	NHL	38	2	3	5	22	—	—	—	—	—
	—Halifax	AHL	16	3	6	9	0	—	—	—	—	—
92-93	—Halifax	AHL	49	6	16	22	18	—	—	—	—	—
NHL totals			**509**	**21**	**76**	**97**	**401**	**44**	**2**	**5**	**7**	**32**

VERBEEK, PAT
RW, WHALERS

PERSONAL: Born May 24, 1964, at Sarnia, Ont. . . . 5-9/190. . . . Shoots right.
TRANSACTIONS/CAREER NOTES: Selected by New Jersey Devils as underage junior in third round (third Devils pick, 43rd overall) of NHL entry draft (June 9, 1982). . . . Suffered severed left thumb between knuckles in a corn-planting machine on his farm and underwent surgery to have thumb reconnected (May 15, 1985). . . . Pulled side muscle (March 1987). . . . Bruised chest (October 28, 1988). . . . Traded by Devils to Hartford Whalers for LW Sylvain Turgeon (June 17, 1989). . . . Missed first three games of 1991-92 season due to contract dispute.
HONORS: Won Emms Family Award (1981-82). . . . Played in NHL All-Star Game (1991).
STATISTICAL NOTES: Only NHL player ever to lead his team in goals scored and penalty minutes (1989-90 and 1990-91).

Season	Team	League	Gms.	G	A	Pts.	Pen.	Gms.	G	A	Pts.	Pen.
80-81	—Petrolia Jr. B.	OPJHL	42	44	44	88	155	—	—	—	—	—
81-82	—Sudbury	OHL	66	37	51	88	180	—	—	—	—	—
82-83	—Sudbury	OHL	61	40	67	107	184	—	—	—	—	—
	—New Jersey	NHL	6	3	2	5	8	—	—	—	—	—
83-84	—New Jersey	NHL	79	20	27	47	158	—	—	—	—	—
84-85	—New Jersey	NHL	78	15	18	33	162	—	—	—	—	—
85-86	—New Jersey	NHL	76	25	28	53	79	—	—	—	—	—
86-87	—New Jersey	NHL	74	35	24	59	120	—	—	—	—	—
87-88	—New Jersey	NHL	73	46	31	77	227	20	4	8	12	51
88-89	—New Jersey	NHL	77	26	21	47	189	—	—	—	—	—
89-90	—Hartford	NHL	80	44	45	89	228	7	2	2	4	26
90-91	—Hartford	NHL	80	43	39	82	246	6	3	2	5	40
91-92	—Hartford	NHL	76	22	35	57	243	7	0	2	2	12
92-93	—Hartford	NHL	84	39	43	82	197	—	—	—	—	—
NHL totals			**783**	**318**	**313**	**631**	**1857**	**40**	**9**	**14**	**23**	**129**

VERMETTE, MARK
RW

PERSONAL: Born October 3, 1967, at Cochenour, Ont. . . . 6-1/203. . . . Shoots right. . . . Name pronounced vuhr-MEHT.
COLLEGE: Lake Superior State (Mich.).
TRANSACTIONS/CAREER NOTES: Selected by Quebec Nordiques in seventh round (eighth

Nordiques pick, 134th overall) of NHL entry draft (June 21, 1986). . . . Signed as free agent by Las Vegas Thunder (July 14, 1993).
HONORS: Named CCHA Player of the Year (1987-88). . . . Named to NCAA All-America West first team (1987-88). . . . Named to CCHA All-Star first team (1987-88).

			REGULAR SEASON					PLAYOFFS				
Season Team	League	Gms.	G	A	Pts.	Pen.	Gms.	G	A	Pts.	Pen.
85-86—Lake Superior State	CCHA	32	1	4	5	7	—	—	—	—	—
86-87—Lake Superior State	CCHA	38	19	17	36	59	—	—	—	—	—
87-88—Lake Superior State	CCHA	46	45	29	74	154	—	—	—	—	—
88-89—Quebec	NHL	12	0	4	4	7	—	—	—	—	—
—Halifax	AHL	52	12	16	28	30	1	0	0	0	0
89-90—Quebec	NHL	11	1	5	6	8	—	—	—	—	—
—Halifax	AHL	47	20	17	37	44	6	1	5	6	6
90-91—Halifax	AHL	46	26	22	48	37	—	—	—	—	—
—Quebec	NHL	34	3	4	7	10	—	—	—	—	—
91-92—Quebec	NHL	10	1	0	1	8	—	—	—	—	—
—Halifax	AHL	44	21	18	39	39	—	—	—	—	—
92-93—Halifax	AHL	67	42	37	79	32	—	—	—	—	—
NHL totals		67	5	13	18	33					

VERNER, ANDREW
G, OILERS

PERSONAL: Born November 10, 1972, at Weston, Ont. . . . 6-0/ 195. . . . Shoots left.
TRANSACTIONS/CAREER NOTES: Selected by Edmonton Oilers in second round (second Oilers pick, 34th overall) of NHL entry draft (June 22, 1991).
HONORS: Named to OHL All-Star second team (1990-91 and 1991-92).

			REGULAR SEASON							PLAYOFFS					
Season Team	League	Gms.	Min.	W	L	T	GA	SO	Avg.	Gms.	Min.	W	L	GA SO	Avg.
89-90—Peterborough	OHL	13	624	7	3	0	38	0	3.65	—	—	—	—	— —	—
90-91—Peterborough	OHL	46	2523	22	14	7	148	0	3.52	3	185	0	3	15 0	4.86
91-92—Peterborough	OHL	53	3123	*34	13	6	190	1	3.65	10	539	5	5	30 0	3.34
92-93—Cape Breton	AHL	36	1974	17	10	6	126	1	3.83	—	—	—	—	— —	—

VERNON, MIKE
G, FLAMES

PERSONAL: Born February 24, 1963, at Calgary, Alta. . . . 5-9/ 170. . . . Shoots left.
TRANSACTIONS/CAREER NOTES: Selected by Calgary Flames in third round (second Flames pick, 56th overall) of NHL entry draft (June 10, 1981). . . . Injured hip (March 2, 1988). . . . Suffered back spasms (February 1989). . . . Suffered back spasms (March 1990); missed 10 games. . . . Suffered lacerated forehead (October 25, 1992); missed five games.
HONORS: Won Most Valuable Player Trophy (1981-82 and 1982-83). . . . Won Top Goaltender Trophy (1981-82 and 1982-83). . . . Won WHL Player of the Year Award (1981-82). . . . Named to WHL All-Star first team (1981-82 and 1982-83). . . . Named to CHL All-Star second team (1983-84). . . . Named to THE SPORTING NEWS All-Star second team (1988-89). . . . Named to NHL All-Star second team (1988-89). . . . Played in NHL All-Star Game (1988 through 1991 and 1993).
RECORDS: Shares NHL single-season playoff record for most wins by a goaltender—16 (1989).
MISCELLANEOUS: Member of Stanley Cup championship team (1989).

			REGULAR SEASON							PLAYOFFS					
Season Team	League	Gms.	Min.	W	L	T	GA	SO	Avg.	Gms.	Min.	W	L	GA SO	Avg.
80-81—Calgary	WHL	59	3154	33	17	1	198	1	3.77	22	1271	. . .	. . .	82 1	3.87
81-82—Calgary	WHL	42	2329	22	14	2	143	*3	*3.68	9	527	. . .	. . .	30 0	*3.42
—Oklahoma City	CHL	—	—	—	—	—	—	—	—	1	70	0	1	4 0	3.43
82-83—Calgary	WHL	50	2856	19	18	2	155	*3	*3.26	16	925	9	7	60 0	3.89
—Calgary	NHL	2	100	0	2	0	11	0	6.60	—	—	—	—	— —	—
83-84—Calgary	NHL	1	11	0	1	0	4	0	21.82	—	—	—	—	— —	—
—Colorado	CHL	*46	*2648	30	13	2	148	1	*3.35	6	347	2	4	21 0	3.63
84-85—Moncton	AHL	41	2050	10	20	4	134	0	3.92	—	—	—	—	— —	—
85-86—Salt Lake City	IHL	10	601	. . .	. . .	. . .	34	1	3.39	—	—	—	—	— —	—
—Moncton	AHL	6	374	3	1	2	21	0	3.37	—	—	—	—	— —	—
—Calgary	NHL	18	921	9	3	3	52	1	3.39	*21	*1229	12	*9	*60 0	2.93
86-87—Calgary	NHL	54	2957	30	21	1	178	1	3.61	5	263	2	3	16 0	3.65
87-88—Calgary	NHL	64	3565	39	16	7	210	1	3.53	9	515	4	4	34 0	3.96
88-89—Calgary	NHL	52	2938	*37	6	5	130	0	2.65	*22	*1381	*16	5	*52 *3	2.26
89-90—Calgary	NHL	47	2795	23	14	9	146	0	3.13	6	342	2	3	19 0	3.33
90-91—Calgary	NHL	54	3121	31	19	3	172	1	3.31	7	427	3	4	21 0	2.95
91-92—Calgary	NHL	63	3640	24	30	9	217	0	3.58	—	—	—	—	— —	—
92-93—Calgary	NHL	64	3732	29	26	9	203	2	3.26	4	150	1	1	15 0	6.00
NHL totals		419	23780	222	138	46	1323	6	3.34	74	4307	40	29	217 3	3.02

VESEY, JIM
C

PERSONAL: Born September 29, 1965, at Charlestown, Mass. . . . 6-1/200. . . . Shoots right. . . . Full name: James Edward Vesey. . . . Name pronounced VEE-SEE.
COLLEGE: Merrimack (Mass.).
TRANSACTIONS/CAREER NOTES: Selected by St. Louis Blues in eighth round (11th Blues pick, 155th overall) of NHL entry draft (June 9, 1984). . . . Broke two bones above right wrist (April 20, 1990). . . . Traded by Blues to Winnipeg Jets (May 24, 1991) to complete deal in which Jets traded G Tom Draper to Blues (February 28, 1991). . . . Traded by Jets to Boston Bruins for future considerations (June 20, 1991). . . . Injured shoulder (November 14, 1991). . . . Underwent shoulder surgery (January 6, 1992); missed remainder of season. . . . Signed as free agent by Phoenix Roadrunners (July 16, 1993).
HONORS: Named to IHL All-Star first team (1988-89).

Season	Team	League	Gms.	G	A	Pts.	Pen.	Gms.	G	A	Pts.	Pen.
				REGULAR SEASON					PLAYOFFS			
84-85—Merrimack College	ECAC-II		33	19	11	30	28	—	—	—	—	—
85-86—Merrimack College	ECAC-II		32	29	32	61	67	—	—	—	—	—
86-87—Merrimack College	ECAC-II		35	22	36	58	57	—	—	—	—	—
87-88—Merrimack College	ECAC-II		40	40	55	95	95	—	—	—	—	—
88-89—St. Louis	NHL		5	1	1	2	7	—	—	—	—	—
—Peoria	IHL		76	47	46	93	137	4	1	2	3	6
89-90—St. Louis	NHL		6	0	1	1	0	—	—	—	—	—
—Peoria	IHL		60	47	44	91	75	5	1	3	4	21
90-91—Peoria	IHL		58	32	41	73	69	19	4	14	18	26
91-92—Maine	AHL		10	6	7	13	13	—	—	—	—	—
—Boston	NHL		4	0	0	0	0	—	—	—	—	—
92-93—Providence	AHL		71	38	39	77	42	6	2	5	7	4
NHL totals			15	1	2	3	7					

VIAL, DENNIS

D, SENATORS

PERSONAL: Born April 10, 1969, at Sault Ste. Marie, Ont.... 6-1/200.... Shoots left. **TRANSACTIONS/CAREER NOTES:** Suspended three games by OHL for spearing (October 1986).... Selected by New York Rangers in sixth round (fifth Rangers pick, 110th overall) of NHL entry draft (June 11, 1988).... Suspended indefinitely by OHL for leaving the bench to fight (March 23, 1989).... Traded by Rangers with C Kevin Miller and RW Jim Cummins to Detroit Red Wings for RW Joe Kocur and D Per Djoos (March 5, 1991).... Injured right knee and ankle (December 7, 1991); missed two games.... Traded by Red Wings with D Doug Crossman to Quebec Nordiques for cash (June 15, 1992).... Traded by Nordiques to Red Wings for cash (September 9, 1992).... Separated right shoulder (January 19, 1993); missed 15 games.... Traded by Red Wings to Tampa Bay Lightning for LW Steve Maltais (June 8, 1993).... Selected by Mighty Ducks of Anaheim in NHL expansion draft (June 24, 1993).... Selected by Ottawa Senators in Phase II of NHL expansion draft (June 25, 1993).

Season	Team	League	Gms.	G	A	Pts.	Pen.	Gms.	G	A	Pts.	Pen.
				REGULAR SEASON					PLAYOFFS			
85-86—Hamilton	OHL		31	1	1	2	66	—	—	—	—	—
86-87—Hamilton	OHL		53	1	8	9	194	8	0	0	0	8
87-88—Hamilton	OHL		52	3	17	20	229	13	2	2	4	49
88-89—Niagara Falls	OHL		50	10	27	37	230	15	1	7	8	44
89-90—Flint	IHL		79	6	29	35	351	4	0	0	0	10
90-91—Binghamton	AHL		40	2	7	9	250	—	—	—	—	—
—New York Rangers	NHL		21	0	0	0	61	—	—	—	—	—
—Detroit	NHL		9	0	0	0	16	—	—	—	—	—
91-92—Detroit	NHL		27	1	0	1	72	—	—	—	—	—
—Adirondack	AHL		20	2	4	6	107	17	1	3	4	43
92-93—Detroit	NHL		9	0	1	1	20	—	—	—	—	—
—Adirondack	AHL		30	2	11	13	177	11	1	1	2	14
NHL totals			66	1	1	2	169					

VILGRAIN, CLAUDE

RW, FLYERS

PERSONAL: Born March 1, 1963, at Port-au-Prince, Haiti.... 6-1/205.... Shoots left.... Name pronounced VIHL-grayn. **COLLEGE:** Moncton (N.B.). **TRANSACTIONS/CAREER NOTES:** Selected by Detroit Red Wings in sixth round (sixth Red Wings pick, 107th overall) of NHL entry draft (June 9, 1982).... Signed as free agent by Vancouver Canucks (June 18, 1987).... Traded by Canucks to New Jersey Devils for C Tim Lenardon (March 7, 1989).... Suffered concussion (December 10, 1991); missed two games.... Injured groin (January 24, 1992); missed one game.... Signed as free agent by Philadelphia Flyers (August 3, 1993).

Season	Team	League	Gms.	G	A	Pts.	Pen.	Gms.	G	A	Pts.	Pen.
				REGULAR SEASON					PLAYOFFS			
80-81—Laval	QMJHL		72	20	31	51	65	—	—	—	—	—
81-82—Laval	QMJHL		58	26	29	55	64	17	14	10	24	22
82-83—Laval	QMJHL		69	46	80	126	72	12	10	4	14	4
83-84—University of Moncton	AUAA		20	11	20	31	8	—	—	—	—	—
84-85—University of Moncton	AUAA		24	35	28	63	20	—	—	—	—	—
85-86—University of Moncton	AUAA		19	17	20	37	25	—	—	—	—	—
86-87—Canadian national team	Int'l		78	28	42	70	38	—	—	—	—	—
87-88—Canadian national team	Int'l		61	21	20	41	41	—	—	—	—	—
—Canadian Olympic Team	Int'l		6	0	0	0	0	—	—	—	—	—
—Vancouver	NHL		6	1	1	2	0	—	—	—	—	—
88-89—Milwaukee	IHL		23	9	13	22	26	—	—	—	—	—
—Utica	AHL		55	23	30	53	41	5	0	2	2	2
89-90—New Jersey	NHL		6	1	2	3	4	4	0	0	0	0
—Utica	AHL		73	37	52	89	32	—	—	—	—	—
90-91—Utica	AHL		59	32	46	78	26	—	—	—	—	—
91-92—New Jersey	NHL		71	19	27	46	74	7	1	1	2	17
92-93—Cincinnati	IHL		57	19	26	45	22	—	—	—	—	—
—New Jersey	NHL		4	0	2	2	0	—	—	—	—	—
—Utica	AHL		22	6	8	14	4	5	0	1	1	0
NHL totals			87	21	32	53	78	11	1	1	2	17

VINCELETTE, DAN

LW, FLYERS

PERSONAL: Born August 1, 1967, at Verdun, Que.... 6-2/200.... Shoots left. **TRANSACTIONS/CAREER NOTES:** Underwent knee surgery (December 1983).... Selected by Chicago Blackhawks as underage junior in fourth round (third Blackhawks pick, 74th overall) of NHL entry draft (June 15, 1985).... Bruised ribs (February 1988)....

Traded by Blackhawks with LW Everett Sanipass and D Mario Doyon to Quebec Nordiques for LW Michel Goulet, G Greg Millen and sixth-round pick in 1991 draft (March 5, 1990).... Separated left shoulder (October 7, 1990); missed 11 games.... Sprained right knee (November 17, 1990).... Traded by Nordiques with C Paul Gillis to Blackhawks for C Mike McNeil and D Ryan McGill (March 5, 1991).... Pulled groin (November 29, 1991); missed four games.... Sprained knee ligaments (January 26, 1992); missed 12 games.... Fractured foot (April 14, 1992).... Selected by Tampa Bay Lightning in NHL expansion draft (June 18, 1992).... Traded by Lightning to Philadelphia Flyers for C Steve Kasper (December 8, 1992).... Loaned to San Diego Gulls (January 20, 1993).

			REGULAR SEASON					PLAYOFFS			
Season Team	League	Gms.	G	A	Pts.	Pen.	Gms.	G	A	Pts.	Pen.
84-85—Drummondville	QMJHL	64	11	24	35	124	12	0	1	1	11
85-86—Drummondville	QMJHL	70	37	47	84	234	22	11	14	25	40
86-87—Drummondville	QMJHL	50	34	35	69	288	8	6	5	11	17
—Chicago	NHL	—	—	—	—	—	3	0	0	0	0
87-88—Chicago	NHL	69	6	11	17	109	4	0	0	0	0
88-89—Chicago	NHL	66	11	4	15	119	5	0	0	0	4
—Saginaw	IHL	2	0	0	0	14	—	—	—	—	—
89-90—Indianapolis	IHL	49	16	13	29	262	—	—	—	—	—
—Chicago	NHL	2	0	0	0	4	—	—	—	—	—
—Quebec	NHL	11	0	1	1	25	—	—	—	—	—
—Halifax	AHL	—	—	—	—	—	2	0	0	0	4
90-91—Halifax	AHL	24	4	9	13	85	—	—	—	—	—
—Quebec	NHL	16	0	1	1	38	—	—	—	—	—
—Indianapolis	IHL	15	5	3	8	51	7	2	1	3	62
91-92—Chicago	NHL	29	3	5	8	56	—	—	—	—	—
—Indianapolis	IHL	16	5	3	8	84	—	—	—	—	—
92-93—Atlanta	IHL	30	5	5	10	126	—	—	—	—	—
—San Diego	IHL	6	0	0	0	6	—	—	—	—	—
NHL totals		193	20	22	42	351	12	0	0	0	4

VINCENT, PAUL
C, MAPLE LEAFS

PERSONAL: Born January 4, 1975, at Utica, N.Y.... 6-4/205.... Shoots left.
HIGH SCHOOL: Cushing Academy (Ashburnham, Mass.).
TRANSACTIONS/CAREER NOTES: Selected by Toronto Maple Leafs in sixth round (fourth Leafs pick, 149th overall) of NHL entry draft (June 26, 1993).

			REGULAR SEASON					PLAYOFFS			
Season Team	League	Gms.	G	A	Pts.	Pen.	Gms.	G	A	Pts.	Pen.
90-91—Cushing Academy	Mass. H.S.	30	4	2	6	8	—	—	—	—	—
91-92—Cushing Academy	Mass. H.S.	30	22	41	63	16	—	—	—	—	—
92-93—Cushing Academy	Mass. H.S.	25	30	32	62	62	—	—	—	—	—

VISHEAU, MARK
D, JETS

PERSONAL: Born June 27, 1973, at Burlington, Ont.... 6-5/200.... Shoots right.... Full name: Mark Andrew Visheau.
HIGH SCHOOL: Saunders Secondary School (London, Ont.).
TRANSACTIONS/CAREER NOTES: Selected by Winnipeg Jets in fourth round (fourth Jets pick, 84th overall) of NHL entry draft (June 20, 1992).

			REGULAR SEASON					PLAYOFFS			
Season Team	League	Gms.	G	A	Pts.	Pen.	Gms.	G	A	Pts.	Pen.
89-90—Burlington Jr. B	OHA	42	11	22	33	53	—	—	—	—	—
90-91—London	OHL	59	4	11	15	40	7	0	1	1	6
91-92—London	OHL	66	5	31	36	104	10	0	4	4	27
92-93—London	OHL	62	8	52	60	88	12	0	5	5	26

VITAKOSKI, VESA
LW, FLAMES

PERSONAL: Born February 13, 1971, at Lappeenranta, Finland.... 6-2/205.... Shoots left.
TRANSACTIONS/CAREER NOTES: Selected by Calgary Flames in second round (third Flames pick, 32nd overall) of NHL entry draft (June 16, 1990).

			REGULAR SEASON					PLAYOFFS			
Season Team	League	Gms.	G	A	Pts.	Pen.	Gms.	G	A	Pts.	Pen.
89-90—SaiPa	Finland	44	24	10	34	...	—	—	—	—	—
90-91—Tappara	Finland	41	17	23	40	14	—	—	—	—	—
91-92—Tappara	Finland	44	19	19	38	39	—	—	—	—	—
92-93—Tappara	Finland	48	27	27	54	28	—	—	—	—	—

VLASAK, TOMAS
C, KINGS

PERSONAL: Born February 1, 1975, at Prague, Czechoslovakia.... 5-10/161.... Shoots right.
TRANSACTIONS/CAREER NOTES: Selected by Los Angeles Kings in fifth round (sixth Kings pick, 120th overall) of NHL entry draft (June 26, 1993).

			REGULAR SEASON					PLAYOFFS			
Season Team	League	Gms.	G	A	Pts.	Pen.	Gms.	G	A	Pts.	Pen.
91-92—Slavia Praha Jrs.	Czech. Jrs.	69	49	43	92	24	—	—	—	—	—
92-93—Slavia Praha	Czech Dv.II	31	17	6	23	6	—	—	—	—	—

VOLEK, DAVID
LW/RW, ISLANDERS

PERSONAL: Born August 16, 1966, at Prague, Czechoslovakia.... 6-0/190.... Shoots right.... Name pronounced VAH-lehk.

TRANSACTIONS/CAREER NOTES: Selected by New York Islanders in 10th round (11th Islanders pick, 208th overall) of NHL entry draft (June 9, 1984).... Suspended six months by International Ice Hockey Federation for steroid use (August 1988).... Separated right shoulder (October 1988).... Injured back (November 16, 1991); missed three games.... Strained lower back (February 17, 1992); missed one game.... Pulled rib cage muscles (March 7, 1992); missed two games.... Suffered from the flu (December 13, 1992); missed two games.

HONORS: Named to NHL All-Rookie team (1988-89).

			REGULAR SEASON					PLAYOFFS			
Season Team	League	Gms.	G	A	Pts.	Pen.	Gms.	G	A	Pts.	Pen.
86-87—Sparta Prague	Czech.	39	27	25	*52	...	—	—	—	—	—
87-88—Sparta Prague	Czech.	30	18	12	30	...	—	—	—	—	—
88-89—New York Islanders	NHL	77	25	34	59	24	—	—	—	—	—
89-90—New York Islanders	NHL	80	17	22	39	41	5	1	4	5	0
90-91—New York Islanders	NHL	77	22	34	56	57	—	—	—	—	—
91-92—New York Islanders	NHL	74	18	42	60	35	—	—	—	—	—
92-93—New York Islanders	NHL	56	8	13	21	34	10	4	1	5	2
NHL totals		364	90	145	235	191	15	5	5	10	2

VON STEFENELLI, PHIL
D, CANUCKS

PERSONAL: Born April 10, 1969, at Vancouver, B.C.... 6-1/183.... Shoots left.... Full name: Philip Von Stefenelli.

COLLEGE: Boston University.

TRANSACTIONS/CAREER NOTES: Selected by Vancouver Canucks in 6th round (5th Canucks pick, 122nd overall) of NHL entry draft (June 11, 1988).

			REGULAR SEASON					PLAYOFFS			
Season Team	League	Gms.	G	A	Pts.	Pen.	Gms.	G	A	Pts.	Pen.
85-86—Richmond	BCJHL	41	6	11	17	28	12	1	1	2	14
86-87—Richmond	BCJHL	52	5	32	37	51	—	—	—	—	—
87-88—Boston University	Hockey East	34	3	13	16	38	—	—	—	—	—
88-89—Boston University	Hockey East	33	2	6	8	34	—	—	—	—	—
89-90—Boston University	Hockey East	44	8	20	28	40	—	—	—	—	—
90-91—Boston University	Hockey East	41	7	23	30	32	—	—	—	—	—
91-92—Milwaukee	IHL	80	2	34	36	40	5	1	2	3	2
92-93—Hamilton	AHL	78	11	20	31	75	—	—	—	—	—

VUJTEK, VLADIMIR
C, OILERS

PERSONAL: Born February 17, 1972, at Ostrava, Severomoravsky, Czechoslovakia. ... 6-1/190.... Shoots left.... Name pronounced VYOO-tehk.

TRANSACTIONS/CAREER NOTES: Selected by Montreal Canadiens in fourth round (fifth Canadiens pick, 73rd overall) of NHL entry draft (June 22, 1991).... Traded by Canadiens with LW Shayne Corson and C Brent Gilchrist to Edmonton Oilers for LW Vincent Damphousse and fourth-round pick (D Adam Wiesel) in 1993 draft (August 27, 1992).... Suffered charley horse (October 6, 1992); missed eight games.... Suspended by Oilers after failing to report to assigned team (January 4, 1993).... Strained lower back (March 17, 1993); missed five games.

HONORS: Named to WHL (West) All-Star first team (1991-92).

			REGULAR SEASON					PLAYOFFS			
Season Team	League	Gms.	G	A	Pts.	Pen.	Gms.	G	A	Pts.	Pen.
90-91—Tri-City	WHL	37	26	18	44	25	—	—	—	—	—
91-92—Tri-City	WHL	53	41	61	102	114	—	—	—	—	—
—Montreal	NHL	2	0	0	0	0	—	—	—	—	—
92-93—Edmonton	NHL	30	1	10	11	8	—	—	—	—	—
—Cape Breton	AHL	20	10	9	19	14	1	0	0	0	0
NHL totals		32	1	10	11	8					

VUKONICH, MIKE
C, KINGS

PERSONAL: Born May 11, 1968, at Duluth, Minn.... 6-2/220.... Shoots left.... Full name: Michael William Vukonich.... Name pronounced VOO-koh-nihch.

HIGH SCHOOL: Denfeld (Duluth, Minn.).

COLLEGE: Harvard.

TRANSACTIONS/CAREER NOTES: Selected by Los Angeles Kings in fifth round (fourth Kings pick, 90th overall) of NHL entry draft (June 13, 1987).... Suffered from mononucleosis (November 1988).

HONORS: Named to ECAC All-Star first team (1989-90 and 1990-91).

			REGULAR SEASON					PLAYOFFS			
Season Team	League	Gms.	G	A	Pts.	Pen.	Gms.	G	A	Pts.	Pen.
85-86—Duluth Denfeld H.S.	Minn. H.S.	24	14	20	34	...	—	—	—	—	—
86-87—Duluth Denfeld H.S.	Minn. H.S.	22	30	23	53	...	—	—	—	—	—
87-88—Harvard University	ECAC	32	9	14	23	24	—	—	—	—	—
88-89—Harvard University	ECAC	27	11	8	19	12	—	—	—	—	—
89-90—Harvard University	ECAC	27	22	29	51	18	—	—	—	—	—
90-91—Harvard University	ECAC	28	32	22	54	28	—	—	—	—	—
91-92—Phoenix	IHL	68	17	11	28	21	—	—	—	—	—
92-93—Phoenix	IHL	70	25	15	40	27	—	—	—	—	—

VUKOTA, MICK
RW, ISLANDERS

PERSONAL: Born September 14, 1966, at Saskatoon, Sask.... 6-2/215.... Shoots right.... Name pronounced vuh-KOH-tuh.

TRANSACTIONS/CAREER NOTES: Signed as free agent by New York Islanders (September 1987).... Suspended six games by AHL for returning from locker room to fight (November 20, 1987).... Suffered sore back (February 1990).... Separated left shoulder (March 18, 1990).... Suspended 10 games by NHL for fighting (April 5, 1990); missed final four games of 1989-90 season and first six games of 1990-91 season.... Injured shoulder prior to 1992-93 season; missed first two games of season.

Season Team	League	REGULAR SEASON					PLAYOFFS				
		Gms.	G	A	Pts.	Pen.	Gms.	G	A	Pts.	Pen.
83-84—Winnipeg	WHL	3	1	1	2	10	—	—	—	—	—
84-85—Kelowna Wings	WHL	66	10	6	16	247	—	—	—	—	—
85-86—Spokane	WHL	64	19	14	33	369	9	6	4	10	68
86-87—Spokane	WHL	61	25	28	53	*337	4	0	0	0	40
87-88—New York Islanders	NHL	17	1	0	1	82	2	0	0	0	23
—Springfield	AHL	52	7	9	16	372	—	—	—	—	—
88-89—Springfield	AHL	3	1	0	1	33	—	—	—	—	—
—New York Islanders	NHL	48	2	2	4	237	—	—	—	—	—
89-90—New York Islanders	NHL	76	4	8	12	290	1	0	0	0	17
90-91—Capital District	AHL	2	0	0	0	9	—	—	—	—	—
—New York Islanders	NHL	60	2	4	6	238	—	—	—	—	—
91-92—New York Islanders	NHL	74	0	6	6	293	—	—	—	—	—
92-93—New York Islanders	NHL	74	2	5	7	216	15	0	0	0	16
NHL totals		349	11	25	36	1356	18	0	0	0	56

VYBORNY, DAVID
C, OILERS

PERSONAL: Born January 22, 1975, at Jihlava, Czechoslovakia.... 5-10/172.... Shoots left.

TRANSACTIONS/CAREER NOTES: Selected by Edmonton Oilers in second round (third Oilers pick, 33rd overall) of NHL entry draft (June 26, 1993).

HONORS: Named Czechoslovakian League Rookie of the Year (1991-92).

Season Team	League	REGULAR SEASON					PLAYOFFS				
		Gms.	G	A	Pts.	Pen.	Gms.	G	A	Pts.	Pen.
90-91—Sparta Prague	Czech.	3	0	0	0	0	—	—	—	—	—
91-92—Sparta Prague	Czech.	32	6	9	15	2	—	—	—	—	—
92-93—Sparta Prague	Czech.	52	20	24	44	...	—	—	—	—	—

WAITE, JIMMY
G, SHARKS

PERSONAL: Born April 15, 1969, at Sherbrooke, Que.... 6-0/163.... Shoots right.

TRANSACTIONS/CAREER NOTES: Selected by Chicago Blackhawks as underage junior in first round (first Blackhawks pick, eighth overall) of NHL entry draft (June 13, 1987).... Broke collarbone (December 6, 1988).... Sprained ankle (October 12, 1991); missed one game.... Loaned to Hershey Bears for part of 1991-92 season.... Traded by Blackhawks to San Jose Sharks for future considerations (June 18, 1993); Sharks sent D Neil Wilkinson to Blackhawks to complete deal (July 9, 1993).

HONORS: Won Raymond Lagace Trophy (1986-87).... Named to QMJHL All-Star second team (1986-87).... Won James Norris Memorial Trophy (1989-90).... Named to IHL All-Star first team (1989-90).

Season Team	League	REGULAR SEASON							PLAYOFFS						
		Gms.	Min.	W	L	T	GA	SO	Avg.	Gms.	Min.	W	L	GA	SO	Avg.
86-87—Chicoutimi	QMJHL	50	2569	23	17	3	209	†2	4.88	11	576	4	6	54	*1	5.63
87-88—Chicoutimi	QMJHL	36	2000	17	16	1	150	0	4.50	4	222	1	2	17	0	4.59
88-89—Chicago	NHL	11	494	0	7	1	43	0	5.22	—	—	—	—	—	—	—
—Saginaw	IHL	5	304	3	1	0	10	0	1.97	—	—	—	—	—	—	—
89-90—Indianapolis	IHL	54	*3207	34	14	5	135	*5	*2.53	†10	*602	9	1	19	†1	*1.89
—Chicago	NHL	4	183	2	0	0	14	0	4.59	—	—	—	—	—	—	—
90-91—Indianapolis	IHL	49	2888	26	18	4	167	3	3.47	6	369	2	4	20	0	3.25
—Chicago	NHL	1	60	1	0	0	2	0	2.00	—	—	—	—	—	—	—
91-92—Chicago	NHL	17	877	4	7	4	54	0	3.69	—	—	—	—	—	—	—
—Indianapolis	IHL	13	702	4	7	1	53	0	4.53	—	—	—	—	—	—	—
—Hershey	AHL	11	631	6	4	1	44	0	4.18	6	360	2	4	19	0	3.17
92-93—Chicago	NHL	20	996	6	7	1	49	2	2.95	—	—	—	—	—	—	—
NHL totals		53	2610	13	21	6	162	2	3.72							

WAKALUK, DARCY
G, STARS

PERSONAL: Born March 14, 1966, at Pincher Creek, Alta.... 5-11/180.... Shoots left.... Name pronounced WAH-kuh-LUHK.

TRANSACTIONS/CAREER NOTES: Selected by Buffalo Sabres as underage junior in seventh round (seventh Sabres pick, 144th overall) of NHL entry draft (June 9, 1984).... Traded by Sabres to Minnesota North Stars for eighth-round pick in 1991 draft (D Jiri Kuntos) and future considerations (May 26, 1991).... Hyperextended knee (February 17, 1993); missed two games.... North Stars franchise moved from Minnesota to Dallas and renamed Stars for 1993-94 season.

HONORS: Shared Harry (Hap) Holmes Memorial Trophy with David Littman (1990-91).

Season Team	League	REGULAR SEASON							PLAYOFFS						
		Gms.	Min.	W	L	T	GA	SO	Avg.	Gms.	Min.	W	L	GA	SO	Avg.
83-84—Kelowna Wings	WHL	31	1555	...	...	...	163	0	6.29	—	—	—	—	—	—	—
84-85—Kelowna Wings	WHL	54	3094	19	30	4	244	0	4.73	5	282	1	4	22	0	4.68
85-86—Spokane	WHL	47	2562	21	22	1	224	1	5.25	7	419	3	4	37	0	5.30

VW

Season	Team	League	Gms.	Min.	W	L	T	GA	SO	Avg.	Gms.	Min.	W	L	GA	SO	Avg.
86-87—Rochester	AHL		11	545	2	2	0	26	0	2.86	5	141	2	0	11	0	4.68
87-88—Rochester	AHL		55	2763	27	16	3	159	0	3.45	6	328	3	3	22	0	4.02
88-89—Buffalo	NHL		6	214	1	3	0	15	0	4.21	—	—	—	—	—	—	—
—Rochester	AHL		33	1566	11	14	0	97	1	3.72	—	—	—	—	—	—	—
89-90—Rochester	AHL		56	3095	31	16	4	173	2	3.35	†17	*1001	10	6	50	0	*3.00
90-91—Buffalo	NHL		16	630	4	5	3	35	0	3.33	2	37	0	1	2	0	3.24
—Rochester	AHL		26	1363	10	10	3	68	*4	*2.99	9	544	6	3	30	0	3.31
91-92—Minnesota	NHL		36	1905	13	19	1	104	1	3.28	—	—	—	—	—	—	—
—Kalamazoo	IHL		1	60	1	0	0	7	0	7.00	—	—	—	—	—	—	—
92-93—Minnesota	NHL		29	1596	10	12	5	97	1	3.65	—	—	—	—	—	—	—
NHL totals			87	4345	28	39	9	251	2	3.47	2	37	0	1	2	0	3.24

WALKER, SCOTT
D, CANUCKS

PERSONAL: Born July 19, 1973, at Montreal.... 5-9/170.... Shoots right.
TRANSACTIONS/CAREER NOTES: Selected by Vancouver Canucks in fifth round (fourth Canucks pick, 124th overall) of NHL entry draft (June 26, 1993).
HONORS: Named to OHL All-Star second team (1992-93).

			REGULAR SEASON					PLAYOFFS			
Season	Team	League	Gms.	G	A	Pts.	Pen.	Gms.	G	A	Pts.	Pen.
89-90—Kitchener-Cambridge Jr.B	OHA		33	7	27	34	91	—	—	—	—	—
90-91—Cambridge Jr. B	OHA		45	10	27	37	241	—	—	—	—	—
91-92—Owen Sound	OHL		53	7	31	38	128	5	0	7	7	8
92-93—Owen Sound	OHL		57	23	68	91	110	8	1	5	6	16
—Canadian national team	Int'l		2	3	0	3	0	—	—	—	—	—

WALTER, RYAN
C/LW, CANUCKS

PERSONAL: Born April 23, 1958, at New Westminster, B.C.... 6-0/200.... Shoots left.... Full name: Ryan William Walter.
TRANSACTIONS/CAREER NOTES: Selected by Washington Capitals from Seattle Breakers in first round (first Capitals pick, second overall) of NHL amateur draft (June 15, 1978).... Traded by Capitals with D Rick Green to Montreal Canadiens for D Rod Langway, D Brian Engblom, C Doug Jarvis and RW Craig Laughlin (September 9, 1982).... Injured groin muscle (November 1983).... Suffered concussion and twisted knee (October 27, 1984).... Suffered back spasms (March 8, 1986).... Broke ankle (March 1986); missed remainder of regular season and 15 playoff games.... Bruised ribs (October 1987).... Suffered back spasms (November 1987).... Suffered concussion (December 9, 1989).... Broke right wrist (October 13, 1990); missed 42 games.... Signed as free agent by Vancouver Canucks (July 26, 1991).
HONORS: Won WCHL Most Valuable Player Award (1977-78).... Won WCHL Player of the Year Award (1977-78).... Named to WCHL All-Star first team (1977-78).... Played in NHL All-Star Game (1983).... Named Bud Light/NHL Man of the Year (1991-92).
MISCELLANEOUS: Member of Stanley Cup championship team (1986).

			REGULAR SEASON					PLAYOFFS			
Season	Team	League	Gms.	G	A	Pts.	Pen.	Gms.	G	A	Pts.	Pen.
73-74—Langley Lords	BCJHL		...	40	62	102	...	—	—	—	—	—
—Kamloops	WCHL		2	0	0	0	0	—	—	—	—	—
74-75—Langley Lords	BCJHL		...	32	60	92	111	—	—	—	—	—
—Kamloops	WCHL		9	8	4	12	2	2	1	1	2	2
75-76—Kamloops	WCHL		72	35	49	84	96	12	3	9	12	10
76-77—Kamloops	WCHL		71	41	58	99	100	5	1	3	4	11
77-78—Seattle	WCHL		62	54	71	125	148	—	—	—	—	—
78-79—Washington	NHL		69	28	28	56	70	—	—	—	—	—
79-80—Washington	NHL		80	24	42	66	106	—	—	—	—	—
80-81—Washington	NHL		80	24	44	68	150	—	—	—	—	—
81-82—Washington	NHL		78	38	49	87	142	—	—	—	—	—
82-83—Montreal	NHL		80	29	46	75	40	3	0	0	0	11
83-84—Montreal	NHL		73	20	29	49	83	15	2	1	3	4
84-85—Montreal	NHL		72	19	19	38	59	12	2	7	9	13
85-86—Montreal	NHL		69	15	34	49	45	5	0	1	1	2
86-87—Montreal	NHL		76	23	23	46	34	17	7	12	19	10
87-88—Montreal	NHL		61	13	23	36	39	11	2	4	6	6
88-89—Montreal	NHL		78	14	17	31	48	21	3	5	8	6
89-90—Montreal	NHL		70	8	16	24	59	11	0	2	2	0
90-91—Montreal	NHL		25	0	1	1	12	5	0	0	0	2
91-92—Vancouver	NHL		67	6	11	17	49	13	0	3	3	8
92-93—Vancouver	NHL		25	3	0	3	10	—	—	—	—	—
NHL totals			1003	264	382	646	946	113	16	35	51	62

WALZ, WES
C

PERSONAL: Born May 15, 1970, at Calgary, Alta.... 5-10/181.... Shoots right.... Name pronounced WAHLS.
TRANSACTIONS/CAREER NOTES: Selected by Boston Bruins in third round (third Bruins pick, 57th overall) of NHL entry draft (June 17, 1989).... Traded by Bruins with D Garry Galley and future considerations to Philadelphia Flyers for D Gord Murphy, RW Brian Dobbin and third-round pick in 1992 draft (LW Sergei Zholtok) (January 2, 1992).
HONORS: Won Jim Piggott Memorial Trophy (1988-89).... Won WHL Player of the Year Award (1989-90).... Named to WHL (East) All-Star first team (1989-90).

W

Season Team	League	Gms.	G	A	Pts.	Pen.	Gms.	G	A	Pts.	Pen.
				REGULAR SEASON					PLAYOFFS		
87-88—Prince Albert	WHL	1	1	1	2	0	—	—	—	—	—
88-89—Lethbridge	WHL	63	29	75	104	32	8	1	5	6	6
89-90—Boston	NHL	2	1	1	2	0	—	—	—	—	—
—Lethbridge	WHL	56	54	86	140	69	19	13	*24	†37	33
90-91—Maine	AHL	20	8	12	20	19	2	0	0	0	21
—Boston	NHL	56	8	8	16	32	2	0	0	0	0
91-92—Boston	NHL	15	0	3	3	12	—	—	—	—	—
—Maine	AHL	21	13	11	24	38	—	—	—	—	—
—Hershey	AHL	41	13	28	41	37	6	1	2	3	0
—Philadelphia	NHL	2	1	0	1	0	—	—	—	—	—
92-93—Hershey	AHL	78	35	45	80	106	—	—	—	—	—
NHL totals		75	10	12	22	44	2	0	0	0	0

WAMSLEY, RICK
G, MAPLE LEAFS

PERSONAL: Born May 25, 1959, at Simcoe, Ont. . . . 5-11/185. . . . Shoots left.
TRANSACTIONS/CAREER NOTES: Selected by Montreal Canadiens in third round (fifth Canadiens pick, 58th overall) of NHL entry draft (August 9, 1979). . . . Traded by Canadiens with second-round (D Brian Benning) and third-round (D Robert Dirk) picks in 1984 draft to St. Louis Blues for first-round (C Shayne Corson) and second-round (C Stephane Richer) picks in 1984 draft (June 9, 1984). . . . Bruised right hand (October 16, 1985); missed nine games. . . . Traded by Blues with D Rob Ramage to Calgary Flames for RW Brett Hull and LW Steve Bozek (March 7, 1988). . . . Pulled groin (March 7, 1988). . . . Broke two bones in left hand (October 10, 1990). . . . Traded by Flames with C Doug Gilmour, LW Kent Manderville, D Jamie Macoun and D Ric Nattress to Toronto Maple Leafs for LW Craig Berube, D Alexander Godynyuk, LW Gary Leeman, D Michel Petit and G Jeff Reese (January 2, 1992). . . . Strained knee (March 5, 1992). . . . Sprained knee (October 11, 1992); missed 12 games.
HONORS: Shared Dave Pinkney Trophy with Al Jensen (1977-78). . . . Shared William M. Jennings Trophy with Denis Herron (1981-82).
MISCELLANEOUS: Member of Stanley Cup championship team (1989).

Season Team	League	Gms.	Min.	W	L	T	GA	SO	Avg.	Gms.	Min.	W	L	GA	SO	Avg.
					REGULAR SEASON								PLAYOFFS			
76-77—St. Catharines	OMJHL	12	647	...	...	...	36	0	3.34	—	—	—	—	—	—	—
77-78—Hamilton Fincups	OMJHL	25	1495	...	...	...	74	2	*2.97	—	—	—	—	—	—	—
78-79—Brantford	OMJHL	24	1444	...	...	...	128	0	5.32	—	—	—	—	—	—	—
79-80—Nova Scotia	AHL	40	2305	19	16	2	125	2	3.25	3	143	1	1	12	0	5.03
80-81—Nova Scotia	AHL	43	2372	17	19	3	155	0	3.92	4	199	2	1	6	†1	*1.81
—Montreal	NHL	5	253	3	0	1	8	1	1.90	—	—	—	—	—	—	—
81-82—Montreal	NHL	38	2206	23	7	7	101	2	2.75	5	300	2	3	11	0	*2.20
82-83—Montreal	NHL	46	2583	27	12	5	151	0	3.51	3	152	0	3	7	0	2.76
83-84—Montreal	NHL	42	2333	19	17	3	144	0	3.70	1	32	0	0	0	0	...
84-85—St. Louis	NHL	40	2319	23	12	5	126	0	3.26	2	120	0	2	7	0	3.50
85-86—St. Louis	NHL	42	2517	22	16	3	144	1	3.43	10	569	4	6	37	0	3.90
86-87—St. Louis	NHL	41	2410	17	15	6	142	0	3.54	2	120	1	1	5	0	2.50
87-88—St. Louis	NHL	31	1818	13	16	1	103	2	3.40	—	—	—	—	—	—	—
—Calgary	NHL	2	73	1	0	0	5	0	4.11	1	33	0	1	2	0	3.64
88-89—Calgary	NHL	35	1927	17	11	4	95	2	2.96	1	20	0	1	2	0	6.00
89-90—Calgary	NHL	36	1969	18	8	6	107	2	3.26	1	49	0	1	9	0	11.02
90-91—Calgary	NHL	29	1670	14	7	5	85	0	3.05	1	2	0	0	1	0	30.00
91-92—Calgary	NHL	9	457	3	4	0	34	0	4.46	—	—	—	—	—	—	—
—Toronto	NHL	8	428	4	3	0	27	0	3.79	—	—	—	—	—	—	—
92-93—Toronto	NHL	3	160	0	3	0	15	0	5.63	—	—	—	—	—	—	—
—St. John's	AHL	2	112	0	1	0	8	0	4.29	—	—	—	—	—	—	—
NHL totals		407	23123	204	131	46	1287	12	3.34	27	1397	7	18	81	0	3.48

WARD, AARON
D, RED WINGS

PERSONAL: Born January 17, 1973, at Windsor, Ont. . . . 6-2/200. . . . Shoots right. . . . Full name: Aaron Christian Ward.
COLLEGE: Michigan.
TRANSACTIONS/CAREER NOTES: Selected by Winnipeg Jets in first round (first Jets pick, fifth overall) of NHL entry draft (June 22, 1991). . . . Traded by Jets with fourth-round pick in 1993 draft (D John Jakopin) and fifth-round pick in 1994 draft to Detroit Red Wings for RW Paul Ysebaert (June 11, 1993).
HONORS: Named to CCHA All-Rookie Team (1990-91). . . . Named to CCHA All-Tournament Team (1990-91).

Season Team	League	Gms.	G	A	Pts.	Pen.	Gms.	G	A	Pts.	Pen.
				REGULAR SEASON					PLAYOFFS		
88-89—Nepean	COJHL	56	2	17	19	44	—	—	—	—	—
89-90—Nepean	COJHL	52	6	33	39	85	—	—	—	—	—
90-91—University of Michigan	CCHA	46	8	11	19	126	—	—	—	—	—
91-92—University of Michigan	CCHA	42	7	12	19	64	—	—	—	—	—
92-93—University of Michigan	CCHA	30	5	8	13	73	—	—	—	—	—
—Canadian national team	Int'l	4	0	0	0	8	—	—	—	—	—

WARD, DIXON
LW, CANUCKS

PERSONAL: Born September 23, 1968, at Edmonton, Alta. . . . 6-0/200. . . . Shoots right.
COLLEGE: North Dakota.
TRANSACTIONS/CAREER NOTES: Selected by Vancouver Canucks in seventh round (sixth Canucks pick, 128th overall) of NHL entry draft (June 11, 1988). . . . Separated left shoulder (December

W

1990).... Sprained ankle (March 14, 1993); missed four games.
HONORS: Named to WCHA All-Star second team (1990-91 and 1991-92).

			REGULAR SEASON					PLAYOFFS				
Season Team	League	Gms.	G	A	Pts.	Pen.	Gms.	G	A	Pts.	Pen.	
86-87—Red Deer	AJHL	59	46	40	86	153	—	—	—	—	—	
87-88—Red Deer	AJHL	51	60	71	131	167	—	—	—	—	—	
88-89—Univ. of North Dakota	WCHA	37	8	9	17	26	—	—	—	—	—	
89-90—Univ. of North Dakota	WCHA	45	35	34	69	44	—	—	—	—	—	
90-91—Univ. of North Dakota	WCHA	43	34	35	69	84	—	—	—	—	—	
91-92—Univ. of North Dakota	WCHA	38	33	31	64	90	—	—	—	—	—	
92-93—Vancouver	NHL	70	22	30	52	82	9	2	3	5	0	
NHL totals		70	22	30	52	82	9	2	3	5	0	

WARD, ED
RW, NORDIQUES
PERSONAL: Born November 10, 1969, at Edmonton, Alta.... 6-3/190.... Shoots right.... Full name: Edward John Ward.
COLLEGE: Northern Michigan.
TRANSACTIONS/CAREER NOTES: Tore knee cartilage (August 1987).... Selected by Quebec Nordiques in sixth round (seventh Nordiques pick, 108th overall) of NHL entry draft (June 11, 1988).

			REGULAR SEASON					PLAYOFFS				
Season Team	League	Gms.	G	A	Pts.	Pen.	Gms.	G	A	Pts.	Pen.	
86-87—Sherwood Park	AJHL	60	18	28	46	272	—	—	—	—	—	
87-88—Northern Michigan Univ.	WCHA	25	0	2	2	40	—	—	—	—	—	
88-89—Northern Michigan Univ.	WCHA	42	5	15	20	36	—	—	—	—	—	
89-90—Northern Michigan Univ.	WCHA	39	5	11	16	77	—	—	—	—	—	
90-91—Northern Michigan Univ.	WCHA	46	13	18	31	109	—	—	—	—	—	
91-92—Halifax	AHL	51	7	11	18	65	—	—	—	—	—	
—Greensboro	ECHL	12	4	8	12	21	—	—	—	—	—	
92-93—Halifax	AHL	70	13	19	32	56	—	—	—	—	—	

WARRINER, TODD
LW/C, NORDIQUES
PERSONAL: Born January 3, 1974, at Chatham, Ont.... 6-1/172.... Shoots left.
HIGH SCHOOL: Herman E. Fawcett (Brantford, Ont.).
TRANSACTIONS/CAREER NOTES: Selected by Quebec Nordiques in first round (first Nordiques pick, fourth overall) of NHL entry draft (June 20, 1992).
HONORS: Won Can.HL Top Draft Prospect Award (1991-92).... Won OHL Top Draft Prospect Award (1991-92).... Named to Can.HL All-Star second team (1991-92).... Named to OHL All-Star first team (1991-92).

			REGULAR SEASON					PLAYOFFS				
Season Team	League	Gms.	G	A	Pts.	Pen.	Gms.	G	A	Pts.	Pen.	
88-89—Blenheim Jr. C	OHA	10	1	4	5	0	—	—	—	—	—	
89-90—Chatham Jr. B	OHA	40	24	21	45	12	—	—	—	—	—	
90-91—Windsor	OHL	57	36	28	64	26	11	6	5	11	12	
91-92—Windsor	OHL	50	41	42	83	66	7	5	4	9	6	
92-93—Windsor	OHL	23	13	21	34	29	—	—	—	—	—	
—Kitchener	OHL	32	19	24	43	35	7	5	14	19	14	

WASHBURN, STEVE
C, PANTHERS
PERSONAL: Born April 10, 1975, at Ottawa, Ont.... 6-1/178.... Shoots left.
TRANSACTIONS/CAREER NOTES: Selected by Florida Panthers in third round (fifth Panthers pick, 78th overall) of NHL entry draft (June 26, 1993).

			REGULAR SEASON					PLAYOFFS				
Season Team	League	Gms.	G	A	Pts.	Pen.	Gms.	G	A	Pts.	Pen.	
90-91—Gloucester	OPJHL	56	21	30	51	47	—	—	—	—	—	
91-92—Ottawa	OHL	59	5	17	22	10	11	2	3	5	4	
92-93—Ottawa	OHL	66	20	38	58	54	—	—	—	—	—	

WATTERS, TIMOTHY
D, KINGS
PERSONAL: Born July 25, 1959, at Kamloops, B.C.... 5-11/185.... Shoots left. ... Full name: Timothy John Watters.
COLLEGE: Michigan Tech.
TRANSACTIONS/CAREER NOTES: Selected by Winnipeg Jets in sixth round (sixth Jets pick, 124th overall) of NHL draft (August 9, 1979).... Pulled hamstring (October 1983).... Broke wrist (December 1984).... Suffered back spasms (February 1986).... Strained knee (December 1987).... Signed as free agent by Los Angeles Kings (July 1988).... Bruised calf (March 1989).... Bruised ankle (December 23, 1989); missed nine games.... Bruised ankle (April 1990).... Bruised ribs (October 14, 1990); missed six games.... Twisted right knee (January 12, 1991).... Injured ankle (October 28, 1991); missed 14 games.... Injured ankle (December 1991).
HONORS: Named to NCAA All-America West team (1980-81).... Named to NCAA All-Tournament team (1980-81).... Named to WCHA All-Star first team (1980-81).

			REGULAR SEASON					PLAYOFFS				
Season Team	League	Gms.	G	A	Pts.	Pen.	Gms.	G	A	Pts.	Pen.	
76-77—Kamloops	BCJHL	60	10	38	48	...	—	—	—	—	—	
77-78—Michigan Tech	WCHA	37	1	15	16	47	—	—	—	—	—	
78-79—Michigan Tech	WCHA	31	6	21	27	48	—	—	—	—	—	
79-80—Canadian national team	Int'l	56	8	21	29	43	—	—	—	—	—	
—Canadian Olympic Team	Int'l	6	1	1	2	0	—	—	—	—	—	
80-81—Michigan Tech	WCHA	43	12	38	50	36	—	—	—	—	—	

Season Team	League	REGULAR SEASON Gms.	G	A	Pts.	Pen.	PLAYOFFS Gms.	G	A	Pts.	Pen.
81-82—Tulsa	CHL	5	1	2	3	0	—	—	—	—	—
—Winnipeg	NHL	69	2	22	24	97	4	0	1	1	8
82-83—Winnipeg	NHL	77	5	18	23	98	3	0	0	0	2
83-84—Winnipeg	NHL	74	3	20	23	169	3	1	0	1	2
84-85—Winnipeg	NHL	63	2	20	22	74	8	0	1	1	16
85-86—Winnipeg	NHL	56	6	8	14	97	—	—	—	—	—
86-87—Winnipeg	NHL	63	3	13	16	119	10	0	0	0	21
87-88—Winnipeg	NHL	36	0	0	0	106	4	0	0	0	4
—Canadian national team	Int'l	2	0	2	2	0	—	—	—	—	—
—Canadian Olympic Team	Int'l	8	0	1	1	2	—	—	—	—	—
88-89—Los Angeles	NHL	76	3	18	21	168	11	0	1	1	6
89-90—Los Angeles	NHL	62	1	10	11	92	4	0	0	0	6
90-91—Los Angeles	NHL	45	0	4	4	92	7	0	0	0	12
91-92—Los Angeles	NHL	37	0	7	7	92	6	0	0	0	6
—Phoenix	IHL	5	0	3	3	6	—	—	—	—	—
92-93—Phoenix	IHL	31	3	3	6	43	—	—	—	—	—
—Los Angeles	NHL	22	0	2	2	18	22	0	2	2	30
NHL totals		680	25	142	167	1222	82	1	5	6	115

WEEKES, KEVIN
G, PANTHERS

PERSONAL: Born April 4, 1975, at Toronto.... 6-0/158.... Shoots left.
HIGH SCHOOL: West Hill (Ont.) Secondary School.
TRANSACTIONS/CAREER NOTES: Selected by Florida Panthers in second round (second Panthers pick, 41st overall) of NHL entry draft (June 26, 1993).

Season Team	League	REGULAR SEASON Gms.	Min.	W	L	T	GA	SO	Avg.	PLAYOFFS Gms.	Min.	W	L	GA	SO	Avg.
91-92—St. Michaels Tier II	Jr. A	2	127	...	...	...	11	0	5.20	—	—	—	—	—	—	—
92-93—Owen Sound	OHL	29	1645	9	12	5	143	0	5.22	1	26	0	0	5	0	11.54

WEEKS, STEVE
G

PERSONAL: Born June 30, 1958, at Scarborough, Ont.... 5-11/170.... Shoots left.
COLLEGE: Northern Michigan.
TRANSACTIONS/CAREER NOTES: Selected by New York Rangers in 11th round (12th Rangers pick, 176th overall) of NHL entry draft (June 15, 1978).... Traded by Rangers to Hartford Whalers for future considerations (September 1984).... Traded by Whalers to Vancouver Canucks for G Richard Brodeur (March 8, 1988).... Traded by Canucks to Buffalo Sabres for cash and future considerations (March 5, 1991); remained in Milwaukee through IHL playoffs.... Signed as free agent by New York Islanders (October 1991).... Traded by Islanders to Los Angeles Kings for seventh-round pick (RW Steve O'Rourke) in 1992 draft (February 18, 1992).... Suffered back spasms (March 3, 1992); missed three games.... Signed as free agent by Washington Capitals (June 16, 1992).... Traded by Capitals to Ottawa Senators for future considerations (August 13, 1992).... Announced retirement and named organizational goaltending instructor of Whalers (February 12, 1993).
HONORS: Named CCHA All-Star second team (1978-79).... Named CCHA Most Valuable Player (1979-80).... Named CCHA Player of the Year (1979-80).... Named to CCHA All-Star first team (1979-80).... Named to NCAA All-Tournament team (1979-80).

Season Team	League	REGULAR SEASON Gms.	Min.	W	L	T	GA	SO	Avg.	PLAYOFFS Gms.	Min.	W	L	GA	SO	Avg.
75-76—Toronto	OHA Mj Jr.A	18	873	...	...	...	73	0	5.02	—	—	—	—	—	—	—
76-77—N. Michigan U.	WCHA	16	811	...	...	...	58	0	4.29	—	—	—	—	—	—	—
77-78—N. Michigan U.	WCHA	19	1015	...	...	...	56	1	3.31	—	—	—	—	—	—	—
78-79—N. Michigan U.	WCHA	25	1437	...	...	...	82	0	3.42	—	—	—	—	—	—	—
79-80—N. Michigan U.	WCHA	36	2133	29	6	1	105	0	*2.95	—	—	—	—	—	—	—
80-81—New Haven	AHL	36	2065	14	17	3	142	1	4.13	—	—	—	—	—	—	—
—New York Rangers	NHL	1	60	0	1	0	2	0	2.00	1	14	0	0	1	0	4.29
81-82—New York Rangers	NHL	49	2852	23	16	9	179	1	3.77	4	127	1	2	9	0	4.25
82-83—Tulsa	CHL	19	1116	8	10	0	60	0	3.23	—	—	—	—	—	—	—
—New York Rangers	NHL	18	1040	9	5	3	68	0	3.92	—	—	—	—	—	—	—
83-84—New York Rangers	NHL	26	1361	10	11	2	90	0	3.97	—	—	—	—	—	—	—
—Tulsa	CHL	3	180	3	0	0	7	0	2.33	—	—	—	—	—	—	—
84-85—Binghamton	AHL	5	303	5	0	0	13	0	2.57	—	—	—	—	—	—	—
—Hartford	NHL	24	1457	10	12	2	93	2	3.83	—	—	—	—	—	—	—
85-86—Hartford	NHL	27	1544	13	13	0	99	1	3.85	3	169	1	2	8	0	2.84
86-87—Hartford	NHL	25	1367	12	8	2	78	1	3.42	1	36	0	0	1	0	1.67
87-88—Hartford	NHL	18	918	6	7	2	55	0	3.59	—	—	—	—	—	—	—
—Vancouver	NHL	9	550	4	3	2	31	0	3.38	—	—	—	—	—	—	—
88-89—Vancouver	NHL	35	2056	11	19	5	102	0	2.98	3	140	1	1	8	0	3.43
89-90—Vancouver	NHL	21	1142	4	11	4	79	0	4.15	—	—	—	—	—	—	—
90-91—Milwaukee	IHL	37	2014	16	19	0	127	0	3.78	3	210	1	2	13	0	3.71
—Vancouver	NHL	1	59	0	1	0	6	0	6.10	—	—	—	—	—	—	—
91-92—New York Islanders	NHL	23	1032	9	4	2	62	0	3.60	—	—	—	—	—	—	—
—Los Angeles	NHL	7	252	1	3	0	17	0	4.05	—	—	—	—	—	—	—
92-93—Ottawa	NHL	7	249	0	5	0	30	0	7.23	—	—	—	—	—	—	—
—New Haven	AHL	6	323	0	6	0	32	0	5.94	—	—	—	—	—	—	—
NHL totals		291	15939	112	119	33	991	5	3.73	12	486	3	5	27	0	3.33

W

WEIGHT, DOUG

C, OILERS

PERSONAL: Born January 21, 1971, at Warren, Mich. . . . 5-11/191. . . . Shoots left. . . . Name pronounced WAYT.
COLLEGE: Lake Superior State (Mich.).
TRANSACTIONS/CAREER NOTES: Selected by New York Rangers in second round (second Rangers pick, 34th overall) of NHL entry draft (June 16, 1990). . . . Sprained elbow (October 14, 1991); missed three games. . . . Damaged ligaments (January 11, 1991). . . . Suspended four off-days and fined $500 by NHL for cross-checking (November 5, 1992). . . . Traded by Rangers to Edmonton Oilers for LW Esa Tikkanen (March 17, 1993).
HONORS: Named to CCHA All-Rookie team (1989-90). . . . Named to NCAA All-America West second team (1990-91). . . . Named to CCHA All-Star first team (1990-91).

			REGULAR SEASON					PLAYOFFS				
Season	Team	League	Gms.	G	A	Pts.	Pen.	Gms.	G	A	Pts.	Pen.
88-89—Bloomfield		NAJHL	34	26	53	79	105	—	—	—	—	—
89-90—Lake Superior State		CCHA	46	21	48	69	44	—	—	—	—	—
90-91—Lake Superior State		CCHA	42	29	46	75	86	—	—	—	—	—
91-92—New York Rangers		NHL	53	8	22	30	23	7	2	2	4	0
—Binghamton		AHL	9	3	14	17	2	4	1	4	5	6
92-93—New York Rangers		NHL	65	15	25	40	55	—	—	—	—	—
—Edmonton		NHL	13	2	6	8	10	—	—	—	—	—
NHL totals			131	25	53	78	88	7	2	2	4	0

WEINRICH, ERIC

D, WHALERS

PERSONAL: Born December 19, 1966, at Roanoke, Va. . . . 6-0/210. . . . Shoots left. . . . Full name: Eric John Weinrich. . . . Name pronounced WIGHN-rihch.
HIGH SCHOOL: North Yarmouth Academy (Yarmouth, Maine).
COLLEGE: Maine.
TRANSACTIONS/CAREER NOTES: Dislocated shoulder (December 1984). . . . Selected by New Jersey Devils in second round (third Devils pick, 32nd overall) of NHL entry draft (June 15, 1985). . . . Traded by Devils with G Sean Burke to Hartford Whalers for RW Bobby Holik, second-round pick in 1993 draft (LW Jay Pandolfo) and future considerations (August 28, 1992). . . . Suffered concussion (November 25, 1992); missed two games.
HONORS: Named to NCAA All-America East second team (1986-87). . . . Named to Hockey East All-Star first team (1986-87). . . . Won Eddie Shore Plaque (1989-90). . . . Named to AHL All-Star first team (1989-90). . . . Named to NHL All-Rookie team (1990-91).

			REGULAR SEASON					PLAYOFFS				
Season	Team	League	Gms.	G	A	Pts.	Pen.	Gms.	G	A	Pts.	Pen.
83-84—North Yarmouth Acad.		Maine H.S.	17	23	33	56	...	—	—	—	—	—
84-85—North Yarmouth Acad.		Maine H.S.	20	6	21	27	...	—	—	—	—	—
85-86—University of Maine		Hockey East	34	0	15	15	26	—	—	—	—	—
86-87—University of Maine		Hockey East	41	12	32	44	59	—	—	—	—	—
87-88—University of Maine		Hockey East	8	4	7	11	22	—	—	—	—	—
—U.S. national team		Int'l	39	3	9	12	24	—	—	—	—	—
—U.S. Olympic Team		Int'l	3	0	0	0	24	—	—	—	—	—
88-89—Utica		AHL	80	17	27	44	70	5	0	1	1	8
—New Jersey		NHL	2	0	0	0	0	—	—	—	—	—
89-90—Utica		AHL	57	12	48	60	38	—	—	—	—	—
—New Jersey		NHL	19	2	7	9	11	6	1	3	4	17
90-91—New Jersey		NHL	76	4	34	38	48	7	1	2	3	6
91-92—New Jersey		NHL	76	7	25	32	55	7	0	2	2	4
92-93—Hartford		NHL	79	7	29	36	76	—	—	—	—	—
NHL totals			252	20	95	115	190	20	2	7	9	27

WEISBROD, JOHN

C, SHARKS

PERSONAL: Born October 8, 1968, at Woodbury, N.Y. . . . 6-3/215. . . . Shoots right. . . . Full name: John Charles Weisbrod Jr. . . . Name pronounced WEIS-brahd.
HIGH SCHOOL: Choate Rosemary Hall (Wallingford, Conn.).
COLLEGE: Harvard.
TRANSACTIONS/CAREER NOTES: Selected by Minnesota North Stars in fourth round (fourth North Stars pick, 73rd overall) of NHL entry draft (June 13, 1987). . . . Injured back; missed most of 1990-91 season. . . . Selected by San Jose Sharks in NHL dispersal draft (May 30, 1991). . . . Injured shoulder; missed 1991-92 season. . . . Injured shoulder (1992-93).

			REGULAR SEASON					PLAYOFFS				
Season	Team	League	Gms.	G	A	Pts.	Pen.	Gms.	G	A	Pts.	Pen.
85-86—Choate Academy		Conn. H.S.	26	21	25	46	...	—	—	—	—	—
86-87—Choate Academy		Conn. H.S.	23	13	14	27	...	—	—	—	—	—
87-88—Harvard University		ECAC	22	8	11	19	16	—	—	—	—	—
88-89—Harvard University		ECAC	31	22	13	35	61	—	—	—	—	—
89-90—Harvard University		ECAC	27	11	21	32	62	—	—	—	—	—
90-91—Harvard University		ECAC	5	2	8	10	8	—	—	—	—	—
91-92—					Did not play—injured.							
92-93—Kansas City		IHL	16	6	2	8	6	—	—	—	—	—

WELLS, JAY

D, RANGERS

PERSONAL: Born May 18, 1959, at Paris, Ont. . . . 6-1/210. . . . Shoots left. . . . Full name: Gordon Jay Wells.
TRANSACTIONS/CAREER NOTES: Selected by Los Angeles Kings in first round (first Kings pick, 16th overall) of NHL entry draft (August 9, 1979). . . . Broke right hand in team practice (October 16, 1981). . . . Tore medial collateral ligament in right knee (December 14, 1982). . . . Sprained ankle (December 1983). . . . Struck in eye during team practice (February 1987). . . . Strained lower back (November 1987). . . . Traded by Kings to Philadelphia

W

Flyers for D Doug Crossman (September 29, 1988).... Bruised right shoulder (October 1988).... Broke knuckle on right hand (January 1989).... Broke toe (November 1989).... Traded by Flyers with fourth-round pick in 1991 draft to Buffalo Sabres for RW Kevin Maguire and second-round pick (RW Mikael Renberg) in 1990 draft (March 5, 1990).... Fractured right ankle (March 6, 1990).... Tore medial collateral ligament of right knee (October 13, 1990); missed 18 games.... Traded by Sabres to New York Rangers for D Randy Moller (March 9, 1992).... Sprained right knee (January 27, 1993); missed 27 games.
HONORS: Named to OMJHL All-Star first team (1978-79).

| Season | Team | League | REGULAR SEASON | | | | | PLAYOFFS | | | | |
			Gms.	G	A	Pts.	Pen.	Gms.	G	A	Pts.	Pen.
76-77	Kingston	OMJHL	59	4	7	11	90	—	—	—	—	—
77-78	Kingston	OMJHL	68	9	13	22	195	5	1	2	3	6
78-79	Kingston	OMJHL	48	6	21	27	100	11	2	7	9	29
79-80	Los Angeles	NHL	43	0	0	0	113	4	0	0	0	11
	Binghamton	AHL	28	0	6	6	48	—	—	—	—	—
80-81	Los Angeles	NHL	72	5	13	18	155	4	0	0	0	27
81-82	Los Angeles	NHL	60	1	8	9	145	10	1	3	4	41
82-83	Los Angeles	NHL	69	3	12	15	167	—	—	—	—	—
83-84	Los Angeles	NHL	69	3	18	21	141	—	—	—	—	—
84-85	Los Angeles	NHL	77	2	9	11	185	3	0	1	1	0
85-86	Los Angeles	NHL	79	11	31	42	226	—	—	—	—	—
86-87	Los Angeles	NHL	77	7	29	36	155	5	1	2	3	10
87-88	Los Angeles	NHL	58	2	23	25	159	5	1	2	3	21
88-89	Philadelphia	NHL	67	2	19	21	184	18	0	2	2	51
89-90	Philadelphia	NHL	59	3	16	19	129	—	—	—	—	—
	Buffalo	NHL	1	0	1	1	0	6	0	0	0	12
90-91	Buffalo	NHL	43	1	2	3	86	1	0	1	1	0
91-92	Buffalo	NHL	41	2	9	11	157	—	—	—	—	—
	New York Rangers	NHL	11	0	0	0	24	13	0	2	2	10
92-93	New York Rangers	NHL	53	1	9	10	107	—	—	—	—	—
NHL totals			**879**	**43**	**199**	**242**	**2133**	**69**	**3**	**13**	**16**	**183**

WERENKA, BRAD
D, OILERS

PERSONAL: Born February 12, 1969, at Two Hills, Alta.... 6-2/204.... Shoots left.... Full name: John Bradley Werenka.... Name pronounced wuh-REHN-kuh.
HIGH SCHOOL: Fort Saskatchewan (Alta.).
COLLEGE: Northern Michigan.

TRANSACTIONS/CAREER NOTES: Selected by Edmonton Oilers as underage junior in second round (second Oilers pick, 42nd overall) of NHL entry draft (June 13, 1987).... Tore stomach muscles (October 1988).... Sprained right knee (November 3, 1989).
HONORS: Named to NCAA All-America West first team (1990-91).... Named to NCAA All-Tournament team (1990-91).... Named to WCHA All-Star first team (1990-91).

| Season | Team | League | REGULAR SEASON | | | | | PLAYOFFS | | | | |
			Gms.	G	A	Pts.	Pen.	Gms.	G	A	Pts.	Pen.
85-86	Fort Saskatchewan	AJHL	29	12	23	35	24	—	—	—	—	—
86-87	Northern Michigan Univ.	WCHA	30	4	4	8	35	—	—	—	—	—
87-88	Northern Michigan Univ.	WCHA	34	7	23	30	26	—	—	—	—	—
88-89	Northern Michigan Univ.	WCHA	28	7	13	20	16	—	—	—	—	—
89-90	Northern Michigan Univ.	WCHA	8	2	5	7	8	—	—	—	—	—
90-91	Northern Michigan Univ.	WCHA	47	20	43	63	36	—	—	—	—	—
91-92	Cape Breton	AHL	66	6	21	27	95	5	0	3	3	6
92-93	Canadian national team	Int'l	18	3	7	10	10	—	—	—	—	—
	Edmonton	NHL	27	5	3	8	24	—	—	—	—	—
	Cape Breton	AHL	4	1	1	2	4	16	4	17	21	12
NHL totals			**27**	**5**	**3**	**8**	**24**					

WERENKA, DARCY
D, RANGERS

PERSONAL: Born May 13, 1973, at Edmonton, Alta.... 6-1/210.... Shoots right.
TRANSACTIONS/CAREER NOTES: Selected by New York Rangers in second round (second Rangers pick, 37th overall) of NHL entry draft (June 22, 1991).
HONORS: Named to WHL (East) All-Star second team (1990-91).

| Season | Team | League | REGULAR SEASON | | | | | PLAYOFFS | | | | |
			Gms.	G	A	Pts.	Pen.	Gms.	G	A	Pts.	Pen.
89-90	Lethbridge	WHL	63	1	18	19	16	19	0	2	2	4
90-91	Lethbridge	WHL	72	13	37	50	39	16	1	7	8	4
91-92	Lethbridge	WHL	69	17	58	75	56	5	2	1	3	0
92-93	Lethbridge	WHL	19	4	17	21	12	—	—	—	—	—
	Brandon	WHL	36	4	25	29	19	3	0	0	0	2
	Binghamton	AHL	3	0	1	1	2	3	0	0	0	0

WESLEY, GLEN
D, BRUINS

PERSONAL: Born October 2, 1968, at Red Deer, Alta.... 6-1/195.... Shoots left.
TRANSACTIONS/CAREER NOTES: Selected by Boston Bruins as underage junior in first round (first Bruins pick, third overall) of NHL entry draft (June 13, 1987).... Sprained left knee (October 1988).... Broke foot (November 24, 1992); missed 14 games.... Injured groin (February 1993); missed one game.... Injured groin (March 1993); missed three games.... Injured groin (April 1993); missed two games.
HONORS: Won WHL West Top Defenseman Trophy (1985-86 and 1986-87).... Named to WHL (West) All-Star first team (1985-86 and 1986-87).... Named to NHL All-Rookie team (1987-88).... Played in NHL All-Star Game (1989).

Season	Team	League	REGULAR SEASON Gms.	G	A	Pts.	Pen.	PLAYOFFS Gms.	G	A	Pts.	Pen.
83-84—Red Deer		AJHL	57	9	20	29	40	—	—	—	—	—
—Portland		WHL	3	1	2	3	0	—	—	—	—	—
84-85—Portland		WHL	67	16	52	68	76	6	1	6	7	8
85-86—Portland		WHL	69	16	75	91	96	15	3	11	14	29
86-87—Portland		WHL	63	16	46	62	72	20	8	18	26	27
87-88—Boston		NHL	79	7	30	37	69	23	6	8	14	22
88-89—Boston		NHL	77	19	35	54	61	10	0	2	2	4
89-90—Boston		NHL	78	9	27	36	48	21	2	6	8	36
90-91—Boston		NHL	80	11	32	43	78	19	2	9	11	19
91-92—Boston		NHL	78	9	37	46	54	15	2	4	6	16
92-93—Boston		NHL	64	8	25	33	47	4	0	0	0	0
NHL totals			**456**	**63**	**186**	**249**	**357**	**92**	**12**	**29**	**41**	**97**

WHITE, PETER
C, OILERS

PERSONAL: Born March 15, 1969, at Montreal.... 5-11/200.... Shoots left.... Full name: Peter Toby White.
COLLEGE: Michigan State.
TRANSACTIONS/CAREER NOTES: Selected by Edmonton Oilers in fifth round (fourth Oilers pick, 92nd overall) of NHL entry draft (June 17, 1989).
HONORS: Named to CCHA All-Rookie team (1988-89).... Named CCHA Playoff Most Valuable Player (1989-90).... Named to CCHA All-Tournament team (1989-90).

Season	Team	League	REGULAR SEASON Gms.	G	A	Pts.	Pen.	PLAYOFFS Gms.	G	A	Pts.	Pen.
87-88—Pembroke		COJHL	56	90	136	226	32	—	—	—	—	—
88-89—Michigan State		CCHA	46	20	33	53	17	—	—	—	—	—
89-90—Michigan State		CCHA	45	22	40	62	6	—	—	—	—	—
90-91—Michigan State		CCHA	37	7	31	38	28	—	—	—	—	—
91-92—Michigan State		CCHA	44	26	51	77	32	—	—	—	—	—
92-93—Cape Breton		AHL	64	12	28	40	10	16	3	3	6	12

WHITMORE, KAY
G, CANUCKS

PERSONAL: Born April 10, 1967, at Sudbury, Ont.... 5-11/185.... Shoots left.
TRANSACTIONS/CAREER NOTES: Selected by Hartford Whalers as underage junior in second round (second Whalers pick, 26th overall) of NHL entry draft (June 15, 1985).... Traded by Whalers to Vancouver Canucks for G Corrie D'Alessio and conditional pick in 1993 draft (October 1, 1992).
HONORS: Shared Dave Pinkney Trophy with Ron Tugnutt (1985-86).... Named to OHL All-Star first team (1985-86).... Won Jack Butterfield Trophy (1990-91).

Season	Team	League	REGULAR SEASON Gms.	Min.	W	L	T	GA	SO	Avg.	PLAYOFFS Gms.	Min.	W	L	GA	SO	Avg.
83-84—Peterborough		OHL	29	1471	17	8	0	110	0	4.49	—	—	—	—	—	—	—
84-85—Peterborough		OHL	*53	*3077	35	16	2	172	†2	3.35	*17	*1020	10	4	58	0	3.41
85-86—Peterborough		OHL	41	2467	27	12	2	114	†3	*2.77	14	837	8	5	40	0	2.87
86-87—Peterborough		OHL	36	2159	14	17	5	118	1	3.28	7	366	3	3	17	1	2.79
87-88—Binghamton		AHL	38	2137	17	15	4	121	3	3.40	2	118	0	2	10	0	5.08
88-89—Binghamton		AHL	*56	*3200	21	29	4	*241	1	4.52	—	—	—	—	—	—	—
—Hartford		NHL	3	180	2	1	0	10	0	3.33	2	135	0	2	10	0	4.44
89-90—Binghamton		AHL	24	1386	3	19	2	109	0	4.72	—	—	—	—	—	—	—
—Hartford		NHL	9	442	4	2	1	26	0	3.53	—	—	—	—	—	—	—
90-91—Hartford		NHL	18	850	3	9	3	52	0	3.67	—	—	—	—	—	—	—
—Springfield		AHL	33	1916	22	9	1	98	1	3.07	*15	*926	11	4	*37	0	*2.40
91-92—Hartford		NHL	45	2567	14	21	6	155	3	3.62	1	19	0	0	1	0	3.16
92-93—Vancouver		NHL	31	1817	18	8	4	94	1	3.10	—	—	—	—	—	—	—
NHL totals			**106**	**5856**	**41**	**41**	**14**	**337**	**4**	**3.45**	**3**	**154**	**0**	**2**	**11**	**0**	**4.29**

WHITNEY, RAY
C, SHARKS

PERSONAL: Born May 8, 1972, at Edmonton, Alta.... 5-9/165.... Shoots right.
TRANSACTIONS/CAREER NOTES: Selected by San Jose Sharks in second round (second Sharks pick, 23rd overall) of NHL entry draft (June 22, 1991).
HONORS: Won Four Broncos Memorial Trophy (1990-91).... Won Bob Clarke Trophy (1990-91).... Won WHL West Player of the Year Award (1990-91).... Won George Parsons Trophy (1990-91).... Named to Memorial Cup All-Star team (1990-91).... Named to WHL (West) All-Star first team (1990-91).

Season	Team	League	REGULAR SEASON Gms.	G	A	Pts.	Pen.	PLAYOFFS Gms.	G	A	Pts.	Pen.
88-89—Spokane		WHL	71	17	33	50	16	—	—	—	—	—
89-90—Spokane		WHL	71	57	56	113	50	6	3	4	*7	6
90-91—Spokane		WHL	72	67	118	*185	36	15	13	18	*31	12
91-92—San Diego		IHL	63	36	54	90	12	4	0	0	0	0
—San Jose		NHL	2	0	3	3	0	—	—	—	—	—
—Koln		Germany	10	3	6	9	4	—	—	—	—	—
92-93—Kansas City		IHL	46	20	33	53	14	12	5	7	12	2
—San Jose		NHL	26	4	6	10	4	—	—	—	—	—
NHL totals			**28**	**4**	**9**	**13**	**4**					

W

WHYTE, SEAN
RW, KINGS

PERSONAL: Born May 4, 1970, at Sudbury, Ont. . . . 6-0/198. . . . Shoots right. . . . Full name: Sean Garnet Whyte. . . . Name pronounced WIGHT.

TRANSACTIONS/CAREER NOTES: Stretched left knee ligaments (October 2, 1988). . . . Selected by Los Angeles Kings in eighth round (seventh Kings pick, 165th overall) of NHL entry draft (June 17, 1989).

Season Team	League	REGULAR SEASON					PLAYOFFS				
		Gms.	G	A	Pts.	Pen.	Gms.	G	A	Pts.	Pen.
86-87—Guelph	OHL	41	1	3	4	13	—	—	—	—	—
87-88—Guelph	OHL	62	6	22	28	71	—	—	—	—	—
88-89—Guelph	OHL	53	20	44	64	57	—	—	—	—	—
89-90—Owen Sound	OHL	54	23	30	53	90	3	0	1	1	10
90-91—Phoenix	IHL	60	18	17	35	61	4	1	0	1	2
91-92—Phoenix	IHL	72	24	30	54	113	—	—	—	—	—
—Los Angeles	NHL	3	0	0	0	0	—	—	—	—	—
92-93—Phoenix	IHL	51	11	35	46	65	—	—	—	—	—
—Los Angeles	NHL	18	0	2	2	12	—	—	—	—	—
NHL totals		21	0	2	2	12					

WIEMER, JIM
D, BRUINS

PERSONAL: Born January 9, 1961, at Sudbury, Ont. . . . 6-4/210. . . . Shoots left. . . . Full name: James Duncan Wiemer. . . . Name pronounced WEE-mer.

TRANSACTIONS/CAREER NOTES: Selected by Buffalo Sabres as underage junior in fourth round (fifth Sabres pick, 83rd overall) of NHL entry draft (June 11, 1980). . . . Traded by Sabres with RW Steve Patrick to New York Rangers for D Chris Renaud and D Dave Maloney (December 6, 1984). . . . Traded by Rangers with rights to D Reijo Ruotsalainen, LW Ville Kentala and LW Clark Donatelli to Edmonton Oilers to complete earlier deal in which Rangers acquired D Don Jackson, D Miroslav Horava and C Mike Golden (October 23, 1986). . . . Traded by Oilers with RW Alan May to Los Angeles Kings for C Brian Wilks and D John English (March 7, 1989). . . . Signed as free agent by Boston Bruins (July 6, 1989). . . . Bruised right leg (November 1989). . . . Pulled groin (January 27, 1992); missed 10 games. . . . Reinjured groin (March 19, 1992); missed six games. . . . Injured groin (December 1992); missed eight games. . . . Injured foot (January 1993); missed two games. . . . Broke foot (January 29, 1993); missed 17 games.

HONORS: Won Eddie Shore Plaque (1985-86). . . . Named to AHL All-Star first team (1985-86).

Season Team	League	REGULAR SEASON					PLAYOFFS				
		Gms.	G	A	Pts.	Pen.	Gms.	G	A	Pts.	Pen.
78-79—Peterborough	OMJHL	63	15	12	27	50	18	4	4	8	15
79-80—Peterborough	OMJHL	53	17	32	49	63	14	6	9	15	19
80-81—Peterborough	OMJHL	65	41	54	95	102	5	1	2	3	15
81-82—Rochester	AHL	74	19	26	45	57	9	0	4	4	2
82-83—Rochester	AHL	74	15	44	59	43	15	5	15	20	22
—Buffalo	NHL	—	—	—	—	—	1	0	0	0	0
83-84—Buffalo	NHL	64	5	15	20	48	—	—	—	—	—
—Rochester	AHL	12	4	11	15	11	18	3	13	16	20
84-85—Rochester	AHL	13	1	9	10	24	—	—	—	—	—
—New Haven	AHL	33	9	27	36	39	—	—	—	—	—
—Buffalo	NHL	10	3	2	5	4	—	—	—	—	—
—New York Rangers	NHL	22	4	3	7	30	1	0	0	0	0
85-86—New Haven	AHL	73	24	49	73	108	—	—	—	—	—
—New York Rangers	NHL	7	3	0	3	2	8	1	0	1	6
86-87—New Haven	AHL	6	0	7	7	6	—	—	—	—	—
—Nova Scotia	AHL	59	9	25	34	72	5	0	4	4	2
87-88—Nova Scotia	AHL	57	11	32	43	99	5	1	1	2	14
—Edmonton	NHL	12	1	2	3	15	2	0	0	0	2
88-89—Cape Breton	AHL	51	12	29	41	80	—	—	—	—	—
—Los Angeles	NHL	9	2	3	5	20	10	2	1	3	19
—New Haven	AHL	3	1	1	2	2	7	2	3	5	2
89-90—Maine	AHL	6	3	4	7	27	—	—	—	—	—
—Boston	NHL	61	5	14	19	63	8	0	1	1	4
90-91—Boston	NHL	61	4	19	23	62	16	1	3	4	14
91-92—Maine	AHL	3	0	1	1	4	—	—	—	—	—
—Boston	NHL	47	1	8	9	84	15	1	3	4	14
92-93—Boston	NHL	28	1	6	7	48	1	0	0	0	4
—Providence	AHL	4	2	1	3	2					
NHL totals		321	29	72	101	376	62	5	8	13	63

WIESEL, ADAM
D, CANADIENS

PERSONAL: Born January 25, 1975, at Holyoke, Mass. . . . 6-3/201. . . . Shoots right. . . . Name pronounced WEE-zul.

HIGH SCHOOL: South Hadley (Mass.).

TRANSACTIONS/CAREER NOTES: Selected by Montreal Canadiens in fourth round (fourth Canadiens pick, 85th overall) of NHL entry draft (June 26, 1993).

Season Team	League	REGULAR SEASON					PLAYOFFS				
		Gms.	G	A	Pts.	Pen.	Gms.	G	A	Pts.	Pen.
90-91—Springfield Jr. B	NEJHL	43	8	17	25	28	—	—	—	—	—
91-92—Springfield Jr. B	NEJHL	47	6	13	19	25	—	—	—	—	—
92-93—Springfield Jr. B	NEJHL	41	11	20	31	34	—	—	—	—	—

WILKIE, BOB
D, FLYERS

PERSONAL: Born February 11, 1969, at Calgary, Alta.... 6-2/220.... Shoots right.
TRANSACTIONS/CAREER NOTES: Selected by Detroit Red Wings as underage junior in second round (third Red Wings pick, 41st overall) of NHL entry draft (June 13, 1987).... Fractured kneecap (January 1990).... Traded by Red Wings to Philadelphia Flyers for future considerations (February 2, 1993).

Season Team	League	REGULAR SEASON					PLAYOFFS				
		Gms.	G	A	Pts.	Pen.	Gms.	G	A	Pts.	Pen.
85-86—Calgary	WHL	63	8	19	27	56	—	—	—	—	—
86-87—Swift Current	WHL	65	12	38	50	50	4	1	3	4	2
87-88—Swift Current	WHL	67	12	68	80	124	10	4	12	16	8
88-89—Swift Current	WHL	62	18	67	85	89	12	1	11	12	47
89-90—Adirondack	AHL	58	5	33	38	64	6	1	4	5	2
90-91—Detroit	NHL	8	1	2	3	2	—	—	—	—	—
—Adirondack	AHL	43	6	18	24	71	2	1	0	1	2
91-92—Adirondack	AHL	7	1	4	5	6	16	2	5	7	12
92-93—Adirondack	AHL	14	0	5	5	20	—	—	—	—	—
—Fort Wayne	IHL	32	7	14	21	82	12	4	6	10	10
—Hershey	AHL	28	7	25	32	18	—	—	—	—	—
NHL totals		8	1	2	3	2					

WILKINSON, NEIL
D, BLACKHAWKS

PERSONAL: Born August 15, 1967, at Selkirk, Man.... 6-3/180.... Shoots right.... Full name: Neil John Wilkinson.
COLLEGE: Michigan State.
TRANSACTIONS/CAREER NOTES: Suffered concussion and broke nose (January 1986). ... Selected by Minnesota North Stars in second round (second North Stars pick, 30th overall) of NHL entry draft (June 21, 1986).... Twisted knee ligaments during training camp (September 1988).... Bruised left instep (November 9, 1989).... Strained back (January 1990).... Tore left thumb ligaments (March 6, 1991); missed five games.... Selected by San Jose Sharks in NHL dispersal draft (May 30, 1991).... Injured groin (December 16, 1991); missed four games.... Injured eye (Janaury 8, 1992); missed three games.... Strained back (February 4, 1992); missed 13 games.... Suffered facial contusions (October 28, 1992); missed two games.... Strained back (November 10, 1992); missed 14 games.... Injured hand (December 18, 1992); missed one game.... Strained back (February 10, 1993); missed six games.... Traded by Sharks to Chicago Blackhawks (July 9, 1993) to complete deal in which Blackhawks sent G Jimmy Waite to Sharks for future considerations (June 18, 1993).

Season Team	League	REGULAR SEASON					PLAYOFFS				
		Gms.	G	A	Pts.	Pen.	Gms.	G	A	Pts.	Pen.
85-86—Selkirk	MJHL	42	14	35	49	91	—	—	—	—	—
86-87—Michigan State	CCHA	19	3	4	7	18	—	—	—	—	—
87-88—Medicine Hat	WHL	55	11	21	32	157	5	1	0	1	2
88-89—Kalamazoo	IHL	39	5	15	20	96	—	—	—	—	—
89-90—Kalamazoo	IHL	20	6	7	13	62	—	—	—	—	—
—Minnesota	NHL	36	0	5	5	100	7	0	2	2	11
90-91—Kalamazoo	IHL	10	0	3	3	38	—	—	—	—	—
—Minnesota	NHL	50	2	9	11	117	22	3	3	6	12
91-92—San Jose	NHL	60	4	15	19	107	—	—	—	—	—
92-93—San Jose	NHL	59	1	7	8	96	—	—	—	—	—
NHL totals		205	7	36	43	420	29	3	5	8	23

WILLIAMS, DARRYL
LW, KINGS

PERSONAL: Born February 29, 1968, at Mount Pearl, Nfld.... 5-11/190.... Shoots left.... Full name: Darryl Clifford Williams.
TRANSACTIONS/CAREER NOTES: Traded by Hamilton Steelhawks with future considerations to Belleville Bulls for C Keith Gretzky (December 1986).... Signed as free agent by Los Angeles Kings (September 1989).

Season Team	League	REGULAR SEASON					PLAYOFFS				
		Gms.	G	A	Pts.	Pen.	Gms.	G	A	Pts.	Pen.
85-86—Victoria	WHL	38	3	2	5	66	—	—	—	—	—
86-87—Hamilton	OHL	24	2	4	6	36	—	—	—	—	—
—Belleville	OHL	34	7	6	13	72	—	—	—	—	—
87-88—Belleville	OHL	63	29	39	68	169	—	—	—	—	—
88-89—New Haven	AHL	15	5	5	10	24	—	—	—	—	—
—Belleville	OHL	45	24	21	45	137	—	—	—	—	—
89-90—New Haven	AHL	51	9	13	22	124	—	—	—	—	—
90-91—New Haven	AHL	57	14	11	25	278	—	—	—	—	—
—Phoenix	IHL	12	2	1	3	53	—	—	—	—	—
91-92—New Haven	AHL	13	0	2	2	69	—	—	—	—	—
—Phoenix	IHL	48	8	19	27	219	—	—	—	—	—
92-93—Phoenix	IHL	61	18	7	25	314	—	—	—	—	—
—Los Angeles	NHL	2	0	0	0	10	—	—	—	—	—
NHL totals		2	0	0	0	10					

WILLIAMS, DAVID
D, MIGHTY DUCKS

PERSONAL: Born August 25, 1967, at Plainfield, N.J.... 6-2/195.... Shoots right.... Full name: David Andrew Williams.
HIGH SCHOOL: Choate Rosemary Hall (Wallingford, Conn.).
COLLEGE: Dartmouth.

W

TRANSACTIONS/CAREER NOTES: Selected by New Jersey Devils as underage junior in 12th round (12th Devils pick, 234th overall) of NHL entry draft (June 15, 1985).... Signed as free agent by San Jose Sharks (August 9, 1991).... Selected by Mighty Ducks of Anaheim in NHL expansion draft (June 24, 1993).
HONORS: Named to NCAA All-America East second team (1988-89).... Named to ECAC All-Star first team (1988-89).

Season Team	League	REGULAR SEASON					PLAYOFFS				
		Gms.	G	A	Pts.	Pen.	Gms.	G	A	Pts.	Pen.
86-87—Dartmouth College...........	ECAC	23	2	19	21	20	—	—	—	—	—
87-88—Dartmouth College...........	ECAC	25	8	14	22	30	—	—	—	—	—
88-89—Dartmouth College...........	ECAC	25	4	11	15	28	—	—	—	—	—
89-90—Dartmouth College...........	ECAC	26	3	12	15	32	—	—	—	—	—
90-91—Knoxville	ECHL	38	12	15	27	40	3	0	0	0	4
—Muskegon......................	IHL	14	1	2	3	4	—	—	—	—	—
91-92—Kansas City...................	IHL	18	2	3	5	22	—	—	—	—	—
—San Jose.......................	NHL	56	3	25	28	40	—	—	—	—	—
92-93—Kansas City...................	IHL	31	1	11	12	28	—	—	—	—	—
—San Jose.......................	NHL	40	1	11	12	49	—	—	—	—	—
NHL totals.................................		96	4	36	40	89					

WILSON, CAREY
C/RW, FLAMES

PERSONAL: Born May 19, 1962, at Winnipeg, Man.... 6-2/205.... Shoots right.... Full name: Carey John Wilson.... Son of Dr. Gerry Wilson, former vice-president and team doctor of Winnipeg Jets of WHA.
COLLEGE: Dartmouth.
TRANSACTIONS/CAREER NOTES: Selected by Chicago Blackhawks in fourth round (eighth Blackhawks pick, 67th overall) of NHL entry draft (June 11, 1980).... Traded by Blackhawks to Calgary Flames for RW Denis Cyr (November 8, 1982).... Suffered ruptured spleen (April 28, 1986); missed remainder of playoffs.... Traded by Flames with D Neil Sheehy and rights to LW Lane MacDonald to Hartford Whalers for RW Shane Churla and D Dana Murzyn (January 3, 1988).... Strained shoulder (October 1987).... Traded by Whalers with fifth-round pick in 1990 draft to New York Rangers for C Brian Lawton, LW Don Maloney and D Norm Maciver (December 26, 1988).... Bruised wrist (February 1989).... Sprained left knee ligaments (October 28, 1989); missed 26 games.... Sprained right knee (March 3, 1990); missed eight games.... Traded by Rangers with future considerations to Whalers for C/RW Jody Hull (July 9, 1990).... Pulled groin in informal skate prior to training camp (September 6, 1990).... Reinjured groin (November 17, 1990); missed eight games.... Tore cartilage (February 15, 1991); missed seven games.... Traded by Whalers to Flames for RW Mark Hunter (March 5, 1991).... Irritated shoulder and ribs (October 20, 1991); missed 14 games.... Suffered reactive tissue irritation (December 1991); missed 17 games.... Injured knee (December 1, 1992); missed one game.... Tore tendon in right knee (December 4, 1992); missed remainder of season.

Season Team	League	REGULAR SEASON					PLAYOFFS				
		Gms.	G	A	Pts.	Pen.	Gms.	G	A	Pts.	Pen.
78-79—Calgary Chinooks	AJHL	60	30	34	64	...	—	—	—	—	—
79-80—Dartmouth College...........	ECAC	31	16	22	38	20	—	—	—	—	—
80-81—Dartmouth College...........	ECAC	21	9	13	22	52	—	—	—	—	—
81-82—Helsinki IFK......................	Finland	39	15	17	32	58	7	1	4	5	6
82-83—Helsinki IFK......................	Finland	36	16	24	40	62	9	1	3	4	12
83-84—Canadian Olympic Team ..	Int'l	59	21	24	45	34	—	—	—	—	—
—Calgary...........................	NHL	15	2	5	7	2	6	3	1	4	2
84-85—Calgary...........................	NHL	74	24	48	72	27	4	0	0	0	0
85-86—Calgary...........................	NHL	76	29	29	58	24	9	0	2	2	2
86-87—Calgary...........................	NHL	80	20	36	56	42	6	1	1	2	6
87-88—Calgary...........................	NHL	34	9	21	30	18	—	—	—	—	—
—Hartford........................	NHL	36	18	20	38	22	6	2	4	6	2
88-89—Hartford........................	NHL	34	11	11	22	14	—	—	—	—	—
—New York Rangers...........	NHL	41	21	34	55	45	4	1	2	3	2
89-90—New York Rangers...........	NHL	41	9	17	26	57	10	2	1	3	0
90-91—Hartford........................	NHL	45	8	15	23	16	—	—	—	—	—
—Calgary...........................	NHL	12	3	3	6	2	7	2	2	4	0
91-92—Calgary...........................	NHL	42	11	12	23	37	—	—	—	—	—
92-93—Calgary...........................	NHL	22	4	7	11	8	—	—	—	—	—
NHL totals.................................		552	169	258	427	314	52	11	13	24	14

WILSON, DOUG
D, SHARKS

PERSONAL: Born July 5, 1957, at Ottawa.... 6-1/187.... Shoots left.
TRANSACTIONS/CAREER NOTES: Underwent knee surgery; missed part of 1976-77 season.... Selected by Chicago Blackhawks from Ottawa 67's in first round (first Blackhawks pick, sixth overall) of NHL amateur draft (June 14, 1977).... Injured shoulder and underwent surgery; missed part of 1978-79 season.... Broke jaw (November 25, 1981).... Injured ankle (November 1983).... Broke nose (February 3, 1984).... Fractured skull (March 4, 1984); missed remainder of season.... Sprained right knee (March 8, 1987).... Underwent shoulder surgery (December 1987).... Fractured right hand (January 25, 1989).... Bruised left shoulder (March 4, 1989).... Pulled left groin (April 9, 1989).... Bruised toe (January 1990).... Pulled groin (March 1990).... Bruised forearm (April 1990).... Underwent surgery to right ankle ligaments (July 27, 1990); missed first 25 games of season.... Aggravated right ankle (December 8, 1990); missed four games.... Traded by Blackhawks to San Jose Sharks for RW Kerry Toporowski and second-round pick in 1992 draft (September 6, 1991).... Dislocated thumb (October 26, 1991); missed 10 games.... Strained back (January 24, 1992); missed three games.... Sprained knee (February 23, 1992); missed remainder of season.... Injured shoulder (October 15, 1992); missed one game.... Strained shoulder (November 8, 1992); missed two games.... Suffered leg contusion (December 9, 1992); missed six games.... Suffered broken bone in foot (January 2, 1993); missed four games.... Strained knee ligaments (February 14, 1993); missed remainder of season.
HONORS: Named to OHA Major Junior A All-Star second team (1975-76).... Named to OMJHL All-Star first team (1976-77). ... Won James Norris Memorial Trophy (1981-82).... Named to THE SPORTING NEWS All-Star first team (1981-82)....

Named to NHL All-Star first team (1981-82). . . . Played in NHL All-Star Game (1982 through 1986, 1990 and 1992). . . . Named to THE SPORTING NEWS All-Star second team (1984-85 and 1989-90). . . . Named to NHL All-Star second team (1984-85 and 1989-90).
MISCELLANEOUS: Does not wear a helmet.

			REGULAR SEASON					PLAYOFFS			
Season Team	League	Gms.	G	A	Pts.	Pen.	Gms.	G	A	Pts.	Pen.
74-75—Ottawa	OHA Mj. Jr. A	55	29	58	87	75	—	—	—	—	—
75-76—Ottawa	OHA Mj. Jr. A	58	26	62	88	142	12	5	10	15	24
76-77—Ottawa	OMJHL	43	25	54	79	85	19	4	20	24	34
77-78—Chicago	NHL	77	14	20	34	72	4	0	0	0	0
78-79—Chicago	NHL	56	5	21	26	37	—	—	—	—	—
79-80—Chicago	NHL	73	12	49	61	70	7	2	8	10	6
80-81—Chicago	NHL	76	12	39	51	80	3	0	3	3	2
81-82—Chicago	NHL	76	39	46	85	54	15	3	10	13	32
82-83—Chicago	NHL	74	18	51	69	58	13	4	11	15	12
83-84—Chicago	NHL	66	13	45	58	64	5	0	3	3	0
84-85—Chicago	NHL	78	22	54	76	44	12	3	10	13	12
85-86—Chicago	NHL	79	17	47	64	80	3	1	1	2	2
86-87—Chicago	NHL	69	16	32	48	36	4	0	0	0	0
87-88—Chicago	NHL	27	8	24	32	28	—	—	—	—	—
88-89—Chicago	NHL	66	15	47	62	69	4	1	2	3	0
89-90—Chicago	NHL	70	23	50	73	40	20	3	12	15	18
90-91—Chicago	NHL	51	11	29	40	32	5	2	1	3	2
91-92—San Jose	NHL	44	9	19	28	26	—	—	—	—	—
92-93—San Jose	NHL	42	3	17	20	40	—	—	—	—	—
NHL totals		1024	237	590	827	830	95	19	61	80	86

WILSON, LANDON
RW, MAPLE LEAFS

PERSONAL: Born March 15, 1975, at St. Louis, Mo. . . . 6-2/202. . . . Shoots right. . . . Son of Rick Wilson, defenseman, Montreal Canadiens, St. Louis Blues, and Detroit Red Wings (1973-74 through 1976-77).
TRANSACTIONS/CAREER NOTES: Selected by Toronto Maple Leafs in first round (second Leafs pick, 19th overall) of NHL entry draft (June 26, 1993).

			REGULAR SEASON					PLAYOFFS			
Season Team	League	Gms.	G	A	Pts.	Pen.	Gms.	G	A	Pts.	Pen.
92-93—Dubuque	USHL	43	29	36	65	284	—	—	—	—	—

WILSON, MIKE
D, CANUCKS

PERSONAL: Born February 26, 1975, at Brampton, Ont. . . . 6-5/180. . . . Shoots left.
TRANSACTIONS/CAREER NOTES: Selected by Vancouver Canucks in first round (first Canucks pick, 20th overall) of NHL entry draft (June 26, 1993).
HONORS: Named to Can.HL All-Rookie team (1992-93). . . . Named to OHL All-Rookie team (1992-93).

			REGULAR SEASON					PLAYOFFS			
Season Team	League	Gms.	G	A	Pts.	Pen.	Gms.	G	A	Pts.	Pen.
91-92—Georgetown Jr. B	OHA	41	9	13	22	65	—	—	—	—	—
92-93—Sudbury	OHL	53	6	7	13	58	14	1	1	2	21

WILSON, RON
C

PERSONAL: Born May 13, 1956, at Toronto. . . . 5-9/180. . . . Shoots left. . . . Full name: Ronald Lee Wilson.
TRANSACTIONS/CAREER NOTES: Selected by Montreal Canadiens from St. Catharines Blackhawks in 15th round (15th Canadiens pick, 133rd overall) of NHL amateur draft (June 1, 1976). . . . Sold by Canadiens to Winnipeg Jets (June 1979). . . . Named player/assistant coach of Moncton Golden Flames (May 1988). . . . Traded by Jets to St. Louis Blues for C Doug Evans (January 22, 1990). . . . Injured knee (October 26, 1992); missed three games. . . . Re-injured knee (December 7, 1992); missed two games. . . . Released by Blues (June 30, 1993).
HONORS: Named to AHL All-Star second team (1988-89).

			REGULAR SEASON					PLAYOFFS			
Season Team	League	Gms.	G	A	Pts.	Pen.	Gms.	G	A	Pts.	Pen.
74-75—Markham Waxers	OPJHL	43	26	28	54	24	—	—	—	—	—
—Toronto	OHA Mj. Jr. A	16	6	12	18	6	23	9	17	26	6
75-76—St. Catharines	OHA Mj. Jr. A	64	37	62	99	44	4	1	6	7	7
76-77—Nova Scotia	AHL	67	15	21	36	18	6	0	0	0	0
77-78—Nova Scotia	AHL	59	15	25	40	17	11	4	4	8	9
78-79—Nova Scotia	AHL	77	33	42	75	91	10	5	6	11	14
79-80—Winnipeg	NHL	79	21	36	57	28	—	—	—	—	—
80-81—Winnipeg	NHL	77	18	33	51	55	—	—	—	—	—
81-82—Tulsa	CHL	41	20	38	58	22	3	1	0	1	2
—Winnipeg	NHL	39	3	13	16	49	—	—	—	—	—
82-83—Sherbrooke	AHL	65	30	55	85	71	—	—	—	—	—
—Winnipeg	NHL	12	6	3	9	4	3	2	2	4	2
83-84—Winnipeg	NHL	51	3	12	15	12	—	—	—	—	—
—Sherbrooke	AHL	22	10	30	40	16	—	—	—	—	—
84-85—Winnipeg	NHL	75	10	9	19	31	8	4	2	6	2
85-86—Winnipeg	NHL	54	6	7	13	16	1	0	0	0	0
—Sherbrooke	AHL	10	9	8	17	9	—	—	—	—	—

W

Season	Team	League	REGULAR SEASON					PLAYOFFS				
			Gms.	G	A	Pts.	Pen.	Gms.	G	A	Pts.	Pen.
86-87	Winnipeg	NHL	80	3	13	16	13	10	1	2	3	0
87-88	Winnipeg	NHL	69	5	8	13	28	1	0	0	0	2
88-89	Moncton	AHL	80	31	61	92	110	8	1	4	5	20
89-90	Moncton	AHL	47	16	37	53	64	—	—	—	—	—
	St. Louis	NHL	33	3	17	20	23	12	3	5	8	18
90-91	St. Louis	NHL	73	10	27	37	54	7	0	0	0	28
91-92	St. Louis	NHL	64	12	17	29	46	6	0	1	1	0
92-93	St. Louis	NHL	78	8	11	19	44	11	0	0	0	12
NHL totals			784	108	206	314	403	59	10	12	22	64

WINNES, CHRIS
RW, FLYERS

PERSONAL: Born February 12, 1968, at Ridgefield, Conn. . . . 6-0/170. . . . Shoots right. . . . Name pronounced WINN-ess.
HIGH SCHOOL: Ridgefield (Conn.), then Northwood School (Lake Placid, N.Y.).
COLLEGE: New Hampshire.
TRANSACTIONS/CAREER NOTES: Selected by Boston Bruins in eighth round (ninth Bruins pick, 161st overall) of NHL entry draft (June 13, 1987). . . . Broke nose (February 23, 1992). . . . Signed as free agent by Philadelphia Flyers (August 4, 1993).
HONORS: Named to Hockey East All-Freshman team (1987-88).

Season	Team	League	REGULAR SEASON					PLAYOFFS				
			Gms.	G	A	Pts.	Pen.	Gms.	G	A	Pts.	Pen.
85-86	Ridgefield H.S.	Conn. H.S.	24	40	30	70	. . .	—	—	—	—	—
86-87	Northwood School	N.Y. H.S.	27	25	25	50	. . .	—	—	—	—	—
87-88	Univ. of New Hampshire	Hockey East	30	17	19	36	28	—	—	—	—	—
88-89	Univ. of New Hampshire	Hockey East	30	11	20	31	22	—	—	—	—	—
89-90	Univ. of New Hampshire	Hockey East	24	10	13	23	12	—	—	—	—	—
90-91	Univ. of New Hampshire	Hockey East	33	15	16	31	24	—	—	—	—	—
	Maine	AHL	7	3	1	4	0	1	0	2	2	0
	Boston	NHL	—	—	—	—	—	1	0	0	0	0
91-92	Maine	AHL	45	12	35	47	30	—	—	—	—	—
	Boston	NHL	24	1	3	4	6	—	—	—	—	—
92-93	Providence	AHL	64	23	36	59	34	4	0	2	2	5
	Boston	NHL	5	0	1	1	0	—	—	—	—	—
NHL totals			29	1	4	5	6	1	0	0	0	0

WITT, BRENDAN
D, CAPITALS

PERSONAL: Born February 20, 1975, at Humboldt, Sask. . . . 6-2/205. . . . Shoots left.
HIGH SCHOOL: Meadowdale (Lynnwood, Wash.).
TRANSACTIONS/CAREER NOTES: Selected by Washington Capitals in first round (first Capitals pick, 11th overall) of NHL entry draft (June 26, 1993).
HONORS: Named to WHL (West) All-Star first team (1922-93).

Season	Team	League	REGULAR SEASON					PLAYOFFS				
			Gms.	G	A	Pts.	Pen.	Gms.	G	A	Pts.	Pen.
90-91	Seattle	WHL	—	—	—	—	—	1	0	0	0	0
91-92	Seattle	WHL	67	3	9	12	212	15	1	1	2	84
92-93	Seattle	WHL	70	2	26	28	239	5	1	2	3	30

WOHLERS, NICK
D, MAPLE LEAFS

PERSONAL: Born July 12, 1970, at Stillwater, Minn. . . . 6-1/210. . . . Shoots right. . . . Name pronounced WOH-luhrs.
HIGH SCHOOL: Stillwater (Minn.).
COLLEGE: St. Thomas (Minn.).
TRANSACTIONS/CAREER NOTES: Selected by Toronto Maple Leafs in NHL supplemental draft (June 19, 1992).

Season	Team	League	REGULAR SEASON					PLAYOFFS				
			Gms.	G	A	Pts.	Pen.	Gms.	G	A	Pts.	Pen.
88-89	University of St. Thomas	MIAC	25	1	9	10	. . .	—	—	—	—	—
89-90	University of St. Thomas	MIAC	24	0	11	11	48	—	—	—	—	—
90-91	University of St. Thomas	MIAC	28	8	11	19	69	—	—	—	—	—
91-92	University of St. Thomas	MIAC	30	25	34	*59	. . .	—	—	—	—	—
92-93	St. John's	AHL	50	1	8	9	70	—	—	—	—	—

WOLANIN, CRAIG
D, NORDIQUES

PERSONAL: Born July 27, 1967, at Grosse Point, Mich. . . . 6-3/205. . . . Shoots left. . . . Name pronounced woh-LAN-ihn.
TRANSACTIONS/CAREER NOTES: Selected by New Jersey Devils as underage junior in first round (first Devils pick, third overall) of NHL entry draft (June 15, 1985). . . . Bruised left shoulder (October 31, 1985). . . . Broke ring finger on left hand (February 1, 1986). . . . Underwent surgery to finger (February 19, 1986). . . . Suffered sore left hip (December 1987). . . . Sprained right knee (November 15, 1988). . . . Underwent surgery to right knee (December 1988). . . . Injured finger (November 22, 1989). . . . Traded by Devils with future considerations to Quebec Nordiques for C Peter Stastny (March 6, 1990); Devils sent D Randy Velischek to Nordiques to complete deal (August 1990). . . . Injured knee (April 1, 1990). . . . Injured groin (October 17, 1991); missed three games. . . . Injured knee (January 8, 1992); missed four games. . . . Pulled muscle in right thigh (October 13, 1992); missed 24 games. . . . Bruised ribs (December 20, 1992); missed six games. . . . Injured groin (January 16, 1993); missed 28 games. . . . Pulled groin (April 1, 1993); missed one game.

Season Team	League	REGULAR SEASON					PLAYOFFS				
		Gms.	G	A	Pts.	Pen.	Gms.	G	A	Pts.	Pen.
84-85—Kitchener	OHL	60	5	16	21	95	4	1	1	2	2
85-86—New Jersey	NHL	44	2	16	18	74	—	—	—	—	—
86-87—New Jersey	NHL	68	4	6	10	109	—	—	—	—	—
87-88—New Jersey	NHL	78	6	25	31	170	18	2	5	7	51
88-89—New Jersey	NHL	56	3	8	11	69	—	—	—	—	—
89-90—Utica	AHL	6	2	4	6	2	—	—	—	—	—
—New Jersey	NHL	37	1	7	8	47	—	—	—	—	—
—Quebec	NHL	13	0	3	3	10	—	—	—	—	—
90-91—Quebec	NHL	80	5	13	18	89	—	—	—	—	—
91-92—Quebec	NHL	69	2	11	13	80	—	—	—	—	—
92-93—Quebec	NHL	24	1	4	5	49	4	0	0	0	4
NHL totals		469	24	93	117	697	22	2	5	7	55

WOOD, DODY
C/LW, SHARKS

PERSONAL: Born May 8, 1972, at Chetwynd, B.C. . . . . 5-11/180. . . . Shoots left.
TRANSACTIONS/CAREER NOTES: Selected by San Jose Sharks in third round (fourth Sharks pick, 45th overall) of NHL entry draft (June 22, 1991).

Season Team	League	REGULAR SEASON					PLAYOFFS				
		Gms.	G	A	Pts.	Pen.	Gms.	G	A	Pts.	Pen.
89-90—Fort St. John	PCJHL	44	51	73	124	270	—	—	—	—	—
—Seattle	WHL	—	—	—	—	—	5	0	0	0	2
90-91—Seattle	WHL	69	28	37	65	272	6	0	1	1	2
91-92—Seattle	WHL	37	13	19	32	232	—	—	—	—	—
—Swift Current	WHL	3	0	2	2	14	7	2	1	3	37
92-93—Kansas City	IHL	36	3	2	5	216	6	0	1	1	15
—San Jose	NHL	13	1	1	2	71	—	—	—	—	—
NHL totals		13	1	1	2	71					

WOOD, RANDY
LW/RW, SABRES

PERSONAL: Born October 12, 1963, at Princeton, N.J. . . . . 6-0/195. . . . Shoots left.
COLLEGE: Yale.
TRANSACTIONS/CAREER NOTES: Signed as free agent by New York Islanders (August 1986). . . . Suspended four games by NHL for stick-swinging incident (October 17, 1989). . . . Strained right shoulder (March 17, 1990). . . . Traded by Islanders with C Pat LaFontaine, D Randy Hillier and future considerations to Buffalo Sabres for C Pierre Turgeon, RW Benoit Hogue, D Uwe Krupp and C Dave McLlwain; Sabres later received fourth-round pick (D Dean Melanson) in 1992 draft (October 25, 1991).
HONORS: Named to ECAC All-Star second team (1984-85). . . . Named to ECAC All-Star first team (1985-86).

Season Team	League	REGULAR SEASON					PLAYOFFS				
		Gms.	G	A	Pts.	Pen.	Gms.	G	A	Pts.	Pen.
82-83—Yale University	ECAC	26	5	14	19	10	—	—	—	—	—
83-84—Yale University	ECAC	18	7	7	14	10	—	—	—	—	—
84-85—Yale University	ECAC	32	25	28	53	23	—	—	—	—	—
85-86—Yale University	ECAC	31	25	30	55	26	—	—	—	—	—
86-87—Springfield	AHL	75	23	24	47	57	—	—	—	—	—
—New York Islanders	NHL	6	1	0	1	4	13	1	3	4	14
87-88—New York Islanders	NHL	75	22	16	38	80	5	1	0	1	6
—Springfield	AHL	1	0	1	1	0	—	—	—	—	—
88-89—Springfield	AHL	1	1	1	2	0	—	—	—	—	—
—New York Islanders	NHL	77	15	13	28	44	—	—	—	—	—
89-90—New York Islanders	NHL	74	24	24	48	39	5	1	1	2	4
90-91—New York Islanders	NHL	76	24	18	42	45	—	—	—	—	—
91-92—New York Islanders	NHL	8	2	2	4	21	—	—	—	—	—
—Buffalo	NHL	70	20	16	36	65	7	2	1	3	6
92-93—Buffalo	NHL	82	18	25	43	77	8	1	4	5	4
NHL totals		468	126	114	240	375	38	6	9	15	34

WOODWARD, ROBERT
LW, CANUCKS

PERSONAL: Born January 15, 1971, at Evanston, Ill. . . . . 6-4/225. . . . Shoots left. . . . Full name: Robert Fairfield Woodward.
HIGH SCHOOL: Deerfield (Ill.).
COLLEGE: Michigan State.
TRANSACTIONS/CAREER NOTES: Bruised kidney playing football (October 1987). . . . Selected by Vancouver Canucks in second round (second Canucks pick, 29th overall) of NHL entry draft (June 17, 1989).

Season Team	League	REGULAR SEASON					PLAYOFFS				
		Gms.	G	A	Pts.	Pen.	Gms.	G	A	Pts.	Pen.
87-88—Deerfield H.S.	Ill. H.S.	25	36	55	91	...	—	—	—	—	—
88-89—Deerfield H.S.	Ill. H.S.	29	46	71	117	12	—	—	—	—	—
89-90—Michigan State	CCHA	44	17	9	26	8	—	—	—	—	—
90-91—Michigan State	CCHA	32	5	13	18	16	—	—	—	—	—
91-92—Michigan State	CCHA	43	14	16	30	64	—	—	—	—	—
92-93—Michigan State	CCHA	36	12	9	21	90	—	—	—	—	—

W

WOOLLEY, JASON

D, CAPITALS

PERSONAL: Born July 27, 1969, at Toronto. . . . 6-0/190. . . . Shoots left. . . . Full name: Jason Douglas Woolley.
COLLEGE: Michigan State.
TRANSACTIONS/CAREER NOTES: Selected by Washington Capitals in third round (fourth Capitals pick, 61st overall) of NHL entry draft (June 17, 1989). . . . Broke wrist (October 12, 1992); missed 24 games.
HONORS: Named to CCHA All-Rookie team (1988-89). . . . Named to NCAA All-America West first team (1990-91). . . . Named to CCHA All-Star first team (1990-91).
MISCELLANEOUS: Member of silver-medal-winning Canadian Olympic team (1992).

Season	Team	League	REGULAR SEASON					PLAYOFFS				
			Gms.	G	A	Pts.	Pen.	Gms.	G	A	Pts.	Pen.
87-88—	St. Michael's Jr. B	ODHA	31	19	37	56	22	—	—	—	—	—
88-89—	Michigan State	CCHA	47	12	25	37	26	—	—	—	—	—
89-90—	Michigan State	CCHA	45	10	38	48	26	—	—	—	—	—
90-91—	Michigan State	CCHA	40	15	44	59	24	—	—	—	—	—
91-92—	Canadian national team	Int'l	60	14	30	44	36	—	—	—	—	—
	—Canadian Olympic Team	Int'l	8	0	5	5	4	—	—	—	—	—
	—Baltimore	AHL	15	1	10	11	6	—	—	—	—	—
	—Washington	NHL	1	0	0	0	0	—	—	—	—	—
92-93—	Baltimore	AHL	29	14	27	41	22	1	0	2	2	0
	—Washington	NHL	26	0	2	2	10	—	—	—	—	—
NHL totals			27	0	2	2	10					

WREGGET, KEN

G, PENGUINS

PERSONAL: Born March 25, 1964, at Brandon, Man. . . . 6-1/195. . . . Shoots left.
TRANSACTIONS/CAREER NOTES: Selected by Toronto Maple Leafs as underage junior in third round (fourth Maple Leafs pick, 45th overall) of NHL entry draft (June 9, 1982). . . . Injured knee (December 26, 1985). . . . Traded by Maple Leafs to Philadelphia Flyers for two first-round picks in 1989 draft (RW Rob Pearson and D Steve Bancroft) (March 6, 1989). . . . Tore hamstring (November 1, 1989); missed seven games. . . . Pulled hamstring (March 24, 1990). . . . Strained right hip flexor (November 4, 1990); missed 15 games. . . . Traded by Flyers with RW Rick Tocchet, D Kjell Samuelsson and third-round pick in 1992 draft to Pittsburgh Penguins for RW Mark Recchi, D Brian Benning and first-round pick in 1992 draft (LW Jason Bowen) previously acquired from Los Angeles Kings (February 19, 1992). . . . Bruised right knee (February 27, 1993); missed one game.
HONORS: Won Top Goaltender Trophy (1983-84). . . . Named to WHL (East) All-Star first team (1983-84).
MISCELLANEOUS: Member of Stanley Cup championship team (1992).

Season	Team	League	REGULAR SEASON								PLAYOFFS						
			Gms.	Min.	W	L	T	GA	SO	Avg.	Gms.	Min.	W	L	GA	SO	Avg.
81-82—	Lethbridge	WHL	36	1713	19	12	0	118	1	4.13	3	84	. .	. .	3	0	2.14
82-83—	Lethbridge	WHL	48	2696	26	17	1	157	1	3.49	*20	*1154	14	5	58	*1	*3.02
83-84—	Lethbridge	WHL	53	*3053	32	20	0	161	0	*3.16	4	210	1	3	18	0	5.14
	—Toronto	NHL	3	165	1	1	1	14	0	5.09	—	—	—	—	—	—	—
84-85—	Toronto	NHL	23	1278	2	15	3	103	0	4.84	—	—	—	—	—	—	—
	—St. Catharines	AHL	12	688	2	8	1	48	0	4.19	—	—	—	—	—	—	—
85-86—	St. Catharines	AHL	18	1058	8	9	0	78	1	4.42	—	—	—	—	—	—	—
	—Toronto	NHL	30	1566	9	13	4	113	0	4.33	10	607	6	4	32	†1	3.16
86-87—	Toronto	NHL	56	3026	22	28	3	200	0	3.97	13	761	7	6	29	1	*2.29
87-88—	Toronto	NHL	56	3000	12	35	4	222	2	4.44	2	108	0	1	11	0	6.11
88-89—	Toronto	NHL	32	1888	9	20	2	139	0	4.42	—	—	—	—	—	—	—
	—Philadelphia	NHL	3	130	1	1	0	13	0	6.00	5	268	2	2	10	0	2.24
89-90—	Philadelphia	NHL	51	2961	22	24	3	169	0	3.42	—	—	—	—	—	—	—
90-91—	Philadelphia	NHL	30	1484	10	14	3	88	0	3.56	—	—	—	—	—	—	—
91-92—	Philadelphia	NHL	23	1259	9	8	3	75	0	3.57	—	—	—	—	—	—	—
	—Pittsburgh	NHL	9	448	5	3	0	31	0	4.15	1	40	0	0	4	0	6.00
92-93—	Pittsburgh	NHL	25	1368	13	7	2	78	0	3.42	—	—	—	—	—	—	—
NHL totals			341	18573	115	169	28	1245	2	4.02	31	1784	15	13	86	2	2.89

WREN, BOB

LW, KINGS

PERSONAL: Born September 16, 1974, at Preston, Ont. . . . 5-10/174. . . . Shoots left.
TRANSACTIONS/CAREER NOTES: Selected by Los Angeles Kings in fourth round (third Kings pick, 94th overall) of NHL entry draft (June 26, 1993).
HONORS: Named to OHL All-Star second team (1992-93).

Season	Team	League	REGULAR SEASON					PLAYOFFS				
			Gms.	G	A	Pts.	Pen.	Gms.	G	A	Pts.	Pen.
90-91—	Kingston Jr. B	OHA	32	27	28	55	85	—	—	—	—	—
91-92—	Detroit	OHL	62	13	36	49	58	7	3	4	7	19
92-93—	Detroit	OHL	63	57	88	145	91	15	4	11	15	20

WRIGHT, TYLER

C, OILERS

PERSONAL: Born April 6, 1973, at Canora, Sask. . . . 5-11/175. . . . Shoots right.
TRANSACTIONS/CAREER NOTES: Selected by Edmonton Oilers in first round (first Oilers pick, 12th overall) of NHL entry draft (June 22, 1991).

Season	Team	League	REGULAR SEASON					PLAYOFFS				
			Gms.	G	A	Pts.	Pen.	Gms.	G	A	Pts.	Pen.
89-90—	Swift Current	WHL	67	14	18	32	119	4	0	0	0	12
90-91—	Swift Current	WHL	66	41	51	92	157	3	0	0	0	6
91-92—	Swift Current	WHL	63	36	46	82	295	8	2	5	7	16

W

Season	Team	League	Gms.	G	A	Pts.	Pen.	Gms.	G	A	Pts.	Pen.
			REGULAR SEASON					**PLAYOFFS**				
92-93—Swift Current..................		WHL	37	24	41	65	76	17	9	17	26	49
—Edmonton.......................		NHL	7	1	1	2	19	—	—	—	—	—
NHL totals.......................................			7	1	1	2	19					

YAKE, TERRY
C, MIGHTY DUCKS

PERSONAL: Born October 22, 1968, at New Westminster, B.C. . . . 5-11/ 175. . . . Shoots right.
TRANSACTIONS/CAREER NOTES: Selected by Hartford Whalers in fourth round (third Whalers pick, 81st overall) of NHL entry draft (June 13, 1987). . . . Selected by Mighty Ducks of Anaheim in NHL expansion draft (June 24, 1993).

Season	Team	League	Gms.	G	A	Pts.	Pen.	Gms.	G	A	Pts.	Pen.
			REGULAR SEASON					**PLAYOFFS**				
84-85—Brandon..........................		WHL	11	1	1	2	0	—	—	—	—	—
85-86—Brandon..........................		WHL	72	26	26	52	49	—	—	—	—	—
86-87—Brandon..........................		WHL	71	44	58	102	64	—	—	—	—	—
87-88—Brandon..........................		WHL	72	55	85	140	59	3	4	2	6	7
88-89—Hartford.........................		NHL	2	0	0	0	0	—	—	—	—	—
—Binghamton		AHL	75	39	56	95	57	—	—	—	—	—
89-90—Hartford.........................		NHL	2	0	1	1	0	—	—	—	—	—
—Binghamton		AHL	77	13	42	55	37	—	—	—	—	—
90-91—Hartford.........................		NHL	19	1	4	5	10	6	1	1	2	16
—Springfield.......................		AHL	60	35	42	77	56	15	9	9	18	10
91-92—Hartford.........................		NHL	15	1	1	2	4	—	—	—	—	—
—Springfield.......................		AHL	53	21	34	55	63	8	3	4	7	2
92-93—Springfield......................		AHL	16	8	14	22	27	—	—	—	—	—
—Hartford........................		NHL	66	22	31	53	46	—	—	—	—	—
NHL totals...			104	24	37	61	60	6	1	1	2	16

YASHIN, ALEXEI
C, SENATORS

PERSONAL: Born November 5, 1973, at Sverdlovsk, U.S.S.R. . . . 6-2/ 189. . . . Shoots right. . . . Name pronounced YA-shin.
TRANSACTIONS/CAREER NOTES: Selected by Ottawa Senators in first round (first Senators pick, second overall) of NHL entry draft (June 20, 1992).
HONORS: Named to CIS All-Star team (1992-93).

Season	Team	League	Gms.	G	A	Pts.	Pen.	Gms.	G	A	Pts.	Pen.
			REGULAR SEASON					**PLAYOFFS**				
90-91—Automobilist Sverdlovsk..		USSR	26	2	1	3	10	—	—	—	—	—
91-92—Dynamo Moscow		CIS	35	7	5	12	19	—	—	—	—	—
92-93—Dynamo Moscow		CIS	27	10	12	22	18	10	7	3	10	18

YAWNEY, TRENT
D, FLAMES

PERSONAL: Born September 29, 1965, at Hudson Bay, Sask. . . . 6-3/ 185. . . . Shoots left.
TRANSACTIONS/CAREER NOTES: Selected by Chicago Blackhawks as underage junior in third round (second Blackhawks pick, 45th overall) of NHL entry draft (June 9, 1984). . . . Bruised left shoulder (March 1989). . . . Strained right knee (April 24, 1989). . . . Bruised kidney (November 11, 1989). . . . Bruised thigh (January 1990). . . . Strained knee (October 1990). . . . Traded by Blackhawks to Calgary Flames for LW Stephane Matteau (December 16, 1991). . . . Fractured right clavicle (September 26, 1992); missed first 20 games of season.

Season	Team	League	Gms.	G	A	Pts.	Pen.	Gms.	G	A	Pts.	Pen.
			REGULAR SEASON					**PLAYOFFS**				
81-82—Saskatoon		WHL	6	1	0	1	0	—	—	—	—	—
82-83—Saskatoon		WHL	59	6	31	37	44	6	0	2	2	0
83-84—Saskatoon		WHL	72	13	46	59	81	—	—	—	—	—
84-85—Saskatoon		WHL	72	16	51	67	158	3	1	6	7	7
85-86—Canadian national team ...		Int'l	73	6	15	21	60	—	—	—	—	—
86-87—Canadian national team ...		Int'l	51	4	15	19	37	—	—	—	—	—
87-88—Canadian national team ...		Int'l	60	4	12	16	81	—	—	—	—	—
—Canadian Olympic Team ..		Int'l	8	1	1	2	6	—	—	—	—	—
—Chicago		NHL	15	2	8	10	15	5	0	4	4	8
88-89—Chicago		NHL	69	5	19	24	116	15	3	6	9	20
89-90—Chicago		NHL	70	5	15	20	82	20	3	5	8	27
90-91—Chicago		NHL	61	3	13	16	77	1	0	0	0	0
91-92—Indianapolis		IHL	9	2	3	5	12	—	—	—	—	—
—Calgary............................		NHL	47	4	9	13	45	—	—	—	—	—
92-93—Calgary..........................		NHL	63	1	16	17	67	6	3	2	5	6
NHL totals...			325	20	80	100	402	47	9	17	26	61

YORK, JASON
D, RED WINGS

PERSONAL: Born May 20, 1970, at Nepean, Ont. . . . 6-2/ 195. . . . Shoots right.
TRANSACTIONS/CAREER NOTES: Selected by Detroit Red Wings in seventh round (sixth Red Wings pick, 129th overall) of NHL entry draft (June 16, 1990).

Season	Team	League	Gms.	G	A	Pts.	Pen.	Gms.	G	A	Pts.	Pen.
			REGULAR SEASON					**PLAYOFFS**				
89-90—Windsor..........................		OHL	39	9	30	39	38	—	—	—	—	—
—Kitchener..........................		OHL	25	11	25	36	17	17	3	19	22	10

WY

Season Team	League	REGULAR SEASON					PLAYOFFS				
		Gms.	G	A	Pts.	Pen.	Gms.	G	A	Pts.	Pen.
90-91—Windsor	OHL	66	13	80	93	40	11	3	10	13	12
91-92—Adirondack	AHL	49	4	20	24	32	5	0	1	1	0
92-93—Adirondack	AHL	77	15	40	55	86	11	0	3	3	18
—Detroit	NHL	2	0	0	0	0	—	—	—	—	—
NHL totals		2	0	0	0	0					

YOUNG, C.J.
RW, BRUINS

PERSONAL: Born January 1, 1968, at Waban, Mass. . . . 5-10/180. . . . Shoots right. . . . Full name: Carl Joshua Young.
COLLEGE: Harvard.
TRANSACTIONS/CAREER NOTES: Selected by New Jersey Devils in NHL supplemental draft (June 16, 1989). . . . Signed as free agent by Calgary Flames (September 9, 1990). . . . Traded by Flames to Boston Bruins for LW Brent Ashton (February 1, 1993).
HONORS: Named to ECAC All-Star second team (1988-89). . . . Named to NCAA All-America East second team (1988-89 and 1989-90). . . . Named to ECAC All-Star first team (1989-90). . . . Won Ken McKenzie Trophy (1990-91).

Season Team	League	REGULAR SEASON					PLAYOFFS				
		Gms.	G	A	Pts.	Pen.	Gms.	G	A	Pts.	Pen.
86-87—Harvard University	ECAC	34	17	12	29	30	—	—	—	—	—
87-88—Harvard University	ECAC	28	13	16	29	40	—	—	—	—	—
88-89—Harvard University	ECAC	34	33	22	55	24	—	—	—	—	—
89-90—Harvard University	ECAC	28	21	28	49	32	—	—	—	—	—
90-91—Salt Lake City	IHL	80	31	36	67	43	4	1	2	3	2
91-92—U.S. national team	Int'l	49	17	17	34	38	—	—	—	—	—
—U.S. Olympic Team	Int'l	8	1	3	4	4	—	—	—	—	—
—Salt Lake City	IHL	9	2	2	4	2	5	0	1	1	4
92-93—Calgary	NHL	28	3	2	5	20	—	—	—	—	—
—Boston	NHL	15	4	5	9	12	—	—	—	—	—
—Providence	AHL	7	4	3	7	26	6	1	0	1	16
NHL totals		43	7	7	14	32					

YOUNG, JASON
LW, SABRES

PERSONAL: Born December 16, 1972, at Sudbury, Ont. . . . 5-10/197. . . . Shoots left.
TRANSACTIONS/CAREER NOTES: Suspended remainder of season by OHL for checking opposing player from behind and breaking his neck (December 4, 1990); reinstated due to career record of 86 penalty minutes in 99 games and also due to the fact that he had no penalties in 71 of the 99 games (March 4, 1991). . . . Selected by Buffalo Sabres in third round (third Sabres pick, 57th overall) of NHL entry draft (June 22, 1991).
HONORS: Named to WCHA All-Star second team (1992-93).

Season Team	League	REGULAR SEASON					PLAYOFFS				
		Gms.	G	A	Pts.	Pen.	Gms.	G	A	Pts.	Pen.
89-90—Sudbury	OHL	62	26	47	73	64	—	—	—	—	—
90-91—Sudbury	OHL	37	21	38	59	22	5	0	4	4	10
91-92—Sudbury	OHL	55	26	56	82	49	11	3	2	5	14
92-93—Rochester	AHL	59	20	20	40	60	14	3	4	7	31

YOUNG, SCOTT
RW, NORDIQUES

PERSONAL: Born October 1, 1967, at Clinton, Mass. . . . 6-0/190. . . . Shoots right. . . . Full name: Scott Allen Young.
HIGH SCHOOL: St. Mark's (Southborough, Mass.).
COLLEGE: Boston University.
TRANSACTIONS/CAREER NOTES: Selected by Hartford Whalers in first round (first Whalers pick, 11th overall) of NHL entry draft (June 21, 1986). . . . Suffered lacerations above right eye (October 8, 1988). . . . Suffered facial lacerations (February 18, 1990). . . . Traded by Whalers to Pittsburgh Penguins for RW Rob Brown (December 21, 1990). . . . Traded by Penguins to Quebec Nordiques for D Bryan Fogarty (March 10, 1992). . . . Injured rib (February 14, 1993); missed one game. . . . Bruised ribs (February 23, 1993); missed one game.
HONORS: Named Hockey East Rookie of the Year (1985-86).
MISCELLANEOUS: Member of Stanley Cup championship team (1991).

Y

Season Team	League	REGULAR SEASON					PLAYOFFS				
		Gms.	G	A	Pts.	Pen.	Gms.	G	A	Pts.	Pen.
84-85—St. Marks H.S.	Mass. H.S.	23	28	41	69	. . .	—	—	—	—	—
85-86—Boston University	Hockey East	38	16	13	29	31	—	—	—	—	—
86-87—Boston University	Hockey East	33	15	21	36	24	—	—	—	—	—
87-88—U.S. Olympic Team	Int'l	59	13	53	66	. . .	—	—	—	—	—
—Hartford	NHL	7	0	0	0	2	4	1	0	1	0
88-89—Hartford	NHL	76	19	40	59	27	4	2	0	2	4
89-90—Hartford	NHL	80	24	40	64	47	7	2	0	2	2
90-91—Hartford	NHL	34	6	9	15	8	—	—	—	—	—
—Pittsburgh	NHL	43	11	16	27	33	17	1	6	7	2
91-92—U.S. national team	Int'l	10	2	4	6	21	—	—	—	—	—
—U.S. Olympic Team	Int'l	8	2	1	3	2	—	—	—	—	—
—Bolzano	Italy	18	22	17	39	6	—	—	—	—	—
92-93—Quebec	NHL	82	30	30	60	20	6	4	1	5	0
NHL totals		322	90	135	225	137	38	10	7	17	8

YOUNG, WENDELL

G, LIGHTNING

PERSONAL: Born August 1, 1963, at Halifax, N.S. . . . . 5-9/181. . . . Shoots left.
TRANSACTIONS/CAREER NOTES: Selected by Vancouver Canucks as underage junior in fourth round (third Canucks pick, 73rd overall) of NHL entry draft (June 10, 1981). . . . Traded by Canucks with third-round pick in 1990 draft (C Kimbi Daniels) to Philadelphia Flyers for D Daryl Stanley and G Darren Jensen (August 28, 1987). . . . Traded by Flyers with seventh-round pick in 1990 draft (C Mike Valila) to Pittsburgh Penguins for Flyers third-round pick in 1990 draft (D Chris Therien)(September 1, 1988). . . . Strained ankle (October 1988). . . . Dislocated right shoulder (February 26, 1991); missed remainder of season. . . . Fractured right hand (February 5, 1992); missed six games. . . . Selected by Tampa Bay Lightning in NHL expansion draft (June 18, 1992). . . . Dislocated shoulder (November 1, 1992); missed five games. . . . Injured shoulder (March 20, 1993); missed remainder of season.
HONORS: Won Baz Bastien Trophy (1987-88). . . . Won Jack Butterfield Trophy (1987-88). . . . Named to AHL All-Star first team (1987-88).
MISCELLANEOUS: Member of Stanley Cup championship teams (1991 and 1992).

						REGULAR SEASON							PLAYOFFS				
Season	Team	League	Gms.	Min.	W	L	T	GA	SO	Avg.	Gms.	Min.	W	L	GA	SO	Avg.
79-80—Cole Harbour		NSJHL	...	1446	...	...	...	94	0	3.90	—	—	—	—	—	—	—
80-81—Kitchener		OMJHL	42	2215	19	15	0	164	1	4.44	14	800	9	1	42	1	3.15
81-82—Kitchener		OHL	*60	*3470	38	17	2	195	1	3.37	15	900	12	1	35	*1	*2.33
82-83—Kitchener		OHL	61	*3611	41	19	0	231	1	3.84	12	720	6	5	43	0	3.58
83-84—Salt Lake City		IHL	20	1094	11	6	0	80	0	4.39	4	122	0	2	11	0	5.41
—Fredericton		AHL	11	569	7	3	0	39	1	4.11	—	—	—	—	—	—	—
—Milwaukee		IHL	6	339	...	...	...	17	0	3.01	—	—	—	—	—	—	—
84-85—Fredericton		AHL	22	1242	7	11	3	83	0	4.01	—	—	—	—	—	—	—
85-86—Fredericton		AHL	24	1457	12	8	4	78	0	3.21	—	—	—	—	—	—	—
—Vancouver		NHL	22	1023	4	9	3	61	0	3.58	1	60	0	1	5	0	5.00
86-87—Fredericton		AHL	30	1676	11	16	0	118	0	4.22	—	—	—	—	—	—	—
—Vancouver		NHL	8	420	1	6	1	35	0	5.00	—	—	—	—	—	—	—
87-88—Philadelphia		NHL	6	320	3	2	0	20	0	3.75	—	—	—	—	—	—	—
—Hershey		AHL	51	2922	33	15	1	135	1	2.77	†12	*767	12	0	28	*1	*2.19
88-89—Pittsburgh		NHL	22	1150	12	9	0	92	0	4.80	1	39	0	0	1	0	1.54
—Muskegon		IHL	2	125	...	...	...	7	0	3.36	—	—	—	—	—	—	—
89-90—Pittsburgh		NHL	43	2318	16	20	3	161	1	4.17	—	—	—	—	—	—	—
90-91—Pittsburgh		NHL	18	773	4	6	2	52	0	4.04	—	—	—	—	—	—	—
91-92—Pittsburgh		NHL	18	838	7	6	0	53	0	3.79	—	—	—	—	—	—	—
92-93—Tampa Bay		NHL	31	1591	7	19	2	97	0	3.66	—	—	—	—	—	—	—
—Atlanta		IHL	3	183	3	0	0	8	0	2.62	—	—	—	—	—	—	—
NHL totals			168	8433	54	77	11	571	1	4.06	2	99	0	1	6	0	3.64

YSEBAERT, PAUL

LW, JETS

PERSONAL: Born May 15, 1966, at Sarnia, Ont. . . . . 6-1/190. . . . Shoots left. . . . Full name: Paul Robert Ysebaert. . . . Name pronounced EYE-suh-BAHRT.
COLLEGE: Bowling Green State.
TRANSACTIONS/CAREER NOTES: Selected by New Jersey Devils in fourth round (fourth Devils pick, 74th overall) of NHL entry draft (June 9, 1984). . . . Pulled stomach and groin muscles (December 1988). . . . Suffered contusion to left thigh (March 1989). . . . Traded by New Jersey Devils to Detroit Red Wings for D Lee Norwood and future considerations; Devils later received fourth-round pick in 1992 draft (D Scott McCabe) to complete deal (November 27, 1990). . . . Injured knee (December 1991); missed one game. . . . Suffered from the flu (December 22, 1992); missed one game. . . . Suffered from the flu (March 5, 1993); missed one game. . . . Suffered from the flu (March 10, 1993); missed one game. . . . Traded by Red Wings to Winnipeg Jets for D Aaron Ward, fourth-round pick in 1993 draft and fifth-round pick in 1994 draft (June 11, 1993).
HONORS: Named CCHA Rookie of the Year (1984-85). . . . Named to CCHA All-Star second team (1985-86 and 1986-87). . . . Won Les Cunningham Plaque (1989-90). . . . Won John B. Sollenberger Trophy (1989-90). . . . Named to AHL All-Star first team (1989-90). . . . Won Alka-Seltzer Plus Award (1991-92).

			REGULAR SEASON					PLAYOFFS			
Season	Team	League	Gms.	G	A	Pts.	Pen.	Gms.	G	A	Pts.	Pen.
83-84—Petrolia Jr. B		OHA	33	35	42	77	20	—	—	—	—	—
84-85—Bowling Green State		CCHA	42	23	32	55	54	—	—	—	—	—
85-86—Bowling Green State		CCHA	42	23	45	68	50	—	—	—	—	—
86-87—Bowling Green State		CCHA	45	27	58	85	44	—	—	—	—	—
—Canadian national team		Int'l	5	1	0	1	4	—	—	—	—	—
87-88—Utica		AHL	78	30	49	79	60	—	—	—	—	—
88-89—Utica		AHL	56	36	44	80	22	5	0	1	1	4
—New Jersey		NHL	5	0	4	4	0	—	—	—	—	—
89-90—New Jersey		NHL	5	1	2	3	0	—	—	—	—	—
—Utica		AHL	74	53	52	*105	61	5	2	4	6	0
90-91—New Jersey		NHL	11	4	3	7	6	—	—	—	—	—
—Detroit		NHL	51	15	18	33	16	2	0	2	2	0
91-92—Detroit		NHL	79	35	40	75	55	10	1	0	1	10
92-93—Detroit		NHL	80	34	28	62	42	7	3	1	4	2
NHL totals			231	89	95	184	119	19	4	3	7	12

YUSHKEVICH, DIMITRI

D, FLYERS

PERSONAL: Born November 19, 1971, at Yaroslavl, U.S.S.R. . . . 5-11/187. . . . Shoots left. . . . Name pronounced yoosh-KEH-vihch.
TRANSACTIONS/CAREER NOTES: Selected by Philadelphia Flyers in sixth round (sixth Flyers pick, 122nd overall) of NHL entry draft (June 22, 1991). . . .
Sprained wrist (January 28, 1993); missed two games.

Season Team	League	Gms.	G	A	Pts.	Pen.	Gms.	G	A	Pts.	Pen.
89-90—Torpedo Yaroslavl	USSR	40	2	3	5	...	—	—	—	—	—
90-91—Torpedo Yaroslavl	USSR	41	10	4	14	...	—	—	—	—	—
91-92—Dynamo Moscow	CIS	41	6	7	13	14	—	—	—	—	—
—Unified Olympic Team	Int'l	8	1	2	3	4	—	—	—	—	—
92-93—Philadelphia	NHL	82	5	27	32	71	—	—	—	—	—
NHL totals		82	5	27	32	71	—	—	—	—	—

YZERMAN, STEVE
C, RED WINGS

PERSONAL: Born May 9, 1965, at Cranbrook, B.C. . . . 5-11/183. . . . Shoots right. . . . Name pronounced EYE-zuhr-muhn.

TRANSACTIONS/CAREER NOTES: Selected by Detroit Red Wings as underage junior in first round (first Red Wings pick, fourth overall) of NHL entry draft (June 8, 1983). . . . Became youngest person (18) to ever play in NHL All-Star Game (January 31, 1984). . . . Fractured collarbone (January 31, 1986). . . . Injured ligaments of right knee and underwent surgery (March 1, 1988). . . . Injured right knee in playoff game (April 8, 1991).

HONORS: Named NHL Rookie of the Year by THE SPORTING NEWS (1983-84). . . . Named to NHL All-Rookie team (1983-84). . . . Played in NHL All-Star Game (1984, 1988 through 1993). . . . Won Lester B. Pearson Award (1988-89).

Season Team	League	Gms.	G	A	Pts.	Pen.	Gms.	G	A	Pts.	Pen.
81-82—Peterborough	OHL	58	21	43	64	65	6	0	1	1	16
82-83—Peterborough	OHL	56	42	49	91	33	4	1	4	5	0
83-84—Detroit	NHL	80	39	48	87	33	4	3	3	6	0
84-85—Detroit	NHL	80	30	59	89	58	3	2	1	3	2
85-86—Detroit	NHL	51	14	28	42	16	—	—	—	—	—
86-87—Detroit	NHL	80	31	59	90	43	16	5	13	18	8
87-88—Detroit	NHL	64	50	52	102	44	3	1	3	4	6
88-89—Detroit	NHL	80	65	90	155	61	6	5	5	10	2
89-90—Detroit	NHL	79	62	65	127	79	—	—	—	—	—
90-91—Detroit	NHL	80	51	57	108	34	7	3	3	6	4
91-92—Detroit	NHL	79	45	58	103	64	11	3	5	8	12
92-93—Detroit	NHL	84	58	79	137	44	7	4	3	7	4
NHL totals		757	445	595	1040	476	57	26	36	62	38

ZALAPSKI, ZARLEY
D, WHALERS

PERSONAL: Born April 22, 1968, at Edmonton, Alta. . . . 6-1/210. . . . Shoots left.

TRANSACTIONS/CAREER NOTES: Selected by Pittsburgh Penguins in first round (first Penguins pick, fourth overall) of NHL entry draft (June 21, 1986). . . . Suffered from Spondylosis, deterioration of the structure of the spine (October 1987). . . . Tore ligaments in right knee (December 29, 1988). . . . Broke right collarbone (October 25, 1989). . . . Sprained right knee (February 24, 1990); missed 13 games. . . . Traded by Penguins with C John Cullen and RW Jeff Parker to Hartford Whalers for C Ron Francis, D Ulf Samuelsson and D Grant Jennings (March 4, 1991). . . . Suffered from the flu (March 3, 1993); missed one game.

HONORS: Named to NHL All-Rookie team (1988-89). . . . Played in NHL All-Star Game (1993).

Season Team	League	Gms.	G	A	Pts.	Pen.	Gms.	G	A	Pts.	Pen.
84-85—Fort Saskatchewan	AJHL	23	17	30	47	14	—	—	—	—	—
85-86—Fort Saskatchewan	AJHL	27	20	33	53	46	—	—	—	—	—
—Canadian national team	Int'l	32	2	4	6	10	—	—	—	—	—
86-87—Canadian national team	Int'l	74	11	29	40	28	—	—	—	—	—
87-88—Canadian national team	Int'l	47	3	13	16	32	—	—	—	—	—
—Canadian Olympic Team	Int'l	8	1	3	4	2	—	—	—	—	—
—Pittsburgh	NHL	15	3	8	11	7	—	—	—	—	—
88-89—Pittsburgh	NHL	58	12	33	45	57	11	1	8	9	13
89-90—Pittsburgh	NHL	51	6	25	31	37	—	—	—	—	—
90-91—Pittsburgh	NHL	66	12	36	48	59	—	—	—	—	—
—Hartford	NHL	11	3	3	6	6	6	1	3	4	8
91-92—Hartford	NHL	79	20	37	57	120	7	2	3	5	6
92-93—Hartford	NHL	83	14	51	65	94	—	—	—	—	—
NHL totals		363	70	193	263	380	24	4	14	18	27

ZAMUNER, ROB
LW/C, LIGHTNING

PERSONAL: Born September 17, 1969, at Oakville, Ont. . . . 6-2/202. . . . Shoots left. . . . Name pronounced ZAM-nuhr.

TRANSACTIONS/CAREER NOTES: Selected by New York Rangers in third round (third Rangers pick, 45th overall) of NHL entry draft (June 17, 1989). . . . Signed as free agent by Tampa Bay Lightning (July 14, 1992); Rangers awarded third-round pick in 1993 draft as compensation (July 23, 1992).

Season Team	League	Gms.	G	A	Pts.	Pen.	Gms.	G	A	Pts.	Pen.
86-87—Guelph	OHL	62	6	15	21	8	—	—	—	—	—
87-88—Guelph	OHL	58	20	41	61	18	—	—	—	—	—
88-89—Guelph	OHL	66	46	65	111	38	7	5	5	10	9
89-90—Flint	IHL	77	44	35	79	32	4	1	0	1	6
90-91—Binghamton	AHL	80	25	58	83	50	9	7	6	13	35
91-92—Binghamton	AHL	61	19	53	72	42	11	8	9	17	8

YZ

Season Team	League	REGULAR SEASON Gms.	G	A	Pts.	Pen.	PLAYOFFS Gms.	G	A	Pts.	Pen.
—New York Rangers	NHL	9	1	2	3	2	—	—	—	—	—
92-93—Tampa Bay	NHL	84	15	28	43	74	—	—	—	—	—
NHL totals		93	16	30	46	76					

ZAYONCE, DEAN
D, NORDIQUES

PERSONAL: Born October 28, 1970, at Kelonwna, B.C. . . . 6-0/200. . . . Shoots right.
TRANSACTIONS/CAREER NOTES: Signed as free agent by Quebec Nordiques (October 8, 1991).

Season Team	League	REGULAR SEASON Gms.	G	A	Pts.	Pen.	PLAYOFFS Gms.	G	A	Pts.	Pen.
90-91—Tri-City	WHL	64	14	37	51	139	7	1	2	3	14
91-92—Greensboro	ECHL	26	2	7	9	151	—	—	—	—	—
—Halifax	AHL	24	0	3	3	26	—	—	—	—	—
92-93—Halifax	AHL	22	0	1	1	6	—	—	—	—	—
—Greensboro	ECHL	26	1	9	10	73	1	0	0	0	0

ZELEPUKIN, VALERI
RW, DEVILS

PERSONAL: Born September 17, 1968, at Voskresensk, U.S.S.R. . . . 5-11/180. . . . Shoots left. . . . Name pronounced ZEHL-ih-POO-kihn.
TRANSACTIONS/CAREER NOTES: Selected by New Jersey Devils in 11th round (13th Devils pick, 221st overall) of NHL entry draft (June 22, 1991). . . . Bruised shoulder (January 22, 1993); missed five games.

Season Team	League	REGULAR SEASON Gms.	G	A	Pts.	Pen.	PLAYOFFS Gms.	G	A	Pts.	Pen.
84-85—Khimik	USSR	5	0	0	0	2	—	—	—	—	—
85-86—Khimik	USSR	33	2	2	4	10	—	—	—	—	—
86-87—Khimik	USSR	19	1	0	1	4	—	—	—	—	—
87-88—SKA Leningrad	USSR	18	18	6	24	. . .	—	—	—	—	—
—CSKA Moscow	USSR	19	3	1	4	8	—	—	—	—	—
88-89—CSKA Moscow	USSR	17	2	3	5	2	—	—	—	—	—
89-90—Khimik	USSR	46	17	14	31	26	—	—	—	—	—
90-91—Khimik	USSR	46	12	19	31	22	—	—	—	—	—
91-92—Utica	AHL	22	20	9	29	8	—	—	—	—	—
—New Jersey	NHL	44	13	18	31	28	4	1	1	2	2
92-93—New Jersey	NHL	78	23	41	64	70	5	0	2	2	0
NHL totals		122	36	59	95	98	9	1	3	4	2

ZENT, JASON
LW, ISLANDERS

PERSONAL: Born April 15, 1971, at Buffalo, N.Y. . . . 5-11/180. . . . Shoots left. . . . Full name: Jason William Zent.
HIGH SCHOOL: Nichols School (Buffalo, N.Y.).
COLLEGE: Wisconsin.
TRANSACTIONS/CAREER NOTES: Selected by New York Islanders in third round (third Islanders pick, 44th overall) of NHL entry draft (June 17, 1989). . . . Sprained ankle while playing racquetball (January 1991).
HONORS: Named to WCHA All-Rookie team (1990-91). . . . Named to NCAA All-Tournament team (1991-92).

Season Team	League	REGULAR SEASON Gms.	G	A	Pts.	Pen.	PLAYOFFS Gms.	G	A	Pts.	Pen.
87-88—Nichols School	N.Y. H.S.	21	20	16	36	28	—	—	—	—	—
88-89—Nichols School	N.Y. H.S.	29	49	32	81	26	—	—	—	—	—
89-90—Nichols School	N.Y. H.S.			Statistics unavailable.							
90-91—University of Wisconsin	WCHA	39	19	18	37	51	—	—	—	—	—
91-92—University of Wisconsin	WCHA	43	27	17	44	134	—	—	—	—	—
92-93—University of Wisconsin	WCHA	40	26	12	38	88	—	—	—	—	—

ZETTLER, ROB
D, SHARKS

PERSONAL: Born March 8, 1968, at Sept Iles, Que. . . . 6-3/195. . . . Shoots left.
TRANSACTIONS/CAREER NOTES: Selected by Minnesota North Stars as underage junior in fifth round (fifth North Stars pick, 55th overall) of NHL entry draft (June 21, 1986). . . . Tore hip flexor (January 21, 1991); missed 11 games. . . . Selected by San Jose Sharks in NHL dispersal draft (May 30, 1991). . . . Strained back (October 20, 1992); missed three games. . . . Injured groin (April 8, 1993); missed one game.

Season Team	League	REGULAR SEASON Gms.	G	A	Pts.	Pen.	PLAYOFFS Gms.	G	A	Pts.	Pen.
84-85—Sault Ste. Marie	OHL	60	2	14	16	37	—	—	—	—	—
85-86—Sault Ste. Marie	OHL	57	5	23	28	92	—	—	—	—	—
86-87—Sault Ste. Marie	OHL	64	13	22	35	89	4	0	0	0	0
87-88—Sault Ste. Marie	OHL	64	7	41	48	77	6	2	2	4	9
—Kalamazoo	IHL	2	0	1	1	0	7	0	2	2	2
88-89—Minnesota	NHL	2	0	0	0	0	—	—	—	—	—
—Kalamazoo	IHL	80	5	21	26	79	6	0	1	1	26
89-90—Minnesota	NHL	31	0	8	8	45	7	0	0	0	6
—Kalamazoo	IHL	41	6	10	16	64	—	—	—	—	—
90-91—Kalamazoo	IHL	1	0	0	0	2	—	—	—	—	—
—Minnesota	NHL	47	1	4	5	119	—	—	—	—	—

Z

Season	Team	League	Gms.	G	A	Pts.	Pen.	Gms.	G	A	Pts.	Pen.
91-92—San Jose	NHL	74	1	8	9	99	—	—	—	—	—
92-93—San Jose	NHL	80	0	7	7	150	—	—	—	—	—
NHL totals			234	2	27	29	413					

ZEZEL, PETER
C, MAPLE LEAFS

PERSONAL: Born April 22, 1965, at Toronto.... 5-11/200.... Shoots left.... Name pronounced ZEH-zuhl.

TRANSACTIONS/CAREER NOTES: Played three games as a striker for Toronto Blizzard in the North American Soccer League (1982).... Selected by Philadelphia Flyers as underage junior in second round (first Flyers pick, 41st overall) of NHL entry draft (June 8, 1983).... Broke hand (November 1984).... Tore medial cartilage in left knee (March 1987).... Sprained right ankle (November 1987).... Separated left shoulder (March 1988).... Traded by Flyers to St. Louis Blues for C Mike Bullard (November 29, 1988).... Pulled groin (December 1988).... Bruised sternum (January 1989).... Sprained right knee (March 5, 1989).... Bruised right hip (March 11, 1990).... Traded by Blues with D Mike Lalor to Washington Capitals for LW Geoff Courtnall (July 13, 1990).... Sprained left ankle (October 23, 1990); missed 23 games.... Reinjured ankle (December 28, 1990); missed two games.... Traded by Capitals with D Bob Rouse to Toronto Maple Leafs for D Al Iafrate (January 16, 1991).... Sprained knee (November 14, 1991); missed five games. ... Strained knee (March 5, 1992).... Bruised knee (November 5, 1992); missed five games.... Sprained wrist (January 6, 1993); missed three games, ... Sprained neck (March 25, 1993); missed five games.

				REGULAR SEASON					PLAYOFFS			
Season	Team	League	Gms.	G	A	Pts.	Pen.	Gms.	G	A	Pts.	Pen.
81-82—Don Mills Flyers	MTHL	40	43	51	94	36	—	—	—	—	—
82-83—Toronto	OHL	66	35	39	74	28	4	2	4	6	0
83-84—Toronto	OHL	68	47	86	133	31	9	7	5	12	4
84-85—Philadelphia	NHL	65	15	46	61	26	19	1	8	9	28
85-86—Philadelphia	NHL	79	17	37	54	76	5	3	1	4	4
86-87—Philadelphia	NHL	71	33	39	72	71	25	3	10	13	10
87-88—Philadelphia	NHL	69	22	35	57	42	7	3	2	5	7
88-89—Philadelphia	NHL	26	4	13	17	15	—	—	—	—	—
—St. Louis	NHL	52	17	36	53	27	10	6	6	12	4
89-90—St. Louis	NHL	73	25	47	72	30	12	1	7	8	4
90-91—Washington	NHL	20	7	5	12	10	—	—	—	—	—
—Toronto	NHL	32	14	14	28	4	—	—	—	—	—
91-92—Toronto	NHL	64	16	33	49	26	—	—	—	—	—
92-93—Toronto	NHL	70	12	23	35	24	20	2	1	3	6
NHL totals			621	182	328	510	351	98	19	35	54	63

ZHAMNOV, ALEXEI
C, JETS

PERSONAL: Born October 1, 1970, at Moscow, U.S.S.R.... 6-1/187.... Shoots left.... Name pronounced ZHAM-nahf.

TRANSACTIONS/CAREER NOTES: Selected by Winnipeg Jets in fourth round (fifth Jets pick, 77th overall) of NHL entry draft (June 16, 1990).... Suffered hip flexor (November 2, 1992); missed two games. ... Suffered back spasms (January 27, 1993); missed one game. ... Suffered back spasms (February 3, 1993); missed one game.... Suffered back spasms (February 12, 1993); missed 12 games.

				REGULAR SEASON					PLAYOFFS			
Season	Team	League	Gms.	G	A	Pts.	Pen.	Gms.	G	A	Pts.	Pen.
88-89—Dynamo Moscow	USSR	4	0	0	0	0	—	—	—	—	—
89-90—Dynamo Moscow	USSR	43	11	6	17	23	—	—	—	—	—
90-91—Dynamo Moscow	USSR	46	16	12	28	24	—	—	—	—	—
91-92—Dynamo Moscow	CIS	39	15	21	36	28	—	—	—	—	—
92-93—Winnipeg	NHL	68	25	47	72	58	6	0	2	2	2
NHL totals			68	25	47	72	58	6	0	2	2	2

ZHITNIK, ALEXEI
D, KINGS

PERSONAL: Born October 10, 1972, at Kiev, U.S.S.R.... 5-11/190.... Shoots left.... Name pronounced DZIHT-nihk.

TRANSACTIONS/CAREER NOTES: Selected by Los Angeles Kings in fourth round (third Kings pick, 81st overall) of NHL entry draft (June 22, 1991).... Suffered from the flu (January 12, 1993); missed five games.

				REGULAR SEASON					PLAYOFFS			
Season	Team	League	Gms.	G	A	Pts.	Pen.	Gms.	G	A	Pts.	Pen.
90-91—Sokol Kiev	USSR	40	1	4	5	46	—	—	—	—	—
91-92—CSKA Moscow	CIS	36	2	7	9	48	—	—	—	—	—
92-93—Los Angeles	NHL	78	12	36	48	80	24	3	9	12	26
NHL totals			78	12	36	48	80	24	3	9	12	26

ZHOLTOK, SERGEI
LW, BRUINS

PERSONAL: Born December 2, 1972, at Riga, U.S.S.R.... 6-0/185.... Shoots right.... Name pronounced ZHOL-tahk.

TRANSACTIONS/CAREER NOTES: Selected by Boston Bruins in third round (second Bruins pick, 56th overall) of NHL entry draft (June 20, 1992).

				REGULAR SEASON					PLAYOFFS			
Season	Team	League	Gms.	G	A	Pts.	Pen.	Gms.	G	A	Pts.	Pen.
90-91—Dynamo Riga	USSR	39	4	0	4	16	—	—	—	—	—
91-92—Riga	CIS	27	6	3	9	6	—	—	—	—	—
92-93—Providence	AHL	64	31	35	66	57	6	3	5	8	4
—Boston	NHL	1	0	1	1	0	—	—	—	—	—
NHL totals			1	0	1	1	0					

Z

ZMOLEK, DOUG
D, SHARKS

PERSONAL: Born November 3, 1970, at Rochester, Minn. . . . 6-1/ 195. . . . Shoots left. . . . Full name: Doug Allan Zmolek. . . . Name pronounced zuh-MOH-lehk.
HIGH SCHOOL: John Marshall (Rochester, Minn.).
COLLEGE: Minnesota.
TRANSACTIONS/CAREER NOTES: Selected by Minnesota North Stars in first round (first North Stars pick, seventh overall) of NHL entry draft (June 17, 1989). . . . Selected by San Jose Sharks in NHL dispersal draft (May 30, 1991).
HONORS: Named to NCAA All-America West second team (1991-92). . . . Named to WCHA All-Star second team (1991-92).

Season	Team	League	REGULAR SEASON					PLAYOFFS				
			Gms.	G	A	Pts.	Pen.	Gms.	G	A	Pts.	Pen.
87-88	Rochester John Marshall HS	Minn. H.S.	27	4	32	36	...	—	—	—	—	—
88-89	Rochester John Marshall HS	Minn. H.S.	29	17	41	58	...	—	—	—	—	—
89-90	University of Minnesota ...	WCHA	40	1	10	11	52	—	—	—	—	—
90-91	University of Minnesota ...	WCHA	42	3	15	18	94	—	—	—	—	—
91-92	University of Minnesota ...	WCHA	44	6	21	27	88	—	—	—	—	—
92-93	San Jose	NHL	84	5	10	15	229	—	—	—	—	—
	NHL totals		84	5	10	15	229	—	—	—	—	—

ZOLOTOV, ROMAN
D, FLYERS

PERSONAL: Born February 13, 1974, at Moscow, U.S.S.R. . . . 6-1/183. . . . Shoots left.
TRANSACTIONS/CAREER NOTES: Selected by Philadelphia Flyers in sixth round (fourth Flyers pick, 127th overall) of NHL entry draft (June 20, 1992).

Season	Team	League	REGULAR SEASON					PLAYOFFS				
			Gms.	G	A	Pts.	Pen.	Gms.	G	A	Pts.	Pen.
91-92	Dynamo Moscow	CIS	1	0	0	0	2	—	—	—	—	—
92-93	Dynamo Moscow	CIS				Statistics unavailable.						

ZOMBO, RICK
D, BLUES

PERSONAL: Born May 8, 1963, at Des Plaines, Ill. . . . 6-1/ 195. . . . Shoots right.
COLLEGE: North Dakota.
TRANSACTIONS/CAREER NOTES: Selected by Detroit Red Wings in eighth round (sixth Red Wings pick, 149th overall) of NHL entry draft (June 10, 1981). . . . Injured knee (December 1984). . . . Injured shoulder (December 1987). . . . Strained knee (December 1988). . . . Suspended three games by NHL for high-sticking (December 27, 1989). . . . Traded by Red Wings to St. Louis Blues for G Vincent Riendeau (October 18, 1991). . . . Fractured bone in left foot (March 14, 1992); missed seven games. . . . Suffered from injury (October 13, 1992); missed one game.
HONORS: Named USHL Best Defenseman (1980-81). . . . Named to USHL All-Star first team (1980-81).

Season	Team	League	REGULAR SEASON					PLAYOFFS				
			Gms.	G	A	Pts.	Pen.	Gms.	G	A	Pts.	Pen.
80-81	Austin	USHL	43	10	26	36	73	—	—	—	—	—
81-82	Univ. of North Dakota	WCHA	45	1	15	16	31	—	—	—	—	—
82-83	Univ. of North Dakota	WCHA	33	5	11	16	41	—	—	—	—	—
83-84	Univ. of North Dakota	WCHA	34	7	24	31	40	—	—	—	—	—
84-85	Adirondack	AHL	56	3	32	35	70	—	—	—	—	—
	Detroit	NHL	1	0	0	0	0	—	—	—	—	—
85-86	Adirondack	AHL	69	7	34	41	94	17	0	4	4	40
	Detroit	NHL	14	0	1	1	16	—	—	—	—	—
86-87	Adirondack	AHL	25	0	6	6	22	—	—	—	—	—
	Detroit	NHL	44	1	4	5	59	7	0	1	1	9
87-88	Detroit	NHL	62	3	14	17	96	16	0	6	6	55
88-89	Detroit	NHL	75	1	20	21	106	6	0	1	1	16
89-90	Detroit	NHL	77	5	20	25	95	—	—	—	—	—
90-91	Detroit	NHL	77	4	19	23	55	7	1	0	1	10
91-92	Detroit	NHL	3	0	0	0	15	—	—	—	—	—
	St. Louis	NHL	64	3	15	18	46	6	0	2	2	12
92-93	St. Louis	NHL	71	0	15	15	78	11	0	1	1	12
	NHL totals		488	17	108	125	566	53	1	11	12	114

ZUBOV, SERGEI
D, RANGERS

PERSONAL: Born July 22, 1970, at Moscow, U.S.S.R. . . . 6-0/ 187. . . . Shoots left. . . . Name pronounced ZOO-bahf.
TRANSACTIONS/CAREER NOTES: Selected by New York Rangers in fifth round (sixth Rangers pick, 85th overall) of NHL entry draft (June 16, 1990). . . . Suffered concussion (February 26, 1993); missed one game.

Season	Team	League	REGULAR SEASON					PLAYOFFS				
			Gms.	G	A	Pts.	Pen.	Gms.	G	A	Pts.	Pen.
88-89	CSKA Moscow	USSR	29	1	4	5	10	—	—	—	—	—
89-90	CSKA Moscow	USSR	48	6	2	8	16	—	—	—	—	—
90-91	CSKA Moscow	USSR	41	6	5	11	12	—	—	—	—	—
91-92	CSKA Moscow	CIS	36	4	7	11	6	—	—	—	—	—
92-93	CSKA Moscow	CIS	1	0	1	1	0	—	—	—	—	—
	Binghamton	AHL	30	7	29	36	14	11	5	5	10	2
	New York Rangers	NHL	49	8	23	31	4	—	—	—	—	—
	NHL totals		49	8	23	31	4	—	—	—	—	—

Z

ARBOUR, AL
ISLANDERS

PERSONAL: Born November 1, 1932, at Sudbury, Ont.... 6-0/180.... Shot left.
TRANSACTIONS/CAREER NOTES: Selected by Chicago Blackhawks from Detroit Red Wings in intraleague draft (June 1958).... Selected by Toronto Maple Leafs from Blackhawks in intraleague draft (June 1961).... Selected by St. Louis Blues from Maple Leafs in NHL expansion draft (June 6, 1967).
HONORS: Won Eddie Shore Plaque (1964-65).... Named to THE SPORTING NEWS West Division All-Star second team (1967-68).... Named to THE SPORTING NEWS West Division All-Star first team (1968-69 and 1969-70).... Played in NHL All-Star Game (1969).
MISCELLANEOUS: Played defense.... Member of Stanley Cup championship teams (1961, 1963 and 1964).

Season	Team	League	REGULAR SEASON					PLAYOFFS				
			Gms.	G	A	Pts.	Pen.	Gms.	G	A	Pts.	Pen.
49-50	Detroit	IHL	33	14	8	22	10	—	—	—	—	—
	Windsor	OHA JR. A	3	0	0	0	0	—	—	—	—	—
50-51	Windsor	OHA JR. A	31	5	4	9	0	—	—	—	—	—
51-52	Windsor	OHA JR. A	52	7	12	19	0	—	—	—	—	—
52-53	Windsor	OHA JR. A	56	5	7	12	0	—	—	—	—	—
	Washington	EHL	4	0	2	2	0	—	—	—	—	—
	Edmonton	WHL	8	0	1	1	2	15	0	5	5	10
53-54	Detroit	NHL	36	0	1	1	18	—	—	—	—	—
	Sherbrooke	QHL	19	1	3	4	24	2	0	0	0	2
54-55	Edmonton	WHL	41	3	9	12	39	—	—	—	—	—
	Quebec	AHL	20	4	5	9	55	4	0	0	0	2
55-56	Edmonton	WHL	70	5	14	19	109	3	0	0	0	4
	Detroit	NHL	—	—	—	—	—	4	0	1	1	0
56-57	Edmonton	WHL	24	2	3	5	24	—	—	—	—	—
	Detroit	NHL	44	1	6	7	38	5	0	0	0	6
57-58	Detroit	NHL	69	1	6	7	104	4	0	1	1	4
58-59	Chicago	NHL	70	2	10	12	86	6	1	2	3	26
59-60	Chicago	NHL	57	1	5	6	66	4	0	0	0	4
60-61	Chicago	NHL	53	3	2	5	40	7	0	0	0	2
61-62	Toronto	NHL	52	1	5	6	68	8	0	0	0	6
62-63	Rochester	AHL	63	6	21	27	97	2	0	2	2	2
	Toronto	NHL	4	1	0	1	4	—	—	—	—	—
63-64	Rochester	AHL	60	3	19	22	62	2	1	0	1	0
	Toronto	NHL	6	0	1	1	0	1	0	0	0	0
64-65	Rochester	AHL	17	1	16	17	88	10	0	1	1	16
	Toronto	NHL	—	—	—	—	—	1	0	0	0	2
65-66	Toronto	NHL	4	0	1	1	2	—	—	—	—	—
	Rochester	AHL	59	2	11	13	86	12	0	2	2	8
66-67	Rochester	AHL	71	3	19	22	48	13	0	1	1	16
67-68	St. Louis	NHL	74	1	10	11	50	14	0	3	3	10
68-69	St. Louis	NHL	67	1	6	7	50	12	0	0	0	10
69-70	St. Louis	NHL	68	0	3	3	85	14	0	1	1	16
70-71	St. Louis	NHL	22	0	2	2	6	6	0	0	0	6
NHL totals			626	12	58	70	617	86	1	8	9	92

HEAD COACHING RECORD

BACKGROUND: Vice president of player development, New York Islanders (1986-87 and 1987-88).
HONORS: Shared Lester Patrick Trophy with Lou Lamoriello and Art Berglund (1991-92).
RECORDS: Holds NHL career regular-season record for games—1,522.

Season	Team	League	REGULAR SEASON					PLAYOFFS		
			W	L	T	Pct.	Finish	W	L	Pct.
70-71	St. Louis	NHL	21	15	14	.560	2nd/West Division	—	—	—
71-72	St. Louis	NHL	19	19	6	.438	3rd/West Division	11	4	.364
72-73	St. Louis	NHL	2	6	5	.346	4th/West Division	—	—	—
73-74	New York Islanders	NHL	19	41	18	.358	8th/East Division	—	—	—
74-75	New York Islanders	NHL	33	25	22	.550	3rd/Patrick Division	9	8	.529
75-76	New York Islanders	NHL	42	21	17	.631	2nd/Patrick Division	7	6	.538
76-77	New York Islanders	NHL	47	21	12	.663	2nd/Patrick Division	8	4	.667
77-78	New York Islanders	NHL	48	17	15	.694	1st/Patrick Division	3	4	.429
78-79	New York Islanders	NHL	51	15	14	.725	1st/Patrick Division	6	4	.600
79-80	New York Islanders	NHL	39	28	13	.569	2nd/Patrick Division	15	6	.714
80-81	New York Islanders	NHL	48	18	14	.688	1st/Patrick Division	15	3	.833
81-82	New York Islanders	NHL	54	16	10	.738	1st/Patrick Division	15	4	.789
82-83	New York Islanders	NHL	42	26	12	.600	2nd/Patrick Division	15	5	.750
83-84	New York Islanders	NHL	50	26	4	.650	1st/Patrick Division	12	9	.571
84-85	New York Islanders	NHL	40	34	6	.538	3rd/Patrick Division	4	6	.400
85-86	New York Islanders	NHL	39	29	12	.563	3rd/Patrick Division	0	3	.000
88-89	New York Islanders	NHL	21	29	3	.425	6th/Patrick Division	—	—	—
89-90	New York Islanders	NHL	31	38	11	.456	4th/Patrick Division	1	4	.200
90-91	New York Islanders	NHL	25	45	10	.375	6th/Patrick Division	—	—	—

Season	Team	League	W	L	T	Pct.	Finish	W	L	Pct.
							REGULAR SEASON		**PLAYOFFS**	
91-92—New York Islanders	NHL		34	35	11	.494	5th/Patrick Division	—	—	—
92-93—New York Islanders	NHL		40	37	7	.518	3rd/Patrick Division	9	9	.500
NHL totals (21 years)			745	541	236	.567	**NHL totals (15 years)**	123	82	.600

NOTES:

1972— Defeated Minnesota in Stanley Cup quarterfinals; lost to Boston in Stanley Cup semifinals.
1975— Defeated New York Rangers in Stanley Cup preliminary round; defeated Pittsburgh in Stanley Cup quarterfinals; lost to Philadelphia in Stanley Cup semifinals.
1976— Defeated Vancouver in Stanley Cup preliminary round; defeated Buffalo in Stanley Cup quarterfinals; lost to Montreal in Stanley Cup semifinals.
1977— Defeated Chicago in Stanley Cup preliminary round; defeated Buffalo in Stanley Cup quarterfinals; lost to Montreal in Stanley Cup semifinals.
1978— Lost to Toronto in Stanley Cup quarterfinals.
1979— Defeated Chicago in Stanley Cup quarterfinals; lost to New York Rangers in Stanley Cup semifinals.
1980— Defeated Los Angeles in Stanley Cup preliminary round; defeated Boston in Stanley Cup quarterfinals; defeated Buffalo in Stanley Cup semifinals; defeated Philadelphia in Stanley Cup finals.
1981— Defeated Toronto in Stanley Cup preliminary round; defeated Edmonton in Stanley Cup quarterfinals; defeated New York Rangers in Stanley Cup semifinals; defeated Minnesota in Stanley Cup finals.
1982— Defeated Pittsburgh in Patrick Division semifinals; defeated New York Rangers in Patrick Division finals; defeated Quebec in Wales Conference finals; defeated Vancouver in Stanley Cup finals.
1983— Defeated Washington in Patrick Division semifinals; defeated New York Rangers in Patrick Division finals; defeated Boston in Wales Conference finals; defeated Edmonton in Stanley Cup finals.
1984— Defeated New York Rangers in Patrick Division semifinals; defeated Washington in Patrick Division finals; defeated Montreal in Wales Conference finals; lost to Edmonton in Stanley Cup finals.
1985— Defeated Washington in Patrick Division semifinals; lost to Philadelphia in Patrick Division finals.
1986— Lost to Washington in Patrick Division semifinals.
1990— Lost to New York Rangers in Patrick Division semifinals.
1993— Defeated Washington in Patrick Division semifinals; defeated Pittsburgh in Patrick Division finals; lost to Montreal in Wales Conference finals.

BERRY, BOB
BLUES

PERSONAL: Born November 29, 1943, at Montreal.... 6-0/190.... Shot left.... Full name: Robert Victor Berry.
COLLEGE: Sir George Williams.
TRANSACTIONS/CAREER NOTES: Sold by Montreal Canadiens to Los Angeles Kings (October 8, 1970).
MISCELLANEOUS: Played professional football with Quebec Rifles of United Football League.... Played left wing.

Season	Team	League	Gms.	G	A	Pts.	Pen.	Gms.	G	A	Pts.	Pen.
				REGULAR SEASON					**PLAYOFFS**			
63-64—Verdun	QJHL		25	38	27	65	93	—	—	—	—	—
—Peterborough	OHA Jr. A		11	4	3	7	0	—	—	—	—	—
64-65—Sir George Williams Univ.	Can. Coll.		17	13	27	40	0	—	—	—	—	—
65-66—Sir George Williams Univ.	Can. Coll.		27	36	48	84	0	—	—	—	—	—
66-67—Sir George Williams Univ.	Can. Coll.		31	48	41	89	0	—	—	—	—	—
67-68—Hull	QSHL		39	32	24	56	0	—	—	—	—	—
68-69—Cleveland	AHL		68	24	29	53	104	—	—	—	—	—
—Montreal	NHL		2	0	0	0	0	—	—	—	—	—
69-70—Montreal	AHL		71	18	41	59	104	8	1	0	1	11
70-71—Los Angeles	NHL		77	25	38	63	52	—	—	—	—	—
71-72—Los Angeles	NHL		78	17	22	39	44	—	—	—	—	—
72-73—Los Angeles	NHL		78	36	28	64	75	—	—	—	—	—
73-74—Los Angeles	NHL		77	23	33	56	56	5	0	0	0	0
74-75—Los Angeles	NHL		80	25	23	48	60	3	1	2	3	2
75-76—Los Angeles	NHL		80	20	22	42	37	9	1	1	2	0
76-77—Fort Worth	CHL		7	4	4	8	0	—	—	—	—	—
—Los Angeles	NHL		69	13	25	38	20	9	0	3	3	4
NHL totals			541	159	191	350	344	26	2	6	8	6

HEAD COACHING RECORD

BACKGROUND: Assistant coach, St. Louis Blues (1988-89 through 1991-92).... Assistant general manager, Blues (1992-93).

Season	Team	League	W	L	T	Pct.	Finish	W	L	Pct.
				REGULAR SEASON					**PLAYOFFS**	
78-79—Los Angeles	NHL		34	34	12	.599	3rd/Norris Division	0	2	.000
79-80—Los Angeles	NHL		30	36	14	.462	2nd/Norris Division	1	3	.250
80-81—Los Angeles	NHL		43	24	13	.619	2nd/Norris Division	1	3	.250
81-82—Montreal	NHL		46	17	17	.681	1st/Adams Division	2	3	.400
82-83—Montreal	NHL		42	24	14	.612	2nd/Adams Division	0	3	.000
83-84—Montreal	NHL		28	30	5	.484		—	—	—
84-85—Pittsburgh	NHL		24	51	5	.331	6th/Patrick Division	—	—	—
85-86—Pittsburgh	NHL		34	38	8	.475	5th/Patrick Division	—	—	—
86-87—Pittsburgh	NHL		30	38	12	.450	5th/Patrick Division	—	—	—
92-93—St. Louis	NHL		33	30	10	.521	4th/Norris Division	7	4	.636
NHL totals (10 years)			344	322	110	.514	**NHL totals (6 years)**	11	18	.379

NOTES:
1979— Lost to New York Rangers in Stanley Cup quarterfinals.
1980— Lost to New York Islanders in Stanley Cup preliminary round.

1981— Lost to New York Rangers in Stanley Cup preliminary round.
1982— Lost to Quebec in Adams Division semifinals.
1983— Lost to Buffalo in Adams Division semifinals.
1992— Defeated Chicago in Norris Division semifinals; lost to Toronto in Norris Division finals.

BOWMAN, SCOTTY
RED WINGS

PERSONAL: Born September 18, 1933, at Montreal. . . . Full name: William Scott Bowman.
HONORS: Inducted into Hall of Fame (1991).

HEAD COACHING RECORD

BACKGROUND: Minor league hockey supervisor, Montreal Canadiens organization (1954-55 through 1956-57). . . . Coach, Team Canada (1976 and 1981). . . . Director of hockey operations/general manager, Buffalo Sabres (1979-80 through 1986-87). . . . Director of player development, Pittsburgh Penguins (1990-91).
HONORS: Won Jack Adams Award (1976-77). . . . Named NHL Executive of the Year by THE SPORTING NEWS (1979-80).
RECORDS: Holds NHL career regular-season record for wins—834; winning percentage—.658. . . . Holds NHL career playoff record for wins—137; games—223.

Season Team	League	REGULAR SEASON					PLAYOFFS		
		W	L	T	Pct.	Finish	W	L	Pct.
67-68—St. Louis	NHL	23	21	14	.517	3rd/Western Division	8	10	.444
68-69—St. Louis	NHL	37	25	14	.579	1st/Western Division	8	4	.667
69-70—St. Louis	NHL	37	27	12	.566	1st/Western Division	8	8	.500
70-71—St. Louis	NHL	13	10	5	.554	2nd/West Division	2	4	.333
71-72—Montreal	NHL	46	16	16	.692	3rd/East Division	2	4	.333
72-73—Montreal	NHL	52	10	16	.769	1st/East Division	12	5	.706
73-74—Montreal	NHL	45	24	9	.635	2nd/East Division	2	4	.333
74-75—Montreal	NHL	47	14	19	.706	1st/Adams Division	6	5	.545
75-76—Montreal	NHL	58	11	11	.794	1st/Adams Division	12	1	.923
76-77—Montreal	NHL	60	8	12	.825	1st/Adams Division	12	2	.857
77-78—Montreal	NHL	59	10	11	.806	1st/Adams Division	12	3	.800
78-79—Montreal	NHL	52	17	11	.719	1st/Adams Division	12	4	.750
79-80—Buffalo	NHL	47	17	16	.688	1st/Adams Division	9	5	.643
81-82—Buffalo	NHL	18	10	7	.614	3rd/Adams Division	1	3	.250
82-83—Buffalo	NHL	38	29	13	.556	3rd/Adams Division	6	4	.600
83-84—Buffalo	NHL	48	25	7	.644	2nd/Adams Division	0	3	.000
84-85—Buffalo	NHL	38	28	14	.563	3rd/Adams Division	2	3	.400
85-86—Buffalo	NHL	18	18	1	.500	5th/Adams Division	—	—	—
86-87—Buffalo	NHL	3	7	2	.333	5th/Adams Division	—	—	—
91-92—Pittsburgh	NHL	39	32	9	.544	3rd/Patrick Division	16	5	.762
92-93—Pittsburgh	NHL	56	21	7	.726	1st/Patrick Division	7	5	.583
NHL totals (21 years)		**834**	**380**	**226**	**.658**	**NHL totals (19 years)**	**137**	**86**	**.614**

NOTES:
1968— Defeated Philadelphia in Western Division finals; defeated Minnesota in Stanley Cup semifinals; lost to Montreal in Stanley Cup finals.
1969— Defeated Philadelphia in Stanley Cup quarterfinals; defeated Los Angeles in Stanley Cup semifinals; lost to Montreal in Stanley Cup finals.
1970— Defeated Minnesota in Stanley Cup quarterfinals; defeated Pittsburgh in Stanley Cup quarterfinals; lost to Boston in Stanley Cup finals.
1971— Lost to Minnesota in Stanley Cup quarterfinals.
1972— Lost to New York Rangers in Stanley Cup quarterfinals.
1973— Defeated Buffalo in Stanley Cup quarterfinals; defeated Philadelphia in Stanley Cup semifinals; defeated Chicago in Stanley Cup finals.
1974— Lost to New York Rangers in Stanley Cup quarterfinals.
1975— Defeated Vancouver in Stanley Cup quarterfinals; lost to Buffalo in Stanley Cup semifinals.
1976— Defeated Chicago in Stanley Cup quarterfinals; defeated New York Islanders in Stanley Cup semifinals; defeated Philadelphia in Stanley Cup finals.
1977— Defeated St. Louis in Stanley Cup quarterfinals; defeated New York Islanders in Stanley Cup semifinals; defeated Boston in Stanley Cup finals.
1978— Defeated Detroit in Stanley Cup quarterfinals; defeated Toronto in Stanley Cup semifinals; defeated Boston in Stanley Cup finals.
1979— Defeated Toronto in Stanley Cup quarterfinals; defeated Boston in Stanley Cup semifinals; defeated New York Rangers in Stanley Cup finals.
1980— Defeated Vancouver in Stanley Cup preliminary round; defeated Chicago in Stanley Cup quarterfinals; lost to New York Islanders in Stanley Cup semifinals.
1982— Lost to Boston in Stanley Cup preliminary rounds.
1983— Defeated Montreal in Adams Division semifinals; lost to Boston in Adams Division finals.
1984— Lost to Quebec in Adams Division semifinals.
1985— Lost to Quebec in Adams Division semifinals.
1992— Defeated Washington in Patrick Division semifinals; defeated New York Rangers in Patrick Division finals; defeated Boston in Wales Conference finals; defeated Chicago in Stanley Cup finals.
1993— Defeated New Jersey in Patrick Division semifinals; lost to New York Islanders in Patrick Division finals.

BOWNESS, RICK
SENATORS

PERSONAL: Born January 25, 1955, at Moncton, N.B. . . . 6-1/185. . . . Shot right. . . . Full name: Richard Gary Bowness.
HIGH SCHOOL: Halifax (N.S.).
COLLEGE: St. Mary's (N.S.).

TRANSACTIONS/CAREER NOTES: Selected by Atlanta Flames from Montreal Juniors in second round (second Flames pick, 26th overall) of NHL amateur draft (June 3, 1975).... Sold by Atlanta Flames to Detroit Red Wings (September 1977).... Sold by Red Wings to St. Louis Blues (September 1978).... Traded by Blues to Winnipeg Jets for D Craig Norwich (June 19, 1980).
MISCELLANEOUS: Played right wing.

Season	Team	League	REGULAR SEASON					PLAYOFFS				
			Gms.	G	A	Pts.	Pen.	Gms.	G	A	Pts.	Pen.
72-73	Quebec	QMJHL	30	2	7	9	2	—	—	—	—	—
73-74	Montreal	QMJHL	67	25	46	71	95	—	—	—	—	—
74-75	Montreal	QMJHL	71	24	76	100	130	—	—	—	—	—
75-76	Tulsa	CHL	64	25	38	63	160	9	4	3	7	12
	Nova Scotia	AHL	2	0	1	1	0	—	—	—	—	—
	Atlanta	NHL	5	0	0	0	0	—	—	—	—	—
76-77	Tulsa	CHL	39	15	15	30	72	8	0	1	1	20
	Atlanta	NHL	28	0	4	4	29	—	—	—	—	—
77-78	Detroit	NHL	61	8	11	19	76	4	0	0	0	2
78-79	St. Louis	NHL	24	1	3	4	30	—	—	—	—	—
	Salt Lake City	CHL	48	25	28	53	92	10	5	4	9	27
79-80	Salt Lake City	CHL	71	25	46	71	135	13	5	9	14	39
	St. Louis	NHL	10	1	2	3	11	—	—	—	—	—
80-81	Tulsa	CHL	35	12	20	32	82	—	—	—	—	—
	Winnipeg	NHL	45	8	17	25	45	1	0	0	0	0
81-82	Tulsa	CHL	79	34	53	87	201	3	0	2	2	2
82-83	Sherbrooke	AHL	65	17	31	48	117	—	—	—	—	—
	NHL totals		173	18	37	55	191	5	0	0	0	2

HEAD COACHING RECORD

BACKGROUND: Player/assistant coach, Sherbrooke, Winnipeg Jets organization (1982-83).... Assistant coach, Jets (1983-84 through 1986-87).... General manager/coach, Moncton, Jets organization (1987-88).

Season	Team	League	REGULAR SEASON					PLAYOFFS		
			W	L	T	Pct.	Finish	W	L	Pct.
87-88	Moncton	AHL	27	45	8	.388	6th/North Division	—	—	—
88-89	Moncton	AHL	37	34	9	.519	3rd/North Division	—	—	—
	Winnipeg	NHL	8	17	3	.339	5th/Smythe Division	—	—	—
89-90	Maine	AHL	31	38	11	.456	5th/North Division	—	—	—
90-91	Maine	AHL	34	34	12	.500	5th/North Division	—	—	—
91-92	Boston	NHL	36	32	12	.525	2nd/Adams Division	8	7	.533
92-93	Ottawa	NHL	10	70	4	.143	6th/Adams Division	—	—	—
	NHL totals (3 years)		54	119	19	.331	NHL totals (1 year)	8	7	.533

NOTES:
1992— Defeated Buffalo in Adams Division semifinals; defeated New York Rangers in Adams Division finals; lost to Pittsburgh in Wales Conference finals.

BURNS, PAT
MAPLE LEAFS

PERSONAL: Born April 4, 1952, at St.-Henri, Que.
MISCELLANEOUS: Served 17 years with the Gastineau (Quebec) and Ottawa Police Departments before assuming a professional hockey career.

HEAD COACHING RECORD

BACKGROUND: Assistant coach, Canadian national team (1986).... Assistant coach, Canadian national junior team (1987).
HONORS: Named NHL Coach of the Year by THE SPORTING NEWS (1988-89 and 1992-93).... Won Jack Adams Award (1988-89 and 1992-93).

Season	Team	League	REGULAR SEASON					PLAYOFFS		
			W	L	T	Pct.	Finish	W	L	Pct.
83-84	Hull	QMJHL	25	45	0	.357	6th/LeBel Division	—	—	—
84-85	Hull	QMJHL	33	34	1	.493	2nd/LeBel Division	1	4	.200
85-86	Hull	QMJHL	54	18	0	.750	1st/LeBel Division	15	0	1.000
86-87	Hull	QMJHL	26	39	5	.407	4th/LeBel Division	4	4	.500
87-88	Sherbrooke	AHL	42	34	4	.550	3rd/North Division	2	4	.333
88-89	Montreal	NHL	53	18	9	.719	1st/Adams Division	14	7	.667
89-90	Montreal	NHL	41	28	11	.581	3rd/Adams Division	5	6	.455
90-91	Montreal	NHL	39	30	11	.556	2nd/Adams Division	6	7	.462
91-92	Montreal	NHL	41	28	11	.581	1st/Adams Division	4	7	.364
92-93	Toronto	NHL	44	29	11	.589	3rd/Norris Division	11	10	.524
	NHL totals (5 years)		218	133	53	.605	NHL totals (5 years)	40	37	.519

NOTES:
1985— Lost to Verdun in President Cup quarterfinals.
1986— Defeated Shawinigan in President Cup quarterfinals; defeated St. Jean in President Cup semifinals; defeated Drummondville in President Cup finals.
1987— Eliminated in President Cup quarterfinal round-robin series.
1988— Lost to Fredericton in Calder Cup quarterfinals.
1989— Defeated Hartford in Adams Division semifinals; defeated Boston in Adams Division finals; defeated Philadelphia in Wales Conference finals; lost to Calgary in Stanley Cup finals.
1990— Defeated Buffalo in Adams Division semifinals; lost to Boston in Adams Division finals.
1991— Defeated Buffalo in Adams Division semifinals; lost to Boston in Adams Division finals.
1992— Defeated Hartford in Adams Division semifinals; lost to Boston in Adams Division finals.
1993— Defeated Detroit in Norris Division semifinals; defeated St. Louis in Norris Division finals; lost to Los Angeles in Campbell Conference finals.

CONSTANTINE, KEVIN

SHARKS

PERSONAL: Born December 27, 1958, at International Falls, Minn. . . . 5-10/165. . . . Full name: Kevin Lars Constantine.
HIGH SCHOOL: International Falls (Minn.).
COLLEGE: Rensselaer Polytechnic Institute (N.Y.), then Nevada-Reno.
TRANSACTIONS/CAREER NOTES: Selected by Montreal Canadiens in ninth round (154th overall) in NHL entry draft (1978). . . . Invited to Canadiens tryout camp (1980).
MISCELLANEOUS: Played goalie.

Season Team	League		REGULAR SEASON								PLAYOFFS					
		Gms.	Min.	W	L	T	GA	SO	Avg.	Gms.	Min.	W	L	GA	SO	Avg.
77-78—R.P.I.	ECAC	6	229	2	2	0	13	0	3.41	—	—	—	—	—	—	—
78-79—R.P.I.	ECAC	5	233	3	2	0	15	0	3.86	—	—	—	—	—	—	—
79-80—R.P.I.	ECAC	24	1342	11	9	0	89	1	3.98	—	—	—	—	—	—	—

HEAD COACHING RECORD

BACKGROUND: Junior varsity coach, Northwood Prep School, New York (1986-87). . . . Assistant coach, Kalamazoo, Minnesota North Stars organization (1988-89 through 1990-91).
HONORS: Won Commisioner's Trophy (1991-92).

Season Team	League		REGULAR SEASON					PLAYOFFS		
		W	L	T	Pct.	Finish		W	L	Pct.
85-86—North Iowa	USHL	17	31	0	.396	6th/USHL		2	3	.400
87-88—Rochester	USHL	39	7	2	.844	T1st/USHL		7	4	.636
91-92—Kansas City	IHL	56	22	4	.707	1st/West Division		12	3	.800
92-93—Kansas City	IHL	46	26	10	.622	2nd/Midwest Division		6	6	.500

NOTES:
1986— Lost to Sioux City in USHL quarterfinals.
1988— Defeated Sioux City in USHL quarterfinals; defeated St. Paul in USHL semifinals; lost to Thunder Bay in USHL finals. Finished first in USA Jr. A National Championships.
1992— Defeated Salt Lake in Turner Cup quarterfinals; defeated Peoria in Turner Cup semifinals; defeated Muskegon in Turner Cup finals.
1993— Defeated Milwaukee in Turner Cup quarterfinals; lost to San Diego in Turner Cup semifinals.

CRISP, TERRY

LIGHTNING

PERSONAL: Born May 28, 1943, at Parry Sound, Ont. . . . 5-10/180. . . . Shot left. . . . Full name: Terrance Arthur Crisp.
TRANSACTIONS/CAREER NOTES: Underwent appendectomy and hernia operation; missed part of 1963-64 season. . . . Selected by St. Louis Blues from Boston Bruins in NHL expansion draft (June 6, 1967). . . . Selected by New York Islanders from Blues in expansion draft (June 6, 1972). . . . Traded by Islanders to Philadelphia Flyers to D Jean Potvin and future considerations (March 5, 1973); Islanders received D Glen Irwin to complete deal (May 18, 1973).
MISCELLANEOUS: Played center. . . . Member of Stanley Cup championship teams (1974 and 1975).

Season Team	League		REGULAR SEASON					PLAYOFFS			
		Gms.	G	A	Pts.	Pen.		Gms.	G	A	Pts.	Pen.
60-61—St. Mary's	OHA					Did not play.					
61-62—Niagara Falls	OHA	50	16	22	38	0		—	—	—	—	—
62-63—Niagara Falls	OHA	50	39	35	74	0		—	—	—	—	—
63-64—Minneapolis	CPHL	42	15	20	35	22		—	—	—	—	—
64-65—Minneapolis	CPHL	70	28	34	62	22		5	0	2	2	0
65-66—Boston	NHL	3	0	0	0	0		—	—	—	—	—
—Oklahoma City	CPHL	61	11	22	33	35		9	1	5	6	0
66-67—Oklahoma City	CPHL	69	31	42	73	37		11	3	7	10	0
67-68—St. Louis	NHL	73	9	20	29	10		18	1	5	6	6
68-69—Kansas City	CHL	4	1	1	2	4		—	—	—	—	—
—St. Louis	NHL	57	6	9	15	14		12	3	4	7	20
69-70—St. Louis	NHL	26	5	6	11	2		16	2	3	5	2
—Buffalo	AHL	51	15	34	49	14		—	—	—	—	—
70-71—St. Louis	NHL	54	5	11	16	13		6	1	0	1	2
71-72—St. Louis	NHL	75	13	18	31	12		11	1	3	4	2
72-73—New York Islanders	NHL	54	4	16	20	6		—	—	—	—	—
—Philadelphia	NHL	12	1	5	6	2		11	3	2	5	2
73-74—Philadelphia	NHL	71	10	21	31	28		17	2	2	4	4
74-75—Philadelphia	NHL	71	8	19	27	20		9	2	4	6	0
75-76—Philadelphia	NHL	38	6	9	15	28		10	0	5	5	2
76-77—Philadelphia	NHL	2	0	0	0	0		—	—	—	—	—
NHL totals		536	67	134	201	135		110	15	28	43	40

HEAD COACHING RECORD

BACKGROUND: Assistant coach, Philadelphia Flyers (1977-78 and 1978-79). . . . Assistant coach, Canadian national team (1990 through 1992).
HONORS: Won Matt Leyden Trophy (1982-83 and 1984-85). . . . Named NHL Coach of the Year by THE SPORTING NEWS (1987-88).

Season Team	League		REGULAR SEASON					PLAYOFFS		
		W	L	T	Pct.	Finish		W	L	Pct.
79-80—Sault Ste. Marie	OHL	22	45	1	.331	6th/Leyden Division		—	—	—
80-81—Sault Ste. Marie	OHL	47	19	2	.706	1st/Leyden Division		8	7	.526
81-82—Sault Ste. Marie	OHL	40	25	3	.610	2nd/Emms Division		4	6	.423
82-83—Sault Ste. Marie	OHL	48	21	1	.693	1st/Emms Division		7	6	.531
83-84—Sault Ste. Marie	OHL	38	28	4	.571	3rd/Emms Division		8	4	.625

Season	Team	League	W	L	T	Pct.	Finish	W	L	Pct.
							—REGULAR SEASON—		**—PLAYOFFS—**	
84-85—Sault Ste. Marie	..............OHL		54	11	1	.826	1st/Emms Division	12	2	.813
85-86—Moncton	......................AHL		34	34	12	.500	3rd/North Division	5	5	.500
86-87—Moncton	......................AHL		43	31	6	.575	3rd/North Division	2	4	.333
87-88—Calgary	..........................NHL		48	23	9	.656	1st/Smythe Division	4	5	.444
88-89—Calgary	..........................NHL		54	17	9	.731	1st/Smythe Division	16	6	.727
89-90—Calgary	..........................NHL		42	23	15	.619	1st/Smythe Division	2	4	.333
92-93—Tampa Bay	....................NHL		23	54	7	.315	6th/Norris Division	—	—	—
NHL totals (4 years)	....		**167**	**117**	**40**	**.577**	**NHL totals (3 years)**	**22**	**15**	**.595**

NOTES:
1981— Sault Ste. Marie had four playoff ties.
1982— Defeated Brantford in Emms Division semifinals; lost to Kitchener in Emms Division finals. Sault Ste. Marie had three playoff ties.
1983— Defeated Brantford in Emms Division semifinals; defeated Kitchener in Emms Division finals; lost to Oshawa in Robertson Cup finals. Sault Ste. Marie had three playoff ties.
1984— Defeated Windsor in Emms Division quarterfinals; defeated Brantford in Emms Division semifinals; lost to Kitchener in Emms Division finals. Sault Ste. Marie had four playoff ties.
1985— Defeated Kitchener in Emms Division quarterfinals; defeated Hamilton in Emms Division finals; defeated Peterborough in Robertson Cup finals. Sault Ste. Marie had two playoff ties.
1986— Defeated Maine in Calder Cup quarterfinals; lost to Adirondack in Calder Cup semifinals.
1987— Lost to Adirondack in Calder Cup quarterfinals.
1988— Defeated Los Angeles in Smythe Division semifinals; lost to Edmonton in Smythe Division finals.
1989— Defeated Vancouver in Smythe Division semifinals; defeated Los Angeles in Smythe Division finals; defeated Chicago in Campbell Conference finals; defeated Montreal in Stanley Cup finals.
1990— Lost to Los Angeles in Smythe Division semifinals.

DEMERS, JACQUES
CANADIENS

PERSONAL: Born August 25, 1944, at Montreal.

HEAD COACHING RECORD

BACKGROUND: Director of player personnel, Chicago Cougars of WHA (1972-73).

HONORS: Won Louis A.R. Pieri Memorial Award (1982-83).... Named NHL Coach of the Year by THE SPORTING NEWS (1985-86 and 1986-87).... Won Jack Adams Award (1986-87 and 1987-88).

Season	Team	League	W	L	T	Pct.	Finish	W	L	Pct.
							—REGULAR SEASON—		**—PLAYOFFS—**	
79-80—Quebec	..............NHL		25	44	11	.381	5th/Adams Division	—	—	—
81-82—Fredericton	..................AHL		20	55	5	.281	5th/Northern Division	—	—	—
82-83—Fredericton	..................AHL		45	27	8	.544	1st/Northern Division	6	6	.500
83-84—St. Louis	........................NHL		32	41	7	.444	2nd/Norris Division	6	5	.545
84-85—St. Louis	........................NHL		37	31	12	.538	1st/Norris Division	0	3	.000
85-86—St. Louis	........................NHL		37	34	9	.519	3rd/Norris Division	10	9	.526
86-87—Detroit	..........................NHL		34	36	10	.488	2nd/Norris Division	9	7	.563
87-88—Detroit	..........................NHL		41	28	11	.581	1st/Norris Division	9	7	.563
88-89—Detroit	..........................NHL		34	34	12	.500	1st/Norris Division	2	4	.333
89-90—Detroit	..........................NHL		28	38	14	.438	5th/Norris Division	—	—	—
92-93—Montreal	......................NHL		48	30	6	.607	3rd/Adams Division	16	4	.800
NHL totals (9 years)	....		**316**	**316**	**92**	**.500**	**NHL totals (7 years)**	**52**	**39**	**.571**

NOTES:
1983— Defeated Adirondack in Calder Cup quarterfinals; lost to Maine in Calder Cup semifinals.
1984— Defeated Detroit in Norris Division semifinals; lost to Minnesota in Norris Division finals.
1985— Lost to Minnesota in Norris Division semifinals.
1986— Defeated Minnesota in Norris Division semifinals; defeated Toronto in Norris Division finals; lost to Calgary in Campbell Conference finals.
1987— Defeated Chicago in Norris Division semifinals; defeated Toronto in Norris Division finals; lost to Edmonton in Campbell Conference finals.
1988— Defeated Toronto in Norris Division semifinals; defeated St. Louis in Norris Division finals; lost to Edmonton in Campbell Conference finals.
1989— Lost to Chicago in Norris Division semifinals.
1993— Defeated Quebec in Adams Division semifinals; defeated Buffalo in Adams Division finals; defeated New York Islanders in Wales Conference finals; defeated Los Angeles in Stanley Cup finals.

GAINEY, BOB
STARS

PERSONAL: Born December 13, 1953, at Peterborough, Ont.... 6-2/195.... Shot left.... Full name: Robert Michael Gainey.

HIGH SCHOOL: Peterborough (Ont.) Secondaire.

TRANSACTIONS/CAREER NOTES: Selected by Montreal Canadiens from Peterborough TPTs in first round (first Canadiens pick, eighth overall) of NHL amateur draft (May 15, 1973).... Separated shoulder; missed part of 1977-78 season.... Tore ligaments in left knee (October 5, 1986).... Pulled groin (March 14, 1987).... Bruised ankle (April 1988).... Bruised left foot (October 15, 1988).... Broke bone in right foot (January 9, 1989); missed two months.... Injured left knee (March 17, 1989).... Reinjured left knee (April 5, 1989).... Released by Canadiens when he announced he would play the 1989-90 season with Epinal Ecureuils (Squirrels), a second-division team in France.

HONORS: Won Frank J. Selke Award (1977-78 through 1980-81).... Played in NHL All-Star Game (1977, 1978, 1980 and 1981).... Won Conn Smythe Trophy (1978-79).... Inducted into Hall of Fame (1992).

MISCELLANEOUS: Played left wing.... Member of Stanley Cup championship teams (1976 through 1979 and 1986).

Season	Team	League	Gms.	G	A	Pts.	Pen.	Gms.	G	A	Pts.	Pen.
							—REGULAR SEASON—			**—PLAYOFFS—**		
70-71—Peterborough	....	OHA Jr. A	4	0	0	0	0	—	—	—	—	—
71-72—Peterborough	....	OHA Mj. Jr. A	4	2	1	3	33	—	—	—	—	—

Season	Team	League	Gms.	G	A	Pts.	Pen.	Gms.	G	A	Pts.	Pen.
			REGULAR SEASON					**PLAYOFFS**				
72-73—Peterborough	OHA Mj. Jr. A	52	22	21	43	99	—	—	—	—	—
73-74—Nova Scotia	AHL	6	2	5	7	4	—	—	—	—	—
—Montreal	NHL	66	3	7	10	34	6	0	0	0	6
74-75—Montreal	NHL	80	17	20	37	49	11	2	4	6	4
75-76—Montreal	NHL	78	15	13	28	57	13	1	3	4	20
76-77—Montreal	NHL	80	14	19	33	41	14	4	1	5	25
77-78—Montreal	NHL	66	15	16	31	57	15	2	7	9	14
78-79—Montreal	NHL	79	20	18	38	44	16	6	10	16	10
79-80—Montreal	NHL	64	14	19	33	32	10	1	1	2	4
80-81—Montreal	NHL	78	23	24	47	36	3	0	0	0	2
81-82—Montreal	NHL	79	21	24	45	24	5	0	1	1	8
82-83—Montreal	NHL	80	12	18	30	43	3	0	0	0	4
83-84—Montreal	NHL	77	17	22	39	41	15	1	5	6	9
84-85—Montreal	NHL	79	19	13	32	40	12	1	3	4	13
85-86—Montreal	NHL	80	20	23	43	20	20	5	5	10	12
86-87—Montreal	NHL	47	8	8	16	19	17	1	3	4	6
87-88—Montreal	NHL	78	11	11	22	14	6	0	1	1	6
88-89—Montreal	NHL	49	10	7	17	34	16	1	4	5	8
89-90—Epinal	France					Statistics unavailable.					
NHL totals		1160	239	262	501	585	182	25	48	73	151

HEAD COACHING RECORD

BACKGROUND: Player/coach for Epinal, a second-division team in France (1989-90).

Season	Team	League	W	L	T	Pct.	Finish	W	L	Pct.
			REGULAR SEASON					**PLAYOFFS**		
90-91—Minnesota	NHL	27	39	14	.425	4th/Norris Division	14	9	.609
91-92—Minnesota	NHL	32	42	6	.438	4th/Norris Division	3	4	.429
92-93—Minnesota	NHL	36	38	10	.488	5th/Norris Division	—	—	—
NHL totals (3 years)		95	119	30	.458	**NHL totals (2 years)**	17	13	.567

NOTES:
1991—Defeated Chicago in Norris Division semifinals; defeated St. Louis in Norris Division finals; defeated Edmonton in Campbell Conference finals; lost to Pittsburgh in Stanley Cup finals.
1992—Lost to Detroit in Norris Division semifinals.

GREEN, TED
OILERS

PERSONAL: Born March 23, 1940, at St. Boniface, Man. . . . 5-11/195. . . . Shot right. . . . Full name: Edward Joseph Green.

TRANSACTIONS/CAREER NOTES: Selected by Boston Bruins from Montreal Canadiens in intraleague draft (June 1960). . . . Underwent surgery on both knees; missed most of 1965-66 and 1966-67 seasons. . . . Sustained skull fracture in preseason game (September 1969); missed entire 1969-70 season. . . . Pulled stomach muscles; missed start of 1971-72 season. . . . Selected by Winnipeg Jets in World Hockey Association player selection draft (February 1972). . . . Rights traded to New England Whalers (May 1972). . . . Suffered back spasms; missed part of 1974-75 season. . . . Traded by Whalers to Jets for future considerations (May 1975). . . . Fractured right ankle; missed final two playoff games (1976).

HONORS: Named to NHL All-Star second team (1968-69).

MISCELLANEOUS: Played defense. . . . Member of Stanley Cup championship team (1972).

Season	Team	League	Gms.	G	A	Pts.	Pen.	Gms.	G	A	Pts.	Pen.
			REGULAR SEASON					**PLAYOFFS**				
58-59—St. Boniface	MJHL					Statistics unavailable.					
59-60—Winnipeg	WHL	70	8	20	28	109	—	—	—	—	—
60-61—Kingston	OMJHL	11	1	5	6	30	5	1	0	1	2
—Boston	NHL	1	0	0	0	2	—	—	—	—	—
—Winnipeg	WHL	57	1	18	19	127	—	—	—	—	—
61-62—Boston	NHL	66	3	8	11	116	—	—	—	—	—
62-63—Boston	NHL	70	1	11	12	117	—	—	—	—	—
63-64—Boston	NHL	70	4	10	14	145	—	—	—	—	—
64-65—Boston	NHL	70	8	27	35	156	—	—	—	—	—
65-66—Boston	NHL	27	5	13	18	113	—	—	—	—	—
66-67—Boston	NHL	47	6	10	16	67	—	—	—	—	—
67-68—Boston	NHL	72	7	36	43	133	4	1	1	2	11
68-69—Boston	NHL	65	8	38	46	99	10	2	7	9	18
69-70—						Did not play.					
70-71—Boston	NHL	78	5	37	42	60	7	1	0	1	25
71-72—Boston	NHL	54	1	16	17	21	10	0	0	0	0
72-73—New England	WHA	78	16	30	46	47	12	1	5	6	25
73-74—New England	WHA	75	7	26	33	42	7	0	4	4	7
74-75—New England	WHA	57	6	14	20	29	—	—	—	—	—
75-76—Winnipeg	WHA	79	5	23	28	73	11	0	2	2	16
76-77—Winnipeg	WHA	70	4	21	25	45	20	1	3	4	12
77-78—Winnipeg	WHA	73	4	22	26	52	8	0	2	2	2
78-79—Winnipeg	WHA	20	0	2	2	16	—	—	—	—	—
WHA totals		452	42	138	180	304	58	2	16	18	62
NHL totals		620	48	206	254	1029	31	4	8	12	54

HEAD COACHING RECORD

BACKGROUND: Assistant coach, Edmonton Oilers (1981-82 through 1985-86 and 1987-88 through 1990-91).... Assistant coach, Team Canada (1984).

Season Team	League	W	L	T	Pct.	Finish	W	L	Pct.
					REGULAR SEASON			**PLAYOFFS**	
91-92—Edmonton	NHL	36	34	10	.513	3rd/Smythe Division	8	8	.500
92-93—Edmonton	NHL	26	50	8	.357	5th/Smythe Division	—	—	—
NHL totals (2 years)		62	84	18	.433	**NHL totals (1 year)**	8	8	.500

NOTES:
1992— Defeated Los Angeles in Smythe Division semifinals; defeated Vancouver in Smythe Division finals; lost to Chicago in Campbell Conference finals.

HOLMGREN, PAUL
WHALERS

PERSONAL: Born December 2, 1955, at St. Paul, Minn.... 6-3/210.... Shot right.... Full name: Paul Howard Holmgren.
COLLEGE: Minnesota.
TRANSACTIONS/CAREER NOTES: Selected by Edmonton Oilers in fifth round (fifth Oilers pick, 67th overall) of WHA amateur draft (May 1974).... WHA rights traded by Oilers to Minnesota Fighting Saints for future considerations (May 1974).... Selected by Philadelphia Flyers from the University of Minnesota in sixth round (fifth Flyers pick, 108th overall) of NHL amateur draft (June 3, 1975).... Signed by Flyers following demise of Minnesota Fighting Saints (March 1976).... Scratched cornea and underwent eye surgery (1976).... Separated right shoulder; missed parts of 1976-77 and 1977-78 seasons.... Separated shoulder during Team U.S.A. training camp (August 1981).... Suspended five games for assaulting referee (December 12, 1981).... Injured knee (January 1982).... Sprained left knee (October 1983).... Bruised left shoulder (January 1984).... Traded by Flyers to Minnesota North Stars for RW Paul Guay and third-round pick in 1985 draft (G Darryl Gilmour) (February 1984).... Injured shoulder (March 1984).... Underwent shoulder surgery (April 1984).... Separated shoulder (October 1984).... Underwent surgery to left shoulder (December 1984).... Announced retirement as a player to become assistant coach of Flyers (July 1985).
HONORS: Played in NHL All-Star Game (1981).
MISCELLANEOUS: Played right wing.

Season Team	League	Gms.	G	A	Pts.	Pen.	Gms.	G	A	Pts.	Pen.
			REGULAR SEASON					**PLAYOFFS**			
73-74—St. Paul Jr. B	OHA	55	22	59	81	183	—	—	—	—	—
74-75—University of Minnesota	WCHA	37	10	21	31	108	—	—	—	—	—
75-76—Johnstown	NAHL	6	3	12	15	12	—	—	—	—	—
—Minnesota	WHA	51	14	16	30	121	—	—	—	—	—
—Richmond	AHL	6	4	4	8	23	—	—	—	—	—
—Philadelphia	NHL	1	0	0	0	2	—	—	—	—	—
76-77—Philadelphia	NHL	59	14	12	26	201	10	1	1	2	25
77-78—Philadelphia	NHL	62	16	18	34	190	12	1	4	5	26
78-79—Philadelphia	NHL	57	19	10	29	168	8	1	5	6	22
79-80—Philadelphia	NHL	74	30	35	65	267	18	10	10	20	47
80-81—Philadelphia	NHL	77	22	37	59	306	12	5	9	14	49
81-82—Philadelphia	NHL	41	9	22	31	183	4	1	2	3	6
82-83—Philadelphia	NHL	77	19	24	43	178	3	0	0	0	6
83-84—Philadelphia	NHL	52	9	13	22	105	—	—	—	—	—
—Minnesota	NHL	11	2	5	7	46	12	0	1	1	6
84-85—Philadelphia	NHL	16	4	3	7	38	3	0	0	0	8
WHA totals		51	14	16	30	121					
NHL totals		527	144	179	323	1684	82	19	32	51	195

HEAD COACHING RECORD

BACKGROUND: Assistant coach, Philadelphia Flyers (1985-86 through 1987-88).

Season Team	League	W	L	T	Pct.	Finish	W	L	Pct.
					REGULAR SEASON			**PLAYOFFS**	
88-89—Philadelphia	NHL	36	36	8	.500	4th/Patrick Division	10	9	.526
89-90—Philadelphia	NHL	30	39	11	.444	6th/Patrick Division	—	—	—
90-91—Philadelphia	NHL	33	37	10	.475	5th/Patrick Division	—	—	—
91-92—Philadelphia	NHL	8	14	2	.380		—	—	—
92-93—Hartford	NHL	26	52	6	.345	5th/Adams Division	—	—	—
NHL totals (5 years)		133	178	37	.435	**NHL totals (1 year)**	10	9	.526

NOTES:
1989— Defeated Washington in Patrick Division semifinals; defeated Pittsburgh in Patrick Division finals; lost to Montreal in Wales Conference finals.

JOHNSTON, EDDIE
PENGUINS

PERSONAL: Born November 24, 1935, at Montreal.... 6-0/190.... Shot left.... Full name: Edward Joseph Johnston.
TRANSACTIONS/CAREER NOTES: Drafted by Boston Bruins from Montreal Canadiens (June 1962).... Traded by Boston to Toronto Maple Leafs to complete earlier deal in which Boston received G Jacques Plante and Toronto's third choice (C Doug Gibson) in 1973 Amateur draft for Boston's first round choice (D Ian Turnbull) in same draft (May 22, 1973).... Traded by Toronto to St. Louis Blues for RW Gary Sabourin (May 27, 1974).... Sold by St. Louis to Chicago Blackhawks (January 27, 1978).
HONORS: Won EPHL Leading Goalie Award (1960-61).
MISCELLANEOUS: Played goalie.

Season	Team	League	REGULAR SEASON								PLAYOFFS						
			Gms.	Min.	W	L	T	GA	SO	Avg.	Gms.	Min.	W	L	GA	SO	Avg.
54-55—Trois Rivieres Flambeaux	QJHL	46	...	...	...	...	169	1	3.67	—	—	—	—	—	—	—
55-56—Chatham	OHA	7	420	...	...	...	31	0	4.43	—	—	—	—	—	—	—
—Amherst	ACSHL	1	60	...	...	...	2	0	2.00	—	—	—	—	—	—	—
56-57—Winnipeg	WHL	50	...	...	...	...	193	2	3.86	—	—	—	—	—	—	—
57-58—Shawinigan Falls	QHL	63	...	...	...	...	230	*5	3.65	14	...	...	...	49	1	3.50
58-59—Edmonton	WHL	49	...	...	...	...	163	1	3.32	3	180	...	...	12	0	4.00
59-60—Johnstown	EHL	63	...	...	...	...	169	4	2.69	—	—	—	—	—	—	—
60-61—Hull-Ottawa	EPHL	70	...	...	...	...	187	*11	*2.67	14	...	...	...	28	0	*2.00
61-62—Spokane	WHL	70	...	...	...	...	237	3	3.30	16	...	...	...	58	*1	3.63
62-63—Boston	NHL	49	2880	11	27	11	196	1	4.08	—	—	—	—	—	—	—
63-64—Boston	NHL	70	*4200	18	*40	12	211	6	3.01	—	—	—	—	—	—	—
64-65—Boston	NHL	47	2820	12	31	4	162	3	3.45	—	—	—	—	—	—	—
65-66—Los Angeles	WHL	5	...	...	...	...	10	1	2.31	—	—	—	—	—	—	—
—Boston	NHL	33	1743	10	19	2	108	1	3.72	—	—	—	—	—	—	—
66-67—Boston	NHL	34	1880	9	21	2	116	0	3.70	—	—	—	—	—	—	—
67-68—Boston	NHL	28	1524	11	8	5	73	...	2.87	—	—	—	—	—	—	—
68-69—Boston	NHL	24	1440	14	6	4	74	2	3.08	1	65	0	1	4	0	3.69
69-70—Boston	NHL	37	2176	16	9	11	108	3	2.98	1	60	0	1	4	0	4.00
70-71—Boston	NHL	38	2280	30	6	2	96	4	2.53	1	60	0	1	7	0	7.00
71-72—Boston	NHL	38	2260	27	8	3	102	2	2.71	7	420	*6	1	13	1	*1.86
72-73—Boston	NHL	45	2510	24	17	1	137	5	3.27	3	160	1	2	9	0	3.38
73-74—Toronto	NHL	26	1516	12	9	4	78	1	3.09	1	60	0	1	6	0	6.00
74-75—St. Louis	NHL	30	1800	12	13	5	93	2	3.10	1	60	0	1	5	0	5.00
75-76—St. Louis	NHL	38	2152	11	17	9	130	1	3.62	—	—	—	—	—	—	—
76-77—St. Louis	NHL	38	2111	13	16	5	108	1	3.07	3	138	0	2	9	0	3.91
77-78—St. Louis	NHL	12	650	5	6	1	45	0	4.15	—	—	—	—	—	—	—
—Chicago	NHL	4	240	1	3	0	17	0	4.25	—	—	—	—	—	—	—
NHL totals		591	34182	236	256	81	1854	32	3.25	18	1023	7	10	57	1	3.34

HEAD COACHING RECORD

BACKGROUND: General manager, Pittsburgh Penguins (1983-84 through 1987-88).... Assistant general manager, Penguins (1988-89).... Vice president/general manager, Hartford Whalers (1989-90 through 1991-92).

Season	Team	League	REGULAR SEASON					PLAYOFFS		
			W	L	T	Pct.	Finish	W	L	Pct.
78-79—New Brunswick	AHL	41	29	10	.575	2nd/Northern Division	2	3	.400
79-80—Chicago	NHL	34	27	19	.544	1st/Smythe Division	3	4	.429
80-81—Pittsburgh	NHL	30	37	13	.456	3rd/Norris Division	2	3	.400
81-82—Pittsburgh	NHL	31	36	13	.469	4th/Patrick Division	2	3	.400
82-83—Pittsburgh	NHL	18	53	9	.281	6th/Patrick Division	—	—	—
NHL totals (4 years)		113	153	54	.438	**NHL totals (3 years)**	7	10	.412

NOTES:
1979— Lost to Nova Scotia in Calder Cup quarterfinals.
1980— Defeated St. Louis in Stanley Cup preliminary round; lost to Buffalo in Stanley Cup quarterfinals.
1981— Lost to St. Louis in Stanley Cup preliminary round.
1982— Lost to New York Islanders in Stanley Cup preliminary round.

KEENAN, MIKE
RANGERS

PERSONAL: Born October 21, 1949, at Whitby, Ont.... 5-10/180.... Shot right.... Full name: Michael Edward Keenan.
HIGH SCHOOL: Denis O'Connor (Ajax, Ont.).
COLLEGE: St. Lawrence (N.Y.).

Season	Team	League	REGULAR SEASON					PLAYOFFS			
			Gms.	G	A	Pts.	Pen.	Gms.	G	A	Pts.	Pen.
69-70—St. Lawrence University	ECAC	10	0	4	4	32	—	—	—	—	—
70-71—St. Lawrence University	ECAC	22	4	12	16	35	—	—	—	—	—
71-72—St. Lawrence University	ECAC	25	13	16	29	52	—	—	—	—	—

HEAD COACHING RECORD

BACKGROUND: Coach, Canadian national junior team (1980).... Coach, NHL All-Star team (1985-86, 1987-88, 1992-93).... Coach, Team Canada (1987).... General manager, Chicago Blackhawks (1989-90 through 1991-92).... General manager/coach, Team Canada (1991).... Coach, Canadian national team (1993)
HONORS: Named NHL Coach of the Year by THE SPORTING NEWS (1984-85).... Won Jack Adams Award (1984-85).

Season	Team	League	REGULAR SEASON					PLAYOFFS		
			W	L	T	Pct.	Finish	W	L	Pct.
79-80—Peterborough	OHL	47	20	1	.699	1st/Leyden Division	15	3	.833
80-81—Rochester	AHL	30	42	8	.425	5th/Southern Division	—	—	—
81-82—Rochester	AHL	40	31	9	.556	2nd/Southern Division	4	5	.444
82-83—Rochester	AHL	46	25	9	.631	1st/Southern Division	12	4	.750
83-84—University of Toronto	OUAA	41	5	3	.867	1st/OUAA	9	0	1.000
84-85—Philadelphia	NHL	53	20	7	.706	1st/Patrick Division	12	7	.632
85-86—Philadelphia	NHL	53	23	4	.688	1st/Patrick Division	2	3	.400
86-87—Philadelphia	NHL	46	26	8	.625	1st/Patrick Division	15	11	.577
87-88—Philadelphia	NHL	38	33	9	.513	3rd/Patrick Division	3	4	.429
88-89—Chicago	NHL	27	41	12	.413	4th/Norris Division	9	7	.563
89-90—Chicago	NHL	41	33	6	.550	1st/Norris Division	10	10	.500

Season	Team	League	REGULAR SEASON					PLAYOFFS		
			W	L	T	Pct.	Finish	W	L	Pct.
75-76—Peterborough	OHA	18	37	11	.356	6th/Leyden Division	—	—	—
76-77—Dallas	CHL	35	25	16	.565	2nd/CHL	1	4	.200
77-78—Toronto	NHL	41	29	10	.575	3rd/Adams Division	6	7	.462
78-79—Toronto	NHL	34	33	13	.506	3rd/Adams Division	2	4	.333
79-80—Buffalo	NHL	14	6	6	.654	1st/Adams Division	—	—	—
80-81—Buffalo	NHL	39	20	21	.619	1st/Adams Division	4	4	.500
81-82—Vancouver	NHL	4	0	1	.900	2nd/Smythe Division	11	6	.647
82-83—Vancouver	NHL	30	35	15	.469	3rd/Smythe Division	1	3	.250
83-84—Vancouver	NHL	17	26	5	.406	3rd/Smythe Division	—	—	—
—Los Angeles	NHL	8	17	3	.339	5th/Smythe Division	—	—	—
89-90—New York Rangers	NHL	36	31	13	.531	1st/Patrick Division	5	5	.500
90-91—New York Rangers	NHL	36	31	13	.531	2nd/Patrick Division	2	4	.333
91-92—New York Rangers	NHL	50	25	5	.656	1st/Patrick Division	6	7	.462
92-93—New York Rangers	NHL	19	17	4	.525		—	—	—
NHL totals (11 years)		328	270	109	.541	NHL totals (8 years)	37	40	.429

NOTES:
1969— Defeated London in OHA quarterfinals; lost to Montreal in OHA semifinals.
1970— Lost to London in OHA quarterfinals.
1971— Lost to Toronto in OHA quarterfinals.
1972— Defeated St. Catherines in OHA quarterfinals; defeated Toronto in OHA semifinals; defeated Ottawa in OHA finals; lost to Cornwall in Memorial Cup finals. Peterborough had two playoff ties.
1973— Defeated Oshawa in OHA quarterfinals; defeated London in OHA semifinals; lost to Toronto in OHA finals. Peterborough had five playoff ties.
1974— Defeated Oshawa in OHA quarterfinals; defeated Kitchener in OHA semifinals; lost to St. Catherines in OHA finals. Peterborough had four playoff ties.
1975— Defeated Oshawa in OHA quarterfinals; lost to Hamilton in OHA finals. Peterborough had two playoff ties.
1977— Lost to Tulsa in Adams Cup semifinals.
1978— Defeated Los Angeles in Stanley Cup preliminary round; defeated New York Islanders in Stanley Cup quarterfinals; lost to Montreal in Stanley Cup semifinals.
1979— Defeated Atlanta in Stanley Cup preliminary round; lost to Montreal in Stanley Cup quarterfinals.
1981— Defeated Vancouver in Stanley Cup preliminary round; lost to Minnesota in Stanley Cup quarterfinals.
1982— Defeated Calgary in Smythe Division semifinals; defeated Los Angeles in Smythe Division finals; defeated Chicago in Campbell Conference finals; lost to New York Islanders in Stanley Cup finals.
1983— Lost to Calgary in Smythe Division semifinals.
1990— Defeated New York Islanders in Patrick Division semifinals; lost to Washington in Patrick Division finals.
1991— Lost to Washington in Patrick Division semifinals.
1992— Defeated New Jersey in Patrick Division semifinals; lost to Pittsburgh in Patrick Division finals.

PADDOCK, JOHN
JETS

PERSONAL: Born June 9, 1954, at Brandon, Man. . . . 6-3/192. . . . Shot right. . . . Full name: Alvin John Paddock.
HIGH SCHOOL: Rivers (Man.) Collegiate.
TRANSACTIONS/CAREER NOTES: Selected by Washington Capitals from Brandon Wheat Kings in third round (third Capitals pick, 37th overall) of NHL amateur draft (May 28, 1974). . . . Traded by Capitals to Philadelphia Flyers to complete earlier deal for LW Bob Sirois (September 1976). . . . Dislocated shoulder (1977-78). . . . Dislocated right elbow (1979-80). . . . Sold by Flyers to Quebec Nordiques (August 1980). . . . Signed as free agent by New Jersey Devils (August 1983).
MISCELLANEOUS: Played right wing.

Season	Team	League	REGULAR SEASON					PLAYOFFS				
			Gms.	G	A	Pts.	Pen.	Gms.	G	A	Pts.	Pen.
72-73—Brandon	WCHL	11	3	2	5	6	—	—	—	—	—
73-74—Brandon	WCHL	68	34	49	83	228	—	—	—	—	—
74-75—Richmond	AHL	72	26	22	48	206	7	5	3	8	38
75-76—Richmond	AHL	42	11	14	25	98	8	0	3	3	5
—Washington	NHL	8	1	1	2	12	—	—	—	—	—
76-77—Springfield	AHL	61	13	16	29	106	—	—	—	—	—
—Philadelphia	NHL	5	0	0	0	9	8	0	0	0	25
77-78—Maine	AHL	61	8	12	20	152	10	*9	1	10	13
78-79—Maine	AHL	79	30	37	67	275	3	2	0	2	0
79-80—Philadelphia	NHL	32	3	7	10	36	8	10	6	16	48
80-81—Maine	AHL	22	8	7	15	53	2	0	0	0	0
—Quebec	NHL	32	2	5	7	25	3	0	1	1	18
81-82—Maine	AHL	39	6	10	16	123	13	2	2	4	18
82-83—Maine	AHL	69	30	23	53	188	—	—	—	—	—
—Philadelphia	NHL	10	2	1	3	4	—	—	—	—	—
83-84—Maine	AHL	17	3	6	9	34	—	—	—	—	—
NHL totals		87	8	14	22	86	5	2	0	2	0

HEAD COACHING RECORD
BACKGROUND: Assistant general manager, Philadelphia Flyers (1989-90).
HONORS: Shared Louis A.R. Pieri Memorial Award with Mike Milbury (1987-88).

Season	Team	League	REGULAR SEASON					PLAYOFFS		
			W	L	T	Pct.	Finish	W	L	Pct.
83-84—Maine	AHL	33	36	11	.481	3rd/North Division	12	5	.706
84-85—Maine	AHL	38	32	10	.538	1st/North Division	5	6	.454

Season	Team	League	W	L	T	Pct.	Finish	W	L	Pct.
							REGULAR SEASON		PLAYOFFS	
85-86—Hershey		AHL	48	29	3	.619	1st/South Division	10	8	.555
86-87—Hershey		AHL	43	36	1	.544	4th/South Division	1	4	.200
87-88—Hershey		AHL	50	27	3	.644	1st/South Division	12	0	.1000
88-89—Hershey		AHL	40	30	10	.563	2nd/South Division	7	5	.583
90-91—Binghamton		AHL	44	30	6	.588	2nd/South Division	4	6	.400
91-92—Winnipeg		NHL	33	32	15	.506	4th/Smythe Division	3	4	.429
92-93—Winnipeg		NHL	40	37	7	.518	4th/Smythe Division	2	4	.333
NHL totals (2 years)			73	69	22	.512	**NHL totals (2 years)**	5	8	.385

NOTES:

1984— Defeated Adirondack in Calder Cup quarterfinals; defeated Nova Scotia in Calder Cup semifinals; defeated Rochester in Calder Cup finals.

1985— Defeated Maine in Calder Cup quarterfinals; lost to Sherbrooke in Calder Cup semifinals.

1986— Defeated New Haven in Calder Cup quarterfinals; defeated St. Catherines in Calder Cup semifinals; lost to Adirondack in Calder Cup finals.

1987— Lost to Rochester in Calder Cup quarterfinals.

1988— Defeated Binghamton in Calder Cup quarterfinals; defeated Adirondack in Calder Cup semifinals; defeated Fredericton in Calder Cup finals.

1989— Defeated Utica in Calder Cup quarterfinals; lost to Adirondack in Calder Cup semifinals.

1991— Defeated Adirondack in Calder Cup qualifying round; defeated Baltimore in Calder Cup quarterfinals; lost to Rochester in Calder Cup semifinals.

1992— Lost to Vancouver in Smythe Division semifinals.

1993— Lost to Vancouver in Smythe Division semifinals.

PAGE, PIERRE

NORDIQUES

PERSONAL: Born April 30, 1948, at St. Hermas, Que.
COLLEGE: Rigaud College, then St. Francis-Xavier (N.S.), then Dalhousie (N.S.).

Season	Team	League	Gms.	G	A	Pts.	Pen.	Gms.	G	A	Pts.	Pen.
							REGULAR SEASON			PLAYOFFS		
69-70—St. Francis-Xavier			22	16	33	49	...	—	—	—	—	—
70-71—St. Francis-Xavier			25	23	54	77	...	—	—	—	—	—

HEAD COACHING RECORD

BACKGROUND: Consultant, Nova Scotia, Montreal Canadiens organization (1973-74 through 1979-80).... Assistant coach, Canadian Olympic team (1980).... Assistant coach, Calgary Flames (1980-81 through 1981-82 and 1985-86 through 1987-88).... General manager/coach, Colorado Flames (1982-83 and 1983-84).... General manager/coach Moncton, Calgary Flames organization (1984-85).... General manager, Quebec Nordiques (1990-91 through 1992-93).

Season	Team	League	W	L	T	Pct.	Finish	W	L	Pct.
							REGULAR SEASON		PLAYOFFS	
71-72—Dalhousie University		AUAA	10	8	0	.556	3rd/AUAA	—	—	—
72-73—Dalhousie University		AUAA	7	14	0	.333	8th/AUAA	—	—	—
73-74—Dalhousie University		AUAA	6	11	4	.381	4th/Kelly Division	—	—	—
74-75—Dalhousie University		AUAA	12	6	0	.667	3rd/AUAA	—	—	—
75-76—Dalhousie University		AUAA	6	9	1	.406	6th/AUAA	—	—	—
76-77—Dalhousie University		AUAA	6	13	1	.325	6th/AUAA	—	—	—
77-78—Dalhousie University		AUAA	9	9	2	.500	5th/AUAA	—	—	—
78-79—Dalhousie University		AUAA	13	7	0	.650	2nd/AUAA	6	2	.750
79-80—Dalhousie University		AUAA	20	1	1	.932	1st/Kelly Division	2	3	.400
82-83—Colorado		CHL	41	36	3	.531	2nd/CHL	2	4	.333
83-84—Colorado		CHL	48	25	3	.619	1st/CHL	2	4	.333
84-85—Moncton		AHL	32	40	8	.450	6th/North Division	—	—	—
88-89—Minnesota		NHL	27	37	16	.438	4th/Norris Division	1	4	.200
89-90—Minnesota		NHL	36	40	4	.475	4th/Norris Division	3	4	.429
91-92—Quebec		NHL	17	34	11	.363	5th/Adams Division	—	—	—
92-93—Quebec		NHL	47	27	10	.619	2nd/Adams Division	2	4	.333
NHL totals (4 years)			127	138	41	.482	**NHL totals (3 years)**	6	12	.333

NOTES:

1979— Defeated Moncton in AUAA semifinals; defeated Saint Mary's in AUAA semifinals; defeated Guelph in CIAU Championship round; defeated Chicoutimi in CIAU Championship round; lost to Alberta in CIAU Championship finals.

1980— Defeated St. Francis-Xavier in AUAA semifinals; lost to Moncton in AUAA finals.

1983— Lost to Birmingham in Adams Cup semifinals.

1984— Lost to Indianapolis in Adams Cup semifinals.

1989— Lost to Chicago in Norris Division semifinals.

1990— Lost to St. Louis in Norris Division semifinals.

1993— Lost to Montreal in Adams Division semifinals.

QUINN, PAT

CANUCKS

PERSONAL: Born January 29, 1943, at Hamilton, Ont.... 6-3/215.... Shot left.... Full name: John Brian Patrick Quinn.
HIGH SCHOOL: Central (Hamilton, Ont.).
COLLEGE: UC San Diego, then Delaware (attended law school).
TRANSACTIONS/CAREER NOTES: Suspended eight games for stick-swinging (November 1960).... Loaned by Detroit Red Wings to Tulsa Oilers for 1964-65 season.... Broke ankle (1965).... Selected by Montreal Canadiens from Red Wings in intraleague draft (June 1966).... Sold by Canadiens to St. Louis Blues (June 1967).... Loaned to Oilers for 1967-68 season.... Sold by Blues to Toronto Maple Leafs for rights to LW Dickie Moore (March 1968).... Selected by Vancouver Canucks in NHL expansion draft (June 1970).... Selected by Atlanta Flames in NHL expansion draft (June 1972).... Broke leg (1976).
MISCELLANEOUS: Played defense.

Season	Team	League	REGULAR SEASON					PLAYOFFS				
			Gms.	G	A	Pts.	Pen.	Gms.	G	A	Pts.	Pen.
58-59—Hamilton Jr. A.	OHA	20	0	1	1	...	—	—	—	—	—
59-60—Hamilton Jr. A.	OHA	27	0	1	1	...	—	—	—	—	—
60-61—Hamilton Jr. B	OHA				Statistics unavailable.						
61-62—					Unknown.						
62-63—Edmonton	CAHL				Statistics unavailable.						
63-64—Knoxville	EHL	72	6	31	37	217	3	0	0	0	9
64-65—Tulsa	CPHL	70	3	32	35	202	—	—	—	—	—
65-66—Memphis	CPHL	67	2	16	18	135	—	—	—	—	—
66-67—Houston	CPHL	15	0	3	3	66	—	—	—	—	—
—Seattle	WHL	35	1	3	4	49	5	0	0	0	2
67-68—Tulsa	CPHL	51	3	15	18	178	11	1	4	5	19
68-69—Tulsa	CHL	17	0	6	6	25	—	—	—	—	—
—Toronto	NHL	40	2	7	9	95	4	0	0	0	13
69-70—Tulsa	CHL	2	0	1	1	6	—	—	—	—	—
—Toronto	NHL	59	0	5	5	88	—	—	—	—	—
70-71—Vancouver	NHL	76	2	11	13	149	—	—	—	—	—
71-72—Vancouver	NHL	57	2	3	5	63	—	—	—	—	—
72-73—Atlanta	NHL	78	2	18	20	113	—	—	—	—	—
73-74—Atlanta	NHL	77	5	27	32	94	4	0	0	0	6
74-75—Atlanta	NHL	80	2	19	21	156	—	—	—	—	—
75-76—Atlanta	NHL	80	2	11	13	134	2	0	1	1	2
76-77—Atlanta	NHL	59	1	12	13	58	1	0	0	0	0
NHL totals			606	18	113	131	950	11	0	1	1	21

HEAD COACHING RECORD

BACKGROUND: Assistant coach, Philadelphia Flyers (1977-78).... Coach, Team Canada (1986).... President/general manager, Vancouver Canucks (1987-88 through 1992-93).

HONORS: Named NHL Coach of the Year by THE SPORTING NEWS (1979-80 and 1991-92).... Won Jack Adams Award (1979-80 and 1991-92).

Season	Team	League	REGULAR SEASON					PLAYOFFS		
			W	L	T	Pct.	Finish	W	L	Pct.
78-79—Philadelphia	NHL	18	8	4	.667	2nd/Patrick Division	3	5	.375
79-80—Philadelphia	NHL	48	12	20	.725	1st/Patrick Division	13	6	.684
80-81—Philadelphia	NHL	41	24	15	.606	2nd/Patrick Division	6	6	.500
81-82—Philadelphia	NHL	34	29	9	.535	3rd/Patrick Division	—	—	—
84-85—Los Angeles	NHL	34	32	14	.513	4th/Smythe Division	0	3	.000
85-86—Los Angeles	NHL	23	49	8	.338	5th/Smythe Division	—	—	—
86-87—Los Angeles	NHL	18	20	4	.476	5th/Smythe Division	—	—	—
90-91—Vancouver	NHL	9	13	4	.423	4th/Smythe Division	2	4	.333
91-92—Vancouver	NHL	42	26	12	.600	1st/Smythe Division	6	7	.462
92-93—Vancouver	NHL	46	29	9	.601	1st/Smythe Division	6	6	.500
NHL totals (10 years)		313	242	99	.554	**NHL totals (7 years)**	36	37	.493

NOTES:
1979— Defeated Vancouver in Stanley Cup preliminary round; lost to New York Rangers in Stanley Cup quarterfinals.
1980— Defeated Edmonton in Stanley Cup preliminary round; defeated New York Rangers in Stanley Cup quarterfinals; defeated Minnesota in Stanley Cup semifinals; lost to New York Islanders in Stanley Cup finals.
1985— Lost to Edmonton in Smythe Division semifinals.
1991— Lost to Los Angeles in Smythe Division semifinals.
1992— Defeated Winnipeg in Smythe Division semifinals; lost to Edmonton in Smythe Division finals.
1993— Defeated Winnipeg in Smythe Division semifinals; lost to Los Angeles in Smythe Division finals.

SIMPSON, TERRY
FLYERS

PERSONAL: Born August 30, 1943, at Brantford, Ont.

HEAD COACHING RECORD

BACKGROUND: Coach, Prince Albert Raiders, Saskatchewan Junior Hockey League (1972-73 through 1981-82).... Assistant coach, Canadian national junior team (1984 and 1985).... Coach, Canadian national junior team (1986).... Assistant coach, Winnipeg Jets (1990-91 through 1992-93).

HONORS: Won Dunc McCallum Memorial Trophy (1983-84 and 1985-86).

Season	Team	League	REGULAR SEASON					PLAYOFFS		
			W	L	T	Pct.	Finish	W	L	Pct.
82-83—Prince Albert	WHL	16	55	1	.229	8th/East Division	—	—	—
83-84—Prince Albert	WHL	41	29	2	.583	5th/East Division	1	4	.200
84-85—Prince Albert	WHL	58	11	3	.826	1st/East Division	12	1	.923
85-86—Prince Albert	WHL	52	17	3	.743	2nd/East Division	6	4	.600
86-87—N.Y. Islanders	NHL	35	33	12	.513	3rd/Patrick Division	7	7	.500
87-88—N.Y. Islanders	NHL	39	31	10	.550	1st/Patrick Division	2	4	.333
88-89—N.Y. Islanders	NHL	7	18	2	.296		—	—	—
NHL totals (3 years)		81	82	24	.497	**NHL totals (2 years)**	9	11	.450

NOTES:
1984— Lost to Medicine Hat in East Division quarterfinals.
1985— Defeated Calgary in East Division semifinals; defeated Medicine Hat in East Division finals; defeated Kamloops in WHL finals.
1986— Defeated Saskatoon in East Division semifinals; lost to Medicine Hat in East Division finals.
1987— Defeated Washington in Patrick Division semifinals; lost to Philadelphia in Patrick Division finals.
1988— Lost to New Jersey in Patrick Division semifinals.

SUTTER, BRIAN

BRUINS

PERSONAL: Born October 7, 1956, at Viking, Alta. . . . 5-11/172. . . . Shot left. . . . Full name: Brian Louis Allen Sutter. . . . Brother of Darryl Sutter, left winger, Chicago Blackhawks (1979-80 through 1986-87) and current head coach, Blackhawks; brother of Brent Sutter, center, Blackhawks; brother of Ron Sutter, center, St. Louis Blues; brother of Rich Sutter, right winger, Blues; and brother of Duane Sutter, right winger, New York Islanders and Blackhawks (1979-80 through 1989-90) and current head coach, Indianapolis Ice of IHL.

TRANSACTIONS/CAREER NOTES: Selected by St. Louis Blues from Lethbridge Broncos in second round (second Blues pick, 20th overall) of NHL amateur draft (June 1, 1976). . . . Suffered hairline fracture of pelvis (November 3, 1983). . . . Broke left shoulder (January 16, 1986). . . . Reinjured left shoulder (March 8, 1986). . . . Damaged left shoulder muscle (November 1986). . . . Sprained ankle (November 1987). . . . Retired as player and signed as head coach of Blues (June 1988).
HONORS: Played in NHL All-Star Game (1982, 1983 and 1985).
MISCELLANEOUS: Played left wing.

			REGULAR SEASON					PLAYOFFS				
Season	Team	League	Gms.	G	A	Pts.	Pen.	Gms.	G	A	Pts.	Pen.
72-73—Red Deer		AJHL	51	27	40	67	54	—	—	—	—	—
73-74—Red Deer		AJHL	59	42	54	96	139	—	—	—	—	—
74-75—Lethbridge		WCHL	53	34	47	81	134	6	0	1	1	39
75-76—Lethbridge		WCHL	72	36	56	92	233	7	3	4	7	45
76-77—Kansas City		CHL	38	15	23	38	47	—	—	—	—	—
—St. Louis		NHL	35	4	10	14	82	4	1	0	1	14
77-78—St. Louis		NHL	78	9	13	22	123	—	—	—	—	—
78-79—St. Louis		NHL	77	41	39	80	165	—	—	—	—	—
79-80—St. Louis		NHL	71	23	35	58	156	3	0	0	0	4
80-81—St. Louis		NHL	78	35	34	69	232	11	6	3	9	77
81-82—St. Louis		NHL	74	39	36	75	239	10	8	6	14	49
82-83—St. Louis		NHL	79	46	30	76	254	4	2	1	3	10
83-84—St. Louis		NHL	76	32	51	83	162	11	1	5	6	22
84-85—St. Louis		NHL	77	37	37	74	121	3	2	1	3	2
85-86—St. Louis		NHL	44	19	23	42	87	9	1	2	3	22
86-87—St. Louis		NHL	14	3	3	6	18	—	—	—	—	—
87-88—St. Louis		NHL	76	15	22	37	147	10	0	3	3	49
NHL totals			779	303	333	636	1786	65	21	21	42	249

HEAD COACHING RECORD

BACKGROUND: Assistant coach, Team Canada (1991).
HONORS: Won Jack Adams Trophy (1990-91).

						REGULAR SEASON			PLAYOFFS		
Season	Team	League	W	L	T	Pct.	Finish		W	L	Pct.
88-89—St. Louis		NHL	33	35	12	.488	2nd/Norris Division		5	5	.500
89-90—St. Louis		NHL	37	34	9	.519	2nd/Norris Division		7	5	.583
90-91—St. Louis		NHL	47	22	11	.656	2nd/Norris Division		6	7	.462
91-92—St. Louis		NHL	36	33	11	.519	3rd/Norris Division		2	4	.333
92-93—Boston		NHL	51	26	7	.649	1st/Adams Division		0	4	.000
NHL totals (5 years)			204	150	50	.567	NHL totals (5 years)		20	25	.444

NOTES:
1989— Defeated Minnesota in Norris Division semifinals; lost to Chicago in Norris Division finals.
1990— Defeated Toronto in Norris Division semifinals; lost to Chicago in Norris Division finals.
1991— Defeated Detroit in Norris Division semifinals; lost to Minnesota in Norris Division finals.
1992— Lost to Chicago in Norris Division semifinals.
1993— Lost to Buffalo in Adams Division semifinals.

SUTTER, DARRYL

BLACKHAWKS

PERSONAL: Born August 19, 1958, at Viking, Alta. . . . 5-10/163. . . . Shot left. . . . Brother of Brian Sutter, left winger, St. Louis Blues (1976-77 through 1987-88) and current head coach, Boston Bruins; brother of Duane Sutter, right winger, New York Islanders and Chicago Blackhawks (1979-80 through 1989-90) and current head coach, Indianapolis Ice of IHL; brother of Rich Sutter, right winger, Blues; brother of Ron Sutter, center, Blues; and brother of Brent Sutter, center, Blackhawks.

TRANSACTIONS/CAREER NOTES: Selected by Chicago Blackhawks in 11th round (11th Blackhawks pick, 179th overall) of NHL amateur draft (June 1978). . . . Lacerated left elbow, developed infection and underwent surgery (November 27, 1981). . . . Broke nose (November 7, 1982). . . . Broke ribs (November 1983). . . . Fracture left cheekbone and injured left eye (January 2, 1984). . . . Underwent arthroscopic surgery to right knee (September 1984). . . . Bruised ribs (October 1984). . . . Broke left ankle (December 26, 1984). . . . Separated right shoulder and underwent surgery (November 13, 1985); missed 30 games. . . . Injured knee (February 1987). . . . Retired as player and signed as assistant coach of Blackhawks (June 1987).
HONORS: Named top rookie of Japan National League (1978-79). . . . Won Dudley (Red) Garrett Memorial Trophy (1979-80). . . . Named to AHL All-Star second team (1979-80).
MISCELLANEOUS: Played left wing.

			REGULAR SEASON					PLAYOFFS				
Season	Team	League	Gms.	G	A	Pts.	Pen.	Gms.	G	A	Pts.	Pen.
74-75—Red Deer		AJHL	60	16	20	36	43	—	—	—	—	—
75-76—Red Deer		AJHL	60	43	93	136	82	—	—	—	—	—
76-77—Red Deer		AJHL	56	55	78	133	131	—	—	—	—	—
—Lethbridge		WCHL	1	1	0	1	0	15	3	7	10	13
77-78—Lethbridge		WCHL	68	33	48	81	119	8	4	9	13	2

Season Team	League	REGULAR SEASON					PLAYOFFS				
		Gms.	G	A	Pts.	Pen.	Gms.	G	A	Pts.	Pen.
78-79—New Brunswick	AHL	19	7	6	13	6	5	1	2	3	0
—Iwakura	Japan	20	28	13	41	0	—	—	—	—	—
79-80—New Brunswick	AHL	69	35	31	66	69	12	6	6	12	8
—Chicago	NHL	8	2	0	2	2	7	3	1	4	2
80-81—Chicago	NHL	76	40	22	62	86	3	3	1	4	2
81-82—Chicago	NHL	40	23	12	35	31	3	0	1	1	2
82-83—Chicago	NHL	80	31	30	61	53	13	4	6	10	8
83-84—Chicago	NHL	59	20	20	40	44	5	1	1	2	0
84-85—Chicago	NHL	49	20	18	38	12	15	12	7	19	12
85-86—Chicago	NHL	50	17	10	27	44	3	1	2	3	0
86-87—Chicago	NHL	44	8	6	14	16	2	0	0	0	0
NHL totals		406	161	118	279	288	51	24	19	43	26

HEAD COACHING RECORD

BACKGROUND: Assistant coach, Chicago Blackhawks (1987-88).... Associate coach, Blackhawks (1991-92).
HONORS: Won Commissioner's Trophy (1989-90).

Season Team	League	REGULAR SEASON					PLAYOFFS		
		W	L	T	Pct.	Finish	W	L	Pct.
88-89—Saginaw	IHL	46	26	10	.622	2nd/East Division	2	4	.333
89-90—Indianapolis	IHL	53	21	8	.695	1st/West Division	12	2	.857
90-91—Indianapolis	IHL	48	29	5	.616	2nd/East Division	3	4	.429
92-93—Chicago	NHL	47	25	12	.631	1st/Norris Division	0	4	.000
NHL totals (1 year)		47	25	12	.631	NHL totals (1 year)	0	4	.000

NOTES:
1989— Lost to Fort Wayne in Turner Cup quarterfinals.
1990— Defeated Peoria in Turner Cup quarterfinals; defeated Salt Lake City in Turner Cup semifinals; defeated Muskegon in Turner Cup finals.
1991— Lost to Fort Wayne in Turner Cup quarterfinals.
1993— Lost to St. Louis in Norris Division semifinals.

WILSON, RON
MIGHTY DUCKS

PERSONAL: Born May 28, 1955, at Windsor, Ont.... 5-11/175.... Shot right.... Full name: Ronald Lawrence Wilson.... Son of Larry Wilson, forward, Detroit Red Wings and Chicago Blawkhawks (1949-50 through 1955-56).
COLLEGE: Providence.
TRANSACTIONS/CAREER NOTES: Selected by Toronto Maple Leafs in seventh round (seventh Maple Leafs pick, 132nd overall) in NHL entry draft (June 1975).... Loaned by Davos club to Minnesota North Stars for remainder of NHL season and playoffs (March 1985).... Loaned by Davos club to Minnesota North Stars for remainder of NHL season and playoffs (March 1986). ... Traded by Davos to Minnesota North Stars for Craig Levie (May 1986).... Separated shoulder (March 9, 1987).
HONORS: Named to NCAA All-America East first team (1974-75 and 1975-76).
MISCELLANEOUS: Played defense.

Season Team	League	REGULAR SEASON					PLAYOFFS				
		Gms.	G	A	Pts.	Pen.	Gms.	G	A	Pts.	Pen.
73-74—Providence College	ECAC	26	16	22	38	...	—	—	—	—	—
74-75—Providence College	ECAC	27	26	61	87	12	—	—	—	—	—
—U.S. national team	Int'l	27	5	32	37	42	—	—	—	—	—
75-76—Providence College	ECAC	28	19	47	66	44	—	—	—	—	—
76-77—Providence College	ECAC	30	17	42	59	62	—	—	—	—	—
—Dallas	CHL	4	1	0	1	2	—	—	—	—	—
77-78—Dallas	CHL	67	31	38	69	18	—	—	—	—	—
—Toronto	NHL	13	2	1	3	0	—	—	—	—	—
78-79—New Brunswick	AHL	31	11	20	31	13	—	—	—	—	—
—Toronto	NHL	5	0	2	2	2	—	—	—	—	—
79-80—New Brunswick	AHL	43	20	43	63	10	—	—	—	—	—
80-81—Davos HC	Switzerland				Statistics unavailable.						
81-82—Davos HC	Switzerland				Statistics unavailable.						
82-83—Davos HC	Switzerland				Statistics unavailable.						
83-84—Davos HC	Switzerland				Statistics unavailable.						
84-85—Davos HC	Switzerland				Statistics unavailable.						
—Minnesota	NHL	13	4	8	12	2	—	—	—	—	—
85-86—Davos HC	Switzerland				Statistics unavailable.						
—Minnesota	NHL	11	1	3	4	8	—	—	—	—	—
86-87—Minnesota	NHL	65	12	29	41	36	—	—	—	—	—
87-88—Minnesota	NHL	24	2	12	14	16	—	—	—	—	—
NHL totals		131	21	55	76	64					

HEAD COACHING RECORD

BACKGROUND: Assistant coach, Milwaukee, Vancouver Canucks organization (1989-90).... Served as interim coach of Milwaukee while Ron Lapointe was hospitalized for cancer treatments (February and March 1990; team was 9-10 during that time).... Assistant coach, Vancouver Canucks (1990-91 through 1992-93).

OTHER BOOKS AVAILABLE
FROM THE SPORTING NEWS LIBRARY

1993 American League Box Scores and Official Averages
Available January 1994. #483 ....$20.95

1993 National League Box Scores and Official Averages
Available January 1994. #482 ....$20.95

Complete Baseball Record Book — 1994
Available January 1994. #484 ....$16.95

1994 Baseball Guide
Available February 1994. #485 ....$12.95

1994 Official Baseball Register
Available February 1994. #486 ....$12.95

American League 1994 Red Book
Available March 1994. #491 ....$11.95

National League 1994 Green Book
Available March 1994. #490 ....$11.95

1994 Official Baseball Rules
Available March 1994. #493 ....$3.95

Complete Super Bowl Book — 1994
Available March 1994. #492 ....$12.95

1993 Pro Football Guide
Available July 1993. #468 ....$12.95

1993 Pro Football Register
Available July 1993. #466 ....$12.95

1993-94 Official NBA Guide
Available September 1993. #474 ....$12.95

1993-94 Official NBA Register
Available September 1993. #472 ....$12.95

1993-94 Official NBA Rules
Available September 1993. #477 ....$3.95

The Series — 1993
Available November 1993. #476 ....$13.95

Call 1-800-825-8508 (or 1-515-246-6911 outside the U.S.) to place an order with your Visa or MasterCard, or send check or money order to:

> The Sporting News
> Attn: Book Dept.
> P.O. Box 11229
> Des Moines, IA 50340

Please include $3.50 for the first book and $1.00 for each additional book to cover the cost of shipping and handling. For Canadian orders, $6.75 for the first book and $1.00 for each additional book. International rates available on request. Please apply sales tax: NY—7.2%; IA—5.0%; IL—6.25%; MO—5.725%. All U.S. and Canadian orders will be shipped UPS. No P.O. boxes, please.